LONGLEY PARK SIXTH FORM COLLEGE

Item

D0833726

DATE REMOVED

- 7 JUL 2021

STOCK

Pocket Oxford Thesaurus

Pocket Oxford Thesaurus

OXFORD
UNIVERSITY PRESS

OXFORD
UNIVERSITY PRESS

Great Clarendon Street, Oxford OX2 6DP

Oxford University Press is a department of the University of Oxford.
It furthers the University's objective of excellence in research, scholarship,
and education by publishing worldwide in

Oxford New York

Auckland Bangkok Buenos Aires Cape Town
Chennai Dar es Salaam Delhi Hong Kong Istanbul Karachi
Kolkata Kuala Lumpur Madrid Melbourne Mexico City Mumbai
Nairobi São Paulo Shanghai Taipei Tokyo Toronto

Oxford is a registered trade mark of Oxford University Press
in the UK and in certain other countries

Published in the United States
by Oxford University Press Inc., New York

© Oxford University Press 2004

The moral rights of the author have been asserted

Database right Oxford University Press (maker)

First published 2004

All rights reserved. No part of this publication may be reproduced,
stored in a retrieval system, or transmitted, in any form or by any means,
without the prior permission in writing of Oxford University Press,
or as expressly permitted by law, or under terms agreed with the appropriate
reprographics rights organization. Enquiries concerning reproduction
outside the scope of the above should be sent to the Rights Department,
Oxford University Press, at the address above

You must not circulate this book in any other binding or cover
and you must impose this same condition on any acquirer

British Library Cataloguing in Publication Data

Data available

Library of Congress Cataloging in Publication Data

Data available

ISBN 0–19–860866–7

1

Typeset in Swift and Arial
by Laserwords Private Ltd.
Printed in Great Britain
by Clays Ltd, Bungay, Suffolk

Contents

Editorial Team

Editor
Maurice Waite

Assistant Editors
Duncan Marshall
Lucy Hollingworth

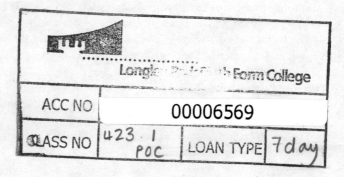

Longl___ ___ __ __ Form College

ACC NO	00006569		
CLASS NO	423.1 POC	LOAN TYPE	7 day

Preface

A thesaurus helps you to express yourself more accurately and in more interesting and varied ways. By listing groups of words that have similar meanings to each other, it offers a choice of alternative words (synonyms) that can be used in place of one that you already have in mind.

It is an invaluable tool for anyone who writes, whether for memos and reports at work, essays and dissertations at school and college, letters to business contacts, friends, or potential employers, or creative writing for a living or for pleasure.

A thesaurus can provide the answer when a word is on the tip of your tongue, or it can expand your vocabulary. It can also help in solving crossword puzzles and with many other word games.

The *Pocket Oxford Thesaurus* is a brand-new thesaurus. Its companion volume, the *Pocket Oxford English Dictionary*, was first published (as the *Pocket Oxford Dictionary*) in 1924, and its current edition is a member of the new generation of Oxford dictionaries, compiled using real, up-to-date evidence in new ways to present the most accurate picture of the language available.

The *Pocket Oxford Thesaurus* also draws on Oxford's unrivalled language research progarmme, to give you the best available choice of alternative words. It also supplies many more invaluable example sentences and phrases than any comparable thesaurus, both to give usage information and to pinpoint the sense that you need.

Unique to this thesaurus are the 1150 Word Links, at 650 entries, giving words which are not synonyms but which have another kind of relation to the headword: for example, at *cat* there are terms for the male and female cat (*tom*, *queen*) as well as the adjective relating to cats (*feline*). Some 'word links' are prefixes or suffixes related to the headword, such as *ichthyo-* at *fish*, *photo-* at *light*, and *-phobic* at *afraid*, to help you understand words like *ichthyology* and *photophobic*.

Guide to the thesaurus

part of speech of the entry word

numbered sense of the entry word

air ▸ noun **1** *hundreds of birds hovered in the air* =**sky**, atmosphere, airspace; ether; *literary* heavens. **2** *open the windows to get some air* =**breeze**, draught, wind; gust/puff of wind. **3** *an air of defiance* =**look**, appearance, impression, aspect, aura, mien, manner, bearing, tone; feel, ambience, atmosphere; *informal* vibe. **4** *a traditional Scottish air* =**tune**, melody, song.
▸ verb **1** *a chance to air your views* =**express**, voice, make public, articulate, state, declare; give expression/voice to; have one's say. **2** *the windows were opened to air the room* =**ventilate**, freshen, refresh, cool. **3** *the film was aired nationwide* =**broadcast**, transmit, screen, show, televise.

example of use, to help distinguish different senses

core synonym—the closest synonym to the entry word

combined synonym group standing for *give expression to* and *give voice to*

> **WORD LINKS**
>
> *relating to air:* **aerial, aero-**
> *study of moving air:* **aerodynamics**

words, prefixes, or suffixes with meanings that are related to the entry word but are not actual synonyms

bag ▸ noun =**suitcase**, case, valise, portmanteau, holdall, grip, overnighter; (**bags**) luggage, baggage.
▸ verb **1** *locals bagged the most fish* =**catch**, land, capture, trap, snare, ensnare. **2** *he bagged seven medals* =**get**, secure, obtain, acquire, pick up; win, achieve, attain; *informal* land, net.

form of the entry word for which the following synonym(s) can be substituted

luxurious ▸ adjective =**opulent**, sumptuous, grand, palatial, magnificent, extravagant, fancy; *Brit.* upmarket; *informal* plush, posh, classy, ritzy, swanky; *Brit. informal* swish; *N. Amer. informal* swank.
−OPPOSITES plain, basic.

label indicating the region of the world in which the following synonym(s) are used (see p.x for abbreviations)

word(s) meaning the opposite of the entry word; most have entries of their own, where a wider choice will be found

night ▶ noun =night-time; (hours of) darkness, dark.
  −OPPOSITES day.
  ■ **night and day** =all the time, around the clock, {morning, noon, and night}, {day in, day out}; ceaselessly, endlessly, incessantly, unceasingly, interminably, constantly, perpetually, continually, relentlessly; *informal* 24-7.

brackets showing that the phrase they contain is one complete synonym

label indicating the style of English in which the following synonym(s) are used

> WORD LINKS
>
> *relating to night:* **nocturnal**
> *fear of the night:* **nyctophobia**

spike ▶ noun =prong, barb, point; skewer, stake, spit; tine, pin; spur; *Mountaineering* piton.
  ▶ verb: *(informal)* =**adulterate**, contaminate, drug, lace; *informal* dope, doctor, cut.

label indicating the specialist field in which the following synonym(s) are used

label indicating the style of English in which this sense of *spike* is used

Most of the synonyms given are part of standard English, but some are suitable only in certain contexts. These are grouped at the end of their synonym set and given the following labels:

formal, e.g. *dwelling* as a synonym for *home*: normally used only in writing, such as official documents.

informal, e.g. *swig* as a synonym for *drink*: normally used only in speech or informal writing.

technical, e.g. *annulus* as a synonym for *ring*: normally used only in technical and specialist language, though not necessarily restricted to any specific field. Words used in specific fields are given appropriate labels, e.g. *Medicine*, *Nautical*.

literary, e.g. *slumber* as a synonym for *sleep*: found only or mainly in literature.

dated, e.g. *capital* as a synonym for *good*: no longer used by most, but still sometimes by older people.

historical, e.g. *minstrel*: still used today, but only to refer to some occupation or article that is no longer part of the modern world.

humorous, e.g. *libation* as a synonym for *drink*: used with the intention of sounding funny or playful.

archaic, e.g. *aliment* as a synonym for *food*: old-fashioned language found in literature of the past, but not in ordinary use today except for an old-fashioned effect.

Synonyms are also labelled if they are used exclusively or mainly in the English spoken in a particular part of the world, namely: British (abbreviated to *Brit.*), northern English (*N. English*), Scottish, North American (*N. Amer.*), United States (*US*), Australian (*Austral.*), New Zealand (*NZ*), and South African (*S. African*).

Note on trademarks and proprietary status

This thesaurus includes some words which have, or are asserted to have, proprietary status as trademarks or otherwise. Their inclusion does not imply that they have acquired for legal purposes a non-proprietary or general significance, nor any other judgement concerning their legal status. In cases where the editorial staff have some evidence that a word has proprietary status this is indicated by the label *trademark*, but no judgement concerning the legal status of such words is made or implied thereby.

Aa

aback ■ **take someone aback**. *See* SURPRISE.

abandon ▶ verb **1** *the party abandoned policies that made it unelectable* =**renounce**, relinquish, dispense with, discard; give up, drop, jettison, do away with, axe; *informal* ditch, scrap, scrub, junk; *formal* forswear. **2** *by that stage, she had abandoned painting* =**give up**, stop, cease, have done with, leave behind, outgrow; *informal* pack in, quit; *Brit. informal* jack in. **3** *he abandoned his wife and children* =**desert**, leave, turn one's back on, cast aside, finish with; jilt, throw over; *informal* walk/run out on, dump, ditch; *literary* forsake. **4** *they abandoned the car and set off on foot* =**leave (behind)**, vacate, dump, quit, evacuate, discard, jettison. **5** *a vast expanse of territory was abandoned to the invaders* =**relinquish**, surrender, give up, cede, yield, leave. **6** *she abandoned herself to the sensuousness of the music* =**give way to**, give oneself up to, yield to, lose oneself to/in.
–OPPOSITES keep, retain, continue.
▶ noun *with reckless abandon* =**uninhibitedness**, recklessness, lack of restraint, lack of inhibition.
–OPPOSITES self-control.

abandoned ▶ adjective **1** *abandoned vehicles* =**discarded**, empty, stranded; *informal* dumped, ditched. **2** *an abandoned tin mine* =**disused**, neglected, idle; deserted, unoccupied, uninhabited, derelict, empty.

abashed ▶ adjective =**embarrassed**, ashamed, shamefaced, mortified, humiliated, humbled, chagrined, crestfallen, sheepish, red-faced, blushing, with one's tail between one's legs.

abate ▶ verb **1** *the storm had abated* =**subside**, die down/away/out, lessen, ease (off), let up, decrease, diminish, fade, dwindle, recede, tail off, peter out, taper off, wane, ebb, weaken. **2** *nothing abated his crusading zeal* =**decrease**, lessen, diminish, reduce, ease, soothe, dampen, calm, tone down, allay, temper.
–OPPOSITES intensify, increase.

abatement ▶ noun **1** *the storm still rages with no sign of abatement* =**subsiding**, dying down/away/out, lessening, easing (off), let-up. **2** *noise abatement* =**reduction**, control.

abattoir ▶ noun =**slaughterhouse**; *archaic* shambles.

abbreviate ▶ verb =**shorten**, reduce, cut, contract, condense, compress, abridge, truncate, prune, shrink, telescope; summarize, abstract, precis, edit.
–OPPOSITES lengthen, expand.

abbreviated ▶ adjective =**shortened**, reduced, cut, condensed, abridged, concise, compact, succinct; thumbnail.
–OPPOSITES long.

abbreviation ▶ noun =**shortened form**, contraction, acronym, initialism.

abdicate ▶ verb **1** *the king abdicated in 1936* =**resign**, retire, stand down, step down, bow out, renounce the throne. **2** *the state abdicated all responsibility for their welfare* =**disown**, reject, renounce, give up, relinquish, abandon, turn one's back on, wash one's hands of; *formal* abjure; *literary* forsake.

abdication ▶ noun **1** *Edward VIII's abdication* =**resignation**, retirement. **2** *an abdication of responsibility* =**disowning**, renunciation, rejection, refusal, relinquishment, repudiation, abandonment.

abdomen ▶ noun =**stomach**, belly, gut, middle, intestines; *informal* tummy, tum, insides, guts, pot, paunch; *Austral. informal* bingy.

> **WORD LINKS**
>
> *relating to the abdomen:* **abdominal, ventral, coeliac**
> *surgical incision of the abdomen:* **laparotomy**

abdominal ▶ adjective =**gastric**, intestinal, stomach, duodenal, visceral, coeliac, ventral.

abduct ▶ verb =**kidnap**, carry off, seize, capture, run away/off with, make off with, spirit away; *informal* snatch.

a

aberrant ▶ adjective =**deviant**, abnormal, atypical, anomalous, irregular, rogue; strange, odd, peculiar, uncommon, freakish; twisted, warped, perverted.
−OPPOSITES normal, typical.

aberration ▶ noun =**anomaly**, deviation, abnormality, irregularity, variation, freak, oddity, peculiarity, curiosity; mistake.

abet ▶ verb =**assist**, aid, help, support, encourage; cooperate with, collaborate with, work with, collude with, side with; endorse, sanction; connive at.
−OPPOSITES hinder.

abeyance ■ in abeyance =**pending**, suspended, deferred, postponed, put off, put to one side, unresolved, up in the air; *informal* in cold storage, on ice, on the back burner.

abhor ▶ verb =**detest**, hate, loathe, despise, regard with disgust, shrink from, recoil from, shudder at; *formal* abominate.
−OPPOSITES love, admire.

abhorrence ▶ noun =**hatred**, loathing, detestation, revulsion, disgust, repugnance, horror, odium, aversion.

abhorrent ▶ adjective =**detestable**, hateful, loathsome, abominable, repellent, repugnant, repulsive, revolting, disgusting, horrible, horrid, horrifying, awful, heinous, reprehensible, obnoxious, odious, nauseating.
−OPPOSITES admirable.

abide ▶ verb **1** *he expected everybody to abide by the rules* =**comply with**, obey, observe, follow, keep to, hold to, conform to, adhere to, stick to, stand by, act in accordance with, uphold, heed, accept, go along with, acknowledge, respect, defer to. **2** (*informal*) *I can't abide the smell of cigarettes* =**stand**, bear; *Brit. informal* stick. **3** *at least one memory will abide* =**continue**, remain, survive, last, persist, stay, live on.
−OPPOSITES flout, disobey.

abiding ▶ adjective =**enduring**, lasting, lifelong, durable, everlasting, perpetual, eternal, unending, constant, permanent, unchanging, steadfast.
−OPPOSITES short-lived, ephemeral.

ability ▶ noun **1** *the ability to read and write* =**capacity**, capability, power, faculty, facility; wherewithal, means. **2** *the president's leadership ability* =**talent**, skill, expertise, aptitude, savoir faire, prowess, accomplishment; competence, proficiency; dexterity, deftness, cleverness, flair, finesse, gift, knack, genius; *informal* know-how.

abject ▶ adjective **1** *abject poverty* =**wretched**, miserable, hopeless, pitiful, sorry, woeful, lamentable, degrading, appalling, atrocious, awful. **2** *an abject failure* =**hopeless**, miserable, disastrous, catastrophic, pathetic; total, utter, complete, unmitigated. **3** *an abject apology* =**grovelling**, cringing, submissive; unreserved, unqualified.

ablaze ▶ adjective **1** *several vehicles were ablaze* =**on fire**, alight, aflame, in flames, flaming, burning, blazing. **2** *every window was ablaze with light* =**lit up**, alight, gleaming, glowing, aglow, bright, shining, glittering, radiant, shimmering, sparkling, flashing, luminous, incandescent.

able ▶ adjective **1** *he will soon be able to resume his duties* =**capable of**, competent to, up to, fit to, qualified to; allowed to, free to, in a position to. **2** *an able student* =**intelligent**, clever, talented, skilful, skilled, accomplished, gifted; proficient, apt, good, adroit, adept; capable, competent, efficient, effective.
−OPPOSITES incompetent, incapable.

able-bodied ▶ adjective =**healthy**, fit, in good health, strong, sound, hale and hearty; in good shape.
−OPPOSITES infirm, frail, disabled.

abnormal ▶ adjective =**unusual**, uncommon, atypical, untypical, unrepresentative, irregular, anomalous, deviant, aberrant, freak, freakish; strange, odd, peculiar, bizarre, weird; eccentric, unconventional, exceptional; unnatural, perverse, perverted, twisted, warped; *informal* funny, freaky, kinky.
−OPPOSITES normal, typical, common.

abnormality ▶ noun *physical or mental abnormalities* =**handicap**, disability, problem; deformity, defect.

abolish ▶ verb =**put an end to**, get rid of, scrap, end, remove, dissolve, stop, ban; *informal* do away with, give something the chop, knock something on the head.
−OPPOSITES retain, create.

abolition ▶ noun =**scrapping**, ending, dissolution, removal.

abominable ▶ adjective =**loathsome**, detestable, hateful, odious, obnoxious, despicable, contemptible, diabolical;

disgusting, revolting, repellent, repulsive, repugnant, abhorrent, reprehensible, atrocious, horrifying, foul, vile, wretched, horrible, awful, dreadful, appalling, nauseating; *informal* terrible, shocking, God-awful; *Brit. informal* beastly.
–OPPOSITES good, admirable.

abomination ▸ noun =**atrocity**, disgrace, horror, obscenity, outrage, evil, crime, monstrosity.

abort ▸ verb **1** *the organism can cause pregnant ewes to abort* =**miscarry**, have a miscarriage. **2** *the crew aborted the take-off* =**halt**, stop, end, call off, abandon, discontinue, terminate, arrest; *informal* pull the plug on.

abortion ▸ noun =**termination**; miscarriage.

abortive ▸ adjective =**unsuccessful**, failed, vain, ineffective, ineffectual, unproductive.
–OPPOSITES successful, fruitful.

abound ▸ verb **1** *cafes abound in the narrow streets* =**be plentiful**, be abundant, be numerous, be thick on the ground; *informal* grow on trees, be two/ten a penny. **2** *a stream which abounded with trout* =**be full of**, overflow with, teem with, be packed with, be crowded with; be crawling with, swarm with, bristle with, be thick with; *informal* be lousy with, be stuffed with, be chock-a-block with.

about ▸ preposition **1** *a book about ancient Greece* =**regarding**, concerning, with reference to, with regard to, with respect to, relating to, on, touching on, dealing with, relevant to, connected with, in connection with, on the subject of. **2** *two hundred people were milling about the room* =**around**, round, throughout, over, through, on every side of.
▸ adverb **1** *there were babies crawling about* =**around**, here and there, to and fro, back and forth, from place to place, hither and thither, in all directions. **2** *I knew he was about somewhere* =**near**, nearby, around, hereabouts, not far off/away, close by, in the vicinity, in the neighbourhood. **3** *about £15,000* =**approximately**, roughly, around, in the region of, circa, of the order of, something like; or so, or thereabouts, more or less, give or take a few, not far off; *Brit.* getting on for; *N. Amer. informal*

in the ballpark of. **4** *there's a lot of flu about* =**around**, in circulation, going on, happening, in the air, abroad; *informal* doing the rounds.
■ **about to** =(just) going to, ready to, all set to, preparing to, intending to; on the point of, on the verge of.

about-turn ▸ noun *(Brit.) the government was forced to make an about-turn* =**volte-face**, U-turn, reversal, retraction, backtracking; change of heart, change of mind.

above ▸ preposition **1** *a tiny window above the door* =**over**, higher (up) than; on top of, on, upon. **2** *those above the rank of Colonel* =**superior to**, senior to, over, higher (up) than, more powerful than; in charge of, commanding. **3** *above suspicion* =**beyond**; immune to, exempt from. **4** *an increase above the rate of inflation* =**greater than**, more than, higher than, exceeding, in excess of, over, over and above, beyond, surpassing, upwards of.
–OPPOSITES below, under, beneath.
▸ adverb **1** *in the darkness above, something moved* =**overhead**, on/at the top, high up, on high, up above, (up) in the sky, above one's head. **2** *the two cases described above* =**earlier**, previously, before, formerly.
▸ adjective *the above example* =**preceding**, previous, earlier, former, foregoing, prior, aforementioned, aforesaid.
■ **above all** =**most importantly**, most of all, chiefly, primarily, first and foremost, essentially, in essence, at bottom; *informal* at the end of the day, when all is said and done.

abrade ▸ verb =**wear away**, wear down, erode.

abrasion ▸ noun **1** *he had abrasions to his forehead* =**graze**, cut, scrape, scratch, gash, laceration, injury, contusion; *Medicine* trauma. **2** *the metal is resistant to abrasion* =**erosion**, wearing away/down.

abrasive ▸ adjective **1** *abrasive kitchen cleaners* =**rough**, coarse, harsh, scratchy. **2** *her abrasive manner* =**curt**, brusque, sharp; **harsh**, rough.
–OPPOSITES kind, gentle.

abreast ■ **abreast of** =**up to date with**, up with, in touch with, informed about, acquainted with, knowledgeable about, conversant with, familiar with, au fait with.

abridge ▸ verb =**shorten**, cut (down),

truncate, trim, crop, clip, prune; abbreviate, condense, contract, compress,
reduce; summarize, sum up, precis, edit.
–OPPOSITES lengthen.

abridged ▸ adjective =**shortened**, cut
(down), concise, condensed, abbreviated; bowdlerized, censored, expurgated; *informal* potted.

abroad ▸ adverb **1** *he regularly travels
abroad* =**overseas**, out of the country,
to/in foreign parts, to/in a foreign coun-
try/land. **2** *rumours were abroad* =**in
circulation**, circulating, everywhere, in
the air, {here, there, and everywhere};
about, around; at large.

abrupt ▸ adjective **1** *an abrupt halt* | *an
abrupt change of subject* =**sudden**, unexpected, unanticipated, unforeseen,
precipitate, surprising, startling; quick,
swift, rapid. **2** *an abrupt manner* =**curt**,
brusque, blunt, short, sharp, terse,
brisk, crisp, unceremonious.
–OPPOSITES gradual, gentle.

abscess ▸ noun =**swelling**, ulcer,
ulceration, cyst, boil, blister, sore, pustule, carbuncle, pimple.

abscond ▸ verb =**run away/off**, escape, bolt, flee, make off, take flight,
take off, decamp; disappear, vanish,
slip away, sneak away; *informal* clear out,
skedaddle, skip, head for the hills, do
a disappearing act, fly the coop, take
French leave, scarper, vamoose; *Brit.
informal* do a bunk, do a runner; *N. Amer.
informal* take a powder.

absence ▸ noun **1** *his absence from the
office* =**non-attendance**, absenteeism;
truancy; leave, holiday, vacation, sabbatical. **2** *the absence of any other suitable
candidate* =**lack**, want, non-existence,
unavailability, shortage.
–OPPOSITES presence.

absent ▸ adjective **1** *she was absent from
work* =**away**, off, out; off duty, on holiday, on leave; gone, missing, unavailable; *informal* AWOL. **2** *an absent look*
=**distracted**, preoccupied, inattentive,
vague, absorbed, dreamy, far away;
blank, empty, vacant.
–OPPOSITES present, attentive, alert.
▸ verb *Rose absented herself* =**stay away**,
be absent, withdraw, retire, take one's
leave, remove oneself.

absent-minded ▸ adjective =**forgetful**, distracted, scatterbrained, preoccupied, inattentive; *informal* having a mind/
memory like a sieve.

absolute ▸ adjective **1** *absolute silence*
| *an absolute disgrace* =**complete**, total,
utter, out-and-out, outright, perfect,
pure; thorough, thoroughgoing, unqualified, unadulterated, unalloyed,
unreserved, downright, consummate,
unmitigated, sheer. **2** *an absolute fact*
=**definite**, certain, unconditional, categorical, unquestionable, incontrovertible, undoubted, unequivocal, conclusive, confirmed. **3** *absolute power*
=**unlimited**, unrestricted, unrestrained, unbounded, boundless, infinite, ultimate, total, supreme, unconditional. **4** *absolute moral standards*
=**universal**, fixed, unchanging.
–OPPOSITES partial, qualified, limited,
conditional.

absolutely ▸ adverb *you're absolutely
right* =**completely**, totally, utterly, perfectly, entirely, wholly, fully, quite,
thoroughly, unreservedly; definitely,
certainly, unquestionably, undoubtedly, without (a) doubt, without question, in every way/respect, one hundred
per cent.
▸ exclamation *(informal)* 'Have I made myself
clear?' 'Absolutely!' =**yes**, indeed, of
course, definitely, certainly, without (a)
doubt, without question, unquestionably, by all means.

absolution ▸ noun =**release**, pardon,
exoneration; deliverance.

absolve ▸ verb =**exonerate**, discharge,
acquit; release, relieve, free, deliver,
clear, exempt, let off.
–OPPOSITES blame, condemn.

absorb ▸ verb **1** *a material which absorbs
water* =**soak up**, suck up, draw up/in,
take up/in, mop up, sop up. **2** *she absorbed the information in silence* =**assimilate**, digest, take in. **3** *the company was
absorbed into the new concern* =**incorporate**, assimilate, integrate, take in, subsume, include, co-opt, swallow up.
4 *these roles absorb most of his time* =**use
(up)**, consume, take up, occupy. **5** *she
was totally absorbed in her book* =**engross**,
captivate, occupy, preoccupy, engage,
rivet, grip, hold, immerse, involve,
enthral, spellbind, fascinate.

absorbent ▸ adjective =**porous**,
sponge-like, permeable.

absorbing ▸ adjective =**fascinating**,
interesting, captivating, gripping, engrossing, compelling, compulsive, enthralling, riveting, spellbinding, thrill-

ing, exciting; *informal* unputdownable.
−OPPOSITES boring, uninteresting.

absorption ▶ noun **1** *the absorption of water* =**soaking up**, sucking up. **2** *the company's absorption into a larger concern* =**incorporation**, assimilation, integration, inclusion. **3** *her total absorption in the music* =**involvement**, immersion, raptness, engrossment, preoccupation, engagement, captivation, fascination, enthralment.

abstain ▶ verb **1** *Benjamin abstained from wine* =**refrain**, desist, hold back, forbear; give up, renounce, avoid, shun, eschew, forgo, go/do without; refuse, decline; *informal* cut out; *formal* abjure. **2** *most pregnant women abstain, or drink very little* =**be teetotal**, take the pledge; *informal* be on the wagon. **3** *262 voted against, 38 abstained* =**not vote**, decline to vote.

abstemious ▶ adjective =**self-denying**, temperate, moderate, self-disciplined, restrained, self-restrained, sober, austere, ascetic, puritanical, spartan.
−OPPOSITES self-indulgent.

abstinence ▶ noun =**self-denial**, self-restraint; teetotalism, temperance, sobriety, abstemiousness.

abstract ▶ adjective **1** *abstract concepts* =**theoretical**, conceptual, intellectual, metaphysical, philosophical, academic. **2** *abstract art* =**non-representational**.
−OPPOSITES actual, concrete.
▶ noun *an abstract of her speech* =**summary**, synopsis, precis, résumé, outline; *N. Amer.* wrap-up.

abstracted ▶ adjective =**absent-minded**, distracted, preoccupied, in a world of one's own, with one's head in the clouds, daydreaming, dreamy, inattentive, pensive, lost in thought, deep/immersed in thought, musing, brooding, absent; *informal* miles away.
−OPPOSITES attentive.

abstraction ▶ noun **1** *philosophical abstractions* =**concept**, idea, notion, thought, theory, hypothesis. **2** *she sensed his momentary abstraction* =**absent-mindedness**, distraction, preoccupation, inattentiveness, inattention, pensiveness.

abstruse ▶ adjective =**obscure**, arcane, esoteric, rarefied, recondite, difficult, hard, cryptic, over/above one's head, incomprehensible, unfathom-able, impenetrable.

absurd ▶ adjective =**preposterous**, ridiculous, ludicrous, farcical, laughable, risible, stupid, foolish, silly, pointless, senseless; *informal* crazy; *Brit. informal* barmy, daft.
−OPPOSITES reasonable, sensible.

absurdity ▶ noun =**preposterousness**, ridiculousness, ludicrousness, stupidity, foolishness, silliness, inanity, pointlessness, senselessness; *informal* craziness.

abundance ▶ noun =**profusion**; host, cornucopia; plenty, multitude; *informal* millions, sea, wealth, lot(s), heap(s), mass(es), stack(s), pile(s), load(s), bags, mountain(s), ton(s), slew, oodles; *Brit. informal* shedload; *N. Amer. informal* gobs.
−OPPOSITES lack, scarcity.

abundant ▶ adjective =**plentiful**, copious, ample, large, huge, great, bumper, overflowing, teeming; in abundance; *informal* a gogo, galore.
−OPPOSITES scarce, sparse.
■ **be abundant** =**abound**, be plentiful, be numerous, be in abundance, be thick on the ground; *informal* be two/ten a penny.

abuse ▶ verb **1** *the judge abused his power* =**misuse**; exploit, take advantage of. **2** *he was accused of abusing children* =**mistreat**, maltreat, ill-treat; molest, interfere with, indecently assault, sexually abuse, sexually assault. **3** *the referee was abused by players from both teams* =**insult**, be rude to, swear at, shout at.
▶ noun **1** *the abuse of power* =**misuse**; exploitation. **2** *the abuse of children* =**mistreatment**, maltreatment, ill-treatment; molestation, indecent assault, sexual abuse, sexual assault. **3** *torrents of abuse* =**insults**, curses, expletives, swear words; swearing, cursing, name-calling; invective.

abusive ▶ adjective =**insulting**, rude, offensive, derogatory, slanderous, libellous.

abysmal ▶ adjective (*informal*) *some of the teaching was abysmal* =**terrible**, dreadful, awful, frightful, atrocious, disgraceful, hopeless, lamentable; *informal* rotten, appalling, pathetic, pitiful, woeful, useless, lousy, dire, poxy, the pits; *Brit. informal* chronic, shocking.

abyss ▶ noun =**chasm**, crevasse, gulf, pit, void.

academic ▶ adjective **1** *an academic*

institution =**educational**, scholastic. **2** *his academic turn of mind* =**scholarly**, literary, intellectual, bookish, cerebral. **3** *the outcome is entirely academic* =**irrelevant**, beside the point; hypothetical, speculative, conjectural.

▶ **noun** *a group of Russian academics* =**scholar**, don, professor, fellow, man/woman of letters, thinker; *informal* egghead.

academy ▶ **noun** =**educational institution**, school, college, university, institute, seminary, conservatory, conservatoire.

accede ▶ **verb** *(formal)* *he acceded to the government's demands* =**agree to**, consent to, accept, assent to, acquiesce in, comply with, go along with, concur with, surrender to, yield to, give in to, give way to, defer to.

accelerate ▶ **verb** **1** *the car accelerated* =**speed up**, go faster, gain momentum, increase speed, pick up speed, gather speed, put on a spurt. **2** *inflation started to accelerate* =**increase**, rise, go up, surge, escalate, spiral. **3** *the university accelerated the planning process* =**hasten**, speed up, step up; *informal* crank up.
−OPPOSITES decelerate, delay.

acceleration ▶ **noun** **1** *the acceleration of the industrial process* =**speeding up**, quickening, stepping up. **2** *an acceleration in the divorce rate* =**increase**, rise, leap, surge, escalation.

accent ▶ **noun** **1** *a Scottish accent* =**pronunciation**, intonation, enunciation, articulation, inflection, tone, modulation, cadence, timbre, delivery. **2** *the accent is on the first syllable* =**stress**, emphasis, accentuation; beat. **3** *the accent is on comfort* =**emphasis**, stress; priority, importance, prominence.

accentuate ▶ **verb** =**focus attention on**, draw attention to, point up, underline, underscore, accent, highlight, spotlight, foreground, feature, bring to the fore, heighten, stress, emphasize.

accept ▶ **verb** **1** *he accepted a pen as a present* =**receive**, take, get, obtain, acquire. **2** *she accepted my invitation to lunch* =**say yes to**, agree to. **3** *she was accepted as one of the family* =**welcome**, receive, embrace, adopt. **4** *he accepted Ellen's explanation* =**believe**; *informal* buy, swallow. **5** *we have to accept his decision* =**go along with**, concur with, comply with, abide by, follow, adhere to, act in accordance

with, defer to, yield to, surrender to, bow to, give in to, submit to, respect. **6** *she will just have to accept the consequences* =**put up with**, take, swallow; reconcile oneself to, resign oneself to, get used to, adjust to, learn to live with, make the best of; face up to.
−OPPOSITES refuse, reject.

acceptable ▶ **adjective 1** *an acceptable standard of living* =**satisfactory**, adequate, reasonable, fair, decent, good enough, sufficient, sufficiently good, tolerable, passable. **2** *an acceptable risk* =**bearable**, tolerable, allowable, admissible, sustainable; *informal* liveable with.

acceptance ▶ **noun 1** *the acceptance of an award* =**receipt**, receiving, taking. **2** *the acceptance of responsibility* =**assumption**, acknowledgement, taking on. **3** *their acceptance of the decision* =**compliance**, acquiescence, deference, submission, respect. **4** *the acceptance of pain* =**toleration**, endurance, forbearance.

accepted ▶ **adjective** =**recognized**, acknowledged, established, traditional, orthodox; usual, customary, normal, standard.

access ▶ **noun 1** *the building has a side access* =**entrance**, entry, way in; door. **2** *they were denied access to the stadium* =**admission**, admittance, entry.
▶ **verb** *the program is used to access the data* =**retrieve**, obtain; read.

accessible ▶ **adjective 1** *the village is only accessible on foot* | *an easily accessible reference tool* =**reachable**, attainable, approachable; obtainable, available; *informal* get-at-able. **2** *his accessible style of writing* =**understandable**, comprehensible, easy to understand, intelligible. **3** *Professor Cooper is very accessible* =**approachable**, friendly, congenial, affable, cordial, welcoming, pleasant.

accessorize ▶ **verb** =**complement**, enhance, set off; go with, accompany; decorate, adorn, ornament.

accessory ▶ **noun 1** *camera accessories* =**attachment**, add-on; supplement; paraphernalia, equipment, gear, stuff. **2** *an accessory to murder* =**accomplice**, collaborator, co-conspirator.

accident ▶ **noun 1** *an accident at work* =**mishap**, misadventure; disaster, tragedy, catastrophe, calamity. **2** *an accident on the motorway* =**crash**, collision, smash, bump; derailment; *N. Amer.*

wreck; *informal* smash-up, pile-up; *Brit. informal* prang, shunt.

accidental ▶ adjective =**fortuitous**, chance, coincidental, serendipitous; unintentional, unintended, inadvertent, unwitting.
–OPPOSITES intentional, deliberate.

accidentally ▶ adverb =**by accident**, by chance, unintentionally, inadvertently, unwittingly.

acclaim ▶ verb *the booklet has been acclaimed by teachers* =**praise**, applaud, cheer, commend, approve, welcome, hail; *formal* laud.
–OPPOSITES criticize.
▶ noun *she has won widespread acclaim* =**praise**, applause, cheers, tributes; approval, admiration, congratulations, commendation.
–OPPOSITES criticism.

acclaimed ▶ adjective =**celebrated**, admired, highly rated, esteemed, exalted, well thought of, well received; eminent, renowned, distinguished, prestigious, illustrious, pre-eminent.

acclimatization ▶ noun =**adjustment**, adaptation, accommodation, habituation, acculturation, familiarization; naturalization; *N. Amer.* acclimation.

acclimatize ▶ verb =**adjust**, adapt; get used; familiarize oneself; find one's feet, get one's bearings; *N. Amer.* acclimate.

accolade ▶ noun =**tribute**, honour, compliment, prize.

accommodate ▶ verb **1** *refugees were accommodated in army camps* =**lodge**, house, put up, billet, board. **2** *the cottages accommodate up to six people* =**hold**, take, have room for, sleep; seat. **3** *we made every effort to accommodate her* =**help**, assist, oblige, cater for, fit in with, satisfy.

accommodating ▶ adjective =**obliging**, cooperative, helpful, amenable, hospitable; flexible.

accommodation ▶ noun **1** *the shortage of accommodation* =**housing**, lodging(s), (living) quarters, rooms; place to stay, billet; shelter, a roof over one's head; *informal* digs, pad; *formal* abode, residence, dwelling. **2** *an accommodation between the two parties was reached* =**arrangement**, understanding, settlement, accord, deal, compromise.

accompaniment ▶ noun **1** *a musical accompaniment* =**backing**, support, background, soundtrack, backing track. **2** *the wine makes a superb accompaniment to cheese* =**complement**, addition, adjunct.

accompany ▶ verb **1** *the driver accompanied her to the door* =**go with**, travel with, keep someone company, tag along with, partner, escort, chaperone, attend, show, see, usher, conduct. **2** *he accompanied the choir on the piano* =**back**, play along with, support.

accomplice ▶ noun =**partner in crime**, associate, accessory, confederate, collaborator, fellow conspirator; henchman; *informal* sidekick.

accomplish ▶ verb =**fulfil**, achieve, succeed in, realize, attain, manage, bring about/off, carry out/through, execute, effect, perform, do, discharge, complete.

accomplished ▶ adjective =**expert**, skilled, skilful, masterly, virtuoso, master, consummate, talented, gifted, able, capable; *informal* mean, nifty, crack, ace, wizard; *N. Amer. informal* crackerjack.

accomplishment ▶ noun **1** *a remarkable accomplishment* =**achievement**, act, deed, exploit, effort, feat, move, coup. **2** *her many accomplishments* =**talent**, skill, gift, ability.

accord ▶ verb **1** *the national assembly accorded him more power* =**give**, grant, present, award, vouchsafe; confer on, bestow on, invest with. **2** *his views accorded with mine* =**correspond**, agree, tally, match, concur, be consistent, be in harmony, be compatible, be in tune.
–OPPOSITES withhold, disagree, differ.
▶ noun **1** *a peace accord* =**pact**, treaty, agreement, settlement, deal, entente, protocol, contract. **2** *the two sides failed to reach accord* =**agreement**, consensus, unanimity, harmony.
■ **of one's own accord** =**voluntarily**, of one's own free will, of one's own volition, by choice; willingly, freely, readily.

accordance ■ **in accordance with** *a ballot held in accordance with trade union rules* =**in agreement with**, in conformity with, in line with, true to, in the spirit of, observing, following, heeding.

according ■ **according to 1** *cook the rice according to the instructions* =**as specified by**, in line with, as per, in accordance with. **2** *salary will be fixed according to experience* =**in proportion**

to, proportional to, commensurate with, in relation to, relative to, in line with, corresponding to.

accordingly ▸ adverb 1 *they recognized the danger and acted accordingly* =**appropriately**, correspondingly. 2 *accordingly, he returned home* =**therefore**, for that reason, consequently, so, as a result, as a consequence, hence, that being the case.

accost ▸ verb =**approach**, stop, confront, detain, speak to; *informal* buttonhole, collar.

account ▸ noun 1 *his account of the incident* =**description**, report, version, story, statement, explanation, tale; chronicle, history, record, log. 2 *the firm's quarterly accounts* =**financial record**, ledger, balance sheet, financial statement; (**accounts**) books. 3 *I pay the account off in full each month* =**bill**, invoice, tally; debt, charges; *N. Amer.* check; *informal* tab. 4 *his background is of no account* =**importance**, import, significance, consequence.
▸ verb *her visit can be accounted a success* =**consider**, regard as, reckon, hold to be, think, look on as, view as, see as, judge, count, deem, rate.
■ **account for 1** *they must account for the delay* =**explain**, answer for, give reasons for, justify. 2 *excise duties account for over half the price* =**constitute**, make up, comprise, form, compose, represent.
■ **on account of** =**because of**, owing to, due to, as a consequence of, thanks to, by virtue of, in view of.
■ **on no account** =**never**, under no circumstances, not for any reason.

accountability ▸ noun =**responsibility**, liability.

accountable ▸ adjective =**responsible**, liable, answerable; to blame.

accoutrements ▸ plural noun =**equipment**, paraphernalia, stuff, things, apparatus, tackle, kit, implements, rig, outfit, regalia, odds and ends, bits and pieces, bits and bobs, trappings, accessories.

accredit ▸ verb 1 *he was accredited with being one of the world's fastest sprinters* =**recognize as**, credit with. 2 *the discovery is usually accredited to the Arabs* =**ascribe**, attribute. 3 *professional bodies accredit these research degrees* =**recognize**, authorize, approve, certify, license.

accredited ▸ adjective =**official**, appointed, recognized, authorized, approved, certified, licensed.

accretion ▸ noun =**accumulation**, formation, collecting, accrual; growth, increase.

accrue ▸ verb 1 *financial benefits will accrue from restructuring* =**result**, arise, follow, ensue; be caused by. 2 *interest is added to the account as it accrues* =**accumulate**, collect, build up, mount up, grow, increase.

accumulate ▸ verb =**gather**, collect, amass, stockpile, pile up, heap up, store (up), hoard, lay in/up; increase, accrue; run up.

accumulation ▸ noun =**mass**, buildup, pile, collection, stock, store, stockpile, reserve, hoard.

accuracy ▸ noun =**correctness**, precision, exactness; fidelity, faithfulness, truth, truthfulness, veracity, authenticity, realism, verisimilitude.

accurate ▸ adjective 1 *accurate information | an accurate representation of the situation* =**correct**, precise, exact, right; factual, literal, faithful, true, truthful, authentic, realistic; *informal* on the mark, on the beam, on the nail; *Brit. informal* spot on, bang on; *N. Amer. informal* on the money, on the button. 2 *an accurate shot* =**well aimed**, on target, unerring, deadly, lethal, sure, true.

accusation ▸ noun =**allegation**, charge, claim, assertion, imputation.

accuse ▸ verb 1 *four people were accused of assault* =**charge with**, indict for, arraign for; *N. Amer.* impeach for. 2 *you accused the companies of causing job losses* =**blame for**, hold responsible for; condemn for, criticize for, denounce for; *informal* point the finger at.
–OPPOSITES absolve, exonerate.

accustom ▸ verb *I soon became accustomed to the heat* =**adapt**, adjust, acclimatize, habituate; become reconciled, get used to, come to terms with, learn to live with; *N. Amer.* acclimate.

accustomed ▸ adjective =**customary**, usual, normal, habitual, regular, routine; *literary* wonted.

ace ▸ adjective *(informal) an ace tennis player* =**excellent**, first-rate, first-class, marvellous, wonderful, magnificent, outstanding, superlative, formidable, virtuoso, expert, champion, consummate; *informal* great, terrific, tremendous, su-

perb, fantastic, sensational, fabulous, fab, crack, hotshot, A1, mean, demon, awesome, magic, tip-top, top-notch; *Brit. informal* smashing, brilliant, brill.
–OPPOSITES mediocre.

acerbic ▸ adjective =**sharp**, sarcastic, sardonic, mordant, trenchant, cutting, razor-edged, biting, stinging, searing, scathing, caustic; *N. Amer. informal* snarky.

ache ▸ noun 1 *a stomach ache* =**pain**, cramp, twinge, pang; gnawing, stabbing, stinging, smarting; soreness, tenderness, irritation, discomfort. 2 *the ache in her heart* =**sorrow**, sadness, misery, grief, anguish, suffering, pain, agony, torture, hurt.
▸ verb *my legs were aching* =**hurt**, be sore, be painful, be in pain, throb, pound; smart, burn, sting; *informal* give someone gyp; *Brit. informal* play up.

achieve ▸ verb =**attain**, reach; realize, bring off/about, pull off, accomplish, carry out/through, fulfil, complete; earn, win, gain, acquire, obtain, come by, get, secure, clinch, net; *informal* wrap up, wangle, swing.

achievement ▸ noun 1 *the achievement of a high rate of economic growth* =**attainment**, realization, accomplishment, fulfilment, implementation, completion. 2 *they were proud of their achievement* =**accomplishment**, feat, act, action, deed, effort, exploit; work, handiwork.

Achilles heel ▸ noun =**weak spot**, weak point, weakness, shortcoming, failing, imperfection, flaw, defect, chink in one's armour.
–OPPOSITES strength.

aching ▸ adjective =**painful**, sore, stiff, tender, uncomfortable; in pain, throbbing, pounding, smarting, burning, stinging.

acid ▸ adjective 1 *a slightly acid flavour* =**acidic**, sour, tart, sharp, acerbic, vinegary. 2 *acid remarks* =**acerbic**, sarcastic, sharp, sardonic, scathing, cutting, biting, stinging, caustic, trenchant, mordant, astringent, harsh, vitriolic, waspish; *N. Amer.* acerb; *informal* bitchy, catty.
–OPPOSITES alkali, sweet, pleasant.

acknowledge ▸ verb 1 *the government acknowledged the need to begin talks* =**admit**, accept, grant, allow, concede, confess, own, recognize. 2 *he did not acknowledge Colin* =**greet**, salute, address;

nod to, wave to, say hello to. 3 *few people acknowledged my letters* =**answer**, reply to, respond to.
–OPPOSITES reject, deny, ignore.

acknowledged ▸ adjective =**recognized**, accepted, confirmed, declared.

acknowledgement ▸ noun 1 *acknowledgement of the need to change* =**acceptance**, admission, recognition. 2 *a smile of acknowledgement* =**greeting**, welcome, salutation. 3 *she left without a word of acknowledgement* =**thanks**, gratitude, appreciation, recognition. 4 *I sent off the form, but there was no acknowledgement* =**answer**, reply, response.

acme ▸ noun =**peak**, pinnacle, zenith, height, high point, crown, crest, summit, top, apex, apogee.
–OPPOSITES nadir.

acolyte ▸ noun =**assistant**, helper, attendant; follower, disciple, supporter; *informal* groupie, hanger-on.

acquaint ▸ verb =**familiarize**, make familiar, make aware of, inform of, advise of, apprise of, get up to date; *informal* fill in on, gen up on, clue in on.

acquaintance ▸ noun 1 *a business acquaintance* =**contact**, associate, colleague. 2 *my acquaintance with George* =**association**, relationship, contact. 3 *the pupils had little acquaintance with the language* =**familiarity with**, knowledge of, experience of, awareness of, understanding of, comprehension of, grasp of.

acquainted ▸ adjective =**familiar**, conversant, at home, up to date, abreast, au fait, versed, knowledgeable, (well) informed; apprised; *informal* genned up, clued in; *formal* cognizant.

acquiesce ▸ verb *he acquiesced in the cover-up* =**accept**, consent to, agree to, allow, assent to, concur with, go along with, give the nod to.

acquiescence ▸ noun =**consent**, agreement, acceptance, concurrence, assent.

acquiescent ▸ adjective =**compliant**, willing, obliging, amenable, unprotesting, docile.

acquire ▸ verb =**obtain**, come by, get, receive, gain, earn, win, come into; buy, purchase, procure, secure, pick up; *informal* get one's hands on, get hold of, land, bag, score.
–OPPOSITES lose.

acquisition ▸ noun **1** *a new acquisition* =**purchase**, addition, investment, possession; *informal* buy. **2** *the acquisition of funds* =**obtaining**, gaining, earning, winning, procurement, collection.

acquisitive ▸ adjective =**greedy**, avaricious, grasping, grabbing, predatory, rapacious, mercenary, materialistic; *informal* money-grubbing.

acquisitiveness ▸ noun =**greed**, greediness, avarice, rapaciousness, rapacity, materialism.

acquit ▸ verb **1** *the jury acquitted her* =**clear**, exonerate, find innocent, absolve; discharge, release, free, set free; *informal* let off (the hook). **2** *the boys acquitted themselves well* =**behave**, conduct oneself, perform, act.
−OPPOSITES convict.

acquittal ▸ noun =**clearing**, exoneration; discharge, release, freeing; *informal* letting off.
−OPPOSITES conviction.

acrid ▸ adjective =**pungent**, bitter, sharp, harsh; stinging, burning.

acrimonious ▸ adjective =**bitter**, angry, rancorous, harsh, vicious, nasty, bad-tempered, ill-natured.

acrimony ▸ noun =**bitterness**, anger, rancour, resentment, ill feeling, bad blood, animosity, antagonism.
−OPPOSITES goodwill.

act ▸ verb **1** *the Government must act to remedy the situation* =**take action**, take steps, take measures, move, react. **2** *he was acting on the orders of the party leader* =**follow**, obey, comply with; fulfil, discharge. **3** *Alison began to act oddly* =**behave**, conduct oneself, react. **4** *the scents act as a powerful aphrodisiac* =**operate**, work, function, serve. **5** *he acted in a highly successful film* =**perform**, play, take part, appear.
▸ noun **1** *acts of kindness | a criminal act* =**deed**, action, feat, exploit, gesture. **2** *the act will raise taxes* =**law**, decree, statute, bill, edict, ruling; *N. Amer. formal* ordinance. **3** *a comedy act* =**performance**, turn, routine, number, sketch. **4** *it was all an act* =**pretence**, show, front, facade, masquerade, charade, pose, sham; *informal* a put-on.

acting ▸ noun *the theory and practice of acting* =**drama**, the theatre, the stage, the performing arts, dramatics, stagecraft; *informal* treading the boards.
▸ adjective *the bank's acting governor* =**temporary**, interim, caretaker, pro tem, provisional, stopgap; deputy, stand-in; *N. Amer. informal* pinch-hitting.
−OPPOSITES permanent.

action ▸ noun **1** *there can be no excuse for their actions* =**deed**, act, undertaking, exploit, manoeuvre, endeavour, effort, exertion; behaviour, conduct, activity. **2** *the need for local action* =**measures**, steps, activism, campaigning; pressure. **3** *the action of hormones on the pancreas* =**effect**, influence, working; power. **4** *he missed all the action while he was away* =**excitement**, activity; *informal* goings-on. **5** *twenty-nine men died in action* =**battle**, combat, hostilities; fighting, active service. **6** *a civil action* =**lawsuit**, suit, case, prosecution, litigation, proceedings.

activate ▸ verb =**operate**, switch on, turn on, start (up), set going, trigger (off), set in motion, actuate, energize; trip.

active ▸ adjective **1** *despite her illness she remained active* =**busy**, mobile; *informal* on the go; full of beans. **2** *an active member of the union* =**hard-working**, industrious, tireless, keen, committed, devoted. **3** *the watermill was active until 1960* =**operative**, working, functioning, operating, operational, in action, in operation; live; *informal* (up and) running.
−OPPOSITES listless, passive.

activity ▸ noun **1** *there was a lot of activity in the area* =**bustle**, action, movement, life; *informal* toing and froing, comings and goings. **2** *a wide range of activities* =**pursuit**, occupation, interest, hobby, pastime, recreation, diversion; venture, undertaking, enterprise, project, scheme; act, action, deed, exploit.

actor, actress ▸ noun =**performer**, player, trouper, thespian; film star, star, starlet; *Brit. informal* luvvy.

> **WORD LINKS**
>
> *relating to actors:* **histrionic, theatrical, thespian**

actual ▸ adjective =**real**, true, genuine, authentic, verified, attested, confirmed, definite, hard; *informal* real live.
−OPPOSITES notional.

actually ▸ adverb *I looked upset but actually I was rather excited* =**really**, in (actual) fact, in point of fact, as a matter of fact, in reality, in actuality, in truth, if truth be told, to tell the truth.

acumen ▸ noun =**astuteness**, shrewd-ness, acuity, sharpness, smartness, brains; judgement, canniness, insight; *informal* nous, savvy, know-how; *N. Amer. informal* smarts; *formal* perspicuity.

acute ▸ adjective **1** *acute food shortages* =**severe**, dire, dreadful, terrible, awful, grave, serious, desperate. **2** *acute stomach pains* =**sharp**, severe, stabbing, excru-ciating, agonizing, racking, searing. **3** *his acute mind* =**astute**, shrewd, sharp, razor-sharp, quick, quick-witted, agile, nimble, intelligent, canny, discerning, perceptive, penetrating, insightful, incisive, piercing, discriminating; *N. Amer. informal* heads-up. **4** *an acute sense of smell* =**keen**, sharp, good, penetrating, discerning, sensitive; discriminating. −OPPOSITES mild, dull.

acutely ▸ adverb =**intensely**, very, severely, deeply, profoundly, keenly, painfully, thoroughly. −OPPOSITES slightly.

adage ▸ noun =**saying**, maxim, axiom, proverb, aphorism, saw, dictum, pre-cept, motto, truism, platitude, cliché, commonplace.

adamant ▸ adjective =**unshakeable**, immovable, unwavering, unswerving, resolute, resolved, determined, firm, steadfast; unrelenting, unyielding, un-bending, dead set.

adapt ▸ verb =**modify**, alter, change, adjust, convert, remodel, revamp, re-work, rejig, reorganize; customize, tailor; amend, refine; *informal* tweak.

adaptable ▸ adjective =**flexible**, ver-satile; accommodating.

adaptation ▸ noun =**adjustment**, alteration, modification, change.

add ▸ verb **1** *the front porch was added later* =**attach**, build on, join, connect; include, incorporate. **2** *they added all the figures up* =**total**, count (up), compute, reckon up, tally; *Brit.* tot up. **3** *the subsidies added up to £1700* =**amount to**, come to, run to, make, total, equal, number. **4** *her decision just added to his woe* =**increase**, magnify, amplify, augment, intensify, heighten, deepen; exacerbate, aggra-vate, compound, reinforce; add fuel to the fire, rub salt in the wound. −OPPOSITES subtract.

addendum ▸ noun =**appendix**, codi-cil, postscript, afterword, tailpiece, rider, coda, supplement; adjunct, ap-pendage, addition, add-on, attachment.

addict ▸ noun **1** *a heroin addict* =**abuser**, user; *informal* junkie, druggy, -freak, -head, pill-popper; *N. Amer. informal* hop-head. **2** *(informal) skiing addicts* =**enthu-siast**, fan, lover, devotee, aficionado, *informal* freak, nut, fiend, fanatic, maniac.

addicted ▸ adjective **1** *he was addicted to tranquillizers* =**dependent on**; *informal* hooked on. **2** *she became addicted to the theatre* =**devoted to**, obsessed with, fixated on, fanatical about, passionate about, a slave to; *informal* hooked on, mad on, crazy about.

addiction ▸ noun **1** *his heroin addiction* =**dependency**, dependence, habit; *infor-mal* monkey. **2** *a slavish addiction to fashion* =**devotion to**, dedication to, obsession with, infatuation with, passion for, love of, mania for, enslavement to.

addictive ▸ adjective =**habit-forming**; compulsive; *Brit. informal* moreish.

addition ▸ noun **1** *the soil is improved by the addition of compost* =**adding**, in-corporation, inclusion, introduction. **2** *an addition to the existing regulations* =**supplement**, adjunct, appendage; add-on, extra; rider. ■ **in addition 1** *conditions were harsh and in addition some soldiers fell victim to snipers* =**additionally**, as well, what's more, furthermore, moreover, also, into the bargain, to boot. **2** *eight presidential can-didates in addition to the General* =**besides**, as well as, on top of, plus, over and above.

additional ▸ adjective =**extra**, added, supplementary, supplemental, further; auxiliary, ancillary; more, other, an-other, new, fresh.

additionally ▸ adverb =**also**, in add-ition, as well, too, besides, on top (of that), moreover, further, furthermore, what's more, over and above that, into the bargain, to boot.

addled ▸ adjective =**muddled**, con-fused, muzzy, fuddled, befuddled, dazed, disoriented, disorientated, fuzzy; *informal* woozy.

address ▸ noun **1** *our officers called at the address* =**house**, flat, apartment, home; *formal* residence, dwelling, abode, domicile. **2** *his address to the European Par-liament* =**speech**, lecture, talk, presen-tation, dissertation; sermon. ▸ verb **1** *the preacher addressed a crowded congregation* =**talk to**, give a talk to, speak to, make a speech to, give a lecture to, lecture, hold forth to; preach to, give a sermon to. **2** *correspondence should be addressed to the Banking Ombudsman* =**direct**, send, communicate, convey. **3** *the minister failed to address the issue of subsidies* =**attend to**, apply oneself to, tackle, see to, deal with, confront, get to grips with, get down to, turn to, take in hand, concentrate on, focus on, devote oneself to.

adept ▸ adjective *an adept negotiator* =**expert**, proficient, accomplished, skilful, talented, masterly, consummate; adroit, dexterous, deft, artful.
−OPPOSITES inept.

▸ noun *kung fu adepts* =**expert**, master; maestro, doyen.
−OPPOSITES amateur.

adequacy ▸ noun **1** *the adequacy of the existing services* =**satisfactoriness**, acceptability; sufficiency. **2** *deep misgivings about his own adequacy* =**capability**, competence, ability; effectiveness, fitness; *formal* efficacy.

adequate ▸ adjective **1** *he lacked adequate financial resources* =**sufficient**, enough, requisite. **2** *the company provides an adequate service* =**acceptable**, passable, reasonable, satisfactory, tolerable, fair, decent, quite good, pretty good, goodish, moderate, unexceptional, unremarkable, undistinguished, ordinary, average, not bad, all right, middling; *informal* OK, so-so, fair-to-middling, nothing to write home about. **3** *the workstations were small but seemed adequate to the task* =**equal to**, up to, capable of, suitable for, able to do, fit for, sufficient for.

adhere ▸ verb **1** *a dollop of cream adhered to her nose* =**stick**, cling, bond, attach; be stuck, be fixed, be glued. **2** *they adhere scrupulously to Judaic law* =**abide by**, stick to, hold to, comply with, live/act in accordance with, conform to, submit to; follow, obey, heed, observe, respect, uphold, fulfil.
−OPPOSITES flout, ignore.

adherent ▸ noun =**follower**, supporter, upholder, defender, advocate, disciple, devotee, partisan, member; believer, worshipper.
−OPPOSITES opponent.

adhesion ▸ noun =**traction**, grip, purchase, hold.

adhesive ▸ noun =**glue**, fixative, gum, paste, cement; *N. Amer.* mucilage; *N. Amer.*

informal stickum.

▸ adjective =**sticky**, tacky, gluey, gummed; viscous; *technical* adherent; *informal* icky.

ad infinitum ▸ adverb =**forever**, for ever and ever, always, all the time, every time, endlessly; *Brit.* for evermore; *informal* until the cows come home.

adjacent ▸ adjective =**adjoining**, neighbouring, next-door, abutting, contiguous; (**adjacent to**) close to, near, next to, by, by the side of, bordering on, beside, alongside, attached to, touching, cheek by jowl with.

adjoin ▸ verb =**be next to**, be adjacent to, border (on), abut; join, connect with, touch, meet.

adjoining ▸ adjective =**connecting**, connected, interconnecting, adjacent, neighbouring, bordering, next-door; contiguous; attached, touching.

adjourn ▸ verb **1** *the hearing was adjourned* =**suspend**, break off, discontinue, interrupt, recess. **2** *sentencing was adjourned until June 9* =**postpone**, put off/back, defer, delay, hold over. **3** *they adjourned to the sitting room* =**withdraw**, retire, retreat; *formal* repair, remove.

adjournment ▸ noun =**suspension**, discontinuation, interruption, postponement, deferment, deferral, stay.

adjudicate ▸ verb =**judge**, try, hear, examine, arbitrate; pronounce on, give a ruling on, pass judgement on, decide, determine, settle, resolve.

adjudication ▸ noun =**judgement**, decision, pronouncement, ruling, settlement, resolution, arbitration, finding, verdict, sentence.

adjudicator ▸ noun =**judge**, arbitrator, arbiter; referee, umpire.

adjunct ▸ noun =**supplement**, addition, extra, add-on, accessory, accompaniment, complement; attachment, appendage, addendum.

adjust ▸ verb **1** *Kate had adjusted to her new life* =**adapt**, become accustomed, get used, accommodate, acclimatize, orient oneself, reconcile oneself, habituate oneself, assimilate; come to terms with, blend in with, fit in with; *N. Amer.* acclimate. **2** *he adjusted the brakes* =**modify**, alter, regulate, tune, fine-tune, balance; arrange, rearrange, change, rejig, rework, revamp, remodel, reshape, tailor, improve, enhance, customize; repair, fix, correct, rectify, overhaul, put right; *informal* tweak.

adjustable ▸ adjective =**alterable**, adaptable, modifiable, variable, multiway, versatile.

adjustment ▸ noun **1** *a period of adjustment* =**adaptation**, acclimatization, habituation, acculturation, naturalization, assimilation; *N. Amer.* acclimation. **2** *the car will run on unleaded petrol with no adjustment* =**modification**, alteration, adaptation, rearrangement, change, customization, refinement; repair, correction, amendment, overhaul, improvement.

ad-lib ▸ verb *she ad-libbed half the speech* =**improvise**, extemporize, speak impromptu, make it up as one goes along; *informal* busk it, wing it.
▸ adverb *she spoke ad lib* =**impromptu**, extempore, spontaneously, extemporaneously; *informal* off the cuff, off the top of one's head.
▸ adjective *a live, ad-lib commentary* =**impromptu**, extempore, extemporary, improvised, unprepared, unrehearsed, unscripted, spontaneous; *informal* off-the-cuff, spur-of-the-moment.

administer ▸ verb **1** *the union is administered by a central executive* =**manage**, direct, control, operate, regulate, coordinate, conduct, handle, run, organize, supervise, superintend, oversee, preside over, govern, rule, lead, head, steer; be in control of, be in charge of, be responsible for, be at the helm of; *informal* head up. **2** *the lifeboat crew administered first aid* =**dispense**, issue, give, provide, apply, offer, distribute, hand out, dole out. **3** *a gym shoe was used to administer punishment* =**inflict**, mete out, deal out, deliver.

administration ▸ noun **1** *the day-to-day administration of the company* =**management**, direction, control, command, charge, conduct, operation, running, leadership, coordination, government, governing, superintendence, supervision, regulation, overseeing. **2** *the previous Labour administration* =**government**, cabinet, regime, executive, authority, directorate, council, leadership, management; parliament, congress, senate; term of office, incumbency.

administrative ▸ adjective =**managerial**, management, directorial, executive, organizational, supervisory, regulatory.

administrator ▸ noun =**manager**, director, executive, controller, coordinator, head, chief, leader, governor, superintendent, supervisor; *informal* boss.

admirable ▸ adjective =**commendable**, praiseworthy, laudable, estimable, creditable, exemplary, honourable, worthy, deserving, respectable, worthwhile, good, sterling, fine.
–OPPOSITES deplorable.

admiration ▸ noun =**respect**, approval, approbation, appreciation, (high) regard, esteem; commendation, acclaim, applause, praise, compliments, tributes, accolades, plaudits.
–OPPOSITES scorn.

admire ▸ verb **1** *I admire your courage* =**respect**, approve of, esteem, think highly of, rate highly, hold in high regard, applaud, praise, commend. **2** *Simon had admired her for a long time* =**adore**, love, worship, dote on, be enamoured of, be infatuated with; be taken with, be attracted to; *informal* carry a torch for, have a thing about.
–OPPOSITES despise.

admirer ▸ noun =**fan**, devotee, enthusiast, aficionado; supporter, adherent, follower, disciple.

admissible ▸ adjective =**valid**, allowable, allowed, permissible, permitted, acceptable, tenable, sound; legitimate; *informal* OK, legit, kosher, pukka.

admission ▸ noun **1** *membership entitles you to free admission* =**admittance**, entry, entrance, right of entry, access, right of access. **2** *admission is fifty pence* =**entrance fee**, entry charge, ticket. **3** *a written admission of liability* =**confession**, acknowledgement, acceptance, concession, disclosure, divulgence.

admit ▸ verb **1** *he was admitted as a scholar to Winchester College* =**accept**, take on, receive, right of entry, enlist, register, sign up. **2** *Paul admitted that he was angry* =**confess**, acknowledge, own, concede, grant, accept, allow; reveal, disclose, divulge. **3** *he admitted three offences of reckless driving* =**confess (to)**, plead guilty to, own up to.
–OPPOSITES exclude, deny.

admittance ▸ noun =**entry**, right of entry, admission, entrance, access, right of access.
–OPPOSITES exclusion.

admonish ▶ verb =**reprimand**, rebuke, scold, reprove, reproach, upbraid, chastise, chide, berate, criticize, take to task, pull up, read the Riot Act to, haul over the coals; *informal* tell off, dress down, bawl out, rap over the knuckles, give someone hell; *Brit. informal* tick off, give someone a rocket, have a go at, carpet, tear someone off a strip; *N. Amer. informal* chew out; *formal* castigate.

adolescence ▶ noun =**teenage years**, teens, youth; pubescence, puberty.

adolescent ▶ noun *an awkward adolescent* =**teenager**, youngster, young person, youth, boy, girl; juvenile, minor; *informal* teen, teeny-bopper.
▶ adjective **1** *an adolescent boy* =**teenage**, pubescent, young; juvenile; *informal* teen. **2** *adolescent silliness* =**immature**, childish, juvenile, infantile, puerile.
–OPPOSITES adult, mature.

adopt ▶ verb **1** *they adopted local customs* =**embrace**, take on/up, espouse, assume, follow. **2** *the people adopted it as their mascot* =**choose**, select, pick, vote for, elect, decide on, opt for.
–OPPOSITES abandon.

adorable ▶ adjective =**lovable**, appealing, charming, cute, sweet, enchanting, bewitching, captivating, engaging, endearing, dear, delightful, lovely, beautiful, attractive, gorgeous, winsome, winning, fetching; *Scottish & N. English* bonny.
–OPPOSITES hateful.

adoration ▶ noun =**love**, devotion, care, fondness; admiration, awe, idolization, worship, hero-worship, adulation.

adore ▶ verb **1** *he adored his mother* =**love dearly**, love, be devoted to, dote on, hold dear, cherish, treasure, prize, think the world of; admire, hold in high regard, look up to, idolize, worship; *informal* put on a pedestal. **2** *(informal) I adore oysters* =**love**, be very fond of, be very keen on, be partial to, have a weakness for; *informal* be wild/crazy/nuts about, have a thing about, be hooked on, go a bundle on.
–OPPOSITES hate.

adorn ▶ verb =**decorate**, embellish, ornament, enhance; beautify, prettify, grace, bedeck, deck (out), dress (up), trim, swathe, wreathe, festoon, garland, array, emblazon.

–OPPOSITES disfigure.

adornment ▶ noun =**decoration**, embellishment, ornamentation, ornament, enhancement; beautification, prettification; frills, accessories, trimmings, finishing touches.

adrift ▶ adjective **1** *(Brit. informal) the pipe of my breathing apparatus came adrift* =**loose**, free; detached, unsecured, unfastened, untied, unknotted, undone. **2** *he was adrift in a strange country* =**lost**, off course; disorientated, disoriented, confused, (all) at sea; drifting, rootless, unsettled.

adroit ▶ adjective =**skilful**, adept, dexterous, deft, nimble, able, capable, skilled, expert, masterly, masterful, practised, polished, slick, proficient, accomplished, gifted, talented; quick-witted, quick-thinking, clever, smart, sharp, cunning, wily, resourceful, astute, shrewd, canny; *informal* nifty.
–OPPOSITES inept, clumsy.

adroitness ▶ noun =**skill**, skilfulness, prowess, expertise, adeptness, dexterity, deftness, nimbleness, ability, capability, mastery, proficiency, accomplishment, artistry, art, facility, aptitude, flair, finesse, talent; quick-wittedness, cleverness, sharpness, cunning, astuteness, shrewdness, resourcefulness, savoir faire; *informal* know-how, savvy.

adulation ▶ noun =**hero-worship**, worship, idolization, adoration, admiration, veneration, awe, devotion, glorification, praise, flattery.

adult ▶ adjective **1** *an adult woman* =**mature**, grown-up, fully grown, fullgrown, fully developed, of age. **2** *an adult movie* =**(sexually) explicit**, pornographic, obscene, smutty, dirty, rude, erotic, sexy; *informal* porn, porno, naughty, blue, X-rated, skin.

adulterate ▶ verb =**dilute**, spoil, taint, contaminate, water down, weaken; *informal* cut.
–OPPOSITES purify.

adulterer ▶ noun =**womanizer**, philanderer, ladies' man, Don Juan, Casanova, Lothario; *informal* cheat, two-timer, love rat; *formal* fornicator.

adulterous ▶ adjective =**unfaithful**, disloyal, deceiving, deceitful; extramarital; *informal* cheating, two-timing.
–OPPOSITES faithful.

adultery ▸ noun =infidelity, unfaithfulness; affair, liaison, amour; *informal* carryings-on, hanky-panky, a bit on the side, playing around; *formal* fornication.
–OPPOSITES fidelity.

advance ▸ verb 1 *the battalion advanced rapidly* =move forward, proceed, press on, push on, push forward, make progress, make headway, gain ground, approach, come closer, draw nearer, near. 2 *the move advanced his career* =promote, further, forward, help, aid, assist, boost, strengthen, improve, benefit; fuel, foster. 3 *technology has advanced in the last few years* =progress, make progress, make headway, develop, evolve, make strides, move forward (in leaps and bounds), move ahead; improve, thrive, flourish, prosper. 4 *a relative advanced him some money* =lend, loan, put up, come up with; *Brit. informal* sub.
–OPPOSITES retreat, hinder, postpone, retract, borrow.
▸ noun 1 *the advance of the aggressors* =progress, (forward) movement; approach. 2 *a significant medical advance* =breakthrough, development, step forward, (quantum) leap; find, discovery, invention.
▸ adjective 1 *an advance party of settlers* =preliminary, first, exploratory; pilot, test, trial. 2 *advance warning* =early, prior.
■ **in advance** =beforehand, before, ahead of time, earlier, previously; in readiness.

advanced ▸ adjective 1 *advanced manufacturing techniques* =state-of-the-art, new, modern, up to date, up to the minute, the newest, cutting edge, the latest; pioneering, innovative, sophisticated. 2 *advanced further-education courses* =higher-level, higher, tertiary.
–OPPOSITES primitive.

advancement ▸ noun *opportunities for advancement* =promotion, (career) development, upgrading, a step up the ladder, progress, improvement, betterment, growth.

advantage ▸ noun 1 *the advantage of belonging to a union* =benefit, value, good/strong point, asset, plus, bonus, boon, blessing, virtue; attraction, beauty; convenience, profit. 2 *they appeared to be gaining the advantage* =upper hand, edge, lead, whip hand; superiority, dominance, ascendancy, supremacy, power, mastery. 3 *there is no advan-*
tage to be gained from delaying the process =benefit, profit, gain, good; *informal* mileage.
–OPPOSITES disadvantage, drawback, detriment.

advantageous ▸ adjective 1 *an advantageous position* =superior, dominant, powerful; good, fortunate, lucky, favourable. 2 *the arrangement is advantageous to both sides* =beneficial, of benefit, helpful, of assistance, useful, of use, of value, profitable, fruitful; convenient, in everyone's interests.
–OPPOSITES disadvantageous, detrimental.

advent ▸ noun =arrival, appearance, emergence, dawn, birth, rise, development; approach, coming.
–OPPOSITES disappearance.

adventure ▸ noun 1 *her recent adventures in Italy* =exploit, escapade, deed, feat, experience; stunt. 2 *they set off in search of adventure* =excitement, thrills, stimulation; risk, danger, hazard, peril, uncertainty, precariousness.

adventurer ▸ noun =daredevil, hero, heroine; swashbuckler; entrepreneur; *informal* adrenalin junkie.

adventurous ▸ adjective 1 *an adventurous traveller* =daring, intrepid, bold, fearless, brave; *informal* gutsy, spunky. 2 *adventurous activities* =risky, dangerous, perilous, hazardous, precarious, uncertain; exciting, thrilling.
–OPPOSITES cautious.

adversary ▸ noun =opponent, rival, enemy, antagonist, combatant, challenger, contender, competitor; opposition, competition; *literary* foe.
–OPPOSITES ally, supporter.

adverse ▸ adjective 1 *adverse weather conditions* =unfavourable, inclement; bad, poor, untoward. 2 *the drug's adverse side effects* =harmful, dangerous, injurious, detrimental, hurtful, deleterious. 3 *an adverse response from the public* =hostile, unfavourable, antagonistic, unfriendly, negative.
–OPPOSITES favourable, auspicious, beneficial.

adversity ▸ noun =misfortune, ill luck, bad luck, trouble, difficulty, hardship, distress, disaster, suffering, sorrow, misery, tribulation, woe, pain, trauma; mishap, misadventure, accident, upset, setback, crisis, catastrophe, tragedy, calamity; trial, burden, blow, vicissitude; hard times, trials and tribulations.

advertise ▶ verb =**publicize**, make public, make known, announce, broadcast, proclaim, trumpet, call attention to, bill; promote, market, beat/bang the drum for, trail; *informal* push, plug, hype, boost; *N. Amer. informal* ballyhoo, flack.

advertisement ▶ noun =**notice**, announcement, bulletin; commercial, promotion, blurb, write-up; poster, leaflet, pamphlet, flyer, handbill, handout, circular, brochure, sign, placard; *informal* ad, push, plug, puff; *Brit. informal* advert.

advice ▶ noun =**guidance**, counselling, counsel, help, direction; information, recommendations, guidelines, suggestions, hints, tips, pointers, ideas.

advisable ▶ adjective =**wise**, desirable, preferable, well, best, sensible, prudent, proper, appropriate, apt, suitable, fitting; expedient, politic, advantageous, beneficial, profitable, in one's (best) interests.

advise ▶ verb **1** *her grandmother advised her about marriage* =**counsel**, give guidance, guide, offer suggestions, give hints/tips/pointers. **2** *he advised caution* =**advocate**, recommend, suggest, urge. **3** *you will be advised of our decision* =**inform**, notify, give notice, apprise, warn; acquaint with, make familiar with, make known to; *informal* fill in on.

adviser ▶ noun =**counsellor**, mentor, guide, consultant, confidant, confidante; coach, teacher, tutor, guru.

advocacy ▶ noun =**support**, backing, promotion, championing; recommendation; *N. Amer.* boosterism.

advocate ▶ noun =**champion**, upholder, supporter, backer, promoter, proponent, exponent, spokesman, spokeswoman, spokesperson, campaigner, lobbyist, fighter, crusader; propagandist, apostle, apologist; *N. Amer.* booster.
–OPPOSITES critic.
▶ verb =**recommend**, prescribe, advise, urge; support, back, favour, uphold, subscribe to; champion, campaign for, speak for, argue for, lobby for, promote.

aesthetic ▶ adjective =**artistic**, tasteful, in good taste, pleasing.

affable ▶ adjective =**friendly**, amiable, genial, congenial, cordial, warm, pleasant, nice, likeable, personable, charming, agreeable, sympathetic, good-humoured, good-natured, kindly, kind, approachable, accessible, amenable, sociable, outgoing, gregarious, clubbable, neighbourly, welcoming, hospitable, obliging; *Scottish* couthy.
–OPPOSITES unfriendly.

affair ▶ noun **1** *what you do is your affair* =**business**, concern, matter, responsibility, province, preserve; problem, worry; *Brit. informal* lookout. **2** (**affairs**) *his financial affairs* =**transactions**, concerns, matters, activities, dealings, undertakings, ventures, business. **3** *the board admitted responsibility for the affair* =**event**, incident, episode; case, matter, business. **4** *his affair with Anthea was over* =**relationship**, romance, fling, dalliance, liaison, involvement, intrigue, amour; *informal* hanky-panky; *Brit. informal* carry-on.

affect[1] ▶ verb **1** *this development may have affected the judge's decision* =**have an effect on**, influence, act on, work on, have an impact on; change, alter, modify, transform, form, shape, sway, bias. **2** *he was visibly affected by the experience* =**move**, touch, make an impression on, hit (hard); **upset**, trouble, distress, disturb, agitate, shake (up). **3** *the disease affected his lungs* =**attack**, infect; hit, strike.

affect[2] ▶ verb *he affected an air of innocence* =**assume**, take on, adopt, feign.

affectation ▶ noun **1** *George had always abhorred affectation* =**pretension**, pretentiousness, affectedness, artificiality, posturing, posing; airs (and graces); *Brit. informal* side. **2** *an affectation of calm* =**facade**, front, show, appearance, pretence.

affected ▶ adjective =**pretentious**, artificial, contrived, unnatural, stagy, studied, mannered, ostentatious; insincere, unconvincing, feigned, false, fake, sham; *informal* phoney.
–OPPOSITES natural, unpretentious, genuine.

affecting ▶ adjective =**touching**, moving, emotional; stirring, heart-warming; poignant, pitiful, piteous, tear-jerking, heart-rending, heartbreaking, disturbing, distressing, upsetting, haunting.

affection ▶ noun =**fondness**, love, liking, tenderness, warmth, devotion, endearment, care, caring, attachment, friendship.

affectionate ▶ adjective =loving, fond, adoring, devoted, caring, doting, tender, warm, warm-hearted, soft-hearted, friendly; demonstrative; *informal* touchy-feely, lovey-dovey.
–OPPOSITES cold.

affiliate ▶ verb =associate with, unite with, combine with, join (up) with, join forces with, link up with, ally with, align with, amalgamate with, merge with; incorporate into.

affiliated ▶ adjective =associated, allied, related, connected, linked; in league, in partnership.

affiliation ▶ noun =association, connection, alliance, alignment, link, attachment, tie, relationship, fellowship, partnership, coalition, union; amalgamation, incorporation, integration.

affinity ▶ noun =empathy, rapport, sympathy, accord, harmony, relationship, bond, closeness, understanding; liking, fondness; *informal* chemistry.
–OPPOSITES aversion, dislike, dissimilarity.

affirm ▶ verb =declare, state, assert, proclaim, pronounce, attest, swear, avow, guarantee, pledge; *formal* aver.
–OPPOSITES deny.

affirmation ▶ noun =declaration, statement, assertion, proclamation, pronouncement, attestation; oath, avowal, guarantee, pledge; deposition.
–OPPOSITES denial.

affirmative ▶ adjective *an affirmative answer* =positive, assenting, consenting, favourable.
–OPPOSITES negative
▶ noun *she took his grunt as an affirmative* =agreement, acceptance, assent, acquiescence, yes; *informal* OK.
–OPPOSITES disagreement.

affix ▶ verb =stick, glue, paste, gum; attach, fasten, fix; clip, tack, pin; tape.
–OPPOSITES detach.

afflict ▶ verb =trouble, burden, distress, beset, harass, worry, oppress; torment, plague, blight, bedevil, rack, curse.

affliction ▶ noun 1 *a herb reputed to cure a variety of afflictions* =disorder, disease, malady, complaint, ailment, illness, handicap; scourge, plague, trouble. 2 *he bore his affliction with great dignity* =suffering, distress, pain, trouble, misery, hardship, misfortune, adversity, sorrow, torment, tribulation, woe.

affluence ▶ noun =wealth, prosperity, fortune; riches, money, resources, assets, possessions, property, substance, means.
–OPPOSITES poverty.

affluent ▶ adjective =wealthy, rich, prosperous, well off, moneyed, well-to-do; propertied, substantial, of means, of substance; *informal* well heeled, rolling in it, made of money, filthy rich, stinking rich, loaded, worth a packet.
–OPPOSITES poor, impoverished.

afford ▶ verb 1 *I can't afford a new car* =pay for; run to, stretch to, manage. 2 *it took more time than he could afford* =spare, allow (oneself). 3 *the rooftop terrace affords beautiful views* =provide, supply, furnish, offer, give, yield.

affront ▶ noun *an affront to public morality* =insult, offence, slight, snub, put-down, provocation, injury; outrage, atrocity, scandal; *informal* slap in the face, kick in the teeth.
▶ verb *she was affronted by his familiarity* =insult, offend, provoke, pique, wound, hurt; put out, irk, displease, bother, rankle, vex, gall; outrage, scandalize; *informal* put someone's back up, needle.

aficionado ▶ noun =connoisseur, expert, authority, specialist, pundit; enthusiast, devotee; *informal* buff, freak, nut, fiend, maniac, fanatic, addict.

afloat ▶ adverb & adjective =buoyant, floating, buoyed up, on/above the surface, (keeping one's head) above water.

afoot ▶ adjective & adverb =in preparation, on the way, brewing, looming, in the offing, in the air/wind, on the horizon; going on, happening, in progress; *informal* on the cards.

afraid ▶ adjective 1 *they ran away because they were afraid* =frightened, scared, terrified, fearful, petrified, shaking in one's shoes, shaking like a leaf; intimidated, alarmed; faint-hearted, cowardly; *informal* scared stiff, in a (blue) funk, in a cold sweat; *N. Amer. informal* spooked. 2 *don't be afraid to ask awkward questions* =reluctant, hesitant, unwilling, slow, chary, shy.
–OPPOSITES brave, confident.

> **WORD LINKS**
> *afraid of ...:* -**phobic**
> *person who is afraid of ...:* -**phobe**

afresh ▶ adverb =anew, again.

after ■ **after all** =most importantly, above all, beyond everything, ultimately; *informal* when all's said and done, at the end of the day, when push comes to shove.

after-effect ▸ noun =repercussion, aftermath, consequence.

aftermath ▸ noun =repercussions, after-effects, consequences, results, fruits.

afterwards ▸ adverb =later, later on, subsequently, then, next, after this/that; at a later time/date, in due course.

again ▸ adverb **1** *her spirits lifted again* =once more, another time, afresh, anew. **2** *this can add half as much again to the price* =extra, in addition, additionally, on top. **3** *again, evidence was not always consistent* =also, furthermore; moreover, besides.
■ **again and again** =repeatedly, over and over (again), time and (time) again, many times, many a time; often, frequently, continually, constantly.

against ▸ preposition **1** *a number of delegates were against the motion* =opposed to, in opposition to, hostile to, averse to, antagonistic towards, unsympathetic to, resistant to, at odds with, in disagreement with, dead set against; *informal* anti, agin. **2** *his age is against him* =disadvantageous to, unfavourable to, damaging to, detrimental to, prejudicial to, deleterious to, harmful to, injurious to, a drawback for. **3** *she leaned against the wall* =touching, in contact with, up against, on.
–OPPOSITES in favour of, pro.

┌─────────────────┐
│ **WORD LINKS** │
│ *related prefix:* **anti-** │
└─────────────────┘

age ▸ noun **1** *her hearing had deteriorated with age* =elderliness, old age, oldness, seniority, maturity; one's advancing/advanced/declining years. **2** *the Elizabethan age* =era, epoch, period, time. **3** *(informal) you haven't been in touch with me for ages* =a long time, days/months/years, an eternity; *informal* ages and ages, donkey's years, a month of Sundays; *Brit. informal* yonks.
▸ verb *Cabernet Sauvignon ages well | the experience has aged her* =mature, mellow, ripen; grow/become/make old, wear out.

agency ▸ noun =business, organiza-

tion, company, firm, office, bureau.

agenda ▸ noun =list, schedule, programme, timetable, line-up, plan.

agent ▸ noun **1** *the sale was arranged through an agent* =representative, emissary, envoy, go-between, proxy, negotiator, intermediary, broker, spokesperson, spokesman, spokeswoman; *informal* rep. **2** *a travel agent* =agency, business, organization, company, firm, bureau. **3** *a CIA agent* =spy, secret agent, undercover agent, operative, mole; *N. Amer. informal* spook, G-man.

agglomeration ▸ noun =collection, mass, cluster, lump, clump, pile, heap; accumulation, build-up; miscellany, jumble, hotchpotch.

aggravate ▸ verb **1** *the new law could aggravate the situation* =worsen, make worse, exacerbate, inflame, compound; add fuel to the fire/flames, add insult to injury, rub salt in the wound. **2** *(informal) you don't have to aggravate people to get what you want* =annoy, irritate, exasperate, put out, nettle, provoke, antagonize, get on someone's nerves, ruffle (someone's feathers), try someone's patience; *Brit.* rub up the wrong way; *informal* needle, bug, hack off, get someone's goat, get under someone's skin, get up someone's nose; *Brit. informal* wind up, nark, get at, get on someone's wick; *N. Amer. informal* tick off.
–OPPOSITES alleviate, improve.

aggravation ▸ noun *(informal)* =nuisance, annoyance, irritation, hassle, trouble, difficulty, inconvenience, bother; *informal* aggro.

aggregate ▸ noun **1** *an aggregate of rock and mineral fragments* =collection, mass, agglomeration; mixture, mix, combination, blend; compound, alloy, amalgam. **2** *he won with an aggregate of 325* =total, sum, grand total.
▸ adjective *an aggregate score* =total, combined, gross, overall, composite.

aggression ▸ noun **1** *an act of aggression* =hostility, belligerence, force, violence. **2** *he played with unceasing aggression* =confidence, self-confidence, boldness, determination, forcefulness, vigour, energy, dynamism, zeal, commitment.

aggressive ▸ adjective **1** *aggressive and disruptive behaviour* =violent, confrontational, antagonistic, truculent, pugnacious, macho; quarrelsome, argumentative. **2** *aggressive foreign policy*

=**warmongering**, warlike, warring, belligerent, bellicose, hawkish, militaristic; expansionist; *informal* gung-ho. **3** *an aggressive promotional drive* =**assertive**, forceful, vigorous, energetic, dynamic, strong; bold, audacious; *informal* in-your-face, feisty.
−OPPOSITES peaceable, peaceful.

aggressor ▸ noun =**attacker**, assaulter, assailant; invader.

aggrieved ▸ adjective =**resentful**, affronted, indignant, disgruntled, discontented, upset, offended, piqued, riled, nettled, vexed, irked, irritated, annoyed, put out; *informal* peeved, miffed, in a huff; *Brit. informal* cheesed off; *N. Amer. informal* sore, steamed.
−OPPOSITES pleased.

aghast ▸ adjective =**horrified**, appalled, dismayed, thunderstruck, stunned, shocked, staggered; *informal* flabbergasted; *Brit. informal* gobsmacked.

agile ▸ adjective **1** *she was as agile as a monkey* =**nimble**, lithe, supple, acrobatic. **2** *an agile mind* =**alert**, sharp, acute, shrewd, astute, perceptive, quick.
−OPPOSITES clumsy, stiff.

agitate ▸ verb **1** *any mention of Clare agitates my grandmother* =**upset**, perturb, fluster, ruffle, disconcert, unnerve, disquiet, disturb, distress, unsettle; *informal* rattle, faze; *N. Amer. informal* discombobulate. **2** *she agitated for the appointment of more women* =**campaign**, push, press, lobby; demonstrate, protest. **3** *agitate the water to disperse the oil* =**stir**, whisk, beat, shake.

agitated ▸ adjective =**upset**, perturbed, flustered, disconcerted, unnerved, disquieted, disturbed, distressed, unsettled; *informal* rattled, fazed, in a dither, in a flap, in a state, in a lather, jittery, in a tizz/tizzy; *Brit. informal* having kittens, in a (flat) spin; *N. Amer. informal* discombobulated.
−OPPOSITES calm, relaxed.

agitation ▸ noun =**anxiety**, disquiet, distress, concern, alarm, worry.

agitator ▸ noun =**troublemaker**, rabble-rouser, agent provocateur, demagogue; insurgent, subversive; *informal* stirrer.

agnostic ▸ noun =**sceptic**, doubter, doubting Thomas.
−OPPOSITES believer, theist.

agonize ▸ verb =**worry**, fret, fuss, brood, wrestle with oneself, be worried/anxious; *informal* stew.

agonizing ▸ adjective =**excruciating**, harrowing, racking, searing, torturous, tormenting, piercing; *informal* hellish, killing.

agony ▸ noun =**torment**, torture, anguish, affliction, trauma.

agree ▸ verb **1** *I agree with you* =**concur**, see eye to eye, be in sympathy, be united, be as one, be unanimous. **2** *they agreed to a ceasefire* =**consent**, assent, acquiesce, accept, approve, say yes, give one's approval, give the nod; *formal* accede. **3** *the plan and the drawing do not agree with each other* =**match (up)**, correspond, conform, coincide, fit, tally, be in harmony/agreement, be consistent; *informal* square. **4** *they agreed on a price* =**settle**, decide, arrive at, negotiate, come to terms, strike a bargain, make a deal, shake hands.
−OPPOSITES differ, contradict, reject.

agreeable ▸ adjective **1** *an agreeable atmosphere of rural tranquillity* =**pleasant**, pleasing, enjoyable, pleasurable, nice, appealing, relaxing, friendly. **2** *an agreeable fellow* =**likeable**, amiable, affable, pleasant, nice, friendly, good-natured, sociable, genial, congenial. **3** *we should get together for a talk, if you're agreeable* =**willing**, amenable, in agreement.
−OPPOSITES unpleasant.

agreement ▸ noun **1** *all heads nodded in agreement* =**accord**, concurrence, consensus; assent, acceptance, consent, acquiescence. **2** *an agreement on imports* =**contract**, compact, treaty, covenant, pact, accord. **3** *there is some agreement between my view and that of the author* =**correspondence**, consistency, compatibility, accord; similarity, resemblance, likeness.
−OPPOSITES discord.

agricultural ▸ adjective =**farm**, farming, agrarian; rural, rustic, pastoral, countryside.
−OPPOSITES urban.

agriculture ▸ noun =**farming**, cultivation, husbandry; agribusiness, agronomy.

> WORD LINKS
>
> *relating to agriculture:* **agrarian, agri-, agro-**

aid ▸ noun **1** *with the aid of his colleagues* =**assistance**, support, help, backing, cooperation. **2** *humanitarian aid* =**relief**,

assistance, support, subsidy, funding, donations, grants; *historical* alms.
–OPPOSITES hindrance.

▶ verb **1** *he provided an army to aid the King of England* =**help**, assist, support, relieve, back (up). **2** *herbal remedies can aid restful sleep* =**facilitate**, promote, encourage, help, further, boost.
–OPPOSITES hinder.

aide ▶ noun =**assistant**, helper, adviser, right-hand man/woman, man/girl Friday, adjutant, deputy, second (in command); lieutenant; *N. Amer.* cohort.

ailing ▶ adjective **1** *the country's ailing economy* =**failing**, weak, poor, tottering, fragile. **2** *his ailing mother* =**(chronically) ill**, sick, sickly, poorly, weak, in poor/bad health, infirm.
–OPPOSITES healthy.

ailment ▶ noun =**illness**, disease, disorder, affliction, malady, complaint, infirmity; *informal* bug, virus.

aim ▶ verb **1** *he aimed the rifle* =**point**, direct, train, sight, line up. **2** *she aimed at the target* =**take aim**, fix on, zero in on, draw a bead on. **3** *undergraduates aiming for a first degree* =**work towards**, be after, set one's sights on, try for, strive for, aspire to; *formal* essay. **4** *this system is aimed at the home entertainment market* =**target**, intend, direct, design, tailor, market, pitch. **5** *we aim to give you the best possible service* =**intend**, mean; plan, resolve, propose.

▶ noun *our aim is to develop gymnasts to the top level* =**objective**, object, goal, end, target, design, desire, intention, intent, plan, purpose, object of the exercise; ambition, aspiration, wish, dream, hope.

aimless ▶ adjective =**purposeless**, directionless, undirected, random.
–OPPOSITES purposeful.

air ▶ noun **1** *hundreds of birds hovered in the air* =**sky**, atmosphere, airspace; ether; *literary* heavens. **2** *open the windows to get some air* =**breeze**, draught, wind; gust/puff of wind. **3** *an air of defiance* =**look**, appearance, impression, aspect, aura, mien, manner, bearing, tone; feel, ambience, atmosphere; *informal* vibe. **4** *a traditional Scottish air* =**tune**, melody, song.

▶ verb **1** *a chance to air your views* =**express**, voice, make public, articulate, state, declare, give expression/voice to; have one's say. **2** *the windows were opened to*

air the room =**ventilate**, freshen, refresh, cool. **3** *the film was aired nationwide* =**broadcast**, transmit, screen, show, televise.

WORD LINKS

relating to air: **aerial, aero-**
study of moving air: **aerodynamics**

airborne ▶ adjective =**flying**, in flight, in the air, on the wing, up, aloft.

aircraft ▶ noun

WORD LINKS

science of aircraft flight: **aeronautics**

airily ▶ adverb =**lightly**, breezily, flippantly, casually, nonchalantly, heedlessly.
–OPPOSITES seriously.

airing ▶ noun **1** *they went to the park for an airing* =**stroll**, walk, turn, amble, promenade; *dated* constitutional. **2** *the airing of different views* =**expression**, voicing, venting, articulating, stating, declaration, communication. **3** *I hope the BBC gives the play another airing* =**broadcast**, transmission, screening, showing, televising.

airless ▶ adjective =**stuffy**, close, stifling, suffocating, oppressive; unventilated.
–OPPOSITES airy.

airtight ▶ adjective **1** *an airtight container* =**sealed**, hermetically sealed. **2** *an airtight alibi* =**indisputable**, cast-iron, solid, incontrovertible, incontestable, irrefutable, watertight.

airy ▶ adjective **1** *the conservatory is light and airy* =**well ventilated**, fresh; spacious, uncluttered; light, bright. **2** *an airy gesture* =**nonchalant**, casual, breezy, flippant, dismissive, insouciant. **3** *airy clouds* =**delicate**, soft, fine, feathery, insubstantial.
–OPPOSITES stuffy.

aisle ▶ noun =**passage**, passageway, gangway, walkway.

akin ▶ adjective =**similar**, related, close, near, comparable, equivalent; connected, alike, analogous.
–OPPOSITES unlike.

alacrity ▶ noun =**eagerness**, willingness, readiness; enthusiasm, keenness; promptness, haste, swiftness, dispatch, speed.

alarm ▶ noun **1** *the girl spun round in alarm* =**fear**, anxiety, apprehension,

nervousness, unease, distress, agitation, consternation, disquiet, fright, panic. **2** *a smoke alarm* =**detector**, sensor; **siren**, signal, bell.
−OPPOSITES calmness, composure.

▶ verb *the news had alarmed her* =**frighten**, scare, panic, unnerve, distress, agitate, upset, disconcert, shock, dismay, disturb; *informal* rattle, spook; *Brit. informal* put the wind up.

alarming ▶ adjective =**frightening**, unnerving, shocking; distressing, upsetting, disconcerting, disturbing; *informal* scary.
−OPPOSITES reassuring.

alcohol ▶ noun =**(intoxicating) liquor**, (strong/alcoholic) drink, spirits; *informal* booze, hooch, the hard stuff, firewater, rotgut, moonshine, grog, the demon drink, the bottle; *Brit. informal* gut-rot; *N. Amer. informal* juice; *technical* ethyl alcohol, ethanol.

WORD LINKS

addiction to alcohol: **alcoholism, dipsomania**
refusal to drink alcohol: **temperance, teetotalism**

alcoholic ▶ adjective =**intoxicating**, inebriating, containing alcohol; strong, hard, stiff.
▶ noun =**dipsomaniac**, drunk, drunkard, heavy/hard/serious drinker, problem drinker, alcohol-abuser; inebriate; *informal* boozer, lush, alky, dipso, soak, wino, barfly; *Austral./NZ informal* hophead.

alcove ▶ noun =**recess**, niche, nook, inglenook, bay.

alert ▶ adjective **1** *police have asked neighbours to keep alert* =**vigilant**, watchful, attentive, observant, wide awake; on the lookout, on one's guard/toes; *informal* keeping one's eyes open/peeled. **2** *mentally alert* =**quick-witted**, sharp, bright, quick, keen, perceptive, on one's toes; *informal* on the ball, quick on the uptake, all there, with it.
−OPPOSITES inattentive.
▶ noun **1** *a state of alert* =**vigilance**, watchfulness, attentiveness, alertness. **2** *a flood alert* =**warning**, notification, notice; siren, alarm, signal.
▶ verb *police were alerted by a phone call* =**warn**, notify, apprise, forewarn, put on one's guard; *informal* tip off.

alias ▶ noun *he is known under several aliases* =**assumed name**, false name,

pseudonym, sobriquet; pen/stage name, nom de plume/guerre.
▶ adverb *Cassius Clay, alias Muhammad Ali* =**also known as**, aka.

alien ▶ adjective **1** *alien cultures* =**foreign**, overseas, non-native. **2** *an alien landscape* =**unfamiliar**, unknown, strange, peculiar; exotic, foreign. **3** *a vicious role alien to his nature* =**incompatible**, opposed, conflicting, contrary, in conflict, at variance. **4** *alien beings* =**extraterrestrial**, unearthly.
−OPPOSITES native, familiar, earthly.
▶ noun **1** *an illegal alien* =**foreigner**, non-native, immigrant, émigré, incomer. **2** *the alien's spaceship crashed* =**extraterrestrial**, ET; *informal* little green man.

alienate ▶ verb =**estrange**, distance, isolate, cut off; set against, turn away, drive apart, set at variance/odds, drive a wedge between.

alienation ▶ noun =**isolation**, detachment, estrangement, separation.

alight[1] ▶ verb **1** *he alighted from the train* =**get off**, step off, disembark, pile out. **2** *a swallow alighted on a branch* =**land**, come to rest, settle, perch.
−OPPOSITES get on, board.

alight[2] ▶ adjective *the stable was alight* =**burning**, ablaze, on fire, in flames, blazing.

align ▶ verb **1** *the desks are aligned with the wall* =**line up**, arrange, position, set, site; coordinate. **2** *he aligned himself with the workers* =**ally**, affiliate, associate, identify, join, side, join forces, team up, band together, throw in one's lot.

alike ▶ adjective *all the doors looked alike* =**similar**, (much) the same, indistinguishable, identical, uniform, interchangeable, cut from the same cloth, like (two) peas in a pod; *informal* much of a muchness.
−OPPOSITES different.
▶ adverb *great minds think alike* =**similarly**, (just) the same, in the same way/manner/fashion, identically.

alive ▶ adjective **1** *the synagogue has kept the Jewish faith alive* =**active**, in existence, functioning, in operation; on the map. **2** *teachers need to be alive to their pupils' needs* =**alert**, awake, aware, conscious, mindful, heedful, sensitive, familiar; *formal* cognizant. **3** *the place was alive with mice* =**teeming**, swarming, overrun, crawling, bristling, infested; crowded, packed.

−OPPOSITES dead, inanimate, inactive, lethargic.

all ▶ determiner **1** *all the children went* =**each of**, every (single), each and every. **2** *the sun shone all week* =**the whole of the**, every bit of the, the complete, the entire.
−OPPOSITES no, none of.
▶ pronoun **1** *all of the cups were broken* =**each one**, the whole lot. **2** *they took all of it* =**everything**, every part, the (whole) lot, the entirety.
−OPPOSITES none, nothing.
▶ adverb *he was dressed all in black* =**completely**, fully, entirely, totally, wholly, utterly.
−OPPOSITES partly.

WORD LINKS
relating to all ...: **omni-, pan-, panto-**

allay ▶ verb =**reduce**, diminish, decrease, lessen, assuage, alleviate, ease, relieve, soothe, soften, calm.
−OPPOSITES increase, intensify.

allegation ▶ noun =**claim**, assertion, charge, accusation, contention.

allege ▶ verb =**claim**, assert, charge, accuse, contend.

alleged ▶ adjective =**supposed**, so-called, claimed, professed, purported, ostensible, putative, unproven.

allegedly ▶ adverb =**reportedly**, supposedly, reputedly, purportedly, ostensibly, apparently, so the story goes.

allegiance ▶ noun =**loyalty**, faithfulness, fidelity, obedience, adherence, devotion.
−OPPOSITES disloyalty, treachery.

allegorical ▶ adjective =**symbolic**, metaphorical, figurative, representative, emblematic.

allegory ▶ noun =**parable**, analogy, metaphor, symbol, emblem.

alleviate ▶ verb =**reduce**, ease, relieve, take the edge off, deaden, dull, diminish, lessen, weaken, lighten, allay, assuage, palliate, damp, soothe, help, soften.
−OPPOSITES aggravate.

alley ▶ noun =**passage**, passageway, alleyway, back alley, backstreet, lane, path, pathway, walk.

alliance ▶ noun =**association**, union, league, confederation, federation, confederacy, coalition, consortium, affiliation, partnership.

allied ▶ adjective *agriculture and allied industries* =**associated**, related, connected, interconnected, linked; similar, equivalent.
−OPPOSITES independent, unrelated.

all-important ▶ adjective =**vital**, essential, indispensable, crucial, key, critical, life-and-death, paramount, pre-eminent, high-priority; urgent, pressing, burning.
−OPPOSITES inessential.

allocate ▶ verb =**allot**, assign, distribute, apportion, share out, portion out, deal out, dole out, give out, dish out, parcel out, ration out, divide out/up; *informal* divvy up.

allocation ▶ noun **1** *the efficient allocation of resources* =**allotment**, assignment, distribution, sharing out, handing out, dealing out, doling out, giving out, dishing out, dividing out/up; *informal* divvying up. **2** *our annual allocation of funds* =**allowance**, allotment, quota, share, ration, grant, slice; *informal* cut; *Brit. informal* whack.

allot ▶ verb =**allocate**, assign, apportion, distribute, issue, grant; earmark, designate, set aside; hand out, deal out, dish out, dole out, give out; *informal* divvy up.

all out ▶ adverb *I'm working all out to finish it* =**as hard as one can**, round the clock, seven/eight days a week, at full throttle, with all one's might (and main); desperately, frantically; *informal* like a madman/lunatic, like mad/crazy, 24-7; *Brit. informal* like billy-o, flat out.
−OPPOSITES lackadaisically.
▶ adjective *an all-out attack* =**full**, total, unequivocal, full-blooded; *informal* full-on, all or nothing, make or break.
−OPPOSITES half-hearted.

allow ▶ verb **1** *the police allowed him to go home* =**permit**, let, authorize, give permission/authorization/leave, grant someone the right, license, entitle; consent, assent, give one's consent/assent/blessing, give the nod, acquiesce, agree, approve; *informal* give the go-ahead, give the thumbs up, OK, give the green light; *formal* accede. **2** *allow an hour or so for driving* =**set aside**, allocate, allot, earmark, designate, assign.
−OPPOSITES prevent, forbid.

allowable ▶ adjective *the maximum allowable number of users* =**permissible**, permitted, allowed, admissible, accept-

LONGLEY PARK SIXTH FORM COLLEGE
HORNINGLOW ROAD
SHEFFIELD

able, legal, lawful, authorized, sanctioned, approved; *informal* OK, legit.
–OPPOSITES forbidden.

allowance ▸ noun **1** *your baggage allowance* =**allocation**, allotment, quota, share, ration, grant, limit. **2** *her father gave her an allowance* =**payment**, pocket money, contribution, grant, subsidy, maintenance.
■ **make allowance(s) for 1** *you must make allowances for delays* =**take into consideration**, take into account, bear in mind, provide for, plan for, cater for, allow for, make provision for, be prepared for. **2** *she always made allowances for him* =**excuse**, make excuses for, forgive, indulge; overlook.

alloy ▸ noun =**mixture**, mix, amalgam, fusion, blend, compound, combination, composite, union; *technical* admixture.

all-powerful ▸ adjective =**omnipotent**, almighty, supreme, absolute, pre-eminent.
–OPPOSITES powerless.

all right ▸ adjective **1** *the tea was all right* =**satisfactory**, acceptable, adequate, passable, reasonable; *informal* so-so, OK. **2** *are you all right?* =**unhurt**, uninjured, unharmed, in one piece, safe (and sound); well, fine, alive and well; *informal* OK. **3** *it's all right for you to go now* =**permissible**, permitted, allowed, acceptable, legal, lawful, authorized, approved, in order; safe; *informal* OK, legit, cool.
–OPPOSITES unsatisfactory, hurt, forbidden.
▸ adverb *the system works all right* =**satisfactorily**, adequately, fairly well, passably, acceptably, reasonably; *informal* OK; well, fine.

allude ▸ verb =**refer**, touch on, suggest, hint, imply, mention (in passing).

allure ▸ noun =**attraction**, lure, draw, pull, appeal, enticement, temptation, charm, seduction, fascination.
▸ verb =**attract**, lure, entice, tempt, captivate, draw, win over, charm, seduce, fascinate, whet the appetite of, make someone's mouth water.
–OPPOSITES repel.

alluring ▸ adjective =**enticing**, tempting, attractive, appealing, inviting, captivating, seductive; enchanting, charming, fascinating.

allusion ▸ noun =**reference**, mention, suggestion, hint, comment, remark.

ally ▸ noun *close political allies* =**associate**, colleague, friend, confederate, partner, supporter.
–OPPOSITES enemy, opponent.
▸ verb **1** *he allied his racing experience with business acumen* =**combine**, marry, couple, merge, amalgamate, join, fuse. **2** *the Catholic powers allied with Philip II* =**unite**, combine, join (up), join forces, band together, team up, collaborate, side, align oneself, form an alliance, throw in one's lot.
–OPPOSITES split.

almighty ▸ adjective **1** *I swear by almighty God* =**all-powerful**, omnipotent, supreme. **2** *(informal) an almighty explosion.* See BIG sense 1.

almost ▸ adverb =**nearly**, (just) about, more or less, practically, virtually, all but, as good as, close to, not quite, not far from/off, to all intents and purposes, quasi-; approaching, bordering on, verging on; *informal* pretty nearly/much/well; *literary* well-nigh, nigh on.

aloft ▸ adjective & adverb **1** *he hoisted the Cup aloft* =**upwards**, up, high, into the air/sky, skyward, heavenward. **2** *the airships stayed aloft for many hours* =**in the air**, in the sky, high up, up (above), on high, overhead.
–OPPOSITES down.

alone ▸ adjective & adverb **1** *she was alone in the house* =**by oneself**, on one's own, all alone, solitary, single, singly, solo; unescorted, companionless; *Brit. informal* on one's tod, on one's lonesome, on one's Jack Jones; *Austral./NZ informal* on one's Pat Malone. **2** *he managed alone* =**unaided**, unassisted, without help/assistance, single-handedly, solo, on one's own. **3** *she felt terribly alone* =**lonely**, isolated, deserted, abandoned, friendless. **4** *a house standing alone* =**apart**, by itself/oneself, separate. **5** *you alone can inspire me* =**only**, solely, just; and no one else, and nothing else, no one but, nothing but.
–OPPOSITES in company, with help, among others.

aloof ▸ adjective =**distant**, detached, unfriendly, remote, unapproachable, formal, stiff, austere, withdrawn, reserved, unforthcoming, uncommunicative; *informal* stand-offish.
–OPPOSITES familiar, friendly.

also ▸ adverb =**too**, as well, besides, in addition, additionally, furthermore,

a

further, moreover, into the bargain, on top (of that), what's more, to boot, equally; *informal* and all; *archaic* withal.

alter ▸ verb **1** *Eliot was persuaded to alter the passage* =**change**, make changes to, adjust, make adjustments to, adapt, amend, modify, revise, revamp, rework, redo, refine; *informal* tweak. **2** *the situation has altered* =**change**, become different, undergo a (sea) change, evolve, move on.
−OPPOSITES preserve, stay the same.

alteration ▸ noun =**change**, adjustment, adaptation, modification, variation, revision, amendment; rearrangement, reordering, restyling, rejigging, reworking, revamping; sea change, transformation; *humorous* transmogrification.

altercation ▸ noun =**argument**, quarrel, squabble, fight, shouting match, disagreement, difference of opinion, falling-out, dispute, wrangle, war of words; *informal* tiff, run-in, slanging match, spat, scrap; *Brit. informal* row, barney, ding-dong, bust-up; *N. Amer. informal* rhubarb.

alternate ▸ verb **1** *rows of trees alternate with dense shrub* =**be interspersed**, follow one another; take turns, take it in turns. **2** *we could alternate the two groups* =**rotate**; swap, exchange, interchange.
▸ adjective **1** *she attended on alternate days* =**every other**, every second. **2** *(N. Amer.) an alternate plan*. See ALTERNATIVE adjective sense 1.

alternative ▸ adjective **1** *an alternative route* =**different**, other, another, second, substitute, replacement; standby, emergency, reserve, backup, auxiliary, fallback; *N. Amer.* alternate. **2** *an alternative lifestyle* =**unorthodox**, unconventional, non-standard, unusual, out of the ordinary; radical, revolutionary, nonconformist, avant-garde; *informal* offbeat, way-out.
▸ noun *we have no alternative* =**option**, choice; substitute, replacement.

altitude ▸ noun =**height**, elevation; distance.

> **WORD LINKS**
>
> *measurement of altitude:* **altimetry**, **hypsometry**

altogether ▸ adverb **1** *he wasn't altogether happy* =**completely**, totally, entirely, absolutely, wholly, fully, thor-

oughly, utterly, perfectly, one hundred per cent, in all respects. **2** *we have five offices altogether* =**in all**, all told, in total.

altruism ▸ noun =**unselfishness**, selflessness, compassion, kindness, public-spiritedness; philanthropy, humanitarianism.
−OPPOSITES selfishness.

always ▸ adverb **1** *he's always late* =**every time**, each time, all the time, without fail, consistently, invariably, regularly, habitually, unfailingly. **2** *she's always complaining* =**continually**, continuously, constantly, forever; all the time, day and night, seven days a week; *informal* 24-7. **3** *the place will always be dear to me* =**forever**, for always, for good (and all), for evermore, for ever and ever, until the end of time, eternally; *informal* for keeps, until the cows come home.
−OPPOSITES never, seldom, sometimes.

amalgamate ▸ verb =**combine**, merge, unite, fuse, blend, meld; join (together), join forces, band (together), link (up), team up, go into partnership.
−OPPOSITES separate.

amalgamation ▸ noun =**combination**, union, blend, mixture, fusion, synthesis, composite, amalgam.

amass ▸ verb =**gather**, collect, assemble; accumulate, stockpile, store (up), accrue, lay in/up, garner; *informal* stash (away).
−OPPOSITES dissipate.

amateur ▸ noun **1** *the crew were all amateurs* =**non-professional**, non-specialist, layman, layperson; dilettante. **2** *what a bunch of amateurs* =**incompetent**, bungler; *Brit. informal* bodger, cowboy, clown.
−OPPOSITES professional, expert.
▸ adjective =**non-professional**, non-specialist, lay; dilettante.

amateurish ▸ adjective =**incompetent**, inept, inexpert, amateur, clumsy, maladroit, bumbling; *Brit. informal* bodged.

amaze ▸ verb =**astonish**, astound, surprise, stun, stagger, nonplus, shock, startle, stupefy, stop someone in their tracks, leave open-mouthed, leave aghast, take someone's breath away, dumbfound; *informal* bowl over, flabbergast; *Brit. informal* knock for six; **(amazed)** thunderstruck, at a loss for words, speechless; *Brit. informal* gobsmacked.

amazement ▸ noun =**astonishment**,

surprise, shock, stupefaction, incredulity, disbelief, speechlessness, awe, wonder, wonderment.

amazing ▶ adjective =**astonishing**, astounding, surprising, stunning, staggering, stupefying, breathtaking; awesome, awe-inspiring, sensational, remarkable, spectacular, stupendous, phenomenal, extraordinary, incredible, unbelievable; *informal* mind-blowing; *literary* wondrous.

ambassador ▶ noun =**envoy**, emissary, representative, diplomat.

ambience ▶ noun =**atmosphere**, air, aura, climate, mood, feel, feeling, vibrations, character, quality, impression, flavour, look, tone; *informal* vibe(s).

ambiguity ▶ noun =**ambivalence**, equivocation; vagueness.

ambiguous ▶ adjective =**equivocal**, ambivalent, unclear, vague, doubtful, dubious, uncertain.
–OPPOSITES clear.

ambition ▶ noun 1 *young people with ambition* =**drive**, determination, enterprise, initiative, eagerness, motivation, a sense of purpose; *informal* get-up-and-go. 2 *her ambition was to become a model* =**aspiration**, intention, goal, aim, objective, object, purpose, intent, plan, desire, wish, target, dream.

ambitious ▶ adjective 1 *an energetic and ambitious politician* =**aspiring**, determined, enterprising, motivated, energetic, committed, purposeful, power-hungry; *informal* go-ahead, go-getting. 2 *an ambitious task* =**challenging**, exacting, demanding, formidable, difficult, hard, tough.
–OPPOSITES laid-back.

ambivalent ▶ adjective =**equivocal**, uncertain, unsure, doubtful, indecisive, inconclusive, in two minds, undecided, torn, in a dilemma, in a quandary, on the fence, hesitating, wavering, vacillating, equivocating, blowing hot and cold; *informal* iffy.
–OPPOSITES unequivocal, certain.

amble ▶ verb =**stroll**, saunter, wander, promenade, walk, take a walk; *informal* mosey, tootle; *Brit. informal* toddle, mooch.

ambush ▶ verb =**surprise**, waylay, attack, jump on, pounce on; *N. Amer.* bushwhack.

amenable ▶ adjective 1 *an amenable child* =**compliant**, biddable, manageable, responsive, reasonable, easy. 2 *many cancers are amenable to treatment* =**susceptible**, receptive, responsive.
–OPPOSITES uncooperative.

amend ▶ verb =**revise**, alter, change, modify, qualify, adapt, adjust; edit, rewrite, redraft, rephrase, reword, rework, revamp.

amends ■ **make amends** =**compensate**, recompense, indemnify; atone for, make up for, make good, expiate.

amenity ▶ noun =**facility**, service, convenience, resource.

America ▶ noun. *See* UNITED STATES OF AMERICA.

amiable ▶ adjective =**friendly**, affable, amicable, cordial; warm, warm-hearted, good-natured, nice, pleasant, agreeable, likeable, genial, good-humoured, easy to get on/along with, companionable, personable; *informal* chummy; *Brit. informal* matey; *N. Amer. informal* regular.
–OPPOSITES unfriendly, disagreeable.

amicable ▶ adjective =**friendly**, good-natured, cordial, easy, neighbourly, harmonious, cooperative, civilized.
–OPPOSITES unfriendly.

amnesty ▶ noun *an amnesty for political prisoners* =**pardon**, reprieve; release, discharge; *informal* let-off.

amok ■ **run amok** =**go berserk**, rampage, riot, run riot, go on the rampage; *informal* raise hell.

amoral ▶ adjective =**unprincipled**, without standards/morals/scruples, unethical; mercenary.
–OPPOSITES principled.

amorous ▶ adjective =**lustful**, sexual, erotic, amatory, ardent, passionate, impassioned; in love, enamoured, love-sick; *informal* lovey-dovey, kissy, smoochy, goo-goo, hot; *Brit. informal* randy.
–OPPOSITES unloving.

amorphous ▶ adjective =**shapeless**, formless, structureless, indeterminate.
–OPPOSITES shaped, definite.

amount ▶ noun =**quantity**, number, total, aggregate, sum, quota, group, size, mass, weight, volume.
■ **amount to** 1 *the bill amounted to £50* =**add up to**, come to, run to, be, total; *Brit.* tot up to. 2 *the delays amounted to maladministration* =**constitute**, comprise, be tantamount, come down,

boil down; signify, signal, indicate, suggest, denote, point to, be evidence, be symptomatic; *literary* betoken.

ample ▸ adjective **1** *there is ample time for discussion* =**enough**, sufficient, adequate, plenty of, more than enough. **2** *an ample supply of wine* =**plentiful**, abundant, copious, profuse, lavish, liberal, generous, bountiful; *informal* a gogo, galore; *literary* plenteous. **3** *his ample tunic* =**spacious**, capacious, roomy; voluminous, loose-fitting, baggy, sloppy.
–OPPOSITES insufficient, meagre.

amplify ▸ verb **1** *many frogs amplify their voices* =**make louder**, louden, turn up, increase, boost, step up, raise. **2** *these notes amplify our statement* =**expand**, enlarge on, elaborate on, develop, flesh out, explain in more detail.
–OPPOSITES reduce, quieten.

amputate ▸ verb =**cut off**, (surgically) remove, saw/chop off, take off.

amulet ▸ noun =**(lucky) charm**, talisman, fetish, mascot, totem.

amuse ▸ verb **1** *her annoyance simply amused him* =**make laugh**, entertain, delight, divert, cheer (up), please, charm, tickle; *informal* crack up; *Brit. informal* crease up. **2** *he amused himself by writing poetry* =**occupy**, engage, busy, absorb, engross, hold someone's attention; interest, entertain, divert.
–OPPOSITES bore.

amusement ▸ noun **1** *we looked with amusement at the cartoon* =**mirth**, merriment, hilarity, glee, delight; enjoyment, pleasure. **2** *I read the book for amusement* =**entertainment**, pleasure, leisure, relaxation, fun, enjoyment, interest; *informal* R & R; *N. Amer. informal* rec. **3** *a wide range of amusements* =**activity**, entertainment, diversion; game, sport.

amusing ▸ adjective =**entertaining**, funny, comical, humorous, lighthearted, jocular, witty, droll, diverting; *informal* rib-tickling.
–OPPOSITES boring, solemn.

anaemic ▸ adjective =**colourless**, bloodless, pale, pallid, wan, ashen, grey, sallow, pasty(-faced), sickly.

analogous ▸ adjective =**comparable**, parallel, similar, like, corresponding, related, equivalent.
–OPPOSITES unrelated.

analogy ▸ noun =**similarity**, parallel, correspondence, likeness, resemblance, correlation, relation, comparison.

–OPPOSITES dissimilarity.

analyse ▸ verb =**examine**, inspect, survey, study, scrutinize; investigate, probe, research, go over (with a fine-tooth comb), review, evaluate, break down, dissect.

analysis ▸ noun =**examination**, investigation, inspection, survey, study, scrutiny; exploration, probe, research, dissection.

analytical, analytic ▸ adjective =**systematic**, logical, scientific, methodical, (well) organized, ordered, orderly, meticulous, rigorous.
–OPPOSITES unsystematic.

anarchic ▸ adjective =**lawless**, unruly, chaotic, turbulent.
–OPPOSITES ordered.

anarchist ▸ noun =**troublemaker**, nihilist, anti-capitalist, agitator, subversive, insurrectionist.

anarchy ▸ noun =**lawlessness**, nihilism, mobocracy, disorder, chaos, tumult.
–OPPOSITES government, order.

anathema ▸ noun =**abhorrent**, hateful, repugnant, repellent, offensive; an abomination, an outrage, someone's bugbear, someone's bête noire.

anatomy ▸ noun =**structure**, make-up, composition, constitution, form, body, physique.

ancestor ▸ noun **1** *he could trace his ancestors back to King James I* =**forebear**, forefather, predecessor, antecedent, progenitor. **2** *the instrument is an ancestor of the lute* =**forerunner**, precursor, predecessor.
–OPPOSITES descendant, successor.

ancestral ▸ adjective =**inherited**, hereditary, familial.

ancestry ▸ noun =**ancestors**, forebears, forefathers, progenitors, antecedents; family tree; lineage, genealogy, roots, blood.

anchor ▸ noun **1** *the anchor of the new coalition* =**mainstay**, cornerstone, linchpin, bulwark, foundation. **2** *a CBS news anchor* =**presenter**, announcer, anchorman, anchorwoman.
▸ verb **1** *the ship was anchored in the bay* =**moor**, berth, be at anchor. **2** *the fish anchors itself to the coral* =**secure**, fasten, attach, fix.

ancient ▸ adjective **1** *ancient civilizations* =**early**, prehistoric, primeval, primor-

dial, primitive. **2** *an ancient custom* =**old**, age-old, archaic, antediluvian, time-worn, time-honoured. **3** *I feel positively ancient* =**antiquated**, decrepit, antediluvian, geriatric; *informal* out of the ark; *Brit. informal* past its/one's sell-by date.
–OPPOSITES recent, contemporary.

> WORD LINKS
>
> *relating to ancient times:* **archaeo-, palaeo-**

ancillary ▸ adjective =**additional**, auxiliary, supporting, helping, extra, supplementary, accessory.

anecdotal ▸ adjective =**unscientific**, unreliable, based on hearsay/rumour, unofficial.

anecdote ▸ noun =**story**, tale, narrative; urban myth; *informal* yarn.

angel ▸ noun *(informal) she's an angel* =**saint**, gem, treasure, darling, dear; *informal* star; *Brit. informal, dated* brick.
–OPPOSITES devil.

angelic ▸ adjective =**innocent**, pure, virtuous, saintly, cherubic.

anger ▸ noun =**annoyance**, vexation, exasperation, irritation, irritability, indignation; rage, fury, wrath, outrage, ill temper/humour.
–OPPOSITES pleasure, good humour.
▸ verb =**annoy**, irritate, exasperate, irk, vex, put out; enrage, incense, infuriate; aggravate, get someone, rile, hack off.
–OPPOSITES pacify, placate.

angle ▸ noun **1** *the wall is sloping at an angle of 33°* =**gradient**, slant, inclination. **2** *consider the problem from a different angle* =**perspective**, point of view, viewpoint, standpoint, position, aspect, slant, direction, approach, tack.
▸ verb *Anna angled her camera upwards* =**tilt**, slant, direct, turn, twist, swivel, lean, tip.

> WORD LINKS
>
> *measurement of angles:* **goniometry**

angry ▸ adjective **1** *Vivienne got angry* =**annoyed**, irate, cross, vexed, irritated, indignant, irked; furious, enraged, infuriated, in a temper, fuming, seething, outraged; *informal* (hopping) mad, hot under the collar, up in arms, foaming at the mouth, steamed up, in a lather/paddy; *Brit. informal* aerated, shirty; *N. Amer. informal* sore, bent out of shape, teed off,

ticked off; *Austral./NZ informal* ropeable, snaky; *literary* wrathful. **2** *an angry debate* =**heated**, passionate, stormy, lively, full and frank; bad-tempered, ill-tempered, acrimonious, bitter. **3** *angry sores* =**inflamed**, red, swollen, sore, painful.
–OPPOSITES pleased, good-humoured.
■ **get angry** =**lose one's temper**, go into a rage, go berserk, flare up; *informal* go mad/crazy/wild, go bananas, hit the roof, go through the roof, go up the wall, see red, go off the deep end, fly off the handle, blow one's top, blow a fuse/gasket, lose one's rag, flip (one's lid), have a fit, foam at the mouth, explode, go ballistic; *Brit. informal* go spare, do one's nut; *N. Amer. informal* flip one's wig, blow one's lid/stack.

angst ▸ noun =**anxiety**, fear, worry, trepidation, malaise, disquiet, unease, anguish.

anguish ▸ noun =**agony**, pain, torment, torture, suffering, distress, angst, misery, sorrow, grief, heartache.
–OPPOSITES happiness.

anguished ▸ adjective =**agonized**, tormented, tortured; grief-stricken, wretched, heartbroken, devastated.

angular ▸ adjective **1** *an angular shape* =**sharp**, pointed, pointy. **2** *an angular face* =**bony**, lean, rangy, spare, thin, gaunt.
–OPPOSITES rounded, curving.

animal ▸ noun **1** *endangered animals* =**creature**, beast, (living) thing; (**animals**) wildlife, fauna; *N. Amer. informal* critter. **2** *the man was an animal* =**beast**, brute, monster, devil, demon, fiend; *informal* swine, bastard, pig.
▸ adjective *animal passion* =**carnal**, fleshly, bodily, physical; brutish, animalistic.

> WORD LINKS
>
> *relating to animals:* **faunal, zoological, zoo-**
> *study of animals:* **zoology**
> *branch of medicine to do with animals:* **veterinary medicine**

animate ▸ verb =**enliven**, energize, invigorate, revive, liven up; inspire, thrill, excite, fire, rouse; *N. Amer.* light a fire under; *informal* buck up, pep up.
–OPPOSITES depress.
▸ adjective =**living**, alive, live, breathing; sentient, aware.
–OPPOSITES inanimate.

a

animated ▸ adjective =**lively**, spirited, high-spirited, energetic, full of life, excited, enthusiastic, eager, alive, vigorous, vibrant, vivacious, buoyant, exuberant, ebullient, effervescent, bouncy, bubbly, perky; *informal* bright-eyed and bushy-tailed, full of beans, bright and breezy, chirpy, chipper, peppy.
−OPPOSITES lethargic, lifeless.

animosity ▸ noun =**antipathy**, hostility, friction, antagonism, enmity, bitterness, rancour, resentment, dislike, ill feeling/will, bad blood, hatred, loathing.
−OPPOSITES goodwill, friendship.

annals ▸ plural noun =**records**, archives, chronicles.

annex ▸ verb =**take over**, appropriate, seize, conquer, occupy, invade.
▸ noun (also **annexe**) =**extension**, addition; wing; *N. Amer.* ell.

annexation ▸ noun =**seizure**, occupation, invasion, conquest, takeover, appropriation.

annihilate ▸ verb =**destroy**, wipe out, obliterate, wipe off the face of the earth; kill, slaughter, exterminate, eliminate, liquidate; *informal* take out, rub out, snuff out, waste, blow away.
−OPPOSITES create.

annotate ▸ verb =**comment on**, add notes/footnotes to, gloss, interpret.

announce ▸ verb **1** *the results were announced* =**make public**, make known, report, declare, state, give out, publicize, broadcast, publish, advertise, circulate, proclaim, release. **2** *Victor announced the guests* =**introduce**, present. **3** *strains of music announced her arrival* =**signal**, indicate, herald, proclaim; *literary* betoken.

announcement ▸ noun **1** *an announcement by the Minister* =**statement**, declaration, proclamation, pronouncement; bulletin, communiqué; *N. Amer.* advisory. **2** *the announcement of the decision* =**declaration**, notification, reporting, publishing, broadcasting.

announcer ▸ noun =**presenter**, anchorman, anchorwoman, anchor; newsreader, newscaster, broadcaster.

annoy ▸ verb =**irritate**, vex, make angry/cross, anger, exasperate, irk, gall, pique, put out, antagonize, get on someone's nerves, ruffle someone's feathers, make someone's hackles rise, nettle; *Brit.* rub up the wrong way; *informal* aggravate, peeve, hassle, miff, rile, needle, get (to), bug, hack off, get up someone's nose, get someone's goat, get someone's back up, give someone the hump, drive mad/crazy, drive round the bend/twist, drive up the wall, get someone's dander up; *Brit. informal* wind up, nark, get on someone's wick; *N. Amer. informal* tee off, tick off, burn up, rankle, gravel; *informal, dated* give someone the pip.
−OPPOSITES please, gratify.

annoyance ▸ noun **1** *much to his annoyance, Louise didn't even notice* =**irritation**, exasperation, vexation, indignation, anger, displeasure, chagrin. **2** *they found him an annoyance* =**nuisance**, pest, bother, irritant, inconvenience, thorn in one's flesh; *informal* pain (in the neck), drag; *N. Amer. informal* nudnik, burr in/under someone's saddle; *Austral./NZ informal* nark.

annoyed ▸ adjective =**irritated**, cross, angry, vexed, exasperated, irked, piqued, displeased, put out, disgruntled, nettled, in a bad mood, in a temper; *informal* aggravated, peeved, miffed, riled, hacked off, hot under the collar; *Brit. informal* narked, shirty; *N. Amer. informal* teed off, ticked off, sore, bent out of shape; *Austral./NZ informal* snaky, crook; *archaic* wroth.

annoying ▸ adjective =**irritating**, infuriating, exasperating, maddening, trying, tiresome, troublesome, bothersome, irksome, vexing, galling; *informal* aggravating.

annual ▸ adjective =**yearly**, once-a-year; year-long, twelve-month.

annually ▸ adverb =**yearly**, once a year, each year, per annum.

annul ▸ verb =**declare invalid**, declare null and void, nullify, invalidate, void; repeal, reverse, rescind, revoke.
−OPPOSITES restore, enact.

anodyne ▸ adjective =**bland**, inoffensive, innocuous, neutral, unobjectionable.

anomalous ▸ adjective =**abnormal**, atypical, irregular, aberrant, exceptional, freak, freakish, odd, bizarre, peculiar, unusual, out of the ordinary.
−OPPOSITES normal, typical.

anomaly ▸ noun =**oddity**, peculiarity, abnormality, irregularity, inconsistency, incongruity, aberration, quirk.

anonymous ▸ adjective **1** *an anonymous donor* =**unnamed**, nameless, unidentified, unknown. **2** *an anonymous letter* =**unsigned**, unattributed. **3** *an anonymous housing estate* =**characterless**, nondescript, impersonal, faceless; grey.
–OPPOSITES known, identified.

answer ▸ noun **1** *her answer was unequivocal* =**reply**, response, rejoinder, reaction; retort, riposte; *informal* comeback. **2** *a new filter is the answer* =**solution**, remedy, way out.
–OPPOSITES question.

▸ verb **1** *Steve was about to answer* =**reply**, respond; rejoin, retort, riposte. **2** *he has yet to answer the charges* =**rebut**, refute, defend oneself against. **3** *a man answering this description* =**match**, fit, correspond to.
■ **answer for** *he will answer for his crime* =**pay for**, be punished for, suffer for; make amends for, make reparation for, atone for.

answerable ▸ adjective =**accountable**, responsible, liable; subject.

ant ▸ noun

> WORD LINKS
>
> *relating to ants:* **formic**
> *study of ants:* **myrmecology**

antagonism ▸ noun =**hostility**, enmity, antipathy, opposition, dissension; bitterness, rancour, resentment, dislike, ill/bad feeling, ill will.
–OPPOSITES rapport, friendship.

antagonist ▸ noun =**adversary**, opponent, enemy, rival.
–OPPOSITES ally.

antagonistic ▸ adjective =**hostile**, against, (dead) set against, opposed, inimical, antipathetic, ill-disposed, resistant, in disagreement; *informal* anti.
–OPPOSITES pro.

antagonize ▸ verb =**arouse hostility in**, alienate; anger, annoy, provoke, vex, irritate; *Brit.* rub up the wrong way; *informal* aggravate, rile, needle, rattle someone's cage, get someone's back up, get someone's dander up; *Brit. informal* nark.
–OPPOSITES pacify, placate.

antediluvian ▸ adjective =**out of date**, outdated, outmoded, old-fashioned, antiquated, behind the times.

antelope ▸ noun

> WORD LINKS
>
> *male:* **buck**
> *female:* **doe**
> *young:* **calf**

anteroom ▸ noun =**antechamber**, vestibule, lobby, foyer.

anthem ▸ noun =**hymn**, song, chorale.

anthology ▸ noun =**collection**, selection, compendium, compilation, miscellany.

anticipate ▸ verb **1** *the police did not anticipate trouble* =**expect**, foresee, predict, be prepared for, bargain on, reckon on; *N. Amer. informal* figure on. **2** *warders can't always anticipate the actions of prisoners* =**pre-empt**, forestall, second-guess. **3** *her plays anticipated his film work* =**foreshadow**, precede, antedate, come/go before.

anticipation ▸ noun =**expectation**, excitement, suspense.
■ **in anticipation of** =**in the expectation of**, in preparation for, ready for.

anticlimax ▸ noun =**let-down**, bathos, disappointment, comedown, non-event; disillusionment; *Brit.* damp squib; *informal* washout.

antics ▸ plural noun =**capers**, pranks, larks, high jinks, skylarking; *Brit. informal* monkey tricks.

antidote ▸ noun *laughter is a good antidote to stress* =**remedy**, cure, solution; coping mechanism.

antipathetic ▸ adjective =**hostile**, against, (dead) set against, opposed, antagonistic, ill-disposed, unsympathetic; *informal* anti, down on.
–OPPOSITES pro.

antipathy ▸ noun =**hostility**, antagonism, animosity, aversion, enmity, dislike, distaste, hatred, abhorrence, loathing.
–OPPOSITES liking, affinity.

antiquated ▸ adjective =**outdated**, out of date, outmoded, outworn, behind the times, old-fashioned, anachronistic; *informal* out of the ark; *N. Amer. informal* horse-and-buggy, mossy, clunky.
–OPPOSITES modern, up to date.

antique ▸ noun =**collector's item**, period piece, bygone, antiquity, object of virtu.

▸ adjective **1** *antique furniture* =**old**, antiquarian, collectable. **2** *antique gods*

=**ancient**, of long ago. **3** *antique work practices. See* ANTIQUATED.
−OPPOSITES modern, state-of-the-art.

antiquity ▶ noun **1** *the civilizations of antiquity* =**long ago**, the past, prehistory, classical/ancient times. **2** *Islamic antiquities* =**antique**, artefact, treasure, object, collector's piece.

antisocial ▶ adjective **1** *antisocial behaviour* =**objectionable**, offensive, unacceptable, disruptive, rowdy. **2** *I'm feeling a bit antisocial* =**unsociable**, unfriendly, uncommunicative, reclusive.

antithesis ▶ noun =(**direct) opposite**, converse, reverse, inverse, obverse, the other side of the coin; *informal* the flip side.

antithetical ▶ adjective =(**directly) opposed**, contrasting, contrary, contradictory, conflicting, incompatible, irreconcilable, inconsistent, poles apart, at variance/odds.
−OPPOSITES identical, like.

anxiety ▶ noun =**worry**, concern, apprehension, apprehensiveness, uneasiness, unease, fearfulness, fear, disquiet, agitation, angst, nervousness, nerves, tenseness; *informal* butterflies (in one's stomach), jitteriness, twitchiness, collywobbles.
−OPPOSITES serenity.

anxious ▶ adjective **1** *I'm anxious about her* =**worried**, concerned, apprehensive, fearful, uneasy, perturbed, troubled, bothered, disturbed, distressed, fretful, agitated, nervous, edgy, unquiet, on edge, tense, worked up, keyed up, jumpy; *informal* uptight, with butterflies in one's stomach, jittery, twitchy, all of a dither, in a tizz/tizzy, het up; *Brit. informal* strung up, windy; *N. Amer. informal* antsy, spooky, squirrelly, in a twit; *Austral./NZ informal* toey. **2** *she was anxious for news* =**eager**, keen, desirous, impatient.
−OPPOSITES carefree, unconcerned.

anyhow ▶ adverb **1** *anyhow, it doesn't really matter* =**anyway**, in any case/event, at any rate; however, be that as it may; *N. Amer. informal* anyways. **2** *her clothes were strewn about anyhow* =**haphazardly**, carelessly, heedlessly, negligently, in a muddle; *informal* all over the place; *Brit. informal* all over the shop; *N. Amer. informal* all over the lot.

apart ■ *apart from* =**except for**, but for, aside from, with the exception of,

excepting, excluding, bar, barring, besides, other than; *informal* outside of; *formal* save.

apartment ▶ noun **1** *a rented apartment* =**flat**, penthouse; *Austral.* home unit; *N. Amer. informal* crib. **2** *the royal apartments* =**suite (of rooms)**, rooms, quarters, accommodation.

apathetic ▶ adjective =**uninterested**, indifferent, unconcerned, unmoved, uninvolved, unemotional, emotionless, dispassionate, lukewarm; *informal* couldn't-care-less.

apathy ▶ noun =**indifference**, lack of interest/enthusiasm/concern, unconcern, unresponsiveness, impassivity, dispassion, dispassionateness, lethargy, languor.
−OPPOSITES enthusiasm, passion.

ape ▶ noun =**primate**; *technical* anthropoid.
▶ verb *he aped Barbara's accent* =**imitate**, mimic, copy, do an impression of; *informal* take off, send up.

┌─────────────────┐
│ **WORD LINKS** │
└─────────────────┘
relating to apes: **simian**
collective noun: **shrewdness**
study of apes: **primatology**

aperture ▶ noun =**opening**, hole, gap, slit, slot, vent, crevice, chink, crack; *technical* orifice.

apex ▶ noun **1** *the apex of a pyramid* =**tip**, peak, summit, pinnacle, top, vertex. **2** *the apex of his career* =**climax**, culmination, apotheosis; peak, pinnacle, zenith, acme, apogee, high(est) point.
−OPPOSITES bottom, nadir.

aphorism ▶ noun =**saying**, maxim, axiom, adage, epigram, dictum, gnome, proverb, saw, tag.

aplomb ▶ noun =**poise**, self-assurance, self-confidence, calmness, composure, collectedness, level-headedness, sangfroid, equilibrium, equanimity; *informal* unflappability.

apocryphal ▶ adjective =**fictitious**, made-up, untrue, fabricated, false, spurious; unverified, unauthenticated, unsubstantiated.
−OPPOSITES authentic.

apologetic ▶ adjective =**regretful**, sorry, contrite, remorseful, penitent, repentant; conscience-stricken, shamefaced, ashamed.
−OPPOSITES unrepentant.

apologist ▶ noun =defender, supporter, upholder, advocate, proponent, exponent, propagandist, champion, campaigner.
–OPPOSITES critic.

apologize ▶ verb =say sorry, express regret, ask forgiveness, ask for pardon, eat humble pie.

apology ▶ noun **1** *I owe you an apology* =expression of regret, one's regrets; *literary* amende honorable. **2** *(informal) an apology for a flat* =travesty, inadequate/poor example; *informal* excuse.

apoplectic ▶ adjective *(informal)* =furious, enraged, infuriated, incensed, raging; incandescent, fuming, seething; *informal* (hopping) mad, livid, foaming at the mouth.

apostle ▶ noun =advocate, apologist, proponent, exponent, promoter, supporter, upholder, champion; convert; *N. Amer.* booster.

apotheosis ▶ noun =culmination, climax, peak, pinnacle, zenith, acme, apogee, high(est) point.
–OPPOSITES nadir.

appal ▶ verb =horrify, shock, dismay, distress, outrage, scandalize; disgust, repel, revolt, sicken, nauseate, offend, make someone's blood run cold.

appalling ▶ adjective **1** *an appalling crime* =shocking, horrific, horrifying, horrible, terrible, awful, dreadful, ghastly, hideous, horrendous, frightful, atrocious, abominable, abhorrent, outrageous, gruesome, grisly, monstrous, heinous. **2** *(informal) your schoolwork is appalling* =dreadful, awful, terrible, frightful, atrocious, disgraceful, deplorable, hopeless, lamentable; *informal* rotten, crummy, pathetic, pitiful, woeful, useless, lousy, abysmal, dire; *Brit. informal* chronic, shocking.

apparatus ▶ noun **1** *laboratory apparatus* =equipment, gear, tackle, paraphernalia, accoutrements; appliances, instruments. **2** *the apparatus of government* =machinery, system, framework, organization.

apparent ▶ adjective **1** *their relief was all too apparent* =evident, plain, obvious, clear, manifest, visible, discernible, perceptible; unmistakable, crystal clear, palpable, patent, blatant, as plain as a pikestaff, writ large; *informal* as plain as the nose on one's face, written all over one's face. **2** *his apparent lack of concern* =seeming, ostensible, outward, superficial.
–OPPOSITES unclear.

apparently ▶ adverb =seemingly, evidently, it seems/appears (that), as far as one knows, by all accounts; ostensibly, outwardly, on the face of it, so the story goes, so I'm told; allegedly, reputedly.

apparition ▶ noun =ghost, phantom, spectre, spirit, wraith; *informal* spook; *literary* phantasm.

appeal ▶ verb **1** *police are appealing for information* =ask, call, plead. **2** *Andrew appealed to me to help them* =implore, beg, entreat, call on, plead with, exhort, ask, request, petition; *literary* beseech. **3** *the thought of travelling appealed to me* =attract, be attractive to, interest, take someone's fancy, fascinate, tempt, entice, allure, lure, draw, whet someone's appetite; *informal* float someone's boat.
▶ noun **1** *an appeal for help* =plea, request, entreaty, cry, call. **2** *the cultural appeal of the island* =attraction, attractiveness, allure, charm; fascination, magnetism, drawing power, pull.

appealing ▶ adjective =attractive, engaging, alluring, enchanting, captivating, bewitching, fascinating, tempting, enticing, seductive, irresistible, winning, winsome, charming, desirable; *Brit. informal* tasty.
–OPPOSITES disagreeable, off-putting.

appear ▶ verb **1** *a cloud of dust appeared on the horizon* =become visible, come into view/sight, materialize, pop up. **2** *fundamental differences were beginning to appear* =be revealed, emerge, surface, manifest itself, become apparent/evident, come to light; arise, crop up. **3** *(informal) Bill still hadn't appeared* =arrive, turn up, put in an appearance, come, get here/there; *informal* show (up), roll up. **4** *they appeared to be completely devoted* =seem, look, give the impression, come across as, strike someone as. **5** *the paperback edition didn't appear for two years* =become available, come on the market, go on sale, come out, be published, be released. **6** *he appeared on Broadway* =perform, play, act.
–OPPOSITES vanish.

appearance ▶ noun **1** *her dishevelled appearance* =look(s), air, aspect, mien. **2** *an appearance of respectability* =impression, air, (outward) show; semblance, facade, veneer, front, pretence. **3** *the* *sudden appearance of her daughter* =**arrival**, advent, coming, emergence, materialization. **4** *the appearance of these symptoms* =**occurrence**, manifestation, development.

appease ▸ verb =**conciliate**, placate, pacify, propitiate, reconcile, win over; *informal* sweeten.
–OPPOSITES provoke, inflame.

appeasement ▸ noun =**conciliation**, placation, pacification, propitiation, reconciliation; peacemaking, peace-mongering.
–OPPOSITES provocation.

append ▸ verb =**add**, attach, affix, tack on, tag on, join on.

appendage ▸ noun =**protuberance**, projection; limb.

appendix ▸ noun =**supplement**, addendum, postscript, codicil; coda, epilogue, afterword, tailpiece.

> WORD LINKS
>
> *surgical removal of the appendix:*
> **appendectomy, appendicectomy**

appetite ▸ noun **1** *a walk sharpens the appetite* =**hunger**, hungriness; taste, palate. **2** *my appetite for learning* =**craving**, longing, yearning, hankering, hunger, thirst, passion; enthusiasm, keenness, eagerness, desire; *informal* yen.

appetizer ▸ noun =**starter**, first course, hors d'oeuvre, amuse-gueule, antipasto.

appetizing ▸ adjective =**mouthwatering**, inviting, tempting; tasty, delicious, flavoursome, toothsome, delectable; *informal* scrumptious, scrummy, yummy, moreish.
–OPPOSITES bland, unappealing.

applaud ▸ verb **1** *the audience applauded* =**clap**, give a standing ovation, put one's hands together; *informal* give someone a big hand. **2** *police have applauded the decision* =**praise**, commend, salute, welcome, celebrate, approve of, sing the praises of, pay tribute to, speak highly of, take one's hat off to.
–OPPOSITES boo, criticize.

applause ▸ noun =**clapping**, (standing) ovation; cheering.

appliance ▸ noun **1** *domestic appliances* =**device**, machine, instrument, gadget, contraption, apparatus, implement, mechanism, contrivance, labour-saving device; *informal* gizmo. **2** *the appliance*

of science =**application**, use, exercise, employment, implementation, utilization, practice, applying, discharge, execution, prosecution, enactment.

applicable ▸ adjective =**relevant**, appropriate, pertinent, apposite, germane, material, significant, related, connected; fitting, suitable, apt.
–OPPOSITES inappropriate, irrelevant.

applicant ▸ noun =**candidate**, interviewee, competitor, contestant, contender, entrant; claimant, petitioner; prospective student/employee, jobseeker.

application ▸ noun **1** *an application for an overdraft* =**request**, appeal, petition, entreaty, plea; approach, claim, demand. **2** *the application of anti-inflation policies* =**implementation**, use, exercise, employment, utilization, applying, discharge, execution, prosecution, enactment. **3** *the argument is clearest in its application to the theatre* =**relevance**, bearing, significance, aptness, importance. **4** *the job requires a great deal of application* =**hard work**, diligence, industriousness, commitment, dedication, devotion, conscientiousness, perseverance, persistence, tenacity, doggedness; concentration, attention, attentiveness, steadiness, patience, endurance; effort, labour, endeavour. **5** *a new graphics application* =**program**, software, routine.

apply ▸ verb **1** *300 people applied for the job* =**bid**, put in, try, petition, register, audition; request, seek, solicit, claim, ask. **2** *the Act did not apply to Scotland* =**be relevant**, have a bearing, pertain, relate, concern, affect, involve, cover, deal with, touch. **3** *she applied some ointment* =**put on**, rub in/on, work in, spread, smear on, slap on. **4** *a steady pressure should be applied* =**exert**, administer, use, exercise, employ, utilize, bring to bear.

■ **apply oneself** =**work hard**, be industrious, show commitment, show dedication; exert oneself, make an effort, try hard, do one's best, give one's all, buckle down, put one's shoulder to the wheel, keep one's nose to the grindstone; strive, endeavour, struggle, labour, toil; pay attention, commit oneself, devote oneself; persevere, persist; *informal* put one's back in it, knuckle down, get stuck in.

appoint ▸ verb =**nominate**, name, designate, install as, commission, engage,

co-opt; select, choose, elect, vote in.
−OPPOSITES reject.

appointed ▶ adjective **1** *at the appointed time* =**scheduled**, arranged, prearranged, specified, agreed, designated, allotted, set, fixed, chosen, established, settled, prescribed, decreed. **2** *a well appointed room* =**furnished**, decorated, fitted out, supplied.

appointment ▶ noun **1** *a six o'clock appointment* =**meeting**, engagement, interview, consultation, session; date, rendezvous, assignation; commitment, fixture. **2** *the appointment of directors* =**nomination**, naming, designation, installation, commissioning, engagement, co-option; selection, choosing, election. **3** *he held an appointment at the university* =**job**, post, position, situation, place, office.

apportion ▶ verb =**share**, divide, allocate, distribute, allot, assign, give out, hand out, mete out, deal out, dish out, dole out; ration, measure out; split; *informal* divvy up.

apposite ▶ adjective =**appropriate**, suitable, fitting, apt, befitting; relevant, pertinent, to the point, applicable, germane, material.
−OPPOSITES inappropriate.

appraisal ▶ noun **1** *an objective appraisal of the book* =**assessment**, evaluation, estimation, judgement, summing-up, consideration. **2** *a free insurance appraisal* =**valuation**, estimate, estimation, quotation.

appraise ▶ verb =**assess**, evaluate, judge, rate, gauge, review, consider; *informal* size up.

appreciable ▶ adjective =**considerable**, substantial, significant, sizeable, goodly, fair, reasonable, marked; perceptible, noticeable, visible; *informal* tidy.
−OPPOSITES negligible.

appreciate ▶ verb **1** *I'd appreciate your advice* =**be grateful**, be thankful, be obliged, be indebted, be in your debt. **2** *I don't feel I'm appreciated here* =**value**, admire, respect, think highly of, think much of. **3** *we appreciate the problems* =**recognize**, acknowledge, realize, know, be aware of, be conscious of, be sensitive to, understand. **4** *a home that will appreciate in value* =**increase**, gain, grow, rise, go up.
−OPPOSITES disparage, depreciate, decrease.

appreciation ▶ noun **1** *he showed his appreciation* =**gratitude**, thanks, gratefulness, thankfulness, recognition. **2** *her appreciation of literature* =**knowledge**, awareness, enjoyment, love; feeling, discrimination, sensitivity. **3** *an appreciation of the value of teamwork* =**acknowledgement**, recognition, realization, knowledge, awareness, consciousness, understanding, comprehension. **4** *the appreciation of the franc against the pound* =**increase**, gain, growth, rise, inflation, escalation. **5** *an appreciation of the professor's work* =**review**, critique, criticism, analysis, assessment, evaluation, judgement; *Brit. informal* crit.
−OPPOSITES ingratitude, unawareness, depreciation, decrease.

appreciative ▶ adjective **1** *we are appreciative of all your efforts* =**grateful**, thankful, obliged, indebted. **2** *an appreciative audience* =**supportive**, encouraging, sympathetic, responsive; receptive, enthusiastic, admiring, approving, complimentary.
−OPPOSITES ungrateful, disparaging.

apprehend ▶ verb **1** *the thieves were quickly apprehended* =**arrest**, catch, capture, seize; take prisoner, take into custody; *informal* collar, nab, nail, run in, bust, pick up, pull in, feel someone's collar; *Brit. informal* nick, do. **2** *they are slow to apprehend danger* =**appreciate**, recognize, discern, perceive, grasp, understand, comprehend; *informal* get the picture; *Brit. informal* twig, suss (out).

apprehension ▶ noun **1** *he was filled with apprehension* =**anxiety**, worry, unease, nervousness, nerves, misgivings, disquiet, concern, tension, trepidation, consternation, angst, dread, fear, foreboding; *informal* butterflies, the willies, the heebie-jeebies. **2** *the apprehension of a perpetrator* =**arrest**, capture, seizure; detention; *informal* bust.
−OPPOSITES confidence.

apprehensive ▶ adjective =**anxious**, worried, uneasy, nervous, concerned, agitated, tense, afraid, scared, frightened, fearful.
−OPPOSITES confident.

apprentice ▶ noun =**trainee**, learner, probationer, novice, beginner, starter; pupil, student; *N. Amer.* tenderfoot; *informal* rookie; *N. Amer. informal* greenhorn.
−OPPOSITES veteran.

apprise ▶ verb =**inform**, tell, notify,

advise, brief, make aware, enlighten, update, keep posted; *informal* clue in, fill in, put wise, put in the picture.

approach ▸ verb **1** *she approached the altar* =**move towards**, come/go/advance towards, near; close in on, gain on. **2** *winter is approaching* =**come**, draw near(er), draw/come/get closer, close in, loom, be on the/its way. **3** *the trade deficit is approaching £20 million* =**border on**, verge on, approximate, touch, nudge, get on for, near, come/be close to. **4** *she approached him about a pay rise* =**speak to**, talk to, sound out, proposition. **5** *he approached the problem in the best way* =**tackle**, address, manage, go about.
–OPPOSITES leave.
▸ noun **1** *the traditional British approach* =**method**, procedure, technique, modus operandi, style, way; strategy, tactic, system, means, line of action. **2** *he considered an approach to the High Court* =**proposal**, submission, application, appeal, plea, request. **3** *the dog barked at the approach of any intruder* =**advance**; arrival, appearance. **4** *the approach to the castle* =**driveway**, drive, road; way.

approachable ▸ adjective **1** *students found the staff approachable* =**friendly**, welcoming, pleasant, agreeable, congenial, affable, cordial; obliging, helpful. **2** *the south landing is approachable by boat* =**accessible**, reachable; *informal* get-at-able.
–OPPOSITES aloof, inaccessible.

approbation ▸ noun =**approval**, acceptance, endorsement, appreciation, respect, admiration, commendation, praise, congratulations, acclaim, esteem, applause.
–OPPOSITES criticism.

appropriate ▸ adjective *this isn't the appropriate time* =**suitable**, proper, fitting, apt, right; relevant, apposite, convenient, opportune; seemly, befitting.
–OPPOSITES unsuitable.
▸ verb **1** *the barons appropriated church lands* =**seize**, commandeer, expropriate, annex, sequestrate, sequester, take over, hijack; steal, take; *informal* swipe, nab; *Brit. informal* pinch, half-inch, nick. **2** *his images have been appropriated by advertisers* =**plagiarize**, copy, poach, steal, swipe, 'borrow'; *informal* rip off, pinch, half-inch, nick.

approval ▸ noun **1** *their proposals went to the ministry for approval* =**acceptance**, agreement, consent, assent, permission, leave, the nod; rubber stamp, sanction, endorsement, ratification, authorization, validation; support, backing; *informal* the go-ahead, the green light, the OK, the thumbs up. **2** *Lily looked at him with approval* =**approbation**, appreciation, admiration, regard, esteem, respect.
–OPPOSITES refusal, dislike.

approve ▸ verb **1** *his boss doesn't approve of his lifestyle* =**agree with**, hold with, endorse, support, be in favour of, favour, think well of, like, take kindly to; admire. **2** *the government approved the proposals* =**accept**, agree to, consent to, assent to, give one's blessing to, bless, rubber-stamp, give the nod; ratify, sanction, endorse, authorize, validate, pass; support, back; *informal* give the go-ahead, give the green light, give the OK, give the thumbs-up.
–OPPOSITES condemn, refuse.

approximate ▸ adjective =**estimated**, rough, imprecise, inexact, broad, loose; *N. Amer. informal* ballpark.
–OPPOSITES precise.
▸ verb =**be/come close to**, be/come near to, approach, border on, verge on; resemble, be similar to.

approximately ▸ adverb =**roughly**, about, around, circa, round about, more or less, in the neighbourhood of, in the region of, of the order of, something like, give or take (a few); near to, close to, nearly, almost, approaching; *Brit.* getting on for; *informal* pushing; *N. Amer. informal* in the ballpark of.
–OPPOSITES precisely.

approximation ▸ noun **1** *the figure is only an approximation* =**estimate**, estimation, guess, rough calculation; *informal* guesstimate; *N. Amer. informal* ballpark figure. **2** *an approximation to the truth* =**semblance**, resemblance, likeness, similarity, correspondence.

apt ▸ adjective **1** *a very apt description* =**suitable**, fitting, appropriate, relevant, applicable, apposite; *Brit. informal* spot on. **2** *they are apt to be a bit slipshod* =**inclined**, given, likely, liable, prone.
–OPPOSITES inappropriate, unlikely, slow.

aptitude ▸ noun =**talent**, gift, flair, bent, skill, knack, facility, ability, capability, potential, capacity, faculty, genius.

aquatic ▸ adjective =marine, water, saltwater, freshwater, seawater, sea, oceanic, river.

arbiter ▸ noun **1** *an arbiter between Moscow and Washington. See* ARBITRATOR. **2** *the great arbiter of fashion* =authority, judge, controller, director; master, expert, pundit.

arbitrary ▸ adjective =capricious, whimsical, random, chance, unpredictable; casual, wanton, motiveless, unreasoned, irrational, illogical, groundless, unjustified.
–OPPOSITES reasoned, democratic.

arbitrate ▸ verb =adjudicate, judge, referee, umpire; mediate, intervene, intercede; settle, decide, resolve, pass judgement.

arbitration ▸ noun =adjudication, judgement; mediation, conciliation, intervention.

arbitrator ▸ noun =adjudicator, arbiter, judge, referee, umpire; mediator, intervenor, go-between.

arc ▸ noun *the arc of a circle* =curve, arch, crescent, semicircle, half-moon; curvature, convexity.
▸ verb *I sent the ball arcing out over the river* =curl, curve; arch.

arcade ▸ noun =shopping centre, shopping precinct, market, galleria; *N. Amer.* plaza, mall, shopping mall.

arcane ▸ adjective =mysterious, secret, covert, clandestine; enigmatic, esoteric, obscure, abstruse, recondite, impenetrable, opaque.

arch¹ ▸ noun *a stone arch* =archway, vault.
▸ verb *she arched her eyebrows* =curve, arc; raise.

arch² ▸ adjective *an arch grin* =mischievous, teasing, knowing, playful, roguish, impish, cheeky.

arch- ▸ combining form *his arch-enemy* =chief, principal, foremost, leading, main, major, prime, premier, greatest; *informal* number-one.
–OPPOSITES minor.

archaic ▸ adjective =obsolete, out of date, old-fashioned, outmoded, behind the times, bygone, anachronistic, antiquated, superannuated, antediluvian, olde worlde; ancient, old, extinct, defunct; *informal* out of the ark.
–OPPOSITES modern.

archetypal ▸ adjective =quintessential, classic, typical, representative, model, exemplary, textbook, copybook; stock, stereotypical, prototypical.
–OPPOSITES atypical.

archetype ▸ noun =quintessence, essence, representative, model, embodiment, prototype, stereotype; original, pattern, standard, paradigm, exemplar.

architect ▸ noun =originator, author, creator, founder, (founding) father; engineer, inventor.

architecture ▸ noun **1** *modern architecture* =building, planning, design, construction. **2** *computer architecture* =structure, construction, organization, layout, design, build, make-up; *informal* set-up.

> **WORD LINKS**
>
> *relating to architecture:* **architectonic**
> *study of architecture:* **architectonics**

archive ▸ noun **1** *she delved into the family archives* =records, annals, chronicles, papers, documents, files; history. **2** *the National Sound Archive* =record office, registry, repository, museum, library.
▸ verb *the videos are archived for future use* =file, log, catalogue, document, record, register; store, cache.

arctic ▸ adjective **1** *Arctic waters* =polar, northern; *literary* hyperborean; *technical* boreal. **2** *arctic weather conditions* =(bitterly) cold, wintry, freezing, frozen, icy, glacial, sub-zero, polar, Siberian.
–OPPOSITES Antarctic, tropical.
▸ noun =far north, North Pole, Arctic circle.
–OPPOSITES Antarctic.

ardent ▸ adjective =passionate, fervent, zealous, wholehearted, intense; enthusiastic, keen, eager, avid, committed, dedicated.
–OPPOSITES apathetic.

ardour ▸ noun =passion, fervour, zeal, intensity; enthusiasm, eagerness, keenness, dedication.

arduous ▸ adjective =onerous, taxing, difficult, hard, heavy, laborious, strenuous, vigorous, back-breaking; demanding, tough, challenging, formidable; exhausting, tiring, punishing, gruelling; *informal* killing; *Brit. informal* knackering.
–OPPOSITES easy.

area ▸ noun **1** *an inner-city area* =district, region, zone, sector, quarter; locality, locale, neighbourhood, parish, patch; tract, belt; *informal* neck of the woods; *Brit. informal* manor; *N. Amer. informal* turf. **2** *specific areas of scientific knowledge* = **field**, sphere, realm, domain, sector, province, territory, line. **3** *the dining area* = **section**, space; place, room.

> **WORD LINKS**
>
> *measurement of area:* **planimetry**

arena ▸ noun **1** *an ice-hockey arena* = **stadium**, amphitheatre; ground, field, ring, rink, pitch, court; *N. Amer.* bowl, park. **2** *the political arena* = **scene**, sphere, realm, province, domain, sector, forum, territory, world.

argot ▸ noun = **jargon**, slang, cant, parlance, vernacular, patois; dialect, speech, language; *informal* lingo.

arguable ▸ adjective = **debatable**, questionable, open to question, controversial, contentious, doubtful, uncertain, moot.
−OPPOSITES untenable, certain.

arguably ▸ adverb = **possibly**, conceivably, feasibly, plausibly, probably, maybe, perhaps.

argue ▸ verb **1** *they argued that the government was to blame* = **contend**, assert, maintain, insist, hold, claim, reason, swear, allege; *formal* aver, opine. **2** *the children are always arguing* = **quarrel**, disagree, row, squabble, fall out, bicker, fight, wrangle, feud, have words, cross swords, lock horns, be at each other's throats.

argument ▸ noun **1** *he had an argument with Tony* = **quarrel**, disagreement, squabble, fight, dispute, wrangle, clash, altercation, feud, contretemps, falling-out; *informal* tiff, slanging match; *Brit. informal* row, barney. **2** *arguments for the existence of God* = **reasoning**, justification, explanation, rationalization; case, defence, vindication; evidence, reasons, grounds.

argumentative ▸ adjective = **quarrelsome**, disputatious, contrary, cantankerous, contentious; belligerent, bellicose, combative, antagonistic, truculent, pugnacious.

arid ▸ adjective **1** *an arid landscape* = **dry**, waterless, parched, scorched, baked, thirsty, desiccated, desert; **barren**, infertile. **2** *an arid documentary* = **dreary**, dull, drab, dry, sterile, colourless, uninspiring, flat, boring, uninteresting, lifeless.
−OPPOSITES wet, fertile, vibrant.

arise ▸ verb **1** *many problems arose* = **come to light**, become apparent, appear, emerge, crop up, turn up, surface, spring up; occur; *literary* come to pass. **2** *injuries arising from defective products* = **result**, proceed, follow, ensue, derive, stem, originate; be caused by.

aristocracy ▸ noun = **nobility**, peerage, gentry, upper class, ruling class, elite, lords, ladies, peers (of the realm), nobles, noblemen, noblewomen; *informal* upper crust, top drawer, aristos; *Brit. informal* nobs, toffs.
−OPPOSITES working class.

aristocrat ▸ noun = **nobleman**, noblewoman, lord, lady, peer (of the realm), peeress; *informal* aristo; *Brit. informal* toff, nob.
−OPPOSITES commoner.

aristocratic ▸ adjective **1** *an aristocratic family* = **noble**, titled, upper-class, blue-blooded, high-born; *informal* upper crust, top drawer; *Brit. informal* posh; *archaic* gentle. **2** *an aristocratic manner* = **refined**, polished, courtly, dignified, decorous, gracious, fine, gentlemanly, ladylike; haughty, proud.
−OPPOSITES working-class, vulgar.

arm[1] ▸ noun *the political arm of the group* = **branch**, section, department, division, wing, sector.

> **WORD LINKS**
>
> *relating to an arm:* **brachial**

arm[2] ▸ verb **1** *he armed himself with a revolver* = **equip**, provide, supply, furnish, issue, fit out. **2** *arm yourself against criticism* = **prepare**, make ready, brace, steel, fortify.

armada ▸ noun = **fleet**, flotilla; *literary* navy.

armaments ▸ plural noun = **arms**, weapons, weaponry, firearms, guns, ordnance, artillery, munitions, materiel.

armistice ▸ noun = **truce**, ceasefire, peace, suspension of hostilities.

armoured ▸ adjective = **armour-plated**, steel-plated, ironclad; bulletproof, bombproof; reinforced, toughened.

arms ▸ plural noun = **weapons**, weaponry, firearms, guns, ordnance, artillery, armaments, munitions.

army ▶ noun **1** *the invading army* =**armed force**, military force, land force(s), military, soldiery, infantry, militia; troops, soldiers. **2** *an army of tourists* =**crowd**, swarm, multitude, horde, mob, gang, throng, mass, flock, herd, pack.

> **WORD LINKS**
>
> relating to armies: **military, martial**

aroma ▶ noun =**smell**, odour, fragrance, scent, perfume, bouquet, nose.

aromatic ▶ adjective =**fragrant**, scented, perfumed, fragranced.

around ▶ preposition *around three miles* =**approximately**, about, round about, circa, roughly, something like, more or less, in the region of, in the neighbourhood of, give or take (a few); nearly, close to, approaching; *Brit.* getting on for; *N. Amer. informal* in the ballpark of.

arouse ▶ verb **1** *they had aroused suspicion* =**provoke**, trigger, stir up, kindle, engender, cause, foster. **2** *his ability to arouse the masses* =**stir up**, rouse, galvanize, excite, electrify, stimulate, inspire, inspirit, move, fire up, whip up, get going, inflame, agitate, goad, incite. **3** *his touch aroused her* =**excite**, stimulate (sexually), titillate; *informal* turn on, get going, give someone a thrill. **4** *she was aroused from her sleep* =**wake (up)**, awaken, bring to/round, rouse; *literary* waken.

–OPPOSITES allay, pacify, turn off.

arraign ▶ verb =**indict**, prosecute, put on trial, bring to trial, take to court, summons, cite; accuse of, charge with; *N. Amer.* impeach; *informal* do.

–OPPOSITES acquit, praise.

arrange ▶ verb **1** *she arranged the flowers in a vase* =**set out**, order, lay out, array, position, present, display, exhibit; group, sort, organize, tidy. **2** *they hoped to arrange a meeting* =**organize**, fix (up), plan, schedule, contrive, settle on, decide, determine, agree. **3** *he arranged the piece for a full orchestra* =**adapt**, set, score, orchestrate.

arrangement ▶ noun **1** *the arrangement of the furniture* =**positioning**, presentation; grouping, organization, alignment. **2** *the arrangements for my trip* =**preparation**, plan, provision; planning. **3** *we had an arrangement* =**agreement**, deal, understanding, bargain, settlement, pact. **4** *an arrangement of Beethoven's symphonies* =**adaptation**, orchestration.

array ▶ noun =**range**, collection, selection, assortment, variety; line-up; display, exhibition.

▶ verb =**arrange**, assemble, group, order, range, place, position, set out, lay out, spread out; display.

arrears ▶ plural noun =**outstanding payment(s)**, debt(s), liabilities, dues.

–OPPOSITES credit.

■ **in arrears** =**behind**, late, overdue, in the red, in debt.

arrest ▶ verb **1** *police arrested him for murder* =**apprehend**, take into custody; *informal* pick up, pull in, pinch, bust, nab, do, collar; *Brit. informal* nick. **2** *the spread of the disease can be arrested* =**stop**, halt, check, block, curb; prevent, obstruct.

–OPPOSITES release, start.

▶ noun =**detention**, apprehension, seizure, capture.

arresting ▶ adjective *an arresting image* =**striking**, eye-catching, conspicuous, engaging, impressive, imposing, spectacular, dramatic, breathtaking, stunning, awe-inspiring; distinctive.

–OPPOSITES inconspicuous.

arrival ▶ noun **1** *they awaited Ruth's arrival* =**coming**, appearance, entrance, entry, approach. **2** *staff greeted the late arrivals* =**comer**, entrant, incomer; visitor, caller, guest. **3** *the arrival of democracy* =**emergence**, appearance, advent, coming, dawn, onset.

–OPPOSITES departure, end.

arrive ▶ verb **1** *more police arrived* =**come**, turn up, get here/there, make it, appear, enter, present oneself, come along, materialize; *informal* show (up), roll in/up, blow in, show one's face. **2** *we arrived at his house* =**reach**, get to, come to, make, make it to, end up at. **3** *they arrived at an agreement* =**reach**, achieve, attain, gain, accomplish; work out, draw up, put together, strike, settle on; *informal* clinch. **4** *virtual reality had arrived* =**emerge**, appear, surface, dawn, be born, come into being, arise.

–OPPOSITES depart, leave.

arrogant ▶ adjective =**haughty**, conceited, self-important, egotistic, full of oneself, superior; overbearing, pompous, bumptious, imperious, overweening; proud, immodest; *informal* high and mighty, too big for one's boots, big-headed.

–OPPOSITES modest.

arrow ▸ noun **1** *a bow and arrow* =**shaft**, bolt, dart. **2** *the arrow pointed right* =**pointer**, indicator, marker, needle.

WORD LINKS

maker or seller of arrows: **fletcher**

art ▸ noun **1** *he studied art* =**fine art**, design; aesthetics. **2** *the art of writing* =**skill**, craft, technique, knack. **3** *she uses art to achieve her aims* =**cunning**, artfulness, slyness, craftiness, guile; deceit, duplicity, artifice, wiles.

artful ▸ adjective =**sly**, crafty, cunning, wily, scheming, devious, Machiavellian, sneaky, tricky, conniving, designing, calculating; canny, shrewd; deceitful, duplicitous, underhand.
–OPPOSITES ingenuous.

article ▸ noun **1** *small household articles* =**object**, thing, item, artefact, commodity, product. **2** *an article in The Times* =**report**, account, story, write-up, feature, item, piece (of writing), column, review, commentary. **3** *the crucial article of the treaty* =**clause**, section, subsection, point, item, paragraph, part, portion.

articulate ▸ adjective *an articulate speaker* =**eloquent**, fluent, effective, persuasive, lucid, expressive, silver-tongued.
–OPPOSITES unintelligible.
▸ verb *they were unable to articulate their emotions* =**express**, voice, vocalize, put in words, communicate, state.

articulated ▸ adjective =**hinged**, jointed, segmented.

artifice ▸ noun =**trickery**, deceit, deception, duplicity, guile, cunning, artfulness, wiliness, craftiness, slyness, chicanery.

artificial ▸ adjective **1** *artificial flowers* =**synthetic**, fake, imitation, mock, ersatz, substitute, replica, reproduction; man-made, manufactured; plastic; *informal* pretend. **2** *an artificial smile* =**insincere**, feigned, false, unnatural, contrived, put-on, exaggerated, forced, laboured, strained, hollow; *informal* pretend, phoney.
–OPPOSITES natural, genuine.

artisan ▸ noun =**craftsman**, craftswoman, craftsperson, technician; smith, wright, journeyman; *archaic* artificer.

artist ▸ noun =**expert**, master, maestro, virtuoso, genius; *informal* pro, ace; *Brit.*

informal dab hand.
–OPPOSITES novice.

artiste ▸ noun =**entertainer**, performer, showman, artist; player, musician, singer, dancer, actor, actress; star.

artistic ▸ adjective =**creative**, imaginative, inventive, expressive; sensitive, perceptive, discerning.
–OPPOSITES unimaginative.

artistry ▸ noun =(**creative) skill**, creativity, art, talent, genius, brilliance, flair, proficiency, virtuosity, finesse, style; craftsmanship, workmanship.

artless ▸ adjective =**natural**, ingenuous, naive, simple, innocent, childlike, guileless; candid, open, sincere, unaffected.
–OPPOSITES scheming.

ascend ▸ verb =**climb**, go up/upwards, move up/upwards, rise (up); mount, scale, conquer.
–OPPOSITES descend.

ascendancy ▸ noun =**dominance**, supremacy, superiority, predominance, primacy, dominion, hegemony, authority, control, command, power, rule, sovereignty.
–OPPOSITES subordination.

ascent ▸ noun **1** *the ascent of the Matterhorn* =**climbing**, scaling, conquest. **2** *the ascent grew steeper* =**slope**, incline, gradient.
–OPPOSITES descent, drop.

ascertain ▸ verb =**find out**, discover, get to know, work out, make out, fathom (out), learn, deduce, divine, discern, see; establish, determine, verify, confirm; *informal* figure out; *Brit. informal* suss (out).

ascetic ▸ adjective =**austere**, self-denying, abstemious, self-disciplined; puritanical, monastic, strict.
–OPPOSITES sybaritic.

ascribe ▸ verb =**attribute**, assign, put down, accredit, credit, impute; blame on, lay at the door of; connect with, associate with.

ash ▸ noun =**cinders**, ashes, clinker.

WORD LINKS

relating to ash: **cinerary**

ashamed ▸ adjective **1** *the poor are made to feel ashamed* =**sorry**, shamefaced, sheepish, guilty, contrite, remorseful, repentant, penitent, regretful, apologetic; embarrassed, mortified. **2** *he was*

ashamed to admit it =**reluctant**, loath, unwilling, disinclined, afraid.
–OPPOSITES proud, pleased.

ashen ▸ adjective =**pale**, wan, pasty, grey, colourless, pallid, white, waxen, ghostly, bloodless.

asinine ▸ adjective =**foolish**, stupid, brainless, mindless, idiotic, ridiculous, absurd, fatuous, silly, inane, witless, empty-headed; *informal* half-witted, dumb, moronic; *Brit. informal* daft; *Scottish & N. English informal* glaikit.
–OPPOSITES intelligent, sensible.

ask ▸ verb **1** *he asked what time we opened* =**enquire**, want to know; question, interrogate, quiz. **2** *they want to ask a few questions* =**put (forward)**, pose, raise, submit. **3** *don't be afraid to ask for advice* =**request**, demand; solicit, seek, crave, apply, petition, call, appeal.
–OPPOSITES answer.

asleep ▸ adjective =**sleeping**, in a deep sleep, napping, catnapping, dozing, drowsing; *informal* snoozing, dead to the world; *Brit. informal* kipping; *humorous* in the land of Nod; *literary* slumbering.
–OPPOSITES awake.

aspect ▸ noun **1** *the photos depict every aspect of life* =**feature**, facet, side, characteristic, particular, detail; angle, slant. **2** *his face had a sinister aspect* =**appearance**, look, air, cast, mien, demeanour, expression; atmosphere, mood, quality, feeling. **3** *a summer house with a southern aspect* =**outlook**, view, exposure; situation, position, location. **4** *the front aspect of the hotel* =**face**, elevation, facade, side.

asperity ▸ noun =**harshness**, sharpness, abrasiveness, severity, acerbity.

aspersions ■ **cast aspersions on** =**vilify**, disparage, denigrate, defame, run down, impugn, belittle, criticize, condemn; malign, slander, libel, discredit; *informal* pull apart, throw mud at, knock, bad-mouth; *Brit. informal* rubbish, slate, slag off.

asphyxiate ▸ verb =**choke (to death)**, suffocate, smother, stifle; throttle, strangle.

aspiration ▸ noun =**desire**, hope, dream, wish, longing, yearning; aim, ambition, expectation, goal, target.

aspire ▸ verb =**desire**, hope, dream, long, yearn, set one's heart on, wish, want; aim, seek, set one's sights on.

aspiring ▸ adjective =**would-be**, hopeful, budding; potential, prospective; *informal* wannabe.

assassin ▸ noun =**murderer**, killer, gunman; executioner; *informal* hit man.

assassinate ▸ verb =**murder**, kill; eliminate, liquidate, execute; *N. Amer.* terminate; *informal* hit.

assassination ▸ noun =**murder**, killing, homicide; execution, elimination; *N. Amer.* termination; *informal* hit.

assault ▸ verb *he assaulted a police officer* =**attack**, hit, strike, punch, beat up, thump; *informal* clout, wallop, belt, clobber, deck, slug, plug, lay into, do over, rough up; *Austral. informal* quilt.
▸ noun **1** *he was charged with assault* =**violence**, battery, indecency, rape, molestation; *Brit.* grievous bodily harm, GBH, actual bodily harm, ABH. **2** *an assault on the city* =**attack**, strike, onslaught, offensive, charge, push, thrust, invasion, bombardment, sortie, incursion, raid, blitz.

assemblage ▸ noun =**collection**, accumulation, conglomeration, gathering, group, grouping, cluster, aggregation, mass, number; assortment, selection, array.

assemble ▸ verb **1** *a crowd had assembled* =**gather**, collect, get together, congregate, convene, meet, muster, rally. **2** *he assembled the suspects* =**bring/call together**, gather, collect, round up, marshal, muster. **3** *how to assemble the kite* =**construct**, build, erect, set up, put together, connect.
–OPPOSITES disperse, dismantle.

assembly ▸ noun **1** *an assembly of dockers* =**gathering**, meeting, congregation, convention, rally, convocation, group, body, crowd, throng, company; *informal* get-together. **2** *car assembly* =**construction**, manufacture, building, fabrication, erection.

assent ▸ noun *they are likely to give their assent* =**agreement**, acceptance, approval, consent, acquiescence; sanction, endorsement, confirmation; permission, leave, blessing; *informal* the go-ahead, the green light, the OK, the thumbs up.
–OPPOSITES dissent, refusal.
▸ verb *he assented to the change* =**agree to**, accept, approve, consent to, give one's blessing to, give the nod; sanction, endorse, confirm; *informal* give the go-

ahead, give the green light, give the OK, OK, give the thumbs up; *formal* accede to. −OPPOSITES refuse.

assert ▸ verb 1 *they asserted that all aboard were safe* =**declare**, maintain, contend, argue, state, claim, announce, pronounce, swear, insist, avow; *formal* aver. 2 *we find it difficult to assert our rights* =**insist on**, stand up for, uphold, defend, press/push for.

assertion ▸ noun =**declaration**, contention, statement, claim, opinion, announcement, pronouncement, protestation, avowal.

assertive ▸ adjective =**confident**, self-confident, bold, decisive, assured, self-assured, self-possessed, strong-willed, forceful, insistent, determined, commanding, pushy; *informal* feisty. −OPPOSITES timid.

assess ▸ verb 1 *the committee's power is hard to assess* =**evaluate**, judge, gauge, rate, estimate, appraise, get the measure of, determine, weigh up, analyse; *informal* size up. 2 *the damage was assessed at £5 billion* =**value**, calculate, work out, determine, cost, price, estimate.

assessment ▸ noun 1 *a teacher's assessment of the pupil's abilities* =**evaluation**, judgement, rating, estimation, appraisal, analysis, opinion. 2 *some assessments valued the estate at £2 million* =**valuation**, calculation, costing, pricing, estimate.

asset ▸ noun 1 *he sees his age as an asset* =**benefit**, advantage, blessing, good/strong point, strength, forte, virtue, recommendation, attraction, resource, boon, merit, bonus, plus, pro. 2 *the seizure of all their assets* =**property**, resources, estate, holdings, possessions, effects, goods, valuables, belongings. −OPPOSITES liability.

assiduous ▸ adjective =**diligent**, careful, meticulous, thorough, sedulous, attentive, conscientious, punctilious, painstaking, rigorous.

assign ▸ verb 1 *a young doctor was assigned the task* =**allocate**, allot, give, set; charge with, entrust with. 2 *she was assigned to a new post* =**appoint**, promote, delegate, commission, post, co-opt; *Military* detail. 3 *we assign large sums of money to travel budgets* =**earmark**, designate, set aside, reserve, appropriate, allot, allocate, apportion.

assignation ▸ noun =**rendezvous**, date, appointment, meeting.

assignment ▸ noun 1 *I'm going to finish this assignment tonight* =**task**, job, duty, chore, mission, errand, undertaking, exercise, business, endeavour, enterprise; project, homework. 2 *the assignment of tasks* =**allocation**, allotment, designation; sharing out, apportionment, distribution, handing out.

assimilate ▸ verb 1 *the amount of information he can assimilate* =**absorb**, take in, acquire, pick up, grasp, comprehend, understand, learn, master; digest. 2 *many tribes were assimilated by Turkic peoples* =**subsume**, incorporate, integrate, absorb.

assist ▸ verb 1 *I spend my time assisting the chef* =**help**, aid, lend a (helping) hand to, work with; support, back (up). 2 *the exchange rates assisted the firm's expansion* =**facilitate**, aid, ease, expedite, spur, promote, boost, benefit, encourage, further. −OPPOSITES hinder, impede.

assistance ▸ noun =**help**, aid, support, backing, reinforcement, succour, relief; a (helping) hand. −OPPOSITES hindrance.

assistant ▸ noun =**subordinate**, deputy, second (in command), number two, right-hand man/woman, aide, personal assistant, PA, attendant, mate, apprentice, junior, auxiliary; hired hand/help, helper, man/girl Friday; *informal* sidekick, gofer; *Brit. informal* dogsbody, skivvy.

associate ▸ verb 1 *the colours that we associate with fire* =**link**, connect, relate, identify, equate. 2 *I was forced to associate with them* =**mix**, keep company, mingle, socialize, go around, rub shoulders, fraternize, consort; *N. Amer.* rub elbows; *informal* hobnob, hang out/around/round; *Brit. informal* hang about. 3 *the firm is associated with a local charity* =**affiliate**, align, connect, ally; merge, integrate.
▸ noun *his business associate* =**partner**, colleague, co-worker, workmate, collaborator, comrade, ally, confederate, acquaintance; *informal* crony; *Austral./NZ informal* offsider.

associated ▸ adjective =**related**, connected, linked, similar, corresponding; attendant, accompanying, incidental. −OPPOSITES unrelated.

association ▸ noun 1 *a trade association* =**alliance**, consortium, coalition, union, league, guild, syndicate, federation, confederation, confederacy, conglomerate, cooperative, partnership, affiliation. **2** *the association between man and environment* =**relationship**, relation, interrelation, connection, interconnection, link, bond, union, tie, attachment, interdependence.

assorted ▶ adjective =**various**, miscellaneous, mixed, varied, varying, diverse, multifarious, sundry; *literary* divers.

assortment ▶ noun =**mixture**, variety, array, mixed bag, mix, miscellany, selection, medley, diversity, ragbag, pot-pourri.

assuage ▶ verb **1** *a pain that could never be assuaged* =**relieve**, ease, alleviate, soothe, mitigate, allay, suppress, subdue, tranquillize; moderate, lessen, diminish, reduce. **2** *her hunger was quickly assuaged* =**satisfy**, gratify, appease, relieve, slake, sate, satiate, quench, check. −OPPOSITES aggravate, intensify.

assume ▶ verb **1** *I assumed he wanted me to keep the book* =**presume**, suppose, take it (as given), take for granted, take as read, conjecture, surmise, conclude, deduce, infer, reason, think, fancy, believe, understand, gather; *N. Amer.* figure. **2** *he assumed a Southern accent* =**affect**, adopt, put on. **3** *they are to assume more responsibility* =**accept**, shoulder, bear, undertake, take on/up. **4** *he assumed control of their finances* =**seize**, take (over), appropriate, wrest, usurp.

assumed ▶ adjective =**false**, fictitious, invented, made-up, fake, bogus, sham, spurious, make-believe; *informal* pretend, phoney; *Brit. informal* cod. −OPPOSITES genuine.

assumption ▶ noun **1** *an assumption about his past* =**supposition**, presumption, conjecture, speculation. **2** *the assumption of power by revolutionaries* =**seizure**, appropriation, expropriation, commandeering, confiscation, hijacking, wresting.

assurance ▶ noun **1** *her calm assurance* =**self-confidence**, confidence, self-assurance, self-possession, nerve, poise, level-headedness; calmness, composure, sangfroid, equanimity; *informal* cool. **2** *you have my assurance* =**word (of honour)**, promise, pledge, vow, oath, undertaking, guarantee, commitment. **3** *life assurance* =**insurance**, indemnity, protection, security, cover. −OPPOSITES self-doubt, uncertainty.

assure ▶ verb **1** *we must assure him of our loyal support* =**reassure**, convince, satisfy, persuade. **2** *he wants to assure a favourable vote* =**ensure**, secure, guarantee, seal, clinch; *informal* sew up. **3** *they guarantee to assure your life* =**insure**, cover, indemnify.

assured ▶ adjective **1** *an assured voice* =**confident**, self-confident, self-assured, self-possessed, poised; calm, composed, imperturbable, unruffled; *informal* unflappable, together. **2** *an assured supply of weapons* =**guaranteed**, certain, sure, secure, reliable, dependable, sound; *informal* sure-fire. −OPPOSITES doubtful, uncertain.

astonish ▶ verb =**amaze**, astound, stagger, startle, stun, confound, dumbfound, nonplus, take aback, leave open-mouthed; *informal* flabbergast, bowl over; *Brit. informal* knock for six.

astonished ▶ adjective =**amazed**, astounded, staggered, surprised, startled, stunned, thunderstruck, aghast, taken aback, dumbfounded, dumbstruck, stupefied, dazed, nonplussed, awestruck; *informal* flabbergasted; *Brit. informal* gobsmacked.

astonishing ▶ adjective =**amazing**, astounding, staggering, surprising, breathtaking, remarkable, extraordinary, incredible, unbelievable, phenomenal; *informal* mind-boggling.

astonishment ▶ noun =**amazement**, surprise, stupefaction, incredulity, disbelief, awe, wonder.

astound ▶ verb =**amaze**, astonish, stagger, surprise, startle, stun, confound, dumbfound, stupefy, daze, take aback, leave open-mouthed; *informal* flabbergast, bowl over; *Brit. informal* knock for six.

astounding ▶ adjective =**amazing**, astonishing, staggering, surprising, breathtaking, remarkable, extraordinary, incredible, unbelievable, phenomenal; *informal* mind-boggling.

astray ▶ adverb **1** *the shots went astray* =**off target**, wide of the mark, awry, off course. **2** *the older boys lead him astray* =**into wrongdoing**, into sin, away from the straight and narrow.

astringent ▶ adjective *her astringent comments* =**severe**, sharp, stern, harsh, acerbic, caustic, mordant, trenchant;

scathing, cutting, incisive, waspish;
N. Amer. acerb.

astronaut ▸ noun = spaceman/
woman, cosmonaut, space traveller,
space cadet; *N. Amer. informal* jock.

astronomical ▸ adjective **1** *astronomical alignments* = **planetary**, stellar, sidereal; celestial. **2** *(informal) the sums he has
paid are astronomical* = **huge**, enormous,
prodigious, monumental, colossal, vast,
gigantic, massive; substantial, considerable, sizeable, hefty, inordinate; *informal*
astronomic, whopping, humongous;
Brit. informal ginormous.
−OPPOSITES tiny.

astute ▸ adjective = **shrewd**, sharp,
acute, quick, clever, intelligent, bright,
smart, canny, perceptive, insightful,
incisive, sagacious, wise; *informal* on the
ball, quick on the uptake, savvy; *Brit.
informal* suss; *N. Amer. informal* heads-up.
−OPPOSITES stupid.

asylum ▸ noun *political asylum* = **refuge**,
sanctuary, shelter, protection, immunity; a safe haven.

asymmetrical ▸ adjective = **lopsided**, unsymmetrical, uneven, unbalanced, crooked, awry, askew, skew,
squint, misaligned; disproportionate,
unequal, irregular; *informal* cock-eyed;
Brit. informal skew-whiff, wonky.

athletic ▸ adjective = **muscular**,
muscly, sturdy, strapping, well built,
strong, powerful, robust, hardy, lusty,
hearty, brawny, burly, broad-
shouldered, Herculean; **fit**, in good
shape, in trim; *informal* sporty, hunky,
beefy.
−OPPOSITES puny.

atmosphere ▸ noun **1** *the gases present
in the atmosphere* = **air**; sky; *literary* the
heavens, the firmament, the ether. **2** *the
hotel has a relaxed atmosphere* = **ambience**,
air, mood, feel, feeling, character, tone,
aura, quality, undercurrent, flavour;
informal vibe.

> **WORD LINKS**
>
> *study of the atmosphere:* **meteorology,
> aerology** *(dated)*
> *study of the upper atmosphere:*
> **aeronomy**

atone ▸ verb = **make amends**, make
reparation, make up for, compensate,
pay, recompense, expiate, make good,
offset; do penance.

atrocious ▸ adjective **1** *atrocious cruel-
ties* = **brutal**, barbaric, barbarous,
savage, vicious; wicked, cruel, nasty,
heinous, monstrous, vile, inhuman,
fiendish, ghastly, horrible; abominable,
disgusting, despicable, contemptible,
loathsome, odious, abhorrent, sickening, horrifying, unspeakable, obscene.
2 *the weather was atrocious* = **appalling**,
dreadful, terrible, unpleasant, miserable; *informal* abysmal, dire, rotten, lousy,
God-awful; *Brit. informal* shocking,
chronic.
−OPPOSITES admirable, superb.

atrocity ▸ noun **1** *press reports detailed
a number of atrocities* = **outrage**, massacre; horror, violation, abuse; crime.
2 *conflict and atrocity around the globe*
= **barbarity**, barbarism, brutality, savagery, inhumanity, cruelty, wickedness,
depravity; viciousness, bestiality.

atrophy ▸ verb **1** *muscles atrophy in zero
gravity* = **waste away**, become emaciated, wither, shrivel (up), shrink; decline, deteriorate, degenerate. **2** *Labour
support atrophied* = **dwindle**, deteriorate,
decline, wane, fade, peter out, crumble,
disintegrate, collapse, slump, go downhill.
−OPPOSITES strengthen, flourish.
▸ noun *muscular atrophy* = **wasting**, emaci-
ation, withering, shrivelling, shrinking;
decay, decline, deterioration, degeneration.
−OPPOSITES strengthening.

attach ▸ verb **1** *a weight is attached to the
cord* = **fasten**, fix, affix, join, connect,
link, secure, make fast, tie, bind, chain;
stick, adhere, glue, fuse. **2** *he attached
himself to the Liberal Party* = **affiliate**, associate, align, ally, join; form an alliance
with. **3** *they attach considerable importance
to research* = **ascribe**, assign, attribute,
accredit, impute. **4** *the medical officer attached to HQ* = **assign**, appoint, allocate,
second; *Military* detail.
−OPPOSITES detach, separate.

attached ▸ adjective *she was very attached to her brother* = **fond of**, devoted
to; *informal* mad about, crazy about.
−OPPOSITES single.

attachment ▸ noun **1** *he has a strong
attachment to his mother* = **bond**, closeness, devotion, loyalty; fondness for,
love for, affection for, feeling for; relationship with. **2** *the shower had a massage
attachment* = **accessory**, fitting, exten-

sion, add-on. **3** *the attachment of safety restraints* =**fixing**, fastening, linking, coupling, connection. **4** *he was on attachment from another regiment* =**assignment**, appointment, secondment, transfer; *Military* detail.

attack ▸ verb **1** *Chris had been brutally attacked* =**assault**, assail, set upon, beat up; batter, punch; *N. Amer.* beat up on; *informal* do over, work over, rough up; *Brit. informal* duff up. **2** *the French had still not attacked* =**strike**, charge, pounce; bomb, shell, strafe, fire. **3** *the clergy attacked government policies* =**criticize**, censure, condemn, pillory, savage, revile, vilify; *informal* knock, slam, lay into; *Brit. informal* slate, slag off, rubbish; *N. Amer. informal* pummel. **4** *they have to attack the problem soon* =**address**, attend to, deal with, confront, apply oneself to, get to work on, embark on; *informal* get stuck into, get cracking on. **5** *the virus attacks the liver* =**affect**, have an effect on, strike; infect, damage, injure; *informal* go for.
−OPPOSITES defend, praise, protect.
▸ noun **1** *an attack on their home* =**assault**, onslaught, offensive, strike, blitz, raid, charge, rush, invasion, incursion. **2** *an outright attack on his style of leadership* =**criticism**, censure, rebuke, admonishment, reprimand, reproof; condemnation, denunciation, revilement, vilification; tirade, diatribe, polemic; *informal* roasting; *Brit. informal* slating, rollicking. **3** *an asthmatic attack* =**fit**, seizure, spasm, convulsion, paroxysm, outburst, bout, episode.
−OPPOSITES defence, commendation.

attacker ▸ noun =**assailant**, assaulter, aggressor; mugger, rapist, killer, murderer.

attain ▸ verb =**achieve**, accomplish, reach, obtain, gain, procure, secure, get, score, net, win, earn, acquire; realize, fulfil; *informal* clinch, bag, wrap up.

attainable ▸ adjective =**achievable**, obtainable, accessible, within reach, securable, realizable; practicable, workable, realistic, reasonable, viable, feasible, possible; *informal* doable, get-at-able.

attainment ▸ noun **1** *the attainment of common goals* =**achievement**, accomplishment, realization, fulfilment, completion. **2** *educational attainment* =**achievement**, accomplishment, proficiency, competence; qualification; skill, aptitude, ability.

attempt ▸ verb *I attempted to answer the question* =**try**, strive, aim, venture, endeavour, seek, undertake, make an effort; have a go at, try one's hand at; *informal* go all out, bend over backwards, bust a gut, have a crack at, have a shot at, have a stab at; *formal* essay.
▸ noun *an attempt to put the economy to rights* =**effort**, endeavour, try, venture, trial, bid; *informal* crack, go, shot, stab; *formal* essay.

attend ▸ verb **1** *they attended a carol service* =**be present at**, sit in on, take part in; appear at, turn up at, visit, go to; *informal* show up at, show one's face at. **2** *he had not attended to the needs of their clients* =**pay attention**, pay heed, be attentive, listen; concentrate, take note, bear in mind, take into consideration, heed, observe, mark. **3** *the wounded were attended to nearby* =**care for**, look after, minister to, see to; tend, treat, nurse, help, aid, assist. **4** *he attended to the boy's education* =**deal with**, see to, manage, organize, sort out, handle, take care of, take charge of, take in hand, tackle. **5** *the queen was attended by an usher* =**escort**, accompany, chaperone, lead, conduct, usher, shepherd; assist, help, serve, wait on. **6** *her giddiness was attended with a fever* =**be accompanied by**, occur with, be associated with, be connected with, be linked with.
−OPPOSITES miss, disregard, ignore, neglect.

attendance ▸ noun **1** *you requested the attendance of a doctor* =**presence**, appearance; attention. **2** *their gig attendances grew* =**audience**, turnout, house, gate; crowd, congregation, gathering; *Austral. informal* muster.
−OPPOSITES absence.
∎ **in attendance** =**present**, here, there, near, nearby, at/on hand, available; assisting, supervising.

attendant ▸ noun **1** *a sleeping car attendant* =**steward**, waiter, waitress, porter, servant; *N. Amer.* waitperson. **2** *a royal attendant* =**escort**, companion, retainer, aide, lady in waiting, equerry, chaperone; servant, manservant, valet, maidservant, maid; *N. Amer.* houseman; *Brit. informal* skivvy; *Military, dated* batman.
▸ adjective *new discoveries and the attendant excitement* =**accompanying**, associated, related, connected, concomitant; resultant, resulting, consequent.

attention ▸ noun **1** *the issue needs fur-*

ther attention =**consideration**, contemplation, deliberation, thought, study, observation, scrutiny, investigation, action. **2** *he tried to attract the attention of a policeman* =**awareness**, notice, scrutiny; eye, gaze. **3** *medical attention* =**care**, treatment, relief, aid, help, assistance.

attentive ▸ adjective **1** *a bright and attentive scholar* =**alert**, perceptive, observant, acute, aware, heedful, vigilant; intent, focused, committed, studious, diligent, conscientious, earnest; *informal* not missing a trick, on the ball. **2** *the most attentive of husbands* =**conscientious**, considerate, thoughtful, kind, caring, solicitous, understanding, sympathetic, obliging, accommodating, gallant, chivalrous; dutiful, responsible.
–OPPOSITES inconsiderate.

attenuated ▸ adjective **1** *attenuated fingers* =**thin**, slender, narrow, slim, skinny, spindly, bony. **2** *his muscle activity was much attenuated* =**weakened**, reduced, lessened, decreased, diminished, impaired.
–OPPOSITES plump, broad, strengthened.

attest ▸ verb =**certify**, corroborate, confirm, verify, substantiate, authenticate, evidence, demonstrate, show, prove; endorse, support, affirm, bear out, give credence to, vouch for; *formal* evince.
–OPPOSITES disprove.

attic ▸ noun =**loft**, roof space, cock loft; garret.

attire ▸ noun *Thomas preferred formal attire* =**clothing**, clothes, garments, dress, wear, garb, costume; *informal* gear, togs, duds, get-up; *Brit. informal* clobber; *N. Amer. informal* threads; *formal* apparel; *archaic* raiment.
▸ verb *she was attired in black crêpe* =**dress (up)**, clothe, garb, robe, array, costume, swathe, deck (out), turn out, fit out, trick out/up, rig out; *informal* get up.

attitude ▸ noun **1** *you seem ambivalent in your attitude* =**view**, viewpoint, outlook, perspective, stance, standpoint, position, orientation, approach, reaction; opinion, ideas, convictions, feelings, thinking. **2** *an attitude of prayer* =**position**, posture, pose, stance.

attorney ▸ noun =**lawyer**, member of the bar, counsel, barrister; *Brit.* Queen's Counsel, QC; *Scottish* advocate; *N. Amer.* counselor(-at-law); *informal* brief.

attract ▸ verb **1** *positive ions are attracted to the negatively charged terminal* =**draw**, pull; suck. **2** *he was attracted by her smile* =**entice**, allure, lure, charm, win over, woo, engage, enchant, entrance, captivate, beguile, bewitch, seduce; excite, titillate, arouse; *informal* turn on.
–OPPOSITES repel.

attraction ▸ noun **1** *the stars are held together by gravitational attraction* =**pull**, draw, force. **2** *she had lost whatever attraction she had ever had* =**appeal**, attractiveness, desirability, seductiveness, allure, animal magnetism; charisma, charm, beauty, good looks. **3** *the park boasts many attractions* =**entertainment**, activity, diversion; amenity, service.
–OPPOSITES repulsion.

attractive ▸ adjective **1** *a more attractive career* =**appealing**, inviting, tempting; agreeable, pleasing, interesting. **2** *she has no idea how attractive she is* =**good-looking**, beautiful, pretty, handsome, lovely, stunning, striking, arresting, gorgeous, prepossessing, fetching, captivating, bewitching, beguiling, engaging, charming, enchanting, appealing, delightful; sexy, seductive, alluring, tantalizing, irresistible, ravishing, desirable; *Scottish & N. English* bonny; *informal* fanciable, tasty, hot, drop-dead gorgeous; *Brit. informal* fit; *N. Amer. informal* cute, foxy; *Austral./NZ informal* spunky; *archaic* comely, fair.
–OPPOSITES uninviting, ugly.

attribute ▸ verb *they attributed their success to him* =**ascribe**, assign, accredit, credit, impute; put down, chalk up, pin on; connect with, associate with.
▸ noun **1** *he has all the attributes of a top player* =**quality**, characteristic, trait, feature, element, aspect, property, sign, hallmark, mark. **2** *the hourglass is the attribute of Father Time* =**symbol**, mark, sign, hallmark, trademark; signature, emblem.

attrition ▸ noun **1** *a gradual attrition of the market economy* =**wearing down/away**, weakening, enfeebling, sapping, attenuation. **2** *the attrition of the edges of the teeth* =**abrasion**, friction, erosion, corrosion, grinding, wearing (down/away); deterioration, damaging.

attune ▸ verb =**accustom**, adjust, adapt, acclimatize, condition, accommodate, assimilate; *N. Amer.* acclimate.

atypical ▸ adjective =**unusual**, untyp-

ical, uncommon, unconventional, unorthodox, irregular, abnormal, aberrant, deviant, unrepresentative; strange, odd, peculiar, bizarre, weird, queer, freakish; exceptional, singular, rare, out of the way, out of the ordinary, extraordinary; informal funny, freaky.
–OPPOSITES normal.

auburn ▸ adjective =**reddish-brown**, russet, chestnut, copper, coppery.

audacious ▸ adjective =**bold**, daring; daredevil, devil-may-care, reckless, madcap; informal gutsy, spunky, ballsy.
–OPPOSITES timid, polite.

audacity ▸ noun **1** *a traveller of extraordinary audacity* =**boldness**, daring, pluck; recklessness; spirit; informal guts, gutsiness, spunk; Brit. informal bottle; N. Amer. informal moxie. **2** *he had the audacity to contradict me* =**impudence**, impertinence, insolence, presumption, cheek, effrontery, nerve, gall, defiance, temerity; informal brass (neck), chutzpah; Brit. informal sauce; N. Amer. informal sass.

audible ▸ adjective =**perceptible**, discernible, detectable; clear, distinct.
–OPPOSITES faint.

audience ▸ noun **1** *the audience applauded* =**spectators**, **listeners**, viewers, onlookers; crowd, throng, congregation, turnout; house, gallery, stalls; Brit. informal punters. **2** *the radio station has a teenage audience* =**public**, market, following, fans; fan base, demographic profile, readership. **3** *an audience with the Pope* =**meeting**, consultation, conference, hearing, reception, interview.

audit ▸ noun *an audit of the party accounts* =**inspection**, examination, scrutiny, probe, investigation, assessment, appraisal, evaluation, review, analysis; informal going-over, once-over.
▸ verb *we audited their accounts* =**inspect**, examine, survey, go through, scrutinize, check, probe, vet, investigate, enquire into, assess, appraise, evaluate, review, analyse, study; informal give something a/the once-over, give something a going-over.

auditorium ▸ noun =**theatre**, hall, assembly room; chamber, room.

au fait ▸ adjective =**familiar**, acquainted, conversant, at home, up to date, in touch; abreast, apprised, in the know, well informed, knowledgeable, well versed, enlightened; informal clued

up, wise to, hip to, plugged/tuned in to, up to speed with.

augment ▸ verb =**increase**, add to, supplement, enhance, build up, enlarge, expand, extend, raise, multiply, swell; magnify, amplify, escalate; improve, boost; informal up, jack up, hike up, bump up, soup up, beef up, turbocharge.
–OPPOSITES decrease.

august ▸ adjective =**distinguished**, respected, eminent, venerable, hallowed, illustrious, prestigious, renowned, celebrated, honoured, acclaimed, esteemed, exalted; great, important, noble, stately, grand, dignified.

aura ▸ noun =**atmosphere**, ambience, air, quality, character, mood, feeling, feel, flavour, tone; emanation, vibration; informal vibe.

auspices ▸ plural noun =**patronage**, aegis, umbrella, protection, keeping, care; support, backing, guardianship, trusteeship, guidance, supervision.

auspicious ▸ adjective =**favourable**, propitious, promising, good, encouraging; opportune, timely, lucky, fortunate, providential, felicitous, advantageous.

austere ▸ adjective **1** *an outwardly austere man* =**severe**, stern, strict, harsh, flinty, dour, grim, cold, frosty, unemotional, unfriendly; formal, stiff, reserved, aloof, forbidding; grave, solemn, serious, unsmiling, unsympathetic, unforgiving; hard, unyielding, unbending; informal hard-boiled. **2** *an austere life* =**ascetic**, self-disciplined, frugal, spartan, puritanical, abstemious, strict, temperate, sober, simple, restrained; chaste. **3** *the buildings were austere* =**plain**, simple, basic, functional, unadorned; bleak, bare, clinical, spartan, ascetic; informal no frills.
–OPPOSITES genial, immoderate, ornate.

Australia ▸ noun =informal Oz, Aussie, down under.

authentic ▸ adjective **1** *an authentic document* =**genuine**, real, bona fide, true; legitimate, lawful, legal, valid; informal the real McCoy, the real thing, pukka, kosher; Austral./NZ informal dinkum. **2** *an authentic depiction of the situation* =**reliable**, dependable, trustworthy, authoritative, honest, faithful; accurate, factual, true, truthful; formal

veracious.
–OPPOSITES fake, unreliable.

authenticate ▶ verb **1** *the evidence will authenticate his claim* =**verify**, validate, prove, substantiate, corroborate, confirm, support, back up, attest to, give credence to. **2** *a mandate authenticated by the popular vote* =**validate**, ratify, confirm, seal, sanction, endorse.

authenticity ▶ noun **1** *the authenticity of the painting* =**genuineness**, bona fides; legitimacy, legality, validity. **2** *the authenticity of this account* =**reliability**, dependability, trustworthiness, credibility; accuracy, truth, veracity, fidelity.

author ▶ noun **1** *modern Canadian authors* =**writer**, wordsmith; novelist, playwright, poet, essayist, biographer; columnist, reporter; *informal* scribe, scribbler. **2** *the author of the peace plan* =**originator**, creator, instigator, founder, father, architect, designer, deviser, producer.

> WORD LINKS
>
> *relating to an author:* **auctorial**

authoritarian ▶ adjective =**autocratic**, dictatorial, despotic, tyrannical, draconian, oppressive, repressive, illiberal, undemocratic; disciplinarian, domineering, overbearing, highhanded, peremptory, imperious, strict, rigid, inflexible; *informal* bossy.
–OPPOSITES democratic, liberal.
▶ noun =**autocrat**, despot, dictator, tyrant; disciplinarian.

authoritative ▶ adjective **1** *authoritative information* =**reliable**, dependable, trustworthy, sound, authentic, valid, attested, verifiable; accurate. **2** *the authoritative edition* =**definitive**, most reliable, best; authorized, accredited, recognized, accepted, approved. **3** *his authoritative manner* =**assured**, confident, assertive; commanding, masterful; domineering, imperious, overbearing, authoritarian; *informal* bossy.
–OPPOSITES unreliable, timid.

authority ▶ noun **1** *a rebellion against those in authority* =**power**, jurisdiction, command, control, charge, dominance, rule, sovereignty, supremacy; influence; *informal* clout. **2** *the authority to arrest drug traffickers* =**authorization**, right, power, mandate, prerogative, licence. **3** *the money was spent without parliamentary authority* =**authorization**, permission, consent, leave, sanction, licence, dispensation, assent, acquiescence, agreement, approval, endorsement, clearance; *informal* the go-ahead, the thumbs up, the OK, the green light. **4** *the authorities* =**officials**, officialdom; government, administration, establishment; police; *informal* the powers that be. **5** *an authority on the stock market* =**expert**, specialist, pundit, doyen(ne), guru, sage, maven; *informal* boffin.

authorization ▶ noun =**permission**, consent, leave, sanction, licence, dispensation, clearance, the nod; assent, agreement, approval, endorsement; authority, right, power, mandate; *informal* the go-ahead, the thumbs up, the OK, the green light.
–OPPOSITES refusal.

authorize ▶ verb **1** *they authorized further action* =**sanction**, permit, allow, approve, consent to, assent to; ratify, endorse, validate; *informal* give the green light, give the go-ahead, OK, give the thumbs up. **2** *the troops were authorized to fire* =**empower**, mandate, commission; entitle.
–OPPOSITES forbid.

authorized ▶ adjective =**approved**, recognized, sanctioned; accredited, licensed, certified; official, lawful, legal, legitimate.
–OPPOSITES unofficial.

autobiography ▶ noun =**memoirs**, life story, own story, personal history.

autocrat ▶ noun =**absolute ruler**, dictator, despot, tyrant.

autocratic ▶ adjective =**despotic**, tyrannical, dictatorial, totalitarian; undemocratic, one-party; domineering, draconian, overbearing, high-handed, peremptory, imperious; harsh, rigid, inflexible, illiberal, oppressive.

automatic ▶ adjective **1** *automatic garage doors* =**mechanized**, mechanical, automated, computerized, electronic, robotic, self-activating, light/heat/motion-sensitive. **2** *an automatic reaction* =**instinctive**, involuntary, unconscious, reflex, knee-jerk, instinctual, subconscious; spontaneous, impulsive, unthinking; mechanical; *informal* gut. **3** *he is the automatic choice for the team* =**inevitable**, unavoidable, inescapable, mandatory, compulsory; certain, definite, obvious, undoubted, assured.
–OPPOSITES manual, deliberate.

autonomous ▸ adjective =self-governing, self-ruling, self-determining, independent, sovereign, free.

autonomy ▸ noun =self-government, self-rule, home rule, self-determination, independence, sovereignty, freedom.

auxiliary ▸ adjective **1** *an auxiliary power source* =**additional**, supplementary, supplemental, extra, reserve, backup, emergency, fallback, second, other. **2** *auxiliary nursing staff* =**ancillary**, assistant, support.
▸ noun *a nursing auxiliary* =**assistant**, helper, ancillary, aid.

avail ■ **to no avail** =in vain, without success, unsuccessfully, fruitlessly, for nothing.

available ▸ adjective **1** *refreshments will be available* =**obtainable**, accessible, to/at hand, at one's disposal, handy, convenient; on sale; untaken, unsold, unused; *informal* up for grabs, on tap. **2** *I'll see if he's available* =**free**, unoccupied; present, here, in, around/about, at work, on duty; contactable.
–OPPOSITES busy, engaged.

avalanche ▸ noun **1** =**snowslide**, icefall; rockslide, landslide, mudslide, landslip. **2** *an avalanche of press comment* =**barrage**, volley, flood, deluge, torrent, tide, wave.

avant-garde ▸ adjective =**experimental**, left-field, modern, cutting edge, progressive, unorthodox, unconventional; *informal* offbeat, way-out.
–OPPOSITES conservative.

avarice ▸ noun =**greed**, acquisitiveness, cupidity, covetousness, rapacity, materialism, mercenariness; *informal* money-grubbing.
–OPPOSITES generosity.

avenge ▸ verb =**requite**, punish, repay, pay back, take revenge for, get even for.

avenue ▸ noun **1** *tree-lined avenues* =**road**, street, drive, parade, boulevard, thoroughfare. **2** *possible avenues of research* =**line**, path; method, approach; angle, tack.

average ▸ noun *the price is above the national average* =**mean**, median, mode; norm, standard, rule, par.
▸ adjective **1** *the average temperature* =**mean**, median, modal. **2** *a woman of average height* =**ordinary**, standard, nor-

mal, typical, regular. **3** *a very average director* =**mediocre**, second-rate, undistinguished, ordinary, middle-of-the-road, unexceptional, unexciting, unremarkable, unmemorable, indifferent, pedestrian, lacklustre, forgettable; *informal* OK, so-so, fair-to-middling, no great shakes, not up to much; *Brit. informal* not much cop; *N. Amer. informal* bush-league; *NZ informal* half-pie.
–OPPOSITES outstanding, exceptional.
■ **on average** =**normally**, usually, ordinarily, generally, in general, for the most part, as a rule, typically; overall, by and large, on the whole.

averse ▸ adjective =**opposed**, against, antipathetic, hostile, ill-disposed, resistant; disinclined, reluctant, loath; *informal* anti.
–OPPOSITES keen.

aversion ▸ noun =**dislike**, antipathy, distaste, abhorrence, hatred, loathing, detestation, hostility; reluctance, disinclination.
–OPPOSITES liking.

avert ▸ verb **1** *she averted her gaze* =**turn aside**, turn away; shift, redirect. **2** *an attempt to avert political chaos* =**prevent**, avoid, stave off, ward off, head off, forestall, preclude.

avid ▸ adjective =**keen**, eager, enthusiastic, ardent, passionate, zealous; devoted, dedicated, wholehearted, earnest.
–OPPOSITES apathetic.

avoid ▸ verb **1** *I avoid situations that cause me stress* =**keep away from**, steer clear of, give a wide berth to. **2** *he is trying to avoid responsibility* =**evade**, dodge, sidestep, escape, run away from, delegate; *informal* duck, wriggle out of, get out of, cop out of; *Austral./NZ informal* duck-shove. **3** *she moved to avoid a blow* =**dodge**, duck, get out of the way of. **4** *you've been avoiding me all evening* =**shun**, stay away from, evade, keep one's distance, elude, hide from; ignore. **5** *he should avoid drinking alcohol* =**refrain from**, abstain from, desist from; steer clear of, eschew.
–OPPOSITES confront, face up to, seek out.

avoidable ▸ adjective =**preventable**; stoppable, escapable.
–OPPOSITES inescapable.

avowed ▸ adjective =**self-confessed**, self-declared, acknowledged, admitted;

a

open, overt.

await ▶ verb **1** *Peter was awaiting news* =**wait for**, expect, anticipate. **2** *many dangers await them* =**be in store for**, lie ahead of, lie in wait for, be waiting for.

awake ▶ verb **1** *she awoke the following morning* =**wake (up)**, awaken, stir, come to, come round; *literary* waken. **2** *they finally awoke to the extent of the problem* =**realize**, become aware of, become conscious of; *informal* get wise to.
▶ adjective **1** *she was still awake* =**wakeful**, sleepless, restless, restive. **2** *too few are awake to the dangers* =**aware of**, conscious of, mindful of, alert to; *formal* cognizant of.
−OPPOSITES asleep, oblivious.

awaken ▶ verb **1** *I awakened early | the jolt awakened her.* See AWAKE verb. **2** *he had awakened strong emotions in her* =**arouse**, rouse, bring out, engender, evoke, trigger, stir up, stimulate, kindle; revive.

award ▶ verb *the society awarded him a medal* =**give**, grant, accord, assign; confer on, bestow on, present to, decorate with.
▶ noun **1** *an award for high-quality service* =**prize**, trophy, medal, decoration; reward; *informal* gong. **2** *a libel award* =**payment**, settlement, compensation. **3** *the Arts Council gave him an award of £1,500* =**grant**, scholarship, endowment; *Brit.* bursary.

aware ▶ adjective **1** *she is aware of the dangers* =**conscious of**, mindful of, informed about, acquainted with, familiar with, alive to, alert to, au fait with; *informal* wise to, in the know about, hip to; *formal* cognizant of. **2** *we need to be more environmentally aware* =**sensitive**, enlightened, knowledgeable, (well) informed, au fait; correct; *informal* clued up, genned up; *Brit. informal* switched-on.
−OPPOSITES ignorant.

awareness ▶ noun =**consciousness**, recognition, realization; understanding, grasp, appreciation, knowledge, insight; familiarity, sensitivity; *formal* cognizance.

awash ▶ adjective **1** *the road was awash* =**flooded**, under water, submerged. **2** *the city was awash with journalists* =**inundated**, flooded, swamped, teeming, swarming, overflowing, overrun; *informal* knee-deep in, buried in.

away ▶ adverb *we'll be away for two weeks* =**elsewhere**, abroad; gone, off (work),

out (of town/the country), absent; on holiday, on vacation.

awe ▶ noun =**wonder**, wonderment; admiration, reverence, respect.

awe-inspiring ▶ adjective. See AWESOME.

awesome ▶ adjective =**breathtaking**, awe-inspiring, magnificent, amazing, stunning, staggering, imposing; formidable, fearsome; *informal* mind-boggling, mind-blowing, brilliant; *literary* wondrous.
−OPPOSITES unimpressive.

awestruck ▶ adjective =**awed**, wonderstruck, amazed, lost for words, open-mouthed; *informal* gobsmacked.

awful ▶ adjective **1** *the place smelled awful* =**disgusting**, terrible, dreadful, ghastly, horrible, vile, foul, revolting, repulsive, repugnant, odious, sickening, nauseating; *informal* sick-making, gross; *Brit. informal* beastly; *literary* noisome. **2** *an awful book* =**dreadful**, terrible, frightful, atrocious; lamentable; *informal* crummy, pathetic, rotten, woeful, lousy, appalling, abysmal, dismal, dire, poxy; *Brit. informal* rubbish. **3** *an awful accident* =**serious**, bad, terrible, dreadful. **4** *you look awful — go and lie down* =**ill**, unwell, sick, nauseous; *Brit.* off colour, poorly; *Brit. informal* grotty, ropy; *Scottish informal* wabbit, peely-wally; *Austral./NZ informal* crook. **5** *I felt awful for getting so angry* =**guilty**, ashamed, contrite, sorry, regretful, repentant; *informal* rotten, terrible, dreadful.
−OPPOSITES wonderful.

awfully ▶ adverb **1** *(informal) an awfully nice man* =**very**, extremely, really, immensely, exceedingly, thoroughly, dreadfully, exceptionally, remarkably, extraordinarily; *N. English* right; *informal* terrifically, terribly, devilishly, seriously, majorly; *Brit. informal* jolly, ever so, dead, well; *N. Amer. informal* real, mighty, awful; *informal, dated* frightfully; *archaic* exceeding. **2** *we played awfully* =**terribly**, dreadfully, atrociously, appallingly; *informal* abysmally, pitifully, diabolically.

awhile ▶ adverb =**for a moment**, for a (little) while, for a short time; *informal* (for) a bit/second/minute.

awkward ▶ adjective **1** *the box was awkward to carry* =**difficult**, tricky; cumbersome, unwieldy; *Brit. informal* fiddly. **2** *an awkward time* =**inconvenient**, in-

appropriate, inopportune, difficult. **3** *he put her in a very awkward position* =**embarrassing**, uncomfortable, unpleasant, delicate, tricky, problematic(al), troublesome, thorny; humiliating, compromising; *informal* sticky, dicey, hairy; *Brit. informal* dodgy. **4** *she felt awkward when alone with him* =**uncomfortable**, uneasy, tense, nervous, edgy; self-conscious, embarrassed. **5** *his awkward movements* =**clumsy**, ungainly, uncoordinated, graceless, inelegant, gauche, gawky, wooden, stiff; unskilful, maladroit, inept, blundering; *informal* clodhopping, ham-fisted, cack-handed; *Brit. informal* all (fingers and) thumbs. **6** *(Brit.) you're being really awkward* =**unreasonable**, uncooperative, unhelpful, difficult, obstructive; contrary, perverse; stubborn, obstinate; *Brit. informal* bloody-minded, bolshie; *N. Amer. informal* balky; *formal* refractory.
–OPPOSITES easy, convenient, at ease, graceful, amenable.

awning ▶ noun =**canopy**, shade, sunshade, shelter, cover; *Brit.* blind.

awry ▶ adjective **1** *something was awry* =**amiss**, wrong; *informal* up. **2** *his wig looked awry* =**askew**, crooked, lopsided, tilted, skewed, skew, squint, to one side, off-centre, uneven; *informal* cock-eyed; *Brit. informal* skew-whiff, wonky.
–OPPOSITES straight.

axe ▶ noun =**hatchet**, cleaver, adze; *Brit.* chopper.
▶ verb **1** *the show was axed* =**cancel**, withdraw, drop, scrap, discontinue, terminate, end; *informal* ditch, dump, pull the plug on. **2** *500 staff were axed* =**dismiss**, make redundant, lay off, let go, discharge, get rid of; *informal* sack, fire, give someone the sack, give someone their marching orders; *Brit. informal* give someone their cards.

axiom ▶ noun =**accepted truth**, general truth, dictum, truism; maxim, adage, aphorism.

axis ▶ noun *an axis of evil* =**alliance**, coalition, bloc, union, confederation, confederacy, league.

axle ▶ noun =**shaft**, spindle, rod.

Bb

babble ▶ verb **1** =**prattle**, rattle on, gabble, chatter, jabber, twitter, go on, run on, prate, ramble, burble, blather; *informal* gab, yak, yabber, yatter, yammer, blabber, jaw, gas, shoot one's mouth off; *Brit. informal* witter, rabbit, chunter, natter, waffle. **2** *a brook babbled gently* =**burble**, murmur, gurgle.

babel ▶ noun =**clamour**, din, racket, tumult, uproar, hubbub; *informal* hullabaloo; *Brit. informal* row.

baby ▶ noun *a newborn baby* =**infant**, newborn, child, tot; *Scottish & N. English* bairn; *technical* neonate; *informal* sprog, tiny; *literary* babe, babe in arms.
▶ adjective *baby carrots* =**miniature**, mini, little, small, small-scale, scaled-down, toy, pocket, midget, dwarf; *Scottish* wee; *N. Amer.* vest-pocket; *informal* teeny, teensy, itsy-bitsy, tiddly, bite-sized; *Brit. informal* titchy; *N. Amer. informal* little-bitty.
–OPPOSITES large.
▶ verb =**pamper**, mollycoddle, spoil, cosset, coddle, indulge, overindulge.

babyish ▶ adjective =**childish**, immature, infantile, juvenile, puerile.
–OPPOSITES mature.

back ▶ noun **1** =**spine**, backbone, spinal column, vertebral column. **2** *the back of the house* =**rear**; *Nautical* stern. **3** *the back of the queue* =**end**, tail end, rear end; *N. Amer.* tag end. **4** *the back of a postcard* =**reverse**, other side, underside; *informal* flip side.
–OPPOSITES front, head, face.
▶ adverb **1** *he pushed his chair back* =**backwards**, behind one, to one's rear, rearwards; away. **2** *a few months back* =**ago**, earlier, previously, before.
–OPPOSITES forward.
▶ verb **1** *companies backed the scheme generously* =**sponsor**, finance, put up the money for, fund, subsidize, underwrite, be a patron of; *informal* foot the bill for, pick up the tab for. **2** *most people backed the idea* =**support**, endorse, sanction, approve of, give one's blessing to, smile on, favour, advocate, promote, uphold, champion; *informal* throw one's weight behind. **3** *he backed the horse at 33–1* =**bet**

on, gamble on, stake money on. **4** *he backed away* =**reverse**, draw back, step back, move backwards, back off, pull back, retreat, withdraw.
–OPPOSITES oppose, advance.
▶ adjective **1** *the back seats* =**rear**, rearmost, hind, hindmost, hinder, posterior. **2** *a back copy* =**past**, old, previous, earlier.
–OPPOSITES front, future.

■ **back down** =**give in**, concede defeat, surrender, yield, submit, climb down, concede.

■ **back out of** =**renege on**, withdraw from, pull out of, retreat from, fail to honour.

■ **back something up** =**substantiate**, corroborate, confirm, support, bear out, endorse, bolster, reinforce, lend weight to.

■ **back someone up** =**support**, stand by, side with, take someone's part.

■ **behind someone's back** =**secretly**, without someone's knowledge, on the sly, sneakily, covertly, surreptitiously.

> **WORD LINKS**
>
> *relating to the back:* **dorsal, lumbar**
> *lying on one's back:* **supine**
> *further back:* **posterior**

backbiting ▶ noun =**malicious talk**, spiteful talk, slander, libel, defamation, abuse; *informal* bitching, cattiness, mudslinging, bad-mouthing; *Brit. informal* slagging off, rubbishing.

backbone ▶ noun **1** =**spine**, spinal column, vertebral column, vertebrae; back. **2** *infantry are the backbone of most armies* =**mainstay**, cornerstone, foundation. **3** *he has enough backbone to see us through* =**strength of character**, strength of will, firmness, resolution, resolve, grit, determination, fortitude, mettle, spirit; *informal* guts, spunk; *Brit. informal* bottle.

back-breaking ▶ adjective =**gruelling**, arduous, strenuous, onerous, punishing, crushing, demanding, exacting, taxing, exhausting, draining; *informal* killing; *Brit. informal* knackering.
–OPPOSITES easy.

backer ▸ noun **1** *£3 million was provided by the project's backers* =**sponsor**, investor, underwriter, financier, patron, benefactor; *informal* angel. **2** *the backers of the proposition* =**supporter**, defender, advocate, promoter, proponent, seconder; *N. Amer.* booster.

backfire ▸ verb *Bernard's plan backfired on him* =**rebound**, boomerang, come back; fail; *informal* blow up in someone's face.

background ▸ noun **1** *a background of trees* =**backdrop**, backcloth, surrounding(s), setting, scene. **2** *students from different backgrounds* =**social circumstances**, family circumstances; environment, class, culture, tradition. **3** *her nursing background* =**experience**, record, history, past, training, education.
–OPPOSITES foreground.
■ **in the background** =**behind the scenes**, out of the public eye, out of the spotlight, out of the limelight, backstage.

backhanded ▸ adjective =**indirect**, ambiguous, oblique, equivocal.
–OPPOSITES direct.

backing ▸ noun **1** *he has the backing of his colleagues* =**support**, help, assistance, aid; approval, endorsement. **2** *financial backing* =**sponsorship**, funding, patronage. **3** *musical backing* =**accompaniment**; harmony, obbligato.

backlash ▸ noun =**adverse reaction**, counterblast, comeback; retaliation, reprisal.

backlog ▸ noun =**accumulation**, logjam, pile-up.

back-pedal ▸ verb *the government has back-pedalled on its plans* =**change one's mind**, go into reverse, backtrack, back down, climb down, do an about-face, do a U-turn, renege, go back on, back out of; *Brit.* do an about-turn.

backslide ▸ verb *many things can cause slimmers to backslide* =**relapse**, lapse, regress, retrogress, weaken, lose one's resolve.
–OPPOSITES persevere.

backup ▸ noun =**help**, support, assistance, aid; reinforcements, reserves.

backward ▸ adjective **1** *a backward look* =**rearward**, to/towards the rear, to/towards the back, behind one, reverse. **2** *the decision was a backward step* =**retrograde**, retrogressive, regressive,

for the worse, in the wrong direction, downhill, negative. **3** *economically backward* =**underdeveloped**, undeveloped; primitive. **4** *he was not backward in displaying his talents* =**hesitant**, reticent, reluctant; shy, diffident, bashful, timid.
–OPPOSITES forward, progressive, advanced, confident.

backwards ▸ adverb **1** *Penny glanced backwards* =**towards the rear**, rearwards, backward, behind one. **2** *count backwards from twenty to ten* =**in reverse**, in reverse order.
–OPPOSITES forwards.

backwoods ▸ plural noun =**the back of beyond**, remote areas, the wilds, the hinterlands, a backwater; *N. Amer.* the backcountry; *informal* the middle of nowhere, the sticks; *N. Amer. informal* the boondocks, the boonies.

bacteria ▸ plural noun =**microorganisms**, microbes, germs, bacilli, pathogens; *informal* bugs.

bad ▸ adjective **1** *bad workmanship* =**substandard**, poor, inferior, second-rate, second-class, unsatisfactory, inadequate, unacceptable, not up to scratch, not up to par, deficient, imperfect, defective, faulty, shoddy, amateurish, careless, negligent; *informal* crummy, rotten, pathetic, useless, woeful, bum, lousy, ropy; *Brit. informal* duff, rubbish. **2** *the alcohol had a bad effect* =**harmful**, damaging, detrimental, injurious, hurtful, destructive, ruinous, deleterious. **3** *the bad guys* =**wicked**, sinful, immoral, evil, morally wrong, corrupt, base, black-hearted, reprobate, amoral; *informal* crooked, bent, dirty. **4** *you bad girl* =**naughty**, badly behaved, disobedient, wayward, wilful, self-willed, defiant, unruly. **5** *bad news* =**unpleasant**, disagreeable, unwelcome; unfortunate; terrible, dreadful, awful, grim, distressing. **6** *a bad time to arrive* =**inauspicious**, unfavourable, inopportune, unpropitious, unfortunate, disadvantageous, inappropriate, unsuitable. **7** *a bad accident* =**severe**, serious, grave, critical, acute; *formal* grievous. **8** *the meat's bad* =**rotten**, off, decayed, decomposed, decomposing, putrid. **9** *a bad knee* =**injured**, wounded, diseased; *Brit. informal* gammy, knackered; *Austral./NZ informal* crook. **10** *I felt bad about leaving them* =**guilty**, conscience-stricken, remorseful, guilt-ridden, ashamed, contrite.
–OPPOSITES good, beneficial, virtuous,

well behaved, minor, slight, fresh, un-repentant.

■ **not bad** =**all right**, adequate, good enough, reasonable, fair, decent, average, tolerable, acceptable; *informal* OK, so-so, fair-to-middling.

badge ▸ noun **1** =**pin**, brooch; *N. Amer.* button. **2** *a badge of success* =**sign**, symbol, indication, signal, mark; hallmark, trademark.

badger ▸ verb =**pester**, harass, bother, plague, torment, hound, nag, chivvy, harry, keep on at, go on at; *informal* hassle, bug.

> **WORD LINKS**
>
> *male:* **boar**
> *female:* **sow**
> *young:* **cub**
> *home:* **sett, earth**
> *collective noun:* **cete**

badinage ▸ noun =**banter**, repartee, witty conversation, wordplay, cut and thrust; *N. Amer. informal* josh.

badly ▸ adverb **1** *the job had very been badly done* =**poorly**, incompetently, ineptly, inexpertly, inefficiently, imperfectly, deficiently, defectively, unsatisfactorily, inadequately, incorrectly, faultily, shoddily, amateurishly, carelessly, negligently; *informal* crummily, pitifully, woefully. **2** *try not to think badly of me* =**unfavourably**, ill, critically, disapprovingly. **3** *stop behaving badly* =**naughtily**, disobediently, wilfully, reprehensibly, mischievously. **4** *he had been badly treated* =**cruelly**, wickedly, unkindly, harshly, shamefully; unfairly, unjustly, wrongly, improperly. **5** *it turned out badly* =**unsuccessfully**, unfavourably, adversely, unfortunately. **6** *some of the victims are badly hurt* =**severely**, seriously, gravely, acutely, critically; *formal* grievously.
–OPPOSITES well, slightly.

bad-tempered ▸ adjective =**irritable**, irascible, tetchy, testy, grumpy, grouchy, crotchety, in a (bad) mood, cantankerous, curmudgeonly, ill-tempered, ill-humoured, peevish, cross, fractious, pettish, crabby; *informal* snappish, on a short fuse; *Brit. informal* shirty, stroppy, ratty; *N. Amer. informal* cranky, ornery; *Austral./NZ informal* snaky.
–OPPOSITES good-humoured, affable.

baffle ▸ verb =**perplex**, puzzle, bewilder, mystify, bemuse, confuse, con-

found, nonplus; *informal* flummox, faze, stump, beat, fox; *N. Amer. informal* discombobulate.
–OPPOSITES enlighten.

baffling ▸ adjective =**puzzling**, bewildering, perplexing, mystifying, bemusing, confusing, unclear.
–OPPOSITES clear, comprehensible.

bag ▸ noun =**suitcase**, case, valise, portmanteau, holdall, grip, overnighter; (**bags**) luggage, baggage.
▸ verb **1** *locals bagged the most fish* =**catch**, land, capture, trap, snare, ensnare. **2** *he bagged seven medals* =**get**, secure, obtain, acquire, pick up; win, achieve, attain; *informal* land, net.

baggage ▸ noun =**luggage**, suitcases, cases, bags.

baggy ▸ adjective =**loose-fitting**, loose, roomy, generously cut, full, ample, voluminous, billowing.
–OPPOSITES tight.

bail ▸ noun *he was released on bail* =**surety**, security, assurance, indemnity; bond, guarantee, pledge.
■ **bail out** *the pilot bailed out* =**eject**, parachute to safety.
■ **bail someone/something out** =**rescue**, save, relieve; finance, help (out), assist, aid.

bait ▸ noun **1** *the fish let go of the bait* =**lure**, decoy, fly. **2** *was she the bait to lure him into a trap?* =**enticement**, lure, decoy, snare, trap, siren, carrot, attraction, draw, magnet; *informal* come-on.
▸ verb *he was baited at school* =**taunt**, tease, goad, pick on, torment, persecute, plague, harry, harass, hound; *informal* needle; *Brit. informal* wind up.

bake ▸ verb *the earth was baked by the sun* =**scorch**, burn, sear, parch, dry (up), desiccate.

balance ▸ noun **1** *I tripped and lost my balance* =**stability**, equilibrium, steadiness, footing. **2** *political balance in broadcasting* =**fairness**, justice, impartiality, egalitarianism; parity, equity, equilibrium, evenness, symmetry, uniformity, comparability. **3** *the food was weighed on a balance* =**scale(s)**, weighing machine, weighbridge. **4** *the balance of the rent* =**remainder**, outstanding amount, rest, residue, difference.
–OPPOSITES instability, bias.
▸ verb **1** *she balanced the book on her head* =**steady**, stabilize, poise, level. **2** *he balanced his radical remarks with more familiar*

declarations =**counterbalance**, balance out, offset, even out/up, counteract, compensate for, make up for. **3** *their income and expenditure do not balance* =**correspond**, agree, tally, match up, concur, coincide, be in agreement, be consistent. **4** *you need to balance cost against benefit* =**weigh (up)**, compare, evaluate, consider, assess, appraise, judge.

■ **in the balance** =**uncertain**, undetermined, unsettled, unresolved, pending, in limbo, up in the air, at a turning point, critical.

■ **on balance** =**overall**, all in all, all things considered, taking everything into consideration/account, by and large.

balanced ▸ adjective **1** *a balanced view* =**fair**, equitable, just, unbiased, unprejudiced, objective, impartial, dispassionate. **2** *a balanced diet* =**mixed**, varied; healthy, sensible. **3** *a balanced individual* =**level-headed**, well adjusted, mature, stable, sensible, practical, pragmatic, reasonable, rational, sane, even-tempered.
–OPPOSITES partial, unhealthy, neurotic.

bald ▸ adjective **1** *a bald head* =**hairless**, smooth, shaven, depilated. **2** *a few bald bushes* =**leafless**, bare, uncovered. **3** *a bald statement* =**plain**, simple, unadorned, unvarnished, unembellished, undisguised; *informal* upfront.
–OPPOSITES hairy, lush, vague.

baldness ▸ noun =**hair loss**, hairlessness; *Medicine* alopecia.

bale¹ ▸ noun *a bale of cotton* =**bundle**, truss, bunch, pack, package, parcel.

bale² ■ **bale out**. See BAIL.

baleful ▸ adjective =**menacing**, threatening, unfriendly, hostile, antagonistic, evil, evil-intentioned, vindictive, malevolent, malicious, malignant, malign, sinister.
–OPPOSITES benevolent, friendly.

balk ▸ verb. See BAULK.

ball¹ ▸ noun =**sphere**, globe, orb, globule.

ball² ▸ noun *a fancy-dress ball* =**dance**, dinner dance, masquerade; *N. Amer.* hoedown, prom.

ballad ▸ noun =**song**, folk song, shanty, ditty, canzone.

balloon ▸ verb **1** *her long skirt ballooned in the wind* =**swell (out)**, puff out/up,

bulge (out), bag, belly (out), fill (out), billow (out). **2** *the company's debt has ballooned* =**increase rapidly**, soar, rocket, shoot up, escalate, mount, spiral; *informal* go through the roof, skyrocket.
–OPPOSITES plummet.

ballot ▸ noun =**vote**, poll, election, referendum, plebiscite.

balm ▸ noun **1** *a skin balm* =**ointment**, lotion, cream, salve, liniment, embrocation, rub, gel, emollient; *technical* demulcent, humectant. **2** *balm for troubled spirits* =**relief**, comfort, ease, succour, consolation, cheer, solace; *literary* easement.
–OPPOSITES astringent, misery.

balmy ▸ adjective =**mild**, gentle, temperate, summery, calm, tranquil, clement, fine, pleasant.
–OPPOSITES harsh, wintry.

ban ▸ verb **1** *smoking was banned* =**prohibit**, forbid, veto, proscribe, disallow, outlaw, make illegal, embargo, bar, debar; *Law* enjoin, restrain. **2** *Gary was banned from the playground* =**exclude**, banish, expel, eject, evict, drive out, force out; *informal* boot out, kick out; *Brit. informal* turf out.
–OPPOSITES permit, admit.

▸ noun **1** *a ban on smoking* =**prohibition**, veto, proscription, embargo, bar, moratorium, injunction. **2** *a ban from international football* =**exclusion**, banishment, expulsion, ejection, eviction.
–OPPOSITES permission, admission.

banal ▸ adjective =**trite**, hackneyed, clichéd, platitudinous, vapid, commonplace, ordinary, common, stock, conventional, stereotyped, overused, overdone, overworked, stale, worn out, time-worn, unimaginative, unoriginal; *informal* old hat, corny, played out.
–OPPOSITES original.

banality ▸ noun **1** *the banality of most sitcoms* =**triteness**, vapidity, staleness, unimaginativeness, prosaicness; *informal* corniness. **2** *they exchanged banalities* =**platitude**, cliché, truism, commonplace.
–OPPOSITES originality, epigram, witticism.

band¹ ▸ noun **1** *a band round her waist* =**belt**, sash, girdle, strap, tape, ring, hoop, loop, circlet, circle, cord, tie; *literary* cincture. **2** *the green band round his pullover* =**stripe**, strip, streak, line, bar.

band² ▸ noun **1** *a band of robbers* =**group**,

gang, mob, pack, troop, troupe, company, party, crew, body, posse; team, side, line-up; association, society, club, circle, fellowship, partnership, guild, lodge, order, fraternity, sorority, union, alliance, institution, league, federation, clique, set, coterie; *informal* bunch. **2** *the band played on* =(**musical**) **group**, pop group, ensemble, orchestra; *informal* combo.

▶ verb =**join** (**up**), team up, join forces, pool resources, club together, get together; amalgamate, unite, form an alliance.

–OPPOSITES split up.

bandage ▶ verb *she bandaged my knee* =**bind**, dress, strap (up).

bandit ▶ noun =**robber**, thief, raider, mugger; freebooter, outlaw, hijacker, looter, marauder, gangster; *dated* desperado; *literary* brigand; *historical* rustler, highwayman.

bandy¹ ▶ adjective *bandy legs* =**bowed**, curved, bent.

–OPPOSITES straight.

bandy² ▶ verb **1** *lots of figures were bandied about* =**spread** (**about/around**), put about, toss about, discuss, rumour, mention, repeat; *literary* bruit about/abroad. **2** *I'm not going to bandy words with you* =**exchange**, swap, trade.

bane ▶ noun =**scourge**, plague, curse, blight, pest, nuisance, headache, nightmare, trial, hardship, burden, thorn in one's flesh/side.

bang ▶ noun **1** *the door slammed with a bang* =**thud**, thump, bump, crack, crash, smack, boom, clang, clap, knock, tap, clunk, clonk; stamp, stomp, clump, clomp; report, explosion, detonation. **2** *a nasty bang on the head* =**blow**, knock, thump, bump, hit, smack, crack; *informal* bash, whack.

▶ verb **1** =**hit**, strike, beat, thump, hammer, knock, rap, pound, thud, punch, bump, smack, crack, slap, slam, welt, cuff, pummel, buffet; *informal* bash, whack, clobber, clout, clip, wallop, belt. **2** *fireworks banged in the air* =**thud**, thump, boom, pound, crack, crash, explode, detonate, burst, blow up.

bangle ▶ noun =**bracelet**, wristlet, armlet.

banish ▶ verb **1** *he was banished for his crime* =**exile**, expel, deport, eject, expatriate, extradite, repatriate, transport; cast out, oust, evict, throw out,

exclude, shut out, ban. **2** *he tried to banish his fear* =**dispel**, dismiss, disperse, scatter, dissipate, drive away, chase away, shut out.

–OPPOSITES admit, engender.

banister ▶ noun =**handrail**; baluster, balustrade.

bank¹ ▶ noun **1** *the banks of Lake Michigan* =**edge**, side, embankment, levee, border, verge, boundary. **2** *a grassy bank* =**slope**, rise, incline, gradient, ramp; mound, ridge, hillock, hummock, knoll; bar, reef, shoal, shelf; pile, heap, mass, drift. **3** *a bank of switches* =**array**, row, line, tier, group, series.

▶ verb **1** *they banked up the earth* =**pile** (**up**), heap (up), stack (up); accumulate, amass. **2** *the aircraft banked* =**tilt**, lean, tip, slant, incline, angle, slope, list, camber, pitch, dip, cant.

> **WORD LINKS**
>
> *relating to a river bank:* **riparian, riverine**

bank² ▶ noun =**store**, reserve, accumulation, stock, stockpile, supply, pool, fund, cache, hoard, deposit; storehouse, reservoir.

▶ verb **1** *I banked the money* =**deposit**, pay in. **2** *they bank with Barclays* =**have an account at**, use, be a customer of.

bankrupt ▶ adjective **1** *the company was declared bankrupt* =**insolvent**, failed, ruined; *Brit.* in administration, in receivership; *informal* bust, belly up; *Brit. informal* skint, stony broke, in Queer Street. **2** *this government is bankrupt of ideas* =**bereft**, devoid, empty, destitute; without, in need of, wanting; *informal* minus, sans.

–OPPOSITES solvent, teeming with.

▶ verb =**ruin**, impoverish, reduce to penury/destitution.

bankruptcy ▶ noun =**insolvency**, liquidation, failure, (financial) ruin; *Brit.* administration, receivership.

–OPPOSITES solvency.

banner ▶ noun **1** *students waved banners* =**placard**, sign, poster, notice. **2** *banners fluttered above the troops* =**flag**, standard, ensign, colour(s), pennant, banderole.

banquet ▶ noun =**feast**, dinner; *informal* spread, blowout; *Brit. informal* nosh-up, slap-up meal.

–OPPOSITES snack.

banter ▶ noun *a brief exchange of banter* =**repartee**, witty conversation, raillery, wordplay, cut and thrust, badinage.

▶ **verb** *sightseers were bantering with the guards* =**joke**, jest, quip; *informal* josh, wisecrack.

baptism ▶ **noun 1** *the baptism ceremony* =**christening**, naming. **2** *his baptism as a politician* =**initiation**, debut, introduction, inauguration, launch, rite of passage.

baptize ▶ **verb 1** *he was baptized as a baby* =**christen**. **2** *they were baptized into the church* =**admit**, initiate, enrol, recruit. **3** *he was baptized Enoch* =**name**, call, dub; *formal* denominate.

bar ▶ **noun 1** *an iron bar* =**rod**, pole, stick, batten, shaft, rail, paling, spar, strut, crosspiece, beam. **2** *a bar of chocolate* =**block**, slab, cake, tablet, wedge, ingot. **3** *your drinks are on the bar* =**counter**, table, buffet. **4** *she had a drink in a bar* =**hostelry**, tavern, inn, taproom; *Brit.* pub, public house; *informal* watering hole; *Brit. informal* local, boozer; *dated* alehouse. **5** *a bar to promotion* =**obstacle**, impediment, hindrance, obstruction, block, hurdle, barrier. **6** *(Brit.)* members of the Bar =**barristers**, advocates, counsel.
–OPPOSITES aid.

▶ **verb 1** *they have barred the door* =**bolt**, lock, fasten, secure, block, barricade, obstruct. **2** *I was barred from entering* =**prohibit**, debar, preclude, forbid, ban, interdict, inhibit; exclude; obstruct, hinder, block.
–OPPOSITES open, admit.

▶ **preposition** *everyone bar me.* See EXCEPT preposition.

barb ▶ **noun 1** =**spike**, prong, spur, thorn, needle, prickle, spine, quill. **2** *the barbs from his critics* =**insult**, sneer, jibe, cutting remark, shaft, slight, brickbat, slur, jeer, taunt; (**barbs**) abuse, disparagement, scoffing, scorn, sarcasm, goading; *informal* dig, put-down.

barbarian ▶ **noun** *the city was besieged by barbarians* =**savage**, heathen, brute, beast; ruffian, thug, lout, vandal, hoodlum, hooligan; *informal* roughneck; *Brit. informal* yob, lager lout.

▶ **adjective** *the barbarian hordes* =**savage**, uncivilized, barbaric, primitive, heathen, wild, brutish, Neanderthal.
–OPPOSITES civilized.

barbaric ▶ **adjective 1** *barbaric crimes* =**brutal**, barbarous, brutish, bestial, savage, vicious, wicked, cruel, ruthless, merciless, villainous, murderous, heinous, monstrous, vile, inhuman, infer-

nal, dark, fiendish, diabolical. **2** *barbaric cultures* =**savage**, barbarian, primitive, heathen, wild, brutish, uncivilized.
–OPPOSITES civilized.

barbarity ▶ **noun 1** *the barbarity of slavery* =**brutality**, brutalism, cruelty, bestiality, barbarism, barbarousness, savagery, viciousness, wickedness, villainy, baseness, inhumanity. **2** *the barbarities of the last war* =**atrocity**, crime, outrage, enormity.
–OPPOSITES benevolence.

barbarous ▶ **adjective.** See BARBARIC sense 1.

barbecue ▶ **noun** =**roast**; *N. Amer.* cookout; *informal* barbie, BBQ.

barbed ▶ **adjective** =**hurtful**, wounding, cutting, stinging, mean, spiteful, nasty, cruel, vicious, unkind, snide, scathing, pointed, bitter, acid, caustic, sharp, vitriolic, venomous, poisonous, hostile, malicious, malevolent, vindictive; *informal* bitchy, catty.
–OPPOSITES kindly.

bare ▶ **adjective 1** *he was bare to the waist* =**naked**, unclothed, undressed, uncovered, stripped, having nothing on, nude; *informal* without a stitch on, in one's birthday suit, in the raw, in the altogether, in the buff; *Brit. informal* starkers; *Scottish informal* in the scud; *N. Amer. informal* buck naked. **2** *a bare room* =**empty**, unfurnished; stark, austere, spartan, unadorned, unembellished, unornamented, plain. **3** *a cupboard bare of food* =**empty**, devoid, bereft; without, lacking. **4** *a bare landscape* =**barren**, bleak, exposed, desolate, stark, arid, desert. **5** *the bare facts* =**basic**, essential, fundamental, plain, straightforward, simple, pure, stark, bald, cold, hard, brutal, harsh.
–OPPOSITES clothed, furnished, embellished, lush.

▶ **verb** =**uncover**, strip, undress, unclothe, denude, expose.
–OPPOSITES cover.

barefaced ▶ **adjective** =**flagrant**, blatant, glaring, obvious, undisguised, unconcealed, naked; shameless, unabashed, unashamed, impudent, audacious, brazen, brass-necked.

barely ▶ **adverb** =**hardly**, scarcely, only just, narrowly, by the skin of one's teeth, by a hair's breadth; almost not; *informal* by a whisker.
–OPPOSITES easily.

bargain ▸ noun **1** *I'll make a bargain with you* =**agreement**, arrangement, understanding, deal; contract, pact; pledge, promise. **2** *this binder is a bargain at £1.98* =**(good) value for money**; *informal* good buy, cheap buy, snip, steal, giveaway.
–OPPOSITES rip-off.

▸ verb =**haggle**, negotiate, discuss terms, deal, barter.

■ **bargain for/on** =**expect**, anticipate, be prepared for, allow for, plan for, reckon with, take into account/consideration, contemplate, imagine, envisage, foresee, predict; count on, rely on, depend on, bank on, plan on, reckon on; *N. Amer. informal* figure on.

■ **into the bargain** =**also**, as well, in addition, besides, on top of (that), over and above that, to boot, for good measure.

barge ▸ noun =**lighter**, canal boat; *Brit.* narrowboat.

▸ verb =**push**, shove, force, elbow, shoulder, jostle, bulldoze, muscle.

■ **barge in** =**burst in**, break in, butt in, cut in, interrupt, intrude, encroach; gatecrash; *informal* horn in.

bark[1] ▸ verb **1** *the dog barked* =**woof**, yap, yelp, bay. **2** *'Okay, outside!' he barked* =**snap**; shout, bawl, cry, yell, roar, bellow, thunder; *informal* holler.
–OPPOSITES whisper.

bark[2] ▸ noun *the bark of a tree* =**rind**, skin, peel, covering.

▸ verb *he barked his shin* =**scrape**, graze, scratch, abrade, scuff, rasp, skin.

> WORD LINKS
> *relating to bark:* **corticate**

barn ▸ noun =**outbuilding**, shed, outhouse, shelter; stable, stall; *Brit.* byre.

baron ▸ noun **1** =**lord**, noble, nobleman, aristocrat, peer. **2** *a press baron* =**magnate**, tycoon, mogul, captain of industry, nabob, mandarin.

baroque ▸ adjective **1** *the baroque exuberance of his printed shirts* =**ornate**, fancy, over-elaborate, extravagant, rococo, fussy, busy, ostentatious, showy. **2** *baroque prose* =**flowery**, florid, flamboyant, high-flown, magniloquent, grandiloquent; *informal* highfalutin, purple.
–OPPOSITES plain.

barrack ▸ verb *(Brit. & Austral./NZ)* =**jeer**, heckle, shout at/down; interrupt, boo, hiss.
–OPPOSITES applaud.

barracks ▸ plural noun =**garrison**, camp, encampment, depot, billet, quarters, fort, cantonment.

barrage ▸ noun **1** *an artillery barrage* =**bombardment**, cannonade; gunfire, shelling; salvo, volley, fusillade; *historical* broadside. **2** *a barrage of criticism* =**deluge**, stream, storm, torrent, onslaught, flood, spate, tide, avalanche, hail, blaze; abundance, mass, profusion. **3** *a barrage across the river* =**dam**, barrier, weir, dyke, embankment, wall.

barrel ▸ noun =**cask**, keg, butt, vat, tun, drum, hogshead, kilderkin, pin, pipe; *historical* firkin.

> WORD LINKS
> *maker of barrels:* **cooper**

barren ▸ adjective **1** *barren land* =**unproductive**, infertile, unfruitful, sterile, arid, desert. **2** *a barren exchange of courtesies* =**pointless**, futile, worthless, profitless, unrewarding, purposeless, useless, vain, aimless, hollow, empty, vacuous, vapid.
–OPPOSITES fertile.

barricade ▸ noun *a barricade across the street* =**barrier**, roadblock, blockade; obstacle, obstruction.

▸ verb *they barricaded the building* =**seal (up)**, close up, block off, shut off/up; defend, protect, fortify, occupy.

barrier ▸ noun **1** =**fence**, railing, barricade, hurdle, bar, blockade, roadblock. **2** *a barrier to international trade* =**obstacle**, obstruction, hurdle, stumbling block, bar, impediment, hindrance, curb.

barring ▸ preposition =**excepting**, with the exception of, discounting, short of, apart from, but for, other than, aside from, excluding, omitting, leaving out, saving; *informal* outside of.

barrister ▸ noun =**counsel**, Queen's Counsel, QC, lawyer; *Scottish* advocate; *N. Amer.* attorney, counselor(-at-law); *informal* brief; (**barristers**) *Brit.* the Bar.

barter ▸ verb **1** *they bartered grain for salt* =**trade**, swap, exchange, sell. **2** *you can barter for souvenirs* =**haggle**, bargain, negotiate, deal, dicker.

▸ noun *an economy based on barter* =**trading**,

exchange, business, commerce, buying and selling, dealing.

base[1] ▸ noun **1** *the base of the tower* =**foundation**, bottom, foot, support, stand, pedestal, plinth. **2** *the system uses existing technology as its base* =**basis**, foundation, bedrock, starting point, source, origin, root(s), core, key component. **3** *the troops returned to their base* =**headquarters**, camp, site, station, settlement, post, centre.
–OPPOSITES top.

▸ verb **1** *he based his idea on a movie* =**found**, build, construct, form, ground, root; (**be based on**) derive from, spring from, stem from, originate in, issue from. **2** *the company was based in London* =**locate**, situate, position, install, station, site.

base[2] ▸ adjective *base motives* =**sordid**, ignoble, low, mean, immoral, improper, unseemly, unscrupulous, unprincipled, dishonest, dishonourable, shameful, bad, wrong, evil, wicked, iniquitous, sinful.
–OPPOSITES noble.

baseless ▸ adjective *baseless accusations* =**groundless**, unfounded, without foundation; unsubstantiated, unproven, unsupported, uncorroborated, unconfirmed, unverified, unattested; unjustified, unwarranted; speculative, conjectural; unsound, unreliable, spurious, specious, trumped up, fabricated, untrue.
–OPPOSITES valid.

basement ▸ noun =**cellar**, vault, crypt, undercroft; *Brit.* lower ground floor, *Scottish* dunny.

bashful ▸ adjective =**shy**, reserved, diffident, inhibited, retiring, reticent, reluctant, shrinking; hesitant, timid, apprehensive, nervous, wary.
–OPPOSITES bold, confident.

basic ▸ adjective **1** *basic human rights* =**fundamental**, essential, primary, principal, cardinal, elementary, quintessential, intrinsic, central, pivotal, critical, key, focal; vital, necessary, indispensable. **2** *basic cooking facilities* =**plain**, simple, unsophisticated, straightforward, adequate; unadorned, undecorated, unornamented; spartan, stark, severe, austere, limited, meagre, rudimentary, patchy, sketchy, minimal; unfussy; crude, makeshift; *informal* bog-

standard.
–OPPOSITES secondary, unimportant, elaborate.

basically ▸ adverb =**fundamentally**, essentially, in essence; firstly, first and foremost, primarily; at heart, at bottom, au fond; principally, chiefly, above all, mostly, mainly, on the whole, by and large, substantially; intrinsically, inherently; *informal* at the end of the day, when all is said and done.

basics ▸ plural noun =**fundamentals**, essentials, rudiments, (first) principles, foundations, preliminaries, groundwork; essence, basis, core; *informal* nitty-gritty, brass tacks, nuts and bolts, ABC.

basin ▸ noun **1** =**bowl**, dish, pan. **2** *a basin among low hills* =**valley**, hollow, dip, depression.

basis ▸ noun **1** *the basis of his method* =**foundation**, support, base; reasoning, rationale, defence; reason, grounds, justification, motivation. **2** *the basis of discussion* =**starting point**, base, point of departure, beginning, premise, fundamental point/principle, principal constituent, cornerstone, core, heart, thrust, essence, kernel, nub. **3** *on a part-time basis* =**footing**, condition, status, position; arrangement.

bask ▸ verb **1** *I basked in the sun* =**laze**, lie, lounge, relax, sprawl, loll. **2** *she's basking in all the glory* =**revel**, delight, luxuriate, wallow, take pleasure, rejoice, glory; enjoy, relish, savour, lap up.

bass ▸ adjective =**low**, deep, resonant, sonorous, rumbling, booming, resounding; baritone.
–OPPOSITES high.

bastard ▸ noun **1** *(archaic) he had fathered a bastard* =**illegitimate child**, child born out of wedlock; *dated* love child. **2** *(informal) he's a real bastard.* See SCOUNDREL.

▸ adjective **1** *(archaic) a bastard child* =**illegitimate**, born out of wedlock. **2** *a bastard Darwinism* =**adulterated**, alloyed, impure, inferior; hybrid, mongrel, patchwork.

bastardize ▸ verb =**adulterate**, corrupt, contaminate, weaken, dilute, taint, pollute, debase, distort.

bastion ▸ noun **1** *the town wall and bastions* =**projection**, outwork, breastwork, barbican. **2** *a bastion of respectabil-*

ity =**stronghold**, bulwark, defender, supporter, guard, protection, protector, defence, prop, mainstay.

batch ▸ noun =**group**, quantity, lot, bunch, mass, cluster, raft, set, collection, bundle, pack; consignment, shipment.

bathe ▸ verb 1 *I bathed in the pool* =**swim**, take a dip. 2 *they bathed his wounds* =**clean**, wash, rinse, wet, soak. 3 *the room was bathed in light* =**suffuse**, permeate, pervade, envelop, flood, cover, wash, fill.

bathing costume *(Brit.)* ▸ noun =**swimsuit**; swimming trunks, bikini; *Brit.* swimming costume; *informal* cossie; *Austral./NZ informal* bathers.

bathos ▸ noun =**anticlimax**, let-down, disappointment, disillusionment; absurdity; *informal* comedown.

baton ▸ noun 1 *the conductor's baton* =**stick**, rod, staff, wand. 2 *police batons* =**truncheon**, club, cudgel, bludgeon, stick, mace, shillelagh; *N. Amer.* nightstick, blackjack; *Brit. informal* cosh.

battalion ▸ noun *a battalion of supporters. See* CROWD noun sense 1.

batten ▸ noun *a timber batten* =**bar**, bolt, rail, shaft; board, strip.
▸ verb *he was battening down the shutters* =**fasten**, fix, secure, clamp, lash, make fast, nail, seal.

batter ▸ verb =**pummel**, pound, hit repeatedly, rain blows on, buffet, belabour, thrash, beat up; *informal* knock about/around, beat the living daylights out of, lay into, lace into, do over, rough up.

battered ▸ adjective =**damaged**, shabby, run down, worn out, falling to pieces, falling apart, dilapidated, rickety, ramshackle, crumbling.

battery ▸ noun 1 *a gun battery* =**emplacement**, artillery unit; cannonry, ordnance. 2 *a battery of equipment* =**array**, set, bank, group, row, line, line-up, collection. 3 *a battery of tests* =**series**, sequence, cycle, string, succession. 4 *assault and battery* =**violence**, mugging; *Brit.* grievous bodily harm, GBH, actual bodily harm, ABH.

battle ▸ noun 1 *he was killed in the battle* =**fight**, armed conflict, clash, struggle, skirmish, engagement, fray, duel; war,

campaign, crusade; warfare, combat, action, hostilities; *informal* scrap, dogfight, shoot-out. 2 *a legal battle* =**conflict**, clash, contest, competition, struggle; disagreement, argument, altercation, dispute, controversy.
▸ verb 1 *he has been battling against illness* =**fight**, combat, contend with; resist, withstand, stand up to, confront; war, feud; struggle, strive, work. 2 *Mark battled his way to the bar* =**force**, push, elbow, shoulder, fight; struggle, labour.

battle cry ▸ noun 1 *the army's battle cry* =**war cry**, war whoop, rallying call/cry. 2 *the battle cry of the feminist movement* =**slogan**, motto, watchword, catchphrase.

battlefield ▸ noun =**battleground**, field of battle, field of operations, combat zone, front.

battlement ▸ noun =**castellation**, crenellation, parapet, rampart, wall.

bauble ▸ noun =**trinket**, knick-knack, ornament, frippery, gewgaw, gimcrack, bibelot.

baulk ▸ verb 1 *I baulk at paying that much* =**be unwilling to**, draw the line at, jib at, be reluctant to, hesitate over; eschew, resist, refuse to, take exception to; draw back from, flinch from, shrink from, recoil from, demur from, not like to, hate to. 2 *they were baulked by traffic* =**impede**, obstruct, thwart, hinder, prevent, check, stop, curb, halt, bar, block, forestall, frustrate.
−OPPOSITES accept, assist.

bawdy ▸ adjective =**ribald**, indecent, risqué, racy, rude, spicy, sexy, suggestive, titillating, naughty, improper, indelicate, indecorous, off colour, earthy, broad, locker-room, Rabelaisian; obscene, vulgar, crude, coarse, gross, lewd, dirty, filthy, smutty, unseemly, salacious, prurient, lascivious, licentious; *informal* X-rated, blue, raunchy; *euphemistic* adult.
−OPPOSITES clean, innocent.

bawl ▸ verb 1 *'Come on!' he bawled* =**shout**, yell, roar, bellow, screech, scream, shriek, howl, whoop, bark, trumpet, thunder; *informal* yammer, holler. 2 *the children continued to bawl* =**cry**, sob, weep, shed tears, wail, whine, howl, squall, ululate; *Scottish informal* greet.
−OPPOSITES whisper.

bay¹ ▸ noun *ships were anchored in the bay* =**cove**, inlet, indentation, gulf, bight, basin, fjord, arm; natural harbour, anchorage.

bay² ▸ noun *there was a bay let into the wall* =**alcove**, recess, niche, nook, opening, hollow, cavity, inglenook.

bay³ ▸ verb **1** *the hounds bayed* =**howl**, bark, yelp, yap, cry, bellow, roar. **2** *the crowd bayed for an encore* =**clamour**, shout, call, press, yell, scream, shriek, roar; demand, insist on.
■ **at bay** =**at a distance**, away, off, at arm's length.

bazaar ▸ noun **1** *a Turkish bazaar* =**market**, souk, mart. **2** *the church bazaar* =**fête**, fair; fund-raiser, charity event; *Brit.* jumble sale, bring-and-buy sale, car boot sale; *N. Amer.* tag sale.

be ▸ verb **1** *there was once a king* =**exist**, have being, have existence; live, be alive, have life, breathe, draw breath, be extant. **2** *the trial is tomorrow* =**occur**, happen, take place, come about, arise, fall, materialize, ensue; *literary* come to pass, befall, betide. **3** *the bed is over there* =**be situated**, be located, be found, be present, be set, be positioned, be placed, be installed; sit, lie, live. **4** *it has been like this for hours* =**remain**, stay, last, continue, persist.

beach ▸ verb *they beached the boat* =**land**, ground, strand, run aground, run ashore.

beachcomber ▸ noun =**scavenger**, forager, collector.

beached ▸ adjective =**stranded**, grounded, aground, ashore, marooned, high and dry, stuck.
–OPPOSITES afloat.

beacon ▸ noun =**signal** (light/fire), danger signal, bonfire; lighthouse.

bead ▸ noun **1** *a string of beads* =**ball**, pellet, pill, globule, sphere, spheroid, oval, ovoid, orb, round; (**beads**) necklace, rosary, chaplet. **2** *beads of sweat* =**droplet**, drop, blob, dot.
■ **draw/get a bead on** =**aim at**, fix on, focus on, zero in on, sight.

beak ▸ noun =**bill**, nib, mandible; *Scottish & N. English* neb.

beaker ▸ noun =**cup**, tumbler, glass, mug, drinking vessel.

beam ▸ noun **1** *an oak beam* =**joist**, lintel, rafter, purlin; spar, girder, baulk, timber, plank; support, strut. **2** *a beam*

of light =**ray**, shaft, stream, streak; flash, gleam, glow, glimmer, glint. **3** *the beam on her face* =**grin**, smile.
–OPPOSITES frown.

▸ verb **1** *the signal is beamed out* =**broadcast**, transmit, relay, send/put out, disseminate; direct, aim. **2** *the sun beamed down* =**shine**, radiate, glare, gleam. **3** *he beamed broadly* =**grin**, smile, smirk; *informal* be all smiles.
–OPPOSITES frown.

bear¹ ▸ verb **1** *she was bearing a box* =**carry**, bring, transport, move, convey, take, fetch; *informal* tote. **2** *the bag bore my name* =**display**, exhibit, be marked with, show, carry, have. **3** *will it bear his weight?* =**support**, carry, hold up, prop up. **4** *they can't bear the cost alone* =**sustain**, carry, support, shoulder, absorb, take on. **5** *she bore no grudge* =**harbour**, foster, entertain, cherish, nurse, nurture. **6** *such a solution does not bear scrutiny* =**withstand**, stand up to, take, cope with, handle, sustain, accept. **7** *I can't bear having him around* =**endure**, tolerate, put up with, stand, abide, submit to, experience, undergo, go through, countenance, brave, weather, stomach; *informal* hack, swallow; *Brit. informal* stick, wear, be doing with; *formal* brook. **8** *she bore a son* =**give birth to**, bring forth, deliver, have, produce, spawn; *informal* drop; *literary* beget. **9** *a shrub that bears berries* =**produce**, yield, give, grow, provide, supply. **10** *bear left at the junction* =**veer**, curve, swerve, fork, diverge, turn, bend.
■ **bear oneself** =**conduct oneself**, carry oneself, acquit oneself, act, behave, perform; *formal* comport oneself.
■ **bear down on** =**advance on**, close in on, move in on, converge on.
■ **bear fruit** =**yield results**, succeed, be effective, be profitable, work; *informal* pay off, come off, do the trick.
■ **bear something in mind** =**take into account**, remember, consider, be mindful of, mark, heed.
■ **bear on** =**be relevant to**, appertain to, relate to, apply to, be pertinent to.
■ **bear something out** =**confirm**, corroborate, substantiate, endorse, vindicate, give credence to, support, ratify, warrant, uphold, justify, prove, authenticate, verify.
■ **bear up** =**remain cheerful**; cope, manage, get by, muddle through; *informal* hack it.
■ **bear with** =**be patient with**, show

forbearance towards, make allowances for, tolerate, put up with, endure.
■ **bear witness/testimony to** =testify to, be evidence of, be proof of, attest to, vouch for; demonstrate, show, establish, indicate, reveal, bespeak.

bear² ▶ noun

> WORD LINKS
>
> relating to bears: **ursine**
> male: **boar**
> female: **sow**
> young: **cub**
> home: **den**
> collective noun: **sloth**

bearable ▶ adjective =**tolerable**, endurable, sustainable.

beard ▶ noun =**facial hair**, whiskers, stubble, five o'clock shadow, bristles.
▶ verb =**confront**, face, challenge, brave, meet head on; defy, oppose, stand up against, square up to, dare.

> WORD LINKS
>
> fear of beards: **pogonophobia**

bearded ▶ adjective =**unshaven**, whiskered; stubbly, bristly.
−OPPOSITES clean shaven.

bearer ▶ noun 1 a lantern-bearer =**carrier**, porter. 2 the bearer of bad news =**messenger**, agent, conveyor, carrier, emissary. 3 the bearer of the documents =**holder**, possessor, owner.

bearing ▶ noun 1 a man of military bearing =**posture**, stance, carriage, gait; Brit. deportment; formal comportment. 2 a rather regal bearing =**demeanour**, manner, air, aspect, attitude, mien, style. 3 this has no bearing on the matter =**relevance**, pertinence, connection, appositeness, germaneness, importance, significance. 4 a bearing of 015° =**direction**, orientation, course, trajectory, heading, tack, path. 5 I lost my bearings =**orientation**, sense of direction; whereabouts, location, position.

beast ▶ noun 1 the beasts of the forest =**animal**, creature, brute; N. Amer. informal critter. 2 he is a cruel beast =**monster**, brute, savage, barbarian, animal, swine, pig, ogre, fiend, sadist, demon, devil.

beat ▶ verb 1 =**hit**, strike, batter, thump, bang, hammer, punch, knock, thrash, pound, pummel, slap, rain blows on; assault, attack, abuse; cudgel, club, birch; informal wallop, belt, bash,

whack, clout, clobber, slug, tan, biff, bop, sock, deck. 2 the waves beat along the shore =**break on/against**, dash against; lash, strike, lap, wash; splash, ripple, roll. 3 the metal is beaten into a die =**hammer**, forge, form, shape, mould, work, stamp, fashion, model. 4 her heart was still beating =**pulsate**, pulse, palpitate, vibrate, throb; pump, pound, thump, thud, hammer, drum. 5 the eagle beat its wings =**flap**, flutter, thrash, wave, vibrate, oscillate. 6 beat the cream into the mixture =**whisk**, mix, blend, whip. 7 she beat a path through the grass =**tread**, tramp, trample, wear, flatten. 8 the team they need to beat =**defeat**, conquer, win against, get the better of, vanquish, trounce, rout, overpower, overcome; informal lick, thrash, whip, clobber. 9 he beat the record =**surpass**, exceed, better, improve on, eclipse, transcend, top, trump, cap.
▶ noun 1 the song has a good beat =**rhythm**, pulse, metre, time, measure, cadence, stress, accent. 2 the beat of hooves =**pounding**, banging, thumping, thudding, booming, hammering, battering, crashing. 3 the beat of her heart =**pulse**, pulsating, vibration, throb, palpitation, reverberation; pounding, thump, thud, hammering, drumming. 4 a policeman on his beat =**circuit**, round, route, path.
■ **beat someone/something off** =**repel**, fight off, fend off, stave off, repulse, drive away/back, force back, push back.
■ **beat someone up** =**assault**, attack, mug; informal knock about/around, do over, work over, rough up, fill in, lay into; Brit. informal duff someone up; N. Amer. informal beat up on.

> WORD LINKS
>
> fear of being beaten: **mastigophobia**

beatific ▶ adjective 1 a beatific smile =**rapturous**, joyful, ecstatic, seraphic, blissful, serene, happy, beaming. 2 a beatific vision =**blessed**, exalted, sublime, heavenly, holy, divine, celestial, paradisical, glorious.

beatify ▶ verb =**canonize**, bless, sanctify, hallow, consecrate.

beatitude ▶ noun =**blessedness**, benediction, grace; bliss, ecstasy, exaltation, supreme happiness, divine joy/rapture; saintliness.

beautiful ▶ adjective =**attractive**,

pretty, handsome, good-looking, alluring, prepossessing; lovely, delightful, appealing, engaging, winsome; ravishing, gorgeous, stunning, arresting, glamorous, bewitching, beguiling; graceful, elegant, exquisite, magnificent; *Scottish & N. English* bonny; *informal* tasty, divine, knockout, drop-dead gorgeous, fanciable; *Brit. informal* smashing; *N. Amer. informal* cute, foxy; *Austral./NZ informal* beaut, spunky; *literary* beauteous.
–OPPOSITES ugly.

beautify ▸ verb =adorn, embellish, enhance, decorate, ornament, garnish, gild, smarten, prettify, enrich, glamorize; *informal* get up, do up, do out, tart up.
–OPPOSITES spoil, uglify.

beauty ▸ noun **1** =attractiveness, prettiness, good looks, comeliness, allure; loveliness, appeal, heavenliness; winsomeness, grace, elegance, exquisiteness; splendour, magnificence, grandeur, impressiveness; gorgeousness, glamour; *Scottish & N. English* bonniness; *literary* beauteousness, pulchritude. **2** *she is a beauty* =beautiful woman, belle, vision, Venus, goddess, picture; *informal* looker, lovely, stunner, knockout, bombshell, dish, cracker, peach, eyeful, bit of all right; *Brit. informal* smasher. **3** *the beauty of this plan* =advantage, attraction, strength, benefit, boon, good thing, strong point, virtue, merit.
–OPPOSITES ugliness, drawback.

becalmed ▸ adjective =motionless, still, at a standstill, at a halt, unmoving.

because ▸ conjunction =since, as, in view of the fact that, seeing that/as; *informal* on account of; *literary* for.
–OPPOSITES despite.
■**because of** =on account of, as a result of, as a consequence of, owing to, due to; thanks to, by/in virtue of; *formal* by reason of.

beckon ▸ verb **1** *the guard beckoned to Benny* =gesture, signal, wave, gesticulate, motion. **2** *the countryside beckons you* =entice, invite, tempt, coax, lure, charm, attract, draw, call.

become ▸ verb **1** *she became rich* =grow, get, turn, come to be, get to be; *literary* wax. **2** *he became a tyrant* =turn into, change into, be transformed into, be converted into. **3** *he became Foreign Secretary* =be appointed (as), be assigned as, be nominated, be elected (as), be made.

4 *the dress becomes her* =suit, flatter, look good on; set off, show to advantage; *informal* do something for. **5** *it ill becomes him to preach the gospel* =befit, suit; *formal* behove.
■**become of** =happen to, be the fate of, be the lot of, overtake; *literary* befall, betide.

becoming ▸ adjective =flattering, fetching, attractive, lovely, pretty, handsome; stylish, elegant, chic, fashionable, tasteful.

bed ▸ noun **1** =couch, berth, billet; *informal* the sack, the hay; *Brit. informal* one's pit; *Scottish informal* one's kip. **2** *a flower bed* =patch, plot, border, strip. **3** *built on a bed of stones* =base, foundation, support, prop, substructure, substratum. **4** *a river bed* =bottom, floor, ground.
▸ verb **1** *the tiles are bedded in mortar* =embed, set, fix, insert, inlay, implant, bury, base, plant, settle. **2** *time to bed out the seedlings* =plant (out), transplant.
■**bed down**. See GO TO BED.
■**go to bed** =retire; *informal* hit the sack, hit the hay, turn in; *Brit. informal* hit the pit.

> ┌─────────────┐
> │ WORD LINKS │
> └─────────────┘
> *fear of beds:* **clinophobia**

bedeck ▸ verb =decorate, adorn, ornament, embellish, furnish, garnish, trim, deck; swathe, wreathe, festoon; *informal* get up, do out.

bedevil ▸ verb =afflict, torment, beset, assail, beleaguer, plague, blight, rack, oppress; harass, distress, trouble, worry, torture.

bedlam ▸ noun =uproar, pandemonium, commotion, mayhem, confusion, disorder, chaos, anarchy, lawlessness; furore, upheaval, hubbub, hurly-burly, turmoil, riot, ruckus, rumpus, tumult; *informal* hullabaloo.
–OPPOSITES calm.

bedraggled ▸ adjective =dishevelled, disordered, untidy, unkempt, tousled, disarranged; *N. Amer. informal* mussed.
–OPPOSITES neat, clean, dry.

bedridden ▸ adjective =immobilized; *informal* laid up, flat on one's back.

bedrock ▸ noun =core, basis, base, foundation, roots, heart, backbone, principle, essence, nitty-gritty; *informal* nuts and bolts.

bedspread ▸ noun =bedcover, coverlet, quilt, throw-over, blanket; *Brit.* eiderdown; *N. Amer.* throw, spread, comforter; *dated* counterpane.

bee ▶ noun

> **WORD LINKS**
>
> *relating to bees:* **apian**
> *home:* **apiary, hive**
> *collective noun:* **swarm, drive, erst**
> *fear of bees:* **apiphobia**

beer ▶ noun =ale, brew; *Brit. informal* wallop, pint, jar; *Austral./NZ informal* hop, sherbet.

beetling ▶ adjective =**projecting**, protruding, prominent, overhanging, sticking out, jutting out.

befitting ▶ preposition =**in keeping with**, appropriate to, fit for, suitable for, suited to, proper to, right for, compatible with, consistent with.

befogged ▶ adjective =**confused**, muddled, befuddled, groggy, dizzy, muzzy; *informal* dopey, woozy, not with it.
−OPPOSITES lucid.

before ▶ preposition 1 *he dressed up before going out* =**prior to**, previous to, earlier than, preparatory to, in preparation for, preliminary to, in anticipation of, in expectation of; in advance of, ahead of; pre-…. 2 *he appeared before the judge* =**in front of**, in the presence of, in the sight of. 3 *death before dishonour* =**in preference to**, rather than, sooner than.
−OPPOSITES after.
▶ adverb 1 *she has ridden before* =**previously**, before now/then, until now/then, up to now/then; earlier, formerly, hitherto, in the past, in days gone by; *formal* heretofore. 2 *a small party went on before* =**ahead**, in front, in advance.
−OPPOSITES behind.

beforehand ▶ adverb =**in advance**, in readiness, ahead of time; before, before now/then, earlier (on), previously, already, sooner.
−OPPOSITES afterwards.

befuddled ▶ adjective =**confused**, muddled, addled, bewildered, disorientated, at sea, fazed, perplexed, dazed, dizzy, stupefied, groggy, muzzy, foggy, fuzzy; *informal* mixed up, dopey, woozy; *N. Amer. informal* discombobulated.
−OPPOSITES clear.

beg ▶ verb 1 *he begged on the streets* =**ask for money**, seek charity, seek alms; *informal* sponge, cadge, scrounge, bum. 2 *we begged for mercy* =**ask for**, request, plead

for, appeal for, call for, sue for, solicit, seek, press for. 3 *he begged her not to go* =**implore**, entreat, plead with, appeal to, supplicate, pray to, importune; ask, request, call on, petition; *literary* beseech.

beggar ▶ noun =**tramp**, vagrant, vagabond, mendicant; *N. Amer.* hobo; *informal* scrounger, sponger, cadger, freeloader; *Brit. informal* dosser; *N. Amer. informal* bum; *Austral./NZ informal* bagman.
▶ verb =**impoverish**, make poor, reduce to penury, pauperize, ruin, wipe out, break, cripple.

beggarly ▶ adjective 1 *a beggarly sum* =**meagre**, paltry, pitiful, miserable, miserly, ungenerous, scant, inadequate, insufficient, insubstantial; *informal* measly, stingy, pathetic, piddling, piffling, mingy; *formal* exiguous. 2 *in beggarly circumstances* =**wretched**, miserable, sordid, squalid, shabby, mean; poor, poverty-stricken, impoverished, distressed, needy, destitute.
−OPPOSITES considerable, affluent.

beggary ▶ noun =**poverty**, penury, destitution, ruin, ruination, indigence, impecuniousness, impoverishment, need, privation, pauperism, mendicity, want, hardship, reduced circumstances.

begin ▶ verb 1 *we began work* =**start**, commence, set about, go about, embark on, launch into, get down to, take up; initiate, set in motion, institute, inaugurate; *informal* get cracking on. 2 *he began by saying hello* =**open**, lead off, get under way, get going, get off the ground, start (off), commence; *informal* start the ball rolling, kick off. 3 *when did the illness begin?* =**appear**, arise, become apparent, spring up, crop up, turn up, come into existence, originate, start, commence, develop.
−OPPOSITES finish, end, disappear.

beginner ▶ noun =**novice**, starter, (raw) recruit, newcomer, tyro, fledgling, neophyte, initiate, fresher, probationer; postulant, novitiate; *N. Amer.* tenderfoot; *informal* rookie, new kid (on the block), newie; *N. Amer. informal* greenhorn.
−OPPOSITES expert, veteran.

beginning ▶ noun 1 *the beginning of socialism* =**dawn**, birth, inception, conception, origination, genesis, emergence, rise, start, commencement, launch, onset, outset; day one; *informal* kick-off. 2 *the beginning of the article* =**opening**, start, commencement, first

part, introduction, preamble. **3** *the therapy has its beginnings in China* =**origin**, source, roots, starting point, birthplace, cradle, spring; genesis, creation.
–OPPOSITES end, conclusion.

begrudge ▶ verb **1** *she begrudged Brian his affluence* =**envy**; resent, be jealous of, be envious of. **2** *don't begrudge the cost* =**resent**, feel aggrieved about, feel bitter about, be annoyed about, be resentful of, mind, object to, take exception to; give unwillingly, give reluctantly.

beguile ▶ verb **1** *she was beguiled by its beauty* =**charm**, attract, entrance, win over, woo, captivate, bewitch, spellbind, dazzle, hypnotize, mesmerize, seduce. **2** *the programme has been beguiling children for years* =**entertain**, amuse, delight, please, occupy, absorb, engage, distract, divert, fascinate, enthral, engross.
–OPPOSITES repel, bore.

beguiling ▶ adjective =**charming**, enchanting, entrancing, charismatic, captivating, bewitching, spellbinding, hypnotizing, mesmerizing, magnetic, alluring, enticing, tempting, inviting, seductive; *informal* come-hither.
–OPPOSITES unappealing.

behalf ■ **on behalf of/on someone's behalf 1** *I am writing on behalf of my client* =**as a representative of**, as a spokesperson for, for, in the name of, in place of, on the authority of, at the behest of. **2** *a campaign on behalf of cycling* =**in the interests of**, in support of, for, for the benefit of, for the good of, for the sake of.

behave ▶ verb **1** *she behaved badly* =**conduct oneself**, act, acquit oneself, bear oneself; *formal* comport oneself. **2** *the children behaved themselves* =**act correctly**, conduct oneself well, be well behaved, be good; be polite, show good manners, mind one's Ps and Qs.
–OPPOSITES misbehave.

behaviour ▶ noun **1** *his behaviour was inexcusable* =**conduct**, deportment, bearing, etiquette; actions, doings; manners, ways; *formal* comportment. **2** *the behaviour of these organisms* =**functioning**, action, performance, operation, working, reaction, response.

WORD LINKS

biological study of behaviour: **ethology**

behead ▶ verb =**decapitate**, cut someone's head off, guillotine.

behind ▶ preposition **1** *he hid behind a tree* =**at the back/rear of**, beyond, on the far/other side of; *N. Amer.* in back of. **2** *a guard ran behind him* =**after**, following, at the back/rear of, hard on the heels of, in the wake of. **3** *you are behind the rest of the class* =**less advanced than**, slower than, weaker than. **4** *he was behind the bombings* =**responsible for**, at the bottom of, the cause of, the source of, the organizer of, to blame for, culpable of, guilty of. **5** *they have the nation behind them* =**supporting**, backing, for, on the side of, in agreement with; financing; *informal* rooting for.
–OPPOSITES in front of, ahead of.
▶ adverb **1** *a man followed behind* =**after**, afterwards, at the back/end, in the rear. **2** *I looked behind* =**over one's shoulder**, to/towards the back, to/towards the rear, backwards. **3** *we're behind, so don't stop* =**(running) late**, behind schedule, behindhand, not on time. **4** *he was behind with his subscription* =**in arrears**, overdue; late, unpunctual, behindhand.
–OPPOSITES in front, ahead.
■ **put something behind one** =**consign to the past**, put down to experience, forget about, ignore.

behindhand ▶ adverb =**behind**, behind schedule/time; late, belated, unpunctual, slow.
–OPPOSITES ahead.

beholden ▶ adjective =**indebted**, in someone's debt, obligated, under an obligation; grateful, owing a debt of gratitude.

beige ▶ adjective =**fawn**, pale brown, buff, sand, sandy, oatmeal, biscuit, coffee-coloured, café au lait, camel.

being ▶ noun **1** *she is warmed by his very being* =**existence**, living, life, reality, actuality, lifeblood, vital force. **2** *God is alive in the being of man* =**soul**, spirit, nature, essence, inner self, psyche; heart, bosom, breast. **3** *an enlightened being* =**creature**, life form, living thing, individual, person, human (being).

belabour ▶ verb **1** =**beat**, hit, strike, smack, batter, pummel, pound, buffet, rain blows on, thrash; *N. Amer.* beat up on; *informal* wallop, whack, clout, clobber, bop, biff, sock, plug. **2** *he was belaboured in the press* =**criticize**, attack, berate, censure, condemn, denounce,

denigrate, revile, pillory, flay, lambaste, savage; *informal* knock, slam, pan, bash, take apart; *Brit. informal* slate, rubbish, slag off; *N. Amer. informal* pummel, cut up; *formal* castigate, excoriate. **3** *don't belabour the point* =**over-elaborate**, labour, dwell on, harp on about, hammer away at; overdo, overplay, overdramatize, make too much of; *informal* flog to death, drag out.
–OPPOSITES praise, understate.

belated ▸ adjective =**late**, overdue, behindhand, delayed, tardy, unpunctual.
–OPPOSITES early.

belch ▸ verb **1** =*informal* **burp**; *Scottish & N. English informal* rift. **2** *the furnace belched flames* =**emit**, give off, pour out, discharge, disgorge, spew out, spit out, vomit, cough up.

beleaguered ▸ adjective **1** *the beleaguered garrison* =**besieged**, blockaded, surrounded, encircled, hemmed in, under attack. **2** *a beleaguered government* =**hard-pressed**, troubled, in difficulties, under pressure, under stress, in a tight corner; *informal* up against it.

belie ▸ verb **1** *his eyes belied his words* =**contradict**, be at odds with, call into question, give the lie to, disprove, debunk, discredit, controvert. **2** *his image belies his talent* =**conceal**, cover, disguise; misrepresent, falsify, give a false idea/account of.
–OPPOSITES testify to, reveal.

belief ▸ noun **1** *it's my belief that age is irrelevant* =**opinion**, view, conviction, judgement, thinking, idea, impression, theory, conclusion, notion. **2** *belief in God* =**faith**, trust, reliance, confidence, credence. **3** *traditional beliefs* =**ideology**, principle, ethic, tenet, canon; doctrine, teaching, dogma, article of faith, creed, credo.
–OPPOSITES disbelief, doubt.

believable ▸ adjective =**credible**, plausible, tenable, conceivable, likely, probable, possible, feasible, reasonable.
–OPPOSITES inconceivable.

believe ▸ verb **1** *I don't believe you* =**trust**, have confidence in, consider honest, consider truthful. **2** *do you believe that story?* =**accept**, be convinced by, give credence to, credit, trust, put confidence in; *informal* swallow, buy, go for. **3** *I believe he worked for you* =**think**, be of the opinion that, have an idea that, imagine, assume, presume, take it,

conjecture, surmise, conclude, deduce, understand, gather; *informal* reckon, figure.
–OPPOSITES doubt.
■ **believe in 1** *she believed in God* =**be convinced of the existence of.** **2** *I believe in lots of exercise* =**have faith in**, trust in, have every confidence in, cling to, set (great) store by, value, be convinced by, be persuaded by; subscribe to, approve of; *informal* swear by, rate.

believer ▸ noun =**devotee**, adherent, disciple, follower, supporter, upholder, worshipper.
–OPPOSITES infidel, sceptic.

belittle ▸ verb =**disparage**, denigrate, run down, deprecate, downgrade, play down, trivialize, minimize, make light of; *informal* do down, pooh-pooh; *formal* derogate.
–OPPOSITES praise, magnify.

bell ▸ noun

> **WORD LINKS**
>
> bell-ringing: **campanology**

belle ▸ noun =**beauty**, vision, picture, pin-up, beauty queen, goddess, Venus; *informal* looker, lovely, stunner, knockout, bombshell, dish, cracker, bobby-dazzler, peach, honey, eyeful, bit of all right; *Brit. informal* smasher.

bellicose ▸ adjective =**belligerent**, aggressive, hostile, antagonistic, pugnacious, truculent, confrontational, contentious, militant, combative; *informal* spoiling for a fight; *Brit. informal* stroppy, bolshie.
–OPPOSITES peaceable.

belligerent ▸ adjective **1** *a belligerent stare* =**hostile**, aggressive, threatening, antagonistic, pugnacious, bellicose, truculent, confrontational, contentious, militant, combative; *informal* spoiling for a fight; *Brit. informal* stroppy, bolshie; *N. Amer. informal* scrappy. **2** *the belligerent states* =**warring**, combatant, fighting, battling.
–OPPOSITES peaceable, neutral.

bellow ▸ verb =**roar**, shout, bawl, thunder, trumpet, boom, bark, yell, shriek, howl, scream; *informal* holler.
–OPPOSITES whisper.

belly ▸ noun =**stomach**, abdomen, paunch, middle, midriff, girth; *informal* tummy, gut, insides.
▸ verb *her skirt bellied out* =**billow (out)**, bulge (out), balloon (out), bag (out), fill

(out); distend.
−OPPOSITES sag, flap.

belong ▸ verb **1** *the house belongs to his mother* =**be owned by**, be the property of, be the possession of, be held by, be in the hands of. **2** *I belong to a union* =**be a member of**, be in, be affiliated to, be allied to, be associated with, be linked to, be an adherent of. **3** *the garden belongs to the flat* =**be part of**, be attached to, be an adjunct of, go with. **4** *these creatures belong with bony fish* =**be classed**, be classified, be categorized, be included, have a place, be located, be situated. **5** *she doesn't belong here* =**fit in**, be suited to, have a rightful place; *informal* go, click.

belonging ▸ noun =**affiliation**, acceptance, association, attachment, integration, closeness; rapport, fellow feeling, fellowship.
−OPPOSITES alienation.

belongings ▸ plural noun =**possessions**, effects, worldly goods, chattels, property; *informal* gear, tackle, kit, things, stuff, bits and pieces; *Brit. informal* clobber, gubbins.

beloved ▸ adjective *her beloved brother* =**darling**, dear, precious, adored, much loved, cherished, treasured, prized, highly regarded, admired, esteemed, idolized.
−OPPOSITES hated.

▸ noun *he watched his beloved* =**sweetheart**, love, darling, dearest, lover, girlfriend, boyfriend, lady friend, man friend; *informal* steady, baby, angel, honey, pet.

below ▸ preposition **1** *the water rushed below them* =**beneath**, under, underneath, further down than, lower than. **2** *the sum is below average* =**less than**, lower than, under, not as much as, smaller than. **3** *a captain is below a major* =**lower than**, under, inferior to, subordinate to, subservient to.
−OPPOSITES above, over, more than.

▸ adverb **1** *I could see what was happening below* =**further down**, lower down, in a lower position, underneath, beneath. **2** *the statements below* =**underneath**, following, further on, at a later point.

> WORD LINKS
> *related prefixes:* **hypo-, sub-**

belt ▸ noun **1** =**girdle**, sash, strap, cummerbund, band; *literary* cincture, baldric. **2** *the commuter belt* =**region**, area, district, zone, sector, territory; tract, strip.

▸ verb *she belted the children in* =**fasten**, tie, bind; *literary* gird.

■ **below the belt** =**unfair**, unjust, unacceptable, inequitable; unethical, unprincipled, immoral, unscrupulous, unsporting, sneaky, dishonourable, underhand; *informal* low-down, dirty; *Brit. informal* out of order, off, not cricket.

bemoan ▸ verb =**lament**, bewail, mourn, grieve over, cry over; deplore, complain about.
−OPPOSITES rejoice at, applaud.

bemused ▸ adjective =**bewildered**, confused, puzzled, perplexed, baffled, mystified, nonplussed, dumbfounded, at sea, at a loss, taken aback, disoriented, disconcerted; *informal* flummoxed, bamboozled, fazed; *N. Amer. informal* discombobulated.

bemusement ▸ noun =**bewilderment**, confusion, puzzlement, perplexity, bafflement, befuddlement, stupefaction, mystification, disorientation; *informal* bamboozlement; *N. Amer. informal* discombobulation.

bench ▸ noun **1** *he sat on a bench* =**pew**, form, stall, settle. **2** *a laboratory bench* =**workbench**, work table, worktop, counter. **3** *the bench heard the evidence* =**judges**, magistrates, judiciary; court.

benchmark ▸ noun =**standard**, point of reference, gauge, criterion, specification, canon, convention, guide, guideline, norm, touchstone, yardstick, barometer, indicator, measure, model, exemplar, pattern.

bend ▸ verb **1** *the frames can be bent to fit your face* =**curve**, crook, flex, angle, hook, bow, arch, buckle, warp, contort, distort, deform, twist. **2** *the highway bent to the left* =**turn**, curve, incline, swing, veer, deviate, diverge, fork, change course, curl, loop. **3** *he bent down to tie his shoe* =**stoop**, bow, crouch, hunch, lean down/over.
−OPPOSITES straighten.

▸ noun *he came to a bend in the road* =**curve**, turn, corner, kink, angle, arc, crescent, twist.
−OPPOSITES straight.

beneath ▸ preposition **1** *we sat beneath the trees* =**under**, underneath, below, at the foot of, at the bottom of; lower than. **2** *the rank beneath theirs* =**inferior to**, below, not so important as, lower than, subordinate to, subservient to. **3** *such an*

attitude was beneath her =**unworthy of**, unbecoming to, degrading to, below.
−OPPOSITES above.

b

▶ **adverb** *sand with rock beneath* =**underneath**, below, further down, lower down.
−OPPOSITES above.

benediction ▶ **noun 1** *the priest said a benediction* =**blessing**, prayer, invocation; grace. **2** *filled with heavenly benediction* =**blessedness**, beatitude, bliss, grace.

benefactor, benefactress
▶ **noun** =**patron**, supporter, backer, sponsor; donor, contributor, subscriber; *informal* angel.

beneficent ▶ **adjective** =**benevolent**, charitable, altruistic, humanitarian, neighbourly, public-spirited, philanthropic; generous, magnanimous, munificent, unselfish, unstinting, open-handed, liberal, lavish, bountiful.
−OPPOSITES unkind, mean.

beneficial ▶ **adjective** =**advantageous**, favourable, helpful, useful, of assistance, valuable, profitable, rewarding, gainful.
−OPPOSITES disadvantageous.

beneficiary ▶ **noun** =**heir**, heiress, inheritor, legatee; recipient.

benefit ▶ **noun 1** *for the benefit of others* =**good**, sake, welfare, well-being, advantage, comfort, ease, convenience; help, aid, assistance, service. **2** *the benefits of working for a large firm* =**advantage**, reward, merit, boon, blessing, virtue; bonus; value; *informal* perk; *formal* perquisite. **3** *state benefit* =**social security payments**, welfare; charity, financial assistance; *informal* the dole; *Scottish informal* the broo.
−OPPOSITES detriment, disadvantage.

▶ **verb 1** *the deal benefited them both* =**be advantageous to**, be beneficial to, profit, do good to, be of service to, serve, be useful to, be helpful to, aid, assist; better, improve, strengthen, boost, advance, further. **2** *they may benefit from drugs* =**profit**, gain, reap reward, make money; make the most of, exploit, turn to one's advantage, put to good use, do well out of; *informal* cash in, make a killing.
−OPPOSITES damage, suffer.

benevolence ▶ **noun** =**kindness**, kind-heartedness, goodness, goodwill, charity, altruism, humanitarianism, compassion, philanthropism; generosity, magnanimity, munificence, unselfishness, beneficence; *literary* bounty, bounteousness.
−OPPOSITES spite, miserliness.

benevolent ▶ **adjective 1** *a benevolent patriarch* =**kind**, kindly, kind-hearted, good-natured, good, benign, compassionate, caring, altruistic, humanitarian, philanthropic; generous, magnanimous, munificent, unselfish, open-handed, beneficent; *literary* bounteous. **2** *a benevolent institution* =**charitable**, non-profit-making, not-for-profit.
−OPPOSITES unkind, tight-fisted.

benighted ▶ **adjective** =**ignorant**, unenlightened, uneducated, uninformed, backward, simple; primitive, uncivilized, unsophisticated, philistine, barbarian, barbaric, barbarous.
−OPPOSITES enlightened.

benign ▶ **adjective 1** *a benign grandfatherly role* =**kindly**, kind, warm-hearted, good-natured, friendly, affectionate, agreeable, genial, congenial, cordial, approachable, tender-hearted, gentle, sympathetic, compassionate, caring, well disposed, benevolent. **2** *a benign climate* =**temperate**, mild, gentle, balmy, soft, pleasant; healthy, wholesome, salubrious. **3** *(Medicine) a benign tumour* =**harmless**, non-malignant, non-cancerous, innocent.
−OPPOSITES unfriendly, hostile, unhealthy, unfavourable, malignant.

bent ▶ **adjective** =**twisted**, crooked, warped, contorted, deformed, misshapen, out of shape, irregular; bowed, arched, curved, angled, hooked, kinked; *N. Amer. informal* pretzeled.
−OPPOSITES straight.

▶ **noun** *an artistic bent* =**inclination**, leaning, tendency, talent, gift, flair, aptitude, facility, skill, capability, capacity; predisposition, disposition, instinct, orientation, predilection, proclivity, propensity.

■ **bent on** =**intent on**, determined on, set on, insistent on, resolved on; committed to, single-minded about, obsessed with, fanatical about, fixated on.

benumbed ▶ **adjective** =**numb**, unfeeling, insensible, stupefied, groggy, foggy, fuzzy, muzzy, dazed, dizzy; befuddled, fuddled, disoriented, confused, bewildered, all at sea; *informal* dopey, woozy, mixed up; *N. Amer. informal* discombobulated.

−OPPOSITES perceptive.

bequeath ▸ verb =leave, will, make over, pass on, hand on/down, entrust, grant, transfer; donate, give; bestow on, confer on, endow with; *Law* demise, devise, convey.

bequest ▸ noun =legacy, inheritance, endowment, settlement; estate, heritage; bestowal, bequeathal; *Law* devise.

berate ▸ verb =scold, rebuke, reprimand, reproach, reprove, admonish, chide, criticize, upbraid, take to task, pull up; *informal* tell off, give someone a talking-to, give someone a telling-off, give someone a dressing-down, give someone a roasting, rap over the knuckles, bawl out, come down on, tear into, slap down, blast; *Brit. informal* tick off, have a go at, carpet, give someone a rocket, give someone a rollicking, tear someone off a strip; *N. Amer. informal* chew out, ream out; *Austral. informal* monster; *formal* castigate; *dated* call down, rate.
−OPPOSITES praise.

bereaved ▸ adjective =orphaned, widowed; mourning, grieving.

bereavement ▸ noun =loss, death, passing (away), demise; *formal* decease.

bereft ▸ adjective =deprived, robbed, stripped, devoid, bankrupt; (**bereft of**) wanting, in need of, lacking, without; *informal* minus, clean out of; *literary* sans.

berserk ▸ adjective =mad, crazy, insane, out of one's mind, hysterical, frenzied, crazed, demented, maniacal, manic, frantic, raving, wild, out of control, amok, on the rampage; *informal* off one's head, off the deep end, ape, bananas, bonkers, nuts, hyper; *Brit. informal* spare, crackers, barmy; *N. Amer. informal* postal.

berth ▸ noun 1 *a 4-berth cabin* =bunk, bed, cot, couch, hammock. 2 *the vessel left its berth* =mooring, dock.
▸ verb 1 *the ship berthed in London Docks* =dock, moor, land, tie up, make fast. 2 *the boats each berth six* =accommodate, sleep.
■ **give someone/something a wide berth** =avoid, shun, keep away from, steer clear of, keep at arm's length, have nothing to do with; dodge, sidestep, circumvent, skirt round.

beset ▸ verb 1 *he is beset by fears* =plague, bedevil, assail, beleaguer, afflict, torment, rack, oppress, trouble, worry, harass, dog. 2 *they were beset by*

enemy forces =surround, besiege, hem in, shut in, fence in, box in, encircle, ring round.

beside ▸ preposition 1 *Kate walked beside him* =alongside, by/at the side of, next to, parallel to, abreast of; adjacent to, next door to; bordering, abutting, neighbouring. 2 *beside Paula, she felt clumsy* =compared with/to, in comparison with/to, next to, against, contrasted with.
■ **beside oneself** =distraught, overcome, out of one's mind, frantic, desperate, distracted, at one's wits' end, frenzied, wound up, worked up; hysterical.
■ **beside the point**. See POINT¹.

┌─────────────────────────┐
│ **WORD LINKS**   │
│ *related prefix:* **para-** │
└─────────────────────────┘

besides ▸ preposition *who did you ask besides Mary?* =in addition to, as well as, over and above, above and beyond, on top of; apart from, other than, aside from, but for, save for, not counting, excluding, not including, except, with the exception of, leaving aside; *N. Amer. informal* outside of.
▸ adverb 1 *there's a lot more besides* =in addition, as well, too, also, into the bargain, on top of that, to boot. 2 *besides, he's a man* =furthermore, moreover, further; anyway, anyhow, in any case; *informal* what's more; *N. Amer. informal* anyways.

besiege ▸ verb 1 *the army besieged Leith* =beleaguer, blockade, surround. 2 *fans besieged his hotel* =surround, mob, crowd round, swarm round, throng round, ring round, encircle. 3 *guilt besieged him* =oppress, torment, torture, rack, plague, afflict, haunt, harrow, beset, beleaguer, trouble, bedevil, prey on. 4 *he was besieged with requests* =overwhelm, inundate, deluge, flood, swamp, snow under; bombard.

besotted ▸ adjective =infatuated, smitten, in love, obsessed; doting on, greatly enamoured of; *informal* bowled over by, swept off one's feet by, struck on, crazy about, mad about, wild about, gone on, carrying a torch for; *Brit. informal* potty about.

bespatter ▸ verb =splatter, spatter, splash, speck, fleck, spot; dirty, soil; *Scottish & Irish* slabber; *informal* splotch, splodge.

bespeak ▸ verb 1 *a tree-lined road which*

bespoke money =**indicate**, be evidence of, be a sign of, denote, point to, testify to, evidence, reflect, demonstrate, show, manifest, display, signify; reveal, betray; *informal* spell. **2** *he had bespoken a room* =**order**, reserve, book; *informal* bag.
–OPPOSITES belie.

best ▶ adjective **1** *the best hotel in Paris* =**finest**, greatest, top, foremost, leading, pre-eminent, premier, prime, first, chief, principal, supreme, of the highest quality, superlative, unrivalled, second to none, without equal, nonpareil, unsurpassed, peerless, matchless, unparalleled, unbeatable, optimum, ultimate, incomparable; highest, record-breaking; *informal* star, number-one, a cut above the rest, top-drawer; *formal* unexampled. **2** *do whatever you think best* =**most advantageous**, most useful, most suitable, most fitting, most appropriate; most prudent, most sensible, most advisable.
–OPPOSITES worst.

▶ adverb **1** *the best-dressed man* =**to the highest standard**, in the best way. **2** *the food he liked best* =**most**, to the highest/greatest degree. **3** *this is best done at home* =**most advantageously**, most usefully, most suitably, most fittingly, most appropriately; most sensibly, most prudently, most wisely; better.
–OPPOSITES worst, least.

▶ noun **1** *only the best will do* =**finest**, choicest, top, cream, choice, prime, elite, crème de la crème, flower, jewel in the crown; *informal* tops, pick of the bunch. **2** *she dressed in her best* =**best clothes**, finery, Sunday best; *informal* best bib and tucker, glad rags. **3** *give her my best* =**best wishes**, regards, greetings, compliments, felicitations, respects; love.

■ **at one's best** =**on top form**, at one's peak, in one's prime, in the pink.

■ **do one's best** =**do one's utmost**, try one's hardest, make every effort, do all one can, give one's all; *informal* bend over backwards, do one's damnedest, go all out, pull out all the stops, bust a gut, break one's neck, move heaven and earth.

■ **had best** =**ought to**, should.

bestial ▶ adjective **1** *Stan's bestial behaviour* =**savage**, brutish, brutal, barbarous, barbaric, cruel, vicious, violent, inhuman, subhuman; depraved, de-generate, perverted, immoral, warped. **2** *man's bestial ancestors* =**animal**, beast-like, animalistic.
–OPPOSITES civilized, humane.

bestir ■ **bestir oneself** =**exert one-self**, make an effort, rouse oneself, get going, get moving, get on with it; *informal* shake a leg, look lively, get cracking, get weaving, get one's finger out, get off one's backside.

bestow ▶ verb =**confer on**, grant, accord, afford, endow someone with, vest in, present, award, give, donate, entrust with, vouchsafe.

bestride ▶ verb **1** *the oilfield bestrides the border* =**extend across**, lie on both sides of, straddle, span, bridge. **2** *he bestrode his horse* =**straddle**, sit/stand astride. **3** *Italy bestrode Europe in opera* =**domin-ate**, tower over/above.

best-seller ▶ noun =**brand leader**; *informal* hit, smash (hit), blockbuster, chart-topper, chartbuster.
–OPPOSITES failure, flop.

best-selling ▶ adjective =**very successful**, very popular; *informal* number-one, chart-topping, hit, smash.

bet ▶ verb **1** *he bet £10 on the favourite* =**wager**, gamble, stake, risk, venture, hazard, chance; put/lay money, speculate; *informal* punt; *Brit. informal* have a flutter, chance one's arm. **2** *(informal) I bet it was your idea* =**be certain**, be sure, be convinced, be confident; expect, predict, forecast, guess.

▶ noun **1** *a £20 bet* =**wager**, gamble, stake, ante; *Brit. informal* flutter, punt. **2** *(informal) my bet is that they'll lose* =**prediction**, forecast, guess; opinion, belief, feeling, view, theory. **3** *(informal) your best bet is to go early* =**option**, choice, alternative, course of action, plan.

bête noire ▶ noun =**bugbear**, pet hate, bogey; a thorn in one's flesh/side, the bane of one's life; *N. Amer.* bugaboo.
–OPPOSITES favourite.

betray ▶ verb **1** *he betrayed his own brother* =**be disloyal to**, be unfaithful to, break faith with, play someone false; inform on/against, give away, denounce, sell out, stab in the back; *informal* split on, rat on, peach on, stitch up, do the dirty on, sell down the river, squeal on; *Brit. informal* grass on, shop, sneak on; *N. Amer. informal* rat out, drop a/the dime on, finger; *Austral./NZ informal* dob on, point the bone at. **2** *he betrayed a secret* =**reveal**,

disclose, divulge, tell, give away, leak; unmask, expose, bring out into the open; let slip, let out, let drop, blurt out; *informal* blab, spill.
−OPPOSITES be loyal to, hide.

betrayal ▶ noun =disloyalty, treachery, bad faith, faithlessness, falseness; duplicity, deception, double-dealing; breach of faith, breach of trust, stab in the back; double-cross, sell-out.
−OPPOSITES loyalty.

betrayer ▶ noun =traitor, backstabber, Judas, double-crosser; renegade, double agent, collaborator, informer, mole, stool pigeon; turncoat, defector; *informal* snake in the grass, rat, scab; *Brit. informal* grass, supergrass, nark.

betrothal ▶ noun *(dated)* =engagement, marriage contract; *archaic* espousal.

betrothed ▶ adjective *(dated)* =engaged (to be married), promised/pledged in marriage, attached; *informal* spoken for; *literary* affianced; *archaic* plighted, espoused.
−OPPOSITES unattached.

better ▶ adjective 1 *better facilities* =superior, finer, of higher quality; preferable; *informal* a cut above, streets ahead, head and shoulders above, ahead of the pack/field. 2 *there couldn't be a better time* =more advantageous, more suitable, more fitting, more appropriate, more useful, more valuable, more desirable. 3 *are you better?* =healthier, fitter, stronger; well, cured, healed, recovered; recovering, on the road to recovery, making progress, improving, on the mend.
−OPPOSITES worse, inferior.
▶ adverb 1 *I played better today* =to a higher standard, in a superior/finer way. 2 *this may suit you better* =more, to a greater degree/extent. 3 *the money could be better spent* =more wisely, more sensibly, more suitably, more fittingly, more advantageously.
▶ verb 1 *he bettered the record* =surpass, improve on, beat, exceed, top, cap, trump, eclipse. 2 *refugees who want to better their lot* =improve, ameliorate, raise, advance, further, lift, upgrade, enhance.
−OPPOSITES worsen.

betterment ▶ noun =improvement, amelioration, advancement, furtherance, upgrading, enhancement.

between ▶ preposition 1 *Philip stood between his parents* =in the middle of, with one on either side; *archaic* betwixt. 2 *the bond between her and her mother* =connecting, linking, joining; uniting, allying.

WORD LINKS

related prefix: **inter-**

bevel ▶ noun =slope, slant, angle, cant, chamfer.

beverage ▶ noun =drink, liquid refreshment; *humorous* libation.

bevy ▶ noun =group, crowd, herd, flock, horde, army, galaxy, assemblage, gathering, band, body, pack; knot, cluster; *informal* bunch, gaggle, posse.

bewail ▶ verb =lament, bemoan, mourn, grieve over, sorrow over, cry over; deplore, complain about.
−OPPOSITES rejoice at, applaud.

beware ▶ verb =watch out, look out, mind out, be alert, keep your eyes open/peeled, keep an eye out, be on the qui vive; take care, be careful, be cautious, have a care, watch your step.

bewilder ▶ verb =baffle, mystify, bemuse, perplex, puzzle, confuse, confound, nonplus; *informal* flummox, faze, stump, beat, fox, be all Greek to, floor; *N. Amer. informal* discombobulate.
−OPPOSITES enlighten.

bewildered ▶ adjective =baffled, mystified, bemused, perplexed, puzzled, confused, nonplussed, at sea, at a loss, disorientated, taken aback; *informal* flummoxed, bamboozled; *N. Amer. Informal* discombobulated.

bewitch ▶ verb 1 *that evil woman bewitched him* =cast/put a spell on, enchant; possess, witch, curse; *N. Amer.* hex, hoodoo; *Austral.* point the bone at. 2 *she was bewitched by her surroundings* =captivate, enchant, entrance, enrapture, charm, beguile, delight, fascinate, enthral.
−OPPOSITES repel.

beyond ▶ preposition 1 *beyond the trees* =on the far side of, on the other side of, further away than, behind, past, after. 2 *beyond six o'clock* =later than, past, after. 3 *inflation beyond 10 per cent* =greater than, more than, exceeding, in excess of, above, upwards of. 4 *little beyond food was provided* =apart from, except, other than, besides; *informal* outside of; *formal* save.

▶ **adverb** *a house with a garden beyond* =**further away**, further off.

bias ▶ **noun 1** *he accused the media of bias* =**prejudice**, partiality, partisanship, favouritism, unfairness, one-sidedness; bigotry, intolerance, discrimination, a jaundiced eye; leaning, tendency, inclination, predilection. **2** *a dress cut on the bias* =**diagonal**, cross, slant, angle.
−OPPOSITES impartiality.

▶ **verb** *this may have biased the result* =**prejudice**, influence, colour, sway, weight, predispose; distort, skew, slant.

biased ▶ **adjective** =**prejudiced**, partial, partisan, one-sided, blinkered; bigoted, intolerant, discriminatory; jaundiced, distorted, warped, twisted, skewed.
−OPPOSITES impartial.

bibliophile ▶ **noun** =**book lover**, avid reader; *informal* bookworm.

bicker ▶ **verb** =**squabble**, argue, quarrel, wrangle, fight, disagree, dispute, spar, have words, be at each other's throats, lock horns; *informal* scrap.
−OPPOSITES agree.

bicycle ▶ **noun** =**cycle**, two-wheeler; *informal* bike, pushbike.

bid¹ ▶ **verb 1** *United bid £1 million for the striker* =**offer**, put up, tender, proffer, propose. **2** *she is bidding for a place in the England team* =**try to obtain**, try to get, make a pitch for.

▶ **noun 1** *a bid of £3,000* =**offer**, tender, proposal. **2** *a bid to cut crime* =**attempt**, effort, endeavour, try; *informal* crack, go, shot, stab; *formal* essay.

bid² ▶ **verb** *she bid him farewell* =**wish**, utter.

biddable ▶ **adjective** =**obedient**, acquiescent, compliant, tractable, amenable, complaisant, cooperative, dutiful, submissive.
−OPPOSITES disobedient, uncooperative.

bidding ▶ **noun** =**command**, order, instruction, decree, injunction, demand, mandate, direction, summons, call; wish, desire; request; *literary* behest.

big ▶ **adjective 1** *a big building* =**large**, sizeable, substantial, great, huge, immense, enormous, extensive, colossal, massive, mammoth, vast, tremendous, gigantic, giant, monumental, mighty, gargantuan, elephantine, titanic, mountainous, Brobdingnagian; towering, tall, high, lofty; outsize, oversized; goodly;

capacious, voluminous, spacious; king-size(d), man-size, family-size(d); *informal* jumbo, whopping, thumping, bumper, mega, humongous, monster, astronomical, almighty, dirty great; *Brit. informal* whacking, ginormous; *formal* commodious. **2** *a big man* =**well built**, sturdy, brawny, burly, broad-shouldered, muscular, muscly, rugged, lusty, Herculean, bulky, hulking, strapping, thickset, stocky, solid, hefty; tall, huge, gigantic; fat, stout, portly, plump, fleshy, paunchy, corpulent, obese; *informal* hunky, beefy, husky. **3** *my big brother* =**grown-up**, adult, mature, grown; elder, older. **4** *a big decision* =**important**, significant, major, momentous, weighty, consequential, far-reaching, key, vital, critical, crucial. **5** *(informal) he has big plans* =**ambitious**, far-reaching, grandiose, on a grand scale. **6** *she's got a big heart* =**generous**, kind, kindly, caring, compassionate, loving. **7** *(informal) African bands are big in Britain* =**popular**, successful, in demand, sought-after, all the rage; *informal* hot, in, cool, trendy, now, hip; *Brit. informal, dated* all the go.
−OPPOSITES small, minor, modest.

big-hearted ▶ **adjective** =**generous**, magnanimous, munificent, open-handed, bountiful, unstinting, unselfish, altruistic, charitable, philanthropic, benevolent; kind, kindly, kind-hearted; *literary* bounteous.
−OPPOSITES mean.

bigot ▶ **noun** =**dogmatist**, partisan, sectarian; racist, sexist, xenophobe, chauvinist, jingoist.

bigoted ▶ **adjective** =**prejudiced**, biased, partial, one-sided, sectarian, discriminatory; opinionated, dogmatic, intolerant, narrow-minded, blinkered, illiberal; racist, sexist, homophobic, xenophobic, chauvinistic, jingoistic; jaundiced, warped, twisted, distorted.
−OPPOSITES open-minded.

bigotry ▶ **noun** =**prejudice**, bias, partiality, partisanship, sectarianism, discrimination; dogmatism, intolerance, narrow-mindedness; racism, sexism, homophobia, xenophobia, chauvinism, jingoism.
−OPPOSITES open-mindedness.

bijou ▶ **adjective** =**small**, little, compact, snug, cosy.

bilious ▶ **adjective 1** *I felt bilious* =**nauseous**, sick, queasy, green about the gills;

N. Amer. informal barfy. **2** *his bilious disposition* =**bad-tempered**, irritable, irascible, tetchy, testy, crotchety, ill-tempered, ill-natured, ill-humoured, peevish, fractious, pettish, crabby, waspish, prickly, crusty, shrewish, quick-tempered; *N. Amer. informal* cranky, ornery. **3** *a bilious green and pink colour scheme* =**lurid**, garish, loud, violent; sickly, nauseating.
–OPPOSITES well, good-humoured, muted.

bill[1] ▶ noun **1** *a bill for £6* =**invoice**, account, statement, list of charges; *humorous* the damage; *N. Amer.* check; *N. Amer. informal* tab. **2** *a parliamentary bill* =**draft law**, proposal, measure. **3** *she was top of the bill* =**programme (of entertainment)**, line-up; *N. Amer.* playbill. **4** *(N. Amer.) a $10 bill* =**banknote**, note; *US informal* greenback. **5** *he had been posting bills* =**poster**, advertisement, public notice, announcement; flyer, leaflet, handbill; *Brit.* fly-poster; *informal* ad; *Brit. informal* advert.
▶ verb **1** *please bill me for the work* =**invoice**, charge, debit, send a statement to. **2** *the concert went ahead as billed* =**advertise**, announce; schedule, programme, timetable; *N. Amer.* slate. **3** *he was billed as the new Sean Connery* =**describe**, call, style, label, dub; promote, publicize, talk up; *informal* hype.

bill[2] ▶ noun *a bird's bill* =**beak**; *Scottish & N. English* neb.

billet ▶ noun *the troops' billets* =**quarters**, rooms; accommodation, lodging, housing; barracks, cantonment.
▶ verb *two soldiers were billeted here* =**accommodate**, quarter, put up, lodge, house; station, garrison.

billow ▶ noun *billows of smoke* =**cloud**, mass.
▶ verb **1** *her dress billowed around her* =**puff up/out**, balloon (out), swell, fill (out), belly out. **2** *smoke billowed from the chimney* =**swirl**, spiral, roll, undulate, eddy; pour, flow.

billowing ▶ adjective =**rolling**, swirling, undulating, surging, heaving, billowy, swelling, rippling.

bin ▶ noun =**container**, receptacle, holder; drum, canister, caddy, can, tin.

bind ▶ verb **1** *they bound her hands* =**tie (up)**, fasten (together), hold together, secure, make fast, attach; rope, strap, lash, truss, tether. **2** *Shelley bound up the*
wound with a dressing =**bandage**, dress, cover, wrap; strap up, tape up. **3** *the experience had bound them together* =**unite**, join, bond, knit together, draw together, yoke together. **4** *we have not bound ourselves to join* =**commit oneself**, undertake, pledge, vow, promise, swear, give one's word. **5** *the edges are bound in a contrasting colour* =**trim**, hem, edge, border, fringe; finish. **6** *they are bound by the agreement* =**constrain**, restrict, restrain, trammel, tie hand and foot, tie down, shackle; hamper, hinder, inhibit.
–OPPOSITES untie, separate.

binding ▶ adjective =**irrevocable**, unalterable, inescapable, unbreakable, contractual; compulsory, obligatory, mandatory, incumbent.

binge ▶ noun *(informal)* =**drinking bout**, debauch; *informal* bender, session, booze-up, blind; *Scottish informal* skite; *N. Amer. informal* jag, toot.

bird ▶ noun =**fowl**; chick, fledgling, nestling; (**birds**) avifauna; *informal* feathered friend, birdie.

> **WORD LINKS**
>
> *relating to birds:* **avian, ornith-**
> *home:* **aviary, nest**
> *collective noun:* **flock, flight, pod**
> *study of birds:* **ornithology**
> *fear of birds:* **ornithophobia**

birth ▶ noun **1** *the birth of a child* =**childbirth**, delivery, nativity; *formal* parturition; *dated* confinement. **2** *the birth of science* =**beginning(s)**, emergence, genesis, dawn, dawning, rise, start. **3** *he is of noble birth* =**ancestry**, lineage, blood, descent, parentage, family, extraction, origin, genealogy, heritage, stock, kinship.
–OPPOSITES death, demise, end.
■ **give birth to** =**have**, bear, produce, be delivered of, bring into the world; *N. Amer.* birth; *informal* drop.

> **WORD LINKS**
>
> *relating to one's birth:* **natal**
> *before birth:* **antenatal**
> *after childbirth:* **post-natal**
> *branch of medicine concerned with birth:* **obstetrics**

birthright ▶ noun =**patrimony**, inheritance, heritage; right, due, prerogative, privilege; primogeniture.

biscuit *(Brit.)* ▶ noun =**cracker**, wafer; *N. Amer.* cookie; *informal* bicky.

bisect ▸ verb =**cut in half**, halve, divide/cut/split in two, split down the middle; cross, intersect.

bisexual ▸ adjective **1** *bisexual crustaceans* =**hermaphrodite**, intersex; androgynous, epicene. **2** *a bisexual actor* =**ambisexual**; *informal* AC/DC, bi, swinging both ways, ambidextrous; *N. Amer. informal* switch-hitting.

bishop ▸ noun =**diocesan**, metropolitan, suffragan; *formal* prelate.

WORD LINKS

relating to a bishop: **episcopal**
---

bishopric ▸ noun =**diocese**, see.

bit ▸ noun **1** *a bit of bread* =**piece**, portion, segment, section, part; chunk, lump, hunk, slice; fragment, scrap, shred, crumb, grain, speck; spot, drop, pinch, dash, soupçon, modicum; morsel, mouthful, bite, sample; iota, jot, tittle, whit, atom, particle, trace, touch, suggestion, hint, tinge; snippet, snatch; *informal* smidgen, tad. **2** *wait a bit* =**moment**, minute, second, (little) while; *informal* sec, jiffy; *Brit. informal* mo, tick.
−OPPOSITES lot.

■ **a bit** =**rather**, fairly, slightly, somewhat, quite, moderately; *informal* pretty, sort of, kind of.

■ **bit by bit** =**gradually**, little by little, in stages, step by step, piecemeal, slowly.

■ **in a bit** =**soon**, in a (little) while, in a second, in a minute, in a moment, shortly; *informal* anon, in a jiffy, in two shakes; *Brit. informal* in a tick, in a mo; *N. Amer. informal* in a snap.

bite ▸ verb **1** =**sink one's teeth into**, chew, munch, crunch, champ, tear at. **2** *the acid bites into the copper* =**corrode**, eat into, burn (into), etch, dissolve. **3** *my boots failed to bite* =**grip**, hold, get a purchase. **4** *the measures begin to bite* =**take effect**, work, act, have results. **5** *a hundred or so retailers should bite* =**accept**, agree, respond; be lured, be enticed, be tempted; take the bait.
▸ noun **1** *he took a bite at his sandwich* =**chew**, munch, nibble, gnaw, nip, snap. **2** *he ate it in two bites* =**mouthful**, piece, bit, morsel. **3** *do you fancy a bite?* =**snack**, light meal, mouthful, soupçon; refreshments; *informal* a little something. **4** *the appetizer had a fiery bite* =**piquancy**, pungency, spiciness, tang, zest, sharpness, tartness; *informal* kick, punch, zing.

biting ▸ adjective **1** *biting comments* =**vicious**, harsh, cruel, savage, cutting, sharp, bitter, scathing, caustic, acid, acrimonious, acerbic, stinging; vitriolic, hostile, spiteful, venomous; *informal* bitchy, catty. **2** *the biting wind* =**freezing**, icy, arctic, glacial; bitter, piercing, penetrating, raw, wintry.
−OPPOSITES mild.

bitter ▸ adjective **1** *bitter coffee* =**sharp**, acidic, acrid, tart, sour, biting, unsweetened, vinegary. **2** *a bitter woman* =**resentful**, embittered, aggrieved, begrudging, rancorous, spiteful, jaundiced, ill-disposed, sullen, sour, churlish. **3** *a bitter blow* =**painful**, unpleasant, disagreeable, nasty, awful, distressing, upsetting, harrowing, heartbreaking, heart-rending, agonizing, traumatic, tragic; *formal* grievous. **4** *a bitter wind* =**freezing**, icy, arctic, glacial; biting, piercing, penetrating, raw, wintry. **5** *a bitter row* =**acrimonious**, virulent, angry, rancorous, spiteful, vicious, vitriolic, savage, ferocious, hate-filled, venomous, poisonous, acrid, nasty, ill-natured.
−OPPOSITES sweet, magnanimous, content, welcome, warm, amicable.

bitterness ▸ noun **1** *the bitterness of the medicine* =**sharpness**, acidity, acridity, tartness, sourness, harshness, vinegariness. **2** *his bitterness grew* =**resentment**, rancour, indignation, grudge, spite, sullenness, sourness, churlishness, moroseness, petulance, pique, peevishness. **3** *the bitterness of war* =**trauma**, pain, agony, grief; unpleasantness, nastiness; heartache, heartbreak, distress, desolation, despair, tragedy. **4** *there was no bitterness between them* =**acrimony**, hostility, antipathy, antagonism, enmity, animus, friction, rancour, vitriol, hatred, loathing, venom, poison, nastiness, ill feeling, bad blood.
−OPPOSITES sweetness, magnanimity, contentment, warmth, goodwill.

bizarre ▸ adjective =**strange**, peculiar, odd, funny, curious, outlandish, outré, eccentric, unconventional, unorthodox, queer, extraordinary; *informal* weird, wacky, oddball, way out, freaky; *Brit. informal* rum; *N. Amer. informal* wacko.
−OPPOSITES normal.

black ▸ adjective **1** *a black horse* =**dark**, pitch-black, jet-black, inky. **2** *a black night* =**unlit**, dark, starless, moonless.

3 *the blackest day of the war* =**tragic**, dark, disastrous, calamitous, catastrophic, cataclysmic, fateful, wretched, woeful; *formal* grievous. **4** *Mary was in a black mood* =**miserable**, unhappy, sad, wretched, heartbroken, grief-stricken, sorrowful, anguished, desolate, despairing, disconsolate, downcast, dejected, cheerless, melancholy, morose, dark, gloomy, glum, mournful, doleful, funereal, forlorn, woeful; *informal* blue; *literary* dolorous. **5** *black humour* =**cynical**, macabre, weird, unhealthy, ghoulish, morbid, gruesome; *informal* sick. **6** *a black look. See* ANGRY *sense 1.*
−OPPOSITES white, clear, bright, joyful.
▸ verb **1** *the steps were neatly blacked* =**blacken**, darken; dirty, make sooty, stain, grime, soil. **2** *she blacked his eye* =**bruise**, contuse.
■ **black out** =**faint**, lose consciousness, pass out, swoon; *informal* flake out.
■ **black and white 1** *a black-and-white picture* =**monochrome**, greyscale. **2** *I wish to see the proposals in black and white* =**in print**, written down, set down, on paper, recorded, documented. **3** *in black-and-white terms* =**categorical**, unequivocal, absolute, uncompromising, unconditional, unqualified, unambiguous, clear.

blackball ▸ verb =**reject**, debar, bar, ban, vote against, blacklist, exclude.
−OPPOSITES admit.

blacken ▸ verb **1** *they blackened their faces* =**black**, darken; dirty, make sooty, stain, grime, soil. **2** *the sky blackened* =**grow/become black**, darken, dim, cloud over. **3** *someone has blackened my name* −**sully**, tarnish, besmirch, drag through the mud/mire, stain, taint, smear, disgrace, dishonour, damage, ruin; slander, defame.
−OPPOSITES whiten, clean, lighten, brighten, clear.

blacklist ▸ verb =**boycott**, ostracize, avoid, embargo, ignore; refuse to employ.

black magic ▸ noun =**sorcery**, witchcraft, wizardry, necromancy, devilry; malediction, voodoo.

blackmail ▸ noun *he was accused of blackmail* =**extortion**, demanding money with menaces; *formal* exaction.
▸ verb **1** *he was blackmailing the murderer* =**extort money from**, threaten, hold to ransom. **2** *she blackmailed me to work for her* =**coerce**, pressurize, pressure, force;

informal lean on, put the screws on, twist someone's arm.

blackout ▸ noun **1** =**power cut**; brown-out. **2** *a news blackout* =**suppression**, silence, censorship. **3** *he had a blackout* =**fainting fit**, loss of consciousness, passing out, swoon, collapse.

blame ▸ verb **1** *he always blames others* =**hold responsible**, hold accountable, condemn, accuse, find/consider guilty, assign fault/liability/guilt to. **2** *they blame youth crime on unemployment* =**ascribe to**, attribute to, impute to, lay at the door of, put down to; *informal* pin.
−OPPOSITES absolve.
▸ noun *he was cleared of all blame* =**responsibility**, guilt, accountability, liability, culpability, fault.

blameless ▸ adjective =**innocent**, guiltless, above reproach, unimpeachable, in the clear, exemplary, perfect, virtuous, pure, impeccable; *informal* squeaky clean.
−OPPOSITES blameworthy.

blameworthy ▸ adjective =**culpable**, reprehensible, indefensible, inexcusable, guilty, wrong, evil, wicked; to blame, at fault, reproachable, responsible, answerable, erring, errant, in the wrong.
−OPPOSITES blameless.

blanch ▸ verb **1** *the sun blanches her hair* =**turn pale**, whiten, lighten, wash out, fade, blench, etiolate. **2** *his face blanched* =**pale**, whiten, lose its colour, lighten, fade, blench. **3** *blanch the spinach leaves* =**scald**, boil briefly.
−OPPOSITES colour, darken.

bland ▸ adjective **1** *bland food* =**tasteless**, flavourless, insipid, weak, watery, mild, wishy-washy. **2** *a bland film* =**uninteresting**, dull, boring, tedious, monotonous, dry, drab, dreary, wearisome; unexciting, unimaginative, uninspired, lacklustre, vapid, flat, stale, trite, vacuous, wishy-washy. **3** *a bland expression* =**unemotional**, emotionless, dispassionate, passionless; unexpressive, cool, impassive; expressionless, blank, wooden, stony, deadpan, hollow, undemonstrative, imperturbable.
−OPPOSITES tangy, interesting, emotional.

blandishments ▸ plural noun =**flattery**, cajolery, coaxing, wheedling, persuasion, honeyed words, smooth talk, blarney; *informal* soft soap, buttering up.

blank ▶ adjective **1** *a blank sheet of paper* =**empty**, unmarked, unused, clear, free, bare, clean, plain. **2** *a blank face* =**expressionless**, deadpan, wooden, stony, impassive, unresponsive, vacuous, empty, glazed, fixed, lifeless, inscrutable. **3** *'What?' said Maxim, looking blank* =**baffled**, mystified, puzzled, perplexed, stumped, at a loss, stuck, bewildered, nonplussed, bemused, lost, uncomprehending, (all) at sea, confused; *informal* flummoxed, bamboozled. **4** *a blank refusal* =**outright**, absolute, categorical, unqualified, complete, flat, straight, positive, certain, explicit, unequivocal, clear.
–OPPOSITES full, expressive, qualified.
▶ noun =**space**, gap, lacuna.

blanket ▶ noun *a blanket of cloud* =**covering**, layer, coating, carpet, overlay, cloak, mantle, veil, pall, shroud.
▶ adjective *blanket coverage* =**complete**, total, comprehensive, overall, general, mass, umbrella, inclusive, all-round, wholesale, outright, across the board, sweeping, indiscriminate, thorough; universal, global, worldwide, international, nationwide, countrywide, coast-to-coast.
–OPPOSITES partial, piecemeal.
▶ verb **1** *snow blanketed the mountains* =**cover**, coat, carpet, overlay; cloak, shroud, swathe, envelop. **2** *double glazing blankets the noise* =**muffle**, deaden, soften, mute, silence, quieten, smother, dampen.
–OPPOSITES amplify.

blare ▶ verb *sirens blared* =**blast**, sound loudly, trumpet, clamour, boom, roar, thunder, bellow, resound.
–OPPOSITES murmur.

blarney ▶ noun =**blandishments**, honeyed words, smooth talk, flattery, cajolery, coaxing, wheedling, persuasion; charm offensive; *informal* sweet talk, soft soap, smarm, buttering up.

blasé ▶ adjective =**indifferent**, unconcerned, uncaring, casual, nonchalant, offhand, uninterested, apathetic, unimpressed, unmoved, unresponsive, phlegmatic; *informal* laid-back.
–OPPOSITES concerned, responsive.

blaspheme ▶ verb =**swear**, curse, take the Lord's name in vain; *informal* cuss.

blasphemous ▶ adjective =**sacrile-**gious, profane, irreligious, irreverent, impious, ungodly, godless.
–OPPOSITES reverent.

blasphemy ▶ noun =**profanity**, sacrilege, irreligion, irreverence, taking the Lord's name in vain, swearing, curse, impiety, desecration.
–OPPOSITES reverence.

blast ▶ noun **1** *the blast from the bomb* =**shock wave**, pressure wave. **2** *Friday's blast killed two people* =**explosion**, detonation, discharge, burst. **3** *a sudden blast of cold air* =**gust**, rush, gale, squall, wind, draught, waft, puff, flurry. **4** *the shrill blast of the trumpets* =**blare**, wail, roar, screech, shriek, hoot, honk, beep.
▶ verb **1** *bombers were blasting airfields* =**blow up**, bomb, blow (to pieces), dynamite, explode. **2** *guns were blasting away* =**fire**, shoot, blaze, let fly, discharge. **3** *he blasted his horn* =**honk**, beep, toot, sound. **4** *radios blasting out pop music* =**blare**, boom, roar, thunder, bellow, pump, shriek, screech. **5** *Fowler was blasted with an air gun* =**shoot**, gun down, mow down, cut down, put a bullet in; *informal* plug.
■**blast off** =**be launched**, take off, lift off, leave the ground, become airborne, take to the air.

blast-off ▶ noun =**launch**, lift-off, take-off, ascent, firing.
–OPPOSITES touchdown.

blatant ▶ adjective =**flagrant**, glaring, obvious, undisguised, unconcealed, open; shameless, barefaced, unabashed, unashamed, unblushing, brazen, brass-necked.
–OPPOSITES inconspicuous, shamefaced.

blather ▶ verb =**prattle**, babble, chatter, twitter, prate, go on, run on, rattle on, yap, maunder, ramble, burble, drivel; *informal* yak, yatter; *Brit. informal* witter, rabbit, chunter, waffle.

blaze ▶ noun **1** =**fire**, flames, conflagration, inferno, holocaust. **2** *a blaze of light* =**glare**, gleam, flash, burst, flare, streak, radiance, brilliance, beam. **3** *a blaze of anger* =**outburst**, burst, eruption, flareup, explosion, outbreak; blast, attack, fit, spasm, paroxysm, access, rush, storm.
▶ verb **1** *the fire blazed merrily* =**burn**, be alight, be on fire, be in flames. **2** *headlights blazed* =**shine**, flash, flare, glare, gleam, glint, dazzle, glitter, glisten.

3 *soldiers blazed away* =**fire**, shoot, blast, let fly.

blazon ▸ verb **1** *their name is blazoned across the sails* =**display**, exhibit, present, spread, emblazon, plaster. **2** *the newspapers blazoned the news abroad* =**publicize**, make known, make public, announce, report, communicate, spread, circulate, give out, publish, broadcast, trumpet, proclaim, promulgate.

bleach ▸ verb **1** *the blinds had been bleached by the sun* =**turn white**, whiten, turn pale, blanch, lighten, fade, decolour, peroxide. **2** *bones bleaching in the sun* =**turn white**, whiten, turn pale, blanch, lose its colour, lighten, fade.
–OPPOSITES darken.

bleak ▸ adjective **1** *a bleak landscape* =**bare**, exposed, desolate, stark, desert, lunar, open, empty, windswept; treeless, without vegetation, denuded. **2** *the future is bleak* =**unpromising**, unfavourable, unpropitious, inauspicious; discouraging, disheartening, depressing, dim, gloomy, black, dark, grim, hopeless.
–OPPOSITES lush, promising.

bleary ▸ adjective =**blurry**, unfocused; fogged, clouded, dull, misty, watery, rheumy.
–OPPOSITES clear.

bleat ▸ verb *don't bleat to me about fairness* =**complain**, grouse, carp, fuss, snivel; *Scottish & Irish* girn; *informal* gripe, beef, whinge, bellyache, moan, go on; *N. English informal* mither; *N. Amer. informal* kvetch.

bleed ▸ verb **1** *his arm was bleeding* =**lose blood**, haemorrhage. **2** *one colour bled into another* =**flow**, run, seep, filter, percolate, leach. **3** *sap was bleeding from the trunk* =**flow**, run, ooze, seep, exude, weep. **4** *the country was bled dry by poachers* =**drain**, sap, deplete, milk, exhaust. **5** *my heart bleeds for them* =**grieve**, ache, sorrow, mourn, lament, feel, suffer; sympathize with, pity.

blemish ▸ noun **1** *not a blemish marred her skin* =**imperfection**, flaw, defect, fault, deformity, discoloration, disfigurement; bruise, scar, pit, pock, scratch, cut, gash; mark, spot, smear, speck, blotch, smudge; birthmark. **2** *government is not without blemish* =**defect**, fault, failing, flaw, imperfection, foible, vice; shortcoming, weakness, deficiency, limitation; taint, stain, dishonour, disgrace.

–OPPOSITES virtue.

▸ verb **1** *nothing blemished the coast* =**mar**, spoil, impair, disfigure, blight, deface, mark, scar; ruin. **2** *his reign was blemished by controversy* =**sully**, tarnish, besmirch, blacken, blot, taint; spoil, mar, ruin, disgrace, damage, undermine, degrade, dishonour; *formal* vitiate.
–OPPOSITES enhance.

blench ▸ verb =**flinch**, start, shy (away), recoil, shrink, pull back, cringe, wince, quail, cower.

blend ▸ verb **1** *blend the ingredients until smooth* =**mix**, mingle, combine, merge, fuse, meld, coalesce, integrate; stir, whisk, fold in. **2** *the new buildings blend with the older ones* =**harmonize**, go (well), fit (in), be in tune, be compatible; coordinate, match, complement.

▸ noun *a blend of bananas and ginger* =**mixture**, mix, combination, amalgamation, amalgam, union, marriage, fusion, meld, synthesis.

bless ▸ verb **1** *the chaplain blessed the couple* =**give a benediction for**. **2** *the Cardinal blessed the memorial plaque* =**consecrate**, sanctify, dedicate (to God), make holy, make sacred; *formal* hallow. **3** *bless the name of the Lord* =**praise**, worship, glorify, honour, exalt, pay homage to, venerate, reverence, hallow. **4** *the gods blessed us with magical voices* =**endow**, bestow, furnish, accord, give, favour, grace; confer on. **5** *I bless the day you came here* =**give thanks for**, be grateful for, thank; appreciate. **6** *the government refused to bless the undertaking* =**sanction**, consent to, endorse, agree to, approve, back, support; *informal* give the thumbs up to, give the green light to, OK.
–OPPOSITES curse, trouble, rue, oppose.

blessed ▸ adjective **1** *a blessed place* =**holy**, sacred, hallowed, consecrated, sanctified; ordained, canonized, beatified. **2** *blessed are the meek* =**favoured**, fortunate, lucky, privileged, enviable. **3** *the fresh air made a blessed change* =**welcome**, pleasant, agreeable, refreshing, favourable, gratifying, heartening, much needed.
–OPPOSITES cursed, wretched, unwelcome.

blessing ▸ noun **1** *may God give us his blessing* =**protection**, favour. **2** *a special blessing from the priest* =**benediction**, invocation, prayer, intercession; grace. **3** *she gave the plan her blessing* =**sanction**,

endorsement, approval, approbation, favour, consent, assent, agreement; backing, support; *informal* the thumbs up. **4** *it was a blessing they didn't have far to go* =**boon**, godsend, advantage, benefit, help, bonus, plus; stroke of luck, windfall.
−OPPOSITES condemnation, affliction.

blight ▸ noun **1** *potato blight* =**disease**, canker, infestation, fungus, mildew, mould. **2** *the blight of aircraft noise* =**affliction**, scourge, bane, curse, plague, menace, misfortune, woe, trouble, ordeal, trial, nuisance, pest.
−OPPOSITES blessing.
▸ verb **1** *a tree blighted by leaf curl* =**infect**, mildew; kill, destroy. **2** *scandal blighted the careers of several politicians* =**ruin**, wreck, spoil, mar, frustrate, disrupt, undo, end, scotch, destroy, shatter, devastate, demolish; *informal* mess up, foul up, put paid to, put the kibosh on, stymie; *Brit. informal* scupper.

blind ▸ adjective **1** *he has been blind since birth* =**sightless**, unsighted, visually impaired, visionless, unseeing. **2** *she was ignorant, but not blind* =**imperceptive**, insensitive, slow, obtuse, uncomprehending; stupid, unintelligent; *informal* dense, dim, thick, dumb, dopey; *Brit. informal* dozy. **3** *you should be blind to failure* =**unmindful of**, mindless of, careless of, heedless of, oblivious to, insensible to, unconcerned about, indifferent to. **4** *blind acceptance of conventional opinion* =**uncritical**, unreasoned, unthinking, unquestioning, mindless, undiscerning, indiscriminate. **5** *a blind rage* =**impetuous**, impulsive, uncontrolled, uncontrollable, unrestrained, immoderate, intemperate, wild, irrational, unbridled. **6** *a blind alley* =**without exit**, blocked, closed, barred, impassable; dead end.
−OPPOSITES sighted, perceptive, mindful, discerning.
▸ verb **1** *he was blinded in a car crash* =**make blind**, deprive of sight, render sightless; put someone's eyes out. **2** *scaffolding blinded the windows* =**obscure**, cover, blot out, mask, shroud, block, eclipse, obstruct. **3** *he was blinded by his faith* =**deprive of judgement**, deprive of perception, deprive of reason, deprive of sense. **4** *they try to blind you with science* =**overawe**, intimidate, daunt, deter, discourage, cow, abash, subdue, dismay; disquiet, discomfit, unsettle, disconcert;

confuse, bewilder, confound, perplex, overwhelm; *informal* faze, psych out.
▸ noun **1** *a window blind* =**screen**, shade, sunshade, curtain, awning, canopy; louvre, jalousie, shutter. **2** *some crook had sent the card as a blind* =**deception**, camouflage, smokescreen, front, facade, cover, pretext, masquerade, feint; trick, ploy, ruse, machination.

blindly ▸ adverb **1** *he stared blindly ahead* =**sightlessly**, unseeingly. **2** *he ran blindly upstairs* =**impetuously**, impulsively, recklessly, heedlessly, uncontrollably. **3** *they blindly followed US policy* =**uncritically**, unquestioningly, unthinkingly, mindlessly, indiscriminately.

blink ▸ verb **1** *his eyes did not blink* =**flutter**, flicker, wink, bat. **2** *several red lights began to blink* =**flash**, flicker, wink.

blinkered ▸ adjective =**narrow-minded**, inward-looking, parochial, provincial, insular, small-minded, short-sighted; hidebound, inflexible, entrenched, prejudiced, bigoted; *Brit.* parish-pump.
−OPPOSITES broad-minded.

bliss ▸ noun **1** *a sigh of bliss* =**joy**, happiness, pleasure, delight, ecstasy, elation, rapture, euphoria. **2** *religions promise perfect bliss after death* =**blessedness**, benediction, beatitude, glory, heavenly joy, divine happiness; heaven, paradise.
−OPPOSITES misery, hell.

blissful ▸ adjective =**ecstatic**, euphoric, joyful, elated, rapturous, on cloud nine, in seventh heaven; delighted, thrilled, overjoyed, joyous; *informal* over the moon, on top of the world.

blister ▸ noun *check for blisters in the roofing felt* =**bubble**, swelling, bulge, protuberance.

blistering ▸ adjective **1** *blistering heat* =**intense**, extreme, ferocious, fierce; **scorching**, searing, blazing, burning, fiery; *informal* boiling, baking, roasting, sweltering. **2** *a blistering attack* =**savage**, vicious, fierce, bitter, harsh, scathing, devastating, caustic, searing, vitriolic. **3** *a blistering pace* =**very fast**, breakneck; *informal* blinding.
−OPPOSITES mild, leisurely.

blithe ▸ adjective *a blithe disregard for the rules* =**casual**, indifferent, unconcerned, unworried, untroubled, uncaring, careless, heedless, thoughtless; nonchalant, blasé.
−OPPOSITES thoughtful.

blitz ▶ noun *the 1940 blitz on London* =**bombardment**, bombing, onslaught, barrage; attack, assault, raid, strike.
▶ verb *the town was blitzed in the war* =**bombard**, attack, bomb, shell, torpedo, strafe; destroy, devastate, ravage.

blizzard ▶ noun =**snowstorm**, white-out.

bloated ▶ adjective =**swollen**, distended, tumefied, bulging, inflated, enlarged, expanded, dilated.

blob ▶ noun **1** *a blob of cold gravy* =**drop**, droplet, globule, bead, bubble; *informal* glob. **2** *a blob of ink* =**spot**, dab, blotch, blot, dot, smudge; *informal* splotch, splodge.

bloc ▶ noun =**alliance**, coalition, federation, confederation, league, union, partnership, axis, body, association, group.

block ▶ noun **1** *a block of cheese* =**chunk**, hunk, lump, wedge, cube, brick, slab, piece; *Brit. informal* wodge. **2** *an apartment block* =**building**, complex, structure, development. **3** *a block of shares* =**batch**, group, set, quantity, tranche. **4** *a sketching block* =**pad**, notepad, jotter, tablet. **5** *a block to development* =**obstacle**, bar, barrier, impediment, hindrance, check, hurdle, deterrent. **6** *a block in the pipe* =**blockage**, obstruction, stoppage, congestion, occlusion, clot.
−OPPOSITES aid.
▶ verb **1** *weeds can block drainage ditches* =**clog (up)**, stop up, choke, plug, bung up, obstruct, gum up, dam up, congest, jam, close; *Brit. informal* gunge up. **2** *picket lines blocked access to the factory* =**hinder**, hamper, obstruct, impede, inhibit, restrict, limit; halt, stop, bar, check, prevent. **3** *he blocked a shot on the goal line* =**parry**, stop, deflect, fend off, hold off, repel, repulse.
−OPPOSITES facilitate.
■ **block something off** =**close up**, shut off, seal off, barricade, bar, obstruct.
■ **block something out 1** *trees blocked out the light* =**conceal**, keep out, blot out, exclude, obliterate, blank out, stop. **2** *block out an area in charcoal* =**rough out**, sketch out, outline, delineate, draft.

blockade ▶ noun **1** *a naval blockade of the island* =**siege**. **2** *they erected blockades* =**barricade**, barrier, roadblock; obstacle, obstruction.
▶ verb *rebels blockaded the capital* =**barricade**, block off, shut off, seal; besiege, surround.

blockage ▶ noun =**obstruction**, stoppage, block, occlusion, congestion.

blonde, blond ▶ adjective =**fair**, light, yellow, flaxen, tow-coloured, golden, platinum; bleached, peroxide.
−OPPOSITES dark.

blood ▶ noun *a woman of noble blood* =**ancestry**, lineage, bloodline, descent, parentage, family, birth, extraction, origin, genealogy, heritage, stock, kinship.

> [!NOTE] WORD LINKS
> *relating to blood:* **haemal, haemic, haematic, sanguineous**
> *branch of medicine relating to blood:* **haematology**
> *fear of blood:* **haemophobia**

blood-curdling ▶ adjective =**terrifying**, frightening, spine-chilling, hair-raising, horrifying, alarming; eerie, sinister, horrible; *informal* scary.

bloodless ▶ adjective **1** *a bloodless revolution* =**non-violent**, peaceful, peaceable, pacifist. **2** *his face was bloodless* =**anaemic**, pale, wan, pallid, ashen, colourless, chalky, waxen, white, grey, pasty, drained, drawn, deathly. **3** *a bloodless Hollywood mogul* =**heartless**, unfeeling, cruel, ruthless, merciless, pitiless, uncharitable; cold, hard, stony-hearted, cold-blooded, callous.
−OPPOSITES bloody, ruddy, charitable.

bloodshed ▶ noun =**slaughter**, massacre, killing, wounding; carnage, butchery, bloodletting, bloodbath; violence, fighting, warfare, battle.

bloodthirsty ▶ adjective =**murderous**, homicidal, violent, vicious, barbarous, barbaric, savage, brutal, cut-throat; fierce, ferocious, inhuman.

bloody ▶ adjective **1** *his bloody nose* =**bleeding**. **2** *bloody medical waste* =**bloodstained**, blood-soaked, gory. **3** *a bloody civil war* =**vicious**, ferocious, savage, fierce, brutal, murderous, gory. **4** *(informal) a bloody nuisance! See* DAMNED.

bloom ▶ noun **1** *orchid blooms* =**flower**, blossom, floweret, floret. **2** *a girl in the bloom of youth* =**prime**, perfection, acme, peak, height, heyday; salad days. **3** *the bloom of her skin* =**radiance**, lustre, sheen, glow, freshness; blush, rosiness, pinkness, colour.
▶ verb **1** *the geraniums bloomed* =**flower**, blossom, open; mature. **2** *the children*

bloomed in the Devonshire air =**flourish**, thrive, prosper, progress, burgeon; *informal* be in the pink.
–OPPOSITES wither, decline.

blossom ▸ noun *pink blossoms* =**flower**, bloom, floweret, floret.
▸ verb 1 *the snowdrops have blossomed* =**bloom**, flower, open, unfold; mature. 2 *the whole region had blossomed* =**develop**, grow, mature, progress, evolve; flourish, thrive, prosper, bloom, burgeon.
–OPPOSITES fade, decline.
■ **in blossom** =**in flower**, flowering, blossoming, blooming, in (full) bloom, open, out.

blot ▸ noun 1 *an ink blot* =**spot**, dot, mark, blotch, smudge, patch, dab; *informal* splotch; *Brit. informal* splodge. 2 *the only blot on a clean campaign* =**blemish**, taint, stain, blight, flaw, fault; disgrace, dishonour. 3 *a blot on the landscape* =**eyesore**, monstrosity, carbuncle, mess; *informal* sight.
▸ verb 1 *blot the excess water* =**soak up**, absorb, sponge up, mop up; dry up/out; dab, pat. 2 *the writing was messy and blotted* =**smudge**, smear, blotch, mark. 3 *he had blotted our name forever* =**tarnish**, taint, stain, blacken, sully, mar; dishonour, disgrace, besmirch.
–OPPOSITES honour.
■ **blot something out** 1 *Mary blotted out her picture* =**erase**, obliterate, delete, efface, rub out, blank out, expunge; cross out, strike out. 2 *clouds were starting to blot out the stars* =**conceal**, hide, obscure, exclude, obliterate, shadow, eclipse. 3 *he urged her to blot out the memory* =**erase**, efface, eradicate, expunge, wipe out.

blotch ▸ noun 1 *pink flowers with dark blotches* =**patch**, smudge, dot, spot, blot, dab, daub; *informal* splotch; *Brit. informal* splodge. 2 *his face was covered in blotches* =**patch**, mark, freckle, birthmark, discoloration.

blotchy ▸ adjective =**mottled**, dappled, patchy, spotty, smudged, marked; *informal* splotchy; *Brit. informal* splodgy.

blow¹ ▸ verb 1 *the icy wind blew around us* =**gust**, puff, flurry, blast, roar, bluster, rush, storm. 2 *his ship was blown on to the rocks* =**sweep**, carry, toss, drive, push, force. 3 *leaves blew across the road* =**drift**, flutter, waft, float, glide, whirl, move. 4 *he blew a smoke ring* =**exhale**, puff; emit, expel, discharge, issue. 5 *Uncle*

Albert was puffing and blowing =**wheeze**, puff, pant, gasp. 6 *he blew a trumpet* =**sound**, blast, toot, pipe, trumpet; play. 7 *a rear tyre had blown* =**burst**, explode, blow out, split, rupture, puncture. 8 *the bulb had blown* =**fuse**, short-circuit, burn out, break, go. 9 *his cover was blown* =**expose**, reveal, uncover, disclose, divulge, unveil, betray.
▸ noun *we're in for a bit of a blow* =**gale**, storm, tempest, hurricane; wind, breeze, gust, draught, flurry.
■ **blow out** 1 *the matches will not blow out in a strong wind* =**be extinguished**, go out, be put out, stop burning. 2 *the front tyre blew out*. See BLOW¹ verb sense 7. 3 *the windows blew out* =**shatter**, rupture, crack, smash, splinter, disintegrate; burst, explode, fly apart; *informal* bust.
■ **blow something out** =**extinguish**, put out, snuff, douse, quench, smother.
■ **blow up** *a lorryload of shells blew up* =**explode**, detonate, go off, ignite, erupt.
■ **blow something up** 1 *they blew the plane up* =**bomb**, blast, destroy; explode, detonate. 2 *blow up the balloons* =**inflate**, pump up, fill up, puff up, swell, expand, aerate.

blow² ▸ noun 1 *a blow on the head* =**knock**, **bang**, hit, punch, thump, smack, crack, rap; *informal* whack, thwack, bash, clout, sock, wallop. 2 *losing his wife must have been a blow* =**shock**, surprise, bombshell, thunderbolt, jolt; calamity, catastrophe, disaster, upset, setback.

blowout ▸ noun *the steering is automatic in the event of blowouts* =**puncture**, flat tyre, burst tyre; *informal* flat.

blowsy ▸ adjective =**untidy**, sloppy, scruffy, messy, dishevelled, unkempt, frowzy, slovenly.
–OPPOSITES tidy, respectable.

blowy ▸ adjective =**windy**, windswept, blustery, gusty, breezy; stormy, squally.
–OPPOSITES still.

bludgeon ▸ noun *hooligans wielding bludgeons* =**cudgel**, club, stick, truncheon, baton; *N. Amer.* nightstick, blackjack; *Brit. informal* cosh.
▸ verb 1 *he was bludgeoned to death* =**batter**, cudgel, club, beat, thrash; *informal* clobber. 2 *I let him bludgeon me into marriage* =**coerce**, force, compel, pressurize, pressure, bully, browbeat, hector, dragoon, steamroller; *informal* strong-arm, railroad.

blue ▸ adjective =sky-blue, azure, cobalt, sapphire, navy, ultramarine, aquamarine, cyan.

blueprint ▸ noun **1** *blueprints of the aircraft* =plan, design, diagram, drawing, sketch, map, layout, representation. **2** *a blueprint for similar measures in other countries* =model, plan, template, framework, pattern, example, guide, prototype, pilot.

bluff[1] ▸ noun *this offer was denounced as a bluff* =deception, subterfuge, pretence, sham, fake, deceit, feint, hoax, fraud, charade; trick, ruse, scheme, machination; *informal* put-on.
▸ verb **1** *they are bluffing to hide their guilt* =pretend, sham, fake, feign, lie, hoax, pose, posture, masquerade, dissemble. **2** *I managed to bluff the board into believing me* =deceive, delude, mislead, trick, fool, hoodwink, dupe, hoax, beguile, gull; *informal* con, kid, have on.

bluff[2] ▸ adjective *a bluff man* =plain-spoken, straightforward, blunt, direct, no-nonsense, frank, open, candid, forthright, unequivocal; hearty, genial, good-natured; *informal* upfront.

bluff[3] ▸ noun =cliff, promontory, headland, crag, bank, peak, escarpment, scarp.

blunder ▸ noun *he shook his head at his blunder* =mistake, error, gaffe, slip, oversight, faux pas; *informal* botch, slip-up, boo-boo; *Brit. informal* clanger, boob; *N. Amer. informal* blooper.
▸ verb **1** *the government admitted it had blundered* =make a mistake, err, miscalculate, bungle, trip up, be wrong; *informal* slip up, screw up, blow it, goof; *Brit. informal* boob. **2** *she blundered down the steps* =stumble, lurch, stagger, flounder, struggle, fumble, grope.

blunt ▸ adjective **1** *a blunt knife* =unsharpened, dull, worn, edgeless. **2** *the leaf is broad with a blunt tip* =rounded, flat, obtuse, stubby. **3** *a blunt message* =straightforward, frank, plain-spoken, candid, direct, bluff, forthright, unequivocal; brusque, abrupt, curt, terse, bald, brutal, harsh; stark; *informal* upfront.
–OPPOSITES sharp, pointed, subtle.
▸ verb **1** *ebony blunts tools very rapidly* =dull, make less sharp. **2** *age hasn't blunted my passion for life* =dull, deaden, dampen, numb, weaken, sap, cool, temper, allay, abate; diminish, reduce, decrease,

lessen, deplete.
–OPPOSITES sharpen, intensify.

blur ▸ verb **1** *she felt tears blur her vision* =cloud, fog, obscure, dim, make hazy, soften. **2** *films blur the difference between villains and victims* =obscure, make vague, confuse, muddle, muddy, obfuscate, cloud, weaken. **3** *memories of the picnic had blurred* =become dim, dull, numb, deaden, mute; lessen, decrease, diminish.
–OPPOSITES sharpen, focus.
▸ noun *a blur on the horizon* =indistinct shape, smudge; haze, cloud, mist.

blurred ▸ adjective =indistinct, fuzzy, hazy, misty, foggy, shadowy, faint; unclear, vague, indefinite, unfocused, obscure, nebulous.

blurt ■ **blurt something out** =burst out with, exclaim, call out; divulge, disclose, reveal, betray, let slip, give away; *informal* blab, gush, let on, spill the beans.

blush ▸ verb *Joan blushed at the compliment* =redden, turn/go pink, turn/go red, flush, colour, burn up.
▸ noun *the darkness hid her fiery blush* =flush, rosiness, pinkness, bloom, high colour.

WORD LINKS
fear of blushing: **erythrophobia**

bluster ▸ verb **1** *he started blustering about the general election* =rant, thunder, bellow, sound off. **2** *storms bluster in from the sea* =blast, gust, storm, roar, rush.
▸ noun *his bluster turned to cooperation* =ranting, thundering, hectoring, bullying, bombast, bumptiousness, braggadocio.

blustery ▸ adjective =stormy, gusty, blowy, windy, squally, wild, tempestuous, turbulent; howling, roaring.
–OPPOSITES calm.

board ▸ noun **1** *a wooden board* =plank, beam, panel, slat, batten, timber, lath. **2** *the board of directors* =committee, council, panel, directorate, commission, group. **3** *your room and board will be free* =food, meals, provisions, refreshments, table, bread; keep, maintenance; *informal* grub, nosh, eats, chow; *Brit. informal* scoff.
▸ verb **1** *he boarded the aircraft* =get on, go aboard, enter, mount, ascend; embark; catch; *informal* hop on. **2** *a number of students boarded with them* =lodge, live, res-

ide, be housed; N. Amer. room; informal put up, have digs. **3** they run a facility for boarding dogs =**accommodate**, lodge, take in, put up, house; keep, feed, cater for.

■ **above board** =**legitimate**, lawful, legal, honest; informal legit, kosher, pukka, by the book, (fair and) square, on the level, upfront.

■ **board something up/over** =**cover up/over**, close up, shut up, seal.

boast ▶ verb **1** his mother had been boasting about him =**brag**, crow, swagger, swank, gloat, show off; exaggerate, overstate; informal talk big, lay it on thick; Austral./NZ informal skite. **2** the hotel boasts a fine restaurant =**possess**, have, own, enjoy, pride oneself/itself on, offer.

▶ noun **1** the government's main boast seemed undone =**brag**, self-praise; exaggeration, overstatement, fanfaronade; informal swank; Austral./NZ informal skite. **2** the hall is the boast of the county =**pride**, joy, wonder, delight, treasure, gem.

boastful ▶ adjective =**bragging**, swaggering, bumptious, puffed up, full of oneself; cocky, conceited, arrogant, egotistical; informal swanky, big-headed.
–OPPOSITES modest.

boat ▶ noun a rowing boat =**vessel**, craft, watercraft, ship; literary keel, barque.
▶ verb he insisted on boating into the lake =**sail**, yacht, cruise.

bob ▶ verb **1** their yacht bobbed about =**move up and down**, bounce, toss, skip, dance, jounce; wobble, jiggle, joggle, jolt, jerk. **2** the bookie's head bobbed =**nod**, incline, dip; wag, waggle. **3** the maid bobbed and left the room =**curtsy**, bow.

bode ▶ verb =**augur**, portend, herald, be a sign of, warn of, foreshadow, be an omen of, presage, indicate, signify, promise, threaten, spell, denote, foretell; prophesy, predict.

bodily ▶ adjective bodily sensations =**physical**, corporeal, corporal, somatic; concrete, real, actual, tangible.
–OPPOSITES spiritual, mental.
▶ adverb he hauled her bodily from the van =**forcefully**, forcibly, violently; wholly, completely, entirely.

body ▶ noun **1** the human body =**figure**, frame, form, physique, anatomy, skeleton; informal bod. **2** he was hit by shrapnel in the head and body =**torso**, trunk. **3** the bodies were put in the fire =**corpse**, car-

cass, skeleton, remains; informal stiff; Medicine cadaver. **4** the body of the article =**main part**, core, heart, hub. **5** the body of the ship =**bodywork**, hull; fuselage. **6** a body of water =**expanse**, mass, area, stretch, tract, sweep, extent. **7** a growing body of evidence =**quantity**, amount, volume, collection, mass, corpus. **8** the representative body of the employers =**association**, organization, group, party, company, society, circle, syndicate, guild, corporation, contingent. **9** a heavenly body =**object**, entity. **10** add body to your hair =**fullness**, thickness, substance, bounce, lift, shape.
■ **body and soul** =**completely**, entirely, totally, utterly, fully, thoroughly, wholeheartedly, unconditionally.

> **WORD LINKS**
>
> relating to the body: **corporal, corporeal, somatic**

bodyguard ▶ noun =**minder**, guard, protector, guardian, defender; informal heavy.

bog ▶ noun =**marsh**, swamp, mire, quagmire, morass, slough, fen, wetland; Brit. carr.
■ **bog someone/something down** =**mire**, stick, entangle, ensnare, embroil; hamper, hinder, impede, obstruct, delay, stall, detain; swamp, overwhelm.

bogey ▶ noun **1** bogies frighten children =**evil spirit**, bogle, spectre, phantom, hobgoblin, demon; informal spook. **2** the guild is the bogey of bankers =**bugbear**, pet hate, bane, anathema, abomination, nightmare, horror, dread, curse; N. Amer. bugaboo.

boggy ▶ adjective =**marshy**, swampy, miry, fenny, muddy, waterlogged, wet, soggy, sodden, squelchy; spongy, heavy, sloughy.
–OPPOSITES dry, firm.

bogus ▶ adjective =**fake**, spurious, false, fraudulent, sham, deceptive; **counterfeit**, forged, feigned; make-believe, dummy, pseudo; informal phoney, pretend.
–OPPOSITES genuine.

bohemian ▶ noun he is an artist and a real bohemian =**nonconformist**, avantgardist, free spirit, dropout; hippy, beatnik.
–OPPOSITES conservative.
▶ adjective a bohemian student life =**uncon-**

ventional, nonconformist, unorthodox, avant-garde, irregular, alternative; artistic; *informal* arty-farty, way-out, offbeat.
−OPPOSITES conventional.

boil[1] ▶ verb **1** *boil the potatoes* =simmer. **2** *the soup is boiling* =simmer, bubble, stew. **3** *a cliff with the sea boiling below* =churn, seethe, froth, foam. **4** *she boiled at his lack of consideration* =fume, seethe, rage, smoulder, bristle, be angry, be furious; get worked up; *informal* see red, get steamed up.
▶ noun *bring the stock to the boil* =boiling point, 100 degrees centigrade.
■ **boil something down** =condense, reduce, concentrate, thicken.

boil[2] ▶ noun *a boil on her neck* =swelling, spot, pimple, blister, pustule, eruption, carbuncle, wen, abscess.

boisterous ▶ adjective **1** *a boisterous game* =lively, animated, exuberant, spirited; rowdy, unruly, wild, uproarious, unrestrained, undisciplined, uninhibited, uncontrolled, rough, disorderly, riotous; noisy, loud, clamorous; *informal* rumbustious. **2** *a boisterous wind* =blustery, gusty, windy, stormy, wild, squally, tempestuous; howling, roaring; *informal* blowy.
−OPPOSITES restrained, calm.

bold ▶ adjective **1** *bold adventurers* =daring, intrepid, brave, courageous, valiant, valorous, fearless, dauntless, audacious, daredevil; adventurous, heroic, plucky, spirited, confident, assured; *informal* gutsy, spunky, feisty. **2** *a bold pattern* =striking, vivid, bright, strong, eye-catching, prominent; gaudy, lurid, garish. **3** *departure times are in bold type* =heavy, thick, pronounced.
−OPPOSITES timid, pale.

bolster ▶ noun =pillow, cushion, pad.
▶ verb *a break would bolster her morale* =strengthen, reinforce, boost, fortify, renew; support, buoy up, shore up, maintain, aid, help; augment, increase.
−OPPOSITES undermine.

bolt ▶ noun **1** *the bolt on the door* =bar, lock, catch, latch, fastener. **2** *nuts and bolts* =rivet, pin, peg, screw. **3** *a bolt whirred over my head* =arrow, quarrel, dart, shaft. **4** *a bolt of lightning* =flash, shaft, streak, burst, flare. **5** *Mark made a bolt for the door* =dash, dart, run, sprint, leap, bound. **6** *a bolt of cloth* =roll, reel, spool.

▶ verb **1** *he bolted the door* =lock, bar, latch, fasten, secure. **2** *the lid was bolted down* =rivet, pin, peg, screw; fasten, fix. **3** *Anna bolted from the room* =dash, dart, run, sprint, hurtle, rush, fly, shoot, bound; flee; *informal* tear, scoot, leg it. **4** *he bolted down his breakfast* =gobble, gulp, wolf, guzzle, devour; *informal* demolish, polish off, shovel down; *N. Amer. informal* scarf, snarf.
■ **a bolt from/out of the blue** =shock, surprise, bombshell, thunderbolt, revelation; *informal* turn-up for the books.
■ **bolt upright** =straight, rigidly, stiffly.

bomb ▶ noun =explosive, incendiary (device); missile, projectile; *dated* blockbuster, bombshell.
▶ verb *their headquarters were bombed* =bombard, blast, shell, blitz, strafe, pound; attack, assault; blow up, destroy, demolish, flatten, devastate.

bombard ▶ verb **1** *gun batteries bombarded the islands* =shell, pound, blitz, strafe, bomb; assail, attack, assault, batter, blast, pelt. **2** *we were bombarded with information* =inundate, swamp, flood, deluge, snow under; besiege, overwhelm.

bombast ▶ noun =bluster, pomposity, empty talk, humbug, turgidity, verbosity, verbiage; pretentiousness, ostentation, grandiloquence; *informal* hot air.

bombastic ▶ adjective =pompous, blustering, turgid, verbose, orotund, high-flown, high-sounding, overwrought, pretentious, ostentatious, grandiloquent; *informal* highfalutin.

bona fide ▶ adjective =authentic, genuine, real, true, actual, legal, legitimate, lawful, valid, proper; *informal* legit, pukka, the real McCoy.
−OPPOSITES bogus.

bonanza ▶ noun =windfall, godsend, boon, blessing, bonus, stroke of luck; *informal* jackpot.

bond ▶ noun **1** *the women forged a close bond* =friendship, relationship, fellowship, partnership, association, affiliation, alliance, attachment. **2** *the prisoner struggled with his bonds* =chains, fetters, shackles, manacles, irons, restraints. **3** *I've broken my bond* =promise, pledge, vow, oath, word (of honour), guarantee, assurance; agreement, contract, pact, bargain, deal.
▶ verb *the extensions are bonded to your hair* =join, fasten, fix, affix, attach, secure,

bind, stick, fuse.

bondage ▶ noun =**slavery**, enslavement, servitude, subjugation, subjection, oppression, domination, exploitation, persecution.
−OPPOSITES liberty.

bone ▶ noun

WORD LINKS

consisting of bone: **osseous**
inflammation of bone: **osteitis**
branch of medicine concerned with bones: **orthopaedics**
surgical incision into bone: **osteotomy**
measurement of bones: **osteometry**

bonhomie ▶ noun =**geniality**, affability, conviviality, cordiality, amiability, sociability, friendliness, warmth, joviality.
−OPPOSITES coldness.

bon mot ▶ noun =**witticism**, quip, pun, pleasantry, jest, joke; informal wisecrack, one-liner.

bonny ▶ adjective (Scottish & N. English) =**beautiful**, attractive, pretty, gorgeous, fetching, prepossessing; lovely, nice, sweet, cute, appealing, endearing, adorable, lovable, charming, winsome; informal divine; Austral./NZ informal beaut.
−OPPOSITES unattractive.

bonus ▶ noun 1 the extra work's a real bonus =**benefit**, advantage, boon, blessing, godsend, stroke of luck, asset, plus, pro, attraction; informal perk; formal perquisite. 2 she's on a good salary and she gets a bonus =**gratuity**, handout, gift, present, reward, prize; incentive, inducement; informal perk, sweetener; formal perquisite.
−OPPOSITES disadvantage.

bon viveur, bon vivant ▶ noun =**hedonist**, pleasure-seeker, sensualist, sybarite, voluptuary; epicure, gourmet, gastronome.
−OPPOSITES puritan.

bony ▶ adjective =**gaunt**, angular, skinny, thin, lean, spare, spindly, skin and bone, skeletal, emaciated, underweight.
−OPPOSITES plump.

book ▶ noun 1 he published his first book in 1610 =**volume**, tome, publication, title; novel, storybook, treatise, manual. 2 he scribbled in his book =**notepad**, notebook, pad, exercise book; logbook, ledger, journal, diary; Brit. jotter, pocketbook;

N. Amer. scratch pad. 3 the council had to balance its books =**accounts**, records; ledger, balance sheet.
▶ verb 1 she booked a table at the restaurant =**reserve**, prearrange, order; informal bag; formal bespeak. 2 we booked a number of events in the Festival =**arrange**, programme, schedule, timetable, line up, lay on; N. Amer. slate.
■ **by the book** =**according to the rules**, within the law, lawfully, legally, legitimately; honestly, fairly; informal on the level, fair and square.
■ **book in** =**register**, check in, enrol.

WORD LINKS

list of books: **bibliography**
book enthusiast: **bibliophile**

booking ▶ noun =**reservation**, prearrangement; appointment, date.

bookish ▶ adjective =**studious**, scholarly, academic, intellectual, highbrow, erudite, learned, educated, knowledgeable; cerebral, serious, earnest, thoughtful.

booklet ▶ noun =**pamphlet**, brochure, leaflet, handbill, flyer, tract; N. Amer. folder, mailer.

boom ▶ noun 1 the boom of the waves on the rocks =**reverberation**, resonance, thunder, echoing, crashing, drumming, pounding, roar, rumble. 2 an unprecedented boom in sales =**upturn**, upsurge, upswing, increase, advance, growth, boost, escalation, improvement.
−OPPOSITES slump.
▶ verb 1 thunder boomed overhead =**reverberate**, resound, resonate; rumble, thunder, blare, echo; crash, roll, clap, explode, bang. 2 a voice boomed at her =**bellow**, roar, thunder, shout, bawl; informal holler. 3 the market continued to boom =**flourish**, burgeon, thrive, prosper, progress, improve, pick up, expand, mushroom, snowball.
−OPPOSITES whisper, slump.

boomerang ▶ verb =**backfire**, recoil, reverse, rebound, come back, ricochet; be self-defeating; informal blow up in one's face.

booming ▶ adjective 1 a booming voice =**resonant**, sonorous, ringing, resounding, reverberating, carrying, thunderous; strident, stentorian, strong, powerful. 2 booming business =**flourishing**, burgeoning, thriving, prospering, prosperous, successful, strong, buoyant;

profitable, fruitful, lucrative; expanding.

boon ▶ noun =**blessing**, godsend, bonus, plus, benefit, advantage, help, aid, asset; stroke of luck; *informal* perk; *formal* perquisite.
–OPPOSITES curse.

boor ▶ noun =**lout**, oaf, ruffian, thug, barbarian, Neanderthal, brute, beast; *informal* yahoo, clod, roughneck, peasant, pig; *Brit. informal* yob, oik.

boorish ▶ adjective =**coarse**, uncouth, rude, ill-bred, uncivilized, unrefined, common, rough, thuggish, loutish; vulgar, unsavoury, gross, brutish, Neanderthal; *informal* cloddish, plebby; *Brit. informal* yobbish; *Austral. informal* ocker.
–OPPOSITES refined.

boost ▶ noun 1 *a boost to one's morale* =**uplift**, lift, spur, encouragement, help, inspiration, stimulus, fillip; *informal* shot in the arm. 2 *a boost in sales* =**increase**, expansion, upturn, upsurge, upswing, rise, escalation, improvement, advance, growth, boom; *informal* hike.
–OPPOSITES decrease.
▶ verb 1 *he phones her to boost her morale* =**improve**, raise, uplift, increase, enhance, encourage, heighten, help, promote, foster, stimulate, invigorate, revitalize; *informal* buck up. 2 *they used advertising to boost sales* =**increase**, raise, escalate, improve, strengthen, inflate, push up, promote, advance, foster, stimulate; facilitate, help, assist, aid; *informal* hike, bump up.
–OPPOSITES decrease.

boot[1] ▶ verb 1 *his shot was booted away by the goalkeeper* =**kick**, punt, tap; propel, drive, knock. 2 *boot up your computer* =**start up**, fire up.

boot[2] ■ **to boot** =**as well**, also, too, besides, into the bargain, in addition, on top, what's more, moreover, furthermore; *informal* and all.

booth ▶ noun 1 *booths for different traders* =**stall**, stand, kiosk. 2 *a phone booth* =**cubicle**, kiosk, box, enclosure, cabin.

bootleg ▶ adjective =**illegal**, illicit, unlawful, unauthorized, unlicensed, pirated; contraband, smuggled, black-market.

booty ▶ noun =**loot**, plunder, pillage, haul, spoils, ill-gotten gains, pickings; *informal* swag.

bordello ▶ noun (*N. Amer.*) =**brothel**, whorehouse; *Law* disorderly house; *Brit. informal* knocking shop; *N. Amer. informal* cathouse; *euphemistic* massage parlour.

border ▶ noun 1 *the border of a medieval manuscript* =**edge**, **margin**, perimeter, circumference, periphery; rim, fringe, verge; sides. 2 *the French border* =**frontier**, boundary, borderline, perimeter.
▶ verb 1 *the fields were bordered by hedges* =**surround**, enclose, encircle, circle, edge, fringe, bound, flank. 2 *the straps are bordered with gold braid* =**edge**, fringe, hem; trim, pipe, finish. 3 *the forest bordered on Broadmoor* =**adjoin**, abut, be next to, be adjacent to, be contiguous with, touch.
■ **border on** =**verge on**, approach, come close to, be comparable to, approximate to, be tantamount to, be similar to, resemble.

borderline ▶ noun *the borderline between old and antique* =**dividing line**, division, line, cut-off point; threshold, margin, border, boundary.
▶ adjective *borderline cases* =**marginal**, uncertain, indefinite, unsettled, undecided, doubtful, indeterminate, unclassifiable; equivocal; questionable, debatable, controversial, contentious, problematic; *informal* iffy.

bore[1] ▶ verb *bore a hole* =**drill**, pierce, perforate, puncture, bore, cut; tunnel, burrow, mine, dig, gouge, sink.
▶ noun 1 *a well bore* =**borehole**, hole, well, shaft, pit. 2 *the canon has a bore of 890 millimetres* =**calibre**, diameter, gauge.

bore[2] ▶ verb *the television news bored Philip* =**stultify**, pall on, stupefy, weary, tire, fatigue, send to sleep, leave cold; *informal* turn off.
–OPPOSITES interest.
▶ noun *you can be such a bore* =**tedious person/thing**, tiresome person/thing, bother, nuisance, pest, annoyance, trial, vexation, thorn in one's flesh/side; *informal* drag, pain (in the neck), headache, hassle.

boredom ▶ noun =**weariness**, ennui, apathy, unconcern; frustration, dissatisfaction, restlessness, restiveness; tedium, dullness, monotony, repetitiveness, flatness, dreariness; *informal* deadliness.

boring ▶ adjective =**tedious**, dull, monotonous, repetitive, unrelieved, unvaried, unimaginative, uneventful; characterless, featureless, colourless, lifeless, insipid, uninteresting, unexciting, uninspiring, unstimulating, jejune, flat, bland, dry, stale, tired, banal, lacklustre, stodgy, dreary, humdrum, mundane; mind-numbing, soul-destroying, wearisome, tiresome; *informal* deadly; *Brit. informal* samey; *N. Amer. informal* dullsville.

borrow ▸ verb 1 *we borrowed a lot of money* =**loan**; lease, hire; *informal* cadge, scrounge, bum; *Brit. informal* scab; *N. Amer. informal* mooch; *Austral./NZ informal* bludge. 2 *adventurous chefs borrow foreign techniques* =**adopt**, take on, acquire, embrace.
−OPPOSITES lend.

bosom ▸ noun 1 *the gown was set low over her bosom* =**bust**, chest; breasts, mammary glands; *informal* boobs, knockers; *Brit. informal* bristols, charlies; *N. Amer. informal* bazooms. 2 *love was kindled within his bosom* =**heart**, breast, soul, core, spirit.
▸ adjective *bosom friends* =**close**, boon, intimate, inseparable, faithful, constant, devoted; good, best, firm, favourite.

boss (*informal*) ▸ noun *the boss of a large company* =**head**, chief, principal, director, president, chief executive, chair, manager(ess); supervisor, foreman, overseer, controller; employer, owner, proprietor, patron; *informal* number one, kingpin, top dog, bigwig; *Brit. informal* gaffer, governor; *N. Amer. informal* head honcho.
▸ verb *you have no right to boss me about* =**order about/around**, dictate to, lord it over, bully, push around/about, domineer, dominate, pressurize, browbeat; call the shots, lay down the law; *informal* bulldoze, walk all over, railroad.

bossy ▸ adjective (*informal*) =**domineering**, pushy, overbearing, imperious, officious, authoritarian, dictatorial; *informal* high and mighty.
−OPPOSITES submissive.

bother ▸ verb 1 *no one bothered her* =**disturb**, trouble, inconvenience, pester, badger, harass, molest, plague, nag, hound, harry, annoy, upset, irritate; *informal* hassle, bug; *N. English informal* mither; *N. Amer. informal* ride. 2 *the incident was too small to bother about* =**mind**, care, concern oneself, trouble oneself, worry oneself; *informal* give a damn, give a hoot. 3 *there was something bothering him* =**worry**, trouble, concern, perturb, disturb, disquiet, disconcert, unnerve, fret, upset, distress, agitate, gnaw at, weigh down; *informal* rattle.
▸ noun 1 *I don't want to put you to any bother* =**trouble**, effort, exertion, inconvenience, fuss, pains; *informal* hassle. 2 *the food was such a bother to cook* =**nuisance**, pest, palaver, rigmarole, job, trial, bind, bore, drag, inconvenience, trouble, problem; *informal* hassle, headache, pain (in the neck). 3 *a spot of bother in the public bar* =**disorder**, fighting, trouble, ado, disturbance, agitation, commotion, uproar; *informal* hoo-ha, aggro, argy-bargy, kerfuffle.

bothersome ▸ adjective =**annoying**, irritating, vexatious, maddening, exasperating; tedious, wearisome, tiresome; troublesome, trying, taxing, awkward; *informal* aggravating, pesky, pestilential.

bottle ▸ noun *a bottle of whisky* =**flask**, carafe, decanter, pitcher, flagon, carboy, demijohn.
■ **bottle something up** =**suppress**, repress, restrain, withhold, hold in, rein in, inhibit, smother, stifle, contain, conceal, hide; *informal* keep a lid on.

bottleneck ▸ noun =**traffic jam**, congestion, hold-up, gridlock, tailback; constriction, narrowing, restriction, obstruction, blockage; *informal* snarl-up.

bottom ▸ noun 1 *the bottom of the stairs* =**foot**, lowest part, base; foundation, substructure, underpinning. 2 *the bottom of the car* =**underside**, underneath, undersurface, undercarriage, underbelly. 3 *the bottom of Lake Ontario* =**floor**, bed, depths. 4 *the bottom of his garden* =**farthest point**, far end, extremity. 5 *the bottom of his class* =**lowest level**. 6 (*Brit.*) *I've got a tattoo on my bottom* =**rear (end)**, rump, seat; buttocks, cheeks; *informal* behind, backside, BTM, sit-upon, derrière; *Brit. informal* bum, botty, jacksie; *N. Amer. informal* butt, fanny, tush, tail, buns, booty, heinie; *humorous* fundament, posterior, stern. 7 *police got to the bottom of the mystery* =**origin**, cause, root, source, basis, foundation; heart, kernel; reality, essence.
−OPPOSITES top, surface.
▸ adjective *she sat on the bottom step* =**lowest**, last, bottommost.
−OPPOSITES top.
■ **from top to bottom** =**thoroughly**, fully, extensively, completely, comprehensively, rigorously, exhaustively, scrupulously, meticulously.

bottomless ▸ adjective 1 *the bottomless pits of hell* =**fathomless**, endless, infinite, immeasurable. 2 *George's appetite was bottomless* =**unlimited**, boundless,

infinite, inexhaustible, endless, everlasting; vast, huge, enormous.
–OPPOSITES limited.

bough ▶ noun =**branch**, limb, arm, offshoot.

boulder ▶ noun =**rock**, stone; *Austral./NZ* gibber.

boulevard ▶ noun =**avenue**, street, road, drive, lane, parade, broadway, thoroughfare.

bounce ▶ verb **1** *the ball bounced* =**rebound**, spring back, ricochet, jounce; *N. Amer.* carom. **2** *William bounced down the stairs* =**bound**, leap, jump, spring, bob, hop, skip, trip, prance.
▶ noun **1** *he reached the door in a single bounce* =**bound**, leap, jump, spring, hop, skip. **2** *the pitch's uneven bounce* =**springiness**, resilience, elasticity, give. **3** *she had lost her bounce* =**vitality**, vigour, energy, vivacity, liveliness, animation, sparkle, verve, spirit, enthusiasm, dynamism; cheerfulness, happiness, buoyancy, optimism; *informal* get-up-and-go, pep, zing.
■ **bounce back** =**recover**, revive, rally, pick up, be on the mend; perk up, cheer up, brighten up, liven up; *informal* buck up.

bouncing ▶ adjective =**vigorous**, thriving, flourishing, blooming; healthy, strong, robust, fit, in fine fettle; *informal* in the pink.

bouncy ▶ adjective **1** *a bouncy bridge* =**springy**, flexible, resilient, elastic, stretchy, rubbery. **2** *a rather bouncy ride* =**bumpy**, jolting, jerky, jumpy, jarring, rough. **3** *she was always bouncy* =**lively**, energetic, perky, frisky, jaunty, dynamic, vital, vigorous, vibrant, animated, spirited, buoyant, bubbly, sparkling, vivacious; enthusiastic, upbeat; *informal* peppy, zingy, chirpy.

bound[1] ▶ adjective **1** *he raised his bound ankles* =**tied**, chained, fettered, shackled, secured. **2** *she seemed bound to win* =**certain**, sure, very likely, destined. **3** *bound by the Official Secrets Act* =**obligated**, obliged, compelled, required, constrained. **4** *religion and morality are bound up with one another* =**connected**, linked, tied, united, allied.

bound[2] ▶ verb =**leap**, jump, spring, bounce, hop; skip, bob, dance, prance, gambol, gallop.

bound[3] ▶ verb **1** *corporate freedom is bounded by law* =**limit**, restrict, confine, circumscribe, demarcate, delimit. **2** *the

heath is bounded by a hedge* =**enclose**, surround, encircle, circle, border; close in/off, hem in. **3** *the garden was bounded by Mill Lane* =**border**, adjoin, abut; be next to, be adjacent to.

boundary ▶ noun **1** *the boundary between Israel and Jordan* =**border**, frontier, borderline, partition. **2** *the boundary between art and advertising* =**dividing line**, division, borderline, cut-off point. **3** *the boundary of his estate* =**bounds**, confines, limits, margins, edges, fringes; border, periphery, perimeter. **4** *the boundaries of accepted behaviour* =**limits**, parameters, bounds, confines.

boundless ▶ adjective =**limitless**, untold, immeasurable, abundant; inexhaustible, endless, infinite, interminable, unfailing, ceaseless, everlasting.
–OPPOSITES limited.

bounds ▶ plural noun **1** *we keep rents within reasonable bounds* =**limits**, confines, proportions. **2** *land within the forest bounds* =**borders**, boundaries, confines, limits, margins, edges; periphery, perimeter.
■ **out of bounds** =**off limits**, restricted; forbidden, banned, proscribed, illegal, illicit, unlawful, unacceptable, taboo; *informal* no go.

bountiful ▶ adjective **1** *their bountiful patron* =**generous**, magnanimous, munificent, open-handed, unselfish, unstinting, lavish; benevolent, beneficent, charitable. **2** *a bountiful supply of fresh food* =**abundant**, plentiful, ample, copious, bumper, superabundant, inexhaustible, prolific, profuse; lavish, generous, handsome, rich; *informal* whopping; *literary* plenteous.
–OPPOSITES mean, meagre.

bounty ▶ noun *a bounty for each man killed* =**reward**, prize, award, commission, premium, dividend, bonus, gratuity, tip, donation, handout; incentive, inducement; *informal* perk, sweetener; *formal* perquisite.

bouquet ▶ noun **1** *her bridal bouquet* =**posy**, nosegay, spray, corsage. **2** *bouquets go to Ann for a well-planned event* =**compliment**, commendation, tribute, accolade; praise, congratulations, applause. **3** *the Chardonnay has a fine bouquet* =**aroma**, nose, smell, fragrance, perfume, scent, odour.

bourgeois ▶ adjective **1** *a bourgeois family* =**middle-class**, propertied; **con-**

ventional, conservative, conformist; provincial, suburban, small-town. **2** *bourgeois decadence* =**capitalistic**, materialistic, money-oriented, commercial.
−OPPOSITES proletarian, communist.

bout ▶ noun **1** *a bout of exercise* =**spell**, period, time, stretch, stint, session; burst, flurry, spurt. **2** *a coughing bout* =**attack**, fit, spasm, paroxysm, convulsion, eruption, outburst. **3** *he is fighting only his fifth bout* =**contest**, match, round, heat, competition, event, meeting, fixture; fight, prizefight.

bovine ▶ adjective **1** *large, bovine eyes* =**cow-like**, taurine. **2** *an expression of bovine amazement* =**stupid**, slow, ignorant, unintelligent, imperceptive, half-baked, vacuous, mindless, witless, doltish; *informal* dumb, dense, dim, dopey, birdbrained; *Brit. informal* dozy, daft.
▶ noun =**cow**, heifer, bull, bullock, calf, ox.

bow¹ ▶ verb **1** *the officers bowed* =**nod**, salaam, bob. **2** *the mast quivered and bowed* =**bend**, buckle, stoop, curve, flex, deform. **3** *the government bowed to foreign pressure* =**yield**, submit, give in, surrender, succumb, capitulate, defer, conform; comply with, accept, heed, observe. **4** *a footman bowed her in* =**usher**, conduct, show, lead, guide, direct, steer, shepherd.
▶ noun *a perfunctory bow* =**obeisance**, salaam, bob, nod.

bow² ▶ noun *the bow of the tanker* =**prow**, front, stem, nose, head, cutwater; *Brit. humorous* sharp end.

bow³ ▶ noun **1** *she tied a bow in her hair* =**loop**, knot; ribbon. **2** *he bent the rod into a bow* =**arc**, curve, bend; crescent, half-moon.

bowdlerize ▶ verb =**expurgate**, censor, blue-pencil, cut, edit; sanitize, water down, emasculate.

bowel ▶ noun **1** *a disorder of the bowels* =**intestine(s)**, small intestine, large intestine, colon; *informal* guts, insides. **2** *the bowels of the ship* =**interior**, inside, core, belly; depths, recesses; *informal* innards.

bower ▶ noun *a rose-scented bower* =**arbour**, pergola, grotto, alcove, sanctuary.

bowl¹ ▶ verb **1** *he bowled a hundred or so balls* =**pitch**, throw, propel, hurl, toss, lob, loft, fling, launch, deliver; spin, roll; *informal* chuck, sling, bung. **2** *the car bowled along the roads* =**hurtle**, speed, shoot, sweep, career, hare, fly; *infor-*

mal belt, tear, scoot; *Brit. informal* bomb; *N. Amer. informal* clip.
■ **bowl someone over** *the explosion bowled us over* =**knock down/over**, fell, floor, prostrate.

bowl² ▶ noun **1** =**dish**, basin, pot, crock, crucible, mortar; container, vessel, receptacle. **2** *the town lay in a shallow bowl* =**valley**, hollow, dip, depression, trough, crater. **3** *(N. Amer.) the Hollywood Bowl* =**stadium**, arena, amphitheatre, colosseum; enclosure, ground; *informal* park.

box¹ ▶ noun **1** =**carton**, pack, packet; case, crate, chest, coffer, casket. **2** *a telephone box* =**booth**, cubicle, kiosk, cabin, hut; compartment, carrel, alcove, bay, recess.
▶ verb *Muriel boxed up his clothes* =**package**, pack, parcel, wrap, bundle, bale, crate.
■ **box something/someone in** =**hem in**, fence in, close in, shut in; trap, confine, imprison, intern; surround, enclose, encircle, circle.

box² ▶ verb **1** *he began boxing professionally* =**fight**, prizefight, spar; battle, brawl; *informal* scrap. **2** *he boxed my ears* =**cuff**, smack, strike, hit, thump, slap, swat, punch, jab, wallop; *informal* belt, bop, biff, sock, clout, clobber, whack, plug, slug.

boxer ▶ noun =**fighter**, pugilist, ringster, prizefighter; *informal* bruiser, scrapper.

boxing ▶ noun =**pugilism**, the noble art, fighting, sparring, fisticuffs; prizefighting.

boy ▶ noun =**lad**, schoolboy, male child, youth, young man, stripling; *Scottish & N. English* laddie; *derogatory* brat. See also CHILD.

boycott ▶ verb *they boycotted the election* =**spurn**, snub, shun, avoid, abstain from, reject, veto.
−OPPOSITES support.
▶ noun *a boycott on the use of tropical timbers* =**ban**, veto, embargo, prohibition, sanction, restriction; avoidance, rejection.

boyfriend ▶ noun =**lover**, sweetheart, beloved, darling, man, escort, suitor; partner, significant other; *informal* fella, flame, fancy man; *N. Amer. informal* squeeze; *dated* beau.

boyish ▶ adjective =**youthful**, young, childlike, adolescent, teenage; immature, juvenile, infantile, childish, babyish, puerile.

brace ▸ noun **1** *the saw is used with a brace* =**vice**, clamp, press. **2** *power drills run faster than a brace* =**drill**, boring tool. **3** *the aquarium is supported by wooden braces* =**prop**, beam, joist, batten, rod, post, strut, stay, support, stanchion, bracket. **4** *a brace on his right leg* =**support**, caliper. **5** *a brace of partridges* =**pair**, couple, duo, twosome; two.
▸ verb **1** *the plane's wing is braced by rods* =**support**, shore up, prop up, hold up, buttress, underpin; strengthen, reinforce. **2** *he braced his hand on the railing* =**steady**, secure, stabilize, fix, poise; tense, tighten. **3** *brace yourself for disappointment* =**prepare**, get ready, gear up, nerve, steel, galvanize, gird, strengthen, fortify; *informal* psych oneself up.

bracelet ▸ noun =**bangle**, band, circlet, armlet, wristlet.

bracing ▸ adjective =**invigorating**, refreshing, stimulating, energizing, exhilarating, reviving, restorative, rejuvenating, revitalizing, rousing, fortifying, strengthening.

bracket ▸ noun **1** *each speaker is fixed on a bracket* =**support**, prop, stay, batten, joist, rest, mounting, rack, frame. **2** *put the words in brackets* =**parenthesis**. **3** *a higher tax bracket* =**group**, category, grade, classification, set, division, order.
▸ verb *women were bracketed with minors* =**group**, classify, class, categorize, grade, list, sort, place, assign; couple, pair, twin; liken, compare.

brackish ▸ adjective =**salty**, saline.

brag ▸ verb =**boast**, crow, swagger, swank, bluster, gloat, show off; blow one's own trumpet, sing one's own praises; *informal* talk big, lay it on thick.

braggart ▸ noun =**boaster**, bragger, swaggerer, poseur, egotist; *informal* bighead, loudmouth, show-off, swank; *N. Amer. informal* showboat, blowhard.

braid ▸ noun **1** *straps bordered with gold braid* =**cord**, thread, tape, binding, rickrack, ribbon; cordon, torsade. **2** *his hair is in braids* =**plait**, pigtail, twist; cornrows, dreadlocks.
▸ verb **1** *she began to braid her hair* =**plait**, entwine, intertwine, interweave, weave, twist, twine. **2** *the sleeves are braided in scarlet* =**trim**, edge, border, pipe, hem, fringe.

brain ▸ noun **1** *the disease attacks cells in the brain* =**cerebrum**, cerebral matter, encephalon. **2** *success requires brains as*

well as brawn =**intelligence**, intellect, brainpower, cleverness, wit(s), reasoning, wisdom, acumen, discernment, judgement, understanding, sense; *informal* nous, grey matter, savvy; *N. Amer. informal* smarts.

WORD LINKS

relating to the brain: **cerebral, encephalic**
inflammation of the brain: **encephalitis**

brainless ▸ adjective =**stupid**, foolish, witless, unintelligent, ignorant, idiotic, simple-minded, empty-headed, half-baked; *informal* dumb, half-witted, brain-dead, moronic, cretinous, thick, dopey, dozy, birdbrained, pea-brained, dippy, wooden-headed; *Brit. informal* divvy; *Scottish & N. English informal* glaikit; *N. Amer. informal* chowderheaded.
−OPPOSITES clever.

brainwash ▸ verb =**indoctrinate**, condition, re-educate, persuade, influence.

brake ▸ noun =**curb**, check, restraint, restriction, constraint, control, limitation.
▸ verb =**slow (down)**, decelerate, reduce speed.
−OPPOSITES accelerate.

branch ▸ noun **1** *the branches of a tree* =**bough**, limb, arm, offshoot. **2** *a branch of the river* =**tributary**, feeder, side stream. **3** *the judicial branch of government* =**division**, subdivision, section, subsection, department, sector, part, side, wing. **4** *the corporation's New York branch* =**office**, bureau, agency; subsidiary, offshoot, satellite.
▸ verb **1** *the place where the road branches* =**fork**, bifurcate, divide, subdivide, split. **2** *narrow paths branched off the road* =**diverge from**, deviate from, split off from; fan out from, radiate from.
■**branch out** =**expand**, open up, extend; diversify, broaden one's horizons.

brand ▸ noun **1** *a new brand of margarine* =**make**, line, label, marque; type, kind, sort, variety; trade name, trademark, proprietary name. **2** *her particular brand of humour* =**type**, kind, sort, variety, class, category, genre, style, ilk; *N. Amer.* stripe. **3** *the brand on a sheep* =**identification**, marker, earmark. **4** *the brand of dipsomania* =**stigma**, shame, disgrace; taint, blot, mark.
▸ verb **1** *the letter M was branded on each*

animal =**mark**, stamp, burn, sear. **2** *the scene was branded on her brain* =**engrave**, stamp, etch, imprint. **3** *the media branded us as communists* =**stigmatize**, mark out; denounce, discredit, vilify; label.

brandish ▶ verb =**flourish**, wave, shake, wield; swing, swish; display, flaunt.

brash ▶ adjective **1** *a brash man* =**self-assertive**, pushy, cocksure, cocky, self-confident, arrogant, bold, audacious, brazen; forward, impudent, insolent, rude. **2** *brash colours* =**garish**, gaudy, loud, flamboyant, showy, tasteless; *informal* flashy, tacky.
–OPPOSITES meek, muted.

brassy ▶ adjective **1** =**brazen**, forward, bold, self-assertive, pushy, cocksure, cocky, brash; shameless, immodest; loud, vulgar, showy, ostentatious; *informal* flashy. **2** *brassy music* =**loud**, blaring, noisy, deafening, strident; raucous, harsh, dissonant, discordant, cacophonous; tinny.
–OPPOSITES demure, soft.

brat ▶ noun *(derogatory)* =**rascal**, wretch, imp; minx, chit; *informal* monster, horror, whippersnapper.

bravado ▶ noun =**boldness**, swaggering, bluster; machismo; boasting, bragging, bombast, braggadocio; *informal* showing off.

brave ▶ adjective =**courageous**, plucky, valiant, valorous, intrepid, heroic, lionhearted, bold, fearless, daring, audacious; unflinching, unshrinking, unafraid, dauntless, doughty, mettlesome, stout-hearted, spirited; *informal* game, gutsy, spunky.
–OPPOSITES cowardly.
▶ noun *(dated) an Indian brave* =**warrior**, soldier, fighter.
▶ verb *fans braved freezing temperatures* =**endure**, put up with, bear, withstand, weather, suffer, go through; face, confront, defy.

bravery ▶ noun =**courage**, pluck, valour, intrepidity, nerve, daring, fearlessness, audacity, boldness, stout-heartedness, heroism; backbone, grit, spine, spirit, mettle; *informal* guts, spunk; *Brit. informal* bottle; *N. Amer. informal* moxie.

bravo ▶ exclamation =**well done**, congratulations; encore.

bravura ▶ noun *a display of bravura* =**skill**, brilliance, virtuosity, expertise, artistry, talent, ability, flair.
▶ adjective *a bravura performance* =**virtuoso**, masterly, outstanding, excellent, superb, brilliant, first-class; *informal* mean, ace, A1.

brawl ▶ noun =**fight**, skirmish, scuffle, tussle, fray, melee, free-for-all, scrum; fisticuffs; *informal* scrap, dust-up, set-to; *Brit. informal* punch-up, ruck.

brawn ▶ noun =**physical strength**, muscle(s), burliness, huskiness, toughness, power, might; *informal* beef.

brawny ▶ adjective =**strong**, muscular, muscly, well built, powerful, mighty, Herculean, strapping, burly, sturdy, husky, rugged; bulky, hefty, meaty, solid; *informal* beefy, hunky, hulking.
–OPPOSITES puny, weak.

bray ▶ verb **1** *a donkey brayed* =**neigh**, whinny, hee-haw. **2** *Billy brayed with laughter* =**roar**, bellow, trumpet.

brazen ▶ adjective =**bold**, shameless, unashamed, unabashed, unembarrassed; defiant, impudent, impertinent, cheeky; barefaced, blatant, flagrant; *Brit. informal* saucy.
–OPPOSITES timid.
■ **brazen it out** =**put on a bold front**, stand one's ground, be defiant, be unrepentant, be unabashed.

breach ▶ noun **1** *a breach of the regulations* =**contravention**, violation, infringement, infraction, transgression, neglect. **2** *a breach between government and Church* =**rift**, schism, division, gulf, chasm; disunion, estrangement, discord, dissension, disagreement; split, break, rupture, scission; *Brit. informal* bust-up. **3** *a breach in the sea wall* =**break**, rupture, split, crack, fracture; opening, gap, hole, fissure.
▶ verb **1** *the river breached its bank* =**break (through)**, burst, rupture; *informal* bust. **2** *the changes breached union rules* =**break**, contravene, violate, infringe; defy, disobey, flout, fly in the face of.

breadth ▶ noun **1** *a breadth of 100 metres* =**width**, broadness, thickness; span; diameter. **2** *the breadth of his knowledge* =**range**, extent, scope, depth, reach, compass, scale, degree.

break ▶ verb **1** *the mirror broke* =**shatter**, smash, crack, snap, fracture, fragment, splinter, fall to bits, fall to pieces; split, burst; *informal* bust. **2** *she had broken her leg* =**fracture**, crack. **3** *the bite had barely broken the skin* =**pierce**, puncture, penetrate, perforate; cut. **4** *the coffee machine*

has broken =**stop working**, break down, give out, go wrong, malfunction, crash; *informal* go kaput, conk out, be on the blink, give up the ghost; *Brit. informal* pack up. **5** *traders who break the law* =**contravene**, violate, infringe, breach; defy, flout, disobey, fly in the face of. **6** *his concentration was broken* =**interrupt**, disturb, interfere with. **7** *they broke for coffee* =**stop**, pause, have a rest; *N. Amer.* recess; *informal* knock off, take five. **8** *a pile of carpets broke his fall* =**cushion**, soften the impact of, take the edge off. **9** *the film broke box-office records* =**exceed**, surpass, beat, better, cap, top, outdo, outstrip, eclipse; *informal* leave standing. **10** *habits are very difficult to break* =**give up**, relinquish, drop; *informal* kick, shake, pack in, quit. **11** *the strategies used to break the union* =**destroy**, crush, quash, defeat, vanquish, overcome, overpower, overwhelm, suppress, cripple; weaken, subdue, cow, undermine. **12** *he tried to break the news gently* =**reveal**, disclose, divulge, impart, tell; announce, release. **13** *he broke the encryption code* =**decipher**, decode, decrypt, unravel, work out; *informal* figure out. **14** *the day broke fair and cloudless* =**dawn**, begin, start, emerge, appear. **15** *waves broke against the rocks* =**crash**, dash, beat, pound, lash. **16** *her voice broke as she relived the experience* =**falter**, quaver, quiver, tremble, shake.
−OPPOSITES repair, keep, resume.

▶ noun **1** *the magazine has been published without a break since 1950* =**interruption**, interval, gap, hiatus; discontinuation, suspension, disruption, cut-off; stop, stoppage, cessation. **2** *let's have a break* =**rest**, respite, recess; stop, pause; interval, intermission; *informal* breather, time out. **3** *a weekend break* =**holiday**; *N. Amer.* vacation; *Brit. informal* vac. **4** *a break in diplomatic relations* =**rift**, schism, split, break-up, severance, rupture; *Brit. informal* bust-up. **5** *a break in the wall* =**gap**, opening, space, hole, breach, chink, crack, fissure; tear, split.

■ **break away 1** *she attempted to break away from his grip* =**escape**, get away, run away, flee, make off; get out of someone's clutches; *informal* leg it, cut and run. **2** *a group broke away from the main party* =**leave**, secede from, split off from, separate from, part company with, defect from; form a splinter group.

■ **break down 1** *his van broke down.* See BREAK verb sense 4. **2** *pay negotiations broke down* =**fail**, collapse, founder, fall

through, disintegrate; *informal* fizzle out. **3** *Vicky broke down, sobbing loudly* =**burst into tears**; lose control, be overcome, go to pieces, crumble, disintegrate; *informal* crack up, lose it.

■ **break something down 1** *the police broke the door down* =**knock down**, kick down, smash in, pull down, tear down, demolish. **2** *break big tasks down into smaller parts* =**divide**, separate, split. **3** *graphs show how the information can be broken down* =**analyse**, categorize, classify, sort, itemize, organize; dissect.

■ **break in 1** *thieves broke in and took her cheque book* =**commit burglary**; force one's way in, burst in. **2** *'I don't want to interfere,' Mrs Hendry broke in* =**interrupt**, butt in, cut in, interject, interpose, intervene, chime in; *Brit. informal* chip in.

■ **break someone in** =**train**, initiate; *informal* show someone the ropes.

■ **break into 1** *thieves broke into a house* =**burgle**, rob; force one's way into, burst into. **2** *Phil broke into the discussion* =**interrupt**, butt into, cut in on, intervene in. **3** *he broke into a song* =**burst into**, launch into.

■ **break off** =**snap off**, come off, become detached, become separated.

■ **break something off 1** *I broke off a branch from the tree* =**snap off**, pull off, sever, detach. **2** *they threatened to break off diplomatic relations* =**end**, terminate, stop, cease, call a halt to, finish, dissolve; **suspend**, discontinue; *informal* pull the plug on.

■ **break out 1** *he broke out of the detention centre* =**escape from**, abscond from, flee from; get free. **2** *fighting broke out* =**flare up**, start suddenly, erupt, burst out.

■ **break up 1** *the meeting broke up* =**end**, finish, stop, terminate; adjourn; *N. Amer.* recess. **2** *the crowd began to break up* =**disperse**, scatter, disband, part company. **3** *Danny and I broke up last year* =**split up**, separate, part (company); divorce.

■ **break something up 1** *police tried to break up the crowd* =**disperse**, scatter, disband. **2** *I'm not going to let you break up my marriage* =**wreck**, ruin, destroy.

breakable ▶ adjective =**fragile**, delicate, flimsy, insubstantial; destructible; *formal* frangible.

breakaway ▶ adjective *a breakaway group* =**separatist**, secessionist, schismatic, splinter; rebel, renegade.

breakdown ▶ noun **1** *the breakdown of*

the negotiations =**failure**, collapse, disintegration. **2** on the death of her father she suffered a breakdown =**nervous breakdown**; informal crack-up. **3** the breakdown of the computer system =**malfunction**, failure, crash. **4** a breakdown of the figures =**analysis**, classification, examination, investigation, dissection.

breaker ▶ noun =**wave**, roller, comber, white horse; informal boomer.

break-in ▶ noun =**burglary**, robbery, theft, raid; informal smash-and-grab.

breakneck ▶ adjective the breakneck pace of change =**rapid**, speedy, high-speed, lightning, whirlwind.
■ **at breakneck speed** =**dangerously fast**, at full tilt, flat out, ventre à terre; informal hell for leather, like the wind, like a bat out of hell, like greased lightning; Brit. informal like the clappers.

breakthrough ▶ noun =**advance**, development, step forward, success, improvement; discovery, innovation, revolution.
–OPPOSITES setback.

break-up ▶ noun **1** the break-up of negotiations =**end**, dissolution; breakdown, failure, collapse, disintegration. **2** their break-up was very amicable =**separation**, split, parting, divorce; estrangement, rift; Brit. informal bust-up. **3** the break-up of the Soviet Union =**division**, partition.

breakwater ▶ noun =**sea wall**, jetty, mole, groyne, pier.

breast ▶ noun **1** the curve of her breasts =**mammary gland**, mamma; (**breasts**) **bosom(s)**, bust, chest; informal boobs, knockers, bubbies; Brit. informal bristols, charlies; N. Amer. informal bazooms. **2** feelings of frustration were rising up in his breast =**heart**, bosom, soul, core.

WORD LINKS
surgical removal of a breast: **mastectomy**
X-ray of a breast: **mammogram**

breath ▶ noun **1** I took a deep breath =**inhalation**, inspiration, gulp of air; exhalation, expiration; Medicine respiration. **2** I had barely enough breath to reply =**wind**; informal puff. **3** a breath of wind =**puff**, waft. **4** a breath of scandal =**hint**, suggestion, trace, touch, whisper, suspicion, whiff, undertone.
■ **take someone's breath away** =**astonish**, astound, amaze, stun, startle, stagger, shock, take aback, dumbfound, jolt, overawe, thrill; informal knock sideways, flabbergast, blow away, bowl over; Brit. informal knock for six.

WORD LINKS
relating to breath: **respiratory**

breathe ▶ verb **1** she breathed deeply =**inhale**, exhale, respire, draw breath; puff, pant, blow, gasp, wheeze; Medicine inspire, expire. **2** at least I'm still breathing =**be alive**, live. **3** he would breathe new life into his firm =**instil**, infuse, inject, impart. **4** 'Together at last,' she breathed =**whisper**, murmur, purr, sigh, say.

breathless ▶ adjective **1** Will arrived flushed and breathless =**out of breath**, panting, puffing, gasping, wheezing; winded; informal out of puff. **2** the crowd were breathless with anticipation =**agog**, open-mouthed, on the edge of one's seat, on tenterhooks, in suspense.

breathtaking ▶ adjective =**spectacular**, magnificent, wonderful, awe-inspiring, awesome, astounding, astonishing, amazing, stunning, incredible; informal sensational, out of this world; literary wondrous.

breed ▶ verb **1** elephants breed readily in captivity =**reproduce**, produce offspring, procreate, multiply; mate. **2** she was born and bred in the village =**bring up**, rear, raise, nurture. **3** the political system bred discontent =**cause**, bring about, give rise to, lead to, produce, generate, foster, result in; stir up; literary beget.
▶ noun **1** a breed of cow =**variety**, stock, strain; type, kind, sort. **2** a new breed of journalist =**type**, kind, sort, variety, class, genre, generation.

breeding ▶ noun **1** individual birds pair for breeding =**reproduction**, procreation; mating. **2** the breeding of rats =**rearing**, raising, nurturing. **3** her aristocratic breeding =**upbringing**, rearing; parentage, family, pedigree, blood, birth. **4** people of rank and breeding =(**good**) **manners**, gentility, refinement, cultivation, polish, urbanity; informal class.

breeding ground ▶ noun the school is a breeding ground for communists =**nursery**, cradle, nest, den; hotbed.

breeze ▶ noun **1** =**gentle wind**, puff of air, gust; literary zephyr. **2** (informal) travelling through London was a breeze =**easy task**, five-finger exercise, walkover; child's play, nothing; informal doodle, piece of cake, cinch, kids' stuff, cake-walk.

breezy ▶ adjective **1** *a breezy day* =**windy**, fresh, brisk, airy; blowy, blustery, gusty. **2** *his breezy manner* =**jaunty**, **cheerful**, cheery, brisk, carefree, easy, casual, relaxed, informal, light-hearted, lively, buoyant, sunny; *informal* upbeat.

brevity ▶ noun **1** *the report is notable for its brevity* =**conciseness**, succinctness, economy of language, pithiness, incisiveness, shortness, compactness. **2** *the brevity of human life* =**shortness**, briefness, transience, ephemerality, impermanence.
–OPPOSITES verbosity.

brew ▶ verb **1** *this beer is brewed in Frankfurt* =**ferment**, make. **2** *I'll brew some tea* =**prepare**, infuse, make, stew; *Brit. informal* mash. **3** *there's trouble brewing* =**develop**, loom, impend, be imminent, be on the horizon, be in the offing, be just around the corner.
▶ noun **1** *home brew* =**beer**, ale. **2** *a hot reviving brew* =**drink**, beverage; tea, coffee. **3** *a dangerous brew of political turmoil and violent conflict* =**mixture**, mix, blend, combination, amalgam, cocktail.

bribe ▶ verb =**buy off**, pay off, suborn; *informal* grease someone's palm, keep someone sweet, fix, square; *Brit. informal* nobble.
▶ noun =**inducement**, incentive, carrot, douceur; *informal* backhander, pay-off, kickback, sweetener; *Brit. informal* bung.

bribery ▶ noun =**subornation**; *N. Amer.* payola; *informal* palm-greasing, graft, hush money.

bric-a-brac ▶ noun =**ornaments**, knick-knacks, trinkets, bibelots, gewgaws, gimcracks; bits and bobs, odds and ends; *informal* junk.

brick ▶ noun *a brick of ice cream* =**block**, cube, bar, cake.

bridal ▶ adjective =**wedding**, nuptial, marriage, matrimonial, marital, conjugal.

bride ▶ noun =**wife**, marriage partner; newly-wed.

bridge ▶ noun **1** *a bridge over the river* =**viaduct**, flyover, overpass, aqueduct. **2** *a bridge between rival groups* =**link**, connection, bond, tie.
▶ verb **1** *a walkway bridged the motorway* =**span**, cross (over), extend across, traverse, arch over. **2** *an attempt to bridge the cultural gap* =**join**, link, connect, unite;

straddle; overcome, reconcile.

| WORD LINKS |

relating to bridges: **pontine**
fear of bridges: **gephyrophobia**

bridle ▶ noun *a horse's bridle* =**harness**, headgear.
▶ verb **1** *she bridled at his tone* =**bristle**, take offence, take umbrage, be affronted, be offended, get angry. **2** *he bridled his indignation* =**curb**, restrain, hold back, control, check, rein in/back; suppress, stifle; *informal* keep a/the lid on.

brief ▶ adjective **1** *a brief account* =**concise**, succinct, short, pithy, incisive, abridged, condensed, compressed, abbreviated, compact, thumbnail, potted; *formal* compendious. **2** *a brief visit* =**short**, flying, fleeting, hasty, hurried, quick, cursory, perfunctory, temporary, short-lived, momentary, transient; *informal* quickie. **3** *a pair of brief shorts* =**skimpy**, scanty, short; revealing. **4** *the boss was rather brief with him* =**brusque**, abrupt, curt, short, blunt, sharp.
–OPPOSITES lengthy.
▶ noun **1** *my brief is to reorganize the project* =**instructions**, directions, directive, remit, mandate. **2** *a barrister's brief* =**case**, summary, argument, contention; dossier.
▶ verb *employees were briefed about the decision* =**inform**, tell, update, notify, advise, apprise; prepare, prime, instruct; *informal* fill in, clue in, put in the picture.

briefing ▶ noun **1** *a press briefing* =**conference**, meeting, interview; *N. Amer.* backgrounder. **2** *this briefing explains the systems* =**information**, rundown, guidance; instructions, directions, guidelines.

briefly ▶ adverb **1** *Henry paused briefly* =**momentarily**, temporarily, for a moment, fleetingly. **2** *briefly, the plot is as follows* =**in short**, in brief, in a word, in sum, in a nutshell, in essence.

briefs ▶ plural noun =**underpants**, pants, knickers, Y-fronts, G-string, thong; *N. Amer.* shorts, undershorts; *informal* panties, undies; *Brit. informal* smalls.

brigade ▶ noun **1** *a brigade of soldiers* =**unit**, contingent, battalion, regiment, division, squadron, company, platoon, section, corps, troop. **2** *the volunteer ambulance brigade* =**squad**, team, group, band, party, crew, force, outfit.

bright ▶ adjective **1** *the bright surface of the metal* =**shining**, brilliant, dazzling, beaming, glaring, sparkling, flashing, glittering, gleaming, glowing, luminous, radiant; shiny, lustrous, glossy. **2** *a bright morning* =**sunny**, cloudless, clear, fair, fine. **3** *bright colours* =**vivid**, brilliant, intense, strong, bold, glowing, rich; gaudy, lurid, garish. **4** *bright flowers* =**colourful**, brightly-coloured, vivid, vibrant; *dated* gay. **5** *a bright guitar sound* =**clear**, vibrant; high-pitched. **6** *a bright young graduate* =**clever**, intelligent, quick-witted, smart, canny, astute, intuitive, perceptive; ingenious, resourceful; *informal* brainy. **7** *a bright smile* =**happy**, cheerful, cheery, jolly, merry, sunny, beaming; lively, exuberant, buoyant, bubbly, bouncy, perky, chirpy. **8** *a bright future* =**promising**, rosy, optimistic, hopeful, favourable, propitious, auspicious, encouraging, good, golden.
–OPPOSITES dull, dark, stupid.

brighten ▶ verb **1** *sunshine brightened the room* =**illuminate**, light up, lighten, cast/shed light on. **2** *you can brighten up the shadiest of corners* =**enhance**, embellish, enrich, dress up, prettify, beautify; *informal* jazz up. **3** *Sarah brightened up as she thought of Emily's words* =**cheer up**, perk up, rally, be enlivened, feel heartened, be uplifted, be encouraged, take heart; *informal* buck up, pep up.

brilliance ▶ noun **1** *a philosopher of great brilliance* =**genius**, talent, ability, prowess, skill, expertise, aptitude, flair, finesse, panache; greatness, distinction; intelligence, wisdom, sagacity, intellect. **2** *the brilliance and beauty of Paris* =**splendour**, magnificence, grandeur, resplendence. **3** *the brilliance of the sunshine* =**brightness**, vividness, intensity; sparkle, glitter, glow, blaze, beam, luminosity, radiance.

brilliant ▶ adjective **1** *a brilliant student* =**gifted**, talented, able, adept, skilful, bright, intelligent, clever, smart, astute, intellectual; elite, superior, first-class, excellent; *informal* brainy. **2** *his brilliant career* =**superb**, glorious, illustrious, impressive, remarkable, exceptional. **3** *a shaft of brilliant light* =**bright**, shining, blazing, dazzling, vivid, intense, gleaming, glaring, luminous, radiant; *literary* irradiant, coruscating. **4** *brilliant green* =**vivid**, intense, bright, bold, dazzling.
–OPPOSITES stupid, bad, dark.

brim ▶ noun **1** *the brim of his hat* =**peak**, visor, shield, shade. **2** *the cup was filled to its brim* =**rim**, lip, brink, edge.
▶ verb **1** *the pan was brimming with water* =**be full (up)**; overflow, run over. **2** *her eyes were brimming with tears* =**fill**; overflow.

brimful ▶ adjective =**full (up)**, brimming, filled to capacity, overfull, running over; *informal* chock-full.
–OPPOSITES empty.

brindle, brindled ▶ adjective =**tawny**, brownish; **dappled**, streaked, mottled, speckled, flecked.

bring ▶ verb **1** *he brought over a tray* =**carry**, fetch, bear, take; convey, transport; move, haul, shift. **2** *Philip brought his bride to his mansion* =**escort**, conduct, guide, lead, usher, show, shepherd. **3** *the wind changed and brought rain* =**cause**, produce, create, generate, precipitate, lead to, give rise to, result in; stir up, whip up, promote. **4** *the police contemplated bringing charges* =**put forward**, prefer, lay, submit, present, initiate, institute. **5** *this job brings him a regular salary* =**earn**, make, fetch, bring in, yield, net, gross, return, produce; command, attract.
■ **bring something about 1** *the affair that brought about her death* =**cause**, produce, give rise to, result in, lead to, occasion, bring on, bring to pass; provoke, generate, engender, precipitate; *formal* effectuate. **2** *he brought the ship about* =**turn (round/around)**, reverse, change the direction of.
■ **bring something back 1** *the smell brought back memories* =**remind one of**, put one in mind of, conjure up, evoke, summon up; take one back. **2** *bring back capital punishment* =**reintroduce**, reinstate, re-establish, revive, resurrect.
■ **bring someone down 1** *he was brought down by a clumsy challenge* =**trip**, knock over/down. **2** *I couldn't bear to bring her down* =**depress**, sadden, upset, get down, dispirit, dishearten, discourage.
■ **bring something down 1** *we will bring down the price* =**decrease**, reduce, lower, cut, drop; *informal* slash. **2** *the unrest brought down the government* =**unseat**, overturn, topple, overthrow, depose, oust.
■ **bring something forward** =**propose**, suggest, advance, raise, table, present, move, submit, lodge.

■ **bring someone in** =**involve**, include, count in.

■ **bring something in 1** *he brought in a private member's bill* =**introduce**, launch, inaugurate, initiate, institute. **2** *the event brings in one million pounds each year. See* BRING *sense 5.*

■ **bring something on.** *See* BRING SOMETHING ABOUT *sense 1.*

■ **bring something out 1** *they were bringing out a new magazine* =**launch**, establish, begin, start, found, set up, instigate, inaugurate, market; publish, print, issue, produce. **2** *the shawl brings out the colour of your eyes* =**accentuate**, highlight, emphasize, accent, set off.

■ **bring someone round 1** *she administered artificial respiration and brought him round* =**wake up**, return to consciousness, rouse, bring to. **2** *we would have brought him round, given time* =**persuade**, convince, talk round, win over, sway, influence.

■ **bring someone up** =**rear**, raise, care for, look after, nurture, provide for.

■ **bring something up** =**mention**, allude to, touch on, raise, broach, introduce; voice, air, suggest, propose, submit, put forward, table.

brink ▶ noun **1** *the brink of the abyss* =**edge**, verge, margin, rim, lip; border, boundary, perimeter, periphery, limit(s). **2** *two countries on the brink of war* =**verge**, threshold, point, edge.

brio ▶ noun =**vigour**, vivacity, gusto, verve, zest, enthusiasm, vitality, dynamism, animation, spirit, energy; *informal* pep, vim, get-up-and-go.

brisk ▶ adjective **1** *a brisk pace* =**quick**, rapid, fast, swift, speedy, hurried; energetic, lively, vigorous; *informal* nippy. **2** *the bar was doing a brisk trade* =**busy**, bustling, lively, hectic; good. **3** *his tone became brisk* =**no-nonsense**, decisive, businesslike; brusque, abrupt, short, sharp, curt, blunt, terse, gruff; *informal* snappy. **4** *a brisk breeze* =**bracing**, fresh, crisp, invigorating, refreshing, stimulating, energizing; biting, keen, chilly, cold; *informal* nippy.
–OPPOSITES slow, quiet.

bristle ▶ noun **1** *the bristles on his chin* =**hair**, whisker; (**bristles**) stubble, five o'clock shadow. **2** *a hedgehog's bristles* =**spine**, prickle, quill, barb.
▶ verb **1** *the hair on the back of his neck bristled* =**rise**, stand up, stand on end. **2** *she bristled at his tone* =**bridle**, take offence, take

umbrage, be affronted, be offended; get angry, be irritated. **3** *the roof bristled with antennae* =**abound**, overflow, be full, be packed, be crowded, be jammed, be covered; *informal* be thick, be chock-full.

bristly ▶ adjective **1** *bristly bushes* =**prickly**, spiky, thorny, scratchy, brambly. **2** *the bristly skin of his cheek* =**stubbly**, hairy, fuzzy, unshaven, whiskery; scratchy, rough, coarse, prickly.
–OPPOSITES smooth.

brittle ▶ adjective **1** *a brittle material* =**breakable**, fragile, delicate; splintery; *formal* frangible. **2** *a brittle laugh* =**harsh**, hard, sharp, grating. **3** *a brittle woman* =**edgy**, nervy, anxious, unstable, highly strung, tense, excitable, jumpy, skittish, neurotic; *informal* uptight.
–OPPOSITES flexible, resilient, soft, relaxed.

broach ▶ verb **1** *I broached the matter with my parents* =**bring up**, raise, introduce, talk about, mention, touch on, air. **2** *he broached a barrel of beer* =**pierce**, puncture, tap; open, uncork; *informal* crack open.

broad ▶ adjective **1** *a broad flight of steps* =**wide**. **2** *the leaves are two inches broad* =**wide**, across, in breadth, in width. **3** *a broad expanse of prairie* =**extensive**, vast, immense, great, spacious, expansive, sizeable, sweeping, rolling. **4** *a broad range of opportunities* =**comprehensive**, inclusive, extensive, wide, all-embracing, eclectic, unlimited. **5** *this report gives a broad outline* =**general**, non-specific, rough, approximate, basic; loose, vague. **6** *a broad hint* =**obvious**, unsubtle, explicit, direct, plain, clear, straightforward, bald, patent, transparent, undisguised, overt. **7** *his broad humour* =**indecent**, coarse, indelicate, ribald, risqué, racy, rude, suggestive, naughty, off colour, earthy, smutty, dirty, filthy, vulgar; *informal* blue, near the knuckle. **8** *a broad Somerset accent* =**pronounced**, noticeable, strong, thick. **9** *he was attacked in broad daylight* =**full**, complete, total; clear, bright.
–OPPOSITES narrow, limited, detailed, subtle.

broadcast ▶ verb **1** *the show will be broadcast worldwide* =**transmit**, relay, air, beam, show, televise, telecast, screen. **2** *the result was broadcast far and wide* =**report**, announce, publicize, proclaim; spread, circulate, air, blazon, trumpet. **3** *don't broadcast too much seed*

=**scatter**, sow, disperse, sprinkle, spread, distribute.
▸ noun =**programme**, show, production, transmission, telecast, screening, videocast; *informal* prog.

broaden ▸ verb **1** *her smile broadened* =**widen**, expand, stretch (out), draw out, spread; deepen. **2** *the government tried to broaden its political base* =**expand**, enlarge, extend, widen, swell; increase, augment, add to, amplify; develop, enrich, improve, build on.

broadly ▸ adverb **1** *the pattern is broadly similar for men and women* =**in general**, on the whole, as a rule, in the main, mainly, predominantly; loosely, roughly, approximately. **2** *he was smiling broadly* =**widely**, openly, from ear to ear.

broad-minded ▸ adjective =**liberal**, tolerant, freethinking, indulgent, progressive, permissive, unshockable; unprejudiced, unbiased.
−OPPOSITES intolerant.

broadside ▸ noun **1** *(historical) the gunners fired broadsides* =**salvo**, volley, cannonade, barrage, blast, fusillade. **2** *a broadside against the economic reforms* =**criticism**, censure, polemic, diatribe, tirade; attack, onslaught.

brochure ▸ noun =**booklet**, prospectus, catalogue; pamphlet, leaflet, handbill, handout; *N. Amer.* folder.

broil ▸ verb *(N. Amer.)* =**grill**, toast, barbecue; cook.

broken ▸ adjective **1** *a broken bottle* =**smashed**, shattered, fragmented, splintered, crushed, snapped; in bits, in pieces; destroyed, disintegrated; cracked, split; *informal* in smithereens. **2** *a broken arm* =**fractured**. **3** *his video's broken* =**damaged**, faulty, defective, not working, malfunctioning, in disrepair, inoperative, out of order, broken-down, down; *informal* on the blink, kaput, bust, conked out, acting up, done for; *Brit. informal* knackered. **4** *broken skin* =**cut**, ruptured, punctured, perforated. **5** *a broken marriage* =**failed**, ended. **6** *broken promises* =**flouted**, violated, infringed, contravened, disregarded, ignored. **7** *he was left a broken man* =**defeated**, beaten, subdued; **demoralized**, dispirited, discouraged, crushed, humbled; dishonoured, ruined. **8** *a night of broken sleep* =**interrupted**, disturbed, fitful, disrupted, discontinuous, intermittent, unsettled, troubled. **9** *she spoke in broken English* =**halting**, hesitating, disjointed, faltering, imperfect.
−OPPOSITES whole, working, uninterrupted, perfect.

broken-down ▸ adjective **1** *a broken-down hotel* =**dilapidated**, run down, ramshackle, tumbledown, in disrepair, battered, crumbling, deteriorated, gone to rack and ruin. **2** *a broken-down car* =**defective**, faulty; not working, malfunctioning, inoperative; *informal* kaput, conked out, clapped out, done for; *Brit. informal* knackered.
−OPPOSITES smart.

broken-hearted ▸ adjective =**heartbroken**, grief-stricken, desolate, devastated, inconsolable, miserable, depressed, melancholy, wretched, sorrowful, forlorn, heavy-hearted, woeful, doleful, downcast, woebegone; *informal* down in the mouth.
−OPPOSITES overjoyed.

broker ▸ noun =**dealer**, agent; middleman, intermediary, mediator; factor, liaison; stockbroker.
▸ verb =**arrange**, organize, orchestrate, work out, settle, clinch; negotiate, mediate.

bronzed ▸ adjective =**tanned**, suntanned, brown.
−OPPOSITES pale.

brooch ▸ noun =**pin**, clip, badge.

brood ▸ noun =**offspring**, young, progeny; family, hatch, clutch; *formal* progeniture.
▸ verb **1** *once the eggs are laid the male broods them* =**incubate**, hatch. **2** *he slumped in his armchair, brooding* =**worry**, fret, agonize, mope, sulk; think, ponder, contemplate, meditate, muse.

brook¹ ▸ noun *a babbling brook* =**stream**, streamlet, rill, runnel, gill; *N. English* beck; *Scottish & N. English* burn; *S. English* bourn; *N. Amer. & Austral./NZ* creek.

brook² ▸ verb *(formal) we brook no violence* =**tolerate**, allow, stand, bear, abide, put up with, endure; accept, permit, countenance; *informal* stomach, hack; *Brit. informal* stick.

brothel ▸ noun =**whorehouse**; *N. Amer.* bordello; *Brit. informal* knocking shop; *N. Amer. informal* cathouse, creep-joint; *euphemistic* massage parlour; *Law* disorderly house; *archaic* bawdy house, house of ill repute.

brother ▸ noun **1** *she had a younger brother* =*informal* bro. **2** *they were brothers* *in crime* =**colleague**, associate, partner, comrade, fellow, friend; *informal* pal, chum; *Brit. informal* mate. **3** *a brother of the Order* =**monk**, cleric, friar, religious, monastic.

> **WORD LINKS**
>
> relating to a brother: **fraternal**
> killing of one's brother or sister:
>   **fratricide**

brotherhood ▸ noun **1** *the ideals of justice and brotherhood* =**comradeship**, fellowship, fraternalism, kinship; camaraderie, friendship. **2** *a Masonic brotherhood* =**society**, fraternity, association, alliance, union, league, guild, order, body, community, club, lodge, circle.

brotherly ▸ adjective **1** *brotherly rivalry* =**fraternal**, sibling. **2** *brotherly love* =**friendly**, comradely; affectionate, amicable, kind, devoted, loyal.

brow ▸ noun **1** =**forehead**, temple. **2** *the brow of the hill* =**summit**, peak, top, crest, crown, head, pinnacle, apex.

browbeat ▸ verb =**bully**, hector, intimidate, force, coerce, compel, dragoon, bludgeon, pressure, pressurize, tyrannize, terrorize, menace; harass, harry, hound; *informal* bulldoze, railroad.

brown ▸ adjective **1** *brown eyes* =**hazel**, chocolate-coloured, coffee-coloured; brunette, sepia, mahogany, umber, burnt sienna; beige, buff, tan, fawn, camel, café au lait, caramel, chestnut. **2** *his skin was brown* =**tanned**, suntanned, bronze; dark, swarthy, dusky. **3** *brown bread* =**wholemeal**.
▸ verb *the grill browns food evenly* =**grill**, toast, singe, sear; barbecue, bake, cook.

browse ▸ verb **1** *I browsed among the shops* =**look around/round**, window-shop, peruse. **2** *she browsed through the newspaper* =**scan**, skim, glance, look, peruse; thumb, leaf, flick; dip into. **3** *cows were browsing in the meadow* =**graze**, feed, crop; ruminate.

bruise ▸ noun *a bruise on her forehead* =**contusion**, lesion, mark, injury; swelling, lump, bump, welt.
▸ verb **1** *her face was badly bruised* =**contuse**, injure, mark, discolour. **2** *every one of the apples is bruised* =**mark**, discolour, blemish; damage, spoil. **3** *Eric's ego was bruised* =**upset**, offend, insult, affront, hurt, wound, injure, crush.

brunette ▸ adjective =**brown-haired**, dark.

brunt ▸ noun =**(full) force**, impact, shock, burden, pressure, weight; effect, repercussions, consequences.

brush¹ ▸ noun **1** *a dustpan and brush* =**broom**, sweeper, besom, whisk. **2** *he gave the seat a brush with his hand* =**clean**, sweep, wipe, dust. **3** *the brush of his lips against her cheek* =**touch**, stroke, skim, graze, nudge, contact; kiss. **4** *a brush with the law* =**encounter**, clash, confrontation, conflict, altercation, incident; *informal* run-in, to-do; *Brit. informal* spot of bother.
▸ verb **1** *he spent his day brushing the floors* =**sweep**, clean, buff, scrub. **2** *she brushed her hair* =**groom**, comb, neaten, tidy, smooth, arrange, fix, do; curry. **3** *she felt his lips brush her cheek* =**touch**, stroke, caress, skim, sweep, graze, contact; kiss. **4** *she brushed a wisp of hair away* =**push**, move, sweep, clear.
■ **brush something aside** =**disregard**, ignore, dismiss, shrug off, wave aside; overlook, pay no attention to, take no notice of, neglect, forget about, turn a blind eye to; reject, spurn; laugh off, make light of, trivialize; *informal* pooh-pooh.
■ **brush someone off** =**rebuff**, dismiss, spurn, reject; slight, scorn, disdain; ignore, disregard, snub, cut, turn one's back on, give someone the cold shoulder, freeze out; jilt, cast aside, discard, throw over, drop, leave; *informal* knock back.

brush² ▸ noun =**undergrowth**, underwood, scrub, brushwood, shrubs, bushes; *N. Amer.* underbrush, chaparral.

brusque ▸ adjective =**curt**, abrupt, blunt, short, sharp, terse, brisk, peremptory, gruff, bluff; offhand, discourteous, impolite, rude; *informal* snappy.
–OPPOSITES polite.

brutal ▸ adjective **1** *a brutal attack* =**savage**, cruel, vicious, ferocious, barbaric, barbarous, wicked, murderous, bloodthirsty, cold-blooded, callous, heartless, merciless, sadistic; heinous, monstrous, abominable, atrocious. **2** *brutal honesty* =**unsparing**, unstinting, unembellished, unvarnished, bald, naked, stark, blunt, direct, straightforward, frank, outspoken, forthright, plain-spoken; complete, total.
–OPPOSITES gentle.

brutalize ▸ verb **1** *the men were brutalized by life in the trenches* =**desensitize**, dehumanize, harden, toughen, inure. **2** *they were brutalized by the police* =**attack**, assault, beat, batter; abuse.

brute ▶ noun **1** *a callous brute* =**savage**, beast, monster, animal, barbarian, fiend, ogre; sadist; thug, lout, ruffian; *informal* swine, pig. **2** *the Alsatian was a vicious-looking brute* =**animal**, beast, creature; *N. Amer. informal* critter.

▶ adjective *brute strength* =**physical**, bodily; crude, violent.

bubble ▶ noun **1** *the bubbles in his mineral water* =**globule**, bead, blister; air pocket; (**bubbles**) sparkle, fizz, effervescence, froth. **2** *a bubble of confidence* =**illusion**, delusion, fantasy, dream, chimera, castle in the air; *informal* pie in the sky.

▶ verb **1** *this wine bubbled nicely on the tongue* =**sparkle**, fizz, effervesce, foam, froth. **2** *the milk was bubbling above the flame* =**boil**, simmer, seethe, gurgle. **3** *she was bubbling over with enthusiasm* =**overflow**, brim over, be filled, gush.

bubbly ▶ adjective **1** *a bubbly wine* =**sparkling**, fizzy, effervescent, gassy, aerated, carbonated; spumante; frothy, foamy. **2** *she was bubbly and full of life* =**vivacious**, animated, ebullient, lively, high-spirited, zestful; sparkling, bouncy, buoyant, carefree; merry, happy, cheerful, perky, sunny, bright; *informal* upbeat, chirpy.
−OPPOSITES still, listless.

buck ▶ verb *it takes guts to buck the system* =**resist**, oppose, defy, fight, kick against.

bucket ▶ noun =**pail**, scuttle, can, tub.

buckle ▶ noun *a belt buckle* =**clasp**, clip, catch, hasp, fastener.

▶ verb **1** *he buckled the belt round his waist* =**fasten**, do up, hook, strap, secure, clasp, clip. **2** *the front axle buckled* =**warp**, bend, twist, curve, distort, contort, deform; bulge, arc, arch; crumple, collapse, give way.

bucolic ▶ adjective =**rustic**, rural, pastoral, country, countryside; *literary* Arcadian, sylvan, georgic.

budding ▶ adjective =**promising**, up-and-coming, rising, in the making, aspiring, future, prospective, potential, fledgling, developing; *informal* would-be, wannabe.

budge ▶ verb **1** *the horses wouldn't budge* =**move**, shift, stir, go. **2** *I couldn't budge the door* =**dislodge**, shift, move, reposition. **3** *they refuse to budge on the issue* =**give way**, yield, change one's mind,

acquiesce, compromise, do a U-turn. **4** *our customers won't be budged on price alone* =**influence**, sway, convince, persuade, induce, entice, tempt, lure, cajole, bring round.

budget ▶ noun **1** *your budget for the week* =**financial plan**, forecast; accounts, statement. **2** *the defence budget* =**allowance**, allocation, quota; grant, award, funds, resources, capital.

▶ verb **1** *we have to budget £7,000 for the work* =**allocate**, allot, allow, earmark, designate, set aside. **2** *budget your finances* =**schedule**, plan, cost, estimate; ration.

▶ adjective *a budget hotel* =**cheap**, inexpensive, economy, low-cost, low-price, cut-price, discount, bargain.
−OPPOSITES expensive.

buff¹ ▶ adjective *a plain buff envelope* =**beige**, yellowish, yellowish-brown, light brown, fawn, sandy, wheaten, biscuit, camel.

▶ verb *he buffed the glass* =**polish**, burnish, shine, clean, rub.

buff² ▶ noun *(informal) a film buff* =**enthusiast**, fan, devotee, lover, admirer; expert, aficionado, authority, pundit; *informal* freak, nut, fanatic, addict.

buffer ▶ noun *a buffer against market fluctuations* =**cushion**, bulwark, shield, barrier, guard, safeguard.

▶ verb *a massage helped to buffer the strain* =**cushion**, absorb, soften, lessen, diminish, moderate, allay.
−OPPOSITES intensify.

buffet¹ ▶ noun **1** *a sumptuous buffet* =**cold table**, self-service meal, smorgasbord. **2** *a station buffet* =**cafe**, cafeteria, snack bar, canteen, restaurant. **3** *the plates are kept in the buffet* =**sideboard**, cabinet, cupboard.

buffet² ▶ verb **1** *rough seas buffeted the coast* =**batter**, pound, lash, strike, hit. **2** *he has been buffeted by bad publicity* =**afflict**, trouble, harm, burden, bother, beset, harass, torment, blight, bedevil.

buffoon ▶ noun *he regarded the chaplain as a buffoon* =**fool**, idiot, dunce, ignoramus, simpleton, jackass; *informal* chump, blockhead, nincompoop, numbskull, dope, twit, nitwit, halfwit, clot, birdbrain, twerp.

bug ▶ noun **1** *bugs were crawling everywhere* =**insect**, mini-beast; *informal* creepy-crawly, beastie. **2** *the bug planted on his phone* =**listening device**, hidden microphone, wire, wiretap, tap. **3** *the*

program developed a bug =**fault**, error, defect, flaw; virus; *informal* glitch, gremlin.
▶ verb *her conversations were bugged* =**record**, eavesdrop on, spy on, overhear; wiretap, tap, monitor.

bugbear ▶ noun =**pet hate**, bête noire, bogey; bane, irritation, vexation, anathema, thorn in one's flesh/side; *informal* peeve, pain (in the neck), hang-up; *N. Amer.* bugaboo.

build ▶ verb 1 *a supermarket had been built* =**construct**, erect, put up, assemble. 2 *they were building a snowman* =**make**, construct, form, create, fashion, model, shape. 3 *they are building a business strategy* =**establish**, found, set up, institute, inaugurate, initiate.
▶ noun *a man of slim build* =**physique**, frame, body, figure, form, shape, stature, proportions; *informal* vital statistics.
■ **build something in/into** =**incorporate in/into**, include in, absorb into, subsume into, assimilate into.
■ **build on** =**expand on**, enlarge on, develop, elaborate, flesh out, embellish, amplify; refine, improve, perfect.
■ **build up** =**increase**, grow, mount up, intensify, escalate; strengthen.
■ **build something up 1** *he built up a huge business* =**establish**, set up, found, institute, start, create; develop, expand, enlarge. 2 *he built up his stamina* =**boost**, strengthen, increase, improve, augment, raise, enhance, swell; *informal* beef up. 3 *I have built up a collection of prints* =**accumulate**, amass, collect, gather; stockpile, hoard.

builder ▶ noun 1 *a canal builder* =**designer**, planner, architect, deviser, creator, maker, constructor. 2 *the builders must finish the job in time* =**construction worker**, bricklayer, labourer; *Brit.* ganger.

building ▶ noun 1 *a brick building* =**structure**, construction, edifice, erection, pile; property, premises, establishment. 2 *the building of power stations* =**construction**, erection, fabrication, assembly.

WORD LINKS
relating to building: **tectonic, architectural**

build-up ▶ noun 1 *the build-up of military strength* =**increase**, growth, expansion, escalation, development, proliferation. 2 *the build-up of carbon dioxide* =accu-

mulation, accretion. 3 *the build-up for the World Cup* =**publicity**, promotion, advertising, marketing; *informal* hype.

built-in ▶ adjective 1 *a built-in cupboard* =**fitted**, integral, integrated, incorporated. 2 *built-in advantages* =**inherent**, intrinsic, inbuilt; essential, implicit, basic, fundamental, deep-rooted.

bulb ▶ noun =**tuber**, corm, rhizome.

bulbous ▶ adjective =**bulging**, protuberant, round, fat, rotund; swollen, tumid, distended, bloated.

bulge ▶ noun =**swelling**, bump, lump, protuberance, prominence.
▶ verb *his eyes were bulging* =**swell**, stick out, puff out, balloon (out), fill out, belly, distend; project, protrude, stand out.

bulk ▶ noun 1 *the sheer bulk of the bags* =**size**, volume, dimensions, proportions, mass, scale, magnitude, immensity, vastness. 2 *the bulk of entrants were British* =**majority**, generality, main part, lion's share, preponderance; most, almost all.
−OPPOSITES minority.
▶ verb *some meals are bulked out with fat* =**expand**, pad out, fill out, eke out; augment, increase.

bulky ▶ adjective 1 *bulky items* =**large**, big, huge, sizeable, substantial, massive; king-size, outsize, oversized, considerable; **cumbersome**, unmanageable, unwieldy, ponderous, heavy, weighty; *informal* jumbo, whopping, hulking; *Brit. informal* ginormous. 2 *a bulky man* =**heavily built**, stocky, thickset, sturdy, well built, burly, strapping, solid, heavy, hefty, meaty; stout, fat, plump, chubby, portly, rotund, round, chunky; overweight, obese, fleshy, corpulent; *informal* tubby, pudgy, roly-poly, beefy, porky, blubbery; *Brit. informal* podgy.
−OPPOSITES small, slight.

bull ▶ noun

WORD LINKS
relating to a bull: **taurine**

bulldoze ▶ verb 1 *they plan to bulldoze the park* =**demolish**, knock down, tear down, pull down, flatten, level, raze, clear. 2 *he bulldozed his way through* =**force**, push, shove, barge, elbow, shoulder, jostle; plunge, crash, sweep.

bullet ▶ noun =**ball**, shot; *informal* slug; (**bullets**) lead.

bulletin ▸ noun **1** *a news bulletin* =**report**, dispatch, story, press release, newscast, flash; statement, announcement, message, communication, communiqué. **2** *the society's monthly bulletin* =**newsletter**, news-sheet, proceedings; newspaper, magazine, digest, gazette, review.

bullish ▸ adjective =**confident**, positive, assertive, assured, bold, determined; optimistic, buoyant, sanguine; *informal* feisty, upbeat.

bully ▸ noun =**persecutor**, oppressor, tyrant, tormentor, intimidator; tough guy, thug.
▸ verb **1** *the others bully him* =**persecute**, oppress, tyrannize, browbeat, intimidate, strong-arm; *informal* push around/about. **2** *she was bullied into helping* =**coerce**, pressure, pressurize, press, push; force, compel; badger, goad, prod, browbeat, bludgeon, intimidate, dragoon, strong-arm; *informal* bulldoze, railroad, lean on.

bulwark ▸ noun **1** *ancient bulwarks* =**wall**, rampart, fortification, parapet, stockade, palisade, barricade, embankment, earthwork. **2** *a bulwark of liberty* =**protector**, defender, protection, guard, defence, supporter, buttress; mainstay, bastion, stronghold.

bumble ▸ verb **1** *they bumbled around the house* =**blunder**, lurch, stumble, stagger, lumber, flounder, totter. **2** *the speakers bumbled* =**mutter**, mumble, stumble, babble, burble, drivel, gibber.

bumbling ▸ adjective =**blundering**, bungling, inept, clumsy, maladroit, awkward, muddled; oafish, clodhopping, lumbering; crude; *informal* botched, ham-fisted, cack-handed.
−OPPOSITES efficient.

bump ▸ noun **1** *I landed with a bump* =**jolt**, crash, smash, smack, crack, bang, thud, thump; *informal* whack, thwack, bash, wallop. **2** *I was woken by a bump* =**bang**, crack, boom, clang, knock, thud, thump, clunk, crash, smash; stomp, clump, clomp. **3** *a bump in the road* =**hump**, lump, ridge, bulge, knob, protuberance. **4** *a bump on his head* =**swelling**, lump, bulge, injury, contusion; outgrowth, growth, carbuncle, protuberance.
▸ verb **1** *cars bumped into each other* =**hit**, crash, smash, slam, bang, knock, run, plough; ram, collide with, strike; *N. Amer.*

impact. **2** *a cart bumping along the road* =**bounce**, jolt, jerk, rattle, shake.

bumper ▸ adjective =**abundant**, rich, bountiful, good, fine; large, big, huge, plentiful, profuse, copious; *informal* whopping; *literary* plenteous, bounteous.
−OPPOSITES meagre.

bumpkin ▸ noun =**yokel**, peasant, provincial, rustic, country cousin, countryman/woman; *N. Amer. informal* hayseed, hillbilly, hick; *Austral. informal* bushy.

bumptious ▸ adjective =**self-important**, conceited, arrogant, self-assertive, pushy, swollen-headed, pompous, overbearing, cocky, swaggering; proud, haughty, egotistical; *informal* snooty, uppity.
−OPPOSITES modest.

bumpy ▸ adjective **1** *a bumpy road* =**uneven**, rough, rutted, pitted, potholed; lumpy, rocky. **2** *a bumpy ride* =**bouncy**, rough, uncomfortable, jolting, lurching, jerky, jarring, bone-shaking. **3** *a bumpy start* =**inconsistent**, variable, irregular, fluctuating, intermittent, erratic, patchy; rocky, unsettled, unstable, turbulent, chaotic.
−OPPOSITES smooth.

bunch ▸ noun **1** *a bunch of flowers* =**bouquet**, posy, nosegay, spray, corsage; wreath, garland. **2** *a bunch of keys* =**cluster**, clump, knot; group.
▸ verb **1** *he bunched the reins in his hand* =**bundle**, clump, cluster, group, gather; pack. **2** *his trousers bunched around his ankles* =**gather**, ruffle, pucker, fold, pleat. **3** *the runners bunched up behind him* =**cluster**, huddle, gather, congregate, collect, amass, group, crowd.

bundle ▸ noun *a bundle of clothes* =**bunch**, roll, clump, wad, parcel, sheaf, bale, bolt; pile, stack, heap, mass; *informal* load, wodge.
▸ verb **1** *she bundled up her things* =**tie**, pack, parcel, wrap, roll, fold, bind, truss, bale. **2** *she was bundled in furs* =**wrap**, envelop, clothe, cover, muffle, swathe, swaddle, shroud, drape, enfold.

bung ▸ noun =**stopper**, plug, cork, spigot, spile, seal; *N. Amer.* stopple.

bungle ▸ verb =**mishandle**, mismanage, mess up, spoil, ruin; *informal* botch, muff, fluff, make a hash of, foul up, screw up; *Brit. informal* make a pig's ear of, cock up; *N. Amer. informal* flub, goof up.

bungler ▸ noun =**blunderer**, incompetent, amateur, bumbler, clown; *informal* botcher; *Brit. informal* bodger; *N. Amer. informal* jackleg.

bungling ▶ adjective =**incompetent**, blundering, amateurish, inept, unskilful, clumsy, awkward, bumbling; *informal* ham-fisted, cack-handed.

bunk ▶ noun =**berth**, cot, bed.

buoy ▶ noun *a mooring buoy* =**float**, marker, beacon.
▶ verb *the party was buoyed by an election victory* =**cheer (up)**, hearten, rally, invigorate, uplift, lift, encourage, stimulate, inspirit; *informal* pep up, perk up, buck up.
−OPPOSITES depress.

buoyancy ▶ noun **1** *the drum's buoyancy* =**lightness**, floatability. **2** *her natural buoyancy* =**cheerfulness**, happiness, light-heartedness, joy, bounce, sunniness, breeziness, jollity; liveliness, ebullience, high spirits, vivacity, vitality, verve, sparkle, zest; optimism; *informal* pep. **3** *the buoyancy of the market* =**vigour**, strength, resilience, growth, improvement, expansion.

buoyant ▶ adjective **1** *a buoyant substance* =**floating**, floatable. **2** *a buoyant mood* =**cheerful**, cheery, happy, lighthearted, carefree, bright, merry, joyful, bubbly, bouncy, sunny, jolly; lively, jaunty, high-spirited, perky; optimistic, confident, positive; *informal* peppy, upbeat. **3** *sales were buoyant* =**booming**, strong, vigorous, thriving; improving, expanding, mushrooming, snowballing.

burble ▶ verb **1** *the exhaust was burbling* =**gurgle**, bubble, murmur, purr, whirr, drone, hum, rumble. **2** *he burbled on* =**prattle**, blather, babble, gabble, prate, drivel, rattle, ramble, maunder, go on, run on; *informal* jabber, blabber, yatter, gab; *Brit. informal* rabbit, witter, waffle, chunter.

burden ▶ noun **1** *they shouldered their burdens* =**load**, cargo, weight; pack, bundle. **2** *a financial burden* =**responsibility**, onus, charge, duty, obligation, liability; trouble, care, problem, worry, difficulty, strain, encumbrance. **3** *the burden of his message* =**gist**, substance, drift, thrust, meaning, significance, essence, import.
▶ verb **1** *he was burdened with a heavy pack* =**load**, charge, weigh down, encumber, hamper; overload, overburden. **2** *avoid*

burdening them with guilt =**oppress**, trouble, worry, harass, upset, distress; haunt, afflict, strain, stress, tax, overwhelm.

burdensome ▶ adjective =**onerous**, oppressive, troublesome, weighty, worrisome, stressful; vexatious, irksome, trying, difficult; arduous, strenuous, hard, laborious, exhausting, tiring, taxing, demanding, punishing, gruelling.

bureau ▶ noun **1** *an oak bureau* =**desk**, writing table, secretaire, escritoire; *Brit.* davenport. **2** *a marriage bureau* =**agency**, service, office, business, company, firm. **3** *the intelligence bureau* =**department**, division, branch, section.

bureaucracy ▶ noun **1** *the ranks of the bureaucracy* =**civil service**, government, administration; establishment, system, powers that be; ministries, authorities. **2** *unnecessary bureaucracy* =**red tape**, rules and regulations, protocol, officialdom, paperwork.

bureaucrat ▶ noun =**official**, administrator, civil servant, minister, functionary, mandarin; *Brit.* jack-in-office; *derogatory* apparatchik.

bureaucratic ▶ adjective **1** *bureaucratic structure* =**administrative**, official, governmental, ministerial, state, civic. **2** *current practice is far too bureaucratic* =**rule-bound**, rigid, inflexible, complicated.

burgeon ▶ verb =**flourish**, thrive, prosper, improve; expand, escalate, swell, grow, boom, mushroom, snowball, rocket.

burglar ▶ noun =**housebreaker**, robber, thief, raider, looter, safe-breaker/cracker; intruder.

burglary ▶ noun **1** *a sentence for burglary* =**housebreaking**, breaking and entering, theft, stealing, robbery, larceny, thievery, looting. **2** *a series of burglaries* =**break-in**, theft, robbery, raid; *informal* smash and grab; *N. Amer. informal* heist.

burgle ▶ verb =**rob**, loot, steal from, plunder, rifle, pillage; break into; *informal* do.

burial ▶ noun =**burying**, interment, committal, inhumation, entombment.
−OPPOSITES exhumation.

┌─────────────────────┐
│ **WORD LINKS**   │
└─────────────────────┘
relating to burial: **funerary**

burial ground ▶ noun =**cemetery**,

graveyard, churchyard, necropolis; *Scottish* kirkyard; *N. Amer.* memorial park; *informal* boneyard.

burlesque ▶ noun =**parody**, caricature, satire, lampoon, skit; *informal* send-up, take-off, spoof.

burly ▶ adjective =**strapping**, well built, sturdy, brawny, strong, muscly, thickset, big, hefty, bulky, stocky, Herculean; *informal* hunky, beefy.
–OPPOSITES puny.

burn ▶ verb **1** *the coal was burning* =**be on fire**, be alight, blaze, go up (in smoke), be in flames, be aflame; smoulder, glow. **2** *he burned the letters* =**set fire to**, set alight, set light to, ignite, touch off; incinerate; *informal* torch. **3** *I burned my dress with the iron* =**scorch**, singe, sear, char, blacken, brand; scald. **4** *her face burned* =**be hot**, be warm, be feverish, be on fire; blush, redden, flush, colour. **5** *she was burning with curiosity* =**be consumed**, be eaten up, be obsessed, be tormented. **6** *Meredith burned to know the secret* =**yearn**, long, ache, desire, want, wish, hanker, crave, hunger, thirst; *informal* yen, itch, be dying. **7** *the energy they burn up* =**consume**, use up, expend, get/go through, eat up; dissipate.

burning ▶ adjective **1** *burning coals* =**blazing**, flaming, fiery, ignited, glowing, red-hot, smouldering; raging, roaring. **2** *burning desert sands* =**extremely hot**, fiery, blistering, scorching, searing, sweltering, torrid; *informal* baking, boiling (hot), roasting, sizzling. **3** *a burning desire* =**intense**, passionate, deep-seated, profound, wholehearted, strong, ardent, fervent, urgent, fierce, eager, frantic, consuming, uncontrollable. **4** *burning issues* =**important**, crucial, significant, vital, essential, pivotal; urgent, pressing, compelling, critical.

burnish ▶ verb =**polish (up)**, shine, buff (up), rub (up).

burrow ▶ noun *a rabbit's burrow* =**warren**, tunnel, hole, dugout; lair, set, den, earth.
▶ verb *the mouse burrows a hole* =**tunnel**, dig (out), excavate, grub, mine, bore, channel; hollow out, gouge out.

burst ▶ verb **1** *one balloon burst* =**split (open)**, rupture, break, tear. **2** *a shell burst* =**explode**, blow up, detonate, go off. **3** *smoke burst through the hole* =**break**, erupt, surge, gush, rush, stream, flow, pour, spill; spout, spurt, jet, spew. **4** *he*

burst into the room =**plunge**, charge, barge, plough, hurtle, career, rush, dash, tear. **5** *she burst into tears* =**break out in**, erupt in, have a fit of.
▶ noun **1** *a burst in the tyre* =**rupture**, puncture, breach, split, blowout. **2** *mortar bursts* =**explosion**, detonation, blast, eruption, bang. **3** *a burst of gunfire* =**volley**, salvo, fusillade, barrage, discharge; hail, rain. **4** *a burst of activity* =**outbreak**, eruption, flare-up, blaze, attack, fit, rush, gale, storm, surge, upsurge, spurt; *informal* splurt.
■ **burst out 1** *'I don't care!' she burst out* =**exclaim**, blurt, cry, shout, yell; *dated* ejaculate. **2** *he burst out crying* =**suddenly start**.

bury ▶ verb **1** *the dead were buried* =**inter**, lay to rest, entomb. **2** *she buried her face in her hands* =**hide**, conceal, cover, enfold, engulf, tuck, cup, sink. **3** *the bullet buried itself in the wood* =**embed**, sink, implant, submerge; drive into; lodge. **4** *he buried himself in his work* =**absorb**, engross, immerse, occupy, engage, busy, involve.
–OPPOSITES exhume.

WORD LINKS

fear of being buried alive: **taphephobia**

bush ▶ noun **1** *a rose bush* =**shrub**; (**bushes**) undergrowth, shrubbery. **2** *the bush* =**wilds**, wilderness; backwoods, hinterland(s); *N. Amer.* backcountry, backland(s); *Austral./NZ* outback, backblocks; *N. Amer. informal* boondocks.

bushy ▶ adjective =**thick**, shaggy, fuzzy, bristly, fluffy, woolly; *informal* jungly.
–OPPOSITES sleek, wispy.

busily ▶ adverb =**actively**, energetically, vigorously, enthusiastically; industriously, purposefully, diligently.

business ▶ noun **1** *she has to smile in her business* =**work**, occupation, profession, career, employment, job, position; field, sphere, trade, craft; *informal* racket, game. **2** *who do you do business with?* =**trade**, commerce, dealing, traffic, merchandising; dealings, transactions, negotiations. **3** *her own business* =**firm**, company, concern, enterprise, venture, organization, operation, undertaking; office, agency, franchise, practice; *informal* outfit, set-up. **4** *none of your business* =**concern**, affair, responsibility, duty, function, obligation; problem, worry; *informal* pigeon, bailiwick; *Brit. informal* lookout. **5** *an odd business* =**affair**, matter, thing, case, circumstance, situation, event, incident, happening, occurrence; episode.

businesslike ▶ adjective =**professional**, efficient, slick, competent, methodical, disciplined, systematic, orderly, organized, structured, practical, pragmatic.

businessman, businesswoman ▶ noun =**entrepreneur**, industrialist, manufacturer, tycoon, magnate, employer; dealer, trader, broker, merchant, buyer, seller, marketeer, merchandiser, vendor, tradesman, retailer, supplier.

bust ▶ noun **1** *her large bust* =**chest**, bosom; breasts, mammary glands, mammae; *informal* boobs, knockers, bubbies; *Brit. informal* bristols, charlies; *N. Amer. informal* bazooms. **2** *a bust of Caesar* =**sculpture**, carving, effigy, statue; head and shoulders.

bustle ▶ verb **1** *people bustled about* =**rush**, dash, hurry, scurry, scuttle, scamper, scramble; run, tear, charge; *informal* scoot, beetle, buzz, zoom. **2** *she bustled us into the kitchen* =**hustle**, sweep, push, whisk; *informal* bundle.
▶ noun *the bustle of the market* =**activity**, action, liveliness, excitement; tumult, hubbub, whirl; *informal* toing and froing, comings and goings.

bustling ▶ adjective =**busy**, crowded, swarming, teeming, thronged; buzzing, hectic, lively.
–OPPOSITES deserted.

busy ▶ adjective **1** *they are busy raising money* =**occupied (in)**, engaged in, involved in, employed in, working at, hard at work (on); rushed off one's feet, hard-pressed; on the job, absorbed, engrossed, immersed, preoccupied; *informal* on the go, hard at it; *Brit. informal* on the hop. **2** *she is busy at the moment* =**unavailable**, engaged, occupied; working; *informal* tied up. **3** *a busy day* =**hectic**, active, lively, full, eventful; energetic, tiring. **4** *the town was busy* =**crowded**, bustling, hectic, swarming, teeming, full, thronged. **5** *a busy design* =**ornate**, overelaborate, overblown, overwrought, overdone, fussy, cluttered, overworked.
–OPPOSITES idle, free, quiet.
▶ verb *he busied himself with paperwork* =**occupy**, involve, engage, concern, absorb, engross, immerse, preoccupy; distract, divert.

busybody ▶ noun =**meddler**, interferer, troublemaker; gossip, scandalmonger; eavesdropper, gawker; *informal* nosy parker, snoop, rubberneck; *Brit. informal* gawper.

but ▶ conjunction **1** *he stumbled but didn't fall* =**yet**, nevertheless, nonetheless, even so, however, still, notwithstanding, despite that, in spite of that, for all that, all the same; though, although. **2** *I am clean but you aren't* =**whereas**, conversely, but then, then again, on the other hand, by/in contrast, on the contrary. **3** *one cannot but sympathize* =**(do) other than**, (do) otherwise than; except.
▶ preposition *everyone but him* =**except (for)**, apart from, other than, besides, aside from, with the exception of, bar, excluding, leaving out, save (for), saving.
▶ adverb *he is but a shadow of his former self* =**only**, just, simply, merely, no more than, nothing but; a mere; *N. English* nobbut.
■ **but for** =**except for**, if it were not for, barring, notwithstanding.

butcher ▶ noun **1** *a butcher's shop* =**meat seller**, slaughterer; *Scottish* flesher. **2** *a Nazi butcher* =**murderer**, slaughterer, killer, assassin; *N. Amer.* terminator; *literary* slayer.
▶ verb **1** *the goat was butchered* =**slaughter**, cut up, carve up, joint. **2** *they butchered 150 people* =**massacre**, murder, slaughter, kill, destroy, exterminate, assassinate; *N. Amer.* terminate; *informal* dispose of; *literary* slay. **3** *the studio butchered the film* =**spoil**, ruin, mutilate, mangle, mess up, wreck; *informal* make a hash of, screw up.

butchery ▶ noun **1** *the butchery trade* =**meat selling**. **2** *(Brit.) the cattle went to the butchery* =**abattoir**, slaughterhouse. **3** *(Brit.) a butchery* =**butcher's (shop)**, meat counter. **4** *the butchery in the war* =**slaughter**, massacre, mass murder, carnage; *literary* slaying.

butt[1] ▶ verb *she butted him* =**ram**, headbutt, bunt; bump, buffet, push, shove; *N. English* tup.

butt[2] ▶ noun *the butt of a joke* =**target**, victim, object, subject; laughing stock.

butt[3] ▶ noun **1** *the butt of a gun* =**stock**, end, handle, hilt, haft, helve. **2** *a cigarette butt* =**stub**, end, stump, remnant; *informal* fag end, dog end.
▶ verb *the shop butts up against the house* =**adjoin**, abut, be next to, be adjacent to,

border (on), neighbour, be connected to; join, touch.

buttocks ▶ plural noun =**cheeks**; rear (end), rump, seat; *Brit.* bottom; *informal* behind, backside, BTM, sit-upon, derrière; *Brit. informal* bum, botty, jacksie; *N. Amer. informal* butt, fanny, tush, tail, buns, booty, heinie; *humorous* fundament, posterior, stern.

WORD LINKS

relating to the buttocks: **natal**

button ▶ noun **1** *shirt buttons* =**fastener**, stud, toggle; hook, catch, clasp. **2** *press the button* =**switch**, knob, control; lever, handle.

buttress ▶ noun **1** *stone buttresses* =**prop**, support, abutment, shore, pier, reinforcement, stanchion. **2** *a buttress against social collapse* =**safeguard**, defence, protection, guard; support, prop; bulwark.
▶ verb =**strengthen**, reinforce, fortify, support, bolster, shore up, underpin, cement, uphold, defend, back up.

buxom ▶ adjective =**large-breasted**, bosomy, big-bosomed; shapely, ample, plump, rounded, full-figured, voluptuous, curvaceous, Rubenesque; *informal* busty, chesty, well endowed, curvy.

buy ▶ verb **1** =**purchase**, acquire, obtain, get, pick up, snap up; take, procure, pay for; invest in; *informal* get hold of, score. **2** *he could not be bought* =**bribe**, buy off, suborn, corrupt; *informal* grease someone's palm, give a backhander to, get at, fix, square; *Brit. informal* nobble.
–OPPOSITES sell.

buyer ▶ noun =**purchaser**, customer, consumer, shopper, investor; (**buyers**) clientele, patronage, market; *Law* vendee.

buzz ▶ noun **1** *the buzz of the bees* =**hum**, murmur, drone. **2** *an insistent buzz from her control panel* =**warning sound**, purr, ring, note, tone, beep, alarm.
▶ verb **1** *bees buzzed* =**hum**, drone, bumble, murmur. **2** *the intercom soon buzzed* =**purr**, warble, sound, ring, beep. **3** *the club is buzzing with excitement* =**hum**, throb, vibrate, pulse, bustle.

by ▶ preposition **1** *I broke it by forcing the lid* =**through**, as a result of, because of, by dint of, by way of, via, by means of; with the help of, with the aid of, by virtue of. **2** *be there by midday* =**no later than**, in good time for, at, before. **3** *a house*

by the lake =**next to**, beside, alongside, by/at the side of, adjacent to; near, close to, neighbouring, adjoining, bordering, overlooking; connected to, contiguous with, attached to. **4** *go by the building* =**past**, in front of, beyond. **5** *all right by me* =**according to**, with, as far as … is concerned.
▶ adverb *people hurried by* =**past**, on, along.
■ **by and by** =**eventually**, ultimately, finally, in the end, one day, sooner or later, in time, in a while, in the long run, in the future, in due course.
■ **by oneself** =**alone**, on one's own, singly, separately, solitarily, unaccompanied, companionless, unattended, unescorted, solo; unaided, unassisted, without help, by one's own efforts, under one's own steam, independently, single-handed(ly), off one's own bat, on one's own initiative; *informal* by one's lonesome; *Brit. informal* on one's tod, on one's Jack Jones.

bygone ▶ adjective =**past**, former, olden, earlier, previous, one-time, long-ago, of old, ancient, antiquated; departed, dead, extinct, defunct, out of date, outmoded; *literary* of yore.
–OPPOSITES present, recent.

by-law ▶ noun *(Brit.)* =**local law**, regulation, rule.

bypass ▶ noun =**ring road**, detour, diversion, alternative route; *Brit.* relief road.
▶ verb **1** *bypass the farm* =**go round**, go past, make a detour round; avoid. **2** *an attempt to bypass the problem* =**avoid**, evade, dodge, escape, elude, circumvent, get round, skirt, sidestep, steer clear of; *informal* duck. **3** *they bypassed the regulations* =**ignore**, pass over, omit, neglect, go over the head of; *informal* short-circuit.

by-product ▶ noun =**side effect**, consequence, entailment, corollary; ramification, repercussion, spin-off, fallout; fruits; *Brit.* knock-on effect.

bystander ▶ noun =**onlooker**, passer-by, non-participant, observer, spectator, eyewitness; *informal* gawper, rubberneck.

byword ▶ noun **1** *the office was a byword for delay* =**perfect example**, classic case, model, exemplar, embodiment, incarnation, personification, epitome, typification. **2** *reality was his byword* =**slogan**, motto, maxim, mantra, catchword, watchword, formula; middle name.

Cc

cab ▸ noun **1** *she hailed a cab* =**taxi**, taxi cab; *Brit.* minicab, hackney carriage; *N. Amer.* hack. **2** *a truck driver's cab* =**driver's compartment**, cabin.

cabal ▸ noun =**clique**, faction, coterie, cell, sect; caucus, lobby, pressure group; *Brit.* ginger group.

cabaret ▸ noun **1** *the evening's cabaret* =**entertainment**, (floor) show, performance. **2** *the cabarets of Montreal* =**nightclub**, club; *N. Amer.* cafe; *informal* nightspot, niterie, clip joint; *N. Amer. informal* honky-tonk.

cabin ▸ noun **1** *a first-class cabin* =**berth**, stateroom, deckhouse. **2** *a cabin by the lake* =**hut**, log cabin, shanty, shack; chalet; *Scottish* bothy; *N. Amer.* cabana; *Austral.* mia-mia. **3** *the driver's cabin* =**cab**, compartment.

cabinet ▸ noun *a walnut cabinet* =**cupboard**, bureau, chest of drawers.

cable ▸ noun **1** *a thick cable moored the ship* =**rope**, cord, line; *Nautical* hawser; *N. Amer.* choker. **2** *electric cables* =**wire**, lead, cord; power line; *Brit.* flex.

cache ▸ noun =**hoard**, store, stockpile, stock, supply, reserve, arsenal; *informal* stash.

cachet ▸ noun =**prestige**, status, standing, kudos, snob value, stature, pre-eminence, eminence; *informal* street cred.
−OPPOSITES stigma.

cackle ▸ verb **1** *the geese cackled at him* =**squawk**, honk, cluck. **2** *Noel cackled with glee* =**laugh**, guffaw, crow, chortle, chuckle.

cacophonous ▸ adjective =**loud**, noisy, ear-splitting, raucous, discordant, unmelodious, tuneless.
−OPPOSITES harmonious.

cacophony ▸ noun =**din**, racket, noise, discord, dissonance; *informal* bedlam.

cadaver ▸ noun *(Medicine)* =**corpse**, (dead) body, remains, carcass; *informal* stiff.

cadaverous ▸ adjective =**(deathly) pale**, pallid, ashen, grey, whey-faced, etiolated, corpse-like; as thin as a rake, bony, skeletal, emaciated, skin and bone, haggard, gaunt, drawn, pinched, hollow-cheeked, hollow-eyed; *informal* like a bag of bones, anorexic; *archaic* starveling.
−OPPOSITES rosy, plump.

cadence ▸ noun =**rhythm**, tempo, metre, beat, pulse; intonation, modulation, lilt.

cadge ▸ verb *(informal)* =**borrow**; *informal* scrounge, bum, touch someone for, sponge; *N. Amer. informal* mooch; *Austral./NZ informal* bludge.

cadre ▸ noun =**corps**, body, team, group, unit.

cafe ▸ noun =**snack bar**, cafeteria; coffee bar/shop, tea room/shop; bistro, brasserie; *N. Amer.* diner; *informal* eatery, noshery; *Brit. informal* caff.

cafeteria ▸ noun =**(self-service) restaurant**, canteen, cafe, buffet, refectory, mess hall.

cage ▸ noun =**enclosure**, pen, pound; coop, hutch; birdcage, aviary.
▸ verb =**confine**, shut in/up, pen, coop up, enclose, lock up.

cagey ▸ adjective *(informal)* =**secretive**, guarded, non-committal, tight-lipped, reticent, evasive; *informal* playing one's cards close to one's chest.
−OPPOSITES open.

cajole ▸ verb =**persuade**, wheedle, coax, talk into, prevail on; *informal* sweet-talk, soft-soap, twist someone's arm.

cake ▸ noun **1** *cream cakes* =**bun**, pastry, gateau, slice. **2** *a cake of soap* =**bar**, tablet, block, slab, lump, wedge, piece.
▸ verb *boots caked with mud* =**coat**, encrust, plaster, cover.

WORD LINKS

maker or seller of cakes: **patissier**
shop selling cakes: **patisserie**

---

calamitous ▸ adjective =**disastrous**, catastrophic, cataclysmic, devastating, dire, tragic.

calamity ▸ noun =**disaster**, catas-

trophe, tragedy, cataclysm, adversity, misfortune, misadventure.
–OPPOSITES godsend.

calculate ▶ verb **1** *the interest is calculated on a daily basis* =**compute**, work out, reckon, figure; add up/together, count up, tally, total; *Brit.* tot up. **2** *his words were calculated to wound her* =**intend**, mean, design. **3** *we had calculated on a quiet Sunday* =**expect**, anticipate, reckon, bargain; *N. Amer. informal* figure on.

calculated ▶ adjective =**deliberate**, premeditated, planned, pre-planned, preconceived, intentional, intended.
–OPPOSITES unintentional.

calculating ▶ adjective =**cunning**, crafty, wily, shrewd, scheming, devious, designing, Machiavellian, disingenuous, contrived.
–OPPOSITES ingenuous.

calculation ▶ noun **1** *the calculation of the overall cost* =**computation**, reckoning, adding up, counting up, working out, figuring; *Brit.* totting up. **2** *political calculations* =**assessment**, judgement; forecast, projection, prediction.

calendar ▶ noun *my social calendar* =**schedule**, programme, diary; timetable, agenda.

calibre ▶ noun **1** *a man of his calibre* =**quality**, merit, distinction, stature, excellence, pre-eminence; ability, expertise, talent, capability, capacity, proficiency. **2** *rugby of this calibre* =**standard**, level, quality. **3** *the calibre of a gun* =**bore**, diameter, gauge.

call ▶ verb **1** *'Wait for me!' she called* =**cry (out)**, shout, yell, bellow, roar, bawl, scream; *informal* holler. **2** *Mum called me in the morning* =**wake (up)**, awaken, rouse; *Brit. informal* knock up; *literary* waken. **3** *I'll call you tomorrow* =**phone**, telephone, get someone on the phone, give someone a call; *Brit.* ring (up), give someone a ring; *informal* call up, give someone a buzz; *Brit. informal* give someone a bell/tinkle, get someone on the blower; *N. Amer. informal* get someone on the horn. **4** *Rose called a taxi* =**summon**, send for, order; phone, telephone. **5** *he called at Ashgrove Cottage* =**pay a (brief) visit to**, visit, pay a call on, call/drop/look in on, drop/stop by, pop into, nip over to. **6** *the prime minister called a meeting* =**convene**, summon, assemble; *formal* convoke. **7** *they called their daughter Hannah* =**name**, christen, baptize; designate, style, term, dub. **8** *I would call him a friend* =**describe as**, regard as, look on as, think of as, consider to be.
▶ noun **1** *I heard calls from the auditorium* =**cry**, shout, yell, roar, scream, exclamation; *informal* holler. **2** *the call of the barn owl* =**cry**, song, sound. **3** *I'll give you a call tomorrow* =**phone call**, telephone call, phone; *Brit.* ring; *informal* buzz; *Brit. informal* bell, tinkle. **4** *a call for party unity* =**appeal**, request, plea. **5** *there's no call for that kind of language* =**need**, necessity, reason, justification, excuse. **6** *there's no call for expensive wine here* =**demand**, desire, market. **7** *the call of the Cairngorms* =**attraction**, appeal, lure, allure, spell, pull, draw.
■ **call something off** =**cancel**, abandon, scrap, drop, axe; *informal* scrub; *N. Amer. informal* redline.
■ **call on 1** *I might call on her later* =**visit**, pay a call on, go and see, look/drop in on; *N. Amer.* visit with; *informal* look up, pop in on. **2** *he called on the government to hold a referendum* =**appeal to**, ask, request, urge.
■ **call someone up 1** *(informal)* *Roland called me up.* See CALL *verb sense 3.* **2** *they called up the reservists* =**enlist**, recruit, conscript; *US* draft. **3** *he was called up for the England team* =**select**, pick, choose; *Brit.* cap.

call girl ▶ noun =**prostitute**, whore, sex worker; *informal* tart, pro, working girl; *N. Amer. informal* hooker, hustler; *euphemistic* escort; *dated* streetwalker.

calling ▶ noun =**profession**, occupation, vocation, career, work, employment, job, business, trade, craft, line (of work).

callous ▶ adjective =**heartless**, unfeeling, uncaring, cold, cold-hearted, hard, as hard as nails, hard-hearted, stony-hearted, insensitive, hardbitten, unsympathetic.
–OPPOSITES kind, compassionate.

callow ▶ adjective =**immature**, inexperienced, naive, green, raw, untried, unworldly, unsophisticated; *informal* wet behind the ears.
–OPPOSITES mature.

calm ▶ adjective **1** *she seemed very calm* =**serene**, tranquil, relaxed, unruffled, unperturbed, unflustered, untroubled; equable, even-tempered; placid, unexcitable, unemotional, phlegmatic; composed, {cool, calm, and collected},

cool-headed, self-possessed; *informal* unflappable, unfazed, laid-back. **2** *the night was calm* =**windless**, still, quiet. **3** *the calm waters of the lake* =**tranquil**, still, smooth, glassy, like a millpond.
−OPPOSITES excited, nervous, stormy.
▶ noun **1** *calm prevailed* =**tranquillity**, stillness, calmness, quiet, quietness, peace, peacefulness. **2** *his usual calm deserted him* =**composure**, coolness, calmness, self-possession, sangfroid; serenity, tranquillity, equanimity, placidity; *informal* cool, unflappability.
■ **calm down 1** *I tried to calm him down* =**soothe**, pacify, placate, mollify, appease, conciliate; *Brit.* quieten (down); *Austral.* square off. **2** *she forced herself to calm down* =**compose oneself**, recover/regain one's composure, control oneself, pull oneself together, simmer down, cool down/off, take it easy; *Brit.* quieten down; *informal* get a grip, keep one's shirt on, wind down; *N. Amer. informal* chill out, hang/stay loose, decompress.

camaraderie ▶ noun =**friendship**, comradeship, fellowship, companionship; mutual support, team spirit, esprit de corps.

camouflage ▶ noun =**disguise**, concealment.
▶ verb =**disguise**, hide, conceal, mask, screen, cover (up).

camp ▶ noun **1** *an army camp* =**bivouac**, encampment; campsite, camping ground. **2** *the liberal and conservative camps* =**faction**, wing, group, lobby, caucus, bloc.
▶ verb *they camped in a field* =**pitch tents**, set up (camp), encamp, bivouac.

campaign ▶ noun **1** *Napoleon's Russian campaign* =**operation(s)**, manoeuvre(s); crusade, war, battle, offensive, attack. **2** *the campaign to reduce vehicle emissions* =**crusade**, drive, push, struggle; operation, strategy, battle plan.
▶ verb **1** *they are campaigning for political reform* =**crusade**, fight, battle, push, press, strive, struggle, lobby, agitate. **2** *she campaigned as a political outsider* =**run/stand (for office)**; canvass, electioneer, lobby; *N. Amer.* stump.

campaigner ▶ noun =**crusader**, fighter, activist; champion, advocate, promoter.

can ▶ noun =**tin**, canister.

cancel ▶ verb **1** *the match was cancelled* =**call off**, abandon, scrap, drop, axe; *informal* scrub; *N. Amer. informal* redline. **2** *his visa has been cancelled* =**annul**, invalidate, nullify, declare null and void, void; revoke, rescind, retract, withdraw. **3** *rising unemployment cancelled out earlier economic gains* =**neutralize**, counterbalance, counteract, balance (out); negate, nullify, wipe out.

cancer ▶ noun **1** *most skin cancers are curable* =**(malignant) growth**, tumour, malignancy; *technical* carcinoma, sarcoma, melanoma, lymphoma, myeloma. **2** *racism is a cancer* =**evil**, blight, scourge, poison, canker, plague; *archaic* pestilence.

> **WORD LINKS**
>
> *relating to cancer:* **carcinomatous, carcin-**
> *causing cancer:* **carcinogenic**
> *fear of cancer:* **carcinophobia**
> *branch of medicine treating cancer:* **oncology**

candid ▶ adjective **1** *his responses were remarkably candid* =**frank**, forthright, blunt, open, honest, truthful, sincere, direct, plain-spoken, bluff; *informal* upfront; *N. Amer. informal* on the up and up. **2** *candid shots* =**unposed**, informal, uncontrived, impromptu, natural.
−OPPOSITES guarded.

candidate ▶ noun **1** *candidates should be computer-literate* =**(job) applicant**, interviewee; contender, nominee, possible; *Brit. informal* runner. **2** *A-level candidates* =**examinee**, entrant; student.

candour ▶ noun =**frankness**, openness, honesty, candidness, truthfulness, sincerity, forthrightness, directness, plain-spokenness, bluffness, bluntness; *informal* telling it like it is.

candy ▶ noun (*N. Amer.*). See CONFECTIONERY.

cane ▶ noun **1** *a silver-topped cane* =**(walking) stick**, staff; crook; *Austral./NZ* waddy. **2** *tie the shoot to a cane* =**stick**, stake, upright, pole.
▶ verb *Matthew was caned for bullying* =**beat**, flog, thrash, lash, birch; *informal* give someone a hiding, larrup; *N. Amer. informal* whale.

canker ▶ noun *racism remains a canker.* See CANCER sense 2.

cannabis ▶ noun =**marijuana**, hashish, bhang, hemp, kif, ganja, sinsemilla; *informal* hash, dope, grass, skunk, pot, blow, draw, weed, reefer; *Brit. informal* wacky baccy; *N. Amer. informal* locoweed.

cannon ▶ noun =**field gun**; mortar, howitzer; machine gun, chain gun.
▶ verb *the couple behind cannoned into us* =**collide with**, hit, run into, crash/smash/plough into.

canny ▶ adjective =**shrewd**, astute, smart, sharp, sharp-witted, discerning, penetrating, discriminating, perceptive, perspicacious; cunning, crafty, wily; *N. Amer.* as sharp as a tack; *informal* savvy; *Brit. informal* suss, sussed; *N. Amer. informal* heads-up.
–OPPOSITES foolish.

canon ▶ noun **1** *the canons of fair play and equal opportunity* =**principle**, rule, law, tenet, precept; standard, convention, criterion, measure. **2** *the Shakespeare canon* =**works**, writings, oeuvre, body of work.

canopy ▶ noun =**awning**, shade.

cant ▶ noun **1** *religious cant* =**hypocrisy**, humbug; *informal* waffle, hot air. **2** *thieves' cant* =**slang**, jargon, idiom, argot, patois, speech, terminology, language; *informal* lingo, -speak, -ese.

cantankerous ▶ adjective =**bad-tempered**, irascible, irritable, grumpy, grouchy, crotchety, tetchy, testy, crusty, curmudgeonly, ill-tempered, ill-humoured, peevish, fractious, pettish, crabby, prickly, touchy; *informal* snappy; *Brit. informal* shirty, narky, ratty; *N. Amer. informal* cranky, ornery; *Austral./NZ informal* snaky.
–OPPOSITES affable.

canteen ▶ noun **1** *the staff canteen* =**restaurant**, cafeteria, refectory, mess hall; *N. Amer.* lunchroom. **2** *a canteen of water* =**container**, flask, bottle.

canvass ▶ verb **1** *he's canvassing for the Green Party* =**campaign**, electioneer; *N. Amer.* stump; *Brit. informal* doorstep. **2** *they promised to canvass all members* =**poll**, question, ask, survey, interview, consult.

canyon ▶ noun =**ravine**, gorge, gully, defile; chasm, abyss, gulf; *N. Amer.* gulch, coulee.

cap ▶ noun **1** *a white plastic cap* =**lid**, top, stopper, cork, bung; *N. Amer.* stopple. **2** *a cap on spending* =**(upper) limit**, ceiling; curb, check.
▶ verb **1** *mountains capped with snow* =**top**, crown, cover, coat, tip; sprinkle, dust, dot, pepper, wreath, ring, shroud. **2** *his*

innings capped a great day =**round off**, crown, be a fitting climax/end/conclusion to. **3** *they tried to cap each other's stories* =**beat**, better, improve on, surpass, outdo, outshine, top. **4** *(Brit.) he was capped for England* =**choose**, select, pick. **5** *budgets will be capped* =**limit**, restrict; curb, control, peg.

capability ▶ noun =**ability**, capacity, power, potential; competence, proficiency, accomplishment, adeptness, aptitude, faculty, experience, skill, talent, flair; *informal* know-how.

capable ▶ adjective *a very capable young woman* =**competent**, able, efficient, effective, proficient, accomplished, adept, handy, experienced, skilful, skilled, talented, gifted; *informal* useful.
–OPPOSITES incompetent.

capacious ▶ adjective =**roomy**, spacious, ample, big, large, sizeable, generous.
–OPPOSITES cramped, small.

capacity ▶ noun **1** *the capacity of the freezer* =**volume**, size, dimensions, measurements, proportions. **2** *his capacity to inspire trust*. See CAPABILITY. **3** *in his capacity as Commander-in-Chief* =**position**, post, job, office; role, function.

cape[1] ▶ noun *a woollen cape* =**cloak**, mantle, cope, stole, poncho.

cape[2] ▶ noun *the ship rounded the cape* =**headland**, promontory, point, head; horn, mull.

caper ▶ verb *children were capering about* =**skip**, dance, romp, frisk, gambol, cavort, prance, frolic, leap, hop, jump.
▶ noun *(informal) I'm too old for this kind of caper* =**business**, stuff, thing; *informal* lark, scene.

capital ▶ noun =**money**, finance(s), funds, the wherewithal, the means, assets, wealth, resources; *informal* dough, bread, loot; *Brit. informal* dosh, brass, lolly, spondulicks; *US informal* greenbacks; *N. Amer. informal* bucks; *Austral./NZ informal* Oscar.

capitalism ▶ noun =**private enterprise**, free enterprise, the free market.
–OPPOSITES communism.

capitalize ■ **capitalize on** =**take advantage of**, profit from, make the most of, exploit, develop; *informal* cash in on.

capitulate ▶ verb =**surrender**, give in, yield, concede defeat, give up (the

struggle), submit; lay down one's arms, raise/show the white flag, throw in the towel/sponge.
–OPPOSITES resist, hold out.

caprice ▶ noun **1** *his wife's caprices* =**whim**, fancy, fad, quirk, eccentricity, foible. **2** *the staff tired of his caprice* =**fickleness**, volatility, capriciousness, unpredictability.

capricious ▶ adjective =**fickle**, changeable, variable, mercurial, volatile, unpredictable, temperamental; whimsical, fanciful, flighty, quirky, faddish.
–OPPOSITES consistent.

capsize ▶ verb =**overturn**, turn over, turn upside down, upend, flip/tip/keel over, turn turtle.
–OPPOSITES right.

capsule ▶ noun **1** *he swallowed a capsule* =**pill**, tablet, lozenge, pastille; *informal* tab. **2** *a space capsule* =**module**, craft, probe.

captain ▶ noun **1** *the ship's captain* =**commander**, master; *informal* skipper. **2** *the team captain* =**leader**, head; *informal* boss, skipper.
▶ verb *a vessel captained by a lunatic* =**command**, run, control, manage, govern; *informal* skipper.

caption ▶ noun =**title**, heading, wording, legend, rubric, slogan, byline.

captivate ▶ verb =**enthral**, charm, enchant, bewitch, fascinate, beguile, entrance, enrapture, delight, attract, allure.
–OPPOSITES repel, bore.

captive ▶ noun =**prisoner**, convict, detainee, inmate; prisoner of war, POW, internee.
▶ adjective =**confined**, caged, incarcerated, locked up; jailed, imprisoned, in prison, interned, detained, in captivity, under lock and key, behind bars.

captivity ▶ noun =**imprisonment**, confinement, internment, incarceration, detention.
–OPPOSITES freedom.

capture ▶ verb **1** *Mark Dawes was captured in Moscow* =**catch**, apprehend, seize, arrest; *informal* nab, collar, lift, pick up, pull in; *Brit. informal* nick. **2** *guerrillas have captured several towns* =**occupy**, invade, conquer, seize, take (possession/control of). **3** *the music captured the atmosphere of a summer morning* =**express**, reproduce, represent, encapsulate, sum

up. **4** *the tales of pirates captured their imagination* =**engage**, attract, catch, seize, hold, grip.
–OPPOSITES free.

▶ noun *he tried to avoid capture* =**arrest**, being taken prisoner/captive, being arrested.

car ▶ noun **1** *he drove up in his car* =**motor (car)**, automobile; *informal* wheels; *N. Amer. informal* auto. **2** *the dining car* =**carriage**, coach; *Brit.* saloon.

carafe ▶ noun =**flask**, jug, pitcher, decanter, flagon.

caravan ▶ noun =**mobile home**; *N. Amer.* trailer.

carcass ▶ noun =**corpse**, (dead) body, remains; *Medicine* cadaver; *informal* stiff.

cardinal ▶ adjective =**fundamental**, basic, main, chief, primary, prime, principal, paramount, pre-eminent, highest, key, essential.
–OPPOSITES unimportant.

care ▶ noun **1** *the care of the child* =**safe keeping**, supervision, custody, charge, protection, control, responsibility; guardianship. **2** *handle with care* =**caution**, respect. **3** *she chose her words with care* =**discretion**, sensitivity, thought; diplomacy, tact; accuracy, precision. **4** *the cares of the day* =**worry**, anxiety, trouble, concern, stress, pressure, strain; sorrow, woe, hardship. **5** *care for others* =**concern**, consideration, thought, regard, solicitude.
–OPPOSITES neglect, carelessness.

▶ verb *the teachers didn't care about our work* =**be concerned**, worry (oneself), trouble/concern oneself, bother, mind, be interested; *informal* give a damn/hoot.
■ **care for 1** *he cares for his children* =**love**, be fond of, be devoted to, treasure, adore, dote on, think the world of, worship, idolize. **2** *would you care for a cup of coffee?* =**like**, want, desire, fancy, feel like. **3** *the hospice cares for the terminally ill* =**look after**, take care of, tend, attend to, minister to, nurse; be responsible for, keep safe, keep an eye on.

career ▶ noun **1** *a business career* =**profession**, occupation, vocation, calling, employment, line (of work), walk of life, métier. **2** *a chequered career* =**history**, life, course, passage, path, existence.
▶ adjective *a career politician* =**professional**, permanent, full-time.
▶ verb *they careered down the hill* =**hurtle**, rush, shoot, race, speed, charge, hare,

fly, pelt, go like the wind; *informal* belt, scoot, tear; *Brit. informal* bucket.

carefree ▸ adjective =**unworried**, untroubled, blithe, airy, nonchalant, insouciant, happy-go-lucky, free and easy, easy-going, relaxed; *informal* laid-back.
–OPPOSITES careworn.

careful ▸ adjective **1** *be careful when you go up the stairs* =**cautious**, alert, attentive, watchful, vigilant, wary, on guard, circumspect. **2** *Roland was careful of his reputation* =**mindful**, heedful, protective, jealous. **3** *careful with money* =**prudent**, thrifty, economical, sparing, frugal, scrimping, abstemious, mean; *informal* stingy. **4** *careful consideration of the facts* =**attentive**, conscientious, painstaking, meticulous, diligent, assiduous, scrupulous, methodical.
–OPPOSITES careless, extravagant.

careless ▸ adjective **1** *careless motorists* =**inattentive**, negligent, remiss; heedless, irresponsible, impetuous, reckless. **2** *careless work* =**shoddy**, slapdash, slipshod, scrappy, slovenly, sloppy, negligent, lax, slack, disorganized, hasty, hurried; *informal* slap-happy. **3** *a careless remark* =**thoughtless**, insensitive, indiscreet, unguarded, incautious, inadvertent.
–OPPOSITES careful, meticulous.

caress ▸ verb =**stroke**, touch, fondle, brush, feel, skim.

caretaker ▸ noun =**janitor**, attendant, porter, custodian, concierge; *N. Amer.* superintendent.
▸ adjective *the caretaker manager* =**temporary**, short-term, provisional, substitute, acting, interim, pro tem, stand-in, fill-in, stopgap; *N. Amer. informal* pinch-hitting.
–OPPOSITES permanent.

careworn ▸ adjective =**worried**, anxious, harassed, strained, stressed; drained, drawn, gaunt, haggard; *informal* hassled.
–OPPOSITES carefree.

cargo ▸ noun =**freight**, load, haul, consignment, delivery, shipment; goods, merchandise.

caricature ▸ noun *a caricature of the Prime Minister* =**cartoon**, parody, satire, lampoon; *informal* send-up, take-off.
▸ verb *she has turned to caricaturing her fellow actors* =**parody**, satirize, lampoon, make fun of; *informal* send up, take off.

caring ▸ adjective =**kind**, kind-hearted, warm-hearted, tender; concerned, at-

tentive, thoughtful, solicitous, considerate; affectionate, loving, doting, fond; sympathetic, understanding, compassionate, feeling.
–OPPOSITES cruel.

carnage ▸ noun =**slaughter**, massacre, butchery, bloodbath, bloodletting, mayhem.

carnal ▸ adjective =**sexual**, sensual, erotic, lustful, lascivious, libidinous, lecherous, licentious; physical, bodily, corporeal, fleshly.
–OPPOSITES spiritual.

carnival ▸ noun **1** *the town's annual carnival* =**festival**, fiesta, fête, gala, Mardi Gras. **2** *(N. Amer.) he worked at a carnival* =**funfair**, circus, fair, amusement show.

carouse ▸ verb =**drink**, go on a drinking bout/spree; revel, celebrate, roister; *informal* booze, go boozing, binge, go on a binge, go on a bender, paint the town red, party, rave, make whoopee, whoop it up; *Brit. informal* go on the bevvy.

carp ▸ verb =**complain**, grumble, grouse, whine, bleat, nag; *informal* gripe, grouch, beef, bellyache, moan, bitch, whinge; *Brit. informal* be on at someone; *N. English informal* mither; *N. Amer. informal* kvetch.
–OPPOSITES praise.

carpenter ▸ noun =**joiner**, cabinetmaker; *Brit. informal* chippy.

carpet ▸ noun **1** *a Turkish carpet* =**rug**, mat. **2** *a carpet of wild flowers* =**covering**, blanket, layer, cover, cloak, mantle.
▸ verb *the ground was carpeted in moss* =**cover**, coat.

carriage ▸ noun **1** *a railway carriage* =**coach**, car; *Brit.* saloon. **2** *a horse and carriage* =**wagon**, coach. **3** *an erect carriage* =**posture**, bearing, stance, gait; attitude, manner, demeanour; *Brit.* deportment.

carrier ▸ noun =**bearer**, conveyor, transporter; porter, courier, haulier.

carry ▸ verb **1** *she carried the box into the kitchen* =**convey**, transfer, move, take, bring, bear, lug, fetch; *informal* cart, hump. **2** *a coach operator carrying 12 million passengers a year* =**transport**, convey, move, handle. **3** *satellites carry the signal over the Atlantic* =**transmit**, conduct, relay, communicate, convey, beam, send. **4** *the dinghy can carry two people* =**support**, sustain, take; accommodate, bear. **5** *managers carry most responsibility* =**undertake**, accept, assume, bear, shoulder, take on (oneself). **6** *she was carrying his baby* =**be pregnant with**, expect. **7** *she carried herself with assurance* =**conduct**, bear, hold; act, behave, acquit; *formal* comport. **8** *a resolution was carried* =**approve**, accept, endorse, ratify; agree to, assent to, rubber-stamp; *informal* OK, give the thumbs up to. **9** *I carried the whole audience* =**win over**, sway, convince, persuade, influence. **10** *today's paper carried an article on housing policy* =**contain**, include, feature; have, bear. **11** *we carry a wide range* =**sell**, stock, keep (in stock), offer, have (for sale), retail, supply. **12** *most medicines carry warnings* =**display**, bear, exhibit, show, be marked/labelled with. **13** *his voice carried across the quay* =**be audible**, travel, reach, be heard.

■ **carry something off 1** *she carried off four awards* =**win**, secure, gain, achieve, collect; *informal* land, net, bag, scoop. **2** *he has carried it off* =**succeed**, triumph, be victorious, be successful, do well, make good; *informal* crack it.

■ **carry on 1** *they carried on arguing* =**continue**, keep (on), go on; persist in, persevere in; *informal* stick with/at. **2** *(informal) the English way of carrying on* =**behave**, act, conduct oneself, acquit oneself; *formal* comport oneself. **3** *(informal) she was carrying on with other men* =**have an affair**, commit adultery, have a fling, sleep, see; *informal* play around, mess about/around; *Brit. informal* play away; *N. Amer. informal* fool around. **4** *(informal) I was always carrying on* =**misbehave**, behave badly, get up to mischief, cause trouble, get up to no good, be naughty; clown about/around, fool about/around, mess about/around; *informal* act up; *Brit. informal* muck about/around, play up.

■ **carry something out 1** *they carried out a Caesarean* =**conduct**, perform, implement, execute. **2** *I carried out my promise* =**fulfil**, carry through, honour, redeem, make good; keep, observe, abide by, comply with, adhere to, stick to, keep faith with.

cart ▶ noun **1** *a horse-drawn cart* =**wagon**, carriage, dray. **2** *a man with a cart took their luggage* =**handcart**, pushcart, trolley, barrow.
▶ verb *(informal) he had the wreckage carted away* =**transport**, haul, move, shift, take; carry.

carton ▶ noun =**box**, package, cardboard box, container, pack, packet.

cartoon ▶ noun **1** *a cartoon of the Prime Minister* =**caricature**, parody, lampoon, satire; *informal* take-off, send-up. **2** *he was reading cartoons* =**comic strip**, comic, graphic novel. **3** *detailed cartoons for a full-size portrait* =**sketch**, rough, outline.

cartridge ▶ noun =**cassette**, magazine, canister, case, container.

carve ▶ verb **1** *he carved horn handles* =**sculpt**; cut, hew, whittle; form, shape, fashion. **2** *I carved my initials on the tree* =**engrave**, incise, score, cut. **3** *he carved the roast chicken* =**slice**, cut up, chop.

■ **carve something up** =**divide**, partition, apportion, subdivide, split up, break up; share out, dole out; *informal* divvy up.

carving ▶ noun =**sculpture**, model, statue, statuette, figure, figurine.

> **WORD LINKS**
>
> relating to carving: **glyptic**

cascade ▶ noun =**waterfall**, cataract, falls, rapids, white water; flood, torrent.
▶ verb *rain cascaded from the roof* =**pour**, gush, surge, spill, stream, flow, issue, spurt, jet.

case[1] ▶ noun **1** *a classic case of overreaction* =**instance**, occurrence, manifestation, demonstration; example, illustration, specimen, sample, exemplar. **2** *if that is the case I will have to find somebody else* =**situation**, position, state of affairs, the lie of the land; circumstances, conditions, facts, how things stand; *Brit.* state of play; *informal* score. **3** *the officers on the case* =**assignment**, job, project, investigation, exercise, enquiry, campaign, affair, examination. **4** *he lost his case* =**lawsuit**, (legal) action, suit, trial, legal/judicial proceedings, litigation. **5** *a strong case* =**argument**, defence, justification, vindication, exposition, thesis.

case[2] ▶ noun **1** *a cigarette case* =**container**, box, canister, holder. **2** *a seed case* =**casing**, cover, sheath, envelope, sleeve, jacket, shell, integument. **3** *(Brit.) she threw some clothes into a case* =**suitcase**, (travelling) bag, valise, portmanteau; (**cases**) luggage, baggage. **4** *a glass display case* =**cabinet**, cupboard.

cash ▶ noun **1** *a wallet stuffed with cash* =**money**, currency, hard cash; (bank) notes, coins, change; *N. Amer.* bills; *informal* dough, bread, loot, moolah; *Brit. informal* dosh, readies, brass, lolly, spondu-

licks; *US informal* greenbacks; *N. Amer. informal* bucks, dinero; *Austral./NZ informal* Oscar. **2** *a lack of cash* =**finance**, money, resources, funds, assets, the means, the wherewithal.
–OPPOSITES cheque, credit.
▶ verb *the bank cashed her cheque* =**exchange**, change, convert into cash/money; honour, pay, accept; *Brit.* encash.
■ **cash in on** =**take advantage of**, exploit, milk; make money from, profit from; *informal* make a killing out of.

cashier ▶ noun =**clerk**, bank clerk, teller, banker, treasurer, bursar, purser.

casing ▶ noun =**cover**, covering, case, shell, envelope, sheath, sleeve, jacket, housing, fairing.

cask ▶ noun =**barrel**, keg, butt, tun, vat, drum, hogshead; *historical* firkin.

casket ▶ noun **1** *a small casket* =**box**, chest, case, container. **2** *(N. Amer.) the casket of a dead soldier* See COFFIN.

cast ▶ verb **1** *he cast the stone into the stream* =**throw**, toss, fling, flick, pitch, hurl, lob; *informal* chuck, sling, bung. **2** *fishermen cast their nets* =**spread**, throw, fling, open (out), extend, reach (out). **3** *she cast a fearful glance over her shoulder* =**direct**, shoot, throw, fling, send. **4** *each citizen cast a vote* =**register**, record, enter, file, deposit. **5** *the fire cast a soft light* =**emit**, give off, throw, send out, radiate. **6** *the figures cast shadows* =**form**, throw, fling, create, produce; project. **7** *the stags' antlers are cast each year* =**shed**, lose, discard, slough off.
▶ noun **1** *a cast of his hand* =**mould**, die, matrix, shape, casting, model. **2** *a cast of the dice* =**throw**, toss, fling, pitch, flick, hurl, lob. **3** *the cast of 'Hamlet'* =**actors**, performers, players; dramatis personae, characters.
■ **cast something aside** =**discard**, reject, throw away/out, get rid of, dispose of, abandon, dump, jettison; *informal* ditch.
■ **cast someone away** =**shipwreck**, wreck; strand, maroon.

caste ▶ noun =**(social) class**, rank, level, stratum, echelon, status.

castigate ▶ verb *(formal)* =**reprimand**, rebuke, admonish, chastise, chide, upbraid, reprove, reproach, scold, berate, take to task, lambaste, haul over the coals, censure; *informal* tell off, give someone an earful, give someone a roasting, dress down, bawl out, give someone

hell, blow up at, pitch into, lay into, blast; *Brit. informal* tear someone off a strip, give someone what for, give someone a rocket; *N. Amer. informal* chew out, ream out; *Austral. informal* monster.
–OPPOSITES praise, commend.

castle ▶ noun =**fortress**, fort, stronghold, fortification, keep, citadel.

castrate ▶ verb =**neuter**, geld, cut, desex, sterilize, fix; *N. Amer. & Austral.* alter; *Brit. informal* doctor; *archaic* emasculate.

casual ▶ adjective **1** *a casual attitude to life* =**indifferent**, uncaring, unconcerned; lackadaisical, blasé, nonchalant, insouciant, offhand, flippant; easy-going, free and easy, blithe, carefree, devil-may-care; *informal* laid-back. **2** *a casual remark* =**offhand**, spontaneous, unthinking, unconsidered, impromptu, throwaway, unguarded; *informal* off-the-cuff. **3** *a casual glance* =**cursory**, perfunctory, superficial, passing, fleeting; hasty, brief, quick. **4** *a casual acquaintance* =**slight**, superficial. **5** *casual work* =**temporary**, part-time, freelance, impermanent, irregular, occasional. **6** *casual sex* =**promiscuous**, recreational, extramarital. **7** *a casual meeting changed his life* =**chance**, accidental, unplanned, unintended, unexpected, unforeseen, unanticipated, fortuitous, serendipitous, adventitious. **8** *a casual shirt* =**informal**, leisure, everyday; *informal* sporty. **9** *the inn's casual atmosphere* =**relaxed**, friendly, informal, easy-going, free and easy; *informal* laid-back.
–OPPOSITES careful, planned, formal.

casualty ▶ noun =**victim**, fatality, loss, MIA; injury; (**casualties**) dead and injured, missing (in action).

cat ▶ noun =**feline**, tomcat, tom, kitten; *informal* pussy (cat), puss, kitty; *Brit. informal* moggie, mog; *archaic* grimalkin.

> **WORD LINKS**
>
> *relating to cats:* **feline**
> *male:* **tom, tomcat**
> *female:* **queen**
> *young:* **kitten**
> *collective noun:* **clowder, glaring**
> *fear of cats:* **ailurophobia**

cataclysm ▶ noun =**disaster**, catastrophe, calamity, tragedy, devastation, upheaval, convulsion.

cataclysmic ▶ adjective =**disastrous**,

catastrophic, calamitous, tragic, devastating, ruinous, terrible, violent, awful.

catalogue ▸ noun **1** *a library catalogue* =**directory**, register, record, list, listing, record, archive, inventory. **2** *a mail-order catalogue* =**brochure**; *N. Amer. informal* wish book.

▸ verb *the collection is fully catalogued* =**classify**, categorize, index, list, archive, inventory, record, itemize.

catapult ▸ noun *a boy fired the catapult* =**sling**, slingshot; *Austral./NZ* shanghai; *historical* ballista, trebuchet.

▸ verb *Sam was catapulted into the sea* =**propel**, launch, hurl, fling, send flying, fire, shoot.

catastrophe ▸ noun =**disaster**, calamity, cataclysm, ruin, tragedy.

catastrophic ▸ adjective =**disastrous**, calamitous, cataclysmic, ruinous, tragic, fatal, dire, awful, terrible, dreadful.

catcall ▸ noun =**whistle**, boo, hiss, jeer, raspberry, hoot, taunt; (**catcalls**) scoffing, abuse, taunting, derision; slow handclap.

catch ▸ verb **1** *he caught the ball* =**seize**, grab, snatch, seize/grab/take hold of, grasp, grip, clutch, clench; receive, get, intercept. **2** *we've caught the thief* =**capture**, seize; apprehend, arrest, take prisoner/captive, take into custody; trap, snare, ensnare; net, hook, land; *informal* nab, collar, run in, bust; *Brit. informal* nick. **3** *her heel caught in a hole* =**become trapped**, become entangled, snag, jam, wedge, lodge, get stuck. **4** *she caught the 7.45 bus* =**be in time for**, make, get; board, get on, leave on **5** *they were caught siphoning petrol* =**discover**, find, come upon/across, stumble on, chance on; surprise, catch in the act (of). **6** *it caught his imagination* =**engage**, capture, attract, draw, grab, grip, seize; hold, absorb, engross. **7** *she caught a whiff of aftershave* =**perceive**, get, pick up, notice, observe, discern, detect, note, make out, glimpse; *Brit. informal* clock. **8** *I couldn't catch what she was saying* =**hear**, perceive, discern, make out; understand, comprehend, grasp, apprehend; *informal* get, get the drift of, figure out; *Brit. informal* twig, suss (out). **9** *it caught the flavour of the sixties* =**evoke**, conjure up, call to mind, recall, encapsulate, capture. **10** *the blow caught her on the side of her face* =**hit**, strike, slap, smack, bang. **11** *he caught*

malaria =**become infected with**, contract, get, be taken ill with, develop, come down with, be struck down with; *Brit.* go down with. **12** *the fire wouldn't catch* =**ignite**, start burning, catch fire, take, kindle; *informal* get going.
–OPPOSITES drop, release, miss.

▸ noun **1** *he inspected the catch* =**haul**, net, bag, yield. **2** *he slipped the catch* =**latch**, lock, fastener, clasp, hasp. **3** *he is always looking for the catch* =**snag**, disadvantage, drawback, stumbling block, hitch, fly in the ointment, pitfall, complication, problem, hiccup, difficulty; trap, trick, snare; *informal* con.

■ **catch on 1** *radio soon caught on* =**become popular**, take off, boom, flourish, thrive. **2** *I caught on fast* =**understand**, comprehend, learn, see the light; *informal* cotton on, latch on, get the picture/message, get wise, wise up.

catching ▸ adjective *(informal)* =**infectious**, contagious, communicable; *dated* infective.

catchphrase ▸ noun =**saying**, jingle, quotation, quote, slogan, catchword; *N. Amer. informal* tag line.

catchword ▸ noun =**motto**, watchword, slogan, byword, catchphrase; *informal* buzzword.

catchy ▸ adjective =**memorable**, unforgettable; appealing, popular.

categorical ▸ adjective =**unqualified**, unconditional, unequivocal, absolute, explicit, unambiguous, definite, direct, downright, outright, emphatic, positive, point-blank, conclusive, out-and-out.
–OPPOSITES qualified, equivocal.

categorize ▸ verb =**classify**, class, group, grade, rate, designate; order, arrange, sort, rank; file, catalogue, list, index.

category ▸ noun =**class**, classification, group, grouping, bracket, heading, set; type, sort, kind, variety, species, breed, brand, make, model; grade, order, rank.

cater ■ **cater for 1** *we cater for vegetarians* =**provide (food) for**, feed, serve, cook for. **2** *a resort catering for older holidaymakers* =**serve**, provide for, meet the needs/wants of, accommodate. **3** *he seemed to cater for all tastes* =**take into account/consideration**, allow for, consider, bear in mind, make provision for, have regard for.

■ **cater to** =satisfy, indulge, pander to, gratify, accommodate, minister to, give in to.

catholic ▸ adjective =diverse, wide, broad, broad-based, eclectic, liberal; comprehensive, all-encompassing, all-embracing, all-inclusive.
−OPPOSITES narrow.

cattle ▸ plural noun =cows, oxen; livestock.

> WORD LINKS
>
> *relating to cattle:* **bovine**
> *male:* **bull**
> *female:* **cow**
> *young:* **calf**
> *collective noun:* **herd, drove**

caucus ▸ noun 1 *(in North America & NZ) caucuses will be held in eleven states* =**meeting**, assembly, gathering, congress, conference, convention, rally, convocation. 2 *(in the UK) the right-wing caucus* =**faction**, camp, bloc, group, set, band, lobby, coterie, pressure group; *Brit.* ginger group.

cause ▸ noun 1 *the cause of the fire* =**source**, root, origin, beginning(s), starting point; basis, foundation; originator, author, creator, agent. 2 *there is no cause for alarm* =**reason**, grounds, justification, call, need, necessity, occasion, excuse. 3 *the cause of human rights | a good cause* =**principle**, ideal, belief, conviction; object, end, aim, objective, purpose; charity, case.
−OPPOSITES effect, result.
▸ verb *this disease can cause blindness* =**bring about**, give rise to, lead to, result in, create, produce, generate, engender, spawn, bring on, precipitate, prompt, provoke, trigger, make happen, induce, inspire, promote, foster; *literary* beget.
−OPPOSITES result from.

caustic ▸ adjective 1 *a caustic cleaner* =**corrosive**. 2 *a caustic comment* =**sarcastic**, cutting, biting, mordant, sharp, scathing, derisive, sardonic, ironic, scornful, trenchant, acerbic, vitriolic; *Brit. informal* sarky.

caution ▸ noun 1 *proceed with caution* =**care**, attention, attentiveness, alertness, watchfulness, vigilance, circumspection, discretion, prudence. 2 *a first offender may receive a caution* =**warning**, admonishment, injunction; reprimand, rebuke, reproof; *informal* telling-off, dressing-down, talking-to; *Brit. informal* ticking-off.
▸ verb 1 *advisers cautioned against tax increases* =**advise**, warn, counsel, urge. 2 *he was cautioned by the police* =**warn**, admonish; reprimand; *informal* tell off, give someone a talking-to; *Brit. informal* give someone a ticking-off.

cautious ▸ adjective =**careful**, attentive, alert, watchful, vigilant, circumspect, prudent.
−OPPOSITES reckless.

cavalier ▸ adjective *a cavalier disregard for danger* =**offhand**, indifferent, casual, dismissive, insouciant, unconcerned.

cave ▸ noun =**cavern**, grotto, pothole, chamber.
■ **cave in 1** *the roof caved in* =**collapse**, fall in/down, give (way), crumble, subside. 2 *the manager caved in to their demands* =**yield**, surrender, capitulate, give in, back down, make concessions, throw in the towel/sponge.

> WORD LINKS
>
> *exploration of caves:* **speleology**;
> *N. Amer.* **spelunking**
> *explorer of caves:* **speleologist,**
> **potholer**

cavern ▸ noun =**cave**, grotto, chamber, gallery.

cavernous ▸ adjective =**vast**, huge, immense, spacious, roomy, capacious, voluminous, extensive, deep; hollow, gaping, yawning.
−OPPOSITES small.

cavity ▸ noun =**space**, chamber, hollow, hole, pocket; orifice, aperture; socket, gap, crater, pit, crack.

cavort ▸ verb =**skip**, dance, romp, jig, caper, frisk, gambol, prance, frolic, lark; bounce, trip, leap, jump, bound, spring, hop.

cease ▸ verb 1 *hostilities had ceased* =**come to an end**, come to a halt, end, halt, stop, conclude, terminate, finish, draw to a close, be over. 2 *they ceased all military activity* =**bring to an end**, bring to a halt, end, halt, stop, conclude, terminate, finish, wind up, discontinue, suspend, break off.
−OPPOSITES start, continue.

ceaseless ▸ adjective =**continual**, constant, continuous; incessant, unceasing, unending, endless, never-ending, interminable, non-stop, uninterrupted, unremitting, relentless, unrelenting, unrelieved, sustained, per-

sistent, eternal, perpetual.
−OPPOSITES intermittent.

cede ▶ verb =**surrender**, concede, relinquish, yield, part with, give up; hand over, deliver up, give over, make over, transfer; abandon, forgo, sacrifice.

ceiling ▶ noun =(upper) limit, maximum.

celebrate ▶ verb 1 *they were celebrating their wedding anniversary* =**commemorate**, observe, mark, keep, honour, remember. 2 *let's all celebrate!* =**enjoy oneself**, make merry, have fun, have a good time, have a party, revel, carouse; *N. Amer.* step out; *informal* party, whoop it up, make whoopee, live it up, have a ball. 3 *the priest celebrated mass* =**perform**, observe, officiate at.

celebrated ▶ adjective =**acclaimed**, admired, highly rated, revered, honoured, esteemed, exalted, vaunted, well thought of; eminent, great, distinguished, prestigious, illustrious, pre-eminent, notable, of note, of repute.
−OPPOSITES unsung.

celebration ▶ noun 1 *the celebration of his 50th birthday* =**commemoration**, observance, marking, keeping. 2 *a cause for celebration* =**jollification**, merrymaking, enjoying oneself, revelry, revels, festivities; *informal* partying. 3 *a birthday celebration* =**party**, function, gathering, festivities, festival, fête, carnival, jamboree; *informal* do, bash, rave; *Brit. informal* rave-up, knees-up, beanfeast, bunfight, beano. 4 *the celebration of the Eucharist* =**observance**, performance, officiation, solemnization.

celebrity ▶ noun 1 *his celebrity grew* =**fame**, prominence, renown, eminence, pre-eminence, stardom, popularity, distinction, note, notability, prestige, stature, repute, reputation. 2 *a sporting celebrity* =**famous person**, VIP, personality, (big) name, household name, star, superstar; *informal* celeb, somebody, someone, megastar.
−OPPOSITES obscurity.

celestial ▶ adjective 1 *a celestial body* =(**in**) **space**, heavenly, astronomical, extraterrestrial, stellar, planetary. 2 *celestial beings* =**heavenly**, holy, saintly, divine, godly, godlike, ethereal; angelic.
−OPPOSITES earthly, hellish.

celibate ▶ adjective =**unmarried**, single; chaste, virginal.

cell ▶ noun 1 *a prison cell* =**room**, cubicle, chamber; dungeon, lock-up. 2 *each cell of the honeycomb* =**compartment**, cavity, hole, hollow, section, unit. 3 *terrorist cells* =**unit**, squad, detachment, group.

cellar ▶ noun =**basement**, vault, lower ground floor; crypt.
−OPPOSITES attic.

cement ▶ noun *polystyrene cement* =**adhesive**, glue, fixative, gum, paste; *N. Amer.* mucilage; *N. Amer. informal* stickum.
▶ verb *he cemented the sample to a microscope slide* =**stick**, bond, fasten, fix, affix, attach, secure, glue, gum, paste.

cemetery ▶ noun =**graveyard**, churchyard, burial ground, necropolis, garden of remembrance; mass grave; *informal* boneyard; *Scottish* kirkyard; *N. Amer.* memorial park; *archaic* God's acre.

censor ▶ verb *letters home were censored* =**cut**; edit, expurgate, sanitize; *informal* clean up.

censorious ▶ adjective =**hypercritical**, overcritical, disapproving, condemnatory, denunciatory, deprecatory, disparaging, reproachful, reproving.
−OPPOSITES complimentary.

censure ▶ verb *he was censured for his conduct*. See REPRIMAND verb.
▶ noun *a note of censure* =**condemnation**, criticism, attack; reprimand, rebuke, admonishment, reproof, upbraiding, disapproval, reproach, obloquy; *formal* excoriation, castigation.
−OPPOSITES approval.

central ▶ adjective 1 *occupying a central position* =**middle**, centre, halfway, midway, mid. 2 *central London* =**inner**, innermost, middle, mid. 3 *their central campaign issue* =**main**, chief, principal, primary, leading, foremost, first, most important, predominant, key, crucial, vital, essential, basic, fundamental, core, prime, premier, paramount, major, overriding; *informal* number one.
−OPPOSITES side, outer, subordinate.

centralize ▶ verb =**concentrate**, consolidate, amalgamate, condense, unify, focus.
−OPPOSITES devolve.

centre ▶ noun *the centre of the town* =**middle**, nucleus, heart, core, hub.
−OPPOSITES edge.
▶ verb *the story centres on a doctor* =**focus**, concentrate, pivot, revolve, be based.

centrepiece ▸ noun =highlight, main feature, high point/spot, climax; focus (of attention), focal point, centre of attention/interest.

ceremonial ▸ adjective =formal, official, state, public; ritual, ritualistic, stately, solemn.
–OPPOSITES informal.

ceremony ▸ noun 1 *a wedding ceremony* =rite, ritual, observance; service, sacrament, liturgy, celebration. 2 *the new Queen was proclaimed with due ceremony* =pomp, protocol, formalities, niceties, decorum, etiquette.

certain ▸ adjective 1 *I'm certain he's guilty* =sure, confident, positive, convinced, in no doubt, satisfied, assured, persuaded. 2 *it is certain that more changes are in the offing* =unquestionable, sure, definite, beyond question, not in doubt, indubitable, undeniable, indisputable; obvious, evident, undisputed. 3 *they are certain to win* =sure, bound, destined. 4 *certain defeat* =inevitable, assured; unavoidable, inescapable, inexorable. 5 *there is no certain cure for this* =reliable, dependable, foolproof, guaranteed, sure, infallible; *informal* sure-fire.
–OPPOSITES doubtful, possible, unlikely.

certainly ▸ adverb 1 *this is certainly a late work* =unquestionably, surely, assuredly, definitely, beyond/without question, without doubt, indubitably, undeniably, irrefutably, indisputably; unmistakably. 2 *our revenues are certainly lower* =admittedly, without question, definitely, undoubtedly, without a doubt.
–OPPOSITES possibly.
▸ exclamation *'Shall we eat now?' 'Certainly.'* =yes, definitely, sure, by all means, indeed, of course, naturally; *informal* absolutely; *Brit. dated* rather.

certainty ▸ noun 1 *she knew with certainty that he was telling the truth* =confidence, sureness, conviction, certitude, assurance. 2 *he accepted defeat as a certainty* =inevitability, foregone conclusion; *informal* sure thing; *Brit. informal* (dead) cert.
–OPPOSITES doubt, possibility.

certificate ▸ noun =guarantee, certification, document, authorization, authentication, accreditation, licence, diploma.

WORD LINKS

collecting old bond and share certificates: **scripophily**

certify ▸ verb 1 *the aircraft was certified as airworthy* =verify, guarantee, attest, validate, confirm, substantiate, endorse, vouch for, testify to. 2 *a certified hospital* =accredit, recognize, license, authorize, approve.

cessation ▸ noun =end, ending, termination, stopping, halting, ceasing, finish, stoppage, conclusion, winding up, discontinuation, abandonment, suspension, breaking off, cutting short.
–OPPOSITES start, resumption.

chafe ▸ verb 1 *the collar chafed his neck* =rub, graze, scrape, scratch; make sore. 2 *I chafed her feet* =rub, warm (up).

chaff[1] ▸ noun 1 *separating the chaff from the grain* =husks, hulls, pods, shells, bran; *N. Amer.* shucks. 2 *the proposals were so much chaff* =rubbish, dross; *N. Amer.* garbage, trash; *Austral./NZ* mullock; *informal* junk.

chaff[2] ▸ noun *good-natured chaff* =banter, repartee, teasing, ragging, joking, jesting, raillery, badinage, wisecracks, witticism(s); *informal* kidding, ribbing; *formal* persiflage.
▸ verb *the pleasures of chaffing your mates* =tease, make fun of, poke fun at, rag; *informal* take the mickey out of, rib, josh, kid, have on, pull someone's leg; *Brit. informal* wind up; *N. Amer. informal* goof on, rag on, razz; *Austral./NZ informal* poke mullock at, poke borak at; *informal, dated* twit; *archaic* make sport of.

chagrin ▸ noun =annoyance, irritation, vexation, exasperation, displeasure, dissatisfaction, discontent; anger, rage, fury, wrath, indignation, resentment; embarrassment, mortification, humiliation, shame.
–OPPOSITES delight.

chain ▸ noun 1 *he was held in chains* =fetters, shackles, irons, leg irons, manacles, handcuffs; *informal* cuffs, bracelets. 2 *a chain of events* =series, succession, string, sequence, train, course.
▸ verb *she chained her bicycle to the railings* =secure, fasten, tie, tether, hitch; restrain, shackle, fetter, manacle, handcuff.

chair ▸ verb *she chairs the economic committee* =preside over; lead, direct, run, manage, control, be in charge of, head.

chairman, chairwoman ▸ noun
=**chair**, chairperson, president, leader, convener; spokesperson, spokesman, spokeswoman.

chalk ■ **chalk something up**
=**achieve**, attain, accomplish, gain, earn, win, make, get, obtain, notch up, rack up.

WORD LINKS
chalky: **calcareous**

chalky ▸ adjective *chalky skin* =**pale**, bloodless, pallid, colourless, wan, ashen, white, pasty.

challenge ▸ noun 1 *he accepted the challenge* =**dare**; summons, offer. 2 *a challenge to his leadership* =**test**, dispute, stand, opposition, confrontation. 3 *it was proving quite a challenge* =**problem**, (difficult) task, test, trial.
▸ verb 1 *we challenged their statistics* =**question**, disagree with, dispute, take issue with, protest against, call into question, object to. 2 *changes that would challenge them* =**test**, tax, strain, make demands on; stretch, stimulate, inspire, excite.

challenging ▸ adjective =**demand**ing, testing, taxing, exacting; difficult, tough, hard, formidable, onerous, arduous, strenuous, gruelling.
–OPPOSITES easy, uninspiring.

champagne ▸ noun =**sparkling wine**; *informal* champers, bubbly, fizz.

champion ▸ noun 1 *the world champion* =**winner**, title-holder, defending champion, gold medallist; prizewinner, victor; *informal* champ, number one. 2 *a champion of change* =**advocate**, proponent, promoter, supporter, defender, upholder, backer, exponent; campaigner, lobbyist, crusader; *N. Amer.* booster.
▸ verb *championing the rights of tribal peoples* =**advocate**, promote, defend, uphold, support, back, stand up for; campaign for, lobby for, fight for, crusade for, stick up for.
–OPPOSITES oppose.

chance ▸ noun 1 *there was a chance he might be released* =**possibility**, prospect, probability, likelihood; risk, threat, danger. 2 *I gave her a chance to answer* =**opportunity**, opening, occasion, turn, time, window (of opportunity); *N. Amer. & Austral./NZ* show; *informal* shot, look-in. 3 *Nigel took an awful chance* =**risk**, gam-

ble, long shot, leap in the dark. 4 *pure chance* =**accident**, coincidence, serendipity, fate, destiny, fortuity, providence, happenstance; good fortune, (good) luck, fluke.
▸ adjective *a chance discovery* =**accidental**, fortuitous, fluky, coincidental, serendipitous; unintentional, unintended, inadvertent, unplanned.
–OPPOSITES intentional.
■ **by chance** =**fortuitously**, by accident, accidentally, coincidentally, serendipitously; unintentionally, inadvertently.
■ **chance on/upon** =**come across/upon**, run across/into, happen on, light on, stumble on, find by chance, meet (by chance); *informal* bump into.

change ▸ verb 1 *this could change the face of Britain* | *things have changed* =**alter**, make/become different, adjust, adapt, amend, modify, revise, refine; reshape, refashion, redesign, restyle, revamp, rework, remodel, reorganize, reorder; vary, transform, transfigure, transmute, metamorphose, evolve; *informal* tweak. 2 *he's changed his job* =**exchange**, substitute, swap, switch, replace, alternate.
–OPPOSITES preserve, keep.
▸ noun 1 *a change of plan* =**alteration**, modification, variation, revision, amendment, adjustment, adaptation; remodelling, reshaping, rearrangement, reordering, restyling, reworking; metamorphosis, transformation, evolution, mutation; *humorous* transmogrification. 2 *a change of government* =**replacement**, exchange, substitution, swap, switch. 3 *I've no change* =**coins**, (hard) cash, silver, coppers.

changeable ▸ adjective =**variable**, inconstant, varying, changing, fluctuating, irregular; erratic, inconsistent, unstable, unsettled, turbulent, changeful; fickle, capricious, temperamental, volatile, mercurial, unpredictable, blowing hot and cold; *informal* up and down.
–OPPOSITES constant.

changeless ▸ adjective =**unchanging**, unvarying, timeless, static, fixed, permanent, constant, unchanged, consistent, uniform, undeviating; stable, steady, unchangeable, unalterable, invariable, immutable.
–OPPOSITES variable.

channel ▸ noun 1 *the English Channel* =**strait(s)**, sound, narrows, passage.

2 *the water ran down a channel* =**duct**, gutter, conduit, trough, culvert, sluice, race, drain. **3** *a channel for their extraordinary energy* =**use**, medium, vehicle, way of harnessing; release (mechanism), safety valve, vent. **4** *a channel of communication* =**means**, medium, instrument, mechanism, agency, vehicle, route, avenue.

▶ verb **1** *she channelled out a groove* =**hollow out**, gouge (out), cut (out). **2** *many countries channel their aid through charities* =**convey**, transmit, conduct, direct, relay, pass on, transfer.

chant ▶ noun =**shout**, cry, call, slogan; chorus, refrain.

▶ verb =**shout**, chorus, repeat, call.

chaos ▶ noun =**disorder**, disarray, disorganization, confusion, mayhem, bedlam, pandemonium, havoc, turmoil, tumult, commotion, disruption, upheaval, uproar; a muddle, a mess, a shambles; anarchy, lawlessness; *informal* hullabaloo, all hell broken loose. −OPPOSITES order.

chaotic ▶ adjective =**disorderly**, disordered, in disorder, in chaos, in disarray, disorganized, topsy-turvy, in pandemonium, in turmoil, in uproar; in a muddle, in a mess, messy, in a shambles; anarchic, lawless; *Brit. informal* shambolic.

chap[1] ▶ verb *my skin chapped in the wind* =**become raw**, become sore, become inflamed, chafe, crack.

chap[2] ▶ noun *(Brit. informal)* *he's a nice chap* =**man**, boy, character; *informal* fellow, guy, geezer; *Brit. informal* bloke, lad, bod; *N. Amer. informal* dude, hombre.

chapter ▶ noun **1** *the first chapter of the book* =**section**, part, division. **2** *a new chapter in our history* =**period**, phase, page, stage, epoch, era. **3** *(N. Amer.) a local chapter of the American Cancer Society* =**branch**, division, subdivision, section, department, lodge, wing, arm.

char ▶ verb =**scorch**, burn, singe, sear, blacken; *informal* toast.

character ▶ noun **1** *a forceful character* | *the character of a town* =**personality**, nature, disposition, temperament, temper, mentality, make-up; features, qualities, properties, traits; spirit, essence, identity, ethos, complexion, tone, feel, feeling. **2** *a woman of character* =**integrity**, honour, moral strength/fibre, rectitude; fortitude, strength, backbone,

resolve, grit, will power; *informal* guts; *Brit. informal* bottle. **3** *a stain on his character* =**reputation**, (good) name, standing, stature, position, status. **4** *(informal) a bit of a character* =**eccentric**, oddity, madcap, crank, individualist, nonconformist; *informal* oddball; *Brit. informal* odd bod. **5** *a boorish character* =**person**, man, woman, soul, creature, individual, customer; *informal* cookie; *Brit. informal* bod, guy. **6** *thirty characters* =**letter**, figure, symbol, sign.

characteristic ▶ noun *interesting characteristics* =**attribute**, feature, (essential) quality, property, trait, aspect, element, facet; mannerism, habit, custom, idiosyncrasy, peculiarity, quirk, oddity, foible.

▶ adjective *his characteristic eloquence* =**typical**, usual, normal; distinctive, particular, special, especial, peculiar, idiosyncratic, singular, unique.

characterize ▶ verb **1** *the period was characterized by scientific advancement* =**distinguish**, mark, typify, set apart. **2** *the women are characterized as prophets of doom* =**portray**, depict, present, represent, describe; categorize, class, style, brand.

charade ▶ noun =**farce**, pantomime, travesty, mockery, parody, act, masquerade.

charge ▶ verb **1** *he didn't charge much* =**ask**, demand; bill, invoice. **2** *the subscription will be charged to your account* =**bill**, debit from, take from. **3** *two men were charged with murder* =**accuse**, indict, arraign; prosecute, try, put on trial; *N. Amer.* impeach. **4** *they charged him with reforming the system* =**entrust**, burden, encumber, saddle, tax. **5** *the cavalry charged the tanks* =**attack**, storm, assault, assail, fall on, swoop on, descend on; *informal* lay into, tear into. **6** *we charged into the crowd* =**rush**, storm, stampede, push, plough, launch oneself, go headlong; *informal* steam; *N. Amer. informal* barrel. **7** *charge your glasses!* | *the guns were charged* =**fill (up)**, top up; load (up), arm. **8** *his work was charged with energy* =**suffuse**, pervade, permeate, saturate, infuse, imbue, fill.

▶ noun **1** *all customers pay a charge* =**fee**, payment, price, tariff, amount, sum, fare, levy. **2** *he pleaded guilty to the charge* =**accusation**, allegation, indictment, arraignment; *N. Amer.* impeachment. **3** *an infantry charge* =**attack**, assault, of-

fensive, onslaught, drive, push, thrust. **4** *the child was in her charge* = **care**, protection, safe keeping, control; custody, guardianship, wardship; hands.
■ **in charge of** = **responsible for**, in control of, at the helm/wheel of, managing, running, administering, directing, supervising, overseeing, controlling; *informal* running the show.

charisma ▶ noun = **charm**, presence, (force of) personality, strength of character; (animal) magnetism, appeal, allure.

charismatic ▶ adjective = **charming**, fascinating; magnetic, captivating, beguiling, appealing, alluring.

charitable ▶ adjective **1** *charitable activities* = **philanthropic**, humanitarian, altruistic, benevolent, public-spirited; non-profit-making. **2** *charitable people* = **big-hearted**, generous, open-handed, free-handed, munificent, bountiful, beneficent; *literary* bounteous. **3** *he was charitable in his judgements* = **magnanimous**, generous, liberal, tolerant, sympathetic, lenient, indulgent, forgiving.

charity ▶ noun **1** *an AIDS charity* = **(voluntary) organization**, (charitable) institution; fund, trust, foundation. **2** *we don't need charity* = **(financial) assistance**, aid, welfare, (financial) relief; handouts, gifts, presents, largesse; *historical* alms. **3** *his actions are motivated by charity* = **philanthropy**, humanitarianism, humanity, altruism, public-spiritedness, social conscience, benevolence. **4** *show a bit of charity* = **goodwill**, compassion, consideration, concern, kindness, kind-heartedness, tenderness, tender-heartedness, sympathy, indulgence, tolerance, leniency.

charlatan ▶ noun = **quack**, sham, fraud, fake, impostor, hoodwinker, hoaxer, cheat, deceiver, double-dealer, (confidence) trickster, swindler, fraudster; *informal* phoney, shark, con man/artist; *N. Amer. informal* bunco artist, gold brick, chiseller; *Austral. informal* magsman, illywhacker.

charm ▶ noun **1** *people were captivated by her charm* = **attractiveness**, beauty, glamour, loveliness; appeal, allure, seductiveness, (sexual/animal) magnetism, charisma; *informal* pulling power. **2** *these traditions retain a lot of charm* = **appeal**, drawing power, attraction, allure, fascination. **3** *magical charms* = **spell**,

incantation, formula; *N. Amer.* mojo, hex. **4** *a lucky charm* = **talisman**, fetish, amulet, mascot, totem.
▶ verb **1** *he charmed them with his singing* = **delight**, please, win (over), attract, captivate, lure, dazzle, fascinate, enchant, enthral, enrapture, seduce, spellbind. **2** *he charmed his mother into agreeing* = **coax**, cajole, wheedle; *informal* sweet-talk, soft-soap.

charming ▶ adjective = **delightful**, pleasing, pleasant, agreeable, likeable, endearing, lovely, lovable, adorable, appealing, attractive, good-looking, prepossessing; alluring, delectable, ravishing, winning, winsome, fetching, captivating, enchanting, entrancing; *informal* heavenly, divine, gorgeous, easy on the eye; *Brit. informal* smashing; *archaic* fair, comely.
– OPPOSITES repulsive.

chart ▶ noun **1** *check your ideal weight on the chart* = **graph**, table, diagram, histogram; bar chart, pie chart, flow chart; *Computing* graphic.
▶ verb **1** *the changes were charted accurately* = **tabulate**, plot, graph, record, register, represent. **2** *the book charted his progress* = **follow**, trace, outline, describe, detail, record, document, chronicle, log.

charter ▶ noun **1** *a Royal charter* = **authority**, authorization, sanction, dispensation, consent, permission; permit, licence, warrant, franchise. **2** *the UN Charter* = **constitution**, code; (fundamental) principles.
▶ verb *they chartered a bus* = **hire**, lease, rent; book, reserve.

chase ▶ verb **1** *the dogs chased the fox* = **pursue**, run after, give chase to, follow; hunt, track, trail; *informal* tail. **2** *she chased away the donkeys* = **drive**, send, scare; *informal* send packing. **3** *she chased away all thoughts of him* = **dispel**, banish, dismiss, drive away, shut out, put out of one's mind. **4** *photographers chased on to the runway* = **rush**, dash, race, speed, shoot, charge, scramble, scurry, hurry; *informal* scoot, belt; *N. Amer. informal* boogie, hightail.
▶ noun *they gave up the chase* = **pursuit**, hunt, trail.

chasm ▶ noun **1** *a deep chasm* = **gorge**, abyss, canyon, ravine, gully, gulf, crevasse, fissure, crevice; *N. Amer.* gulch. **2** *the chasm between their views* = **breach**, gulf, rift; difference, separation, division, schism.

chassis ▸ noun =**framework**, frame, structure, substructure.

chasten ▸ verb *both men were chastened* =**subdue**, humble, cow, squash, deflate, flatten, take down a peg or two, put someone in their place; *informal* cut down to size, settle someone's hash.

chat ▸ noun *I popped in for a chat* =**talk**, conversation, gossip, heart-to-heart, tête-à-tête; *informal* jaw, gas, confab; *Brit. informal* natter, chinwag.
▸ verb *they chatted with the guests* =**talk**, gossip; *informal* gas, jaw, chew the rag/fat; *Brit. informal* natter, have a chinwag; *N. Amer. informal* shoot the breeze/bull; *Austral./NZ informal* mag.

chatter ▸ noun *she tired him with her chatter* =**chat**, talk, gossip, chit-chat, patter, jabbering, prattling, babbling, tittle-tattle, blathering; *informal* yabbering, yammering, yattering, yapping; *Brit. informal* nattering, chuntering, rabbiting on.
▸ verb *they chattered excitedly.* See CHAT verb.

chatty ▸ adjective **1** *he was a chatty person* =**talkative**, communicative, expansive, unreserved, gossipy, gossiping, garrulous, loquacious, voluble, verbose; *informal* mouthy, gabby, gassy. **2** *a chatty letter* =**conversational**, gossipy, informal, casual, familiar, friendly; *informal* newsy.
−OPPOSITES taciturn.

chauvinist ▸ adjective =**jingoistic**, chauvinistic, flag-waving, xenophobic, racist, ethnocentric; sexist, misogynist.
▸ noun =**sexist**, misogynist; *informal* male chauvinist pig, MCP.

cheap ▸ adjective **1** *cheap tickets* =**inexpensive**, low-priced, low-cost, economical, competitive, affordable, reasonable, reasonably priced, budget, economy, bargain, cut-price, reduced, discounted, discount, rock-bottom, giveaway, bargain-basement; *informal* dirt cheap. **2** *plain without looking cheap* =**poor-quality**, second-rate, third-rate, substandard, inferior, vulgar, shoddy, trashy, tawdry, cheap and nasty, cheapjack; *informal* rubbishy, cheapo, junky, tacky, kitsch; *Brit. informal* naff, duff, ropy, grotty; *N. Amer. informal* two-bit, dime-store. **3** *a cheap remark* =**despicable**, contemptible, immoral, unscrupulous, unprincipled, cynical.
−OPPOSITES expensive.

cheapen ▸ verb **1** *cheapening the cost of exports* =**reduce**, lower (in price), cut, mark down, discount; *informal* slash. **2** *Hetty never cheapened herself* =**demean**, debase, degrade, lower, humble, devalue, compromise, discredit, disgrace, dishonour, shame.

cheat ▸ verb =**swindle**, defraud, deceive, trick, dupe, hoodwink, double-cross, gull; *informal* diddle, rip off, con, fleece, shaft, sting, put one over on, pull a fast one on; *N. Amer. informal* sucker, gold-brick, stiff; *Austral. informal* pull a swifty on.
▸ noun =**swindler**, cheater, fraudster, (confidence) trickster, deceiver, hoaxer, double-dealer, double-crosser, sham, fraud, fake, charlatan; *informal* con artist; *N. Amer. informal* grifter, bunco artist, gold brick, chiseller; *Austral. informal* magsman, illywhacker.

check ▸ verb **1** *troops checked all vehicles | I checked her background* =**examine**, inspect, look at/over, scrutinize; study, investigate, research, probe, look into, enquire into; *informal* check out, give something a/the once-over. **2** *he checked that the gun was cocked* =**make sure**, confirm, verify. **3** *two defeats checked their progress* =**halt**, stop, arrest; bar, obstruct, foil, thwart, curb, block.
▸ noun **1** *a check of the records* =**examination**, inspection, scrutiny, perusal, study, investigation; test, trial, monitoring; check-up; *informal* once-over, look-see. **2** *a check on the abuse of authority* =**control**, restraint, constraint, curb, limitation. **3** *(N. Amer.) the waitress arrived with the check* =**bill**, account, invoice, statement; *N. Amer. informal* tab.
■ **check in** =**report** (one's arrival), book in, register.
■ **check out** =**leave**, depart; pay the bill, settle up.

check-up ▸ noun =**examination**, inspection, evaluation, analysis, survey, test, appraisal, check; *informal* once-over, going-over.

cheek ▸ noun =**impudence**, impertinence, insolence, cheekiness, impoliteness, disrespect, bad manners, rudeness, cockiness; answering back, talking back; *informal* brass (neck), lip, mouth, chutzpah; *Brit. informal* backchat; *N. Amer. informal* sass, sassiness, nerviness, back talk.

┌─────────────────────────┐
│ **WORD LINKS** │
│ *relating to the cheek:* **buccal, malar** │
└─────────────────────────┘

cheeky ▶ adjective =**impudent**, impertinent, insolent, presumptuous, cocky, overfamiliar, discourteous, disrespectful, impolite, rude; *informal* brass-necked, lippy, mouthy, fresh, saucy; *N. Amer. informal* sassy, nervy.
–OPPOSITES respectful, polite.

cheer ▶ noun *the cheers of the crowd* =**hurrah**, hurray, whoop, bravo, shout; (**cheers**) acclaim, clamour, applause, ovation.
–OPPOSITES boo.
▶ verb **1** *they cheered their team* =**applaud**, hail, salute, shout for, clap, put one's hands together for; bring the house down; *informal* holler for, give someone a big hand; *N. Amer. informal* ballyhoo. **2** *the bad weather did little to cheer me* =**raise/lift someone's spirits**, brighten, buoy up, enliven, hearten, gladden, uplift, perk up, encourage; *informal* buck up.
–OPPOSITES boo, depress.
■ **cheer up** =**perk up**, brighten (up), liven up, rally, revive, bounce back, take heart; *informal* buck up.
■ **cheer someone up.** See CHEER verb sense 2.

cheerful ▶ adjective **1** *he arrived looking cheerful* =**happy**, jolly, merry, bright, glad, sunny, joyful, joyous, light-hearted, in good/high spirits, full of the joys of spring, exuberant, buoyant, ebullient, cheery, jaunty, animated, smiling; jovial, genial, good-humoured; carefree, unworried, untroubled, without a care in the world; *informal* upbeat, chipper, chirpy, peppy, bright-eyed and bushy-tailed, full of beans. **2** *a cheerful room* =**pleasant**, attractive, agreeable, bright, sunny, happy, friendly, welcoming.
–OPPOSITES sad.

cheerless ▶ adjective =**gloomy**, dreary, dull, dismal, bleak, drab, sombre, dark, dim, dingy, funereal; austere, stark, bare, comfortless, unwelcoming, uninviting; miserable, wretched, joyless, depressing, disheartening, dispiriting.

cheery ▶ adjective. See CHEERFUL sense 1.

cherish ▶ verb **1** *a woman he could cherish* =**adore**, hold dear, love, dote on, be devoted to, revere, esteem, admire; think the world of, hold in high esteem; care for, look after, protect, preserve, keep safe. **2** *I cherish her letters* =**treasure**, prize, hold dear. **3** *they cherished dreams*

of glory =**harbour**, entertain, cling to, foster, nurture.

chest ▶ noun **1** *a bullet wound in the chest* =**breast**, upper body, torso, trunk; *technical* thorax. **2** *she had a large chest* =**bust**, bosom. **3** *an oak chest* =**box**, case, casket, crate, trunk, coffer, strongbox.

> **WORD LINKS**
> relating to the chest: **pectoral, thoracic**
> surgical incision of the chest:
> **thoracotomy**

chew ▶ verb *Carolyn chewed a mouthful of toast* =**munch**, masticate, champ, crunch, gnaw, eat, consume.

chic ▶ adjective =**stylish**, smart, elegant, sophisticated, dressy, dapper, dashing; fashionable, in vogue, up to date, up to the minute, à la mode; *informal* trendy, snappy, snazzy, natty; *Brit. informal* swish; *N. Amer. informal* fly, spiffy, kicky, tony.
–OPPOSITES unfashionable.

chicanery ▶ noun =**trickery**, deception, deceit, deceitfulness, duplicity, dishonesty, deviousness, unscrupulousness, underhandedness, subterfuge, fraud, fraudulence, sharp practice, skulduggery, swindling, cheating, duping; *informal* crookedness, monkey business, hanky-panky, shenanigans; *Brit. informal* jiggery-pokery; *N. Amer. informal* monkeyshines; *archaic* knavery.

chicken ▶ noun

> **WORD LINKS**
> male: **cock, rooster**
> female: **hen**
> young: **chick**

chief ▶ noun **1** *a Highland chief* =**leader**, chieftain, head, headman, ruler, overlord, master, commander, potentate. **2** *the chief of the central bank* =**head**, principal, chief executive, president, chair, chairman, chairwoman, chairperson, governor, director, manager, manageress; *N. Amer.* chief executive officer, CEO; *informal* skipper, (head) honcho, boss; *Brit. informal* gaffer, guv'nor; *N. Amer. informal* padrone, sachem.
▶ adjective **1** *the chief rabbi* =**head**, leading, principal, premier, highest, supreme, arch. **2** *their chief aim* =**main**, principal, primary, prime, first, cardinal, central, key, crucial, essential, predominant, pre-eminent, overriding; *informal* number-one.
–OPPOSITES subordinate, minor.

chiefly ▸ adverb =**mainly**, in the main, primarily, principally, predominantly, mostly, for the most part; usually, habitually, typically, commonly, generally, on the whole, largely, by and large, as a rule, almost always.

child ▸ noun =**youngster**, little one, boy, girl; baby, newborn, infant, toddler; schoolboy, schoolgirl, minor, junior; son, daughter, descendant; (**children**) offspring, progeny; Scottish & N. English bairn, laddie, lassie, lass; informal kid, kiddie, kiddiewink, nipper, tiny, tot, lad; Brit. informal sprog; N. Amer. informal rug rat; Austral./NZ informal ankle-biter; derogatory brat, guttersnipe.

> WORD LINKS
>
> relating to children: **paedo-**
> fear of children: **paedophobia**
> branch of medicine dealing with
> children: **paediatrics**
> killing of a young child: **infanticide**

childbirth ▸ noun

> WORD LINKS
>
> relating to childbirth: **obstetric**
> fear of childbirth: **tocophobia**

childhood ▸ noun =**youth**, early years/life, infancy, babyhood, boyhood, girlhood, prepubescence, minority.
−OPPOSITES adulthood.

childish ▸ adjective **1** childish behaviour =**immature**, babyish, infantile, juvenile, puerile; silly. **2** a round childish face =**childlike**, youthful, young, young-looking, girlish, boyish.
−OPPOSITES mature, adult.

childlike ▸ adjective =**innocent**, artless, guileless, unworldly; unsophisticated, naive, trusting, unsuspicious; unaffected, uninhibited, natural, spontaneous.

chill ▸ noun **1** a chill in the air =**coldness**, chilliness, coolness, nip. **2** he had a chill =**cold**, dose of flu/influenza.
−OPPOSITES warmth.
▸ verb his quiet tone chilled Ruth =**scare**, frighten, petrify, terrify, alarm; make someone's blood run cold, chill to the bone/marrow, make someone's flesh crawl; informal scare the pants off; Brit. informal put the wind up; archaic affright.
−OPPOSITES warm.
▸ adjective a chill wind =**cold**, chilly, cool, fresh; wintry, frosty, icy, ice-cold, gla-

cial, polar, arctic, bitter, biting, freezing; informal nippy; Brit. informal parky.
■ **chill out** (informal). See RELAX sense 1.

chilly ▸ adjective **1** the weather had turned chilly =**cold**, cool, crisp, fresh, wintry, frosty, icy; informal nippy; Brit. informal parky. **2** a chilly reception =**unfriendly**, unwelcoming, cold, cool, frosty; informal stand-offish.
−OPPOSITES warm.

chimera ▸ noun =**illusion**, fantasy, delusion, dream, fancy.

China ▸ noun

> WORD LINKS
>
> study of China: **sinology**

china ▸ noun **1** a china cup =**porcelain**. **2** a table laid with the best china =**dishes**, plates, cups and saucers, crockery, tableware, dinnerware, dinner service, tea service.

chink¹ ▸ noun a chink in the curtains =**opening**, gap, space, hole, aperture, crack, fissure, cranny, cleft, split, slit.

chink² ▸ verb the glasses chinked =**jingle**, jangle, clink, tinkle.

chip ▸ noun **1** wood chips =**fragment**, sliver, splinter, shaving, paring, flake. **2** a chip in the glass =**nick**, crack, scratch; flaw, fault. **3** gambling chips =**counter**, token; N. Amer. check.
▸ verb **1** the teacup was chipped =**nick**, crack, scratch. **2** the plaster had chipped =**break (off)**, crack, crumble.
■ **chip in 1** 'He's right,' Gloria chipped in =**interrupt**, interject, interpose, cut in, chime in, butt in. **2** parents and staff chipped in to raise the cash =**contribute**, club together, pay; informal fork out, shell out, cough up; Brit. informal stump up; N. Amer. informal kick in.

chirpy ▸ adjective (informal). See CHEERFUL sense 1.

chivalrous ▸ adjective =**gallant**, gentlemanly, honourable, respectful, considerate; courteous, polite, gracious, well mannered.
−OPPOSITES rude, cowardly.

chivalry ▸ noun =**gallantry**; courtesy, politeness, graciousness, good manners.
−OPPOSITES rudeness.

chivvy ▸ verb =**nag**, badger, hound, harass, harry, pester, keep on at, go on at; informal hassle, bug, breathe down someone's neck; N. Amer. informal ride.

choice ▶ noun **1** *their choice of candidate | freedom of choice* =**selection**, choosing, picking; decision, say, vote. **2** *you have no other choice* =**option**, alternative, course of action; way (out). **3** *an extensive choice of wines* =**range**, variety, selection, assortment. **4** *the perfect choice* =**appointee**, nominee, candidate, selection.
▶ adjective *choice plums* =**superior**, first-class, first-rate, prime, premier, grade A, best, finest, excellent, select, quality, top, top-quality, high-grade, prize, fine, special; *informal* A1, top-notch.
−OPPOSITES inferior.

choke ▶ verb **1** *Christopher started to choke* =**gag**, retch, cough, fight for breath. **2** *thick dust choked her* =**suffocate**, asphyxiate, smother, stifle. **3** *she had been choked to death* =**strangle**, throttle; asphyxiate, suffocate; *informal* strangulate. **4** *the guttering was choked with leaves* =**clog (up)**, bung up, stop up, block, obstruct; *technical* occlude.

choose ▶ verb **1** *we chose a quiet country hotel* =**select**, pick (out), opt for, plump for, settle on, decide on, fix on; appoint, name, nominate, vote for. **2** *I'll stay as long as I choose* =**wish**, want, desire, feel/be inclined, please, like, see fit.

choosy ▶ adjective *(informal)* =**fussy**, finicky, fastidious, over-particular, difficult/hard to please, exacting, demanding; *informal* picky, pernickety; *N. Amer. informal* persnickety.

chop ▶ verb =**cut (up)**, cube, dice, hew, split; fell; *N. Amer.* hash.
■ **chop something off** =**cut off**, sever, lop, shear.

choppy ▶ adjective =**rough**, turbulent, heavy, heaving, stormy, tempestuous, squally.
−OPPOSITES calm.

chore ▶ noun =**task**, job, duty, errand.

chortle ▶ verb =**chuckle**, laugh, giggle, titter, tee-hee, snigger; guffaw.

christen ▶ verb **1** *she was christened Sara* =**baptize**, name, give the name of, call. **2** *a group who were christened 'The Magic Circle'* =**call**, name, dub, style, term, designate, label, nickname.

Christmas ▶ noun =**Noel**; *informal* Xmas; *Brit. informal* Chrimbo; *archaic* Yule, Yuletide.

chronic ▶ adjective **1** *a chronic illness* =**persistent**, long-standing, long-term; incurable. **2** *chronic economic problems* =**constant**, continuing, ceaseless, persistent, long-lasting; severe, serious, acute, grave, dire. **3** *a chronic liar* =**inveterate**, hardened, dyed-in-the-wool, incorrigible; compulsive; *informal* pathological.
−OPPOSITES acute, temporary.

chronicle ▶ noun *a chronicle of the region's past* =**record**, account, history, annals, archive(s); log, diary, journal.
▶ verb *the events that followed have been chronicled* =**record**, put on record, write down, set down, document, report.

chronological ▶ adjective =**sequential**, consecutive, in sequence, in order; linear.

chubby ▶ adjective =**plump**, tubby, rotund, portly, dumpy, chunky, well upholstered, well covered, well rounded; *informal* roly-poly, pudgy, blubbery; *Brit. informal* podgy; *N. Amer. informal* zaftig, corn-fed.
−OPPOSITES skinny.

chuck ▶ verb *(informal)* **1** *he chucked the letter onto the table* =**throw**, toss, fling, hurl, pitch, cast, lob; *informal* sling, bung; *Austral. informal* hoy; *NZ informal* bish. **2** *I chucked the rubbish* =**throw away/out**, discard, dispose of, get rid of, dump, bin, jettison; *informal* ditch, junk; *N. Amer. informal* trash. **3** *I've chucked my job* =**give up**, leave, resign from; *informal* quit, pack in; *Brit. informal* jack in. **4** *Mary chucked him for another guy* =**leave**, finish with, break off with, jilt; *informal* dump, ditch, give someone the elbow; *Brit. informal* give someone the push, give someone the big E.

chuckle ▶ verb −**chortle**, giggle, titter, snicker, snigger.

chum ▶ noun *(informal)* =**friend**, companion, intimate; playmate, classmate, schoolmate, workmate; *informal* pal, crony; *Brit. informal* mate, china, mucker; *N. Amer. informal* buddy, amigo, compadre, homeboy.
−OPPOSITES enemy, stranger.

chunk ▶ noun =**lump**, hunk, wedge, block, slab, square, nugget, brick, cube, bar, cake; *informal* wodge; *N. Amer. informal* gob.

chunky ▶ adjective **1** *a chunky young man* =**stocky**, sturdy, thickset, heavily built, well built, burly, bulky, brawny, solid; *Austral./NZ* nuggety. **2** *a chunky sweater* =**thick**, bulky, heavy.
−OPPOSITES slight, light.

churchyard ▸ noun =graveyard, cemetery, necropolis, burial ground, garden of remembrance; *Scottish* kirkyard; *N. Amer.* memorial park; *archaic* God's acre.

churlish ▸ adjective =rude, ill-mannered, discourteous, impolite; inconsiderate, uncharitable, surly, sullen; *informal* ignorant.
−OPPOSITES polite.

churn ▸ verb *the propellers churned up the water* =disturb, stir up, agitate.
■ **churn something out** =produce, make, turn out; *informal* crank out, bang out.

chute ▸ noun **1** *a refuse chute* =channel, slide, shaft, funnel, conduit, tube. **2** *water chutes* =(water) slide, flume.

cigarette ▸ noun =*informal* ciggy, cig, smoke, cancer stick; *Brit. informal* fag, snout.

cinema ▸ noun **1** *the local cinema* =*N. Amer.* movie theatre/house; *dated* picture palace/theatre. **2** *I often go to the cinema* =the pictures, the movies; *informal* the flicks. **3** *British cinema* =films, film, movies, motion pictures.

WORD LINKS
relating to the cinema: **cinematographic**

circa ▸ preposition =approximately, (round) about, around, in the region of, roughly, something like, or so, or thereabouts, more or less; *informal* as near as dammit; *N. Amer. informal* in the ballpark of.
−OPPOSITES exactly.

circle ▸ noun **1** *a circle of gold stars* =ring, band, hoop, circlet; halo, disc; *technical* annulus. **2** *her circle of friends* =group, set, company, coterie, clique; crowd, band; *informal* gang, bunch, crew, posse. **3** *illustrious circles* =sphere, world, milieu; society.
▸ verb **1** *seagulls circled above* =wheel, revolve, rotate, whirl, spiral. **2** *satellites circling the earth* =go round, travel round, circumnavigate; orbit. **3** *the abbey was circled by a wall* =surround, encircle, ring, enclose, encompass; *literary* gird.

circuit ▸ noun =lap, turn, round, circle.

circuitous ▸ adjective =roundabout, indirect, winding, meandering, serpentine.
−OPPOSITES direct.

circular ▸ noun =leaflet, pamphlet, handbill, flyer; *N. Amer.* mailer, folder, dodger.

circulate ▸ verb **1** *the news was widely circulated* =spread (about/around), communicate, disseminate, make known, make public, broadcast, publicize, advertise; distribute, give out, pass around. **2** *they circulated among the guests* =socialize, mingle; mix; wander, stroll.

circumference ▸ noun =perimeter, border, boundary; edge, rim, margin, fringe.

circumspect ▸ adjective =cautious, wary, careful, chary, guarded, on one's guard; watchful, alert, attentive, heedful, vigilant, leery; *informal* cagey.
−OPPOSITES unguarded.

circumstances ▸ plural noun **1** *favourable economic circumstances* =situation, conditions, state of affairs, position; (turn of) events; factors, context, background, environment. **2** *Jane explained the circumstances to him* =the facts, the details, the particulars, things, the lie of the land; *Brit.* the state of play; *N. Amer.* the lay of the land; *informal* what's what, the score, the situation. **3** *his circumstances have changed* =(financial) position, situation, lifestyle; conditions, resources, means, finances, income.

circumvent ▸ verb =avoid, get round/past, evade, bypass, sidestep, dodge; *N. Amer.* end-run; *informal* duck.

citation ▸ noun **1** *a citation from an eighteenth-century text* =quotation, quote, extract, excerpt, passage, line; reference, allusion; *N. Amer.* cite. **2** *a citation for gallantry* =commendation, (honourable) mention.

cite ▸ verb **1** *cite the passage in full* =quote, reproduce. **2** *he cited the case of Leigh v. Gladstone* =refer to, make reference to, mention, allude to, instance; specify, name.

citizen ▸ noun **1** *a British citizen* =subject, national, passport holder, native. **2** *the citizens of Edinburgh* =inhabitant, resident, native, townsman, townswoman, taxpayer, people; *formal* denizen; *archaic* burgher.

city ▸ noun =town, municipality, metropolis, megalopolis; conurbation; *Scottish* burgh; *informal* big smoke; *N. Amer. informal* burg.

WORD LINKS

relating to cities: **urban, civic, metropolitan**

civic ▶ adjective =**municipal**, city, town, urban, metropolitan; public, civil, community.

civil ▶ adjective **1** *a civil marriage* =**secular**, non-religious, lay; *formal* laic. **2** *civil aviation* =**non-military**, civilian. **3** *he behaved in a civil manner* =**polite**, courteous, well mannered, gentlemanly, chivalrous, gallant, ladylike.
–OPPOSITES religious, military, rude.

civilian ▶ noun =**non-combatant**, ordinary/private citizen.

civility ▶ noun =**courtesy**, courteousness, politeness, good manners, graciousness, consideration, respect.
–OPPOSITES rudeness.

civilization ▶ noun **1** *a higher stage of civilization* =(**human**) **development**, advancement, progress, enlightenment, culture, refinement, sophistication. **2** *ancient civilizations* =**culture**, society, nation, people.

civilize ▶ verb =**enlighten**, improve, educate, instruct, refine, cultivate, polish, socialize, humanize; *formal* edify.

civilized ▶ adjective =**polite**, courteous, well mannered, civil; cultured, cultivated, refined, polished, sophisticated; enlightened, educated, advanced, developed.
–OPPOSITES rude, unsophisticated.

clad ▶ adjective =**dressed**, clothed, attired, got up, garbed, rigged out; wearing, sporting; *archaic* apparelled.

claim ▶ verb **1** *he claimed that she was lying* =**assert**, declare, profess, maintain, state, hold, affirm, avow; argue, contend, allege; *formal* aver. **2** *you can claim compensation* =**request**, ask for, apply for; demand, exact.
▶ noun **1** *her claim that she was raped* =**assertion**, declaration, profession, avowal, protestation; contention, allegation. **2** *a claim for damages* =**request**, application; demand, petition.

claimant ▶ noun =**applicant**, candidate; petitioner, plaintiff, litigant, appellant.

clamber ▶ verb =**scramble**, climb, scrabble.

clammy ▶ adjective **1** *his clammy hands* =**moist**, damp, sweaty, sticky; slimy, slippery. **2** *the clammy atmosphere* =**damp**, dank, wet; humid, close, muggy, heavy.
–OPPOSITES dry.

clamour ▶ noun =**din**, racket, rumpus, uproar, tumult, shouting, yelling, screaming, baying, roaring; commotion, hubbub; *informal* hullabaloo; *Brit. informal* row.
▶ verb =**demand**, call, press, push, lobby.

clamp ▶ noun *a clamp was holding the wood* =**brace**, vice, press.
▶ verb **1** *the sander is clamped on to the workbench* =**fasten**, secure, fix, attach; screw, bolt. **2** *a pipe was clamped between his teeth* =**clench**, grip, hold, press, clasp. **3** *his car was clamped* =**immobilize**, wheel-clamp; *N. Amer.* boot.
■ **clamp down on** =**suppress**, prevent, stop, put a stop/end to, stamp out; crack down on, limit, restrict, control.

clampdown ▶ noun *(informal)* =**suppression**, prevention; crackdown, restriction, curb.

clan ▶ noun =**family**, house, dynasty, tribe; *Anthropology* kinship group.

clandestine ▶ adjective =**secret**, covert, furtive, surreptitious, stealthy, cloak-and-dagger; *informal* hush-hush.

clang ▶ noun =**reverberation**, ring, peal, chime.
▶ verb =**reverberate**, resound, ring, peal, chime, toll.

clank ▶ noun & verb =**jangle**, rattle, clink, clang, jingle.

clannish ▶ adjective =**cliquey**, cliquish, insular, exclusive; unfriendly, unwelcoming.

clap ▶ verb **1** *the audience clapped* =**applaud**, give someone a round of applause, put one's hands together; *informal* give someone a (big) hand; *N. Amer. informal* give it up. **2** *he clapped Owen on the back* =**slap**, strike, hit, smack, thump, pat; *informal* whack.
▶ noun **1** *everybody gave him a clap* =**round of applause**, handclap; *informal* hand. **2** *a clap of thunder* =**crack**, crash, bang, boom; peal.

claptrap ▶ noun. See NONSENSE *sense* 1.

clarify ▶ verb =**make clear**, shed/throw light on, illuminate; **explain**, define, spell out, clear up.
–OPPOSITES confuse.

clarity ▶ noun **1** *the clarity of his explanation* =**lucidity**, clearness, coherence, transparency. **2** *the clarity of the image* =**sharpness**, clearness, crispness, definition. **3** *the clarity of the water* =**limpidity**, clearness, transparency, translucence. –OPPOSITES vagueness, blurriness, opacity.

clash ▶ noun **1** *clashes between armed gangs* =**confrontation**, skirmish, fight, battle, engagement, encounter, conflict. **2** *an angry clash* =**argument**, altercation, confrontation, shouting match; contretemps, quarrel, disagreement, dispute; *informal* run-in, slanging match. **3** *the clash of cymbals* =**crash**, clang, bang.
▶ verb **1** *protesters clashed with police* =**fight**, battle, confront, skirmish, contend, come to blows, come into conflict. **2** *the prime minister clashed with union leaders* =**disagree**, differ, wrangle, dispute, cross swords, lock horns, be at loggerheads. **3** *the dates clash* =**conflict**, coincide, overlap. **4** *she clashed the cymbals together* =**bang**, strike, clang, crash.

clasp ▶ verb **1** *Ruth clasped his hand* =**grasp**, grip, clutch, hold tightly, squeeze; take hold of, seize, grab. **2** *he clasped Joanne in his arms* =**embrace**, hug, envelop; hold, squeeze.
▶ noun **1** *a gold clasp* =**fastener**, fastening, catch, clip, pin; buckle, hasp. **2** *his tight clasp* =**embrace**; grip, grasp.

class ▶ noun **1** *a hotel of the first class* =**category**, grade, rating, classification, group, grouping. **2** *a new class of heart drug* =**kind**, sort, type, variety, genre, brand; species, genus, breed, strain; *N. Amer.* stripe. **3** *mixing with people of her own class* =**rank**, stratum, level, echelon, group, grouping; status, caste. **4** *there are 30 pupils in the class* =**form**, group, set, stream. **5** *a maths class* =**lesson**, period; seminar, tutorial, workshop. **6** *(informal) a woman of class* =**style**, elegance, chic, sophistication, taste, refinement, quality.
▶ verb *the 12-seater is classed as a commercial vehicle* =**classify**, categorize, group, grade; order, sort, codify; bracket, designate, label, pigeonhole.

classic ▶ adjective **1** *the classic work on the subject* =**definitive**, authoritative, outstanding, first-rate, first-class, best, finest, excellent, superior, masterly. **2** *a classic example of Norman design* =**typical**, archetypal, quintessential, vintage; model, representative, perfect, prime, textbook. **3** *a classic look* =**simple**, elegant, understated; traditional, time-

less, ageless.
–OPPOSITES atypical.
▶ noun *a classic of the genre* =**definitive example**, model, epitome, paradigm, exemplar; masterpiece.

classical ▶ adjective **1** *classical mythology* =(ancient) Greek, Hellenic; Latin, Roman. **2** *a classical style* =**simple**, pure, restrained, plain, austere; harmonious, balanced, symmetrical, elegant.
–OPPOSITES modern.

classification ▶ noun **1** *the classification of diseases* =**categorization**, classifying, grouping, grading, ranking, organization, sorting, codification, systematization. **2** *a series of classifications* =**category**, class, group, grouping, grade, grading, ranking, bracket.

classify ▶ verb =**categorize**, group, grade, rank, order, organize, range, sort, type, codify, bracket; catalogue, list, file, index.

classy ▶ adjective *(informal)* =**stylish**, high-class, superior, exclusive, chic, elegant, smart, sophisticated; *Brit.* upmarket; *N. Amer.* high-toned; *informal* posh, ritzy, plush, swanky; *Brit. informal* swish.

clatter ▶ verb =**rattle**, clank, clang.

clause ▶ noun =**section**, paragraph, article, subsection; condition, proviso, rider.

claw ▶ noun **1** *a bird's claw* =**talon**, nail. **2** *a crab's claw* =**pincer**, nipper.
▶ verb *her fingers clawed his shoulders* =**scratch**, lacerate, tear, rip, scrape, dig into.

clean ▶ adjective **1** *keep the wound clean* =**washed**, scrubbed, cleansed, cleaned; spotless, unsoiled, unstained, unsullied, unblemished, immaculate, pristine, dirt-free; hygienic, sanitary, disinfected, sterilized, sterile, aseptic, decontaminated; laundered. **2** *a clean sheet of paper* =**blank**, empty, clear, plain; unused, new, pristine, fresh, unmarked. **3** *clean air* =**pure**, clear, fresh; unpolluted, uncontaminated. **4** *a clean life* =**virtuous**, good, upright, upstanding; honourable, respectable, reputable, decent, righteous, moral, exemplary; innocent, pure, chaste. **5** *the firm is clean* =**innocent**, guiltless, blameless, guilt-free, above suspicion; *informal* squeaky clean. **6** *a good clean fight* =**fair**, honest, sporting, sportsmanlike, honourable, by the rules/book; *informal* on the level. **7** *a clean cut* =**neat**, smooth, crisp, straight,

precise. **8** *clean lines* =**simple**, elegant, graceful, streamlined, smooth.
−OPPOSITES dirty, polluted.

▶ **verb 1** *Dad cleaned the windows* =**wash**, cleanse, wipe, sponge, scrub, mop, rinse, scour, swab, hose down, sluice (down), disinfect; shampoo. **2** *I got my clothes cleaned* =**launder**, wash, dry-clean. **3** *she cleaned the fish* =**gut**, draw, dress; *formal* eviscerate.
−OPPOSITES dirty.

■ **clean someone out** (*informal*) =**bankrupt**, ruin, make insolvent, make penniless, wipe out.

cleanse ▶ **verb 1** *the wound was cleansed* =**clean (up)**, wash, bathe, rinse, disinfect. **2** *cleansing the environment of traces of lead* =**rid**, clear, free, purify, purge.

clear ▶ **adjective 1** *clear instructions* =**understandable**, comprehensible, intelligible, plain, uncomplicated, explicit, lucid, coherent, simple, straightforward, unambiguous, clear-cut. **2** *a clear case of harassment* =**obvious**, evident, plain; sure, definite, unmistakable, manifest, indisputable, unambiguous, patent, incontrovertible, irrefutable, beyond doubt, beyond question; palpable, visible, discernible, conspicuous, overt, blatant, glaring. **3** *clear water* =**transparent**, limpid, translucent, crystal clear. **4** *a clear sky* =**bright**, cloudless, unclouded; blue, sunny, starry. **5** *the road was clear | a clear view* =**unobstructed**, passable, open; unrestricted, unhindered. **6** *the algae were clear of toxins* =**free**, devoid, without, unaffected by; rid. **7** *two clear days' notice* =**whole**, full, entire, complete.
−OPPOSITES vague, opaque, cloudy, obstructed.

▶ **verb 1** *the smoke had cleared* =**disappear**, go away, stop; die away, fade, wear off, lift, settle, evaporate, dissipate, decrease, lessen, shift. **2** *they cleared the table* =**empty**, unload, strip. **3** *clearing drains* =**unblock**, unstop. **4** *staff cleared the building* =**evacuate**, empty; leave. **5** *Karen cleared the dirty plates* =**remove**, take away, carry away, tidy away/up. **6** *I cleared the bar at my first attempt* =**go over**, pass over, sail over; jump (over), vault (over), leap (over), hurdle. **7** *he was cleared by the court* =**acquit**, declare innocent, find not guilty; absolve, exonerate; *informal* let off (the hook). **8** *I was cleared to work on the atomic project* =**authorize**, permit, allow, pass, accept, endorse, license, sanction; *informal* OK, give the OK, give the thumbs up, give the green light, give the go-ahead. **9** *I cleared £50,000 profit* =**net**, make/realize a profit of, take home, pocket; gain, earn, make, get, bring in, pull in.

■ **clear off/out** (*informal*) =**go away**, get out, leave; be off with you, shoo, on your way; *informal* beat it, push off, shove off, scram, scoot, buzz off; *Brit. informal* hop it, sling your hook; *Austral./NZ informal* rack off; *N. Amer. informal* bug off, take a hike; *literary* begone.

■ **clear something out 1** *we cleared out the junk room* =**empty (out)**; tidy (up), clear up. **2** *clear out the rubbish* =**get rid of**, throw out/away, discard, dispose of, dump, bin, scrap, jettison; *informal* chuck (out/away), ditch, get shut of; *Brit. informal* get shot of; *N. Amer. informal* trash.

■ **clear up** *my health problems cleared up.* See CLEAR verb sense 1.

■ **clear something up 1** *clear up the garden* =**tidy (up)**, put in order, straighten up, clean up, fix. **2** *we've cleared up the problem* =**solve**, resolve, straighten out, find an/the answer to; get to the bottom of, explain; *informal* crack, figure out, suss out.

clearance ▶ **noun 1** *slum clearance* =**removal**, clearing, demolition. **2** *you must have Home Office clearance* =**authorization**, permission, consent, approval, leave, sanction, licence, dispensation, assent, agreement, endorsement; *informal* the green light, the go-ahead, the thumbs up, the OK, the say-so. **3** *there is plenty of clearance* =**space**, room (to spare), headroom, margin, leeway.

clear-cut ▶ **adjective** =**definite**, distinct, clear, well defined, precise, specific, explicit, unambiguous, unequivocal, black and white, cut and dried.
−OPPOSITES vague.

clearing ▶ **noun** =**glade**, dell, gap, opening.

clearly ▶ **adverb 1** *write clearly* =**intelligibly**, plainly, distinctly, comprehensibly; legibly, audibly. **2** *clearly, substantial changes are needed* =**obviously**, evidently, patently, unquestionably, undoubtedly, without doubt, plainly, undeniably, incontrovertibly, doubtless, it goes without saying, needless to say.

cleave ■ **cleave to** (*literary*) **1** *her tongue clove to the roof of her mouth* =**stick (fast)** to, adhere to, be attached to. **2** *cleaving too closely to Moscow's line* =**adhere to**, hold to, abide by, be loyal/faithful to.

cleaver ▸ noun =**chopper**, hatchet, axe, knife; butcher's knife, kitchen knife.

cleft ▸ noun **1** *a deep cleft in the rocks* =**split**, crack, fissure, crevice, rift, break, fracture, rent, breach. **2** *the cleft in his chin* =**dimple**.
▸ adjective *a cleft tail* =**split**, divided, cloven.

clemency ▸ noun =**mercy**, mercifulness, leniency, mildness, indulgence, quarter; compassion, humanity, pity, sympathy.
–OPPOSITES ruthlessness.

clench ▸ verb **1** *he clenched his hands* =**squeeze (together)**, clamp (together), close/shut (tightly), clasp. **2** *he clenched the back of the chair* =**grip**, grasp, grab, clutch, clasp, hold tightly, seize, press, squeeze.

clergy ▸ noun =**clergymen**, clergywomen, churchmen, churchwomen, clerics, priests, ecclesiastics, men/women of God; ministry, priesthood, holy orders, the church, the cloth.
–OPPOSITES laity.

WORD LINKS

relating to clergy: **clerical**

clergyman, clergywoman ▸ noun =**priest**, churchman, churchwoman, man/woman of the cloth, man/woman of God; cleric, minister, preacher, chaplain, father, ecclesiastic, pastor, vicar, rector, parson, curate, deacon, deaconess; *Scottish* kirkman; *N. Amer.* dominie; *informal* reverend, padre, Holy Joe, sky pilot; *Austral. informal* josser.

clerical ▸ adjective **1** *clerical jobs* =**office**, desk; administrative, secretarial; white-collar. **2** *a clerical matter* =**ecclesiastical**, church, priestly, religious, spiritual; holy.
–OPPOSITES secular.

clerk ▸ noun =**office worker**, clerical worker, administrator; bookkeeper; cashier, teller; *informal* pen-pusher.

clever ▸ adjective **1** *a clever young woman* =**intelligent**, bright, smart, astute, quick-witted, shrewd; talented, gifted, capable, able, competent; educated, learned, knowledgeable, wise; *informal* brainy, savvy. **2** *a clever scheme* =**ingenious**, canny, cunning, crafty, artful, slick, neat; *informal* nifty. **3** *she was clever*

with her hands =**skilful**, dexterous, adroit, adept, deft, nimble, handy; skilled, talented, gifted. **4** *a clever remark* =**witty**, amusing, droll, humorous, funny; facetious, sarcastic, cheeky.
–OPPOSITES stupid.

cliché ▸ noun =**platitude**, hackneyed phrase, commonplace, banality, truism, stock phrase; *informal* old chestnut.

click ▸ verb **1** *(informal) that night it clicked* =**become clear**, fall into place, come home, make sense, dawn, register, get through, sink in. **2** *(informal) we just clicked* =**take to each other**, get along, be compatible, be like-minded, feel a rapport, see eye to eye, be on the same wavelength; *informal* hit it off. **3** *(informal) this issue hasn't clicked with the voters* =**go down well**, prove popular, be a hit, succeed, resonate, work, take off.

client ▸ noun =**customer**, buyer, purchaser, shopper, consumer, user; patient; patron, regular; (**clients**) clientele, patronage, public, market; *Brit. informal* punter.

clientele ▸ noun =**clients**. *See* CLIENT.

cliff ▸ noun =**precipice**, rock face, crag, bluff, ridge, escarpment, scar, scarp, overhang.

climactic ▸ adjective =**final**, ending, closing, concluding, ultimate; exciting, thrilling, gripping, riveting, dramatic, hair-raising; crucial, decisive, critical.

climate ▸ noun **1** *a mild climate* =**(weather) conditions**, weather. **2** *they come from colder climates* =**region**, area, zone, country, place; *literary* clime. **3** *the political climate* =**atmosphere**, mood, feeling, ambience; ethos, attitude; milieu; *informal* vibe(s).

WORD LINKS

study of climate: **climatology**

climax ▸ noun **1** *the climax of his career* =**peak**, pinnacle, height, high(est) point, top; acme, zenith; culmination, crowning point, crown, crest; highlight, high spot. **2** =**orgasm**; ejaculation.
–OPPOSITES nadir.
▸ verb **1** *the event will climax with a concert* =**culminate**, peak, reach a pinnacle, come to a crescendo, come to a head. **2** =**orgasm**; ejaculate; *informal* come, feel the earth move.

climb ▸ verb **1** *we climbed the hill* =**ascend**, mount, scale, scramble up, clam-

ber up, shin up; go up, walk up; con-quer, gain. **2** *the plane climbed* =**rise**, ascend, go up, gain height/altitude. **3** *the road climbs steeply* =**slope (up-wards)**, rise, go uphill, incline. **4** *the shares climbed to 550 pence* =**increase**, rise, go up; shoot up, soar, rocket. **5** *he climbed through the ranks* =**advance**, rise, move up, progress, work one's way. **6** *he climbed out of his car* =**clamber**, scramble; step.
−OPPOSITES descend, drop, fall.
▶ noun *a steep climb* =**ascent**, route; walk.
−OPPOSITES descent.
■ **climb down 1** *Sandy climbed down the ladder* =**descend**, go/come down. **2** *the Government had to climb down* =**back down**, admit defeat, surrender, capitu-late, yield, give in, give way, submit; re-treat, backtrack; eat one's words, eat humble pie; do a U-turn; *Brit.* do an about-turn; *N. Amer. informal* eat crow.

clinch ▶ verb **1** *he clinched the deal* =**se-cure**, settle, conclude, close, pull off, bring off, complete, confirm, seal, final-ize; *informal* sew up, wrap up. **2** *these find-ings clinched the matter* =**settle**, decide, determine; resolve. **3** *they clinched the title* =**win**, secure.
−OPPOSITES lose.

cling ▶ verb *rice grains tend to cling to-gether* =**stick**, adhere, hold.
■ **cling (on) to 1** *she clung to him* =**hold on**, clutch, grip, grasp, clasp, hang on; embrace, hug. **2** *they clung to their beliefs* =**adhere to**, hold to, stick to, stand by, abide by, cherish, remain true to, have faith in; *informal* stick with.

clinic ▶ noun =**medical centre**, health centre, surgery, doctor's; workshop, session.

clinical ▶ adjective **1** *he seemed so clinical* =**detached**, impersonal, dispassionate, uninvolved, distant, remote, aloof, re-moved, cold, indifferent, neutral, un-sympathetic, unfeeling, unemotional. **2** *the room was very clinical* =**plain**, stark, austere, spartan, bleak, bare; func-tional, basic, institutional, impersonal, characterless.
−OPPOSITES emotional, luxurious.

clip¹ ▶ noun **1** *the clip on his briefcase* =**fas-tener**, clasp, hasp, catch, hook, buckle, lock. **2** *his clip was empty* =**magazine**, cartridge.
▶ verb *he clipped the pages together* =**fasten**, attach, fix, join; pin, staple, tack.

clip² ▶ verb **1** *I clipped the hedge* =**trim**, prune, cut, snip, crop, shear, pare; lop; neaten, shape. **2** *clip the coupon below* =**remove**, cut out, tear out, detach. **3** *his lorry clipped a van* =**hit**, strike, touch, graze, glance off, nudge, dent, scrape.
▶ noun **1** *a film clip* =**extract**, excerpt, snip-pet, fragment; trailer. **2** *I gave the dog a clip* =**trim**, cut, crop, haircut; shear.

clipping ▶ noun =**cutting**, snippet, ex-tract, excerpt; article, report, feature, review.

clique ▶ noun =**coterie**, set, circle, ring, in-crowd, group; club, society, frater-nity, sorority; cabal, caucus; *informal* gang, posse.

cloak ▶ noun **1** *the cloak over his shoulders* =**cape**, robe, mantle. **2** *a cloak of secrecy* =**cover**, veil, mantle, shroud, screen, mask, shield, blanket.
▶ verb *a peak cloaked in mist* =**conceal**, hide, cover, veil, shroud, mask, obscure, cloud; envelop, swathe, surround.

clock ▶ noun =**timepiece**, timer, chron-ometer, chronograph.

clod ▶ noun =**lump**, clump, chunk, hunk, wedge, slab.

clog ▶ verb =**block**, obstruct, congest, jam, choke, bung up, plug, stop up, fill up; *Brit. informal* gunge up.

cloister ▶ verb *they were cloistered at home* =**confine**, isolate, shut away, se-quester, seclude, closet.

cloistered ▶ adjective =**secluded**, sheltered, protected, insulated; shut off, isolated; solitary, monastic, reclusive, hermit-like.

close¹ ▶ adjective **1** *the town is close to Leeds* =**near**, adjacent; in the vicinity of, in the neighbourhood of, within reach of; neighbouring, adjoining, abutting, alongside, on the doorstep, a stone's throw away; nearby, at hand, at close quarters; *informal* within spitting dis-tance. **2** *flying in close formation* =**dense**, compact, tight, solid. **3** *I was close to tears* =**near**, on the verge of, on the brink of, on the point of. **4** *a very close match* =**evenly matched**, even, neck and neck. **5** *close relatives* =**immediate**, direct, near. **6** *close friends* =**intimate**, dear, bosom; close-knit, inseparable, de-voted, faithful; special, good, best, fast, firm; *informal* (as) thick as thieves. **7** *a close resemblance* =**strong**, marked, dis-tinct, pronounced. **8** *a close examination*

=**careful**, detailed, thorough, minute, searching, painstaking, meticulous, rigorous, scrupulous, conscientious. **9** *the weather was close* =**humid**, muggy, stuffy, airless, heavy, sticky, sultry, oppressive, stifling.
−OPPOSITES far, distant, one-sided, slight, fresh.
▶ noun *(Brit.) a small close of houses* =**cul-de-sac**, street; courtyard.

close² ▶ verb **1** *she closed the door* =**shut**, pull to, push to, slam. **2** *close the hole* =**block (up/off)**, stop up, plug, seal (up /off), shut up/off, bung (up); clog (up), choke, obstruct. **3** *the enemy were closing fast* =**catch up**, creep up, near, approach, gain on someone. **4** *the gap is closing* =**narrow**, reduce, shrink, lessen, get smaller, diminish, contract. **5** *his arms closed around her* =**meet**, join, connect; form a circle. **6** *he closed the meeting* =**end**, conclude, finish, terminate, wind up. **7** *the factory is to close* =**shut down**, close down, cease production, cease trading, be wound up, go out of business, go bankrupt, go into receivership, go into liquidation; *informal* fold, go to the wall, go bust. **8** *he closed a deal* =**clinch**, settle, secure, seal, confirm, establish; transact, pull off; complete, conclude, fix, agree, finalize; *informal* wrap up.
−OPPOSITES open, widen, begin.
▶ noun *the close of the talks* =**end**, finish, conclusion.
−OPPOSITES beginning.
■ **close down**. See CLOSE² verb sense 7.

closet ▶ noun *a clothes closet* =**cupboard**, wardrobe, cabinet, locker.
▶ adjective *a closet revolutionary* =**secret**, covert, private; surreptitious, clandestine.
▶ verb *David was closeted in his den* =**shut away**, sequester, seclude, cloister, confine, isolate.

closure ▶ noun =**closing down**, shutdown, winding up.

clot ▶ noun =**lump**, clump, mass; thrombosis; *informal* glob; *Brit. informal* gob.
▶ verb =**coagulate**, set, congeal, thicken, solidify.

> WORD LINKS
> surgical removal of a blood clot: **embolectomy, thrombectomy**

cloth ▶ noun **1** *a maker of cloth* =**fabric**, material, textile(s). **2** *a cloth to wipe the* *table* =**rag**, wipe, duster; flannel, towel; *Austral.* washer. **3** *a gentleman of the cloth* =**the clergy**, the priesthood, the ministry; clergymen, clerics, priests.

> WORD LINKS
> seller of cloth: **clothier, draper**

clothe ▶ verb =**dress**, attire, robe, garb, array, costume, swathe, deck (out), turn out, fit out, rig (out); *informal* get up.

clothes ▶ plural noun =**clothing**, garments, attire, garb, dress, wear, costume; *informal* gear, togs, duds, get-up; *Brit. informal* clobber; *N. Amer. informal* threads; *formal* apparel; *archaic* raiment.

> WORD LINKS
> relating to clothes: **sartorial**
> maker or seller of clothes: **clothier, outfitter, couturier, tailor**

clothing ▶ noun. See CLOTHES.

cloud ▶ noun *a cloud of exhaust smoke* =**mass**, billow; pall, mantle, blanket.
▶ verb **1** *the sand is churned up, clouding the water* =**dirty**, muddy. **2** *anger clouded my judgement* =**confuse**, muddle, obscure.

cloudy ▶ adjective **1** *a cloudy sky* =**overcast**, clouded; dark, grey, black, leaden; murky; sombre, dismal, heavy, gloomy; sunless, starless; hazy, misty, foggy. **2** *cloudy water* =**murky**, muddy, milky, dirty, turbid.
−OPPOSITES clear.

cloven ▶ adjective =**split**, divided, cleft.

clown ▶ noun **1** *the class clown* =**joker**, comedian, comic, wag, wit, jester, buffoon; *Austral./NZ informal* hard case. **2** *bureaucratic clowns* =**fool**, idiot, dolt, ass, simpleton, ignoramus; *informal* moron, numbskull, nincompoop, halfwit, bonehead, fathead, birdbrain; *Brit. informal* prat, berk, twit, nitwit, twerp.
▶ verb *Harvey clowned around* =**fool around/about**, play the fool, play about/around, monkey about/around; joke; *informal* mess about/around, lark (about/around); *Brit. informal* muck about/ around.

cloying ▶ adjective =**sickly**, syrupy, saccharine; sickening, nauseating; mawkish, sentimental, mushy, slushy, sloppy; *Brit.* twee; *informal* over the top, OTT, gooey, cheesy, corny; *N. Amer. informal* cornball, sappy.

club¹ ▶ noun **1** *a canoeing club* =**society**,

association, organization, institution, group, circle, band, body, ring, crew; alliance, league, union. **2** *the city has great clubs* = nightclub, bar; *informal* disco, niterie. **3** *the top club in the league* = team, squad, side.

■ **club together** = pool resources, join forces, team up, band together, get together, pull together, collaborate; *informal* have a whip-round.

club² ▶ noun *a wooden club* = cudgel, truncheon, bludgeon, baton, stick, mace, bat; *N. Amer.* blackjack, nightstick; *Brit. informal* cosh.

▶ verb *he was clubbed with an iron bar* = cudgel, bludgeon, bash, beat, hit, strike, batter, belabour; *informal* clout, clobber; *Brit. informal* cosh.

clue ▶ noun **1** *police are searching for clues* = hint, indication, sign, signal, pointer, trace, indicator; lead, tip; evidence, information. **2** *a crossword clue* = question, problem, puzzle, riddle, poser.

clump ▶ noun **1** *a clump of trees* = cluster, thicket, group, bunch. **2** *a clump of earth* = lump, clod, mass, chunk.

▶ verb **1** *galaxies clump together* = cluster, group, collect, gather, assemble, congregate, mass. **2** *they were clumping around upstairs* = stamp, stomp, clomp, tramp, lumber; thump, bang; *informal* galumph.

clumsy ▶ adjective **1** *she was terribly clumsy* = awkward, uncoordinated, ungainly, graceless, inelegant; inept, maladroit, unskilful, accident-prone, like a bull in a china shop, all fingers and thumbs; *informal* cack-handed, ham fisted, butterfingered, having two left feet; *N. Amer. informal* klutzy. **2** *a clumsy contraption* = unwieldy, cumbersome, bulky, awkward. **3** *a clumsy remark* = gauche, awkward, graceless; unsubtle, crass; tactless, insensitive, thoughtless, undiplomatic, indelicate, ill-judged. –OPPOSITES graceful, elegant, tactful.

cluster ▶ noun **1** *clusters of berries* = bunch, clump, mass, knot, group, clutch. **2** *a cluster of spectators* = crowd, group, knot, huddle, bunch, throng, flock, pack; *informal* gaggle.

▶ verb *they clustered around the television* = congregate, gather, collect, group, assemble; huddle, crowd.

clutch ▶ verb = grip, grasp, clasp, cling to, hang on to, clench, hold, grab.
■ **clutch at** = reach for, snatch at, grab

at, claw at, scrabble for.

clutches ▶ plural noun = power, control; hands, hold, grip, grasp; custody.

clutter ▶ noun = disorder, chaos, disarray, untidiness, mess, confusion; litter, rubbish, junk.

▶ verb = litter, mess up; be strewn, be scattered; cover, bury.

coach¹ ▶ noun **1** *a journey by coach* = bus. **2** *a railway coach* = carriage, wagon, compartment, van, Pullman; *N. Amer.* car.

coach² ▶ noun *a football coach* = instructor, trainer; teacher, tutor, mentor, guru.

▶ verb *he coached Richard in maths* = instruct, teach, tutor, school, educate; drill; train.

coagulate ▶ verb = congeal, clot, thicken, gel; solidify, harden, set, dry.

coal ▶ noun

> **WORD LINKS**
>
> *coal mine:* **colliery**
> *coal miner:* **collier**

coalesce ▶ verb = merge, unite, join/come together, combine, fuse, mingle, blend; amalgamate, consolidate, integrate, converge.

coalition ▶ noun = alliance, union, partnership, bloc, caucus; federation, league, association, confederation, consortium, syndicate, combine; amalgamation, merger.

coarse ▶ adjective **1** *coarse blankets* = rough, scratchy, prickly, wiry, harsh. **2** *his coarse features* = rough, heavy; ugly. **3** *a coarse boy* = oafish, loutish, boorish, uncouth, rude, impolite, ill-mannered; vulgar, common, rough. **4** *a coarse remark* = vulgar, crude, rude, off colour, lewd, smutty, indelicate, improper, unseemly, crass, tasteless.
–OPPOSITES soft, delicate, refined.

coarsen ▶ verb **1** *hands coarsened by work* = roughen, toughen, harden, callus. **2** *I had been coarsened by the army* = desensitize, dehumanize, harden; dull, deaden.
–OPPOSITES soften, refine.

coast ▶ noun *the west coast* = seaboard, coastline, seashore, shore, shoreline, seaside, waterfront.

▶ verb *the car coasted down a hill* = freewheel, cruise, taxi, drift, glide, sail.

c

WORD LINKS

relating to a coast: **littoral**

coat ▸ noun **1** *a winter coat* =overcoat, raincoat; parka, jacket. **2** *a dog's coat* =fur, hair, wool, fleece; hide, pelt, skin. **3** *a coat of paint* =layer, covering, coating, skin, film, wash; glaze, veneer, patina; deposit.
▸ verb *the tube was coated with wax* =cover, paint, glaze, varnish; surface, veneer, laminate, plate, face; daub, smear, cake, plaster.

coating ▸ noun. See COAT *noun sense 3.*

coax ▸ verb =persuade, wheedle, cajole, get round; beguile, seduce, inveigle, manoeuvre; *informal* sweet-talk, softsoap, butter up, twist someone's arm.

cobble ■ **cobble something together** =throw/fling together; improvise, contrive, rig (up), whip up; *informal* rustle up; *Brit. informal* knock up.

cock ▸ noun =rooster, cockerel, capon.
▸ verb **1** *he cocked his head* =tilt, tip, angle, incline, dip. **2** *she cocked her little finger* =bend, flex, crook, curve. **3** *the dog cocked its leg* =lift, raise, hold up.

cock-eyed ▸ adjective *(informal)* **1** *that picture is cock-eyed* =crooked, awry, askew, lopsided, tilted, off-centre, skewed, skew, squint, misaligned; *Brit. informal* skew-whiff, wonky. **2** *a cock-eyed scheme* =absurd, ridiculous, idiotic, stupid, foolish, silly, half-baked, hare-brained; *informal* crazy; *Brit. informal* barmy, daft.

cocksure ▸ adjective =arrogant, conceited, overconfident, cocky, proud, vain, self-important, swollen-headed, egotistical, presumptuous.
–OPPOSITES modest.

cocky ▸ adjective =arrogant, conceited, overconfident, cocksure, swollen-headed, self-important, egotistical, presumptuous, boastful.
–OPPOSITES modest.

cocoon ▸ verb =protect, shield, shelter, screen, cushion, insulate, isolate, cloister.

coddle ▸ verb =pamper, cosset, mollycoddle, spoil, indulge, overindulge, pander to; mother, wait on hand and foot.
–OPPOSITES neglect.

code ▸ noun **1** *a secret code* =cipher. **2** *a strict social code* =convention, etiquette, protocol, ethic. **3** *the penal code* =law(s),

rules, regulations; constitution, system.

WORD LINKS

study of codes: **cryptology**
writing or cracking of codes: **cryptography**
writer or cracker of codes: **cryptographer**
put into code: **encipher, encode, encrypt**
solve a code: **decipher, decrypt, crack**

codify ▸ verb =systematize, organize, arrange, order, structure; tabulate, catalogue, list, sort, index, classify, categorize, file, log.

coerce ▸ verb =pressure, pressurize, press, push, constrain; force, compel, oblige, browbeat, bludgeon, bully, threaten, intimidate, dragoon, twist someone's arm; *informal* railroad, squeeze, steamroller, lean on.

coercion ▸ noun =force, compulsion, constraint, duress, oppression, enforcement, harassment, intimidation, threats, arm-twisting, pressure.

coffer ▸ noun =fund(s), reserves, resources, money, finances, wealth, capital, purse.

coffin ▸ noun =sarcophagus; *N. Amer.* casket; *informal* box; *humorous* wooden overcoat.

cogent ▸ adjective =convincing, compelling, strong, forceful, powerful, potent, effective; valid, sound, plausible, telling; impressive, persuasive, eloquent, credible; conclusive; logical, reasoned, rational, reasonable, lucid, coherent, clear.

cognition ▸ noun =perception, discernment, apprehension, learning, understanding, comprehension, insight; reasoning, thinking, thought.

cognizance ▸ noun *(formal)*. See AWARENESS.

cognizant ▸ adjective *(formal)*. See AWARE *sense 1.*

coherent ▸ adjective =logical, reasoned, rational, sound, cogent, consistent; clear, lucid, articulate; intelligible, comprehensible.
–OPPOSITES muddled.

cohesion ▸ noun =unity, togetherness, solidarity, bond, coherence; connection, linkage.

coil ▸ noun =loop, twist, turn, curl; spiral.

▶ verb =**wind**, loop, twist, curl, twine, wrap.

coin ▶ verb *he coined the term* =**invent**, create, make up, conceive, originate, think up, dream up.

> **WORD LINKS**
>
> *relating to coins:* **numismatic**
> *collector of coins:* **numismatist**

coincide ▶ verb **1** *the events coincided* =**occur simultaneously**, happen together, co-occur, coexist. **2** *their interests do not always coincide* =**tally**, correspond, agree, accord, match up, fit, be consistent, be compatible, dovetail, mesh; *informal* square.
  –OPPOSITES differ.

coincidence ▶ noun =**accident**, chance, serendipity, providence, happenstance, fate, luck; fortune; a fluke.

coincidental ▶ adjective =**accidental**, chance, fluky, random; fortuitous, adventitious, serendipitous.

coitus ▶ noun *(technical).* See SEX noun sense 1.

cold ▶ adjective **1** *a cold day* =**chilly**, chill, cool, freezing, icy, snowy, wintry, frosty, frigid; bitter, biting, raw; *informal* nippy, arctic; *Brit. informal* parky. **2** *I'm cold* =**freezing**, frozen, numb; chilly, cool. **3** *a cold reception* =**unfriendly**, inhospitable, unwelcoming, cool, frigid, frosty; distant, formal, stiff.
  –OPPOSITES hot, warm.

> **WORD LINKS**
>
> *relating to cold:* **cryo-**
> *fear of cold:* **cheimaphobia**

cold-blooded ▶ adjective =**cruel**, callous, sadistic, inhuman, inhumane, pitiless, merciless, ruthless, unfeeling, uncaring, heartless.

cold-hearted ▶ adjective =**unfeeling**, unloving, uncaring, unsympathetic, unemotional, unfriendly, uncharitable, unkind, insensitive; hard-hearted, stony-hearted, heartless, hard, cold.

collaborate ▶ verb **1** *they collaborated on the project* =**cooperate**, join forces, work together, combine; pool resources, club together. **2** *they collaborated with the enemy* =**fraternize**, conspire, collude, cooperate, consort.

collaborator ▶ noun **1** *his collaborator on the book* =**co-worker**, partner, associate, colleague, confederate; assistant.

2 *a wartime collaborator* =**sympathizer**; traitor, quisling, fifth columnist.

collapse ▶ verb **1** *the roof collapsed* =**cave in**, fall in, subside, fall down, give (way), crumple, crumble, disintegrate. **2** *he collapsed last night* =**faint**, pass out, black out, lose consciousness, keel over; *informal* flake out, conk out. **3** *she collapsed in tears* =**break down**; go to pieces, be overcome; *informal* crack up. **4** *peace talks collapsed* =**break down**, fail, fall through, fold, founder; *informal* flop, fizzle out.
▶ noun **1** *the collapse of the roof* =**cave-in**, disintegration. **2** *the collapse of the talks* =**breakdown**, failure.

collar ▶ noun *a collar round the pipe* =**ring**, band, sleeve, flange.
▶ verb *(informal)* **1** *he collared a thief* =**apprehend**, arrest, catch, capture, seize; *informal* nab, pick up, pull in, feel someone's collar; *Brit. informal* nick. **2** *she collared me in the street* =**accost**, waylay, approach, detain, stop, halt, catch, confront, importune; *informal* buttonhole; *Brit. informal* nobble.

collate ▶ verb =**collect**, gather, accumulate, assemble; combine, put together; arrange, organize.

collateral ▶ noun =**security**, surety, guarantee, insurance, indemnity; backing.

colleague ▶ noun =**co-worker**, fellow worker, workmate, teammate, associate, partner, collaborator, ally, confederate; *Brit. informal* oppo.

collect ▶ verb **1** *he collected the rubbish* –**gather**, accumulate, assemble; amass, stockpile, pile up, heap up, store (up), hoard, save; mass, accrue. **2** *a crowd soon collected* =**gather**, assemble, meet, muster, congregate, convene, converge. **3** *I must collect the children* =**fetch**, pick up, go/come and get, call for, meet. **4** *they collect money for charity* =**raise**, ask for, solicit; obtain, acquire, gather.
  –OPPOSITES disperse, distribute.

collected ▶ adjective =**calm**, cool, self-possessed, self-controlled, composed, poised; serene, tranquil, relaxed, unruffled, unperturbed, untroubled; placid, quiet, sedate, phlegmatic; *informal* unfazed, laid-back.
  –OPPOSITES excited, hysterical.

collection ▶ noun **1** *a collection of stolen items* =**hoard**, pile, heap, stack, stock, store, stockpile; accumulation, reserve, supply, bank, pool, fund, mine, reservoir; *informal* stash. **2** *a collection of shoppers* =**group**, crowd, body, gathering; knot, cluster. **3** *his collection of Victorian dolls* =**array**, display; hoard. **4** *a collection of short stories* =**anthology**, selection, compendium, compilation, miscellany. **5** *a collection for famine relief* =**appeal**; *informal* whip-round.

collective ▸ adjective =**common**, shared, joint, combined, mutual, communal, pooled; united, allied, cooperative, collaborative.
−OPPOSITES individual.

college ▸ noun =**school**, academy, university, institute.

collide ▸ verb *the train collided with a lorry* =**crash**; hit, strike, run into, bump into, meet head-on.

collision ▸ noun **1** *a collision on the ring road* =**crash**, accident, smash; *Brit.* RTA (road traffic accident); *N. Amer.* wreck; *informal* pile-up; *Brit. informal* shunt. **2** *a collision between two ideas* =**conflict**, clash.

colloquial ▸ adjective =**informal**, conversational, everyday; unofficial, idiomatic, slangy, vernacular, popular, demotic.
−OPPOSITES formal.

collude ▸ verb =**conspire**, connive, collaborate, plot, scheme; *informal* be in cahoots.

colon ▸ noun

WORD LINKS

surgical removal of colon: **colectomy**
surgical opening of colon: **colostomy**

colonize ▸ verb =**settle (in)**, people, populate; occupy, take over, invade.

colony ▸ noun **1** *a French colony* =**territory**, dependency, protectorate, satellite, settlement, outpost, province. **2** *the British colony in New York* =**population**, community. **3** *an artists' colony* =**community**, commune; quarter, district, ghetto.

colossal ▸ adjective =**huge**, massive, enormous, gigantic, giant, mammoth, vast, immense, monumental, prodigious, mountainous, titanic, towering, king-size(d); *informal* monster, whopping, humongous, jumbo; *Brit. informal* ginormous.
−OPPOSITES tiny.

colour ▸ noun **1** *the lights changed colour* =**hue**, shade, tint, tone; coloration. **2** *oil*

colour =**paint**, pigment, colourant, dye, stain. **3** *the colour in her cheeks* =**redness**, pinkness, rosiness, ruddiness, blush, flush, bloom, glow, radiance. **4** *people of every colour* =**race**, ethnic group. **5** *anecdotes add colour to the text* =**vividness**, life, liveliness, vitality, excitement, interest, richness, zest, spice, piquancy, impact, immediacy; *informal* oomph, pizzazz, punch, kick. **6** *the colours of the Oxford City club* =**strip**, kit, uniform, costume, livery, regalia. **7** *the regimental colours.* See FLAG[1] noun.

▸ verb **1** *the wood was coloured blue* =**tint**, dye, stain, paint, bleach. **2** *she coloured with embarrassment* =**blush**, redden, go pink, go red, flush. **3** *the experience coloured her outlook* =**influence**, affect, taint, warp, skew, distort.

WORD LINKS

relating to colour: **chromatic**
fear of colour: **chromophobia**
measurement of colour: **colorimetry**

colourful ▸ adjective **1** *a colourful picture* =**brightly coloured**, vivid, vibrant, brilliant, radiant, rich; gaudy, glaring, garish; multicoloured, multicolour, rainbow, psychedelic; *informal* jazzy. **2** *a colourful account* =**vivid**, graphic, lively, animated, dramatic, fascinating, interesting, stimulating, scintillating, evocative.

colourless ▸ adjective **1** *a colourless liquid* =**transparent**, clear; translucent. **2** *her colourless face* =**pale**, pallid, wan, anaemic, bloodless, ashen, white, waxen, pasty, sickly, drained, drawn, ghostly, deathly.
−OPPOSITES colourful, rosy.

column ▸ noun **1** *arches supported by massive columns* =**pillar**, post, support, upright, pier, pile, pilaster, stanchion. **2** *a column in the paper* =**article**, piece, feature, review, editorial, leader. **3** *we walked in a column* =**line**, file, queue, procession, train, convoy; *informal* crocodile.

columnist ▸ noun =**writer**, contributor, journalist, correspondent, newspaperman, newspaperwoman, newsman, newswoman; wordsmith; critic, reviewer, commentator; *informal* scribbler, hack, journo.

comatose ▸ adjective =**unconscious**, in a coma, insensible.

comb ▸ verb **1** *she combed her hair* =**groom**, brush, untangle, smooth, straighten, neaten, tidy, arrange. **2** *police combed the area* =**search**, scour, explore, sweep, examine, check.

combat ▸ noun *he was killed in combat* =**battle**, fighting, action, hostilities, conflict, war, warfare.
▸ verb *they tried to combat the disease* =**fight**, battle, tackle, attack, counter, resist; impede, block; stop, halt, prevent, check, curb.

combative ▸ adjective =**pugnacious**, aggressive, antagonistic, quarrelsome, argumentative, hostile, truculent, belligerent; *informal* spoiling for a fight.
−OPPOSITES conciliatory.

combination ▸ noun =**amalgamation**, amalgam, merger, blend, mixture, mix, fusion, marriage, coalition, integration, incorporation, synthesis, composite.

combine ▸ verb **1** *he combines comedy with tragedy* =**amalgamate**, integrate, incorporate, merge, mix, fuse, blend; join, marry. **2** *teachers combined to tackle the problem* =**unite**, collaborate, join forces, get together, team up.

combustible ▸ adjective =**inflammable**, flammable.

come ▸ verb **1** *come and listen* =**approach**, advance, draw close/closer, draw near/nearer. **2** *they came last night* =**arrive**, get here/there, make it, appear, come on the scene; turn up, materialize; *informal* show (up), roll in/up. **3** *they came to a stream* =**reach**, arrive at, get to; come across, run across, happen on, chance on, come upon, stumble on; end up at; *informal* wind up at. **4** *the dress comes to her ankles* =**extend**, stretch, reach, hang. **5** *she comes from Belgium* =**be from**, be a native of, hail from, originate in; live in, reside in. **6** *attacks came without warning* =**happen**, occur, take place, come about, fall, present itself, crop up, materialize, arise, arrive, appear.
−OPPOSITES go, leave.

■ **come about** =**happen**, occur, take place, transpire, fall; arise; *literary* come to pass.

■ **come across** *they came across his friends* =**meet**, run into, run across, come upon, chance on, stumble on, happen on; discover, encounter, find; *informal* bump into.

■ **come along 1** *the puppies are coming along nicely* =**progress**, develop, shape

up; come on, turn out; improve, get better, pick up, rally, recover. **2** *Come along!* =**hurry (up)**, be quick, get a move on, look lively, speed up, move faster; *informal* get moving, get cracking, step on it, move it, buck up, shake a leg, make it snappy; *Brit. informal* get your skates on; *N. Amer. informal* get a wiggle on; *dated* make haste.

■ **come apart** =**break up**, fall to bits, fall to pieces, disintegrate, come unstuck, separate, split, tear.

■ **come between** =**alienate**, estrange, separate, divide, split up, break up, disunite, set at odds.

■ **come by** =**obtain**, acquire, gain, get, find, pick up, procure, secure; buy, purchase; *informal* get one's hands on, get hold of, bag, score, swing.

■ **come in for** =**receive**, experience, sustain, undergo, go through, encounter, face, be subjected to, bear, suffer.

■ **come on** =**progress**, develop, shape up, take shape, come along, turn out; improve.

■ **come round 1** *Friday the 13th comes round every few months* =**occur**, take place, happen, come up, crop up, arise; recur, reoccur, return, reappear. **2** *come round for a drink* =**visit**, call (in/round), look in, stop by, drop by/in/round/over, come over; *informal* pop in/round/over.

■ **come to 1** *the bill came to £17.50* =**amount to**, add up to, run to, total, equal. **2** *I came to in the hospital* =**regain consciousness**, come round, awake, wake up.

■ **come up with** =**produce**, devise, think up; propose, put forward, submit, suggest, recommend, advocate, introduce.

comeback ▸ noun =**return**, recovery, resurgence, rally, upturn; *Brit.* fightback.

comedian ▸ noun **1** *a famous comedian* =**comic**, comedienne, funny man/woman, humorist, gagster, stand-up; *N. Amer.* tummler. **2** *Dad was such a comedian* =**joker**, wit, wag, comic, clown; *informal* laugh, hoot, case.

comedienne ▸ noun. *See* COMEDIAN *sense 1.*

comedy ▸ noun *the comedy in their work* =**humour**, funny side, laughs, jokes.
−OPPOSITES tragedy.

comfort ▸ noun **1** *travel in comfort* =**ease**, repose; luxury, prosperity. **2** *words of comfort* =**consolation**, condolence, sympathy, commiseration; sup-

comfortable | commensurate

▶ verb *a friend tried to comfort her* =**console**; support, reassure, soothe, calm; cheer, hearten.
–OPPOSITES distress, depress.

comfortable ▶ adjective **1** *a comfortable lifestyle* =**pleasant**; affluent, well-to-do, luxurious, opulent. **2** *a comfortable room* =**cosy**, snug, warm, pleasant, agreeable; restful, homely; *informal* comfy. **3** *comfortable clothes* =**loose**, casual; *informal* comfy. **4** *a comfortable pace* =**leisurely**, unhurried, relaxed, easy, gentle, sedate, undemanding, slow; *informal* laid-back. **5** *they feel comfortable with each other* =**at ease**, relaxed, secure, safe, contented, happy.
–OPPOSITES hard, spartan, tense.

comforting ▶ adjective =**soothing**, reassuring, calming; heartening, cheering.

comic ▶ adjective =**humorous**, funny, amusing, hilarious; comical; zany; witty.
–OPPOSITES serious.
▶ noun =**comedian**, comedienne, funny man/woman, humorist, wit; joker.

comical ▶ adjective **1** *he could be quite comical* =**funny**, humorous, droll, witty, amusing, entertaining; *informal* wacky, waggish. **2** *they look comical in those suits* =**silly**, absurd, ridiculous, laughable, ludicrous, preposterous, foolish; *informal* crazy.
–OPPOSITES sensible.

coming ▶ adjective *the coming election* =**forthcoming**, imminent, impending, approaching.
▶ noun *the coming of spring* =**approach**, advance, advent, arrival, appearance, emergence, onset.

command ▶ verb **1** *he commanded his men to retreat* =**order**, tell, direct, instruct, call on, require. **2** *Jones commanded a tank squadron* =**be in charge of**, be in command of; head, lead, control, direct, manage, supervise, oversee; *informal* head up.
▶ noun **1** *officers shouted commands* =**order**, instruction, direction. **2** *he had 160 men under his command* =**authority**, control, charge, power, direction, dominion, guidance; leadership, rule, government, management, supervision, jurisdiction. **3** *a brilliant command of English* =**knowledge**, mastery, grasp, comprehension, understanding.

commandeer ▶ verb =**seize**, take, requisition, appropriate, expropriate, sequestrate, sequester, confiscate, annex, take over, claim; hijack, help oneself to; *informal* walk off with.

commander ▶ noun =**leader**, head, chief, overseer, controller; commander-in-chief, C.-in-C., commanding officer, CO, officer; *informal* boss, boss man, skipper, numero uno, number one, top dog, kingpin, head honcho; *Brit. informal* gaffer, guv'nor.

commanding ▶ adjective **1** *a commanding position* =**dominant**, superior, powerful, prominent, advantageous, favourable. **2** *a commanding voice* =**authoritative**, masterful, assertive, firm, emphatic.

commemorate ▶ verb =**celebrate**, pay tribute to, pay homage to, honour, salute, toast; remember, recognize, acknowledge, observe, mark.

commence ▶ verb =**begin**, start; get the ball rolling, get going, get under way, get off the ground, set about, embark on, launch into; open, initiate, inaugurate; *informal* kick off, get the show on the road.
–OPPOSITES conclude.

commencement ▶ noun =**beginning**, start, opening, outset, onset, launch, inception; *informal* kick-off.

commend ▶ verb **1** *we should commend him* =**praise**, compliment, congratulate, applaud, salute, honour; sing the praises of, pay tribute to, take one's hat off to, pat on the back. **2** *I commend her to you without reservation* =**recommend**; endorse, vouch for, speak for, support, back. **3** *(formal) I commend them to your care* =**entrust**, trust, deliver, commit, hand over, give, turn over, consign, assign.
–OPPOSITES criticize.

commendable ▶ adjective =**admirable**, praiseworthy, creditable, laudable, estimable, meritorious, exemplary, noteworthy, honourable, respectable, fine, excellent.
–OPPOSITES reprehensible.

commendation ▶ noun **1** *letters of commendation* =**praise**, congratulation, appreciation; recognition, tribute. **2** *a commendation for bravery* =**award**, prize, honour, citation.

commensurate ▶ adjective *a salary commensurate with your qualifications* =**appropriate to**, in keeping with, in line with, consistent with, corresponding to, according to, relative to; dependent on, based on.

comment ▸ noun **1** *their comments on her appearance* =**remark**, observation, statement; pronouncement, judgement, reflection, opinion, view; criticism. **2** *a great deal of comment* =**discussion**, debate; interest. **3** *a comment in the margin* =**note**, annotation, footnote, gloss, explanation.
▸ verb **1** *they commented on the food* =**remark on**, speak about, talk about, discuss, mention. **2** '*It will soon be night,*' *he commented* =**remark**, observe, say, state, declare, announce.

commentary ▸ noun **1** *the test match commentary* =**narration**, description, report, review. **2** *textual commentary* =**explanation**, elucidation, interpretation, exegesis, analysis; assessment, appraisal, criticism; notes, comments.

commentator ▸ noun **1** *a television commentator* =**narrator**, announcer, presenter, anchor, anchorman, anchorwoman; reporter, journalist, newscaster, sportscaster. **2** *a political commentator* =**analyst**, pundit, monitor, observer.

commerce ▸ noun =**trade**, trading, business, dealing, traffic; (financial) transactions, dealings.

commercial ▸ adjective **1** *a vessel built for commercial purposes* =**trade**, trading, business, private enterprise, mercantile, sales. **2** *we turn good ideas into commercial products* =**lucrative**, moneymaking, money-spinning, profitable, remunerative, fruitful; viable, successful.
▸ noun *a TV commercial* =**advertisement**, promotion, display; *informal* ad, plug; *Brit. informal* advert.

commercialized ▸ adjective =**profit-orientated**, money-orientated, commercial, materialistic, mercenary.

commiserate ▸ verb –**sympathize**, empathize; (**commiserate with**) offer sympathy to, offer condolences to, comfort, console.

commiseration ▸ noun =**condolence(s)**, sympathy, pity.

commission ▸ noun **1** *the dealer's commission* =**percentage**, share, portion, dividend, premium, fee, bonus; *informal* cut, take, rake-off, slice; *Brit. informal* whack, divvy. **2** *a commission to design a monument* =**contract**, engagement, assignment, booking; appointment, job. **3** *an independent commission* =**committee**, board, council, panel, body.
▸ verb **1** *he was commissioned to paint a portrait* =**engage**, contract, charge, employ, hire, recruit, retain, appoint, enlist, co-opt, book, sign up. **2** *they commissioned a sculpture* =**order**; authorize.
■ **out of commission** =**not in service**, not in use, unserviceable; not working, inoperative, out of order; broken (down); *informal* knackered.

commit ▸ verb **1** *he committed a murder* =**carry out**, do, perpetrate, engage in, execute, accomplish; be responsible for; *informal* pull off. **2** *she was committed to their care* =**entrust**, consign, assign, deliver, give, hand over, relinquish; *formal* commend. **3** *they committed themselves to the project* =**pledge**, devote, apply, give, dedicate. **4** *the judge committed him to prison* =**consign**, send, deliver, confine.

commitment ▸ noun **1** *the pressure of his commitments* =**responsibility**, obligation, duty, tie, liability; task; engagement, arrangement. **2** *her commitment to her students* =**dedication**, devotion, allegiance, loyalty, faithfulness, fidelity. **3** *he made a commitment* =**vow**, promise, pledge, oath; contract, pact, deal; decision, resolution.

committed ▸ adjective =**devout**, devoted, dedicated, loyal, faithful, staunch, firm, steadfast, unwavering, wholehearted, keen, passionate, ardent, fervent, sworn; *informal* card-carrying, true blue.
–OPPOSITES apathetic.

commodity ▸ noun –**item**, material, product, article, object; import, export.

common ▸ adjective **1** *the common people* =**ordinary**, normal, average, unexceptional; simple. **2** *a very common occurrence* =**usual**, ordinary, familiar, regular, frequent, recurrent, everyday; standard, typical, conventional, commonplace. **3** *a common belief* =**widespread**, general, universal, popular, mainstream, prevalent, prevailing, rife, established, conventional, traditional, orthodox, accepted. **4** *the common good* =**collective**, communal, community, public, popular, general; shared, combined. **5** *they are far too common* =**uncouth**, vulgar, coarse, rough, unladylike, ungentlemanly, uncivilized, unsophisticated, unrefined; lowly, inferior, proletarian, plebeian; *informal* plebby.

–OPPOSITES unusual, rare, individual, refined.

commonly ▸ adverb =often, frequently, regularly, repeatedly, time and (time) again, all the time, routinely, habitually, customarily; N. Amer. oftentimes; informal lots.

commonplace ▸ adjective **1** a commonplace occurrence =**common**, normal, usual, ordinary, familiar, routine, standard, everyday, daily, regular, frequent, habitual, typical. **2** a commonplace writing style =**ordinary**, run-of-the-mill, unremarkable, unexceptional, average, mediocre, pedestrian, prosaic, lacklustre, dull, bland, uninteresting, mundane; hackneyed, trite, banal, clichéd, predictable, stale, tired, unoriginal; informal bog-standard, a dime a dozen; Brit. informal common or garden; N. Amer. informal ornery, bush-league.
–OPPOSITES original, unusual.

common sense ▸ noun =**sensibleness**, (good) sense, (native) wit, judgement, level-headedness, prudence, discernment, canniness, astuteness, shrewdness, wisdom, insight, perception; practicality, capability, resourcefulness, enterprise; informal horse sense, gumption, nous, savvy; Brit. informal common; N. Amer. informal smarts.
–OPPOSITES folly.

commotion ▸ noun =**disturbance**, uproar, tumult, rumpus, ruckus, furore, hue and cry, fuss, stir, storm; turmoil, disorder, confusion, chaos, mayhem, havoc, pandemonium; unrest, fracas, riot; Irish, N. Amer., & Austral. donnybrook; informal ruction(s), ballyhoo, kerfuffle, hoo-ha, to-do, hullabaloo; Brit. informal carry-on, row, aggro, argy-bargy.

communal ▸ adjective **1** a communal kitchen =**shared**, joint, common. **2** they farm on a communal basis =**collective**, cooperative, community.
–OPPOSITES private, individual.

commune ▸ noun she lives in a commune =**collective**, cooperative, kibbutz.
▸ verb =**bond**, identify, empathize, have a rapport, feel at one; relate to, feel close to.

communicable ▸ adjective =**contagious**, infectious, transmittable, transmissible, transferable, spreadable; informal catching.

communicate ▸ verb **1** he communicated the news to his boss =**convey**, tell, impart, relay, transmit, pass on, announce, report, recount, relate, present; divulge, disclose, mention; spread, disseminate, broadcast. **2** they communicate daily =**liaise**, be in touch, be in contact, have dealings, interface, commune, meet; talk, speak. **3** learn how to communicate better =**get one's message across**, explain oneself, express oneself, make oneself understood, get through to someone. **4** the disease is communicated easily =**transmit**, transfer, spread, carry, pass on.

communication ▸ noun **1** the communication of news =**transmission**, divulgence, disclosure; dissemination, promulgation, broadcasting. **2** there was no communication between them =**contact**, dealings, relations, connection, association, socializing, intercourse; correspondence, dialogue, talk, conversation, discussion; dated commerce. **3** an official communication =**message**, statement, announcement, report, dispatch, communiqué, letter, bulletin, correspondence. **4** road and rail communications =**links**, connections; services, routes; systems, networks.

communicative ▸ adjective =**forthcoming**, expansive, expressive, unreserved, uninhibited, vocal, outgoing, frank, open, candid; talkative, chatty, loquacious; informal gabby.

communion ▸ noun =**affinity**, fellowship, kinship, friendship, fellow feeling, togetherness, closeness, harmony, understanding, rapport, connection, communication, empathy, accord, unity.

communiqué ▸ noun =(official) **communication**, press release, bulletin, message, missive, dispatch, statement, report, announcement, declaration, proclamation; N. Amer. advisory; informal memo.

communism ▸ noun =**collectivism**, state ownership; Bolshevism, Marxism, Maoism.

communist ▸ noun & adjective =**collectivist**, leftist; Bolshevik, Bolshevist, Marxist, Maoist; informal, derogatory Commie, Bolshie, red, lefty; dated East European, Soviet.

community ▸ noun **1** work done for the community =**population**, populace, people, citizenry, (general) public; residents, inhabitants, citizens. **2** a monastic community =**brotherhood**, sisterhood, fraternity, sorority; colony, order. **3** *community of interests* =**similarity**, likeness, comparability, correspondence, agreement, closeness, affinity.

commute ▶ verb **1** *they commute by train* =**go to work**, travel to work. **2** *his sentence was commuted* =**reduce**, lessen, lighten, shorten, cut.
−OPPOSITES increase.

compact[1] ▶ adjective =**neat**, small, handy, petite; fiddly; pocket size, mini; *Scottish* wee; *Brit. informal* dinky.
−OPPOSITES bulky.
▶ verb =**compress**, condense, pack down, press down, tamp (down), flatten.

compact[2] ▶ noun *the warring states signed a compact* =**treaty**, pact, accord, agreement, contract, bargain, deal, settlement, covenant, concordat.

companion ▶ noun **1** *Harry and his companion* =**associate**, partner, escort, compatriot, confederate; friend, intimate, confidant(e), comrade; *informal* pal, chum, crony, sidekick; *Brit. informal* mate; *N. Amer. informal* buddy; *Austral./NZ informal* offsider. **2** *the tape is a companion to the book* =**complement**; accompaniment, supplement, addition, adjunct, accessory. **3** *The Gardener's Companion* =**handbook**, manual, guide, reference book, ABC, primer; *informal* bible.

companionable ▶ adjective =**friendly**, affable, cordial, genial, congenial, amiable, easy-going, good-natured; sociable, convivial, outgoing, gregarious; *informal* chummy, pally; *Brit. informal* matey; *N. Amer. informal* clubby.

companionship ▶ noun =**friendship**, fellowship, closeness, togetherness, amity, intimacy, rapport, camaraderie, brotherhood, sisterhood.

company ▶ noun **1** *an oil company* =**firm**, business, corporation, establishment, agency, office, bureau, institution, organization, concern, enterprise; conglomerate, consortium, syndicate, multinational; *informal* outfit. **2** *I enjoy his company* =**companionship**, friendship, fellowship; society. **3** *I'm expecting company* =**guests**, visitors, callers, people; someone. **4** *a company of poets* =**group**, crowd, party, band, assembly, troupe, throng; *informal* bunch, gang. **5** *a company of infantry* =**unit**, section, detachment, corps, squad, platoon.

comparable ▶ adjective **1** *comparable*

incomes =**similar**, close, near, approximate, equivalent, commensurate, proportional, proportionate; like, matching. **2** *nobody is comparable with him* =**equal to**, as good as, in the same league as, able to hold a candle to, on a par with, on a level with; a match for.

compare ▶ verb **1** *we compared the two portraits* =**contrast**; examine, assess, weigh up. **2** *he was compared to Wagner* =**liken**, equate; class with, bracket with. **3** *the porcelain compares with Dresden china* =**be as good as**, be comparable to, bear comparison with, be the equal of, match up to, be on a par with, be in the same league as, come close to, hold a candle to; match, resemble, rival, approach.
■ **beyond compare** =**without equal**, second to none, in a class of one's own; peerless, matchless, unmatched, incomparable, inimitable, outstanding, consummate, unique, singular, perfect.

comparison ▶ noun *there's no comparison between them* =**resemblance**, likeness, similarity, correspondence.

compartment ▶ noun =**section**, part, recess, chamber, cavity; pocket.

compartmentalize ▶ verb =**categorize**, pigeonhole, bracket, group, classify, characterize, stereotype, label, brand; sort, rank, rate.

compass ▶ noun =**scope**, range, extent, reach, span, breadth, ambit, limits, parameters, bounds.

compassion ▶ noun =**pity**, sympathy, empathy, fellow feeling, care, concern, solicitude, sensitivity, warmth, love, tenderness, mercy, leniency, tolerance, kindness, humanity, charity.
−OPPOSITES indifference, cruelty.

compassionate ▶ adjective =**sympathetic**, empathetic, understanding, caring, sensitive, warm, loving; merciful, lenient, tolerant, considerate, kind, humane, charitable, big-hearted.

compatibility ▶ noun =**like-mindedness**, similarity, affinity, closeness, fellow feeling, harmony, rapport, empathy, sympathy.

compatible ▶ adjective =**(well) suited**, well matched, like-minded, in tune, in harmony; *informal* on the same wavelength.

compatriot ▶ noun =**(fellow) countryman/woman**, comrade, countryman, countrywoman, fellow citizen.

compel ▸ verb =force, pressurize, pressure, press, push; oblige, require, make; *informal* lean on, put the screws on.

compelling ▸ adjective **1** *a compelling performance* =enthralling, captivating, gripping, riveting, spellbinding, mesmerizing, absorbing. **2** *a compelling argument* =convincing, persuasive, cogent, irresistible, powerful, strong.
−OPPOSITES boring, weak.

compendium ▸ noun =collection, compilation, anthology, digest.

compensate ▸ verb **1** *we agreed to compensate him for his loss* =recompense, repay, pay back, reimburse, remunerate, recoup, indemnify. **2** *his flair compensated for his faults* =balance (out), counterbalance, counteract, offset, make up for, cancel out.

compensation ▸ noun =recompense, repayment, reimbursement, remuneration, indemnification, indemnity, redress; damages; *N. Amer. informal* comp.

compère ▸ noun =host, presenter, anchor, anchorman/woman, master of ceremonies, MC, announcer; *N. Amer. informal* emcee.

compete ▸ verb **1** *they competed in a tennis tournament* =take part, participate, play, be involved; enter, go in for. **2** *they had to compete with other firms* =contend, vie, battle, jockey, go head to head, pit oneself against; challenge, take on. **3** *no one can compete with him* =rival, challenge, keep up with, keep pace with, compare with, match, be in the same league as, come near to, come close to, touch; *informal* hold a candle to.

competence ▸ noun **1** *my technical competence* =capability, ability, competency, proficiency, accomplishment, expertise, skill, prowess, talent; *informal* savvy, know-how. **2** *the competence of the system* =adequacy, suitability, fitness; effectiveness; *formal* efficacy. **3** *matters within the competence of the courts* =authority, power, control, jurisdiction, ambit, scope, remit.

competent ▸ adjective **1** *a competent carpenter* =capable, able, proficient, adept, accomplished, complete, skilful, skilled, gifted, talented, expert; good. **2** *the court was not competent to hear the case* =fit, suitable, suited, appropriate; qualified, empowered, authorized.
−OPPOSITES inadequate, unfit.

competition ▸ noun **1** *Stephanie won the competition* =contest, tournament, match, game, heat, fixture, event; trial. **2** *I'm not interested in competition* =rivalry, competitiveness; conflict; *informal* keeping up with the Joneses. **3** *we must stay ahead of the competition* =opposition, other side, field; enemy; *informal* other guy; *literary* foe.

competitive ▸ adjective **1** *a competitive player* =ambitious, zealous, keen, combative, aggressive; *informal* go-ahead. **2** *a highly competitive industry* =ruthless, aggressive, fierce; *informal* dog-eat-dog, cut-throat. **3** *competitive prices* =reasonable, moderate, keen; low, inexpensive, cheap, budget, bargain; rock-bottom, bargain-basement.
−OPPOSITES apathetic, exorbitant.

competitor ▸ noun **1** *the competitors in the race* =contestant, contender, challenger, participant, entrant; runner, player. **2** *our European competitors* =rival, challenger, opponent, adversary; competition, opposition.
−OPPOSITES ally.

compilation ▸ noun =collection, selection, anthology, compendium, corpus.

compile ▸ verb =assemble, put together, make up, collate, compose, organize, arrange; gather, collect.

complacency ▸ noun =smugness, self-satisfaction, self-congratulation, self-regard.

complacent ▸ adjective =smug, self-satisfied, self-congratulatory, self-regarding.

complain ▸ verb =protest, grumble, whine, bleat, carp, cavil, grouse, make a fuss, object, speak out, criticize, find fault; *informal* whinge, gripe, bellyache, moan, beef, bitch, sound off; *Brit. informal* create; *N. Amer. informal* kvetch.

complaint ▸ noun **1** *they lodged a complaint* =protest, objection, grievance, grouse, quibble, grumble; charge, accusation, allegation, criticism; *informal* beef, gripe, whinge. **2** *a kidney complaint* =disorder, disease, infection, illness, ailment, sickness; condition, problem, upset, trouble; *informal* bug, virus.

complement ▸ noun **1** *the perfect complement to the food* =accompaniment, companion, addition, supplement, accessory. **2** *a full complement of lifeboats* =amount, contingent, capacity, allowance, quota.

▶ verb *this sauce complements the dessert* =**accompany**, go with, round off, set off, suit, harmonize with; enhance, complete.

complementary ▶ adjective =**harmonious**, compatible, corresponding, matching; reciprocal.
–OPPOSITES incompatible.

complete ▶ adjective **1** *the complete interview* =**entire**, whole, full, total; uncut, unabridged, unexpurgated. **2** *their research was complete* =**finished**, ended, concluded, completed; discharged, settled, done; *informal* wrapped up, sewn up. **3** *a complete fool* =**absolute**, out-and-out, utter, total, real, downright, thoroughgoing, veritable, prize, perfect, unqualified, unmitigated, sheer; *N. Amer.* full-bore; *Brit. informal* right.
–OPPOSITES partial, unfinished.

▶ verb **1** *he had to complete his training* =**finish**, end, conclude, finalize, wind up; *informal* wrap up. **2** *the outfit was completed with a veil* =**finish off**, round off, top off, crown, cap. **3** *complete the application form* =**fill in/out**, answer.

completely ▶ adverb =**totally**, entirely, wholly, thoroughly, fully, utterly, absolutely, perfectly, unreservedly, unconditionally, quite, altogether, downright; in every way, in every respect, one hundred per cent, every inch, to the hilt.

completion ▶ noun =**realization**, accomplishment, achievement, fulfilment, consummation, finalization, resolution; finish, end, conclusion.

complex ▶ adjective **1** *a complex situation* =**complicated**, involved, intricate, convoluted, elaborate, difficult, knotty, tricky, thorny; *Brit. informal* fiddly. **2** *a complex structure* =**compound**, composite, multiplex.
–OPPOSITES simple.

▶ noun **1** *a complex of roads* =**network**, system, nexus, web. **2** *(informal)* he had a complex about losing his hair =**obsession**, fixation, preoccupation; neurosis; *informal* hang-up, thing, bee in one's bonnet.

complexion ▶ noun **1** *a pale complexion* =**skin**, skin colour/tone. **2** *governments of all complexions* =**type**, kind, sort; colour, persuasion.

complexity ▶ noun =**complication**, problem, difficulty, intricacy.

compliance ▶ noun *compliance with international law* =**obedience to**, observance of, adherence to, conformity to, respect for. **2** *he mistook her silence for compliance* =**acquiescence**, agreement, assent, consent, acceptance.
–OPPOSITES violation, defiance.

compliant ▶ adjective =**acquiescent**, amenable, biddable, tractable, accommodating, cooperative; obedient, docile, malleable, pliable; submissive, tame.
–OPPOSITES recalcitrant.

complicate ▶ verb =**make (more) difficult**, make complicated, mix up, confuse, muddle; *informal* mess up, screw up.
–OPPOSITES simplify.

complicated ▶ adjective =**complex**, intricate, involved, convoluted, tangled, impenetrable, knotty, tricky, thorny, labyrinthine, tortuous; confusing, bewildering, perplexing; *Brit. informal* fiddly.
–OPPOSITES straightforward.

complication ▶ noun **1** *a complication concerning ownership* =**difficulty**, problem, obstacle, hurdle, stumbling block; drawback, snag, catch, hitch; *Brit.* spanner in the works; *informal* headache. **2** *the complication of life in our society* =**complexity**, complicatedness, intricacy, convolutedness.

complicity ▶ noun =**collusion**, involvement, collaboration, connivance; conspiracy.

compliment ▶ noun **1** *an unexpected compliment* =**flattering remark**, tribute, accolade, commendation, pat on the back; (**compliments**) praise, acclaim, admiration, flattery, blandishments. **2** *my compliments on your cooking* =**congratulations**. **3** *Margaret sends her compliments* =**greetings**, regards, respects, good wishes, best wishes.
–OPPOSITES insult.

▶ verb *they complimented his performance* =**praise**, pay tribute to, speak highly/well of, flatter, wax lyrical about, make much of, commend, acclaim, applaud; salute; congratulate.
–OPPOSITES criticize.

complimentary ▶ adjective **1** *complimentary remarks* =**flattering**, appreciative, congratulatory, admiring, approving, commendatory, favourable, glowing, adulatory. **2** *complimentary tickets* =**free (of charge)**, gratis, for noth-

ing; courtesy; *informal* on the house.
–OPPOSITES derogatory.

comply ▶ verb *Myra complied with his wishes* =**abide by**, observe, obey, adhere to, conform to, follow, respect; agree to, assent to, go along with, yield to, submit to, defer to.
–OPPOSITES ignore, disobey.

component ▶ noun =**part**, piece, bit, element, constituent, ingredient; unit, module, section.
▶ adjective =**constituent**; basic, essential.

compose ▶ verb **1** *a poem composed by Shelley* =**write**, devise, make up, think up, produce, invent, concoct; pen, author. **2** *how to compose a photograph* =**organize**, arrange, set out. **3** *the congress is composed of ten senators* =**make up**, constitute, form, comprise.
■ **compose oneself** =**calm down**, control oneself, regain one's composure, pull oneself together, steady oneself, keep one's head; *informal* get a grip, keep one's cool; *N. Amer. informal* decompress.

composed ▶ adjective =**calm**, collected, cool (as a cucumber), self-controlled, self-possessed; serene, tranquil, relaxed, at ease, unruffled, unperturbed, untroubled; equable, even-tempered, imperturbable; *informal* unflappable, together, laid-back.
–OPPOSITES excited.

composer ▶ noun =**melodist**, symphonist, songwriter, songster; *informal* tunesmith, songsmith.

composite ▶ adjective =**compound**, complex; combined, blended, mixed.
▶ noun =**amalgamation**, amalgam, combination, compound, fusion, synthesis, mixture, blend; alloy.

composition ▶ noun **1** *the composition of the council* =**make-up**, constitution, configuration, structure, formation, form, fabric, anatomy, organization; *informal* set-up. **2** *a literary composition* =**work (of art)**, creation, opus, piece. **3** *the composition of a poem* =**writing**, creation, formulation, compilation. **4** *a school composition* =**essay**, paper, study, piece of writing; *N. Amer.* theme. **5** *the composition of the painting* =**arrangement**, layout; proportions, balance, symmetry.

composure ▶ noun =**self-control**, self-possession, calm, equanimity, equilibrium, serenity, tranquillity; poise, presence of mind, sangfroid, placid-

ness, impassivity; *informal* cool.

compound ▶ noun *a compound of two materials* =**amalgam**, blend, mixture, mix, alloy.
▶ adjective *a compound substance* =**composite**, complex.
–OPPOSITES simple.
▶ verb **1** *a smell compounded of dust and mould* =**be composed of**, be made up of, be formed from. **2** *soap compounded with disinfectant* =**mix**, combine, blend. **3** *his illness compounds their problems* =**aggravate**, exacerbate, worsen, add to, augment, intensify, heighten, increase.
–OPPOSITES alleviate.

comprehend ▶ verb =**understand**, grasp, take in, apprehend, follow, make sense of, fathom; *informal* work out, figure out, make head or tail of, get one's head around, take on board, get the drift of, catch on to, get; *Brit. informal* twig, suss (out).

comprehensible ▶ adjective =**intelligible**, understandable, accessible; lucid, coherent, clear, plain, straightforward.
–OPPOSITES opaque.

comprehension ▶ noun =**understanding**, grasp, conception, apprehension, cognition, ken, knowledge, awareness.
–OPPOSITES ignorance.

comprehensive ▶ adjective =**inclusive**, all-inclusive, complete; thorough, full, extensive, all-embracing, exhaustive, detailed, in-depth, encyclopedic, universal; radical, sweeping, across the board, wholesale; broad, wide-ranging; *informal* wall-to-wall.
–OPPOSITES limited.

compress ▶ verb =**squeeze**, press, squash, crush, compact; *informal* scrunch.
–OPPOSITES expand.

comprise ▶ verb **1** *the country comprises twenty states* =**consist of**, be made up of, be composed of, contain, encompass, incorporate; include. **2** *this breed comprises half the herd* =**make up**, constitute, form, compose; account for.

compromise ▶ noun **1** *they reached a compromise* =**agreement**, understanding, settlement, terms, deal, trade-off, bargain; middle ground, happy medium, balance.
–OPPOSITES intransigence.
▶ verb **1** *we compromised* =**meet each other halfway**, come to an understanding,

make a deal, make concessions, find a happy medium, strike a balance. **2** *his actions could compromise his reputation* =**undermine**, weaken, damage, harm; jeopardize, prejudice.

compulsion ▸ noun **1** *he is under no compulsion to go* =**obligation**, duress, pressure. **2** *a compulsion to tell the truth* =**urge**, impulse, need, desire, drive; obsession, fixation, addiction.

compulsive ▸ adjective **1** *a compulsive desire* =**irresistible**, uncontrollable, compelling, overwhelming, urgent. **2** *compulsive eating* =**obsessive**, obsessional, addictive, uncontrollable. **3** *a compulsive liar* =**inveterate**, chronic, incorrigible, incurable, hopeless, persistent, habitual; *informal* pathological. **4** *it's compulsive viewing* =**fascinating**, compelling, gripping, riveting, engrossing, enthralling, captivating.

compulsory ▸ adjective =**obligatory**, mandatory, required, requisite, necessary, essential; imperative, unavoidable, enforced, prescribed.
–OPPOSITES optional.

compunction ▸ noun =**scruples**, misgivings, qualms, worries, unease, doubts, reluctance, reservations.

compute ▸ verb =**calculate**, work out, reckon, determine, evaluate, quantify; add up, count up, tally, total; *Brit.* tot up.

computer ▸ noun

WORD LINKS

fear of computers: **cyberphobia**

comrade ▸ noun =**companion**, friend; colleague, associate, partner, co-worker, workmate; *informal* pal, chum, crony; *Brit. informal* mate; *N. Amer. informal* buddy.

con (*informal*) ▸ verb & noun. *See* SWINDLE.

concave ▸ adjective =**hollow**, depressed, sunken; indented, recessed; curved.
–OPPOSITES convex.

conceal ▸ verb **1** *clouds concealed the sun* =**hide**, screen, cover, obscure, block out, blot out, mask, shroud. **2** *he concealed his true feelings* =**hide**, cover up, disguise, mask, veil; keep secret; suppress, repress, bottle up; *informal* keep a/the lid on.
–OPPOSITES reveal, confess.

concealed ▸ adjective =**hidden**, out of sight, invisible, covered, disguised, camouflaged, obscured; private, secret.

concealment ▸ noun **1** *the concealment of the bushes* =**cover**, shelter, protection, screen; privacy, seclusion; secrecy. **2** *the deliberate concealment of facts* =**suppression**, hiding, covering up, hushing up.

concede ▸ verb **1** *I had to concede that I'd overreacted* =**admit**, acknowledge, accept, allow, grant, recognize, own, confess; agree. **2** *he eventually conceded the title to Ali* =**surrender**, yield, give up, relinquish, hand over.
–OPPOSITES deny, retain.
■ **concede defeat** =**capitulate**, admit defeat, give in, surrender, yield, give up, submit, raise the white flag; back down, climb down, throw in the towel.

conceit ▸ noun **1** *his extraordinary conceit* =**vanity**, narcissism, conceitedness, egotism, self-admiration, self-regard; pride, arrogance, self-importance; *informal* big-headedness. **2** *the conceits of Shakespeare's verse* =**image**, imagery, metaphor, simile, trope.
–OPPOSITES humility.

conceited ▸ adjective =**vain**, narcissistic, self-centred, egotistic, egocentric; proud, arrogant, boastful, full of oneself, self-important, immodest; self-satisfied; supercilious, haughty, snobbish; *informal* big-headed, too big for one's boots, stuck-up, high and mighty.

conceivable ▸ adjective =**imaginable**, possible; plausible, credible, believable, feasible.

conceive ▸ verb **1** *the project was conceived in 1977* =**think up**, think of, dream up, devise, formulate, design, originate, create, develop; hatch; *informal* cook up. **2** *I could hardly conceive what it must be like* =**imagine**, envisage, visualize, picture, think; grasp, appreciate.

concentrate ▸ verb **1** *the government concentrated its efforts on staying in power* =**focus**, direct, centre. **2** *she concentrated on the film* =**focus on**, pay attention to, keep one's mind on, devote oneself to; be absorbed in, be engrossed in, be immersed in; *informal* get stuck into. **3** *troops concentrated on the horizon* =**collect**, gather, congregate, converge, mass, rally. **4** *the liquid is filtered and concentrated* =**condense**, boil down, reduce.
–OPPOSITES disperse, dilute.
▸ noun *a fruit concentrate* =**extract**, distillation.

concentrated ▸ adjective **1** *a con-*

centrated effort =**strenuous**, concerted, intensive, all-out, intense. **2** *a concentrated solution* =**condensed**, reduced; undiluted; strong.

–OPPOSITES half-hearted, diluted.

concentration ▶ noun **1** *a task requiring concentration* =**close attention**, attentiveness, application, single-mindedness, absorption. **2** *the concentration of effort* =**focusing**, centralization. **3** *a high concentration of sodium* =**density**, level; presence; amount, volume.

–OPPOSITES inattention.

concept ▶ noun =**idea**, notion, conception, abstraction; theory, hypothesis.

conception ▶ noun **1** *the fertility treatment resulted in conception* =**pregnancy**, fertilization, impregnation, insemination. **2** *the product's conception* =**inception**, genesis, origination, creation, invention; beginning, origin. **3** *his original conception* =**plan**, scheme, project, proposal; intention, aim, idea. **4** *my conception of democracy* =**idea**, concept, notion, understanding; perception, image, impression. **5** *they had no conception of our problems* =**understanding**, comprehension, appreciation, grasp, knowledge; idea, inkling; *informal* clue.

concern ▶ verb **1** *the report concerns the war* =**be about**, deal with, cover; relate to, pertain to. **2** *that doesn't concern you* =**affect**, involve, be relevant to, apply to, have a bearing on, impact on; be important to, interest. **3** *one thing still concerns me* =**worry**, disturb, trouble, bother, perturb, unsettle.

▶ noun **1** *a voice full of concern* =**anxiety**, worry, disquiet, apprehensiveness, unease, consternation. **2** *his concern for others* =**solicitude**, consideration, care, sympathy, regard. **3** *housing is the concern of the council* =**responsibility**, business, affair, charge, duty, job; province, preserve; problem, worry; *informal* bailiwick; *Brit. informal* lookout. **4** *issues of concern to women* =**interest**, importance, relevance, significance. **5** *a publishing concern* =**company**, business, firm, organization, operation, corporation, establishment, house, office, agency; *informal* outfit, set-up.

–OPPOSITES indifference.

concerned ▶ adjective **1** *her mother looked concerned* =**worried**, anxious, upset, perturbed, troubled, uneasy, apprehensive. **2** *all concerned parties* =**inter-**

ested, involved, affected; connected, related, implicated.

concerning ▶ preposition =**about**, regarding, relating to, with reference to, referring to, with regard to, as regards, with respect to, respecting, dealing with, on the subject of, in connection with, re, apropos of.

concert ▶ noun =**performance**, show, production; recital; *informal* gig.
■ **in concert** =**together**, jointly, in combination, in collaboration, in cooperation, in league, side by side; in unison.

concerted ▶ adjective **1** *a concerted effort* =**strenuous**, vigorous, intensive, all-out, intense, concentrated. **2** *concerted action* =**joint**, united, collaborative, collective, combined, cooperative.
–OPPOSITES half-hearted, individual.

concession ▶ noun **1** *the government made several concessions* =**compromise**; sop. **2** *tax concessions* =**reduction**, cut, discount, deduction, decrease; rebate; *informal* break. **3** *a logging concession* =**right**, privilege; licence, permit, franchise, warrant.

conciliate ▶ verb **1** *he tried to conciliate the workforce* =**appease**, placate, pacify, mollify, assuage, soothe, win over, make peace with. **2** *he conciliated in the dispute* =**mediate**, act as peacemaker, arbitrate.
–OPPOSITES provoke.

conciliator ▶ noun =**peacemaker**, mediator, go-between, middleman, intermediary.
–OPPOSITES troublemaker.

conciliatory ▶ adjective =**propitiatory**, placatory, appeasing, pacifying, mollifying, peacemaking.

concise ▶ adjective =**succinct**, pithy, incisive, brief, short and to the point, short and sweet; abridged, condensed, compressed, abbreviated, compact, potted; *informal* snappy.
–OPPOSITES lengthy, wordy.

conclude ▶ verb **1** *the meeting concluded at ten* =**finish**, end, draw to a close, stop, cease. **2** *he concluded the press conference* =**bring to an end**, close, wind up, terminate, dissolve; round off; *informal* wrap up. **3** *an attempt to conclude a deal* =**negotiate**, broker, agree, come to terms on, settle, clinch, finalize, tie up; bring about, arrange, effect, engineer. **4** *I concluded that he was rather unpleasant* =**deduce**, infer, gather, judge, decide, con-

jecture, surmise; *N. Amer.* figure.
–OPPOSITES commence.

conclusion ▶ noun **1** *the conclusion of his speech* =**end**, ending, finish, close. **2** *the conclusion of a trade agreement* =**negotiation**, brokering, settlement, completion, arrangement, resolution. **3** *his conclusions have been verified* =**deduction**, inference, interpretation, judgement, verdict.
–OPPOSITES beginning.
■ **in conclusion** =**finally**, in closing, to conclude, last but not least; to sum up.

conclusive ▶ adjective **1** *conclusive proof* =**incontrovertible**, undeniable, indisputable, irrefutable, unquestionable, convincing, certain, decisive, definitive, definite, positive, categorical, unequivocal. **2** *a conclusive win* =**emphatic**, resounding, convincing; decisive.
–OPPOSITES unconvincing.

concoct ▶ verb **1** *this story she has concocted* =**make up**, dream up, fabricate, invent; formulate, hatch, brew; *informal* cook up. **2** *she concocted a salad* =**put together**, assemble; *informal* fix, rustle up; *Brit. informal* knock up, throw together.

concoction ▶ noun **1** *a concoction containing gin and vodka* =**mixture**, brew, preparation, potion. **2** *a strange concoction of styles* =**blend**, mixture, mix, combination, hybrid. **3** *her story is an improbable concoction* =**fabrication**, invention, falsification; *informal* fairy story, fairy tale.

concord ▶ noun *(formal)* **1** *council meetings rarely ended in concord* =**agreement**, harmony, accord, consensus, concurrence, unity. **2** *a concord was to be drawn up* =**treaty**, agreement, accord, pact, compact, settlement.
–OPPOSITES discord.

concourse ▶ noun =**entrance**, foyer, lobby, hall.

concrete ▶ adjective **1** *concrete objects* =**solid**, material, real, physical, tangible, palpable, substantial. **2** *concrete proof* =**definite**, firm, positive, conclusive, definitive; real, genuine, bona fide.
–OPPOSITES abstract, imaginary.

concur ▶ verb **1** *we concur with this view* =**agree**, be in agreement, go along, fall in, be in sympathy; see eye to eye, be of the same mind, be of the same opinion. **2** *the two events concurred* =**coincide**, be simultaneous, co-occur.

–OPPOSITES disagree.

concurrent ▶ adjective =**simultaneous**, contemporaneous, parallel.

condemn ▶ verb **1** *he condemned the suspended players* =**censure**, criticize, denounce, revile; *informal* slam, blast, lay into; *Brit. informal* slate, slag off, have a go at. **2** *he was condemned to death* =**sentence**. **3** *his illness condemned him to a lonely life* =**doom**, destine, damn; consign, assign.
–OPPOSITES praise.

condemnation ▶ noun =**censure**, criticism, denunciation, vilification; *informal* flak, a bad press.

condense ▶ verb **1** *the water vapour condenses* =**precipitate**, liquefy, become liquid; deliquesce. **2** *he condensed the play* =**abridge**, shorten, cut, abbreviate, edit.
–OPPOSITES vaporize, expand.

condensed ▶ adjective **1** *a condensed text* =**abridged**, shortened, cut, compressed, abbreviated, reduced, truncated, concise; *informal* potted. **2** *condensed soup* =**concentrated**, evaporated, reduced; strong, undiluted.
–OPPOSITES diluted.

condescend ▶ verb **1** *don't condescend to your reader* =**patronize**, talk down to, look down one's nose at, look down on. **2** *he condescended to see us* =**deign**, stoop, lower oneself, demean oneself, consent.

condescending ▶ adjective =**patronizing**, supercilious, superior, disdainful, lofty, haughty; *informal* snooty, stuck-up; *Brit. informal* toffee-nosed.

condition ▶ noun **1** *check the condition of your wiring* =**state**, shape, order; *Brit. informal* nick. **2** *they lived in appalling conditions* =**circumstances**, surroundings, environment, situation, set-up. **3** *she was in tip-top condition* =**fitness**, health, form, shape. **4** *a liver condition* =**disorder**, problem, complaint, illness, disease, ailment, sickness, affliction, infection, upset; *informal* bug, virus. **5** *a condition of employment* =**stipulation**, constraint, prerequisite, precondition, requirement, rule, term, specification, provision, proviso.
▶ verb **1** *their choices are conditioned by the economy* =**constrain**, control, govern, determine, decide; affect, shape. **2** *our minds are conditioned by habit* =**train**, teach, educate, guide; accustom, adapt, habituate, mould. **3** *condition the boards with water* =**treat**, prepare, prime, tem-

per, process, acclimatize, acclimate, season. **4** *a product to condition your skin* =**improve**, nourish, tone (up).

conditional ▶ adjective **1** *their approval is conditional on success* =**subject to**, dependent on, contingent on, based on, determined by, tied to. **2** *a conditional offer* =**qualified**, dependent, contingent, with reservations, limited, provisional, provisory.

condolences ▶ plural noun =**sympathy**, commiseration(s).

condom ▶ noun =**contraceptive**, sheath; *N. Amer.* prophylactic; *Brit. trademark* Durex; *Brit. informal* johnny; *N. Amer. informal* rubber, safe; *Brit. informal, dated* French letter.

condone ▶ verb =**disregard**, accept, allow, let pass, turn a blind eye to, overlook, forget; forgive, pardon, excuse, let go.
−OPPOSITES condemn.

conducive ▶ adjective =**favourable**, beneficial, advantageous, opportune, encouraging, promising, convenient, good, helpful, instrumental, productive, useful.
−OPPOSITES unfavourable.

conduct ▶ noun **1** *they complained about her conduct* =**behaviour**, performance; actions, activities, deeds, doings, exploits; habits, manners. **2** *the conduct of the elections* =**management**, running, direction, control, supervision, regulation, administration, organization, coordination, handling.
▶ verb **1** *the election was conducted lawfully* =**manage**, direct, run, administer, organize, coordinate, orchestrate, handle, control, oversee, supervise, regulate, carry out/on. **2** *he was conducted through the corridors* =**escort**, guide, lead, usher, show; shepherd, see, bring, take, help. **3** *aluminium conducts heat* =**transmit**, convey, carry, channel, relay.
■ **conduct oneself** =**behave**, act, acquit oneself, bear oneself.

conduit ▶ noun =**channel**, duct, pipe, tube, gutter, trench, culvert, sluice, chute.

confectionery ▶ noun =**sweets**, chocolates, bonbons; *N. Amer.* candy; *informal* sweeties.

confederacy ▶ noun =**federation**, confederation, alliance, league, association, coalition, consortium, syndicate, group, circle; bloc, axis.

confederate ▶ adjective *confederate councils* =**federal**, federated, allied, associated, united.
−OPPOSITES split.
▶ noun *he met his confederate in the street* =**associate**, partner, accomplice, helper, assistant, ally, collaborator, colleague; *Austral./NZ informal* offsider.

confederation ▶ noun =**alliance**, league, confederacy, federation, association, coalition, consortium, conglomerate, syndicate, group, circle; society, union.

confer ▶ verb **1** *she conferred a knighthood on him* =**bestow on**, present to, grant to, award to, decorate with, honour with, give to, endow with, extend to, vouchsafe to. **2** *she went to confer with her colleagues* =**consult**, talk, speak, converse, have a chat, have a tête-à-tête, parley.

conference ▶ noun =**congress**, meeting, convention, seminar, colloquium, symposium, forum, summit.

confess ▶ verb **1** *he confessed that he had done it* =**admit**, acknowledge, reveal, disclose, divulge; own up; *informal* fess up. **2** *they could not make him confess* =**own up**, plead guilty, accept the blame; tell the truth, tell all; *informal* come clean, spill the beans, let the cat out of the bag. **3** *I confess I don't know* =**acknowledge**, admit, concede, grant, allow, own.
−OPPOSITES deny.

confession ▶ noun =**admission**, acknowledgement.

confidant, confidante ▶ noun =**close friend**, bosom friend, best friend; intimate, familiar; *informal* chum, pal, crony; *Brit. informal* mate, mucker; *N. Amer. informal* buddy.

confide ▶ verb =**reveal**, disclose, divulge, impart, declare, vouchsafe, tell; confess.

confidence ▶ noun **1** *I have little confidence in these figures* =**trust**, belief, faith. **2** *she's brimming with confidence* =**self-assurance**, self-confidence, self-possession, assertiveness, self-belief; conviction.
−OPPOSITES scepticism, doubt.

confident ▶ adjective **1** *we are confident that business will improve* =**optimistic**, hopeful; sure, certain, positive, convinced, in no doubt, satisfied. **2** *a confident girl* =**self-assured**, assured, self-confident, positive, assertive, self-possessed.

confidential ▶ adjective =private, personal, intimate, quiet; secret, sensitive, classified, restricted, unofficial, undisclosed, unpublished; *informal* hush-hush.

confidentially ▶ adverb =privately, in private, in confidence, between ourselves/themselves, off the record, quietly, secretly, in secret, behind closed doors.

configuration ▶ noun =arrangement, layout, geography, design, organization, order, grouping, positioning, disposition, alignment; shape, form, array, formation, structure, format.

confine ▶ verb 1 *they were confined in the house* =enclose, incarcerate, imprison, intern, impound, hold captive, trap; shut in/up, keep, lock in/up, coop (up); fence in, hedge in. 2 *he confined his remarks to the weather* =restrict, limit.

confined ▶ adjective =cramped, constricted, restricted, limited, small, narrow, compact, tight, poky, uncomfortable, inadequate.
–OPPOSITES roomy.

confinement ▶ noun =imprisonment, internment, incarceration, custody, captivity, detention, restraint; house arrest.

confines ▶ plural noun =limits, margins, extremities, edges, borders, boundaries, fringes; periphery, perimeter.

confirm ▶ verb 1 *records confirm the latest evidence* =corroborate, verify, prove, validate, authenticate, substantiate, justify, vindicate; support, uphold, back up. 2 *he confirmed that help was on the way* =affirm, reaffirm, assert, assure someone, repeat. 3 *his appointment was confirmed by the President* =ratify, validate, sanction, endorse, formalize, authorize, warrant, accredit, approve, accept.
–OPPOSITES contradict, deny.

confirmation ▶ noun 1 *independent confirmation of the deaths* =corroboration, verification, proof, testimony, endorsement, authentication, substantiation, evidence. 2 *confirmation of your appointment* =ratification, approval, authorization, validation, sanction, endorsement, formalization, acceptance.

confirmed ▶ adjective =established, long-standing, committed, dyed-in-the-wool, through and through; staunch, loyal, faithful, devoted, dedicated, stead-

fast; habitual, compulsive, persistent; unapologetic, unashamed, inveterate, chronic, incurable; *informal* card-carrying.

confiscate ▶ verb =impound, seize, commandeer, requisition, appropriate, expropriate, sequester, sequestrate, take (away).
–OPPOSITES return.

confiscation ▶ noun =seizure, requisition, appropriation, expropriation, sequestration.

conflagration ▶ noun =fire, blaze, flames, inferno, firestorm.

conflict ▶ noun 1 *industrial conflicts* =dispute, quarrel, squabble, disagreement, clash; discord, friction, strife, antagonism, hostility; feud, schism. 2 *the Vietnam conflict* =war, campaign, fighting, engagement, encounter, struggle, hostilities; warfare, combat. 3 *a conflict between work and home life* =clash, incompatibility, friction; mismatch, variance, divergence, contradiction.
–OPPOSITES agreement, peace, harmony.
▶ verb *their interests sometimes conflict* =clash, be incompatible, vary, be at odds, be in conflict, differ, diverge, disagree, contrast, collide.

conflicting ▶ adjective =contradictory, incompatible, inconsistent, irreconcilable, contrary, opposite, opposing, antithetical, clashing, divergent; at odds.

confluence ▶ noun =convergence, meeting, junction.

conform ▶ verb 1 *visitors have to conform to our rules* =comply with, abide by, obey, observe, follow, keep to, stick to, adhere to, uphold, heed, accept, go along with, fall in with, respect, defer to; satisfy, meet, fulfil. 2 *they refuse to conform* =fit/blend in; behave (oneself), toe the line, obey the rules; *informal* play it by the book, play by the rules. 3 *goods must conform to their description* =match, fit, suit, answer, agree with, be like, correspond to, be consistent with, measure up to, tally with, square with.
–OPPOSITES flout, rebel.

conformist ▶ noun =traditionalist, conservative, diehard, reactionary; *informal* stick-in-the-mud, stuffed shirt.
–OPPOSITES eccentric, rebel.

confound ▶ verb 1 *the figures confounded analysts* =amaze, astonish, dumbfound, stagger, surprise, startle, stun, nonplus; throw, shake, discompose, bewilder, baffle, mystify, bemuse, perplex, puzzle, confuse; take aback, catch off balance; *informal* flabbergast, blow someone's mind, blow away, flummox, faze, stump, beat; *N. Amer. informal* discombobulate. **2** *he has always confounded expectations* =**contradict**, counter, invalidate, negate, go against, explode, demolish, shoot down, destroy, disprove; *informal* shoot full of holes.

confront ▸ verb **1** *Martin confronted the burglar* =**challenge**, square up to, face (up to), come face to face with, meet, accost; stand up to, tackle. **2** *the problems that confront us* =**face**, plague, bother, beset, threaten. **3** *they must confront these issues* =**tackle**, address, face, get to grips with, grapple with, take on, attend to, see to, deal with. **4** *she confronted him with the evidence* =**present**, face.
−OPPOSITES avoid.

confrontation ▸ noun =**conflict**, clash, fight, battle, encounter, head-to-head, face-off, engagement, skirmish; hostilities, fighting; *informal* set-to, run-in, dust-up, showdown.

confuse ▸ verb **1** *don't confuse students with too much detail* =**bewilder**, baffle, mystify, bemuse, perplex, puzzle, confound, nonplus; *informal* flummox, faze, stump; *N. Amer. informal* discombobulate. **2** *the authors have confused the issue* =**complicate**, muddle, blur, obscure, cloud. **3** *some confuse strokes with heart attacks* =**mix up**, muddle up, mistake for.
−OPPOSITES enlighten, simplify.

confused ▸ adjective **1** *they are confused about what is going on* =**bewildered**, bemused, puzzled, perplexed, baffled, mystified, muddled, dumbfounded, at sea, at a loss, taken aback, disoriented; *informal* flummoxed; *N. Amer. informal* discombobulated. **2** *her confused elderly mother* =**demented**, bewildered, muddled, addled, befuddled, disoriented, disorientated; senile. **3** *a confused recollection* =**vague**, unclear, indistinct, imprecise, blurred, hazy, dim; imperfect, sketchy. **4** *a confused mass of bones* =**disorderly**, disordered, disorganized, untidy, muddled, jumbled, mixed up, chaotic, topsy-turvy, tangled; *informal* higgledy-piggledy; *Brit. informal* shambolic.
−OPPOSITES lucid, clear, precise, neat.

confusing ▸ adjective =**bewildering**, baffling, perplexing, puzzling, mystifying; ambiguous, misleading, inconsistent, contradictory.

confusion ▸ noun **1** *there is confusion about the new system* =**uncertainty**, doubt, ignorance. **2** *she stared in confusion* =**bewilderment**, bafflement, perplexity, puzzlement, befuddlement; *N. Amer. informal* discombobulation. **3** *her life was in utter confusion* =**disorder**, disarray, chaos, mayhem; turmoil, tumult, uproar, hurly-burly, muddle, mess; *informal* shambles. **4** *a confusion of boxes* =**jumble**, muddle, mess, heap, tangle.
−OPPOSITES certainty, order.

congeal ▸ verb =**coagulate**, clot, thicken, gel, cake, set.

congenial ▸ adjective **1** *very congenial people* =**sociable**, sympathetic, convivial, hospitable, genial, personable, agreeable, friendly, pleasant, likeable, amiable, nice. **2** *a congenial environment* =**pleasant**, pleasing, agreeable, enjoyable, pleasurable, nice, appealing, satisfying, relaxing, welcoming, hospitable, favourable.
−OPPOSITES unpleasant.

congenital ▸ adjective **1** *congenital defects* =**inborn**, innate, constitutional, inbuilt, natural, inherent. **2** *a congenital liar* =**inveterate**, compulsive, persistent, chronic, regular, habitual, obsessive, confirmed; incurable, incorrigible, irredeemable, hopeless; *informal* pathological.
−OPPOSITES acquired.

congested ▸ adjective =**crowded**, overcrowded, full, overflowing, packed, jammed, thronged, teeming, swarming; obstructed, blocked, clogged, choked; *informal* snarled up, gridlocked, jam-packed.
−OPPOSITES clear.

congestion ▸ noun =**crowding**, overcrowding; obstruction, blockage; traffic jam, bottleneck; *informal* snarl-up, gridlock.

conglomerate ▸ noun **1** *the conglomerate was broken up* =**corporation**, combine, group, consortium, partnership, federation. **2** *a conglomerate of disparate peoples* =**mixture**, mix, combination, amalgamation, union, composite, synthesis; miscellany, hotchpotch.

congratulate ▸ verb *they are to be congratulated* =**praise**, commend, applaud, salute, honour; pay tribute to, pat on the back, take one's hat off to.
−OPPOSITES criticize.

congratulations ▶ plural noun = best wishes, compliments; felicitations.

congregate ▶ verb = assemble, gather, collect, come together, convene, rally, muster, meet, cluster, group. –OPPOSITES disperse.

congregation ▶ noun = parishioners, parish, churchgoers, flock, faithful, believers; audience.

congress ▶ noun = legislature, assembly, parliament, council, senate, chamber, house.

conical ▶ adjective = cone-shaped, tapered, tapering, pointed; informal pointy.

conjectural ▶ adjective = speculative, theoretical, hypothetical, putative, notional; postulated, inferred, presumed, assumed.

conjecture ▶ noun = speculation, guesswork, surmise, fancy, theory, supposition, a shot in the dark. –OPPOSITES fact.
▶ verb = guess, speculate, surmise, infer, assume, suppose. –OPPOSITES know.

conjugal ▶ adjective = marital, matrimonial, nuptial, marriage, bridal; literary connubial.

conjunction ▶ noun = co-occurrence, concurrence, coincidence, coexistence, synchronicity, synchrony.

conjure ▶ verb 1 he conjured a cigarette out of the air = produce, magic, summon. 2 the picture that his words conjured up = bring to mind, call to mind, evoke, summon up, suggest.

conjuring ▶ noun = magic, illusion, sleight of hand, legerdemain; formal prestidigitation.

conjuror ▶ noun = magician, illusionist; formal prestidigitator.

connect ▶ verb 1 electrodes were connected to the device = attach, join, fasten, fix, link, secure, hitch; stick, pin, screw, bolt, clamp, clip, hook (up). 2 customs connected with Easter = associate, link, couple; identify, relate to. –OPPOSITES detach.

connection ▶ noun 1 the connection between commerce and art = link, relationship, relation, interconnection, interdependence, association; bond, tie, tie-in, correspondence, parallel, analogy. 2 he has the right connections = contact, friend, acquaintance, ally, colleague, associate; relation, relative.
■ **in connection with** = regarding, concerning, with reference to, with regard to, with respect to, relating to, in relation to, on, connected with, on the subject of, in the matter of, apropos, re.

connivance ▶ noun = collusion, complicity, collaboration, involvement, assistance.

connive ▶ verb 1 wardens connived at offences = ignore, overlook, disregard, pass over, take no notice of, turn a blind eye to. 2 the government connived with security forces = conspire, collude, collaborate, plot, scheme.

conniving ▶ adjective = scheming, cunning, calculating, devious, wily, sly, tricky, artful, guileful; manipulative, Machiavellian, deceitful, underhand, treacherous.

connoisseur ▶ noun = expert, authority, specialist, pundit, aesthete; gourmet, epicure, gastronome; informal buff; N. Amer. informal maven.

connotation ▶ noun = overtone, undertone, undercurrent, implication, nuance, hint, echo, association.

connote ▶ verb = imply, suggest, indicate, signify, hint at, give the impression of, smack of.

conquer ▶ verb 1 the Franks conquered the Visigoths = defeat, beat, vanquish, triumph over, be victorious over, get the better of; overcome, overwhelm, overpower, overthrow, subdue, subjugate, quell, quash, crush. 2 Peru was conquered by Spain = seize, take (over), appropriate, subjugate, capture, occupy, invade, annex, overrun. 3 the first men to conquer Mount Everest = climb, ascend, mount, scale. 4 the way to conquer fear = overcome, get the better of, control, master, deal with, cope with, rise above; quell, quash, beat, triumph over; informal lick. –OPPOSITES lose.

conquest ▶ noun 1 the conquest of the Aztecs = defeat, overthrow, subjugation; victory over, triumph over. 2 their conquest of the valley = seizure, takeover, capture, occupation, invasion, acquisition, appropriation. 3 the conquest of Everest = ascent, climbing. –OPPOSITES victory, surrender.

conscience ▶ noun = sense of right and wrong; morals, standards, values, principles, ethics, beliefs; scruples, qualms.

conscientious ▶ adjective =diligent, industrious, punctilious, painstaking, sedulous, assiduous, dedicated, careful, meticulous, thorough, attentive, hard-working, studious, rigorous, particular; religious, strict.
–OPPOSITES casual.

conscious ▶ adjective 1 *the patient was conscious* =aware, awake; *informal* with us. 2 *a conscious decision* =deliberate, purposeful, knowing, considered, calculated, wilful, premeditated.
–OPPOSITES unaware.

conscript ▶ verb *they were conscripted into the army* =call up, enlist, recruit; *US* draft.
▶ noun *an army conscript* =enlisted soldier/man/woman, recruit; *US* draftee.
–OPPOSITES volunteer.

consecrate ▶ verb =sanctify, bless; dedicate, devote.

consecutive ▶ adjective =successive, succeeding, in succession, running, in a row, one after the other, back-to-back, straight, uninterrupted; *informal* on the trot.

consensus ▶ noun 1 *there was consensus among delegates* =agreement, harmony, concurrence, accord, unity, unanimity, solidarity. 2 *the consensus was that they should act* =general opinion, common view.
–OPPOSITES disagreement.

consent ▶ noun *the consent of all members* =agreement, assent, acceptance, approval; permission, authorization, sanction, leave; backing, endorsement, support; *informal* go-ahead, thumbs up, green light, OK.
–OPPOSITES dissent.
▶ verb *she consented to surgery* =agree, assent, submit; allow, give permission, sanction, accept, approve, go along with.
–OPPOSITES forbid.

consequence ▶ noun 1 *a consequence of inflation* =result, upshot, outcome, effect, repercussion, ramification, corollary, concomitant; fruit(s), product, by-product, end result. 2 *the past is of no consequence* =importance, import, significance, account, substance, note, value, concern, interest.
–OPPOSITES cause.

consequent ▶ adjective =resulting, resultant, ensuing, consequential; following, subsequent, successive; attend-

ant, accompanying, concomitant; collateral, associated, related.

consequential ▶ adjective 1 *a fire and the consequential smoke damage* =resulting, resultant, ensuing, consequent; subsequent; attendant, accompanying, concomitant; collateral. 2 *one of his more consequential initiatives* =important, significant, momentous.
–OPPOSITES insignificant.

consequently ▶ adverb =as a result, as a consequence, so, thus, therefore, ergo, accordingly, hence, for this/that reason, because of this/that.

conservation ▶ noun =preservation, protection, safeguarding, safe keeping; care, guardianship, husbandry, supervision; upkeep, maintenance, repair, restoration; ecology, environmentalism.

conservative ▶ adjective 1 *the conservative wing of the party* =right-wing, reactionary, traditionalist; *Brit.* Tory; *US* Republican. 2 *the conservative trade-union movement* =traditionalist, old-fashioned, dyed-in-the-wool, hidebound, unadventurous, reactionary, set in one's ways; moderate, middle-of-the-road; *informal* stick in the mud. 3 *a conservative suit* =conventional, sober, modest, sensible, restrained, low-key, demure; *informal* square, straight.
–OPPOSITES socialist, radical, ostentatious.
▶ noun *liberals and conservatives have found common ground* =right-winger, reactionary; *Brit.* Tory; *US* Republican.

conservatory ▶ noun *a teaching job at the Moscow Conservatory* =conservatoire, music school, drama school; academy.

conserve ▶ verb *fossil fuel should be conserved* =preserve, protect, save, safeguard, keep, look after; sustain, husband.
–OPPOSITES squander.
▶ noun *cherry conserve* =jam, preserve, jelly.

consider ▶ verb 1 *Isabel considered her choices* =think about, contemplate, reflect on, review, mull over, ponder, deliberate on, chew over, meditate on, ruminate on; assess, evaluate, weigh up, appraise; *informal* size up. 2 *I consider him irresponsible* =deem, think, believe, judge, rate, count, find; regard as, hold to be, reckon to be, view as, see as. 3 *he considered the ceiling* =look at, contemplate, observe, regard, survey,

examine, inspect. **4** *the inquiry will consider those issues* = **take into consideration**, take account of, make allowances for, bear in mind, be mindful of, note.
−OPPOSITES ignore.

considerable ▶ adjective = **sizeable**, substantial, appreciable, significant; *informal* tidy.
−OPPOSITES paltry.

considerably ▶ adverb = **greatly**, (very) much, a great deal, a lot, lots; significantly, substantially, appreciably, markedly, noticeably; *informal* plenty.

considerate ▶ adjective = **attentive**, thoughtful, solicitous; kind, unselfish, caring; polite, sensitive.

consideration ▶ noun **1** *your case needs careful consideration* = **thought**, deliberation, reflection, contemplation; examination, inspection, scrutiny, analysis, discussion; attention. **2** *his health is the prime consideration* = **factor**, issue, matter, concern, aspect, feature. **3** *firms should show more consideration* = **attentiveness**, concern, care, thoughtfulness, solicitude; understanding, respect, sensitivity.

considering ▶ preposition = **bearing in mind**, taking into consideration, taking into account, in view of, in the light of.

consign ▶ verb *I consigned her picture to the dustbin* = **deposit**, commit, banish, relegate.

consignment ▶ noun = **delivery**, shipment, load, boatload, truckload, cargo; batch.

consist ▶ verb = **be composed**, be made up of, be formed; comprise, contain, incorporate.

consistency ▶ noun **1** *the trend shows a degree of consistency* = **uniformity**, constancy, regularity, evenness, steadiness; dependability, reliability. **2** *cream of pouring consistency* = **thickness**, density, viscosity; texture.

consistent ▶ adjective **1** *consistent opinion-poll evidence* = **constant**, regular, uniform, steady, stable, even, unchanging; dependable, reliable, predictable. **2** *her injuries were consistent with a knife attack* = **compatible**, in tune, in line; corresponding to, conforming to.
−OPPOSITES irregular, incompatible.

consolation ▶ noun = **comfort**, sol-

ace, sympathy, pity, commiseration; relief, encouragement, reassurance.

console¹ ▶ verb *she tried to console him* = **comfort**, sympathize with, commiserate with, show compassion for; help, support, cheer (up), hearten, encourage, reassure, soothe.
−OPPOSITES upset.

console² ▶ noun *a digital console* = **control panel**, instrument panel, dashboard, keyboard, array; *informal* dash.

consolidate ▶ verb **1** *we consolidated our position in the market* = **strengthen**, secure, stabilize, reinforce, fortify. **2** *consolidate the results into an action plan* = **combine**, unite, merge, integrate, amalgamate, fuse, synthesize, bring together.

consonance ▶ noun = **agreement**, accord, harmony, unison; compatibility, congruity, congruence.

consort ▶ noun *the queen and her consort* = **partner**, companion, mate; spouse, husband, wife.
▶ verb *he consorted with other women* = **associate**, keep company, mix, go around, spend time, socialize, fraternize, have dealings; *informal* run around, hang around/round, hang out; *Brit. informal* hang about.

conspicuous ▶ adjective = **easily seen**, clear, visible, noticeable, discernible, perceptible, detectable; obvious, manifest, evident, apparent, marked, pronounced, prominent; striking, eye-catching, overt, blatant, writ large; distinct, recognizable, unmistakable, inescapable; *informal* as plain as the nose on one's face, standing out like a sore thumb, standing out a mile.

conspiracy ▶ noun **1** *a conspiracy to manipulate the race results* = **plot**, scheme, plan, ploy, trick, ruse, subterfuge. **2** *conspiracy to murder* = **plotting**, collusion, intrigue, connivance.

conspirator ▶ noun = **plotter**, schemer, colluder, collaborator, conniver.

conspire ▶ verb **1** *they admitted conspiring to steal cars* = **plot**, scheme, plan, intrigue. **2** *circumstances conspired against them* = **combine**, unite, join forces; *informal* gang up.

constancy ▶ noun **1** *constancy between lovers* = **fidelity**, faithfulness, loyalty, commitment, dedication, devotion. **2** *the constancy of Henry's views* = **steadfastness**, resolution, resolve, firmness,

fixedness; determination, perseverance, tenacity, doggedness, staunchness, staying power. **3** *the constancy of
human nature* =**consistency**, permanence, durability; uniformity, immutability, regularity, stability.

constant ▸ adjective **1** *the constant background noise* =**continual**, continuous,
persistent, sustained, round-the-clock;
ceaseless, unceasing, perpetual, incessant, never-ending, eternal, endless,
unabating, non-stop, unrelieved; interminable, unremitting, relentless. **2** *a
constant speed* =**consistent**, regular,
steady, uniform, even, invariable, unvarying, unchanging, undeviating. **3** *a
constant friend* =**faithful**, loyal, devoted,
true, fast, firm, unswerving; steadfast,
staunch, dependable, trustworthy,
trusty, reliable. **4** *maintain constant vigilance* =**steadfast**, steady, resolute, determined, tenacious, dogged, unwavering,
unflagging.
–OPPOSITES fitful, variable, fickle.

constantly ▸ adverb =**always**, all the
time, continually, continuously, persistently; round the clock, night and day,
{morning, noon, and night}; endlessly,
non-stop, incessantly, unceasingly, perpetually, eternally, forever; interminably, unremittingly, relentlessly; *Scottish*
aye; *informal* 24-7.
–OPPOSITES occasionally.

consternation ▸ noun =**dismay**, distress, disquiet, discomposure; surprise;
alarm, fear, fright, shock.
–OPPOSITES satisfaction.

constituent ▸ adjective *constituent
parts* =**component**, integral; elemental,
basic, essential.
▸ noun **1** *MPs must listen to their constituents*
=**voter**, elector. **2** *the constituents of tobacco* =**component**, ingredient, element; part, piece, bit, unit; section, portion.

constitute ▸ verb **1** *farmers constituted
10 per cent of the population* =**amount to**,
add up to, account for, form, make up,
compose, comprise. **2** *this constitutes a
breach of copyright* =**be equivalent to**, be,
be tantamount to, be regarded as. **3** *the
courts were constituted in 1875* =**inaugurate**, establish, initiate, found, create,
set up, start, form, organize, develop;
commission, charter, invest, appoint,
install.

constitution ▸ noun **1** *the constitution*

guarantees our rights =**charter**, social
code, law; bill of rights; rules, regulations. **2** *the chemical constitution of the dye*
=**composition**, make-up, structure,
construction, arrangement, configuration, formation, anatomy. **3** *she has the
constitution of an ox* =**health**, physique;
strength, stamina, energy.

constitutional ▸ adjective **1** *constitutional powers* =**legal**, lawful, legitimate, authorized, permitted; sanctioned,
ratified, warranted, constituted, statutory, chartered, official. **2** *a constitutional
weakness* =**inherent**, intrinsic, innate,
fundamental, essential, inborn, inbred.

constrain ▸ verb **1** *he felt constrained to
explain* =**compel**, force, drive, impel, oblige, require. **2** *prices were constrained by
state controls* =**restrict**, limit, curb,
check, restrain, contain, hold back,
keep down.

constraint ▸ noun **1** *financial constraints* =**restriction**, limitation, curb,
check, restraint, control; hindrance,
impediment, obstruction, handicap.
2 *they were able to talk without constraint*
=**inhibition**, uneasiness, embarrassment; self-consciousness, forcedness,
awkwardness.

constrict ▸ verb =**narrow**, tighten,
compress, contract, squeeze, strangle;
archaic straiten.
–OPPOSITES expand, dilate.

constriction ▸ noun =**tightness**,
pressure, compression, contraction; obstruction, blockage, impediment; *Medicine* stricture.

construct ▸ verb **1** *a new motorway was
being constructed* =**build**, erect, put up,
set up, assemble, manufacture, fabricate, create, make. **2** *he constructed a
faultless argument* =**formulate**, form, put
together, create, devise, compose, work
out; fashion, mould, shape, frame.
–OPPOSITES demolish.

construction ▸ noun **1** *the construction of a new airport* =**building**, erection,
putting up, setting up, establishment;
assembly, manufacture, fabrication,
creation. **2** *the station was a spectacular
construction* =**structure**, building, edifice, work.

constructive ▸ adjective =**useful**,
helpful, productive, positive, encouraging; practical, valuable, profitable,
worthwhile.

construe ▸ verb =**interpret**, understand, read, see, take, take to mean, regard.

consul ▸ noun =**ambassador**, diplomat, chargé d'affaires, attaché, envoy, emissary.

consult ▸ verb **1** *you need to consult a solicitor* =**seek advice from**, ask, see, call (on), speak to, turn to, contact, get in touch with; *informal* pick someone's brains. **2** *the government must consult with interested parties* =**confer**, talk things over, communicate, parley, deliberate; *informal* put their heads together. **3** *she consulted her diary* =**refer to**, turn to, look at, check.

consultant ▸ noun **1** *an engineering consultant* =**adviser**, expert, specialist, pundit. **2** *a consultant at Guy's hospital* =**senior doctor**, specialist.

consultation ▸ noun **1** *the need for further consultation with industry* =**discussion**, dialogue, debate, negotiation, deliberation. **2** *a 30-minute consultation* =**meeting**, talk, discussion, interview, audience, hearing; appointment, session.

consume ▸ verb **1** *vast amounts of food and drink were consumed* =**eat**, devour, ingest, swallow, gobble up, wolf down, guzzle, feast on, snack on; **drink**, gulp down, imbibe, sup; *informal* tuck into, put away, polish off, dispose of, pig oneself on, down, neck, sink, swill; *Brit. informal* scoff, shift; *N. Amer. informal* scarf (down/up), snarf (down/up). **2** *natural resources are being consumed at an alarming rate* =**use (up)**, utilize, expend; deplete, exhaust. **3** *the fire consumed fifty houses* =**destroy**, demolish, lay waste, wipe out, annihilate, devastate, gut, ruin, wreck. **4** *Carolyn was consumed with guilt* =**eat up**, devour, grip, overwhelm; absorb, preoccupy.

consumer ▸ noun =**purchaser**, buyer, customer, shopper, user, end-user; client; (**the consumer** or **consumers**) the public, the market, people.

consuming ▸ adjective =**absorbing**, compelling, compulsive, obsessive, overwhelming; intense, powerful, burning, raging, profound, deep-seated.

consummate ▸ verb *the deal was finally consummated* =**complete**, conclude, finish, accomplish, achieve; execute, carry out, perform; *informal* sew up, wrap up.
▸ adjective *his consummate skill | a consum-*

mate politician =**supreme**, superb, superlative, superior, accomplished, expert, proficient, skilful, skilled, masterly, master, first-class, polished, practised, perfect, ultimate; complete, total, utter, absolute, pure.

consumption ▸ noun **1** *food unfit for human consumption* =**eating**, drinking, ingestion. **2** *the consumption of fossil fuels* =**use**, using up, utilization, depletion.

contact ▸ noun **1** *a disease transmitted through contact with rats* =**touch**, touching; proximity, exposure, intimacy. **2** *diplomats were asked to avoid all contact with him* =**communication**, correspondence; association, connection, intercourse, relations, dealings. **3** *he had many contacts in Germany* =**connection**, acquaintance, associate, friend.
▸ verb *anyone with information should contact the police* =**get in touch with**, communicate with, approach, notify; telephone, phone, call, ring up, speak to, talk to, write to; *informal* get hold of.

contagious ▸ adjective =**infectious**, communicable, transmittable, transmissible; *informal* catching; *dated* infective.

contain ▸ verb **1** *the archive contains much unpublished material* =**include**, comprise, take in, incorporate, involve, encompass, embrace; consist of, be made up of, be composed of =**hold**. **2** *the boat contained four people* =**hold**, carry, accommodate, seat; sleep. **3** *he must contain his anger* =**restrain**, curb, rein in, suppress, repress, stifle, subdue, quell, swallow, bottle up, hold in, keep in check.

container ▸ noun =**receptacle**, vessel, holder, repository; box, canister.

contaminate ▸ verb =**pollute**; defile, debase, corrupt, taint, infect, spoil, soil, stain; poison.
−OPPOSITES purify.

contemplate ▸ verb **1** *she contemplated her image in the mirror* =**look at**, view, regard, examine, inspect, observe, survey, study, scrutinize, stare at, gaze at, eye. **2** *he contemplated his fate* =**think about**, ponder, reflect on, consider, mull over, muse on, dwell on, deliberate over, meditate on, ruminate on, chew over, brood on/about, turn over in one's mind; *formal* cogitate. **3** *he was contemplating action for damages* =**consider**, think about, have in mind, intend, plan, propose.

contemplation ▶ noun **1** *the contemplation of beautiful objects* =**viewing**, examination, inspection, observation, survey, study, scrutiny. **2** *a time for contemplation* =**thought**, reflection, meditation, consideration, deliberation, introspection.

contemplative ▶ adjective =**thoughtful**, pensive, reflective, meditative, ruminative, introspective, brooding, deep/lost in thought.

contemporary ▶ adjective **1** *contemporary sources* =**of the time**, of the day, contemporaneous, concurrent, coexisting. **2** *contemporary society* =**modern**, present-day, present, current. **3** *a very contemporary design* =**modern**, up to date, up to the minute, fashionable; modish, latest, recent; *informal* trendy, hip.
−OPPOSITES old-fashioned, out of date.
▶ noun *Chaucer's contemporaries* =**peer**, fellow.

contempt ▶ noun =**scorn**, disdain, derision; disgust, loathing, hatred, abhorrence.
−OPPOSITES respect.

contemptible ▶ adjective =**despicable**, detestable, hateful, reprehensible, deplorable, unspeakable, disgraceful, shameful, ignominious, abject, low, mean, cowardly, discreditable, worthless, shabby, cheap; *archaic* scurvy.
−OPPOSITES admirable.

contemptuous ▶ adjective =**scornful**, disdainful, insulting, insolent, derisive, mocking, sneering, scoffing, withering, scathing; condescending, supercilious, haughty, superior, arrogant, dismissive, aloof; *informal* high and mighty, snotty, sniffy.
−OPPOSITES respectful.

contend ▶ verb **1** *the pilot had to contend with torrential rain* =**cope with**, face, grapple with, deal with, take on, handle. **2** *three main groups were contending for power* =**compete**, vie, contest, fight, battle, tussle; strive, struggle. **3** *he contends that the judge was wrong* =**assert**, maintain, hold, claim, argue, insist, state, declare, profess, affirm; allege; *formal* aver.

content[1] ▶ adjective *she seemed content with life* =**contented**, satisfied, pleased, fulfilled, happy, cheerful, glad; unworried, untroubled, at ease, at peace, tranquil, serene.

−OPPOSITES discontented, dissatisfied.
▶ verb *her reply seemed to content him* =**satisfy**, please; soothe, pacify, placate, appease, mollify.

content[2] ▶ noun **1** *foods with a high fibre content* =**amount**, proportion, level. **2** (**contents**) *the contents of a vegetarian sausage* =**constituents**, ingredients, components. **3** *the content of the essay* =**subject matter**, theme, argument, thesis, message, thrust, substance, text, ideas.

contented ▶ adjective *a contented man.* See CONTENT[1] adjective.

contention ▶ noun **1** *a point of contention* =**disagreement**, dispute, argument, discord, conflict, friction, strife, dissension, disharmony. **2** *the Marxist contention that capitalism equals exploitation* =**argument**, claim, submission, allegation, assertion, declaration; opinion, position, view, belief, thesis, case.
−OPPOSITES agreement.

contentious ▶ adjective **1** *a contentious issue* =**controversial**, debatable, disputed, open to debate, moot, vexed. **2** *a contentious debate* =**heated**, vehement, fierce, violent, intense, impassioned. **3** *contentious people.* See QUARRELSOME.

contentment ▶ noun =**contentedness**, content, satisfaction, fulfilment, happiness, pleasure, cheerfulness; ease, comfort, well-being, peace, equanimity, serenity, tranquillity.

contest ▶ noun **1** *a boxing contest* =**competition**, match, tournament, game, meet, trial, bout, heat, fixture, tie, race. **2** *the contest for the party leadership* =**fight**, battle, tussle, struggle, competition, race.
▶ verb **1** *he intended to contest the seat* =**compete for**, contend for, vie for, fight for, go for. **2** *we contested the decision* =**oppose**, object to, challenge, take issue with, question, call into question. **3** *the issues have been hotly contested* =**debate**, argue about, dispute, quarrel over.

contestant ▶ noun =**competitor**, participant, player, contender, candidate, aspirant, entrant.

context ▶ noun =**circumstances**, conditions, factors, state of affairs, situation, background, scene, setting.

contingency ▶ noun =**eventuality**, (chance) event, incident, happening, occurrence, juncture, possibility, accident, chance, emergency.

contingent ▸ adjective **1** *the merger is contingent on government approval* =**dependent on**, conditional on, subject to, determined by, hinging on, resting on. **2** *contingent events* =**chance**, accidental, fortuitous, possible, unforeseeable, unpredictable, random, haphazard.
▸ noun **1** *a contingent of Japanese businessmen* =**group**, party, body, band, company, cohort, deputation, delegation; *informal* bunch. **2** *a contingent of marines* =**detachment**, unit, group.

continual ▸ adjective **1** *a service disrupted by continual breakdowns* =**frequent**, repeated, constant, recurrent, recurring, regular. **2** *she was in continual pain* =**constant**, continuous, unremitting, unrelenting, unrelieved, chronic, uninterrupted, unbroken, round-the-clock.
–OPPOSITES occasional, temporary.

continuance ▸ noun. See CONTINUATION.

continuation ▸ noun =**carrying on**, continuance, extension, prolongation, protraction, perpetuation.
–OPPOSITES end.

continue ▸ verb **1** *he was unable to continue with his job* =**carry on**, proceed, pursue, go on, keep on, persist, press on, persevere, keep at; *informal* stick at. **2** *discussions continued throughout the year* =**go on**, carry on, last, extend, run on, drag on. **3** *we are keen to continue this relationship* =**maintain**, keep up, sustain, keep going, keep alive, preserve. **4** *his willingness to continue in office* =**remain**, stay, carry on, keep going. **5** *we continued our conversation after supper* =**resume**, pick up, take up, carry on with, return to, revisit.
–OPPOSITES stop, break off.

continuing ▸ adjective =**ongoing**, continuous, sustained, persistent, steady, relentless, uninterrupted, unabating, unremitting, unceasing.
–OPPOSITES sporadic.

continuous ▸ adjective =**continual**, uninterrupted, unbroken, constant, ceaseless, incessant, steady, sustained, solid, continuing, ongoing, unceasing, without a break, non-stop, round-the-clock, persistent, unremitting, relentless, unrelenting, unabating, unrelieved, endless, unending, never-ending, perpetual, everlasting, eternal, interminable; running; *N. Amer.* without surcease.
–OPPOSITES intermittent.

contort ▸ verb =**twist**, bend out of shape, distort, misshape, warp, buckle, deform.

contour ▸ noun =**outline**, shape, form; lines, curves; silhouette, profile.

contraband ▸ adjective =**smuggled**, black-market, bootleg, under the counter, illegal, illicit, unlawful; prohibited, banned, proscribed; *informal* hot.

contract ▸ noun *a legally binding contract* =**agreement**, commitment, arrangement, settlement, understanding, compact, covenant, bond; deal, bargain.
▸ verb **1** *the market for such goods began to contract* =**shrink**, get smaller, decrease, diminish, reduce, dwindle, decline; collapse. **2** *her stomach muscles contracted* =**tighten**, tense, flex, constrict, draw in, narrow. **3** *his name was soon contracted to 'Jack'* =**shorten**, abbreviate, cut, reduce; elide. **4** *the company was contracted to build the stadium* =**engage**, take on, hire, commission; employ. **5** *she contracted German measles* =**develop**, catch, get, pick up, come down with, succumb to; *Brit.* go down with.
–OPPOSITES expand, relax, lengthen.

contraction ▸ noun **1** *the contraction of the industry* =**shrinking**, shrinkage, decline, decrease, diminution, dwindling; collapse. **2** *the contraction of muscles* =**tightening**, tensing, flexing. **3** *my contractions started at midnight* =**labour pains**, labour; cramps. **4** *'goodbye' is a contraction of 'God be with you'* –**abbreviation**, short form, shortened form, elision, diminutive.

contradict ▸ verb **1** *he contradicted the government's account of the affair* =**deny**, refute, rebut, dispute, challenge, counter. **2** *nobody dared to contradict him* =**argue with**, go against, challenge, oppose; *formal* gainsay. **3** *this research contradicts previous computer models* =**conflict with**, be at odds with, be at variance with, be inconsistent with, run counter to, disagree with; challenge, undermine.
–OPPOSITES confirm, agree with.

contradiction ▸ noun **1** *the contradiction between his faith and his lifestyle* =**conflict**, clash, disagreement, opposition, inconsistency, mismatch, variance. **2** *a*

contradiction of his statement =**denial**, refutation, rebuttal, countering.
–OPPOSITES confirmation, agreement.

contradictory ▸ adjective =**opposed**, in opposition, opposite, antithetical, contrary, contrasting, conflicting, at variance, at odds, opposing, clashing, divergent, different; inconsistent, incompatible, irreconcilable.

contraption ▸ noun =**device**, gadget, apparatus, machine, appliance, mechanism, invention, contrivance; *informal* gizmo, widget; *Brit. informal* gubbins; *Austral. informal* bitzer.

contrary ▸ adjective **1** *contrary views* =**opposite**, opposing, opposed, contradictory, clashing, conflicting, antithetical, incompatible, irreconcilable. **2** *she was sulky and contrary* =**perverse**, awkward, difficult, uncooperative, unhelpful, obstructive, recalcitrant, wilful, self-willed, stubborn, obstinate, mulish, pig-headed, intractable; *informal* cussed; *Brit. informal* bloody-minded, bolshie, stroppy; *N. Amer. informal* balky; *formal* refractory.
–OPPOSITES compatible, accommodating.
▸ noun *in fact, the contrary is true* =**opposite**, reverse, converse, antithesis.
■ **contrary to** =**in conflict with**, against, at variance with, at odds with, in opposition to, counter to, incompatible with.

contrast ▸ noun **1** *the contrast between rural and urban trends* =**difference**, dissimilarity, disparity, distinction, divergence, variance, variation, differentiation; contradiction, incongruity, opposition. **2** *Jane was a complete contrast to Sarah* =**opposite**, antithesis; foil, complement.
–OPPOSITES similarity.
▸ verb *a view which contrasts with his earlier opinion* =**differ from**, be at variance with, be contrary to, conflict with, go against, be at odds with, be in opposition to, disagree with, clash with. **2** *people contrasted her with her sister* =**compare**, juxtapose; measure against; distinguish from, differentiate from.
–OPPOSITES resemble, liken.

contravene ▸ verb =**break**, breach, violate, infringe; defy, disobey, flout.
–OPPOSITES comply with.

contravention ▸ noun =**breach**, violation, infringement.

contribute ▸ verb **1** *the government contributed a million pounds* =**give**, donate, put up, grant, bestow, present, provide, supply, furnish; *informal* chip in, pitch in, fork out, shell out, cough up; *Brit. informal* stump up; *N. Amer. informal* kick in, ante up, pony up. **2** *an article contributed by Dr Clouson* =**supply**, provide, submit. **3** *numerous factors contribute to job satisfaction* =**play a part in**, be instrumental in, be a factor in, have a hand in, be conducive to, make for, lead to, cause.

contribution ▸ noun **1** *voluntary financial contributions* =**donation**, gift, offering, present, handout, grant, subsidy, allowance, endowment, subscription. **2** *contributions from local authors* =**article**, piece, story, item, paper, essay.

contributor ▸ noun **1** *the magazine's regular contributors* =**writer**, columnist, correspondent. **2** *campaign contributors* =**donor**, benefactor, subscriber, supporter, backer, subsidizer, patron, sponsor.

contrite ▸ adjective =**remorseful**, repentant, penitent, regretful, sorry, apologetic, rueful, sheepish, hangdog, ashamed, chastened, shamefaced.

contrition ▸ noun =**remorse**, remorsefulness, repentance, penitence, sorrow, sorrowfulness, regret, ruefulness, pangs of conscience; shame, guilt.

contrivance ▸ noun **1** *a mechanical contrivance* =**device**, gadget, machine, appliance, contraption, apparatus, mechanism, implement, tool, invention; *informal* gizmo, widget; *Austral. informal* bitzer. **2** *her matchmaking contrivances* =**scheme**, stratagem, tactic, manoeuvre, move, plan, ploy, gambit, wile, trick, ruse, plot, machination.

contrive ▸ verb =**bring about**, engineer, manufacture, orchestrate, stage-manage, create, devise, concoct, construct, plan, fabricate, plot, hatch; *informal* wangle, set up.

contrived ▸ adjective =**forced**, strained, studied, artificial, affected, put-on, pretended, false, manufactured, unnatural; laboured, overdone.
–OPPOSITES natural.

control ▸ noun **1** *China retained control over the region* =**jurisdiction**, power, authority, command, dominance, government, mastery, leadership, rule, sovereignty, supremacy; charge, management, direction, supervision, superintendence. **2** *strict import controls* =**restraint**, constraint, limitation, restriction, check, curb; regulation. **3** *her control deserted her* =**self-control**, self-restraint, self-possession, composure, calmness; *informal* cool.

▶ verb **1** *one family had controlled the company since its formation* =**be in charge of**, run, manage, direct, administer, head, preside over, supervise, steer; command, rule, govern, lead, dominate, hold sway over, be at the helm; *informal* head up, be in the driving seat. **2** *she struggled to control her temper* =**restrain**, keep in check, curb, check, contain, hold back, bridle, rein in, suppress, repress, master. **3** *public spending was controlled* =**limit**, restrict, curb, cap, constrain.

controversial ▶ adjective =**contentious**, disputed, moot, disputable, debatable, arguable, vexed, tendentious.

controversy ▶ noun =**disagreement**, dispute, argument, debate, dissension, contention, wrangling, quarrelling, war of words, storm; *Brit. informal* row.

conundrum ▶ noun =**problem**, question, difficulty, quandary, dilemma.

convalesce ▶ verb =**recuperate**, get better, recover, get well, get back on one's feet.

convalescence ▶ noun =**recuperation**, recovery, return to health, rehabilitation, improvement.

convene ▶ verb **1** *he convened a secret meeting* =**summon**, call, call together, order; *formal* convoke. **2** *the committee convened for its final session* =**assemble**, gather, meet, come together, congregate; *formal* foregather.

convenience ▶ noun **1** *the convenience of the arrangement* =**expedience**, advantageousness, advantage, propitiousness, timeliness; suitability, appropriateness. **2** *for convenience, the handset is wall-mounted* =**ease of use**, usability, usefulness, utility, serviceability, practicality. **3** *the kitchen has all the modern conveniences* =**appliance**, (labour-saving) device, gadget; amenity, facility; *informal* mod con.

convenient ▶ adjective **1** *a convenient time* =**suitable**, appropriate, fitting, fit, suited, opportune, timely, favourable, advantageous, seasonable, expedient. **2** *a hotel that's convenient for the beach* =**near (to)**, close to, within easy reach of, well situated for, handy for, not far

from, just round the corner from; *informal* a stone's throw from, within spitting distance of.

convention ▶ noun **1** *social conventions* =**custom**, usage, practice, tradition, way, habit, norm; rule, code, canon; propriety, etiquette, protocol; *formal* praxis; (**conventions**) mores. **2** *a convention signed by 74 countries* =**agreement**, accord, protocol, compact, pact, treaty, concordat; contract, bargain, deal. **3** *the party's biennial convention* =**conference**, meeting, congress, assembly, gathering, summit, convocation, synod, conclave.

conventional ▶ adjective **1** *the conventional wisdom of the day* =**orthodox**, traditional, established, accepted, received, mainstream, prevailing, prevalent. **2** *a conventional railway* =**normal**, standard, regular, ordinary, usual, traditional, typical, common. **3** *a very conventional woman* =**conservative**, traditional, conformist, bourgeois, old-fashioned, of the old school, small-town; *informal* straight, square, stick-in-the-mud, fuddy-duddy. **4** *a conventional piece of work* =**unoriginal**, formulaic, predictable, unadventurous, unremarkable.
–OPPOSITES unorthodox, original.

converge ▶ verb =**meet**, intersect, cross, connect, link up, coincide, join, unite, merge.
–OPPOSITES diverge.

conversant ▶ adjective =**familiar**, acquainted, au fait, at home, well versed, well informed, knowledgeable, informed, abreast, up to date; *informal* up to speed, clued up, genned up; *formal* cognizant.

conversation ▶ noun =**discussion**, talk, chat, gossip, tête-à-tête, heart-to-heart, head-to-head, exchange, dialogue; *informal* confab, jaw, chit-chat; *Brit. informal* chinwag, natter; *N. Amer. informal* gabfest, schmooze; *Austral./NZ informal* yarn; *formal* colloquy.

conversational ▶ adjective =**informal**, chatty, relaxed, friendly; colloquial, idiomatic, everyday.

converse[1] ▶ verb *they conversed in low voices* =**talk**, speak, chat, discourse, communicate; *informal* chew the fat, jaw; *Brit. informal* natter; *N. Amer. informal* visit, shoot the breeze/bull; *Austral./NZ informal* mag.

converse[2] ▶ noun *the converse is also*

true =**opposite**, reverse, obverse, contrary, antithesis, other side of the coin; *informal* flip side.

conversion ▸ noun **1** *the conversion of waste into energy* =**change**, changing, transformation, metamorphosis, transmutation; *humorous* transmogrification. **2** *the conversion of the building* =**adaptation**, alteration, modification, redevelopment, redesign, renovation. **3** *his religious conversion* =**rebirth**, regeneration, reformation; transformation.

convert ▸ verb **1** *plants convert the sun's energy into chemical energy* =**change**, turn, transform, metamorphose, transfigure, transmute; *humorous* transmogrify. **2** *the factory was converted into flats* =**adapt**, turn, change, alter, modify, redevelop, redesign, restyle, revamp, renovate, rehabilitate; *N. Amer.* bring up to code; *informal* do up; *N. Amer. informal* rehab. **3** *they sought to convert sinners* =**proselytize**, evangelize, redeem, save, reform, re-educate.

convey ▸ verb **1** *taxis conveyed guests to the station* =**transport**, carry, bring, take, fetch, bear, move, ferry, shuttle, shift, transfer. **2** *he conveyed the information to me* =**communicate**, pass on, make known, impart, relay, transmit, send, hand on, relate, tell, reveal, disclose. **3** *it's impossible to convey how I felt* =**express**, communicate, get across/over, put across/over, indicate, say; articulate. **4** *he conveys an air of competence* =**project**, exude, emit, emanate.

convict ▸ verb =**find guilty**, sentence; *Brit. informal* be done for.
−OPPOSITES acquit.
▸ noun =**prisoner**, inmate; criminal, offender, lawbreaker, felon; *informal* jailbird, con, (old) lag, crook; *N. Amer. informal* yardbird.

conviction ▸ noun **1** *his conviction for murder* =**judgement**, sentence. **2** *his political convictions* =**beliefs**, opinions, views, persuasion, ideals, position, stance, values. **3** *she spoke with conviction* =**certainty**, certitude, assurance, confidence, sureness.
−OPPOSITES acquittal, uncertainty.

convince ▸ verb **1** *he convinced me that I was wrong* =**make certain**, persuade, satisfy, prove to; assure. **2** *I convinced her to marry me* =**persuade**, induce, prevail on, get, talk into, win over, cajole, inveigle.

convincing ▸ adjective **1** *a convincing argument* =**cogent**, persuasive, plausible, powerful, potent, strong, forceful, compelling, irresistible, telling, conclusive. **2** *a convincing 5–0 win* =**resounding**, emphatic, decisive, conclusive.

convivial ▸ adjective =**friendly**, genial, affable, amiable, congenial, agreeable, good-humoured, cordial, warm, sociable, outgoing, gregarious, clubbable, companionable, cheerful, jolly, jovial, lively; enjoyable, festive; *Scottish* couthy.

conviviality ▸ noun =**friendliness**, geniality, affability, amiability, bonhomie, congeniality, cordiality, warmth, good nature, sociability, gregariousness, cheerfulness, good cheer, joviality, jollity, gaiety, liveliness.

convocation ▸ noun =**assembly**, gathering, meeting, conference, convention, congress, council, symposium, colloquium, conclave, synod.

convoluted ▸ adjective =**complicated**, complex, involved, elaborate, serpentine, labyrinthine, tortuous, tangled, Byzantine; confused, confusing, bewildering, baffling.
−OPPOSITES straightforward.

convolution ▸ noun **1** *crosses adorned with elaborate convolutions* =**twist**, turn, coil, spiral, twirl, curl, helix, whorl, loop, curlicue. **2** *the convolutions of the plot* =**complexity**, intricacy, complication, twist, turn, entanglement.

convoy ▸ noun =**group**, fleet, cavalcade, motorcade, cortège, caravan, line, train.

convulsion ▸ noun **1** *she had convulsions* =**fit**, seizure, paroxysm, spasm, attack. **2** (**convulsions**) *the audience collapsed in convulsions* =**fits (of laughter)**, paroxysms (of laughter), uncontrollable laughter; *informal* hysterics. **3** *the political convulsions of the period* =**upheaval**, eruption, cataclysm, turmoil, turbulence, tumult, disruption, agitation, disturbance, unrest, disorder.

convulsive ▸ adjective =**spasmodic**, jerky, paroxysmal, violent, uncontrollable.

cook ▸ verb =**prepare**, make, put together; *informal* fix, rustle up; *Brit. informal* knock up.
■ **cook something up** *(informal)* =**concoct**, devise, contrive, fabricate, trump up, hatch, plot, plan, invent, make up, think up, dream up.

cooking ▸ noun =**cuisine**, cookery, baking; food.

> WORD LINKS
>
> *relating to cooking:* **culinary**

cool ▸ adjective **1** *a cool breeze* =**chilly**, chill, cold, bracing, brisk, crisp, fresh, refreshing, invigorating; draughty; *informal* nippy; *Brit. informal* parky. **2** *a cool response* =**unenthusiastic**, lukewarm, tepid, indifferent, uninterested, apathetic, half-hearted; unfriendly, distant, remote, aloof, cold, chilly, frosty, unwelcoming, unresponsive, offhand, uncommunicative, undemonstrative; *informal* stand-offish. **3** *his ability to keep cool in a crisis* =**calm**, composed, as cool as a cucumber, collected, level-headed, self-possessed, controlled, self-controlled, poised, serene, tranquil, unruffled, unperturbed, unmoved, untroubled, imperturbable, placid, phlegmatic; *informal* unflappable, together, laid-back. **4** *(informal) she thinks she's so cool* =**fashionable**, stylish, chic, up to the minute, sophisticated; *informal* trendy, funky, with it, hip, big, happening, groovy; *N. Amer. informal* kicky, tony, fly.
> −OPPOSITES warm, enthusiastic, agitated.
▸ noun **1** *the cool of the evening* =**chill**, chilliness, coldness, coolness. **2** *Ken lost his cool* =**self-control**, control, composure, self-possession, calmness, equilibrium, calm; aplomb, poise, sangfroid.
> −OPPOSITES warmth.
▸ verb **1** *cool the sauce in the fridge* =**chill**, refrigerate. **2** *her reluctance did nothing to cool his interest* =**lessen**, moderate, diminish, reduce, dampen. **3** *Simpson's ardour had cooled* =**subside**, lessen, diminish, decrease, abate, moderate, die down, fade, dwindle, wane. **4** *after a while, she cooled off* =**calm down**, recover/ regain one's composure, compose oneself, control oneself, pull oneself together, simmer down.
> −OPPOSITES heat, inflame, intensify.

coop ▸ noun *a hen coop* =**pen**, run, cage, hutch, enclosure.
▸ verb *he hates being cooped up at home* =**confine**, shut in/up, cage (in), pen up/in, keep, detain, trap, incarcerate, immure.

cooperate ▸ verb **1** *police and social services cooperated in the operation* =**collaborate**, work together, work side by side, pull together, join forces, team up, unite, combine, pool resources, liaise. **2** *he was happy to cooperate* =**be of assistance**, assist, help, lend a hand, be of service, do one's bit; *informal* play ball.

cooperation ▸ noun **1** *cooperation between management and workers* =**collaboration**, joint action, combined effort, teamwork, partnership, coordination, liaison, association, synergy, give and take, compromise. **2** *thank you for your cooperation* =**assistance**, helpfulness, help, aid.

cooperative ▸ adjective **1** *a cooperative effort* =**collaborative**, collective, combined, common, joint, shared, mutual, united, concerted, coordinated. **2** *pleasant and cooperative staff* =**helpful**, eager to help, obliging, accommodating, willing, amenable.

coordinate ▸ verb **1** *exhibitions coordinated by a team of international scholars* =**organize**, arrange, order, synchronize, bring together; curate, manage, oversee. **2** *care workers coordinate at a local level* =**cooperate**, liaise, collaborate, work together, communicate, be in contact. **3** *floral designs coordinate with the decor* =**match**, complement, set off; harmonize, blend, fit in, go.

cope ▸ verb **1** *she couldn't cope on her own* =**manage**, survive, subsist, look after oneself, fend for oneself, shift for oneself, carry on, get by/through, bear up, hold one's own, keep one's end up, keep one's head above water; *informal* make it, hack it. **2** *his inability to cope with the situation* =**deal with**, handle, manage, address, face (up to), confront, tackle, get to grips with, get through, weather, come to terms with.

copious ▸ adjective =**abundant**, plentiful, ample, profuse, full, extensive, generous, lavish, fulsome, liberal, overflowing, in abundance, many, numerous; *informal* a gogo, galore; *literary* plenteous.
−OPPOSITES sparse.

copse ▸ noun =**thicket**, grove, wood, coppice, clump; *Brit.* spinney; *N. Amer. & Austral./NZ* brush; *archaic* holt.

copulate ▸ verb. *See* HAVE SEX *at* SEX.

copulation ▸ noun. *See* SEX *sense* 1.

copy ▸ noun **1** *a copy of the report* =**duplicate**, facsimile, photocopy; transcript; reprint; *trademark* Xerox. **2** *a copy of a sketch by Leonardo da Vinci* =**replica**, re-

production, print, imitation, likeness; counterfeit, forgery, fake.
▶ verb **1** *each form had to be copied* = **duplicate**, photocopy, xerox, photostat, run off, reproduce. **2** *portraits copied from original paintings by Reynolds* = **reproduce**, replicate; forge, fake, counterfeit. **3** *their sound was copied by a lot of jazz players* = **imitate**, reproduce, emulate, follow, echo, mirror, parrot, mimic, ape; plagiarize, steal; *informal* rip off.

coquettish ▶ adjective = **flirtatious**, flirty, provocative, seductive, inviting, kittenish, coy, arch, teasing, playful; *informal* come-hither, vampish.

cord ▶ noun = **string**, thread, thong, lace, ribbon, strap, tape, tie, line, rope, cable, wire, ligature; twine, yarn, elastic, braid.

cordial ▶ adjective *a cordial welcome* = **friendly**, warm, genial, affable, amiable, pleasant, fond, affectionate, warmhearted, good-natured, gracious, hospitable, welcoming, hearty.
▶ noun *fruit cordial* = **squash**, crush, concentrate; juice.

cordon ▶ noun = **barrier**, line, row, chain, ring, circle.
▶ verb = **close off**, shut off, seal off, fence off, separate off, isolate, enclose, surround.

core ▶ noun **1** *the earth's core* = **centre**, interior, middle, nucleus; recesses, bowels, depths; *informal* innards. **2** *the core of the argument* = **heart**, heart of the matter, nucleus, nub, kernel, marrow, meat, essence, quintessence, crux, gist, pith, substance, basis, fundamentals; *informal* nitty-gritty, brass tacks.
−OPPOSITES periphery.
▶ adjective *the core issue* = **central**, key, basic, fundamental, principal, primary, main, chief, crucial, vital, essential; *informal* number-one.
−OPPOSITES peripheral.

cork ▶ noun = **stopper**, stop, plug, bung, peg; *N. Amer.* stopple.

corn ▶ noun = **grain**, cereal (crop); wheat, barley, oats, rye; maize; *Brit.* corn on the cob, sweetcorn.

cornea ▶ noun

> **WORD LINKS**
> surgical incision of the cornea: **keratotomy**

corner ▶ noun **1** *the cart lurched round the corner* = **bend**, curve, dog-leg; turn, turning, junction, fork, intersection; *Brit.* hairpin bend. **2** *a charming corner of Italy* = **district**, region, area, section, quarter, part; *informal* neck of the woods. **3** *he found himself in a bit of a corner* = **predicament**, plight, tight spot, mess, muddle, difficulty, problem, dilemma, quandary; *informal* pickle, jam, stew, fix, hole, hot water, bind.
▶ verb **1** *he was eventually cornered by police dogs* = **surround**, trap, hem in, pen in, enclose, isolate, cut off; capture, catch. **2** *crime syndicates have cornered the stolen car market* = **gain control of**, take over, control, dominate, monopolize; capture; *informal* sew up.

cornerstone ▶ noun = **foundation**, basis, keystone, mainspring, mainstay, linchpin, bedrock, base, backbone, key, centrepiece, core, heart, centre, crux.

corny ▶ adjective *(informal)* = **banal**, trite, hackneyed, clichéd, predictable, stereotyped, platitudinous, tired, stale, overworked, overused, well worn; mawkish, sentimental, mushy, slushy, sloppy, cloying, syrupy, sugary, saccharine; *Brit.* twee; *informal* cheesy, schmaltzy, cutesy, toe-curling; *Brit. informal* soppy; *N. Amer. informal* cornball, hokey.

corollary ▶ noun = **consequence**, (end) result, upshot, effect, repercussion, product, by-product; *Brit.* knock-on effect.

corporation ▶ noun **1** *the chairman of the corporation* = **company**, firm, business, concern, operation, organization, agency, trust, partnership; conglomerate, group, chain, multinational; *informal* outfit, set-up. **2** *(Brit.) the corporation refused two planning applications* = **(town/city) council**, local authority.

corporeal ▶ adjective = **bodily**, fleshly, carnal, human, mortal, earthly, physical, material.

corps ▶ noun **1** *an army corps* = **unit**, division, detachment, section, company, contingent, squad, squadron, regiment, battalion, brigade, platoon. **2** *a corps of trained engineers* = **group**, body, band, party, gang, pack; team, crew.

corpse ▶ noun = **dead body**, body, carcass, remains; *informal* stiff; *Medicine* cadaver.

> **WORD LINKS**
> relating to corpses: **necro-**
> fear of corpses: **necrophobia**

corpulent ▶ adjective =fat, obese, overweight, plump, portly, stout, chubby, paunchy, beer-bellied, heavy, bulky, chunky, well padded, well covered, meaty, fleshy, rotund, broad in the beam; *informal* tubby, pudgy, beefy, porky, roly-poly, blubbery; *Brit. informal* podgy; *N. Amer. informal* corn-fed.
−OPPOSITES thin.

correct ▶ adjective **1** *the correct answer* =**right**, accurate, true; *informal* on the mark, on the beam, on the nail; *Brit. informal* spot on, bang on; *N. Amer. informal* on the money, on the button. **2** *correct behaviour* =**proper**, seemly, decorous, decent, respectable, right, suitable, fit, fitting, befitting, appropriate; approved, accepted, conventional, customary, traditional, orthodox.
−OPPOSITES wrong, improper.
▶ verb **1** *correct any mistakes* =**rectify**, put right, set right, amend, emend, remedy, repair. **2** *an attempt to correct the trade imbalance* =**counteract**, offset, counterbalance, compensate for, make up for, neutralize. **3** *the brakes need correcting* =**adjust**, fix, set, reset, standardize, normalize, calibrate, fine-tune.

correction ▶ noun =**rectification**, righting, amendment, repair, remedy.

corrective ▶ adjective =**remedial**, therapeutic, restorative, curative.

correctly ▶ adverb **1** *the questions were answered correctly* =**accurately**, right, without error. **2** *she behaved correctly at all times* =**properly**, decorously, with decorum, decently, fittingly, appropriately, well.

correlate ▶ verb **1** *social status often correlates with wealth* =**correspond**, match, parallel, agree, tally, tie in, be consistent, be compatible, coordinate, dovetail, relate, conform; *informal* square; *N. Amer. informal* jibe. **2** *fat intake was correlated with heart disease* =**connect**, link, associate, relate.
−OPPOSITES contrast.

correlation ▶ noun =**connection**, association, link, tie-in, tie-up, relation, relationship, interrelationship, interdependence, interconnection, interaction; correspondence.

correspond ▶ verb **1** *their actions do not correspond with their statements* =**correlate**, agree, be in agreement, be consistent, be compatible, accord, be in tune, concur, coincide, tally, tie in, dovetail, fit in; match; *informal* square; *N. Amer. informal* jibe. **2** *a rank corresponding to the British rank of sergeant* =**be equivalent**, be analogous, be comparable, equate. **3** *Debbie and I corresponded for years* =**exchange letters**, write, communicate, keep in touch/contact.

correspondence ▶ noun **1** *there is some correspondence between the two variables* =**correlation**, agreement, consistency, compatibility, conformity, similarity, resemblance, parallel, comparability, accord, concurrence, coincidence. **2** *his private correspondence* =**letters**, messages, missives, mail, post; communication.

correspondent ▶ noun =**reporter**, journalist, columnist, writer, contributor, commentator.

corresponding ▶ adjective =**commensurate**, parallel, correspondent, matching, correlated, relative, proportional, proportionate, comparable, equivalent, analogous.

corridor ▶ noun =**passage**, passageway, aisle, gangway, hall, hallway, gallery, arcade.

corroborate ▶ verb =**confirm**, verify, endorse, ratify, authenticate, validate, certify; support, back up, uphold, bear out, bear witness to, attest to, testify to, vouch for, substantiate, sustain.
−OPPOSITES contradict.

corrode ▶ verb **1** *the iron had corroded* =**rust**, tarnish; wear away, disintegrate, crumble, perish, rot; oxidize. **2** *acid rain corrodes buildings* =**wear away**, eat away (at), consume, destroy; dissolve.

corrosive ▶ adjective =**caustic**, burning, stinging; destructive, damaging, harmful, harsh.

corrugated ▶ adjective =**ridged**, fluted, grooved, furrowed, crinkled, crinkly, puckered, creased, wrinkled, wrinkly, crumpled; *technical* striated.

corrupt ▶ adjective **1** *a corrupt official* | *corrupt practices* =**dishonest**, unscrupulous, unprincipled, unethical, amoral, untrustworthy, venal, underhand, double-dealing, fraudulent; criminal, illegal, unlawful, nefarious; *informal* crooked, shady, dirty, sleazy; *Brit. informal* bent, dodgy. **2** *he is utterly corrupt* =**immoral**, depraved, degenerate, vice-ridden, perverted, debauched, dissolute, dissipated, bad, wicked, evil, base, sinful, ungodly, profane, impious, im-

pure; *informal* warped.
–OPPOSITES honest, ethical, pure.
▶ verb =**deprave**, pervert, warp, lead astray, defile, pollute, sully.

corruption ▶ noun **1** *political corruption* =**dishonesty**, unscrupulousness, double-dealing, fraud, misconduct, crime, criminality, wrongdoing; bribery, subornation, venality, extortion, profiteering; *N. Amer.* payola; *informal* graft, crookedness, sleaze. **2** *his fall into corruption* =**immorality**, depravity, vice, degeneracy, perversion, debauchery, dissoluteness, decadence, wickedness, evil, sin, sinfulness, ungodliness; *formal* turpitude.
–OPPOSITES honesty, morality, purity.

cortège ▶ noun *the funeral cortège* =**procession**, parade, cavalcade, motorcade, convoy, train, column, file, line.

cosmetic ▶ adjective *most of the changes were merely cosmetic* =**superficial**, surface, skin-deep, outward, exterior, external.
–OPPOSITES fundamental.
▶ noun (**cosmetics**) *a new range of cosmetics* =**make-up**, beauty products; *informal* warpaint, paint, slap.

cosmic ▶ adjective **1** *cosmic bodies* =**extraterrestrial**, space, astral, planetary, stellar; sidereal. **2** *a tale on a cosmic scale* =**epic**, huge, immense, enormous, massive, colossal, prodigious; fathomless, measureless, infinite, limitless, boundless.

cosmonaut ▶ noun =**astronaut**, spaceman/woman, space traveller, space cadet; *N. Amer. informal* jock.

cosmopolitan ▶ adjective **1** *the student body has a cosmopolitan character* =**multicultural**, multiracial, international, worldwide, global. **2** *a cosmopolitan audience* =**worldly**, worldly-wise, cultivated, cultured, sophisticated, suave, urbane, glamorous, fashionable; *informal* jet-setting.

cosset ▶ verb =**pamper**, indulge, overindulge, mollycoddle, coddle, baby, pet, mother, nanny, pander to, featherbed, spoil; wrap in cotton wool, wait on someone hand and foot.

cost ▶ noun **1** *the cost of the equipment* =**price**, fee, tariff, fare, toll, levy, charge, rental; value, valuation, quotation, rate; *humorous* damage. **2** *the human cost of the conflict* =**sacrifice**, loss, expense, penalty, toll, price. **3** (**costs**) *we need to make*

£10,000 *to cover our costs* =**expenses**, outgoings, overheads; expenditure, outlay.
▶ verb **1** *the chair costs £186* =**be priced at**, sell for, be valued at, fetch, come to, amount to; *informal* set someone back, go for; *Brit. informal* knock someone back. **2** *the proposal has not yet been costed* =**price**, value, put a price/value/figure on, itemize.

costly ▶ adjective **1** *costly machinery* =**expensive**, dear, high-cost, overpriced; *Brit.* over the odds; *informal* steep, pricey. **2** *a costly mistake* =**catastrophic**, disastrous, calamitous, ruinous; damaging, harmful, injurious, deleterious.
–OPPOSITES cheap.

costume ▶ noun **1** *Elizabethan costumes* =**(set of) clothes**, garments, robes, outfit, ensemble; dress, clothing, attire, garb, uniform, livery; *informal* get-up, gear, togs; *Brit. informal* clobber, kit; *N. Amer. informal* threads; *formal* apparel; *archaic* raiment. **2** (*Brit.*) *if you'd like a dip, we can lend you a costume.* See SWIMSUIT.

cosy ▶ adjective **1** *a cosy country cottage* =**snug**, comfortable, warm, homey, homely, welcoming; safe, sheltered, secure; *N. Amer.* down-home, homestyle; *informal* comfy, snug as a bug (in a rug). **2** *a cosy chat* =**intimate**, relaxed, informal, friendly.

coterie ▶ noun =**clique**, set, circle, inner circle, crowd, in-crowd, band, community; *informal* gang, posse.

cottage ▶ noun =**lodge**, chalet, cabin; shack, shanty; *(in Russia)* dacha; *Scottish* bothy, but and ben; *Austral. informal* weekender; *literary* bower.

couch ▶ noun *she seated herself on the couch* =**settee**, sofa, divan, chaise longue, chesterfield, love seat, settle, ottoman; *Brit.* put-you-up; *N. Amer.* daybed, davenport.
▶ verb *his reply was couched in deferential terms* =**express**, phrase, word, frame, put, formulate, style, convey, say, state, utter.

cough ▶ verb *he coughed loudly* =**hack**, hawk, bark; splutter, clear one's throat.
▶ noun *a loud cough* =**bark**, splutter; *informal* frog in one's throat.
 ■ **cough up** =**pay (up)**, come up with, hand over, dish out, part with; *informal* fork out, shell out, lay out; *Brit. informal* stump up; *N. Amer. informal* ante up, pony up.

WORD LINKS

relating to coughing: **tussive**

council ▸ noun **1** *the town council* =**local authority**, local government, municipal authority, administration, executive, chamber, assembly; *Brit.* corporation. **2** *the Schools Council* =**advisory body**, board, committee, commission, assembly, panel; synod. **3** *that evening, she held a family council* =**meeting**, gathering, conference, assembly.

counsel ▸ noun **1** *his wise counsel* =**advice**, guidance, counselling, direction; recommendations, suggestions, guidelines, hints, tips, pointers, warnings. **2** *the counsel for the defence* =**barrister**, lawyer; *Scottish* advocate; *N. Amer.* attorney, counselor(-at-law); *informal* brief.
▸ verb *he counselled the team to withdraw from the deal* =**advise**, recommend, direct, advocate, encourage, warn, caution; guide.

counsellor ▸ noun =**adviser**, consultant, guide, mentor.

count ▸ verb **1** *she counted the money again* =**add up**, add together, reckon up, figure up, total, tally, calculate, compute; *Brit.* tot up. **2** *a company with 250 employees, not counting overseas staff* =**include**, take into account/consideration, take account of, allow for. **3** *I count it a privilege to be asked* =**consider**, think, feel, regard, look on as, view as, hold to be, judge, deem, account. **4** *it's your mother's feelings that count* =**matter**, be of consequence, be of account, be significant, signify, be important, carry weight; *informal* cut any ice.
▸ noun *her white blood cell count* =**amount**, number, total; level, reading, index; density, concentration.
■ **count on/upon 1** *you can count on me* =**rely on**, depend on, bank on, trust (in), be sure of, have (every) confidence in, believe in, put one's faith in, take for granted, take as read. **2** *they hadn't counted on Rangers' indomitable spirit* =**expect**, reckon on, anticipate, envisage, allow for, be prepared for, bargain for/on; *N. Amer. informal* figure on.

countenance ▸ noun *his strikingly handsome countenance* =**face**, features, physiognomy, profile; (facial) expression, look, appearance, aspect, mien; *informal* mug; *Brit. informal* mush, phizog, phiz, clock, boat race; *N. Amer. informal* puss; *literary* visage.
▸ verb *he would not countenance the use of force* =**tolerate**, permit, allow, agree to, consent to, go along with, hold with, put up with, accept; *Scottish* thole; *informal* stand for; *formal* brook.

counter[1] ▸ noun *a pile of counters* =**token**, chip, disc; piece, man, marker; *N. Amer.* check.

counter[2] ▸ verb **1** *workers countered accusations of dishonesty with claims of oppression* =**respond to**, parry, hit back at, answer, retort to. **2** *the second argument is more difficult to counter* =**oppose**, dispute, argue against/with, contradict, controvert, negate, counteract; challenge, contest; *formal* gainsay.
–OPPOSITES support.
▸ adjective *a counter bid* =**opposing**, opposed; retaliatory, contrary.
■ **counter to** =**against**, in opposition to, contrary to, at variance with, in defiance of, in contravention of, in conflict with, at odds with.

counteract ▸ verb **1** *new measures to counteract drug trafficking* =**prevent**, thwart, frustrate, foil, impede, curb, hinder, hamper, check, put a stop/end to, defeat. **2** *a drug to counteract the possible effect on her heart* =**offset**, counterbalance, balance (out), cancel out, even out, countervail, compensate for, make up for, remedy; neutralize, nullify, negate, invalidate.
–OPPOSITES encourage, exacerbate.

counterbalance ▸ verb =**compensate for**, make up for, offset, balance (out), even out, counteract, equalize, neutralize, nullify, negate, undo.

counterfeit ▸ adjective *counterfeit cassettes* =**fake**, pirate, bogus, forged, imitation; *informal* phoney.
–OPPOSITES genuine.
▸ noun *the notes were counterfeits* =**fake**, forgery, copy, reproduction, imitation; fraud, sham; *informal* phoney.
–OPPOSITES original.
▸ verb *his signature was hard to counterfeit* =**fake**, forge, copy, reproduce, imitate.

countermand ▸ verb =**revoke**, rescind, reverse, undo, repeal, retract, withdraw, quash, overturn, overrule, cancel, annul, invalidate, nullify, negate.
–OPPOSITES uphold.

counterpart ▸ noun =**equivalent**, opposite number, peer, equal, parallel, complement, analogue, match, twin, mate, fellow, brother, sister.

countless ▶ adjective =**innumerable**, numerous, untold, legion, without number, numberless, limitless, multitudinous, incalculable; *informal* umpteen, no end of, loads of, stacks of, heaps of, masses of, oodles of, zillions of; *N. Amer. informal* gazillions of; *literary* myriad.
−OPPOSITES few.

countrified ▶ adjective =**rural**, rustic, pastoral, bucolic, country; idyllic, unspoilt; *literary* Arcadian, sylvan.
−OPPOSITES urban.

country ▶ noun 1 *foreign countries* =**nation**, (sovereign) state, kingdom, realm, territory, province, principality. 2 *he risked his life for his country* =**homeland**, native land, fatherland, motherland. 3 *the country took to the streets* =**people**, public, population, populace, citizenry, nation; electorate, voters, taxpayers, grass roots; *Brit. informal* Joe Public. 4 *thickly forested country* =**terrain**, land, territory; landscape, scenery, setting, surroundings, environment. 5 *she hated living in the country* =**countryside**, green belt, great outdoors; provinces, rural areas, backwoods, back of beyond, hinterland; *Austral./NZ* outback, bush, back country, backblocks, booay; *informal* sticks, middle of nowhere; *N. Amer. informal* boondocks, boonies, tall timbers; *Austral. informal* beyond the black stump.
▶ adjective *country pursuits* =**rural**, countryside, outdoor, rustic, pastoral, bucolic; *literary* sylvan, Arcadian.
−OPPOSITES urban.

countryman, countrywoman ▶ noun =**compatriot**, fellow citizen; brother, sister, comrade.

countryside ▶ noun 1 *beautiful unspoilt countryside* =**landscape**, scenery, surroundings, setting, environment; country, terrain, land. 2 *I was brought up in the countryside.* See COUNTRY noun *sense 5.*

county ▶ noun =**shire**, province, territory, region, district, area.

coup ▶ noun 1 *a violent military coup* =**coup d'état**, overthrow, takeover; (palace) revolution, rebellion, revolt, insurrection, uprising. 2 *a major publishing coup* =**success**, triumph, feat, accomplishment, achievement, scoop.

coup de grâce ▶ noun =**death blow**, finishing blow, kiss of death; *informal* KO, kayo.

coup d'état ▶ noun. See COUP *sense 1.*

couple ▶ noun 1 *a couple of girls* =**pair**, duo, twosome, two, brace. 2 *a honeymoon couple* =**husband and wife**, twosome, partners, lovers; *informal* item.
▶ verb 1 *a sense of hope is coupled with a sense of loss* =**combine**, accompany, mix, incorporate, link, associate, connect, ally; add to, join to; *formal* conjoin. 2 *a cable is coupled to one of the wheels* =**connect**, attach, join, fasten, fix, link, secure, tie, bind, strap, rope, tether, truss, lash, hitch, yoke, chain, hook (up).
−OPPOSITES detach.

coupon ▶ noun 1 *money-off coupons* =**voucher**, token, ticket, slip; *N. Amer. informal* ducat, comp, rain check. 2 *fill in the coupon below* =**form**, (tear-off) slip.

courage ▶ noun =**bravery**, courageousness, pluck, valour, fearlessness, nerve, daring, audacity, boldness, grit, heroism, gallantry; *informal* guts, spunk; *Brit. informal* bottle; *N. Amer. informal* moxie, cojones, sand.
−OPPOSITES cowardice.

courageous ▶ adjective =**brave**, plucky, fearless, valiant, intrepid, heroic, undaunted, unflinching, unshrinking, unafraid, dauntless, indomitable, doughty, mettlesome, stout-hearted, gallant, death-or-glory; *N. Amer.* rock-ribbed; *informal* game, gutsy, spunky, ballsy, have-a-go.
−OPPOSITES cowardly.

courier ▶ noun 1 *the documents were sent by courier* =**messenger**, dispatch rider, runner. 2 *a courier for a package holiday company* =**representative**, (tour) guide; *N. Amer.* tour director; *informal* rep.

course ▶ noun 1 *the island was not far off our course* =**route**, way, track, path, line, trail, trajectory, bearing, heading. 2 *the course of history* =**progression**, development, progress, advance, evolution, flow, movement, sequence, order, succession, rise, march, passage, passing. 3 *the best course to adopt* =**procedure**, plan (of action), course/line of action, modus operandi, practice, approach, technique, way, means, policy, strategy, tactic, programme. 4 *a waterlogged course* =**racecourse**, racetrack, track, ground. 5 *a French course* =**programme/course of study**; curriculum, syllabus; classes, lectures, studies. 6 *a course of antibiotics* =**programme**, series, sequence, system, schedule, regime.

▶ verb *tears coursed down her cheeks* =**flow**, pour, stream, run, rush, gush, cascade, flood, roll.

■ **of course** =**naturally**, as might be expected, as you/one would expect, needless to say, certainly, to be sure, as a matter of course, obviously, it goes without saying; *informal* natch.

court ▶ noun **1** *the court found him guilty* =**court of law**, law court; bench, bar, tribunal, chancery, assizes. **2** *the King's court* =**(royal) household**, retinue, entourage, train, suite, courtiers, attendants.
▶ verb **1** *a newspaper editor who was courted by senior politicians* =**cultivate**, wine and dine; *informal* butter up. **2** *he was busily courting public attention* =**seek**, pursue, go after, strive for, solicit. **3** *he's often courted controversy* =**risk**, invite, attract, bring on oneself.

┌─────────────────┐
│ **WORD LINKS** │
└─────────────────┘
relating to law courts: **forensic**

courteous ▶ adjective =**polite**, well mannered, civil, respectful, well behaved; gentlemanly, chivalrous, gallant, gracious, obliging, considerate.
–OPPOSITES rude.

courtesy ▶ noun =**politeness**, courteousness, good manners, civility, respect; chivalry, gallantry; graciousness, consideration, thought.

courtier ▶ noun =**attendant**, lord, lady, lady-in-waiting, steward, equerry, page, squire.

courtship ▶ noun **1** *a whirlwind courtship* =**romance**, (love) affair; engagement. **2** *his courtship of Emma* =**wooing**, courting, suit, pursuit.

courtyard ▶ noun =**quadrangle**, cloister, square, plaza, piazza, close, enclosure, yard; *informal* quad.

cove ▶ noun *a small sandy cove* =**bay**, inlet, fjord; *Scottish* (sea) loch; *Irish* lough.

covenant ▶ noun =**contract**, agreement, undertaking, commitment, guarantee, warrant, pledge, promise, bond, indenture; pact, deal, settlement, arrangement, understanding.

cover ▶ verb **1** *she covered her face with a towel* =**protect**, shield, shelter; hide, conceal, mask. **2** *his car was covered in mud* =**cake**, coat, encrust, plaster, smother; daub, smear, splatter. **3** *snow covered the fields* =**blanket**, carpet, coat,

shroud, smother. **4** *a course covering all aspects of the business* =**deal with**, consider, take in, include, involve, incorporate, embrace. **5** *the trial was covered by a range of newspapers* =**report on**, write about, describe, commentate on, deal with. **6** *he turned on the radio to cover the sound of their conversation* =**mask**, disguise, hide, camouflage. **7** *I'm covering for Jill* =**stand in for**, fill in for, deputize for, take over from, relieve, take the place of, sit in for, hold the fort; *informal* sub for; *N. Amer. informal* pinch-hit for. **8** *can you make enough to cover your costs?* =**pay (for)**, be enough for, fund, finance; pay back, make up for, offset. **9** *your home is covered against damage and loss* =**insure**, protect, secure, underwrite, assure, indemnify. **10** *we covered ten miles each day* =**travel**, journey, go, do.
–OPPOSITES expose.
▶ noun **1** *a protective cover* =**covering**, sleeve, wrapping, wrapper, envelope, sheath, housing, jacket, casing, cowling; awning, canopy, tarpaulin, fairing. **2** *a manhole cover* =**lid**, top, cap. **3** *a book cover* =**binding**, jacket, dust jacket, dust cover, wrapper. **4** (**covers**) *she pulled the covers over her head* =**bedclothes**, bedding, sheets, blankets. **5** *a thick cover of snow* =**coating**, coat, covering, layer, carpet, blanket; film, sheet, veneer, crust, skin, cloak, mantle, veil, pall, shroud. **6** *panicking onlookers ran for cover* =**shelter**, protection, refuge, sanctuary, haven, hiding place. **7** *the company was a cover for an international swindle* =**front**, facade, smokescreen, screen, blind, camouflage, disguise, mask, cloak. **8** (*Brit.*) *your policy provides cover against damage by subsidence* =**insurance**, protection, security, assurance, indemnification, indemnity.
■ **cover something up** =**conceal**, hide, keep secret/dark, hush up, draw a veil over, suppress, sweep under the carpet, gloss over; *informal* whitewash, keep a/the lid on.

coverage ▶ noun =**reporting**, description, treatment, handling, presentation, investigation, commentary; reports, articles, pieces, stories; portrayal.

covering ▶ noun **1** *a canvas covering* =**awning**, canopy, tarpaulin, cowling, casing, housing, fairing; wrapping, wrapper, cover, envelope, sheath, sleeve, jacket, lid, top, cap. **2** *a covering of snow* =**layer**, coating, coat, carpet,

blanket, overlay, topping, dusting, film, sheet, veneer, crust, skin, cloak, mantle, veil.
▶ adjective *a covering letter* =**accompanying**, explanatory, supplementary.

coverlet ▶ noun =**bedspread**, bedcover, cover, throw, duvet, quilt; *Brit.* eiderdown; *N. Amer.* spread, comforter; *dated* counterpane.

covert ▶ adjective =**secret**, furtive, clandestine, surreptitious, stealthy, cloak-and-dagger, backstairs, under-the-table, hidden, concealed, private, undercover, underground; *informal* hush-hush.
–OPPOSITES overt.

cover-up ▶ noun =**whitewash**, concealment, facade, camouflage, disguise, mask.
–OPPOSITES exposé.

covet ▶ verb =**desire**, yearn for, crave, have one's heart set on, want, wish for, long for, hanker after/for, hunger after/for, thirst for.

covetous ▶ adjective =**grasping**, greedy, acquisitive, desirous, possessive, envious, green with envy.

cow ▶ verb =**intimidate**, daunt, browbeat, bully, tyrannize, scare, terrorize, frighten, dishearten, subdue; *informal* psych out, bulldoze, steamroller.

coward ▶ noun =**weakling**, milksop, namby-pamby, mouse; *informal* chicken, scaredy-cat, yellow-belly, sissy, baby; *Brit. informal* big girl's blouse; *N. Amer. informal* pantywaist, pussy; *Austral./NZ informal* dingo, sook.
–OPPOSITES hero.

cowardly ▶ adjective =**faint-hearted**, lily-livered, spineless, chicken-hearted, craven, timid, timorous, fearful, pusillanimous; *informal* yellow, chicken, weak-kneed, gutless, yellow-bellied, wimpish, wimpy; *Brit. informal* wet.
–OPPOSITES brave.

cowboy ▶ noun =**cattleman**, cowhand, cowman, cowherd, herder, herdsman, drover, stockman, rancher, gaucho, vaquero; *N. Amer. informal* cowpuncher, cowpoke; *N. Amer. dated* buckaroo.

cower ▶ verb =**cringe**, shrink, crouch, tremble, shake, quake, blench, quail, grovel.

coy ▶ adjective =**demure**, shy, modest, bashful, reticent, diffident, self-effacing, shrinking, timid.
–OPPOSITES brazen.

crabbed ▶ adjective *her crabbed handwriting* =**cramped**, ill-formed, bad, illegible, unreadable, indecipherable; shaky, spidery.

crabby ▶ adjective =**irritable**, cantankerous, irascible, bad-tempered, grumpy, grouchy, crotchety, tetchy, testy, crusty, curmudgeonly, ill-tempered, ill-humoured, peevish, cross, fractious, pettish, crabbed, prickly, waspish; *informal* snappy; *Brit. informal* shirty, stroppy, narky, ratty; *N. Amer. informal* cranky, ornery; *Austral./NZ informal* snaky.
–OPPOSITES affable.

crack ▶ noun **1** *a crack in the glass* =**split**, break, chip, fracture, rupture; crazing; flaw, imperfection. **2** *a crack between two rocks* =**space**, gap, crevice, fissure, cleft, breach, rift, cranny, chink. **3** *the crack of a rifle* =**bang**, report, explosion, detonation, pop; clap, crash. **4** *a crack on the head* =**blow**, bang, hit, knock, rap, punch, bump, smack, slap; *informal* bash, whack, thwack, clout, wallop, biff, bop. **5** *(informal) we'll have a crack at it* =**attempt**, try; *informal* go, shot, stab, bash. **6** *(informal) cheap cracks about her clothes* =**joke**, witticism, quip, jibe, taunt, sneer, insult; *informal* gag, wisecrack, dig.
▶ verb **1** *the glass cracked in the heat* =**break**, split, fracture, rupture, snap. **2** *she cracked him across the forehead* =**hit**, strike, smack, slap, beat, thump, knock, rap, punch; *informal* bash, whack, thwack, clobber, clout, clip, wallop, belt, biff, bop, sock; *Brit. informal* slosh; *N. Amer. informal* boff, bust, slug. **3** *he finally cracked* =**break down**, give way, cave in, go to pieces, crumble, lose control, yield, succumb. **4** *(informal) the code proved hard to crack* =**decipher**, interpret, decode, break, solve, work out; *informal* figure out, suss out.
▶ adjective *a crack shot* =**expert**, formidable, virtuoso, masterly, consummate, excellent, first-rate, first-class, marvellous, wonderful, magnificent, outstanding, superlative; deadly; *informal* great, superb, fantastic, ace, hotshot, mean, demon; *Brit. informal* brilliant; *N. Amer. informal* crackerjack.
–OPPOSITES incompetent.
■ **crack down on** =**suppress**, prevent, stop, put a stop to, put an end to, stamp out, eliminate, eradicate; clamp down on, get tough on, come down hard on, limit, restrain, restrict, check, keep in

check, control, keep under control.

cracked ▸ adjective =**chipped**, broken, crazed, fractured, splintered, split; damaged, defective, flawed, imperfect.

crackle ▸ verb =**sizzle**, fizz, hiss, crack, snap, sputter, splutter.

cradle ▸ noun **1** *the baby's cradle* =**crib**, Moses basket, cot, carrycot. **2** *the cradle of democracy* =**birthplace**, fount, fountainhead, source, spring, fountain, origin, place of origin, seat; *literary* wellspring.
▸ verb *she cradled his head in her arms* =**hold**, support, pillow, cushion, shelter, protect; rest, prop (up).

craft ▸ noun **1** *the historian's craft* =**activity**, occupation, trade, profession, work, line of work, job. **2** *she used craft and diplomacy* =**cunning**, craftiness, guile, wiliness, artfulness, deviousness, slyness, trickery, duplicity, dishonesty, deceit, deceitfulness, deception, intrigue, subterfuge; wiles, ploys, ruses, schemes, tricks. **3** *a sailing craft* =**vessel**, ship, boat.

craftsman, craftswoman
▸ noun =**artisan**, artist, skilled worker; expert, master.

craftsmanship ▸ noun =**workmanship**, artistry, art, handiwork, work; skill, expertise, technique.

crafty ▸ adjective =**cunning**, wily, guileful, artful, devious, sly, tricky, scheming, calculating, sharp, shrewd, astute, canny; duplicitous, dishonest, deceitful; *archaic* subtle.
–OPPOSITES honest.

crag ▸ noun =**cliff**, bluff, ridge, precipice, height, peak, tor, escarpment, scarp.

craggy ▸ adjective **1** *the craggy cliffs* =**steep**, sheer, perpendicular; rocky, rugged. **2** *his craggy face* =**rugged**, rough-hewn, strong; weather-beaten, weathered.

cram ▸ verb **1** *wardrobes crammed with clothes* =**fill**, stuff, pack, jam, fill to overflowing, fill to the brim, overload; crowd, throng. **2** *they all crammed into the car* =**crowd**, pack, pile, squash. **3** *he crammed his clothes into a suitcase* =**thrust**, push, shove, force, ram, jam, stuff, pack, pile, squash, squeeze, wedge. **4** *most of the students are cramming for exams* =**revise**; *informal* swot, mug up, bone up.

cramp ▸ noun *stomach cramps* =**muscle/**muscular spasm, pain, shooting pain, pang.
▸ verb *tighter rules will cramp economic growth* =**hinder**, impede, inhibit, hamper, constrain, hamstring, interfere with, restrict, limit, shackle; slow down, check, arrest, curb, retard.

cramped ▸ adjective **1** *cramped accommodation* =**poky**, uncomfortable, confined, restricted, constricted, small, tiny, narrow, crowded, congested. **2** *cramped handwriting* =**small**, crabbed, illegible, unreadable, indecipherable.
–OPPOSITES spacious.

crane ▸ noun =**derrick**, winch, hoist, windlass; block and tackle.

crank¹ ▸ verb *you crank the engine by hand* =**start**, turn (over), get going.
■ **crank something up** (*informal*) =**increase**, intensify, heighten, escalate, add to, augment, build up, expand, extend, raise; speed up, accelerate; *informal* up, jack up, hike up, step up, bump up, pump up.

crank² ▸ noun *a bunch of cranks* =**eccentric**, oddity, madman/madwoman, lunatic; *informal* oddball, freak, weirdo, crackpot, loony, nut, nutcase, head case, maniac; *Brit. informal* nutter; *N. Amer. informal* screwball, kook.

cranky ▸ adjective **1** (*informal*) *a cranky diet* =**eccentric**, bizarre, weird, peculiar, odd, strange, unconventional, left-field, unorthodox, outlandish; silly, stupid, mad, crazy, idiotic; *informal* wacky, crackpot, nutty; *Brit. informal* daft, potty. **2** (*N. Amer. informal*) *the children were tired and cranky*. See IRRITABLE.

cranny ▸ noun =**chink**, crack, crevice, slit, split, fissure, rift, cleft, opening, gap, aperture, cavity, hole, hollow, niche, corner, nook.

crash ▸ verb **1** *the car crashed into a tree* =**smash into**, collide with, be in collision with, hit, strike, ram, cannon into, plough into, meet head-on, run into; *N. Amer.* impact. **2** *he crashed his car* =**smash**, wreck; *Brit.* write off; *Brit. informal* prang; *N. Amer. informal* total. **3** *waves crashed against the shore* =**dash**, batter, pound, lash, slam, thunder. **4** *thunder crashed overhead* =**boom**, crack, roll, explode, bang, blast, blare, resound, reverberate, rumble, thunder, echo. **5** (*informal*) *his company crashed* =**collapse**, fold, fail, go under, go bankrupt, cease trading, go into receivership, go into liquidation, be wound up; *informal* go broke, go bust, go to the wall, go belly up.

▶ noun **1** *a crash on the motorway* = **accident**, collision, smash, road traffic accident, RTA; derailment; *N. Amer.* wreck; *informal* pile-up; *Brit. informal* prang, shunt. **2** *a loud crash* = **bang**, smash, smack, crack, bump, thud, clatter, clang; report, detonation, explosion; noise, racket, din, **3** *the crash of her company* = **collapse**, failure, liquidation.

crass ▶ adjective = **stupid**, insensitive, mindless, thoughtless, witless, oafish, boorish, asinine, coarse, gross, graceless, tasteless, tactless, clumsy, heavy-handed, blundering; *informal* ignorant.
−OPPOSITES intelligent.

crate ▶ noun = **(packing) case**, chest, tea chest, box; container, receptacle.

crater ▶ noun = **hollow**, bowl, basin, hole, cavity, depression; *Geology* caldera.

crave ▶ verb = **long for**, yearn for, desire, want, wish for, hunger for, thirst for, sigh for, pine for, hanker after, covet, lust after, ache for, set one's heart on, dream of, be bent on; *informal* have a yen for, itch for, be dying for.

craven ▶ adjective = **cowardly**, lily-livered, faint-hearted, chicken-hearted, spineless, timid, timorous, fearful, pusillanimous, weak, feeble; *informal* yellow, chicken, weak-kneed, gutless, yellow-bellied, wimpish; contemptible, abject, ignominious; *Brit. informal* wet.
−OPPOSITES brave.

craving ▶ noun = **longing**, yearning, desire, want, wish, hankering, hunger, thirst, appetite, greed, lust, ache, need, urge; *informal* yen, itch.

crawl ▶ verb **1** *they crawled under the table* = **creep**, worm one's way, go on all fours, go on hands and knees, wriggle, slither, squirm, scrabble. **2** *(informal) I'm not going to go crawling to him* = **grovel to**, kowtow to, pander to, toady to, bow and scrape to, dance attendance on, make up to, fawn on/over; *informal* suck up to, lick someone's boots, butter up. **3** *the place was crawling with soldiers* = **be full of**, overflow with, teem with, be packed with, be crowded with, be alive with, be overrun with, swarm with, be bristling with, be infested with, be thick with; *informal* be stuffed with, be jam-packed with, be chock-a-block with, be chock-full of.

craze ▶ noun = **fad**, fashion, trend,

vogue, enthusiasm, mania, passion, rage, obsession, compulsion, fixation, fetish, fancy, taste, fascination, preoccupation; *informal* thing.

crazed ▶ adjective = **mad**, insane, deranged, demented, certifiable, lunatic, psychopathic; wild, raving, berserk, manic, maniac, frenzied; *informal* crazy, mental, off one's head, out of one's head, raving mad. *See also* CRAZY *sense* 1.
−OPPOSITES sane.

crazy ▶ adjective *(informal)* **1** *a crazy old man* = **mad**, insane, out of one's mind, deranged, demented, not in one's right mind, crazed, lunatic, non compos mentis, unhinged, mad as a hatter, mad as a March hare; *informal* mental, off one's head, nutty (as a fruitcake), off one's rocker, not right in the head, round the bend, raving mad, bats, batty, bonkers, cuckoo, loopy, loony, bananas, loco, with a screw loose, touched, gaga, doolally, not all there, out to lunch, away with the fairies; *Brit. informal* barmy, crackers, barking (mad), potty, round the twist, off one's trolley, not the full shilling; *N. Amer. informal* nutso, out of one's tree, meshuga, wacko, gonzo; *Austral./NZ informal* bushed. **2** *a crazy idea* = **stupid**, foolish, idiotic, silly, absurd, ridiculous, ludicrous, preposterous, farcical, laughable, nonsensical, imbecilic, hare-brained, half-baked, impracticable, unworkable, ill-conceived, senseless; *informal* cock-eyed; *Brit. informal* barmy, daft. **3** *he's crazy about her* = **passionate about**, very keen on, enamoured of, infatuated with, smitten with, devoted to; very enthusiastic about, fanatical about; *informal* wild/mad/nuts about, gone on; *Brit. informal* potty about.
−OPPOSITES sane, sensible, apathetic.

creak ▶ verb = **squeak**, squeal; groan; whine, complain.

cream ▶ noun **1** *skin cream* = **lotion**, ointment, moisturizer, emollient, unguent, cosmetic; salve, rub, embrocation, balm, liniment. **2** *the cream of the world's photographers* = **best**, finest, pick, flower, crème de la crème, elite.
−OPPOSITES dregs.
▶ adjective *a cream dress* = **off-white**, cream-coloured, creamy, ivory.

creamy ▶ adjective = **smooth**, thick, velvety; rich, buttery.
−OPPOSITES lumpy.

crease ▶ noun **1** *trousers with knife-edge*

creases =**fold**, line, ridge; pleat, tuck; furrow, groove, corrugation. **2** *the creases at the corners of her eyes* =**wrinkle**, line, crinkle, pucker; (**creases**) crow's feet.
▶ **verb** *her skirt was creased and stained* =**crumple**, wrinkle, crinkle, line, scrunch up, rumple.

create ▶ **verb 1** *she has created a work of stunning originality* =**produce**, generate, bring into being, make, fashion, build, construct; design, devise, frame, develop, shape, form, forge. **2** *regular socializing creates a good team spirit* =**bring about**, give rise to, lead to, result in, cause, breed, generate, engender, produce, make for, promote, foster, sow the seeds of, contribute to. **3** *the government planned to create a free-trade zone* =**establish**, found, initiate, institute, constitute, inaugurate, launch, set up, form, organize, develop. **4** *she was created a life peer in 1990* =**appoint**, make; invest as, install as.
−OPPOSITES destroy.

creation ▶ **noun 1** *the creation of a coalition government* =**establishment**, formation, foundation, initiation, institution, inauguration, constitution; production, generation, fashioning, building, construction, development, setting up. **2** *the whole of creation* =**the world**, the universe, the cosmos; the living world, the natural world, nature, life, living things. **3** *Dickens's literary creations* =**work**, work of art, production, opus; achievement.
−OPPOSITES destruction.

creative ▶ **adjective** =**inventive**, imaginative, innovative, experimental, original; artistic; inspired, visionary; enterprising, resourceful.

creativity ▶ **noun** =**inventiveness**, imagination, innovation, innovativeness, originality, individuality; artistry, inspiration, vision; enterprise, initiative, resourcefulness.

creator ▶ **noun 1** *the creator of the series* =**author**, writer, designer, deviser, maker, producer; originator, inventor, architect, mastermind, prime mover; *literary* begetter. **2** *the Sabbath is kept to honour the Creator. See* GOD *sense* 1.

creature ▶ **noun 1** *the earth and its creatures* =**animal**, beast; living thing, living being; *N. Amer. informal* critter. **2** *you're such a lazy creature!* =**person**, individual, human being, character, soul, wretch,

customer; *informal* devil, beggar, sort, type. **3** *she was denounced as a creature of the liberals* =**lackey**, minion, hireling, servant, puppet, tool, cat's paw, pawn; *informal* stooge, yes-man; *Brit. informal* poodle.

credence ▶ **noun 1** *the government placed little credence in the scheme* =**belief**, faith, trust, confidence, reliance. **2** *later reports lent credence to this view* =**credibility**, plausibility.

credentials ▶ **plural noun** =**documents**, documentation, papers, identity papers, bona fides, ID, ID card, identity card, passport, proof of identity; certification.

credibility ▶ **noun 1** *the whole tale lacks credibility* =**plausibility**, believability, credence; authority, cogency. **2** *the party lacked moral credibility* =**trustworthiness**, reliability, dependability, integrity.

credible ▶ **adjective** =**believable**, plausible, tenable, able to hold water, conceivable, likely, probable, possible, feasible, reasonable, with a ring of truth, persuasive, convincing.

credit ▶ **noun** *he never got much credit for the show's success* =**praise**, commendation, acclaim, acknowledgement, recognition, kudos, glory, esteem, respect, admiration, tributes, bouquets, thanks, gratitude, appreciation; *informal* brownie points.
▶ **verb** =**believe**, accept, give credence to, trust, have faith in; *informal* buy, swallow, fall for, take something as gospel.
■ **on credit** =**on hire purchase**, on (the) HP, by instalments, on account; *informal* on tick, on the slate; *Brit. informal* on the never-never.

creditable ▶ **adjective** =**commendable**, praiseworthy, laudable, admirable, honourable, estimable, meritorious, worthy, deserving, respectable.
−OPPOSITES deplorable.

credulous ▶ **adjective** =**gullible**, naive, easily taken in, impressionable, unsuspecting, unsuspicious, unwary, unquestioning; innocent, ingenuous, inexperienced, unsophisticated, unworldly, wide-eyed.
−OPPOSITES suspicious.

creed ▶ **noun 1** *people of many creeds and cultures* =**faith**, religion, (religious) belief, (religious) persuasion, denomination, sect. **2** *his political creed* =**system (of belief)**, (set of) beliefs, principles, articles of faith, ideology, credo, doctrine, teaching, dogma, tenets.

creek ▶ noun **=inlet**, bay, estuary, bight, fjord, sound; *Scottish* firth, frith; *(in Orkney & Shetland)* voe.

creep ▶ verb **1** *Tim crept out of the house* **=tiptoe**, steal, sneak, slip, slink, pad, edge, inch; skulk, prowl. **2** *(informal) they're always creeping to the boss* **=grovel to**, ingratiate oneself with, curry favour with, toady to, kowtow to, bow and scrape to, pander to, fawn on/over, make up to; *informal* crawl to, suck up to, lick someone's boots, butter up.

creepy ▶ adjective *(informal)* **=frightening**, eerie, disturbing, sinister, weird, hair-raising, menacing, threatening; *Scottish* eldritch; *informal* spooky, scary.

crescent ▶ noun **=half-moon**, sickle, arc, curve, bow.

crest ▶ noun **1** *the bird's crest* **=comb**, plume, tuft. **2** *the crest of the hill* **=summit**, peak, top, tip, pinnacle, brow, crown, apex. **3** *the Duke of Wellington's crest* **=insignia**, regalia, badge, emblem, coat of arms, arms.

crestfallen ▶ adjective **=downhearted**, downcast, despondent, disappointed, disconsolate, disheartened, discouraged, dispirited, dejected, sad, dismayed, unhappy, forlorn.
–OPPOSITES cheerful.

crevasse ▶ noun **=chasm**, abyss, fissure, cleft, crack, split, breach, rift, hole, cavity.

crevice ▶ noun **=crack**, fissure, cleft, chink, cranny, nook, slit, split, rift, fracture, breach; opening, gap, hole.

crew ▶ noun **1** *the ship's crew* **=sailors**, mariners, hands, ship's company, ship's complement. **2** *a crew of cameramen and sound engineers* **=team**, company, unit, corps, party, gang.

crib ▶ noun **=cot**, cradle, Moses basket, carrycot.
▶ verb *(informal) she cribbed the plot from a Shakespeare play* **=copy**, plagiarize, poach, appropriate, steal, 'borrow'; *informal* rip off, lift; *Brit. informal* nick, pinch.

crick ▶ verb **=strain**, twist, rick, sprain, pull, wrench; injure, hurt, damage.

crime ▶ noun **1** *kidnapping is a very serious crime* **=offence**, unlawful act, illegal act, felony, misdemeanour, misdeed; *Law* tort. **2** *the increase in crime* **=lawbreaking**, delinquency, wrongdoing, criminality, misconduct, illegality, villainy; *Law* malfeasance.

WORD LINKS

study of crime: **criminology**

criminal ▶ noun *a convicted criminal* **=lawbreaker**, offender, villain, delinquent, felon, convict, miscreant; thief, burglar, robber, armed robber, gunman, gangster, terrorist; *informal* crook, con, jailbird, (old) lag; *N. Amer. informal* hood, yardbird; *Austral./NZ informal* crim; *Law* malfeasant.
▶ adjective **1** *criminal conduct* **=unlawful**, illegal, illicit, lawless, felonious, delinquent, fraudulent, actionable, culpable; villainous, nefarious, corrupt, wrong; *informal* crooked; *Brit. informal* bent; *Law* malfeasant. **2** *(informal) a criminal waste of taxpayer's money* **=deplorable**, shameful, reprehensible, disgraceful, inexcusable, unforgivable, unpardonable, outrageous, monstrous, shocking, scandalous, wicked.
–OPPOSITES lawful.

WORD LINKS

study of criminals: **criminology**

crimp ▶ verb **=pleat**, flute, corrugate, ruffle, fold, crease, crinkle, pucker, gather; pinch, compress, press/squeeze together.

cringe ▶ verb **1** *she cringed as he bellowed in her ear* **=cower**, shrink, recoil, shy away, flinch, blench; shake, tremble, quiver, quake. **2** *I cringe when I think of it* **=wince**, shudder, squirm, feel embarrassed/mortified.

crinkle ▶ verb **=wrinkle**, crease, pucker, furrow, corrugate, line; rumple, scrunch up.

crinkly ▶ adjective **=wrinkled**, wrinkly, crinkled, creased, crumpled, rumpled, crimped, corrugated, fluted, puckered, furrowed; wavy.

cripple ▶ verb **1** *the accident crippled her* **=disable**, paralyse, immobilize, lame, incapacitate, handicap. **2** *the company had been crippled by the recession* **=devastate**, ruin, destroy, wipe out; paralyse, bring to a standstill, put out of action, put out of business, bankrupt, break, bring someone to their knees.

crippled ▶ adjective **=disabled**, paralysed, incapacitated, (physically) handicapped, lame, immobilized, bedridden, confined to a wheelchair; *euphemistic* physically challenged.

crisis ▸ noun **1** *the situation had reached a crisis* =**critical point**, turning point, crossroads, head, moment of truth, zero hour, point of no return, Rubicon; *informal* crunch. **2** *the current economic crisis* =**emergency**, disaster, catastrophe, calamity; predicament, plight, mess, trouble, dire straits, difficulty, extremity.

crisp ▸ adjective **1** *crisp bacon* =**crunchy**, crispy, brittle, breakable; dry. **2** *a crisp autumn day* =**invigorating**, brisk, fresh, refreshing, exhilarating; cool, chill, chilly; *informal* nippy; *Brit. informal* parky. **3** *her answer was crisp* =**brisk**, businesslike, no-nonsense, incisive, to the point, matter of fact, brusque; terse, succinct, concise, brief, short, short and sweet, laconic; *informal* snappy. **4** *crisp white bedlinen* =**smooth**, fresh, ironed; starched.
–OPPOSITES soft, sultry, rambling.

criterion ▸ noun =**standard**, specification, measure, gauge, test, scale, benchmark, yardstick, touchstone, barometer; principle, rule, law, canon.

critic ▸ noun **1** *a literary critic* =**reviewer**, commentator, analyst, judge, pundit. **2** *critics of the government* =**detractor**, attacker, fault-finder.

critical ▸ adjective **1** *a highly critical report* =**censorious**, condemnatory; disparaging, disapproving, fault-finding, judgemental, negative, unfavourable; *informal* nit-picking, picky. **2** *a critical essay* =**analytical**, interpretative, expository, explanatory. **3** *the situation is critical* =**grave**, serious, dangerous, risky, perilous, hazardous, precarious, touch-and-go, in the balance, uncertain, desperate, dire, acute, life-and-death. **4** *the choice of materials is critical for product safety* =**crucial**, vital, essential, of the essence, all-important, paramount, fundamental, key, pivotal, decisive, deciding.
–OPPOSITES complimentary, unimportant.

criticism ▸ noun **1** *she was stung by his criticism* =**censure**, condemnation, denunciation, disapproval, disparagement, opprobrium, fault-finding, attack, brickbats, recrimination; *informal* flak, a bad press, panning; *Brit. informal* stick, slating; *formal* excoriation. **2** *literary criticism* =**evaluation**, assessment, appraisal, analysis, judgement; commentary, interpretation, explanation.

criticize ▸ verb =**find fault with**, censure, denounce, condemn, attack, lambaste, pillory, rail against, inveigh against, cast aspersions on, pour scorn on, disparage, denigrate, give a bad press to, run down; *informal* knock, pan, slam, hammer, lay into, pull to pieces, pick holes in; *Brit. informal* slag off, slate, rubbish; *N. Amer. informal* pummel, trash; *Austral./NZ informal* bag, monster; *formal* excoriate.
–OPPOSITES praise.

critique ▸ noun =**analysis**, evaluation, assessment, appraisal, appreciation, criticism, review, study, commentary.

crock ▸ noun =**pot**, jar; jug, pitcher, ewer; container, receptacle, vessel.

crockery ▸ noun =**dishes**, crocks, china, tableware; plates, bowls, cups, saucers.

crony ▸ noun *(informal)* =**friend**, companion, bosom friend/pal/buddy, intimate, confidant(e), familiar, associate, comrade; *informal* pal, chum, sidekick; *Brit. informal* mate; *N. Amer. informal* buddy, amigo, compadre.

crook ▸ noun **1** *(informal) a small-time crook* =**criminal**, lawbreaker, villain, delinquent, felon, convict, malefactor, wrongdoer; rogue, scoundrel, cheat, swindler, racketeer; thief, robber, burglar; *informal* (old) lag, shark, con man, con, jailbird; *N. Amer. informal* hood, yardbird; *Austral./NZ informal* crim; *Law* malfeasant. **2** *the crook of a tree branch* =**bend**, fork, curve, angle.
▸ verb *he crooked his finger and called the waiter* =**cock**, flex, bend, curve, curl.

crooked ▸ adjective **1** *narrow, crooked streets* =**winding**, twisting, zigzag, meandering, tortuous, serpentine. **2** *a crooked spine* =**bent**, twisted, misshapen, deformed, malformed, contorted, warped, bowed, distorted; *Scottish* thrawn. **3** *the picture over the bed looked crooked* =**lopsided**, askew, awry, off-centre, uneven, out of true, out of line, at an angle, aslant, slanting, squint; *Scottish* agley; *informal* cock-eyed; *Brit. informal* skew-whiff, wonky. **4** *(informal) a crooked cop* | *crooked deals* =**dishonest**, unscrupulous, unprincipled, untrustworthy, corrupt, venal; criminal, illegal, unlawful, nefarious, fraudulent; *Brit. informal* bent, dodgy.
–OPPOSITES straight, honest.

crop ▸ noun **1** *some farmers lost their entire*

crop =**harvest**, yield; fruits, produce. **2** *a bumper crop of mail* =**batch**, lot, collection, supply, intake.

▶ **verb 1** *she's had her hair cropped* =**cut (short)**, clip, shear, shave, lop off, chop off, hack off; dock. **2** *a flock of sheep were cropping the turf* =**graze on**, browse on, feed on, nibble, eat.

■ **crop up** =**happen**, occur, arise, turn up, spring up, pop up, emerge, materialize, surface, appear, come to light, present itself; *literary* come to pass, befall.

WORD LINKS

science of crop production: **agronomy**

cross ▶ **noun 1** *a bronze cross* =**crucifix**, rood. **2** *we all have our crosses to bear* =**burden**, trouble, worry, trial, tribulation, affliction, curse, misfortune, adversity, hardship, vicissitude; millstone, albatross, thorn in one's flesh/side; misery, woe, pain, sorrow, suffering; *informal* hassle, headache. **3** *a cross between a yak and a cow* =**hybrid**, cross-breed, half-breed, mongrel; mixture, amalgam, blend, combination.

▶ **verb 1** *they crossed the hills on foot* =**travel across**, traverse; negotiate, navigate, cover. **2** *the point where the two roads cross* =**intersect**, meet, join, connect, crisscross. **3** *no one dared cross him* =**oppose**, resist, defy, obstruct; contradict, argue with, quarrel with, stand up to, take a stand against, take issue with. **4** *the breed was crossed with the similarly coloured Friesian* =**hybridize**, cross-breed, interbreed, cross-fertilize, cross-pollinate.

▶ **adjective** *Jane was getting cross* =**angry**, annoyed, irate, irritated, in a bad mood, vexed, irked, piqued, put out, displeased; irritable, short-tempered, bad-tempered, snappish, crotchety, grouchy, grumpy, fractious, testy, tetchy, crabby; *informal* mad, hot under the collar, peeved, riled, snappy, up in arms, steamed up, in a paddy; *Brit. informal* aerated, shirty, stroppy, ratty; *N. Amer. informal* sore, bent out of shape, teed off, ticked off; *Austral./NZ informal* ropeable, snaky, crook.
−OPPOSITES pleased.

■ **cross something out** =**delete**, strike out, score out, put a line through, cancel, obliterate.

cross-examine ▶ **verb** =**interrogate**, question, quiz, give someone the third degree; *informal* grill, pump, put someone through the wringer/mangle.

crossing ▶ **noun 1** *a busy road crossing* =**junction**, crossroads, intersection, interchange; level crossing. **2** *a short ferry crossing* =**journey**, passage, voyage.

crosswise, crossways ▶ **adverb** =**diagonally**, obliquely, transversely, aslant, cornerwise, at an angle, on the bias; *N. Amer.* cater-cornered, kitty-corner.

crotch ▶ **noun** =**groin**, crutch; lap.

crotchety ▶ **adjective** =**bad-tempered**, irascible, irritable, grumpy, grouchy, cantankerous, short-tempered, tetchy, testy, curmudgeonly, ill-tempered, ill-humoured, peevish, cross, fractious, pettish, waspish, crabbed, crabby, prickly, touchy; *informal* snappy; *Brit. informal* narky, ratty; *N. Amer. informal* cranky, ornery; *Austral./NZ informal* snaky.
−OPPOSITES good-humoured.

crouch ▶ **verb** =**squat**, bend (down), hunker down, hunch over, stoop, kneel (down); duck, cower.

crow ▶ **verb 1** *a cock crowed* =**cry**, squawk, screech, caw. **2** *try to avoid crowing about your success* =**boast**, brag, trumpet, swagger, swank, gloat.

crowd ▶ **noun 1** *a crowd of people* =**throng**, horde, mass, multitude, host, army, herd, flock, drove, swarm, sea, troupe, pack, mob, rabble; collection, company, gathering, assembly, congregation; *informal* gaggle, bunch, gang, posse. **2** *he's been hanging round with Hurley's crowd* =**set**, group, circle, clique, coterie; camp; *informal* gang, crew, lot, posse. **3** *the final attracted a capacity crowd* =**audience**, spectators, listeners, viewers; house, turnout, attendance, gate; congregation; *Brit. informal* punters.

▶ **verb 1** *reporters crowded round her* =**cluster**, flock, swarm, mill, throng, huddle, gather, assemble, congregate, converge. **2** *the guests all crowded into the dining room* =**surge**, push one's way, jostle, elbow one's way; squeeze, pile, cram. **3** *the quayside was crowded with holidaymakers* =**throng**, pack, jam, cram, fill. **4** *stop crowding me* =**pressurize**, pressure; harass, hound, pester, harry, badger, nag; *informal* hassle, lean on.

WORD LINKS

fear of crowds: **demophobia, ochlophobia**

crowded ▶ **adjective** =**packed**, full, filled to capacity, full to bursting, congested, overflowing, teeming, swarming, thronged, populous, overpopulated; busy; *informal* jam-packed, stuffed, chock-a-block, chock-full, bursting at the seams, full to the gunwales, wall-to-wall, mobbed; *Austral./NZ informal* chocker. –OPPOSITES deserted.

crown ▸ noun **1** *a jewelled crown* =**coronet**, diadem, circlet. **2** *the world heavyweight crown* =**title**, award; trophy, cup, medal, plate, shield, belt, prize. **3** *loyal servants of the Crown* =**monarch**, sovereign, king, queen, emperor, empress; monarchy, royalty. **4** *the crown of the hill* =**top**, crest, summit, peak, pinnacle, tip, brow, apex.
▸ verb **1** *a teaching post at Harvard crowned his career* =**round off**, cap, be the climax of, be the culmination of, top off, complete. **2** *a steeple crowned by a gilded weathercock* =**top**, cap, tip, head, surmount.

crucial ▸ adjective **1** *negotiations were at a crucial stage* =**pivotal**, critical, key, decisive, deciding; life-and-death. **2** *confidentiality is crucial in this case* =**all-important**, of the utmost importance, of the essence, critical, pre-eminent, paramount, essential, vital.
–OPPOSITES unimportant.

crude ▸ adjective **1** *crude oil* =**unrefined**, unpurified, unprocessed, untreated; coarse, raw, natural. **2** *a crude barricade* =**primitive**, simple, basic, homespun, rudimentary, rough, rough and ready, rough-hewn, makeshift, improvised. **3** *crude jokes* =**vulgar**, rude, naughty, suggestive, bawdy, off colour, indecent, obscene, offensive, lewd, salacious, licentious, ribald, coarse, uncouth, indelicate, tasteless, smutty, dirty, filthy, scatological; *informal* blue.
–OPPOSITES refined, sophisticated.

cruel ▸ adjective **1** *a cruel man* =**brutal**, savage, inhuman, barbaric, barbarous, brutish, bloodthirsty, vicious, sadistic, wicked, fiendish, diabolical, monstrous; callous, ruthless, merciless, pitiless, remorseless, uncaring, heartless, stony-hearted, hard-hearted, cold-blooded, cold-hearted, unfeeling, unkind, inhumane. **2** *her death was a cruel blow* =**harsh**, severe, bitter, heartbreaking, heart-rending, painful, agonizing, traumatic; *formal* grievous.
–OPPOSITES compassionate.

cruelty ▸ noun =**brutality**, savagery, inhumanity, barbarity, barbarousness, brutishness, bloodthirstiness, viciousness, sadism, wickedness; callousness, ruthlessness.

cruise ▸ noun *a cruise down the Nile* =**(boat) trip**; voyage, journey.
▸ verb **1** *she cruised across the Atlantic* =**sail**, voyage, journey. **2** *a taxi cruised past* =**drive slowly**, drift, sail; *informal* mosey, tootle; *Brit. informal* pootle.

crumb ▸ noun =**fragment**, bit, morsel, particle, speck, scrap, shred, sliver, atom, grain, trace, tinge, mite, jot, ounce; *informal* smidgen, tad.

crumble ▸ verb =**disintegrate**, fall apart, fall to pieces, fall down, break up, collapse, fragment; decay, fall into decay, deteriorate, degenerate, go to rack and ruin, decompose, rot, perish.

crumbly ▸ adjective =**friable**, powdery, granular; short; soft.

crumple ▸ verb **1** *she crumpled the note in her fist* =**crush**, scrunch up, screw up, squash, squeeze. **2** *his trousers were dirty and crumpled* =**crease**, wrinkle, crinkle, rumple. **3** *her resistance crumpled* =**collapse**, give way, cave in, go to pieces, break down, crumble, be overcome.

crunch ▸ verb =**munch**, chomp, champ, bite into; crush, grind, break, smash.

crusade ▸ noun =**campaign**, drive, push, movement, effort, struggle; battle, war, offensive.
▸ verb =**campaign**, fight, battle, take up arms, take up the cudgels, work, strive, struggle, agitate, lobby.

crusader ▸ noun =**campaigner**, fighter, champion, advocate; reformer.

crush ▸ verb **1** *essential oils are released when the herbs are crushed* =**squash**, squeeze, press, compress; pulp, mash, mangle; flatten, trample on, tread on; *informal* squidge; *N. Amer. informal* smush. **2** *your dress will get crushed* =**crease**, crumple, rumple, wrinkle, crinkle, scrunch up. **3** *crush the biscuits with a rolling pin* =**pulverize**, pound, grind, break up, smash, crumble; mill; *technical* comminute. **4** *he crushed her in his arms* =**hug**, squeeze, hold tight, embrace, enfold. **5** *the new regime crushed all opposition* =**suppress**, put down, quell, quash, stamp out, repress, subdue, extinguish. **6** *Alan was crushed by her words* =**mortify**, humiliate, chagrin, deflate, demoralize, flatten, squash; devastate, shatter.
▸ noun **1** *the crush of people* =**crowd**, throng, horde, swarm, press, mob. **2** *(informal) a*

crust | cultivate

teenage crush =**infatuation**, obsession, fixation; *informal* pash, puppy love, calf love. **3** *lemon crush* =**squash**, fruit juice, cordial, drink.

crust ▶ noun =**covering**, layer, coating, cover, coat, sheet, thickness, film, skin, topping; encrustation, scab.

crusty ▶ adjective =**irritable**, cantankerous, irascible, bad-tempered, ill-tempered, grumpy, grouchy, crotchety, short-tempered, tetchy, testy, crabby, curmudgeonly, peevish, cross, fractious, pettish, crabbed, prickly, waspish; *informal* snappy; *Brit. informal* narky, ratty; *N. Amer. informal* cranky, ornery; *Austral./NZ informal* snaky.
–OPPOSITES good-natured.

crux ▶ noun =**nub**, heart, essence, central point, main point, core, centre, nucleus, kernel.

cry ▶ verb **1** *Mandy started to cry* =**weep**, shed tears, sob, wail, bawl, howl, snivel, whimper; lament, grieve, mourn; *Scottish* greet; *informal* boohoo, blub, blubber, turn on the waterworks; *Brit. informal* grizzle. **2** *'Wait!' he cried* =**call**, shout, exclaim, sing out, yell, shriek, scream, screech, bawl, bellow, roar, squeal, yelp; *informal* holler.
–OPPOSITES laugh, whisper.
▶ noun =**call**, shout, exclamation, yell, shriek, scream, screech, bawl, bellow, roar, howl; *informal* holler.
■ **cry off** *(informal)* =**back out**, pull out, cancel, withdraw, change one's mind; *informal* get cold feet, cop out.

crypt ▶ noun =**tomb**, vault, burial chamber, sepulchre, catacomb.

cryptic ▶ adjective =**enigmatic**, mysterious, confusing, mystifying, puzzling, obscure, abstruse, arcane, elliptical, oblique.
–OPPOSITES clear.

cubbyhole ▶ noun =**booth**, cubicle; den, snug; cabin, hole; *N. Amer.* cubby.

cube ▶ noun =**block**, lump, chunk, brick.

cuddle ▶ verb **1** *she picked up the baby and cuddled her* =**hug**, embrace, clasp, hold tight, hold in one's arms. **2** *the pair were kissing and cuddling* =**embrace**, hug, caress, pet, fondle; *informal* canoodle, smooch; *informal, dated* spoon, bill and coo. **3** *I cuddled up to him* =**snuggle**, nestle, curl, nuzzle.

cuddly ▶ adjective =**huggable**, cuddlesome; plump, curvaceous, rounded,

buxom, soft, warm; *N. Amer. informal* zaftig.

cudgel ▶ noun =**club**, bludgeon, truncheon, baton, shillelagh, mace; *N. Amer.* blackjack, billy, nightstick; *Brit.* life preserver; *Brit. informal* cosh.
▶ verb =**bludgeon**, club, beat, batter, bash; *Brit. informal* cosh.

cue ▶ noun =**signal**, sign, indication, prompt, reminder.

cuff ▶ verb =**hit**, strike, slap, smack, thump, beat, punch; *informal* clout, wallop, belt, whack, bash, clobber, bop, biff, sock; *Brit. informal* slosh; *N. Amer. informal* boff, slug.
■ **off the cuff** *(informal)* *an off-the-cuff remark* =**impromptu**, extempore; unrehearsed, unscripted, unprepared, improvised, spontaneous, unplanned.

cuisine ▶ noun =**cooking**, cookery; food.

cul-de-sac ▶ noun =**no through road**, blind alley, dead end.

cull ▶ verb =**slaughter**, kill, destroy; put down.

culminate ▶ verb *the festival culminated in a dramatic fire-walking ceremony* =**come to a climax**, come to a head, climax; build up to, lead up to; end with, finish with, conclude with.

culmination ▶ noun =**climax**, pinnacle, peak, high point, height, summit, crest, zenith, crowning moment, apotheosis, apex, apogee; consummation.
–OPPOSITES nadir.

culpable ▶ adjective =**to blame**, guilty, at fault, in the wrong, answerable, accountable, responsible, blameworthy.
–OPPOSITES innocent.

culprit ▶ noun =**guilty party**, offender, wrongdoer, miscreant; criminal, malefactor, lawbreaker, felon, delinquent; *informal* baddy, crook.

cult ▶ noun **1** *a religious cult* =**sect**, group, movement. **2** *the cult of youth in Hollywood* =**obsession with**, fixation on, mania for, idolization of, devotion to, worship of, veneration of.

cultivate ▶ verb **1** *the peasants cultivated the land* =**till**, plough, dig, hoe, farm, work. **2** *they were encouraged to cultivate basic food crops* =**grow**, raise, rear, plant, sow. **3** *Tessa tried to cultivate her* =**woo**, court, curry favour with, ingratiate oneself with; *informal* get in someone's good books, butter up, suck up to; *N. Amer. informal* shine up to. **4** *he wants to cultivate his mind* =**improve**, better, refine, elevate; educate, train, develop, enrich.

cultivated ▶ adjective =**cultured**, educated, well read, civilized, enlightened, refined, polished; sophisticated, urbane, cosmopolitan.

cultural ▶ adjective **1** *cultural differences* =**social**, lifestyle; sociological, anthropological. **2** *cultural achievements* =**aesthetic**, artistic, intellectual; educational.

culture ▶ noun **1** *a lover of culture* =**the arts**, the humanities; high art. **2** *a man of culture* =**education**, cultivation, enlightenment, discernment, discrimination, taste, refinement, sophistication. **3** *Afro-Caribbean culture* =**civilization**, society, way of life, lifestyle; customs, traditions, heritage, habits, ways, conventions, values. **4** *a corporate culture of greed and envy* =**philosophy**, outlook, approach, modus operandi, ethic, rationale.

cultured ▶ adjective =**cultivated**, artistic, enlightened, civilized, educated, well educated, well read, well informed, learned, knowledgeable, discerning, discriminating, refined, sophisticated; *informal* arty.
–OPPOSITES ignorant.

cumbersome ▶ adjective **1** *a cumbersome diving suit* =**unwieldy**, unmanageable, awkward, clumsy, inconvenient; bulky, large, heavy, weighty; *informal* hulking, clunky. **2** *cumbersome procedures* =**complicated**, complex, involved, inefficient, unwieldy, slow.
–OPPOSITES manageable, straightforward.

cumulative ▶ adjective =**increasing**, growing, mounting; collective, aggregate, amassed; *Brit.* knock-on.

cunning ▶ adjective *a cunning scheme* =**crafty**, wily, artful, devious, sly, scheming, designing, calculating, Machiavellian; shrewd, astute, clever, canny; deceitful, deceptive, duplicitous; *archaic* subtle.
–OPPOSITES honest.
▶ noun *his political cunning* =**guile**, craftiness, deviousness, slyness, trickery, duplicity; shrewdness, astuteness.

cupboard ▶ noun =**closet**, cabinet, armoire.

cupidity ▶ noun =**greed**, avarice, avariciousness, acquisitiveness, covetousness, rapacity, materialism, mercenariness, Mammonism; *informal* money-grubbing.
–OPPOSITES generosity.

curable ▶ adjective =**treatable**, operable.

curative ▶ adjective =**healing**, therapeutic, medicinal, remedial, corrective, restorative, health-giving.

curator ▶ noun =**custodian**, keeper, conservator, guardian, caretaker, steward.

curb ▶ noun =**restraint**, restriction, check, brake, rein, control, limitation, limit, constraint; *informal* crackdown.
▶ verb =**restrain**, hold back/in, keep back, repress, suppress, fight back, keep in check, check, control, rein in, contain, bridle, subdue; *informal* keep a/the lid on.

curdle ▶ verb =**go off**, turn, sour, ferment.

cure ▶ verb **1** *he was cured of the disease* =**heal**, restore to health, make well/better. **2** *economic equality cannot cure all social ills* =**rectify**, remedy, put/set right, right, fix, mend, repair, heal, make better; solve, sort out; eliminate, end, put an end to. **3** *some farmers cured their own bacon* =**preserve**, smoke, salt, dry.
▶ noun **1** *a cure for cancer* =**remedy**, medicine, medication, antidote; treatment, therapy. **2** *interest rate cuts are not the cure for the problem* =**solution**, answer, antidote, panacea, cure-all.

curio ▶ noun =**trinket**, knick-knack, ornament, bauble, oddity; objet d'art, rarity, curiosity, conversation piece.

curiosity ▶ noun **1** *his evasiveness roused my curiosity* =**interest**, inquisitiveness. **2** *the shop is full of curiosities* =**oddity**, curio; knick-knack, ornament, bauble, trinket; objet d'art, rarity; *N. Amer.* kickshaw.

curious ▶ adjective **1** *she was curious to know what had happened* =**intrigued**, interested, eager/dying to know; inquisitive. **2** *her curious behaviour* =**strange**, odd, peculiar, funny, unusual, bizarre, weird, eccentric, queer, extraordinary, abnormal, out of the ordinary, anomalous, surprising, incongruous; *informal* offbeat; *Scottish* unco; *Brit. informal* rum.
–OPPOSITES uninterested, ordinary.

curl ▶ verb **1** *smoke curled up from his cigarette* =**spiral**, coil, wreathe, twirl, swirl;

wind, curve, bend, twist (and turn), loop, meander, snake, corkscrew, zigzag. **2** *Ruth curled her arms around his neck* =**wind**, twine, entwine, wrap. **3** *they curled up together on the sofa* =**nestle**, snuggle, cuddle; *N. Amer.* snug down.
▶ noun **1** *the tangled curls of her hair* =**ringlet**, corkscrew, kink. **2** *a curl of smoke* =**spiral**, coil, twirl, swirl, twist, corkscrew, curlicue.

curly ▶ adjective =**wavy**, curling, curled, frizzy, kinky, corkscrew.
–OPPOSITES straight.

currency ▶ noun **1** *foreign currency* =**money**, legal tender, cash, banknotes, notes, coins; *N. Amer.* bills. **2** *a term which has gained new currency* =**prevalence**, circulation, exposure; acceptance, popularity.

current ▶ adjective **1** *current events* =**contemporary**, present-day, modern, present, contemporaneous; topical, in the news, live, burning. **2** *the idea is still current* =**prevalent**, prevailing, common, accepted, in circulation, popular, widespread. **3** *a current driving licence* =**valid**, usable, up to date. **4** *the current prime minister* =**incumbent**, present, in office, in power; reigning.
–OPPOSITES past, out of date, former.
▶ noun **1** *a current of air* =**flow**, stream, slipstream; thermal, updraught, draught; undercurrent, undertow, tide. **2** *the current of human life* =**course**, progress, progression, flow, tide, movement.

WORD LINKS

instrument for measuring electric currents: **galvanometer**

curriculum ▶ noun =**syllabus**, study programme; subjects.

curse ▶ noun **1** *the curse of racism* =**evil**, blight, scourge, plague, cancer, canker, poison. **2** *the curse of unemployment* =**affliction**, burden, bane. **3** *muffled curses* =**swear word**, expletive, oath, profanity, four-letter word, dirty word, obscenity; *informal* cuss, cuss word; *formal* imprecation.
▶ verb **1** *she was cursed with feelings of inadequacy* =**afflict**, trouble, plague, bedevil. **2** *drivers cursed and sounded their horns* =**swear**, take the Lord's name in vain; *informal* cuss, turn the air blue, eff and blind.

cursed ▶ adjective =**damned**, doomed, ill-fated, ill-starred; *informal* jinxed; *literary* accursed, star-crossed.

cursory ▶ adjective =**perfunctory**, desultory, casual, superficial, token; hasty, quick, hurried, rapid, brief, passing, fleeting.
–OPPOSITES thorough.

curt ▶ adjective =**terse**, brusque, abrupt, clipped, blunt, short, monosyllabic, sharp; gruff, rude, impolite, discourteous.
–OPPOSITES expansive.

curtail ▶ verb **1** *economic policies designed to curtail spending* =**reduce**, cut, cut down, decrease, lessen, trim; restrict, limit, curb, rein in/back; *informal* slash. **2** *his visit was curtailed* =**shorten**, cut short, truncate.
–OPPOSITES increase, lengthen.

curtains ▶ noun =*N. Amer.* drapes.

curvaceous ▶ adjective =**shapely**, voluptuous, sexy, full-figured, buxom, full-bosomed, bosomy, Junoesque; *informal* curvy, well endowed, pneumatic, busty.
–OPPOSITES skinny.

curve ▶ noun *the serpentine curves of the river* =**bend**, turn, loop, curl, twist; arc, arch, bow, half-moon, undulation, curvature.
▶ verb *the road curved back on itself* =**bend**, turn, loop, wind, meander, undulate, snake, spiral, twist, coil, curl; arc, arch.

curved ▶ adjective =**bent**, arched, bowed, crescent, curving, wavy, sinuous, serpentine, meandering, undulating, curvy.
–OPPOSITES straight.

cushion ▶ noun *a cushion against inflation* =**protection**, buffer, shield, defence, bulwark.
▶ verb **1** *she cushioned her head on her arms* =**support**, cradle, prop (up), rest. **2** *to cushion the blow, pensions were increased* =**soften**, lessen, diminish, decrease, mitigate, alleviate, take the edge off; dull, deaden. **3** *residents are cushioned from the outside world* =**protect**, shield, shelter, cocoon.

cushy ▶ adjective *(informal)* =**easy**, undemanding; comfortable.
–OPPOSITES difficult.

custodian ▶ noun =**curator**, keeper, conservator, guardian, overseer, superintendent; caretaker, steward, protector.

custody ▶ noun *the parent who has cus-*

tody of the child =**care**, guardianship, charge, keeping, safe keeping, wardship, responsibility, protection, tutelage.

■ **in custody** =**in prison**, in jail, imprisoned, incarcerated, locked up, under lock and key, interned, detained; on remand; *informal* behind bars, doing time, inside; *Brit. informal* banged up.

custom ▸ noun **1** *his unfamiliarity with local customs* =**tradition**, practice, usage, way, convention, formality, ceremony, ritual; shibboleth, sacred cow, unwritten rule; mores. **2** *it is our custom to visit the Lake District in October* =**habit**, practice, routine, way; policy, rule; *formal* wont.

customarily ▸ adverb =**usually**, traditionally, normally, as a rule, generally, ordinarily, commonly, habitually, routinely.
–OPPOSITES occasionally.

customary ▸ adjective **1** *customary social practices* =**usual**, traditional, normal, conventional, familiar, accepted, routine, established, time-honoured, prevailing. **2** *her customary good sense* =**usual**, accustomed, habitual; *literary* wonted.
–OPPOSITES unusual.

customer ▸ noun =**consumer**, buyer, purchaser, patron, client; shopper; *Brit. informal* punter.

customs ▸ plural noun. See TAX noun sense 1.

cut ▸ verb **1** *he cut his finger* =**gash**, slash, lacerate, slit, wound, injure; scratch, graze, nick, incise, score. **2** *cut the pepper into small pieces* =**chop**, cut up, slice, dice, cube; carve; *N. Amer.* hash. **3** *the name that had been cut into the stone* =**carve**, engrave, incise, etch, score; chisel, whittle. **4** *the government will cut public expenditure* =**reduce**, cut back/down on, decrease, lessen, retrench, trim; rationalize, downsize; mark down, discount, lower; *informal* slash. **5** *the text has been substantially cut* =**shorten**, abridge, condense, abbreviate, truncate; edit; censor, expurgate. **6** *you need to cut ten lines per page* =**delete**, remove, take out, excise; *informal* chop. **7** *oil supplies had been cut* =**discontinue**, break off, suspend, interrupt; stop, end. **8** *where the line cuts the vertical axis* =**cross**, intersect, bisect; meet, join.

▸ noun **1** *a cut on his jaw* =**gash**, slash, lacer-

ation, incision, wound, injury; scratch, graze, nick. **2** *a cut of beef* =**piece**, joint, fillet, steak; section. **3** *(informal) they want their cut* =**share**, portion, bit, quota, percentage; *informal* slice (of the cake), rake-off, piece of the action; *Brit. informal* whack. **4** *his hair was in need of a cut* =**haircut**, trim, clip. **5** *a cut in interest rates* =**reduction**, cutback, decrease, lessening; *N. Amer.* rollback. **6** *the cut of his jacket* =**style**, design; tailoring, line, fit.

■ **cut back** *companies cut back on foreign investment* **1** =**reduce**, cut, decrease, lessen, retrench, economize on, trim, slim down, scale down; rationalize, downsize, pull/draw in one's horns, tighten one's belt; *informal* slash. **2** *cut back any new growth* =**trim**, snip, clip, crop, shear, shave; pare; prune, lop, dock; mow.

■ **cut someone/something down 1** *24 trees were cut down* =**fell**, chop down. **2** *he was cut down in his prime* =**kill**, slaughter, shoot down, mow down, gun down; *informal* take out, blow away; *literary* slay.

■ **cut in** =**interrupt**, butt in, break in, interject, interpose, chime in; *Brit. informal* chip in.

■ **cut someone/something off 1** *they cut off his finger* =**sever**, chop off, hack off; amputate. **2** *oil and gas supplies were cut off* =**discontinue**, break off, disconnect, suspend; stop, end, bring to an end. **3** *people cut off by the flood* =**isolate**, separate; trap, strand, maroon.

■ **cut out** =**stop working**, stop, fail, give out, break down; *informal* die, give up the ghost, conk out; *Brit. informal* pack up.

■ **cut someone/something out 1** *cut out all the diseased wood* =**remove**, take out, excise, extract. **2** *it's best to cut out alcohol altogether* =**give up**, refrain from, abstain from, go without; *informal* quit, leave off, pack in, lay off, knock off. **3** *his mother cut him out of her will* =**exclude**, leave out, omit, eliminate.

■ **cut something short** =**break off**, shorten, truncate, curtail, terminate, end, stop, abort, bring to an untimely end.

cutback ▸ noun =**reduction**, cut, decrease; economy, saving; *N. Amer.* rollback.
–OPPOSITES increase.

cute ▸ adjective =**endearing**, adorable, lovable, sweet, lovely, appealing, engaging, delightful, dear, darling, winning, winsome, attractive, pretty; *informal* twee; *Brit. informal* dinky.

cut-price ▸ adjective =**cheap**, marked down, reduced, on (special) offer, discount; *N. Amer.* cut-rate.

cut-throat ▸ adjective =**ruthless**, merciless, fierce, intense, aggressive, dog-eat-dog.

cutting ▸ noun *a newspaper cutting* =**clipping**; article, piece, column, paragraph.
▸ adjective *a cutting remark* =**hurtful**, wounding, barbed, pointed, scathing, acerbic, caustic, acid, sarcastic, sardonic, snide, spiteful, malicious, mean, nasty, cruel, unkind; *informal* bitchy, catty; *Brit. informal* sarky; *N. Amer. informal* snarky.
–OPPOSITES friendly, warm.

cycle ▸ noun **1** *the cycle of birth, death, and rebirth* =**circle**, round, rotation; pattern, rhythm; loop. **2** *the painting is one of a cycle of seven* =**series**, sequence, succession, run; set.

cyclical ▸ adjective =**recurrent**, recurring, regular, repeated; periodic, seasonal, circular.

cyclone ▸ noun =**hurricane**, typhoon, storm, tornado, whirlwind, tempest; *Austral.* willy-willy; *N. Amer. informal* twister.

cynic ▸ noun =**sceptic**, doubter, doubting Thomas; pessimist, prophet of doom; *informal* doom (and gloom) merchant.
–OPPOSITES idealist.

cynical ▸ adjective =**sceptical**, doubtful, distrustful, suspicious, disbelieving; pessimistic, negative, world-weary, disillusioned, disenchanted, jaundiced.
–OPPOSITES idealistic.

cynicism ▸ noun =**scepticism**, doubt, distrust, mistrust, suspicion, disbelief; pessimism, negativity, world-weariness, disenchantment.
–OPPOSITES idealism.

cyst ▸ noun =**growth**, lump; abscess, boil, carbuncle.

dab ▸ verb *she dabbed disinfectant on the cut* =**pat**, press, touch, swab; daub, apply, wipe.
▸ noun *a dab of glue* =**drop**, spot, smear, splash, bit; *informal* smidgen, lick.

dabble ▸ verb **1** *they dabbled their feet in the pool* =**splash**, dip, paddle, trail. **2** *he dabbled in politics* =**toy with**, dip into, flirt with, tinker with, play with.

dabbler ▸ noun =**amateur**, dilettante.
–OPPOSITES professional.

daft ▸ adjective (*Brit. informal*) **1** *a daft idea* =**absurd**, preposterous, ridiculous, ludicrous, laughable; idiotic, stupid, foolish, silly, hare-brained, half-baked; *informal* crazy, cock-eyed; *Brit. informal* barmy. **2** *he's really daft* =**stupid**, idiotic, empty-headed; unhinged, insane, mad; *informal* thick, dim, dopey, dumb, dim-witted, half-witted, birdbrained, pea-brained, slow on the uptake, soft in the head, brain-dead, touched, crazy, mental, nuts, batty, bonkers; *Brit. informal* potty, barmy, crackers; *N. Amer. informal* dumb-ass. **3** *she's daft about him* =**infatuated with**, smitten with, besotted by; *informal* crazy, mad, nuts; *Brit. informal* potty.
–OPPOSITES sensible.

daily ▸ adjective *a daily event* =**everyday**, day-to-day; quotidian, diurnal, circadian.
▸ adverb *the museum is open daily* =**every day**, once a day, day after day.

dainty ▸ adjective **1** *a dainty china cup* =**delicate**, fine, elegant, exquisite; *Brit. informal* dinky. **2** *a dainty eater* =**fastidious**, fussy, finicky; particular; *informal* choosy, pernickety, picky; *Brit. informal* faddy.
–OPPOSITES unwieldy, undiscriminating.

dais ▸ noun =**platform**, stage, podium, rostrum, stand; soapbox.

dam ▸ noun =**barrage**, barrier, wall, embankment, barricade, obstruction.
▸ verb =**block (up)**, obstruct, bung up, close; *technical* occlude.

damage ▸ noun **1** *did the thieves do any damage?* =**harm**, destruction, vandal-ism; injury, desecration; ruin, havoc, devastation. **2** *she won £4,300 damages* =**compensation**, recompense, restitution, redress, reparation(s); indemnification, indemnity; *N. Amer. informal* comp.
▸ verb *the parcel had been damaged* =**harm**, deface, mutilate, mangle, impair, injure, disfigure, vandalize; tamper with, sabotage; ruin, destroy, wreck; *N. Amer. informal* trash.
–OPPOSITES repair.

damaging ▸ adjective =**harmful**, detrimental, injurious, hurtful, inimical, dangerous, destructive, ruinous, deleterious; bad, malign, adverse, undesirable, prejudicial, unfavourable; unhealthy, unwholesome.
–OPPOSITES beneficial.

damn ▸ verb =**condemn**, censure, criticize, attack, denounce, revile; find fault with, give something a bad press, deprecate, disparage; *informal* slam, lay into, blast; *Brit. informal* slate, slag off.
–OPPOSITES bless, praise.
▸ noun (*informal*) *I don't care a damn* =**jot**, whit, iota, rap, scrap, bit; *informal* hoot, two hoots.

damnation ▸ noun condemnation, eternal punishment, perdition, doom, hellfire; *informal* fire and brimstone.

damned ▸ adjective **1** *damned souls* =**cursed**, doomed, lost, condemned; *literary* accursed. **2** (*informal*) *this damned car won't start* =**blasted**, damn, damnable, confounded, rotten, wretched; *informal* bloody; *Brit. informal* blessed, flaming, flipping, blinking, blooming, bleeding, ruddy; *dated* accursed.

damning ▸ adjective =**incriminating**; damaging, derogatory; conclusive, irrefutable.

damp ▸ adjective *her hair was damp* =**moist**; humid, steamy, muggy, clammy, sweaty, sticky, dank, wet, rainy, drizzly, showery, misty, foggy, dewy.
–OPPOSITES dry.
▸ noun *the damp in the air* =**moisture**, dampness, humidity, wetness, wet, water, condensation, steam, vapour;

clamminess, dankness; rain, dew, drizzle, precipitation; perspiration, sweat.
−OPPOSITES dryness.

> WORD LINKS
>
> *fear of damp:* **hygrophobia**

dampen ▸ verb **1** *the rain dampened her face* =**moisten**, damp, wet; *literary* bedew. **2** *nothing could dampen her enthusiasm* =**lessen**, decrease, diminish, reduce, moderate, damp, put a damper on, cool, discourage; suppress, extinguish, quench, stifle, curb, limit, check, restrain, inhibit, deter.
−OPPOSITES dry, heighten.

damper ■ **put a damper on something** =**curb**, check, restrain, restrict, limit, constrain, rein in/back, control, impede.

dampness ▸ noun. *See* DAMP noun.

dance ▸ verb **1** *he danced with her* sway, trip, twirl, whirl, pirouette, gyrate; *informal* bop, trip the light fantastic; *N. Amer. informal* get down. **2** *the girls danced round me* =**caper**, cavort, frisk, frolic, skip, prance, gambol; leap, jump, hop, bounce. **3** *flames danced in the fireplace* =**flicker**, leap, dart, play, flit, quiver; twinkle, shimmer, glitter.
▸ noun *the school dance* =**ball**; masquerade; *N. Amer.* prom, hoedown; *informal* disco, rave, hop, bop.

danger ▸ noun **1** *an element of danger* =**peril**, hazard, risk, jeopardy. **2** *he is a danger to society* =**menace**, hazard, threat, risk. **3** *a serious danger of fire* =**possibility**, chance, risk, probability, likelihood, prospect.
−OPPOSITES safety.

dangerous ▸ adjective **1** *a dangerous animal* =**menacing**, threatening, treacherous; savage, wild, vicious, murderous, desperate. **2** *dangerous wiring* =**hazardous**, perilous, risky, unsafe, unpredictable, precarious, insecure, touch-and-go, chancy, treacherous, unstable, volatile; *informal* dicey, hairy; *Brit. informal* dodgy.
−OPPOSITES harmless, safe.

dangle ▸ verb **1** *a chain dangled from his belt* =**hang** (down), droop, swing, sway, wave, trail, stream. **2** *he dangled the keys* =**wave**, swing, jiggle, brandish, flourish.

dangling ▸ adjective =**hanging**, drooping, droopy, suspended, pendulous, trailing, flowing, tumbling.

dank ▸ adjective =**damp**, musty, chilly, clammy, moist, wet, humid.
−OPPOSITES dry.

dapper ▸ adjective =**smart**, spruce, trim, debonair, neat, well dressed, well groomed, well turned out, elegant, chic, dashing; *informal* snazzy, snappy, natty, sharp; *N. Amer. informal* spiffy, fly.
−OPPOSITES scruffy.

dappled ▸ adjective =**speckled**, blotched, blotchy, spotted, spotty, dotted, mottled, marbled, flecked, freckled; piebald, brindle(d); patchy, variegated; *informal* splotchy, splodgy.

dare ▸ verb **1** *nobody dared to say a word* =**be brave enough**, have the courage; venture, have the nerve, have the temerity, be so bold as, have the audacity; risk, take the liberty of; *N. Amer.* take a flyer; *informal* stick one's neck out, go out on a limb. **2** *she dared him to go* =**challenge**, defy, invite, bid, provoke, goad; throw down the gauntlet.
▸ noun *she accepted the dare* =**challenge**, invitation; wager, bet.

daredevil ▸ noun *a young daredevil crashed his car* =**madcap**, hothead, adventurer, exhibitionist; *Brit.* tearaway; *informal* show-off, adrenalin junkie.
▸ adjective *a daredevil skydiver* =**daring**, bold, audacious, intrepid, fearless, madcap; reckless, rash, impulsive, impetuous, foolhardy; *Brit.* tearaway.
−OPPOSITES cowardly, cautious.

daring ▸ adjective *a daring attack* =**bold**, audacious, intrepid, fearless, brave, valiant, heroic, dashing; madcap, rash, reckless, heedless; *informal* gutsy, spunky.
▸ noun *his sheer daring* =**boldness**, audacity, temerity, fearlessness, intrepidity, bravery, courage, valour, heroism, pluck, spirit, mettle; recklessness, rashness, foolhardiness; *informal* nerve, guts, spunk, grit; *Brit. informal* bottle; *N. Amer. informal* moxie, sand.

dark ▸ adjective **1** *a dark night* =**black**, pitch-black, jet-black, inky; starless, moonless; dingy, gloomy, shadowy, shady. **2** *a dark secret* =**terrible**, awful, dreadful, hideous, ghastly, gruesome; mysterious, secret, hidden, concealed, veiled, covert, clandestine. **3** *dark hair* =**brunette**, dark brown, sable, jet-black, ebony. **4** *dark skin* =**swarthy**, dusky, olive, black, ebony. **5** *dark days* =**difficult**, dangerous, challenging, hard, grim, desperate; dire, awful, terrible,

dreadful, horrible, horrendous, atrocious, nightmarish, harrowing; wretched, woeful; **tragic**, disastrous, calamitous, catastrophic, cataclysmic. **6** *dark thoughts* =**gloomy**, dismal, negative, downbeat, bleak, grim, fatalistic, black; despairing, despondent, hopeless, cheerless, melancholy; glum, grave, morose, mournful, doleful. **7** *a dark look* =**moody**, brooding, sullen, dour, scowling, glowering, angry, forbidding, threatening, ominous. **8** *dark deeds* =**evil**, wicked, sinful, bad, iniquitous, ungodly, unholy, base; vile, unspeakable, foul, monstrous, shocking, atrocious, abominable, hateful, despicable, horrible, heinous, diabolical, fiendish, murderous, barbarous, black; sordid, degenerate, depraved; dishonourable, dishonest, unscrupulous; *informal* low-down, dirty, crooked, shady.
−OPPOSITES bright, blonde, pale, happy, good.
▶ noun *night in the dark* =**night**, nighttime, darkness; nightfall; blackout.
−OPPOSITES light, day.
■ **in the dark** *(informal)* =**unaware**, ignorant, oblivious, uninformed, unenlightened, unacquainted.

darken ▶ verb =**grow dark**, blacken, grow dim, cloud over, lour.

darkness ▶ noun **1** *lights shone in the darkness* =**dark**, blackness; gloom, dimness, murkiness, shadow, shade. **2** *darkness fell* =**night**, night-time, dark. **3** *the forces of darkness* =**evil**; wickedness, sin, ungodliness; the Devil.

WORD LINKS

fear of darkness: **scotophobia**

darling ▶ noun **1** *good night, darling* =**dear**, dearest, love, lover, sweetheart, sweet, beloved; *informal* honey, angel, pet, sweetie, sugar, babe, baby, poppet, treasure. **2** *the darling of the media* =**favourite**, idol, hero, heroine; *Brit. informal* blue-eyed boy/girl.
▶ adjective **1** *his darling wife* =**dear**, dearest, precious, beloved; esteemed. **2** *a darling little hat* =**adorable**, charming, cute, sweet, enchanting, bewitching, dear, delightful, lovely, beautiful, attractive, gorgeous, fetching; *Scottish & N. English* bonny.

darn ▶ verb *he was darning his socks* =**mend**, repair; sew up, stitch, patch.

dart ▶ noun *she made a dart for the door*
=**dash**, rush, run, bolt, break, charge, sprint, bound, leap, dive; scurry, scamper, scramble.
▶ verb **1** *Karl darted across the road* =**dash**, rush, tear, run, bolt, fly, shoot, charge, race, sprint, bound, leap, dive, gallop, scurry, scamper, scramble; *informal* scoot. **2** *he darted a glance at her* =**direct**, cast, throw, shoot, send, flash.

dash ▶ verb **1** *he dashed home* =**rush**, race, run, sprint, gallop, career, charge, shoot, hurtle, hare, fly, speed, zoom; *informal* tear, belt, pelt, zip, whip, hotfoot it, leg it; *Brit. informal* bomb, go like the clappers; *N. Amer. informal* barrel. **2** *he dashed the glass to the ground* =**hurl**, smash, fling, slam, throw, toss, cast, propel, send; *informal* chuck, heave, sling, bung; *N. Amer. informal* peg. **3** *rain dashed against the walls* =**be hurled**, crash, smash; batter, strike, beat, pound, lash, drum. **4** *her hopes were dashed* =**shatter**, destroy, wreck, ruin, crush, demolish, blight, overturn, scotch, spoil, frustrate, thwart, check; *informal* do for, blow a hole in, put paid to; *Brit. informal* scupper.
−OPPOSITES dawdle, raise.
▶ noun **1** *a dash for the door* =**rush**, race, run, sprint, bolt, dart, leap, charge, bound, break; scramble. **2** *a dash of salt* =**pinch**, touch, sprinkle, taste, spot, drop, dab, speck, sprinkling, splash, bit, modicum, little; *informal* smidgen, tad, lick. **3** *he led off with such dash* =**verve**, style, flamboyance, gusto, zest, confidence, self-assurance, elan, flair, vigour, vivacity, sparkle, brio, panache, éclat, vitality, dynamism; *informal* pizzazz, pep, oomph.

dashing ▶ adjective **1** *a dashing pilot* =**debonair**, devil-may-care, raffish, flamboyant, bold, swashbuckling; romantic, gallant. **2** *he looked very dashing* =**stylish**, smart, elegant, dapper, spruce, trim, debonair; *informal* snazzy, natty, swish; *N. Amer. informal* spiffy.

dastardly ▶ adjective *(dated)* =**wicked**, evil, heinous, villainous, diabolical, fiendish, barbarous, cruel, dark, rotten, vile, monstrous, abominable, despicable, degenerate, sordid; bad, base, mean, low, dishonourable, dishonest, unscrupulous, unprincipled; *informal* low-down, dirty, shady, rascally, scoundrelly, crooked; *Brit. informal* beastly.
−OPPOSITES noble.

data ▶ noun =**facts**, figures, statistics, details, particulars, specifics; information, intelligence, material, input; *informal* info, gen.

date ▸ noun **1** *the only date he has to remember* =**day (of the month)**, occasion, time; year; anniversary. **2** *a later date seems likely for the megaliths* =**time**, age, period, era, epoch, century, decade, year. **3** *a lunch date* =**appointment**, meeting, engagement, rendezvous; commitment. **4** *(informal) a date for tonight* =**partner**, escort, girlfriend, boyfriend; *informal* bird, fella.
▸ verb **1** *the building dates from the 16th century* =**is from**, was built in, originates in, comes from, belongs to, goes back to. **2** *the best films don't date* =**age**, grow old, become dated, show its age; be of its time. **3** *(informal) he's dating Jill* =**go out with**, take out, go with, see; *informal* go steady with; *dated* court.

WORD LINKS
relating to dates: **chronological**

dated ▸ adjective =**old-fashioned**, outdated, outmoded, passé, behind the times, archaic, obsolete, antiquated; unfashionable, unstylish, crusty, olde worlde, prehistoric, antediluvian; *informal* old hat, out, out of the ark.
–OPPOSITES modern.

daub ▸ verb *he daubed a rock with paint* =**smear**, plaster, splash, spatter, splatter, cake, cover, smother, coat.
▸ noun *daubs of paint* =**smear**, smudge, splash, blot, spot, patch, blotch; *informal* splodge, splotch.

daughter ▸ noun =**girl**, little/baby girl.

WORD LINKS
relating to a daughter or son: **filial**
killing of one's daughter: **filicide**

daunt ▸ verb =**discourage**, deter, demoralize, put off, dishearten, dispirit; intimidate, abash, throw, cow, overawe, awe; *informal* rattle, faze.
–OPPOSITES hearten.

dauntless ▸ adjective =**fearless**, determined, resolute, indomitable, intrepid, doughty, plucky, spirited, mettlesome; *informal* gutsy.

dawdle ▸ verb **1** *they dawdled over breakfast* =**linger**, take one's time, be slow, waste time, idle, delay, procrastinate, stall; *informal* dilly-dally; *archaic* tarry. **2** *Ruth dawdled home* =**amble**, stroll, trail, move at a snail's pace; *informal*

mosey, tootle; *Brit. informal* pootle, mooch.
–OPPOSITES hurry.

dawn ▸ noun **1** *we got up at dawn* =**daybreak**, sunrise, first light, daylight, cockcrow; first thing (in the morning); *N. Amer.* sunup. **2** *the dawn of civilization* =**beginning**, start, birth, inception, genesis, emergence, advent, appearance, arrival, dawning, rise, origin, onset; unfolding, development, infancy; *informal* kick-off.
–OPPOSITES dusk, end.
▸ verb **1** *Thursday dawned crisp and sunny* =**begin**, break, arrive, emerge. **2** *a bright new future has dawned* =**begin**, start, commence, be born, appear, arrive, emerge; arise, rise, break, unfold, develop. **3** *the reality dawned on him* =**occur to**, come to, strike, hit, register with, cross someone's mind, suggest itself.
–OPPOSITES end.

WORD LINKS
fear of dawn: **eosophobia**

day ▸ noun **1** *I stayed for a day* =**twenty-four hours**. **2** *enjoy the beach during the day* =**daytime**, daylight; waking hours. **3** *the leading architect of the day* =**period**, time, age, era, generation. **4** *in his day he had great influence* =**heyday**, prime, time; peak, height, zenith, ascendancy.
–OPPOSITES night, decline.
■ **day after day** =**repeatedly**, again and again, over and over (again), time and (time) again, frequently, often, time after time, {day in, day out}, night and day, all the time; persistently, recurrently, constantly, continuously, continually, relentlessly, regularly, habitually, unfailingly, always; *N. Amer.* oftentimes; *informal* 24-7.
■ **day by day** =**gradually**, slowly, progressively; bit by bit, inch by inch, little by little.
■ **day in, day out.** *See* DAY AFTER DAY.

WORD LINKS
relating to the day: **diurnal**

daybreak ▸ noun =**dawn**, the crack of dawn, sunrise, first light, first thing (in the morning), cockcrow; daylight; *N. Amer.* sunup.
–OPPOSITES nightfall.

daydream ▸ noun **1** *she was lost in a daydream* =**reverie**, trance, fantasy, vision, dream. **2** *a big house was one of her daydreams* =**dream**, pipe dream, fantasy, castle in the air, castle in Spain, fond hope; wishful thinking; *informal* pie in the sky.

▸ **verb** *stop daydreaming!* =**dream**, stare into space; fantasize, be in cloud cuckoo land, build castles in the air, build castles in Spain.

daydreamer ▸ **noun** =**dreamer**, fantasist, fantasizer, romantic, wishful thinker, idealist; visionary, theorizer, utopian, Walter Mitty.

daylight ▸ **noun 1** *do the test in daylight* =**natural light**, sunlight. **2** *she only went there in daylight* =**(the) daytime**, day; broad daylight.
 −OPPOSITES darkness, night-time, nightfall.

day-to-day ▸ **adjective** =**regular**, everyday, daily, routine, habitual, frequent, normal, standard, usual, typical.

daze ▸ **verb 1** *he was dazed by his fall* =**stun**, confuse, disorient, stupefy; knock unconscious, knock out. **2** *she was dazed by the revelations* =**astound**, amaze, astonish, startle, dumbfound, stupefy, overwhelm, stagger, shock, confound, bewilder, take aback, nonplus, shake up; *informal* flabbergast, knock sideways, bowl over, blow away; *Brit. informal* knock for six.
▸ **noun** *she is in a daze* =**stupor**, trance, haze; spin, whirl, muddle, jumble.

dazzle ▸ **verb 1** *she was dazzled by the headlights* =**blind**; confuse, disorient. **2** *I was dazzled by the exhibition* =**overwhelm**, overcome, impress, move, stir, affect, touch, awe, overawe, leave speechless, take someone's breath away; spellbind, hypnotize; *informal* bowl over, blow away, knock out.
▸ **noun** *the dazzle of the limelight* =**sparkle**, glitter, brilliance, glory, splendour, magnificence, glamour; attraction, lure, allure, draw, appeal; *informal* razzle-dazzle, razzmatazz.

dazzling ▸ **adjective 1** *the sunlight was dazzling* =**bright**, blinding, glaring, brilliant. **2** *a dazzling performance* =**remarkable**, extraordinary, outstanding, exceptional; incredible, amazing, astonishing, phenomenal, breathtaking, thrilling; excellent, wonderful, magnificent, marvellous, superb, first-rate, superlative, virtuoso; *informal* mind-blowing, out of this world, fabulous, fab, super, sensational, ace, A1, cool, awesome; *Brit. informal* smashing, brill.

dead ▸ **adjective 1** *my parents are dead* =**passed on/away**, expired, departed, no more; late, lost; perished, fallen, slain, killed, murdered; lifeless, extinct; *informal* (as) dead as a doornail, six feet under, pushing up daisies; *formal* deceased. **2** *patches of dead ground* =**barren**, lifeless, bare, desolate, sterile. **3** *a dead language* =**obsolete**, extinct, defunct, disused, abandoned, discarded, superseded, vanished, forgotten; archaic, ancient. **4** *the phone was dead* =**not working**, out of order, inoperative, inactive, broken, defective; *informal* kaput, conked out, on the blink, bust; *Brit. informal* knackered. **5** *a dead arm* =**numb**, numbed, deadened, unfeeling; paralysed, crippled, incapacitated, immobilized, frozen. **6** *her dead eyes* =**emotionless**, unemotional, unfeeling, impassive, unresponsive, inexpressive, wooden, stony, cold; deadpan, flat; blank, vacant. **7** *his affection for her was dead* =**extinguished**, quashed, stifled; finished, over, gone, no more; (ancient) history. **8** *a dead town* =**boring**, uninteresting, unexciting, uninspiring, dull, flat, quiet, sleepy, slow, lifeless; *informal* one-horse; *N. Amer. informal* dullsville.
 −OPPOSITES alive, fertile, modern, working, lively.
▸ **adverb 1** *he was dead serious* =**completely**, absolutely, totally, utterly, deadly, perfectly, entirely, quite, thoroughly; in every way, one hundred per cent. **2** *flares were seen dead ahead* =**directly**, exactly, precisely, immediately, right, straight, due, squarely; *informal* bang, slap bang.

deadbeat ▸ **noun** (*informal*) =**layabout**, loafer, idler, good-for-nothing; *informal* waster, slacker; *Brit. informal* skiver; *N. Amer. informal* bum; *literary* wastrel.

deaden ▸ **verb 1** *surgeons tried to deaden the pain* =**numb**, dull, blunt, suppress; alleviate, mitigate, diminish, reduce, lessen, ease, soothe, relieve, assuage. **2** *the wood panelling deadened any noise* =**muffle**, mute, smother, stifle, dull, damp (down); soften; cushion, buffer, absorb.
 −OPPOSITES intensify, amplify, emphasize.

deadline ▸ **noun** =**time limit**, limit, finishing date, target date, cut-off point.

deadlock ▸ **noun** =**stalemate**, impasse, checkmate, stand-off; standstill, halt, (full) stop, dead end, gridlock.

deadly ▸ **adjective 1** *these drugs can be*

deadly =fatal, lethal, mortal, life-threatening; dangerous, injurious, harmful, detrimental, deleterious, unhealthy; noxious, toxic, poisonous; *literary* deathly. **2** *deadly enemies* =**mortal**, irreconcilable, implacable; bitter, sworn. **3** *his aim is deadly* =**unerring**, unfailing, perfect; sure, true, precise, accurate, exact; *Brit. informal* spot on, bang on.
–OPPOSITES harmless, mild, inaccurate.

▶ adverb *deadly serious* =**completely**, absolutely, totally, utterly, perfectly, entirely, wholly, quite, dead, thoroughly; in every way, one hundred per cent, to the hilt.

deadpan ▶ adjective =**blank**, expressionless, unexpressive, impassive, inscrutable, poker-faced, straight-faced; stony, wooden, vacant, fixed, lifeless.
–OPPOSITES expressive.

deaf ▶ adjective **1** *she is deaf and blind* =**hard of hearing**, hearing impaired, deafened; *informal* deaf as a post. **2** *she was deaf to their pleading* =**unmoved by**, untouched by, unaffected by, indifferent to, unresponsive to, unconcerned by; unaware of, oblivious to, impervious to.

deafening ▶ adjective =**ear-splitting**, overwhelming, almighty, mighty, tremendous; booming, thunderous.
–OPPOSITES low, soft.

deal ▶ noun *completion of the deal* =**agreement**, understanding, pact, bargain, covenant, contract, treaty; arrangement, compromise, settlement; terms; transaction, sale, account; *Law* indenture.

▶ verb **1** *how to deal with difficult children* =**cope with**, handle, manage, treat, take care of, take charge of, take in hand, sort out, tackle, take on; control; act/behave towards. **2** *the article deals with advances in biochemistry* =**concern**, be about, have to do with, discuss, consider, cover; tackle, study, explore, investigate, examine, review, analyse. **3** *the company deals in high-tech goods* =**trade in**, buy and sell; sell, purvey, supply, stock, market, merchandise; traffic, smuggle; *informal* push; *Brit. informal* flog. **4** *the cards were dealt* =**distribute**, give out, share out, divide out, hand out, pass out, pass round, dispense, allocate; *informal* divvy up. **5** *the court dealt a blow to government reforms* =**deliver**, administer, inflict, give, impose; aim.

dealer ▶ noun **1** *an antique dealer*

=**trader**, tradesman, tradesperson, merchant, salesman/woman, seller, vendor, purveyor, pedlar; buyer, merchandiser, distributor, supplier, shopkeeper, retailer, wholesaler; *Brit.* stockist. **2** *a dealer in a bank* =**stockbroker**, broker-dealer, broker, agent.

dealing ▶ noun **1** *dishonest dealing* =**business methods/practices**, business, commerce, trading, transactions; behaviour, conduct, actions. **2** *the UK's dealings with China* =**relations**, relationship, association, connections, contact, intercourse; negotiations, transactions; trade, trading, business, commerce, traffic; *informal* truck, doings.

dear ▶ adjective **1** *a dear friend* =**beloved**, loved, cherished, precious; esteemed, respected; close, intimate, bosom, boon, best. **2** *her pictures were too dear to part with* =**precious**, treasured, valued, prized, cherished, special. **3** *such a dear man* =**endearing**, adorable, lovable, appealing, engaging, charming, captivating, winsome, lovely, nice, pleasant, delightful, sweet, darling. **4** *rather dear meals* =**expensive**, costly, high-priced, overpriced, exorbitant, extortionate; *Brit.* over the odds; *informal* pricey, steep, stiff.
–OPPOSITES hated, disagreeable, cheap.

▶ noun **1** *don't worry, my dear* =**darling**, dearest, love, beloved, sweetheart, sweet, precious, treasure; *informal* sweetie, sugar, honey, baby, pet, sunshine, poppet. **2** *he's such a dear* =**darling**, pet, angel, gem, treasure; *informal* star, hero.

dearly ▶ adverb *I love him dearly* =**very much**, a great deal, greatly, deeply, profoundly; to distraction.

dearth ▶ noun =**lack**, scarcity, shortage, shortfall, want, deficiency, insufficiency, inadequacy, sparseness, scantiness, rareness; absence.
–OPPOSITES surfeit.

death ▶ noun **1** *her father's death* =**demise**, dying, end, passing, loss of life; murder, assassination, execution, slaughter, massacre; *formal* decease. **2** *the death of their dream* =**end**, finish, termination, extinction, extinguishing, collapse, destruction, obliteration.
–OPPOSITES life, birth.

WORD LINKS

fear of death: **thanatophobia**
---

deathless ▶ adjective =**immortal**, undying, imperishable, indestructible; enduring, everlasting, eternal; timeless, ageless.
−OPPOSITES mortal, ephemeral.

deathly ▶ adjective =**deathlike**, deadly, ghostly, ghastly; ashen, chalky, white, pale, pallid, bloodless, wan, anaemic, pasty.

debacle ▶ noun =**fiasco**, failure, catastrophe, disaster, mess, ruin; downfall, collapse, defeat; informal foul-up, screwup, hash, botch, washout; Brit. informal cock-up, pig's ear, bodge; N. Amer. informal snafu.

debase ▶ verb =**degrade**, devalue, demean, cheapen, prostitute, discredit, drag down, tarnish, blacken; disgrace, dishonour, shame; damage, harm, undermine.
−OPPOSITES enhance.

debased ▶ adjective **1** their debased amusements =**immoral**, debauched, dissolute, perverted, degenerate, wicked, sinful, vile, base, iniquitous, corrupt; lewd, lascivious, lecherous, prurient, indecent. **2** the myth lives on in a debased form =**corrupt**, corrupted, bastardized, adulterated, diluted, tainted.
−OPPOSITES honourable, original.

debatable ▶ adjective =**arguable**, disputable, questionable, open to question, controversial, contentious; doubtful, dubious, uncertain, unsure, unclear; borderline, inconclusive, moot, unsettled, unresolved, unconfirmed, undetermined, undecided, up in the air; informal iffy.

debate ▶ noun a debate on the reforms =**discussion**, discourse, parley, dialogue; argument, dispute, wrangle, war of words, dissension, disagreement, contention, conflict; negotiations, talks; informal confab, powwow.
▶ verb **1** MPs will debate our future =**discuss**, talk over/through, talk about, thrash out, argue, dispute; informal kick around/about. **2** he debated whether to call her =**consider**, think over/about, chew over, mull over, weigh up, ponder, deliberate, contemplate, muse, meditate; formal cogitate.

debauched ▶ adjective =**dissolute**, dissipated, degenerate, corrupt, depraved, sinful, unprincipled, immoral; lascivious, lecherous, lewd, lustful, libidinous, licentious, promiscuous,
loose, wanton, abandoned; decadent, profligate, intemperate, sybaritic.
−OPPOSITES wholesome.

debauchery ▶ noun =**dissipation**, degeneracy, corruption, vice, depravity; immodesty, indecency, perversion, iniquity, wickedness, sinfulness, impropriety, immorality; lasciviousness, salaciousness, lechery, lewdness, lust, promiscuity, wantonness; decadence, intemperance; formal turpitude.

debilitate ▶ verb =**weaken**, enfeeble, enervate, sap, drain, exhaust, weary, fatigue, prostrate; undermine, impair, indispose, incapacitate, cripple, disable, paralyse, immobilize, lay low; informal knock out, do in.
−OPPOSITES invigorate.

debonair ▶ adjective =**suave**, urbane, sophisticated, cultured, self-possessed, self-assured, confident, charming, gracious, courteous, gallant, gentlemanly, refined, polished, well bred, genteel, dignified, courtly; well groomed, elegant, stylish, smart, dashing; informal smooth, sharp; Brit. informal swish.
−OPPOSITES unsophisticated.

debrief ▶ verb =**question**, quiz, interview, examine, cross-examine, interrogate, probe, sound out; informal grill, pump.

debris ▶ noun =**detritus**, refuse, rubbish, waste, litter, scrap, dross, chaff, flotsam and jetsam; rubble, wreckage; remains, scraps, dregs; N. Amer. trash, garbage; Austral./NZ mullock; informal junk.

debt ▶ noun **1** he couldn't pay his debts =**bill**, account, dues, arrears, charges; N. Amer. check; informal tab. **2** his debt to the author =**indebtedness**, obligation; gratitude, appreciation, thanks.
■ **in debt** =**owing money**, in arrears, behind, overdrawn; insolvent, bankrupt, ruined; Brit. in liquidation; informal in the red, in Queer Street, on the rocks.

debtor ▶ noun =**borrower**; bankrupt, insolvent, defaulter.
−OPPOSITES creditor.

debunk ▶ verb =**explode**, deflate, quash, discredit, disprove, refute, contradict, controvert, invalidate, negate; challenge, call into question; informal shoot full of holes, blow sky-high; formal confute.
−OPPOSITES confirm.

debut ▶ noun =**first appearance**, first

performance, launch, entrance, premiere, introduction, inception, inauguration; *informal* kick-off.

decadence ▸ noun =**dissipation**, degeneracy, debauchery, corruption, depravity, vice, sin, moral decay, immorality, amorality; intemperance, licentiousness, self-indulgence, hedonism.
−OPPOSITES morality.

decadent ▸ adjective =**dissolute**, dissipated, degenerate, corrupt, depraved, sinful, unprincipled, immoral, amoral; licentious, abandoned, profligate, intemperate; sybaritic, hedonistic, pleasure-seeking, self-indulgent.

decant ▸ verb =**pour out/off**, draw off, siphon off, drain, tap; transfer.

decay ▸ verb **1** *the corpses had decayed* =**decompose**, rot, putrefy, go bad, go off, spoil, fester, perish, deteriorate; break down, moulder, shrivel, wither. **2** *the cities continue to decay* =**deteriorate**, degenerate, decline, go downhill, slump, slide, go to rack and ruin, go to seed; disintegrate, fall to pieces, fall into disrepair; collapse; *informal* go to pot, go to the dogs, go down the toilet/pan; *Austral./NZ informal* go to the pack.
▸ noun **1** *signs of decay* =**decomposition**, putrefaction; rot, mould, mildew, fungus. **2** *the decay of American values* =**deterioration**, degeneration, debasement, degradation, decline, weakening, atrophy; crumbling, disintegration, collapse.

decayed ▸ adjective =**decomposed**, decomposing, rotten, putrescent, putrid, bad, off, spoiled, perished; mouldy, festering, fetid, rancid, rank.

decaying ▸ adjective **1** *decaying fish* =**decomposing**, decomposed, rotting, rotten, putrescent, putrid, bad, off, perished; mouldy, festering, fetid, rancid, rank. **2** *a decaying city* =**declining**, degenerating, dying, crumbling; run down, tumbledown, ramshackle, shabby, decrepit; *informal* on the way out.

deceased ▸ adjective *(formal)* =**dead**, expired, departed, gone, no more, passed on/away; late, lost, late lamented; perished, fallen, slain, slaughtered, killed, murdered; lifeless, extinct; *informal* (as) dead as a doornail, six feet under, pushing up daisies.

deceit ▸ noun =**deception**, deceitfulness, duplicity, double-dealing, lies, fraud, cheating, trickery, chicanery, deviousness, slyness, guile, bluff, lying, pretence, treachery; *informal* crookedness, monkey business, jiggery-pokery; *N. Amer. informal* monkeyshines.
−OPPOSITES honesty.

deceitful ▸ adjective **1** *a deceitful woman* =**dishonest**, untruthful, insincere, false, disingenuous, untrustworthy, unscrupulous, unprincipled, two-faced, duplicitous, double-dealing, underhand, crafty, cunning, sly, scheming, calculating, treacherous, Machiavellian; *informal* sneaky, tricky, crooked; *Brit. informal* bent. **2** *a deceitful allegation* =**fraudulent**, fabricated, invented, concocted, made up, trumped up, untrue, false, bogus, fake, spurious, fallacious, deceptive, misleading.
−OPPOSITES honest, true.

deceive ▸ verb *she was deceived by a con man* =**swindle**, defraud, cheat, trick, hoodwink, hoax, dupe, take in, mislead, delude, fool, outwit, lead on, inveigle, beguile, double-cross, gull; *informal* con, bamboozle, do, diddle, swizzle, rip off, shaft, pull a fast one on, take for a ride, pull the wool over someone's eyes, sell a pup to; *N. Amer. informal* sucker, snooker, stiff.

decelerate ▸ verb =**slow down/up**, ease up, reduce speed, brake.
−OPPOSITES accelerate.

decency ▸ noun **1** *standards of taste and decency* =**propriety**, decorum, good taste, respectability, dignity, correctness, good form, etiquette; morality, virtue, modesty, delicacy. **2** *he didn't have the decency to tell me* =**courtesy**, politeness, good manners, civility; consideration, thoughtfulness.

decent ▸ adjective **1** *a decent burial* =**proper**, correct, appropriate, suitable; respectable, dignified, decorous, seemly; nice, right, tasteful; conventional, accepted, standard, traditional, orthodox; comme il faut; *informal* pukka. **2** *(Brit. informal) a very decent chap* =**honourable**, honest, trustworthy, dependable; respectable, upright, clean-living, virtuous, good; obliging, helpful, accommodating, generous, kind, thoughtful, considerate; neighbourly, hospitable, pleasant, agreeable, amiable. **3** *a job with decent pay* =**satisfactory**, reasonable, fair, acceptable, adequate, sufficient; not bad, all right, tolerable, passable, suitable; *informal* OK, okay.

–OPPOSITES unpleasant, unsatisfactory.

deception ▸ noun **1** *they obtained money by deception* =**deceit**, deceitfulness, duplicity, double-dealing, fraud, cheating, trickery, chicanery, deviousness, guile, bluff, lying, pretence, treachery; *informal* crookedness, monkey business, jiggery-pokery; *N. Amer. informal* monkeyshines. **2** *it was all a deception* =**trick**, deceit, sham, fraud, pretence, hoax, fake, artifice; stratagem, device, ruse, scheme, dodge, machination, subterfuge; cheat, swindle; *informal* con, set-up, scam, flimflam; *N. Amer. informal* bunco.

deceptive ▸ adjective **1** *distances are very deceptive* =**misleading**; illusory; ambiguous. **2** *deceptive practices* =**deceitful**, duplicitous, fraudulent, counterfeit, underhand, scheming, treacherous, Machiavellian; disingenuous, untrustworthy, unscrupulous, unprincipled, dishonest, insincere, false; *informal* crooked, sharp, shady, sneaky, tricky; *Brit. informal* bent.

decide ▸ verb **1** *she decided to become a writer* =**resolve**, determine, make up one's mind, make a decision; elect, choose, opt, plan, aim, have the intention, have in mind, set one's sights on. **2** *research to decide a variety of questions* =**settle**, resolve, determine, work out, answer; *informal* sort out, figure out. **3** *the court is to decide the case* =**adjudicate**, arbitrate, judge; hear, try, examine; sit in judgement on, pronounce on, give a verdict on, rule on.

decided ▸ adjective **1** *they have a decided advantage* =**distinct**, clear, marked, pronounced, obvious, striking, noticeable, unmistakable, patent, manifest; definite, certain, positive, emphatic, undeniable, indisputable, unquestionable; assured, guaranteed. **2** *he was very decided* =**determined**, resolute, firm, strong-minded, strong-willed, emphatic, dead set, unwavering, unyielding, unbending, inflexible, unshakeable, unrelenting; *N. Amer.* rock-ribbed. **3** *our future is decided* =**settled**, established, resolved, determined, agreed, designated, chosen, ordained, prescribed; set, fixed; *informal* sewn up, wrapped up.

decidedly ▸ adverb =**distinctly**, clearly, markedly, obviously, noticeably, unmistakably, patently, manifestly; definitely, certainly, positively,

absolutely, downright, undeniably, unquestionably; extremely, exceedingly, exceptionally, particularly, especially, very; *N. English* right; *informal* terrifically, devilishly, ultra, mega, majorly; *Brit. informal* jolly, ever so, dead, well; *N. Amer. informal* real, mighty, awful.

deciding ▸ adjective =**determining**, decisive, conclusive, key, pivotal, crucial, critical, significant.

decipher ▸ verb **1** *he deciphered the code* =**decode**, decrypt, break, work out, solve, interpret, translate; make sense of, get to the bottom of, unravel; *informal* crack, figure out; *Brit. informal* twig, suss (out). **2** *his writing was hard to decipher* =**make out**, discern, perceive, read, follow.
–OPPOSITES encode.

decision ▸ noun **1** *they came to a decision* =**resolution**, conclusion, settlement; choice, option, selection. **2** *the judge's decision* =**verdict**, finding, ruling, recommendation, judgement, pronouncement, adjudication; order, rule; result; *Law* determination; *N. Amer.* resolve.

decisive ▸ adjective **1** *a decisive man* =**resolute**, firm, strong-minded, strong-willed, determined; purposeful. **2** *the decisive factor* =**deciding**, conclusive, determining; key, pivotal, critical, crucial, significant, influential, major, chief, principal, prime.

deck ▸ verb **1** *the street was decked with bunting* =**decorate**, bedeck, adorn, ornament, trim, trick out, garnish, cover, hang, festoon, garland, swathe, wreathe; *informal* get up, do up, do out, tart up; *literary* bedizen. **2** *Ingrid was decked out in blue* =**dress (up)**, clothe, attire, garb, robe, drape, turn out, fit out, rig out, outfit, costume; *informal* doll up, get up, do up.

declaim ▸ verb =**make a speech**, give an address, give a lecture, deliver a sermon; speak, hold forth, orate, preach, lecture, sermonize, moralize; *informal* sound off, spout; speak out, rail, inveigh, fulminate, rage, thunder; rant.

declaration ▸ noun **1** *they issued a declaration* =**announcement**, statement, communication, pronouncement, proclamation, communiqué, edict; *N. Amer.* advisory. **2** *a declaration of faith* =**assertion**, profession, affirmation, acknowledgement, revelation, disclosure, manifestation, confirmation, testimony, validation, certification, attestation; pledge, avowal, vow, oath, protestation.

declare ▶ verb **1** *she declared her political principles* =**proclaim**, announce, state, reveal, air, voice, articulate, express, vent, set forth, publicize, broadcast. **2** *he declared that they were guilty* =**assert**, maintain, state, affirm, contend, argue, insist, hold, profess, claim, avow, swear; *formal* aver.

decline ▶ verb **1** *she declined all invitations* =**turn down**, reject, brush aside, refuse, rebuff, spurn, repulse, dismiss; forgo, pass up; abstain from, say no; *informal* give the thumbs down to, give something a miss, give someone the brush-off; *Brit. informal* knock back. **2** *the number of traders has declined* =**decrease**, reduce, lessen, diminish, dwindle, contract, shrink, fall off, tail off; drop, fall, go down, slump, plummet; *informal* nosedive, crash. **3** *standards steadily declined* =**deteriorate**, degenerate, decay, crumble, collapse, slump, slip, slide, go downhill, worsen; weaken, wane, ebb; *informal* go to pot, go to the dogs, go down the toilet/pan; *Austral./NZ informal* go to the pack.
–OPPOSITES accept, increase, rise.
▶ noun **1** *a decline in profits* =**reduction**, decrease, downturn, downswing, depreciation, diminution, ebb, drop, slump, plunge; *informal* nosedive, crash. **2** *habitat decline* =**deterioration**, degeneration, degradation, shrinkage; erosion.
■ **in decline** =**declining**, decaying, crumbling, collapsing, failing; disappearing, dying, moribund; *informal* on its last legs, on the way out.

decode ▶ verb =**decipher**, decrypt, work out, solve, interpret, translate; make sense of, get to the bottom of, unravel, find the key to; *informal* crack, figure out; *Brit. informal* twig, suss (out).

decompose ▶ verb =**decay**, rot, putrefy, go bad, go off, spoil, perish, deteriorate; degrade, break down.

decomposition ▶ noun =**decay**, putrefaction, putrescence.

decontaminate ▶ verb =**sanitize**, sterilize, disinfect, clean, cleanse, purify; fumigate.

decor ▶ noun =**decoration**, furnishing; colour scheme.

decorate ▶ verb **1** *the door was decorated with a wreath* =**ornament**, adorn, trim, embellish, garnish, furnish, enhance, grace, prettify; festoon, garland, bedeck. **2** *he started to decorate his home* =**paint**, **wallpaper**, paper; refurbish, furbish, renovate, redecorate; *informal* do up, spruce up, do over, fix up, give something a facelift, make over. **3** *he was decorated for courage* =**give a medal to**, honour, cite, reward.

decoration ▶ noun **1** *a ceiling with rich decoration* =**ornamentation**, adornment, trimming, embellishment, gilding; beautification, prettification; enhancements, frills, accessories, trimmings, finery, frippery. **2** *a Christmas tree decoration* =**ornament**, bauble, trinket, knick-knack. **3** *a decoration won on the battlefield* =**medal**, award, prize; *Brit. informal* gong.

decorative ▶ adjective =**ornamental**; fancy, ornate, attractive, pretty, showy.
–OPPOSITES functional.

decorum ▶ noun **1** *he had acted with decorum* =**propriety**, seemliness, decency, good taste, correctness; politeness, courtesy, good manners. **2** *a breach of decorum* =**etiquette**, protocol, good form, custom, convention.
–OPPOSITES impropriety.

decrease ▶ verb **1** *pollution levels decreased* =**lessen**, reduce, drop, diminish, decline, dwindle, fall off; die down, abate, subside, tail off, ebb, wane; plummet, plunge. **2** *decrease the amount of fat in your body* =**reduce**, lessen, lower, cut; slim down, tone down, deplete, minimize; *informal* slash.
–OPPOSITES increase.
▶ noun *a decrease in crime* =**reduction**, drop, decline, downturn, cut, cutback, diminution, ebb, wane.
–OPPOSITES increase.

decree ▶ noun **1** *a presidential decree* =**order**, edict, command, commandment, mandate, proclamation, dictum; law, statute, act; *formal* ordinance. **2** *a court decree* =**judgement**, verdict, adjudication, ruling, resolution, decision.
▶ verb *he decreed that a stadium should be built* =**order**, command, rule, dictate, pronounce, proclaim, ordain; direct, decide, determine.

decrepit ▶ adjective **1** *a decrepit old man* =**feeble**, infirm, weak, frail; disabled, incapacitated, crippled, doddering, tottering; old, elderly, aged, ancient, senile; *informal* past it, over the hill. **2** *a decrepit house* =**dilapidated**, rickety, run

down, tumbledown, ramshackle, derelict, ruined, in (a state of) disrepair, gone to rack and ruin; decayed, crumbling.
–OPPOSITES strong, sound.

decry ▸ verb =**denounce**, condemn, criticize, censure, attack, rail against, run down, pillory, lambaste, vilify, revile; disparage, deprecate; *informal* slam, blast, knock; *Brit. informal* slate.
–OPPOSITES praise.

dedicate ▸ verb **1** *she dedicated her life to the sick* =**devote**, commit, pledge, give (up), sacrifice; set aside, allocate, consign. **2** *the chapel was dedicated to the Virgin Mary* =**devote**, assign; bless, consecrate, sanctify.

dedicated ▸ adjective **1** *a dedicated socialist* =**committed**, devoted, staunch, firm, steadfast, resolute, loyal, faithful, true, dyed-in-the-wool; wholehearted, single-minded, earnest, ardent, passionate, fervent; *informal* card-carrying. **2** *data is accessed by a dedicated search engine* =**exclusive**, custom built, customized, special, purpose built; built-in, inbuilt, onboard, in-house.
–OPPOSITES indifferent.

dedication ▸ noun **1** *sport requires dedication* =**commitment**, application, diligence, industry, resolve, enthusiasm, conscientiousness, perseverance, persistence, tenacity, drive, staying power; hard work, effort. **2** *her dedication to the job* =**devotion**, commitment, loyalty, allegiance. **3** *the book has a dedication to his wife* =**inscription**, message. **4** *the dedication of the church* =**blessing**, consecration, sanctification.
–OPPOSITES apathy.

deduce ▸ verb =**conclude**, reason, work out, infer; glean, divine, intuit, understand, assume, presume, conjecture, surmise, reckon; *informal* figure out; *Brit. informal* suss out.

deduct ▸ verb =**subtract**, take away, take off, debit, dock, discount; remove; *informal* knock off.
–OPPOSITES add.

deduction ▸ noun **1** *the deduction of tax* =**subtraction**, removal, debit. **2** *gross pay, before deductions* =**stoppage**, tax; expenses. **3** *she was right in her deduction* =**conclusion**, inference, supposition, hypothesis, assumption, presumption; suspicion, conviction, belief, reasoning.

deed ▸ noun **1** *heroic deeds* =**act**, action; feat, exploit, achievement, accomplishment, endeavour, undertaking, enterprise. **2** *unity must be established in deed and word* =**fact**, reality, actuality.

deem ▸ verb =**consider**, regard as, judge, hold to be, view as, see as, take for, class as, count, find, esteem, suppose, reckon; think, believe, feel.

deep ▸ adjective **1** *a deep ravine* =**cavernous**, yawning, gaping, huge, extensive; bottomless, fathomless, unfathomable. **2** *two inches deep* =**in depth**, downwards, inwards. **3** *deep affection* =**intense**, heartfelt, wholehearted, deep-seated, deep-rooted; sincere, genuine, earnest, enthusiastic, great. **4** *a deep sleep* =**sound**, heavy. **5** *a deep thinker* =**profound**, serious, philosophical; intelligent, intellectual, learned, wise, scholarly; discerning, penetrating, perceptive, insightful. **6** *he was deep in concentration* =**rapt**, absorbed, engrossed, preoccupied, immersed, lost, gripped, intent, engaged. **7** *a deep mystery* =**obscure**, complex, mysterious, secret, unfathomable, opaque, abstruse, recondite, esoteric, enigmatic, arcane; puzzling, baffling, mystifying, inexplicable. **8** *his deep voice* =**low-pitched**, low, bass, rich, powerful, resonant, booming, sonorous. **9** *a deep red* =**dark**, intense, rich, strong.
–OPPOSITES shallow, superficial, high, light.
▸ adverb **1** *I dug deep* =**far down**, way/right/a long way down. **2** *he took them deep into the forest* =**far**, a long way; *informal* miles.

deepen ▸ verb **1** *his love for her had deepened* =**grow**, increase, intensify, strengthen; *informal* step up; *Brit. informal* hot up. **2** *they deepened the hole* =**dig out**, dig deeper, excavate.

deeply ▸ adverb =**profoundly**, greatly, enormously, extremely, very much; strongly, intensely, keenly, acutely; thoroughly, completely, entirely; *informal* well, seriously, majorly.

deep-rooted ▸ adjective =**deep-seated**, deep, profound, fundamental, basic; established, ingrained, entrenched, unshakeable, inbuilt; persistent, abiding, lingering.
–OPPOSITES superficial.

deep-seated ▸ adjective. See DEEP-ROOTED.

deer ▶ noun

WORD LINKS

relating to deer: **cervine**
male: **stag**
female: **doe**
collective noun: **herd, mob**

deface ▶ verb =**vandalize**, disfigure, spoil, ruin, damage; *N. Amer. informal* trash.

defamation ▶ noun =**libel**, slander, calumny, character assassination, vilification; scandalmongering, aspersions, muckraking, abuse; disparagement, denigration; smear, slur; *informal* mudslinging.

defamatory ▶ adjective =**libellous**, slanderous, malicious, vicious, backbiting, muckraking; abusive, disparaging, denigrating, insulting; *informal* mudslinging, bitchy, catty.

defame ▶ verb =**libel**, slander, malign, cast aspersions on, smear, traduce, give someone a bad name, run down, speak ill of, vilify, besmirch, disparage, denigrate, discredit; *informal* do a hatchet job on, drag through the mud; *N. Amer.* slur; *informal* bad-mouth; *Brit. informal* slag off.
−OPPOSITES compliment.

defeat ▶ verb 1 *the army which defeated the Scots* =**beat**, conquer, win against, triumph over, get the better of, vanquish; rout, trounce, overcome, overpower, crush, subdue; *informal* lick, thrash, whip, wipe the floor with, make mincemeat of, clobber, slaughter, demolish, cane; *Brit. informal* stuff; *N. Amer. informal* cream, skunk. 2 *this defeats the original point of the plan* =**thwart**, frustrate, foil, ruin, scotch, derail; *informal* put the kibosh on, put paid to, stymie; *Brit. informal* scupper, nobble. 3 *the motion was defeated* =**reject**, overthrow, throw out, dismiss, outvote, turn down; *informal* give the thumbs down.
▶ noun 1 *a crippling defeat* =**loss**, conquest; rout, trouncing; *informal* thrashing, hiding, drubbing, licking, pasting, massacre, slaughter. 2 *the defeat of his plans* =**failure**, downfall, collapse, ruin; rejection, frustration, abortion, miscarriage; undoing.
−OPPOSITES victory, success.

defeatist ▶ adjective *a defeatist attitude* =**pessimistic**, fatalistic, negative, despondent, despairing, hopeless, gloomy.
−OPPOSITES optimistic.
▶ noun =**pessimist**, fatalist, prophet of doom, doomster; misery, killjoy, worrier; *informal* quitter, wet blanket, loser.
−OPPOSITES optimist.

defecate ▶ verb =**excrete (faeces)**, have a bowel movement, evacuate one's bowels, relieve oneself, go to the lavatory/toilet; *informal* do a number two, do/have a poo.

defect¹ ▶ noun *he spotted a defect in my work* =**fault**, flaw, imperfection, deficiency, weakness, inconsistency, weak spot, inadequacy, shortcoming, limitation, failing, deformity, blemish; mistake, error; *informal* glitch, gremlin, bug.

defect² ▶ verb *his chief intelligence officer defected* =**desert**, change sides, turn traitor, rebel, renege; *Military* go AWOL; *literary* forsake.

defection ▶ noun =**desertion**, absconding, decamping, flight; treason, betrayal, disloyalty.

defective ▶ adjective =**faulty**, flawed, imperfect, shoddy, inoperative, malfunctioning, out of order, unsound; broken; *informal* on the blink; *Brit. informal* knackered, duff.
−OPPOSITES perfect.

defector ▶ noun =**deserter**, turncoat, traitor, renegade, Judas, quisling; *informal* rat.

defence ▶ noun 1 *the defence of the fortress* =**protection**, guarding, security, fortification; resistance, deterrent. 2 *more spending on defence* =**armaments**, weapons, weaponry, arms; the military, the armed forces. 3 *the prisoner's defence* =**vindication**, explanation, mitigation, justification, rationalization, excuse, alibi, reason; plea, pleading; testimony, declaration, case.

defenceless ▶ adjective 1 *defenceless animals* =**vulnerable**, helpless, powerless, weak. 2 *the country is wholly defenceless* =**undefended**, unprotected, unguarded, unarmed; vulnerable, exposed, insecure.
−OPPOSITES resilient.

defend ▶ verb 1 *a fort built to defend Ireland* =**protect**, guard, safeguard, secure, shield; fortify; uphold, support, watch over. 2 *he defended his policy* =**justify**, vindicate, argue for, support, make a case for, plead for; explain. 3 *the manager defended his players* =**support**, back, stand by, stick up for, stand up for.

−OPPOSITES attack, criticize.

defendant ▶ noun =**accused**, prisoner (at the bar); appellant, litigant, respondent; suspect.
−OPPOSITES plaintiff.

defender ▶ noun **1** *defenders of the environment* =**protector**, guard, guardian, preserver; custodian, watchdog, keeper, overseer, superintendent, caretaker. **2** *a defender of colonialism* =**supporter**, upholder, backer, champion, advocate, apologist, proponent, exponent, promoter; adherent, believer.

defensive ▶ adjective **1** *troops in defensive positions* =**defending**, protective. **2** *a defensive response* =**self-justifying**, oversensitive, prickly, paranoid, neurotic; *informal* uptight, twitchy.

defer[1] ▶ verb *the committee will defer their decision* =**postpone**, put off, delay, hold over/off, put back; shelve, suspend, stay, mothball; *N. Amer.* put over, table, take a rain check on; *informal* put on ice, put on the back burner, put in cold storage.

defer[2] ▶ verb *they deferred to Joseph's judgement* =**yield**, submit, give way, give in, surrender, capitulate, acquiesce.

deference ▶ noun =**respect**, respectfulness; submissiveness, submission, obedience, accession, capitulation, acquiescence, compliance.
−OPPOSITES disrespect.

deferential ▶ adjective =**respectful**, humble, obsequious; dutiful, obedient, submissive, subservient, yielding, acquiescent, compliant.

defiance ▶ noun =**resistance**, opposition, non-compliance, disobedience, insubordination, dissent, recalcitrance, rebellion; contempt, disregard, scorn, insolence.
−OPPOSITES obedience.

defiant ▶ adjective =**intransigent**, resistant, obstinate, uncooperative, non-compliant, recalcitrant; insubordinate, rebellious, mutinous; *informal* feisty; *Brit. informal* stroppy, bolshie.
−OPPOSITES cooperative.

deficiency ▶ noun **1** *a vitamin deficiency* =**insufficiency**, lack, shortage, want, deficit, shortfall; scarcity. **2** *the team's big deficiency* =**defect**, fault, flaw, imperfection, weakness, weak point, inadequacy, shortcoming, limitation, failing.

−OPPOSITES surplus, strength.

deficient ▶ adjective **1** *a diet deficient in vitamin A* =**lacking**, wanting, inadequate, insufficient, limited, poor; short of/on, low on. **2** *deficient leadership* =**defective**, faulty, flawed, inadequate, imperfect, shoddy, weak, inferior, unsound, substandard, poor; *Brit. informal* duff.

deficit ▶ noun =**shortfall**, deficiency, shortage, undersupply; debt, arrears; loss.
−OPPOSITES surplus.

defile ▶ verb =**desecrate**, profane, violate; contaminate, pollute, debase, degrade, dishonour.
−OPPOSITES sanctify.

definable ▶ adjective =**determinable**, ascertainable, definite, clear-cut, precise, exact, specific.

define ▶ verb **1** *the dictionary defines it succinctly* =**explain**, expound, interpret, describe. **2** *he defined the limits of the middle class* =**determine**, establish, fix, specify, designate, decide, stipulate, set out.

definite ▶ adjective **1** *a definite answer* =**explicit**, specific, express, precise, exact, clear-cut, direct, plain, outright; fixed. **2** *definite evidence* =**certain**, sure, positive, conclusive, decisive, firm, concrete, unambiguous, unequivocal, clear, unmistakable, proven; guaranteed, assured, cut and dried. **3** *she had a definite dislike for Robert* =**unmistakable**, unequivocal, unambiguous, certain, undisputed, decided, marked, distinct. **4** *a definite geographical area* =**fixed**, marked, specific, identifiable.
−OPPOSITES vague, ambiguous, indeterminate.

definitely ▶ adverb =**certainly**, surely, for sure, unquestionably, without doubt, without question, undoubtedly, indubitably, positively, absolutely; undeniably, unmistakably, as sure as eggs is eggs.

definition ▶ noun **1** *the definition of 'intelligence'* =**meaning**, sense; interpretation, explanation, description. **2** *the definition of the picture* =**clarity**, visibility, sharpness, crispness; resolution.

definitive ▶ adjective **1** *a definitive decision* =**conclusive**, final; unconditional, unqualified, absolute, categorical, positive, definite. **2** *the definitive guide* =**authoritative**, exhaustive, best, finest;

classic, standard, recognized, accepted, official.

deflate ▶ verb **1** *he deflated the tyres* =**let down**, flatten; puncture. **2** *the balloon deflated* =**go down**, collapse, shrink, contract. **3** *the news had deflated him* =**subdue**, humble, cow, chasten; dispirit, dismay, discourage, dishearten; squash, crush, bring down, take the wind out of someone's sails. **4** *the budget deflated the economy* =**reduce**, slow down; devalue, depreciate, depress.
−OPPOSITES inflate.

deflect ▶ verb **1** *she wanted to deflect attention from herself* =**turn away**, divert, draw away; fend off, parry, stave off. **2** *the ball deflected off the wall* =**bounce**, glance, ricochet.

deform ▶ verb =**disfigure**, bend out of shape, contort, buckle, warp; damage, impair.

deformed ▶ adjective =**misshapen**, distorted, malformed, contorted, out of shape; twisted, crooked, warped, buckled, gnarled; crippled, disfigured, grotesque; injured, damaged, mutilated, mangled.

deformity ▶ noun =**malformation**, misshapenness, distortion, crookedness; imperfection, abnormality, irregularity; disfigurement; defect, flaw, blemish.

defraud ▶ verb =**swindle**, cheat, rob; deceive, dupe, hoodwink, double-cross, trick; *informal* con, do, sting, diddle, rip off, shaft, pull a fast one on, put one over on, sell a pup to; *N. Amer. informal* sucker, snooker, stiff; *Austral. informal* pull a swifty on.

deft ▶ adjective =**skilful**, adept, adroit, dexterous, agile, nimble, handy; able, capable, skilled, proficient, accomplished, expert, polished, slick, professional, masterly; clever, shrewd, astute, canny, sharp; *informal* nifty, nippy.
−OPPOSITES clumsy.

defunct ▶ adjective =**disused**, inoperative, non-functioning, unusable, obsolete; no longer existing, discontinued; extinct.
−OPPOSITES working, extant.

defuse ▶ verb **1** *he tried to defuse the grenade* =**deactivate**, disarm, disable, make safe. **2** *an attempt to defuse the tension* =**reduce**, lessen, diminish, lighten, relieve, ease, alleviate.
−OPPOSITES activate, intensify.

defy ▶ verb **1** *he defied European law* =**disobey**, go against, flout, fly in the face of, disregard, ignore; break, violate, contravene, breach, infringe; *informal* cock a snook at. **2** *he scowled, defying her to mock him* =**challenge**, dare.
−OPPOSITES obey.

degeneracy ▶ noun =**corruption**, decadence, moral decay, dissipation, dissolution, profligacy, vice, immorality, sin, sinfulness, ungodliness; debauchery; *formal* turpitude.

degenerate ▶ adjective **1** *a degenerate form of classicism* =**debased**, degraded, corrupt, impure. **2** *her degenerate brother* =**corrupt**, decadent, dissolute, dissipated, debauched, reprobate, profligate; sinful, ungodly, immoral, unprincipled, amoral, dishonourable, disreputable, unsavoury.
−OPPOSITES pure, moral.
▶ noun *a bunch of degenerates* =**reprobate**, debauchee, profligate, libertine, roué.
▶ verb **1** *their quality of life had degenerated* =**deteriorate**, decline, slip, slide, worsen, lapse, slump, go downhill, regress; go to rack and ruin; *informal* go to pot, go to the dogs, hit the skids, go down the toilet/pan. **2** *the muscles started to degenerate* =**waste (away)**, atrophy, weaken, break down, deteriorate; collapse.
−OPPOSITES improve.

degradation ▶ noun **1** *poverty brings with it degradation* =**humiliation**, shame, loss of self-respect, indignity, ignominy. **2** *the degradation of women* =**demeaning**, debasement, belittling. **3** *the degradation of the tissues* =**deterioration**, degeneration, atrophy, decay; breakdown, wasting (away), collapse.

degrade ▶ verb **1** *prisons should not degrade prisoners* =**demean**, debase, humiliate, dehumanize, brutalize. **2** *the polymer will not degrade* =**break down**, deteriorate, degenerate, decay.
−OPPOSITES dignify.

degrading ▶ adjective =**humiliating**, demeaning, shameful, mortifying, ignominious, undignified.

degree ▶ noun =**level**, standard, grade, mark; amount, extent, measure; magnitude, intensity, strength; proportion, ratio.
■ **by degrees** =**gradually**, little by little, bit by bit, inch by inch, step by step, slowly; piecemeal.

deign ▸ verb =**condescend**, stoop, lower oneself, demean oneself, humble oneself; consent, vouchsafe.

deity ▸ noun =**god**, goddess, divine being, supreme being, divinity, immortal; creator, demiurge; godhead.

dejected ▸ adjective =**downcast**, downhearted, despondent, disconsolate, dispirited, crestfallen, disheartened; depressed, crushed, desolate, heartbroken, in the doldrums, sad, unhappy, doleful, melancholy, miserable, woebegone, forlorn, wretched, glum, gloomy; *informal* fed up, blue, down in the mouth, down in the dumps.
　–OPPOSITES cheerful.

delay ▸ verb 1 *we were delayed by the traffic* =**detain**, hold up, make late, slow up/down, bog down; hinder, hamper, impede, obstruct. 2 *don't delay* =**linger**, drag one's feet, hold back, dawdle, waste time; procrastinate, stall, hang fire, mark time, hesitate, dither, shilly-shally; *informal* dilly-dally. 3 *he may delay the cut in interest rates* =**postpone**, put off, defer, hold over, shelve, suspend, stay; reschedule; *N. Amer.* put over, table; *informal* put on ice, put on the back burner, put in cold storage.
　–OPPOSITES hurry, advance.
▸ noun 1 *drivers will face lengthy delays* =**hold-up**, wait. 2 *the delay of his trial* =**postponement**, deferral, deferment; adjournment.

delectable ▸ adjective 1 *a delectable meal* =**delicious**, mouth-watering, appetizing, flavoursome, toothsome; succulent, luscious, tasty; *informal* scrumptious, scrummy, yummy; *N. Amer. informal* finger-licking, nummy. 2 *the delectable Ms Davis* =**delightful**, lovely, captivating, charming, enchanting, appealing, beguiling; beautiful, attractive, ravishing, gorgeous, stunning, alluring, sexy, seductive, desirable, luscious; *informal* divine, heavenly, dreamy; *Brit. informal* tasty.
　–OPPOSITES unpalatable, unattractive.

delegate ▸ noun *trade union delegates* =**representative**, envoy, emissary, commissioner, agent, deputy, commissary; spokesperson, spokesman/woman; ambassador.
▸ verb 1 *she must delegate routine tasks* =**assign**, entrust, pass on, hand on/over, turn over, devolve, transfer. 2 *they were delegated to negotiate with the States* =**authorize**, commission, appoint, nomin-

ate, mandate, empower, charge, choose, designate, elect.

delegation ▸ noun 1 *the delegation from South Africa* =**deputation**, (diplomatic) mission, commission; delegates, representatives, envoys, emissaries, deputies. 2 *the delegation of tasks to others* =**assignment**, entrusting, giving, devolution, transference.

delete ▸ verb =**remove**, cut out, take out, edit out, expunge, excise, eradicate, cancel; cross out, strike out, ink out, scratch out, obliterate, white out; rub out, erase, efface, wipe out, blot out.
　–OPPOSITES add.

deliberate ▸ adjective 1 *a deliberate attempt to provoke him* =**intentional**, calculated, conscious, intended, planned, studied, knowing, wilful, wanton, purposeful, purposive, premeditated, preplanned; voluntary. 2 *small, deliberate steps* =**careful**, cautious; measured, regular, even, steady. 3 *a deliberate worker* =**methodical**, systematic, careful, painstaking, meticulous, thorough.
　–OPPOSITES accidental, hasty, careless.
▸ verb *she deliberated on his words* =**think about/over**, ponder, consider, contemplate, reflect on, muse on, meditate on, ruminate on, mull over, weigh up; brood over, dwell on; *N. Amer.* think on.

deliberately ▸ adverb 1 *he deliberately hurt me* =**intentionally**, on purpose, purposely, by design, knowingly, wittingly, consciously, purposefully; wilfully, wantonly; *Law* with malice aforethought. 2 *he walked deliberately down the aisle* =**carefully**, cautiously, slowly, steadily, evenly.

deliberation ▸ noun 1 *after much deliberation, I accepted* =**thought**, consideration, reflection, contemplation, meditation, rumination; *formal* cogitation. 2 *he replaced the glass with deliberation* =**care**, carefulness, caution.

delicacy ▸ noun 1 *the delicacy of the fabric* =**fineness**, delicateness, fragility; thinness, lightness, flimsiness. 2 *the delicacy of the situation* =**difficulty**, trickiness; sensitivity, ticklishness, awkwardness. 3 *treat this matter with delicacy* =**care**, sensitivity, tact, discretion, diplomacy, subtlety, sensibility. 4 *an Australian delicacy* =**treat**, luxury; speciality.

delicate ▸ adjective 1 *delicate embroidery* =**fine**, intricate, dainty. 2 *a delicate shade of blue* =**subtle**, soft, muted; pastel,

pale, light. **3** *delicate china cups* =**fragile**, frail. **4** *his wife is very delicate* =**sickly**, unhealthy, frail, feeble, weak; unwell, infirm. **5** *a delicate issue* =**difficult**, tricky, sensitive, ticklish, awkward; embarrassing; *informal* sticky, dicey. **6** *the matter required delicate handling* =**careful**, sensitive, tactful, diplomatic, discreet, kid-glove, softly-softly. **7** *a delicate mechanism* =**sensitive**, light, precision.
–OPPOSITES coarse, lurid, strong, robust, clumsy.

delicious ▸ adjective =**delectable**, mouth-watering, appetizing, tasty, flavoursome, toothsome, succulent, luscious; *informal* scrumptious, scrummy, yummy; *N. Amer. informal* finger-licking, nummy.
–OPPOSITES unpalatable.

delight ▸ verb **1** *her manners delighted him* =**charm**, enchant, captivate, entrance, thrill; entertain, amuse, divert; *informal* send, tickle pink, bowl over.
2 *Fabia delighted in his touch* =**take pleasure**, revel, luxuriate, wallow, glory; adore, love, relish, savour, lap up; *informal* get a kick out of, get a buzz out of, get a thrill out of, dig; *N. Amer. informal* get a charge out of, get off on.
–OPPOSITES dismay, disgust, dislike.
▸ noun *she squealed with delight* =**pleasure**, happiness, joy, glee, gladness; excitement, amusement; bliss, rapture, elation.
–OPPOSITES displeasure.

delighted ▸ adjective =**pleased**, glad, happy, thrilled, overjoyed, ecstatic, elated; on cloud nine, walking on air, in seventh heaven, jumping for joy; enchanted, charmed; amused, diverted; gleeful, cock-a-hoop; *informal* over the moon, tickled pink, as pleased as Punch, on top of the world, as happy as Larry; *Brit. informal* chuffed; *N. English informal* made up; *Austral. informal* wrapped.

delightful ▸ adjective **1** *a delightful evening* =**lovely**, enjoyable; amusing, entertaining; marvellous, wonderful, splendid, thrilling; *informal* great, super, fabulous, fab, terrific, heavenly, divine, grand; *Brit. informal* brilliant, brill, smashing; *N. Amer. informal* peachy, ducky; *Austral./NZ informal* beaut, bonzer. **2** *the delightful Sally* =**charming**, enchanting, captivating, bewitching, appealing; sweet, endearing, cute, lovely, adorable, delectable, delicious, gorgeous, ravishing, beautiful; *Scottish & N. English* bonny;

informal divine.

delimit ▸ verb =**determine**, establish, set, fix, demarcate, define, delineate.

delineate ▸ verb **1** *the aims of the study as delineated by the boss* =**describe**, set forth/out, present, outline, depict, represent; map out, define, specify, identify. **2** *a section delineated in red marker pen* =**outline**, trace, block in, mark (out/off), delimit.

delinquency ▸ noun =**crime**, wrongdoing, lawbreaking, lawlessness, misconduct, misbehaviour; misdemeanours, offences, misdeeds.

delinquent ▸ adjective =**lawless**, lawbreaking, criminal; errant, badly behaved, troublesome, difficult, unruly, disobedient, uncontrollable.
▸ noun =**offender**, wrongdoer, malefactor, lawbreaker, criminal; hooligan, vandal, ruffian, hoodlum; young offender; *informal* tearaway.

delirious ▸ adjective **1** *she was delirious most of the time* =**incoherent**, raving, babbling, irrational; feverish, frenzied; deranged, demented, out of one's mind. **2** *the crowd was delirious* =**ecstatic**, elated, thrilled, overjoyed, beside oneself, walking on air, on cloud nine, in seventh heaven, transported, rapturous; hysterical, wild, frenzied; *informal* blissed out, over the moon.
–OPPOSITES lucid.

delirium ▸ noun =**derangement**, dementia, madness, insanity; incoherence, irrationality, hysteria, feverishness, hallucination.
–OPPOSITES lucidity.

deliver ▸ verb **1** *the parcel was delivered to his house* =**bring**, take, convey, carry, transport; send, dispatch. **2** *the money was delivered up to the official* =**hand over**, turn over, make over, sign over; surrender, give up, yield, cede; consign, commit, entrust, trust. **3** *he was delivered from his enemies* =**save**, rescue, free, liberate, release, extricate, emancipate, redeem. **4** *the court delivered its verdict* =**utter**, give, make, read, broadcast; pronounce, announce, declare, proclaim, hand down, return, set forth. **5** *she delivered a blow to his head* =**administer**, deal, inflict, give; *informal* land. **6** *he delivered the first ball* =**bowl**, pitch, hurl, throw, cast, lob. **7** *the trip delivered everything she wanted* =**provide**, supply, furnish. **8** *we must deliver on our commitments* =**fulfil**, live up to, carry out, carry through, make good.

deliverance ▸ noun =**liberation**, release, delivery, discharge, rescue, emancipation; salvation.

delivery ▸ noun **1** *the delivery of the goods* =**conveyance**, carriage, transportation, transport, distribution; dispatch, remittance; freightage, haulage, shipment. **2** *we get several deliveries a day* =**consignment**, load, shipment. **3** *her delivery was stilted* =**speech**, pronunciation, enunciation, articulation, elocution.

delude ▸ verb =**mislead**, deceive, fool, take in, trick, dupe, hoodwink, gull, lead on; *informal* con, pull the wool over someone's eyes, lead up the garden path, take for a ride; *N. Amer. informal* sucker, snooker; *Austral. informal* pull a swifty on.

deluge ▸ noun **1** *homes were swept away by the deluge* =**flood**, torrent, water(s); tidal wave; *Brit.* spate. **2** *the deluge turned the pitch into a swamp* =**downpour**, torrential rain; thunderstorm, rainstorm, cloudburst. **3** *a deluge of complaints* =**barrage**, volley; flood, torrent, avalanche, stream.
▸ verb **1** *homes were deluged by the rains* =**flood**, inundate, submerge, swamp, drown. **2** *we have been deluged with calls* =**inundate**, overwhelm, overrun, flood, swamp, snow under, engulf, bombard.

delusion ▸ noun =**misapprehension**, misconception, misunderstanding, mistake, error, misconstruction, misbelief; fallacy, illusion, fantasy.

de luxe ▸ adjective =**luxurious**, luxury, sumptuous, palatial, opulent, lavish; grand, high-class, quality, exclusive, choice, fancy; expensive, costly; *Brit.* upmarket; *informal* plush, posh, classy, ritzy, swanky; *Brit. informal* swish; *N. Amer. informal* swank.
−OPPOSITES basic, cheap.

delve ▸ verb **1** *she delved in her pocket* =**rummage**, search, hunt, scrabble about/around, root about/around, ferret, fish about/around in, dig; go through, rifle through. **2** *we must delve deeper into the matter* =**investigate**, enquire, probe, explore, research, look into, go into.

demand ▸ noun **1** *I gave in to her demands* =**request**, call, command, order, dictate. **2** *the demands of a young family* =**requirement**, need; claim; commit-

ment, imposition. **3** *the big demand for such toys* =**market**, call, appetite, desire.
▸ verb **1** *workers demanded wage increases* =**call for**, ask for, request, push for, hold out for; insist on, claim. **2** *Harvey demanded that I tell him the truth* =**order**, command, enjoin, urge, insist. **3** *'Where is she?' he demanded* =**ask**, inquire; say. **4** *an activity demanding detailed knowledge* =**require**, need, necessitate, call for, involve, entail. **5** *they demanded complete anonymity* =**insist on**, stipulate; expect, look for.
■ **in demand** =**sought-after**, desired, coveted, wanted, desirable, popular, all the rage, at a premium, like gold dust; *informal* big, trendy, hot.

demanding ▸ adjective **1** *a demanding task* =**difficult**, challenging, taxing, exacting, tough, hard, onerous, formidable; arduous, rigorous, gruelling, backbreaking, punishing. **2** *a demanding child* =**nagging**, importunate; trying, tiresome, hard to please.
−OPPOSITES easy.

demarcation ▸ noun **1** *clear demarcation of function* =**separation**, distinction, differentiation, division, delimitation, definition. **2** *territorial demarcations* =**boundary**, border, borderline, frontier; dividing line, divide.

demean ▸ verb =**discredit**, lower, degrade, debase, devalue; cheapen, abase, humiliate.
−OPPOSITES dignify.

demeaning ▸ adjective =**degrading**, humiliating, shameful, mortifying, undignified.

demeanour ▸ noun =**manner**, air, attitude, appearance, look; bearing, carriage; behaviour, conduct.

demented ▸ adjective =**mad**, insane, deranged, out of one's mind, crazed, lunatic, unbalanced, unhinged, disturbed, non compos mentis; *informal* crazy, mental, off one's head, off one's rocker, nutty, round the bend, raving mad, batty, cuckoo, loopy, loony, bananas, screwy, touched, gaga, not all there, out to lunch; *Brit. informal* barmy, bonkers, crackers, barking (mad), round the twist, off one's trolley, not the full shilling; *N. Amer. informal* buggy, nutso, squirrelly, wacko.
−OPPOSITES sane.

dementia ▸ noun =**mental illness**, madness, insanity, derangement, lunacy; Alzheimer's (disease).

demise ▸ noun 1 *her tragic demise* =**death**, dying, passing, end; *formal* decease; *archaic* expiry. 2 *the demise of the Ottoman empire* =**end**, break-up, disintegration, fall, downfall, collapse.
−OPPOSITES birth.

demobilize ▸ verb =**disband**, decommission, discharge; *Brit. informal* demob.

democratic ▸ adjective =**elected**, representative, parliamentary, popular; egalitarian.

demolish ▸ verb 1 *they demolished a block of flats* =**knock down**, pull down, tear down, bring down, destroy, flatten, raze (to the ground), level, bulldoze; blow up. 2 *he demolished her credibility* =**destroy**, ruin, wreck; overturn, explode, drive a coach and horses through; *informal* shoot full of holes.
−OPPOSITES construct, strengthen.

demolition ▸ noun 1 *the demolition of the building* =**destruction**, levelling, bulldozing, clearance. 2 *the demolition of his theory* =**destruction**, refutation.

demon ▸ noun 1 *demons from hell* =**devil**, evil spirit. 2 *the man was a demon* =**monster**, fiend, devil, brute, savage, beast, barbarian, animal. 3 *Surrey's fast-bowling demon* =**genius**, expert, master, virtuoso, maestro; *informal* hotshot, whizz, buff, pro, ace.
−OPPOSITES angel, saint.

> **WORD LINKS**
>
> *study of demons:* **demonology**

demonic, demoniac, demoniacal ▸ adjective 1 *demonic powers* =**devilish**, fiendish, diabolical, satanic, hellish, infernal; evil. 2 *the demonic intensity of his playing* =**frenzied**, wild, feverish, frenetic, frantic, furious, manic, like one possessed.

demonstrable ▸ adjective =**verifiable**, provable; verified, proven, confirmed; obvious, clear, clear-cut, evident, apparent, manifest, patent, distinct, noticeable; unmistakable, undeniable.

demonstrate ▸ verb 1 *his findings demonstrate that boys commit more crimes* =**show**, indicate, establish, prove, confirm, verify. 2 *she demonstrated various drawing techniques* =**show**, display; present, illustrate, exemplify. 3 *his work demonstrated an analytical ability* =**reveal**,

bespeak, indicate, signify, signal, denote, show, display, exhibit; bear witness to, testify to. 4 *they demonstrated against the Government* =**protest**, rally, march; picket, strike.

demonstration ▸ noun 1 *a demonstration of woodcarving* =**exhibition**, presentation, display. 2 *his paintings are a demonstration of his talent* =**manifestation**, indication, sign, mark, token, embodiment; expression. 3 *an anti-racism demonstration* =**protest**, march, rally, lobby, sit-in; *informal* demo.

demonstrative ▸ adjective =**expressive**, open, forthcoming, communicative, unreserved, emotional, effusive; affectionate, cuddly, loving, warm, friendly, approachable; *informal* touchy-feely, lovey-dovey.
−OPPOSITES reserved.

demoralize ▸ verb =**dishearten**, dispirit, deject, cast down, depress, dismay, daunt, discourage, unnerve, crush, shake, throw, cow, subdue; break someone's spirit; *informal* knock the stuffing out of, knock sideways; *Brit. informal* knock for six.
−OPPOSITES hearten.

demoralized ▸ adjective =**dispirited**, disheartened, downhearted, dejected, downcast, low, depressed; disconsolate, crestfallen, disappointed, dismayed, daunted, discouraged; crushed, humbled, subdued.

demote ▸ verb =**downgrade**, relegate, reduce; depose, unseat, displace, oust; *Military* cashier.
−OPPOSITES promote.

demure ▸ adjective =**modest**, reserved, shy, reticent; decorous, decent, seemly, ladylike, respectable, proper, virtuous, pure, innocent, chaste; sober, sedate, staid, prim, goody-goody, strait-laced; *informal* butter-wouldn't-melt.
−OPPOSITES brazen.

den ▸ noun 1 *the mink left its den* =**lair**, burrow, hole, shelter, hiding place, hideout. 2 *a notorious drinking den* =**haunt**, site, hotbed, nest, pit, hole; *informal* joint, dive. 3 *sulking in his den* =**study**, studio, workshop; retreat, sanctuary, hideaway; *informal* hidey-hole.

denial ▸ noun 1 *the reports met with a denial* =**contradiction**, refutation, rebuttal, repudiation, disclaimer; negation. 2 *the denial of insurance to certain people* =**refusal**, withholding; rejection, turndown; *informal* knock-back; *N. Amer. formal* declination. **3** *the denial of worldly values* =**renunciation**, eschewal, repudiation, disavowal, rejection, abandonment, relinquishment.

denigrate ▶ verb =**disparage**, belittle, deprecate, decry, cast aspersions on, criticize, attack; speak ill of, give someone a bad name, defame, slander, libel; run down, abuse, insult, revile, malign, vilify; *N. Amer.* slur; *informal* bad-mouth, pull to pieces; *Brit. informal* rubbish, slate, slag off.

–OPPOSITES extol.

denizen ▶ noun *(formal)* =**inhabitant**, resident, townsman/woman, native, local; occupier, occupant, dweller.

denomination ▶ noun **1** *a Christian denomination* =**religious group**, sect, cult, movement, body, branch, order, school; church. **2** *banknotes in a number of denominations* =**value**, unit, size.

denote ▶ verb **1** *the headdress denoted high status* =**designate**, indicate, be a mark of, signify, signal, symbolize, represent, mean; distinguish, mark, identify. **2** *his manner denoted an inner strength* =**suggest**, point to, smack of, indicate, show, reveal, intimate, imply, convey, betray, bespeak; *informal* spell.

denouement ▶ noun =**resolution**, outcome, ending, end, finish, close; culmination, climax, conclusion, solution.

denounce ▶ verb **1** *the pope denounced his critics* =**condemn**, criticize, attack, censure, decry, revile, damn; proscribe, rail against, run down; *N. Amer.* slur; *informal* slam, hit out at, lay into; *Brit. informal* slate, slag off; *formal* castigate. **2** *he was denounced as a traitor* =**expose**, betray, inform on; incriminate, implicate, cite, name, accuse.

–OPPOSITES praise.

dense ▶ adjective **1** *a dense forest* =**thick**, crowded, compact, solid, tight; overgrown, impenetrable, impassable. **2** *dense smoke* =**thick**, heavy, opaque, murky; concentrated, condensed. **3** *(informal) they were dense enough to believe me* =**stupid**, brainless, mindless, foolish, slow, simple-minded, empty-headed, idiotic; *informal* thick, dim, moronic, dumb, dopey, dozy; *Brit. informal* daft.

–OPPOSITES sparse, thin, clever.

density ▶ noun =**solidity**, solidness, denseness, thickness, substance, mass; compactness, tightness, hardness.

WORD LINKS

instrument for measuring the density of liquids: **hydrometer**

dent ▶ noun **1** *a dent in his car* =**knock**, indentation, dint, dimple, depression, hollow, crater, pit. **2** *a dent in their finances* =**hole**; gap, reduction, cut.

–OPPOSITES increase.

▶ verb **1** *Jamie dented his car* =**knock**, dint, mark. **2** *the experience dented her confidence* =**diminish**, reduce, lessen, weaken, erode, undermine, sap, shake, damage.

deny ▶ verb **1** *the report was denied by witnesses* =**contradict**, repudiate, challenge, contest. **2** *he denied the request* =**refuse**, turn down, reject, rebuff, repulse, decline, veto, dismiss; *informal* knock back, give the thumbs down to. **3** *she had to deny her culture* =**renounce**, repudiate, disavow, disown, wash one's hands of, reject, discard, cast aside, abandon, give up; *literary* forsake.

–OPPOSITES confirm, accept.

depart ▶ verb **1** *James departed after lunch* =**leave**, go (away), withdraw, absent oneself, quit, exit, decamp, retreat, retire; make off, run off/away; set off/out, get under way, be on one's way; *informal* make tracks, up sticks, clear off/out, take off, split; *Brit. informal* sling one's hook. **2** *the budget departed from the norm* =**deviate**, diverge, digress, drift, stray, veer; differ, vary.

–OPPOSITES arrive.

departed ▶ adjective =**dead**, expired, passed on/away; fallen; *formal* deceased.

department ▶ noun **1** *the public health department* =**division**, section, sector, unit, branch, wing; office, bureau, agency, ministry. **2** *the food is Kay's department* =**domain**, territory, province, area, line; responsibility, business, affair, charge, task, concern; *informal* pigeon, baby, bailiwick.

departure ▶ noun **1** *he tried to delay her departure* =**leaving**, going, leave-taking, withdrawal, exit. **2** *a departure from normality* =**deviation**, divergence, digression, shift; variation, change. **3** *an exciting departure for film-makers* =**change**, innovation, novelty.

depend ▶ verb **1** *her career depends on this reference* =**be dependent on**, hinge on, hang on, rest on, rely on. **2** *my family depends on me* =**rely on**, lean on; count on, bank on, trust (in), have faith in, believe in; pin one's hopes on.

dependable ▶ adjective =reliable, trustworthy, trusty, faithful, loyal, stable; sensible, responsible.

dependant ▶ noun =child, minor; ward, charge, protégé; relative; (**dependants**) offspring, children, progeny.

dependence ▶ noun. See DEPENDENCY senses 1, 2, 3.

dependency ▶ noun 1 *her dependency on her husband* =**dependence**, reliance; need for. 2 *the association of retirement with dependency* =**helplessness**, dependence, weakness, defencelessness, vulnerability. 3 *drug dependency* =**addiction**, dependence; reliance; craving, compulsion, fixation, obsession; abuse. 4 *a British dependency* =**colony**, protectorate, province, outpost; holding, possession.
–OPPOSITES independence.

dependent ▶ adjective 1 *your placement is dependent on her decision* =**conditional**, contingent, based; subject to, determined by, influenced by. 2 *the army is dependent on volunteers* =**reliant on**, relying on, counting on; sustained by. 3 *she is dependent on drugs* =**addicted to**, reliant on; *informal* hooked on. 4 *he is ill and dependent* =**reliant**, needy; helpless, weak, infirm, invalid, incapable, debilitated, disabled. 5 *a UK dependent territory* =**subsidiary**, subject; ancillary.

depict ▶ verb 1 *the painting depicts the Last Supper* =**portray**, show, represent, picture, illustrate, reproduce, render. 2 *the process depicted by Darwin's theory* =**describe**, detail, relate; present, set forth, set out, outline, delineate; represent, portray, characterize.

depiction ▶ noun 1 *a depiction of Aphrodite* =**picture**, painting, portrait, drawing, sketch, study, illustration; image, likeness. 2 *the film's depiction of women* =**portrayal**, representation, presentation, characterization.

deplete ▶ verb =**exhaust**, use up, consume, expend, drain, empty; reduce, decrease, diminish.
–OPPOSITES augment.

depletion ▶ noun =**exhaustion**, use, consumption, expenditure; reduction, decrease, diminution; impoverishment.

deplorable ▶ adjective 1 *your conduct is deplorable* =**disgraceful**, shameful,

inexcusable, unpardonable, atrocious, awful, terrible, dreadful, diabolical, unforgivable, despicable, abominable, contemptible, beyond the pale. 2 *the garden is in a deplorable state* =**lamentable**, regrettable, unfortunate, wretched, atrocious, awful, terrible, dreadful, diabolical; sorry, poor; *informal* appalling, dire, abysmal, woeful, lousy; *formal* grievous.
–OPPOSITES admirable.

deplore ▶ verb 1 *we deplore violence* =**abhor**, find unacceptable, frown on, disapprove of, take a dim view of, take exception to; detest, despise; condemn, denounce. 2 *he deplored their lack of flair* =**regret**, lament, mourn, bemoan, bewail, complain about, grieve over, sigh over.
–OPPOSITES applaud.

deploy ▶ verb 1 *forces were deployed at strategic points* =**position**, station, post, place, install, locate, situate, site, establish; base; distribute. 2 *she deployed all her skills* =**use**, utilize, employ, take advantage of, exploit; bring into service, call on, turn to, resort to.

deport ▶ verb =**expel**, banish, extradite, repatriate; throw out; *informal* kick out, boot out, send packing; *Brit. informal* turf out.
–OPPOSITES admit.

depose ▶ verb =**overthrow**, unseat, dethrone, topple, remove, supplant, displace; dismiss, oust, throw out; *informal* chuck out, boot out, get rid of, show someone the door; *Brit. informal* turf out.

deposit ▶ noun 1 *a thick deposit of ash* =**accumulation**, sediment; layer, covering, coating, blanket. 2 *a copper deposit* =**seam**, vein, lode, layer, stratum, bed. 3 *they paid a deposit* =**down payment**, advance payment, prepayment, instalment, retainer.
▶ verb 1 *she deposited her books on the table* =**put (down)**, place, set (down), unload, rest; drop; *informal* dump, park, plonk; *N. Amer. informal* plunk. 2 *the silt deposited by flood water* =**leave (behind)**, precipitate, dump; wash up, cast up. 3 *the gold was deposited at the bank* =**lodge**, bank, house, store, stow, leave, put away; *informal* stash.

depot ▶ noun 1 *the bus depot* =**terminal**, terminus, station, garage; headquarters, base. 2 *an arms depot* =**storehouse**, warehouse, store, repository, depository, cache; arsenal, armoury, dump.

depraved ▸ adjective =**corrupt**, perverted, deviant, degenerate, debased, immoral, unprincipled; debauched, dissolute, licentious, lecherous, prurient, indecent, sordid; wicked, sinful, vile, iniquitous, nefarious; *informal* warped, twisted, pervy, sick.

depravity ▸ noun =**corruption**, vice, perversion, deviance, degeneracy, immorality, debauchery, dissipation, profligacy, licentiousness, lechery, prurience, obscenity, indecency; wickedness, sin, iniquity; *informal* perviness; *formal* turpitude.

depreciate ▸ verb =**decrease (in value)**, lose value, fall/drop (in price).

depress ▸ verb **1** *the news depressed him* =**sadden**, dispirit, cast down, get down, dishearten, demoralize, crush, shake, weigh down on; upset, distress, grieve; *informal* give someone the blues, make someone fed up. **2** *new economic policies depressed sales* =**slow down**, reduce, lower, weaken, impair; inhibit, restrict. **3** *imports will depress farm prices* =**reduce**, lower, cut, cheapen, keep down, discount, deflate, depreciate, devalue, diminish. **4** *depress each key in turn* =**press**, push, hold down; tap.
–OPPOSITES encourage, raise.

depressed ▸ adjective **1** *he felt lonely and depressed* =**sad**, unhappy, miserable, gloomy, melancholy, dejected, disconsolate, downhearted, downcast, down, despondent, dispirited, low, heavyhearted, morose, dismal, desolate; tearful, upset; *informal* blue, down in the dumps, down in the mouth, fed up. **2** *a depressed economy* =**weak**; inactive, flat, slow, slack, sluggish, stagnant. **3** *a depressed area* =**poverty-stricken**, poor, disadvantaged, deprived, needy, distressed; run down; *informal* slummy.
–OPPOSITES cheerful, strong, inflated, prosperous.

depressing ▸ adjective **1** *depressing thoughts* =**upsetting**, distressing, painful, heartbreaking; dismal, bleak, black, sombre, gloomy, grave, unhappy, melancholy, sad; wretched, doleful; *informal* morbid. **2** *a depressing place* =**gloomy**, melancholy, bleak, dreary, grim, drab, sombre, dark, dingy, funereal, cheerless, joyless, comfortless, uninviting.

depression ▸ noun **1** *she ate to ease her depression* =**unhappiness**, sadness, melancholy, melancholia, misery, sorrow, gloom, despondency, low spirits, heavy heart, despair, desolation, hopelessness. **2** *an economic depression* =**recession**, slump, decline, downturn, standstill; stagnation. **3** *a depression in the ground* =**hollow**, indentation, dent, dint, cavity, concavity, dip, pit, hole, trough, crater; basin, bowl.

deprivation ▸ noun **1** *unemployment and deprivation* =**poverty**, impoverishment, privation, hardship, destitution; need, want. **2** *deprivation of political rights* =**dispossession**, withholding, withdrawal, removal, divestment, expropriation, seizure.
–OPPOSITES wealth.

deprive ▸ verb =**dispossess**, strip, divest, relieve; cheat out of; *informal* do out of.

deprived ▸ adjective =**disadvantaged**, underprivileged, poverty-stricken, impoverished, poor, destitute, needy.

depth ▸ noun **1** *the depth of the caves* =**deepness**. **2** *the depth of his knowledge* =**extent**, range, scope, breadth, width. **3** *her lack of depth* =**profundity**, wisdom, understanding, intelligence, discernment, penetration, insight, awareness. **4** *a work of great depth* =**complexity**, intricacy; profundity, gravity, weight. **5** *depth of colour* =**intensity**, richness, deepness, vividness, strength, brilliance. **6** *the depths of the sea* =**bottom**, floor, bed.
–OPPOSITES shallowness, triviality, surface.
■ **in depth** =**thoroughly**, extensively, comprehensively, rigorously, exhaustively, completely, fully; meticulously, scrupulously, painstakingly.

> **WORD LINKS**
>
> *measurement of depth of seas and lakes:* **bathymetry**
> *fear of depth:* **bathophobia**

deputation ▸ noun =**delegation**, commission, committee, (diplomatic) mission; contingent, group, party.

deputize ▸ verb =**stand in**, sit in, fill in, cover, substitute, replace, take someone's place, relieve, take over; hold the fort, step into the breach; act for, act on behalf of; *informal* sub.

deputy ▸ noun *he handed over to his deputy* =**second (in command)**, number two, assistant, aide, right-hand man/woman, man/girl Friday; substitute,

stand-in, understudy; representative, proxy, agent, spokesperson; *Scottish* depute; *informal* sidekick, locum.
▸ adjective *her deputy editor* =**assistant**, substitute, acting, reserve, fill-in, caretaker.

deranged ▸ adjective =**insane**, mad, disturbed, unbalanced, unhinged, unstable, irrational; crazed, demented, berserk, frenzied, lunatic; non compos mentis; *informal* touched, crazy, mental; *Brit. informal* barmy, barking (mad), round the twist.
−OPPOSITES rational.

derelict ▸ adjective **1** *a derelict building* =**dilapidated**, ramshackle, run down, tumbledown, in ruins, falling down. **2** *a derelict airfield* =**disused**, abandoned, deserted. **3** *he was derelict in his duty* =**negligent**, neglectful, remiss, lax, careless, sloppy, slipshod, slack, irresponsible.
▸ noun *the derelicts who survive on the streets* =**tramp**, vagrant, down and out, homeless person, drifter; beggar; outcast; *informal* dosser, bag lady; *N. Amer. informal* hobo, bum.

dereliction ▸ noun **1** *buildings were reclaimed from dereliction* =**dilapidation**, disrepair, deterioration, ruin, rack and ruin; abandonment, neglect, disuse. **2** *dereliction of duty* =**negligence**, neglect, failure.

deride ▸ verb =**ridicule**, mock, scoff at, jibe at, make fun of, poke fun at, laugh at, hold up to ridicule, pillory; disdain, disparage, denigrate, dismiss, slight; sneer at, scorn, insult; *informal* knock, pooh-pooh, take the mickey out of.
−OPPOSITES praise.

derision ▸ noun =**mockery**, ridicule, jeers, sneers, taunts; disdain, disparagement, denigration, disrespect, insults; scorn, contempt.

derisive ▸ adjective =**mocking**, jeering, scoffing, teasing, derisory, snide, sneering; disdainful, scornful, contemptuous, taunting, insulting; scathing, sarcastic; *informal* snidey; *Brit. informal* sarky.

derisory ▸ adjective **1** *a derisory sum* =**inadequate**, insufficient, tiny; trifling, paltry, pitiful, miserly, miserable; negligible; ridiculous, laughable, insulting; *informal* measly, stingy, lousy, pathetic, piddling, piffling, mingy, poxy. **2** *derisory calls from the crowd*. See DERISIVE.

derivation ▸ noun =**origin**, etymol-

ogy, root, provenance, source; origination, basis, cause.

derivative ▸ adjective *her poetry was derivative* =**imitative**, unoriginal, uninventive, unimaginative, uninspired; plagiaristic; trite, hackneyed, clichéd, stale; *informal* copycat, cribbed, old hat.
−OPPOSITES original.
▸ noun =**by-product**, extract; spin-off.

derive ▸ verb **1** *he derives consolation from his poetry* =**obtain**, get, take, gain, acquire, procure, extract. **2** *'coffee' derives from the Turkish 'kahveh'* =**originate in**, stem from, come from, descend from, spring from, be taken from. **3** *his fortune derives from property* =**originate in**, be rooted in; stem from, come from, spring from, proceed from, issue from.

derogatory ▸ adjective =**disparaging**, disrespectful, demeaning; critical, pejorative, negative, unfavourable, uncomplimentary, unflattering, insulting; offensive, personal, abusive, rude, nasty, mean, hurtful; defamatory, slanderous, libellous; *informal* bitchy, catty.
−OPPOSITES complimentary.

descend ▸ verb **1** *the plane started descending* =**go down**, come down; drop, fall, sink, dive, plummet, plunge, nosedive. **2** *she descended the stairs* =**climb down**, go down, come down; shin down, slide down. **3** *the road descends to a village* =**slope**, dip, slant, go down, fall away. **4** *she saw Leo descend from the bus* =**alight**, disembark, get down, get off, dismount. **5** *they would not descend to such mean tricks* =**stoop**, lower oneself, demean oneself, debase oneself; resort, be reduced. **6** *the situation descended into chaos* =**degenerate**, deteriorate, decline, sink, slide, slip. **7** *they descended on his house* =**flock to**, besiege, surround, take over, invade, swoop on, occupy.
−OPPOSITES ascend, climb, board.

descendant ▸ noun =**successor**; heir; (**descendants**) offspring, progeny, family, lineage; *Law* issue.
−OPPOSITES ancestor.

descent ▸ noun **1** *the plane began its descent* =**dive**, drop; fall. **2** *a steep descent* =**slope**, incline, dip, drop, gradient, slant; hill. **3** *his descent into alcoholism* =**decline**, slide, fall, degeneration, deterioration. **4** *she is of Italian descent* =**ancestry**, parentage, ancestors, family; extraction, origin, derivation, birth; lineage, stock, blood; roots, origins.

5 *the sudden descent of the cavalry* =**attack**, assault, onslaught, charge, thrust, push, drive, incursion, foray.

describe ▸ verb **1** *he described his experiences* =**report**, recount, relate, tell of, set out, chronicle; detail, catalogue, give a rundown of; explain, illustrate, discuss, comment on. **2** *she described him as a pathetic figure* =**designate**, pronounce, call, label, style, dub; characterize, class; portray, depict, brand, paint. **3** *the pen described a circle* =**delineate**, mark out, outline, trace, draw.

description ▸ noun **1** *a description of my travels* =**account**, report, rendition, explanation, illustration; chronicle, narrative, story; portrayal, portrait; details. **2** *the description of oil as 'black gold'* =**designation**, labelling, naming, dubbing; characterization, classification, branding; portrayal, depiction. **3** *vehicles of every description* =**sort**, variety, kind, type, category, order, breed, class, designation, specification, genre, genus, brand, make, character, ilk; *N. Amer.* stripe.

descriptive ▸ adjective =**illustrative**, expressive, graphic, detailed, lively, vivid, striking; explanatory.

desecrate ▸ verb =**violate**, profane, defile, debase, degrade, dishonour; vandalize, damage, destroy, deface.

desert[1] ▸ verb **1** *his wife deserted him* =**abandon**, leave, turn one's back on; throw over, jilt, break up with; leave high and dry, leave in the lurch, leave behind, strand, maroon; *informal* walk/run out on, drop, dump, ditch; *literary* forsake. **2** *his allies were deserting the cause* =**renounce**, repudiate, relinquish, wash one's hands of, abandon, turn one's back on, betray, disavow; *literary* forsake. **3** *soldiers deserted in droves* =**abscond**, defect, run away, make off, decamp, flee, turn tail, take French leave, depart, quit; *Military* go AWOL.

desert[2] ▸ noun *an African desert* =**wasteland**, wastes, wilderness; dust bowl.

deserted ▸ adjective **1** *a deserted wife* =**abandoned**, jilted, cast aside; neglected, stranded, marooned; forlorn, bereft, dropped; *literary* forsaken. **2** *a deserted village* =**empty**, uninhabited, unoccupied, abandoned, evacuated, vacant; neglected; desolate, lonely, godforsaken.
–OPPOSITES populous.

deserter ▸ noun =**absconder**, runaway, fugitive, truant, escapee; renegade, defector, turncoat, traitor.

deserve ▸ verb =**merit**, earn, warrant, rate, justify, be worthy of, be entitled to, have a right to, be qualified for.

deserved ▸ adjective =**well earned**, merited, warranted, justified, justifiable; rightful, due, right, just, fair, fitting, appropriate, suitable, proper, apt.

deserving ▸ adjective **1** *a deserving cause* =**worthy**, commendable, praiseworthy, admirable, estimable, creditable; respectable, decent, honourable, righteous. **2** *a lapse deserving of punishment* =**meriting**, warranting, justifying, suitable for, worthy of.

design ▸ noun **1** *a design for the offices* =**plan**, blueprint, drawing, sketch, outline, map, plot, diagram, draft, representation, scheme, model. **2** *a Celtic design* =**pattern**, motif, device; style, theme, layout, form, shape.
▸ verb **1** *they designed a new engine* =**invent**, create, think up, come up with, devise, formulate, conceive; make, produce, develop, fashion; *informal* dream up. **2** *this paper is designed to provoke discussion* =**intend**, aim; mean.
■ **by design** =**deliberately**, intentionally, on purpose, purposefully; knowingly, wittingly, consciously, calculatedly.

designate ▸ verb **1** *some firms designate a press officer* =**appoint**, nominate, depute, delegate; select, choose, pick, elect, name, identify, assign. **2** *the rivers are designated 'Sites of Special Scientific Interest'* =**classify**, class, label, tag; name, call, term, dub.

designation ▸ noun **1** *the designation of a leader* =**appointment**, nomination, naming, selection, election. **2** *the designation of nature reserves* =**classification**, specification, definition, earmarking, pinpointing. **3** *the designation 'Generalissimo'* =**title**, name, epithet, tag; nickname, byname, sobriquet; *informal* moniker, handle; *formal* appellation.

desirability ▸ noun **1** *the desirability of the property* =**appeal**, attractiveness, allure; attraction. **2** *the desirability of a different approach* =**advisability**, advantage, benefit, merit, value, profitability. **3** *her obvious desirability* =**attractiveness**, sexual attraction, beauty, good looks; charm, seductiveness; *informal* sexiness.

desirable ▸ adjective **1** *a desirable location* =**attractive**, sought-after, in demand, popular, enviable; appealing, agreeable, pleasant; valuable, good, excellent; *informal* to die for, must-have. **2** *it is desirable that they should meet* =**advantageous**, advisable, wise, sensible, recommended; helpful, useful, beneficial, worthwhile, profitable, preferable. **3** *a very desirable woman* =**(sexually) attractive**, beautiful, pretty, appealing; seductive, alluring, enchanting, beguiling, captivating, bewitching, irresistible; *informal* sexy, beddable.
–OPPOSITES unattractive, unwise, ugly.

desire ▸ noun **1** *a desire to see the world* =**wish**, want, aspiration, fancy, inclination, impulse, yearning, longing, craving, hankering, hunger; eagerness, enthusiasm, determination; *informal* yen, itch. **2** *his eyes glittered with desire* =**lust**, passion, sensuality, sexuality, hunger; lasciviousness, lechery, salaciousness, libidinousness; *informal* raunchiness, horniness; *Brit. informal* randiness.
▸ verb **1** *they desired peace* =**want**, wish for, long for, yearn for, crave, hanker after, be desperate for, be bent on, covet, aspire to; fancy; *informal* have a yen for, yen for. **2** *she desired him* =**be attracted to**, lust after, burn for, be infatuated by; *informal* fancy, have the hots for, have a crush on, be mad/crazy/nuts about.

desired ▸ adjective **1** *cut the cloth to the desired length* =**required**, necessary, proper, right, correct; appropriate, suitable; preferred, chosen, selected. **2** *the desired outcome* =**wished for**, wanted, sought-after, longed for.

desist ▸ verb =**abstain**, refrain, forbear, hold back, keep; stop, cease, discontinue, give up, break off, drop, dispense with, eschew; *informal* lay off, give over, quit, pack in.
–OPPOSITES continue.

desolate ▸ adjective **1** *desolate moorlands* =**bleak**, stark, bare, dismal, grim; wild, inhospitable; deserted, uninhabited, godforsaken, abandoned, empty; unfrequented, unvisited, isolated, remote. **2** *she is desolate* =**miserable**, despondent, depressed, disconsolate, devastated, despairing, inconsolable, broken-hearted, grief-stricken, bereft.
–OPPOSITES populous, joyful.
▸ verb **1** *droughts desolated the plains* =**devastate**, ravage, ruin, lay waste to. **2** *she was desolated by the loss of her husband*

=**dishearten**, depress, sadden, cast down, make miserable, weigh down, crush; *informal* shatter.

desolation ▸ noun **1** *the desolation of the Gobi desert* =**bleakness**, starkness, barrenness; wildness; isolation, loneliness, remoteness. **2** *a feeling of utter desolation* =**misery**, sadness, unhappiness, despondency, sorrow, depression, grief, woe; broken-heartedness, wretchedness, dejection, devastation, despair, anguish, distress.

despair ▸ noun =**hopelessness**, discouragement, desperation, distress, anguish, unhappiness; despondency, depression, disconsolateness, misery, wretchedness; defeatism, pessimism.
–OPPOSITES hope, joy.
▸ verb =**lose hope**, give up, lose heart, be discouraged, be despondent, be demoralized, resign oneself; be pessimistic.

despairing ▸ adjective =**hopeless**, in despair, dejected, depressed, despondent, disconsolate, gloomy, miserable, wretched, desolate, inconsolable; disheartened, discouraged, demoralized, devastated; defeatist, pessimistic.
–OPPOSITES hopeful, joyous.

despatch ▸ verb & noun. *See* DISPATCH.

desperate ▸ adjective **1** *a desperate look* =**despairing**, hopeless; anguished, distressed, wretched, desolate, forlorn, distraught; out of one's mind, at one's wits' end, beside oneself, at the end of one's tether. **2** *a desperate attempt to escape* =**last-ditch**, last-gasp, eleventh-hour, do-or-die, final; frantic, frenzied, wild. **3** *a desperate shortage of teachers* =**grave**, serious, critical, acute; dire, awful, terrible, dreadful; urgent, pressing, drastic, extreme; *informal* chronic. **4** *they were desperate for food* =**eager**, longing, yearning, hungry, crying out; *informal* dying. **5** *a desperate act* =**violent**, dangerous, lawless; reckless, rash, hasty, impetuous, foolhardy, risky; do-or-die.

desperately ▸ adverb **1** *he screamed desperately for help* =**in desperation**, in despair, despairingly, in anguish, in distress; wretchedly, hopelessly, desolately, forlornly. **2** *they are desperately ill* =**seriously**, critically, gravely, severely, acutely, dangerously, perilously; very, extremely, dreadfully; hopelessly; *informal* terribly. **3** *he desperately wanted to talk* =**urgently**; intensely, eagerly.

desperation ▸ noun = **hopelessness**, despair, distress; anguish, agony, torment, misery, wretchedness; discouragement.

despicable ▸ adjective = **contemptible**, loathsome, hateful, detestable, reprehensible, abhorrent, abominable, awful, heinous; odious, vile, low, mean, abject, shameful, ignominious, shabby, ignoble, disreputable, discreditable, unworthy; *informal* dirty, rotten, low-down; *Brit. informal* beastly; *archaic* scurvy.
−OPPOSITES admirable.

despise ▸ verb = **detest**, hate, loathe, abhor, deplore; scorn, disdain, look down on, deride, sneer at, revile; spurn, shun.
−OPPOSITES adore.

despite ▸ preposition = **in spite of**, notwithstanding, regardless of, in the face of, for all, even with.

despondency ▸ noun = **hopelessness**, despair, discouragement, low spirits, wretchedness; melancholy, gloom, misery, desolation, disappointment, dejection, sadness, unhappiness; *informal* heartache.

despondent ▸ adjective = **disheartened**, discouraged, dispirited, downhearted, downcast, crestfallen, down, low, disconsolate, despairing, wretched; melancholy, gloomy, morose, dismal, woebegone, miserable, depressed, dejected, sad; *informal* down in the mouth, down in the dumps.
−OPPOSITES hopeful, cheerful.

despot ▸ noun = **tyrant**, oppressor, dictator, autocrat.

despotic ▸ adjective = **autocratic**, dictatorial, totalitarian, absolutist, undemocratic; one-party, tyrannical, tyrannous, oppressive, repressive, draconian, illiberal.
−OPPOSITES democratic.

dessert ▸ noun = **pudding**, sweet; *Brit. informal* afters, pud.

destabilize ▸ verb = **undermine**, weaken, damage, subvert, sabotage, unsettle, upset, disrupt.
−OPPOSITES strengthen.

destination ▸ noun = **journey's end**, end of the line; terminus, stop, stopping place, port of call; goal, target, end.

destined ▸ adjective **1** *he is destined to lead a troubled life* = **fated**, ordained, predestined, meant; doomed. **2** *computers destined for Pakistan* = **heading**, bound, en route, scheduled, headed; intended, meant, designated.

destiny ▸ noun **1** *master of his own destiny* = **future**, fate, fortune, doom; lot. **2** *she was sent by destiny* = **fate**, providence; God, the stars; luck, fortune, chance; karma.

destitute ▸ adjective = **penniless**, poor, impoverished, poverty-stricken, without a penny to one's name; *Brit.* on the breadline; *informal* hard up, (flat) broke, strapped (for cash), without two pennies to rub together, without a bean, on one's uppers; *Brit. informal* stony broke, skint; *N. Amer. informal* stone broke, without a red cent.
−OPPOSITES rich.

destitution ▸ noun = **poverty**, impoverishment, penury, pennilessness, privation; hardship, need, want, straitened circumstances, dire straits, deprivation, (financial) distress.

destroy ▸ verb **1** *their offices were destroyed by bombing* = **demolish**, knock down, level, raze (to the ground), fell; wreck, ruin, shatter; blast, blow up. **2** *traffic would destroy the conservation area* = **spoil**, ruin, wreck, blight, devastate, wreak havoc on. **3** *illness destroyed his career chances* = **wreck**, ruin, spoil, undo, put an end to, put a stop to, terminate, frustrate, blight, crush, quash, dash, scotch; devastate, demolish, sabotage; *Brit.* throw a spanner in the works of; *informal* mess up, muck up, foul up, put paid to, put the kibosh on, do for, queer, blow a hole in; *Brit. informal* scupper. **4** *the horse had to be destroyed* = **kill**, put down, put to sleep, slaughter; exterminate. **5** *we had to destroy the enemy* = **annihilate**, wipe out, obliterate, wipe off the face of the earth, eradicate, eliminate, eradicate, liquidate, finish off, erase; kill, slaughter, massacre, exterminate; *informal* take out, rub out, snuff out; *N. Amer. informal* waste.
−OPPOSITES build, preserve, raise, spare.

destruction ▸ noun **1** *the destruction caused by allied bombers* = **devastation**, carnage, ruin, chaos; wreckage; mess, disorder. **2** *the destruction of the countryside* = **wrecking**, burning, digging up, pulling down, bombing, annihilation, obliteration, devastation, ruining. **3** *the destruction of cattle* = **slaughter**, killing, putting down, extermination, culling.

destructive ▸ adjective **1** *the most destructive war* =**devastating**, ruinous, disastrous, catastrophic, calamitous; damaging, crippling; violent, savage, fierce, brutal, deadly, lethal. **2** *destructive criticism* =**negative**, hostile, vicious, unfriendly; unhelpful, obstructive, discouraging.

detach ▸ verb **1** *he detached the lamp from its bracket* =**unfasten**, disconnect, disengage, separate, uncouple, remove, loose, unhitch, unhook, free; pull off, cut off, break off. **2** *he detached himself from the crowd* =**free**, separate; move away, split off; leave, abandon. **3** *he has detached himself from his family* =**dissociate**, divorce, alienate, separate, segregate, isolate, cut off; break away, disaffiliate; withdraw from, break with.
−OPPOSITES attach, join.

detached ▸ adjective **1** *a detached collar* =**unfastened**, disconnected, separated, separate, loosened; untied, unhitched, undone, unhooked, unbuttoned; free, severed, cut off. **2** *a detached observer* =**dispassionate**, disinterested, objective, uninvolved, outside, neutral, unbiased, unprejudiced, impartial, nonpartisan; indifferent, aloof, remote, distant, impersonal.

detachment ▸ noun **1** *she looked on with detachment* =**objectivity**, dispassion, disinterest, open-mindedness, neutrality, impartiality; indifference, aloofness. **2** *a detachment of soldiers* =**unit**, detail, squad, troop, contingent, outfit, task force, patrol, crew; platoon, company, corps, brigade, battalion.

detail ▸ noun **1** *the picture is correct in every detail* =**particular**, respect, feature, characteristic, specific, aspect, facet, part, constituent; fact, piece of information, point, element, circumstance, consideration. **2** *that's just a detail* =**triviality**, technicality, nicety, trifle, fine point, incidental, inessential. **3** *records with a considerable degree of detail* =**precision**, exactness, accuracy, thoroughness, carefulness, scrupulousness. **4** *a guard detail* =**unit**, detachment, squad, troop, contingent, outfit, task force, patrol. **5** *I got the toilet detail* =**duty**, task, job, chore, charge, responsibility, assignment, function, mission, engagement, occupation, undertaking, errand.
▸ verb **1** *the report details our objections* =**describe**, explain, expound, relate, catalogue, list, spell out, itemize, identify, specify; state, declare, present, set out, frame; cite, quote, instance =**mention**, name. **2** *troops were detailed to prevent the escape* =**assign**, allocate, appoint, delegate, commission, charge; send, post; nominate, vote, elect, co-opt.
■ **in detail** =**thoroughly**, in depth, exhaustively, minutely, closely, meticulously, rigorously, scrupulously, painstakingly, carefully; completely, comprehensively, fully, extensively.

detailed ▸ adjective =**comprehensive**, full, complete, thorough, exhaustive, all-inclusive; elaborate, minute, intricate; explicit, specific, precise, exact, accurate, meticulous, painstaking; itemized, blow-by-blow.
−OPPOSITES general.

detain ▸ verb **1** *they were detained for questioning* =**hold**, take into custody, take (in), confine, intern; arrest, apprehend, seize; *informal* pick up, run in, haul in, nab, collar; *Brit. informal* nick. **2** *don't let me detain you* =**delay**, hold up, make late, keep, slow up/down; hinder.
−OPPOSITES release.

detect ▸ verb **1** *I detected a note of urgency in her voice* =**notice**, perceive, discern, become aware of, note, make out, spot, recognize, pick up, register, distinguish, identify; catch, sense, see, smell, taste, feel, hear; *Brit. informal* clock. **2** *they are responsible for detecting fraud* =**discover**, uncover, find out, turn up, unearth, dig up, root out, expose, reveal. **3** *the hackers were detected* =**catch**, hunt down, track down, find (out), expose, reveal, unmask, smoke out; apprehend, arrest; *informal* nail.

detection ▸ noun **1** *the detection of methane* =**discernment**, perception, awareness, recognition, identification, diagnosis; sensing, sight, smelling, tasting, noticing. **2** *the detection of insider dealing* =**discovery**, uncovering, unearthing, exposure, revelation. **3** *he managed to escape detection* =**capture**, identification, exposure, discovery; arrest.

detective ▸ noun =**investigator**, private investigator, private detective, operative; police officer; *informal* private eye, PI, sleuth, snoop; *N. Amer. informal* shamus, gumshoe.

detention ▸ noun =**custody**, imprisonment, confinement, incarceration, internment, detainment, captivity; arrest; quarantine.

deter ▸ verb **1** *the high cost deterred many* =**discourage**, dissuade, put off, scare off; dishearten, demoralize, daunt, intimidate. **2** *the presence of a caretaker deters crime* =**prevent**, stop, avert, stave off, ward off.
−OPPOSITES encourage.

deteriorate ▸ verb **1** *his health deteriorated* =**worsen**, decline, degenerate; fail, slump, slip, go downhill, go backwards, wane, ebb; *informal* go to pot. **2** *these materials deteriorate if stored wrongly* =**decay**, degrade, degenerate, break down, decompose, rot, go off, spoil, perish.
−OPPOSITES improve.

deterioration ▸ noun **1** *a deterioration in law and order* =**decline**, collapse, failure, drop, downturn, slump. **2** *deterioration of the roof structure* =**decay**, degradation, degeneration, breakdown, decomposition, rotting; weakening.
−OPPOSITES improvement.

determination ▸ noun =**resolution**, resolve, will power, strength of character, single-mindedness, purposefulness; staunchness, perseverance, persistence, tenacity, staying power; strong-mindedness, backbone; stubbornness, doggedness, obstinacy; spirit, courage, pluck, grit, stout-heartedness; *informal* guts, spunk.

determine ▸ verb **1** *chromosomes determine the sex of the embryo* =**control**, decide, regulate, direct, dictate, govern; affect, influence. **2** *he determined to sell up* =**resolve**, decide, make up one's mind, choose, elect, opt. **3** *the rent shall be determined by an accountant* =**specify**, set, fix, decide on, settle, assign, designate, arrange, choose, establish, ordain, prescribe, decree. **4** *determine the composition of the fibres* =**ascertain**, find out, discover, learn, establish, calculate, work out, make out, deduce, diagnose, discern; check, verify, confirm; *informal* figure out.

determined ▸ adjective **1** *he was determined to have his way* =**intent on**, bent on, set on, insistent on, resolved to. **2** *a very determined man* =**resolute**, purposeful, adamant, single-minded, unswerving, unwavering, intent, insistent; persevering, persistent, tenacious; strong-minded, strong-willed, steely, four-square, dedicated, committed; stubborn, dogged, obstinate.

determining ▸ adjective =**deciding**, decisive, conclusive, final, definitive, key, pivotal, crucial, critical, major, chief, prime.

deterrent ▸ noun =**disincentive**, discouragement, damper, curb, check, restraint; inhibition.
−OPPOSITES incentive.

detest ▸ verb =**abhor**, hate, loathe, despise, shrink from, be unable to bear, find intolerable, disdain, have an aversion to.
−OPPOSITES love.

detestable ▸ adjective =**abhorrent**, hateful, loathsome, despicable, abominable, repellent, repugnant, repulsive, revolting, disgusting, distasteful, horrible, horrid, awful.

detonate ▸ verb **1** *the charge detonated in deep water* =**explode**, go off, blow up; ignite. **2** *they detonated the bomb* =**set off**, explode, discharge, let off, touch off, trigger; ignite.

detonation ▸ noun =**explosion**, discharge, blowing up; blast, bang, report.

detour ▸ noun =**diversion**, roundabout route, indirect route, scenic route; bypass, ring road; digression, deviation; *Brit.* relief road.

detract ▸ verb **1** *my reservations should not detract from the book's excellence* =**belittle**, take away from, diminish, reduce, lessen, minimize, play down, trivialize, decry, devalue. **2** *the patterns will detract attention from each other* =**divert**, distract, draw away, deflect, avert, shift.

detractor ▸ noun =**critic**, attacker, fault-finder, backbiter; *informal* knocker.

detriment ▸ noun =**harm**, damage, injury, hurt, impairment, loss.
−OPPOSITES benefit.

detrimental ▸ adjective =**harmful**, damaging, injurious, hurtful, inimical, deleterious, destructive, ruinous, disastrous, bad, malign, adverse, undesirable, unfavourable, unfortunate; unhealthy, unwholesome.
−OPPOSITES beneficial.

detritus ▸ noun =**debris**, waste, refuse, rubbish, litter, scrap, flotsam and jetsam, rubble; remains, remnants, fragments, scraps, dregs, leavings, sweepings, dross, scum; *N. Amer.* trash, garbage; *Austral./NZ* mullock; *informal* dreck.

devalue ▸ verb =**belittle**, disparage, denigrate, discredit, diminish, trivialize, reduce, undermine.

devastate ▸ verb **1** *the city was devastated by an earthquake* =**destroy**, ruin, wreck, lay waste, ravage, demolish, raze (to the ground), level, flatten. **2** *he was devastated by the news* =**shatter**, shock, stun, daze, dumbfound, traumatize, crush, overwhelm, overcome, distress; *informal* knock sideways; *Brit. informal* knock for six.

devastating ▸ adjective **1** *a devastating cyclone* =**destructive**, ruinous, disastrous, catastrophic, calamitous, cataclysmic; damaging, injurious; crippling, violent, savage, fierce, dangerous, fatal, deadly, lethal. **2** *devastating news* =**shattering**, shocking, traumatic, overwhelming, crushing, distressing, terrible. **3** *(informal) a devastating critique* =**incisive**, highly effective, penetrating, cutting, withering, blistering, searing, scathing, fierce, savage, stinging, biting, caustic, harsh.

devastation ▸ noun **1** *the hurricane left a trail of devastation* =**destruction**, ruin, desolation, havoc, wreckage; ruins. **2** *the devastation of Prussia* =**destruction**, wrecking, ruination; demolition, annihilation. **3** *the devastation you have caused the family* =**shock**, trauma, distress, stress, strain, pain, anguish, suffering, upset, agony, misery, heartache.

develop ▸ verb **1** *the industry developed rapidly* =**grow**, expand, spread; advance, progress, evolve, mature. **2** *a plan was developed* =**initiate**, instigate, set in motion; originate, invent, form, establish, generate. **3** *children should develop their talents* =**expand**, augment, broaden, supplement, reinforce; enhance, refine, improve = polish, perfect. **4** *a row developed* =**start**, begin, emerge, erupt, break out, arise, break, unfold, happen. **5** *he developed the disease last week* =**fall ill with**, be stricken with, succumb to; contract, catch, get, pick up, come down with, become infected with.

development ▸ noun **1** *the development of the firm* =**evolution**, growth, expansion, enlargement, spread, progress; success. **2** *there have been a number of developments* =**event**, change, circumstance, thing; incident, occurrence. **3** *a housing development* =**estate**, complex, site.

deviant ▸ adjective =**aberrant**, abnormal, atypical, anomalous, irregular, non-standard; nonconformist, perverse, uncommon, unusual; freakish, strange, odd, peculiar, bizarre, eccentric, idiosyncratic, unorthodox, exceptional; warped, perverted; *informal* kinky, quirky.
−OPPOSITES normal.
▸ noun =**nonconformist**, eccentric, maverick, individualist; outsider, misfit; *informal* oddball, weirdo, freak; *N. Amer. informal* screwball, kook.

deviate ▸ verb =**diverge**, digress, drift, stray, veer, swerve; get sidetracked, branch off; differ, vary.

deviation ▸ noun =**divergence**, digression, departure; difference, variation, variance; aberration, abnormality, irregularity, anomaly, inconsistency, discrepancy.

device ▸ noun **1** *a device for measuring pressure* =**implement**, gadget, utensil, tool, appliance, apparatus, instrument, machine, mechanism, contrivance, contraption; *informal* gizmo, widget. **2** *an ingenious legal device* =**ploy**, tactic, move, stratagem, scheme, plot, trick, ruse, manoeuvre, dodge; *Brit. informal* wheeze. **3** *their shields bear his device* =**emblem**, symbol, logo, badge, crest, insignia, coat of arms, seal, mark, design, motif; monogram, trademark.

devil ▸ noun **1** *God and the Devil* =**Satan**, Beelzebub, Lucifer, the Prince of Darkness; *informal* Old Nick. **2** *they drove out the devils from their bodies* =**evil spirit**, demon. **3** *he was a devil* =**brute**, beast, monster, fiend; villain, sadist, barbarian, ogre. **4** *a naughty little devil* =**rascal**, rogue, imp, fiend, monkey, wretch; *informal* monster, horror, scamp, tyke; *Brit. informal* perisher; *N. Amer. informal* varmint.

WORD LINKS
relating to the Devil: **diabolical, diabolic**

devilish ▸ adjective **1** *a devilish grin* =**diabolical**, fiendish, demonic, satanic; hellish. **2** *a devilish torture* =**wicked**, evil, vile, foul, abominable, loathsome, monstrous, hideous, horrible, appalling, dreadful, awful, terrible, ghastly, despicable, depraved, dark, black, immoral; vicious, cruel, savage, barbaric. **3** *a devilish job* =**difficult**, tricky, ticklish, troublesome, thorny, awkward, problematic.

devil-may-care ▸ adjective =**reckless**, rash, impetuous, impulsive, daredevil, hot-headed, wild, foolhardy; nonchalant, casual, breezy, flippant, insouciant, happy-go-lucky, easy-going, unworried, untroubled, unconcerned.

devious ▸ adjective **1** *the devious ways in which they bent the rules* =**underhand**, deceitful, dishonest, dishonourable, unethical, unprincipled, immoral, unscrupulous, unfair, treacherous, duplicitous; crafty, cunning, calculating, artful, conniving, scheming, sly, wily; sneaky, furtive, secret, clandestine, surreptitious, covert; *N. Amer.* snide, snidey; *informal* crooked, shady, dirty, low-down; *Brit. informal* dodgy. **2** *a devious route around the coast* =**circuitous**, roundabout, indirect, meandering, tortuous.
–OPPOSITES open, honest, direct.

devise ▸ verb =**conceive**, think up, dream up, work out, formulate, concoct; design, invent, coin, originate; compose, construct, fabricate, create, produce, develop; discover, hit on; hatch, contrive; *informal* cook up.

devoid ■ **devoid of** =**empty of**, free of, bereft of, denuded of, lacking, without, wanting; *informal* minus.

devolution ▸ noun =**decentralization**, delegation; transfer; surrender, relinquishment.

devolve ▸ verb =**delegate**, pass (down/ on), hand down/over/on, transfer, transmit, assign, consign, convey, entrust, turn over, give, cede, surrender, relinquish, deliver; bestow, grant.

devote ▸ verb =**allocate**, assign, allot, commit, give (over), apportion, consign, pledge; dedicate, consecrate; set aside, earmark, reserve.

devoted ▸ adjective =**loyal**, faithful, true (blue), staunch, steadfast, constant, committed, dedicated, devout; fond, loving.

devotee ▸ noun **1** *a devotee of rock music* =**enthusiast**, fan, lover, aficionado, admirer; *informal* buff, freak, nut, fiend, fanatic, addict. **2** *devotees thronged the temple* =**follower**, adherent, supporter, disciple, member; believer, worshipper.

devotion ▸ noun **1** *her devotion to her husband* =**loyalty**, faithfulness, fidelity, commitment, allegiance, dedication; fondness, love, care. **2** *a life of devotion* =**piety**, spirituality, godliness, holiness, sanctity.

devour ▸ verb **1** *he devoured his meal* =**eat hungrily**, eat greedily, gobble (up/down), guzzle, gulp (down), bolt (down), cram down, gorge oneself on, wolf (down), feast on, consume, eat up; *informal* pack away, demolish, dispose of, make short work of, polish off, shovel down, stuff oneself with, pig oneself on, put away; *Brit. informal* scoff. **2** *flames devoured the house* =**consume**, engulf, envelop.

devout ▸ adjective =**dedicated**, devoted, committed, loyal, faithful, staunch, genuine, firm, steadfast, unwavering, sincere, wholehearted, keen, enthusiastic, zealous, passionate, ardent, fervent, active; pious, reverent, God-fearing, dutiful, churchgoing.

dexterity ▸ noun =**deftness**, adeptness, adroitness, agility, ability, talent, skill, proficiency, expertise, experience, efficiency, mastery, finesse.

dexterous ▸ adjective =**deft**, adept, adroit, agile, nimble, neat, handy, able, capable, skilful, skilled, proficient, expert, practised, polished; efficient, effortless, slick, professional, masterly; *informal* nifty, mean, ace.
–OPPOSITES clumsy.

diabolical, diabolic ▸ adjective **1** *diabolical forces* =**devilish**, satanic, demonic, hellish, infernal, evil, wicked, ungodly, unholy. **2** *(informal) a diabolical performance* =**dreadful**, awful, terrible, disgraceful, shameful, lamentable, deplorable, appalling, atrocious; *informal* crummy, dire, dismal, God-awful, abysmal, rotten, pathetic, pitiful, lousy; *Brit. informal* rubbish.

diagnose ▸ verb =**identify**, determine, distinguish, recognize, detect, pinpoint.

diagnosis ▸ noun **1** *the diagnosis of coeliac disease* =**identification**, detection, recognition, determination, discovery, pinpointing. **2** *the results confirmed his diagnosis* =**opinion**, judgement, verdict, conclusion.

diagonal ▸ adjective =**crosswise**, crossways, slanting, slanted, aslant, squint, oblique, angled, at an angle, cornerways, cornerwise; *N. Amer.* cater-cornered, kitty-cornered.

diagram ▸ noun =**drawing**, representation, plan, outline, figure.

dial ▸ verb =**phone**, telephone, call, ring, make/place a call (to).

dialogue ▸ noun **1** *a book consisting of a series of dialogues* =**conversation**, talk, discussion, interchange; chat, tête-à-tête; *informal* confab; *formal* colloquy. **2** *a serious political dialogue* =**discussion**, exchange, debate, exchange of views, talk, head-to-head, consultation, conference; talks, negotiations; *informal* powwow; *N. Amer. informal* skull session.

diameter ▶ noun =**breadth**, width, thickness; calibre, bore, gauge.

diametrical, diametric ▶ adjective =**direct**, absolute, complete, exact, extreme, polar.

diarrhoea ▶ noun =*informal* the runs, the trots, gippy tummy, holiday tummy, Delhi belly, Montezuma's revenge; *Brit. informal* the squits; *N. Amer. informal* turista; *archaic* the flux.
–OPPOSITES constipation.

diary ▶ noun **1** *he put the date in his diary* =**appointment book**, engagement book, personal organizer; *trademark* Filofax. **2** *her World War II diaries* =**journal**, memoir, chronicle, log, logbook, history, annal, record; *N. Amer.* daybook.

diatribe ▶ noun =**tirade**, harangue, onslaught, attack, polemic, denunciation, broadside, fulmination; *informal* blast.

dictate ▶ verb **1** *his attempts to dictate policy* =**prescribe**, lay down, impose, set down, order, command, decree, ordain, direct, determine, decide, control, govern. **2** *you are in no position to dictate to me* =**give orders to**, order about/around, lord it over; lay down the law; *informal* boss about/around, push around/about, throw one's weight about/around. **3** *choice is often dictated by availability* =**determine**, control, govern, decide, influence, affect.
▶ noun *the dictates of his superior* =**order**, command, commandment, decree, edict, ruling, dictum, diktat, directive, direction, instruction, pronouncement, mandate, requirement, stipulation, injunction, demand; *formal* ordinance; *literary* behest.

dictator ▶ noun =**autocrat**, despot, tyrant.
–OPPOSITES democrat.

dictatorial ▶ adjective =**domineering**, autocratic, authoritarian, oppressive, imperious, officious, overweening, overbearing, peremptory; *informal* bossy, high-handed.

dictatorship ▶ noun =**despotism**, tyranny, autocracy, authoritarianism, totalitarianism, fascism; oppression, repression.

–OPPOSITES democracy.

diction ▶ noun **1** *his careful diction* =**enunciation**, articulation, pronunciation, speech, intonation, inflection; delivery. **2** *the need for contemporary diction in poetry* =**phrasing**, turn of phrase, wording, language, usage, vocabulary, terminology, expressions, idioms.

dictionary ▶ noun =**lexicon**, glossary.

> **WORD LINKS**
>
> *relating to dictionaries:* **lexicographic**
> *writing of dictionaries:* **lexicography**
> *writer of dictionaries:* **lexicographer**

didactic ▶ adjective =**instructive**, instructional, educational, educative, informative, informational, edifying, moralistic.

die ▶ verb **1** *her father died last year* =**pass away**, pass on, lose one's life, expire, breathe one's last, meet one's end, meet one's death, lay down one's life, perish, go to meet one's maker, cross the great divide; *informal* give up the ghost, kick the bucket, croak, buy it, turn up one's toes, cash in one's chips, shuffle off this mortal coil; *Brit. informal* snuff it, peg out, pop one's clogs; *N. Amer. informal* bite the big one, buy the farm. **2** *the wind had died down* =**abate**, subside, drop, lessen, ease (off), let up, moderate, fade, peter out, wane, ebb, relent, weaken; melt away, dissolve, vanish, disappear. **3** *(informal) the engine died* =**fail**, cut out, give out, stop; *informal* conk out, go kaput, give up the ghost; *Brit. informal* pack up. **4** *(informal) she's dying to meet you* =**long**, yearn, burn, ache; *informal* itch.
–OPPOSITES live, intensify.

diehard ▶ adjective =**hard-line**, reactionary, ultra-conservative, traditionalist, dyed-in-the-wool, intransigent, inflexible, uncompromising, rigid, entrenched; staunch.

diet ▶ noun =**food**, eating habits; nutrition; *informal* grub, nosh.
▶ verb =**be on a diet**; slim, lose weight, watch one's weight; *N. Amer.* reduce; *N. Amer. informal* slenderize.

differ ▶ verb **1** *the second set of data differed from the first* =**contrast with**, be different/dissimilar to, be unlike, vary from, diverge from, deviate from, conflict with, run counter to, be incompatible with, be at odds with, go against, contradict. **2** *the two sides differed over this issue* =**disagree**, conflict, be at vari-

ance/odds, be in dispute, not see eye to eye.
–OPPOSITES resemble, agree.

difference ▸ noun **1** *the difference between the two sets of data* =**dissimilarity**, contrast, distinction, differentiation, variance, variation, divergence, disparity, deviation, polarity, gap, imbalance, contradiction. **2** *we've had our differences in the past* =**disagreement**, difference of opinion, dispute, argument, quarrel, wrangle, contretemps, altercation; *informal* tiff, set-to, run-in, spat; *Brit. informal* row. **3** *I am willing to pay the difference* =**balance**, remainder, rest.
–OPPOSITES similarity.

different ▸ adjective **1** *people with different lifestyles* =**dissimilar**, unlike, contrasting, divergent, differing, varying, disparate; poles apart, incompatible, mismatched, conflicting, clashing; *informal* like chalk and cheese. **2** *suddenly everything in her life was different* =**changed**, altered, transformed, new, unfamiliar, unknown, strange. **3** *two different occasions* =**distinct**, separate, individual, independent. **4** *(informal) he wanted to try something different* =**unusual**, out of the ordinary, unfamiliar, novel, new, fresh, original, unconventional, exotic, uncommon.
–OPPOSITES similar, related, ordinary.

differentiate ▸ verb **1** *he cannot differentiate between fantasy and reality* =**distinguish**, discriminate, make/draw a distinction, tell the difference, tell apart. **2** *this differentiates their business from all other booksellers* =**make different**, distinguish, set apart, single out, separate, mark out.

differentiation ▸ noun =**distinction**, distinctness, difference; separation, demarcation, delimitation.

difficult ▸ adjective **1** *a very difficult job* =**hard**, strenuous, arduous, laborious, tough, demanding, punishing, gruelling, back-breaking, exhausting, tiring; *informal* hellish, killing, no picnic. **2** *she found maths very difficult* =**hard**, complicated, impenetrable, unfathomable, over/above one's head, beyond one, puzzling, baffling, perplexing, confusing, mystifying; problematic, intricate, knotty, thorny, ticklish. **3** *a difficult child* =**troublesome**, tiresome, trying, exasperating, awkward, demanding, perverse, contrary, recalcitrant, unmanageable, obstreperous, unhelpful,

uncooperative, disobliging; hard to please, fussy, finicky; *formal* refractory. **4** *you've come at a difficult time* =**inconvenient**, awkward, inopportune, unfavourable, unfortunate, inappropriate, unsuitable, untimely, ill-timed. **5** *the family have been through very difficult times* =**bad**, tough, grim, dark, black, hard, distressing, upsetting, traumatic.
–OPPOSITES easy, simple, accommodating.

difficulty ▸ noun **1** *the difficulty of balancing motherhood with a career* =**strain**, trouble, problems, struggle, laboriousness, arduousness; *informal* hassle, stress. **2** *practical difficulties* =**problem**, complication, snag, hitch, fly in the ointment, pitfall, handicap, impediment, hindrance, obstacle, hurdle, stumbling block, obstruction, barrier; *Brit.* spanner in the works; *informal* headache, hiccup. **3** *Charles got into difficulties* =**trouble**, predicament, plight, hard times, dire straits; quandary, dilemma; *informal* deep water, a fix, a jam, a spot, a scrape, a stew, a hole, a pickle.
–OPPOSITES ease.

diffidence ▸ noun =**shyness**, bashfulness, modesty, self-effacement, meekness, unassertiveness, timidity, humility, hesitancy, reticence.

diffident ▸ adjective =**shy**, bashful, modest, self-effacing, unassuming, meek, unconfident, unassertive, timid, timorous, humble, shrinking, reticent.
–OPPOSITES confident.

diffuse ▸ verb =**spread**, spread around, disseminate, disperse, distribute, put about, circulate, communicate, purvey, propagate, transmit, broadcast, promulgate.
▸ adjective =**spread out**, scattered.

diffusion ▸ noun =**spread**, dissemination, scattering, dispersal, distribution, circulation, propagation, transmission, broadcasting, promulgation.

dig ▸ verb **1** *she began to dig the soil* =**turn over**, work, break up. **2** *he dug a hole* =**excavate**, dig out, quarry, hollow out, scoop out, gouge out; cut, bore, tunnel, burrow, mine. **3** *the bodies were hastily dug up* =**exhume**, disinter, unearth. **4** *Winnie dug her elbow into his ribs* =**poke**, prod, jab, stab, shove, ram, push, thrust, drive, stick. **5** *he'd been digging into my past* =**delve**, probe, search, inquire, look, investigate, research, examine, scrutinize, check up on; *informal* check out. **6** *I dug up some disturbing information* =**uncover**, discover, find (out), unearth, dredge up, root out, ferret out, turn up, reveal, bring to light, expose.

▶ noun **1** *a dig in the ribs* =**poke**, prod, jab, stab, shove, push. **2** (*informal*) *they're always making digs at each other* =**snide remark**, cutting remark, jibe, jeer, taunt, sneer, insult, barb, insinuation; *informal* wisecrack, crack, put-down.

digest ▶ verb *Liz digested this information* =**assimilate**, absorb, take in, understand, comprehend, grasp; consider, think about, reflect on, ponder, contemplate, mull over.

▶ noun *a digest of their findings* =**summary**, synopsis, abstract, precis, résumé, summation; compilation; *N. Amer. informal* wrap-up.

digit ▶ noun **1** *the door code has ten digits* =**numeral**, number, figure, integer. **2** *our frozen digits* =**finger**, thumb, toe; extremity.

dignified ▶ adjective =**stately**, noble, courtly, majestic, distinguished, proud, august, lofty, exalted, regal, lordly, imposing, impressive, grand; solemn, serious, grave, formal, ceremonious, decorous, sedate.

dignify ▶ verb =**ennoble**, enhance, distinguish, add distinction to, honour, grace, exalt, magnify, glorify, elevate.

dignitary ▶ noun =**worthy**, VIP, pillar of society, luminary, leading light, big name; *informal* heavyweight, bigwig, big gun, big shot.

dignity ▶ noun =**self-respect**, pride, self-esteem, self-worth.

digress ▶ verb =**deviate**, go off at a tangent, get off the subject, get sidetracked, lose the thread, diverge, turn aside/away, depart, drift, stray, wander.

digression ▶ noun =**deviation**, detour, diversion, departure, divergence; aside.

dilapidated ▶ adjective =**run down**, tumbledown, ramshackle, brokendown, in disrepair, shabby, battered, rickety, shaky, crumbling, in ruins, ruined, decayed, decaying, decrepit; neglected, uncared-for, untended, the worse for wear, falling to pieces, falling apart, gone to rack and ruin.

dilate ▶ verb =**enlarge**, widen, expand, distend.
  –OPPOSITES contract.

dilemma ▶ noun =**quandary**, predicament, catch-22, vicious circle, plight, mess, muddle; difficulty, problem, trouble, perplexity, confusion, conflict; *informal* fix, tight spot/corner; *Brit. informal* sticky wicket.

dilettante ▶ noun =**dabbler**, amateur, non-professional, non-specialist, layman, layperson.

diligence ▶ noun =**conscientiousness**, assiduousness, hard work, application, concentration, effort, care, industriousness, rigour, meticulousness, thoroughness; perseverance, persistence, tenacity, dedication, commitment.

diligent ▶ adjective =**industrious**, hard-working, assiduous, conscientious, particular, punctilious, meticulous, painstaking, rigorous, careful, thorough, sedulous; dedicated, committed.
  –OPPOSITES lazy.

dilute ▶ verb **1** *strong bleach can be diluted with water* =**make weaker**, weaken, water down; thin out, thin; doctor, adulterate; *informal* cut. **2** *the original plans have been diluted* =**weaken**, moderate, tone down, water down, compromise.
  –OPPOSITES concentrate.

▶ adjective *a dilute acid. See* DILUTED.

diluted ▶ adjective =**weak**, dilute, thin, watered down, watery; adulterated.
  –OPPOSITES concentrated.

dim ▶ adjective **1** *the dim light* =**faint**, weak, feeble, soft, pale, dull, subdued, muted, wishy-washy. **2** *long dim corridors* =**dark**, badly lit, dingy, dismal, gloomy, murky. **3** *a dim figure* =**indistinct**, ill-defined, unclear, vague, shadowy, nebulous, blurred, blurry, fuzzy. **4** *dim memories* =**vague**, imprecise, imperfect, unclear, indistinct, sketchy, hazy, blurred, shadowy. **5** *their prospects for the future looked dim* =**gloomy**, unpromising, bleak, unfavourable, discouraging, disheartening, depressing, dispiriting, hopeless.
  –OPPOSITES bright, distinct, encouraging.

▶ verb **1** *the lights were dimmed* =**turn down**, lower, dip, soften, subdue. **2** *my memories have not dimmed with time* =**fade**, dwindle.
  –OPPOSITES brighten, sharpen, intensify.

dimension ▶ noun **1** *the dimensions of*

the room =**size**, measurements, proportions, extent; length, width, breadth, depth, area, volume, capacity; footage, acreage. **2** *the dimension of the problem* =**size**, scale, extent, scope, magnitude; importance, significance. **3** *the cultural dimensions of the problem* =**aspect**, feature, element, facet, side.

diminish ▸ verb **1** *the pain will gradually diminish* =**decrease**, lessen, decline, reduce, subside, die down, abate, dwindle, fade, slacken off, let up, ebb, wane, recede, die away/out, peter out. **2** *new legislation diminished the courts' authority* =**reduce**, decrease, lessen, curtail, cut, cut down/back, constrict, restrict, limit, curb, check; weaken, blunt, erode, undermine, sap.
–OPPOSITES increase.

diminution ▸ noun =**reduction**, decrease, lessening, decline, dwindling, fading, weakening, ebb.

diminutive ▸ adjective =**tiny**, small, little, petite, elfin, minute, miniature, minuscule, compact, pocket, toy, midget, undersized, short; *Scottish* wee; *informal* teeny, weeny, teeny-weeny, teensy-weensy, itty-bitty, itsy-bitsy, tiddly, dinky, baby, pint-sized; *Brit. informal* titchy; *N. Amer. informal* little-bitty.
–OPPOSITES enormous.

dimple ▸ noun =**indentation**, hollow, cleft, dint.

din ▸ noun =**noise**, racket, rumpus, cacophony, babel, hubbub, tumult, uproar, commotion, clangour, clatter; shouting, yelling, screaming, caterwauling, clamour, outcry; *Scottish & N. English* stramash; *informal* hullabaloo; *Brit. informal* row.
–OPPOSITES silence.

dine ▸ verb **1** *we dined at a restaurant* =**have dinner**, have supper, eat; *dated* sup. **2** *they dined on lobster* =**eat**, feed on, feast on, banquet on, partake of; *informal* tuck into.

dingy ▸ adjective =**gloomy**, dark, dull, badly/poorly lit, murky, dim, dismal, dreary, drab, sombre, grim, cheerless; dirty, grimy, shabby, faded, worn, dowdy, seedy, run down.
–OPPOSITES bright.

dinner ▸ noun =**evening meal**, supper, main meal; lunch; feast, banquet; *Brit.* tea; *informal* spread, blowout; *Brit. informal* nosh-up, slap-up meal; *formal* repast.

> **WORD LINKS**
> *relating to dinner:* **prandial**

dint ▸ noun =**dent**, indentation, hollow, depression, dip, dimple, cleft, pit.
■ **by dint of** =**by means of**, by virtue of, on account of, as a result of, as a consequence of, owing to, on the strength of, due to, thanks to, by; *formal* by reason of.

dip ▸ verb **1** *he dipped a rag in the water* =**immerse**, submerge, plunge, duck, dunk, lower, sink. **2** *the sun dipped below the horizon* =**sink**, set, go/drop (down), fall, descend; disappear, vanish. **3** *the president's popularity has dipped* =**decrease**, fall, drop, fall off, decline, diminish, dwindle, slump, plummet, plunge. **4** *the road dipped* =**slope down**, descend, go down; drop (away), fall away. **5** *you might have to dip into your savings* =**draw on**, use, make use of, have recourse to, spend. **6** *an interesting book to dip into* =**browse through**, skim through, look through, flick through, glance at, peruse, run one's eye over.
–OPPOSITES rise, increase.
▸ noun **1** *a relaxing dip in the pool* =**swim**, bathe; paddle. **2** *chicken satay with peanut dip* =**sauce**, relish, chutney. **3** *the hedge at the bottom of the dip* =**slope**, incline, decline, descent; hollow, depression, basin. **4** *a dip in sales* =**decrease**, fall, drop, downturn, decline, falling-off, slump, reduction, diminution.

diplomacy ▸ noun **1** *diplomacy failed to win them independence* =**statesmanship**, statecraft, negotiation(s), discussion(s), talks, dialogue; international relations, foreign affairs. **2** *Jack's quiet diplomacy* =**tact**, tactfulness, sensitivity, discretion, delicacy, politeness, thoughtfulness, judiciousness, prudence.

diplomat ▸ noun =**ambassador**, attaché, consul, chargé d'affaires, envoy, emissary, plenipotentiary.

diplomatic ▸ adjective =**tactful**, sensitive, subtle, delicate, polite, discreet, thoughtful, careful, judicious, prudent, politic.
–OPPOSITES tactless.

dire ▸ adjective **1** *the dire economic situation* =**terrible**, dreadful, appalling, frightful, awful, atrocious, grim, alarming; grave, serious, disastrous, ruinous, hopeless, wretched, desperate, parlous. **2** *he was in dire need of help* =**urgent**, desperate, pressing, crying, sore, grave, serious, extreme, acute. **3** *dire warnings* =**ominous**, gloomy, grim, dismal.

direct ▶ adjective **1** *the most direct route* =**straight**; short, quick. **2** *a direct flight* =**non-stop**, unbroken, uninterrupted, through. **3** *he is very direct* =**frank**, candid, straightforward, honest, open, blunt, plain-spoken, outspoken, forthright, no-nonsense, matter-of-fact, not afraid to call a spade a spade; *informal* upfront. **4** *direct contact with the president* =**face to face**, personal, head-on, firsthand, tête-à-tête. **5** *a direct quotation* =**verbatim**, word for word, to the letter, faithful, exact, precise, accurate, correct. **6** *the direct opposite* =**exact**, absolute, complete, diametrical.
▶ verb **1** *an economic elite directed the nation's affairs* =**manage**, govern, run, administer, control, conduct, handle, be in charge/control of, preside over, lead, head, rule; supervise, superintend, oversee, regulate, orchestrate, coordinate. **2** *was that remark directed at me?* =**aim at**, target at, address to, intend for, mean for, design for. **3** *a man in uniform directed them to the hall* =**give directions**, show the way, guide, lead, conduct, accompany, usher, escort. **4** *the judge directed the jury to return a not guilty verdict* =**instruct**, tell, command, order, charge, require.

direction ▶ noun **1** *a northerly direction* =**way**, route, course, line, bearing, orientation. **2** *the newspaper's political direction* =**orientation**, inclination, leaning, tendency, bent, bias; tack, attitude. **3** *his direction of the project* =**administration**, management, conduct, handling, running, supervision, superintendence, regulation, orchestration; control, command, rule, leadership, guidance. **4** *explicit directions about nursing care* =**instruction**, order, command, rule, regulation, requirement.

directive ▶ noun =**instruction**, direction, command, order, charge, injunction, rule, ruling, regulation, law, dictate, decree, dictum, edict, mandate, fiat; *formal* ordinance.

directly ▶ adverb **1** *they flew directly to New York* =**straight**, right, as the crow flies, by a direct route. **2** *I went directly after breakfast* =**immediately**, at once, instantly, right (away), straight (away), post-haste, without delay, forthwith; quickly, speedily, promptly; *informal* pronto. **3** *the houses directly opposite*

=**exactly**, right, immediately; diametrically, *informal* bang. **4** *she spoke simply and directly* =**frankly**, candidly, openly, bluntly, forthrightly, without beating around the bush.

director ▶ noun =**administrator**, manager, chairman, chairwoman, chairperson, chair, head, chief, principal, leader, governor, president; managing director, MD, chief executive, CEO; *informal* boss, kingpin, top dog, gaffer, head honcho, numero uno; *N. Amer. informal* Mister Big.

directory ▶ noun =**index**, list, listing, register, catalogue, record, archive, inventory.

dirt ▶ noun **1** *his face was streaked with dirt* =**grime**, filth; dust, soot; muck, mud, mire, sludge, slime, ooze; smudges, stains; *informal* crud, yuck, grunge; *Brit. informal* grot, gunge. **2** *the packed dirt of the road* =**earth**, soil, clay; ground.

> **WORD LINKS**
> *fear of dirt:* **mysophobia**

dirty ▶ adjective **1** *a dirty sweatshirt | dirty water* =**soiled**, grimy, grubby, filthy, mucky, stained, unwashed, greasy, cloudy, muddy, dusty, sooty; unclean, sullied, impure, tarnished, polluted, contaminated, defiled, foul, unhygienic, insanitary, unsanitary; *informal* cruddy, yucky, icky; *Brit. informal* manky, gungy, grotty. **2** *a dirty joke* =**indecent**, obscene, rude, naughty, vulgar, smutty, coarse, crude, filthy, bawdy, suggestive, ribald, racy, salacious, risqué, offensive, off colour, lewd, pornographic, explicit, X-rated; *informal* blue; *euphemistic* adult. **3** *a dirty look* =**malevolent**, resentful, hostile, black, dark; angry, disapproving.
−OPPOSITES clean, innocent.
▶ verb *the dog had dirtied her dress* =**soil**, stain, muddy, blacken, mess (up), mark, spatter, smudge, smear, splatter; sully, pollute, foul, defile.
−OPPOSITES clean.

disability ▶ noun =**handicap**, incapacity, impairment, infirmity, defect, abnormality; condition, disorder, affliction.

disable ▶ verb **1** *an injury that could disable somebody for life* =**incapacitate**, put out of action, debilitate; handicap, cripple, lame, maim, immobilize, paralyse. **2** *the bomb squad disabled the device* =**de-**

activate, defuse, disarm, make safe.

disabled ▶ adjective = handicapped, incapacitated; debilitated, infirm; crippled, lame, paralysed, immobilized, bedridden; *euphemistic* physically challenged, differently abled.
−OPPOSITES able-bodied.

disadvantage ▶ noun = drawback, snag, downside, stumbling block, fly in the ointment, catch, hindrance, obstacle, impediment; flaw, defect, weakness, fault, handicap, con, trouble, difficulty, problem, complication; *informal* minus.
−OPPOSITES benefit.

disadvantaged ▶ adjective = deprived, underprivileged, depressed, in need, needy, poor, impoverished, indigent, hard up; *Brit.* on the breadline.

disadvantageous ▶ adjective = unfavourable, bad; detrimental, prejudicial, deleterious, harmful, damaging, injurious.

disaffected ▶ adjective = dissatisfied, disgruntled, discontented, frustrated, alienated, resentful, embittered.
−OPPOSITES contented.

disagree ▶ verb 1 *no one was willing to disagree with him* = take issue, challenge, contradict, oppose; be at variance/odds, not see eye to eye, differ, dissent, be in dispute, debate, argue, quarrel, wrangle, clash, be at loggerheads, cross swords, lock horns; *formal* gainsay. 2 *their accounts disagree on details* = differ, be dissimilar, be different, vary, diverge; contradict each other, conflict, clash. 3 *the spicy food disagreed with her* = make ill, make unwell, nauseate, sicken, upset.

disagreeable ▶ adjective 1 *a disagreeable smell* = unpleasant, nasty, offensive, off-putting, obnoxious, objectionable, horrible, horrid, dreadful, frightful, abominable, odious, repulsive, repellent, revolting, disgusting, foul, vile, nauseating, sickening, unpalatable. 2 *a disagreeable man* = bad-tempered, grumpy, sullen; unfriendly, unpleasant, nasty, mean, rude, surly, discourteous, impolite, brusque, abrupt.
−OPPOSITES pleasant.

disagreement ▶ noun 1 *there was some disagreement over possible solutions* = dissent, dispute, difference of opinion, controversy, discord, contention, division. 2 *a heated disagreement* = argument, debate, quarrel, wrangle, squab-ble, falling-out, altercation, dispute, war of words, contretemps; *informal* tiff, set-to, spat, ding-dong; *Brit. informal* row, barney; *Scottish informal* rammy. 3 *the disagreement between the results of the two assessments* = difference, dissimilarity, variation, variance, discrepancy, disparity, divergence, contradiction, conflict, clash, contrast.

disallow ▶ verb = reject, refuse, dismiss, say no to; ban, bar, block, forbid, prohibit; cancel, invalidate, overrule, quash, overturn, countermand, reverse, throw out, set aside.

disappear ▶ verb 1 *by 4 o'clock the mist had disappeared* = vanish, be lost to view/sight, recede; fade (away), melt away, clear, dissolve, disperse, evaporate. 2 *this way of life has disappeared* = die out, cease to exist, end, go, pass away, pass into oblivion, perish, vanish.
−OPPOSITES materialize.

disappoint ▶ verb = let down, fail, dissatisfy; upset, dismay, sadden, disenchant, disillusion, shatter someone's illusions.
−OPPOSITES delight.

disappointed ▶ adjective = upset, saddened, let down, cast down, disheartened, downhearted, downcast, dispirited, discouraged, despondent, dismayed, crestfallen; disenchanted, disillusioned; *informal* choked, miffed, cut up; *Brit. informal* gutted, as sick as a parrot.
−OPPOSITES delighted.

disappointing ▶ adjective = regrettable, unfortunate, discouraging, disheartening, dispiriting, dismaying, unsatisfactory.

disappointment ▶ noun 1 *she tried to hide her disappointment* = sadness, regret, dismay, sorrow; disenchantment, disillusionment. 2 *the trip was a bit of a disappointment* = let-down, non-event, anticlimax; *Brit.* damp squib; *informal* washout.
−OPPOSITES delight.

disapproval ▶ noun = disapprobation, objection, dislike; dissatisfaction, disfavour, displeasure, distaste; criticism, censure, condemnation, denunciation, deprecation; *informal* the thumbs down.

disapprove ▶ verb = object to, have a poor opinion of, look down one's nose at, take exception to, dislike, take a dim view of, look askance at, frown on, be against, not believe in; deplore, criticize, censure, condemn, denounce, decry.

disapproving ▶ adjective =reproachful, reproving, critical, censorious, condemnatory, disparaging, denigratory, deprecatory, unfavourable; hostile.

disarm ▶ verb 1 *the militia refused to disarm* =lay down one's arms/weapons; surrender; demobilize, demilitarize. 2 *police disarmed the bomb* =defuse, disable, deactivate, make safe. 3 *the warmth in his voice disarmed her* =win over, charm, persuade; mollify, appease, placate, pacify, conciliate, propitiate.

disarmament ▶ noun =demilitarization, demobilization, decommissioning, arms reduction, arms limitation, arms control.

disarming ▶ adjective =winning, charming, irresistible, persuasive, beguiling; conciliatory, mollifying.

disarray ▶ noun =disorder, confusion, chaos, untidiness, disorganization, dishevelment, a mess, a muddle, a shambles.
–OPPOSITES tidiness.

disaster ▶ noun 1 *a railway disaster* =catastrophe, calamity, cataclysm, tragedy, act of God; accident. 2 *a string of personal disasters* =misfortune, mishap, misadventure, setback, reversal, stroke of bad luck, blow. 3 *(informal) the film was a disaster* =failure, fiasco, catastrophe; *informal* flop, dud, washout, dead loss.
–OPPOSITES success, triumph.

disastrous ▶ adjective =catastrophic, calamitous, cataclysmic, tragic; devastating, ruinous, dire, terrible, awful, shocking, appalling, dreadful; black, dark, unfortunate, unlucky, ill-fated, ill-starred, inauspicious.

disavow ▶ verb =deny, disclaim, disown, wash one's hands of, repudiate, reject, renounce.

disband ▶ verb =break up, disperse, demobilize, dissolve, scatter, separate, go separate ways, part company.
–OPPOSITES assemble.

disbelief ▶ noun =incredulity, incredulousness, scepticism, doubt, doubtfulness, dubiousness, cynicism, suspicion, distrust, mistrust; *formal* dubiety.

disbelieving ▶ adjective =incredu-

lous, doubtful, dubious, unconvinced; distrustful, mistrustful, suspicious, cynical, sceptical.

disc, disk ▶ noun 1 *the sun was a huge scarlet disc* =circle, round. 2 *computer disks* =diskette, floppy disk, floppy; hard disk; CD-ROM. 3 *(dated) an old T-Rex disc* =record, album, LP, single, 45.

discard ▶ verb =dispose of, throw away/out, get rid of, toss out, jettison, scrap, dispense with, cast aside/off, throw on the scrap heap; reject, repudiate, abandon, drop, have done with, shed; *informal* chuck (away/out), dump, ditch, bin, junk, get shut of; *Brit. informal* get shot of; *N. Amer. informal* trash.
–OPPOSITES keep.

discern ▶ verb =perceive, make out, pick out, detect, recognize, notice, observe, see, spot; identify, determine, distinguish; *literary* espy.

discernible ▶ adjective =visible, detectable, noticeable, perceptible, observable, identifiable; apparent, evident, clear, obvious.

discerning ▶ adjective =discriminating, judicious, shrewd, astute, intelligent, sharp, selective, sophisticated, tasteful, sensitive, perceptive, knowing.

discharge ▶ verb 1 *he was discharged from the RAF* =dismiss, eject, expel, throw out, make redundant; release, let go; *Military* cashier; *informal* sack, give someone the sack, fire, kick/boot out, give someone the boot, turf out, give someone their cards, give someone their marching orders, give someone the push. 2 *he was discharged from prison* =release, free, let out. 3 *oil is routinely discharged from ships* =release, eject, let out, pour out, void, give off, dump. 4 *the swelling will burst and discharge pus* =emit, exude, ooze, leak, drip. 5 *he accidentally discharged a pistol* =fire, shoot, let off; set off, loose off, trigger, explode, detonate. 6 *the ferry was discharging passengers* =unload, offload, put off; remove. 7 *they discharged their duties efficiently* =carry out, perform, execute, conduct, do; fulfil, accomplish, achieve, complete.
–OPPOSITES recruit, imprison, absorb.

▶ noun 1 *his discharge from the service* =dismissal, release, removal, ejection, expulsion; *Military* cashiering; *informal* the sack, the boot. 2 *her discharge from prison* =release. 3 *a discharge of diesel oil into the river* =leak, leakage, emission, release, outflow. **4** *a watery discharge from the eyes* =**emission**, secretion, excretion, suppuration; pus. **5** *the discharge of their duties* =**carrying out**, performance, performing, execution, conduct; fulfilment, accomplishment, completion.

disciple ▶ noun =**follower**, adherent, believer, admirer, devotee, acolyte, apostle; pupil, student; supporter, advocate, proponent, apologist.

disciplinarian ▶ noun =**martinet**, hard taskmaster, authoritarian; tyrant, despot; *N. Amer.* ramrod; *informal* slavedriver.

discipline ▶ noun **1** *parental discipline* =**control**, training, teaching, instruction, regulation, direction, order, authority, rule, strictness, a firm hand. **2** *he was able to maintain discipline among his men* =**good behaviour**, order, control, obedience. **3** *sociology is a fairly new discipline* =**field (of study)**, branch of knowledge, subject, area; speciality.
▶ verb **1** *she had disciplined herself to ignore the pain* =**train**, drill, teach, school, coach. **2** *he was disciplined by the management* =**punish**, penalize, bring to book; reprimand, rebuke, reprove, chastise, upbraid; *informal* dress down, give someone a dressing-down, give someone a roasting; *Brit. informal* carpet; *formal* castigate.

disclaim ▶ verb =**deny**, refuse to accept/acknowledge, reject, wash one's hands of.
–OPPOSITES accept.

disclose ▶ verb **1** *the information must not be disclosed to anyone* =**reveal**, make known, divulge, tell, impart, communicate, pass on, vouchsafe; release, make public, broadcast, publish, report; leak, betray, let slip, let drop, give away. **2** *exploratory surgery disclosed an aneurysm* =**uncover**, reveal, show, bring to light.
–OPPOSITES conceal.

disclosure ▶ noun **1** *she was embarrassed by this unexpected disclosure* =**revelation**, declaration, announcement, news, report, leak. **2** *the disclosure of official information* =**publishing**, broadcasting; revelation, communication, release, uncovering, unveiling, exposure; leaking.

discoloration ▶ noun =**stain**, mark, patch, streak, spot, blotch, tarnishing; blemish, flaw, defect, bruise, contusion; birthmark; *informal* splodge, splotch.

discolour ▶ verb =**stain**, mark, soil, dirty, streak, smear, spot, tarnish, spoil, blemish; blacken, char; fade, bleach.

discoloured ▶ adjective =**stained**, marked, spotted, dirty, soiled, tarnished, blackened; bleached, faded, yellowed.

discomfort ▶ noun **1** *discomfort caused by indigestion* =**pain**, aches and pains, soreness; aching, twinge, pang, throb, cramp; *Brit. informal* gyp. **2** *the discomforts of life at sea* =**inconvenience**, difficulty, problem, trial, tribulation, hardship; *informal* hassle. **3** *Ruth flushed and Thomas noticed her discomfort* =**embarrassment**, discomfiture, unease, awkwardness, discomposure, confusion, nervousness, distress, anxiety.
▶ verb *his purpose was to discomfort the Prime Minister* =**embarrass**, disconcert, nonplus, discomfit, take aback, unsettle, unnerve, ruffle, confuse, fluster; *informal* faze, rattle; *N. Amer. informal* discombobulate.

disconcerting ▶ adjective =**unsettling**, unnerving, discomfiting, disturbing, perturbing, troubling, upsetting, worrying, alarming; confusing, bewildering, perplexing.

disconnect ▶ verb **1** *the trucks were disconnected from the train* =**detach**, disengage, uncouple, decouple, unhook, unhitch, undo, unfasten, unyoke. **2** *she felt as if she had been disconnected from the real world* =**separate**, cut off, divorce, sever, isolate, divide, part, disengage, dissociate, remove. **3** *an engineer disconnected the appliance* =**deactivate**, shut off, turn off, switch off, unplug, isolate.
–OPPOSITES attach, connect.

disconnected ▶ adjective **1** *a world that seemed disconnected from reality* =**detached**, separate, separated, divorced, cut off, isolated, dissociated, disengaged. **2** *a disconnected narrative* =**disjointed**, incoherent, garbled, confused, jumbled, mixed up, rambling, wandering, disorganized, uncoordinated, ill-thought-out.

disconsolate ▶ adjective =**sad**, unhappy, doleful, woebegone, dejected, downcast, downhearted, despondent, dispirited, crestfallen, cast down, down, disheartened, discouraged, demoralized.
–OPPOSITES cheerful.

discontent ▶ noun =**dissatisfaction**,

disaffection, grievances, unhappiness, displeasure, bad feelings, resentment, envy; restlessness, unrest, uneasiness, unease, frustration, irritation, annoyance; *informal* a chip on one's shoulder.
−OPPOSITES satisfaction.

discontented ▸ adjective =dissatisfied, disgruntled, disaffected, unhappy, aggrieved, displeased, resentful, envious; restless, frustrated, irritated, annoyed; *informal* fed up.
−OPPOSITES satisfied.

discontinue ▸ verb =stop, end, terminate, put an end/stop to, wind up, finish, call a halt to, cancel, drop, abandon, dispense with, do away with, get rid of, axe, abolish; suspend, interrupt, break off, withdraw; *informal* cut, pull the plug on, scrap, knock something on the head.

discontinuity ▸ noun =disconnectedness, disconnection, break, disruption, interruption, disjointedness.

discontinuous ▸ adjective =intermittent, sporadic, broken, fitful, interrupted, on and off, disrupted, erratic, disconnected.

discord ▸ noun **1** *stress resulting from family discord* =strife, conflict, friction, hostility, antagonism, antipathy, enmity, bad feeling, ill feeling, bad blood, argument, quarrelling, squabbling, bickering, wrangling, feuding, disagreement, dissension, dispute, disunity, division. **2** *the music faded in discord* =dissonance, discordance, disharmony, cacophony.
−OPPOSITES accord, harmony.

discordant ▸ adjective =inharmonious, tuneless, off-key, dissonant, harsh, jarring, grating, jangling, jangly, strident, shrill, screeching, screechy, cacophonous; sharp, flat.
−OPPOSITES harmonious.

discount ▸ noun *students get a 10 per cent discount* =reduction, deduction, markdown, price cut, cut, concession; rebate.
▸ verb **1** *I'd heard rumours, but discounted them* =disregard, pay no attention to, take no notice of, dismiss, ignore, overlook, reject; *informal* take with a pinch of salt, pooh-pooh. **2** *the RRP is discounted in many stores* =reduce, mark down, cut, lower; *informal* knock down. **3** *top Paris hotels discounted 20 per cent off published room rates* =deduct, take off; *informal* knock

off, slash.
−OPPOSITES believe, increase.

discourage ▸ verb **1** *we want to discourage children from smoking* =deter, dissuade, put off, talk out of. **2** *she was discouraged by his hostile tone* =dishearten, dispirit, demoralize, cast down, disappoint; put off, unnerve, daunt, intimidate. **3** *he sought to discourage further speculation* =prevent, stop, put a stop to, avert; inhibit, hinder, curb, put a damper on, throw cold water on.
−OPPOSITES encourage.

discouraged ▸ adjective =disheartened, dispirited, demoralized, deflated, disappointed, let down, disconsolate, despondent, dejected, cast down, downcast, crestfallen, dismayed, low-spirited, gloomy, glum, unenthusiastic; put off, daunted, intimidated, cowed, crushed; *informal* down in the mouth, down in the dumps, fed up, unenthused.

discouraging ▸ adjective =depressing, demoralizing, disheartening, dispiriting, disappointing, gloomy, off-putting; unfavourable, unpromising, inauspicious.
−OPPOSITES encouraging.

discourse ▸ noun **1** *they prolonged their discourse outside the door* =discussion, conversation, talk, dialogue, conference, debate, consultation; parley, powwow, chat; *informal* confab; *formal* confabulation, colloquy. **2** *a discourse on critical theory* =essay, treatise, dissertation, paper, study, critique, monograph, disquisition, tract; lecture, address, speech, oration; sermon, homily.
▸ verb **1** *he discoursed at length on his favourite topic* =hold forth, expatiate, pontificate; talk, give a talk, give a speech, lecture, sermonize, preach; *informal* spout, sound off. **2** *Edward was discoursing with his friends* =converse, talk, speak, debate, confer, consult, parley, chat.

discourteous ▸ adjective =rude, impolite, ill-mannered, bad-mannered, disrespectful, uncivil, ungentlemanly, unladylike, ill-bred, boorish, crass, ungracious, uncouth; insolent, impudent, cheeky, audacious, presumptuous; curt, brusque, blunt, abrupt, offhand, short, sharp; *informal* ignorant.
−OPPOSITES polite, courteous.

discourtesy ▸ noun =rudeness, impoliteness, ill manners, bad manners, incivility, disrespect, ungraciousness, boorishness, uncouthness; insolence, impudence, impertinence; curtness, brusqueness, abruptness.

discover ▸ verb **1** *firemen discovered a body in the debris* =**find**, locate, come across/upon, stumble on, chance on, uncover, unearth, turn up. **2** *eventually, I discovered the truth* =**find out**, learn, realize, ascertain, work out, fathom out, dig out, ferret out, root out; *informal* figure out, tumble to; *Brit. informal* twig, rumble, suss out; *N. Amer. informal* dope out. **3** *scientists discovered a new way of dating fossils* =**hit on**, find.

discovery ▸ noun **1** *the discovery of the body* =**finding**, location, uncovering, unearthing. **2** *the discovery that she was pregnant* =**realization**, recognition; revelation, disclosure. **3** *he failed to take out a patent on his discoveries* =**find**, finding, breakthrough, innovation.

discredit ▸ verb **1** *an attempt to discredit him* =**bring into disrepute**, disgrace, dishonour, damage (the reputation of), blacken the name of, put/show in a bad light, reflect badly on, compromise, smear, tarnish, taint; *N. Amer. slur.* **2** *that theory has been discredited* =**disprove**, invalidate, explode, refute; *informal* debunk.
▸ noun =**dishonour**, disgrace, shame, humiliation, ignominy.
–OPPOSITES honour, glory.

discreditable ▸ adjective =**dishonourable**, reprehensible, shameful, deplorable, disgraceful, disreputable, blameworthy, ignoble, shabby, regrettable.
–OPPOSITES creditable.

discreet ▸ adjective **1** *discreet enquiries* =**careful**, circumspect, cautious; tactful, diplomatic, judicious, strategic, sensitive. **2** *discreet lighting* =**unobtrusive**, inconspicuous, subtle, low-key, understated, subdued, muted, soft, restrained.

discrepancy ▸ noun =**difference**, disparity, variation, deviation, divergence, disagreement, inconsistency, dissimilarity, mismatch, discordance, incompatibility, conflict.
–OPPOSITES correspondence.

discrete ▸ adjective =**separate**, distinct, individual, detached, unattached, disconnected, discontinuous.
–OPPOSITES connected.

discretion ▸ noun **1** *you can rely on his*

discretion =**circumspection**, carefulness; tact, tactfulness, diplomacy, delicacy, sensitivity, prudence, judiciousness. **2** *honorary fellowships awarded at the discretion of the council* =**choice**, option, preference, disposition; pleasure, will, inclination.

discretionary ▸ adjective =**optional**, voluntary, at one's discretion.
–OPPOSITES compulsory.

discriminate ▸ verb **1** *he cannot discriminate between fact and opinion* =**differentiate**, distinguish, draw a distinction, tell the difference, tell apart; separate. **2** *policies that discriminate against women* =**be biased**, be prejudiced; treat differently, treat unfairly, put at a disadvantage, pick on.

discriminating ▸ adjective =**discerning**, perceptive, astute, shrewd, judicious, insightful; selective, tasteful, refined, sensitive, cultivated, cultured, artistic, aesthetic.
–OPPOSITES indiscriminate.

discrimination ▸ noun **1** *racial discrimination* =**prejudice**, bias, bigotry, intolerance, favouritism, partisanship; sexism, chauvinism, racism, racialism, anti-Semitism, ageism, classism; positive discrimination, affirmative action; *(in S. Africa, historical)* apartheid. **2** *a man with no discrimination* =**discernment**, judgement, perceptiveness, acumen, astuteness, shrewdness, judiciousness, insight; (good) taste, refinement, sensitivity, cultivation.
–OPPOSITES impartiality.

discriminatory ▸ adjective =**prejudicial**, biased, prejudiced, preferential, unfair, unjust, inequitable, weighted, one-sided, partisan; sexist, chauvinistic, chauvinist, racist, racialist, anti-Semitic, ageist, classist.
–OPPOSITES impartial.

discuss ▸ verb **1** *I discussed the matter with my wife* =**talk over**, talk about, talk through, converse about, debate, confer about, deliberate about, chew over, consider, weigh up, thrash out; *informal* kick around/about. **2** *chapter three discusses this topic in detail* =**examine**, explore, study, analyse, go into, deal with, treat, consider, concern itself with, tackle.

discussion ▸ noun **1** *a long discussion with her husband* =**conversation**, talk, dialogue, discourse, conference, debate, exchange of views, consultation, deliberation; powwow, chat, tête-à-tête, heart-to-heart; negotiations, parley; *informal* confab, chit-chat, rap; *N. Amer. informal* skull session, bull session; *formal* confabulation, colloquy. **2** *the book's candid discussion of sexual matters* =**examination**, exploration, analysis, study; treatment, consideration.

disdain ▶ noun *she looked at him with disdain* =**contempt**, scorn, scornfulness, contemptuousness, derision, disrespect; disparagement, condescension, superciliousness, hauteur, haughtiness, dismissiveness; distaste.
−OPPOSITES respect.
▶ verb *she disdained exhibitionism* =**scorn**, deride, pour scorn on, regard with contempt, sneer at, sniff at, curl one's lip at, look down one's nose at, look down on; despise.

disdainful ▶ adjective =**contemptuous**, scornful, derisive, sneering, withering, disparaging, condescending, patronizing, supercilious, haughty, superior, arrogant, dismissive; *informal* high and mighty, sniffy, snotty.
−OPPOSITES respectful.

disease ▶ noun =**illness**, sickness, ill health; infection, ailment, malady, disorder, condition, problem; pestilence, plague, cancer, canker, blight; *informal* bug, virus; *Brit. informal* lurgy; *dated* contagion.

WORD LINKS

relating to disease: **pathological**
branches of medicine to do with diseases: **epidemiology, pathology, therapeutics**
fear of disease: **pathophobia, nosophobia**

diseased ▶ adjective =**unhealthy**, ill, sick, unwell, ailing, sickly, unsound; infected, septic, contaminated, blighted, rotten, bad.

disembark ▶ verb =**get off**, alight, step off, leave; go ashore; land, arrive; *N. Amer.* deplane; *informal* pile out.

disembodied ▶ adjective =**bodiless**, incorporeal, discarnate, spiritual; intangible, insubstantial, impalpable; ghostly, spectral, phantom, wraithlike.

disembowel ▶ verb =**gut**, draw; *formal* eviscerate.

disenchanted ▶ adjective =**disillusioned**, disappointed, let down, discontented; *informal* fed up.

disenchantment ▶ noun =**disillusionment**, disappointment, dissatisfaction, discontent.

disengage ▶ verb **1** *I disengaged his hand from mine* =**remove**, detach, disentangle, extricate, separate, release, free, loosen, loose, disconnect, unfasten, unclasp, uncouple, undo, unhook, unhitch, untie, unyoke, disentwine. **2** *American forces disengaged from the country* =**withdraw**, leave, pull out of, quit, retreat from.
−OPPOSITES attach, enter.

disentangle ▶ verb **1** *Allen was disentangling a coil of rope* =**untangle**, unravel, untwist, unwind, undo, untie, straighten out, smooth out. **2** *he disentangled his fingers from her hair* =**extricate**, extract, free, remove, disengage, untwine, disentwine, release, loosen, detach, unfasten, unclasp, disconnect.

disfigure ▶ verb =**mar**, spoil, deface, scar, blemish; damage, mutilate, deform, maim, ruin; vandalize.
−OPPOSITES adorn.

disfigurement ▶ noun **1** *the disfigurement of Victorian buildings* =**defacement**, spoiling, scarring, mutilation, damaging, vandalizing, ruin. **2** *a facial disfigurement* =**blemish**, defect, discoloration, blotch; scar, pockmark; deformity, malformation, abnormality, injury, wound.

disgorge ▶ verb =**pour out**, discharge, eject, throw out, emit, expel, spit out, spew out, belch forth, spout; vomit.

disgrace ▶ noun **1** *he brought disgrace on the family* =**dishonour**, shame, discredit, ignominy, degradation, disrepute, infamy, scandal, stigma, condemnation, vilification; humiliation, embarrassment, loss of face; *Austral.* strife. **2** *the unemployment figures are a disgrace* =**scandal**, outrage, affront, insult; *informal* crime, sin.
−OPPOSITES honour.
▶ verb **1** *you have disgraced the family name* =**bring shame on**, shame, dishonour, discredit, bring into disrepute, degrade, debase, defame, stigmatize, taint, sully, tarnish, besmirch, stain, blacken, drag through the mud/mire. **2** *he was publicly disgraced* =**discredit**, dishonour, stigmatize; humiliate, chasten, humble, demean, put someone in their place, take down a peg or two, cut down to size.

disgraceful | disillusion

–OPPOSITES honour.

■ **in disgrace** =out of favour, unpopular, under a cloud, disgraced; *Informal* in someone's bad/black books, in the doghouse; *NZ informal* in the dogbox.

disgraceful ▶ adjective =shameful, shocking, scandalous, deplorable, despicable, contemptible, beyond contempt, beyond the pale, dishonourable, discreditable, reprehensible, base, mean, low, blameworthy, unworthy, ignoble, shabby, inglorious, outrageous, abominable, atrocious, appalling, dreadful, terrible.

–OPPOSITES admirable.

disgruntled ▶ adjective =dissatisfied, discontented, aggrieved, resentful, displeased, unhappy, disappointed, disaffected; annoyed, irked, put out; *informal* hacked off, browned off, peed off; *Brit. informal* cheesed off, narked; *N. Amer. informal* fed up, sore, teed off, ticked off.

disguise ▶ verb *he disguised his true feelings* =camouflage, conceal, hide, cover up, mask, screen, veil; paper over, gloss over.

–OPPOSITES expose.

disgust ▶ noun =revulsion, repugnance, aversion, distaste, abhorrence, loathing, detestation.
▶ verb =revolt, repel, repulse, sicken, horrify, appal, turn someone's stomach; *N. Amer. informal* gross out.

–OPPOSITES delight.

disgusting ▶ adjective 1 *the food was disgusting* =revolting, repulsive, sickening, nauseating, stomach-churning, stomach-turning, off-putting, unpalatable, distasteful, foul, abominable; *N. Amer.* vomitous; *informal* yucky, icky, gross, sick-making. 2 *I find racism disgusting* =abhorrent, repellent, loathsome, offensive, appalling, outrageous, objectionable, shocking, horrifying, scandalous, monstrous, vile, odious, obnoxious, detestable, hateful, sickening, beyond the pale; *informal* gross, ghastly, sick.

–OPPOSITES delicious, delightful.

dish ▶ noun 1 *a china dish* =bowl, plate, platter, casserole. 2 *vegetarian dishes* =recipe, meal, course; (**dishes**) food; fare, cuisine.

■ **dish something out** =distribute, dispense, issue, hand out/round, give out, pass out/round; deal out, dole out, share out, allocate, allot, apportion.

■ **dish something up** =serve (up), spoon out, ladle out.

disharmony ▶ noun =discord, friction, strife, conflict, hostility, acrimony, bad blood, bad feeling, enmity, dissension, disagreement, feuding, quarrelling; disunity, division, divisiveness.

dishearten ▶ verb =discourage, dispirit, demoralize, cast down, depress, disappoint, dismay; put off, deter, unnerve, daunt.

–OPPOSITES encourage.

disheartened ▶ adjective =discouraged, dispirited, demoralized, deflated, disappointed, let down, despondent, dejected, cast down, downcast, depressed, crestfallen, dismayed; daunted; *informal* fed up, down in the mouth, down in the dumps.

dishevelled ▶ adjective =untidy, unkempt, scruffy, messy, in a mess, disordered, disarranged, rumpled, bedraggled; uncombed, tousled, tangled, shaggy, straggly, windswept; *N. Amer. informal* mussed (up).

–OPPOSITES tidy.

dishonest ▶ adjective =fraudulent, corrupt, swindling, cheating, double-dealing; underhand, crafty, cunning, devious, treacherous, unfair, unjust, dirty, unethical, immoral, unscrupulous, unprincipled; criminal, illegal, unlawful; false, untruthful, deceitful, deceiving, lying; *informal* crooked, shady, tricky, sharp; *Brit. informal* bent, dodgy; *Austral./NZ informal* shonky.

dishonesty ▶ noun =fraud, fraudulence, sharp practice, corruption, cheating, chicanery, double-dealing, deceit, deception, duplicity, lying, falseness, falsity, falsehood, untruthfulness, trickery, underhandedness, subterfuge, skulduggery, treachery, unscrupulousness, criminality, misconduct; *informal* crookedness, dirty tricks, shenanigans; *Brit. informal* jiggery-pokery.

–OPPOSITES probity.

dishonour ▶ noun =disgrace, shame, discredit; stigma.
▶ verb =disgrace, shame, discredit, bring into disrepute, debase.

dishonourable ▶ adjective =disgraceful, shameful, disreputable, discreditable, ignoble, reprehensible, shabby, shoddy, base, low, improper, unseemly, unworthy.

disillusion ▶ verb =disabuse, en-

lighten, set straight, open someone's eyes; disenchant, shatter someone's illusions, disappoint.
–OPPOSITES deceive.

disillusioned ▶ adjective =**disenchanted**, disappointed, let down, discouraged; cynical, sour, negative.

disincentive ▶ noun =**deterrent**, discouragement; obstacle, impediment, hindrance, obstruction, block, barrier.

disinclined ▶ adjective =**reluctant**, unwilling, unenthusiastic, hesitant.
–OPPOSITES willing.

disinfect ▶ verb =**sterilize**, sanitize, clean, cleanse, purify, decontaminate.
–OPPOSITES contaminate.

disingenuous ▶ adjective =**insincere**, dishonest, deceitful, duplicitous; hypocritical, cynical.

disinherit ▶ verb =**cut someone out of one's will**, cut off.

disintegrate ▶ verb =**break up**, break apart, fall apart, fall to pieces, fragment, fracture, shatter, splinter; crumble, deteriorate, decay, decompose, collapse.

disinter ▶ verb =**exhume**, unearth, dig up.

disinterest ▶ noun **1** *scholarly disinterest* =**impartiality**, neutrality, objectivity, detachment. **2** *he looked at us with complete disinterest* =**indifference**, lack of interest, unconcern, impassivity.
–OPPOSITES bias.

disinterested ▶ adjective **1** *disinterested advice* =**unbiased**, unprejudiced, impartial, neutral, non-partisan, detached, uninvolved, objective, dispassionate, impersonal, clinical; with no axe to grind. **2** *he looked at her with disinterested eyes* =**uninterested**, indifferent, incurious, unconcerned, impassive, detached; *informal* couldn't-care-less.

disjointed ▶ adjective =**unconnected**, disconnected, discontinuous, fragmented, disordered, muddled, mixed up, jumbled, garbled.

dislike ▶ verb *a man she had always disliked* =**find distasteful**, regard with distaste, be averse to, have an aversion to, disapprove of, object to, take exception to.
▶ noun *she viewed the other woman with dislike* =**distaste**, aversion, disfavour, antipathy; disgust, repugnance, abhorrence.

dislodge ▶ verb **1** *replace any stones*

you dislodge =**displace**, knock out of place/position, move, shift; knock over, upset. **2** *economic sanctions failed to dislodge the dictator* =**remove**, force out, drive out, oust, eject, get rid of, evict, unseat, depose, topple.

disloyal ▶ adjective =**unfaithful**, false, untrue, inconstant; treacherous, subversive, seditious, unpatriotic, twofaced, double-dealing, double-crossing, deceitful; *informal* back-stabbing, two-timing; *literary* perfidious.

disloyalty ▶ noun =**unfaithfulness**, infidelity, inconstancy, faithlessness, betrayal; duplicity, double-dealing, treachery, treason, subversion, sedition; *informal* back-stabbing, two-timing; *literary* perfidy, perfidiousness.

dismal ▶ adjective **1** *a dismal look* =**gloomy**, glum, melancholy, morose, doleful, woebegone, forlorn, dejected, dispirited, downcast, despondent, disconsolate, miserable, sad, unhappy, sorrowful, wretched; *informal* fed up, down in the dumps/mouth. **2** *a dismal hall* =**dingy**, dim, dark, gloomy, dreary, drab, dull, bleak, cheerless, depressing, uninviting, unwelcoming. **3** (*informal*) *a dismal performance*. See POOR sense 2.
–OPPOSITES cheerful, bright.

dismantle ▶ verb =**take apart**, take to pieces/bits, pull to pieces, disassemble, break up, strip (down).
–OPPOSITES assemble, build.

dismay ▶ verb =**appal**, horrify, shock, shake (up); disconcert, take aback, alarm, unnerve, unsettle, throw off balance, discompose; disturb.
–OPPOSITES encourage, please.
▶ noun =**alarm**, shock, surprise, consternation, concern, perturbation, disquiet, discomposure.
–OPPOSITES pleasure, relief.

dismember ▶ verb =**cut up**, chop up, carve up, joint; pull apart, butcher.

dismiss ▶ verb **1** *the president dismissed five ministers* =**give someone their notice**, get rid of, discharge; lay off, make redundant; *informal* sack, give someone the sack, fire, boot out, give someone the boot/elbow/push, give someone their marching orders, show someone the door; *Brit. informal* give someone their cards; *Military* cashier. **2** *the guards were dismissed* =**send away**, let go. **3** *he dismissed all morbid thoughts* =**banish**, set aside, put out of one's mind; reject,

deny, repudiate, spurn.
−OPPOSITES engage.

dismissal ▸ noun **1** *the threat of dismissal* = **one's notice**, discharge; redundancy, laying off; *informal* the sack, sacking, firing, the boot, the axe, the elbow, one's marching orders; *Brit. informal* one's cards, the chop. **2** *a condescending dismissal* = **rejection**, repudiation, repulse, non-acceptance.
−OPPOSITES recruitment.

dismissive ▸ adjective = **contemptuous**, disdainful, scornful, sneering, disparaging; *informal* sniffy.
−OPPOSITES admiring.

dismount ▸ verb = **alight**, get off/down, climb off/down, hop off/down.

disobedient ▸ adjective = **insubordinate**, unruly, wayward, badly behaved, naughty, delinquent, troublesome, rebellious, defiant, mutinous, recalcitrant, wilful, intractable, obstreperous; *Brit. informal* bolshie.

disobey ▸ verb = **defy**, go against, flout, contravene, infringe, transgress, violate; disregard, ignore, pay no heed to.

disorder ▸ noun **1** *he hates disorder* = **untidiness**, disorderliness, mess, disarray, chaos, confusion; clutter, jumble; a muddle, a shambles. **2** *incidents of public disorder* = **unrest**, disturbance, disruption, upheaval, turmoil, mayhem, pandemonium; violence, fighting, rioting, lawlessness, anarchy; breach of the peace, fracas, rumpus, melee; *informal* aggro. **3** *a blood disorder* = **disease**, infection, complaint, condition, affliction, malady, sickness, illness, ailment, infirmity.
−OPPOSITES tidiness, peace.

disordered ▸ adjective **1** *her grey hair was disordered* = **untidy**, unkempt, messy, in a mess; disorganized, chaotic, confused, jumbled, muddled; *N. Amer. informal* mussed (up); *Brit. informal* shambolic. **2** *a disordered digestive system* = **dysfunctional**, disturbed, unsettled, unbalanced, upset, poorly.

disorderly ▸ adjective **1** *a disorderly desk* = **untidy**, disorganized, messy, cluttered; in disarray, in a mess, in a jumble, in a muddle, at sixes and sevens; *informal* like a bomb's hit it, higgledy-piggledy; *Brit. informal* shambolic. **2** *disorderly behaviour* = **unruly**, boisterous, rough, rowdy, wild, riotous; disruptive, troublesome, lawless.
−OPPOSITES tidy, peaceful.

disorganized ▸ adjective **1** *a disorganized tool box* = **disorderly**, disordered, jumbled, muddled, untidy, messy, chaotic, topsy-turvy, haphazard; in disorder, in disarray, in a mess, in a muddle, in a shambles; *informal* higgledy-piggledy; *Brit. informal* shambolic. **2** *muddled and disorganized* = **unmethodical**, unsystematic, undisciplined, badly organized, inefficient; haphazard, hit-or-miss, careless, sloppy, slapdash.
−OPPOSITES orderly.

disorientated, disoriented
▸ adjective = **confused**, bewildered, (all) at sea; lost, adrift, off-course, having lost one's bearings; *informal* not knowing whether one is coming or going.

disown ▸ verb = **reject**, cast off/aside, abandon, renounce, deny; turn one's back on, wash one's hands of, have nothing more to do with.

disparage ▸ verb = **belittle**, denigrate, deprecate, play down, trivialize; ridicule, deride, mock, scorn, scoff at, sneer at; run down, defame, discredit, speak badly of, cast aspersions on, impugn, vilify, traduce, criticize; *N. Amer.* slur; *informal* do down, pick holes in, knock, slam, pan, bad-mouth, pooh-pooh; *Brit. informal* rubbish, slate.
−OPPOSITES praise.

disparaging ▸ adjective = **derogatory**, deprecatory, denigratory, belittling; critical, scathing, negative, unfavourable, uncomplimentary, uncharitable; contemptuous, scornful, snide, disdainful; *informal* bitchy, catty.
−OPPOSITES complimentary.

disparate ▸ adjective = **contrasting**, different, differing, dissimilar; varying, various, diverse, diversified, heterogeneous, distinct, separate, divergent; *literary* divers.
−OPPOSITES homogeneous.

disparity ▸ noun = **discrepancy**, inconsistency, imbalance; variance, variation, divergence, gap, gulf; difference, dissimilarity, contrast.
−OPPOSITES similarity.

dispassionate ▸ adjective = **objective**, detached, neutral, disinterested, impartial, non-partisan, unbiased, unprejudiced; scientific, analytical.
−OPPOSITES biased.

dispatch ▸ verb **1** *all the messages were dispatched* = **send (off)**, post, mail, for-

ward. **2** *the business was dispatched in the morning* =**deal with**, finish, conclude, settle, discharge, perform; expedite, push through; *informal* make short work of. **3** *the good guy dispatched a host of villains* =**kill**, put to death; slaughter, butcher, massacre, wipe out, exterminate, eliminate; murder, assassinate, execute; *informal* bump off, do in, do away with, top, take out, blow away; *N. Amer. informal* ice, rub out, waste; *literary* slay.
▶ noun **1** *goods ready for dispatch* =**sending**, posting, mailing. **2** *the latest dispatch from the front* =**communication**, communiqué, bulletin, report, statement, letter, message; news, intelligence; *informal* memo, info, low-down; *literary* tidings.

dispel ▶ verb =**banish**, eliminate, drive away/off, get rid of; relieve, allay, ease, quell.

dispensable ▶ adjective =**expendable**, disposable, replaceable, inessential, non-essential; unnecessary, redundant, superfluous, surplus to requirements.

dispense ▶ verb **1** *servants dispensed the drinks* =**distribute**, pass round, hand out, dole out, dish out, share out. **2** *the soldiers dispensed summary justice* =**administer**, deliver, issue, discharge, deal out, mete out. **3** *dispensing medicines* =**prepare**, make up; supply, provide, sell.
■ **dispense with 1** *let's dispense with the formalities* =**waive**, omit, drop, leave out, forgo; do away with; *informal* give something a miss. **2** *he dispensed with his crutches* =**get rid of**, throw away/out, dispose of, discard; *informal* ditch, scrap, dump, chuck out/away, get shut of; *Brit. informal* get shot of.

disperse ▶ verb **1** *the crowd began to disperse | police dispersed the demonstrators* =**break up**, split up, disband, scatter, leave, go their separate ways; drive away/off, chase away. **2** *the fog finally dispersed* =**dissipate**, dissolve, melt away, fade away, clear, lift. **3** *seeds dispersed by birds* =**scatter**, disseminate, distribute, spread.
–OPPOSITES assemble, gather.

dispirited ▶ adjective =**disheartened**, discouraged, demoralized, downcast, low, low-spirited, dejected, downhearted, depressed, disconsolate; *informal* fed up.
–OPPOSITES heartened.

dispiriting ▶ adjective =**disheartening**, depressing, discouraging, daunting, demoralizing.

displace ▶ verb **1** *roof tiles displaced by gales* =**dislodge**, dislocate, move, shift; move out of place, knock out of place/position. **2** *English displaced the local language* =**replace**, take the place of, supplant, supersede.
–OPPOSITES replace.

display ▶ noun **1** *a display of dolls and puppets | a motorcycle display* =**exhibition**, exposition, array, arrangement, presentation, demonstration; spectacle, show, parade, pageant. **2** *his display of concern* =**manifestation**, expression, show.
▶ verb **1** *the Crown Jewels are displayed in London* =**exhibit**, show, put on show/view; arrange, array, present, lay out, set out. **2** *the play displays his many theatrical talents* =**show off**, parade, highlight, reveal; publicize, make known, call/draw attention to. **3** *she displayed a vein of sharp humour* =**manifest**, show evidence of, reveal; demonstrate, show; *formal* evince.
–OPPOSITES conceal.

displease ▶ verb =**annoy**, irritate, anger, irk, vex, pique, gall, nettle; put out, upset.

displeasure ▶ noun =**annoyance**, irritation, crossness, anger, vexation, pique; dissatisfaction, discontent, disgruntlement, disapproval.
–OPPOSITES satisfaction.

disposable ▶ adjective =**throwaway**, single-use.

disposal ▶ noun =**throwing away**, discarding, removal, collection, uplifting; *informal* dumping, ditching, chucking (out/away).

dispose ▶ verb *tradition would dispose us to keep going* =**incline**, encourage, persuade, predispose, make willing, prompt, lead, motivate; sway, influence.
■ **dispose of** =**throw away/out**, get rid of, discard, jettison, scrap; *informal* dump, ditch, chuck (out/away), get shut of; *Brit. informal* get shot of; *N. Amer. informal* trash.

disposed ▶ adjective **1** *they are philanthropically disposed* =**inclined**, predisposed, minded. **2** *we are not disposed to argue* =**willing**, inclined, prepared, ready, minded, in the mood.

disposition ▶ noun **1** *a nervous disposition* =**temperament**, nature, character, constitution, make-up, mentality. **2** *the* *disposition of the armed forces* =**arrangement**, positioning, placement, configuration; set-up, line-up, layout.

dispossess ▸ verb =**divest**, strip, rob, cheat out of, deprive; *informal* do out of.

disproportionate ▸ adjective =**out of proportion** to, not appropriate to, not commensurate with, too large/small for; inordinate, unreasonable, excessive, undue.

disprove ▸ verb =**refute**, prove false, rebut, falsify, debunk, negate, invalidate; *informal* shoot full of holes, blow out of the water.

disputable ▸ adjective =**debatable**, open to debate/question, arguable, contentious, contestable, moot, questionable, doubtful; *informal* iffy.

dispute ▸ noun **1** *a subject of dispute* =**debate**, discussion, disputation, argument, controversy, disagreement, dissension, conflict, friction, strife, discord. **2** *they have settled their dispute* =**quarrel**, argument, altercation, squabble, falling-out, disagreement, difference of opinion, clash, wrangle; *informal* tiff, spat, scrap; *Brit. informal* row, barney, ding-dong; *N. Amer. informal* rhubarb.
–OPPOSITES agreement.
▸ verb **1** *George disputed with him* =**debate**, discuss, exchange views; quarrel, argue, disagree, clash, fall out, wrangle, bicker, squabble; *informal* have words, have a tiff/spat. **2** *they disputed his proposals* =**challenge**, contest, question, call into question, impugn, quibble over, contradict, argue about, disagree with, take issue with.
–OPPOSITES accept.

disqualified ▸ adjective =**banned**, barred, debarred; ineligible.
–OPPOSITES allowed.

disquiet ▸ noun *grave public disquiet* =**unease**, uneasiness, worry, anxiety, anxiousness, concern; consternation, upset, angst; agitation, restlessness, fretfulness; *informal* jitteriness.
–OPPOSITES calm.
▸ verb *I was disquieted by the news* =**perturb**, agitate, upset, disturb, unnerve, unsettle, discompose, disconcert; make uneasy, worry, make anxious; trouble, concern, make fretful, make restless.

disregard ▸ verb *Annie disregarded the remark* =**ignore**, take no notice of, pay no attention/heed to; overlook, turn a blind eye to, turn a deaf ear to, shut one's eyes to, gloss over, brush off/aside, shrug off.
–OPPOSITES heed.
▸ noun *blithe disregard for the rules* =**indifference**, non-observance, inattention, heedlessness, neglect.
–OPPOSITES attention.

disrepair ▸ noun =**dilapidation**, decrepitude, shabbiness, ricketiness, collapse, ruin, neglect, disuse.

disreputable ▸ adjective =**bad**, unwholesome, villainous; unsavoury, slippery, seedy, sleazy; *informal* crooked, shady, shifty; *Brit. informal* dodgy.
–OPPOSITES respectable.

disrepute ▸ noun =**disgrace**, shame, dishonour, infamy, notoriety, ignominy, bad reputation.
–OPPOSITES honour.

disrespect ▸ noun **1** *disrespect for authority* =**contempt**, lack of respect, scorn, disregard, disdain. **2** *he meant no disrespect to anybody* =**discourtesy**, rudeness, impoliteness, incivility, ill/bad manners; insolence, impudence, impertinence.
–OPPOSITES esteem.

disrespectful ▸ adjective =**discourteous**, rude, impolite, uncivil, ill-mannered, bad-mannered; insolent, impudent, impertinent, cheeky, flippant, insubordinate.
–OPPOSITES polite.

disrupt ▸ verb =**throw into confusion/disorder/disarray**, cause confusion/turmoil in, play havoc with; disturb, interfere with, upset, unsettle; obstruct, impede, hold up, delay, interrupt.

disruptive ▸ adjective =**troublesome**, unruly, badly behaved, rowdy, disorderly, undisciplined, wild; unmanageable, uncontrollable, uncooperative, out of control/hand, obstreperous, truculent; *formal* refractory.
–OPPOSITES well behaved.

dissatisfaction ▸ noun =**discontent**, discontentment, disaffection, disquiet, unhappiness, disgruntlement, vexation, annoyance, irritation.

dissatisfied ▸ adjective =**discontented**, malcontent, unsatisfied, disappointed, disaffected, unhappy, displeased; disgruntled, aggrieved, vexed, annoyed, irritated.
–OPPOSITES contented.

d

dissect ▶ verb **1** *the body was dissected* =**cut up/open**, dismember. **2** *the text of the gospels was dissected* =**analyse**, examine, study, scrutinize, pore over, investigate, go over with a fine-tooth comb.

dissection ▶ noun **1** *the dissection of corpses* =**cutting up/open**, dismemberment; autopsy, post-mortem. **2** *a thorough dissection of their policies* =**analysis**, examination, study, scrutinization, investigation; evaluation, assessment.

disseminate ▶ verb =**spread**, circulate, distribute, disperse, promulgate, propagate, publicize, communicate, pass on, put about, make known.

dissent ▶ verb =**differ**, disagree, demur, fail to agree, be at variance/odds, take issue; protest, object.
−OPPOSITES agree, conform.
▶ noun =**disagreement**, difference of opinion, argument, dispute; disapproval, objection, protest, opposition; friction, strife.
−OPPOSITES agreement.

dissenter ▶ noun =**dissident**, objector, protester, disputant; rebel, renegade, maverick, independent; heretic.

dissertation ▶ noun =**essay**, thesis, treatise, paper, study, discourse, tract, monograph.

disservice ▶ noun =**unkindness**, bad/ill turn, disfavour; injury, harm, hurt, damage, wrong, injustice.
−OPPOSITES favour.

dissident ▶ noun =**dissenter**, objector, protester; rebel, revolutionary, subversive, agitator, insurgent, insurrectionist; refusenik.
−OPPOSITES conformist.
▶ adjective =**dissenting**, disagreeing; opposing, objecting, protesting, rebellious, rebelling, revolutionary, nonconformist.
−OPPOSITES conforming.

dissimilar ▶ adjective =**different**, differing, unalike, variant, diverse, divergent, heterogeneous, disparate, unrelated, distinct, contrasting.

dissimilarity ▶ noun =**difference(s)**, variance, diversity, heterogeneity, disparateness, disparity, distinctness, contrast, non-uniformity, divergence.

dissipate ▶ verb **1** *his anger dissipated* =**disappear**, vanish, evaporate, dissolve, melt away, melt into thin air, be

dispelled; disperse, scatter. **2** *he dissipated his fortune* =**squander**, fritter (away), misspend, waste, be prodigal with, spend recklessly/freely, spend like water; use up, consume, run through, go through; *informal* blow, splurge.

dissipated ▶ adjective =**dissolute**, debauched, decadent, intemperate, profligate, self-indulgent, wild, depraved; licentious, promiscuous; drunken.
−OPPOSITES ascetic.

dissipation ▶ noun **1** *drunken dissipation* =**debauchery**, decadence, dissoluteness, dissolution, intemperance, excess, profligacy, self-indulgence, wildness; depravity, degeneracy; licentiousness, promiscuity; drunkenness. **2** *the dissipation of our mineral wealth* =**squandering**, frittering (away), waste, misspending.
−OPPOSITES asceticism, consolidation.

dissociate ▶ verb *the word 'spiritual' has become dissociated from religion* =**separate**, detach, disconnect, sever, cut off, divorce; isolate, alienate.
−OPPOSITES relate.

dissociation ▶ noun =**separation**, disconnection, detachment, severance, divorce, split; segregation, division; *literary* sundering.
−OPPOSITES union.

dissolute ▶ adjective =**dissipated**, debauched, decadent, intemperate, profligate, self-indulgent, wild, depraved; licentious, promiscuous; drunken.
−OPPOSITES ascetic.

dissolution ▶ noun **1** *the dissolution of parliament* =**cessation**, conclusion, end, ending, termination, winding up/down, discontinuation, suspension, disbanding. **2** *a life of dissolution.* See DISSIPATION sense 1.

dissolve ▶ verb **1** *sugar dissolves in water* =**break down**; liquefy, deliquesce, disintegrate. **2** *his fears dissolved* =**disappear**, vanish, melt away, evaporate, disperse, dissipate; dwindle, fade (away), wither. **3** *the crowd dissolved* =**disperse**, disband, break up, scatter. **4** *the assembly was dissolved* =**disband**, bring to an end, end, terminate, discontinue, close down, wind up/down, suspend; adjourn. **5** *their marriage was dissolved* =**annul**, nullify, void, invalidate, revoke.

dissonant ▶ adjective =**inharmonious**, discordant, unmelodious, atonal,

off-key, cacophonous.
–OPPOSITES harmonious.

dissuade ▶ verb =**discourage**, deter, prevent, divert, stop; talk out of, persuade against, advise against, argue out of.
–OPPOSITES encourage.

distance ▶ noun **1** *they measured the distance* =**interval**, space, span, gap, extent; length, width, breadth, depth; range, reach. **2** *our perception of distance* =**remoteness**; closeness. **3** *a mix of warmth and distance* =**aloofness**, remoteness, detachment, unfriendliness; reserve, reticence, restraint, formality; *informal* stand-offishness.

distant ▶ adjective **1** *distant parts of the world* =**faraway**, far-off, far-flung, remote, out of the way, outlying. **2** *the distant past* =**remote**, bygone; ancient, prehistoric. **3** *half a mile distant* =**away**, off, apart. **4** *a distant memory* =**vague**, faint, dim, indistinct, unclear, indefinite, sketchy, hazy. **5** *a distant family connection* =**remote**, indirect, slight. **6** *father was always very distant* =**aloof**, reserved, remote, detached, unapproachable; withdrawn, taciturn, uncommunicative, undemonstrative, unforthcoming, unresponsive, unfriendly; *informal* standoffish. **7** *a distant look in his eyes* =**distracted**, absent, faraway, detached, vague.
–OPPOSITES near, close, recent.

distaste ▶ noun =**dislike**, aversion, disapproval, disapprobation, disdain, repugnance.
–OPPOSITES liking.

distasteful ▶ adjective =**unpleasant**, disagreeable, displeasing, undesirable; objectionable, offensive, unsavoury, unpalatable, obnoxious.
–OPPOSITES agreeable.

distended ▶ adjective =**swollen**, bloated, dilated, engorged, enlarged, inflated, expanded, extended, bulging, protuberant.

distil ▶ verb =**purify**, refine, filter, treat, process.

distinct ▶ adjective **1** *two distinct categories* =**discrete**, separate, different, unconnected; distinctive, contrasting. **2** *the tail has distinct black tips* =**clear**, well defined, unmistakable, easily distinguishable; recognizable, visible, obvious, pronounced, prominent, striking.

–OPPOSITES overlapping, indefinite.

distinction ▶ noun **1** *distinctions that we observed* =**difference**, contrast, variation; division, differentiation, dividing line, gulf, gap. **2** *a painter of distinction* =**importance**, significance, note, consequence; renown, prominence, eminence, pre-eminence, repute, reputation; merit, worth, greatness, excellence, quality. **3** *he had served with distinction* =**honour**, credit, excellence, merit.
–OPPOSITES similarity, mediocrity.

distinctive ▶ adjective =**distinguishing**, characteristic, typical, individual, particular, peculiar, unique, exclusive, special.
–OPPOSITES common.

distinctly ▶ adverb **1** *there's something distinctly odd about him* =**decidedly**, markedly, definitely; unmistakably, manifestly, patently; *Brit. informal* dead. **2** *Laura spoke quite distinctly* =**clearly**, plainly, intelligibly, audibly.

distinguish ▶ verb **1** *distinguishing reality from fantasy* =**differentiate**, tell apart, discriminate between, tell the difference between. **2** *he could distinguish shapes in the dark* =**discern**, see, perceive, make out; detect, recognize, identify. **3** *this is what distinguishes history from other disciplines* =**separate**, set apart, make distinctive, make different; single out, mark off, characterize.

distinguishable ▶ adjective =**discernible**, recognizable, identifiable, detectable.

distinguished ▶ adjective =**eminent**, famous, renowned, prominent, well known; esteemed, respected, illustrious, acclaimed, celebrated, great; notable, important, influential.
–OPPOSITES unknown, obscure.

distinguishing ▶ adjective =**distinctive**, differentiating, characteristic, typical, peculiar, singular, unique.

distorted ▶ adjective **1** *a distorted face* =**twisted**, warped, contorted, buckled, deformed, malformed, misshapen, disfigured, crooked, awry, out of shape. **2** *a distorted version* =**misrepresented**, perverted, twisted, falsified, misreported, misstated, garbled, inaccurate; biased, prejudiced, slanted, coloured, loaded, weighted.

distract ▶ verb =**divert**, sidetrack, draw away, disturb, put off.

distracted ▸ adjective =**preoccupied**, inattentive, vague, abstracted, absent-minded, faraway, in a world of one's own; bemused, confused, bewildered; troubled, harassed, worried; *informal* miles away, not with it.
−OPPOSITES attentive.

distracting ▸ adjective =**disturbing**, unsettling, intrusive, disconcerting, bothersome, off-putting.

distraction ▸ noun 1 *a distraction from the real issues* =**diversion**, interruption, disturbance, interference, hindrance. 2 *frivolous distractions* =**amusement**, entertainment, diversion, recreation, leisure pursuit.

distraught ▸ adjective =**worried**, upset, distressed, fraught; overcome, overwrought, beside oneself, out of one's mind, desperate, hysterical, worked up, at one's wits' end; *informal* in a state.

distress ▸ noun 1 *she concealed her distress* =**anguish**, suffering, pain, agony, torment, heartache, heartbreak; sorrow, sadness, unhappiness. 2 *a ship in distress* =**danger**, peril, difficulty, trouble, jeopardy, risk.
−OPPOSITES happiness, safety.
▸ verb *he was distressed by the trial* =**upset**, pain, make miserable; trouble, worry, bother, perturb, disturb, disquiet, agitate; *informal* cut up.
−OPPOSITES calm, please.

distressing ▸ adjective =**upsetting**, worrying, disturbing, disquieting, painful, traumatic, agonizing, harrowing; sad, saddening, heartbreaking, heart-rending.
−OPPOSITES comforting.

distribute ▸ verb 1 *the proceeds were distributed among his creditors* =**give out**, deal out, dole out, dish out, hand out/round; share out, divide out/up, parcel out. 2 *the newsletter is distributed free* =**circulate**, issue, hand out, deliver, disseminate. 3 *a hundred and thirty different species are distributed worldwide* =**disperse**, scatter, spread.
−OPPOSITES collect.

distribution ▸ noun 1 *the distribution of aid* =**giving out**, dealing out, doling out, handing out/round, issuing; allocation, sharing out, dividing up/out, parcelling out. 2 *the geographical distribution of plants* =**dispersal**, dissemination, spread, arrangement; placement, pos-

ition, location. 3 *centres of food distribution* =**supply**, delivery, dispersal, transportation. 4 *the statistical distribution of the problem* =**frequency**, prevalence, incidence, commonness.

district ▸ noun =**neighbourhood**, area, region, locality, locale, community, quarter, sector, zone, territory; ward, parish; *informal* neck of the woods.

distrust ▸ noun =**mistrust**, suspicion, wariness, chariness, lack of trust, lack of confidence; scepticism, doubt, doubtfulness, cynicism; misgivings, qualms, disbelief.
▸ verb =**mistrust**, be suspicious of, be wary/chary of, be leery of, regard with suspicion, suspect; be sceptical of, have doubts about, doubt, be unsure of/about, have misgivings about, wonder about.

disturb ▸ verb 1 *somewhere where we won't be disturbed* =**interrupt**, intrude on, butt in on, barge in on; distract, disrupt, bother, trouble, pester, harass; *informal* hassle. 2 *don't disturb his papers* =**move**, rearrange, mix up, interfere with, mess up, muddle. 3 *waters disturbed by winds* =**agitate**, churn up, stir up; cloud, muddy. 4 *he wasn't disturbed by the allegations* =**perturb**, trouble, concern, worry, upset; agitate, fluster, discomfit, disconcert, dismay, distress, discompose, unsettle, ruffle.

disturbance ▸ noun 1 *a disturbance to local residents* =**disruption**, distraction, interference; bother, trouble, inconvenience, upset, annoyance, irritation, intrusion; *informal* hassle. 2 *disturbances in the town centre* =**riot**, fracas, upheaval, brawl, street fight, melee, free-for-all, ruckus, rumpus; *informal* ruction. 3 *emotional disturbance* =**trouble**, perturbation, distress, worry, upset, agitation, discomposure, discomfiture.

disturbed ▸ adjective 1 *disturbed sleep* =**disrupted**, interrupted, fitful, intermittent, broken. 2 *disturbed children* =**troubled**, distressed, upset, distraught; unbalanced, unstable, disordered, dysfunctional, maladjusted, neurotic, unhinged, damaged; *informal* screwed up, mixed up.

disturbing ▸ adjective =**worrying**, troubling, upsetting, distressing, discomfiting, disconcerting, disquieting, unsettling, dismaying, alarming, frightening.

disunity ▸ noun =**disagreement**, dissent, dissension, argument, arguing, quarrelling, feuding; conflict, strife, friction, discord.

disuse ▸ noun =**non-use**, lack of use, neglect, abandonment, desertion, obsolescence.

disused ▸ adjective =**unused**, idle; abandoned, deserted, vacated, unoccupied, uninhabited.

ditch ▸ noun =**trench**, trough, channel, dyke, drain, gutter, gully, watercourse, conduit.

dither ▸ verb =**hesitate**, falter, waver, vacillate, change one's mind, be in two minds, be indecisive, be undecided; *Brit.* haver; *informal* shilly-shally, dilly-dally.

dive ▸ verb **1** *they dived into the clear water | the plane was diving towards the ground* =**plunge**, nosedive, jump head first, bellyflop; plummet, fall, drop, pitch. **2** *they dived for cover* =**leap**, jump, lunge, throw/fling oneself, go headlong, duck.
▸ noun **1** *a dive into the pool* =**plunge**, nosedive, jump, bellyflop; fall, drop, swoop, pitch. **2** *a sideways dive* =**lunge**, spring, jump, leap.

diverge ▸ verb **1** *the two roads diverged* =**separate**, part, fork, divide, split, bifurcate, go in different directions. **2** *areas where our views diverge* =**differ**, be different, be dissimilar; disagree, be at variance/odds, conflict, clash.
–OPPOSITES converge, agree.

divergence ▸ noun **1** *the divergence of the human and ape lineages* =**separation**, dividing, parting, forking, bifurcation. **2** *a marked political divergence* =**difference**, dissimilarity, variance, disparity; disagreement, incompatibility, mismatch.

divergent ▸ adjective =**differing**, varying, different, dissimilar, unalike, disparate, contrasting, contrastive; conflicting, incompatible, contradictory, at odds, at variance.
–OPPOSITES similar.

diverse ▸ adjective =**various**, sundry, manifold, multiple; varied, varying, miscellaneous, assorted, mixed, diversified, divergent, heterogeneous, a mixed bag of; different, differing, distinct, unlike, dissimilar; *literary* divers, myriad.

diversify ▸ verb **1** *farmers looking for ways to diversify* =**branch out**, expand; develop. **2** *a plan aimed at diversifying the economy* =**vary**, bring variety to; modify, alter, change, transform; expand, enlarge.

diversion ▸ noun **1** *the diversion of 19 rivers* =**re-routing**, redirection, deflection, deviation, divergence. **2** *traffic diversions* =**detour**, deviation, alternative route. **3** *the noise created a diversion* =**distraction**, disturbance, smokescreen; *informal* red herring. **4** *a city full of diversions* =**entertainment**, amusement, pastime, delight; fun, recreation, pleasure.

diversity ▸ noun =**variety**, miscellany, assortment, mixture, mix, melange, range, array, multiplicity; variation, variance, diverseness, diversification, heterogeneity, difference.
–OPPOSITES uniformity.

divert ▸ verb **1** *a plan to divert Siberia's rivers* =**re-route**, redirect, change the course of, deflect, channel. **2** *he diverted her from her studies* =**distract**, sidetrack, disturb, draw away, be a distraction, put off. **3** *the story diverted them* =**amuse**, entertain, distract, delight, enchant, interest, fascinate, absorb, engross, rivet, grip, hold the attention of.

diverting ▸ adjective =**entertaining**, amusing, enjoyable, pleasing, agreeable, delightful, appealing; interesting, fascinating, intriguing, absorbing, riveting, compelling; humorous, funny, witty, comical.
–OPPOSITES boring.

divest ▸ verb =**deprive**, strip, dispossess, rob, cheat/trick out of.

divide ▸ verb **1** *he divided his kingdom into four* =**split (up)**, cut up, carve up; dissect, bisect, halve, quarter. **2** *a curtain divided her cabin from the galley* =**separate**, segregate, partition, screen off, section off, split off. **3** *the stairs divide at the mezzanine* =**diverge**, separate, part, branch (off), fork, split (in two), bifurcate. **4** *Jack divided the cash* =**share out**, portion out, ration out, parcel out, deal out, dole out, dish out, distribute, dispense; *informal* divvy up. **5** *he aimed to divide his opponents* =**disunite**, drive apart, drive a wedge between, break up, split (up), set at variance/odds; separate, isolate, estrange, alienate. **6** *living things are divided into three categories* =**classify**, sort (out), categorize, order, group, arrange, grade, rank.
–OPPOSITES unify, join, converge.
▸ noun *the sectarian divide* =**breach**, gulf,

gap, split; borderline, boundary, dividing line.

dividend ▶ noun **1** *an annual dividend* =**share**, portion, premium, return, gain, profit; *informal* cut, rake-off; *Brit. informal* divvy. **2** *the research will produce dividends in the future* =**benefit**, advantage, gain; bonus.

divination ▶ noun =**fortune telling**, divining, prophecy, prediction, soothsaying; clairvoyance.

> [!NOTE] WORD LINKS
> *to do with divination:* **mantic, -mancy**

divine¹ ▶ adjective **1** *a divine being* =**godly**, angelic; heavenly, celestial, holy. **2** *divine worship* =**religious**, holy, sacred, sanctified, consecrated, blessed, devotional.
–OPPOSITES mortal, infernal.

divine² ▶ verb *Fergus divined how afraid she was* =**guess**, surmise, conjecture, deduce, infer; discern, intuit, perceive, recognize, see, realize, appreciate, understand, grasp, comprehend; *informal* figure (out); *Brit. informal* twig, suss.

divinity ▶ noun **1** *they denied Christ's divinity* =**divine nature**, divineness, godliness, deity, godhead. **2** *the study of divinity* =**theology**, religious studies, religion, scripture. **3** *a female divinity* =**deity**, god, goddess, divine being.

division ▶ noun **1** *the division of the island | cell division* =**dividing (up)**, breaking up, break-up, carving up, splitting, dissection, bisection; partitioning, separation, segregation. **2** *the division of his estates* =**sharing out**, dividing up, parcelling out, dishing out, allocation, allotment, apportionment; splitting up, carving up; *informal* divvying up. **3** *the division between nomadic and urban cultures* =**dividing line**, divide, boundary, borderline, border, demarcation line; gap, gulf. **4** *each class is divided into nine divisions* =**section**, subsection, subdivision, category, class, group, grouping, set. **5** *an independent division of the executive* =**department**, branch, arm, wing, sector, section, subsection, subdivision, subsidiary. **6** *the causes of social division* =**disunity**, disunion, conflict, discord, disagreement, alienation, isolation.

> [!NOTE] WORD LINKS
> *relating to division:* **schizo-**

divisive ▶ adjective =**alienating**, estranging, isolating, schismatic.
–OPPOSITES unifying.

divorce ▶ noun **1** *she wants a divorce* =**dissolution**, annulment, (official/judicial) separation. **2** *a growing divorce between the church and people* =**separation**, division, split, disunity, estrangement, alienation; schism, gulf, chasm.
–OPPOSITES marriage, unity.
▶ verb **1** *her parents have divorced* =**dissolve one's marriage**, annul one's marriage, end one's marriage, get a divorce. **2** *religion cannot be divorced from morality* =**separate**, disconnect, divide, dissociate, detach, isolate, alienate, set apart, cut off.

divulge ▶ verb =**disclose**, reveal, tell, communicate, pass on, publish, broadcast, proclaim; expose, uncover, make public, give away, let slip; *informal* spill the beans about, let on about.
–OPPOSITES conceal.

dizzy ▶ adjective =**giddy**, light-headed, faint, unsteady, shaky, muzzy, wobbly; *informal* woozy.

do ▶ verb **1** *she does most of the manual work* =**carry out**, undertake, discharge, execute, perform, accomplish, achieve; bring about, engineer; *informal* pull off; *formal* effectuate. **2** *they can do as they please* =**act**, behave, conduct oneself, acquit oneself. **3** *regular coffee will do* =**suffice**, be adequate, be satisfactory, fill/fit the bill, serve one's purpose, meet one's needs, suit one. **4** *the boys will do the dinner* =**prepare**, make, get ready, see to, arrange, organize, be responsible for, be in charge of; *informal* fix. **5** *the company is doing a new range | a portrait I am doing* =**make**, create, produce, work on, design, manufacture. **6** *each room was done in a different style* =**decorate**, furnish, deck out, finish; *Brit. informal* do out. **7** *her maid did her hair* =**style**, arrange, adjust, prepare; *informal* fix. **8** *I am doing a show to raise money* =**put on**, present, produce; perform in, act in, take part in, participate in. **9** *you've done me a favour* =**grant**, pay, render, give. **10** *show me how to do these equations* =**work out**, figure out, calculate; solve, resolve. **11** *she's doing archaeology* =**study**, read, learn, take a course in. **12** *he is doing well at college* =**get on/along**, progress, fare, manage, cope. **13** *he was doing 80mph* =**drive at**, travel at, move at. **14** *the cyclists do 30 miles per day* =**travel (over)**, journey,

cover, achieve, notch up, log; *informal* chalk up, clock up.
▸ **noun** (*Brit. informal*) *he invited us to a do* =**party**, reception, gathering, celebration, function, social event/occasion, social; *informal* bash, shindig; *Brit. informal* knees-up, beanfeast, bunfight; *Austral./ NZ informal* rage, jollo.
■ **do away with 1** *they want to do away with the old customs* =**abolish**, get rid of, discard, remove, eliminate, discontinue, stop, end, terminate, put an end/ stop to, dispense with, drop, abandon, give up; *informal* scrap, ditch, dump. **2** (*informal*) *she tried to do away with her husband. See* KILL *verb sense 1.*
■ **do something out** (*Brit. informal*) =**decorate**, furnish, ornament, deck out, trick out; *informal* do up.
■ **do something up 1** *she did her bootlace up* =**fasten**, tie (up), lace, knot; make fast, secure. **2** (*informal*) *he's had his house done up* =**renovate**, refurbish, refit, redecorate, decorate, revamp, make over, modernize, improve, spruce up, smarten up; *informal* give something a facelift; *N. Amer. informal* rehab.
■ **do without** =**forgo**, dispense with, abstain from, refrain from, eschew, give up, cut out, renounce, manage without; *formal* forswear.

docile ▸ **adjective** =**compliant**, obedient, pliant, submissive, deferential, unassertive, cooperative, amenable, accommodating, biddable.
−OPPOSITES disobedient, wilful.

dock[1] ▸ **noun** *his boat was moored at the dock* =**harbour**, marina, port; wharf, quay, pier, jetty, landing stage
▸ **verb** *the ship docked* =**moor**, berth, put in, tie up, anchor.

dock[2] ▸ **verb 1** *they docked the money from his salary* =**deduct**, subtract, remove, debit, take off/away; *informal* knock off. **2** *workers had their pay docked* =**reduce**, cut, decrease. **3** *the dog's tail was docked* =**cut off**, cut short, shorten, crop, lop; remove, amputate, detach, sever, chop off, take off.

docket (*Brit.*) ▸ **noun** =**document**, chit, coupon, voucher, certificate, counterfoil, bill, receipt, ticket; *Brit. informal* chitty.

doctor ▸ **noun** =**physician**, clinician; general practitioner, GP, consultant, registrar; *Brit.* house officer, houseman; *N. Amer.* intern, extern; *informal* doc,

medic, medico; *Brit. informal* quack.
▸ **verb 1** *he doctored Stephen's drink* =**adulterate**, tamper with, lace; *informal* spike, dope. **2** *the reports have been doctored* =**falsify**, tamper with, interfere with, alter, change; forge, fake; *Brit. informal* fiddle (with).

> WORD LINKS

related prefix: **iatro-**

doctrinaire ▸ **adjective** =**dogmatic**, rigid, inflexible, uncompromising; authoritarian, intolerant, fanatical, zealous, extreme.

doctrine ▸ **noun** =**creed**, credo, dogma, belief, teaching, ideology; tenet, maxim, canon, principle, precept.

document ▸ **noun** =**paper**, certificate, deed, contract, agreement.
▸ **verb** =**record**, register, report, log, chronicle, put on record, write down; detail, note, describe.

documentary ▸ **adjective 1** *documentary evidence* =**recorded**, documented, registered, written, chronicled, archived, on record/paper, in writing. **2** *a documentary film* =**factual**, nonfictional.

doddery ▸ **adjective** =**tottering**, staggering, shuffling, shambling, shaky, unsteady, wobbly; feeble, frail, weak.

dodge ▸ **verb 1** *she dodged into a telephone booth* =**dart**, bolt, dive, slip. **2** *he could easily dodge the two coppers* =**elude**, evade, avoid, escape, run away from, lose, shake (off); *informal* give someone the slip. **3** *the minister tried to dodge the debate* =**avoid**, evade, get out of, back out of, sidestep; *N. Amer.* end-run; *informal* duck, wriggle out of; *Austral./NZ informal* duck-shove.
▸ **noun 1** *a dodge to the right* =**dart**, dive, lunge, leap, spring. **2** *a clever dodge | a tax dodge* =**ruse**, ploy, scheme, tactic, stratagem, subterfuge, trick, hoax, wile, cheat, deception, blind; swindle, fraud; *informal* scam, con (trick); *Brit. informal* wheeze; *N. Amer. informal* bunco, grift; *Austral. informal* lurk, rort.

dodgy ▸ **adjective** (*Brit. informal*) **1** *a dodgy second-hand car salesman. See* DISHONEST. **2** *dodgy champagne* =**second-rate**, third-rate, substandard, low-quality; poor, cheap; *N. Amer.* cheapjack; *Brit. informal* ropy, grotty.

dog ▸ **noun** *she went for a walk with her dog*

=**hound**, canine, mongrel; pup, puppy; *informal* doggy, pooch; *Austral. informal* bitzer.

▶ **verb** *the scheme was dogged by bad weather* =**plague**, beset, bedevil, beleaguer, blight, trouble.

> **WORD LINKS**
>
> relating to dogs: **canine**
> male: **dog**
> female: **bitch**
> young: **pup, puppy**
> collective noun: **pack**
> fear of dogs: **cynophobia**

dogged ▶ adjective =**tenacious**, determined, resolute, resolved, purposeful, persistent, persevering, single-minded, tireless; strong-willed, steadfast, staunch.
−OPPOSITES half-hearted.

dogma ▶ noun =**teaching**, belief, tenet, principle, precept, maxim, article of faith, canon; creed, credo, doctrine, ideology.

dogmatic ▶ adjective =**opinionated**, assertive, insistent, emphatic, adamant, doctrinaire, authoritarian, imperious, dictatorial, uncompromising, unyielding, inflexible, rigid.

dogsbody ▶ noun *(Brit. informal)* =**drudge**, menial (worker), factotum, servant, slave, lackey, minion, man/girl Friday; *informal* gofer; *Brit. informal* skivvy; *N. Amer. informal* peon.

doing ▶ noun **1** *the doing of the act constitutes the offence* =**performance**, performing, carrying out, execution, implementation, implementing, achievement, accomplishment, realization, completion. **2** *an account of his doings in Paris* =**exploit**, activity, act, action, deed, feat, achievement, accomplishment. **3** *that would take some doing* =**effort**, exertion, (hard) work, application, labour, toil, struggle.

doldrums ▶ plural noun =**depression**, melancholy, gloom, downheartedness, dejection, despondency, low spirits, despair; inertia, apathy, listlessness; *N. Amer.* blahs; *informal* blues.
■ **in the doldrums** =**inactive**, quiet, slow, slack, sluggish, stagnant.

dole ■ **dole something out** =**deal out**, share out, divide up, allocate, distribute, dispense, hand out, give out, dish out/up; *informal* divvy up.

doleful ▶ adjective =**mournful**, woeful, sorrowful, sad, unhappy, depressed, gloomy, melancholy, miserable, forlorn, wretched, woebegone, despondent, dejected, disconsolate, downcast, downhearted; *informal* blue, down in the mouth/dumps.
−OPPOSITES cheerful.

dollop ▶ noun *(informal)* =**blob**, gobbet, lump, ball; *informal* glob; *Brit. informal* gob, wodge.

dolt ▶ noun. See IDIOT.

doltish ▶ adjective. See STUPID sense 1.

domain ▶ noun **1** *they extended their domain* =**realm**, kingdom, empire, dominion, province, territory, land. **2** *the domain of art* =**field**, area, sphere, discipline, province, world.

domestic ▶ adjective **1** *domestic commitments* =**family**, home, household. **2** *she was not at all domestic* =**domesticated**, homely. **3** *small domestic animals* =**domesticated**, tame, pet, household. **4** *the domestic car industry* =**national**, state, home, internal. **5** *domestic plants* =**native**, indigenous.
▶ noun *they worked as domestics* =**servant**, home help, maid, housemaid, cleaner, housekeeper; *Brit. dated* charwoman, charlady, char; *Brit. informal* daily (help).

domesticated ▶ adjective **1** *domesticated animals* =**tame**, tamed, pet, domestic, trained. **2** *domesticated crops* =**cultivated**, naturalized. **3** *I'm quite domesticated really* =**home-loving**, homely.
−OPPOSITES wild.

dominance ▶ noun =**supremacy**, superiority, ascendancy, pre-eminence, domination, dominion, mastery, power, authority, rule, command, control, sway.

dominant ▶ adjective **1** *the dominant classes* =**presiding**, ruling, governing, controlling, commanding, ascendant, supreme, authoritative. **2** *he has a dominant personality* =**assertive**, authoritative, forceful, domineering, commanding, controlling, pushy. **3** *the dominant issues in psychology* =**main**, principal, prime, premier, chief, foremost, primary, predominant, paramount, prominent; central, key, crucial, core; *informal* number-one.
−OPPOSITES subservient.

dominate ▶ verb **1** *the Russians dominated Iran in the nineteenth century* =**control**, influence, exercise control over, command, be in command of, be in charge of, rule, govern, direct, have ascendancy over, have mastery over; be in the driver's seat, be at the helm; *N. Amer. informal* have someone in one's hip pocket; *literary* sway. **2** *the Puritan work ethic still dominates* =**predominate**, prevail, reign, be prevalent, be paramount, be pre-eminent. **3** *the village is dominated by the viaduct* =**overlook**, command, tower above/over, loom over.

domination ▶ noun =**rule**, government, sovereignty, control, command, authority, power, dominion, dominance, mastery, supremacy, superiority, ascendancy, sway.

domineering ▶ adjective =**overbearing**, authoritarian, imperious, high-handed, autocratic; masterful, dictatorial, despotic, oppressive, strict, harsh; *informal* bossy.

dominion ▶ noun =**supremacy**, ascendancy, dominance, domination, superiority, predominance, pre-eminence, hegemony, authority, mastery, control, command, power, sway, rule, government, jurisdiction, sovereignty.

don[1] ▶ noun *an Oxford don* =**university teacher**, (university) lecturer, fellow, professor, reader, academic, scholar.

don[2] ▶ verb *he donned an overcoat* =**put on**, get dressed in, dress (oneself) in, get into, slip into/on.

donate ▶ verb =**give**, give/make a donation of, contribute, make a contribution of, gift, subscribe, grant, bestow; *informal* chip in, pitch in; *Brit. informal* stump up; *N. Amer. informal* kick in.

donation ▶ noun =**gift**, contribution, subscription, present, handout, grant, offering.

done ▶ adjective **1** *the job is done* =**finished**, ended, concluded, complete, completed, accomplished, achieved, fulfilled, discharged, executed; *informal* wrapped up, sewn up, polished off. **2** *is the meat done?* =**cooked (through)**, ready. **3** *those days are done* =**over (and done with)**, at an end, finished, ended, concluded, terminated, no more, dead, gone, in the past. **4** *(informal) that's just not done* =**proper**, seemly, decent, respectable, right, correct, in order, fitting, appropriate, acceptable, the done thing. –OPPOSITES incomplete, underdone, ongoing.

donnish ▶ adjective =**scholarly**, stu-

dious, academic, bookish, intellectual, learned, highbrow.

donor ▶ noun =**giver**, contributor, benefactor, benefactress, subscriber; supporter, backer, patron, sponsor.

doom ▶ noun =**destruction**, downfall, ruin, ruination; extinction, annihilation, death, nemesis.
▶ verb =**destine**, fate, predestine, preordain, mean; condemn, sentence.

doomed ▶ adjective =**ill-fated**, ill-starred, cursed, jinxed, damned.

door ▶ noun =**doorway**, portal, opening, entrance, entry, exit.
■ **out of doors** =**outside**, outdoors, in/into the open air, alfresco.

dope ▶ noun *(informal) he was caught smuggling dope* =**(illegal) drugs**, narcotics; cannabis, heroin.
▶ verb **1** *the horse was doped* =**drug**, tamper with, interfere with; sedate; *Brit. informal* nobble. **2** *they doped his drink* =**add drugs to**, tamper with, adulterate, contaminate, lace; *informal* spike, doctor.

dopey ▶ adjective *(informal)* **1** *feeling a bit dopey* =**stupefied**, confused, muddled, befuddled, disorientated, groggy, muzzy; *informal* woozy, not with it. **2** *he's really dopey. See* STUPID *sense* 1.
–OPPOSITES alert, intelligent.

dormant ▶ adjective =**sleeping**, resting; **inactive**, passive, inert, latent, idle, quiescent.
–OPPOSITES awake, active.

dose ▶ noun =**measure**, portion, dosage; *informal* hit.
▶ verb =**drug**, fill (up); pump, prime, load, stuff, cram.

dossier ▶ noun =**file**, report, case history; account, notes, document(s), documentation, data, information, evidence.

dot ▶ noun *a pattern of tiny dots* =**spot**, speck, fleck, speckle; full stop, decimal point.
▶ verb **1** *spots of rain dotted his shirt* =**spot**, fleck, mark, spatter. **2** *restaurants are dotted around the site* =**scatter**, pepper, sprinkle, strew; spread, disperse, distribute.
■ **on the dot** *(informal)* =**precisely**, exactly, sharp, prompt, dead on, on the stroke of …; *informal* bang on; *N. Amer. informal* on the button, on the nose.

dote ■ **dote on** =**adore**, love dearly, be devoted to, idolize, treasure, cherish, worship, hold dear.

doting ▸ adjective =**adoring**, loving, besotted, infatuated; affectionate, fond, devoted, caring.

double ▸ adjective *a double garage | double yellow lines* =**dual**, duplex, twin, binary, duplicate, in pairs, coupled, twofold.
–OPPOSITES single.
▸ adverb *we had to pay double* =**twice (over)**, twice the amount, doubly.
▸ noun **1** *if it's not her, it's her double* =**look-alike**, twin, clone, duplicate, exact likeness, replica, copy, facsimile, Doppelgänger; *informal* spitting image, dead ringer, dead spit. **2** *she used a double for the stunts* =**stand-in**, substitute.
▸ verb **1** *they doubled his salary* =**multiply by two**, increase twofold. **2** *the bottom sheet had been doubled up* =**fold (back/up/down/over/under)**, turn back/up/down/over/under, tuck back/up/down/under.
■ **at/on the double** =**very quickly**, as fast as one's legs can carry one, at a run, at a gallop, fast, swiftly, rapidly, speedily, at (full) speed, at full tilt, as fast as possible; *informal* double quick, like (greased) lightning, like the wind, like a scalded cat, like a bat out of hell; *Brit. informal* like the clappers, at a rate of knots; *N. Amer. informal* lickety-split.

WORD LINKS

related prefixes: **bi-, di-, diplo-**

double-cross ▸ verb =**betray**, cheat, defraud, trick, hoodwink, mislead, deceive, swindle, be disloyal to, be unfaithful to, play false; *informal* do the dirty on, sell down the river.

double-dealing ▸ noun =**duplicity**, treachery, betrayal, double-crossing, unfaithfulness, untrustworthiness, infidelity, bad faith, disloyalty, fraud, underhandedness, cheating, dishonesty, deceit, deceitfulness, deception, falseness; *informal* crookedness.
–OPPOSITES honesty.

doubly ▸ adverb =**twice as**, even more, especially, extra.

doubt ▸ noun **1** *there was some doubt as to the caller's identity* =**uncertainty**, confusion; controversy; queries, questions. **2** *a weak leader racked by doubt* =**indecision**, hesitation, uncertainty, insecurity, unease, apprehension; hesitancy, vacillation, irresolution. **3** *there is doubt about their motives* =**scepticism**, distrust, mistrust, suspicion, cynicism, uneasiness, apprehension, wariness, chariness; reservations, misgivings, suspicions.
–OPPOSITES certainty, conviction.
▸ verb *they doubted my story* =**disbelieve**, distrust, mistrust, suspect, have doubts about, be suspicious of, have misgivings about, feel uneasy about, feel apprehensive about, query, question, challenge.
–OPPOSITES trust.
■ **in doubt 1** *the issue was in doubt* =**doubtful**, uncertain, open to question, unconfirmed, unknown, undecided, unresolved, in the balance, up in the air; *informal* iffy. **2** *if you are in doubt, ask for advice* =**irresolute**, hesitant, ambivalent; doubtful, unsure, uncertain, in two minds, undecided, in a quandary/dilemma.
■ **no doubt** =**doubtless**, undoubtedly, indubitably, without (a) doubt; unquestionably, undeniably, incontrovertibly, irrefutably; unequivocally, clearly, plainly, obviously, patently.

doubter ▸ noun =**sceptic**, doubting Thomas, non-believer, unbeliever, disbeliever, cynic, scoffer, dissenter.
–OPPOSITES believer.

doubtful ▸ adjective **1** *I was doubtful about going* =**hesitant**, in doubt, unsure, uncertain, in two minds, in a quandary/dilemma. **2** *it is doubtful whether he will come* =**in doubt**, uncertain, open to question, unsure, debatable, up in the air. **3** *the whole trip is looking rather doubtful* =**unlikely**, improbable, dubious. **4** *they are doubtful of the methods used* =**distrustful**, mistrustful, suspicious, wary, chary, leery, apprehensive; sceptical, unsure, ambivalent, dubious. **5** *this decision is of doubtful validity* =**questionable**, arguable, debatable, controversial, contentious; *informal* iffy; *Brit. informal* dodgy.
–OPPOSITES confident, certain, probable, trusting.

doubtless ▸ adverb =**undoubtedly**, indubitably, no doubt; unquestionably, indisputably, undeniably, incontrovertibly, irrefutably; certainly, surely, of course.

dour ▸ adjective =**stern**, unsmiling, unfriendly, severe, forbidding, gruff, surly, grim, sullen, austere, stony.
–OPPOSITES cheerful, friendly.

douse ▸ verb **1** *a mob doused the thieves with petrol* =**drench**, soak, saturate, wet, slosh. **2** *a guard doused the flames* =**ex-**

tinguish, put out, quench, smother, dampen down.

dovetail ▸ verb =fit in, go together, be consistent, match, conform, harmonize, be in tune, correspond; *informal* square; *N. Amer. informal* jibe.

dowdy ▸ adjective =unfashionable, frumpy, old-fashioned, inelegant, shabby, frowzy; *Brit. informal* mumsy; *Austral./NZ informal* daggy.
−OPPOSITES fashionable.

down¹ ▸ adverb 1 *they went down in the lift* =downwards, downstairs. 2 *she fell down* =to the ground/floor, over.
−OPPOSITES up.
▸ preposition 1 *the lift plunged down the shaft* =to the bottom of. 2 *I walked down the street* =along, to the other end of, from one end of … to the other. 3 *down the years* =throughout, through, during.
▸ adjective 1 *I'm feeling a bit down* =depressed, sad, unhappy, melancholy, miserable, wretched, sorrowful, gloomy, dejected, downhearted, despondent, dispirited, low; *informal* blue, down in the dumps/mouth, fed up. 2 *the computer is down* =not working, inoperative, malfunctioning, out of order, broken; not in service, out of action, out of commission; *informal* conked out, bust, (gone) kaput; *N. Amer. informal* on the fritz.
−OPPOSITES elated, working.
▸ verb *(informal)* 1 *he struck Slater, downing him* =knock down/over, knock to the ground, bring down, topple; *informal* deck, floor, flatten. 2 *he downed his beer* =drink (up/down), gulp (down), guzzle, quaff, drain, toss off, slug, finish off; *informal* sink, knock back, put away; *N. Amer. informal* scarf (down/up), snarf (down/up).

down² ▸ noun *goose down* =feathers, hair; fluff, fuzz, floss, lint.

down and out ▸ adjective =destitute, poverty-stricken, impoverished, penniless, insolvent; needy, in straitened circumstances, distressed, badly off; homeless, on the streets, vagrant, sleeping rough; *informal* hard up, (flat) broke, strapped (for cash), without a brass farthing, without two pennies to rub together; *Brit. informal* stony broke, skint; *N. Amer. informal* without a red cent, on skid row.
−OPPOSITES wealthy.
▸ noun (**down-and-out**) beggar, homeless person, vagrant, tramp, derelict, vagabond; *N. Amer.* hobo; *Austral.* bagman;

informal have-not, bag lady; *Brit. informal* dosser; *N. Amer. informal* bum.

down at heel ▸ adjective 1 *the resort looks down at heel* =run down, dilapidated, neglected, uncared-for; seedy, insalubrious, squalid, slummy, wretched; *informal* scruffy, scuzzy; *Brit. informal* grotty; *N. Amer. informal* shacky. 2 *a down-at-heel labourer* =scruffy, shabby, ragged, tattered, mangy, sorry; unkempt, bedraggled, dishevelled, ungroomed, seedy, untidy; *informal* tatty, scuzzy, grungy; *Brit. informal* grotty; *N. Amer. informal* raggedy.
−OPPOSITES smart.

downbeat ▸ adjective =pessimistic, gloomy, negative, defeatist, cynical, bleak, fatalistic, dark, black; despairing, despondent, depressing, demoralizing, hopeless, melancholy, glum.

downcast ▸ adjective =despondent, disheartened, discouraged, dispirited, downhearted, crestfallen, down, low, disconsolate, despairing; sad, melancholy, gloomy, glum, morose, doleful, dismal, woebegone, miserable, depressed, dejected; *informal* blue, down in the mouth/dumps.
−OPPOSITES elated.

downfall ▸ noun =undoing, ruin, ruination; defeat, conquest, overthrow; nemesis, destruction, annihilation; elimination; end, collapse, fall, crash, failure; Waterloo.
−OPPOSITES rise.

downgrade ▸ verb 1 *plans to downgrade three workers* =demote, reduce/lower in rank; relegate. 2 *I won't downgrade their achievement* =disparage, denigrate, detract from, run down, belittle; *informal* bad-mouth.
−OPPOSITES promote, praise.

downhearted ▸ adjective =despondent, disheartened, discouraged, dispirited, downcast, crestfallen, down, low, disconsolate, wretched; melancholy, gloomy, glum, doleful, dismal, woebegone, miserable, depressed, dejected, sorrowful, sad; *informal* blue, down in the mouth/dumps.
−OPPOSITES elated.

downmarket ▸ adjective *(Brit.)* =cheap, cheap and nasty, inferior; low-class, lowbrow, unsophisticated, rough, insalubrious; *informal* tacky, rubbishy, dumbed down.

downpour ▸ noun =rainstorm, cloudburst, deluge; thunderstorm; torrential/pouring rain.

downright ▶ adjective *downright lies*
=**complete**, total, absolute, utter, thorough, out-and-out, outright, sheer, arrant, pure, real, veritable, categorical,
unmitigated, unadulterated, unalloyed,
unequivocal; *Brit. informal* proper.
▶ adverb *that's downright dangerous* =**thoroughly**, utterly, positively, profoundly,
really, completely, totally, entirely; in
every respect, through and through;
informal plain, just.

downside ▶ noun =**drawback**, disadvantage, snag, stumbling block, catch,
pitfall, fly in the ointment; handicap,
limitation, trouble, difficulty, problem,
complication, nuisance; hindrance;
weak spot/point; *informal* minus, flip
side.
−OPPOSITES advantage.

down-to-earth ▶ adjective =**practical**, sensible, realistic, matter-of-fact,
rational, logical, balanced, sober, pragmatic, level-headed, commonsensical,
sane.
−OPPOSITES idealistic.

downtrodden ▶ adjective
=**oppressed**, persecuted, repressed, tyrannized, crushed, enslaved, exploited,
victimized, bullied; disadvantaged,
underprivileged, powerless, helpless;
abused, maltreated.

downy ▶ adjective =**soft**, velvety,
smooth, fleecy, fluffy, fuzzy, feathery,
furry, woolly, silky.

doze ▶ verb =**catnap**, nap, drowse, sleep
lightly, rest; *informal* snooze, snatch forty
winks, get some shut-eye; *Brit. informal*
kip; *N. Amer. informal* catch some Zs.
▶ noun =**catnap**, nap, siesta, rest; *informal*
snooze, forty winks; *Brit. informal* kip, zizz.
■ **doze off** =**fall asleep**, go to sleep,
drop off; *informal* nod off, drift off; *N. Amer.
informal* sack out, zone out.

dozy ▶ adjective **1** *feeling really dozy*
=**drowsy**, sleepy, half asleep, heavy-
eyed, somnolent; weary, tired, fatigued;
N. Amer. logy; *informal* dopey, yawny. **2** *the
dozy woman at reception* =**slow-witted**,
unobservant, stupid, forgetful, useless,
hopeless, incompetent; *informal* dopey.

drab ▶ adjective **1** *a drab interior* =**colourless**, grey, dull, washed out, muted;
dingy, dreary, dismal, cheerless,
gloomy, sombre. **2** *a drab existence* =**uninteresting**, dull, boring, tedious, monotonous, dry, dreary; unexciting, unin-

spiring, insipid, flat, stale, wishy-washy,
colourless; lame, tired, sterile, anaemic,
barren, tame; run-of-the-mill, mediocre,
nondescript, characterless, mundane,
unremarkable, humdrum.
−OPPOSITES bright, cheerful, interesting.

draconian ▶ adjective =**harsh**, severe,
strict, extreme, drastic, stringent,
tough; cruel, oppressive, ruthless, relentless, punitive; authoritarian, despotic, tyrannical, repressive; *Brit.* swingeing.
−OPPOSITES lenient.

draft ▶ noun **1** *the first draft of his speech*
=**version**, attempt, effort. **2** *a draft of
the building* =**plan**, blueprint, design,
diagram, drawing, sketch, map, layout,
representation. **3** *a banker's draft*
=**cheque**, order, money order, bill of
exchange.

drag ▶ verb **1** *she dragged the chair backwards* =**haul**, pull, tug, heave, lug, draw;
trail. **2** *the day dragged* =**become tedious**, pass slowly, creep by, hang heavy,
wear on, go on too long, go on and on.
▶ noun **1** *the drag from the parachute* =**pull**,
resistance, tug. **2** *(informal) work can be a
drag* =**bore**, nuisance, bother, trouble,
pest, annoyance, trial; *informal* pain (in
the neck), bind, headache, hassle.
■ **drag on** =**persist**, continue, go on,
carry on, extend, run on, endure, prevail.
■ **drag something out** =**prolong**, protract, draw out, spin out, string out,
extend, lengthen, carry on, keep going,
continue.

drain ▶ verb **1** *a valve for draining the
tank* =**empty (out)**, void, clear (out),
evacuate, unload. **2** *drain off any surplus
liquid* =**draw off**, extract, withdraw,
remove, siphon off, pour out, pour
off; bleed, tap, void, filter, discharge.
3 *the water drained away to the sea* =**flow**,
pour, trickle, stream, run, rush, gush,
flood, surge; leak, ooze, seep, dribble,
issue, filter, bleed, leach. **4** *more people
would just drain our resources* =**use up**,
exhaust, deplete, consume, expend, get
through, sap, strain, tax; milk, bleed.
5 *he drained his drink* =**drink (up/down)**,
gulp (down), guzzle, quaff, swallow,
finish off, toss off, slug; *informal* sink,
down, swig, swill (down), polish off,
knock back, put away.
−OPPOSITES fill.
▶ noun **1** *the drain filled with water* =**sewer**,

channel, conduit, ditch, culvert, duct, pipe, gutter. **2** *a drain on the battery* =**strain**, pressure, burden, load, tax, demand.

drama ▸ noun **1** *a television drama* =**play**, show, piece, (theatrical) work, dramatization. **2** *he is studying drama* =**acting**, the theatre, the stage, the performing arts, dramatic art, stagecraft, performance. **3** *she liked to create a drama* =**incident**, scene, spectacle, crisis; excitement, thrill, sensation; disturbance, row, commotion, turmoil; dramatics, theatrics, histrionics.

dramatic ▸ adjective **1** *dramatic art* =**theatrical**, theatric, thespian, stage, dramaturgical. **2** *a dramatic increase* =**considerable**, substantial; significant, remarkable, extraordinary, exceptional, phenomenal; *informal* tidy. **3** *there were dramatic scenes in the city* =**exciting**, stirring, action-packed, sensational, spectacular; startling, unexpected, tense, gripping, riveting, thrilling, hair-raising; rousing, lively, electrifying, impassioned, moving. **4** *dramatic headlands* =**striking**, impressive, imposing, spectacular, breathtaking, dazzling, sensational, awesome, awe-inspiring, remarkable, outstanding, incredible, phenomenal. **5** *a dramatic gesture* =**exaggerated**, theatrical, ostentatious, actressy, stagy, showy, melodramatic, overdone, histrionic, affected, mannered, artificial; *informal* hammy, ham. –OPPOSITES insignificant, boring, restrained.

dramatist ▸ noun =**playwright**, scriptwriter, screenwriter.

dramatize ▸ verb **1** *the novel was dramatized for television* =**turn into a play/film**, adapt (for the stage/screen). **2** *the tabloids dramatized the event* =**exaggerate**, overdo, overstate, hyperbolize, magnify, amplify, inflate; sensationalize, embroider, colour, aggrandize, embellish, elaborate; *informal* blow up (out of all proportion).

drape ▸ verb **1** *she draped a shawl round her* =**wrap**, wind, swathe, sling, hang. **2** *the chair was draped with blankets* =**cover**, envelop, swathe, shroud, deck, festoon, overlay, cloak, wind, enfold. **3** *he draped one leg over the arm of his chair* =**dangle**, hang, suspend, droop, drop, swing.

drastic ▸ adjective =**extreme**, serious,

desperate, radical, far-reaching, momentous, substantial; heavy, severe, harsh, rigorous; oppressive, draconian. –OPPOSITES moderate.

draught ▸ noun **1** *the draught made Robin shiver* =**current of air**, rush of air; waft, wind, breeze, gust, puff, blast. **2** *a deep draught of beer* =**gulp**, drink, swallow, mouthful, slug; *informal* swig, swill.

draw ▸ verb **1** *he drew the house* =**sketch**, make a drawing (of), delineate, outline, rough out, illustrate, render, represent, trace; portray, depict. **2** *she drew her chair in to the table* =**pull**, haul, drag, tug, heave, lug, trail, tow; *informal* yank. **3** *the train drew into the station* =**move**, go, come, proceed, progress, travel, advance, pass, drive; inch, roll, glide, cruise; sweep; back. **4** *she drew the curtains* –**close**, shut, pull to; open, part, pull back, pull open, fling open. **5** *he drew some fluid off the knee joint* =**drain**, extract, withdraw, remove, suck, pump, siphon, bleed, tap. **6** *he drew his gun* =**pull out**, take out, produce, fish out, extract, withdraw; unsheathe. **7** *I drew £50 out of the bank* =**withdraw**, take out. **8** *she was drawing huge audiences* =**attract**, win, capture, catch, engage, lure, entice, bring in. **9** *what conclusion can we draw?* =**deduce**, infer, conclude, derive, gather, glean.
▸ noun **1** *she won the Christmas draw* =**raffle**, lottery, sweepstake, sweep, tombola, ballot; *N. Amer.* lotto. **2** *the match ended in a draw* =**tie**, dead heat, stalemate. **3** *the draw of central London* =**attraction**, lure, allure, pull, appeal, glamour, enticement, temptation, charm, seduction, fascination, magnetism.
■ **draw on** =**call on**, have recourse to, avail oneself of, turn to, look to, fall back on, rely on, exploit, use, employ, utilize, bring into play.
■ **draw something out 1** *he drew out a gun. See* DRAW *verb sense 6.* **2** *they always drew their parting out* =**prolong**, protract, drag out, spin out, string out, extend, lengthen; *Brit. informal* make a meal of.
■ **draw up** =**stop**, pull up, halt, come to a standstill, brake, park; arrive.
■ **draw something up** =**compose**, formulate, frame, write down, draft, prepare, think up, devise, work out; create, invent, design.

drawback ▸ noun =**disadvantage**, snag, downside, stumbling block, catch,

hitch, pitfall, fly in the ointment; weak spot/point, weakness, imperfection; handicap, limitation, trouble, difficulty, problem, complication; hindrance, obstacle, impediment, obstruction, inconvenience, discouragement; *Brit.* spanner in the works; *informal* minus, hiccup.
–OPPOSITES benefit.

drawing ▶ noun =**sketch**, picture, illustration, representation, portrayal, depiction, composition, study; diagram, outline, design, plan.

WORD LINKS

to do with drawing: **graphic**

drawn ▶ adjective *she looked pale and drawn* =**pinched**, haggard, drained, wan, hollow-cheeked; fatigued, tired, exhausted; tense, stressed, strained, worried, anxious, harassed; *informal* hassled.

dread ▶ verb *I used to dread going to school* =**fear**, be afraid of, worry about, be anxious about, have forebodings about; be terrified by, tremble/shudder at.
▶ noun *she was filled with dread* =**fear**, apprehension, trepidation, anxiety, worry, concern, foreboding, disquiet, unease, angst; fright, panic, alarm; terror, horror; *informal* the jitters, the heebie-jeebies.
–OPPOSITES confidence.

dreadful ▶ adjective **1** *a dreadful accident* =**terrible**, frightful, horrible, grim, awful, dire; horrifying, shocking, distressing, appalling, harrowing; ghastly, fearful, horrendous; tragic, calamitous; *formal* grievous. **2** *a dreadful meal* =**frightful**; shocking, awful, abysmal, atrocious, disgraceful, deplorable; *informal* pathetic, woeful, crummy, rotten, sorry, third-rate, lousy, ropy, God-awful; *Brit. informal* duff, chronic, rubbish. **3** *you're a dreadful flirt* =**outrageous**, shocking; inordinate, immoderate, unrestrained; incorrigible.
–OPPOSITES pleasant, agreeable.

dreadfully ▶ adverb **1** *I'm dreadfully hungry* =**extremely**, very, really, exceedingly, tremendously, exceptionally, extraordinarily; decidedly; *N. English* right; *informal* terrifically, terribly, desperately, awfully, devilishly, mega, seriously, majorly; *Brit. informal* jolly, ever so, dead, well; *N. Amer. informal* real, mighty, awful; *informal, dated* frightfully. **2** *she missed James dreadfully* =**very much**,

much, lots, a lot, a great deal, intensely, desperately; *informal* loads, tons. **3** *the company performed dreadfully* =**terribly**, awfully, atrociously, appallingly, abominably, poorly; *informal* abysmally, pitifully, diabolically.

dream ▶ noun **1** *she went around in a dream* =**daydream**, reverie, trance, daze, stupor, haze; *Scottish* dwam. **2** *he realized his childhood dream* =**ambition**, aspiration, hope; goal, aim, objective, grail, intention, intent, target; desire, wish, yearning; daydream, fantasy. **3** *he's an absolute dream* =**delight**, joy, marvel, wonder, gem, treasure; beauty, vision.
▶ verb **1** *I dreamed of making the Olympic team* =**fantasize about**, daydream about; wish for, hope for, long for, yearn for, hanker after, set one's heart on; aspire to, aim for, set one's sights on. **2** *she's always dreaming* =**daydream**, be in a trance, be lost in thought, be preoccupied, be abstracted, stare into space, be in cloud cuckoo land; muse. **3** *I wouldn't dream of being late* =**think**, consider, contemplate, conceive.
▶ adjective *his dream home* =**ideal**, perfect, ultimate, fantasy.
■ **dream something up** =**think up**, invent, concoct, devise, hatch, contrive, create, work out, come up with; *informal* cook up.

WORD LINKS

relating to dreams: **oneiric**
interpretation of dreams: **oneiromancy**
fear of dreams: **oneirophobia**

dreamer ▶ noun =**fantasist**, daydreamer; romantic, sentimentalist, idealist, wishful thinker, Don Quixote; Utopian, visionary.
–OPPOSITES realist.

dreamlike ▶ adjective =**ethereal**, phantasmagorical, trance-like; surreal; nightmarish, Kafkaesque; hazy, shadowy, faint, indistinct, unclear.

dreamy ▶ adjective *a dreamy expression* =**daydreaming**, dreaming; pensive, thoughtful, reflective, meditative, ruminative; preoccupied, distracted, rapt, inattentive, vague, absorbed, absent-minded, with one's head in the clouds, in a world of one's own; *informal* miles away.
–OPPOSITES alert.

dreary ▶ adjective =**dull**, uninteresting,

flat, tedious, wearisome, boring, unexciting, unstimulating, uninspiring,
soul-destroying; humdrum, monotonous, uneventful, unremarkable, featureless.
−OPPOSITES exciting.

dregs ▸ plural noun **1** *the dregs from a
bottle of wine* =**sediment**, deposit, residue, sludge, lees, grounds, settlings;
remains. **2** *the dregs of humanity* =**scum**,
refuse, riff-raff, outcasts, deadbeats; the
underclass, the untouchables, the lowest of the low, the great unwashed, the
hoi polloi; *informal* trash.
−OPPOSITES elite.

drench ▸ verb =**soak**, saturate, wet
through, permeate, douse, souse; steep,
bathe.

dress ▸ verb **1** *he dressed quickly* =**put
on clothes**, clothe oneself, get dressed.
2 *she was dressed in a suit* =**clothe**, attire,
garb, deck out, trick out/up, costume,
array, robe; *informal* get up, doll up. **3** *she
enjoyed dressing the tree* =**decorate**, trim,
deck, adorn, ornament, embellish,
beautify, prettify; festoon, garland.
4 *they dressed his wounds* =**bandage**,
cover, bind, wrap.
▸ noun **1** *a long blue dress* =**frock**, gown,
robe, shift. **2** *full evening dress* =**clothes**,
clothing, garments, attire; costume,
outfit, ensemble, garb, turnout; *informal*
gear, get-up, togs, duds, glad rags; *Brit.
informal* clobber; *N. Amer. informal* threads;
formal apparel; *archaic* raiment.

> **WORD LINKS**
>
> to do with dress: **sartorial**

dressmaker ▸ noun =**tailor**, seamstress, needlewoman; outfitter, costumier, clothier; couturier, designer; *dated*
modiste.

dressy ▸ adjective =**smart**, formal;
elaborate, ornate; stylish, elegant, chic,
fashionable; *informal* snappy, snazzy,
natty, trendy.
−OPPOSITES casual.

dribble ▸ verb **1** *the baby started to dribble* =**drool**, slaver, slobber, salivate,
drivel, water at the mouth; *Scottish & Irish*
slabber. **2** *rainwater dribbled down her face*
=**trickle**, drip, fall, run, drizzle; ooze,
seep.
▸ noun **1** *there was dribble on his chin* =**saliva**,
spittle, spit, slaver, slobber, drool. **2** *a
dribble of sweat* =**trickle**, drip, stream;
drop, splash, fleck.

dried ▸ adjective =**dehydrated**, desiccated, dry, dried up.

drift ▸ verb **1** *his raft drifted down the river*
=**be carried**, be borne; float, bob, waft,
meander. **2** *the guests drifted away* =**wander**, meander, stray, potter, dawdle,
float; *Brit. informal* mooch. **3** *don't allow
your attention to drift* =**stray**, digress,
wander, deviate, diverge, veer. **4** *snow
drifted over the path* =**pile up**, bank up,
heap up, accumulate, gather, amass.
▸ noun **1** *a drift from the country to urban
areas* =**movement**, shift, flow, transfer,
gravitation. **2** *the pilot had not noticed any
drift* =**deviation**, movement, digression.
3 *he caught the drift of her thoughts* =**gist**,
essence, meaning, sense, substance,
significance; thrust, import, tenor; implication, intention; direction. **4** *a drift
of deep snow* =**pile**, heap, bank, mound,
mass, accumulation

drifter ▸ noun =**wanderer**, traveller,
transient, roamer, tramp, vagabond,
vagrant; *N. Amer.* hobo.

drill ▸ noun **1** *military drill* =**training**, instruction, coaching, teaching; (physical)
exercises, workout; *informal* square-
bashing. **2** *Estelle knew the drill* =**procedure**, routine, practice, programme,
schedule; method, system.
▸ verb **1** *drill the piece of wood* =**bore a
hole in**, make a hole in; bore, pierce,
puncture, perforate. **2** *a sergeant drilling
new recruits* =**train**, instruct, coach,
teach, discipline; exercise, put someone
through their paces. **3** *his mother had
drilled politeness into him* =**instil**, hammer, drive, drum, din, implant, ingrain;
teach, indoctrinate, brainwash.

drink ▸ verb **1** *she drank her coffee* =**swallow**, gulp (down), quaff, guzzle, sup;
imbibe, sip, consume, drain, toss off,
slug; *informal* swig, down, knock back,
put away, neck, sink, swill. **2** *he never
drank* =**drink alcohol**, tipple, indulge,
carouse; *informal* hit the bottle, booze,
have one over the eight, get tanked up,
go on a bender; *Brit. informal* bevvy; *N. Amer.
informal* bend one's elbow.
▸ noun **1** *he took a sip of his drink* =**beverage**, dram, nightcap, nip, tot; pint; *Brit.
informal* bevvy; *humorous* libation. **2** *she
turned to drink* =**alcohol**, (intoxicating)
liquor, alcoholic drink; *informal* booze,
hooch, the hard stuff, firewater, rotgut,
moonshine, the bottle, the sauce, grog,
Dutch courage. **3** *she took a drink of her
wine* =**swallow**, gulp, sip, mouthful,

draught, slug; *informal* swig, swill. **4** *a drink of orange juice* =**glass**, cup, mug.
■ **drink something in** =**absorb**, assimilate, digest, ingest, take in; be rapt in, be lost in, be fascinated by, pay close attention to.

WORD LINKS

fear of drink: **potophobia**

drinker ▶ noun =**drunkard**, drunk, inebriate, tippler; alcoholic, dipsomaniac; *informal* boozer, soak, lush, wino, alky, sponge, barfly; *Austral./NZ informal* hophead.
−OPPOSITES teetotaller.

drip ▶ verb **1** *there was a tap dripping* =**dribble**, leak. **2** *sweat dripped from his chin* =**drop**, dribble, trickle, run, splash, plop; leak, emanate, issue.
▶ noun **1** *a bucket to catch the drips* =**drop**, dribble, spot, trickle, splash. **2** *(informal) that drip who fancies you* =**weakling**, ninny, milksop, namby-pamby, crybaby, softie, doormat; *informal* wimp, weed, sissy; *Brit. informal* wet, big girl's blouse; *N. Amer. informal* pantywaist, pussy, wuss.

drive ▶ verb **1** *I can't drive a car* =**operate**, handle, manage; pilot, steer; sail, fly; work. **2** *he drove to the police station* =**travel (by car)**, motor; go. **3** *I'll drive you to the airport* =**run**, chauffeur, give someone a lift, take, ferry, transport, convey, carry. **4** *the engine drives the front wheels* =**power**, propel, move, push. **5** *he drove a nail into the boot* =**hammer**, screw, ram, sink, plunge, thrust, propel, knock. **6** *a desperate mother driven to crime* =**force**, compel, prompt, precipitate; oblige, coerce, pressure, goad, spur, prod. **7** *he drove his staff extremely hard* =**work**, push, tax, exert.
▶ noun **1** *an afternoon drive* =**excursion**, outing, trip, jaunt, tour; ride, run, journey; *informal* spin. **2** *the house has a long drive* =**driveway**, approach, access road. **3** *sexual drive* =**urge**, appetite, desire, need; impulse, instinct. **4** *she lacked the drive to succeed* =**motivation**, ambition, single-mindedness, will power, dedication, doggedness, tenacity; enthusiasm, zeal, commitment, aggression, spirit; energy, vigour, verve, vitality, pep; *informal* get-up-and-go. **5** *an anti-corruption drive* =**campaign**, crusade, movement, effort, push, appeal, initiative. **6** *(Brit.) a whist drive* =**tournament**, competition,

contest, event, match.
■ **drive at** =**suggest**, imply, hint at, allude to, intimate, insinuate, indicate; refer to, mean, intend; *informal* get at.

drivel ▶ noun *he was talking complete drivel* =**nonsense**, twaddle, claptrap, balderdash, gibberish, rubbish, mumbo-jumbo; *N. Amer.* garbage; *informal* rot, poppycock, phooey, piffle, tripe, bosh, bull, hogwash, baloney; *Brit. informal* cobblers, codswallop, waffle, tosh, double Dutch; *N. Amer. informal* flapdoodle, bushwa; *informal, dated* bunkum.
▶ verb *you always drivel on* =**talk nonsense**, talk rubbish, babble, ramble, gibber, blather, blether, prattle, gabble; *Brit. informal* waffle, witter.

driver ▶ noun =**motorist**, chauffeur; pilot, operator.

drizzle ▶ noun *a drizzle of olive oil* =**trickle**, dribble, drip, stream, rivulet; sprinkle, sprinkling.
▶ verb *drizzle the cream over the fruit* =**trickle**, drip, dribble, pour, splash, sprinkle.

droll ▶ adjective =**funny**, humorous, amusing, comic, comical, mirthful, hilarious; zany, quirky; jocular, light-hearted, witty, whimsical, wry, tongue-in-cheek; *informal* waggish, wacky, side-splitting, rib-tickling.
−OPPOSITES serious.

drone ▶ verb **1** *a plane droned overhead* =**hum**, buzz, whirr, vibrate, murmur, rumble, purr. **2** *he droned on about right and wrong* =**go on and on**, talk at length; pontificate, hold forth; *informal* spout, sound off.
▶ noun **1** *the drone of aircraft taking off* =**hum**, buzz, whirr, vibration, murmur, purr.

drool ▶ verb *his mouth was drooling* =**salivate**, dribble, slaver, slobber; *Scottish & Irish* slabber.
▶ noun *a fine trickle of drool* =**saliva**, spit, spittle, dribble, slaver, slobber.

droop ▶ verb **1** *the dog's tail is drooping* =**hang (down)**, dangle, sag, flop; wilt, sink, slump, drop. **2** *his eyelids were drooping* =**close**, shut, fall.

droopy ▶ adjective =**hanging (down)**, dangling, falling, dropping, draped; bent, bowed, stooping; sagging, flopping, wilting.

drop ▶ verb **1** *Eric dropped the box* =**let**

fall, let go of, lose one's grip on; release, unhand, relinquish. **2** *water drops from the cave roof* =**drip**, fall, dribble, trickle, run, leak. **3** *a plane dropped out of the sky* =**fall**, descend, plunge, plummet, dive, nosedive, tumble. **4** *she dropped to her knees* =**fall**, sink, collapse, slump, tumble. **5** *(informal) I was dropping with exhaustion* =**collapse**, faint, pass out, black out, swoon, keel over; *informal* flake out, conk out. **6** *the track dropped from the ridge* =**slope downwards**, slant downwards, descend, go down, fall away, sink, dip. **7** *the exchange rate dropped* =**decrease**, lessen, reduce, diminish, depreciate; fall, decline, dwindle, sink, slump, plunge, plummet. **8** *pupils can drop history if they wish* =**give up**; discontinue, end, stop, cease, halt; abandon, forgo, relinquish, dispense with, have done with; *informal* pack in, quit. **9** *he was dropped from the team* =**exclude**, discard, expel, throw out, leave out; dismiss, discharge, let go; *informal* boot out, kick out, turf out. **10** *he dropped his unsuitable friends* =**abandon**, desert; renounce, disown, turn one's back on, wash one's hands of; reject, give up, cast off; neglect, shun; *literary* forsake. **11** *he dropped all reference to compensation* =**omit**, leave out, eliminate, take out, miss out, delete, cut, erase. **12** *the taxi dropped her at the station* =**deliver**, bring, take, convey, carry, transport; leave, unload. **13** *drop the gun on the ground* =**put**, place, deposit, set, lay, leave; *informal* pop, plonk. **14** *the team has yet to drop a point* =**lose**, concede, give away.
 –OPPOSITES lift, rise, increase, keep, win.

▶ noun **1** *a drop of water* =**droplet**, blob, globule, bead; *informal* glob. **2** *it needs a drop of oil* =**small amount**, little, bit, dash, spot; dribble, sprinkle, trickle, splash; dab, speck, smattering, sprinkling, modicum; *informal* smidgen, tad. **3** *a small drop in profits* =**decrease**, reduction, decline, fall-off, downturn, slump; cut, cutback, curtailment; depreciation. **4** *I walked to the edge of the drop* =**cliff**, abyss, chasm, gorge, gully, precipice; slope, descent, incline.
 –OPPOSITES increase.

■ **drop off 1** *trade dropped off sharply.* See DROP verb sense 7. **2** *she kept dropping off* =**fall asleep**, doze (off), nap, catnap, drowse; *informal* nod off, drift off, snooze, take forty winks.

■ **drop out of** *he dropped out of university*

=**leave**; *informal* quit, pack in, jack in.

dropout ▶ noun =**nonconformist**, hippy, beatnik, bohemian, free spirit, rebel; idler, layabout, loafer; *informal* oddball, deadbeat, waster.

droppings ▶ plural noun =**excrement**, excreta, faeces, stools, dung, ordure, manure; *informal* poo.

dross ▶ noun =**rubbish**, junk; debris, chaff, detritus, flotsam and jetsam; *N. Amer.* garbage, trash; *informal* dreck.

drowsy ▶ adjective =**sleepy**, dozy, heavy-eyed, groggy, somnolent; tired, weary, fatigued, exhausted, yawning, nodding; lethargic, sluggish, torpid, listless, languid; *informal* snoozy, dopey, yawny, dead beat, all in, dog-tired; *Brit. informal* knackered.
 –OPPOSITES alert.

drudgery ▶ noun =**hard work**, menial work, donkey work, toil, labour; chores; *informal* skivvying; *Brit. informal* graft; *Austral./NZ informal* (hard) yakka.

drug ▶ noun **1** *drugs prescribed by doctors* =**medicine**, medication; remedy, cure, antidote. **2** *she was under the influence of drugs* =**narcotic**, stimulant, hallucinogen; *informal* dope, gear; recreational drug.
▶ verb **1** *he was drugged* =**anaesthetize**; poison; knock out; *informal* dope. **2** *she drugged his coffee* =**tamper with**, lace, poison; *informal* dope, spike, doctor.

> ### WORD LINKS
> *relating to drugs:* **pharmaceutical**
> *branch of medicine to do with drugs:*
>   **pharmacology**
> *fear of drugs:* **pharmacophobia**
> *shop selling drugs: Brit.* **pharmacy, chemist's;** *N. Amer.* **drugstore**
> *seller of drugs: Brit.* **pharmacist, chemist;** *N. Amer.* **druggist**

drugged ▶ adjective =**stupefied**, insensible, befuddled; delirious, hallucinating, narcotized; anaesthetized, knocked out; *informal* stoned, high (as a kite), doped, tripping, spaced out, wasted, wrecked, off one's head/trolley/face, out of it.
 –OPPOSITES sober.

drum ▶ noun *a drum of radioactive waste* =**canister**, barrel, cylinder, tank, bin, can; container.
▶ verb **1** *she drummed her fingers on the desk*

=**tap**, beat, rap, thud, thump; tattoo; thrum. **2** *the rules were drummed into us at school* =**instil**, drive, din, hammer, drill, implant, ingrain, inculcate.

■ **drum someone out** =**expel**, dismiss, throw out, oust; drive out, get rid of; exclude, banish; *informal* give someone the boot, boot out, kick out, give someone their marching orders, give someone the push, show someone the door, send packing; *Military* cashier.

■ **drum something up** =**round up**, gather, collect; summon, attract; canvass, solicit, petition.

> WORD LINKS
>
> *player of drums:* **drummer, timpanist, percussionist**

drunk ▶ adjective =**intoxicated**, inebriated, drunken, incapable, tipsy, the worse for drink, under the influence; *informal* tight, merry, in one's cups, three sheets to the wind, pie-eyed, plastered, smashed, wrecked, wasted, sloshed, soused, sozzled, blotto, stewed, pickled, tanked (up), off one's face, out of one's head, ratted; *Brit. informal* legless, bevvied, paralytic, Brahms and Liszt, half cut, out of it, bladdered, trolleyed, squiffy, tiddly; *N. Amer. informal* loaded, trashed, juiced, sauced, out of one's gourd, in the bag, zoned; *euphemistic* tired and emotional.
–OPPOSITES sober.
▶ noun =**drunkard**, inebriate, drinker, tippler, sot; heavy drinker, problem drinker, alcoholic, dipsomaniac; *informal* boozer, soak, lush, wino, alky, sponge, barfly, tosspot; *Austral./NZ informal* hophead, metho.
–OPPOSITES teetotaller.

drunken ▶ adjective **1** *a drunken driver.* See DRUNK adjective. **2** *a drunken all-night party* =**debauched**, dissipated, unrestrained, uninhibited, abandoned; *informal* boozy.

drunkenness ▶ noun =**intoxication**, inebriation, tipsiness; intemperance, overindulgence, debauchery; heavy drinking, alcoholism, alcohol abuse, dipsomania.

dry ▶ adjective **1** *the dry desert* =**arid**, parched, scorched, baked; waterless, moistureless, rainless; dehydrated, desiccated, thirsty. **2** *dry leaves* =**parched**, dried, withered, shrivelled, wilted, wiz-

ened; crisp, crispy, brittle; dehydrated, desiccated. **3** *a dry debate* =**dull**, uninteresting, boring, unexciting, tedious, tiresome, wearisome, dreary, monotonous; unimaginative, sterile, flat, bland, lacklustre, prosaic, humdrum, mundane; *informal* deadly. **4** *a dry sense of humour* =**wry**, subtle, laconic, sharp; ironic, sardonic, sarcastic, cynical; satirical.
–OPPOSITES wet, moist, fresh, lively.
▶ verb **1** *the sun dried the ground* =**parch**, scorch, bake; dehydrate, desiccate. **2** *dry the leaves completely* =**dehydrate**, desiccate; wither, shrivel. **3** *he dried the dishes* =**towel**, rub, wipe; mop up, blot up, soak up, absorb. **4** *she dried her eyes* =**wipe**, dab. **5** *methods of drying meat* =**desiccate**, dehydrate; preserve.
–OPPOSITES moisten.

■ **dry up 1** *(informal) he dried up and didn't say another thing* =**stop speaking**, stop talking, fall silent, shut up; forget one's words. **2** *investment may dry up* =**dwindle**, subside, peter out, wane, taper off, ebb, come to a halt/end, run out, give out, disappear, vanish.

dual ▶ adjective =**double**, twofold, binary; twin, matching, paired, coupled.
–OPPOSITES single.

dub ▶ verb *he was dubbed 'the world's sexiest man'* =**nickname**, call, name, label, christen, term, tag, entitle, style; designate, characterize, nominate.

dubious ▶ adjective **1** *I was rather dubious about the idea* =**doubtful**, uncertain, unsure, hesitant; sceptical, suspicious; *informal* iffy. **2** *a dubious businessman* =**suspicious**, suspect, untrustworthy, unreliable, questionable; *informal* shady, fishy; *Brit. informal* dodgy.
–OPPOSITES certain, trustworthy.

duck¹ ▶ noun

> WORD LINKS
>
> *male:* **drake**
> *female:* **duck**
> *young:* **duckling**

duck² ▶ verb **1** *he ducked behind the wall* =**bob down**, bend (down), stoop (down), crouch (down), squat (down), hunch down, hunker down. **2** *she was ducked in the river* =**dip**, dunk, plunge, immerse, submerge, lower, sink. **3** *(informal) they cannot duck the issue forever* =**shirk**, dodge, evade, avoid, elude, escape, back out of, shun, sidestep, bypass, circumvent; *informal* cop out of, get out of, wriggle out of, funk; *Austral./NZ informal* duck-shove.

duct ▸ noun =**tube**, channel, canal, vessel; conduit; pipe, outlet, inlet, flue, shaft, vent.

dud (*informal*) ▸ noun *their new product is a dud* =**failure**, flop, let-down, disappointment; *Brit.* damp squib; *informal* washout, lemon, no-hoper, non-starter, dead loss, lead balloon; *N. Amer. informal* clinker.
–OPPOSITES success.

▸ adjective **1** *a dud computer* =**defective**, faulty, unsound, inoperative, broken, malfunctioning; *informal* bust, busted, kaput, conked out; *Brit. informal* duff, knackered. **2** *a dud £50 note* =**counterfeit**, fraudulent, forged, fake, false, bogus; invalid, worthless; *informal* phoney.
–OPPOSITES sound, genuine.

due ▸ adjective **1** *their fees were due* =**owing**, owed, payable; outstanding, overdue, unpaid, unsettled, undischarged; *N. Amer.* delinquent. **2** *the chancellor's statement is due today* =**expected**, anticipated, scheduled for, awaited; required. **3** *the respect due to a great artist* =**deserved by**, merited by, warranted by; appropriate to, fit for, fitting for, right for, proper to. **4** *he drove without due care* =**proper**, correct, rightful, suitable, appropriate, apt; adequate, sufficient, enough, satisfactory, requisite.

▸ noun *members have paid their dues* =**fee**, subscription, charge; payment, contribution.

▸ adverb *he hiked due north* =**directly**, straight, exactly, precisely, dead.
■ **due to 1** *her death was due to an infection* =**attributable to**, caused by, ascribed to, because of, put down to. **2** *the train was cancelled due to staff shortages* =**because of**, owing to, on account of, as a consequence of, as a result of, thanks to, in view of; *formal* by reason of.

duel ▸ noun **1** *he was killed in a duel* =**single combat**, fight, confrontation, head-to-head; *informal* face-off, shoot-out. **2** *a snooker duel* =**contest**, match, game, meet, encounter, clash.

dulcet ▸ adjective =**sweet**, soothing, mellow, honeyed, mellifluous, pleasant, agreeable; melodious, melodic, lilting, lyrical, silvery, golden.
–OPPOSITES harsh.

dull ▸ adjective **1** *a dull novel* =**uninteresting**, boring, tedious, monotonous, unimaginative, uneventful; characterless, featureless, colourless, lifeless, insipid, unexciting, uninspiring, flat, bland, dry, stale, tired, banal, lacklustre, stodgy, dreary, humdrum, mundane; mind-numbing, soul-destroying, wearisome, tiring, tiresome, irksome; *informal* deadly, not up to much; *Brit. informal* samey; *N. Amer. informal* dullsville. **2** *a dull morning* =**overcast**, cloudy, gloomy, dark, dismal, dreary, sombre, grey, murky, sunless. **3** *dull colours* =**drab**, dreary, sombre, dark, subdued, muted, faded, washed out, muddy. **4** *a dull sound* =**muffled**, muted, quiet, soft, faint, indistinct, stifled. **5** *the chisel became dull* =**blunt**, worn. **6** *a rather dull child* =**unintelligent**, stupid, slow, witless, vacuous, empty-headed, brainless, mindless, foolish, idiotic; *informal* dense, dim, half-witted, thick, dumb, dopey, dozy, slow on the uptake, wooden-headed, fat-headed.
–OPPOSITES interesting, bright, loud, resonant, sharp, clever.

▸ verb **1** *the pain was dulled by drugs* =**lessen**, decrease, diminish, reduce, dampen, blunt, deaden, allay, ease, soothe, assuage, alleviate. **2** *sleep dulled his mind* =**numb**, benumb, deaden, desensitize, stupefy, daze. **3** *the sombre atmosphere dulled her spirit* =**dampen**, lower, depress, crush, sap, extinguish, smother, stifle.
–OPPOSITES intensify, enliven, enhance, brighten.

duly ▸ adverb **1** *the document was duly signed* =**properly**, correctly, appropriately, suitably, fittingly. **2** *he duly arrived to collect Alice* =**at the right time**, on time, punctually.

dumb ▸ adjective **1** *she stood dumb while he shouted* =**mute**, speechless, tongue-tied, silent, at a loss for words; taciturn, uncommunicative, untalkative, tight-lipped, close-mouthed. **2** (*informal*) *he is not as dumb as you'd think* =**stupid**, unintelligent, ignorant, dense, brainless, mindless, foolish, slow, dull, simple, empty-headed, vacuous, vapid, idiotic, half-baked; *informal* thick, dim, moronic, cretinous, dopey, dozy, thickheaded, wooden-headed, fat-headed, birdbrained, pea-brained; *Brit. informal* daft.
–OPPOSITES clever.

dumbfound ▸ verb =astonish, astound, amaze, stagger, surprise, startle, stun, confound, stupefy, daze, nonplus, take aback, stop someone in their tracks, strike dumb, leave open-mouthed, leave aghast; *informal* flabbergast, floor, knock sideways, bowl over; *Brit. informal* knock for six.

dumbfounded ▸ adjective =astonished, astounded, amazed, staggered, startled, stunned, confounded, nonplussed, stupefied, dazed, dumbstruck, open-mouthed, speechless, thunderstruck; taken aback, disconcerted; *informal* flabbergasted, flummoxed; *Brit. informal* gobsmacked.

dummy ▸ noun *a shop-window dummy* =mannequin, model, figure.
▸ adjective *a dummy attack* =simulated, practice, trial, mock, make-believe; *informal* pretend, phoney.
–OPPOSITES real.

dump ▸ noun **1** *take the rubbish to the dump* =tip, rubbish dump, rubbish heap, dumping ground; dustheap, slag heap. **2** *(informal) the house is a dump* =hovel, shack, slum; mess; *informal* hole, pigsty.
▸ verb **1** *he dumped his bag on the table* =put down, set down, deposit, place, shove, unload; drop, throw down; *informal* stick, park, plonk; *Brit. informal* bung; *N. Amer. informal* plunk. **2** *they will dump asbestos at the site* =dispose of, get rid of, throw away/out, discard, bin, jettison; *informal* ditch, junk. **3** *(informal) he dumped her* =abandon, desert, leave, jilt, break up with, finish with, throw over; *informal* walk out on, drop, ditch, chuck, give someone the elbow; *Brit. informal* give someone the big E.

dumpy ▸ adjective =short, squat, stubby; **plump**, stout, chubby, chunky, portly, fat, bulky; *informal* tubby, roly-poly, pudgy, porky; *Brit. informal* podgy.
–OPPOSITES tall, slender.

dun[1] ▸ adjective *a dun cow* =greyish-brown, brownish, mousy, muddy, khaki, umber.

dun[2] ▸ verb *you can't dun me for her debts* =importune, press, plague, pester, nag, harass, hound, badger; *informal* hassle, bug; *N. English informal* mither.

dune ▸ noun =bank, mound, hillock, hummock, knoll, ridge, heap, drift.

dung ▸ noun =manure, muck; excrement, faeces, droppings, ordure, cowpats; *informal* poo.

WORD LINKS

dung-eating: **coprophagous**

dupe ▸ verb *they were duped by a con man* =deceive, trick, hoodwink, hoax, swindle, defraud, cheat, double-cross; gull, mislead, take in, fool, inveigle; *informal* con, do, rip off, diddle, shaft, pull the wool over someone's eyes, pull a fast one on, sell a pup to; *N. Amer. informal* sucker, snooker; *Austral. informal* pull a swifty on.
▸ noun *an innocent dupe in her game* =victim, pawn, puppet, instrument; fool, innocent; *informal* sucker, stooge, sitting duck, muggins, fall guy; *Brit. informal* mug; *N. Amer. informal* pigeon, patsy, sap.

duplicate ▸ noun *a duplicate of the invoice* =copy, photocopy, facsimile, reprint; replica, reproduction, clone; *trademark* Xerox, photostat.
▸ adjective *duplicate keys* =matching, identical, twin, corresponding, equivalent.
▸ verb **1** *she will duplicate the newsletter* =copy, photocopy, photostat, xerox, reproduce, replicate, reprint, run off. **2** *a feat difficult to duplicate* =repeat, do again, redo, replicate.

duplicity ▸ noun =deceitfulness, deceit, deception, double-dealing, underhandedness, dishonesty, fraud, fraudulence, sharp practice, chicanery, trickery, subterfuge, skulduggery, treachery; *informal* crookedness, shadiness, dirty tricks, shenanigans, monkey business.
–OPPOSITES honesty.

durability ▸ noun =imperishability, longevity; resilience, strength, sturdiness, toughness, robustness.
–OPPOSITES fragility.

durable ▸ adjective **1** *durable carpets* =hard-wearing, long-lasting, heavy-duty, tough, resistant, imperishable, indestructible, strong, sturdy, robust. **2** *a durable peace* =lasting, long-lasting, long-term, enduring, persistent, abiding; stable, secure, firm, deep-rooted, permanent, undying, everlasting.
–OPPOSITES delicate, short-lived.

duration ▸ noun =full length, time, time span, time scale, period, term, span, fullness, length, extent.

duress ▸ noun =**coercion**, compulsion, force, pressure, intimidation, constraint; threats; *informal* arm-twisting.

during ▸ conjunction =**throughout**, through, in, in the course of, for the time of.

dusk ▸ noun =**twilight**, nightfall, sunset, sundown, evening, close of day; semi-darkness, gloom, murkiness; *literary* gloaming, eventide.
–OPPOSITES dawn.

dust ▸ noun 1 *the desk was covered in dust* =**dirt**, grime, filth, smut, soot. 2 *they fought in the dust* =**earth**, soil, dirt.
▸ verb 1 *she dusted her mantelpiece* =**wipe**, clean, brush, sweep. 2 *dust the cake with icing sugar* =**sprinkle**, scatter, powder, dredge, sift, cover, strew.

> **WORD LINKS**
> *fear of dust:* **koniophobia**

dusty ▸ adjective 1 *the floor was dusty* =**dirty**, grimy, grubby, unclean, mucky, sooty; undusted; *informal* grungy, cruddy; *Brit. informal* grotty. 2 *dusty sandstone* =**powdery**, crumbly, chalky, friable; granular, gritty, sandy.
–OPPOSITES clean.

dutiful ▸ adjective =**conscientious**, responsible, dedicated, devoted, attentive; obedient, compliant; deferential, reverent, reverential, respectful.
–OPPOSITES remiss.

duty ▸ noun 1 *a misguided sense of duty* =**responsibility**, obligation, commitment; allegiance, loyalty, faithfulness, fidelity, homage. 2 *it was his duty to attend the king* =**job**, task, assignment, mission, function, charge, role, responsibility, obligation; *dated* office. 3 *the duty was raised on alcohol* =**tax**, levy, tariff, excise, toll, fee, payment, rate; dues.
■ **off duty** =**not working**, at leisure, on holiday, on leave, off (work), free.
■ **on duty** =**working**, at work, busy, occupied, engaged; *informal* on the job, tied up.

dwarf ▸ noun 1 =**person of restricted growth**, small person, short person; midget, pygmy, manikin, homunculus. 2 *the wizard captured the dwarf* =**gnome**, goblin, hobgoblin, troll, imp, elf, brownie, leprechaun.
▸ adjective *dwarf conifers* =**miniature**, small, little, tiny, toy, pocket, diminutive, baby, pygmy, undersized; *Scottish*

wee; *informal* mini, teeny, teeny-weeny, itsy-bitsy, tiddly, pint-sized; *Brit. informal* titchy; *N. Amer. informal* little-bitty.
–OPPOSITES giant.
▸ verb 1 *the buildings dwarf the trees* =**dominate**, tower over, loom over, overshadow. 2 *her progress was dwarfed by her sister's success* =**overshadow**, outshine, surpass, exceed, outclass, outstrip, outdo, top, trump, transcend; diminish.

dwell ▸ verb *(formal) gypsies dwell in these caves* =**reside**, live, be settled, be housed, lodge, stay; *informal* put up; *formal* abide.
■ **dwell on** =**linger over**, mull over, muse on, brood about/over, think about; be preoccupied by, obsess about, eat one's heart out over; harp on about, discuss at length.

dwelling ▸ noun *(formal)* =**residence**, home, house, accommodation; lodgings, quarters, rooms; *informal* place, pad, digs; *formal* abode, domicile, habitation.

dwindle ▸ verb =**diminish**, decrease, reduce, lessen, shrink, wane; fall off, tail off, drop, fall, slump, plummet; *informal* nosedive.
–OPPOSITES increase.

dye ▸ noun *a blue dye* =**colourant**, colouring, colour, dyestuff, pigment, tint, stain, wash.
▸ verb *the gloves were dyed* =**colour**, tint, pigment, stain, wash.

dyed-in-the-wool ▸ adjective =**inveterate**, confirmed, entrenched, established, long-standing, deep-rooted, diehard; complete, absolute, thorough, thoroughgoing, out-and-out, true blue; firm, unshakeable, staunch, steadfast, committed, devoted, dedicated, loyal, unswerving; *N. Amer.* full-bore; *informal* card-carrying.

dying ▸ adjective 1 *his dying aunt* =**terminally ill**, at death's door, on one's deathbed, near death, fading fast, expiring, moribund, not long for this world; *informal* on one's last legs, having one foot in the grave. 2 *a dying art form* =**declining**, vanishing, fading, ebbing, waning; *informal* on the way out. 3 *her dying words* =**final**, last.
–OPPOSITES thriving, first.

dynamic ▸ adjective =**energetic**, spirited, active, lively, zestful, vital, vigorous, forceful, powerful, positive; high-powered, aggressive, bold, enterprising; magnetic, passionate, fiery,

dynamism | dyspeptic

high-octane; *informal* go-getting, peppy, full of get-up-and-go, full of vim and vigour, gutsy, spunky, feisty, go-ahead.
–OPPOSITES half-hearted.

dynamism ▶ noun =energy, spirit, liveliness, zestfulness, vitality, vigour, forcefulness, power, potency, positivity; aggression, drive, ambition, enterprise; magnetism, passion, fire; *informal* pep, get-up-and-go, vim and vigour, guts, feistiness.

dynasty ▶ noun =bloodline, line, lineage, house, family; regime, empire.

dyspeptic ▶ adjective =bad-tempered, short-tempered, irritable, snappish, testy, tetchy, touchy, crabby, crotchety, grouchy, cantankerous, peevish, cross, disagreeable, waspish, prickly; *informal* snappy, on a short fuse; *Brit. informal* stroppy, ratty, eggy, like a bear with a sore head; *N. Amer. informal* cranky, ornery.

Ee

each ▶ pronoun *there are 5000 books and each must be cleaned* =**every one**, each one, each and every one, all, the whole lot.
▶ determiner *he visited each month* =**every**, each and every, every single.
▶ adverb *they gave a tenner each* =**apiece**, per person, per capita.

eager ▶ adjective **1** *small eager faces* =**keen**, enthusiastic, avid, fervent, ardent; highly motivated, committed, earnest; *informal* mad keen, (as) keen as mustard. **2** *we were eager for news* =**anxious**, impatient, longing, yearning, wishing, hoping; desirous of, hankering after; *informal* itching, gagging, dying.
–OPPOSITES apathetic.

eagerness ▶ noun =**keenness**, enthusiasm, fervour, zeal, earnestness, commitment, dedication; impatience, desire, longing, yearning, hunger, appetite; *informal* yen.

eagle ▶ noun

> WORD LINKS
>
> young: **eaglet**
> nest: **eyrie**

ear ▶ noun **1** *he had the ear of the president* =**attention**, notice. **2** *he has an ear for a good song* =**appreciation**, feel, instinct, intuition, sense.
■ **play it by ear**. See PLAY.

> WORD LINKS
>
> to do with the ear: **aural, auricular, otic**
> to do with hearing: **auditory**
> branch of medicine concerning the ear:
>   **audiology, otology**
> branch of medicine concerning the ears
>   and throat: **otolaryngology**
> branch of medicine concerning the ears,
>   nose, and throat:
>   **otorhinolaryngology**
> inflammation of the ear: **otitis**
> surgery to repair an ear: **otoplasty**

early ▶ adjective **1** *early copies of the book* =**advance**, forward; initial, preliminary, first; pilot, trial. **2** *an early death* =**untimely**, premature, unseasonable.

3 *early man* =**primitive**, ancient, prehistoric, primeval. **4** *an early response* =**prompt**, timely, quick, speedy, rapid, fast.
–OPPOSITES late, modern, overdue.
▶ adverb **1** *Rachel has to get up early* =**in the early morning**; at dawn, at daybreak, at cockcrow, with the lark. **2** *they hoped to leave school early* =**before the usual/appointed time**; prematurely, too soon, ahead of time/schedule.
–OPPOSITES late.

earmark ▶ verb =**set aside**, keep (back), reserve, designate, assign, mark; allocate, allot, devote, pledge, give over.

earn ▶ verb **1** *they earned £20,000* =**be paid**, take home, gross; receive, get, make, obtain, collect, bring in; *informal* pocket, bank, rake in, net, bag. **2** *he has earned their trust* =**deserve**, merit, warrant, justify, be worthy of; gain, win, secure, establish, obtain, procure, get, acquire.
–OPPOSITES lose.

earnest ▶ adjective **1** *he is dreadfully earnest* =**serious**, solemn, grave, sober, humourless, staid, intense; committed, dedicated, keen, diligent, zealous. **2** *earnest prayer* =**devout**, heartfelt, wholehearted, sincere, impassioned, fervent, ardent, intense, urgent.
–OPPOSITES frivolous, half-hearted.
■ **in earnest 1** *we are in earnest about stopping burglaries* =**serious**, sincere, wholehearted, genuine; committed, firm, resolute, determined. **2** *he started writing in earnest* =**zealously**, purposefully, determinedly, resolutely; passionately, wholeheartedly.

earnestly ▶ adverb =**seriously**, solemnly, gravely, intently; sincerely, resolutely, firmly, ardently, fervently, eagerly.

earnings ▶ plural noun =**income**, wages, salary, stipend, pay, payment, fees; revenue, yield, profit, takings, proceeds, dividends, return, remuneration.

earth ▶ noun **1** *the moon orbits the earth* =**world**, globe, planet. **2** *a trembling of the earth* =**land**, ground, terra firma;

floor. **3** *he ploughed the earth* =**soil**, clay, loam; dirt, sod, turf; ground.

> **WORD LINKS**
>
> *to do with the earth:* **terrestrial, telluric**
> *study of the earth:* **geography, geology, geochemistry, geomorphology**

earthly ▶ adjective =**worldly**, temporal, mortal, human; material; carnal, fleshly, bodily, physical, corporeal, sensual.
−OPPOSITES extraterrestrial, heavenly.

earthquake ▶ noun =**(earth) tremor**, shock, convulsion; *informal* quake.

> **WORD LINKS**
>
> *to do with earthquakes:* **seismic**
> *study of earthquakes:* **seismology**

earthy ▶ adjective **1** *earthy peasant food* =**down-to-earth**, unsophisticated, unrefined, simple, plain, unpretentious, natural; honest. **2** *earthy language* =**bawdy**, ribald, off colour, racy, rude, vulgar, lewd, crude, foul, coarse, uncouth, unseemly, indelicate, indecent, obscene; *informal* blue, locker-room, X-rated; *Brit. informal* fruity, near the knuckle.

ease ▶ noun **1** *he defeated them all with ease* =**effortlessness**, no trouble, simplicity. **2** *his ease of manner* =**naturalness**, casualness, informality, amiability, affability; unconcern, composure, nonchalance, insouciance. **3** *a life of ease* =**affluence**, wealth, prosperity, luxury, plenty; comfort, contentment, enjoyment, well-being.
−OPPOSITES difficulty, formality, trouble, hardship.
▶ verb **1** *the alcohol eased his pain* =**relieve**, alleviate, mitigate, soothe, palliate, moderate, dull, deaden, numb; reduce, lighten, diminish. **2** *the rain eased off* =**abate**, subside, die down, let up, slacken off, diminish, lessen, peter out, relent, come to an end. **3** *work helped to ease her mind* =**calm**, quieten, pacify, soothe, comfort, console; hearten, gladden, uplift, encourage. **4** *he eased out the cork* =**slide**, slip, squeeze; guide, manoeuvre, inch, edge.
−OPPOSITES aggravate, worsen, hinder.

easily ▶ adverb **1** *I overcame this problem easily* =**effortlessly**, comfortably, simply; with ease, without difficulty, without a hitch; *informal* no problem/sweat. **2** *he's easily the best* =**undoubtedly**, without doubt, without question, indisputably, undeniably, definitely, certainly, clearly, obviously, patently; by far, far and away, by a mile.

east ▶ adjective =**eastern**, easterly; oriental.

easy ▶ adjective **1** *the task was very easy* =**uncomplicated**, undemanding, unchallenging, effortless, painless, trouble-free, simple, straightforward, elementary, plain sailing; *informal* a piece of cake, child's play, kids' stuff, a cinch, no sweat, a doddle, a breeze; *Brit. informal* easy-peasy; *N. Amer. informal* duck soup, a snap. **2** *an easy baby* =**docile**, manageable, placid, compliant, acquiescent, obliging, cooperative, easy-going. **3** *an easy target* =**vulnerable**, susceptible, defenceless; naive, gullible, trusting. **4** *Vic's easy manner* =**natural**, casual, informal, unceremonious, unreserved, unaffected, easy-going, amiable, affable, genial, good-humoured; carefree, nonchalant, unconcerned; *informal* laid-back. **5** *an easy life* =**quiet**, tranquil, serene, peaceful, untroubled, contented, relaxed, comfortable, secure, safe; *informal* cushy. **6** *an easy pace* =**leisurely**, unhurried, comfortable, undemanding, easy-going, gentle, sedate, moderate, steady.
−OPPOSITES difficult, demanding, formal.

easy-going ▶ adjective =**relaxed**, even-tempered, placid, mellow, mild, happy-go-lucky, carefree, free and easy, nonchalant, insouciant, imperturbable; amiable, considerate, undemanding, patient, tolerant, lenient, broad-minded, understanding; good-natured, pleasant, agreeable; *informal* laid-back, unflappable.
−OPPOSITES intolerant.

eat ▶ verb **1** *we ate a hearty breakfast* =**consume**, devour, ingest, partake of; gobble (up/down), bolt (down), wolf (down); munch, chomp; *informal* guzzle, put away, demolish, dispose of, polish off, pig out on; *Brit. informal* scoff; *N. Amer. informal* scarf, snarf. **2** *we ate at a local restaurant* =**have a meal**, feed, snack; breakfast, lunch, dine; feast, banquet; *informal* graze, nosh. **3** *acidic water can eat away at pipes* =**erode**, corrode, burn through, consume, dissolve, decay, rot; damage, destroy.

eavesdrop ▶ verb =**listen in**, spy; overhear; *informal* snoop, earwig.

ebb ▸ verb **1** *the tide ebbed* =**recede**, go out, retreat. **2** *his courage began to ebb* =**diminish**, dwindle, wane, fade (away), peter out, decline, flag.
–OPPOSITES increase.

ebony ▸ adjective =**black**, jet black, pitch black, coal black, sable, inky, sooty, raven.

ebullience ▸ noun =**exuberance**, buoyancy, cheerfulness, cheeriness, merriment, jollity, sunniness, jauntiness, high spirits; animation, sparkle, vivacity, enthusiasm, perkiness; *informal* bubbliness, chirpiness, bounciness.

ebullient ▸ adjective =**exuberant**, buoyant, cheerful, joyful, cheery, merry, jolly, sunny, jaunty; animated, sparkling, vivacious, irrepressible; *informal* bubbly, bouncy, upbeat, chirpy, full of beans.
–OPPOSITES depressed.

eccentric ▸ adjective *eccentric behaviour* =**unconventional**, abnormal, irregular, aberrant, anomalous, odd, queer, strange, peculiar, weird, bizarre, outlandish; idiosyncratic, quirky, nonconformist; *informal* way out, offbeat, freaky, oddball, wacky, cranky; *Brit. informal* rum; *N. Amer. informal* kooky, wacko.
–OPPOSITES conventional.
▸ noun *he was something of an eccentric* =**oddity**, free spirit; misfit; *informal* oddball, weirdo, freak, nut, crank; *Brit. informal* one-off, odd bod, nutter; *N. Amer. informal* wacko, screwball.

eccentricity ▸ noun =**unconventionality**, singularity, oddness, strangeness, weirdness, quirkiness, freakishness; peculiarity, foible, idiosyncrasy, whimsy, quirk; *informal* nuttiness, screwiness, freakiness; *N. Amer. informal* kookiness.

ecclesiastical ▸ adjective =**priestly**, ministerial, clerical, canonical, sacerdotal; church, churchly, religious, spiritual, holy, divine; *informal* churchy.

echelon ▸ noun =**level**, rank, grade, step, rung, tier, position, order.

echo ▸ noun *a faint echo of my shout* =**reverberation**, reflection, ringing, repetition, repeat.
▸ verb **1** *his laughter echoed round the room* =**reverberate**, resonate, resound, reflect, ring, vibrate. **2** *Bill echoed Rex's words* =**repeat**, restate, reiterate; copy, imitate, parrot, mimic; reproduce, recite, quote, regurgitate; *informal* recap.

3 *the garden echoes the relaxed style of the interior* =**repeat**, reflect, continue, complement.

eclectic ▸ adjective =**wide-ranging**, broad-based, extensive, comprehensive, encyclopedic; varied, diverse, catholic, all-embracing, multifaceted, multifarious, heterogeneous, miscellaneous, assorted.

eclipse ▸ verb *she was eclipsed by her brother* =**outshine**, overshadow, surpass, exceed, outclass, outstrip, outdo, top, trump, transcend, upstage.

economic ▸ adjective **1** *economic reform* =**financial**, monetary, budgetary, fiscal; commercial. **2** *the firm cannot remain economic* =**profitable**, moneymaking, lucrative, remunerative, fruitful, productive; solvent, viable, cost-effective. **3** *an economic alternative to carpeting* =**cheap**, inexpensive, low-cost, budget, economy, economical, cut-price, discount, bargain.
–OPPOSITES unprofitable, expensive.

economical ▸ adjective **1** *an economical car* =**cheap**, inexpensive, low-cost, budget, economy, economic; cut-price, discount, bargain. **2** *a very economical shopper* =**thrifty**, provident, prudent, sensible, frugal, sparing, abstemious, mean, parsimonious, penny-pinching, miserly; *N. Amer.* forehanded; *informal* stingy.
–OPPOSITES expensive, spendthrift.

economize ▸ verb =**save (money)**, cut costs; cut back, make cutbacks, retrench, budget, make economies, be thrifty, be frugal, scrimp, cut corners, tighten one's belt, draw in one's horns, watch the/your pennies.

economy ▸ noun **1** *the nation's economy* =**wealth**, (financial) resources; financial system, financial management. **2** *one can combine good living with economy* =**thrift**, thriftiness, prudence, careful budgeting, economizing, saving, restraint, frugality, abstemiousness; *N. Amer.* forehandedness.
–OPPOSITES extravagance.

ecstasy ▸ noun =**rapture**, bliss, elation, euphoria, transports, rhapsodies; joy, jubilation, exultation.
–OPPOSITES misery.

ecstatic ▸ adjective =**enraptured**, elated, euphoric, rapturous, joyful, overjoyed, blissful; on cloud nine, in seventh heaven, beside oneself with joy, jumping for joy, delighted, thrilled, exultant; *informal* over the moon, on top of the world, blissed out.

ecumenical ▸ adjective =**non-denominational**, universal, all-embracing, all-inclusive.
−OPPOSITES denominational.

eddy ▸ noun *eddies at the river's edge* =**swirl**, whirlpool, vortex.
▸ verb *the snow eddied around her* =**swirl**, whirl, spiral, wind, circulate, twist; flow, ripple, stream, surge.

edge ▸ noun **1** *the edge of the lake* =**border**, boundary, extremity, fringe, margin, side; lip, rim, brim, brink, verge; perimeter, circumference, periphery, limits, bounds. **2** *she had an edge in her voice* =**sharpness**, severity, bite, sting, acerbity, acidity, trenchancy; sarcasm, malice, spite, venom. **3** *they have an edge over their rivals* =**advantage**, lead, head start, the whip hand, the upper hand; superiority, dominance, ascendancy, supremacy, primacy.
−OPPOSITES middle, disadvantage.
▸ verb **1** *poplars edged the orchard* =**border**, fringe, skirt; surround, enclose, encircle, circle, encompass, bound. **2** *a frock edged with lace* =**trim**, decorate, finish; border, fringe; hem. **3** *he edged closer to the fire* =**creep**, inch, work one's way, ease oneself; sidle, steal, slink.
■ **on edge.** See EDGY.

edgy ▸ adjective =**tense**, nervous, on edge, anxious, apprehensive, uneasy, unsettled; twitchy, jumpy, nervy, keyed up, restive, skittish, neurotic, insecure; *informal* uptight, wired; *Brit. informal* strung up.
−OPPOSITES calm.

edible ▸ adjective =**safe/fit to eat**, fit for human consumption; digestible, palatable.

edict ▸ noun =**decree**, order, command, commandment, mandate, proclamation, pronouncement, dictate; law, statute, act, bill, ruling, injunction; *formal* ordinance.

edifice ▸ noun =**building**, structure, construction, complex; property, development, premises.

edify ▸ verb *(formal)* =**educate**, instruct, teach, school, tutor, train, guide; enlighten, inform, cultivate, develop, improve, better.

edit ▸ verb **1** *she edited the text* =**correct**, check, copy-edit, improve, emend, pol-

ish; modify, adapt, revise, rewrite, reword, rework, redraft; shorten, condense, cut, abridge; *informal* clean up. **2** *an anthology edited by Mark Dawes* =**select**, choose, assemble, organize, put together, compile.

edition ▸ noun =**issue**, number, volume, impression, publication; version.

educate ▸ verb =**teach**, school, tutor, instruct, coach, train, drill; guide, inform, enlighten; inculcate, indoctrinate; *formal* edify.

educated ▸ adjective =**informed**, literate, schooled, tutored, well read, learned, knowledgeable, enlightened; intellectual, academic, erudite, scholarly, cultivated, cultured.

education ▸ noun **1** *the education of young children* =**teaching**, schooling, tuition, tutoring, instruction, coaching, training, tutelage, guidance; indoctrination, inculcation, enlightenment; *formal* edification. **2** *a woman of some education* =**learning**, knowledge, literacy, scholarship, enlightenment.

> **WORD LINKS**
>
> *to do with education:* **pedagogic**

educational ▸ adjective **1** *an educational establishment* =**academic**, scholastic, learning, teaching, pedagogic. **2** *an educational experience* =**instructive**, instructional, educative, informative, illuminating, enlightening; *formal* edifying.

educative ▸ adjective. See EDUCATIONAL sense 2.

educator ▸ noun =**teacher**, tutor, instructor, schoolteacher, schoolmaster, schoolmistress; educationalist; lecturer, professor; guide, mentor, guru; *N. Amer. informal* schoolmarm; *formal* pedagogue.

eerie ▸ adjective =**uncanny**, sinister, ghostly, unnatural, unearthly, supernatural, other-worldly; strange, abnormal, odd, weird, freakish; *informal* creepy, scary, spooky, freaky.

efface ▸ verb =**erase**, eradicate, expunge, blot out, rub out, wipe out, remove, eliminate; delete, cancel, obliterate, blank out.

effect ▸ noun **1** *the effect of these changes* =**result**, consequence, upshot, outcome, repercussions, ramifications; end result, conclusion, culmination, corollary, concomitant, aftermath; fruit(s),

product, by-product; *informal* pay-off.
2 *the effect of the drug* =**impact**, action, effectiveness, influence; power, potency, strength; success; *formal* efficacy.
3 *the dead man's effects* =**belongings**, possessions, (worldly) goods, chattels; property, paraphernalia; *informal* gear, tackle, things, stuff, bits and pieces; *Brit. informal* clobber.
–OPPOSITES cause.

▶ verb *they effected many changes* =**achieve**, accomplish, carry out, realize, manage, bring off, execute, conduct, engineer, perform, do, perpetrate, discharge, complete; cause, bring about, create, produce, make; provoke, occasion, generate, engender, actuate, initiate; *formal* effectuate.

■ **in effect** =**really**, in reality, in truth, in (actual) fact, effectively, essentially, in essence, practically, to all intents and purposes, all but, as good as, more or less, almost, nearly, just about; *informal* pretty much; *literary* well-nigh, nigh on.

■ **take effect 1** *these measures will take effect in May* =**come into force**, come into operation, begin, become valid, become law, apply, be applied. **2** *the drug started to take effect* =**work**, act, be effective, produce results.

effective ▶ adjective **1** *an effective treatment* =**successful**, effectual, potent, powerful; helpful, beneficial, advantageous, valuable; *formal* efficacious. **2** *an effective argument* =**convincing**, compelling, strong, forceful, sound, valid; impressive, persuasive, plausible, credible, authoritative; logical, reasonable, lucid, coherent, cogent, eloquent. **3** *the new law will be effective from next week* =**operative**, in force, in effect; valid, official, lawful, legal, binding; *Law* effectual. **4** *Korea was under effective Japanese control* =**virtual**, practical, essential, actual, implicit, tacit.
–OPPOSITES weak, invalid, theoretical.

effectiveness ▶ noun =**success**, productiveness, potency, power; *formal* efficacy.

effectual ▶ adjective =**effective**, successful, productive, constructive; worthwhile, helpful, beneficial, advantageous, valuable, useful; *formal* efficacious.

effeminate ▶ adjective =**womanish**, effete, foppish, mincing; *informal* camp, limp-wristed.
–OPPOSITES manly.

effervesce ▶ verb =**fizz**, sparkle, bubble; froth, foam.

effervescence ▶ noun **1** *wines full of effervescence* =**fizz**, fizziness, sparkle, bubbliness. **2** *his cheeky effervescence* =**vivacity**, liveliness, high spirits, ebullience, exuberance, buoyancy, sparkle, gaiety, jollity, cheerfulness, perkiness, breeziness, enthusiasm, irrepressibility, vitality, zest, energy, dynamism; *informal* pep, bounce.

effervescent ▶ adjective **1** *an effervescent drink* =**fizzy**, sparkling, carbonated, aerated, gassy, bubbly. **2** *effervescent young people* =**vivacious**, lively, animated, high-spirited, bubbly, ebullient, buoyant, sparkling, scintillating, light-hearted, jaunty, happy, jolly, cheery, cheerful, perky, sunny, enthusiastic, irrepressible, vital, zestful, energetic, dynamic; *informal* peppy, bouncy, upbeat, chirpy, full of beans.
–OPPOSITES still, depressed.

effete ▶ adjective **1** *effete trendies* =**affected**, pretentious, precious, mannered, over-refined; ineffectual; *informal* la-di-da; *Brit. informal* poncey. **2** *an effete young man* =**effeminate**, girlish, feminine; soft, timid, cowardly, lily-livered, spineless, pusillanimous; *informal* sissy, wimpish, wimpy.
–OPPOSITES manly, powerful.

efficacious ▶ adjective *(formal)* =**effective**, effectual, successful, productive, constructive; helpful, beneficial, advantageous, valuable, useful.

efficacy ▶ noun *(formal)* =**effectiveness**, success, productiveness, power; benefit, advantage, value, virtue, usefulness.

efficiency ▶ noun **1** *we need reforms to bring efficiency* =**organization**, order, orderliness, regulation, coherence; productivity, effectiveness. **2** *I compliment you on your efficiency* =**competence**, capability, ability, proficiency, adeptness, expertise, professionalism, skill, effectiveness.

efficient ▶ adjective **1** *efficient techniques* =**organized**, methodical, systematic, logical, orderly, businesslike, streamlined, productive, effective, cost-effective. **2** *an efficient secretary* =**competent**, capable, able, proficient, adept, skilful, skilled, effective, productive, organized, businesslike.
–OPPOSITES disorganized, incompetent.

effigy ▶ noun =**statue**, statuette, sculpture, model, dummy; guy; likeness, image; bust.

effluent ▶ noun =**(liquid) waste**, sewage, effluvium, outflow, discharge, emission.

effort ▶ noun **1** *an effort to work together* =**attempt**, try, endeavour; *informal* crack, shot, stab, bash. **2** *a fine effort* =**achievement**, accomplishment, feat; undertaking, enterprise, work; result, outcome. **3** *the job requires little effort* =**exertion**, energy, work, application, labour, muscle, toil, strain; *informal* sweat, elbow grease; *Brit. informal* graft; *Austral./NZ informal* (hard) yakka.

effortless ▶ adjective =**easy**, undemanding, unchallenging, painless, simple, uncomplicated, straightforward, elementary; fluent, natural; *informal* as easy as pie, child's play, kids' stuff, a cinch, no sweat, a doddle, a breeze; *Brit. informal* easy-peasy; *N. Amer. informal* duck soup, a snap.
−OPPOSITES difficult.

effrontery ▶ noun =**impudence**, impertinence, cheek, insolence, audacity, temerity, presumption, nerve, gall, shamelessness, impoliteness, disrespect, bad manners; *informal* brass (neck), face, chutzpah; *Brit. informal* sauce; *N. Amer. informal* sass.

effusive ▶ adjective =**gushing**, gushy, unrestrained, extravagant, fulsome, demonstrative, lavish, enthusiastic, lyrical; expansive, wordy, verbose.
−OPPOSITES restrained.

egg ▶ noun =**ovum**; gamete, germ cell; **(eggs)** roe, spawn.
■ **egg someone on** =**urge**, goad, incite, provoke, push, drive, prod, prompt, induce, impel, spur on; encourage, exhort, motivate, galvanize.

WORD LINKS

egg-shaped: **ovate, ovoid, oviform**
batch of eggs: **clutch**

ego ▶ noun =**self-esteem**, self-importance, self-worth, self-respect, self-image, self-confidence.

egocentric ▶ adjective =**self-centred**, egomaniacal, self-interested, selfish, self-seeking, self-absorbed, self-obsessed; narcissistic, vain, self-important.
−OPPOSITES altruistic.

egotism, egoism ▶ noun =**self-centredness**, egomania, egocentricity, self-interest, selfishness, self-seeking, self-serving, self-regard, self-obsession; narcissism, vanity, conceit, self-importance; boastfulness.

egotist, egoist ▶ noun =**self-seeker**, egocentric, egomaniac, narcissist; boaster, braggart; *informal* swank, show-off, big-head; *N. Amer. informal* showboat.

egotistic, egoistic ▶ adjective =**self-centred**, selfish, egocentric, egomaniacal, self-interested, self-seeking, self-absorbed, self-obsessed; narcissistic, vain, conceited, self-important; boastful.

egress ▶ noun **1** *the egress from the gallery was blocked* =**exit**, way out, escape route. **2** *a means of egress* =**departure**, exit, withdrawal, retreat, exodus; escape; vacation.
−OPPOSITES entrance.

eight ▶ cardinal number =**octet**, eightsome, octuplets.

WORD LINKS

relating to eight: **octo-, octa-**

eject ▶ verb **1** *the volcano ejected ash* =**emit**, spew out, discharge, give off, send out, belch, vent; expel, release, disgorge, spout, vomit, throw up. **2** *the pilot had time to eject* =**bail out**, escape, get out. **3** *they were ejected from the hall* =**expel**, throw out, turn out, remove, oust; evict, banish; *informal* chuck out, kick out, turf out, boot out; *N. Amer. informal* give someone the bum's rush.
−OPPOSITES admit, appoint.

ejection ▶ noun **1** *the ejection of electrons* =**emission**, discharge, expulsion, release; elimination. **2** *their ejection from the ground* =**expulsion**, removal, eviction.

eke ▶ verb *I had to eke out my remaining funds* =**husband**, use sparingly, be thrifty with, be frugal with, be sparing with, use economically; *informal* go easy on.
−OPPOSITES squander.

elaborate ▶ adjective **1** *an elaborate plan* =**complicated**, complex, intricate, involved; detailed, painstaking, careful; tortuous, convoluted, Byzantine. **2** *an elaborate plasterwork ceiling* =**ornate**, decorated, embellished, adorned, ornamented, fancy, fussy, busy, ostentatious, extravagant, showy, baroque, rococo.

–OPPOSITES simple, plain.

▶ **verb** *both sides refused to elaborate on their reasons* =**expand on**, enlarge on, add to, flesh out; develop, fill out, amplify.

elan ▶ **noun** =**flair**, style, panache, confidence, dash, éclat; energy, vigour, vitality, liveliness, brio, esprit, animation, vivacity, zest, verve, spirit, pep, sparkle, enthusiasm, gusto, eagerness, feeling, fire; *informal* pizzazz, zing, zip, vim, oomph.

elapse ▶ **verb** =**pass**, go by/past, wear on, slip by/away/past, roll by/past, slide by/past, steal by/past, tick by/past.

elastic ▶ **adjective 1** *elastic material* =**stretchy**, elasticated, springy, flexible, pliant, pliable, supple. **2** *an elastic concept of nationality* =**adaptable**, flexible, adjustable, accommodating, variable, fluid, versatile.
–OPPOSITES rigid.

elasticity ▶ **noun 1** *the skin's natural elasticity* =**stretchiness**, flexibility, pliancy, suppleness, springiness; *informal* give. **2** *the elasticity of the term* =**adaptability**, flexibility, adjustability, fluidity, versatility.

elated ▶ **adjective** =**thrilled**, delighted, overjoyed, ecstatic, euphoric, jubilant, beside oneself, exultant, rapturous, in raptures, walking on air, on cloud nine/seven, in seventh heaven, jumping for joy, in transports of delight; *informal* on top of the world, over the moon, on a high, tickled pink; *Austral. informal* wrapped.
–OPPOSITES miserable.

elation ▶ **noun** =**euphoria**, ecstasy, happiness, delight, joy, jubilation, exultation, bliss, rapture.

elbow ▶ **verb** =**push**, shove, force, shoulder, jostle, barge, muscle, bulldoze.

elder ▶ **adjective** *his elder brother* =**older**, senior, big.
▶ **noun** *the church elders* =**leader**, patriarch, father.

elderly ▶ **adjective** *her elderly mother* =**aged**, old, advanced in years, ageing, long in the tooth, past one's prime; grey-haired, grey-bearded, grizzled, hoary; in one's dotage, decrepit, doddering, senescent; *informal* getting on, past it, over the hill.
–OPPOSITES youthful.
▶ **noun** (**the elderly**) =**old people**, senior citizens, (old-age) pensioners, OAPs, re-

tired people; geriatrics; *N. Amer.* seniors, retirees, golden agers; *informal* (golden) oldies, wrinklies; *N. Amer. informal* oldsters, woopies.

elect ▶ **verb 1** *a new president was elected* =**vote for**, vote in, return, cast one's vote for; choose, pick, select. **2** *she elected to stay behind* =**choose**, decide, opt, vote.

election ▶ **noun** =**ballot**, vote, popular vote; poll; *Brit.* by-election; *US* primary.

> [!NOTE] WORD LINKS
> study of elections: **psephology**

electioneer ▶ **verb** =**campaign**, canvass, go on the hustings, doorstep.

elector ▶ **noun** =**voter**, member of the electorate, constituent.

electric ▶ **adjective** *the atmosphere was electric* =**exciting**, charged, electrifying, thrilling, dramatic, intoxicating, dynamic, stimulating, galvanizing, rousing, stirring, moving; tense.

electricity ▶ **noun** =**power**, energy, current, voltage, static; *Brit.* mains; *Canadian* hydro; *Brit. informal* leccy.

> [!NOTE] WORD LINKS
> fear of electricity: **electrophobia**

electrify ▶ **verb** =**excite**, thrill, stimulate, arouse, rouse, inspire, stir (up), exhilarate, intoxicate, galvanize, move, fire (with enthusiasm), fire someone's imagination, invigorate, animate; startle, jolt, shock; *N. Amer.* light a fire under; *informal* give someone a buzz, give someone a kick; *N. Amer. informal* give someone a charge.

elegance ▶ **noun 1** *he was attracted by her elegance* =**style**, stylishness, grace, gracefulness, taste, tastefulness, sophistication; refinement, dignity, beauty, poise; suaveness, urbanity. **2** *the elegance of the idea* =**neatness**, simplicity.

elegant ▶ **adjective 1** *an elegant black outfit* =**stylish**, graceful, tasteful, sophisticated, classic, chic, smart; refined, poised; cultivated, polished, cultured; dashing, debonair, suave, urbane. **2** *an elegant solution* =**neat**, simple.
–OPPOSITES gauche.

elegiac ▶ **adjective** =**mournful**, melancholic, melancholy, plaintive, sorrowful, sad, lamenting; funereal; nostalgic, poignant.
–OPPOSITES cheerful.

elegy ▶ noun =**lament**, requiem, funeral poem/song; *Irish* keen; *Irish & Scottish* coronach.

element ▶ noun 1 *an essential element of the local community* =**component**, constituent, part, section, portion, piece, segment, bit; aspect, feature, facet, ingredient, strand, detail, point; member, unit, module, item. 2 *there is an element of truth in this stereotype* =**trace**, touch, hint, smattering, soupçon. 3 (**elements**) *I braved the elements* =**the weather**, the climate, the (weather) conditions.

elemental ▶ adjective =**natural**; primal, mythic, fundamental, essential, basic; rudimentary, profound, deep-rooted.

elementary ▶ adjective 1 *an elementary astronomy course* =**basic**, rudimentary; preparatory, introductory. 2 *a lot of the work is elementary* =**easy**, simple, straightforward, uncomplicated, undemanding, painless, child's play, plain sailing; *informal* as easy as falling off a log, as easy as pie, as easy as ABC, a piece of cake, no sweat, kids' stuff; *Brit. informal* easy-peasy.
–OPPOSITES advanced, difficult.

elevate ▶ verb 1 *we need a breeze to elevate the kite* =**raise**, lift (up), raise up/aloft, upraise; hoist, hike up, haul up. 2 *he was elevated to Secretary of State* =**promote**, upgrade, move up; raise; exalt; *informal* kick upstairs, move up the ladder.
–OPPOSITES lower, demote.

elevated ▶ adjective 1 *an elevated section of motorway* =**raised**; up in the air, high up; overhead. 2 *elevated language* =**lofty**, grand, exalted, fine, sublime; inflated, pompous, bombastic. 3 *his elevated status* =**high**, high-ranking, lofty, exalted; grand, noble.
–OPPOSITES lowly.

elevation ▶ noun 1 *his elevation to the peerage* =**promotion**, upgrading, advancement, advance. 2 *1500 to 3000 metres in elevation* =**altitude**, height.

elf ▶ noun =**pixie**, fairy, sprite, imp, brownie; dwarf, gnome, goblin, hobgoblin; leprechaun, puck, troll.

elfin ▶ adjective =**elf-like**, elfish, pixie-like; puckish, impish, playful, mischievous; dainty, delicate, small, petite, slight, little, tiny, diminutive.

elicit ▶ verb =**obtain**, draw out, extract, bring out, evoke, call forth, bring forth, induce, prompt, generate, engender, trigger, provoke.

eligible ▶ adjective 1 *those people eligible to vote* =**entitled**, permitted, allowed, qualified, able. 2 *an eligible bachelor* =**desirable**, suitable; available, single, unmarried, unattached.

eliminate ▶ verb 1 *a policy that would eliminate inflation* =**remove**, get rid of, put an end to, do away with, end, stop, eradicate, destroy, annihilate, stamp out, wipe out, extinguish; *informal* knock something on the head. 2 *he was eliminated from the title race* =**knock out**, beat; exclude, rule out, disqualify. 3 *his critics were eliminated* =**kill**, assassinate, murder, execute, do away with, liquidate.

elite ▶ noun =**best**, pick, cream, crème de la crème, flower; high society, jet set, beautiful people.
–OPPOSITES dregs.

elixir ▶ noun =**potion**, concoction, brew, mixture; medicine, tincture; extract, essence, concentrate, distillation; *literary* draught.

elliptical ▶ adjective 1 *an elliptical shape* =**oval**, egg-shaped, ovoid. 2 *elliptical comments* =**cryptic**, abstruse, ambiguous, obscure, oblique.

elongate ▶ verb =**lengthen**, extend, stretch (out), draw out.
–OPPOSITES shorten.

eloquence ▶ noun =**fluency**, articulacy, articulateness, expressiveness, silver tongue, persuasiveness, effectiveness; oratory, rhetoric; *informal* gift of the gab, way with words, blarney.

eloquent ▶ adjective =**fluent**, articulate, expressive, silver-tongued; persuasive, well expressed, effective, lucid, vivid; smooth-tongued.
–OPPOSITES inarticulate.

elsewhere ▶ adverb =**somewhere else**, in/at/to another place, in/at/to a different place, hence; not here, not present, absent, away, abroad, out.
–OPPOSITES here.

elucidate ▶ verb =**explain**, make clear, illuminate, throw/shed light on, clarify, clear up, sort out, unravel, spell out; interpret.
–OPPOSITES confuse.

elude ▶ verb =**evade**, avoid, get away from, dodge, escape from, run (away) from; lose, shake off, give the slip to, slip away from, throw off the scent; *informal* slip through someone's fingers, slip through the net.

elusive ▸ adjective **1** *her elusive husband* =difficult to find/locate/track down; slippery. **2** *an elusive quality* =indefinable, intangible, impalpable; fugitive; ambiguous.

emaciated ▸ adjective =thin, skeletal, bony, gaunt, wasted, thin as a rake; scrawny, skinny, scraggy, skin and bone, raw-boned, stick-like; starved, underfed, undernourished, underweight, half-starved; cadaverous, shrivelled, shrunken, withered; *informal* anorexic, like a bag of bones.
–OPPOSITES fat.

emanate ▸ verb **1** *warmth emanated from the fireplace* =issue, spread, radiate. **2** *the proposals emanated from a committee* =originate, stem, derive, proceed, spring, issue, emerge, flow, come. **3** *he emanated an air of power* =exude, emit, radiate, give off/out, send out/forth.

emancipated ▸ adjective =liberated, independent, unconstrained, uninhibited; free.

embankment ▸ noun =bank, mound, ridge, earthwork, causeway, barrier, levee, dam, dyke.

embargo ▸ noun *an embargo on oil sales* =ban, bar, prohibition, stoppage, interdict, veto, moratorium; restriction, restraint, block, barrier; boycott.
▸ verb *arms sales were embargoed* =ban, bar, prohibit, stop, outlaw; restrict, restrain, block; boycott.
–OPPOSITES allow.

embark ▸ verb **1** *he embarked at Dover* =board (ship), go on board, go aboard; *informal* hop on, jump on. **2** *he embarked on a new career* =begin, start, commence, undertake, set out on, take up, turn one's hand to, get down to; enter into, venture into, launch into, plunge into, engage in, settle down to; *informal* get cracking on, get going on.

embarrass ▸ verb =mortify, shame, put someone to shame, humiliate, abash, make uncomfortable; discomfit; *informal* show up.

embarrassed ▸ adjective =mortified, red-faced, blushing, abashed, shamed, ashamed, shamefaced, humiliated, chagrined, self-conscious, uncomfortable, not knowing where to look, sheepish; discomfited, disconcerted;

flustered, agitated; tongue-tied; *informal* with egg on one's face, wishing the earth would swallow one up.

embarrassing ▸ adjective =humiliating, shameful, mortifying, ignominious; awkward, uncomfortable, compromising; discomfiting; *informal* cringeworthy, cringe-making, toe-curling.

embarrassment ▸ noun **1** *he was scarlet with embarrassment* =mortification, humiliation, shame, shamefacedness, awkwardness, self-consciousness, sheepishness, discomfort, discomfiture; ignominy. **2** *his current financial embarrassment* =difficulty, predicament, plight, problem, mess; *informal* bind, jam, pickle, fix, scrape. **3** *an embarrassment of riches* =surplus, excess, over-abundance, superabundance, glut, surfeit, superfluity.

embed, imbed ▸ verb =implant, plant, set, fix, lodge, root, insert, place; sink, drive in, hammer in, ram in.

embellish ▸ verb **1** *weapons embellished with precious metal* =decorate, adorn, ornament; beautify, enhance, grace; trim, garnish, gild; deck, bedeck, festoon, emblazon. **2** *the legend was embellished by an American academic* =elaborate, embroider, expand on, exaggerate.

embellishment ▸ noun **1** *architectural embellishments* =decoration, ornamentation, adornment; enhancement. **2** *we wanted the truth, not romantic embellishments* =elaboration, addition, exaggeration.

embezzle ▸ verb =misappropriate, steal, thieve, pilfer, purloin, appropriate, defraud someone of, siphon off, pocket, help oneself to; put one's hand in the till; *informal* rob, rip off, skim, line one's pockets; *Brit. informal* pinch, nick, half-inch.

embezzlement ▸ noun =misappropriation, theft, stealing, robbery, thieving, pilfering, purloining, pilferage, appropriation, swindling; fraud, larceny.

embittered ▸ adjective =bitter, resentful, rancorous, jaundiced, aggrieved, sour, frustrated, dissatisfied, alienated, disaffected.

emblazon ▸ verb **1** *shirts emblazoned with the company name* =adorn, decorate, ornament, embellish; inscribe. **2** *a flag with a hammer and sickle emblazoned on it* =display, depict, show.

emblem ▸ noun =symbol, representation, token, image, figure, mark, sign; crest, badge, device, insignia, stamp, seal, coat of arms, shield; logo, trademark.

emblematic ▸ adjective =symbolic, representative, demonstrative, suggestive, indicative.

embodiment ▸ noun =personification, incarnation, realization, manifestation, expression, representation, actualization, symbol; paradigm, epitome, paragon, soul, model; type, essence, quintessence, exemplification, exemplar, ideal; *formal* reification.

embody ▸ verb 1 *Gradgrind embodies the spirit of industrial capitalism* =personify, realize, manifest, symbolize, represent, express, incarnate, epitomize, stand for, typify, exemplify. 2 *the changes embodied in the Act* =incorporate, include, contain, encompass.

embolden ▸ verb =fortify, make brave/braver, encourage, hearten, strengthen, brace, stiffen the resolve of, lift the morale of; rouse, stir, stimulate, cheer, rally, fire, animate, inspirit, invigorate; *informal* buck up.
–OPPOSITES dishearten.

embrace ▸ verb 1 *he embraced her warmly* =hug, take/hold in one's arms, hold, cuddle, clasp to one's bosom, squeeze, clutch; caress; enfold; *informal* canoodle, smooch. 2 *most western European countries have embraced the concept* =welcome, welcome with open arms, accept, take up, take to one's heart, adopt; espouse. 3 *the faculty embraces a wide range of disciplines* =include, take in, comprise, contain, incorporate, encompass, cover, involve, subsume.
▸ noun *a fond embrace* =hug, cuddle, squeeze, clinch, caress; bear hug.

embroider ▸ verb 1 *a cushion embroidered with a pattern of golden keys* =sew, stitch; decorate, adorn, ornament, embellish. 2 *she embroidered her stories with colourful detail* =elaborate, embellish, enlarge on, exaggerate, dress up, gild, colour; *informal* jazz up.

embroidery ▸ noun 1 =needlework, needlepoint, needlecraft, sewing. 2 *fanciful embroidery of the facts* =elaboration, embellishment, adornment, ornamentation, colouring, enhancement; exaggeration, overstatement.

embroil ▸ verb =involve, entangle, ensnare, enmesh, catch up, mix up, bog down, mire.

embryonic ▸ adjective =rudimentary, undeveloped, unformed, immature, incomplete, incipient; fledgling, budding, nascent, emerging, developing.
–OPPOSITES mature.

emerge ▸ verb 1 *a policeman emerged from the alley* =come out, appear, come into view, become visible, surface, materialize, issue, come forth. 2 *several unexpected facts emerged* =become known, become apparent, be revealed, come to light, come out, turn up, transpire, unfold, turn out, prove to be the case.

emergence ▸ noun =appearance, arrival, coming, materialization; advent, inception, dawn, birth, origination, start, development.

emergency ▸ noun *a military emergency* =crisis; extremity; disaster, catastrophe, calamity; *informal* panic stations.
▸ adjective 1 *an emergency meeting* =urgent, crisis; extraordinary. 2 *emergency supplies* =reserve, standby, backup, fallback.

emergent ▸ adjective =emerging, developing, rising, dawning, budding, embryonic, infant, fledgling, nascent, incipient.

emigrate ▸ verb =move abroad, move overseas, leave one's country, migrate; relocate, resettle.
–OPPOSITES immigrate.

emigration ▸ noun =migration; exodus, diaspora; relocation, resettling.

eminence ▸ noun =fame, celebrity, illustriousness, distinction, renown, pre-eminence, greatness, prestige, importance, reputation, note; prominence, superiority, stature, standing.

eminent ▸ adjective 1 *an eminent man of letters* =illustrious, distinguished, renowned, esteemed, pre-eminent, notable, noteworthy, great, prestigious, important, influential, outstanding, noted, of note; famous, celebrated, prominent, well known, acclaimed, exalted, revered, venerable. 2 *the eminent reasonableness of their claims* =obvious, clear, conspicuous, marked, singular, signal; total, complete, utter, absolute, thorough, perfect, downright, sheer.
–OPPOSITES unknown.

eminently ▸ adverb =very, greatly,

highly, exceedingly, extremely, particularly, exceedingly, supremely, uniquely; conspicuously, singularly; totally, completely, utterly, absolutely, thoroughly, perfectly, downright.

emissary ▶ noun =envoy, ambassador, delegate, attaché, consul; agent, representative.

emission ▶ noun =discharge, release, outpouring, outflow, outrush, leak, excretion, secretion, ejection.

emit ▶ verb 1 *hydrocarbons emitted from vehicle exhausts* =discharge, release, give out/off, pour out, send forth, throw out, issue; leak, ooze, excrete, disgorge, secrete, eject; spout, belch, spew out; emanate, radiate, exude. 2 *he emitted a loud cry* =utter, voice, let out, produce, give vent to, come out with.
–OPPOSITES absorb.

emotion ▶ noun 1 *she was good at hiding her emotions* =feeling, sentiment; reaction, response. 2 *overcome by emotion, she turned away* =passion, strength of feeling. 3 *responses based purely on emotion* =instinct, intuition, gut feeling; sentiment, the heart.

emotional ▶ adjective 1 *an emotional young man* =passionate, hot-blooded, ardent, fervent, excitable, temperamental, melodramatic, tempestuous; demonstrative, responsive, sentimental, sensitive. 2 *he paid an emotional tribute to his wife* =poignant, moving, touching, affecting, powerful, stirring, emotive, heart-rending, heart-warming, impassioned, dramatic; *informal* tear-jerking.
–OPPOSITES unfeeling.

emotionless ▶ adjective =unemotional, unfeeling, dispassionate, passionless, unexpressive, cool, cold, cold-blooded, impassive, indifferent, detached, remote, aloof; toneless, flat, dead, expressionless, blank, wooden, stony, deadpan.

emotive ▶ adjective =controversial, contentious, inflammatory; sensitive, delicate, difficult, problematic, touchy, awkward, prickly, ticklish.

empathize ▶ verb =identify, sympathize, understand, share someone's feelings, be in tune; relate to, feel for, have insight into; *informal* put oneself in someone else's shoes.

emperor ▶ noun =ruler, sovereign, king, monarch, potentate.

WORD LINKS
relating to an emperor: **imperial**

emphasis ▶ noun 1 *the curriculum gave more emphasis to reading and writing* =prominence, importance, significance, value; stress, weight, accent, attention, priority, pre-eminence, urgency, force. 2 *the emphasis is on the word 'little'* =stress, accent, weight, prominence; beat.

emphasize ▶ verb =stress, underline, highlight, focus attention on, point up, lay stress on, draw attention to, spotlight, foreground; bring to the fore, belabour; accentuate, underscore; *informal* press home, rub it in.
–OPPOSITES understate.

emphatic ▶ adjective =vehement, firm, wholehearted, forceful, energetic, vigorous, direct, insistent; certain, definite, out-and-out, one hundred per cent; decided, determined, categorical, unqualified, unconditional, unequivocal, unambiguous, absolute, explicit, downright, outright, clear.
–OPPOSITES hesitant.

empire ▶ noun 1 *the Ottoman Empire* =kingdom, realm, domain, territory; commonwealth; power, world power, superpower. 2 *a worldwide shipping empire* =organization, corporation, multinational, conglomerate, consortium, company, business, firm, operation.

WORD LINKS
relating to an empire: **imperial**

empirical ▶ adjective =experiential, practical, first-hand, hands-on; observed, seen.
–OPPOSITES theoretical.

employ ▶ verb 1 *she employed a chauffeur* =hire, engage, recruit, take on, sign up, put on the payroll, enrol, appoint; retain. 2 *Sam was employed in carving a stone figure* =occupy, engage, involve, keep busy, tie up; absorb, engross, immerse. 3 *the team employed subtle psychological tactics* =use, utilize, make use of, avail oneself of; apply, exercise, practise, put into practice, exert, bring into play, bring to bear; draw on, resort to, turn to, have recourse to.
–OPPOSITES dismiss.

employed ▶ adjective =working, in work, in employment, holding down a job; earning, waged.

employee ▶ noun =**worker**, member of staff; blue-collar worker, white-collar worker, workman, labourer, (hired) hand; (**employees**) personnel, staff, workforce.

employment ▶ noun =**work**, labour, service; job, post, position, situation, occupation, profession, trade, métier, business, line, line of work, calling, vocation, craft.

emporium ▶ noun =**shop**, store, outlet, retail outlet; department store, chain store, supermarket, hypermarket, superstore, megastore; establishment.

empower ▶ verb **1** *the act empowered Henry to punish heretics* =**authorize**, entitle, permit, allow, license, enable. **2** *movements to empower the poor* =**emancipate**, unshackle, set free, liberate.
−OPPOSITES forbid.

empress ▶ noun =**ruler**, sovereign, queen, monarch, potentate.

emptiness ▶ noun =**void**, vacuum, empty space, gap, hole.

empty ▶ adjective **1** *an empty house* =**vacant**, unoccupied, uninhabited, untenanted, bare, desolate, deserted, abandoned; clear, free. **2** *an empty threat* =**meaningless**, hollow, idle, vain, futile, worthless, useless, ineffectual. **3** *without her my life is empty* =**futile**, pointless, purposeless, worthless, meaningless, valueless, of no value, useless, of no use, aimless, senseless, inconsequential. **4** *his eyes were empty* =**blank**, expressionless, vacant, wooden, stony, impassive, absent, glazed, fixed, lifeless, emotionless, unresponsive.
−OPPOSITES full, serious, worthwhile.
▶ verb **1** *I emptied the dishwasher* =**unload**, unpack; clear, evacuate. **2** *he emptied out the contents of the case* =**remove**, take out, extract, tip out, pour out.
−OPPOSITES fill.

emulate ▶ verb =**imitate**, copy, mirror, echo, follow, model oneself on, take a leaf out of someone's book; match, equal, parallel, be on a par with, be in the same league as, come close to; compete with, contend with, rival, surpass.

enable ▶ verb =**allow**, permit, let, equip, empower, make able, fit; authorize, qualify.
−OPPOSITES prevent.

enact ▶ verb =**act out**, act, perform, appear in, stage, mount, put on, present.
−OPPOSITES repeal.

enactment ▶ noun =**acting**, performing, performance, staging, presentation.

enamoured ▶ adjective =**in love**, infatuated, besotted, smitten, captivated, enchanted, fascinated, bewitched, beguiled; keen on, taken with; *informal* mad about, crazy about, wild about, bowled over by, struck on, sweet on, carrying a torch for.

encampment ▶ noun =**camp**, military camp, bivouac; campsite; tents.

encapsulate ▶ verb =**summarize**, sum up, put in a nutshell; capture, express.

enchant ▶ verb =**captivate**, charm, delight, enrapture, entrance, enthral, beguile, bewitch, spellbind, fascinate, hypnotize, mesmerize, rivet, grip, transfix; *informal* bowl someone over.
−OPPOSITES bore.

enchanting ▶ adjective =**captivating**, charming, delightful, bewitching, beguiling, adorable, lovely, attractive, appealing, engaging, winning, fetching, winsome, alluring, disarming, irresistible, fascinating.

enchantment ▶ noun =**allure**, delight, charm, beauty, attractiveness, appeal, fascination, irresistibility, magnetism, pull, draw, lure.

encircle ▶ verb =**surround**, enclose, circle, girdle, ring, encompass; close in, shut in, fence in, wall in, hem in, confine; *literary* gird.

enclose ▶ verb **1** *tall trees enclosed the garden* =**surround**, circle, ring, girdle, encompass, encircle; close in, shut in, fence in, wall in, hedge in, hem in. **2** *please enclose a stamped addressed envelope* =**include**, insert, put in; send.

> WORD LINKS
>
> *fear of enclosed spaces:* **claustrophobia**

enclosure ▶ noun =**paddock**, fold, pen, compound, stockade, ring, yard; sty, coop; *N. Amer.* corral.

encompass ▶ verb =**cover**, embrace, include, incorporate, take in, contain, comprise, involve, deal with.

encounter ▶ verb **1** *I encountered a girl I used to know* =**meet**, run into, come across/upon, stumble across/on, chance on, happen on; *informal* bump into. **2** *we encountered a slight problem* =**experience**, run into, come up against, face, be faced with, confront.

▶ noun **1** *an unexpected encounter* =**meeting**, chance meeting. **2** *a violent encounter between police and demonstrators* =**battle**, fight, clash, confrontation, struggle, skirmish, engagement; *informal* run-in, set-to, dust-up, scrap.

encourage ▶ verb **1** *the players were encouraged by the crowd's response* =**hearten**, cheer, buoy up, uplift, inspire, motivate, spur on, stir, stir up, fire up, stimulate, invigorate, vitalize, revitalize, embolden, fortify; *informal* buck up, pep up, give a shot in the arm to. **2** *she had encouraged him to go* =**persuade**, coax, urge, press, push, pressure, pressurize, prod, goad, egg on, prompt, influence, sway. **3** *the Government was keen to encourage local businesses* =**support**, back, champion, promote, further, foster, nurture, cultivate, strengthen, stimulate; help, assist, aid, boost, fuel.
–OPPOSITES discourage, dissuade, hinder.

encouragement ▶ noun **1** *she needed a bit of encouragement* =**support**, cheering up, inspiration, motivation, stimulation; morale-boosting; *informal* a shot in the arm. **2** *they required no encouragement to get back to work* =**persuasion**, coaxing, urging, prodding, prompting, inducement, incentive, carrot. **3** *the encouragement of foreign investment* =**support**, backing, championship, championing, sponsoring, promotion, furtherance, furthering, fostering, nurture, cultivation; help, assistance; *N. Amer.* boosterism.

encouraging ▶ adjective **1** *an encouraging start* =**promising**, hopeful, auspicious, favourable; heartening, reassuring, cheering, comforting, welcome, pleasing, gratifying. **2** *my parents were very encouraging* =**supportive**, understanding, helpful; positive, responsive, enthusiastic.

encroach ▶ verb =**intrude**, trespass, impinge, invade, infiltrate, interrupt, infringe, violate, interfere with, disturb; tread/step on someone's toes; *informal* horn in on, muscle in on.

encroachment ▶ noun =**intrusion**, trespass, invasion, infiltration, incursion, obtrusion, infringement, impingement.

encumber ▶ verb **1** *her movements were encumbered by her heavy skirts* =**hamper**, hinder, obstruct, impede, cramp, inhibit, restrict, limit, constrain, restrain, bog down, retard, slow (down); inconvenience, disadvantage, handicap. **2** *they are encumbered with debt* =**burden**, load, weigh down, saddle; overwhelm, tax, overload; *Brit. informal* lumber.

encumbrance ▶ noun =**burden**, responsibility, obligation, liability, weight, load, pressure, trouble, worry; millstone, albatross.

encyclopedic ▶ adjective =**comprehensive**, complete, thorough, thoroughgoing, full, exhaustive, in-depth, wide-ranging, all-inclusive, all-embracing, all-encompassing, universal, vast; *formal* compendious.

end ▶ noun **1** *the end of the road* =**extremity**, furthermost part, limit; margin, edge, border, boundary, periphery; point, tip, tail end; *N. Amer.* tag end. **2** *the end of the novel* =**conclusion**, termination, ending, finish, close, resolution, climax, finale, culmination, denouement. **3** *a cigarette end* =**butt**, stub, stump. **4** *wealth is a means and not an end in itself* =**aim**, goal, purpose, objective, object, holy grail, target; intention, intent; aspiration, wish, desire, ambition. **5** *the commercial end of the business* =**aspect**, side, section, area, field, part, share, portion, segment, province. **6** *his end might come at any time* =**death**, dying, demise, passing, expiry; doom, extinction, annihilation, extermination, destruction; downfall, ruin, ruination, Waterloo; *formal* decease.
–OPPOSITES beginning.

▶ verb **1** *the show ended with a wedding scene* =**finish**, conclude, terminate, come to an end, draw to a close, close, stop, cease; culminate, climax. **2** *she ended their relationship* =**break off**, call off, bring to an end, put an end to, stop, finish, terminate, discontinue; dissolve, cancel.
–OPPOSITES begin.

endanger ▶ verb =**imperil**, jeopardize, risk, put at risk, put in danger; threaten, pose a threat to, be a danger to.

endearing ▶ adjective =**lovable**, adorable, cute, sweet, dear, delightful, lovely, charming, appealing, attractive, engaging, winning, captivating, enchanting, beguiling, winsome.

endeavour ▶ verb *the company endeavoured to expand its activities* =**try**, attempt, seek, undertake, aspire, aim, set out;

strive, struggle, labour, toil, work.
▶ noun **1** *an endeavour to build a more buoy-ant economy* =**attempt**, try, bid, effort, venture; *informal* go, crack, shot, stab, bash. **2** *an extremely unwise endeavour* =**undertaking**, enterprise, venture, exercise, activity, exploit, deed, act, action, move; scheme, plan, project; *informal* caper.

ending ▶ noun =**end**, finish, close, closing, conclusion, resolution, summing-up, denouement, finale; cessation, stopping, termination, discontinuation.
–OPPOSITES beginning.

endless ▶ adjective **1** *a woman with endless energy* =**unlimited**, limitless, infinite, inexhaustible, boundless, unbounded, untold, immeasurable, measureless, incalculable; abundant, abounding, great; ceaseless, unceasing, unending, without end, everlasting, constant, continuous, continual, interminable, unfading, unfailing, perpetual, eternal, enduring, lasting. **2** *as children we played endless games* =**countless**, innumerable, untold, legion, numberless, unnumbered, numerous, very many, manifold, multitudinous, multifarious; a great number of, infinite numbers of, a multitude of; *informal* umpteen, no end of, loads of, stacks of, heaps of, masses of, oodles of, zillions of; *N. Amer. informal* gazillions of; *literary* myriad, divers.
–OPPOSITES limited, few.

endorse ▶ verb =**support**, back, agree with, approve (of), favour, subscribe to, recommend, champion, stick up for, uphold, affirm, sanction; *informal* throw one's weight behind.
–OPPOSITES oppose.

endorsement ▶ noun =**support**, backing, approval, seal of approval, agreement, recommendation, championship, patronage, affirmation, sanction.

endow ▶ verb =**provide**, supply, furnish, equip, invest, favour, bless, grace, gift; give, bestow.

endowment ▶ noun **1** *a generous endowment* =**bequest**, legacy, inheritance; gift, present, grant, award, donation, contribution, subsidy, settlement. **2** *his natural endowments* =**quality**, characteristic, feature, attribute, faculty, ability, talent, gift, strength, aptitude, capability, capacity.

endurable ▶ adjective =**bearable**, tol-erable, supportable, manageable, sustainable.
–OPPOSITES unbearable.

endurance ▶ noun **1** *she pushed him beyond the limit of his endurance* =**toleration**, tolerance, sufferance, forbearance, patience, acceptance, resignation, stoicism. **2** *the race is a test of endurance* =**stamina**, staying power, fortitude, perseverance, persistence, tenacity, doggedness, grit, indefatigability, resolution, determination; *informal* stickability.

endure ▶ verb **1** *he endured years of pain* =**undergo**, go through, live through, experience; cope with, deal with, face, suffer, tolerate, put up with, brave, bear, withstand, sustain, weather; *Scottish* thole. **2** *our love will endure for ever* =**last**, live, live on, go on, survive, abide, continue, persist, remain.
–OPPOSITES fade.

enduring ▶ adjective =**lasting**, long-lasting, abiding, durable, continuing, persisting, eternal, perennial, permanent, unending, everlasting; constant, stable, steady, steadfast, fixed, firm, unwavering, unfaltering, unchanging.
–OPPOSITES short-lived.

enemy ▶ noun =**opponent**, adversary, rival, antagonist, combatant, challenger, competitor, opposition, competition, other side; *literary* foe.
–OPPOSITES ally.

energetic ▶ adjective **1** *an energetic woman* =**active**, lively, dynamic, spirited, animated, vital, vibrant, bouncy, bubbly, exuberant, sprightly, tireless, indefatigable, enthusiastic; *informal* peppy, sparky, feisty, full of beans, full of the joys of spring, bright-eyed and bushy-tailed. **2** *energetic exercises* =**vigorous**, strenuous, brisk; hard, arduous, demanding, taxing, tough, rigorous. **3** *an energetic advertising campaign* =**forceful**, vigorous, high-powered, all-out, determined, bold, powerful, potent; intensive, hard-hitting, pulling no punches, aggressive, high-octane; *informal* punchy, in-your-face.
–OPPOSITES lethargic, gentle, half-hearted.

energize ▶ verb =**enliven**, liven up, animate, vitalize, invigorate, perk up, excite, electrify, stimulate, stir up, fire up, rouse, motivate, move, drive, spur on, encourage, galvanize; *informal* pep up, buck up, give a shot in the arm to.

energy ▸ noun =**vitality**, vigour, life, liveliness, animation, vivacity, spirit, verve, enthusiasm, zest, vibrancy, spark, sparkle, effervescence, exuberance, buoyancy, sprightliness; dynamism, drive; fire, passion; *informal* zip, zing, pep, pizzazz, punch, bounce, oomph, go, get-up-and-go; *N. Amer. informal* feistiness.

enfeeble ▸ verb =**weaken**, debilitate, incapacitate, lay low; drain, sap, exhaust, tire.
−OPPOSITES strengthen.

enfold ▸ verb =**envelop**, engulf, sheathe, swathe, swaddle, cocoon, shroud, veil, cloak, drape, cover; surround, enclose, encase, encircle.

enforce ▸ verb **1** *the sheriff enforced the law* =**impose**, apply, administer, implement, bring to bear, discharge, execute. **2** *they cannot enforce cooperation between the parties* =**force**, compel, coerce, exact.

enforced ▸ adjective =**compulsory**, obligatory, mandatory, involuntary, forced, imposed, required, prescribed, contractual, binding.
−OPPOSITES voluntary.

engage ▸ verb **1** *tasks which engage children's interest* =**capture**, catch, arrest, grab, draw, attract, gain, win, hold, grip, absorb, occupy. **2** *he engaged a secretary* =**employ**, hire, recruit, take on, enrol, appoint. **3** *the chance to engage in a wide range of pursuits* =**participate in**, take part in, partake in/of, enter into. **4** *infantry units engaged the enemy* =**fight**, do battle with, attack, take on, clash with; encounter, meet.
−OPPOSITES lose, dismiss.

engagement ▸ noun **1** *a business engagement* =**appointment**, meeting, arrangement, commitment; date, assignation, rendezvous. **2** *Britain's continued engagement in open trading* =**participation**, involvement, association. **3** *the first engagement of the war* =**battle**, fight, clash, confrontation, encounter, conflict, skirmish; action, combat, hostilities.

engaging ▸ adjective =**charming**, appealing, attractive, pleasing, pleasant, agreeable, likeable, lovable, sweet, winning, winsome, fetching; *Scottish & N. English* bonny.
−OPPOSITES unappealing.

engender ▸ verb =**cause**, be the cause of, give rise to, bring about, occasion, lead to, result in, produce, create, generate, arouse, rouse, inspire, provoke, kindle, trigger, spark, stir up, whip up.

engine ▸ noun **1** *a car engine* =**motor**; turbine. **2** *the main engine of change* =**cause**, agent, instrument, originator, initiator, generator.

engineer ▸ noun **1** *a structural engineer* =**designer**, planner, builder. **2** *a ship's engineer* =**operator**, driver, controller.
▸ verb *he engineered a takeover deal* =**bring about**, arrange, pull off, bring off, contrive, manoeuvre, manipulate, negotiate, organize, orchestrate, choreograph, mount, stage, mastermind, originate, manage, stage-manage, coordinate, direct.

England ▸ noun =*Brit. informal* Blighty; *Austral./NZ informal* Old Dart; *literary* Albion.

> **WORD LINKS**
>
> mania for English things: **Anglomania**
> fear of English people and things:
> **Anglophobia**

engrave ▸ verb **1** *my name was engraved on the trophy* =**carve**, inscribe, cut (in), incise, chisel, score. **2** *the image was engraved in his memory* =**fix**, set, imprint, stamp, brand, impress, embed, etch.

engraving ▸ noun =**etching**, print; plate, picture, illustration.

engross ▸ verb =**absorb**, engage, rivet, grip, hold, interest, involve, occupy, preoccupy; fascinate, captivate, enthral, intrigue.

engrossed ▸ adjective =**absorbed**, involved, interested, occupied, preoccupied, immersed, caught up, riveted, gripped, rapt, fascinated, intent, captivated, enthralled.

engrossing ▸ adjective =**absorbing**, interesting, riveting, gripping, captivating, compelling, compulsive, fascinating, enthralling; *informal* unputdownable.

engulf ▸ verb =**inundate**, flood, deluge, immerse, swamp, swallow up, submerge; bury, envelop, overwhelm.

enhance ▸ verb =**increase**, add to, intensify, heighten, magnify, amplify, inflate, strengthen, build up, supplement, augment, boost, raise, lift, elevate, exalt; improve, enrich, complement.
−OPPOSITES diminish.

enigma ▸ noun =**mystery**, puzzle, riddle, conundrum, paradox.

enigmatic ▶ adjective =mysterious, inscrutable, puzzling, mystifying, baffling; cryptic, elliptical, paradoxical, obscure, oblique.

enjoin ▶ verb =urge, encourage, admonish, press; instruct, direct, require, order, command, tell, call on, demand, charge; *literary* bid.

enjoy ▶ verb **1** *he enjoys playing the piano* =like, be fond of, take pleasure in, be keen on, delight in, appreciate, relish, revel in, adore, lap up, savour, luxuriate in, bask in; *informal* get a kick out of, get a thrill out of, get a buzz out of, go a bundle on. **2** *she had always enjoyed good health* =benefit from, have the benefit of; be blessed with, be favoured with, be endowed with, possess, own, boast.
–OPPOSITES dislike, lack.
■ **enjoy oneself** =have fun, have a good time, have the time of one's life; make merry, celebrate, revel; *informal* party, have a ball, have a whale of a time, whoop it up, let one's hair down.

enjoyable ▶ adjective =entertaining, amusing, delightful, pleasant, congenial, convivial, fine, good, agreeable, pleasurable, satisfying, gratifying.

enjoyment ▶ noun =pleasure, fun, entertainment, amusement, recreation, relaxation; happiness, merriment, joy, jollity; satisfaction, gratification, liking; *humorous* delectation.

enlarge ▶ verb **1** *they enlarged the scope of their research* =extend, expand, grow, add to, amplify, augment, magnify, build up, supplement; widen, broaden, stretch, lengthen; elongate, deepen, thicken. **2** *the lymph glands had enlarged* =swell, distend, bloat, bulge, dilate, blow up, puff up, balloon. **3** *he enlarged on this subject* =elaborate on, expand on, add to, build on, flesh out, add detail to; develop, fill out, embellish, embroider.
–OPPOSITES reduce, shrink.

enlargement ▶ noun =expansion, extension, growth, amplification, augmentation, addition, magnification, widening, broadening, lengthening; elongation, deepening, thickening; swelling, dilation.

enlighten ▶ verb =inform, tell, make aware, open someone's eyes, illuminate, apprise, brief, update, bring up to date; *informal* put in the picture, clue in, fill in, put wise, bring up to speed.

enlightened ▶ adjective =informed, well informed, aware, sophisticated, advanced, developed, liberal, open-minded, broad-minded, educated, knowledgeable, wise; civilized, refined, cultured, cultivated.
–OPPOSITES benighted.

enlightenment ▶ noun =insight, understanding, awareness, wisdom, education, learning, knowledge; illumination, awakening, instruction, teaching; open-mindedness, broad-mindedness; culture, refinement, cultivation, civilization.

enlist ▶ verb **1** *he enlisted in the Royal Engineers* =join up, join, enrol in, sign up for, volunteer for. **2** *he was enlisted in the army* =recruit, call up, enrol, sign up; conscript; *US* draft. **3** *he enlisted the help of a friend* =obtain, engage, secure, win, get, procure.

enliven ▶ verb **1** *a meeting enlivened by her wit* =liven up, spice up, ginger up, leaven; *informal* perk up, pep up. **2** *the visit had enlivened my mother* =cheer up, brighten up, liven up, perk up, raise someone's spirits, uplift, gladden, buoy up, animate, vivify, vitalize, invigorate, restore, revive, refresh, stimulate, rouse, boost; *informal* buck up, pep up.

en masse ▶ adverb =(all) together, as a group, as one, en bloc, as a whole, in a body, wholesale.

enmesh ▶ verb =embroil, entangle, ensnare, snare, trap, entrap, ensnarl, involve, catch up, mix up, bog down, mire.

enmity ▶ noun =hostility, animosity, antagonism, friction, antipathy, animus, acrimony, bitterness, rancour, resentment, ill feeling, bad feeling, ill will, bad blood, hatred, loathing, odium.
–OPPOSITES friendship.

ennoble ▶ verb =dignify, honour, exalt, elevate, raise, enhance, distinguish.
–OPPOSITES demean.

enormity ▶ noun **1** *the enormity of the task* =immensity, hugeness; size, extent, magnitude, greatness. **2** *the enormity of his crimes* =wickedness, vileness, baseness, depravity; outrageousness, monstrousness, hideousness, heinousness, brutality, savagery, viciousness.

enormous ▶ adjective =huge, vast, immense, gigantic, great, giant, massive, colossal, mammoth, tremendous, mighty, monumental, epic, prodigious,

mountainous, king-size(d), titanic, towering, gargantuan; *informal* mega, monster, whopping (great), humongous, jumbo, astronomical; *Brit. informal* whacking (great), ginormous.
–OPPOSITES tiny.

enormously ▸ adverb **1** *an enormously important factor* =**very**, extremely, really, exceedingly, exceptionally, tremendously, immensely, hugely; *informal* terrifically, awfully, terribly, seriously, desperately, ultra, damn, damned; *Brit. informal* ever so, well, dead, jolly; *N. Amer. informal* real, mighty, darned; *informal, dated* frightfully. **2** *prices vary enormously* =**considerably**, greatly, a great deal, a lot.
–OPPOSITES slightly.

enough ▸ determiner *they had enough food* =**sufficient**, adequate, ample, the necessary; *informal* plenty of.
–OPPOSITES insufficient.
▸ pronoun *there's enough for everyone* =**sufficient**, plenty, a sufficient amount, an adequate amount, as much as necessary; a sufficiency, an ample supply; one's fill.

enquire, inquire ▸ verb **1** *I enquired about part-time training courses* =**ask**, make enquiries. **2** *the commission is to enquire into alleged illegal payments* =**investigate**, probe, look into; research, examine, explore, delve into; *informal* check out.

enquiring, inquiring ▸ adjective =**inquisitive**, curious, interested, questioning, probing, searching; investigative.

enquiry, inquiry ▸ noun **1** *telephone enquiries* =**question**, query. **2** *an enquiry into alleged security leaks* =**investigation**, probe, examination, exploration; inquest, hearing.

enrage ▸ verb =**anger**, infuriate, incense, madden, inflame; antagonize, provoke, exasperate; *informal* drive mad/crazy, drive up the wall, make someone see red, make someone's blood boil, make someone's hackles rise, get someone's back up; *N. Amer. informal* burn up.
–OPPOSITES placate.

enraged ▸ adjective =**furious**, infuriated, irate, incensed, raging, incandescent, fuming, ranting, raving, seething, beside oneself; *informal* mad, hopping mad, wild, livid, boiling, apoplectic, hot under the collar, foaming at the mouth, steamed up, in a paddy, fit to be tied.

–OPPOSITES calm.

enrich ▸ verb =**enhance**, improve, better, add to, augment; supplement, complement; boost, elevate, raise, lift, refine.
–OPPOSITES spoil.

enrol ▸ verb **1** *they both enrolled for the course* =**register**, sign on/up, put one's name down, apply, volunteer; enter, join. **2** *280 new members were enrolled* =**accept**, admit, take on, register, sign on/up, recruit, engage.

en route ▸ adverb =**along/on the way**, in transit, during the journey, along/on the road, on the move; coming, going, proceeding, travelling.

ensemble ▸ noun **1** *a Bulgarian folk ensemble* =**group**, band; company, troupe, cast, chorus, corps; *informal* combo. **2** *the buildings present a charming provincial ensemble* =**whole**, entity, unit, body, set, combination, composite, package; sum, total, totality, entirety, aggregate. **3** *a pink and black ensemble* =**outfit**, costume, suit; *informal* get-up.

enshrine ▸ verb =**set down**, set out, express, lay down, embody, realize, manifest, incorporate, represent, contain, include, preserve, treasure, immortalize.

ensign ▸ noun =**flag**, standard, colour(s), banner.

enslavement ▸ noun =**slavery**, servitude; exploitation, oppression.
–OPPOSITES liberation.

ensnare ▸ verb =**capture**, catch, trap, entrap, snare, net; entangle, embroil, enmesh.

ensue ▸ verb =**result**, follow, develop, proceed, succeed, emerge, arise, derive, issue.

ensure ▸ verb **1** *ensure that the surface is completely clean* =**make sure**, make certain, see to it; check, confirm, establish, verify. **2** *legislation to ensure equal opportunities for all* =**secure**, guarantee, assure, certify.

entail ▸ verb =**involve**, necessitate, require, need, demand, call for; mean, imply; cause, produce, result in, lead to, give rise to, occasion.

entangle ▸ verb **1** *their parachutes became entangled* =**twist**, intertwine, entwine, tangle, snarl, knot, coil. **2** *he was entangled in a lawsuit* =**involve**, embroil, mix up, catch up, bog down, mire.

enter ▶ verb **1** *police entered the house* =**go in/into**, come in/into, get in/into, set foot in, gain access to. **2** *a bullet entered his chest* =**penetrate**, pierce, puncture, perforate. **3** *he entered politics in 1979* =**get involved in**, join, throw oneself into, engage in, embark on, take up. **4** *the planning entered a new phase* =**reach**, move into, get to, begin, start, commence. **5** *they entered the Army at eighteen* =**join**, enrol in/for, enlist in, volunteer for, sign up for. **6** *she entered a cookery competition* =**go in for**, register for, enrol for, sign on/up for; compete in, take part in, participate in. **7** *the cashier entered the details in a ledger* =**record**, write, put down, take down, note, jot down; register, log. **8** *please enter your password* =**key (in)**, type (in), tap in. **9** *(Law) he entered a plea of guilty* =**submit**, register, lodge, record, file, put forward, present.
–OPPOSITES leave.

enterprise ▶ noun **1** *a joint enterprise* =**undertaking**, endeavour, venture, exercise, activity, operation, task, business; project, scheme, plan, programme, campaign. **2** *a woman with enterprise* =**initiative**, resourcefulness, entrepreneurialism, imagination, ingenuity, inventiveness, originality, creativity; dynamism, drive, ambition, energy; *informal* get-up-and-go, oomph. **3** *a profit-making enterprise* =**business**, company, firm, venture, organization, operation, concern, corporation, establishment, partnership; *informal* outfit, set-up.

enterprising ▶ adjective =**resourceful**, entrepreneurial, imaginative, ingenious, inventive, creative; dynamic, ambitious, energetic, adventurous; *informal* go-ahead.
–OPPOSITES unimaginative.

entertain ▶ verb **1** *he wrote stories to entertain them* =**amuse**, please, charm, cheer, interest; engage, occupy. **2** *he entertains foreign visitors* =**receive**, play host/hostess to, invite (round/over), throw a party for; wine and dine, cater for, feed, fête. **3** *we don't entertain much* =**receive guests**, have people round/over, have company, hold/throw a party. **4** *I would never entertain such an idea* =**consider**, give consideration to, contemplate, think of; countenance; *formal* brook.
–OPPOSITES bore, reject.

entertainer ▶ noun =**performer**, artiste, artist.

entertaining ▶ adjective =**delightful**, enjoyable, amusing, pleasing, agreeable, appealing, engaging, interesting, fascinating, absorbing, compelling; humorous, funny, comical; *informal* fun.

entertainment ▶ noun =**amusement**, pleasure, leisure, recreation, relaxation, fun, enjoyment, interest; *N. Amer. informal* rec.

enthral ▶ verb =**captivate**, charm, enchant, bewitch, fascinate, beguile, entrance, delight; absorb, engross, rivet, grip, transfix, hypnotize, mesmerize, spellbind.
–OPPOSITES bore.

enthralling ▶ adjective =**fascinating**, entrancing, enchanting, bewitching, captivating, delightful; absorbing, engrossing, compelling, riveting, gripping, exciting, spellbinding; *informal* unputdownable.

enthuse ▶ verb **1** *I enthused about the idea* =**rave**, be enthusiastic, wax lyrical, get all worked up; praise to the skies; *informal* go wild/mad/crazy; *N. Amer. informal* ballyhoo. **2** *he enthuses people* =**motivate**, inspire, stimulate, encourage, spur (on), galvanize, rouse, excite, stir (up), fire.

enthusiasm ▶ noun =**eagerness**, keenness, ardour, fervour, passion, zeal, zest, gusto, energy, verve, vigour, vehemence, fire, spirit; wholeheartedness, commitment, devotion, earnestness; *informal* get-up-and-go.
–OPPOSITES apathy.

enthusiast ▶ noun =**fan**, devotee, aficionado, lover, admirer, follower; expert, connoisseur, authority, pundit; *informal* buff, freak, fanatic, nut, fiend, addict, maniac.

enthusiastic ▶ adjective =**eager**, keen, avid, ardent, fervent, passionate, zealous, vehement; excited, wholehearted, committed, devoted, fanatical, earnest.

entice ▶ verb =**tempt**, lure, attract, appeal to; invite, persuade, convince, beguile, coax, woo; seduce; *informal* sweet-talk.

enticement ▶ noun =**lure**, temptation, attraction, appeal, draw, pull; charm, seduction.

enticing ▶ adjective =**tempting**, alluring, attractive, appealing, inviting, seductive, beguiling, charming.

entire ▶ adjective =**whole**, complete,

total, full.

entirely ▶ adverb **1** *that's entirely out of the question* =**absolutely**, completely, totally, wholly, utterly, quite; altogether, in every respect, thoroughly. **2** *a gift entirely for charitable purposes* =**solely**, only, exclusively, purely, merely, just, alone.

entirety ■ **in its entirety** =**completely**, entirely, totally, fully, wholly.

entitle ▶ verb **1** *this pass entitles you to visit the museum* =**qualify**, make eligible, authorize, allow, permit; enable, empower. **2** *a chapter entitled 'Comedy and Tragedy'* =**name**, title, call, label, designate, dub.

entitlement ▶ noun **1** *their entitlement to benefits* =**right**, claim. **2** *your holiday entitlement* =**allowance**, allocation, quota, ration, limit.

entity ▶ noun =**being**, creature, individual, organism, life form; body, object, article, thing.

entourage ▶ noun =**retinue**, staff, bodyguards; attendants, minders; *informal* people, posse.

entrails ▶ plural noun =**intestines**, bowels, guts, viscera, internal organs, vital organs; offal; *informal* insides, innards.

entrance[1] ▶ noun **1** *the main entrance* =**entry**, way in, access, approach; door, portal, gate; opening, mouth; entrance hall, foyer, porch; *N. Amer.* entryway. **2** *the entrance of Mrs Knight* =**appearance**, arrival, entry, coming. **3** *he was refused entrance* =**admission**, admittance, (right of) entry, access.
−OPPOSITES exit, departure.

entrance[2] ▶ verb *I was entranced by her beauty* =**enchant**, bewitch, beguile, captivate, mesmerize, hypnotize, spellbind, transfix; enthral, engross, absorb, fascinate; stun, electrify; charm, delight; *informal* bowl over, knock out.

entrant ▶ noun =**competitor**, contestant, contender, participant; candidate, applicant.

entreat ▶ verb =**implore**, beg, plead with, pray, ask, request; bid, enjoin, appeal to, call on; *literary* beseech.

entrenched, intrenched ▶ adjective =**ingrained**, established, fixed, firm, deep-seated, deep-rooted; unshakeable, ineradicable.

entrepreneur ▶ noun =**businessman/woman**; dealer, trader, promoter,

impresario; *informal* wheeler-dealer, whizz-kid, mover and shaker, go-getter.

entrust ▶ verb **1** *he was entrusted with the task* =**charge**, invest, endow. **2** *the powers entrusted to the Home Secretary* =**assign**, confer on, bestow on, vest in, consign; delegate; give, grant, vouchsafe.

entry ▶ noun **1** *my moment of entry* =**appearance**, arrival, entrance, coming. **2** *the entry to the flats* =**entrance**, way in, access, approach; door, portal, gate; entrance hall, foyer, lobby; *N. Amer.* entryway. **3** *he was refused entry* =**admission**, admittance, entrance, access. **4** *entries in the cash book* =**item**, record, note; memo, memorandum. **5** *data entry* =**recording**, archiving, logging, documentation, capture. **6** *we must pick a winner from the entries* =**submission**, entry form, application.
−OPPOSITES departure, exit.

entwine ▶ verb =**wind round**, twist round, coil round; weave, intertwine, interlace; entangle, tangle; twine.

enumerate ▶ verb =**list**, itemize, set out, give; cite, name, specify, identify, spell out, detail, particularize.

enunciate ▶ verb =**pronounce**, articulate; say, speak, utter, voice, vocalize, sound, mouth.

envelop ▶ verb =**surround**, cover, enfold, engulf, encircle, encompass, cocoon, sheathe, swathe, enclose; cloak, screen, shield, veil, shroud.

enviable ▶ adjective =**desirable**, desired, favoured, sought-after, attractive; fortunate, lucky; *informal* to die for.

envious ▶ adjective –**jealous**, covetous, desirous; grudging, begrudging, resentful.

environment ▶ noun **1** *the hospital environment* =**situation**, setting, milieu, background, backdrop, scene, location, context, framework; sphere, world, realm; ambience, atmosphere. **2** *the impact of pesticides on the environment* –**the natural world**, nature, the earth, the ecosystem, the biosphere, Mother Nature; wildlife, flora and fauna, the countryside.

> **WORD LINKS**
>
> study of the environment: **ecology**
> destruction of the environment: **ecocide**

environmentalist ▶ noun =**conservationist**, ecologist, nature-lover; *infor-*

mal eco-warrior, tree-hugger.

environs ▸ plural noun =**surroundings**, surrounding area, vicinity; locality, neighbourhood, district, region; precincts; *N. Amer.* vicinage.

envisage ▸ verb **1** *it was envisaged that the hospital would open soon* =**foresee**, predict, forecast, anticipate, expect, think likely. **2** *I cannot envisage what the future holds* =**imagine**, contemplate, picture; conceive of, think of.

envoy ▸ noun =**ambassador**, emissary, diplomat, consul, attaché, chargé d'affaires; representative, delegate, spokesperson; agent, intermediary, mediator; *informal* go-between.

envy ▸ noun =**jealousy**, covetousness; resentment, bitterness, discontent.
▸ verb **1** *I admired and envied her* =**be envious of**, be jealous of, be resentful of. **2** *we envied her lifestyle* =**covet**, desire, aspire to, wish for, want, long for, yearn for, hanker after, crave.

ephemeral ▸ adjective =**transitory**, transient, fleeting, passing, short-lived, momentary, brief, short; temporary, impermanent, short-term.
–OPPOSITES permanent.

epic ▸ adjective *their epic journey* =**ambitious**, heroic, grand, great; monumental.

epidemic ▸ noun **1** *an epidemic of typhoid* =**outbreak**, plague, pandemic. **2** *a joyriding epidemic* =**spate**, rash, wave, eruption, outbreak, craze; flood, torrent; upsurge, upturn, increase, growth, rise.
▸ adjective *the craze is now epidemic* =**rife**, rampant, widespread, wide-ranging, extensive, pervasive; global, universal, ubiquitous; endemic, pandemic.

epilogue ▸ noun =**afterword**, postscript, PS, coda, codicil, appendix, tailpiece, supplement, addendum, rider.
–OPPOSITES prologue.

episode ▸ noun **1** *the best episode of his career* =**incident**, event, occurrence, happening; occasion, interlude, chapter, experience, adventure, exploit; matter, affair, thing. **2** *the final episode of the series* =**instalment**, chapter, passage; part, portion, section; programme, show. **3** *an episode of illness* =**period**, spell, bout, attack, phase; *informal* dose.

episodic ▸ adjective =**in episodes**, in instalments, in sections, in parts.
–OPPOSITES continuous.

epitaph ▸ noun =**elegy**, commemoration, obituary; inscription.

epithet ▸ noun =**sobriquet**, nickname, byname, title, name, label, tag; description, designation; *informal* moniker, handle.

epitome ▸ noun =**personification**, embodiment, incarnation, paragon; essence, quintessence, archetype, paradigm, typification; exemplar, model, soul, example; height.

epitomize ▸ verb =**embody**, encapsulate, typify, exemplify, represent, manifest, symbolize, illustrate, sum up; personify.

epoch ▸ noun =**era**, age, period, time, span, stage; aeon.

equable ▸ adjective **1** *an equable man* =**even-tempered**, calm, composed, collected, self-possessed, relaxed, easygoing; mellow, mild, tranquil, placid, stable, level-headed; imperturbable, unexcitable, untroubled, well balanced; *informal* unflappable, together, laid-back. **2** *an equable climate* =**stable**, constant, uniform, unvarying, consistent, unchanging, changeless; moderate, temperate.
–OPPOSITES temperamental, extreme.

equal ▸ adjective **1** *lines of equal length* =**identical**, uniform, alike, like, the same; matching, corresponding. **2** *fares equal to a fortnight's wages* =**equivalent**, identical, amounting; on a par with. **3** *equal treatment before the law* =**impartial**, non-partisan, fair, just, equitable; unprejudiced, non-discriminatory. **4** *an equal contest* =**evenly matched**, even, balanced, level, on an equal footing; *informal* fifty-fifty, level pegging, neck and neck.
–OPPOSITES different, discriminatory.
▸ noun *they did not treat him as their equal* =**equivalent**, peer, fellow, like; counterpart, match, parallel.
▸ verb **1** *two plus two equals four* =**be equal to**, be equivalent to, be the same as; come to, amount to, make, total, add up to. **2** *he equalled the world record* =**match**, reach, parallel, be level with.
■ **equal to** =**capable of**, fit for, up to, good/strong enough for; suitable for, suited to, appropriate for; *informal* having what it takes.

equality ▸ noun =**fairness**, equal rights, equal opportunities, equitability; impartiality, even-handedness; justice.

equalize ▸ verb **1** *attempts to equalize their earnings* =**make equal**, make even, even out/up, level, regularize, standardize, balance, square, match; bring into line. **2** *Villa equalized in the second half* =**level the score**, draw.

equanimity ▸ noun =**composure**, calm, level-headedness, self-possession, cool-headedness, presence of mind; serenity, tranquillity, imperturbability, equilibrium; poise, assurance, self-confidence, aplomb, sangfroid, nerve; *informal* cool.
−OPPOSITES anxiety.

equate ▸ verb **1** *he equates criticism with treachery* =**identify**, compare, bracket, class, associate, connect, link, relate, ally. **2** *moves to equate supply and demand* =**equalize**, balance, even out/up, level, square, tally, match; make equal, make even, make equivalent.

equation ▸ noun **1** *the equation of success with riches* =**identification**, association, connection, matching. **2** *other factors came into the equation* =**situation**, problem, case, question, issue.

equestrian ▸ adjective =**on horseback**, mounted, riding.

equilibrium ▸ noun **1** *the equilibrium of the economy* =**balance**, symmetry; harmony, stability. **2** *his equilibrium was never shaken* =**composure**, calm, equanimity, sangfroid; poise, presence of mind; self-possession, self-command; tranquillity, serenity; *informal* cool.
−OPPOSITES imbalance, agitation.

equip ▸ verb **1** *the boat was equipped with a flare gun* =**provide**, furnish, supply, issue, kit out, stock, provision, arm, endow. **2** *the course will equip them for the workplace* =**prepare**, qualify, ready, suit; train.

equipment ▸ noun =**apparatus**, paraphernalia; tools, utensils, implements, instruments, hardware, gadgets, gadgetry; stuff, things; kit, tackle; resources, supplies; trappings, appurtenances, accoutrements; *informal* gear; *Military* materiel, baggage.

equitable ▸ adjective =**fair**, just, impartial, even-handed, unbiased, unprejudiced, egalitarian; *informal* fair and square.
−OPPOSITES unfair.

equity ▸ noun **1** *the equity of Finnish society* =**fairness**, justness, impartiality, egalitarianism. **2** *he owns 25% of the equity in the property* =**value**, worth; ownership, rights, proprietorship.

equivalence ▸ noun =**equality**, sameness, interchangeability, comparability, correspondence; uniformity, similarity, likeness, nearness.

equivalent ▸ adjective *a degree or equivalent qualification* =**equal**, identical; similar, parallel, analogous, comparable, corresponding, commensurate.
▸ noun *Denmark's equivalent of the Daily Mirror* =**counterpart**, parallel, alternative, analogue, twin, opposite number; equal, peer.

equivocal ▸ adjective =**ambiguous**, indefinite, non-committal, vague, imprecise, inexact, inexplicit, hazy; unclear; ambivalent, uncertain, unsure, indecisive.
−OPPOSITES definite.

equivocate ▸ verb =**prevaricate**, be evasive, be non-committal, be vague, be ambiguous, dodge the issue, beat about the bush, hedge one's bets, pussyfoot around; vacillate, shilly-shally, waver, hesitate, stall; *Brit.* hum and haw; *informal* sit on the fence, duck the issue.

era ▸ noun =**epoch**, age, period, time, span, aeon; generation.

eradicate ▸ verb =**eliminate**, get rid of, remove, obliterate; exterminate, destroy, annihilate, kill, wipe out; abolish, stamp out, extinguish, quash; erase, efface, excise, expunge.

erase ▸ verb **1** *they erased his name from all lists* =**delete**, rub out, wipe off, blank out; expunge, excise, remove, obliterate. **2** *the tape had been erased* =**wipe (clean)**, record over, clear.

erect ▸ adjective **1** *she held her body erect* =**upright**, straight, vertical, perpendicular; standing. **2** *an erect penis* =**engorged**, enlarged, swollen, tumescent; hard, stiff. **3** *the dog's fur was erect* =**bristling**, standing on end, upright.
−OPPOSITES bent, flaccid, flat.
▸ verb =**build**, construct, put up; assemble, put together, fabricate.
−OPPOSITES demolish, dismantle, lower.

erection ▸ noun **1** *the erection of a house* =**construction**, building, assembly, fabrication, elevation. **2** *a bleak concrete erection* =**building**, structure, edifice, construction, pile. **3** =**erect penis**, phallus.

erode ▸ verb =**wear away/down**, abrade, grind down, crumble; weather;

undermine, weaken, deteriorate, destroy.

erosion ▶ noun =**wearing away**, abrasion, attrition; weathering; dissolution; deterioration, disintegration, destruction.

erotic ▶ adjective =**(sexually) arousing**, (sexually) stimulating, titillating, suggestive; pornographic, (sexually) explicit, lewd, smutty, hard-core, soft-core, dirty, racy, risqué, ribald, naughty; sexual, sexy, sensual, amatory; seductive, alluring, tantalizing; *informal* blue, X-rated, steamy, raunchy; *euphemistic* adult.

err ▶ verb =**make a mistake**, be wrong, be in error, be mistaken, blunder, be incorrect, miscalculate, get it wrong; *informal* slip up, screw up, foul up, goof, make a boo-boo.

errand ▶ noun =**task**, job, chore, assignment.

erratic ▶ adjective =**unpredictable**, inconsistent, changeable, variable, inconstant, irregular, fitful, unstable, turbulent, unsettled, changing, varying, fluctuating, mutable; unreliable, undependable, volatile, mercurial, capricious, fickle, temperamental.
−OPPOSITES consistent.

erroneous ▶ adjective =**wrong**, incorrect, mistaken, in error, inaccurate, untrue, false, fallacious; unsound, specious, faulty, flawed; *informal* off beam, way out.
−OPPOSITES correct.

error ▶ noun =**mistake**, inaccuracy, miscalculation, blunder, oversight; fallacy, misconception, delusion; misprint; *informal* slip-up, bloomer, boo-boo; *Brit. informal* boob.
■ **in error** =**wrongly**, by mistake, mistakenly, incorrectly; accidentally, by accident, inadvertently, unintentionally, by chance.

ersatz ▶ adjective =**artificial**, substitute, imitation, synthetic, fake, false, mock, simulated; pseudo, sham, bogus, spurious, counterfeit; manufactured, man-made; *informal* phoney.
−OPPOSITES genuine.

erudite ▶ adjective =**learned**, scholarly, educated, knowledgeable, well read, well informed, intellectual; intelligent, clever, academic, literary; highbrow, cerebral; *informal* brainy.
−OPPOSITES ignorant.

erupt ▶ verb **1** *the volcano erupted* =**give out lava**, become active, explode. **2** *fighting erupted* =**break out**, flare up; start.

eruption ▶ noun **1** *a volcanic eruption* =**discharge**, explosion, lava flow, pyroclastic flow. **2** *an eruption of violence* =**outbreak**, flare-up, upsurge, outburst, explosion; wave, spate.

escalate ▶ verb **1** *prices have escalated* =**increase rapidly**, soar, rocket, shoot up, mount, spiral, climb, go up; *informal* go through the roof, skyrocket. **2** *the dispute escalated* =**grow**, develop, mushroom, increase, heighten, intensify, accelerate.
−OPPOSITES plunge, shrink.

escalation ▶ noun **1** *an escalation in oil prices* =**increase**, rise, hike, growth, leap, upsurge, upturn. **2** *an escalation of the conflict* =**intensification**, aggravation, exacerbation; expansion, build-up, increase; deterioration.

escapade ▶ noun =**exploit**, stunt, caper, antic(s); adventure, venture; deed, feat, experience; incident, occurrence, event.

escape ▶ verb **1** *he escaped from prison* =**run away/off**, get out, break out, break free, bolt, make one's getaway; disappear, vanish, slip away, sneak away; *informal* do a vanishing act, fly the coop, leg it; *Brit. informal* do a bunk, do a runner; *N. Amer. informal* go on the lam. **2** *he escaped his pursuers* =**get away from**, escape from, elude, avoid, dodge, shake off; *informal* give someone the slip. **3** *they escaped injury* =**avoid**, evade, elude, cheat, sidestep, circumvent, steer clear of; shirk; *informal* duck. **4** *lethal gas escaped* =**leak (out)**, seep (out), discharge, flow (out), pour (out), gush (out), spurt (out), spew (out).
▶ noun **1** *his escape from prison* =**getaway**, breakout, flight; *Brit. informal* flit. **2** *a gas escape* =**leak**, leakage, spill, seepage, discharge, outflow, outpouring.

escapee ▶ noun =**runaway**, escaper, absconder; jailbreaker, fugitive; truant; deserter, defector.

escapism ▶ noun =**fantasy**, fantasizing, daydreaming, daydreams, reverie; imagination, flight(s) of fancy, pipe dreams, wishful thinking; *informal* pie in the sky.
−OPPOSITES realism.

escort ▶ noun *a police escort* =**guard**, bodyguard, protector, minder, custo-

dian; attendant, chaperone; entourage, retinue; protection, convoy.
▶ verb **1** *he was escorted home by the police* =**conduct**, accompany, guide, usher, shepherd, take. **2** *he escorted her in to dinner* =**accompany**, partner, take, bring.

esoteric ▶ adjective =**abstruse**, obscure, arcane, rarefied, recondite, abstract; enigmatic, inscrutable, cryptic; complex, complicated, incomprehensible, impenetrable, mysterious.

especially ▶ adverb **1** *work poured in, especially from Kent* =**mainly**, mostly, chiefly, principally, largely; substantially, particularly, primarily. **2** *a committee especially for the purpose* =**expressly**, specially, specifically, exclusively, just, particularly, explicitly. **3** *he is especially talented* =**exceptionally**, particularly, specially, extremely, singularly, distinctly, unusually, extraordinarily, uncommonly, uniquely, remarkably, outstandingly; *informal* seriously, majorly; *Brit. informal* jolly, dead, well.

espionage ▶ noun =**spying**, infiltration; surveillance, reconnaissance.

espousal ▶ noun =**adoption**, embracing, acceptance; support, championship, encouragement, defence; sponsorship, promotion, endorsement, advocacy, approval.

espouse ▶ verb =**adopt**, embrace, take up, accept; support, back, champion.
–OPPOSITES reject.

essay ▶ noun =**article**, composition, paper, dissertation, thesis, discourse, treatise; commentary, critique, polemic; piece, feature; *N. Amer.* theme.

essence ▶ noun **1** *the very essence of economics* =**quintessence**, soul, spirit, nature; core, heart, substance; basis, principle, reality; *informal* nitty-gritty. **2** *essence of ginger* =**extract**, concentrate, elixir, juice; oil.
■ **in essence** =**essentially**, basically, fundamentally, primarily, principally, chiefly, predominantly, substantially; above all, first and foremost; effectively, virtually, to all intents and purposes.
■ **of the essence**. See ESSENTIAL adjective sense 1.

essential ▶ adjective **1** *it is essential to remove the paint* =**crucial**, key, vital, indispensable, all-important, of the essence, critical, imperative; urgent, pressing, high-priority. **2** *the essential simplicity of his style* =**basic**, inherent,

fundamental, quintessential, intrinsic, underlying, characteristic, innate, primary.
–OPPOSITES unimportant, secondary.
▶ noun **1** *an essential for broadcasters* =**necessity**, prerequisite, requisite; *informal* must, must have. **2** *the essentials of the job* =**fundamentals**, basics, rudiments, first principles, foundations; essence, basis, core, kernel, crux; *informal* nitty-gritty, nuts and bolts.

establish ▶ verb **1** *they established an office in Moscow* =**set up**, start, initiate, institute, form, found, create, inaugurate; build, construct, install. **2** *evidence to establish his guilt* =**prove**, demonstrate, show, indicate, determine, confirm.

established ▶ adjective **1** *established practice* =**accepted**, traditional, orthodox, habitual, set, fixed, official; usual, customary, common, normal, general, prevailing, accustomed, familiar, expected, conventional, standard. **2** *an established composer* =**well known**, recognized, esteemed, respected, famous, prominent, noted, renowned.

establishment ▶ noun **1** *the establishment of a democracy* =**foundation**, institution, formation, inception, creation, installation; inauguration, start, initiation. **2** *a dressmaking establishment* =**business**, firm, company, concern, enterprise, venture, organization, operation; factory, plant, shop; *informal* outfit, set-up. **3** *educational establishments* =**institution**, place, premises, institute. **4** *they dare to poke fun at the Establishment* =**the authorities**, the powers that be, the system, the ruling class; *informal* Big Brother.

estate ▶ noun **1** *the Balmoral estate* =**property**, grounds, garden(s), park, parkland, land(s); territory. **2** *a housing estate* =**area**, development, complex; *Scottish* scheme. **3** *a coffee estate* =**plantation**, farm, holding; forest, vineyard; *N. Amer.* ranch. **4** *he left an estate worth £610,000* =**assets**, capital, wealth, riches, holdings, fortune; property, effects, possessions, belongings.

esteem ▶ noun *she was held in high esteem* =**respect**, admiration, acclaim, approbation, appreciation, favour, recognition, honour, reverence; estimation, regard.
▶ verb *such ceramics are highly esteemed* =**respect**, **admire**, value, regard, appreciate, like, prize, treasure, favour, revere.

estimate ▶ verb **1** *estimate the cost* =**calculate roughly**, approximate, guess; evaluate, judge. **2** *we estimate it to be worth £50,000* =**consider**, believe, reckon, deem, judge, rate, gauge.
▶ noun *an estimate of the cost* =**rough calculation**, approximation, estimation, rough guess; costing, quotation, valuation, evaluation; *informal* guesstimate.

estimation ▶ noun **1** *an estimation of economic growth* =**estimate**, approximation, rough calculation, rough guess, evaluation; *informal* guesstimate. **2** *he rated highly in Carl's estimation* =**assessment**, judgement; esteem, opinion, view.

estrange ▶ verb =**alienate**, antagonize, turn away, drive away, distance; drive a wedge between.

estrangement ▶ noun =**alienation**, disaffection, unfriendliness; difference; parting, separation, divorce, break-up, split, breach, schism.

estuary ▶ noun =**(river) mouth**, firth; delta.

et cetera ▶ adverb =**and so on**, and so forth, and the rest, and/or the like, and suchlike, etc.; *informal* and what have you, and whatnot.

etch ▶ verb =**engrave**, carve, inscribe, incise, score, mark; scratch, scrape.

etching ▶ noun =**engraving**, print, plate.

eternal ▶ adjective **1** *eternal happiness* =**everlasting**, never-ending, endless, perpetual, undying, immortal, abiding, permanent, enduring, timeless. **2** *eternal vigilance* =**constant**, continual, continuous, perpetual, persistent, sustained, unremitting, unrelieved, uninterrupted, unbroken, never-ending, non-stop, round-the-clock, endless, ceaseless.
−OPPOSITES transient, intermittent.

eternally ▶ adverb **1** *I shall be eternally grateful* =**forever**, permanently, perpetually, (for) evermore, for ever and ever, for eternity, in perpetuity, enduringly; *N. Amer.* forevermore; *informal* until doomsday, until the cows come home. **2** *the tenants complain eternally* =**constantly**, continually, continuously, always, all the time, persistently, repeatedly, regularly; day and night, non-stop, endlessly, incessantly, perpetually; interminably; *informal* 24-7.

eternity ▶ noun **1** *the memory will remain for eternity* =**ever**, all time, perpetuity. **2** *(informal) I waited an eternity for you* =**a long time**, an age, ages, a lifetime; hours, years, aeons; forever; *informal* donkey's years, a month of Sundays; *Brit. informal* yonks.

ethereal ▶ adjective **1** *her ethereal beauty* =**delicate**, exquisite; fragile, airy, fine, subtle. **2** *ethereal beings* =**celestial**, heavenly, spiritual, other-worldly.
−OPPOSITES substantial, earthly.

ethical ▶ adjective **1** *an ethical dilemma* =**moral**. **2** *an ethical investment policy* =**morally correct**, right-minded, principled, good, moral; just, honourable, fair.

ethics ▶ plural noun =**morals**, morality, values, principles, ideals, standards (of behaviour).

ethnic ▶ adjective =**racial**, race-related, ethnological; national, tribal.

ethos ▶ noun =**spirit**, character, atmosphere, climate, mood, feeling, essence; disposition, rationale, morality, moral code.

etiquette ▶ noun =**protocol**, manners, accepted behaviour, the rules, decorum, good form; courtesy, propriety, formalities, niceties; custom, convention; *informal* the done thing.

etymology ▶ noun =**derivation**, (word) history, origin, source.

eulogize ▶ verb =**extol**, acclaim, sing the praises of, praise to the skies, wax lyrical about, rave about, enthuse about; *N. Amer. informal* ballyhoo.
−OPPOSITES criticize.

eulogy ▶ noun =**accolade**, tribute, compliment, commendation; praise, acclaim.
−OPPOSITES attack.

euphemism ▶ noun =**polite term**, indirect term, substitute, alternative.

euphemistic ▶ adjective =**polite**, substitute, understated, indirect, neutral, evasive; diplomatic, alternative, nice.

euphoria ▶ noun =**elation**, happiness, joy, delight, glee; excitement, exhilaration, jubilation, exultation; ecstasy, bliss, rapture.
−OPPOSITES misery.

euphoric ▶ adjective =**elated**, happy, joyful, delighted, gleeful; excited, exhilarated, jubilant, exultant; ecstatic, blissful, rapturous, on cloud nine, in seventh heaven; *informal* on the top of the world, over the moon, on a high.

euthanasia ▶ noun =**mercy killing**, assisted suicide.

evacuate ▶ verb **1** *local residents were evacuated* =**removed**, move out, take away. **2** *they evacuated the building* =**leave**, vacate, abandon, move out of, quit, withdraw from, retreat from, decamp from, flee, depart from. **3** *police evacuated the area* =**clear**, empty.

evacuation ▶ noun **1** *the evacuation of civilians* =**removal**, clearance, movement; deportation. **2** *the evacuation of military bases* =**clearance**; abandonment, vacation, desertion.

evade ▶ verb **1** *they evaded the guards* =**elude**, avoid, dodge, escape (from), steer clear of, sidestep; lose, leave behind, shake off; *N. Amer.* end-run; *informal* give someone the slip. **2** *he evaded the question* =**avoid**, dodge, sidestep, bypass, skirt round, fudge, be evasive about; *informal* duck, cop out of.
−OPPOSITES confront.

evaluate ▶ verb =**assess**, judge, gauge, rate, estimate, appraise, analyse, weigh up, get the measure of; *informal* size up, check out.

evaluation ▶ noun =**assessment**, appraisal, judgement, consideration, analysis.

evangelical ▶ adjective **1** *evangelical Christianity* =**scriptural**, biblical; fundamentalist. **2** *an evangelical socialist* =**evangelistic**, evangelizing, passionate, crusading, proselytizing, fanatical, ardent, zealous.

evangelist ▶ noun =**preacher**, missionary, proselytizer, crusader, propagandist.

evangelistic ▶ adjective. *See* EVANGELICAL *sense* 2.

evaporate ▶ verb **1** *the water evaporated* =**vaporize**; dry up. **2** *the feeling has evaporated* =**end**, pass (away), fizzle out, peter out, wear off, vanish, fade, disappear, melt away.
−OPPOSITES condense, wet, materialize.

evasion ▶ noun **1** *the evasion of immigration control* =**avoidance**, circumvention, dodging, sidestepping. **2** *she grew tired of all the evasion* =**prevarication**, evasiveness, beating about the bush, hedging,

pussyfooting, equivocation, vagueness; *Brit.* humming and hawing.

evasive ▶ adjective =**equivocal**, prevaricating, elusive, ambiguous, noncommittal, vague, inexplicit, unclear; roundabout, indirect; *informal* cagey.

eve ▶ noun *the eve of the election* =**day before**, evening before, night before; the run-up to.
−OPPOSITES morning.

even ▶ adjective **1** *an even surface* =**flat**, smooth, uniform; level, plane. **2** *an even temperature* =**uniform**, constant, steady, stable, consistent, unvarying, unchanging, regular. **3** *the score was even* =**level**, drawn, tied, all square, balanced; neck and neck; *Brit.* level pegging; *informal* even-steven(s). **4** *an even disposition* =**even-tempered**, balanced, stable, equable, placid, calm, composed, poised, cool, relaxed, easy, imperturbable, unexcitable, unruffled, untroubled; *informal* together, laid-back, unflappable.
−OPPOSITES bumpy, irregular, unequal, moody.
▶ verb **1** *the canal bottom was evened out* =**flatten**, level (off/out), smooth (off/out). **2** *the union wants to even up our wages* =**equalize**, make equal, level up, balance, square; standardize, regularize.
▶ adverb **1** *it got even colder* =**still**, yet, more, all the more. **2** *she is afraid, even ashamed, to ask for help* =**indeed**, you could say, in truth, actually, or rather.
■ **even so** =**nevertheless**, nonetheless, all the same, just the same, anyway, anyhow, still, yet, however, notwithstanding, despite that, in spite of that, for all that, be that as it may, in any event, at any rate.
■ **get even** =**have one's revenge**, avenge oneself, even the score, settle the score, pay someone back, reciprocate, retaliate; *informal* get one's own back, give someone a taste of their own medicine, settle someone's hash; *literary* be revenged.

even-handed ▶ adjective =**fair**, just, equitable, impartial, unbiased, unprejudiced, non-partisan, non-discriminatory.
−OPPOSITES biased.

evening ▶ noun =**night**; twilight, dusk, nightfall, sunset, sundown.

event ▶ noun **1** *an annual event* =**occurrence**, happening, incident, affair, occasion, phenomenon; function, gathering; *informal* bash, do. **2** *a team event* =**competition**, contest, tournament, match, fixture; race, game.

■ **in any event/at all events** =**regardless**, whatever happens, come what may, no matter what, at any rate, in any case, anyhow, anyway, even so, still, nevertheless, nonetheless; *N. Amer. informal* anyways.

■ **in the event** =**as it turned out**, as it happened, in the end; as a result, as a consequence.

even-tempered ▸ adjective =**serene**, calm, composed, tranquil, relaxed, easygoing, unworried, untroubled, unruffled, imperturbable, placid, stable, level-headed; *informal* unflappable, laid-back.
–OPPOSITES excitable.

eventful ▸ adjective =**busy**, action-packed, full, lively, active, hectic.
–OPPOSITES dull.

eventual ▸ adjective =**final**, ultimate, resulting, ensuing, consequent, subsequent.

eventuality ▸ noun =**event**, situation, circumstance, case, contingency, chance; outcome, result.

eventually ▸ adverb =**in the end**, in due course, by and by, in time, after some time, after a bit, finally, at last; ultimately, in the long run, at the end of the day, one day, some day, sometime, sooner or later.

ever ▸ adverb **1** *the best I've ever done* =**at any time**, at any point, on any occasion, under any circumstances, on any account; up till now, until now. **2** *he was ever the optimist* =**always**, forever, eternally. **3** *an ever increasing rate of crime* =**continually**, constantly, always, endlessly, perpetually, incessantly, unremittingly. **4** *will she ever learn?* =**at all**, in any way.

■ **ever so** (*Brit. informal*) =**very**, extremely, exceedingly, especially, immensely, particularly, really, truly; *N. English* right; *informal* awfully, terribly, desperately, mega, ultra; *Brit. informal* well, dead, jolly; *N. Amer. informal* real, mighty, awful.

everlasting ▸ adjective =**eternal**, endless, never-ending, perpetual, undying, abiding, enduring, infinite.
–OPPOSITES transient, occasional.

evermore ▸ adverb =**always**, forever, ever, for always, for all time, until hell freezes over, eternally, in perpetuity; ever after, henceforth; *Brit.* for evermore, forever more; *N. Amer.* forevermore; *informal* until the cows come home, until the twelfth of never.

every ▸ determiner **1** *he exercised every day* =**each**, each and every, every single. **2** *we make every effort to satisfy our clients* =**all possible**, the utmost.

everybody ▸ pronoun =**everyone**, every person, each person, all, one and all, all and sundry, the whole world, the public; *informal* {every Tom, Dick, and Harry}, every man jack, every mother's son.

everyday ▸ adjective **1** *the everyday demands of a baby* =**daily**, day-to-day, quotidian; ongoing. **2** *everyday drugs like aspirin* =**commonplace**, ordinary, common, usual, regular, familiar, conventional, run-of-the-mill, standard, stock; household, domestic; *Brit.* common or garden; *informal* bog-standard.
–OPPOSITES unusual.

everyone ▸ pronoun =**everybody**, every person, each person, all, one and all, all and sundry, the whole world, the public; *informal* {every Tom, Dick, and Harry}, every man jack, every mother's son.

everything ▸ pronoun =**each thing**, every single thing, the (whole) lot; all; *informal* the whole caboodle, the whole shebang, the works; *Brit. informal* the full monty; *N. Amer. informal* the whole ball of wax.
–OPPOSITES nothing.

WORD LINKS

fear of everything: **panphobia, panophobia, pantophobia**

everywhere ▸ adverb =**all over**, all around, in every nook and cranny, far and wide, near and far, high and low, {here, there, and everywhere}; throughout the land, the world over, worldwide; *informal* all over the place; *Brit. informal* all over the shop; *N. Amer. informal* all over the map.
–OPPOSITES nowhere.

evict ▸ verb =**expel**, eject, remove, dislodge, turn out, throw out, drive out; dispossess; *informal* chuck out, kick out, boot out, bounce, give someone the (old) heave-ho, throw someone out on their ear; *Brit. informal* turf out; *N. Amer. informal* give someone the bum's rush.

eviction ▶ noun =**expulsion**, ejection, removal, dislodgement, displacement.

evidence ▶ noun **1** *evidence of his infidelity* =**proof**, confirmation, verification, substantiation, corroboration. **2** *the court accepted her evidence* =**testimony**, statement, declaration, submission; *Law* deposition, representation, affidavit. **3** *evidence of a struggle* =**signs**, indications, pointers, marks, traces, suggestions, hints; manifestation.
■ **in evidence** =**noticeable**, conspicuous, obvious, perceptible, visible, on view, plain to see.

evident ▶ adjective =**obvious**, apparent, noticeable, conspicuous, perceptible, visible, discernible, clear, plain, manifest, patent; palpable, tangible, distinct; *informal* as plain as the nose on your face, sticking out like a sore thumb, sticking out a mile, as clear as day.

evidently ▶ adverb **1** *he was evidently upset* =**obviously**, clearly, plainly; unmistakably, undeniably, undoubtedly. **2** *evidently, she believed him* =**seemingly**, apparently, as far as one can tell, from/by all appearances, on the face of it; it seems (that), it appears (that).

evil ▶ adjective **1** *an evil deed* =**wicked**, bad, wrong, immoral, sinful, foul, vile, iniquitous, depraved, villainous, vicious, malicious; malevolent, sinister, demonic, devilish, diabolical, fiendish, dark; monstrous, shocking, despicable, atrocious, heinous, odious, contemptible, horrible. **2** *an evil spirit* =**harmful**, bad, malign; unclean. **3** *evil weather* =**unpleasant**, disagreeable, nasty, horrible, foul, filthy, vile.
–OPPOSITES good, beneficial, pleasant.
▶ noun **1** *the evil in our midst* =**wickedness**, badness, wrongdoing, sin, sinfulness, immorality, vice, iniquity, degeneracy, corruption, depravity, villainy; *formal* turpitude. **2** *nothing but evil will result* =**harm**, pain, misery, sorrow, suffering, trouble, disaster, misfortune, catastrophe, affliction, woe. **3** *the evil of war* =**abomination**, atrocity, obscenity, outrage, monstrosity, barbarity.

evocative ▶ adjective =**reminiscent**, suggestive, redolent; expressive, vivid, powerful, haunting, moving, poignant.

evoke ▶ verb =**bring to mind**, put one in mind of, conjure up, summon (up), invoke, elicit, stimulate, stir up, awaken, arouse.

evolution ▶ noun **1** *the evolution of Bolshevism* =**development**, growth, rise, progress, expansion. **2** *his interest in evolution* =**Darwinism**, natural selection.

evolve ▶ verb =**develop**, progress, advance; mature, grow, expand, spread; change, transform, adapt, metamorphose; *humorous* transmogrify.

exacerbate ▶ verb =**aggravate**, worsen, inflame, compound; intensify, increase, heighten, magnify, add to.
–OPPOSITES reduce.

exact ▶ adjective **1** *an exact description* =**precise**, accurate, correct, faithful, close, true; literal, strict, perfect; detailed, minute, meticulous, thorough; *informal* on the nail, on the mark; *Brit. informal* spot on, bang on; *N. Amer. informal* on the money, on the button. **2** *an exact record keeper* =**careful**, meticulous, painstaking, punctilious, conscientious, scrupulous, exacting.
–OPPOSITES inaccurate, careless.
▶ verb *they exacted a terrible vengeance on him* =**inflict**, impose, administer, apply, wreak.

exacting ▶ adjective *an exacting training routine* =**demanding**, stringent, testing, challenging, arduous, laborious, taxing, gruelling, punishing, hard, tough.
–OPPOSITES easy, easy-going.

exactly ▶ adverb **1** *it's exactly as I expected* =**precisely**, entirely, absolutely, completely, totally, just, quite, in every way, in every respect, one hundred per cent, every inch, to the hilt; *informal* to a T. **2** *write it out exactly* =**accurately**, precisely, unerringly, faultlessly, perfectly; verbatim, word for word, letter for letter, faithfully.
▶ exclamation *'She escaped?' 'Exactly.'* =**precisely**, yes, that's right, just so, quite (so), indeed; *informal* you got it, absolutely.

exaggerate ▶ verb =**overstate**, overemphasize, overestimate, inflate; embellish, embroider, elaborate, overplay, dramatize, stretch the truth; *Brit. informal* make a mountain out of a molehill, blow out of all proportion, make a big thing of.
–OPPOSITES understate.

exaggerated ▶ adjective =**overstated**, inflated, magnified, excessive, over-elaborate, overdone, overplayed, overdramatized, highly coloured, melodramatic; *informal* over the top, OTT.

exaggeration ▶ noun =**overstatement**, overemphasis; dramatization, elaboration, embellishment, embroidery, hyperbole, overkill, gilding the lily.

exalted ▶ adjective **1** *his exalted office* =**high**, high-ranking, elevated, superior, lofty, eminent, prestigious, illustrious, distinguished, esteemed. **2** *his exalted aims* =**noble**, lofty, high-minded, elevated, ambitious.

exam ▶ noun =**test**, examination; assessment; paper; *N. Amer.* quiz.

examination ▶ noun **1** *artefacts spread out for examination* =**scrutiny**, inspection, perusal, study, investigation, consideration, analysis, appraisal, evaluation. **2** *a medical examination* =**inspection**, check-up, assessment, appraisal; probe, test, scan; *informal* once-over, overhaul. **3** *a school examination* =**test**, exam, assessment; *N. Amer.* quiz.

examine ▶ verb **1** *they examined the bank records* =**inspect**, scrutinize, investigate, look at, study, sift (through), appraise, analyse, review, survey; *informal* check out. **2** *students were examined after a year* =**test**, quiz, question; assess, appraise.

examiner ▶ noun =**tester**, questioner, interviewer, assessor, marker, inspector; adjudicator, scrutineer.

example ▶ noun **1** *a fine example of Chinese porcelain* =**specimen**, sample, exemplar, instance, case, illustration. **2** *we must follow their example* =**precedent**, lead, model, pattern, exemplar, ideal. **3** *he was hanged as an example to others* =**warning**, lesson, deterrent; moral; disincentive.
■ **for example** =**for instance**, e.g., such as, like.

exasperate ▶ verb =**infuriate**, anger, annoy, irritate, madden, provoke, irk, vex, get on someone's nerves, ruffle someone's feathers; *Brit.* rub up the wrong way; *informal* aggravate, rile, bug, needle, hack off, get up someone's nose, get someone's back up, get someone's goat, give someone the hump; *Brit. informal* nark, wind up, get on someone's wick; *N. Amer. informal* tee off, tick off.
−OPPOSITES please.

exasperating ▶ adjective =**infuriating**, annoying, irritating, maddening, trying; *informal* aggravating.

exasperation ▶ noun =**irritation**, annoyance, vexation, anger, fury; *informal* aggravation.

excavate ▶ verb =**unearth**, dig up, uncover, reveal; disinter, exhume.

excavation ▶ noun =**hole**, pit, trench, trough; (archaeological) site; dig.

exceed ▶ verb =**be more than**, be greater than, be over, go beyond, top; surpass.

exceeding (*archaic*) ▶ adjective *his exceeding kindness* =**great**, considerable, exceptional, tremendous, immense, extreme, supreme, outstanding.
▶ adverb *the Lord has been exceeding gracious*. See EXCEEDINGLY.

exceedingly ▶ adverb =**extremely**, exceptionally, especially, tremendously, very, really, truly, most; *informal* terribly, awfully, seriously, mega, ultra; *Brit. informal* ever so, well, dead, jolly; *N. Amer. informal* real, mighty; *archaic* exceeding.

excel ▶ verb **1** *he excelled at football* =**shine**, be excellent, be outstanding, be skilful, be talented; stand out, be second to none. **2** *she excelled him in her work* =**surpass**, outdo, outshine, outclass, outstrip, beat, top, transcend, better, pass, eclipse, overshadow.

excellence ▶ noun =**distinction**, quality, superiority, brilliance, greatness, calibre, eminence; skill, talent, virtuosity, accomplishment, mastery.

excellent ▶ adjective =**very good**, superb, outstanding, exceptional, marvellous, wonderful; perfect, matchless, peerless, supreme, first-rate, first-class, superlative, splendid, fine; *informal* A1, ace, great, terrific, tremendous, fantastic, fabulous, fab, top-notch, class, awesome, magic, wicked, cool, out of this world; *Brit. informal* brilliant, brill, smashing; *Austral. informal* bonzer.
−OPPOSITES inferior.

except ▶ preposition =**excluding**, not including, excepting, omitting, not counting, but, besides, apart from, aside from, barring, bar, other than, saving; with the exception of; *informal* outside of; *formal* save.
−OPPOSITES including.

exception ▶ noun *this case is an exception* =**anomaly**, irregularity, deviation, special case, peculiarity, abnormality, oddity; misfit; *informal* freak.
■ **take exception** =**object**, take of-

fence, take umbrage, demur, disagree; resent; *informal* kick up a fuss, kick up a stink.

■ **with the exception of.** See EXCEPT preposition.

exceptional ▶ adjective **1** *the drought was exceptional* =**unusual**, uncommon, abnormal, atypical, out of the ordinary, rare, unprecedented, unexpected, surprising; strange, odd, freakish, anomalous, peculiar. **2** *her exceptional ability* =**outstanding**, extraordinary, remarkable, special, phenomenal, prodigious; unequalled, unparalleled, unsurpassed, peerless, matchless.
–OPPOSITES normal, average.

exceptionally ▶ adverb =**exceedingly**, outstandingly, extraordinarily, remarkably, especially, phenomenally, prodigiously.

excerpt ▶ noun =**extract**, part, section, piece, portion, snippet, clip, bit; reading, citation, quotation, quote, line, passage; *N. Amer.* cite.

excess ▶ noun **1** *an excess of calcium* =**surplus**, surfeit, over-abundance, superabundance, superfluity, glut; too much. **2** *the excess is turned into fat* =**remainder**, rest, residue; leftovers, remnants; surplus, extra, difference. **3** *a life of excess* =**overindulgence**, intemperance, immoderation, profligacy, extravagance, decadence, self-indulgence.
–OPPOSITES lack, restraint.

▶ adjective *excess oil* =**surplus**, superfluous, redundant, unwanted, unneeded, excessive; extra.

■ **in excess of** =**more than**, over, above, upwards of, beyond.

excessive ▶ adjective **1** *excessive alcohol consumption* =**immoderate**, intemperate, overindulgent, unrestrained, uncontrolled; lavish, extravagant. **2** *the cost is excessive* =**exorbitant**, extortionate, unreasonable, outrageous, uncalled for, extreme, unwarranted, disproportionate, too much; *informal* over the top, OTT.

excessively ▶ adverb =**inordinately**, unduly, unnecessarily, unreasonably, ridiculously, overly; very, extremely, exceedingly, exceptionally, impossibly; immoderately, too much.

exchange ▶ noun **1** *the exchange of ideas* =**interchange**, trade, trading, swapping, traffic, trafficking. **2** *a brief exchange* =**conversation**, dialogue, chat, talk, discussion; debate, argument, altercation; *Brit. informal* row, barney.

▶ verb *we exchanged shirts* =**trade**, swap, switch, change.

excise[1] ▶ noun *the excise on spirits* =**duty**, tax, levy, tariff.

excise[2] ▶ verb **1** *the tumours were excised* =**cut out/off/away**, take out, extract, remove. **2** *all unnecessary detail was excised* =**delete**, cross out/through, strike out, score out, cancel, put a line through; erase.

excitable ▶ adjective =**temperamental**, mercurial, volatile, emotional, sensitive, highly strung, unstable, nervous, tense, edgy, jumpy, twitchy, neurotic; *informal* uptight, wired.
–OPPOSITES placid.

excite ▶ verb **1** *the prospect of a holiday excited me* =**thrill**, exhilarate, animate, enliven, rouse, stir, stimulate, galvanize, electrify, inspirit; *informal* buck up, pep up, ginger up, give someone a buzz/kick; *N. Amer. informal* give someone a charge. **2** *she wore stockings to excite him* =**arouse (sexually)**, stimulate, titillate; *informal* turn someone on, get someone going, float someone's boat. **3** *his clothes excited envy* =**provoke**, stir up, rouse, arouse, kindle, trigger (off), spark off, incite, cause.
–OPPOSITES bore, depress.

excited ▶ adjective **1** *they were excited about the holiday* =**thrilled**, exhilarated, animated, enlivened, electrified; enraptured, intoxicated, feverish, enthusiastic; *informal* high (as a kite), fired up. **2** *he made her feel excited* =**(sexually) aroused**, stimulated, titillated; *informal* turned on, hot, horny, sexed up; *Brit. informal* randy.

excitement ▶ noun **1** *the excitement of seeing a leopard in the wild* =**thrill**, pleasure, delight, joy; *informal* kick, buzz; *N. Amer. informal* charge. **2** *excitement in her eyes* =**exhilaration**, elation, animation, enthusiasm, eagerness, anticipation, feverishness; *informal* pep, vim, zing. **3** *bringing new excitement into their love life* =**(sexual) arousal**, passion, stimulation, titillation.

exciting ▶ adjective **1** *an exciting story* =**thrilling**, exhilarating, stirring, rousing, stimulating, intoxicating, electrifying, invigorating; gripping, compelling, powerful, dramatic. **2** *he found her kisses exciting* =**(sexually) arousing**, (sexually) stimulating, titillating, erotic, sexual, sexy; *informal* raunchy, steamy, horny.

exclaim ▸ verb =cry (out), declare, blurt out; call (out), shout (out), yell.

exclamation ▸ noun =cry, call, shout, yell.

exclude ▸ verb **1** *women were excluded from the club* =keep out, deny access to, shut out, bar, ban, prohibit. **2** *the clause excluded any judicial review* =rule out, preclude. **3** *the price excludes postage* =be exclusive of, not include.
–OPPOSITES admit, include.

exclusion ▸ noun **1** *the exclusion of women from the society* =barring, keeping out, banning, prohibition. **2** *the exclusion of other factors* =elimination, ruling out, precluding. **3** *the exclusion of pupils* =expulsion, ejection, throwing out; suspension.
–OPPOSITES acceptance, inclusion.

exclusive ▸ adjective **1** *an exclusive club* =select, chic, high-class, elite, fashionable, stylish, elegant, premier; expensive; *Brit.* upmarket; *N. Amer.* high-toned; *informal* posh, ritzy, classy; *Brit. informal* swish; *N. Amer. informal* tony. **2** *a room for your exclusive use* =sole, unshared, unique, individual, personal, private. **3** *prices exclusive of VAT* =not including, excluding, leaving out, omitting, excepting.
–OPPOSITES inclusive.
▸ noun *a six-page exclusive* =scoop, exposé, special.

excrement ▸ noun =faeces, excreta, stools, droppings; ordure, dung, manure; dirt, muck, mess; *informal* poo, turds, doings, doo-doo; *Brit. informal* cack, whoopsies, jobbies; *N. Amer. informal* poop.

WORD LINKS

relating to excrement: **copro-, scato-**
medical study of excrement: **scatology**
fear of excrement: **coprophobia**
excrement-eating: **coprophagous**

excrescence ▸ noun *the new buildings were an excrescence* =eyesore, blot on the landscape, monstrosity.

excrete ▸ verb =expel, pass, void, discharge, eject, evacuate; defecate, urinate.
–OPPOSITES ingest.

excruciating ▸ adjective =agonizing, severe, acute, intense, violent, racking, searing, piercing, stabbing, raging; unbearable, unendurable; *informal* splitting, killing.

excursion ▸ noun =trip, outing, jaunt, expedition, journey, tour; day trip/out, drive, run, ride; *informal* junket, spin.

excusable ▸ adjective =forgivable, pardonable, defensible, justifiable.
–OPPOSITES unforgivable.

excuse ▸ verb **1** *please excuse me* =forgive, pardon. **2** *such conduct cannot be excused* =justify, defend, condone; forgive, overlook, disregard, ignore, tolerate. **3** *she was excused from her duties* =let off, release, relieve, exempt, absolve, free.
–OPPOSITES punish, blame, condemn.
▸ noun **1** *that's no excuse for stealing* =justification, defence, reason, explanation, mitigating circumstances, mitigation. **2** *an excuse to get away* =pretext, pretence; *Brit.* get-out; *informal* story, alibi. **3** *(informal) that pathetic excuse for a man!* =travesty of; *informal* apology for.

execute ▸ verb **1** *he was finally executed* =put to death, kill. **2** *he executed a series of financial deals* =carry out, accomplish, bring off/about, achieve, complete, engineer; *informal* pull off.

execution ▸ noun **1** *the execution of the plan* =implementation, carrying out, accomplishment, bringing off/about, attainment, realization. **2** *the execution of the play* =performance, presentation, rendition, rendering, staging, delivery. **3** *a public execution|sentenced to execution* =killing; capital punishment, the death penalty.

executive ▸ adjective *executive powers* =administrative, decision-making, managerial; law-making.
▸ noun **1** *top-level executives* =chief, head, director, senior official, senior manager; *informal* boss, exec, suit. **2** *the future role of the executive* =administration, management, directorate; government.

exemplary ▸ adjective **1** *her exemplary behaviour* =perfect, ideal, model, faultless, flawless, impeccable, irreproachable; excellent, outstanding, above/beyond reproach. **2** *exemplary jail sentences* =(serving as a) deterrent, cautionary, warning.
–OPPOSITES deplorable.

exemplify ▸ verb **1** *this story exemplifies current trends* =typify, epitomize, be an example of, be representative of, symbolize. **2** *he exemplified his point with an anecdote* =illustrate, give an example of, demonstrate.

exempt ▶ adjective =**free**, not liable/subject, exempted, excepted, excused, absolved.
−OPPOSITES subject to.
▶ verb =**excuse**, free, release, exclude, give/grant immunity, spare, absolve; *informal* let off; *N. Amer. informal* grandfather.

exemption ▶ noun =**immunity**, exception, dispensation, indemnity, exclusion, freedom, release, relief, absolution; *informal* let-off.

exercise ▶ noun **1** *exercise improves your heart* =**physical activity**, a workout, working out. **2** *translation exercises* =**task**, piece of work, problem, assignment. **3** *military exercises* =**manoeuvres**, operations.
▶ verb **1** *she exercised every day* =**work out**, do exercises, train. **2** *he must learn to exercise patience* =**use**, employ, make use of, utilize; practise, apply. **3** *the problem continued to exercise him* =**worry**, trouble, concern, bother, disturb, perturb, distress, preoccupy, prey on someone's mind, make uneasy; *informal* bug, do someone's head in.

exert ▶ verb **1** *he exerted considerable pressure on me* =**bring to bear**, apply, use, utilize, deploy. **2** *he had clearly been exerting himself* =**push oneself**, work hard.

exertion ▶ noun **1** *she was panting with the exertion* =**effort**, strain. **2** *the exertion of pressure* =**use**, application, exercise, employment, utilization.

exhale ▶ verb =**breathe out**, blow out, puff out; sigh.
−OPPOSITES inhale.

exhaust ▶ verb **1** *the effort had exhausted him* =**tire (out)**, wear out, overtire, fatigue, weary, drain, run someone into the ground; *informal* do in, take it out of one, wipe out, knock out, shatter; *Brit. informal* knacker; *N. Amer. informal* poop, tucker out. **2** *the country has exhausted its reserves* =**use up**, run through, go through, consume, finish, deplete, spend, empty, drain; *informal* blow. **3** *we've exhausted the subject* =**deal with**, do to death.
−OPPOSITES invigorate, replenish.

exhausted ▶ adjective **1** *I'm exhausted* =**tired out**, worn out, weary, dog-tired, ready to drop, drained, fatigued; *informal* done in, all in, dead beat, shattered, bushed, knocked out, wiped out; *Brit. informal* knackered, whacked (out), jig-

gered; *N. Amer. informal* pooped, tuckered out, fried, whipped; *Austral./NZ informal* stonkered. **2** *exhausted reserves* =**used up**, consumed, finished, spent, depleted; empty, drained.

exhausting ▶ adjective =**tiring**, wearying, taxing, wearing, draining; arduous, strenuous, onerous, demanding, gruelling; *informal* killing, murderous; *Brit. informal* knackering.

exhaustion ▶ noun **1** *sheer exhaustion forced Paul to give up* =**(extreme) tiredness**, overtiredness, fatigue, weariness. **2** *the exhaustion of fuel reserves* =**consumption**, depletion, using up; draining, emptying.

exhaustive ▶ adjective =**comprehensive**, all-inclusive, complete, full, encyclopedic, thorough, in-depth; detailed, meticulous, painstaking.
−OPPOSITES perfunctory.

exhibit ▶ verb **1** *the paintings were exhibited in Glasgow* =**put on display/show**, display, show. **2** *Luke exhibited signs of jealousy* =**show**, reveal, display, manifest; indicate, demonstrate, present; *formal* evince.
▶ noun **1** *an exhibit at the British Museum* =**item**, piece, artefact. **2** *(N. Amer.) people flocked to the exhibit*. See EXHIBITION sense 1.

exhibition ▶ noun **1** *a photography exhibition* =**display**, show, showing, presentation, demonstration, exposition; *N. Amer.* exhibit. **2** *a convincing exhibition of concern* =**display**, show, demonstration, manifestation, expression.

exhibitionist ▶ noun =**poser**, self-publicist; extrovert; *informal* show-off; *N. Amer. informal* showboat.

exhilarate ▶ verb =**thrill**, excite, intoxicate, elate, delight, enliven, animate, invigorate, energize, stimulate; *informal* give someone a thrill/buzz; *N. Amer. informal* give someone a charge.

exhilarating ▶ adjective =**thrilling**, exciting, invigorating, stimulating; electrifying.

exhilaration ▶ noun =**elation**, euphoria, exultation, exaltation, joy, happiness, delight, joyousness, jubilation, rapture, ecstasy.

exhort ▶ verb =**urge**, encourage, call on, enjoin, charge, press; bid, appeal to, entreat, implore; *literary* beseech.

exhortation ▶ noun =**entreaty**, appeal, call, charge.

exhume ▶ verb =**disinter**, dig up, disentomb.
−OPPOSITES bury.

exile ▶ noun 1 *his exile from his homeland* =**banishment**, isolation. 2 *political exiles* =**émigré**, expatriate; displaced person, DP, refugee, deportee; *informal* expat.

exist ▶ verb 1 *animals that existed long ago* =**live**, be alive, be living. 2 *the liberal climate that now exists* =**prevail**, occur, be found, be in existence. 3 *she had to exist on a low income* =**survive**, subsist, live, support oneself; manage, make do, get by, scrape by, make ends meet.

existence ▶ noun 1 *the industry's continued existence* =**survival**, continuation. 2 *her suburban existence* =**way of life/living**, life, lifestyle.
■ **in existence** 1 *there are many species in existence* =**alive**, existing, extant, existent. 2 *the only copy still in existence* =**surviving**, remaining, in circulation.

existing ▶ adjective =**present**, current, available; in existence, surviving, remaining, extant.

exit ▶ noun 1 *the fire exit* =**way out**, door, egress, escape route. 2 *take the second exit* =**turning**, turn-off, turn; *N. Amer.* turnout. 3 *his sudden exit* =**departure**, leaving, withdrawal, going, decamping, retreat; flight, exodus, escape.
−OPPOSITES entrance, arrival.
▶ verb *the doctor had just exited* =**leave**, go (out), depart, withdraw, retreat.
−OPPOSITES enter.

exodus ▶ noun =**mass departure**, withdrawal, evacuation; migration, emigration; flight, escape.

exonerate ▶ verb =**absolve**, clear, acquit, find innocent, discharge; *formal* exculpate.
−OPPOSITES convict.

exorbitant ▶ adjective =**extortionate**, excessive, prohibitive, outrageous, unreasonable, inflated, huge, enormous; *Brit.* over the odds; *informal* steep, stiff, over the top, a rip-off; *Brit. informal* daylight robbery.
−OPPOSITES reasonable.

exotic ▶ adjective 1 *exotic birds* =**foreign**, non-native, tropical. 2 *exotic places* =**foreign**, faraway, far-off, far-flung, distant. 3 *Linda's exotic appearance* =**striking**, colourful, eye-catching; unusual, unconventional, extravagant, outlandish.
−OPPOSITES native, nearby, conventional.

expand ▶ verb 1 *metals expand when heated* =**increase in size**, become larger, enlarge; swell; lengthen, stretch, thicken, fill out. 2 *the company is expanding* =**grow**, become/make larger, become/make bigger, increase in size/scope; extend, augment, broaden, widen, develop, diversify, build up; branch out, spread, proliferate. 3 *the minister expanded on the proposals* =**elaborate on**, enlarge on, go into detail about, flesh out, develop.
−OPPOSITES shrink, contract.

expanse ▶ noun =**area**, stretch, sweep, tract, swathe, belt, region; sea, carpet, blanket, sheet.

expansion ▶ noun 1 *expansion and contraction* =**enlargement**, increase, swelling; lengthening, elongation, stretching, thickening. 2 *the expansion of the company* =**growth**, increase, enlargement, extension, development; spread, diversification.
−OPPOSITES contraction.

expansive ▶ adjective 1 *expansive moorland* =**extensive**, sweeping, rolling. 2 *expansive coverage* =**wide-ranging**, extensive, broad, wide, comprehensive, thorough. 3 *Cara grew more expansive* =**communicative**, forthcoming, sociable, friendly, outgoing, affable, chatty, talkative.

expatriate ▶ noun *expatriates working overseas* =**emigrant**, émigré, (economic) migrant; *informal* expat.
−OPPOSITES national.
▶ adjective *expatriate workers* =**emigrant**, living abroad, émigré; *informal* expat.
−OPPOSITES indigenous.

expect ▶ verb 1 *I expect she'll be late* =**suppose**, presume, imagine, assume, surmise; *informal* guess, reckon; *N. Amer. informal* figure. 2 *a 10 per cent rise was expected* =**anticipate**, await, look for, hope for, look forward to; contemplate, bargain for/on, bank on; predict, forecast, envisage. 3 *we expect total loyalty* =**require**, ask for, call for, want, insist on, demand.

expectancy ▶ noun =**anticipation**, expectation, eagerness, excitement.

expectant ▶ adjective 1 *expectant fans* =**eager**, excited, waiting with bated breath, hopeful. 2 *an expectant mother* =**pregnant**; *informal* expecting, in the family way, preggers.

expectation ▸ noun 1 *her expectations were unrealistic* =**supposition**, assumption, presumption, conjecture, calculation, prediction. 2 *tense with expectation* =**anticipation**, expectancy, eagerness, excitement, suspense.

expecting ▸ adjective (informal). See EXPECTANT sense 2.

expedient ▸ adjective =**convenient**, advantageous, useful, of use, beneficial, of benefit, helpful; practical, pragmatic, politic, prudent, judicious.
▸ noun =**measure**, means, method, stratagem, scheme, plan, move, tactic, manoeuvre, device, contrivance, ploy, dodge; *Austral. informal* lurk.

expedite ▸ verb =**speed up**, accelerate, hurry, hasten, step up, quicken, precipitate, dispatch; advance, facilitate, ease, make easier, further, promote, aid, push through, urge on, boost, stimulate, spur on, help along.
–OPPOSITES delay.

expedition ▸ noun 1 *an expedition to the South Pole* =**journey**, voyage, tour, odyssey; safari, trek, hike. 2 *(informal) a shopping expedition* =**trip**, excursion, outing. 3 *all members of the expedition* =**group**, team, party, crew, squad.

expel ▸ verb =**throw out**, bar, ban, debar, drum out, get rid of, dismiss; *Military* cashier; *informal* chuck out, sling out, kick/boot out; *Brit. informal* turf out; *N. Amer. informal* give someone the bum's rush.
–OPPOSITES admit.

expend ▸ verb =**use (up)**, utilize, consume, eat up, deplete, get through.
–OPPOSITES save, conserve.

expendable ▸ adjective =**dispensable**, replaceable, non-essential, inessential, unnecessary, not required, superfluous.
–OPPOSITES indispensable.

expenditure ▸ noun =**outgoings**, costs, payments, expenses, overheads, spending.
–OPPOSITES income.

expense ▸ noun 1 *Nigel resented the expense* =**cost**, price, charge(s), outlay, fee(s), tariff(s). 2 *regular expenses* =**outgoing**, payment, outlay, expenditure, charge, bill, overhead.

expensive ▸ adjective =**costly**, dear, high-priced, overpriced, exorbitant, extortionate; *informal* steep, pricey, costing an arm and a leg, costing the earth, costing a bomb.
–OPPOSITES cheap, economical.

experience ▸ noun 1 *qualifications and experience* =**skill**, (practical) knowledge, understanding; background, record, history; maturity, worldliness, sophistication; *informal* know-how. 2 *an enjoyable experience* =**incident**, occurrence, event, happening, episode; adventure, exploit, escapade. 3 *his first experience of business* =**involvement in**, participation in, contact with, acquaintance with, exposure to.
▸ verb *they experience daily harassment* =**undergo**, encounter, meet, come into contact with, come across, come up against, face, be faced with.

experienced ▸ adjective 1 *an experienced pilot* =**knowledgeable**, skilful, skilled, expert; proficient, trained, competent, capable, well trained, well versed; seasoned, practised, mature, veteran. 2 *she deluded herself that she was experienced* =**worldly (wise)**, sophisticated, mature, knowing; *informal* streetwise.
–OPPOSITES novice, naive.

experiment ▸ noun 1 *carrying out experiments* =**test**, investigation, trial, examination, observation; assessment, evaluation, appraisal, analysis, study. 2 *these results have been established by experiment* =**research**, experimentation, observation, analysis, testing.
▸ verb *they experimented with new ideas* =**carry out trials/tests**, conduct research/experiments; test, trial, try out, assess, appraise, evaluate.

WORD LINKS

relating to experiment: **empirical**

experimental ▸ adjective 1 *the experimental stage* =**exploratory**, investigational, trial, test, pilot; speculative, conjectural, hypothetical, tentative, preliminary. 2 *experimental music* =**new**, radical, avant-garde, alternative; unorthodox, unconventional, left-field; *informal* way-out.

expert ▸ noun =**specialist**, authority, pundit; adept, maestro, virtuoso, master, wizard; connoisseur, aficionado; *informal* ace, buff, pro, whizz, hotshot; *Brit. informal* dab hand; *N. Amer. informal* maven, crackerjack.
▸ adjective =**skilful**, skilled, adept, accom-

plished, talented, fine; masterly, virtuoso, great, excellent, first-class, first-
rate, superb; proficient, good, able,
capable, experienced, practised, knowledgeable; *informal* wizard, ace, crack,
mean.
−OPPOSITES incompetent.

expertise ▶ noun =**skill**, skilfulness,
prowess, proficiency, competence;
knowledge, ability, aptitude, capability;
informal know-how.

expire ▶ verb **1** *my contract has expired*
=**run out**, become invalid, become void,
lapse; end, finish, stop, come to an end,
terminate. **2** *the spot where he expired*
=**die**, pass away/on, breathe one's last;
informal kick the bucket, bite the dust,
croak, buy it; *Brit. informal* snuff it, peg
out, pop one's clogs.

expiry ▶ noun **1** *the expiry of the lease*
=**lapse**. **2** *the expiry of his term of office*
=**end**, finish, termination, conclusion.

explain ▶ verb **1** *he explained the procedure* =**describe**, give an explanation of,
make clear/intelligible, spell out, put
into words; elucidate, expound, clarify,
throw light on. **2** *that could explain his behaviour* =**account for**, give an explanation for, give a reason for.

explanation ▶ noun **1** *an explanation
of his theory* =**clarification**; description,
statement; interpretation, commen-
tary. **2** *I owe you an explanation* =**account**,
reason; justification, excuse, defence,
vindication.

explanatory ▶ adjective =**explaining**,
descriptive, describing, illustrative, elucidatory.

expletive ▶ noun =**swear word**, oath,
curse, obscenity, profanity, four-letter
word, dirty word; *informal* cuss word,
cuss; *formal* imprecation; (**expletives**)
bad language, foul language, strong language, swearing.

explicable ▶ adjective =**explainable**,
understandable, comprehensible, accountable, intelligible, interpretable.

explicit ▶ adjective **1** *explicit instructions*
=**clear**, plain, straightforward, crystal
clear, easily understandable; precise,
exact, specific, unequivocal, unambiguous; detailed, comprehensive, exhaustive. **2** *sexually explicit material* =**uncen-
sored**, graphic, candid, full-frontal.
−OPPOSITES vague.

explode ▶ verb **1** *a bomb has exploded*
=**blow up**, detonate, go off, burst

(apart), fly apart. **2** *exploding an atomic device* =**set off**, let off, discharge.
3 *he just exploded* =**lose one's temper**,
blow up; *informal* fly off the handle, hit
the roof, blow one's cool/top, go wild, go
bananas, see red, go off the deep end;
Brit. informal go spare, go crackers; *N. Amer.
informal* blow one's lid/stack. **4** *the city's exploding population* =**increase suddenly/
rapidly**, mushroom, snowball, escalate,
burgeon, rocket. **5** *exploding the myths
about men* =**disprove**, refute, rebut, repudiate, debunk, give the lie to; *informal*
shoot full of holes, blow out of the
water.
−OPPOSITES defuse.

exploit ▶ verb **1** *we should exploit this opportunity* =**utilize**, use, make use of,
turn/put to good use, make the most of,
capitalize on, benefit from; *informal* cash
in on. **2** *exploiting the workers* =**take advantage of**, abuse, impose on, treat unfairly, misuse, ill-treat; *informal* walk (all)
over, take for a ride, rip off.
▶ noun *his exploits brought him notoriety*
=**feat**, deed, act, adventure, stunt, escapade; achievement.

exploitation ▶ noun **1** *the exploitation
of mineral resources* =**utilization**, use,
making use of, making the most of, cap-
italization on; *informal* cashing in on.
2 *the exploitation of the poor* =**taking advantage**, abuse, misuse, ill-treatment,
unfair treatment, oppression.

exploration ▶ noun =**investigation**,
study, survey, research, inspection,
examination, scrutiny, observation.

exploratory ▶ adjective =**investigative**, explorative, probing, fact-finding;
trial, test, preliminary, provisional.

explore ▶ verb **1** *they explored the possibilities* =**investigate**, look into, consider,
examine, research, survey, scrutinize,
study, review, go over with a fine-tooth
comb; *informal* check out. **2** *exploring Ice-
land* =**travel (over)**, tour; survey, take a
look at, inspect, investigate, reconnoitre; *informal* recce, give something a/
the once-over.

explorer ▶ noun =**traveller**, discov-
erer, voyager, adventurer; surveyor,
scout, prospector.

explosion ▶ noun **1** *Ed heard the explosion* =**detonation**, eruption; bang, blast,
boom. **2** *an explosion of anger* =**outburst**,
flare-up, outbreak, eruption, storm,
rush, surge; fit, paroxysm, attack. **3** *a*

population explosion =**sudden/rapid increase**, mushrooming, snowballing, escalation, multiplication, burgeoning, rocketing.

explosive ▶ adjective **1** *explosive gases* =**volatile**, inflammable, flammable, combustible, incendiary. **2** *Marco's explosive temper* =**fiery**, stormy, violent, volatile, passionate, tempestuous, turbulent, touchy, irascible, hot-headed, short-tempered. **3** *an explosive situation* =**tense**, (highly) charged, overwrought; dangerous, perilous, hazardous, sensitive, delicate, unstable, volatile.
▶ noun *stocks of explosives* =**bomb**, incendiary (device).

exponent ▶ noun **1** *an exponent of free trade* =**advocate**, supporter, proponent, upholder, backer, defender, champion; promoter, propagandist, campaigner, fighter, crusader, enthusiast, apologist. **2** *a karate exponent* =**practitioner**, performer, player.
−OPPOSITES critic, opponent.

export ▶ verb **1** *exporting raw materials* =**sell overseas/abroad**, send overseas/abroad, trade internationally. **2** *he is trying to export his ideas to America* =**transmit**, spread, disseminate, circulate, communicate, pass on.
−OPPOSITES import.

expose ▶ verb **1** *at low tide the rocks are exposed* =**reveal**, uncover, lay bare. **2** *he was exposed to radiation* =**subject**. **3** *they were exposed to new ideas* =**introduce to**, bring into contact with, make aware of, familiarize with, acquaint with. **4** *he was exposed as a liar* =**uncover**, reveal, unveil, unmask, detect, find out; discover, bring to light, make known; denounce, condemn; *informal* spill the beans on, blow the whistle on.
−OPPOSITES cover.

exposé ▶ noun =**revelation**, disclosure, exposure; report, feature, piece, column; *informal* scoop.
−OPPOSITES cover-up.

exposed ▶ adjective =**unprotected**, unsheltered, open to the elements/weather; vulnerable, defenceless, undefended.
−OPPOSITES sheltered.

exposition ▶ noun =**explanation**, description, elucidation, explication, interpretation; account, commentary, appraisal, assessment, discussion.

expository ▶ adjective =**explanatory**, descriptive, describing, elucidatory, explicatory, explicative, interpretative.

expostulate ▶ verb =**remonstrate**, disagree, argue, take issue, protest, reason, express disagreement, raise objections.

exposure ▶ noun **1** *the exposure of fossils in the cliffs* =**revealing**, revelation, uncovering, baring, laying bare. **2** *exposure to toxins* =**subjection**. **3** *suffering from exposure* =**frostbite**, cold, hypothermia. **4** *exposure to great literature* =**introduction to**, experience of, contact with, acquaintance with, awareness of. **5** *the exposure of a banking fraud* =**uncovering**, revelation, disclosure, unveiling, unmasking, discovery, detection. **6** *we're getting a lot of exposure* =**publicity**, advertising, public interest/attention, media interest/attention; *informal* hype. **7** *how many exposures are left?* =**picture**, photograph; *informal* photo.

expound ▶ verb =**present**, put forward, set forth, propose, propound; explain, give an explanation of, detail, spell out, describe.

express¹ ▶ verb =**communicate**, convey, indicate, show, demonstrate, reveal, put across/over, get across/over; articulate, put into words, voice, give voice to; state, assert, air, make public, give vent to.
■ **express oneself** =**communicate one's thoughts/opinions/views**, put thoughts into words, speak one's mind, say what's on one's mind.

express² ▶ adjective *an express train* =**rapid**, swift, fast, high-speed; nonstop, direct.
−OPPOSITES slow.
▶ noun *an overnight express* =**express train**, fast train, direct train.

expression ▶ noun **1** *the free expression of their views* =**utterance**, uttering, voicing, declaration, articulation, assertion, setting forth. **2** *an expression of sympathy* =**indication**, demonstration, show, exhibition, token; communication, illustration, revelation. **3** *a sad expression* =**look**, appearance, air, manner, countenance, mien. **4** *a well-known expression* =**idiom**, phrase; proverb, saying, adage, maxim, axiom, aphorism; platitude, cliché. **5** *put more expression into it* =**emotion**, feeling, spirit, passion, intensity; style, intonation, tone.

expressionless ▶ adjective **1** *his face*

was expressionless =**inscrutable**, dead-pan, poker-faced; blank, vacant, emotionless, unemotional, inexpressive; glazed, stony, wooden, impassive. **2** *a flat, expressionless tone* =**dull**, dry, toneless, monotonous, flat, wooden, unmodulated, unvarying, devoid of feeling/emotion.
–OPPOSITES expressive, lively.

expressive ▶ adjective **1** *an expressive shrug* =**eloquent**, meaningful, demonstrative, suggestive. **2** *an expressive song* =**emotional**, passionate, poignant, moving, stirring, emotionally charged.
–OPPOSITES expressionless, unemotional.

expressly ▶ adverb **1** *he was expressly forbidden to see her* =**explicitly**, clearly, directly, plainly, distinctly; absolutely; specifically, categorically, pointedly, emphatically. **2** *a machine expressly built for speed* =**solely**, specifically, particularly, specially, exclusively, just, only, explicitly.

expropriate ▶ verb =**seize**, take (away/over), appropriate, take possession of, requisition, commandeer, claim, acquire, sequestrate, confiscate.

expulsion ▶ noun **1** *expulsion from the party* =**removal**, debarment, dismissal, exclusion, discharge, ejection, drumming out. **2** *the expulsion of bodily waste* =**discharge**, ejection, excretion, voiding, evacuation, elimination, passing.
–OPPOSITES admission.

expunge ▶ verb =**erase**, remove, delete, rub out, wipe out, efface; cross out, strike out, blot out, blank out; destroy, obliterate, eradicate, eliminate.

expurgate ▶ verb =**censor**, bowdlerize, cut, edit; clean up, sanitize.

exquisite ▶ adjective **1** *exquisite antiques* =**beautiful**, lovely, elegant, fine; magnificent, superb, wonderful; delicate, fragile, dainty, subtle. **2** *exquisite taste* =**discriminating**, discerning, sensitive, fastidious; refined.

extant ▶ adjective =**(still) existing**, in existence, existent, surviving, remaining.

extemporary, extemporaneous ▶ adjective *an extemporary prayer.* See EXTEMPORE.

extempore ▶ adjective =**impromptu**, spontaneous, unscripted, ad lib, extemporary, extemporaneous; improvised, unrehearsed, unplanned, unprepared,

off the top of one's head; *informal* off-the-cuff.
–OPPOSITES rehearsed.
▶ adverb =**spontaneously**, extemporaneously, ad lib, without preparation, without rehearsal, off the top of one's head; *informal* off the cuff.

extemporize ▶ verb =**improvise**, ad lib, play it by ear, think on one's feet, do something off the top of one's head; *informal* busk it, wing it, do something off the cuff.

extend ▶ verb **1** *we've extended the kitchen* =**expand**, enlarge, increase; lengthen, widen, broaden. **2** *the garden extends as far as the road* =**continue**, carry on, run on, stretch (out), reach. **3** *we have extended our range of services* =**widen**, expand, broaden; augment, supplement, increase, add to, enhance, develop. **4** *extending the life of parliament* =**prolong**, lengthen, increase; stretch out, protract, spin out, string out. **5** *extend your arms and legs* =**stretch out**, spread out, reach out, straighten out. **6** *he extended a hand in greeting* =**hold out**, reach out, hold forth; offer, give, outstretch, proffer. **7** *we wish to extend our thanks to Mr Bayes* =**offer**, proffer, give, accord.
–OPPOSITES reduce, narrow, shorten.
■ **extend to** =**include**, take in, incorporate, encompass.

extended ▶ adjective =**prolonged**, protracted, long-lasting, long-drawn-out, long.

extension ▶ noun **1** *they are planning a new extension* =**addition**, add-on, adjunct, annex, wing; *N. Amer.* ell. **2** *an extension of our knowledge* =**expansion**, increase, enlargement, widening, broadening, deepening; augmentation, enhancement, development, growth, continuation. **3** *an extension of opening hours* =**prolongation**, lengthening, increase.

extensive ▶ adjective **1** *a mansion with extensive grounds* =**large**, sizeable, substantial, considerable, ample, great, vast. **2** *extensive knowledge* =**comprehensive**, thorough, exhaustive; broad, wide, wide-ranging, catholic.

extent ▶ noun **1** *two acres in extent* =**area**, size, expanse, length; proportions, dimensions. **2** *the full extent of her illness* =**degree**, scale, level, magnitude, scope; size, breadth, width, reach, range.

extenuating ▸ adjective =mitigating, excusing, justifying, vindicating.

exterior ▸ adjective =outer, outside, outermost, outward, external.
−OPPOSITES interior.
▸ noun =outside, external surface, outward appearance, facade.

WORD LINKS

related prefixes: ecto-, exo-, extra-

exterminate ▸ verb =kill, put to death, take/end the life of, dispatch; slaughter, butcher, massacre, wipe out; eliminate, eradicate, annihilate; murder, assassinate, execute; informal do away with, bump off, do in, top, take out, blow away; N. Amer. informal ice, rub out, waste; literary slay.

extermination ▸ noun =killing, murder, assassination, putting to death, execution, dispatch, slaughter, massacre, liquidation, elimination, eradication, annihilation; literary slaying.

external ▸ adjective 1 an external wall =outer, outside, outermost, outward, exterior. 2 an external examiner =outside, independent.
−OPPOSITES internal, in-house.

WORD LINKS

related prefixes: ecto-, exo-, extra-

extinct ▸ adjective 1 an extinct species =vanished, lost, died out, wiped out, destroyed, gone. 2 an extinct volcano =inactive.
−OPPOSITES extant, dormant.

extinction ▸ noun =dying out, disappearance, vanishing; extermination, destruction, elimination, eradication, annihilation.

extinguish ▸ verb =douse, put out, stamp out, smother.
−OPPOSITES light.

extirpate ▸ verb =weed out, destroy, eradicate, stamp out, root out, wipe out, eliminate, suppress, crush, put down, put an end to, get rid of.

extol ▸ verb =praise, go into raptures about/over, wax lyrical about, sing the praises of, praise to the skies, acclaim, eulogize, rave about, enthuse about/over; informal go wild about, go on about; N. Amer. informal ballyhoo; formal laud; archaic panegyrize.
−OPPOSITES criticize.

extort ▸ verb =obtain by force, extract, exact, wring, wrest, screw, squeeze; N. Amer. & Austral. informal put the bite on someone for.

extortion ▸ noun =demanding money with menaces, blackmail, N. Amer. informal shakedown.

extortionate ▸ adjective =exorbitant, excessively high, excessive, outrageous, unreasonable, inordinate, inflated; informal over the top, OTT.

extra ▸ adjective =additional, more, added, supplementary, further, auxiliary, ancillary, subsidiary, secondary.
▸ adverb =exceptionally, particularly, specially, especially, very, extremely; unusually, extraordinarily, uncommonly, remarkably, outstandingly, amazingly, incredibly, really; informal seriously, mucho, awfully, terribly; Brit. jolly, dead, well; informal, dated frightfully.
▸ noun =addition, supplement, adjunct, addendum, add-on.

extract ▸ verb 1 he extracted the cassette =take out, draw out, pull out, remove, withdraw; release, extricate. 2 they extracted a confession =wrest, exact, wring, screw, squeeze, obtain by force, obtain by threat(s), extort; N. Amer. & Austral. informal put the bite on someone for. 3 the roots are crushed to extract the juice =squeeze out, press out, obtain, get (out). 4 data extracted from the report =excerpt, select, reproduce, copy, take.
−OPPOSITES insert.
▸ noun 1 an extract from his article =excerpt, passage, citation, quotation. 2 an extract of ginseng =distillation, distillate, concentrate, essence, juice, derivative.

extraction ▸ noun 1 the extraction of gall stones =removal, taking out, drawing out, pulling out, withdrawal; extrication. 2 the extraction of grape juice =squeezing, pressing, obtaining. 3 a man of Irish extraction =descent, ancestry, parentage, ancestors, family, antecedents; lineage, line, origin, birth; genealogy, heredity, stock, pedigree, blood; roots, origins.
−OPPOSITES insertion.

extradite ▸ verb 1 he was extradited to Germany =deport, send back. 2 a bid to extradite her from Belgium =have someone deported, bring back.

extradition ▸ noun =deportation, repatriation, expulsion.

extraneous ▸ adjective =irrelevant, immaterial, beside the point, unrelated, unconnected, inapposite, inapplicable.

extraordinary ▸ adjective **1** *an extraordinary coincidence* =**remarkable**, exceptional, amazing, astonishing, astounding, sensational, stunning, incredible, unbelievable, phenomenal; striking, outstanding, momentous, impressive, singular, memorable, unforgettable, unique, noteworthy; out of the ordinary, unusual, uncommon, rare, surprising; *informal* fantastic, terrific, tremendous, stupendous; *literary* wondrous. **2** *extraordinary speed* =**very great**, tremendous, enormous, immense, prodigious, stupendous, monumental; *informal* almighty.

extravagance ▸ noun **1** *a fit of extravagance* =**profligacy**, improvidence, wastefulness, prodigality, lavishness. **2** *the wine was an extravagance* =**luxury**, indulgence, self-indulgence, treat, extra, non-essential. **3** *the extravagance of the decor* =**ornateness**, elaborateness; ostentation. **4** *the extravagance of his compliments* =**excessiveness**, exaggeration, outrageousness, immoderation.

extravagant ▸ adjective **1** *an extravagant lifestyle* =**spendthrift**, profligate, wasteful, prodigal, lavish, expensive, costly. **2** *extravagant praise* =**excessive**, immoderate, exaggerated, gushing, unrestrained, effusive, fulsome. **3** *decorated in an extravagant style* =**ornate**, elaborate, fancy; over-elaborate, ostentatious, exaggerated, baroque, rococo; *informal* flash, flashy.
−OPPOSITES thrifty, cheap, plain.

extravaganza ▸ noun =**spectacular**, display, spectacle, show, pageant.

extreme ▸ adjective **1** *extreme danger* =**utmost**, (very) great, greatest (possible), maximum, great, acute, enormous, severe, high, exceptional, extraordinary, serious. **2** *extreme measures* =**drastic**, serious, desperate, dire, radical, far-reaching; heavy, sharp, severe, austere, harsh, tough, strict, rigorous, oppressive, draconian; *Brit.* swingeing. **3** *extreme views* =**radical**, extremist, immoderate, fanatical, revolutionary, subversive, militant. **4** *extreme sports* =**dangerous**, hazardous, risky, high-risk, adventurous; *informal* white-knuckle. **5** *the extreme north-west* =**furthest**, farthest, furthermost, farthermost, very, utmost, ultra-.
−OPPOSITES slight, moderate.
▸ noun **1** *the two extremes | extremes of tem-*

perature =**opposite**, antithesis, side of the coin, (opposite) pole, limit, extremity; contrast.
■ **in the extreme**. *See* EXTREMELY.

extremely ▸ adverb =**very**, exceedingly, exceptionally, especially, extraordinarily, in the extreme, tremendously, immensely, hugely, supremely, highly, really, mightily; *informal* terrifically, awfully, fearfully, terribly, devilishly, majorly, seriously, mega, ultra, damn, damned; *Brit. informal* ever so, well, hellish, dead, jolly; *N. Amer. informal* real, mighty, awful, darned; *informal, dated* devilish, frightfully; *archaic* exceeding.
−OPPOSITES slightly.

extremist ▸ noun =**fanatic**, radical, zealot, fundamentalist, hardliner, militant, activist.
−OPPOSITES moderate.

extremity ▸ noun **1** *the eastern extremity* =**limit**, end, edge, side, boundary, border, frontier; perimeter, periphery, margin, tip. **2** *she lost feeling in her extremities* =**hands and feet**, fingers and toes, limbs. **3** *the extremity of the violence* =**intensity**, magnitude, acuteness, ferocity, vehemence, fierceness, violence, severity, seriousness, strength, power, powerfulness, vigour, force, forcefulness.

extricate ▸ verb =**extract**, free, release, disentangle, get out, remove, withdraw, disengage; *informal* get someone/oneself off the hook.

extrovert ▸ noun *like most extroverts he was a good dancer* =**outgoing person**, sociable person, socializer, life and soul of the party.
−OPPOSITES introvert.
▸ adjective *his extrovert personality* =**outgoing**, extroverted, sociable, gregarious, genial, affable, friendly, unreserved.
−OPPOSITES introverted.

extrude ▸ verb =**force out**, thrust out, squeeze out, express, eject, expel, release, emit.

exuberant ▸ adjective =**ebullient**, buoyant, cheerful, high-spirited, exhilarated, excited, elated, exultant, euphoric, joyful, cheery, merry, jubilant, vivacious, enthusiastic, irrepressible, energetic, animated, full of life, lively, vigorous; *informal* bubbly, bouncy, full of beans; *literary* blithe.
−OPPOSITES gloomy.

exude ▸ verb **1** *milkweed exudes a milky sap* =**give off/out**, discharge, release, emit, issue; ooze, secrete. **2** *he exuded self-confidence* =**emanate**, radiate, ooze, emit; display, show, exhibit, manifest.

exult ▸ verb =**rejoice**, be joyful, be happy, be delighted, be elated, be ecstatic, be overjoyed, be cock-a-hoop, be jubilant, be rapturous, be in raptures, be thrilled, jump for joy, be on cloud nine, be in seventh heaven; celebrate, cheer; *informal* be over the moon, be on top of the world; *Austral. informal* be wrapped; *literary* joy; *archaic* jubilate.
■**exult in** =**rejoice at/in**, take delight in, find/take pleasure in, enjoy, revel in, glory in, delight in, relish, savour; be/feel proud of, congratulate oneself on.
–OPPOSITES sorrow.

exultant ▸ adjective =**jubilant**, thrilled, triumphant, delighted, exhilarated, happy, overjoyed, joyous, joyful, gleeful, cock-a-hoop, excited, rejoicing, ecstatic, euphoric, elated, rapturous, in raptures, enraptured, on cloud nine, in seventh heaven; *informal* over the moon; *N. Amer. informal* wigged out.

exultation ▸ noun =**jubilation**, rejoicing, happiness, pleasure, joy, gladness, delight, glee, elation, cheer, euphoria, exhilaration, delirium, ecstasy, rapture, exuberance.

eye ▸ noun **1** *he rubbed his eyes* =**eyeball**; *informal* peeper. **2** *sharp eyes* =**eyesight**, vision, sight, powers of observation, (visual) perception. **3** *an eye for a bargain* =**appreciation**, awareness, alertness, perception, consciousness, feeling, instinct, intuition, nose. **4** *his watchful eye* =**watch**, gaze, stare, regard; observation, surveillance, vigilance, contemplation, scrutiny. **5** *killing was wrong in their eyes* =**opinion**, (way of) thinking, mind, view, viewpoint, attitude, standpoint, perspective, belief, judgement, assessment, analysis, estimation.
▸ verb **1** *he eyed me suspiciously* =**look at**, observe, view, gaze at, stare at, regard, contemplate, survey, scrutinize, consider, glance at; watch; *informal* have/take a gander at, check out, size up; *Brit. informal* have/take a butcher's at, have/take a dekko at, have/take a shufti at, clock; *N. Amer. informal* eyeball. **2** *eyeing young women in the street* =**ogle**, leer at, stare at,

make eyes at; *informal* eye up; *Brit. informal* gawp at, gawk at; *Austral./NZ informal* perv on.
■**clap/lay/set eyes on** (*informal*) =**see**, observe, notice, spot, spy, catch sight of, glimpse, catch/get a glimpse of; *literary* behold, espy.
■**see eye to eye** =**agree**, concur, be in agreement, be of the same mind/opinion, be in accord, think as one; be on the same wavelength, get on/along.
■**up to one's eyes** (*informal*) =**busy**, (fully) occupied; overloaded, overburdened, overworked, under pressure, hard-pressed, rushed/run off one's feet; *informal* pushed, up against it.

> WORD LINKS
>
> *relating to the eye:* **ocular, ophthalmic, optic**
> *inflammation of the eye:* **ophthalmitis**
> *branch of medicine concerning the eye:* **ophthalmology**
> *measurement of the eye:* **ophthalmometry**

eye-catching ▸ adjective =**striking**, arresting, conspicuous, dramatic, impressive, spectacular, breathtaking, dazzling, amazing, stunning, sensational, remarkable, distinctive, unusual, out of the ordinary.

eyelash ▸ noun =**lash**; *Anatomy* cilium.

> WORD LINKS
>
> *relating to eyelashes:* **ciliary**

eyelid ▸ noun

> WORD LINKS
>
> *relating to the eyelids:* **palpebral, ciliary**
> *inflammation of the eyelid:* **blepharitis**
> *surgery to repair eyelids:* **blepharoplasty**

eyesight ▸ noun =**sight**, vision, faculty of sight, ability to see, (visual) perception.

> WORD LINKS
>
> *measurement of eyesight:* **optometry**

eyesore ▸ noun =**ugly sight**, blot (on the landscape), mess, scar, blight, excrescence, blemish, monstrosity; *informal* sight.

eyewitness ▸ noun =**observer**, onlooker, witness, bystander, passer-by.

Ff

fable ▸ noun =parable, allegory.

fabled ▸ adjective **1** *a fabled giant of Irish myth* =**legendary**, mythical, fabulous, fairy-tale. **2** *the fabled quality of French wine* =**celebrated**, renowned, famed, famous, well known, prized, noted, notable, acclaimed, esteemed.

fabric ▸ noun **1** *the finest fabrics* =**cloth**, material, textile. **2** *the fabric of the building* =**structure**, material.

> WORD LINKS
>
> *seller of fabrics:* **clothier, draper**

fabricate ▸ verb =falsify, fake, counterfeit; invent, make up.

fabrication ▸ noun =invention, concoction, (piece of) fiction, falsification, lie, untruth, falsehood, fib, myth, made-up story, fairy story/tale, cock-and-bull story; *Brit. informal* porky (pie).

fabulous ▸ adjective **1** *fabulous salaries* =**stupendous**, prodigious, phenomenal, remarkable, exceptional; astounding, amazing, fantastic, breathtaking, staggering, unthinkable, unimaginable, incredible, unbelievable, unheard of, untold, undreamed of, beyond one's wildest dreams; *informal* mind-boggling, mind-blowing. **2** *(informal) we had a fabulous time.* See EXCELLENT.

facade ▸ noun **1** *a half-timbered facade* =**front**, frontage, face, elevation, exterior, outside. **2** *a facade of bonhomie* =**show**, front, appearance, pretence, simulation, affectation, semblance, illusion, act, masquerade, charade, mask, veneer.

face ▸ noun **1** *a beautiful face* =**countenance**, physiognomy, features; *informal* mug; *Brit. informal* mush, dial, clock, phiz, phizog, boat race; *N. Amer. informal* puss, pan; *literary* visage. **2** *her face grew sad* =**expression**, look, appearance, countenance. **3** *he made a face* =**grimace**, scowl, wince, frown, pout. **4** *a cube has six faces* =**side**, aspect, surface, plane, facet, wall, elevation. **5** *a watch face* =**dial**, display. **6** *he put on a brave face* =**front**, show, display, act, appearance, facade, exterior, mask.

▸ verb **1** *the hotel faces the sea* =**look out on**, front on to, look towards, look over/across, overlook, be opposite (to). **2** *you'll just have to face the truth* =**accept**, become reconciled to, get used to, become accustomed to, adjust to, acclimatize oneself to; learn to live with, cope with, deal with, come to terms with, become resigned to. **3** *he faced a tough choice* =**be confronted by**, be faced with. **4** *the problems facing our police force* =**beset**, worry, trouble, confront; torment, plague, bedevil, curse. **5** *he faced the challenge* =**brave**, face up to, encounter, meet (head-on), confront. **6** *a wall faced with flint* =**cover**, clad, veneer, overlay, surface, dress, laminate, coat, line.

■ **face to face** =facing (each other), opposite (each other), across from each other.

■ **on the face of it** =ostensibly, to all appearances, to all intents and purposes, at first glance, on the surface, superficially; apparently, seemingly, outwardly, it seems (that), it would seem (that), it appears (that), it would appear (that), as far as one can see/tell, by all accounts.

facelift ▸ noun **1** *she's planning to have a facelift* =**cosmetic surgery**, plastic surgery. **2** *(informal) the theatre is reopening after a facelift* =**renovation**, redecoration, refurbishment, revamp, makeover, reconditioning, overhaul, modernization, restoration, repairs, redevelopment, rebuilding, reconstruction, refit.

facet ▸ noun **1** *the facets of the gem* =**surface**, face, side, plane. **2** *facets of his character* =**aspect**, feature, side, dimension, strand; component, constituent, element.

facetious ▸ adjective =flippant, flip, glib, frivolous, tongue-in-cheek, joking, jokey, jocular, playful, mischievous. −OPPOSITES serious.

facile ▸ adjective =simplistic, superficial, oversimplified; shallow, glib, naive; *N. Amer.* dime-store.

facilitate ▶ verb = make easy/easier, ease, make possible, smooth the way for; enable, assist, help (along), aid, oil the wheels of, expedite, speed up.
– OPPOSITES impede.

facility ▶ noun 1 *car-parking facilities* = provision, space, means, equipment. 2 *the camera has a zoom facility* = feature, setting, mode, option. 3 *a wealth of local facilities* = amenity, resource, service. 4 *a medical facility* = establishment, centre, station, location, premises, site, post, base; *informal* joint, outfit, set-up.

facing ▶ noun = cladding, veneer, skin, surface, facade, front, coating, covering, dressing, overlay; *N. Amer.* siding.

facsimile ▶ noun = copy, reproduction, duplicate, photocopy, replica, likeness, carbon copy, print, reprint, off-print; fax; *trademark* Xerox.
– OPPOSITES original.

fact ▶ noun 1 *a fact that we cannot ignore* = reality, actuality, certainty; truth, verity, gospel. 2 *every fact was double-checked* = detail, piece of information, particular, item, element, point, factor, feature, characteristic, circumstance, aspect, facet; (**facts**) information, findings, data.
– OPPOSITES lie, fiction.
■ **in fact** = actually, in actual fact, really, in reality, in point of fact, as a matter of fact, in truth, to tell the truth.

faction ▶ noun 1 *a faction of the Liberal Party* = clique, coterie, caucus, cabal, bloc, camp, group, grouping, sector, section, wing, arm, branch, set; pressure group, splinter group; *Brit.* ginger group. 2 *the council was split by faction* = infighting, dissension, dissent, dispute, discord, strife, conflict, friction, argument, disagreement, controversy, quarrelling, wrangling, bickering, squabbling, disharmony, disunity, schism.

factor ▶ noun = element, part, component, ingredient, strand, constituent, point, detail, item, feature, facet, aspect, characteristic, consideration, influence, circumstance.

factory ▶ noun = works, plant, yard, mill, (industrial) unit; workshop, shop.

factual ▶ adjective = truthful, true, accurate, authentic, historical, genuine, fact-based; true-to-life, correct, exact, honest, faithful, literal, verbatim, word for word, unbiased, objective.
– OPPOSITES fictitious.

faculty ▶ noun 1 *the faculty of speech* = power, capability, capacity, facility, wherewithal, means; (**faculties**) senses, wits, reason, intelligence. 2 *the arts faculty* = department, school, division, section.

fad ▶ noun = craze, vogue, trend, fashion, mode, enthusiasm, passion, obsession, mania, rage, compulsion, fixation, fetish, fancy, whim, fascination; *informal* thing.

fade ▶ verb 1 *the paintwork has faded* = become pale, become bleached, become washed out, lose colour, discolour. 2 *sunlight had faded the picture* = bleach, wash out, make pale, blanch. 3 *remove the flower heads as they fade* = wither, wilt, droop, shrivel, die. 4 *the afternoon light began to fade* = (grow) dim, grow faint, fail, dwindle, die away, wane, disappear, vanish, decline, melt away. 5 *Communism was fading away* = decline, die out, diminish, deteriorate, decay, crumble, collapse, fail, fall, sink, slump, go downhill.
– OPPOSITES brighten, increase.

faeces ▶ plural noun = excrement, bodily waste, waste matter, ordure, dung, manure; excreta, stools, droppings; dirt, filth, muck, mess; *informal* poo, doo-doo, doings, turds; *Brit. informal* cack, whoopsies, jobbies; *N. Amer. informal* poop.

> **WORD LINKS**
>
> *relating to faeces:* **copro-, scato-**
> *medical study of faeces:* **scatology**
> *fear of faeces:* **coprophobia**
> *faeces-eating:* **coprophagous**

fail ▶ verb 1 *the scheme had failed* = be unsuccessful, not succeed, fall through, fall flat, collapse, founder, backfire, meet with disaster, come to nothing/naught; *informal* flop, bomb. 2 *he failed his examination* = be unsuccessful in, not pass; not make the grade; *informal* flunk. 3 *his friends had failed him* = let down, disappoint; desert, abandon, betray, be disloyal to; *literary* forsake. 4 *the ventilation system has failed* = break (down), stop working, cut out, crash; malfunction, go wrong, develop a fault; *informal* conk out, go on the blink; *Brit. informal* pack up, play up. 5 *Ceri's health was failing* = deteriorate, degenerate, decline, fade, wane, ebb. 6 *900 businesses are failing a week* = collapse, crash, go under, go bankrupt, go into receivership, go into

liquidation, cease trading, be wound up; *informal* fold, flop, go bust, go broke, go to the wall.
−OPPOSITES succeed, pass, thrive, work.
■ **without fail** = without exception, unfailingly, regularly, invariably, predictably, conscientiously, religiously, whatever happened.

failing ▶ noun *Jeanne accepted him despite his failings* = fault, shortcoming, weakness, imperfection, defect, flaw, frailty, vice.
−OPPOSITES strength.

failure ▶ noun 1 *the failure of the escape attempt* = lack of success, defeat, collapse, foundering. 2 *the scheme had been a failure* = fiasco, debacle, catastrophe, disaster; *informal* flop, washout, dead loss; *N. Amer. informal* snafu, clinker. 3 *she was a failure* = loser, underachiever, ne'er-do-well, disappointment; *informal* no-hoper, dead loss. 4 *a failure on my part* = negligence, dereliction, omission, oversight. 5 *the failure of the heating system* = breaking down, breakdown, malfunction; crash. 6 *company failures* = collapse, crash, bankruptcy, insolvency, liquidation, closure.
−OPPOSITES success.

> [!NOTE] WORD LINKS
> *fear of failure:* kakorrhaphiaphobia

faint ▶ adjective 1 *a faint mark* = indistinct, vague, unclear, indefinite, ill-defined, imperceptible, unobtrusive; pale, light, faded. 2 *a faint cry* = quiet, muted, muffled, stifled; feeble, weak, whispered, murmured, indistinct; low, soft, gentle. 3 *a faint possibility* = slight, slender, slim, small, tiny, negligible, remote, vague. 4 *I suddenly felt faint* = dizzy, giddy, light-headed, unsteady; *informal* woozy.
−OPPOSITES clear, loud, strong.
▶ verb *he nearly fainted* = pass out, lose consciousness, black out, keel over, swoon; *informal* flake out, conk out, zonk out.
▶ noun *a dead faint* = blackout, fainting fit, loss of consciousness, swoon.

faint-hearted ▶ adjective = timid, timorous, nervous, nervy, easily scared, fearful, afraid; cowardly, craven, spineless, pusillanimous, lily-livered; *informal* yellow, yellow-bellied, chicken, chicken-hearted, gutless, sissy, wimpy, wimpish.
−OPPOSITES brave.

faintly ▶ adverb 1 *Maria called his name faintly* = indistinctly, softly, gently, weakly; in a whisper, in a murmur, in a low voice. 2 *he looked faintly bewildered* = slightly, vaguely, somewhat, quite, fairly, rather, a little, a bit, a touch, a shade; *informal* sort of, kind of.
−OPPOSITES loudly, extremely.

fair[1] ▶ adjective 1 *the courts were generally fair* = just, equitable, honest; impartial, unbiased, unprejudiced, non-partisan, neutral, even-handed. 2 *fair weather* = fine, dry, bright, clear, sunny, cloudless; warm, balmy, clement, benign, pleasant. 3 *fair hair* = blond(e), yellow, golden, flaxen, light; fair-haired, light-haired, golden-haired. 4 *fair skin* = pale, light, light-coloured, white, creamy. 5 *a fair achievement* = reasonable, passable, tolerable, satisfactory, acceptable, respectable, decent, all right, good enough, pretty good, not bad, average, middling; *informal* OK, so-so.
−OPPOSITES inclement, unfavourable, dark.
■ **fair and square** = honestly, fairly, by the book; lawfully, legally, legitimately; *informal* on the level; *N. Amer. informal* on the up and up.

fair[2] ▶ noun 1 *a country fair* = fête, gala, festival, carnival. 2 *an antiques fair* = market, bazaar, mart, exchange, sale. 3 *a new art fair* = exhibition, display, show, exposition; *N. Amer.* exhibit.

fairly ▶ adverb 1 *we were treated fairly* = justly, equitably, impartially, without bias, without prejudice, even-handedly; equally, the same. 2 *in fairly good condition* = reasonably, passably, tolerably, adequately, moderately, quite, relatively, comparatively; *informal* pretty. 3 *he fairly hauled her along the street* = positively, really, veritably, simply, actually, absolutely; practically, almost, nearly, all but; *informal* plain.

fairy ▶ noun = sprite, pixie, elf, imp, brownie, puck, leprechaun; *literary* faerie, fay.

faith ▶ noun 1 *our faith in him* = trust, belief, confidence, conviction. 2 *she died for her faith* = religion, (religious) belief, church, sect, denomination, (religious) persuasion, ideology, creed, teaching, doctrine.
−OPPOSITES mistrust.
■ **break faith with** = be disloyal to, be unfaithful to, be untrue to, betray,

break one's promise to, fail, let down; double-cross, deceive, cheat, stab in the back; *informal* do the dirty on.

■ **keep faith with** =**be loyal to**, be faithful to, be true to, stand by, stick by, keep one's promise to.

faithful ▶ adjective **1** *his faithful assistant* =**loyal**, constant, true, devoted, true-blue, unswerving, staunch, steadfast, dedicated, committed; trusty, dependable, reliable. **2** *a faithful copy* =**accurate**, precise, exact, unerring, faultless, true, close, strict; realistic, authentic; *informal* on the mark, on the nail; *Brit. informal* spot on, bang on; *N. Amer. informal* on the money.
−OPPOSITES inaccurate.

faithless ▶ adjective =**unfaithful**, disloyal, inconstant, false, untrue, adulterous, traitorous; deceitful, two-faced, double-crossing; *informal* cheating, two-timing, back-stabbing; *literary* perfidious.

fake ▶ noun **1** *the sculpture was a fake* =**forgery**, counterfeit, copy, pirate(d) copy, sham, fraud, hoax, imitation, reproduction; *informal* phoney, rip-off, dupe. **2** *that doctor is a fake* =**charlatan**, quack, sham, fraud, humbug, impostor, hoaxer, cheat, (confidence) trickster, fraudster; *informal* phoney, con man, con artist.

▶ adjective **1** *fake banknotes* =**counterfeit**, forged, fraudulent, sham, imitation, pirate(d), false, bogus; invalid; *informal* phoney, dud. **2** *fake diamonds* =**imitation**, artificial, synthetic, simulated, reproduction, replica, ersatz, man-made, dummy, false, mock, bogus; *informal* pretend, phoney, pseudo. **3** *a fake accent* =**feigned**, faked, put-on, assumed, invented, affected; unconvincing, artificial, mock; *informal* phoney, pseud; *Brit. informal* cod.
−OPPOSITES genuine, authentic.

▶ verb **1** *the certificate was faked* =**forge**, counterfeit, falsify, copy, pirate, reproduce, replicate. **2** *he faked a yawn* =**feign**, pretend, simulate, put on, affect.

fall ▶ verb **1** *bombs began to fall* =**drop**, descend, come down, go down; plummet, plunge, sink, dive, tumble; cascade. **2** *he tripped and fell* =**topple over**, tumble over, keel over, fall down/over, go head over heels, go headlong, collapse, take a spill, pitch forward; trip (over), stumble, slip; *informal* come a cropper. **3** *the water level began to fall* =**subside**, recede, drop, retreat, fall

away, go down, sink. **4** *inflation will fall* =**decrease**, decline, diminish, fall off, drop off, lessen, dwindle, plummet, plunge, slump, sink; depreciate; *informal* go through the floor, nosedive, take a header, crash. **5** *those who fell in the war* =**die**, perish, lose one's life, be killed, be slain, be lost, meet one's death; *informal* bite the dust, croak, buy it; *Brit. informal* snuff it. **6** *the town fell to the barbarians* =**surrender**, yield, submit, give in, capitulate, succumb; be taken by, be defeated by, be conquered by, be overwhelmed by. **7** *Easter falls on 23rd April* =**occur**, take place, happen, come about; arise. **8** *night fell* =**come**, arrive, appear, arise. **9** *she fell ill* =**become**, grow, get, turn. **10** *the task fell to him* =**be the responsibility of**, be the duty of, be one's job; come someone's way.
−OPPOSITES rise, flood, increase, flourish.

▶ noun **1** *an accidental fall* =**tumble**, trip, spill, topple, slip; *informal* nosedive. **2** *a fall in sales* =**decline**, fall-off, drop, decrease, cut, dip, reduction, downswing; plummet, plunge, slump; *informal* nosedive, crash. **3** *the fall of the Roman Empire* =**downfall**, collapse, failure, decline, deterioration, degeneration; destruction, overthrow, demise. **4** *the fall of Berlin* =**surrender**, capitulation, yielding, submission; defeat. **5** *a steep fall down to the ocean* =**descent**, declivity, slope, slant, incline; *N. Amer.* downgrade. **6** *trips below the falls* =**waterfall**, cascade, cataract; rapids, white water.
−OPPOSITES increase, rise, ascent.

■ **fall apart** =**fall/come to pieces**, fall/come to bits, come apart (at the seams); disintegrate, fragment, break up, break apart, crumble, decay, perish; *informal* bust.

■ **fall back** =**retreat**, withdraw, back off, draw back, pull back, pull away, move away.

■ **fall back on** =**resort to**, turn to, look to, call on, have recourse to; rely on, depend on, lean on.

■ **fall behind 1** *the other walkers fell behind* =**lag (behind)**, trail (behind), be left behind, drop back, bring up the rear; straggle, dally, dawdle, hang back. **2** *they fell behind on their payments* =**get into debt**, get into arrears, default, be in the red.

■ **fall down 1** *I spin round till I fall down.* See FALL *verb sense* 2. **2** *his work fell down in some areas* =**fail**, be unsuccessful, not succeed, not make the grade, fall short, fall flat, disappoint; miss the mark; *informal* come a cropper, flop.

■ **fall for** (*informal*) **1** *she fell for John* =**fall in love with**, become infatuated with, lose one's heart to, take a fancy to, be smitten by, be attracted to. **2** *she won't fall for that trick* =**be deceived by**, be duped by, be fooled by, be taken in by, believe, trust, be convinced by; *informal* go for, buy, swallow (hook, line, and sinker).

■ **fall in** =**collapse**, cave in, crash in, fall down; give way, crumble, disintegrate.

■ **fall off**. *See* FALL *verb sense 4.*

■ **fall out** =**quarrel**, argue, row, fight, squabble, bicker, have words, disagree, be at odds, clash, wrangle, cross swords, lock horns, be at loggerheads, be at each other's throats; *informal* scrap, argufy, argy-bargy.

■ **fall through** =**fail**, be unsuccessful, come to nothing, miscarry, abort, go awry, collapse, founder, come to grief; *informal* fizzle out, flop, fold, come a cropper, go down like a lead balloon.

fallacious ▶ adjective =**erroneous**, false, untrue, wrong, incorrect, flawed, inaccurate, mistaken, misinformed, misguided; specious, spurious, bogus, fictitious, fabricated, made up; groundless, unfounded, unproven, unsupported, uncorroborated; *informal* phoney, full of holes, off beam.
–OPPOSITES correct.

fallacy ▶ noun =**misconception**, misbelief, delusion, misapprehension, misinterpretation, misconstruction, error, mistake; untruth, inconsistency, myth.

fallen ▶ adjective =**dead**, perished, killed, slain, slaughtered, murdered; lost, late, lamented, departed, gone; *formal* deceased.

fallible ▶ adjective =**error-prone**, errant, liable to err, open to error; imperfect, flawed, weak.

false ▶ adjective **1** *a false report* =**incorrect**, untrue, wrong, erroneous, fallacious, flawed, distorted, inaccurate, imprecise; untruthful, fictitious, concocted, fabricated, invented, made up, trumped up, unfounded, spurious; counterfeit, forged, fraudulent. **2** *a false friend* =**faithless**, unfaithful, disloyal, untrue, inconstant, treacherous, traitorous, two-faced, double-crossing, deceitful, dishonest, duplicitous, untrustworthy, unreliable; untruthful; *informal*

cheating, two-timing, back-stabbing. **3** *false pearls* =**fake**, artificial, imitation, synthetic, simulated, reproduction, replica, ersatz, man-made, dummy, mock; *informal* phoney, pretend, pseudo.
–OPPOSITES correct, truthful, faithful, genuine.

falsehood ▶ noun **1** *a downright falsehood* =**lie**, untruth, fib, falsification, fabrication, invention, fiction, story, cock and bull story, flight of fancy; *informal* tall story, tall tale, fairy story, fairy tale, whopper; *Brit. informal* porky (pie); *humorous* terminological inexactitude. **2** *he accused me of falsehood* =**lying**, untruthfulness, fibbing, fabrication, invention, perjury, telling stories; deceit, deception, pretence, artifice, double-crossing, treachery.
–OPPOSITES truth, honesty.

falsify ▶ verb =**forge**, fake, counterfeit, fabricate; alter, change, doctor, tamper with, fudge, manipulate, adulterate, misrepresent, misreport, distort, warp, embellish, embroider.

falter ▶ verb =**hesitate**, delay, drag one's feet, stall; waver, vacillate, be indecisive, be irresolute, blow hot and cold; *Brit.* haver, hum and haw; *informal* sit on the fence, dilly-dally, shilly-shally.

fame ▶ noun =**renown**, celebrity, stardom, popularity, prominence; note, distinction, esteem, importance, account, consequence, greatness, eminence, prestige, stature, repute; notoriety, infamy.
–OPPOSITES obscurity.

famed ▶ adjective =**famous**, celebrated, well known, prominent, noted, notable, renowned, respected, esteemed, acclaimed; notorious, infamous.
–OPPOSITES unknown.

familiar ▶ adjective **1** *a familiar task* =**well known**, recognized, accustomed; common, commonplace, everyday, day-to-day, ordinary, habitual, usual, customary, routine, standard, stock, mundane, run-of-the-mill. **2** *are you familiar with the subject?* =**acquainted**, conversant, versed, knowledgeable, well informed; at home with, no stranger to, au fait with; *informal* well up on, in the know about, genned up on, clued up on, up to speed with. **3** *he is too familiar with the teachers* =**overfamiliar**, presumptuous, disrespectful, forward, bold, impudent, impertinent.

–OPPOSITES formal.

familiarity ▸ noun **1** *a familiarity with politics* =**acquaintance with**, awareness of, experience of, insight into; knowledge of, understanding of, comprehension of, grasp of, skill in, proficiency in. **2** *she was affronted by his familiarity* =**overfamiliarity**, presumption, presumptuousness, forwardness, boldness, audacity, cheek, impudence, impertinence, disrespect. **3** *our familiarity allows us to tease each other* =**closeness**, intimacy, attachment, affinity, friendliness, friendship, amity; *informal* chumminess, palliness; *Brit. informal* mateyness.

familiarize ▸ verb =**make conversant**, make familiar, acquaint; accustom to, habituate to, instruct in, teach in, educate in, school in, prime in, introduce to; *informal* gen up on, clue up on, put in the picture about, give the gen about, give the low-down on, fill in on.

family ▸ noun **1** *I met his family* =**relatives**, relations, (next of) kin, kinsfolk, kindred, one's (own) flesh and blood, nearest and dearest, people, connections; extended family; clan, tribe; *informal* folks. **2** *she is married with a family* =**children**, little ones, youngsters; offspring, progeny, descendants, heirs; brood; *Law* issue; *informal* kids, kiddies, tots. **3** *the cat family* =**(taxonomic) group**; order, class, genus, species; stock, strain, line; *Zoology* phylum.

family tree ▸ noun =**ancestry**, genealogy, descent, lineage, line, bloodline, pedigree, background, extraction, derivation; family, dynasty, house; forebears, forefathers, antecedents, roots, origins.

famine ▸ noun **1** *a nation threatened by famine* =**food shortages**. **2** *the cotton famine* =**shortage**, scarcity, lack, dearth, deficiency, insufficiency, shortfall, drought.
–OPPOSITES plenty.

famished ▸ adjective =**ravenous**, hungry, starving, starved, empty, unfed; *informal* peckish.
–OPPOSITES full.

famous ▸ adjective =**well known**, prominent, famed, popular; renowned, noted, eminent, distinguished, esteemed, celebrated, respected; of distinction, of repute; illustrious, acclaimed, great, legendary; notorious, infamous.

–OPPOSITES unknown.

fan¹ ▸ noun *a ceiling fan* =**air-cooler**, air conditioner, ventilator, blower.
▸ verb **1** *she fanned her face* =**cool**, ventilate. **2** *they fanned public fears* =**intensify**, increase, agitate, inflame, exacerbate; stimulate, stir up, whip up, fuel, kindle, arouse. **3** *the police squad fanned out* =**spread**, branch; split up, divide up.

fan² ▸ noun *a basketball fan* =**enthusiast**, devotee, admirer, lover; supporter, follower, disciple, adherent, zealot; expert, connoisseur, aficionado; *informal* buff, fiend, freak, nut, addict, fanatic, groupie; *N. Amer. informal* jock.

fanatic ▸ noun **1** *a religious fanatic* =**zealot**, extremist, militant, dogmatist, devotee, adherent; sectarian, bigot, partisan, radical, diehard; *informal* maniac, nutter. **2** *(informal) a keep-fit fanatic. See* FAN².

fanatical ▸ adjective **1** *they are fanatical about their faith* =**zealous**, extremist, extreme, militant, dogmatic, radical, diehard; intolerant, single-minded, blinkered, inflexible, uncompromising. **2** *he was fanatical about tidiness* =**enthusiastic**, eager, keen, fervent, passionate; obsessive, obsessed, fixated, compulsive; *informal* wild, gung-ho, nuts, crazy; *Brit. informal* potty.

fanciful ▸ adjective **1** *a fanciful story* =**fantastic**, far-fetched, unbelievable, extravagant; ridiculous, absurd, preposterous; imaginary, made-up; *informal* tall, hard to swallow. **2** *a fanciful girl* =**imaginative**, inventive; whimsical, impractical, dreamy, quixotic; out of touch with reality, in a world of one's own.
–OPPOSITES literal, practical.

fancy ▸ verb **1** *(Brit. informal) I fancied a change of scene* =**wish for**, want, desire; long for, yearn for, crave, thirst for, hanker after, dream of, covet; *informal* have a yen for; *archaic* be desirous of. **2** *(Brit. informal) she fancied him* =**be attracted to**, find attractive, be infatuated with, be taken with, desire; lust after, burn for; *informal* have a crush on, have the hots for, be crazy about, have a thing about, carry a torch for. **3** *I fancied I could see lights* =**think**, imagine, believe, be of the opinion, be under the impression; *informal* reckon.
▸ adjective *fancy clothes* =**elaborate**, ornate, ornamental, decorative, embellished,

intricate; ostentatious, showy, flamboyant; luxurious, lavish, extravagant, expensive; *informal* flash, flashy, jazzy, ritzy, snazzy, posh, classy; *Brit. informal* swish.
–OPPOSITES plain.

▶ noun *his fancy to own a farm* =**desire**, urge, wish; inclination, whim, impulse, notion, whimsy; yearning, longing, hankering, craving; *informal* yen, itch.

fantasize ▶ verb =**daydream**, dream, muse, make-believe, pretend, imagine, live in a dream world.

fantastic ▶ adjective **1** *a fantastic notion* =**fanciful**, extravagant, extraordinary, irrational, wild, absurd, far-fetched, nonsensical, incredible, unbelievable, unthinkable, implausible, improbable, unlikely, doubtful, dubious; strange, peculiar, odd, queer, weird, eccentric, whimsical; *informal* crazy, cock-eyed, off the wall. **2** *fantastic shapes* =**strange**, weird, bizarre, outlandish, peculiar, grotesque, freakish, surreal, exotic. **3** *(informal) a fantastic car* =**marvellous**, wonderful, sensational, outstanding, superb, excellent, first-rate, first-class, dazzling, out of this world, breathtaking; *informal* great, terrific, fabulous, fab, mega, super, ace, magic, cracking, cool, wicked, awesome; *Brit. informal* brilliant, brill, smashing; *Austral./NZ informal* bonzer.
–OPPOSITES rational, ordinary.

fantasy ▶ noun **1** *a mix of fantasy and realism* =**imagination**, fancy, invention, make-believe, creativity, vision; daydreaming, reverie. **2** *his fantasy about being famous* =**dream**, daydream, pipe dream, fanciful notion, wish; fond hope, delusion, illusion; *informal* pie in the sky.
–OPPOSITES realism.

far ▶ adverb **1** *far from the palace* =**a long way**, a great distance, a good way; afar. **2** *her charm far outweighs any flaws* =**much**, considerably, markedly, immeasurably, greatly, significantly, substantially, appreciably, noticeably; to a great extent, by a long way, by far, by a mile, easily.
–OPPOSITES near.

▶ adjective **1** *far places* =**distant**, faraway, far-off, remote, out of the way, far-flung, outlying. **2** *the far side of the campus* =**further**, more distant; opposite.
–OPPOSITES near.

■ **by far** =**by a great amount**, by a good deal, by a long way, by a mile, far and away; undoubtedly, without doubt, without question, positively, absolutely, easily; significantly, substantially, appreciably, much; *Brit.* by a long chalk.

■ **far and away**. *See* BY FAR.

■ **far from** *staff were far from happy* =**not**, not at all, nowhere near; the opposite of.

■ **go far** =**be successful**, succeed, prosper, flourish, thrive, get on (in the world), make good, set the world on fire; *informal* make a name for oneself, make one's mark, go places, do all right for oneself.

■ **so far 1** *nobody has noticed so far* =**until now**, up to now, up to this point, as yet, thus far, hitherto, up to the present, to date. **2** *his liberalism only extends so far* =**to a certain extent**, up to a point, to a degree, within reason, within limits.

faraway ▶ adjective **1** *faraway places* =**distant**, far off, far, remote, far-flung, outlying; obscure, out of the way, off the beaten track. **2** *a faraway look in her eyes* =**dreamy**, daydreaming, abstracted, absent-minded, distracted, preoccupied, vague; lost in thought, somewhere else, not with us, in a world of one's own; *informal* miles away.
–OPPOSITES nearby.

farce ▶ noun *the trial was a farce* =**mockery**, travesty, absurdity, sham, pretence, masquerade, charade, joke, waste of time; *informal* shambles.
–OPPOSITES tragedy.

farcical ▶ adjective =**ridiculous**, preposterous, ludicrous, absurd, laughable, risible, nonsensical; senseless, pointless, useless, silly, foolish, idiotic, stupid, hare-brained; *informal* crazy; *Brit. informal* barmy, daft.

fare ▶ noun **1** *we paid the fare* =**price**, cost, charge, fee, toll, tariff. **2** *the taxi picked up a fare* =**passenger**, traveller, customer; *Brit. informal* punter. **3** *they eat simple fare* =**food**, meals, sustenance, nourishment, nutriment, foodstuffs, provender, provisions; cooking, cuisine; diet, table; *informal* grub, nosh, eats, chow; *Brit. informal* scoff; *formal* victuals.

▶ verb *how are you faring?* =**get on**, get along, cope, manage, do, survive; *informal* make out.

farewell ▶ exclamation *farewell, Patrick!* =**goodbye**, so long, adieu; au revoir, ciao; *informal* bye, bye-bye, cheerio, see you (later), later(s); *Brit. informal* ta-ta,

cheers; *informal, dated* toodle-oo, toodle-pip.
▶ **noun** *an emotional farewell* = **goodbye**, valediction, adieu; leave-taking, parting, departure; send-off.

far-fetched ▶ **adjective** = **improbable**, unlikely, implausible, unconvincing, dubious, doubtful, incredible, unbelievable, unthinkable; contrived, fanciful, unrealistic, ridiculous, absurd, preposterous; *informal* hard to swallow, fishy.
−OPPOSITES likely.

farm ▶ **noun** = **smallholding**, farmstead, plantation, estate; farmland; *Brit.* grange, croft; *Scottish* steading; *N. Amer.* ranch; *Austral./NZ* station.
▶ **verb** = **breed**, rear, keep, raise, tend.
■ **farm something out** = **contract out**, outsource, subcontract, delegate.

farmer ▶ **noun** = **agriculturalist**, agronomist, smallholder, breeder; *Brit.* crofter; *N. Amer.* rancher.

farming ▶ **noun** = **agriculture**, cultivation, land management, farm management; husbandry; agriscience, agronomy, agribusiness; *Brit.* crofting.

> **WORD LINKS**
>
> *relating to agriculture:* **agrarian, agri-, agro-**

far-reaching ▶ **adjective** = **extensive**, wide-ranging, comprehensive, widespread, all-embracing, overarching, sweeping, blanket, wholesale; important, significant, radical, major.
−OPPOSITES limited.

far-sighted ▶ **adjective** = **prescient**, visionary, shrewd, discerning, judicious, canny, prudent.

farther ▶ **adverb & adjective.** *See* FURTHER.

farthest ▶ **adjective.** *See* FURTHEST.

fascinate ▶ **verb** = **interest**, captivate, engross, absorb, enchant, enthral, entrance, transfix, rivet, mesmerize, engage, compel; lure, tempt, entice, draw; charm, attract, intrigue.
−OPPOSITES bore.

fascinating ▶ **adjective** = **interesting**, captivating, engrossing, absorbing, enchanting, enthralling, spellbinding, riveting, engaging, compelling, compulsive, gripping, thrilling; alluring, tempting, irresistible; charming, attractive, intriguing, diverting, entertaining.

fascination ▶ **noun** = **interest**, pre-

occupation, passion, obsession, compulsion; allure, lure, charm, attraction, intrigue, appeal, pull, draw.

fascism ▶ **noun** = **authoritarianism**, totalitarianism, dictatorship, despotism; Nazism; nationalism, xenophobia, racism, anti-Semitism; neo-fascism, neo-Nazism.

fascist ▶ **noun** = **authoritarian**, totalitarian, autocrat, extreme right-winger; Nazi, blackshirt; nationalist, xenophobe, racist, anti-Semite; neo-fascist, neo-Nazi.
−OPPOSITES liberal.
▶ **adjective** = **authoritarian**, totalitarian, dictatorial, despotic, autocratic, undemocratic, illiberal; Nazi, extreme right-wing, militarist; nationalist(ic), xenophobic, racist.
−OPPOSITES democratic.

fashion ▶ **noun 1** *the fashion for tight clothes* = **vogue**, trend, craze, rage, mania, fad; style, look; tendency, convention, custom, practice; *informal* thing. **2** *the world of fashion* = **clothes**, clothing design, couture; *informal* the rag trade. **3** *it needs to be run in a sensible fashion* = **manner**, way, method, mode, style; system, approach.
▶ **verb** *fashioned from clay* = **construct**, build, make, manufacture, contrive; cast, shape, form, mould, sculpt; forge, hew, carve.
■ **in fashion** = **fashionable**, in vogue, up to date, up to the minute, all the rage, chic, à la mode; *informal* trendy, with it, cool, in, the in thing, hot, big, hip, happening, now, sharp, groovy; *N. Amer. informal* tony, fly
■ **out of fashion** = **unfashionable**, dated, old-fashioned, out of date, outdated, outmoded, behind the times; unstylish, unpopular, passé, démodé; *informal* old hat, out, square, out of the ark.

fashionable ▶ **adjective** = **in vogue**, voguish, in fashion, popular, (bang) up to date, up to the minute, modern, all the rage, modish, à la mode, trendsetting; stylish, chic; *informal* trendy, classy, with it, cool, in, the in thing, hot, big, hip, happening, now, sharp, groovy, snazzy; *N. Amer. informal* tony, fly.

fast¹ ▶ **adjective 1** *a fast pace* = **speedy**, quick, swift, rapid; fast-moving, high-speed; accelerated, express, blistering, breakneck, pell-mell; hasty, hurried; *informal* nippy, zippy, scorching, supersonic; *Brit. informal* cracking. **2** *he held the*

door fast =**secure**, fastened, tight, firm, closed, shut, to; immovable. **3** *a fast colour* =**indelible**, lasting, permanent, stable. **4** *fast friends* =**loyal**, devoted, faithful, firm, steadfast, staunch, true, boon, bosom, inseparable; constant, enduring, unswerving.
–OPPOSITES slow, loose, temporary.
▶ adverb **1** *she drove fast* =**quickly**, rapidly, swiftly, speedily, briskly, at speed, at full tilt; hastily, hurriedly, in a hurry, post-haste, pell-mell; like a shot, like a flash, on the double, at the speed of light; *informal* double quick, p.d.q. (pretty damn quick), nippily, like (greased) lightning, hell for leather, like mad, like the wind, like a scalded cat, like a bat out of hell; *Brit. informal* like the clappers, at a rate of knots, like billy-o; *N. Amer. informal* lickety-split; *literary* apace. **2** *his wheels were stuck fast* =**securely**, firmly; tight. **3** *he's fast asleep* =**deeply**, sound, completely. **4** *live fast, die young* =**wildly**, dangerously, dissolutely, intemperately, immoderately, recklessly, self-indulgently, extravagantly.
–OPPOSITES slowly.

fast² ▶ verb *we must fast and pray* =**eat nothing**, refrain from eating, go without food, go hungry, starve oneself; go on hunger strike.
–OPPOSITES eat.
▶ noun *a five-day fast* =**period of fasting**, period of abstinence; hunger strike; diet.
–OPPOSITES feast.

fasten ▶ verb **1** *he fastened the door* =**bolt**, lock, secure, make fast, chain, seal. **2** *they fastened splints to his leg* =**attach**, fix, affix, clip, pin, tack; stick, bond, join. **3** *he fastened his horse to a tree* =**tie (up)**, bind, tether, truss, fetter, lash, hitch, anchor, strap, rope. **4** *the dress fastens at the front* =**button (up)**, zip (up), do up, close. **5** *his gaze fastened on me* =**focus**, fix, be riveted, concentrate, zero in, zoom in, direct at.
–OPPOSITES unlock, remove, open, untie, undo.

fastidious ▶ adjective =**scrupulous**, punctilious, painstaking, meticulous; perfectionist, fussy, finicky, particular; critical, overcritical, hard to please, exacting, demanding; *informal* pernickety, nit-picking, choosy, picky; *N. Amer. informal* persnickety.
–OPPOSITES lax.

fat ▶ adjective **1** *a fat man* =**plump**, stout, overweight, large, chubby, portly, flabby, paunchy, pot-bellied, meaty, of ample proportions; obese, corpulent, gross, fleshy; *informal* tubby, roly-poly, beefy, porky, blubbery, chunky; *Brit. informal* podgy. **2** *fat bacon* =**fatty**, greasy, oily. **3** *a fat book* =**thick**, big, chunky, substantial; long.
–OPPOSITES thin, lean, small.
▶ noun **1** *whale fat* =**blubber**, fatty tissue, adipose tissue. **2** *eggs in sizzling fat* =**oil**, grease; lard, suet, butter, margarine.

WORD LINKS
relating to fat: **lipo-**

fatal ▶ adjective **1** *a fatal disease* =**deadly**, lethal, mortal, death-dealing; terminal, incurable, untreatable, inoperable; *literary* deathly. **2** *a fatal mistake* =**disastrous**, devastating, ruinous, catastrophic, calamitous, dire; costly; *formal* grievous.
–OPPOSITES harmless, beneficial.

fatalism ▶ noun =**acceptance**, passivity, resignation, stoicism.

fatality ▶ noun =**death**, casualty, mortality, victim.

fate ▶ noun **1** *what has fate in store for me?* =**destiny**, providence, the stars, chance, luck, serendipity, fortune, karma. **2** *my fate was in their hands* =**future**, destiny, outcome, end, lot. **3** *a similar fate would befall Harris* =**death**, demise, end; retribution, sentence.
▶ verb *she was fated to face the same problem* =**be predestined**, be preordained, be destined, be meant, be doomed; be bound, be guaranteed.

fateful ▶ adjective **1** *that fateful day* =**decisive**, critical, crucial, pivotal; momentous, important, key, significant, historic, portentous. **2** *the fateful defeat of 1402* =**disastrous**, ruinous, calamitous, devastating, tragic, terrible.
–OPPOSITES unimportant.

father ▶ noun **1** *his mother and father* =**male parent**, patriarch; *informal* dad, daddy, pop, pa, old man; *Brit. informal, dated* pater. **2** *(literary) the religion of my fathers* =**ancestors**, forefathers, forebears, predecessors, antecedents, progenitors. **3** *the father of democracy* =**originator**, initiator, founder, inventor, creator, maker, author, architect.
–OPPOSITES child, mother, descendant.
▶ verb =**be the father of**, sire, spawn, breed; *literary* beget.

WORD LINKS

relating to a father: **paternal, patri-**
killing of one's father: **patricide**

fathom ▸ verb =**understand**, comprehend, work out, make sense of, grasp,
divine, puzzle out, get to the bottom of;
interpret, decipher, decode; *informal*
make head or tail of, tumble to, crack;
Brit. informal twig, suss (out), savvy.

fatigue ▸ noun =**tiredness**, weariness,
exhaustion.
–OPPOSITES energy.
▸ verb =**tire (out)**, exhaust, wear out,
drain, weary, wash out, overtire, prostrate; *informal* knock out, take it out of, do
in, fag out, whack, poop, shatter, bush,
wear to a frazzle; *Brit. informal* knacker.
–OPPOSITES invigorate.

fatness ▸ noun =**plumpness**, stout-
ness, heaviness, chubbiness, portliness,
rotundity, flabbiness, paunchiness;
obesity, corpulence; *informal* tubbiness,
podginess.
–OPPOSITES thinness.

fatty ▸ adjective =**greasy**, oily.
–OPPOSITES lean.

fatuous ▸ adjective =**silly**, foolish, stupid, inane, idiotic, vacuous, asinine;
pointless, senseless, ridiculous, ludicrous, absurd; *informal* dumb, gormless;
Brit. informal daft.
–OPPOSITES sensible.

fault ▸ noun 1 *he has his faults* =**defect**,
failing, imperfection, flaw, blemish,
shortcoming, weakness, frailty, foible,
vice. 2 *engineers have located the fault* =**defect**, flaw, imperfection, bug; error, mistake, inaccuracy; *informal* glitch, gremlin.
3 *it was not my fault* =**responsibility**, liability, culpability, guilt. 4 *don't blame
one child for another's faults* =**misdeed**,
wrongdoing, offence, misdemeanour,
misconduct, indiscretion, peccadillo,
transgression.
–OPPOSITES merit, strength.
▸ verb *you can't fault their commitment* =**find
fault with**, criticize, attack, condemn,
reproach; complain about, moan about;
informal knock, gripe about, beef about,
pick holes in; *Brit. informal* slag off, have a
go at.
■ **at fault** =**to blame**, blameworthy,
culpable; responsible, guilty, in the
wrong.
■ **to a fault** =**excessively**, unduly, immoderately, overly, needlessly.

faultless ▸ adjective =**perfect**, flawless, without fault, error-free, impeccable, accurate, precise, exact, correct,
exemplary.
–OPPOSITES flawed.

faulty ▸ adjective 1 *a faulty electric blanket*
=**malfunctioning**, broken, damaged,
defective, not working, out of order; *informal* on the blink, acting up, kaput,
bust; *Brit. informal* knackered, playing up,
duff; *N. Amer. informal* on the fritz. 2 *her
logic is faulty* =**defective**, flawed, unsound, inaccurate, incorrect, erroneous, fallacious, wrong.
–OPPOSITES working, sound.

faux pas ▸ noun =**gaffe**, blunder, mistake, indiscretion, impropriety; *informal*
boo-boo; *Brit. informal* boob; *N. Amer. informal*
blooper.

favour ▸ noun 1 *will you do me a favour?*
=**good turn**, service, good deed, (act of)
kindness, courtesy. 2 *she looked on him
with favour* =**approval**, approbation,
goodwill, kindness, benevolence.
–OPPOSITES disservice, disapproval.
▸ verb 1 *the party favours electoral reform*
=**advocate**, recommend, approve of, be
in favour of, support, back, champion;
campaign for, stand up for, press for,
lobby for, promote; *informal* plug, push
for. 2 *Robyn favours loose clothes* =**prefer**,
go (in) for, choose, opt for, select, pick,
plump for, be partial to, like. 3 *father always favoured George* =**prefer**, be biased
towards, like more/better. 4 *the conditions favoured the other team* =**benefit**, be
to the advantage of, help, assist, aid, be
of service to. 5 *he did it to favour Lucy* =**oblige**, honour, gratify, humour, indulge.
–OPPOSITES oppose, dislike, hinder.
■ **in favour of** =**on the side of**, pro, (all)
for, giving support to, approving of,
sympathetic to.

favourable ▸ adjective 1 *a favourable
review* =**approving**, complimentary,
flattering, glowing, enthusiastic; good,
pleasing, positive. 2 *conditions are favourable* =**advantageous**, beneficial, in one's
favour, good, right, suitable, fitting, appropriate; propitious, auspicious, promising, encouraging. 3 *a favourable reply*
=**positive**, affirmative, assenting, agreeing, approving; encouraging, reassuring.
–OPPOSITES critical, disadvantageous,
negative.

favourably ▸ adverb =**positively**, approvingly, sympathetically, enthusiastically, appreciatively.

favoured ▸ adjective =preferred, favourite, recommended, chosen, choice.

favourite ▸ adjective =best-loved, most-liked, favoured, dearest; preferred, chosen, choice.

▸ noun =(first) choice, pick, preference, pet, darling, the apple of one's eye; *informal* golden boy; *Brit. informal* blue-eyed boy/girl; *N. Amer. informal* fair-haired boy/girl.

favouritism ▸ noun =partiality, partisanship, preferential treatment, favour, nepotism, prejudice, bias, inequality, unfairness, discrimination.

fawn[1] ▸ adjective *a fawn carpet* =beige, buff, sand, oatmeal, café au lait, camel, taupe, stone, mushroom.

fawn[2] ▸ verb *they were fawning over the President* =be obsequious to, be sycophantic to, curry favour with, pay court to, play up to, crawl to, ingratiate oneself with, dance attendance on; *informal* suck up to, grovel to, make up to, be all over; *Austral./NZ informal* smoodge to.

fawning ▸ adjective =obsequious, servile, sycophantic, flattering, ingratiating, unctuous, grovelling, crawling; *informal* bootlicking, smarmy.

fear ▸ noun 1 *she felt fear at entering the house* =terror, fright, fearfulness, horror, alarm, panic, agitation, trepidation, dread, consternation, dismay, distress; anxiety, worry, angst, unease, uneasiness, apprehension, apprehensiveness, nervousness, nerves, foreboding; *informal* the creeps, the willies, the heebie-jeebies, jitteriness, twitchiness, butterflies (in the stomach), (blue) funk. 2 *a fear of heights* =phobia, aversion, antipathy, dread; nightmare, horror, terror; anxiety, neurosis; *informal* hang-up.

▸ verb 1 *she feared her husband* =be afraid of, be fearful of, be scared of, be apprehensive of, dread, live in fear of, be terrified of; be anxious about, worry about, feel apprehensive about. 2 *he fears heights* =have a phobia about, have a horror of, take fright at; *informal* have a thing about, have a hang-up about. 3 *he feared to tell them* =be too afraid, be too scared, hesitate, dare not. 4 *they feared for his health* =worry about, feel anxious about, feel concerned about, have anxieties about. 5 *I fear you may be right* =suspect, have a (sneaking) suspicion, be inclined

to think, be afraid, have a hunch, think it likely.

fearful ▸ adjective 1 *they are fearful of being overheard* =afraid, frightened, scared (stiff), scared to death, terrified, petrified; alarmed, panicky, nervy, nervous, tense, apprehensive, uneasy, worried (sick), anxious; *informal* jittery, jumpy, in a (blue) funk. 2 *a fearful accident* =terrible, dreadful, awful, appalling, frightful, ghastly, horrific, horrible, horrifying, horrendous, terribly bad, shocking, atrocious, abominable, hideous, gruesome. 3 *(informal) he was in a fearful hurry* =(very) great, extreme, real, dreadful; *informal* terrible.

fearfully ▸ adverb 1 *she opened the door fearfully* =apprehensively, uneasily, nervously, timidly, timorously, hesitantly, with one's heart in one's mouth. 2 *(informal) Stephanie looked fearfully cross* =extremely, exceedingly, exceptionally, remarkably, uncommonly, extraordinarily, tremendously, incredibly, very, really; *Scottish* unco; *informal* awfully, terribly, dreadfully, seriously, majorly; *Brit.* well, ever so, dead; *N. Amer. informal* real, mighty, awful; *dated* frightfully.

fearless ▸ adjective =bold, brave, courageous, intrepid, valiant, valorous, gallant, plucky, heroic, daring, indomitable, doughty; unafraid, undaunted, unflinching; *informal* gutsy, spunky, ballsy, feisty.
 −OPPOSITES timid, cowardly.

fearsome ▸ adjective =frightening, horrifying, terrifying, menacing, chilling, spine-chilling, hair-raising, alarming, unnerving, daunting, formidable, forbidding, dismaying, disquieting, disturbing; *informal* scary.

feasible ▸ adjective =practicable, practical, workable, achievable, attainable, realizable, viable, realistic, sensible, reasonable, within reason; suitable, possible; *informal* doable.
 −OPPOSITES impractical.

feast ▸ noun 1 *a wedding feast* =banquet, meal, dinner; treat, entertainment; revels, festivities; *informal* blowout, spread; *Brit. informal* nosh-up, beanfeast, bunfight, beano, slap-up meal. 2 *a feast for the eyes* =treat, delight, joy, pleasure.

▸ verb *they feasted on lobster* =gorge on, dine on, eat one's fill of, binge on; eat, devour, consume, partake of; *informal* stuff one's face with, stuff oneself with, pig oneself on, pig out on.

feat ▸ noun =**achievement**, accomplishment, attainment, coup, triumph; undertaking, enterprise, venture, operation, exercise, endeavour, effort, performance, exploit.

feather ▸ noun =**plume**, quill; (**feathers**) plumage, down.

> WORD LINKS
>
> *fear of feathers:* **pteronophobia**

feature ▸ noun **1** *a feature of Indian music* =**characteristic**, attribute, quality, property, trait, hallmark, trademark; aspect, facet, factor, ingredient, component, element, theme; peculiarity, idiosyncrasy, quirk. **2** *her delicate features* =**face**, countenance, physiognomy; *informal* mug, kisser; *Brit. informal* mush, phiz, phizog; *N. Amer. informal* puss, pan; *literary* visage. **3** *she made a feature of her sculptures* =**centrepiece**, (special) attraction, highlight, focal point, focus (of attention), conversation piece. **4** *a series of short features* =**article**, piece, item, report, story, column, review, commentary, write-up.
▸ verb **1** *Radio 3 is featuring a week of live concerts* =**present**, promote, make a feature of, give prominence to, spotlight, highlight, showcase. **2** *she is to feature in a new movie* =**star**, appear, participate, be.

feckless ▸ adjective =**useless**, worthless, incompetent, inept, good-for-nothing, ne'er-do-well; lazy, idle, slothful, indolent, shiftless; *informal* no-good.

fecund ▸ adjective =**fertile**, fruitful, productive, high-yielding; rich, lush, flourishing, thriving.
–OPPOSITES barren.

federal ▸ adjective =**confederate**, federated; combined, allied, united, amalgamated, integrated.

federation ▸ noun =**confederation**, confederacy, league; combination, alliance, coalition, union, syndicate, guild, consortium, partnership, cooperative, association, amalgamation.

fee ▸ noun =**payment**, wage, salary, allowance; price, cost, charge, tariff, rate, amount, sum, figure; (**fees**) remuneration, dues, earnings, pay; *formal* emolument.

feeble ▸ adjective **1** *old and feeble* =**weak**, weakened, frail, infirm, delicate, sickly, ailing, unwell, poorly, enfeebled, debilitated, incapacitated, decrepit. **2** *a feeble argument* =**ineffective**, ineffectual, inadequate, unconvincing, implausible, unsatisfactory, poor, weak, flimsy. **3** *he's too feeble to stand up to her* =**cowardly**, faint-hearted, spineless, lily-livered; timid, timorous, fearful, unassertive, weak, ineffectual; *informal* wimpy, sissy, gutless, chicken; *Brit. informal* wet. **4** *a feeble light* =**faint**, dim, weak, pale, soft, subdued, muted.
–OPPOSITES strong, brave.

feed ▸ verb **1** *a large family to feed* =**give food to**, provide for, cater for, cook for; suckle, breastfeed, bottle-feed. **2** *the baby spends all day feeding* =**eat**, have a meal, snack; *informal* nosh, graze. **3** *too many cows feeding in a small area* =**graze**, browse, crop. **4** *the birds feed on nuts* =**live on/off**, exist on, subsist on, eat, consume. **5** *feeding her anger* =**strengthen**, fortify, support, bolster, reinforce, boost, fuel, encourage, nurse. **6** *she fed secrets to the Russians* =**supply**, provide, give, deliver, furnish, issue, leak.
▸ noun *animal feed* =**fodder**, food, provender.

feel ▸ verb **1** *she felt the fabric* =**touch**, stroke, caress, fondle, finger, handle. **2** *she felt a breeze on her back* =**perceive**, sense, detect, discern, notice, be aware of, be conscious of. **3** *he will not feel any pain* =**experience**, undergo, go through, bear, endure, suffer. **4** *he felt his way towards the door* =**grope**, fumble, scrabble. **5** *feel the temperature of the water* =**test**, try (out), gauge, assess. **6** *he feels that he should go* =**believe**, think, consider (it right), be of the opinion, hold, maintain, judge; *informal* reckon, figure. **7** *the air feels damp* =**seem**, appear, strike one as.
▸ noun **1** *the divers worked by feel* =**(sense of) touch**, feeling (one's way). **2** *the feel of the paper* =**texture**, finish; weight, thickness, consistency. **3** *the feel of the house* =**atmosphere**, ambience, aura, mood, feeling, air, impression, character, spirit, flavour; *informal* vibrations, vibe(s). **4** *a feel for languages* =**aptitude**, knack, flair, bent, talent, gift, faculty, ability.
■ **feel for** =**sympathize with**, be sorry for, pity, feel pity for, feel sympathy for, feel compassion for, be moved by; commiserate with, condole with.

■ **feel like** =want, would like, wish for, desire, fancy, feel in need of, long for; *informal* yen for, be dying for.

feeler ▸ noun =antenna, tentacle.

feeling ▸ noun **1** *assess the fabric by feeling* =(sense of) **touch**, feel, hand. **2** *a feeling of nausea* =**sensation**, sense. **3** *I had a feeling that I would win* =(sneaking) **suspicion**, notion, inkling, hunch, intuition, funny feeling, fancy, idea; presentiment, premonition; *informal* gut feeling. **4** *the strength of her feeling* =**love**, affection, fondness, tenderness, warmth, warmness, emotion, sentiment; passion, ardour, desire. **5** *public feeling* =**sentiment**, emotion; opinion, attitude, belief, ideas, views, consensus. **6** *show some feeling* =**compassion**, sympathy, empathy, fellow feeling, concern, solicitude, solicitousness, tenderness; pity, sorrow, commiseration, charity. **7** *he had hurt her feelings* =**sensibilities**, sensitivities, self-esteem, pride. **8** *my feeling is that it is true* =**opinion**, belief, view, impression, intuition, instinct, hunch, estimation, guess. **9** *a feeling of peace* =**atmosphere**, ambience, aura, air, feel, mood, impression, spirit, quality, flavour; *informal* vibrations, vibe(s). **10** *a remarkable feeling for language* =**aptitude**, knack, flair, bent, talent, feel, gift, faculty, ability.
▸ adjective *a feeling man* =**sensitive**, warm, warm-hearted, tender, tender-hearted, caring, sympathetic, kind, compassionate, understanding, thoughtful.

feign ▸ verb =**simulate**, fake, affect, give the appearance of, make a pretence of.

feigned ▸ adjective =**pretended**, simulated, affected, artificial, insincere, put-on, fake, false, sham; *informal* pretend, phoney.
–OPPOSITES sincere.

feint ▸ noun =**bluff**, blind, ruse, deception, subterfuge, hoax, trick, ploy, device, dodge, sham, pretence, cover, smokescreen, distraction, contrivance; *informal* red herring.

felicitations ▸ plural noun =**congratulations**, good/best wishes, (kind) regards, blessings, compliments, respects.

felicitous ▸ adjective =**apt**, well chosen, fitting, suitable, appropriate, apposite, pertinent, germane, relevant.

–OPPOSITES inappropriate, unfortunate.

feline ▸ adjective =**catlike**, graceful, sleek, sinuous.
▸ noun =**cat**, kitten; *informal* puss, pussy (cat); *Brit. informal* moggie, mog; *archaic* grimalkin.

fell[1] ▸ verb **1** *the dead trees had to be felled* =**cut down**, chop down, hack down, saw down, clear. **2** *she felled him with one punch* =**knock down/over**, knock to the ground, floor, strike down, bring down, bring to the ground, prostrate; knock out, knock unconscious; *informal* deck, flatten, down, lay out, KO; *Brit. informal* knock for six.

fell[2] ▸ adjective *(literary)* ■ **at/in one fell swoop** =**all at once**, together, at the same time, in one go.

fellow ▸ noun **1** *(informal) he's a decent sort of fellow* =**man**, boy; person, individual, soul; *informal* guy, geezer, lad, fella, character, customer, devil, bastard; *Brit. informal* chap, bloke; *N. Amer. informal* dude, hombre; *Austral./NZ informal* digger; *informal, dated* body, dog, cove. **2** *he exchanged glances with his fellows* =**companion**, friend, comrade, partner, associate, co-worker, colleague; *informal* chum, pal, buddy; *Brit. informal* mate. **3** *some workers were wealthier than their fellows* =**peer**, equal, contemporary.
■ **fellow feeling** =**sympathy**, empathy, feeling, compassion, care, concern, solicitude, solicitousness, warmth, tenderness, (brotherly) love; pity, sorrow, commiseration.

fellowship ▸ noun **1** *a community bound together in fellowship* =**companionship**, sociability, comradeship, camaraderie, friendship, mutual support; togetherness, solidarity; *informal* chumminess, palliness; *Brit. informal* mateyness. **2** *the church fellowship* =**association**, society, club, league, union, guild, alliance, fraternity, brotherhood, sorority, sodality.

female ▸ adjective =**feminine**, womanly, ladylike.
–OPPOSITES male.
▸ noun. See WOMAN sense 1.

feminine ▸ adjective **1** *a very feminine young woman* =**womanly**, ladylike, girlish, girlie. **2** *he seemed slightly feminine* =**effeminate**, womanish, unmanly, effete; *informal* sissy, wimpy, limp-wristed.

–OPPOSITES masculine, manly.

femininity ▶ noun = womanliness, feminineness.

feminism ▶ noun = the women's **movement**, women's liberation, women's rights; *informal, dated* women's lib.

femme fatale ▶ noun = seductress, temptress, siren; *informal* vamp.

fen ▶ noun = marsh, marshland, salt marsh, fenland, wetland, (peat) bog, swamp, swampland; *N. Amer.* moor.

fence ▶ noun 1 *a gap in the fence* = barrier, paling, railing, enclosure, barricade, stockade, palisade.
▶ verb 1 *they fenced off the meadow* = enclose, surround, encircle, circle, encompass. 2 *he fenced in his chickens* = confine, pen in, coop up, shut in/up; enclose, surround; *N. Amer.* corral.

fend ▶ verb *they were unable to fend off the invasion* = ward off, head off, stave off, hold off, repel, repulse, resist, fight off, defend oneself against, prevent, stop, block.
■ **fend for oneself** = take care of oneself, look after oneself, provide for oneself, shift for oneself, manage by oneself, cope alone, stand on one's own two feet.

feral ▶ adjective 1 *feral dogs* = wild, untamed, undomesticated, untrained. 2 *a feral snarl* = fierce, ferocious, vicious, savage, predatory, menacing, bloodthirsty; atavistic.
–OPPOSITES tame, pet.

ferment ▶ verb 1 *the beer continues to ferment* = brew; effervesce, fizz, foam, froth. 2 *an environment that ferments disorder* = cause, bring about, give rise to, generate, engender, spawn, instigate, provoke, incite, excite, stir up, whip up, foment.

WORD LINKS

science of fermentation: **zymology**

ferocious ▶ adjective 1 *ferocious animals* = fierce, savage, wild, predatory, aggressive, dangerous. 2 *a ferocious attack* = brutal, vicious, violent, bloody, barbaric, savage, sadistic, ruthless, cruel, merciless, heartless, bloodthirsty, murderous, frenzied.
–OPPOSITES gentle, mild.

ferocity ▶ noun = savagery, brutality, barbarity, fierceness, violence, blood-

thirstiness, murderousness; ruthlessness, cruelty, pitilessness, mercilessness, heartlessness.

ferret ▶ verb 1 *she ferreted in her handbag* = rummage, feel around, grope around, forage around, fish about/around, poke about/around; search through, hunt through, rifle through; *Austral./NZ informal* fossick through. 2 *ferreting out injustice* = unearth, uncover, discover, detect, search out, bring to light, track down, dig up, root out, nose out; *informal* get wise to; *Brit. informal* rumble.

WORD LINKS

male: **jack**
female: **jill**
young: **kit**
collective noun: **busyness**

ferry ▶ verb = transport, convey, carry, ship, run, take, bring, shuttle.

fertile ▶ adjective 1 *the soil is fertile* = fecund, fruitful, productive, rich, lush. 2 *fertile couples* = able to conceive, able to have children. 3 *a fertile imagination* = creative, inventive, innovative, visionary, original, ingenious; productive, prolific.
–OPPOSITES barren.

fertilization ▶ noun = conception, impregnation, insemination; pollination.

fertilize ▶ verb 1 *the field was fertilized* feed, mulch, compost, manure, dress, top-dress. 2 *these orchids are fertilized by insects* = pollinate.

fervent ▶ adjective = impassioned, passionate, intense, vehement, ardent, sincere, heartfelt; enthusiastic, zealous, fanatical, wholehearted, avid, eager, keen, committed, dedicated, devout; *informal* mad keen.
–OPPOSITES apathetic.

fervour ▶ noun = passion, ardour, intensity, zeal, vehemence, emotion, warmth, earnestness, avidity, eagerness, keenness, enthusiasm, excitement, animation, vigour, energy, fire, spirit, zest.
–OPPOSITES apathy.

fester ▶ verb 1 *the wound festered* = suppurate, become septic, weep; *Medicine* maturate, be purulent. 2 *rubbish festered in the streets* = rot, moulder, decay, decompose, putrefy. 3 *their resentment festered* = rankle, eat/gnaw away at one's mind, brew, smoulder.

festival ▶ noun =fête, fair, gala (day), carnival, fiesta, jamboree, celebrations, festivities.

festive ▶ adjective =jolly, merry, joyous, joyful, happy, jovial, light-hearted, cheerful, jubilant, convivial, high-spirited, mirthful, uproarious; celebratory, holiday, carnival; Christmassy.

festivity ▶ noun =celebration, festival, entertainment, party; merrymaking, feasting, revelry, jollification; revels, fun and games; informal bash, shindig, shindy; Brit. informal rave-up, knees-up, beanfeast, bunfight, beano.

festoon ▶ verb =decorate, adorn, ornament, trim, deck (out), hang, loop, drape, swathe, garland, wreathe, bedeck; informal do up/out, get up, trick out.

fetch ▶ verb 1 he went to fetch a doctor =(go and) get, go for, call for, summon, pick up, collect, bring, carry, convey, transport. 2 the land could fetch millions =sell for, bring in, raise, realize, yield, make, command, cost, be priced at; informal go for, pull in; Brit. informal knock someone back.

fetching ▶ adjective =attractive, appealing, sweet, pretty, lovely, delightful, charming, prepossessing, captivating, enchanting, irresistible; Scottish & N. English bonny; informal divine, heavenly; Brit. informal fit, smashing; archaic comely, fair.

fête ▶ noun (Brit.) =gala (day), bazaar, fair, festival, fiesta, jubilee, carnival; fund-raiser.

fetid ▶ adjective =stinking, smelly, foul-smelling, malodorous, reeking, pungent, acrid, high, rank, foul, noxious; Brit. informal niffy, pongy, whiffy, humming; N. Amer. informal funky; literary noisome.
–OPPOSITES fragrant.

fetish ▶ noun 1 a rubber fetish =fixation, obsession, compulsion, mania; weakness, fancy, fascination; informal thing, hang-up. 2 an African fetish totem, talisman, charm, amulet; idol, image, effigy.

fetter ▶ verb fettered by legislation =restrict, restrain, constrain, limit; hinder, hamper, impede, obstruct, hamstring, inhibit, check, curb, trammel.

fettle ▶ noun =shape, trim, (physical) fitness, (state of) health; condition,

form, (state of) repair, (working) order; Brit. informal nick.

fetus ▶ noun embryo, unborn baby/child.

> **WORD LINKS**
>
> killing of a fetus: **feticide**

feud ▶ noun =vendetta, conflict; rivalry, hostility, enmity, strife, discord; quarrel, argument.
▶ verb =quarrel, fight, argue, bicker, squabble, fall out, dispute, clash, differ, be at odds; informal scrap.

fever ▶ noun 1 he developed fever =feverishness, high temperature; Medicine pyrexia; informal temperature. 2 a fever of excitement =ferment, frenzy, furore; ecstasy, rapture. 3 World Cup fever =excitement, mania, frenzy, agitation, passion.

> **WORD LINKS**
>
> relating to fever: **febrile**
> fear of fever: **febriphobia**
> medicine for fever: **febrifuge**

fevered ▶ adjective 1 her fevered brow =feverish, febrile, hot, burning. 2 a fevered imagination =excited, agitated, frenzied, overwrought.

feverish ▶ adjective 1 she's really feverish =febrile, fevered, hot, burning; informal having a temperature. 2 feverish excitement =frenzied, frenetic, hectic, agitated, excited, restless, nervous, worked up, overwrought, frantic, furious, hysterical, wild, uncontrolled, unrestrained.

few ▶ determiner police are revealing few details =not many, hardly any, scarcely any; a small number of, a small amount of, one or two, a handful of; little.
–OPPOSITES many.
▶ adjective comforts here are few =scarce, scant, meagre, in short supply; thin on the ground, few and far between, infrequent, uncommon, rare.
–OPPOSITES plentiful.
■ a few =a small number, a handful, one or two, a couple, two or three; not many, hardly any.

fiancé, fiancée ▶ noun =betrothed, husband-to-be, wife-to-be, bride-to-be, future husband/wife; informal intended.

fiasco ▶ noun =failure, disaster, catastrophe, debacle, shambles, farce, mess, wreck; informal flop, washout; Brit. informal cock-up; N. Amer. informal snafu; Austral./NZ

informal fizzer.
−OPPOSITES success.

fib ▶ noun =**lie**, untruth, falsehood, made-up story, invention, fabrication, deception, (piece of) fiction; (little) white lie, half-truth; *informal* tall story/ tale, whopper; *Brit. informal* porky (pie).
−OPPOSITES truth.

▶ verb =**lie**, tell a fib, tell a lie, invent/make up a story.

fibre ▶ noun **1** *fibres from the murderer's jumper* =**thread**, strand, filament. **2** *natural fibres* =**material**, cloth, fabric. **3** *a man with no fibre*. See MORAL FIBRE. **4** *fibre in the diet* =**roughage**, bulk.

fickle ▶ adjective =**capricious**, changeable, variable, volatile, mercurial; inconstant, undependable, unsteady, unfaithful, faithless, flighty, giddy, skittish; *literary* mutable.
−OPPOSITES constant.

fiction ▶ noun **1** *the traditions of British fiction* =**novels**, stories, (creative) writing, (prose) literature. **2** *this is an absolute fiction* =**fabrication**, invention, lie, fib, untruth, falsehood, fantasy, nonsense.
−OPPOSITES fact.

fictional ▶ adjective =**fictitious**, invented, imaginary, made up, make-believe, unreal, fabricated, mythical.
−OPPOSITES real.

fictitious ▶ adjective **1** *a fictitious name* =**false**, fake, fabricated, sham; bogus, spurious, assumed, affected, adopted, invented, made up; *informal* pretend, phoney. **2** *a fictitious character*. See FICTIONAL.
−OPPOSITES genuine.

fiddle (*informal*) ▶ noun **1** *she played the fiddle* =**violin**, viola. **2** *a VAT fiddle* =**fraud**, swindle, confidence trick; *informal* racket, con trick.

▶ verb **1** *he fiddled with a beer mat* =**fidget**, play, toy, twiddle, fuss, fool about/ around; finger, handle; *informal* mess about/around; *Brit. informal* muck about/ around. **2** *he fiddled with the dials* =**adjust**, tinker, play about/around, meddle, interfere; *informal* tweak. **3** *fiddling the figures* =**falsify**, manipulate, massage, rig, distort, misrepresent, doctor, alter, tamper with, interfere with; *informal* fix, cook (the books).

fidelity ▶ noun **1** *fidelity to her husband* =**faithfulness**, loyalty, constancy; trustworthiness, dependability, reliability; *formal* troth. **2** *the fidelity of the reproduction* =**accuracy**, exactness, precision, preciseness, correctness, strictness, closeness, faithfulness, authenticity.
−OPPOSITES disloyalty.

fidget ▶ verb **1** *the audience began to fidget* =**move restlessly**, wriggle, squirm, twitch, jiggle, shuffle, be agitated; *informal* be jittery. **2** *she fidgeted with her scarf* =**play**, fuss, toy, twiddle, fool about/ around; *informal* fiddle, mess about/ around.

▶ noun **1** *what a fidget you are!* =**restless person**, bundle of nerves. **2** *that woman gives me the fidgets* =**restlessness**, nervousness, fidgetiness; *informal* the jitters, twitchiness.

fidgety ▶ adjective =**restless**, restive, on edge, uneasy, nervous, nervy, keyed up, anxious, agitated; *informal* jittery, twitchy.

field ▶ noun **1** *a large ploughed field* =**meadow**, pasture, paddock, grassland, pastureland, sward. **2** *a football field* =**pitch**, ground, sports field, playing field, recreation ground. **3** *the field of biotechnology* =**area**, sphere, discipline, province, department, domain, sector, branch, subject; *informal* bailiwick. **4** *your field of vision* =**scope**, range, sweep, reach, extent. **5** *she is well ahead of the field* =**competitors**, entrants, competition; applicants, candidates, possibles.

▶ verb **1** *she fielded the ball* =**catch**, stop, retrieve; return, throw back. **2** *fielding a great team* =**send out**, play, put up; assemble, offer. **3** *he fielded some awkward questions* =**deal with**, handle, cope with, answer, reply to, respond to.

fiend ▶ noun *a heartless fiend* =**brute**, beast, villain, barbarian, monster, ogre, sadist; *informal* swine.

fiendish ▶ adjective **1** *a fiendish act* =**wicked**, cruel, vicious, evil, malevolent, villainous; brutal, savage, barbaric, barbarous, inhuman, murderous, ruthless, merciless. **2** *a fiendish plot* =**cunning**, clever, ingenious, crafty, canny, wily, devious, shrewd; *informal* sneaky. **3** *a fiendish puzzle* =**difficult**, complex, challenging, complicated, intricate, involved, knotty, thorny.

fierce ▶ adjective **1** *a fierce black mastiff* =**ferocious**, savage, vicious, aggressive. **2** *fierce competition* =**aggressive**, cutthroat; keen, intense, strong, relentless. **3** *fierce jealousy* =**intense**, powerful, vehement, passionate, impassioned,

fervent, ardent. **4** *a fierce wind* =**power-ful**, strong, violent, forceful; stormy, blustery, gusty, tempestuous. **5** *a fierce pain* =**severe**, extreme, intense, acute, awful, dreadful; excruciating, agonizing, piercing.
–OPPOSITES gentle, mild.

fiery ▶ adjective **1** *a fiery blast* =**burning**, blazing, flaming; on fire, ablaze. **2** *a fiery red* =**bright**, brilliant, vivid, intense, rich. **3** *her fiery spirit* =**passionate**, impassioned, ardent, fervent, spirited; quick-tempered, volatile, explosive.

fight ▶ verb **1** *two men were fighting* =**brawl**, exchange blows, attack/assault each other, hit/punch each other; struggle, grapple, wrestle; *informal* scrap, have a dust-up, have a set-to; *Brit. informal* have a punch-up; *N. Amer. informal* rough-house; *Austral./NZ informal* stoush, go the knuckle. **2** *he fought in Vietnam* =(do) battle, go to war, take up arms, be a soldier; engage, meet, clash, skirmish. **3** *a war fought for freedom* =**engage in**, wage, conduct, prosecute, undertake. **4** *they are always fighting* =**quarrel**, argue, row, bicker, squabble, fall out, have a row/fight, wrangle, be at odds, disagree, differ, have words, bandy words, be at each other's throats, be at loggerheads; *informal* scrap. **5** *fighting against injustice* =**campaign**, strive, battle, struggle, contend, crusade, agitate, lobby, push, press. **6** *they will fight the decision* =**oppose**, contest, contend with, confront, challenge, appeal (against), combat, dispute, quarrel with, argue against/with, strive against, struggle against. **7** *Don fought the urge to cry* =**repress**, restrain, suppress, stifle, smother, hold back, fight back, keep in check, curb, control, rein in, choke back; *informal* keep the lid on, cork up.
▶ noun **1** *a fight outside a club* =**brawl**, fracas, melee, rumpus, skirmish, sparring match, struggle, scuffle, altercation, scrum, clash, disturbance; fisticuffs; *informal* scrap, dust-up, set-to, shindy, shindig; *Brit. informal* punch-up, bust-up, ruck; *N. Amer. informal* rough house, brannigan; *Austral./NZ informal* stoush; *Law, dated* affray. **2** *a heavyweight fight* =**boxing match**, bout, match, contest. **3** *the fight against terrorism* =**battle**, engagement, conflict, struggle; war, campaign, crusade, action, hostilities. **4** *a fight with my girlfriend* =**argument**, quarrel, squabble, row, wrangle, disagreement, falling-out,

contretemps, altercation, dispute; *informal* tiff, spat, scrap, slanging match; *Brit. informal* barney, ding-dong, bust-up. **5** *their fight for control of the company* =**struggle**, battle, campaign, push, effort. **6** *she had no fight left in her* =**will**, resistance, spirit, courage, pluck, pluckiness, grit, strength, backbone, determination, resolution, resolve, resoluteness, aggression, aggressiveness; *informal* guts, spunk; *Brit. informal* bottle; *N. Amer. informal* sand, moxie.
■ **fight back 1** *use your anger to fight back* =**retaliate**, counter-attack, strike back, hit back, respond, reciprocate, return fire. **2** *she fought back tears.* See FIGHT verb sense 7.
■ **fight someone/something off** =**repel**, repulse, beat off/back, ward off, fend off, keep/hold at bay, drive away/back, force back.

fighter ▶ noun **1** *a guerrilla fighter* =**soldier**, fighting man/woman, warrior, combatant, serviceman/woman; troops, personnel, militia; *Brit. informal* squaddie. **2** *the fighter was knocked to the ground* =**boxer**, pugilist, prizefighter; wrestler.

fighting ▶ adjective =**violent**, combative, aggressive, pugnacious, truculent, belligerent, bellicose.
–OPPOSITES peaceful.
▶ noun =**violence**, hostilities, conflict, action, combat; warfare, war, battles, skirmishing, rioting; *Law, dated* affray.
–OPPOSITES peace.

figment ▶ noun =**invention**, creation, fabrication; hallucination, illusion, delusion, fancy, vision.

figurative ▶ adjective =**metaphorical**, non-literal, symbolic, allegorical, representative, emblematic.
–OPPOSITES literal.

figure ▶ noun **1** *the figure for April* =**statistic**, number, quantity, amount, level, total, sum; (**figures**) data, statistics, information. **2** *the second figure was 9* =**digit**, numeral, character, symbol. **3** *he can't put a figure on it* =**price**, cost, amount, value, valuation. **4** *I'm good at figures* =**arithmetic**, mathematics, sums, calculations, computation, numbers; *Brit. informal* maths; *N. Amer. informal* math. **5** *her petite figure* =**physique**, build, frame, body, proportions, shape, form. **6** *a dark figure emerged* =**silhouette**, outline, shape, form. **7** *a figure of authority* =**person**, personage, individual, man, woman, character, personality; representative, embodiment, personification, epitome. **8** *life-size figures* =**model**, effigy, representation, carving, image. **9** *geometrical figures* =**shape**, pattern, design, motif. **10** *see figure 4* =**diagram**, illustration, drawing, picture, plate.

▶ verb **1** *he figures in many myths* =**feature**, appear, be featured, be mentioned, be referred to, have prominence. **2** (*informal*) *I figured that Ed had won* =**suppose**, think, believe, consider, expect, take it, suspect, sense; assume, dare say, conclude, take it as read, presume, deduce, infer, gather; *N. Amer.* guess.

■ **figure on** (*N. Amer. informal*) *I figured on paying about $10* =**plan on**, count on, rely on, bank on, bargain on, depend on, pin one's hopes on; anticipate, expect to.

■ **figure something out** (*informal*) *he's figured out how to work the lamp* =**work out**, fathom, puzzle out, decipher, ascertain, make sense of, think through, get to the bottom of; understand, comprehend, see, grasp, get the hang of, get the drift of; *informal* twig, crack; *Brit. informal* suss out.

filament ▶ noun =**fibre**, thread, strand.

file[1] ▶ noun **1** *he opened the file* =**folder**, portfolio, binder. **2** *we have files on all of you* =**dossier**, document, record, report; data, information, documentation, annals, archives. **3** *the files had been deleted* =**document**; data, information, material; text.

▶ verb **1** *file the documents correctly* =**categorize**, classify, organize, put in place/order, order, arrange, catalogue, store, archive. **2** *Debbie has filed for divorce* =**apply**, register, ask. **3** *two women have filed a civil suit* =**bring**, press, lodge, place; *formal* prefer.

file[2] ▶ noun *a file of boys* =**line**, column, row, string, chain, procession; *Brit. informal* crocodile.

▶ verb *we filed out into the park* =**walk in a line**, march, parade, troop.

file[3] ▶ verb *she filed her nails* =**smooth**, buff, rub (down), polish, shape; scrape, abrade, rasp, sandpaper; manicure.

filigree ▶ noun =**tracery**, fretwork, latticework, scrollwork, lacework.

fill ▶ verb **1** *he filled a bowl with cereal* =**make/become full**, fill up, top up, charge. **2** *guests filled the parlour* =**crowd into**, throng, pack (into), occupy, squeeze into, cram (into); overcrowd.

3 *he began filling his shelves* =**stock**, pack, load, supply, replenish, restock, refill. **4** *fill all the holes with putty* =**block up**, stop (up), plug, seal. **5** *the perfume filled the room* =**pervade**, permeate, suffuse, be diffused through, penetrate, infuse. **6** *the person who fills this vacancy* =**occupy**, hold, take up; *informal* hold down.

−OPPOSITES empty.

■ **fill in** =**substitute**, deputize, stand in, cover, take over, act as stand-in, take the place of; *informal* sub, step into someone's shoes/boots; *N. Amer. informal* pinch-hit.

■ **fill someone in** =**inform**, advise, tell, acquaint with, apprise, brief, update; *informal* put in the picture, bring up to speed.

■ **fill something in** (*Brit.*) =**complete**, answer, fill up; *N. Amer.* fill out.

■ **fill out** =**grow fatter**, become plumper, flesh out, put on weight, get heavier.

■ **fill something out 1** *this account needs to be filled out* =**expand**, enlarge, add to, elaborate on, flesh out; supplement, extend, develop, amplify. **2** (*N. Amer.*) *he filled out the forms. See* FILL SOMETHING IN.

filling ▶ noun *filling for cushions* =**stuffing**, padding, wadding, filler.

▶ adjective *a filling meal* =**substantial**, hearty, ample, satisfying, square; heavy, stodgy.

film ▶ noun **1** *a film of sweat* =**layer**, coat, coating, covering, cover, sheet, patina, overlay. **2** *Emma was watching a film* =**movie**, picture, feature (film), motion picture; video; *informal* flick, pic; *dated* moving picture. **3** *she would like to work in film* =**cinema**, movies, the pictures, films; the silver screen, the big screen.

▶ verb **1** *he filmed the next scene* =**record (on film)**, shoot, capture on film, video. **2** *his eyes had filmed over* =**cloud**, mist, haze; become blurred, blur.

> WORD LINKS
> *relating to film:* **cinematographic**

film star ▶ noun =**(film) actor/actress**, movie star, leading man/woman, lead; celebrity, star, starlet, superstar; *informal* celeb; *informal, dated* matinee idol.

filmy ▶ adjective =**diaphanous**, transparent, see-through, translucent, sheer, gossamer; delicate, fine, light, thin, silky.

−OPPOSITES thick, opaque.

filter ▶ noun *a carbon filter* =**strainer**,

sifter; sieve; gauze; net.
▶ verb **1** *the farmers filter the water* =**sieve**, strain, sift, filtrate; clarify, purify, refine, treat. **2** *the rain had filtered through her jacket* =**seep**, percolate, leak, trickle, ooze, leach.

filth ▶ noun **1** *stagnant pools of filth* = **dirt**, muck, grime, mud, mire, sludge, slime, ooze; excrement, excreta, dung, manure, ordure, sewage; rubbish, refuse, dross; pollution, contamination, filthiness, foulness, nastiness; *N. Amer.* garbage; *informal* crud, grunge; *Brit. informal* grot, gunge; *N. Amer. informal* trash. **2** *I felt sick after reading that filth* =**pornography**, dirty books, obscenity; smut; *informal* porn, porno.

filthy ▶ adjective **1** *the room was filthy* =**dirty**, mucky, grimy, muddy, slimy, unclean; foul, squalid, sordid, nasty, soiled, sullied; polluted, contaminated, unhygienic, unsanitary; *informal* cruddy, grungy; *Brit. informal* grotty; *literary* besmirched. **2** *his face was filthy* =**unwashed**, unclean, dirty, grimy, smeared, grubby, muddy, mucky, black, blackened, stained; *literary* begrimed. **3** *filthy jokes* =**obscene**, indecent, dirty, smutty, rude, improper, coarse, bawdy, vulgar, lewd, racy, off colour, earthy, ribald, risqué, pornographic, explicit; *informal* blue, porn, porno, X-rated; *N. Amer. informal* raw; *euphemistic* adult. **4** *you filthy brute!* =**despicable**, contemptible, nasty, low, base, mean, vile, obnoxious; *informal* dirty (rotten), low-down, no-good. **5** *he was in a filthy mood* =**bad**, foul, bad-tempered, irritable, grumpy, grouchy, cross, fractious, peevish; *informal* snappish, snappy; *Brit. informal* shirty, stroppy, narky, ratty; *N. Amer. informal* cranky, ornery.
–OPPOSITES clean.
▶ adverb *filthy rich* =**very**, extremely, tremendously, immensely, remarkably, excessively, exceedingly; *informal* stinking, awfully, terribly, seriously, mega, ultra, damn.

final ▶ adjective **1** *the final year of study* =**last**, closing, concluding, finishing, end, ultimate, eventual. **2** *their decisions are final* =**irrevocable**, unalterable, absolute, conclusive, irrefutable, incontrovertible, indisputable, unchallengeable, binding.
–OPPOSITES first, provisional.

finale ▶ noun =**climax**, culmination; end, ending, finish, close, conclusion,

termination; denouement.
–OPPOSITES beginning.

finality ▶ noun =**conclusiveness**, decisiveness, decision, definiteness, definitiveness, certainty, certitude; irrevocability, irrefutability, incontrovertibility.

finalize ▶ verb =**conclude**, complete, clinch, settle, work out, secure, wrap up, wind up, put the finishing touches to; reach an agreement on, agree on, come to terms on; *informal* sew up.

finally ▶ adverb **1** *she finally got married* =**eventually**, ultimately, in the end, after a long time, at (long) last; in the long run, in the fullness of time. **2** *finally, attach the ribbon* =**lastly**, last, in conclusion. **3** *this should finally dispel that myth* =**conclusively**, irrevocably, decisively, definitively, for ever, for good, once and for all.

finance ▶ noun **1** *he knows about finance* =**financial affairs**, money matters, economics, commerce, business, investment. **2** *short-term finance* =**funds**, assets, money, capital, resources, cash, reserves, revenue, income; funding, backing, sponsorship.
▶ verb *a project financed by grants* =**fund**, pay for, back, capitalize, endow, subsidize, invest in; underwrite, guarantee, sponsor, support; *N. Amer. informal* bankroll.

WORD LINKS
relating to finance: **fiscal**

financial ▶ adjective =**monetary**, money, economic, pecuniary, fiscal, banking, commercial, business, investment.

financier ▶ noun =**investor**, speculator, banker, capitalist, industrialist, businessman, businesswoman, stockbroker; *informal* money man.

finch ▶ noun

WORD LINKS
collective noun: **charm**

find ▶ verb **1** *I found the book I wanted* =**locate**, spot, pinpoint, unearth, obtain; search out, track down, root out; come across/upon, run across/into, chance on, light on, happen on, stumble on, encounter; *informal* bump into. **2** *they found a cure for rabies* =**discover**, invent, come up with, hit on. **3** *the police found her purse* =**retrieve**, recover, get back, regain, repossess. **4** *I hope you find peace* =**obtain**, acquire, get, procure, come by, secure, gain, earn, achieve, attain. **5** *I found the courage to speak* =**summon (up)**, gather, muster (up), screw up, call up. **6** *caffeine is found in coffee* =**be (present)**, occur, exist, appear. **7** *you'll find that it's a lively area* =**discover**, become aware, realize, observe, notice, note, learn. **8** *I find this strange* =**consider**, think, believe to be, feel to be, look on as, view as, see as, judge, deem, regard as. **9** *he was found guilty* =**judge**, deem, rule, declare, pronounce. **10** *her barb found its mark* =**arrive at**, reach, attain, achieve; hit, strike. −OPPOSITES lose.

▶ noun **1** *an archaeological find* =**discovery**, acquisition. **2** *this table is a real find* =**bargain**; godsend, boon; *informal* good buy.

■ **find out** =**discover**, become aware, learn, detect, discern, observe, notice, note, get/come to know, realize; bring to light, reveal, expose, unearth, disclose; *informal* figure out, cotton on, catch on, tumble, get wise; *Brit. informal* twig, rumble, suss.

finding ▶ noun **1** *the finding of the leak* =**discovery**, location, locating, detection, detecting, uncovering. **2** *the tribunal's findings* =**conclusion**, decision, verdict, pronouncement, judgement, ruling, rule, decree, recommendation; *Law* determination; *N. Amer.* resolve.

fine[1] ▶ adjective **1** *fine wines* =**good**, choice, select, prime, quality, the best, the finest, special, superior, of distinction, premium, premier, classic, vintage. **2** *a really fine piece of work* =**excellent**, first-class, first-rate, great, exceptional, outstanding, splendid, magnificent, exquisite, supreme, superb, wonderful, superlative, second to none; *informal* A1, top-notch, splendiferous. **3** *a fine fellow* =**worthy**, admirable, praiseworthy, laudable, estimable, upright, upstanding, respectable. **4** *that's fine, but it's not enough* =**all right**, acceptable, suitable, good (enough), passable, satisfactory, adequate, reasonable, tolerable; *informal* OK. **5** *I feel fine* =**good**, well, healthy, all right, (fighting) fit, blooming, thriving, in good shape/condition, in fine fettle; *informal* OK, great, in the pink. **6** *a fine day* =**fair**, dry, bright, clear, sunny, without a cloud in the sky, warm, balmy, summery. **7** *fine clothes* =**elegant**, stylish, expensive, smart, chic, fashionable; fancy, sumptuous,

lavish, opulent; *informal* flashy, swanky, ritzy, plush. **8** *a fine mind* =**keen**, quick, alert, sharp, bright, brilliant, astute, clever, intelligent. **9** *fine china* =**delicate**, fragile, dainty; thin, light. **10** *fine hair* =**thin**, light, delicate, wispy, flyaway. **11** *a fine point* =**sharp**, keen, acute, razor-sharp. **12** *fine material* =**sheer**, light, lightweight, thin, flimsy; diaphanous, filmy, gossamer, silky, transparent, translucent, see-through. **13** *fine sand* =**fine-grained**, powdery; dusty, ground, crushed. **14** *fine details* =**intricate**, delicate, detailed, elaborate, dainty, meticulous. **15** *a fine distinction* =**subtle**, ultra-fine, nice, hair-splitting. −OPPOSITES poor, unsatisfactory, ill, inclement, thick, coarse.

▶ adverb *(informal)* *you're doing fine* =**well**, all right, not badly, satisfactorily, adequately, nicely, tolerably; *informal* OK, good, great. −OPPOSITES badly.

fine[2] ▶ noun *heavy fines* =**(financial) penalty**, sanction, fee, charge.

▶ verb *I was fined* =**penalize**, impose a fine on, charge.

finery ▶ noun =**regalia**, best clothes, (Sunday) best; *informal* glad rags, best bib and tucker.

finesse ▶ noun **1** *masterly finesse* =**skill**, skilfulness, expertise, subtlety, flair, panache, elan, polish, artistry, virtuosity, mastery. **2** *a modicum of finesse* =**tact**, tactfulness, discretion, diplomacy, delicacy, sensitivity.

finger ▶ noun *he raised his finger* =**digit**.
▶ verb **1** *she fingered her brooch* =**touch**, feel, handle, stroke, rub, caress, fondle, toy with, play (about/around) with, fiddle with. **2** *(N. Amer. informal)* *no one fingered the culprit* =**identify**, recognize, pick out, spot; inform on, point the finger at; *informal* rat on, squeal on, tell on, blow the whistle on, snitch on, peach on; *Brit. informal* grass on.

┌──────────────┐
│ **WORD LINKS** │
└──────────────┘
relating to fingers: **digital**

finicky ▶ adjective =**fussy**, fastidious, punctilious, over-particular, difficult, exacting, demanding; *informal* picky, choosy, pernickety; *N. Amer. informal* persnickety.

finish ▶ verb **1** *Pam finished her work* =**complete**, end, conclude, terminate, bring to a conclusion/end/close, wind

up; crown, cap, round off, put the finishing touches to; accomplish, discharge, carry out, do, get done, fulfil; *informal* wrap up, sew up, polish off. **2** *Hitch finished his dinner* =**consume**, eat, devour, drink, finish off, polish off, gulp (down); use (up), exhaust, empty, drain, get through; *informal* down. **3** *the programme has finished* =**end**, come to an end, stop, conclude, come to a conclusion/close, cease. **4** *finished in a black lacquer* =**varnish**, lacquer, veneer, coat, stain, wax, enamel, glaze, paint.
–OPPOSITES start, begin, continue.

▶ noun **1** *the finish of filming* =**end**, ending, completion, conclusion, close, closing, termination; final part/stage, finale, denouement. **2** *a race to the finish* =**finishing line/post**, tape, line. **3** *a shiny finish* =**veneer**, lacquer, lamination, glaze, coating, covering; gloss, patina, sheen, lustre; surface, texture.
–OPPOSITES start, beginning.

■ **finish someone/something off 1** *the hunters finished them off* =**kill**, take/end the life of, execute, terminate, exterminate, liquidate, get rid of; *informal* wipe out, do in, bump off, take out, dispose of, do away with, put down; *N. Amer. informal* ice, rub out, waste. **2** *financial difficulties finished us off* =**overwhelm**, overcome, defeat, get the better of, bring down; *informal* drive to the wall.

finished ▶ adjective **1** *the finished job* =**completed**, concluded, terminated, over (and done with), at an end; accomplished, executed, discharged, fulfilled, done; *informal* wrapped up, sewn up, polished off. **2** *he was finished* =**ruined**, defeated, beaten, wrecked, doomed, bankrupt, broken; *informal* washed up, through.
–OPPOSITES incomplete.

finite ▶ adjective =**limited**, restricted, determinate, fixed.

fire ▶ noun **1** *a fire broke out* =**blaze**, conflagration, inferno; flames, burning, combustion. **2** *an electric fire* =**heater**, radiator, convector; boiler, furnace. **3** *he lacked fire* =**dynamism**, energy, vigour, animation, vitality, vibrancy, exuberance, zest, elan; passion, ardour, zeal, spirit, verve, vivacity, vivaciousness; enthusiasm, eagerness, gusto, fervour; *informal* pep, vim, go, get-up-and-go, oomph. **4** *machine-gun fire* =**gunfire**, firing, bombardment; volley, salvo. **5** *they directed their fire at the prime minister*

=**criticism**, censure, condemnation, denunciation, opprobrium, admonishments; hostility, antagonism, animosity.

▶ verb **1** *howitzers firing shells* =**launch**, shoot, discharge, let fly with. **2** *someone fired a gun* =**shoot**, discharge, let off, set off. **3** *(informal) he was fired* =**dismiss**, discharge, give someone their notice, lay off, let go, get rid of, axe, cashier; *informal* sack, give someone the sack, boot out, give someone the boot, give someone the elbow/push, give someone their marching orders; *Brit. informal* give someone their cards. **4** *the engine fired* =**start**, get started, get going. **5** *the story fired my imagination* =**stimulate**, stir up, excite, awaken, arouse, rouse, inflame, animate, inspire, motivate.

■ **catch fire** =**ignite**, catch light, burst into flames, go up in flames.

■ **on fire** =**burning**, alight, ablaze, blazing, aflame, in flames.

> **WORD LINKS**
>
> relating to fire: **pyro-**
> fear of fire: **pyrophobia**
> obsession with fire: **pyromania**

firearm ▶ noun =**gun**, weapon; *informal* shooter; *N. Amer. informal* piece, rod, shooting iron.

firebrand ▶ noun =**radical**, revolutionary, agitator, rabble-rouser, incendiary, subversive, troublemaker.

fireproof ▶ adjective =**non-flammable**, incombustible, fire resistant, flame resistant, flame retardant, heatproof.
–OPPOSITES inflammable.

fireworks ▶ plural noun *his stubbornness has produced some fireworks* =**uproar**, trouble, mayhem, fuss; tantrums, hysterics.

firm¹ ▶ adjective **1** *the ground is fairly firm* =**hard**, solid, unyielding, resistant; solidified, hardened, compacted, compressed, dense, stiff, rigid, set. **2** *firm foundations* =**secure**, stable, steady, strong, fixed, fast, taut, tight; immovable, stationary, motionless. **3** *a firm handshake* =**strong**, vigorous, sturdy, forceful. **4** *I was very firm | a firm supporter* =**resolute**, determined, decided, resolved, steadfast; adamant, emphatic, insistent, single-minded, in earnest, wholehearted; unfaltering, unwavering, unflinching, unswerving, unbending; committed. **5** *firm friends* =**close**,

good, boon, intimate, inseparable, dear, special, fast; constant, devoted, loving, faithful, long-standing, steady, steadfast. **6** *firm plans* =**definite**, fixed, settled, decided, established, confirmed, agreed; unalterable, unchangeable, irreversible.
–OPPOSITES soft, unstable, limp, indefinite.

firm² ▶ noun *an accountancy firm* =**company**, business, concern, enterprise, organization, corporation, conglomerate, office, bureau, agency, consortium; *informal* outfit, set-up, operation.

first ▶ adjective **1** *the first chapter* =**earliest**, initial, opening, introductory. **2** *first principles* =**fundamental**, basic, rudimentary, primary; key, cardinal, central, chief, vital, essential. **3** *our first priority* =**foremost**, principal, highest, greatest, paramount, top, uppermost, prime, chief, leading, main, major; overriding, predominant, prevailing, central, core, dominant; *informal* number-one. **4** *first prize* =**top**, best, prime, premier, winner's, winning.
–OPPOSITES last, closing.
▶ adverb **1** *the room they had first entered* =**at first**, to begin with, first of all, at the outset, initially. **2** *I'd like to eat first* =**before anything else**, now. **3** *she wouldn't go—she'd die first!* =**in preference**, sooner, rather.
▶ noun *from the first* =**the (very) beginning**, the start, the outset; *informal* the word go, the off.

first-class ▶ adjective **1** *a first-class carriage* =**superior**, top-quality, high-grade, prime, premier, premium, grade A, the best, the finest, select, exclusive, five-star; *informal* tip-top. **2** *a first-class effort* =**excellent**, first-rate, marvellous, heroic, superb; *informal* A1, top-notch.
–OPPOSITES poor.

first-hand ▶ adjective =**direct**, immediate, personal, hands-on.
–OPPOSITES vicarious, indirect.

first name ▶ noun =**forename**, Christian name, given name.
–OPPOSITES surname.

first-rate ▶ adjective =**top-quality**, high-quality, top-grade, first-class, second to none, fine; superlative, excellent, superb, outstanding, exceptional, exemplary, marvellous, magnificent, splendid; *informal* tip-top, top-notch, ace, A1, super, great, terrific, tremendous,

fantastic; *Brit. informal* top-hole, smashing; *informal, dated* capital.

fiscal ▶ adjective =**tax**, budgetary; financial, economic, monetary, money.

fish ▶ verb **1** *some people were fishing in the lake* =**go fishing**, angle, trawl. **2** *she fished for her purse* =**search**, delve, look, hunt; grope, fumble, ferret (about/around), root about/around, rummage (about/around/round).
■ **fish someone/something out** =**pull out**, haul out, remove, extricate, extract, retrieve; rescue from, save from.

> [!NOTE] WORD LINKS
> young: **fry**
> *collective noun*: **school, run**
> *study of fish*: **ichthyology**
> *fish farming*: **pisciculture, mariculture**
> *fish-eating*: **piscivorous**
> *fear of fish*: **ichthyophobia**

fisherman ▶ noun =**angler**.

fishing ▶ noun =**angling**, trawling, catching fish.

> [!NOTE] WORD LINKS
> *relating to fishing*: **halieutic**

fishy ▶ adjective *(informal)* *there's something fishy here* =**suspicious**, questionable, dubious, doubtful, suspect; odd, queer, peculiar, strange; *informal* funny, shady, crooked, bent; *Brit. informal* dodgy, iffy; *Austral./NZ informal* shonky.

fission ▶ noun =**splitting**, division, dividing, rupture, breaking, severance.
–OPPOSITES fusion.

fissure ▶ noun =**opening**, crevice, crack, cleft, breach, crevasse, chasm; break, fracture, fault, rift, rupture, split.

fit¹ ▶ adjective **1** *not fit to eat* | *a fit subject for a book* =**suitable**, good enough, -worthy; relevant, pertinent, apt, appropriate, suited, apposite, fitting. **2** *not fit to look after children* =**competent**, able, capable; ready, prepared, equipped. **3** *(informal) fit to drop* =**ready**, prepared, all set, likely, about. **4** *tanned and fit* =**healthy**, well, in good health, in (good) shape, in trim, in good condition, fighting fit, as fit as a fiddle/flea; athletic, muscular, strong, robust, hale and hearty.
–OPPOSITES unsuitable, incapable, unwell.
▶ verb **1** *my coat should fit you* =**be the right/correct size (for)**, be big/small

enough (for), fit like a glove. **2** *having carpets fitted* =**lay**, install, put in; position, place, fix, arrange. **3** *cameras fitted with autofocus* =**equip**, provide, supply, fit out, furnish. **4** *they fitted the slabs together* =**join**, connect, put together, piece together, attach, unite, link. **5** *a sentence that fits his crime* =**be appropriate to**, suit, match, correspond to, tally with, go with, accord with, correlate to, be congruous with, be congruent with, be consonant with. **6** *an MSc fits you for a scientific career* =**qualify**, prepare, make ready, train.

▶ noun *the fit between philosophy and practice* =**correlation**, correspondence, agreement, consistency, equivalence, match, similarity, compatibility, concurrence.
■ **fit in** =**conform**, be in harmony, blend in, be in line, be assimilated into.
■ **fit someone/something out/up** =**equip**, provide, supply, furnish, kit out, rig out.

fit² ▶ noun **1** *an epileptic fit* =**convulsion**, spasm, paroxysm, seizure, attack. **2** *a fit of the giggles* =**outbreak**, outburst, attack, bout, spell. **3** *mum would have a fit* =**tantrum**, frenzy; *informal* paddy, stress; heart attack; *N. Amer. informal* blowout.
■ **in/by fits and starts** =**spasmodically**, intermittently, sporadically, erratically, irregularly, fitfully, haphazardly.

fitful ▶ adjective =**intermittent**, sporadic, spasmodic, broken, disturbed, disrupted, patchy, irregular, uneven, unsettled.

fitness ▶ noun **1** *polo requires tremendous fitness* =**good health**, strength, robustness, vigour, athleticism, toughness, physical fitness, stamina. **2** *his fitness for active service* =**suitability**, capability, competence, ability, aptitude; readiness, preparedness.

fitted ▶ adjective **1** *a fitted sheet* =**shaped**, contoured; tailored, bespoke. **2** *a fitted wardrobe* =**built-in**, integral, integrated. **3** *he wasn't fitted for the job* =**(well) suited**, right, suitable; equipped, fit; *informal* cut out.

fitting ▶ noun **1** *a light fitting* =**attachment**, connection, part, piece, component, accessory. **2** *bathroom fittings* =**furnishings**, furniture, fixtures, fitments, equipment. **3** *the fitting of catalytic converters* =**installation**, installing, putting in, fixing.
▶ adjective *a fitting conclusion* =**apt**, appropriate, suitable, apposite; fit, proper, right, seemly, correct; *archaic* meet.
−OPPOSITES unsuitable.

five ▶ cardinal number =**quintet**, fivesome; quintuplets.

> **WORD LINKS**
>
> relating to five: **quin-, quinque-, penta-**

fix ▶ verb **1** *signs were fixed to lamp posts* =**fasten**, attach, affix, secure; join, connect, couple, link; install, implant, embed; stick, glue, pin, nail, screw, bolt, clamp, clip. **2** *his words are fixed in my memory* =**stick**, lodge, embed. **3** *his eyes were fixed on the ground* =**focus**, direct, level, point, train. **4** *he fixed my car* =**repair**, mend, put right, get working, restore; overhaul, service, renovate, recondition. **5** *Jim fixed it for us to see the show* =**arrange**, organize, contrive, manage, engineer; *informal* swing, wangle. **6** *(informal) Laura was fixing her hair* =**arrange**, put in order, adjust; style, groom, comb, brush; *informal* do. **7** *(informal) I'll fix supper* =**prepare**, cook, make, get; *informal* rustle up; *Brit. informal* knock up. **8** *let's fix a date* =**decide on**, select, choose, resolve on; determine, settle, set, arrange, establish, allot; designate, name, appoint, specify. **9** *chemicals that fix the dye* =**make permanent**, make fast, set. **10** *(informal) the fight was fixed* =**rig**; tamper with, skew, influence; *informal* fiddle.
−OPPOSITES remove.

▶ noun *(informal)* **1** *they are in a bit of a fix* =**predicament**, plight, difficulty, awkward situation, corner, tight spot; mess, dire straits; *informal* pickle, jam, hole, scrape, bind, sticky situation. **2** *a quick fix for the coal industry* =**solution**, answer, resolution, way out, remedy, cure; *informal* magic bullet. **3** *the result was a fix* =**fraud**, swindle, trick, charade, sham; *informal* set-up, fiddle.
■ **fix someone up** *(informal)* =**provide**, supply, furnish.
■ **fix something up** =**organize**, arrange, make arrangements for, fix, sort out.

fixated ▶ adjective =**obsessed**, preoccupied, obsessive; focused, keen, gripped, engrossed, immersed, wrapped up in, enthusiastic, fanatical; *informal* hooked, wild, nuts, crazy; *Brit. informal* potty.

fixation ▶ noun =**obsession**, preoccupation, mania, addiction, compulsion;

informal thing, bug, craze, fad.

fixed ▸ adjective =**predetermined**, set, established, arranged, specified, decided, agreed, determined, confirmed, prescribed, definite, defined, explicit, precise.

fixture ▸ noun **1** *fixtures and fittings* =**fixed appliance**, installation, unit. **2** (*Brit.*) *their first fixture of the season* =**match**, race, game, competition, contest, event.

fizz ▸ verb *the mixture fizzed like mad* =**effervesce**, sparkle, bubble, froth.
▸ noun **1** *the fizz in champagne* =**effervescence**, sparkle, fizziness, bubbles, bubbliness, gassiness, carbonation, froth. **2** *the fizz of the static* =**crackle**, crackling, buzz, buzzing, hiss, hissing, white noise.

fizzle ■ **fizzle out** =**peter out**, die off, ease off, cool off; tail off, wither away.

fizzy ▸ adjective =**effervescent**, sparkling, carbonated, gassy, bubbly, frothy.
–OPPOSITES still, flat.

flab ▸ noun (*informal*) =**fat**, excess weight, plumpness; paunch, (pot) belly, (beer) gut.

flabbergast ▸ verb (*informal*). *See* ASTONISH.

flabbiness ▸ noun =**fat**, fatness, fleshiness, plumpness, chubbiness, corpulence; softness, looseness, flaccidity, droopiness, sag; *informal* flab, tubbiness.

flabby ▸ adjective **1** *his flabby stomach* =**soft**, loose, flaccid, slack, untoned, drooping, sagging. **2** *a flabby woman* =**fat**, fleshy, overweight, plump, chubby, portly, rotund, broad in the beam, of ample proportions, corpulent; *informal* tubby, roly-poly, well covered, well upholstered.
–OPPOSITES firm, thin.

flaccid ▸ adjective **1** *flaccid muscles* =**soft**, loose, flabby, slack, lax; drooping, sagging. **2** *a flaccid performance* =**lacklustre**, lifeless, listless, uninspiring, unanimated, tame.
–OPPOSITES firm, spirited.

flag[1] ▸ noun *the Irish flag* =**banner**, standard, ensign, pennant, streamer; colours; *Brit.* pendant.
▸ verb *flag the misspelt words* =**indicate**, identify, point out, mark, label, tag, highlight.
■ **flag someone/something down** =**hail**, wave down, stop, halt.

WORD LINKS

relating to flags: **vexillary**
study of flags: **vexillology**

flag[2] ▸ noun *stone flags* =**flagstone**, (paving) slab, (paving) stone.

flag[3] ▸ verb **1** *they were flagging towards the finish* =**tire**, grow tired/weary, weaken, grow weak, wilt, droop. **2** *my energy flags in the afternoon* =**fade**, decline, wane, ebb, diminish, decrease, lessen, dwindle; wither, melt away, die away/down.
–OPPOSITES revive.

flagrant ▸ adjective =**blatant**, glaring, obvious, overt, conspicuous, barefaced, shameless, brazen, undisguised, unconcealed.

flagstone ▸ noun =**(paving) slab**, (paving) stone, flag.

flail ▸ verb **1** *he fell headlong, his arms flailing* =**wave**, swing, thrash about, flap about. **2** *I was flailing about in the water* =**flounder**, struggle, thrash, writhe, splash.

flair ▸ noun **1** *a flair for publicity* =**aptitude**, talent, gift, instinct, (natural) ability, facility, skill, bent, feel. **2** *she dressed with flair* =**style**, stylishness, panache, dash, elan, poise; *informal* class.

flak ▸ noun (*informal*) *he's come in for a lot of flak* =**criticism**, censure, disapproval, hostility, complaints; vilification, abuse, brickbats; *Brit. informal* stick, verbal; *formal* castigation, excoriation.

flake[1] ▸ noun =**sliver**, wafer, shaving, paring; chip; fragment, scrap, shred.
▸ verb =**peel (off)**, chip, blister, come off (in layers).

flake[2] ▸ verb ■ **flake out** (*informal*) *she flaked out in her chair* =**fall asleep**, go to sleep, drop off; collapse, faint, pass out, lose consciousness, black out, swoon; *informal* conk out, nod off; *N. Amer. informal* sack out, zone out.

flaky ▸ adjective –**flaking**, peeling, scaly, blistering, scabrous.

flamboyant ▸ adjective **1** *her flamboyant personality* =**ostentatious**, exuberant, confident, lively, animated, vibrant, vivacious. **2** *a flamboyant cravat* =**colourful**, brightly coloured, bright, vibrant, vivid; dazzling, eye-catching, bold; showy, gaudy, garish, lurid, loud; *informal* jazzy, flashy.
–OPPOSITES restrained.

flame ▶ noun **1** *a sheet of flames* =**fire**; blaze, conflagration, inferno. **2** (*informal*) *an old flame* =**sweetheart**, boyfriend, girlfriend, lover, partner.

▶ verb **1** *logs crackled and flamed* =**burn**, blaze, flare; flicker. **2** *Erica's cheeks flamed* =**go red**, blush, flush, redden, go pink/crimson/scarlet, colour, glow.
–OPPOSITES extinguish.

■ **in flames** =**on fire**, burning, alight, flaming, blazing, ignited, aflame; *literary* afire.

flameproof ▶ adjective =**non-flammable**, non-inflammable, flame-resistant, fire-resistant, flame-retardant.
–OPPOSITES flammable.

flaming ▶ adjective **1** *a flaming bonfire* =**blazing**, burning. **2** *flaming hair* =**bright**, brilliant, vivid; red, ginger. **3** *a flaming row* =**furious**, violent, vehement, frenzied, angry, passionate. **4** (*informal*) *where's that flaming ambulance?* =**wretched**; *informal* damned, damnable, blasted, blessed, confounded; *Brit. informal* flipping, blinking, blooming, effing; *Brit. informal, dated* bally, ruddy.

flammable ▶ adjective =**inflammable**, combustible.

flank ▶ noun **1** *the horse's flanks* =**side**, haunch, quarter, thigh. **2** *the southern flank of the Eighth Army* =**side**, wing; face, aspect.

▶ verb *the garden is flanked by two rivers* =**edge**, bound, line, border, fringe.

flannel ▶ noun **1** (*Brit.*) *she dabbed her face with a flannel* =**facecloth**, cloth; *N. Amer.* washcloth, washrag; *Austral.* washer. **2** (*Brit. informal*) *all that flannel from salespeople* =**smooth talk**, flattery, blarney, blandishments, honeyed words; prevarication, equivocation, evasion, doublespeak; *informal* spiel, soft soap, sweet talk, baloney, hot air; *Brit. informal* waffle; *Austral./NZ informal* guyver.

flap ▶ verb **1** *the mallards flapped their wings* =**beat**, flutter, agitate, wave, wag, swing. **2** *the flag flapped in the breeze* =**flutter**, fly, blow, swing, sway, ripple, stir.

▶ noun **1** *pockets with buttoned flaps* =**fold**, covering, top, overlap. **2** *a few flaps of its wing* =**flutter**, stroke, beat, movement. **3** (*informal*) *in a flap* =**panic**, fluster; *informal* state, dither, blue funk, stew, tizzy; *N. Amer. informal* twit.

flare ▶ noun **1** *the flare of the match* =**blaze**, flash, burst, flicker. **2** *a flare set*

off by the crew =**distress signal**, rocket, beacon, light, signal, maroon. **3** *a flare of anger* =**burst**, rush, eruption, explosion, spasm.

▶ verb **1** *the match flared* =**blaze**, flash, flare up, flame, burn; flicker. **2** *her nostrils flared* =**spread**, broaden, widen; dilate.

■ **flare up 1** *his injury has flared up again* =**recur**, reoccur, reappear; break out, erupt. **2** *I flared up at him* =**lose one's temper**, become enraged, fly into a temper, go berserk; *informal* blow one's top, fly off the handle, go mad, go bananas, hit the roof, go up the wall, go off the deep end, lose one's rag, flip (one's lid), explode, have a fit; *Brit.* go spare, go crackers, do one's nut; *N. Amer. informal* flip one's wig, blow one's lid/stack.

flash ▶ verb **1** *a torch flashed* =**shine**, flare, blaze, gleam, glint, sparkle, burn; blink, wink, flicker, shimmer, twinkle, glimmer, glisten, scintillate; *literary* glister. **2** (*informal*) *flashing his money about* =**show off**, flaunt, flourish, display, parade. **3** *racing cars flashed past* =**zoom**, streak, tear, shoot, dash, dart, fly, whistle, hurtle, rush, bolt, race, speed, career, whizz, whoosh, buzz; *informal* belt, zap; *Brit. informal* bomb, bucket; *N. Amer. informal* barrel.

▶ noun **1** *a flash of light* =**flare**, blaze, burst; gleam, glint, sparkle, flicker, shimmer, twinkle, glimmer. **2** *a shoulder flash* =**emblem**, insignia, badge; stripe, bar, chevron. **3** *a sudden flash of inspiration* =**burst**, outburst, wave, rush, surge, flush.

▶ adjective (*informal*) *a flash sports car.* See FLASHY.

■ **in/like a flash** =**instantly**, suddenly, abruptly, immediately, all of a sudden; quickly, rapidly, swiftly, speedily; in an instant/moment, in a (split) second, in a trice, in the blink of an eye; *informal* in a jiffy, before you can say Jack Robinson.

flashy ▶ adjective (*informal*) =**ostentatious**, flamboyant, showy, conspicuous, extravagant, expensive; vulgar, tasteless, brash, lurid, garish, loud, gaudy; *informal* snazzy, fancy, swanky, flash, jazzy, glitzy.
–OPPOSITES understated.

flask ▶ noun =**bottle**, container; hip flask, vacuum flask; *trademark* Thermos.

flat¹ ▶ adjective **1** *a flat surface* =**level**, horizontal; smooth, even, uniform, regular, plane. **2** *the sea was flat* =**calm**, still, glassy, smooth, placid, like a millpond. **3** *a flat wooden box* =**shallow**, low-

sided. **4** *flat sandals* =**low**, low-heeled, without heels. **5** *his voice was flat* =**monotonous**, toneless, droning, boring, dull, tedious, uninteresting, unexciting, soporific; bland, dreary, colourless, featureless, emotionless, expressionless, lifeless, spiritless, lacklustre. **6** *he felt flat and weary* =**depressed**, dejected, dispirited, despondent, downhearted, disheartened, low, low-spirited, down, unhappy, blue; without energy, weary, tired out, worn out, exhausted, drained; *informal* down in the mouth/dumps. **7** *the market was flat* =**slow**, inactive, sluggish, slack, quiet, depressed. **8** *(Brit.) a flat battery* =**expired**, dead, finished, used up, run out. **9** *a flat tyre* =**deflated**, punctured, burst; perished, blown. **10** *a flat fee* =**fixed**, set, regular, unchanging, unvarying, invariable. **11** *a flat denial* =**outright**, direct, absolute, definite, positive, straight, plain, explicit; firm, resolute, adamant, assertive, emphatic, categorical, unconditional, unqualified, unequivocal.
−OPPOSITES vertical, uneven.

▶ **adverb** *she lay flat on the floor* =**stretched out**, outstretched, spreadeagled, sprawling, prone, supine, prostrate, recumbent.

■ **flat out** =**hard**, as hard as possible, for all one's worth, to the full/limit, all out; at full speed, as fast as possible, at full tilt; *informal* like crazy, like mad, like the wind, like a bomb; *Brit. informal* like billy-o, like the clappers.

flat² ▶ noun *a two-bedroom flat* =**apartment**, penthouse; rooms; *Austral.* home unit; *N. Amer. informal* crib.

flatten ▶ verb **1** *Tom flattened the crumpled paper* =**make/become flat**, make/become even, smooth (out/off), level (out/off). **2** *the cows flattened the grass* =**compress**, press down, crush, squash, compact, trample. **3** *tornadoes can flatten buildings in seconds* =**demolish**, raze (to the ground), tear down, knock down, destroy, wreck, devastate, obliterate; *N. Amer. informal* total.
−OPPOSITES crumple, raise, build.

flatter ▶ verb **1** *it amused him to flatter her* =**compliment**, praise, express admiration for, say nice things about, pay court to, fawn on; humour, flannel, blarney; *informal* sweet-talk, soft-soap, butter up, play up to. **2** *I was flattered to be asked* =**honour**, gratify, please, delight; *informal* tickle pink. **3** *a hairstyle that* *flattered her* =**suit**, become, look good on, go well with; *informal* do something/a lot for.
−OPPOSITES insult, offend.

flatterer ▶ noun =**sycophant**, groveller, fawner, lackey; *informal* crawler, toady, bootlicker, yes man.

flattering ▶ adjective **1** *flattering remarks* =**complimentary**, praising, favourable, commending, admiring, applauding, appreciative, good; honeyed, sugary, silver-tongued, honey-tongued; fawning, oily, obsequious, ingratiating, servile, sycophantic; *informal* sweet-talking, soft-soaping, crawling, bootlicking. **2** *it was very flattering to be nominated* =**pleasing**, gratifying, honouring. **3** *her most flattering dress* =**becoming**, enhancing.
−OPPOSITES unflattering.

flattery ▶ noun =**praise**, adulation, compliments, blandishments, honeyed words; fawning, blarney; *informal* sweet talk, soft soap, buttering up, toadying; *Brit. informal* flannel.

flatulence ▶ noun =**(intestinal) gas**, wind; *informal* farting.

flaunt ▶ verb =**show off**, display, make a (great) show of, put on show/display, parade; brag about, crow about, vaunt; *informal* flash.

flavour ▶ noun **1** *the flavour of basil* =**taste**, savour, tang. **2** *salami can give extra flavour* =**flavouring**, seasoning, tastiness, tang, relish, bite, piquancy, pungency, spice, spiciness, zest; *informal* zing, zip. **3** *a strong international flavour* =**character**, quality, feel, feeling, ambience, atmosphere, aura, air, mood, tone; spirit, essence, nature; *informal* vibe. **4** *this excerpt will give you a flavour of the report* =**impression**, suggestion, hint, taste.

▶ **verb** *spices for flavouring food* =**add flavour to**, add flavouring to, season, spice (up), add piquancy to, ginger up, enrich; *informal* pep up.

flavouring ▶ noun **1** *combined with other flavourings* =**seasoning**, spice, herb, additive; condiment; dressing. **2** *vanilla flavouring* =**essence**, extract, concentrate, distillate.

flaw ▶ noun =**defect**, blemish, fault, imperfection, deficiency, weakness, weak spot/point, inadequacy, shortcoming, limitation, failing, foible; *Computing* bug; *informal* glitch.

–OPPOSITES strength.

flawed ▸ adjective **1** *a flawed mirror* =**faulty**, defective, unsound, imperfect; broken, cracked, scratched; *Brit. informal* duff. **2** *the findings were flawed* =**unsound**, defective, faulty, distorted, inaccurate, incorrect, erroneous, fallacious.

–OPPOSITES flawless, sound.

flawless ▸ adjective =**perfect**, unblemished, unmarked, unimpaired; whole, intact, sound, unbroken, undamaged, mint, pristine; impeccable, immaculate, consummate, accurate, correct, faultless, error-free, unerring; exemplary, model, ideal, copybook.

–OPPOSITES flawed.

fleck ▸ noun *flecks of pale blue* =**spot**, mark, dot, speck, speckle, freckle, patch, smudge, streak, blotch, dab; *informal* splash, splodge.

▸ verb *flecked with white* =**spot**, mark, dot, speckle, bespeckle, freckle, stipple, stud, bestud, blotch, mottle, streak, splash, spatter, bespatter, scatter, sprinkle, dust, pepper; *Scottish & Irish* slabber; *informal* splosh, splodge.

fledgling ▸ adjective *fledgling industries* =**emerging**, emergent, sunrise, dawning, embryonic, infant, nascent; developing, in the making, budding, up-and-coming, rising.

–OPPOSITES declining, mature.

flee ▸ verb **1** *she fled to her room* =**run (away/off)**, run for it, make a run for it, take flight, be gone, make off, take off, take to one's heels, make a break for it, bolt, beat a (hasty) retreat, make a quick exit, make one's getaway, escape; *informal* beat it, clear off/out, vamoose, skedaddle, split, leg it, turn tail, scram; *Brit. informal* scarper; *N. Amer. informal* light out, bug out, cut out, peel out; *Austral. informal* shoot through; *archaic* fly. **2** *they fled the country* =**run away from**, leave hastily, escape from; *informal* skip; *archaic* fly.

fleece ▸ noun =**wool**, coat.

▸ verb *(informal).* See SWINDLE verb.

fleecy ▸ adjective =**fluffy**, woolly, downy, soft, fuzzy, furry, shaggy.

–OPPOSITES coarse.

fleet[1] ▸ noun *the fleet set sail* =**navy**, naval force, (naval) task force, armada, flotilla, squadron, convoy.

fleet[2] ▸ adjective *(literary) as fleet as a greyhound* =**nimble**, agile, lithe, lissom, acrobatic, supple, light-footed, light

on one's feet, spry, sprightly; quick, fast, swift, rapid, speedy, brisk, smart; *informal* nippy, zippy, twinkle-toed.

fleeting ▸ adjective =**brief**, short, short-lived, quick, momentary, cursory, transient, ephemeral, fugitive, passing, transitory.

–OPPOSITES lasting.

flesh ▸ noun **1** *his smooth, white flesh* =**tissue**, skin, body; muscle, fat; *informal* blubber, flab. **2** *strip the flesh away from the bone* =**meat**, muscle. **3** *a fruit with juicy flesh* =**pulp**, marrow, meat. **4** *the pleasures of the flesh* =**the body**, human nature, physicality, carnality, animality; sensuality, sexuality.

■ **one's (own) flesh and blood** =**family**, relative(s), relation(s), kin, kinsfolk, kinsman, kinsmen, kinswoman, kinswomen, kindred, nearest and dearest, people; *informal* folks.

■ **flesh out** =**put on weight**, gain weight, get heavier, grow fat/fatter, fatten up, get fat, fill out.

■ **flesh something out** =**expand (on)**, elaborate on, add to, build on, add flesh to, put flesh on (the bones of), add detail to, expatiate on, supplement, reinforce, augment, fill out, enlarge on.

■ **in the flesh** =**in person**, before one's (very) eyes, in front of one; in real life, live; physically, bodily, in bodily/human form, incarnate.

> **WORD LINKS**
>
> *related prefix:* **carn-**
> *fear of flesh:* **selaphobia**

fleshy ▸ adjective =**plump**, chubby, portly, fat, obese, overweight, stout, corpulent, paunchy, well padded, well covered, well upholstered, rotund; *informal* tubby, pudgy, beefy, porky, roly-poly, blubbery; *Brit. informal* podgy; *N. Amer. informal* corn-fed; *Austral./NZ* nuggety.

–OPPOSITES thin.

flex[1] ▸ verb **1** *you must flex your elbow* =**bend**, crook, hook, cock, angle, double up. **2** *Rachel flexed her cramped muscles* =**tighten**, tauten, tense (up), tension, contract.

–OPPOSITES straighten, relax.

flex[2] ▸ noun *(Brit.) an electric flex* =**cable**, wire, lead; *N. Amer. informal* cord.

flexibility ▸ noun **1** *the flexibility of wood* =**pliability**, suppleness, pliancy, plasticity; elasticity, stretchiness, springiness, spring, resilience, bounce; *informal*

give. **2** *the flexibility of an endowment loan* =**adaptability**, adjustability, variability, versatility, open-endedness, freedom, latitude. **3** *the flexibility shown by the local authority* =**willingness to compromise**, accommodation, amenability, cooperation, tolerance.
–OPPOSITES rigidity, inflexibility, intransigence.

flexible ▶ adjective **1** *flexible tubing* =**pliable**, supple, bendable, pliant, plastic; elastic, stretchy, springy, resilient, bouncy; *informal* bendy. **2** *a flexible arrangement* =**adaptable**, adjustable, variable, versatile, open-ended, open, free. **3** *the need to be flexible towards tenants* =**accommodating**, amenable, willing to compromise, cooperative, tolerant.
–OPPOSITES rigid, inflexible, intransigent.

flick ▶ noun *a flick of the wrist* =**jerk**, snap, flip, whisk.
▶ verb **1** *he flicked the switch* =**click**, snap, flip, jerk; throw, pull, push. **2** *the horse flicked its tail* =**swish**, twitch, wave, wag, waggle, jiggle, shake.
■ **flick through** =**thumb (through)**, leaf through, flip through, skim through, scan, look through, browse through, dip into, glance at/through, peruse, run one's eye over.

flicker ▶ verb **1** *the lights flickered* =**glimmer**, flare, dance, gutter; twinkle, sparkle, blink, wink, flash. **2** *his eyelids flickered* =**flutter**, quiver, tremble, shiver, shudder, jerk, twitch.

flier ▶ noun. *See* FLYER.

flight ▶ noun **1** *the history of flight* =**aviation**, flying, air transport, aeronautics. **2** *a flight to Rome* =**plane trip/journey**, air trip/journey; service, ticket. **3** *the flight of the ball* =**trajectory**, path (through the air), track, orbit. **4** *a flight of birds* =**flock**, swarm, cloud, throng. **5** *his headlong flight from home* =**escape**, getaway, hasty departure, exit, exodus, breakout, bolt, disappearance; *Brit. informal* flit. **6** *a flight of stairs* =**staircase**, set of steps/stairs.
■ **put someone to flight** =**chase away/off**, drive back/away/off/out, scatter (to the four winds), disperse, repel, repulse, rout, stampede, scare off; *Brit.* see off; *informal* send packing.
■ **take flight** =**flee**, run (away/off), run for it, make a run for it, be gone, make off, take off, take to one's heels, make a break for it, bolt, beat a (hasty) retreat,

make a quick exit, make one's getaway, escape; *informal* beat it, clear off/out, vamoose, skedaddle, split, leg it, turn tail, scram; *Brit. informal* scarper; *N. Amer. informal* light out, bug out, cut out, peel out; *Austral. informal* shoot through; *archaic* fly.

flighty ▶ adjective =**fickle**, inconstant, mercurial, whimsical, capricious, skittish, volatile, impulsive; irresponsible, giddy, wild, careless, thoughtless.
–OPPOSITES steady, responsible.

flimsy ▶ adjective **1** *a flimsy building* =**insubstantial**, fragile, frail, shaky, unstable, wobbly, tottery, rickety, ramshackle, makeshift; jerry-built, badly built, shoddy, gimcrack. **2** *a flimsy dress* =**thin**, light, fine, filmy, floaty, diaphanous, sheer, delicate, gossamer, gauzy. **3** *flimsy evidence* =**weak**, feeble, poor, inadequate, insufficient, thin, unsubstantial, unconvincing, implausible, unsatisfactory.
–OPPOSITES sturdy, thick, sound.

flinch ▶ verb **1** *he flinched at the noise* =**wince**, start, shudder, quiver, jerk. **2** *he never flinched from his duty* =**shrink from**, recoil from, shy away from, swerve from, demur from; dodge, evade, avoid, duck, baulk at, fight shy of.

fling ▶ verb *he flung the axe into the river* =**throw**, toss, sling, hurl, cast, pitch, lob; *informal* chuck, heave, bung.
▶ noun **1** *a birthday fling* =**good time**, spree, bit of fun; fun and games, revels, larks; *informal* binge, night on the town. **2** *she had a brief fling with him* =**affair**, love affair, relationship, romance, liaison, entanglement, involvement, attachment.

flip ▶ verb **1** *the wave flipped the dinghy over | the plane flipped on to its back* =**overturn**, turn over, tip over, roll (over), upturn, capsize; upend, invert, knock over; keel over, topple over, turn turtle. **2** *he flipped the key through the air* =**throw**, flick, toss, fling, sling, pitch, cast, spin, lob; *informal* chuck, bung. **3** *I flipped the transmitter switch* =**flick**, click; throw, push, pull.
■ **flip through** =**thumb (through)**, leaf through, flick through, skim through, scan, look through, browse through, dip into, glance at/through, peruse, run one's eye over.

flippancy ▶ noun =**frivolity**, levity, facetiousness; disrespect, irreverence, cheek, impudence, impertinence; *Brit. informal* sauce; *N. Amer. informal* sassiness.

−OPPOSITES seriousness, respect.

flippant ▶ adjective =frivolous, facetious, tongue-in-cheek; disrespectful, irreverent, cheeky, impudent, impertinent; informal flip, saucy, waggish; N. Amer. informal sassy.

−OPPOSITES serious, respectful.

flirt ▶ verb 1 he liked to flirt with her =tease, lead on. 2 those who flirt with fascism =dabble in, toy with, trifle with, play with, tinker with, dip into, scratch the surface of.

▶ noun Anna was quite a flirt =tease, philanderer, coquette, heartbreaker.

flirtation ▶ noun =coquetry, teasing, trifling.

flirtatious ▶ adjective =coquettish, flirty, kittenish, teasing.

flit ▶ verb =dart, dance, skip, play, dash, trip, flutter, bob, bounce.

float ▶ verb 1 oil floats on water =stay afloat, stay on the surface, be buoyant, be buoyed up. 2 the balloon floated in the air =hover, levitate, be suspended, hang, defy gravity. 3 a cloud floated across the moon =drift, glide, sail, slip, slide, waft. 4 they have floated an idea or two =suggest, put forward, come up with, submit, propose, advance, test; informal run something up the flagpole (to see who salutes). 5 the company was floated on the Stock Exchange =launch, offer, sell, introduce.

−OPPOSITES sink, rush, withdraw.

floating ▶ adjective 1 floating seaweed =buoyant, afloat, drifting. 2 floating gas balloons =hovering, levitating, suspended, hanging. 3 floating voters =uncommitted, undecided, uncertain, unsure, undeclared. 4 a floating population =unsettled, transient, temporary, variable, fluctuating; migrant, wandering, nomadic, on the move, migratory, travelling, drifting, roving, roaming, itinerant. 5 a floating exchange rate =variable, changeable, changing, fluid, fluctuating.

−OPPOSITES sunken, grounded, committed, settled, fixed.

flock ▶ noun 1 a flock of sheep =herd, drove. 2 a flock of birds =flight, swarm, cloud. 3 flocks of people =crowd, throng, horde, mob, rabble, mass, multitude, host, army, pack, swarm, sea; informal gaggle.

▶ verb 1 people flocked around her =gather, collect, congregate, assemble, converge, mass, crowd, throng, cluster, swarm. 2 tourists flock to the place =stream, go in large numbers, swarm, crowd, troop.

flog ▶ verb 1 he was flogged =whip, scourge, birch, cane, beat. 2 (Brit. informal) he's flogging his car =sell, put on sale, put up for sale, offer for sale, trade in, deal in, peddle; informal push.

flood ▶ noun 1 a severe flood =inundation, deluge; torrent, overflow, flash flood; Brit. spate. 2 a flood of tears =outpouring, torrent, rush, stream, gush, surge, cascade. 3 a flood of complaints =succession, series, string; barrage, volley, battery; avalanche, torrent, stream, storm.

−OPPOSITES trickle.

▶ verb 1 the whole town was flooded =inundate, swamp, deluge, immerse, submerge, drown, engulf. 2 the river could flood =overflow, burst its banks, brim over, run over. 3 cheap goods flooding the market =glut, swamp, saturate. 4 refugees flooded in =pour, stream, flow, surge, swarm, pile, crowd.

−OPPOSITES trickle.

WORD LINKS

relating to floods: **diluvial**
fear of floods: **antlophobia**

---

floor ▶ noun 1 he sat on the floor =ground, flooring. 2 the second floor =storey, level, deck, tier.

▶ verb 1 he floored his attacker =knock down, knock over, bring down, fell, prostrate; informal lay out. 2 (informal) the question floored him =baffle, defeat, confound, perplex, puzzle, nonplus, mystify; informal beat, flummox, stump, fox, make someone scratch their head; N. Amer. informal buffalo.

flop ▶ verb 1 he flopped into a chair =collapse, slump, crumple, sink, drop. 2 his hair flopped over his eyes =hang (down), dangle, droop, sag, loll. 3 (informal) the play flopped =be unsuccessful, fail, not work, fall flat, founder, misfire, backfire, be a disappointment, do badly, lose money, be a disaster; informal bomb, go to the wall, come a cropper, bite the dust; N. Amer. informal tank.

−OPPOSITES succeed.

▶ noun (informal) the play was a flop =failure, disaster, debacle, catastrophe; Brit. damp squib; informal washout, also-ran, dog, lemon, non-starter; N. Amer. informal clinker.

–OPPOSITES success.

floppy ▸ adjective =**limp**, flaccid, slack, flabby, relaxed; drooping, droopy; loose, flowing.
–OPPOSITES erect, stiff.

florid ▸ adjective **1** *a florid complexion* =**ruddy**, red, red-faced, rosy, rosy-cheeked, pink; flushed, blushing, high-coloured. **2** *florid English* =**flowery**, flamboyant, high-flown, high-sounding, grandiloquent, ornate, fancy, bombastic, elaborate; *informal* highfalutin, purple.
–OPPOSITES pale, plain.

flotsam ▸ noun =**wreckage**; rubbish, debris, detritus, waste, dross, refuse, scrap; *N. Amer.* trash, garbage; *informal* dreck, junk; *Brit. informal* grot.

flounce¹ ▸ verb *she flounced off to her room* =**storm**, stride, sweep, stomp, stamp, march, strut, stalk.

flounce² ▸ noun *a lace flounce* =**frill**, ruffle, ruff, ruche.

flounder ▸ verb **1** *floundering in the water* =**struggle**, thrash, flail, twist and turn, splash, stagger, stumble, reel, lurch, blunder, squirm, writhe. **2** *she floundered, not knowing what to say* =**struggle**, be out of one's depth, have difficulty, be confounded, be confused; *informal* scratch one's head, be flummoxed, be clueless, be foxed, be fazed, be floored, be beaten. **3** *more firms are floundering* =**struggle (financially)**, be in dire straits, face (financial) ruin, be in difficulties, face bankruptcy/insolvency.
–OPPOSITES prosper.

flourish ▸ verb **1** *ferns flourish in the shade* =**grow**, thrive, prosper, do well, burgeon, increase, multiply, proliferate; spring up, shoot up, bloom, blossom, bear fruit, burst forth, run riot. **2** *the arts flourished* =**thrive**, prosper, bloom, be in good health, be vigorous, be in its heyday; progress, make progress, advance, make headway, develop, improve; evolve, make strides, move forward (in leaps and bounds), expand; *informal* be in the pink, go places, go great guns, get somewhere. **3** *he flourished a sword* =**brandish**, wave, shake, wield; swing, twirl; display, show off.
–OPPOSITES die, wither, decline.

flout ▸ verb =**defy**, refuse to obey, disobey, break, violate, fail to comply with, fail to observe, contravene, infringe,

breach, commit a breach of, transgress against; ignore, disregard; *informal* cock a snook at.
–OPPOSITES observe.

flow ▸ verb **1** *the water flowed down the channel* =**run**, course, glide, drift, circulate; trickle, seep, ooze, dribble, drip, drizzle, spill; stream, swirl, surge, sweep, gush, cascade, pour, roll, rush. **2** *many questions flow from today's announcement* =**result**, proceed, arise, follow, ensue, derive, stem, accrue; originate, emanate, spring, emerge; be caused by, be generated by, be produced by, be consequent on.
▸ noun *a good flow of water* =**movement**, motion, current, circulation; trickle, ooze; stream, swirl, surge, gush, rush, spate, tide.

flower ▸ noun **1** *blue flowers* =**bloom**, blossom. **2** *the flower of the nation's youth* =**best**, finest, pick, choice, cream, the crème de la crème, elite.
–OPPOSITES dregs.

> **WORD LINKS**
>
> relating to flowers: **floral, flor-, antho-**
> fear of flowers: **anthophobia**
> seller of flowers: **florist**

flowery ▸ adjective **1** *flowery fabrics* =**floral**. **2** *flowery language* =**florid**, flamboyant, ornate, fancy, convoluted; high-flown, high-sounding, grandiloquent, overblown; *informal* highfalutin, purple.
–OPPOSITES plain.

flowing ▸ adjective **1** *long flowing hair* =**loose**, free. **2** *soft, flowing lines* =**sleek**, streamlined, aerodynamic, smooth, clean; elegant, graceful. **3** *he writes in an easy, flowing style* =**fluent**, fluid, free-flowing, effortless, easy, natural, smooth.
–OPPOSITES stiff, curly, jagged, halting.

fluctuate ▸ verb =**vary**, change, differ, shift, alter, waver, swing, oscillate, alternate, rise and fall, go up and down, see-saw, yo-yo, be unstable.

fluctuation ▸ noun =**variation**, change, shift, alteration, swing, movement, oscillation, alternation, rise and fall, see-sawing, yo-yoing, instability, unsteadiness.
–OPPOSITES stability.

flue ▸ noun =**duct**, tube, shaft, vent, pipe, passage, channel, conduit; funnel, chimney, smokestack.

fluent ▸ adjective **1** *a fluent speech* =**ar-**

fluff ▸ noun **1** *fluff on her sleeve* =**fuzz**, lint, dust; *N. Amer.* dustballs, dust bunnies. **2** *(informal) he only made a few fluffs* =**mistake**, error, slip, slip of the tongue; wrong note; *informal* slip-up.
▸ verb *(informal) he fluffed his only line* =**bungle**, make a mess of, fumble, miss, deliver badly, muddle up, forget; *informal* mess up, make a hash of, make a botch of, foul up, screw up; *Brit. informal* make a muck of, make a pig's ear of, cock up, make a Horlicks of; *N. Amer. informal* flub, goof up.
−OPPOSITES succeed in.

fluffy ▸ adjective =**fleecy**, woolly, fuzzy, hairy, feathery, downy, furry; soft.
−OPPOSITES rough.

fluid ▸ noun *the fluid seeps up the tube* =**liquid**, watery substance, solution; **gas**, gaseous substance, vapour.
−OPPOSITES solid.
▸ adjective **1** *a fluid substance* =**free-flowing**; liquid, liquefied, melted, molten, runny, running; gaseous, gassy. **2** *his plans were still fluid* =**adaptable**, flexible, adjustable, open-ended, open, open to change, changeable, variable. **3** *this fluid state of affairs* =**fluctuating**, changeable, subject/likely to change, (ever-)shifting, inconstant; unstable, unsettled, turbulent, volatile. **4** *he stood up in one fluid movement* =**smooth**, fluent, flowing, effortless, easy, continuous; graceful, elegant.
−OPPOSITES solid, firm, static, jerky.

fluke ▸ noun =**chance**, coincidence, accident, twist of fate; piece of luck, stroke of good luck/fortune.

flummox ▸ verb *(informal)* =**baffle**, perplex, puzzle, bewilder, mystify, bemuse, confuse, confound, nonplus; *informal* faze, stump, beat, fox, floor; *N. Amer. informal* discombobulate, buffalo.

flurried ▸ adjective =**agitated**, flustered, ruffled, in a panic, worked up, beside oneself, overwrought, perturbed, frantic; *informal* in a flap, in a state, in a twitter, in a fluster, in a dither, all of a dither, all of a lather, in a tizz/tizzy, in a tiz-woz; *Brit. informal* in a (flat) spin, having kittens; *N. Amer. informal* in a twit.
−OPPOSITES calm.

flurry ▸ noun **1** *a flurry of snow* =**swirl**, whirl, eddy, flurry, shower, gust. **2** *a flurry of activity* =**burst**, outbreak, spurt, fit, spell, bout, rash, eruption. **3** *a flurry of imports* =**spate**, wave, flood, deluge, torrent, stream, tide, avalanche; series, succession, string, outbreak, rash, explosion, run, rush.
−OPPOSITES dearth, trickle.

flush¹ ▸ verb **1** *she flushed in embarrassment* =**blush**, redden, go pink, go red, go crimson, go scarlet, colour (up). **2** *flushing toxins from the body* =**rinse**, wash, sluice, swill, cleanse, clean; *Brit. informal* sloosh. **3** *they flushed out the snipers* =**drive**, chase, force, dislodge, expel.
−OPPOSITES pale.
▸ noun **1** *a flush crept over her face* =**blush**, colour, rosiness, pinkness, ruddiness, bloom. **2** *the first flush of manhood* =**bloom**, glow, freshness, radiance, vigour, rush.
−OPPOSITES paleness.

flush² ▸ adjective *(informal) flush with cash* =**well supplied**, well provided, well stocked, replete, overflowing, bursting, brimful, brimming, loaded, overloaded, teeming, stuffed, swarming, thick, solid; full of, abounding in, rich in, abundant in; *informal* awash, jam-packed, chock-full of; *Austral./NZ informal* chocker.
−OPPOSITES lacking, low (on).

flushed ▸ adjective **1** *flushed faces* =**red**, pink, ruddy, glowing, rosy, florid, high-coloured, healthy-looking, aglow, burning, feverish; blushing, red-faced, embarrassed, shamefaced. **2** *flushed with success* =**elated**, excited, thrilled, exhilarated, happy, delighted, overjoyed, joyous, gleeful, jubilant, exultant, ecstatic, euphoric, rapturous; *informal* blissed out, over the moon, high, on a high; *N. Amer. informal* wigged out.
−OPPOSITES pale, dismayed.

fluster ▸ verb *she was flustered by his presence* =**unsettle**, unnerve, agitate, ruffle, upset, bother, put on edge, disquiet, disturb, worry, perturb, disconcert, confuse, throw off balance, confound, nonplus; *informal* rattle, faze, put into a flap, throw into a tizzy; *Brit. informal* send into a spin; *N. Amer. informal* discombobulate.
−OPPOSITES calm.
▸ noun *in a terrible fluster* =**state of agitation**, state of anxiety, nervous state, panic, frenzy, fret; *informal* dither, flap, tizz, tizzy, tiz-woz, state, sweat; *N. Amer. informal* twit.

–OPPOSITES state of calm.

fluted ▸ adjective =**grooved**, channelled, furrowed, ribbed, corrugated, ridged.
–OPPOSITES smooth, plain.

flutter ▸ verb **1** *butterflies fluttered around* =**flit**, hover, dance. **2** *a tern was fluttering its wings* =**flap**, beat, quiver, agitate, vibrate. **3** *she fluttered her eyelashes* =**flicker**, bat. **4** *flags fluttered* =**flap**, wave, ripple, undulate, quiver; fly. **5** *her heart fluttered* =**beat weakly**, beat irregularly, palpitate, miss/skip a beat, quiver, go pit-a-pat.
▸ noun **1** *the flutter of wings* =**beating**, flapping, quivering, agitation, vibrating. **2** *a flutter of nervousness* =**tremor**, wave, rush, surge, flash, stab, flush, tremble, quiver, shiver, frisson, chill, thrill, tingle, shudder, ripple, flicker.

flux ▸ noun =**continuous change**, changeability, variability, inconstancy, fluidity, instability, unsteadiness, fluctuation, variation, shift, movement, oscillation, alternation, rise and fall, see-sawing, yo-yoing.
–OPPOSITES stability.

fly¹ ▸ verb **1** *a bird flew overhead* =**travel through the air**, wing its way, wing, glide, soar, wheel; hover, hang; take wing, take to the air, mount. **2** *they flew to Paris* =**travel by plane/air**, jet. **3** *we flew in supplies* =**transport (by plane/ air)**, airlift, lift, jet, drop, parachute. **4** *he can fly a plane* =**pilot**, operate, control, manoeuvre, steer. **5** *the ship was flying a French flag* =**display**, show, exhibit. **6** *flags flew in the town* =**flutter**, flap, wave. **7** *doesn't time fly?* =**go quickly**, fly by/past, pass swiftly, slip past, rush past. **8** *the runners flew by.* See SPEED verb sense 1.
■ **fly at** =**attack**, assault, pounce on, set upon, set about, weigh into, let fly at, turn on, round on, lash out at, hit out at, belabour; *informal* lay into, tear into, sail into, pitch into, wade into, let someone have it, jump; *Brit. informal* have a go at; *N. Amer. informal* light into.
■ **let fly.** See LET.

fly² ▸ adjective (*Brit. informal*) =**shrewd**, sharp, astute, acute, canny, worldly-wise, knowing, clever; *informal* streetwise, not born yesterday, smart, no fool, nobody's fool; *Brit. informal* suss; *Scottish & N. English informal* pawky.
–OPPOSITES naive.

fly-by-night ▸ adjective =**unreliable**,

undependable, untrustworthy, disreputable; **dishonest**, deceitful, dubious, unscrupulous; *informal* iffy, shady, shifty, slippery, crooked; *Brit. informal* dodgy, bent; *Austral./NZ informal* shonky.
–OPPOSITES reliable, honest.

flyer, flier ▸ noun **1** *frequent flyers* =**air traveller**, air passenger, airline customer. **2** *flyers promoting a new bar* =**handbill**, bill, handout, leaflet, circular, advertisement; *N. Amer.* dodger.

flying ▸ adjective **1** *a flying beetle* =**airborne**, in the air, in flight; **winged**. **2** *a flying visit* =**brief**, short, lightning, fleeting, hasty, rushed, hurried, quick, whistle-stop, cursory, perfunctory; *informal* quickie.
–OPPOSITES long.

foam ▸ noun *the foam on the waves* =**froth**, spume, surf; fizz, effervescence, bubbles, head; lather, suds.
▸ verb *the water foamed* =**froth**; fizz, effervesce, bubble; lather; ferment, rise; boil, seethe.

foamy ▸ adjective =**frothy**, foaming, bubbly, aerated, bubbling; sudsy; whipped, whisked.

fob ■ **fob someone off** *I'm not going to be fobbed off* =**put off**, stall, give someone the runaround, deceive; placate, appease.
■ **fob something off on** *he fobbed off the kids on Cliff* =**impose**, palm off, unload, dump, get rid of, foist, offload; saddle someone with something, land someone with something, lumber someone with something.

focus ▸ noun **1** *a focus of community life* =**centre**, focal point, central point, centre of attention, hub, pivot, nucleus, heart, cornerstone, linchpin. **2** *the focus is on helping people* =**emphasis**, accent, priority, attention, concentration. **3** *the main focus of this chapter* =**subject**, theme, concern, subject matter, topic, issue, thesis, point, thread; substance, essence, gist, matter.
▸ verb **1** *he focused his binoculars on the tower* =**bring into focus**; aim, point, turn. **2** *the investigation will focus on areas of need* =**concentrate**, centre, zero in, zoom in; address itself to, pay attention to, pinpoint, revolve around, have as its starting point.
■ **in focus** =**sharp**, crisp, distinct, clear, well defined, well focused.
■ **out of focus** =**blurred**, unfocused,

indistinct, blurry, fuzzy, hazy, misty, cloudy, lacking definition, nebulous.

foe ▶ noun *(literary)* =**enemy**, adversary, opponent, rival, antagonist, combatant, challenger, competitor, opposer, opposition, competition, other side.
−OPPOSITES friend.

fog ▶ noun =**mist**, smog, murk, haze, haar; *N. English* (sea) fret; *informal* pea-souper.
▶ verb *the windscreen fogged up* | *his breath fogged the glass* =**steam up**, mist over, cloud over, film over, make/become misty.
−OPPOSITES demist, clear.

foggy ▶ adjective **1** *the weather was foggy* =**misty**, smoggy, hazy, murky. **2** *a foggy memory* =**muddled**, confused, dim, hazy, shadowy, cloudy, blurred, obscure, vague, indistinct, unclear.
−OPPOSITES clear.

foible ▶ noun =**weakness**, failing, shortcoming, flaw, imperfection, blemish, fault, defect, limitation; quirk, kink, idiosyncrasy, eccentricity, peculiarity.
−OPPOSITES strength.

foil¹ ▶ verb *the escape attempt was foiled* =**thwart**, frustrate, obstruct, hamper, hinder, snooker, cripple, scotch, derail; stop, block, prevent, defeat; *informal* do for, put paid to, stymie; *Brit. informal* scupper, nobble, queer, put the mockers on.
−OPPOSITES assist.

foil² ▶ noun *the wine was a perfect foil to pasta* =**contrast**, complement; antithesis.

foist ▶ verb =**impose**, force, thrust, offload, unload, dump, palm off, fob off; pass off, get rid of; saddle someone with, land someone with, lumber someone with.

fold¹ ▶ verb **1** *I folded the cloth* =**double (over/up)**, crease, turn under/up/over, bend, tuck, gather, pleat. **2** *fold the cream into the mixture* =**mix**, blend, stir gently. **3** *he folded her in his arms* =**enfold**, wrap, envelop; take, gather, clasp, squeeze, clutch; embrace, hug, cuddle, cradle. **4** *the firm folded last year* =**fail**, collapse, founder; go bankrupt, become insolvent, cease trading, go into receivership, go into liquidation, be wound up, be closed (down), be shut (down); *informal* crash, go bust, go broke, go under, go to the wall, go belly up.
▶ noun *there was a fold in the paper* =**crease**, knife-edge; wrinkle, crinkle, pucker, furrow; pleat, gather.

fold² ▶ noun =**enclosure**, pen, paddock, pound, compound, ring; *N. Amer.* corral.

folder ▶ noun =**file**, binder, ring binder, portfolio, document case, envelope, sleeve, wallet.

foliage ▶ noun =**leaves**, leafage; greenery, vegetation, verdure.

folk ▶ noun *(informal)* **1** *the local folk* =**people**, individuals, {men, women, and children}, (living) souls, mortals; citizenry, inhabitants, residents, populace, population; *informal* peeps; *formal* denizens. **2** *my folks live in Hull* =**relatives**, relations, family, nearest and dearest, people, kinsfolk, kinsmen, kinswomen, kin, kith and kin, kindred, flesh and blood.

folklore ▶ noun =**mythology**, lore, tradition; legends, fables, myths, folk tales, folk stories, old wives' tales.

follow ▶ verb **1** *we'll let the others follow* =**come behind**, come after, go behind, go after, walk behind. **2** *people who follow the band around* =**accompany**, go along with, go around with, travel with, escort, attend, trail around with, string along with; *informal* tag along with. **3** *the police followed her everywhere* =**shadow**, trail, stalk, track; *informal* tail. **4** *follow the instructions* =**obey**, comply with, conform to, adhere to, stick to, keep to, act in accordance with, abide by, observe, heed, pay attention to. **5** *I couldn't follow what he said* =**understand**, comprehend, apprehend, take in, grasp, fathom, appreciate, see; *informal* make head or tail of, get, figure out, savvy, get one's head around, get one's mind around, get the drift of; *Brit. informal* suss out. **6** *he follows Manchester United* =**be a fan of**, be a supporter of, support, watch.
−OPPOSITES lead, flout, misunderstand.

■ **follow something through** =**complete**, bring to completion, see through; stay/continue with, carry on with, keep on/going with; *informal* stick something out.

■ **follow something up** =**investigate**, research, look into, dig into, delve into, make enquiries into, enquire about, ask questions about, pursue, chase up; *informal* check out; *N. Amer. informal* scope out.

follower ▶ noun **1** *the president's followers* =**assistant**, attendant, compan-

ion, henchman, minion, lackey, servant; *informal* hanger-on, sidekick; entourage, staff. **2** *a follower of Christ* =**disciple**, apostle, supporter, defender, champion; believer, worshipper. **3** *followers of Scottish football* =**fan**, enthusiast, admirer, devotee, lover, supporter, adherent; *N. Amer. informal* rooter.
–OPPOSITES leader, opponent.

following ▸ noun *his devoted following* =**admirers**, supporters, backers, fans, adherents, devotees, public, audience; circle, retinue, train.
–OPPOSITES opposition.
▸ adjective **1** *the following day* =**next**, ensuing, succeeding, subsequent. **2** *the following questions* =**below**, underneath; these.
–OPPOSITES preceding, aforementioned.

folly ▸ noun =**foolishness**, foolhardiness, stupidity, idiocy, lunacy, madness, rashness, recklessness, imprudence, injudiciousness, irresponsibility, thoughtlessness, indiscretion; *informal* craziness; *Brit. informal* daftness.
–OPPOSITES wisdom.

foment ▸ verb =**instigate**, incite, provoke, agitate, excite, stir up, whip up, encourage, urge, fan the flames of.

fond ▸ adjective **1** *she was fond of dancing* =**keen on**, partial to, addicted to, enthusiastic about, passionate about; attached to, attracted to, enamoured of, in love with, having a soft spot for; *informal* into, hooked on, gone on, sweet on, struck on. **2** *his fond father* =**adoring**, devoted, doting, loving, caring, affectionate, kind, attentive. **3** *a fond hope* =**unrealistic**, naive, foolish, overoptimistic, deluded, delusory, absurd, vain.
–OPPOSITES indifferent, unfeeling, realistic.

fondle ▸ verb =**caress**, stroke, pat, pet, finger, tickle, play with; maul, molest; *informal* paw, grope, feel up, touch up, cop a feel of.

fondness ▸ noun **1** *they look at each other with fondness* =**affection**, love, liking, warmth, tenderness, kindness, devotion, endearment, attachment, friendliness. **2** *a fondness for spicy food* =**liking**, love, taste, partiality, keenness, inclination, penchant, predilection, passion, appetite; weakness, soft spot; *informal* thing, yen.
–OPPOSITES hatred.

food ▸ noun **1** *French food* =**nourishment**, sustenance, nutriment, fare; cooking, cuisine; foodstuffs, provender, refreshments, meals, provisions, rations; solids; *informal* eats, eatables, nosh, grub, chow, nibbles; *Brit. informal* scoff, tuck; *N. Amer. informal* chuck; *formal* comestibles; *dated* victuals. **2** *food for the cattle* =**fodder**, feed, provender, forage.

> WORD LINKS
>
> relating to food: **alimentary, culinary**
> fear of food: **cibophobia, sitophobia**

fool ▸ noun **1** *acting like a fool* =**idiot**, ass, halfwit, blockhead, dunce, simpleton, clod; *informal* dope, ninny, nincompoop, chump, dimwit, dumbo, dummy, dum-dum, fathead, numbskull, dunderhead, pudding-head, thickhead, airhead, lamebrain, cretin, moron, nerd, imbecile, pea-brain, birdbrain, jerk, dipstick, donkey, noodle; *Brit. informal* nit, nitwit, twit, clot, goat, plonker, berk, prat, pillock, wally, dork, twerp, charlie, mug; *Scottish informal* nyaff, balloon, sumph, gowk; *N. Amer. informal* schmuck, bozo, boob; turkey, schlepper, chowderhead, dumbhead, goofball, goof, goofus, galoot, lummox, klutz, putz, schlemiel, sap, meatball; *Austral./ NZ informal* drongo, dill, alec, galah, boofhead. **2** *she made a fool of me* =**laughing stock**, dupe, gull; *informal* stooge, sucker, mug, fall guy; *N. Amer. informal* sap.
▸ verb **1** *he'd been fooled* =**deceive**, trick, hoax, dupe, take in, mislead, delude, hoodwink, bluff, gull; swindle, defraud, cheat, double-cross; *informal* con, bamboozle, pull a fast one on, take for a ride, pull the wool over someone's eyes, put one over on, have on, diddle, fiddle, rip off, do, sting, shaft; *Brit. informal* sell a pup to; *N. Amer. informal* sucker, snooker, stiff, euchre, hornswoggle; *Austral. informal* pull a swifty on; *literary* cozen. **2** *I'm not fooling, I promise* =**pretend**, make believe, put on an act, act, sham, fake; joke, jest; *informal* kid; *Brit. informal* have someone on.
■ **fool around** =**fiddle**, play (about/ around), toy, trifle, meddle, tamper, interfere, monkey about/around; *informal* mess about/around; *Brit. informal* muck about/around.

foolhardy ▸ adjective =**reckless**, rash, irresponsible, impulsive, hot-headed, impetuous, daredevil, devil-may-care, death-or-glory, madcap, hare-brained, precipitate, hasty, overhasty.

–OPPOSITES prudent.

foolish ▸ adjective =**stupid**, silly, idiotic, witless, brainless, mindless, unintelligent, thoughtless, half-baked, imprudent, incautious, injudicious, unwise; ill-advised, ill-considered, impolitic, rash, reckless, foolhardy; *informal* dumb, dim, dim-witted, half-witted, thick, gormless, hare-brained, crackbrained, pea-brained, woodenheaded; *Brit. informal* barmy, daft; *Scottish & N. English informal* glaikit; *N. Amer. informal* dumb-ass, chowderheaded.
–OPPOSITES sensible, wise.

foolishness ▸ noun =**folly**, stupidity, idiocy, imbecility, silliness, inanity, thoughtlessness, imprudence, injudiciousness, lack of caution/foresight/sense, irresponsibility, indiscretion, foolhardiness, rashness, recklessness; *Brit. informal* daftness.
–OPPOSITES sense, wisdom.

foolproof ▸ adjective =**infallible**, dependable, reliable, trustworthy, certain, sure, guaranteed, safe, sound, tried and tested; watertight, airtight, flawless, perfect; *informal* sure-fire.
–OPPOSITES flawed.

foot ▸ noun 1 *my feet hurt* =*informal* tootsies, trotters; *N. Amer. informal* dogs. 2 *the animal's foot* =paw, hoof, trotter, pad. 3 *the foot of the hill* =**bottom**, base, lowest part; end; foundation.
■ **foot the bill** (*informal*) =**pay (the bill)**, settle up; *informal* pick up the tab, cough up, fork out, shell out, come across; *N. Amer. informal* pick up the check.

> [!NOTE] WORD LINKS
> relating to feet: **pedi-, -pod(e)**
> medical treatment of the feet: **chiropody**

football (*Brit.*) ▸ noun =**soccer**, Association football; *informal* footie.

footing ▸ noun 1 *Jenny lost her footing* =**foothold**, toehold, grip, purchase. 2 *a solid financial footing* =**basis**, base, foundation. 3 *on an equal footing* =**standing**, status, position; condition, arrangement, basis; relationship, terms.

footnote ▸ noun =**note**, annotation, comment, gloss; aside, incidental remark, digression.

footprint ▸ noun =**footmark**, mark, impression; (**footprints**) track(s), spoor.

footstep ▸ noun =**footfall**, step, tread, stomp, stamp.

foppish ▸ adjective =**dandyish**, dandified, dapper, dressy; affected, vain; *informal* natty; *Brit. informal* poncey.

forage ▸ verb =**hunt**, search, look, rummage (about/around/round), ferret (about/around), root about/around, scratch about/around, nose around/about/round, scavenge.
▸ noun =**hunt**, search, look, quest, rummage, scavenge.

foray ▸ noun =**raid**, attack, assault, incursion, swoop, strike, onslaught, sortie, sally, push, thrust.

forbear ▸ verb =**refrain**, abstain, desist, keep, restrain oneself, stop oneself, hold back, withhold; resist the temptation to; eschew, avoid, decline to.
–OPPOSITES persist.

forbearance ▸ noun =**tolerance**, patience, resignation, endurance, fortitude, stoicism; leniency, clemency, indulgence; restraint, self-restraint, self-control.

forbearing ▸ adjective =**patient**, tolerant, easy-going, lenient, clement, forgiving, understanding, accommodating, indulgent; long-suffering, resigned, stoic; restrained, self-controlled.
–OPPOSITES impatient, intolerant.

forbid ▸ verb =**prohibit**, ban, outlaw, make illegal, veto, proscribe, disallow, embargo, bar, debar, interdict.
–OPPOSITES permit.

forbidden ▸ adjective =**prohibited**, verboten, taboo; illegal, illicit, against the law; *informal* not on, out.
–OPPOSITES permitted.

forbidding ▸ adjective 1 *a forbidding manner* =**hostile**, unwelcoming, unfriendly, off-putting, unsympathetic, unapproachable, grim, stern, hard, tough, frosty. 2 *the castle looked forbidding* =**threatening**, ominous, menacing, sinister, brooding, daunting, fearsome, frightening, chilling, disturbing, disquieting.
–OPPOSITES friendly, inviting.

force ▸ noun 1 *he pushed with all his force* =**strength**, power, energy, might, effort, exertion; impact, pressure, weight, impetus. 2 *they used force to achieve their aims* =**coercion**, compulsion, constraint, duress, oppression, harassment, intimidation, violence; *informal* armtwisting. 3 *the force of the argument* =**cogency**, weight, effectiveness, sound-

ness, validity, strength, power, significance, influence, authority; *informal* punch; *formal* efficacy. **4** *a force for good* =**agency**, power, influence, instrument, vehicle, means. **5** *a peacekeeping force* =**body**, group, outfit, party, team; detachment, unit, squad.
−OPPOSITES weakness.
▶ verb **1** *he was forced to pay* =**compel**, coerce, make, constrain, oblige, impel, drive, pressurize, pressure, press, push, press-gang, bully, dragoon, bludgeon; *informal* put the screws on, lean on, twist someone's arm. **2** *the door had to be forced* =**break open**, knock/smash/break down, kick in. **3** *water was forced through a hole* =**propel**, push, thrust, shove, drive, press, pump. **4** *they forced a confession out of the kids* =**extract**, exact, extort, wrest, wring, drag, screw, squeeze, beat.
■ **in force 1** *the law is now in force* =**effective**, in operation, operative, operational, in action, valid. **2** *her fans were out in force* =**in great numbers**, in hordes/droves, in their hundreds/thousands.

forced ▶ adjective **1** *forced entry* =**violent**, forcible. **2** *forced repatriation* =**enforced**, compulsory, obligatory, mandatory, involuntary, imposed, required. **3** *a forced smile* =**strained**, unnatural, artificial, false, feigned, simulated, contrived, laboured, stilted, studied, mannered, affected, unconvincing, insincere, hollow; *informal* phoney, pretend, put on.
−OPPOSITES voluntary, natural.

forceful ▶ adjective **1** *a forceful personality* =**dynamic**, energetic, assertive, authoritative, vigorous, powerful, strong, pushy, driving, determined, insistent, commanding, dominant, domineering; *informal* bossy, in-your-face, go-ahead, feisty. **2** *a forceful argument* =**cogent**, convincing, compelling, strong, powerful, potent, weighty, effective, well founded, telling, persuasive, irresistible, eloquent, coherent.
−OPPOSITES weak, submissive, unconvincing.

forcible ▶ adjective **1** *forcible entry* =**forced**, violent. **2** *forcible repatriation.* See FORCED sense 2. **3** *a forcible argument.* See FORCEFUL sense 2.

forebear ▶ noun =**ancestor**, forefather, antecedent, progenitor.
−OPPOSITES descendant.

foreboding ▶ noun **1** *a feeling of foreboding* =**apprehension**, anxiety, trepidation, disquiet, unease, uneasiness, misgiving, suspicion, worry, fear, fearfulness, dread, alarm; *informal* the willies, the heebie-jeebies, the jitters. **2** *their forebodings proved justified* =**premonition**, presentiment, bad feeling, sneaking suspicion, funny feeling, intuition.
−OPPOSITES calm.

forecast ▶ verb *they forecast record profits* =**predict**, prophesy, foretell, foresee; estimate, reckon.
▶ noun *a gloomy forecast* =**prediction**, prophecy, prognostication, prognosis; estimate.

forefather ▶ noun =**forebear**, ancestor, antecedent, progenitor.
−OPPOSITES descendant.

forefront ▶ noun =**vanguard**, spearhead, head, lead, front, fore, front line, cutting edge, leading edge.
−OPPOSITES rear, background.

forego ▶ verb. See FORGO.

foregone ■ *a foregone conclusion* =**certainty**, inevitability, matter of course, predictable result; *informal* sure thing; *Brit.* cert, dead cert.

foreground ▶ noun **1** *the foreground of the picture* =**front**, fore. **2** *keep himself in the foreground* =**front**, limelight, spotlight, fore, front line, vanguard.

forehead ▶ noun =**brow**, temple.

WORD LINKS

relating to the forehead: **frontal**

foreign ▶ adjective **1** *foreign investors* =**overseas**, external. **2** *foreign lands* =**distant**, far-off, exotic, alien; non-native. **3** *the concept is foreign to us* =**unfamiliar**, unknown, unheard of, strange, alien; novel, new.
−OPPOSITES domestic, native, familiar.

foreigner ▶ noun =**alien**, non-native, stranger, outsider; immigrant, settler, newcomer, incomer.
−OPPOSITES native.

WORD LINKS

fear of foreigners: **xenophobia**

foreman, forewoman ▶ noun =**supervisor**, overseer, superintendent, team leader; foreperson; *Brit.* chargehand, captain, ganger; *Scottish* grieve; *N. Amer. informal* ramrod, straw boss; *Austral. informal* pannikin boss; *Mining* overman.

foremost ▶ adjective =**leading**, principal, premier, prime, top, greatest, best,

supreme, pre-eminent, outstanding, most important, most notable; *N. Amer.* ranking; *informal* number-one.
−OPPOSITES minor.

forerunner ▶ noun **1** *the forerunners of the dinosaurs* =**predecessor**, precursor, antecedent, ancestor, forebear. **2** *headaches may be the forerunner of other complaints* =**prelude**, herald, harbinger, precursor.
−OPPOSITES descendant.

foresee ▶ verb =**anticipate**, predict, forecast, expect, envisage, envision, see; foretell, prophesy; *Scottish* spae.

foreshadow ▶ verb =**signal**, indicate, signify, mean, be a sign of, suggest, herald, be a harbinger of, warn of, portend, prefigure, presage, promise, point to, anticipate; *informal* spell; *literary* betoken.

foresight ▶ noun =**forethought**, planning, far-sightedness, vision, anticipation, prudence, care, caution; *N. Amer.* forehandedness.
−OPPOSITES hindsight.

forest ▶ noun =**wood(s)**, woodland, trees, plantation; jungle, rainforest.

> **WORD LINKS**
> *relating to forests:* **sylvan**

forestall ▶ verb =**pre-empt**, get in before, steal a march on; anticipate, second-guess; nip in the bud, thwart, frustrate, foil, stave off, ward off, fend off, avert, preclude, obviate, prevent; *informal* beat someone to it.

forestry ▶ noun =**forest management**, tree growing; *technical* arboriculture, silviculture.

foretaste ▶ noun =**sample**, taster, taste, preview, specimen, example; indication, suggestion, hint, whiff; warning, forewarning, omen.

foretell ▶ verb =**predict**, forecast, prophesy, prognosticate; foresee, anticipate, envisage, envision, see; warn of, point to, signal; *Scottish* spae.

forethought ▶ noun =**anticipation**, planning, forward planning, provision, precaution, prudence, care, caution; foresight, far-sightedness, vision.
−OPPOSITES impulse, recklessness.

forever ▶ adverb **1** *their love would last forever* =**for always**, evermore, for ever and ever, for good, for all time, until the end of time, until hell freezes over, eternally; *N. Amer.* forevermore; *informal* until

the cows come home, until doomsday, until kingdom come. **2** *he was forever banging into things* =**always**, continually, constantly, perpetually, incessantly, endlessly, persistently, repeatedly, regularly; non-stop, day and night, {morning, noon, and night}; all the time, the whole time; *Scottish* aye; *informal* 24-7.
−OPPOSITES never, occasionally.

forewarn ▶ verb =**warn**, warn in advance, give advance warning, give notice, apprise, inform; alert, caution, put someone on their guard; *informal* tip off; *Brit. informal* tip someone the wink.

foreword ▶ noun =**preface**, introduction, prologue, preamble; *informal* intro.
−OPPOSITES conclusion.

forfeit ▶ verb =**lose**, be deprived of, surrender, relinquish, sacrifice, give up, yield, renounce, forgo; *informal* pass up, lose out on.
−OPPOSITES retain.
▶ noun =**penalty**, sanction, punishment, penance; fine; confiscation, loss, relinquishment, forfeiture, surrender.

forge¹ ▶ verb **1** *he forged a huge sword* =**hammer out**, beat out, fashion. **2** *they forged a partnership* =**build**, construct, form, create, establish, set up. **3** *he forged her signature* =**fake**, falsify, counterfeit, copy, imitate, reproduce, replicate, simulate; *informal* pirate.

forge² ▶ verb *they forged on through swamps* =**advance**, press on, push on, soldier on, march on, push forward, make progress, make headway.
■ **forge ahead** =**advance**, progress, make progress, put a spurt on.

forged ▶ adjective =**fake**, faked, false, counterfeit, imitation, copied, pirate(d); sham, bogus; *informal* phoney, dud.
−OPPOSITES genuine.

forger ▶ noun =**counterfeiter**, faker, imitator, pirate.

forgery ▶ noun **1** *guilty of forgery* =**counterfeiting**, falsification, faking, copying, pirating. **2** *the painting was a forgery* =**fake**, counterfeit, fraud, imitation, replica, copy, pirate copy; *informal* phoney.

forget ▶ verb **1** *he forgot where he was* =**fail to remember**, be unable to remember. **2** *I never forget my briefcase* =**leave behind**, fail to take/bring, travel/leave home without. **3** *I forgot to close the door* =**neglect**, fail, omit. **4** *you* *can forget that idea* =**stop thinking about**, put out of one's mind; shut out, blank out, pay no heed to, not worry about, ignore, overlook, take no notice of.

−OPPOSITES remember.

■ **forget oneself** =misbehave, behave badly, get up to mischief, get up to no good; be rude; *informal* carry on, act up.

forgetful ▸ adjective **1** *I'm so forgetful these days* =**absent-minded**, amnesic, amnesiac, vague, scatterbrained, disorganized, dreamy, abstracted, with a mind/memory like a sieve; *informal* scatty. **2** *forgetful of the time* =**heedless**, careless; inattentive to, negligent about, oblivious to, unconcerned about, indifferent to.

−OPPOSITES reliable, heedful.

forgetfulness ▸ noun =**absent-mindedness**, amnesia, poor memory, a lapse of memory, vagueness, abstraction; *informal* scattiness.

−OPPOSITES reliability, heed.

forgivable ▸ adjective =**pardonable**, excusable, understandable, tolerable, permissible, allowable, justifiable.

forgive ▸ verb **1** *she would not forgive him* =**pardon**, excuse, exonerate, absolve; *formal* exculpate. **2** *you must forgive his rude conduct* =**excuse**, overlook, disregard, ignore, pass over, make allowances for, allow; turn a blind eye to, turn a deaf ear to, indulge, tolerate.

−OPPOSITES blame, resent, punish.

forgiveness ▸ noun =**pardon**, absolution, exoneration, dispensation, indulgence, clemency, mercy; reprieve, amnesty; *informal* let-off.

−OPPOSITES mercilessness, punishment.

forgiving ▸ adjective **1** *she is very forgiving* =**merciful**, lenient, compassionate, magnanimous, humane, soft-hearted, forbearing, tolerant, indulgent, understanding. **2** *a very forgiving aircraft* =**robust**, tough; resilient, strong.

−OPPOSITES merciless, vindictive.

forgo, forego ▸ verb =**do without**, go without, give up, waive, renounce, surrender, relinquish, part with, drop, sacrifice, abstain from, refrain from, eschew, cut out; *informal* swear off; *formal* forswear, abjure.

−OPPOSITES keep.

forgotten ▸ adjective =**unremembered**, out of mind, consigned to obliv-ion; left behind; neglected, overlooked, ignored, disregarded, unrecognized.

−OPPOSITES remembered.

fork ▸ verb =**split**, branch (off), divide, subdivide, separate, part, diverge, go in different directions, bifurcate.

forked ▸ adjective =**split**, branching, branched, bifurcated, Y-shaped, V-shaped, divided.

−OPPOSITES straight.

forlorn ▸ adjective **1** *he sounded forlorn* =**unhappy**, sad, miserable, sorrowful, dejected, despondent, disconsolate, wretched, down, downcast, dispirited, downhearted, crestfallen, depressed, melancholy, gloomy, glum, mournful, despairing, doleful; *informal* blue, down in the mouth, down in the dumps, fed up. **2** *a forlorn attempt* =**hopeless**; useless, futile, pointless, purposeless, vain, unavailing.

−OPPOSITES happy, sure-fire.

form ▸ noun **1** *the form of the landscape | form is less important than content* =**shape**, configuration, formation, structure, construction, arrangement, appearance, exterior, outline, format, layout, design. **2** *the human form* =**body**, shape, figure, frame, physique, anatomy; *informal* vital statistics. **3** *the infection takes different forms* =**manifestation**, appearance, embodiment, incarnation, semblance, shape, guise. **4** *sponsorship is a form of advertising* =**kind**, sort, type, class, category, variety, genre, brand, style; species, genus, family. **5** *you have to fill in a form* =**questionnaire**, document, coupon, slip. **6** *what form is your daughter in?* =**class**, year; *N. Amer.* grade. **7** *in good form* =**condition**, fettle, shape, health; *Brit. informal* nick. **8** (*Brit.*) *a wooden form* =**bench**, pew, stall.

−OPPOSITES content.

▸ verb **1** *formed from mild steel* =**make**, construct, build, manufacture, fabricate, assemble, put together; create, produce, concoct, devise, contrive, fashion, shape. **2** *he formed a plan* =**formulate**, devise, conceive, work out, think up, lay, draw up, put together, produce, fashion, concoct, forge, hatch, develop; *informal* dream up. **3** *they formed a company* =**set up**, establish, found, launch, create, bring into being, institute, start, get going, initiate, bring about, inaugurate. **4** *a mist was forming* =**materialize**, come into being/existence, emerge, develop; take shape, gather, accumulate, collect,

amass; crystallize, precipitate, condense. **5** *his men formed themselves into a line* =**arrange**, draw up, line up, assemble, organize, sort, order, range, array, dispose, marshal, deploy. **6** *these parts form an integrated whole* =**comprise**, make, make up, constitute, compose, add up to. **7** *the city formed a natural meeting point* =**constitute**, serve as, act as, function as, make.
–OPPOSITES dissolve, disappear.

■ **good form** =**good manners**, manners, convention, etiquette, protocol; *informal* the done thing.

formal ▸ adjective **1** *a formal dinner* =**ceremonial**, ritualistic, ritual, conventional, traditional; stately, courtly, solemn, dignified; elaborate, ornate, dressy. **2** *a very formal manner* =**aloof**, reserved, remote, detached, unapproachable; stiff, prim, stuffy, staid, ceremonious, correct, proper, decorous, conventional, precise, exact, punctilious, unbending, inflexible, straitlaced; *informal* stand-offish. **3** *a formal garden* =**symmetrical**, regular, orderly, geometric. **4** *formal permission* =**official**, legal, authorized, approved, validated, certified, endorsed, documented, sanctioned, licensed, recognized, authoritative. **5** *formal education* =**conventional**, mainstream; school, institutional.
–OPPOSITES informal, casual, colloquial, unofficial.

formality ▸ noun **1** *the formality of the occasion* =**ceremony**, ritual, red tape, protocol, decorum; stateliness, courtliness, solemnity. **2** *his formality was off-putting* =**aloofness**, reserve, remoteness, detachment, unapproachability; stiffness, primness, stuffiness, staidness, correctness, decorum, punctiliousness, inflexibility; *informal* standoffishness. **3** *we keep the formalities to a minimum* =**official procedure**, bureaucracy, red tape, paperwork. **4** *the interview is just a formality* =**routine**, routine practice, normal procedure.
–OPPOSITES informality.

format ▸ noun =**design**, style, presentation, appearance, look; form, shape, size; arrangement, plan, structure, scheme, composition, configuration.

formation ▸ noun **1** *the formation of the island* =**emergence**, coming into being, genesis, development, evolution, shaping, origin. **2** *the formation of a new government* =**establishment**, setting up,

institution, foundation, inception, creation, inauguration. **3** *fighters flying in a V formation* =**configuration**, arrangement, pattern, array, alignment; order.
–OPPOSITES destruction, disappearance, dissolution.

formative ▸ adjective **1** *at a formative stage* =**developmental**, early, fluid, experimental, trial. **2** *a formative influence* =**determining**, controlling, influential, guiding, decisive, forming, shaping, determinative.

former ▸ adjective **1** *the former bishop* =**one-time**, erstwhile, sometime, ex-; previous, foregoing, preceding, earlier, prior, last. **2** *in former times* =**earlier**, old, past, bygone, olden, long-ago, gone by, long past, of old; *literary* of yore. **3** *the former view* =**first-mentioned**, first.
–OPPOSITES future, next, latter.

formerly ▸ adverb =**previously**, earlier, before, until now/then, hitherto, née, once, once upon a time, at one time, in the past.

formidable ▸ adjective **1** *a formidable beast* =**intimidating**, forbidding, alarming, frightening, awesome, fearsome, threatening, dangerous. **2** *a formidable task* =**onerous**, arduous, taxing, difficult, hard, heavy, laborious, strenuous, back-breaking, uphill, Herculean, monumental, colossal; demanding, tough, challenging, exacting. **3** *a formidable pianist* =**accomplished**, masterly, virtuoso, expert; impressive, powerful, mighty, terrific, superb, great, complete, redoubtable; *informal* tremendous, nifty, crack, ace, wizard, magic, mean, wicked, deadly; *N. Amer. informal* crackerjack.
–OPPOSITES pleasant-looking, comforting, easy, poor, weak.

formless ▸ adjective =**shapeless**, amorphous, unshaped, indeterminate; structureless, unstructured.
–OPPOSITES shaped, definite.

formula ▸ noun **1** *a legal formula* =**form of words**, set expression, phrase, saying. **2** *a peace formula* =**recipe**, prescription, blueprint, plan; method, procedure, technique, system. **3** *a formula for removing grease* =**preparation**, concoction, mixture, compound, creation, substance.

formulate ▸ verb **1** *the miners formulated a plan* =**devise**, conceive, work out, think up, lay, draw up, put together, form, produce, fashion, concoct, contrive, forge, hatch, prepare, develop; *informal* dream up. **2** *how Marx formulated his question* =**express**, phrase, word, put into words, frame, couch, put, articulate, say, state, utter.

fornication ▸ noun *(formal)* =**extramarital sex**, extramarital relations, adultery, infidelity, unfaithfulness, cuckoldry; *informal* hanky-panky, a bit on the side.

forte ▸ noun =**strength**, strong point, speciality, strong suit, talent, skill, bent, gift, métier; *informal* thing.
–OPPOSITES weakness.

forth ▸ adverb **1** *smoke billowed forth* =**out**, into view; into existence. **2** *from that day forth* =**onwards**, onward, on, forward.

forthcoming ▸ adjective **1** *forthcoming events* =**imminent**, impending, coming, upcoming, approaching, future; close, (close) at hand, in store, in the wind, in the air, in the offing, in the pipeline, on the horizon, on the way, on us, about to happen. **2** *no reply was forthcoming* =**available**, on offer; offered. **3** *he was not very forthcoming about himself* =**communicative**, talkative, chatty; expansive, expressive, frank, open, candid.
–OPPOSITES past, current, unavailable, uncommunicative.

forthright ▸ adjective =**frank**, direct, straightforward, honest, candid, open, sincere, outspoken, straight, blunt, plain-spoken, no-nonsense, bluff, matter-of-fact, to the point; *informal* upfront.
–OPPOSITES secretive, evasive.

forthwith ▸ adverb =**immediately**, at once, instantly, directly, right away, straight away, post-haste, without delay, without hesitation; quickly, speedily, promptly; *informal* pronto.
–OPPOSITES sometime.

fortification ▸ noun =**rampart**, wall, defence, palisade, stockade, earthwork, parapet, barricade.

fortify ▸ verb **1** *measures to fortify the building* =**strengthen**, secure, barricade, protect. **2** *I'll have a drink to fortify me* =**invigorate**, strengthen, energize, enliven, liven up, animate, vitalize, rejuvenate, restore, revive, refresh; *informal* pep up, buck up.
–OPPOSITES weaken, sedate, subdue.

fortitude ▸ noun =**courage**, bravery,

endurance, resilience, mettle, moral fibre, strength of mind, strength of character, backbone, spirit, grit, steadfastness; *informal* guts; *Brit. informal* bottle.
–OPPOSITES faint-heartedness.

fortress ▸ noun =**fort**, castle, citadel, bunker, stronghold, fortification.

fortuitous ▸ adjective =**lucky**, fortunate, providential, chance, advantageous, timely, opportune, adventitious, serendipitous; inadvertent, unintentional, unintended, unplanned, unexpected, unanticipated, unforeseen.
–OPPOSITES predictable, lucky.

fortunate ▸ adjective **1** *he was fortunate enough to survive* =**lucky**, favoured, blessed, blessed with good luck, in luck. **2** *in a fortunate position* =**favourable**, advantageous, happy.
–OPPOSITES unfortunate, unfavourable.

fortunately ▸ adverb =**luckily**, by good luck, by good fortune, as luck would have it; mercifully, thankfully.

fortune ▸ noun **1** *fortune favoured him* =**chance**, accident, coincidence, serendipity, destiny, providence; *N. Amer.* happenstance. **2** *a change of fortune* =**luck**, fate, destiny, predestination, the stars, karma, lot. **3** *an upswing in Sheffield's fortunes* =**circumstances**, state of affairs, condition, position, situation; plight, predicament. **4** *he made his fortune in steel* =**wealth**, money, riches, assets, resources, means, possessions, estate. **5** *(informal) this dress cost a fortune* =**huge amount**, king's ransom, millions, billions; *informal* small fortune, packet, mint, bundle, pile, wad, arm and a leg, pretty penny, tidy sum, big money; *Brit. informal* bomb, shedloads; *N. Amer. informal* big bucks, gazillions.
–OPPOSITES pittance.

forum ▸ noun **1** *forums were held for staff* =**meeting**, assembly, gathering, rally, conference, seminar, convention, symposium, colloquium; *N. Amer. & NZ* caucus; *informal* get-together. **2** *a forum for discussion* =**setting**, place, context, stage, framework, backdrop.

forward ▸ adverb **1** *the traffic moved forward* =**ahead**, forwards, onwards, onward, on, further. **2** *the winner stepped forward* =**towards the front**, out, forth, into view, up. **3** *from that day forward* =**onward**, onwards, on, forth; for ever.
–OPPOSITES backwards.

▶ adjective **1** *a forward movement* =**onward**, advancing. **2** *the Red Army's forward bridgehead* =**front**, advance, foremost, leading. **3** *forward planning* =**future**, forward-looking, for the future, anticipatory. **4** *the girls were very forward* =**bold**, **brazen**, brazen-faced, shameless, familiar, overfamiliar; *informal* fresh.
−OPPOSITES backward, rear, shy, late.

▶ verb **1** *my mother forwarded your letter* =**send on**, post on, redirect, readdress, pass on. **2** *the goods were forwarded by sea* =**send**, dispatch, transmit, carry, convey, deliver, ship.

forward-looking ▶ adjective =**progressive**, enlightened, bold, enterprising, ambitious, pioneering, innovative, modern, positive, reforming, radical.
−OPPOSITES backward-looking.

forwards ▶ adverb. See FORWARD adverb.

fossilized ▶ adjective **1** *fossilized remains* =**petrified**. **2** *a fossilized idea* =**archaic**, antiquated, antediluvian, old-fashioned, outdated, outmoded, behind the times, anachronistic, stuck in time; *informal* prehistoric.

foster ▶ verb **1** *he fostered the arts* =**encourage**, promote, further, stimulate, cultivate, nurture, strengthen, enrich; help, aid, assist, support, back. **2** *they fostered two children* =**bring up**, rear, raise, care for, take care of, look after, provide for.
−OPPOSITES neglect, suppress.

foul ▶ adjective **1** *a foul smell* =**disgusting**, revolting, repulsive, repugnant, abhorrent, loathsome, offensive, sickening, nauseating, nauseous, stomach-churning, stomach-turning, distasteful, obnoxious, objectionable, odious, noxious; *N. Amer.* vomitous; *informal* ghastly, gruesome, gross, putrid, yucky, sick-making; *Brit. informal* beastly; *Austral. informal* on the nose; *literary* noisome. **2** *a foul shirt* =**horrible**, awful, hideous, revolting, dreadful, ghastly, terrible, ugly, tasteless; *informal* gross. **3** *he had been foul to her* =**unkind**, malicious, mean, nasty, unpleasant, unfriendly, spiteful, cruel, vicious, malevolent, despicable, contemptible; *informal* horrible, horrid, rotten; *Brit. informal* beastly. **4** *foul weather* =**inclement**, unpleasant, awful, terrible, disagreeable, bad; rough, stormy, squally, gusty, windy, blustery, wild, blowy, rainy, wet; *Brit. informal* filthy. **5** *foul drinking water* =**contaminated**, polluted, infected, tainted, impure, filthy, dirty, unclean. **6** *foul language* =**vulgar**, crude, coarse, filthy, dirty, obscene, indecent, naughty, lewd, suggestive, smutty, ribald, salacious, scatological, offensive, abusive; *informal* blue.
−OPPOSITES pleasant, kind, fair, clean, righteous, mild, fair.

▶ verb **1** *the river had been fouled* =**dirty**, infect, pollute, contaminate, poison, taint, sully, soil, stain, blacken, muddy, splash, spatter, smear, blight, defile, make filthy. **2** *allowing dogs to foul the pavement* =**mess**, dirty; *informal* poo on, dump on, do one's business on, do jobbies on. **3** *the trawler had fouled its nets* =**tangle up**, entangle, snarl, catch, entwine, enmesh, twist.
−OPPOSITES clean up, disentangle.

foul-mouthed ▶ adjective =**vulgar**, crude, coarse; obscene, rude, smutty, dirty, filthy, indecent, indelicate, offensive, lewd, X-rated, scatological, abusive; *informal* blue.

found ▶ verb **1** *he founded his company in 1989* =**establish**, set up, start, begin, get going, institute, inaugurate, launch, form, create, bring into being, originate, develop. **2** *they founded a new city* =**build**, establish; construct, erect, put up. **3** *their relationship was founded on trust* =**base**, build, construct; ground in, root in; rest, hinge, depend.
−OPPOSITES dissolve, liquidate, abandon, demolish.

foundation ▶ noun **1** *the foundations of the wall* =**footing**, foot, base, substructure, underpinning; bottom. **2** *there was no foundation for the claim* =**justification**, grounds, evidence, basis. **3** *an educational foundation* =**(endowed) institution**, (charitable) body/panel, (funding) agency.

founder[1] ▶ noun *the founder of modern physics* =**originator**, creator, (founding) father, architect, engineer, designer, developer, pioneer, author, planner, inventor, mastermind.

founder[2] ▶ verb **1** *the ship foundered* =**sink**, go to the bottom, go down, be lost at sea; *informal* go to Davy Jones's locker. **2** *the scheme foundered* =**fail**, be unsuccessful, not succeed, fall flat, fall through, collapse, backfire, meet with disaster, come to nothing/naught; *informal* flop, bomb.
−OPPOSITES succeed.

fountain ▶ noun **1** *a fountain of water*

=jet, spray, spout, spurt, well, cascade. **2** *a fountain of knowledge* =**source**, fount, well; reservoir, fund, mass, mine.

four ▸ cardinal number =**quartet**, foursome, tetralogy, quadruplets.

> **WORD LINKS**
>
> *relating to four:* **quadri-, tetra-**

fox ▸ noun

> **WORD LINKS**
>
> *relating to foxes:* **vulpine**
> *male:* **fox**
> *female:* **vixen**
> *young:* **cub**
> *collective noun:* **skulk**
> *home:* **earth, hole, burrow**

foyer ▸ noun =**entrance hall**, hall, hallway, entrance, entry, porch, reception area, atrium, concourse, lobby; *N. Amer.* entryway.

fracas ▸ noun =**disturbance**, brawl, melee, rumpus, skirmish, struggle, scuffle, scrum, clash, fisticuffs, altercation; *informal* scrap, dust-up, set-to, shindy, shindig; *Brit. informal* punch-up, bust-up, ruck; *N. Amer. informal* rough house, brannigan; *Austral./NZ informal* stoush; *Law, dated* affray.

fraction ▸ noun **1** *a fraction of the population* =**tiny part**, fragment, snippet, snatch. **2** *he moved a fraction closer* =**tiny amount**, little, bit, touch, soupçon, trifle, mite, shade, jot; *informal* smidgen, smidge, tad.
−OPPOSITES whole.

fractious ▸ adjective **1** *fractious children* =**grumpy**, bad-tempered, irascible, irritable, crotchety, grouchy, cantankerous, tetchy, testy, ill-tempered, illhumoured, peevish, cross, pettish, waspish, crabby, crusty, prickly; *Brit. informal* shirty, stroppy, narky, ratty; *N. Amer. informal* cranky, ornery; *Austral./NZ informal* snaky. **2** *the fractious parliamentary party* =**wayward**, unruly, uncontrollable, unmanageable, out of hand, obstreperous, difficult, headstrong, recalcitrant, intractable; disobedient, insubordinate, disruptive, disorderly, undisciplined; contrary, wilful.
−OPPOSITES contented, affable, dutiful.

fracture ▸ noun =**break**, crack.
▸ verb =**break**, crack, snap, shatter, splinter.

fragile ▸ adjective **1** *fragile vases* =**break-able**, easily broken; delicate, dainty, fine, brittle, flimsy. **2** *the fragile ceasefire* =**tenuous**, shaky, insecure, vulnerable, flimsy. **3** *she is still very fragile* =**weak**, delicate, frail, debilitated; ill, unwell, ailing, poorly, sickly, infirm.
−OPPOSITES strong, durable, robust.

fragment ▸ noun **1** *meteorite fragments* =**piece**, bit, particle, speck; chip, shard, sliver, splinter; shaving, paring, snippet, scrap, offcut, flake, shred, wisp, morsel; *Scottish* skelf. **2** *a fragment of conversation* =**snatch**, snippet, scrap, bit.
▸ verb *explosions caused the chalk to fragment* =**break up**, break (into pieces), crack open/apart, shatter, splinter, fracture; disintegrate, fall to pieces, fall apart.

fragmentary ▸ adjective =**incomplete**, fragmented, disconnected, disjointed, broken, discontinuous, piecemeal, scrappy, bitty, sketchy, uneven.

fragrance ▸ noun **1** *the fragrance of spring flowers* =**sweet smell**, scent, perfume, bouquet; aroma, nose. **2** *a daring new fragrance* =**perfume**, scent, eau de toilette, toilet water; eau de cologne, cologne.

fragrant ▸ adjective =**sweet-scented**, sweet-smelling, scented, perfumed, aromatic.
−OPPOSITES smelly.

frail ▸ adjective **1** *a frail old lady* =**weak**, delicate, feeble, enfeebled, debilitated; infirm, ill, ailing, unwell, sickly, poorly, in poor health. **2** *a frail structure* =**fragile**, easily damaged, delicate, flimsy, insubstantial, unsteady, unstable, rickety.
−OPPOSITES strong, robust.

frailty ▸ noun **1** *the frailty of old age* =**infirmity**, weakness, enfeeblement, debility; fragility, delicacy; ill health, sickliness. **2** *his many frailties* =**weakness**, fallibility; weak point, flaw, imperfection, defect, failing, fault, shortcoming, deficiency, inadequacy, limitation.
−OPPOSITES strength.

frame ▸ noun **1** *a tubular metal frame* =**framework**, structure, substructure, skeleton, chassis, shell; support, scaffolding, foundation. **2** *his tall, slender frame* =**body**, figure, form; shape, physique, build, proportions.
▸ verb **1** *he had the picture framed* =**mount**, set in a frame. **2** *those who frame the regulations* =**formulate**, draw up, draft, plan, shape, compose, put together,

form, devise, create.
■ **frame of mind** = mood, state of mind, humour, temper, disposition.

framework ▶ noun = frame, substructure, structure, skeleton, chassis; support, scaffolding, foundation.

France ▶ noun

> WORD LINKS
>
> fear of French people and things:
> **Francophobia, Gallophobia**
> lover of French people and things:
> **Francophile**

franchise ▶ noun 1 *the extension of the franchise to women* = suffrage, the vote, the right to vote, voting rights, enfranchisement. 2 *the company lost its TV franchise* = warrant, charter, licence, permit, authorization, permission, sanction.

frank[1] ▶ adjective 1 *he was quite frank with me* = candid, direct, forthright, plain, plain-spoken, straight, straightforward, straight from the shoulder, explicit, to the point, matter-of-fact; open, honest, truthful, sincere; bluff, blunt, unsparing, not afraid to call a spade a spade; *informal* upfront. 2 *she looked at Sam with frank admiration* = open, undisguised, unconcealed, naked, unmistakable, clear, obvious, transparent, patent, manifest, evident, perceptible, palpable.
−OPPOSITES evasive.

frank[2] ▶ verb *the envelope had not been franked* = stamp, postmark.

frankly ▶ adverb 1 *frankly, I'm not interested* = to be frank, to be honest, to tell you the truth, to be truthful, in all honesty, as it happens. 2 *he stated the case quite frankly* = candidly, directly, plainly, straightforwardly, straight from the shoulder, forthrightly, openly, honestly, without beating about the bush, without mincing one's words; bluntly, with no holds barred.

frantic ▶ adjective = panic-stricken, panicky, beside oneself, at one's wits' end, distraught, overwrought, worked up, agitated, distressed; frenzied, wild, frenetic, feverish, hysterical, desperate; *informal* in a state, in a tizzy/tizz, wound up, het up, in a flap, tearing one's hair out; *Brit. informal* having kittens, in a flat spin.
−OPPOSITES calm.

fraternity ▶ noun 1 *a spirit of fraternity* = brotherhood, fellowship, kinship, friendship, (mutual) support, solidarity,

community, union, togetherness; sisterhood. 2 *the teaching fraternity* = profession, community, trade, set, circle. 3 *(N. Amer.) a college fraternity* = society, club, association; group, set.

fraternize ▶ verb = associate, mix, consort, socialize, keep company, rub shoulders; *N. Amer.* rub elbows; *informal* hang around/round, hang out, run around, knock about/around, hobnob.

fraud ▶ noun 1 *he was arrested for fraud* = fraudulence, sharp practice, cheating, swindling, embezzlement, deceit, deception, double-dealing, chicanery. 2 *social security frauds* = swindle, racket, deception, trick, cheat, hoax; *informal* scam, con, con trick, rip-off, sting, diddle, fiddle; *N. Amer. informal* bunco, hustle, grift. 3 *they exposed him as a fraud* = impostor, fake, sham, charlatan, quack; swindler, fraudster, racketeer, cheat, confidence trickster; *informal* phoney, con man, con artist.

fraudulent ▶ adjective = dishonest, cheating, swindling, corrupt, criminal, illegal, unlawful, illicit; deceitful, double-dealing, duplicitous, dishonourable, unscrupulous, unprincipled; *informal* crooked, shady, dirty; *Brit. informal* bent, dodgy; *Austral./NZ informal* shonky.
−OPPOSITES honest.

fraught ▶ adjective 1 *their world is fraught with danger* = full of, filled with, rife with; attended by. 2 *she sounded a bit fraught* = anxious, worried, stressed, upset, distraught, overwrought, worked up, agitated, distressed, distracted, desperate, frantic, panic-stricken, panicky; beside oneself, at one's wits' end, at the end of one's tether; *informal* wound up, in a state, in a flap, tearing one's hair out; *Brit. informal* having kittens, in a flat spin.

fray ▶ verb 1 *cheap fabric soon frays* = unravel, wear, wear thin, wear out/through. 2 *her nerves were frayed* = strain, tax, overtax, put on edge.

frayed ▶ adjective 1 *a frayed shirt collar* = worn, threadbare, tattered, ragged, holey, moth-eaten, in holes, the worse for wear; *informal* tatty; *N. Amer. informal* raggedy. 2 *his frayed nerves* = strained, fraught, tense, edgy, stressed.

freak ▶ noun 1 *a genetically engineered freak* = aberration, abnormality, irregularity, oddity; monster, monstrosity, mutant. 2 *the accident was a freak* = anomaly, aberration, rarity, oddity, one-off;

fluke, twist of fate. **3** *(informal) a bunch of freaks* =**oddity**, eccentric, misfit; crank, lunatic; *informal* oddball, weirdo, nutcase, nut; *Brit. informal* nutter; *N. Amer. informal* wacko, kook. **4** *(informal) a fitness freak* =**enthusiast**, fan, devotee, lover, aficionado; *informal* fiend, nut, fanatic, addict, maniac.

▶ adjective *a freak storm | a freak result* =**unusual**, anomalous, aberrant, atypical, unrepresentative, irregular, exceptional, unaccountable; unpredictable, unforeseeable, unexpected, unanticipated, surprising; isolated.
–OPPOSITES normal.

freakish ▶ adjective *freakish weather.* See FREAK adjective.

free ▶ adjective **1** *admission is free* =**without charge**, free of charge, for nothing; complimentary, gratis; *informal* for free, on the house. **2** *free of any pressures* =**unencumbered by**, unaffected by, clear of, without, rid of; exempt from, not liable to, safe from, immune to, excused of; *informal* sans, minus. **3** *I'm free this afternoon* =**unoccupied**, not busy, available; off duty, off work, off, on holiday, on leave; at leisure, with time on one's hands, with time to spare. **4** *the bathroom's free* =**vacant**, empty, available, unoccupied, not taken, not in use. **5** *a proud, free nation* =**independent**, self-governing, self-governed, self-ruling, self-determining, sovereign, autonomous; democratic. **6** *the killer is still free* =**on the loose**, at liberty, at large, loose; unconfined, unbound, untied, unchained, unrestrained. **7** *you are free to leave* =**able to**, in a position to, capable of; allowed, permitted. **8** *the free flow of water* =**unimpeded**, unobstructed, unrestricted, unhampered, clear, open. **9** *she was free with her money* =**generous**, liberal, open-handed, unstinting, bountiful; lavish, extravagant, prodigal. **10** *his free and open manner* =**frank**, open, candid, direct, plain-spoken; unrestrained, unconstrained, free and easy, uninhibited.
–OPPOSITES busy, occupied, captive, mean.

▶ verb **1** *the hostages were freed* =**release**, set free, let go, liberate, discharge, deliver; set loose, let loose, turn loose, untie, unchain, unfetter, unshackle, unleash. **2** *victims were freed by firefighters* =**extricate**, release, get out, pull out, pull free; rescue. **3** *they wish to be freed from all legal*

ties =**exempt**, except, excuse, relieve, unburden.
–OPPOSITES confine, trap.

■ **free and easy** =**easy-going**, relaxed, casual, informal, unceremonious, unforced, natural, open, spontaneous, uninhibited, friendly; tolerant, liberal; *informal* laid-back.

freedom ▶ noun **1** *a desperate bid for freedom* =**liberty**, liberation, release, deliverance, delivery. **2** *the fight for freedom* =**independence**, self-government, self-determination, self rule, home rule, sovereignty, autonomy; democracy. **3** *freedom from political accountability* =**exemption**, immunity, dispensation; impunity. **4** *patients have more freedom to choose who treats them* =**right**, entitlement, privilege, prerogative; scope, latitude, leeway, flexibility, space, breathing space, room, elbow room; licence, leave, free rein, a free hand, carte blanche.
–OPPOSITES captivity, subjection, liability.

> **WORD LINKS**
>
> *fear of freedom:* **eleutherophobia**

free-for-all ▶ noun =**brawl**, fight, scuffle, tussle, struggle, confrontation, clash, altercation, fray, fracas, melee, rumpus, disturbance; breach of the peace; *informal* dust-up, scrap, set-to, shindy; *Brit. informal* punch-up, bust-up, barney; *Scottish informal* rammy.

freely ▶ adverb **1** *may I speak freely?* =**openly**, candidly, frankly, directly, without constraint, without inhibition; truthfully, honestly, without beating about the bush, without mincing one's words, without prevarication. **2** *they gave their time and labour freely* =**voluntarily**, willingly, readily; of one's own volition, of one's own accord, of one's own free will, without compulsion.

free will ▶ noun =**self-determination**, freedom of choice, autonomy, liberty, independence.

■ **of one's own free will** =**voluntarily**, willingly, readily, freely, without reluctance, without compulsion, of one's own accord, of one's own volition, of one's own choosing.

freeze ▶ verb **1** *the stream had frozen* =**ice over**, ice up, solidify. **2** *we froze in winter* =**be very cold**, be numb with cold, turn blue with cold, shiver, be chilled to the bone/marrow. **3** *she froze in*

horror =**stop dead**, stop in one's tracks, stop, stand (stock) still, go rigid, become motionless, become paralysed. **4** *the prices of basic foodstuffs were frozen* =**fix**, hold, peg, set; limit, restrict, cap, confine, regulate; hold/keep down.
–OPPOSITES thaw.

■**freeze someone out** (*informal*) =**exclude**, leave out, shut out, cut out, ignore, ostracize, spurn, snub, shun, cut, cut dead, turn one's back on, cold-shoulder, leave out in the cold; *Brit.* send to Coventry; *Brit. informal* blank.

WORD LINKS

related prefix: **cryo-**

freezing ▸ adjective **1** *a freezing wind* =**bitter**, bitterly cold, icy, chill, frosty, glacial, wintry, sub-zero; raw, biting, piercing, penetrating, cutting, numbing; arctic, polar, Siberian. **2** *you must be freezing* =**frozen**, numb with cold, chilled to the bone/marrow, frozen stiff, shivering; *informal* frozen to death.
–OPPOSITES balmy, hot.

freight ▸ noun =**goods**, cargo, merchandise.

frenetic ▸ adjective =**frantic**, wild, frenzied, hectic, fraught, feverish, fevered, mad, manic, hyperactive, energetic, intense, fast and furious, turbulent, tumultuous.
–OPPOSITES calm.

frenzied ▸ adjective =**frantic**, wild, frenetic, hectic, fraught, feverish, fevered, mad, crazed, manic, intense, furious, uncontrolled, out of control.
–OPPOSITES calm.

frenzy ▸ noun =**fit**, paroxysm, spasm, fever, delirium.

frequency ▸ noun =**rate of occurrence**, incidence, amount, commonness, prevalence; *Statistics* distribution.

frequent ▸ adjective **1** *frequent bouts of infection* =**recurrent**, recurring, repeated, periodic, continual, successive; many, numerous, lots of, several. **2** *a frequent traveller* =**habitual**, regular; experienced.
–OPPOSITES occasional.
▸ verb *he frequented chic clubs* =**visit**, patronize, spend time in, visit regularly, be a regular visitor to, haunt; *informal* hang out at.

frequently ▸ adverb =**regularly**, often, very often, all the time, habitually, customarily, routinely; many times, many a time, lots of times, again and again, time and again, over and over again, repeatedly, recurrently, continually; *N. Amer.* oftentimes.

fresh ▸ adjective **1** *fresh fruit* =**newly picked**, crisp; raw, natural, unprocessed. **2** *a fresh sheet of paper* =**clean**, blank, empty, clear, white; unused, new, pristine, unmarked, untouched. **3** *a fresh approach* =**new**, modern; original, novel, different, innovative, unusual, unconventional, unorthodox; radical, revolutionary; *informal* offbeat. **4** *fresh recruits* =**young**, youthful; new, inexperienced, naive, untrained, unqualified, untried, raw. **5** *her fresh complexion* =**healthy**, healthy-looking, clear, bright, youthful, blooming, glowing, unblemished; fair, rosy, rosy-cheeked, pink, ruddy. **6** *the night air was fresh* =**cool**, crisp, refreshing, invigorating; pure, clean, clear, uncontaminated, untainted, raw. **7** *a fresh wind* =**chilly**, chill, cool, cold, brisk, bracing, invigorating, strong; *informal* nippy; *Brit. informal* parky. **8** (*informal*) *he's getting a little too fresh* =**impudent**, impertinent, insolent, presumptuous, forward, cheeky, disrespectful, rude, lippy, mouthy, saucy; *N. Amer. informal* sassy.
–OPPOSITES stale, old, tired, warm.

freshen ▸ verb **1** *the cold water freshened him* =**refresh**, revitalize, restore, revive, wake up, rouse, enliven, liven up, energize, brace, invigorate; *informal* buck up, pep up. **2** *he opened a window to freshen the room* =**ventilate**, air, aerate; deodorize, purify, cleanse; refresh, cool. **3** (*N. Amer.*) *the waitress freshened their coffee* =**refill**, top up, fill up, replenish.
■**freshen up** =**have a wash**, wash oneself, bathe, shower, tidy oneself (up), spruce oneself up, smarten oneself up, groom oneself, primp oneself; *N. Amer.* wash up; *informal* titivate oneself, do oneself up, doll oneself up; *Brit. informal* tart oneself up; *formal or humorous* perform one's ablutions.

freshman, freshwoman ▸ noun =**first year student**, undergraduate; newcomer, new recruit, starter, probationer; beginner, learner, novice; *N. Amer.* tenderfoot; *informal* undergrad, rookie; *Brit. informal* fresher; *N. Amer. informal* greenhorn.

fret ▸ verb =**worry**, get anxious, feel uneasy, get distressed, get upset, upset oneself, concern oneself; agonize, sigh, pine, brood, eat one's heart out.

fretful ▶ adjective =**distressed**, upset, miserable, unsettled, uneasy, ill at ease, uncomfortable, edgy, agitated, worked up, tense, stressed, restive, fidgety; *informal* het up, uptight, twitchy.

friable ▶ adjective =**crumbly**, easily crumbled, powdery, dusty, chalky, soft; dry.

friction ▶ noun **1** *the lubrication reduces friction* =**abrasion**, rubbing, chafing, grating, rasping, scraping; resistance, drag. **2** *friction between father and son* =**discord**, strife, conflict, disagreement, dissension, dissent, opposition, contention, dispute, disputation, arguing, argument, quarrelling, bickering, squabbling, wrangling, fighting, feuding, rivalry, hostility, animosity, antipathy, enmity, antagonism, resentment, acrimony, bitterness, bad feeling, ill feeling, ill will, bad blood.
–OPPOSITES harmony.

friend ▶ noun **1** *a close friend* =**companion**, best friend, intimate, confidante, confidant, familiar, soul mate, playmate, playfellow, classmate, schoolmate, workmate; ally, associate; sister, brother; *informal* pal, chum, sidekick, crony; *Brit. informal* mate, mucker; *N. English informal* marrow, marrer; *N. Amer. informal* buddy, amigo, compadre, homeboy. **2** *the friends of the Opera* =**patron**, backer, supporter, benefactor, benefactress, sponsor; well-wisher, defender, champion.
–OPPOSITES enemy.

friendless ▶ adjective =**alone**, all alone, by oneself, solitary, lonely, with no one to turn to, lone, without friends, companionless, unwanted, unloved, abandoned, rejected, forsaken, shunned, spurned, forlorn; *N. Amer.* lonesome.
–OPPOSITES popular.

friendliness ▶ noun =**affability**, amiability, geniality, congeniality, bonhomie, cordiality, good nature, good humour, warmth, affection, conviviality, joviality, companionability, sociability, gregariousness, camaraderie, neighbourliness, hospitableness, approachability, accessibility, openness, kindness, kindliness, sympathy, amenability, benevolence.

friendly ▶ adjective **1** *a friendly woman* =**affable**, amiable, genial, congenial, cordial, warm, affectionate, demonstrative, convivial, companionable, sociable, gregarious, outgoing, clubbable, comradely, neighbourly, hospitable, approachable, easy to get on with, accessible, communicative, open, unreserved, easy-going, good-natured, kindly, amenable, agreeable; *Scottish* couthy; *informal* chummy, pally, clubby; *Brit. informal* matey; *N. Amer. informal* buddy-buddy. **2** *friendly conversation* =**amicable**, congenial, cordial, pleasant, easy, relaxed, casual, informal, unceremonious; close, intimate, familiar.
–OPPOSITES hostile.

friendship ▶ noun **1** *lasting friendships* =**relationship**, attachment, association, bond, tie, link, union. **2** *ties of love and friendship* =**amity**, camaraderie, friendliness, comradeship, companionship, fellowship, closeness, affinity, rapport, understanding, harmony, unity; intimacy, affection.
–OPPOSITES enmity.

fright ▶ noun **1** *she was paralysed with fright* =**fear**, terror, horror, alarm, panic, dread, trepidation, dismay, nervousness, apprehension, disquiet. **2** *the experience gave everyone a fright* =**scare**, shock, surprise, turn, jolt, start; the shivers, the shakes; *informal* the jitters, the heebie-jeebies, the willies, the creeps, the collywobbles, a cold sweat; *Brit. informal* the (screaming) abdabs, butterflies (in one's stomach).

frighten ▶ verb =**scare**, startle, alarm, terrify, petrify, shock, chill, panic, shake, disturb, dismay, unnerve, unman, intimidate, terrorize, cow, daunt; strike terror into, put the fear of God into, chill someone to the bone/marrow, make someone's blood run cold; *informal* scare the living daylights out of, scare stiff, scare someone out of their wits, scare witless, scare to death, scare the pants off, spook, make someone's hair stand on end, make someone jump out of their skin; *Brit. informal* put the wind up, give someone the heebie-jeebies; *Irish informal* scare the bejesus out of; *archaic* affright.

frightening ▶ adjective =**terrifying**, horrifying, alarming, startling, chilling, spine-chilling, hair-raising, blood-curdling, disturbing, unnerving, intimidating, daunting, upsetting, traumatic; eerie, sinister, fearsome, nightmarish, macabre, menacing; *Scottish* eldritch; *informal* scary, spooky, creepy, hairy.

frightful ▶ adjective **1** *a frightful accident* =**horrible**, horrific, ghastly, horrendous, serious, awful, dreadful, terrible, nasty, grim, dire, unspeakable; alarming, shocking, terrifying, appalling, fearful; hideous, gruesome, grisly; *informal* horrid. **2** *(informal) a frightful racket* =**awful**, terrible, dreadful, appalling, ghastly, abominable; insufferable, unbearable; *informal* God-awful; *Brit. informal* beastly.

frigid ▶ adjective **1** *a frigid January night* =**very cold**, bitterly cold, bitter, freezing, frozen, frosty, icy, chilly, chill, wintry, bleak, sub-zero, arctic, Siberian, polar, glacial; *informal* nippy; *Brit. informal* parky. **2** *frigid politeness* =**stiff**, formal, stony, wooden, unemotional, passionless, unfeeling, distant, aloof, remote, reserved, unapproachable; frosty, cold, icy, cool, unsmiling, forbidding, unfriendly, unwelcoming; *informal* offish, stand-offish.
–OPPOSITES hot, friendly.

frill ▶ noun =**ruffle**, flounce, ruff, ruche, fringe.
■ **no-frills** =**plain**, simple, basic, straightforward, unpretentious, down to earth; **practical**, serviceable; economical, cheap; workaday, modest, utilitarian, minimalist, functional; spartan, austere, impersonal, characterless, soulless, institutional, clinical.

frilly ▶ adjective =**ruffled**, flounced, frilled, crimped, ruched, trimmed, lacy, frothy; fancy, ornate.

fringe ▶ noun **1** *the city's northern fringe* =**perimeter**, periphery, border, margin, rim, outer edge, edge, extremity, limit; outer limits, limits, borders, bounds, outskirts. **2** *blue curtains with a yellow fringe* =**edging**, edge, border, trimming, frill, flounce, ruffle.
–OPPOSITES middle.
▶ adjective *fringe theatre* =**alternative**, avant-garde, experimental, left-field, radical, extreme.
–OPPOSITES mainstream.
▶ verb **1** *a robe of gold, fringed with black* =**trim**, edge, hem, border, braid; decorate, adorn, ornament, embellish, finish. **2** *the lake is fringed by trees* =**border**, edge, bound, skirt, line, surround, enclose, encircle, circle, ring.

fringe benefit ▶ noun =**extra**, added

extra, additional benefit, privilege; *informal* perk; *formal* perquisite.

frisk ▶ verb **1** *the spaniels frisked around my ankles* =**frolic**, gambol, cavort, caper, scamper, skip, dance, romp, prance, leap, spring, hop, jump, bounce. **2** *the officer frisked him* =**search**, body-search, check.

frisky ▶ adjective =**lively**, bouncy, bubbly, perky, active, energetic, animated, zestful; playful, coltish, skittish, spirited, high-spirited, in high spirits, exuberant; *informal* full of beans, sparky; *literary* frolicsome.

fritter ▶ verb =**squander**, waste, misuse, misspend, dissipate; overspend, spend like water, be prodigal with, run through, get through; *informal* blow, splurge, pour/chuck something down the drain.
–OPPOSITES save.

frivolity ▶ noun =**light-heartedness**, levity, joking, jocularity, gaiety, fun, frivolousness, silliness, foolishness, flightiness, skittishness; superficiality, shallowness, vacuity, empty-headedness.

frivolous ▶ adjective **1** *a frivolous girl* =**skittish**, flighty, giddy, silly, foolish, superficial, shallow, feather-brained, empty-headed, pea-brained, bird-brained, vacuous, vapid; *informal* dizzy, dippy; *N. Amer. informal* ditzy. **2** *frivolous remarks* =**flippant**, glib, facetious, joking, jokey, light-hearted; fatuous, inane, senseless, thoughtless; *informal* flip. **3** *new rules to stop frivolous lawsuits* =**time-wasting**, pointless, trivial, trifling, minor.
–OPPOSITES sensible, serious.

frizzy ▶ adjective =**curly**, curled, corkscrew, ringlety, crimped, crinkly, kinky, frizzed; permed; *N. Amer. informal* nappy.
–OPPOSITES straight.

frock ▶ noun =**dress**, gown, robe, shift; garment, costume.

frog ▶ noun

WORD LINKS
young: **tadpole**

frolic ▶ verb =**play**, amuse oneself, romp, disport oneself, frisk, gambol, cavort, caper, scamper, skip, dance, prance, leap about, jump about; *dated* sport.

front ▶ noun **1** *the front of the boat* =**fore**,

foremost part, forepart, anterior, nose, head; bow, prow; foreground. **2** *a shop front* =**frontage**, face, facing, facade; window. **3** *the front of the queue* =**head**, beginning, start, top, lead. **4** *she kept up a brave front* =**appearance**, air, face, manner, demeanour, bearing, pose, exterior, veneer, (outward) show, act, pretence. **5** *the shop was a front for his real business* =**cover**, blind, disguise, facade, mask, cloak, screen, smokescreen, camouflage.
–OPPOSITES rear, back.
▶ adjective =**leading**, lead, first, foremost.
–OPPOSITES last.
▶ verb *the houses fronted on a reservoir* =**overlook**, look out on/over, face (towards), lie opposite (to); have a view of, command a view of.
■ **in front** =**ahead**, to/at the fore, at the head, up ahead, in the vanguard, in the van, in the lead, leading, coming first; at the head of the queue; *informal* up front.

frontier ▶ noun =**border**, boundary, borderline, dividing line; perimeter, limit, edge, rim; marches, bounds.

frost ▶ noun =**ice**, rime, verglas; *informal* Jack Frost; *archaic* hoar.

frosty ▶ adjective **1** *a frosty morning* =**freezing**, cold, icy-cold, bitter, bitterly cold, chill, wintry, frigid, glacial, arctic; frozen, icy; *informal* nippy; *Brit. informal* parky; *literary* rimy. **2** *a frosty look* =**cold**, frigid, icy, glacial, unfriendly, inhospitable, unwelcoming, forbidding, hostile, stony, stern, hard.

froth ▶ noun =**foam**, head; bubbles, frothiness, fizz, effervescence; lather, suds; scum.
▶ verb =**bubble**, fizz, effervesce, foam, lather; churn, seethe.

frothy ▶ adjective **1** *a frothy liquid* =**foaming**, foamy, bubbling, bubbly, fizzy, sparkling, effervescent, gassy, carbonated; sudsy. **2** *a frothy pink evening dress* =**frilly**, flouncy, lacy. **3** *a frothy woman's magazine* =**lightweight**, light, superficial, shallow, slight, insubstantial; trivial, trifling, frivolous.

frown ▶ verb **1** *she frowned at him* =**scowl**, glower, glare, lour, make a face, look daggers, give someone a black look; knit/furrow one's brows; *informal* give someone a dirty look. **2** *public displays of affection were frowned on* =**disapprove of**, view with disfavour, dislike, look askance at, not take kindly to, take a

dim view of, take exception to, object to, have a low opinion of.
–OPPOSITES smile.

frozen ▶ adjective **1** *the frozen ground* =**icy**, ice-covered, ice-bound, frosty, frosted; frozen solid, hard, (as) hard as iron. **2** *they were frozen* =**freezing**, icy, cold, chilled to the bone/marrow, numb, numbed, frozen stiff.
–OPPOSITES boiling.

frugal ▶ adjective **1** *a hard-working, frugal man* =**thrifty**, economical, careful, cautious, prudent, provident, unwasteful, sparing; abstemious, austere, self-denying, ascetic, monkish, spartan; parsimonious, miserly, niggardly, cheese-paring, penny-pinching, close-fisted; *N. Amer.* forehanded; *informal* tight-fisted, tight, stingy. **2** *their frugal breakfast* =**meagre**, scanty, scant, paltry, skimpy; plain, simple, spartan, inexpensive, cheap, economical.
–OPPOSITES extravagant, lavish.

fruit ▶ noun *the fruits of their labours* =**reward**, benefit, profit, product, return, yield, legacy, issue; result, outcome, upshot, consequence, effect.

***

WORD LINKS

seller of fruit: **fruiterer**;
(*Brit.*) **greengrocer**;
(*Brit. dated*) **costermonger**
fruit-growing: **pomiculture, orcharding, citriculture**
science of fruit-growing: **pomology**
fruit-eating: **frugivorous**
study of fruit and seeds: **carpology**

***

fruitful ▶ adjective **1** *a fruitful tree* =**fertile**, fecund, prolific, high-yielding. **2** *fruitful discussions* =**productive**, constructive, useful, of use, worthwhile, helpful, beneficial, valuable, rewarding, profitable, advantageous, successful.
–OPPOSITES barren, futile.

fruition ▶ noun =**fulfilment**, realization, actualization, materialization, achievement, attainment, accomplishment, resolution; success, completion, consummation, conclusion, close, finish, perfection, maturity.

fruitless ▶ adjective =**futile**, vain, in vain, to no avail, to no effect, idle; pointless, useless, worthless, wasted, hollow; ineffectual, ineffective; unproductive, unrewarding, profitless, unsuccessful, unavailing, barren, for naught; abortive.

−OPPOSITES productive.

fruity ▶ adjective *his fruity voice* =**deep**, rich, resonant, full, mellow, clear, strong, vibrant.

frumpy ▶ adjective =**dowdy**, frumpish, unfashionable, old-fashioned; drab, dull, shabby, scruffy; *Brit. informal* mumsy.
−OPPOSITES fashionable.

frustrate ▶ verb **1** *his plans were frustrated* =**thwart**, defeat, foil, block, stop, put a stop to, counter, spoil, check, disappoint, forestall, dash, scotch, quash, crush, derail, snooker; obstruct, impede, hamper, hinder, hamstring, stand in the way of; *informal* stymie, foul up, screw up, put the kibosh on, banjax, do for; *Brit. informal* scupper. **2** *the delays frustrated him* =**exasperate**, infuriate, annoy, anger, vex, irritate, irk, try someone's patience; *informal* aggravate, bug, miff, hack off.
−OPPOSITES help, facilitate.

frustration ▶ noun **1** *he clenched his fists in frustration* =**exasperation**, annoyance, anger, vexation, irritation; disappointment, dissatisfaction, discontentment, discontent; *informal* aggravation. **2** *the frustration of his plans* =**thwarting**, defeat, prevention, foiling, blocking, spoiling, forestalling, derailment; obstruction, hampering, hindering; failure, collapse.

fuddled ▶ adjective =**stupefied**, addled, befuddled, confused, muddled, bewildered, dazed, stunned, muzzy, groggy, foggy, fuzzy, vague, disorientated, disoriented, all at sea; *informal* dopey, woozy, woolly-minded, fazed, not with it; *N. Amer. informal* discombobulated.

fuddy-duddy ▶ noun *(informal)* =**(old)** fogey, conservative, traditionalist, conformist; fossil, dinosaur, troglodyte; *Brit.* museum piece; *informal* stick-in-the-mud, square, stuffed shirt, dodo.

fudge ▶ verb =**evade**, avoid, dodge, skirt, duck, gloss over; hedge, prevaricate, be non-committal, beat about the bush, equivocate; *Brit.* hum and haw; *informal* cop out, sit on the fence.
▶ noun =**compromise**, cover-up; spin; *informal* cop-out.

fuel ▶ noun **1** *the car ran out of fuel* =**petrol**, diesel; power; *N. Amer.* gasoline, gas. **2** *she added more fuel to the fire* =**firewood**, wood, kindling, logs; coal, coke, anthracite; oil, paraffin, kerosene.

▶ verb **1** *power stations fuelled by coal* =**power**, fire; drive, run. **2** *the rumours fuelled anxiety among MPs* =**fan**, feed, stoke up, inflame, intensify, stimulate, encourage, provoke, incite, whip up; sustain, keep alive.

fugitive ▶ noun =**escapee**, runaway, deserter, absconder; refugee.
▶ adjective =**escaped**, runaway, on the run, on the loose, at large; wanted; *informal* AWOL; *N. Amer. informal* on the lam.

fulfil ▶ verb **1** *he fulfilled a lifelong ambition* =**achieve**, attain, realize, actualize, make happen, succeed in, bring to completion, bring to fruition, satisfy. **2** *she failed to fulfil her duties* =**carry out**, perform, accomplish, execute, do, discharge, conduct; complete, finish, conclude. **3** *they fulfilled the criteria* =**meet**, satisfy, comply with, conform to, fill, answer.

fulfilled ▶ adjective =**satisfied**, content, contented, happy, pleased; serene, placid, untroubled, at ease, at peace.
−OPPOSITES discontented.

full ▶ adjective **1** *her glass was full* =**filled**, filled up, filled to capacity, brimming, brimful. **2** *streets full of people* =**crowded**, packed, crammed, congested; teeming, swarming, thronged, overrun; abounding, bursting, overflowing; *informal* jam-packed, wall-to-wall, stuffed, chock-a-block, chock-full, bursting at the seams, packed to the gunwales, awash. **3** *all the seats were full* =**occupied**, taken, in use. **4** *I'm full* =**replete**, full up, satisfied, sated, satiated; gorged, glutted; *informal* stuffed, pigged out. **5** *she'd had a full life* =**eventful**, interesting, exciting, lively, action-packed, busy, active. **6** *a full list of facilities* =**comprehensive**, thorough, exhaustive, all-inclusive, all-encompassing, all-embracing, in-depth; complete, entire, whole, unabridged, uncut. **7** *driving at full speed* =**maximum**, top. **8** *a full figure* =**plump**, (well) rounded, buxom, shapely, ample, curvaceous, voluptuous, womanly, Junoesque; *informal* busty, curvy, well upholstered, well endowed; *N. Amer. informal* zaftig. **9** *a full skirt* =**loose-fitting**, loose, baggy, voluminous, roomy, capacious, billowing.
−OPPOSITES empty, hungry, selective, thin.
▶ adverb **1** *she looked full into his face* =**directly**, right, straight, squarely, square,

dead, point-blank; *informal* bang, slap (bang), plumb. **2** *you knew full well I was leaving* =**very**, perfectly, quite; *informal* darn, damn, damned; *Brit. informal* jolly; *N. Amer. informal* darned.

■ **in full** =**in its entirety**, in toto, in total, unabridged, uncut.

■ **to the full** =**fully**, thoroughly, completely, to the utmost, to the limit, to the maximum, for all one's worth.

full-blooded ▶ adjective =**uncompromising**, all-out, out and out, committed, vigorous, strenuous, intense; unrestrained, uncontrolled, unbridled, hard-hitting, no-holds-barred.
–OPPOSITES half-hearted.

full-blown ▶ adjective =**fully developed**, full-scale, full-blooded, fully fledged, complete, total, thorough, entire; advanced.

full-grown ▶ adjective =**adult**, mature, grown-up, of age; fully grown, fully developed, fully fledged, ripe.
–OPPOSITES infant.

fullness ▶ noun **1** *the fullness of the information they provide* =**comprehensiveness**, completeness, thoroughness, exhaustiveness. **2** *the fullness of her body* =**plumpness**, roundedness, roundness, shapeliness, curvaceousness, voluptuousness, womanliness; *informal* curviness. **3** *the recording has a fullness and warmth* =**resonance**, richness, intensity, depth, vibrancy, strength, clarity.

■ **in the fullness of time** =**in due course**, eventually, in time, one day, some day, sooner or later; ultimately, finally, in the end.

full-scale ▶ adjective **1** *a full-scale model* =**full-size**, life-size. **2** *a full-scale public inquiry* =**thorough**, comprehensive, extensive, exhaustive, complete, all-out, all-encompassing, all-inclusive, all-embracing, thoroughgoing, wide-ranging, sweeping, in-depth.
–OPPOSITES small-scale.

fully ▶ adverb =**completely**, entirely, wholly, totally, quite, thoroughly, in all respects, in every respect, without reservation, without exception, to the hilt.
–OPPOSITES partly, nearly.

fully fledged ▶ adjective =**trained**, qualified, proficient, experienced; mature, fully developed, full grown; *Brit.* time-served.
–OPPOSITES novice.

fulminate ▶ verb =**protest**, rail, rage, rant, thunder, storm, declaim, inveigh, speak out, make/take a stand; denounce, decry, condemn, criticize, censure, disparage, attack, arraign; *informal* mouth off about, kick up a stink about.

fulsome ▶ adjective =**excessive**, extravagant, immoderate, over-appreciative, flattering, adulatory, fawning, unctuous, ingratiating, cloying, saccharine; enthusiastic, effusive, rapturous, glowing, gushing, profuse, generous, lavish; *informal* over the top, OTT, smarmy.

fumble ▶ verb =**grope**, fish, scrabble, feel.

fume ▶ noun *toxic fumes* =**smoke**, vapour, gas; pollution.
▶ verb *Ella was fuming at his arrogance* =**be furious**, be enraged, seethe, be livid, be incensed, boil, be beside oneself, spit; rage, rant and rave; *informal* be hot under the collar, foam at the mouth, see red.

fumigate ▶ verb =**disinfect**, purify, sterilize, sanitize, decontaminate, cleanse, clean out.
–OPPOSITES soil.

fun ▶ noun **1** *I joined in with the fun* =**enjoyment**, entertainment, amusement, pleasure; jollification, merrymaking; recreation, leisure, relaxation; good time, great time; *informal* R & R, living it up, a ball, beer and skittles. **2** *she's full of fun* =**merriment**, cheerfulness, cheeriness, jollity, joviality, jocularity, high spirits, gaiety, mirth, laughter, hilarity, glee, gladness, light-heartedness, levity. **3** *he became a figure of fun* =**ridicule**, derision, mockery, laughter, scorn, contempt.
–OPPOSITES boredom, misery.
▶ adjective *(informal) a fun evening* =**enjoyable**, entertaining, amusing, pleasurable, pleasing, agreeable, interesting.

■ **in fun** =**playfully**, in jest, as a joke, tongue in cheek, light-heartedly, for a laugh, teasingly.

■ **make fun of** =**tease**, poke fun at, rag, ridicule, mock, laugh at, taunt, jeer at, scoff at, deride; parody, lampoon, caricature, satirize; *informal* take the mickey out of, rib, kid, have on, pull someone's leg, send up; *Brit. informal* wind up; *N. Amer. informal* goof on, rag on, razz.

function ▶ noun **1** *the main function of the machine* =**purpose**, task, use, role. **2** *my function was to train the recruits* =**responsibility**, duty, role, concern, prov-

ince, activity, assignment, obligation, charge; task, job, mission, undertaking, commission. **3** *a function attended by local dignitaries* =(**social**) **event**, party, (social) occasion, affair, gathering, reception, soirée, jamboree, gala; *N. Amer.* levee; *informal* do, bash, shindig; *Brit. informal* bean-feast.
▶ **verb 1** *the system had ceased to function* =**work**, go, run, be in working/running order, operate, be operative. **2** *the museum functions as an education centre* =**act**, serve, operate, perform, work, play the role of.

functional ▶ adjective **1** *a small functional kitchen* =**practical**, useful, utilitarian, workaday, serviceable; minimalist, plain, simple, basic, modest, unadorned, unpretentious, no-frills; impersonal, characterless, soulless, institutional, clinical, austere, spartan. **2** *the machine is now fully functional* =**working**, in working order, functioning, in service, in use; going, running, operative, operating, in operation, in commission, in action, active; *informal* up and running.

functionary ▶ noun =**official**, public servant, civil servant, bureaucrat, administrator, apparatchik.

fund ▶ noun **1** *an emergency fund* =**collection**, kitty, reserve, pool, purse; endowment, foundation, trust, grant, investment; savings, nest egg; *informal* stash. **2** *short of funds* =**money**, cash; wealth, means, assets, resources, savings, capital, reserves, the wherewithal; *informal* dough, bread, loot, dosh; *Brit. informal* lolly, spondulicks, readies. **3** *his fund of stories* =**stock**, store, supply, accumulation, collection, bank, pool; mine, reservoir, storehouse, treasury, treasure house, hoard, repository.
▶ **verb** *we were funded by the Treasury* =**finance**, pay for, back, capitalize, sponsor, put up the money for, subsidize, underwrite, endow, support, maintain; *informal* foot the bill for, pick up the tab for; *N. Amer. informal* bankroll, stake.

fundamental ▶ adjective =**basic**, underlying, core, rudimentary, elemental, elementary, root; primary, prime, cardinal, first, principal, chief, key, central, vital, essential, important, indispensable, necessary, crucial, pivotal, critical.
–OPPOSITES secondary, unimportant.

fundamentally ▶ adverb =**essentially**, in essence, basically, at heart, at

bottom, deep down; primarily, above all, first and foremost, first of all; *informal* at the end of the day, when all is said and done.

fundamentals ▶ plural noun =**basics**, essentials, rudiments, foundations, basic principles, first principles, preliminaries; crux, heart of the matter, essence, core, heart, base, bedrock; *informal* nuts and bolts, nitty-gritty, brass tacks, ABC.

funeral ▶ noun =**burial**, interment, entombment, committal, inhumation, laying to rest; cremation.

funereal ▶ adjective =**sombre**, gloomy, mournful, melancholy, lugubrious, sepulchral, miserable, doleful, woeful, sad, sorrowful, cheerless, joyless, bleak, dismal, depressing, dreary.
–OPPOSITES cheerful.

fungus ▶ noun =**mushroom**, toadstool; mould, mildew, rust.

> **WORD LINKS**
>
> *science of fungi:* **mycology**
> *fungus-eating:* **fungivorous**
> *chemical that destroys fungus:*
>   **fungicide**

funnel ▶ noun **1** *we poured it through a funnel* =**tube**, pipe, conduit. **2** *smoke poured from the ship's funnels* =**chimney**, flue.
▶ **verb** *money was funnelled back into Europe* =**channel**, feed, direct, convey, move, pass; pour, filter.

funny ▶ adjective **1** *a very funny film* =**amusing**, humorous, witty, comic, comical, droll, facetious, jocular, jokey; hilarious, hysterical, riotous, uproarious; entertaining, diverting, sparkling, scintillating; silly, farcical, slapstick; *informal* side-splitting, rib-tickling, laugh-a-minute, wacky, zany, waggish, off the wall, a scream, rich, priceless. **2** *a funny coincidence* =**strange**, peculiar, odd, queer, weird, bizarre, curious, freakish, freak, quirky; mysterious, mystifying, puzzling, perplexing; unusual, uncommon, anomalous, irregular, abnormal, exceptional, singular, out of the ordinary, extraordinary; *Brit. informal, dated* rum. **3** *there's something funny about him* =**suspicious**, suspect, dubious, untrustworthy, questionable; *informal* shady, fishy; *Brit. informal* dodgy.
–OPPOSITES serious, unsurprising, trustworthy.

fur ▸ noun =hair, wool; coat, fleece, pelt.

WORD LINKS

fear of fur: **doraphobia**

furious ▸ adjective **1** *he was furious when we told him* =**enraged**, infuriated, irate, incensed, raging, incandescent, fuming, ranting, raving, seething, beside oneself, outraged; *informal* mad, hopping mad, wild, livid, boiling, apoplectic, on the warpath, foaming at the mouth, steamed up, in a paddy, fit to be tied; *literary* wrathful. **2** *a furious debate* =**heated**, hot, passionate, fiery; fierce, vehement, violent, wild, tumultuous, turbulent, tempestuous, stormy, acrimonious.
−OPPOSITES calm.

furnish ▸ verb **1** *the bedrooms are elegantly furnished* =**fit out**, appoint, outfit; *Brit. informal* do out. **2** *they furnished us with waterproofs* =**supply**, provide, equip, issue, kit out, present, give; *informal* fix up.

furniture ▸ noun =**furnishings**, effects; *Law* chattels; *informal* stuff, things.

furore ▸ noun =**commotion**, uproar, outcry, fuss, upset, brouhaha, palaver, pother, tempest, agitation, pandemonium, disturbance, hubbub, rumpus, tumult, turmoil; stir, excitement; *informal* song and dance, to-do, hoo-ha, hullabaloo, ballyhoo, kerfuffle, flap, stink; *Brit. informal* carry-on.

furrow ▸ noun **1** *furrows in a field* =**groove**, trench, rut, trough, channel. **2** *the furrows on either side of her mouth* =**wrinkle**, line, crease, crinkle, crow's foot.
▸ verb *his brow furrowed* =**wrinkle**, crease, line, crinkle, pucker, screw up, scrunch up.

furry ▸ adjective =**hairy**, downy, fleecy, soft, fluffy, fuzzy, woolly.

further ▸ adverb *further, it gave him an alibi* =**furthermore**, moreover, what's more, also, additionally, in addition, besides, as well, too, to boot, on top of that, over and above that, into the bargain, by the same token.
▸ adjective **1** *the further side of the field* =**more distant**, remoter, outer, farther (away/off); far, other, opposite. **2** *further information* =**additional**, more, extra, supplementary; new, fresh.
▸ verb *attempts to further his career* =**promote**, advance, forward, develop, facili-

tate, aid, assist, help, help along, boost, encourage.
−OPPOSITES impede.

furthermore ▸ adverb =**moreover**, further, what's more, also, additionally, in addition, besides, as well, too, on top of that, over and above that, into the bargain, by the same token.

furthest ▸ adjective =**most distant**, most remote, remotest, furthest/farthest away, farthest, furthermost, farthermost; outlying, outer, outermost, extreme, uttermost.
−OPPOSITES nearest.

furtive ▸ adjective =**secretive**, secret, surreptitious, clandestine, hidden, covert, conspiratorial, cloak-and-dagger, backstairs; sly, sneaky, under-the-table; *informal* hush-hush, shifty.
−OPPOSITES open.

fury ▸ noun **1** *she exploded with fury* =**rage**, anger, wrath, outrage, temper; indignation, umbrage, annoyance, exasperation; *literary* ire. **2** *the fury of the storm* =**fierceness**, ferocity, violence, turbulence, tempestuousness, savagery; severity, intensity, vehemence, force, forcefulness, power, strength.
−OPPOSITES good humour, mildness.

fuse ▸ verb **1** *a band which fuses rap with rock* =**combine**, amalgamate, put together, join, unite, marry, blend, merge, meld, mingle, integrate, intermix, intermingle, synthesize; coalesce, compound, alloy. **2** *metal fused to coloured glass* =**bond**, stick, bind, weld, solder. **3** *(Brit.) a light had fused* =**short-circuit**, stop working, trip; *informal* go, blow.
−OPPOSITES separate.

fusion ▸ noun =**blend**, combination, amalgamation, union, marrying, bonding, merging, melding, mingling, integration, intermingling, synthesis.

fuss ▸ noun **1** *what's all the fuss about?* =**ado**, excitement, agitation, stir, commotion, confusion, disturbance, brouhaha, uproar, furore, palaver, storm in a teacup; bother; *informal* hoo-ha, to-do, ballyhoo, song and dance, performance, pantomime, kerfuffle; *Brit. informal* carry-on; *N. Amer. informal* fuss and feathers. **2** *they settled in with very little fuss* =**bother**, trouble, inconvenience, effort, exertion, labour; *informal* hassle. **3** *he didn't cause any fuss* =**protest**, complaint, objection.
▸ verb *he was still fussing about his clothes* =**worry**, fret, be anxious, be agitated,

make a big thing out of; make a mountain out of a molehill; *informal* flap, be in a tizzy, be in a stew, make a meal of.

fussy ▸ adjective **1** *he's very fussy about what he eats* =**finicky**, particular, fastidious, discriminating, selective; hard to please, difficult, exacting, demanding; faddish; *informal* pernickety, choosy, picky; *Brit. informal* faddy; *N. Amer. informal* persnickety. **2** *a fussy bridal gown* =**over-elaborate**, ornate, fancy, overdone; busy, cluttered.

fusty ▸ adjective **1** *the room smelt fusty* =**stale**, musty, dusty; stuffy, airless, unventilated; damp, mildewy. **2** *a fusty conservative* =**old-fashioned**, out of date, outdated, behind the times, antediluvian, backward-looking; fogeyish; *informal* square, out of the ark.
–OPPOSITES fresh.

futile ▸ adjective =**fruitless**, vain, pointless, useless, ineffectual, ineffective, to no effect, of no use, in vain, to no avail, unavailing; unsuccessful, failed, thwarted; unproductive, unprofitable, abortive; impotent, hollow, empty, forlorn, idle, hopeless.
–OPPOSITES useful.

futility ▸ noun =**fruitlessness**, pointlessness, uselessness, ineffectiveness, inefficacy; failure, unprofitability; hollowness, emptiness, forlornness, hopelessness.

future ▸ noun **1** *plans for the future* =**time to come**, time ahead; what lies ahead. **2** *her future lay in acting* =**destiny**, fate, fortune; prospects; chances.
–OPPOSITES past.

▸ adjective **1** *a future date* =**later**, to come, following, ensuing, succeeding, subsequent, coming. **2** *his future wife* =**to be**, destined; intended, planned, prospective.

■ **in future** =**from now on**, after this, in the future, from this day forward, hence, henceforward, subsequently, in time to come; *formal* hereafter.

fuzz ▸ noun *the soft fuzz on his cheeks* =**hair**, down; fur, fluff.

fuzzy ▸ adjective **1** *her fuzzy hair* =**frizzy**, fluffy, woolly; downy, soft; *N. Amer. informal* nappy. **2** *a fuzzy picture* =**blurry**, blurred, indistinct, unclear, out of focus, misty. **3** *a fuzzy concept* =**imprecise**, unfocused, nebulous; ill-defined, indefinite, vague, hazy, loose, woolly. **4** *my mind was fuzzy* =**confused**, muddled, addled, fuddled, befuddled, groggy, disoriented, disorientated, mixed up; foggy, dizzy, bleary.

Gg

gab *(informal)* ■ **the gift of the gab** =eloquence, fluency, expressiveness, a silver tongue; persuasiveness; *informal* a way with words, blarney.

gabble ▶ verb =jabber, babble, prattle, rattle, drivel, twitter; *Brit. informal* waffle, rabbit, chunter, witter.

gadget ▶ noun =appliance, apparatus, instrument, implement, tool, utensil, contrivance, contraption, machine, mechanism, device, labour-saving device, convenience, invention; *informal* gizmo, gimmick, widget.

gaffe ▶ noun =blunder, mistake, error, slip, faux pas, indiscretion, impropriety, miscalculation, solecism; *informal* slip-up, howler, boo-boo, boner, fluff; *Brit. informal* boob, bloomer, clanger; *N. Amer. informal* blooper, goof.

gag[1] ▶ verb **1** *the government tried to gag its critics* =silence, muzzle, mute, suppress, stifle; censor, curb, check, restrain, restrict. **2** *the stench made her gag* =retch, heave.

gag[2] ▶ noun *(informal)* *he told a few gags* =joke, jest, witticism, quip, pun, double entendre; *informal* crack, wisecrack, one-liner, funny.

gaily ▶ adverb **1** *she skipped gaily along the path* =merrily, cheerfully, cheerily, happily, joyfully, joyously, light-heartedly, blithely, jauntily, gleefully. **2** *gaily painted boats* =brightly, colourfully, brilliantly. **3** *she plunged gaily into teaching* =heedlessly, unthinkingly, thoughtlessly, without thinking, carelessly; casually, nonchalantly, airily, breezily, lightly.

gain ▶ verb **1** *he gained a scholarship* =obtain, get, secure, acquire, come by, procure, attain, achieve, earn, win, capture, clinch, pick up, carry off; *informal* land, net, bag, scoop, wangle, swing, walk away/off with. **2** *they stood to gain from the deal* =profit, make money, benefit, do well out of; *informal* make a killing, milk. **3** *she gained weight* =put on, increase in. **4** *they were gaining on us* =catch up with/on, catch someone up, catch, close in on, near, approach.
−OPPOSITES lose.

gainful ▶ adjective =profitable, paid, well paid, remunerative, lucrative, moneymaking; rewarding, fruitful, worthwhile, useful, productive, constructive, beneficial, advantageous, valuable.

gait ▶ noun =walk, step, stride, pace, tread, way of walking; bearing, carriage; *Brit.* deportment.

gala ▶ noun =fête, fair, festival, carnival, pageant, jubilee, jamboree, party, celebration.

galaxy ▶ noun **1** *a distant galaxy* =star system; constellation; stars. **2** *a galaxy of TV's biggest stars* =host, multitude, array, gathering, assemblage, assembly, company, group.

gale ▶ noun **1** *a howling gale* =wind, high wind, hurricane, tornado, cyclone, whirlwind; storm, squall, tempest, typhoon; *N. Amer.* windstorm; *informal* burster, buster. **2** *gales of laughter* =peal, howl, hoot, shriek, scream, roar; outburst, burst, fit, paroxysm.

gall[1] ▶ noun *she had the gall to ask for money* =effrontery, impudence, impertinence, cheek, cheekiness, insolence, audacity, temerity, presumption, cockiness, nerve, shamelessness, disrespect, bad manners; *informal* brass neck, face, chutzpah; *Brit. informal* sauce; *N. Amer. informal* sass.

gall[2] ▶ verb *it galled him to have to sit in silence* =irritate, annoy, vex, anger, infuriate, exasperate, irk, pique, nettle, put out, displease, antagonize; *informal* aggravate, peeve, miff, rile, needle, get (to), bug, hack off, get up someone's nose, get someone's goat, get/put someone's back up, get someone's dander up, drive mad/crazy, drive round the bend/twist, drive up the wall; *Brit. informal* wind up, nark, get on someone's wick, give someone the hump; *N. Amer. informal* tee off, tick off, rankle.

gallant ▶ adjective **1** *his gallant comrades* =**brave**, courageous, valiant, bold, plucky, daring, fearless, intrepid, heroic, stout-hearted; *informal* gutsy, spunky. **2** *her gallant companion* =**chivalrous**, gentlemanly, courteous, polite, attentive, respectful, gracious, considerate, thoughtful.
−OPPOSITES cowardly, discourteous.

gallantry ▶ noun =**bravery**, courage, courageousness, valour, pluck, nerve, daring, boldness, fearlessness, heroism, stout-heartedness, mettle, grit; *informal* guts, spunk; *Brit. informal* bottle; *N. Amer. informal* moxie.

gallery ▶ noun **1** *the National Gallery* =**art gallery**, museum. **2** *they sat up in the gallery* =**balcony**, circle, upper circle; *informal* gods. **3** *a long gallery with doors along each side* =**passage**, passageway, corridor, walkway, arcade.

galling ▶ adjective =**annoying**, irritating, vexing, vexatious, infuriating, maddening, irksome, provoking, exasperating, trying, tiresome, troublesome, bothersome, displeasing, disagreeable; *informal* aggravating.

gallop ▶ verb =**rush**, race, run, sprint, bolt, dart, dash, career, charge, shoot, hurtle, hare, fly, speed, zoom, streak; *informal* tear, belt, pelt, scoot, zip, whip, hotfoot it, leg it; *Brit. informal* bomb, go like the clappers; *N. Amer. informal* barrel.
−OPPOSITES amble.

galvanize ▶ verb =**jolt**, shock, startle, impel, stir, spur, prod, urge, motivate, stimulate, electrify, excite, rouse, arouse, awaken; invigorate, fire, animate, vitalize, energize, exhilarate, thrill, dynamize, inspire; *N. Amer.* light a fire under; *informal* give someone a shot in the arm.

gambit ▶ noun =**stratagem**, scheme, plan, tactic, manoeuvre, move, course/ line of action, device; machination, ruse, trick, ploy; *Brit. informal* wheeze, wangle.

gamble ▶ verb **1** *he started to gamble* =**bet**, place/lay a bet on something; *Brit. informal* punt, have a flutter. **2** *investors are gambling that the pound will fall* =**take a chance**, take a risk; *N. Amer.* take a flyer; *informal* stick one's neck out, go out on a limb; *Brit. informal* chance one's arm.
▶ noun *I took a gamble and it paid off* =**risk**, chance, leap in the dark; pot luck.

game ▶ noun **1** *the children invented a new* game =**pastime**, diversion, entertainment, amusement, distraction, recreation, sport, activity. **2** *we haven't lost a game all season* =**match**, contest, fixture, meeting; tie, play-off. **3** *he's in the banking game* =**business**, profession, occupation, trade, industry, line (of work/business); *informal* racket.
▶ adjective *I need a bit of help — are you game?* =**willing**, prepared, ready, disposed, of a mind; eager, keen, enthusiastic.

gamut ▶ noun =**range**, spectrum, span, scope, sweep, compass, area, breadth, reach, extent, catalogue, scale; variety.

gang ▶ noun **1** *a gang of teenagers* =**band**, group, crowd, pack, horde, throng, mob, herd, swarm, troop; company, gathering; *informal* posse, bunch, gaggle, load. **2** *(informal) John's one of our gang* =**circle**, set, group, clique, in-crowd, coterie, lot, ring; *informal* crew. **3** *a gang of workmen* =**crew**, team, group, squad, shift, detachment, unit.
■ **gang up** =**conspire**, cooperate, work together, act together, combine, join forces, team up, get together, unite, ally.

gangling, gangly ▶ adjective =**lanky**, rangy, tall, thin, skinny, spindly, stringy, bony, angular, scrawny, spare; awkward, uncoordinated, ungainly, gawky, inelegant, graceless, ungraceful.
−OPPOSITES squat.

gangster ▶ noun =**hoodlum**, racketeer, thug, villain, criminal; Mafioso; *informal* mobster, crook, tough; *N. Amer. informal* hood.

gaol ▶ noun *(Brit. dated)*. See JAIL.

gaoler ▶ noun *(Brit. dated)*. See JAILER.

gap ▶ noun **1** *a gap in the shutters* =**opening**, aperture, space, breach, chink, slit, crack, crevice, cranny, cavity, hole, orifice, perforation, break, fracture, rift, rent, fissure, cleft, divide. **2** *a gap between meetings* =**pause**, intermission, interval, interlude, break, breathing space, breather, respite, hiatus; *N. Amer.* recess. **3** *a gap in our records* =**omission**, blank, lacuna. **4** *the gap between rich and poor* =**chasm**, gulf, rift, split, separation, breach; contrast, difference, disparity, divergence, imbalance.

gape ▶ verb **1** *she gaped at him in astonishment* =**stare**, stare open-mouthed, goggle, gaze, ogle; *informal* rubberneck; *Brit. informal* gawk, gawp. **2** *a jacket which gaped* *at every seam* =**open**, yawn; part, split.

gaping ▶ adjective =**cavernous**, yawning, wide, broad; vast, huge, enormous, immense.

garbage (N. Amer.) ▶ noun **1** *the garbage was taken away* =**rubbish**, refuse, waste, detritus, litter, junk, scrap; scraps, scourings, leftovers, remains; *N. Amer.* trash; *Austral./NZ* mullock. **2** *what he says is garbage* =**rubbish**, nonsense, balderdash, claptrap, twaddle; dross; *informal* hogwash, baloney, tripe, bilge, bull, bunk, poppycock, rot, piffle, dreck; *Brit. informal* tosh, codswallop, cobblers, stuff and nonsense.

garble ▶ verb =**mix up**, muddle, jumble, confuse, obscure, distort.

garden ▶ noun (**gardens**) =**park**, estate, grounds.
  ■ **lead someone up the garden path** (*informal*) =**deceive**, mislead, delude, hoodwink, dupe, trick, beguile, take in, fool, pull the wool over someone's eyes, gull; *informal* con, pull a fast one on, string along, take for a ride, put one over on.

WORD LINKS

relating to gardens: **horticultural**

gargantuan ▶ adjective =**huge**, enormous, vast, gigantic, giant, massive, colossal, mammoth, immense, mighty, monumental, mountainous, titanic, towering, tremendous, king-size(d), prodigious; *informal* mega, monster, whopping, humongous, jumbo; *Brit. informal* whacking, ginormous.
  –OPPOSITES tiny.

garish ▶ adjective =**gaudy**, lurid, loud, harsh, glaring, showy, glittering, brassy, brash; tasteless, vulgar; *informal* flash, flashy, tacky.
  –OPPOSITES drab.

garland ▶ noun =**wreath**, ring, circle, crown.
  ▶ verb =**festoon**, wreathe, swathe, hang; adorn, deck, bedeck, array.

garment ▶ noun =**item/article of clothing**; (**garments**) clothes, clothing, dress, garb, outfit, costume, attire; *informal* get-up, rig-out, gear, togs, duds; *N. Amer. informal* threads; *formal* apparel.

garner ▶ verb =**gather**, collect, accumulate, amass, get together, assemble.

garnish ▶ verb =**decorate**, adorn, ornament, trim, dress, embellish.

▶ noun =**decoration**, adornment, ornament, embellishment, enhancement, finishing touch.

garrison ▶ noun **1** *the English garrison had left* =**troops**, militia, soldiers, forces; force, detachment, unit. **2** *forces from three garrisons* =**fortress**, fort, camp, command post, base, station; barracks.
  ▶ verb *troops were garrisoned in York* =**station**, post, deploy, assign; base, site, place, position; billet.

garrulous ▶ adjective =**talkative**, loquacious, voluble, verbose, chatty, gossipy; effusive, expansive, forthcoming, conversational, communicative; *informal* mouthy, gabby, having the gift of the gab; *Brit. informal* able to talk the hind legs off a donkey.
  –OPPOSITES taciturn.

gash ▶ noun =**laceration**, cut, wound, injury, slash, tear; slit, split, rip, rent; scratch; *Medicine* lesion.
  ▶ verb =**lacerate**, cut (open), wound, injure, hurt, slash, tear, gouge, puncture, slit, split, rend; scratch.

gasp ▶ verb **1** *I gasped in surprise* =**catch/draw in one's breath**, gulp. **2** *he fell on the ground, gasping* =**pant**, puff, puff and blow, wheeze, breathe hard/heavily, choke, fight for breath.
  ▶ noun *a gasp of dismay* =**gulp**; exclamation, cry.

gate ▶ noun **1** *wooden gates* =**barrier**, turnstile. **2** *she went through the gate* =**gateway**, doorway, entrance, exit; door, portal; *N. Amer.* entryway.

gather ▶ verb **1** *we gathered in the hotel lobby* =**congregate**, assemble, meet, collect, come/get together, convene, muster, rally, converge. **2** *he gathered his family together* =**summon**, call together, bring together, assemble, convene, rally, round up, muster, marshal. **3** *they gathered the crops* =**harvest**, reap, crop; pick, pluck; collect. **4** *I gather he's a footballer* =**understand**, believe, be led to believe, conclude, deduce, infer, assume, take it, surmise; hear, learn, discover. **5** *her dress was gathered at the waist* =**pleat**, pucker, tuck, fold, ruffle.
  –OPPOSITES disperse.

gathering ▶ noun **1** *she addressed the gathering* =**assembly**, meeting, convention, rally, council, congress; congregation, audience, crowd, group, throng, mass, multitude; *informal* get-together. **2** *the gathering of information* =**collecting**, collection, garnering, amassing, accumulation, accrual.

gauche ▸ adjective =**awkward**, gawky, inelegant, graceless, ungraceful, ungainly, maladroit, inept; unsophisticated, uncultured, uncultivated, unrefined.
−OPPOSITES elegant, sophisticated.

gaudy ▸ adjective =**garish**, lurid, loud, glaring, harsh, showy, glittering, brassy, ostentatious; tasteless, vulgar, unattractive; informal flash, flashy, tacky.
−OPPOSITES drab, tasteful.

gauge ▸ noun **1** the temperature gauge =**meter**, measure; indicator, dial, scale, display. **2** an important gauge of economic activity =**measure**, indicator, barometer, point of reference, guide, guideline, touchstone, yardstick, benchmark, criterion, test. **3** guitar strings of different gauges =**size**, diameter, thickness; bore, calibre.
▸ verb **1** astronomers can gauge the star's brightness =**measure**, calculate, compute, work out, determine, ascertain; count, weigh, quantify, put a figure on. **2** it is hard to gauge how effective the ban was =**assess**, evaluate, determine, estimate, form an opinion of, appraise, weigh up, get the measure of, judge, guess; informal size up.

gaunt ▸ adjective =**haggard**, drawn, thin, lean, skinny, spindly, spare, bony, angular, raw-boned, pinched, hollow-cheeked, scrawny, scraggy, as thin as a rake, cadaverous, skeletal, emaciated, skin and bone; wasted, withered; informal like a bag of bones.
−OPPOSITES plump.

gauzy ▸ adjective =**translucent**, transparent, sheer, see-through, fine, delicate, flimsy, filmy, gossamer, diaphanous, wispy, thin, light, floaty, insubstantial.
−OPPOSITES opaque, thick.

gawky ▸ adjective =**awkward**, ungainly, gangling, gauche, maladroit, clumsy, inelegant, uncoordinated, graceless, ungraceful; unsophisticated, unconfident.
−OPPOSITES graceful.

gay ▸ adjective **1** gay men and women =**homosexual**, lesbian; informal queer, pink, swinging the other way, homo. **2** (dated) her children were carefree and gay =**cheerful**, cheery, merry, jolly, carefree, jovial, glad, happy, in good/high

spirits, joyful, exuberant, animated, lively, vivacious, buoyant, bouncy, bubbly, perky, effervescent, playful; informal chirpy. **3** (dated) having a gay old time =**jolly**, merry, uproarious, rollicking, entertaining, enjoyable, convivial. **4** (dated) gay checked curtains =**bright**, brightly coloured, vivid, vibrant; multicoloured; flamboyant, showy, gaudy.
−OPPOSITES heterosexual, gloomy.
▸ noun gays were accepted =**homosexual**, lesbian; informal queer, homo, queen, pansy, nancy, dyke, butch, femme.

gaze ▸ verb =**stare**, gape, goggle, eye, look, study, scrutinize, take a good look; ogle, leer; informal gawk, rubberneck; Brit. informal gawp; N. Amer. informal eyeball.
▸ noun =**stare**, fixed look, gape; regard, inspection, scrutiny.

gazebo ▸ noun =**summer house**, pavilion, belvedere.

gear ▸ noun (informal) **1** his fishing gear =**equipment**, apparatus, paraphernalia, articles, appliances; tools, utensils, implements, instruments; stuff, things; kit, rig, tackle; trappings, appurtenances, accoutrements, regalia; Brit. informal clobber, gubbins. **2** I'll go back to my hotel and pick up my gear =**belongings**, possessions, effects, paraphernalia, bits and pieces, bits and bobs, bags, baggage; informal things, stuff, kit; Brit. informal clobber. **3** the best designer gear =**clothes**, clothing, garments, outfits, attire, garb; dress, wear; informal togs, duds, get-up; Brit. informal clobber, kit; N. Amer. informal threads; formal apparel.

gel, jell ▸ verb **1** leave the mixture to gel =**set**, stiffen, solidify, thicken, harden. **2** things started to gel very quickly =**take shape**, fall into place, come together, take form, work out; crystallize.

gelatinous ▸ adjective =**jelly-like**, glutinous, viscous, sticky, gluey, gummy, slimy; informal gooey, gunky.

gem ▸ noun **1** rubies and other gems =**jewel**, precious stone, semi-precious stone, stone. **2** she's a real gem =**treasure**, prize, find; informal one in a million, the bee's knees, the best/greatest.

genealogy ▸ noun =**lineage**, line (of descent), family tree, bloodline; pedigree, ancestry, heritage, parentage, family, stock, blood, roots.

general ▸ adjective **1** suitable for general use =**widespread**, common, extensive, universal, wide, popular, public, main-

stream; established, conventional, traditional, orthodox, accepted. **2** *a general pay increase* = **comprehensive**, overall, across the board, blanket, umbrella, mass, wholesale, sweeping, broadranging, inclusive, company-wide; universal, global, worldwide, nationwide. **3** *the general practice* = **usual**, customary, habitual, traditional, normal, conventional, typical, standard, regular; familiar, accepted, prevailing, routine, runof-the-mill, established, everyday, ordinary, common. **4** *a general description* = **broad**, imprecise, inexact, rough, loose, approximate, unspecific, vague, woolly, indefinite; *N. Amer. informal* ballpark.
−OPPOSITES restricted, localized, specialist, exceptional, detailed.

generality ▶ noun = **generalization**, general statement, general principle, sweeping statement; abstraction.
−OPPOSITES specific.

generally ▶ adverb **1** *summers were generally hot* = **normally**, in general, as a rule, by and large, more often than not, almost always, mainly, mostly, for the most part, predominantly, on the whole; usually, habitually, customarily, typically, ordinarily, commonly. **2** *the idea was generally accepted* = **widely**, commonly, extensively, universally, popularly.

generate ▶ verb = **cause**, give rise to, lead to, result in, bring about, create, make, produce, engender, spawn, precipitate, prompt, provoke, trigger, spark off, stir up, induce, promote, foster.

generation ▶ noun **1** *people of the same generation* = **age**, age group, peer group. **2** *generations ago* = **ages**, years, aeons, a long time, an eternity; *informal* donkey's years; *Brit. informal* yonks. **3** *the next generation of computers* = **crop**, batch, wave, range. **4** *the generation of new ideas* = **creation**, production, initiation, origination, inception.

generic ▶ adjective **1** *a generic term* = **general**, common, collective, nonspecific, inclusive, all-encompassing, broad, comprehensive, blanket, umbrella. **2** *generic drugs* = **unbranded**, nonproprietary.
−OPPOSITES specific.

generosity ▶ noun **1** *the generosity of our host* = **liberality**, lavishness, magnanimity, munificence, open-handedness, unselfishness; kindness, benevolence, altruism, charity, big-heartedness, goodness. **2** *the generosity of the portions* = **abundance**, plentifulness, lavishness, liberality, largeness, size.

generous ▶ adjective **1** *she is generous with money* = **liberal**, lavish, magnanimous, giving, open-handed, bountiful, unselfish, ungrudging, free, indulgent. **2** *a generous amount of fabric* = **lavish**, plentiful, copious, ample, liberal, large, great, abundant, profuse, bumper, prolific; *informal* a gogo, galore.
−OPPOSITES mean, selfish, meagre.

genesis ▶ noun = **origin**, source, root, beginning, start.

genial ▶ adjective = **friendly**, affable, cordial, amiable, warm, easy-going, approachable, sympathetic; good-natured, good-humoured, cheerful; neighbourly, hospitable, companionable, sociable, convivial, outgoing, gregarious; *informal* chummy, pally; *Brit. informal* matey.
−OPPOSITES unfriendly.

genitals ▶ plural noun = **private parts**, genitalia, sexual organs, reproductive organs, pudenda; crotch, groin; *informal* naughty bits, privates; *euphemistic* nether regions.

genius ▶ noun **1** *the world knew of his genius* = **brilliance**, intelligence, intellect, ability, cleverness, brains. **2** *he has a genius for organization* = **talent**, gift, flair, aptitude, facility, knack, bent, ability, expertise, capacity, faculty; strength, forte, brilliance. **3** *he is a genius* = **brilliant person**, gifted person, mastermind, Einstein, intellectual, brain; prodigy; *informal* egghead, bright spark; *Brit. informal* brainbox, clever clogs; *N. Amer. informal* brainiac.
−OPPOSITES stupidity, dunce.

genocide ▶ noun = **mass murder**, annihilation, extermination, elimination, liquidation, eradication, butchery; ethnic cleansing, holocaust.

genre ▶ noun = **category**, class, classification, group, set, list; type, sort, kind, variety, style, model, school, ilk.

genteel ▶ adjective = **refined**, respectable, well mannered, courteous, polite, proper, correct, seemly; well bred, cultured, sophisticated, ladylike, gentlemanly, dignified, gracious; affected; *Brit. informal* posh.
−OPPOSITES uncouth.

gentle ▶ adjective **1** *his manner was gentle*

=**kind**, tender, sympathetic, considerate, understanding, compassionate, benevolent; humane, lenient, merciful, clement; mild, placid, serene, sweet-tempered. **2** *a gentle breeze* =**light**, soft. **3** *a gentle slope* =**gradual**, slight, easy. –OPPOSITES brutal, strong, steep.

gentleman ▶ noun =**man**; nobleman; *informal* gent.

genuine ▶ adjective **1** *a genuine Picasso* =**authentic**, real, actual, original, bona fide, true, veritable; attested, undisputed; *informal* pukka, the real McCoy, the real thing, kosher; *Austral./NZ informal* dinkum. **2** *a very genuine person* =**sincere**, honest, truthful, straightforward, direct, frank, candid, open; artless, natural, unaffected; *informal* straight, upfront, on the level; *N. Amer. informal* on the up and up. –OPPOSITES bogus, insincere.

genus ▶ noun =**type**, sort, kind, genre, style, variety, category, class; breed, brand, family.

germ ▶ noun **1** *this detergent kills germs* =**microbe**, micro-organism, bacillus, bacterium, virus; *informal* bug. **2** *the germ of an idea* =**start**, beginning(s), seed, embryo, bud, root, rudiment; origin, source, potential; core, nucleus, kernel, essence.

> WORD LINKS
>
> *substance that destroys germs:* **germicide**

germane ▶ adjective =**relevant**, pertinent, applicable, apposite. –OPPOSITES irrelevant.

Germany ▶ noun

> WORD LINKS
>
> *relating to Germany:* **Germanic, Teutonic**
> *fear of German people and things:* **Germanophobia, Teutophobia**

germinate ▶ verb **1** *the grain is allowed to germinate* =**sprout**, shoot (up), bud; develop, grow, spring up. **2** *the idea began to germinate* =**develop**, take root, grow, emerge, evolve, mature, expand, advance, progress.

gestation ▶ noun =**pregnancy**, incubation; development, maturation.

gesticulate ▶ verb =**gesture**, signal, motion, wave, sign.

gesticulation ▶ noun =**gesturing**, gesture, hand movement, signals, signs; wave, indication; body language.

gesture ▶ noun **1** *a gesture of surrender* =**signal**, sign, motion, indication, gesticulation. **2** *a symbolic gesture* =**action**, act, deed, move.
▶ verb *he gestured to her* =**signal**, motion, gesticulate, wave, indicate, give a sign.

get ▶ verb **1** *where did you get that hat?* =**acquire**, obtain, come by, receive, gain, earn, win, come into, be given; buy, purchase, procure, secure; gather, collect, pick up, hook, net, land; achieve, attain; *informal* get one's hands on, get one's mitts on, get hold of, grab, bag, score. **2** *I got your letter* =**receive**. **3** *your tea's getting cold* =**become**, grow, turn, go. **4** *get the children from school* =**fetch**, collect, go/come for, call for, pick up, bring, deliver, convey, ferry, transport. **5** *the chairman gets £650,000 a year* =**earn**, be paid, take home, bring in, make, receive, collect, gross; *informal* pocket, bank, rake in, net, bag. **6** *did the police get him?* =**apprehend**, catch, arrest, capture, seize; *informal* collar, grab, nab, nail, run in, pinch, bust, pick up, pull in; *Brit. informal* nick. **7** *I got a taxi* =**travel by/on/in**; take, catch, use. **8** *she got flu* =**succumb to**, develop, go/come down with, fall victim to, be struck down with, be afflicted by/with; become infected with, catch, contract, fall ill with; *Brit.* go down with; *informal* take ill with; *N. Amer. informal* take sick with. **9** *I got him on the phone* =**contact**, get in touch with, communicate with, make contact with, reach; speak to, talk to; *informal* get hold of. **10** *I didn't get what he said* =**hear**, catch, make out, follow, take in. **11** *I don't get the joke* =**understand**, comprehend, grasp, see, fathom, follow, perceive, apprehend, unravel, decipher; *informal* get the drift of, catch on to, latch on to, figure out; *Brit. informal* twig, suss. **12** *we got there early* =**arrive**, reach, come, make it, turn up, appear, enter, present oneself, come along, materialize, show one's face; *informal* show (up), roll in/up. **13** *we got her to agree* =**persuade**, induce, prevail on, influence; talk into, cajole into. **14** *I'll get supper* =**prepare**, get ready, cook, make; *informal* fix, rustle up; *Brit. informal* knock up. **15** *what gets me is how selfish she is* =**annoy**, irritate, exasperate, anger, irk, vex, provoke, incense, infuriate,

madden, try someone's patience, ruffle someone's feathers; *informal* aggravate, peeve, miff, rile, get to, needle, hack off, get someone's back up, get on someone's nerves, get up someone's nose, get someone's goat, drive mad, make someone see red; *Brit. informal* wind up, nark, get someone's wick; *N. Amer. informal* tee off, tick off.
−OPPOSITES give, send, take, leave.
■ **get about** =move about, move around, travel.
■ **get something across** =communicate, get over, impart, convey, transmit, make clear, express.
■ **get ahead** =prosper, flourish, thrive, do well; succeed, make it, advance, get on/go up in the world, make good; *informal* go places, get somewhere, make the big time.
■ **get along** =be friendly, be compatible, get on; agree, see eye to eye, concur, be in accord, be on the same wavelength; *informal* hit it off.
■ **get around** =travel, circulate, socialize.
■ **get at** =access, get to, reach, touch.
■ **get away** =escape, run away/off, break out, break free, break loose, bolt, flee, take flight, make off, take off, decamp, abscond, make a run for it; slip away, sneak away; *informal* skedaddle, do a disappearing act, scarper, leg it; *Brit. informal* do a bunk, do a runner.
■ **get someone down** =depress, sadden, make unhappy, dishearten, demoralize, discourage, crush, weigh down, oppress, upset, distress; *informal* give someone the blues, make someone fed up.
■ **get by** =manage, cope, survive, exist, subsist, muddle through/along, scrape by, make ends meet, make do, keep the wolf from the door; *informal* make out.
■ **get off** *Sally got off the bus* =alight (from), step off, dismount (from), descend (from), disembark (from), leave, exit.
■ **get on 1** *we got on the train* =board, enter, step aboard, climb on, mount, ascend, catch; *informal* hop on, jump on. **2** *how are you getting on?* =fare, manage, progress, get along, do, cope, survive; *informal* make out. **3** *he got on with his job* =continue, proceed, go ahead, carry/go/press on, persist, persevere; keep at; *informal* stick with/at. **4** *we don't get on. See* GET ALONG.
■ **get out of** =evade, dodge, shirk,

avoid, escape, sidestep; *informal* duck (out of), wriggle out of, cop out of; *Austral./NZ informal* duck-shove.
■ **get something over**. *See* GET SOMETHING ACROSS.
■ **get round someone** =cajole, persuade, wheedle, coax, prevail on, win over, bring round, sway, beguile, charm, inveigle, influence, won; *informal* sweet-talk, soft-soap, butter up, twist someone's arm.
■ **get together 1** *get together the best people* =collect, gather, assemble, bring together, rally, muster, marshal, convene. **2** *we must get together soon* =meet (up), rendezvous, see each other, socialize.
■ **get up** =get out of bed, rise, stir, rouse oneself; *informal* surface; *formal* arise.

getaway ▶ noun =escape, breakout, bolt for freedom, flight; disappearance, vanishing act; *Brit. informal* flit.

get-together ▶ noun =party, meeting, gathering, social event; *informal* do, bash; *Brit. informal* rave-up, knees-up, jolly, bunfight, beano.

ghastly ▶ adjective **1** *a ghastly murder* =terrible, frightful, horrible, grim, awful; horrifying, shocking, appalling; dreadful, horrendous, monstrous, gruesome, grisly. **2** *(informal) a ghastly building* =unpleasant, objectionable, disagreeable, distasteful, awful, terrible, dreadful, frightful, detestable, insufferable, vile; *informal* horrible, horrid.
−OPPOSITES pleasant, charming.

ghost ▶ noun =spectre, phantom, wraith, spirit, presence; apparition; *informal* spook.

> WORD LINKS
> *fear of ghosts:* **phasmophobia**

ghostly ▶ adjective =spectral, ghost-like, phantom, wraithlike; unearthly, unnatural, supernatural; insubstantial, shadowy; eerie, weird, uncanny; frightening, spine-chilling, hair-raising, blood-curdling, terrifying, chilling, sinister; *informal* creepy, scary, spooky.

ghoulish ▶ adjective =macabre, grisly, gruesome, grotesque, ghastly; unhealthy, unwholesome.

giant ▶ noun =colossus, behemoth, mammoth, monster; *informal* jumbo.

–OPPOSITES dwarf.

▶ adjective =**huge**, colossal, massive, enormous, gigantic, mammoth, vast, immense, monumental, mountainous, titanic, towering, king-size(d), gargantuan; *informal* mega, monster, whopping, humongous, jumbo, hulking, bumper; *Brit. informal* ginormous.
–OPPOSITES miniature.

gibber ▶ verb =**prattle**, babble, ramble, drivel, jabber, gabble, burble, twitter, mutter, mumble; *informal* blabber, blather, blether; *Brit. informal* witter, chunter.

gibberish ▶ noun =**nonsense**, rubbish, balderdash, blather, blether; *informal* drivel, gobbledegook, mumbo-jumbo, tripe, hogwash, baloney, bilge, bull, bunk, guff, eyewash, piffle, twaddle, poppycock; *Brit. informal* cobblers, codswallop, double Dutch, tosh; *N. Amer. informal* garbage, blathers, applesauce.

gibe ▶ noun & verb. See JIBE.

giddiness ▶ noun =**dizziness**, lightheadedness; faintness, unsteadiness, shakiness, wobbliness; *informal* wooziness, legs like jelly.

giddy ▶ adjective **1** *she felt giddy* =**dizzy**, light-headed, faint, weak, vertiginous; unsteady, shaky, wobbly, reeling; *informal* woozy. **2** *she was young and giddy* =**flighty**, silly, frivolous, skittish, irresponsible, flippant; feather-brained, scatty, thoughtless, heedless, carefree; *informal* dippy; *N. Amer. informal* ditzy.
–OPPOSITES steady, sensible.

gift ▶ noun **1** *he gave the staff a gift* =**present**, handout, donation, offering, bonus, award, endowment; tip, gratuity; *informal* prezzie, freebie, perk. **2** *a gift for music* =**talent**, flair, aptitude, facility, knack, bent, ability, expertise, capacity, capability, faculty; endowment, strength, genius, brilliance, skill.

gifted ▶ adjective =**talented**, skilful, skilled, accomplished, expert, consummate, master(ly), first-rate, able, apt, adept, proficient; intelligent, clever, bright, brilliant; precocious; *informal* crack, top-notch, ace.
–OPPOSITES inept.

gigantic ▶ adjective =**huge**, enormous, vast, giant, massive, colossal, mammoth, immense, monumental, mountainous, titanic, towering, king-size(d), gargantuan; *informal* mega, monster,

whopping, humongous, jumbo, hulking, bumper; *Brit. informal* ginormous.
–OPPOSITES tiny.

giggle ▶ verb =**titter**, snigger, snicker, tee-hee, chuckle, chortle, laugh.
▶ noun =**titter**, snigger, snicker, tee-hee, chuckle, chortle, laugh.

gimmick ▶ noun =**publicity device**, stunt, contrivance, scheme, stratagem, ploy; *informal* shtick.

gingerly ▶ adverb =**cautiously**, carefully, with care, warily, charily, delicately; hesitantly, timidly.
–OPPOSITES recklessly.

girl ▶ noun **1** *a five-year-old girl* =**female child**, daughter; schoolgirl; *Scottish & N. English* lass, lassie. See also CHILD. **2** *a tall dark girl* =**young woman**, young lady, miss; *Scottish* lass, lassie; *Irish* colleen; *informal* chick, girlie, filly; *Brit. informal* bird, bint; *N. Amer. informal* gal, broad, dame, jane, babe; *Austral./NZ informal* sheila; *literary* maid, damsel; *archaic* wench. **3** *his girl left him.* See GIRLFRIEND.

girlfriend ▶ noun =**sweetheart**, lover, partner, significant other, girl, woman; fiancée; *informal* steady; *Brit. informal* bird; *N. Amer. informal* squeeze; *dated* lady (friend), lady-love, betrothed.

girlish ▶ adjective =**girlie**, youthful, childish, immature; feminine.

gist ▶ noun =**essence**, substance, central theme, heart of the matter, nub, kernel, marrow, meat, crux; thrust, drift, sense, meaning, significance, import; *informal* nitty-gritty.

give ▶ verb **1** *he gave them £2000* =**present with**, provide with, supply with, furnish with, let someone have; hand (over), offer, proffer; award, grant, bestow, accord, confer, make over; donate, contribute, put up. **2** *can I give him a message?* =**convey**, pass on, impart, communicate, transmit; send, deliver, relay; tell. **3** *a baby given into their care* =**entrust**, commit, consign, assign; *formal* commend. **4** *he gave his life for them* =**sacrifice**, give up, relinquish; devote, dedicate. **5** *he gave her time to think* =**allow**, permit, grant, accord; offer. **6** *this leaflet gives our opening times* =**show**, display, set out, indicate, detail, list. **7** *garlic gives flavour* =**produce**, yield, afford, impart, lend. **8** *he gave a party* =**organize**, arrange, lay on, throw, host, hold, have, provide. **9** *Dominic gave a bow*

=**perform**, execute, make, do. **10** *she gave a shout* =**utter**, let out, emit, produce, make. **11** *he gave Harry a black eye* =**administer**, deliver, deal, inflict, impose. **12** *the door gave* =**give way**, cave in, collapse, break, fall apart; bend, buckle.
–OPPOSITES receive, take.

▶ **noun** *(informal) there isn't enough give in the jacket* =**elasticity**, flexibility, stretch; slack, play.

■ **give someone away** =**betray**, inform on; *informal* split on, rat on, peach on, do the dirty on, blow the whistle on, sell down the river; *Brit. informal* grass on, shop; *N. Amer. informal* rat out, finger; *Austral./NZ informal* dob on.

■ **give in** =**capitulate**, concede defeat, admit defeat, give up, surrender, yield, submit, back down, give way, defer, relent, throw in the towel/sponge.

■ **give something off/out** =**emit**, produce, send out, throw out; discharge, release, exude, vent.

■ **give something out** =**distribute**, issue, hand out, pass round, dispense; dole out, dish out, mete out; allocate, allot, share out.

■ **give up**. See GIVE IN.

■ **give something up** =**stop**, cease, discontinue, desist from, abstain from, cut out, renounce, forgo, resign from, stand down from; *informal* quit, kick, swear off, leave off, pack in, lay off; *Brit. informal* jack in.

give and take ▶ **noun** =**compromise**, concession; cooperation, reciprocity, teamwork, interplay.

given ▶ **adjective** *a given number of years* =**specified**, stated, designated, set, particular, specific; prescribed, agreed, appointed, prearranged, predetermined.
–OPPOSITES unspecified.

▶ **preposition** *given the issue's complexity, a summary is difficult* =**considering**, in view of, bearing in mind, in the light of; assuming.

■ **given to** =**prone**, liable, inclined, disposed, predisposed.

glad ▶ **adjective 1** *I'm really glad you're coming* =**pleased**, happy, delighted, thrilled, overjoyed, cock-a-hoop, elated; gratified, grateful, thankful; *informal* tickled pink, over the moon; *Brit. informal* chuffed; *N. English informal* made up; *Austral. informal* wrapped. **2** *I'd be glad to help* =**willing**, eager, happy, pleased, delighted; ready, prepared.
–OPPOSITES dismayed, reluctant.

gladden ▶ **verb** =**delight**, please, make happy, elate; cheer (up), hearten, buoy up, give someone a lift, uplift; gratify; *informal* tickle someone pink, buck up.
–OPPOSITES sadden.

gladly ▶ **adverb** =**with pleasure**, happily, cheerfully; willingly, readily, eagerly, freely, ungrudgingly.

glamorous ▶ **adjective 1** *a glamorous woman* =**beautiful**, elegant, chic, stylish, fashionable; *informal* classy, glam. **2** *a glamorous lifestyle* =**exciting**, glittering, glossy, colourful, exotic; *informal* ritzy, glitzy, jet-setting.
–OPPOSITES dowdy, dull.

glamour ▶ **noun 1** *she had undeniable glamour* =**beauty**, allure, elegance, chic, style; charisma, charm, magnetism. **2** *the glamour of TV* =**allure**, attraction, fascination, charm, magic, romance, mystique, spell; excitement, thrill, glitter, the bright lights; *informal* glitz, glam.

glance ▶ **verb 1** *Rachel glanced at him* =**look briefly**, look quickly, peek, peep; glimpse; *Scottish* keek; *informal* have a gander; *Brit. informal* take a dekko, have a shufti, have a butcher's; *Austral./NZ informal* squiz. **2** *I glanced through the report* =**read quickly**, scan, skim, leaf, flick, flip, thumb, browse; dip into. **3** *a bullet glanced off the wall* =**ricochet**, rebound, be deflected, bounce.

▶ **noun** *a glance at his watch* =**peek**, peep, brief look, quick look, glimpse; *Scottish* keek; *informal* gander; *Brit. informal* dekko, shufti, butcher's; *Austral./NZ informal* squiz, geek.

glare ▶ **verb** *she glared at him* =**scowl**, glower, look daggers, frown, lour, give someone a black look, look threateningly; *informal* give someone a dirty look.

▶ **noun 1** *a cold glare* =**scowl**, glower, angry stare, frown, black look, threatening look; *informal* dirty look. **2** *the glare of the lights* =**blaze**, dazzle, shine, beam; brilliance.

glaring ▶ **adjective 1** *glaring lights* =**dazzling**, blinding, blazing, strong, harsh. **2** *a glaring omission* =**obvious**, conspicuous, unmistakable, inescapable, unmissable, striking; flagrant, blatant, outrageous, gross, overt, patent, transparent, manifest; *informal* standing/sticking out like a sore thumb.
–OPPOSITES soft, minor.

glass ▶ noun **1** *a glass of water* =**tumbler**. **2** *we sell china and glass* =**glassware**, crystal, crystalware.

┌─────────────────────────────────┐
│ **WORD LINKS** │
│ *relating to glass:* **vitreous** │
│ *fear of glass:* **nerophobia** │
│ *glass-fitter:* **glazier** │
└─────────────────────────────────┘

glasses ▶ plural noun =**spectacles**; *N. Amer.* eyeglasses; *informal* specs.

glasshouse ▶ noun =**greenhouse**, hothouse, conservatory.

glassy ▶ adjective **1** *the glassy surface of the lake* =**smooth**, mirror-like, gleaming, shiny, glossy, vitreous; slippery, icy; calm, still, flat. **2** *a glassy stare* =**expressionless**, glazed, blank, vacant, fixed, motionless; emotionless, impassive, lifeless, wooden.
–OPPOSITES rough, expressive.

glaze ▶ verb **1** *pastry glazed with caramel* =**cover**, coat, brush; ice, frost. **2** *his eyes glazed over* =**become glassy**, go blank; mist over, film over.
▶ noun *a cake with an apricot glaze* =**coating**, topping; icing, frosting.

gleam ▶ verb =**shine**, glimmer, glint, glitter, shimmer, sparkle, twinkle, flicker, wink, glisten, flash.
▶ noun **1** *a gleam of light* =**glimmer**, glint, shimmer, twinkle, sparkle, flicker, flash; beam, ray, shaft. **2** *the gleam of brass* =**shine**, lustre, gloss, sheen; glint, glitter, glimmer, sparkle; brilliance, radiance, glow.

glean ▶ verb =**obtain**, get, take, draw, derive, extract, cull, garner, gather; learn, find out.

glee ▶ noun =**delight**, pleasure, happiness, joy, gladness; amusement, mirth, merriment; excitement; triumph, jubilation, relish, satisfaction, gratification.
–OPPOSITES disappointment.

gleeful ▶ adjective =**delighted**, pleased, joyful, happy, glad, overjoyed; amused, mirthful, merry, exuberant; cock-a-hoop, jubilant; *informal* over the moon.

glib ▶ adjective =**slick**, pat, plausible; smooth-talking, fast-talking, silver-tongued, smooth; disingenuous, insincere, facile, shallow, superficial, flippant; *informal* flip, sweet-talking.
–OPPOSITES sincere.

glide ▶ verb **1** *a gondola glided past* =**slide**, slip, sail, float, drift, flow; coast, freewheel, roll; skim, skate. **2** *seagulls gliding*

over the waves =**soar**, wheel, plane; fly.

glimmer ▶ noun **1** *a glimmer of light* =**gleam**, glint, flicker, shimmer, glow, twinkle, ray. **2** *a glimmer of hope* =**gleam**, flicker, ray, trace, sign, suggestion, hint.

glimpse ▶ noun *a glimpse of her face* =**brief/quick look**; glance, peek, peep.
▶ verb *he glimpsed a figure* =**catch sight of**, notice, discern, spot, spy, sight, pick out, make out; *Brit. informal* clock.

glint ▶ verb =**shine**, catch the light, glitter, sparkle, twinkle, shimmer, flash.
▶ noun =**glitter**, gleam, sparkle, twinkle, glimmer, flash.

glisten ▶ verb =**shine**, sparkle, twinkle, glitter, glimmer, shimmer, wink, flash.

glitter ▶ verb *crystal glittered in the candlelight* =**shine**, sparkle, twinkle, glint, shimmer, glimmer, wink, flash, catch the light.
▶ noun *the glitter of light on the water* =**sparkle**, twinkle, glint, shimmer, glimmer, flicker, flash.

gloat ▶ verb =**delight**, relish, revel, rejoice, glory, exult, triumph, crow.

global ▶ adjective **1** *the global economy* =**worldwide**, international, world, intercontinental. **2** *a global view of the problem* =**comprehensive**, overall, general, all-inclusive, all-encompassing, universal, blanket; broad.

globe ▶ noun **1** *every corner of the globe* =**world**, earth, planet. **2** *the sun is a globe* =**sphere**, orb, ball.

gloom ▶ noun **1** *she peered into the gloom* =**darkness**, dark, dimness, blackness, shadows, shade. **2** *his gloom deepened* =**despondency**, depression, dejection, melancholy, unhappiness, sadness, glumness, gloominess, misery, sorrow, woe, wretchedness; despair, pessimism, hopelessness.
–OPPOSITES light, happiness.

gloomy ▶ adjective **1** *a gloomy room* =**dark**, shadowy, sunless, dim, sombre, dingy, dismal, dreary, murky, unwelcoming, cheerless, comfortless, funereal. **2** *Joanna looked gloomy* =**despondent**, downcast, downhearted, dejected, dispirited, disheartened, discouraged, demoralized, crestfallen; depressed, desolate, low, sad, unhappy, glum, melancholy, miserable, fed up, mournful, forlorn, morose; *informal* blue, down in the mouth, down in the dumps. **3** *gloomy forecasts about the economy* =**pessimistic**,

depressing, downbeat, disheartening, disappointing; unfavourable, bleak, bad, black, sombre, grim, cheerless, hopeless.
–OPPOSITES bright, cheerful, optimistic.

glorify ▶ verb =ennoble, exalt, elevate, dignify, enhance, promote; praise, celebrate, honour, extol, acclaim, applaud; glamorize, idealize, romanticize.

glorious ▶ adjective =wonderful, marvellous, magnificent, superb, sublime, spectacular, lovely, fine, delightful; *informal* super, great, stunning, fantastic, terrific, tremendous, sensational, heavenly, divine, gorgeous, fabulous, fab, awesome, ace; *Brit. informal* smashing; *literary* wondrous.
–OPPOSITES undistinguished, horrid.

glory ▶ noun **1** *a sport that won him glory* =renown, fame, prestige, honour, distinction, kudos, eminence, acclaim, praise; celebrity, recognition, reputation. **2** *a house restored to its former glory* =magnificence, splendour, grandeur, majesty, greatness, nobility, opulence, beauty, elegance. **3** *the glories of Vermont* =wonder, beauty, delight, marvel.
–OPPOSITES shame, obscurity, modesty.
▶ verb *we gloried in our independence* =take pleasure in, revel in, rejoice in, delight in; relish, savour; be proud of; *informal* get a kick out of, get a thrill out of.

gloss ▶ noun *the gloss of her hair* =shine, sheen, lustre, gleam, patina, brilliance, shimmer.
▶ verb *he tried to gloss over his problems* =conceal, cover up, hide, disguise, mask, veil; shrug off, brush aside, play down, minimize, understate, make light of; *informal* brush under the carpet.

glossy ▶ adjective **1** *a glossy wooden floor* =shiny, gleaming, lustrous, brilliant, glistening, satiny, smooth; polished, lacquered, glazed. **2** *a glossy magazine* =expensive, high-quality, stylish, fashionable, glamorous; *Brit.* upmarket, coffee-table; *informal* classy, glitzy.
–OPPOSITES dull, cheap.

glove ▶ noun =mitten, mitt, gauntlet.

glow ▶ verb **1** *lights glowed from the windows* =shine, gleam, glimmer, flicker, flare. **2** *a fire glowed in the hearth* =smoulder, burn. **3** *she glowed with pride* =tingle, thrill; beam.
▶ noun *the glow of the fire* =radiance, light, gleam, glimmer, incandescence; warmth, heat.

glower ▶ verb =scowl, glare, look daggers, frown, lour, give a someone black look; *informal* give someone a dirty look.

glowing ▶ adjective **1** *glowing coals* =bright, shining, radiant, incandescent, luminous; smouldering. **2** *his glowing cheeks* =rosy, pink, red, flushed, blushing; radiant, blooming, ruddy, burning. **3** *glowing colours* =vivid, vibrant, bright, brilliant, rich, intense, strong, radiant, warm. **4** *a glowing report* =complimentary, favourable, enthusiastic, admiring, rapturous; fulsome; *informal* rave.

glue ▶ noun *a tube of glue* =adhesive, gum, paste, cement; *N. Amer.* mucilage; *N. Amer. informal* stickum.
▶ verb **1** *the planks were glued together* =stick, gum, paste; fix, cement. **2** *(informal) she was glued to the television* =be riveted to, be gripped by, be hypnotized by, be mesmerized by.

glum ▶ adjective =gloomy, downcast, downhearted, dejected, despondent, crestfallen, disheartened; depressed, desolate, unhappy, doleful, melancholy, miserable, mournful, forlorn, in the doldrums, morose; *informal* fed up, blue, down in the mouth, down in the dumps.
–OPPOSITES cheerful.

glut ▶ noun =surplus, excess, surfeit, superfluity, over-abundance, superabundance.
–OPPOSITES dearth.
▶ verb =cram full, overfill, overload, oversupply, saturate, flood, inundate, deluge, swamp; *informal* stuff.

glutinous ▶ adjective =sticky, viscous; thick, stodgy; *informal* gooey, gloopy; *N. Amer. informal* gloppy.

glutton ▶ noun =gourmand, big eater; *informal* (greedy) pig, gannet, greedy guts.

gluttonous ▶ adjective =greedy, voracious, insatiable, wolfish; *informal* piggish.

gluttony ▶ noun =greed, greediness, overeating; *informal* piggishness.

gnarled ▶ adjective **1** *a gnarled tree trunk* =knobbly, knotty, knotted, gnarly, lumpy, bumpy; twisted, bent, crooked, distorted, contorted. **2** *gnarled hands* =twisted, bent, misshapen; arthritic; rough, wrinkled, wizened.

gnash ▶ verb =grind, grate, rasp, grit.

gnaw ▶ verb **1** *the dog gnawed at a bone*

=**chew**, champ, chomp, bite, munch, crunch; nibble, worry. **2** *the doubts gnawed at her* =**nag**, plague, torment, torture, trouble, distress, worry, haunt, oppress, burden, hang over, bother, fret; niggle.

go ▸ verb **1** *he's gone into town* =**move**, proceed, make one's way, advance, progress, pass; travel, journey. **2** *the road goes to London* =**extend**, stretch, reach; lead. **3** *the money will go to charity* =**be given**, be donated, be granted, be presented, be awarded; be devoted; be handed (over). **4** *it's time to go* =**leave**, depart, take oneself off, go away, withdraw, absent oneself, make an exit, exit; set off, start out, get under way, be on one's way; decamp, retreat, retire, make off, clear out, run off/away, flee; *Brit.* make a move; *informal* make tracks, push off, beat it, take off, skedaddle, scram, split, scoot; *Brit. informal* sling one's hook. **5** *all our money had gone* =**be used up**, be spent, be exhausted, be consumed, be drained, be depleted. **6** *I'd like to see my grandchildren before I go* =**die**, pass away, pass on, lose one's life, expire, breathe one's last, perish, go to meet one's maker; *informal* give up the ghost, kick the bucket, croak, buy it, turn up one's toes; *Brit. informal* snuff it, pop one's clogs; *N. Amer. informal* bite the big one, buy the farm. **7** *the bridge went* =**collapse**, give way, fall down, cave in, crumble, disintegrate. **8** *his hair had gone grey* =**become**, get, turn, grow. **9** *he heard the bell go* =**make a sound**, sound, reverberate, resound; ring, chime, peal, toll, clang. **10** *everything went well* =**turn out**, work out, develop, come out; result, end (up); *informal* pan out. **11** *those colours don't go* =**match**, harmonize, blend, be suited, be complementary, coordinate, be compatible. **12** *my car won't go* =**function**, work, run, operate.

−OPPOSITES arrive, come, return, clash.

▸ noun *(informal)* =**attempt**, try, effort, bid; *informal* shot, stab, crack, bash, whirl, whack.

■ **go about** =**set about**, begin, embark on, start, commence, address oneself to, get down to, get to work on, get going on, undertake; approach, tackle, attack; *informal* get cracking on/with.

■ **go along with** =**agree to/with**, fall in with, comply with, cooperate with, acquiesce in, assent to, follow; submit to, yield to, defer to.

■ **go away**. See GO verb sense 4.

■ **go back on** =**renege on**, break, fail to honour, default on, repudiate, retract; do an about-face; *informal* cop out (of), rat on.

■ **go down 1** *the ship went down* =**sink**, founder. **2** *interest rates are going down* =**decrease**, get lower, fall, drop, decline; plummet, plunge, slump. **3** *his name will go down in history* =**be remembered**, be recorded, be commemorated.

■ **go for 1** *I went for the tuna* =**choose**, pick, opt for, select, plump for, decide on. **2** *the man went for her* =**attack**, assault, hit, strike, beat up, assail, set upon, rush at, lash out at; *informal* lay into; *Brit. informal* have a go at, duff up; *N. Amer. informal* beat up on. **3** *he goes for older women* =**be attracted to**, like, fancy; prefer, favour, choose; *informal* have a thing about.

■ **go in for** =**take part in**, participate in, engage in, get involved in, join in, enter into, undertake, pursue; espouse, adopt, embrace.

■ **go into** =**investigate**, examine, enquire into, look into, research, probe, explore, delve into; consider, review, analyse.

■ **go off 1** *the bomb went off* =**explode**, detonate, blow up. **2** *(Brit.) the milk's gone off* =**go bad**, go stale, go sour, turn, spoil, go rancid.

■ **go on 1** *the lecture went on for hours* =**last**, continue, carry on, run on, proceed; endure, persist; take. **2** *she went on about the sea* =**talk at length**, ramble, rattle on, chatter, prattle, gabble, blether, blather, twitter; *informal* gab, yak; *Brit. informal* witter, rabbit, natter, waffle, chunter; *N. Amer. informal* run off at the mouth. **3** *I'm not sure what went on* =**happen**, take place, occur, transpire; *N. Amer. informal* go down.

■ **go out 1** *the lights went out* =**be turned off**, be extinguished; stop burning. **2** *he's going out with Kate* =**see**, take out, be someone's boyfriend/girlfriend, be involved with; *informal* date, go with; *N. Amer. informal, dated* step out with; *dated* court.

■ **go over 1** *go over the figures* =**examine**, study, scrutinize, inspect, look at/over, scan, check; analyse, appraise, review. **2** *we are going over our lines* =**rehearse**, practise, read through, run through.

■ **go round 1** *the wheels were going round* =**spin**, revolve, turn, rotate, whirl. **2** *a nasty rumour going round* =**be spread**, be circulated, be put about, circulate, pass round, be broadcast.

■ **go through 1** *the terrible things she has gone through* =**undergo**, experience, face, suffer, be subjected to, live through, endure, brave, bear, tolerate, withstand, put up with, cope with, weather. **2** *he went through hundreds of pounds* =**spend**, use up, run through, get through; waste, squander, fritter away. **3** *he went through Susie's bag* =**search**, look, hunt, rummage, rifle. **4** *I went through the report* =**examine**, study, scrutinize, inspect, look over, scan, check. **5** *the deal has gone through* =**be completed**, be concluded, be brought off; be approved.

■ **go under** =**go bankrupt**, cease trading, go into receivership, go into liquidation, become insolvent, be liquidated, be wound up, be shut (down); fail; *informal* go broke, go to the wall, go belly up, fold.

■ **go without 1** *I went without breakfast* =**do without**, deny oneself. **2** *the children did not go without* =**be deprived**, be in want, go short, go hungry, be in need.

goad ▶ verb =**provoke**, spur, prod, egg on, hound, badger, rouse, stir, move, stimulate, motivate, prompt, induce, encourage, urge, inspire; impel, pressure.

go-ahead (*informal*) ▶ noun =**permission**, consent, leave, licence, clearance; authorization, assent, agreement, approval, endorsement, sanction, blessing, the nod; *informal* the thumbs up, the OK, the green light.
▶ adjective =**enterprising**, resourceful; progressive, pioneering, forward-looking, enlightened; enthusiastic, ambitious, entrepreneurial; adventurous, dynamic; *informal* go-getting.

goal ▶ noun =**objective**, aim, end, target, design, intention, intent, plan, purpose; (holy) grail; ambition, aspiration, wish, dream, desire, hope.

goat ▶ noun

> **WORD LINKS**
>
> *relating to goats:* **caprine**
> *male:* **billygoat**
> *female:* **nannygoat**
> *young:* **kid**
> *collective noun:* **flock, herd, trip**

gobble ▶ verb =**guzzle**, bolt, gulp, devour, wolf, cram, gorge (oneself) on; *informal* tuck into, put away, demolish,

polish off, shovel down, stuff one's face (with), pig oneself (on); *Brit. informal* scoff, gollop, shift; *N. Amer. informal* scarf (down/up).

gobbledegook ▶ noun (*informal*) =**gibberish**, nonsense, rubbish, mumbo-jumbo; *N. Amer.* garbage; *Brit. informal* double Dutch; *N. Amer. informal* bushwa, applesauce.

go-between ▶ noun =**intermediary**, middleman, agent, broker, liaison, linkman, contact; negotiator, interceder, intercessor, mediator.

goblet ▶ noun =**wine glass**, chalice; glass, beaker, tumbler, cup.

goblin ▶ noun =**hobgoblin**, gnome, dwarf, troll, imp, elf, brownie, fairy, pixie, leprechaun.

god ▶ noun **1** *a gift from God* =**the Lord**, the Almighty, the Creator, the Maker, the Godhead; Allah, Jehovah, Yahweh; (God) the Father, (God) the Son, the Holy Ghost/Spirit, the Holy Trinity. **2** *sacrifices to appease the gods* =**deity**, goddess, divine being, celestial being, divinity, immortal, avatar. **3** *wooden gods* =**idol**, graven image, icon, totem, talisman, fetish, juju.

> **WORD LINKS**
>
> *relating to gods:* **divine**
> *study of God:* **theology**
> *fear of God:* **theophobia**

godforsaken ▶ adjective =**wretched**, miserable, dreary, dismal, depressing, grim, cheerless, bleak, desolate, gloomy; deserted, neglected, isolated, remote, backward; *Brit. informal* grotty.
–OPPOSITES charming.

godless ▶ adjective **1** *a godless society* =**atheistic**, unbelieving, agnostic, sceptical, heretical, faithless, irreligious, ungodly, unholy, impious, profane; infidel, heathen, idolatrous, pagan; satanic, devilish. **2** *godless pleasures* =**immoral**, wicked, sinful, wrong, evil, bad, iniquitous, corrupt; irreligious, sacrilegious, profane, blasphemous, impious; depraved, degenerate, debauched, perverted, decadent; impure.
–OPPOSITES religious, virtuous.

godly ▶ adjective =**religious**, devout, pious, reverent, believing, God-fearing, saintly, holy, prayerful, churchgoing.
–OPPOSITES irreligious.

godsend ▶ noun =**boon**, blessing,

bonus, plus, benefit, advantage, help, aid, asset; stroke of luck; *informal* perk; *formal* perquisite.
−OPPOSITES curse.

goggle ▸ verb =**stare**, gape, gaze, ogle; *informal* gawk, rubberneck; *Brit. informal* gawp.

going-over ▸ noun *(informal)* **1** *his work was subjected to a going-over* =**examination**, inspection, investigation, probe, check-up; assessment, review, analysis, appraisal, critique; *informal* once-over. **2** *the flat needs a going-over* =**clean**, dust, mop, scrub; *informal* vacuum, once-over. **3** *the thugs gave him a going-over* =**beating**, thrashing, thumping, pummelling, battering, pelting; assault, attack; *informal* doing-over, belting, bashing, pasting, walloping, clobbering, hiding.

goings-on ▸ plural noun =**events**, happenings, affairs, business; mischief, misbehaviour, misconduct, funny business; *informal* monkey business, hanky-panky, shenanigans; *Brit. informal* jiggery-pokery, carry-on; *N. Amer. informal* monkeyshines.

gold ▸ noun

> **WORD LINKS**
>
> *relating to gold:* **auric, aurous**
> *containing gold:* **auriferous**
> *fear of gold:* **aurophobia, chrysophobia**

golden ▸ adjective **1** *her golden hair* =**blond(e)**, yellow, fair, flaxen. **2** *a golden opportunity* =**excellent**, fine, superb, splendid; special, unique; favourable, opportune, promising, bright, full of promise; advantageous, profitable, valuable, providential.
−OPPOSITES dark, unhappy.

gone ▸ adjective **1** *I wasn't gone long* =**away**, absent, off, out; missing, unavailable. **2** *those days are gone* =**past**, over (and done with), no more, done, finished, ended; forgotten, dead and buried. **3** *the milk's all gone* =**used up**, consumed, finished, spent, depleted. **4** *an aunt of mine, long since gone* =**dead**, expired, departed, no more, passed on/away; *formal* deceased.
−OPPOSITES present, here, alive.

good ▸ adjective **1** *a good product* =**fine**, superior, quality, excellent, superb, outstanding, magnificent, exceptional, marvellous, wonderful, first-rate, first-class, sterling; *informal* great, OK, A1, ace, terrific, fantastic, fabulous, fab, topnotch, class, awesome, wicked; *informal,*

dated capital; *Brit. informal* smashing, brilliant, brill; *Austral. informal* beaut, bonzer; *Brit. informal, dated* spiffing, top hole. **2** *a good person* =**virtuous**, righteous, upright, upstanding, moral, ethical, principled; exemplary, law-abiding, blameless, guiltless, honourable, reputable, decent, respectable, noble, trustworthy; whiter than white, saintly, saintlike, angelic; *informal* squeaky clean. **3** *the children are good at school* =**well behaved**, obedient, dutiful, polite, courteous, respectful. **4** *a good suggestion* =**right**, correct, proper, decorous, seemly; appropriate, fitting, apt, suitable. **5** *a good driver* =**capable**, able, proficient, adept, adroit, accomplished, skilful, skilled, talented, masterly, expert; *informal* great, mean, wicked, nifty, ace; *N. Amer. informal* crackerjack. **6** *a good friend* =**close**, intimate, dear, bosom, special, best, firm, valued, treasured; loving, devoted, loyal, faithful, constant, reliable, dependable, trustworthy, trusty, true, unfailing, staunch. **7** *we had a good time* =**enjoyable**, pleasant, agreeable, pleasurable, delightful, great, nice, lovely; amusing; *informal* super, fantastic, fabulous, fab, terrific, grand; *Brit. informal* brilliant, brill, smashing; *N. Amer. informal* peachy, ducky; *Austral./NZ informal* beaut, bonzer. **8** *it was good of you to come* =**kind**, kind-hearted, generous, charitable, magnanimous, gracious; altruistic, unselfish, selfless. **9** *a good time to call* =**convenient**, suitable, appropriate, fitting, fit; opportune, timely, favourable, advantageous, expedient. **10** *milk is good for you* =**wholesome**, healthy, healthful, nourishing, nutritious, nutritional, beneficial, salubrious. **11** *good food* =**tasty**, appetizing, flavoursome, flavourful, palatable; succulent; *informal* scrumptious, delish, scrummy, yummy; *Brit. informal* moreish; *N. Amer. informal* finger-licking, nummy. **12** *a good reason* =**valid**, genuine, authentic, legitimate, sound, bona fide; convincing, persuasive, telling, potent, cogent, compelling. **13** *we waited a good hour* =**whole**, full, entire, complete, solid. **14** *a good number of them* =**considerable**, sizeable, substantial, significant; goodly, fair, reasonable; plentiful, abundant, great, large, generous; *informal* tidy. **15** *wear your good clothes* =**best**, smart, smartest, finest, nicest; special, party, Sunday, formal, dressy. **16** *good weather* =**fine**, fair, dry; bright, clear, sunny, cloudless; calm, windless; warm,

mild, balmy, clement, pleasant, nice.
−OPPOSITES bad, wicked, naughty,
poor, terrible, inconvenient, small,
scruffy.
▶ noun **1** *issues of good and evil* =**virtue**,
righteousness, goodness, morality, integrity, rectitude; honesty, truth, hon-
our, probity. **2** *it's all for your own good* =**benefit**, advantage, profit, gain, interest,
welfare, well-being.
−OPPOSITES wickedness, disadvantage.
■ **for good** *those days are gone for good*
=**forever**, permanently, for always, (for)
evermore, for ever and ever, for eternity, never to return; *N. Amer.* forevermore; *informal* for keeps.

goodbye ▶ exclamation =**farewell**,
adieu, au revoir, ciao, auf Wiedersehen,
adios; *Austral./NZ* hooray; *informal* bye, bye-
bye, so long, see you (later), later(s); *Brit.
informal* cheers, cheerio, ta-ta; *N. English
informal* ta-ra; *informal, dated* toodle-oo,
toodle-pip.

good-humoured ▶ adjective =**genial**, affable, cordial, friendly, amiable,
easy-going, approachable, good-
natured, cheerful, cheery.
−OPPOSITES grumpy.

good-looking ▶ adjective =**attractive**,
beautiful, pretty, handsome, lovely,
stunning, striking, arresting, gorgeous,
prepossessing, fetching, captivating, bewitching, beguiling, charming, enchanting, appealing, delightful; sexy,
seductive, alluring, tantalizing, irresistible, ravishing, desirable; *Scottish & N. English* bonny; *informal* fanciable, tasty, hot,
easy on the eye, drop-dead gorgeous; *Brit.
informal* fit; *N. Amer. informal* cute, foxy; *Austral./NZ informal* spunky; *literary* beauteous;
archaic comely, fair.
−OPPOSITES ugly.

good-natured ▶ adjective =**warm-
hearted**, friendly, amiable; understanding, sympathetic, easy-going, accommodating; *Brit. informal* decent.
−OPPOSITES malicious.

goodness ▶ noun **1** *he had some goodness in him* =**virtue**, good, righteousness,
morality, integrity, rectitude; honesty,
truth, truthfulness, honour; propriety,
decency, respectability, nobility,
worthiness, worth, merit; blamelessness, purity. **2** *his goodness towards us*
=**kindness**, humanity, benevolence,
graciousness; tenderness, warmth, affection, love, goodwill; sympathy, compassion, care, concern, understanding,

tolerance, generosity, charity, leniency,
clemency, magnanimity.

goods ▶ plural noun **1** *he dispatched the
goods* =**merchandise**, wares, stock, commodities, produce, products, articles.
2 *(Brit.)* *most goods went by train* =**freight**,
cargo.

goodwill ▶ noun =**benevolence**, compassion, goodness, kindness, consideration, charity, thoughtfulness, decency,
sympathy, understanding, neighbourliness.
−OPPOSITES hostility.

goose ▶ noun

┌─────────────┐
│ WORD LINKS │
└─────────────┘
male: **gander**
female: **goose**
young: **gosling**
collective noun: **gaggle** *(on land)*,
    skein/team/wedge *(in flight)*
relating to geese: **anserine**

gore[1] ▶ noun =**blood**; bloodshed,
slaughter, carnage, butchery; violence.

gore[2] ▶ verb =**pierce**, stab, stick, impale, spear.

gorge ▶ noun =**ravine**, canyon, gully,
defile, couloir; chasm, gulf; *N. English*
clough, gill; *N. Amer.* gulch, coulee.
■ **gorge oneself** =**stuff**, cram, fill; satiate, overindulge; *informal* pig.

gorgeous ▶ adjective **1** *a gorgeous girl*
=**good-looking**, attractive, beautiful,
pretty, handsome, lovely, stunning,
striking, arresting, prepossessing, fetching, captivating, charming, enchanting,
appealing, delightful; sexy, seductive,
alluring, irresistible, ravishing, desirable; *Scottish & N. English* bonny; *informal*
fanciable, tasty, hot; *Brit. informal* fit; *N.
Amer. informal* cute, foxy; *Austral./NZ informal*
spunky; *literary* beauteous; *archaic* comely,
fair. **2** *a gorgeous view* =**spectacular**,
splendid, superb, wonderful, grand, impressive, awe-inspiring, awesome,
amazing, stunning, breathtaking, incredible; *informal* sensational, fabulous,
fantastic. **3** *gorgeous uniforms* =**resplendent**, magnificent, sumptuous, luxurious, elegant, opulent; dazzling, brilliant. **4** *(informal)* *gorgeous weather*
=**excellent**, marvellous, superb, very
good, first-rate, first-class, wonderful,
magnificent, splendid; *informal* great,
glorious, terrific, fantastic, fabulous,
fab, ace; *Brit. informal* smashing, brilliant,
brill; *Austral./NZ informal* bonzer.

–OPPOSITES ugly, drab, terrible.

gory ▸ adjective =grisly, gruesome, violent, bloody, brutal, savage; ghastly, frightful, horrid, fearful, hideous, macabre, horrible, horrific.

gospel ▸ noun 1 *preaching the Gospel* =**Christianity**; the word of God, the New Testament. 2 *don't treat this as gospel* =**the truth**; fact, actual fact, a certainty.

gossamer ▸ adjective =gauzy, fine, diaphanous, delicate, filmy, floaty, wispy, thin, light, insubstantial, flimsy; translucent, transparent, see-through, sheer.

gossip ▸ noun 1 *tell me all the gossip* =news, rumour(s); scandal, hearsay; *informal* dirt, buzz; *Brit. informal* goss; *N. Amer. informal* scuttlebutt. 2 *they went for a gossip* =chat, talk, conversation, chatter, heart-to-heart, tête-à-tête, blether, blather; *informal* chit-chat, jaw, gas, confab, goss; *Brit. informal* natter, chinwag; *N. Amer. informal* gabfest; *Austral./NZ informal* yarn. 3 *she's such a gossip* =busybody, muckraker.
▸ verb 1 *she gossiped about his wife* =talk, whisper, tell tales; *informal* dish the dirt. 2 *people sat around gossiping* =chat, talk, converse, speak to each other, discuss things; *informal* gas, chew the fat, chew the rag, jaw, yak, yap; *Brit. informal* natter, chinwag; *N. Amer. informal* shoot the breeze.

gouge ▸ verb =scoop out, hollow out, excavate; cut (out), dig (out), scrape (out), scratch (out).

gourmet ▸ noun =gastronome, epicure, epicurean; connoisseur; *informal* foodie.

govern ▸ verb 1 *he governs the province* =rule, preside over, control, be in charge of; run, head, administer, manage, regulate, oversee, supervise. 2 *the rules governing social behaviour* =determine, decide, control, regulate, direct, rule, dictate, shape; affect.

government ▸ noun =administration, executive, regime, authority, council; powers that be; cabinet, ministry.

governor ▸ noun =leader, ruler, chief, head; premier, president, chancellor; administrator, principal, director, chairman/woman, chair, superintendent, commissioner, controller; *informal* boss.

WORD LINKS

relating to a governor: **gubernatorial**

gown ▸ noun =dress, frock, robe.

grab ▸ verb =seize, grasp, snatch, take hold of, grip, clasp, clutch; take; dive for, lunge for.
▸ noun =lunge, snatch, dive.

grace ▸ noun 1 *the grace of a ballerina* =elegance, poise, gracefulness, finesse. 2 *he had the grace to apologize* =courtesy, decency, (good) manners, politeness, respect, tact. 3 *he fell from grace* =favour, approval, approbation, acceptance, esteem, regard, respect.
–OPPOSITES inelegance, effrontery, disfavour.
▸ verb *a mosaic graced the floor* =adorn, embellish, decorate, ornament, enhance.

graceful ▸ adjective =elegant, fluid, fluent, natural; agile, supple, nimble, light-footed.

graceless ▸ adjective =gauche, maladroit, inept, awkward, unsure, unpolished, unsophisticated, uncultured, unrefined; clumsy, ungainly, ungraceful, inelegant, uncoordinated, gawky, gangling, bumbling; tactless, thoughtless, inconsiderate; *informal* cack-handed.

gracious ▸ adjective 1 *a gracious hostess* =courteous, polite, civil, well mannered; tactful, diplomatic; kind, considerate, thoughtful, obliging, accommodating, indulgent; hospitable. 2 *gracious buildings* =elegant, stylish, tasteful, graceful; comfortable, luxurious, sumptuous, opulent, grand, high-class; *informal* swanky, plush.
–OPPOSITES rude, crude.

gradation ▸ noun 1 *a gradation of ability* =range, scale, spectrum, compass, span; progression, hierarchy, ladder, pecking order. 2 *each pay band has a number of gradations* =level, grade, rank, position, stage, standard, rung, step, notch; class, stratum, group, grouping, set.

grade ▸ noun 1 *hotels within the same grade* =category, set, class, classification, grouping, group, bracket. 2 *his job is of the lowest grade* =rank, level, standing, position, class, status, order; step, rung, stratum, tier. 3 *(N. Amer.) the best grades in the school* =mark, score; assessment, evaluation, appraisal. 4 *(N. Amer.) the fifth grade* =year, form, class.
▸ verb 1 *eggs are graded by size* =classify, class, categorize, bracket, sort, group, arrange, pigeonhole; rank, evaluate, rate, value. 2 *(N. Amer.) the essays have been graded* =assess, mark, score, judge,

evaluate, appraise.

■ **make the grade** *(informal)* =**come up to standard**, come up to scratch, qualify, pass, pass muster, measure up; succeed, win through; *informal* be up to snuff, cut it, cut the mustard.

gradient ▸ noun =**slope**, incline, hill, rise, ramp, bank; *N. Amer.* grade.

gradual ▸ adjective **1** *a gradual transition* =**slow**, measured, unhurried, cautious; piecemeal, step-by-step, little-by-little; bit-by-bit; progressive, continuous, steady. **2** *a gradual slope* =**gentle**, moderate, slight, easy.
–OPPOSITES abrupt, steep.

gradually ▸ adverb =**slowly**, slowly but surely, cautiously, gently, gingerly; piecemeal, little by little, bit by bit, inch by inch, by degrees; progressively, systematically; regularly, steadily.

graduate ▸ verb **1** *when he graduates* =**qualify**, get one's degree, complete one's studies. **2** *she graduated to serious drama* =**progress**, advance, move up/on. **3** *a proposal to graduate income tax* =**rank**, grade, order, group, classify, categorize.

graft ▸ noun *a skin graft* =**transplant**, implant.
▸ verb **1** *graft a bud onto the stem* =**affix**, join, insert, splice. **2** *tissue is grafted on to the cornea* =**transplant**, implant.

grain ▸ noun **1** *fields of grain* =**cereal**. **2** *a grain of corn* =**kernel**, seed. **3** *grains of sand* =**granule**, particle, speck; bit, piece; scrap, crumb, fragment, morsel. **4** *a grain of truth* =**trace**, hint, tinge, suggestion, shadow; bit, soupçon; ounce, iota, jot, whit, scrap, shred; *informal* smidgen, smidge, tad. **5** *the grain of the timber* =**texture**; weave, pattern.

grammar ▸ noun =**syntax**, rules of language; morphology; linguistics.

grammatical ▸ adjective **1** *the grammatical structure of a sentence* =**syntactic**, morphological; linguistic. **2** *a grammatical sentence* =**well formed**, correct, idiomatic; proper.

grand ▸ adjective **1** *a grand hotel* =**magnificent**, imposing, impressive, awe-inspiring, splendid, resplendent, majestic, monumental; palatial, stately, large; luxurious, sumptuous, lavish, opulent; *Brit.* upmarket; *N. Amer.* upscale; *informal* fancy, posh, plush, classy, swanky; *Brit. informal* swish. **2** *a grand scheme* =**ambitious**, bold, epic, big, extravagant. **3** *a grand old lady* =**august**, distinguished,

illustrious, eminent, esteemed, honoured, venerable, dignified, respectable; pre-eminent, prominent, notable, renowned, celebrated, famous. **4** *the grand staircase* =**main**, principal, central, prime. **5** *(informal) you're doing a grand job* =**excellent**, very good, marvellous, splendid, first-class, first-rate, wonderful, outstanding, sterling, fine; *informal* superb, terrific, great, super, ace; *Brit. informal* smashing, brilliant, brill.
–OPPOSITES inferior, humble, minor, poor.
▸ noun *(informal) a cheque for ten grand* =**thousand pounds/dollars**; *informal* thou, K; *N. Amer. informal* G, gee.

grandeur ▸ noun =**splendour**, magnificence, impressiveness, glory, resplendence, majesty, greatness; stateliness, pomp, ceremony.

grandfather ▸ noun =*informal* grandad, grandpa, gramps, grampy; *N. Amer. informal* grandaddy.

grandiose ▸ adjective **1** *the court's grandiose facade* =**magnificent**, impressive, grand, imposing, splendid, majestic, glorious, elaborate; palatial, stately, luxurious, opulent; *informal* plush, swanky, flash. **2** *a grandiose plan* =**ambitious**, bold, overambitious, extravagant, high-flown, flamboyant; *informal* over the top, OTT.
–OPPOSITES humble, modest.

grandmother ▸ noun =*informal* grandma, granny, nana; *Brit. informal* gran, nan, nanna, nanny; *N. Amer. informal* gramma.

grant ▸ verb **1** *he granted them leave of absence* =**allow**, accord, permit, afford, vouchsafe. **2** *he granted them £20,000* =**give**, award, bestow on, confer on, present with, provide with, endow with, supply with. **3** *I grant that the difference is slight* =**admit**, accept, concede, yield, allow, appreciate, recognize, acknowledge, confess; agree.
–OPPOSITES refuse, deny.
▸ noun *a grant from the council* =**endowment**, award, donation, bursary, allowance, subsidy, contribution, handout, allocation, gift; scholarship.

granular ▸ adjective =**powder**, powdered, powdery, grainy, granulated, gritty.

granulated ▸ adjective =**powdered**, crushed, ground, minced, grated, pulverized.

granule ▶ noun =**grain**, particle, fragment, bit, crumb, morsel, mote, speck.

grape ▶ noun

> WORD LINKS
>
> *farming of grapes:* **viticulture, viniculture**

graph ▶ noun =**chart**, diagram.

graphic ▶ adjective **1** *a graphic representation* =**visual**, pictorial, illustrative, diagrammatic; drawn. **2** *a graphic account* =**vivid**, explicit, detailed; powerful, colourful, lurid, shocking; realistic, descriptive, illustrative.
–OPPOSITES vague.
▶ noun *(Computing)* *add some graphics* =**picture**, illustration, image; diagram, graph, chart.

grapple ▶ verb **1** *the police grappled with him* =**wrestle**, struggle, tussle; scuffle, battle. **2** *grappling with addiction* =**tackle**, confront, face, deal with, cope with, get to grips with.

grasp ▶ verb **1** *she grasped his hand* =**grip**, clutch, clasp, hold, clench; catch, seize, grab, snatch. **2** *he grasped the important points* =**understand**, comprehend, take in, perceive, see, apprehend, assimilate, absorb; *informal* get, catch on to, figure out, get one's head around, take on board; *Brit. informal* twig, suss (out). **3** *he grasped the opportunity* =**take advantage of**, act on; seize, leap at, snatch, jump at.
–OPPOSITES release, overlook.
▶ noun **1** *his grasp on her hand* =**grip**, hold; clutch, clasp. **2** *a prize lay within their grasp* =**reach**, scope, power, range; sights. **3** *a grasp of history* =**understanding**, comprehension, apprehension, awareness, grip, knowledge; mastery, command.

grasping ▶ adjective =**avaricious**, acquisitive, greedy, rapacious, mercenary, materialistic; mean, miserly, parsimonious, niggardly, hoarding, selfish, possessive, close; *informal* tight-fisted, tight, stingy, money-grubbing; *N. Amer. informal* cheap, grabby.

grass ▶ noun =**turf**; lawn, green; *literary* sward.
▶ verb **1** *the hill is completely grassed* =**grass over**, turf. **2** *(Brit. informal) he grassed on them* =**inform**, tell; give away, betray, sell out; *informal* split, blow the whistle, rat, squeal, do the dirty, stitch up, sell down the river; *Brit. informal* shop; *N. Amer.*

informal finger; *Austral./NZ informal* dob, pimp.

> WORD LINKS
>
> *relating to grass:* **graminaceous**
> *study of grasses:* **agrostology**
> *grass-eating:* **graminivorous**

grate ▶ verb **1** *grate the cheese* =**shred**, pulverize, mince, grind, granulate, crush, crumble. **2** *her bones grated together* =**grind**, rub, rasp, scrape, jar, creak. **3** *the tune grates slightly* =**irritate**, set someone's teeth on edge, jar; annoy, nettle, chafe.

grateful ▶ adjective =**thankful**, appreciative; indebted, obliged, obligated, in your debt, beholden.

gratification ▶ noun =**satisfaction**, fulfilment, indulgence, relief, appeasement; pleasure, enjoyment.

gratify ▶ verb **1** *it gratified him* =**please**, gladden, make happy, delight, make someone feel good, satisfy; *informal* tickle pink, give someone a kick. **2** *he gratified his desires* =**satisfy**, fulfil, indulge, give in to, satiate, feed.
–OPPOSITES displease, frustrate.

grating[1] ▶ adjective **1** *a grating noise* =**scraping**, scratching, grinding, rasping. **2** *a grating voice* =**harsh**, raucous, strident, piercing, shrill, screechy; discordant, jarring.
–OPPOSITES harmonious, pleasing.

grating[2] ▶ noun *an iron grating* =**grid**, grate, grille, lattice, trellis.

gratis ▶ adverb =**free (of charge)**, without charge, for nothing, at no cost; *informal* on the house, for free.

gratitude ▶ noun =**gratefulness**, thankfulness, thanks, appreciation, indebtedness; recognition, acknowledgement, credit.

gratuitous ▶ adjective =**unjustified**, uncalled for, unwarranted, unprovoked, undue; indefensible, unjustifiable; needless, unnecessary, inessential, unmerited, groundless, senseless, wanton, indiscriminate; excessive, immoderate, inordinate, inappropriate.
–OPPOSITES necessary, paid.

grave[1] ▶ noun *she left flowers at his grave* =**burying place**; tomb; (last) resting place.

grave[2] ▶ adjective **1** *a grave matter* =**serious**, important, weighty, profound,

significant, momentous; critical, urgent, pressing; dire, terrible, awful, dreadful. **2** *Jackie looked grave* =**solemn**, serious, sober, unsmiling, grim, sombre; severe, stern, dour.
–OPPOSITES trivial, cheerful.

gravel ▶ noun =**shingle**, grit, pebbles, stones.

gravelly ▶ adjective **1** *a gravelly beach* =**shingly**, pebbly, stony, gritty. **2** *his gravelly voice* =**husky**, gruff, throaty, deep, croaky, rasping, grating, harsh, rough.

gravestone ▶ noun =**headstone**, tombstone, stone, monument, memorial.

graveyard ▶ noun =**cemetery**, churchyard, burial ground, necropolis.

gravitate ▶ verb =**move**, head, drift, be drawn, be attracted; tend, lean, incline.

gravity ▶ noun **1** *the gravity of the situation* =**seriousness**, importance, significance, weight, consequence, magnitude; acuteness, urgency; awfulness, dreadfulness. **2** *the gravity of his demeanour* =**solemnity**, seriousness, sombreness, sobriety, soberness, severity, grimness, dourness; gloominess.

graze[1] ▶ verb *the deer grazed* =**feed**, eat, crop, nibble, browse.

graze[2] ▶ verb **1** *he grazed his arm* =**scrape**, skin, scratch, chafe, scuff, rasp; cut, nick. **2** *his shot grazed the bar* =**touch**, brush, shave, skim, kiss, scrape, clip, glance off.
▶ noun *grazes on the skin* =**scratch**, scrape, abrasion, cut.

grease ▶ noun *guns packed in grease* =**oil**, fat; lubricant, lubrication.
▶ verb *grease a baking dish* =**lubricate**, oil, butter.

greasy ▶ adjective **1** *a greasy supper* =**fatty**, oily, buttery. **2** *greasy hair* =**oily**. **3** *the pitch was very greasy* =**slippery**, slick, slimy, slithery, oily; *informal* slippy. **4** *a greasy little man* =**ingratiating**, obsequious, sycophantic, fawning, toadying, grovelling; effusive, gushing; unctuous, oily; *informal* smarmy, slimy.
–OPPOSITES lean, dry.

great ▶ adjective **1** *they showed great interest* =**considerable**, substantial, significant, serious; exceptional, extraordinary. **2** *a great expanse of water* =**large**, big, extensive, expansive, broad, wide, ample; vast, immense, huge, enormous, massive; *informal* humongous, whopping; *Brit. informal* ginormous. **3** *great writers* =**prominent**, eminent, distinguished, illustrious, celebrated, acclaimed, admired, esteemed, renowned, notable, famous, well known; leading, top, major, principal. **4** *a great castle* =**magnificent**, imposing, impressive, awe-inspiring, grand, splendid, majestic. **5** *a great sportsman* =**expert**, skilful, skilled, adept, accomplished, talented, fine, masterly, master, brilliant, virtuoso, marvellous, outstanding, first class, superb; *informal* crack, ace, A1, class. **6** *a great fan of rugby* =**enthusiastic**, eager, keen, zealous, devoted, ardent, fanatical, passionate, dedicated, committed. **7** *we had a great time* =**enjoyable**, delightful, lovely; excellent, marvellous, wonderful, fine, splendid; *informal* terrific, fantastic, fabulous, fab, super, grand, cool; *Brit. informal* smashing, brilliant, brill; *Austral./NZ informal* bonzer, beaut.
–OPPOSITES little, small, minor, modest, poor, unenthusiastic, bad.
▶ adverb *a great big house* =**very**, extremely, exceedingly, really; *informal* dirty, whopping.

greatly ▶ adverb =**very much**, considerably, substantially, appreciably, significantly, markedly, sizeably, seriously, materially, profoundly; enormously, vastly, immensely, tremendously, mightily, extremely, exceedingly; *informal* plenty, majorly.
–OPPOSITES slightly.

greatness ▶ noun **1** *a woman destined for greatness* =**eminence**, distinction; importance, significance; celebrity, fame, prominence, renown. **2** *his greatness as a writer* =**brilliance**, genius, prowess, talent, expertise, mastery, artistry, virtuosity, skill, proficiency; flair, finesse; calibre, distinction.

greed, greediness ▶ noun **1** *human greed* =**avarice**, acquisitiveness, covetousness, rapacity; materialism, mercenariness; *informal* money-grubbing, money-grabbing. **2** *her mouth watered with greed* =**gluttony**, hunger, voracity, insatiability, self-indulgence; *informal* piggishness. **3** *their greed for power* =**desire**, appetite, hunger, thirst, craving, longing, yearning, hankering; *informal* yen, itch.

–OPPOSITES generosity, temperance, indifference.

greedy ▸ adjective **1** *a greedy eater* = **gluttonous**, ravenous, voracious, insatiable; *informal* piggish, piggy. **2** *his greedy manager* = **avaricious**, acquisitive, covetous, grasping, materialistic, mercenary; *informal* money-grubbing, money-grabbing; *N. Amer. informal* grabby.

green ▸ adjective **1** *a green scarf* = **viridescent**; olive green, pea green, emerald green, lime green, bottle green, Lincoln green, sea green. **2** *a green island* = **verdant**, grassy, leafy. **3** *Green issues* = **environmental**, ecological, conservation, eco-. **4** *a green alternative to diesel* = **environmentally friendly**, eco-friendly. **5** *green bananas* = **unripe**, immature. **6** *the new supervisor was very green* = **inexperienced**, callow, raw, unseasoned, untried; ignorant; unsophisticated, unpolished; naive, innocent, unworldly; *informal* wet behind the ears.
–OPPOSITES barren, ripe, experienced.
▸ noun **1** *a canopy of green over the road* = **foliage**, greenery, plants, leaves, vegetation. **2** *the village green* = **lawn**, common. **3** *they had roast beef and greens* = **vegetables**; *informal* veg. **4** *Greens are against the bypass* = **environmentalist**, conservationist; *informal* eco-warrior, tree-hugger.

greenery ▸ noun = **foliage**, vegetation, plants, green, leaves, undergrowth, plant life, flora, verdure.

greenhouse ▸ noun = **hothouse**, glasshouse, conservatory.

greet ▸ verb **1** *she greeted Hank cheerily* = **say hello to**, address, salute, hail; welcome, meet, receive. **2** *the decision was greeted with outrage* = **receive**, respond to, react to, take.

greeting ▸ noun **1** *he shouted a greeting* = **hello**, salutation, address; welcome; acknowledgement. **2** *birthday greetings* = **best wishes**, good wishes, congratulations, felicitations; compliments, regards, respects.
–OPPOSITES farewell.

gregarious ▸ adjective = **sociable**, convivial, companionable, outgoing.
–OPPOSITES unsociable.

grey ▸ adjective **1** *a grey suit* = **silvery**, gunmetal, slate, charcoal, smoky. **2** *his grey hair* = **white**, silver, hoary. **3** *a grey day* = **cloudy**, overcast, dull, sunless, gloomy, dreary, dismal, sombre, bleak, murky. **4** *her face looked grey* = **ashen**, wan, pale, pasty, pallid, colourless, bloodless, white, waxen; sickly, peaky, drained, drawn, deathly. **5** *his grey existence* = **characterless**, colourless, nondescript, flat, bland; dull, boring, tedious, monotonous; soulless. **6** *a grey area* = **ambiguous**, doubtful, unclear, uncertain, indefinite, open to question, debatable.
–OPPOSITES sunny, ruddy, lively, certain.

grid ▸ noun **1** *a metal grid* = **grating**, mesh, grille, gauze, lattice. **2** *the grid of streets* = **network**, matrix.

grief ▸ noun = **sorrow**, misery, sadness, anguish, pain, distress, heartache, heartbreak, agony, woe, desolation; mourning, mournfulness, bereavement.
–OPPOSITES joy.
■ **come to grief** = **fail**, meet with disaster, fall through, fall flat, founder; *informal* come unstuck, come a cropper, flop.

grief-stricken ▸ adjective = **sorrowful**, sorrowing, heartbroken, brokenhearted, anguished, distressed, despairing, devastated, upset, inconsolable; mourning, grieving, mournful, bereaved.
–OPPOSITES joyful.

grievance ▸ noun = **complaint**, criticism, objection, grumble, grouse; ill feeling, bad feeling, resentment, bitterness; *informal* gripe, beef.

grieve ▸ verb **1** *she grieved for her father* = **mourn**, sorrow; cry, sob, weep. **2** *it grieved me to leave her* = **sadden**, upset, distress, pain, hurt, wound, break someone's heart.
–OPPOSITES rejoice, please.

grievous *(formal)* ▸ adjective = **serious**, severe, grave, bad, critical, dreadful, terrible, awful, crushing.
–OPPOSITES slight, trivial.

grim ▸ adjective **1** *his grim expression* = **stern**, forbidding, uninviting, unsmiling, dour, formidable, harsh, steely, flinty, stony. **2** *grim humour* = **black**, dark, bleak, cynical. **3** *grim secrets* = **dreadful**, ghastly, horrible, terrible, awful, appalling, frightful, shocking, grisly, gruesome, hideous, macabre; depressing, distressing, upsetting, worrying, unpleasant. **4** *a grim little hovel* = **bleak**, dismal, dingy, wretched, miserable, depressing, cheerless, joyless, gloomy, uninviting; *informal* God-awful. **5** *grim determination* = **resolute**, firm,

determined, steadfast; obstinate, stubborn, unyielding, intractable, uncompromising, unshakeable, unrelenting, relentless, dogged, tenacious.
–OPPOSITES amiable, pleasant.

grimace ▶ noun *his mouth twisted into a grimace* =**scowl**, frown, sneer; face.
▶ verb *Nina grimaced at Joe* =**scowl**, frown, sneer, glower; make a face, make faces, pull a face.
–OPPOSITES smile.

grime ▶ noun =**dirt**, smut, soot, dust, mud, filth, mire; *informal* muck, crud; *Brit. informal* grot, gunge.

grimy ▶ adjective =**dirty**, grubby, mucky, soiled, stained, filthy, smutty, sooty, dusty, muddy; *informal* yucky, cruddy; *Brit. informal* manky, grotty, gungy; *Austral./NZ* scungy.
–OPPOSITES clean.

grin ▶ verb =**smile**, beam; smirk.
▶ noun =**smile**, beam; smirk.
–OPPOSITES frown, scowl.

grind ▶ verb 1 *the ore is ground into powder* =**crush**, pound, pulverize, mill, crumble. 2 *one stone grinds against another* =**rub**, grate, scrape.
▶ noun *the daily grind* =**drudgery**, toil, labour, donkey work, exertion, chores, slog.
■ **grind someone down** =**oppress**, crush, break.

grip ▶ verb 1 *she gripped the edge of the table* =**grasp**, clutch, hold, clasp, take hold of, clench, grab, seize, cling to; squeeze, press. 2 *Jo was gripped by a sneezing fit* =**afflict**, affect, take over, beset, rack, convulse. 3 *we were gripped by the drama* =**engross**, enthral, absorb, rivet, spellbind, hold spellbound, bewitch, fascinate, mesmerize.
–OPPOSITES release.
▶ noun 1 *a tight grip* =**grasp**, hold. 2 *the wheels lost their grip on the road* =**traction**, purchase, friction, adhesion. 3 *in the grip of an obsession* =**control**, power, hold, stranglehold, clutches, influence.
■ **come/get to grips with** =**deal with**, cope with, handle, grasp, tackle, take on, grapple with, face, face up to, confront.

gripping ▶ adjective =**engrossing**, enthralling, absorbing, riveting, captivating, spellbinding, bewitching, fascinating, compelling, mesmerizing; thrilling, exciting, action-packed, dramatic, stimulating; *informal* unputdownable, page-turning.
–OPPOSITES boring.

grisly ▶ adjective =**gruesome**, ghastly, frightful, horrid, horrifying, fearful, hideous, macabre, horrible, grim, awful, dreadful, terrible, horrific, shocking, appalling, abominable, loathsome, abhorrent, odious, monstrous.

gristly ▶ adjective =**stringy**, sinewy, fibrous; tough, leathery, chewy.

grit ▶ noun =**gravel**, pebbles, stones, shingle, sand; dust, dirt.

gritty ▶ adjective =**sandy**, gravelly, pebbly, stony; powdery, dusty.

grizzled ▶ adjective =**grey**, greying, silver, silvery, snowy, white, salt-and-pepper; grey-haired.

groan ▶ verb 1 *she groaned and rubbed her stomach* =**moan**, cry. 2 *the tree groaned* =**creak**; grate, rasp.
▶ noun 1 *a groan of anguish* =**moan**, cry. 2 *the groan of the timbers* =**creaking**, creak, grating, grinding.

groggy ▶ adjective =**dazed**, muzzy, in a stupor, befuddled, disoriented, disorientated, dizzy, punch-drunk, unsteady, wobbly, weak, faint; *informal* dopey, woozy, not with it.

groin ▶ noun =**crotch**, crutch, genitals.

> **WORD LINKS**
> *relating to the groin:* **inguinal**

groom ▶ verb 1 *she groomed her pony* =**curry**, brush, clean, rub down. 2 *his hair was carefully groomed* =**brush**, comb, arrange, do; *informal* fix. 3 *groomed for stardom* =**prepare**, prime, condition, tailor; coach, train, drill, teach, school.
▶ noun *the bride and groom* =**bridegroom**.

groove ▶ noun =**furrow**, channel, trench, trough, canal, hollow, indentation, rut, gutter, fissure.

grooved ▶ adjective =**furrowed**, fluted, corrugated, ribbed, ridged.

grope ▶ verb 1 *she groped for her glasses* =**fumble**, scrabble, fish, ferret, rummage, feel, search, hunt. 2 *(informal) one of the men groped her* =**fondle**, touch; *informal* paw, maul, feel up, touch up.

gross ▶ adjective 1 *(informal) the place smelled gross* =**disgusting**, revolting, foul, nasty, obnoxious, sickening, nauseating, stomach-churning; tasteless; *N. Amer.* vomitous; *informal* yucky, icky, sick-making, gut-churning. 2 *a gross distortion of the truth* =**flagrant**, blatant,

glaring, obvious, overt, naked, bare-faced, shameless, brazen, patent, transparent, manifest, palpable; out and out, utter, complete. **3** *gross income* =**total**, full, overall, combined, aggregate; before deductions, before tax.
–OPPOSITES pleasant, net.

▶ verb *he grosses over a million a year* =**earn**, make, bring in, take, get, receive, collect; *informal* rake in.

grotesque ▶ adjective **1** *a grotesque creature* =**malformed**, deformed, misshapen, distorted, twisted; ugly, monstrous, hideous, freakish, unnatural, abnormal, strange, odd, peculiar; *informal* weird, freaky. **2** *grotesque mismanagement of funds* =**outrageous**, monstrous, shocking, appalling, preposterous; ridiculous, ludicrous, farcical, unbelievable, incredible.
–OPPOSITES normal.

grotto ▶ noun =**cave**, cavern, hollow.

ground ▶ noun **1** *she collapsed on the ground* =**floor**, earth, terra firma; *informal* deck. **2** *soggy ground* =**earth**, soil, turf; land, terrain. **3** *the team's home ground* =**stadium**, pitch, field, arena, track. **4** *the mansion's grounds* =**estate**, gardens, park, parkland, land, property, surroundings, territory. **5** *grounds for dismissal* =**reason**, cause, basis, foundation, justification, rationale, argument, premise, occasion, excuse, pretext, motive, motivation.

▶ verb *the boat grounded on a mud bank* =**run aground**, run ashore, beach, land.

groundless ▶ adjective =**baseless**, without basis, without foundation, ill-founded, unfounded, unsupported, uncorroborated, unproven, empty, idle, unsubstantiated, unwarranted, unjustified, unjustifiable.

groundwork ▶ noun =**preliminary work**, preliminaries, preparations, spadework, legwork, donkey work; planning, arrangements, organization, homework; basics, essentials, fundamentals.

group ▶ noun **1** *the exhibits were divided into three groups* =**category**, class, classification, grouping, set, batch, type, sort, kind, variety, family, species, genus; grade, grading, rank. **2** *a group of tourists* =**crowd**, party, body, band, company, gathering, congregation, assembly, collection, cluster, flock, pack, troop, gang; *informal* bunch. **3** *a group within the party*

=**faction**, division, section, clique, coterie, circle, set, ring, camp, bloc, caucus, fringe movement, splinter group. **4** *the women's group* =**association**, club, society, league, guild, circle, union. **5** *a small group of trees* =**cluster**, knot, collection, mass, clump. **6** *a folk group* =**band**, ensemble, act; *informal* line-up, combo, outfit.

▶ verb **1** *patients were grouped according to age* =**categorize**, classify, class, catalogue, sort, bracket, pigeonhole, grade, rate, rank. **2** *chairs were grouped round the table* =**place**, arrange, assemble, organize, range, line up, lay out. **3** *the two parties grouped together* =**unite**, join together/up, team up, join forces, get together, affiliate, combine; collaborate, work together, pull together, cooperate.

grouse ▶ verb *she groused about the food.* See COMPLAIN.

▶ noun *our biggest grouse was about the noise.* See COMPLAINT.

> **WORD LINKS**
>
> *male:* **cock**
> *female:* **hen**
> *young:* **cheeper**
> *collective noun:* **pack, covey**

grove ▶ noun =**copse**, wood, thicket, coppice; orchard, plantation; *Brit.* spinney.

grovel ▶ verb **1** *George grovelled at her feet* =**prostrate oneself**, lie, kneel, cringe. **2** *she was not going to grovel to him* =**be obsequious**, fawn on, kowtow, bow and scrape, toady, dance attendance on, ingratiate oneself with; *informal* crawl, creep, suck up to, lick someone's boots.

grow ▶ verb **1** *the boys had grown* =**get bigger**, get taller, get larger, increase in size. **2** *profits continue to grow* =**increase**, swell, multiply, snowball, mushroom, balloon, build up, mount up, pile up; *informal* skyrocket. **3** *flowers grew among the rocks* =**sprout**, germinate, spring up, develop, bud, burst forth, bloom, flourish, thrive, run riot. **4** *he grew vegetables* =**cultivate**, produce, propagate, raise, rear; farm. **5** *the family business grew* =**expand**, extend, develop, progress; flourish, thrive, burgeon, prosper, succeed, boom. **6** *Leonora grew bored* =**become**, get, turn, begin to feel.
–OPPOSITES shrink, decline.

growl ▶ verb =**snarl**, bark, yap, bay.

grown-up ▶ noun *she wanted to be*

treated like a grown-up =**adult**, (grown) woman, (grown) man.
–OPPOSITES child.

▶ **adjective** *she has two grown-up daughters* =**adult**, mature, of age; fully grown, full-grown.

growth ▶ **noun 1** *population growth* =**increase**, expansion, proliferation, multiplication, enlargement, mushrooming, snowballing, rise, escalation, build-up. **2** *the growth of plants* =**development**, growing, sprouting; blooming. **3** *the growth of local enterprises* =**expansion**, extension, development, progress, advance, advancement, spread; rise, success, boom, upturn, upswing. **4** *a growth on his jaw* =**tumour**, malignancy, cancer; lump, swelling, nodule; cyst, polyp.
–OPPOSITES decrease, decline.

grub ▶ **noun** =**larva**; maggot; caterpillar.

grubby ▶ **adjective** =**dirty**, grimy, filthy, mucky, unwashed, stained, soiled, smeared, spotted; *informal* cruddy, yucky; *Brit. informal* manky, grotty, gungy.
–OPPOSITES clean.

grudge ▶ **noun** =**grievance**, resentment, bitterness, rancour, dissatisfaction, ill will, animosity, antipathy, antagonism; *informal* a chip on one's shoulder.

grudging ▶ **adjective** =**reluctant**, unwilling, forced, half-hearted, unenthusiastic, hesitant; begrudging, resentful.
–OPPOSITES eager.

gruelling ▶ **adjective** =**exhausting**, tiring, wearying, taxing, draining; demanding, exacting, difficult, hard, arduous, strenuous, laborious, backbreaking, harsh, severe, stiff, punishing, crippling; *informal* murderous, hellish; *Brit. informal* knackering.

gruesome ▶ **adjective** =**grisly**, ghastly, frightful, horrid, horrifying, hideous, horrible, grim, awful, dreadful, terrible, horrific, shocking, appalling, disgusting, revolting, sickening, unspeakable; *informal* sick, sick-making, gross.
–OPPOSITES pleasant.

gruff ▶ **adjective 1** *a gruff reply* | *his gruff exterior* =**abrupt**, brusque, curt, short, blunt; taciturn; surly, grumpy, crusty, ungracious; *informal* grouchy. **2** *a gruff voice* =**rough**, guttural, throaty, gravelly, husky, croaking, rasping, hoarse, harsh; low.
–OPPOSITES friendly, soft.

grumble ▶ **verb** =**complain**, grouse,

whine, mutter, bleat, carp, protest, make a fuss; *informal* moan, bellyache, beef, bitch, grouch, gripe, whinge; *Brit. informal* chunter, create; *N. English informal* mither; *N. Amer. informal* kvetch.

▶ **noun** =**complaint**, grouse, grievance, protest, cavil, criticism; *informal* grouch, moan, whinge, beef, gripe.

grumpy ▶ **adjective** =**bad-tempered**, crabby, short-tempered, crotchety, tetchy, crabbed, touchy, irascible, crusty, cantankerous, curmudgeonly, surly, ill-humoured, cross, fractious, disagreeable; *informal* grouchy; *Brit. informal* narky, ratty, like a bear with a sore head; *N. Amer. informal* cranky, ornery, soreheaded.
–OPPOSITES good-humoured.

guarantee ▶ **noun 1** *a one-year guarantee* =**warranty**. **2** *a guarantee that the hospital will stay open* =**promise**, assurance, word (of honour), pledge, vow, oath, commitment, covenant. **3** *a guarantee for loans* =**collateral**, security, surety.

▶ **verb 1** *he agreed to guarantee the loan* =**underwrite**. **2** *I guarantee he will accept* =**promise**, swear, pledge, vow, give one's word, give an assurance, give an undertaking, cross one's heart (and hope to die).

guard ▶ **verb 1** *troops guarded the bridge* =**protect**, stand guard over, watch over, keep an eye on; cover, patrol, police, defend. **2** *the men were guarded by armed officers* =**watch**, mind; protect. **3** *we must guard against poachers* =**beware of**, keep watch for, be alert to, keep an eye out for, be on the alert/lookout for.

▶ **noun 1** *border guards* =**sentry**, sentinel, nightwatchman; protector, defender, guardian; lookout, watch. **2** *a prison guard* =**warder**, warden, keeper; jailer; *informal* screw. **3** *a metal guard* =**cover**, shield, screen, fender; bumper, buffer.

■ **off (one's) guard** =**unprepared**, unready, inattentive, unwary, unsuspecting; *informal* napping, asleep at the wheel, on the hop.

■ **on one's guard** =**vigilant**, alert, on the alert, wary, watchful, cautious, careful, heedful, chary, circumspect, on the lookout, on one's toes, prepared, ready, wideawake, attentive, observant, keeping one's eyes peeled.

guarded ▶ **adjective** =**cautious**, careful, circumspect, wary, chary, reluctant, non-committal; *informal* cagey.

guardian ▶ **noun** =**protector**,

defender, preserver, custodian, warden, guard, keeper; curator, caretaker, steward, trustee.

WORD LINKS

relating to a guardian: **tutelary**

guerrilla ▶ noun =**freedom fighter**, irregular, partisan; rebel, revolutionary; terrorist.

guess ▶ verb **1** *he guessed that she was about 40* =**estimate**, reckon, judge; postulate, speculate, conjecture, surmise. **2** *(informal) I guess I owe you an apology* =**suppose**, think, imagine, expect, suspect, dare say; *informal* reckon, figure.
▶ noun *my guess was right* =**hypothesis**, theory, postulation, conjecture, surmise, estimate, belief, opinion, supposition, speculation, suspicion, impression, feeling.

guesswork ▶ noun =**guessing**, conjecture, surmise, supposition, assumptions, presumptions, speculation, hypothesizing, theorizing; approximation.

guest ▶ noun **1** *we have guests* =**visitor**, caller; company. **2** *hotel guests* =**resident**, boarder, lodger; patron, client; *N. Amer.* roomer.
−OPPOSITES host.

guest house ▶ noun =**boarding house**, bed and breakfast, B & B, hotel.

guffaw ▶ verb =**roar (with laughter)**, laugh heartily/loudly, bellow, cackle.

guidance ▶ noun **1** *she looked to him for guidance* =**advice**, counsel, direction, instruction; suggestions, tips, hints, pointers, guidelines. **2** *under the guidance of an expert* =**direction**, control, leadership, management, supervision, charge.

guide ▶ noun **1** *our guide took us back to the hotel* =**escort**, attendant, courier; usher; chaperone. **2** *he is my inspiration and my guide* =**adviser**, mentor, counsellor; guru. **3** *the techniques given serve as a guide* =**outline**, template, example, exemplar; introduction, overview. **4** *a guide to Paris* =**guidebook**, travelogue; companion, handbook, directory, A to Z; *informal* bible.
▶ verb **1** *he guided her to her seat* =**lead**, conduct, show, show someone the way, usher, shepherd, direct, steer, pilot, escort; see, take, help, assist. **2** *the chairman guides the meeting* =**direct**, steer, manage, conduct, run, be in charge of, govern, preside over, supervise, over-

see; handle, regulate. **3** *he was always there to guide me* =**advise**, counsel, direct.

guidebook ▶ noun =**guide**, travel guide, travelogue; companion, handbook, directory, A to Z; *informal* bible.

guideline ▶ noun =**recommendation**, instruction, direction, suggestion, advice; regulation, rule, principle; standard, criterion.

guild ▶ noun =**association**, society, union, league, organization, company, cooperative, fellowship, club, order, lodge, brotherhood, fraternity, sisterhood, sorority.

guile ▶ noun =**cunning**, craftiness, craft, artfulness, artifice, wiliness, slyness, deviousness; deception, deceit, duplicity, underhandedness, double-dealing, trickery.
−OPPOSITES honesty.

guileless ▶ adjective =**artless**, naive, open, simple, childlike, innocent, unsophisticated, unworldly, trusting.
−OPPOSITES scheming.

guilt ▶ noun **1** *the proof of his guilt* =**culpability**, guiltiness, blameworthiness. **2** *a terrible feeling of guilt* =**self-reproach**, shame, a guilty conscience, pangs of conscience; remorse, regret, contrition.
−OPPOSITES innocence.

guiltless ▶ adjective =**innocent**, blameless, not to blame, without fault; *informal* squeaky clean, whiter than white, as pure as the driven snow.
−OPPOSITES guilty.

guilty ▶ adjective **1** *the guilty party* =**culpable**, to blame, at fault, in the wrong. **2** *I still feel guilty about it* =**ashamed**, guilt-ridden, conscience-stricken, remorseful, sorry, contrite, repentant, penitent, regretful, rueful, abashed, shamefaced, sheepish, hangdog.
−OPPOSITES innocent, unrepentant.

guise ▶ noun **1** *Zeus appeared in the guise of a swan* =**likeness**, appearance, semblance, form, shape, image; disguise. **2** *sums paid under the guise of consultancy fees* =**pretence**, disguise, front, facade, cover, blind, screen, smokescreen.

gulf ▶ noun **1** *the ice gave way and the gulf widened* =**hole**, crevasse, fissure, cleft, split, rift, pit, chasm, abyss, void; ravine, gorge, canyon, gully. **2** *a gulf between rich and poor* =**divide**, division, separation, gap; difference, contrast, polarity.

gullet ▶ noun =**oesophagus**, throat, pharynx; crop, craw.

WORD LINKS

relating to the gullet: **oesophageal**

gullible ▶ adjective =**credulous**, naive, easily deceived, impressionable, unsuspecting, ingenuous, innocent, inexperienced, green; *informal* wet behind the ears.
–OPPOSITES suspicious.

gully ▶ noun **1** *a steep icy gully* =**ravine**, canyon, gorge, pass, defile, couloir; *S. English* chine; *N. English* clough, gill; *N. Amer.* gulch, coulee. **2** *water runs from the drainpipe into a gully* =**channel**, conduit, trench, ditch, drain, culvert, gutter.

gulp ▶ verb **1** *she gulped her juice* =**swallow**, quaff, swill down; *informal* swig, down, knock back. **2** *he gulped down the rest of his meal* =**gobble**, guzzle, devour, bolt, wolf; *informal* put away, demolish, polish off, shovel down; *Brit. informal* scoff. **3** *Jenny gulped back her tears* =**choke back**, fight/hold back, suppress, stifle, smother.
–OPPOSITES sip.
▶ noun *a gulp of cold beer* =**mouthful**, swallow, draught; *informal* swig.

gum[1] ▶ noun *stuck down with gum* =**glue**, adhesive, paste; *N. Amer.* mucilage.
▶ verb *the receipts were gummed into a book* =**stick**, glue, paste; fix, affix, attach, fasten.
■ **gum something up** =**clog (up)**, choke (up), stop up, plug; obstruct; *informal* bung up.

gum[2] ▶ noun (Anatomy)

WORD LINKS

relating to the gums: **gingival**
inflammation of the gums: **gingivitis**

gumption ▶ noun (*informal*) =**initiative**, resourcefulness, enterprise, imagination; sense, common sense, wit; *informal* get-up-and-go, spunk, nous, savvy, horse sense; *N. Amer. informal* smarts.

gun ▶ noun =**firearm**; pistol, revolver, handgun, rifle, shotgun, machine gun; weapon; *informal* shooter; *N. Amer. informal* piece, shooting iron.

gunfire ▶ noun =**gunshots**, shots, shooting, firing, shelling.

gunman ▶ noun =**robber**, gangster, terrorist; sniper, gunfighter; assassin, murderer, killer; *informal* hit man, gunslinger, mobster; *N. Amer. informal* shootist, hood.

gurgle ▶ verb *the water swirled and gurgled* =**babble**, burble, tinkle, bubble, ripple, murmur, purl, splash.
▶ noun *the gurgle of a small brook* =**babbling**, tinkling, bubbling, murmur, purling, splashing.

guru ▶ noun **1** *a Hindu guru and mystic* =**(spiritual) teacher**, tutor, sage, mentor, (spiritual) leader, leader, master; *Hinduism* swami, Maharishi. **2** *a management guru* =**expert**, authority, pundit, leading light, master, specialist.
–OPPOSITES disciple.

gush ▶ verb =**surge**, burst, spout, spurt, jet, stream, rush, pour, spill, cascade, flood; flow, run, issue; *Brit. informal* sloosh.
▶ noun =**surge**, stream, spurt, jet, spout, outpouring, outflow, burst, rush, cascade, flood, torrent; *technical* efflux.

gushing, gushy ▶ adjective =**effusive**, enthusiastic, overenthusiastic, unrestrained, extravagant, fulsome, lavish; *informal* over the top, OTT, laid on with a trowel.
–OPPOSITES restrained.

gust ▶ noun =**flurry**, blast, puff, blow, rush; squall.
▶ verb =**blow**, bluster, roar.

gusto ▶ noun =**enthusiasm**, relish, appetite, enjoyment, delight, glee, pleasure; zest, zeal, fervour, verve, keenness.
–OPPOSITES apathy, distaste.

gusty ▶ adjective =**blustery**, windy, breezy; squally, stormy, tempestuous, wild, turbulent; *informal* blowy.
–OPPOSITES calm.

gut ▶ noun **1** *an ache in his gut* =**stomach**, belly, abdomen; intestines, bowels; *informal* tummy, tum, insides, innards. **2** *fish guts* =**entrails**; intestines, viscera; offal; *informal* insides, innards. **3** (*informal*) *Nicola has a lot of guts* =**courage**, bravery, backbone, nerve, pluck, spirit, boldness, daring, grit, fearlessness, toughness, determination; *informal* spunk; *Brit. informal* bottle; *N. Amer. informal* moxie.
▶ adjective (*informal*) *a gut feeling* =**instinctive**, intuitive, deep-seated; knee-jerk, automatic, involuntary, spontaneous, unthinking.
▶ verb **1** *gut the sardines* =**clean (out)**, disembowel, draw; *formal* eviscerate. **2** *the church was gutted by fire* =**devastate**, destroy, lay waste, ravage, ruin, wreck.

WORD LINKS

relating to the gut: **visceral, enteric, entero-**

gutless ▸ adjective (*informal*). See COW-ARDLY.

gutsy ▸ adjective (*informal*). See BRAVE.

gutter ▸ noun =**drain**, sluice, culvert, sewer; channel, conduit, pipe; trough, trench, ditch.

guttural ▸ adjective =**throaty**, husky, gruff, gravelly, growly, growling, croaky, croaking, harsh, rough, rasping; deep, low, thick.

guy ▸ noun (*informal*) =**man**, fellow; youth, boy; *informal* lad, fella, geezer, gent; *Brit.*

informal chap, bloke; *N. Amer. informal* dude, hombre.

guzzle ▸ verb **1** *he guzzled his burger* =**gobble**, bolt, wolf, devour; *informal* tuck into, demolish, polish off, pig oneself on, shovel down; *Brit. informal* scoff, shift; *N. Amer. informal* snarf down/up, scarf down/up. **2** *she guzzled down the orange juice* =**gulp down**, swallow, quaff, swill; *informal* knock back, swig, down, slug down.

gypsy, gipsy ▸ noun =**Romany**; traveller; nomad, rover, wanderer.

gyrate ▸ verb =**rotate**, revolve, wheel, turn, whirl, circle, pirouette, twirl, swirl, spin, swivel.

Hh

habit ▶ noun **1** =**custom**, practice, routine, way; *formal* wont. **2** *(informal) his cocaine habit* =**addiction**, dependence, craving, fixation. **3** *a monk's habit* =**garments**, dress, garb, clothing, attire, outfit, costume; *formal* apparel.
■ **in the habit of** =**accustomed to**, used to, given to, inclined to; *literary* wont to.

habitable ▶ adjective =**fit to live in**, inhabitable, in good repair, liveable-in.

habitat ▶ noun =**natural environment**, home, domain, haunt.

habitation ▶ noun **1** *fit for human habitation* =**occupancy**, occupation, residence, living in, tenancy. **2** *(formal) his principal habitation* =**residence**, house, home, dwelling, seat; *formal* dwelling place, abode, domicile.

habitual ▶ adjective **1** =**constant**, persistent, continual, continuous, perpetual, non-stop, endless, never-ending; *informal* eternal. **2** *habitual drinkers* =**inveterate**, confirmed, compulsive, incorrigible, hardened, ingrained, chronic, regular. **3** *his habitual secretiveness* =**customary**, accustomed, regular, usual, normal, characteristic; *literary* wonted.
−OPPOSITES occasional, unaccustomed.

habituate ▶ verb =**accustom**, make used, familiarize, adapt, adjust, attune, acclimatize, condition; *N. Amer.* acclimate.

habitué ▶ noun =**frequent visitor**, regular customer, familiar face, regular, patron.

hack¹ ▶ verb =**cut**, chop, hew, lop, saw, slash.
■ **hack it** *(informal)* =**cope**, manage; stand it, tolerate it, bear it, put up with it; *informal* handle it, abide it, stick it.

hack² ▶ noun =**journalist**, reporter, newspaperman, newspaperwoman, writer; *informal* scribbler.

hackle ■ **make someone's hackles rise** =**annoy**, irritate, exasperate, anger, incense, infuriate, irk, nettle, vex, put out, provoke, gall, antagonize, get on someone's nerves, ruffle someone's feathers, rankle with; *Brit.* rub up the wrong way; *informal* aggravate, peeve, needle, rile, make someone see red, make someone's blood boil, hack off, get someone's back up, get someone's goat, get up someone's nose, get someone's dander up, bug, miff; *Brit. informal* wind up, nark, get on someone's wick; *N. Amer. informal* tee off, tick off, burn up; *informal, dated* give someone the pip.

hackneyed ▶ adjective =**overused**, overdone, overworked, worn out, time-worn, stale, tired, threadbare; trite, banal, clichéd.
−OPPOSITES original.

Hades ▶ noun. See HELL *sense* 1.

haft ▶ noun =**handle**, grip, hilt, shaft, butt, stock.

hag ▶ noun =**crone**, old woman, gorgon; *informal* witch, cow, old bag.

haggard ▶ adjective =**drawn**, tired, exhausted, drained, careworn; gaunt, pinched, hollow-cheeked, hollow-eyed.
−OPPOSITES healthy.

haggle ▶ verb =**barter**, bargain, negotiate, wrangle.

hail¹ ▶ verb **1** *a friend hailed him* =**call out to**, shout to, address; greet, say hello to, salute. **2** *he hailed a cab* =**flag down**, wave down. **3** *critics hailed the film as a masterpiece* =**acclaim**, praise, applaud. **4** *Rick hails from Australia* =**come from**, be from, be a native of.

hail² ▶ noun *a hail of bullets* =**barrage**, volley, shower, stream, salvo.
▶ verb =**beat**, shower, rain, fall, pour.

hair ▶ noun **1** =**head of hair**, shock of hair, mane, mop; locks, tresses, curls, ringlets. **2** =**hairstyle**, haircut; *informal* hairdo. **3** =**fur**, wool, coat, fleece, mane.

> **WORD LINKS**
>
> relating to hair: **capillaceous**
> fear of hair: **trichophobia**

hairdresser ▶ noun =**hairstylist**, stylist, coiffeur, coiffeuse; barber.

hairless ▶ adjective =**bald**; shaven, shorn, clean-shaven, beardless, smooth-faced.
−OPPOSITES hairy.

hairpiece ▸ noun =wig, toupee; *informal* rug.

hair-raising ▸ adjective =terrifying, frightening, petrifying, chilling, horrifying, spine-chilling, blood-curdling; *informal* hairy, spooky, scary, creepy.

hair-splitting ▸ adjective =pedantic; quibbling, niggling; *informal* nit-picking; *Brit. informal* pernickety, picky; *N. Amer. informal* persnickety.

hairstyle ▸ noun =haircut, cut, style, hair, coiffure; *informal* hairdo.

hairy ▸ adjective **1** *animals with hairy coats* =shaggy, bushy, long-haired; woolly, furry, fleecy. **2** *his hairy face* =bearded, bewhiskered, stubbly, bristly; *formal* hirsute. **3** *(informal) a hairy situation* =risky, dangerous, perilous, hazardous; tricky; *informal* dicey, sticky; *Brit. informal* dodgy.

hale ▸ adjective =healthy, fit, fighting fit, well, in good health, bursting with health, in fine fettle, as fit as a fiddle/flea; strong, robust, vigorous, hardy, sturdy, hearty, lusty, able-bodied; *informal* in the pink, as right as rain.
−OPPOSITES unwell.

half ▸ adverb **1** *half-cooked chicken* =partially. **2** *I'm half inclined to believe you* =to a certain extent/degree, (up) to a point, in part, in some measure.
−OPPOSITES fully, completely.

half-baked ▸ adjective =ill-conceived, hare-brained, ill-judged, impractical, unrealistic, unworkable, ridiculous; *informal* crackpot.

half-hearted ▸ adjective =unenthusiastic, cool, lukewarm, tepid, apathetic.
−OPPOSITES enthusiastic.

halfway ▸ adjective *the halfway point* =midway, middle, mid, central, centre, intermediate.
▸ adverb **1** *he stopped halfway down the passage* =midway, in the middle, in the centre; part of the way, part-way. **2** *halfway decent* =relatively, fairly, comparatively, moderately.
∎ **meet someone halfway** =compromise, reach an agreement, make a deal, find the middle ground, strike a balance.

hall ▸ noun **1** =entrance hall, hallway, entry, entrance, lobby, foyer, vestibule. **2** *the village hall* =assembly room, meeting room, chamber; auditorium, theatre, house.

hallmark ▸ noun *the tiny bubbles are the hallmark of fine champagnes* =mark, distinctive feature, characteristic, sign, sure sign, telltale sign, badge, stamp, trademark, indication, indicator.

hallucinate ▸ verb =have hallucinations, see things, be delirious; *informal* trip.

hallucination ▸ noun =delusion, illusion, figment of the imagination, mirage, chimera, fantasy.

halo ▸ noun =aura, nimbus, corona, aureole.

halt ▸ verb **1** =stop, come to a halt, come to a stop, come to a standstill; pull up, draw up. **2** *a strike has halted production* =stop, bring to a stop, put a stop to; suspend, arrest; check, curb, stem, staunch, block, stall; *informal* pull the plug on, put the kibosh on.
−OPPOSITES start, continue.
▸ noun **1** =stop, standstill. **2** *a halt in production* =stoppage, break, pause, interval, interruption, hiatus.

halting ▸ adjective *a halting conversation | halting English* =hesitant, faltering, hesitating, stumbling, stammering, stuttering; broken, imperfect.
−OPPOSITES fluent.

ham-fisted ▸ adjective =clumsy, bungling, incompetent, amateurish, inept, inexpert, maladroit, gauche, bumbling; *informal* cack-handed; *Brit. informal* all fingers and thumbs.
−OPPOSITES skilful.

hammer ▸ noun =mallet, gavel, sledgehammer.
▸ verb **1** =beat, forge, shape, form, mould, fashion. **2** *Sally hammered at the door* =batter, pummel, beat, bang, pound; knock on, thump on; *informal* bash, wallop, clobber.

hamper[1] ▸ noun =basket, pannier.

hamper[2] ▸ verb =hinder, obstruct, impede, inhibit, curb, delay, slow down, hold up, interfere with; restrict, constrain, block, check, curtail, handicap, hamstring; *informal* stymie.
−OPPOSITES help.

hamstring ▸ verb =handicap, hamper, cripple, hinder, obstruct, impede, inhibit, constrain, restrict, shackle, fetter, encumber, block, frustrate; *informal* stymie.
−OPPOSITES help.

hand ▸ noun **1** =palm, fist; *informal* paw,

mitt. **2** *the clock's second hand* =**pointer**, indicator, needle. **3** *in government hands* =**control**, power; command, management, care, supervision, jurisdiction; possession, custody. **4** *written in his own hand* =**handwriting**, writing, script. **5** *a factory hand* =**worker**, manual worker, unskilled worker, blue-collar worker, workman, labourer, operative, roustabout.
▶ verb =**pass**, give, let someone have, throw, toss; present to; *informal* chuck, bung.

■ **at hand 1** *close at hand* =**readily available**, handy, within reach, accessible, close (by), nearby, at the ready, at one's fingertips, at one's disposal. **2** *the time for action is at hand* =**imminent**, approaching, coming, about to happen, on the horizon.

■ **hand something down** =**pass on**, pass down; bequeath, leave, make over, give, transfer.

■ **hand in glove** =**in collaboration**, in close association, in partnership, in league, in collusion; *informal* in cahoots.

■ **hand something on** =**give**, pass, hand, transfer, grant.

■ **hand something out** =**distribute**, hand round, give out/round, pass out/round, share out, dole out, dish out, deal out, issue, dispense.

■ **hand something over** =**yield**, give, give up, pass, grant, entrust, surrender, relinquish, turn over, deliver up, forfeit, sacrifice.

■ **to hand** =**readily available**, handy, within reach, accessible, ready, close (by), nearby, at the ready, at one's fingertips, convenient.

■ **try one's hand** =**make an attempt**; *informal* have a go, have a stab, have a shot, have a bash, give something a whirl.

WORD LINKS

relating to the hands: **manual**

handbag ▶ noun =**bag**, shoulder bag, clutch bag; *N. Amer.* purse, pocketbook.

handbill ▶ noun =**notice**, advertisement, flyer, leaflet, circular, handout, brochure; *N. Amer.* dodger; *informal* ad; *Brit. informal* advert.

handbook ▶ noun =**manual**, instructions, ABC, A to Z; almanac, companion, guide, guidebook.

handcuff ▶ verb =**manacle**, shackle; restrain, clap/put someone in irons; *informal* cuff.

handcuffs ▶ plural noun =**manacles**, shackles, irons, restraints; *informal* cuffs, bracelets; *archaic* darbies.

handful ▶ noun =**a few**, a small number, a small amount, a small quantity, one or two, some, not many.

handgun ▶ noun =**pistol**, revolver, side arm, six-shooter; *N. Amer. informal* piece, Saturday night special.

handicap ▶ noun **1** =**disability**, infirmity, defect, impairment, affliction. **2** *a handicap to industrial competitiveness* =**impediment**, hindrance, obstacle, barrier, encumbrance, constraint; disadvantage, stumbling block.
–OPPOSITES benefit, advantage.
▶ verb *handicapped by lack of funding* =**hamper**, impede, hinder, impair, hamstring; restrict, constrain; *informal* stymie.
–OPPOSITES help.

handicapped ▶ adjective =**disabled**, incapacitated, disadvantaged; infirm, invalid; *euphemistic* physically challenged, differently abled.

handicraft ▶ noun =**craft**, handiwork, craftwork.

handiwork ▶ noun =**creation**, product, work, achievement.

handkerchief ▶ noun =**tissue**; *trademark* Kleenex; *informal* hanky, nose rag, snot rag; *literary* kerchief.

handle ▶ verb **1** =**hold**, pick up, grasp, grip, lift. **2** *a car which is easy to handle* =**control**, drive, steer, operate, manoeuvre. **3** *she handled the job well* =**deal with**, manage, tackle, take care of, take charge of, attend to, see to, sort out. **4** *the company handling the account* =**administer**, manage, control, conduct, direct, supervise, oversee, be in charge of, take care of, look after. **5** *the traders handled imported goods* =**trade in**, deal in, buy, sell, supply, peddle, traffic in.
▶ noun *the knife's handle* =**haft**, grip, hilt, stock, shaft, butt.

handout ▶ noun **1** *she existed on handouts* =**charity**, benefit, donations, subsidies; *historical* alms. **2** *a xeroxed handout* =**leaflet**, pamphlet, brochure; handbill, flyer, circular, mailshot.

hand-picked ▶ adjective =**specially chosen**, selected, invited; select, elite; choice.

handsome ▸ adjective **1** *a handsome man* =**good-looking**, attractive, personable, striking; *informal* hunky, dishy, tasty, fanciable; *Brit. informal* fit; *N. Amer. informal* cute; *Austral./NZ informal* spunky. **2** *a handsome woman* =**striking**, imposing, prepossessing, good-looking, attractive, personable. **3** *a handsome profit* =**substantial**, considerable, sizeable, princely, large, big, ample, bumper; *informal* tidy, whopping; *Brit. informal* whacking, ginormous.
−OPPOSITES ugly, meagre.

handwriting ▸ noun =**writing**, script, hand; *informal* scrawl, scribble.

WORD LINKS

study of handwriting: **graphology**

handy ▸ adjective **1** =**useful**, convenient, practical, easy-to-use, user-friendly, helpful. **2** *keep your credit card handy* =**readily available**, to hand, within reach, accessible, ready, close (by), nearby, at the ready, at one's fingertips. **3** *he's handy with a needle* =**skilful**, skilled, dexterous, deft, able, adept, proficient; good with one's hands.
−OPPOSITES inconvenient, inept.

handyman ▸ noun =**odd-job man**, odd-jobber, jack of all trades; *informal* Mr Fixit.

hang ▸ verb **1** *lights hung from the trees* =**be suspended**, dangle, swing, sway. **2** *hang the picture at eye level* =**put up**, pin up, display. **3** *the room was hung with streamers* =**decorate**, adorn, drape, festoon, deck out. **4** *he was hanged for murder* =**send to the gallows**, execute; *informal* string up. **5** *a pall of smoke hung over the city* =**hover**, float, be suspended.
■ **hang about** *(Brit.)* **1** *See* HANG AROUND. **2** *(informal) hang about, what's this?* See HANG ON sense 4.
■ **hang around/round** *(informal)* **1** *I've seen him hanging around outside her house* =**loiter**, skulk. **2** *they spent their time hanging around in bars* kill time, kick one's heels, twiddle one's thumbs; *informal* hang out. **3** *she's hanging around with a bunch of hippies* =**associate**, mix, socialize, fraternize, rub shoulders; *N. Amer.* rub elbows; *informal* hang out, run around, knock about/around, hobnob.
■ **hang fire** =**delay**, hold back, stall, pause; *informal* sit tight.
■ **hang on 1** *he hung on to her coat* =**hold on**, grip, clutch, grasp, hold tightly,

cling. **2** *her future hung on his decision* =**depend on**, turn on, hinge on, rest on. **3** *I'll hang on as long as I can* =**persevere**, hold on, keep going, keep at it, continue; *informal* soldier on, stick at it, stick it out. **4** *(informal) hang on, let me think* =**wait a minute**, hold on, stop; hold the line; *informal* hold your horses; *Brit. informal* hang about.
■ **hang out.** *See* HANG AROUND senses 2, 3.

hangdog ▸ adjective =**shamefaced**, sheepish, guilty-looking, cowed, dejected, downcast.
−OPPOSITES defiant.

hanger-on ▸ noun =**follower**, toady, camp follower, parasite, leech, dependant; *N. Amer.* cohort; *informal* groupie, sponger, freeloader, passenger.

hanging ▸ noun *silk wall hangings* =**drape**, tapestry; drapery.
▸ adjective *hanging fronds of honeysuckle* =**dangling**, trailing, drooping, pendent, pendulous.

hang-out ▸ noun =**haunt**, stamping ground, meeting place, watering hole; *N. Amer.* stomping ground.

hang-up ▸ noun =**neurosis**, phobia, preoccupation, fixation, obsession; inhibition, mental block; *informal* complex, thing, issue, bee in one's bonnet.

hank ▸ noun =**coil**, length, loop, twist, skein.

hanker ▸ verb =**yearn**, long, wish, hunger, thirst, lust, ache; *informal* have a yen, itch.

hankering ▸ noun =**longing**, yearning, craving, hunger, thirst, ache, lust; *informal* yen, itch.
−OPPOSITES aversion.

hanky-panky ▸ noun *(informal)* =**goings-on**, funny business, mischief, chicanery, skulduggery; *informal* monkey business, shenanigans, carryings-on; *Brit. informal* jiggery-pokery.

haphazard ▸ adjective =**random**, disorderly, indiscriminate, chaotic, hit-and-miss, aimless; chance; *informal* higgledy-piggledy.
−OPPOSITES methodical.

hapless ▸ adjective =**unfortunate**, unlucky, unhappy, wretched, miserable.
−OPPOSITES lucky.

happen ▸ verb **1** *remember what happened last time* =**occur**, take place, come about; *N. Amer. informal* go down; *literary* come to pass. **2** *I wonder what happened to Susie?* = **become of;** *literary* befall. **3** *they happened to be in London* = **chance,** have the good/bad luck.

happening ▸ noun *bizarre happenings* = **occurrence,** event, incident, episode.
▸ adjective *(informal) a happening nightclub* = **fashionable,** popular; *informal* trendy, funky, hot, cool, with it, hip, in, now, groovy; *N. Amer. informal* tony.
−OPPOSITES unfashionable.

happily ▸ adverb **1** = **contentedly,** cheerfully, cheerily, merrily, joyfully. **2** *I will happily do as you ask* = **gladly,** willingly, readily, freely. **3** *happily, we arrived just in time* = **fortunately,** luckily, thankfully, mercifully, as luck would have it.

happiness ▸ noun = **pleasure,** contentment, satisfaction, cheerfulness, merriment, joy, well-being.

happy ▸ adjective **1** = **cheerful,** cheery, merry, joyful, jovial, jolly, carefree, smiling, beaming, grinning, in good spirits, in a good mood, pleased, contented, content, satisfied, sunny. **2** *we will be happy to advise you* = **glad,** pleased, delighted, more than willing. **3** *a happy coincidence* = **fortunate,** lucky, timely, convenient.
−OPPOSITES sad, unwilling, unfortunate.

happy-go-lucky ▸ adjective = **easygoing,** carefree, casual, free and easy, blithe, nonchalant; *informal* laid-back.
−OPPOSITES anxious.

harangue ▸ noun = **tirade,** diatribe, lecture, rant, polemic.
▸ verb = **rant at,** lecture, shout at; berate.

harass ▸ verb = **persecute,** intimidate, hound; pester, bother; *informal* hassle, bug, give someone a hard time; *N. Amer. informal* devil, ride.

harassed ▸ adjective = **stressed,** hard-pressed, careworn, worried, troubled, beleaguered; *informal* hassled.
−OPPOSITES carefree.

harassment ▸ noun = **persecution,** intimidation, victimization; *informal* hassle.

harbour ▸ noun = **port,** dock, marina; mooring, waterfront.
▸ verb **1** *he is harbouring a dangerous criminal* = **shelter,** conceal, hide, shield, protect. **2** *Rose harboured a grudge against him* = **bear,** hold, nurse.

hard ▸ adjective **1** *hard ground* = **firm,** solid, rigid, stiff, unbreakable, inflexible, impenetrable, unyielding, compacted; tough, strong. **2** *hard physical work* = **arduous,** strenuous, tiring, exhausting, back-breaking, gruelling, heavy, laborious; difficult, taxing, exacting, challenging, demanding, punishing, tough, formidable; *Brit. informal* knackering. **3** *hard workers* = **industrious,** diligent, assiduous, conscientious, energetic, keen, enthusiastic, indefatigable; studious. **4** *a hard problem* = **difficult,** puzzling, perplexing, baffling, bewildering, mystifying, thorny, problematic. **5** *times are hard* = **harsh,** grim, difficult, bad, bleak, tough, austere, dark. **6** *a hard taskmaster* = **strict,** harsh, severe, stern, tough, demanding, exacting; uncompromising, implacable, unrelenting; ruling with a rod of iron. **7** *a hard winter* = **cold,** bitter, harsh, severe, bleak, freezing, icy. **8** *a hard blow* = **forceful,** heavy, strong, sharp, violent, powerful. **9** *hard facts* = **reliable,** definite, undeniable, indisputable, verifiable.
−OPPOSITES soft, easy, lazy, gentle.
▸ adverb **1** *George pushed her hard* = **forcefully,** forcibly, roughly, heavily, sharply, violently, with all one's might. **2** *they worked hard* = **diligently,** industriously, assiduously, conscientiously, energetically, doggedly; *informal* like mad, like crazy. **3** *she looked hard at me* = **closely,** intently, critically, carefully, searchingly.
■ **hard and fast** = **definite,** fixed, set, strict, rigid, clear-cut, cast-iron.
■ **hard up** *(informal)* = **poor,** short of money, badly off, impoverished; *formal* impecunious, in reduced circumstances; *informal* broke, strapped (for cash); *Brit. informal* skint.

hardbitten ▸ adjective = **hardened,** tough, cynical, unsentimental, hardheaded; *informal* hard-nosed, hard-boiled.
−OPPOSITES sentimental.

hard-boiled ▸ adjective *(informal).* See HARDBITTEN.

hard-core ▸ adjective = **diehard,** staunch, dedicated, committed, dyed-in-the-wool; hard-line.

harden ▸ verb **1** *this glue hardens in four hours* = **solidify,** set, stiffen, thicken. **2** *their suffering had hardened them* = **toughen,** desensitize, inure, harden someone's heart; numb.
−OPPOSITES liquefy, soften.

hardened ▶ adjective *a hardened criminal* =**inveterate**, seasoned, habitual, chronic, compulsive, confirmed, dyed-in-the-wool; incorrigible.

hard-headed ▶ adjective =**unsentimental**, practical, businesslike, realistic, down-to-earth, matter-of-fact, no-nonsense; *informal* hard-nosed.
−OPPOSITES idealistic.

hard-hearted ▶ adjective =**unfeeling**, heartless, cold, hard, callous, unsympathetic, uncaring, having a heart of stone, as hard as nails.
−OPPOSITES compassionate.

hard-hitting ▶ adjective =**uncompromising**, forthright, frank, direct, tough; unsparing, pulling no punches, not mincing one's words.

hardiness ▶ noun =**robustness**, strength, toughness, ruggedness, sturdiness, resilience.
−OPPOSITES frailty.

hard-line ▶ adjective =**uncompromising**, strict, extreme, diehard.
−OPPOSITES moderate.

hardly ▶ adverb *we hardly know each other* =**scarcely**, barely, only just.

hard-nosed ▶ adjective *(informal)* =**tough-minded**, unsentimental, no-nonsense, hard-headed, hardbitten, down-to-earth.
−OPPOSITES sentimental.

hard-pressed ▶ adjective =**troubled**, beleaguered, ailing, harassed; overburdened.

hardship ▶ noun =**difficulty**, privation, destitution, poverty, austerity, penury, need; distress, suffering, adversity, trials and tribulations, dire straits.
−OPPOSITES prosperity, ease.

hardware ▶ noun =**equipment**, apparatus, gear, paraphernalia, tackle, kit, machinery.

hard-wearing ▶ adjective =**durable**, strong, tough, resilient, stout, rugged.
−OPPOSITES flimsy.

hard-working ▶ adjective =**diligent**, industrious, conscientious, assiduous, persevering, studious.
−OPPOSITES lazy.

hardy ▶ adjective =**robust**, healthy, fit, strong, sturdy, tough, rugged; *dated* stalwart.
−OPPOSITES delicate.

hare ▶ noun

> **WORD LINKS**
>
> *male:* **buck**
> *female:* **doe**
> *young:* **leveret**
> *home:* **form**
> *collective noun:* **down, mute, husk**

hare-brained ▶ adjective *a hare-brained scheme* =**foolish**, madcap, stupid, ridiculous, idiotic, half-baked; *informal* crackpot, crazy; *Brit. informal* daft, barmy.
−OPPOSITES sensible, intelligent.

hark ■ **hark back to** =**recall**, call/bring to mind, evoke, put one in mind of.

harm ▶ noun *it won't do you any harm* =**injury**, damage, mischief.
−OPPOSITES benefit.
▶ verb **1** *he's never harmed anybody in his life* =**hurt**, lay a finger on, mistreat, ill-treat. **2** *this could harm his World Cup prospects* =**damage**, spoil, affect, undermine.

harmful ▶ adjective =**damaging**, injurious, detrimental, dangerous; *formal* deleterious, negative, unhealthy, unwholesome, hurtful, destructive; noxious, hazardous.
−OPPOSITES beneficial.

harmless ▶ adjective **1** *a harmless substance* =**safe**, innocuous. **2** *he seems harmless enough* =**inoffensive**, innocuous.
−OPPOSITES dangerous.

harmonious ▶ adjective **1** *a harmonious relationship* =**friendly**, amicable, cordial, amiable, congenial, easy. **2** *a harmonious blend of traditional and modern* =**balanced**, coordinated, pleasing, tasteful.
−OPPOSITES discordant, hostile, incongruous.

harmonize ▶ verb **1** *colours which harmonize* =**coordinate**, go together, match, blend, mix, balance, tone in; be compatible, be harmonious, suit each other, set each other off. **2** *the need to harmonize tax laws across Europe* =**standardize**, coordinate, integrate, synchronize, make consistent, bring into line, systematize.
−OPPOSITES clash.

harmony ▶ noun **1** *musical harmony* =**tunefulness**, euphony, melodiousness. **2** *the harmony of the whole design* =**balance**, symmetry, congruity, coordination. **3** *the villagers live together in harmony* =**accord**, agreement, peace, amity,

friendship, fellowship, cooperation, understanding, unity, like-mindedness; *formal* concord.
–OPPOSITES dissonance, disagreement.

harness ▶ noun =tack, tackle, equipment; yoke; *archaic* equipage.
▶ verb **1** *he harnessed his horse* =hitch up, put in harness, yoke. **2** *attempts to harness solar energy* =exploit, utilize, use, make use of, put to use.

harp ∎ **harp on about** =keep on about, go on about, dwell on, make an issue of.

harrowing ▶ adjective =distressing, traumatic, upsetting; shocking, disturbing.

harry ▶ verb *they were constantly harried by an unseen foe* =harass, hound, torment, pester, worry, badger, nag, plague; *informal* hassle, bug, lean on, give someone a hard time.

harsh ▶ adjective **1** *a harsh voice* =grating, rasping, strident, raucous, discordant; screeching, shrill; rough. **2** *harsh colours* =glaring, loud, garish, gaudy, lurid. **3** *his harsh treatment of captives* =cruel, savage, barbarous, merciless, inhumane; ruthless, pitiless, severe, hard-hearted. **4** *they took harsh measures to end the crisis* =severe, stringent, firm, stiff, hard, stern, rigorous. **5** *harsh words* =rude, discourteous, impolite; unfriendly, sharp, bitter, unkind, disparaging. **6** *harsh conditions* =austere, grim, spartan, hard, inhospitable. **7** *a harsh winter* =hard, severe, cold, bitter, bleak, freezing, icy. **8** *harsh cream cleaners* =abrasive, coarse, rough.
–OPPOSITES soft, subdued, kind, friendly, comfortable, mild.

harvest ▶ noun *a poor harvest* =yield, crop, vintage.
▶ verb *he harvested the wheat* =gather (in), bring in, reap, pick, collect.

hash¹ ∎ **make a hash of** (*informal*) =make a mess of; *informal* botch, bungle, muck up, foul up, ruin, wreck, screw up; *Brit. informal* make a pig's ear of, cock up; *N. Amer. informal* flub.

hash² ▶ noun (*informal*) *she smokes a lot of hash. See* CANNABIS.

hassle (*informal*) ▶ noun *parking is such a hassle* =inconvenience, bother, nuisance, trouble, annoyance, irritation, fuss; *informal* aggravation, aggro, stress, headache, pain (in the neck).
▶ verb *don't hassle me!* =harass, pester, be on at, badger, hound, bother, torment; *informal* bug, give someone a hard time, be on someone's back; *N. English informal* mither.

hassled ▶ adjective (*informal*) =harassed, agitated, stressed (out), flustered; beleaguered; under pressure, hot and bothered; *informal* up against it.
–OPPOSITES calm.

haste ▶ noun =speed, hurriedness, swiftness, rapidity, quickness, briskness.
–OPPOSITES delay.
∎ **in haste** =quickly, rapidly, fast, speedily, in a rush, in a hurry.

hasten ▶ verb **1** *we hastened back* =hurry, rush, dash, race; go quickly; *informal* scoot, zip, hotfoot it, leg it; *N. Amer. informal* hightail; *dated* make haste. **2** *chemicals can hasten ageing* =bring on, precipitate, advance.
–OPPOSITES dawdle, delay.

hastily ▶ adverb *Meg retreated hastily* =hurriedly, quickly, swiftly, rapidly, speedily, briskly, without delay, posthaste; on the double; *informal* double quick, p.d.q. (pretty damn quick); *Brit. informal* at a rate of knots; *N. Amer. informal* lickety-split.

hasty ▶ adjective **1** *a hasty departure* =hurried, quick, swift, speedy, brisk. **2** *a hasty decision* =rash, impetuous, impulsive, reckless, precipitate, spur-of-the-moment.
–OPPOSITES slow, considered.

hate ▶ verb **1** *they hate each other* =loathe, detest, despise, dislike, abhor, be unable to bear/stand. **2** *I hate to bother you* =be sorry, be reluctant, be loath.
–OPPOSITES love.
▶ noun *feelings of hate* =hatred, loathing, detestation, abhorrence, abomination, execration, revulsion; disgust.
–OPPOSITES love.
∎ **pet hate** =bugbear, bane, bête noire, thorn in one's flesh/side; *N. Amer.* bugaboo.

hateful ▶ adjective =detestable, horrible, despicable, objectionable, revolting, loathsome, abhorrent, abominable, odious, disgusting, obnoxious, vile.
–OPPOSITES delightful.

hatred ▶ noun =loathing, hate, detestation, abhorrence, execration; *formal* odium.

haughtiness ▶ noun =arrogance, pride, hauteur, condescension; superciliousness; *informal* snootiness.

–OPPOSITES modesty.

haughty ▶ adjective =**arrogant**, proud, superior, supercilious, condescending; above oneself; *informal* stuck-up, snooty, high and mighty, la-di-da; *Brit. informal* toffee-nosed; *N. Amer. informal* chesty.
–OPPOSITES humble.

haul ▶ verb **1** *she hauled the basket upstairs* =**drag**, pull, heave, lug, hump. **2** *a contract to haul coal* =**transport**, carry, ship, ferry, move, shift.

haunches ▶ plural noun =**hindquarters**, rump, rear (end).

haunt ▶ verb *the sight haunted me for years* =**torment**, disturb, trouble, worry, plague; prey on, weigh on, nag at, obsess; *informal* bug.
▶ noun *a favourite haunt of artists* =**hang-out**, stamping ground, meeting place; spot, venue; *N. Amer.* stomping ground.

haunted ▶ adjective **1** *the church is haunted* =**possessed**, cursed, jinxed. **2** *his haunted eyes* =**tormented**, anguished, tortured, troubled, worried.

haunting ▶ adjective =**evocative**, affecting, stirring, powerful; poignant; memorable.

hauteur ▶ noun =**haughtiness**, superciliousness, arrogance, pride, superiority; condescension; airs and graces; *informal* snootiness.

have ▶ verb **1** *he had a new car* =**own**, be in possession of; be blessed with, boast, enjoy. **2** *the flat has five rooms* =**comprise**, consist of, contain, include, incorporate, be composed of, be made up of. **3** *they had tea together* =**eat**, partake of; drink, take, imbibe, quaff. **4** *to have a party* =**organize**, hold, give, throw, put on, lay on. **5** *we are having guests for dinner* =**entertain**, be host to, receive; invite round/over. **6** *he had trouble finding the restaurant* =**experience**, encounter, meet with, run into. **7** *I have a headache* =**be suffering from**, be afflicted by/with, be affected by, be troubled with. **8** *many of them have doubts* =**harbour**, entertain, feel, nurse. **9** *he had them throw Chris out* =**make**, ask to, get to, tell to, order to, force to. **10** *I can't have you insulting me* =**put up with**, go along with; *informal* stand for, be doing with. **11** *I have to get up at six* =**must**, be obliged to, be required to, be compelled to, be forced to, be bound to. **12** *(informal)* *I've been had* =**trick**, fool, deceive, dupe, take in; *informal* do, con; *N. Amer.*

informal sucker.

■ **have done with** =**have finished with**, be done with, be through with, want no more to do with.

■ **have had it** *(informal)* **1** *they admit that they've had it* =**have no chance**, have no hope, have failed, be finished, be defeated. **2** *if you tell anyone, you've had it* =**will be in trouble**; *informal* will be for the high jump; *Brit. informal* will be for it.

■ **have someone on** *(Brit. informal)* =**play a trick on**, play a joke on, pull someone's leg; *Brit. informal* wind up; *N. Amer. informal* put on.

■ **have something on 1** *she had a hat on* =**be wearing**, be dressed in, be clothed in, be decked out in. **2** *(Brit.)* *I've got a lot on at the moment* =**have arranged**, have planned, have organized, have on the go.

haven ▶ noun *a safe haven* =**refuge**, retreat, shelter, sanctuary; oasis.

haversack ▶ noun =**knapsack**, rucksack, backpack.

havoc ▶ noun *hyperactive children create havoc* =**chaos**, mayhem, bedlam, pandemonium.

hawk[1] ▶ noun

> **WORD LINKS**
>
> young: **chick, eyas**
> collective noun: **cast**

hawk[2] ▶ verb =**peddle**, sell, trade in, traffic in, deal in; *Brit. informal* flog.

hazard ▶ noun *the hazards of radiation* =**danger**, risk, peril, threat.

hazardous ▶ adjective =**risky**, dangerous, unsafe, perilous, fraught with danger; high-risk; *informal* dicey; *Brit. informal* dodgy.
–OPPOSITES safe, certain.

haze ▶ noun =**mist**, fog, haar, cloud.

hazy ▶ adjective **1** *a hazy day* =**misty**, foggy; smoggy, murky. **2** *hazy memories* =**vague**, dim, nebulous, blurred, fuzzy.

head ▶ noun **1** *her head hit the wall* =**skull**, cranium; *informal* nut, noggin; *informal, dated* noddle. **2** *he had to use his head* =**brain(s)**, brainpower, intellect, intelligence; grey matter; *Brit. informal* loaf; *N. Amer. informal* smarts. **3** *she had a head for business* =**aptitude**, talent, gift, capacity. **4** *the head of the church* =**leader**, chief, controller, governor, superintendent; commander, captain; director, manager; principal, president; *informal* boss,

Mr Big, head honcho; *Brit. informal* gaffer, guv'nor; *N. Amer. informal* big kahuna.
5 *the head of the queue* =**front**, beginning, start; top.
−OPPOSITES back.
▶ adjective *the head waiter* =**chief**, principal, leading, main, first, top, highest; *N. Amer.* ranking.
▶ verb *a team headed by a manager* =**command**, control, lead, manage, direct, supervise, superintend, oversee, preside over.
■ **at the head of** =**in charge of**, controlling, leading, managing, running, directing; at the wheel of, at the helm of.
■ **head across/along/towards** =**move**, make one's way, travel, pass, proceed, go.
■ **head first**. *See* HEADLONG adverb.
■ **head someone/something off 1** *he went to head off the visitors* =**intercept**, divert, redirect, re-route, turn away. **2** *they headed off an argument* =**forestall**, avert, stave off, nip in the bud; prevent, avoid, stop.
■ **keep one's head** =**keep/stay/remain calm**, keep one's self-control; *informal* keep one's cool.
■ **lose one's head** =**lose control**, lose one's composure, go to pieces; panic, get hysterical; *informal* lose one's cool, freak out, crack up; *Brit. informal* throw a wobbly.

WORD LINKS
relating to the head: **cephalic**

headache ▶ noun **1** *I've got a headache* =**sore head**, migraine, hangover. **2** *(informal)* *it was a real headache* =**problem**, worry, hassle, pain (in the neck), bind.

head case ▶ noun *(informal)* =**maniac**, lunatic, madman, madwoman; *informal* loony; *Brit. informal* nutter; *N. Amer. informal* crazy, wacko.

heading ▶ noun **1** *chapter headings* =**title**, caption, legend, rubric, headline. **2** *this topic falls under four main headings* =**category**, division, class, section, group, topic, area.

headland ▶ noun =**cape**, promontory, point, foreland, peninsula, ness, spit, horn, bill, bluff; *Scottish* mull.

headlong ▶ adverb **1** *he fell headlong into the water* =**head first**, on one's head. **2** *she rushed headlong into marriage* =**without thinking**, precipitously, impetuously, rashly, recklessly, hastily.

−OPPOSITES cautiously.
▶ adjective *a headlong dash* =**breakneck**, whirlwind; reckless, precipitous.
−OPPOSITES cautious.

head-on ▶ adjective *a head-on confrontation* =**direct**, face to face, eyeball to eyeball, personal, open.
▶ adverb *we must meet this issue head-on* =**directly**, face to face, eyeball to eyeball, personally, openly.

headquarters ▶ plural noun =**head office**, HQ, base, nerve centre, mission control.

headstone ▶ noun =**gravestone**, tombstone, memorial.

headstrong ▶ adjective =**wilful**, strong-willed, stubborn, obstinate, obdurate; contrary, perverse, wayward.

head teacher ▶ noun =**head**, headmaster, headmistress, principal, director.

headway ■ **make headway** =**make progress**, make strides, gain ground, advance, come along.

heady ▶ adjective **1** *heady wine* =**potent**, intoxicating, strong. **2** *the heady days of my youth* =**exhilarating**, exciting, thrilling, intoxicating.
−OPPOSITES boring.

heal ▶ verb **1** *he heals the sick* =**make better**, cure, treat, restore to health. **2** *his knee had healed* =**get better**, be cured, recover, mend. **3** *time will heal the pain* =**alleviate**, ease, assuage, lessen, allay. **4** *we tried to heal the rift* =**put right**, repair, resolve, settle; *informal* patch up.
−OPPOSITES aggravate, worsen.

healing ▶ adjective =**curative**, therapeutic, medicinal, restorative.
−OPPOSITES harmful.

WORD LINKS
related prefix: **iatro-**

health ▶ noun **1** *he was restored to health* =**well-being**, fitness, good condition; strength, vigour. **2** *poor health* =**condition**, physical shape, constitution.
−OPPOSITES illness.

WORD LINKS
health-giving: **salubrious**
relating to health: **sanitary**

healthful ▶ adjective =**healthy**, beneficial, wholesome, nourishing, nutritious.
−OPPOSITES unhealthy.

healthy ▶ adjective **1** *a healthy baby* =**well**, fit, in good shape, in fine fettle, in tip-top condition; strong, fighting fit. **2** *a healthy diet* =**health-giving**, good for one; wholesome, nutritious, nourishing.
–OPPOSITES ill, unwholesome.

heap ▶ noun **1** *a heap of boxes* =**pile**, stack, mound, mountain. **2** *(informal) we have heaps of room* =**lots**, plenty, an abundance, (a great) many, a large number; *informal* hundreds, thousands, millions, loads, piles, oodles, stacks, masses, reams, wads, pots, oceans, miles, tons, zillions; *Brit. informal* lashings.
▶ verb *she heaped logs on the fire* =**pile (up)**, stack (up), make a mound of.
■ **heap something on/upon** *they heaped praise on her* =**shower on**, lavish on, load on.

hear ▶ verb **1** *she could hear voices* =**make out**, catch, get, perceive; overhear. **2** *they heard that I had moved* =**learn**, find out, discover, gather, glean. **3** *a jury heard the case* =**try**, judge; adjudicate (on).

hearing ▶ noun **1** *she moved out of hearing* =**earshot**, hearing distance. **2** *I had a fair hearing* =**chance to speak**, opportunity to be heard. **3** *he gave evidence at the hearing* =**trial**, court case, inquiry, inquest, tribunal.

> WORD LINKS
>
> *relating to hearing:* **auditory, aural, acoustic**
> *branch of medicine to do with hearing:* **audiology**
> *measurement of hearing:* **audiometry**

hearsay ▶ noun =**rumour**, gossip, tittle-tattle, idle talk; stories, tales.

heart ▶ noun **1** *he poured out his heart* =**emotions**, feelings, sentiments; soul, mind. **2** *he has no heart* =**compassion**, sympathy, humanity, feeling(s), empathy, understanding; soul, goodwill. **3** *they lost heart* =**enthusiasm**, spirit, determination, resolve, nerve; *Brit. informal* bottle. **4** *the heart of the city* =**centre**, middle, hub, core. **5** *the heart of the matter* =**essence**, crux, core, nub, root, meat, substance, kernel; *informal* nitty-gritty.
–OPPOSITES edge.
■ **after one's own heart** =**like-minded**, kindred, congenial, on the same wavelength.
■ **at heart** =**deep down**, basically, fundamentally, essentially, in essence,

intrinsically; *informal* when you get right down to it.
■ **(off) by heart** =**from memory**, off pat, word for word, verbatim, parrot-fashion, word-perfect.
■ **do one's heart good** =**cheer (up)**, please, gladden, make one happy, delight, hearten, gratify, make one feel good, give one a lift.
■ **eat one's heart out** =**pine**, long, ache, brood, mope, fret, sigh.
■ **from the (bottom of one's) heart** =**sincerely**, earnestly, truly, genuinely, heartily, deeply.
■ **give/lose one's heart to** =**fall in love with**, be smitten by; *informal* fall for, fall head over heels for, be swept off one's feet by.
■ **have a change of heart** =**change one's mind**, have second thoughts, have a rethink, think again; *informal* get cold feet.
■ **have a heart** =**show compassion**, be kind, be merciful.
■ **heart and soul** =**wholeheartedly**, absolutely, completely, entirely, fully, utterly, to the hilt, one hundred per cent.
■ **take heart** =**be encouraged**, be heartened, be comforted, be consoled.
■ **with one's heart in one's mouth** =**with bated breath**, fearfully, apprehensively, with trepidation, nervously, anxiously.

> WORD LINKS
>
> *relating to the heart:* **cardiac**
> *relating to the arteries of the heart:* **coronary**
> *branch of medicine to do with the heart:* **cardiology**
> *inflammation of the heart:* **carditis**
> *fear of heart disease:* **cardiophobia**

heartache ▶ noun =**anguish**, suffering, distress, unhappiness, misery, sorrow, sadness, heartbreak, pain, hurt, woe.
–OPPOSITES happiness.

heartbreak ▶ noun. See HEARTACHE.

heartbreaking ▶ adjective =**distressing**, upsetting, disturbing, heart-rending, tragic, painful, sad, agonizing, harrowing.
–OPPOSITES comforting.

heartbroken ▶ adjective =**anguished**, devastated, broken-hearted, heavy-hearted, grieving, grief-stricken, inconsolable, crushed, shattered, desolate, despairing; miserable, sorrowful, sad, despondent; *informal* choked.

heartburn ▸ noun =**indigestion**, dyspepsia, pyrosis.

hearten ▸ verb =**cheer (up)**, encourage, raise someone's spirits, boost, buoy up, perk up; *informal* buck up, pep up.

heartfelt ▸ adjective =**sincere**, genuine, from the heart; earnest, profound, deep, wholehearted; honest.
–OPPOSITES insincere.

heartily ▸ adverb 1 *we heartily welcome the changes* =**wholeheartedly**, warmly, profoundly, with all one's heart; eagerly, enthusiastically. 2 *they were heartily sick of her* =**thoroughly**, completely, absolutely, exceedingly, downright; *N. Amer.* quite; *informal* seriously; *Brit. informal* jolly, well; *N. Amer. informal* real, mighty.

heartless ▸ adjective =**unfeeling**, unsympathetic, unkind, uncaring, hard-hearted; cold, callous, cruel, merciless, pitiless, inhuman.
–OPPOSITES compassionate.

heart-rending ▸ adjective =**distressing**, upsetting, disturbing, heartbreaking, tragic, painful, sad, agonizing, harrowing.

heart-throb ▸ noun *(informal)* =**idol**, pin-up, hero; *informal* dreamboat.

heart-to-heart ▸ adjective *a heart-to-heart chat* =**intimate**, man-to-man, woman-to-woman; candid, honest.
▸ noun *they had a long heart-to-heart* =**private conversation**, tête-à-tête, one-to-one, head-to-head; talk, word; *informal* confab.

heart-warming ▸ adjective =**touching**, heartening, stirring, uplifting, cheering, gratifying.
–OPPOSITES distressing.

hearty ▸ adjective 1 *a hearty character* =**exuberant**, jovial, ebullient, cheerful, uninhibited, effusive, lively, loud, animated, vivacious, energetic, spirited. 2 *hearty congratulations* =**wholehearted**, heartfelt, sincere, genuine, real, true. 3 *a hearty woman of sixty-five* =**robust**, healthy, hardy, fit; vigorous, sturdy, strong. 4 *a hearty meal* =**substantial**, large, ample, satisfying, filling, generous.
–OPPOSITES introverted, half-hearted, frail, light.

heat ▸ noun 1 *a plant sensitive to heat* =**warmth**, hotness, warmness, high temperature. 2 *the summer heat* =**hot weather**, sultriness, mugginess, humidity; heatwave, hot spell. 3 *he took the heat out of the dispute* =**passion**, intensity, vehemence, warmth, fervour, excitement, agitation; anger.
–OPPOSITES cold, apathy.
▸ verb 1 *the food was heated* =**warm (up)**, reheat, cook, keep warm. 2 *the pipes expand as they heat up* =**get hot**, get warm, warm up; *Brit. informal* hot up.
–OPPOSITES cool.

WORD LINKS
relating to heat: **thermal**
fear of heat: **thermophobia**

heated ▸ adjective 1 *a heated swimming pool* =**warm**, hot. 2 *a heated argument* =**vehement**, passionate, impassioned, animated, 'lively', acrimonious; angry, bitter, furious, fierce. 3 *Robert grew heated as he spoke of the risks* =**excited**, animated, worked up, wound up, keyed up; *informal* het up.

heater ▸ noun =**radiator**, convector, fire, brazier.

heave ▸ verb 1 *she heaved the sofa backwards* =**haul**, pull, drag, tug; *informal* yank. 2 *(informal) she heaved a brick at him* =**throw**, fling, cast, hurl, lob, pitch; *informal* chuck, sling; *N. English & Austral. informal* hoy; *NZ informal* bish. 3 *he heaved a sigh of relief* =**let out**, breathe, give; emit, utter. 4 *the sea heaved* =**rise and fall**, roll, swell, surge, churn, seethe. 5 *she heaved into the sink* =**retch**; vomit, cough up; *Brit.* be sick; *N. Amer.* get sick; *informal* throw up, puke, chunder, chuck up, hurl, spew; *Scottish informal* boke; *N. Amer. informal* barf, upchuck.

heaven ▸ noun 1 *the good will have a place in heaven* =**paradise**, Zion; the hereafter, the next world, the afterworld; Elysium, Valhalla; *literary* the empyrean. 2 *a good book is my idea of heaven* =**bliss**, ecstasy, rapture, contentment, happiness, delight, joy; paradise. 3 *(literary) he observed the heavens* =**the sky**, the skies, the upper atmosphere; *literary* the firmament, the vault of heaven, the blue, the (wide) blue yonder.
–OPPOSITES hell, misery.
■ **in seventh heaven** =**ecstatic**, euphoric, thrilled, elated, delighted, overjoyed, on cloud nine, walking on air, jumping for joy, transported, delirious, blissful; *informal* over the moon, on top

of the world, on a high, tickled pink, as pleased as Punch, cock-a-hoop.

■ **move heaven and earth** =try one's hardest, do one's best, do one's utmost, do all one can, spare no effort; *informal* bend over backwards, do one's damnedest, go all out, bust a gut.

> **WORD LINKS**
>
> *relating to heaven:* **celestial, empyrean**
> *fear of heaven:* **uranophobia**

heavenly ▸ adjective **1** *heavenly choirs* =**divine**, holy, celestial; angelic; *literary* empyrean. **2** *heavenly constellations* =**celestial**, cosmic, stellar; sidereal. **3** *(informal) a heavenly morning* =**delightful**, wonderful, glorious, sublime; exquisite, beautiful, lovely, gorgeous, enchanting; *informal* divine, super, great, fantastic, fabulous, terrific.
–OPPOSITES mortal, infernal, terrestrial, dreadful.

heaven-sent ▸ adjective =**auspicious**, providential, propitious, felicitous, opportune, golden, favourable, serendipitous, lucky, fortunate.
–OPPOSITES inopportune.

heavily ▸ adverb **1** *Dad walked heavily* =**laboriously**, slowly, ponderously, awkwardly, clumsily. **2** *we were heavily defeated* =**decisively**, conclusively, roundly, soundly, utterly, completely, thoroughly. **3** *he drank heavily* =**excessively**, immoderately, copiously, intemperately, too much. **4** *the area is heavily planted with trees* =**densely**, closely, thickly. **5** *I became heavily involved* =**deeply**, very, extremely, greatly, exceedingly, tremendously, profoundly.
–OPPOSITES easily, narrowly, moderately.

heavy ▸ adjective **1** *a heavy box* =**weighty**, hefty, substantial, ponderous; solid, dense, leaden. **2** *a heavy man* =**big**, fat, obese, corpulent, large, bulky, stout, overweight, portly, plump, fleshy; *informal* tubby. **3** *a heavy blow to the head* =**forceful**, hard, strong, violent, powerful, mighty, sharp, severe. **4** *a gardener did the heavy work for me* =**strenuous**, hard, physical, difficult, arduous, demanding, back-breaking, gruelling; *archaic* toilsome. **5** *a heavy burden of responsibility* =**onerous**, burdensome, demanding, difficult, weighty; oppressive. **6** *heavy fog* =**dense**, thick, soupy, murky, impenetrable. **7** *a heavy sky* =**overcast**,

cloudy, grey, murky, dark, black, stormy, leaden, louring. **8** *heavy rain* =**torrential**, relentless, teeming, severe. **9** *heavy soil* =**clay**, muddy, sticky, wet; *Brit.* claggy. **10** *a heavy fine* =**sizeable**, hefty, substantial, colossal, big; stiff; whopping. **11** *heavy seas* =**tempestuous**, turbulent, rough, wild, stormy, choppy. **12** *heavy fighting* =**intense**, fierce, relentless, severe, serious. **13** *a heavy drinker* =**immoderate**, excessive, intemperate, chronic. **14** *a heavy meal* =**substantial**, filling, stodgy, rich, big. **15** *he felt heavy and very tired* =**lethargic**, listless, sluggish, torpid, languid, apathetic. **16** *these poems are rather heavy* =**tedious**, difficult, dull, dry, serious, heavy going, dreary, boring, turgid, uninteresting; *informal* deadly. **17** *branches heavy with blossom* =**laden**, loaded, covered, filled, groaning, bursting. **18** *he has heavy features* =**coarse**, rough, rough-hewn, unrefined; rugged, craggy.
–OPPOSITES light, thin, gentle, easy, bright, friable, small, calm, moderate, energetic, cheerful, meagre, delicate.

heavy-handed ▸ adjective **1** *they are heavy-handed with the equipment* =**clumsy**, awkward, maladroit; *informal* ham-fisted, cack-handed; *Brit. informal* all (fingers and) thumbs. **2** *heavy-handed policing* =**insensitive**, oppressive, overbearing, harsh, severe; tactless, undiplomatic, inept.
–OPPOSITES dexterous, sensitive.

heavy-hearted ▸ adjective =**melancholy**, sad, sorrowful, mournful, gloomy, depressed, despondent, dejected, downhearted, downcast, disconsolate, miserable, wretched, woebegone, doleful, unhappy; *literary* dolorous.
–OPPOSITES cheerful.

heckle ▸ verb =**jeer**, shout down, boo, hiss; *Brit. & Austral./NZ* barrack; *informal* give someone a hard time.
–OPPOSITES cheer.

hectic ▸ adjective =**frantic**, frenetic, frenzied, feverish, manic, busy, active, fast and furious.
–OPPOSITES leisurely.

hector ▸ verb =**bully**, intimidate, browbeat, harass, torment, plague; coerce, pressurize, strong-arm.

hedge ▸ noun **1** *an excellent hedge against a fall in sterling* =**safeguard**, protection, shield, screen, guard, buffer, cushion. **2** *his analysis is full of hedges* =**equivo-**

cation, evasion, fudge, qualification; ambiguity, vagueness.
▶ verb **1** *fields hedged with hawthorn* =**surround**, enclose, border, edge, bound. **2** *she was hedged in by her education* =**confine**, restrict, limit, hinder, obstruct, impede, constrain. **3** *he hedged at every new question* =**prevaricate**, equivocate, dodge the issue, be non-committal, be evasive, be vague; *Brit.* hum and haw; *informal* sit on the fence, duck the question. **4** *the company hedged its position on the market* =**safeguard**, protect, shield, guard, cushion.

hedonism ▶ noun =**self-indulgence**, pleasure-seeking, self-gratification, sybaritism; decadence, intemperance, extravagance, high living.
−OPPOSITES self-restraint.

hedonist ▶ noun =**sybarite**, sensualist, voluptuary, pleasure-seeker, bon viveur.
−OPPOSITES ascetic.

hedonistic ▶ adjective =**self-indulgent**, pleasure-seeking, sybaritic; unrestrained, intemperate, immoderate, decadent.

heed ▶ verb *heed the warnings* =**pay attention to**, take notice of, take note of, pay heed to, attend to, listen to; be mindful of, consider, take into account, obey, adhere to, abide by, observe, take to heart, be alert to.
−OPPOSITES disregard.
▶ noun *he paid no heed* =**attention**, notice, note, regard.

heedful ▶ adjective =**attentive**, careful, mindful, cautious, prudent, circumspect; alert, aware, wary, chary.

heedless ▶ adjective =**unmindful**, taking no notice, neglectful, oblivious, inattentive, blind, deaf; incautious, imprudent, rash, reckless, foolhardy.

heft ▶ verb =**lift (up)**, raise (up), heave, hoist, haul; carry, lug; *informal* cart, tote, hump.

hefty ▶ adjective **1** *a hefty young man* =**burly**, heavy, sturdy, strapping, bulky, strong, muscular, large, big, solid, well built; *informal* hulking, beefy. **2** *a hefty kick* =**powerful**, violent, hard, forceful. **3** *a hefty fine* =**substantial**, sizeable, considerable, stiff, large, heavy; *informal* astronomical, whopping.
−OPPOSITES slight, feeble, light, small.

hegemony ▶ noun =**leadership**, dominance, supremacy, authority, mastery,

control, power, rule.

height ▶ noun **1** *the height of the wall* =**highness**, tallness, elevation, stature, altitude. **2** *the mountain heights* =**summit**, top, peak, crest, crown, tip, cap, pinnacle. **3** *the height of their fame* =**highest point**, peak, acme, zenith, apogee, pinnacle, climax. **4** *the height of bad manners* =**epitome**, acme, quintessence; ultimate, utmost.
−OPPOSITES width, nadir.

> WORD LINKS
>
> measurement of height: **altimetry, hypsometry**
> fear of heights: **acrophobia**

heighten ▶ verb **1** *the roof had to be heightened* =**make higher**, raise, lift (up), elevate. **2** *her pleasure was heightened by guilt* =**intensify**, increase, enhance, add to, augment, boost, strengthen, deepen, magnify, reinforce.
−OPPOSITES lower, reduce.

heinous ▶ adjective =**odious**, wicked, evil, atrocious, monstrous, abominable, detestable, despicable, horrific, terrible, awful, abhorrent, loathsome, hideous, unspeakable, execrable.
−OPPOSITES admirable.

heir, heiress ▶ noun =**successor**, next in line, inheritor, beneficiary, legatee.

> WORD LINKS
>
> relating to an heir: **hereditary**

helix ▶ noun =**spiral**, coil, corkscrew, twist, gyre.

hell ▶ noun **1** *they feared hell* =**the netherworld**, the Inferno; eternal damnation, perdition; hellfire, fire and brimstone; Hades; *literary* the pit. **2** *he made her life hell* =**a misery**, torture, agony, a torment, a nightmare, woe.
−OPPOSITES heaven, paradise.
■ **give someone hell** *(informal)* **1** *when I found out I gave him hell* =**give someone what for**, rebuke, admonish, chastise, chide, upbraid, reprove, scold, berate, remonstrate with, take to task, lambaste; haul over the coals; *informal* tell off, dress down, give someone a roasting, let someone have it, bawl out, come down hard on, lay into, blast; have a go at, carpet, give someone a rollicking, give someone a mouthful, tear someone off a strip; *N. Amer. informal* chew out; *formal* castigate. **2** *she gave me hell when*

I was her junior =**harass**, hound, bully, intimidate, pick on, victimize, terrorize; *informal* hassle, give someone a hard time.

■ **hell for leather** =**at top speed**, rapidly, speedily, swiftly, full pelt, headlong, hotfoot, post-haste, helter-skelter, at the speed of light; *informal* like a bat out of hell, like the wind, like greased lightning, like a bomb; *Brit. informal* like the clappers, at a rate of knots; *N. Amer. informal* lickety-split.

■ **raise hell** (*informal*) **1** *they were raising hell* =**cause a disturbance**, be noisy, run riot, run wild, go on the rampage; *informal* raise the roof. **2** *he raised hell with the planners* =**remonstrate**, expostulate, be furious; argue; *informal* kick up a stink.

> **WORD LINKS**
>
> *relating to hell:* **infernal**
> *fear of hell:* **hadephobia, stygiophobia**

hell-bent ▶ adjective =**intent**, determined, (dead) set, insistent, fixed, resolved.
–OPPOSITES half-hearted.

hellish ▶ adjective **1** *the hellish face of Death* =**infernal**; diabolical, fiendish, satanic, demonic. **2** (*informal*) *a hellish week* =**horrible**, rotten, awful, terrible, dreadful, ghastly, vile, foul, appalling, atrocious, horrendous, frightful, nasty, disagreeable; tough, hard, traumatic, gruelling; *informal* murderous, lousy; *Brit. informal* beastly; *N. Amer. informal* hellacious.
–OPPOSITES angelic, wonderful.
▶ adverb (*Brit. informal*) *it's hellish hard work* =**extremely**, very, exceedingly, exceptionally, tremendously, immensely, intensely, really, mightily; *informal* terrifically, awfully, fearfully, terribly, devilishly, majorly, seriously, ultra, damn; *Brit. informal* ever so, well, bloody, dead; *N. Amer. informal* real, mighty, awful.
–OPPOSITES moderately.

helm ■ **at the helm** =**in charge**, in command, in control, responsible, in authority, at the wheel, in the driving seat, in the saddle; *informal* holding the reins.

help ▶ verb **1** =**assist**, aid, lend a hand (to), give assistance to, come to the aid of; be of service to, be of use to; do someone a favour, do someone a service, do someone a good turn, give someone a leg up; rally round, pitch in. **2** *this credit card helps cancer research* =**support**, contribute to, give money to, donate to; promote, boost, back. **3** *sore throats are helped by lozenges* =**relieve**, soothe, ease, alleviate, improve, assuage, lessen.
–OPPOSITES hinder, impede, worsen.
▶ noun **1** *this could be of help to you* =**assistance**, aid, support, succour; benefit, use, advantage, service, comfort. **2** *he sought help for his eczema* =**relief**, alleviation, improvement, assuagement, healing.
■ **cannot help** *he could not help laughing* =**be unable to stop**, be unable to refrain from, be unable to keep from.
■ **help oneself to** =**steal**, take, appropriate, 'borrow', 'liberate', pocket, purloin; *informal* swipe, nab, filch, snaffle, walk off with; *Brit. informal* nick, pinch, whip, knock off.

helper ▶ noun =**assistant**, aide, deputy, auxiliary, second, right-hand man/woman, attendant.

helpful ▶ adjective **1** *the staff are very helpful* =**obliging**, eager to please, kind, accommodating, supportive; sympathetic, neighbourly. **2** *we found your comments helpful* =**useful**, beneficial, valuable, constructive; informative, instructive. **3** *a helpful new tool* =**handy**, useful, convenient, practical, easy-to-use, serviceable; *informal* neat, nifty.
–OPPOSITES unsympathetic, useless, inconvenient.

helping ▶ noun =**portion**, serving, piece, slice, share; *informal* dollop.

helpless ▶ adjective =**dependent**, incapable, powerless, weak; defenceless, vulnerable, exposed, unprotected.
–OPPOSITES independent.

helter-skelter ▶ adverb *they ran helter-skelter down the hill* =**headlong**, pell-mell, hotfoot, post-haste, at full pelt, at full tilt, hell for leather; *informal* like a bat out of hell, like the wind, like greased lightning, like a bomb; *Brit. informal* like the clappers, at a rate of knots; *N. Amer. informal* lickety-split.
▶ adjective *a helter-skelter collection of houses* =**disordered**, chaotic, muddled, jumbled, untidy, haphazard, disorganized; *informal* higgledy-piggledy; *Brit. informal* shambolic.
–OPPOSITES orderly.

hence ▶ adverb =**consequently**, as a consequence, for this reason, therefore, ergo, so, accordingly, as a result, because of that, that being so.

henceforth, henceforward
▶ adverb = **from now on**, as of now, in (the) future, subsequently, from this day on; *formal* hereafter.

henchman ▶ noun = **right-hand man**, assistant, aide, helper; bodyguard, minder; *informal* sidekick, crony, heavy.

henpecked ▶ adjective = **browbeaten**, downtrodden, bullied, dominated, subjugated, oppressed, intimidated.
−OPPOSITES domineering.

herald ▶ noun 1 *(historical) a herald announced the armistice* = **messenger**, courier. 2 *the first herald of spring* = **harbinger**, sign, indicator, signal, portent, omen; *literary* foretoken.
▶ verb 1 *shouts heralded their approach* = **proclaim**, announce, broadcast, publicize, declare, advertise. 2 *the speech heralded a policy change* = **signal**, indicate, announce; usher in, pave the way for, be a harbinger of; *literary* foretoken, betoken.

Herculean ▶ adjective 1 *a Herculean task* = **superhuman**, heroic, formidable, tough, huge, massive. 2 *his Herculean build* = **strong**, muscular, powerful, solid, strapping, brawny, burly; *informal* hunky, beefy, hulking.
−OPPOSITES easy, puny.

herd ▶ noun 1 *a herd of cows* = **drove**, flock, pack, fold; collection. 2 *a herd of tourists* = **crowd**, group, bunch, horde, mob, pack, swarm, company. 3 *they consider themselves above the herd* = **the common people**, the masses, the crowd; the hoi polloi, the mob, the proletariat, the rabble, the riff-raff, the great unwashed; *informal* the proles, the plebs.
▶ verb 1 *we herded the sheep into the pen* = **drive**, shepherd, guide; round up, gather, collect. 2 *we all herded into the room* = **crowd**, pack, flock; cluster, huddle.

hereafter ▶ adverb *(formal) nothing I say hereafter is intended to offend* = **from now on**, after this, from this moment forth, subsequently, hence, henceforth, henceforward; *formal* hereinafter.
▶ noun *our preparation for the hereafter* = **life after death**, the afterlife, the afterworld, the next world; eternity, heaven, paradise.

hereditary ▶ adjective 1 *a hereditary right* = **inherited**; bequeathed, willed, handed down, passed down, passed on. 2 *a hereditary disease* = **genetic**, inborn, inherited, inbred, innate; in the family, in the blood, in the genes.

heresy ▶ noun = **dissension**, dissent, nonconformity, heterodoxy, unorthodoxy, apostasy, blasphemy.

heretic ▶ noun = **dissenter**, nonconformist, apostate, iconoclast.
−OPPOSITES conformist, believer.

heritage ▶ noun 1 *Europe's cultural heritage* = **tradition**, history, past, background; culture, customs. 2 *his Greek heritage* = **ancestry**, lineage, descent, extraction, parentage, roots, heredity.

hermetic ▶ adjective = **airtight**, sealed; watertight, waterproof.

hermit ▶ noun = **recluse**, loner, ascetic; *historical* anchorite, anchoress; *archaic* eremite.

> **WORD LINKS**
>
> *relating to a hermit:* **eremitic**

hero ▶ noun 1 *a sporting hero* = **star**, superstar, megastar, idol, celebrity; favourite, darling; *informal* celeb. 2 *the hero of the film* = **(male) protagonist**, main character/role, starring role; (male) lead, lead (actor/role), leading man.
−OPPOSITES coward, loser, villain.

heroic ▶ adjective 1 *heroic rescuers* = **brave**, courageous, valiant, intrepid, bold, fearless, daring; doughty, plucky, stout-hearted, mettlesome; gallant, chivalrous; *informal* gutsy, spunky. 2 *obelisks on a heroic scale* = **prodigious**, grand, enormous, huge, massive, titanic, colossal, monumental; epic; *informal* mega.

heroine ▶ noun 1 *a sporting heroine* = **star**, superstar, megastar, idol, celebrity, luminary, exemplar; favourite, darling; *informal* celeb. 2 *the film's heroine* = **female protagonist**, main (female) character/role; (female) lead, lead (role/actress), leading lady; prima donna, diva.

heroism ▶ noun = **bravery**, courage, valour, daring, fearlessness, pluck; backbone, spine, grit, mettle; gallantry, chivalry; *informal* guts, spunk; *Brit. informal* bottle; *N. Amer. informal* moxie.

hero-worship ▶ noun = **idolization**, adulation, admiration, idealization, worship, adoration, veneration, lionization.

hesitancy ▶ noun. See HESITATION.

hesitant ▶ adjective 1 *she is hesitant about buying* = **uncertain**, undecided, unsure, doubtful, dubious, nervous,

reluctant; ambivalent, in two minds; *Brit.* havering, humming and hawing; *informal* iffy. **2** *a hesitant child* = **timid**, diffident, shy, bashful, insecure.
−OPPOSITES certain, decisive, confident.

hesitate ▸ verb **1** *she hesitated, unsure of what to say* = **pause**, delay, wait, stall; be uncertain, be unsure, be doubtful, be indecisive, equivocate, vacillate, waver; *Brit.* haver, hum and haw; *informal* dilly-dally. **2** *don't hesitate to contact me* = **be reluctant**, be unwilling, be disinclined, scruple; have misgivings about, have qualms about, shrink from, think twice about.

hesitation ▸ noun = **uncertainty**, doubt, dubiousness; irresolution, indecision; equivocation, vacillation; dithering, stalling, delay; reluctance, disinclination, unease, ambivalence.

heterodox ▸ adjective = **unorthodox**, nonconformist, dissenting, dissident, rebellious, renegade.
−OPPOSITES orthodox.

heterogeneous ▸ adjective = **diverse**, varied, varying, miscellaneous, assorted, mixed, sundry, disparate, different, differing, unrelated.
−OPPOSITES homogeneous.

hew ▸ verb = **chop**, hack, cut, lop; carve, shape, fashion, sculpt, model.

heyday ▸ noun = **prime**, peak, height, pinnacle, acme, zenith; day, time.

hiatus ▸ noun = **pause**, break, gap, lacuna, interval, intermission, interlude, interruption.

hidden ▸ adjective **1** *a hidden camera* = **concealed**, secret, invisible, unseen; camouflaged. **2** *a hidden meaning* = **obscure**, unclear, concealed; cryptic, mysterious, secret, covert, abstruse, arcane; ulterior, deep, subliminal, coded.
−OPPOSITES visible, obvious.

hide¹ ▸ verb **1** *he hid the money* = **conceal**, secrete, put out of sight, cache; *informal* stash. **2** *they hid in an air vent* = **conceal oneself**, secrete oneself, take cover; lie low, go to ground; *informal* hole up; *Brit. informal, dated* lie doggo. **3** *clouds hid the moon* = **obscure**, block out, blot out, obstruct, cloud, shroud, veil, eclipse. **4** *he could not hide his dislike* = **conceal**, keep secret, cover up, keep quiet about, bottle up, suppress; disguise, mask; *informal* keep a/the lid on.
−OPPOSITES flaunt, reveal.

hide² ▸ noun *the hide will be tanned* = **skin**, pelt, coat.

hideaway ▸ noun = **retreat**, refuge, hiding place, hideout, den, bolt-hole; *informal* hidey-hole.

hidebound ▸ adjective = **conservative**, reactionary, conventional, orthodox; set in one's ways, rigid.
−OPPOSITES liberal.

hideous ▸ adjective **1** *a hideous face* = **ugly**, repulsive, repellent, unsightly, revolting, gruesome, grotesque, monstrous. **2** *hideous cases of torture* = **horrific**, terrible, appalling, awful, dreadful, frightful, horrible, horrendous, horrifying, shocking, sickening, gruesome, ghastly.
−OPPOSITES beautiful, pleasant.

hideout ▸ noun = **hiding place**, hideaway, retreat, shelter, bolt-hole, safe house; *informal* hidey-hole.

hiding¹ ▸ noun *(informal)* *they gave him a hiding* = **beating**, battering, thrashing, thumping, drubbing; *informal* licking, belting, bashing, pasting, walloping, clobbering.

hiding² ◼ **in hiding** *the fugitive is in hiding* = **hidden**, concealed, lying low, gone to ground; *Brit. informal, dated* lying doggo.

hiding place ▸ noun = **hideaway**, hideout, retreat, refuge, shelter, sanctuary, sanctum, bolt-hole, safe house; *informal* hidey-hole.

hierarchy ▸ noun = **pecking order**, ranking, grading, ladder, scale.

hieroglyphic ▸ noun **1** *hieroglyphics on a stone monument* = **symbols**, signs, ciphers, sigils. **2** *notebooks filled with hieroglyphics* = **scribble**, scrawl, code; shorthand.

higgledy-piggledy *(informal)* ▸ adjective *a higgledy-piggledy pile of papers* = **disorderly**, disorganized, untidy, messy, chaotic, jumbled, muddled, confused, unsystematic, irregular; *Brit. informal* shambolic.
−OPPOSITES tidy.

▸ adverb *the cars were parked higgledy-piggledy* = **in disorder**, in a muddle, in a jumble, in disarray, untidily, haphazardly; *informal* all over the place, topsy-turvy, every which way, any old how.

high ▸ adjective **1** *a high mountain* = **tall**, lofty, towering, giant, big; multi-storey, high-rise. **2** *a high position in the govern-*

ment =**high-ranking**, leading, top, prominent, senior; influential, powerful, important, prime, premier, exalted; *N. Amer.* ranking; *informal* top-notch. **3** *high principles* =**noble**, lofty, moral, ethical, honourable, admirable, upright. **4** *high prices* =**inflated**, excessive, unreasonable, expensive, exorbitant, extortionate; *informal* steep, stiff. **5** *high standards* =**excellent**, outstanding, exemplary, exceptional, admirable, fine, first-class, superior, superlative, superb; impeccable, unimpeachable; *informal* A1, top-notch. **6** *high winds* =**strong**, powerful, violent, intense, stiff; blustery, gusty, tempestuous, turbulent. **7** *the high life* =**luxurious**, lavish, extravagant, grand, opulent; *Brit.* upmarket; *N. Amer.* upscale. **8** *I have a high opinion of you* =**favourable**, good, positive, approving, admiring, complimentary. **9** *a high note* =**high-pitched**; soprano, treble, falsetto, shrill, sharp, piercing, penetrating. **10** (*informal*) *high on drugs* =**intoxicated**, befuddled, delirious, hallucinating; *informal* high as a kite, stoned, tripping, spaced out, wasted, wrecked, off one's head, wired. **11** *the partridges were high* =**gamy**, smelly, strong-smelling.
−OPPOSITES short, lowly, amoral, cheap, low, light, abstemious, unfavourable, deep, sober, fresh.
▶ noun *prices were at a rare high* =**high point**, peak; zenith, acme, height.
−OPPOSITES low.
▶ adverb *a jet flew high overhead* =**at great height**, high up, far up, way up, at altitude; in the air, in the sky, on high, aloft, overhead.
−OPPOSITES low.
■ **high and dry** =**destitute**, bereft, helpless, in the lurch, stranded, marooned.
■ **high and low** =**everywhere**, all around, far and wide, {here, there, and everywhere}, in every nook and cranny; *informal* all over the place; *Brit. informal* all over the shop; *N. Amer. informal* all over the map.
■ **high and mighty** (*informal*) =**self-important**, disdainful, supercilious, superior, snobbish, conceited, above oneself; *informal* stuck-up, snooty, hoity-toity, la-di-da; *Brit. informal* toffee-nosed.
■ **on a high** (*informal*) =**ecstatic**, euphoric, delirious, elated, thrilled, overjoyed, walking on air, on cloud nine, in seventh heaven, jumping for joy, in raptures; *informal* blissed out, over the moon, on top of the world; *Austral./NZ*

informal wrapped.

> **WORD LINKS**
> *fear of high places:* **acrophobia**, **hypsophobia**
> *fear of high buildings:* **batophobia**

highbrow ▶ adjective =**intellectual**, scholarly, bookish, academic, educated, donnish, bluestocking; erudite, learned; *informal* brainy.
−OPPOSITES lowbrow.

high-class ▶ adjective =**superior**, first-rate; excellent, select, choice, premier, top, top-flight; de luxe, top-quality; *Brit.* upmarket; *informal* top-notch, top-drawer, A1, classy, posh.

highfalutin ▶ adjective (*informal*). See PRETENTIOUS.

high-flown ▶ adjective =**grand**, extravagant, elaborate, flowery, ornate, overblown, overdone, overwrought, grandiloquent, grandiose, inflated; *informal* windy, purple.
−OPPOSITES plain.

high-handed ▶ adjective =**imperious**, peremptory, arrogant, haughty, domineering, overbearing; autocratic, authoritarian, dictatorial; *informal* bossy, high and mighty.
−OPPOSITES liberal.

high jinks ▶ plural noun =**antics**, pranks, stunts, tricks; skylarking, mischief, horseplay, tomfoolery, clowning; *informal* shenanigans, monkey business.

highland ▶ noun =**uplands**, mountains, hills, heights, moors; plateau; *Brit.* wolds.

highlight ▶ noun *the highlight of his career* =**high point**, climax, peak, pinnacle, height, acme, zenith, summit.
−OPPOSITES nadir.
▶ verb *he has highlighted shortcomings in the plan* =**spotlight**, call attention to, focus on, underline, show up, bring out, accentuate, accent, give prominence to, stress, emphasize.

highly ▶ adverb **1** *a highly dangerous substance* =**very**, extremely, exceedingly, particularly, most, really, thoroughly, decidedly, distinctly, exceptionally, immensely, inordinately, singularly, extraordinarily; *N. English* right; *informal* awfully, terribly, majorly, seriously, mega, ultra, oh-so, damn; *Brit. informal* ever so, well, dead, jolly; *N. Amer. informal* real, mighty, awful; *dated* frightfully. **2** *he was*

highly regarded =**favourably**, well, approvingly, positively, enthusiastically.
−OPPOSITES slightly, unfavourably.

highly strung ▶ adjective =**nervous**, nervy, excitable, temperamental, sensitive, unstable, brittle, edgy, jumpy, anxious, overwrought, neurotic; *informal* uptight.
−OPPOSITES easy-going.

high-minded ▶ adjective =**principled**, honourable, moral, upright, noble, righteous, virtuous, worthy.
−OPPOSITES unprincipled.

high-pitched ▶ adjective =**high**, shrill, sharp, piercing; soprano, treble, falsetto.
−OPPOSITES deep.

high-powered ▶ adjective =**dynamic**, demanding, challenging, high-level, fast-moving, high-pressure.

high-pressure ▶ adjective. See HIGH-POWERED.

high-sounding ▶ adjective =**grand**, high-flown, extravagant, elaborate, grandiose, inflated.
−OPPOSITES plain.

high-speed ▶ adjective =**fast**, quick, rapid, speedy, swift, breakneck, lightning; express, whistle-stop, supersonic; *literary* fleet.
−OPPOSITES slow.

high-spirited ▶ adjective =**lively**, full of fun, fun-loving, animated, bouncy, bubbly, sparkling, vivacious, buoyant, exuberant, ebullient, irrepressible; *informal* chirpy, sparky, bright and breezy, full of beans; *literary* frolicsome.

high spirits ▶ plural noun =**liveliness**, vitality, spirit, energy, bounce, sparkle, vivacity, cheerfulness, exuberance, ebullience, joie de vivre.

hijack ▶ verb =**commandeer**, seize, take over; appropriate, expropriate.

hike ▶ noun =**walk**, trek, tramp, trudge, slog, footslog, march; ramble; *Brit. informal* yomp.
▶ verb =**walk**, trek, tramp, trudge, slog, march; ramble; *Brit. informal* yomp.
∎ **hike something up 1** *Roy hiked up his trousers* =**hitch up**, pull up, hoist; *informal* yank up. **2** *they hiked up the price* =**increase**, raise, up, put up, push up; *informal* jack up, bump up.

hilarious ▶ adjective **1** *a hilarious story* =**very funny**, hysterical, uproarious, rib-tickling; *informal* side-splitting, price-

less, a scream, a hoot. **2** *a hilarious evening* =**amusing**, entertaining, animated, high-spirited, lively, funny, merry, jolly, mirthful, uproarious.
−OPPOSITES sad, serious.

hilarity ▶ noun =**amusement**, mirth, laughter, merriment, light-heartedness, fun, humour, jollity, gaiety, exuberance, high spirits.

hill ▶ noun =**high ground**, prominence, hillock, hillside, rise, mound, knoll, hummock, tor, fell, pike, mesa; ridge, slope, incline, gradient; *Scottish & Irish* drum; *Scottish* brae; *Geology* drumlin; *formal* eminence.

hillock ▶ noun =**mound**, prominence, rise, knoll, hummock, hump; bank, ridge; *N. English* howe; *N. Amer.* knob; *formal* eminence.

hilt ▶ noun =**handle**, haft, grip, shaft, shank, stock.
∎ **to the hilt** =**completely**, fully, wholly, totally, entirely, utterly, unreservedly, unconditionally, in every respect, one hundred per cent, every inch, to the full, all the way.

hind ▶ adjective =**back**, rear, hinder, hindmost, posterior.
−OPPOSITES fore, front.

hinder ▶ verb =**hamper**, impede, inhibit, retard, thwart, foil, curb, delay, interfere with, set back, slow down, hold back, hold up; restrict, restrain, constrain, curtail, frustrate, cramp, handicap, cripple, hamstring; *Brit.* throw a spanner in the works; *informal* stymie.
−OPPOSITES facilitate.

hindrance ▶ noun =**impediment**, obstacle, barrier, obstruction, handicap, hurdle, restraint, restriction, encumbrance; complication, delay, drawback, setback, difficulty, inconvenience, hitch, stumbling block, fly in the ointment, hiccup; *Brit.* spanner in the works.
−OPPOSITES help.

hinge ▶ verb *our future hinges on the election* =**depend**, hang, rest, turn, centre, be contingent, be dependent; be determined by.

hint ▶ noun **1** *a hint that he would leave* =**clue**, inkling, suggestion, indication, sign, signal, pointer, intimation, insinuation, mention. **2** *handy hints about painting* =**tip**, suggestion, pointer, clue, guideline, recommendation. **3** *a hint of garlic* =**trace**, touch, suspicion, suggestion, dash, soupçon, modicum; *informal*

smidgen, tad.
▸ **verb** *what are you hinting at?* =**imply**, insinuate, intimate, suggest; refer to, drive at, mean; *informal* get at.

hinterland ▸ **noun** =**the backwoods**, the back of beyond; *Austral./NZ* the outback, the backblocks, the booay; *informal* the sticks, the middle of nowhere; *N. Amer. informal* the boondocks.

hip[1] ▸ **noun**

- -
| **WORD LINKS** |
relating to the hips: **sciatic**
- -

hip[2] ▸ **adjective** *(informal).* *See* FASHIONABLE.

hippy ▸ **noun** =**dropout**, bohemian, free spirit, nonconformist.

hire ▸ **verb 1** *we hired a car* =**rent**, lease, charter. **2** *they hire labour in line with demand* =**employ**, engage, recruit, appoint, take on, sign up, commission.
−OPPOSITES dismiss.
▸ **noun** *the hire of the machine* =**rental**, rent, hiring, lease.

hire purchase ▸ **noun** =**instalment plan**, deferred payment, HP, easy terms; *Brit. informal* the never-never.

hirsute ▸ **adjective** *(formal)* =**hairy**, shaggy, bushy; woolly, furry, fleecy; bearded, unshaven.

hiss ▸ **verb 1** *the escaping gas hissed* =**fizz**, whistle, wheeze. **2** *the audience hissed* =**jeer**, catcall, whistle, hoot.
▸ **noun 1** *the hiss of steam* =**fizz**, whistle, sibilance, wheeze. **2** *the speaker received hisses* =**jeer**, catcall, whistle; abuse, derision.

historian ▸ **noun** =**chronicler**, annalist, archivist, recorder; antiquarian.

historic ▸ **adjective** =**significant**, notable, important, momentous, memorable, remarkable; groundbreaking, epoch-making, red-letter; *informal* earth-shattering.
−OPPOSITES insignificant.

historical ▸ **adjective 1** *historical evidence* =**documented**, recorded, chronicled; authentic, factual, actual. **2** *historical figures* =**past**, bygone, ancient, old, former; *literary* of yore.
−OPPOSITES contemporary.

history ▸ **noun 1** *my interest in history* =**the past**, former times, the olden days, yesterday, antiquity; *literary* days of yore, yesteryear. **2** *a history of the Civil War* =**chronicle**, archive, record, report, narrative, account, study. **3** *she gave details of her history* =**background**, past, life story, experiences, record.

histrionic ▸ **adjective** =**melodramatic**, theatrical, dramatic, exaggerated, stagy, showy, affected, overacted; *informal* hammy.

histrionics ▸ **plural noun** =**dramatics**, theatrics, tantrums; affectation.

hit ▸ **verb 1** =**strike**, slap, smack, cuff, punch, thump, swat; beat, thrash, batter, belabour, pound, pummel, box someone's ears; *informal* whack, wallop, bash, biff, bop, clout, clip, sock, crown, beat the living daylights out of, give someone a (good) hiding, belt, tan, lay into, deck; *Brit. informal* stick one on, slosh; *N. Amer. informal* slug, boff; *Austral./NZ informal* dong; *literary* smite. **2** *a car hit the barrier* =**crash into**, run into, smash into, knock into, bump into, plough into, collide with, meet head-on. **3** *the tragedy hit her hard* =**devastate**, affect badly; upset, shatter, crush, shock, traumatize; *informal* knock sideways, knock the stuffing out of; *Brit. informal* knock for six. **4** *(informal) spending will hit £1,800 million* =**reach**, arrive at, rise to, climb to. **5** *it hit me that I had forgotten* =**occur to**, strike, dawn on, come to; enter one's head, cross one's mind.
▸ **noun 1** =**blow**, punch, knock, bang, cuff, slap, smack, tap, crack; *informal* whack, wallop, bash, belt, clout, sock; *N. Amer. informal* boff, slug; *Austral./NZ* dong. **2** *he directed many big hits* =**success**, sell-out, winner, triumph, sensation; best-seller; *informal* smash (hit), knock-out, crowd-puller, biggie.
−OPPOSITES failure.
■ **hit back** =**retaliate**, respond, reply, react, counter, defend oneself.
■ **hit home** =**strike home**, hit the mark, register, be understood, get through, sink in.
■ **hit it off** *(informal)* =**get on (well)**, get along, be compatible, be on the same wavelength, see eye to eye, take to each other, warm to each other, make friends; *informal* click.
■ **hit on/upon** =**discover**, come up with, think of, conceive of, dream up, invent, create, devise.
■ **hit out at** =**criticize**, attack, censure, denounce, condemn, lambaste, rail against, inveigh against, arraign; *informal* pan, slam, hammer, lay into; *Brit. informal* slate, rubbish; *N. Amer. informal* trash; *formal* excoriate.

hitch ▸ verb **1** *she hitched the blanket around her* =**pull**, hike, lift, raise; *informal* yank. **2** *Tom hitched the pony to his cart* =**harness**, yoke, couple, fasten, connect, attach.
▸ noun *it went without a hitch* =**problem**, difficulty, snag, setback, obstacle, obstruction, complication; *informal* glitch, hiccup.

hit-or-miss, hit-and-miss ▸ adjective =**erratic**, haphazard, disorganized, sloppy, unmethodical, uneven, inconsistent, random; *informal* slap-happy.
–OPPOSITES meticulous.

hoard ▸ noun *a secret hoard* =**cache**, stockpile, stock, store, collection, supply, reserve, fund; *informal* stash.
▸ verb *they hoarded their rations* =**stockpile**, store (up), put aside, put by, lay by, set aside, stow away; cache, amass, collect, save, accumulate, squirrel away; *informal* stash away, salt away.
–OPPOSITES squander.

hoarse ▸ adjective =**rough**, harsh, croaky, throaty, gruff, husky, grating, rasping.
–OPPOSITES mellow, clear.

hoax ▸ noun *the call was a hoax* =**practical joke**, prank, trick; deception, fraud; *informal* con, spoof, wind-up, scam.
▸ verb *Travis often hoaxed his listeners* =**play a (practical) joke on**, trick, fool; deceive, hoodwink, dupe, take in, lead on, gull; *informal* con, kid, have on, pull a fast one on, put one over on, wind up; *N. Amer. informal* sucker, snooker.

hoaxer ▸ noun =**(practical) joker**, prankster, trickster; *informal* con man.

hobble ▸ verb =**limp**, shamble, totter, dodder, stagger, stumble; *Scottish* hirple.

hobby ▸ noun =**pastime**, leisure activity; sideline, diversion; recreation, amusement.

hobgoblin ▸ noun =**goblin**, imp, gremlin, demon, bogey.

hobnob ▸ verb *(informal)* =**associate**, mix, fraternize, socialize, spend time, go around, mingle, consort, rub shoulders; *N. Amer.* rub elbows; *informal* hang around/round/out, knock about/around.

hocus-pocus ▸ noun =**jargon**, mumbo-jumbo, gibberish, balderdash, claptrap, nonsense, rubbish, twaddle, garbage; *informal* gobbledegook, double Dutch; *N. Amer. informal* flapdoodle; *informal, dated* bunkum.

hodgepodge ▸ noun *(N. Amer.)*. See HOTCHPOTCH.

hog ▸ verb *(informal)* *he hogged the limelight* =**monopolize**, dominate, corner, control, take over.

hoist ▸ verb *we hoisted the mainsail* =**raise**, lift (up), haul up, heave up, winch up, pull up, upraise, uplift, elevate, erect.
–OPPOSITES lower.
▸ noun *a mechanical hoist* =**crane**, winch, block and tackle, pulley, windlass.

hold ▸ verb **1** *she held a suitcase* =**clasp**, clutch, grasp, grip, clench, cling to, hold on to; carry, bear. **2** *I wanted to hold her* =**embrace**, hug, clasp, cradle, enfold, squeeze, cuddle. **3** *do you hold a driving licence?* =**possess**, have, own, bear, carry. **4** *the branch held my weight* =**support**, bear, carry, take, keep up, sustain. **5** *the police were holding him* =**detain**, imprison, lock up, keep behind bars, put in prison, put in jail, incarcerate, confine, intern; *informal* put away, put inside. **6** *he held a senior post* =**occupy**, have, fill; *informal* hold down. **7** *the tank held 250 gallons* =**take**, contain, accommodate, fit; have a capacity of, have room for. **8** *the court held that there was no evidence* =**maintain**, consider, take the view, believe, think, feel, deem, be of the opinion; judge, rule, decide; *informal* reckon; *formal* opine. **9** *the offer still holds* =**stand**, be valid, apply, remain, exist, be in force, be in effect. **10** *they held a meeting* =**convene**, call, summon; conduct, have, organize, run; *formal* convoke.
–OPPOSITES release, lose, end.
▸ noun **1** *she kept a hold on my hand* =**grip**, grasp, clasp, clutch. **2** *Tom had a hold over his father* =**influence**, power, control, dominance, authority. **3** *the military tightened their hold on the capital* =**control**, grip, power, stranglehold, dominion.
■ **hold back** =**hesitate**, pause, stop oneself, desist, forbear.
■ **hold someone back** =**hinder**, hamper, impede, obstruct, check, curb, block, thwart, frustrate, stand in someone's way.
■ **hold something back 1** *Jane held back the tears* =**suppress**, fight back, choke back, stifle, smother, subdue, rein in, repress, curb, control; *informal* keep a/the lid on. **2** *don't hold anything back from me* =**withhold**, hide, conceal; *informal* sit on, keep under one's hat.
■ **hold someone down** =**oppress**,

repress, suppress, subdue, subjugate, keep down, keep under, tyrannize, dominate.

■ **hold something down 1** *they will hold down inflation* =**keep down**, keep low, freeze, fix. **2** *(informal) she held down two jobs* =**occupy**, hold, have, do, fill.

■ **hold forth** =**speak at length**, talk at length, go on, sound off; declaim, spout, pontificate, orate, preach, sermonize; *informal* speechify, preachify, drone on.

■ **hold something off** =**resist**, repel, repulse, rebuff, parry, deflect, fend off, stave off, ward off, keep at bay.

■ **hold on** *if only they could hold on a while* =**keep going**, persevere, survive, last, continue, struggle on, carry on, hold out, see it through, stay the course; *informal* soldier on, stick at it, hang in there.

■ **hold on to** *he held on to the chair* =**clutch**, hold, hang on to, clasp, grasp, grip, cling to.

■ **hold one's own**. See OWN.

■ **hold something out** =**extend**, proffer, offer, present; outstretch, reach out, stretch out, put out.

■ **hold something up 1** *they held up the trophy* =**display**, hold aloft, exhibit, show (off), flourish, brandish; *informal* flash. **2** *concrete pillars hold up the bridge* =**support**, hold, bear, carry, take, keep up, prop up, shore up, buttress. **3** *our flight was held up* =**delay**, detain, make late, set back. **4** *a lack of cash has held up progress* =**obstruct**, impede, hinder, hamper, inhibit, thwart, curb; *informal* stymie.

■ **hold with** =**approve of**, agree with, be in favour of, endorse, accept, countenance, support, subscribe to, give one's blessing to, take kindly to; *informal* stand for.

holder ▸ noun *a knife holder* =**container**, receptacle, case, cover, housing, sheath.

holdings ▸ plural noun =**assets**, funds, capital, resources, savings, investments, securities, equities, bonds, stocks and shares, reserves.

hold-up ▸ noun =**delay**, setback, hitch, snag, difficulty, problem, glitch, hiccup; traffic jam, tailback; *informal* snarl-up.

hole ▸ noun 1 *a hole in the roof* =**opening**, aperture, gap, space, vent, chink; breach, crack, rupture; puncture, perforation, split, gash, slit, crevice, fissure. **2** *a hole in the ground* =**pit**, crater, depression, hollow; well, borehole, excavation, dugout; pothole. **3** *the badger's hole* =**burrow**, lair, den, earth, sett; retreat, shelter. **4** *(informal) I was living in a real hole* =**hovel**, slum, shack, mess; *informal* dump, dive, pigsty, tip.

▸ **verb** *a fuel tank was holed* =**puncture**, perforate, pierce, penetrate, rupture, split, lacerate, gash.

holiday ▸ noun =**vacation**, break, rest, recess; time off, time out, leave, furlough, sabbatical; trip, tour, journey, voyage.

holier-than-thou ▸ adjective =**sanctimonious**, self-righteous, smug, self-satisfied; priggish, pious; *informal* goody-goody, preachy.
−OPPOSITES humble.

hollow ▸ adjective 1 *hollow cheeks* =**sunken**, deep-set, concave, depressed, recessed. **2** *a hollow voice* =**dull**, low, flat, toneless, expressionless.

▸ **noun 1** *a hollow under the tree* −**hole**, pit, cavity, crater, trough; depression, indentation, dip; niche, nook, cranny, recess. **2** *the village lay in a hollow* =**valley**, vale, dale; *Brit.* dene, combe; *N. English* clough; *Scottish* glen, strath; *literary* dell.

▸ **verb** *a tunnel hollowed out of a mountain* =**gouge**, scoop, dig, cut; excavate, channel.

holocaust ▸ noun =**slaughter**, mass murder, genocide; massacre, carnage.

holy ▸ adjective 1 *holy men* =**saintly**, godly, pious, religious, devout, God-fearing, spiritual; righteous, good, virtuous, pure; canonized, beatified; ordained. **2** *a Jewish holy place* =**sacred**, consecrated, hallowed, sanctified, venerated, revered, religious, dedicated.
−OPPOSITES sinful, irreligious, cursed.

homage ▸ noun =**respect**, honour, reverence, worship, admiration, esteem, adulation, acclaim; tribute, acknowledgement, recognition.

■ **pay homage to** =**honour**, acclaim, applaud, salute, praise, commend, pay tribute to, take one's hat off to; *formal* laud.

home ▸ noun 1 *they fled their homes* =**residence**, place of residence, house; flat, apartment, bungalow, cottage; accommodation, property, quarters, lodgings, rooms; address, *informal* pad, digs; *formal* domicile, abode, dwelling (place), habitation. **2** *I am far from my home* =**homeland**, native land, home town, birthplace, roots, fatherland, mother

country, motherland, country of origin, the old country. **3** *a home for the elderly* =**institution**; nursing home, retirement home, rest home; children's home; hospice, shelter, refuge, retreat, asylum, hostel.
▸ **adjective** *the UK home market* =**domestic**, internal, local, national.
–OPPOSITES foreign, international.
■ **at home** *I was at home all day* =**in**, in one's house, present, available, indoors, inside, here.
■ **hit home.** See HIT.
■ **home in on** =**focus on**, concentrate on, zero in on, centre on, fix on; highlight, spotlight, underline, pinpoint; *informal* zoom in on.

homeland ▸ **noun** =**native land**, country of origin, home, fatherland, motherland, mother country, the old country.

homeless ▸ **adjective** *homeless people* =**of no fixed abode**, without a roof over one's head, on the streets, vagrant, sleeping rough; destitute, down and out.

homely ▸ **adjective 1** *a homely atmosphere* =**cosy**, comfortable, snug, welcoming, friendly, congenial, intimate, warm, hospitable, informal, relaxed, pleasant, cheerful; *informal* comfy. **2** *(N. Amer.) she's rather homely* =**unattractive**, plain, unprepossessing, ugly; *informal* not much to look at; *Brit. informal* no oil painting.
–OPPOSITES uncomfortable, attractive.

homespun ▸ **adjective** =**unsophisticated**, plain, simple, unpolished, unrefined, rustic, folksy; coarse, rough, crude, rudimentary.
–OPPOSITES sophisticated.

homicidal ▸ **adjective** =**murderous**, violent, brutal, savage, ferocious, vicious, bloody, bloodthirsty, barbarous, barbaric, psychopathic.

homicide ▸ **noun** =**murder**, killing, slaughter, butchery, massacre; assassination, execution, extermination; patricide, matricide, infanticide; *literary* slaying.

homily ▸ **noun** =**sermon**, lecture, discourse, address, lesson, talk, speech, oration.

homogeneous ▸ **adjective 1** *a homogeneous group* =**uniform**, identical, unvaried, consistent, undistinguishable; alike, similar, (much) the same, all of a piece; *informal* much of a muchness. **2** *we have to compete with homogeneous products*

=**similar**, comparable, equivalent, like, analogous, corresponding, parallel, matching, related.
–OPPOSITES different.

homogenize ▸ **verb** =**make uniform**, make similar, unite, integrate, fuse, merge, blend, meld, coalesce, amalgamate, combine.
–OPPOSITES diversify.

homologous ▸ **adjective** =**similar**, comparable, equivalent, like, analogous, corresponding, correspondent, parallel, matching, related, congruent.
–OPPOSITES different.

hone ▸ **verb** =**sharpen**, whet, strop, grind, file.
–OPPOSITES blunt.

honest ▸ **adjective 1** *an honest man* =**upright**, honourable, principled, righteous, right-minded, respectable; virtuous, good, decent, law-abiding, upstanding, incorruptible, truthful, trustworthy, reliable, conscientious, scrupulous. **2** *I haven't been honest with you* =**truthful**, sincere, candid, frank, open, forthright, straight; straightforward; *informal* upfront. **3** *an honest mistake* =**genuine**, real, actual, true, bona fide, legitimate, fair and square; *informal* legit, kosher, on the level, honest-to-goodness.
–OPPOSITES unscrupulous, insincere.

honestly ▸ **adverb 1** *he earned the money honestly* =**fairly**, lawfully, legally, legitimately, honourably, decently, ethically, in good faith, by the book; *informal* on the level. **2** *we honestly believe this is for the best* =**sincerely**, genuinely, truthfully, truly, wholeheartedly; really, actually, to be honest, to tell you the truth, to be frank, in all honesty, in all sincerity.

honesty ▸ **noun 1** *I can attest to his honesty* =**integrity**, uprightness, honourableness, honour, righteousness; virtue, goodness, probity, high-mindedness, fairness, incorruptibility, truthfulness, trustworthiness, reliability, dependability. **2** *they spoke with honesty about their fears* =**sincerity**, candour, frankness, directness, truthfulness, truth, openness, straightforwardness.

honey ▸ **noun**

WORD LINKS

honey production: **apiculture**
honey-eating: **mellivorous**

honeyed ▶ adjective =sweet, sugary, saccharine, pleasant, flattering, unctuous; dulcet, soothing, soft, mellow, mellifluous.
–OPPOSITES harsh.

honorary ▶ adjective **1** *an honorary doctorate* =titular, nominal, in name only, unofficial, token. **2** *(Brit.) an honorary treasurer* =unpaid, unsalaried, voluntary, volunteer; *N. Amer.* pro bono (publico).

honour ▶ noun **1** *a man of honour* =integrity, honesty, uprightness, morals, morality, (high) principles, righteousness, high-mindedness; virtue, goodness, decency, probity, scrupulousness, fairness, justness, trustworthiness. **2** *a mark of honour* =distinction, privilege, glory, kudos, cachet, prestige. **3** *our honour is at stake* =reputation, (good) name, character, repute, image, standing, status. **4** *the honour of meeting the Queen* =privilege, pleasure; compliment.
–OPPOSITES unscrupulousness, shame.
▶ verb **1** *we should honour our parents* =esteem, respect, admire, defer to, look up to; appreciate, value, cherish; revere, venerate. **2** *they were honoured at a special ceremony* =applaud, acclaim, praise, salute, recognize, celebrate, commemorate, commend, hail, eulogize, pay homage to, pay tribute to; *formal* laud. **3** *he honoured the contract* =fulfil, observe, keep, obey, heed, follow, carry out; keep to, abide by, adhere to, comply with, conform to, be true to. **4** *the cheque was not honoured* =accept, take, clear, pass, cash; *Brit.* encash.
–OPPOSITES disgrace, criticize, disobey.

honourable ▶ adjective **1** *an honourable man* =honest, moral, principled, righteous, right-minded; decent, respectable, virtuous, good, upstanding, upright, noble, fair, just, truthful, trustworthy, law-abiding, reputable, dependable. **2** *an honourable career* =illustrious, distinguished, eminent, great, glorious, prestigious.
–OPPOSITES crooked, deplorable.

hoodlum ▶ noun =gangster, mobster, Mafioso, heavy, hit man, thug, criminal; *N. Amer. informal* hood.

hoodwink ▶ verb =deceive, trick, dupe, fool, delude, cheat, take in, hoax, mislead, defraud, double-cross, swindle,

gull; *informal* con, bamboozle, do, have, sting, diddle, rip off, pull a fast one on, put one over on, take for a ride; *N. Amer. informal* sucker, snooker; *Austral. informal* pull a swifty on; *literary* cozen.

hoof ▶ noun =trotter, foot; *Zoology* ungula.

hook ▶ noun **1** *she hung her jacket on the hook* =peg, nail. **2** *the dress has six hooks* =fastener, clasp, hasp, clip.
▶ verb **1** *they hooked baskets onto the ladder* =attach, hitch, fasten, fix, secure, hang, clasp. **2** *he hooked his thumbs in his belt* =curl, bend, crook, loop, curve. **3** *he hooked a 24 lb pike* =catch, land, net, take, bag.
■ **by hook or by crook** =by any means, somehow (or other), no matter how, in one way or another, by fair means or foul, come hell or high water.
■ **hook, line, and sinker** =completely, totally, utterly, entirely, wholly, absolutely, one hundred per cent, {lock, stock, and barrel}.
■ **off the hook** *(informal)* =out of trouble, in the clear, free; *informal* let off.

hooked ▶ adjective **1** *a hooked nose* =curved, hook-shaped, aquiline, angular, bent; *Biology* falcate, falciform, uncinate. **2** *(informal) hooked on cocaine* =addicted to, dependent on; *informal* using, heavily/seriously into; *N. Amer. informal* have a jones for. **3** *(informal) he is hooked on crosswords* =keen on, enthusiastic about, addicted to, obsessed with, fanatical about; *informal* mad about, crazy about, wild about, nuts about.
–OPPOSITES straight.

hooligan ▶ noun =lout, thug, tearaway, vandal, ruffian, troublemaker; *Austral.* larrikin; *informal* tough, rough, bruiser, roughneck; *Brit. informal* yob, yobbo, bovver boy, lager lout; *Scottish informal* ned.

hoop ▶ noun =ring, band, circle, circlet, loop; *technical* annulus.

hoot ▶ noun **1** *the hoot of an owl* =screech, shriek, call, cry; tu-whit tu-whoo. **2** *the hoot of a horn* =beep, honk, toot, blast, blare. **3** *hoots of derision* =shout, yell, cry, howl, shriek, whoop, whistle; boo, jeer, catcall. **4** *(informal) your mum's a real hoot* =character, clown; *informal* scream, laugh, case, one, riot, giggle.
▶ verb **1** *an owl hooted* =screech, shriek, cry, call. **2** *a car horn hooted* =beep, honk, toot, blare, blast, sound. **3** *they hooted in*

disgust =**shout**, yell, cry, howl, shriek, whistle; boo, jeer, catcall.

hop ▸ verb 1 *he hopped along the road* =**jump**, bound, spring, bounce, skip, leap; prance, dance, frolic, gambol. **2** (*informal*) *she hopped over to France* =**go**, travel; *informal* pop, whip; *Brit. informal* nip.
▸ noun *the rabbit had a hop around* =**jump**, bounce, prance, leap, spring, gambol.
■ **on the hop** (*Brit. informal*) *he was caught on the hop* =**unprepared**, unready, off guard, unawares, by surprise, with one's defences down; *informal* napping; *Brit. informal* with one's trousers down.

hope ▸ noun **1** *I had high hopes* =**aspiration**, desire, wish, expectation, ambition, aim, plan; dream. **2** *a life filled with hope* =**hopefulness**, optimism, expectation, expectancy; confidence, faith, belief.
–OPPOSITES pessimism.
▸ verb **1** *he's hoping for a medal* =**expect**, anticipate, look for, be hopeful of, want; dream of. **2** *we're hoping to address this issue* =**aim**, intend, be looking, have the intention, have in mind, plan.

hopeful ▸ adjective **1** *he remained hopeful* =**optimistic**, full of hope, confident, positive, buoyant, sanguine, bullish, cheerful. **2** *hopeful signs* =**promising**, encouraging, heartening, reassuring, favourable, optimistic.

hopefully ▸ adverb **1** *he rode on hopefully* =**optimistically**, full of hope, confidently, buoyantly, sanguinely. **2** *hopefully it should finish soon* =**all being well**, if all goes well, God willing, with luck; most likely, probably; touch wood, fingers crossed.

hopeless ▸ adjective **1** *a hopeless case* =**irremediable**, beyond hope, lost, irreparable, irreversible; incurable; impossible, futile, forlorn, unworkable, impracticable; *archaic* bootless. **2** *Joseph was hopeless at maths* =**bad**, poor, awful, terrible, dreadful, appalling, atrocious; inferior, incompetent, unskilled; *informal* pathetic, useless, lousy, rotten; *Brit. informal* rubbish.

hopelessly ▸ adverb *she was hopelessly lost* =**utterly**, completely, irretrievably, impossibly; extremely, very, desperately, totally, dreadfully; *informal* terribly.

horde ▸ noun =**crowd**, mob, pack, gang, troop, army, swarm, mass; throng, multitude, host, flock; *informal* load.

horizontal ▸ adjective **1** *a horizontal surface* =**level**, flat, plane, smooth, even; straight, parallel. **2** *she was stretched horizontal on a sunbed* =**flat**, supine, prone, prostrate.
–OPPOSITES vertical.

horrendous ▸ adjective. See HORRIBLE.

horrible ▸ adjective **1** *a horrible murder* =**dreadful**, awful, terrible, shocking, appalling, horrifying, horrific, horrendous, grisly, ghastly, gruesome, harrowing, unspeakable; macabre, spine-chilling; loathsome, monstrous, abominable, atrocious, sickening. **2** (*informal*) *a horrible little man* =**nasty**, horrid, disagreeable, awful, dreadful, terrible, appalling, repulsive, ghastly; obnoxious, hateful, odious, objectionable, insufferable, vile, loathsome; *informal* frightful, God-awful; *Brit. informal* beastly.
–OPPOSITES pleasant, agreeable.

horrid ▸ adjective. See HORRIBLE.

horrific ▸ adjective =**dreadful**, horrendous, horrible, frightful, awful, terrible, atrocious; horrifying, shocking, appalling, harrowing; hideous, grisly, ghastly, unspeakable, sickening.

horrify ▸ verb *he was horrified by her remarks* =**shock**, appal, outrage, scandalize, offend; disgust, revolt, nauseate, sicken.

horror ▸ noun **1** *children screamed in horror* =**terror**, fear, fright, alarm, panic; dread. **2** *to her horror she found herself alone* =**dismay**, consternation, alarm, distress; disgust, shock. **3** *the horror of the tragedy* =**awfulness**, frightfulness, savagery, hideousness, ghastliness. **4** (*informal*) *he's a little horror* =**rascal**, devil, imp, monkey, monster; *informal* terror, scamp, scallywag, tyke; *Brit. informal* perisher; *N. Amer. informal* varmint.
–OPPOSITES delight, satisfaction.
■ **have a horror of** =**hate**, detest, loathe, abhor; *formal* abominate.

horse ▸ noun =**mount**, charger, cob, nag, hack; pony, foal, yearling, colt, stallion, gelding, mare, filly; *N. Amer.* bronco; *Austral./NZ* moke, yarraman; *informal* geegee; *archaic* steed.
■ **horse around/about** (*informal*) =**fool around/about**, play the fool, act the clown, clown about/around, monkey about/around; *informal* mess about/around, lark about/around; *Brit. informal* muck about/around.

WORD LINKS

relating to horses: **equine**
male: **stallion**
castrated male: **gelding**
female: **mare**
young: **foal**
young male: **colt**
young female: **filly**
collective noun: **drove, string, stud, team**
relating to riding horses: **equestrian**
fear of horses: **hippophobia**
seller of horses: Brit. archaic **horse-coper**

horseman, horsewoman ▸ noun =**rider**, jockey; cavalryman, trooper; *historical* hussar, dragoon, knight; *archaic* cavalier.

horseplay ▸ noun =**tomfoolery**, fooling around, clowning, buffoonery; antics, high jinks; *informal* shenanigans, monkey business.

horticulture ▸ noun =**gardening**, floriculture, arboriculture, agriculture, cultivation.

hose ▸ noun =**pipe**, tube, duct, outlet, pipeline, siphon.

hosiery ▸ noun =**stockings**, tights, hold-ups, nylons, hose; socks; *N. Amer.* pantyhose.

hospitable ▸ adjective =**welcoming**, friendly, congenial, sociable, convivial, cordial; gracious, helpful, obliging, accommodating, warm, kind, generous, bountiful.

hospital ▸ noun =**infirmary**, sanatorium, hospice; *Brit.* cottage hospital; *Military* field hospital.

hospitality ▸ noun **1** *he is renowned for his hospitality* =**friendliness**, helpfulness, warmth, kindness, congeniality, cordiality, generosity. **2** *corporate hospitality* =**entertainment**; catering, food.

host[1] ▸ noun *the host of a TV series* =**presenter**, compère, anchor, anchorman, anchorwoman, announcer.
−OPPOSITES guest.
▸ verb *the show is hosted by Angus* =**present**, introduce, compère, front, anchor.

host[2] ▸ noun **1** *a host of memories* =**multitude**, abundance, wealth, profusion; *informal* load, heap, mass, pile, ton; *Brit. informal* shedload; *literary* myriad. **2** *a host of well-wishers* =**crowd**, throng, flock, swarm, horde, mob, army, legion.

hostage ▸ noun =**captive**, prisoner, detainee, internee.

hostel ▸ noun =**hotel**, YMCA, YWCA, bed and breakfast, B & B, boarding house, guest house.

hostile ▸ adjective **1** *a hostile attitude* =**unfriendly**, unkind, unsympathetic, rancorous; antagonistic, aggressive, confrontational, belligerent, truculent. **2** *hostile conditions* =**unfavourable**, adverse, bad, harsh, grim, inhospitable, forbidding. **3** *they are hostile to the idea* =**opposed**, averse, antagonistic, ill-disposed, unsympathetic, antipathetic, against; *informal* anti, down on.
−OPPOSITES friendly, favourable.

hostility ▸ noun **1** *he glared at her with hostility* =**antagonism**, unfriendliness, malevolence, unkindness, rancour, venom, hatred; aggression, belligerence. **2** *their hostility to the present regime* =**opposition**, antagonism, animosity, antipathy, ill feeling, resentment, enmity. **3** *a cessation of hostilities* =**fighting**, (armed) conflict, combat, warfare, war, bloodshed, violence.

hot ▸ adjective **1** *hot food* =**heated**, piping (hot), sizzling, steaming, roasting, boiling (hot), scorching, scalding, red-hot. **2** *a hot day* =**very warm**, balmy, summery, tropical, scorching, searing, blistering; sweltering; *informal* boiling, baking, roasting. **3** *she felt very hot* =**feverish**, febrile; burning, flushed. **4** *a hot chilli* =**spicy**, peppery, fiery, strong; piquant, powerful. **5** *the competition was hot* =**fierce**, intense, keen, competitive, cut-throat, ruthless, aggressive, strong. **6** *(informal) hot news* =**breaking**, recent, late, up to date, up to the minute; just out. **7** *(informal) a hot new act* =**popular**, in demand, sought-after; fashionable, in vogue, all the rage; *informal* big, in, now, hip, trendy, cool. **8** *(informal) she is hot on local history* =**knowledgeable about**, well informed about, au fait with, up on, well versed in; *informal* clued up about, genned up about.
−OPPOSITES cold, chilly, mild, dispassionate, weak, old.

■ **hot under the collar** *(informal)*. See ANGRY *sense* 1.

hot air ▸ noun *(informal)* =**nonsense**, rubbish, garbage, empty talk, claptrap, drivel, balderdash, gibberish; *informal* guff, bosh, hogwash, poppycock, bilge, twaddle; *Brit. informal* cobblers, codswallop, tosh; *N. Amer. informal* flapdoodle.

hotbed ▶ noun *a hotbed of crime* =**breeding ground**, den, cradle, nest.

hot-blooded ▶ adjective =**passionate**, amorous, lustful, libidinous, lecherous; *informal* horny, randy.
−OPPOSITES cold.

hotchpotch ▶ noun =**mixture**, mixed bag, assortment, jumble, ragbag, miscellany, medley, pot-pourri; melange, mishmash; *N. Amer.* hodgepodge.

hotel ▶ noun =**inn**, motel, boarding house, guest house, bed and breakfast, B & B, hostel.

hotfoot ▶ adverb =**hastily**, hurriedly, speedily, quickly, fast, rapidly, swiftly, without delay, post-haste, helter-skelter; *N. Amer. informal* lickety-split.
−OPPOSITES slowly.
■ **hotfoot it** *(informal)* =**hurry**, dash, run, race, sprint, bolt, dart, charge, shoot, hare, fly, speed, zoom, streak; *informal* tear, belt, pelt, scoot, clip, leg it; *Brit. informal* bomb; *N. Amer. informal* hightail it.

hot-headed ▶ adjective =**impetuous**, impulsive, rash, irresponsible, foolhardy; excitable, volatile, fiery, hot-tempered.

hothouse ▶ noun =**greenhouse**, glasshouse, conservatory, orangery, vinery, winter garden.

hotly ▶ adverb **1** *the rumours were hotly denied* =**vehemently**, vigorously, strenuously, fiercely, heatedly; angrily, indignantly. **2** *hotly pursued by Boris* =**closely**, swiftly, quickly.
−OPPOSITES calmly.

hot-tempered ▶ adjective =**irascible**, quick-tempered, short-tempered, irritable, fiery, bad-tempered; touchy, volatile, testy, tetchy; *informal* on a short fuse.
−OPPOSITES easy-going.

hound ▶ noun =(**hunting**) **dog**, canine, mongrel, cur; *informal* doggy, pooch, mutt; *Austral./NZ informal* mong, bitzer.
▶ verb **1** *she was hounded by the press* =**pursue**, chase, follow, shadow, stalk, track, trail; harass, persecute, pester, badger, torment. **2** *they hounded him out of office* =**force**, drive, push, urge, coerce, dragoon, strong-arm; *informal* bulldoze, railroad; *Brit. informal* bounce; *N. Amer. informal* hustle.

> WORD LINKS
> collective noun: **pack, cry**

house ▶ noun **1** *an estate of 200 houses* =**residence**, home; homestead; a roof over one's head; *formal* habitation, dwelling (place), abode, domicile. **2** *you'll wake the whole house!* =**household**, family, clan, tribe; *informal* brood. **3** *the house of Stewart* =**family**, clan, tribe; dynasty, line, bloodline, lineage. **4** *a printing house* =**firm**, business, company, corporation, enterprise, establishment, institution, concern, organization, operation; *informal* outfit, set-up. **5** *the country's upper house* assembly, legislative body, chamber, council, parliament, congress, senate, diet. **6** *the house applauded* =**audience**, crowd, spectators, viewers; congregation; gallery, stalls; *Brit. informal* punters.
▶ verb **1** *we can house twelve adults* =**accommodate**, give someone a roof over their head, lodge, quarter, board, billet, take in, sleep, put up. **2** *this panel houses the main switch* =**contain**, hold, store; cover, protect, enclose.

household ▶ noun *the household was asleep* =**family**, house, occupants; clan, tribe; *informal* brood.
▶ adjective *household goods* =**domestic**, family; everyday, workaday.

householder ▶ noun =**homeowner**, owner, occupant, resident; leaseholder; proprietor, freeholder; *Brit.* occupier, owner-occupier.

houseman ▶ noun *(Brit.)* =**junior doctor**; *N. Amer.* intern, resident.

house-trained *(Brit.)* ▶ adjective =**domesticated**, trained; *N. Amer.* housebroken.

housing ▶ noun **1** =**houses**, homes, residences; accommodation, living quarters; *formal* dwellings. **2** =**casing**; covering, case, cover, holder, fairing, sleeve.

hovel ▶ noun =**shack**, slum, shanty, hut; *informal* dump, hole.

hover ▶ verb **1** *helicopters hovered overhead* =**hang**, be poised, be suspended, float; fly. **2** *a servant hovered nearby* =**wait**, linger.

however ▶ adverb *however, this is not inevitable* =**nevertheless**, nonetheless, even so, for all that, despite that, in spite of that; be that as it may, having said that.

howl ▶ noun **1** *the howl of a wolf* =**baying**, cry, bark, yelp. **2** *a howl of anguish* =**wail**, cry, yell, yelp; bellow, roar, shout, shriek, scream, screech.

▶ verb **1** *dogs howled in the distance* =**bay**, cry, bark, yelp. **2** *a baby started to howl* =**wail**, cry, yell, bawl, bellow, shriek, scream, screech, caterwaul; *informal* holler. **3** *we howled with laughter* =**laugh**, guffaw, roar; be doubled up, split one's sides; *informal* fall about, crack up, be in stitches.

howler ▶ noun *(informal)* =**mistake**, error, blunder, gaffe, slip; *informal* slip-up, boo-boo, clanger; *Brit. informal* boob; *N. Amer. informal* blooper.

hub ▶ noun *the hub of family life* =**centre**, core, heart, focus, focal point, nucleus, kernel, nerve centre.
–OPPOSITES periphery.

hubbub ▶ noun **1** *her voice was lost in the hubbub* =**noise**, din, racket, commotion, clamour, cacophony, babel, rumpus; *Brit. informal* row. **2** *she fought through the hubbub* =**confusion**, chaos, pandemonium, bedlam, mayhem, tumult, fracas, hurly-burly.

huckster ▶ noun =**trader**, dealer, vendor, salesman, pedlar, hawker; *informal* pusher.

huddle ▶ verb **1** *they huddled together* =**crowd**, cluster, gather, bunch, throng, flock, collect, group, congregate; press, pack, squeeze. **2** *he huddled beneath the sheets* =**curl up**, snuggle, nestle, hunch up.
–OPPOSITES disperse.
▶ noun *a huddle of passengers* =**group**, cluster, bunch; collection; *informal* gaggle.

hue ▶ noun **1** *paints in a variety of hues* =**colour**, shade, tone, tint. **2** *men of all political hues* =**complexion**, type, kind, sort, cast, stamp, character, persuasion, nature.

hue and cry ▶ noun =**commotion**, outcry, uproar, fuss, clamour, furore, ruckus, rumpus; *informal* hoo-ha, hullabaloo, ballyhoo, kerfuffle, to-do, song and dance; *Brit. informal* row.

huff ▶ noun =**bad mood**, sulk, pet; temper; *informal* grump; *Brit. informal* strop; *N. Amer. informal* snit.

huffy ▶ adjective =**irritable**, irritated, annoyed, cross, grumpy, bad-tempered, crotchety, crabby, cantankerous, moody; *Brit. informal* narky, miffed, shirty.

hug ▶ verb **1** *they hugged each other* =**embrace**, cuddle, squeeze, clasp, clutch, hold tight. **2** *our route hugged the coast* =**follow**, stick to, run along.
▶ noun *there were hugs as we left* =**embrace**, cuddle, squeeze, bear hug.

huge ▶ adjective =**enormous**, vast, immense, great, massive, colossal, prodigious, gigantic, gargantuan, mammoth, monumental; giant, towering, mountainous, titanic; epic, Herculean; *informal* jumbo, mega, monster, whopping, humongous, hulking, bumper, astronomical; *Brit. informal* ginormous.
–OPPOSITES tiny.

hugely ▶ adverb =**very**, extremely, exceedingly, most, really, tremendously, greatly, decidedly, exceptionally, immensely, inordinately, extraordinarily, vastly; very much, to a great extent; *N. English* right; *informal* terrifically, awfully, terribly, majorly, seriously, mega, ultra, oh-so, damn; *Brit. informal* ever so, well, dead, jolly; *N. Amer. informal* real, mighty, awful; *informal, dated* frightfully; *archaic* exceeding.

hulk ▶ noun **1** *the rusting hulks of ships* =**wreck**, ruin; shell, skeleton, hull. **2** *a great hulk of a man* =**giant**, lump; *informal* clodhopper, ape, gorilla; *N. Amer. informal* lummox.

hull[1] ▶ noun *the ship's hull* =**framework**, body, shell, frame, skeleton, structure.

hull[2] ▶ noun *separate the nut from its hull* =**shell**, husk, pod, case, covering, integument; *Botany* pericarp.
▶ verb =**shell**, husk, peel, pare, skin; *technical* decorticate.

hum ▶ verb **1** *the engine was humming* =**purr**, drone, murmur, buzz, thrum, whirr, throb, vibrate. **2** *she hummed a tune* =**sing**, croon, murmur. **3** *the workshops are humming* =**be busy**, be active, be lively, buzz, bustle, be a hive of activity, throb. **4** *(Brit. informal) this stuff really hums.* See REEK verb.
▶ noun *a low hum of conversation* =**murmur**, drone, purr, buzz.
■ **hum and haw** *(Brit.)* =**hesitate**, dither, vacillate, be indecisive, equivocate, prevaricate, waver, blow hot and cold; *Brit.* haver; *Scottish* swither; *informal* shilly-shally.

human ▶ adjective **1** *they're only human* =**mortal**, flesh and blood; fallible, weak, frail, imperfect, vulnerable; physical, bodily, fleshly. **2** *his human side* =**compassionate**, humane, kind, considerate, understanding, sympathetic; approachable, accessible.
–OPPOSITES infallible.
▶ noun *the link between humans and animals* =**person**, human being, Homo sapiens,

man, woman, individual, mortal, (living) soul; earthling; (**humans**) the human race, humanity, humankind, mankind, man, people.

WORD LINKS

study of humankind: **anthropology**
measurement of the human body:
  anthropometry
eating other humans:
  anthropophagous, cannibalistic

---

humane ▸ adjective =**compassionate**, kind, considerate, understanding, sympathetic, tolerant; lenient, forbearing, forgiving, merciful, humanitarian, charitable.
–OPPOSITES cruel.

humanitarian ▸ adjective **1** *a humanitarian act* =**compassionate**, humane; unselfish, altruistic, generous. **2** *a humanitarian organization* =**charitable**, philanthropic, public-spirited, socially concerned, welfare, aid.
–OPPOSITES selfish.
▸ noun =**philanthropist**, altruist, benefactor, social reformer, good Samaritan; do-gooder.

humanities ▸ plural noun =**(liberal) arts**, literature; classics, classical studies, classical literature.

humanity ▸ noun **1** *humanity evolved from the apes* =**humankind**, mankind, man, people, the human race; Homo sapiens. **2** *he praised them for their humanity* =**compassion**, brotherly love, fellow feeling, humaneness, kindness, consideration, understanding, sympathy, tolerance; leniency, mercy, pity, tenderness; benevolence, charity.

humanize ▸ verb =**civilize**, improve, better; educate, enlighten; socialize; *formal* edify.

humble ▸ adjective **1** *she was very humble* =**meek**, deferential, respectful, submissive, self-effacing, unassertive; unpresuming, modest, unassuming, self-deprecating; *Scottish* mim. **2** *a humble background* =**lowly**, poor, undistinguished, mean; common, ordinary, simple, unremarkable, insignificant, inconsequential. **3** *my humble abode* =**modest**, plain, simple, ordinary, little, wee.
–OPPOSITES proud, noble, grand.
▸ verb **1** *it humbled him to ask for help* =**humiliate**, demean, lower, degrade, debase; mortify, shame. **2** *Wales were humbled by Romania* =**defeat**, beat, trounce,

rout, overwhelm, get the better of, bring to one's knees; *informal* lick, clobber, slaughter, massacre, crucify, walk all over; *N. Amer. informal* shellac, cream.

humbug ▸ noun **1** *that is sheer humbug* =**hypocrisy**, posturing, cant, empty talk. **2** *you see what a humbug I am?* =**hypocrite**, fraud, fake, plaster saint; charlatan, cheat, deceiver, dissembler; *informal* phoney.

humdrum ▸ adjective =**mundane**, dull, dreary, boring, tedious, monotonous, prosaic; routine, ordinary, everyday, run-of-the-mill, workaday, pedestrian.
–OPPOSITES remarkable, exciting.

humid ▸ adjective =**muggy**, close, sultry, sticky, steamy, oppressive, airless, stifling, suffocating, stuffy, clammy, heavy.
–OPPOSITES fresh.

WORD LINKS

measurement of humidity: **hygrometry, psychrometry**

---

humiliate ▸ verb =**embarrass**, mortify, humble, shame, put to shame, disgrace; discomfit, chasten, deflate, crush, squash; demean, degrade; cause to feel small, cause to lose face, take down a peg or two; *informal* show up, put down, cut down to size, settle someone's hash; *N. Amer. informal* make someone eat crow.

humiliating ▸ adjective =**embarrassing**, mortifying, humbling, ignominious, inglorious, shameful; discreditable, undignified, chastening, demeaning, degrading, deflating.

humiliation ▸ noun =**embarrassment**, mortification, shame, indignity, ignominy, disgrace, dishonour, degradation, discredit, obloquy, opprobrium; loss of pride, loss of face; blow to one's pride, slap in the face, kick in the teeth.
–OPPOSITES honour.

humility ▸ noun =**modesty**, humbleness, meekness, diffidence, unassertiveness; lack of pride, lack of vanity.
–OPPOSITES pride.

hummock ▸ noun =**hillock**, hump, mound, knoll, prominence, elevation, rise, dune; *N. Amer.* knob; *formal* eminence.

humorist ▸ noun =**wit**, wag; comic, funny man/woman, comedian, comedienne, joker.

humorous ▸ adjective =**amusing**, funny, comic, comical, entertaining, diverting, witty, jocular, light-hearted,

tongue-in-cheek, wry; hilarious, up-roarious, riotous, zany, farcical, droll.
–OPPOSITES serious.

humour ▸ noun 1 *the humour of the situation* =**comedy**, funny side, hilarity; absurdity, ludicrousness, drollness; satire, irony. 2 *the stories are spiced up with humour* =**jokes**, jests, quips, witticisms, funny remarks, puns; wit, comedy, drollery; *informal* gags, wisecracks, waggishness, one-liners. 3 *his good humour was infectious* =**mood**, temper, disposition, temperament, state of mind; spirits.
▸ verb *she was always humouring him* =**indulge**, accommodate, pander to, cater to, yield to, give way to, give in to, go along with; mollify, placate.

humourless ▸ adjective =**serious**, solemn, sober, sombre, grave, grim, dour, unsmiling, stony-faced; gloomy, glum, sad, melancholy, dismal, joyless, cheerless, lugubrious; dry.
–OPPOSITES jovial.

hump ▸ noun *a hump at the base of the spine* =**protuberance**, prominence, lump, bump, knob, protrusion, projection, bulge, swelling, hunch; growth, outgrowth.
▸ verb *(informal) he humped boxes up the stairs* =**heave**, carry, lug, lift, hoist, heft; *informal* schlep, tote.
■ **give someone the hump** *(informal)*. See ANNOY.

hunch ▸ noun 1 *the hunch on his back* =**protuberance**, hump, lump, bump, knob, protrusion, prominence, bulge, swelling; growth. 2 *my hunch is that he'll be back* =**feeling**, guess, suspicion, impression, inkling, idea, notion, fancy, intuition; *informal* gut feeling.

hundred ▸ cardinal number century; *informal* ton.

┌─────────────────────┐
│ **WORD LINKS** │
│ *relating to a hundred:* **centenary,** │
│ **centennial, centi-, hecto-** │
└─────────────────────┘

hunger ▸ noun 1 *she was faint with hunger* =**lack of food**, hungriness, emptiness; starvation, malnutrition, malnourishment, undernourishment. 2 *a hunger for news* =**desire**, craving, longing, yearning, hankering, appetite, thirst; *informal* itch, yen.
■ **hunger after/for** =**desire**, crave; long for, yearn for, pine for, ache for, hanker after, thirst for, lust for; want, need;

informal have a yen for, itch for, be dying for, be gagging for.

hungry ▸ adjective 1 *I was really hungry* =**ravenous**, starving, starved, famished; malnourished, undernourished, underfed; *informal* peckish. 2 *they are hungry for success* =**eager**, keen, avid, longing, yearning, aching, greedy; craving, desirous of, hankering after; *informal* itching, dying, gagging.
–OPPOSITES full.

hunk ▸ noun 1 *a hunk of bread* =**chunk**, wedge, block, slab, lump, square, gobbet; *Brit. informal* wodge. 2 *(informal) he's a real hunk* =**muscleman**, strongman, macho man, Adonis; *informal* he-man, stud.
–OPPOSITES wimp.

hunt ▸ verb 1 *they hunted deer* =**chase**, stalk, pursue, course; track, trail. 2 *police are hunting for her* =**search**, look (high and low), scour the area; seek, try to find.
▸ noun 1 *the thrill of the hunt* =**chase**, pursuit. 2 *police have stepped up their hunt* =**search**, quest.

hunted ▸ adjective =**harassed**, persecuted, harried, hounded, beleaguered, troubled, tormented; *informal* hassled.
–OPPOSITES carefree.

hunter ▸ noun =**huntsman**, huntswoman, trapper, stalker, woodsman; predator, raptor, carnivore, meat eater.

hunting ▸ noun =**blood sports**, field sports, shooting, coursing; the chase.

hurdle ▸ noun 1 *his leg hit a hurdle* =**fence**, jump, barrier, barricade, bar, railing, rail. 2 *the final hurdle to overcome* =**obstacle**, difficulty, problem, barrier, bar, snag, stumbling block, impediment, obstruction, complication, hindrance.

hurl ▸ verb. See THROW.

hurly-burly ▸ noun. See CONFUSION.

hurricane ▸ noun =**cyclone**, typhoon, tornado, storm, windstorm, whirlwind, gale; *Austral.* willy-willy; *N. Amer. informal* twister.

hurried ▸ adjective 1 *hurried glances* =**quick**, fast, swift, rapid, speedy, brisk, hasty; cursory, perfunctory, brief, short, fleeting. 2 *a hurried decision* =**hasty**, rushed, speedy, quick; precipitate, spur-of-the-moment.
–OPPOSITES slow, considered.

hurriedly ▸ adverb =**hastily**, speedily,

quickly, rapidly, swiftly, briskly; without delay.

hurry ▶ verb **1** *hurry or you'll be late* = **be quick**, hurry up, hasten, speed up; run, dash, rush, race, fly; scurry, scramble, scuttle, sprint; *informal* get a move on, step on it, get cracking, get moving, shake a leg; *Brit. informal* shift, get one's skates on; *N. Amer. informal* get the lead out, get a wiggle on; *dated* make haste. **2** *she hurried him out* = **hustle**, hasten, push, urge, usher.
–OPPOSITES dawdle, delay.
▶ noun *in all the hurry, we forgot* = **rush**, haste, hustle and bustle, confusion, commotion, hubbub.

h

hurt ▶ verb **1** *my back hurts* = **be painful**, be sore, be tender, cause pain, cause discomfort; ache, smart, sting, burn, throb; *informal* be killing; *Brit. informal* be playing up. **2** *Dad hurt his leg* = **injure**, wound, damage, disable; bruise, cut, gash, graze, scrape, scratch, lacerate. **3** *his words hurt her* = **distress**, pain, wound, sting, upset, sadden, devastate, grieve, mortify. **4** *high interest rates are hurting the economy* = **harm**, damage, weaken, blight, impede, jeopardize, undermine, ruin, wreck, sabotage, cripple.
–OPPOSITES heal, comfort, benefit.
▶ noun *all the hurt he had caused* = **distress**, pain, suffering, grief, misery, anguish, trauma, woe, upset, sadness, sorrow; harm, damage, trouble.
–OPPOSITES joy.
▶ adjective **1** *my hurt hand* = **injured**, wounded, bruised, grazed, cut, gashed, sore, painful, aching, smarting, throbbing. **2** *Anne's hurt expression* = **pained**, distressed, anguished, upset, sad, mortified, offended; *informal* miffed, peeved.
–OPPOSITES pleased.

hurtful ▶ adjective *hurtful words* = **upsetting**, distressing, wounding, painful; unkind, cruel, nasty, mean, malicious, spiteful.

hurtle ▶ verb = **speed**, rush, run, race, career, whizz, zoom, charge, shoot, streak, gallop, hare, fly, go like the wind; *informal* belt, pelt, tear, go like a bat out of hell; *Brit. informal* bomb, bucket, go like the clappers; *N. Amer. informal* barrel.

husband ▶ noun = **spouse**, partner, mate, consort, man; *informal* hubby, old man, one's better half; *Brit. informal* other half.

hush ▶ verb **1** *he tried to hush her* = **silence**, quieten (down), shush; gag, muzzle; *informal* shut up. **2** *they hushed up the dangers* = **keep secret**, conceal, hide, suppress, cover up, keep quiet about; obscure, veil, sweep under the carpet.
–OPPOSITES disclose.
▶ exclamation *Hush! Someone will hear you* = **be quiet**, keep quiet, quieten down, hold your tongue; *informal* shut up, shut your mouth, shut your face, shut your trap, button your lip, pipe down, put a sock in it, give it a rest, not another word; *Brit. informal* shut your gob.
▶ noun *a hush descended* = **silence**, quiet; stillness, peace, calm, tranquillity.
–OPPOSITES noise.

husk ▶ noun = **shell**, hull, pod, case, covering, integument; *Botany* pericarp.

husky ▶ adjective *a husky voice* = **throaty**, gruff, gravelly, hoarse, croaky, rough, guttural, harsh, rasping, raspy.
–OPPOSITES shrill, soft.

hustle ▶ verb *I was hustled away* = **manhandle**, push, shove, thrust, frogmarch; rush, hurry, whisk, usher, show; *informal* bundle.
■ **hustle and bustle** = **confusion**, bustle, tumult, hubbub, activity, action, liveliness, excitement, whirl; *informal* toing and froing, comings and goings, ballyhoo, hoo-ha, hullabaloo.

hut ▶ noun = **shack**, shanty, (log) cabin, shelter, shed, lean-to; hovel; *Scottish* bothy, shieling; *N. Amer.* cabana.

hybrid ▶ noun = **cross**, cross-breed; mixture, blend, amalgamation, combination, composite, fusion.
▶ adjective *hybrid roses* = **composite**, crossbred, interbred; mixed, blended, compound.

hybridize ▶ verb = **cross-breed**, cross, interbreed, cross-fertilize, cross-pollinate; mix, blend, combine, amalgamate.

hygiene ▶ noun = **cleanliness**, sanitation, sterility, purity, disinfection; public health, environmental health.

hygienic ▶ adjective = **sanitary**, clean, germ-free, disinfected, sterilized, sterile, antiseptic, aseptic, unpolluted, uncontaminated; *informal* squeaky clean.
–OPPOSITES insanitary.

hyperbole ▶ noun = **exaggeration**, overstatement, magnification, embroidery, embellishment, excess, overkill.

−OPPOSITES understatement.

hypercritical ▶ adjective. *See* OVER-CRITICAL.

hypnosis ▶ noun =mesmerism, hypnotism, hypnotic suggestion, autosuggestion.

hypnotic ▶ adjective =mesmerizing, mesmeric, spellbinding, entrancing, bewitching, irresistible, compelling; soporific, sedative, numbing.

hypnotize ▶ verb *they were hypnotized by the dancers* =entrance, spellbind, enthral, transfix, captivate, bewitch, enrapture, grip, rivet, absorb.

hypocrisy ▶ noun =sanctimoniousness, piousness, cant, posturing, humbug, pretence; insincerity, falseness; *informal* phoneyness.
−OPPOSITES sincerity.

hypocrite ▶ noun =pretender, humbug, deceiver, dissembler; *informal* phoney.

hypocritical ▶ adjective =sanctimo-nious, pious, self-righteous, holier-than-thou, superior; insincere, false; two-faced; *informal* phoney.

hypothesis ▶ noun =theory, theorem, thesis, conjecture, supposition, postulate, proposition, premise, assumption; notion, concept, idea.

hypothetical ▶ adjective =theoretical, speculative, conjectured, notional, supposed, assumed; academic, imaginary.
−OPPOSITES actual.

hysteria ▶ noun =frenzy, feverishness, hysterics, derangement, mania; panic, alarm, distress.
−OPPOSITES calm.

hysterical ▶ adjective **1** *Janet became hysterical* =overwrought, overemotional, out of control, frenzied, frantic, wild; beside oneself, driven to distraction, manic, delirious, unhinged, deranged, out of one's mind, raving; *informal* in a state. **2** (*informal*). *See* HILARIOUS.

ice ▶ noun **1** *a lake covered with ice* =icicles; black ice, verglas, frost, rime, permafrost, hoar (frost); *N. Amer.* glaze. **2** *assorted ices* =ice cream, water ice, sorbet; *N. Amer.* sherbet. **3** *the ice in her voice* =coldness, coolness, frostiness, iciness; hostility, unfriendliness.

■ **on ice** *(informal).* See PENDING adjective sense 1.

WORD LINKS

relating to ice: **gelid, glacial**
fear of ice: **cryophobia**

ice-cold ▶ adjective =icy, freezing, glacial, sub-zero, frozen, wintry; arctic, polar, Siberian; bitter, biting, raw.
–OPPOSITES hot.

icon ▶ noun =image, idol, portrait, representation, symbol.

iconoclast ▶ noun =dissenter, sceptic; heretic, dissident; rebel, renegade, mutineer.

icy ▶ adjective **1** *icy roads* =frosty, frozen (over), iced over, ice-bound, ice-covered; slippery; *literary* rimy. **2** *an icy wind* =freezing, chill, biting, bitter, raw, arctic, glacial, Siberian, polar. **3** *an icy voice* =unfriendly, hostile, forbidding; cold, chilly, frosty, glacial; haughty, stern, hard.

idea ▶ noun **1** *the idea of death scares her* =concept, notion, conception, thought. **2** *our idea is to open a new shop* =plan, scheme, design, proposal, proposition, suggestion; aim, intention, objective, object, goal, target, concept. **3** *Liz had various ideas on the subject* =thought, theory, view, opinion, feeling, belief, conclusion. **4** *I had an idea that it might happen* =sense, feeling, suspicion, fancy, inkling, hunch, notion, impression. **5** *an idea of the cost* =estimate, approximation, guess, conjecture; *informal* guesstimate.

ideal ▶ adjective **1** *ideal flying weather* =perfect, faultless, exemplary, classic, model, ultimate, quintessential. **2** *an ideal world* =unattainable, unachievable, impracticable; unreal, hypothetical, theoretical, Utopian.

–OPPOSITES bad, concrete, real.

▶ noun **1** *an ideal to aim at* =model, pattern, exemplar, example, paradigm. **2** *liberal ideals* =principle, standard, value, belief, conviction; (**ideals**) morals, ethics, ideology, creed.

idealist ▶ noun =Utopian, visionary, romantic, dreamer.
–OPPOSITES realist.

idealistic ▶ adjective =Utopian, visionary, romantic, unrealistic, impractical.

idealize ▶ verb =romanticize, glamorize, sentimentalize.

identical ▶ adjective =(exactly) the same, indistinguishable, twin, interchangeable; alike, matching.
–OPPOSITES different.

identifiable ▶ adjective =distinguishable, recognizable; noticeable, perceptible, discernible, detectable, observable, perceivable, visible.
–OPPOSITES unrecognizable.

identification ▶ noun **1** *the identification of the suspect* =recognition, singling out, pinpointing, naming. **2** *early identification of problems* =determination, establishment, ascertainment, discovery, diagnosis. **3** *may I see your identification?* =ID, papers, documents, credentials; card, pass, badge. **4** *the identification of the party with high taxes* =association, linking, connection. **5** *his identification with the music* =empathy, rapport, sympathy, understanding.

identify ▶ verb **1** *Gail identified her attacker* =recognize, pick out, spot, point out, pinpoint, put one's finger on, name. **2** *I identified four problem areas* =determine, establish, ascertain, make out, discern, distinguish. **3** *we identify sport with glamour* =associate, link, connect, relate. **4** *Peter identifies with the team captain* =empathize, sympathize; understand, relate to, feel for.

identity ▶ noun *she was afraid of losing her identity* =individuality, self; personality, character, originality, distinctiveness, uniqueness.

ideology ▸ noun =belief; doctrine, creed, theory.

idiocy ▸ noun. See STUPIDITY.

idiom ▸ noun =expression, phrase, turn of phrase.

idiomatic ▸ adjective =colloquial, everyday, conversational, vernacular; natural.

idiosyncrasy ▸ noun =peculiarity, oddity, eccentricity, mannerism, quirk, characteristic.

idiosyncratic ▸ adjective =distinctive, individual, individualistic, characteristic, peculiar, typical, special, specific, unique, personal; eccentric, unconventional, quirky.

idiot ▸ noun. See FOOL.

idiotic ▸ adjective. See STUPID.

idle ▸ adjective **1** *an idle fellow* =lazy, indolent, slothful, work-shy, shiftless. **2** *I was bored with being idle* =unemployed, jobless, out of work, redundant, unoccupied; *Brit. informal* on the dole, resting. **3** *their idle hours* =unoccupied, spare, empty, unfilled. **4** *idle remarks* =frivolous, trivial, trifling, minor, insignificant, unimportant. **5** *idle threats* =empty, meaningless, worthless, vain.
−OPPOSITES industrious, employed, working, busy, serious.

> ### WORD LINKS
> *fear of being idle:* **thassophobia**

idler ▸ noun =loafer, layabout, good-for-nothing, ne'er-do-well; *informal* skiver, waster, slacker, slob, lazybones; *N. Amer. informal* slowpoke; *literary* wastrel.
−OPPOSITES workaholic.

idol ▸ noun **1** *an idol in a shrine* =icon, effigy, statue, figure, figurine, totem. **2** *the pop world's latest idol* =hero, heroine, star, superstar, icon, celebrity; darling; *informal* pin-up, heart throb.

idolize ▸ verb =hero-worship, worship, revere, venerate, look up to, exalt; *informal* put on a pedestal.

idyllic ▸ adjective =perfect, wonderful, blissful, halcyon, happy; *literary* Arcadian.

if ▸ conjunction **1** *if the weather is fine, we can walk* =on condition that, provided (that), presuming (that), supposing (that), assuming (that), as long as, in the event that. **2** *if I go out she gets nasty* =whenever, every time. **3** *I wonder if he*

noticed =whether, whether or not.

ignite ▸ verb **1** *moments before the petrol ignited* =catch fire, burst into flames, explode. **2** *a cigarette ignited the fumes* =light, set fire to, set alight. **3** *the campaign failed to ignite voter interest* =arouse, kindle, trigger, spark, excite, provoke, stimulate, stir up, incite.
−OPPOSITES go out, extinguish.

ignoble ▸ adjective =dishonourable, unworthy, base, shameful, contemptible, despicable, shabby.

ignominious ▸ adjective =humiliating, undignified, embarrassing, inglorious.
−OPPOSITES glorious.

ignominy ▸ noun =shame, humiliation, embarrassment; disgrace, dishonour, indignity.

ignorance ▸ noun **1** *his ignorance of economics* =incomprehension, unfamiliarity, inexperience, innocence, lack of knowledge. **2** *their attitudes are based on ignorance* =lack of knowledge; unenlightenment, benightedness.
−OPPOSITES knowledge, education.

ignorant ▸ adjective **1** *an ignorant country girl* =uneducated, unschooled, untutored, illiterate, uninformed, unenlightened, benighted; inexperienced, unsophisticated. **2** *ignorant of working-class life* =unaware, unconscious, unfamiliar, unacquainted, uninformed.
−OPPOSITES educated, knowledgeable.

ignore ▸ verb **1** *he ignored her* =take no notice of, pay no attention to; snub, look right through, cold-shoulder; *Brit. informal* blank. **2** *doctors ignored her husband's instructions* =disregard, take no account of; fail to observe, disobey, defy.
−OPPOSITES acknowledge, obey.

ill ▸ adjective **1** *she was feeling rather ill* =unwell, sick, poorly; bad; *informal* under the weather, lousy, rough; *Brit. informal* ropy, grotty; *Austral./NZ informal* crook. **2** *the ill effects of smoking* =harmful, damaging, detrimental, deleterious, adverse, injurious, pernicious, dangerous; *archaic* baneful.
−OPPOSITES well, healthy, beneficial, auspicious.
▸ noun **1** *the ills of society* =problems, troubles, difficulties, misfortunes, trials, tribulations; *informal* headaches, hassles. **2** *he wished them no ill* =harm, hurt, injury, pain, trouble, misfortune, distress.

▶ adverb 1 *he can ill afford the loss of income* =**barely**, scarcely, hardly, only just. 2 *we are ill prepared* =**inadequately**, insufficiently, poorly, badly.
−OPPOSITES well.

■ **ill at ease** =**awkward**, uneasy, uncomfortable, embarrassed, self-conscious, out of place; restless, restive, fidgety, worried, anxious, on edge, edgy, nervous, tense; *informal* twitchy, jittery; *N. Amer. informal* discombobulated, antsy.

ill-advised ▶ adjective =**unwise**, misguided, imprudent, ill-considered, ill-judged; foolhardy, hare-brained, rash, reckless.
−OPPOSITES judicious.

ill-considered ▶ adjective =**rash**, ill-advised, ill-judged, injudicious, imprudent, unwise, hasty; ill-conceived, badly thought out.
−OPPOSITES judicious.

ill-defined ▶ adjective =**vague**, indistinct, unclear, imprecise; blurred, fuzzy, hazy, woolly, nebulous.

ill-disposed ▶ adjective =**hostile**, antagonistic, unfriendly, unsympathetic, antipathetic, inimical, unfavourable.
−OPPOSITES friendly.

illegal ▶ adjective =**unlawful**, illicit, criminal, felonious; unlicensed, unauthorized; outlawed, banned, forbidden, prohibited, proscribed.
−OPPOSITES lawful, legitimate.

illegible ▶ adjective =**unreadable**, indecipherable, unintelligible.

illegitimate ▶ adjective =**illegal**, unlawful, illicit, criminal, felonious; fraudulent, corrupt, dishonest; *informal* crooked, shady; *Brit. informal* bent, dodgy.
−OPPOSITES legal, lawful.

ill-fated ▶ adjective =**doomed**, blighted, damned, cursed, ill-starred, jinxed; *literary* star-crossed.

ill-founded ▶ adjective =**baseless**, groundless, without foundation, unjustified; misinformed, misguided.

ill-humoured ▶ adjective =**bad-tempered**, ill-tempered, cross; irritable, irascible, tetchy, crotchety, touchy, cantankerous, curmudgeonly, peevish, fractious, waspish, prickly, grumpy, grouchy, crabby, splenetic; *N. Amer. informal* cranky, ornery, peckish; *Austral./NZ informal* snaky.
−OPPOSITES amiable.

illiberal ▶ adjective =**intolerant**, conservative, reactionary, undemocratic, authoritarian, repressive, oppressive.

illicit ▶ adjective =**illegal**, unlawful, criminal; outlawed, banned, forbidden, prohibited, proscribed; unlicensed, unauthorized; contraband, black-market, bootleg.
−OPPOSITES lawful, legal.

illiterate ▶ adjective *politically illiterate* =**ignorant**, unaware, uneducated.

ill-judged ▶ adjective =**ill-considered**, unwise, ill-thought-out; imprudent, incautious, injudicious, misguided, ill-advised, impolitic.
−OPPOSITES judicious.

ill-mannered ▶ adjective =**bad-mannered**, discourteous, rude, impolite, abusive; insolent, impertinent, impudent, cheeky, loutish, uncouth; *informal* ignorant.
−OPPOSITES polite.

illness ▶ noun =**sickness**, disease, ailment, complaint, malady, affliction, infection; *informal* bug, virus; *dated* contagion.
−OPPOSITES good health.

| WORD LINKS |
fear of illness: **nosophobia**

illogical ▶ adjective =**irrational**, unreasonable, unsound, unreasoned; erroneous, invalid, spurious, fallacious.

ill-tempered ▶ adjective. *See* ILL-HUMOURED.

ill-timed ▶ adjective =**untimely**, mistimed, badly timed.
−OPPOSITES timely.

ill-treat ▶ verb =**abuse**, mistreat, maltreat, ill-use, misuse.
−OPPOSITES pamper.

ill-treatment ▶ noun =**abuse**, mistreatment, maltreatment, misuse.

illuminating ▶ adjective =**informative**, enlightening, revealing, explanatory, instructive, helpful, educational.

illumination ▶ noun =**light**, lighting, radiance, gleam, glow, glare.

illusion ▶ noun 1 *the lighting increases the illusion of depth* =**appearance**, impression, semblance. 2 *it's just an illusion* =**mirage**, hallucination, apparition, figment of the imagination, trick of the light, chimera.

illusory ▶ adjective =**false**, imagined,

imaginary, fanciful, unreal; sham, fallacious.
−OPPOSITES genuine.

illustrate ▸ verb **1** *the photographs that
illustrate the text* =**decorate**, adorn, ornament, accompany, support. **2** *this can
be illustrated through a brief example* =**explain**, elucidate, clarify, demonstrate,
show; *informal* get across/over.

illustration ▸ noun **1** *the illustrations
in children's books* =**picture**, drawing,
sketch, figure, plate, print. **2** *by way of illustration* =**exemplification**, demonstration; example, analogy.

illustrious ▸ adjective =**eminent**, distinguished, acclaimed, notable, noteworthy, prominent, pre-eminent, foremost, leading, important; renowned,
famous, well known, celebrated.
−OPPOSITES unknown.

ill will ▸ noun =**animosity**, hostility,
enmity, antipathy; ill feeling, bad blood,
antagonism, resentment, bitterness.
−OPPOSITES goodwill.

image ▸ noun **1** *images of the Queen*
=**likeness**; depiction, portrayal, representation; painting, picture, portrait,
drawing, photograph. **2** *images of the
planet Neptune* =**picture**, photograph.
3 *the image of this country as a democracy*
=**conception**, impression, idea, perception, notion. **4** *his public image* =**persona**,
profile, face.

> WORD LINKS
>
> *study of images:* **iconography,
> iconology**

Imaginable ▸ adjective = thinkable,
conceivable.

imaginary ▸ adjective =**unreal**, non-
existent, fictional, pretend, make-
believe, illusory; made-up.
−OPPOSITES real.

imagination ▸ noun =**creativity**, vision, inventiveness, resourcefulness,
ingenuity; originality.

imaginative ▸ adjective =**creative**,
visionary, inventive, resourceful, ingenious; original, innovative.

imagine ▸ verb **1** *you can imagine the
scene* =**visualize**, envisage, picture, see
in the mind's eye; dream up, think up/
of, conceive. **2** *I imagine he was at home*
=**assume**, presume, expect, take it (as
read), suppose.

imbalance ▸ noun =**disparity**, variation, contrast, lack of harmony; gap.

imbed ▸ verb. *See* EMBED.

imbue ▸ verb =**permeate**, saturate,
suffuse; inject, inculcate; fill.

imitate ▸ verb **1** *other artists have imi-
tated his style* =**emulate**, copy, follow,
echo, parrot; *informal* rip off. **2** *he could
imitate Winston Churchill* =**mimic**, do an
impression of, impersonate; *informal* take
off, send up; *N. Amer. informal* make like.

imitation ▸ noun **1** *an imitation of a
sailor's hat* =**copy**, simulation, reproduction, replica. **2** *learning by imitation*
=**emulation**, copying. **3** *a perfect imitation of Francis* =**impersonation**, impression, parody, caricature; *informal* send-up,
take-off, spoof.
▸ adjective *imitation ivory* =**artificial**, synthetic, simulated, man-made, manufactured, ersatz, substitute; mock, fake.
−OPPOSITES real, genuine.

immaculate ▸ adjective **1** *an immaculate white shirt* =**clean**, spotless, pristine;
shining, shiny, gleaming. **2** *immaculate
condition* =**perfect**, pristine, mint; flawless, faultless, unblemished; *informal*
tip-top, A1. **3** *his immaculate record* =**unblemished**, spotless, impeccable, unsullied, untarnished; *informal* squeaky
clean.
−OPPOSITES dirty, damaged.

immaterial ▸ adjective =**irrelevant**,
unimportant, inconsequential, insignificant, of no matter/moment, of little
account, beside the point, neither here
nor there.
−OPPOSITES significant.

immature ▸ adjective *an extremely immature girl* =**childish**, babyish, infantile,
juvenile, puerile, callow.

immeasurable ▸ adjective =**incalculable**, inestimable, innumerable;
limitless, boundless, unbounded; vast,
immense.

immediate ▸ adjective **1** *the UN called
for immediate action* =**instant**, instantaneous, prompt, swift, speedy, rapid,
quick. **2** *their immediate concerns* =**current**, present; urgent, pressing. **3** *our
immediate neighbours* =**nearest**, close,
next-door; adjacent, adjoining.
−OPPOSITES delayed, distant.

immediately ▸ adverb **1** *it was necessary to make a decision immediately*
=**straight away**, at once, right away, in-

stantly, now, directly, forthwith, this/ that (very) minute, this/that instant, there and then, without delay, post-haste. **2** *I sat immediately behind him* =**directly**, right, exactly, precisely, squarely, just, dead; *informal* slap bang; *N. Amer. informal* smack dab.

immense ▸ adjective =**huge**, vast, massive, enormous, gigantic, colossal, great, very large/big, monumental, towering, tremendous; giant, monstrous, mammoth, titanic, king-sized; *informal* mega, monster, whopping (great), thumping (great), humongous, jumbo; *Brit. informal* whacking (great), ginormous.
–OPPOSITES tiny.

immensely ▸ adverb =**extremely**, very, exceedingly, exceptionally, extraordinarily, tremendously, hugely, outstandingly, uncommonly, supremely, highly, really, truly, mightily, thoroughly, in the extreme; *informal* terrifically, awfully, fearfully, terribly, devilishly, seriously, mega, damn; *Brit. informal* ever so, well, bloody, hellish, dead, jolly; *N. Amer. informal* mighty, powerful, awful; *informal, dated* devilish, frightfully; *archaic* exceeding.
–OPPOSITES slightly.

immerse ▸ verb **1** *the metal was immersed in acid* =**submerge**, dip, dunk, duck, sink. **2** *Elliot was immersed in his work* =**absorb**, engross, occupy, engage, involve, bury; preoccupy; *informal* lose oneself in.

immigrant ▸ noun =**newcomer**, settler, incomer, migrant; non-native, foreigner, alien.
–OPPOSITES native.

imminent ▸ adjective =**impending**, close (at hand), near, (fast) approaching, coming, forthcoming, on the way, expected, looming; *informal* on the cards.

immobile ▸ adjective =**motionless**, without moving, still, stock-still, static, stationary; rooted to the spot, rigid, frozen, transfixed, like a statue, not moving a muscle.

immobilize ▸ verb =**put out of action**, disable, deactivate, paralyse, cripple; bring to a standstill, halt, stop; clamp, wheel-clamp.

immoderate ▸ adjective =**excessive**, heavy, intemperate, unrestrained, unrestricted, uncontrolled, unbridled, overindulgent; undue, inordinate; extravagant, lavish, prodigal, profligate.

immodest ▸ adjective =**indecorous**, improper, indecent, indelicate, immoral; forward, bold, brazen, shameless, loose, wanton; *informal* fresh, cheeky, saucy.

immoral ▸ adjective =**unethical**, bad, wrong, wicked, unprincipled, unscrupulous, dishonourable, dishonest, corrupt; sinful, impure, unchaste, promiscuous.
–OPPOSITES ethical, chaste.

immorality ▸ noun =**wickedness**, badness, corruption, dishonesty, sin, vice, debauchery, dissolution, perversion, promiscuity.

immortal ▸ adjective **1** *our immortal souls* =**undying**, deathless, eternal, everlasting; imperishable, indestructible. **2** *an immortal classic* =**timeless**, perennial, classic, time-honoured, enduring, evergreen.
▸ noun *one of the immortals of soccer* =**great**, hero, myth, legend, demigod, superstar.

immortality ▸ noun **1** *the dream of immortality* =**eternal life**, everlasting life; indestructibility, imperishability. **2** *the book has achieved immortality* =**timelessness**, legendary status, classic status, lasting fame/renown.

immortalize ▸ verb =**commemorate**; celebrate, eulogize, pay tribute to, honour, salute, exalt, glorify.

immovable ▸ adjective **1** *lock your bike to something immovable* =**fixed**, secure, set firm, set fast; stuck, jammed, stiff. **2** *he sat immovable* =**motionless**, unmoving, stationary, still, stock-still, not moving a muscle, rooted to the spot; transfixed, paralysed, frozen. **3** *she was immovable in her loyalty* =**steadfast**, unwavering, unswerving, resolute, determined, firm, unshakeable, unfailing, dogged, tenacious, inflexible, unyielding, unbending, uncompromising.
–OPPOSITES mobile, moving.

immune ▸ adjective =**resistant**, not subject, not liable, not vulnerable; protected from, safe from, secure against.
–OPPOSITES susceptible.

immunity ▸ noun **1** *immunity to malaria* =**resistance**; protection, defence. **2** *immunity from prosecution* =**exemption**, exception, freedom. **3** *diplomatic immunity* =**indemnity**, privilege, prerogative, licence; exemption, impunity, protection.

WORD LINKS

branch of medicine to do with immunity:
immunology

immunize ▶ verb =vaccinate, inoculate, inject.

immutable ▶ adjective =fixed, set, rigid, inflexible, permanent, established; unchanging, unvarying, constant.
–OPPOSITES variable.

imp ▶ noun **1** =demon, devil; hobgoblin, goblin. **2** *a cheeky young imp* =rascal, monkey, devil, wretch; *informal* scamp, brat, horror, tyke; *Brit. informal* perisher; *N. Amer. informal* hellion, varmint; *archaic* scapegrace, rapscallion.

impact ▶ noun **1** *the force of the impact* =collision, crash, smash, bump, knock. **2** *the job losses will have a major impact* =effect, influence; consequences, repercussions, ramifications.
▶ verb **1** (*N. Amer.*) =crash into, smash into, collide with, hit, strike, smack into, bang into. **2** *interest rates have impacted on spending* =affect, influence, have an effect, make an impression; hit.

impair ▶ verb =have a negative effect on, damage, harm, diminish, reduce, weaken, lessen, decrease, impede, hinder.
–OPPOSITES improve, enhance.

impaired ▶ adjective =disabled, handicapped, incapacitated; *euphemistic* challenged.

impairment ▶ noun =disability, handicap, defect, dysfunction.

impale ▶ verb =stick, skewer, spear, spike, transfix; pierce, run through.

impalpable ▶ adjective =intangible, insubstantial, incorporeal; indefinable.

impart ▶ verb **1** *she had news to impart* =communicate, pass on, convey, transmit, relay, relate, recount, tell, make known, make public, report, announce; disclose, reveal, divulge. **2** *the brush imparts a good sheen* =give, bestow, confer, grant, lend, afford, provide, supply.

impartial ▶ adjective =unbiased, unprejudiced, neutral, non-partisan, disinterested, detached, dispassionate, objective, open-minded.
–OPPOSITES biased, partisan.

impassable ▶ adjective =unpassable, unnavigable, untraversable; closed (off), blocked.

impasse ▶ noun =deadlock, dead end, stalemate, checkmate, stand-off; standstill.

impassioned ▶ adjective =emotional, heartfelt, earnest, sincere, fervent, passionate.

impassive ▶ adjective =expressionless, inexpressive, inscrutable, blank, poker-faced, straight-faced; stony.
–OPPOSITES expressive.

impatience ▶ noun **1** *he was shifting in his seat with impatience* =restlessness, agitation, nervousness; eagerness, keenness. **2** *a burst of impatience* =irritability, tetchiness, irascibility, peevishness, frustration, exasperation, annoyance.

impatient ▶ adjective **1** *Melissa grew impatient* =restless, agitated, nervous, anxious, ill at ease, edgy, jumpy; *informal* twitchy, jittery, uptight. **2** *they are impatient to get back home* =anxious, eager, keen; *informal* itching, dying. **3** *an impatient gesture* =irritated, annoyed, angry, tetchy, snappy, cross; abrupt, curt, brusque, terse, short.
–OPPOSITES calm, reluctant.

impeach ▶ verb (*N. Amer.*) =indict, charge, accuse, arraign, prosecute.

impeccable ▶ adjective =flawless, faultless, unblemished, spotless, stainless, perfect, exemplary; irreproachable; *informal* squeaky clean.
–OPPOSITES imperfect, sinful.

impede ▶ verb =hinder, obstruct, hamper, hold back/up, delay, interfere with, disrupt, retard, slow (down).
–OPPOSITES facilitate.

impediment ▶ noun **1** *an impediment to economic improvement* =hindrance, obstruction, obstacle, barrier, bar, block, check, curb, restriction. **2** *a speech impediment* =defect, impairment; stammer, stutter, lisp.

impel ▶ verb *financial difficulties impelled her to seek work* =force, compel, oblige, require, make, urge, drive, push, prompt.

impending ▶ adjective =imminent, close (at hand), near, approaching, coming, brewing, looming, threatening.

impenetrable ▶ adjective **1** *impenetrable armour* =unbreakable, indestructible, solid, thick, unyielding. **2** *impenetrable forest* =impassable; dense, thick, overgrown. **3** *impenetrable statistics* =incomprehensible, unfathomable, unintelligible, baffling, bewildering, confusing, opaque.

imperative ▶ adjective =vital, crucial, critical, essential, urgent.
−OPPOSITES unimportant.

imperceptible ▶ adjective =unnoticeable, undetectable, indiscernible, invisible, inaudible, impalpable; slight, small, subtle, faint.
−OPPOSITES noticeable.

imperfect ▶ adjective =faulty, flawed, defective, shoddy, unsound, inferior, second-rate, substandard; damaged, blemished, torn, broken, cracked, scratched; Brit. informal duff.

imperfection ▶ noun 1 the glass is free from imperfections =defect, fault, flaw, deformity, discoloration; crack, scratch, chip, dent, blemish, stain, spot, mark. 2 he was aware of his imperfections =flaw, fault, failing, deficiency, weakness, weak point, shortcoming, inadequacy, limitation.
−OPPOSITES strength.

WORD LINKS
fear of imperfection: **atelophobia**

imperial ▶ adjective =royal, regal, monarchic, sovereign, kingly, queenly, princely.

imperil ▶ verb =endanger, jeopardize, risk; threaten.

imperious ▶ adjective =peremptory, high-handed, overbearing, domineering, authoritarian, dictatorial, authoritative, bossy, arrogant; informal pushy, high and mighty.

imperishable ▶ adjective =enduring, everlasting, undying, immortal, perennial, long-lasting; indestructible, inextinguishable, unfading.

impermanent ▶ adjective =temporary, transient, transitory, passing, fleeting, momentary, ephemeral; short-lived, brief, here today, gone tomorrow; literary evanescent.

impermeable ▶ adjective =watertight, waterproof, damp-proof, airtight, (hermetically) sealed.

impersonal ▶ adjective =aloof, distant, remote, detached, anonymous; unemotional, unsentimental, cold, cool, indifferent, unconcerned; formal, stiff, businesslike; informal starchy, standoffish.

−OPPOSITES warm.

impersonate ▶ verb =imitate, mimic, do an impression of, ape; parody, caricature, satirize, lampoon; masquerade as, pose as, pass oneself off as; informal take off, send up; N. Amer. informal make like.

impersonation ▶ noun =impression, imitation; parody, caricature, pastiche; informal take-off, send-up.

impertinence ▶ noun =rudeness, insolence, impoliteness, bad manners, disrespect; impudence, cheek; informal brass (neck); N. Amer. informal sass, sassiness, chutzpah.

impertinent ▶ adjective =rude, insolent, impolite, ill-mannered, bad-mannered, disrespectful; impudent, cheeky, presumptuous, forward; informal brass-necked, saucy; N. Amer. informal sassy.
−OPPOSITES polite.

impervious ▶ adjective 1 he seemed impervious to criticism =unaffected, untouched, immune, indifferent. 2 an impervious damp-proof course =impermeable, impenetrable, waterproof, watertight.
−OPPOSITES susceptible, permeable.

impetuous ▶ adjective =impulsive, rash, hasty, reckless, foolhardy, imprudent, injudicious, ill-considered; spontaneous, impromptu, spur-of-the-moment.
−OPPOSITES considered.

impetus ▶ noun 1 the flywheel lost its impetus =momentum, drive, thrust; energy, force, power, push. 2 the sales force were given fresh impetus =motivation, stimulus, incentive, inspiration.

impinge ▶ verb =affect, have an effect, touch, impact on.

impious ▶ adjective =godless, ungodly, irreligious, sinful, immoral, sacrilegious, profane, blasphemous, irreverent.

impish ▶ adjective =mischievous, roguish, wicked, rascally, naughty, playful, puckish.

implacable ▶ adjective =unforgiving; intransigent, inflexible, unyielding, unbending, uncompromising, unrelenting, ruthless, remorseless, merciless.

implant ▶ verb 1 the collagen is implanted under the skin =insert, embed, bury, lodge, place. **2** *he implanted the idea in my mind* =**instil**, inculcate, introduce, inject, plant, sow.

▸ noun *a silicone implant* =**transplant**, graft, implantation, insert.

implausible ▸ adjective =**unlikely**, improbable, questionable, doubtful, debatable; unconvincing, far-fetched.
−OPPOSITES convincing.

implement ▸ noun *garden implements* =**tool**, utensil, instrument, device, apparatus, gadget, contraption, appliance, contrivance; *informal* gizmo.

▸ verb *the cost of implementing the new law* =**execute**, apply, put into effect/action, put into practice, carry out/through, perform, enact; fulfil, discharge, bring about.

implicate ▸ verb **1** *he had been implicated in a financial scandal* =**incriminate**; involve, connect, embroil, enmesh. **2** *viruses are implicated in the development of cancer* =**involve in**, concern with, associate with, connect with.

implication ▸ noun **1** *he was smarting at their implication* =**suggestion**, inference, insinuation, innuendo, intimation, imputation. **2** *important political implications* =**consequence**, result, ramification, repercussion, reverberation, effect. **3** *his implication in the murder* =**incrimination**, involvement, connection, entanglement, association.

implicit ▸ adjective **1** *implicit assumptions* =**implied**, inferred, understood, hinted at, suggested; unspoken, unstated, tacit, taken for granted. **2** *assumptions implicit in the way questions are asked* =**inherent**, latent, underlying, inbuilt, incorporated. **3** *an implicit trust in human nature* =**absolute**, complete, total, wholehearted, utter; unqualified, unconditional; unshakeable, unquestioning, firm.
−OPPOSITES explicit.

implicitly ▸ adverb =**completely**, absolutely, totally, wholeheartedly, utterly, unconditionally, unreservedly, without reservation.

implied ▸ adjective. See IMPLICIT *sense* 1.

implore ▸ verb *his mother implored him to continue studying* =**plead with**, beg, entreat, appeal to, ask, request, call on; exhort, urge; *literary* beseech.

imply ▸ verb **1** *are you implying he is mad?* =**insinuate**, suggest, hint, intimate, give someone to understand, indicate,

make out. **2** *the forecast traffic increase implies more roads* =**involve**, entail; mean, point to, signify, indicate, signal.

impolite ▸ adjective =**rude**, bad-mannered, ill-mannered, discourteous, uncivil, disrespectful, inconsiderate, boorish, ungentlemanly, unladylike; insolent, impudent, impertinent, cheeky; *informal* ignorant, lippy.

impolitic ▸ adjective =**imprudent**, unwise, injudicious, incautious, irresponsible; ill-judged, ill-advised; undiplomatic, tactless.
−OPPOSITES prudent.

import ▸ verb *the UK imports iron ore* =**bring in**, buy in, ship in.
−OPPOSITES export.

▸ noun *a matter of great import* =**importance**, significance, consequence, momentousness, magnitude, substance, weight, note, gravity, seriousness. **2** *the full import of her words* =**meaning**, sense, essence, gist, drift, message, thrust, substance, implication.
−OPPOSITES insignificance.

importance ▸ noun **1** *an event of immense importance* =**significance**, momentousness, import, consequence, note; seriousness, gravity. **2** *she had an exaggerated sense of her own importance* =**power**, influence, authority; prominence, eminence, pre-eminence, notability, worth.
−OPPOSITES insignificance.

important ▸ adjective **1** *an important meeting* =**significant**, consequential, momentous, of great import, major; critical, crucial, vital, pivotal, decisive, urgent, historic. **2** *the important thing is that you do your best* =**main**, chief, principal, key, major, salient, prime, foremost, paramount, overriding, crucial, vital, critical, essential, significant; central, fundamental; *informal* number-one. **3** *the school was important to the community* =**valuable**, necessary, essential, indispensable, vital. **4** *he was an important man* =**powerful**, influential, well-connected, high-ranking; prominent, eminent, pre-eminent, notable; distinguished, esteemed, respected, prestigious, great; *informal* major league.
−OPPOSITES trivial, insignificant.

impose ▸ verb **1** *he imposed his ideas on everyone* =**foist**, force, inflict, press, urge. **2** *new taxes will be imposed* =**levy**, charge, apply, enforce, set, establish, institute, introduce, bring into effect. **3** *how dare you impose on me like this!* =**take advantage of,** exploit, take liberties with; bother, trouble, disturb, inconvenience, put out, put to trouble.

imposing ▸ adjective =**impressive,** striking, arresting, eye-catching, dramatic, spectacular, stunning, awesome, formidable, splendid, grand, majestic.
–OPPOSITES modest.

imposition ▸ noun **1** *the imposition of an alien culture* =**imposing,** foisting, forcing, inflicting. **2** *the imposition of VAT* =**levying,** charging, application, enforcement, enforcing; setting, establishment, introduction, institution. **3** *it would be no imposition* =**burden,** encumbrance, bother, worry; *informal* hassle.

impossible ▸ adjective **1** *the winds made fishing impossible* =**out of the question,** impracticable, non-viable, unworkable. **2** *an impossible dream* =**unattainable,** unachievable, unobtainable, hopeless, impracticable, unworkable. **3** *food shortages made life impossible* =**unbearable,** intolerable, unendurable. **4** *(informal)* *an impossible woman* =**unreasonable,** difficult, awkward; intolerable, unbearable; exasperating, maddening, infuriating.
–OPPOSITES attainable, bearable.

impostor ▸ noun =**impersonator,** deceiver, hoaxer, fraudster; fake, fraud; *informal* phoney.

impotent ▸ adjective =**powerless,** ineffective, ineffectual; useless, feeble; emasculated.
–OPPOSITES powerful, effective.

impound ▸ verb =**confiscate,** appropriate, take possession of, seize, commandeer, expropriate, requisition, take over, sequester, sequestrate; *Law* distrain.

impoverish ▸ verb **1** *the widow had been impoverished by debt* =**make poor,** make penniless, reduce to penury, bankrupt, ruin. **2** *the trees were impoverishing the soil* =**weaken,** exhaust, deplete.

impoverished ▸ adjective **1** *an impoverished peasant farmer* =**poor,** poverty-stricken, penniless, destitute, indigent, needy, on the breadline; bankrupt, ruined, insolvent; *informal* on one's uppers, on skid row; *formal* penurious. **2** *the soil is impoverished* =**weakened,** exhausted, drained, sapped, depleted, spent; barren, unproductive, infertile.

–OPPOSITES rich.

impracticable ▸ adjective =**unworkable,** unfeasible, non-viable, unachievable, unattainable, unrealizable; impractical.
–OPPOSITES workable, feasible.

impractical ▸ adjective **1** *an impractical suggestion* =**unrealistic,** unworkable, unfeasible, non-viable; ill-thought-out, absurd; idealistic, fanciful, romantic; *informal* cock-eyed, crackpot, crazy. **2** *impractical white ankle boots* =**unsuitable,** not sensible, inappropriate, unserviceable.
–OPPOSITES practical, sensible.

imprecise ▸ adjective **1** *a rather imprecise definition* =**vague,** loose, indistinct, inaccurate, non-specific, sweeping, broad, general; hazy, fuzzy, woolly, nebulous, ambiguous, equivocal, uncertain. **2** *an imprecise estimate* =**inexact,** approximate, rough; *N. Amer. informal* ballpark.
–OPPOSITES exact.

impregnable ▸ adjective **1** *an impregnable castle* =**invulnerable,** impenetrable, unassailable, inviolable, secure, strong, well fortified, well defended; invincible, unconquerable. **2** *an impregnable parliamentary majority* =**unassailable,** unbeatable, undefeatable, unshakeable, invincible, invulnerable.
–OPPOSITES vulnerable.

impregnate ▸ verb =**infuse,** soak, steep, saturate, drench; marinate.

impresario ▸ noun =**organizer,** (stage) manager, producer; promoter, publicist, showman; director, conductor, maestro.

impress ▸ verb **1** *Hazel had impressed him mightily* =**make an impression on,** have an impact on, influence, affect, move, stir, rouse, excite, inspire; dazzle, awe; *informal* grab. **2** *goldsmiths impressed his likeness on the medallions* =**imprint,** print, stamp, mark, emboss, punch. **3** *impress upon her the need to save* =**emphasize to,** stress to, bring home to, instil in, inculcate into, drum into, knock into.
–OPPOSITES disappoint.

impression ▸ noun **1** *he got the impression she was hiding something* =**feeling,** sense, fancy, (sneaking) suspicion, inkling, intuition, hunch; notion, idea, funny feeling; *informal* gut feeling. **2** *a favourable impression* =**opinion,** view, image, picture, perception, judgement, verdict, estimation. **3** *school made a profound impression on me* =**impact**, effect, influence. **4** *the lid had left a circular impression* =**indentation**, dent, mark, outline, imprint. **5** *he did a good impression of their science teacher* =**impersonation**, imitation; parody, caricature; *informal* take-off, send-up, spoof. **6** *an artist's impression of the gardens* =**representation**, portrayal, depiction, rendition, interpretation, picture. **7** *a revised impression of the 1981 edition* =**print run**, imprint, reprint, issue, edition.

impressionable ▶ adjective =**easily influenced**, suggestible, susceptible, persuadable, pliable, malleable, pliant, ingenuous, trusting, naive, gullible.

impressive ▶ adjective **1** *an impressive building* =**magnificent**, majestic, imposing, splendid, spectacular, grand, awe-inspiring, stunning, breathtaking. **2** *they played some impressive football* =**admirable**, masterly, accomplished, expert, skilled, skilful, consummate; excellent, outstanding, first-class, first-rate, fine; *informal* great, mean, nifty, cracking, ace, wizard; *N. Amer. informal* crackerjack.
–OPPOSITES ordinary, mediocre.

imprint ▶ verb **1** *patterns can be imprinted in the clay* =**stamp**, print, impress, mark. **2** *the image was imprinted on his mind* =**fix**, establish, stick, lodge, implant, embed.
▶ noun **1** *her feet left imprints on the floor* =**impression**, print, mark, indentation. **2** *colonialism has left its imprint* =**impact**, effect, influence, impression.

imprison ▶ verb =**incarcerate**, send to prison, jail, lock up, put away, intern, detain, hold prisoner, hold captive; *informal* send down, put behind bars, put inside; *Brit. informal* bang up.
–OPPOSITES free, release.

imprisoned ▶ adjective =**incarcerated**, in prison, in jail, jailed, locked up, interned, detained, held prisoner, held captive; *informal* sent down, behind bars, doing time, inside; *Brit. informal* doing porridge, banged up.

imprisonment ▶ noun =**incarceration**, internment, confinement, detention, captivity; *informal* time; *Brit. informal* porridge.

improbability ▶ noun =**unlikelihood**, implausibility; doubtfulness, uncertainty, dubiousness.

improbable ▶ adjective **1** *it seemed improbable that the hot weather would continue* =**unlikely**, doubtful, dubious, debatable, questionable, uncertain. **2** *an improbable exaggeration* =**unconvincing**, unbelievable, implausible, unlikely.
–OPPOSITES certain, believable.

impromptu ▶ adjective *an impromptu lecture* =**unrehearsed**, unprepared, unscripted, extempore, extemporized, improvised, spontaneous, unplanned; *informal* off-the-cuff.
–OPPOSITES prepared, rehearsed.

improper ▶ adjective **1** *it is improper for policemen to accept gifts* =**inappropriate**, unacceptable, unsuitable, unprofessional, irregular; unethical, dishonest, dishonourable; *informal* not cricket. **2** *it was improper for young ladies to drive a young man home* =**unseemly**, unfitting, unladylike, ungentlemanly, inappropriate, indelicate, impolite; indecent, immodest, indecorous, immoral. **3** *an extremely improper poem* =**indecent**, risqué, off colour, suggestive, naughty, ribald, earthy, smutty, dirty, filthy, vulgar, crude, rude, obscene, lewd; *informal* blue, raunchy, steamy; *Brit. informal* fruity, saucy.
–OPPOSITES acceptable, decent.

impropriety ▶ noun **1** *a suggestion of impropriety* =**wrongdoing**, misconduct, dishonesty, corruption, unscrupulousness, unprofessionalism, irregularity; unseemliness, indelicacy, indecency, immorality. **2** *fiscal improprieties* =**transgression**, misdemeanour, offence, misdeed, crime; indiscretion, mistake, peccadillo.

improve ▶ verb **1** *ways to improve the service* =**make better**, ameliorate, upgrade, refine, enhance, boost, build on, raise; *informal* tweak, fine tune. **2** *communications improved during the 18th century* =**get better**, advance, progress, develop; make headway, make progress, pick up, look up, move forward. **3** *the patient is improving* =**recover**, get better, recuperate, gain strength, rally, revive, get back on one's feet, get over something; be on the mend. **4** *they need to improve their offer* =**increase**, make larger, raise, augment, supplement, top up; reconsider; *informal* up, bump up.
–OPPOSITES worsen, deteriorate.
■ **improve on** =**surpass**, better, do better than, outdo, exceed, beat, top, cap.

improvement ▶ noun =advance, development, upgrade, refinement, enhancement, amelioration; boost, augmentation; rally, recovery, upswing; step forward.

improvise ▶ verb **1** *she was improvising in front of the cameras* =**extemporize**, ad-lib; *informal* speak off the cuff, speak off the top of one's head, wing it. **2** *she improvised a sandpit* =**contrive**, devise, throw together, cobble together, rig up; *informal* whip up, rustle up; *Brit. informal* knock up.

improvised ▶ adjective **1** *an improvised speech* =**impromptu**, unrehearsed, unprepared, unscripted, extempore, spontaneous, unplanned; *informal* off-the-cuff. **2** *an improvised shelter* =**makeshift**, cobbled-together, rough and ready, make-do.
–OPPOSITES prepared, rehearsed.

imprudent ▶ adjective =**unwise**, injudicious, incautious, misguided, ill-advised, improvident, irresponsible, short-sighted, foolish.
–OPPOSITES sensible.

impudence ▶ noun =**impertinence**, insolence, effrontery, cheek, cockiness, brazenness; presumption, disrespect, flippancy; rudeness, impoliteness, ill manners, discourteousness, gall; *informal* brass neck, chutzpah, nerve; *N. Amer. informal* sassiness.

impudent ▶ adjective =**impertinent**, insolent, cheeky, cocky, brazen; presumptuous, forward, disrespectful, insubordinate; rude, impolite, ill-mannered, discourteous; *informal* brass-necked, saucy, lippy; *N. Amer. informal* sassy.
–OPPOSITES polite.

impulse ▶ noun **1** *she had an impulse to run and hide* =**urge**, instinct, drive, compulsion, itch; whim, desire, fancy, notion. **2** *a man of impulse* =**spontaneity**, impetuosity, recklessness, rashness. **3** *passions provide the main impulse of poetry* =**inspiration**, stimulation, stimulus, incitement, motivation, encouragement, spur, catalyst. **4** *impulses from the spinal cord to the muscles* =**pulse**, current, wave, signal.
■ **on (an) impulse** =**impulsively**, spontaneously, on the spur of the moment, without thinking.

impulsive ▶ adjective **1** *he had an impulsive nature* =**impetuous**, spontan-

eous, hasty, passionate, emotional. **2** *an impulsive decision* =**impromptu**, snap, spontaneous, unpremeditated, spur-of-the-moment, extemporaneous.
–OPPOSITES cautious, premeditated.

impunity ▶ noun *the impunity enjoyed by military officers* =**immunity**, indemnity, exemption (from punishment), licence; privilege, liberty.
–OPPOSITES liability.
■ **with impunity** =**without punishment**, scot-free, unpunished.

impure ▶ adjective **1** *impure gold* =**unrefined**, crude, raw; adulterated, blended, diluted, alloyed. **2** *the water was impure* =**contaminated**, polluted, tainted, unwholesome, poisoned; dirty; unhygienic, unsanitary. **3** *impure thoughts* =**immoral**, sinful, wrongful, wicked; unchaste, lustful, lecherous, lewd, lascivious, obscene, indecent, ribald, risqué, improper, crude, coarse.
–OPPOSITES clean, chaste.

impurity ▶ noun **1** *the impurity of the air* =**contamination**, pollution; dirtiness, filthiness, foulness, unwholesomeness. **2** *the impurities in beer* =**contaminant**, pollutant, foreign body; dross, dirt, filth. **3** *sin and impurity* =**immorality**, sin, sinfulness, wickedness; lustfulness, lechery, lewdness, lasciviousness, obscenity, crudeness, indecency, impropriety, vulgarity, coarseness.

impute ▶ verb =**attribute**, ascribe, assign, credit; connect with, associate with.

in ▶ preposition **1** *she was hiding in a wardrobe* =**inside**, within, in the middle of; surrounded by, enclosed by, among. **2** *he was covered in mud* =**with**, by. **3** *he put a fruit gum in his mouth* =**into**, inside. **4** *they met in 1921* =**during**, in the course of, over. **5** *I'll see you in half an hour* =**after**, at the end of, following; within, in less than, in under. **6** *a tax of ten pence in the pound* =**to**, per, every, each.
–OPPOSITES outside.
▶ adverb *his mum walked in* =**inside**, indoors, into the room.
–OPPOSITES out.
▶ adjective **1** *there was no one in* =**present**, (at) home; inside, indoors, in the house/room. **2** *(informal) beards are in* =**fashionable**, in fashion, in vogue, popular, chic, à la mode, de rigueur; *informal* trendy, all the rage, cool, the in thing, hip. **3** *(informal) I was in with all the right people* =**in favour**, popular, friendly, friends; ac-

cepted; *informal* in someone's good books.
–OPPOSITES out, unfashionable, unpopular.

■ **in for** =due for, in line for; expecting, about to receive.

■ **in for it** =in trouble, about to be punished; *informal* for the high jump, in hot/deep water, in shtook; *Brit. informal* for it.

■ **in on** =privy to, aware of, acquainted with, informed about/of, apprised of; *informal* wise to, in the know about, hip to.

■ **ins and outs** *(informal)* =details, particulars, facts, features, characteristics, nuts and bolts; *informal* nitty gritty.

inability ▸ noun =lack of ability, incapability, incapacity, powerlessness, impotence, helplessness.

inaccessible ▸ adjective **1** *an inaccessible woodland site* =unreachable; cut-off, isolated, remote, in the back of beyond, out of the way. **2** *the book was elitist and inaccessible* =esoteric, obscure, abstruse, recondite, arcane; elitist, exclusive, difficult.

inaccuracy ▸ noun **1** *the inaccuracy of recent opinion polls* =incorrectness, inexactness, imprecision, erroneousness, fallaciousness, faultiness. **2** *the article contained a number of inaccuracies* =error, mistake, fault; erratum; *Brit. literal*; *informal* howler, boo-boo, typo; *N. Amer. informal* blooper, goof.
–OPPOSITES correctness.

inaccurate ▸ adjective =inexact, imprecise, incorrect, wrong, erroneous, faulty, imperfect, flawed, defective, unsound, unreliable; false, mistaken, untrue; *informal* off beam; *Brit. informal* adrift.

inaction ▸ noun =inactivity, nonintervention; apathy, inertia, indolence.

inactive ▸ adjective **1** *over the next few days I remained inactive* =idle, indolent, lazy, slothful, lethargic, inert, sluggish, unenergetic, listless, torpid. **2** *the device remains inactive until the computer starts up* =inoperative, idle; not working, out of service, unused, not in use.

inactivity ▸ noun **1** *years of inactivity* =idleness, indolence, laziness, slothfulness, lethargy, inertia, sluggishness, listlessness. **2** *government inactivity* =inaction, non-intervention; neglect, negligence, apathy, inertia.
–OPPOSITES action.

inadequacy ▸ noun **1** *the inadequacy*
of available resources =insufficiency, deficiency, scarcity, scarceness, sparseness, dearth, paucity, shortage, want, lack; paltriness, meagreness. **2** *her feelings of personal inadequacy* =incompetence, incapability, unfitness, ineffectiveness, inefficiency, inefficacy, ineptness, uselessness, impotence, powerlessness. **3** *the inadequacies of the present system* =shortcoming, defect, fault, failing, weakness, limitation, flaw, imperfection.
–OPPOSITES abundance, competence.

inadequate ▸ adjective **1** *inadequate water supplies* =insufficient, deficient, poor, scant, scarce, sparse, in short supply; paltry, meagre, limited. **2** *he's a bit inadequate* =incapable; immature, juvenile; *informal* sad.
–OPPOSITES sufficient.

inadmissible ▸ adjective =unallowable, invalid, unacceptable, impermissible, disallowed, forbidden, prohibited, precluded.

inadvertent ▸ adjective =unintentional, unintended, accidental, unplanned.
–OPPOSITES deliberate.

inadvertently ▸ adverb =accidentally, by accident, unintentionally, unwittingly.

inadvisable ▸ adjective =unwise, illadvised, imprudent, ill-judged, illconsidered, injudicious, impolitic.
–OPPOSITES shrewd.

inalienable ▸ adjective =inviolable, absolute, sacrosanct; non-negotiable.

inane ▸ adjective =silly, foolish, stupid, fatuous, idiotic, asinine, frivolous, vapid; *informal* dumb, moronic; *Brit. informal* daft.
–OPPOSITES sensible.

inanimate ▸ adjective =lifeless, inert, insentient.
–OPPOSITES living.

inapplicable ▸ adjective =irrelevant, immaterial, not germane, unrelated, extraneous, beside the point.
–OPPOSITES relevant.

inapposite ▸ adjective =inappropriate, unsuitable, inapt, out of place, infelicitous, misplaced, ill-judged, illadvised.
–OPPOSITES appropriate.

inappreciable ▸ adjective =imperceptible, minute, tiny, slight, small; in-

significant, inconsequential, unimportant, negligible; *informal* piddling, piffling.
−OPPOSITES considerable.

inappropriate ▸ adjective =unsuitable, unfitting, unseemly, unbecoming, improper; out of place/keeping, inapposite, inapt; *informal* out of order.
−OPPOSITES suitable.

inapt ▸ adjective. *See* INAPPROPRIATE.

inattention ▸ noun =distraction, inattentiveness, preoccupation, absent-mindedness, daydreaming, abstraction.
−OPPOSITES concentration.

inattentive ▸ adjective 1 *an inattentive pupil* =distracted, preoccupied, absent-minded, daydreaming, dreamy, abstracted; *informal* miles away. 2 *inattentive service* =negligent, neglectful, slack, sloppy, slapdash, lax.
−OPPOSITES alert.

inaudible ▸ adjective =unclear, indistinct; faint, muted, soft, low, muffled, whispered, muttered, murmured, mumbled.

inaugural ▸ adjective =first, opening, initial, introductory.
−OPPOSITES final.

inaugurate ▸ verb 1 *he inaugurated a new policy* =initiate, begin, start, institute, launch, get going, get under way, establish, lay the foundations of; bring in, usher in; *informal* kick off. 2 *the new President will be inaugurated* =admit to office, install, instate, swear in; invest, ordain, crown.

inauspicious ▸ adjective =unpromising, unpropitious, unfavourable, unfortunate, infelicitous, ominous.
−OPPOSITES promising.

inborn ▸ adjective =innate, congenital; inherent, natural, inbred, inherited, hereditary, in one's genes.

inbred ▸ adjective. *See* INBORN.

inbuilt ▸ adjective 1 *an inbuilt CD-ROM drive* =built-in, integral, incorporated, inboard, on-board, hardwired. 2 *our inbuilt survival instinct* =inherent, intrinsic, innate, congenital, natural.

incalculable ▸ adjective =inestimable, indeterminable, untold, immeasurable, incomputable; enormous, immense, huge, vast, innumerable.

incandescent ▸ adjective 1 *incandescent fragments of lava* =white-hot, red-hot, burning, fiery, blazing; glowing, aglow, radiant, bright, brilliant. 2 *the minister was incandescent* =furious, incensed, seething, infuriated, enraged, raging, fuming, irate, beside oneself; *informal* livid, foaming at the mouth, (hopping) mad, wild, apoplectic.

incantation ▸ noun 1 *he muttered some weird incantations* =chant, invocation, spell, formula; *NZ* makutu; *informal* mumbo-jumbo, hocus-pocus. 2 *ritual incantation* =chanting, intonation, recitation.

incapable ▸ adjective 1 *an incapable government* =incompetent, inept, inadequate, ineffective, ineffectual, unfit, unqualified, unequal to the task; *informal* not up to it, not up to snuff, a dead loss. 2 *he was mentally incapable* =incapacitated, helpless, powerless, incompetent.
−OPPOSITES competent.

incapacitated ▸ adjective =disabled, debilitated, indisposed, unfit; immobilized, out of action, out of commission; *informal* laid up.
−OPPOSITES fit.

incapacity ▸ noun =disability, incapability, debility, impairment, indisposition; incompetence, inadequacy, ineffectiveness.
−OPPOSITES capability.

incarcerate ▸ verb =imprison, put in prison, send to prison, jail, lock up, put under lock and key, put away, intern, confine, detain, hold, put in chains, clap in irons, hold prisoner, hold captive; *Brit.* detain at Her Majesty's pleasure; *informal* send down, put behind bars, put inside; *Brit. informal* bang up.
−OPPOSITES release.

incarceration ▸ noun =imprisonment, internment, confinement, detention, custody, captivity, restraint; *informal* time; *Brit. informal* porridge.

incarnate ▸ adjective =made flesh, personified, in bodily form; corporeal, embodied, made manifest.

incarnation ▸ noun 1 *the incarnation of artistic genius* =embodiment, personification, exemplification, epitome; manifestation; archetype, exemplar. 2 *a previous incarnation* =lifetime, life, existence.

incautious ▸ adjective =rash, unwise, careless, thoughtless, reckless, unthinking, imprudent, ill-advised, ill-judged, injudicious.
−OPPOSITES circumspect.

incendiary ▶ adjective **1** *an incendiary device* =**combustible**, flammable, inflammable. **2** *an incendiary speech* =**inflammatory**, rabble-rousing, provocative; contentious, controversial.

incense ▶ verb *his taunts incensed me* =**enrage**, infuriate, anger, madden, outrage, exasperate, antagonize, provoke; *informal* make someone see red, make someone's blood boil, make someone's hackles rise, drive mad/crazy; *N. Amer. informal* burn up.
−OPPOSITES placate, please.

incensed ▶ adjective =**enraged**, furious, infuriated, irate, raging, incandescent, fuming, seething, beside oneself, outraged; *informal* mad, hopping mad, wild, livid, apoplectic, foaming at the mouth.

incentive ▶ noun =**inducement**, motivation, motive, reason, stimulus, spur, impetus, encouragement, impulse, carrot; incitement; *informal* sweetener.
−OPPOSITES deterrent.

inception ▶ noun =**establishment**, institution, foundation, founding, formation, initiation, setting up, start-up, origination, constitution, inauguration, opening, day one; beginning, commencement, start, birth; *informal* kick-off.
−OPPOSITES end.

incessant ▶ adjective =**ceaseless**, unceasing, constant, continual, unabating, interminable, endless, unending, never-ending, perpetual, continuous, nonstop, uninterrupted, unbroken, unremitting, unrelenting, sustained.
−OPPOSITES intermittent.

incessantly ▶ adverb =**constantly**, continually, all the time, non-stop, without stopping, without a break, round the clock, {morning, noon, and night}, interminably, unremittingly, ceaselessly, endlessly; *informal* 24-7.
−OPPOSITES occasionally.

incidence ▶ noun =**occurrence**, prevalence; rate, frequency; amount, degree, extent.

incident ▶ noun **1** *incidents in his youth* =**event**, occurrence, episode, experience, happening, occasion, affair, business; adventure, exploit, escapade; matter, development. **2** *police are investigating another incident* =**disturbance**, clash, confrontation, accident, shooting, explosion; situation; *Law, dated* affray. **3** *the journey was not without incident* =**excitement**, adventure, drama; danger, peril.

incidental ▶ adjective **1** *incidental details* =**secondary**, subsidiary, minor, peripheral, background, by-the-by, unimportant, insignificant, inconsequential, tangential, extraneous. **2** *an incidental discovery* =**chance**, accidental, random; fluky, fortuitous, serendipitous, coincidental, unlooked-for.
−OPPOSITES essential, deliberate.

incidentally ▶ adverb **1** *incidentally, I haven't had a reply yet* =**by the way**, by the by(e), in passing, en passant, speaking of which; *informal* btw, as it happens. **2** *the infection was discovered incidentally* =**by chance**, by accident, accidentally, fortuitously, by a fluke, by happenstance.

incinerate ▶ verb =**burn**, reduce to ashes, carbonize; cremate.

incipient ▶ adjective =**developing**, growing, emerging, emergent, dawning, initial; nascent, embryonic, fledgling, in its infancy.
−OPPOSITES full-blown.

incision ▶ noun **1** *a surgical incision* =**cut**, opening, slit. **2** *incisions on the marble* =**notch**, nick, scratch, carving; scarification.

incisive ▶ adjective =**penetrating**, acute, sharp, razor-sharp, keen, astute, trenchant, shrewd, piercing, perceptive, insightful, perspicacious; concise, succinct, pithy, to the point, crisp, clear; *informal* punchy.
−OPPOSITES rambling, vague.

incite ▶ verb **1** *he was arrested for inciting racial hatred* =**stir up**, whip up, encourage, stoke up, fuel, kindle, ignite, inflame, stimulate, instigate, provoke, excite, arouse, awaken, inspire, trigger, spark off. **2** *she incited him to commit murder* =**egg on**, encourage, urge, goad, provoke, spur on, drive, push, prod, prompt, induce, impel; *informal* put up to.
−OPPOSITES discourage, deter.

incivility ▶ noun =**rudeness**, discourtesy, impoliteness, bad manners, disrespect, boorishness, ungraciousness.
−OPPOSITES politeness.

inclement ▶ adjective =**cold**, chilly, bleak, wintry, freezing, snowy, icy; wet, rainy, drizzly, damp; stormy, blustery, wild, rough, squally, windy; unpleasant, bad, foul, nasty, filthy, severe, extreme, harsh.

–OPPOSITES fine.

inclination ▶ noun **1** *his political inclinations* =**tendency**, propensity, proclivity, leaning, predisposition, predilection, impulse, bent; penchant, preference, appetite, affinity; taste. **2** *an inclination of his head* =**nod**, bow, bending, lowering, movement.
–OPPOSITES aversion.

incline ▶ verb **1** *his prejudice inclines him to overlook obvious facts* =**predispose**, lead, make, dispose, prejudice; prompt, induce. **2** *I incline to the opposite view* =**prefer**, favour, go for; tend, lean, swing, veer, gravitate, be drawn. **3** *he inclined his head* =**bend**, nod, bob, lower, dip. **4** *the columns incline away from the vertical* =**lean**, tilt, angle, tip, slope, slant, bend, curve; list.
▶ noun *a steep incline* =**slope**, gradient, pitch, ramp, bank, ascent, rise, dip, descent; hill; *N. Amer.* grade, downgrade, upgrade.

inclined ▶ adjective **1** *I'm inclined to believe her* =**disposed**, minded, of a mind. **2** *she's inclined to gossip* =**prone**, given, in the habit of, liable, apt; *literary* wont.

include ▶ verb **1** *activities include drama and music* =**incorporate**, comprise, encompass, cover, embrace, take in, number, contain. **2** *don't forget to include the cost of repairs* =**allow for**, count, take into account, take into consideration.
–OPPOSITES exclude.

including ▶ preposition =**inclusive of**, counting; as well as, plus, together with.

inclusive ▶ adjective **1** *an inclusive price | an inclusive definition* =**all-in**, comprehensive, overall, full, all-round, umbrella, catch-all, all-encompassing. **2** *prices are inclusive of VAT* =**including**, incorporating, taking in, counting, covering.

incoherent ▶ adjective **1** *a long, incoherent speech* =**unclear**, confused, muddled, incomprehensible, hard to follow, disjointed, disconnected, disordered, garbled, jumbled, scrambled; rambling, wandering, discursive, disorganized, illogical; inarticulate; mumbling, slurred. **2** *she was incoherent and shivering violently* =**delirious**, raving, babbling, hysterical, irrational.
–OPPOSITES lucid.

income ▶ noun =**earnings**, salary, pay, remuneration, wages, stipend; revenue, receipts, takings, profits, proceeds, turnover, yield, dividend; *N. Amer.* take;

formal emolument.
–OPPOSITES expenditure, outgoings.

incoming ▶ adjective *the incoming president* =**new**, next, future; ... elect, ...-to-be, ... designate.
–OPPOSITES outgoing.

incomparable ▶ adjective =**without equal**, beyond compare, unparalleled, matchless, peerless, unmatched, without parallel, beyond comparison, second to none, in a class of its own, unequalled, unrivalled, inimitable.

incomparably ▶ adverb =**far and away**, by far, infinitely, immeasurably, easily.

incompatible ▶ adjective **1** *she and McBride are totally incompatible* =**unsuited**, mismatched, ill-matched, poles apart, worlds apart, like day and night; *Brit.* like chalk and cheese. **2** *incompatible economic objectives* =**irreconcilable**, conflicting, opposed, opposite, contradictory, antagonistic, antipathetic; clashing, inharmonious, discordant; mutually exclusive. **3** *a theory incompatible with that of his predecessor* =**inconsistent with**, at odds with, out of keeping with, at variance with, contrary to, in conflict with, in opposition to, (diametrically) opposed to, counter to, irreconcilable with.
–OPPOSITES well matched, harmonious, consistent.

incompetent ▶ adjective =**inept**, unskilled, inexpert, amateurish, unprofessional, bungling, blundering, clumsy, inadequate, ineffective, inefficient, ineffectual; *informal* useless, pathetic, cack-handed, ham-fisted, not up to it.

incomplete ▶ adjective **1** *the manuscript is still incomplete* =**unfinished**, uncompleted, partial, half-finished. **2** *inaccurate or incomplete information* =**deficient**, insufficient, partial, sketchy, fragmentary, scrappy, bitty; expurgated, bowdlerized, censored.

incomprehensible ▶ adjective =**unintelligible**, impossible to understand, impenetrable, unclear, indecipherable; baffling, bewildering; abstruse, esoteric, recondite, arcane; *Brit. informal* double Dutch.
–OPPOSITES intelligible, clear.

inconceivable ▶ adjective =**unbelievable**, beyond belief, incredible, unthinkable, unimaginable, out of the question; *informal* hard to swallow.

—OPPOSITES likely.

inconclusive ▶ adjective =indecisive; indefinite, indeterminate, unresolved, unproved, unsettled, still open to question/doubt; *informal* up in the air, left hanging.

incongruous ▶ adjective **1** *the women looked somewhat incongruous in their fur coats* =out of place; wrong, strange, odd, absurd, bizarre. **2** *an incongruous collection of objects* =ill-matched, ill-assorted, mismatched, disparate.
—OPPOSITES appropriate, harmonious.

inconsequential ▶ adjective =insignificant, unimportant, of little/no consequence, neither here nor there, incidental, immaterial, irrelevant; negligible, slight, minor, trivial, trifling, petty; *informal* piddling, piffling.
—OPPOSITES important.

inconsiderate ▶ adjective =thoughtless, unthinking, insensitive, selfish, self-centred, impolite, discourteous, rude; tactless, undiplomatic; *informal* ignorant.
—OPPOSITES thoughtful.

inconsistent ▶ adjective **1** *his inconsistent behaviour* =erratic, changeable, unpredictable, variable, unstable, unsettled, uneven; capricious, fickle, unreliable, mercurial, volatile; *informal* up and down; *technical* labile. **2** *he had done nothing inconsistent with his morality* =incompatible with, conflicting with, at odds with, at variance with, contrary to, irreconcilable with, out of keeping with; antithetical to.

inconsolable ▶ adjective =heartbroken, broken-hearted, grief stricken, beside oneself, devastated, distraught; *informal* gutted.

inconspicuous ▶ adjective =unobtrusive, unnoticeable, unremarkable, unexceptional, modest, unassuming, discreet, low-profile.
—OPPOSITES noticeable.

incontestable ▶ adjective =incontrovertible, indisputable, undeniable, irrefutable, unassailable, beyond dispute, unquestionable, beyond question, indubitable, beyond doubt.
—OPPOSITES questionable.

incontinent ▶ adjective =unrestrained, uncontrolled, unbridled, unchecked.

incontrovertible ▶ adjective =indisputable, incontestable, undeniable, irrefutable, unassailable, beyond dispute, unquestionable, beyond question, indubitable, beyond doubt, unarguable; conclusive, categorical.
—OPPOSITES questionable.

inconvenience ▶ noun **1** *we apologize for any inconvenience caused* =trouble, bother, problems, disruption, difficulty, disturbance; *informal* aggravation, hassle. **2** *his early arrival was clearly an inconvenience* =nuisance, trouble, bother, problem; *informal* headache, pain, pain in the neck, pain in the backside, drag, hassle; *N. Amer. informal* pain in the butt.
▶ verb *I don't want to inconvenience you* =trouble, bother, put out, put to any trouble, disturb, impose on.

inconvenient ▶ adjective =awkward, difficult, inopportune, untimely, ill-timed, unsuitable, inappropriate, unfortunate.

incorporate ▶ verb **1** *the region was incorporated into Moldavian territory* =absorb, include, subsume, assimilate, integrate, take in, swallow up. **2** *the model incorporates some advanced features* =include, contain, embrace, build in; offer, boast. **3** *a small amount of salt is incorporated with the butter* =blend, mix, combine; fold in, stir in.

incorporeal ▶ adjective =intangible, impalpable; disembodied; spiritual, ethereal; insubstantial, transcendental; ghostly, spectral, supernatural.
—OPPOSITES tangible.

incorrect ▶ adjective **1** *an incorrect answer* =wrong, erroneous, in error, mistaken; untrue, false; *informal* off beam, out, way out. **2** *incorrect behaviour* =inappropriate, wrong, unsuitable, inapt, inapposite; ill-advised, ill-considered, ill-judged, unacceptable, improper, unseemly; *informal* out of order.

incorrigible ▶ adjective =inveterate, habitual, confirmed, hardened, incurable, irredeemable, hopeless; unrepentant, unapologetic, unashamed.

incorruptible ▶ adjective =honest, honourable, trustworthy, principled, good, upright, virtuous.
—OPPOSITES venal.

increase ▶ verb **1** *demand is likely to increase* =grow, get bigger, get larger, enlarge, expand, swell; rise, climb; intensify, strengthen, extend, spread, widen; mount, accumulate; *literary* wax. **2** *higher expectations will increase user de-*

mand =**add to**, make larger, make bigger, augment, supplement, top up, build up, extend, raise, swell, inflate; magnify, intensify, strengthen, heighten; *informal* up, jack up, bump up, crank up.
–OPPOSITES decrease, reduce.
▶ noun *the increase in size | an increase in demand* =**growth**, rise, enlargement, expansion, extension, elevation; increment, addition, augmentation; magnification, intensification, amplification, escalation, surge; *informal* hike.

incredible ▶ adjective **1** *I find his story incredible* =**unbelievable**, hard to believe, unconvincing, far-fetched, implausible, improbable, highly unlikely, dubious, doubtful; inconceivable, unthinkable, unimaginable. **2** *an incredible feat of engineering* =**magnificent**, wonderful, marvellous, spectacular, remarkable, phenomenal, prodigious, breathtaking, extraordinary, unbelievable, amazing, stunning, astounding, astonishing, awe-inspiring, staggering, formidable, awesome, superhuman; *informal* fantastic, terrific, tremendous, stupendous, mind-boggling, mind-blowing, out of this world; *literary* wondrous.

incredulity ▶ noun =**disbelief**, scepticism, mistrust, suspicion, doubt; cynicism.

incredulous ▶ adjective =**disbelieving**, sceptical, distrustful, suspicious, doubtful, dubious, unconvinced; cynical.

increment ▶ noun =**increase**, addition, supplement, gain, augmentation.
–OPPOSITES reduction.

incriminate ▶ verb =**implicate**, involve, enmesh; point the finger at.

inculcate ▶ verb =**instil**, implant, fix, impress, imprint; hammer into, drum into, drill into.

incumbent ▶ adjective **1** *it is incumbent on the government to give a clear lead* =**necessary**, essential, imperative. **2** *the incumbent president* =**current**, present, in office; reigning.
▶ noun *the first incumbent of the post* =**holder**, bearer, occupant.

incur ▶ verb =**bring upon oneself**, expose oneself to, lay oneself open to; run up; sustain, experience.

incurable ▶ adjective **1** *an incurable illness* =**untreatable**, inoperable, irremediable; terminal, fatal; chronic. **2** *an incurable romantic* =**inveterate**, dyed-in-the-wool, confirmed, established, absolute, complete, utter, thoroughgoing, out-and-out; incorrigible, hopeless.

incursion ▶ noun =**attack**, assault, raid, invasion, foray, blitz, sortie, sally, advance, push, thrust.
–OPPOSITES retreat.

indebted ▶ adjective =**beholden**, obliged, grateful, in someone's debt.

indecent ▶ adjective **1** *indecent photographs* =**obscene**, dirty, filthy, rude, naughty, vulgar, crude, lewd, smutty, off colour, pornographic, offensive; ribald, risqué, racy; *informal* blue, porn, X-rated, raunchy, skin; *Brit. informal* saucy; *euphemistic* adult. **2** *indecent clothes* =**revealing**, skimpy, scanty, low-cut; erotic, arousing, sexy, provocative, titillating. **3** *indecent haste* =**unseemly**, improper, unbecoming, inappropriate.

indecipherable ▶ adjective =**illegible**, unreadable, unintelligible, unclear.

indecision ▶ noun =**indecisiveness**, hesitation, tentativeness; ambivalence, doubt, uncertainty; vacillation, equivocation; shilly-shallying, dithering; *Brit.* humming and hawing; *Scottish* swithering; *informal* dilly-dallying, sitting on the fence.

indecisive ▶ adjective **1** *an indecisive result* =**inconclusive**, proving nothing, open, indeterminate, unclear, ambiguous. **2** *an indecisive leader* =**irresolute**, hesitant, tentative, weak; vacillating, dithering, wavering; blowing hot and cold, unsure, uncertain; undecided.

indeed ▶ adverb **1** *there was, indeed, quite a furore* =**as expected**, to be sure; in truth. **2** *'May I join you?' 'Indeed you may.'* =**yes**, certainly, of course, by all means; *informal* you bet.

indefatigable ▶ adjective =**tireless**, untiring, unwearying, unflagging, dogged, unshakeable, indomitable.

indefensible ▶ adjective **1** *indefensible cruelty* =**inexcusable**, unjustifiable, unpardonable, unforgivable. **2** *an indefensible point of view* =**untenable**, unsustainable, insupportable, unjustifiable, unacceptable.

indefinable ▶ adjective =**hard to define**, hard to describe, indescribable; vague, elusive.

indefinite ▶ adjective **1** *an indefinite period* =**indeterminate**, unspecified, undefined, unlimited; limitless, infinite, endless. **2** *an indefinite meaning* =**vague**, ill-defined, unclear, loose, imprecise, nebulous, blurred, fuzzy.
–OPPOSITES fixed, clear.

indelible ▶ adjective =**ineradicable**, permanent, lasting, enduring, unfading, unforgettable.

indelicate ▶ adjective =**insensitive**, tactless, undiplomatic, impolitic, indiscreet, improper, indecent, rude.

indemnity ▶ noun **1** *no indemnity will be given for loss of cash* =**insurance**, assurance, protection, security, indemnification, surety. **2** *the company was paid $100,000 in indemnity* =**compensation**, reimbursement, recompense, repayment, restitution, redress, reparation(s), damages.

indent ▶ verb =**notch**, make an indentation in, scallop, groove, furrow.

indentation ▶ noun =**hollow**, depression, dip, dent, cavity, concavity, pit; dimple; recess, bay, inlet, cove.

independence ▶ noun **1** *the struggle for American independence* =**self-government**, self-rule, home rule, self-determination, sovereignty, autonomy. **2** *the adviser's independence* =**impartiality**, neutrality, disinterestedness, detachment, objectivity. **3** *independence of spirit* =**freedom**, individualism, unconventionality, unorthodoxy.

independent ▶ adjective **1** *an independent country* =**self-governing**, self-ruling, self-determining, sovereign, autonomous, non-aligned. **2** *two independent groups verified the results* =**separate**, different, unconnected, unrelated, discrete. **3** *an independent school* =**private**, non-state-run, private-sector, fee-paying; privatized, deregulated, denationalized. **4** *independent advice* =**impartial**, unbiased, unprejudiced, neutral, disinterested, uninvolved, detached, dispassionate, objective, nonpartisan, with no axe to grind. **5** *an independent spirit* =**freethinking**, free, individualistic, unconventional, maverick, bold, unconstrained, uninhibited.
–OPPOSITES subservient, related, public, biased.

independently ▶ adverb =**alone**, on one's own, separately, unaccompanied, solo; unaided, unassisted, without help, by one's own efforts, under one's own steam, single-handed(ly), off one's own bat, on one's own initiative.

indescribable ▶ adjective =**inexpressible**, indefinable, beyond words/description, incommunicable; unutterable, unspeakable; intense, extreme, acute, strong, powerful, profound; incredible, extraordinary, remarkable.

indestructible ▶ adjective =**unbreakable**, shatterproof, vandal-proof, durable; lasting, enduring, everlasting, undying, immortal, imperishable; *literary* adamantine.
–OPPOSITES fragile.

indeterminate ▶ adjective **1** *an indeterminate period of time* =**undetermined**, uncertain, unknown, unspecified, unstipulated, indefinite, unfixed. **2** *some indeterminate background noise* =**vague**, indefinite, unclear, nebulous, indistinct.

index ▶ noun =**list**, listing, inventory, catalogue, register, directory, database.

indicate ▶ verb **1** *sales indicate a growing market for such art* =**point to**, be a sign of, be evidence of, demonstrate, show, testify to, be symptomatic of, denote, mark, signal, reflect, signify, suggest, imply; *literary* betoken. **2** *the president indicated his willingness to use force* =**state**, declare, make known, communicate, announce, mention; put it on record. **3** *please indicate your choice of prize on the form* =**specify**, designate, stipulate, show.

indication ▶ noun =**sign**, signal, indicator, symptom, mark, demonstration; pointer, guide, hint, clue, intimation, omen, warning.

indicative ▶ adjective =**symptomatic**, expressive, suggestive, representative, emblematic, symbolic.

indicator ▶ noun **1** *these tests are a reliable indicator of performance* =**measure**, gauge, barometer, guide, index, mark, sign, signal. **2** *the depth indicator* =**meter**, measuring device, measure, gauge, dial.

indict ▶ verb =**charge**, accuse, arraign, take to court, put on trial, prosecute; summons, cite, prefer charges against; *N. Amer.* impeach.
–OPPOSITES acquit.

indictment ▶ noun =**charge**, accusation, arraignment; citation, summons; *N. Amer.* impeachment.

indifference ▸ noun =lack of concern, disinterest, lack of interest, nonchalance; boredom, unresponsiveness, impassivity, detachment, coolness.

indifferent ▸ adjective **1** *an indifferent shrug* =**unconcerned**, uninterested, uncaring, casual, nonchalant, offhand, unenthusiastic; unimpressed, bored, unmoved, impassive, detached, cool. **2** *an indifferent performance* =**mediocre**, ordinary, average, middle-of-the-road, uninspired, undistinguished, unexceptional, unexciting, unremarkable, run-of-the-mill, pedestrian, prosaic, lacklustre, forgettable, amateurish; *informal* OK, so-so, fair-to-middling, no great shakes, not up to much; *Brit. informal* not much cop; *N. Amer. informal* bush-league; *NZ informal* half-pie.
−OPPOSITES enthusiastic, brilliant.

indigenous ▸ adjective =**native**, original, aboriginal.

indigestion ▸ noun =**dyspepsia**, heartburn, pyrosis, acidity.

indignant ▸ adjective =**aggrieved**, affronted, displeased, cross, angry, annoyed, offended, exasperated, piqued, in high dudgeon; *informal* peeved, irked, put out, miffed, riled, in a huff; *Brit. informal* narked; *N. Amer. informal* sore.

indignation ▸ noun =**resentment**, umbrage, affront, displeasure, anger, annoyance, exasperation, offence, pique.

indignity ▸ noun =**shame**, humiliation, loss of self-respect, embarrassment, mortification; disgrace, dishonour; abuse, offence, injustice, slight, snub, discourtesy, disrespect; *informal* slap in the face, kick in the teeth.

indirect ▸ adjective **1** *an indirect effect* =**incidental**, secondary, subordinate, ancillary, collateral, concomitant, contingent. **2** *an indirect route* =**roundabout**, circuitous, meandering, serpentine, winding, tortuous. **3** *an indirect attack* =**oblique**, implicit, implied.

indirectly ▸ adverb **1** *I heard of the damage indirectly* =**second-hand**; *informal* on the grapevine, on the bush/jungle telegraph. **2** *he referred to the subject indirectly* =**obliquely**, by implication, tangentially.

indiscernible ▸ adjective **1** *an almost indiscernible change* =**unnoticeable**, imperceptible, undetectable, indistinguishable; tiny, minute, minuscule, microscopic, infinitesimal, negligible. **2** *an indiscernible shape* =**indistinct**, nebulous, unclear, fuzzy, vague, indefinite, amorphous, shadowy, dim.
−OPPOSITES distinct.

indiscreet ▸ adjective =**imprudent**, unwise, impolitic, injudicious, incautious, irresponsible, ill-judged, careless, rash; undiplomatic, indelicate, tactless.

indiscretion ▸ noun **1** *he was prone to indiscretion* =**imprudence**, injudiciousness, irresponsibility; tactlessness, insensitivity. **2** *his past indiscretions* =**blunder**, lapse, gaffe, mistake, faux pas, error, slip, impropriety; misdemeanour, transgression, peccadillo, misdeed.

indiscriminate ▸ adjective =**nonselective**, undiscriminating, uncritical, aimless, hit-or-miss, haphazard, random, arbitrary, unsystematic; wholesale, general, sweeping, blanket; casual, careless.
−OPPOSITES selective.

indispensable ▸ adjective =**essential**, necessary, all-important, of the utmost importance, vital, crucial, key; invaluable.
−OPPOSITES superfluous.

indisposed ▸ adjective =**ill**, unwell, sick, poorly, not (very) well; out of action.
−OPPOSITES well.

indisposition ▸ noun =**illness**, malady, ailment, disorder, sickness; condition, complaint, problem.

indisputable ▸ adjective =**incontrovertible**, incontestable, undeniable, irrefutable, beyond dispute, unquestionable, beyond question, indubitable, beyond doubt, unarguable; demonstrable, self-evident, clear, clear-cut.
−OPPOSITES questionable.

indistinct ▸ adjective **1** *the shoreline was indistinct* =**blurred**, fuzzy, hazy, misty, foggy, cloudy, shadowy, dim; unclear, obscure, faint, hard to make out. **2** *indistinct sounds* =**muffled**, muted, low, quiet, soft, faint; muttered, mumbled, whispered.
−OPPOSITES clear.

indistinguishable ▸ adjective **1** *the two girls were indistinguishable* =**identical**, impossible to tell apart, like (two) peas in a pod; *informal* dead ringers. **2** *his words were indistinguishable* =**unintelligible**, incomprehensible; unclear.
−OPPOSITES unalike, clear.

individual ▶ adjective **1** *exhibitions devoted to individual artists* =**single**, separate, discrete, independent; sole, lone. **2** *he had his own individual style of music* =**unique**, characteristic, distinctive, distinct, particular, idiosyncratic, peculiar, personal, special. **3** *a highly individual apartment* =**original**, unique, exclusive, singular, different, unusual, novel, unorthodox, out of the ordinary.
▶ noun **1** *Peter was a rather stuffy individual* =**person**, human being, soul, creature; man, woman, boy, girl; character; *informal* type, sort, beggar, cookie, customer, guy, geezer, devil; *Brit. informal* bod, gent. **2** *she was a real individual* =**individualist**, free spirit, nonconformist, original, eccentric, character, maverick; *Brit. informal* one-off.

individualism ▶ noun =**independence**, freedom of thought, originality; unconventionality, eccentricity.

individualist ▶ noun =**free spirit**, individual, nonconformist, original, eccentric, maverick; *Brit. informal* one-off.
–OPPOSITES conformist.

individualistic ▶ adjective =**unconventional**, unorthodox, atypical, singular, unique, original, nonconformist, independent, freethinking; eccentric, maverick, idiosyncratic.

individuality ▶ noun =**distinctiveness**, uniqueness, originality, singularity, particularity, peculiarity; personality, character, identity, self.

individually ▶ adverb =**one at a time**, one by one, singly, separately, independently.
–OPPOSITES together.

indoctrinate ▶ verb =**brainwash**, propagandize, proselytize, inculcate, re-educate, condition, mould; instruct, teach, school, drill.

indolence ▶ noun =**laziness**, idleness, slothfulness, shiftlessness, inactivity, lethargy, languor, torpor.

indolent ▶ adjective =**lazy**, idle, slothful, work-shy, sluggardly, shiftless, lackadaisical, languid, inactive, lethargic; slack, good-for-nothing, feckless; *informal* bone idle.
–OPPOSITES industrious, energetic.

indomitable ▶ adjective =**invincible**, unconquerable, unbeatable, unassailable, invulnerable, unshakeable; indefatigable, unyielding, unbending, steadfast, staunch, resolute, firm; unflinching, intrepid.
–OPPOSITES submissive.

indubitable ▶ adjective =**unquestionable**, undoubtable, indisputable, unarguable, incontestable, undeniable, irrefutable, incontrovertible, unequivocal, absolute, conclusive; beyond doubt, beyond dispute, not in doubt.
–OPPOSITES doubtful.

induce ▶ verb **1** *the pickets induced many workers to stay away* =**persuade**, convince, prevail upon, get, make, prompt, encourage, cajole into, talk into. **2** *these activities induce a feeling of togetherness* =**bring about**, cause, produce, effect, create, give rise to, generate, instigate, engender, set in motion, trigger off, arouse, foster, promote, encourage; *literary* beget.
–OPPOSITES dissuade, prevent.

inducement ▶ noun =**incentive**, encouragement, attraction, stimulus, carrot, motivation; bribe; *informal* sweetener.
–OPPOSITES deterrent.

induct ▶ verb =**admit to**, introduce to, initiate into, install in, instate in, swear into; appoint to.

indulge ▶ verb **1** *Sally indulged her passion for chocolate* =**satisfy**, gratify, fulfil, feed; yield to, give in to. **2** *she indulged in a series of drinking bouts* =**carry out**, become involved in, participate in, commit, yield to. **3** *she did not like her children to be indulged* =**pamper**, spoil, overindulge, coddle, mollycoddle, cosset; pander to, wait on hand and foot.
–OPPOSITES frustrate.
■ **indulge oneself** =**treat oneself**, splash out; *informal* go to town, splurge.

indulgence ▶ noun **1** *the indulgence of all his desires* =**satisfaction**, gratification, fulfilment. **2** *indulgence contributed to his ill-health* =**self-gratification**, self-indulgence, overindulgence, intemperance, excess, lack of restraint, extravagance, hedonism. **3** *they viewed holidays as an indulgence* =**extravagance**, luxury, treat, non-essential, extra, frill. **4** *her indulgence left him spoilt* =**pampering**, coddling, mollycoddling, cosseting. **5** *his parents view his lapses with indulgence* =**tolerance**, forbearance, understanding, compassion, sympathy, leniency.

indulgent ▶ adjective =**generous**, permissive, easy-going, liberal, tolerant, forgiving, forbearing, lenient, kind,

kindly, soft-hearted.
—OPPOSITES strict.

industrialist ▶ noun =manufacturer, factory owner; captain of industry, magnate, tycoon.

industrious ▶ adjective =hardworking, diligent, assiduous, dedicated, conscientious, studious; busy, active, bustling, energetic, productive; with one's shoulder to the wheel, with one's nose to the grindstone.
—OPPOSITES indolent.

industry ▶ noun **1** British industry =manufacturing, production; construction. **2** the publishing industry =business, trade, field, line (of business); informal racket. **3** the kitchen was a hive of industry =activity, energy, productiveness; hard work, industriousness, diligence, application, dedication.

inebriated ▶ adjective. See DRUNK.

inedible ▶ adjective =uneatable, indigestible, unsavoury, unpalatable; stale, rotten, off, bad.

ineffable ▶ adjective =indescribable, inexpressible, beyond words; undefinable, unutterable; overwhelming, breathtaking, awesome, staggering, amazing.

ineffective ▶ adjective **1** an ineffective scheme =unsuccessful, unproductive, unprofitable, ineffectual. **2** an ineffective president =ineffectual, inefficient, inadequate, incompetent, incapable, unfit, inept, weak, poor; informal useless, hopeless.

ineffectual ▶ adjective. See INEFFECTIVE senses 1, 2.

inefficacious ▶ adjective. See INEFFECTIVE sense 1.

inefficient ▶ adjective **1** an inefficient worker =ineffective, ineffectual, incompetent, inept; disorganized, unprepared. **2** inefficient processes =uneconomical, wasteful, unproductive, time-wasting, slow; deficient, disorganized, unsystematic.

inelegant ▶ adjective **1** an inelegant bellow of laughter =unrefined, uncouth, unsophisticated, coarse, vulgar. **2** inelegant dancing =graceless, ungraceful, ungainly, uncoordinated, awkward, clumsy, lumbering.
—OPPOSITES refined, graceful.

inept ▶ adjective =incompetent, unskilful, unskilled, inexpert, amateurish;

clumsy, awkward, maladroit, bungling, blundering.
—OPPOSITES competent.

inequality ▶ noun =imbalance, inequity, inconsistency, variation, variability; divergence, disparity, discrepancy, dissimilarity, difference; bias, prejudice, discrimination, unfairness.

inequitable ▶ adjective =unfair, unjust, unequal, uneven, discriminatory, preferential, biased, partisan, prejudiced.
—OPPOSITES fair.

inequity ▶ noun =unfairness, injustice, discrimination, partisanship, favouritism, bias, prejudice.

inert ▶ adjective =unmoving, motionless, immobile, inanimate, still, stationary, static; dormant, sleeping; unconscious, comatose, lifeless, insensible.
—OPPOSITES active.

inertia ▶ noun =inactivity, inaction, inertness; apathy, lethargy, listlessness; motionlessness, immobility, lifelessness; formal stasis.

inescapable ▶ adjective =unavoidable, inevitable, ineluctable, inexorable; assured, sure, certain.
—OPPOSITES avoidable.

inessential ▶ adjective =unnecessary, non-essential, unwanted, uncalled-for, needless, redundant, superfluous, expendable; unimportant, peripheral, minor.

inestimable ▶ adjective =immeasurable, incalculable, innumerable; limitless, boundless.
—OPPOSITES few.

inevitable ▶ adjective =unavoidable, inescapable, inexorable, ineluctable; assured, certain, sure.
—OPPOSITES uncertain.

inevitably ▶ adverb =naturally, necessarily, automatically, as a matter of course, of necessity, inescapably, unavoidably, certainly, surely; informal like it or not; formal perforce.

inexact ▶ adjective =imprecise, approximate, rough, crude, general, vague; N. Amer. informal ballpark.

inexcusable ▶ adjective =indefensible, unjustifiable, unwarranted, unpardonable, unforgivable; unacceptable, unreasonable; uncalled-for.

inexhaustible ▶ adjective **1** her patience is inexhaustible =unlimited, limit-

less, infinite, boundless, endless, never-ending, unfailing, everlasting. **2** *the dancers were inexhaustible* =**tireless**, indefatigable, untiring, unfaltering, unflagging.
–OPPOSITES limited, weary.

inexorable ▸ adjective =**relentless**, unstoppable, inescapable, inevitable, unavoidable, persistent, continuous, non-stop, steady, unceasing, unremitting, unrelenting.

inexpensive ▸ adjective =**cheap**, low-priced, low-cost, economical, competitive, affordable, reasonable, budget, economy, bargain, cut-price, reduced, discounted, discount.

inexperience ▸ noun =**ignorance**, naivety, innocence, immaturity.

inexperienced ▸ adjective =**inexpert**, unpractised, untrained, unschooled, unqualified, unskilled; ignorant, unseasoned, naive, unsophisticated, callow, immature; *informal* wet behind the ears, wide-eyed.

inexpert ▸ adjective =**unskilled**, unskilful, amateurish, unprofessional, inexperienced; inept, incompetent, maladroit, clumsy, bungling, blundering; *informal* cack-handed, ham-fisted, butterfingered.

inexplicable ▸ adjective =**unaccountable**, unexplainable, incomprehensible, baffling, puzzling, perplexing, mystifying, bewildering; mysterious.
–OPPOSITES understandable.

inexpressible ▸ adjective =**indescribable**, undefinable, unutterable, unspeakable, beyond words; unimaginable, inconceivable, unthinkable.

inexpressive ▸ adjective =**expressionless**, impassive, emotionless; inscrutable, blank, vacant, glazed, lifeless, deadpan, wooden, stony; poker-faced.

inextinguishable ▸ adjective =**irrepressible**, unquenchable, indestructible, undying, unfailing, enduring, everlasting, eternal.

infallible ▸ adjective **1** *an infallible sense of timing* =**unerring**, unfailing, faultless, flawless, impeccable, perfect, precise, accurate, meticulous, scrupulous; *Brit. informal* spot on. **2** *infallible cures* =**unfailing**, guaranteed, dependable, trustworthy, reliable, sure, certain, safe, foolproof, effective; *informal* sure-fire; *formal* efficacious.

infamous ▸ adjective =**notorious**, disreputable; legendary, fabled.
–OPPOSITES reputable.

infamy ▸ noun =**notoriety**, ill fame, disgrace, discredit, shame, dishonour, ignominy, scandal, censure, blame, disapprobation, condemnation.

infancy ▸ noun **1** *she died in infancy* =**babyhood**, early childhood. **2** *the infancy of broadcasting* =**beginnings**, early days, early stages; seeds, roots; start, emergence, dawn, birth, inception.
–OPPOSITES end.

infant ▸ noun *a sickly infant* =**baby**, newborn, (young) child, (tiny) tot, little one; *Medicine* neonate; *Scottish & N. English* bairn, wean; *informal* tiny, sprog; *literary* babe.
▸ adjective *infant companies* =**developing**, emergent, emerging, embryonic, nascent, new, fledgling, budding, up-and-coming.

infantile ▸ adjective =**childish**, babyish, immature, puerile, juvenile, adolescent; silly, inane, fatuous.

infatuated ▸ adjective =**besotted**, in love, obsessed, taken; captivated by, enchanted by, bewitched by, under the spell of; *informal* smitten with, sweet on, mad about, crazy about, stuck on.

infatuation ▸ noun =**passion**, adoration, desire, devotion; obsession, fixation; *informal* crush, thing, hang-up, pash.

infect ▸ verb **1** *they can infect their children* =**pass infection to**, contaminate. **2** *nitrates were infecting rivers* =**contaminate**, pollute, taint, foul, dirty, blight, damage, ruin; poison. **3** *his high spirits infected everyone* =**affect**, influence, touch; excite, inspire, stimulate, animate.

infection ▸ noun **1** *a kidney infection* =**disease**, virus; illness, ailment, sickness, infirmity; *informal* bug. **2** *the infection in his wounds* =**contamination**, poison; septicaemia, suppuration, inflammation; germs; *Medicine* sepsis.

infectious ▸ adjective **1** *infectious diseases* =**contagious**, communicable, transmittable, transmissible, transferable, spreadable; epidemic; *informal* catching. **2** *her laughter is infectious* =**irresistible**, compelling, contagious, catching.

infelicitous ▸ adjective =**unfortunate**, unsuitable, inappropriate, inapposite, inapt; untimely, inopportune.

–OPPOSITES appropriate.

infer ▸ verb =deduce, conclude, surmise, reason; gather, understand, presume, assume, take it; read between the lines; N. Amer. figure; Brit. informal suss (out).

inference ▸ noun =deduction, conclusion, reasoning, presumption, assumption, supposition, reckoning, extrapolation; guesswork.

inferior ▸ adjective **1** she regards him as inferior =second-class, lower-ranking, subordinate, junior, minor, lowly, humble, menial, beneath one. **2** inferior accommodation =second-rate, substandard, low-quality, low-grade, unsatisfactory, shoddy, deficient; poor, bad, awful, dreadful, wretched; informal crummy, dire, rotten, lousy, third-rate.
–OPPOSITES superior, luxury.
▸ noun how dare she treat him as an inferior? =subordinate, junior, underling, minion.

infernal ▸ adjective **1** the infernal regions =hellish, lower, nether, subterranean, underworld. **2** (informal) an infernal nuisance =damnable, wretched; informal damned, damn, blasted, blessed, pesky; Brit. informal blinking, blooming, flaming, flipping; Brit. informal, dated bally, ruddy.

infertile ▸ adjective **1** infertile soil =barren, unproductive; sterile, impoverished, arid. **2** she was infertile =sterile, barren; childless; Medicine infecund.

infest ▸ verb =overrun, spread through, invade, infiltrate, pervade, permeate, inundate, overwhelm; beset, plague.

infested ▸ adjective =overrun, swarming, teeming, crawling, alive, ridden; plagued, beset.

infidel ▸ noun =unbeliever, nonbeliever; heathen, pagan, idolater, heretic.

infidelity ▸ noun =unfaithfulness, adultery; disloyalty, treachery, doubledealing, duplicity, deceit; affair; informal playing around, fooling around, cheating, two-timing; formal fornication.

infiltrator ▸ noun =spy, (secret) agent, plant, intruder, interloper, subversive, informer, mole, entryist, fifth columnist; N. Amer. informal spook.

infinite ▸ adjective **1** the universe is infinite =boundless, unbounded, unlimited, limitless, never-ending; immeasurable,

fathomless. **2** an infinite number of birds =countless, uncountable, innumerable, numberless, immeasurable, incalculable, untold; great, huge, enormous. **3** she bathed him with infinite care =great, immense, extreme, supreme, absolute.
–OPPOSITES limited, small.

infinitesimal ▸ adjective =minute, tiny, minuscule, very small; microscopic, imperceptible, indiscernible; Scottish wee; informal teeny, teeny-weeny, itsy-bitsy, tiddly; Brit. informal titchy; N. Amer. informal little-bitty.
–OPPOSITES huge.

infinity ▸ noun **1** the infinity of space =endlessness, infiniteness, boundlessness, limitlessness; vastness, immensity. **2** an infinity of different molecules =infinite number; abundance, profusion, host, multitude, mass, wealth; informal heap, load.

infirm ▸ adjective =frail, weak, debilitated, disabled; ill, unwell, sick, sickly, poorly, ailing.
–OPPOSITES healthy.

infirmity ▸ noun **1** they were excused due to infirmity =frailty, weakness, delicacy, debility; disability, impairment; illness, sickness, poor health. **2** the infirmities of old age =ailment, malady, illness, disorder, sickness, affliction, complaint.

inflame ▸ verb **1** he inflamed a sensitive situation =aggravate, exacerbate, intensify, worsen, compound. **2** his opinions inflamed his rival =enrage, incense, anger, madden, infuriate, exasperate, provoke, antagonize, rile; informal make someone see red, make someone's blood boil.
–OPPOSITES calm, soothe, placate.

inflamed ▸ adjective =swollen, puffed up; red, hot, burning, itchy; raw, sore, painful, tender; infected.

inflammable ▸ adjective =flammable, combustible, incendiary, ignitable; volatile, unstable.
–OPPOSITES fireproof.

inflammation ▸ noun =swelling, puffiness; redness, heat, burning; rawness, soreness, tenderness; infection.

inflammatory ▸ adjective =provocative, incendiary, stirring, rousing, rabble-rousing, seditious, mutinous; like a red rag to a bull; fiery, passionate; controversial, contentious.

inflate ▸ verb **1** the mattress inflated =blow up, fill up, fill with air, puff up/

out; dilate, distend, swell. **2** *the demand inflated prices* =**increase**, raise, boost, escalate, put up; *informal* hike up, jack up, bump up. **3** *the figures were inflated by the press* =**exaggerate**, overplay, overstate, enhance, embellish; increase, augment.
–OPPOSITES decrease, understate.

inflated ▸ adjective **1** *an inflated balloon* =**blown up**, filled, puffed up/out, pumped up; distended, expanded, engorged, swollen. **2** *inflated prices* =**high**, sky-high, excessive, unreasonable, prohibitive, outrageous, exorbitant, extortionate; *Brit.* over the odds; *informal* steep. **3** *an inflated opinion of himself* =**exaggerated**, immoderate, overblown, overstated. **4** *inflated language* =**high-flown**, extravagant, exaggerated, elaborate, overblown, overwrought, grandiose.

inflection ▸ noun =**stress**, cadence, rhythm, accentuation, intonation, emphasis, modulation, lilt.

inflexible ▸ adjective **1** *his inflexible attitude* =**stubborn**, obstinate, intransigent, unbending, immovable, unyielding; pig-headed, uncompromising. **2** *inflexible rules* =**unalterable**, unchangeable, immutable; fixed, set, strict. **3** *an inflexible structure* =**rigid**, stiff, unyielding, unbending; hard, firm.
–OPPOSITES accommodating, pliable.

inflict ▸ verb **1** *he inflicted an injury on Frank* =**impose**, exact, wreak, deal out, mete out. **2** *I won't inflict my views on my children* =**impose**, force, thrust, foist.

infliction ▸ noun =**administration**, delivery, application; imposition, perpetration.

influence ▸ noun **1** *the influence of parents on their children* =**effect**, impact; control, sway, hold, power. **2** *a bad influence on young girls* =**example to**, (role) model for, inspiration to. **3** *political influence* =**power**, authority, sway, leverage, weight, pull; *informal* clout, muscle, teeth; *N. Amer. informal* drag.
▸ verb **1** *bosses can influence our careers* =**affect**, have an impact on, determine, guide, control, shape, govern, decide; change, alter. **2** *an attempt to influence the jury* =**sway**, bias, prejudice, suborn; pressurize, coerce; intimidate, browbeat; *informal* lean on; *Brit. informal* nobble.

influential ▸ adjective =**powerful**, controlling; important.

influx ▸ noun **1** *an influx of tourists* =**in-**

undation, rush, stream, flood, incursion; invasion. **2** *an influx of river water* =**inflow**, inrush, flood, inundation.

inform ▸ verb **1** *she informed him that she was ill* =**tell**, notify, apprise, advise, impart to, communicate to, let someone know; brief, enlighten, send word to. **2** *he informed on two colleagues* =**denounce**, give away, betray, incriminate, report; sell out, stab in the back; *informal* rat, squeal, split, tell, blow the whistle, snitch, stitch up; *Brit. informal* grass, shop; *Scottish informal* clype; *N. Amer. informal* rat out, finger; *Austral./NZ informal* dob. **3** *the articles were informed by feminism* =**suffuse**, pervade, permeate, infuse, imbue.

informal ▸ adjective **1** *an informal discussion* =**unofficial**, casual, relaxed, easy-going; low key. **2** *informal language* =**colloquial**, vernacular, idiomatic, demotic, popular; familiar, everyday; simple, natural, unpretentious; *informal* slangy, chatty, folksy. **3** *informal clothes* =**casual**, relaxed, comfortable, everyday, sloppy, leisure; *informal* comfy.
–OPPOSITES formal, official, literary, smart.

informality ▸ noun =**lack of ceremony**, casualness, unpretentiousness; homeliness; ease, naturalness, approachability.

information ▸ noun =**details**, particulars, facts, figures, statistics, data; knowledge, intelligence; advice, guidance, direction, counsel, enlightenment; news; *informal* info, gen, the lowdown, the dope, the inside story.

informative ▸ adjective =**instructive**, illuminating, enlightening, revealing, explanatory; factual, educational, edifying, didactic; *informal* newsy.

informed ▸ adjective =**knowledgeable**, enlightened, educated; briefed, up to date, up to speed, in the picture, in the know, au fait; *informal* clued up, genned up; *Brit. informal* switched-on, sussed.
–OPPOSITES ignorant.

informer ▸ noun =**informant**, betrayer, traitor, Judas, collaborator, stool pigeon, fifth columnist, spy, double agent, infiltrator, plant; telltale; *N. Amer.* tattletale; *informal* rat, squealer, whistleblower, snitch; *Brit. informal* grass, supergrass, nark, snout; *Scottish informal* clype; *N. Amer. informal* fink, stoolie.

infraction ▸ noun =infringement, contravention, breach, violation, transgression.

infrequent ▸ adjective =rare, uncommon, unusual, exceptional, few (and far between), like gold dust, as scarce as hens' teeth; unaccustomed, unwonted; isolated, scarce, scattered; sporadic, intermittent; *informal* once in a blue moon.
–OPPOSITES common.

infringe ▸ verb **1** *the bid infringed EU rules* =contravene, violate, transgress, break, breach. **2** *surveillance could infringe personal liberties* =undermine, erode, diminish, weaken, impair, damage, compromise, encroach on.
–OPPOSITES obey, preserve.

infuriate ▸ verb =enrage, incense, anger, madden, inflame; exasperate; *informal* make someone see red, get someone's back up, make someone's blood boil, get up someone's nose; *Brit. informal* wind up, get to.
–OPPOSITES please.

infuriating ▸ adjective =exasperating, maddening.

infuse ▸ verb **1** *she was infused with a sense of hope* =fill, suffuse, imbue, inspire, charge, pervade, permeate. **2** *he infused new life into the group* =instil, breathe, inject, impart, introduce. **3** *infuse the dried leaves* =steep, brew, stew, soak, immerse, souse; *Brit. informal* mash.

ingenious ▸ adjective =inventive, creative, imaginative, original, innovative, pioneering, resourceful, enterprising, inspired; clever.
–OPPOSITES unimaginative.

ingenuous ▸ adjective =naive, innocent, simple, childlike, trusting, trustful; wide-eyed, inexperienced; open, artless, guileless.
–OPPOSITES artful.

inglorious ▸ adjective =shameful, dishonourable, ignominious, discreditable, disgraceful, scandalous; ignoble, undignified, wretched.

ingrained ▸ adjective **1** *ingrained attitudes* =entrenched, established, deeprooted, deep-seated, fixed, firm, unshakeable, abiding, enduring, stubborn. **2** *ingrained dirt* =ground-in, fixed, deep; permanent, indelible.
–OPPOSITES transient, superficial.

ingratiate ◼ ingratiate oneself =curry favour, cultivate, win over, get in someone's good books; toady to, crawl to, grovel to, kowtow to, play up to, flatter, court; *informal* suck up to.

ingratiating ▸ adjective =sycophantic, toadying, fawning, unctuous, obsequious; flattering; *informal* smarmy, slimy, creepy.

ingratitude ▸ noun =ungratefulness, thanklessness, unthankfulness.

ingredient ▸ noun =constituent, component, element; part, piece, bit, strand, portion, unit, feature, aspect, attribute.

inhabit ▸ verb =live in, occupy; settle (in), people, populate, colonize; dwell in, reside in, have one's home in; *formal* abide in.

inhabitable ▸ adjective =habitable, fit to live in, usable; *informal* liveable-in.

inhabitant ▸ noun =resident, occupant, occupier, dweller, settler; local, native; (**inhabitants**) population, populace, people, public, community, citizenry, townsfolk, townspeople; *formal* denizen.

inhale ▸ verb =breathe in, draw in, suck in, sniff in, drink in.

inherent ▸ adjective =intrinsic, innate, immanent, built-in, inborn, ingrained, deep-rooted; essential, fundamental, basic, structural, organic; natural, instinctive, instinctual.
–OPPOSITES acquired.

inherit ▸ verb **1** *she inherited the farm* =come into/by, be bequeathed, be left, be willed. **2** *Richard inherited the title* =succeed to, assume, take over, come into; *formal* accede to.

inheritance ▸ noun **1** *a comfortable inheritance* =legacy, bequest, endowment; birthright, heritage, patrimony. **2** *his inheritance of the title* =succession to, accession to, assumption of, elevation to.

> **WORD LINKS**
> *relating to inheritance:* **hereditary**

inhibit ▸ verb =impede, hinder, hamper, hold back, discourage, interfere with, obstruct, slow down, retard.
–OPPOSITES assist allow.

inhibited ▸ adjective =shy, reticent, reserved, self-conscious, diffident, bashful, coy; hesitant, insecure, unconfident, unassertive, timid; withdrawn, repressed, undemonstrative; *informal* uptight.

inhibition ▸ noun =**shyness**, reticence, self-consciousness, reserve, diffidence; wariness, hesitance, hesitancy; insecurity; unassertiveness, timidity; repression, reservation; *informal* problem, phobia, hang-up.

inhospitable ▸ adjective **1** *the inhospitable climate* =**hostile**, bleak, forbidding, cheerless, harsh, desolate, stark. **2** *forgive me if I seem inhospitable* =**unwelcoming**, unfriendly, unsociable, unsocial, unneighbourly, uncongenial; cold, frosty, aloof, distant, remote, offhand; uncivil, discourteous, ungracious.
−OPPOSITES welcoming.

inhuman ▸ adjective **1** *inhuman treatment* =**cruel**, harsh, inhumane, brutal, callous, sadistic, savage, vicious, barbaric. **2** *hellish and inhuman shapes* =**monstrous**, devilish, ghostly, demonic, animal, bestial; unearthly.
−OPPOSITES humane.

inhumane ▸ adjective. See INHUMAN sense 1.

inimical ▸ adjective =**harmful**, injurious, detrimental, deleterious, prejudicial, damaging; antagonistic, hostile, contrary.
−OPPOSITES advantageous.

inimitable ▸ adjective =**unique**, exclusive, distinctive, individual, special, idiosyncratic; incomparable, in a class of one's own.

iniquity ▸ noun **1** *the iniquity of his conduct* =**wickedness**, sinfulness, immorality. **2** *I will forgive their iniquities* =**sin**, crime, transgression, wrongdoing, wrong, offence.
−OPPOSITES goodness, virtue.

initial ▸ adjective =**beginning**, opening, commencing, starting, embryonic; first, early, primary, preliminary, preparatory; introductory, inaugural.
−OPPOSITES final.

initially ▸ adverb =**at first**, at the start, at the outset, in/at the beginning, to begin with, to start with, originally.

initiate ▸ verb **1** *the government initiated the scheme* =**begin**, start (off), commence; institute, inaugurate, launch, instigate, establish, set up. **2** *he was initiated into a religious cult* =**introduce**, admit, induct, install, incorporate,

swear in; ordain, invest.
−OPPOSITES finish, expel.

initiative ▸ noun **1** *employers are looking for initiative* =**enterprise**, resourcefulness, inventiveness, imagination, ingenuity, originality, creativity. **2** *he has lost the initiative* =**advantage**, upper hand, edge, lead. **3** *a recent initiative on recycling* =**plan**, scheme, strategy, measure, proposal, step, action, approach.

inject ▸ verb **1** *he injected the codeine* =**administer**, take; *informal* shoot (up), mainline, fix (up). **2** *a pump injects air into the valve* =**insert**, introduce, feed, push, force, shoot. **3** *he injected new life into the team* =**introduce**, instil, infuse, imbue, breathe.

injection ▸ noun =**inoculation**, vaccination, immunization, booster; dose; *informal* jab, shot.

injudicious ▸ adjective =**imprudent**, unwise, inadvisable, ill-advised, misguided; ill-considered, ill-judged, foolish.
−OPPOSITES prudent.

injunction ▸ noun =**order**, ruling, direction, directive, command, instruction; decree, edict, dictum, dictate, fiat, mandate.

injure ▸ verb **1** *he injured his foot* =**hurt**, wound, damage, harm; cripple, lame, disable; break; *Brit. informal* knacker. **2** *a libel injured her reputation* =**damage**, mar, spoil, ruin, blight, blemish, tarnish, blacken.

injured ▸ adjective **1** *his injured arm* =**hurt**, wounded, damaged, sore, bruised; broken, fractured; *Brit. informal* gammy. **2** *an injured tone* =**upset**, hurt, wounded, offended, reproachful, pained, aggrieved.
−OPPOSITES healthy.

injurious ▸ adjective =**harmful**, damaging, deleterious, detrimental, hurtful; disadvantageous, unfavourable, undesirable, adverse, inimical.

injury ▸ noun **1** *minor injuries* =**wound**, bruise, cut, gash, scratch, graze, abrasion, contusion, lesion; *Medicine* trauma. **2** *they escaped without injury* =**harm**, hurt, damage, pain, suffering.

WORD LINKS
fear of injury: **traumatophobia**

injustice ▸ noun **1** *the injustice of the world* =**unfairness**, unjustness, inequity; cruelty, tyranny, repression, exploitation, corruption; bias, prejudice, discrimination, intolerance. **2** *his sacking was an injustice* =**wrong**, offence, crime, sin, outrage, atrocity, scandal, disgrace, affront.

inkling ▸ noun =**idea**, notion, sense, impression, suggestion, indication; clue, intimation.

inlaid ▸ adjective =**inset**, set, studded, lined, panelled; ornamented, decorated.

inland ▸ adjective =**interior**, inshore, central, internal, upcountry.
–OPPOSITES coastal.
▸ adverb =**upcountry**, inshore, ashore.

inlet ▸ noun **1** =**cove**, bay, bight, creek, estuary, fjord, sound; *Scottish* firth. **2** *an air inlet* =**vent**, flue, shaft, duct, channel, pipe.

inmate ▸ noun **1** *the inmates of the hospital* =**patient**, inpatient; resident, occupant. **2** *the prison's inmates* =**prisoner**, convict, captive, detainee, internee, occupant.

inmost ▸ adjective. *See* INNERMOST.

inn ▸ noun =**tavern**, bar, hostelry; hotel, guest house; *Brit.* pub, public house; *Canadian* beer parlour; *informal* watering hole; *dated* alehouse.

innards ▸ plural noun *(informal)* =**entrails**, internal organs, viscera, intestines, bowels, guts; *informal* insides.

innate ▸ adjective =**inborn**, inbred, inherent, natural, intrinsic, instinctive, intuitive; hereditary, inherited, in the blood, in the family; inbuilt, deep-rooted, deep-seated.
–OPPOSITES acquired.

inner ▸ adjective **1** *inner London* =**central**, downtown, innermost. **2** *the inner gates* =**internal**, interior, inside, innermost. **3** *the Queen's inner circle* =**private**, restricted, exclusive, intimate. **4** *the inner meaning* =**hidden**, secret, deep, underlying; veiled, esoteric. **5** *one's inner life* =**mental**, intellectual, psychological, spiritual, emotional.
–OPPOSITES external, apparent.

innermost ▸ adjective **1** *the innermost shrine* =**central**, internal, interior. **2** *her innermost feelings* =**deepest**, deep-seated, underlying, intimate, private, personal, secret, hidden, concealed; true, real, honest.

innocence ▸ noun **1** *he protested his in-*nocence =**guiltlessness**, blamelessness. **2** *she took advantage of his innocence* =**naivety**, credulity, inexperience, gullibility, guilelessness, ingenuousness.

innocent ▸ adjective **1** *he was entirely innocent* =**guiltless**, blameless, faultless; honest, upright, law-abiding. **2** *innocent fun* =**harmless**, innocuous, safe, inoffensive. **3** *innocent foreign students* =**naive**, ingenuous, trusting, credulous; impressionable, easily led; inexperienced, unsophisticated; artless, guileless.
–OPPOSITES guilty, sinful, worldly.

innocuous ▸ adjective **1** *an innocuous fungus* =**harmless**, safe, non-toxic; edible. **2** *an innocuous comment* =**inoffensive**, unobjectionable, unexceptionable, harmless; anodyne.
–OPPOSITES harmful, offensive.

innovation ▸ noun =**change**, alteration, upheaval; reorganization, restructuring; novelty.

innovative ▸ adjective =**original**, new, novel, fresh, unusual, experimental, inventive, ingenious; pioneering, groundbreaking, revolutionary, radical.

innovator ▸ noun =**pioneer**, trailblazer, pathfinder, groundbreaker; modernizer, progressive; experimenter, inventor.

innuendo ▸ noun =**insinuation**, suggestion, intimation, implication; aspersion, slur.

innumerable ▸ adjective =**countless**, numerous, untold, legion, numberless, limitless; *informal* umpteen, no end of, loads of, masses of, oodles of, zillions of; *N. Amer. informal* gazillions of; *literary* myriad.
–OPPOSITES few.

inoculate ▸ verb =**immunize**, vaccinate, inject; protect against; *informal* give someone a jab/shot.

inoculation ▸ noun =**immunization**, vaccination, vaccine; injection, booster; *informal* jab, shot.

WORD LINKS

fear of inoculation: **trypanophobia, vaccinophobia**
---

inoffensive ▸ adjective =**harmless**, innocuous, unobjectionable, unexceptionable; mild, peaceful, peaceable, gentle; tame, innocent.

inoperable ▸ adjective **1** *an inoperable*

tumour =**untreatable**, incurable, irremediable. **2** *the airfield was left inoperable* =**unusable**, out of action, out of service. **3** *the agreement is now inoperable* =**impractical**, unworkable, unfeasible, non-viable, impracticable.
–OPPOSITES curable, workable.

inoperative ▶ adjective **1** *the fan is inoperative* =**out of order**, out of service, broken, out of commission, unserviceable, faulty, defective; down; *informal* bust, kaput, on the blink, shot; *Brit. informal* knackered. **2** *the contract is inoperative* =**void**, null and void, invalid, ineffective, non-viable; cancelled, revoked, terminated.
–OPPOSITES working, valid.

inopportune ▶ adjective =**inconvenient**, unsuitable, inappropriate, unfavourable, unfortunate; untimely, ill-timed.
–OPPOSITES convenient.

inordinate ▶ adjective =**excessive**, undue; massive, huge; disproportionate, extreme; immoderate, extravagant.
–OPPOSITES moderate.

inorganic ▶ adjective =**inanimate**, inert; mineral.

input ▶ noun =**contribution**, feedback, comments, response, participation, say, effort.
▶ verb =**enter**, put in, load, insert; key in, type in.

inquest ▶ noun =**inquiry**, investigation, probe, examination, review; hearing.

inquire ▶ verb. *See* ENQUIRE.

inquiring ▶ adjective. *See* ENQUIRING.

inquiry ▶ noun. *See* ENQUIRY.

inquisition ▶ noun =**interrogation**, cross-examination; investigation, inquiry, inquest; *informal* grilling.

inquisitive ▶ adjective =**curious**, interested; prying; *informal* nosy.
–OPPOSITES indifferent.

insane ▶ adjective **1** *she was declared insane* =**of unsound mind**, certifiable; psychotic, schizophrenic; mad, deranged, demented, out of one's mind, non compos mentis, sick in the head, unhinged, crazed; *informal* crazy, (stark) raving mad, bonkers, cracked, batty, loony, loopy, nuts, screwy, bananas, wacko, off one's rocker, off one's head, round the bend; *Brit. informal* crackers, barmy, barking (mad), off one's trolley,

round the twist; *N. Amer. informal* buggy, nutso, out of one's tree; *Austral./NZ informal* bushed. **2** *an insane suggestion* =**stupid**, idiotic, nonsensical, absurd, ridiculous, ludicrous, preposterous; *informal* crazy, mad; *Brit. informal* daft, barmy
–OPPOSITES sensible, calm.

insanitary ▶ adjective =**unhygienic**, unsanitary, unhealthy, dirty, filthy, contaminated; infected, germ-ridden.
–OPPOSITES hygienic.

insanity ▶ noun **1** *insanity runs in her family* =**mental illness**, madness, dementia; lunacy; mania, psychosis; *informal* craziness. **2** *it would be insanity to take this loan* =**folly**, madness, idiocy, stupidity, lunacy; *informal* craziness.

> WORD LINKS
> *fear of insanity:* **lyssophobia, maniphobia**

insatiable ▶ adjective =**unquenchable**, uncontrollable; voracious, ravenous, wolfish; avid, eager, keen.

inscribe ▶ verb =**carve**, write, engrave, incise, cut; imprint, stamp.

inscription ▶ noun **1** *the inscription on the sarcophagus* =**lettering**, wording, writing, legend; epitaph. **2** *the book had an inscription* =**dedication**, message; signature, autograph.

inscrutable ▶ adjective =**enigmatic**, unreadable, mysterious; inexpressive, expressionless, impassive, blank, deadpan, poker-faced, dispassionate.
–OPPOSITES expressive.

insect ▶ noun

> WORD LINKS
> *study of insects:* **entomology**
> *collective noun:* **flight, swarm**
> *insect-eating:* **insectivorous, entomophagous**
> *fear of insects:* **entomophobia**
> *substance that kills insects:* **insecticide**

insecure ▶ adjective **1** *an insecure young man* =**unconfident**, uncertain, unsure, doubtful, hesitant, self-conscious, inhibited; anxious, fearful. **2** *insecure windows* =**unprotected**, unguarded, vulnerable, unsecured. **3** *an insecure footbridge* =**unstable**, rickety, wobbly, shaky, unsteady, precarious.
–OPPOSITES confident, stable.

insecurity ▶ noun **1** *he hid his insecurity* =**lack of confidence**, self-doubt, diffidence, timidity, uncertainty, nervousness, inhibition; anxiety, worry, unease. **2** *the insecurity of our situation* =**vulnerability**; instability, fragility, frailty, shakiness.

insensible ▶ adjective =**unconscious**, senseless, inert, comatose, passed out, blacked out; *informal* out (cold), out for the count, out of it, dead to the world; *Brit. informal* spark out.
−OPPOSITES conscious.

insensitive ▶ adjective **1** *an insensitive bully* =**heartless**, unfeeling, inconsiderate, thoughtless, thick-skinned; hard-hearted, uncaring, unsympathetic, unkind. **2** *he was insensitive to her feelings* =**impervious to**, oblivious to, unaware of, unresponsive to, indifferent to.
−OPPOSITES compassionate.

insentient ▶ adjective =**inanimate**, lifeless, inorganic, inert; unconscious, unaware, unfeeling.

insert ▶ verb **1** *he inserted a tape in the machine* =**put**, place, push, thrust, slide, slip, load, fit, slot, install; *informal* pop, stick, bung. **2** *she inserted an extra clause* =**enter**, introduce, incorporate, interpose, interject; add.
−OPPOSITES extract, remove.
▶ noun *the newspaper carried an insert* =**enclosure**, supplement; circular, advertisement, pamphlet, leaflet; *informal* ad, flyer.

inside ▶ noun **1** *the inside of the volcano* =**interior**; centre, core, middle, heart, bowels. **2** *(informal) my insides are out of order* =**stomach**, gut, bowels, intestines; *informal* belly, tummy, guts.
−OPPOSITES exterior.
▶ adjective **1** *his inside pocket* =**inner**, interior, internal, innermost. **2** *inside information* =**confidential**, classified, restricted, privileged, private, secret, exclusive; *informal* hush-hush.
−OPPOSITES outer, public.
▶ adverb **1** *she ushered me inside* =**indoors**, within, in. **2** *how do you feel inside?* =**inwardly**, within, privately, deep down, at heart, emotionally, mentally, psychologically, spiritually. **3** *(informal) if I burgle again I'll be back inside* =**in prison**, in jail, in custody; locked up, imprisoned, incarcerated; *informal* behind bars, doing time; *Brit. informal* banged up.
−OPPOSITES outside.

insider ▶ noun =**member**, worker, employee, representative; person in the know; mole.

insidious ▶ adjective =**stealthy**, subtle, cunning, crafty, artful, sly, wily, underhand, indirect; *informal* sneaky.

insight ▶ noun **1** *your insight has been invaluable* =**intuition**, perception, understanding, comprehension, appreciation, penetration, acumen, perspicacity, judgement, acuity; vision, imagination; *informal* nous, savvy. **2** *an insight into the government* =**understanding of**, appreciation of; introduction to; *informal* eye-opener.

insignia ▶ noun =**badge**, crest, emblem, symbol, sign, mark, seal, coat of arms, logo.

insignificant ▶ adjective =**unimportant**, trivial, trifling, negligible, inconsequential, of no account, paltry, petty, insubstantial, worthless, irrelevant, immaterial, peripheral; *informal* piddling.

insincere ▶ adjective =**false**, fake, hollow, artificial, feigned, pretended, put-on; disingenuous, hypocritical, cynical, deceitful, duplicitous, double-dealing, two-faced, untruthful; *informal* phoney, pretend, pseud.

insinuate ▶ verb =**imply**, suggest, hint, intimate; *informal* make out.
■ **insinuate oneself into** =**worm one's way into**, ingratiate oneself with, curry favour with; infiltrate, impinge on; *informal* muscle in on.

insinuation ▶ noun =**implication**, inference, suggestion, hint, intimation, innuendo; undertone; aspersion.

insipid ▶ adjective **1** *insipid coffee* =**tasteless**, flavourless, bland, weak, wishy-washy; unappetizing. **2** *insipid pictures* =**unimaginative**, uninspired, uninspiring, characterless, flat, uninteresting, bland, run-of-the-mill, pedestrian, tired, lame, tame, anaemic.
−OPPOSITES tasty, interesting.

insist ▶ verb **1** *be prepared to insist* =**stand firm**, stand one's ground, be resolute, be determined, hold out, be emphatic, not take no for an answer; persevere, persist; *informal* stick to one's guns. **2** *she insisted that they pay up* =**demand**, command; urge, exhort. **3** *he insisted that he knew nothing* =**maintain**, assert, protest, swear, declare, repeat, reiterate; *formal* aver.

insistence ▶ noun **1** *she sat down at Anne's insistence* =**demand**, bidding, command, dictate, instruction, requirement, request, entreaty, exhortation; *informal* say-so; *literary* behest. **2** *his insistence that he loved her* = **assertion**, contention, assurance, affirmation, avowal.

insistent ▸ adjective **1** *Tony's insistent questioning* = **persistent**, determined, tenacious, unyielding, dogged, unrelenting, inexorable. **2** *an insistent buzzing* = **incessant**, constant, unremitting.

insolent ▸ adjective = **impertinent**, impudent, cheeky, ill-mannered, bad mannered, rude, impolite, discourteous, disrespectful, insubordinate; cocky; *informal* fresh, lippy, saucy; *N. Amer. informal* sassy. −OPPOSITES polite.

insoluble ▸ adjective *some problems are insoluble* = **unsolvable**, unanswerable, unresolvable; unworkable.

insolvency ▸ noun = **bankruptcy**, liquidation, failure, collapse, (financial) ruin; pennilessness, penury; *Brit.* receivership.

insolvent ▸ adjective = **bankrupt**, ruined, liquidated; penniless; *Brit.* in receivership, without a penny (to one's name); *informal* bust, (flat) broke, belly up, gone to the wall, on the rocks, in the red, hard up, strapped for cash.

insomnia ▸ noun = **sleeplessness**, wakefulness, restlessness.

insouciance ▸ noun = **nonchalance**, unconcern, indifference; *informal* cool. −OPPOSITES anxiety.

insouciant ▸ adjective = **nonchalant**, untroubled, unworried, unruffled, unconcerned, indifferent, blasé, carefree, free and easy; *informal* laid-back.

inspect ▸ verb = **examine**, check, scrutinize, investigate, vet, test, monitor, survey, study, look over, probe; *informal* check out, give something a/the once-over.

inspection ▸ noun = **examination**, check-up, survey, scrutiny, probe, exploration, investigation; *informal* once-over, going-over, look-see.

inspector ▸ noun = **examiner**, scrutineer, investigator, surveyor, assessor, reviewer, analyst; observer, overseer, supervisor, monitor, watchdog, ombudsman; auditor.

inspiration ▸ noun **1** *she's an inspiration to others* = **stimulus**, motivation, encouragement, influence, spur; example, model; exemplar. **2** *his work lacks inspiration* = **creativity**, inventiveness,

innovation, ingenuity, imagination, originality; insight, vision. **3** *she had a sudden inspiration* = **bright idea**, revelation; *informal* brainwave; *N. Amer. informal* brainstorm.

inspire ▸ verb **1** *the landscape inspired him to write* = **stimulate**, motivate, encourage, influence, rouse, move, stir, energize, galvanize, incite. **2** *the film inspired a musical* = **give rise to**, lead to, bring about, cause, prompt, spawn, engender; *literary* beget. **3** *Charles inspired awe in her* = **arouse**, awaken, prompt, induce, ignite, trigger, kindle, produce, bring out.

inspired ▸ adjective = **outstanding**, wonderful, marvellous, excellent, magnificent, exceptional, first-class, first-rate, virtuoso, superlative; *informal* tremendous, superb, ace, wicked, awesome, out of this world; *Brit. informal* brilliant. −OPPOSITES poor.

inspiring ▸ adjective = **inspirational**, encouraging, heartening, uplifting, stirring, rousing, electrifying; moving.

instability ▸ noun **1** *the instability of political life* = **unreliability**, uncertainty, unpredictability, insecurity, volatility, capriciousness; changeability, mutability. **2** *emotional instability* = **volatility**, unpredictability, variability, inconsistency; frailty, weakness. **3** *the instability of the foundations* = **unsteadiness**, unsoundness, shakiness, weakness, fragility. −OPPOSITES steadiness.

install ▸ verb **1** *a photocopier was installed in the office* = **put**, place, station, site; insert. **2** *they installed a new president* = **swear in**, induct, instate, inaugurate, invest; appoint, ordain, consecrate, anoint; enthrone, crown. **3** *she installed herself behind the table* = **ensconce**, position, settle, seat, plant; sit (down); *informal* plonk, park. −OPPOSITES remove.

installation ▸ noun **1** *the installation of radiators* = **installing**, fitting, putting in. **2** *the installation of the chancellor* = **swearing in**, induction, inauguration, investiture; ordination, consecration; enthronement, coronation. **3** *a new computer installation* = **unit**, system, set-up. **4** *an army installation* = **base**, camp, post, depot, centre, facility.

instalment ▸ noun = **part**, episode,

chapter, issue, programme, section, volume.

instance ▸ noun =**example**, occasion, occurrence, case; illustration.
■ **in the first instance** =initially, at first, at the start, at the outset, in/at the beginning, to begin with, to start with, originally.

instant ▸ adjective **1** *instant access to your money* =**immediate**, instantaneous, on-the-spot, prompt, swift, speedy, rapid, quick; *informal* snappy. **2** *instant meals* =**prepared**, pre-cooked; microwaveable, convenience.
–OPPOSITES delayed.
▸ noun **1** *come here this instant!* =**moment**, minute, second. **2** *it all happened in an instant* =**trice**, moment, minute, (split) second, twinkling of an eye, flash, no time (at all); *informal* jiffy, the blink of an eye.

instantaneous ▸ adjective =**immediate**, instant, on-the-spot, prompt, swift, speedy, quick.
–OPPOSITES delayed.

instantly ▸ adverb =**immediately**, at once, straight away, right away, instantaneously; forthwith, there and then, here and now, this/that minute, this/that instant.

instead ■ **instead of** =**as an alternative to**, as a substitute for, as a replacement for, in place of, in lieu of, in preference to; rather than.

instigate ▸ verb =**set in motion**, get under way, get off the ground, start, commence, begin, initiate, launch, institute, set up, inaugurate, establish, organize; *informal* kick off.
–OPPOSITES halt.

instigation ▸ noun =**prompting**, suggestion; request, entreaty, demand, insistence.

instigator ▸ noun =**initiator**, prime mover, architect, designer, planner, inventor, mastermind, originator, author, creator, agent; founder, founding father; ringleader.

instil ▸ verb =**inculcate**, implant, ingrain, impress; engender, produce, induce, foster; drum into.

instinct ▸ noun **1** *some instinct told me to be careful* =**inclination**, urge, drive, compulsion; intuition, feeling, sixth sense; nose. **2** *a good instinct for acting* =**talent**, gift, ability, aptitude, skill, flair, feel, knack.

instinctive ▸ adjective =**intuitive**, natural, instinctual, innate, inborn, inherent; unconscious, subconscious; automatic, reflex, knee-jerk; *informal* gut.
–OPPOSITES learned.

institute ▸ noun =**organization**, establishment, institution, foundation, centre; academy, school, college, university; society, association, federation, body, guild.
▸ verb =**initiate**, set in motion, get under way, get off the ground, start, commence, begin, launch; set up, inaugurate, found, establish, organize.
–OPPOSITES end.

institution ▸ noun **1** *an academic institution* =**establishment**, organization, institute, foundation, centre; academy, school, college, university; society, association, body, guild. **2** *they spent their lives in institutions* =(**residential**) **home**, hospital; asylum; prison. **3** *the institution of marriage* =**practice**, custom, convention, tradition; phenomenon. **4** *the institution of legal proceedings* =**initiation**, instigation, launch, start, commencement.

institutional ▸ adjective =**organized**, established, bureaucratic, conventional, procedural, set, formal, formalized, systematic, systematized, structured, regulated.

instruct ▸ verb **1** *the union instructed them to strike* =**order**, direct, command, tell, enjoin, call on, mandate, charge. **2** *nobody instructed him in how to operate it* =**teach**, school, coach, train, educate, tutor, guide, show. **3** *the bank was instructed that money would be withdrawn* =**inform**, tell, notify, apprise, advise.

instruction ▸ noun **1** *do not disobey my instructions* =**order**, command, directive, direction, decree, edict, injunction, mandate, dictate, commandment. **2** *read the instructions* =**directions**, key, specification; handbook, manual, guide; *informal* spec. **3** *he gave instruction in self defence* =**tuition**, teaching, coaching, schooling, tutelage; lessons, classes, lectures; training, drill, guidance.

instructive ▸ adjective =**informative**, instructional, illuminating, enlightening, explanatory; educational, educative, edifying; useful, helpful.

instructor ▸ noun =**trainer**, coach, teacher, tutor; adviser, counsellor, guide.

instrument ▸ noun **1** *a wound made with a sharp instrument* =**implement**, tool, utensil; device, apparatus, contrivance, gadget. **2** *check all the cockpit instruments* =**gauge**, meter; indicator, dial, display. **3** *an instrument of learning* =**agent**, agency, cause, channel, medium, means, vehicle. **4** *a mere instrument acting under coercion* =**pawn**, puppet, creature, dupe, cog; tool; *informal* stooge.

instrumental ■ **be instrumental in** =**play a part in**, contribute to, be a factor in, have a hand in; add to, promote, advance, further.

insubordinate ▸ adjective =**disobedient**, unruly, wayward, errant, badly behaved, disorderly, undisciplined, delinquent, troublesome, rebellious, defiant; *Brit. informal* bolshie.
−OPPOSITES obedient.

insubordination ▸ noun =**disobedience**, unruliness, indiscipline, bad behaviour, misbehaviour, misconduct; rebellion, defiance, mutiny, revolt.

insubstantial ▸ adjective **1** *an insubstantial structure* =**flimsy**, slight, fragile, breakable, weak, frail, unstable, shaky, wobbly, rickety, ramshackle, jerry-built. **2** *insubstantial evidence* =**weak**, flimsy, feeble, poor, inadequate, insufficient, tenuous, inconsequential, unconvincing, implausible, unsatisfactory.
−OPPOSITES sturdy, sound, tangible.

insufferable ▸ adjective **1** *the heat was insufferable* =**intolerable**, unbearable, unendurable, oppressive, overwhelming, overpowering; more than flesh and blood can stand; *informal* too much. **2** *his win made him insufferable* =**conceited**, arrogant, boastful, cocky, cocksure, full of oneself, swollen-headed, self-important; vain, self-satisfied, self-congratulatory, smug; *informal* big-headed, too big for one's boots.
−OPPOSITES bearable, modest.

insufficient ▸ adjective =**inadequate**, deficient, poor, scant, scanty; not enough, too little, too few, too small; limited.

insular ▸ adjective **1** *insular people* =**narrow-minded**, blinkered, inward-looking, parochial. **2** *an insular existence* =**isolated**, cut off, segregated, detached, solitary, lonely.
−OPPOSITES broad-minded, cosmopolitan.

insulate ▸ verb **1** *pipes must be insulated*
=**wrap**, sheathe, cover, encase, enclose; lag, heatproof, soundproof. **2** *they were insulated from the impact of the war* =**protect**, save, shield, shelter, screen, cushion, cocoon.

insulation ▸ noun **1** *a layer of insulation* =**lagging**; protection, padding. **2** *insulation from the rigours of city life* =**protection**, defence, shelter; separation.

insult ▸ verb =**abuse**, be rude to, call someone names, slight, disparage, discredit, libel, slander, malign, defame, denigrate, cast aspersions on; offend, hurt, humiliate; *informal* bad-mouth; *Brit. informal* slag off.
−OPPOSITES compliment.
▸ noun =**jibe**, affront, slight, slur, indignity; abuse, aspersions; *informal* dig, put-down.

insulting ▸ adjective =**abusive**, rude, offensive, disparaging, belittling, derogatory, deprecating, disrespectful, uncomplimentary, pejorative; defamatory, slanderous, libellous, scurrilous, blasphemous; *informal* bitchy, catty.

insuperable ▸ adjective =**insurmountable**, invincible, unassailable; overwhelming.

insurance ▸ noun =**indemnity**, assurance, (financial) protection, security, cover.

insure ▸ verb =**provide insurance for**, indemnify, cover, assure, protect, underwrite.

insurgent ▸ adjective =**rebellious**, rebel, mutinous, insurrectionist; renegade, seditious, subversive.
−OPPOSITES loyal.
▸ noun =**rebel**, revolutionary, mutineer, insurrectionist, agitator, subversive, renegade; guerrilla, terrorist.
−OPPOSITES loyalist.

insurmountable ▸ adjective =**insuperable**, unconquerable, invincible, unassailable; overwhelming, hopeless, impossible.

insurrection ▸ noun =**rebellion**, revolt, uprising, mutiny, revolution, insurgence, sedition; civil disorder, unrest, anarchy.

intact ▸ adjective =**whole**, entire, complete, unbroken, undamaged, unscathed, untouched, unspoiled, unblemished, unmarked; undefiled, unsullied; in one piece.
−OPPOSITES damaged.

intangible ▶ adjective =**indefinable**, indescribable, inexpressible, nameless; vague, obscure, unclear, indefinite, subtle, elusive.

integral ▶ adjective 1 *an integral part of human behaviour* =**essential**, fundamental, basic, intrinsic, inherent; vital, necessary. 2 *the dryer has an integral heat sensor* =**built-in**, inbuilt, integrated, inboard, fitted. 3 *an integral approach to learning* =**unified**, integrated, comprehensive, holistic, all-embracing.
–OPPOSITES peripheral, fragmented.

integrate ▶ verb =**combine**, amalgamate, merge, unite, fuse, blend, consolidate, meld, mix; incorporate, unify, assimilate, homogenize; desegregate.
–OPPOSITES separate.

integrated ▶ adjective 1 *an integrated package of services* =**unified**, united, consolidated, amalgamated, combined, homogeneous, assimilated, cohesive. 2 *an integrated school* =**desegregated**, unsegregated, mixed; multi-faith, multiracial.

integrity ▶ noun 1 *I never doubted his integrity* =**honesty**, probity, rectitude, honour, sincerity, truthfulness, trustworthiness. 2 *the integrity of the federation* =**unity**, coherence, cohesion; solidity. 3 *the structural integrity of the aircraft* =**soundness**, strength, sturdiness, solidity, durability, stability, rigidity.
–OPPOSITES dishonesty, division, fragility.

intellect ▶ noun 1 *a film that appeals to the intellect* =**mind**, brain(s), intelligence, reason, judgement; grey matter, brain cells. 2 *one of the finest intellects* =**thinker**, intellectual; mind, brain.

intellectual ▶ adjective 1 *his intellectual capacity* =**mental**; rational, conceptual, theoretical, analytical, logical. 2 *an intellectual man* =**cerebral**, academic, erudite, bookish, highbrow, scholarly.
–OPPOSITES physical.

intelligence ▶ noun 1 *a man of great intelligence* =**cleverness**, intellect, brainpower, judgement, reasoning; acumen, wit, insight, perception, smartness. 2 *intelligence from our agents* =**information**, facts, details, particulars, data, knowledge, material; *informal* info, gen, dope.

intelligent ▶ adjective 1 *an intelligent woman* =**clever**, bright, quick-witted, smart, astute, insightful, perceptive; *informal* brainy. 2 *intelligent life* =**rational**, reasoning, thinking. 3 *intelligent machines* =**self-regulating**, capable of learning, smart.

intelligible ▶ adjective =**comprehensible**, understandable; accessible, digestible, user-friendly; lucid, clear, coherent, plain, unambiguous.

intemperance ▶ noun =**over-indulgence**, immoderation, excess, extravagance; overindulgence, gratification.

intemperate ▶ adjective =**immoderate**, excessive, uncontrolled; overindulgent, extravagant, unrestrained, prodigal, profligate.
–OPPOSITES moderate.

intend ▶ verb =**plan**, mean, have in mind, aim, propose; hope, expect, envisage.

intended ▶ adjective =**deliberate**, intentional, calculated, conscious, planned, knowing, wilful, wanton, done on purpose, premeditated, pre-planned; *Law* aforethought.
–OPPOSITES accidental.

intense ▶ adjective 1 *intense heat* =**extreme**, great, acute, fierce, severe, high; exceptional, extraordinary; harsh, strong, powerful; *informal* serious. 2 *a very intense young man* =**passionate**, impassioned, zealous, vehement; earnest, eager, committed.
–OPPOSITES mild, apathetic.

intensify ▶ verb =**escalate**, increase, step up, raise, strengthen, reinforce; pick up, build up, heighten, deepen, extend, expand, amplify, magnify; aggravate, exacerbate, worsen, inflame, compound.
–OPPOSITES abate.

intensity ▶ noun 1 *the intensity of the sun* =**strength**, power, force; severity, ferocity, vehemence, fierceness, harshness. 2 *his eyes had a glowing intensity* =**passion**, ardour, fervour, vehemence, fire, emotion; eagerness, animation.

intensive ▶ adjective =**thorough**, thoroughgoing, in-depth, rigorous, exhaustive; vigorous, detailed, minute, close, meticulous, scrupulous, painstaking, methodical; extensive.
–OPPOSITES cursory.

intent ▶ noun *he tried to divine his father's intent* =**aim**, intention, purpose, objective, object, goal, target.
▶ adjective 1 *he was intent on proving his point* =**bent**, set, determined, insistent, re-

solved, hell-bent, keen; committed to; determined to. **2** *an intent expression* = **attentive**, absorbed, engrossed, fascinated, enthralled, rapt; focused, studious, preoccupied.

■ **to all intents and purposes** = in effect, effectively, in essence, essentially, virtually, practically; more or less, just about, all but, as good as, in all but name, as near as dammit; almost, nearly; *informal* pretty much, pretty well; *literary* nigh on.

intention ▶ noun = aim, purpose, intent, objective, object, goal, target.

intentional ▶ adjective = deliberate, calculated, conscious, intended, planned, meant, knowing, wilful, purposeful, premeditated, done on purpose, pre-planned, preconceived; *Law* aforethought.

intently ▶ adverb = attentively, closely, keenly, earnestly, hard, carefully, fixedly.

inter ▶ verb = bury, lay to rest, entomb; *literary* inhume.
– OPPOSITES exhume.

intercede ▶ verb = mediate, arbitrate, conciliate, negotiate, moderate.

intercept ▶ verb = stop, head off, cut off; catch, seize, grab, snatch; block.

intercession ▶ noun = mediation, arbitration, conciliation, negotiation.

interchange ▶ verb **1** *they interchange ideas* = exchange, trade, swap, barter, bandy. **2** *the terms are often interchanged* = substitute, transpose, exchange, switch, swap (round), change (round).
▶ noun **1** *the interchange of ideas* = exchange, trade, swapping, give and take, traffic. **2** *a motorway interchange* = junction, intersection; *N. Amer.* cloverleaf.

interchangeable ▶ adjective = identical, indistinguishable, the same; *informal* much of a muchness.

intercourse ▶ noun **1** *social intercourse* = dealings, relations, relationships, association, contact; interchange, communication, communion. **2** *she did not consent to intercourse* = sexual intercourse, sex, sexual relations, intimacy, coupling, copulation; *informal* nooky; *Brit. informal* bonking, rumpy pumpy, how's your father; *technical* coitus; *formal* fornication; *dated* carnal knowledge.

interdict ▶ noun = prohibition, ban,

bar, veto, embargo, moratorium, injunction.
– OPPOSITES permission.

interest ▶ noun **1** *we listened with interest* = attentiveness, attention; regard, notice; curiosity; enjoyment, delight. **2** *places of interest* = attraction, appeal, fascination, charm, beauty, allure. **3** *this will be of interest to those involved* = concern, consequence, importance, import, significance, note, relevance, value. **4** *her interests include reading* = hobby, pastime, leisure pursuit, recreation, diversion; passion, love, obsession; *informal* thing, bag, cup of tea. **5** *a financial interest in the firm* = stake, share, claim, investment; involvement, concern. **6** *his attorney guarded his interests* = concern, business, affair. **7** *her savings earned interest* = dividends, profits, returns; a percentage.
– OPPOSITES boredom.
▶ verb *a topic that interests you* = appeal to, be of interest to, attract, intrigue; amuse, divert, entertain; arouse one's curiosity, whet one's appetite; *informal* tickle someone's fancy.
– OPPOSITES put off.

interested ▶ adjective **1** *an interested crowd* = attentive, fascinated, riveted, gripped, captivated, agog; intrigued, curious; keen, eager; *informal* all ears. **2** *the government consulted with interested bodies* = concerned, involved, affected.

interesting ▶ adjective = absorbing, engrossing, fascinating, riveting, gripping, compelling, captivating, engaging, enthralling; appealing; amusing, entertaining, stimulating, thought-provoking, diverting, intriguing.

interfere ▶ verb **1** *don't let emotion interfere with duty* = impede, obstruct, stand in the way of, hinder, inhibit, restrict, constrain, hamper, handicap; disturb, disrupt, influence, affect, confuse. **2** *she tried not to interfere* = butt in, barge in, intrude, encroach; *informal* poke one's nose in, stick one's oar in. **3** *(Brit. euphemistic) he interfered with local children* = (sexually) abuse, (sexually) assault, indecently assault, molest, grope; *informal* feel up, touch up.

interference ▶ noun **1** *they resent state interference* = intrusion, intervention, involvement; meddling, prying. **2** *radio interference* = disruption, disturbance, static, noise.

interfering ▸ adjective =**meddlesome**, meddling, intrusive, prying; *informal* nosy-parker.

interim ▸ adjective =**provisional**, temporary, pro tem, stopgap, short-term, caretaker, acting, intervening, transitional.
–OPPOSITES permanent.

interior ▸ adjective **1** *the house has interior panelling* =**inside**, inner, internal. **2** *the interior deserts of the US* =**inland**, upcountry, inner, innermost, central. **3** *the country's interior affairs* =**internal**, home, domestic, national, state, civil, local. **4** *an interior monologue* =**inner**, mental, spiritual, psychological; private, personal, secret.
–OPPOSITES exterior, outer, foreign.
▸ noun **1** *the interior of the castle* =**inside**, depths, recesses, bowels, belly; heart. **2** *the country's interior* =**centre**, heartland.
–OPPOSITES exterior, outside.

interject ▸ verb **1** *she interjected a comment* =**interpose**, introduce, throw in, add. **2** *he interjected before anyone could say anything* =**interrupt**, intervene, cut in, butt in, chime in; *Brit. informal* chip in; *N. Amer. informal* put in one's two cents.

interjection ▸ noun =**exclamation**; cry, shout, vociferation, utterance; *dated* ejaculation.

interlock ▸ verb =**interconnect**, interlink, engage, mesh, join, unite, connect, couple.

interloper ▸ noun =**intruder**, trespasser, invader, infiltrator; uninvited guest; *informal* gatecrasher.

interlude ▸ noun =**interval**, intermission, break, recess, pause, rest, breathing space, gap, hiatus, lull; *informal* breather, let-up, time out.

intermediary ▸ noun =**mediator**, go-between, negotiator, arbitrator, peacemaker; middleman, broker.

intermediate ▸ adjective =**halfway**, in-between, middle, mid, midway, intervening, transitional.

interment ▸ noun =**burial**, burying, committal, entombment, inhumation; funeral.

interminable ▸ adjective =**(seemingly) endless**, never-ending, unending, ceaseless, unceasing, incessant, constant, continual.

intermingle ▸ verb =**mix**, intermix, mingle, blend, fuse, merge, combine, amalgamate; associate, fraternize; *literary* commingle.

intermission ▸ noun =**interval**, interlude, break, recess, time out.

intermittent ▸ adjective =**sporadic**, irregular, fitful, spasmodic, discontinuous, isolated, random, patchy, scattered; occasional, periodic.
–OPPOSITES continuous.

intern ▸ verb *they were interned without trial* =**imprison**, incarcerate, impound, jail, put behind bars, detain, hold (captive), lock up, confine; *Brit. informal* bang up.
▸ noun *an intern at a local firm* =**trainee**, apprentice, probationer, student.

internal ▸ adjective **1** *an internal courtyard* =**inner**, interior, inside; central. **2** *the state's internal affairs* =**domestic**, home, interior, civil, local; national, state. **3** *an internal struggle* =**mental**, psychological, emotional; personal, private, inner.
–OPPOSITES external, foreign.

international ▸ adjective =**global**, worldwide, intercontinental, universal; cosmopolitan, multiracial, multinational.
–OPPOSITES national, local.

interplay ▸ noun =**interaction**, interchange; reciprocity, give and take.

interpolate ▸ verb =**insert**, interpose, enter, add, incorporate, introduce.

interpret ▸ verb **1** *the rabbis interpret the Jewish law* =**explain**, elucidate, expound, clarify. **2** *the remark was interpreted as an invitation* =**understand**, construe, take (to mean), see, regard. **3** *the symbols are difficult to interpret* =**decipher**, decode, translate; understand.

interpretation ▸ noun **1** *the interpretation of the Bible's teachings* =**explanation**, elucidation, exposition, exegesis, clarification. **2** *she did not care what interpretation he put on her haste* =**meaning**, understanding, explanation, inference. **3** *the interpretation of experimental findings* =**analysis**, evaluation. **4** *his interpretation of Mozart* =**rendition**, execution, presentation, performance, reading, playing, singing.

interrogate ▸ verb =**question**, cross-examine, quiz; interview, examine, debrief, give someone the third degree; *informal* pump, grill.

interrupt ▸ verb **1** *she opened her mouth to interrupt* =**cut in (on)**, break in (on), barge in (on); *N. Amer.* put one's two cents in; *informal* butt in (on), chime in (on); *Brit. informal* chip in (on). **2** *the band had to interrupt their tour* =**suspend**, adjourn, break off; stop, halt; *informal* put on ice. **3** *their view was interrupted by houses* =**obstruct**, impede, block, restrict.

interruption ▸ noun **1** *he was not pleased at her interruption* =**cutting in**, barging in, intervention, intrusion; *informal* butting in. **2** *an interruption of the power supply* =**suspension**, breaking off, cutting.

intersection ▸ noun **1** *the intersection of the two curves* =**crossing**, meeting. **2** *the driver stopped at an intersection* =**(road) junction**, T-junction, interchange, crossroads; *Brit.* roundabout.

intersperse ▸ verb **1** *alpine plants were interspersed among the rocks* =**scatter**, spread, arrange, dot. **2** *the beech trees are interspersed with conifers* =**mix**, alternate, punctuate.

intertwine ▸ verb =**entwine**, interweave, interlace, twist, coil.

interval ▸ noun =**intermission**, interlude, break, recess, time out.

intervene ▸ verb =**intercede**, involve oneself, get involved, step in; interfere, intrude.

intervention ▸ noun =**involvement**, intercession; interference, intrusion.

interview ▸ noun *all applicants will be called for an interview* =**meeting**, discussion; interrogation, cross-examination, debriefing; audience, talk, chat; *informal* grilling.
▸ verb *we interviewed seventy subjects for the survey* =**talk to**, question, interrogate, cross-examine, debrief; poll, canvass, sound out; *informal* grill, pump; *Law* examine.

interviewer ▸ noun =**questioner**, interrogator, examiner, assessor; journalist, reporter; inquisitor.

interweave ▸ verb **1** *the threads are interwoven* =**intertwine**, interlace, splice, braid, plait; twist together, weave together, wind together. **2** *their fates were interwoven* =**interlink**, link, connect; intertwine.

intestines ▸ plural noun =**gut**, guts, entrails, viscera; small intestine, large intestine; *informal* insides, innards.

━━━━━━━━━━━━━━━━━━━━
WORD LINKS

relating to the intestines: **enteric, entero-, visceral**
incision into the intestine: **enterotomy**
inflammation of the intestines: **enteritis**
━━━━━━━━━━━━━━━━━━━━

intimacy ▸ noun =**closeness**, togetherness, rapport, attachment, familiarity, friendliness, affection, warmth.

intimate[1] ▸ adjective **1** *an intimate friend* =**close**, bosom, dear, cherished, fast, firm. **2** *an intimate atmosphere* =**friendly**, warm, welcoming, hospitable, relaxed, informal; cosy, comfortable. **3** *intimate thoughts* =**personal**, private, confidential, secret; inward. **4** *an intimate knowledge* =**detailed**, thorough, exhaustive, deep, in-depth, profound. **5** *intimate relations* =**sexual**, carnal, amorous, amatory.
–OPPOSITES distant, formal.

intimate[2] ▸ verb **1** *he intimated his decision* =**announce**, state, proclaim, make known, make public, disclose, reveal, divulge. **2** *her feelings were subtly intimated* =**imply**, suggest, hint at, indicate.

intimation ▸ noun =**suggestion**, hint, indication, sign, signal, inkling, suspicion, impression.

intimidate ▸ verb =**frighten**, menace, scare, terrorize; threaten, browbeat, bully, harass, harry, hound; *informal* lean on.

intolerable ▸ adjective =**unbearable**, insufferable, insupportable, unendurable, more than flesh and blood can stand, too much to bear.
–OPPOSITES bearable.

intolerant ▸ adjective **1** *intolerant in religious matters* =**bigoted**, narrowminded, illiberal; prejudiced. **2** *foods to which you are intolerant* =**allergic**, sensitive, hypersensitive.

intonation ▸ noun **1** *she read the sentence with the wrong intonation* =**inflection**, pitch, tone, cadence, lilt, modulation. **2** *the intonation of hymns* =**chanting**, recitation, singing.

intone ▸ verb =**chant**, sing, recite.

intoxicate ▸ verb **1** *one glass of wine intoxicated him* =**inebriate**, make drunk, befuddle, go to someone's head. **2** *he was intoxicated by cinema* =**exhilarate**, thrill, elate, delight, captivate, enthral, entrance, enrapture.

intoxicated ▸ adjective. *See* DRUNK.

intoxicating ▸ adjective **1** *intoxicating drink* =**alcoholic**, strong, hard. **2** *an intoxicating sense of freedom* =**heady**, exhilarating, thrilling, stirring, stimulating, invigorating, electrifying; powerful, potent; *informal* mind-blowing.
–OPPOSITES non-alcoholic.

intoxication ▸ noun. See DRUNKENNESS.

intractable ▸ adjective **1** *intractable problems* =**unmanageable**, uncontrollable, insurmountable. **2** *an intractable man* =**stubborn**, obstinate, obdurate, inflexible, unbending, unyielding, uncompromising, unaccommodating, difficult, awkward, pig-headed.
–OPPOSITES manageable, compliant.

intransigent ▸ adjective =**uncompromising**, inflexible, unbending, unyielding, unwavering, stubborn, obstinate, pig-headed.
–OPPOSITES compliant.

intrenched ▸ adjective. See ENTRENCHED.

intrepid ▸ adjective =**fearless**, unflinching, bold, daring, heroic, dynamic, indomitable; brave, valiant, doughty.
–OPPOSITES fearful.

intricate ▸ adjective =**complex**, complicated, convoluted, tangled; elaborate, ornate, detailed.

intrigue ▸ verb *her answer intrigued him* =**interest**, fascinate, arouse someone's curiosity, attract; engage.
▸ noun *the intrigue that accompanied the selection of a new leader* =**plotting**, conniving, scheming, machination, double-dealing, subterfuge.

intriguing ▸ adjective =**interesting**, fascinating, absorbing, engaging.

intrinsic ▸ adjective =**inherent**, innate, inborn, inbred, congenital, natural; integral, basic, fundamental, essential.

introduce ▸ verb **1** *he has introduced a new system* =**institute**, initiate, launch, inaugurate, establish, found; bring in, set in motion, start, begin, get going. **2** *she introduced Lindsey to the young man* =**present (formally)**, make known, acquaint with. **3** *introducing nitrogen into canned beer* =**insert**, inject, put, force, shoot, feed. **4** *she introduced a note of seriousness* =**instil**, infuse, inject, add. **5** *the same presenter introduces the programme each week* =**announce**, present; host; open.

introduction ▸ noun **1** *the introduction of democratic reforms* =**institution**, establishment, initiation, launch, inauguration, foundation; pioneering. **2** *an introduction to the king* =(**formal**) **presentation**; meeting, audience. **3** *the introduction to the catalogue* =**foreword**, preface, preamble, prologue, prelude; *informal* intro. **4** *an introduction to the history of the period* =**basic explanation/account**, way in, overview; the basics, the rudiments, the fundamentals.
–OPPOSITES afterword.

introductory ▸ adjective **1** *the introductory chapter* =**opening**, initial, starting, initiatory, first, preliminary. **2** *an introductory course* =**elementary**, basic, rudimentary, entry-level.
–OPPOSITES final, advanced.

introspection ▸ noun =**self-analysis**, soul-searching, introversion; contemplation, reflection; *informal* navel-gazing.

introspective ▸ adjective =**inward-looking**, self-analysing, introverted, introvert; contemplative, thoughtful, reflective; *informal* navel-gazing.

introverted ▸ adjective =**shy**, reserved, withdrawn, reticent, diffident, retiring, quiet; introspective, introvert, inward-looking; pensive.
–OPPOSITES extroverted.

intrude ▸ verb =**encroach**, impinge, trespass, infringe; invade, violate, disturb, disrupt.

intruder ▸ noun =**trespasser**, interloper, invader, infiltrator; burglar, housebreaker.

intrusion ▸ noun =**encroachment**; invasion, incursion, intervention, disruption, impingement.

intrusive ▸ adjective **1** *an intrusive journalist* =**intruding**, invasive, inquisitive, prying; *informal* nosy. **2** *intrusive questions* =**personal**, prying, impertinent.

intuition ▸ noun **1** *he works by intuition* =**instinct**, feeling; spirit, soul. **2** *this confirms an intuition I had* =**hunch**, feeling (in one's bones), inkling, (sneaking) suspicion; premonition; *informal* gut feeling.

intuitive ▸ adjective =**instinctive**, innate, inborn, inherent, natural; unconscious, subconscious; *informal* gut.

inundate ▸ verb **1** *many buildings were inundated* =**flood**, deluge, swamp, submerge, engulf. **2** *we have been inundated* by complaints =**overwhelm**, overrun, overload, swamp, besiege, snow under.

inure ▸ verb =**harden**, toughen, desensitize, condition; accustom, habituate.
−OPPOSITES sensitize.

invade ▸ verb **1** the island was invaded =**occupy**, conquer, capture, seize, take (over), annex, overrun, storm. **2** someone had invaded our privacy =**intrude on**, violate, encroach on, infringe on, trespass on, disturb, disrupt. **3** the feeling of betrayal invaded my being =**permeate**, pervade, fill, overtake.
−OPPOSITES withdraw.

invader ▸ noun =**attacker**, raider, marauder; occupier, conqueror; intruder.

invalid[1] ▸ adjective her invalid husband =**ill**, sick, ailing, unwell, infirm; incapacitated, bedridden, frail, sickly, poorly.
−OPPOSITES healthy.
▸ verb an officer invalided by a chest wound =**disable**, incapacitate, hospitalize, put out of action, lay up.

invalid[2] ▸ adjective **1** the law was invalid =**(legally) void**, null and void, not binding, illegitimate, inapplicable. **2** the whole theory is invalid =**false**, fallacious, spurious, unsound, wrong; untenable.
−OPPOSITES binding, true.

invalidate ▸ verb **1** a low turnout invalidated the ballot =**render invalid**, void, nullify, annul, negate, cancel, overturn, overrule. **2** this invalidates your argument =**disprove**, refute, explode, negate; undermine.

invaluable ▸ adjective =**indispensable**, crucial, key, vital, irreplaceable, all-important.
−OPPOSITES dispensable.

invariable ▸ adjective =**unvarying**, unchanging, unvaried; constant, stable, set, steady; unchangeable, unalterable.
−OPPOSITES varied.

invariably ▸ adverb =**always**, at all times, without fail, without exception; consistently, habitually, unfailingly.
−OPPOSITES sometimes, never.

invasion ▸ noun **1** the invasion of the islands =**occupation**, conquering, capture, seizure, annexation, takeover. **2** an invasion of my privacy =**violation**, infringement, interruption, encroachment, disturbance, disruption, breach.
−OPPOSITES withdrawal.

invective ▸ noun =**abuse**, insults, expletives, swear words, swearing, curses,

bad/foul language.
−OPPOSITES praise.

inveigle ▸ verb =**cajole**, wheedle, coax, persuade, talk; informal sweet-talk, soft-soap, con; N. Amer. informal sucker.

invent ▸ verb **1** Louis Braille invented an alphabet to help blind people =**originate**, create, design, devise, contrive, develop. **2** they invented the story for a laugh =**make up**, fabricate, concoct, hatch, dream up; informal cook up.

invention ▸ noun **1** the invention of the telescope =**origination**, creation, development, design. **2** medieval inventions =**innovation**, creation, contraption, contrivance, device, gadget. **3** a journalistic invention =**fabrication**, concoction, (piece of) fiction, story, tale; lie, untruth, falsehood, fib.

inventive ▸ adjective **1** the most inventive composer of his time =**creative**, original, innovative, imaginative, resourceful. **2** a fresh, inventive comedy =**original**, innovative, unusual, fresh, novel, new; groundbreaking, unorthodox, unconventional.
−OPPOSITES unimaginative, hackneyed.

inventor ▸ noun =**originator**, creator; designer, deviser, developer, maker, producer; author, architect; father.

inventory ▸ noun =**list**, listing, catalogue, record, register, checklist, log, archive.

inverse ▸ adjective =**reverse**, reversed, inverted, opposite, converse, contrary, counter, antithetical.

inversion ▸ noun =**reversal**, transposition, turning upside down; reverse, antithesis, converse.

invert ▸ verb =**turn upside down**, upturn, upend, flip/turn (over).

invest ▸ verb **1** he invested in a steel mill =**put/plough money into**, fund, back, finance, underwrite. **2** they invested £18 million =**spend**, expend, put in, plough in; informal lay out. **3** the powers invested in the bishop =**vest in**, confer on, bestow on, grant to. **4** bishops whom the king had invested =**instate**, install, induct, swear in; ordain, crown.

investigate ▸ verb =**enquire into**, look into, go into, probe, explore, scrutinize; analyse, study, examine; informal check out, suss out; N. Amer. informal scope out.

investigation ▶ noun =examination, inquiry, study, inspection, exploration, analysis; research, scrutiny; probe, review.

investigator ▶ noun =inspector, examiner, analyst; researcher, factfinder, scrutineer; detective.

investiture ▶ noun =inauguration, appointment, installation, initiation, swearing in; ordination, consecration, crowning.

investment ▶ noun 1 *it's a good investment* =**venture**, proposition. 2 *an investment of £305,000* =**stake**, payment, outlay. 3 *a substantial investment of time* =**sacrifice**, commitment, input.

inveterate ▶ adjective 1 *an inveterate gambler* =**confirmed**, hardened, incorrigible, addicted, compulsive, obsessive; *informal* pathological, chronic. 2 *an inveterate Democrat* =**staunch**, steadfast, committed, devoted, dedicated, dyed-in-the-wool, diehard.

invidious ▶ adjective 1 *that put her in an invidious position* =**unpleasant**, awkward, difficult; undesirable, unenviable. 2 *an invidious comparison* =**unfair**, unjust, unwarranted.
–OPPOSITES pleasant, fair.

invigorate ▶ verb =revitalize, energize, refresh, revive, enliven, liven up, perk up, wake up, animate, galvanize, fortify, rouse, exhilarate; *informal* buck up, pep up.
–OPPOSITES tire.

invincible ▶ adjective =invulnerable, indestructible, unconquerable, unbeatable, indomitable, unassailable; impregnable.
–OPPOSITES vulnerable.

inviolable ▶ adjective =inalienable, absolute, unalterable, unchallengeable; sacrosanct, sacred.

inviolate ▶ adjective =untouched, undamaged, unharmed, unscathed; unspoiled, unsullied, unstained, undefiled; intact.

invisible ▶ adjective =not visible; undetectable; inconspicuous, imperceptible; unseen, unnoticed, unobserved, hidden, out of sight.

invitation ▶ noun 1 *an invitation to dinner* =**call**, summons; *informal* invite. 2 *an open door is an invitation to a thief* =**encouragement**, magnet, enticement; *informal* come-on.

invite ▶ verb 1 *they invited us to lunch* =**ask**, summon, have someone over/round. 2 *applications are invited for the post* =**ask for**, request, call for, appeal for, solicit, seek. 3 *airing such views invites trouble* =**cause**, induce, provoke, ask for, encourage, lead to; bring on oneself, arouse.

inviting ▶ adjective =tempting, enticing, alluring, beguiling; attractive, appealing; appetizing, mouth-watering; intriguing, seductive.
–OPPOSITES repellent.

invoice ▶ noun *an invoice for the goods* =**bill**, account, statement (of charges); *N. Amer.* check; *informal* tab.
▶ verb *we'll invoice you for the damage* =**bill**, charge.

invoke ▶ verb 1 *he invoked his statutory rights* =**cite**, refer to; resort to, have recourse to, turn to. 2 *I invoked the Madonna* =**pray to**, call on, appeal to. 3 *middle-class morality invokes many anxieties* =**bring forth**, bring out, elicit, conjure up, generate.

involuntary ▶ adjective 1 *an involuntary shudder* =**reflex**, automatic; instinctive, unintentional, uncontrollable. 2 *involuntary repatriation* =**compulsory**, obligatory, mandatory, forced, prescribed.
–OPPOSITES deliberate, optional.

involve ▶ verb 1 *the inspection involved a lot of work* =**require**, necessitate, demand, call for; entail. 2 *I try to involve everyone in key decisions* =**include**, bring in, consult.
–OPPOSITES preclude, exclude.

involved ▶ adjective 1 *social workers involved in the case* =**associated**, connected, concerned. 2 *he had been involved in burglaries* =**implicated**, caught up, mixed up. 3 *a long and involved story* =**complicated**, intricate, complex; convoluted. 4 *they were totally involved in their work* =**engrossed**, absorbed, immersed, caught up, preoccupied, intent.
–OPPOSITES unconnected, straightforward.

involvement ▶ noun 1 *his involvement in the plot* =**participation**; collaboration, collusion, complicity; association, connection, entanglement. 2 *emotional involvement* =**attachment**, friendship, intimacy; commitment.

invulnerable ▶ adjective =impervious, immune; indestructible, impregnable, unassailable, invincible, secure.

inward ▸ adverb *the door opened inward.*
See INWARDS.

inwardly ▸ adverb =(on the) inside, internally, within, deep down (inside), in
one's heart (of hearts).

inwards ▸ adverb =inside, into the interior, inward, within.

iota ▸ noun =(little) bit, mite, speck,
scrap, shred, ounce, jot.

irascible ▸ adjective =irritable, quick-
tempered, short-tempered, snappy,
tetchy, touchy, crabby, waspish;
grouchy, cantankerous, curmudgeonly,
peevish, querulous, fractious; *informal*
prickly, ratty.

irate ▸ adjective =angry, furious, infuriated, enraged, fuming, seething; raging,
outraged, up in arms; indignant, irritated; *literary* wrathful.

iridescent ▸ adjective =shimmering,
shining, gleaming, glowing, lustrous,
opalescent.

irk ▸ verb =irritate, annoy, pique, nettle,
vex; anger; peeve, miff, needle, get (to),
bug, hack off; *Brit. informal* get on someone's wick; *N. Amer. informal* tee off.
−OPPOSITES please.

irksome ▸ adjective =irritating, annoying, vexing, galling; tiresome, trying, difficult.

iron ▸ noun **1** *a ship built of iron* =metal,
pig iron, cast iron, wrought iron; steel;
rust. **2** *she needed some iron in her soul*
=strength, toughness, resilience, steel;
stone. **3** *leg irons* =manacles, shackles,
fetters, chains, handcuffs; *informal* cuffs.
▸ adjective **1** *an iron bar* =made of iron, fer-
ric, ferrous; steel. **2** *an iron law of politics*
=inflexible, unbreakable, absolute, incontrovertible, immutable. **3** *an iron will*
=uncompromising, unrelenting, unyielding, unbending, rigid, unwavering;
steely.
−OPPOSITES flexible.

■ **iron something out 1** *John had ironed
out all the minor snags* =resolve,
straighten out, sort out, clear up, put
right, solve, rectify; *informal* fix. **2** *ironing
out differences in national systems* =elimin-
ate, eradicate; reconcile; resolve.

> WORD LINKS
>
> *containing iron:* **ferro-**

ironic ▸ adjective **1** *Edward's tone was
ironic* =sarcastic, sardonic, dry, caustic,

scathing, acerbic, bitter, trenchant;
mocking, derisive, scornful; *Brit. informal*
sarky. **2** *it's ironic that I've ended up writing*
=paradoxical, funny, strange; typical.
−OPPOSITES sincere.

irony ▸ noun **1** *that note of irony in her voice*
=sarcasm, bitterness; mockery, ridi-
cule, derision, scorn; *Brit. informal* sarki-
ness. **2** *the irony of the situation* =paradox.
−OPPOSITES sincerity.

irrational ▸ adjective =unreasonable,
illogical; groundless, baseless, unfounded, unjustifiable.
−OPPOSITES logical.

irreconcilable ▸ adjective =incom-
patible, at odds, at variance, conflicting, antagonistic, mutually exclusive,
diametrically opposed; poles apart.
−OPPOSITES compatible.

irrecoverable ▸ adjective
=unrecoverable, unreclaimable, irretrievable, irredeemable, unsalvageable,
gone for ever.

irrefutable ▸ adjective =indisput-
able, undeniable, unquestionable, incontrovertible, incontestable, beyond
question, beyond doubt; conclusive,
definite, definitive, decisive.

irregular ▸ adjective **1** *irregular features
| an irregular coastline* =asymmetrical,
uneven, crooked, misshapen, lopsided,
twisted. **2** *irregular surfaces* =rough,
bumpy, uneven, pitted, rutted; lumpy,
knobbly, gnarled. **3** *an irregular heart-
beat* =inconsistent, unsteady, uneven,
fitful, patchy, variable, varying, changeable, inconstant, erratic, unstable, unsettled, spasmodic, intermittent. **4** *irregular financial dealings* =improper,
illegitimate, unethical, unprofessional;
informal shady, dodgy. **5** *an irregular army*
=guerrilla, underground; paramilitary;
partisan, mercenary, terrorist.
−OPPOSITES straight, smooth.
▸ noun *gun-toting irregulars* =guerrilla;
paramilitary; resistance fighter, partisan, mercenary, terrorist.

irregularity ▸ noun **1** *the irregularity of
the coastline* =asymmetry, non-uniformity, unevenness, crookedness, lopsided-
ness. **2** *the irregularity of the surface*
=roughness, bumpiness, unevenness.
3 *irregularities in the concrete* =bump,
lump, bulge, hump, protuberance,
kink; hole, hollow, pit, crater; crack,
chink, fissure. **4** *the irregularity of the bus
service* =inconsistency, unevenness, fit-

fulness, patchiness, inconstancy, variability, changeableness, unpredictability, unreliability. **5** *financial irregularities* =**impropriety**, wrongdoing, misconduct, dishonesty.

irregularly ▸ adverb =**erratically**, intermittently, in/by fits and starts, fitfully, haphazardly, inconsistently, unsteadily, unevenly, variably, spasmodically.

irrelevance ▸ noun =**inapplicability**; unimportance, inconsequentiality, insignificance.

irrelevant ▸ adjective =**beside the point**, immaterial, unconnected, unrelated, peripheral, extraneous; unimportant, inconsequential, insignificant, trivial.

irreligious ▸ adjective =**atheistic**, non-believing, agnostic, faithless, godless, ungodly, impious, profane.
–OPPOSITES pious.

irreparable ▸ adjective =**irreversible**, irrevocable, irrecoverable, unrepairable, beyond repair.
–OPPOSITES repairable.

irreplaceable ▸ adjective =**unique**, unrepeatable, incomparable.

irrepressible ▸ adjective =**ebullient**, exuberant, buoyant, breezy, jaunty, high-spirited, vivacious, animated, full of life, lively; *informal* bubbly, bouncy, peppy, chipper, chirpy, full of beans.

irreproachable ▸ adjective =**impeccable**, exemplary, immaculate, outstanding, exceptional, admirable, perfect; above/beyond reproach, blameless; *informal* squeaky clean, whiter than white.
–OPPOSITES reprehensible.

irresistible ▸ adjective **1** *her irresistible smile* =**captivating**, enticing, alluring; enchanting. **2** *an irresistible impulse* =**uncontrollable**, overwhelming, overpowering, ungovernable.

irrespective ▸ adjective =**regardless of**, without regard to/for, notwithstanding, whatever, no matter what.

irresponsible ▸ adjective **1** *irresponsible behaviour* =**reckless**, rash, careless, unwise, imprudent, ill-advised, injudicious, hasty, foolhardy, impetuous. **2** *an irresponsible teenager* =**immature**, foolish; unreliable, undependable, untrustworthy.
–OPPOSITES sensible.

irretrievable ▸ adjective =**irreversible**, unrectifiable, irrecoverable, irreparable.
–OPPOSITES reversible.

irreverent ▸ adjective =**disrespectful**; impertinent, cheeky, flippant, rude, discourteous.
–OPPOSITES respectful.

irreversible ▸ adjective =**irreparable**, unrepairable, unrectifiable, irrevocable, permanent; unalterable.

irrevocable ▸ adjective =**irreversible**, unalterable, unchangeable, immutable, final, binding, permanent.

irritability ▸ noun =**irascibility**, tetchiness, testiness, cantankerousness, short temper, ill humour, peevishness, fractiousness, crabbiness, waspishness, prickliness; *Brit. informal* shirtiness, rattiness; *N. Amer. informal* crankiness; *Austral./ NZ informal* snakiness.

irritable ▸ adjective =**bad-tempered**, short-tempered, irascible, tetchy, testy, grumpy, grouchy, crotchety, cantankerous, peevish, fractious, pettish, crabby, waspish, prickly, splenetic, dyspeptic; *informal* on a short fuse; *Brit. informal* shirty, ratty; *N. Amer. informal* cranky, ornery; *Austral./NZ informal* snaky.
–OPPOSITES good-humoured.

irritant ▸ noun =**annoyance**, (source of) irritation, thorn in someone's side/ flesh, nuisance; *informal* pain (in the neck), headache; *N. Amer. informal* nudnik, burr in/under someone's saddle; *Austral./ NZ informal* nark.

irritate ▸ verb **1** See ANNOY. **2** *some sand irritated my eyes* =**inflame**, hurt, chafe, scratch, scrape, rub.

irritated ▸ adjective. See ANNOYED.

irritating ▸ adjective. See ANNOYING.

irritation ▸ noun. See ANNOYANCE.

island ▸ noun =**isle**, islet; atoll; *Brit.* holm; (**islands**) archipelago.

> **WORD LINKS**
>
> *relating to an island:* **insular**

isolate ▸ verb **1** *she isolated herself from her family* | *the contaminated area was isolated* =**separate**, segregate, detach, cut off, shut away, alienate, distance; cloister, seclude; cordon off, seal off, close off, fence off. **2** *the computer can isolate the offending vehicles* =**identify**, single out, pick out, point out, pinpoint.
–OPPOSITES integrate.

isolated ▸ adjective **1** *isolated communities* =**remote**, out of the way, outlying, off the beaten track, in the back of beyond, godforsaken, inaccessible, cut-off; *informal* in the middle of nowhere, in the sticks; *N. Amer. informal* jerkwater, in the tall timbers; *Austral./NZ informal* Barcoo, beyond the black stump. **2** *he lived a very isolated existence* =**solitary**, lonely, secluded, reclusive, hermit-like; *N. Amer.* lonesome. **3** *an isolated incident* =**unique**, lone, solitary; unusual, exceptional, untypical, freak; *informal* one-off.
–OPPOSITES accessible, sociable, common.

isolation ▸ noun **1** *their feeling of isolation* =**solitariness**, loneliness, friendlessness. **2** *the isolation of some mental hospitals* =**remoteness**, inaccessibility.
–OPPOSITES contact.

issue ▸ noun **1** *the committee discussed the issue* =**matter (in question)**, question, point (at issue), affair, case, subject, topic; problem, situation. **2** *the latest issue of our magazine* =**edition**, number, instalment, copy. **3** *the issue of a special stamp* =**issuing**, release, publication.
▸ verb **1** *the minister issued a statement* =**release**, put out, deliver, publish, broadcast, circulate, distribute. **2** *the captain issued the crew with guns* =**supply**, provide, furnish, arm, equip, fit out, rig out, kit out; *informal* fix up. **3** *delicious smells issued from the kitchen* =**emanate**, emerge, exude, flow (out/forth), pour (out/forth); waft, drift, drip, seep.
–OPPOSITES withdraw.
■ **at issue** =**in question**, in dispute, under discussion, under consideration, up for debate.

■ **take issue** =**disagree**; challenge, dispute, (call into) question.

Italy ▸ noun

> WORD LINKS
>
> *fear of Italian people and things:*
> **Italophobia**
> *lover of Italian people and things:*
> **Italophile**

itch ▸ noun *I have an itch on my back* =**tingling**, irritation, itchiness.
▸ verb *my chilblains really itch* tingle, be irritated, be itchy; sting, hurt, be sore.

> WORD LINKS
>
> *fear of itching:* **acarophobia**

item ▸ noun **1** *an item of farm equipment | the main item in a badger's diet* =**thing**, article, object, artefact, piece, product; element, constituent, component, ingredient. **2** *the meeting discussed the item* =**issue**, matter, affair, case, situation, subject, topic, question, point. **3** *a news item* =**report**, story, article, piece, write-up, bulletin, feature, review. **4** *items in the profit and loss account* =**entry**, record, statement.

itemize ▸ verb *Steinburg itemized thirty-two design faults* =**list**, catalogue, record, document, register, detail, specify, identify.

iterate ▸ verb =**repeat**, recapitulate; restate, reiterate; *informal* recap.

itinerant ▸ adjective =**travelling**, peripatetic, wandering, roving, roaming, touring, nomadic, migrant, homeless, vagrant; of no fixed address/abode.

itinerary ▸ noun =**route**, plan, schedule, timetable, programme.

Jj

jab ▶ verb *he jabbed the Englishman with his finger* =**poke**, prod, dig, nudge; thrust, stab, push.
▶ noun *a jab in the ribs* =**poke**, prod, nudge; thrust, stab, push.

jabber ▶ verb =**prattle**, babble, chatter, gabble, rattle on/away, blather; *informal* yak, yap, blabber; *Brit. informal* witter, rabbit, natter.

jack ■ **jack something up** *they jacked up the car* =**raise**, hoist, lift (up), winch up, hitch up, elevate.

jacket ▶ noun =**wrapping**, wrapper, sleeve, cover, covering, sheath.

jaded ▶ adjective **1** *a jaded palate* =**satiated**, sated, glutted; dulled, blunted, deadened. **2** *she felt really jaded* =**tired (out)**, weary, wearied, worn out, exhausted, fatigued, drained; *informal* all in, done (in), dead (beat), dead on one's feet, bushed; *Brit. informal* knackered, whacked; *N. Amer. informal* tuckered out.
−OPPOSITES fresh.

jag ▶ noun =**point**, barb, thorn; spike, spine.

jagged ▶ adjective =**spiky**, barbed, ragged, rough, uneven, irregular, broken; serrated, spiny, sawtooth.
−OPPOSITES smooth.

jail ▶ noun *he was thrown into jail* =**prison**, lock-up, detention centre; *N. Amer.* penitentiary, jailhouse, correctional facility; *informal* clink, cooler, the slammer, inside, jug; *Brit. informal* nick; *N. Amer. informal* can, pen, slam, pokey.
▶ verb *she was jailed for killing her husband* =**send to prison/jail**, put in prison/jail, imprison, incarcerate, lock up, put away, detain; *informal* send down, put behind bars, put inside; *Brit. informal* bang up.
−OPPOSITES acquit, release.

jailer ▶ noun =**prison officer**, warder, warden, guard; *informal* screw; *archaic* turnkey.

jam¹ ▶ verb **1** *he jammed a finger in each ear* =**stuff**, shove, force, ram, thrust, press, push, stick, cram. **2** *hundreds of people jammed into the hall* =**crowd**, pack, pile, press, squeeze, cram; throng, mob, fill, block, clog, congest. **3** *the rudder had jammed* =**stick**, become stuck, catch, seize (up). **4** *dust can jam the mechanism* =**immobilize**, paralyse, disable, cripple; clog (up), block (up); *informal* bung up.
▶ noun *a traffic jam* =**tailback**, hold-up, queue, congestion, bottleneck; *N. Amer.* gridlock; *informal* snarl-up.

jam² ▶ noun *raspberry jam* =**preserve**, conserve, jelly, marmalade.

jamb ▶ noun =**post**, doorpost, upright, frame.

jamboree ▶ noun =**rally**, gathering, convention, conference; festival, fête, fiesta, gala, carnival; *informal* bash, shindig, do.

jangle ▶ verb **1** *keys jangled at his waist* =**clank**, clink, jingle, tinkle. **2** *the noise jangled her nerves* =**grate on**, jar on, irritate, disturb, fray, put/set on edge.

janitor ▶ noun =**caretaker**, custodian, porter, concierge, doorkeeper, doorman, warden; cleaner; *N. Amer.* superintendent.

jar¹ ▶ noun *a jar of honey* =**pot**, container, crock.

jar² ▶ verb **1** *each step jarred my whole body* =**jolt**, jerk, shake, vibrate. **2** *her shrill voice jarred on him* =**grate**, set someone's teeth on edge, irritate, annoy, get on someone's nerves. **3** *the verse jars with the words that follow* =**clash**, conflict, contrast, be incompatible, be at variance, be at odds, be inconsistent.

jargon ▶ noun =**slang**, cant, argot, patter; gobbledegook; *informal* lingo, -speak, -ese.

jarring ▶ adjective =**clashing**, conflicting, contrasting, incompatible, incongruous; discordant, dissonant, harsh, grating, strident, shrill.
−OPPOSITES harmonious.

jaundiced ▶ adjective =**bitter**, resentful, cynical, soured, disenchanted, disillusioned, pessimistic, sceptical, distrustful, suspicious.

jaunt ▶ noun =(pleasure) trip, outing, excursion, day trip, day out; tour, drive, ride, run; *informal* spin.

jaunty ▶ adjective =cheerful, cheery, happy, merry, jolly, joyful; lively, perky, bright, buoyant, bubbly, bouncy, breezy, exuberant, ebullient; carefree, light-hearted; *informal* full of beans, chirpy; *literary* blithe.
–OPPOSITES depressed, serious.

javelin ▶ noun =spear, harpoon, dart.

jaw ▶ noun **1** *a broken jaw* =jawbone; *Anatomy* mandible, maxilla. **2** *the whale seized a seal in its jaws* =mouth, maw, muzzle; *informal* chops.

> WORD LINKS
>
> *relating to the jaw:* **mandibular, maxillary**

jazzy ▶ adjective =bright, colourful, eye-catching, vivid, lively, vibrant, bold, flamboyant, showy; *informal* flashy.
–OPPOSITES dull.

jealous ▶ adjective **1** *jealous of his brother* =envious, covetous; resentful, grudging, green with envy. **2** *a jealous lover* =suspicious, distrustful; possessive, proprietorial, overprotective. **3** *jealous of their rights* =protective, vigilant, watchful, mindful, careful.
–OPPOSITES proud, trusting.

jealousy ▶ noun **1** *consumed with jealousy* =envy; resentment, bitterness. **2** *an intense jealousy of their status* =protectiveness, vigilance, watchfulness, care.

jeans ▶ plural noun =denims, blue jeans; *trademark* Levi's, Wranglers.

jeer ▶ verb *the demonstrators jeered the police* =taunt, mock, scoff at, ridicule, sneer at, deride, insult, abuse, jibe (at); heckle, catcall (at), boo (at), whistle at.
–OPPOSITES applaud, cheer.

▶ noun *the jeers of the crowd* =taunt, sneer, insult, shout, jibe, boo, catcall; derision, teasing, scoffing, abuse, scorn, heckling, catcalling; *Brit. & Austral./NZ* barracking.
–OPPOSITES applause, cheer.

jell ▶ verb. See GEL.

jeopardize ▶ verb =threaten, endanger, imperil, risk, put in danger/jeopardy; compromise, prejudice.
–OPPOSITES safeguard.

jeopardy ▶ noun =danger, peril; risk.

jerk ▶ noun **1** *she gave the reins a jerk* =yank, tug, pull, wrench. **2** *he let the clutch in with a jerk* =jolt, lurch, bump, judder, jump; bounce, shake.

▶ verb **1** *she jerked her arm free* =yank, tug, pull, wrench, wrest, drag, snatch. **2** *the car jerked along* =jolt, lurch, bump, judder, bounce.

jerky ▶ adjective =convulsive, spasmodic, fitful, twitchy, shaky.
–OPPOSITES smooth.

jerry-built ▶ adjective =shoddy, gimcrack, rickety, ramshackle, flimsy; second-rate, third-rate.
–OPPOSITES sturdy.

jersey ▶ noun =pullover, sweater; *Brit.* jumper; *informal* woolly.

jet¹ ▶ noun **1** *a jet of water* =stream, spurt, spray, spout; gush, surge, burst. **2** *carburettor jets* =nozzle, head, spout.

jet² ▶ adjective *her glossy jet hair* =black, pitch-black, coal-black, ebony, raven, sable, sooty.

jettison ▶ verb **1** *six aircraft jettisoned their loads* =dump, drop, ditch, discharge, throw out, tip out, unload. **2** *he jettisoned his unwanted papers | the scheme was jettisoned* =discard, dispose of, throw away/out, get rid of; reject, scrap, axe, abandon, drop; *informal* chuck (away/out), dump, ditch, bin, junk, get shut of.
–OPPOSITES retain.

jetty ▶ noun =pier, landing (stage), quay, wharf, dock; *N. Amer.* dockominium, levee.

jewel ▶ noun **1** *priceless jewels* =gem, gemstone, (precious) stone; *informal* sparkler, rock. **2** *the jewel of his collection* =showpiece, pride (and joy), cream, crème de la crème, jewel in the crown, prize, pick. **3** *the girl is a jewel* =treasure, angel, gem, marvel, find, godsend; *informal* one in a million, a star.

jewellery ▶ noun =jewels, gems, gemstones, precious stones, costume jewellery.

jibe ▶ noun *cruel jibes* =snide remark, taunt, sneer, jeer, insult, barb; *informal* dig, put-down.

jig ▶ verb =bob, jump, spring, skip, hop, prance, bounce.

jiggle ▶ verb =shake, waggle, wiggle.

jilt ▶ verb =leave, walk out on, throw over, finish with, break up with; *informal* chuck, ditch, dump, drop, run out on, give someone the push/elbow, give someone the big E; *literary* forsake.

jingle ▸ noun **1** *the jingle of money in the till* =**clink**, chink, tinkle, jangle. **2** *advertising jingles* =**slogan**, catchphrase; song, rhyme, tune; *N. Amer. informal* tag line.
▸ verb **1** *her bracelets jingled noisily* =**clink**, chink, tinkle, jangle. **2** *the bell jingled* =**tinkle**, ring, ding, ping, chime.

jingoism ▸ noun =**chauvinism**, ultranationalism, xenophobia.

jinx ▸ noun *the jinx struck six days later* =**curse**, spell, hoodoo, malediction; the evil eye, black magic, voodoo, bad luck; *N. Amer.* hex; *archaic* malison.
▸ verb *the family is jinxed* =**curse**, cast a spell on, put the evil eye on; *Austral.* point the bone at; *N. Amer.* hex.

job ▸ noun **1** *my job involves a lot of travelling* =**position**, post, situation, appointment; occupation, profession, trade, career, (line of) work, métier, craft; vocation, calling; vacancy, opening; *Austral. informal* grip. **2** *this job will take three months* =**task**, piece of work, assignment, project; chore, errand; undertaking, venture, operation. **3** *it's your job to protect her* =**responsibility**, duty, charge, task; role, function, mission; *informal* department.

> WORD LINKS
>
> relating to a job: **vocational**

jobless ▸ adjective =**unemployed**, out of work, out of a job, unwaged, redundant, laid off; *Brit. informal* signing on, on the dole, resting; *Austral./NZ informal* on the wallaby track.
−OPPOSITES employed.

jockey ▸ noun =**rider**, horseman, horsewoman, equestrian; *Austral. informal* hoop.
▸ verb **1** *he jockeyed himself into the team* =**manoeuvre**, ease, edge, work, steer; inveigle, insinuate, ingratiate. **2** *ministers began jockeying for position* =**compete**, contend, vie; struggle, fight, scramble, jostle.

jocular ▸ adjective =**humorous**, funny, witty, comic, comical, amusing, droll, jokey, facetious, tongue-in-cheek, teasing, playful; light-hearted, jovial, cheerful, cheery, merry.
−OPPOSITES solemn.

jog ▸ verb **1** *he jogged along the road* =**run**, trot, lope. **2** *a hand jogged his elbow* =**nudge**, prod, poke, push, bump, jar.
▸ noun *he set off at a jog* =**run**, trot, lope.

joie de vivre ▸ noun =**gaiety**, cheerfulness, cheeriness, light-heartedness, happiness, joy, joyfulness, high spirits, jollity, exuberance, ebullience, liveliness, vivacity, verve, effervescence, buoyancy, zest, zestfulness; *informal* pep, zing.
−OPPOSITES sobriety.

join ▸ verb **1** *the two parts of the mould are joined with clay* =**connect**, unite, couple, fix, affix, attach, fasten, stick, glue, fuse, weld, amalgamate, bond, link, merge, secure, make fast, tie, bind. **2** *here the path joins a major road* =**meet**, touch, reach, abut, adjoin. **3** *I'm off to join the search party* =**help in**, participate in, get involved in, contribute to; enlist in, join up, sign up; band together, get together, team up.
−OPPOSITES separate, leave.
▸ noun. See JOINT sense 1.

joint ▸ noun **1** *a leaky joint* =**join**, junction, intersection, link, connection; weld, seam. **2** *(informal) a classy joint* =**place**, establishment; restaurant, bar, club, nightclub, venue.
▸ adjective *matters of joint interest* | *a joint effort* =**common**, shared, communal, collective; mutual, cooperative, collaborative, concerted, combined, united.
−OPPOSITES separate.

> WORD LINKS
>
> relating to joints: **arthro-**

jointly ▸ adverb =**together**, in partnership, in cooperation, cooperatively, in conjunction, in combination, mutually.

joke ▸ noun **1** *telling jokes* =**funny story**, jest, witticism, quip; pun; *informal* gag, wisecrack, crack, funny, one-liner; *N. Amer. informal* boffola. **2** *playing stupid jokes* =**trick**, prank, stunt, hoax, jape; *informal* leg-pull, spoof, wind-up. **3** *(informal) he soon became a joke* =**laughing stock**, figure of fun, object of ridicule. **4** *(informal) the present system is a joke* =**farce**, travesty, waste of time; shambles; *N. Amer. informal* shuck.
▸ verb *she joked with the guests* =**tell jokes**, jest, banter, quip; *informal* wisecrack, josh.

joker ▸ noun =**humorist**, comedian, comedienne, comic, wit, jester; prankster, practical joker, hoaxer, trickster, clown; *informal* card; *informal, dated* wag.

jolly ▸ adjective =**cheerful**, happy, cheery, good-humoured, jovial, merry,

sunny, joyful, joyous, light-hearted, in high spirits, bubbly, exuberant, ebullient, genial, fun-loving; *informal* chipper, chirpy, perky, bright-eyed and bushytailed; *formal* jocund; *literary* blithe.
—OPPOSITES miserable.
▶ **adverb** *(Brit. informal)* *a jolly good idea. See* VERY adverb.

jolt ▶ **verb 1** *the train jolted the passengers to one side* =**push**, thrust, jar, bump, knock, bang; shake, jog. **2** *the car jolted along* =**bump**, bounce, jerk, rattle, lurch, shudder, judder. **3** *she was jolted out of her reverie* =**startle**, surprise, shock, stun, shake, take aback; *informal* rock, floor, knock sideways; *Brit. informal* knock for six.
▶ **noun 1** *a series of sickening jolts* =**bump**, bounce, shake, jerk, lurch. **2** *he woke up with a jolt* =**start**, jerk, jump. **3** *the sight of the dagger gave him a jolt* =**fright**, shock, scare, surprise; *informal* turn.

jostle ▶ **verb 1** *she was jostled by noisy students* =**push**, shove, elbow; barge. **2** *people jostled for the best position* =**struggle**, vie, jockey, scramble, fight.

jot ▶ **verb** *I've jotted down a few details* =**write**, note, take down; scribble, sketch.

journal ▶ **noun 1** *a medical journal* =**periodical**, magazine, gazette, digest, review, newsletter, news-sheet, bulletin; newspaper, paper; daily, weekly, monthly, quarterly. **2** *he keeps a journal* =**diary**, log, logbook, chronicle; *N. Amer.* daybook.

journalism ▶ **noun 1** *a career in journalism* =**newspapers**, magazines, the press; *Brit.* Fleet Street. **2** *his incisive style of journalism* =**reporting**, writing, reportage, coverage; articles, reports, features, pieces, stories, reviews.

journalist ▶ **noun** =**reporter**, correspondent, newspaperman, newspaperwoman, newsman, newswoman, columnist, writer, commentator, reviewer; *informal* news hound, hack, hackette, stringer, journo; *N. Amer. informal* newsy.

journey ▶ **noun** *his journey round the world* =**trip**, expedition, tour, trek, voyage, cruise, ride, drive; crossing, passage, flight; odyssey, pilgrimage; *archaic* peregrination.
▶ **verb** *they journeyed south* =**travel**, go, voyage, sail, cruise, fly, hike, trek, ride, drive, make one's way.

jovial ▶ **adjective** =**cheerful**, jolly, happy, cheery, good-humoured, convivial, genial, good-natured, affable, outgoing; smiling, merry, sunny, joyful, joyous, high-spirited, exuberant; *formal* jocund; *literary* blithe.
—OPPOSITES miserable.

joy ▶ **noun 1** *whoops of joy* =**delight**, pleasure, joyfulness, jubilation, triumph, exultation, rejoicing, happiness, gladness, elation, euphoria, bliss, ecstasy, rapture. **2** *it was a joy to be with her* =**pleasure**, delight, treat, thrill; *informal* buzz, kick.
—OPPOSITES misery, trial.

joyful ▶ **adjective 1** *his joyful mood* =**cheerful**, happy, jolly, merry, sunny, joyous, light-hearted, bubbly, exuberant, ebullient, cheery, smiling, mirthful; jubilant, gleeful; jovial, genial, good-humoured, full of the joys of spring; *formal* jocund; *literary* blithe. **2** *joyful news* =**pleasing**, happy, good, cheering, gladdening, welcome, heart-warming. **3** *a joyful occasion* =**happy**, cheerful, merry, jolly, festive, joyous.
—OPPOSITES sad, distressing.

joyless ▶ **adjective 1** *a joyless man* =**gloomy**, melancholy, morose, lugubrious, glum, sombre, saturnine, sullen, dour, humourless. **2** *a joyless place* =**depressing**, cheerless, gloomy, dreary, bleak, drab, dismal, desolate, austere, sombre; *literary* drear.
—OPPOSITES cheerful, welcoming.

joyous ▶ **adjective** *See* JOYFUL *senses* 1, 3.

jubilant ▶ **adjective** =**overjoyed**, exultant, triumphant, joyful, cock-a-hoop, exuberant, elated, thrilled, gleeful, euphoric, ecstatic, enraptured, in raptures, walking on air, in seventh heaven, on cloud nine; *informal* over the moon, on top of the world; *N. Amer. informal* wigged out; *Austral. informal* wrapped.
—OPPOSITES despondent.

jubilation ▶ **noun** =**exultation**, joy, joyousness, elation, euphoria, ecstasy, rapture, glee, exuberance.

jubilee ▶ **noun** =**anniversary**, commemoration; celebration, festival.

judge ▶ **noun 1** *the judge sentenced him to five years* =**justice**, magistrate, recorder, sheriff; *N. Amer.* jurist; *Brit. informal* beak. **2** *a panel of judges will select the winner* =**adjudicator**, arbiter, assessor, examiner, moderator, scrutineer.
▶ **verb 1** *I judged that she was simply exhausted*

=**conclude**, decide; consider, believe, think, deem; deduce, gather, infer, gauge, estimate, guess, surmise, conjecture; regard as, look on as, take to be, rate as, class as; *informal* reckon, figure. **2** *the case was judged by a tribunal* =**try**, hear; adjudicate, decide. **3** *she was judged innocent of murder* =**pronounce**, decree, rule, find. **4** *the competition will be judged by Alan Amey* =**adjudicate**, arbitrate, moderate. **5** *entries were judged by a panel of experts* =**assess**, appraise, evaluate; examine, review.

judgement ▸ noun **1** *his temper could affect his judgement* =**discernment**, perception, discrimination, powers of reasoning, reason, logic; mind. **2** *I am relying on your judgement* =**acumen**, shrewdness, astuteness, (common) sense, perspicacity, acuity, discrimination, wisdom, wit, judiciousness, prudence, canniness, sharpness; *informal* nous, savvy, horse sense, gumption; *N. Amer. informal* smarts. **3** *a court judgement* =**verdict**, decision, adjudication, ruling, pronouncement, decree, finding; sentence.

judgemental ▸ adjective =**critical**, censorious, disapproving, disparaging, deprecating, negative, overcritical.

judicial ▸ adjective =**legal**, juridical; official.

judicious ▸ adjective =**wise**, sensible, prudent, shrewd, astute, canny, discerning.
–OPPOSITES ill-advised.

jug ▸ noun =**pitcher**, ewer, crock, jar, urn; carafe, flask, flagon, decanter; *N. Amer.* creamer.

juice ▸ noun *the juice from two lemons* =**liquid**, fluid, sap, milk, gum; extract; concentrate, essence.

juicy ▸ adjective =**succulent**, tender, moist; ripe.
–OPPOSITES dry.

jumble ▸ noun **1** *the books were in a jumble* =**heap**, muddle, mess, tangle; confusion, disarray, chaos; hotchpotch, mishmash, miscellany, mixed bag, medley; *N. Amer.* hodgepodge. **2** *(Brit.) bags of jumble* =**junk**, bric-a-brac; *Brit.* lumber.
▸ verb *the photographs are all jumbled up* =**mix up**, muddle up, disorganize, disorder.

jumbo ▸ adjective *(informal)*. See HUGE.

jump ▸ verb **1** *the cat jumped off his lap* | *Flora began to jump about* =**leap**, spring,

bound, hop; skip, caper, dance, prance, frolic, cavort. **2** *he jumped the fence* =**vault (over)**, leap over, clear, sail over, hop over, hurdle. **3** *pre-tax profits jumped* =**rise**, go up, shoot up, soar, surge, climb, increase; *informal* skyrocket. **4** *the noise made her jump* =**start**, jolt, flinch, recoil, shudder.
▸ noun **1** *the short jump across the gully* =**leap**; gap, distance. **2** *the horse cleared the last jump* =**obstacle**, barrier; fence, hurdle. **3** *a jump in profits* =**rise**, leap, increase, upsurge, upswing; *informal* hike. **4** *I woke up with a jump* =**start**, jerk, spasm, shudder.

jumper ▸ noun *(Brit.)* =**sweater**, pullover, jersey; *informal* woolly.

jumpy ▸ adjective *(informal)* =**nervous**, on edge, edgy, tense, nervy, anxious, ill at ease, uneasy, restless, fidgety, keyed up, overwrought; *informal* a bundle of nerves, jittery, like a cat on a hot tin roof, uptight, het up, in a tizz/tizzy; *Brit. informal* like a cat on hot bricks; *N. Amer. informal* spooky, squirrelly, antsy; *Austral./NZ informal* toey.
–OPPOSITES calm.

junction ▸ noun =**crossroads**, intersection, interchange, T-junction; turn, turn-off, exit; *Brit.* roundabout; *N. Amer.* turnout, cloverleaf.

jungle ▸ noun =**rainforest**, forest.

junior ▸ adjective **1** *the junior members of the family* =**younger**, youngest. **2** *a junior minister* =**low-ranking**, subordinate, lesser, lower, minor, secondary. **3** *John White Junior* =**the Younger**; *Brit.* minor; *N. Amer.* II.
–OPPOSITES senior, older.

junk *(informal)* ▸ noun *an attic full of junk* =**rubbish**, clutter, odds and ends, bits and pieces, bric-a-brac; refuse, litter, scrap, waste, debris, detritus, dross; *Brit.* lumber; *N. Amer.* trash; *Austral./NZ* mullock; *Brit. informal* odds and sods.
▸ verb *junk all the rubbish* =**throw away/out**, discard, get rid of, dispose of, scrap, toss out, jettison; *informal* chuck (away/out), dump, ditch, bin, get shut of; *Brit. informal* get shot of.

jurisdiction ▸ noun **1** *an area under French jurisdiction* =**authority**, control, power, dominion, rule, administration, command, sway, leadership, sovereignty. **2** =**territory**, region, province, district, area, domain, realm.

just ▸ adjective *a just and democratic society*

=**fair**, fair-minded, equitable, even-handed, impartial, unbiased, objective, neutral, disinterested, unprejudiced, open-minded, non-partisan; honourable, upright, decent, honest, righteous, moral, virtuous, principled.
–OPPOSITES unfair.
▸ adverb **1** *she's just right for him* =**exactly**, precisely, absolutely, completely, totally, entirely, perfectly, utterly, wholly, thoroughly, in all respects; *informal* down to the ground, to a T, dead. **2** *we just made it* =**narrowly**, only just, by a hair's breadth, by the skin of one's teeth; barely, scarcely, hardly; *informal* by a whisker. **3** *she's just a child* =**only**, merely, simply, (nothing) but, no more than. **4** *the colour's just fantastic* =**really**, absolutely, completely, entirely, totally, quite; indeed, truly, utterly.
–OPPOSITES hardly, easily.

justice ▸ noun **1** *I appealed to his sense of justice* =**fairness**, justness, fair play, fair-mindedness, equity, even-handedness, impartiality, objectivity, neutrality, disinterestedness, honesty, righteousness, morality. **2** *the justice of his case* =**validity**, justification, soundness, well-foundedness, legitimacy. **3** =**judge**, magistrate, recorder, sheriff; *N. Amer.* jurist; *Brit. informal* beak.

WORD LINKS

relating to a system of justice: **judicial**
fear of justice: **dikephobia**

justifiable ▸ adjective =**valid**, legitimate, warranted, well founded, justified,
just, reasonable; defensible, tenable, supportable, acceptable.
–OPPOSITES indefensible.

justification ▸ noun =**grounds**, reason, basis, rationale, premise, vindication, explanation; defence, argument; case.

justify ▸ verb **1** *directors must justify the expenditure* =**give grounds for**, give reasons for, explain, account for; defend, vindicate, back up, support. **2** *the situation justified further investigation* =**warrant**, be good reason for, be a justification for.

justly ▸ adverb **1** *he is justly proud of his achievement* =**justifiably**, with (good) reason, legitimately, rightly, rightfully, deservedly. **2** *they were treated justly* =**fairly**, with fairness, equitably, even-handedly, impartially, without bias, objectively, without prejudice.
–OPPOSITES unjustifiably.

jut ▸ verb =**stick out**, project, protrude, bulge out, overhang.

juvenile ▸ adjective **1** *juvenile offenders* =**young**, teenage, adolescent, junior, pubescent, prepubescent. **2** *juvenile behaviour* =**childish**, immature, puerile, infantile, babyish; foolish, silly.
–OPPOSITES adult, mature.
▸ noun *many victims are juveniles* =**young person**, youngster, child, teenager, adolescent, minor, junior; *informal* kid.
–OPPOSITES adult.

juxtapose ▸ verb =**put together**; compare, contrast.

kaleidoscopic ▶ adjective =**multi-coloured**, many-hued, variegated, psychedelic, rainbow; ever-changing.
–OPPOSITES monochrome, constant.

kangaroo ▶ noun

WORD LINKS

male: **buck**
female: **doe**
young: **joey**
collective noun: **mob, troop**

keel ▶ noun *the upturned keel of the boat* =**base**, bottom (side), underside.
■ **keel over 1** *the boat keeled over* =**capsize**, turn turtle, turn upside down, founder; overturn, turn over, tip over. **2** *the slightest activity made him keel over* =**collapse**, faint, pass out, black out, lose consciousness, swoon.

keen ▶ adjective **1** *his publishers were keen to capitalize on his success* =**eager**, anxious, intent, impatient, determined; *informal* raring, itching, dying. **2** *a keen birdwatcher* =**enthusiastic**, avid, eager, ardent, fervent; conscientious, committed, dedicated, zealous, obsessive. **3** *they are keen on horses | a girl he was keen on* =**enthusiastic**, interested, passionate; attracted to, fond of, taken with, smitten with, enamoured of, infatuated with; *informal* struck on, gone on, mad about, crazy about, nuts about. **4** *a keen cutting edge* =**sharp**, well-honed, razor-sharp. **5** *keen eyesight* =**acute**, sharp, discerning, sensitive, perceptive, clear. **6** *a keen mind* =**acute**, penetrating, astute, incisive, sharp, perceptive, piercing, razor-sharp, shrewd, discerning, clever, intelligent, brilliant, bright, smart, wise, insightful. **7** *a keen wind* =**cold**, icy, freezing, harsh, raw, bitter; penetrating, piercing, biting. **8** *a keen sense of duty* =**intense**, acute, fierce, passionate, burning, fervent, ardent, strong, powerful.
–OPPOSITES reluctant, unenthusiastic.

keenness ▶ noun **1** *the company's keenness to sign a deal* =**eagerness**, willingness, readiness, impatience; enthusiasm, fervour, wholeheartedness, zest, zeal, ardour, passion. **2** *keenness of hearing* =**acuteness**, sharpness, sensitivity, perceptiveness, clarity. **3** *the keenness of his mind* =**acuity**, sharpness, incisiveness, astuteness, perceptiveness, shrewdness, insight, cleverness, discernment, intelligence, brightness, brilliance. **4** *the keenness of his sense of loss* =**intensity**, acuteness, strength, power; depth.

keep ▶ verb **1** *you should keep all the old forms* =**retain (possession of)**, hold on to, not part with; save, store, put by/aside, set aside; *N. Amer.* set by; *informal* hang on to. **2** *I tried to keep calm* =**remain**, stay, carry on being. **3** *he keeps going on about the murder* =**persist in**, keep on, carry on, continue, insist on. **4** *I shan't keep you long* =**detain**, keep waiting, delay, hold up, slow down. **5** *most people kept the rules | he had to keep his promise* =**comply with**, obey, observe, conform to, abide by, adhere to, stick to, heed, follow; carry out, act on, make good, honour, keep to, stand by. **6** *keeping the old traditions* =**preserve**, keep alive/up, keep going, carry on, perpetuate, maintain, uphold, sustain. **7** *where is her umbrella kept?* =**store**, house, stow, put (away), place, deposit. **8** *the shop keeps a good stock of wallpaper* =**(have in) stock**, carry, have (for sale), hold; offer, boast. **9** *he stole to keep his family* =**provide for**, support, feed, maintain, sustain; take care of, look after. **10** *she keeps rabbits* =**breed**, rear, raise, farm; own. **11** *his parents kept a shop* =**manage**, run, own, operate.
–OPPOSITES throw away, break, abandon.
▶ noun *money to pay for his keep* =**maintenance**, upkeep, sustenance, board (and lodging), food, livelihood.
■ **keep off** =**avoid**, steer clear of, stay away from, not go near.
■ **keep on at** =**nag**, go on at, badger, chivvy, harass, hound, pester; *informal* hassle.
■ **keep to 1** *I've got to keep to the rules* =**obey**, abide by, observe, follow, comply with, adhere to, respect, stick to, be bound by. **2** *please keep to the point* =**stick**

to, restrict oneself to, confine oneself to.

keeper ▸ noun =**curator**, custodian, guardian, administrator, overseer, steward, caretaker.

keeping ▸ noun *the document is in the keeping of the county archivist* =**care**, custody, charge, possession, trust, protection.

■ **in keeping with** =**consistent with**, in harmony with, in accord with, in agreement with, in line with, in character with, compatible with; appropriate to, befitting, suitable for.

keepsake ▸ noun =**memento**, souvenir, reminder, remembrance, token.

keg ▸ noun =**barrel**, cask, vat, butt, hogshead; *historical* firkin.

kernel ▸ noun **1** *the kernel of a nut* =**seed**, grain, core, centre. **2** *the kernel of the argument* =**essence**, core, heart, essentials, quintessence, fundamentals, basics, nub, gist, substance; *informal* nitty-gritty. **3** *a kernel of truth* =**nucleus**, germ, grain, nugget.

key ▸ noun *the key to the mystery | the key to success* =**answer**, clue, solution, explanation; basis, foundation, requisite, precondition, means, way, route, path, passport, secret, formula.
▸ adjective *a key figure* =**crucial**, central, essential, indispensable, pivotal, critical, dominant, vital, principal, prime, chief, major, leading, main, important, significant.
−OPPOSITES peripheral.

keynote ▸ noun =**theme**, gist, substance, burden, tenor, pith, marrow, essence, heart, core, basis.

keystone ▸ noun =**foundation**, basis, linchpin, cornerstone, base, (guiding) principle, core, heart, centre, crux.

kick ▸ verb **1** *her attacker kicked her* =**boot**; *Brit. informal* put the boot in on. **2** *the gun kicked hard* =**recoil**; jump, jerk, pull; judder, vibrate.
▸ noun **1** *a kick on the knee* =**blow**, crack; *informal* boot. **2** *(informal) I get a kick out of driving* =**thrill**, excitement, stimulation, tingle, frisson; *informal* buzz, high; *N. Amer. informal* charge. **3** *(informal) a drink with a powerful kick to it* =**effect**, strength, power; tang, zest, bite, edge; *informal* punch, hit. **4** *(informal) a health kick* =**craze**, obsession, mania; *informal* fad, trip, thing.
■ **kick someone/something around** *(informal) kick a few ideas around* =**discuss**,
talk over, debate, thrash out, consider, play with, think about.
■ **kick back** *(N. Amer. informal)* =**relax**, unwind, take it easy, slow down, let up, ease up/off, sit back; *informal* chill out.
■ **kick off** *(informal)* =**start**, commence, begin, get going, get off the ground, get under way; open, start off, set in motion, launch, initiate, introduce, inaugurate, usher in.
■ **kick someone out** *(informal)* =**expel**, eject, throw out, oust, evict, get rid of, axe; dismiss, discharge; *informal* chuck out, send packing, boot out, give someone their marching orders, sack, fire; *Brit. informal* turf out; *N. Amer. informal* give someone the bum's rush.

kickback ▸ noun *(informal)* =**bribe**, inducement; *N. Amer.* payola; *informal* payoff, sweetener, backhander.

kick-off ▸ noun *(informal)* =**beginning**, start, commencement, outset, opening.

kid ▸ noun *(informal)* =**child**, youngster, little one, baby, toddler, tot, infant, boy/girl, young person, minor, juvenile, adolescent, teenager, youth, stripling; offspring, son/daughter; *Scottish* bairn; *informal* kiddie, nipper, kiddiewink, shaver; *Brit. informal* sprog; *N. Amer. informal* rug rat; *Austral./NZ* ankle-biter; *derogatory* brat; *literary* babe.

kidnap ▸ verb =**abduct**, carry off, capture, seize, snatch, take hostage.

kidney ▸ noun

> **WORD LINKS**
>
> branch of medicine concerning the kidneys: **nephrology**
> inflammation of the kidneys: **nephritis**
> removal of a kidney: **nephrectomy**
> removal of a kidney stone: **lithotomy**

kill ▸ verb **1** *gangs killed twenty-seven people* =**murder**, take the life of, assassinate, eliminate, terminate, dispatch, finish off, put to death, execute; slaughter, butcher, massacre, wipe out, annihilate, exterminate, liquidate, mow down; *informal* bump off, polish off, do away with, do in, knock off, top, take out, blow away, dispose of; *N. Amer. informal* rub out, waste; *literary* slay. **2** *this would kill all hopes of progress* =**destroy**, put an end to, end, extinguish, dash, quash, ruin, wreck, shatter, smash, crush, scotch, thwart; *informal* put paid to, put the kibosh on, stymie; *Brit. informal* scupper. **3** *we had a few hours to kill at the airport* =**while away**, fill (up), occupy, beguile, pass, spend, waste. **4** *a shot to kill the pain* =**alleviate**, assuage, soothe, allay, dull, blunt, deaden, stifle, suppress, subdue. **5** *(informal) Congress killed the bill* =**veto**, defeat, vote down, rule against, reject, throw out, overrule, overturn, put a stop to, quash. **6** *(informal) Noel killed the engine* =**turn off**, switch off, stop, shut off/down, cut.

killer ▶ noun =**murderer**, assassin, butcher, serial killer, gunman; executioner; *informal* hit man; *literary* slayer.

killing ▶ noun =**murder**, assassination, homicide, manslaughter, elimination, execution; slaughter, massacre, butchery, carnage, bloodshed, extermination, annihilation; *literary* slaying.

killjoy ▶ noun =**spoilsport**, prophet of doom; *informal* wet blanket, party-pooper, misery; *Austral./NZ informal* wowser.

kin ▶ noun =**relatives**, relations, family (members), kindred; kinsfolk, kinsmen, kinswomen, people; *informal* folks.

kind[1] ▶ noun **1** *all kinds of gifts | the kinds of bird that could be seen* =**sort**, type, variety, style, form, class, category, genre; genus, species, race, breed. **2** *they were different in kind | the first of its kind* =**character**, nature, essence, quality, disposition, make-up; type, style, manner, description, temperament, ilk; *N. Amer.* stripe.

■ **kind of** *(informal)* =**rather**, quite, fairly, somewhat, a little, slightly, a shade; *informal* sort of, a bit, kinda, pretty, a touch, a tad.

kind[2] ▶ adjective *a kind and caring person* =**kindly**, good-natured, kind-hearted, warm-hearted, caring, affectionate, loving, warm; considerate, helpful, thoughtful, obliging, unselfish, selfless, altruistic, good, attentive; compassionate, sympathetic, understanding, big-hearted, benevolent, benign, friendly, neighbourly, hospitable, well meaning, public-spirited; generous, liberal, open-handed, bountiful, munificent; *Brit. informal* decent.
−OPPOSITES inconsiderate, mean.

kind-hearted ▶ adjective =**kind**, caring, warm-hearted, kindly, benevolent, good-natured, tender, warm, compassionate, sympathetic, understanding; indulgent, altruistic, benign.

kindle ▶ verb **1** *he kindled a fire* =**light**, ignite, get going, set light to, set fire to,

put a match to. **2** *Elvis kindled my interest in music* =**rouse**, arouse, wake, awaken; stimulate, inspire, stir (up), excite, evoke, provoke, fire, inflame, trigger, activate, spark off.
−OPPOSITES extinguish.

kindliness ▶ noun =**kindness**, benevolence, warmth, gentleness, tenderness, care, humanity, sympathy, compassion, understanding; generosity, charity, kind-heartedness, warm-heartedness, thoughtfulness.

kindly ▶ adjective *a kindly old lady* =**benevolent**, kind, kind-hearted, warm-hearted, generous, good-natured; gentle, warm, compassionate, caring, loving, benign, well meaning; helpful, thoughtful, considerate, good-hearted, nice, friendly, neighbourly.
−OPPOSITES unkind, cruel.
▶ adverb =**nicely**, warmly, affectionately, tenderly, lovingly, compassionately; considerately, thoughtfully, helpfully, obligingly, generously, selflessly, unselfishly.
−OPPOSITES unkindly, harshly.

kindness ▶ noun =**kindliness**, kind-heartedness, warm-heartedness, affection, warmth, gentleness, concern, care; consideration, helpfulness, thoughtfulness, unselfishness, selflessness, altruism, compassion, sympathy, understanding, big-heartedness, benevolence, friendliness, neighbourliness, hospitality; generosity, magnanimity.

king ▶ noun **1** *the king of France* =**ruler**, sovereign, monarch, Crown, emperor, prince, potentate. **2** *(informal) the king of world football* =**number one**, leading light, master, leader; *informal* supremo, maestro, boss (man), top dog.

┌─────────────┐
│ WORD LINKS │
└─────────────┘
relating to a king: **regal**

kingdom ▶ noun **1** *his kingdom stretched to the sea* =**realm**, domain, dominion, country, empire, land, territory; nation, (sovereign) state, province. **2** *Henry's little kingdom* =**domain**, province, realm, sphere, dominion, territory, fiefdom, zone.

kink ▶ noun =**curl**, twist, twirl, loop, knot, tangle, entanglement, bend.

kinky ▶ adjective **1** *(informal) a kinky relationship* =**perverted**, abnormal, deviant, unnatural, depraved, degenerate, perverse; *informal* pervy. **2** *(informal) kinky* *underwear* =**sexy**, provocative, arousing, erotic, titillating, naughty, rude; *Brit. informal* saucy.

kinship ▸ noun 1 *ties of kinship* =**relationship**, family, blood, ancestry, kindred. 2 *she felt kinship with the others* =**affinity**, sympathy, rapport, harmony, understanding, empathy, closeness, bond, compatibility; similarity, likeness, correspondence.

kiosk ▸ noun =**booth**, stand, stall, counter, news-stand.

kiss ▸ verb 1 *he kissed her* =**give someone a kiss**; *informal* peck, smooch, canoodle, neck, pet; *Brit. informal* snog; *N. Amer. informal* buss; *informal, dated* spoon. 2 *the ball just kissed the crossbar* =**brush (against)**, caress, touch, stroke, skim.
▸ noun =*informal* peck, smack, smacker, smooch; *Brit. informal* snog; *N. Amer. informal* buss.

kit ▸ noun 1 *his tool kit* =**equipment**, tools, implements, instruments, gadgets, utensils, appliances, tools of the trade, gear, tackle, hardware, paraphernalia; *informal* things, stuff; *Military* accoutrements. 2 *(Brit. informal) their football kit* =**clothes**, clothing, rig, outfit, dress, costume, garments, attire, garb, gear, get-up, rig-out; *formal* apparel. 3 *a model aircraft kit* =**set**, pack, flat-pack.
■ **kit someone/something out** =**equip**, fit (out/up), furnish, supply, provide, issue; dress, clothe, array, attire, rig out, deck out; *informal* fix up.

kitchen ▸ noun =**kitchenette**, kitchen-diner, cooking area, galley, cookhouse; *N. Amer.* cookery.

kittenish ▸ adjective =**playful**, lighthearted, skittish, lively, coquettish, flirtatious, frivolous, flippant, superficial, trivial, shallow, silly; *informal* flirty, dizzy; *literary* frolicsome.
–OPPOSITES serious.

knack ▸ noun 1 *a knack for making money | it takes practice to acquire the knack* =**gift**, talent, flair, genius, instinct, faculty, ability, capability, capacity, aptitude, bent, forte, facility; technique, method, trick, skill, art, expertise; *informal* the hang of something. 2 *he has a knack of getting injured at the wrong time* =**tendency**, propensity, habit, proneness, liability, predisposition.

knapsack ▸ noun =**rucksack**, backpack, haversack, pack, kitbag.

knead ▸ verb 1 *kneading the dough* =**pummel**, work, pound, squeeze, shape, mould. 2 *she kneaded the base of his neck* =**massage**, press, manipulate, rub.

kneel ▸ verb =**fall to one's knees**, get down on one's knees, genuflect; *historical* kowtow.

knickers ▸ plural noun *(Brit.)* =**underpants**, briefs, French knickers, camiknickers; underwear, lingerie, underclothes, undergarments; *Brit.* pants; *informal* panties, undies; *Brit. informal* knicks, smalls; *dated* drawers; *historical* bloomers.

knick-knack ▸ noun =**ornament**, novelty, trinket, trifle, bauble, curio; memento, souvenir; *N. Amer.* kickshaw; *N. Amer. informal* tchotchke; *archaic* bijou.

knife ▸ verb *he was knifed in the back* =**stab**, hack, gash, slash, lacerate, cut, bayonet.

knight ▸ noun =**cavalier**, cavalryman, horseman; lord, noble, nobleman; *historical* chevalier, paladin.

knit ▸ verb 1 *disparate regions began to knit together* =**unite**, unify, come together, bond, fuse, coalesce, merge, meld, blend. 2 *we expect broken bones to knit* =**heal**, mend, join, fuse. 3 *Marcus knitted his brows* =**furrow**, contract, gather, wrinkle.

knob ▸ noun 1 *a black rod with a knob at the base* =**lump**, bump, protuberance, protrusion, bulge, swelling, knot, node, nodule, ball; *informal* boss. 2 *the knobs on the radio* =**dial**, button. 3 *a knob of butter* =**lump**, nugget, pat, ball, dollop, piece; *N. Amer. informal* gob.

knock ▸ verb 1 *he knocked on the door* =**bang**, tap, rap, thump, pound, hammer; strike, beat. 2 *she knocked her knee on the table* =**bump**, bang, hit, strike, crack; injure, hurt, bruise; *informal* bash, whack. 3 *he knocked into an elderly man* =**collide with**, bump into, bang into, run into, crash into, smash into, plough into; *N. Amer.* impact; *informal* bash into. 4 *(informal) I'm not knocking the company.* See CRITICIZE.
▸ noun 1 *a knock at the door* =**tap**, rap, rat-tat, knocking, bang, banging, pounding, hammering, thump, thud. 2 *the casing is tough enough to withstand knocks* =**bump**, blow, bang, jolt, jar, shock; collision, crash, smash, impact. 3 *a knock on the head* =**blow**, bang, hit, slap, smack, crack, punch, cuff, thump; *informal* clip,

clout, wallop, thwack, belt, bash. **4** *life's hard knocks* =**setback**, reversal, defeat, failure, difficulty, misfortune, bad luck, mishap, (body) blow, disaster, calamity, disappointment, sorrow, trouble, hardship; *informal* kick in the teeth.

■ **knock about/around** *(informal)* **1** *knocking around the area* =**wander (around)**, roam (around), rove (around), range over, travel (around), journey around, voyage around, drift around, potter around; *informal* gad about, gallivant around. **2** *she knocks around with artists* =**associate**, consort, keep company, go around, mix, socialize, be friends, be friendly; *informal* hobnob, hang out, run around.

■ **knock someone/something about/around** =**beat (up)**, batter, hit, punch, thump, thrash, slap; maltreat, mistreat, abuse, ill-treat, assault, attack; *N. Amer.* beat up on; *informal* rough up, do over, give someone a hiding, clobber, clout, bash, belt, whack, wallop.

■ **knock someone down** =**fell**, floor, flatten, bring down, knock to the ground; knock over, run over/down.

■ **knock something down** =**demolish**, pull down, tear down, destroy; raze (to the ground), level, flatten, bulldoze.

■ **knock off** *(informal)* =**stop work**, finish (work), clock off, leave work, go home.

■ **knock someone off** *(informal)*. See KILL verb *sense* 1.

■ **knock something off 1** *(Brit. informal)* *someone knocked off the video.* See STEAL verb *sense* 1. **2** *(informal)* *we expect you to knock off three stories a day* =**produce**, make, turn out, create, construct, assemble, put together; complete, finish. **3** *(informal)* *knock off 10% from the bill* =**deduct**, take off/away, subtract, dock.

■ **knock someone out 1** *I hit him and knocked him out* =**knock unconscious**, knock senseless; floor, prostrate; *informal* lay out, KO, fell. **2** *England was knocked out* =**eliminate**, beat, defeat, vanquish, overwhelm, trounce. **3** *(informal) walking that far knocked her out* =**exhaust**, wear out, tire (out), fatigue, weary, drain; *informal* do in, take it out of; *Brit. informal* knacker; *N. Amer. informal* poop. **4** *(informal) the view knocked me out* =**overwhelm**, stun, stupefy, amaze, astound, astonish, stagger, take someone's breath away; impress, dazzle, enchant, entrance; *informal* bowl over, flabbergast, knock sideways, blow away; *Brit. informal* knock for six.

■ **knock something up** *(Brit. informal)* =**improvise**, contrive; *informal* whip up, rig up, throw together, cobble together, rustle up.

knoll ▸ noun =**hillock**, mound, rise, hummock, hill, hump, tor, bank, ridge, elevation; *Scottish* brae; *literary* eminence.

knot ▸ noun **1** *a knot in the wood* =**nodule**, gnarl, node; lump, knob, swelling, protuberance, bump. **2** *a small knot of people* =**cluster**, group, band, huddle, bunch, circle, ring, gathering.
▸ verb *a scarf knotted round her throat* =**tie**, fasten, secure, bind, do up.

knotted ▸ adjective =**tangled**, knotty, matted, snarled, unkempt, uncombed, tousled; *informal* mussed up.

knotty ▸ adjective *a knotty problem* =**complex**, complicated, involved, intricate, convoluted; difficult, hard, thorny, taxing, awkward, tricky, problematic, troublesome.
−OPPOSITES straightforward.

know ▸ verb **1** *she doesn't know I'm here* =**be aware**, realize, be conscious; notice, perceive, see, sense, recognize. **2** *I don't know his address* =**have**, be apprised of; *formal* be cognizant of. **3** *do you know the rules* =**be familiar with**, be conversant with, be acquainted with, be versed in, have mastered, have a grasp of, understand, comprehend; have learned; *informal* be clued up on. **4** *I don't know many people here* =**be acquainted with**, have met, be familiar with; *Scottish* ken.

know-all ▸ noun *(informal)* =**wiseacre**; *informal* smart alec, wise guy, smarty-pants; *Brit. informal* clever clogs, clever Dick; *N. Amer. informal* know-it-all.

know-how ▸ noun *(informal)* =**knowledge**, expertise, skill, proficiency, understanding, mastery, technique; ability, capability, competence, capacity, adeptness, dexterity, deftness, adroitness; *informal* savvy.

knowing ▸ adjective **1** *a knowing smile* =**significant**, meaningful, expressive, suggestive; arch, sly, mischievous, impish, superior. **2** *she's a very knowing child* =**sophisticated**, worldly, worldly-wise, urbane, experienced; knowledgeable, well informed, enlightened; shrewd, astute, canny, sharp, wily, perceptive; *informal* streetwise. **3** *a knowing infringement of the rules* =**deliberate**, intentional, conscious, calculated, wilful, done on purpose, premeditated, planned; cynical.

knowingly ▸ adverb =**deliberately**, intentionally, consciously, wittingly, on purpose, by design, premeditatedly, wilfully; cynically.

knowledge ▸ noun **1** *his knowledge of history | technical knowledge* =**understanding**, comprehension, grasp, command, mastery; expertise, skill, proficiency, expertness, accomplishment, adeptness, capacity, capability; *informal* know-how. **2** *people anxious to display their knowledge* =**learning**, erudition, education, scholarship, schooling, wisdom. **3** *he slipped away without my knowledge* =**awareness**, consciousness, realization, cognition, apprehension, perception, appreciation; *formal* cognizance. **4** *an intimate knowledge of the countryside* =**familiarity**, acquaintance, conversance, intimacy.
–OPPOSITES ignorance.

WORD LINKS

relating to knowledge: **gnostic**
---

knowledgeable ▸ adjective **1** *a knowledgeable old man* =**well informed**, learned, well read, (well) educated, erudite, scholarly, cultured, cultivated, enlightened. **2** *he is knowledgeable about modern art* =**conversant**, familiar, well acquainted, au fait; up on, up to date with, abreast of; *informal* clued up, genned up; *Brit. informal* switched on.
–OPPOSITES ill-informed.

known ▸ adjective *a known criminal* =**recognized**, well known, widely known, noted, celebrated, notable, notorious; acknowledged, self-confessed, declared, overt.

kowtow ▸ verb =**grovel**, be obsequious, be servile, be sycophantic, fawn on, bow and scrape, toady, abase oneself; curry favour with, dance attendance on, ingratiate oneself with; *informal* crawl, creep, suck up, lick someone's boots; *Austral./NZ informal* smoodge to.

kudos ▸ noun =**prestige**, cachet, glory, honour, status, standing, distinction, fame, celebrity; admiration, respect, esteem, acclaim, praise, credit.

k

label ▸ noun **1** *the price is clearly stated on the label* =**tag**, ticket, tab, sticker, marker, docket. **2** *a designer label* =**brand (name)**, (trade) name, trademark, make, logo. **3** *the label the media came up with for me* =**designation**, description, tag; name, epithet, nickname, title, sobriquet, pet name; *formal* appellation.
▸ verb **1** *label each jar with the date* =**tag**, ticket, mark. **2** *tests labelled him an underachiever* =**categorize**, classify, class, describe, designate, identify; mark, stamp, brand, condemn, pigeonhole, stereotype, typecast; call, name, term, dub, nickname.

> **WORD LINKS**
>
> *matchbox label collector:* **phillumenist**

laborious ▸ adjective **1** *a laborious job* =**arduous**, hard, heavy, difficult, strenuous, gruelling, punishing, exacting, tough, onerous, burdensome, backbreaking, trying, challenging; wearing; tedious, boring. **2** *Doug's laborious style* =**laboured**, strained, forced, stiff, stilted, unnatural, artificial, overwrought, heavy, ponderous.
−OPPOSITES easy, effortless.

labour ▸ noun **1** *manual labour* =**(hard) work**, toil, exertion, industry, drudgery, effort, donkey work; *informal* slog, grind, sweat, elbow grease; *Brit. informal* graft; *literary* travail. **2** *the conflict between capital and labour* =**workers**, employees, workforce, staff, working people, labourers, labour force, proletariat. **3** *a difficult labour* =**childbirth**, birth, delivery; contractions; *literary* travail; *dated* confinement.
−OPPOSITES rest, management.
▸ verb **1** *a project on which he had laboured for many years* =**work (hard)**, toil, slave (away), grind away, struggle, strive, exert oneself, work one's fingers to the bone, work like a Trojan/slave; *informal* slog away, plug away; *Brit. informal* graft. **2** *Newcastle laboured to break down their defence* =**strive**, struggle, endeavour, work, try hard, make every effort, do one's best, do one's utmost, do all one can,

give one's all, go all out, fight, exert oneself; *informal* bend/lean over backwards, pull out all the stops.

laboured ▸ adjective **1** *laboured breathing* =**strained**, difficult, forced, laborious. **2** *a rather laboured joke* =**contrived**, strained, forced, unnatural, artificial, overdone, ponderous, laborious, unconvincing.

labourer ▸ noun =**workman**, worker, working man, manual worker, unskilled worker, blue-collar worker, (hired) hand, roustabout, drudge, menial; *Austral./NZ* rouseabout; *Brit. dated* navvy.

labyrinth ▸ noun **1** *a labyrinth of little streets* =**maze**, warren, network, complex, web, entanglement. **2** *the labyrinth of conflicting regulations* =**tangle**, web, maze, morass, jungle; jumble, mishmash.

labyrinthine ▸ adjective **1** *labyrinthine corridors* =**maze-like**, winding, twisting, serpentine, meandering. **2** *a labyrinthine system* =**complicated**, intricate, complex, involved, tortuous, convoluted, tangled, elaborate; confusing, puzzling, mystifying, bewildering, baffling.

lace ▸ verb **1** *he laced up his running shoes* =**fasten**, do up, tie up, secure, knot. **2** *tea laced with rum* =**flavour**, mix, blend, fortify, strengthen, stiffen, season, spice (up), liven up; doctor, adulterate; *informal* spike.
−OPPOSITES untie.

lacerate ▸ verb =**cut (open)**, gash, slash, tear, rip, rend, shred, score, scratch; wound, hurt.

laceration ▸ noun =**gash**, cut, wound, injury, tear, slash, scratch, scrape, abrasion, graze.

lack ▸ noun *a lack of cash* =**absence**, want, need, deficiency, dearth, shortage, shortfall, scarcity, paucity, scarceness, deficit.
−OPPOSITES abundance.
▸ verb *she's immature and lacks judgement* =**be without**, be in need of, need, be

lacking, require, want, be short of, be deficient in, be low on, be pressed for, have insufficient; *informal* be strapped for.
–OPPOSITES have, possess.

lacking ▸ adjective **1** *proof was lacking* =**absent**, missing, non-existent, un-available. **2** *the advocate general found the government lacking* =**deficient**, defective, inadequate, wanting, flawed, faulty, un-acceptable. **3** *the game was lacking in atmosphere* =**without**, devoid of, bereft of; deficient in, low on, short on, in need of.
–OPPOSITES present, plentiful.

lacklustre ▸ adjective =**uninspired**, uninspiring, unimaginative, dull, hum-drum, colourless, characterless, bland, insipid, flat, dry, lifeless, tame, prosaic; dreary, tedious.
–OPPOSITES inspired.

laconic ▸ adjective =**brief**, concise, terse, brusque, succinct, short, pithy.
–OPPOSITES verbose.

lad ▸ noun *(informal)* **1** *a young lad* =**boy**, schoolboy, youth, youngster, juvenile, stripling; *informal* kid, nipper, whipper-snapper; *Scottish informal* laddie; *derogatory* brat. **2** *a hard-working lad* =**(young) man**; *informal* guy, fellow, geezer; *Brit. informal* chap, bloke; *N. Amer. informal* dude, hombre; *Austral./NZ informal* digger.

ladder ▸ noun *the academic ladder* =**hier-archy**, scale, ranking, pecking order.

laden ▸ adjective =**loaded**, burdened, weighed down, overloaded, piled high; full, filled, packed, stuffed, crammed; *informal* chock-full, chock-a-block.

ladle ▸ verb =**spoon out**, scoop out, dish up/out, serve, distribute.

lady ▸ noun **1** *several ladies were present* =**woman**, female; *Scottish & N. English* lass, lassie; *Brit. informal* bird, bint; *N. Amer. informal* dame, broad, jane; *Austral./NZ informal* sheila; *literary* maid, damsel; *archaic* wench. **2** *lords and ladies* =**noblewoman**, duchess, countess, peeress, viscountess, baroness; *archaic* gentlewoman.

ladylike ▸ adjective =**genteel**, polite, refined, well bred, cultivated, polished, decorous, proper, respectable, seemly, well mannered, cultured, sophisticated, elegant; *Brit. informal* posh.
–OPPOSITES coarse.

lag ▸ verb =**fall behind**, straggle, fall back, trail (behind), hang back, not keep pace, bring up the rear.
–OPPOSITES keep up.

laid-back ▸ adjective *(informal)* =**re-laxed**, easy-going, equable, free and easy, casual, nonchalant, insouciant, unexcitable, blasé, cool, calm, uncon-cerned; leisurely, unhurried; *informal* unflappable.
–OPPOSITES uptight.

laid up ▸ adjective *(informal)* =**bedridden**, housebound, incapacitated, injured, disabled; ill, sick, unwell, poorly, ailing, indisposed.
–OPPOSITES healthy, active.

lair ▸ noun **1** *the lair of a large python* =**den**, burrow, hole, tunnel, cave. **2** *a villain's lair* =**hideaway**, hiding place, hideout, den, base; *informal* hidey-hole.

lake ▸ noun =**pond**, pool, tarn, reservoir, lagoon, waterhole, inland sea; *Scottish* loch, lochan; *Anglo-Irish* lough; *N. Amer.* bayou, pothole (lake); *literary* mere.

WORD LINKS

relating to lakes: **lacustrine**
study of lakes: **limnology**

lambaste ▸ verb =**criticize**, chastise, censure, take to task, harangue; up-braid, scold, reprimand, rebuke, chide, reprove, admonish, berate; *informal* lay into, pitch into, tear into, give someone a dressing-down, carpet, tell off, bawl out; *Brit. informal* tick off, have a go at, slam; *N. Amer. informal* chew out; *formal* cas-tigate, excoriate.

lame ▸ adjective **1** *the mare was lame* =**limping**, hobbling; crippled, disabled, incapacitated; *informal* gammy; *dated* game; *archaic* halt. **2** *a lame excuse* =**fee-ble**, weak, thin, flimsy, poor; unconvin-cing, implausible, unlikely.
–OPPOSITES convincing.

lament ▸ verb =**bemoan**, bewail, com-plain about, deplore; protest against, object to, oppose, fulminate against, inveigh against, denounce.
–OPPOSITES celebrate.

lamentable ▸ adjective =**deplorable**, regrettable, terrible, awful, wretched, woeful, dire, disastrous, desperate, grave, appalling, dreadful; pitiful, shameful, unfortunate; *formal* egregious.
–OPPOSITES wonderful.

lamentation ▸ noun =**weeping**, wail-ing, crying, sobbing, moaning, grieving, mourning.

lamp ▸ noun =**light**, lantern; torch.

lampoon ▸ verb *he was mercilessly*

lampooned =**satirize**, mock, ridicule, make fun of, caricature, parody, tease; *informal* send up.

▶ noun *a lampoon of student life* =**satire**, burlesque, parody, skit, caricature, mockery; *informal* send-up, take-off, spoof.

lance ▶ noun *a knight with a lance* =**spear**, pike, javelin; harpoon.

land ▶ noun **1** *Lyme Park has 1323 acres of land* | *publicly owned land* =**grounds**, fields, open space; property, territory, acres, acreage, estate, lands, real estate; countryside, rural area, green belt; *historical* demesne. **2** *fertile land* =**soil**, earth, loam, topsoil, humus. **3** *many people are leaving the land* =**the countryside**, the country, rural areas; farming, agriculture. **4** *Tunisia is a land of variety* =**country**, nation, (nation) state, realm, kingdom, province; region, area, place, domain. **5** *the lookout sighted land to the east* =**terra firma**, dry land; coast, coastline, shore.

▶ verb **1** *Allied troops landed in France* =**disembark**, go ashore, debark, alight, get off. **2** *the ship landed at Le Havre* =**berth**, dock, moor, (drop) anchor, tie up, put in. **3** *their plane landed at Chicago* =**touch down**, make a landing, come in to land, come down. **4** *a bird landed on the branch* =**perch**, settle, come to rest, alight. **5** *(informal) Nick landed the job of editor* =**get**, obtain, acquire, secure, gain, net, win, achieve, attain, bag, carry off; *informal* swing. **6** *(informal) that habit landed her in trouble* =**get**, bring, lead. **7** *(informal) they landed her with the bill* =**burden**, leave, saddle, encumber; *informal* dump; *Brit. informal* lumber. **8** *(informal) John landed a punch on Brian's chin* =**inflict**, deal, deliver, administer, dispense, mete out; *informal* fetch.

−OPPOSITES sail, take off.

■ **land up** =**finish up**, find oneself, end up; *informal* wind up, fetch up.

WORD LINKS

relating to land: **terrestrial**

landlady, landlord ▶ noun **1** *the landlord of the pub* =**publican**, licensee, innkeeper, owner, hotelier, restaurateur; manager, manageress. **2** *the landlady had objected to the noise* =**owner**, proprietor, proprietress, lessor, householder, landowner.

−OPPOSITES tenant.

landmark ▶ noun **1** *one of London's most* famous landmarks =**monument**, feature; building. **2** *the ruling was hailed as a landmark* =**turning point**, milestone, watershed, critical point.

landscape ▶ noun =**scenery**, countryside, topography, country, terrain, land.

landslide ▶ noun **1** *floods and landslides* =**landslip**, mudslide; avalanche. **2** *the Labour landslide* =**victory**, overwhelming majority, triumph; *informal* whitewash.

lane ▶ noun **1** *country lanes* =**byroad**, byway, track, road; alley, alleyway. **2** *cycle lanes* =**track**, way, course.

language ▶ noun **1** *the structure of language* =**speech**, writing, communication, conversation, speaking, talking, talk, discourse; words, vocabulary, text. **2** *the English language* =**tongue**, mother tongue, native tongue; *informal* lingo; lingua franca, Creole, dialect. **3** *the booklet is written in simple, everyday language* =**wording**, phrasing, phraseology, style, vocabulary, terminology, expressions, turn of phrase, parlance, form of expression, usage, idiolect, choice of words; speech, dialect, patois, slang, idiom, jargon, argot, cant; *informal* lingo.

WORD LINKS

relating to language: **linguistic**
scientific study of language: **linguistics**

languid ▶ adjective **1** *a languid wave of the hand* =**relaxed**, unhurried, languorous, slow; listless, lethargic, sluggish, lazy, idle, indolent, apathetic; *informal* laid-back. **2** *she was pale and languid* =**sickly**, weak, faint, feeble, frail, delicate; tired, weary, fatigued.

−OPPOSITES energetic.

languish ▶ verb **1** *the plants languished and died* =**weaken**, deteriorate, decline, go downhill; wither, droop, wilt, fade, waste away. **2** *the general is now languishing in prison* =**waste away**, rot, be abandoned, be neglected, be forgotten, suffer; lie.

−OPPOSITES thrive.

languor ▶ noun =**lassitude**, lethargy, listlessness, torpor, fatigue, weariness, sleepiness, drowsiness; laziness, idleness, indolence, inertia, sluggishness, apathy.

−OPPOSITES vigour.

lank ▶ adjective **1** *lank, greasy hair* =**limp**, lifeless, lustreless, dull; straggling; straight, long. **2** *his lank figure. See* LANKY.

lanky ▶ adjective =tall, **thin**, slender, slim, lean, lank, skinny, spindly, spare, gangling, gangly, gawky, rangy.
–OPPOSITES stocky.

lap[1] ▶ noun *Henry sat on his gran's lap* =**knee**, knees, thighs.

lap[2] ▶ noun *a race of eight laps* =**circuit**, leg, circle, revolution, round.
▶ verb *she lapped the other runners* =**overtake**, outstrip, leave behind, pass, go past; catch up with.

lap[3] ▶ verb **1** *waves lapped against the sea wall* =**splash**, wash, swish, slosh, break; *literary* plash. **2** *the dog lapped water out of a puddle* =**drink**, lick up, sup, swallow, slurp, gulp.
■ **lap something up** =relish, revel in, savour, delight in, wallow in, glory in, enjoy.

lapse ▶ noun **1** *a lapse of concentration* =**failure**, slip, error, mistake, blunder, fault, omission; *informal* slip-up. **2** *his lapse into petty crime* =**decline**, fall, falling, slipping, drop, deterioration, degeneration, backsliding, regression, descent, sinking, slide. **3** *a lapse of time* =**interval**, gap, pause, interlude, lull, hiatus, break.
▶ verb **1** *the planning permission has lapsed* =**expire**, become void, become invalid, run out. **2** *do not let friendships lapse* =**(come to an) end**, cease, stop, terminate, pass, fade, wither, die. **3** *she lapsed into silence* =**revert**, relapse; drift, slide, slip, sink.

lapsed ▶ adjective **1** *a lapsed Catholic* =**non-practising**, backsliding, apostate. **2** *a lapsed season ticket* =**expired**, void, invalid, out of date.
–OPPOSITES practising, valid.

larceny ▶ noun. *See* THEFT.

larder ▶ noun =**pantry**, (food) store, (food) cupboard; cooler, scullery.

large ▶ adjective **1** *a large house | large numbers of people* =**big**, sizeable, substantial, considerable, good; tall, high; voluminous. **2** *a large red-faced man* =**big**, burly, heavy, tall, bulky, thickset, chunky, hefty, muscular, brawny, solid, powerful, sturdy, strong; fat, plump, overweight, chubby, stout, meaty, fleshy, portly, rotund, flabby, paunchy, obese, corpulent; *informal* beefy, tubby, pudgy; *Brit. informal* podgy; *N. Amer. informal* zaftig, corn-fed. **3** *a large supply of wool* =**abundant**, copious, plentiful, ample, liberal, generous, lavish, bountiful, good, considerable, superabundant; *literary* plenteous.
–OPPOSITES small, meagre.

WORD LINKS
related prefixes: **macro-, mega-**

largely ▶ adverb =**mostly**, mainly, to a large/great extent, chiefly, predominantly, primarily, principally, for the most part, in the main; typically, commonly.

largesse ▶ noun =**generosity**, liberality, munificence, bountifulness, beneficence, altruism, charity, philanthropy, magnanimity, benevolence, charitableness, open-handedness, kindness.
–OPPOSITES meanness.

lark (*informal*) ▶ noun **1** *we were just having a bit of a lark* =**laugh**, giggle, joke; prank, trick, jape. **2** *I've got this snowboarding lark sussed* =*informal* **thing**, business, racket, caper, trip.
▶ verb *he's always larking about* =**fool about/around**, play tricks, make mischief, monkey about/around, clown about/around, have fun, skylark; *informal* mess about/around; *Brit. informal* muck about/around.

lascivious ▶ adjective =**lecherous**, lewd, lustful, licentious, libidinous, salacious, lubricious, prurient, dirty, smutty, naughty, suggestive, indecent; *informal* horny; *Brit. informal* randy; *formal* concupiscent.

lash ▶ verb **1** *rain lashed the window panes* =**beat against**, dash against, pound, batter, strike, drum. **2** *the tiger began to lash his tail* =**swish**, flick, twitch, whip. **3** *two boats were lashed together* =**fasten**, bind, tie (up), tether, hitch, knot, rope, make fast.
▶ noun **1** *he brought the lash down upon the prisoner's back* =**whip**, scourge, flail, birch, cane; *historical* knout, cat-o'-nine-tails, cat. **2** *twenty lashes* =**stroke**, blow; *archaic* stripe.
■ **lash out 1** *the president lashed out at the opposition* =**criticize**, attack, condemn, denounce, lambaste, harangue, pillory; berate, upbraid, rebuke, reproach; *informal* lay into; *formal* castigate. **2** *Norman lashed out at Terry with a knife* =**hit out**, strike, let fly, take a swing; set upon/about, turn on, round on, attack; *informal* lay into, pitch into.

lass ▶ noun (*Scottish & N. English*) =**girl**, young woman, young lady; *Scottish* lassie; *Irish* colleen; *informal* chick, girlie; *Brit.*

informal bird, bint; *N. Amer. informal* dame, babe, doll, gal, broad; *Austral./NZ informal* sheila; *literary* maid, maiden, damsel; *archaic* wench.

lassitude ▶ noun =**lethargy**, listlessness, weariness, languor, sluggishness, tiredness, fatigue, torpor, apathy.
–OPPOSITES vigour.

last¹ ▶ adjective **1** *the last woman in the queue* =**rearmost**, hindmost, endmost, furthest (back), final, ultimate. **2** *Rembrandt spent his last years in Amsterdam* =**closing**, concluding, final, end, terminal; later, latter. **3** *we met last year* =**previous**, preceding; prior, former. **4** *this was his last chance* =**final**, only remaining.
–OPPOSITES first, early, next.
▶ adverb *the candidate coming last is eliminated* =**at the end**, at/in the rear, at the back.
▶ noun *the most important business was left to the last* =**end**, ending, finish, close, conclusion, finale.
–OPPOSITES beginning.
■ **at last** =**finally**, in the end, eventually, ultimately, at long last, after a long time, in (the fullness of) time.
■ **the last word** *the last word in luxury* =**the best**, the peak, the acme, the epitome, the latest; the pinnacle, the apex, the apogee, the ultimate, the height, the zenith, the crème de la crème.

last² ▶ verb **1** *the hearing lasted for six days* =**continue**, go on, carry on, keep on/going, proceed, take; stay, remain, persist. **2** *how long will he last as manager?* =**survive**, endure, hold on/out, keep going, persevere; *informal* stick it out, hang on, hack it. **3** *the car is built to last* =**endure**, wear well, stand up, bear up; *informal* go the distance.

last-ditch ▶ adjective =**last-minute**, last-chance, eleventh-hour, last-resort, desperate, final; *informal* last-gasp.

lasting ▶ adjective =**enduring**, long-lasting, long-lived, abiding, continuing, long-term, permanent; durable, stable, secure, long-standing; eternal, undying, everlasting, unending, never-ending.
–OPPOSITES ephemeral.

lastly ▶ adverb =**finally**, in conclusion, to conclude, to sum up, to end, last, ultimately.
–OPPOSITES firstly.

late ▶ adjective **1** *the train was late* =**behind time**, behind schedule; tardy, overdue, delayed. **2** *her late husband* =**dead**, departed, lamented, passed on/away; *formal* deceased.
–OPPOSITES punctual, early.
▶ adverb **1** *she had arrived late* =**behind schedule**, behind time, belatedly, tardily, at the last minute. **2** *I was working late* =**after hours**, overtime; into the night.

lately ▶ adverb =**recently**, of late, latterly.

lateness ▶ noun =**unpunctuality**, tardiness, delay.

latent ▶ adjective =**dormant**, untapped, unused, undiscovered, hidden, concealed, unseen, undeveloped, unrealized, unfulfilled, potential.

later ▶ adjective *a later chapter* =**subsequent**, following, succeeding, future, upcoming, to come, ensuing, next.
–OPPOSITES earlier.
▶ adverb **1** *later, the film rights were sold* =**subsequently**, eventually, then, next, later on, after this/that, afterwards, at a later date, in the future, in due course, by and by, in a while, in time. **2** *two days later a letter arrived* =**afterwards**, later on, after (that), subsequently, following; *formal* thereafter.

lateral ▶ adjective **1** *lateral movements* =**sideways**, sideward, to the side, edgeways, oblique. **2** *lateral thinking* =**unorthodox**, creative, imaginative, original, innovative; new, novel, different.

latest ▶ adjective =**most recent**, newest, just out, just released, fresh, (bang) up to date, up to the minute, state-of-the-art, cutting-edge, leading-edge, current, modern, contemporary, fashionable, in fashion, in vogue; *informal* in, with it, trendy, hip, hot, happening, cool.
–OPPOSITES old.

lather ▶ noun **1** *a rich, soapy lather* =**foam**, froth, suds, bubbles; *literary* spume. **2** *(informal) Dad was in a lather* =**panic**, fever; *informal* flap, sweat, tizzy, dither, state, stew; *N. Amer. informal* twit.

latitude ▶ noun =**freedom**, scope, leeway, (breathing) space, flexibility, liberty, independence, free rein, licence, room to manoeuvre, slack.
–OPPOSITES restriction.

latter ▶ adjective **1** *the latter half of the season* =**later**, closing, end, concluding, final. **2** *Russia chose the latter option* =**last-mentioned**, second, last, final.

–OPPOSITES former.

latter-day ▶ adjective =**modern**, present-day, current, contemporary.

latterly ▶ adverb **1** *latterly, she has been in more pain* =**recently**, lately, of late. **2** *latterly he worked as a political editor* =**ultimately**, finally, towards the end.

lattice ▶ noun =**grid**, framework, trellis, network, mesh; matrix.

laudable ▶ adjective =**praiseworthy**, commendable, admirable, worthy, deserving, creditable, estimable, exemplary.
–OPPOSITES shameful.

laugh ▶ verb **1** *he started to laugh* =**chuckle**, chortle, guffaw, giggle, titter, snigger, snicker, burst out laughing, roar, hoot, dissolve into laughter, split one's sides, be doubled up; *informal* be in stitches, be rolling in the aisles, crease up, fall about, crack up. **2** *people laughed at his theories* =**ridicule**, mock, deride, scoff at, jeer at, sneer at, jibe at, make fun of, poke fun at, scorn; lampoon, satirize; *informal* take the mickey out of, pooh-pooh; *Austral./NZ informal* poke mullock at.
▶ noun **1** *he gave a short laugh* =**chuckle**, chortle, guffaw, giggle, titter, snigger, snicker, roar, hoot, shriek, belly laugh. **2** *(informal) he was a laugh* =**joker**, wag, wit, clown, jester, prankster, character; *informal* card, case, hoot, scream, riot, barrel of laughs; *Austral./NZ informal* hard case. **3** *(informal) I entered the contest for a laugh* =**joke**, prank, bit of fun, jest; *informal* lark.
■ **laugh something off** =**dismiss**, make a joke of, make light of, shrug off, brush aside, scoff at; *informal* pooh-pooh.

laughable ▶ adjective =**ridiculous**, ludicrous, absurd, risible, preposterous; foolish, silly, idiotic, stupid, nonsensical, crazy, insane, outrageous; *Brit. informal* daft.

laughing stock ▶ noun =**figure of fun**, dupe, butt, stooge.

laughter ▶ noun **1** *the laughter subsided* =**laughing**, chuckling, chortling, guffawing, giggling, tittering, sniggering. **2** *a source of laughter* =**amusement**, entertainment, humour, mirth, merriment, gaiety, hilarity, jollity, fun.

launch ▶ verb **1** *a chair was launched at him* =**throw**, hurl, fling, pitch, lob, let fly; fire, shoot; *informal* chuck, heave, sling. **2** *the government launched a new cam-*paign =**initiate**, get going, get under way, start, commence, begin, present, inaugurate, set up, introduce; *informal* kick off.

lavatory ▶ noun =**toilet**, WC, water closet, (public) convenience, cloakroom, powder room, urinal, privy, latrine; *N. Amer.* washroom, bathroom, rest room, men's/ladies' room, commode, comfort station; *Nautical* head; *informal* little girls'/boys' room, smallest room; *Brit. informal* loo, bog, the Ladies, the Gents, khazi, lav; *N. Amer. informal* can, john; *Austral./NZ informal* dunny; *archaic* closet, garderobe, jakes.

lavish ▶ adjective **1** *a lavish apartment* =**sumptuous**, luxurious, gorgeous, costly, expensive, opulent, grand, splendid, rich, fancy; *informal* posh. **2** *he was lavish with his hospitality* =**generous**, liberal, bountiful, unstinting, unsparing, free, munificent, extravagant, prodigal. **3** *lavish amounts of champagne* =**abundant**, copious, plentiful, liberal, prolific, generous; *literary* plenteous.
–OPPOSITES meagre, frugal.
▶ verb *she lavished money on her children* =**shower**, heap, throw at.

law ▶ noun **1** *the law* =**rules (and regulations)**, constitution, legislation, legal code; rubric. **2** *a new law* =**regulation**, statute, act, bill, decree, edict, rule, ruling, resolution, dictum, command, order, directive, dictate, diktat, fiat, bylaw; *N. Amer. formal* ordinance. **3** *(informal) on the run from the law.* See POLICE noun. **4** *the laws of the game* =**rule**, regulation, principle, convention, instruction, guideline. **5** *a moral law* =**principle**, rule, precept, commandment, belief, creed, credo, maxim, tenet, doctrine, canon.

┌─────────────────────────────────────┐
│ **WORD LINKS** │
│ *relating to laws:* **legal, judicial, juridical** │
└─────────────────────────────────────┘

law-abiding ▶ adjective =**honest**, lawful, righteous, upright, upstanding, good, decent, virtuous, moral, dutiful, obedient, compliant.
–OPPOSITES criminal.

lawbreaker ▶ noun =**criminal**, felon, wrongdoer, evil-doer, offender, transgressor, miscreant; villain, rogue; *informal* crook; *formal* malefactor.

lawful ▶ adjective =**legitimate**, legal, licit, just, permissible, permitted, allowable, allowed, rightful, sanctioned,

authorized, warranted, within the law; *informal* legit.
–OPPOSITES illegal.

lawless ▸ adjective =**anarchic**, disorderly, wild, ungovernable, unruly, rebellious, insubordinate, riotous, mutinous.
–OPPOSITES orderly.

lawlessness ▸ noun =**anarchy**, disorder, chaos, unruliness, criminality, crime.

lawyer ▸ noun =**solicitor**, barrister, advocate, counsel, Queen's Counsel, QC; *N. Amer.* attorney, counselor(-at-law); *informal* brief.

lax ▸ adjective =**slack**, slipshod, negligent, remiss, careless, sloppy, slapdash, offhand, casual; easy-going, permissive, overindulgent.
–OPPOSITES strict.

lay¹ ▸ verb **1** *Curtis laid the newspaper on the table* =**put (down)**, place, set (down), deposit, rest, position, shove; *informal* stick, dump, park, plonk; *Brit. informal* bung. **2** *they are going to lay charges* =**bring (forward)**, press, prefer, lodge, register, place, file. **3** *we laid plans for the next voyage* =**devise**, arrange, make (ready), prepare, work out, hatch, design, plan, scheme, plot, conceive, put together, draw up, produce, develop, formulate; *informal* cook up.

■ **lay something down 1** *they were forced to lay down their weapons* =**relinquish**, surrender, give up, abandon. **2** *the ground rules have been laid down* =**formulate**, set down, draw up, frame; prescribe, ordain, dictate, decree; enact, pass, decide, determine.

■ **lay something in** =**stock up with/on**, stockpile, store (up), amass, hoard, stow (away), put aside/away/by, garner, collect, squirrel away; *informal* salt away, stash (away).

■ **lay into** *(informal)* **1** *a policeman laying into a protestor.* See ASSAULT verb sense 1. **2** *he laid into her with a string of insults.* See CRITICIZE.

■ **lay off** *(informal)* =**give up**, stop, refrain from, abstain from, desist from, cut out; *informal* pack in, leave off, quit.

■ **lay someone off** =**make redundant**, dismiss, let go, discharge, give notice to; *informal* sack, fire, give someone their cards, give someone their marching orders, give someone the boot/push, give someone the (old) heave-ho.

■ **lay something on** =**provide**, supply,

furnish, line up, organize, prepare, produce, make available; *informal* fix up.

■ **lay someone out** *(informal)* =**knock out/down**, knock unconscious, fell, floor, flatten; *informal* KO, kayo; *Brit. informal* knock for six.

■ **lay something out 1** *Robyn laid the plans out on the desk* =**spread out**, set out, display; unfold, unroll, open. **2** *a paper laying out our priorities* =**outline**, sketch out, detail, draw up, formulate, work out, frame, draft. **3** *(informal) he had to lay out £70.* See PAY verb sense 2.

■ **lay waste** =**devastate**, wipe out, destroy, demolish, annihilate, raze, ruin, wreck, level, flatten, ravage, pillage, sack, despoil.

lay² ▸ adjective *a lay audience* =**nonprofessional**, non-specialist, non-technical, untrained, unqualified.

layabout ▸ noun =**idler**, good-for-nothing, loafer, lounger, shirker, sluggard, laggard, malingerer; *informal* skiver, waster, slacker, lazybones; *Austral./NZ informal* bludger; *literary* wastrel.

layer ▸ noun =**coating**, sheet, coat, film, covering, blanket, skin.

layman ▸ noun. See LAYPERSON senses 1, 2.

lay-off ▸ noun =**redundancy**, dismissal, discharge; *informal* sacking, firing, the sack, the boot, the axe, the elbow.
–OPPOSITES recruitment.

layout ▸ noun **1** *the layout of the house* =**arrangement**, geography, design, organization; plan. **2** *the magazine's layout* =**design**, arrangement, presentation, style, format; structure, organization, composition, configuration.

layperson ▸ noun **1** *a prayer book for laypeople* =**member of the congregation**, layman, laywoman; (**laypeople**) the laity. **2** *engineering sounds highly specialized to the layperson* =**non-expert**, layman, non-professional, non-specialist.

laze ▸ verb =**relax**, unwind, idle, do nothing, loaf (around/about), lounge (around/about), loll (around/about), lie (around/about), take it easy; *informal* hang around/round, veg (out).

lazy ▸ adjective =**(bone) idle**, indolent, slothful, work-shy, shiftless, inactive, sluggish, lethargic; slack, lax.
–OPPOSITES industrious.

lazybones ▸ noun *(informal)* =**idler**, loafer, layabout, good-for-nothing, shirker, sluggard, laggard; *informal* skiver, waster, slacker; *Austral./NZ informal* bludger; *literary* wastrel.

leach ▸ verb =drain, filter, percolate, strain.

lead[1] ▸ **verb 1** *Michelle led them into the house* =**guide**, conduct, show (the way), usher, escort, steer, shepherd; accompany, see, take. **2** *he led us to believe they were lying* =**cause**, induce, prompt, move, persuade, drive, make; incline, predispose. **3** *she led a coalition of radicals* =**be the leader of**, be the head of, preside over, head, command, govern, rule, be in charge of, be in command of, be in control of, run, control, be at the helm of; administer, organize, manage; reign over; *informal* head up. **4** *Rangers were leading at half-time* =**be ahead**, be winning, be (out) in front, be in the lead, be first. **5** *the champion was leading the field* =**be ahead of**, head; outrun, outstrip, outpace, leave behind; outdo, outclass, beat. **6** *I just want to lead a normal life* =**live**, have, spend, pass, enjoy.
–OPPOSITES follow.

▸ **noun 1** *I was in the lead early on* =**first place**, van, vanguard; ahead, in front, winning. **2** *they took the lead in the personal computer market* =**first position**, forefront, primacy, dominance, superiority, ascendancy; pre-eminence, supremacy, advantage. **3** *playing the lead* =**leading role**, star/starring role, title role, principal role. **4** *a labrador on a lead* =**leash**, tether, cord, rope, chain. **5** *detectives were following up a new lead* =**clue**, pointer, hint, tip, tip-off, suggestion, indication, sign.

▸ **adjective** *the lead position* =**leading**, first, top, foremost, front, head; chief, principal, premier; pole.

■ **lead someone on** =**deceive**, mislead, delude, hoodwink, dupe, trick, fool; tease, flirt with; *informal* string along, lead up the garden path, take for a ride.

■ **lead to** *this might lead to job losses* =**result in**, cause, bring on/about, give rise to, make happen, create, produce, occasion, effect, generate, contribute to, promote; provoke, stir up, spark off, arouse, foment, instigate; involve.

lead[2] ▸ **noun** *a lead-lined box*.

┌─────────────┐
│ **WORD LINKS** │
└─────────────┘
relating to lead: **plumbic, plumbous**

leaden ▸ **adjective 1** *his eyes were leaden with sleep* =**dull**, heavy; listless, lifeless. **2** *leaden prose* =**boring**, dull, unimagina-

tive, uninspired, heavy, laboured, wooden. **3** *a leaden sky* =**grey**, black, dark; cloudy, gloomy, overcast, dull, murky, sunless, louring, oppressive, threatening.

leader ▸ **noun 1** *the leader of the Democratic Party* =**chief**, head, principal; commander, captain; controller, superior, headman; chairman, chairwoman, chairperson, chair; (managing) director, MD, manager, superintendent, supervisor, overseer, master, mistress; president, premier, governor; ruler, monarch, king, queen, sovereign, emperor; *informal* boss, skipper, gaffer, guv'nor, number one, numero uno, honcho; *N. Amer. informal* sachem, padrone. **2** *a world leader in the use of video conferencing* =**pioneer**, front runner, innovator, trailblazer, groundbreaker, trendsetter.
–OPPOSITES follower, supporter.

leadership ▸ **noun 1** *the leadership of the Conservative Party* =**control**, rule, command, dominion; directorship, premiership, governorship, captaincy. **2** *firm leadership* =**guidance**, direction, control, management, supervision; organization, governance.

leading ▸ **adjective 1** *he played the leading role in his team's victory* =**main**, chief, major, prime, principal, foremost, key, central, focal, paramount, dominant, essential. **2** *the leading industrialized countries* =**most powerful**, most important, greatest, chief, pre-eminent, principal, dominant. **3** *last season's leading scorer* =**top**, highest, best, first; front, lead; star.
–OPPOSITES subordinate, minor.

leaf ▸ **noun** *a folder of loose leaves* =**page**, sheet, folio.

▸ **verb** *he leafed through the documents* =**flick**, flip, thumb, skim, browse, glance, riffle; scan, run one's eye over, peruse.

┌─────────────┐
│ **WORD LINKS** │
└─────────────┘
relating to leaves: **foliar**
resembling leaves: **foliaceous**
decorated like leaves: **foliate**
leaf-eating: **folivorous**

leaflet ▸ **noun** =**pamphlet**, booklet, brochure, handbill, circular, flyer, handout, bulletin; *N. Amer.* folder, dodger.

league ▸ **noun 1** *a league of nations* =**alliance**, confederation, confederacy, federation, union, association, coalition, consortium, affiliation, cooperative, guild, partnership, fellowship, syndicate. **2** *the store is not in the same league* =**class**, group, category, level.

■ **in league with** =**collaborating with**, cooperating with, in alliance with, allied with, conspiring with, hand in glove with; *informal* in cahoots with.

leak ▶ verb **1** *oil was leaking from the tanker* =**seep (out)**, escape, ooze (out), issue, drip, dribble, drain, bleed. **2** *the tanks are leaking gasoline* =**discharge**, exude, emit, release, drip, dribble, ooze, secrete. **3** *civil servants leaking information* =**disclose**, divulge, reveal, make public, tell, impart, pass on, relate, communicate, expose, release, bring into the open.
▶ noun **1** *check that there are no leaks in the bag* =**hole**, opening, puncture, perforation, gash, slit, nick, rent, break, crack, fissure, rupture, tear. **2** *a gas leak* =**discharge**, leakage, seepage, escape. **3** *leaks to the media* =**disclosure**, revelation, exposé.

leaky ▶ adjective =**leaking**, dripping; cracked, split, punctured, perforated.
–OPPOSITES watertight.

lean¹ ▶ verb **1** *Polly leaned against the door* =**rest**, recline. **2** *trees leaning in the wind* =**slant**, incline, bend, tilt, slope, tip, list. **3** *he leans towards existentialist philosophy* =**tend**, incline, gravitate; have a preference for, have a penchant for, be partial to, have a liking for, have an affinity with. **4** *someone to lean on* =**depend**, rely, count, bank, trust in.

lean² ▶ adjective **1** *a tall, lean man* =**slim**, thin, slender, spare, wiry, lanky. **2** *a lean harvest* =**meagre**, sparse, poor, mean, inadequate, insufficient, paltry. **3** *lean times* =**unproductive**, barren; hard, bad, difficult, tough; austere.
–OPPOSITES fat, abundant, prosperous.

leaning ▶ noun =**inclination**, tendency, bent, proclivity, propensity, penchant, predisposition, predilection, partiality, preference, bias, attraction, liking, fondness, taste.

leap ▶ verb **1** *he leapt over the gate* =**jump (over)**, vault (over), spring over, bound over, hop (over), hurdle, clear. **2** *Claudia leapt to her feet* =**spring**, jump, bound. **3** *profits leapt by 55%* =**jump**, soar, rocket, skyrocket, shoot up; rise.
▶ noun *a leap of 33%* =**sudden rise**, surge, upsurge, upswing, upturn.
■ **in/by leaps and bounds** =**rapidly**, swiftly, quickly, speedily, at a rate of knots.

learn ▶ verb **1** *learn a foreign language* =**acquire**, grasp, master, take in, absorb, assimilate, digest, familiarize oneself with; study, read up on, be taught; *informal* get the hang of. **2** *she learnt the poem* =**memorize**, learn by heart, commit to memory, learn parrot-fashion, get off/down pat. **3** *he learned that the school would be closing* =**discover**, find out, become aware, be informed, hear (tell); *informal* get wind of the fact.

learned ▶ adjective =**scholarly**, erudite, knowledgeable, widely read, cultured, intellectual, academic, literary, bookish, highbrow; *informal* brainy.
–OPPOSITES ignorant.

learner ▶ noun =**beginner**, trainee, apprentice, pupil, student, novice, newcomer, starter, probationer, tyro, fledgling, neophyte; *N. Amer.* tenderfoot; *N. Amer. informal* greenhorn.
–OPPOSITES veteran.

learning ▶ noun **1** *a centre of learning* =**study**, education, schooling, tuition, teaching; research, investigation. **2** *the astonishing range of his learning* =**scholarship**, knowledge, education, erudition; understanding, wisdom.
–OPPOSITES ignorance.

lease ▶ noun *a 15-year lease* =**leasehold**, agreement, charter; rental, tenancy, tenure.
–OPPOSITES freehold.
▶ verb **1** *the film crew leased a large hangar* =**rent**, hire, charter. **2** *they leased the mill to a reputable family* =**rent (out)**, let (out), hire (out), sublet, sublease.

leash ▶ noun *keep your dog on a leash* =**lead**, tether, rope, chain; restraint.

leather ▶ noun *a leather jacket* =**skin**, hide; suede.
▶ verb *he caught me and leathered me* =**beat**, belt, thrash; *informal* wallop, whack, tan someone's hide, give someone a (good) hiding.

leathery ▶ adjective *leathery skin* =**rough**, rugged, wrinkled, wrinkly, furrowed, lined, wizened, weather-beaten, calloused, gnarled.

leave¹ ▶ verb **1** *I left the hotel* =**depart from**, go (away) from, withdraw from, retire from, take oneself off from, take one's leave of, pull out of, quit, abandon, desert, decamp from, vacate, absent oneself from; say one's farewells/goodbyes, make oneself scarce; *informal* push off, shove off, clear out/off, split,

vamoose, scoot, make tracks, up sticks; *Brit. informal* sling one's hook. **2** *the next morning we left for Leicester* =**set off**, head, make; set sail, get going. **3** *he's left his wife* =**abandon**, desert, jilt, leave in the lurch, leave high and dry, throw over; *informal* dump, ditch, chuck, drop, walk/run out on; *literary* forsake. **4** *he left his job in November* =**resign from**, retire from, step down from, withdraw from, pull out of, give up; *informal* quit, jack in. **5** *she left her handbag on a bus* =**leave behind**, forget, lose, mislay. **6** *I thought I'd leave it to the experts* =**entrust**, hand over, pass on, refer; delegate; defer. **7** *he left her £100,000* =**bequeath**, will, endow, hand down.
–OPPOSITES arrive.

■ **leave someone in the lurch** =**leave stranded**, leave high and dry, abandon, desert, let down.

■ **leave off** (*informal*) =**stop**, cease, finish, desist from, break off, lay off, give up, refrain from, eschew; *informal* quit, knock off, jack in, swear off; *formal* forswear.

■ **leave someone/something out 1** *Adam left out the address* =**miss out**, omit, overlook, forget; skip, miss. **2** *he was left out of the England squad* =**exclude**, omit, drop, pass over.

leave² ▶ noun **1** *the judge granted leave to appeal* =**permission**, consent, authorization, sanction, dispensation, approval, clearance, blessing, agreement, backing, assent, acceptance, licence; *informal* the go-ahead, the green light, the OK, the thumbs-up. **2** *he was on leave* =**holiday**, vacation, break, furlough, sabbatical, leave of absence; *informal* hols, vac.

leaven ▶ verb *formal proceedings leavened by humour* =**permeate**, infuse, pervade, imbue, suffuse; enliven, liven up, invigorate, energize, electrify, ginger up, perk up, brighten up, season, spice up; *informal* pep up.

lecher ▶ noun =**womanizer**, libertine, debauchee, rake, roué; Don Juan, Casanova, Lothario, Romeo; *informal* lech, dirty old man; *formal* fornicator.

lecherous ▶ adjective =**lustful**, licentious, lascivious, libidinous, prurient, lewd, salacious, debauched, dissolute, wanton, dissipated, degenerate, depraved, dirty, filthy; *informal* randy, horny; *formal* concupiscent.
–OPPOSITES chaste.

lecture ▶ noun **1** *a lecture on children's literature* =**speech**, talk, address, discourse, presentation, oration, lesson. **2** *Dave got a severe lecture* =**scolding**, reprimand, rebuke, reproof, reproach, upbraiding, berating, admonishment; *informal* dressing-down, telling-off, talking-to, tongue-lashing; *formal* castigation.
▶ verb **1** *lecturing on the dangers of drugs* =**talk**, speak, discourse, hold forth, declaim; *informal* spout, sound off. **2** *she lectures at university* =**teach**, tutor; work. **3** *he was lectured by the headmaster* =**scold**, reprimand, rebuke, reproach, upbraid, berate, chastise, admonish, lambaste, haul over the coals, take to task; *informal* give someone a dressing-down, give someone a talking-to, tell off, bawl out; *Brit. informal* tick off, carpet; *formal* castigate.

lecturer ▶ noun =(**university/college**) **teacher**, tutor, scholar, don, professor, fellow; academic; *formal* pedagogue.

ledge ▶ noun =**shelf**, sill, mantel, mantelpiece; projection, protrusion, overhang, ridge, prominence.

ledger ▶ noun =(**account**) **book**, record book, register, log; records, books; balance sheet, financial statement.

leech ▶ noun =**parasite**, bloodsucker, passenger; *informal* scrounger, sponger, freeloader.

leer ▶ verb *Henry leered at her* =**ogle**, eye; *informal* give someone a/the once-over, lech.

leery ▶ adjective =**wary**, cautious, careful, guarded, chary, suspicious, distrustful; worried, anxious, apprehensive.

leeway ▶ noun =**freedom**, scope, latitude, space, room, liberty, flexibility, licence, free hand, free rein.

left ▶ adjective =**left-hand**, sinistral; *Nautical* port; *Nautical, archaic* larboard; *Heraldry* sinister.
–OPPOSITES right, starboard.

leftover ▶ noun **1** *a leftover from the 60s* =**residue**, survivor, vestige, legacy. **2** *put the leftovers in the fridge* =**remainder**, scraps, remnants, remains; excess, surplus.
▶ adjective *leftover food* =**remaining**, left, uneaten; excess, surplus, superfluous, unused, unwanted, spare.

left-wing ▶ adjective =**socialist**, communist, leftist, Labour, Marxist–

Leninist, Bolshevik, Trotskyite, Maoist; *informal* Commie, lefty, red, pinko.
–OPPOSITES right-wing, conservative.

leg ▶ noun **1** *Lee broke his leg* =(lower) limb, shank; *informal* peg, pin; femur, tibia, fibula. **2** *a table leg* =upright, support. **3** *the first leg of a European tour* =part, stage, section, phase, stretch, lap.

■ **leg it** (*informal*) **1** *if the dog starts barking, leg it!* =run (away), flee, make off, make a break for it, escape, hurry; *informal* hightail it, hotfoot it, run for it, skedaddle, vamoose, split, scoot, scram; *Brit. informal* scarper. **2** *legging it around London* =walk, march, tramp, trek, trudge, plod, wander.

> WORD LINKS
>
> *relating to a leg:* **crural**

legacy ▶ noun **1** *a legacy from a great aunt* =bequest, inheritance, endowment, gift, birthright; *formal* benefaction. **2** *the legacy of the war* =consequence, effect, repercussion, aftermath, by-product, result.

legal ▶ adjective =lawful, legitimate, within the law, legalized, valid; permissible, permitted, allowable, allowed, above board, admissible, acceptable; constitutional; *informal* legit, kosher.
–OPPOSITES criminal.

legality ▶ noun =lawfulness, legitimacy, validity, admissibility, permissibility, constitutionality; justice.

legalize ▶ verb =make legal, decriminalize, legitimize, permit, allow, authorize, sanction, license; regularize, normalize.
–OPPOSITES prohibit.

legend ▶ noun **1** *the Arthurian legends* =myth, saga, epic, (folk) tale, (folk) story, fable; folklore, lore, mythology, (folk) tradition. **2** *pop legends* =celebrity, star, superstar, icon, phenomenon, luminary, giant, hero; *informal* celeb, megastar. **3** *the wording of the legend* =caption, inscription, dedication, slogan, heading, title. **4** *the legend to Figure 5* =explanation, key, guide.

legendary ▶ adjective **1** *legendary kings* =fabled, heroic, traditional, fairy-tale, storybook, mythical, mythological. **2** *a legendary figure in the trade-union movement* =famous, celebrated, famed, renowned, acclaimed, illustrious, esteemed, honoured, exalted, venerable,

distinguished, great, eminent, pre-eminent.
–OPPOSITES historical.

legibility ▶ noun =readability, clarity, clearness, neatness.

legible ▶ adjective =readable, easy to read, clear, plain, neat, intelligible.

legion ▶ noun *the legions of TV cameras* =horde, throng, multitude, crowd, mass, mob, gang, swarm, flock, herd, army.
▶ adjective *her fans are legion* =numerous, countless, innumerable, incalculable, many, abundant, plentiful; *literary* myriad.

legislation ▶ noun =law, rules, rulings, regulations, acts, bills, statutes; *N. Amer. formal* ordinances.

legislative ▶ adjective =law-making, judicial, parliamentary, governmental, policy-making.

legislator ▶ noun =lawmaker, lawgiver, parliamentarian, Member of Parliament, MP, congressman, congresswoman, senator.

legitimate ▶ adjective **1** *the only form of legitimate gambling* =legal, lawful, authorized, permitted, permissible, allowable, allowed, sanctioned, approved, licensed, statutory, constitutional; *informal* legit. **2** *the legitimate heir* =rightful, lawful, genuine, authentic, real, true, proper. **3** *legitimate grounds for unease* =valid, sound, admissible, acceptable, well founded, justifiable, reasonable, sensible, just, fair, bona fide.
–OPPOSITES illegal, invalid.

legitimize ▶ verb =validate, legitimate, permit, authorize, sanction, license, condone, justify, endorse, support; legalize.
–OPPOSITES outlaw.

leisure ▶ noun *the balance between leisure and work* =free time, spare time, time off; recreation, relaxation; *informal* R & R.
–OPPOSITES work.
■ **at your leisure** =at your convenience, when it suits you, in your own (good) time; *informal* whenever.

leisurely ▶ adjective =unhurried, relaxed, easy, gentle, sedate, comfortable, restful, undemanding, slow.
–OPPOSITES hurried.

lend ▶ verb **1** *I'll lend you my towel* =loan, let someone use; advance; *Brit. informal* sub. **2** *these examples lend weight to his*

assertions =**add**, impart, give, bestow, confer, provide, supply, furnish, contribute.
–OPPOSITES borrow.

length ▶ noun **1** *a length of three or four metres* | *the whole length of the valley* =**extent**, distance, span, reach; area, expanse, stretch, range, scope. **2** *a considerable length of time* =**period**, duration, stretch, span. **3** *a length of blue silk* =**piece**, strip. **4** *MPs criticized the length of the speech* =**protractedness**, lengthiness, extent, extensiveness; prolixity, wordiness, verboseness, long-windedness.
■ **at length 1** *he spoke at length* =**for a long time**, for ages, for hours, interminably, endlessly, ceaselessly, unendingly. **2** *he was questioned at length* =**thoroughly**, fully, in detail, in depth, comprehensively, exhaustively, extensively. **3** *his search led him, at length, to Seattle* =**eventually**, in time, finally, at (long) last, in the end, ultimately.

lengthen ▶ verb **1** *he lengthened his stride* =**elongate**, make longer, extend; expand, widen, broaden, enlarge. **2** *you'll need to lengthen the cooking time* =**prolong**, make longer, increase, extend, expand, protract, stretch out.
–OPPOSITES shorten.

lengthy ▶ adjective **1** *a lengthy civil war* =**(very) long**, long-lasting; prolonged. **2** *lengthy discussions* =**protracted**, long-drawn-out; time-consuming.
–OPPOSITES short.

leniency ▶ noun =**mercifulness**, mercy, clemency, forgiveness; tolerance, forbearance, charity, indulgence, mildness.

lenient ▶ adjective =**merciful**, forgiving, forbearing, tolerant, charitable, humane, indulgent, magnanimous.
–OPPOSITES severe.

lesion ▶ noun =**wound**, injury, bruise, abrasion, contusion; ulcer, sore, abscess.

lessen ▶ verb **1** *exercise lessens the risk of heart disease* =**reduce**, make less/smaller, minimize, decrease; allay, assuage, alleviate, attenuate, ease, dull, deaden, blunt, moderate, mitigate, dampen, soften, tone down, dilute, weaken. **2** *the pain began to lessen* =**grow less**, grow smaller, decrease, diminish, decline, subside, abate; fade, die down/off, let up, ease off, tail off, drop (off/away), fall, dwindle, ebb, wane, recede.

3 *his behaviour lessened him in their eyes* =**diminish**, degrade, discredit, devalue, belittle.
–OPPOSITES increase.

lesser ▶ adjective **1** *a lesser offence* =**less important**, minor, secondary, subsidiary, marginal, ancillary, auxiliary, supplementary, peripheral. **2** *you look down at us lesser mortals* =**subordinate**, minor, inferior, second-class, subservient, lowly, humble.
–OPPOSITES greater, superior.

lesson ▶ noun **1** *a maths lesson* =**class**, session, seminar, tutorial, lecture, period. **2** *they try harder in their lessons* =**classwork**, schoolwork, work, classes. **3** *Stuart's accident should be a lesson to all parents* =**warning**, deterrent, caution; example, message; moral.

lest ▶ conjunction =**(just) in case**, for fear that, in order to avoid.

let ▶ verb **1** *let him sleep for now* =**allow**, permit, give permission to, give leave to, authorize, license; empower, enable, entitle; assent to, consent to, agree to; *informal* give the green light to, give the go-ahead to, give the thumbs up to, OK; *formal* accede to; *archaic* suffer. **2** *they've let their flat* =**rent (out)**, let out, lease, hire (out), sublet, sublease.
–OPPOSITES prevent, prohibit.
■ **let someone down** =**fail**, disappoint, disillusion; abandon, desert, leave stranded, leave in the lurch.
■ **let go** =**release (one's hold on)**, loose/loosen one's hold on, relinquish; *archaic* unhand.
■ **let someone go** =**make redundant**, dismiss, discharge, lay off, give notice to, axe; *informal* sack, fire, give someone their cards, give someone their marching orders, send packing, give someone the boot/push.
■ **let something off** =**detonate**, discharge, explode, set off, fire (off).
■ **let someone off 1** (*informal*) *I'll let you off this time* =**pardon**, forgive; deal leniently with; acquit, absolve, exonerate, clear, vindicate; *informal* let someone off the hook; *formal* exculpate. **2** *he let me off work* =**excuse from**, exempt from, spare from.
■ **let on** (*informal*) **1** *I never let on that I felt anxious* =**reveal**, make known, tell, disclose, mention, divulge, let slip, give away, make public; blab; *informal* let the cat out of the bag, give the game away. **2** *they all let on that they didn't hear me*

=**pretend**, feign, affect, make out, make believe.

■ **let something out 1** *I let out a cry of triumph* =**utter**, emit, give (vent to), produce, issue, express, voice, release. **2** *she let out that he'd given her a lift home* =**reveal**, make known, tell, disclose, mention, divulge, let slip, give away, let it be known, blurt out.

■ **let someone out** =**release**, liberate, (set) free, let go, discharge; set/turn loose.

■ **let up** (*informal*) **1** *the rain has let up* =**abate**, lessen, decrease, diminish, subside, relent, slacken, die down/off, ease (off), tail off; ebb, wane, dwindle, fade; stop. **2** *you never let up, do you?* =**relax**, ease up/off, slow down; pause, break (off), take a break, rest, stop.

let-down ▶ noun =**disappointment**, anticlimax, comedown, non-event, fiasco, setback, blow; *informal* washout, downer, damp squib.

lethal ▶ adjective =**fatal**, deadly, mortal, life-threatening; poisonous, toxic, noxious, venomous; dangerous, destructive, harmful; *literary* deathly, nocuous; *archaic* baneful.
−OPPOSITES harmless, safe.

lethargic ▶ adjective =**sluggish**, inert, inactive, slow, lifeless; languid, listless, apathetic, weary, tired, fatigued.

lethargy ▶ noun =**sluggishness**, inertia, inactivity, inaction, slowness, torpor, lifelessness, listlessness, languor, languidness, apathy, passivity, weariness, tiredness.
−OPPOSITES vigour, energy.

letter ▶ noun **1** *capital letters* =**character**, sign, symbol, mark, figure, rune. **2** *she received a letter* =**message**, (written) communication, note, line, missive, dispatch; correspondence; post, mail; *formal* epistle. **3** *a man of letters* =**learning**, scholarship, erudition, education.

■ **to the letter** =**strictly**, precisely, exactly, accurately, closely, faithfully, religiously, punctiliously, literally, in every detail.

> **WORD LINKS**
>
> *relating to alphabetical letters:* **literal**
> *relating to letters (correspondence):*
> **epistolary**

let-up ▶ noun (*informal*) =**abatement**, lessening, decrease, decline, relenting, remission, slackening, weakening, relaxation, dying down, easing off, tailing off, dropping away/off; respite, break, interval, hiatus, stop, pause.

level ▶ adjective **1** *a smooth and level surface* =**flat**, smooth, even, uniform, plane, flush. **2** *he kept his voice level* =**steady**, even, uniform, regular, constant; calm. **3** *the scores were level* =**equal**, even, drawn, tied, all square, neck and neck, level pegging, on a par, evenly matched; *informal* even-steven(s). **4** *his eyes were level with hers* =**at the same height**, on a level, in line.
−OPPOSITES uneven, unsteady, unequal.

▶ noun **1** *the post is at research-officer level* =**rank**, position; degree, grade, stage, standard; class, group, set, classification. **2** *a high level of employment* =**quantity**, amount, extent, measure, degree, volume. **3** *the sixth level* =**floor**, storey, deck.

▶ verb **1** *tilt the tin to level the mixture* =**even off/out**, flatten, smooth (out). **2** *bulldozers levelled the building* =**raze (to the ground)**, demolish, flatten, bulldoze; destroy. **3** *he levelled his opponent with a single blow* =**knock down/out**, lay out, prostrate, flatten, floor, fell; *informal* KO. **4** *Carl levelled the score* =**equalize**, equal, even (up), make level. **5** *he levelled his pistol at me* =**aim**, point, direct, train, focus, turn. **6** (*informal*) *I'd like to level with you* =**be frank**, be open, be honest, be straight, lay one's cards on the table; *informal* be upfront.

■ **on the level** (*informal*) =**genuine**, straight, honest, above board, fair, true, sincere, straightforward; *informal* upfront; *N. Amer. informal* on the up and up.

level-headed ▶ adjective =**sensible**, practical, realistic, prudent, pragmatic, reasonable, rational, mature, sound, sober, businesslike, no-nonsense, {cool, calm, and collected}, having one's feet on the ground; *informal* unflappable, together.
−OPPOSITES excitable.

lever ▶ noun **1** *you can insert a lever and prise the rail off* =**crowbar**, bar, jemmy. **2** *he pulled the lever* =**handle**, arm, switch.
▶ verb *he levered the door open* =**prise**, force, wrench, pull, wrest; *N. Amer.* pry; *informal* jemmy.

leverage ▶ noun **1** *the long handles provide increased leverage* =**grip**, purchase, hold; support, anchorage. **2** *they have* *significant leverage in negotiations* =**influence**, power, authority, weight, sway, pull, control, say, advantage, pressure; *informal* clout, muscle, teeth.

levitate ▸ noun =**float**, rise (into the air), hover, be suspended, glide, hang, fly.

levity ▸ noun =**light-heartedness**, high spirits, cheerfulness, humour, gaiety, hilarity, frivolity, amusement, mirth, laughter, merriment, glee, jollity.
–OPPOSITES seriousness.

levy ▸ verb =**impose**, charge, exact, raise, collect.
▸ noun =**tax**, tariff, toll, excise, duty.

lewd ▸ adjective **1** *a lewd old man* =**lecherous**, lustful, licentious, lascivious, dirty, prurient, salacious, lubricious, libidinous; debauched, depraved, degenerate, perverted; *informal* horny; *Brit. informal* randy; *formal* concupiscent. **2** *a lewd song* =**vulgar**, crude, smutty, dirty, filthy, obscene, coarse, off colour, indecent, salacious; rude, racy, risqué, naughty, earthy, spicy, bawdy, ribald; *informal* blue, raunchy, X-rated; *N. Amer. informal* raw.
–OPPOSITES chaste, clean.

liability ▸ noun **1** *they have big liabilities* =**(financial) obligations**, debts, arrears, dues, (financial) commitments. **2** *he's become a bit of a liability* =**hindrance**, encumbrance, burden, handicap, nuisance, inconvenience, embarrassment; impediment, disadvantage; millstone (round one's neck).
–OPPOSITES asset.

liable ▸ adjective **1** *they are liable for negligence* =**(legally) responsible**, accountable, answerable, chargeable, blameworthy, at fault, culpable, guilty. **2** *my income is liable to fluctuate wildly* =**likely**, inclined, tending, disposed, apt, predisposed, prone, given. **3** *areas liable to flooding* =**exposed**, prone, subject, susceptible, vulnerable, in danger of, at risk of.

liaise ▸ verb =**cooperate**, collaborate; communicate, network, interface, link up.

liaison ▸ noun **1** *the branches work in close liaison* =**cooperation**, contact, association, connection, collaboration, communication, alliance, partnership.
2 *Dave was my White House liaison* =**intermediary**, mediator, middleman, contact, link, go-between, representative, agent. **3** *a secret liaison* =(**love**) **affair**, relationship, romance, attachment, fling, tryst; *informal* hanky-panky.

liar ▸ noun =**fibber**, deceiver, perjurer, fabricator; *informal* storyteller.

WORD LINKS
compulsive liar: **mythomaniac**

libel ▸ noun *she sued two newspapers for libel* =**defamation (of character)**, character assassination, calumny, misrepresentation, scandalmongering; aspersions, denigration, vilification, disparagement, insult, malicious gossip; lie, slur, smear, untruth; *informal* mudslinging, bad-mouthing.
▸ verb *she claimed the magazine had libelled her* =**defame**, malign, blacken someone's name, sully someone's reputation, smear, cast aspersions on, drag someone's name through the mud/mire, besmirch, tarnish, taint, stain, vilify, denigrate, disparage; *N. Amer.* slur.

libellous ▸ adjective =**defamatory**, denigratory, disparaging, derogatory, false, untrue, insulting, scurrilous.

liberal ▸ adjective **1** *the values of a liberal society* =**tolerant**, unprejudiced, broad-minded, open-minded, enlightened; permissive, free (and easy), easy-going, libertarian, indulgent, lenient. **2** *a liberal social agenda* =**progressive**, advanced, modern, forward-looking, forward-thinking, enlightened, reformist, radical; *informal* go-ahead. **3** *a liberal interpretation of divorce laws* =**flexible**, broad, loose, rough, free, non-literal, imprecise, vague, indefinite. **4** *liberal coatings of paint* =**abundant**, copious, ample, plentiful, generous, lavish; *literary* plenteous. **5** *they were liberal with their cash* =**generous**, open-handed, unsparing, unstinting, lavish, free, munificent, bountiful, benevolent, big-hearted, philanthropic, charitable.
–OPPOSITES reactionary, strict, miserly.

liberate ▸ verb =**(set) free**, release, let out/go, set/let loose, save, rescue; emancipate, enfranchise.
–OPPOSITES imprison, enslave.

liberation ▸ noun **1** *the liberation of prisoners* =**freeing**, release, rescue; emancipation. **2** *women's liberation* =**freedom**, equality, (equal) rights, emancipation, enfranchisement.
–OPPOSITES confinement, oppression.

liberator ▸ noun =**rescuer**, saviour, deliverer, emancipator.

libertine ▶ noun =**philanderer**, playboy, rake, roué, Don Juan, Lothario, Casanova, Romeo; lecher, seducer, womanizer, adulterer, debauchee, profligate, wanton; *informal* ladykiller, lech.

liberty ▶ noun **1** *personal liberty* =**freedom**, independence, self-determination, latitude. **2** *the essence of British liberty* =**independence**, freedom, autonomy, sovereignty, self government, self rule, self determination; civil liberties, human rights. **3** *the liberty to go where one pleases* =**right**, prerogative, entitlement, privilege, permission, sanction, authorization, authority, licence.
–OPPOSITES constraint, slavery.
■ **at liberty 1** *he was at liberty for three months* =**free**, (on the) loose, at large, on the run, unconfined. **2** *I am not at liberty to say* =**free**, able, entitled, eligible.

libidinous ▶ adjective =**lustful**, lecherous, lascivious, lewd, salacious, prurient, licentious, lubricious, dissolute, debauched, depraved, degenerate, dissipated, wanton, promiscuous; *informal* horny; *Brit. informal* randy; *formal* concupiscent.

libido ▶ noun =**sex drive**, sexual appetite; (sexual) desire.

licence ▶ noun **1** *a driving licence* =**permit**, certificate, document, documentation, authorization, warrant; credentials; pass, papers. **2** *they manufacture footwear under licence* =**franchise**, consent, sanction, warrant, warranty, charter. **3** *the army have too much licence* =**freedom**, liberty, free rein, latitude, independence, scope, carte blanche; *informal* a blank cheque. **4** *poetic licence* =**disregard**, inventiveness, invention, creativity, imagination, fancy, freedom, looseness.

license ▶ verb =**permit**, allow, authorize, grant/give authority to, grant/give permission to; certify, empower, entitle, enable, let, qualify, sanction.
–OPPOSITES ban.

licentious ▶ adjective =**dissolute**, dissipated, debauched, degenerate, immoral, wanton, decadent, depraved, corrupt; lustful, lecherous, lascivious, libidinous, prurient, lubricious, lewd, promiscuous; *formal* concupiscent.
–OPPOSITES moral.

lick ▶ verb **1** *the spaniel licked his face* =**tongue**, wash; lap, slurp; slobber over. **2** *flames licking round the coal* =**flicker**, play, dance.

lid ▶ noun *the lid of a saucepan* =**cover**, top, cap, covering.
■ **put a/the lid on** *(informal)* =**stop**, control, end, put an end/stop to, put paid to.
■ **lift the lid off/on** *(informal)* =**expose**, reveal, make known, go public on/with, bring into the open, disclose, divulge; *informal* spill the beans, blow the gaff.

lie¹ ▶ noun *it was a lie* =**untruth**, falsehood, fib, fabrication, deception, invention, (piece of) fiction, falsification, white lie; *informal* tall story, whopper; *Brit. informal* porky (pie); *humorous* terminological inexactitude.
–OPPOSITES truth.
▶ verb *he had lied to the police* =**tell an untruth/lie**, fib, dissemble, dissimulate, tell a white lie, perjure oneself, commit perjury; *formal* forswear oneself.

> **WORD LINKS**
>
> *lying:* **mendacious**
> *compulsion to lie:* **mythomania**

lie² ▶ verb **1** *he was lying on the bed* =**recline**, lie down/back, be recumbent, be prostrate, be supine, be prone, be stretched out, sprawl, rest, repose, lounge, loll. **2** *her handbag lay on the chair* =**be**, be situated, be positioned, be arranged, be displayed, rest. **3** *lying on the border of Switzerland and Austria* =**be situated**, be located, be placed, be found, be sited. **4** *his body lies in a crypt* =**be buried**, be interred, be laid to rest, rest, be entombed. **5** *the difficulty lies in convincing people* =**consist**, be inherent, be present, be contained, exist, reside.
–OPPOSITES stand.
■ **lie low** =**hide (out)**, go into hiding, conceal oneself, keep out of sight, go to earth/ground; *informal* hole up; *Brit. informal*, dated lie doggo.

lieutenant ▶ noun =**deputy**, second in command, right-hand man/woman, number two, assistant, aide; *informal* sidekick.

life ▶ noun **1** *the joy of giving life to a child* =**existence**, being, living, animation; sentience, creation, viability. **2** *life on Earth* =**living beings/creatures**; human/animal/plant life, fauna, flora, the ecosystem, the biosphere, the ecosphere; human beings, humanity, humankind, mankind, man. **3** *an easy life* =**way of life**, lifestyle, situation, fate, lot. **4** *the last nine months of his life* =**life-**

time, life span, days, time (on earth), existence. **5** *the life of a Parliament* =**duration**, lifetime, existence. **6** *he is full of life* =**vivacity**, animation, liveliness, vitality, verve, high spirits, exuberance, zest, buoyancy, dynamism, elan, gusto, bounce, spirit, fire; (hustle and) bustle, movement; *informal* oomph, pizzazz, pep, zing, zip. **7** *the life of the party* =**(vital) spirit**, life force, lifeblood, heart, soul. **8** *more than 1,500 lives were lost in the accident* =**person**, human being, individual, soul. **9** *a life of Chopin* =**biography**, autobiography, life story/history, profile, chronicle, account, portrait; *informal* biog, bio.
−OPPOSITES death.

> WORD LINKS
>
> *relating to life:* **bio-**
> *having life:* **animate**
> *essential for life:* **vital**

life-and-death ▸ adjective =**vital**, of vital importance, crucial, critical, urgent, pivotal, momentous, key, serious, grave, significant; *informal* earth-shattering.
−OPPOSITES trivial.

lifeblood ▸ noun =**life (force)**, driving force, vital spark, inspiration, stimulus, essence, crux, heart, soul, core.

life-giving ▸ adjective =**vitalizing**, animating, energizing, invigorating, stimulating; life preserving, life-sustaining.

lifeless ▸ adjective **1** *a lifeless body* =**dead**, stiff, cold, inert; *formal* deceased. **2** *a lifeless landscape* =**barren**, sterile, bare, desolate, stark, arid, infertile, uninhabited; bleak, colourless, characterless, soulless. **3** *a lifeless performance* =**lacklustre**, apathetic, lethargic; expressionless, emotionless, colourless, characterless, wooden, blank.
−OPPOSITES alive, lively.

lifelike ▸ adjective =**realistic**, true to life, faithful, detailed, vivid, graphic, natural, naturalistic; representational.
−OPPOSITES unrealistic.

lifelong ▸ adjective =**lasting**, longlasting, long-term, constant, enduring, permanent.
−OPPOSITES ephemeral.

lifestyle ▸ noun =**way of life**, life, situation; conduct, behaviour, habits, mores.

lifetime ▸ noun **1** *during his lifetime* =**lifespan**, life, days, time (on earth),

existence, career. **2** *the lifetime of workstations* =**duration**, (active) life, life expectancy. **3** *it would take a lifetime* =**a long time**, an eternity, forever, years, aeons; *informal* ages (and ages), an age.

lift ▸ verb **1** *lift the pack on to your back* =**raise**, hoist, heave, haul up, heft, raise up/aloft, elevate, hold high; pick up, grab, take up; winch up, jack up; *informal* hump. **2** *the news lifted his spirits* =**boost**, raise, buoy up, cheer up, perk up, brighten up, gladden, encourage, stimulate, revive; *informal* buck up. **3** *the fog had lifted* =**clear**, rise, disperse, dissipate, disappear, vanish, dissolve. **4** *the ban has been lifted* =**cancel**, remove, withdraw, revoke, rescind, end, stop, terminate. **5** *the RAF lifted them to safety* =**airlift**, transport, fly; winch; whisk. **6** *(informal) he lifted sections from a 1986 article* =**copy**, plagiarize, reproduce, borrow, steal; *informal* nick, crib, rip off.
−OPPOSITES drop, put down.

▸ noun **1** *give me a lift up* =**push**, hand, heave, thrust, shove. **2** *he gave me a lift to the airport* =**ride**; run, drive. **3** *that goal will give his confidence a real lift* =**boost**, fillip, impetus, encouragement, spur, push; improvement, enhancement; *informal* shot in the arm.

∎ **lift off** =**take off**, become airborne, take to the air, blast off.

light[1] ▸ noun **1** *the light of the candles* =**illumination**, brightness, shining, gleam, brilliance, radiance, glow, blaze, glare; sunlight, moonlight, starlight, lamplight, firelight; *literary* effulgence. **2** *there was a light on in the hall* =**lamp**; headlight, sidelight, street light, floodlight; lantern; torch, flashlight, bulb. **3** *we'll be driving in the light* =**daylight**, daytime, day; natural light, sunlight. **4** *he saw the problem in a different light* =**aspect**, angle, slant, approach, viewpoint, standpoint, context, hue, complexion.
−OPPOSITES darkness.

▸ adjective **1** *a light bedroom* =**bright**, well lit, sunny. **2** *light blue* =**pale**, pastel; faded, washed out, insipid.
−OPPOSITES dark, gloomy.

∎ **come to light** =**be discovered**, be uncovered, be unearthed, come out, become known, become apparent, appear, emerge.

∎ **in the light of** =**taking into consideration**, considering, bearing in mind, in view of.

∎ **light something up** =**brighten**,

illuminate, throw/cast light on, shine on; floodlight; *literary* illumine.
■ **throw/cast/shed light on** =explain, elucidate, clarify, clear up.

WORD LINKS

related prefix: **photo-, lumin-, luc-**
study of behaviour of light: **optics**
measurement of the intensity of light:
   photometry
fear of light: **photophobia**

light² ▶ adjective **1** *it's light and compact* =**lightweight**; portable. **2** *a light cotton dress* =**flimsy**, lightweight, thin; floaty, gauzy, diaphanous. **3** *she is light on her feet* =**nimble**, agile, lithe, graceful; quick; sprightly; *informal* twinkle-toed; *literary* fleet. **4** *a light soil* =**crumbly**, friable, loose, workable, sandy. **5** *a light dinner* =**small**, modest, simple; quick. **6** *light duties* =**easy**, simple, undemanding, untaxing; *informal* cushy. **7** *light reading* =**entertaining**, lightweight, diverting, undemanding; middle-of-the-road, mainstream; frivolous, superficial, trivial. **8** *light footsteps | a light touch* =**gentle**, delicate, dainty, soft, faint; careful, sensitive, subtle.
–OPPOSITES heavy.

light³ ■ **light on/upon** =come across, chance on, hit on, happen on, stumble on/across, find, discover, uncover, come up with.

lighten¹ ▶ verb **1** *the sky was beginning to lighten* =**become/grow/get lighter**, brighten. **2** *the first touch of dawn lightened the sky* =**brighten**, make brighter, light up, illuminate; *literary* illumine. **3** *he used lemon juice to lighten his hair* =**make lighter**, whiten, bleach, blanch; fade.
–OPPOSITES darken.

lighten² ▶ verb **1** *lightening the burden of taxation* =**make lighter**, lessen, reduce, decrease, diminish, ease; alleviate, relieve. **2** *an attempt to lighten her mood* =**cheer (up)**, brighten, gladden, lift, boost, buoy (up), revive, restore, revitalize.
–OPPOSITES increase, depress.

light-headed ▶ adjective =**dizzy**, giddy, faint; muzzy, feverish; *informal* woozy.

light-hearted ▶ adjective =**carefree**, cheerful, cheery, happy, merry, glad, playful, blithe, bright, vivacious, bubbly, jaunty, bouncy, breezy; entertaining, amusing, diverting; *informal* chirpy,

upbeat; *dated* gay.
–OPPOSITES miserable.

lightly ▶ adverb **1** *Maisie kissed him lightly on the cheek* =**softly**, gently, faintly, delicately. **2** *season very lightly* =**sparingly**, sparsely, moderately, delicately; subtly.
–OPPOSITES hard, heavily.

lightweight ▶ adjective **1** *a lightweight jacket* =**thin**, light, flimsy, insubstantial; summery. **2** *lightweight entertainment* =**trivial**, insubstantial, superficial, shallow, undemanding, frivolous.
–OPPOSITES heavy.

like¹ ▶ verb **1** *I like him* =**be fond of**, have a soft spot for, think well/highly of, admire, respect; be attracted to, fancy, find attractive, be keen on, be taken with; *informal* rate. **2** *Maisie likes veal | she likes gardening* =**enjoy**, have a taste for, have a liking for, be partial to, find/take pleasure in, be keen on, find agreeable, have a penchant/passion for; appreciate, love, adore, relish; *informal* have a thing about, be into, be mad about/for, be hooked on, go a bundle on. **3** *feel free to say what you like* =**choose**, please, wish, want, see/think fit, care to, will.
–OPPOSITES hate.

like² ▶ preposition **1** *you're just like a teacher* =**similar to**, the same as, identical to, analogous to, akin to, resembling. **2** *the figure landed like a cat* =**in the same way/manner as**, in the manner of, in a similar way to. **3** *cities like Birmingham* =**such as**, for example, for instance; in particular, namely, viz. **4** *Richard sounded mean, which isn't like him* =**characteristic of**, typical of, in character with.
▶ noun *we shan't see his like again* =**equal**, match, equivalent, counterpart, twin, parallel.
▶ adjective *a like situation* =**similar**, comparable, corresponding, analogous, parallel, equivalent; related, kindred; matching.
–OPPOSITES dissimilar.

likeable ▶ adjective =**pleasant**, nice, friendly, agreeable, affable, amiable, genial, personable, good-natured, engaging, appealing, endearing, convivial, congenial.
–OPPOSITES unpleasant.

likelihood ▶ noun =**probability**, chance, prospect, possibility, odds; risk, threat, danger; hope, promise.

likely ▶ adjective **1** *it seemed likely that a scandal would break* =**probable**, (distinctly) possible, odds-on, plausible, imaginable; predictable, foreseeable; *informal* on the cards. **2** *a likely explanation* =**plausible**, reasonable, feasible, acceptable, believable, credible, tenable. −OPPOSITES improbable, unbelievable.

liken ▸ verb =**compare**, equate. −OPPOSITES contrast.

likeness ▸ noun **1** *her likeness to Anne is quite uncanny* =**resemblance**, similarity, correspondence. **2** *a likeness of the president* =**representation**, image, depiction, portrayal; picture, drawing, sketch, painting, portrait, photograph, study. −OPPOSITES dissimilarity.

likewise ▸ adverb **1** *an ambush was out of the question, likewise poison* =**also**, equally, in addition, too, as well, to boot; besides, moreover, furthermore. **2** *encourage your family and friends to do likewise* =**the same**, similarly, correspondingly.

liking ▸ noun =**fondness**, love, affection, penchant, attachment; enjoyment, taste, passion; preference, partiality, predilection. −OPPOSITES dislike.

lilt ▸ noun =**cadence**, inflection, intonation, rhythm, swing, beat, pulse, tempo.

limb ▸ noun =**arm**, **leg**, appendage; *archaic* member.

limber ■ limber up =**warm up**, loosen up, get into shape, practise, train, stretch.

limbo ■ in limbo =**in abeyance**, unattended to, unfinished; suspended, deferred, postponed, put off, pending, on ice, in cold storage; unresolved, undetermined, up in the air; *informal* on the back burner, on hold.

limelight ▸ noun =**attention**, interest, scrutiny, the public eye/gaze, the glare of publicity, prominence, the spotlight; fame, celebrity. −OPPOSITES obscurity.

limit ▸ noun **1** *the city limits* =**boundary (line)**, border, frontier, edge; perimeter, margin. **2** *a limit of 4,500 supporters* =**maximum**, ceiling, upper limit.
▸ verb *the pressure to limit costs* =**restrict**, curb, cap, (hold in) check, restrain; regulate, control, govern.

limitation ▸ noun **1** *a limitation on the number of newcomers* =**restriction**, curb, restraint, control, check. **2** *he is aware of*

his own limitations =**imperfection**, flaw, defect, failing, shortcoming, weak point, deficiency, failure, frailty, weakness, inconsistency. −OPPOSITES increase, strength.

limited ▸ adjective =**restricted**, finite, small, tight, slight, in short supply, short; meagre, scanty, sparse, inadequate, insufficient, paltry, poor, minimal. −OPPOSITES limitless, ample.

limitless ▸ adjective =**boundless**, unbounded, unlimited; infinite, endless, never-ending, unending, everlasting, untold, immeasurable, bottomless, interminable, perpetual. −OPPOSITES limited.

limp¹ ▸ verb *she limped out of the house* =**hobble**; lurch, stagger.

limp² ▸ adjective **1** *a limp handshake* =**soft**, flaccid, loose, slack, lax; floppy, drooping, droopy, sagging. **2** *we were all limp with exhaustion* =**weak**; comatose, prostrate, on one's knees. **3** *a rather limp speech* =**uninspired**, uninspiring, insipid, flat, lifeless, vapid, tepid. −OPPOSITES firm, energetic.

limpid ▸ adjective **1** *a limpid pool* =**clear**, transparent, glassy, crystal clear, translucent, unclouded. **2** *his limpid prose style* =**lucid**, clear, transparent, plain, unambiguous, simple; accessible. −OPPOSITES opaque.

line¹ ▸ noun **1** *he drew a line through the name* =**stroke**, **dash**, score, underline, underscore; slash, solidus; stripe, strip, band, belt; *technical* striation; *Brit.* oblique. **2** *there were lines round her eyes* =**wrinkle**, furrow, crease, crinkle, crow's foot. **3** *the classic lines of the Bentley* =**contour**, outline, configuration, shape, design, profile. **4** *he headed the ball over the line* | *the county line* =**boundary (line)**, limit, border, frontier, touchline, margin, perimeter. **5** *the clothes line* =**cord**, rope, cable, wire. **6** *a line of soldiers* =**file**, rank, column, string, train, procession; row, queue; *Brit. informal* crocodile. **7** *a line of figures* =**column**, row. **8** *the line of flight of some bees* =**course**, route, track, path. **9** *they took a very tough line with the industry* | *the party line* =**course (of action)**, procedure; policy, practice, approach, programme, position, stance, philosophy, way. **10** *her own line of thought* =**course**, direction, drift, tack, tendency, trend;

avenue. **11** *he couldn't remember his lines* =**words**, part, script, speech. **12** *a new line of convenience food* =**brand**, kind, sort, type, variety. **13** *the opening line of the poem* =**sentence**, phrase, clause; passage, extract, quotation, quote, citation.

▶ verb **1** *her face was lined with age* =**furrow**, wrinkle, crease. **2** *the driveway was lined by poplars* =**border**, edge, fringe, bound.
■ **draw the line at** =**stop short of**, refuse to accept, baulk at.
■ **in line 1** *standing in line for food* =**in a queue**, in a row, in a file. **2** *the adverts are in line with the editorial style* =**in agreement**, in accord, in accordance, in harmony, in step, in compliance. **3** *in line with the goal* =**aligned**, level; alongside, abreast, side by side. **4** *the referee kept him in line* =**under control**, in order, in check.
■ **in line for** =**a candidate for**, in the running for; due for; *informal* up for.
■ **line up** =**form a queue/line**, queue up, fall in.
■ **line someone/something up** *we've lined up an all-star cast* =**assemble**, get together, organize, prepare, arrange, fix up, lay on; book, schedule, timetable.

line² ▶ verb *a cardboard box lined with a blanket* =**cover**, back, pad; insulate, lag, seal.

lineage ▶ noun =**ancestry**, family, parentage, birth, descent, line, extraction, genealogy, roots, origin, background; stock, bloodline, breeding, pedigree.

lined¹ ▶ adjective **1** *lined paper* =**ruled**, feint, striped, banded. **2** *his lined face* =**wrinkled**, wrinkly, furrowed, wizened.
–OPPOSITES plain, smooth.

lined² ▶ adjective *lined curtains* =**covered**, backed; padded, insulated; sealed.

liner ▶ noun =**ship**, ocean liner, passenger vessel, boat.

line-up ▶ noun **1** *a star-studded line-up* =**cast**, bill, programme. **2** *United's line-up* =**team**, squad, side; configuration.

linger ▶ verb **1** *the crowd lingered* =**wait (around)**, stand (around), remain; loiter; *informal* stick around, hang around/round; *archaic* tarry. **2** *the infection can linger for years* =**persist**, continue, remain, stay, endure, carry on, last.
–OPPOSITES vanish.

lingerie ▶ noun =**women's underwear**, underclothes, underclothing, undergarments; nightwear, night-

clothes; *informal* undies, frillies, underthings, unmentionables; *Brit. informal* smalls.

lingering ▶ adjective **1** *lingering doubts* =**remaining**, surviving, persisting, abiding, nagging, niggling. **2** *a slow, lingering death* =**protracted**, prolonged, long-drawn-out; agonizing.

linguistic ▶ adjective =semantic, rhetorical, verbal, phonetic; grammatical.

lining ▶ noun =**backing**, facing, padding, insulation.

link ▶ noun **1** *a chain of steel links* =**loop**, ring. **2** *the links between transport and the environment* =**connection**, relationship, association, linkage, tie-up. **3** *their links with the labour movement* =**bond**, tie, attachment, connection, association, affiliation.
▶ verb **1** *four boxes were linked together* =**join**, connect, fasten, attach, bind; secure, fix, tie, couple, yoke. **2** *the evidence linking him with the body* =**associate**, connect, relate; bracket.

lion ▶ noun

> **WORD LINKS**
>
> *relating to lions:* **leonine**
> *collective noun:* **pride, sawt**
> *home:* **den**

lip ▶ noun *the lip of the crater* =**edge**, rim, brim, border, verge, brink.

> **WORD LINKS**
>
> *relating to the lips:* **labial, labio-**

liquefy ▶ verb =**liquidize**, purée; pulp; condense; melt.

liquid ▶ adjective *liquid fuels* =**fluid**, liquefied; melted, molten, thawed, dissolved; *Chemistry* hydrous.
–OPPOSITES solid.
▶ noun *a vat of liquid* =**fluid**; moisture; liquor, solution, juice, sap.

> **WORD LINKS**
>
> *science of moving liquids:* **hydraulics**

liquidate ▶ verb *the company was liquidated* =**close down**, wind up, put into liquidation, dissolve, disband.

liquidize ▶ verb =**purée**, cream, liquefy, blend.

liquor ▶ noun **1** *alcoholic liquor* =**alcohol**, spirits, (alcoholic) drink; *informal* booze, the hard stuff, hooch; moonshine. **2** *strain the liquor into the sauce* =**stock**, broth, bouillon, juice, liquid.

list[1] ▸ noun *a list of the world's wealthiest people* = **catalogue**, inventory, record, register, roll, file, index, directory, checklist.

▸ verb *the accounts are listed below* = **record**, register, enter; itemize, enumerate, catalogue, file, log, minute, categorize, inventory; classify, group, sort, rank, index.

list[2] ▸ verb *the boat listed to one side* = **lean (over)**, tilt, tip, heel (over), careen, pitch, incline, slant, slope, bank.

listen ▸ verb **1** *are you listening?* = **pay attention**, be attentive, attend, concentrate; keep one's ears open, prick up one's ears; *informal* be all ears; *literary* hark. **2** *policy-makers should listen to popular opinion* = **heed**, take heed of, take notice/note of, bear in mind, take into consideration/account.
■ **listen in** = **eavesdrop**, spy, overhear, tap, bug, monitor.

listless ▸ adjective = **lethargic**, lifeless; languid, inactive, inert, sluggish.
–OPPOSITES energetic.

literal ▸ adjective *the literal sense of the word 'dreadful'* = **strict**, technical, concrete, original, true.
–OPPOSITES figurative.

literary ▸ adjective **1** *literary works* = **artistic**, poetic, dramatic. **2** *her literary friends* = **scholarly**, intellectual, academic.

literate ▸ adjective = **(well) educated**, well read, widely read, scholarly, learned, knowledgeable, cultured, cultivated, well informed.
–OPPOSITES ignorant.

literature ▸ noun **1** *English literature* = **writing**; poetry, drama, prose. **2** *the literature on prototype theory* = **publications**, reports, studies; material. **3** *election literature* = **documentation**, material, publicity, blurb, propaganda, advertising; *informal* bumf.

lithe ▸ adjective = **agile**, graceful, supple, loose-limbed, nimble, deft, flexible.
–OPPOSITES clumsy.

litigation ▸ noun = **(legal/judicial) proceedings**, (legal) action, lawsuit, legal dispute, (legal) case, prosecution, indictment.

litter ▸ noun **1** *never drop litter* = **rubbish**, refuse, junk, waste, debris, detritus; *N. Amer.* trash, garbage. **2** *the litter of glasses*

around her = **clutter**, jumble, muddle, mess, heap; *informal* shambles.
▸ verb *clothes littered the floor* = **cover**, clutter up; pepper.

little ▸ adjective **1** *a little writing desk* = **small**, small-scale, compact; miniature, tiny; toy, baby, undersized, dwarf, midget; *Scottish* wee; *informal* teeny-weeny, teensy-weensy, itsy-bitsy, tiddly; *Brit. informal* titchy, dinky; *N. Amer. informal* vest-pocket. **2** *a little man* = **short**, small, slight, petite, diminutive, tiny; *Scottish* wee; *informal* teeny-weeny, pint-sized. **3** *my little sister* = **young**, younger, baby. **4** *a little while* = **brief**, short; quick, hasty, cursory. **5** *a few little problems* = **minor**, unimportant, insignificant, trivial, trifling, petty, paltry, inconsequential.
–OPPOSITES big, large, elder, important.

▸ determiner *they have little political influence* = **hardly any**, not much, scant, limited, restricted, modest, little or no, minimal, negligible.
–OPPOSITES considerable.

▸ adverb **1** *he is little known as a teacher* = **hardly**, barely, scarcely, not much, (only) slightly. **2** *this disease is little seen nowadays* = **rarely**, seldom, infrequently, hardly (ever), scarcely (ever), not much.
–OPPOSITES well, often.
■ **a little 1** *add a little water* = **some**, a bit of, a touch of, a soupçon of, a dash of, a taste of, a spot of; a hint of; a dribble of, a splash of, a pinch of, a sprinkling of, a speck of; *informal* a smidgen of, a tad of. **2** *after a little, Oliver came in* = **a short time**, a while, a bit, an interval, a short period; a minute, a moment, a second, an instant; *informal* a sec, a mo, a jiffy. **3** *this reminds me a little of the Adriatic* = **slightly**; somewhat, a little bit, quite, to some degree.
■ **little by little** = **gradually**, slowly, by degrees, by stages, step by step, bit by bit, progressively; imperceptibly.

live[1] ▸ verb **1** *the greatest mathematician who ever lived* = **exist**, be alive, be, have life; breathe, draw breath, walk the earth. **2** *I live in London* = **reside**, have one's home, lodge; inhabit, occupy, populate; *Scottish* stay; *formal* dwell. **3** *she had lived a difficult life* = **experience**, spend, pass, lead, have, go through, undergo. **4** *Freddy lived by scavenging* = **survive**, make a living, eke out a living; subsist, support oneself, sustain oneself, make ends meet, keep body

and soul together.
–OPPOSITES die, be dead.

■ **live it up** *(informal)* =**enjoy oneself**, live in the lap of luxury, have a good time, go on a spree; *informal* party, push the boat out, have a ball, make whoopee; *N. Amer. informal* live high on/off the hog.

■ **live off/on** =**subsist on**, feed on/off, eat, consume.

live² ▸ adjective **1** *live bait* =**living**, (still) alive, (still) conscious. **2** *a live rail* =**electrified**, charged, powered (up), active, (switched) on. **3** *a live grenade* =**unexploded**, explosive, active, primed. **4** *a live issue* =**topical**, current, controversial; burning, pressing, important, relevant.
–OPPOSITES dead, inanimate, recorded.

livelihood ▸ noun =**(source of) income**, means of support, living, subsistence, daily bread, bread and butter; job, work, employment, occupation.

lively ▸ adjective **1** *a lively young woman* =**energetic**, active, animated, dynamic, full of life, outgoing, spirited, high-spirited, vivacious, enthusiastic, vibrant, buoyant, exuberant, effervescent, cheerful; bouncy, bubbly, sparkling; *informal* full of beans, chirpy, chipper. **2** *a lively bar* =**busy**, crowded, bustling, buzzing; vibrant, boisterous, jolly. **3** *a lively debate* =**heated**, vigorous, animated, spirited, enthusiastic, forceful; exciting, interesting, memorable. **4** *a lively portrait of the local community* =**vivid**, colourful, striking, graphic. **5** *he bowled at a lively pace* =**brisk**, quick, fast, rapid, swift, speedy, smart.
–OPPOSITES quiet, dull.

liven ■ **liven up** =**brighten up**, cheer up, perk up, revive, rally, pick up, bounce back; *informal* buck up.

■ **liven someone/something up** =**brighten up**, cheer up, enliven, animate, raise someone's spirits, perk up, spice up, wake up, invigorate, revive, refresh, galvanize, stimulate, stir up, get going; *informal* buck up, pep up.

liver ▸ noun

> **WORD LINKS**
>
> *relating to the liver:* **hepatic**
> *inflammation of the liver:* **hepatitis**
> *removal of the liver:* **hepatectomy**

livery ▸ noun =**uniform**, regalia, costume, dress, attire, garb, clothing, outfit, ensemble; *informal* get-up, gear, kit;

formal apparel; *archaic* raiment, vestments.

livid ▸ adjective **1** *(informal)* *Mum was absolutely livid.* See FURIOUS sense 1. **2** *a livid bruise* =**purplish**, bluish, dark, purple; angry.

living ▸ noun **1** *she cleaned floors for a living* =**livelihood**, (source of) income, means of support, subsistence, keep, daily bread, bread and butter; job, work, employment, occupation. **2** *healthy living* =**way of life**, lifestyle, life; conduct, behaviour, activities, habits.
▸ adjective **1** *living organisms* =**alive**, live, animate, sentient; breathing, existing. **2** *a living language* =**current**, contemporary; active.
–OPPOSITES dead, extinct.

living room ▸ noun =**sitting room**, lounge, front room.

load ▸ noun **1** *MacDowell's got a load to deliver* =**cargo**, freight, consignment, delivery, shipment, goods, merchandise; pack, bundle, parcel; lorryload, truckload, shipload, boatload, vanload. **2** *(informal)* *I bought a load of clothes* =**a lot**, a great deal, a large amount/number; many, plenty; *informal* a heap, a mass, a pile, a stack, a ton, lots, heaps, masses, piles, stacks, tons. **3** *a heavy teaching load* =**commitment**, responsibility, duty, obligation, burden.
▸ verb **1** *we quickly loaded the van* =**fill (up)**, pack, lade, charge, stock, stack. **2** *Larry loaded boxes into the jeep* =**pack**, stow, store, stack, bundle; place, deposit, put away. **3** *loading the committee with responsibilities* =**burden**, weigh down, saddle, charge; overburden, overwhelm, encumber, tax, strain, trouble, worry. **4** *Richard loaded Marshal with honours* =**reward**, ply, regale, shower. **5** *he loaded a gun* =**prime**, charge; set up, prepare. **6** *load the cassette into the camcorder* =**insert**, put, place, slot, slide.

loaded ▸ adjective **1** *a loaded freight train* =**full**, filled, laden, packed, stuffed, crammed, brimming, stacked; *informal* chock-full, chock-a-block. **2** *a politically loaded word* =**charged**, emotive, sensitive, delicate.

loaf ▸ verb *he was just loafing around* =**laze**, lounge, loll, idle; *informal* hang around/round; *Brit. informal* hang about, mooch about/around; *N. Amer. informal* bum around.

loan ▸ noun *a loan of £7,000* =**credit**,

advance; mortgage, overdraft; *Brit. informal* sub.

loath ▶ adjective =**reluctant**, unwilling, disinclined; averse, opposed, resistant.
−OPPOSITES willing.

loathe ▶ verb =**hate**, detest, abhor, not be able to bear/stand; *formal* abominate.
−OPPOSITES love.

loathing ▶ noun =**hatred**, hate, abhorrence, odium; antipathy, dislike, hostility, animosity, ill feeling, bad feeling, malice, enmity; repugnance.

loathsome ▶ adjective =**hateful**, detestable, abhorrent, repulsive, odious, repugnant, repellent, disgusting, revolting, sickening, abominable, despicable, contemptible, reprehensible; vile, horrible, nasty, obnoxious, gross, foul; *informal* horrid; *literary* noisome.

lob ▶ verb =**throw**, toss, fling, pitch, hurl, sling, launch, propel; *informal* chuck, bung, heave.

lobby ▶ noun 1 *the hotel lobby* =**entrance** (**hall**), hallway, hall, vestibule, foyer, reception area. **2** *the anti-hunt lobby* =**pressure group**, interest group, movement, campaign, crusade; faction, camp, contingent.
▶ verb **1** *readers are urged to lobby their MPs* =**approach**, contact, importune, sway; petition, solicit, appeal to, pressurize. **2** *a group lobbying for better rail services* =**campaign**, crusade, press, push, ask, call, demand; promote, advocate, champion.

local ▶ adjective **1** *the local council* =**community**, district, neighbourhood, regional, town, municipal, provincial, village, parish. **2** *a local restaurant* =**neighbourhood**, nearby, near, at hand, close by; handy, convenient. **3** *a local infection* =**confined**, restricted, contained, localized; limited.
−OPPOSITES national.
▶ noun *complaints from the locals* =**local person**, native, inhabitant, resident, parishioner.
−OPPOSITES outsider.

locale ▶ noun =**place**, site, spot, area; position, location, setting, scene, venue, background, backdrop, environment; neighbourhood, district, region, locality.

locality ▶ noun *other schools in the locality* =**vicinity**, neighbourhood, area, district, region; *informal* neck of the woods.

localize ▶ verb =**limit**, restrict, confine, contain, circumscribe, concentrate.
−OPPOSITES generalize, globalize.

locate ▶ verb **1** *spotter planes located the submarines* =**find**, pinpoint, track down, unearth, sniff out, smoke out, search out, uncover. **2** *a company located near Pittsburgh* =**situate**, site, position, place, base; put, build, establish, found, station, install.

location ▶ noun =**position**, place, situation, site, locality, locale, spot, whereabouts; scene, setting, area, environment; venue, address; *technical* locus.

lock¹ ▶ noun *the lock on the door* =**bolt**, catch, fastener, clasp, hasp, latch.
▶ verb **1** *he locked the door* =**bolt**, fasten, secure; padlock, latch, chain. **2** *she locked her legs* =**join**, interlock, link, engage, combine, connect; couple. **3** *the wheels locked* =**become stuck**, stick, jam, seize. **4** *he locked her in an embrace* =**clasp**, clench, grasp, embrace, hug, squeeze.
−OPPOSITES unlock, open, separate, divide.
■ **lock someone up** =**imprison**, jail, incarcerate, intern, send to prison, put behind bars, put under lock and key, put in chains, clap in irons, cage, pen, coop up; *informal* send down, put away, put inside.

lock² ▶ noun *a lock of hair* =**tress**, tuft, curl, ringlet, hank, strand, wisp, coil.

locker ▶ noun =**cupboard**, cabinet, chest, safe, box, case, coffer; storeroom.

lock-up ▶ noun *they stored spare furniture in a lock-up* =**storeroom**, store, warehouse, depository; garage.

locomotion ▶ noun =**movement**, motion; travel, mobility, motility; walking, running; progress, passage, transport; *formal* perambulation.

lodge ▶ noun **1** *the porter's lodge* =**gatehouse**, cottage. **2** *a hunting lodge* =**house**, cottage, cabin, chalet; *Brit.* shooting box. **3** *a Masonic lodge* =**section**, branch, wing; hall, clubhouse, meeting room; *N. Amer.* chapter.
▶ verb **1** *William lodged at our house* =**reside**, board, stay, live, stop; *N. Amer.* room; *informal* have digs; *formal* dwell; *archaic* abide. **2** *the government lodged a protest* =**submit**, register, enter, put forward, advance, lay, present, tender, proffer, put on record, record, table, file. **3** *the money was lodged in a bank* =**deposit**, put, bank; stash, store, stow, put away. **4** *the bullet*

lodged in his back =**become embedded**, get/become stuck, stick, catch, become caught, wedge.

lodger ▸ noun =**boarder**, paying guest, tenant; *N. Amer.* roomer.

lodging ▸ noun =**accommodation**, rooms, chambers, living quarters, place to stay, a roof over one's head, housing, shelter; *informal* digs; *formal* abode, residence, dwelling, dwelling place, habitation.

lofty ▸ adjective **1** *a lofty tower* =**tall**, high. **2** *lofty ideals* =**noble**, exalted, high, high-minded, worthy, grand, fine, elevated. **3** *lofty disdain* =**haughty**, arrogant, disdainful, supercilious, condescending, scornful, contemptuous, self-important, conceited, snobbish; *informal* stuck-up, snooty; *Brit. informal* toffee-nosed.
−OPPOSITES low, short, base, lowly, modest.

log ▸ noun *a log of phone calls* =**record**, register, logbook, journal, diary, minutes, chronicle, record book, ledger, account, tally.
▸ verb **1** *all complaints are logged* =**register**, record, note down, write down, jot down, put in writing, enter, file, minute. **2** *the pilot had logged 95 hours* =**attain**, achieve, chalk up, make, do, go, cover, clock up.

loggerheads ■ **at loggerheads** =in **disagreement**, at odds, at variance, in dispute, at daggers drawn, in conflict, at war; *informal* at each other's throats.

logic ▸ noun **1** *this case appears to defy all logic* =**reason**, judgement, rationality, wisdom, sense, good sense, common sense, sanity. **2** *the logic of their argument* =**reasoning**, line, rationale, argument.

logical ▸ adjective **1** *information displayed in a logical fashion* =**reasoned**, rational, sound, cogent, valid; coherent, clear, systematic, orderly, methodical, analytical, consistent, objective. **2** *the logical outcome* =**natural**, reasonable, sensible, understandable; predictable, unsurprising, only to be expected, likely.
−OPPOSITES illogical, irrational, unlikely, surprising.

logistics ▸ plural noun =**organization**, planning, plans, management, arrangement, administration, orchestration, coordination, execution, handling, running.

logo ▸ noun =**emblem**, trademark, device, symbol, design, sign, mark; insignia, crest, seal, coat of arms, shield, badge, motif, monogram.

loiter ▸ verb =**linger**, wait, skulk; loaf, lounge, idle, laze; *informal* hang around/round; *Brit. informal* hang about, mooch about/around.

loll ▸ verb **1** *he lolled in an armchair* =**lounge**, sprawl; slouch, slump; recline, relax. **2** *her head lolled to one side* =**hang**, droop, sag, drop, flop.

lone ▸ adjective **1** *a lone police officer* =**solitary**, single, solo, unaccompanied, sole; isolated. **2** *a lone parent* =**single**, unmarried; separated, divorced, widowed.

loneliness ▸ noun **1** *his loneliness was unbearable* =**isolation**, friendlessness, abandonment, rejection; *N. Amer.* lonesomeness. **2** *the enforced loneliness of a prison cell* =**solitariness**, solitude, aloneness, separation. **3** *the loneliness of the village* =**isolation**, remoteness, seclusion.

> **WORD LINKS**
>
> *fear of loneliness:* **autophobia, ermitophobia**

lonely ▸ adjective **1** *I felt very lonely* =**isolated**, alone, friendless, with no one to turn to, abandoned, rejected, unloved, unwanted; *N. Amer.* lonesome. **2** *the lonely life of a writer* =**solitary**, isolated. **3** *a lonely road* =**deserted**, uninhabited, desolate, isolated, remote, out of the way, secluded, in the back of beyond, godforsaken; *informal* in the middle of nowhere.
−OPPOSITES popular, sociable, crowded.

loner ▸ noun =**recluse**, introvert, lone wolf, hermit, misanthrope, outsider; *historical* anchorite.

long¹ ▸ adjective *a long silence* =**lengthy**, extended, prolonged, protracted, long-lasting, drawn-out, endless, lingering, interminable.
−OPPOSITES short, brief.

long² ▸ verb *I longed for the holidays* =**yearn**, pine, ache, hanker for/after, hunger, thirst, itch, be eager, be desperate; crave, dream of; *informal* have a yen, be dying.

longing ▸ noun *a longing for the countryside* =**yearning**, craving, ache, burning, hunger, thirst, hankering; *informal* yen, itch.

▸ adjective *a longing look* =**yearning**, hungry, thirsty, wistful, covetous, desperate.

long-lasting ▸ adjective =**enduring**, lasting, abiding, long-lived, long-term, permanent.
–OPPOSITES short-lived, ephemeral.

long-lived ▸ adjective. *See* LONG-LASTING.

long-standing ▸ adjective =**well established**, long-established, time-honoured, traditional; abiding, enduring.
–OPPOSITES new, recent.

long-suffering ▸ adjective =**patient**, forbearing, tolerant, uncomplaining, stoical; accommodating, forgiving.
–OPPOSITES impatient, complaining.

long-winded ▸ adjective =**verbose**, wordy, lengthy, long, overlong, prolix, interminable; discursive, rambling, tortuous, meandering, repetitious; *Brit. informal* waffly.
–OPPOSITES concise, succinct, laconic.

look ▸ verb **1** *Mrs Wright looked at him* =**glance**, gaze, stare, gape, peer; peep, peek, take a look; watch, observe, view, regard, examine, inspect, eye, scan, scrutinize, survey, study, contemplate, take in, ogle; *informal* take a gander, rubberneck, give someone/something a/ the once-over, get a load of; *Brit. informal* take a dekko, take a butcher's, take a shufti, clock, gawp; *N. Amer. informal* eyeball. **2** *her room looked out on Broadway* =**overlook**, face, front. **3** *they looked shocked* =**seem (to be)**, appear (to be); come across/over as.
–OPPOSITES ignore.

▸ noun **1** *have a look at this report* =**glance**, examination, study, inspection, scrutiny, peep, peek, glimpse; *informal* eyeful, gander, look-see, once-over, squint, recce; *Brit. informal* shufti, dekko, butcher's. **2** *the look on her face* =**expression**, mien. **3** *that rustic look* =**appearance**, air, aspect, manner, mien, demeanour, impression, effect, ambience. **4** *this season's look* =**fashion**, style; *informal* thing, groove.

■ **look after** =**take care of**, care for, attend to, minister to, tend, mind, keep an eye on, keep safe, be responsible for, protect; nurse, babysit, childmind.

■ **look back on** =**reflect on**, think back to, remember, recall, reminisce about.

■ **look down on** =**disdain**, scorn, look

down one's nose at, sneer at, despise.

■ **look for** =**search for**, hunt for, try to find, seek, cast about/around/round for, try to track down, forage for.

■ **look forward to** =**await with pleasure**, eagerly anticipate, lick one's lips over, be unable to wait for, count the days until.

■ **look into** =**investigate**, enquire into, go into, probe, explore, follow up, research, study, examine; *informal* check out; *N. Amer. informal* scope out.

■ **look like** =**resemble**, bear a resemblance to, look similar to, take after, have the look of, have the appearance of, remind one of, make one think of; *informal* be the (spitting) image of, be a dead ringer for.

■ **look on/upon** =**regard**, consider, think of, deem, judge, see, view, count, reckon.

■ **look out** =**beware**, watch out, mind out, be on (one's) guard, be alert, be wary, be vigilant, be careful, take care, be cautious, pay attention, take heed, keep one's eyes open/peeled, keep an eye out; watch one's step.

■ **look something over** =**inspect**, examine, scrutinize, cast an eye over, take stock of, vet, view, peruse, read through; *informal* take a dekko at, give something a/the once-over; *N. Amer.* check out; *N. Amer. informal* eyeball.

■ **look to 1** *we must look to the future* =**consider**, think about, turn one's thoughts to, focus on, take heed of, pay attention to, attend to, address. **2** *they look to the government for help* =**turn to**, resort to, have recourse to, fall back on, rely on.

■ **look up** =**improve**, get better, pick up, come along/on, progress, make progress, make headway, perk up, rally, take a turn for the better.

■ **look someone up** (*informal*) =**visit**, pay a visit to, call on, go to see, look in on; *N. Amer.* visit with, go see; *informal* drop in on.

■ **look up to** =**admire**, have a high opinion of, think highly of, hold in high regard, regard highly, respect, esteem, venerate, idolize.

lookalike ▸ noun =**double**, twin, clone, duplicate, exact likeness, replica, copy, facsimile, Doppelgänger; *informal* spitting image, dead ringer.

lookout ▸ noun **1** *the lookout sighted sails* =**watchman**, watch, guard, sentry, sentinel; observer. **2** (Brit. informal) that's your lookout =**problem**, concern, business, affair, responsibility, worry; informal pigeon.

■ **be on the lookout/keep a lookout** =**keep watch**, keep an eye out, keep one's eyes peeled, be alert.

loom ▸ verb **1** ghostly shapes loomed out of the fog =**emerge**, appear, materialize, reveal itself. **2** the church loomed above him =**soar**, tower, rise, rear up; hang, overshadow. **3** without reforms, disaster looms =**be imminent**, be on the horizon, impend, threaten, brew, be just around the corner.

loop ▸ noun a loop of rope =**coil**, ring, circle, noose, spiral, curl, bend, curve, arc, twirl, whorl, twist, helix.
▸ verb **1** Dave looped rope around their hands =**coil**, wind, twist, snake, spiral, curve, bend, turn. **2** he looped the cables together =**fasten**, tie, join, connect, knot, bind.

loophole ▸ noun =**flaw**, discrepancy, inconsistency, ambiguity, omission; Brit. get-out.

loose ▸ adjective **1** a loose floorboard =**not secure**, unsecured, unattached; detached; wobbly, unsteady; dangling, free. **2** she wore her hair loose =**untied**, free, down. **3** there's a wolf loose =**free**, at large, at liberty, on the loose, on the rampage. **4** a loose interpretation =**vague**, imprecise, approximate; broad, general, rough; liberal. **5** a loose jacket =**baggy**, generously cut, slack, roomy; oversized, shapeless, sagging, sloppy, big.
–OPPOSITES secure, literal, narrow, tight.
▸ verb **1** the hounds have been loosed =**free**, let loose, release; untie, unchain, unfasten, unleash. **2** the fingers loosed their hold =**relax**, slacken, loosen; lessen. **3** Brian loosed off a shot =**fire**, discharge, shoot, let off.
–OPPOSITES confine, tighten.
■ **let loose.** See LOOSE verb sense 1.
■ **on the loose** =**free**, at liberty, at large, escaped; on the run, on the rampage; N. Amer. informal on the lam.

loose-limbed ▸ adjective =**supple**, limber, lithe, willowy; agile, nimble.

loosen ▸ verb **1** you simply loosen two screws =**undo**, slacken; unfasten, detach, release, disconnect. **2** her fingers loosened =**slacken**, become loose, let go, ease. **3** Philip loosened his grip =**weaken**, relax, slacken, loose, lessen, reduce.

■ **loosen up** =**relax**, unwind, ease up/off; informal let up, hang loose, lighten up, go easy.
–OPPOSITES tighten.

loot ▸ noun a bag full of loot =**booty**, spoils, plunder, stolen goods, contraband; informal swag, ill-gotten gains.
▸ verb troops looted the cathedral =**plunder**, pillage, ransack, sack, rifle, rob; strip, clear out, gut.

lop ▸ verb =**cut**, chop, hack, saw, hew; prune, clip, trim, snip.

lope ▸ verb =**stride**, run, bound; lollop.

lopsided ▸ adjective =**crooked**, askew, awry, off-centre, uneven, out of true, out of line, asymmetrical, tilted, at an angle, slanting, squint; Scottish agley; informal cock-eyed; Brit. informal skew-whiff, wonky.
–OPPOSITES even, level, balanced.

loquacious ▸ adjective =**talkative**, voluble, garrulous, chatty, gossipy; informal gabby, gassy; Brit. informal able to talk the hind legs off a donkey.
–OPPOSITES reticent, taciturn.

lord ▸ noun **1** lords and ladies =**noble**, nobleman, peer, aristocrat. **2** it is my duty to obey my lord's wishes =**master**, ruler, leader, chief, superior, monarch, sovereign, king, emperor, prince, governor, commander.
–OPPOSITES commoner, servant, inferior.

lore ▸ noun **1** Arthurian lore =**mythology**, myths, legends, stories, traditions, folklore. **2** cricket lore =**knowledge**, learning, wisdom; tradition; informal know-how.

lorry ▸ noun =**truck**, wagon, van, juggernaut, trailer; articulated lorry, heavy-goods vehicle, HGV; dated pantechnicon.

lose ▸ verb **1** I've lost my watch =**mislay**, misplace, be unable to find, lose track of. **2** he lost his pursuers =**escape from**, evade, elude, dodge, avoid, give someone the slip, shake off, throw off; leave behind, outdistance, outstrip, outrun. **3** you've lost your opportunity =**waste**, squander, fail to take advantage of, let pass, miss; informal pass up, lose out on, blow. **4** they always lose at football =**be defeated**, be/get beaten; informal come a cropper, go down.
–OPPOSITES find, seize, win.

loser ▸ noun **1** the loser still gets a medal =**runner-up**, also-ran. **2** (informal) he's a complete loser =**failure**, underachiever,

ne'er-do-well, dead loss; write-off, has-been; *informal* flop, non-starter, no-hoper, washout.
–OPPOSITES winner, success.

loss ▸ noun **1** *the loss of the papers* =mislaying, misplacement; destruction, theft, selling. **2** *loss of earnings* =forfeiture, diminution, erosion, reduction, depletion. **3** *the loss of her husband* =death, demise, passing (away/on), end; *formal* decease. **4** *British losses in the war* =casualty, fatality, victim; dead. **5** *a loss of £15,000* =deficit, debit, debt.
–OPPOSITES recovery, profit.
■ **at a loss** =baffled, nonplussed, mystified, puzzled, perplexed, bewildered, bemused, confused, dumbfounded, stumped, stuck; *informal* flummoxed, beaten.

lost ▸ adjective **1** *her lost keys* =missing, mislaid, misplaced; stolen. **2** *I think we're lost* =off course, going round in circles, adrift, at sea. **3** *a lost opportunity* =missed, wasted, squandered, gone by the board; *informal* down the drain. **4** *lost traditions* =bygone, past, former, old, vanished, forgotten, consigned to oblivion, extinct, dead, gone. **5** *lost species and habitats* =extinct, died out, defunct, vanished, gone; **destroyed**, wiped out, exterminated. **6** *a lost cause* =hopeless, futile, forlorn, failed, beyond recovery. **7** *lost souls* =damned, fallen, condemned, cursed, doomed; *literary* accursed. **8** *lost in thought* =engrossed, absorbed, rapt, immersed, deep, intent, engaged, wrapped up.
–OPPOSITES current, saved.

lot ▸ pronoun *a lot of money* | *lots of friends* =a large amount, a good/great deal, an abundance, a wealth, a profusion, plenty; many, a great many, a large number, a considerable number, scores; *informal* hundreds, thousands, millions, billions, loads, masses, heaps, piles, oodles, stacks, reams, wads, pots, oceans, mountains, miles, tons, zillions; *Brit. informal* a shedload, lashings.
–OPPOSITES a little, not much, a few, not many.
▸ adverb *I work in pastels a lot* =a great deal, a good deal, much; often, frequently, regularly.
–OPPOSITES a little, not much.
▸ noun **1** *(informal) what do your lot think?* =group, crowd, circle, crew; *informal* bunch, gang, mob, posse; *Brit. informal* shower. **2** *the books were auctioned in lots*

| *lot 69* =item, article; batch, group, bundle, parcel. **3** *his lot in life* =fate, destiny, fortune; situation, circumstances, state, condition, position, plight, predicament. **4** *(N. Amer.) some youngsters playing ball in a vacant lot* =piece/patch of ground, plot; *N. Amer.* plat.

lotion ▸ noun =ointment, cream, salve, balm, rub, moisturizer, lubricant, unguent, liniment, embrocation.

lottery ▸ noun =raffle, (prize) draw, sweepstake, sweep, tombola, pools.

loud ▸ adjective **1** *loud music* =noisy, blaring, booming, deafening, roaring, thunderous, ear-splitting, piercing; powerful, stentorian; *Music* forte, fortissimo. **2** *loud complaints* =vociferous, clamorous, insistent, vehement, emphatic. **3** *a loud T-shirt* =garish, gaudy, lurid, showy, ostentatious; vulgar, tasteless; *informal* flashy, naff, tacky.
–OPPOSITES quiet, soft, gentle, sober, tasteful.

loudly ▸ adverb =at high volume, at the top of one's voice; noisily; stridently, vociferously, shrilly; *Music* forte, fortissimo.
–OPPOSITES quietly, softly.

loudspeaker ▸ noun =speaker, monitor; loudhailer, megaphone; public address system, PA (system); *Brit. trademark* tannoy; *N. Amer.* bullhorn.

lounge ▸ verb =laze, lie, loll, lie back, lean back, recline, relax, rest, repose, take it easy; sprawl, slump, slouch; loaf, idle, do nothing.
▸ noun =living room, sitting room, front room, drawing room, morning room; *dated* parlour.

lour, lower ▸ verb =scowl, frown, glower, glare, look daggers; *informal* give someone dirty looks.
–OPPOSITES smile.

louring, lowering ▸ adjective =overcast, dark, leaden, grey, cloudy, clouded, gloomy, threatening, menacing.
–OPPOSITES sunny, bright.

louse ▸ noun

> **WORD LINKS**
>
> *fear of lice:* **pediculophobia**
> *chemical used to kill lice:* **pediculicide**

lout ▸ noun =hooligan, ruffian, thug, boor, oaf, rowdy; *informal* tough, roughneck, bruiser; *Brit. informal* yob, yobbo.

–OPPOSITES smoothie, gentleman.

loutish ▸ adjective =**uncouth**, rude, ill-mannered, coarse; thuggish, boorish, uncivilized, rough; *informal* slobbish; *Brit. informal* yobbish.
–OPPOSITES polite, well behaved.

lovable ▸ adjective =**adorable**, dear, sweet, cute, charming, lovely, likeable, engaging, endearing.
–OPPOSITES hateful, loathsome.

love ▸ noun 1 *a friendship that blossomed into love* =**infatuation**, adoration, attachment, devotion, fondness, tenderness, warmth, intimacy, passion, desire, lust, yearning, besottedness. 2 *her love of fashion* =**liking**, taste, passion, zeal, zest, enthusiasm, keenness, fondness, weakness, partiality, predilection, penchant. 3 *their love for their fellow human beings* =**compassion**, care, regard, solicitude, concern, altruism, unselfishness, philanthropy, benevolence, humanity. 4 *he was her one true love* =**beloved**, loved one; dearest, darling, sweetheart, sweet, angel, honey. 5 *my mother sends her love* =**best wishes**, regards, greetings, kind regards.
–OPPOSITES hatred.

▸ verb 1 *she loves him dearly* =**be in love with**, be infatuated with, be smitten with, be besotted with, adore, idolize, worship, think the world of, be devoted to, dote on, care for, hold dear; *informal* be mad/crazy/nuts/wild/potty about, carry a torch for. 2 *Laura loved painting* =**like**, delight in, enjoy, have a passion for, take pleasure in; have a weakness for, be partial to, be taken with; *informal* have a thing about, be mad/crazy/nuts/wild/potty about, be hooked on, go a bundle on, get off on, get a buzz out of.
–OPPOSITES hate.

■ **in love with** =**infatuated with**, besotted with, enamoured of, smitten with; captivated by, bewitched by, enthralled by, entranced by; devoted to; *informal* mad/crazy/nuts/wild/potty about.

WORD LINKS
relating to love: **amatory, phil-**

love affair ▸ noun 1 *he had a love affair with a teacher* =**relationship**, affair, romance, liaison, fling; *Brit. informal* carry-on. 2 *a love affair with the motor car* =**enthusiasm**, mania, devotion, passion, obsession.

loveless ▸ adjective =**passionless**, un-

loving, sterile, empty, barren, hollow.
–OPPOSITES loving, passionate.

lovely ▸ adjective 1 *a lovely young woman* =**beautiful**, pretty, attractive, good-looking, handsome, adorable; enchanting, gorgeous, alluring, ravishing, glamorous; *Scottish & N. English* bonny; *informal* tasty, stunning, drop-dead gorgeous; *Brit. informal* fit; *N. Amer. informal* cute, foxy; *archaic* comely. 2 *a lovely view* =**scenic**, picturesque, pleasing; magnificent, stunning, splendid. 3 *(informal) we had a lovely day* =**delightful**, very pleasant, very nice, marvellous, wonderful, sublime, superb; *informal* terrific, fabulous, heavenly, divine, amazing, glorious.
–OPPOSITES ugly, horrible.

lover ▸ noun 1 *she had a secret lover* =**boyfriend**, **girlfriend**, beloved, sweetheart; mistress; partner; *informal* bit on the side, bit of fluff, toy boy, fancy man, fancy woman; *dated* beau; *archaic* paramour. 2 *a dog lover* =**devotee**, admirer, fan, enthusiast, aficionado; *informal* buff, freak, nut.

WORD LINKS
lover of …: **-phile**

lovesick ▸ adjective =**lovelorn**, pining, languishing, longing, yearning, infatuated.

loving ▸ adjective =**affectionate**, fond, devoted, adoring, doting, solicitous; caring, tender, warm, close; amorous, passionate.
–OPPOSITES cold, cruel.

low¹ ▸ adjective 1 *a low fence* =**short**, small, little; squat, stubby, stunted. 2 *she was wearing a low dress* =**low-cut**, skimpy, revealing, plunging. 3 *low prices* =**cheap**, economical, moderate, reasonable, modest, bargain, bargain-basement, rock-bottom. 4 *supplies were low* =**scarce**, scant, meagre, sparse, few, little; reduced, depleted, diminished. 5 *low quality* =**inferior**, substandard, poor, bad, low-grade, second-rate, unsatisfactory. 6 *of low birth* =**humble**, lowly, low-ranking, poor; common, ordinary. 7 *low expectations* =**unambitious**, unaspiring, modest. 8 *a low opinion* =**unfavourable**, poor, bad, adverse, negative. 9 *a low voice* =**quiet**, soft, faint, gentle, muted, subdued, muffled, hushed. 10 *a low note* =**bass**, low-pitched, deep, rumbling, booming, sonorous. 11 *she was feeling low* =**depressed**, dejected, despondent,

downhearted, downcast, down, miserable, dispirited; flat, weary; *informal* fed up, down in the mouth, down in the dumps, blue.
–OPPOSITES high, expensive, plentiful, superior, noble, favourable, exalted, loud, cheerful, lively.
▸ noun *the dollar fell to an all-time low* =**nadir**, low point, lowest level; rock bottom.
–OPPOSITES high.

low² ▸ verb *cattle were lowing* =**moo**, bellow.

lowbrow ▸ adjective =**mass-market**, tabloid, popular, lightweight, unsophisticated, trashy, simplistic; *Brit.* downmarket; *informal* dumbed-down, rubbishy.
–OPPOSITES highbrow, intellectual.

lower¹ ▸ adjective **1** *the lower house of parliament* =**subordinate**, inferior, lesser, junior, minor, secondary, subsidiary, subservient. **2** *her lower lip* =**bottom**, bottommost, nether, under. **3** *a lower price* =**cheaper**, reduced, cut.
–OPPOSITES upper, higher, increased.

lower² ▸ verb **1** *she lowered the mask* =**let down**, take down, drop, let fall. **2** *lower your voice* =**soften**, modulate, quieten, hush, tone down, muffle, turn down. **3** *they are lowering their prices* =**reduce**, decrease, lessen, bring down, cut, slash. **4** *the water level lowered* =**subside**, fall (off), recede, ebb, wane; abate.
–OPPOSITES raise, increase.

lower³ ▸ verb *he lowered at her. See* LOUR.

low-key ▸ adjective =**restrained**, modest, understated, muted, subtle, quiet, low-profile, inconspicuous, unostentatious, unobtrusive, discreet.
–OPPOSITES ostentatious, obtrusive.

lowly ▸ adjective =**humble**, low, low-ranking; common, ordinary, plain, modest, simple; obscure.
–OPPOSITES aristocratic, exalted.

loyal ▸ adjective =**faithful**, true, devoted; constant, steadfast, staunch, dependable, reliable, trustworthy, trusty; patriotic.
–OPPOSITES treacherous.

loyalty ▸ noun =**allegiance**, faithfulness, obedience, adherence, devotion; steadfastness, staunchness, dedication, commitment; patriotism.
–OPPOSITES treachery.

lozenge ▸ noun **1** *the pattern consists of overlapping lozenges* =**diamond**, rhombus. **2** *a throat lozenge* =**pastille**, drop;

cough sweet; *dated* cachou.

lubricant ▸ noun =**grease**, oil, lubrication, lotion, unguent; *informal* lube.

lubricate ▸ verb =**grease**, oil.

lucid ▸ adjective **1** *a lucid description* =**intelligible**, comprehensible, understandable, cogent, coherent, articulate; clear, transparent; plain, straightforward. **2** *he was not lucid enough to explain* =**rational**, sane, in possession of one's faculties, compos mentis, clear-headed, sober; *informal* all there.
–OPPOSITES confusing, confused.

luck ▸ noun **1** *with luck you'll make it* =**good fortune**, good luck; stroke of luck; *informal* lucky break. **2** *I wish you luck* =**success**, prosperity, good fortune, good luck. **3** *it is a matter of luck whether it hits or misses* =**fortune**, fate, serendipity; chance, accident, a twist of fate; *Austral./NZ informal* mozzle.
–OPPOSITES bad luck, misfortune.

luckily ▸ adverb =**fortunately**, happily, providentially, by good fortune, as luck would have it; mercifully, thankfully.
–OPPOSITES unfortunately.

luckless ▸ adjective =**unlucky**, unfortunate, unsuccessful, hapless, doomed, ill-fated; *literary* star-crossed.
–OPPOSITES lucky.

lucky ▸ adjective **1** *the lucky winner* =**fortunate**, in luck, favoured, charmed; successful; *Brit. informal* jammy. **2** *a lucky escape* =**providential**, fortunate, timely, opportune, serendipitous; chance, fortuitous, accidental.
–OPPOSITES unfortunate.

lucrative ▸ adjective =**profitable**, gainful, remunerative, moneymaking, paying, well paid; rewarding, worthwhile; thriving, flourishing, successful, booming.
–OPPOSITES unprofitable.

ludicrous ▸ adjective =**absurd**, ridiculous, farcical, laughable, risible, preposterous, mad, insane, idiotic, stupid, asinine, nonsensical; *informal* crazy.
–OPPOSITES sensible.

lug ▸ verb =**carry**, lift, heave, hoist, manhandle; haul, drag, tug, tow; *informal* hump, schlep, tote; *Scottish informal* humph.

luggage ▸ noun =**baggage**; bags, suitcases, cases. *See also* BAG *noun.*

lugubrious ▸ adjective =**mournful**, gloomy, sad, unhappy, melancholy,

doleful, woeful, miserable, forlorn, sombre, solemn, sorrowful, morose, dour, cheerless, joyless, dismal; *literary* dolorous.
–OPPOSITES cheerful.

lukewarm ▸ adjective **1** *lukewarm coffee* =**tepid**, warmish, at room temperature. **2** *a lukewarm response* =**indifferent**, cool, half-hearted, apathetic, unenthusiastic, tepid, offhand, perfunctory, non-committal.
–OPPOSITES hot, cold, enthusiastic.

lull ▸ verb **1** *the sound of the bells lulled us to sleep* =**soothe**, calm, hush; rock to sleep. **2** *his suspicions were soon lulled* =**allay**, ease, alleviate, quiet, quieten; reduce, diminish; quell, banish, dispel. **3** *the noise had lulled* =**abate**, die down, subside, let up, moderate, lessen, dwindle, decrease, diminish.
–OPPOSITES waken, agitate, arouse, intensify.
▸ noun **1** *a lull in the fighting* =**pause**, respite, interval, break, suspension, breathing space; *informal* let-up, breather. **2** *the lull before the storm* =**calm**, stillness, quiet, tranquillity, peace, silence, hush.
–OPPOSITES agitation, activity.

lumber[1] ▸ verb *elephants lumbered past* =**lurch**, stumble, trundle, shamble, shuffle; trudge, clump.

lumber[2] ▸ noun **1** *a spare room packed with lumber* =**jumble**, clutter, odds and ends, bits and pieces; rubbish; *informal* junk, odds and sods. **2** *the lumber trade* =**timber**, wood.
▸ verb *(Brit. informal) she was lumbered with a husband and child* =**burden**, saddle, encumber.
–OPPOSITES free.

lumbering ▸ adjective =**clumsy**, awkward, slow, blundering, bumbling, inept; ponderous; *informal* clodhopping.
–OPPOSITES nimble, agile.

luminary ▸ noun =**leading light**, inspiration, hero, heroine, leader, expert, master; legend, great, giant.
–OPPOSITES nobody.

luminous ▸ adjective =**shining**, bright, brilliant, radiant, dazzling, glowing, scintillating; luminescent, phosphorescent, fluorescent, incandescent.
–OPPOSITES dark.

lump ▸ noun **1** *a lump of coal* =**chunk**, hunk, piece, block, wedge, slab, ball, knob, clod, gobbet, dollop; *informal* glob; *N. Amer. informal* gob. **2** *a lump on his head* =**swelling**, bump, bulge, protuberance, protrusion, growth, nodule.
▸ verb *it is convenient to lump them together* =**combine**, put, group, bunch.

lumpy ▸ adjective =**bumpy**, knobbly, uneven, rough, gnarled.

lunacy ▸ noun =**folly**, foolishness, madness, stupidity, silliness, idiocy, recklessness, irresponsibility; *informal* craziness; *Brit. informal* daftness.
–OPPOSITES sense, prudence.

lunatic ▸ noun *he drives like a lunatic* =**maniac**, madman, madwoman; fool, idiot; *informal* loony, nutcase, head case, psycho; *Brit. informal* nutter; *N. Amer. informal* screwball.
▸ adjective *a lunatic idea. See* MAD *sense* 3.

lunch ▸ noun =**midday meal**, luncheon; *Brit.* dinner.

WORD LINKS

relating to a meal: **prandial**

lung ▸ noun

WORD LINKS

relating to the lungs: **pulmonary, pneumo-**
measurement of lung capacity: **spirometry**
removal of a lung: **pneumonectomy**

lunge ▸ noun *Darren made a lunge at his attacker* =**thrust**, dive, rush, charge, grab.
▸ verb *he lunged at Finn with a knife* =**thrust**, dive, spring, launch oneself, rush.

lurch ▸ verb **1** *he lurched into the kitchen* =**stagger**, stumble, sway, reel, roll, totter. **2** *the car lurched to the left* =**swing**, list, roll, pitch, veer, swerve.

lure ▸ verb *consumers are frequently lured into debt* =**tempt**, entice, attract, induce, coax, persuade, inveigle, seduce, beguile.
–OPPOSITES deter, put off.
▸ noun *the lure of the stage* =**temptation**, attraction, pull, draw, appeal; inducement, allure, fascination, interest, glamour.

lurid ▸ adjective **1** *lurid colours* =**bright**, vivid, glaring, fluorescent, intense, gaudy, loud. **2** *lurid details of the murder* =**sensational**, extravagant, colourful; salacious, graphic, explicit, prurient, shocking; gruesome, gory, grisly; *informal* juicy.
–OPPOSITES muted, restrained.

lurk ▶ verb =skulk, loiter, lie in wait, hide.

luscious ▶ adjective **1** *luscious fruit* =delicious, succulent, juicy, mouth-watering, sweet, tasty, appetizing; *informal* scrumptious, yummy; *N. Amer. informal* nummy. **2** *a luscious Swedish starlet* =gorgeous, nubile, ravishing, alluring, sultry, beautiful, stunning; *informal* fanciable, tasty, curvy; *Brit. informal* fit; *N. Amer. informal* foxy, cute; *Austral./NZ informal* spunky.
–OPPOSITES unappetizing, plain, scrawny.

lush ▶ adjective **1** *lush vegetation* =luxuriant, rich, abundant, profuse, riotous, vigorous; dense, thick, rampant. **2** *a lush apartment* =luxurious, sumptuous, palatial, opulent, lavish, elaborate, extravagant, fancy; *informal* plush, ritzy, posh, swanky; *Brit. informal* swish; *N. Amer. informal* swank.
–OPPOSITES barren, sparse, shrivelled, austere.

lust ▶ noun **1** *his lust for her* =desire, longing, passion; libido, sex drive, sexuality; lechery, lecherousness, lasciviousness; *informal* horniness; *Brit. informal* randiness. **2** *a lust for power* =greed, desire, craving, eagerness, longing, yearning, hunger, thirst, appetite, hankering.
–OPPOSITES dread, aversion.
▶ verb **1** *he lusted after his employer's wife* =desire, be consumed with desire for; *informal* have the hots for, lech after/over, fancy, have a thing about/for, drool over, have the horn for. **2** *she lusted after adventure* =crave, desire, want, long for, yearn for, dream of, hanker for/after, hunger for, thirst for, ache for.
–OPPOSITES dread, avoid.

lustful ▶ adjective =lecherous, lascivious, libidinous, licentious, salacious; wanton, immodest, indecent, dirty, prurient; passionate, sensual; *informal* horny, randy, raunchy; *formal* concupiscent.
–OPPOSITES chaste, pure.

lustily ▶ adverb =heartily, vigorously, loudly, at the top of one's voice, powerfully, forcefully, strongly.
–OPPOSITES feebly, quietly.

lustre ▶ noun =sheen, gloss, shine, gleam, patina.
–OPPOSITES dullness.

lustreless ▶ adjective =dull, lack-

lustre, matt, unpolished, tarnished, dingy, flat.
–OPPOSITES lustrous, bright.

lustrous ▶ adjective =shiny, shining, satiny, silky, glossy, gleaming, burnished, polished; bright, brilliant, luminous.
–OPPOSITES dull, dark.

lusty ▶ adjective **1** *lusty young men* =healthy, strong, fit, vigorous, robust, energetic; rugged, sturdy, muscular, muscly, strapping, hefty, burly; *informal* beefy; *dated* stalwart. **2** *lusty singing* =loud, vigorous, hearty; enthusiastic.
–OPPOSITES feeble, quiet.

luxuriant ▶ adjective =lush, rich, abundant, profuse, riotous, prolific, vigorous; dense, thick, rampant.
–OPPOSITES barren, sparse.

luxuriate ▶ verb =revel, bask, delight, wallow; (**luxuriate in**) enjoy, relish, savour.
–OPPOSITES dislike.

luxurious ▶ adjective =opulent, sumptuous, grand, palatial, magnificent, extravagant, fancy; *Brit.* upmarket; *informal* plush, posh, classy, ritzy, swanky; *Brit. informal* swish; *N. Amer. informal* swank.
–OPPOSITES plain, basic.

luxury ▶ noun **1** *we'll live in luxury* =opulence, sumptuousness, grandeur, magnificence, splendour, lavishness. **2** *a TV is his only luxury* =indulgence, extravagance, treat, extra, frill.
–OPPOSITES simplicity, necessity.

lying ▶ noun *she was no good at lying* =untruthfulness, fabrication, fibbing, perjury; dishonesty, mendacity, telling lies, misrepresentation, deceit, duplicity; *literary* perfidy.
–OPPOSITES honesty.
▶ adjective *he was a lying womanizer* =untruthful, false, dishonest, mendacious, deceitful, deceiving, duplicitous, double-dealing, two-faced; *literary* perfidious.
–OPPOSITES truthful.

lyrical ▶ adjective **1** *a subtle, lyrical film* =expressive, emotional, deeply felt, personal, passionate. **2** *she was lyrical about her success* =enthusiastic, effusive, rapturous, ecstatic, euphoric.
–OPPOSITES unenthusiastic.

lyrics ▶ plural noun =words; libretto, text, lines.

macabre ▶ adjective =gruesome, grisly, grim, gory, ghastly, grotesque.

macerate ▶ verb =pulp, soften, liquefy, soak.

Machiavellian ▶ adjective =devious, cunning, crafty, wily, sly, scheming, treacherous, unscrupulous, deceitful, dishonest; *literary* perfidious.
−OPPOSITES straightforward, ingenuous.

machinations ▶ plural noun =scheming, plotting, intrigue, conspiracies, tricks, stratagems, manoeuvring.

machine ▶ noun 1 *a machine that is cheap to run* =device, appliance, apparatus, engine, gadget, mechanism. 2 *an efficient publicity machine* =organization, system, structure; *informal* set-up.

machinery ▶ noun 1 *road-making machinery* =equipment, apparatus, plant, hardware, gear; gadgetry, technology. 2 *the machinery of local government* =workings, organization, system, structure, institution; *informal* set-up.

machinist ▶ noun =operator, operative.

machismo ▶ noun =(aggressive) masculinity, toughness, male chauvinism, sexism, laddishness, maleness; virility, manliness.

macho ▶ adjective =(aggressively) male, (aggressively) masculine; manly, virile, red-blooded; *informal* butch, laddish.
−OPPOSITES wimpish.

mackintosh ▶ noun =raincoat, gaberdine, trench coat, waterproof; *Brit.* pakamac; *N. Amer.* slicker; *Brit. informal* mac.

mad ▶ adjective 1 *he was killed by his mad brother* =insane, mentally ill, certifiable, deranged, demented, of unsound mind, out of one's mind, sick in the head, crazy, crazed, lunatic, non compos mentis, unhinged, disturbed, raving, psychotic, mad as a hatter, mad as a March hare, away with the fairies; *informal* mental, off one's head, off one's nut, nuts, off one's rocker, not right in the head, round the bend, stark staring/raving mad, batty, bonkers, dotty, cuckoo, cracked, loopy, loony, doolally, bananas, loco, screwy, schizoid, touched, gaga, not all there; *Brit. informal* barmy, crackers, barking, barking mad, round the twist, off one's trolley, not the full shilling; *N. Amer. informal* nutso, out of one's tree, meshuga, wacko, gonzo; *Austral./NZ informal* bushed; *NZ informal* porangi; (**be mad**) *informal* have a screw loose, have bats in the/one's belfry; *Austral. informal* have kangaroos in the/one's top paddock; (**go mad**) lose one's mind, take leave of one's senses; *informal* lose one's marbles, crack up. 2 *(informal) I'm still mad at him* =angry, furious, infuriated, enraged, fuming, incensed, beside oneself; *informal* livid, spare; *N. Amer. informal* sore; *literary* wrathful; (**go mad**) lose one's temper, get in a rage, rant and rave; *informal* explode, go off the deep end, go ape, flip, flip one's lid; *Brit. informal* do one's nut; *N. Amer. informal* flip one's wig. 3 *some mad scheme* =foolish, insane, stupid, lunatic, idiotic, absurd, silly, inane, asinine, wild; *informal* crazy, crackpot; *Brit. informal* daft. 4 *(informal) he's mad about jazz* =passionate, fanatical; ardent, fervent, avid; devoted to, infatuated with, in love with; *informal* crazy, dotty, nuts, wild, hooked on; *Brit. informal* potty; *N. Amer. informal* nutso. 5 *it was a mad dash to get ready* =frenzied, frantic, frenetic, feverish, hysterical, wild, hectic, manic.
−OPPOSITES sane, pleased, sensible, indifferent, calm.

madcap ▶ adjective 1 *a madcap scheme* =reckless, rash, foolhardy, foolish, hare-brained, wild; *informal* crazy, crackpot. 2 *a madcap comedy* =zany, eccentric; *informal* wacky.

madden ▶ verb 1 *what maddens people most is his vagueness* =infuriate, exasperate, irritate; incense, anger, enrage, provoke, upset, agitate, vex, irk, make someone's hackles rise, make someone see red; *informal* aggravate, make someone's blood boil, get up someone's nose, get someone's goat, get someone's back up; *Brit. informal* nark; *N. Amer. informal* tee off, tick off. **2** *they were maddened with pain* =**drive mad**, derange, unhinge, unbalance; *informal* drive round the bend.

made-up ▸ adjective =**invented**, fabricated, trumped up, concocted, fictitious, fictional, false, untrue, specious, spurious, bogus, apocryphal.

madhouse ▸ noun *(informal)* =**bedlam**, mayhem, chaos, pandemonium, uproar, turmoil, madness; *N. Amer.* three-ring circus.

madly ▸ adverb **1** *she was smiling madly* =**insanely**, wildly; *informal* crazily. **2** *it was fun, hurtling madly downhill* =**furiously**, hurriedly, speedily, energetically; *informal* like mad, like crazy. **3** *(informal) he loved her madly* =**intensely**, fervently, wildly, to distraction. **4** *(informal) his job isn't madly exciting* =**very**, tremendously, wildly, all that, hugely; *informal* awfully, terribly, terrifically, fantastically.
–OPPOSITES sanely, slowly, slightly.

madman, madwoman ▸ noun =**lunatic**, maniac, psychotic, psychopath; *informal* loony, nut, nutcase, head case, psycho; *Brit. informal* nutter; *N. Amer. informal* screwball.

madness ▸ noun **1** *today madness is called mental illness* =**insanity**, mental illness, dementia, derangement; lunacy; mania, psychosis; *informal* craziness. **2** *it would be madness to do otherwise* =**folly**, foolishness, idiocy, stupidity, insanity, lunacy. **3** *it's absolute madness in here* =**bedlam**, mayhem, chaos, pandemonium, uproar, turmoil, all hell broken loose; *N. Amer.* three-ring circus.
–OPPOSITES sanity, common sense, good sense, calm.

maelstrom ▸ noun *the maelstrom of war* =**turbulence**, tumult, turmoil, chaos, confusion, upheaval, pandemonium, bedlam, whirlwind.

maestro ▸ noun =**virtuoso**, master, expert, genius, wizard; *informal.*ace, whizz, hotshot.
–OPPOSITES tyro, beginner.

magazine ▸ noun =**journal**, periodical, supplement, colour supplement; *informal* glossy, mag, 'zine.

maggot ▸ noun =**grub**, larva.

magic ▸ noun **1** *do you believe in magic?* =**sorcery**, witchcraft, necromancy, enchantment, the supernatural, occultism, the occult, black magic, the black arts; voodoo. **2** *he does magic at children's parties* =**conjuring (tricks)**, illusion; *formal* prestidigitation. **3** *the magic of the stage* =**allure**, excitement, fascination, charm, glamour. **4** *the old Liverpool magic* =**brilliance**, skill, accomplishment, adroitness, deftness, dexterity, expertise, art, finesse, talent.
▸ adjective **1** *a magic spell* =**supernatural**, enchanted. **2** *a magic place* =**fascinating**, captivating, charming, glamorous, magical, enchanting, entrancing, spellbinding, magnetic, irresistible, hypnotic. **3** *(informal) we had a magic time* =**marvellous**, wonderful, excellent; *informal* terrific, fabulous, fab, brilliant, brill.

magical ▸ adjective **1** *magical powers* =**supernatural**, magic, mystical, otherworldly. **2** *the news had a magical effect* =**extraordinary**, remarkable, incredible, amazing, astonishing, astounding, staggering, miraculous; *literary* wondrous. **3** *this magical island* =**enchanting**, entrancing, spellbinding, bewitching, beguiling, fascinating, captivating, alluring, enthralling, charming, lovely, delightful, beautiful; *informal* heavenly, divine, gorgeous.
–OPPOSITES predictable, boring.

magician ▸ noun **1** =**sorcerer**, sorceress, witch, wizard, warlock, enchanter, enchantress, necromancer. **2** =**conjuror**, illusionist; *formal* prestidigitator.

magisterial ▸ adjective **1** *a magisterial performance* =**authoritative**, masterful, assured, commanding. **2** *his magisterial style of questioning* =**domineering**, dictatorial, autocratic, imperious, overbearing; *informal* bossy.
–OPPOSITES untrustworthy, humble, hesitant, tentative.

magnanimity ▸ noun =**generosity**, charity, benevolence, beneficence, bigheartedness, altruism, philanthropy, humanity, chivalry, nobility.
–OPPOSITES meanness, selfishness.

magnanimous ▸ adjective =**generous**, charitable, benevolent, beneficent, big-hearted, handsome, philanthropic, chivalrous, noble.
–OPPOSITES mean-spirited, selfish.

magnate ▸ noun =**tycoon**, mogul, captain of industry; baron, lord, king; *informal* big shot; *derogatory* fat cat.

magnet ▸ noun *a magnet for tourists* =**attraction**, focus, draw, lure.

magnetic ▸ adjective *a magnetic personality* =**alluring**, attractive, fascinating, captivating, enchanting, enthralling, entrancing, seductive, irresistible, charismatic.

magnetism ▸ noun *his sheer magnetism* =**allure**, attraction, fascination, appeal, draw, charm, magic, spell, charisma.

WORD LINKS

measurement of magnetic force: **magnetometry**

magnification ▸ noun =**enlargement**, enhancement, increase, augmentation, extension, expansion, amplification, intensification.
–OPPOSITES reduction, understatement.

magnificence ▸ noun =**splendour**, resplendence, grandeur, impressiveness, glory, majesty, nobility, pomp, stateliness, elegance, sumptuousness, opulence, luxury, lavishness, richness, brilliance.
–OPPOSITES modesty, tawdriness, weakness.

magnificent ▸ adjective 1 *a magnificent view of the mountains* =**splendid**, spectacular, impressive, striking, glorious, superb, majestic, awesome, awe-inspiring, breathtaking. 2 *a magnificent apartment overlooking the lake* =**sumptuous**, grand, impressive, imposing, monumental, palatial, opulent, luxurious, lavish, rich, dazzling, beautiful; *informal* splendiferous, ritzy, posh. 3 *a magnificent performance* =**masterly**, skilful, virtuoso, brilliant; outstanding.
–OPPOSITES uninspiring, modest, tawdry, poor, weak.

magnify ▸ verb =**enlarge**, boost, enhance, maximize, increase, augment, extend, expand, amplify, intensify; *informal* blow up.
–OPPOSITES reduce, minimize, understate.

magnitude ▸ noun 1 *the magnitude of the task* =**immensity**, vastness, hugeness, enormity; size, extent. 2 *events of such magnitude* =**importance**, import, significance, consequence.
–OPPOSITES smallness, triviality.

maid ▸ noun 1 *the maid cleared the table* =**female servant**, housemaid, chambermaid, domestic; (home) help, cleaner, cleaning woman/lady; *Brit. informal* daily, Mrs Mop; *Brit. dated* charwoman, charlady. 2 *(literary) a beautiful maid* =**girl**, young woman, young lady, lass, miss; *Scottish* (wee) lassie; *literary*

maiden, damsel, nymph; *archaic* wench.

maiden ▸ noun *(literary)*. See MAID *sense 2*.
▸ adjective 1 *a maiden aunt* =**unmarried**, spinster, unwed, single. 2 *a maiden voyage* =**first**, inaugural, introductory.

mail ▸ noun *the mail arrived* =**post**, letters, correspondence; postal system, postal service, post office; email; *informal* snail mail; *N. Amer.* the mails.
▸ verb *we mailed the parcels* =**send**, post, dispatch, forward, redirect, ship; email.

maim ▸ verb =**injure**, wound, cripple, disable, incapacitate, mutilate, lacerate, disfigure, deform, mangle.

main ▸ adjective *the main item* =**principal**, chief, leading, foremost, most important, major, ruling, dominant, central, focal, key, prime, primary, first, fundamental, predominant, pre-eminent.
–OPPOSITES subsidiary, minor.

mainly ▸ adverb =**mostly**, for the most part, in the main, on the whole, largely, by and large, to a large extent, predominantly, chiefly, principally, primarily.

mainspring ▸ noun =**motive**, motivation, impetus, driving force, incentive, impulse, reason, root.

mainstay ▸ noun =**foundation**, base, prop, linchpin, cornerstone, pillar, bulwark, buttress, backbone, anchor.

mainstream ▸ adjective =**normal**, conventional, ordinary, orthodox, accepted, established, common, prevailing, popular.
–OPPOSITES fringe.

maintain ▸ verb 1 *they wanted to maintain peace* =**preserve**, conserve, keep, retain, keep going, prolong, perpetuate, sustain, carry on, continue. 2 *the council maintains the roads* =**look after**, service, care for, take care of. 3 *the costs of maintaining a family* =**support**, provide for, keep, sustain. 4 *he always maintained his innocence | he maintains that he is innocent* =**insist (on)**, declare, assert, protest, affirm, avow, profess, claim, allege, contend, argue; *formal* aver.
–OPPOSITES break, discontinue, neglect, deny.

maintenance ▸ noun 1 *the maintenance of peace* =**preservation**, conservation, keeping, perpetuation, carrying on, continuation. 2 *car maintenance* =**upkeep**, service, servicing, repair(s), care, aftercare. 3 *the maintenance of his children* =**support**, keeping, upkeep, susten-

ance. **4** *absent fathers are forced to pay maintenance* =**financial support**, child support, alimony; upkeep.
–OPPOSITES breakdown, discontinuation, neglect.

majestic ▶ adjective =**stately**, dignified, distinguished, solemn, magnificent, grand, splendid, glorious, impressive, noble, awe-inspiring, monumental, palatial; imposing, heroic.
–OPPOSITES modest, wretched.

majesty ▶ noun =**stateliness**, dignity, solemnity, magnificence, pomp, grandeur, grandness, splendour, glory, impressiveness, nobility.
–OPPOSITES modesty, wretchedness.

major ▶ adjective **1** *the major English poets* =**greatest**, best, finest, most important, chief, main, prime, principal, leading, foremost, outstanding, pre-eminent. **2** *an issue of major importance* =**crucial**, vital, great, considerable, paramount, utmost, prime. **3** *a major factor* =**important**, big, significant, weighty, crucial, key. **4** *major surgery* =**serious**, radical, complicated, difficult.
–OPPOSITES minor, little, trivial.

majority ▶ noun **1** *the majority of cases* =**larger part/number**, greater part/number, best/better part, most, more than half; bulk, (main) body, preponderance, predominance. **2** *a majority in the election* =**(winning) margin**; landslide, whitewash.
–OPPOSITES minority.

make ▶ verb **1** *he makes models* =**construct**, build, assemble, put together, manufacture, produce, fabricate, create, form, fashion, model; improvise. **2** *she made me drink it* =**force**, compel, coerce, press, drive, pressurize, oblige, require; have someone do something, prevail on, bludgeon, strong-arm, impel, constrain; *informal* railroad, bulldoze, steamroller. **3** *don't make such a noise* =**cause**, create, produce, generate, effect, set up, establish, institute, found, develop, originate; *literary* beget. **4** *she made a little bow* =**perform**, execute, give, do, accomplish, achieve, bring off, carry out, effect. **5** *they made him chairman* =**appoint**, designate, name, nominate, select, elect, vote in, install; induct, institute, invest, ordain. **6** *he had made a will* =**formulate**, frame, draw up, devise, make out, prepare, compile, compose, put together; draft, write, pen. **7** *I've made a mistake* =**perpetrate**, commit, be responsible for, be guilty of. **8** *he's made a lot of money* =**acquire**, obtain, gain, get, secure, win, earn; bring in. **9** *he made tea* =**prepare**, get ready, put together, concoct, cook, dish up, throw together, whip up, brew; *informal* fix. **10** *we've got to make a decision* =**reach**, come to, settle on, conclude. **11** *she made a short announcement* =**utter**, give, deliver, recite, pronounce. **12** *the sofa makes a good bed* =**be**, act as, serve as, function as, constitute. **13** *he'll make the first team* =**gain/get a place in**, get into, enter. **14** *he just made his train* =**catch**, get, arrive/be in time for, reach.
–OPPOSITES destroy, lose, miss.
▶ noun =**brand**, marque, label.
■ **make believe** =**pretend**, fantasize, daydream, dream, imagine, play.
■ **make do** =**scrape by**, get by/along, manage, cope, survive, muddle through/along, improvise, make ends meet, keep the wolf from the door, keep one's head above water; *informal* make out.
■ **make for** *constant arguing doesn't make for a happy marriage* =**contribute to**, be conducive to, produce, promote, facilitate, foster.
■ **make it 1** *he never made it as a singer* =**succeed**, be a success, make good; *informal* make the grade, arrive, crack it. **2** *she's very ill—is she going to make it?* =**survive**, pull through, get better, recover.
■ **make off** =**run away/off**, take to one's heels, beat a hasty retreat, flee, make a run for it, take off, take flight, bolt, make oneself scarce, do a disappearing act; *informal* clear off/out, beat it, leg it, skedaddle, vamoose, hightail it, hotfoot it, split, scoot, scram; *Brit. informal* scarper, do a runner; *N. Amer. informal* take a powder.
■ **make off with** =**take**, steal, purloin, pilfer, abscond with, run away/off with, carry off, snatch; *informal* walk away/off with, swipe, filch, snaffle, nab, lift, 'liberate', 'borrow'; *Brit. informal* pinch, half-inch, nick, whip, knock off; *N. Amer. informal* heist, glom.
■ **make out** (*informal*) *how did you make out?* =**get on/along**, fare, do, go, manage.
■ **make something out 1** *I could just make out a figure in the distance* =**see**, discern, distinguish, detect, observe, recognize; *literary* espy. **2** *he couldn't make out what she was saying* =**understand**, grasp,

follow, work out, make sense of, interpret, decipher, make head or tail of, get, catch. **3** *she made out that he was violent* =**allege**, claim, suggest, imply, hint, insinuate, indicate, intimate; *formal* aver. **4** *he made out a cheque for $20* =**write (out)**, fill out, fill in, complete, draw up.
■ **make up** *let's kiss and make up* =**be friends again**, bury the hatchet, make peace, forgive and forget, shake hands, settle one's differences.
■ **make something up 1** *exports make up 42% of earnings* =**comprise**, form, compose, constitute, account for. **2** *the pharmacist made up the prescription* =**prepare**, mix, concoct, put together. **3** *he made up an excuse* =**invent**, fabricate, concoct, think up; devise, manufacture, formulate; *informal* cook up.
■ **make up for 1** *she tried to make up for what she'd said* =**atone for**, make amends for, compensate for; expiate. **2** *job satisfaction can make up for low pay* =**offset**, counterbalance, counteract, compensate for; cancel out.

make-believe ▸ noun =**fantasy**, pretence, daydreaming, invention, fancy, fabrication, play-acting, charade, masquerade.
–OPPOSITES reality.
▸ adjective =**imaginary**, imagined, made-up, fantasy, dreamed-up, fanciful, fictitious, fake, mock, sham, simulated; *informal* pretend, phoney.
–OPPOSITES real, actual.

maker ▸ noun =**creator**, manufacturer, constructor, builder, producer.

makeshift ▸ adjective =**temporary**, provisional, stopgap, standby, rough and ready, improvised, ad hoc, extempore, thrown together.
–OPPOSITES permanent.

make-up ▸ noun **1** *she used too much make-up* =**cosmetics**; *informal* warpaint, slap. **2** *the cellular make-up of plants* =**composition**, constitution, structure, configuration, arrangement. **3** *jealousy isn't part of his make-up* =**character**, nature, temperament, personality, disposition, mentality, persona, psyche.

making ▸ noun **1** *the making of cars* =**manufacture**, mass production, building, construction, assembly, production, creation, putting together, fabrication. **2** *she has the makings of a champion* =**qualities**, characteristics, ingredients; potential, capacity, capability; stuff.
–OPPOSITES destruction.

maladjusted ▸ adjective =**disturbed**, unstable, neurotic, dysfunctional; *informal* mixed up, screwed up, hung up, messed up.
–OPPOSITES normal, stable.

maladministration ▸ noun *(formal)* =**mismanagement**, mishandling, incompetence; malpractice, misconduct; *Law* malfeasance.
–OPPOSITES probity, efficiency.

maladroit ▸ adjective =**bungling**, awkward, inept, clumsy, bumbling, incompetent, heavy-handed, gauche; *informal* ham-fisted, cack-handed.
–OPPOSITES adroit, skilful.

malady ▸ noun =**illness**, sickness, disease, infection, ailment, disorder, complaint, affliction, infirmity; *informal* bug, virus.

malaise ▸ noun =**unhappiness**, discomfort, melancholy, depression, despondency, dejection, angst, ennui; lassitude, listlessness, weariness; infirmity, illness, sickness, disease.
–OPPOSITES comfort, well-being.

malapropism ▸ noun =**wrong word**, solecism, misuse; slip of the tongue.

malcontent ▸ noun =**troublemaker**, mischief-maker, agitator, dissident, rebel; moaner; *informal* stirrer, whinger; *N. Amer. informal* kvetch.

male ▸ adjective *male sexual jealousy* =**masculine**; virile, manly, macho.
–OPPOSITES female.
▸ noun *two males walked past. See* MAN noun sense 1.

┌─────────────────────┐
│ **WORD LINKS**   │
├─────────────────────┤
│ *related prefix:* **andro-** │
└─────────────────────┘

malevolence ▸ noun =**malice**, hostility, hate, hatred, ill will, enmity, ill feeling, venom, rancour, vindictiveness, vengefulness; *literary* maleficence.
–OPPOSITES benevolence.

malevolent ▸ adjective =**malicious**, hostile, baleful, venomous, evil, malign, malignant, rancorous, vicious, vindictive, vengeful; *literary* maleficent.
–OPPOSITES benevolent.

malformation ▸ noun =**deformity**, distortion, crookedness, disfigurement, abnormality.

malformed ▸ adjective =**deformed**, misshapen, ill-proportioned, disfigured, distorted, crooked, contorted, twisted, warped; abnormal; *Scottish*

thrawn.
–OPPOSITES perfect, normal, healthy.

malfunction ▸ verb *the computer has malfunctioned* =**crash**, go wrong, break down, fail, stop working; *informal* conk out, go kaput, fall over, act up; *Brit. informal* play up, pack up.
▸ noun *a computer malfunction* =**crash**, breakdown, fault, failure, bug; *informal* glitch.

malice ▸ noun =**spite**, malevolence, ill will, vindictiveness, vengefulness, malignity, animus, enmity, rancour; *literary* maleficence.
–OPPOSITES benevolence.

malicious ▸ adjective =**spiteful**, malevolent, vindictive, vengeful, malign, nasty, hurtful, mischievous, cruel; *literary* maleficent.
–OPPOSITES benevolent.

malign ▸ adjective *a malign influence* =**harmful**, evil, bad, baleful, destructive, malignant, injurious.
–OPPOSITES beneficial.
▸ verb *he maligned an innocent man* =**defame**, slander, libel, blacken someone's name/character, smear, vilify, cast aspersions on, run down, denigrate, disparage, slur, abuse; *informal* bad-mouth, knock; *Brit. informal* rubbish, slag off.
–OPPOSITES praise.

malignant ▸ noun **1** *a malignant disease* =**virulent**, invasive, uncontrollable, dangerous, deadly, fatal, life-threatening. **2** *a malignant growth* =**cancerous**; *technical* metastatic. **3** *a malignant thought* =**spiteful**, malicious, malevolent, vindictive, vengeful, malign, nasty, hurtful, mischievous, cruel.
–OPPOSITES benign, benevolent.

malinger ▸ verb =**pretend to be ill**, sham; shirk; *informal* put it on, fake it; *Brit. informal* skive, swing the lead; *N. Amer. informal* gold-brick.

malingerer ▸ noun =**shirker**, idler, layabout; *informal* slacker; *Brit. informal* skiver; *N. Amer. informal* gold brick.

mall ▸ noun =**shopping precinct**, shopping centre, arcade, galleria; *N. Amer.* plaza.

malleable ▸ adjective **1** *a malleable substance* =**pliable**, ductile, plastic, pliant, soft, workable. **2** *a malleable young woman* =**easily influenced**, suggestible, susceptible, impressionable, easily led; vulnerable.
–OPPOSITES hard, intractable.

malnutrition ▸ noun =**undernourishment**, malnourishment, poor diet.

malodorous ▸ adjective =**foul-smelling**, evil-smelling, fetid, smelly, stinking (to high heaven), reeking, rank, high, putrid, noxious; *informal* stinky; *Brit. informal* niffy, pongy, whiffy, humming; *N. Amer. informal* funky; *literary* noisome.
–OPPOSITES fragrant.

malpractice ▸ noun =**wrongdoing**, (professional) misconduct, unprofessionalism; negligence, carelessness, incompetence, corruption.

maltreat ▸ verb =**ill-treat**, mistreat, abuse, ill-use, mishandle; knock about/around, hit, beat, manhandle, persecute, molest; *informal* beat up, rough up, do over.

maltreatment ▸ noun =**ill-treatment**, mistreatment, abuse; violence, harm, persecution, molestation.

mammoth ▸ adjective. *See* HUGE.

man ▸ noun **1** *a handsome man* =**male**, adult (male), gentleman; youth; *informal* guy, fellow, geezer, gent; *Brit. informal* bloke, chap, lad, cove; *Scottish & Irish informal* bodach; *N. Amer. informal* dude, hombre; *Austral./NZ informal* digger. **2** *all men are mortal* =**human being**, human, person, mortal, individual, personage, soul. **3** *the evolution of man* =**the human race**, the human species, Homo sapiens, humankind, humanity, human beings, humans, people, mankind. **4** *the men voted to strike* =**workers**, workforce, employees, staff, personnel, human resources, manpower, labour force; troops; *informal* liveware. **5** *have you met her new man?* =**boyfriend**, partner, husband, spouse, lover, fiancé; common-law husband, live-in lover, significant other, cohabitee; *informal* fancy man, toy boy, sugar daddy, intended; *N. Amer. informal* squeeze; *dated* beau, steady, young man. **6** *his man brought him a cocktail* =**manservant**, valet, attendant, retainer; page, footman, flunkey; *N. Amer.* houseman; *Military, dated* batman.
▸ verb **1** *the office is manned from 9 a.m. to 5 p.m.* =**staff**, crew, occupy, people. **2** *firemen manned the pumps* =**operate**, work, use.

■ **man to man** =**frankly**, openly, honestly, directly, candidly, plainly, without beating about the bush; woman to woman.

■ **to a man** =without exception, bar none, one and all, everyone, unanimously, as one.

WORD LINKS

relating to men: **male, masculine, virile, andro-**
centred on men: **androcentric**
fear of men: **androphobia**
hatred of men: **misandry**
government by men: **androcracy**

manacle ▶ verb =shackle, fetter, chain, put/clap in irons, handcuff, restrain; secure; *informal* cuff.

manacles ▶ plural noun =handcuffs, shackles, chains, irons, fetters, restraints, bonds; *informal* cuffs, bracelets.

manage ▶ verb **1** *she manages a staff of 80* =be in charge of, run, head, direct, control, preside over, lead, govern, rule, command, supervise, oversee, administer, organize, conduct, handle, be at the helm of; *informal* head up. **2** *how much work can you manage this week?* =accomplish, achieve, do, carry out, perform, undertake, bring about, finish, deal with, get through. **3** *will you be able to manage without him?* =cope, get along/on, make do, be/fare/do all right, carry on, survive, get by, muddle through/along, fend for oneself, shift for oneself, make ends meet; *informal* make out, hack it. **4** *she can't manage that horse* =control, handle, master; cope with, deal with.

manageable ▶ adjective **1** *a manageable amount of work* =achievable, doable, practicable, feasible, reasonable, attainable, viable. **2** *a manageable child* =compliant, tractable, pliant, biddable, docile, amenable, accommodating, acquiescent. **3** *a manageable tool* =user-friendly, easy to use, handy.
–OPPOSITES difficult, impossible.

management ▶ noun **1** *he's responsible for the management of the firm* =administration, running, managing, organization; direction, leadership, control, governance, rule, command, supervision, handling, guidance, operation. **2** *workers are in dispute with the management* =managers, employers, directors, board of directors, board, directorate, executive, administration, leadership; owners, proprietors; *informal* bosses, top brass.

manager ▶ noun =executive, head of department, line manager, supervisor, principal, administrator, head, director, managing director, superintendent, foreman, forewoman, overseer; *informal* boss, chief, governor; *Brit. informal* gaffer, guv'nor.

mandate ▶ noun **1** *he called an election to seek a mandate for his policies* =authority, approval, ratification, endorsement, sanction, authorization. **2** *a mandate from the UN* =instruction, directive, decree, command, order, injunction, edict, ruling, fiat; *formal* ordinance.

mandatory ▶ adjective =obligatory, compulsory, binding, required, requisite, necessary, essential, imperative.
–OPPOSITES optional.

manfully ▶ adverb =bravely, courageously, gallantly, heroically, valiantly; determinedly, hard, strongly, vigorously; with all one's strength, to the best of one's abilities, desperately.

mangle ▶ verb =mutilate, disfigure, damage, injure, crush; cut up, tear apart, butcher, maul.

mangy ▶ adjective =scruffy, moth-eaten, shabby, worn; dirty, squalid, sleazy, seedy; *informal* tatty, the worse for wear, ratty, scuzzy; *Brit. informal* grotty.

manhandle ▶ verb **1** *he was manhandled by a gang of youths* =push, shove, jostle, hustle; maul, molest; *informal* paw, rough up; *N. Amer. informal* roust. **2** *we manhandled the piano down the stairs* =heave, haul, push, shove; pull, tug, drag, lug, manoeuvre; *informal* hump.

manhood ▶ noun **1** *the transition from boyhood to manhood* =maturity, sexual maturity, adulthood. **2** *an insult to his manhood* =virility, manliness, machismo, masculinity, maleness.

mania ▶ noun **1** *fits of mania* =madness, derangement, dementia, insanity, lunacy, psychosis, mental illness; delirium, frenzy, hysteria, raving, wildness. **2** *his mania for gadgets* =obsession, compulsion, fixation, fetish, fascination, preoccupation, passion, enthusiasm, desire, urge, craving, craze, fad, rage; *informal* thing.

maniac ▶ noun **1** *a homicidal maniac* =lunatic, madman, madwoman, psychopath; *informal* loony, nutcase, nut, psycho, head case, headbanger, sicko; *Brit. informal* nutter; *N. Amer. informal* crazy, meshuggener. **2** *(informal) a football maniac* =enthusiast, fan, devotee, aficionado;

informal freak, fiend, fanatic, nut, buff, addict.

manic ▶ adjective **1** *a manic grin* =**mad**, insane, deranged, demented, maniacal, wild, crazed, demonic, hysterical, raving, unhinged; *informal* crazy. **2** *manic activity* =**frenzied**, feverish, frenetic, hectic, intense; *informal* mad.
–OPPOSITES sane, calm.

manifest ▶ verb =**display**, show, exhibit, demonstrate, betray, present, reveal; *formal* evince.
–OPPOSITES hide.
▶ adjective =**obvious**, clear, plain, apparent, evident, patent, palpable, distinct, definite, blatant, overt, transparent, conspicuous, undisguised.
–OPPOSITES secret.

manifestation ▶ noun **1** *the manifestation of anxiety* =**display**, demonstration, show, exhibition, presentation. **2** *manifestations of global warming* =**sign**, indication, evidence, symptom, testimony, proof, mark, reflection, example, instance.

manifesto ▶ noun =**policy statement**, mission statement, platform, programme, declaration, proclamation, pronouncement.

manifold ▶ adjective =**many**, numerous, multiple, multifarious, legion, diverse, various, several, varied, different, miscellaneous, assorted, sundry; *literary* myriad, divers.

manipulate ▶ verb **1** *he manipulated some knobs and levers* =**operate**, work; turn, pull, push, twist, slide. **2** *she manipulated the muscles of his back* =**massage**, rub, knead, press, squeeze; palpate. **3** *the government tried to manipulate the situation* =**control**, influence, use to one's advantage, exploit; twist. **4** *they accused him of manipulating the data* =**falsify**, rig, distort, alter, change, doctor, massage, juggle, tamper with, tinker with, interfere with, misrepresent; *informal* cook, fiddle.

manipulative ▶ adjective =**scheming**, calculating, cunning, crafty, wily, shrewd, devious, designing, conniving, Machiavellian, artful, slippery, sly, unscrupulous, disingenuous.

manipulator ▶ noun =**exploiter**, user, conniver, wheeler-dealer; *informal* operator.

mankind ▶ noun =**the human race**, man, humanity, human beings, humans, Homo sapiens, humankind, people, men and women.

manly ▶ adjective **1** *his manly physique* =**virile**, masculine, strong, all-male, muscular, muscly, strapping, well built, sturdy, robust; rugged, tough, powerful, brawny; *informal* hunky. **2** *their manly deeds* =**brave**, courageous, bold, valiant, valorous, fearless, plucky, macho, intrepid, daring, heroic, gallant, chivalrous, swashbuckling.
–OPPOSITES effeminate, cowardly.

man-made ▶ adjective =**artificial**, synthetic, manufactured; imitation, ersatz, simulated, mock, fake.
–OPPOSITES natural, real.

manner ▶ noun **1** *it was dealt with in a very efficient manner* =**way**, fashion, mode, means, method, system, style, approach, technique, procedure, process. **2** *(archaic)* *what manner of person is he?* =**kind**, sort, type, variety, breed, brand, class, category, order. **3** *her rather unfriendly manner* =**demeanour**, air, aspect, attitude, bearing, cast, behaviour, conduct; mien. **4** *the life and manners of Victorian society* =**customs**, habits, ways, practices, conventions, usages. **5** *you ought to teach him some manners* =**etiquette**, social graces, protocol, politeness, decorum, propriety, civility, Ps and Qs.

mannered ▶ adjective =**affected**, pretentious, unnatural, artificial, contrived, stilted, stiff, forced, put-on, theatrical, precious, stagy, camp.
–OPPOSITES natural.

mannerism ▶ noun =**idiosyncrasy**, quirk, oddity, foible, trait, peculiarity, habit, characteristic.

mannish ▶ adjective =**unfeminine**, masculine, unladylike; *informal* butch.
–OPPOSITES feminine, girlish.

manoeuvre ▶ verb **1** *I manoeuvred the car into the space* =**steer**, guide, drive, negotiate, navigate, pilot, direct, manipulate, move, work. **2** *he manoeuvred things to suit himself* =**manipulate**, contrive, manage, engineer, devise, plan, fix, organize, arrange, set up, orchestrate, choreograph, stage-manage; *informal* wangle. **3** *he began manoeuvring for the party leadership* =**intrigue**, plot, scheme, plan, conspire, pull strings.
▶ noun **1** *a tricky parking manoeuvre* =**operation**, exercise, move, movement, action. **2** *diplomatic manoeuvres* =**strata-**

gem, tactic, gambit, ploy, trick, dodge, ruse, scheme, device, plot, machination, artifice, subterfuge, intrigue.

manservant ▶ noun =**valet**, attendant, retainer, equerry, gentleman's gentleman, man; steward, butler, footman, flunkey, page, houseboy, lackey; *N. Amer.* houseman; *Military, dated* batman.

mansion ▶ noun =**country house**, stately home, hall, manor house; *informal* palace, pile.
−OPPOSITES hovel.

mantle ▶ noun **1** *a dark green velvet mantle* =**cloak**, cape, shawl, wrap, stole. **2** *a thick mantle of snow* =**covering**, layer, blanket, sheet, veil, canopy, cover, cloak, pall, shroud. **3** *the mantle of leadership* =**role**, burden, onus, duty, responsibility.

manual ▶ adjective **1** *manual work* =**physical**, labouring, blue-collar. **2** *a manual typewriter* =**hand-operated**, hand.
▶ noun *a training manual* =**handbook**, instruction book, instructions, guide, companion, ABC, guidebook; *informal* bible.

manufacture ▶ verb **1** *the company manufactures laser printers* =**make**, produce, mass-produce, build, construct, assemble, put together, create, turn out. **2** *a story manufactured by the press* =**make up**, invent, fabricate, concoct, hatch, dream up, think up, trump up, devise, formulate, contrive; *informal* cook up.
▶ noun *the manufacture of aircraft engines* =**production**, making, manufacturing, mass production, construction, building, assembly.

manufacturer ▶ noun =**maker**, producer; industrialist, captain of industry.

manure ▶ noun =**dung**, muck, excrement, droppings, ordure, guano, cowpats; fertilizer; *N. Amer. informal* cow chips, horse apples.

manuscript ▶ noun =**document**, text, script, paper, typescript.

WORD LINKS
study of manuscripts: **codicology**

many ▶ determiner & adjective **1** *many animals were killed* =**numerous**, a great/good deal of, a lot of, plenty of, countless, innumerable, scores of, crowds of, droves of, an army of, a horde of, a multitude of, a multiplicity of, untold; diverse, multifarious; copious, abundant, profuse, an abundance of, a profusion of; frequent; *informal* lots of, umpteen, loads of, masses of, stacks of, heaps of, piles of, bags of, tons of, oodles of, dozens of, hundreds of, thousands of, millions of, billions of, zillions of, a slew of; *Brit. informal* a shedload of; *N. Amer. informal* gazillions of; *Austral./NZ informal* a swag of; *literary* myriad, divers. **2** *sacrificing the individual for the sake of the many* =**the people**, the common people, the masses, the populace, the public, the rank and file; *derogatory* the hoi polloi, the common herd, the mob, the proletariat, the riff-raff, the great unwashed, the proles, the plebs.
−OPPOSITES few.

WORD LINKS
related prefixes: **multi-, poly-**

map ▶ noun =**plan**, chart; A to Z, street plan, guide; atlas.
▶ verb *the region was mapped from the air* =**chart**, plot, delineate, draw, record.
■ **map something out** =**outline**, set out, lay out, sketch out, trace out, delineate, detail, draw up, formulate, work out, frame, draft, plan, plot out.

WORD LINKS
relating to maps: **cartographic**
making of maps: **cartography**

mar ▶ verb **1** *an ugly bruise marred his features* =**spoil**, impair, disfigure, blemish, scar. **2** *the celebrations were marred by violence* =**spoil**, ruin, damage, wreck; taint, tarnish.
−OPPOSITES enhance.

marauder ▶ noun =**raider**, plunderer, looter, robber, pirate, freebooter, bandit, rustler; *literary* brigand; *archaic* buccaneer, corsair.

marauding ▶ adjective =**predatory**, rapacious, thieving, plundering, looting.

march ▶ verb **1** *the men marched past* =**stride**, walk, troop, step, pace, tread; slog, tramp, hike, trudge; parade, file. **2** *she marched in without even knocking* =**stride**, stalk, strut, flounce, storm, stomp, sweep, sail, steam.
▶ noun **1** *a 20-mile march* =**hike**, trek, slog, walk. **2** *police sought to ban the march* =**parade**, procession, cortège; demonstration; *informal* demo. **3** *the march of technology* =**progress**, advance; development, evolution; passage.

margin ▶ noun **1** *the margin of the lake*

=edge, side, verge, border, perimeter, brink, brim, rim, fringe, boundary, periphery, bound, extremity. **2** *there's no margin for error* **=leeway**, latitude, scope, room, space; slack, excess, allowance. **3** *they won by a narrow margin* **=gap**, majority, amount.

marginal ▶ adjective **1** *the difference is marginal* **=slight**, small, tiny, minute, insignificant, minimal, negligible. **2** *a very marginal case* **=borderline**, disputable, questionable, doubtful.

marijuana ▶ noun **=cannabis**, hashish, bhang, hemp, kif, ganja, sinsemilla; *informal* dope, hash, grass, pot, blow, draw, the weed, skunk; *Brit. informal* wacky baccy; *N. Amer. informal* locoweed.

marinate ▶ verb **=souse**, soak, steep, immerse, marinade.

marine ▶ adjective **1** *marine plants* **=seawater**, sea, saltwater; aquatic; *technical* pelagic, thalassic. **2** *a marine insurance company* **=maritime**, nautical, naval; seafaring, seagoing, ocean-going.

mariner ▶ noun **=sailor**, seaman, seafarer.

marital ▶ adjective **=matrimonial**, married, wedded, conjugal, nuptial, marriage, wedding; *literary* connubial.

maritime ▶ adjective **=naval**, marine, nautical; seafaring, seagoing, sea, ocean-going.

mark ▶ noun **1** *a dirty mark* **=blemish**, streak, spot, fleck, dot, blot, stain, smear, speck, speckle, blotch, smudge, smut, fingermark, fingerprint; bruise, discoloration; *informal* splotch, splodge. **2** *a punctuation mark* **=symbol**, sign, character; diacritic. **3** *books bearing the mark of a well-known bookseller* **=logo**, seal, stamp, symbol, emblem, device, insignia, badge, brand, trademark, monogram, hallmark, logotype, watermark, coat of arms. **4** *unemployment passed the three million mark* **=point**, level, stage. **5** *a mark of respect* **=sign**, token, symbol, indication, badge, emblem; symptom, proof. **6** *the war left its mark on him* **=impression**, imprint; effect, impact, influence. **7** *the mark of a civilized society* **=characteristic**, feature, trait, attribute, quality, hallmark, indicator. **8** *he got a good mark for maths* **=grade**, grading, rating, score, percentage.

▶ verb **1** *be careful not to mark the paintwork* **=discolour**, stain, smear, smudge, streak; dirty, bruise; *informal* splotch,

splodge; *literary* smirch. **2** *her possessions were clearly marked* **=name**, initial, label. **3** *I've marked the relevant passages* **=indicate**, label, tick; show, identify, highlight. **4** *a festival to mark the town's 200th anniversary* **=celebrate**, observe, recognize, acknowledge, keep, honour, commemorate, remember. **5** *the incidents marked a new phase in their campaign* **=represent**, signify, indicate, herald. **6** *his style is marked by simplicity and concision* **=characterize**, distinguish, identify, typify. **7** *I have a pile of essays to mark* **=assess**, evaluate, appraise, correct; *N. Amer.* grade.

marked ▶ adjective **=noticeable**, pronounced, decided, distinct, striking, clear, glaring, blatant, unmistakable, obvious, plain, manifest, patent, palpable, prominent, significant, conspicuous, notable, recognizable, identifiable, distinguishable, discernible.
−OPPOSITES imperceptible.

market ▶ noun **1** **=shopping centre**, marketplace, mart, flea market, bazaar, souk, fair; *archaic* emporium. **2** *there's no market for such goods* **=demand**, call, want, desire, need, requirement. **3** *the market is sluggish* **=trade**, trading, business, things.
▶ verb *the product was marketed worldwide* **=sell**, retail, merchandise, trade, peddle, hawk; advertise, promote.
■ **on the market** **=on sale**, (up) for sale, on offer, available, obtainable; *N. Amer.* on the block.

marksman, markswoman ▶ noun **=sniper**, sharpshooter; good shot; *informal* crack shot; *N. Amer. informal* deadeye, shootist.

maroon ▶ verb **=strand**, cast away, cast ashore; abandon, leave behind, leave.

marriage ▶ noun **1** *a proposal of marriage* **=(holy) matrimony**, wedlock. **2** *the marriage took place at St Margaret's* **=wedding**, (wedding/marriage) ceremony, nuptials, union. **3** *a marriage of jazz, pop, and gospel* **=union**, fusion, mixture, mix, blend, amalgamation, combination, hybrid.
−OPPOSITES divorce, separation.

WORD LINKS

to do with marriage: **conjugal, marital, matrimonial, nuptial, connubial**
fear of marriage: **gamophobia**
obsession with marriage: **gamomania**

married ▸ adjective **1** *a married couple* =**wedded**, wed; *informal* spliced, hitched. **2** *married life* =**marital**, matrimonial, conjugal, nuptial; *literary* connubial.
–OPPOSITES single.

marry ▸ verb **1** *the couple married last year* =**get/be married**, wed, be wed, become man and wife, plight/pledge one's troth; *informal* tie the knot, walk down the aisle, take the plunge, get spliced, get hitched, say 'I do'. **2** *John wanted to marry her* =**wed**; *informal* make an honest woman of. **3** *the show marries poetry with art* =**join**, unite, combine, fuse, mix, blend, merge, amalgamate, link, connect, couple, knit, yoke.
–OPPOSITES divorce, separate.

marsh ▸ noun =**swamp**, marshland, bog, swampland, morass, mire, quagmire, slough, fen, fenland; *Scottish & N. English* moss.

WORD LINKS
relating to marshes: **paludal**

marshal ▸ verb =**assemble**, gather (together), collect, muster, call together, draw up, line up, array, organize, group, arrange, deploy, position; mobilize, summon, round up.

marshy ▸ adjective =**boggy**, swampy, muddy, squelchy, soggy, waterlogged; *Scottish & N. English* mossy.
–OPPOSITES dry, firm.

martial ▸ adjective =**military**, soldierly, army; warlike, fighting, militaristic; *informal* gung-ho.

martinet ▸ noun =**disciplinarian**, slave-driver, (hard) taskmaster, authoritarian, tyrant.

marvel ▸ verb *she marvelled at their courage* =**be amazed**, be astonished, be awed, wonder; *informal* be gobsmacked.
▸ noun *a marvel of technology* =**wonder**, miracle, sensation, spectacle, phenomenon.

marvellous ▸ adjective =**excellent**, splendid, wonderful, magnificent, superb, glorious, sublime, lovely, delightful; *informal* super, great, amazing, fantastic, terrific, tremendous, sensational, heavenly, divine, gorgeous, grand, fabulous, fab, awesome, magic, ace, mind-blowing, far out, out of this world; *Brit. informal* smashing, brilliant, brill; *N. Amer. informal* boss, bonzer; *Brit. informal, dated* cham-

pion, wizard, ripping, spiffing, top-hole; *N. Amer. informal, dated* swell.
–OPPOSITES commonplace, awful.

masculine ▸ adjective **1** *a masculine trait* =**male**, man's, men's; male-oriented. **2** *a powerfully masculine man* =**virile**, macho, manly, all-male; muscular, muscly, strong, strapping, well built, rugged, robust, brawny, powerful, red-blooded, vigorous; *informal* hunky. **3** *a rather masculine woman* =**mannish**, unfeminine, unladylike; *informal* butch.
–OPPOSITES feminine, effeminate.

masculinity ▸ noun =**virility**, manliness, maleness, machismo.

mash ▸ verb =**pulp**, crush, purée, cream, pound, beat.

mask ▸ noun **1** *she wore a mask to conceal her face* =**disguise**; *historical* visor; *archaic* vizard. **2** *he dropped his mask of good humour* =**pretence**, semblance, veil, screen, front, facade, veneer, disguise, cover, cloak, camouflage.
▸ verb *poplar trees masked the factory* =**hide**, conceal, disguise, cover up, obscure, screen, cloak, camouflage.

masquerade ▸ noun *he couldn't keep up the masquerade much longer* =**pretence**, deception, pose, act, front, facade, disguise, cover-up, play-acting, make-believe; *informal* put-on.
▸ verb =**pretend to be**, pose as, pass oneself off as, impersonate, disguise oneself as.

mass ▸ noun **1** *a soggy mass of fallen leaves* =**pile**, heap; accumulation. **2** *a mass of cyclists* =**crowd**, horde, throng, host, troop, army, herd, flock, swarm, mob, pack, flood, multitude. **3** *the mass of the population* =**majority**, greater part/number, best/better part, major part, bulk, main body, lion's share. **4** *the masses* =**the common people**, the populace, the public, the people, the rank and file, the crowd; *derogatory* the hoi polloi, the mob, the proletariat, the common herd, the great unwashed, the plebs.
▸ adjective *mass hysteria* =**widespread**, general, wholesale, universal.
▸ verb *they began massing troops in the region* =**assemble**, gather together.

massacre ▸ noun *a cold-blooded massacre* =**slaughter**, killing, murder, execution, annihilation, liquidation, extermination; carnage, butchery, bloodbath, bloodletting.
▸ verb *thousands were massacred* =**slaugh-**

ter, butcher, murder, kill, annihilate, exterminate, execute, liquidate, eliminate, mow down, cut down.

massage ▶ noun =**rub**, rub-down; shiatsu, reflexology, acupressure, osteopathy.
▶ verb **1** *he massaged her tired muscles* =**rub**, knead, manipulate, pummel, work. **2** *the statistics have been massaged* =**alter**, tamper with, manipulate, doctor, falsify, juggle, fiddle with, tinker with, distort, change, rig, interfere with; *informal* fix, cook, fiddle.

massive ▶ adjective =**huge**, enormous, vast, immense, mighty, great, colossal, tremendous, prodigious, gigantic, gargantuan, mammoth, monstrous, monumental, giant, mountainous, titanic, epic, Herculean; *informal* monster, jumbo, mega, whopping, humongous, astronomical; *Brit. informal* whacking, ginormous.
–OPPOSITES tiny.

master ▶ noun **1** *(historical) he acceded to his master's wishes* =**lord**, ruler, sovereign, monarch. **2** *the dog's master* =**owner**, keeper, handler. **3** *a chess master* =**expert**, adept, genius, maestro, virtuoso, authority; *informal* ace, wizard, whizz, hotshot; *Brit. informal* dab hand; *N. Amer. informal* maven, crackerjack. **4** *the master of the ship* =**captain**, commander; *informal* skipper. **5** *the geography master* =**teacher**, schoolteacher, schoolmaster, tutor, instructor. **6** *their spiritual master* =**guru**, teacher, leader, guide, mentor.
–OPPOSITES servant, amateur, pupil.
▶ verb **1** *I managed to master my fears* =**overcome**, conquer, beat, quell, suppress, control, triumph over, subdue, vanquish, subjugate, curb, check, defeat, get the better of, get a grip on, get over; *informal* lick. **2** *it took ages to master the technique* =**learn**, become proficient in; pick up, grasp, understand; *informal* get the hang of.
▶ adjective *a master craftsman* =**expert**, adept, proficient, skilled, skilful, deft, dexterous, adroit, practised, experienced, masterly, accomplished; *informal* crack, ace; *N. Amer. informal* crackerjack.

masterful ▶ adjective **1** *a masterful man* =**commanding**, powerful, imposing, authoritative. **2** *their masterful handling of the situation* =**expert**, adept, masterly, skilful, skilled, adroit, proficient, deft, dexterous, accomplished, polished, consummate.

–OPPOSITES weak, inept.

masterly ▶ adjective. *See* MASTERFUL *sense 2.*

mastermind ▶ verb *he masterminded the whole campaign* =**plan**, control, direct, be in charge of, run, conduct, organize, arrange, preside over, orchestrate, stage-manage, engineer, manage, coordinate.
▶ noun *the mastermind behind the project* =**genius**, intellect; *informal* brain, brains.

masterpiece ▶ noun =**chef-d'œuvre**, pièce de résistance, masterwork, magnum opus, tour de force.

master stroke ▶ noun =**stroke of genius**, coup, triumph, tour de force.

mastery ▶ noun **1** *her mastery of the language* =**proficiency**, ability, capability; knowledge, understanding, comprehension, familiarity, command, grasp, grip. **2** *man's mastery over nature* =**control**, domination, command, supremacy, pre-eminence, superiority; power, authority, jurisdiction, dominion, sovereignty.

masticate ▶ verb =**chew**, munch, champ, chomp; ruminate.

mat ▶ noun **1** *the hall mat* =**rug**, carpet; doormat. **2** *he placed his glass on the mat* =**coaster**, beer mat, doily; *Brit.* drip mat. **3** *a thick mat of hair* =**mass**, tangle, mop, thatch, shock, mane.
▶ verb *his hair was matted with blood* =**tangle**, entangle, knot, snarl up.

match ▶ noun **1** *a football match | a boxing match* =**contest**, competition, game, tournament, tie, fixture, trial, test, meet, bout, fight; friendly, (local) derby; play-off, replay, rematch. **2** *the vase was an exact match of the one she already owned* =**lookalike**, double, twin, duplicate, mate, companion, counterpart, pair; replica, copy; *informal* spitting image, dead ringer. **3** *a love match* =**marriage**, betrothal, relationship, partnership, union.
▶ verb **1** *the curtains matched the duvet cover* =**go with**, coordinate with, complement, suit. **2** *did their statements match?* =**correspond**, be in agreement, tally, agree, match up, coincide, square. **3** *no one can match him at chess* =**equal**, compare with, be in the same league as, touch, keep up with, rival, compete with; *informal* hold a candle to.

matching ▶ adjective =**corresponding**, equivalent, parallel, analogous;

coordinating, complementary; paired, twin, identical, like, alike.
–OPPOSITES different, clashing.

matchless ▶ adjective =**incomparable**, unrivalled, beyond compare/comparison, unparalleled, unequalled, peerless, second to none, unsurpassed, unsurpassable.

mate ▶ noun 1 *(Brit. informal) he's gone out with his mates* =**friend**, companion, schoolmate, classmate, workmate; *informal* pal, chum; *Brit. informal* mucker; *N. English informal* marrer; *N. Amer. informal* buddy, amigo, compadre, homeboy. 2 *she's finally found her ideal mate* =**partner**, husband, wife, spouse, lover, significant other, companion; *informal* better half, hubby, missus, missis; *Brit. informal* other half. 3 *a plumber's mate* =**assistant**, helper, apprentice.
▶ verb *pandas rarely mate in captivity* =**breed**, couple, copulate.

material ▶ noun 1 *the decomposition of organic material* =**matter**, substance, stuff. 2 *the materials for a new building* =**constituent**, raw material, component. 3 *cleaning materials* =**things**, items, articles, stuff; *Brit. informal* gubbins. 4 *curtain material* =**fabric**, cloth, textiles. 5 *material for a magazine article* =**information**, data, facts, facts and figures, statistics, evidence, details, particulars, background, notes; *informal* info, gen, dope.
▶ adjective 1 *the material world* =**physical**, corporeal, tangible, mundane, worldly, earthly, secular, temporal, concrete, real. 2 *she was too fond of material pleasures* =**sensual**, physical, carnal, corporal, fleshly, bodily. 3 *information that could be material to the inquiry* =**relevant**, pertinent, applicable, germane; vital, essential, key.
–OPPOSITES spiritual, aesthetic, irrelevant.

materialistic ▶ adjective =**consumerist**, acquisitive, greedy; worldly, capitalistic, bourgeois.

materialize ▶ verb 1 *the forecast investment boom did not materialize* =**happen**, occur, come about, take place, transpire; *literary* come off; *literary* come to pass. 2 *Harry materialized at the door* =**appear**, turn up, arrive, emerge, surface, pop up; *informal* show up, fetch up.

maternal ▶ adjective 1 *her maternal instincts* =**motherly**, protective, caring,

nurturing. 2 *his maternal grandparents* =**on one's mother's side**, on the distaff side.

mathematical ▶ adjective 1 *mathematical symbols* =**arithmetical**, numerical; statistical, algebraic, geometric, trigonometric. 2 *with mathematical precision* =**rigorous**, meticulous, scrupulous, strict, pinpoint, unerring.

matrimonial ▶ adjective =**marital**, conjugal, married, wedded; nuptial; *literary* connubial.

matrimony ▶ noun =**marriage**, wedlock, union; nuptials.
–OPPOSITES divorce.

matted ▶ adjective =**tangled**, knotted, tousled, dishevelled, uncombed, unkempt, ratty; *black English* natty.

matter ▶ noun 1 *decaying vegetable matter* =**material**, stuff. 2 *the heart of the matter* =**affair**, business, proceedings, situation, events, incident, episode, experience; subject, topic, issue, question, point, point at issue, case.
▶ verb *it doesn't matter what you wear* =**be important**, make any difference, be of consequence, be relevant, count.

matter-of-fact ▶ adjective =**unemotional**, practical, down-to-earth, sensible, realistic, unsentimental, pragmatic, businesslike, commonsensical, level-headed, hard-headed, no-nonsense, straightforward.

mature ▶ adjective 1 *a mature woman* =**adult**, grown, fully grown, full-grown, in one's prime. 2 *he's very mature for his age* =**grown-up**, sensible, responsible, adult, level-headed, reliable, dependable; wise, sophisticated. 3 *mature cheese* =**ripe**, mellow; rich, strong, flavoursome, full-bodied.
–OPPOSITES adolescent, childish.
▶ verb 1 *kittens mature when they are about a year old* =**be fully grown**; come of age, reach adulthood, reach maturity. 2 *he's matured since he left home* =**grow up**; blossom. 3 *leave the cheese to mature* =**ripen**, mellow; age. 4 *their friendship didn't have time to mature* =**develop**, grow, evolve, bloom, blossom, flourish, thrive.

maturity ▶ noun 1 *her progress from childhood to maturity* =**adulthood**, coming of age, manhood/womanhood. 2 *he displayed a maturity beyond his years* =**responsibility**, sense, level-headedness; wisdom, sophistication.

maudlin ▶ adjective =**mawkish**, sentimental, mushy, slushy, sloppy; *Brit.* twee; *informal* schmaltzy, cheesy, corny, toe-curling; *Brit. informal* soppy; *N. Amer. informal* cornball, three-hankie.

maul ▶ verb **1** *he had been mauled by a lion* =**savage**, attack, lacerate, claw, scratch. **2** *she hated being mauled by men* =**molest**, feel, fondle, manhandle; *informal* grope, paw, touch up. **3** *his book was mauled by the critics. See* CRITICIZE.

maverick ▶ noun =**individualist**, nonconformist, free spirit, original, eccentric; rebel, dissenter, dissident. −OPPOSITES conformist.

mawkish ▶ adjective =**sentimental**, maudlin, mushy, slushy, sloppy, cloying, saccharine, sugary, syrupy, nauseating; *Brit.* twee; *informal* schmaltzy, weepy, cutesy, lovey-dovey, cheesy, corny, sick-making, toe-curling; *Brit. informal* soppy; *N. Amer. informal* cornball, hokey.

maxim ▶ noun =**saying**, adage, aphorism, proverb, motto, saw, axiom, dictum, precept, epigram.

maximum ▶ adjective *the maximum amount* =**greatest**, highest, biggest, largest, top, most, utmost. −OPPOSITES minimum. ▶ noun *production levels are near their maximum* =**upper limit**, limit, utmost, greatest, most, peak, height, ceiling, top. −OPPOSITES minimum.

maybe ▶ adverb =**perhaps**, possibly; for all one knows; *N. English* happen; *literary* peradventure, perchance.

mayhem ▶ noun =**chaos**, havoc, bedlam, pandemonium, uproar, turmoil, a riot, anarchy; *informal* a madhouse.

maze ▶ noun =**labyrinth**, network, warren; web, tangle, jungle.

meadow ▶ noun =**field**, paddock; pasture; *literary* lea, mead.

meagre ▶ adjective =**inadequate**, scant, paltry, limited, restricted, modest, sparse, negligible, skimpy, slender, miserable, pitiful, puny, miserly, niggardly; *informal* measly, stingy, pathetic, piddling. −OPPOSITES abundant.

meal ▶ noun =**snack**, feast, banquet; *informal* bite (to eat), spread, blowout, feed; *Brit. informal* nosh-up; *formal* repast.

WORD LINKS

relating to meals: **prandial**

mean[1] ▶ verb **1** *flashing lights mean the road is blocked* =**signify**, denote, indicate, connote, show, express, spell out; stand for, represent, symbolize; imply, suggest, intimate, refer to, allude to; *literary* betoken. **2** *she didn't mean to break it* =**intend**, aim, plan, have in mind, set out, aspire, desire, want, wish, expect. **3** *the closures will mean a rise in unemployment* =**entail**, involve, necessitate, lead to, result in, give rise to, bring about, cause, engender, produce. **4** *a red sky in the morning usually means rain* =**presage**, portend, foretell, augur, promise, foreshadow, herald, signal, bode; *literary* betoken.

mean[2] ▶ adjective **1** *he's too mean to leave a tip* =**miserly**, niggardly, parsimonious, penny-pinching, cheese-paring; *informal* tight-fisted, stingy, tight, mingy; *N. Amer. informal* cheap. **2** *a mean trick* =**unkind**, nasty, unpleasant, spiteful, malicious, unfair, cruel, shabby, despicable, contemptible, obnoxious, vile, odious, loathsome, base, low; *informal* horrible, horrid, hateful, rotten, low-down; *Brit. informal* beastly. −OPPOSITES generous, kind.

mean[3] ▶ noun *a mean between saving and splashing out* =**middle course**, middle way, midpoint, happy medium, golden mean, compromise, balance; median, norm, average. ▶ adjective *the mean temperature* =**average**, median, normal, standard.

meander ▶ verb **1** *the river meandered gently* =**zigzag**, wind, twist, turn, curve, bend, snake. **2** *we meandered along the path* =**stroll**, saunter, amble, wander, drift; *Scottish* stravaig; *informal* mosey, tootle.

meandering ▶ adjective **1** *a meandering stream* =**winding**, windy, zigzag, twisting, turning, serpentine, sinuous, twisty. **2** *a meandering letter* =**rambling**, circuitous, roundabout, digressive, discursive, convoluted. −OPPOSITES straight, succinct.

meaning ▶ noun **1** *the meaning of his remark* =**significance**, sense, signification, import, gist, thrust, drift, implication, tenor, message. **2** *the word has several different meanings* =**definition**, sense, explanation, denotation, connotation, interpretation. **3** *my life has no meaning* =**value**, validity, worth, significance, point.

WORD LINKS

relating to meaning: **semantic**
study of meaning: **semantics**

meaningful ▶ adjective **1** *a meaningful remark* =**significant**, relevant, important, telling. **2** *a meaningful relationship* =**sincere**, deep, serious, earnest, significant, important. **3** *a meaningful glance* =**expressive**, eloquent, pointed; pregnant, revealing, suggestive.
–OPPOSITES inconsequential.

meaningless ▶ adjective **1** *a jumble of meaningless words* =**unintelligible**, incomprehensible, incoherent. **2** *she felt her life was meaningless* =**futile**, pointless, aimless, empty, hollow, vain, purposeless, valueless, useless, worthless, senseless, unimportant, insignificant, inconsequential.
–OPPOSITES worthwhile.

means ▶ plural noun **1** *the best means to achieve your goal* =**method**, way, manner, course, procedure. **2** *she doesn't have the means to support herself* =**money**, resources, capital, income, finance, funds, cash, the wherewithal, assets; *informal* dough, bread; *Brit. informal* dosh, brass, lolly, spondulicks, ackers. **3** *a man of means* =**wealth**, riches, affluence, substance, fortune, property.

meantime ▶ adverb. *See* MEANWHILE.

meanwhile ▶ adverb **1** *meanwhile, I'll stay here* =**for now**, for the moment, for the present, for the time being, meantime, in the meantime, in the interim, in the interval **2** *cook for a further half hour; meanwhile, make the stuffing* =**at the same time**, simultaneously, concurrently.

measurable ▶ adjective **1** *a measurable amount* =**quantifiable**, assessable. **2** *a measurable improvement* =**appreciable**, noticeable, significant, visible, perceptible, definite, obvious.

measure ▶ verb =**calculate**, compute, count, quantify, weigh, size, evaluate, assess, gauge, determine.
▶ noun **1** *cost-cutting measures* =**action**, act, course (of action), deed, procedure, step, expedient; manoeuvre, initiative, programme, operation. **2** *the Senate passed the measure* =**statute**, act, bill, law. **3** *use a measure to check the size* =**ruler**, tape measure, gauge, meter, scale, level. **4** *one measure of rice to two of water* =**portion**, unit. **5** *sales are the measure of the company's success* =**yardstick**, test, standard, barometer, touchstone, benchmark.
■ **get the measure of** =**evaluate**, assess, gauge, judge, weigh up; understand, fathom, read, be wise to, see through; *informal* suss out, have someone's number.
■ **measure up** =**pass muster**, match up, come up to standard, fit/fill the bill, be acceptable; *informal* come up to scratch, make the grade, cut the mustard, be up to snuff.
■ **measure up to** =**meet**, come up to, equal, match, bear comparison with, be on a level with; achieve, satisfy, fulfil.

measured ▶ adjective **1** *his measured tread* =**regular**, steady, even, rhythmic, unfaltering; slow, dignified, stately, sedate, leisurely, unhurried. **2** *his measured tones* =**thoughtful**, careful, considered, deliberate, restrained.

measureless ▶ adjective =**boundless**, limitless, unlimited, unbounded, immense, vast, endless, infinite, immeasurable, incalculable.
–OPPOSITES limited.

measurement ▶ noun **1** *measurement of the effect is difficult* =**quantification**, computation, calculation; evaluation, assessment. **2** *all measurements are in metric units* =**size**, dimension, proportions; value, amount, quantity.

meat ▶ noun =**flesh**.

WORD LINKS

meat-eating: **carnivorous**

meaty ▶ adjective **1** *a tall, meaty young man* =**beefy**, brawny, burly, muscular, muscly. **2** *a good, meaty story* =**solid**, substantial, satisfying, thought-provoking.

mechanical ▶ adjective **1** *a mechanical device* =**mechanized**, machine-driven, automated, automatic. **2** *a mechanical response* =**automatic**, unthinking, habitual, routine; unemotional, unfeeling, lifeless.
–OPPOSITES manual.

mechanism ▶ noun **1** *an electrical mechanism* =**machine**, appliance, apparatus, device, instrument, contraption, gadget; *informal* gizmo. **2** *the train's safety mechanism* =**machinery**, gear, system, equipment. **3** *a formal mechanism for citizens to lodge complaints* =**procedure**, process, system, method, means, medium, channel.

mechanize ▸ verb =automate, industrialize, motorize, computerize.

medal ▸ noun =decoration, ribbon, star, badge, award; honour; *Brit. informal* gong.

meddle ▸ verb **1** *don't meddle in my affairs* =interfere, intrude, intervene, pry; *informal* poke one's nose in; *N. Amer. informal* kibitz. **2** *someone had been meddling with her things* =fiddle, interfere, tamper, mess; *Brit. informal* muck about/around.

meddlesome ▸ adjective =interfering, meddling, prying; *informal* nosy, nosy-parker.

mediate ▸ verb **1** *Austria tried to mediate between the two sides* =arbitrate, conciliate, moderate, make peace; intervene, intercede, act as an intermediary, liaise. **2** *a tribunal was set up to mediate disputes* =resolve, settle, arbitrate in, umpire, reconcile, referee; mend, clear up; *informal* patch up.

mediation ▸ noun =arbitration, conciliation, reconciliation, intervention, intercession; negotiation, shuttle diplomacy.

mediator ▸ noun =arbitrator, arbiter, negotiator, conciliator, peacemaker, go-between, middleman, intermediary, moderator, broker, liaison officer; umpire, referee, adjudicator, judge.

medicinal ▸ adjective =curative, healing, remedial, therapeutic, restorative, health-giving.

> **WORD LINKS**
>
> *related prefix:* **iatro-**

medicine ▸ noun =medication, drug, prescription, treatment, remedy, cure; nostrum, panacea, cure-all.

> **WORD LINKS**
>
> *relating to medicines:* **pharmaceutical**
> *seller of medicines:* **pharmacist**; *Brit.* **chemist;** *N. Amer.* **druggist**
> *shop selling medicines:* **pharmacy;** *Brit.* **chemist's;** *N. Amer.* **drugstore**

medieval ▸ adjective **1** *medieval times* =Middle-Age; Dark-Age; Gothic. **2** *(informal) the plumbing's a bit medieval* =primitive, antiquated, archaic, antique, antediluvian, old-fashioned, outdated, outmoded; *informal* out of the ark; *N. Amer. informal* horse-and-buggy, clunky.
–OPPOSITES modern.

mediocre ▸ adjective =ordinary, average, uninspired, undistinguished, indifferent, unexceptional, unexciting, unremarkable, run-of-the-mill, pedestrian, prosaic, lacklustre, forgettable, amateurish; *informal* OK, so-so.
–OPPOSITES excellent.

meditate ▸ verb =contemplate, think, consider, ponder, muse, reflect, deliberate, ruminate, brood, mull over; *formal* cogitate.

meditation ▸ noun =contemplation, thought, musing, consideration, reflection, deliberation, rumination, brooding, reverie, concentration; *formal* cogitation.

meditative ▸ adjective =pensive, contemplative, reflective, ruminative, introspective, brooding.

medium ▸ noun =means, method, avenue, channel, vehicle, organ, instrument, mechanism.
▸ adjective =average, middling, medium-sized, middle-sized, moderate, normal, standard.

medley ▸ noun =assortment, miscellany, mixture, melange, variety, mixed bag, mix, collection, selection, potpourri, patchwork.

meek ▸ adjective =submissive, obedient, compliant, tame, biddable, acquiescent, timid, unprotesting; quiet, mild, gentle, docile, shy, diffident, unassuming, self-effacing.
–OPPOSITES assertive.

meet ▸ verb **1** *I met an old friend on the train* =encounter, come face to face with, run into, run across, come across/upon, chance on, happen on, stumble across; *informal* bump into. **2** *she first met Paul at a party* =get to know, be introduced to, make the acquaintance of. **3** *the committee met on Saturday* =assemble, gather, come together, get together, congregate, convene. **4** *the place where three roads meet* =converge, connect, touch, link up, intersect, cross, join. **5** *the announcement was met with widespread hostility* =greet, receive, treat. **6** *he does not meet our requirements* =fulfil, satisfy, measure up to, match (up to), conform to, come up to, comply with, answer.
▸ noun *an athletics meet. See* MEETING *sense 5.*

meeting ▸ noun **1** *he stood up to address the meeting* =gathering, assembly, conference, congregation, convention, summit, rally; *N. Amer.* caucus; *informal* get-together. **2** *she demanded a meeting with the minister* =**consultation**, audience, interview. **3** *he intrigued her on their first meeting* =**encounter**, contact; appointment, assignation, rendezvous. **4** *the meeting of land and sea* =**convergence**, coming together, confluence, conjunction, union; intersection, crossing. **5** *an athletics meeting* =**event**, tournament, meet, rally, competition, match, game, contest.

melancholy ▸ adjective =**sad**, sorrowful, unhappy, mournful, lugubrious, gloomy, despondent, downhearted, downcast, disconsolate, glum, miserable, morose, woeful, doleful, joyless; *informal* down in the dumps, down in the mouth, blue.
–OPPOSITES cheerful.
▸ noun *a feeling of melancholy* =**sadness**, sorrow, unhappiness, melancholia, dejection, depression, despondency, gloom, misery; *informal* the blues.

melange ▸ noun =**mixture**, medley, assortment, blend, variety, mixed bag, mix, miscellany, selection, pot-pourri, patchwork.

melee, mêlée ▸ noun =**fracas**, disturbance, rumpus, tumult, commotion, disorder, fray; brawl, fight, scuffle, struggle, skirmish, free-for-all, tussle; *informal* scrap, set-to; *N. Amer. informal* rough house.

mellifluous ▸ adjective =**sweet-sounding**, dulcet, honeyed, mellow, soft, liquid, silvery, soothing, rich, smooth, euphonious, harmonious, tuneful.
–OPPOSITES cacophonous.

mellow ▸ adjective **1** *the mellow tone of his voice* =**dulcet**, sweet-sounding, tuneful, melodious, mellifluous; soft, smooth, warm, full, rich. **2** *a mellow wine* =**full-bodied**, mature, full-flavoured, rich, smooth. **3** *a mellow mood* =**genial**, affable, amiable, good-humoured, good-natured, pleasant, relaxed, easygoing.

melodious ▸ adjective =**tuneful**, melodic, musical, mellifluous, dulcet, sweet-sounding, silvery, harmonious, euphonious, lyrical; *informal* easy on the ear.
–OPPOSITES discordant.

melodramatic ▸ adjective =**exaggerated**, histrionic, extravagant, over-

dramatic, overdone, sensationalized, overemotional; theatrical, stagy, actressy; *informal* hammy.

melody ▸ noun **1** *familiar melodies* =**tune**, air, strain, theme, song, refrain. **2** *his unique gift for melody* =**melodiousness**, tunefulness, musicality.

melt ▸ verb **1** *the snow was beginning to melt* =**liquefy**, thaw, defrost, soften, dissolve. **2** *his anger melted away* =**vanish**, disappear, fade, dissolve, evaporate.

member ▸ noun =**subscriber**, associate, fellow.

membrane ▸ noun =**layer**, sheet, skin, film, tissue.

memento ▸ noun =**souvenir**, keepsake, reminder, remembrance, token, memorial; trophy, relic.

memoir ▸ noun **1** *a touching memoir of her childhood* =**account**, history, record, chronicle, narrative, story, portrayal, depiction, portrait, profile. **2** *he published his memoirs in 1955* =**autobiography**, life story; journal, diary.

memorable ▸ adjective =**unforgettable**, indelible, catchy, haunting; momentous, significant, historic, notable, noteworthy, important, special, outstanding, arresting, impressive, distinctive, distinguished.

memorandum ▸ noun =**message**, communication, note, email, letter, missive; *informal* memo.

memorial ▸ noun **1** *the war memorial* =**monument**, cenotaph, mausoleum; statue, plaque, cairn; shrine. **2** *the festival is a memorial to his life's work* =**tribute**, testimonial; remembrance, memento.
▸ adjective *a memorial service* =**commemorative**, remembrance.

memorize ▸ verb =**commit to memory**, remember, learn (by heart), become word-perfect in.

memory ▸ noun **1** *happy memories of her childhood* =**recollection**, remembrance, reminiscence; impression. **2** *the town built a statue in memory of him* =**commemoration**, remembrance; honour, tribute, recognition, respect.

> **WORD LINKS**
> *relating to memory:* **mnemonic**

menace ▸ noun **1** *an atmosphere full of menace* =**threat**, intimidation; malevolence, oppression. **2** *a menace to society* =**danger**, peril, risk, hazard, threat.

3 *that child is a menace* =**nuisance**, pest, troublemaker, mischief-maker; *informal* bad news.
▶ verb **1** *the elephants are still menaced by poaching* =**threaten**, endanger, put at risk, jeopardize, imperil. **2** *a gang of skinheads menaced local residents* =**intimidate**, threaten, terrorize, frighten, scare, terrify.

menacing ▶ adjective =**threatening**, ominous, intimidating, frightening, forbidding, hostile, sinister, baleful.
–OPPOSITES friendly.

mend ▶ verb =**repair**, fix, restore; sew (up), stitch, darn, patch; renew, renovate, fill in; *informal* patch up.
–OPPOSITES break.

menial ▶ adjective =**unskilled**, lowly, humble, low-grade, low-status, degrading.

mental ▶ adjective **1** *mental faculties* =**intellectual**, cerebral, rational, cognitive. **2** *a mental disorder* =**psychiatric**, psychological; behavioural.
–OPPOSITES physical.

mentality ▶ noun =**way of thinking**, mind set, mind, psychology, attitude, outlook, make-up.

mentally ▶ adverb =**in one's mind**, in one's head, inwardly, internally.

mention ▶ verb **1** *don't mention the war* =**allude to**, refer to, touch on/upon; bring up, raise, broach. **2** *Jim mentioned that he'd met them before* =**state**, say, indicate, let someone know, disclose, divulge, reveal. **3** *I'll gladly mention your work to my friends* =**recommend**, commend, put in a (good) word for; *informal* plug.
▶ noun =**reference**, allusion, comment; citation; *informal* namecheck, plug.

mentor ▶ noun **1** *his political mentors* =**adviser**, guide, guru, consultant; confidant(e). **2** *regular meetings between mentor and trainee* =**trainer**, teacher, tutor, instructor, counsellor.

menu ▶ noun =**bill of fare**, carte du jour, set menu, table d'hôte.

mephitic ▶ adjective *(literary)*. See MAL ODOROUS.

mercantile ▶ adjective =**commercial**, trade, trading, business, merchant, sales.

mercenary ▶ adjective =**grasping**, greedy, acquisitive, avaricious, venal, materialistic; *informal* money-grubbing.

merchandise ▶ noun =**goods**, wares, stock, commodities, produce, products.
▶ verb =**promote**, market, sell, retail; advertise, publicize, push; *informal* hype, plug.

merchant ▶ noun =**trader**, dealer, wholesaler, broker, agent, seller, buyer, vendor, distributor.

WORD LINKS

relating to merchants: **mercantile, commercial**

merciful ▶ adjective =**forgiving**, compassionate, pitying, forbearing, lenient, humane, mild, kind, soft-hearted, tender-hearted, gracious, sympathetic, humanitarian, liberal, tolerant, indulgent, generous, magnanimous, benign, benevolent.
–OPPOSITES cruel.

mercifully ▶ adverb =**luckily**, fortunately, happily, thankfully, thank goodness/God/heavens.

merciless ▶ adjective =**ruthless**, remorseless, pitiless, unforgiving, implacable, inexorable, relentless, inhumane, inhuman, unfeeling, intolerant, severe, cold-blooded, hard-hearted, stony-hearted, heartless, harsh, callous, cruel, brutal, barbarous, cut-throat.
–OPPOSITES compassionate.

mercurial ▶ adjective =**volatile**, capricious, temperamental, excitable, fickle, changeable, unpredictable, variable, mutable, erratic, inconstant, inconsistent, unstable, unsteady, fluctuating, ever-changing, moody, flighty, wayward, impulsive; *technical* labile.
–OPPOSITES stable.

mercy ▶ noun **1** *he showed no mercy to the others* =**leniency**, clemency, compassion, pity, charity, forgiveness, forbearance, quarter, humanity; soft-heartedness, tender-heartedness, kindness, sympathy, indulgence, tolerance, generosity, magnanimity, beneficence.
–OPPOSITES ruthlessness, cruelty.
■ **at the mercy of 1** *they found themselves at the mercy of a tyrant* =**in the power of**, under/in the control of, in the clutches of, under the heel of, subject to. **2** *he was at the mercy of the elements* =**defenceless against**, vulnerable to, exposed to, susceptible to, prey to, (wide) open to.

merely ▶ adverb =**only**, purely, solely, simply, just, but.

merge ▶ verb **1** *the company merged with*

a European firm =**join (together)**, join forces, amalgamate, unite, affiliate, team up, link (up). **2** the two organizations were merged =**amalgamate**, bring together, join, consolidate, conflate, unite, unify, combine, incorporate, integrate, link (up), yoke. **3** the two colours merged =**mingle**, blend, fuse, mix, intermix, intermingle, coalesce; literary commingle.
–OPPOSITES separate.

merger ▸ noun =**amalgamation**, combination, union, fusion, coalition, affiliation, unification, incorporation, consolidation, link-up, alliance.
–OPPOSITES split.

merit ▸ noun **1** composers of outstanding merit =**excellence**, quality, calibre, worth, worthiness, value, distinction, eminence. **2** the merits of the scheme =**good point**, strong point, advantage, benefit, value, asset, plus.
–OPPOSITES inferiority, fault, disadvantage.
▸ verb the accusation did not merit a response =**deserve**, earn, be deserving of, warrant, rate, justify, be worthy of, be entitled to, have a right to, have a claim to/on.

meritorious ▸ adjective =**praiseworthy**, laudable, commendable, admirable, estimable, creditable, worthy, deserving, excellent, exemplary, good.
–OPPOSITES discreditable.

merriment ▸ noun =**high spirits**, exuberance, cheerfulness, gaiety, fun, buoyancy, levity, liveliness, cheer, joy, joyfulness, joyousness, jollity, happiness, gladness, jocularity, conviviality, festivity, merrymaking, revelry, mirth, glee, laughter, hilarity, light-heartedness, amusement, pleasure.
–OPPOSITES misery.

merry ▸ adjective **1** merry throngs of students =**cheerful**, cheery, in high spirits, bright, sunny, smiling, light-hearted, buoyant, lively, carefree, joyful, joyous, jolly, convivial, festive, mirthful, gleeful, happy, glad, laughing; informal chirpy; formal jocund; literary blithe. **2** (Brit. informal) after three beers he began to feel quite merry =**tipsy**, mellow; Brit. informal tiddly, squiffy.
–OPPOSITES miserable.

mesh ▸ noun wire mesh =**netting**, net; grille, screen, lattice, gauze.
▸ verb **1** one gear meshes with the input gear =**engage**, connect, lock, interlock. **2** our ideas just do not mesh =**harmonize**, fit together, match, dovetail, connect, interconnect.

mesmerize ▸ verb =**enthral**, spellbind, entrance, dazzle, bewitch, charm, captivate, enchant, fascinate, transfix, grip, hypnotize.

mesmerizing ▸ adjective =**enthralling**, spellbinding, entrancing, dazzling, captivating, enchanting, fascinating, gripping, hypnotic, compelling, bewitching.

mess ▸ noun **1** please clear up the mess =**untidiness**, disorder, disarray, clutter, shambles, muddle, chaos; Brit. informal tip. **2** dog mess =**excrement**, muck, faeces, excreta, dirt; informal poo. **3** I've got to get out of this mess =**plight**, predicament, (tight) spot/corner, difficulty, trouble, quandary, dilemma, problem, muddle, mix-up; informal jam, fix, pickle, stew, hole, scrape. **4** it's all a bit of a mess =**muddle**, bungle; informal botch, foul-up; Brit. informal cock-up; N. Amer. informal snafu.
■ **make a mess of** =**mismanage**, mishandle, bungle, fluff, spoil, ruin, wreck; informal mess up, botch, make a hash of, muck up, foul up; Brit. informal make a pig's ear of, make a Horlicks of, cock up.
■ **mess about/around** =**potter about**, fiddle about/around, footle about/around, play about/around, fool about/around; fidget, toy, trifle, tamper, tinker, interfere, meddle, monkey (about/around); informal piddle about/around; Brit. informal muck about/around.
■ **mess something up** he messed up my kitchen =**dirty**, clutter up, jumble, dishevel, rumple; N. Amer. informal muss up.

message ▸ noun **1** are there any messages for me? =**communication**, news, note, memo, email, letter, missive, report, bulletin, communiqué, dispatch; information. **2** the message of his teaching =**meaning**, sense, import, idea; point, thrust, gist, essence, content, subject (matter), substance, implication, drift, lesson.
■ **get the message** (informal) =**understand**, get the point, realize, comprehend; informal twig, catch on, latch on, get the picture.

messenger ▸ noun =**courier**, postman, runner, dispatch rider, envoy, emissary, agent, go-between; historical herald; archaic legate.

messy ▸ adjective **1** messy oil spills | messy

hair =**dirty**, filthy, grubby, soiled, grimy; mucky, muddy, slimy, sticky, sullied, stained, smeared, smudged; dishevelled, scruffy, unkempt, rumpled, matted, tousled, bedraggled, tangled; *informal* yucky; *Brit. informal* gungy. **2** *a messy kitchen* =**untidy**, disordered, in a muddle, chaotic, confused, disorganized, in disarray; cluttered; in a jumble; *informal* like a bomb's hit it; *Brit. informal* shambolic. **3** *a messy legal battle* =**complex**, tangled, confused, convoluted; unpleasant, nasty, bitter, acrimonious.
–OPPOSITES clean, tidy.

metallic ▸ adjective **1** *a metallic sound* =**tinny**, jangling, jingling; grating, screeching, grinding; harsh, jarring. **2** *metallic paint* =**sparkly**, glittery; lustrous, shiny, glossy.

metamorphose ▸ verb =**transform**, change, mutate, transmute, convert, alter, modify; morph; *humorous* transmogrify.

metamorphosis ▸ noun =**transformation**, mutation, transmutation, change, alteration; *humorous* transmogrification.

metaphor ▸ noun =**figure of speech**, image, trope, analogy, comparison, symbol.

metaphorical ▸ adjective =**figurative**, allegorical, symbolic; imaginative, extended.
–OPPOSITES literal.

metaphysical ▸ adjective **1** *metaphysical questions* =**abstract**, theoretical, conceptual, philosophical; speculative, intellectual, academic. **2** *a metaphysical battle between Good and Evil* =**transcendental**, spiritual, supernatural.

mete ■ **mete something out** =**dispense**, hand out, allocate, allot, apportion, issue, deal out, dole out, dish out, assign, administer.

meteoric ▸ adjective =**rapid**, lightning, swift, fast, speedy, instant, sudden, spectacular, dramatic, overnight.
–OPPOSITES gradual.

method ▸ noun **1** *they use very old-fashioned methods* =**procedure**, technique, system, practice, routine, modus operandi, process; strategy, tactic, approach. **2** *there's no method in his approach* =**order**, organization, structure, form, system, logic, planning, design, consistency.
–OPPOSITES disorder.

methodical ▸ adjective =**orderly**, well ordered, well organized, (well) planned, efficient, businesslike, systematic, structured, logical, analytical, disciplined; consistent, scientific.

meticulous ▸ adjective =**careful**, conscientious, diligent, scrupulous, punctilious, painstaking; thorough, studious, rigorous, detailed, perfectionist, fastidious, methodical, particular.
–OPPOSITES careless.

métier ▸ noun **1** *he had another métier besides the priesthood* =**occupation**, job, profession, business, employment, career, vocation, trade, craft, line (of work); *N. Amer.* specialty. **2** *television is more my métier* =**forte**, strong point, strength, speciality, talent, bent; *informal* thing, cup of tea.

metropolis ▸ noun =**capital (city)**, chief town, county town; big city, conurbation, megalopolis.

mettle ▸ noun =**spirit**, fortitude, strength of character, moral fibre, steel, determination, resolve, resolution, backbone, grit, courage, courageousness, bravery, valour, fearlessness, daring; *informal* guts, spunk; *Brit. informal* bottle.

miasma ▸ noun *(literary)* =**stink**, reek, stench, smell, odour; *Brit. informal* pong, niff, whiff.

microbe ▸ noun

> WORD LINKS
>
> *fear of microbes:* **microphobia, bacillophobia**

microscopic ▸ adjective =**tiny**, minute, infinitesimal, minuscule; micro, diminutive; *Scottish* wee; *informal* teeny, weeny, teeny-weeny, teensy-weensy, itsy-bitsy; *Brit. informal* titchy, tiddly.
–OPPOSITES huge.

midday ▸ noun =**noon**, twelve noon, high noon, noonday.
–OPPOSITES midnight.

> WORD LINKS
>
> *relating to midday:* **meridional**

middle ▸ noun **1** *a shallow dish with a spike in the middle* =**centre**, midpoint, halfway point, dead centre, focus, hub; eye, heart, core, kernel. **2** *he had a towel round his middle* =**midriff**, waist, belly, stomach; *informal* tummy, tum.
–OPPOSITES edge.

▶ **adjective 1** *the middle point* =**central**, mid, mean, medium, median, midway, halfway. **2** *the middle level* =**intermediate**, intermediary.

> **WORD LINKS**
> related prefix: **meso-**

middleman ▶ noun =**intermediary**, go-between; dealer, broker, agent, factor, wholesaler, distributor.

middling ▶ adjective =**average**, standard, normal, middle-of-the-road; moderate, ordinary, commonplace, everyday, workaday, tolerable, passable; run-of-the-mill, fair; *informal* OK, so-so, bog-standard, fair-to-middling; *NZ informal* half-pie.

midget ▶ noun *(offensive)* =**dwarf**, manikin, gnome, pygmy; *informal* shrimp.

midnight ▶ noun =**twelve midnight**, the middle of the night, the witching hour.
–OPPOSITES midday.

mien ▶ noun =**appearance**, look, expression, countenance, aura, demeanour, attitude, air, manner, bearing; *formal* comportment.

might ▶ noun =**strength**, force, power, vigour, energy, brawn, powerfulness, forcefulness.

mightily ▶ adverb =**extremely**, exceedingly, enormously, immensely, tremendously, hugely, dreadfully, very (much); *informal* awfully, majorly, mega, seriously; *N. Amer. informal* mighty.

mighty ▶ adjective **1** *a mighty blow* =**powerful**, forceful, violent, vigorous, hefty, thunderous. **2** *a mighty warrior* =**fearsome**, ferocious; awesome, heroic, great; renowned, legendary. **3** *mighty oak trees* =**huge**, enormous, massive, gigantic, giant, colossal, mammoth, immense, titanic; *informal* monster, whopping (great), thumping (great), humongous, jumbo(-sized); *Brit. informal* whacking (great), ginormous.
–OPPOSITES feeble, puny, tiny.
▶ adverb *(N. Amer. informal)* *I'm mighty pleased to see you* =**extremely**, exceedingly, enormously, immensely, tremendously, hugely, mightily, very (much); *informal* awfully, dreadfully, majorly, mega; *Brit. informal* well, jolly; *informal, dated* frightfully.

migrant ▶ noun =**immigrant**, emigrant; nomad, itinerant, traveller,

transient, wanderer, drifter.
▶ adjective =**travelling**, mobile, wandering, drifting, nomadic, itinerant, transient.

migrate ▶ verb **1** *rural populations migrated to urban areas* =**relocate**, resettle, move (house); emigrate, go abroad. **2** *wildebeest migrate across the Serengeti* =**roam**, wander, drift, rove, travel.

mild ▶ adjective **1** *a mild tone of voice* =**gentle**, tender, soft, sympathetic, peaceable, quiet; reasonable. **2** *a mild punishment* =**lenient**, light. **3** *he was eyeing her with mild interest* =**slight**, faint, vague. **4** *mild weather* =**warm**, balmy, temperate, clement. **5** *a mild curry* =**bland**, light; insipid.
–OPPOSITES harsh, strong, severe.

milieu ▶ noun =**environment**, sphere, background, backdrop, setting, context, atmosphere, ambience; location, conditions, surroundings, environs.

militant ▶ adjective =**hard-line**, extreme, active, extremist, committed, zealous, fanatical, radical.
▶ noun =**activist**, extremist, radical, zealot.

militaristic ▶ adjective =**warmongering**, warlike, martial, hawkish, pugnacious, combative, aggressive, belligerent, bellicose; *informal* gung-ho.
–OPPOSITES peaceable.

military ▶ adjective =**fighting**; service, army, armed, defence, martial.
–OPPOSITES civilian.
▶ noun *the military took power* =**(armed) forces**, services, militia; army, navy, air force, marines, generals.

militate ■ **militate against** =**work against**, hinder, discourage, be prejudicial to, be detrimental to.

milk ▶ verb *milking rich clients* =**exploit**, take advantage of, suck dry; *informal* bleed, squeeze, fleece.

> **WORD LINKS**
> relating to milk: **dairy, lactic**

milky ▶ adjective =**pale**, white, milk-white, chalky, pearly, ivory, alabaster.
–OPPOSITES swarthy.

mill ▶ noun *a steel mill* =**factory**, (processing) plant, works, workshop, shop, foundry.
▶ verb *the wheat is milled into flour* =**grind**, pulverize, powder, granulate, pound, crush, press; *technical* comminute.

■ **mill around/about** =wander, drift, swarm; crowd, pack, fill.

mime ▶ noun *a mime of someone fencing* =**dumb show**, pantomime, action.
▶ verb *she mimed picking up a phone* =**act out**, gesture, simulate, pretend, represent.

mimic ▶ verb =**imitate**, copy, impersonate, do an impression of, ape, caricature, parody; *informal* send up, take off, spoof.
▶ noun =**impersonator**, impressionist; *informal* copycat.

mimicry ▶ noun =**imitation**, impersonation, copying.

mince ▶ verb =**grind**, chop up, cut up; *N. Amer.* hash.

mind ▶ noun **1** *a good teacher must stretch pupils' minds* =**brain**, intelligence, intellect, brains, brainpower, wits, understanding, reasoning, judgement, sense, head; *informal* grey matter, brainbox, brain cells; *Brit. informal* loaf; *N. Amer. informal* smarts. **2** *he kept his mind on the job* =**attention**, thoughts, concentration. **3** *the tragedy affected her mind* =**sanity**, (mental) faculties, senses, wits, reason, reasoning, judgement. **4** *a great mind* =**intellect**, thinker, brain, scholar.
▶ verb **1** *do you mind if I smoke?* =**object**, care, be bothered, be annoyed, be upset, take offence, disapprove, look askance; *informal* give/care a damn, give/care a toss, give/care a hoot. **2** *mind the step!* =**be careful of**, watch out for, look out for, beware of. **3** *mind you wipe your feet* =**be/make sure (that)**, see (that); remember to, don't forget to. **4** *her husband was minding the baby* =**look after**, take care of, keep an eye on, attend to, care for.
■ **be in two minds** =**be undecided**, be uncertain, be unsure, hesitate, waver, vacillate, dither; *Brit.* haver, hum and haw; *informal* dilly-dally, shilly-shally.
■ **mind out** =**take care**, be careful, watch out, look out, beware.

> [!NOTE] **WORD LINKS**
> to do with the mind: **mental, cognitive**
> study of the mind: **psychology**
> branch of medicine to do with the mind: **psychiatry**

mindful ▶ adjective =**aware**, conscious, sensible, alive, alert, acquainted; *informal* wise, hip; *formal* cognizant.
−OPPOSITES heedless.

mindless ▶ adjective **1** *a mindless idiot* =**stupid**, idiotic, brainless, asinine, witless, empty-headed, slow-witted, feather-brained; *informal* dumb, pig-ignorant, brain-dead, cretinous, moronic, thick, birdbrained, pea-brained, dopey, dim, half-witted, dippy, fatheaded, boneheaded; *N. Amer. informal* chowderheaded. **2** *mindless acts of vandalism* =**unthinking**, thoughtless, senseless, gratuitous, wanton, indiscriminate. **3** *a mindless task* =**mechanical**, routine; tedious, boring, monotonous, brainless, mind-numbing.

mine ▶ noun **1** *a coal mine* =**pit**, excavation, quarry, workings, diggings; strip mine; *Brit.* opencast mine; *N. Amer.* open-pit mine. **2** *a mine of information* =**store**, storehouse, reservoir, repository, gold mine, treasure house, treasury.
▶ verb *the iron ore was mined from shallow pits* =**quarry**, excavate, dig (up), extract, remove.

mingle ▶ verb **1** *fact and fiction are skilfully mingled in his novels* =**mix**, blend, intermingle, intermix, interweave, interlace, combine, merge, fuse, unite, join, amalgamate, meld, mesh; *literary* commingle. **2** *wedding guests mingled in the marquee* =**socialize**, circulate, fraternize, get together; *informal* hobnob.
−OPPOSITES separate.

miniature ▶ adjective *a miniature railway* =**small-scale**, mini; little, small, baby, toy, pocket, dwarf, pygmy, diminutive; *Scottish* wee; *N. Amer.* vest-pocket.
−OPPOSITES giant.

minimal ▶ adjective =**very little/small**, minimum, the least (possible); nominal, token, negligible.
−OPPOSITES maximum.

minimize ▶ verb **1** *the aim is to minimize costs* =**keep down**, keep at/to a minimum, reduce, decrease, cut (down), lessen, curtail, diminish, prune; *informal* slash. **2** *we should not minimize his contribution* =**belittle**, make light of, play down, underestimate, underrate, downplay, undervalue, understate.
−OPPOSITES maximize, exaggerate.

minimum ▶ noun *costs will be kept to the minimum* =**lowest level**, lower limit, rock bottom; least, lowest, slightest.
−OPPOSITES maximum.
▶ adjective *the minimum amount of effort* =**minimal**, least, smallest, least possible, slightest, lowest, minutest.

minion ▸ noun =**underling**, flunkey, lackey, hanger-on, follower, servant, stooge.

minister ▸ noun **1** *a government minister* =**member of the government**, cabinet minister, secretary of state. **2** *a minister of religion* =**clergyman**, clergywoman, cleric, pastor, vicar, rector, priest, parson, father, man/woman of the cloth, man/woman of God, churchman, churchwoman; curate, chaplain; *informal* reverend, padre. **3** *the British minister in Egypt* =**ambassador**, chargé d'affaires, envoy, emissary, consul, representative; *archaic* legate.
▸ verb *doctors were ministering to the injured* =**tend**, care for, take care of, look after, nurse, treat, attend to, see to, help, assist.

ministry ▸ noun **1** *the ministry for foreign affairs* =**department**, bureau, agency, office. **2** *he's training for the ministry* =**holy orders**, the priesthood, the cloth, the church.

minor ▸ adjective **1** *a minor problem* =**slight**, small; unimportant, insignificant, inconsequential, subsidiary, negligible, trivial, trifling, paltry, petty; *N. Amer.* nickel-and-dime; *informal* piffling, piddling. **2** *a minor poet* =**little known**, unknown, lesser, unimportant, insignificant, obscure; *N. Amer.* minor-league; *informal* small-time; *N. Amer. informal* two-bit.
–OPPOSITES major, important.
▸ noun *the accused was a minor* =**child**, infant, youth, adolescent, teenager, boy, girl; *informal* kid.
–OPPOSITES adult.

mint ▸ noun *(informal) they made a mint out of the deal* =**millions**, billions, a king's ransom; *informal* **a (small) fortune**, a bundle, a packet, a pile; *Brit. informal* a bomb, big money; *N. Amer. informal* big bucks; *Austral. informal* big bickies, motser.
▸ verb *the shilling was minted in 1742* =**coin**, stamp, strike, cast, forge, manufacture. ■ **in mint condition** =**brand new**, pristine, perfect, immaculate, unblemished, undamaged, unmarked, unused, first-class, excellent.

minuscule ▸ adjective =**tiny**, minute, microscopic, micro, baby, dwarf; *Scottish* wee; *informal* teeny, teeny-weeny, teensy, teensy-weensy, itsy-bitsy, eensy, eensy-weensy, tiddly; *Brit. informal* titchy.
–OPPOSITES huge.

minute¹ ▸ noun **1** *it'll only take a minute* =**moment**, short time, little while, second, bit, instant; *informal* sec, jiffy; *Brit. informal* tick, mo, two ticks. **2** *at that minute, Tony walked in* =**point (in time)**, moment, instant, second, juncture. **3** *their objection was noted in the minutes* =**record(s)**, proceedings, log, notes; transcript, summary.
■ **in a minute** =**very soon**, in a moment/second/instant, in a trice, shortly, any minute (now), in a short time, in (less than) no time, before long; *N. Amer.* momentarily; *informal* anon, in a jiffy, in two shakes, before you can say Jack Robinson; *Brit. informal* in a tick, in a mo, in two ticks; *N. Amer. informal* in a snap; *literary* ere long.
■ **this minute** =**at once**, immediately, directly, this second, instantly, straight away, right away/now, forthwith; *informal* pronto, straight off, right off, toot sweet.
■ **up to the minute** =**latest**, newest, up to date, modern, fashionable, chic, stylish, all the rage, in vogue; *informal* trendy, with it, in.

minute² ▸ adjective **1** *minute particles* =**tiny**, minuscule, microscopic, micro, diminutive, miniature; *Scottish* wee; *informal* teeny, teeny-weeny, teensy, teensy-weensy, itsy-bitsy, eensy, eensy-weensy; *Brit. informal* titchy, tiddly. **2** *a minute chance of success* =**negligible**, slight, infinitesimal, minimal. **3** *minute detail* =**exhaustive**, painstaking, meticulous, rigorous, scrupulous, punctilious.
–OPPOSITES huge.

WORD LINKS
measurement of minute objects: **micrometry**

minutely ▸ adverb =**exhaustively**, painstakingly, meticulously, rigorously, scrupulously, punctiliously.

minutiae ▸ plural noun =**details**, niceties, finer points, particulars, trivia.

miracle ▸ noun *Germany's economic miracle* =**wonder**, marvel, sensation, phenomenon.

miraculous ▸ adjective *a miraculous escape* =**amazing**, astounding, remarkable, extraordinary, incredible, unbelievable, sensational.

mirage ▸ noun =**optical illusion**, hallucination, apparition, fantasy, chimera, figment of the imagination, vision; *literary* phantasm.

mire ▶ noun *it's a mire out there* =**swamp**, bog, morass, quagmire.
▶ verb *he has become mired in lawsuits* =**entangle**, tangle up, embroil, bog down, catch up, mix up, involve.

mirror ▶ noun **1** *a quick look in the mirror* =**looking glass**, wing mirror, rear-view mirror; *Brit.* glass. **2** *the Frenchman's life was a mirror of his own* =**reflection**, replica, copy, match, parallel.
▶ verb *pop music mirrored the mood of desperation* =**reflect**, match, reproduce, imitate, copy, mimic, echo, parallel.

┌─────────────────────────────────────┐
│ **WORD LINKS**   │
│   │
│ relating to mirrors: **catoptric, specular** │
│ fear of mirrors: **eisoptrophobia** │
└─────────────────────────────────────┘

mirth ▶ noun =**merriment**, high spirits, cheerfulness, hilarity, glee, laughter, gaiety, euphoria, exhilaration, light-heartedness, joviality, joy.
−OPPOSITES misery.

mirthless ▶ adjective =**humourless**, grim, sour, surly, dour, sullen, sulky, gloomy, mournful, doleful, miserable.
−OPPOSITES cheerful.

misadventure ▶ noun =**accident**, difficulty, misfortune, mishap; setback, reversal (of fortune), stroke of bad luck; failure, disaster, tragedy, calamity, woe, tribulation, catastrophe.

misanthropic ▶ adjective =**unsociable**, antisocial, unfriendly, reclusive, uncongenial, cynical, jaundiced.

misapply ▶ verb =**misuse**, misemploy, abuse; distort, warp, misinterpret, misconstrue, misrepresent.

misapprehension ▶ noun =**misunderstanding**, misinterpretation, misreading, misjudgement, misconception, misbelief, the wrong idea, false impression, delusion.

misappropriate ▶ verb =**embezzle**, expropriate, steal, thieve, pilfer, pocket, help oneself to; *informal* swipe, filch, rip off; *Brit. informal* pinch, nick, whip, knock off.

misappropriation ▶ noun =**embezzlement**, expropriation, stealing, theft, thieving, pilfering.

misbehave ▶ verb =**behave badly**, be naughty, be disobedient, get up to mischief, get up to no good; be rude; *informal* carry on, act up.

misbehaviour ▶ noun =**bad behaviour**, misconduct, naughtiness, disobedience, mischief; bad manners, rudeness.

miscalculate ▶ verb =**misjudge**, make a mistake (about), overestimate, underestimate, overvalue, undervalue; go wrong, err, be wide of the mark.

miscalculation ▶ noun =**error of judgement**, misjudgement, mistake, overestimate, underestimate.

miscarry ▶ verb *our plan miscarried* =**go wrong**, go awry, go amiss, be unsuccessful, fail, misfire, abort, founder, come to nothing, fall through, fall flat; *informal* flop.
−OPPOSITES succeed.

miscellaneous ▶ adjective =**various**, varied, different, assorted, mixed, sundry, diverse, disparate; diversified, motley, multifarious, heterogeneous; *literary* divers.

miscellany ▶ noun =**assortment**, mixture, melange, blend, variety, mixed bag, mix, medley, diversity, collection, selection, assemblage, pot-pourri, mishmash, hotchpotch, ragbag; *N. Amer.* hodgepodge.

mischance ▶ noun =**accident**, misfortune, mishap, misadventure, disaster, tragedy, calamity, catastrophe, upset, blow; bad luck, ill fortune.

mischief ▶ noun **1** *the boys are always getting up to mischief* =**naughtiness**, bad behaviour, misbehaviour, mischievousness, misconduct, disobedience; pranks, tricks, capers, nonsense, devilry, funny business; *informal* monkey business, shenanigans, hanky-panky; *Brit. informal* carryings-on, jiggery-pokery. **2** *the mischief in her eyes* =**impishness**, roguishness, devilment; glint, twinkle.

mischievous ▶ adjective **1** *a mischievous child* =**naughty**, badly behaved, troublesome; rascally, roguish. **2** *a mischievous smile* =**playful**, wicked, impish, roguish. **3** *a mischievous allegation* =**malicious**, malevolent, spiteful, vindictive, vengeful, malign, pernicious, mean, nasty, harmful, hurtful, cruel, unkind.
−OPPOSITES well behaved.

misconceive ▶ verb =**misunderstand**, misinterpret, misconstrue, misapprehend, mistake, misread; miscalculate, be mistaken, get the wrong idea.

misconception ▶ noun =**misappre-hension**, misunderstanding, mistake, error, misinterpretation, misconstruction, misreading, misjudgement, misbelief, miscalculation, false impression, illusion, fallacy, delusion.

misconduct ▶ noun **1** *allegations of misconduct* =**wrongdoing**, unlawfulness, criminality; unprofessionalism, malpractice, negligence, impropriety; *formal* maladministration. **2** *misconduct in the classroom* =**misbehaviour**, bad behaviour, mischief, naughtiness, rudeness.

misconstrue ▶ verb =**misunderstand**, misinterpret, misconceive, misapprehend, mistake, misread; be mistaken about, get the wrong idea about, get it/someone wrong.

miscreant ▶ noun =**criminal**, culprit, wrongdoer, malefactor, offender, villain, lawbreaker, evil-doer, delinquent, reprobate.

misdeed ▶ noun =**wrong**, crime, felony, misdemeanour, misconduct, offence, error, transgression, sin; *archaic* trespass.

misdemeanour ▶ noun =**wrongdoing**, crime, felony; misdeed, misconduct, offence, error, peccadillo, transgression, sin; *archaic* trespass.

miser ▶ noun =**penny-pincher**, niggard, cheese-parer, Scrooge; *informal* skinflint, meanie, money-grubber, cheapskate; *N. Amer. informal* tightwad.
–OPPOSITES spendthrift.

miserable ▶ adjective **1** *I'm too miserable to eat* =**unhappy**, sad, sorrowful, dejected, depressed, downcast, downhearted, down, despondent, disconsolate, wretched, glum, gloomy, dismal, melancholy, woebegone, doleful, forlorn, heartbroken; *informal* blue, down in the mouth/dumps. **2** *their miserable surroundings* =**dreary**, dismal, gloomy, drab, wretched, depressing, grim, cheerless, bleak, desolate; poor, shabby, squalid, seedy, dilapidated. **3** *miserable weather* =**unpleasant**, disagreeable, depressing; wet, rainy, stormy; *informal* rotten, foul. **4** *a miserable old man* =**grumpy**, sullen, bad-tempered, dour, surly, sour, glum, moody, unsociable, lugubrious, irritable, churlish, cantankerous, crotchety, cross, crabby, grouchy, testy, peevish, crusty, waspish. **5** *miserable wages* =**inadequate**, meagre, scanty, paltry, small, poor, pitiful, niggardly; *infor-*

mal measly, stingy, pathetic. **6** *all that fuss about a few miserable pounds* =**wretched**, confounded, stupid; *informal* blithering, blessed, damned, blasted; *Brit. informal* flaming; *dated* accursed.
–OPPOSITES cheerful, lovely.

miserliness ▶ noun =**meanness**, niggardliness, closeness, parsimoniousness; *informal* stinginess, tight-fistedness; *N. Amer.* cheapness.

miserly ▶ adjective **1** *his miserly great-uncle* =**mean**, niggardly, parsimonious, close-fisted, penny-pinching, cheese-paring, grasping, Scrooge-like; *informal* stingy, tight, tight-fisted; *N. Amer. informal* cheap. **2** *the prize is a miserly £300* =**meagre**, paltry, negligible, miserable, pitiful, niggardly; *informal* measly, stingy, pathetic.
–OPPOSITES generous.

misery ▶ noun **1** *periods of intense misery* =**unhappiness**, distress, wretchedness, suffering, anguish, anxiety, angst, torment, pain, grief, heartache, heartbreak, despair, despondency, dejection, depression, desolation, gloom, melancholy, woe, sadness, sorrow; *informal* the blues. **2** *the miseries of war* =**affliction**, misfortune, difficulty, problem, ordeal, trouble, hardship; sorrow, trial, tribulation, woe. **3** *(Brit. informal) he's a real old misery* =**killjoy**, dog in the manger, spoilsport; *informal* sourpuss, grouch, grump, party-pooper.
–OPPOSITES contentment, pleasure.

misfire ▶ verb =**go wrong**, go awry, fail, founder, fall through/flat; backfire; *informal* flop, go up in smoke.

misfit ▶ noun =**nonconformist**, eccentric, maverick, individualist, square peg in a round hole; *informal* oddball, weirdo, freak; *N. Amer. informal* screwball.

misfortune ▶ noun =**problem**, difficulty, setback, trouble, adversity, (stroke of) bad luck, misadventure, mishap, blow, failure, accident, disaster; sorrow, misery, woe, trial, tribulation.

misgiving ▶ noun =**qualm**, doubt, reservation; suspicion; second thoughts; trepidation, scepticism, unease, anxiety, apprehension, disquiet.

misguided ▶ adjective =**erroneous**, fallacious, unsound, misplaced, misconceived, ill-advised, ill-considered, ill-judged, inappropriate, unwise, injudicious, imprudent.

mishandle ▸ verb =mismanage, make a mess of; *informal* botch; *Brit. informal* make a pig's ear of, make a Horlicks of.

mishap ▸ noun =accident, trouble, problem, difficulty, setback, adversity, misfortune, blow; disaster, tragedy, catastrophe, calamity.

mishmash ▸ noun =jumble, confusion, hotchpotch, ragbag, patchwork, assortment, medley, miscellany, mixture, melange, blend, mix, pot-pourri, conglomeration; *N. Amer.* hodgepodge.

misinform ▸ verb =mislead, misguide, delude, deceive, lie to, hoodwink; *informal* lead up the garden path, take for a ride; *N. Amer. informal* give someone a bum steer.

misinformation ▸ noun =disinformation; propaganda, spin; lies, fibs, half-truths.

misinterpret ▸ verb =misunderstand, misconceive, misconstrue, misapprehend, mistake, misread.

misjudge ▸ verb =get the wrong idea about, get wrong, miscalculate, misread; overestimate, underestimate, overvalue, undervalue, underrate.

mislay ▸ verb =lose, misplace, be unable to find.
–OPPOSITES find.

mislead ▸ verb =deceive, delude, take in, lie to, fool, hoodwink, throw off the scent, pull the wool over someone's eyes, misinform, give wrong information to; *informal* lead up the garden path, take for a ride; *N. Amer. informal* give someone a bum steer.

misleading ▸ adjective =deceptive, confusing, deceiving, equivocal, ambiguous.

mismanage ▸ verb =bungle, fluff, make a mess of, mishandle, spoil, ruin, wreck; *informal* botch, make a hash of, mess up, muck up; *Brit. informal* make a pig's ear of, make a Horlicks of.

mismatch ▸ noun =discrepancy, inconsistency, contradiction, incongruity, conflict, discord, clash.

mismatched ▸ adjective =unsuited, incongruous, incompatible, inconsistent, at odds; out of keeping, clashing, dissimilar, different, at variance, disparate, unrelated, divergent, contrasting.
–OPPOSITES matching.

misplace ▸ verb =lose, mislay, be unable to find.

–OPPOSITES find.

misplaced ▸ adjective **1** *his comments were misplaced* =misguided, unwise, ill-advised, ill-considered, ill-judged, inappropriate. **2** *misplaced keys* =lost, mislaid, missing.

misprint ▸ noun =mistake, error, erratum; *Brit. literal; informal* typo.

misquote ▸ verb =misreport, misrepresent, take/quote out of context, distort, twist, slant, put a spin on, falsify.

misrepresent ▸ verb =misreport, misquote, quote/take out of context, misinterpret, put a spin on, falsify, distort.

miss¹ ▸ verb **1** *the shot missed her by inches* =be/go wide of, fall short of, pass, overshoot. **2** *I left early to miss the traffic* =avoid, beat, evade, escape, dodge, sidestep, elude, circumvent, bypass. **3** *she missed him when he was away* =pine for, yearn for, ache for, long for.
–OPPOSITES hit, catch.
▸ noun *one hit and three misses* =failure, omission, slip, blunder, error, mistake.
■ **miss someone/something out** =leave out, exclude, miss (off), fail to mention, pass over, skip, omit, ignore.

miss² ▸ noun *a headstrong young miss* =young woman, young lady, girl, schoolgirl; *Scottish* lass, lassie; *Irish* colleen; *informal* girlie, chick, bit, doll; *Brit. informal* bird; *N. Amer. informal* broad, dame; *Austral./NZ informal* sheila; *literary* maiden, maid, damsel; *archaic* wench.

misshapen ▸ adjective =deformed, malformed, distorted, crooked, twisted, warped, out of shape, bent, disfigured, grotesque.

missing ▸ adjective **1** *his wallet is missing* =lost, mislaid, misplaced, absent, gone (astray), unaccounted for. **2** *passion was missing from her life* =absent, lacking, gone, wanting.
–OPPOSITES present.

mission ▸ noun **1** *a mercy mission to Romania* =assignment, commission, expedition, journey, trip, undertaking, operation, project. **2** *her mission in life* =vocation, calling, goal, aim, quest, purpose, function; task, job, labour, work, duty. **3** *a trade mission* =delegation, deputation, commission. **4** *a bombing mission* =sortie, operation, raid; job, assignment, shift.

missionary ▸ noun =evangelist, apostle, proselytizer, preacher; zealot.

missive ▸ noun =message, communication, letter, word, note, memorandum, line, communiqué, dispatch, news; *informal* memo; *formal* epistle; *literary* tidings.

misspent ▸ adjective =wasted, dissipated, squandered, thrown away, frittered away, misused, misapplied.

misstate ▸ verb =misreport, misrepresent, take/quote out of context, distort, twist, put a spin on, falsify.

mist ▸ noun =haze, fog, smog, murk, cloud; *Scottish* haar.
■ **mist over/up** =steam up, become misty, cloud over.

mistake ▸ noun 1 *I assumed it had been a mistake* =error, fault, inaccuracy, omission, slip, blunder, miscalculation, misunderstanding, oversight, misinterpretation, gaffe, faux pas, solecism; *informal* slip-up, boo-boo, howler; *Brit. informal* boob, clanger, bloomer; *N. Amer. informal* goof. 2 *spelling mistakes* =misprint, error, erratum; *Brit. literal; informal* typo.
▸ verb 1 *men are apt to mistake their own feelings* =misunderstand, misinterpret, get wrong, misconstrue, misread. 2 *children often mistake pills for sweets* =confuse with, mix up with, take for.
■ **make a mistake** =go wrong, err, make an error, blunder, miscalculate; *informal* slip up, make a boo-boo, make a howler; *Brit. informal* boob; *N. Amer. informal* drop the ball, screw up, goof (up).

mistaken ▸ adjective =wrong, erroneous, inaccurate, incorrect, off beam, false, fallacious, unfounded, misguided, misinformed.
■ **be mistaken** =be wrong, be in error, be under a misapprehension, be misinformed, be misguided; *informal* be barking up the wrong tree, get the wrong end of the stick.
–OPPOSITES correct.

mistakenly ▸ adverb =wrongly, in error, erroneously, incorrectly, falsely, fallaciously, inaccurately.
–OPPOSITES correctly.

mistimed ▸ adjective =ill-timed, badly timed, inopportune, inappropriate, untimely.
–OPPOSITES opportune.

mistreat ▸ verb =ill-treat, maltreat, abuse, knock about/around, hit, beat, strike, molest, injure, harm, hurt; misuse, mishandle; *informal* beat up, rough up.

mistreatment ▸ noun =ill-treatment, maltreatment, abuse, beating, molestation, injury, harm; mishandling, manhandling.

mistress ▸ noun =lover, girlfriend, kept woman; *informal* fancy woman, bit on the side; *archaic* paramour.

mistrust ▸ verb =be suspicious of, be mistrustful of, be distrustful of, be sceptical of, be wary of, be chary of, distrust, have doubts about, have misgivings about, have reservations about, suspect.
▸ noun =suspicion, distrust, doubt, misgivings, wariness, reservations.

mistrustful ▸ adjective =suspicious, chary, wary, distrustful, doubtful, dubious, uneasy, sceptical, leery.

misty ▸ adjective =hazy, foggy, cloudy.
–OPPOSITES clear.

misunderstand ▸ verb =misapprehend, misinterpret, misconstrue, misconceive, mistake, misread; be mistaken, get the wrong idea; *informal* be barking up the wrong tree, get (hold of) the wrong end of the stick.

misunderstanding ▸ noun 1 *a fundamental misunderstanding of juvenile crime* =misinterpretation, misreading, misapprehension, misconception, false impression. 2 *we have had some misunderstandings* =disagreement, difference (of opinion), dispute, falling-out, quarrel, argument, altercation, wrangle, row, clash; *informal* spat, scrap, tiff.

misuse ▸ verb 1 *misusing public funds* =embezzle, misappropriate, abuse; waste, squander. 2 *she had been misused by her husband* =ill-treat, maltreat, mistreat, abuse, knock about/around, hit, beat, molest, injure, harm, hurt; manhandle; *informal* beat up, rough up.
▸ noun *a misuse of company assets* =embezzlement, fraud; squandering, waste.

mitigate ▸ verb =alleviate, reduce, diminish, lessen, weaken, lighten, attenuate, take the edge off, allay, ease, assuage, palliate, relieve, tone down.
–OPPOSITES aggravate.

mitigating ▸ adjective =extenuating, justifying, vindicating, qualifying; *formal* exculpatory.

mitigation ▸ noun 1 *the mitigation of the problems* =alleviation, reduction, diminution, lessening, easing, weakening, assuagement, relief. 2 *what did she say in mitigation?* =extenuation, explanation, excuse; justification.

mix ▶ verb **1** *mix all the ingredients together*
=**blend**, mingle, combine, put together,
jumble; beat, fold, whisk, stir, toss; fuse,
unite, join, amalgamate, incorporate,
meld, marry, coalesce, homogenize,
intermingle, intermix; *technical* admix;
literary commingle. **2** *she mixes with all
sorts* =**associate**, socialize, fraternize,
keep company, consort; mingle, circulate; *Brit.* rub shoulders; *N. Amer.* rub elbows; *informal* hang out/around, knock
about/around, hobnob; *Brit. informal* hang
about.
−OPPOSITES separate.
▶ noun *a mix of ancient and modern* =**mixture**, blend, combination, compound,
fusion, alloy, union, amalgamation, hybrid; medley, melange, collection, selection, assortment, variety, mixed bag,
miscellany, pot-pourri, jumble, hotchpotch, ragbag, patchwork; *N. Amer.*
hodgepodge.
■ **mixed up in** =**involved in**, embroiled
in, caught up in, entangled in.

mixed ▶ adjective **1** *a mixed collection* =**assorted**, varied, variegated, miscellan-
eous, disparate, diverse, diversified,
motley, sundry, jumbled, heterogeneous. **2** *mixed reactions* =**ambivalent**,
equivocal, contradictory, conflicting,
confused, muddled.
−OPPOSITES homogeneous.

mixed up ▶ adjective *(informal)* =**confused**, (all) at sea, befuddled, bemused,
bewildered, muddled; maladjusted, disturbed, neurotic, unbalanced; *informal*
hung up, messed up.

mixer ▶ noun **1** *a kitchen mixer* =**blender**,
food processor, liquidizer, beater. **2** *she
was never really a mixer* =**socializer**, extrovert, socialite.

mixture ▶ noun **1** *the pudding mixture*
=**blend**, mix, brew, combination, concoction; composition, compound, alloy,
amalgam. **2** *a strange mixture of people*
=**assortment**, miscellany, medley,
melange, blend, variety, mixed bag,
mix, diversity, collection, selection, pot-
pourri, mishmash, hotchpotch, ragbag,
patchwork; *N. Amer.* hodgepodge. **3** *the
animal was a mixture of breeds* =**cross**,
cross-breed, mongrel, hybrid.

mix-up ▶ noun =**confusion**, muddle,
misunderstanding, mistake, error.

moan ▶ noun **1** *moans of pain* =**groan**,
wail, whimper, sob, cry. **2** *(informal) there
were moans about the delay* =**complaint**,
grouse, grumble, whine, carping; *informal*
gripe, bellyache, bitch, whingeing, beef.
▶ verb **1** *he moaned in agony* =**groan**, wail,
whimper, sob, cry. **2** *(informal) you're always moaning about the weather* =**complain**, grouse, grumble, whine, carp; *informal* gripe, grouch, bellyache, bitch,
beef, whinge; *N. English informal* mither.

mob ▶ noun **1** *troops dispersed the mob*
=**crowd**, horde, multitude, rabble,
mass, throng, gathering, assembly. **2** *the
mob were excluded from political life* =**the
common people**, the masses, the rank
and file, the proletariat; the hoi polloi,
the lower classes, the rabble, the riff-
raff, the great unwashed; *informal* the
proles, the plebs.
▶ verb **1** *the Chancellor was mobbed when he
visited Berlin* =**surround**, besiege, jostle;
heckle. **2** *reporters mobbed her hotel*
=**crowd (into)**, fill, pack, throng; invade,
occupy, besiege.

WORD LINKS
fear of mobs: **demophobia, ochlophobia**

mobile ▶ adjective **1** *both patients are mobile* =**able to move (around)**, able to
walk, walking; *informal* up and about;
Medicine ambulant. **2** *her mobile face*
=**expressive**, animated. **3** *a mobile library*
=**travelling**, transportable, portable,
movable; itinerant, peripatetic. **4** *mobile young people* =**able to travel**, car-
owning; flexible, independent.
−OPPOSITES motionless, static.

mobility ▶ noun **1** *the mobility of Billy's
face* =**expressiveness**, animation. **2** *mobility in the workforce* =**adaptability**, flexibility, versatility.

mobilize ▶ verb **1** *the government mobil-
ized the troops* =**marshal**, deploy, muster,
rally, call up, assemble, mass, organize,
prepare. **2** *mobilizing support for the party*
=**generate**, arouse, awaken, excite, incite, provoke, foment, prompt, stimulate, stir up, galvanize, encourage, inspire, whip up.

mock ▶ verb **1** *the local children mocked
the old people* =**ridicule**, jeer at, sneer at,
deride, scorn, make fun of, laugh at,
scoff at, tease, taunt; *informal* take the
mickey out of; *N. Amer. informal* goof on,
rag on, pull someone's chain; *Austral./NZ
informal* poke mullock at, sling off at.
2 *they mocked the way he speaks* =**parody**,

ape, take off, imitate, mimic; *informal* send up.

▶ adjective *mock leather* =**imitation**, artificial, man-made, simulated, synthetic, ersatz, fake, reproduction, false, counterfeit; *informal* pretend, phoney.
−OPPOSITES genuine.

mockery ▶ noun 1 *the mockery in his voice* =**ridicule**, derision, jeering, sneering, contempt, scorn, scoffing, teasing, taunting, sarcasm. 2 *the trial was a mockery* =**travesty**, charade, farce, parody; joke.

mocking ▶ adjective =**sneering**, derisive, contemptuous, scornful, sardonic, ironic, sarcastic.

mode ▶ noun 1 *an informal mode of policing* =**manner**, way, fashion, means, method, system, style, approach. 2 *the camera is in manual mode* =**function**, position, operation, setting; option. 3 *the mode for active wear* =**fashion**, vogue, style, look, trend; craze, rage, fad.

model ▶ noun 1 *a working model* =**replica**, copy, representation, mock-up, dummy, imitation, duplicate, reproduction, facsimile. 2 *the American model of airline deregulation* =**prototype**, archetype, type, version; mould, template, framework, pattern, design, blueprint. 3 *she was a model as a teacher* =**ideal**, paragon, perfect example/specimen, exemplar; perfection, acme, epitome. 4 *a top model* =**fashion model**, supermodel, mannequin; *informal* clothes horse. 5 *the latest model of car* =**version**, type, design, variety, kind, sort.

▶ adjective 1 *model trains* =**replica**, toy, miniature, dummy, imitation, duplicate, reproduction, facsimile. 2 *a model teacher* =**ideal**, perfect, exemplary, classic; flawless, faultless.

moderate ▶ adjective 1 *moderate success* =**average**, modest, medium, middling, tolerable, passable, adequate, fair; indifferent, unexceptional, unremarkable; *informal* OK, so-so, bog-standard, fair-to-middling. 2 *moderate prices* =**reasonable**, acceptable; inexpensive, fair, modest. 3 *moderate views* =**middle-of-the-road**, non-extremist; liberal, pragmatic.
−OPPOSITES great, unreasonable, extreme.

▶ verb 1 *the wind has moderated* =**die down**, abate, let up, calm down, lessen, decrease, diminish; recede, weaken, subside. 2 *you can help her moderate her temper* =**curb**, control, check, temper, restrain,

subdue; repress, tame, lessen, decrease, lower, reduce, diminish, alleviate, allay, appease, assuage, ease, soothe, calm, tone down.
−OPPOSITES increase.

moderately ▶ adverb =**somewhat**, quite, fairly, reasonably, comparatively, relatively, to some extent; tolerably, passably, adequately; *informal* pretty.

moderation ▶ noun 1 *he urged them to show moderation* =**self-restraint**, restraint, self-control, self-discipline; temperance, leniency. 2 *a moderation of their confrontational style* =**relaxation**, easing (off), reduction, abatement, weakening, slackening, tempering, softening, diminution, lessening; modulation, modification; *informal* let-up.

modern ▶ adjective 1 *modern times* =**present-day**, contemporary, present, current, twenty-first-century, latter-day, recent. 2 *her clothes are very modern* =**fashionable**, up to date, trendsetting, stylish, voguish, modish, chic, à la mode; the latest, new, newest, newfangled, modernistic, advanced; *informal* trendy, cool, in, with it, now, hip, happening.
−OPPOSITES past, old-fashioned.

modernity ▶ noun =**contemporaneity**, modernness; *informal* trendiness, hipness.

modernize ▶ verb 1 *they are modernizing their manufacturing facilities* =**update**, bring up to date, streamline, rationalize, overhaul; renovate, remodel, refashion, revamp. 2 *we must modernize to survive* =**get up to date**, move with the times, innovate, adapt; *informal* get in the swim, get with it.

modest ▶ adjective 1 *she was modest about her poetry* =**self-effacing**, self-deprecating, humble, unassuming; shy, diffident, reserved, reticent, coy. 2 *modest success* =**moderate**, fair, limited, tolerable, passable, adequate, satisfactory, acceptable, unexceptional. 3 *a modest house* =**small**, ordinary, simple, plain, humble, inexpensive, unostentatious, unpretentious. 4 *her modest dress* =**decorous**, decent, seemly, demure, proper; appropriate, sensitive, sensible.
−OPPOSITES conceited, great, grand.

modesty ▶ noun 1 *Hannah's modesty cloaks many talents* =**self-effacement**, humility; shyness, bashfulness, self-consciousness, reserve, reticence, timidity. 2 *the modesty of his home* =**unpretentiousness**, simplicity, plainness, ordinariness.

modicum ▸ noun =**small amount**, particle, speck, fragment, scrap, crumb, grain, morsel, shred, dash, drop, pinch, jot, iota, whit, atom, smattering, scintilla, hint; *informal* smidgen, tad.

modification ▸ noun **1** *the design is undergoing modification* =**alteration**, adjustment, change, adaptation, refinement, revision. **2** *some minor modifications were made* =**revision**, refinement, improvement, amendment, adaptation, adjustment, change, alteration.

modify ▸ verb **1** *their economic policy has been modified* =**alter**, change, adjust, adapt, amend, revise, reshape, refashion, restyle, revamp, rework, remodel, refine; *informal* tweak. **2** *he modified his more extreme views* =**moderate**, revise, temper, soften, tone down, qualify.

modish ▸ adjective =**fashionable**, stylish, chic, modern, contemporary, voguish, up to the minute, à la mode; *informal* trendy, cool, with it, in, now, hip, happening; *N. Amer. informal* kicky.

modulate ▸ verb **1** *the cells modulate the body's response* =**regulate**, adjust, set, modify, moderate. **2** *she modulated her voice* =**adjust**, change the tone of; alter, lower.

modus operandi ▸ noun =**method** (of working), way, manner, technique, style, approach, methodology, strategy, plan, formula; *formal* praxis.

mogul ▸ noun =**magnate**, tycoon, VIP, notable, personage, baron, captain, king, lord, grandee; *informal* bigwig, big shot, big noise, top dog; *N. Amer. informal* top banana, big enchilada.

moist ▸ adjective **1** *the air was moist* =**damp**, steamy, humid, muggy, clammy, dank, wet, soggy, sweaty, sticky. **2** *a moist fruitcake* =**succulent**, juicy; soft, tender.
 −OPPOSITES dry.

moisten ▸ verb =**dampen**, wet, damp, water, humidify.

moisture ▸ noun =**wetness**, wet, water, liquid, condensation, steam, vapour, dampness, damp, humidity, clamminess, mugginess, dankness.

WORD LINKS

related prefix: hygro-*instrument for measuring moisture in the air:* **hygrometer, hygroscope**

moisturizer ▸ noun =**lotion**, cream,

balm, emollient, salve, unguent, lubricant; *technical* humectant.

mole¹ ▸ noun *the mole on his left cheek* =**mark**, freckle, blotch, spot, blemish.

mole² ▸ noun **1** *moles have burrowed under the lawn* =*dialect* mouldwarp, mouldywarp. **2** *a well-placed mole* =**spy**, (secret) agent, undercover agent, operative, plant, infiltrator; *N. Amer. informal* spook.

WORD LINKS

collective noun: **labour**

molest ▸ verb **1** *stop molesting him, you big bully!* =**harass**, harry, pester, persecute, torment; *N. Amer. informal* roust. **2** *he molested a ten-year-old boy* =**(sexually) abuse**, (sexually) assault, interfere with, rape, violate; *informal* grope, paw, touch up; *literary* ravish.

mollify ▸ verb **1** *they mollified the protesters* =**appease**, placate, pacify, soothe, calm (down). **2** *mollifying the fears of the public* =**allay**, assuage, alleviate, mitigate, ease, reduce.
 −OPPOSITES enrage.

mollycoddle ▸ verb *his parents mollycoddle him* =**pamper**, cosset, coddle, spoil, indulge, overindulge, pet, baby, nanny, wait on hand and foot, wrap in cotton wool.

molten ▸ adjective =**liquefied**, liquid, fluid, melted, flowing.

moment ▸ noun **1** *he thought for a moment* =**little while**, short time, bit, minute, instant, (split) second; *informal* sec, jiffy; *Brit. informal* tick, mo, two ticks. **2** *the moment they met* =**point (in time)**, time, hour; instant, second, minute, day.
 ■ **in a moment** =**very soon**, in a minute, in a second, in a trice, shortly, any minute (now), in the twinkling of an eye, in (less than) no time, in no time at all; *N. Amer.* momentarily; *informal* in a jiffy, in two shakes (of a lamb's tail), before you can say Jack Robinson, in the blink of an eye; *Brit. informal* in a tick, in two ticks, in a mo; *N. Amer. informal* in a snap; *literary* ere long.

momentarily ▸ adverb **1** *he paused momentarily* =**briefly**, fleetingly, for a moment, for a second, for an instant. **2** *(N. Amer.) my husband will be here momentarily*. *See* IN A MOMENT.

momentary ▸ adjective =**brief**, short, short-lived, fleeting, passing, transient, ephemeral; *literary* evanescent.

–OPPOSITES lengthy.

momentous ▸ adjective =important, significant, historic, portentous, critical, crucial, life-and-death, decisive, pivotal, consequential, of consequence, far-reaching; informal earth-shattering.
–OPPOSITES insignificant.

momentum ▸ noun =impetus, energy, force, power, strength, thrust, speed, velocity.

monarch ▸ noun =sovereign, ruler, Crown, crowned head, potentate; king, queen, emperor, empress.

monastery ▸ noun =friary, abbey, priory.

monastic ▸ adjective a monastic existence =austere, ascetic, simple, solitary, monkish, celibate, quiet, cloistered, sequestered, secluded, reclusive, hermit-like.

monetary ▸ adjective =financial, fiscal, pecuniary, money, cash, economic, budgetary.

money ▸ noun **1** I haven't got enough money =(hard) cash, ready money; the means, the wherewithal, funds, capital, finances, (filthy) lucre; banknotes, notes, coins, change, currency; Brit. sterling; N. Amer. bills; N. Amer. & Austral. roll; informal dough, bread, loot, shekels, moolah, the necessary; Brit. informal dosh, brass, lolly, readies, spondulicks; N. Amer. informal dinero, bucks, mazuma; US informal greenbacks, simoleons, jack, rocks; Austral./NZ informal Oscar. **2** she married him for his money =wealth, riches, fortune, affluence, (liquid) assets, resources, means. **3** the money here is better =pay, salary, wages, remuneration.
■ in the money (informal) =rich, wealthy, affluent, well-to-do, well off, prosperous, moneyed, in clover, opulent; informal rolling in it, loaded, stinking rich, well heeled, made of money.

WORD LINKS

relating to money: **pecuniary, monetary**
collector of notes and coins: **numismatist**
fear of money: **chrematophobia**

moneyed ▸ adjective =rich, wealthy, affluent, well-to-do, well off, prosperous, opulent, of means, of substance; informal rolling in it, loaded, stinking/filthy rich, well heeled, made of money.
–OPPOSITES poor.

money-grubbing ▸ adjective (informal) =acquisitive, avaricious, grasping, money-grubbing, rapacious, mercenary, materialistic; N. Amer. informal grabby.

moneymaking ▸ adjective =profitable, profit-making, remunerative, lucrative, successful, financially rewarding.
–OPPOSITES loss-making.

mongrel ▸ noun =cross-breed, cross, mixed breed, half-breed; tyke, cur, mutt; NZ kuri; Austral. informal mong, bitzer.

monitor ▸ noun **1** monitors covered all entrances =detector, scanner, recorder, sensor, (security) camera, CCTV. **2** UN monitors =observer, watchdog, overseer, supervisor; scrutineer. **3** a computer monitor =screen, display, VDU.
▸ verb his movements were closely monitored =observe, watch, track, keep an eye on, keep under surveillance, record, note, oversee; informal keep tabs on.

monkey ▸ noun =simian, primate, ape.
■ monkey with =tamper with, fiddle with, interfere with, meddle with, tinker with, play with; informal mess with; Brit. informal muck about/around with.

WORD LINKS

relating to monkeys: **simian**
collective noun: **troop**
study of monkeys: **primatology**

monolith ▸ noun =standing stone, menhir, megalith.

monolithic ▸ adjective **1** a monolithic building =massive, huge, vast, colossal, gigantic, immense, giant, enormous; featureless, characterless. **2** the old monolithic Communist party =inflexible, rigid, unbending, unchanging, fossilized; faceless, impersonal.

monologue ▸ noun =soliloquy; speech, address, lecture, sermon; formal oration.

monopolize ▸ verb **1** the company has monopolized the market =corner, control, take over, dominate, gain a stranglehold over, gain control/dominance over. **2** he monopolized the conversation =dominate, take over; informal hog.

monotonous ▸ adjective **1** a monotonous job =tedious, boring, dull, uninteresting, unexciting, repetitive, repetitious, unvarying, unchanging, humdrum, routine, mechanical, mind-numbing, soul-destroying; colourless,

featureless, dreary; *informal* deadly; *Brit. informal* samey; *N. Amer. informal* dullsville. **2** *a monotonous voice* = **toneless**, flat, featureless, soporific; robotic, mechanical.
−OPPOSITES interesting.

monotony ▸ noun **1** *the monotony of everyday life* = **tedium**, tediousness, dullness, boredom, repetitiveness, uniformity, routineness; uneventfulness, dreariness, colourlessness, featurelessness. **2** *the monotony of her voice* = **tonelessness**, flatness.

monster ▸ noun **1** *legendary sea monsters* = **creature**, beast, being; giant, demon, dragon. **2** *her husband is a monster* = **animal**, fiend, beast, devil, demon, barbarian, savage, brute; *informal* swine, pig, psycho. **3** *the boy's little monster* = **horror**, imp, monkey, wretch, devil, rascal; *informal* scamp, scallywag, tyke; *Brit. informal* perisher; *N. Amer. informal* varmint, hellion; *archaic* rapscallion. **4** *he's a monster of a man* = **giant**, mammoth, colossus, leviathan, titan.

monstrosity ▸ noun = **eyesore**, blot on the landscape, carbuncle, excrescence.

monstrous ▸ adjective **1** *a monstrous creature* = **grotesque**, hideous, ugly, ghastly, gruesome, horrible, horrific, horrifying, grisly, disgusting, repulsive, dreadful, frightening, terrible, terrifying. **2** *a monstrous tidal wave.* See HUGE. **3** *monstrous acts of violence* = **appalling**, wicked, abominable, terrible, horrible, dreadful, vile, outrageous, shocking, disgraceful; unspeakable, despicable, vicious, savage, barbaric, barbarous, inhuman; *Brit. informal* beastly.
−OPPOSITES lovely, small.

monument ▸ noun **1** *a stone monument* = **memorial**, statue, pillar, column, obelisk, cross; cenotaph, tomb, mausoleum, shrine. **2** *a monument was placed over the grave* = **gravestone**, headstone, tombstone. **3** *a monument to a past era* = **testament**, record, reminder, remembrance, memorial, commemoration.

monumental ▸ adjective **1** *a monumental task* = **huge**, enormous, gigantic, massive, colossal, mammoth, immense, tremendous, mighty, stupendous. **2** *a monumental error of judgement* = **terrible**, dreadful, awful, colossal, staggering, huge, enormous, unforgivable. **3** *monumental works of art* = **vast**, huge, majestic, grand, awe-inspiring, heroic, epic.

mood ▸ noun **1** *she's in a good mood* = **frame/state of mind**, humour, temper; disposition, spirit. **2** *he's obviously in a mood* = **bad mood**, (bad) temper, sulk; low spirits, the doldrums, the blues; *Brit. informal* paddy. **3** *the mood of the film* = **atmosphere**, feeling, spirit, ambience, aura, character, tenor, flavour, feel, tone.
■ **in the mood** = **in the right frame of mind**, feeling like, wanting to, inclined to, disposed to, minded to, eager to, willing to.

moody ▸ adjective = **temperamental**, emotional, volatile, capricious, changeable, mercurial; sullen, sulky, morose, glum, miserable, dejected, despondent, doleful.
−OPPOSITES cheerful.

moon ▸ noun = **satellite**.
▸ verb **1** *stop mooning about* = **waste time**, loaf, idle, mope; *Brit. informal* mooch; *N. Amer. informal* lollygag. **2** *he's mooning over her photograph* = **mope**, pine, brood, daydream.

WORD LINKS

relating to the moon: **lunar**
scientific study of the moon: **selenology**

---

moonshine ▸ noun. See RUBBISH noun sense 2.

moor[1] ▸ verb *a boat was moored to the quay* = **tie (up)**, secure, make fast, fix, berth, dock.

moor[2] ▸ noun *a walk on the moor* = **upland**, heath, moorland; *Brit.* fell, wold.

moot ▸ adjective *a moot point* = **debatable**, open to discussion/question, arguable, questionable, open to doubt, disputable, contentious, disputed, unresolved, unsettled, up in the air.
▸ verb *the idea was first mooted in the 1930s* = **raise**, bring up, broach, mention, put forward, introduce, advance, propose, suggest.

mop ▸ noun *her tousled mop of hair* = **shock**, mane, tangle, mass.
▸ verb *a man was mopping the floor* = **wash**, clean, wipe.
■ **mop something up 1** *I mopped up the spilt coffee* = **wipe up**, clean up, sponge up. **2** *troops mopped up the last pockets of resistance* = **finish off**, deal with, dispose of, take care of, clear up, eliminate.

mope ▸ verb **1** *it's no use moping* = **brood**, sulk, be miserable, be despondent, pine, eat one's heart out, fret, grieve; *informal* be down in the dumps/mouth. **2** *she was moping about the house* =**languish**, moon, loaf; *Brit. informal* mooch; *N. Amer. informal* lollygag.

moral ▶ adjective **1** *moral issues* =**ethical**. **2** *a very moral man* =**virtuous**, good, righteous, upright, upstanding, high-minded, principled, honourable, honest, just, noble, respectable, decent, clean-living, law-abiding. **3** *moral support* =**psychological**, emotional, mental.
−OPPOSITES dishonourable.
▶ noun **1** *the moral of the story* =**lesson**, message, meaning, significance, import, point, teaching. **2** *he has no morals* =**moral code**, code of ethics, values, principles, standards, (sense of) morality, scruples.

morale ▶ noun =**confidence**, self-confidence, self-esteem, spirit(s), team spirit; motivation.

moral fibre ▶ noun =**strength of character**, fibre, fortitude, resolve, backbone, spine, mettle.

morality ▶ noun **1** *the morality of nuclear weapons* =**ethics**, rights and wrongs; whys and wherefores; *informal* ins and outs. **2** *a sharp decline in morality* =**virtue**, goodness, good behaviour, righteousness, uprightness; morals, principles, honesty, integrity, propriety, honour, justice, decency. **3** *Christian morality* =**morals**, standards, ethics, principles; mores.

moralize ▶ verb =**pontificate**, sermonize, lecture, preach.

morass ▶ noun =**confusion**, chaos, muddle, tangle, entanglement; quagmire.

moratorium ▶ noun =**embargo**, ban, prohibition, suspension, postponement, stay, halt, freeze, respite; hiatus.

morbid ▶ adjective **1** *a morbid fascination with contemporary warfare* =**ghoulish**, macabre, unhealthy, gruesome, unwholesome; *informal* sick. **2** *I felt decidedly morbid* =**gloomy**, glum, melancholy, morose, dismal, sombre, despondent, dejected, depressed, downcast, down, disconsolate, miserable, unhappy, downhearted, dispirited, low; *informal* blue, down in the dumps/mouth.
−OPPOSITES wholesome, cheerful.

mordant ▶ adjective =**caustic**, trenchant, biting, cutting, acerbic, sardonic, sarcastic, scathing, acid, sharp, keen;

critical, bitter, virulent, vitriolic.

more ▶ determiner *I could do with some more clothes* =**additional**, further, added, extra, increased, new, other, supplementary.
−OPPOSITES less, fewer.
■ **more or less** =**approximately**, roughly, nearly, almost, close to, about, of the order of, in the region of.

moreover ▶ adverb =**besides**, furthermore, what's more, in addition, also, as well, too, to boot, additionally, on top of that, into the bargain; *archaic* withal.

mores ▶ plural noun =**customs**, conventions, ways, traditions, practices, habits.

moribund ▶ adjective **1** *the patient was moribund* =**dying**, expiring, on one's deathbed, near death, at death's door, not long for this world. **2** *the moribund shipbuilding industry* =**declining**, in decline, waning, dying, stagnating, stagnant, crumbling, on its last legs.
−OPPOSITES thriving.

morning ▶ noun **1** *I've got a meeting this morning* =**before lunch(time)**, a.m.; *literary* morn; *Nautical & N. Amer.* forenoon. **2** *morning is on its way* =**dawn**, daybreak, sunrise, first light; *N. Amer.* sunup; *literary* cockcrow.

> WORD LINKS
>
> *relating to the morning:* **matutinal, antemeridian**

morose ▶ adjective =**sullen**, sulky, gloomy, bad-tempered, ill-tempered, surly, sour, glum, moody, ill-humoured, grumpy, irritable, cantankerous, crotchety, crabby, grouchy, testy, snappish, peevish, crusty.
−OPPOSITES cheerful.

morsel ▶ noun =**mouthful**, bite, nibble, bit, taste, spoonful, forkful, sliver, drop, dollop, spot, gobbet; titbit; *informal* smidgen.

mortal ▶ adjective **1** *mortal remains* | *all men are mortal* =**perishable**, physical, bodily, corporeal, fleshly, earthly; human, impermanent, transient, ephemeral. **2** *a mortal blow* =**deadly**, fatal, lethal, death-dealing, murderous, terminal. **3** *mortal enemies* =**irreconcilable**, deadly, sworn, bitter, out-and-out, implacable. **4** *living in mortal fear* =**extreme**, (very) great, terrible, awful, dreadful, intense, severe, dire, unbearable.
−OPPOSITES venial.

▶ noun *we are mere mortals* =**human (being)**, person, man/woman; earthling.

mortality ▶ noun **1** *a sense of his own mortality* =**impermanence**, transience, ephemerality, perishability; humanity; corporeality. **2** *the causes of mortality* =**death**, loss of life, dying.

mortification ▶ noun =**embarrassment**, humiliation, chagrin, discomfiture, discomposure, shame.

mortify ▶ verb **1** *I'd be mortified if my friends found out* =**embarrass**, humiliate, chagrin, discomfit, shame, abash, horrify, appal. **2** *he was mortified at being excluded* =**hurt**, wound, affront, offend, put out, pique, irk, annoy, vex; *informal* rile.

mortuary ▶ noun =**morgue**, funeral parlour; *Brit.* chapel of rest.

most ▶ pronoun *most of the guests brought flowers* =**nearly all**, almost all, the greatest part/number, the majority, the bulk, the preponderance.
–OPPOSITES little, few.
■ **for the most part** =**mostly**, mainly, in the main, on the whole, largely, by and large, to a large extent, predominantly, chiefly, principally, generally, usually, typically, commonly, as a rule.

mostly ▶ adverb **1** *the other passengers were mostly businessmen* =**mainly**, for the most part, on the whole, in the main, largely, chiefly, predominantly, principally, primarily. **2** *I mostly wear jeans* =**usually**, generally, in general, as a rule, ordinarily, normally, customarily, typically, most of the time, almost always.

moth-eaten ▶ adjective =**threadbare**, worn (out), old, ancient, shabby, scruffy, tattered, ragged; *informal* tatty, ratty, the worse for wear; *N. Amer. informal* raggedy.

mother ▶ noun *I will ask my mother* =*informal* ma, mam, mammy; *Brit. informal* mum, mummy; *N. Amer. informal* mom, mommy; matriarch; *Brit. informal, dated* mater.
–OPPOSITES child, father.
▶ verb =**look after**, care for, take care of, nurse, protect, tend, raise, rear; pamper, coddle, cosset, fuss over.
–OPPOSITES neglect.

> WORD LINKS
>
> *relating to a mother:* **maternal, matrikilling of one's mother:* **matricide**

motherly ▶ adjective =**maternal**, maternalistic, protective, caring, loving, nurturing.

motif ▶ noun **1** *a colourful tulip motif* =**design**, pattern, decoration, figure, shape, device, emblem. **2** *a recurring motif in Pinter's work* =**theme**, idea, concept, subject, topic, leitmotif.

motion ▶ noun **1** *the rocking motion of the boat | a planet's motion around the sun* =**movement**, moving, locomotion, rise and fall, shifting; progress, passage, transit, course, travel; orbit. **2** *a motion of the hand* =**gesture**, movement, signal, sign, indication; wave, nod, gesticulation. **3** *the motion failed to obtain a majority* =**proposal**, proposition, recommendation.
▶ verb *he motioned her to sit down* =**gesture**, signal, direct, indicate; wave, beckon, nod.
■ **in motion** =**moving**, on the move, going, travelling, running, functioning, operational.
■ **set in motion** =**start**, commence, begin, activate, initiate, launch, get under way, get going, get off the ground; trigger off, set off, spark off, generate, cause.

> WORD LINKS
>
> *relating to motion:* **kinetic**
> *fear of motion:* **kinetophobia**

motionless ▶ adjective =**unmoving**, still, stationary, stock-still, immobile, static, not moving a muscle, rooted to the spot, transfixed, paralysed, frozen, petrified.
–OPPOSITES moving.

motivate ▶ verb **1** *motivated by greed* =**prompt**, drive, move, inspire, stimulate, influence, activate, impel, propel, spur (on). **2** *it's the teacher's job to motivate the child* =**inspire**, stimulate, encourage, spur (on), excite, incentivize, fire (with enthusiasm).

motivation ▶ noun **1** *his motivation was financial* =**motive**, motivating force, incentive, stimulus, stimulation, inspiration, inducement, incitement, spur. **2** *staff motivation* =**enthusiasm**, drive, determination, commitment, enterprise; *informal* get-up-and-go.

motive ▶ noun =**reason**, motivation, motivating force, rationale, grounds, cause, basis.
▶ adjective *motive force* =**kinetic**, driving,

propulsive, dynamic.

motley ▶ adjective = **miscellaneous**, disparate, diverse, assorted, varied, heterogeneous.
–OPPOSITES homogeneous.

mottled ▶ adjective = **blotchy**, blotched, streaked, streaky, marbled, dappled; informal splotchy.

motto ▶ noun = **maxim**, saying, proverb, aphorism, adage, saw, axiom, formula, expression, phrase, dictum, precept; slogan, catchphrase.

mould ▶ noun 1 the molten metal is poured into a mould = **cast**, die, form, matrix, shape, template, pattern, frame. 2 an actress in the traditional Hollywood mould = **pattern**, form, type, style, tradition, school.
▶ verb 1 a figure moulded from clay = **shape**, form, fashion, model, work, construct, make, create, sculpt, cast. 2 the ideas that are moulding US policy = **determine**, direct, control, guide, influence, shape, form, fashion, make.

moulder ▶ verb = **decay**, decompose, rot (away), go mouldy, go off, go bad, spoil, putrefy.

mouldy ▶ adjective = **mildewed**, mildewy, musty, mouldering, fusty; decaying, decayed, rotting, rotten, bad, spoiled, decomposing.

mound ▶ noun 1 a mound of books = **heap**, pile, stack, mountain. 2 high on the mound = **hillock**, hill, knoll, rise, hummock, hump; Scottish brae; Geology drumlin.

mount ▶ verb 1 he mounted the stairs = **go up**, ascend, climb (up), scale. 2 they mounted their horses = **get on to**, bestride, climb on to, leap on to, hop on to. 3 the museum is mounting an exhibition = **put on**, present, install; organize, stage, set up. 4 the company mounted a takeover bid = **organize**, stage, prepare, arrange; launch, set in motion, initiate. 5 their losses mounted rapidly = **increase**, grow, rise, escalate, soar, spiral, shoot up, rocket, climb, accumulate, build up, multiply. 6 cameras were mounted above the door = **install**, place, fix, set, put, position.
–OPPOSITES descend.
▶ noun = **setting**, backing, support, mounting, frame, stand.

mountain ▶ noun 1 climb a mountain = **peak**, summit; (**mountains**) range, massif, sierra; Scottish ben, Munro. 2 a mountain of work = **a lot**; informal heap, pile, stack, slew, lots, loads, tons, masses. 3 a butter mountain = **surplus**, surfeit, glut.

WORD LINKS

relating to mountains: **orographic, oro-**

mountainous ▶ adjective 1 a mountainous region = **hilly**, craggy, rocky, alpine. 2 mountainous waves = **huge**, enormous, gigantic, massive, giant, colossal, immense, tremendous, mighty; informal whopping, thumping, humongous; Brit. informal whacking, ginormous.
–OPPOSITES flat, tiny.

mourn ▶ verb 1 Isobel mourned her husband = **grieve for**, sorrow over, lament for, weep for. 2 he mourned the loss of the beautiful buildings = **deplore**, bewail, bemoan, rue, regret.

mournful ▶ adjective = **sad**, sorrowful, doleful, melancholy, woeful, griefstricken, miserable, heartbroken, broken-hearted, gloomy, dismal, desolate, dejected, despondent, depressed, downcast, disconsolate, woebegone, forlorn, rueful.
–OPPOSITES cheerful.

mourning ▶ noun = **grief**, grieving, sorrowing, lamentation.

mouse ▶ noun

WORD LINKS

relating to mice: **murine**
fear of mice: **musophobia**

mousy ▶ adjective a small, mousy woman = **timid**, quiet, timorous, shy, selfeffacing, diffident.

mouth ▶ noun 1 open your mouth = **lips**, jaws; muzzle; informal trap, chops, kisser; Brit. informal gob, cakehole; N. Amer. informal pie-hole, puss, bazoo. 2 the mouth of the cave = **entrance**, opening. 3 the mouth of the river outlet; estuary, delta, firth. 4 (informal) he's all mouth = **talk**, threats, promises, bluster; informal hot air. 5 (informal) less of your mouth = **impudence**, cheek, insolence, impertinence, effrontery, presumption, presumptuousness, rudeness, disrespect; informal lip, (brass) neck; Brit. informal sauce, backchat; N. Amer. informal sass, sassiness, back talk.
▶ verb he mouthed platitudes = **utter**, speak; pronounce, enunciate, articulate, voice, express; churn out.

WORD LINKS

relating to the mouth: **oral, buccal**
scientific study of the mouth:
  stomatology

---

mouthful ▸ noun **1** *a mouthful of pizza*
=**bite**, nibble, taste, bit, piece; spoonful,
forkful. **2** *a mouthful of beer* =**draught**,
sip, swallow, drop, gulp, slug; *informal*
swig.

mouthpiece ▸ noun =**spokesperson**,
spokesman, spokeswoman, agent, representative, propagandist, voice; *informal*
spin doctor.

movable ▸ adjective =**portable**, transportable, transferable; mobile.
−OPPOSITES fixed.

move ▸ verb **1** *she moved to the door* | *don't
move!* =**go**, walk, step, proceed, progress, advance, jump; shrink; budge,
stir, shift, change position. **2** *he moved
the chair closer to the fire* =**carry**, transfer,
shift, push, pull, lift, slide. **3** *things were
moving too fast* =**go**, progress, advance,
develop, evolve, change, happen. **4** *he
urged the council to move quickly* =**act**, take
steps, do something, take measures; *informal* get moving. **5** *she's moved to Cam-
bridge* =**relocate**, move house, move
away/out, change address, leave, go
(away), decamp; *Brit. informal* up sticks; *N.
Amer. informal* pull up stakes. **6** *I was deeply
moved by the story* =**affect**, touch, impress, shake, upset, disturb. **7** *she was
moved to find out more about it* =**inspire**,
prompt, stimulate, motivate, provoke,
influence, rouse, induce, incite. **8** *they
are not prepared to move on this issue*
=**change**, budge, shift one's ground,
change one's mind, have second
thoughts; do a U-turn, do an about-face;
Brit. do an about-turn. **9** *she moves in rarefied circles* =**circulate**, mix, socialize,
keep company, associate; *informal* hang
out/around; *Brit. informal* hang about. **10** *I
move that we adjourn* =**propose**, submit,
suggest, advocate, recommend, urge.
▸ noun **1** *his eyes followed her every move*
=**movement**, motion, action; gesture.
2 *his recent move to London* =**relocation**,
change of house/address, transfer, posting. **3** *the latest move in the war against
drugs* =**initiative**, step, action, measure,
manoeuvre, tactic, stratagem. **4** *it's your
move* =**turn**, go; *Scottish* shot.
■ **get a move on** (*informal*) =**hurry up**,
speed up; *informal* get cracking, get moving, step on it, shake a leg; *Brit. informal* get

one's skates on, stir one's stumps; *N.
Amer. informal* get a wiggle on; *dated* make
haste.
■ **make a move 1** *waiting for the other
side to make a move* =**do something**, act,
take the initiative; *informal* get moving.
2 (*Brit.*) *I'd better be making a move* =**leave**,
take one's leave, be on one's way, get
going, depart, be off; *informal* push off,
shove off, split.

movement ▸ noun **1** *Rachel made a sud-
den movement* | *there was almost no move-
ment* =**motion**, move; gesture, sign, signal; action, activity. **2** *the movement of
supplies* =**transportation**, shifting, conveyance, moving, transfer. **3** *a political
movement* =**group**, party, faction, wing,
lobby, camp; division, sect, cult. **4** *a
movement to declare war on poverty* =**campaign**, crusade, drive, push, initiative.
5 *there have been movements in the financial
markets* =**development**, change, fluctuation, variation. **6** *the movement towards
equality* =**trend**, tendency, drift, swing,
shift; march. **7** *there should be some movement by the end of the month* =**progress**,
development, change, advance,
improvement. **8** *a symphony in three movements* =**part**, section, division; act.

WORD LINKS

relating to movement: **kinetic**
fear of movement: **kinetophobia**

---

movie ▸ noun **1** *a horror movie* =**film**,
picture, feature (film); *informal* flick. **2** *let's
go to the movies* =**the cinema**, the pictures, the silver screen; *informal* the flicks,
the big screen.

moving ▸ adjective **1** *moving parts* | *a
moving train* =**in motion**, operating, operational, working, on the move, active; movable, mobile. **2** *a moving book*
=**affecting**, touching, poignant, heart-
warming, heart-rending, emotional; inspiring, inspirational, stimulating, stirring.
−OPPOSITES fixed, stationary.

mow ▸ verb *she had mown the grass* =**cut**,
trim; crop, clip.
■ **mow someone/something down**
=**kill**, gun down, shoot (down), cut
down, butcher, slaughter, massacre, annihilate, wipe out; *informal* blow away.

much ▸ determiner *is there much food?* =**a
lot of**, a great/good deal of, a great/large
amount of, plenty of, ample, abundant,
plentiful; *informal* lots of, loads of, heaps

of, masses of, tons of, stacks of.
−OPPOSITES little.

▶ **adverb 1** *it didn't hurt much* =**greatly**, a great deal, a lot, considerably, appreciably. **2** *does he come here much?* =**often**, frequently, many times, regularly, habitually, routinely, usually, normally, commonly; *informal* a lot.

▶ **pronoun** *he did much for our team* =**a lot**, a great/good deal, plenty; *informal* lots, loads, heaps, masses, tons.

muck ▶ **noun 1** *I'll just clean off the muck* =**dirt**, grime, filth, mud, slime, mess; *informal* crud, gunk, grunge, gloop; *Brit. informal* gunge, grot; *N. Amer. informal* guck, glop. **2** *spreading muck on the fields* =**dung**, manure, ordure, excrement, excreta, droppings, faeces; *N. Amer. informal* cow chips, horse apples.

■ **muck something up** (*informal*) =**make a mess of**, mess up, bungle, spoil, ruin, wreck; *informal* botch, make a hash of, muff, fluff, foul up, louse up; *Brit. informal* make a pig's ear of, make a Horlicks of; *N. Amer. informal* goof up.

■ **muck about/around** (*Brit. informal*) **1** *he was mucking about with his mates* =**fool about/around**, play about/around, clown about/around; *informal* mess about/around, horse about/around, lark (about/around). **2** *someone's been mucking about with the video* =**interfere**, fiddle (about/around), play about/around, tamper, meddle, tinker; *informal* mess (about/around).

mucky ▶ **adjective** =**dirty**, filthy, grimy, muddy, grubby, messy, soiled, stained, smeared, slimy, sticky; *informal* cruddy, grungy, gloopy; *Brit. informal* gungy, grotty; *Austral./NZ informal* scungy; *literary* besmirched, begrimed, befouled.
−OPPOSITES clean.

mud ▶ **noun** =**mire**, sludge, ooze, silt, clay, dirt, soil.

muddle ▶ **verb 1** *the papers have got muddled up* =**confuse**, mix up, jumble (up), disarrange, disorganize, disorder, mess up. **2** *it would only muddle you* =**bewilder**, confuse, bemuse, perplex, puzzle, baffle, nonplus, mystify.

▶ **noun 1** *the files are in a muddle* =**mess**, confusion, jumble, tangle, hotchpotch, mishmash, chaos, disorder, disarray, disorganization; *N. Amer.* hodgepodge. **2** *a bureaucratic muddle* =**bungle**, mix-up, misunderstanding; *informal* foul-up; *N. Amer. informal* snafu.

■ **muddle along/through** =**cope**, man-

age, get by/along, scrape by/along, make do.

muddled ▶ **adjective 1** *a muddled pile of photographs* =**jumbled**, in a muddle, in a mess, chaotic, in disarray, topsy-turvy, disorganized, disordered, disorderly, mixed up, at sixes and sevens; *informal* higgledy-piggledy. **2** *she felt muddled* =**confused**, bewildered, bemused, perplexed, disoriented, in a muddle; *N. Amer. informal* discombobulated. **3** *muddled thinking* =**incoherent**, confused, muddle-headed, woolly, vague.
−OPPOSITES orderly, clear.

muddy ▶ **adjective 1** *muddy ground* =**waterlogged**, boggy, marshy, swampy, squelchy, squishy, mucky, slimy, spongy, wet, soft. **2** *muddy boots* =**dirty**, filthy, mucky, grimy, soiled. **3** *muddy water* =**murky**, cloudy, turbid; *N. Amer.* riled, roily. **4** *a muddy pink* =**dingy**, dirty, drab, dull, sludgy.
−OPPOSITES clean, clear.

▶ **verb** =**get muddy**, dirty, soil, spatter; *literary* besmirch.

muff ▶ **verb** (*informal*) =**mishandle**, mismanage, mess up, make a mess of, bungle; *informal* botch, make a hash of, fluff, foul up, louse up; *Brit. informal* make a pig's ear of, make a Horlicks of; *N. Amer. informal* goof up.

muffle ▶ **verb 1** *everyone was muffled up in coats* =**wrap (up)**, swathe, enfold, envelop, cloak. **2** *the sound of their footsteps was muffled* =**deaden**, dull, dampen, mute, soften, quieten, mask, stifle, smother.

muffled ▶ **adjective** =**indistinct**, faint, muted, dull, soft, stifled, smothered.
−OPPOSITES loud.

mug[1] ▶ **noun** *a china mug* =**beaker**, cup; tankard, glass, stein, flagon.

▶ **verb** (*informal*) *he was mugged by three youths* =**assault**, attack, set upon, beat up, rob; *informal* jump, rough up, lay into; *Brit. informal* duff up, do over.

mug[2] ■ **mug something up** (*informal*) =**study**, read up, cram; *informal* bone up (on); *Brit. informal* swot.

muggy ▶ **adjective** =**humid**, close, sultry, sticky, oppressive, airless, stifling, suffocating, stuffy, clammy, damp, heavy, fuggy.
−OPPOSITES fresh.

mull ■ **mull something over** =**ponder**, consider, think over/about, reflect on, contemplate, turn over in one's mind, chew over, cogitate on, give some thought to; *archaic* pore on.

multicoloured ▸ adjective =kaleido-scopic, psychedelic, colourful, multi-colour, many-coloured, many-hued, rainbow, jazzy, variegated.
–OPPOSITES monochrome.

multifarious ▸ adjective =diverse, many, numerous, various, varied, mul-tiple, multitudinous, multiplex, mani-fold, multifaceted, different, heteroge-neous, miscellaneous, assorted; *literary* myriad, divers.
–OPPOSITES homogeneous.

multiple ▸ adjective =numerous, many, various, different, diverse, sev-eral, manifold, multifarious, multitudi-nous; *literary* myriad, divers.
–OPPOSITES single.

> WORD LINKS
> *related prefixes:* **multi-, poly-**

multiplicity ▸ noun =abundance, mass, host, array, variety; range, diver-sity, heterogeneity, plurality, profu-sion; *informal* load, stack, heap, ton; *literary* myriad.

multiply ▸ verb =increase, grow, accu-mulate, proliferate, mount up, mush-room, snowball.
–OPPOSITES decrease.

multitude ▸ noun 1 *a multitude of birds* =host, horde, mass, swarm, abundance, profusion; scores, droves; *informal* loads, masses, stacks, heaps, tons, hundreds, thousands, millions; *N. Amer. informal* gazillions. 2 *Father Peter addressed the multitude* =crowd, gathering, assembly, congregation, throng, horde, mob.

multitudinous ▸ adjective =numer-ous, many, abundant, profuse, prolific, copious, multifarious; *literary* divers, myriad.

mumble ▸ verb =mutter, murmur, talk under one's breath.

mumbo-jumbo ▸ noun =nonsense, gibberish, claptrap, rubbish, balder-dash, hocus-pocus; *informal* gobblede-gook, double Dutch.

munch ▸ verb =chew, champ, chomp, masticate, crunch, eat.

mundane ▸ adjective 1 *her mundane life* =humdrum, dull, boring, tedious, mon-otonous, tiresome, unexciting, un-interesting, uneventful, unremarkable, routine, ordinary, everyday, day-to-day,

run-of-the-mill, commonplace, work-aday. 2 *the mundane world* =earthly, worldly, terrestrial, material, temporal, secular; *literary* sublunary.
–OPPOSITES extraordinary, spiritual.

municipal ▸ adjective =civic, civil, metropolitan, urban, city, town, bor-ough.
–OPPOSITES rural.

municipality ▸ noun =borough, town, city, district; *N. Amer.* precinct, township; *Scottish* burgh.

munificence ▸ noun =generosity, bountifulness, open-handedness, mag-nanimity, lavishness, liberality, philan-thropy, largesse, big-heartedness, be-neficence; *literary* bounty.

munificent ▸ adjective =generous, bountiful, open-handed, magnanimous, philanthropic, princely, handsome, lav-ish, liberal, charitable, big-hearted, be-neficent; *literary* bounteous.
–OPPOSITES mean.

murder ▸ noun 1 *a brutal murder* =kil-ling, homicide, assassination, exter-mination, execution, slaughter, butch-ery, massacre; manslaughter; *informal* liquidation; *literary* slaying. 2 *(informal) driving there was murder* =hell (on earth), a nightmare, misery, torture, agony; *informal* the worst, the pits.
▸ verb *someone tried to murder him* =kill, put/do to death, assassinate, execute, eliminate, dispatch, butcher, slaughter, massacre, wipe out; *informal* bump off, do in, do away with, knock off, blow away, blow someone's brains out, take out, dispose of, liquidate; *N. Amer. informal* ice, rub out, waste; *literary* slay.

murderer, murderess ▸ noun =killer, assassin, serial killer, butcher; *informal* hit man, hired gun; *dated* homi-cide; *literary* slayer.

murderous ▸ adjective *a murderous at-tack* =homicidal, brutal, violent, sav-age, ferocious, fierce, vicious, blood-thirsty, barbarous, barbaric; fatal, lethal, deadly, mortal, death-dealing; *archaic* sanguinary.

murky ▸ adjective 1 *a murky winter after-noon* =dark, gloomy, grey, leaden, dull, dim, overcast, cloudy, clouded, sunless, dismal, dreary, bleak. 2 *murky water* =dirty, muddy, cloudy, turbid; *N. Amer.* riled, roily. 3 *her murky past* =question-able, suspicious, suspect, dubious, dark, mysterious, secret; *informal* shady.

–OPPOSITES bright, clear.

murmur ▸ noun **1** *his voice was a murmur* =**whisper**, mutter, mumble. **2** *there were murmurs in Tory ranks* =**complaint**, grumble, grouse; *informal* gripe, moan. **3** *the murmur of bees* =**hum**, buzz, drone; sigh, rustle; *literary* susurration.

▸ verb **1** *he heard them murmuring in the hall* =**mutter**, mumble, whisper, talk under one's breath. **2** *no one murmured at the delay* =**complain**, mutter, grumble, grouse; *informal* gripe, moan. **3** *the wind was murmuring through the trees* =**rustle**, sigh; burble; *literary* whisper, purl.

muscle ▸ noun **1** *he had muscle but no brains* =**strength**, power, muscularity, brawn; *informal* beef, beefiness. **2** *financial muscle* =**influence**, power, strength, might, force, forcefulness, weight; *informal* clout.

■ **muscle in** (*informal*) =**interfere**, force one's way in, impose oneself, encroach; *informal* horn in.

WORD LINKS

relating to muscles: **myo-**
branch of medicine to do with muscles: **orthopaedics**
incision into muscle: **myotomy**

muscular ▸ adjective **1** *he's very muscular* =**strong**, brawny, muscly, well built, burly, strapping, sturdy, powerful, athletic; *Physiology* mesomorphic; *informal* hunky, beefy. **2** *a muscular economy* =**vigorous**, robust, strong, powerful, dynamic, potent, active.

muse[1] ▸ noun *the poet's muse* =**inspiration**, creativity, stimulus.

muse[2] ▸ verb *I mused on Toby's story* =**ponder**, consider, think over/about, mull over, reflect on, contemplate, turn over in one's mind, chew over, cogitate on; think, be lost in contemplation/thought, daydream; *archaic* pore on.

mush ▸ noun **1** *some sort of greyish mush* =**pulp**, slop, paste, purée, mash; *informal* gloop, goo, gook; *N. Amer. informal* glop. **2** *romantic mush* =**rubbish**, garbage; *informal* schmaltz, corn, slush; *N. Amer. informal* slop.

mushroom ▸ verb *ecotourism mushroomed in the 1980s* =**proliferate**, burgeon, spread, increase, expand, boom, explode, snowball, rocket, skyrocket; thrive, flourish, prosper.
–OPPOSITES contract.

mushy ▸ adjective **1** *cook until the fruit is*

mushy =**soft**, pulpy, sloppy, spongy, squashy, squelchy, squishy; *informal* gooey, gloopy; *Brit. informal* squidgy. **2** *a mushy film* =**sentimental**, mawkish, slushy, emotional, saccharine; *informal* schmaltzy, weepy, corny; *Brit. informal* soppy; *N. Amer. informal* cornball, sappy, hokey.
–OPPOSITES firm.

musical ▸ adjective =**tuneful**, melodic, melodious, harmonious, sweet-sounding, sweet, mellifluous, euphonious.
–OPPOSITES discordant.

musician ▸ noun =**player**, performer, instrumentalist, accompanist, soloist, virtuoso, maestro; *historical* minstrel.

musing ▸ noun =**meditation**, thinking, contemplation, deliberation, pondering, reflection, rumination, introspection, daydreaming, reverie, dreaming, preoccupation, brooding; *formal* cogitation.

must ▸ verb *I must go* =**ought to**, should, have (got) to, need to, be obliged to, be required to, be compelled to.

muster ▸ verb **1** *they mustered 50,000 troops* =**assemble**, mobilize, rally, raise, summon, gather (together), mass, collect, convene, call up, call to arms, recruit, conscript; *US* draft. **2** *reporters mustered outside her house* =**congregate**, assemble, gather (together), come together, collect, convene, mass, rally. **3** *she mustered her courage* =**summon (up)**, screw up, call up, rally.

■ **pass muster** =**be good enough**, come up to standard, come up to scratch, measure up, be acceptable/adequate, fill/fit the bill; *informal* make the grade, come/be up to snuff, cut the mustard, do the business.

musty ▸ adjective =**mouldy**, stale, fusty, damp, dank, mildewy, smelly, stuffy, airless, unventilated; *N. Amer. informal* funky.
–OPPOSITES fresh.

mutable ▸ adjective =**changeable**, variable, varying, fluctuating, shifting, inconsistent, unpredictable, inconstant, uneven, unstable, protean.
–OPPOSITES invariable.

mutant ▸ noun =**freak (of nature)**, deviant, monstrosity, monster, mutation.

mutate ▸ verb =**change**, metamorphose, evolve; transmute, transform; *humorous* transmogrify.

mutation ▸ noun **1** =alteration, change, transformation, metamorphosis, transmutation; *humorous* transmogrification. **2** *a genetic mutation* =mutant, freak (of nature), deviant, monstrosity, monster.

mute ▸ adjective **1** *Yasmin remained mute* =silent, speechless, dumb, unspeaking, tight-lipped, taciturn; *informal* mum. **2** *a mute appeal* =wordless, silent, dumb, unspoken. **3** *the church was mute* =quiet, silent, hushed.
–OPPOSITES voluble, spoken.
▸ verb **1** *the noise was muted by the heavy curtains* =deaden, muffle, dampen, soften; stifle, smother, suppress. **2** *Bruce muted his criticisms* =restrain, soften, tone down, moderate, temper.
–OPPOSITES intensify.

muted ▸ adjective **1** *the muted hum of traffic* =muffled, faint, indistinct, quiet, soft, low; distant, faraway. **2** *muted tones* =subdued, pastel, delicate, subtle, understated, restrained.

mutilate ▸ verb **1** *the bodies had been mutilated* =mangle, maim, disfigure, dismember; slash, hack. **2** *the carved screen had been mutilated* =vandalize, damage, deface, violate, desecrate; slash, hack.

mutinous ▸ adjective =rebellious, insubordinate, subversive, seditious, insurgent, insurrectionary.

mutiny ▸ noun =insurrection, rebellion, revolt, riot, uprising, insurgence, insubordination.
▸ verb =rise up, rebel, revolt, riot; strike.

mutt ▸ noun *(informal)* *a long-haired mutt* =dog, hound, mongrel, cur; *Austral. informal* mong, bitzer.

mutter ▸ verb **1** *a group of men stood muttering* =talk under one's breath, murmur, mumble, whisper. **2** *backbenchers muttered about the reshuffle* =grumble, complain, grouse, carp, whine; *informal* moan, gripe, beef, whinge; *Brit. informal* chunter; *N. Amer. informal* kvetch.

mutual ▸ adjective =reciprocal, reciprocated, requited, returned; common, joint, shared.

muzzle ▸ noun *the dog's velvety muzzle* =snout, nose, mouth, maw.
▸ verb *attempts to muzzle the media* =gag, silence, censor, stifle, restrain, check, curb, fetter.

muzzy ▸ adjective **1** *she felt muzzy* =groggy, light-headed, faint, dizzy, befuddled; *informal* dopey, woozy. **2** *a slightly muzzy picture* =blurred, blurry, fuzzy, unfocused, unclear, ill-defined, foggy.
–OPPOSITES clear.

myopic ▸ adjective **1** *a myopic patient* =short-sighted; *N. Amer.* nearsighted. **2** *the government's myopic attitude* =unimaginative, short-sighted, narrow-minded, small-minded, short-term.
–OPPOSITES long-sighted, far-sighted.

myriad *(literary)* ▸ noun *myriads of insects* =multitude, scores, mass, host, droves, hordes; *informal* lots, loads, masses, stacks, tons, hundreds, thousands, millions; *N. Amer. informal* gazillions.
▸ adjective *the myriad lights of the city* =innumerable, countless, infinite, numberless, untold, unnumbered, immeasurable, multitudinous.

mysterious ▸ adjective **1** *he vanished in mysterious circumstances* =puzzling, strange, peculiar, curious, funny, queer, odd, weird, bizarre, mystifying, inexplicable, baffling, perplexing. **2** *he was being very mysterious* =enigmatic, inscrutable, secretive, reticent, evasive, furtive, surreptitious.
–OPPOSITES straightforward.

mystery ▸ noun **1** *his death remains a mystery* =puzzle, enigma, conundrum, riddle, secret; paradox. **2** *her past is shrouded in mystery* =secrecy, obscurity, uncertainty, mystique.

mystic, mystical ▸ adjective =spiritual, religious, transcendental, paranormal, other-worldly, supernatural, occult, metaphysical.

mystify ▸ verb =bewilder, puzzle, perplex, baffle, confuse, confound, bemuse, nonplus, throw; *informal* flummox, stump, bamboozle, faze, fox.

mystique ▸ noun =charisma, glamour, romance, mystery, magic, charm, appeal, allure.

myth ▸ noun **1** *ancient Greek myths* =(folk) tale, (folk) story, legend, fable, saga; lore, folklore. **2** *the myths surrounding childbirth* =misconception, fallacy, old wives' tale, fairy story/tale, fiction; *informal* (tall) story, cock and bull story.

WORD LINKS

study of myths: **mythology**

mythical ▸ adjective **1** *mythical beasts* =legendary, mythological, fabled, fabulous, fairy-tale, storybook; fantastical, imaginary, imagined, fictitious. **2** *her* *mythical child* =**imaginary**, fictitious, make-believe, fantasy, invented, made-up, non-existent; *informal* pretend.

mythological ▶ adjective =**fabled**, fabulous, fairy-tale, legendary, mythical, mythic, traditional; fictitious, imaginary.

mythology ▶ noun =**myth(s)**, legend(s), folklore, folk tales/stories, lore, tradition.

Nn

nadir ▶ noun =**low point**, all-time low, bottom, rock bottom; *informal* the pits.
−OPPOSITES zenith.

nag ▶ verb **1** *she's constantly nagging me* =**harass**, keep on at, go on at, badger, give someone a hard time, chivvy, hound, criticize, find fault with, moan at, grumble at; *informal* hassle; *N. Amer. informal* ride; *Austral. informal* heavy. **2** *this has been nagging me for weeks* =**trouble**, worry, bother, plague, torment, niggle, prey on one's mind; *informal* bug, aggravate.
▶ noun *she's such a nag* =**bully**; shrew, harpy, harridan; *archaic* scold.

nagging ▶ adjective **1** *his nagging wife* =**bullying**, shrewish, complaining, grumbling, fault-finding, scolding, carping, bossy. **2** *a nagging pain* =**persistent**, continuous, niggling, unrelenting, unremitting; chronic.

nail ▶ noun **1** *fastened with nails* =**tack**, pin, staple. **2** *biting her nails* =**fingernail**, thumbnail, toenails.
▶ verb **1** *a board was nailed to the wall* =**fasten**, attach, fix, affix, secure, tack, hammer, pin. **2** *(informal) efforts to nail the suspects* =**catch**, capture, apprehend, arrest, seize; *informal* collar, nab, pull in, pick up; *Brit. informal* nick. **3** *the pictures had nailed the lie* =**expose**, reveal, uncover, unmask, bring to light, identify.
■ **on the nail** =**immediately**, at once, without delay, straight away, right away, promptly, directly, now, this minute; *N. Amer.* on the barrelhead.

WORD LINKS

relating to finger- and toenails: **ungual**

naive ▶ adjective =**innocent**, unsophisticated, artless, ingenuous, inexperienced, guileless, unworldly, trusting, gullible, credulous, immature, callow, raw, green; *informal* wet behind the ears.
−OPPOSITES worldly.

naivety ▶ noun =**innocence**, ingenuousness, guilelessness, unworldliness, trustfulness; gullibility, credulousness, credulity, immaturity, callowness.

naked ▶ adjective **1** *a naked woman* =**nude**, bare, in the nude, stark naked, having nothing on, stripped, unclothed, undressed, in a state of nature; *informal* without a stitch on, in one's birthday suit, in the raw/buff, in the altogether, in the nuddy, mother naked; *Brit. informal* starkers; *N. Amer. informal* buck naked. **2** *a naked flame* =**unprotected**, uncovered, exposed, unguarded. **3** *the naked branches of the trees* =**bare**, barren, denuded, stripped, uncovered. **4** *I felt naked and exposed* =**vulnerable**, helpless, weak, powerless, defenceless, exposed, open to attack. **5** *the naked truth | naked hostility* =**undisguised**, plain, unadorned, unvarnished, unqualified, stark, bald; overt, obvious, open, patent, evident, manifest, unmistakable, blatant.
−OPPOSITES clothed, covered.

WORD LINKS

fear of being naked: **gymnophobia**

nakedness ▶ noun =**nudity**, state of undress, bareness.

name ▶ noun **1** *her name's Gemma* =**designation**, honorific, title, tag, epithet, label; *informal* moniker, handle; *formal* appellation. **2** *the top names in the fashion industry* =**celebrity**, star, superstar, VIP, leading light, big name, luminary; expert, authority; *informal* celeb, somebody, megastar, big noise, big shot, bigwig, big gun. **3** *the good name of the firm* =**reputation**, character, repute, standing, stature, esteem, prestige, cachet, kudos; renown, popularity, distinction.
▶ verb **1** *they named the child Pamela* =**call**, dub; label, style, term, title; baptize, christen; *formal* denominate. **2** *the driver was named as Jason Penter* =**identify**, specify; give. **3** *he has named his successor* =**choose**, select, pick, decide on, nominate, designate.

WORD LINKS

relating to names: **nominal, onomastic**
study of place names: **toponymy**
fear of names: **onomatophobia**

named ▶ adjective **1** *a girl named Anne*

=**called**, by the name of, baptized, christened, known as; dubbed, entitled, styled, termed, labelled. **2** *named individuals* =**specified**, designated, identified, cited, mentioned, singled out; specific, particular.

nameless ▶ adjective **1** *a nameless photographer* =**unnamed**, unidentified, anonymous, unspecified, unacknowledged, uncredited; unknown, unsung. **2** *nameless fears* =**unspeakable**, unutterable, inexpressible, indescribable; indefinable, vague, unspecified.

namely ▶ adverb =**that is (to say)**, to be specific, specifically, viz, to wit; in other words.

nanny ▶ noun *the children's nanny* =**nursemaid**, au pair, childminder, carer; *dated* nurse.
▶ verb *stop nannying me* =**mollycoddle**, cosset, coddle, wrap in cotton wool, baby, feather-bed; spoil, pamper, indulge, overindulge.

nap ▶ verb *they were napping on the sofa* =**doze**, sleep, take a nap, catnap, rest, take a siesta; *informal* snooze, snatch forty winks, get some shut-eye; *Brit. informal* have a kip; *N. Amer. informal* catch some Zs.
▶ noun *she is taking a nap* =**sleep**, catnap, siesta, doze, lie-down, rest; *informal* snooze, forty winks, shut-eye; *Brit. informal* kip.
■ **catch someone napping** =**catch off guard**, catch unawares, (take by) surprise, catch out, find unprepared; *informal* catch someone with their trousers/pants down; *Brit. informal* catch on the hop.

narcissism ▶ noun =**vanity**, self-love, self-admiration, self-absorption, self-obsession, conceit, self-centredness, self-regard, egotism.
–OPPOSITES modesty.

narcissistic ▶ adjective =**vain**, self-absorbed, self-obsessed, conceited, self-centred, self-regarding, egotistic, egotistical.

narcotic ▶ noun =**drug**, opiate; painkiller, analgesic, anodyne, palliative.
▶ adjective =**soporific**, sleep-inducing, opiate; painkilling, pain-relieving, analgesic, anodyne.

narrate ▶ verb =**tell**, relate, recount, describe, chronicle, report; voice-over, commentate, present, deliver.

narration ▶ noun **1** *a narration of past events* =**account**, narrative, chronicle, description, report, relation. **2** *his narra-tion of the story* =**voice-over**, commentary; delivery, presentation.

narrative ▶ noun =**account**, chronicle, history, description, record, report; story, tale.

narrator ▶ noun **1** *the narrator of 'the Arabian Nights'* =**storyteller**, relater, chronicler, presenter, author; *Austral. informal* magsman. **2** *the film's narrator* =**voice-over**, commentator; presenter.
–OPPOSITES listener, audience.

narrow ▶ adjective **1** *the path became narrower* =**small**, tapered, tapering; *archaic* strait. **2** *her narrow waist* =**slender**, slim, small, slight, attenuated, thin, tiny. **3** *a narrow space* =**confined**, cramped, tight, restricted, limited, constricted, small, tiny. **4** *a narrow range of products* =**limited**, restricted, small, inadequate, insufficient, deficient. **5** *a narrow view of the world.* See NARROW-MINDED. **6** *in a narrow sense of the word* =**strict**, literal, exact, precise. **7** *a narrow escape* =**close**, near, by a hair's breadth; *informal* by a whisker.
–OPPOSITES wide, broad.
▶ verb *the path narrowed | narrowing the gap between rich and poor* =**get/become/make narrower**, get/become/make smaller, taper, diminish, decrease, reduce, contract, shrink, constrict; *archaic* straiten.

narrowly ▶ adverb **1** *one bullet narrowly missed him* =**(only) just**, barely, scarcely, hardly, by a hair's breadth; *informal* by a whisker. **2** *she looked at me narrowly* =**closely**, carefully, searchingly, attentively.

narrow-minded ▶ adjective =**intolerant**, illiberal, reactionary, conservative, parochial, provincial, insular, small-minded, petty, blinkered, inward-looking, narrow, hidebound, prejudiced, bigoted; *N. Amer. informal* jerkwater.
–OPPOSITES tolerant.

nastiness ▶ noun =**unkindness**, unpleasantness, unfriendliness, disagreeableness, rudeness, spitefulness, maliciousness, meanness, ill temper, offensiveness, viciousness, malevolence, vileness; *informal* bitchiness, cattiness.

nasty ▶ adjective **1** *a nasty smell* =**unpleasant**, disagreeable, disgusting, distasteful, awful, dreadful, horrible, terrible, vile, foul, abominable, frightful, loathsome, revolting, repulsive, odious, sickening, nauseating, repellent, repug-

nant, horrendous, appalling, atrocious, obnoxious, unsavoury, unappetizing, off-putting; noxious, foul-smelling, smelly, stinking, rank, fetid, malodorous; *informal* ghastly, horrid, diabolical, yucky, God-awful; *Brit. informal* whiffy, pongy, niffy; *N. Amer. informal* lousy, funky; *Austral. informal* on the nose; *literary* noisome. **2** *the weather turned nasty* =**unpleasant**, disagreeable, foul, filthy, inclement; wet, stormy, cold. **3** *she can be really nasty* =**unkind**, unpleasant, unfriendly, disagreeable, rude, spiteful, malicious, mean, ill-tempered, vicious, malevolent, obnoxious, hateful, hurtful; *informal* bitchy, catty. **4** *a nasty accident* | *a nasty cut* =**serious**, dangerous, bad, awful, dreadful, terrible, severe; painful, ugly. **5** *she had the nasty habit of appearing unannounced* =**annoying**, irritating, infuriating, unpleasant, maddening, exasperating.
−OPPOSITES nice.

nation ▸ noun =**country**, (sovereign/nation) state, land, realm, kingdom, republic; fatherland, motherland; people, race, tribe, clan.

WORD LINKS
relating to a nation: **ethnic**

national ▸ adjective **1** *national politics* =**state**, public, federal, governmental; civic, civil, domestic, internal. **2** *a national strike* =**nationwide**, countrywide, state, general, widespread.
−OPPOSITES local, international.
▸ noun *a French national* =**citizen**, subject, native; voter, passport holder.

nationalism ▸ noun =**patriotism**, xenophobia, chauvinism, jingoism.

nationalistic ▸ adjective =**patriotic**, nationalist, xenophobic, chauvinistic, jingoistic.

nationality ▸ noun **1** *British nationality* =**citizenship**. **2** *people of different nationalities* =**country**, ethnic group, ethnic minority, race, nation.

nationwide ▸ adjective =**national**, countrywide, state, general, widespread, extensive.
−OPPOSITES local.

native ▸ noun *a native of Sweden* =**inhabitant**, resident, local; citizen, national; *formal* dweller.
−OPPOSITES foreigner.
▸ adjective **1** *the native population* =**indigenous**, original. **2** *native produce* | *native*

plants =**domestic**, home-grown, home-made, local; indigenous. **3** *a native instinct for politics* =**innate**, inherent, inborn, instinctive, intuitive, natural. **4** *her native tongue* =**mother**; home, local.
−OPPOSITES immigrant.

natter (*Brit. informal*) ▸ verb *they nattered away*. See CHAT verb.
▸ noun *she rang up for a natter*. See CHAT noun.

natty ▸ adjective (*informal*) =**smart**, stylish, fashionable, dapper, debonair, dashing, spruce, well dressed, chic, elegant, trim; *N. Amer.* trig; *informal* snazzy, trendy, snappy, nifty; *N. Amer. informal* sassy, spiffy, fly, kicky.
−OPPOSITES scruffy.

natural ▸ adjective **1** *a natural occurrence* =**normal**, ordinary, everyday, usual, regular, common, commonplace, typical, routine, standard. **2** *natural products* =**unprocessed**, organic, pure, unrefined, high-fibre, additive-free; green, GM-free, ecologically sound. **3** *Alex is a natural leader* =**born**, instinctive; congenital, pathological. **4** *his natural instincts* =**innate**, inborn, inherent, native; hereditary, inherited, inbred, congenital. **5** *she seemed very natural* =**unaffected**, spontaneous, uninhibited, relaxed, unselfconscious, genuine, open, artless, guileless, unpretentious. **6** *it was quite natural to think she admired him* =**reasonable**, logical, understandable, (only) to be expected, predictable.
−OPPOSITES abnormal, artificial, affected.

naturalist ▸ noun =**natural historian**, scientist; biologist, botanist, zoologist, ornithologist, entomologist; ecologist, conservationist.

naturalistic ▸ adjective =**realistic**, real-life, true-to-life, lifelike, representational, photographic; graphic, down-to-earth, gritty, unsentimental, unflinching, unsparing.
−OPPOSITES abstract.

naturally ▸ adverb **1** *he's naturally shy* =**by nature**, by character, inherently, innately, congenitally, pathologically. **2** *try to act naturally* =**normally**, in a natural manner/way, spontaneously, genuinely, unpretentiously; *informal* natural. **3** *naturally, they wanted kept quiet* =**of course**, as might be expected, needless to say; obviously, clearly, it goes without saying.

–OPPOSITES self-consciously.

naturalness ▶ noun =**unselfcon-sciousness**, spontaneity, straightfor-wardness, genuineness, openness, un-pretentiousness.

nature ▶ noun **1** *the beauty of nature* =**the natural world**, Mother Nature, Mother Earth, the environment; the universe, the cosmos; wildlife, flora and fauna, the countryside, the land, the landscape. **2** *such crimes are, by their very nature, difficult to hide* =**essence**, inherent/basic/essential features, character, complexion. **3** *it was not in Daisy's nature to be negative* =**character**, personality, disposition, temperament, make-up, psyche, constitution. **4** *experiments of a similar nature* =**kind**, sort, type, variety, category, ilk, class, species, genre, style, cast, order, mould, stamp; *N. Amer.* stripe.

naturist ▶ noun =**nudist**.
–OPPOSITES textile.

naughty ▶ adjective **1** *a naughty boy* =**badly behaved**, disobedient, bad, way-ward, defiant, unruly, insubordinate, wilful, delinquent, undisciplined, disor-derly, disruptive, fractious, recalcitrant, wild, obstreperous, difficult, trouble-some, awkward, contrary, perverse; mischievous, impish, roguish, rascally; *informal* brattish; *formal* refractory. **2** *naughty jokes* =**indecent**, risqué, rude, racy, ribald, bawdy, suggestive, im-proper, indelicate, indecorous; vulgar, dirty, filthy, smutty, crude, coarse, ob-scene, lewd, pornographic; *informal* raunchy; *Brit. informal* fruity, saucy; *N. Amer. informal* gamy; *euphemistic* adult.
–OPPOSITES well behaved, decent.

nausea ▶ noun **1** *symptoms include nau-sea* =**sickness**, biliousness, queasiness; vomiting, retching; travel-sickness, sea-sickness, carsickness, airsickness. **2** *it in-duces a feeling of nausea* =**disgust**, revul-sion, repugnance, repulsion, distaste, aversion, loathing, abhorrence.

nauseate ▶ verb =**make someone sick**, sicken, turn someone's stomach; disgust, revolt; *N. Amer. informal* gross out.

nauseating ▶ adjective *some nauseating song* =**sickening**, stomach-churning, nauseous, emetic; disgusting, revolting, loathsome, foul; *N. Amer.* vomitous; *infor-mal* sick-making, gross.

nauseous ▶ adjective *the food made her feel nauseous* =**sick**, nauseated, queasy, bilious, green about/at the gills, ill, un-well; seasick, carsick, airsick, travel-sick; *N. Amer. informal* barfy.

nautical ▶ adjective =**maritime**, mar-ine, naval, seafaring; boating, sailing.

navel ▶ noun =*informal* belly button, tummy button; *Anatomy* umbilicus.

> **WORD LINKS**
>
> relating to the navel: **umbilical**
> related prefix: **omphalo-**

navigable ▶ adjective =**passable**, ne-gotiable, traversable; clear, open, un-obstructed, unblocked.

navigate ▶ verb **1** *he navigated the yacht across the Atlantic* =**steer**, pilot, guide, direct, captain; *Nautical* con; *informal* skip-per. **2** *the upper reaches are dangerous to navigate* =**sail (across/over)**, cross, tra-verse, negotiate. **3** *I'll drive—you can navigate* =**map-read**, give directions.

navigation ▶ noun **1** *the navigation of the ship* =**steering**, piloting, sailing, guiding, directing, guidance. **2** *the skills of navigation* =**helmsmanship**, steersmanship, seamanship, map-reading.

navy ▶ noun **1** *a 600-ship navy* =**fleet**, flo-tilla, armada. **2** *a navy suit* =**navy blue**, dark blue, indigo.

near ▶ adverb **1** *her children all live near* =**close (by)**, nearby, (close/near) at hand, in the neighbourhood, in the vicinity, within reach, on the doorstep, a stone's throw away; *informal* in spitting distance. **2** *near perfect conditions* =**almost**, just about, nearly, practically, virtually; *literary* well-nigh.
▶ preposition *a hotel near the seafront* =**close to**, a short distance from, in the vicin-ity/neighbourhood of, within reach of, a stone's throw away from; *informal* within spitting distance of.
▶ adjective **1** *the house is near here* =**close**, nearby, (close/near) at hand, a stone's throw away, within reach, accessible, handy, convenient; *informal* within spit-ting distance. **2** *the final judgement is near* =**imminent**, in the offing, (close/near) at hand, (just) around the corner, on its way, coming, impending, looming. **3** *a near escape* =**narrow**, close; by a hair's breadth; *informal* by a whisker.
–OPPOSITES far, distant.
▶ verb **1** *by dawn we were nearing Moscow* =**approach**, draw near/nearer to, get close/closer to, advance towards, close in on. **2** *the death toll is nearing 3,000*

=**verge on**, border on, approach; *informal* be getting on for.

nearby ▸ adjective *one of the nearby villages* =**not far away/off**, (close/near) at hand, close (by), near, within reach, neighbouring, local; accessible, handy, convenient.
–OPPOSITES faraway.

▸ adverb *her mother lives nearby* =**close (by)**, (close/near) at hand, near, a short distance away, in the neighbourhood, in the vicinity, within reach, on the doorstep, (just) round the corner, locally.

nearly ▸ adverb =**almost**, (just) about, more or less, practically, virtually, all but, as good as, not far off, to all intents and purposes; not quite; *informal* pretty much, pretty well; *literary* well-nigh.

near miss ▸ noun =**close thing**, near thing, narrow escape; *informal* close shave.

nearness ▸ noun **1** *the town's nearness to Rome* =**closeness**, proximity; accessibility, handiness. **2** *the nearness of death* =**imminence**, closeness, immediacy.

nearsighted ▸ adjective *(N. Amer.)* =**short-sighted**, myopic.
–OPPOSITES long-sighted

neat ▸ adjective **1** *the bedroom was neat and clean* =**tidy**, orderly, well ordered, in (good) order, shipshape (and Bristol fashion), in apple-pie order, spick and span, uncluttered, straight, trim. **2** *he's very neat* =**smart**, spruce, dapper, trim, well groomed, well turned out; *N. Amer.* trig; *informal* natty. **3** *her neat handwriting* =**clear**, regular, precise, elegant; *informal* easy-to-read. **4** *this neat little gadget* =**compact**, well designed, handy; *Brit. informal* dinky, nifty. **5** *his neat footwork* =**skilful**, deft, dexterous, adroit, adept, expert; *informal* nifty. **6** *a neat solution* =**clever**, ingenious, inventive; imaginative. **7** *neat gin* =**undiluted**, straight, unmixed; *N. Amer. informal* straight up.
–OPPOSITES untidy.

neaten ▸ verb =**tidy (up)**, straighten (up), smarten (up), spruce up, put in order; *N. Amer. informal* fix up.

neatly ▸ adverb **1** *neatly arranged papers* =**tidily**, methodically, systematically; smartly; in order. **2** *the point was neatly put* =**cleverly**, aptly, elegantly, well, effectively. **3** *a neatly executed header* =**skilfully**, deftly, adroitly, adeptly, expertly.

neatness ▸ noun =**tidiness**, orderliness, trimness; smartness.

nebulous ▸ adjective **1** *a nebulous figure* =**indistinct**, indefinite, unclear, vague, hazy, fuzzy, blurred, blurry, foggy; faint, shadowy, obscure. **2** *nebulous ideas* =**vague**, ill-defined, unclear, hazy, uncertain, imprecise, muddled, confused, ambiguous; woolly, fuzzy.
–OPPOSITES clear.

necessarily ▸ adverb =**as a consequence**, as a result, automatically, as a matter of course, certainly, incontrovertibly, inevitably, unavoidably, inescapably, of necessity; *formal* perforce.

necessary ▸ adjective **1** *planning permission is necessary* =**obligatory**, requisite, required, compulsory, mandatory, imperative, needed, de rigueur; essential, vital. **2** *a necessary consequence* =**inevitable**, unavoidable, inescapable, inexorable.

necessitate ▸ verb =**make necessary**, entail, involve, mean, require, demand, call for, be grounds for, force.

necessity ▸ noun **1** *the VCR is now regarded as a necessity* =**essential**, requisite, prerequisite, necessary, basic, sine qua non; *Informal* must-have. **2** *political necessity forced him to resign* =**force of circumstance**, obligation, need, call, exigency. **3** *the necessity of growing old* =**inevitability**, certainty, inescapability, inexorability. **4** *necessity made them steal* =**poverty**, need, neediness, deprivation, privation, destitution; desperation.

■ **of necessity** =**necessarily**, inevitably, unavoidably, inescapably; as a matter of course, naturally, automatically, certainly, surely, definitely, incontrovertibly, undoubtedly; *formal* perforce.

neck ▸ noun =*technical* cervix; *archaic, informal* scrag.

▸ verb *(informal)* =**kiss**, caress, pet; *informal* smooch, canoodle; *Brit. informal* snog; *N. Amer. informal* make out; *informal, dated* spoon.

■ **neck and neck** =**level**, equal, tied, side by side; *Brit.* level pegging; *informal* even-steven(s).

> **WORD LINKS**
>
> *relating to the neck:* **cervical, jugular**

necklace ▸ noun =**chain**, choker, necklet; beads, pearls; pendant, locket; *historical* torc.

necromancy ▸ noun =**sorcery**,

(black) magic, witchcraft, witchery, wizardry, the occult, occultism, voodoo, hoodoo; divination; spiritualism.

née ▸ adjective *Jill Wyatt, née Peters* =**born**, formerly, previously.

need ▸ verb 1 *do you need money?* =**require**, be in/have need of, want; be crying out for, be desperate for; demand, call for, necessitate, entail, involve; lack, be without, be short of. **2** *do I need to come?* =**have to**; be meant to, be supposed to; be expected to. **3** *she needed him so much* =**yearn for**, pine for, long for, desire, miss.
▸ noun **1** *there's no need to apologize* =**necessity**, requirement, call, demand. **2** *basic human needs* =**requirement**, necessity, want, requisite, prerequisite. **3** *your need is greater than mine* =**neediness**, want, poverty, deprivation, privation, hardship, destitution. **4** *my hour of need* =**difficulty**, trouble, distress; crisis, emergency, urgency, extremity.
∎ **in need** =**needy**, deprived, disadvantaged, underprivileged, poor, impoverished, poverty-stricken, destitute, impecunious ▸ indigent; *Brit.* on the breadline.

needed ▸ adjective =**necessary**, required, wanted, desired, lacking.
–OPPOSITES optional.

needle ▸ noun **1** *the virus is transmitted via needles* =**hypodermic needle**; *informal* spike; syringe. **2** *the needle on the meter* =**indicator**, pointer, marker, arrow, hand.
▸ verb *(informal) he needled her all the time.* See ANNOY.

WORD LINKS

fear of needles: **belonephobia**

needless ▸ adjective =**unnecessary**, unneeded, uncalled for; gratuitous, pointless; dispensable, superfluous, redundant, excessive.
–OPPOSITES necessary.

needy ▸ adjective =**poor**, deprived, disadvantaged, underprivileged, in need, needful, hard up, poverty-stricken, indigent, impoverished, destitute, impecunious, penniless; *Brit.* on the breadline; *informal* on one's uppers, broke, strapped (for cash), without two pennies to rub together; *Brit. informal* skint, stony broke, in Queer Street; *N. Amer. informal* stone broke; *formal* penurious.
–OPPOSITES wealthy.

negate ▸ verb **1** *they negated the court's*

ruling =**invalidate**, nullify, neutralize, cancel; undo, reverse, annul, void, revoke, rescind, repeal, retract, countermand, overrule, overturn. **2** *he negates the political nature of education* =**deny**, dispute, contradict, rebut, reject, repudiate; *formal* gainsay.
–OPPOSITES validate, confirm.

negation ▸ noun =**denial**, contradiction, repudiation, refutation, rebuttal; nullification, cancellation, revocation, repeal, retraction; *formal* abrogation.

negative ▸ adjective **1** *a negative reply* =**opposing**, opposed, contrary, anti-, dissenting; in the negative. **2** *stop being so negative* =**pessimistic**, defeatist, gloomy, cynical, fatalistic, dismissive; unenthusiastic, apathetic, unresponsive. **3** *a negative effect on the economy* =**harmful**, bad, adverse, damaging, detrimental, unfavourable, disadvantageous.
–OPPOSITES positive, optimistic, favourable.

negativity ▸ noun =**pessimism**, defeatism, gloom, cynicism, hopelessness, despair, despondency; apathy, indifference.

neglect ▸ verb **1** *she neglected the children* =**fail to look after**, leave alone, abandon; *literary* forsake. **2** *he's neglecting his work* =**pay no attention to**, let slide/ slip, not attend to, be remiss about, be lax about, leave undone. **3** *I neglected to inform her* =**fail**, omit, forget.
–OPPOSITES cherish, heed, remember.
▸ noun **1** *the place had an air of neglect* =**disrepair**, dilapidation, shabbiness, disuse, abandonment. **2** *her doctor was guilty of neglect* =**negligence**, dereliction (of duty), carelessness, laxity, slackness, irresponsibility. **3** *the neglect of women* =**disregard**, ignoring, overlooking; inattention to, indifference to; exclusion.
–OPPOSITES care, attention.

neglected ▸ adjective **1** *neglected animals* =**uncared for**, abandoned; mistreated, maltreated; *literary* forsaken. **2** *a neglected cottage* =**derelict**, dilapidated, tumbledown, ramshackle, untended. **3** *a neglected masterpiece* =**disregarded**, forgotten, overlooked, ignored, unrecognized, unnoticed, unsung, underrated.

neglectful ▸ adjective. See NEGLIGENT.

negligent ▸ adjective =**neglectful**, remiss, careless, lax, irresponsible,

inattentive, thoughtless, unmindful, forgetful; slack, sloppy; N. Amer. derelict.
–OPPOSITES dutiful.

negligible ▸ adjective =trivial, trifling, insignificant, unimportant, minor, inconsequential; minimal, small, slight, inappreciable, infinitesimal; informal minuscule, piddling.
–OPPOSITES significant.

negotiable ▸ adjective 1 the salary will be negotiable =open to discussion, flexible. 2 the path was negotiable =passable, navigable, crossable, usable, traversable; clear, unblocked, unobstructed; open. 3 negotiable cheques =transferable; valid.

negotiate ▸ verb 1 she refused to negotiate =discuss (terms), talk, consult, parley, confer, debate; compromise; mediate, intercede, arbitrate, moderate, conciliate; bargain, haggle. 2 he negotiated a new contract =arrange, broker, work out, thrash out, agree on; settle, clinch, conclude, pull off, bring off, transact; informal sort out, swing. 3 I negotiated the obstacles =get round, get past, get over, clear, cross; surmount, overcome, deal with, cope with.

negotiation ▸ noun 1 the negotiations resume next week =discussion(s), talks; conference, debate, dialogue, consultation. 2 the negotiation of a deal =arrangement, brokering; settlement, conclusion, completion, transaction.

negotiator ▸ noun =mediator, arbitrator, go-between, middleman, intermediary; representative, spokesperson, broker.

neigh ▸ verb =whinny, bray, snicker.

neighbourhood ▸ noun 1 a quiet neighbourhood =district, area, locality, locale, quarter, community; part, region, zone; informal neck of the woods; Brit. informal manor; N. Amer. informal hood, nabe. 2 in the neighbourhood of Canterbury =vicinity, environs; purlieus.

neighbouring ▸ adjective =adjacent, adjoining, bordering, connecting, next-door, nearby.
–OPPOSITES remote.

neighbourly ▸ adjective =obliging, helpful, friendly, kind, amiable, amicable, affable, genial, agreeable, hospitable, companionable, civil, cordial, good-natured, nice, pleasant, generous; considerate, thoughtful, unselfish; Brit.

informal decent.
–OPPOSITES unfriendly.

nemesis ▸ noun this could be the bank's nemesis =downfall, undoing; ruin, ruination, destruction, Waterloo.

nepotism ▸ noun =favouritism, preferential treatment, the old boy network, looking after one's own, bias, partiality, partisanship; Brit. jobs for the boys, the old school tie.
–OPPOSITES impartiality.

nerve ▸ noun 1 the nerves that transmit pain =nerve fibre, neuron, axon; Physiology dendrite. 2 the match will be a test of nerve =confidence, assurance, cool-headedness, self-possession; courage, bravery, pluck; determination, will power, spirit, backbone, fortitude, mettle, grit; informal guts, spunk; Brit. informal bottle; N. Amer. informal moxie. 3 he had the nerve to chat her up =audacity, cheek, effrontery, gall, temerity, presumption, impudence, impertinence, arrogance; informal face, front, brass neck, chutzpah; Brit. informal sauce. 4 pre-wedding nerves =anxiety, tension, nervousness, stress, worry, cold feet, apprehension; informal butterflies (in one's stomach), collywobbles, jitters, shakes; Brit. informal the (screaming) abdabs.

■ **get on someone's nerves** =irritate, annoy, irk, anger, bother, vex, provoke, displease, exasperate, infuriate, gall, pique, needle, ruffle someone's feathers, try someone's patience; jar on, grate on, rankle; Brit. rub up the wrong way; informal aggravate, get to, bug, miff, peeve, rile, nettle, get up someone's nose, hack off, get someone's goat; Brit. informal nark, get on someone's wick, wind up.

> **WORD LINKS**
>
> relating to nerves in the body: **neural**
> related prefix: **neuro-**
> inflammation of a nerve: **neuritis**
> branches of medicine to do with the nerves: **neurology, neuropathology, neurosurgery**
> surgical removal of a nerve: **neurectomy**
> surgical cutting of a nerve: **neurotomy**

nerve-racking ▸ adjective =stressful, anxious, worrying, fraught, nail-biting, tense, difficult, trying, worrisome, daunting, frightening; informal scary, hairy.

nervous ▸ adjective 1 a nervous woman

=**highly strung**, anxious, edgy, nervy, tense, excitable, jumpy, skittish, brittle, neurotic; timid. **2** *he was so nervous he couldn't eat* =**anxious**, worried, apprehensive, on edge, edgy, tense, stressed, agitated, uneasy, restless, worked up, keyed up, overwrought, jumpy; fearful, frightened, scared, shaky, in a cold sweat; *informal* with butterflies in one's stomach, jittery, twitchy, in a state, uptight, wired, in a flap, het up; *Brit. informal* strung up/out, having kittens; *N. Amer. informal* spooky, squirrelly. **3** *a nervous disorder* =**neurological**, neural; mental.
−OPPOSITES relaxed, calm.

nervousness ▸ noun =**anxiety**, edginess, tension, agitation, stress, worry, apprehension, uneasiness, disquiet, fear, trepidation, alarm; *Brit.* nerviness; *informal* butterflies (in one's stomach), collywobbles, the jitters, the willies, the heebie-jeebies, the shakes; *Brit. informal* the (screaming) abdabs.

nervy ▸ adjective. See NERVOUS senses 1, 2.

nestle ▸ verb =**snuggle**, cuddle, huddle, nuzzle, settle, burrow.

net[1] ▸ noun *a dress of green net* =**netting**, meshwork, tulle, fishnet, lace.
▸ verb *they netted some big criminals* =**catch**, capture, trap, snare, bag, get; *informal* nab, collar, bust; *British informal* nick.

net[2] ▸ adjective **1** *net earnings* =**after tax**, after deductions, take-home, final; *informal* bottom line. **2** *the net result* =**final**, end, ultimate, closing; overall, actual, effective.
−OPPOSITES gross.
▸ verb *she netted £50,000* =**earn**, make, get, take home, bring in, pocket, realize, be paid; *informal* walk away with.

nether ▸ adjective =**lower**, low, bottom, under; underground.
−OPPOSITES upper.

nettle ▸ verb =**irritate**, annoy, irk, gall, vex, anger, exasperate, infuriate, provoke; upset, displease, offend, pique, get on someone's nerves, try someone's patience, ruffle someone's feathers; *Brit.* rub up the wrong way; *N. Amer.* rankle; *informal* aggravate, rile, needle, get to, bug, get up someone's nose, hack off, get someone's goat; *Brit. informal* nark, get on someone's wick, wind up; *N. Amer. informal* tick off.

network ▸ noun **1** *a network of arteries* =**web**, lattice, net, matrix, mesh, criss-cross, grid, reticulation; *Anatomy* plexus. **2** *a network of lanes* =**maze**, labyrinth, warren, tangle.

neurosis ▸ noun =**obsession**, phobia, fixation, mania; fetish.

neurotic ▸ adjective =**overanxious**, oversensitive, nervous, nervy, tense, highly strung, paranoid; obsessive, fixated, hysterical, overwrought, irrational; *informal* twitchy.
−OPPOSITES stable, calm.

neuter ▸ adjective =**asexual**, sexless; androgynous.
▸ verb *have your pets neutered* =**sterilize**, castrate, spay, geld, cut, fix; *N. Amer. & Austral.* alter; *Brit. informal* doctor.

neutral ▸ adjective **1** *she's neutral on this issue* =**impartial**, unbiased, unprejudiced, objective, open-minded, non-partisan, disinterested, dispassionate, detached, impersonal, indifferent, uncommitted. **2** *Switzerland remained neutral* =**unaligned**, non-aligned, unaffiliated; uninvolved. **3** *a neutral topic of conversation* =**inoffensive**, bland, unobjectionable, unexceptionable, anodyne, uncontroversial; safe, harmless, innocuous. **4** *a neutral background* =**pale**, light, colourless, indeterminate, drab, insipid, nondescript, dull.
−OPPOSITES biased, partisan, provocative, colourful.

neutralize ▸ verb =**counteract**, offset, counterbalance, balance, counterpoise, countervail, compensate for, make up for; cancel out, nullify, negate.

never-ending ▸ adjective **1** *never-ending noise* =**incessant**, continuous, unceasing, ceaseless, constant, continual, perpetual, uninterrupted, unbroken, steady, unremitting, relentless, persistent, interminable, non-stop, endless, unending, everlasting, eternal. **2** *never-ending tasks* =**endless**, countless, innumerable, limitless, boundless; *literary* myriad.

nevertheless ▸ adverb =**nonetheless**, even so, however, still, yet, though; in spite of that, despite that, be that as it may, for all that, that said, just the same, all the same; notwithstanding, regardless, anyway, anyhow.

new ▸ adjective **1** *new technology* =**recent**, up to date, the latest, current, state-of-the-art, contemporary, advanced, cutting edge, modern. **2** *new ideas* =**novel**, original, fresh; imaginative, creative, experimental; newfangled, ultra-modern, avant-garde, futuristic; *informal* way out, far out. **3** *is your boat new?* = **unused**, brand new, pristine, fresh. **4** *new neighbours moved in* = **different**, another, alternative; unfamiliar, unknown, strange; unaccustomed, untried. **5** *they had a new classroom built* = **additional**, extra, supplementary, further, another, fresh. **6** *I came back a new woman* = **reinvigorated**, restored, revived, improved, refreshed, regenerated, reborn. −OPPOSITES old, hackneyed, second-hand, present.

> WORD LINKS
> *related prefix:* **neo-**
> *fear of new things:* **neophobia**

newcomer ▶ noun **1** *a newcomer to the village* = **(new) arrival**, immigrant, in-comer, settler, stranger, outsider, for-eigner, alien; *N. English* offcomer; *informal* johnny-come-lately, new kid on the block; *Austral. informal* blow-in. **2** *photography tips for the newcomer* = **beginner**, novice, learner; trainee, apprentice, probationer, tyro, initiate, neophyte; *N. Amer.* tenderfoot; *informal* rookie, newbie; *N. Amer. informal* greenhorn.

newfangled ▶ adjective = **new**, the latest, modern, ultra-modern, up to the minute, state-of-the-art, advanced, con-temporary; *informal* trendy, flash. −OPPOSITES dated.

newly ▶ adverb = **recently**, (only) just, lately, freshly; not long ago, a short time ago, only now, of late; new-.

news ▶ noun = **report**, announcement, story, account; article, news flash, news-cast, headlines, press release, commu-nication, communiqué, bulletin; mes-sage, dispatch, statement, intelligence; disclosure, revelation, word, talk, gos-sip; *informal* scoop; *literary* tidings.

newspaper ▶ noun = **paper**, journal, gazette, news-sheet; tabloid, broad-sheet, quality (paper), national (paper), local (paper), daily (paper), weekly (paper); free sheet, scandal sheet; *informal* rag; *N. Amer. informal* tab.

newsworthy ▶ adjective = **interest-ing**, topical, notable, noteworthy, im-portant, significant, momentous, his-toric, remarkable, sensational. −OPPOSITES unremarkable.

next ▶ adjective **1** *the next chapter* = **fol-lowing**, succeeding, upcoming, to come. **2** *the next house in the street* = **neigh-bouring**, adjacent, adjoining, next-door, bordering on, connected to, at-tached to; closest, nearest. −OPPOSITES previous.
▶ adverb *where shall we go next?* = **then**, after, afterwards, after this/that, follow-ing that/this, later, subsequently; *formal* thereafter. −OPPOSITES before.
■ **next to** = **beside**, by, alongside, by the side of, next door to, adjacent to, side by side with; close to, near, neighbouring, adjoining.

nibble ▶ verb **1** *they nibbled at mangoes* = **pick**, peck, gnaw, snack on; toy with; taste, sample; *informal* graze (on). **2** *the mouse nibbled his finger* = **bite**, nip, peck.
▶ noun **1** *the hamster enjoyed a nibble on the lettuce* = **bite**, gnaw; taste. **2** *nuts and nib-bles* = **morsel**, mouthful, bite; snack, tit-bit, canapé, hors d'oeuvre.

nice ▶ adjective **1** *have a nice time* = **enjoy-able**, pleasant, agreeable, good, satisfy-ing, gratifying; entertaining, amusing, diverting; *informal* lovely, great; *N. Amer. in-formal* neat. **2** *nice people* = **pleasant**, like-able, agreeable, personable, congenial, amiable, affable, genial, friendly, charming, delightful, engaging; sympa-thetic, compassionate, good. **3** *nice man-ners* = **polite**, courteous, civil, refined, polished, genteel, elegant. **4** *that's a ra-ther nice distinction* = **subtle**, fine, deli-cate, precise, strict, close; careful, me-ticulous, scrupulous. **5** *it's a nice day* = **fine**, pleasant, agreeable; dry, sunny, warm, mild. −OPPOSITES unpleasant, nasty, rough.

nicety ▶ noun *legal niceties* = **subtlety**, fine point, nuance, refinement, detail.

niche ▶ noun **1** *a niche in the wall* = **recess**, alcove, nook, cranny, hollow, bay, cav-ity, cubbyhole, pigeonhole. **2** *he found his niche in life* = **(ideal) position**, place, function, vocation, calling, métier, sta-tion, job, level.

nick ▶ noun **1** *a slight nick in the blade* = **cut**, scratch, incision, snick, notch, chip; dent, indentation. **2** *(Brit. informal)* she's in the nick. See PRISON. **3** *(Brit. informal)* he's at the nick = **police station**, station; *N. Amer.* precinct, station house; *informal* cop shop. **4** *(Brit. informal) the car's in good nick* = **condition**, repair, shape, state,

order, form, fettle, trim.
▶ verb **1** *I nicked my toe* =**cut**, scratch, snick, graze. **2** *(Brit. informal) she nicked his wallet.* See STEAL verb sense 1. **3** *(Brit. informal) Steve's been nicked.* See ARREST verb sense 1.

nickname ▶ noun =**sobriquet**, by-name, tag, label, epithet, cognomen; pet name, diminutive, endearment; *informal* moniker; *formal* appellation.

nifty ▶ adjective *(informal)* **1** *nifty camerawork* =**skilful**, deft, agile, adroit, nice; *informal* fancy, classy. **2** *a nifty little gadget* =**useful**, handy, practical, neat; compact. **3** *a nifty suit* =**fashionable**, stylish, smart, nice; *informal* classy.
–OPPOSITES clumsy.

niggle ▶ verb =**irritate**, annoy, bother, provoke, exasperate, upset, gall, irk, rankle with; *informal* rile, get to, bug.
▶ noun =**quibble**, complaint, criticism, grumble, grouse, cavil; *informal* gripe, moan, beef, grouch.

night ▶ noun =**night-time**; (hours of) darkness, dark.
–OPPOSITES day.
■ **night and day** =**all the time**, around the clock, {morning, noon, and night}, {day in, day out}, ceaselessly, endlessly, incessantly, unceasingly, interminably, constantly, perpetually, continually, relentlessly; *informal* 24-7.

WORD LINKS
relating to night: **nocturnal**
fear of the night: **nyctophobia**

nightclub ▶ noun =**discotheque**, night spot, club, bar; *N. Amer.* cafe; *informal* disco, niterie.

nightfall ▶ noun =**sunset**, sundown, dusk, twilight, evening, dark; *literary* eventide.
–OPPOSITES dawn.

nightly ▶ adjective **1** *nightly raids* =**every night**, each night, night after night. **2** *his nightly wanderings* =**nocturnal**, night-time.
▶ adverb *a band plays there nightly* =**every night**, each night, night after night.

nightmare ▶ noun *the journey was a nightmare* =**hell**, misery, agony, torture, murder, purgatory, disaster; *informal* the pits.

nightmarish ▶ adjective =**unearthly**, spine-chilling, hair-raising, horrific, macabre, hideous, unspeakable, gruesome, grisly, ghastly, harrowing, disturbing; *informal* scary, creepy.

nihilism ▶ noun =**scepticism**, disbelief, unbelief, agnosticism, atheism; negativity, cynicism, pessimism; rejection, denial; despair.

nihilist ▶ noun =**sceptic**, disbeliever, unbeliever; atheist; cynic, pessimist.

nihilistic ▶ adjective =**negative**, pessimistic, bleak, hopeless, cynical, destructive, despairing; atheistic.

nil ▶ noun =**nothing**, none; nought, zero, 0; *Tennis* love; *Cricket* a duck; *N. English* nowt; *informal* zilch, nix, not a dicky bird; *Brit. informal* sweet Fanny Adams, sweet FA, not a sausage; *N. Amer. informal* zip, nada, a goose egg; *archaic* naught.

nimble ▶ adjective **1** *he was nimble on his feet* =**agile**, sprightly, light, spry, quick, lithe, limber; skilful, deft, dexterous, adroit; *informal* nippy, twinkle-toed. **2** *a nimble mind* =**quick**, alert, lively, wide awake, observant, astute, perceptive, penetrating, discerning, shrewd, sharp; intelligent, bright, smart, clever, brilliant; *informal* quick on the uptake.
–OPPOSITES clumsy, dull.

nine ▶ cardinal number =**nonet**.

WORD LINKS
relating to nine: **nonary**
related prefix: **nona-**

nip ▶ verb *the child nipped her* =**bite**, nibble, peck; pinch, tweak, squeeze.
▶ noun *penguins can give a serious nip* =**bite**, peck, nibble; pinch, tweak.

nipple ▶ noun =**teat**; *Anatomy* mamilla.

WORD LINKS
relating to a nipple: **mamillary**

nippy ▶ adjective *(informal)* **1** *a nippy little hatchback* =**fast**, quick, lively, speedy; *informal* zippy. **2** *it's a bit nippy in here* =**chilly**, cold, frosty.
–OPPOSITES lumbering, slow, warm.

nit-picking ▶ adjective *(informal).* See PEDANTIC.

nitty-gritty ▶ noun *(informal)* =**basics**, essentials, fundamentals, substance, quintessence, heart of the matter; nub, crux, gist, meat, kernel; *informal* brass tacks, nuts and bolts.

no ▶ adverb =**absolutely not**, definitely not, most certainly not, of course not, under no circumstances, by no means,

not at all, negative, never, not really; *informal* nope, nah, not on your life, no way, not a chance; *Brit. informal* no fear, not on your nelly; *archaic* nay.
–OPPOSITES yes.

nobility ▸ noun 1 *a member of the nobility* =**aristocracy**, peerage, peers (of the realm), lords, nobles, noblemen, noblewomen; *informal* aristos; *Brit. informal* nobs. 2 *the nobility of his deed* =**virtue**, goodness, honour, decency, integrity; magnanimity, generosity, selflessness.

noble ▸ adjective 1 *a noble family* =**aristocratic**, blue-blooded, high-born, titled; *archaic* gentle. 2 *a noble cause* =**righteous**, virtuous, good, honourable, worthwhile; upright, decent, worthy, moral, ethical, reputable. 3 *a noble pine forest* =**magnificent**, splendid, grand, stately, imposing, dignified, proud, striking, majestic, glorious, awesome, monumental, regal.
–OPPOSITES humble, dishonourable, base.
▸ noun *Scottish nobles* =**aristocrat**, nobleman, noblewoman, lord, lady, peer (of the realm), peeress; *informal* aristo; *Brit. informal* nob.

nod ▸ verb 1 *she nodded her head* =**incline**, bob, bow, dip. 2 *he nodded to me to start* =**signal**, gesture, gesticulate, motion, sign, indicate.
▸ noun 1 *she gave a nod to the manager* =**signal**, indication, sign, cue; gesture. 2 *a quick nod of his head* =**inclination**, bob, bow, dip.
■ **nod off** =**fall asleep**, go to sleep, doze off, drop off; *informal* drift off, flake out, go out like a light; *N. Amer. informal* sack out.

node ▸ noun =**junction**, intersection, interchange, fork, confluence, convergence, meeting.

noise ▸ noun =**sound**, din, hubbub, clamour, racket, uproar, tumult, commotion, pandemonium, babel; *informal* hullabaloo; *Brit. informal* row.
–OPPOSITES silence.

noisy ▸ adjective 1 *a noisy crowd* =**rowdy**, raucous, clamorous, boisterous; chattering, talkative, vociferous, shouting, screaming. 2 *noisy music* =**loud**, blaring, booming, deafening, thunderous, ear-splitting, piercing, strident, cacophonous.
–OPPOSITES quiet, soft.

nomad ▸ noun =**itinerant**, traveller,

migrant, wanderer; gypsy; transient, drifter.

nominal ▸ adjective 1 *the nominal head of the campaign* =**in name only**, titular, formal, official; theoretical, supposed, ostensible, so-called. 2 *a nominal rent* =**token**, symbolic; minimal, small; *Brit.* peppercorn; *N. Amer. informal* nickel-and-dime.
–OPPOSITES real, considerable.

nominate ▸ verb =**propose**, recommend, suggest, name, put forward, present, submit.

nonchalant ▸ adjective =**calm**, composed, unconcerned, cool; indifferent, blasé, dispassionate, casual, insouciant; *informal* laid-back.
–OPPOSITES anxious.

non-committal ▸ adjective =**evasive**, equivocal, guarded, circumspect, reserved; vague; *informal* cagey.

nonconformist ▸ noun =**dissenter**, protester, rebel, renegade, schismatic; freethinker, apostate, heretic; individualist, free spirit, maverick, eccentric, original, deviant, misfit, dropout, outsider; *informal* freak, oddball; *N. Amer. informal* screwball, kook.

nondescript ▸ adjective =**undistinguished**, unremarkable, unexceptional, featureless, characterless, unmemorable; ordinary, commonplace, average, run-of-the-mill, mundane; uninteresting, uninspiring, colourless, bland.
–OPPOSITES distinctive.

nonentity ▸ noun =**nobody**, cipher, nothing, small fry, lightweight; *informal* no-hoper, non-starter, no-mark.
–OPPOSITES celebrity.

non-essential ▸ adjective =**unnecessary**, inessential, unneeded, superfluous, uncalled for, redundant, dispensable, expendable, unimportant, extraneous.

nonetheless ▸ adverb =**nevertheless**, even so, however, still, yet, though; in spite of that, despite that, be that as it may, for all that, that said, just the same, all the same; notwithstanding, regardless, anyway, anyhow.

non-existent ▸ adjective =**imaginary**, imagined, unreal, fictional, fictitious, made up, invented, fanciful; fantastic, mythical; illusory.
–OPPOSITES real.

non-observance ▸ noun =**infringe-**

ment, breach, violation, contravention, transgression, non-compliance, infraction.

nonplus ▸ verb =**surprise**, stun, dumbfound, confound, take aback, disconcert, throw (off balance); puzzle, perplex, baffle, bemuse, bewilder; *informal* faze, flummox, stump, bamboozle, fox; *N. Amer. informal* discombobulate.

nonsense ▸ noun **1** *he was talking nonsense* =**rubbish**, balderdash, gibberish, claptrap, blarney, garbage; *informal* hogwash, rot, guff, baloney, tripe, drivel, gobbledegook, bilge, bosh, bunk, hot air, piffle, poppycock, phooey, twaddle; *Brit. informal* cobblers, codswallop, tosh, double Dutch; *Scottish & N. English informal* havers; *N. Amer. informal* flapdoodle, bushwa, applesauce; *informal, dated* bunkum, tommyrot. **2** *she stands no nonsense* =**mischief**, messing about, misbehaviour, funny business; *informal* tomfoolery, monkey business, shenanigans, hankypanky; *Brit. informal* monkey tricks, jiggery-pokery. **3** *the whole thing is a nonsense* =**joke**, farce, travesty, sham; insanity, madness.
–OPPOSITES sense, wisdom.

nonsensical ▸ adjective **1** *her nonsensical way of talking* =**meaningless**, illogical. **2** *a nonsensical scheme* =**foolish**, insane, stupid, idiotic, absurd, silly, inane, hare-brained, ridiculous, ludicrous, preposterous; *informal* crazy, crackpot, nutty; *Brit. informal* daft.
–OPPOSITES logical, sensible.

non-stop ▸ adjective *non-stop entertainment* =**continuous**, constant, continual, perpetual, incessant, unceasing, ceaseless, uninterrupted, round-the-clock; unremitting, relentless, persistent.
–OPPOSITES occasional.

▸ adverb *we worked non-stop* =**continuously**, continually, incessantly, unceasingly, ceaselessly, all the time, constantly, perpetually, round the clock, steadily, relentlessly, persistently; *informal* 24-7.
–OPPOSITES occasionally.

noon ▸ noun =**midday**, twelve o'clock, twelve hundred hours, twelve noon, high noon, noonday; *literary* noontide, noontime.

WORD LINKS
relating to noon: **meridional**

norm ▸ noun **1** *norms of diplomatic behav-*

iour =**convention**, standard; criterion, yardstick, benchmark, touchstone, rule, formula, pattern, guide, guideline, model, exemplar. **2** *such teams are now the norm* =**standard**, usual, the rule; normal, typical, average, par for the course, expected.

normal ▸ adjective **1** *they issue books in the normal way* =**usual**, standard, ordinary, customary, conventional, habitual, accustomed, expected; typical, common, everyday, regular, routine, traditional; *literary* wonted. **2** *a normal couple* =**ordinary**, average, typical, run-of-the-mill, middle-of-the-road, common, conventional, mainstream, unremarkable, unexceptional; *N. Amer. informal* garden-variety; *informal* bog-standard, a dime a dozen; *Brit. informal* common or garden. **3** *the man was not normal* =**sane**, in one's right mind, right in the head, of sound mind, compos mentis; *informal* all there.
–OPPOSITES unusual, insane.

normality ▸ noun =**normalcy**, business as usual, the daily round; routine, order, regularity.

normally ▸ adverb **1** *she wanted to be able to walk normally* =**naturally**, conventionally, like everyone else. **2** *normally we'd keep quiet about this* =**usually**, ordinarily, as a rule, generally, in general, mostly, for the most part, by and large, mainly, most of the time, on the whole; typically, traditionally.

north ▸ adjective =**northern**, northerly, boreal.

nose ▸ noun **1** *a punch on the nose* =**snout**, muzzle, proboscis, trunk; *informal* beak, conk, schnozz, schnozzle, hooter, sniffer. **2** *he has a good nose* =**sense of smell**. **3** *a nose for scandal* =**instinct**, feeling, sixth sense, intuition, insight, feel. **4** *wine with a fruity nose* =**smell**, bouquet, aroma, fragrance, perfume, scent, odour.

▸ verb **1** *the dog nosed the ball* =**nuzzle**, nudge, push. **2** *she's nosing into my business* =**pry**, inquire, poke about/around, interfere (in), meddle (in); be a busybody, stick/poke one's nose in; *informal* be nosy (about), snoop; *Austral./NZ informal* stickybeak. **3** *he nosed the car into the traffic* =**ease**, inch, edge, move, manoeuvre, steer, guide.

■ **nose around/about/round** =**investigate**, explore, ferret (about/around), rummage, search; delve into, peer into;

prowl around; *informal* snoop about/around/round.

WORD LINKS

relating to the nose: **nasal, rhinal**
related prefixes: **naso-, rhino-**
inflammation of the nose: **rhinitis**
surgical repair of the nose: **rhinoplasty**
branch of medicine concerning the ears, nose, and throat:
   otorhinolaryngology

nosedive (*informal*) ▶ noun *sterling took a nosedive* =**tumble**, drop, plunge, decline, slump; *informal* crash.
−OPPOSITES climb, rise.
▶ verb *costs have nosedived* =**fall**, drop, sink, plunge, plummet, tumble, slump, go down, decline; *informal* crash.
−OPPOSITES soar.

nostalgia ▶ noun =**reminiscence**, remembrance, recollection; wistfulness, regret, sentimentality.

nostalgic ▶ adjective =**wistful**, romantic, sentimental; regretful, dewy-eyed, maudlin.

nosy ▶ adjective (*informal*) =**prying**, inquisitive, curious, busybody, spying, eavesdropping, intrusive; *informal* snooping.

notable ▶ adjective **1** *notable examples of workmanship* =**noteworthy**, remarkable, outstanding, important, significant, memorable; marked, striking, impressive. **2** *a notable author* =**prominent**, important, well known, famous, famed, noted, distinguished, eminent, illustrious, respected, esteemed, renowned, celebrated, acclaimed, influential, prestigious, of note.
−OPPOSITES unremarkable, unknown.
▶ noun *movie stars and other notables* =**celebrity**, public figure, VIP, dignitary, worthy, luminary; star, superstar, (big) name; *informal* celeb, bigwig, big shot, big cheese, big fish, megastar; *Brit. informal* nob; *N. Amer. informal* kahuna, high muckamuck.
−OPPOSITES nonentity.

notably ▶ adverb **1** *other countries, notably the USA* =**in particular**, particularly, especially; primarily, principally. **2** *these are notably short-lived birds* =**remarkably**, especially, exceptionally, singularly, particularly, peculiarly, distinctly, significantly, unusually, uncommonly, decidedly, conspicuously.

notation ▶ noun **1** *algebraic notation*

=**symbols**, characters; alphabet, script; code. **2** *notations in the margin* =**annotation**, jotting, comment, footnote, entry, memo, gloss.

notch ▶ noun =**nick**, cut, incision, score, scratch, slit, snick, slot, groove, cleft, indentation.
■ **notch something up** =**score**, achieve, attain, gain, earn, make; rack up, chalk up; register, record.

note ▶ noun **1** *a note in her diary* =**record**, entry, reminder; *informal* memo. **2** *he will take notes of the meeting* =**minutes**, record, details; report, account, transcript; synopsis, summary, outline. **3** *notes in the margins* =**annotation**, footnote, comment. **4** *he wrote me a note* =**message**, letter, line; *formal* epistle, missive. **5** (*Brit.*) *a £20 note* =**banknote**; *N. Amer.* bill; *US informal* greenback; (**notes**) paper money. **6** *this is worthy of note* =**attention**, consideration, notice; comment. **7** *a composer of note* =**distinction**, importance, renown, repute, stature, standing, consequence, account. **8** *a note of hopelessness in her voice* =**tone**, intonation, inflection, sound; hint, indication, sign, element, suggestion, sense.
▶ verb **1** *we will note your suggestion* =**bear in mind**, be mindful of, consider, take notice of; register, record, enter. **2** *the letter noted the ministers' concern* =**mention**, refer to, touch on, indicate, point out, make known, state. **3** *note the date in your diary* =**write down**, put down, jot down, take down, enter, mark, record, register, pencil.

notebook ▶ noun =**notepad**, exercise book; register, logbook, log, diary, journal, record; *Brit.* jotter, pocketbook; *N. Amer.* scratch pad.

noted ▶ adjective =**renowned**, well known, famous, famed, prominent, celebrated; notable, of note, important, eminent, distinguished, illustrious, acclaimed, esteemed; of distinction, of repute.
−OPPOSITES unknown.

noteworthy ▶ adjective =**notable**, interesting, significant, important; remarkable, striking, outstanding, memorable, unique, special; unusual, extraordinary, singular.
−OPPOSITES unexceptional.

nothing ▶ noun **1** *there's nothing I can do* =**not a thing**, not anything, nil, zero; *N. English* nowt; *informal* zilch, sweet Fanny

Adams, sweet FA, nix, not a dicky bird; *Brit. informal* damn all, not a sausage, not a bean; *N. Amer. informal* zip, nada, diddly squat; *archaic* naught. **2** *he treats her as nothing* =**a nobody**, a nonentity, a cipher, a non-person. **3** *the share value fell to nothing* =**zero**, nought, 0; *Tennis* love; *Cricket* a duck.
−OPPOSITES something.

■**for nothing 1** *she hosted the show for nothing* =**free (of charge)**, gratis, at no cost; *informal* for free, on the house. **2** *all this trouble for nothing* =**in vain**, to no avail, to no purpose, with no result, needlessly, pointlessly.

■**nothing but** *he's nothing but a nuisance* =**merely**, only, just, solely, simply, purely, no more than.

nothingness ▶ noun =**oblivion**, blankness, darkness, blackness, emptiness; void, vacuum, abyss.

notice ▶ noun **1** *nothing escaped his notice* =**attention**, observation, awareness, consciousness, perception; regard, consideration, scrutiny; watchfulness, vigilance, attentiveness. **2** *a notice on the wall* =**poster**, bill, handbill, advertisement, announcement, bulletin; flyer, leaflet, pamphlet; sign, card; *informal* ad; *Brit. informal* advert. **3** *we will give you notice of any changes* =**notification**, (advance) warning; news, word. **4** *the film got bad notices* =**review**, write-up, report; *Brit. informal* crit.

▶ verb *I noticed that the door was open* =**observe**, note, see, discern, detect, spot, distinguish; *Brit. informal* clock.
−OPPOSITES overlook.

noticeable ▶ adjective =**distinct**, evident, obvious, apparent, manifest, plain, clear, marked, conspicuous, unmistakable, pronounced, prominent, striking; perceptible, discernible, detectable, observable, visible, appreciable.

notification ▶ noun =**information**, word, advice, news, intelligence; communication, message; *literary* tidings.

notify ▶ verb =**inform**, tell, advise, apprise, let someone know; alert, warn.

notion ▶ noun **1** *he had a notion that something was wrong* =**idea**, belief, conviction, opinion, view, thought, impression, perception; hypothesis, theory; (funny) feeling, (sneaking) suspicion, intuition, hunch. **2** *Claire had no notion of what he meant* =**understanding**, idea,

clue, inkling. **3** *he got a notion to return* =**impulse**, inclination, whim, desire, wish, fancy.

notoriety ▶ noun =**infamy**, disrepute, bad name, dishonour, discredit.

notorious ▶ adjective =**infamous**, scandalous; well known, famous, famed, legendary.

nought ▶ noun =**nil**, zero, 0, nothing (at all); *Tennis* love; *Cricket* a duck; *informal* zilch; *Brit. informal* not a sausage; *N. Amer. informal* zip, nada.

nourish ▶ verb **1** *patients must be well nourished* =**feed**, provide for, sustain, maintain. **2** *we nourish the talents of children* =**encourage**, promote, foster, nurture, cultivate, boost, strengthen, enrich. **3** *the hopes Ursula nourished* =**cherish**, nurture, foster, harbour, nurse, entertain, maintain, hold, have, keep.

nourishing ▶ adjective =**nutritious**, wholesome, good for one, healthy, health-giving, healthful, beneficial.
−OPPOSITES unhealthy.

nourishment ▶ noun =**food**, sustenance, nutriment, nutrition, provisions, provender, fare; *informal* grub, nosh, chow, eats; *Brit. informal* scoff; *N. Amer. informal* chuck; *formal* comestibles; *dated* victuals.

novel¹ ▶ noun *curl up with a good novel* =**book**, paperback, hardback; story, tale, narrative, romance; best-seller; *informal* blockbuster.

novel² ▶ adjective *a novel way of making money* =**new**, original, unusual, unfamiliar, unconventional, unorthodox; different, fresh, imaginative, innovative, inventive, modern; avant-garde, pioneering, groundbreaking, revolutionary; unprecedented; experimental, untested, untried; strange, exotic, newfangled.
−OPPOSITES traditional.

novelist ▶ noun =**writer**, author; *informal* scribbler.

novelty ▶ noun **1** *the novelty of our approach* =**originality**, newness, freshness, unconventionality, unfamiliarity; imaginativeness, creativity; uniqueness. **2** *we sell seasonal novelties* =**knick-knack**, trinket, bauble, toy, trifle, ornament; *N. Amer.* kickshaw.

novice ▶ noun =**beginner**, learner, newcomer, fledgling; apprentice, trainee, probationer, student, pupil;

N. Amer. tenderfoot; *informal* rookie, newie; *N. Amer. informal* greenhorn.
−OPPOSITES expert, veteran.

now ▸ adverb **1** *I'm extremely busy now* =**at the moment**, at present, at the present (time/moment), at this (moment in) time, currently; *N. Amer.* presently; *Brit. informal* at the minute. **2** *television is now the main source of news* =**nowadays**, today, these days, in this day and age. **3** *you must leave now* =**at once**, straight away, right away, this minute, this instant, immediately, instantly, directly, without further ado, promptly, without delay, as soon as possible; *informal* pronto, straight off, asap.
■ **now and again** =**occasionally**, (every) now and then, from time to time, sometimes, every so often, (every) now and again, at times, on occasion(s), (every) once in a while; periodically.

nowadays ▸ adverb =**these days**, today, at the present time, in these times, in this day and age, now, currently, at the moment, at present, at this moment in time; *N. Amer.* presently.

noxious ▸ adjective =**poisonous**, toxic, deadly, harmful, dangerous, damaging, destructive; unpleasant, nasty, disgusting, awful, dreadful, horrible, terrible, vile, revolting, foul, nauseating, appalling, offensive; malodorous, fetid, putrid; *informal* ghastly, horrid; *literary* noisome.
−OPPOSITES innocuous.

nuance ▸ noun =**(fine) distinction**, (subtle) difference; shade, gradation, variation, degree; subtlety, nicety.

nub ▸ noun =**crux**, central/main point, core, heart (of the matter), nucleus, essence, quintessence, kernel, meat, pith; gist, substance; *informal* nitty-gritty.

nucleus ▸ noun **1** *the nucleus of the banking world* =**core**, centre, heart, hub, middle, focal point, pivot, crux. **2** *a nucleus of union men supported him* =**(hard) core**, caucus, coterie, clique, faction.

nude ▸ adjective =**(stark) naked**, bare, unclothed, undressed, unclad, with nothing on, as nature intended, au naturel; *informal* without a stitch on, in one's birthday suit, in the raw/buff, in the altogether, in the nuddy; *Brit. informal* starkers; *Scottish informal* in the scud; *N. Amer. informal* buck naked.
−OPPOSITES clothed.

┌─────────────────────┐
│ **WORD LINKS** │
└─────────────────────┘
fear of nudity: **gymnophobia**

nudge ▸ verb **1** *he nudged Ben* =**poke**, elbow, dig, prod, jab. **2** *the canoe nudged the bank* =**touch**, bump (against), push (against), run into. **3** *we nudged them towards a decision* =**prompt**, encourage, prod. **4** *unemployment was nudging 3,000,000* =**approach**, near, come close to, touch, be verging on, border on.
▸ noun *Maggie gave him a nudge* =**poke**, dig (in the ribs), prod, jab, push.

nugget ▸ noun =**lump**, chunk, piece, hunk, gobbet; *N. Amer. informal* gob.

nuisance ▸ noun =**annoyance**, inconvenience, bore, bother, irritation, trial, burden; pest, thorn in one's side/flesh; *informal* pain (in the neck), hassle, bind, drag, aggravation, headache; *Scottish informal* nyaff, skelf; *N. Amer. informal* nudnik; *Austral./NZ informal* nark.
−OPPOSITES blessing.

nullify ▸ verb =**annul**, render null and void, void, invalidate; repeal, reverse, rescind, revoke, cancel, abolish; do away with, terminate, quash.
−OPPOSITES ratify.

numb ▸ adjective *his fingers were numb* =**without sensation**, dead, without feeling, numbed, desensitized, unfeeling, frozen; anaesthetized; dazed, stunned, stupefied, paralysed, immobilized.
−OPPOSITES sensitive.
▸ verb *the cold numbed her senses* =**deaden**, desensitize, dull; anaesthetize; daze, stupefy, paralyse, immobilize, freeze.
−OPPOSITES sensitize.

number ▸ noun **1** *a whole number* =**numeral**, integer, figure, digit; character, symbol; decimal, unit; cardinal number, ordinal number. **2** *a large number of complaints* =**amount**, quantity; total, aggregate, tally; quota, average. **3** *the wedding of one of their number* =**group**, company, crowd, circle, party, band, crew, set; *informal* gang. **4** *the band performed another number* =**song**, piece (of music), tune, track; routine, sketch, dance, act.
▸ verb **1** *visitors numbered more than two million* =**add up to**, amount to, total, come to. **2** *he numbers the fleet at a thousand* =**calculate**, count, total, compute, reckon, estimate, tally; assess; *Brit.* tot up; *formal* enumerate. **3** *he numbers her among his friends* =**include**, count,

reckon, deem.

■ **a number of** =several, various, (quite) a few, sundry, some.

■ **without number** =countless, innumerable, unlimited, limitless, untold, numberless, uncountable, uncounted; numerous, many, legion; *informal* more ... than one can shake a stick at; *literary* myriad.

> WORD LINKS
>
> *relating to numbers:* **numerical**

numberless ▸ adjective =innumerable, countless, unlimited, endless, limitless, untold, uncountable, uncounted; numerous, legion; *informal* more ... than one can shake a stick at; *literary* myriad.

numbing ▸ adjective **1** *menthol has a numbing action* =desensitizing, deadening, benumbing, anaesthetic, anaesthetizing; paralysing. **2** *numbing cold* =freezing, raw, bitter, biting, arctic.

numeral ▸ noun =number, integer, figure, digit; character, symbol, unit.

numerous ▸ adjective =many, a number of, a lot of; several, plenty of, copious, an abundance of; frequent; *informal* umpteen.
–OPPOSITES few.

nuptial ▸ adjective =matrimonial, marital, marriage, wedding, conjugal, bridal; married, wedded; *Law* spousal; *literary* connubial.

nuptials ▸ plural noun =wedding (ceremony), marriage, union; *archaic* espousal.

nurse ▸ noun **1** *skilled nurses* =carer; *informal* Florence Nightingale, nursey; *N. Amer. informal* candy-striper. **2** *(dated) she had been his nurse in childhood* =nanny, nursemaid, nursery nurse, childminder, au pair, childcarer, babysitter, ayah.
▸ verb **1** *they nursed smallpox patients* =care for, take care of, look after, tend, minister to. **2** *Rosa was nursing her baby* =breastfeed, suckle, feed. **3** *they nursed old grievances* =harbour, foster, bear, have, hold (on to), retain.

nursemaid ▸ noun. *See* NURSE noun sense 2.

nurture ▸ verb **1** *she nurtured her children into adulthood* =bring up, care for, take care of, look after, tend, rear, raise, support. **2** *we nurtured these plants* =cultivate, grow, keep, tend. **3** *he nurtured my love of art* =encourage, promote, stimulate, develop, foster, cultivate, boost, strengthen, fuel.
–OPPOSITES neglect, hinder.

nut ▸ noun **1** *(informal) he smacked her on the nut* =head, skull, cranium, crown; *informal* noodle, noggin; *Brit. informal* bonce; *informal, dated* conk, noddle. **2** *(informal) some nut arrived at the office* =maniac, lunatic, madman, madwoman, eccentric; *informal* loony, nutcase, fruitcake, head case, crank, crackpot, weirdo; *Brit. informal* nutter; *N. Amer. informal* screwball, crazy; *N. Amer. & Austral./NZ informal* dingbat. **3** *(informal) a movie nut* =enthusiast, fan, devotee, aficionado; *informal* freak, fiend, fanatic, addict, buff; *N. Amer. informal* jock.
■ **do one's nut** *(informal)* =be furious, lose one's temper; *informal* go mad, go crazy, go wild, go bananas, have a fit, blow one's top, hit the roof, go off the deep end, go ape, freak out, flip, lose one's rag; *Brit. informal* go spare.

nutrition ▸ noun =nourishment, nutriment, nutrients, sustenance, food; *informal* grub, chow, nosh; *Brit. informal* scoff; *literary* viands; *dated* victuals.

nutritious ▸ adjective =nourishing, good for one, full of goodness; wholesome, healthy, healthful, beneficial, sustaining.

nuts ▸ adjective *(informal)* **1** *they thought we were nuts. See* MAD *sense* 1. **2** *he's nuts about her* =infatuated with, devoted to, in love with, smitten with, enamoured of, hot for; *informal* mad, crazy, nutty, wild, hooked on, gone on, dead keen on; *Brit. informal* potty.

nuts and bolts ▸ plural noun =basics, fundamentals, practicalities, essentials, mechanics; *informal* nitty-gritty, ins and outs, brass tacks.

nutty ▸ adjective *(informal)* **1** *they're all nutty. See* MAD *sense* 1. **2** *she's nutty about Elvis. See* NUTS *sense* 2.

Oo

oaf ▶ noun = **lout**, boor, barbarian, Neanderthal, yokel; fool, idiot, imbecile; *informal* cretin, ass, goon, yahoo, ape, lump, meathead, bonehead, lamebrain; *Brit. informal* clot, plonker, berk, pillock, yob, yobbo; *Scottish informal* nyaff, gowk; *N. Amer. informal* bozo, dumbhead, lummox, klutz, goofus, clunk, turkey; *Austral. informal* hoon, dingbat, galah, drongo; *archaic* lubber.

oafish ▶ adjective = **stupid**, foolish, idiotic; loutish, awkward, gawkish, clumsy, lumbering, ape-like, Neanderthal, uncouth, boorish, rough, brutish, ill-mannered, unrefined; *informal* clodhopping, blockheaded, boneheaded, thickheaded; *Brit. informal* yobbish.

oasis ▶ noun = **refuge**, haven, retreat, sanctuary.

oath ▶ noun 1 *an oath of allegiance* = **vow**, pledge, promise, affirmation, word (of honour), guarantee. 2 *a stream of oaths* = **swear word**, profanity, expletive, four-letter word, dirty word, obscenity, curse; *formal* imprecation.

obdurate ▶ adjective = **stubborn**, obstinate, intransigent, inflexible, unyielding, unbending, pig-headed, stiff-necked; headstrong; *Brit. informal* bloody-minded.
   −OPPOSITES malleable.

obedient ▶ adjective = **compliant**, biddable, acquiescent, tractable, amenable, pliant; dutiful, good, law-abiding, deferential, respectful, manageable, governable, docile, tame, meek, passive, submissive.
   −OPPOSITES rebellious.

obelisk ▶ noun = **column**, pillar, needle, shaft, monolith, monument.

obese ▶ adjective = **fat**, overweight, corpulent, gross, stout, fleshy, heavy, portly, pot-bellied, bloated, flabby; *informal* porky, roly-poly, blubbery.
   −OPPOSITES thin.

obey ▶ verb 1 *I obeyed him* = **do what someone says**; submit to, defer to. 2 *he refused to obey the order* = **carry out**, perform, act on, execute, discharge, implement. 3 *the rules have to be obeyed* = **comply with**, adhere to, observe, abide by, act in accordance with, conform to, respect, follow, keep to, stick to.
   −OPPOSITES defy, ignore.

object ▶ noun 1 *wooden objects* = **thing**, article, item; *informal* doodah, thingamajig, thingummy, whatsit, whatchamacallit; *Brit. informal* gubbins; *N. Amer. informal* doodad. 2 *he became the object of criticism* = **target**, butt, focus, recipient, victim. 3 *his object was to resolve the crisis* = **objective**, aim, goal, target, purpose, end, plan, point; ambition, design, intention, idea.
   ▶ verb *teachers objected to the scheme* = **protest about**, oppose, take exception to, take issue with, take a stand against, argue against, quarrel with, condemn, draw the line at, demur at, mind, complain about; beg to differ; *informal* kick up a fuss/stink about.
   −OPPOSITES approve, accept.

objection ▶ noun = **protest**, protestation, demurral, complaint, cavil; opposition, counter-argument, disagreement, disapproval, dissent.

objectionable ▶ adjective = **unpleasant**, disagreeable, distasteful, undesirable, obnoxious, offensive, nasty, horrible, horrid, disgusting, awful, dreadful, appalling, insufferable, odious, vile, foul, unsavoury, repulsive, repellent, repugnant, revolting, abhorrent, loathsome, detestable; *informal* ghastly; *Brit. informal* beastly.
   −OPPOSITES pleasant.

objective ▶ adjective 1 *try to be objective* = **impartial**, unbiased, unprejudiced, non-partisan, disinterested, neutral, uninvolved, even-handed, equitable, fair, open-minded, dispassionate, detached. 2 *objective knowledge* = **factual**, actual, real, empirical, verifiable.
   −OPPOSITES biased, subjective.
   ▶ noun *our objective is to make a profit* = **aim**, intention, purpose, target, goal, intent, object, point; idea, plan.

objectively ▶ adverb = **impartially**, without bias/prejudice, even-handedly, dispassionately, with an open mind, without fear or favour.

objectivity ▸ noun =**impartiality**, lack of bias/prejudice, fairness, fair-mindedness, neutrality, even-handedness, open-mindedness, disinterest, detachment.

obligation ▸ noun **1** *his professional obligations* =**duty**, commitment, responsibility; function, task, job, burden, charge, onus, liability, requirement, debt. **2** *a sense of obligation* =**duty**, compulsion, indebtedness; duress, necessity, pressure, constraint.

obligatory ▸ adjective =**compulsory**, mandatory, prescribed, required, demanded, statutory, enforced, binding, incumbent; requisite, necessary, imperative, unavoidable, inescapable, essential.
–OPPOSITES optional.

oblige ▸ verb **1** *we are obliged to accept the decision* =**require**, compel, bind, constrain, leave someone no option, force. **2** *I'll be happy to oblige you* =**do someone a favour**, accommodate, help, assist; indulge, humour.

obliged ▸ adjective =**thankful**, grateful, appreciative; beholden, indebted, in someone's debt.

obliging ▸ adjective =**helpful**, accommodating, cooperative, agreeable, amenable, generous, kind, hospitable, amiable, gracious, unselfish; *Brit. informal* decent.
–OPPOSITES unhelpful.

oblique ▸ adjective **1** *an oblique line* =**slanting**, slanted, sloping, at an angle, angled, diagonal, askew, squint; *N. Amer.* cater-cornered. **2** *an oblique reference* =**indirect**, roundabout, circuitous, implicit, implied, elliptical, evasive.
–OPPOSITES straight, direct.
▸ noun =**slash**, solidus, backslash.

obliquely ▸ adverb **1** *the sun shone obliquely across the tower* =**diagonally**, at an angle, slantwise, sideways, sidelong. **2** *he referred obliquely to the war* =**indirectly**, in a roundabout way, circuitously, evasively.

obliterate ▸ verb **1** *he tried to obliterate the memory* =**erase**, eradicate, expunge, wipe out, blot out, remove all traces of. **2** *a bomb that would obliterate a city* =**destroy**, wipe out, annihilate, demolish, wipe off the face of the earth; *informal* zap. **3** *clouds obliterated the sun* =**hide**,

obscure, blot out, block, cover, screen.

oblivion ▸ noun **1** *I drank myself into oblivion* =**unconsciousness**, insensibility, stupor; coma, blackout. **2** *rescued from artistic oblivion* =**obscurity**, limbo, anonymity.
–OPPOSITES consciousness, fame.

oblivious ▸ adjective =**unaware**, unconscious, heedless, unmindful, insensible, ignorant, blind, deaf; unconcerned, impervious.
–OPPOSITES conscious.

obnoxious ▸ adjective =**unpleasant**, disagreeable, nasty, offensive, objectionable, unsavoury, revolting, repulsive, repellent, repugnant, disgusting, odious, vile, foul, loathsome, nauseating, sickening, hateful, insufferable, intolerable; *informal* horrible, horrid, ghastly, gross, sick-making, yucky, God-awful; *Brit. informal* beastly.
–OPPOSITES delightful.

obscene ▸ adjective **1** *obscene literature* =**pornographic**, indecent, smutty, dirty, filthy, X-rated, adult, explicit, lewd, rude, vulgar, coarse, immoral, improper, off colour; scatological; *informal* blue, porn. **2** *an obscene amount* =**scandalous**, shocking, outrageous, immoral.

obscenity ▸ noun **1** *they were prosecuted for obscenity* =**indecency**, immorality, impropriety, lewdness. **2** *the men muttered obscenities* =**expletive**, swear word, oath, profanity, curse, four-letter word, dirty word, blasphemy; *informal* cuss; *formal* imprecation. **3** *the obscenity of the arms trade* =**scandal**, outrage, immorality.

obscure ▸ adjective **1** *his origins remain obscure* =**unclear**, uncertain, unknown, mysterious, hazy, vague, indeterminate. **2** *obscure references to Proust* =**cryptic**, oblique, opaque, elliptical, unintelligible, incomprehensible, impenetrable, unfathomable; recondite, arcane, esoteric. **3** *an obscure Peruvian painter* =**little known**, unknown, unheard of; unsung, unrecognized, forgotten.
–OPPOSITES clear, plain, famous, distinct.
▸ verb **1** *clouds obscured the sun* =**hide**, conceal, cover, veil, shroud, screen, mask, cloak, block, obliterate, eclipse. **2** *recent events have obscured the issue* =**confuse**, complicate, obfuscate, cloud, blur, muddy.
–OPPOSITES reveal, clarify.

obscurity ▸ noun =insignificance, inconspicuousness, unimportance, anonymity; limbo, twilight, oblivion.
–OPPOSITES fame.

obsequious ▸ adjective =servile, ingratiating, sycophantic, fawning, unctuous, oily, grovelling, cringing, subservient, submissive, slavish; *informal* slimy, bootlicking, smarmy.

observable ▸ adjective =noticeable, visible, perceptible, perceivable, detectable, distinguishable, discernible, recognizable.

observance ▸ noun =compliance, adherence, accordance, respect, observation, fulfilment, obedience; keeping, obeying.

observant ▸ adjective =alert, sharp-eyed, sharp, eagle-eyed, keen-eyed, watchful; *informal* beady-eyed, not missing a trick, on the ball.
–OPPOSITES inattentive.

observation ▸ noun 1 *detailed observation of their behaviour* =monitoring, watching, scrutiny, survey, surveillance, attention, study. 2 *his observations were correct* =remark, comment; opinion, impression, thought, reflection.

observe ▸ verb 1 *she observed that he was drunk* =notice, see, note, perceive, discern, spot. 2 *he had been observing her* =watch, look at, contemplate, view, survey, regard, keep an eye on, scrutinize, keep under observation/surveillance, keep watch on, monitor; *informal* keep tabs on, keep a beady eye on. 3 *'You look tired,' she observed* =remark, comment, say, mention, declare, announce, state, pronounce. 4 *they agreed to observe the ceasefire* =comply with, abide by, keep, obey, adhere to, heed, honour, fulfil, respect, follow, consent to, accept.

observer ▸ noun 1 *the casual observer* =spectator, onlooker, watcher, fly on the wall, viewer, witness. 2 *industry observers are worried* =commentator, reporter; monitor.

obsess ▸ verb 1 *it obsessed him for years* =preoccupy, prey on (someone's mind), possess, haunt, consume, plague, torment, hound, bedevil, take over, eat up, grip. 2 *stop obsessing about it* =worry, go on, dwell, brood.

obsessed ▸ adjective =fixated, possessed, consumed; infatuated, besotted; *informal* smitten, hung up; *N. Amer. informal* hipped.

obsession ▸ noun =fixation, passion, mania, compulsion, preoccupation, infatuation, addiction, fetish, craze; hobby horse; phobia, complex, neurosis; *informal* bee in one's bonnet, hang-up, thing.

obsessive ▸ adjective =(all-)consuming, compulsive, controlling, fanatical, neurotic, excessive; *informal* pathological.

obsolescent ▸ adjective =dying out, on the decline/wane, disappearing, moribund, out of date, outdated, old-fashioned, outmoded; *informal* on the way out.

obsolete ▸ adjective =out of date, outdated, outmoded, old-fashioned, passé; superannuated, outworn, antiquated, antediluvian, anachronistic, discontinued, old, dated, archaic, ancient, fossilized, extinct, defunct, dead, bygone; *informal* out of the ark, prehistoric; *Brit. informal* past its sell-by date.
–OPPOSITES current, modern.

obstacle ▸ noun =barrier, hurdle, stumbling block, obstruction, bar, block, impediment, hindrance, snag, catch, drawback, hitch, fly in the ointment, handicap, difficulty, problem, disadvantage; *Brit.* spanner in the works.
–OPPOSITES advantage, aid.

obstinacy ▸ noun =stubbornness, inflexibility, intransigence, pig-headedness, wilfulness, recalcitrance, implacability; persistence, tenacity, doggedness.

obstinate ▸ adjective =stubborn, unyielding, inflexible, unbending, intransigent, intractable, obdurate, stubborn as a mule, pig-headed, self-willed, headstrong, stiff-necked, uncompromising, implacable, immovable, unshakeable; persistent, tenacious, dogged.
–OPPOSITES compliant.

obstreperous ▸ adjective =unruly, disorderly, rowdy, disruptive, difficult, riotous, wild, turbulent, boisterous; noisy, loud; *informal* rumbustious; *Brit. informal* stroppy, bolshie; *N. Amer. informal* rambunctious.
–OPPOSITES quiet, restrained.

obstruct ▸ verb 1 *ensure that vents are not obstructed* =block (up), clog (up), occlude, cut off, bung up, choke, dam up. 2 *he was obstructing the traffic* =hold up, bring to a standstill, stop, halt, block. 3 *they may obstruct aid distribution* =impede, hinder, interfere with, hamper,

block, interrupt, hold up, stand in the way of, frustrate, sabotage; slow down, delay, stonewall, stop, halt, restrict, limit, curb.
–OPPOSITES clear, facilitate.

obstruction ▸ noun =**obstacle**, barrier, stumbling block, impediment, hindrance, difficulty, check, restriction; blockage, stoppage, congestion, bottleneck, hold-up; *Medicine* occlusion.

obstructive ▸ adjective =**unhelpful**, uncooperative, awkward, difficult, perverse, contrary; *Brit. informal* bloody-minded, bolshie; *N. Amer. informal* balky.
–OPPOSITES helpful.

obtain ▸ verb =**get**, acquire, come by, secure, procure, pick up, be given; gain, earn, achieve, attain; *informal* get hold of, get/lay one's hands on, land.
–OPPOSITES lose.

obtainable ▸ adjective =**available**, to be had, in circulation, on the market, on offer, in season, at one's disposal, at hand, accessible; *informal* up for grabs, on tap, get-at-able.

obtrusive ▸ adjective =**conspicuous**, prominent, noticeable, obvious, unmistakable, out of place; *informal* sticking out a mile, sticking out like a sore thumb.
–OPPOSITES inconspicuous.

obtuse ▸ adjective =**stupid**, foolish, slow-witted, slow, unintelligent, simple-minded; *informal* dim, dim-witted, dense, dumb, slow on the uptake, half-witted, brain-dead, moronic, cretinous, thick, dopey, dozy; *Brit. informal* divvy; *Scottish & N. English informal* glaikit; *N. Amer. informal* dumb-ass, chowderheaded.
–OPPOSITES clever.

obviate ▸ verb =**preclude**, prevent, remove, get rid of, do away with, get round, rule out, eliminate.

obvious ▸ adjective =**clear**, crystal clear, plain, evident, apparent, manifest, patent, conspicuous, pronounced, transparent, palpable, prominent, marked, decided, distinct, noticeable, perceptible, visible, discernible; *informal* as plain as the nose on your face, sticking out like a sore thumb, sticking out a mile.
–OPPOSITES imperceptible.

obviously ▸ adverb =**clearly**, evidently, plainly, patently, visibly, discernibly, manifestly, noticeably; of course, naturally, needless to say, it goes without saying.

–OPPOSITES perhaps.

occasion ▸ noun **1** *a previous occasion* =**time**, instance, juncture, point, episode, experience; situation, case, circumstance. **2** *a special occasion* =**event**, affair, function, celebration, party, get-together, gathering; *informal* do, bash.
■ **on occasion.** *See* OCCASIONALLY.

occasional ▸ adjective =**infrequent**, intermittent, irregular, periodic, sporadic, odd; *N. Amer.* sometime.
–OPPOSITES regular, frequent.

occasionally ▸ adverb =**sometimes**, from time to time, (every) now and then, (every) now and again, at times, every so often, (every) once in a while, on occasion, periodically, at intervals, intermittently, on and off, off and on.
–OPPOSITES often.

occult ▸ adjective =**supernatural**, magic, magical, satanic, mystical; psychic.
■ **the occult** =**the supernatural**, magic, black magic, witchcraft, necromancy, the black arts, occultism, devil worship, satanism, Wicca, voodoo, white magic; *NZ* makutu.

occupancy ▸ noun =**occupation**, tenancy, residence, residency, inhabitation, habitation, living, owner-occupancy; *formal* dwelling.

occupant ▸ noun =**resident**, inhabitant, owner, householder, tenant, leaseholder, lessee; *Brit.* occupier, owner-occupier.

occupation ▸ noun **1** *his father's occupation* =**job**, profession, (line) of work, trade, employment, business, career, métier, vocation, calling, craft; *Austral. informal* grip. **2** *a property suitable for immediate occupation* =**residence**, residency, habitation, inhabitation, occupancy, tenancy, living in. **3** *the Roman occupation of Britain* =**conquest**, capture, invasion, seizure; colonization, rule, control.

occupational ▸ adjective =**job-related**, work, professional, vocational, employment, business, career.

occupied ▸ adjective **1** *tasks which kept her occupied* =**busy**, working, at work, active; *informal* tied up, hard at it, on the go. **2** *the tables was occupied* =**in use**, full, engaged, taken. **3** *only two flats are occupied* =**inhabited**, lived-in.
–OPPOSITES free, vacant.

occupy ▸ verb **1** *Carol occupied the basement flat* =**live in**, inhabit, lodge in;

move into; people, populate, settle; *Scottish* stay in. **2** *he occupies a post at the Treasury* =**hold**, fill, have; *informal* hold down. **3** *something to occupy my mind* =**engage**, busy, distract, absorb, engross, preoccupy, hold, interest, involve, entertain. **4** *the region was occupied by Japan* =**capture**, seize, take possession of, conquer, invade, take over, colonize, annex, subjugate.

occur ▶ verb **1** *an accident occurred at 3.30* =**happen**, take place, come about; *N. Amer. informal* go down. **2** *the disease occurs in the tropics* =**be found**, be present, exist, appear. **3** *an idea occurred to her* =**enter one's head/mind**, cross one's mind, come/spring to mind, strike one, hit one, come to one, dawn on one, suggest itself.

occurrence ▶ noun **1** *a rare occurrence* =**event**, incident, happening, phenomenon. **2** *the occurrence of cancer* =**existence**, instance, appearance; frequency, incidence, rate, prevalence; *Statistics* distribution.

ocean ▶ noun =**the sea**; *informal* the drink; *Brit. informal* the briny; *literary* the deep, the waves.

> **WORD LINKS**
>
> *relating to the ocean:* **oceanic, marine, maritime, pelagic, thalassic**

odd ▶ adjective **1** *an odd man* =**strange**, peculiar, queer, funny, bizarre, eccentric, unusual, weird, unconventional, quirky, zany; *informal* wacky, kooky, screwy, offbeat, off the wall. **2** *some odd things had happened* =**strange**, unusual, peculiar, funny, curious, weird, bizarre, uncanny, queer, unexpected, abnormal, atypical, anomalous, different, puzzling, mystifying, baffling, unaccountable. **3** *we have the odd drink together | he does odd jobs for friends* =**occasional**, casual, irregular, isolated, sporadic, periodic; miscellaneous, various, varied, sundry. **4** *odd shoes* =**mismatched**, unmatched, unpaired; single, lone, solitary, extra, leftover.
−OPPOSITES normal, ordinary, regular.

oddity ▶ noun **1** *she was a bit of an oddity* =**eccentric**, crank, misfit, maverick, nonconformist, individualist; *informal* character, oddball, weirdo; *N. Amer. informal* kook. **2** *the oddities of human nature* =**peculiarity**, idiosyncrasy, eccentricity, quirk, twist.

oddments ▶ plural noun **1** *oddments of material* =**scraps**, remnants, odds and ends, bits, pieces, bits and bobs, leftovers, fragments, snippets, offcuts. **2** *a cellar full of oddments. See* ODDS AND ENDS *at* ODDS.

odds ▶ plural noun *the odds are that he is still alive* =**likelihood**, probability, chances.
■ **at odds 1** *he was at odds with his colleagues* =**in conflict**, in disagreement, at loggerheads, quarrelling, arguing; *N. Amer.* on the outs. **2** *behaviour at odds with the interests of the company* =**at variance**, conflicting, contrary, incompatible, inconsistent, irreconcilable.
■ **odds and ends** =**bits and pieces**, bits and bobs, bits, pieces, stuff, paraphernalia, things, sundries, bric-a-brac, knick-knacks, oddments; *informal* junk; *Brit. informal* odds and sods, clobber, gubbins.

odious ▶ adjective =**revolting**, repulsive, repellent, repugnant, disgusting, offensive, objectionable, vile, foul, abhorrent, loathsome, nauseating, sickening, hateful, detestable, abominable, monstrous, appalling, insufferable, intolerable, despicable, contemptible, unspeakable, atrocious, awful, terrible, dreadful, frightful, obnoxious, unpleasant, disagreeable, nasty; *informal* ghastly, horrible, horrid, God-awful; *Brit. informal* beastly.
−OPPOSITES delightful.

odour ▶ noun =**smell**, stench, stink, reek; *Brit. informal* pong, whiff, niff, hum; *N. Amer. informal* funk; *literary* miasma.

> **WORD LINKS**
>
> *relating to odour:* **osmic, olfactory**

odyssey ▶ noun =**journey**, voyage, trek, travels, quest, crusade, pilgrimage.

off ▶ adjective **1** *Kate's off today* =**away**, absent, not at work, off duty, on holiday, on leave; free; *N. Amer.* on vacation. **2** *the game's off* =**cancelled**, postponed, called off. **3** *the fish was off* =**rotten**, bad, stale, mouldy, sour, rancid, turned, spoiled. **4** *(Brit. informal) I felt decidedly off. See* OFF COLOUR *sense 1*. **5** *(Brit. informal) that remark was a bit off* =**unfair**, unjust, uncalled for, below the belt, unjustified, unreasonable, unwarranted, unnecessary; *informal* a bit much; *Brit. informal* out of order.
■ **off and on** =**periodically**, at intervals, on and off, (every) once in a while, every

so often, (every) now and then/again, from time to time, occasionally, sometimes, intermittently, irregularly.

offbeat ▶ adjective *(informal)* =**unconventional**, unorthodox, unusual, eccentric, idiosyncratic, strange, bizarre, weird, peculiar, odd, freakish, outlandish, out of the ordinary, Bohemian, alternative, left-field, zany, quirky; *informal* wacky, freaky, way-out, off the wall, kooky, oddball.
–OPPOSITES conventional.

off colour ▶ adjective **1** *(Brit.) I'm feeling a bit off colour* =**unwell**, ill, poorly, out of sorts, not oneself, sick, queasy, nauseous, peaky, run down, washed out, below par; *informal* under the weather, rough; *Brit. informal* ropy, off; *Scottish informal* wabbit, peely-wally; *Austral./NZ informal* crook. **2** *off-colour jokes* =**smutty**, dirty, rude, crude, suggestive, indecent, indelicate, risqué, racy, bawdy, naughty, blue, vulgar, ribald, coarse; *informal* raunchy; *Brit. informal* fruity, saucy; *euphemistic* adult.
–OPPOSITES well.

offence ▶ noun **1** *he has committed an offence* =**crime**, illegal/unlawful act, misdemeanour, breach of the law, felony, infringement. **2** *an offence to natural justice* =**affront**, slap in the face, insult, outrage, violation. **3** *I do not want to cause offence* =**annoyance**, resentment, indignation, displeasure, hard/bad/ill feelings, animosity.
■ **take offence** =**be offended**, take exception, take something personally, take something amiss, get upset/annoyed/angry; *Brit. informal* get the hump.

offend ▶ verb **1** *I'm sorry if I offended him* =**hurt someone's feelings**, give offence to, affront, displease, upset, distress, hurt, wound; *Brit.* rub up the wrong way. **2** *criminals who offend repeatedly* =**break the law**, commit a crime, do wrong.

offended ▶ adjective =**affronted**, insulted, aggrieved, displeased, upset, hurt, wounded, put out, indignant.
–OPPOSITES pleased.

offender ▶ noun =**wrongdoer**, criminal, lawbreaker, miscreant, felon, delinquent, culprit, guilty party; *informal* malefactor.

offensive ▶ adjective **1** *offensive remarks* =**insulting**, rude, derogatory, disrespectful, personal, hurtful, wounding, abusive; *formal* exceptionable. **2** *an offen-*

sive smell =**unpleasant**, disagreeable, nasty, distasteful, objectionable, off-putting, awful, terrible, dreadful, frightful, obnoxious, abominable, disgusting, repulsive, repellent, vile, foul, sickening, nauseating; *informal* ghastly, horrible, horrid, gross, God-awful; *Brit. informal* beastly.
–OPPOSITES complimentary, pleasant.
▶ noun *a military offensive* =**attack**, assault, onslaught, drive, invasion, push, thrust, charge, sortie, sally, foray, raid, incursion, blitz, campaign.

offer ▶ verb **1** *Frank offered a suggestion* =**put forward**, proffer, give, present, come up with, suggest, propose, advance, submit, tender. **2** *she offered to help* =**volunteer**, step/come forward, show willing. **3** *he offered $200* =**bid**, tender, put in a bid/offer of. **4** *a job offering good prospects* =**provide**, afford, supply, give, furnish, present, hold out. **5** *she offered no resistance* =**attempt**, try, give, show, express.
–OPPOSITES withdraw, refuse.
▶ noun **1** *offers of help* =**proposal**, proposition, suggestion, submission, approach, overture. **2** *the highest offer* =**bid**, tender, (bidding) price.

offering ▶ noun =**contribution**, donation.

offhand ▶ adjective =**casual**, careless, uninterested, unconcerned, indifferent, cool, nonchalant, blasé, insouciant, cavalier, glib, perfunctory, cursory, dismissive; *informal* couldn't-care-less, take-it-or-leave-it.
▶ adverb =**on the spur of the moment**, without consideration, spontaneously; *informal* off the cuff, off the top of one's head, just like that.

office ▶ noun **1** *we met at her office* =**place of work**, place of business, workplace, workroom. **2** *the company's Paris office* =**branch**, division, section, bureau, department. **3** *the office of President* =**post**, position, appointment, job, occupation, role, situation, function, capacity.

officer ▶ noun **1** *officers and men* =**army officer**. **2** *all officers carry warrant cards.* See POLICE OFFICER. **3** *the officers of the society* =**official**, office-holder, committee member, board member.

official ▶ adjective **1** *an official inquiry* =**authorized**, approved, validated, authenticated, certified, accredited, endorsed, sanctioned, licensed, recognized, legitimate, legal, lawful, valid, bona fide, proper; *informal* kosher. **2** *an official function* =**ceremonial**, formal, solemn; bureaucratic.

–OPPOSITES unauthorized, informal.

▶ noun *a union official* =**officer**, administrator, executive, functionary; bureaucrat, mandarin; representative, agent; *derogatory* apparatchik.

officiate ▶ verb =**be in charge of**, take charge of, preside over; oversee, superintend, supervise, conduct, run.

officious ▶ adjective =**self-important**, bumptious, self-assertive, overbearing, interfering, intrusive, meddlesome, meddling; *informal* bossy.

–OPPOSITES self-effacing.

off-key ▶ adjective =**out of tune**, flat, tuneless, discordant.

–OPPOSITES harmonious.

offload ▶ verb **1** *the cargo was being offloaded* =**unload**, remove, empty (out), tip (out). **2** *he offloaded 5,000 of the shares* =**dispose of**, dump, jettison, get rid of, transfer, shift; palm off, foist, fob off.

off-putting ▶ adjective **1** *an off-putting aroma* =**unpleasant**, unattractive, disagreeable, offensive, distasteful, unappetizing, objectionable, nasty, disgusting, repellent; *informal* horrid, horrible. **2** *her manner was most off-putting* =**discouraging**, disheartening, daunting, disconcerting, unnerving, unsettling.

offset ▶ verb =**counterbalance**, balance (out), cancel (out), even out/up, counteract, countervail, neutralize, compensate for, make up for.

offshoot ▶ noun =**outcome**, result, effect, consequence, upshot, product, by-product, spin-off, development, ramification.

offspring ▶ noun =**children**, sons and daughters, progeny, youngsters, babies, infants, brood; descendants, heirs, successors; *Law* issue; *informal* kids; *Brit. informal* sprogs, brats; *derogatory* spawn.

often ▶ adverb =**frequently**, many times, on many/numerous occasions, a lot, as often as not, repeatedly, again and again; regularly, routinely, usually, habitually, commonly, generally, in many cases/instances, ordinarily; *N. Amer.* oftentimes.

–OPPOSITES seldom.

ogle ▶ verb =**leer at**, stare at, eye, make

eyes at; *informal* eye up; *Austral./NZ informal* perv on.

ogre ▶ noun =**monster**, **brute**, fiend, beast, barbarian, savage, animal, tyrant, bogeyman.

oily ▶ adjective **1** *oily substances* =**greasy**, oleaginous; *technical* sebaceous; *formal* pinguid. **2** *oily food* =**greasy**, fatty, buttery. **3** *an oily man* =**unctuous**, ingratiating, smooth-talking, fulsome, flattering; obsequious, sycophantic; *informal* smarmy, slimy.

ointment ▶ noun =**lotion**, cream, salve, liniment, embrocation, rub, gel, balm, emollient, unguent.

OK, okay *(informal)* ▶ exclamation *OK, I'll go with him* =**all right**, right, right then, right you are, very well, very good, fine; *informal* okey-doke(y); *Brit. informal* righto, righty-ho.

▶ adjective **1** *the film was OK* =**satisfactory**, all right, acceptable, competent; adequate, tolerable, passable, reasonable, fair, decent, not bad, average, middling, moderate, unremarkable, unexceptional; *informal* so-so, fair-to-middling. **2** *Jo's feeling OK now* =**fine**, all right, well, better. **3** *it is OK for me to come?* =**permissible**, allowable, acceptable, all right, in order, permitted, fitting, suitable, appropriate.

–OPPOSITES unsatisfactory, ill.

▶ noun *he's given me the OK* =**authorization**, approval, seal of approval, agreement, consent, assent, permission, endorsement, ratification, sanction, confirmation, blessing, leave; *informal* the go-ahead, the green light, the thumbs up, say-so.

–OPPOSITES refusal.

▶ verb *the move must be okayed by the president* =**authorize**, approve, agree to, consent to, sanction, pass, ratify, endorse, allow, give something the nod; *informal* give the go-ahead, give the green light, give the thumbs up; *formal* accede to.

–OPPOSITES refuse, veto.

old ▶ adjective **1** *old people* =**elderly**, aged, older, senior, advanced in years, venerable; in one's dotage, long in the tooth, grey-haired, grizzled, past one's prime, not as young as one was, ancient, decrepit, doddery, senescent, senile, superannuated; *informal* getting on, past it, over the hill. **2** *old farm buildings* =**dilapidated**, broken-down, run down, tumbledown, ramshackle, decaying, crumbling, disintegrating. **3** *old clothes*

=**worn**, worn out, shabby, threadbare, frayed, patched, tattered, moth-eaten, ragged; old-fashioned, out of date, outmoded; cast-off, hand-me-down; *informal* tatty. **4** *old cars* =**antique**, veteran, vintage, classic. **5** *she's old for her years* =**mature**, wise, sensible, experienced, worldly-wise. **6** *the old days* =**bygone**, past, former, olden, of old, previous, early, earlier, earliest. **7** *the same old phrases* =**hackneyed**, banal, trite, overused, overworked, tired, worn out, stale, clichéd, stock; *informal* corny. **8** *an old girlfriend* =**former**, previous, ex-, one-time, sometime, erstwhile.
–OPPOSITES young, new, modern.
■ **old age** =**age**, declining years, advanced years, senescence, senility, dotage.
■ **old man 1** =**senior citizen**, pensioner, OAP, elder, grandfather; patriarch; *informal* greybeard, codger; *Brit. informal* buffer, geezer; *archaic* grandsire, ancient. **2** *(informal) her old man was away.* See HUSBAND noun.
■ **old person** =**senior citizen**, senior, (old-age) pensioner, OAP, elder, geriatric; *N. Amer.* golden ager; *informal* old stager, old-timer, oldie, wrinkly, crumbly; *N. Amer. informal* oldster, woopie.
■ **old woman 1** =**senior citizen**, pensioner, OAP, crone; *informal* old dear, old biddy; *archaic* beldam. **2** *(informal) his old woman threw him out.* See WIFE.

WORD LINKS

relating to old age: **gerontic**
relating to old people: **geriatric**
branch of medicine concerning old people: **geriatrics**
study of old age: **gerontology**
government by old people: **gerontocracy**
deteriorate with old age: **senesce**

old-fashioned ▶ adjective =**out of date**, outdated, dated, out of fashion, outmoded, unfashionable, passé, frumpy; outworn, old, behind the times, archaic, obsolescent, obsolete, ancient, antiquated, superannuated, defunct; medieval, prehistoric, antediluvian, old-fogeyish, backward-looking, quaint, anachronistic, fusty, moth-eaten, olde worlde; *informal* old hat, square, not with it, out of the ark; *N. Amer. informal* horse-and-buggy, clunky, rinky-dink.
–OPPOSITES modern.

old-time ▶ adjective =**former**, bygone, past, old-fashioned; traditional, folk, old-world, quaint.
–OPPOSITES modern.

omen ▶ noun =**portent**, sign, signal, token, forewarning, warning, harbinger, auspice, presage, indication; *literary* foretoken.

ominous ▶ adjective =**threatening**, menacing, baleful, forbidding, sinister; black, dark, gloomy.
–OPPOSITES promising.

omission ▶ noun **1** *the omission of certain news items* =**exclusion**, leaving out. **2** *I regret any omission on my part* =**negligence**, neglect, dereliction, oversight, lapse, failure.

omit ▶ verb **1** *they omitted his name from the list* =**leave out**, exclude, leave off, miss out, miss, cut. **2** *I omitted to mention this* =**forget**, neglect, fail.
–OPPOSITES add, include, remember.

omnipotence ▶ noun =**all-powerfulness**, supremacy, pre-eminence, supreme power; invincibility.

omnipotent ▶ adjective =**all-powerful**, almighty, supreme, pre-eminent; invincible.

omnipresent ▶ adjective =**ubiquitous**, all-pervasive, everywhere; rife, pervasive, prevalent.

omniscient ▶ adjective =**all-knowing**, all-wise, all-seeing.

on ▶ adjective *the computer's on* =**functioning**, working, in use, operating, online, up, running.
–OPPOSITES off.
■ **on and off.** See OFF AND ON *at* OFF.

once ▶ adverb **1** *I only met him once* =**on one occasion**, one time. **2** *he didn't help once* =**ever**, at any time, on any occasion, at all. **3** *they were friends once* =**formerly**, previously, in the past, at one time, at one point, once upon a time, in days/times gone by, in the (good) old days, long ago; *literary* in days/times of yore.
–OPPOSITES often, now.
▶ conjunction *once she's gone* =**as soon as**, when, after.
■ **at once 1** *leave at once* =**immediately**, right away, right now, this moment/instant/second/minute, now, straight away, instantly, directly, forthwith, without delay/hesitation, without further ado; quickly, as fast as possible, as soon as possible, asap. **2** *they all arrived at once* =**at the same time**, (all) together, simultaneously; as a group, in unison.

■ **once and for all** =**conclusively**, decisively, finally, positively, definitely, definitively, irrevocably; for good, for always, forever, permanently.

■ **once in a while** =**occasionally**, from time to time, (every) now and then/again, every so often, on occasion, at times, sometimes, off and on, at intervals, periodically, sporadically, intermittently.

oncoming ▶ adjective =**approaching**, advancing.

one ▶ cardinal number **1** =**unit**, item; *technical* monad. **2** *only one person came* =**a single**, a solitary, a sole, a lone. **3** *her one concern* =**only**, single, solitary, sole. **4** *they have become one* =**united**, a unit, amalgamated, consolidated, integrated, combined, incorporated, allied, affiliated, linked, joined, unified, in league, in partnership; wedded, married.

WORD LINKS

related prefixes: **mono-, uni-**
obsession with one thing: **monomania**

onerous ▶ adjective =**burdensome**, arduous, strenuous, difficult, hard, severe, heavy, back-breaking, oppressive, weighty, exhausting, tiring, taxing, demanding, punishing, gruelling.
–OPPOSITES easy.

one-sided ▶ adjective **1** *a one-sided account* =**biased**, prejudiced, partisan, partial, slanted, unfair. **2** *a one-sided game* =**unequal**, uneven, unbalanced.
–OPPOSITES impartial.

one-time ▶ adjective =**former**, ex-, old, previous, sometime, erstwhile.

ongoing ▶ adjective **1** *negotiations are ongoing* =**in progress**, under way, going on, continuing, proceeding. **2** *an ongoing struggle* =**continuous**, continuing, nonstop, constant, ceaseless, unceasing, unending, endless, never-ending, unremitting.

onlooker ▶ noun =**eyewitness**, witness, observer, spectator, bystander; sightseer; *informal* rubberneck.

only ▶ adverb **1** *only enough for two* =**at most**, at best, just, no/not more than. **2** *for your eyes only* =**exclusively**, solely. **3** *you're only saying that* =**merely**, simply, just.
▶ adjective *their only son* =**sole**, single, one (and only), solitary, lone, unique; exclusive.

onset ▶ noun =**start**, beginning, commencement, arrival, (first) appearance, inception, day one; outbreak.
–OPPOSITES end.

onslaught ▶ noun =**assault**, attack, offensive, advance, charge, rush, foray, push, thrust, drive, blitz, bombardment, barrage.

onus ▶ noun =**burden**, responsibility, obligation, duty, weight, load, charge.

ooze ▶ verb **1** *blood oozed from the wound* =**seep**, discharge, flow, exude, trickle, drip, dribble, issue, leak, drain, bleed. **2** *positively oozing charm* =**exude**, gush, drip, emanate, radiate.

opaque ▶ adjective **1** *opaque glass* =**non-transparent**, cloudy, filmy, blurred, smeared, misty. **2** *opaque language* =**obscure**, unclear, unfathomable, incomprehensible, unintelligible, impenetrable; *informal* as clear as mud.
–OPPOSITES transparent, clear.

open ▶ adjective **1** *the door's open* =**not shut**, not closed, unlocked, off the latch; ajar, gaping, yawning. **2** *a silk shirt, open at the neck* =**unfastened**, not done up, undone, unbuttoned, unzipped. **3** *the roads are open* =**clear**, passable, navigable. **4** *open countryside* | *open spaces* =**unenclosed**, rolling, sweeping, wide (open), exposed; spacious, uncluttered; undeveloped. **5** *a map was open beside him* =**spread out**, unfolded, unfurled, unrolled, extended, stretched out. **6** *the bank wasn't open* =**open for business**, open to the public. **7** *the position is still open* =**available**, vacant, free, unfilled; *informal* up for grabs. **8** *open to abuse* =**vulnerable**, subject, susceptible, liable, exposed. **9** *she was very open* =**frank**, candid, honest, forthcoming, communicative, forthright, direct, unreserved, plain-spoken, outspoken; *informal* upfront. **10** *open hostility* =**overt**, manifest, palpable, conspicuous, plain, undisguised, unconcealed, clear, naked; blatant, flagrant, barefaced, brazen. **11** *I'm open to suggestions* =**receptive**, amenable, willing/ready to listen, responsive. **12** *what other options are open to us?* =**available**, accessible, on hand, on offer. **13** *an open meeting* =**public**, general, unrestricted.
–OPPOSITES shut.
▶ verb **1** *she opened the front door* =**unfasten**, unlock; throw wide. **2** *Katherine opened the parcel* =**unwrap**, undo, untie. **3** *shall I open another bottle?* =**uncork**,

crack (open). **4** *Adam opened the map* =**spread out**, unfold, unfurl, unroll, straighten out. **5** *we'll be opening next week* =**start trading**, set up shop. **6** *Bryan opened the meeting* =**begin**, start, commence, initiate, set in motion, get going, get under way, get off the ground; *informal* kick off. **7** *the lounge opens on to a patio* =**give access**, lead.
−OPPOSITES close, shut, end.

> **WORD LINKS**
>
> *fear of open places:* **agoraphobia**

open air ▶ adjective =**outdoor**, out-of-doors, outside, alfresco.
−OPPOSITES indoor.

opening ▶ noun **1** *an opening in the roof* =**hole**, gap, aperture, orifice, vent, crack, slit, chink; spyhole, peephole. **2** *United created openings but were unable to score* =**opportunity**, chance, window (of opportunity), possibility. **3** *the opening of the session* =**beginning**, start, commencement, outset; *informal* kick-off. **4** *a gallery opening* =**launch**, inauguration; opening/first night, premiere.

openly ▶ adverb **1** *drugs were openly on sale* =**publicly**, blatantly, flagrantly, overtly. **2** *he spoke openly of his problems* =**frankly**, candidly, explicitly, honestly, sincerely, forthrightly, freely.
−OPPOSITES secretly.

open-minded ▶ adjective =**unbiased**, unprejudiced, neutral, objective, disinterested; tolerant, liberal, permissive, broad-minded.
−OPPOSITES prejudiced, narrow-minded.

open-mouthed ▶ adjective =**astounded**, amazed, stunned, staggered, thunderstruck, aghast, stupefied, shocked, speechless, dumbstruck; *informal* flabbergasted; *Brit. informal* gobsmacked.

operate ▶ verb **1** *he can operate the crane* =**work**, run, use, handle, control, manage; drive, steer, manoeuvre. **2** *the machine ceased to operate* =**function**, work, go, run. **3** *the way the law operates* =**take effect**, act, apply, work, function. **4** *we operated the mines until 1979* =**direct**, control, manage, run, be in control/charge of.

operation ▶ noun **1** *the sliders ensure smooth operation* =**functioning**, working, running, performance, action. **2** *the operation of the factory* =**management**, running, administration, supervision. **3** *a heart bypass operation* =**surgery**, surgical intervention. **4** *a military operation* =**action**, exercise, undertaking, enterprise, manoeuvre, campaign. **5** *their mining operation* =**business**, enterprise, company, firm; *informal* outfit.
■ **in operation.** See OPERATIONAL.

operational ▶ adjective =**(up and) running**, working, functioning, operative, in operation, in use, in action; in working order, serviceable, functional, usable.

operative ▶ adjective **1** *the steam railway is operative.* See OPERATIONAL. **2** *the operative word* =**key**, significant, relevant, crucial, critical.
−OPPOSITES invalid.
▶ noun **1** *the operatives clean the machines* =**machinist**, (machine) operator, mechanic, engineer, worker, workman, (factory) hand. **2** *a CIA operative* =**(secret/ undercover) agent**, spy, mole, plant; *N. Amer. informal* spook.

operator ▶ noun **1** *a machine operator* =**machinist**, mechanic, operative, engineer, worker. **2** *a tour operator* =**contractor**, entrepreneur, promoter.

opiate ▶ noun =**drug**, narcotic, sedative, anaesthetic, painkiller, analgesic; morphine, heroin, opium; *informal* dope.

opinion ▶ noun =**belief**, judgement, thought(s), (way of) thinking, mind, (point of) view, viewpoint, position, standpoint.

opinionated ▶ adjective =**dogmatic**, pushy.

opponent ▶ noun **1** *his Republican opponent* =**rival**, adversary, (fellow) competitor, enemy, antagonist, combatant, contender, challenger. **2** *an opponent of the reforms* =**critic**; objector, dissenter.
−OPPOSITES ally, supporter.

opportune ▶ adjective =**auspicious**, propitious, favourable, advantageous, felicitous; timely, convenient, suitable, appropriate, apt, fitting.
−OPPOSITES disadvantageous.

opportunism ▶ noun =**expediency**, pragmatism; striking while the iron is hot, making hay while the sun shines.

opportunity ▶ noun =**(lucky) chance**; time, occasion, moment, opening, option, window (of opportunity), possibility, scope, freedom; *informal* shot, break, look-in.

oppose ▶ verb =**be against**, object to, be hostile to, disagree with, dislike, disapprove of; resist, take a stand against, put up a fight against, fight, challenge; argue with/against; *informal* be anti.
−OPPOSITES support.

opposed ■ opposed to =**against**, (dead) set against; averse to, hostile to, antagonistic to, antipathetic to; *informal* anti.
■ as opposed to =**in contrast with**, as against, as contrasted with, rather than, instead of.

opposing ▶ adjective **1** *opposing points of view* =**conflicting**, contrasting, opposite, incompatible, irreconcilable, contradictory, antithetical, clashing, at variance, at odds, divergent, opposed. **2** *opposing sides* =**rival**, opposite, enemy. **3** *the opposing page* =**opposite**, facing.

opposite ▶ adjective **1** *they sat opposite each other* =**facing**, face to face with, across from. **2** *the opposite page* =**facing**, opposing. **3** *opposite views* =**conflicting**, contrasting, incompatible, irreconcilable, antithetical, contradictory, at variance, at odds, different, differing, divergent, opposing. **4** *opposite sides* =**rival**, opposing, enemy.
−OPPOSITES same.
▶ noun *the opposite was true* =**reverse**, converse, antithesis, contrary, inverse, obverse.

opposition ▶ noun **1** *the proposal met with opposition* =**resistance**, hostility, antagonism, antipathy, objection, dissent, disapproval. **2** *they beat the opposition* =**opponents**, opposing side, other side/team, competition, rivals, adversaries. **3** *the opposition between the public and the private* =**conflict**, clash, disparity, antithesis, polarity.

oppress ▶ verb =**persecute**, tyrannize, crush, repress, subjugate, subdue, keep down.

oppressed ▶ adjective =**persecuted**, downtrodden, abused, ill-treated, subjugated, tyrannized, repressed, subdued; disadvantaged, underprivileged.

oppression ▶ noun =**persecution**, abuse, ill-treatment, tyranny, repression, suppression, subjection, subjugation; cruelty, brutality, injustice.

oppressive ▶ adjective **1** *an oppressive dictatorship* =**harsh**, cruel, brutal, repressive, tyrannical, despotic; ruthless, merciless, pitiless. **2** *an oppressive silence* =**overwhelming**, overpowering, unbearable, unendurable, intolerable. **3** *it was overcast and oppressive* =**muggy**, close, heavy, hot, humid, sticky, airless, stuffy, stifling, sultry.
−OPPOSITES lenient.

oppressor ▶ noun =**persecutor**, ruler.

opt ▶ verb =**choose**, select, pick (out), decide on, go for, settle on, plump for.

optimism ▶ noun =**hopefulness**, hope, confidence, buoyancy, positivity, positive attitude.
−OPPOSITES pessimism.

optimistic ▶ adjective **1** *she felt optimistic about the future* =**positive**, confident, hopeful, sanguine, bullish, buoyant; *informal* upbeat. **2** *the forecast is optimistic* =**encouraging**, promising, hopeful, reassuring, favourable.
−OPPOSITES pessimistic.

optimum ▶ adjective =**best**, most favourable, most advantageous, ideal, perfect, prime, optimal.

option ▶ noun =**choice**, alternative, possibility, course of action.

optional ▶ adjective =**voluntary**, discretionary, non-compulsory.
−OPPOSITES compulsory.

opulence ▶ noun =**luxuriousness**, sumptuousness, lavishness, richness, luxury, luxuriance, splendour, magnificence, grandeur, splendidness; *informal* plushness.
−OPPOSITES poverty.

opulent ▶ adjective =**luxurious**, sumptuous, palatial, lavishly appointed, rich, splendid, magnificent, grand, grandiose, fancy; *informal* plush, swanky; *Brit. informal* swish; *N. Amer. informal* swank.
−OPPOSITES spartan.

opus ▶ noun =**composition**, work (of art), piece.

oral ▶ adjective =**spoken**, verbal, unwritten, vocal, uttered, said.
−OPPOSITES written.
▶ noun =**oral examination**; *Brit.* viva (voce).

orator ▶ noun =**(public) speaker**, speech-maker, lecturer.

orb ▶ noun =**sphere**, globe, ball, circle.

orbit ▶ noun =**course**, path, circuit, track, trajectory, rotation, revolution, circle.
▶ verb =**revolve round**, circle round, go round, travel round.

orchestra ▶ noun =**ensemble**; *informal* band.

orchestrate ▶ verb **1** *the piece was orchestrated by Mozart* =**arrange**, adapt, score. **2** *orchestrating a protest campaign* =**organize**, arrange, plan, set up, bring about, mobilize, mount, stage, mastermind, coordinate, direct, engineer.

ordain ▶ verb **1** *the decision to ordain women* =**confer holy orders on**, appoint, anoint, consecrate. **2** *the path ordained by God* =**predetermine**, predestine, preordain, determine, prescribe, designate.

ordeal ▶ noun =**unpleasant experience**, trial, nightmare, trauma, hell (on earth), torture, torment, agony.

order ▶ noun **1** *alphabetical order* =**sequence**, arrangement, organization, system, series, succession. **2** *some semblance of order* =**tidiness**, neatness, orderliness. **3** *the police managed to keep order* =**peace**, control, law (and order), lawfulness, calm, (peace and) quiet. **4** *his sense of order* =**orderliness**, organization, method; symmetry, uniformity, regularity; routine. **5** *in good order* =**condition**, state, repair, shape. **6** *I had to obey his orders* =**command**, instruction, directive, direction, decree, edict, injunction, dictate. **7** *the company has won the order* =**commission**, request, requisition. **8** *the lower orders of society* =**class**, level, rank, grade, caste. **9** *the established order* =**(class) system**, hierarchy, pecking order. **10** *a religious order* =**community**, brotherhood, sisterhood. **11** *the Orange Order* =**organization**, association, society, fellowship, fraternity, lodge, guild, league, union, club. **12** *skills of a very high order* =**type**, kind, sort, nature, variety; quality, calibre, standard. −OPPOSITES chaos.

▶ verb **1** *he ordered me to return* =**instruct**, command, direct, enjoin, tell. **2** *he ordered that their assets be confiscated* =**decree**, ordain, rule. **3** *order your tickets by phone* =**request**, apply for; book, reserve. **4** *the messages are ordered chronologically* =**organize**, arrange, sort out, lay out; group, classify, categorize, catalogue.

■ **in order 1** *list the dates in order* =**in sequence**, in alphabetical order, in numerical order, in order of priority. **2** *everything is in order* =**tidy**, neat, orderly, straight, trim, shipshape, in apple-pie order; in position, in place. **3** *I think a drink is in order* =**appropriate**,

fitting, suitable, acceptable, (all) right, permissible, permitted, allowable; *informal* okay.

■ **out of order 1** *the lift's out of order* =**not working**, broken (down), out of service/commission/action, inoperative; down; *informal* conked out, bust, (gone) kaput; *N. Amer. informal* on the fritz. **2** *(Brit. informal) that's really out of order* =**unacceptable**, unfair, unjust, unjustified, uncalled for, below the belt, unreasonable, unwarranted, beyond the pale; *informal* not on, a bit much; *Brit. informal* a bit thick, off; *Austral./NZ informal* over the fence.

orderly ▶ adjective **1** *an orderly room* =**neat**, tidy, well ordered, in order, trim, in apple-pie order, spick and span. **2** *the orderly presentation of information* =**(well) organized**, efficient, methodical, systematic, meticulous; coherent, structured, logical. **3** *the crowd was orderly* =**well behaved**, law-abiding, disciplined, peaceful, peaceable, non-violent. −OPPOSITES untidy, disorganized.

ordinarily ▶ adverb =**usually**, normally, as a (general) rule, generally, in general, for the most part, mainly, mostly, most of the time, typically, commonly, routinely.

ordinary ▶ adjective **1** *the ordinary course of events* =**usual**, normal, standard, typical, common, customary, habitual, everyday, regular, routine, day-to-day. **2** *my life seemed very ordinary* =**average**, normal, run-of-the-mill, standard, typical, middle-of-the-road, conventional, unremarkable, unexceptional, workaday, undistinguished, nondescript, colourless, commonplace, humdrum, mundane, unmemorable, pedestrian, prosaic, uninteresting, uneventful, dull, boring, bland; *informal* bog-standard, nothing to write home about, no great shakes; *Brit. informal* common or garden; *N. Amer. informal* ornery. −OPPOSITES unusual.

ordnance ▶ noun =**guns**, cannon, artillery, weapons, arms; munitions.

organ ▶ noun *the official organ of the Communist Party* =**newspaper**, paper, journal, periodical, magazine, newsletter, mouthpiece.

organic ▶ adjective **1** *organic matter* =**living**, live, animate, biological. **2** *organic vegetables* =**pesticide-free**, additive-free, natural. **3** *an organic part of the drama* =**essential**, fundamental, integral, intrinsic, vital, indispensable, inherent. **4** *a organic whole* =**structured**, organized, coherent, integrated, coordinated, ordered, harmonious.

organism ▸ noun **1** *fish and other organisms* =**living thing**, being, creature, animal, plant, life form. **2** *a complex political organism* =**structure**, system, organization, entity.

organization ▸ noun **1** *the organization of conferences* =**planning**, arrangement, coordination, organizing, running, management. **2** *the overall organization of the book* =**structure**, arrangement, plan, pattern, order, form, format, framework, composition, constitution. **3** *his lack of organization* =**efficiency**, order, orderliness, planning. **4** *a large organization* =**company**, firm, corporation, institution, group, consortium, conglomerate, agency, association, society; *informal* outfit.

organize ▸ verb **1** *organize the information* =**(put in) order**, arrange, sort (out), assemble, marshal, put straight, group, classify, collate, categorize, catalogue. **2** *they organized a search party* =**arrange**, coordinate, sort out, put together, fix up, set up, lay on, orchestrate, take care of, see to/about, deal with, mobilize.

organized ▸ adjective =**(well) ordered**, well run, well regulated, structured; orderly, efficient, neat, tidy, methodical; *informal* together.
—OPPOSITES inefficient.

orgiastic ▸ adjective =**debauched**, wild, riotous, wanton, dissolute, depraved.

orgy ▸ noun **1** *a drunken orgy* =**wild party**; *informal* binge, booze-up, bender; *Brit. informal* rave-up; *N. Amer. informal* toot. **2** *an orgy of violence* =**bout**, spree; *informal* binge.

orient, orientate ▸ verb **1** *she found it hard to orient herself* =**get/find one's bearings**. **2** *oriented to the business community* =**aim**, direct, pitch, design, intend. **3** *the stones are oriented from north to south* =**align**, place, position, arrange.

oriental ▸ adjective =**eastern**, Far Eastern.

orientation ▸ noun **1** *the orientation of the radar station* =**positioning**, location, position, situation, placement, alignment. **2** *broadly Marxist in orientation* =attitude, inclination. **3** *orientation courses* =**induction**, training, initiation, briefing.

orifice ▸ noun =**opening**, hole, aperture, slot, slit, cleft.

origin ▸ noun **1** *the origins of life* =**beginning**, start, genesis, birth, dawning, dawn, emergence, creation; source, basis, cause, root(s). **2** *the origin of the word* =**source**, derivation, root(s), provenance, etymology; *N. Amer.* provenience. **3** *his Scottish origins* =**descent**, ancestry, parentage, pedigree, lineage, line (of descent), heritage, birth, extraction, family; roots.

original ▸ adjective **1** *the original inhabitants* =**indigenous**, native; first, earliest, early. **2** *an original Rembrandt* =**authentic**, genuine, actual, true, bona fide. **3** *a highly original film* =**innovative**, creative, imaginative, inventive; new, novel, fresh; unusual, unconventional, unorthodox, groundbreaking, pioneering, unique, distinctive.
▸ noun **1** *a copy of the original* =**prototype**, source, master. **2** *he really is an original* =**individual**, eccentric, nonconformist, free spirit, maverick; *informal* character, oddball; *Brit. informal* one-off.

originality ▸ noun =**inventiveness**, ingenuity, creativeness, creativity, innovation, novelty, freshness, imagination, individuality, unconventionality, uniqueness, distinctiveness.

originally ▸ adverb =**(at) first**, in/at the beginning, to begin with, initially, in the first place, at the outset.

originate ▸ verb **1** *the disease originates from Africa* =**arise**, have its origin, begin, start, stem, spring, emerge, emanate. **2** *Bill originated the idea* =**invent**, create, initiate, devise, think up, dream up, conceive, formulate, form, develop, generate, engender, produce, mastermind, pioneer.

originator ▸ noun =**inventor**, creator, architect, author, father, mother, initiator, innovator, founder, pioneer, mastermind.

ornament ▸ noun =**knick-knack**, trinket, bauble; *informal* whatnot, doodah; *N. Amer. informal* tchotchke, kickshaw, bijou.

ornamental ▸ adjective =**decorative**, fancy; ornate, ornamented.

ornamentation ▸ noun =decoration, adornment, embellishment, ornament, trimming, accessories.

ornate ▶ adjective **1** *an ornate mirror* =**elaborate**, decorated, embellished, adorned, ornamented, fancy, fussy, ostentatious, showy; *informal* flash, flashy. **2** *ornate language* =**elaborate**, flowery, florid; grandiose, pompous, pretentious, high-flown, bombastic, overwrought, overblown; *informal* highfalutin.
–OPPOSITES plain.

orthodox ▶ adjective **1** *orthodox views* =**conventional**, mainstream, conformist, (well) established, traditional, traditionalist, prevalent, popular, conservative, unoriginal. **2** *an orthodox Hindu* =**conservative**, traditional, observant, devout, strict.
–OPPOSITES unconventional.

orthodoxy ▶ noun =**conventionality**, conventionalism, conformism, conservatism, traditionalism, conformity.

oscillate ▶ verb **1** *the pendulum started to oscillate* =**swing (to and fro)**, swing back and forth, sway; *N. Amer. informal* wigwag. **2** *oscillating between fear and bravery* =**waver**, swing, fluctuate, alternate, see-saw, yo-yo, sway, vacillate, hover; *informal* wobble.

oscillation ▶ noun =**swinging (to and fro)**, swing, swaying.

ostensible ▶ adjective =**apparent**, outward, superficial, professed, supposed, alleged, purported.
–OPPOSITES genuine.

ostensibly ▶ adverb =**apparently**, seemingly, on the face of it, to all intents and purposes, outwardly, superficially, allegedly, supposedly, purportedly.

ostentation ▶ noun =**showiness**, show, ostentatiousness, pretentiousness, vulgarity, conspicuousness, display, flamboyance, gaudiness, brashness, extravagance, ornateness, exhibitionism; *informal* flashiness, glitz, glitziness, ritziness.

ostentatious ▶ adjective =**showy**, pretentious, conspicuous, flamboyant, gaudy, brash, vulgar, loud, extravagant, fancy, ornate, over-elaborate; *informal* flash, flashy, over the top, OTT, glitzy, ritzy; *N. Amer. informal* superfly.
–OPPOSITES restrained.

ostracize ▶ verb =**exclude**, shun, spurn, cold-shoulder, reject, shut out, ignore, snub, cut dead; blackball, blacklist; *Brit.* send to Coventry; *informal* freeze out; *Brit. informal* blank.
–OPPOSITES welcome.

other ▶ adjective **1** *these homes use other fuels* =**alternative**, different; various. **2** *are there any other questions?* =**more**, further, additional, extra, added, supplementary.

otherwise ▶ adverb **1** *hurry up, otherwise we'll be late* =**or (else)**, if not. **2** *she's exhausted, but otherwise she's fine* =**in other respects**, apart from that. **3** *he could not have acted otherwise* =**in any other way**, differently.

otter ▶ noun

> **WORD LINKS**
>
> male: **dog**
> female: **bitch**
> home: **holt**

ounce ▶ noun =**particle**, scrap, bit, speck, iota, jot, trace, atom, shred, crumb, fragment, grain, drop, spot; *informal* smidgen.

oust ▶ verb =**drive out**, expel, force out, remove (from office/power), eject, get rid of, depose, topple, unseat, overthrow, bring down, overturn, dismiss, dislodge, displace.

out ▶ adjective & adverb **1** *she's out at the moment* =**not here**, not at home, not in, (gone) away, elsewhere. **2** *the secret was out* =**revealed**, (out) in the open, common/public knowledge. **3** *the roses are out* =**in flower**, flowering, in (full) bloom, blooming, in blossom, blossoming. **4** *the book should be out soon* =**available**, obtainable, in the shops, published, in print. **5** *(informal) grunge is out* =**unfashionable**, out of fashion, dated, outdated, passé; *informal* old hat. **6** *smoking is out* =**forbidden**, not permitted, not allowed, unacceptable; *informal* not on. **7** *he was slightly out in his calculations* =**mistaken**, inaccurate, incorrect, wrong, in error.
–OPPOSITES in.
▶ verb *(informal) it was not our intention to out him* =**expose**, unmask.
■ **out cold** =**unconscious**, knocked out, out for the count; *informal* KO'd.

out-and-out ▶ adjective =**utter**, downright, thoroughgoing, absolute, complete, thorough, total, unmitigated, outright, real, perfect; *N. Amer.* full-bore; *informal* deep-dyed; *Brit. informal* right;

Austral./NZ informal fair.
–OPPOSITES partial.

outbreak ▶ noun **1** *outbreaks of violence* =**eruption**, flare-up, upsurge, rash, wave, spate, burst, flurry. **2** *the outbreak of war* =**start**, beginning, commencement, onset.

outburst ▶ noun =**eruption**, explosion, flare-up, flood, storm, outpouring, surge, fit.

outcast ▶ noun =**pariah**, persona non grata, reject, outsider.

outclass ▶ verb =**surpass**, be superior to, be better than, outshine, overshadow, eclipse, outdo, outplay, outstrip, get the better of, upstage; beat, defeat; *informal* be a cut above, be head and shoulders above, run rings round.

outcome ▶ noun =(**end**) **result**, consequence, net result, upshot, conclusion, issue, end (product).

outcry ▶ noun =**protest(s)**, protestation(s), complaints, objections, furore, fuss, commotion, uproar, outbursts, opposition, dissent; *informal* hullabaloo, ballyhoo, ructions, stink.

outdated ▶ adjective =**old-fashioned**, out of date, outmoded, out of fashion, unfashionable, dated, passé, old, behind the times, obsolete, antiquated; *informal* out, old hat, square, out of the ark; *N. Amer. informal* horse-and-buggy, clunky.
–OPPOSITES modern.

outdistance ▶ verb =**outrun**, outstrip, outpace, leave behind, get ahead of; overtake, pass.

outdo ▶ verb =**surpass**, outshine, overshadow, eclipse, outclass, outmanoeuvre, get the better of, put in the shade, upstage; exceed, transcend, top, cap, beat, better, leave behind, get ahead of; *informal* be a cut above, be head and shoulders above, run rings round.

outdoor ▶ adjective =**open air**, out-of-doors, outside, al fresco.
–OPPOSITES indoor.

outer ▶ adjective =**outside**, outermost, outward, exterior, external, surface.
–OPPOSITES inner.

outface ▶ verb =**stand up to**, face down.

outfit ▶ noun **1** *a new outfit* =**costume**, suit, uniform, ensemble, attire, clothes, clothing, dress, garb; *informal* get-up, gear, togs; *Brit. informal* kit, rig-out; *formal* apparel. **2** *(informal) a local manufacturing outfit* =**organization**, enterprise, company, firm, business; group, body, team; *informal* set-up.
▶ verb *enough swords to outfit an army* =**equip**, kit out, fit out/up, rig out, supply, arm; dress, clothe, deck out.

outflow ▶ noun =**discharge**, outflowing, outpouring, rush, flood, deluge, spurt, jet, cascade, stream, torrent, gush, outburst; flow.

outgoing ▶ adjective **1** *outgoing children* =**extrovert**, uninhibited, unreserved, demonstrative, affectionate, warm, sociable, convivial, lively, gregarious; communicative, responsive, open, forthcoming, frank. **2** *the outgoing president* =**departing**, retiring, leaving.
–OPPOSITES introverted, incoming.

outgoings ▶ plural noun =**expenses**, expenditure, spending, outlay, payments, costs, overheads.

outgrowth ▶ noun =**protuberance**, swelling, excrescence, growth, lump, bump, bulge.

outing ▶ noun =(**pleasure**) **trip**, excursion, jaunt, expedition, day out, (mystery) tour, drive, ride, run; *informal* junket, spin.

outlandish ▶ adjective =**weird**, queer, far out, eccentric, unconventional, unorthodox, funny, bizarre, unusual, strange, peculiar, odd, curious; *informal* offbeat, off the wall, way-out, wacky, freaky, kinky, oddball.
–OPPOSITES ordinary.

outlast ▶ verb =**outlive**, survive, live/last longer than.

outlaw ▶ noun =**fugitive**, (wanted) criminal; bandit, robber; *dated* desperado.
▶ verb =**ban**, bar, prohibit, forbid, veto, make illegal, proscribe.
–OPPOSITES permit.

outlay ▶ noun =**expenditure**, expenses, spending, outgoings, payment, investment.
–OPPOSITES profit.

outlet ▶ noun **1** *a central-heating outlet* =**vent (hole)**, way out; outfall, opening, channel, conduit, duct. **2** *an outlet for farm produce* =**market**, retail outlet, shop, store. **3** *an outlet for their energies* =**means of expression**, (means of) release, vent, avenue, channel.

outline ▶ noun **1** *the outline of the building*

=**silhouette**, profile, shape, contours, form, lines. **2** *an outline of our proposal* =**rough idea**, thumbnail sketch, (quick) rundown, summary, synopsis, résumé, precis; essence, main points, gist, (bare) bones.

▶ verb *she outlined the plan briefly* =**rough out**, sketch out, draft, give a rough idea of, summarize, precis.

outlive ▶ verb =**live on after**, live longer than, outlast, survive.

outlook ▶ noun **1** *a positive outlook* =**point of view**, viewpoint, (way of) thinking, perspective, attitude, standpoint, stance, frame of mind. **2** *a lovely open outlook* =**view**, vista, prospect, panorama. **3** *the outlook for the economy* =**prospects**, future.

outlying ▶ adjective =**distant**, remote, out of the way, faraway, far-flung, inaccessible, off the beaten track.

outmanoeuvre ▶ verb =**outwit**, outsmart, out-think, steal a march on, trick, get the better of.

outmoded ▶ adjective =**out of date**, old-fashioned, outdated, dated, behind the times, antiquated, obsolete, passé, anachronistic; *informal* old hat.

out of date ▶ adjective **1** *the design is so out of date* =**old-fashioned**, outmoded, outdated, dated, old, passé, behind the times, obsolete, antiquated, anachronistic; *informal* out, old hat, not with it, out of the ark; *N. Amer. informal* horse-and-buggy, clunky. **2** *your ticket is out of date* =**expired**, lapsed, invalid, (null and) void. **3** *your information is out of date* =**obsolete**, no longer valid/relevant/true; incorrect, inaccurate.
–OPPOSITES fashionable, current.

out of the way ▶ adjective =**outlying**, distant, remote, faraway, far-flung, isolated, lonely, godforsaken, inaccessible, off the beaten track.
–OPPOSITES accessible.

out of work ▶ adjective =**unemployed**, jobless; redundant, laid off; *Brit. informal* on the dole; *Austral. informal* on the wallaby track.

outpouring ▶ noun =**outflow**, outrush, rush, flood, deluge, jet, cascade, stream, torrent, gush, outburst, flow.

output ▶ noun =**production**, yield, gross domestic product; work.

outrage ▶ noun **1** *public outrage* =**indignation**, fury, anger, rage, wrath. **2** *it is an outrage* =**scandal**, offence, insult, affront, disgrace.

▶ verb *his remarks outraged everyone* =**enrage**, infuriate, incense, anger, scandalize, offend, affront, shock, horrify, disgust, appal.

outrageous ▶ adjective **1** *outrageous behaviour* =**shocking**, disgraceful, scandalous, atrocious, appalling, dreadful; attention-seeking, controversial. **2** *outrageous clothes* =**eye-catching**, flamboyant, showy, gaudy, ostentatious; *informal* saucy, flashy.

outright ▶ adverb **1** *he rejected the proposal outright* =**completely**, entirely, wholly, totally, categorically, absolutely, utterly, flatly, unreservedly, out of hand. **2** *I told her outright* =**explicitly**, directly, frankly, candidly, bluntly, plainly, in plain language, to someone's face, straight from the shoulder; *Brit. informal* straight up. **3** *they were killed outright* =**instantly**, instantaneously, immediately, at once, straight away, then and there, on the spot. **4** *paintings have to be bought outright* =**all at once**, in one go.

▶ adjective **1** *an outright lie* =**out-and-out**, absolute, complete, downright, utter, sheer, categorical. **2** *the outright winner* =**definite**, unequivocal, clear, unmistakable; overall.

outrun ▶ verb =**run faster than**, outstrip, outdistance, outpace, leave behind, lose; *informal* leave standing.

outset ▶ noun =**start**, starting point, beginning; *informal* the word go.
–OPPOSITES end.

outshine ▶ verb =**surpass**, overshadow, eclipse, outclass, put in the shade, beat, better; *informal* be a cut above, be head and shoulders above, run rings round.

outside ▶ noun *the outside of the building* =**outer/external surface**, exterior, case, skin, shell, covering, facade.

▶ adjective **1** *outside lights* =**exterior**, external, outer, outdoor, out-of-doors. **2** *outside contractors* =**independent**, freelance, casual, external.

▶ adverb *they went outside | shall we eat outside?* =**outdoors**, out of doors, alfresco.
–OPPOSITES inside.

WORD LINKS

related prefixes: **ecto-, exo-, extra-**

outsider ▶ noun =**stranger**, visitor,

non-member; foreigner, alien, immigrant, emigrant, émigré; incomer, newcomer.

outsize ▶ adjective =huge, oversized, enormous, gigantic, great, giant, colossal, massive, mammoth, vast, immense, tremendous, monumental, prodigious, king-sized; *informal* mega, monster, whopping (great), thumping (great), humongous, jumbo, bumper; *Brit. informal* whacking (great), ginormous.

outskirts ▶ plural noun =edges, fringes, suburbs, suburbia.

outsmart ▶ verb =outwit, outmanoeuvre, steal a march on, trick, get the better of; *informal* pull a fast one on, put one over on.

outspoken ▶ adjective =forthright, direct, candid, frank, straightforward, open, straight from the shoulder, plainspoken; blunt.

outspread ▶ adjective =fully extended, outstretched, spread out, unfolded, unfurled, (wide) open, opened out.

outstanding ▶ adjective 1 *an outstanding painter* =excellent, marvellous, magnificent, superb, fine, wonderful, superlative, exceptional, first-class, first-rate; *informal* great, terrific, tremendous, super, amazing, fantastic, sensational, fabulous, ace, cracking, A1, mean, awesome, out of this world; *Brit. informal* smashing, brilliant; *N. Amer. informal* neat; *Austral. informal* bonzer. 2 *how much work is still outstanding?* =to be done, undone, unfinished, incomplete, remaining, pending. 3 *outstanding debts* =unpaid, unsettled, owing, owed, to be paid, payable, due, overdue; *N. Amer.* delinquent.

outstrip ▶ verb 1 *he outstripped the police cars* =go faster than, outrun, outdistance, outpace, leave behind, get (further) ahead of, lose; *informal* leave standing. 2 *demand far outstrips supply* =surpass, exceed, be more than, top.

outward ▶ adjective =external, outer, outside, exterior; surface, superficial, seeming, apparent, ostensible. –OPPOSITES inward.

outwardly ▶ adverb =externally, on the surface, superficially, on the face of it, to all intents and purposes, apparently, ostensibly, seemingly.

outweigh ▶ verb =be greater than, exceed, be superior to, prevail over, have the edge on/over, override, supersede, offset, cancel out, (more than) make up for, outbalance, compensate for.

outwit ▶ verb =outsmart, outmanoeuvre, steal a march on, trick, get the better of; *informal* pull a fast one on, put one over on.

outworn ▶ adjective =out of date, outdated, old-fashioned, outmoded, dated, antiquated, obsolete, defunct. –OPPOSITES up to date.

oval ▶ adjective =egg-shaped, ovoid, elliptical.

ovation ▶ noun =(round of) applause, cheers, bravos, acclaim, standing ovation; *informal* (big) hand.

oven ▶ noun =(kitchen) stove, microwave (oven); rotisserie.

over ▶ preposition 1 *there was cloud over the hills* =above, on top of, higher (up) than, atop, covering. 2 *he walked over the grass* =across, on. 3 *he has three people over him* =superior to, above, higher up than, in charge of, responsible for. 4 *over 2,000 people* =more than, above, in excess of, upwards of. 5 *an argument over money* =on the subject of, about, concerning, with reference to, regarding, relating to, in connection with. –OPPOSITES under.
▶ adverb 1 *a plane flew over* =overhead, past, by. 2 *the relationship is over* =at an end, finished, concluded, terminated, ended, no more, a thing of the past.
■ **over and above** =in addition to, on top of, plus, as well as, besides, along with.
■ **over and over** =repeatedly, again and again, time and (time) again, many times, frequently, constantly, continually, persistently, ad nauseam.

overact ▶ verb =exaggerate, overdo it, overplay it; *informal* ham it up, camp it up.

overall ▶ adjective *the overall cost* =total, all-inclusive, gross, final, inclusive.
▶ adverb *overall, things are better* =generally (speaking), in general, altogether, all in all, on balance, on average, for the most part, in the main, on the whole, by and large, to a large extent.

overawe ▶ verb =intimidate, daunt, cow, disconcert, unnerve, subdue, dismay, frighten, alarm, scare; *informal* psych out; *N. Amer. informal* buffalo.

overbalance ▶ verb =fall over, topple over, lose one's balance, tip over.

overbearing ▸ adjective =**domineer-ing**, dominating, autocratic, tyrannical, despotic, oppressive, high-handed, bullying; *informal* bossy.

overblown ▸ adjective =**florid**, grandiose, pompous, flowery, overwrought, pretentious, high-flown; *informal* highfalutin.

overcast ▸ adjective =**cloudy**, clouded (over), sunless, darkened, dark, grey, black, leaden, heavy, dull, murky.
–OPPOSITES bright.

overcharge ▸ verb =**swindle**, charge too much, cheat, defraud, fleece, short-change; *informal* rip off, sting, screw, rob, diddle, do; *N. Amer. informal* gouge.

overcome ▸ verb =**get the better of**, prevail over, control, get/bring under control, master, conquer, defeat, beat; *informal* lick, best.
▸ adjective =**overwhelmed**, moved, affected, speechless.
■ **overcome by** =**overwhelm**, overpower, asphyxiate, render unconscious, suffocate, poison.

overconfident ▸ adjective =**cock-sure**, cocky, smug, conceited, self-assured, brash, blustering, overbearing; *informal* too big for one's boots.

overcrowded ▸ adjective =**overfull**, overflowing, full to overflowing/bursting, crammed full, congested, over-populated, crowded, swarming, teeming; *informal* bursting/bulging at the seams, full to the gunwales, jam-packed.
–OPPOSITES empty.

overdo ▸ verb **1** *she overdoes the sex scenes* =**exaggerate**, overstate, overemphasize, overplay, go overboard with, over-dramatize. **2** *don't overdo the drink* =**have/use/eat/drink too much of**, overindulge in, have/use/eat/drink to excess.
–OPPOSITES understate.
■ **overdo it** =**work too hard**, overwork, do too much, burn the candle at both ends, drive/push oneself too hard, work/run oneself into the ground, wear oneself to a shadow, wear oneself out, strain oneself; *informal* kill oneself, knock oneself out.

overdue ▸ adjective **1** *the ship is overdue* =**late**, behind schedule, behind time, delayed. **2** *overdue payments* =**unpaid**, unsettled, owing, owed, payable, due, outstanding, undischarged; *N. Amer.* delinquent.
–OPPOSITES early, punctual.

overeat ▸ verb =**eat too much**, be greedy, gorge (oneself), overindulge (oneself), feast, gourmandize; *informal* binge, make a pig of oneself, pig out; *N. Amer. informal* scarf out.
–OPPOSITES starve.

overemphasize ▸ verb =**place/lay too much emphasis/stress on**, over-stress, exaggerate, make too much of, overplay, overdo; *informal* make a big thing about/of, blow up out of all proportion.
–OPPOSITES understate, play down.

overflow ▸ verb =**spill over**, flow over, brim over, well over, flood.
▸ noun =**surplus**, excess, additional people/things, extra people/things, remainder, overspill.

overflowing ▸ adjective =**overfull**, full to overflowing/bursting, spilling over, running over, crammed full, over-crowded, overloaded; *informal* bursting/bulging at the seams, jam-packed.
–OPPOSITES empty.

overhaul ▸ verb =**service**, maintain, repair, mend, fix up, rebuild, renovate, recondition, refit, refurbish; *informal* do up, patch up.

overhead ▸ adverb *a burst of thunder erupted overhead* =**(up/directly) above**, high up, (up) in the sky, on high, above/over one's head.
–OPPOSITES below.
▸ adjective *overhead lines* =**aerial**, elevated, raised.
–OPPOSITES underground.

overheads ▸ plural noun =**(running) costs**, operating costs, fixed costs, expenses.
–OPPOSITES profit.

overindulge ▸ verb **1** *we all overindulge at Christmas* =**drink/eat too much**, overeat, be greedy, be intemperate, overindulge oneself, overdo it, drink/eat to excess, gorge (oneself), feast, gourmandize; *informal* binge, stuff oneself, go overboard, make a pig of oneself, pig oneself; *N. Amer. informal* scarf out. **2** *his mother had overindulged him* =**spoil**, give in to, indulge, humour, pander to, pamper, mollycoddle, baby.
–OPPOSITES abstain.

overindulgence ▸ noun =**intemperance**, immoderation, excess, over-eating.
–OPPOSITES abstinence.

overjoyed ▶ adjective =ecstatic, euphoric, thrilled, elated, delighted, on cloud nine/seven, in seventh heaven, jubilant, rapturous, jumping for joy, delirious, blissful, in raptures, as pleased as Punch, cock-a-hoop, as happy as a sandboy, as happy as Larry; *informal* over the moon, on top of the world, tickled pink; *N. Amer. informal* as happy as a clam; *Austral. informal* wrapped.
−OPPOSITES unhappy.

overload ▶ verb =strain, overtax, overwork, overuse, swamp, overwhelm.

overlook ▶ verb 1 *he overlooked the mistake* =fail to notice, fail to spot, miss. 2 *his work has been overlooked* =disregard, neglect, ignore, pass over, forget. 3 *she was willing to overlook his faults* =ignore, disregard, take no notice of, make allowances for, turn a blind eye to, excuse, pardon, forgive. 4 *the lounge overlooks the garden* =have a view of, look over/across, look on to, look out on/over.

overly ▶ adverb =unduly, excessively, inordinately, too.

overpower ▶ verb =overwhelm, get the better of, overthrow, subdue, suppress, subjugate, repress, bring someone to their knees.

overpowering ▶ adjective 1 *overpowering grief* =overwhelming, oppressive, unbearable, unendurable, intolerable, shattering. 2 *an overpowering smell* =stifling, suffocating, strong, pungent, powerful; nauseating, offensive, acrid, fetid.

overrate ▶ verb =overestimate, overvalue, think too much of.
−OPPOSITES underestimate.

overreact ▶ verb =react disproportionately, blow something up out of all proportion; *Brit. informal* go over the top.

override ▶ verb =disallow, overrule, countermand, veto, quash, overturn, overthrow; cancel, reverse, rescind, revoke, repeal, annul, nullify, invalidate, negate, void.

overriding ▶ adjective =most important, uppermost, top, first (and foremost), highest, pre-eminent, predominant, principal, primary, paramount, chief, main, major, foremost, central, key; *informal* number-one.

overrule ▶ verb =countermand, cancel, reverse, rescind, repeal, revoke, retract, disallow, override, veto, quash, overturn, overthrow, annul, nullify, invalidate, negate, void.

overrun ▶ verb =invade, storm, occupy, swarm into, surge into, inundate, overwhelm, descend on.

oversee ▶ verb =supervise, superintend, be in charge/control of, be responsible for, look after, keep an eye on, inspect, administer, organize, manage, direct, preside over.

overseer ▶ noun =supervisor, foreman, forewoman, team leader, controller, (line) manager, manageress, head (of department), superintendent, captain; *informal* boss, chief, governor; *Brit. informal* gaffer, guv'nor; *N. Amer. informal* straw boss; *Austral. informal* pannikin boss.

overshadow ▶ verb 1 *the trees that overshadow the square* =tower over, dominate, overlook. 2 *a childhood overshadowed by illness* =blight, take the edge off, mar, spoil, ruin. 3 *he was overshadowed by his brother* =outshine, eclipse, surpass, exceed, outclass, outstrip, outdo, upstage; *informal* be head and shoulders above.

oversight ▶ noun 1 *a stupid oversight* =mistake, error, omission, lapse, slip, blunder; *informal* slip-up, boo-boo; *Brit. informal* boob; *N. Amer. informal* goof. 2 *the omission was due to oversight* =carelessness, inattention, negligence, forgetfulness.

overstate ▶ verb =exaggerate, overdo, overemphasize, overplay, dramatize; *informal* blow up out of all proportion.
−OPPOSITES understate.

overstatement ▶ noun =exaggeration, overemphasis, dramatization, hyperbole.

overt ▶ adjective =undisguised, unconcealed, plain (to see), clear, conspicuous, obvious, noticeable, manifest, patent, open, blatant.
−OPPOSITES covert.

overtake ▶ verb 1 *a green car overtook us* =pass, go past/by, get/pull ahead of. 2 *Goa overtook Ibiza as their favourite destination* =outstrip, surpass, overshadow, eclipse, outshine, outclass; exceed, top, cap. 3 *the calamity which overtook us* =befall, happen to, come upon, hit, strike, overwhelm, overcome.

overthrow ▶ verb 1 *the President was overthrown* =remove (from office/

power), bring down, topple, depose, oust, displace, unseat. **2** *an attempt to overthrow Soviet rule* =**put an end to**, defeat, conquer.
▶ noun **1** *the overthrow of the Shah* =**removal (from office/power)**, downfall, toppling, deposition, ousting, displacement, supplanting, unseating. **2** *the overthrow of capitalism* =**ending**, defeat, displacement, fall, collapse, downfall, demise.

overtone ▶ noun =**connotation**, hidden meaning, implication, association, undercurrent, undertone, echo, vibrations, hint, suggestion, insinuation, intimation, suspicion, feeling, nuance.

overture ▶ noun **1** *the overture to Don Giovanni* =**prelude**, introduction, opening, introductory movement. **2** *the overture to a long debate* =**preliminary**, prelude, introduction, lead-in, precursor, start, beginning. **3** *peace overtures* =**(opening) move**, approach, advances, feeler, signal.

overturn ▶ verb **1** *the boat overturned* =**capsize**, turn turtle, keel over, tip over, topple over, turn over. **2** *I overturned the stool* =**upset**, tip over, topple over, turn over, knock over, upend. **3** *the Senate may overturn this ruling* =**cancel**, reverse, rescind, repeal, revoke, retract, countermand, disallow, override, overrule, veto, quash, overthrow, annul, nullify, invalidate, negate, void.

overused ▶ adjective =**hackneyed**, overworked, worn out, time-worn, tired, played out, clichéd, stale, trite, banal, stock, unoriginal.

overweight ▶ adjective =**fat**, obese, stout, corpulent, gross, fleshy, plump, portly, chubby, pot-bellied, flabby, well padded, broad in the beam; *informal* tubby, blubbery; *Brit. informal* podgy.
–OPPOSITES skinny.

overwhelm ▶ verb **1** *huge waves overwhelmed the ship* =**swamp**, submerge, engulf, deluge, flood, inundate. **2** *Spain overwhelmed Russia in the hockey* =**defeat (utterly/heavily)**, trounce, rout, beat (hollow), conquer, vanquish, be victorious over, triumph over, overcome, overthrow, crush; *informal* thrash, lick, best, clobber, wipe the floor with. **3** *she was overwhelmed by a sense of tragedy* =**overcome**, move, stir, affect, touch, strike, dumbfound, shake, devastate, leave speechless; *informal* bowl over,

knock sideways, floor; *Brit. informal* knock/hit for six.

overwhelming ▶ adjective **1** *an overwhelming number of people* =**very large**, enormous, immense, inordinate, massive, huge. **2** *an overwhelming desire to laugh* =**very strong**, powerful, uncontrollable, irrepressible, irresistible, overpowering, compelling.

overwork ▶ verb =**work too hard**, work/run oneself into the ground, work one's fingers to the bone, burn the candle at both ends, overtax oneself, burn oneself out, do too much, overdo it, strain oneself, overload oneself, drive/push oneself too hard; *informal* kill oneself, knock oneself out.

overworked ▶ adjective **1** *overworked staff* =**stressed (out)**, overtaxed, overburdened, overloaded, exhausted, worn out. **2** *an overworked phrase* =**hackneyed**, overused, worn out, tired, played out, clichéd, threadbare, stale, trite, banal, stock, unoriginal.
–OPPOSITES relaxed, original.

overwrought ▶ adjective =**tense**, agitated, nervous, on edge, edgy, keyed up, worked up, highly strung, neurotic, overexcited, beside oneself, distracted, distraught, frantic, hysterical; *informal* in a state, in a tizzy, uptight, wound up, het up.
–OPPOSITES calm.

owe ▶ verb =**be in debt (to)**, be indebted (to), be in arrears (to), be under an obligation (to).

owing ▶ adjective *the rent was owing* =**unpaid**, to be paid, payable, due, overdue, undischarged, owed, outstanding, in arrears; *N. Amer.* delinquent.
–OPPOSITES paid.
■ **owing to** =**because of**, as a result of, on account of, due to, as a consequence of, thanks to, in view of.

own ▶ adjective *he has his own reasons* =**personal**, individual, particular, private, personalized, unique.
▶ verb **1** *I own this house* =**be the owner of**, possess, have (to one's name). **2** *(formal) she had to own that she agreed* =**admit**, concede, grant, accept, acknowledge, agree, confess.
■ **hold one's own** =**stand firm**, stand one's ground, keep one's end up, keep one's head above water, compete, survive, cope, get on/along.
■ **on one's own 1** *I am all on my own*

=**(all) alone**, (all) by oneself, solitary, unaccompanied, companionless; *informal* by one's lonesome; *Brit. informal* on one's tod. **2** *she works well on her own* =**unaided**, unassisted, without help, without assistance, (all) by oneself, independently.

■ **own up** =**confess** (to), admit to, admit guilt, plead guilty, accept blame/responsibility, tell the truth (about), make a clean breast of it, tell all; *informal* come clean (about).

owner ▶ noun =**possessor**, holder, proprietor/proprietress, homeowner, freeholder, landlord, landlady.

ownership ▶ noun =**(right of) possession**, freehold, proprietorship, proprietary rights, title.

Pp

pace ▶ noun 1 *ten paces* =**step**. 2 *a slow, steady pace* =**gait**, stride, walk, march. 3 *a furious pace* =**speed**, rate, velocity.
▶ verb *she paced up and down* =**walk**, stride, march, pound.

pacifism ▶ noun =**non-violence**; peacemaking.

pacifist ▶ noun =**peace-lover**, conscientious objector, dove.
–OPPOSITES warmonger.

pacify ▶ verb =**placate**, appease, calm (down), conciliate, propitiate, assuage, mollify, soothe.
–OPPOSITES enrage.

pack ▶ noun 1 *a pack of cigarettes* =**packet**, container, package, box, carton, parcel. 2 *a pack of wolves* =**group**, herd, troop. 3 *a pack of hooligans* =**crowd**, mob, group, band, party, set, gang, rabble, horde, throng, huddle, mass, assembly, gathering, host; *informal* crew, bunch.
▶ verb 1 *she helped pack the car* =**fill (up)**, put things in, load. 2 *they packed their belongings* =**stow**, put away, store, box up. 3 *the glasses were packed in straw* =**wrap (up)**, package, parcel, swathe, swaddle, encase, envelop, bundle. 4 *shoppers packed the store* =**throng**, crowd (into), fill (to overflowing), cram, jam, squash into, squeeze into.
■ **pack something in** (informal) =**resign from**, leave, give up; *informal* quit, chuck; *Brit. informal* jack in.
■ **pack someone off** (informal) =**send off**, dispatch, bundle off.
■ **pack up** (Brit. informal) =**break (down)**, stop working, fail; *informal* conk out, go on the blink.
■ **pack something up** =**put away**, tidy up/away, clear up/away.

package ▶ noun 1 *the delivery of a package* =**parcel**, packet, box. 2 *a package of services* =**collection**, bundle, combination, range, complement, raft, platform.
▶ verb *goods packaged in recyclable materials* =**wrap (up)**, gift-wrap; pack (up), box, sealed.

packaging ▶ noun =**wrapping**, packing, covering.

packed ▶ adjective =**crowded**, full, filled (to capacity), crammed, jammed, solid, teeming, seething, swarming; *informal* jam-packed, chock-full, chock-a-block, full to the gunwales, bursting/bulging at the seams.

packet ▶ noun 1 *a packet of cigarettes* =**pack**, carton, container, case, package. 2 (informal) *it cost a packet* =**a lot of money**, a king's ransom, millions, billions; *informal* a (small) fortune, pots/heaps of money, a mint, a bundle, a pile, a tidy sum, a pretty penny, big money; *Brit. informal* a bomb; *N. Amer. informal* big bucks, gazillions; *Austral. informal* big bickies, motser.

pact ▶ noun =**agreement**, treaty, entente, protocol, deal, settlement; armistice, truce; *formal* concord.

pad[1] ▶ noun 1 *a pad over the eye* =**dressing**, pack, wad. 2 *making notes on a pad* =**notebook**, notepad, writing pad, jotter; *N. Amer.* scratch pad.
■ **pad something out** =**expand**, fill out, amplify, increase, flesh out, lengthen, spin out.

pad[2] ▶ verb *he padded along the landing* =**walk**, lope, trot; creep, tiptoe, steal, pussyfoot.

padded ▶ adjective =**quilted**, insulated, lined, cushioned, stuffed; thick; lagged.

padding ▶ noun 1 *padding around the ankle* =**wadding**, cushioning, stuffing, packing, filling, lining. 2 *a concise style with no padding* =**verbiage**, wordiness; *Brit. informal* waffle.

paddle[1] ▶ noun *use the paddles to row ashore* =**oar**, scull.
▶ verb *we paddled around the bay* =**row gently**, pull, scull.

paddle[2] ▶ verb *children were paddling in the water* =**splash about**; dabble.

padlock ▶ verb =**lock (up)**, fasten, secure.

padre ▶ noun =**priest**, chaplain, minister, pastor, father, parson, clergyman, cleric, man of the cloth, vicar, rector, curate; *informal* reverend, Holy Joe, sky pilot; *Austral. informal* josser.

pagan ▶ noun =**heathen**, infidel; pantheist.

▶ adjective =**heathen**, ungodly, irreligious, infidel; non-Christian, pre-Christian.

page[1] ▶ noun =**folio**, sheet, side, leaf.

page[2] ▶ noun =**errand boy**, messenger (boy); *N. Amer.* bellboy, bellhop.

▶ verb =**call (for)**, summon, send for, buzz.

pageant ▶ noun =**parade**, procession, cavalcade, tableau; spectacle, extravaganza, show.

pageantry ▶ noun =**spectacle**, display, ceremony, magnificence, pomp, splendour, grandeur, show; *informal* razzle-dazzle, razzmatazz.

pain ▶ noun **1** *she endured great pain* =**suffering**, agony, torture, torment, discomfort. **2** *a pain in the stomach* =**ache**, aching, soreness, throbbing, sting, twinge, shooting pain, stab, pang; discomfort, irritation. **3** *the pain of losing a loved one* =**sorrow**, grief, heartache, heartbreak, sadness, unhappiness, distress, misery, wretchedness, despair; agony, torment, torture. **4** *(informal) that child is a pain.* See NUISANCE. **5** *he took great pains to hide his feelings* =**care**, effort, bother, trouble.

▶ verb =**sadden**, grieve, distress, trouble, perturb, oppress, cause anguish to.

■ **be at pains** =**try hard**, make a great effort, put oneself out; strive, endeavour, try, do one's best, do one's utmost, go all out; *informal* bend/fall/lean over backwards.

> **WORD LINKS**
>
> *pain in a part of the body:* **-algia**
> *medicine for reducing pain:* **analgesic**
> *drug making one unable to feel pain:*
>   **anaesthetic**
> *branch of medicine concerning*
>   *insensitivity to pain:* **anaesthesiology**

pained ▶ adjective =**upset**, hurt, wounded, injured, insulted, offended, aggrieved, displeased, disgruntled, annoyed, indignant, irritated, resentful; *informal* riled, miffed, aggravated, peeved, hacked off, browned off; *Brit. informal* narked, cheesed off; *N. Amer. informal* teed off, ticked off, sore.

painful ▶ adjective **1** *a painful arm* =**sore**, hurting, tender, aching, throbbing. **2** *a painful experience* =**disagreeable**, unpleasant, nasty, distressing, upsetting,

traumatic, miserable, sad, heartbreaking, agonizing, harrowing.

painfully ▶ adverb =**distressingly**, disturbingly, uncomfortably, unpleasantly; dreadfully; *informal* terribly, awfully; *informal, dated* frightfully.

painkiller ▶ noun =**analgesic**, anaesthetic, narcotic; palliative.

painless ▶ adjective **1** *a simple, painless operation* =**pain-free**. **2** *getting rid of him proved painless* =**easy**, trouble-free, straightforward, simple, uncomplicated.

−OPPOSITES painful, difficult.

painstaking ▶ adjective =**careful**, meticulous, thorough, assiduous, attentive, diligent, industrious, conscientious, punctilious, scrupulous, rigorous, particular; pedantic, fussy.

−OPPOSITES slapdash.

paint ▶ noun =**colouring**, colourant, tint, dye, stain, pigment, colour.

▶ verb **1** *I painted the ceiling* =**colour**, decorate, whitewash, emulsion, gloss, spray-paint, airbrush. **2** *painting slogans on a wall* =**daub**, smear, spray-paint, airbrush. **3** *Rembrandt painted his mother* =**portray**, picture, paint a picture/portrait of, depict, represent.

painting ▶ noun =**picture**, illustration, portrayal, depiction, representation, image, artwork; oil (painting), watercolour, canvas.

pair ▶ noun **1** *a pair of gloves* =**set (of two)**, matching set, brace. **2** *the pair were arrested* =**two**, couple, duo.

▶ verb *a cardigan paired with a matching skirt* =**match**, put together, couple, combine.

■ **pair off/up** =**get together**, team up, form a couple, make a twosome.

palace ▶ noun =**royal/official residence**, castle, château, mansion, stately home.

> **WORD LINKS**
>
> *like a palace:* **palatial**

palatable ▶ adjective **1** *palatable meals* =**edible**, tasty, appetizing, delicious, mouth-watering, toothsome, succulent; *informal* scrumptious, yummy, scrummy, moreish. **2** *the truth is not always palatable* =**pleasant**, acceptable, agreeable, to one's liking.

−OPPOSITES disagreeable.

palate ▶ noun =**(sense of) taste**, appetite, stomach.

palatial ▶ adjective =**luxurious**, magnificent, sumptuous, splendid, grand, opulent, lavish, stately, fancy; *Brit.* upmarket; *informal* plush, swanky, posh, ritzy; *Brit. informal* swish.
−OPPOSITES modest.

palaver ▶ noun *(informal)* =**fuss**, bother, commotion, trouble, rigmarole; *informal* song and dance, performance, to-do, carrying-on, kerfuffle, hoo-ha, hullabaloo, ballyhoo.

pale ▶ adjective **1** *she looked pale* =**white**, pallid, pasty, wan, colourless, anaemic, bloodless, washed out, peaky, ashen, grey, whey-faced, drained, sickly, sallow, as white as a sheet; milky, ivory, milk-white, alabaster; *informal* like death warmed up. **2** *pale colours* =**light**, light-coloured, pastel, muted, subtle, soft; faded, bleached, washed out. **3** *the pale light of morning* =**dim**, faint, weak, feeble. **4** *a pale imitation* =**feeble**, weak, insipid, poor, inadequate; *informal* pathetic.
−OPPOSITES dark.
▶ verb =**go/turn white**, grow/turn pale, blanch, lose colour.

pall¹ ▶ noun *a pall of smoke* =**cloud**, covering, cloak, shroud, layer, blanket.
■ **cast a pall over** =**spoil**, cast a shadow over, overshadow, cloud, put a damper on.

pall² ▶ verb *the high life was beginning to pall* =**become/grow tedious**, become/grow boring, lose its/their attraction, wear off.

pallid ▶ adjective **1** *a pallid child* =**pale**, white, pasty, wan, colourless, anaemic, washed out, peaky, whey-faced, ashen, grey, drained, sickly, sallow; *informal* like death warmed up. **2** *pallid watercolours* =**insipid**, uninspired, colourless, uninteresting, unexciting, unimaginative, lifeless, sterile, bland.

pallor ▶ noun =**paleness**, pallidness, lack of colour, wanness, ashen hue, pastiness, peakiness, greyness, sickliness, sallowness.

palm ■ **grease someone's palm** *(informal)* =**bribe**, buy (off), corrupt, suborn; *informal* give a backhander to, give a sweetener to.
■ **have someone in the palm of one's hand** =**have control over**.
■ **palm something off** =**foist**, fob off, get rid of, dispose of, unload.

palpable ▶ adjective **1** *a palpable bump* =**tangible**, touchable, noticeable, detectable. **2** *his reluctance was palpable* =**perceptible**, visible, noticeable, discernible, detectable, observable, tangible, unmistakable, transparent; obvious, clear, plain (to see), evident, apparent, manifest, staring one in the face, written all over someone.
−OPPOSITES imperceptible.

palpitate ▶ verb **1** *her heart began to palpitate* =**beat rapidly**, pound, throb, thud, thump, hammer, race. **2** *palpitating with terror* =**tremble**, quiver, quake, shake (like a leaf).

paltry ▶ adjective =**small**, meagre, trifling, insignificant, negligible, inadequate, insufficient, derisory, pitiful, pathetic, miserable, niggardly, beggarly; *informal* measly, piddling, poxy; *formal* exiguous.
−OPPOSITES considerable.

pamper ▶ verb =**spoil**, indulge, overindulge, cosset, mollycoddle, coddle, baby, wait on someone hand and foot.

pamphlet ▶ noun =**brochure**, leaflet, booklet, circular, flyer, handbill; *N. Amer.* mailer, folder, dodger.

pan¹ ▶ noun =**saucepan**, frying pan, skillet.
▶ verb *(informal)*. See CRITICIZE.
−OPPOSITES praise.
■ **pan out** =**turn out**, work out, end (up), come out, fall out, evolve.

pan² ▶ verb *the camera panned to the building* =**swing (round)**, sweep, move, turn.

panacea ▶ noun =**universal cure**, cure-all, elixir, wonder drug; *informal* magic bullet.

panache ▶ noun =**flamboyance**, confidence, self-assurance, style, flair, elan, dash, verve, zest, spirit, brio, éclat, vivacity, gusto, liveliness, vitality, energy; *informal* pizzazz, oomph, zip, zing.

pancake ▶ noun =**crêpe**, tortilla, tostada, chapatti, dosa, latke; *N. Amer.* flapjack, slapjack.

pandemic ▶ adjective =**widespread**, prevalent, pervasive, rife, rampant.

pandemonium ▶ noun =**bedlam**, chaos, mayhem, uproar, turmoil, tumult, commotion, confusion, anarchy, furore, hubbub, rumpus; *informal* hullabaloo.
−OPPOSITES peace.

pander ■ **pander to** =**indulge**, gratify, satisfy, cater to, accommodate, give in to, comply with.

panel ▸ noun **1** *a control panel* =console, instrument panel, dashboard; instruments, controls, dials; array. **2** *a panel of judges* =group, team, body, committee, board.

pang ▸ noun **1** *hunger pangs* =(sharp) pain, shooting pain, twinge, stab, spasm. **2** *a pang of remorse* =qualm, twinge, prick.

panic ▸ noun *a wave of panic* =alarm, anxiety, nervousness, fear, fright, trepidation, dread, terror, agitation, hysteria, consternation, dismay, apprehension; *informal* flap, fluster, cold sweat, funk, tizzy; *N. Amer. informal* swivet.
−OPPOSITES calm.

▸ verb **1** *there's no need to panic* =be alarmed, be scared, be nervous, be afraid, take fright, be agitated, be hysterical, lose one's nerve, get overwrought, get worked up; *informal* get in a flap, lose one's cool, get into a tizzy, run around like a headless chicken, freak out, get in a stew; *Brit. informal* get the wind up, go into a (flat) spin, have kittens. **2** *talk of love panicked her* =frighten, alarm, scare, unnerve; *informal* throw into a tizzy, freak out; *Brit. informal* put the wind up.

panic-stricken ▸ adjective =alarmed, frightened, scared (stiff), terrified, terror-stricken, petrified, horrified, horror-stricken, panicky, frantic, frenzied, nervous, agitated, hysterical, beside oneself, worked up, overwrought; *informal* in a cold sweat, in a (blue) funk, in a flap, in a fluster, in a tizzy; *Brit. informal* in a flat spin.

panorama ▸ noun =(scenic) view, vista, prospect, scene, scenery, landscape, seascape, cityscape, skyline.

panoramic ▸ adjective =sweeping, wide, extensive, scenic, commanding.

pant ▸ verb =breathe heavily, breathe hard, puff (and blow), huff and puff, gasp, wheeze.

panting ▸ adjective =out of breath, breathless, short of breath, puffed out, puffing (and blowing), huffing and puffing, gasping (for breath), wheezing, wheezy.

pants ▸ plural noun **1** *(Brit.)* =underpants, briefs, Y-fronts, boxer shorts, boxers, long johns, (French) knickers, bikini briefs; *Brit.* camiknickers; *N. Amer.* shorts, undershorts; *informal* panties; *Brit.*

informal smalls; *dated* drawers, bloomers, unmentionables; *N. Amer. dated* step-ins. **2** *(N. Amer.). See* TROUSERS.

pap ▸ noun =rubbish, nonsense, froth; *Brit.* candyfloss; *informal* dreck, drivel, trash, twaddle.

paper ▸ noun **1** *a sheet of paper* =writing paper, notepaper, foolscap. **2** *the local paper* =newspaper, journal, gazette, periodical; tabloid, broadsheet, daily, weekly; *informal* rag; *N. Amer. informal* tab. **3** *the paper was peeling off the walls* =wallpaper, wallcovering; *Brit.* woodchip; *trademark* Anaglypta. **4** *toffee papers* =wrapper, wrapping. **5** *a three-hour paper* =exam, examination, test. **6** *he has just published a paper* =essay, article, monograph, thesis, work, dissertation, treatise, study, report, analysis, tract, critique, review; *N. Amer.* theme. **7** *personal papers* =documents, certificates, letters, files, deeds, records, archives, paperwork, documentation. **8** *they asked us for our papers* =identification papers/documents, identity card, ID, credentials.

▸ verb *we papered the hall* =wallpaper, decorate.

■ **paper something over** =cover up, hide, conceal, disguise, camouflage, gloss over.

■ **on paper 1** *he put his thoughts down on paper* –in writing, in black and white, in print. **2** *the teams were evenly matched on paper* =in theory, theoretically, supposedly.

par ■ **below par 1** *their performances have been below par* =substandard, inferior, not up to scratch, below average, second-rate, mediocre, poor, undistinguished; *informal* not up to snuff; *N. Amer. informal* bush-league. **2** *I'm feeling below par* =unwell, not (very) well, not oneself, out of sorts; ill, poorly, washed out, run down, peaky; *Brit.* off (colour); *informal* under the weather, lousy, rough; *Brit. informal* ropy, grotty; *Austral./NZ informal* crook; *dated* queer.

■ **on a par with** =as good as, comparable with, in the same class/league as, equivalent to, equal to, on a level with, of the same standard as.

■ **par for the course** =normal, typical, standard, usual, what one would expect.

■ **up to par** =good enough, up to the mark, satisfactory, acceptable, adequate, up to scratch; *informal* up to snuff.

parable ▸ noun =allegory, moral story/

tale, fable.

parade ▸ noun **1** *a victory parade* =**procession**, march, cavalcade, motorcade, spectacle, display, pageant; review, tattoo; *Brit.* march past. **2** *she walked along the parade* =**promenade**, walkway, esplanade, mall; *N. Amer.* boardwalk; *Brit. informal* prom.
▸ verb **1** *the teams paraded through the city* =**march**, process, file, troop. **2** *she paraded up and down* =**strut**, swagger, stride. **3** *he was keen to parade his knowledge* =**display**, exhibit, make a show of, flaunt, show (off), demonstrate.

paradigm ▸ noun =**model**, pattern, example, exemplar, standard, prototype, archetype.

paradise ▸ noun **1** *souls in paradise* =**(the kingdom of) heaven**, Elysium, Valhalla. **2** *a tropical paradise* =**utopia**, Shangri-La, heaven, idyll. **3** *this is sheer paradise!* =**bliss**, heaven, ecstasy, delight, joy, happiness, heaven on earth.
−OPPOSITES hell.

paradox ▸ noun =**contradiction (in terms)**, self-contradiction, inconsistency, incongruity, conflict; enigma, puzzle, mystery, conundrum.

paradoxical ▸ adjective =**contradictory**, self-contradictory, inconsistent, incongruous; illogical, puzzling, baffling, incomprehensible, inexplicable.

paragon ▸ noun =**perfect/shining example**, model, epitome, archetype, ideal, exemplar, embodiment, personification, quintessence, acme.

paragraph ▸ noun =**section**, subdivision, part, subsection, division, portion, segment, passage.

parallel ▸ adjective **1** *parallel lines* =**side by side**, aligned, collateral, equidistant. **2** *parallel careers* =**similar**, analogous, comparable, corresponding, like, of a kind, akin, related, equivalent, matching. **3** *a parallel universe* =**coexisting**, concurrent; contemporaneous, simultaneous.
−OPPOSITES divergent.
▸ noun **1** *an exact parallel* =**counterpart**, analogue, equivalent, likeness, match, twin, duplicate, mirror. **2** *there is an interesting parallel between these figures* =**similarity**, likeness, resemblance, analogy, correspondence, equivalence, correlation, relation, symmetry.
▸ verb **1** *his experiences parallel mine* =**resemble**, be similar to, be like, bear a resem-

blance to; correspond to, be analogous to, be comparable/equivalent to, equate with/to, correlate with, imitate, echo, remind one of, duplicate, mirror, follow, match. **2** *her performance has never been paralleled* =**equal**, match, rival, emulate.

paralyse ▸ verb **1** *both of his legs were paralysed* =**disable**, cripple, immobilize, incapacitate, debilitate. **2** *the capital was paralysed by a strike* =**bring to a standstill**, immobilize, bring to a (grinding) halt, freeze, cripple, disable.

paralysed ▸ adjective =**disabled**, crippled, handicapped, incapacitated, powerless, immobilized, useless; *Medicine* paraplegic, quadriplegic, tetraplegic, monoplegic, hemiplegic.

paralysis ▸ noun **1** *the disease can cause paralysis* =**immobility**, powerlessness, incapacity, debilitation; *Medicine* paraplegia, quadriplegia, tetraplegia, monoplegia, hemiplegia. **2** *complete paralysis of the ports* =**shutdown**, immobilization, stoppage, gridlock.

parameter ▸ noun =**framework**, variable, limit, boundary, limitation, restriction, criterion, guideline.

paramount ▸ adjective =**most important**, uppermost, supreme, chief, overriding, predominant, foremost, prime, primary, principal, highest, main, key, central, leading, major, top, greatest; *informal* number-one.

paranoia ▸ noun =**persecution complex**, delusions, obsession, psychosis.

paranoid ▸ adjective =**over-suspicious**, paranoiac, suspicious, mistrustful, fearful, insecure.

parapet ▸ noun =**balustrade**, barrier, wall.

paraphernalia ▸ plural noun =**equipment**, stuff, things, apparatus, kit, implements, tools, utensils, material(s), appliances, accoutrements, appurtenances, odds and ends, bits and pieces; *informal* gear; *Brit. informal* clobber.

paraphrase ▸ verb =**reword**, rephrase, put/express differently, rewrite, gloss.
▸ noun =**rewording**, rephrasing, rewriting, rewrite, gloss.

parasite ▸ noun =**hanger-on**, cadger, leech, passenger; *informal* bloodsucker, sponge, scrounger, freeloader; *N. Amer. informal* mooch; *Austral./NZ informal* bludger.

WORD LINKS

fear of parasites: **parasitophobia**

parcel ▸ noun **1** *a parcel of clothes* =**package**, packet; pack, bundle, box, case, bale. **2** *a parcel of land* =**plot**, piece, patch, tract; *Brit.* allotment; *N. Amer.* lot, plat.
▸ verb *she parcelled up the papers* =**pack (up)**, package, wrap (up), gift-wrap, tie up, bundle up.

parched ▸ adjective **1** *the parched earth* =**(bone) dry**, dried up/out, arid, desiccated, dehydrated, baked, burned, scorched; withered, shrivelled. **2** *(informal) I'm parched. See* THIRSTY *sense 1.*
–OPPOSITES soaking.

pardon ▸ noun **1** *pardon for your sins* =**forgiveness**, absolution. **2** *he offered them a full pardon* =**reprieve**, amnesty, exoneration, release, acquittal, discharge; *formal* exculpation.
▸ verb **1** *I know she will pardon me* =**forgive**, absolve. **2** *they were subsequently pardoned* =**exonerate**, acquit; reprieve; *informal* let off; *formal* exculpate.
–OPPOSITES blame, punish.
▸ exclamation *Pardon?* =**what (did you say)**, eh, pardon me, I beg your pardon, sorry, excuse me; *informal* come again.

pare ▸ verb =**cut (off)**, trim (off), peel (off), strip (off), skin; *technical* decorticate.
■ pare down =**reduce**, diminish, decrease, cut (back/down), trim, slim down, prune, curtail.

parent ▸ verb =**bring up**, look after, take care of, rear, raise.

WORD LINKS

killing of one's parent: **parricide**

parentage ▸ noun =**origins**, extraction, birth, family, ancestry, lineage, heritage, pedigree, descent, blood, stock, roots.

parenthood ▸ noun =**childcare**, child-rearing, motherhood, fatherhood, parenting.

pariah ▸ noun =**outcast**, persona non grata, leper, undesirable, unperson.

parish ▸ noun **1** *the parish of Upton* =**district**, community. **2** *the vicar scandalized the parish* =**parishioners**, churchgoers, congregation, fold, flock, community.

WORD LINKS

relating to a parish: **parochial**

parity ▸ noun =**equality**, equivalence, uniformity, consistency, correspondence, congruity, levelness, unity.

park ▸ noun **1** *we were playing in the park* =**public garden**, recreation ground, playground, play area. **2** *fifty acres of park* =**parkland**, grassland, woodland, garden(s), lawns, grounds, estate. **3** *the liveliest player on the park* =**(playing) field**, football field, pitch.
▸ verb **1** *he parked his car* =**leave**, position; stop, pull up. **2** *(informal) park your bag by the door* =**put (down)**, place, deposit, leave, stick, shove, dump; *informal* plonk; *Brit. informal* bung.
■ park oneself *(informal)* =**sit down**, seat oneself, settle (oneself), install oneself; *informal* plonk oneself.

parlance ▸ noun =**jargon**, language, phraseology, talk, speech, argot, patois, cant; *informal* lingo, -ese, -speak.

parliament ▸ noun **1** *the Queen's Speech to Parliament* =**the Houses of Parliament**, Westminster, the (House of) Commons. **2** *the Russian parliament* =**legislature**, congress, senate, (upper/lower) house, (upper/lower) chamber, diet, assembly.

parliamentary ▸ adjective =**legislative**, law-making, governmental, congressional, senatorial, democratic, elected, representative.

parochial ▸ adjective =**narrow-minded**, small-minded, provincial, narrow, small-town, conservative, illiberal, intolerant; *N. Amer. informal* jerkwater.
–OPPOSITES broad-minded.

parochialism ▸ noun =**narrow-mindedness**, provincialism, small-mindedness.

parody ▸ noun **1** *a parody of the news* =**satire**, burlesque, lampoon, pastiche, caricature, imitation; *informal* spoof, take-off, send-up. **2** *a parody of the truth* =**distortion**, travesty, caricature, misrepresentation, perversion, corruption, debasement.
▸ verb *parodying science fiction* =**satirize**, lampoon, caricature, mimic, imitate, ape, copy, make fun of, take off; *informal* send up.

paroxysm ▸ noun =**spasm**, attack, fit, burst, bout, convulsion, seizure, outburst, eruption, explosion.

parrot ▸ verb =**repeat (mindlessly/mechanically)**, echo; chant, intone.

WORD LINKS

relating to parrots: **psittacine**

parrot ▶ noun =psittacine.
▶ verb *they parroted slogans without appreciating their significance* =repeat (mindlessly), repeat mechanically, echo.

parrot-fashion ▶ adverb =mechanically, by rote, mindlessly, automatically.

parry ▶ verb **1** *Sharpe parried the blow* =ward off, fend off; deflect, block. **2** *I parried her questions* =evade, sidestep, avoid, dodge, field.

parsimonious ▶ adjective =mean, miserly, niggardly, close, penny-pinching, Scrooge-like; *informal* tight-fisted, tight, stingy, mingy; *N. Amer. informal* cheap.
–OPPOSITES generous.

parson ▶ noun =vicar, rector, clergyman, cleric, chaplain, pastor, curate, man of the cloth, minister, priest; *informal* reverend, padre; *Austral. informal* josser.

part ▶ noun **1** *the last part of the cake | a large part of their life* =bit, slice, chunk, lump, hunk, wedge, piece; portion, proportion, percentage, fraction. **2** *car parts* =component, bit, constituent, element, module. **3** *body parts* =organ, limb, member. **4** *the third part of the book* =section, division, volume, chapter, act, scene, instalment. **5** *another part of the country* =district, neighbourhood, quarter, section, area, region. **6** *the part of Juliet* =(theatrical) role, character. **7** *he's learn- ing his part* =lines, words, script, speech; libretto, lyrics, score. **8** *he was jailed for his part in the affair* =involvement, role, function, hand, work, responsibility, capacity, position, participation, contribution; *informal* bit.
–OPPOSITES whole.
▶ verb **1** *the curtains parted* =separate, divide (in two), split (in two), move apart. **2** *we parted on bad terms* =leave, take one's leave, say goodbye/farewell, say one's goodbyes/farewells, go one's (separate) ways, go away, depart.
–OPPOSITES join, meet.
▶ adjective *a part payment* =incomplete, partial, half, semi-, limited.
–OPPOSITES complete.
▶ adverb *it is part finished* =to a certain extent/degree, to some extent/degree, partly, partially, in part, half, relatively, comparatively, (up) to a point, some-

what; not totally, not entirely, (very) nearly, almost, just about, all but.
–OPPOSITES completely.
■ **for the most part**. *See* MOST.
■ **in part** =to a certain extent/degree, to some extent/degree, partly, partially, slightly, in some measure, (up) to a point.
■ **part with** =give up/away, relinquish, forgo, surrender, hand over, deliver up.
■ **take part** =participate, join in, get involved, enter, play a part/role, be a participant, contribute, have a hand, help, assist, lend a hand; *informal* get in on the act.
■ **take part in** =participate in, engage in, join in, get involved in, share in, play a part/role in, be a participant in, contribute to, be associated with, have a hand in.
■ **take someone's part** =support, give one's support to, take the side of, side with, stand by, stick up for, be supportive of, back (up), give one's backing to, be loyal to, defend, come to the defence of, champion.

partake ▶ verb **1** *(formal) visitors can partake in golf* =participate in, take part in, engage in, join in, get involved in. **2** *she had partaken of lunch* =consume, have, eat, drink, devour. **3** *Bohemia partakes of both East and West* =have the qualities/attributes of, suggest, evoke, be characterized by.

partial ▶ adjective **1** *a partial recovery* =incomplete, limited, qualified, imperfect, fragmentary, unfinished. **2** *a very partial view of the situation* =biased, prejudiced, partisan, one-sided, slanted, skewed, coloured, unbalanced.
–OPPOSITES complete, unbiased.
■ **be partial to** =like, love, enjoy, have a liking for, be fond of, be keen on, have a soft spot for, have a taste for, have a penchant for; *informal* adore, be mad about/on, have a thing about, be crazy about, be nutty about; *Brit. informal* be potty about; *N. Amer. informal* cotton to; *Austral./NZ informal* be shook on.

partially ▶ adverb =to a limited extent/degree, to a certain extent/degree, partly, in part, (up) to a point, somewhat, comparatively, slightly.

participant ▶ noun =participator, contributor, party, member; entrant, competitor, player, contestant, candidate.

participate ▶ verb =take part, join,

engage, get involved, share, play a part/role, be a participant, partake, have a hand in, be associated with.

participation ▸ noun =involvement, part, contribution, association.

particle ▸ noun =(tiny) bit, (tiny) piece, speck, spot; fragment, sliver, splinter.

particular ▸ adjective **1** *a particular group of companies* =specific, certain, distinct, separate, discrete, definite, precise; single, individual. **2** *an issue of particular importance* =(extra) special, especial, exceptional, unusual, singular, uncommon, notable, noteworthy, remarkable, unique. **3** *he was particular about what he ate* =fussy, fastidious, finicky, meticulous, discriminating, selective, painstaking, exacting, demanding; *informal* pernickety, choosy, picky; *Brit. informal* faddy.
–OPPOSITES general, careless.
▸ noun *the same in every particular* =detail, item, point, element, fact, feature.
■ **in particular 1** *nothing in particular* =specific, special. **2** *the poor, in particular, were hit by rising prices* =particularly, specifically, especially, specially.

particularly ▸ adverb **1** *the acoustics are particularly good* =especially, specially, extremely, exceptionally, singularly, unusually, remarkably, outstandingly, amazingly, incredibly, really. **2** *he particularly asked that I should help you* =specifically, explicitly, expressly, in particular, especially, specially.

parting ▸ noun *an emotional parting* =farewell, leave-taking, goodbye, adieu, departure.
▸ adjective *a parting kiss* =farewell, goodbye, last, final.

partisan ▸ noun =guerrilla, freedom fighter, resistance fighter, irregular (soldier).
▸ adjective =biased, prejudiced, one-sided, discriminatory, partial, sectarian, factional.
–OPPOSITES unbiased.

partition ▸ noun **1** *the partition of Palestine* =dividing (up), partitioning, separation, division, splitting (up), breaking up, break-up. **2** *room partitions* =screen, (room) divider, (dividing) wall, barrier, panel.
▸ verb **1** *moves to partition Poland* =divide (up), separate, split (up), break up. **2** *the hall was partitioned* =subdivide, divide

(up); separate (off), section off, screen off.

partly ▸ adverb =to a certain extent/degree, to some extent/degree, in part, partially, a little, somewhat, not entirely, relatively, moderately, (up) to a point, in some measure, slightly.
–OPPOSITES completely.

partner ▸ noun **1** *business partners* =colleague, associate, co-worker, fellow worker, collaborator, comrade, teammate; *Brit. informal* oppo; *Austral./NZ informal* offsider. **2** *his partner in crime* =accomplice, confederate, accessory, collaborator, fellow conspirator, helper; *informal* sidekick. **3** *your relationship with your partner* =spouse, husband, wife; lover, girlfriend, boyfriend, fiancé, fiancée, significant other, live-in lover, common-law husband/wife, man, woman, mate; *informal* hubby, missus, old man, old lady/woman, better half; *Brit. informal* other half.

partnership ▸ noun **1** *close partnership* =cooperation, association, collaboration, coalition, alliance, union, affiliation, connection. **2** *thriving partnerships* =company, firm, business, corporation, organization, association, consortium, syndicate.

partridge ▸ noun

> **WORD LINKS**
>
> *collective noun:* **covey**

party ▸ noun **1** *150 people attended the party* =(social) gathering, (social) function, get-together, celebration, reunion, festivity, reception, soirée, social; *N. Amer.* fête, hoedown; *Austral./NZ* corroboree; *informal* bash, shindig, rave, do; *Brit. informal* rave-up, knees-up, beanfeast, beano, bunfight; *N. Amer. informal* blast, wingding, kegger; *Austral./NZ informal* shivoo, rage, ding, jollo, rort. **2** *a party of visitors* =group, company, body, gang, band, crowd, pack, contingent; *informal* bunch, crew, load. **3** *a left-wing party* =faction, group, bloc, camp, caucus; alliance. **4** *don't mention a certain party* =person, individual, somebody, someone.
▸ verb *(informal) let's party!* =celebrate, have fun, enjoy oneself, have a party, have a good/wild time, rave it up, make merry; *informal* go out on the town, paint the town red, whoop it up, let one's hair

down, make whoopee, live it up, have a ball.

■ **be a party to** =get involved in/with, be associated with, be a participant in.

pass[1] ▶ verb **1** *the traffic passing through the village* =**go**, proceed, move, progress, make one's way, travel. **2** *a car passed him* =**overtake**, go past/by, pull ahead of, leave behind. **3** *time passed* =**elapse**, go by/past, advance, wear on, roll by, tick by. **4** *he passed the time reading* =**occupy**, spend, fill, use (up), employ, while away. **5** *pass the salt* =**hand (over)**, let someone have, give, reach. **6** *he passed the ball* =**kick**, hit, throw, lob. **7** *her estate passed to her grandson* =**be transferred**, go, be left, be bequeathed, be handed down/on, be passed on; *Law* devolve. **8** *his death passed unnoticed* =**happen**, occur, take place. **9** *the storm passed* =**come to an end**, fade (away), blow over, run its course, die out/down, finish, end, cease. **10** *he passed the exam* =**be successful in**, succeed in, gain a pass in, get through; *informal* sail through, scrape through. **11** *the Senate passed the bill* =**approve**, vote for, accept, ratify, adopt, agree to, authorize, endorse, legalize, enact; *informal* OK. **12** *she could not let that comment pass* =**go (unnoticed)**, stand, go unremarked, go undisputed. **13** *passing urine* =**discharge**, excrete, evacuate, expel, emit, release.

–OPPOSITES stop, fail, reject.

▶ noun **1** *you must show your pass* =**permit**, warrant, authorization, licence. **2** *a cross-field pass* =**kick**, hit, throw, shot.

■ **make a pass at** =make (sexual) advances to, proposition; *informal* come on to, make a play for; *N. Amer. informal* hit on, make time with, put the make on.

■ **pass away/on**. See DIE sense 1.

■ **pass as/for** =be mistaken for, be taken for, be accepted as.

■ **pass out** =faint, lose consciousness, black out.

■ **pass something up** =turn down, reject, refuse, decline, give up, forgo, let pass, miss (out on); *informal* give something a miss.

pass[2] ▶ noun *a mountain pass* =**route**, way, road, passage; *N. Amer.* notch.

passable ▶ adjective **1** *the beer was passable* =**adequate**, all right, acceptable, satisfactory, not (too) bad, average, tolerable, fair; mediocre, middling, ordinary, indifferent, unremarkable, unexceptional; *informal* OK, so-so; *NZ informal*

half-pie. **2** *the road is still passable* =**navigable**, traversable, negotiable, open, clear.

passably ▶ adverb =**quite**, rather, somewhat, fairly, reasonably, moderately, comparatively, relatively, tolerably; *informal* pretty.

passage ▶ noun **1** *their passage through the country* =**transit**, progress. **2** *the passage of time* =**passing**, advance, course, march. **3** *clearing a passage to the front door* =**way (through)**, route, path. **4** *a passage to the kitchen*. See PASSAGEWAY sense 1. **5** *a passage between the buildings*. See PASSAGEWAY sense 2. **6** *the nasal passages* =**duct**, orifice, opening, channel; inlet, outlet. **7** *the passage to democracy* =**transition**, development, progress, move, change, shift. **8** *the passage of the bill* =**enactment**, passing, ratification, approval, adoption, authorization, legalization. **9** *a passage from 'Macbeth'* =**extract**, excerpt, quotation, quote.

passageway ▶ noun **1** *secret passageways* =**corridor**, hall, passage, hallway. **2** *a narrow passageway off the main street* =**alley**, alleyway, passage, lane, path, pathway, footpath, track, thoroughfare; *N. Amer.* areaway.

passé ▶ adjective. See OLD-FASHIONED.

passenger ▶ noun =**traveller**, commuter, fare payer; consumer.

passing ▶ adjective **1** *of passing interest* =**fleeting**, transient, transitory, ephemeral, brief, short-lived, temporary, momentary. **2** *a passing glance* =**hasty**, rapid, hurried, brief, quick; cursory, superficial, casual, perfunctory.

▶ noun **1** *the passing of time* =**passage**, course, progress, advance. **2** *Jack's passing* =**death**, demise, passing away/on, end, loss, quietus; *formal* decease. **3** *the passing of the new bill* =**enactment**, ratification, approval, adoption, authorization, legalization, endorsement.

■ **in passing** =incidentally, by the by/way.

passion ▶ noun **1** *the passion of activists* =**fervour**, ardour, enthusiasm, eagerness, zeal, zealousness, vigour, fire, energy, animation, spirit, fanaticism. **2** *he worked himself up into a passion* =**(blind) rage**, fit of anger/temper, temper, tantrum, fury, frenzy; *Brit. informal* paddy. **3** *hot with passion* =**love**, (sexual) desire, lust, ardour, lasciviousness, lustfulness. **4** *his passion for football* =**enthusiasm**,

love, mania, fascination, obsession, fanaticism, fixation, compulsion, appetite, addiction; *informal* thing. **5** *wine is a passion with me* =**obsession**, preoccupation, craze, mania, hobby horse.
–OPPOSITES apathy.

passionate ▶ adjective **1** *a passionate entreaty* =**intense**, impassioned, ardent, fervent, vehement, fiery, heated, emotional, heartfelt, excited, animated, spirited. **2** *McGregor is passionate about sport* =**very keen**, very enthusiastic, addicted; *informal* mad, crazy, hooked, nuts; *N. Amer. informal* nutso; *Austral./NZ informal* shook. **3** *a passionate kiss* =**amorous**, ardent, hot-blooded, loving, sexy, sensual, erotic, lustful; *informal* steamy, hot, turned on. **4** *a passionate woman* =**excitable**, emotional, fiery, volatile, mercurial, quick-tempered, highly strung, impulsive, temperamental.
–OPPOSITES apathetic.

passionless ▶ adjective =**unemotional**, cold, cold-blooded, emotionless, frigid, cool, unfeeling, unloving, unresponsive, undemonstrative, impassive.

passive ▶ adjective **1** *a passive role* =**inactive**, non-active, non-participative, uninvolved. **2** *passive victims* =**submissive**, acquiescent, unresisting, compliant, pliant, obedient, docile, malleable, pliable.
–OPPOSITES active.

passport ▶ noun **1** =**travel permit**, (travel) papers, visa. **2** *a passport to fame* =**key**, path, way, route, avenue, door, doorway.

past ▶ adjective **1** *times past* =**gone (by)**, bygone, former, (of) old, olden, long-ago. **2** *the past few months* =**last**, recent, preceding. **3** *a past chairman* =**previous**, former, foregoing, erstwhile, one-time, sometime, ex-.
–OPPOSITES present, future.
▶ noun *details of her past* =**history**, background, life (story).
▶ preposition **1** *I drove past the cafe* =**in front of**, by. **2** *it's past 9 o'clock* =**beyond**, after, later than.
▶ adverb *they hurried past* =**along**, by, on.
■ **in the past** =**formerly**, previously, in days/years/times gone by, in former times, in the (good) old days, in days of old, in olden times, once (upon a time).

paste ▶ noun **1** *blend the ingredients to a paste* =**purée**, pulp, mush. **2** *wallpaper paste* =**adhesive**, glue, gum; *N. Amer.*

mucilage. **3** *fish paste* =**spread**, pâté.
▶ verb *a notice was pasted on the door* =**glue**, stick, gum, fix, affix.

pastel ▶ adjective =**pale**, soft, light.
–OPPOSITES dark, bright.

pastiche ▶ noun =**imitation**, parody; *informal* take-off.

pastille ▶ noun =**lozenge**, sweet, drop; tablet, pill.

pastime ▶ noun =**hobby**, leisure activity/pursuit, sport, game, recreation, amusement, diversion, entertainment, interest, sideline.

past master ▶ noun =**expert**, master, wizard, genius, old hand, veteran, maestro, authority; *Brit. informal* dab hand; *N. Amer. informal* maven, crackerjack.

pastor ▶ noun =**priest**, minister, parson, clergyman, cleric, chaplain, padre, man of the cloth, vicar, rector, curate; *informal* reverend; *Austral. informal* josser.

pastoral ▶ adjective =**rural**, country, countryside, rustic, agricultural, bucolic; *literary* sylvan, Arcadian.
–OPPOSITES urban.

pasture ▶ noun =**grazing (land)**, grassland, grass; meadow, field; *Austral./NZ* run.

┌─────────────────┐
│ **WORD LINKS** │
└─────────────────┘
relating to pasture: **pastoral**

pasty ▶ adjective =**pale**, pallid, wan, colourless, anaemic, ashen, white, grey, washed out, sallow.

pat[1] ▶ verb *Brian patted her on the shoulder* =**tap**, clap, touch.
▶ noun **1** *a pat on the cheek* =**tap**, clap, touch. **2** *a pat of butter* =**piece**, lump, portion, knob, mass, ball, curl.
■ **pat someone on the back** =**congratulate**, praise, take one's hat off to; commend, compliment, applaud, acclaim.

pat[2] ▶ adjective *pat answers* =**glib**, simplistic, facile, unconvincing.
■ **off pat** =**word-perfect**, by heart, by rote, by memory, parrot-fashion.
■ **get something off pat** =**memorize**, commit to memory, remember, learn by heart, learn (by rote).

patch ▶ noun **1** *a patch over one eye* =**cover**, eyepatch, covering, pad. **2** *a reddish patch on her wrist* =**blotch**, mark, spot, smudge, smear, stain, streak, blemish; *informal* splodge, splotch. **3** *a patch of ground* =**plot**, area, piece, strip,

p

tract, parcel; bed; *Brit.* allotment; *N. Amer.* lot. **4** (*Brit. informal*) *going through a difficult patch* =**period**, time, spell, phase, stretch; *Brit. informal* spot.
▶ **verb** *her jeans were neatly patched* =**mend**, repair, put a patch on, sew (up), stitch (up).
■ **patch something up** (*informal*) **1** *the houses were being patched up* =**repair**, mend, fix. **2** *he's trying to patch things up with his wife* =**reconcile**, make up, settle, put to rights, rectify, clear up, set right, make good, resolve, square.

patchwork ▶ **noun** =**assortment**, miscellany, mixture, melange, medley, blend, mixed bag, mix, collection, selection, combination, pot-pourri, jumble, mishmash, ragbag, hotchpotch; *N. Amer.* hodgepodge.

patchy ▶ **adjective 1** *their teaching has been patchy* =**uneven**, bitty, varying, variable, intermittent, fitful, sporadic, erratic, irregular. **2** *patchy evidence* =**fragmentary**, inadequate, insufficient, rudimentary, limited, sketchy.
–OPPOSITES uniform, comprehensive.

patent ▶ **adjective 1** *patent nonsense* =**obvious**, clear, plain, evident, manifest, transparent, overt, conspicuous, blatant, downright, barefaced, flagrant, undisguised, unconcealed, unmistakable. **2** *patent medicines* =**proprietary**, patented, licensed, branded.

path ▶ **noun 1** *the path to the beach* =**footpath**, pathway, track, trail, bridle path, lane; cycle path/track; *N. Amer.* bikeway. **2** *journalists blocked his path* =**route**, way, course. **3** *the best path to follow* =**course of action**, route, road, avenue, line, approach, tack.

pathetic ▶ **adjective 1** *a pathetic sight* =**pitiful**, moving, touching, poignant, plaintive, wretched, forlorn. **2** (*informal*) *a pathetic excuse* =**feeble**, woeful, sorry, poor, pitiful, lamentable, deplorable, contemptible.

pathological ▶ **adjective 1** *a pathological condition* =**morbid**, diseased. **2** (*informal*) *a pathological liar* =**compulsive**, obsessive, inveterate, habitual, persistent, chronic, hardened, confirmed.

pathos ▶ **noun** =**poignancy**, tragedy, sadness, pitifulness.

patience ▶ **noun 1** *she tried everyone's patience* =**forbearance**, tolerance, restraint, stoicism; composure, equanimity, understanding, indulgence. **2** *a task*

requiring patience =**perseverance**, persistence, endurance, tenacity, application, staying power, doggedness.

patient ▶ **adjective 1** *I must ask you to be patient* =**forbearing**, uncomplaining, tolerant; calm, composed, even-tempered, accommodating, understanding, indulgent. **2** *patient research* =**persevering**, persistent, tenacious, dogged, determined.
▶ **noun** *a doctor's patient* =**sick person**, case.

patio ▶ **noun** =**terrace**; courtyard, quadrangle, quad; *N. Amer.* sun deck.

patriot ▶ **noun** =**nationalist**, loyalist; chauvinist, jingoist, flag-waver.

patriotic ▶ **adjective** =**nationalist**, nationalistic, loyalist, loyal; chauvinistic, jingoistic, flag-waving.
–OPPOSITES traitorous.

patriotism ▶ **noun** =**nationalism**; chauvinism, jingoism, flag-waving.

patrol ▶ **noun 1** *anti-poaching patrols* =**vigil**, guard, watch. **2** *the patrol stopped a woman* =**squad**, detachment, party, force.
▶ **verb** *a guard was patrolling the estate* =(**keep**) **guard** (**on**), keep watch (on); police, make the rounds (of); stand guard (over), defend, safeguard.

patron ▶ **noun 1** *a patron of the arts* =**sponsor**, backer, benefactor, benefactress, contributor, subscriber, donor; philanthropist, promoter, friend, supporter. **2** *club patrons* =**customer**, client, consumer, user, visitor, guest; *informal* regular.

patronage ▶ **noun 1** *arts patronage* =**sponsorship**, backing, funding, financing, assistance, support. **2** *political patronage* =**power of appointment**, favouritism, nepotism. **3** *thank you for your patronage* =**custom**, trade, business.

patronize ▶ **verb 1** *don't patronize me!* =**talk down to**, treat like a child. **2** *they patronized local tradesmen* =**use**, buy from, shop at, be a customer/client of, deal with, frequent, support.

patronizing ▶ **adjective** =**condescending**, supercilious, superior, imperious, scornful; *informal* uppity, high and mighty.

patter¹ ▶ **verb 1** *raindrops pattered against the window* =**go pitter-patter**, tap, drum, beat, pound, go pit-a-pat. **2** *she pattered across the floor* =**scurry**, scuttle, skip, trip.

▸ noun *the patter of rain* =**pitter-patter**, tapping, pattering, drumming, beating, pounding, rat-a-tat, pit-a-pat.

patter² ▸ noun *the salesmen's patter* =**(sales) pitch**; *informal* line, spiel.

pattern ▸ noun **1** *the pattern on the wallpaper* =**design**, decoration, motif, marking. **2** *working patterns* =**system**, order, arrangement, form, method, structure, scheme, plan, format. **3** *this set the pattern for a generation* =**model**, example, criterion, standard, basis, point of reference, norm, yardstick, touchstone, benchmark; blueprint.

patterned ▸ adjective =**decorated**, ornamented, fancy, adorned, embellished.
–OPPOSITES plain.

paunch ▸ noun =**pot/beer belly**; *informal* beer gut, pot.

pauper ▸ noun =**poor person**, down-and-out; *informal* have-not.

pause ▸ noun =**break**, interruption, lull, respite, breathing space, hiatus, gap, interlude; adjournment, rest, wait, hesitation; *informal* let-up, breather.
▸ verb =**stop**, break off, take a break; adjourn, rest, wait, hesitate, falter, waver; *informal* take a breather.

pave ▸ verb *the yard was paved* =**tile**, surface, flag.
■ **pave the way for** =**prepare (the way) for**, make preparations for, get ready for, lay the foundations for.

pavement ▸ noun =**footpath**, walkway; *N. Amer.* sidewalk.

paw ▸ verb **1** *the puppies pawed each other* =**pull**, grab, maul. **2** *Barry tried to paw her* =**fondle**, feel, molest; *informal* grope, feel up, touch up, goose.

pawn ▸ noun *the parents may use the child as a pawn* =**puppet**, dupe, hostage, tool, cat's paw, instrument.

pay ▸ verb **1** *I must pay him for his work* =**reward**, reimburse, recompense, remunerate. **2** *I paid £7 for a ticket* =**spend**, pay out; *informal* lay/shell/fork out, cough up; *N. Amer. informal* ante up, pony up. **3** *he paid his debts* =**discharge**, settle, pay off, clear. **4** *he made the buses pay* =**be profitable**, make money, make a profit. **5** *it may pay you to be early* =**be advantageous to**, benefit, be of advantage to, be beneficial to. **6** *he will pay for his mistakes* =**suffer (the consequences)**, be punished, atone, pay the penalty/price.
▸ noun *equal pay* =**salary**, wages, payment;

earnings, remuneration, reimbursement, income, revenue.
■ **pay someone back** =**get one's revenge on**, get back at, get even with, settle the score.
■ **pay something back** =**repay**, pay off, give back, return, reimburse, refund.
■ **pay for** =**finance**, fund; treat someone to; *informal* foot the bill for, shell out for, fork out for, cough up for; *N. Amer. informal* ante up for, pony up for.
■ **pay something off** =**pay (in full)**, settle, discharge, clear, liquidate.
■ **pay off** *(informal)* =**meet with success**, be successful, be effective, get results, work.
■ **pay something out** =**spend**, pay, dish out, put up, part with, hand over; *informal* shell out, fork out/up, lay out, cough up.
■ **pay up** =**settle up**, pay (in full); *informal* cough up.

payable ▸ adjective =**due**, owed, owing, outstanding, unpaid, overdue; *N. Amer.* delinquent.

payment ▸ noun **1** *discounts for early payment* =**remittance**, settlement, discharge, clearance. **2** *monthly payments* =**instalment**, premium. **3** *extra payment for good performance* =**salary**, wages, pay, earnings, fee(s), remuneration, reimbursement, income.

pay-off ▸ noun *(informal)* =**outcome**, denouement, culmination, conclusion, development, result.

peace ▸ noun **1** *peace of mind* =**serenity**, peacefulness, tranquillity, calm, calmness, composure, ease, contentment. **2** *we pray for peace* =**order**, harmony; *formal* concord. **3** *a lasting peace* =**treaty**, truce, ceasefire, armistice.
–OPPOSITES noise, war.

peaceable ▸ adjective =**peace-loving**, non-violent, non-aggressive, easy-going, placid, gentle, good-natured, even-tempered, amiable, affable, genial.
–OPPOSITES aggressive.

peaceful ▸ adjective **1** *everything was quiet and peaceful* =**tranquil**, calm, restful, quiet, still, relaxing, soothing, undisturbed, untroubled, private, secluded. **2** *his peaceful mood* =**serene**, calm, tranquil, composed, placid, at ease, untroubled, unworried, content. **3** *peaceful relations* =**harmonious**, on good terms, amicable, friendly, cordial, non-violent.

–OPPOSITES noisy, agitated, hostile.

peacemaker ▶ noun =arbitrator, arbiter, mediator, negotiator, conciliator, go-between, intermediary.

peacock ▶ noun

WORD LINKS

species: **peacock**
female: **peahen**
young: **peachick**
collective noun: **muster**

peak ▶ noun **1** *the peaks of the mountains* =**summit**, top, crest, pinnacle, cap. **2** *the highest peak* =**mountain**, hill, height. **3** *the peak of a cap* =**brim**, visor. **4** *the peak of his career* =**height**, high point/spot, pinnacle, summit, top, climax, culmination, apex, zenith, crowning point, acme, apogee, prime, heyday.
▶ verb *Labour support has peaked* =**reach its height**, climax.
▶ adjective *peak times* =**maximum**, greatest, busiest, highest.

peaky ▶ adjective =**pale**, pasty, wan, drained, washed out, drawn, pallid, anaemic, ashen, grey, sickly, sallow; ill, unwell, poorly, run down; *Brit.* off (colour); *informal* under the weather, rough; *Brit. informal* grotty, ropy.

peal ▶ noun **1** *a peal of bells* =**chime**, ring. **2** *peals of laughter* =**shriek**, shout, scream, howl, gale, fit, roar, hoot. **3** *a peal of thunder* =**rumble**, roar, boom, crash, clap, crack.

peasant ▶ noun **1** *peasants working the land* =**agricultural worker**, labourer. **2** *(informal) you peasants!* See BOOR.

peck ▶ verb **1** *the budgie pecked me* =**bite**, nip. **2** *he pecked her on the cheek* =**kiss**. **3** *(informal) the old lady pecked at her food* =**nibble**, pick at, toy with, play with.

peculiar ▶ adjective **1** *something peculiar happened* =**strange**, unusual, odd, funny, curious, bizarre, weird, queer; extraordinary; suspicious, eerie, unnatural; *informal* fishy, creepy, spooky. **2** *peculiar behaviour* =**bizarre**, eccentric, strange, odd, weird, funny, unusual, abnormal, unconventional, outlandish, quirky; *informal* wacky, freaky, oddball, offbeat, off the wall; *N. Amer. informal* wacko. **3** *(informal) I feel a bit peculiar.* See UNWELL. **4** *customs peculiar to this area* =**characteristic of**, typical of, exclusive to. **5** *their own peculiar contribution* =**distinctive**, characteristic, distinct, individual, special, unique, personal.

–OPPOSITES ordinary.

peculiarity ▶ noun **1** *a legal peculiarity* =**oddity**, anomaly, abnormality. **2** *a physical peculiarity* =**idiosyncrasy**, mannerism, quirk, foible. **3** *the peculiarity of this notion* =**strangeness**, oddness, bizarreness, weirdness, queerness, unexpectedness, incongruity. **4** *the peculiarity of her appearance* =**outlandishness**, bizarreness, unconventionality, weirdness, oddness, eccentricity, strangeness, quirkiness; *informal* wackiness, freakiness.

pedant ▶ noun =**dogmatist**, purist, literalist, formalist; quibbler, hair-splitter; *informal* nit-picker.

pedantic ▶ adjective =**overscrupulous**, precise, exact, punctilious, fussy, fastidious, finicky; dogmatic, purist; hair-splitting, quibbling; *informal* nit-picking, pernickety.

pedantry ▶ noun =**dogmatism**, purism; overscrupulousness, perfectionism, fastidiousness, punctiliousness, hair-splitting, casuistry, sophistry; *informal* nit-picking.

peddle ▶ verb **1** *they are peddling water filters* =**sell (from door to door)**, hawk, tout; trade (in), deal in, traffic in. **2** *peddling unorthodox views* =**advocate**, champion, preach, put forward, proclaim, propound, promote.

pedestal ▶ noun *a bust on a pedestal* =**plinth**, base, support, mount, stand, pillar, column.
■ **put someone on a pedestal** =**idealize**, look up to, hold in high regard, think highly of, admire, esteem, revere, worship.

pedestrian ▶ noun =**walker**, person on foot.
–OPPOSITES driver.
▶ adjective =**dull**, boring, tedious, monotonous, uneventful, unremarkable, uninspired, unimaginative, unexciting, routine; commonplace, workaday; ordinary, everyday, run-of-the-mill, mundane, humdrum; *informal* bog-standard.
–OPPOSITES exciting.

pedigree ▶ noun =**ancestry**, lineage, line (of descent), genealogy, extraction, derivation, origin(s), heritage, parentage, bloodline, background, roots.
▶ adjective =**pure-bred**, thoroughbred.

pedlar ▶ noun **1** *an old pedlar* =**travelling salesman**, door-to-door salesman, huckster; street trader, hawker. **2** *a drug* *pedlar* =**trafficker**, dealer; *informal* pusher.

peek ▶ verb **1** *they peeked from behind the curtains* =**(have a) peep**, sneak a look; *informal* take a gander, have a squint; *Brit. informal* have a dekko, have/take a butcher's, take a shufti. **2** *the deer's antlers peeked out from the trees* =**appear (slowly/partly)**, show, peep (out).
▶ noun *a peek at the map* =**secret/sly look**, peep, glance, glimpse, hurried/quick look; *informal* gander, squint; *Brit. informal* dekko, butcher's, shufti.

peel ▶ verb **1** *peel and core the fruit* =**pare**, skin; hull, shell. **2** *the wallpaper was peeling* =**flake (off)**, come off in layers/strips.
▶ noun *orange peel* =**rind**, skin, covering, zest.
∎ **peel something off** *(Brit. informal)* =**take off**, strip off, remove.

peep ▶ verb **1** *I peeped through the keyhole* =**look quickly**, sneak a look, (have a) peek, glance; *informal* take a gander, have a squint; *Brit. informal* have a dekko, have/take a butcher's, take a shufti. **2** *the moon peeped through the clouds* =**appear (slowly/partly)**, show, come into view/sight, emerge, peek, peer out.
▶ noun *I'll just take a peep* =**quick/brief look**, peek, glance; *informal* gander, squint; *Brit. informal* dekko, butcher's, shufti.

peer¹ ▶ verb *he peered at the manuscript* =**look closely**, squint.

peer² ▶ noun **1** *hereditary peers* =**aristocrat**, lord, lady, noble, nobleman, noblewoman. **2** *his academic peers* =**equal**, fellow; contemporary.

peerage ▶ noun =**aristocracy**, nobility; the House of Lords, the Lords.

peerless ▶ adjective =**incomparable**, matchless, unrivalled, beyond compare/comparison, unparalleled, without equal, second to none, unsurpassed; unique, consummate.

peeve ▶ verb *(informal)* =**irritate**, annoy, vex, anger, irk, gall, pique, nettle, put out; *informal* aggravate, rile, needle, get to, bug, hack off, get someone's goat, get/put someone's back up; *N. Amer. informal* tee off, tick off.

peeved ▶ adjective *(informal)* =**irritated**, annoyed, cross, angry, vexed, displeased, disgruntled, indignant, galled, irked, put out, aggrieved, offended, affronted, piqued, nettled, in high

dudgeon; *informal* aggravated, miffed, riled; *Brit. informal* narked, cheesed off, brassed off; *N. Amer. informal* teed off, ticked off, sore.

peg ▶ noun =**pin**, nail, dowel; *Mountaineering* piton.
▶ verb **1** *the flysheet is pegged to the ground* =**fix**, pin, attach, fasten, secure. **2** *we decided to peg our prices* =**hold down**, keep down, fix, set, hold, freeze.

pejorative ▶ adjective =**disparaging**, derogatory, defamatory, slanderous, libellous, abusive, insulting.
–OPPOSITES complimentary.

pellet ▶ noun **1** *a pellet of mud* =**ball**, piece. **2** *pellet wounds* =**bullet**, shot, lead shot, buckshot. **3** *rabbit pellets* =**excrement**, excreta, droppings, faeces, dung.

pelt¹ ▶ verb **1** *they pelted him with snowballs* =**bombard**, shower, attack, assail, pepper. **2** *rain was pelting down* =**pour down**, teem down, stream down, tip down, rain cats and dogs; *Brit. informal* bucket down. **3** *(informal) they pelted into the factory* =**dash**, run, race, rush, sprint, bolt, dart, career, charge, shoot, hurtle, hare, fly, speed, zoom, streak; hurry; *informal* tear, belt, hotfoot it, scoot, leg it; *Brit. informal* bomb; *N. Amer. informal* hightail it.

pelt² ▶ noun *an animal's pelt* =**skin**, hide, fleece, coat, fur.

pen¹ ▶ verb *he penned a number of articles* =**write**, compose, draft, dash off.

pen² ▶ noun *a sheep pen* =**enclosure**, fold, pound, compound, stockade; sty, coop; *N. Amer.* corral.
▶ verb *the hostages were penned up in a basement* =**confine**, coop (up), cage, shut in, box up/in, lock up/in, trap, imprison, incarcerate.

penal ▶ adjective **1** *a penal institution* =**disciplinary**, punitive, correctional. **2** *penal rates of interest* =**exorbitant**, extortionate, excessive, outrageous, preposterous, unreasonable, inflated, sky-high.

penalize ▶ verb **1** *if you break the rules you will be penalized* =**punish**, discipline. **2** *blind people would be penalized* =**handicap**, disadvantage, discriminate against.
–OPPOSITES reward.

penalty ▶ noun **1** *increased penalties for speeding* =**punishment**, sanction; fine, forfeit, sentence. **2** *the penalties of old age* =**disadvantage**, difficulty, drawback, handicap, downside, minus; burden,

trouble.
–OPPOSITES reward.

penance ▶ noun =**atonement**, expiation, amends; punishment, penalty.

penchant ▶ noun =**liking**, fondness, preference, taste, appetite, partiality, love, passion, weakness, inclination, bent, proclivity, predilection, predisposition.

pencil ▶ verb =**write (down)**, jot (down), scribble, note, take down.

pendant ▶ noun =**necklace**, locket, medallion.

pending ▶ adjective **1** *nine cases were still pending* =**unresolved**, undecided, unsettled, (up) in the air, ongoing, outstanding, not done, unfinished, incomplete; *informal* on the back burner. **2** *with a general election pending* =**imminent**, impending, about to happen/take place, forthcoming, on the way, coming, approaching, looming, near, close (at hand), in the offing.
▶ preposition *they were released on bail pending an appeal* =**awaiting**, until, till.

pendulous ▶ adjective =**drooping**, dangling, droopy, sagging, floppy; hanging.

penetrate ▶ verb **1** *the knife penetrated his lungs* =**pierce**, puncture, enter, perforate. **2** *they penetrated enemy lines* =**infiltrate**, slip/get into, enter. **3** *his words finally penetrated* =**register**, sink in, become clear, fall into place; *informal* click.

penetrating ▶ adjective **1** *a penetrating wind* =**piercing**, cutting, biting, stinging, keen, sharp, harsh, raw, freezing, chill, bitter, cold. **2** *a penetrating voice* =**shrill**, strident, piercing, ear-splitting. **3** *her penetrating gaze* =**piercing**, searching, intent, probing, sharp, keen. **4** *a penetrating analysis* =**perceptive**, insightful, keen, sharp, intelligent, clever, smart, incisive, trenchant, astute, shrewd, clear, acute.
–OPPOSITES mild, soft.

penetration ▶ noun =**perforation**, piercing, puncturing, entry.

peninsula ▶ noun =**cape**, promontory, point, head, headland, ness, horn, bluff, mull.

penitence ▶ noun =**repentance**, contrition, regret, remorse, sorrow, pangs of conscience, shame, sackcloth and ashes.

penitent ▶ adjective =**repentant**, contrite, remorseful, sorry, apologetic, regretful, conscience-stricken, shame-faced, abject, in sackcloth and ashes.
–OPPOSITES unrepentant.

pen name ▶ noun =**pseudonym**, nom de plume; assumed name, alias.

pennant ▶ noun =**flag**, standard, ensign, colour(s), banner.

penniless ▶ adjective =**destitute**, poverty-stricken, impoverished, poor, impecunious, needy; bankrupt, insolvent; *Brit.* on the breadline, without a penny (to one's name); *informal* (flat) broke, cleaned out, on one's uppers, without a brass farthing, bust; *Brit. informal* stony broke, skint; *N. Amer. informal* stone broke.
–OPPOSITES wealthy.

penny-pinching ▶ adjective =**mean**, miserly, niggardly, parsimonious, cheese-paring, grasping, Scrooge-like; *informal* stingy, mingy, tight, tight-fisted, money-grubbing.
–OPPOSITES generous.

pension ▶ noun =**old-age pension**, retirement pension, superannuation; allowance, benefit, support, welfare.

pensioner ▶ noun =**retired person**, old-age pensioner, OAP, senior citizen; *N. Amer.* senior, retiree.

pensive ▶ adjective =**thoughtful**, reflective, contemplative, meditative, introspective, ruminative, absorbed, preoccupied, deep/lost in thought, brooding.

pent-up ▶ adjective =**repressed**, suppressed, stifled, smothered, restrained, confined, bottled up.

people ▶ noun **1** *crowds of people* =**human beings**, persons, individuals, humans, mortals, (living) souls, personages, {men, women, and children}; *informal* folk. **2** *the British people* =**citizens**, subjects, electors, voters, taxpayers, residents, inhabitants, (general) public, citizenry, nation, population, populace. **3** *a man of the people* =**the common people**, the proletariat, the masses, the populace, the rank and file; *derogatory* the hoi polloi, the common herd, the great unwashed; *informal, derogatory* the proles, the plebs. **4** *her people don't live far away* =**family**, parents, relatives, relations, folk, kinsfolk, flesh and blood, nearest and dearest; *informal* folks. **5** *the peoples of Africa* =**race**, (ethnic) group, tribe, clan, nation.

▶ **verb** *those who once peopled Newfoundland* =**populate**, settle (in), colonize, inhabit, live in, occupy; *formal* reside in, dwell in.

WORD LINKS

relating to (ordinary) people: **demotic, plebeian, demo-**
relating to a people: **ethnic**
study of people: **anthropology**
study of different peoples: **ethnology**
fear of people: **anthropophobia**
killing of a people: **ethnocide**

pep (informal) ■ **pep something up** =**enliven**, animate, liven up, put some/new life into, invigorate, revitalize, ginger up, energize, galvanize, put some spark into, stimulate, get something going, perk up; brighten up, cheer up; *informal* buck up.

pepper ▶ **verb 1** *stars peppered the desert skies* =**sprinkle**, fleck, dot, spot, stipple. **2** *gunfire peppered the area* =**bombard**, pelt, shower, rain down on, strafe, rake, blitz.

peppery ▶ **adjective** =**spicy**, hot, fiery, piquant, pungent, sharp.
−OPPOSITES mild, bland.

perceive ▶ **verb 1** *he perceived a tear in her eye* =**see**, discern, detect, catch sight of, spot, observe, notice. **2** *he was perceived as too negative* =**regard**, look on, view, consider, think of, judge, deem.

perceptible ▶ **adjective** =**noticeable**, detectable, discernible, visible, observable, recognizable, appreciable; obvious, apparent, clear, distinct.

perception ▶ **noun 1** *popular perceptions about old age* =**impression**, idea, conception, notion, thought, belief. **2** *he talks with great perception* =**insight**, perceptiveness, understanding, intelligence, intuition, incisiveness, trenchancy, astuteness, shrewdness, acuteness, acuity, penetration, thoughtfulness.

perceptive ▶ **adjective** =**insightful**, discerning, sensitive, intuitive, observant; piercing, penetrating, clear-sighted, far-sighted, intelligent, clever, canny, keen, sharp, astute, shrewd, quick, smart, acute; *informal* on the ball; *N. Amer. informal* heads-up.
−OPPOSITES obtuse.

perch ▶ **verb 1** *a swallow perched on the telegraph wire* =**sit**, rest; alight, settle, land. **2** *she perched her glasses on her nose* =**put**, place, set, rest, balance.

percolate ▶ **verb 1** *chemicals percolated through the soil* =**filter**, drain, drip, ooze, seep, trickle, dribble, leak, leach. **2** *these views began to percolate through society* =**spread**, be disseminated, filter, pass; permeate.

peremptory ▶ **adjective** =**brusque**, imperious, high-handed, abrupt, summary.

perennial ▶ **adjective** =**abiding**, enduring, lasting, everlasting, perpetual, eternal, continuing, unending, unceasing, never-ending, endless, ceaseless, constant, continual.

perfect ▶ **adjective 1** *a perfect wife* =**ideal**, model, faultless, flawless, consummate, exemplary, best, ultimate, copybook. **2** *in perfect condition* =**flawless**, mint, as good as new, pristine, immaculate; superb, optimum, prime, peak, excellent; *informal* tip-top, A1. **3** *a perfect copy* =**exact**, precise, accurate, faithful, true; *Brit. informal* spot on; *N. Amer. informal* on the money. **4** *the perfect Christmas present* =**ideal**, just right, appropriate, fitting, fit, suitable, apt, tailor-made; very; *Brit. informal* spot on, just the job. **5** *she felt a perfect idiot* =**absolute**, complete, total, real, out-and-out, thorough, downright, utter, in every respect, unalloyed; *Brit. informal* right; *Austral./NZ informal* fair.
▶ **verb** *he's perfecting his style* =**improve**, polish (up), hone, refine, brush up, fine-tune.

perfection ▶ **noun 1** *the perfection of his technique* =**improvement**, refining, honing. **2** *for her, he was perfection* =**the ideal**, a paragon, the last word, the ultimate; *informal* the tops, the best/greatest thing since sliced bread, the bee's knees.

perfectionist ▶ **noun** =**purist**, stickler for perfection, idealist.

perfectly ▶ **adverb 1** *a perfectly cooked meal* =**superbly**, superlatively, excellently, flawlessly, faultlessly, to perfection, immaculately, exquisitely, consummately; *N. Amer.* to a fare-thee-well; *informal* like a dream, to a T. **2** *we understand each other perfectly* =**absolutely**, completely, altogether, entirely, wholly, totally, fully, in every respect. **3** *you know perfectly well what I mean* =**very**, quite, full; *informal* damn.

perforate ▶ **verb** =**pierce**, penetrate, enter, puncture, prick, bore through, riddle.

perform ▸ verb **1** *duties to perform* =**carry out**, do, execute, discharge, conduct, implement; *informal* pull off; *formal* effectuate. **2** *the car performs well* =**function**, work, operate, run, go, respond, behave, act. **3** *the play was performed in Britain* =**stage**, put on, present, mount, act, produce. **4** *the band performed live* =**play**, sing.
–OPPOSITES neglect.

performance ▸ noun **1** *the evening performance* =**show**, production, showing, presentation, staging; concert, recital; *informal* gig. **2** *their performance was excellent* =**rendition**, interpretation, playing, acting. **3** *the performance of his duty* =**carrying out**, execution, discharge, completion, fulfilment; *formal* effectuation. **4** *the performance of the processor* =**functioning**, working, operation, running, behaviour; response, economy. **5** *(informal) he made a great performance about it* =**fuss**, palaver, scene, issue; *NZ* bobsy-die; *informal* song and dance, to-do, hoo-ha, business, pantomime.

performer ▸ noun =**actor**, actress, artiste, artist, entertainer, trouper, player, musician, singer, dancer, comic, comedian, comedienne.

perfume ▸ noun **1** *a bottle of perfume* =**scent**, fragrance, eau de toilette, toilet water. **2** *the heady perfume of lilacs* =**smell**, scent, fragrance, aroma, bouquet.

perfumed ▸ adjective =**sweet-smelling**, scented, fragrant, fragranced, perfumy, aromatic.

perfunctory ▸ adjective =**cursory**, desultory, quick, brief, hasty, hurried, rapid, fleeting, token, casual, superficial, offhand.
–OPPOSITES careful, thorough.

perhaps ▸ adverb =**maybe**, for all one knows, it could be, it may be, it's possible, possibly, conceivably; *N. English* happen; *literary* perchance.

peril ▸ noun =**danger**, jeopardy, risk, hazard, menace, threat.

perilous ▸ adjective =**dangerous**, hazardous, risky, unsafe, treacherous.
–OPPOSITES safe.

perimeter ▸ noun **1** *the perimeter of a circle* =**circumference**, outside, outer edge. **2** *the perimeter of the camp* =**boundary**, border, limits, bounds, edge, margin, fringe(s), periphery.

period ▸ noun **1** *a six-week period* =**time**, spell, interval, stretch, term, span, phase, bout, chapter, stage; while; *Brit. informal* patch. **2** *the post-war period* =**era**, age, epoch, time, days, years; *Geology* aeon. **3** *a double Maths period* =**lesson**, class, session. **4** *women who suffer from painful periods* =**menstruation**, menstrual flow; *informal* monthlies, time of the month; *technical* menses. **5** *(N. Amer.) a comma instead of a period* =**full stop**, (full) point, stop.

periodic ▸ adjective =**regular**, periodical, at fixed intervals, recurrent, recurring, repeated, cyclical, seasonal; occasional, infrequent, intermittent, sporadic, spasmodic, odd.

periodical ▸ noun =**journal**, publication, magazine, newspaper, paper, review, digest, gazette, newsletter, organ, quarterly; *informal* mag, book, glossy.

peripatetic ▸ adjective =**nomadic**, itinerant, travelling, wandering, roving, roaming, migrant, migratory, unsettled.

peripheral ▸ adjective **1** *the city's peripheral housing estates* =**outlying**, outer. **2** *peripheral issues* =**secondary**, subsidiary, incidental, tangential, marginal, minor, unimportant, lesser, ancillary.
–OPPOSITES central.

periphery ▸ noun =**edge**, margin, fringe, boundary, border, perimeter, rim; outskirts, outer limits/reaches.
–OPPOSITES centre.

perish ▸ verb **1** *millions of soldiers perished* =**die**, lose one's life, be killed, fall, expire, meet one's death, be lost; *informal* buy it. **2** *the wood had perished* =**go bad**, spoil, rot, decay, decompose.

perk¹ ■ **perk up** =**cheer up**, brighten up, liven up, revive, bounce back, rally; *informal* buck up.
■ **perk someone/something up** =**cheer up**, liven up, brighten up, raise someone's spirits, give someone a boost/lift, revitalize, reinvigorate, put new life/heart into, rejuvenate, refresh; *informal* buck up, pep up.

perk² ▸ noun *a job with a lot of perks* =**fringe benefit**, advantage, bonus, extra, plus; *informal* freebie; *formal* perquisite.

perky ▸ adjective =**cheerful**, lively, vivacious, bubbly, effervescent, bouncy, spirited, cheery, merry, buoyant, exuberant, jaunty, frisky, sprightly, spry, bright, sunny, jolly, full of the joys of

p

spring; *informal* full of beans, bright-eyed and bushy-tailed, chirpy, chipper; *N. Amer. informal* peppy; *dated* gay.

permanence ▶ noun =**stability**, durability, fixity, changelessness, immutability, endurance, constancy, continuity, immortality, indestructibility.

permanent ▶ adjective **1** *permanent brain damage* =**lasting**, enduring, indefinite, continuing, constant, irreparable, irreversible, lifelong, indelible, standing. **2** *a permanent job* =**long-term**, stable, secure.
–OPPOSITES temporary.

permanently ▶ adverb **1** *the attack left her permanently disabled* =**for all time**, forever, for good, for always, for ever and ever, (for) evermore, indelibly; *informal* for keeps. **2** *I was permanently hungry* =**continually**, constantly, perpetually, always.

permeable ▶ adjective =**porous**, absorbent.

permeate ▶ verb **1** *the smell permeated the entire flat* =**pervade**, spread through, fill; filter through, penetrate, pass through, percolate through, suffuse, steep, impregnate. **2** *these resins permeate the timber* =**soak through**, penetrate, seep through, saturate, percolate through, leach through.

permissible ▶ adjective =**permitted**, allowable, allowed, acceptable, legal, lawful, legitimate, admissible, licit, authorized; *informal* legit, OK.
–OPPOSITES forbidden.

permission ▶ noun =**authorization**, consent, leave, authority, sanction, licence, dispensation, assent, acquiescence, agreement, approval, seal of approval, approbation, endorsement, blessing, clearance; *informal* the go-ahead, the thumbs up, the OK, the green light, say-so.

permissive ▶ adjective =**liberal**, broad-minded, open-minded, free (and easy), easy-going, live-and-let-live, libertarian, tolerant, indulgent, lenient; overindulgent, lax, soft.
–OPPOSITES intolerant, strict.

permit ▶ verb =**allow**, let, authorize, sanction, grant, license, empower, enable, entitle; consent to, assent to, give one's blessing to, agree to, tolerate; legalize, legitimatize; *informal* give the go-ahead to, give the thumbs up to, OK,

give the OK to, give the green light to; *formal* accede to; *archaic* suffer.
–OPPOSITES ban, forbid.

▶ noun =**authorization**, licence, pass, ticket, warrant, documentation, certification; passport, visa.

permutation ▶ noun =**variation**, alteration, modification, change, shift, transformation, mutation; *humorous* transmogrification.

pernicious ▶ adjective =**harmful**, damaging, destructive, injurious, hurtful, detrimental, deleterious, dangerous, adverse, unhealthy, unfavourable, bad, malign, malignant, noxious, corrupting.
–OPPOSITES beneficial.

pernickety ▶ adjective *(informal)* =**fussy**, difficult to please, finicky, fastidious, particular, punctilious, hairsplitting; *informal* nit-picking, picky; *N. Amer. informal* persnickety.
–OPPOSITES easy-going.

perpendicular ▶ adjective **1** *the perpendicular stones* =**upright**, vertical, erect, straight (up and down), standing, upended. **2** *lines perpendicular to each other* =**at right angles**, at 90 degrees.
–OPPOSITES horizontal.

perpetrate ▶ verb =**commit**, carry out, perform, execute, do, effect; inflict, wreak; *informal* pull off.

perpetual ▶ adjective **1** *in perpetual darkness* =**everlasting**, eternal, permanent, unending, without end, lasting, abiding, unchanging. **2** *a perpetual state of fear* =**constant**, permanent, uninterrupted, continuous, unremitting, unending, unceasing, persistent, abiding. **3** *her mother's perpetual nagging* =**interminable**, incessant, ceaseless, endless, relentless, unrelenting, persistent, continual, continuous, non-stop, never-ending, repeated, unremitting, round-the-clock, unabating; *informal* eternal.
–OPPOSITES temporary, intermittent.

perpetuate ▶ verb =**keep alive**, keep going, preserve, conserve, sustain, maintain, continue, extend.

perplex ▶ verb =**puzzle**, baffle, mystify, bemuse, bewilder, confound, confuse, nonplus, disconcert.

perplexing ▶ adjective =**puzzling**, baffling, mystifying, mysterious, bewildering, confusing, disconcerting, worrying.

perplexity ▶ noun =**confusion**, bewil-

P

derment, puzzlement, bafflement, incomprehension, mystification, bemusement.

per se ▶ adverb = **in itself**, of itself, by itself, as such, intrinsically; by its very nature, in essence, by definition, essentially.

persecute ▶ verb **1** *they were persecuted for their beliefs* = **oppress**, abuse, victimize, ill-treat, mistreat, maltreat, torment, torture. **2** *she was persecuted by the press* = **harass**, hound, plague, badger, harry, intimidate, pick on, pester, bother, bedevil; *informal* hassle, give someone a hard time, get on someone's back; *Austral. informal* heavy.

persecution ▶ noun **1** *religious persecution* = **oppression**, victimization, ill-treatment, mistreatment, abuse, discrimination. **2** *the persecution I endured at school* = **harassment**, hounding, intimidation, bullying.

perseverance ▶ noun = **persistence**, tenacity, determination, staying power; patience, endurance, application, dedication, commitment, doggedness, stamina; *informal* stickability; *N. Amer. informal* stick-to-it-iveness.

persevere ▶ verb = **persist**, continue, carry on, go on, keep on, keep going, struggle on, hammer away, be persistent, keep at it, not take no for an answer, be tenacious, plod on, plough on; *informal* soldier on, hang on, plug away, stick to one's guns, stick it out, hang in there.
–OPPOSITES give up.

persist ▶ verb **1** *Corbett persisted with his questioning.* See PERSEVERE. **2** *if dry weather persists, water the lawn thoroughly* = **continue**, hold, carry on, last, keep on, remain, linger, stay, endure.

persistence ▶ noun. See PERSEVERANCE.

persistent ▶ adjective **1** *a very persistent man* = **tenacious**, determined, resolute, dogged, tireless, indefatigable, patient, untiring, insistent, unrelenting. **2** *persistent rain* = **constant**, continuous, continuing, continual, non-stop, never-ending, steady, uninterrupted, unbroken, interminable, incessant, endless, unending, unrelenting. **3** *a persistent cough* = **chronic**, nagging, frequent; repeated, habitual.
–OPPOSITES irresolute, intermittent.

person ▶ noun = **human being**, individual, man/woman, human, being, (living) soul, mortal, creature; personage, character, customer; *informal* type, sort, beggar, cookie; *Brit. informal* bod; *informal, dated* body.
■ **in person** = **physically**, in the flesh, personally; oneself.

> [!NOTE] **WORD LINKS**
> *killing of a person:* **homicide**

persona ▶ noun = **image**, face, public face, character, identity; front, facade, exterior.

personable ▶ adjective = **pleasant**, agreeable, likeable, nice, amiable, affable, congenial, pleasing; attractive, presentable, good-looking, nice-looking, pretty, appealing; *Scottish* couthy; *Scottish & N. English* bonny.
–OPPOSITES disagreeable, unattractive.

personage ▶ noun = **important person**, VIP, luminary, celebrity, personality, famous name, household name, public figure, star, dignitary, notable, worthy; *informal* celeb, somebody, big shot.

personal ▶ adjective **1** *a highly personal style* = **distinctive**, characteristic, unique, individual, idiosyncratic. **2** *a personal appearance* = **in person**, in the flesh, actual, live, physical. **3** *his personal life* = **private**, intimate. **4** *a personal friend* = **intimate**, close, dear, bosom. **5** *personal knowledge* = **direct**, empirical, first-hand, immediate. **6** *personal remarks* = **derogatory**, disparaging, belittling, insulting, rude, disrespectful, offensive, pejorative.
–OPPOSITES public, general.

personality ▶ noun **1** *her cheerful personality* = **character**, nature, disposition, temperament, make-up, psyche. **2** *she had loads of personality* = **charisma**, magnetism, character, charm, presence. **3** *a famous personality* = **celebrity**, VIP, star, superstar, big/famous name, somebody, leading light, luminary, notable, personage; *informal* celeb.

personalize ▶ verb = **customize**, individualize.

personally ▶ adverb **1** *I'd like to thank him personally* = **in person**, oneself. **2** *personally, I like it* = **for my part**, for myself, to my way of thinking, to my mind, in my estimation, as far as I am concerned, in my view/opinion, from my point of view, from where I stand, as I see it, if you ask me, for my money, in my book.

personification ▸ noun =embodiment, incarnation, epitome, quintessence, essence, type, symbol, soul, model, exemplification, exemplar, image, representation.

personify ▸ verb =epitomize, embody, be the incarnation of, typify, exemplify, represent, symbolize.

personnel ▸ noun =staff, employees, workforce, workers, labour force, manpower, human resources.

perspective ▸ noun =outlook, view, viewpoint, point of view, standpoint, position, stand, stance, angle, slant, attitude, frame of mind, frame of reference.

perspiration ▸ noun =sweat, moisture; *Medicine* diaphoresis, hidrosis.

perspire ▸ verb =sweat, be dripping/pouring with sweat, glow.

persuadable ▸ adjective =malleable, tractable, pliable, compliant, amenable, adaptable, accommodating, cooperative, flexible, acquiescent, biddable, complaisant, like putty in one's hands, suggestible.

persuade ▸ verb **1** *he persuaded her to go with him* =prevail on, talk into, coax, convince, get, induce, win over, bring round, influence, sway; *informal* sweet-talk. **2** *lack of money persuaded them to abandon the scheme* =cause, lead, move, dispose, incline.
–OPPOSITES dissuade, deter.

persuasion ▸ noun **1** *Monica needed a lot of persuasion* =coaxing, persuading, inducement, convincing, encouragement, urging, enticement; *informal* sweet-talking. **2** *various religious persuasions* =group, grouping, sect, denomination, party, camp, side, faction, affiliation, school of thought, belief, creed, faith.

persuasive ▸ adjective =convincing, cogent, compelling, forceful, powerful, eloquent, impressive, sound, valid, strong, effective, telling; plausible, credible.
–OPPOSITES unconvincing.

pert ▸ adjective =jaunty, neat, trim, stylish, smart, perky, rakish; *informal* natty; *N. Amer. informal* saucy.

pertain ▸ verb **1** *developments pertaining to the economy* =concern, relate to, be connected with, be relevant to, apply to, refer to, have a bearing on, affect, involve, touch on; *archaic* regard. **2** *the economic situation that pertained in Britain* =exist, be the order of the day, be the case, prevail; *formal* obtain.

pertinent ▸ adjective =relevant, to the point, apposite, appropriate, suitable, fitting, fit, apt, applicable, material, germane.
–OPPOSITES irrelevant.

perturb ▸ verb =worry, upset, unsettle, disturb, concern, trouble, disquiet; disconcert, discomfit, unnerve, alarm, bother; *informal* rattle.
–OPPOSITES reassure.

perturbed ▸ adjective =upset, worried, unsettled, disturbed, concerned, troubled, anxious, ill at ease, uneasy, disquieted, fretful; disconcerted, discomposed, agitated, flustered, ruffled; *informal* twitchy, rattled, fazed; *N. Amer. informal* discombobulated.
–OPPOSITES calm.

peruse ▸ verb =read, study, scrutinize, inspect, examine, wade through, look through; browse through, leaf through, scan, run one's eye over, glance through, flick through, skim through, thumb through.

pervade ▸ verb =permeate, spread through, fill, suffuse, imbue, penetrate, filter through, infuse, inform.

pervasive ▸ adjective =prevalent, pervading, extensive, ubiquitous, omnipresent, universal, widespread, general.

perverse ▸ adjective **1** *he is being deliberately perverse* =awkward, contrary, difficult, unreasonable, uncooperative, unhelpful, obstructive, stubborn, obstinate, obdurate; *informal* cussed; *Brit. informal* bloody-minded; *formal* refractory. **2** *a verdict that is manifestly perverse* =illogical, irrational, wrong-headed. **3** *perverse forms of pleasure* =perverted, depraved, unnatural, abnormal, deviant, warped, twisted; *informal* kinky, sick, pervy.
–OPPOSITES accommodating, reasonable.

perversion ▸ noun **1** *a perversion of the truth* =distortion, misrepresentation, travesty, twisting, corruption, misuse. **2** *sexual perversion* =deviance, abnormality; depravity.

perversity ▸ noun **1** *out of sheer perversity* =contrariness, awkwardness, recalcitrance, stubbornness, obstinacy, obduracy; *informal* cussedness; *Brit. informal* bloody-mindedness. **2** *the perversity of the decision* =unreasonableness, irrationality, illogicality, wrong-headedness.

pervert ▶ verb =**corrupt**, lead astray, debase, warp, pollute, poison, deprave, debauch.
▶ noun =**deviant**, degenerate; *informal* perv, dirty old man, sicko.

perverted ▶ adjective =**unnatural**, deviant, warped, twisted, abnormal, unhealthy, depraved, perverse, aberrant, debased, degenerate, wrong, bad; *informal* sick, kinky, pervy.

pessimism ▶ noun =**defeatism**, negativity, doom and gloom, gloominess, cynicism, fatalism; hopelessness, depression, despair, despondency.
−OPPOSITES optimism.

pessimist ▶ noun =**defeatist**, fatalist, prophet of doom, cynic; sceptic, doubter; misery, killjoy; *informal* doom (and gloom) merchant, wet blanket; *N. Amer. informal* gloomy Gus.
−OPPOSITES optimist.

pessimistic ▶ adjective =**gloomy**, negative, defeatist, downbeat, cynical, bleak, fatalistic, dark, black, despairing, despondent, depressed, hopeless.
−OPPOSITES optimistic.

pest ▶ noun =**nuisance**, annoyance, irritant, thorn in one's flesh/side, trial, the bane of one's life, menace, trouble, problem, worry, bother; *informal* pain (in the neck), headache; *Scottish informal* skelf; *N. Amer. informal* nudnik; *Austral./NZ informal* nark.

pester ▶ verb =**badger**, hound, harass, plague, annoy, bother, trouble, persecute, torment, bedevil, harry, worry; *informal* hassle, bug, get on someone's back; *N. English informal* mither; *N. Amer. informal* devil.

pet ▶ adjective 1 *a pet lamb* =**tame**, domesticated, domestic; *Brit.* housetrained; *N. Amer.* housebroken. 2 *his pet theory* =**favourite**, favoured, cherished; particular, special, personal.
▶ verb 1 *the cats came to be petted* =**stroke**, caress, fondle, pat. 2 *couples petting in their cars* =**kiss and cuddle**, kiss, cuddle, embrace, caress; *informal* canoodle, neck, smooch; *Brit. informal* snog; *N. Amer. informal* make out, get it on; *informal, dated* spoon.

peter ■ **peter out** =**fizzle out**, fade (away), die away/out, dwindle, diminish, taper off, tail off, trail away/off, wane, ebb, melt away, evaporate, disappear.

petite ▶ adjective =**small**, dainty,

diminutive, slight, little, elfin, delicate, small-boned; *Scottish* wee.

petition ▶ noun =**appeal**, round robin.
▶ verb =**appeal to**, request, ask, call on, entreat, beg, implore, plead with, apply to, press, urge; *literary* beseech.

petrified ▶ adjective 1 *she looked petrified* =**terrified**, horrified, scared/frightened out of one's wits, scared/frightened to death. 2 *petrified remains of prehistoric animals* =**ossified**, fossilized, calcified.

petrify ▶ verb =**terrify**, horrify, scare/frighten to death, scare/frighten the living daylights out of; paralyse, transfix; *informal* scare the pants off; *Irish informal* scare the bejesus out of.

petrol ▶ noun =**fuel**; *N. Amer.* gasoline, gas; *informal* juice.

petticoat ▶ noun =**slip**, underskirt, half-slip, underslip.

petty ▶ adjective 1 *petty regulations* =**trivial**, trifling, minor, insignificant, inconsequential, paltry, footling, pettifogging; *informal* piffling, piddling. 2 *a petty form of revenge* =**small-minded**, mean, shabby, spiteful.
−OPPOSITES important, magnanimous.

petulant ▶ adjective =**peevish**, badtempered, querulous, pettish, fretful, irritable, sulky, crotchety, touchy, tetchy, testy, fractious; *informal* grouchy; *Brit. informal* ratty; *N. English informal* mardy; *N. Amer. informal* cranky.
−OPPOSITES good-humoured.

phantasmagorical ▶ adjective =**dreamlike**, psychedelic, kaleidoscopic, surreal, unreal, hallucinatory, fantastic.

phantom ▶ noun =**ghost**, apparition, spirit, spectre, wraith; *informal* spook; *literary* phantasm, shade.

phase ▶ noun 1 *the final phase of the campaign* =**stage**, period, chapter, episode, part, step. 2 *he's going through a difficult phase* =**period**, stage, time, spell; *Brit. informal* patch.
■ **phase something in** =**introduce** (gradually), ease in.
■ **phase something out** =**withdraw** (gradually), discontinue, stop using, run down, wind down.

phenomenal ▶ adjective =**remarkable**, exceptional, extraordinary, amazing, astonishing, astounding, stunning, incredible, unbelievable; marvellous, magnificent, wonderful, outstanding,

unprecedented; *informal* fantastic, terrific, tremendous, stupendous, awesome, out of this world; *literary* wondrous.
−OPPOSITES ordinary.

phenomenon ▶ noun **1** *a rare phenomenon* =**occurrence**, event, happening, fact, situation, circumstance, experience, case, incident, episode. **2** *a pop phenomenon* =**marvel**, sensation, wonder, prodigy.

philander ▶ verb =**womanize**, have affairs, flirt; *informal* play around, carry on, play the field, play away, sleep around; *N. Amer. informal* fool around.

philanderer ▶ noun =**womanizer**, Casanova, Don Juan, Lothario, flirt, ladies' man, playboy; *informal* stud, ladykiller.

philanthropic ▶ adjective =**charitable**, generous, benevolent, humanitarian, public-spirited, altruistic, magnanimous; unselfish, kind.
−OPPOSITES selfish, mean.

philanthropist ▶ noun =**benefactor**, good Samaritan; do-gooder.

philanthropy ▶ noun =**benevolence**, generosity, humanitarianism, public-spiritedness, altruism, social conscience, charity, fellow feeling, magnanimity, unselfishness, humanity, kindness, kind-heartedness, compassion.

philistine ▶ adjective =**uncultured**, lowbrow, uncultivated, uncivilized, uneducated, unenlightened, commercial, materialist, bourgeois; ignorant, crass, boorish, barbarian.
▶ noun =**barbarian**, boor, yahoo, materialist.

philosopher ▶ noun =**thinker**, theorist, theoretician; scholar, intellectual, sage.

philosophical ▶ adjective **1** *a philosophical question* =**theoretical**, metaphysical. **2** *a philosophical mood* =**thoughtful**, reflective, pensive, meditative, contemplative, introspective. **3** *he was very philosophical about it* =**stoical**, self-possessed, serene, dispassionate, phlegmatic, forbearing, long-suffering, resigned.

philosophize ▶ verb =**theorize**, speculate; pontificate, preach, sermonize, moralize.

philosophy ▶ noun **1** *the philosophy of Aristotle* =**thinking**, thought, reasoning. **2** *her political philosophy* =**beliefs**, credo, ideology, ideas, thinking, notions, theories, doctrine, tenets, principles, views.

phlegm ▶ noun **1** =**mucus**, catarrh. **2** *British phlegm* =**calmness**, coolness, composure, equanimity, placidity, impassivity, imperturbability, impassiveness; *informal* cool, unflappability.

phlegmatic ▶ adjective =**calm**, cool, composed, controlled, serene, tranquil, placid, impassive, imperturbable, unruffled, philosophical; *informal* unflappable.
−OPPOSITES excitable.

phobia ▶ noun =**fear**, dread, horror, terror, aversion, antipathy, revulsion; complex, neurosis; *informal* thing, hang-up.

phone ▶ noun **1** *she spent hours on the phone* =**telephone**; *Brit. informal* blower; *Brit.* rhyming slang dog and bone. **2** *give me a phone sometime* =**call**, telephone call; *Brit.* ring; *informal* buzz; *Brit. informal* tinkle, bell.
▶ verb *I'll phone you later* =**telephone**, call; *Brit.* ring, ring up, give someone a ring; *informal* call up, give someone a buzz; *Brit. informal* give someone a bell/tinkle, get on the blower to; *N. Amer. informal* get someone on the horn.

phoney (*informal*) ▶ adjective *a phoney address* =**bogus**, false, fake, fraudulent, spurious; counterfeit, forged, imitation; pretended, contrived, affected, insincere; *informal* pretend, put-on; *Brit. informal* cod.
−OPPOSITES authentic.
▶ noun **1** *he's nothing but a phoney* =**impostor**, sham, fake, fraud, charlatan; *informal* con artist. **2** *the diamond's a phoney* =**fake**, imitation, counterfeit, forgery.

photocopy ▶ noun *a photocopy of the letter* =**copy**, duplicate, reproduction, facsimile; *trademark* Xerox, photostat.
▶ verb *I photocopied the form* =**copy**, duplicate, xerox, photostat, reproduce.

photograph ▶ noun =**picture**, photo, snap, snapshot, shot, likeness, print, still.
▶ verb =**take someone's picture/photo**, snap, shoot, film.

photographer ▶ noun =**lensman**, paparazzo; cameraman; *N. Amer. informal* shutterbug.

photographic ▶ adjective **1** *a photographic record* =**pictorial**, in photographs. **2** *a photographic memory* =**detailed**, exact, precise, accurate, vivid; *Psychology* eidetic.

phrase ▸ noun =**expression**, construction, term, turn of phrase; idiom; saying.
▸ verb =**express**, put into words, put, word, formulate, couch, frame, articulate, verbalize.

phraseology ▸ noun =**wording**, choice of words, phrasing, way of speaking/writing, usage, idiom, diction, parlance, words, language, vocabulary, terminology; jargon; *informal* lingo, -speak, -ese.

physical ▸ adjective **1** *physical pleasure* =**bodily**, corporeal, corporal; carnal, fleshly, non-spiritual. **2** *physical work* =**manual**, labouring, blue-collar. **3** *the physical universe* =**material**, concrete, tangible, palpable, solid, substantial, real, actual, visible.
−OPPOSITES mental, spiritual.

physician ▸ noun =**doctor**, medical practitioner, general practitioner, GP, clinician; specialist, consultant; *informal* doc, medic.

physiognomy ▸ noun =**face**, features, countenance, expression, look, mien; *informal* mug; *Brit. informal* phizog, phiz; *Brit. rhyming slang* boat race; *N. Amer. informal* puss; *literary* visage.

physique ▸ noun =**body**, build, figure, frame, anatomy, shape, form, proportions; muscles, musculature; *informal* vital statistics, bod.

pick ▸ verb **1** *picking apples* =**harvest**, gather (in), collect, pluck. **2** *pick a time that suits you* =**choose**, select, single out, take, opt for, plump for, elect, decide on, settle on, fix on, sift out, sort out; name, nominate. **3** *Beth picked at her food* =**nibble**, toy with, play with. **4** *people were singing and picking guitars* =**pluck**, twang. **5** *he tried to pick a fight* =**provoke**, start, cause, incite, instigate, prompt, bring about.
▸ noun *the pick of the crop* =**best**, finest, choice, choicest, prime, cream, flower, pearl, gem, jewel, crème de la crème, elite.
■ **pick on** =**bully**, victimize, torment, persecute, criticize, taunt, tease; *informal* get at, needle.
■ **pick something out 1** *one painting was picked out for special mention* =**choose**, select, single out, elect, settle on; name,

nominate. **2** *she picked out Jessica in the crowd* =**see**, make out, distinguish, discern, spot, perceive, detect, notice, recognize, identify, catch sight of, glimpse; *literary* espy.

■ **pick up** =**improve**, recover, rally, make a comeback, bounce back, perk up, look up, take a turn for the better, turn the/a corner, be on the mend, make headway, make progress.

■ **pick someone/something up** =**lift**, take up, raise, hoist, scoop up, gather up, snatch up.

■ **pick someone up 1** *I'll pick you up after lunch* =**fetch**, collect, call for. **2** *(informal) he was picked up by the police* =**arrest**, apprehend, detain, take into custody, seize; *informal* nab, run in, bust; *Brit. informal* nick. **3** *(informal) he picked her up in a club* =**meet**; *informal* get off with, pull, cop off with.

■ **pick something up 1** *we picked it up at a flea market* =**find**, discover, come across, stumble across, happen on, chance on; acquire, obtain, come by, get; purchase, buy; *informal* get hold of, get/lay one's hands on, bag, land. **2** *he picked up the story in the 1950s* =**resume**, take up, start again, recommence, continue, carry/go on with. **3** *she picked up a virus* =**catch**, contract, get, go/come down with. **4** *all the gossip he'd picked up* =**hear**, hear tell, get wind of, be told, learn; glean, garner. **5** *we're picking up a distress signal* =**receive**, detect, get, hear.

picket ▸ noun **1** *forty pickets were arrested* =**striker**, demonstrator, protester. **2** *fences made of cedar pickets* =**stake**, post, paling; upright.
▸ verb *workers picketed the factory* =**demonstrate at**; blockade.

pickle ▸ noun **1** *a jar of pickle* =**relish**, chutney. **2** *(informal) they got into an awful pickle* =**plight**, predicament, mess, difficulty, trouble, dire/desperate straits, problem; *informal* tight corner, tight spot, jam, fix, scrape, bind, hole, hot water.
▸ verb *fish pickled in brine* =**preserve**, souse, marinate.

pickup ▸ noun =**improvement**, recovery, revival, upturn, upswing, rally, comeback, resurgence, renewal, turnaround.
−OPPOSITES slump.

pictorial ▸ adjective =**illustrated**, in pictures, photographic, graphic.

picture ▸ noun **1** *pictures in an art gallery* =**painting**, drawing, sketch, watercolour, print, canvas, portrait, portrayal, illustration, artwork, depiction, likeness, representation, image; fresco, mural. **2** *we were told not to take pictures* =**photograph**, photo, snap, snapshot, shot, exposure, still, enlargement. **3** *my picture of the ideal woman* =**concept**, idea, impression, (mental) image, vision, visualization, notion. **4** *the picture of health* =**personification**, embodiment, epitome, essence, quintessence, soul, model. **5** *a picture starring Robert De Niro* =**film**, movie, feature (film), motion picture; video; *informal* flick. **6** *we went to the pictures* =**the cinema**, the movies, the silver screen, the big screen; *informal* the flicks.

▶ **verb 1** *they were pictured playing in the snow* =**paint**, draw, sketch, photograph, depict, portray, show. **2** *Anne still pictured Richard as he had been* =**visualize**, see (in one's mind's eye), imagine, remember.

picturesque ▶ adjective =**attractive**, pretty, beautiful, lovely, scenic, charming, quaint, pleasing, delightful.
–OPPOSITES ugly.

piddling ▶ adjective *(informal)* =**trivial**, trifling, petty, tiny, insignificant, unimportant, inconsequential; meagre, inadequate, insufficient, paltry, derisory, pitiful, miserable, puny, niggardly, mere; *informal* measly, pathetic, piffling, mingy, poxy; *N. Amer. informal* nickel-and-dime.

piece ▶ noun **1** *a piece of cheese | a piece of wood* =**bit**, slice, chunk, segment, section, lump, hunk, wedge, slab, block, cake, bar, cube, stick, length; fragment, sliver, splinter, wafer, chip, crumb, scrap, remnant, shred, shard, snippet; mouthful, morsel; *Brit. informal* wodge. **2** *the pieces of a clock* =**component**, part, bit, section, constituent, element; unit, module. **3** *a piece of furniture* =**item**, article, specimen. **4** *a piece of the profit* =**share**, portion, slice, quota, part, bit, percentage, amount, quantity, ration, fraction; *informal* cut, rake-off; *Brit. informal* whack. **5** *pieces from his collection* =**work** (of art), artwork, artefact; composition, opus. **6** *the reporter who wrote the piece* =**article**, item, story, report, essay, feature, review, column. **7** *the pieces on a chess board* =**token**, counter, man, disc, chip, tile.
■ **in one piece 1** *the camera was still in one piece* =**unbroken**, entire, whole, intact, undamaged, unharmed. **2** *I'll bring her back in one piece* =**unhurt**, unscathed, safe (and sound).
■ **in pieces** =**broken**, in bits, shattered, smashed; *informal* bust.
■ **go/fall to pieces** =**have a breakdown**, break down, go out of one's mind, lose control, lose one's head, fall apart; *informal* crack up, lose it, come/fall apart at the seams, freak (out).

pièce de résistance ▶ noun =**masterpiece**, magnum opus, chef-d'œuvre, masterwork, tour de force, showpiece, prize, jewel in the crown.

piecemeal ▶ adverb =**a little at a time**, bit by bit, gradually, slowly, in stages/steps, step by step, little by little, by degrees, in fits and starts.

pier ▶ noun =**jetty**, quay, wharf, dock, landing stage.

pierce ▶ verb =**penetrate**, puncture, perforate, prick.

piercing ▶ adjective **1** *a piercing shriek* =**shrill**, ear-splitting, high-pitched, penetrating, strident. **2** *a piercing pain* =**intense**, excruciating, agonizing, sharp, stabbing, shooting, severe, fierce, searing. **3** *his piercing gaze* =**searching**, probing, penetrating, sharp, keen.

piety ▶ noun =**devoutness**, devotion, piousness, holiness, godliness; reverence, faith, spirituality.

piffle ▶ noun *(informal)*. See NONSENSE sense 1.

piffling ▶ adjective *(informal)* =**inadequate**, tiny, minimal, trifling, paltry, pitiful, negligible; miserly, miserable; *informal* measly, stingy, lousy, pathetic, piddling, mingy, poxy.

pig ▶ noun **1** *a herd of pigs* =**hog**, boar, sow, porker, swine; piglet; *children's word* piggy. **2** *(informal) he's such a pig* =**glutton**; *informal* hog, greedy guts; *Brit. informal* gannet.

> **WORD LINKS**
>
> male: **boar**
> female: **sow**
> young: **piglet**
> relating to pigs: **porcine**
> home: **sty**

pigeon ▶ noun

> **WORD LINKS**
>
> young: **squab**

pigeonhole ▶ noun *convenient pigeonholes* =**category**, class, group, designation.

▶ verb **1** *they were pigeonholed as an indie guitar band* = **categorize**, compartmentalize, classify, characterize, label, brand, tag, designate. **2** *the plan was pigeonholed last year* = **postpone**, put off, put back, defer, shelve, hold over, put to one side, put on ice, mothball, put in cold storage; *N. Amer.* table; *informal* put on the back burner.

pig-headed ▶ adjective = **obstinate**, stubborn (as a mule), obdurate, headstrong, self-willed, wilful, perverse, contrary, recalcitrant, stiff-necked, intransigent, unyielding; *Brit. informal* bloody-minded; *formal* refractory.

pigment ▶ noun = **colouring**, colour, tint, dye.

pile¹ ▶ noun **1** *a pile of stones* = **heap**, stack, mound, pyramid, mass; collection, accumulation, assemblage, stockpile, hoard. **2** *(informal) I've a pile of work to do* = **lot**, reams, mountain; abundance, cornucopia, plethora; *informal* load, heap, mass, slew, ocean, stack, ton; *Brit. informal* shedload; *Austral./NZ informal* swag.

▶ verb **1** *he piled up the plates* = **heap (up)**, stack (up), put on top of each other. **2** *he piled his plate with salad* = **load**, heap, fill (up), stack, charge. **3** *we piled into the car* = **crowd**, climb, pack, squeeze.

■ **pile up** = **accumulate**, grow, mount up, escalate, soar, spiral, rocket, increase, accrue, build up, multiply.

pile² ▶ noun *a carpet with a short pile* = **nap**, fibres, threads.

pile-up ▶ noun = **crash**, collision, smash, (road) accident; *Brit.* RTA (road traffic accident); *N. Amer.* wreck; *Brit. informal* shunt.

pilfer ▶ verb = **steal**, thieve, take, snatch, purloin, loot; *informal* swipe, rob, nab, rip off, lift, 'liberate', 'borrow', filch, snaffle; *Brit. informal* pinch, half-inch, nick, whip, knock off, nobble; *N. Amer. informal* heist.

pilgrimage ▶ noun = **journey**, expedition, visit, trek; odyssey.

pill ▶ noun = **tablet**, capsule, pellet, lozenge, pastille.

pillage ▶ verb **1** *the abbey was pillaged* = **ransack**, rob, plunder, raid, loot; sack, devastate, lay waste, ravage. **2** *coins pillaged from an ancient tomb* = **steal**, pilfer, take, purloin, loot; *informal* swipe, rob, nab, rip off, lift, 'liberate', 'borrow', filch, snaffle; *Brit. informal* pinch, half-

inch, nick, whip, knock off; *N. Amer. informal* heist.

pillar ▶ noun **1** *stone pillars* = **column**, post, support, upright, pier, pile, pilaster, stanchion, prop; obelisk, monolith. **2** *a pillar of the community* = **stalwart**, mainstay, bastion, rock; leading light, worthy, backbone, support, upholder, champion.

pillory ▶ verb = **attack**, criticize, censure, condemn, lambaste, savage, denounce; *informal* knock, slam, pan, bash, crucify, hammer; *Brit. informal* slate, rubbish, slag off; *N. Amer. informal* pummel; *Austral./NZ informal* bag, monster; *formal* excoriate.

pillow ▶ noun = **cushion**, bolster, pad; headrest.

pilot ▶ noun **1** *a fighter pilot* = **airman**, **airwoman**, flyer; captain; *informal* skipper; *N. Amer. informal* jock; *dated* aviator, aeronaut. **2** *a harbour pilot* = **navigator**, helmsman, steersman, coxswain. **3** *a pilot for a TV series* = **trial**; sample, experiment.

▶ adjective *a pilot project* = **experimental**, exploratory, trial, test, sample, speculative; preliminary.

▶ verb *he piloted the jet to safety* = **navigate**, guide, manoeuvre, steer, control, direct, captain; fly, aviate; drive; sail; *informal* skipper.

pimp ▶ noun = **procurer**, procuress; brothel-keeper, madam; *Brit. informal* ponce; *archaic* bawd.

pimple ▶ noun = **spot**, pustule, boil, swelling, eruption, blackhead, carbuncle; **(pimples)** acne; *informal* whitehead, zit; *Scottish informal* plook.

pin ▶ noun **1** *fasten the hem with a pin* = **tack**, safety pin, nail, staple, fastener. **2** *a broken pin in the machine* = **bolt**, peg, rivet, dowel. **3** *they wore name pins* = **badge**, brooch.

▶ verb **1** *she pinned the brooch to her dress* = **attach**, fasten, affix, fix, clip; join, secure. **2** *they pinned him to the ground* = **hold (down)**, press, hold fast; pinion.

■ **pin someone/something down** = **confine**, trap, hem in, corner, close in, shut in, hedge in, pen in, entangle, enmesh, immobilize.

■ **pin something on someone** = **blame for**, hold responsible for, attribute to, impute to, ascribe to; lay something at someone's door; *informal* stick on.

pinch ▶ verb **1** *he pinched my arm* = **nip**,

tweak, squeeze, grasp. **2** *my new shoes pinch my toes* =**hurt**, pain; squeeze, crush, cramp. **3** *(Brit. informal) you pinched his biscuits* =**steal**, take, snatch, pilfer, purloin; *informal* swipe, rob, nab, lift, 'liberate', 'borrow', filch; *Brit. informal* nick, half-inch, whip, knock off; *N. Amer. informal* heist.

▸ **noun 1** *he gave her arm a pinch* =**nip**, tweak, squeeze. **2** *a pinch of salt* =**bit**, touch, dash, spot, trace, soupçon, speck, taste; *informal* smidgen, tad.

■ **at a pinch** =**if necessary**, if need be, in an emergency; *N. Amer.* in a pinch; *Brit. informal* at a push.

■ **feel the pinch** =**suffer (hardship)**, be short of money, be poor.

pinched ▸ adjective =**strained**; tired, worn; thin, drawn, haggard, gaunt.
–OPPOSITES healthy.

pine ▸ verb =**yearn**, long, ache, sigh, hunger, languish; miss, mourn.

pinion ▸ verb =**hold down**, pin down, restrain, hold fast, immobilize; tie, bind, truss (up), shackle, fetter, hobble, manacle, handcuff; *informal* nail.

pink ▸ adjective =**rose**, rosy, rosé, pale red, salmon, coral; flushed, blushing.

■ **in the pink** *(informal)* =**in good health**, healthy, well, hale and hearty; blooming, flourishing, thriving, vigorous, strong, lusty, robust, in fine fettle, in excellent shape.

pinnacle ▸ noun **1** *pinnacles of rock* =**peak**, needle, crag, tor; summit, crest, apex, tip. **2** *the pinnacle of the sport* =**highest level**, peak, height, high point, top, apex, zenith, apogee, acme.
–OPPOSITES nadir.

pinpoint ▸ noun =**point**, spot, speck, dot.

▸ **adjective** =**precise**, strict, exact, meticulous, scrupulous.

▸ **verb** =**identify**, determine, distinguish, discover, find, locate, detect, track down, spot, diagnose, recognize, pin down, home in on, put one's finger on

pioneer ▸ noun **1** *the pioneers of the Wild West* =**settler**, colonist, colonizer, frontiersman/woman, explorer. **2** *a pioneer of motoring* =**developer**, innovator, trailblazer, groundbreaker; founding father, architect, creator.

▸ **verb** *he pioneered the sale of insurance* =**introduce**, develop, launch, instigate, initiate, spearhead, institute, establish, found, be the father/mother of, originate, set in motion, create; lay the groundwork, prepare the way, blaze a trail, break new ground.

pious ▸ adjective **1** *a pious family* =**religious**, devout, God-fearing, church-going, holy, godly, saintly, reverent, righteous. **2** *a pious platitude* =**sanctimonious**, hypocritical, insincere, self-righteous, holier-than-thou, churchy; *informal* goody-goody. **3** *a pious hope* =**forlorn**, vain, doomed, hopeless, desperate; unlikely, unrealistic.
–OPPOSITES irreligious, sincere.

pip ▸ noun =**seed**, stone, pit.

pipe ▸ noun **1** *a central-heating pipe* =**tube**, conduit, hose, main, duct, line, channel, pipeline, drain; tubing, piping. **2** *she was playing a pipe* =**whistle**, penny whistle, flute, recorder, fife; chanter. **3** *the sound of the pipes* =**bagpipes**, uillean pipes, Northumberland pipes.

▸ **verb 1** *the beer is piped into barrels* =**siphon**, feed, channel, run, convey. **2** *programmes piped in from London* =**transmit**, feed, patch.

■ **pipe down** *(informal)* =**be quiet**, be silent, hush, stop talking, hold one's tongue; *informal* shut up, shut one's mouth, button it, button one's lip, belt up, put a sock in it.

pipe dream ▸ noun =**fantasy**, false hope, illusion, delusion, daydream, chimera; castle in the air; *informal* pie in the sky.

pipeline ▸ noun *a gas pipeline* =**pipe**, conduit, main, line, duct, tube.

■ **in the pipeline** =**on the way**, coming, forthcoming, upcoming, imminent, about to happen, near, close, brewing, in the offing, in the wind.

piquant ▸ adjective **1** *a piquant sauce* =**spicy**, tangy, peppery, hot; tasty, flavoursome, savoury; pungent, sharp, tart, zesty, strong, salty. **2** *a piquant story* =**intriguing**, stimulating, interesting, fascinating, colourful, exciting, lively; spicy, provocative, racy; *informal* juicy.
–OPPOSITES bland, dull.

pique ▸ noun *a fit of pique* =**irritation**, annoyance, resentment, anger, displeasure, indignation, petulance, ill humour, vexation, exasperation, disgruntlement, discontent.

▸ **verb 1** *his curiosity was piqued* =**stimulate**, arouse, rouse, provoke, whet, awaken, excite, kindle, stir, galvanize. **2** *she was piqued by his neglect* =**irritate**, annoy, bother, vex, displease, upset, offend, affront, anger, gall, irk, nettle; *informal* peeve, aggravate, miff, rile, bug, needle, get someone's back up, hack off, get someone's goat; *Brit. informal* nark; *N. Amer. informal* tick off, tee off.

piracy ▶ noun **1** *piracy on the high seas* =**robbery**, freebooting, hijacking; *archaic* buccaneering. **2** *software piracy* =**(illegal) copying**, plagiarism, copyright infringement, bootlegging.

pirate ▶ noun **1** *pirates boarded the ship* =**freebooter**, hijacker, marauder, raider; *historical* privateer; *archaic* buccaneer, corsair. **2** *software pirates* =**copyright infringer**, plagiarist, copyist.
▶ verb *designers may pirate good ideas* =**steal**, copy, plagiarize, poach, appropriate, bootleg; *informal* crib, lift, rip off; *Brit. informal* nick, pinch.

pirouette ▶ noun =**spin**, twirl, whirl, turn.
▶ verb =**spin round**, twirl, whirl, turn round, revolve.

pistol ▶ noun =**handgun**, gun, revolver, side arm; six-shooter; *informal* gat; *N. Amer. informal* shooting iron.

pit¹ ▶ noun **1** *we dug a pit* =**hole**, trough, hollow, excavation, cavity, crater, pothole; shaft. **2** *pit closures* =**coal mine**, colliery, quarry.
▶ verb **1** *his skin had been pitted by acne* =**mark**, pock(mark), scar. **2** *craters pitted the landscape* =**make holes in**, make hollows in, pock(mark), scar.

■ **pit someone/something against** =**set against**, match against, put in opposition to, put in competition with.
■ **the pits** *(informal)* =**the worst**, the lowest of the low; rock-bottom, awful, terrible, dreadful, deplorable; *informal* appalling, lousy, abysmal, dire; *Brit. informal* chronic.

pit² ▶ noun *cherry pits* =**stone**, pip, seed.

pitch¹ ▶ noun **1** *the pitch was unfit for cricket* =**(playing) field**, ground, sports field; *Brit.* park. **2** *her voice rose in pitch* =**tone**, key, modulation, frequency. **3** *the pitch of the roof* =**gradient**, slope, slant, angle, steepness, tilt, incline. **4** *her anger reached such a pitch that she screamed* =**level**, intensity, point, degree, height, extent. **5** *his sales pitch* =**patter**, talk; *informal* spiel, line. **6** *street traders reserved their pitches* =**site**, place, spot, station; *Scottish* stance; *Brit. informal* patch.
▶ verb **1** *he pitched the note into the fire*

=**throw**, toss, fling, hurl, cast, lob, flip; *informal* chuck, sling, heave, bung; *N. Amer. informal* peg; *Austral. informal* hoy; *NZ informal* bish. **2** *he pitched overboard* =**fall**, tumble, topple, plunge, plummet. **3** *they pitched their tents* =**put up**, set up, erect, raise. **4** *the boat pitched* =**lurch**, toss (about), plunge, roll, reel, sway, rock, list.

■ **pitch in** =**help (out)**, assist, lend a hand, join in, participate, contribute, do one's bit, chip in, cooperate, collaborate; *Brit. informal* muck in.
■ **pitch into** =**attack**, turn on, lash out at, set upon, assault, fly at, tear into, weigh into, belabour; *informal* lay into; *N. Amer. informal* light into.

pitch² ▶ noun *cement coated with pitch* =**bitumen**, asphalt, tar.

pitch-black ▶ adjective =**black**, dark, inky, jet-black, coal-black, ebony; starless.

pitcher ▶ noun =**jug**, ewer, jar; *N. Amer.* creamer.

pitfall ▶ noun =**hazard**, danger, risk, peril, difficulty, catch, snag, stumbling block, drawback.

pith ▶ noun =**essence**, main point, fundamentals, heart, substance, nub, core, quintessence, crux, gist, meat, kernel, marrow, burden; *informal* nitty-gritty.

pithy ▶ adjective =**succinct**, terse, concise, compact, short (and sweet), brief, condensed, to the point, epigrammatic, crisp; significant, meaningful, telling.
−OPPOSITES verbose.

pitiful ▶ adjective **1** *in a pitiful state* =**distressing**, sad, piteous, pitiable, pathetic, heart-rending, moving, touching, tear-jerking; plaintive, poignant, forlorn; poor, sorry, wretched, abject, miserable. **2** *a pitiful £50 a month* =**paltry**, miserable, meagre, trifling, negligible, pitiable, derisory; *informal* pathetic, measly, piddling, mingy; *Brit. informal* poxy. **3** *his performance was pitiful* =**dreadful**, awful, terrible, lamentable, hopeless, feeble, pitiable, woeful, inadequate, deplorable, laughable; *informal* pathetic, useless, appalling, lousy, abysmal, dire.

pitiless ▶ adjective =**merciless**, unmerciful, ruthless, cruel, heartless, remorseless, hard-hearted, cold-hearted, harsh, callous, severe, unsparing, unforgiving, unfeeling, uncaring, unsympathetic, uncharitable.

–OPPOSITES merciful.

pittance ▶ noun = a tiny amount, next to nothing, very little; *informal* peanuts, chicken feed; *N. Amer. informal* chump change.

pitted ▶ adjective **1** *his skin was pitted* = **pockmarked**, pocked, scarred, marked, blemished. **2** *the pitted lane* = **potholed**, rutted, bumpy, rough, uneven.

–OPPOSITES smooth.

pity ▶ noun **1** *a voice full of pity* = **compassion**, commiseration, condolence, sympathy, fellow feeling, understanding. **2** *it's a pity he never had children* = **shame**, too bad, misfortune; *informal* crime, bummer, sin.

–OPPOSITES indifference, cruelty.

▶ verb *they pitied me* = **feel sorry for**, feel for, sympathize with, empathize with, commiserate with, take pity on, be moved by.

■ **take pity on** = **feel sorry for**, be compassionate towards, be sympathetic towards, have mercy on, help (out).

pivot ▶ noun = **fulcrum**, axis, axle, swivel; pin, shaft, hub, spindle, hinge, kingpin.

▶ verb **1** *the panel pivots inwards* = **rotate**, turn, swivel, revolve, spin. **2** *it all pivoted on his response* = **depend**, hinge, turn, centre, hang, rely, rest; revolve around.

pivotal ▶ adjective = **central**, crucial, vital, critical, focal, essential, key, decisive.

pixie ▶ noun = **elf**, fairy, sprite, imp, brownie, puck, leprechaun.

placard ▶ noun = **notice**, poster, sign, bill, advertisement; banner; *informal* ad; *Brit. informal* advert.

placate ▶ verb = **pacify**, calm, appease, mollify, soothe, win over, conciliate, propitiate, make peace with, humour; *Austral./NZ* square someone off.

–OPPOSITES provoke.

place ▶ noun **1** *an ideal place for dinner* = **location**, site, spot, setting, position, situation, area, region, locale; venue; *technical* locus. **2** *foreign places* = **country**, state, area, region, town, city; district; *literary* clime. **3** *a place of her own* = **home**, house, flat, apartment; accommodation, property, pied-à-terre; rooms, quarters; *informal* pad, digs; *Brit. informal* gaff; *formal* residence, abode, dwelling (place), domicile, habitation. **4** *in your place, I'd agree* = **situation**, position, circumstances; *informal* shoes. **5** *a place was reserved for her* = **seat**, chair, space. **6** *I offered him a place in the company* = **job**, position, post, appointment, situation; employment. **7** *I know my place* = **status**, position, standing, rank, niche. **8** *it was not her place to sort it out* = **responsibility**, duty, job, task, role, function, concern, affair, charge.

▶ verb **1** *books were placed on the table* = **put (down)**, set (down), lay, deposit, position, plant, rest, stand, station, situate, leave; *informal* stick, dump, bung, park, plonk, pop; *N. Amer. informal* plunk. **2** *the trust you placed in me* = **put**, lay, set, invest. **3** *a survey placed the company sixth* = **rank**, order, grade, class, classify; put, set, assign. **4** *Joe couldn't quite place her* = **identify**, recognize, remember, put a name to, pin down; locate, pinpoint. **5** *we were placed with foster parents* = **accommodate**, house; allocate, assign.

■ **in place 1** *the veil was held in place by pearls* = **in position**, in situ. **2** *the plans are in place* = **ready**, set up, all set, established, arranged, in order.

■ **in place of** = **instead of**, rather than, as a substitute for, as a replacement for, in exchange for, in lieu of; in someone's stead.

■ **out of place 1** *he said something out of place* = **inappropriate**, unsuitable, unseemly, improper, untoward, out of keeping, unbecoming, wrong. **2** *she seemed out of place in a launderette* = **incongruous**, out of one's element, like a fish out of water; uncomfortable, uneasy.

■ **put someone in their place** = **humiliate**, take down a peg or two, deflate, crush, squash, humble; *informal* cut down to size, settle someone's hash.

■ **take place** = **happen**, occur, come about, transpire, crop up, materialize, arise; *N. Amer. informal* go down; *literary* come to pass.

■ **take the place of** = **replace**, stand in for, substitute for, act for, fill in for, cover for, relieve.

placement ▶ noun **1** *the placement of the chairs* = **positioning**, placing, arrangement, position, deployment, location. **2** *teaching placements* = **job**, post, assignment, posting, position, appointment, engagement.

placid ▶ adjective **1** *she's normally very placid* = **even-tempered**, calm, tranquil, equable, unexcitable, serene, mild, composed, self-possessed, poised, easy-

going, level-headed, steady, unruffled, unperturbed, phlegmatic; *informal* unflappable. **2** *a placid village* =**quiet**, calm, tranquil, still, peaceful, undisturbed, restful, sleepy.
–OPPOSITES excitable, bustling.

plagiarism ▸ noun =**copying**, infringement of copyright, piracy, theft, stealing; *informal* cribbing.

plagiarize ▸ verb =**copy**, pirate, steal, poach, appropriate; *informal* rip off, crib, 'borrow'; *Brit. informal* pinch, nick.

plague ▸ noun **1** *they died of the plague* =**bubonic plague**, pneumonic plague, Black Death; disease, sickness, epidemic; *dated* contagion; *archaic* pestilence. **2** *a plague of fleas* =**infestation**, epidemic, invasion, swarm, multitude, host. **3** *theft is the plague of restaurants* =**bane**, curse, scourge, affliction, blight.
▸ verb **1** *he was plagued by poor health* =**afflict**, bedevil, torment, trouble, beset, dog, curse. **2** *he plagued her with questions* =**pester**, harass, badger, bother, torment, persecute, bedevil, harry, hound, trouble, nag, molest; *informal* hassle, bug, aggravate; *N. English informal* mither; *N. Amer. informal* devil.

plain ▸ adjective **1** *it was plain that something was wrong* =**obvious**, (crystal) clear, evident, apparent, manifest; unmistakable, transparent; pronounced, marked, striking, conspicuous, self-evident, indisputable; as plain as a pikestaff, writ large; *informal* standing/sticking out like a sore thumb, standing/sticking out a mile. **2** *plain English* =**intelligible**, comprehensible, understandable, clear, lucid, simple, straightforward, user-friendly. **3** *plain speaking* =**candid**, frank, outspoken, forthright, direct, honest, truthful, blunt, bald, unequivocal; *informal* upfront. **4** *a plain dress* =**simple**, ordinary, unadorned, unfussy, homely, basic, modest, unsophisticated; restrained, muted; everyday, workaday. **5** *a plain girl* =**unattractive**, unprepossessing, ugly, ordinary; *N. Amer.* homely; *informal* not much to look at; *Brit. informal* no oil painting. **6** *it was plain bad luck* =**sheer**, pure, downright, out-and-out.
–OPPOSITES obscure, fancy, attractive, pretentious.
▸ adverb *plain stupid* =**downright**, utterly, absolutely, completely, totally, really, thoroughly, unquestionably, positively; *informal* plumb.
▸ noun *the plains of North America* =**grass-**

land, flatland, prairie, savannah, steppe; tundra, pampas, veld.

plain-spoken ▸ adjective =**candid**, frank, outspoken, forthright, direct, honest, truthful, open, blunt, straightforward, explicit, unequivocal, unambiguous, not afraid to call a spade a spade; *informal* upfront.
–OPPOSITES evasive.

plaintive ▸ adjective =**mournful**, sad, pathetic, pitiful, melancholy, sorrowful, unhappy, wretched, woeful, forlorn.

plan ▸ noun **1** *a plan for raising money* =**scheme**, idea, proposal, proposition, project, programme, system, method, strategy, stratagem, formula, recipe. **2** *her plan was to break even* =**intention**, aim, idea, intent, objective, object, goal, target, ambition. **3** *plans for the clubhouse* =**blueprint**, drawing, diagram, sketch; *N. Amer.* plat.
▸ verb **1** *plan your route in advance* =**organize**, arrange, work out, design, outline, map out, prepare, formulate, frame, develop, devise, concoct. **2** *he plans to buy a house* =**intend**, aim, propose, mean, hope. **3** *I'm planning a new garden* =**design**, draw up, sketch out, map out; *N. Amer.* plat.

plane[1] ▸ noun **1** *a horizontal plane* =**(flat) surface**, level surface; the flat, horizontal. **2** *a higher plane of achievement* =**level**, degree, standard, stratum; dimension.
▸ adjective *a plane surface* =**flat**, level, horizontal, even; smooth, regular, uniform.
▸ verb *boats planed across the water* =**skim**, glide.

plane[2] ▸ noun *the plane took off* =**aircraft**, airliner; flying machine; *Brit.* aeroplane; *N. Amer.* airplane, ship.

┌─────────────────────────┐
│ **WORD LINKS** │
└─────────────────────────┘
science of flight: **aeronautics**

planet ▸ noun =**celestial body**, heavenly body, satellite, asteroid; *literary* orb, sphere.

plank ▸ noun =**board**, floorboard, timber.

planning ▸ noun =**preparation(s)**, organization, arrangement, design; forethought, groundwork.

plant ▸ noun **1** *garden plants* =**flower**, vegetable, herb, shrub, weed; (**plants**) vegetation, greenery, flora. **2** *a CIA plant* =**spy**, informant, informer, (secret) agent, mole, infiltrator, operative; *N. Amer. informal* spook. **3** *a chemical plant* =**factory**, works; refinery, mill.

▶ verb **1** *plant the seeds* =**sow**, scatter; transplant. **2** *he planted his feet on the ground* =**place**, put, set, position, situate, settle; *informal* plonk. **3** *she planted the idea in his mind* =**instil**, implant, put, place, introduce, fix, establish, lodge. **4** *letters were planted to embarrass them* =**place**, leave.

> **WORD LINKS**
>
> *study of plants:* **botany**
> *plant-eating:* **herbivorous**
> *substance used to kill plants:* **herbicide**

plaque ▶ noun =**plate**, tablet, panel, sign.

plaster ▶ noun **1** *the plaster covering the bricks* =**plasterwork**, stucco. **2** *a statuette made of plaster* =**plaster of Paris**, gypsum. **3** *waterproof plasters* =**sticking plaster**, (adhesive) dressing; *trademark* Elastoplast, Band-Aid.

▶ verb **1** *bread plastered with butter* =**spread**, smother, smear, cake, coat. **2** *his hair was plastered down with sweat* =**flatten (down)**, smooth down, slick down.

plastic ▶ adjective **1** *at high temperatures the rocks become plastic* =**malleable**, mouldable, pliable, ductile, flexible, soft, workable, bendable; *informal* bendy. **2** *the plastic minds of children* =**impressionable**, malleable, receptive, pliable, pliant, flexible; persuadable, susceptible, manipulable. **3** *a plastic smile* =**artificial**, false, fake, superficial, bogus, unnatural, insincere; *informal* phoney, pretend.

–OPPOSITES rigid, intractable, genuine.

plate ▶ noun **1** *a dinner plate* =**dish**, platter, salver; *historical* trencher; *archaic* charger. **2** *a plate of spaghetti* =**plateful**, helping, portion, serving. **3** *steel plates* =**panel**, sheet, slab. **4** *a brass plate on the door* =**plaque**, sign, tablet. **5** *the book has colour plates* =**picture**, print, illustration, photograph, photo.

▶ verb *the roof was plated with steel* =**cover**, coat, overlay, laminate, veneer, armour.

plateau ▶ noun =**upland**, mesa, highland.

platform ▶ noun **1** *he made a speech from the platform* =**stage**, dais, rostrum, podium. **2** *the Democratic Party's platform* =**policy**, programme, party line, manifesto.

platitude ▶ noun =**cliché**, truism,

commonplace, old chestnut.

platonic ▶ adjective =**non-sexual**, non-physical, chaste; intellectual.
–OPPOSITES sexual, physical.

platoon ▶ noun =**unit**, patrol, troop, squad, squadron, team, company, corps, outfit, detachment, contingent.

platter ▶ noun =**plate**, dish, salver, tray; *historical* trencher; *archaic* charger.

plaudits ▶ plural noun =**praise**, acclaim, commendation, congratulations, accolades, compliments, cheers, applause, tributes.
–OPPOSITES criticism.

plausible ▶ adjective =**credible**, reasonable, believable, likely, feasible, tenable, possible, conceivable, imaginable; convincing.
–OPPOSITES unlikely.

play ▶ verb **1** *the children played with toys* =**amuse oneself**, entertain oneself, enjoy oneself, have fun; relax, occupy oneself, divert oneself; frolic, romp; *informal* mess about/around, lark (about/around). **2** *I used to play football* =**take part in**, participate in, be involved in, compete in, do. **3** *Liverpool play Oxford on Sunday* =**compete against**, take on, meet. **4** *he was to play Macbeth* =**act (the part of)**, take the role of, appear as, portray, perform; be. **5** *he learned to play the flute* =**perform on**, make music on. **6** *the sunlight played on the water* =**dance**, glitter; sparkle, glint.

▶ noun **1** *work and play* =**amusement**, relaxation, recreation, diversion, leisure; enjoyment, pleasure, fun; *informal* living it up. **2** *a Shakespeare play* =**drama**, theatrical work; comedy, tragedy; production, performance. **3** *there was no play in the rope* =**movement**, slack, give.

■ **play around** *(informal)* =**womanize**, philander, have affairs, flirt; *informal* carry on, mess about/around, play the field, sleep around; *Brit. informal* play away; *N. Amer. informal* fool around.

■ **play ball** *(informal)* =**cooperate**, collaborate, play the game, show willing, help, lend a hand, assist.

■ **play something down** =**make light of**, make little of, gloss over, downplay, understate; soft-pedal, diminish, trivialize, underrate, underestimate, undervalue.

■ **play for time** =**stall**, temporize, delay, hold back, hang fire, procrastinate, drag one's feet.

■ **play it by ear** =**improvise**, extemporize, ad lib, make it up as one goes along, think on one's feet; *informal* busk it, wing it.

■ **play on** =**exploit**, take advantage of, use, turn to (one's) account, profit by, capitalize on, trade on, milk, abuse.

■ **play the game** =**play fair**, be fair, play by the rules, conform, be a good sport, toe the line.

■ **play up** (*Brit. informal*) **1** *the boys really did play up* =**misbehave**, be bad, be naughty. **2** *the boiler's playing up* =**malfunction**, not work, be defective, be faulty; *informal* go on the blink, act up. **3** *his leg was playing up* =**be painful**, hurt, ache, be sore; *informal* kill someone, give someone gyp.

■ **play up to** =**ingratiate oneself with**, curry favour with, court, fawn over, make up to, toady to, crawl to, pander to, flatter; *informal* soft-soap, suck up to, butter up, lick someone's boots.

playboy ▶ noun =**socialite**, pleasure-seeker; ladies' man, womanizer, philanderer, rake, roué; *informal* ladykiller.

player ▶ noun **1** *a tournament for young players* =**participant**, contestant, competitor, contender. **2** *the players in the orchestra* =**musician**, performer, instrumentalist. **3** *the players of the Royal Shakespeare Company* =**actor**, **actress**, performer, thespian, entertainer, artist(e), trouper.

playful ▶ adjective **1** *a playful mood* =**frisky**, lively, full of fun, frolicsome, high-spirited, exuberant; mischievous, impish, rascally, tricksy; *informal* full of beans. **2** *a playful remark* =**light-hearted**, jokey, teasing, humorous, jocular, facetious, frivolous, flippant; *informal* waggish.

–OPPOSITES serious.

playground ▶ noun =**play area**, park, playing field, recreation ground.

playmate ▶ noun =**friend**, playfellow, companion; *informal* chum, pal; *Brit. informal* mate; *N. Amer. informal* buddy.

playwright ▶ noun =**dramatist**; scriptwriter, screenwriter, writer.

plea ▶ noun =**appeal**, entreaty, supplication, petition, request, call, suit, solicitation.

plead ▶ verb **1** *he pleaded with her to stay* =**beg**, implore, entreat, appeal to, ask; *literary* beseech. **2** *she pleaded ignorance* =**claim**, use as an excuse, assert, allege, argue.

pleasant ▶ adjective **1** *a pleasant evening* =**enjoyable**, pleasurable, nice, agreeable; entertaining, amusing, delightful, charming; fine, balmy; *informal* lovely, great. **2** *the staff are pleasant* =**friendly**, agreeable, amiable, nice, genial, cordial, likeable, good-natured, personable; hospitable, approachable, gracious, courteous, polite, obliging, helpful, considerate; charming, lovely, delightful, sweet.

–OPPOSITES disagreeable.

pleasantry ▶ noun =**banter**, badinage; polite/casual remark.

please ▶ verb **1** *he'd do anything to please her* =**make happy**, give pleasure to, make someone feel good; delight, charm, amuse; satisfy, gratify, humour, oblige; *informal* tickle someone pink. **2** *do as you please* =**like**, want, wish, desire, see fit, think fit, choose, will, prefer.

–OPPOSITES annoy.

▶ adverb *please sit down* =**if you please**, if you wouldn't mind, if you would be so good; kindly.

pleased ▶ adjective =**happy**, glad, delighted, gratified, grateful, thankful, content, contented, satisfied; thrilled; *informal* over the moon, tickled pink, on cloud nine; *Brit. informal* chuffed; *N. English informal* made up; *Austral. informal* wrapped.

–OPPOSITES unhappy.

pleasing ▶ adjective **1** *a pleasing result* =**good**, agreeable, pleasant, pleasurable, satisfying, gratifying, great. **2** *her pleasing manner* =**friendly**, amiable, pleasant, agreeable, affable, nice, genial, likeable, charming, engaging, delightful; *informal* lovely.

pleasurable ▶ adjective =**pleasant**, enjoyable, nice, pleasing, agreeable, gratifying; fun, entertaining, amusing, diverting.

pleasure ▶ noun **1** *she smiled with pleasure* =**happiness**, delight, joy, gladness, glee, satisfaction, gratification, contentment, enjoyment, amusement. **2** *his greatest pleasure in life* =**joy**, amusement, diversion, recreation, pastime; treat, thrill. **3** *don't mix business and pleasure* =**enjoyment**, fun, entertainment; recreation, leisure, relaxation. **4** *a life of pleasure* =**hedonism**, indulgence, self-indulgence, gratification.

■ **take pleasure in** =**enjoy**, delight in, love, like, appreciate, relish, savour, revel in, glory in; *informal* get a kick out of, get a thrill out of.

■ **with pleasure** =**gladly**, willingly, happily, readily; by all means, of course.

> WORD LINKS
>
> *pursuit of pleasure:* **hedonism**

pleat ▶ noun =**fold**, crease, gather, tuck.
▶ verb =**fold**, crease, gather, tuck, crimp.

plebeian ▶ noun *plebeians and gentry lived together* =**proletarian**, commoner, working-class person, worker; peasant; *informal* pleb, prole.
–OPPOSITES aristocrat.
▶ adjective **1** *people of plebeian descent* =**lower-class**, working-class, proletarian, common, peasant; mean, humble, lowly. **2** *plebeian tastes* =**uncultured**, uncultivated, unrefined, lowbrow, philistine, uneducated; coarse, uncouth, common, vulgar; *informal* plebby; *Brit. informal* non-U.
–OPPOSITES noble, refined.

plebiscite ▶ noun =**vote**, referendum, ballot, poll.

pledge ▶ noun *his election pledge* =**promise**, undertaking, vow, word (of honour), commitment, assurance, oath, guarantee.
▶ verb **1** *he pledged to root out corruption* =**promise**, vow, swear, undertake, commit oneself, declare, affirm. **2** *they pledged £100 million* =**promise (to give)**, donate, contribute, give, put up.

plenary ▶ adjective =**full**, complete, entire.

plentiful ▶ adjective =**abundant**, copious, ample, profuse, rich, lavish, generous, bountiful, large, great, bumper, prolific; *informal* a gogo, galore; *literary* plenteous.
–OPPOSITES scarce.

plenty ▶ noun *times of plenty* =**prosperity**, affluence, wealth, opulence, comfort, luxury; plentifulness, abundance.
▶ pronoun *there are plenty of books* =**a lot of**, many, a great deal of, a plethora of, enough (and to spare), no lack of, sufficient, a wealth of; *informal* loads of, lots of, heaps of, stacks of, masses of, tons of, oodles of.

plethora ▶ noun =**excess**, abundance, superabundance, surplus, glut, surfeit, profusion, too many, too much, enough and to spare.
–OPPOSITES dearth.

pliable ▶ adjective **1** *leather is pliable*

=**flexible**, pliant, bendable, supple, workable, plastic; *informal* bendy. **2** *pliable teenage minds* =**malleable**, impressionable, flexible, adaptable, pliant, biddable, tractable, suggestible, persuadable, manipulable.
–OPPOSITES rigid, obdurate.

pliant ▶ adjective. See PLIABLE senses 1, 2.

plight ▶ noun =**predicament**, difficult situation, dire straits, trouble, difficulty, extremity, bind; *informal* dilemma, tight corner, tight spot, hole, pickle, jam, fix.

plod ▶ verb =**trudge**, walk heavily, clump, stomp, tramp, lumber, slog; *Brit. informal* trog.

plot ▶ noun **1** *a plot to overthrow him* =**conspiracy**, intrigue, plan. **2** *the plot of her novel* =**storyline**, story, scenario, action, thread. **3** *a three-acre plot* =**piece of ground**, patch, area, tract, acreage; *Brit.* allotment; *N. Amer.* lot, plat; *N. Amer. & Austral./NZ* homesite.
▶ verb **1** *he plotted their downfall* =**plan**, scheme, arrange, organize, hatch, concoct, devise, dream up; *informal* cook up. **2** *his brother was plotting against him* =**conspire**, scheme, intrigue, connive. **3** *the points were plotted on a graph* =**mark**, chart, map.

plotter ▶ noun =**conspirator**, schemer, intriguer.

plough ▶ verb **1** *the fields were ploughed* =**till**, furrow, harrow, cultivate, work. **2** *the car ploughed into a wall* =**crash**, smash, career, plunge, bulldoze, hurtle, cannon, run, drive; *N. Amer. informal* barrel.

ploy ▶ noun =**ruse**, tactic, move, device, stratagem, scheme, trick, gambit, plan, manoeuvre, dodge, subterfuge; *Brit. informal* wheeze.

pluck ▶ verb **1** *he plucked a thread from his lapel* =**remove**, pick (off), pull (off/out), extract, take (off). **2** *she plucked at his T-shirt* =**pull (at)**, tug (at), clutch (at), snatch (at), grab, catch (at), tweak, jerk; *informal* yank. **3** *she plucked the guitar strings* =**strum**, pick, thrum, twang.
▶ noun *it took a lot of pluck* =**courage**, bravery, nerve, backbone, spine, daring, spirit, grit; *informal* guts, spunk; *Brit. informal* bottle; *N. Amer. informal* moxie.

plucky ▶ adjective =**brave**, courageous, spirited, game; *informal* gutsy, spunky.
–OPPOSITES timid.

plug ▶ noun **1** *she pulled out the plug* =**stop-**

per, bung, cork, seal; *N. Amer.* stopple.
2 (*informal*) *a plug for his new book* =**adver-tisement**, promotion, commercial, rec-ommendation, mention, good word; *informal* hype, push, puff, ad, boost; *Brit. informal* advert.
▶ verb **1** *plug the holes* =**stop (up)**, seal (up/off), close (up/off), block (up/off), fill (up). **2** (*informal*) *she plugged her new film* =**publicize**, promote, advertise, mention, bang the drum for, draw attention to; *informal* hype (up), push.
■ **plug away** (*informal*) =**toil**, labour, slave away, soldier on, persevere, persist, keep on, plough on; *informal* slog away, beaver away, peg away.

plumb[1] ▶ verb *an attempt to plumb her psyche* =**explore**, probe, delve into, search, examine, investigate, fathom, penetrate, understand.
▶ adverb **1** (*informal*) *it went plumb through the screen* =**right**, exactly, precisely, directly, dead, straight; *informal* (slap) bang. **2** (*N. Amer. informal*) *he's plumb crazy* =**utterly**, absolutely, completely, downright, totally, quite, thoroughly.

plumb[2] ▶ verb *he plumbed in the washing machine* =**install**, put in, fit.

plume ▶ noun =**feather**, quill.

plummet ▶ verb **1** *the plane plummeted to the ground* =**plunge**, dive, drop, fall, hurtle. **2** *share prices plummeted* =**fall (steeply)**, plunge, tumble, drop (rapidly), go down, slump; *informal* crash, nosedive.

plump[1] ▶ adjective *a plump child* =**chubby**, fat, rotund, well padded, ample, round, chunky, portly, overweight, fleshy, paunchy, bulky, corpulent; *informal* tubby, roly-poly, pudgy; *Brit. informal* podgy; *N. Amer. informal* zaftig, corn-fed.
−OPPOSITES thin.

plump[2] ▶ verb **1** *Jack plumped down on to a chair* =**flop**, collapse, sink, fall, drop, slump; *informal* plonk oneself; *N. Amer. informal* plank oneself. **2** *she plumped her bag on the table* =**put (down)**, set (down), place, deposit, dump, stick; *informal* plonk; *Brit. informal* bung; *N. Amer. informal* plunk.
■ **plump for** =**choose**, decide on, go for, opt for, pick, settle on, select, take, elect.

plunder ▶ verb **1** *they plundered the countryside* =**pillage**, loot, rob, raid, ransack, despoil, strip, ravage, lay waste, sack,

devastate. **2** *money plundered from pension funds* =**steal**, purloin, seize, pillage; embezzle.
▶ noun *huge quantities of plunder* =**booty**, loot, stolen goods, spoils, ill-gotten gains; *informal* swag.

plunge ▶ verb **1** *Joy plunged into the sea* =**dive**, jump, throw oneself. **2** *the aircraft plunged to the ground* =**plummet**, nosedive, drop, fall, tumble, descend. **3** *the car plunged down an alley* =**charge**, hurtle, career, plough, tear; *N. Amer. informal* barrel. **4** *oil prices plunged* =**fall sharply**, plummet, drop, go down, tumble, slump; *informal* crash, nosedive. **5** *he plunged the dagger into her back* =**thrust**, stab, sink, stick, ram, drive, push, shove, force. **6** *plunge the pears into water* =**immerse**, submerge, dip, dunk. **7** *the room was plunged into darkness* =**throw**, cast.
▶ noun **1** *a plunge in the pool* =**dive**, jump, dip. **2** *a plunge in profits* =**fall**, drop, slump; *informal* nosedive, crash.
■ **take the plunge** =**commit oneself**, go for it; *informal* go for broke.

plurality ▶ noun =**(wide) variety**, diversity, range, multitude, multiplicity, wealth, profusion, abundance, plethora, host; *informal* load, stack, heap, mass.

plus ▶ preposition **1** *three plus three makes six* =**and**, added to. **2** *four novels plus various poems* =**as well as**, together with, along with, in addition to, and, not to mention.
−OPPOSITES minus.
▶ noun *one of the pluses of the job* =**advantage**, good point, asset, pro, (fringe) benefit, bonus, extra, attraction; *informal* perk.
−OPPOSITES disadvantage.

plush ▶ adjective (*informal*) =**luxurious**, luxury, de luxe, sumptuous, palatial, lavish, opulent, magnificent, rich, expensive, fancy, grand; *Brit.* upmarket; *informal* posh, ritzy, swanky, classy; *Brit. informal* swish; *N. Amer. informal* swank.
−OPPOSITES austere.

ply[1] ▶ verb **1** *he plied a profitable trade* =**engage in**, carry on, pursue, conduct, practise. **2** *ferries ply between all lake resorts* =**go (regularly)**, travel, shuttle, go back and forth. **3** *she plied me with scones* =**provide**, supply, shower. **4** *he plied her with questions* =**bombard**, assail, pester, plague, harass; *informal* hassle.

ply[2] ▶ noun *a three-ply tissue* =**layer**, thickness, strand, sheet, leaf.

poach ▸ verb **1** *he's been poaching salmon* =**hunt (illegally)**, catch (illegally); steal. **2** *workers were poached by other firms* =**steal**, appropriate, purloin, take; headhunt; *informal* nab, swipe; *Brit. informal* nick, pinch.

pocket ▸ noun **1** *a bag with two pockets* =**pouch**, compartment. **2** *pockets of resistance* =**(isolated) area**, patch, region, island, cluster.
▸ adjective *a pocket dictionary* =**small**, miniature, mini, compact, concise, abridged, potted, portable; *N. Amer.* vest-pocket.
▸ verb *he pocketed $900,000* =**steal**, take, appropriate, purloin, misappropriate, embezzle; *informal* filch, swipe, snaffle; *Brit. informal* pinch, nick, whip.

pockmark ▸ noun =**scar**, pit, pock, mark, blemish.

pod ▸ noun =**shell**, husk, hull, case; *N. Amer.* shuck; *Botany* pericarp, capsule.

podgy ▸ adjective *(Brit. informal)* =**chubby**, plump, fat, well padded, ample, round, chunky, portly, overweight, fleshy, paunchy, bulky, corpulent; *informal* tubby, roly-poly, pudgy, beefy, porky, blubbery; *N. Amer. informal* zaftig, corn-fed.
–OPPOSITES thin.

podium ▸ noun =**platform**, stage, dais, rostrum, stand.

poem ▸ noun =**verse**, rhyme, piece of poetry; ode, sonnet, ballad.

poet ▸ noun =*literary* bard; *derogatory* poetaster.

poetic ▸ adjective **1** *poetic compositions* =**poetical**, verse, metrical. **2** *poetic language* =**expressive**, figurative, symbolic, flowery, artistic, imaginative, creative.

poetry ▸ noun =**poems**, verse, versification, rhyme.

poignancy ▸ noun =**pathos**, pitifulness, sadness, sorrow, mournfulness, wretchedness, misery, tragedy.

poignant ▸ adjective =**touching**, moving, sad, affecting, pitiful, pathetic, sorrowful, mournful, wretched, miserable, distressing, heart-rending, tear-jerking, plaintive, tragic.

point¹ ▸ noun **1** *the point of a needle* =**tip**, (sharp) end, extremity; prong, spike, tine, nib, barb. **2** *points of light* =**pinpoint**, dot, spot, speck. **3** *a meeting point* =**place**, position, location, site, spot. **4** *this point in her life* =**time**, stage, juncture, period, phase. **5** *the tension had reached such a high point* =**level**, degree, stage, pitch, extent. **6** *an important point* =**detail**, item, fact, thing, argument, consideration, factor, element; subject, issue, topic, question, matter. **7** *get to the point* =**heart of the matter**, essence, nub, core, crux; *informal* brass tacks, nitty-gritty. **8** *what's the point of this?* =**purpose**, aim, object, objective, goal, intention; use, sense, value, advantage. **9** *he had his good points* =**attribute**, characteristic, feature, trait, quality, property, aspect, side.
▸ verb **1** *she pointed the gun at him* =**aim**, direct, level, train. **2** *the evidence pointed to his guilt* =**indicate**, suggest, evidence, signal, signify, denote.
∎ **beside the point** =**irrelevant**, immaterial, unimportant, neither here nor there, inconsequential, incidental, unconnected, peripheral, tangential.
∎ **make a point of** =**make an effort to**, go out of one's way to, put emphasis on.
∎ **on the point of** =**(just) about to**, on the verge of, on the brink of, going to, all set to.
∎ **point of view** =**opinion**, view, belief, attitude, feeling, sentiment, thoughts; position, perspective, viewpoint, standpoint, outlook.
∎ **point something out** =**identify**, show, draw attention to, indicate, specify, detail, mention.
∎ **point something up** =**emphasize**, highlight, draw attention to, accentuate, underline, spotlight, foreground, bring to the fore.
∎ **to the point** =**relevant**, pertinent, apposite, germane, applicable, apropos, appropriate, apt.
∎ **up to a point** =**partly**, to some extent, to a certain degree, in part, partially

point² ▸ noun *the ship rounded the point* =**promontory**, headland, foreland, cape, peninsula, bluff, ness, horn.

point-blank ▸ adverb **1** *he fired the pistol point-blank* =**at close range**, close up/to. **2** *she couldn't say it point-blank* =**bluntly**, directly, straight, frankly, candidly, openly, explicitly, unequivocally, unambiguously, plainly, flatly, categorically, outright.
▸ adjective *a point-blank refusal* =**blunt**, direct, straight, straightforward, frank, candid, forthright, explicit, unequivocal, plain, clear, flat, decisive, unqualified, categorical, outright.

pointed ▸ adjective **1** *a pointed stick* =**sharp**, tapering, tapered, spiked, barbed; *informal* pointy. **2** *a pointed remark* =**cutting**, trenchant, biting, incisive, acerbic, caustic, scathing, venomous, sarcastic; *informal* sarky; *N. Amer. informal* snarky.

pointer ▶ noun **1** *the pointer moved to 100rpm* =**indicator**, needle, arrow, hand. **2** *he used a pointer on the chart* =**stick**, rod, cane; cursor. **3** *a pointer to the outcome of the election* =**indication**, indicator, clue, hint, sign, signal, evidence, intimation, inkling, suggestion. **4** *I can give you a few pointers* =**tip**, hint, suggestion, guideline, recommendation.

pointless ▶ adjective =**senseless**, futile, hopeless, unavailing, aimless, idle, worthless, valueless; absurd, insane, stupid, silly, foolish.
−OPPOSITES valuable.

poise ▶ noun **1** *poise and good deportment* =**grace**, gracefulness, elegance, balance, control. **2** *in spite of the setback she retained her poise* =**composure**, equanimity, self-possession, aplomb, self-assurance, self-control, sangfroid, dignity; *informal* cool.
▶ verb **1** *she was poised on one foot* =**balance**, hold (oneself) steady, be suspended, remain motionless, hang, hover. **2** *he was poised for action* =**prepare oneself**, ready oneself, brace oneself, gear oneself up, stand by.

poison ▶ noun =**toxin**, venom.
▶ verb **1** *her mother poisoned her* =**give poison to**; murder. **2** *a blackmailer poisoning baby foods* =**contaminate**, put poison in, adulterate, spike, lace, doctor. **3** *the Amazon is being poisoned* =**pollute**, contaminate, taint, spoil. **4** *they poisoned his mind* =**twist**, warp, corrupt.

WORD LINKS
study of poisons: **toxicology**

poisonous ▶ adjective **1** *a poisonous snake* =**venomous**, deadly. **2** *a poisonous chemical* =**toxic**, noxious, deadly, fatal, lethal, mortal, death-dealing. **3** *a poisonous glance* =**malicious**, malevolent, hostile, spiteful, bitter, venomous, vindictive, vitriolic, rancorous, malign.
−OPPOSITES harmless, non-toxic, benevolent.

poke ▶ verb **1** *she poked him in the ribs* =**prod**, jab, dig, nudge, shove, jolt, stab, stick. **2** *leave the cable poking out* =**stick out**, jut out, protrude, project, extend.

▶ noun *Carrie gave him a poke* =**prod**, jab, dig, elbow, nudge.
■ **poke about/around** =**search**, hunt, rummage (around), forage, grub, root about/around, scavenge, nose around, ferret (about/around); sift through, rifle through, scour, comb.
■ **poke fun at** =**mock**, make fun of, ridicule, laugh at, jeer at, sneer at, deride, scorn, scoff at, pillory, lampoon; *informal* send up, take the mickey out of; *Austral./NZ informal* poke mullock at.
■ **poke one's nose into** =**pry into**, interfere in, intrude on, butt into, meddle with; *informal* snoop into.

poky ▶ adjective =**small**, little, tiny, cramped, confined, restricted, boxy; *euphemistic* compact, bijou.
−OPPOSITES spacious.

polar ▶ adjective =**opposite**, opposed, dichotomous, extreme, contrary, contradictory, antithetical.

polarity ▶ noun =**difference**, dichotomy, separation, opposition, contradiction, antithesis, antagonism.

pole¹ ▶ noun =**post**, pillar, stanchion, stake, stick, support, prop, batten, bar, rail, rod, beam; staff, stave, cane, baton.

pole² ▶ noun =**extremity**, extreme, limit, antipode.
■ **poles apart** =**completely different/opposite**, directly opposed, antithetical, incompatible, irreconcilable, worlds apart, at opposite extremes; *Brit.* like chalk and cheese.

WORD LINKS
relating to both the North and South Poles: **bipolar**

polemic ▶ noun =**diatribe**, invective, rant, tirade, broadside, attack, harangue.

police ▶ noun =**police force/service**, police officers, policemen, policewomen, officers of the law, the forces of law and order; *Brit.* constabulary; *informal* the cops, the fuzz, (the long arm of) the law, the boys in blue; *Brit. informal* the (Old) Bill, coppers, bobbies, busies, the force; *N. Amer. informal* the heat; *informal, derogatory* pigs.
▶ verb **1** *we must police the area* =**guard**, watch over, protect, defend, patrol; control, regulate. **2** *the regulations will be policed by the ministry* =**enforce**, regulate, oversee, supervise, monitor, observe, check.

police officer ▸ noun =policeman, policewoman, officer (of the law); *Brit.* constable; *N. Amer.* patrolman, trooper, roundsman; *informal* cop; *Brit. informal* copper, bobby, rozzer, busy, (PC) plod; *N. Amer. informal* uniform; *informal, derogatory* pig.

policy ▸ noun =plans, approach, code, system, guidelines, theory; line, position, stance.

polish ▸ verb 1 *I polished his shoes* =shine, wax, buff, rub up/down; gloss, burnish. 2 *polish up your essay* =perfect, refine, improve, hone, enhance; brush up, revise, edit, correct, rewrite, go over, touch up; *informal* clean up.
▸ noun =sophistication, refinement, urbanity, suaveness, elegance, style, grace, finesse; *informal* class.
■ **polish something off** *(informal)* 1 *he polished off an apple pie* =eat, finish, consume, devour, guzzle, wolf down, down, bolt; drink up, drain, quaff, gulp (down); *informal* put away, scoff, shovel down, sink, swill, knock back; *Brit. informal* shift, gollop; *N. Amer. informal* scarf (down/up), snarf (down/up). 2 *I'll polish off the last few pages* =complete, finish, deal with, accomplish, discharge, do.

polished ▸ adjective 1 *a polished table* =shiny, glossy, gleaming, lustrous, glassy; waxed, buffed, burnished. 2 *a polished performance* =expert, accomplished, masterly, masterful, skilful, adept, adroit, dexterous; consummate, superb, superlative, first-rate, fine.
–OPPOSITES dull, inexpert.

polite ▸ adjective 1 *a very polite girl* =well mannered, civil, courteous, respectful, well behaved, well bred, gentlemanly, ladylike, genteel, gracious; tactful, diplomatic. 2 *polite society* =civilized, refined, cultured, sophisticated.
–OPPOSITES rude, uncivilized.

politic ▸ adjective =wise, prudent, sensible, judicious; advantageous, beneficial, profitable; appropriate, suitable, fitting, apt.
–OPPOSITES unwise.

political ▸ adjective =governmental, government, constitutional, ministerial, parliamentary; diplomatic, legislative, administrative.

politician ▸ noun =legislator, Member of Parliament, MP, minister, statesman, stateswoman; senator, congressman/woman; *informal* politico.

politics ▸ noun 1 *a career in politics* =government, affairs of state, public affairs; diplomacy. 2 *he studies politics* =political science. 3 *what are his politics?* =political views, political leanings. 4 *office politics* =power struggles, machinations, manoeuvring, realpolitik.

poll ▸ noun 1 *a second-round poll* =vote, ballot, show of hands, referendum, plebiscite; election. 2 *the poll was unduly low* =voting figures, vote, returns, count, turnout. 3 *a poll to investigate holiday choices* =survey, opinion poll; market research, census.
▸ verb 1 *most of those polled supported him* =canvass, survey, ask, question, interview, ballot. 2 *she polled 119 votes* =get, gain, register, record, return.

pollute ▸ verb =contaminate, taint, poison, foul, dirty, soil, infect.
–OPPOSITES purify.

pollution ▸ noun =contamination, impurity; dirt, filth, infection.

pomp ▸ noun =ceremony, solemnity, ritual, display, spectacle, pageantry; show, ostentation, splendour, grandeur, magnificence, majesty, stateliness, glory; *informal* razzmatazz.

pompous ▸ adjective =self-important, imperious, overbearing, sententious, grandiose, affected, pretentious, puffed up, haughty, proud, conceited, supercilious, condescending, patronizing; *informal* snooty, uppity.
–OPPOSITES modest.

pond ▸ noun =pool, waterhole; *Scottish* lochan; *N. Amer.* pothole; *Austral./NZ* tank.

ponder ▸ verb =think about, contemplate, consider, review, reflect on, mull over, meditate on, muse on, deliberate about, cogitate on, dwell on, brood on, ruminate on, chew over, turn over in one's mind.

ponderous ▸ adjective 1 *a ponderous procession* =slow, awkward, lumbering, cumbersome, ungainly, graceless. 2 *a ponderous speech* =laboured, laborious, lifeless, plodding, pedestrian, boring, dull, tedious, monotonous.
–OPPOSITES light, lively.

pontificate ▸ verb =hold forth, expound, declaim, preach, lay down the law, sound off, lecture; *informal* mouth off.

pooh-pooh ▸ verb *(informal)* =dismiss, reject, wave aside, disregard, discount; play down, make light of, belittle, deride, sneer at; *Austral./NZ informal* wipe.

pool[1] ▶ noun **1** *pools of water* =**puddle**, pond. **2** *the hotel has a pool* =**swimming pool**, baths, lido; *Brit.* swimming bath(s); *N. Amer.* natatorium.

pool[2] ▶ noun **1** *a pool of skilled labour* =**supply**, reserve(s), reservoir, fund; store, bank, stock, cache. **2** *a pool of money for emergencies* =**fund**, reserve, kitty, pot, bank, purse.
▶ verb *they pooled their skills* =**combine**, group, join, unite, merge; share.

poor ▶ adjective **1** *a poor family* =**poverty-stricken**, penniless, impoverished, impecunious, needy, destitute, unable to make ends meet; insolvent; *Brit.* on the breadline, without a penny (to one's name); *informal* (flat) broke, hard up, cleaned out, strapped, on one's uppers, without two pennies to rub together; *Brit. informal* skint. **2** *poor workmanship* =**substandard**, bad, deficient, defective, faulty, imperfect, inferior; unsatisfactory, second-rate, third-rate, shoddy, crude, inadequate, unacceptable; *informal* crummy, rubbishy, rotten, tenth-rate; *Brit. informal* ropy, duff, rubbish, dodgy. **3** *a poor crop* =**meagre**, scanty, scant, paltry, disappointing, limited, reduced, modest, sparse, spare, deficient, insubstantial, skimpy, small, lean, slender; *informal* measly, stingy, pathetic, piddling. **4** *the poor thing* =**unfortunate**, unlucky, unhappy, hapless, pitiful, wretched.
–OPPOSITES rich, superior, good, lucky.

poorly ▶ adverb *the text is poorly written* =**badly**, imperfectly, incompetently; crudely, shoddily, inadequately.
▶ adjective *she felt poorly* =**ill**, unwell, not (very) well, ailing, indisposed, out of sorts, under/below par, peaky; sick, queasy, nauseous; *Brit.* off colour; *informal* under the weather, funny, peculiar, rough; *Brit. informal* ropy, grotty; *Scottish informal* wabbit; *Austral./NZ informal* crook.

pop ▶ verb **1** *champagne corks popped* =**go bang**, go off; crack, snap, burst, explode. **2** *I'm just popping home* =**go**, visit; *informal* tootle, whip; *Brit. informal* nip. **3** *pop a bag over the pot* =**put**, place, slip, throw, slide, stick, set, lay, position, arrange.
▶ noun *the balloons burst with a pop* =**bang**, crack, snap; explosion, report.
■ **pop up** =**appear (suddenly)**, occur (suddenly), arrive, materialize, come along, happen, emerge, arise, crop up, turn up, present itself, come to light;

informal show up.

pope ▶ noun =**pontiff**, Bishop of Rome, Holy Father, Vicar of Christ, His Holiness.

> **WORD LINKS**
>
> *relating to a pope:* **papal, pontifical**
> *position of pope:* **papacy**

populace ▶ noun =**population**, inhabitants, residents, natives; community, country, (general) public, people, nation; common people, man/woman in the street, masses, multitude, rank and file; *Brit. informal* Joe Public; *derogatory* the hoi polloi, common herd, rabble, riff-raff.

popular ▶ adjective **1** *the restaurant is very popular* =**well liked**, sought-after, in demand; commercial, marketable, fashionable, in vogue, all the rage, hot; *informal* in, cool, big. **2** *popular science* =**nonspecialist**, non-technical, amateur, lay person's, general, middle-of-the-road; accessible, simplified, plain, simple, easy, straightforward, understandable; mass-market, middlebrow, lowbrow. **3** *popular opinion* =**widespread**, general, common, current, prevailing, standard; ordinary, conventional. **4** *a popular movement for independence* =**mass**, general, communal, collective, social, group, civil, public.
–OPPOSITES highbrow.

popularize ▶ verb **1** *tobacco was popularized by Sir Walter Raleigh* =**make popular**, make fashionable; market, publicize; *informal* hype. **2** *he popularized physics* =**simplify**, make accessible, demystify.

popularly ▶ adverb **1** *old age is popularly associated with illness* =**widely**, generally, commonly, usually, habitually, conventionally, traditionally. **2** *the rock was popularly known as 'Arthur's Seat'* =**informally**, unofficially.

populate ▶ verb **1** *the island is populated by goats* =**inhabit**, occupy, people; live in/on. **2** *an attempt to populate the island* =**settle**, colonize, people, occupy.

population ▶ noun =**inhabitants**, residents, people, citizens, citizenry, public, community, populace, society, natives, occupants; *formal* denizens.

populous ▶ adjective =**densely populated**, congested, crowded, packed, teeming.
–OPPOSITES deserted.

porch ▶ noun =**vestibule**, foyer,

entrance (hall), entry, lobby; *N. Amer.* ramada, stoop.

pore ■ pore over =**study**, read intently, peruse, scrutinize, scan, examine, go over.

pornographic ▶ adjective =**obscene**, indecent, lewd, dirty, smutty, filthy; erotic, titillating, arousing, suggestive, sexy, risqué; off colour, X-rated, hardcore, soft-core; *informal* porno, blue; *euphemistic* adult.

pornography ▶ noun =**erotica**, pornographic material, dirty books/videos; smut, filth; *informal* (hard/soft) porn, girlie magazines, skin flicks.

porous ▶ adjective =**permeable**, penetrable; absorbent, spongy.
–OPPOSITES impermeable.

porpoise ▶ noun

WORD LINKS

collective noun: **pod, school**

port[1] ▶ noun **1** *the port of Kiel* =**seaport**. **2** *shells exploded down by the port* =**harbour**, dock(s), marina.

port[2] ▶ noun *the exhaust port* =**aperture**, opening, outlet, inlet, vent, duct.

portable ▶ adjective =**transportable**, movable, mobile; lightweight, compact, handy, convenient.

portal ▶ noun =**doorway**, gateway, entrance, exit, opening; door, gate; *N. Amer.* entryway.

portend ▶ verb =**presage**, augur, foreshadow, foretell, prophesy; be a sign, warn, be an omen, indicate, herald, signal, bode, promise, threaten, signify, spell, denote; *literary* betoken.

portent ▶ noun =**omen**, sign, signal, token, warning, foreshadowing, prediction, prophesy, harbinger, augury, auspice, presage; writing on the wall, indication, hint; *literary* foretoken.

portentous ▶ adjective =**pompous**, bombastic, self-important, solemn, sonorous, grandiloquent.

porter[1] ▶ noun *a porter helped with the bags* =**carrier**, bearer; *N. Amer.* redcap, skycap.

porter[2] ▶ noun *(Brit.) the college porter* =**doorman**, doorkeeper, commissionaire, gatekeeper.

portion ▶ noun **1** *the upper portion of the chimney* =**part**, piece, bit, section, segment. **2** *her portion of the allowance*

=**share**, slice, quota, part, percentage, amount, quantity, fraction, division, allocation, tranche, measure; *informal* cut, rake-off; *Brit. informal* whack. **3** *a portion of cake* =**helping**, serving; slice, piece, chunk, wedge, slab, hunk; *Brit. informal* wodge.

▶ verb *she portioned out the food* =**share out**; distribute, hand out, deal out, dole out, give out, dispense.

portly ▶ adjective =**stout**, plump, fat, overweight, heavy, corpulent, fleshy, pot-bellied, well padded, rotund, stocky, bulky; *informal* tubby, roly-poly, beefy, porky; *Brit. informal* podgy; *N. Amer. informal* corn-fed.
–OPPOSITES slim.

portrait ▶ noun **1** *a portrait of the King* =**picture**, likeness; painting, drawing, photograph; image. **2** *a vivid portrait of Italy* =**description**, portrayal, representation, depiction, impression, account.

portray ▶ verb **1** *he always portrays Windermere in sunny weather* =**paint**, draw, sketch, picture, depict, represent, illustrate, render, show. **2** *the man portrayed by Waugh* =**describe**, depict, characterize, represent. **3** *he portrays her as a doormat* =**represent**, depict, characterize, describe, present. **4** *the actor portrays a spy* =**play**, act the part of, take the role of, represent, appear as.

portrayal ▶ noun **1** *her portrayal of adolescence* =**description**, representation, characterization, depiction, evocation. **2** *Brando's portrayal of Corleone* =**performance as**, representation, interpretation, rendering.

pose ▶ verb **1** *pollution poses a threat to health* =**constitute**, present, offer, be. **2** *the question posed earlier* =**raise**, ask, put, submit, advance, propose, suggest, moot. **3** *the guys posing at the bar* =**posture**, attitudinize, put on airs; *informal* show off, ponce about/up and down.
▶ noun **1** *a sexy pose* =**posture**, position, stance, attitude. **2** *her pose of aggrieved innocence* =**act**, affectation, show, display, posture, expression.
■ **pose as** =**pretend to be**, impersonate, pass oneself off as, masquerade as.

poser[1] ▶ noun *this situation's a bit of a poser* =**difficult question**, problem, tough one, puzzle, mystery, riddle; *informal* dilemma, toughie.

poser[2] ▶ noun *he's such a poser* =**exhibitionist**, poseur, poseuse; *informal* show-off, pseud.

poseur ▸ noun. *See* POSEUR².

posh ▸ adjective **1** *(informal) a posh hotel* =**smart**, stylish, fancy, high-class, fashionable, chic, luxurious, luxury, de luxe, exclusive; *Brit.* upmarket; *informal* classy, swanky, snazzy, plush, ritzy, flash; *Brit. informal* swish; *N. Amer. informal* swank, tony. **2** *(Brit. informal) a posh accent* =**upper-class**, aristocratic; *Brit. informal* plummy, Sloaney.

posit ▸ verb =**postulate**, put forward, advance, propound, submit, propose, assert.

position ▸ noun **1** *the aircraft's position* =**location**, place, situation, spot, site, locality, setting, area; whereabouts, bearings, orientation. **2** *a standing position* =**posture**, stance, attitude, pose. **3** *our financial position* =**situation**, state, condition, circumstances; predicament, plight. **4** *their position in society* =**status**, place, level, rank, standing; stature, prestige, reputation, importance. **5** *a secretarial position* =**job**, post, situation, appointment; opening, vacancy, placement. **6** *the government's position on the matter* =**viewpoint**, opinion, outlook, attitude, stand, standpoint, stance, perspective, thinking, policy, feelings.
▸ verb *he positioned a chair between them* =**put**, place, locate, situate, set, site, stand, station; plant, stick, install; arrange; *informal* plonk, park.

positive ▸ adjective **1** *a positive response* =**affirmative**, favourable, good, enthusiastic, supportive, encouraging. **2** *say something positive* =**constructive**, useful, productive, helpful, worthwhile, beneficial. **3** *she seems a lot more positive* =**optimistic**, hopeful, confident, cheerful, sanguine, buoyant; *informal* upbeat. **4** *positive economic signs* =**favourable**, good, promising, encouraging, heartening, propitious, auspicious. **5** *positive proof* =**definite**, certain, reliable, concrete, tangible, clear-cut, explicit, firm, decisive, real, actual. **6** *I'm positive he's coming back* =**certain**, sure, convinced, confident, satisfied.
−OPPOSITES negative, pessimistic, doubtful, unsure.

positively ▸ adverb **1** *I could not positively identify the voice* =**confidently**, definitely, with certainty, conclusively. **2** *he was positively livid* =**absolutely**, downright; virtually; *informal* plain.

possess ▸ verb **1** *the only hat she possessed* =**own**, have (to one's name). **2** *he did not possess a sense of humour* =**have**, be blessed with, be endowed with; enjoy, boast. **3** *an evil force possessed him* =**take control of**, take over; bewitch, enchant, enslave.

possessed ▸ adjective =**mad**, demented, insane, crazed, berserk; bewitched, enchanted, under a spell.

possession ▸ noun **1** *the estate came into their possession* =**ownership**, control, hands, keeping, care, custody, charge. **2** *she packed her possessions* =**belongings**, things, property, (worldly) goods, (personal) effects, assets, valuables; stuff, bits and pieces; luggage, baggage; *informal* gear, junk; *Brit. informal* clobber.

possessive ▸ adjective =**proprietorial**, overprotective, controlling, dominating, jealous, clingy.

possibility ▸ noun **1** *a possibility that he might be alive* =**chance**, likelihood, probability, hope; risk, hazard, danger, fear. **2** *buying a smaller house is one possibility* =**option**, alternative, choice, course of action, solution. **3** *the idea has distinct possibilities* =**potential**, promise, prospects.

possible ▸ adjective **1** *it's not possible to check the figures* =**feasible**, practicable, viable, attainable, achievable, workable; *informal* on, doable. **2** *a possible reason for his disappearance* =**likely**, plausible, imaginable, believable; potential, probable, credible. **3** *a possible future leader* =**potential**, prospective, likely, probable.
−OPPOSITES unlikely.

possibly ▸ adverb **1** *possibly he took her with him* =**perhaps**, maybe, it is possible. **2** *you can't possibly refuse* =**conceivably**, under any circumstances, by any means. **3** *could you possibly help me?* =**please**, kindly, be so good as to.

post¹ ▸ noun *wooden posts* =**pole**, stake, upright, shaft, prop, support, picket, strut, pillar.
▸ verb **1** *the notice posted on the wall* =**affix**, attach, fasten, display, pin (up), put up, stick (up). **2** *the group posted a net profit* =**announce**, report, make known, publish.

post² ▸ noun *(Brit.)* **1** *the winners will be notified by post* =**mail**; *informal* snail mail. **2** *did we get any post?* =**letters**, correspondence, mail.

▶ verb *(Brit.) post the order form today* =send (off), mail, put in the post/mail, get off.
■ **keep someone posted** =keep informed, keep up to date, keep in the picture.

post³ ▶ noun **1** *there were seventy candidates for the post* =job, position, appointment, situation, place; vacancy, opening; *Austral. informal* grip. **2** *back to your posts* =(assigned) position, station.
▶ verb **1** *he'd been posted to Berlin* =send, assign, dispatch. **2** *armed guards were posted* =put on duty, mount, station.

poster ▶ noun =notice, placard, bill, sign, advertisement, playbill; *Brit.* flyposter.

posterior ▶ adjective *the posterior part of the skull* =rear, hind, back.
–OPPOSITES anterior.
▶ noun *(humorous) her soft, plump posterior. See* BOTTOM noun *sense 6.*

posterity ▶ noun =future generations, the future.

post-haste ▶ adverb =as quickly as possible, without delay, without further/more ado, with all speed, promptly, immediately, at once, straight away, right away; *informal* pronto, straight off.

postman, postwoman ▶ noun =N. Amer. mailman; *Brit. informal* postie.

post-mortem ▶ noun **1** *the hospital carried out a post-mortem* =autopsy, PM, necropsy. **2** *a post-mortem of the interview* =analysis, evaluation, assessment, examination, review; debriefing.

postpone ▶ verb =put off/back, delay, defer, reschedule, adjourn, shelve; *N. Amer.* put over, take a rain check on; *informal* put on ice, put on the back burner.
–OPPOSITES bring forward.

postponement ▶ noun =deferral, deferment, delay, putting off/back, rescheduling, adjournment, shelving.

postulate ▶ verb =put forward, suggest, advance, posit, hypothesize, propose.

posture ▶ noun **1** *a kneeling posture* =position, pose, attitude, stance. **2** *good posture* =bearing, carriage, stance, comportment; *Brit.* deportment. **3** *trade unions adopted a militant posture* =attitude, stance, standpoint, point of view, opinion, position.
▶ verb *Keith postured, flexing his biceps* =pose, strike an attitude, strut.

posy ▶ noun =bouquet, bunch (of flowers), spray, nosegay, corsage; buttonhole.

pot ▶ noun **1** *a pot of soup* =pan, saucepan, casserole. **2** *Neolithic pots* =vessel; bowl, cooking pot; earthenware, pottery. **3** *Jim raked in half the pot* =bank, kitty, pool, purse, jackpot.
■ **go to pot** *(informal)* =deteriorate, decline, degenerate, go to (rack and) ruin, go downhill, go to seed; *informal* go to the dogs, go down the tubes; *Austral./NZ informal* go to the pack.

pot-bellied ▶ adjective =portly, rotund; *informal* tubby, roly-poly.

pot belly ▶ noun =paunch, (beer) belly; *informal* beer gut, pot, tummy.

potency ▶ noun **1** *the potency of his words* =forcefulness, force, effectiveness, persuasiveness, cogency, authoritativeness, authority, power, powerfulness. **2** *the potency of the drugs* =strength, powerfulness, power, effectiveness; *formal* efficacy.

potent ▶ adjective **1** *a potent political force* =powerful, strong, mighty, formidable, influential, dominant. **2** *a potent argument* =forceful, convincing, cogent, compelling, persuasive, powerful, strong. **3** *a potent drug* =strong, powerful, effective; *formal* efficacious.
–OPPOSITES weak.

potential ▶ adjective =possible, likely, prospective, future, probable.
▶ noun =possibilities, potentiality, prospects; promise, capability, capacity.

potion ▶ noun =concoction, mixture, brew, elixir, drink; medicine, tonic; *literary* draught.

pot-pourri ▶ noun =mixture, assortment, collection, selection, assemblage, medley, miscellany, mix, variety, mixed bag, patchwork; ragbag, hotchpotch, mishmash, jumble; *N. Amer.* hodgepodge.

potter ▶ verb =amble, wander, meander, stroll, saunter; *informal* mosey, tootle, toddle; *N. Amer. informal* putter.

pottery ▶ noun =ceramics, crockery, earthenware, terracotta, stoneware, china.

> **WORD LINKS**
>
> *relating to pottery:* **ceramic**

potty ▶ adjective *(Brit. informal)* **1** *I'm going potty. See* CRAZY *sense 1.* **2** *she's potty about you. See* CRAZY *sense 3.*

pouch ▶ noun =**bag**, purse, sack, sac, pocket; *Scottish* sporran.

pounce ▶ verb =**jump**, spring, leap, dive, lunge, attack.

pound[1] ▶ verb **1** *the two men pounded him with their fists* =**beat**, strike, hit, batter, thump, pummel, punch, rain blows on, belabour, hammer, set on, tear into; *informal* bash, clobber, wallop, beat the living daylights out of, whack, thwack, lay into; *N. Amer. informal* light into, whale. **2** *waves pounded the seafront* =**beat against**, crash against, batter, dash against, lash, buffet. **3** *gunships pounded the capital* =**bombard**, bomb, shell. **4** *pound the garlic to a paste* =**crush**, grind, pulverize, mash, pulp. **5** *I heard him pounding along the gangway* =**stomp**, lumber, clomp, clump, tramp. **6** *her heart was pounding* =**throb**, thump, thud, hammer, pulse, race, go pit-a-pat.

pound[2] ▶ noun *ten pounds* pound sterling, £; *Brit. informal* quid, smacker, nicker.

pound[3] ▶ noun *a dog pound* =**enclosure**, compound, pen, yard.

pour ▶ verb **1** *blood was pouring from his nose* =**stream**, flow, run, gush, course, jet, spurt, surge, spill. **2** *Amy poured wine into his glass* =**tip**, splash, spill, decant; *informal* slosh, slop. **3** *it was pouring* =**rain heavily/hard**, teem down, pelt down, tip down, come down in torrents/sheets, rain cats and dogs; *informal* be chucking it down; *Brit. informal* bucket down; *N. Amer. informal* rain pitchforks. **4** *people poured off the train* =**throng**, crowd, swarm, stream, flood.

poverty ▶ noun **1** *abject poverty* =**penury**, destitution, indigence, penniless-ness, impoverishment, neediness, hardship, impecuniousness. **2** *the poverty of choice* =**scarcity**, deficiency, dearth, shortage, paucity, absence, lack. **3** *the poverty of her imagination* =**inferiority**, mediocrity, poorness, sterility.
–OPPOSITES wealth, abundance.

> **WORD LINKS**
> *fear of poverty:* **peniaphobia**

poverty-stricken ▶ adjective =**(extremely) poor**, impoverished, destitute, penniless, in penury, impecunious, indigent, needy, in need/want; *Brit.* on the breadline, without a penny (to one's name); *informal* on one's uppers, without two pennies/farthings to rub together.
–OPPOSITES wealthy.

powder ▶ noun =**dust**; *historical* pounce. ▶ verb *the grains are powdered* =**crush**, grind, pulverize, pound, mill.

powdered ▶ adjective =**dried**, freeze-dried.

powdery ▶ adjective =**fine**, dry, fine-grained, powder-like, dusty, chalky, floury, sandy, crumbly, friable.

power ▶ noun **1** *the power of speech* =**ability**, capacity, capability, potential, faculty. **2** *the union has enormous power* =**control**, authority, influence, dominance, mastery, domination, dominion, sway, weight, leverage; *informal* clout, teeth; *N. Amer. informal* drag. **3** *the power to stop and search* =**authority**, right, authorization. **4** *a major European power* =**state**, country, nation. **5** *he hit the ball with as much power as he could* =**strength**, powerfulness, might, force, forcefulness, vigour, energy; *Brit. informal* welly. **6** *the power of his arguments* =**forcefulness**, powerfulness, potency, strength, force, cogency, persuasiveness. **7** *the new engine has more power* =**(driving) force**, horsepower, hp, acceleration, torque; *informal* oomph, poke. **8** *generating power from waste* =**energy**, electricity.
–OPPOSITES inability, weakness.

■ **have someone in/under one's power** =**have control over**, have influence over, have under one's thumb, have at one's mercy, have in one's clutches, have in the palm of one's hand; *N. Amer.* have in one's hip pocket; *informal* have over a barrel.

■ **the powers that be** =**the authorities**, the people in charge, the government.

> **WORD LINKS**
> *obsession with power:* **megalomania**

powerful ▶ adjective **1** *powerful shoulders* =**strong**, muscular, muscly, sturdy, strapping, robust, brawny, burly, athletic, manly, well built, solid; *informal* beefy, hunky; *dated* stalwart. **2** *a powerful drink* =**intoxicating**, hard, strong, stiff. **3** *a powerful blow* =**violent**, forceful, hard, mighty. **4** *he felt a powerful urge to kiss her* =**intense**, keen, fierce, strong, irresistible, overpowering, overwhelming. **5** *a powerful nation* =**influential**, strong, important, dominant, commanding, formidable. **6** *a powerful critique* =**cogent**, compelling, convincing, persuasive, forceful.

–OPPOSITES weak, gentle.

powerless ▸ adjective =**impotent**, helpless, ineffectual, ineffective, useless, defenceless, vulnerable.

practicable ▸ adjective =**realistic**, feasible, possible, within the bounds/realms of possibility, viable, reasonable, sensible, workable, achievable; *informal* doable.

practical ▸ adjective **1** *practical experience* =**empirical**, hands-on, actual, experiential. **2** *there are no practical alternatives* =**feasible**, practicable, realistic, viable, workable, possible, reasonable, sensible; *informal* doable. **3** *practical clothes* =**functional**, sensible, utilitarian. **4** *try to be more practical* =**realistic**, sensible, down-to-earth, businesslike, commonsensical, hard-headed, no-nonsense; *informal* hard-nosed. **5** *a practical certainty* =**virtual**, effective, near.
–OPPOSITES theoretical.

practicality ▸ noun **1** *the practicality of the proposal* =**feasibility**, practicability, viability, workability. **2** *practicality of design* =**functionalism**, functionality, serviceability, utility. **3** *his calm practicality* =(**common**) **sense**, realism, pragmatism. **4** *the practicalities of army life* =**practical details**; *informal* nitty gritty, nuts and bolts.

practical joke ▸ noun =**trick**, joke, prank, jape, hoax; *informal* leg-pull.

practically ▸ adverb **1** *the cinema was practically empty* =**almost**, (very) nearly, virtually, just about, all but, more or less, as good as, to all intents and purposes, verging on, bordering on; *informal* pretty nearly, pretty well; *literary* well-nigh. **2** *'You can't afford it,' he pointed out practically* =**realistically**, sensibly, reasonably.

practice ▸ noun **1** *the practice of radiotherapy* =**application**, exercise, use, operation, implementation, execution. **2** *common practice* =**custom**, procedure, policy, convention, tradition; *formal* praxis. **3** *it takes lots of practice | the team's final practice* =**training**, rehearsal, repetition, preparation, dummy run, runthrough; *informal* dry run. **4** *the practice of medicine* =**profession**, career, business, work. **5** *a small legal practice* =**business**, firm, office, company; *informal* outfit.
■ **in practice** =**in reality**, realistically, practically.
■ **out of practice** =**rusty**, unpractised.

■ **put something into practice** =**use**, make use of, put to use, utilize, apply.

practise ▸ verb **1** *he practised the songs every day* =**rehearse**, run through, go over/through, work on/at; polish, perfect. **2** *the performers were practising* =**train**, rehearse, prepare, go through one's paces. **3** *we still practise these rituals today* =**carry out**, perform, observe. **4** *she practises medicine* =**work at/in**, pursue a career in.

practised ▸ adjective =**expert**, experienced, seasoned, skilled, skilful, accomplished, proficient, talented, able, adept.

pragmatic ▸ adjective =**practical**, matter of fact, sensible, down-to-earth, commonsensical, businesslike, having both/one's feet on the ground, hard-headed, no-nonsense; *informal* hard-nosed.
–OPPOSITES impractical.

praise ▸ verb =**commend**, applaud, pay tribute to, speak highly of, compliment, congratulate, sing the praises of, rave about, go into raptures about, heap praise on, wax lyrical about, make much of, pat on the back, take one's hat off to, hail, eulogize; *N. Amer. informal* ballyhoo.
–OPPOSITES criticize.
▸ noun =**approval**, acclaim, admiration, approbation, plaudits, congratulations, commendation; tribute, accolade, compliment, a pat on the back, eulogy.

> **WORD LINKS**
> *expressing praise:* **laudatory**

praiseworthy ▸ adjective =**commendable**, admirable, laudable, worthy (of admiration), meritorious, estimable.

prance ▸ verb =**cavort**, dance, jig, trip, caper, jump, leap, spring, bound, skip, hop, frisk, romp, frolic.

prank ▸ noun =(**practical**) **joke**, trick, escapade, stunt, caper, jape, game, hoax; *informal* lark, leg-pull.

prattle ▸ verb. *See* CHAT verb.
▸ noun. *See* CHATTER noun.

preach ▸ verb **1** *he preached to a large congregation* =**give a sermon**, sermonize, address, speak. **2** *preaching the gospel* =**proclaim**, teach, spread, propagate, expound. **3** *they preach toleration* =**advocate**, recommend, advise, urge, teach, counsel. **4** *who are you to preach?* =**moralize**, sermonize, pontificate, lecture, harangue; *informal* preachify.

WORD LINKS

relating to preaching: **homiletic**
art of preaching: **homiletics**

preamble ▶ noun =**introduction**, preface, prologue; foreword, prelude; *informal* intro.

prearranged ▶ adjective =**arranged beforehand**, agreed in advance, predetermined, pre-established, pre-planned.

precarious ▶ adjective =**uncertain**, insecure, unpredictable, risky, parlous, hazardous, dangerous, unsafe; unsettled, unstable, unsteady, shaky; *informal* dicey, chancy, iffy; *Brit. informal* dodgy. –OPPOSITES safe.

precaution ▶ noun =**safeguard**, preventative/preventive measure, safety measure, insurance; *informal* backstop.

precautionary ▶ adjective =**preventative**, preventive, safety.

precede ▶ verb **1** *adverts preceded the film* =**go/come before**, lead (up) to, pave/prepare the way for, herald, introduce, usher in. **2** *Catherine preceded him into the studio* =**go ahead of**, go in front of, go before, go first, lead the way. –OPPOSITES follow.

precedence ■ **take precedence over** =**take priority over**, outweigh, prevail over, come before.

precedent ▶ noun =**model**, exemplar, example, pattern; paradigm, criterion, yardstick, standard.

preceding ▶ adjective =**foregoing**, previous, prior, former, earlier, above, aforementioned; *formal* anterior.

precinct ▶ noun **1** *a pedestrian precinct* =**area**, zone, sector. **2** *within the precincts of the City* =**bounds**, boundaries, limits, confines. **3** *the cathedral precinct* =**enclosure**, close, court.

precious ▶ adjective **1** *precious works of art* =**valuable**, costly, expensive; invaluable, priceless. **2** *her most precious possession* =**valued**, cherished, treasured, prized, favourite, dear, dearest, beloved, special. **3** *his precious manners* =**affected**, pretentious; *informal* la-di-da; *Brit. informal* poncey.

precipice ▶ noun =**cliff (face)**, rock face, sheer drop, crag, bluff, escarpment.

precipitate ▶ verb **1** *the incident precipitated a crisis* =**bring about/on**, cause, lead to, give rise to, instigate, trigger, spark, touch off, provoke. **2** *they were precipitated down the mountain* =**hurl**, catapult, throw, plunge, launch, fling, propel.
▶ adjective **1** *their actions were precipitate* =**hasty**, overhasty, rash, hurried, rushed; impetuous, impulsive, precipitous, incautious, imprudent, injudicious, ill-advised, reckless. **2** *a precipitate decline.* See PRECIPITOUS sense 2.

precipitous ▶ adjective **1** *a precipitous drop* =**steep**, sheer, perpendicular, abrupt, sharp, vertical. **2** *his precipitous fall from power* =**sudden**, rapid, swift, abrupt, headlong, speedy, quick, fast. **3** *he was too precipitous.* See PRECIPITATE adjective sense 1.

precis ▶ noun =**summary**, synopsis, résumé, abstract, outline, summarization, summation; abridgement, digest, overview, epitome; *N. Amer.* wrap-up.
▶ verb =**summarize**, sum up, give the main points of; abridge, condense, shorten, abstract, outline.

precise ▶ adjective **1** *precise measurements* =**exact**, accurate, correct, specific, detailed, explicit. **2** *at that precise moment* =**exact**, particular, very, specific. **3** *precise attention to detail* =**meticulous**, careful, exact, scrupulous, punctilious, conscientious, particular, methodical, strict, rigorous. –OPPOSITES inaccurate.

precisely ▶ adverb **1** *at 2 o'clock precisely* =**exactly**, sharp, on the dot; promptly, prompt, dead (on), on the stroke of …; *informal* bang (on); *Brit. informal* spot on; *N. Amer. informal* on the button/nose. **2** *precisely the man I am looking for* =**exactly**, just, in all respects; *informal* to a T. **3** *fertilization can be timed precisely* =**accurately**, exactly. **4** *'So you knew?' 'Precisely.'* =**yes**, exactly, absolutely, (that's) right, quite so.

precision ▶ noun =**exactness**, exactitude, accuracy, correctness, preciseness; care, carefulness, meticulousness, scrupulousness, punctiliousness, rigour, rigorousness.

preclude ▶ verb =**prevent**, make it impossible for, rule out, stop, prohibit, debar, bar, hinder, impede, inhibit, exclude.

preconceived ▶ adjective =**predetermined**, prejudged; prejudiced, biased.

preconception ▸ noun =precon-
ceived idea/notion, presupposition, assumption, presumption, prejudgement;
prejudice.

precondition ▸ noun =prerequisite,
(necessary/essential) condition, requirement, necessity, essential, imperative,
sine qua non; *informal* must.

precursor ▸ noun **1** *a precursor of the
guitar* =forerunner, predecessor, forefather, father, antecedent, ancestor,
forebear. **2** *a precursor of disasters to come*
=harbinger, herald, sign, indication,
portent, omen.

precursory ▸ adjective =preliminary,
prior, previous, introductory, preparatory, prefatory.

predatory ▸ adjective **1** *predatory birds*
=predacious, carnivorous, hunting; of
prey. **2** *his predatory appetites* =exploit-
ative, wolfish, rapacious, manipulative.

predecessor ▸ noun **1** *the Prime Minister's predecessor* =forerunner, precursor, antecedent. **2** *our Victorian predecessors* =ancestor, forefather, forebear,
antecedent.
–OPPOSITES successor, descendant.

predestined ▸ adjective =preor-
dained, ordained, predetermined, destined, fated.

predetermined ▸ adjective **1** *a predetermined location* =prearranged, established in advance, preset, agreed. **2** *our
predetermined fate* =predestined, preordained.

predicament ▸ noun =difficult situation, mess, difficulty, plight, quandary,
muddle; *informal* hole, fix, jam, pickle,
scrape, bind, tight spot/corner, dilemma.

predicate ▸ verb =base, be dependent, found, establish, rest, ground,
premise.

predict ▸ verb =forecast, foretell, foresee, prophesy, anticipate, tell in advance, envision, envisage.

predictable ▸ adjective =foreseeable,
(only) to be expected, anticipated, foreseen, unsurprising; *informal* inevitable.

prediction ▸ noun =forecast, prophecy, prognosis, prognostication; projection, conjecture, guess.

predilection ▸ noun =liking, fondness, preference, partiality, taste, penchant, weakness, soft spot, fancy, inclination, leaning, bias, propensity,

bent, proclivity, predisposition, appetite.
–OPPOSITES dislike.

predispose ▸ verb **1** *lack of exercise may
predispose you to obesity* =make susceptible, make liable, make prone, make
vulnerable, put at risk of. **2** *attitudes that
predispose people to behave badly* =lead, influence, induce, prompt, dispose.

predisposed ▸ adjective =inclined,
prepared, ready, of a mind, disposed,
minded, willing.

predisposition ▸ noun **1** *a predisposition to heart disease* =susceptibility,
proneness, tendency, liability, inclination, vulnerability. **2** *their political pre-
dispositions* =preference, predilection,
inclination, leaning.

predominance ▸ noun **1** *the predominance of women carers* =prevalence,
dominance, preponderance. **2** *military
predominance* =supremacy, mastery,
control, power, ascendancy, dominance, pre-eminence, superiority.

predominant ▸ adjective **1** *our predominant objectives* =main, chief, principal, most important, primary, prime,
central, leading, foremost, key, paramount; *informal* number-one. **2** *the predominant political forces* =controlling,
dominant, predominating, more/most
powerful, pre-eminent.
–OPPOSITES subsidiary.

predominantly ▸ adverb =mainly,
mostly, for the most part, chiefly, principally, primarily, in the main, on the
whole, largely, by and large, typically,
generally, usually.

predominate ▸ verb **1** *small-scale producers predominate* =be in the majority,
be predominant, prevail. **2** *private interest predominates over the public good* =pre-
vail; override, outweigh.

pre-eminence ▸ noun =superiority,
supremacy, greatness, excellence, distinction, prominence, predominance,
eminence, importance, prestige, stature, fame, renown.

pre-eminent ▸ adjective =greatest,
leading, foremost, best, finest, chief,
outstanding, excellent, distinguished,
prominent, eminent, important, top,
famous, renowned, celebrated, illustrious; *N. Amer.* marquee.
–OPPOSITES undistinguished.

pre-empt ▸ verb =forestall, prevent,
beat, anticipate.

preen ▶ verb **1** *the robin preened its feathers* =**clean**, tidy, groom, smooth, arrange. **2** *she preened before the mirror* =**admire oneself**, primp oneself, groom oneself, spruce oneself up; *informal* titivate oneself, doll oneself up; *Brit. informal* tart oneself up; *N. Amer. informal* gussy oneself up.

preface ▶ noun =**introduction**, foreword, preamble, prologue, prelude; front matter; *informal* prelims, intro.
▶ verb =**precede**, introduce, begin, open, start.

prefer ▶ verb **1** *I prefer white wine to red* =**like better**, would rather (have), would sooner (have), favour, be more partial to; choose, select, pick, opt for, go for, plump for. **2** *(formal) do you want to prefer charges?* =**bring**, press, file, lodge, lay.

preferable ▶ adjective =**better**, best, more desirable, more suitable, advantageous, superior, preferred, recommended.

preferably ▶ adverb =**ideally**, if possible.

preference ▶ noun **1** *her preference for gin* =**liking**, partiality, fondness, taste, inclination, leaning, bent, penchant, predisposition. **2** *preference was given to female applicants* =**priority**, favour, precedence, preferential treatment.
■ **in preference to** =**rather than**, instead of, in place of, sooner than.

preferential ▶ adjective =**special**, better, privileged, superior, favourable, partial, discriminatory, partisan, biased.

prefigure ▶ verb =**foreshadow**, presage, be a harbinger of, herald; *literary* foretoken.

pregnancy ▶ noun =**gestation**, maternity.

> **WORD LINKS**
>
> *relating to pregnancy:* **antenatal, prenatal, gestational**

pregnant ▶ adjective **1** *she is pregnant* =**expecting a baby**, expectant, carrying a child; *informal* expecting, in the family way, preggers, with a bun in the oven; *Brit. informal* up the duff, in the (pudding) club, up the spout; *N. Amer. informal* knocked up, having swallowed a watermelon seed; *Austral. informal* with a joey in the pouch; *archaic* with child. **2** *a pregnant pause* =**meaningful**, significant, suggestive, expressive, charged.

prehistoric ▶ adjective **1** *prehistoric times* =**primitive**, primeval, primordial, primal, ancient, early. **2** *the special effects look prehistoric* =**out of date**, outdated, outmoded, old-fashioned, passé, antiquated, archaic, behind the times, primitive, antediluvian; *informal* out of the ark; *N. Amer. informal* horse and buggy, clunky.
–OPPOSITES modern.

prejudice ▶ noun **1** *male prejudices about women* =**preconceived idea**, preconception. **2** *they are motivated by prejudice* =**bigotry**, bias, partisanship, partiality, intolerance, discrimination, unfairness, inequality.
▶ verb **1** *the article could prejudice the jury* =**bias**, influence, sway, predispose, make biased, make partial, colour. **2** *this could prejudice his chances* =**damage**, be detrimental to, be prejudicial to, injure, harm, hurt, spoil, impair, undermine, hinder, compromise.

prejudiced ▶ adjective =**biased**, bigoted, discriminatory, partisan, intolerant, narrow-minded, unfair, unjust, inequitable, coloured.
–OPPOSITES impartial.

prejudicial ▶ adjective =**detrimental**, damaging, injurious, harmful, disadvantageous, hurtful, deleterious.
–OPPOSITES beneficial.

preliminary ▶ adjective *the discussions are still at a preliminary stage* =**preparatory**, introductory, initial, opening; early, exploratory.
–OPPOSITES final.
▶ noun *he began without any preliminaries* =**introduction**, preamble, opening remarks, formalities.

prelude ▶ noun =**preliminary**, overture, opening, preparation, introduction, start, commencement, beginning, lead-in, precursor.

premature ▶ adjective **1** *his premature death* =**untimely**, (too) early, unseasonable. **2** *such a step would be premature* =**rash**, overhasty, hasty, precipitate, precipitous, impulsive, impetuous; *informal* previous.
–OPPOSITES overdue.

prematurely ▶ adverb *don't act prematurely* =**rashly**, overhastily, hastily, precipitately, precipitously.

premeditated ▶ adjective =**planned**, intentional, deliberate, pre-planned, calculated, cold-blooded, conscious,

prearranged.
–OPPOSITES spontaneous.

premeditation ▸ noun =(advance) **planning**, forethought, pre-planning, (criminal) intent; *Law* malice aforethought.

premier ▸ adjective =**leading**, foremost, chief, principal, head, top-ranking, top, prime, primary, first, highest, pre-eminent, senior, outstanding, master; *N. Amer.* ranking.
▸ noun =**head of government**, prime minister, PM, president, chancellor.

premiere ▸ noun =**first performance**, first night, opening night.

premise ▸ noun =**proposition**, assumption, hypothesis, thesis, presupposition, postulate, supposition, presumption, surmise, conjecture, speculation, assertion, belief.

premises ▸ plural noun =**building(s)**, property, site, office.

premium ▸ noun 1 *monthly premiums of £30* =(**regular**) **payment**, instalment. 2 *you must pay a premium for organic fruit* =**surcharge**, additional payment, extra amount.
■ **at a premium** =**scarce**, in great demand, hard to come by, in short supply, thin on the ground.
■ **put/place a premium on** =**value greatly**, attach great/special importance to, set great store by, put a high value on.

premonition ▸ noun =**foreboding**, presentiment, intuition, (funny) feeling, hunch, suspicion, feeling in one's bones.

preoccupation ▸ noun 1 *an air of preoccupation* =**pensiveness**, concentration, engrossment, absorption, self-absorption, thinking, deep thought, brooding; abstraction. 2 *their main preoccupation was food* =**obsession**, concern; passion, enthusiasm, hobby horse.

preoccupied ▸ adjective 1 *he's preoccupied with work* =**obsessed**, concerned, absorbed, engrossed, intent, involved, wrapped up. 2 *she looked preoccupied* =**lost/deep in thought**, pensive, distracted.

preoccupy ▸ verb =**engross**, concern, absorb, take up someone's attention, distract, obsess, occupy, prey on someone's mind.

preordain ▸ verb =**predestine**, destine, ordain, fate, predetermine.

preparation ▸ noun 1 *the preparation of a plan* =**devising**, putting together, drawing up, construction, composition, production, getting ready, development. 2 *preparations for the party* =**arrangements**, planning, plans. 3 *a preparation to kill mites* =**mixture**, compound, concoction, solution, medicine, potion, cream, ointment, lotion.

preparatory ▸ adjective =**preliminary**, initial, introductory, opening, precursory.

prepare ▸ verb 1 *I will prepare a report* =**make/get ready**, put together, draw up, produce, arrange, assemble, construct, compose, formulate. 2 *the meal is easy to prepare* =**cook**, make, get, put together, concoct; *informal* fix, rustle up; *Brit. informal* knock up. 3 *preparing for war* =**get ready**, make preparations, arrange things, make provision, get everything set. 4 *athletes preparing for the Olympics* =**train**, get into shape, practise, get ready. 5 *I must prepare for my exams* =**study**, revise; *Brit. informal* swot. 6 *prepare yourself for a shock* =**brace**, make ready, tense, steel, steady.

prepared ▸ adjective 1 *prepared for action* =**ready**, (all) set, equipped, primed; waiting, poised. 2 *I'm prepared to negotiate* =**willing**, ready, disposed, (favourably) inclined, of a mind, minded.

preponderance ▸ noun 1 *the preponderance of women among older people* =**prevalence**, predominance, dominance. 2 *the preponderance of the evidence* =**bulk**, majority, greater quantity, larger part, best/better part, most.

prepossessing ▸ adjective =**attractive**, beautiful, pretty, handsome, good-looking, fetching, charming.
–OPPOSITES ugly.

preposterous ▸ adjective =**absurd**, ridiculous, foolish, stupid, ludicrous, farcical, laughable, comical, risible, nonsensical, senseless, insane; outrageous, monstrous; *informal* crazy.
–OPPOSITES sensible.

prerequisite ▸ noun =(**necessary**) **condition**, precondition, essential, requirement, requisite, necessity, sine qua non; *informal* must.
▸ adjective =**necessary**, required, called for, essential, requisite, obligatory, compulsory.
–OPPOSITES unnecessary.

prerogative ▶ noun =**entitlement**, right, privilege, advantage, due, birthright.

prescience ▶ noun =**far-sightedness**, foresight, foreknowledge; insight, intuition, perception.

prescient ▶ adjective =**prophetic**, predictive, visionary; far-sighted; insightful, intuitive, perceptive.

prescribe ▶ verb 1 *traditional values prescribe a life of domesticity* =**advise**, recommend, advocate, suggest, endorse, champion, promote. 2 *rules prescribing your duty* =**stipulate**, lay down, dictate, specify, determine.

prescriptive ▶ adjective =**dictatorial**, narrow, rigid, authoritarian, arbitrary, repressive, dogmatic.

presence ▶ noun 1 *the presence of an intruder* =**existence**. 2 *I requested the presence of a lawyer* =**attendance**, appearance. 3 *a woman of great presence* =**aura**, charisma, (strength/force of) personality.
–OPPOSITES absence.
■ **presence of mind** =**composure**, equanimity, self-possession, level-headedness, self-assurance, calmness, sangfroid, imperturbability; alertness, quick-wittedness; *informal* cool, unflappability.

present¹ ▶ adjective 1 *a doctor must be present* =**in attendance**, here, there, near, nearby, (close/near) at hand, available. 2 *organic compounds are present* =**in existence**; detectable, occurring, there, here. 3 *the present economic climate* =**current**, present-day, existing.
–OPPOSITES absent.
▶ noun *think about the present* =**now**, today, the present time/moment, the here and now.
–OPPOSITES past, future.
■ **at present** =**at the moment**, just now, right now, at the present time, currently, at this moment in time.
■ **for the present** =**for the time being**, for now, for the moment.
■ **the present day** =**modern times**, nowadays.

present² ▶ verb 1 *Eddy presented a cheque to the winner* =**hand over/out**, give (out), confer, bestow, award, grant, accord. 2 *the committee presented its report* =**submit**, set forth, put forward, offer, tender, table. 3 *may I present my wife?* =**introduce**, make known, acquaint someone with. 4 *I called to present my compliments* =**offer**, give, express. 5 *presenting good quality opera* =**stage**, put on, produce, perform. 6 *she presents a TV show* =**host**, introduce, compère; *N. Amer. informal* emcee. 7 *they present him as a criminal* =**represent**, describe, portray, depict.
■ **present oneself 1** *he presented himself at ten* =**be present**, make an appearance, appear, turn up, arrive. 2 *an opportunity that presented itself* =**occur**, arise, happen, come about/up, appear, crop up, turn up.

present³ ▶ noun *a birthday present* =**gift**, donation, offering, contribution; *informal* prezzie.

presentable ▶ adjective 1 *I'm making the place look presentable* =**tidy**, neat, straight, clean, spick and span, in good order, shipshape (and Bristol fashion). 2 *make yourself presentable* =**smart**, tidy, neat, decent.

presentation ▶ noun 1 *the presentation of his certificate* =**awarding**, presenting, giving, handing over/out, bestowal, granting. 2 *the presentation of food* =**appearance**, arrangement, packaging, layout. 3 *the presentation of new proposals* =**submission**, proffering, offering, tendering, advancing, proposal, suggestion, mooting, tabling. 4 *a sales presentation* =**demonstration**, talk, lecture, address, speech, show, exhibition, display, introduction, launch, launching, unveiling. 5 *a presentation of his latest play* =**staging**, production, performance, mounting, showing.

present-day ▶ adjective =**current**, present, contemporary, latter-day, present-time, modern, twenty-first-century.

presentiment ▶ noun =**premonition**, foreboding, intuition, (funny) feeling, hunch, feeling in one's bones, sixth sense.

presently ▶ adverb 1 *I shall see you presently* =**soon**, shortly, quite soon, in a short time, in a little while, at any moment/minute/second, before long; *N. Amer.* momentarily; *informal* pretty soon; *Brit. informal* in a mo. 2 *he is presently abroad* =**at present**, currently, at the/this moment.

preservation ▶ noun 1 *wood preservation* =**conservation**, protection, care. 2 *the preservation of the status quo* =**continuation**, conservation, maintenance, upholding, sustaining, perpetuation. **3** *the preservation of food* =**conserving**.

preserve ▶ verb *oil preserves the wood* =**conserve**, protect, maintain, care for, look after. **2** *the wish to preserve the status quo* =**continue (with)**, conserve, keep going, maintain, uphold, sustain, perpetuate. **3** *preserving him from harm* =**guard**, protect, keep, defend, safeguard, shelter, shield. **4** *spices enable us to preserve food* =**conserve**.

▶ noun **1** *strawberry preserve* =**jam**, jelly, marmalade, conserve. **2** *the preserve of the rich* =**domain**, area, field, sphere, orbit, realm, province, territory; *informal* turf, bailiwick. **3** *a game preserve* =**sanctuary**, (game) reserve, reservation.

preside ▶ verb *the chairman presides at the meeting* =**chair**, be chairman/chairwoman/chairperson, officiate (at), conduct, lead.

■ **preside over** =**be in charge of**, be responsible for, be at the head/helm of, head, be head of, manage, administer, be in control of, control, direct, lead, govern, rule, command, supervise, oversee; *informal* head up.

president ▶ noun **1** *terrorists assassinated the president* =**head of state**. **2** *the president of the society* =**head**, chief, director, leader, governor, principal, master; *N. Amer. informal* prexy. **3** *the president of the company* =**chairman**, chairwoman; managing director, MD, chief executive (officer), CEO.

press ▶ verb **1** *press the paper down firmly* =**push (down)**, press down, depress, hold down, force, thrust, squeeze, compress. **2** *his shirt was pressed* =**iron**. **3** *she pressed the child to her bosom* =**clasp**, hold close, hug, cuddle, squeeze, clutch, grasp, embrace. **4** *Winnie pressed his hand* =**squeeze**, grip, clutch. **5** *the crowd pressed round* =**cluster**, gather, converge, congregate, flock, swarm, throng, crowd. **6** *the government pressed its claim* =**plead**, urge, advance, present, submit, put forward. **7** *they pressed him to agree* =**urge**, put pressure on, pressurize, force, push, coerce, dragoon, steamroller, browbeat; *informal* lean on, put the screws on, twist someone's arm, railroad, bulldoze. **8** *they pressed for a ban* =**call**, ask, clamour, push, campaign, demand.

▶ noun **1** *a private press* =**publishing house**, printing company; printing press. **2** *the freedom of the press* =**the media**, the newspapers, the papers, the news media, the fourth estate; journalism, reporters; *Brit. dated* Fleet Street. **3** *the company had some bad press* =**(press) reports**, press coverage, press articles, press reviews.

■ **be pressed for** =**have too little**, be short of, have insufficient, lack, be lacking (in), be deficient in, need, be/stand in need of; *informal* be strapped for.

■ **press on** =**proceed**, keep going, continue, carry on, make progress, make headway, press ahead, forge on/ahead, push on, keep on, persevere, keep at it, stay with it, plod on, plough on; *informal* soldier on, plug away, stick at it.

pressing ▶ adjective **1** *a pressing problem* =**urgent**, critical, crucial, acute, desperate, serious, grave, life-and-death. **2** *a pressing engagement* =**important**, high-priority, critical, crucial, unavoidable.

pressure ▶ noun **1** *atmospheric pressure* =**force**, load, stress, thrust; compression, weight. **2** *they put pressure on us* =**duress**, coercion, force, compulsion; pestering, harassment, nagging, badgering, intimidation. **3** *she had a lot of pressure from work* =**strain**, stress, tension, trouble, difficulty; *informal* hassle.

▶ verb *they pressured him into resigning.* See PRESSURIZE.

> **WORD LINKS**
>
> *device for measuring atmospheric pressure:* **barometer**

pressurize ▶ verb *he pressurized us into selling* =**coerce**, pressure, push, persuade, force, bulldoze, hound, nag, badger, browbeat, bully, bludgeon, intimidate, dragoon, twist someone's arm; *informal* railroad, lean on; *N. Amer. informal* hustle.

prestige ▶ noun =**status**, standing, stature, prestigiousness, reputation, repute, note, renown, honour, esteem, importance, prominence, influence, eminence; kudos, cachet.

prestigious ▶ adjective **1** *prestigious journals* =**reputable**, distinguished, respected, esteemed, eminent, august, highly regarded, illustrious, leading, renowned. **2** *a prestigious job* =**impressive**, important, prominent, high-ranking, influential, powerful.

−OPPOSITES obscure, minor.

presumably ▶ adverb =**I presume**, I expect, I assume, I take it, I imagine, I dare say, I guess, doubtless, no doubt.

presume ▸ verb *I presume it was once an attic* =**assume**, suppose, imagine, take it, expect.

presumption ▸ noun **1** *this presumption may be easily rebutted* =**assumption**, supposition, presupposition, belief, judgement, hypothesis, inference, deduction, conclusion. **2** *he apologized for his presumption* =**brazenness**, audacity, boldness, temerity, arrogance, presumptuousness, forwardness; impudence, impertinence, effrontery.

presumptuous ▸ adjective =**brazen**, audacious, forward, familiar, impertinent, insolent, impudent, rude.

presuppose ▸ verb =**presume**, assume, take it for granted, take it as read, suppose, surmise, think, accept, consider.

presupposition ▸ noun =**presumption**, assumption, supposition.

pretence ▸ noun **1** *cease this pretence* =**make-believe**, acting, dissembling, faking, simulation, play-acting, posturing; deception, deceit, trickery, dishonesty, hypocrisy. **2** *he made a pretence of being concerned* =**(false) show**, semblance, affectation, (false) appearance, outward appearance, impression, (false) front, guise, facade, display.
−OPPOSITES honesty.

pretend ▸ verb **1** *they pretend to listen* =**make as if**, act like, affect; go through the motions, fake it. **2** *I'll pretend to be the dragon* =**make believe**, play at, act, impersonate.
▸ adjective *(informal)* =**mock**, fake, sham, simulated, artificial, ersatz, false, pseudo; *informal* phoney.

pretended ▸ adjective =**fake**, faked, affected, professed, spurious, mock, simulated, make-believe, pseudo, sham, false, bogus; *informal* pretend, phoney.

pretender ▸ noun =**claimant**, aspirant.

pretension ▸ noun =**pretentiousness**, affectation, artificiality, airs, posing, posturing, show, flashiness; pomposity.

pretentious ▸ adjective =**affected**, ostentatious, showy; pompous, overblown, high-sounding, flowery, grandiose; *informal* pseudo; *Brit. informal* poncey.

preternatural ▸ adjective =**extraordinary**, exceptional, unusual, uncommon, singular, unprecedented, remarkable, phenomenal, abnormal, inexplicable, unaccountable.

pretext ▸ noun =**(false) excuse**; guise, ploy, pretence, ruse.

prettify ▸ verb =**beautify**, titivate, smarten (up); *informal* doll up, do up, give something a facelift; *Brit. informal* tart up.

pretty ▸ adjective =**attractive**, good-looking, nice-looking, personable, fetching, prepossessing, appealing, charming, delightful, cute; *Scottish & N. English* bonny; *archaic* fair.
−OPPOSITES plain, ugly.
▸ adverb =**quite**, rather, somewhat, fairly.

prevail ▸ verb **1** *common sense will prevail* =**win (out/through)**, triumph, be victorious, carry the day, come out on top, succeed; rule, reign. **2** *the conditions that prevailed in the 1950s* =**exist**, be present, be the case, occur, be prevalent, be in force/effect; *formal* obtain.
■ **prevail on/upon** =**persuade**, induce, talk someone into, coax, convince, make, get, urge, coerce; *informal* sweet-talk, soft-soap.

prevailing ▸ adjective =**current**, existing, prevalent, usual, common, general, widespread.

prevalence ▸ noun =**commonness**, currency, widespread presence, popularity, pervasiveness, extensiveness.

prevalent ▸ adjective =**widespread**, frequent, usual, common, current, popular, general.
−OPPOSITES rare.

prevaricate ▸ verb =**be evasive**, beat about the bush, hedge, shilly-shally, equivocate; temporize, stall (for time); *Brit.* hum and haw.

prevent ▸ verb =**stop**, avert, nip in the bud; foil, thwart; prohibit, forbid.
−OPPOSITES allow.

preventive ▸ adjective **1** *preventive maintenance* =**pre-emptive**, precautionary, protective. **2** *preventive medicine* =**prophylactic**; proactive.
▸ noun *a preventive against crime* =**precautionary measure**, deterrent, safeguard, security, protection, defence.

previous ▸ adjective **1** *the previous five years | her previous boyfriend* =**foregoing**, preceding; old, earlier, prior, former, ex-, past, last, sometime, one-time, erstwhile. **2** *(informal) I was a bit previous* =**overhasty**, hasty, premature; *informal* ahead of oneself.

−OPPOSITES next.

■ **previous to** =before, prior to, until.

previously ▶ adverb =formerly, earlier (on), before, hitherto, at one time, in the past, in days/times gone by, in bygone days, in times past, in former times.

prey ▶ noun 1 *the lions killed their prey* =quarry. 2 *she was easy prey* =victim, target.

−OPPOSITES predator.

■ **prey on 1** *the larvae prey on aphids* =hunt, catch; eat, feed on, live on/off. **2** *they prey on the elderly* =exploit, victimize, pick on, take advantage of. **3** *the problem preyed on his mind* =oppress, weigh (heavily) on, gnaw at; trouble, worry, disturb, distress, haunt, nag, torment, plague, obsess.

price ▶ noun 1 *the purchase price* =cost, charge, fee, fare, amount, sum. 2 *the price of success* =consequence, result, cost, penalty, sacrifice; downside, drawback, disadvantage, minus.

■ **at a price** =at a high price/cost, at considerable cost; expensively.

■ **at any price** =whatever the price, at whatever cost.

■ **be priced at** =fix/set the price of, cost, value, rate; estimate.

■ **beyond price.** See PRICELESS sense 1.

priceless ▶ adjective *priceless works of art* =of incalculable value/worth, invaluable, beyond price; irreplaceable.

−OPPOSITES worthless, cheap.

pricey ▶ adjective *(informal)*. See EXPENSIVE.

prick ▶ verb 1 *prick the potatoes* =pierce, puncture, make holes in, stab, perforate, nick, jab. 2 *his conscience pricked him* =trouble, worry, distress, perturb, disturb. 3 *the horse pricked its ears* =raise, erect. 4 *its ears pricked up* =rise, stand up.

▶ noun 1 *a prick in the leg* =jab, sting, pinprick, stab.

■ **prick up one's ears** =listen carefully, pay attention, become attentive, begin to take notice, attend; *informal* be all ears.

prickle ▶ noun 1 *the cactus is covered with prickles* =thorn, needle, barb, spike, point, spine. 2 *a cold prickle of fear* =tingle, chill, thrill, rush.

prickly ▶ adjective 1 *a prickly cactus* =spiky, spiked, thorny, barbed, spiny.

2 *my skin feels prickly* =tingly, tingling, prickling. **3** *a prickly character.* See IRRITABLE. **4** *a prickly question* =problematic, awkward, ticklish, tricky, delicate, sensitive, difficult, knotty, thorny, troublesome.

pride ▶ noun 1 *a source of pride* =self-esteem, dignity, honour, self-respect. 2 *pride in a job well done* =pleasure, joy, delight, gratification, fulfilment, satisfaction, sense of achievement. 3 *he refused out of pride* =arrogance, vanity, self-importance, hubris, conceitedness, egotism, snobbery.

−OPPOSITES shame, humility.

■ **the pride of** =best, finest, top, cream, pick, choice, prize, the jewel in the crown.

■ **pride oneself on** =be proud of, take pride in, take satisfaction in.

priest ▶ noun =clergyman, clergywoman, minister (of religion), cleric, pastor, vicar, rector, parson, churchman, churchwoman, man/woman of the cloth, man/woman of God, father, curate, chaplain; *Scottish* kirkman; *N. Amer.* dominie; *informal* reverend, padre.

> **WORD LINKS**
>
> *relating to priests:* **clerical, hieratic, sacerdotal**
> *fear of priests:* **hierophobia**

prig ▶ noun =prude, puritan, killjoy; *informal* goody-goody, holy Joe; *N. Amer. informal* bluenose.

priggish ▶ adjective =self-righteous, holier-than-thou, sanctimonious, moralistic, prudish, puritanical, prim, strait-laced, stuffy, prissy, narrow-minded; *informal* goody-goody, starchy.

−OPPOSITES broad-minded.

prim ▶ adjective =demure, formal, stuffy, strait-laced, prudish; prissy, mimsy, priggish, puritanical; *Brit.* po-faced; *informal* starchy.

primacy ▶ noun =priority, precedence, pre-eminence, superiority, supremacy, ascendancy, dominance.

primal ▶ adjective =basic, fundamental, essential, elemental.

primarily ▶ adverb 1 *he was primarily a singer* =first (and foremost), firstly, essentially, in essence, fundamentally, principally, predominantly. 2 *work is done primarily for large institutions* =mostly, for the most part, chiefly, mainly, in the main, on the whole,

P

largely, to a large extent, especially, generally, usually, typically, commonly, as a rule.

primary ▸ adjective =**main**, chief, key, prime, central, principal, foremost, first, most important, predominant, paramount; *informal* number-one.
–OPPOSITES secondary.

prime[1] ▸ adjective **1** *his prime reason for leaving* =**main**, chief, key, primary, central, principal, foremost, first, most important, paramount, major; *informal* number-one. **2** *the prime cause of flooding* =**fundamental**, basic, essential, primary, central. **3** *prime agricultural land* =**top-quality**, top, best, first-class, first-rate, grade A, superior, choice, select, finest; *informal* tip-top, A1, top-notch. **4** *a prime example* =**archetypal**, typical, classic, characteristic, quintessential.
–OPPOSITES secondary, inferior.
▸ noun *he is in his prime* =**heyday**, peak, pinnacle, high point/spot, zenith.

prime[2] ▸ verb **1** *he primed the gun* =**prepare**, load. **2** *Lucy had primed him carefully* =**brief**, fill in, prepare, advise, instruct, coach, drill.

prime minister ▸ noun =**premier**, first minister.

primeval ▸ adjective **1** *primeval forest* =**ancient**, earliest, first, prehistoric, primordial; pristine, virgin. **2** *primeval fears* =**instinctive**, primitive, basic, primal, primordial, intuitive, inborn, innate, inherent.

primitive ▸ adjective **1** *primitive times* =**ancient**, earliest, first, prehistoric, primordial, primeval. **2** *a primitive people* =**preliterate**, non-industrial. **3** *primitive tools* =**crude**, simple, rough (and ready), basic, rudimentary, rude, makeshift. **4** *primitive art* =**simple**, natural, naive.
–OPPOSITES sophisticated, civilized.

primordial ▸ adjective **1** *the primordial oceans* =**ancient**, earliest, first, prehistoric, primeval. **2** *their primordial desires* =**instinctive**, primitive, basic, primal, primeval, intuitive, inborn.

primp ▸ verb =**groom**, tidy, arrange, brush, comb; smarten (up), spruce up; *informal* titivate, doll up; *Brit. informal* tart up; *N. Amer. informal* gussy up.

prince ▸ noun =**ruler**, sovereign, monarch.

princely ▸ adjective *a princely sum. See* HANDSOME *sense* 3.

principal ▸ adjective =**main**, chief, primary, leading, foremost, first, most important, predominant, dominant, pre-eminent, highest, top, topmost; *informal* number-one.
–OPPOSITES minor.
▸ noun =**head (teacher)**, headmaster, headmistress; dean, rector, chancellor, vice-chancellor, president, provost; *N. Amer. informal* prexy.

principally ▸ adverb =**mainly**, mostly, chiefly, for the most part, in the main, on the whole, largely, predominantly, primarily.

principle ▸ noun **1** *elementary principles* =**truth**, concept, idea, theory, fundamental, essential. **2** *the principle of laissez-faire* =**doctrine**, belief, creed, credo, code, ethic, dictum, canon, law. **3** *a woman of principle* | *sticking to one's principles* =**morals**, morality, (code of) ethics, beliefs, ideals, standards; integrity, righteousness, virtue, probity, (sense of) honour, decency, conscience, scruples.
■ **in principle 1** *there is no reason, in principle, why not* =**in theory**, theoretically, on paper. **2** *he accepted the idea in principle* =**in general**, in essence, on the whole, in the main.

principled ▸ adjective =**moral**, ethical, virtuous, righteous, upright, upstanding, honourable, honest.

print ▸ verb **1** *patterns were printed on the cloth* =**imprint**, impress, stamp, mark. **2** *they printed 30,000 copies* =**publish**, issue, release, circulate. **3** *the incident is printed on her memory* =**register**, record, impress, imprint, engrave, etch, stamp, mark.
▸ noun **1** *small print* =**type**, printing, letters, lettering, characters, type size, typeface, font. **2** *prints of his left hand* =**impression**, fingerprint, footprint. **3** *sporting prints* =**picture**; engraving, etching, lithograph, linocut, woodcut. **4** *prints and negatives* =**photograph**, photo, snap, snapshot, picture, still; *Brit.* enprint. **5** *soft floral prints* =**printed cloth/fabric**, patterned cloth/fabric.
■ **in print** =**published**, printed, available, obtainable.
■ **out of print** =**no longer available**, unavailable, unobtainable.

prior ▸ adjective =**earlier**, previous, preceding, advance.
–OPPOSITES subsequent.
■ **prior to** =**before**, until, till, up to,

previous to, earlier than.

priority ▸ noun **1** *safety is our priority* =**prime concern**, main consideration. **2** *giving priority to education* =**precedence**, preference, pre-eminence, predominance, primacy. **3** *oncoming traffic has priority* =**right of way**.

prise ▸ verb **1** *I prised the lid off* =**lever**, jemmy; wrench, wrest, twist; *N. Amer.* pry, jimmy. **2** *he had to prise information from them* =**wring**, wrest, winkle out, screw, squeeze, force.

prison ▸ noun =**jail**, lock-up, penal institution; *N. Amer.* jailhouse, penitentiary, correctional facility; *informal* clink, slammer, stir, jug, brig; *Brit. informal* nick; *N. Amer. informal* can, pen, cooler, pokey, slam; *Brit. Military* glasshouse.
■ **be in prison** =**be behind bars**; *informal* be inside, do time; *Brit. informal* do bird, do porridge.

┌─────────────────┐
│ **WORD LINKS** │
└─────────────────┘
relating to prison: **custodial**

prisoner ▸ noun **1** *a prisoner serving a life sentence* =**convict**, detainee, inmate; *informal* jailbird, con; *N. Amer. informal* yardbird. **2** *the army took many prisoners* =**prisoner of war**, POW, internee, captive.

prissy ▸ adjective =**prudish**, priggish, prim (and proper), strait-laced, Victorian, schoolmarmish; *Brit.* po-faced; *informal* starchy.
−OPPOSITES broad-minded.

pristine ▸ adjective =**immaculate**, perfect, in mint condition, as new, unspoilt, spotless, flawless, clean, fresh, new, virgin, pure.
−OPPOSITES dirty, spoilt.

privacy ▸ noun =**seclusion**, solitude, isolation.

private ▸ adjective **1** *his private plane* =**personal**, own, special, exclusive. **2** *private talks* =**confidential**, secret, classified. **3** *private thoughts* =**intimate**, personal, secret; innermost, undisclosed, unspoken, unvoiced. **4** *a very private man* =**reserved**, introverted, self-contained, reticent, retiring, unsociable, withdrawn, solitary, reclusive. **5** *somewhere private to talk* =**secluded**, undisturbed, remote, isolated. **6** *in a private capacity* =**unofficial**, personal. **7** *private industry* =**independent**, non-state; privatized; commercial, private-enterprise.
−OPPOSITES public, open, extrovert,

busy, crowded, official, state, nationalized.
▸ noun *a private in the army* =**private soldier**; trooper; *Brit.* sapper, gunner; *US* GI; *Brit. informal* Tommy, squaddie.
■ **in private** =**in secret**, secretly, privately, behind closed doors, in camera.

private detective ▸ noun =**private investigator**; *informal* private eye, PI, sleuth, snoop; *N. Amer. informal* shamus, gumshoe; *informal, dated* private dick.

privately ▸ adverb **1** *we must talk privately* =**in private**, behind closed doors, in camera. **2** *privately, I was glad* =**secretly**, inwardly, deep down. **3** *he lived very privately* =**out of the public eye**, out of public view.
−OPPOSITES publicly.

privation ▸ noun =**deprivation**, hardship, destitution, impoverishment, need.
−OPPOSITES plenty, luxury.

privilege ▸ noun **1** *senior pupils have certain privileges* =**advantage**, benefit; prerogative, entitlement, right; concession, freedom, liberty. **2** *it was a privilege to meet her* =**honour**, pleasure.

privileged ▸ adjective **1** *a privileged background* =**wealthy**, rich, affluent, prosperous. **2** *privileged information* =**confidential**, private, secret, restricted, classified, not for publication, off the record, inside; *informal* hush-hush.
−OPPOSITES underprivileged, disadvantaged, public.

privy ■ **privy to** =**in the know about**, acquainted with, in on, apprised of; *formal* cognizant of.

prize ▸ noun **1** *an art prize* =**award**, reward, purse; trophy, medal. **2** *the prizes of war* =**spoils**, booty, plunder, loot, pickings, trophy.
▸ adjective **1** *a prize bull* =**champion**, award-winning, top, best. **2** *a prize idiot* =**utter**, complete, total, absolute, real, perfect; *Brit. informal* right, bloody; *Austral./NZ informal* fair.
−OPPOSITES second-rate.

prized ▸ adjective =**treasured**, precious, cherished, much loved, beloved, valued, esteemed, highly regarded.

prizewinner ▸ noun =**champion**, winner, gold medallist, victor; *informal* champ, number one.

probability ▸ noun **1** *the probability of winning* =**likelihood**, prospect, expectation, chance(s), odds. **2** *relegation is a* *distinct probability* =**prospect**, possibility.

probable ▶ adjective =**likely**, odds-on, expected, anticipated; *informal* on the cards, a safe bet.
–OPPOSITES unlikely.

probably ▶ adverb =**in all likelihood**, in all probability, as like(ly) as not, ten to one, the chances are.

probation ▶ noun =**trial (period)**, test period.

probe ▶ noun =**investigation**, enquiry, examination, inquest, study.
▶ verb =**examine**, feel, explore, prod, poke.

probity ▶ noun =**integrity**, honesty, uprightness, decency, morality, rectitude, goodness, virtue.
–OPPOSITES untrustworthiness.

problem ▶ noun 1 *there's been a problem* =**difficulty**, worry, complication; snag, hitch, drawback, stumbling block, obstacle, hiccup, setback, catch; misfortune, mishap, misadventure; *informal* dilemma, headache. 2 *I don't want to be a problem* =**nuisance**, bother; *informal* drag, pain (in the neck). 3 *arithmetical problems* =**puzzle**, question, poser, riddle, conundrum; *informal* brain-teaser.
▶ adjective *a problem child* =**troublesome**, difficult, unmanageable, unruly, disobedient, uncontrollable, recalcitrant, delinquent.
–OPPOSITES well behaved, manageable.

problematic ▶ adjective =**difficult**, troublesome, tricky, awkward, controversial, ticklish, complicated, complex, knotty, thorny, prickly, vexed; *informal* sticky; *Brit. informal* dodgy.
–OPPOSITES easy, simple, straightforward.

procedure ▶ noun =**course/line of action**, policy, method, system, strategy, way, approach, formula, mechanism, methodology, technique; routine, drill, practice.

proceed ▶ verb 1 *she was uncertain how to proceed* =**begin**, make a start, get going, move. 2 *he proceeded down the road* =**go**, make one's way, advance, move, progress, carry on, press on, push on. 3 *we should proceed with the talks* =**go ahead**, carry on, go on, continue, keep on, get on; pursue, prosecute.
–OPPOSITES stop.

proceedings ▶ plural noun 1 *the evening's proceedings* =**events**, activities, happenings, goings-on. 2 *the proceedings of the meeting* =**report**, transactions, minutes, account, record(s); annals, archives. 3 *legal proceedings* =**legal action**, litigation; lawsuit, case, prosecution.

proceeds ▶ plural noun =**profits**, earnings, receipts, returns, takings, income, revenue; *Sport* gate (money/receipts); *N. Amer.* take.

process ▶ noun 1 *investigation is a long process* =**procedure**, operation, action, activity, exercise, affair, business, job, task, undertaking. 2 *a new canning process* =**method**, system, technique, means, practice, way, approach, methodology.
▶ verb *applications are processed rapidly* =**deal with**, attend to, see to, sort out, handle, take care of.
■ **in the process of** =**in the middle of**, in the course of, in the midst of, in the throes of, busy with, occupied in/with, taken up with/by, involved in.

procession ▶ noun 1 *a procession through the town* =**parade**, march, march past, motorcade, cortège; column, file. 2 *a procession of dance routines* =**series**, succession, stream, string, sequence.

proclaim ▶ verb 1 *messengers proclaimed the good news* =**declare**, announce, pronounce, state, make known, give out, advertise, publish, broadcast, trumpet. 2 *the men proclaimed their innocence* =**assert**, declare, profess, maintain, protest. 3 *he proclaimed himself president* =**declare**, pronounce, announce.

proclamation ▶ noun =**declaration**, announcement, pronouncement, statement, notification, broadcast; assertion, profession, protestation; decree, order, edict, ruling.

proclivity ▶ noun =**inclination**, tendency, leaning, disposition, proneness, propensity, bent, bias, penchant, predisposition; predilection, partiality, liking, preference, taste, fondness.

procrastinate ▶ verb =**delay**, put off doing something, postpone action, defer action, play for time.

procreate ▶ verb =**produce offspring**, reproduce, multiply, propagate, breed.

procure ▶ verb =**obtain**, acquire, get, find, come by, secure, pick up; buy, purchase; *informal* get hold of, get one's hands on.

prod ▶ verb =**poke**, jab, dig, elbow, stab.

▶ noun =**poke**, jab, dig, elbow, thrust.

prodigal ▶ adjective =**wasteful**, extravagant, spendthrift, profligate.
–OPPOSITES thrifty.

prodigious ▶ adjective =**enormous**, huge, colossal, immense, vast, great, massive, gigantic, mammoth, tremendous, inordinate, monumental; amazing, astonishing, astounding, staggering, stunning, remarkable, phenomenal, spectacular, extraordinary, exceptional, breathtaking, incredible; *informal* humongous, stupendous, fantastic, fabulous, mega, awesome; *Brit. informal* ginormous.
–OPPOSITES small, unexceptional.

prodigy ▶ noun =**genius**, mastermind, virtuoso, wunderkind; *informal* whizz-kid, whizz, wizard.

produce ▶ verb **1** *the company produces furniture* =**manufacture**, make, construct, build, fabricate, put together, assemble, turn out, create; mass-produce; *informal* churn out. **2** *the vineyards produce excellent wines* =**yield**, grow, give, supply, provide, furnish, bear. **3** *she produced ten puppies* =**give birth to**, bear, deliver, bring forth, bring into the world. **4** *he produced five novels* =**create**, fashion, turn out; compose, write, pen; paint. **5** *she produced an ID card* =**pull out**, extract, fish out; present, offer, proffer, show. **6** *no evidence was produced* =**present**, offer, provide, furnish, advance, put forward, bring forward, come up with. **7** *that will produce a reaction* =**give rise to**, bring about, cause, occasion, generate, engender, lead to, result in, effect, induce, set off; provoke, precipitate, breed, spark off, trigger. **8** *James produced the play* =**stage**, put on, mount, present.
▶ noun *local produce* =**food**, foodstuff(s), products; fruit, vegetables.

producer ▶ noun **1** *a car producer* =**manufacturer**, maker, builder, constructor. **2** *coffee producers* =**grower**, farmer. **3** *the producer of the show* =**impresario**, manager, administrator, promoter.

product ▶ noun **1** *household products* =**artefact**, commodity; (**products**) goods, ware(s), merchandise, produce. **2** *a product of experience* =**result**, consequence, outcome, effect, upshot.

production ▶ noun **1** *the production of cars* =**manufacture**, making, construction, building, fabrication, assembly, creation; mass production. **2** *the production of literary works* =**creation**, origination, fashioning; composition, writing. **3** *agricultural production* =**output**, yield; productivity. **4** *admission only on production of a ticket* =**presentation**, showing. **5** *a theatre production* =**performance**, staging, presentation, show, piece, play.

productive ▶ adjective **1** *a productive artist* =**prolific**, inventive, creative. **2** *productive talks* =**useful**, constructive, profitable, fruitful, gainful, valuable, effective, worthwhile, helpful. **3** *productive land* =**fertile**, fruitful, rich, fecund.
–OPPOSITES sterile, barren.

productivity ▶ noun **1** *workers have boosted productivity* =**efficiency**, work rate; output, yield, production. **2** *the productivity of the soil* =**fruitfulness**, fertility, richness, fecundity.
–OPPOSITES sterility, barrenness.

profane ▶ adjective **1** *subjects both sacred and profane* =**secular**, lay, non-religious. **2** *profane language* =**obscene**, blasphemous, indecent, foul, vulgar, crude, filthy, dirty, coarse, rude, offensive.
–OPPOSITES religious, reverent, decorous.
▶ verb *invaders profaned our temples* =**desecrate**, violate, defile.

profanity ▶ noun **1** *he hissed a profanity | an outburst of profanity* =**oath**, swear word, expletive, curse, obscenity, four-letter word, dirty word; blasphemy, swearing, foul language, bad language, cursing. **2** *acts of profanity* =**sacrilege**, blasphemy, ungodliness, impiety, irreverence, disrespect.

profess ▶ verb **1** *he professed his love* =**declare**, announce, proclaim, assert, state, affirm, avow, maintain, protest. **2** *she professed to loathe publicity* =**claim**, pretend, purport, affect; make out.

professed ▶ adjective =**claimed**, supposed, ostensible, self-styled, apparent, pretended, purported.

profession ▶ noun **1** *his chosen profession* =**career**, occupation, calling, vocation, métier, line (of work), job, business, trade, craft; *informal* racket. **2** *a profession of allegiance* =**declaration**, affirmation, statement, announcement, proclamation, assertion, avowal, vow, claim, protestation.

professional ▶ adjective **1** *professional occupations* =**white-collar**, non-manual.

2 *a professional cricketer* =**paid**, salaried. **3** *a very professional job* =**expert**, accomplished, skilful, masterly, masterful, fine, polished, skilled, proficient, competent, able, businesslike, deft. **4** *not a professional way to behave* =**appropriate**, fitting, proper, honourable, ethical.
—OPPOSITES manual, amateur, amateurish, inappropriate, unethical.
▶ noun **1** *affluent young professionals* =**white-collar worker**, office worker. **2** *his first season as a professional* =**professional player**, paid player, salaried player; *informal* pro. **3** *she was a real professional* =**expert**, virtuoso, old hand, master, maestro, past master; *informal* pro, ace.
—OPPOSITES manual worker, amateur.

proffer ▶ verb =**offer**, tender, submit, extend, volunteer, suggest, propose, put forward.
—OPPOSITES refuse, withdraw.

proficiency ▶ noun =**skill**, expertise, accomplishment, competence, mastery, prowess, professionalism, ability; *informal* know-how.
—OPPOSITES incompetence.

proficient ▶ adjective =**skilled**, skilful, expert, accomplished, competent, masterly, adept, adroit, deft, dexterous, able, professional; *informal* crack, ace, mean.
—OPPOSITES incompetent.

profile ▶ noun **1** *his handsome profile* =**side view**, outline, silhouette, contour, shape, form, lines. **2** *a profile of the organization* =**description**, account, study, portrait, rundown, sketch, outline.
▶ verb *he was profiled in the Times* =**describe**, write about, give an account of, portray, depict, outline.

profit ▶ noun **1** *the firm made a profit* =**(financial) gain**, return(s), yield, proceeds, earnings, winnings, surplus, excess; *informal* pay dirt, bottom line. **2** *there was little profit in going on* =**advantage**, benefit, value, use, good, avail; *informal* mileage.
—OPPOSITES loss, disadvantage.
▶ verb **1** *we will not profit from the deal* =**make money**; *informal* rake it in, clean up, make a packet, make a killing, make a bundle; *N. Amer. informal* make big bucks, make a fast/quick buck. **2** *how will that profit us?* =**benefit**, be advantageous to, be of use/value to, do someone good, help, be of service to, serve, assist, aid.
—OPPOSITES lose, disadvantage.
■ **profit by/from** =**benefit from**, take advantage of, derive benefit from, capitalize on, make the most of, turn to one's advantage, put to good use, do well out of, exploit, gain from; *informal* cash in on.

profitable ▶ adjective **1** *a profitable company* =**moneymaking**, profit-making, commercial, successful, money-spinning, solvent, in the black, gainful, remunerative, financially rewarding, paying, lucrative, bankable. **2** *profitable study* =**beneficial**, useful, advantageous, valuable, productive, worthwhile; rewarding, fruitful, illuminating, informative, well spent.
—OPPOSITES loss-making, fruitless, useless.

profligate ▶ adjective **1** *profligate local authorities* =**wasteful**, extravagant, spendthrift, improvident, prodigal. **2** *a profligate lifestyle* =**dissolute**, degenerate, debauched; promiscuous, loose, wanton, licentious, decadent, abandoned.
—OPPOSITES thrifty, frugal, moral, upright.

profound ▶ adjective **1** *profound relief* =**heartfelt**, intense, keen, great, extreme, acute, severe, sincere, earnest, deep, deep-seated, overpowering, overwhelming. **2** *a profound change* =**far-reaching**, radical, extensive, sweeping, exhaustive, thoroughgoing. **3** *a profound analysis* =**wise**, learned, intelligent, scholarly, discerning, penetrating, perceptive, astute, thoughtful, insightful. **4** *profound truths* =**complex**, abstract, deep, weighty, difficult.
—OPPOSITES superficial, mild, slight, simple.

profuse ▶ adjective **1** *profuse apologies* =**copious**, prolific, abundant, liberal, unstinting, fulsome, effusive, extravagant, lavish, gushing. **2** *profuse blooms* =**luxuriant**, plentiful, copious, abundant, lush, rich, exuberant, riotous, teeming, rank, rampant.
—OPPOSITES meagre, sparse.

profusion ▶ noun =**abundance**, mass, host, cornucopia, riot, plethora, superabundance; *informal* sea, wealth.

progeny ▶ noun =**offspring**, young, babies, children, sons and daughters, family, brood; descendants, heirs; *Law* issue.

prognosis ▶ noun =**forecast**, prediction, prognostication.

prognosticate ▶ verb =**forecast**, predict, prophesy.

prognostication ▶ noun =predic-tion, forecast, prophecy, prognosis.

programme ▶ noun 1 *our programme for the day* =**schedule**, agenda, calendar, timetable; order of events, line-up. 2 *the government's reform programme* =**scheme**, plan, package, strategy. 3 *a television programme* =**broadcast**, production, show, presentation, transmission, performance; *informal* prog. 4 *a programme of study* =**course**, syllabus, curriculum. 5 *a theatre programme* =**guide**, list of performers; *N. Amer.* playbill.
▶ verb *they programmed the day well* =**arrange**, organize, schedule, plan, map out, timetable, line up; *N. Amer.* slate.

progress ▶ noun 1 *snow made progress difficult* =(forward) movement, advance, going, headway, passage. 2 *scientific progress* =**development**, advance, advancement, headway, step(s) forward; improvement, growth.
–OPPOSITES relapse.
▶ verb 1 *they progressed slowly down the road* =**go**, make one's way, move, proceed, advance, go on, continue, make headway, work one's way. 2 *the school has progressed rapidly* =**develop**, make progress, advance, make headway, take steps forward, move on, get on, gain ground; improve, get better, come on, come along, make strides; thrive, prosper, blossom, flourish; *informal* be getting there.
–OPPOSITES relapse.
■ in progress =under way, going on, ongoing, happening, occurring, taking place, proceeding, continuing; *N. Amer.* in the works.

progression ▶ noun 1 *progression to the next stage* =**progress**, advancement, movement, passage; development, evolution, growth. 2 *a progression of peaks on the graph* =**succession**, series, sequence, string, stream, chain, train, row, cycle.

progressive ▶ adjective 1 *progressive deterioration* =**continuing**, continuous, ongoing; gradual, step-by-step, cumulative. 2 *progressive views* =**modern**, liberal, advanced, forward-thinking, enlightened, enterprising, innovative, pioneering, dynamic, bold, reforming, reformist, radical; *informal* go-ahead.
–OPPOSITES conservative, reactionary.
▶ noun *he is very much a progressive* =**innovator**, reformer, reformist, liberal.

prohibit ▶ verb 1 *state law prohibits gambling* =**forbid**, ban, bar, interdict, proscribe, make illegal, embargo, outlaw,

disallow; *Law* enjoin. 2 *a cash shortage prohibited the visit* =**prevent**, stop, rule out, preclude, make impossible.
–OPPOSITES allow.

prohibited ▶ adjective =**illegal**, illicit, against the law; *Islam* haram; *informal* not on, out, no go.
–OPPOSITES permitted.

prohibition ▶ noun 1 *the prohibition of cannabis* =**banning**, forbidding, prohibiting, barring, proscription, outlawing. 2 *a prohibition was imposed* =**ban**, bar, interdict, veto, embargo, injunction, moratorium.

prohibitive ▶ adjective 1 *prohibitive costs* =**excessively high**, sky-high, overinflated; out of the question, beyond one's means; extortionate, unreasonable, exorbitant; *informal* steep, criminal. 2 *prohibitive regulations* =**proscriptive**, restrictive, repressive.

project ▶ noun 1 *an engineering project* =**scheme**, plan, programme, enterprise, undertaking, venture; proposal, idea, concept. 2 *a history project* =**assignment**, piece of work, piece of research, task.
▶ verb 1 *profits are projected to rise* =**forecast**, predict, expect, estimate, calculate, reckon. 2 *his projected book* =**intend**, plan, propose, devise, design, outline. 3 *balconies projected over the lake* =**stick out**, jut (out), protrude, extend, stand out, bulge out, poke out, thrust out. 4 *the sun projected his shadow on the wall* =**cast**, throw, send, shed, shine. 5 *she tried to project a calm image* =**convey**, put across, put over, communicate, present, promote.

projectile ▶ noun =**missile**.

projecting ▶ adjective =**sticking out**, protuberant, protruding, prominent, jutting, overhanging, proud, bulging.
–OPPOSITES sunken, flush.

projection ▶ noun 1 *a sales projection* =**forecast**, prediction, prognosis, expectation, estimate. 2 *tiny projections on the cliff face* =**protuberance**, protrusion, sticking-out bit, prominence, eminence, outcrop, outgrowth; overhang, ledge, shelf.

proletarian ▶ adjective *a proletarian background* =**working-class**, plebeian, cloth-cap, common.
–OPPOSITES aristocratic.

proletariat ▶ noun =**the workers**, working-class people, wage-earners, the labouring classes, the common people,

the lower classes, the masses, the commonalty, the rank and file; *derogatory* the hoi polloi, the great unwashed, the mob, the rabble; *informal, derogatory* the plebs, the proles.
–OPPOSITES aristocracy.

proliferate ▶ verb =increase rapidly, grow rapidly, multiply, rocket, mushroom, snowball, burgeon, run riot.
–OPPOSITES decrease, dwindle.

prolific ▶ adjective 1 *a prolific crop of tomatoes* =**plentiful**, abundant, bountiful, profuse, copious, luxuriant, rich, lush; fruitful; *literary* plenteous. 2 *a prolific composer* =**productive**, fertile.

prologue ▶ noun =**introduction**, foreword, preface, preamble, prelude; *informal* intro.
–OPPOSITES epilogue.

prolong ▶ verb =**lengthen**, extend, draw/drag out, protract, spin/stretch out; carry on, continue, keep up, perpetuate.
–OPPOSITES shorten.

promenade ▶ noun 1 *the tree-lined promenade* =**esplanade**, front, seafront, parade, walk, boulevard, avenue; *N. Amer.* boardwalk; *Brit. informal* prom. 2 *our nightly promenade* =**walk**, stroll, turn, amble, airing; *dated* constitutional.
▶ verb *we promenaded in the park* =**walk**, stroll, saunter, wander, amble, stretch one's legs, take a turn.

prominence ▶ noun 1 *his rise to prominence* =**fame**, celebrity, eminence, pre-eminence, importance, distinction, greatness, note, notability, prestige, stature, standing. 2 *the press gave prominence to the reports* =**(good) coverage**, importance, precedence, weight, a high profile, top billing. 3 *a rocky prominence* =**hillock**, hill, hummock, mound; outcrop, crag, spur, rise; ridge; peak, pinnacle; promontory, cliff, headland.

prominent ▶ adjective 1 *a prominent surgeon* =**important**, well known, leading, eminent, distinguished, notable, noteworthy, noted, illustrious, celebrated, famous, renowned; *N. Amer.* major-league. 2 *prominent cheekbones* =**protuberant**, protruding, projecting, jutting (out), standing out, sticking out, proud, bulging. 3 *a prominent feature of the landscape* =**conspicuous**, noticeable, easily seen, obvious, unmistakable, eye-catching, pronounced, salient, striking, dominant; obtrusive.

–OPPOSITES unimportant, unknown, inconspicuous.

promiscuity ▶ noun =**licentiousness**, wantonness, immorality; *informal* sleeping around.
–OPPOSITES chastity, virtue.

promiscuous ▶ adjective 1 *sexually promiscuous* =**licentious**, indiscriminate, wanton, immoral; *dated* loose. 2 *promiscuous reading* =**indiscriminate**, undiscriminating, unselective, catholic, eclectic, wide-ranging.
–OPPOSITES chaste, virtuous, selective.

promise ▶ noun 1 *you broke your promise* =**word (of honour)**, assurance, pledge, vow, guarantee, oath, bond, undertaking, agreement, commitment, contract, covenant. 2 *he shows promise* =**potential**, possibility. 3 *a promise of fine weather* =**indication**, hint, suggestion, sign.
▶ verb 1 *she promised to go* =**give one's word**, swear, pledge, vow, undertake, guarantee, contract, engage, give an assurance, commit oneself, bind oneself, swear/take an oath, covenant. 2 *the skies promised sunshine* =**indicate**, lead one to expect, point to, be a sign of, be evidence of, give hope of, bespeak, presage, augur, herald, bode, portend.

promising ▶ adjective 1 *a promising start* =**good**, encouraging, favourable, hopeful, full of promise, auspicious, propitious, bright, rosy, heartening, reassuring. 2 *a promising actor* =**with potential**, budding, up-and-coming, rising, coming, in the making.
–OPPOSITES unfavourable, hopeless.

promontory ▶ noun =**headland**, point, cape, head, horn, bill, ness, peninsula; *Scottish* mull.

promote ▶ verb 1 *she's been promoted* =**upgrade**, give promotion to, elevate, advance, move up. 2 *an organization promoting justice* =**encourage**, further, advance, foster, develop, boost, stimulate, forward, work for. 3 *she is promoting her new film* =**advertise**, publicize, give publicity to, beat/bang the drum for, market, merchandise; *informal* push, plug, hype; *N. Amer. informal* ballyhoo, flack.
–OPPOSITES demote, obstruct, play down.

promoter ▶ noun =**advocate**, champion, supporter, backer, proponent, protagonist, campaigner; *N. Amer.* booster.

promotion ▶ noun 1 *her promotion at*

work =**upgrading**, preferment, elevation, advancement, step up (the ladder).
2 *the promotion of justice* =**encouragement**, furtherance, furthering, advancement, contribution to, fostering, boosting, stimulation; *N. Amer.* boosterism.
3 *the promotion for her new film* =**advertising**, publicizing, marketing; publicity, campaign, propaganda; *informal* hard sell, plug, hype, puff; *N. Amer. informal* ballyhoo.

prompt ▶ verb **1** *curiosity prompted him to look* =**induce**, make, move, motivate, lead, dispose, persuade, incline, encourage, stimulate, prod, impel, spur on, inspire. **2** *the statement prompted a hostile reaction* =**give rise to**, bring about, cause, occasion, result in, lead to, elicit, produce, engender, induce, precipitate, trigger, spark off, provoke. **3** *the actors needed prompting* =**remind**, cue, feed, help out; jog someone's memory.
–OPPOSITES deter.
▶ adjective *a prompt reply* =**quick**, swift, rapid, speedy, fast, direct, immediate, instant, early, punctual, in good time, on time.
–OPPOSITES slow, late.
▶ adverb *at 3.30 prompt* =**exactly**, precisely, sharp, on the dot, dead, punctually, on the nail; *informal* bang on; *N. Amer. informal* on the button/nose.

promptly ▶ adverb **1** *William arrived promptly at 7.30* =**punctually**, on time; *informal* on the dot, bang on; *Brit. informal* spot on; *N. Amer. informal* on the button/nose. **2** *I expect the matter to be dealt with promptly* =**without delay**, straight/right away, at once, immediately, now, as soon as possible; **quickly**, swiftly, rapidly, speedily, fast; *informal* pronto, a.s.a.p., p.d.q. (pretty damn quick).
–OPPOSITES late, slowly.

promulgate ▶ verb =**make known**, make public, publicize, spread, communicate, propagate, disseminate, broadcast, promote, preach.

prone ▶ adjective **1** *softwood is prone to rotting* | *prone to rot* =**susceptible**, vulnerable, subject, open, liable, given, predisposed, likely, disposed, inclined, apt. **2** *his prone body* =**(lying) face down**, on one's stomach/front; **lying flat/down**, horizontal, prostrate.
–OPPOSITES resistant, immune, upright.

prong ▶ noun =**tine**, spike, point, tip, projection.

pronounce ▶ verb **1** *his name is difficult to pronounce* =**say**, enunciate, utter, voice, sound, vocalize, get one's tongue round. **2** *the doctor pronounced her fit for work* =**declare**, proclaim; judge, rule, decree.

pronounced ▶ adjective =**noticeable**, marked, strong, conspicuous, striking, distinct, prominent, unmistakable, obvious.
–OPPOSITES slight.

pronouncement ▶ noun =**announcement**, proclamation, declaration, assertion; judgement, ruling.

pronunciation ▶ noun =**accent**, diction, delivery, intonation; articulation, enunciation, vocalization.

> WORD LINKS
>
> *study of correct pronunciation:* **orthoepy**

proof ▶ noun =**evidence**, verification, corroboration, authentication, confirmation, certification, documentation.
▶ adjective =**resistant**, immune, unaffected, impervious.

prop ▶ noun **1** *the roof is held up by props* =**pole**, post, support, upright, brace, buttress, stay, strut. **2** *a prop for the economy* =**mainstay**, pillar, anchor, support.
▶ verb *he propped his bike against the wall* =**lean**, rest, stand, balance.
■ **prop something up 1** *this post is propping the wall up* =**hold up**, shore up, buttress, support, brace, underpin. **2** *they prop up loss-making industries* =**subsidize**, underwrite, fund, finance.

propaganda ▶ noun =**information**, promotion, advertising, publicity; disinformation; *informal* hype

propagate ▶ verb **1** *an easy plant to propagate* =**breed**, grow, cultivate. **2** *these shrubs propagate easily* =**reproduce**, multiply, proliferate, increase, spread. **3** *they propagated socialist ideas* =**spread**, disseminate, communicate, make known, promulgate, circulate, broadcast, publicize, proclaim, preach, promote.

propel ▶ verb **1** *a boat propelled by oars* =**move**, power, push, drive. **2** *the impact propelled him into the street* =**throw**, thrust, toss, fling, hurl, pitch, send, shoot.

propeller ▶ noun =**rotor**, screw; *informal* prop.

propensity ▶ noun =**tendency**, inclination, predisposition, proneness, proclivity, readiness, liability, disposition, leaning, weakness.

proper ▸ adjective **1** *he's not a proper scientist* =**real**, genuine, actual, true, bona fide; *informal* kosher. **2** *the proper channels* =**right**, correct, accepted, conventional, established, official, regular, acceptable, appropriate. **3** *they were terribly proper* =**formal**, conventional, correct, orthodox, polite, punctilious, respectable. **4** *(Brit. informal) a proper mess* =**complete**, absolute, real, perfect, total, thorough, utter, out-and-out; *Brit. informal* right; *Austral./NZ informal* fair.
–OPPOSITES fake, inappropriate, wrong, unconventional.

property ▸ noun **1** *lost property* =**possessions**, belongings, things, effects, stuff, goods; *informal* gear. **2** *private property* =**building(s)**, premises, house(s), land; *Law* realty; *N. Amer.* real estate. **3** *healing properties* =**quality**, attribute, characteristic, feature, power, trait, mark, hallmark.

prophecy ▸ noun =**prediction**, forecast, prognostication, prognosis, divination.

prophesy ▸ verb =**predict**, foretell, forecast, foresee, prognosticate.

prophet, prophetess ▸ noun =**seer**, soothsayer, fortune teller, clairvoyant; oracle.

prophetic ▸ adjective =**prescient**, predictive, far-seeing.

propitiate ▸ verb =**appease**, placate, mollify, pacify, make peace with, conciliate, soothe, calm.
–OPPOSITES provoke.

propitious ▸ adjective =**favourable**, auspicious, promising, providential, advantageous, optimistic, bright, rosy, heaven-sent, hopeful; opportune, timely.
–OPPOSITES inauspicious, unfortunate.

proponent ▸ noun =**advocate**, champion, supporter, promoter, protagonist, campaigner; *N. Amer.* booster.

proportion ▸ noun **1** *a proportion of the land* =**part**, portion, amount, quantity, bit, piece, percentage, fraction, section, segment, share. **2** *the proportion of water to alcohol* =**ratio**, distribution, relative amount/number. **3** *a sense of proportion* =**balance**, symmetry, harmony, correspondence, correlation, agreement. **4** *men of huge proportions* =**size**, dimen-

sions, magnitude, measurements; mass, volume, bulk; expanse, extent, width, breadth.

proportional ▸ adjective =**corresponding**, proportionate, comparable, in proportion, pro rata, commensurate, equivalent.
–OPPOSITES disproportionate.

proposal ▸ noun **1** *the proposal was rejected* =**scheme**, plan, idea, project, programme, motion, proposition, suggestion, submission. **2** *the proposal of a new constitution* =**putting forward**, proposing, submission.
–OPPOSITES withdrawal.

propose ▸ verb **1** *he proposed a solution* =**put forward**, suggest, submit, advance, offer, present, move, come up with. **2** *do you propose to go?* =**intend**, mean, plan, have in mind/view, aim. **3** *he proposed to her!* =**ask someone to marry you**; *informal* pop the question.
–OPPOSITES withdraw.

proposition ▸ noun **1** *a business proposition* =**proposal**, scheme, plan, project, idea, programme. **2** *doing it for real is a very different proposition* =**task**, job, undertaking, venture, activity, affair.
▸ verb *he never dared proposition her* =**propose sex with**, make advances to; *informal* come on to.

propound ▸ verb =**put forward**, advance, offer, proffer, present, set forth, submit, tender, suggest, postulate, propose, posit.

proprietor, proprietress ▸ noun =**owner**, possessor, holder, master, mistress; landowner, landlord, landlady; innkeeper, shopkeeper; *Brit.* publican.

propriety ▸ noun =**decorum**, respectability, decency, correctness, good manners, courtesy, politeness, rectitude.
–OPPOSITES indecorum.

propulsion ▸ noun =**thrust**, motive force, impetus, impulse, drive, driving force, actuation, push, pressure, power.

prosaic ▸ adjective =**ordinary**, everyday, commonplace, conventional, straightforward, routine, run-of-the-mill; **unimaginative**, uninspired, uninspiring, matter-of-fact, dull, dreary, humdrum, mundane, pedestrian, tame, plodding.
–OPPOSITES interesting, imaginative, inspired.

proscribe ▸ verb =**forbid**, prohibit, ban, bar, make illegal, embargo, out-

law, disallow, veto.
−OPPOSITES allow, authorize, accept.

prosecute ▸ verb 1 *they prosecute offenders* =**take to court**, bring/institute legal proceedings against, take legal action against, sue, try, bring to trial, put on trial, put in the dock, indict, arraign; *N. Amer.* impeach. 2 *they helped him prosecute the war* =**pursue**, fight, wage, carry on, conduct, direct, engage in, proceed with.
−OPPOSITES defend, let off, give up.

proselytize ▸ verb =**evangelize**, convert, win over, preach (to), recruit, act as a missionary.

prospect ▸ noun 1 *there is little prospect of success* =**likelihood**, hope, expectation, (good/poor) chance, odds, probability, possibility, promise, lookout; fear, danger. 2 *her job prospects* =**possibilities**, potential, expectations, outlook. 3 *a daunting prospect* =**vision**, thought, idea; task, undertaking.
▸ verb *prospecting for oil* =**search**, look, explore, survey, scout, hunt.

prospective ▸ adjective =**potential**, possible, probable, likely, future, eventual, -to-be, soon-to-be, in the making; intending, aspiring, would-be.

prospectus ▸ noun =**brochure**, pamphlet, description; syllabus, curriculum, catalogue, programme, list, schedule.

prosper ▸ verb =**flourish**, thrive, do well, bloom, blossom, burgeon, progress, do all right for oneself, get ahead, get on (in the world), be successful; *informal* go places.
−OPPOSITES fail, flounder.

prosperity ▸ noun =**success**, affluence, wealth, ease, plenty.
−OPPOSITES hardship, failure.

prosperous ▸ adjective =**thriving**, flourishing, successful, strong, vigorous, profitable, lucrative, expanding, booming, burgeoning, **affluent**, wealthy, rich, moneyed, well off, well-to-do; *informal* in the money.
−OPPOSITES ailing, poor.

prostitute ▸ noun =**whore**, sex worker, call girl; rent boy; *informal* working girl; *N. Amer. informal* hooker, hustler.
▸ verb *they prostituted their art* =**betray**, sacrifice, sell, sell out, debase, degrade, demean, devalue, cheapen, lower, shame, misuse.

prostrate ▸ adjective 1 *the prostrate figure on the ground* =**prone**, lying flat, lying down, stretched out, spreadeagled, sprawling, horizontal, recumbent. 2 *his wife was prostrate with grief* =**overwhelmed**, overcome, overpowered, stunned, dazed; speechless, helpless; *informal* knocked/hit for six.
−OPPOSITES upright.
■ **prostrate oneself** =**throw oneself flat/down**, lie down, stretch oneself out, throw oneself at someone's feet.

protagonist ▸ noun 1 *the protagonist in the plot* =**chief/central/principal/main/leading character**, hero/heroine, leading man/lady, title role, lead. 2 *a protagonist of deregulation* =**champion**, advocate, upholder, supporter, backer, promoter, proponent, exponent, campaigner, fighter, crusader; apostle, apologist; *N. Amer.* booster.
−OPPOSITES opponent.

protean ▸ adjective =**ever-changing**, variable, changeable, mutable, kaleidoscopic, unstable, shifting, fluctuating, fluid.
−OPPOSITES constant, consistent.

protect ▸ verb =**keep safe**, keep from harm, save, safeguard, preserve, defend, shield, cushion, insulate, shelter, screen, guard, watch over, look after, take care of, keep.
−OPPOSITES expose, neglect, attack, harm.

protection ▸ noun 1 *protection against frost* =**defence**, security, safe keeping, safety, sanctuary, shelter, refuge, immunity, insurance, indemnity. 2 *the protection of the Church* =**safe keeping**, care, charge, keeping, aegis, auspices, umbrella, guardianship, support, patronage. 3 *a good protection against noise* =**barrier**, buffer, shield, screen, cushion, bulwark.

protective ▸ adjective 1 *protective clothing* =**special**, safety; thick, heavy, insulated; -proof, -resistant. 2 *he felt protective towards her* =**solicitous**, caring, paternal/maternal; overprotective, possessive, jealous.

protector ▸ noun 1 *a protector of the environment* =**defender**, preserver, guardian, champion, patron, custodian. 2 *ear protectors* =**guard**, shield, buffer, cushion, pad, screen.

protégé, protégée ▸ noun =**pupil**, student, trainee, apprentice; disciple, follower; ward.

protest ▶ noun **1** *a storm of protest* =**objection**, complaint, challenge, dissent, demurral, remonstration, fuss, outcry. **2** *the women staged a protest* =**demonstration**, rally, vigil; sit-in, occupation; work-to-rule, stoppage, strike, walkout, mutiny, picket, boycott; *informal* demo.
–OPPOSITES support, approval.
▶ verb **1** *residents protested at the plans* =**express opposition**, object, dissent, take issue, make/take a stand, put up a fight, take exception, complain, express disapproval, disagree, demur, make a fuss; cry out, speak out, rail, inveigh, fulminate; *informal* kick up a fuss/stink. **2** *people protested outside the cathedral* =**demonstrate**, march, hold a rally. **3** *he protested his innocence* =**insist on**, maintain, assert, affirm, announce, proclaim, declare, profess.
–OPPOSITES acquiesce, support, deny.

protestation ▶ noun **1** *his protestations of innocence* =**declaration**, announcement, profession, assertion, insistence, claim, affirmation, assurance. **2** *we helped him despite his protestations* =**objection**, protest, exception, complaint, disapproval, opposition, dissent, demurral.
–OPPOSITES denial, acquiescence, support.

protester ▶ noun =**demonstrator**, marcher; striker, picket.

protocol ▶ noun **1** *a stickler for protocol* =**etiquette**, convention, formalities, custom, the rules, procedure, ritual, decorum, the done thing. **2** *the two countries signed a protocol* =**agreement**, treaty, entente, concordat, convention, deal, pact, contract, compact.

prototype ▶ noun **1** *a prototype of the weapon* =**original**, master, template, pattern, sample. **2** *the prototype of an ideal wife* =**typical example**, paradigm, archetype, exemplar.

protract ▶ verb =**prolong**, lengthen, extend, draw out, drag out, spin out, stretch out, string out.
–OPPOSITES curtail, shorten.

protracted ▶ adjective =**prolonged**, extended, long-drawn-out, lengthy, long.
–OPPOSITES short.

protrude ▶ verb =**stick out**, jut (out), project, extend, stand out, bulge out, poke out.

protruding ▶ adjective =**sticking out**, protuberant, projecting, prominent, overhanging, proud, bulging.
–OPPOSITES sunken, flush.

protrusion ▶ noun =**bump**, lump, knob; protuberance, projection, swelling, outcrop, outgrowth.

protuberance ▶ noun =**bump**, lump, knob, projection, protrusion, prominence, swelling, outcrop, outgrowth.

proud ▶ adjective **1** *the proud parents* =**pleased**, glad, happy, delighted, thrilled, satisfied, gratified. **2** *a proud day* =**pleasing**, gratifying, satisfying, cheering, heart-warming; happy, good, glorious, memorable, notable. **3** *they were poor but proud* =**dignified**, noble; independent. **4** *leave the filler proud of the wall surface* =**projecting**, sticking out/up, jutting (out), protruding, prominent, raised.
–OPPOSITES ashamed, shameful, humble, modest, flush.

prove ▶ verb **1** *that proves I'm right* =**show (to be true)**, demonstrate (the truth of), provide proof/evidence; substantiate, verify, validate, authenticate. **2** *the rumour proved to be correct* =**turn out**, be found.
–OPPOSITES disprove.
■ **prove oneself** =**demonstrate one's abilities/qualities**, show one's (true) mettle, show what one is made of.

provenance ▶ noun =**origin**, source, pedigree, derivation; *N. Amer.* provenience.

proverb ▶ noun =**saying**, adage, saw, maxim, axiom, motto, aphorism, epigram, dictum, precept.

proverbial ▶ adjective =**well known**, famous, famed, renowned, traditional, time-honoured, legendary.

provide ▶ verb **1** *we will provide funds* =**supply**, give, issue, furnish, come up with, dispense, bestow, impart, produce, yield, deliver, donate, contribute, allocate, distribute, allot, put up; *informal* fork out, lay out; *N. Amer. informal* ante up, pony up. **2** *he was provided with tools* =**equip**, furnish, issue, supply, outfit; fit out, rig out, kit out, arm, provision; *informal* fix up. **3** *he had to provide for his family* =**feed**, nurture, nourish; support, maintain, keep, sustain. **4** *the test may provide the answer* =**offer**, present, af-

ford, give, add, bring, yield, impart, reveal. **5** *we have provided for further restructuring* = **prepare**, allow, make provision, arrange, plan, cater. **6** *the banks have to provide against bad debts* = **take precautions**, take steps/measures, guard; make provision for.
−OPPOSITES refuse, withhold, deprive, neglect.

provided ▶ conjunction = **if**, on condition that, providing (that), provided that, presuming (that), assuming (that), on the assumption that, as long as, given (that), with/on the understanding that.

providence ▶ noun = **fate**, destiny, nemesis, predestination, predetermination, the stars; one's lot (in life).

provident ▶ adjective = **prudent**, farsighted, judicious, circumspect, wise, sensible; thrifty, economical.
−OPPOSITES improvident.

providential ▶ adjective = **opportune**, advantageous, favourable, auspicious, propitious, welcome, lucky, happy, fortunate, felicitous, timely, well timed, seasonable, convenient.
−OPPOSITES inopportune.

provider ▶ noun = **supplier**, donor, giver, contributor, source.

providing ▶ conjunction. *See* PROVIDED.

province ▶ noun **1** *a province of the Roman Empire* = **territory**, region, state, department, canton, area, district, sector, zone, division. **2** *people in the provinces* = **the regions**, the rest of the country, rural areas/districts, the countryside, the backwoods, the wilds; *informal* the sticks, the middle of nowhere; *N. Amer. informal* the boondocks.

provincial ▶ adjective **1** *the provincial government* = **regional**, state, territorial, district, local, county. **2** *provincial areas* = **non-metropolitan**, small-town, non-urban, outlying, rural, country, rustic, backwoods, backwater; *informal* one-horse; *N. Amer. informal* hick, freshwater. **3** *they're so dull and provincial* = **unsophisticated**, narrow-minded, parochial, small-town, suburban, insular, inward-looking, conservative; small-minded, blinkered, bigoted, prejudiced; *N. Amer. informal* jerkwater, corn-fed.
−OPPOSITES national, metropolitan, cosmopolitan, sophisticated, broad-minded.

provision ▶ noun **1** *the provision of*

weapons to guerrillas = **supplying**, supply, providing, giving, donation; equipping, furnishing. **2** *limited provision for young children* = **facilities**, services, amenities, resource(s), arrangements; means, funds, assistance, allowance(s). **3** *provisions for the trip* = **supplies**, food and drink, stores, groceries, foodstuff(s), rations; *informal* grub, eats, nosh; *N. Amer. informal* chuck; *formal* comestibles; *dated* victuals. **4** *he made no provision for the future* = **preparations**, plans, arrangements, precautions, contingency. **5** *the provisions of the Act* = **term**; requirement, specification, stipulation.

provisional ▶ adjective = **interim**, temporary; transitional, changeover, stopgap, short-term, fill-in, acting, caretaker; working, tentative.
−OPPOSITES permanent, definite.

provisionally ▶ adverb = **temporarily**, short-term, for the interim, for the present, for the time being, for now, subject to confirmation, conditionally, tentatively.

proviso ▶ noun = **condition**, stipulation, provision, clause, rider, qualification, restriction, caveat.

provocation ▶ noun = **goading**, prodding, incitement, pressure; harassment; teasing, taunting, torment; *informal* hassle, aggravation.

provocative ▶ adjective **1** *provocative remarks* = **annoying**, irritating, exasperating, infuriating, maddening, vexing, galling, insulting, offensive, inflammatory, incendiary, controversial; *informal* aggravating. **2** *a provocative pose* = **sexy**, sexually arousing/exciting, alluring, seductive, suggestive, inviting, tantalizing, titillating; indecent, pornographic, indelicate, immodest, shameless; erotic, sensuous, slinky, coquettish, amorous, flirtatious; *informal* tarty, come-hither.
−OPPOSITES soothing, calming, modest, decorous.

provoke ▶ verb **1** *the plan has provoked outrage* = **arouse**, produce, evoke, cause, give rise to, occasion, call forth, elicit, induce, excite, spark off, touch off, kindle, generate, engender, instigate, result in, lead to, bring on, precipitate, prompt, trigger. **2** *he was provoked into replying* = **goad**, spur, prick, sting, prod, incite, rouse, stir, move, stimulate, inflame, impel. **3** *he's dangerous if provoked* = **annoy**, anger, enrage, irritate, mad-

den, nettle, ruffle; harass, harry, molest; *Brit.* rub up the wrong way; *informal* peeve, aggravate, hassle, miff, rile, needle, hack off, get/put someone's back up, get up someone's nose; *Brit. informal* wind up, nark; *N. Amer. informal* rankle, ride, gravel.
–OPPOSITES allay, deter, pacify, appease.

prow ▸ noun =bow(s), stem, front, nose, head; *Brit. humorous* sharp end.

prowess ▸ noun =skill, expertise, mastery, ability, capability, capacity, talent, aptitude, dexterity, competence, proficiency, finesse; *informal* know-how.
–OPPOSITES inability, ineptitude.

prowl ▸ verb =steal, slink, skulk, sneak, stalk, creep; *informal* snoop.

proximity ▸ noun =closeness, nearness; accessibility, handiness.

proxy ▸ noun =deputy, representative, substitute, delegate, agent, surrogate, stand-in, go-between.

prude ▸ noun =puritan, prig, killjoy, moralist; *informal* goody-goody; *N. Amer. informal* bluenose.

prudence ▸ noun **1** *beyond the bounds of prudence* =wisdom, good judgement, common sense. **2** *financial prudence* =caution, care, providence, foresight, circumspection; thrift, economy.
–OPPOSITES folly, recklessness, extravagance.

prudent ▸ adjective **1** *it is prudent to obtain consent* =wise, sensible, politic, judicious, shrewd, advisable, well advised. **2** *a prudent approach to borrowing* =cautious, careful, provident, far-sighted, judicious, shrewd, circumspect; thrifty, economical.
–OPPOSITES unwise, reckless, extravagant.

prudish ▸ adjective =puritanical, priggish, prim, prim and proper, moralistic, sententious, censorious, strait-laced, Victorian, stuffy; *informal* goody-goody.
–OPPOSITES permissive.

prune ▸ verb **1** *I pruned the roses* =cut back, trim, thin, clip, shear, pollard, top. **2** *prune any new shoots* =cut off, lop (off), chop off, clip, snip (off). **3** *staff numbers have been pruned* =reduce, cut (back/down), pare (down), slim down, trim, downsize, axe, shrink; *informal* slash.
–OPPOSITES increase.

prurient ▸ adjective =salacious, licentious, voyeuristic, lascivious, lecherous, lustful, lewd, libidinous.

pry ▸ verb =be inquisitive, poke about/around, ferret (about/around), spy, be a busybody; *informal* stick/poke one's nose in/into, be nosy, snoop; *Austral./NZ informal* stickybeak.
–OPPOSITES mind one's own business.

pseud ▸ noun =poser, poseur, fraud; *informal* show-off, phoney.

pseudo ▸ adjective =bogus, sham, phoney, mock, ersatz, quasi-, fake, false, spurious, contrived, affected, insincere; *informal* pretend, put-on; *Brit. informal* cod.
–OPPOSITES genuine.

pseudonym ▸ noun =pen name, nom de plume, assumed name, alias, sobriquet, stage name, nom de guerre.

psych *(informal)* ■ **psych someone out** =intimidate, daunt, cow, scare, terrorize, frighten, dishearten, unnerve, subdue.

■ **psych oneself up** =nerve oneself, steel oneself, brace oneself, prepare oneself, gird (up) one's loins.

psyche ▸ noun =soul, spirit, (inner) self, ego, persona, subconscious, mind, intellect.
–OPPOSITES body.

psychiatrist ▸ noun =psychotherapist, psychoanalyst; *informal* shrink.

psychic ▸ adjective **1** *psychic powers* =supernatural, paranormal, otherworldly, preternatural, metaphysical, extrasensory, magic(al), mystic(al), occult. **2** *I'm not psychic* =clairvoyant, telepathic. **3** *psychic development* =emotional, spiritual, inner; mental.
–OPPOSITES normal, physical.
▸ noun *she is a psychic* =clairvoyant, fortune teller; medium, spiritualist; telepath, mind-reader.

psychological ▸ adjective **1** *his psychological state* =mental, emotional, inner. **2** *her pain was psychological* =(all) in the mind, psychosomatic, emotional, subjective, subconscious.
–OPPOSITES physical.

psychology ▸ noun **1** *a degree in psychology* =study of the mind, science of the mind. **2** *the psychology of the road user* =mindset, mind, thought processes, way of thinking, mentality, psyche, attitude(s), make-up, character; *informal* what makes someone tick.

psychopath ▶ noun =**madman**, **madwoman**, maniac, lunatic, psychotic, sociopath; *informal* loony, nutcase, nut, psycho, head case, sicko; *Brit. informal* nutter; *N. Amer. informal* screwball, crazy, meshuggener.

psychopathic ▶ adjective. *See* MAD *sense* 1.

psychosomatic ▶ adjective =(**all**) **in the mind**, psychological, subjective, subconscious, unconscious.

psychotic ▶ adjective. *See* MAD *sense* 1.

pub ▶ noun *(Brit.)* =**bar**, inn, tavern, hostelry, taproom, roadhouse; *Brit.* public house; *Austral./NZ* hotel; *informal* watering hole; *Brit. informal* local, boozer; *dated* alehouse; *N. Amer. historical* saloon.

puberty ▶ noun =**adolescence**, pubescence, growing up; youth, young adulthood, teenage years, teens; *formal* juvenescence.

public ▶ adjective **1** *public affairs* =**state**, national, government; constitutional, civic, civil, official, social, municipal, community, communal, local; nationalized. **2** *by public demand* =**popular**, general, common, communal, collective, shared, joint, universal, widespread. **3** *a public figure* =**prominent**, well known, important, leading, eminent, distinguished, celebrated, household, famous; *N. Amer.* major-league. **4** *public places* =**open (to the public)**, communal, available, free, unrestricted, community. **5** *the news became public* =**known**, published, publicized, in circulation.
–OPPOSITES private, obscure, unknown, restricted, secret.
▶ noun **1** *the British public* =**people**, citizens, subjects, general public, electors, electorate, voters, taxpayers, residents, inhabitants, citizenry, population, populace, community, society, country, nation; everyone. **2** *his adoring public* =**audience**, spectators, followers, following, fans, devotees, admirers; patrons, clientele, market, consumers, buyers, customers, readers.
■ **in public** =**publicly**, in full view, openly, in the open, for all to see, blatantly, flagrantly, brazenly, overtly.

> **WORD LINKS**
>
> *fear of public places:* **agoraphobia**

publication ▶ noun **1** *the author of this*

publication =**book**, volume, title, work, tome, opus; newspaper, paper, magazine, periodical, newsletter, bulletin, journal, report; *informal* rag, mag, 'zine. **2** *the publication of her new book* =**issuing**, publishing, printing, distribution, spreading, dissemination, promulgation, appearance.

publicity ▶ noun **1** *the blaze of publicity* =**public attention/interest**, media attention/interest, exposure, glare, limelight. **2** *publicity should boost sales* =**promotion**, advertising, propaganda; boost, push; *informal* hype, ballyhoo, puff(ery), build-up, razzmatazz; plug.

publicize ▶ verb **1** *I never publicize this fact* =**make known**, make public, announce, broadcast, spread, promulgate, disseminate, circulate, air. **2** *he just wants to publicize his book* =**advertise**, promote, build up, talk up, push, beat the drum for, boost; *informal* hype, plug, puff (up).
–OPPOSITES conceal, suppress.

public-spirited ▶ adjective =**community-minded**, (socially) concerned, philanthropic, charitable; altruistic, humanitarian, generous, unselfish.

publish ▶ verb **1** *we publish novels* =**issue**, bring out, produce, print. **2** *he ought to publish his views* =**make known**, make public, publicize, announce, broadcast, issue, put out, distribute, spread, promulgate, disseminate, circulate, air.

pucker ▶ verb =**wrinkle**, crinkle, crease, furrow, crumple, rumple, ruck up, scrunch up, ruffle, screw up, shrivel.
▶ noun =**wrinkle**, crinkle, crumple, furrow, line, fold.

puckish ▶ adjective =**mischievous**, naughty, impish, roguish, playful; *informal* waggish.

pudding ▶ noun =**dessert**, sweet, last course; *Brit. informal* afters, pud.

puddle ▶ noun =**pool**, spill.

puerile ▶ adjective =**childish**, immature, infantile, juvenile, babyish; silly, inane, fatuous, foolish.
–OPPOSITES mature, sensible.

puff ▶ noun **1** *a puff of wind* =**gust**, blast, flurry, rush, draught, waft, breeze, breath. **2** *he took a puff at his cigar* =**pull**; *informal* drag, toke.
▶ verb **1** *he walked fast, puffing a little* =**breathe heavily**, pant, blow; gasp. **2** *she puffed at her cigarette* =**smoke**, draw on, drag on, suck at/on.

p

■ **puff out/up** =bulge, swell (out), stick out, distend, balloon (up/out), expand, inflate, enlarge.

■ **puff something out/up** =distend, expand, dilate, inflate, blow up, pump up, enlarge, bloat.

puffed ▶ adjective =out of breath, breathless, short of breath; panting, puffing, gasping, wheezing, wheezy, winded.

puffed-up ▶ adjective =self-important, conceited, arrogant, bumptious, pompous, overbearing; affected, vain; informal snooty, uppity, uppish.

puffy ▶ adjective =swollen, puffed up, distended, enlarged, inflated, dilated, bloated, engorged, bulging.

pugnacious ▶ adjective =combative, aggressive, antagonistic, belligerent, quarrelsome, argumentative, hostile, truculent.
–OPPOSITES peaceable.

puke ▶ verb (informal). See VOMIT verb senses 1, 2.

pull ▶ verb 1 *he pulled the box towards him* =tug, haul, drag, draw, tow, heave, jerk, wrench; informal yank. **2** *she pulled a muscle* =strain, sprain, wrench, tear. **3** *race day pulled big crowds* =attract, draw, bring in, pull in, lure, seduce, entice, tempt, beckon, interest, fascinate.
–OPPOSITES push, repel.
▶ noun **1** *give the chain a pull* =tug, jerk, heave; informal yank. **2** *she took a pull on her beer* =gulp, draught, drink, swallow, mouthful, slug; informal swig. **3** *a pull on a cigarette* =puff; informal drag. **4** *the pull of the theatre* =attraction, draw, lure, magnetism, fascination, appeal, allure.

■ **pull back** =withdraw, retreat, fall back, back off; pull out, retire, disengage.

■ **pull something down** =demolish, knock down, tear down, dismantle, raze (to the ground), level, flatten, bulldoze, destroy.

■ **pull in** =stop, halt, come to a halt, pull over, pull up, pull off the road, draw up, brake, park.

■ **pull someone/something in 1** *they pulled in big audiences*. See PULL verb sense 3. **2** (informal) *the police pulled him in* =arrest, apprehend, detain, take into custody, seize, capture, catch; informal collar, nab, nick, pinch, run in, bust, feel someone's collar.

■ **pull something off** =achieve, fulfil,

succeed in, accomplish, bring off, carry off, clinch, fix, effect, engineer.

■ **pull out** =withdraw, resign, leave, retire, step down, bow out, back out, give up; informal quit.

■ **pull over**. See PULL IN.

■ **pull through** =get better, get well again, improve, recover, rally, come through, recuperate.

■ **pull oneself together** =regain one's composure, recover, get a grip (on oneself), get over it; informal snap out of it, get one's act together, buck up.

■ **pull up**. See PULL IN.

■ **pull someone up** =reprimand, rebuke, scold, chide, chastise, upbraid, berate, reprove, reproach, censure, take to task, admonish, lecture, read someone the Riot Act; informal tell off; Brit. informal tick off.

pulp ▶ noun **1** *he ground it into a pulp* =mush, mash, paste, purée, slop, slush, mulch; informal gloop, goo; N. Amer. informal glop. **2** *the sweet pulp on cocoa seeds* =flesh, marrow, meat.
▶ verb *pulp the gooseberries* =mash, purée, cream, crush, press, liquidize, liquefy, sieve.
▶ adjective *pulp fiction* =trashy, cheap, sensational, lurid, tasteless; informal tacky, rubbishy.

pulpit ▶ noun =stand, lectern, platform, podium, dais, rostrum.

pulsate ▶ verb =palpitate, pulse, throb, pump, undulate, surge, heave, rise and fall; beat, thump.

pulse¹ ▶ noun **1** *the pulse in her neck* =heartbeat, heart rate. **2** *the pulse of the engine* =rhythm, beat, tempo, pounding, throbbing, thudding, drumming. **3** *pulses of ultrasound* =burst, blast, surge.
▶ verb *music pulsed through the building* =throb, pulsate, vibrate, beat, pound, thud, thump, drum, reverberate, echo.

pulse² ▶ noun *eat plenty of pulses* =legume; bean, lentil.

pulverize ▶ verb **1** *the seeds are pulverized* =grind, crush, pound, powder, mill, press, pulp, mash; technical comminute. **2** (informal) *he pulverized the opposition*. See TROUNCE.

pummel ▶ verb =batter, pound, belabour, beat; punch, strike, hit, thump; informal clobber, wallop, bash, whack, beat the living daylights out of, give someone a (good) hiding, belt, biff, lay into.

pump ▶ verb **1** *they pumped air down the*

tube =**force**, drive, push; suck, draw. **2** *she pumped up the tyre* =**inflate**, blow up, fill up; swell, enlarge, distend, expand, dilate, puff up. **3** *blood was pumping from his leg* =**spurt**, spout, squirt, jet, surge, spew, gush, stream, flow, pour, spill, well, cascade, run, course.

pun ▶ noun =**play on words**, wordplay, double entendre, innuendo, witticism.

punch[1] ▶ verb *Jim punched him in the face* =**hit**, strike, thump, jab, smash; batter, buffet, pound, pummel; *informal* sock, slug, biff, bop, wallop, clobber, bash, whack, thwack, clout; *Brit. informal* stick one on, dot, slosh; *N. Amer. informal* boff, bust; *Austral./NZ informal* quilt.
▶ noun *a punch on the nose* =**blow**, hit, knock, thump, box, jab, clip, welt; uppercut, hook; *informal* sock, slug, biff, bop, wallop, bash, whack, clout, belt; *N. Amer. informal* boff, bust.

punch[2] ▶ verb *he punched her ticket* =**make a hole in**, perforate, puncture, pierce, prick, hole, spike, skewer.

punch-up ▶ noun (*Brit. informal*). See FIGHT noun sense 1.

punchy ▶ adjective =**forceful**, incisive, strong, powerful, vigorous, dynamic, effective; dramatic, passionate, vivid.
–OPPOSITES languid.

punctilious ▶ adjective –**meticulous**, conscientious, diligent, scrupulous, careful, painstaking, rigorous, perfectionist; fussy, fastidious, finicky, pedantic; *informal* nit-picking, pernickety; *N. Amer. informal* persnickety.
–OPPOSITES careless.

punctual ▶ adjective =**on time**, prompt, on schedule, in (good) time; *informal* on the dot.
–OPPOSITES late.

punctuate ▶ verb **1** *how to punctuate direct speech* =**add punctuation to**, put punctuation marks in; mark. **2** *a talk punctuated by slides* =**break up**, interrupt, intersperse, pepper, sprinkle, scatter.

puncture ▶ noun **1** *the tyre developed a puncture* =**hole**, perforation, rupture; cut, gash, slit; leak. **2** *my car has a puncture* =**flat tyre**; *informal* flat.
▶ verb **1** *he punctured the balloon* =**make a hole in**, pierce, rupture, perforate, stab, cut, slit, prick; deflate.

pundit ▶ noun =**expert**, authority, specialist, doyen(ne), master, guru, sage, savant; *informal* buff, whizz.

pungent ▶ adjective =**strong**, powerful, pervasive, penetrating; sharp, acid, sour, biting, bitter, tart, vinegary, tangy; aromatic, spicy, piquant, peppery, hot, garlicky.
–OPPOSITES bland, mild.

punish ▶ verb **1** *they punished their children* =**discipline**, teach someone a lesson; tan someone's hide; *informal* murder, wallop, come down on (like a ton of bricks), have someone's guts for garters; *Brit. informal* give someone what for; *dated* chastise. **2** *higher charges would punish the poor* =**penalize**, disadvantage, handicap, hurt.

punishing ▶ adjective =**arduous**, demanding, taxing, strenuous, rigorous, stressful, trying; hard, heavy, difficult, tough, exhausting, tiring, gruelling, relentless.
–OPPOSITES easy.

punishment ▶ noun **1** *the punishment of the guilty* =**penalizing**, punishing, disciplining. **2** *the teacher imposed punishments* =**penalty**, sanction, sentence; discipline, justice, judgement. **3** *the van takes a lot of punishment* –**maltreatment**, mistreatment, abuse, heavy use; *informal* hammer.

┌─────────────────────────────────┐
│ **WORD LINKS**   │
│   │
│ *relating to punishment:* **punitive, penal** │
│ *study of punishment:* **penology** │
│ *fear of punishment:* **poinephobia** │
└─────────────────────────────────┘

punitive ▶ adjective **1** *punitive measures* =**penal**, disciplinary, corrective, retributive. **2** *punitive taxes* =**harsh**, severe, stiff, stringent, crushing, crippling; high, sky-high, inflated, exorbitant, extortionate, excessive; *Brit.* swingeing.

punter ▶ noun (*Brit. informal*) =**customer**, client, patron; buyer, purchaser, shopper, consumer; (**punters**) clientele, audience, trade, business; *Brit. informal* bums on seats.

puny ▶ adjective **1** *a puny boy* =**undersized**, stunted, slight, small, little; weak, feeble, sickly, delicate, frail, fragile; *informal* weedy. **2** *their puny efforts* =**pitiful**, pitiable, miserable, sorry, meagre, paltry, trifling, inconsequential; *informal* pathetic, measly, piddling.
–OPPOSITES sturdy, substantial.

pupil ▶ noun **1** *former pupils of the school* =**student**, scholar; schoolchild, schoolboy, schoolgirl. **2** *the guru's pupils* =**disciple**, follower, student, protégé, apprentice, trainee, novice.

puppet ▶ noun **1** *a show with puppets* =**marionette**; glove puppet, finger puppet. **2** *a puppet of the government* =**pawn**, tool, instrument, cat's paw, poodle; mouthpiece, minion, stooge.

purchase ▶ verb *we purchased new software* =**buy**, acquire, obtain, pick up, procure; invest in; *informal* get hold of, score.
−OPPOSITES sell.
▶ noun **1** *he's happy with his purchase* =**acquisition**, buy, investment, order, bargain; shopping, goods. **2** *he could get no purchase on the wall* =**grip**, grasp, hold, foothold, toehold, anchorage, support; traction, leverage.
−OPPOSITES sale.

purchaser ▶ noun =**buyer**, shopper, customer, consumer, patron.

pure ▶ adjective **1** *pure gold* =**unadulterated**, undiluted; sterling, solid, 100%; flawless, perfect, genuine, real. **2** *the air is so pure* =**clean**, clear, fresh, sparkling, unpolluted, uncontaminated, untainted; wholesome, natural, healthy; uninfected, disinfected, germ-free, sterile, sterilized, aseptic. **3** *pure in body and mind* =**virtuous**, moral, good, righteous, saintly, honourable, reputable, wholesome, clean, honest, upright, upstanding, exemplary; chaste; decent, worthy, noble, blameless, guiltless, spotless, unsullied, uncorrupted, undefiled; *informal* squeaky clean. **4** *pure maths* =**theoretical**, abstract, conceptual, academic. **5** *three hours of pure magic* =**sheer**, utter, absolute, out-and-out, complete, total, perfect.
−OPPOSITES adulterated, polluted, immoral, practical.

purely ▶ adverb =**entirely**, wholly, exclusively, solely, only, just, merely.

purgatory ▶ noun =**torment**, torture, misery, suffering, affliction, anguish, agony, woe, hell; an ordeal, a nightmare.
−OPPOSITES paradise.

purge ▶ verb =**cleanse**, clear, purify.
▶ noun =**removal**, expulsion, ejection, exclusion, eviction, dismissal, sacking, ousting, eradication.

purify ▶ verb =**clean**, cleanse, refine, decontaminate; filter, clear, freshen, deodorize; sanitize, disinfect, sterilize.

purist ▶ noun =**pedant**, perfectionist, formalist, literalist, stickler, traditionalist, dogmatist; *informal* nit-picker.

puritan ▶ noun =**moralist**, prude, prig, killjoy; ascetic; *informal* goody-goody, Holy Joe; *N. Amer. informal* bluenose.

puritanical ▶ adjective =**moralistic**, puritan, strait-laced, stuffy, prudish, prim, priggish; narrow-minded, sententious, censorious, austere, severe, ascetic, abstemious; *informal* goody-goody, starchy.
−OPPOSITES permissive.

purity ▶ noun **1** *the purity of our tap water* =**cleanness**, freshness. **2** *they sought purity in a foul world* =**virtue**, morality, goodness, righteousness, piety, honour, honesty, integrity, decency; innocence, chastity.

purloin ▶ verb *(formal)* =**steal**, thieve, rob, take, snatch, pilfer, loot, appropriate; *informal* swipe, nab, rip off, lift, 'liberate', 'borrow', filch, snaffle; *Brit. informal* pinch, half-inch, nick, whip, knock off, nobble; *N. Amer. informal* heist.

purport ▶ verb *this work purports to be objective* =**claim**, profess, pretend.

purpose ▶ noun **1** *the purpose of his visit* =**motive**, motivation, grounds, cause, occasion, reason, point, basis, justification. **2** *their purpose was to subvert the economy* =**intention**, aim, object, objective, goal, end, plan, scheme, target; ambition, aspiration. **3** *I cannot see any purpose in it* =**advantage**, benefit, good, use, value, merit, worth, profit; *informal* mileage. **4** *the original purpose of the porch* =**function**, role, use. **5** *they started with some purpose* =**determination**, resolution, resolve, enthusiasm, ambition, motivation, commitment, conviction, dedication; *informal* get-up-and-go.
■ **on purpose** =**deliberately**, intentionally, purposely, by design, wilfully, knowingly, consciously; expressly, specifically, especially, specially.

purposeful ▶ adjective =**determined**, resolute, steadfast, single-minded, committed.
−OPPOSITES aimless.

purposely ▶ adverb. See ON PURPOSE at PURPOSE.

purse ▶ noun **1** *the money fell out of her purse* =**wallet**, money bag; *N. Amer.* change purse, billfold. **2** *(N. Amer.) a woman's purse.* See HANDBAG. **3** *the fight will net him a $75,000 purse* =**prize**, reward; winnings, stake(s).
▶ verb *he pursed his lips* =**press together**, compress, tighten, pucker, pout.

pursue ▶ verb **1** *I pursued him down the garden* =**follow**, run after, chase; hunt, stalk, track, trail, hound. **2** *pursue the goal of political union* =**strive for**, work towards, seek, search for, aim at/for, aspire to. **3** *she pursued a political career* =**engage in**, be occupied in, practise, follow, conduct, ply, take up, undertake, carry on. **4** *we will not pursue the matter* =**investigate**, research, inquire into, look into, examine, scrutinize, analyse, delve into, probe.
−OPPOSITES avoid, shun.

pursuit ▶ noun **1** *the pursuit of profit* =**striving for**, quest after/for, search for. **2** *a worthwhile pursuit* =**activity**, hobby, pastime, diversion, recreation, amusement; occupation, trade, vocation, business, work, job, employment.

purvey ▶ verb =**sell**, supply, provide, furnish, cater, retail, deal in, trade, stock, offer; peddle, tout, traffic in; *informal* flog.

purveyor ▶ noun =**seller**, vendor, retailer, supplier, stockist, trader, pedlar.

pus ▶ noun =**suppuration**, discharge, secretion.

push ▶ verb **1** *she tried to push him away* =**shove**, thrust, propel; send, drive, force, prod, poke, nudge, elbow, shoulder; sweep, bundle, hustle, manhandle, ram. **2** *she pushed her way into the flat* =**force**, shove, thrust, squeeze, jostle, elbow, shoulder, bundle, hustle; work, inch. **3** *he pushed the panic button* =**press**, depress, hold down, squeeze; operate, activate. **4** *don't push her to join in* =**urge**, press, pressure, pressurize, force, coerce, nag; browbeat into; *informal* lean on, twist someone's arm, bulldoze. **5** *they push their own products* =**advertise**, publicize, promote, bang the drum for; sell, market, merchandise; *informal* plug, hype (up), flog; *N. Amer. informal* ballyhoo.
−OPPOSITES pull.

▶ noun **1** *I felt a push in the back* =**shove**, thrust, nudge, bump, jolt, prod, poke. **2** *the army's eastward push* =**advance**, drive, thrust, charge, attack, assault, onslaught, onrush, offensive, sortie, sally, incursion.

■ **push someone around** =**bully**, domineer, trample on, bulldoze, browbeat, tyrannize, intimidate, threaten, victimize, pick on; *informal* lean on, boss about/around.

■ **push for** =**demand**, call for, request, press for, campaign for, lobby for, speak up for; urge, promote, advocate, champion.

■ **push off** *(informal)* =**go away**, depart, leave, get out; go, get moving, be off (with you), shoo; *informal* skedaddle, split, scram, run along, beat it, get lost, shove off, buzz off, clear off, on your bike; *Brit. informal* get stuffed, sling your hook, hop it, bog off, naff off; *N. Amer. informal* bug off, take a powder, take a hike; *Austral./NZ informal* rack off, nick off.

■ **push on** =**press on**, continue, carry on, advance, proceed, go on, forge ahead.

pushover ▶ noun **1** *the teacher was a pushover* =**weakling**, man of straw; *informal* soft touch, easy meat. **2** *this course is a pushover* =**gift**, five-finger exercise; child's play; *informal* doddle, piece of cake, money for old rope, cinch, breeze; *Brit. informal* doss; *N. Amer. informal* duck soup, snap; *Austral./NZ informal* bludge.

pushy ▶ adjective =**assertive**, overbearing, domineering, aggressive, forceful, forward; thrusting, ambitious, overconfident, cocky; *informal* bossy.
−OPPOSITES submissive.

pusillanimous ▶ adjective =**timid**, timorous, cowardly, fearful, faint-hearted, lily-livered, spineless, craven; *informal* chicken, gutless, wimpy, wimpish, sissy, yellow, yellow-bellied.
−OPPOSITES brave.

pussyfoot ▶ verb =**equivocate**, be evasive, be non-committal, sidestep the issue, prevaricate, quibble, hedge, beat about the bush; *Brit.* hum and haw; *informal* duck the question, sit on the fence, shilly-shally.

pustule ▶ noun =**pimple**, spot, boil, swelling, eruption, carbuncle, blister, abscess; *informal* zit; *Scottish informal* plook.

put ▶ verb **1** *she put the parcel on a chair* =**place**, set (down), lay (down), deposit, position; leave, plant; *informal* stick, dump, bung, park, plonk, pop; *N. Amer. informal* plunk. **2** *he didn't want to be put in a category* =**assign to**, consign to, allocate to, place in. **3** *don't put the blame on me* =**lay**, pin, place, fix; attribute to, impute to, assign to, allocate to, ascribe to. **4** *the proposals put to the committee* =**submit**, present, tender, offer, advance, suggest, propose. **5** *she put it bluntly* =**express**, word, phrase, frame, formulate, render, convey, couch; state, say, utter. **6** *he put the cost at £8,000* =**estimate**, calculate, reckon, gauge, assess, evaluate, value, judge, measure, compute, fix, set.

■ **put about** *the ship put about* =**turn round**, come about, change course.

■ **put something about** *the rumour had been put about* =**spread**, circulate, make public, disseminate, broadcast, publicize, pass on, propagate, bandy about.

■ **put something across/over** =**communicate**, convey, get across/over, explain, make clear, spell out.

■ **put something aside 1** *we've got a bit put aside in the bank* =**save**, put by, set aside, deposit, reserve, store, stockpile, hoard, stow, cache; *informal* salt away, squirrel away, stash away. **2** *they put aside their differences* =**disregard**, set aside, ignore, forget, discount, bury.

■ **put someone away** (*informal*) =**jail**, imprison, put in prison, put behind bars, lock up, incarcerate; *informal* cage; *Brit. informal* bang up, send down; *N. Amer. informal* jug.

■ **put something away 1** *I put away some money.* See PUT SOMETHING ASIDE *sense 1.* **2** *she never puts her things away* =**replace**, put back, tidy away/up, clear away/up. **3** (*informal*) *she can put away a lot of food.* See EAT *sense 1.*

■ **put something back 1** *he put the books back* =**replace**, return, restore, put away, tidy away. **2** *they put back the film's release date.* See PUT SOMETHING OFF.

■ **put someone down** (*informal*) =**criticize**, belittle, disparage, deprecate, denigrate, slight, humiliate; *informal* show up, cut down to size.

■ **put something down 1** *he put his ideas down on paper* =**write down**, note down, jot down, take down, set down; list, record, register, log. **2** *they put down the rebellion* =**suppress**, check, crush, quash, squash, quell, overthrow, stamp out, repress, subdue. **3** *the horse had to be put down* =**destroy**, put to sleep, put out of its misery, put to death, kill. **4** *put it down to the heat* =**attribute**, ascribe, impute; blame on.

■ **put something forward.** See PUT *sense 4.*

■ **put in for** =**apply for**, try for; request, seek, ask for.

■ **put someone off** =**deter**, discourage, dissuade, daunt, unnerve, intimidate, scare off; distract, disturb, divert, sidetrack; *informal* turn off.

■ **put something off** =**postpone**, defer, delay, put back, adjourn, hold over, reschedule, shelve, table; *informal* put on

ice, put on the back burner.

■ **put something on 1** *she put on jeans* =**dress in**, don, pull on, throw on, slip into, change into. **2** *I put the light on* =**switch on**, turn on, activate. **3** *they put on an extra train* =**provide**, lay on, supply, make available. **4** *the museum put on an exhibition* =**organize**, stage, mount, present, produce. **5** *she put on an American accent* =**feign**, fake, simulate, affect, assume. **6** *he put a fiver on Oxford United* =**bet**, gamble, stake, wager; place, lay.

■ **put someone out 1** *Maria was put out by the slur* =**annoy**, anger, irritate, offend, affront, displease, irk, vex, pique, nettle, gall, upset; *informal* rile, miff, peeve; *Brit. informal* nark. **2** *I don't want to put you out* =**inconvenience**, trouble, bother, impose on.

■ **put something out 1** *firemen put out the blaze* =**extinguish**, quench, douse, smother; blow out, snuff out. **2** *he put out a press release* =**issue**, publish, release, bring out, circulate, publicize, post.

■ **put someone up 1** *we can put him up for a few days* =**accommodate**, house, take in; give someone a roof over their head. **2** *they put up a candidate* =**nominate**, propose, put forward, recommend.

■ **put something up 1** *the building was put up 100 years ago* =**build**, construct, erect, raise. **2** *she put up a poster* =**display**, pin up, stick up, hang up, post. **3** *we put up alternative schemes* =**propose**, put forward, present, submit, suggest, tender. **4** *the Chancellor put up taxes* =**increase**, raise; *informal* jack up, hike, bump up. **5** *he put up most of the funding* =**provide**, supply, furnish, give, contribute, donate, pledge, pay; *informal* fork out, cough up, shell out; *N. Amer. informal* ante up, pony up.

■ **put someone up to something** (*informal*) =**persuade**, encourage to, urge to, egg on to, incite to, goad into.

■ **put up with** =**tolerate**, take, stand (for), accept, stomach, swallow, endure, bear, support, take something lying down; *informal* abide, lump it; *Brit. informal* stick, be doing with; *formal* brook; *archaic* suffer.

putative ▸ adjective =**supposed**, assumed, presumed; accepted, recognized; alleged, reputed, reported, rumoured.

put-down ▸ noun (*informal*) =**snub**, slight, affront, rebuff, sneer, rejoinder, barb, jibe, criticism; *informal* dig.

putrefy ▶ verb = decay, rot, decompose, go bad, go off, spoil, fester, perish, deteriorate; moulder.

putrid ▶ adjective = decomposing, decaying, rotting, rotten, bad, off, putrefied, putrescent, rancid, mouldy; foul, fetid, rank.

puzzle ▶ verb **1** *her decision puzzled me* = perplex, confuse, bewilder, bemuse, baffle, mystify, confound, nonplus; *informal* flummox, faze, stump, beat; *N. Amer. informal* discombobulate. **2** *she puzzled over the problem* = think hard about, mull over, muse over, ponder, contemplate, meditate on, consider, deliberate on, chew over, wonder about.
▶ noun *the poem has always been a puzzle* = enigma, mystery, paradox, conundrum, poser, riddle, problem.

puzzled ▶ adjective = perplexed, confused, bewildered, bemused, baffled, mystified, confounded, nonplussed, at a loss; *informal* flummoxed, stumped, fazed; *N. Amer. informal* discombobulated.

puzzling ▶ adjective = baffling, perplexing, bewildering, confusing, complicated, unclear, mysterious, enigmatic, ambiguous, obscure, abstruse, unfathomable, incomprehensible, impenetrable, cryptic.
−OPPOSITES clear.

pygmy ▶ noun = lightweight, nonentity, nobody, cipher; small fry; *informal* pipsqueak, no-hoper.
−OPPOSITES giant.

pyromaniac ▶ noun = arsonist, incendiary; *Brit.* fire-raiser; *N. Amer.* fire starter; *informal* firebug; *N. Amer. informal* torch.

Qq

quack ▸ noun *a quack selling fake medicines* =**swindler**, charlatan, mountebank, trickster, fraudster, impostor, hoaxer, sharper; *informal* con man, shark.

quadrangle ▸ noun =**courtyard**, quad, court, cloister, precinct; square, plaza, piazza.

quaff ▸ verb =**drink**, swallow, gulp (down), guzzle, slurp, down, drain, empty; imbibe, partake of, consume, sup, sip; *informal* sink, kill, glug, swig, swill, slug, knock back; *Brit. informal* get outside (of), shift, murder.

quagmire ▸ noun **1** *the field became a quagmire* =**swamp**, morass, bog, marsh, mire, slough. **2** *a judicial quagmire* =**muddle**, mix-up, mess, predicament, mare's nest, quandary, tangle, imbroglio; *informal* sticky situation, pickle, stew, dilemma, fix, bind.

quail ▸ verb =**cower**, cringe, flinch, shrink, recoil, shy (away), pull back; shiver, tremble, shake, quake, blench.

quaint ▸ adjective **1** *a quaint town* =**picturesque**, charming, sweet, attractive, old-fashioned, old-world; *Brit.* twee; *N. Amer.* cunning; *pseudo-archaic* olde (worlde). **2** *quaint customs* =**unusual**, different, out of the ordinary, curious, eccentric, quirky, bizarre, whimsical, unconventional; *informal* offbeat.
−OPPOSITES ugly, ordinary.

quake ▸ verb **1** *the ground quaked* =**shake**, tremble, quiver, shudder, sway, rock, wobble, move, heave, convulse. **2** *we quaked when we saw the soldiers* =**tremble**, shake, quiver, shiver; blench, blanch, flinch, shrink, recoil, cower, cringe.

qualification ▸ noun **1** *a teaching qualification* =**certificate**, diploma, degree, licence, document, warrant; eligibility, acceptability, adequacy; proficiency, skill, ability, capability, aptitude. **2** *I can't accept it without qualification* =**modification**, limitation, reservation, stipulation; alteration, amendment, revision, moderation, mitigation; condition, proviso, caveat.

qualified ▸ adjective =**certified**, certificated, chartered, licensed, professional; trained, fit, competent, accomplished, proficient, skilled, experienced, expert.

qualify ▸ verb **1** *I qualify for free travel* =**be eligible**, meet the requirements; be entitled to, be permitted. **2** *they qualify as refugees* =**count**, be considered, be designated, be eligible. **3** *she qualified as a solicitor* =**be certified**, be licensed; pass, graduate, succeed. **4** *the course qualified them to teach* =**authorize**, empower, allow, permit, license; equip, prepare, train, educate, teach. **5** *they qualified their findings* =**modify**, limit, restrict, make conditional; moderate, temper, modulate, mitigate.

quality ▸ noun **1** *a poor quality of signal* =**standard**, grade, class, calibre, condition, character, nature, form, rank, value, level; sort, type, kind, variety. **2** *work of such quality* =**excellence**, superiority, merit, worth, value, virtue, calibre, eminence, distinction, incomparability; talent, skill, virtuosity, craftsmanship. **3** *her good qualities* =**feature**, trait, attribute, characteristic, point, aspect, facet, side, property.

qualm ▸ noun =**misgiving**, doubt, reservation, second thought, worry, concern, anxiety; (**qualms**) hesitation, demur, reluctance, disinclination, apprehension, trepidation, unease; scruples, remorse, compunction.

quandary ▸ noun =**predicament**, plight, difficult situation; trouble, muddle, mess, confusion, difficulty, mare's nest; *informal* dilemma, sticky situation, pickle, hole, stew, fix, bind, jam.

quantity ▸ noun **1** *the quantity of food collected* =**amount**, total, aggregate, sum, quota, mass, weight, volume, bulk; quantum, proportion, portion, part. **2** *a quantity of ammunition* =**amount**, lot, great deal, an abundance, a wealth, a profusion, plenty; *informal* piles, oodles, tons, lots, loads, heaps, masses, stacks; *Brit. informal* shedloads.

quarrel ▸ noun *they had a quarrel about money* =**argument**, disagreement, squabble, fight, dispute, wrangle, clash, altercation, feud, contretemps, disputation, falling-out, war of words, shouting match; *informal* tiff, slanging match, run-in; *Brit. informal* barney, row, bust-up.
▸ verb *don't quarrel over it* =**argue**, fight, disagree, fall out; differ, be at odds; bicker, squabble, cross swords, lock horns, be at each other's throats; *Brit. informal* row.
■ **quarrel with** *you can't quarrel with the verdict* =**fault**, criticize, object to, oppose, take exception to; attack, take issue with, impugn, contradict, dispute, controvert; *informal* knock; *formal* gainsay.

quarrelsome ▸ adjective =**argumentative**, disputatious, confrontational, captious, pugnacious, combative, antagonistic, bellicose, belligerent, cantankerous, choleric; *Brit. informal* stroppy; *N. Amer. informal* scrappy.
–OPPOSITES peaceable.

quarry ▸ noun =**prey**, victim; object, goal, target; kill, game.

quarter ▸ noun 1 *the Latin quarter* =**district**, area, region, part, side, neighbourhood, precinct, locality, sector, zone; ghetto, community, enclave. **2** *help from an unexpected quarter* =**source**, direction, place, location; person. **3** *the servants' quarters* =**accommodation**, lodgings, rooms, chambers; home; *informal* pad, digs; *formal* abode, residence, domicile. **4** *the riot squads gave no quarter* =**mercy**, leniency, clemency, compassion, pity, charity, sympathy, tolerance.
▸ verb **1** *they were quartered in a villa* =**accommodate**, house, board, lodge, put up, take in, install, shelter; *Military* billet. **2** *I quartered the streets* =**patrol**, range over, tour, reconnoitre, traverse, survey, scout; *Brit. informal* recce.

quash ▸ verb **1** *he may quash the sentence* =**cancel**, reverse, rescind, repeal, revoke, retract, countermand, withdraw, overturn, overrule, veto, annul, nullify, invalidate, negate, void; *formal* abrogate. **2** *we want to quash these rumours* =**put an end to**, put a stop to, stamp out, crush, put down, check, curb, nip in the bud, squash, quell, subdue, suppress, extinguish, stifle.
–OPPOSITES validate.

quasi- ▸ combining form **1** *quasi-scientific* =**supposedly**, seemingly, apparently, allegedly, ostensibly, on the face of it, on the surface, to all intents and purposes, outwardly, superficially, purportedly, nominally; pseudo-. **2** *a quasi-autonomous organization* =**partly**, partially, half, relatively, comparatively, (up) to a point; almost, nearly, just about, all but.

quaver ▸ verb =**tremble**, waver, quiver, shake, vibrate, oscillate, fluctuate, falter, warble.

quay ▸ noun =**wharf**, pier, jetty, landing stage, berth; marina, dock, harbour.

queasy ▸ adjective =**nauseous**, bilious, sick; ill, unwell, poorly, green about the gills; *Brit.* off colour.

queen ▸ noun **1** *the Queen was crowned* =**monarch**, sovereign, ruler, head of state; Her Majesty; king's consort, queen consort. **2** *(informal) the queen of soul music* =**doyenne**, star, leading light, big name, prima donna, idol, heroine, favourite, darling, goddess.

queer ▸ adjective *it seemed queer to see him here* =**odd**, strange, unusual, funny, peculiar, curious, bizarre, weird, uncanny, freakish, eerie, unnatural; unconventional, unorthodox, unexpected, unfamiliar, abnormal, anomalous, atypical, out of the ordinary, incongruous, irregular; *informal* fishy, creepy, spooky, freaky; *Brit. informal* rum.
–OPPOSITES normal.
▸ verb *he queered the whole deal* =**spoil**, ruin, wreck, destroy, scotch, disrupt, undo, thwart, foil, blight, cripple, jeopardize, threaten, undermine, compromise; *informal* botch, blow, put the kibosh on; *Brit. informal* scupper.

quell ▸ verb **1** *troops quelled the unrest* =**put an end to**, put a stop to, end, crush, put down, check, crack down on, curb, nip in the bud, squash, quash, subdue, suppress, overcome; *informal* squelch. **2** *he quelled his misgivings* =**calm**, soothe, pacify, settle, quieten, silence, allay, assuage, mitigate, moderate; *literary* stay.

quench ▸ verb **1** *they quenched their thirst* =**satisfy**, slake, sate, satiate, gratify, relieve, assuage, take the edge off, indulge; lessen, reduce, diminish, check, suppress, extinguish, overcome. **2** *the flames were quenched* =**extinguish**, put out, snuff out, smother, douse.

querulous ▸ adjective =**petulant**, peevish, pettish, complaining, fractious, fretful, irritable, testy, tetchy, cross,

q

snappish, crabby, crotchety, cantankerous, miserable, moody, grumpy, bad-tempered, sullen, sulky, sour, churlish; *informal* snappy, grouchy, whingy; *Brit. informal* ratty, cranky; *N. English informal* mardy; *N. Amer. informal* soreheaded.

query ▶ noun **1** *we are happy to answer any queries* =**question**, enquiry; *Brit. informal* quiz. **2** *there was a query as to who owned the hotel* =**doubt**, uncertainty, question (mark), reservation.
▶ verb **1** *'Why do that?' queried Isobel* =**ask**, enquire, question; *Brit. informal* quiz. **2** *folk may query his credentials* =**question**, challenge, dispute, cast aspersions on, doubt, have suspicions about.

quest ▶ noun **1** *their quest for her killer* =**search**, hunt; pursuance of. **2** *Sir Galahad's quest* =**expedition**, journey, voyage, trek, travels, odyssey, adventure, exploration, search; crusade, mission, pilgrimage.
■ **in quest of** =**in search of**, in pursuit of, seeking, looking for, on the lookout for, after.

question ▶ noun **1** *please answer my question* =**enquiry**, query; interrogation; *Brit. informal* quiz. **2** *there is no question that he is ill* =**doubt**, dispute, argument, debate, uncertainty, dubiousness, reservation; *formal* dubiety. **3** *the political questions of the day* =**issue**, matter, business, problem, concern, topic, theme, case; debate, argument, dispute, controversy.
–OPPOSITES answer, certainty.
▶ verb **1** *the magistrate questions the suspect* =**interrogate**, cross-examine, cross-question, quiz, catechize; interview, debrief, examine; *informal* grill, pump. **2** *she questioned his motives* =**query**, challenge, dispute, cast aspersions on, doubt, suspect.
■ **beyond question 1** *her loyalty is beyond question* =**undoubted**, certain, indubitable, indisputable, incontrovertible, unquestionable, undeniable, clear, patent, manifest. **2** *the results demonstrated this beyond question* =**indisputably**, irrefutably, incontestably, incontrovertibly, unquestionably, undeniably, beyond doubt, clearly, patently, obviously.
■ **in question** =**at issue**, under discussion, under consideration, on the agenda, to be decided.
■ **out of the question** =**impossible**, impracticable, unfeasible, unworkable, inconceivable, unimaginable, unrealizable, unsuitable; *informal* not on.

WORD LINKS

relating to questions: **interrogative**

questionable ▶ adjective **1** *jokes of questionable taste* =**controversial**, contentious, doubtful, dubious, uncertain, debatable, arguable; unverified, unprovable, unresolved, unconvincing, implausible, improbable; borderline, marginal, moot; *informal* iffy; *Brit. informal* dodgy. **2** *questionable financial dealings* =**suspicious**, suspect, dubious, irregular, odd, strange, murky, dark, unsavoury, disreputable; *informal* funny, fishy, shady, iffy; *Brit. informal* dodgy.
–OPPOSITES indisputable, honest.

questionnaire ▶ noun =**question sheet**, survey form, opinion poll; test, quiz.

queue ▶ noun **1** *a queue of people* =**line**, row, column, file, chain, string; procession, train, cavalcade; waiting list; *N. Amer.* wait list; *Brit. informal* crocodile. **2** *a traffic queue* =**(traffic) jam**, tailback, gridlock; *N. Amer.* backup; *informal* snarl-up.
▶ verb *we queued for ice creams* =**line up**, wait in line, fall in.

quibble ▶ noun *I have just one quibble* =**criticism**, objection, complaint, protest, argument, exception, grumble, grouse, cavil; *informal* niggle, moan, gripe, beef, grouch.
▶ verb *no one quibbled with the title* =**object to**, find fault with, complain about, cavil at; split hairs, chop logic; criticize, query, fault, pick holes in; *informal* nitpick.

quick ▶ adjective **1** *a quick worker* =**fast**, swift, rapid, speedy, expeditious, brisk, smart; lightning, whirlwind, fast-track, whistle-stop, breakneck; *informal* nippy, zippy. **2** *a quick look* =**hasty**, hurried, cursory, perfunctory, desultory, superficial, summary; brief, short, fleeting, transient, transitory, short-lived, lightning, momentary. **3** *a quick end to the recession* =**sudden**, instantaneous, immediate, abrupt, precipitate. **4** *she isn't as quick as the others* =**intelligent**, bright, clever, gifted, able, astute, sharp-witted, smart; observant, alert, sharp, perceptive; *informal* brainy, on the ball.
–OPPOSITES slow, long.

quicken ▶ verb **1** *she quickened her pace* =**speed up**, accelerate, step up, hasten, hurry (up); *informal* gee up. **2** *the film quick-*

ened his interest in nature =**stimulate**, excite, arouse, rouse, stir up, activate, galvanize, whet, inspire, kindle; invigorate, revive, revitalize.

quickly ▶ adverb **1** *he walked quickly* =**fast**, swiftly, briskly, rapidly, speedily, at full tilt, at a gallop, at the double, post-haste, hotfoot; *informal* double quick, p.d.q. (pretty damn quick), like (greased) lightning, hell for leather, like mad, like blazes, like the wind; *Brit. informal* like the clappers, like billy-o; *N. Amer. informal* lickety-split; *literary* apace. **2** *you'd better leave quickly* =**immediately**, directly, at once, now, straight away, right away, instantly, forthwith, without delay, without further ado; soon, promptly, early; *N. Amer.* momentarily; *informal* like a shot, a.s.a.p., p.d.q., pronto, straight off. **3** *he quickly inspected it* =**briefly**, fleetingly, briskly; hastily, hurriedly, cursorily, perfunctorily, superficially, desultorily.

quick-tempered ▶ adjective =**irritable**, irascible, hot-tempered, short-tempered, snappish, fiery, touchy, volatile; cross, crabby, crotchety, cantankerous, grumpy, ill-tempered, bad-tempered, testy, tetchy, prickly, choleric; *informal* snappy, grouchy, cranky, on a short fuse; *Brit. informal* narky, ratty, eggy; *N. Amer. informal* soreheaded.
−OPPOSITES placid.

quick-witted ▶ adjective =**intelligent**, bright, clever, gifted, able, astute, quick, smart, sharp-witted; observant, alert, sharp, perceptive; *informal* brainy, on the ball, quick on the uptake.
−OPPOSITES slow.

quid pro quo ▶ noun =**exchange**, trade, swap, switch, barter, substitute, reciprocation, return; amends, compensation, recompense, restitution, reparation.

quiescent ▶ adjective =**inactive**, inert, idle, dormant, at rest, inoperative, deactivated, quiet; still, motionless, immobile, passive.
−OPPOSITES active.

quiet ▶ adjective **1** *the whole pub went quiet* =**silent**, still, hushed, noiseless, soundless; mute, dumb, speechless. **2** *a quiet voice* =**soft**, low, muted, muffled, faint, indistinct, inaudible, hushed, whispered, suppressed. **3** *a quiet village* =**peaceful**, sleepy, tranquil, calm, still, restful, undisturbed, untroubled;

unfrequented. **4** *can I have a quiet word?* =**private**, confidential, secret, discreet, unofficial, off the record, between ourselves. **5** *you can't keep it quiet for long* =**secret**, confidential, classified, unrevealed, undisclosed, unknown, under wraps; *informal* hush-hush, mum. **6** *business is quiet* =**slow**, stagnant, slack, sluggish, inactive, idle.
−OPPOSITES loud, busy, public.
▶ noun *the quiet of the countryside* =**peace**, restfulness, calm, tranquillity, serenity; silence, still, hush.

quieten ▶ verb **1** *quieten the children down* =**silence**, hush, shush; *informal* shut up. **2** *her companions quietened* =**fall silent**, stop talking, break off, shush, hold one's tongue; *informal* shut up, clam up, pipe down.

quietly ▶ adverb **1** *she quietly entered the room* =**silently**, noiselessly, soundlessly, inaudibly. **2** *he spoke quietly* =**softly**, in a low voice, in a whisper, in a murmur, under one's breath, in an undertone, sotto voce, gently, faintly, weakly, feebly. **3** *some bonds were sold quietly* =**discreetly**, privately, confidentially, secretly, unofficially, off the record. **4** *she is quietly confident* =**calmly**, patiently, placidly, serenely.

quilt ▶ noun =**duvet**, cover(s); *Brit.* eiderdown; *N. Amer.* comforter, puff; *Austral. trademark* Doona.

quintessence ▶ noun **1** *it's the quintessence of the modern home* =**perfect example**, exemplar, prototype, stereotype, picture, epitome, embodiment, ideal. **2** *the quintessence of intelligence* =**essence**, soul, spirit, nature, core, heart, crux, kernel, marrow, substance; *informal* nitty-gritty.

quintessential ▶ adjective =**typical**, prototypical, stereotypical, archetypal, classic, model, standard, stock, representative, conventional; ideal, consummate, exemplary, best, ultimate.

quip ▶ noun =**joke**, witticism, jest, pun, sally, pleasantry, bon mot; *informal* one-liner, gag, wisecrack, funny.

quirk ▶ noun **1** *they all know his quirks* =**idiosyncrasy**, peculiarity, oddity, eccentricity, foible, whim, vagary, caprice, fancy, crotchet, habit, characteristic, trait, fad. **2** *a quirk of fate* =**chance**, fluke, freak, anomaly, twist.

quirky ▶ adjective =**eccentric**, idiosyncratic, unconventional, unorthodox,

unusual, strange, bizarre, peculiar, odd, outlandish, zany; *informal* wacky, freaky, way-out, far out, offbeat.
–OPPOSITES conventional.

quit ▸ verb **1** *he quit the office at 12.30* =**leave**, vacate, exit, depart from. **2** *(informal) he quit his job* =**resign from**, leave, give up, hand in one's notice; *informal* chuck, pack in. **3** *(informal) quit living in the past* =**give up**, stop, discontinue, drop, abandon, abstain from; *informal* pack in, leave off.

quite ▸ adverb **1** *two quite different types* =**completely**, entirely, totally, wholly, absolutely, utterly, thoroughly, altogether. **2** *red hair was quite common* =**fairly**, rather, somewhat, slightly, relatively, comparatively, moderately, reasonably, to a certain extent; *informal* pretty, kind of, sort of.

quiver ▸ verb **1** *I quivered with terror* =**tremble**, shake, shiver, quaver, quake, shudder. **2** *the bird quivers its wings* =**flutter**, flap, beat, agitate, vibrate.

quixotic ▸ adjective =**idealistic**, romantic, visionary, Utopian, extravagant, starry-eyed, unrealistic, unworldly; impracticable, unworkable, impossible.

quiz ▸ noun =**competition**, test of knowledge.
▸ verb *a man was being quizzed by police* =**question**, interrogate, cross-examine, cross-question, interview, sound out, give someone the third degree; *informal* grill, pump.

quizzical ▸ adjective =**enquiring**, questioning, curious; puzzled, perplexed, baffled, mystified; amused, mocking, teasing.

quota ▸ noun =**allocation**, share, allowance, limit, ration, portion, dispensation, slice (of the cake); percentage, commission; proportion, fraction, bit, amount, quantity; *informal* cut, rake-off; *Brit. informal* whack.

quotation ▸ noun **1** *a quotation from Dryden* =**citation**, quote, excerpt, extract, passage, line, paragraph, verse, phrase; reference, allusion; *N. Amer.* cite. **2** *a quotation for the building work* =**estimate**, quote, price, tender, bid, costing, charge, figure.

quote ▸ verb **1** *he quoted from the book* =**recite**, repeat, reproduce, retell, echo, iterate; take, extract. **2** *she quoted one case in which a girl died* =**cite**, mention, refer to, name, instance, specify, identify; relate, recount; allude to, point out, present, offer, advance.
▸ noun **1** *a Shakespeare quote.* See QUOTATION sense 1. **2** *ask the contractor for a quote.* See QUOTATION sense 2.

quotidian ▸ adjective **1** *the quotidian routine* =**daily**, everyday, day-to-day, diurnal. **2** *her dreadfully quotidian car* =**ordinary**, average, run-of-the-mill, everyday, standard, typical, middle-of-the-road, common, conventional, mainstream, unremarkable, unexceptional, workaday, commonplace, mundane, uninteresting; *informal* bog-standard, a dime a dozen; *Brit. informal* common or garden.
–OPPOSITES unusual.

q

rabbit ▸ noun = *Brit.* coney; *informal* bunny.

> **WORD LINKS**
>
> male: **buck**
> female: **doe**
> young: **kitten**
> home: **warren, burrow, hutch**

rabble ▸ noun **1** *a rabble of youths* =**mob**, crowd, throng, gang, swarm, horde, pack, mass, group. **2** *rule by the rabble* =**the common people**, the masses, the populace, the multitude, the rank and file, the commonality, the plebeians, the proletariat, the peasantry, the lower classes; *derogatory* the hoi polloi, the riff-raff; *informal, derogatory* the proles, the plebs.
−OPPOSITES nobility.

rabble-rouser ▸ noun =**agitator**, troublemaker, instigator, firebrand, revolutionary, demagogue.

rabid ▸ adjective **1** *a rabid anti-royalist* =**extreme**, fanatical, overzealous, extremist, maniacal, passionate, fervent, diehard, uncompromising, illiberal; *informal* gung-ho.
−OPPOSITES moderate.

race[1] ▸ noun **1** *Dave won the race* =**contest**, competition, event, fixture, heat, trial(s). **2** *the race for naval domination* =**competition**, rivalry, contention; quest. **3** *the mill race* =**channel**, waterway, conduit, sluice, spillway.
▸ verb **1** *he will race in the final* =**compete**, contend; run. **2** *Claire raced after him* =**hurry**, dash, rush, run, sprint, bolt, dart, gallop, career, charge, shoot, hurtle, hare, fly, speed, scurry; *informal* tear, belt, pelt, scoot, hotfoot it, leg it; *Brit. informal* bomb. **3** *her heart was racing* =**pound**, throb, pulsate, thud, thump, hammer, palpitate, flutter, pitter-patter, quiver, pump.

race[2] ▸ noun **1** *pupils of different races* =**ethnic group**, racial type, origin. **2** *a bloodthirsty race* =**people**, nation.

> **WORD LINKS**
>
> killing of a race: **ethnocide, genocide**

racial ▸ adjective =**ethnic**, ethnological, race-related; cultural, national, tribal.

racism ▸ noun =**racial discrimination**, racialism, xenophobia, chauvinism, bigotry.

racist ▸ noun *he was a racist* =**racial bigot**, racialist, xenophobe, chauvinist.
▸ adjective *a racist society* =**(racially) discriminatory**, racialist, prejudiced, bigoted.

rack ▸ noun =**frame**, framework, stand, holder, trestle, support, shelf.
▸ verb =**torment**, afflict, torture, agonize, harrow; plague, bedevil, persecute, trouble, worry.

racket ▸ noun =**noise**, din, hubbub, clamour, uproar, tumult, commotion, rumpus, pandemonium, babel; *informal* hullabaloo; *Brit. informal* row.

raconteur ▸ noun =**storyteller**, narrator, anecdotalist.

racy ▸ adjective =**risqué**, suggestive, naughty, sexy, spicy, ribald; indecorous, indecent, immodest, off colour, dirty, rude, smutty, crude, salacious; *informal* raunchy, blue; *Brit. informal* saucy; *euphemistic* adult.
−OPPOSITES prim.

raddled ▸ adjective =**haggard**, gaunt, drawn, tired, fatigued, drained, exhausted, worn out, washed out; unwell, unhealthy; *informal* the worse for wear.

radiance ▸ noun **1** *the radiance of the sun* =**light**, brightness, brilliance, luminosity, beams, rays, illumination, blaze, glow, gleam, lustre, glare; luminescence, incandescence. **2** *her face flooded with radiance* =**joy**, elation, jubilation, ecstasy, rapture, euphoria, delirium, happiness, delight, pleasure.

radiant ▸ adjective **1** *the radiant moon* =**shining**, bright, illuminated, brilliant, gleaming, glowing, ablaze, luminous, lustrous, incandescent, dazzling, shimmering. **2** *she looked radiant* =**joyful**, elated, thrilled, overjoyed, jubilant, rapturous, ecstatic, euphoric, in seventh heaven, on cloud nine, delighted, very happy; *informal* on top of the world, over

the moon.
−OPPOSITES dark, gloomy.

radiate ▸ verb 1 *stars radiate energy* =**emit**, give off, discharge, diffuse; shed, cast. 2 *light radiated from the hall* =**shine**, beam, emanate. 3 *their faces radiate hope* =**display**, show, exhibit. 4 *four spokes radiate from the hub* =**fan out**, spread out, branch out/off, extend, issue.

radical ▸ adjective 1 *radical reform* =**thorough**, complete, total, comprehensive, exhaustive, sweeping, far-reaching, wide-ranging, extensive, profound, major, stringent, rigorous. 2 *radical differences between the two theories* =**fundamental**, basic, essential, quintessential; structural, deep-seated, intrinsic, organic, constitutive. 3 *a radical political movement* =**revolutionary**, progressive, reformist, revisionist, progressivist; extreme, fanatical, militant, diehard.
−OPPOSITES superficial, minor, conservative.

raffish ▸ adjective =**rakish**, unconventional, bohemian; devil-may-care, casual, careless.
−OPPOSITES staid.

raffle ▸ noun =**lottery**, (prize) draw, sweepstake, sweep, tombola; *N. Amer.* lotto.

rag ▸ noun 1 *an oily rag* =**cloth**; *N. Amer. informal* schmatte. 2 *a man dressed in rags* =**tatters**, torn clothing.

ragamuffin ▸ noun =**urchin**, waif, guttersnipe; *informal* scarecrow.

ragbag ▸ noun =**jumble**, hotchpotch, mishmash, mess, hash; assortment, mixture, miscellany, medley, melange, variety, diversity, pot-pourri.

rage ▸ noun 1 *his rage is due to frustration* =**fury**, anger, wrath, outrage, indignation, temper, spleen, resentment, pique, annoyance, vexation, displeasure; *informal* grump, strop; *literary* ire, choler. 2 *the current rage for DIY* =**craze**, passion, fashion, taste, trend, vogue, fad, enthusiasm, obsession, compulsion, fixation, fetish, mania, preoccupation; *informal* thing.
▸ verb 1 *she raged silently* =**be angry**, be furious, be enraged, be incensed, seethe, be beside oneself, rave, storm, fume, spit; *informal* be livid, be wild, be steamed up. 2 *he raged against the reforms* =**protest about**, complain about, oppose, denounce; fulminate, storm, rail; *informal*

kick up a stink about. 3 *a storm was raging* =**be violent**, be turbulent, be tempestuous; thunder, rampage.
■ **(all) the rage** =**popular**, fashionable, in vogue, the (latest) thing, in great demand; *informal* in, cool, big, trendy, hot, hip.

ragged ▸ adjective 1 *ragged jeans* =**tattered**, torn, ripped, holey, moth-eaten, frayed, worn (out), falling to pieces, threadbare, scruffy, shabby; *informal* tatty. 2 *a ragged child* =**shabby**, scruffy, down at heel, unkempt. 3 *a ragged coastline* =**jagged**, craggy, rugged, uneven, rough, irregular; serrated, sawtooth, indented.
−OPPOSITES smart.

raging ▸ adjective 1 *a raging mob* =**angry**, furious, enraged, incensed, infuriated, irate, fuming, seething, ranting; *informal* livid; *literary* wrathful. 2 *raging seas* =**stormy**, violent, wild, turbulent, tempestuous. 3 *a raging headache* =**excruciating**, agonizing, painful, throbbing, acute, bad. 4 *her raging thirst* =**severe**, extreme, great, excessive.

raid ▸ noun 1 *the raid on Dieppe* =**attack**, assault, descent, blitz, incursion, sortie; onslaught, storming, charge, offensive, invasion, blitzkrieg. 2 *a raid on a shop* =**robbery**, burglary, hold-up, break-in, ram raid; looting, plunder; *informal* smash-and-grab, stick-up; *Brit. informal* blag; *N. Amer. informal* heist. 3 *a police raid on the flat* =**swoop**, search; *N. Amer. informal* bust, takedown.
▸ verb 1 *they raided shipping in the harbour* =**attack**, assault, set upon, descend on, swoop on, blitz, assail, storm, rush. 2 *armed men raided the store* =**rob**, hold up, break into; plunder, steal from, pillage, loot, ransack, sack; *informal* stick up. 3 *homes were raided by police* =**search**, swoop on; *N. Amer. informal* bust.

raider ▸ noun =**robber**, burglar, thief, housebreaker, plunderer, pillager, looter, marauder; attacker, assailant, invader.

rail ▸ verb =**protest**, fulminate, inveigh, rage, speak out, make a stand; expostulate, criticize, denounce, condemn; *informal* kick up a fuss about.

railing ▸ noun =**fence**, fencing, rail(s), paling, palisade, balustrade, banister, hurdle.

raillery ▸ noun =**teasing**, mockery, chaff, ragging, joshing; banter, badinage; *informal* leg-pulling, ribbing, kidding.

rain ▸ noun **1** *the rain had stopped* =**rainfall**, precipitation, raindrops, wet weather; drizzle, mizzle, shower, rainstorm, cloudburst, torrent, downpour, deluge, storm. **2** *a rain of hot ash* =**shower**, deluge, flood, torrent, avalanche, flurry; storm, hail.
▸ verb **1** *it rained heavily* =**pour (down)**, pelt down, tip down, teem down, beat down, lash down, sheet down; fall, drizzle, spit; *informal* be chucking it down; *Brit. informal* bucket down. **2** *bombs rained on the city* =**fall**, hail, drop, shower.

WORD LINKS

relating to rain: **pluvial, pluvious**

rainy ▸ adjective =**wet**, showery, drizzly, damp, inclement.

raise ▸ verb **1** *he raised a hand* =**lift (up)**, hold aloft, elevate, uplift, upraise, upthrust; hoist, haul up, hitch up; *Brit. informal* hoick up. **2** *he raised himself in the bed* =**set upright**, set vertical; sit up, stand up. **3** *they raised prices* =**increase**, put up, push up, up, mark up, escalate, inflate; *informal* hike (up), jack up, bump up. **4** *he raised his voice* =**amplify**, louden, magnify, intensify, boost, lift, increase, heighten, augment. **5** *how will you raise the money?* =**get**, obtain, acquire; accumulate, amass, collect, fetch, net, make. **6** *the city raised troops to fight for them* =**recruit**, enlist, sign up, conscript, call up, mobilize, rally, assemble; *US* draft. **7** *a tax raised on imports* =**levy**, impose, exact, demand, charge. **8** *he raised several objections* =**bring up**, air, ventilate; present, table, propose, submit, advance, suggest, moot, put forward. **9** *the disaster raised doubts about safety* =**give rise to**, occasion, cause, produce, engender, elicit, create, result in, lead to, prompt, awaken, arouse, induce, kindle, incite, stir up, trigger, spark off, provoke, instigate, foment, whip up; *literary* beget. **10** *most parents raise their children well* =**bring up**, rear, nurture, look after, care for, provide for, mother, parent, tend, cherish; educate, train. **11** *he raised cattle* =**breed**, rear, nurture, keep, tend; grow, farm, cultivate, produce.
−OPPOSITES lower, reduce, demolish.

raised ▸ adjective =**embossed**, relief, relievo, die-stamped.

rake¹ ▸ verb **1** *he raked the leaves into a pile* =**scrape up**, collect, gather. **2** *she*

raked the gravel =**smooth (out)**, level, even out, flatten, comb. **3** *the cat raked his arm with its claws* =**scratch**, lacerate, scrape, rasp, graze, grate. **4** *she raked a hand through her hair* =**drag**, pull, scrape, tug, comb. **5** *I raked through my pockets* =**rummage**, search, hunt, sift, rifle.
■ **rake something up** =**remind people of**, recollect, remember, call to mind; drag up, dredge up.

rake² ▸ noun =**playboy**, libertine, profligate; degenerate, roué, debauchee; lecher, seducer, womanizer, philanderer, adulterer, Don Juan, Lothario, Casanova; *informal* ladykiller, ladies' man, lech.

rakish ▸ adjective =**dashing**, debonair, stylish, jaunty, devil-may-care; raffish, disreputable, louche; *informal* sharp.

rally ▸ verb **1** *the troops rallied and held their ground* =**regroup**, reassemble, reform, reunite. **2** *he rallied an army* =**muster**, marshal, mobilize, raise, call up, recruit, enlist, conscript; assemble, gather, round up; *US* draft; *formal* convoke. **3** *ministers rallied to denounce the rumours* =**get together**, band together, assemble, join forces, unite, ally, collaborate, cooperate, pull together. **4** *share prices rallied* =**recover**, improve, get better, pick up, revive, bounce back, perk up, look up, turn a corner.
−OPPOSITES disperse, disband, slump.
▸ noun **1** *a rally in support of the strike* =**(mass) meeting**, gathering, assembly; demonstration, (protest) march; *informal* demo. **2** *a rally in oil prices* =**recovery**, upturn, improvement, comeback, resurgence.
−OPPOSITES slump.

ram ▸ verb **1** *he rammed his sword into its sheath* =**force**, thrust, plunge, stab, push, sink, dig, stick, cram, jam, stuff, pack. **2** *a van rammed the car* =**hit**, strike, crash into, collide with, impact, run into, smash into, bump (into), butt.

ramble ▸ verb **1** *we rambled around the lanes* =**walk**, hike, tramp, trek, backpack; wander, stroll, saunter, amble, roam, range, rove, traipse; *Scottish & Irish* stravaig; *informal* mosey, tootle; *formal* perambulate. **2** *she does ramble on* =**chatter**, babble, prattle, prate, blather, gabble, jabber, twitter, rattle, maunder; *informal* jaw, gas, gab, yak, yabber; *Brit. informal* witter, chunter, natter, waffle, rabbit.

rambler ▸ noun =**walker**, hiker, backpacker, wanderer, rover; *literary* way-farer.

rambling ▸ adjective **1** *a rambling speech* =**long-winded**, verbose, wordy, prolix; digressive, maundering, roundabout, circuitous, circumlocutory; discon-nected, disjointed, incoherent. **2** *rambling streets* =**winding**, twisting, labyrin-thine; sprawling. **3** *a rambling rose* =**trailing**, creeping, climbing, vining. –OPPOSITES concise.

ramification ▸ noun =**consequence**, result, aftermath, outcome, effect, up-shot; development, implication.

ramp ▸ noun =**slope**, bank, incline, gra-dient, tilt; rise, ascent, acclivity; drop, descent, declivity.

rampage ▸ verb =**riot**, run amok, go berserk; storm, charge, tear.
■ **go on the rampage** =**riot**, go ber-serk, get out of control, run amok; *N. Amer. informal* go postal.

rampant ▸ adjective **1** *rampant inflation* =**uncontrolled**, unrestrained, un-checked, unbridled, widespread; out of control, out of hand, rife. **2** *rampant dis-like* =**vehement**, strong, violent, force-ful, intense, passionate, fanatical. **3** *ram-pant vegetation* =**luxuriant**, exuberant, lush, rich, riotous, rank, profuse, vigor-ous; *informal* jungly.
–OPPOSITES controlled, mild.

rampart ▸ noun =**defensive wall**, em-bankment, earthwork, parapet, breast-work, battlement, bulwark, outwork.

ramshackle ▸ adjective =**tumble-down**, dilapidated, derelict, decrepit, neglected, run down, gone to rack and ruin, crumbling, decaying; rickety, shaky, unsound; *informal* shambly; *N. Amer. informal* shacky.
–OPPOSITES sound.

rancid ▸ adjective =**sour**, stale, turned, rank, putrid, foul, rotten, bad, off; gamy, high, fetid.
–OPPOSITES fresh.

rancorous ▸ adjective =**bitter**, spite-ful, hateful, resentful, acrimonious, ma-licious, malevolent, hostile, venomous, vindictive, baleful, vitriolic, vengeful, pernicious, mean, nasty; *informal* bitchy, catty.
–OPPOSITES amicable.

rancour ▸ noun =**bitterness**, spite, hate, hatred, resentment, malice, ill will, malevolence, animosity, antipathy, enmity, hostility, acrimony, venom, vitriol.

random ▸ adjective *random checks* =**un-systematic**, unmethodical, arbitrary, unplanned, undirected, casual, indis-criminate, non-specific, haphazard, stray, erratic.
–OPPOSITES systematic.
■ **at random** =**unsystematically**, arbi-trarily, randomly, unmethodically, hap-hazardly.

range ▸ noun **1** *his range of vision* =**span**, scope, compass, sweep, extent, area, field, orbit, ambit, horizon, latitude; limits, bounds, confines, parameters. **2** *a range of mountains* =**row**, chain, si-erra, ridge, massif; line, string, series. **3** *a range of foods* =**assortment**, variety, diversity, mixture, collection, array, se-lection, choice. **4** *she put the dish into the range* =**stove**, cooker.
▸ verb **1** *charges range from 1% to 5%* =**vary**, fluctuate, differ; extend, stretch, reach, cover, go, run. **2** *on the stalls are ranged fresh foods* =**arrange**, line up, order, pos-ition, dispose, set out, array. **3** *they ranged over the steppes* =**roam**, rove, tra-verse, travel, journey, wander, drift, ramble, meander, stroll, traipse, walk, hike, trek.

rangy ▸ adjective =**long-legged**, long-limbed, leggy, tall; slender, slim, lean, thin, gangly, lanky, spindly, skinny, spare.
–OPPOSITES squat.

rank[1] ▸ noun **1** *he was elevated to ministe-rial rank* =**position**, level, grade, echelon; class, status, standing; *dated* station. **2** *a family of rank* =**high standing**, blue blood, high birth, nobility, aristocracy; eminence, distinction, prestige; prom-inence, influence, consequence, power. **3** *a rank of riflemen* =**row**, line, file, col-umn, string, train, procession.
▸ verb **1** *the plant is ranked as endangered* =**classify**, class, categorize, rate, grade, bracket, group, pigeonhole, designate; catalogue, file, list. **2** *he ranked below the others* =**be graded**, have a status, be classed, be classified, be categorized; be-long. **3** *tulips ranked like guardsmen* =**line up**, align, order, arrange, dispose, set out, array, range.
■ **the rank and file 1** *the officers and the rank and file* =**other ranks**, soldiers, NCOs, lower ranks; men, troops. **2** *a speech appealing to the rank and file* =**the (common) people**, the proletariat, the

masses, the populace, the rabble, the commonality, the third estate, the plebeians, the great unwashed; *derogatory* the hoi polloi, the riff-raff; *informal, derogatory* the proles, the plebs.

rank² ▸ adjective **1** *rank vegetation* =**abundant**, lush, luxuriant, dense, profuse, vigorous, overgrown; *informal* jungly. **2** *a rank smell* =**offensive**, unpleasant, nasty, revolting, sickening, obnoxious, noxious; foul, fetid, smelly, stinking, reeking, high, off, rancid, putrid, malodorous; *Brit. informal* niffy, pongy, whiffy, humming; *literary* noisome. **3** *rank stupidity* =**downright**, utter, outright, out-and-out, absolute, complete, sheer, arrant, thoroughgoing, unqualified, unmitigated, positive.
–OPPOSITES sparse, pleasant.

rankle ▸ verb =**annoy**, upset, anger, irritate, offend, affront, displease, provoke, irk, vex, pique, nettle, gall; *informal* rile, miff, peeve, aggravate, hack off; *Brit. informal* nark; *N. Amer. informal* tick off.

ransack ▸ verb =**plunder**, pillage, raid, rob, loot, sack, strip, despoil; ravage, devastate, turn upside down; scour, rifle, comb, search.

ransom ▸ noun =**pay-off**, payment, sum, price.
▸ verb =**release**, free, deliver, liberate, rescue; buy the freedom of.

rant ▸ verb *she ranted on about the unfairness* =**hold forth**, go on, fulminate, vociferate, sound off, spout, pontificate, bluster, declaim; shout, yell, bellow; *informal* mouth off.
▸ noun *he went into a rant about them* =**tirade**, diatribe, broadside.

rap¹ ▸ verb **1** *she rapped his fingers with a ruler* =**hit**, strike; *informal* whack, thwack, bash, wallop; *literary* smite. **2** *I rapped on the door* =**knock**, tap, bang, hammer, pound.

rap² ▸ noun *they didn't care a rap* =**whit**, iota, jot, hoot, scrap, bit, fig; *informal* damn, monkey's.

rapacious ▸ adjective =**grasping**, greedy, avaricious, acquisitive, covetous; mercenary, materialistic; *informal* money-grubbing; *N. Amer. informal* grabby.
–OPPOSITES generous.

rape ▸ noun *he was charged with rape* =**sexual assault**; *archaic* ravishment, defilement. **2** *the rape of rainforests* =**destruction**, violation, ravaging, pillaging, plundering, desecration, defilement,

sacking, sack.
▸ verb **1** *he raped her at knifepoint* =**sexually assault**, violate, force oneself on; *literary* ravish; *archaic* defile. **2** *they raped our country* =**ravage**, violate, desecrate, defile, plunder, pillage, despoil; lay waste, ransack, sack.

rapid ▸ adjective =**quick**, fast, swift, speedy, expeditious, express, brisk; lightning, meteoric, whirlwind; sudden, instantaneous, instant, immediate; hurried, hasty, precipitate; *informal* p.d.q. (pretty damn quick).
–OPPOSITES slow.

rapidly ▸ adverb =**quickly**, fast, swiftly, speedily, post-haste, hotfoot, at full tilt, briskly; hurriedly, hastily, in haste, in a rush, precipitately; *informal* like a shot, double quick, p.d.q. (pretty damn quick), in a flash, hell for leather, at the double, like (greased) lightning, like mad, like the wind; *Brit. informal* like the clappers, at a rate of knots, like billy-o; *N. Amer. informal* lickety-split; *literary* apace.
–OPPOSITES slowly.

rapport ▸ noun =**affinity**, close relationship, (mutual) understanding, bond, empathy, sympathy, accord.

rapt ▸ adjective =**fascinated**, enthralled, spellbound, captivated, riveted, gripped, mesmerized, enchanted, entranced, bewitched; transported, enraptured, thrilled, ecstatic.
–OPPOSITES inattentive.

rapture ▸ noun =**ecstasy**, bliss, exaltation, euphoria, elation, joy, enchantment, delight, happiness, pleasure.
■ **go into raptures** =**enthuse**, rhapsodize, rave, gush, wax lyrical.

rapturous ▸ adjective =**ecstatic**, joyful, elated, euphoric, enraptured, on cloud nine, in seventh heaven, transported, enchanted, blissful, happy; enthusiastic, delighted, thrilled, overjoyed, rapt; *informal* over the moon, on top of the world, blissed out; *Austral. informal* wrapped.

rare ▸ adjective **1** *rare moments of privacy* =**infrequent**, scarce, sparse, few and far between, thin on the ground, like gold dust; occasional, limited, odd, isolated, unaccustomed, unwonted; *Brit.* out of the common. **2** *rare stamps* =**unusual**, recherché, uncommon, unfamiliar, atypical, singular. **3** *a man of rare talent* =**exceptional**, outstanding, unparalleled, peerless, matchless, unique, un-

rivalled, inimitable, beyond compare, without equal, second to none, unsurpassed; consummate, superior, superlative, first-class; *informal* A1, top-notch.
–OPPOSITES common, commonplace.

rarefied ▸ adjective =**esoteric**, exclusive, select; elevated, lofty.

rarely ▸ adverb =**seldom**, infrequently, hardly (ever), scarcely, not often; once in a while, now and then, occasionally; *informal* once in a blue moon.
–OPPOSITES often.

raring ▸ adjective =**eager**, keen, enthusiastic; impatient, longing, desperate; ready; *informal* dying, itching, gagging.

rarity ▸ noun **1** *the rarity of earthquakes in the UK* =**infrequency**, unusualness, scarcity. **2** *this book is a rarity* =**collector's item**, rare thing, rare bird, rara avis; wonder, nonpareil, one of a kind; curiosity, oddity; *Brit. informal* one-off.

rascal ▸ noun =**scallywag**, imp, monkey, mischief-maker, wretch; *informal* scamp, tyke, horror, monster; *Brit. informal* perisher.

rash¹ ▸ noun **1** *he broke out in a rash* =**spots**, breakout, eruption; hives. **2** *a rash of articles in the press* =**series**, succession, spate, wave, flood, deluge, torrent; outbreak, epidemic, flurry.

rash² ▸ adjective =**reckless**, impulsive, impetuous, hasty, foolhardy, incautious, precipitate; careless, heedless, thoughtless, imprudent, foolish; ill-advised, injudicious, ill-judged, misguided, hare-brained.
–OPPOSITES prudent.

rasp ▸ verb **1** *enamel is rasped off the teeth* =**scrape**, rub, abrade, grate, grind, sand, file, scratch, scour. **2** *'Help!' he rasped* =**croak**, squawk, caw.

rasping ▸ adjective =**harsh**, grating, jarring, scratchy, hoarse, rough, gravelly, croaky, gruff, husky, throaty, guttural.

rate ▸ noun **1** *a fixed rate of interest* =**percentage**, ratio, proportion; scale, standard. **2** *an hourly rate of £30* =**charge**, price, cost, tariff, fare, levy, toll; fee, remuneration, payment, wage, allowance. **3** *the rate of change* =**speed**, pace, tempo, velocity, momentum.
▸ verb **1** *they rated their ability at driving* =**assess**, evaluate, appraise, judge, weigh up, estimate, calculate, gauge, measure, adjudge; grade, rank, classify, categorize. **2** *the scheme was rated effective* =**con-**

sider, judge, reckon, think, hold, deem, find; regard as, look on as, count as. **3** *he rated only a brief mention* =**merit**, deserve, warrant, be worthy of, be deserving of. **4** *(informal) Ben doesn't rate him* =**think highly of**, set much store by; admire, esteem, value.
■ **at any rate** =**in any case**, anyhow, anyway, in any event, nevertheless; whatever happens, come what may, regardless, notwithstanding.

rather ▸ adverb **1** *I'd rather you went* =**sooner**, by preference, by choice. **2** *it's rather complicated* =**quite**, a bit, a little, fairly, slightly, somewhat, relatively, to some degree, comparatively; *informal* pretty, sort of, kind of. **3** *her true feelings — or rather, lack of feelings* =**more precisely**, to be exact, strictly speaking. **4** *she seemed sad rather than angry* =**more**; as opposed to, instead of. **5** *it was not impulsive, but rather a considered decision* =**on the contrary**, instead.

ratify ▸ verb =**confirm**, approve, sanction, endorse, agree to, accept, uphold, authorize, formalize, validate, recognize; sign.
–OPPOSITES reject.

rating ▸ noun =**grade**, classification, ranking, category, designation; assessment, evaluation, appraisal; mark, score.

ratio ▸ noun =**proportion**, comparative number, correlation, relationship, correspondence; percentage, fraction, quotient.

ration ▸ noun **1** *a daily ration of chocolate* =**allowance**, allocation, quota, quantum, share, portion, helping; amount, quantity, measure, proportion, percentage. **2** *the garrison ran out of rations* =**supplies**, provisions, food, foodstuffs, eatables, edibles, provender; stores; *informal* grub, eats; *N. Amer. informal* chuck; *formal* comestibles.
▸ verb *fuel supplies were rationed* =**control**, limit, restrict; conserve.

rational ▸ adjective **1** *a rational approach* =**logical**, reasoned, sensible, reasonable, cogent, intelligent, judicious, shrewd, common-sense, sound, prudent; down-to-earth, practical, pragmatic. **2** *she was not rational at the time of signing* =**sane**, compos mentis, of sound mind; normal, balanced, lucid, coherent; *informal* all there. **3** *man is a rational being* =**intelligent**, thinking, reasoning;

cerebral, logical, analytical.
−OPPOSITES illogical, insane.

rationale ▶ noun =reason(s), thinking, logic, grounds, sense; principle, theory, argument, case; motive, explanation, justification, excuse; the whys and wherefores.

rationalize ▶ verb 1 *he tried to rationalize his behaviour* =justify, explain (away), account for, defend, vindicate, excuse. 2 *an attempt to rationalize the industry* =streamline, reorganize, modernize, update; trim, hone, simplify, downsize, prune.

rattle ▶ verb 1 *hailstones rattled against the window* =clatter, patter; clink, clunk. 2 *he rattled some coins* =jingle, jangle, clink, tinkle. 3 *the bus rattled along* =jolt, bump, bounce, jounce, shake, judder. 4 *the government was rattled by the strike* =unnerve, disconcert, disturb, fluster, shake, perturb, discompose, discomfit, ruffle, throw; *informal* faze.

raucous ▶ adjective 1 *raucous laughter* =harsh, strident, screeching, piercing, shrill, grating, discordant, dissonant; noisy, loud, cacophonous. 2 *a raucous hen night* =rowdy, noisy, boisterous, roisterous, wild.
−OPPOSITES soft, quiet.

raunchy ▶ adjective *(informal)*. See SEXY sense 2.

ravage ▶ verb =lay waste, devastate, ruin, destroy, wreak havoc on; pillage, plunder, despoil, ransack, sack, loot; *literary* rape.

ravages ▶ plural noun 1 *the ravages of time* =damaging effects, ill effects. 2 *the ravages of man* =(acts of) destruction, damage, devastation, ruin, havoc, depredation(s).

rave ▶ verb 1 *he was raving about the fires of hell* =talk wildly, babble, jabber. 2 *I raved and swore at them* =rant (and rave), rage, lose one's temper, storm, fulminate, fume; shout, roar, thunder, bellow; *informal* fly off the handle, blow one's top, go up the wall, hit the roof; *Brit. informal* go spare; *N. Amer. informal* flip one's wig. 3 *he raved about her talent* =praise enthusiastically, go into raptures about/over, wax lyrical about, sing the praises of, rhapsodize over, enthuse about/over, acclaim, eulogize, extol; *N. Amer. informal* ballyhoo; *formal* laud.
−OPPOSITES criticize.

raven ▶ adjective *raven hair* =black, jet-black, ebony; *literary* sable.

WORD LINKS

relating to ravens: **corvine**
collective noun: **unkindness**
---

ravenous ▶ adjective 1 *I'm absolutely ravenous* =very hungry, starving, famished. 2 *her ravenous appetite* =voracious, insatiable; greedy, gluttonous.

ravine ▶ noun =gorge, canyon, gully, defile, couloir; chasm, abyss, gulf; *S. English* chine; *N. English* clough, gill, thrutch; *N. Amer.* gulch, coulee.

raving ▶ adjective 1 *a raving beauty* =very great, remarkable, extraordinary, singular, striking, outstanding, stunning. 2 *she's raving mad.* See MAD sense 1.

ravings ▶ plural noun =gibberish, rambling, babbling, wild/incoherent talk.

ravishing ▶ adjective =very beautiful, gorgeous, stunning, wonderful, lovely, striking, magnificent, dazzling, radiant, delightful, charming, enchanting; *informal* amazing, sensational, fantastic, fabulous, terrific; *Brit. informal* smashing.
−OPPOSITES hideous.

raw ▶ adjective 1 *raw carrot* =uncooked, fresh. 2 *raw materials* =unprocessed, untreated, unrefined, crude, natural. 3 *raw recruits* =inexperienced, new, untrained, untried, untested; callow, immature, green, naive. 4 *his skin is raw* =sore, red, painful, tender; abraded, chafed. 5 *a raw morning* =bleak, cold, chilly, freezing, icy, wintry, bitter; *informal* nippy; *Brit. informal* parky. 6 *raw emotions* =strong, intense, passionate, fervent, powerful, violent.
−OPPOSITES cooked, processed.

ray ▶ noun 1 *rays of light* =beam, shaft, streak, stream. 2 *a ray of hope* =glimmer, flicker, spark, hint, suggestion, sign.

raze ▶ verb =destroy, demolish, tear down, pull down, knock down, level, flatten, bulldoze, wipe out, lay waste.

re ▶ preposition =about, concerning, regarding, relating to, apropos (of), on the subject of, in respect of, with reference to, in connection with.

reach ▶ verb 1 *Travis reached out a hand* =stretch out, hold out, extend, out-stretch, thrust out, stick out. 2 *she reached Helen's house* =arrive at, get to, come to; end up at. 3 *the temperature reached 94 degrees* =attain, get to; rise to,

climb to; fall to, sink to, drop to; *informal* hit. **4** *the leaders reached an agreement* =**achieve**, work out, draw up, put together, negotiate, thrash out, hammer out. **5** *I have been trying to reach you all day* =**get in touch with**, contact, get through to, get, speak to; *informal* get hold of. **6** *our concern is to reach more people* =**influence**, sway, get (through) to, have an impact on.
▶ noun **1** *Bobby moved out of her reach* =**grasp**, range. **2** *small goals within your reach* =**capabilities**, capacity. **3** *beyond the reach of the law* =**jurisdiction**, authority, influence; scope, range, compass, ambit.

react ▶ verb **1** *how he would react if she told him?* =**behave**, act, take it, conduct oneself; respond, reply, answer. **2** *he reacted against the regulations* =**rebel against**, oppose, rise up against.

reaction ▶ noun **1** *his reaction bewildered her* =**response**, answer, reply, rejoinder, retort, riposte; *informal* comeback. **2** *a reaction against modernism* =**backlash**, counteraction.

reactionary ▶ adjective *a reactionary policy* =**right-wing**, conservative, rightist, traditionalist, conventional.
–OPPOSITES progressive.
▶ noun *an extreme reactionary* =**right-winger**, conservative, rightist, traditionalist, conventionalist.
–OPPOSITES radical.

read ▶ verb **1** *he was reading the newspaper* =**peruse**, study, scrutinize, look through, pore over, be absorbed in; run one's eye over, cast an eye over, leaf through, scan. **2** *he read a passage of the letter* =**read out/aloud**, recite, declaim. **3** *I can't read my writing* =**decipher**, make out, make sense of, interpret, understand. **4** *his remark could be read as a criticism* =**interpret**, take (to mean), construe, see, understand. **5** *he read history* =**study**, take; *N. Amer. & Austral./NZ* major in.

■ **read something into something** =**infer from**, interpolate from, assume from, attribute to.

■ **read up on** =**study**; *informal* bone up on; *Brit. informal* mug up on, swot.

> WORD LINKS
>
> *readable:* **legible**
> *unreadable:* **illegible**
> *ability to read:* **literacy**
> *inability to read:* **illiteracy**

readable ▶ adjective **1** *the inscription is readable* =**legible**, decipherable, clear, intelligible, comprehensible. **2** *her novels are immensely readable* =**enjoyable**, entertaining, interesting, absorbing, gripping, enthralling, engrossing; *informal* unputdownable.
–OPPOSITES illegible.

readily ▶ adverb **1** *Durkin readily offered to drive* =**willingly**, unhesitatingly, ungrudgingly, gladly, happily, eagerly, promptly. **2** *the island is readily accessible* =**easily**, without difficulty.
–OPPOSITES reluctantly.

readiness ▶ noun **1** *their readiness to accept change* =**willingness**, enthusiasm, eagerness, keenness; promptness, quickness, alacrity. **2** *a state of readiness* =**preparedness**. **3** *the readiness of his reply* =**promptness**, quickness, rapidity, swiftness, speediness.

■ **in readiness** =**(at the) ready**, available, on hand, accessible, handy.

reading ▶ noun **1** *a cursory reading of the page* =**perusal**, study, scanning; browse (through), look (through), glance (through), leaf (through). **2** *a man of wide reading* =**(book) learning**, scholarship, education, erudition. **3** *readings from the Bible* =**passage**, lesson; section, piece. **4** *my reading of the situation* =**interpretation**, construal, understanding, explanation, analysis. **5** *a meter reading* =**record**, figure, indication, measurement.

ready ▶ adjective **1** *are you ready?* =**prepared**, (all) set, organized, primed; *informal* fit, psyched up, geared up. **2** *everything is ready* =**completed**, finished, prepared, organized, done, arranged, fixed. **3** *he's always ready to help* =**willing**, prepared, pleased, inclined, disposed; eager, keen, happy, glad; *informal* game. **4** *she looked ready to collapse* =**about to**, on the point of, on the verge of, close to, liable to, likely to. **5** *a ready supply of food* =**(easily) available**, accessible, handy, close/near at hand, to/on hand, convenient, within reach, near, at one's fingertips. **6** *a ready answer* =**prompt**, quick, swift, speedy, fast, immediate, unhesitating; clever, sharp, astute, shrewd, keen, perceptive, discerning.
▶ verb =**prepare**, organize, gear oneself up; *informal* psych oneself up.

■ **at the ready** =**in position**, poised, waiting.

■ **make ready** =**prepare**, gear up for.

ready-made ▸ adjective =pre-assembled, pre-cooked, oven-ready, convenience, ready-to-wear, off-the-peg.

real ▸ adjective **1** *is she a fictional character or a real person?* =**actual**, non-fictional, factual; historical; material, physical, tangible, concrete, palpable. **2** *real gold* =**genuine**, authentic, bona fide; *informal* pukka, kosher. **3** *my real name* =**true**, actual. **4** *tears of real grief* =**sincere**, genuine, true, unfeigned, heartfelt, unaffected. **5** *a real man* =**proper**, true; *informal* regular. **6** *you're a real idiot* =**complete**, utter, thorough, absolute, total, prize, perfect; *Brit. informal* right, proper.
−OPPOSITES imaginary, imitation.

realism ▸ noun **1** *optimism tinged with realism* =**pragmatism**, practicality, common sense, level-headedness. **2** *a degree of realism* =**authenticity**, fidelity, verisimilitude, truthfulness.

realistic ▸ adjective **1** *you've got to be realistic* =**practical**, pragmatic, matter-of-fact, down-to-earth, sensible, commonsensical; rational, reasonable, level-headed, clear-sighted; *informal* no-nonsense. **2** *a realistic aim* =**achievable**, attainable, feasible, practicable, viable, reasonable, sensible, workable; *informal* doable. **3** *a realistic portrayal of war* =**true (to life)**, lifelike, truthful, faithful, graphic.
−OPPOSITES idealistic, impracticable.

reality ▸ noun **1** *distinguishing fantasy from reality* =**the real world**, real life, actuality; truth. **2** *the harsh realities of life* =**fact**, actuality, truth. **3** *the reality of the detail* =**verisimilitude**, authenticity, fidelity.
−OPPOSITES fantasy.
▪ **in reality** =**in (actual) fact**, actually, really, in truth; in practice.

realization ▸ noun **1** *a growing realization of the danger* =**awareness**, understanding, comprehension, consciousness, appreciation, recognition, discernment; *formal* cognizance. **2** *the realization of our dreams* =**fulfilment**, achievement, accomplishment, attainment; *formal* effectuation.

realize ▸ verb **1** *he suddenly realized what she meant* =**register**, perceive, discern, notice; understand, grasp, comprehend, see, recognize, work out, fathom (out), apprehend; *informal* latch on to, cotton on to, tumble to, savvy, figure out, get (the message); *Brit. informal* twig, suss. **2** *they*

realized their dream =**fulfil**, achieve, accomplish, make a reality, make happen, bring to fruition, bring about/off, carry out/through; *formal* effectuate. **3** *the company realized significant profits* =**make**, clear, gain, earn, return, produce. **4** *the goods realized £30* =**be sold for**, fetch, go for, make, net. **5** *he realized his assets* =**cash in**, liquidate, capitalize.

really ▸ adverb **1** *he is really very wealthy* =**in (actual) fact**, actually, in reality, in truth. **2** *he really likes her* =**genuinely**, truly, honestly; undoubtedly, certainly, assuredly, unquestionably. **3** *they were really kind* =**very**, extremely, thoroughly, decidedly, dreadfully, exceptionally, exceedingly, immensely, tremendously, uncommonly, remarkably, eminently, extraordinarily, most; *N. Amer.* quite; *informal* awfully, terribly, terrifically, right, ultra; *Brit. informal* jolly, ever so, dead; *N. Amer. informal* real, mighty, awful.
▸ exclamation *'They've split up.' 'Really?'* =**is that so**, is that a fact, well I never (did); *Brit. informal* {well, I'll be blowed}.

realm ▸ noun **1** *peace in the realm* =**kingdom**, country, land, dominion, nation. **2** *the realm of academia* =**domain**, sphere, area, field, world, province, territory.

reap ▸ verb **1** *the corn was reaped* =**harvest**, garner, gather in, bring in. **2** *reaping the benefits* =**receive**, obtain, get, acquire, secure, realize.

rear¹ ▸ verb **1** *I was reared in Newcastle* =**bring up**, care for, look after, nurture, parent; *N. Amer.* raise. **2** *he reared cattle* =**breed**, raise, keep. **3** *laboratory-reared plants* =**grow**, cultivate. **4** *Harry reared his head* =**raise**, lift (up), hold up.

rear² ▸ noun **1** *the rear of the building* =**back (part)**, hind part; *Nautical* stern. **2** *the rear of the queue* =**(tail) end**, back end.
−OPPOSITES front.
▸ adjective *the rear bumper* =**back**, end, rearmost; hind; *technical* posterior.

rearrange ▸ verb **1** *the furniture has been rearranged* =**reposition**, move round, change round. **2** *Tony had rearranged his schedule* =**reorganize**, alter, adjust, change (round), reschedule; *informal* jigger.

reason ▸ noun **1** *the main reason for his decision* =**cause**, ground(s), basis, rationale; motive, purpose, point, aim, intention, objective, goal; explanation, justification, argument, defence, vindication, excuse. **2** *postmodern voices railing against reason* =**rationality**, logic, cognition. **3** *he was losing his reason* =**sanity**, mind, mental faculties; senses, wits; *informal* marbles.

▶ **verb 1** *a young child is unable to reason* =**think rationally**, think logically; *formal* cogitate. **2** *Scott reasoned that Annabel might be ill* =**calculate**, conclude, reckon, think, judge, deduce, infer, surmise; *informal* figure.

■ **by reason of** *(formal)* =**because of**, on account of, as a result of, owing to, due to, by virtue of, thanks to.

■ **reason something out** =**work out**, think through, make sense of, get to the bottom of, puzzle out; *informal* figure out.

■ **reason with someone** =**talk round**, bring round, persuade, prevail on, convince; make someone see the light.

■ **with reason** =**justifiably**, justly, legitimately, rightly.

WORD LINKS

relating to reason: **rational**

reasonable ▶ **adjective 1** *a reasonable man* | *a reasonable explanation* =**sensible**, rational, logical, fair, just, equitable; intelligent, wise, level-headed, practical, realistic; sound, valid, commonsensical; tenable, plausible, credible, believable. **2** *take reasonable precautions* =**practicable**, sensible; appropriate, suitable. **3** *cars in reasonable condition* =**fairly good**, acceptable, satisfactory, average, adequate, fair, all right, tolerable, passable; *informal* OK. **4** *reasonable prices* =**inexpensive**, moderate, low, cheap, budget, bargain.

reasoned ▶ **adjective** =**logical**, rational, well thought out, clear, lucid, coherent, cogent, considered, sensible.

reasoning ▶ **noun** =**thinking**, (train of) thought, logic, analysis, interpretation, explanation, rationalization.

reassure ▶ **verb** =**put someone's mind at rest**, encourage, inspirit, hearten, buoy up, cheer up; comfort, soothe.
–OPPOSITES alarm.

rebate ▶ **noun** =**(partial) refund**, repayment; discount, deduction, reduction, decrease.

rebel ▶ **noun 1** *the rebels took control of the capital* =**revolutionary**, insurgent, mutineer, insurrectionist, guerrilla, terrorist, freedom fighter. **2** *the concept of*

the artist as a rebel =**nonconformist**, dissenter, dissident, iconoclast, maverick.

▶ **verb 1** *the citizens rebelled* =**revolt**, mutiny, riot, rise up, take up arms. **2** *his stomach rebelled at the thought of food* =**recoil**, show/feel repugnance. **3** *teenagers rebelling against their parents* =**defy**, disobey, kick against, challenge, oppose, resist.
–OPPOSITES obey.

▶ **adjective 1** *rebel troops* =**insurgent**, revolutionary, mutinous, insurrectionary. **2** *rebel MPs* =**rebellious**, defiant, disobedient, insubordinate, subversive, resistant, recalcitrant; nonconformist, maverick, iconoclastic.
–OPPOSITES compliant.

rebellion ▶ **noun 1** *troops suppressed the rebellion* =**uprising**, revolt, insurrection, mutiny, revolution, insurgence; riot, disorder, unrest. **2** *an act of rebellion* =**defiance**, disobedience, insubordination, subversion, resistance.

rebellious ▶ **adjective 1** *rebellious troops* =**rebel**, insurgent, mutinous, riotous, insurrectionary, revolutionary. **2** *a rebellious adolescent* =**defiant**, disobedient, insubordinate, unruly, mutinous, wayward, obstreperous, recalcitrant, intractable; *Brit. informal* bolshie.

rebirth ▶ **noun** =**revival**, renaissance, resurrection, reawakening, renewal, regeneration; revitalization, rejuvenation.

rebound ▶ **verb 1** *the ball rebounded* =**bounce (back)**, spring back, ricochet, boomerang; *N. Amer.* carom. **2** *later, sterling rebounded* =**recover**, rally, pick up. **3** *Thomas's tactics rebounded on him* =**backfire**, boomerang.

rebuff ▶ **verb** *his offer was rebuffed* =**reject**, turn down, spurn, refuse, decline, repudiate; snub, slight, dismiss, brush off.
–OPPOSITES accept.

▶ **noun** *the rebuff did little to dampen his ardour* =**rejection**, snub, slight; refusal, spurning; *informal* brush-off, kick in the teeth, slap in the face.

rebuild ▶ **verb** =**reconstruct**, renovate, restore, remodel, remake, reassemble.
–OPPOSITES demolish.

rebuke ▶ **verb** *she never rebuked him* =**reprimand**, reproach, scold, admonish, reprove, upbraid, berate, take to task, criticize, censure; *informal* tell off, give someone a talking-to, give someone a dressing-down; *Brit. informal* give

someone a rocket, tick off; *N. Amer. informal* chew out; *formal* castigate.
−OPPOSITES praise.
▶ noun *a severe rebuke* =**reprimand**, reproach, scolding, admonition, reproof, criticism, recrimination, censure; *informal* telling-off, dressing-down, talking-to; *Brit. informal* rocket, ticking-off; *formal* castigation.
−OPPOSITES praise.

rebut ▶ verb =**refute**, deny, disprove; invalidate, negate, contradict, controvert, counter, discredit, give the lie to, explode; *informal* shoot full of holes; *formal* confute.
−OPPOSITES confirm.

rebuttal ▶ noun =**refutation**, denial, countering, invalidation, negation, contradiction.

recalcitrant ▶ adjective =**uncooperative**, intractable, insubordinate, defiant, rebellious, wilful, wayward, headstrong, self-willed, contrary, perverse, difficult, awkward; *Brit. informal* bloody-minded, bolshie, stroppy; *formal* refractory.
−OPPOSITES amenable.

recall ▶ verb 1 *he recalled his student days* =**remember**, recollect, call to mind; think back on/to, reminisce about. 2 *their exploits recall the days of chivalry* =**bring to mind**, call up, conjure up, evoke. 3 *the ambassador was recalled* =**summon back**, order back, call back.
−OPPOSITES forget.
▶ noun 1 *the recall of the ambassador* =**summoning back**, ordering back, calling back. 2 *their recall of dreams* =**recollection**, remembrance, memory.

recant ▶ verb 1 *he was forced to recant his beliefs* =**renounce**, disavow, deny, repudiate, renege on; *formal* forswear, abjure. 2 *he refused to recant* =**change one's mind**, be apostate. 3 *he recanted his testimony* =**retract**, take back, withdraw.

recantation ▶ noun =**renunciation**, renouncement, disavowal, denial, repudiation, retraction, withdrawal.

recapitulate ▶ verb =**summarize**, sum up; restate, repeat, reiterate, go over, review; *informal* recap.

recede ▶ verb 1 *the waters receded* =**retreat**, go back/down, move back/away, withdraw, ebb, subside, abate. 2 *the lights receded into the distance* =**disappear from view**, be lost to view. 3 *fears of violence have receded* =**diminish**, lessen, decrease, dwindle, fade, abate, subside,

ebb, wane.
−OPPOSITES advance, grow.

receipt ▶ noun 1 *the receipt of a letter* =**receiving**, getting, obtaining, gaining; arrival, delivery. 2 *make sure you get a receipt* =**proof of purchase**, sales ticket. 3 *receipts from house sales* =**proceeds**, takings, income, revenue, earnings; profits, (financial) return(s); *N. Amer.* take.

receive ▶ verb 1 *Tony received an award | they received £650 in damages* =**be given**, be presented with, be awarded, collect; get, obtain, gain, acquire; win, be paid, earn, gross, net. 2 *she received a letter* =**be sent**, accept (delivery of). 3 *Alec received the news on Monday* =**be told**, be informed of, be notified of, hear, discover, find out (about), learn; *informal* get wind of. 4 *he received her suggestion with a lack of interest* =**hear**, listen to; respond to, react to. 5 *she received an injury* =**experience**, sustain, undergo, meet with; suffer, bear.
−OPPOSITES give, send.

recent ▶ adjective 1 *recent research* =**new**, the latest, current, fresh, modern, contemporary, up to date, up to the minute. 2 *his recent visit* =**not long past**, just gone.
−OPPOSITES old.

recently ▶ adverb =**not long ago**, a little while back; lately, latterly, just now.

receptacle ▶ noun =**container**, holder, repository.

reception ▶ noun 1 *the reception of foreign diplomats* =**greeting**, welcoming, entertaining. 2 *a chilly reception* =**response**, reaction, treatment. 3 *a wedding reception* =**(formal) party**, function, social occasion, soirée; *N. Amer.* levee; *informal* do, bash; *Brit. informal* knees-up, beanfeast, bunfight.

receptive ▶ adjective =**open-minded**, responsive, amenable, well disposed, flexible, approachable, accessible.
−OPPOSITES unresponsive.

recess ▶ noun 1 *two recesses fitted with bookshelves* =**alcove**, bay, niche, nook, corner, hollow, oriel. 2 *the deepest recesses of Broadcasting House* =**innermost parts/ reaches**, remote/secret places, heart, depths, bowels. 3 *the Christmas recess* =**adjournment**, break, interlude, interval, rest; holiday, vacation.

recession ▶ noun =**downturn**, depression, slump, slowdown.

–OPPOSITES boom.

recherché ▸ adjective =obscure, rare, esoteric, abstruse, arcane, recondite, exotic, strange, unusual, unfamiliar.

recipe ▸ noun *a recipe for success* =formula, prescription, blueprint.

recipient ▸ noun =receiver, beneficiary, legatee, donee.
–OPPOSITES donor.

reciprocal ▸ adjective =mutual, common, shared, joint, corresponding, complementary.

reciprocate ▸ verb 1 *I was happy to reciprocate* =do the same (in return), return the favour. 2 *love that was not reciprocated* =requite, return, give back.

recital ▸ noun 1 *a piano recital* =concert, (musical) performance, solo (performance). 2 *her recital of Adam's failures* =enumeration, list, litany, catalogue, detailing; account, report, description, recapitulation, recounting. 3 *a recital of the Lord's Prayer. See* RECITATION *sense 1.*

recitation ▸ noun 1 *the recitation of his poem* =recital, saying aloud, declamation, rendering, rendition, delivery, performance. 2 *a recitation of her life story* =account, description, narration, story. 3 *songs and recitations* =reading, passage; poem, verse, monologue.

recite ▸ verb 1 *he began to recite the Koran* =quote, say aloud, declaim, deliver, render. 2 *Sir John recited the facts they knew* =enumerate, list, detail, reel off; recount, relate, describe, narrate, recapitulate, repeat.

reckless ▸ adjective =rash, careless, thoughtless, heedless, precipitate, impetuous, impulsive, daredevil, devil-may-care; irresponsible, foolhardy, audacious.
–OPPOSITES careful.

reckon ▸ verb 1 *the cost was reckoned at £60* =calculate, compute, work out, figure; count (up), add up, total; *Brit.* tot up. 2 *Anselm reckoned Hugh among his friends* =include, count, regard as, look on as. 3 *it was reckoned a failure* =regard as, consider, judge, hold to be, think of as; deem, rate, gauge, count. 4 *I reckon to get value for money* =expect, anticipate, hope to, be looking to; count on, rely on, depend on, bank on; *N. Amer. informal* figure on.

■ **to be reckoned with** =important, significant; influential, powerful,

strong, potent, formidable, redoubtable.

■ **reckon with** 1 *it's her mother you'll have to reckon with* =deal with, contend with, face (up to). 2 *they hadn't reckoned with her burning ambition* =take into account, take into consideration, bargain for/on, anticipate, foresee, be prepared for, consider; *formal* take cognizance of.

■ **reckon without** =overlook, fail to take account of, disregard.

reckoning ▸ noun 1 *by my reckoning, this comes to £2 million* =calculation, estimation, computation, working out, summation, addition. 2 *by her reckoning, the train was late* =opinion, view, judgement, evaluation, estimate. 3 *the terrible reckoning that he deserved* =retribution, fate, doom, nemesis, punishment.

■ **day of reckoning** =judgement day, day of retribution, doomsday.

reclaim ▸ verb 1 *expenses can be reclaimed* =get back, claim back, recover, regain, retrieve, recoup. 2 *Henrietta had reclaimed him from a life of vice* =save, rescue, redeem; reform.

recline ▸ verb =lie (down/back), lean back; be recumbent; relax, repose, loll, lounge, sprawl, stretch out.

recluse ▸ noun 1 *a religious recluse* =hermit, ascetic, eremite; *historical* anchorite. 2 *a natural recluse* =loner, solitary, lone wolf.

reclusive ▸ adjective =solitary, secluded, isolated, hermitic, eremitic, cloistered.
–OPPOSITES gregarious.

recognition ▸ noun 1 *there was no sign of recognition on his face* =identification, recollection, remembrance. 2 *his recognition of his lack of experience* =acknowledgement, acceptance, admission; realization, awareness, consciousness, knowledge, appreciation; *formal* cognizance. 3 *official recognition* =official approval, certification, accreditation, endorsement, validation. 4 *you deserve recognition for the great job you are doing* =appreciation, gratitude, thanks, congratulations, credit, commendation, acclaim, acknowledgement.

recognizable ▸ adjective =identifiable, noticeable, perceptible, discernible, detectable, distinguishable, observable, perceivable; distinct, unmistakable, clear.
–OPPOSITES imperceptible.

recognize ▸ verb 1 *Hannah recognized him at once* =**identify**, place, know, put a name to; remember, recall, recollect; *Scottish & N. English* ken. 2 *they recognized Alan's ability* =**acknowledge**, accept, admit; realize, be aware of, be conscious of, perceive, discern, appreciate; *formal* be cognizant of. 3 *psychotherapists who are recognized* =**officially approve**, certify, accredit, endorse, sanction, validate. 4 *the Trust recognized their hard work* =**pay tribute to**, appreciate, be grateful for, acclaim, commend.

recoil ▸ verb 1 *she instinctively recoiled* =**draw back**, jump back, pull back; flinch, shy away, shrink (back), blench. 2 *he recoiled from the thought* =**feel revulsion at**, feel disgust at, shrink from, baulk at. 3 *his rifle recoiled* =**kick (back)**, jerk back, spring back. 4 *this will eventually recoil on him* =**rebound on**, backfire, boomerang.

recollect ▸ verb =**remember**, recall, call to mind, think of; think back to, reminisce about.
–OPPOSITES forget.

recollection ▸ noun =**memory**, remembrance, impression, reminiscence.

recommend ▸ verb 1 *his former employer recommended him for the post* =**advocate**, endorse, commend, suggest, put forward, propose, nominate, put up; speak favourably of, put in a good word for, vouch for; *informal* plug. 2 *the committee recommended a cautious approach* =**advise**, counsel, urge, exhort, enjoin, prescribe, argue for, back, support; suggest, advocate, propose. 3 *there was little to recommend her* =**have in one's favour**, give an advantage to; *informal* have going for one.

recommendation ▸ noun 1 *the adviser's recommendations* =**advice**, counsel, guidance, direction, enjoinder; suggestion, proposal. 2 *a personal recommendation* =**commendation**, endorsement, good word, testimonial; suggestion, tip; *informal* plug. 3 *the pillow's only recommendation was that it matched the upholstery* =**advantage**, good point/feature, benefit, asset, boon, attraction, appeal.

recompense ▸ verb 1 *offenders should recompense their victims* =**compensate**, indemnify, repay, reimburse, make reparation to, make restitution to, make amends to. 2 *she wanted to recompense him* =**reward**, pay back. 3 *nothing could recompense her loss* =**make up for**, compensate for, make amends for, make restitution for, make reparation for, redress, make good.
▸ noun *damages were paid in recompense* =**compensation**, reparation, restitution, indemnification; reimbursement, repayment, redress.

reconcilable ▸ adjective =**compatible**, consistent, congruous.

reconcile ▸ verb 1 *the news reconciled us* =**reunite**, bring (back) together (again); pacify, appease, placate, mollify; *formal* conciliate. 2 *trying to reconcile his religious beliefs with his career* =**make compatible**, harmonize, square, make congruent, balance. 3 *the quarrel was reconciled* =**settle**, resolve, sort out, smooth over, iron out, mend, remedy, heal, rectify; *informal* patch up. 4 *they had to reconcile themselves to drastic losses* =**(come to) accept**, resign oneself to, come to terms with, learn to live with, get used to, make the best of.
–OPPOSITES estrange.

reconciliation ▸ noun 1 *the reconciliation of the disputants* =**reunion**, bringing together (again), conciliation; pacification, appeasement, placating, mollification. 2 *a reconciliation of their differences* =**resolution**, settlement, resolving, mending. 3 *there was little hope of reconciliation* =**agreement**, compromise, understanding, peace; *formal* concord. 4 *the reconciliation of theory with practice* =**harmonization**, squaring, balancing.

recondite ▸ adjective =**obscure**, abstruse, arcane, esoteric, recherché, profound, difficult, complex, complicated, involved.

recondition ▸ verb =**overhaul**, rebuild, renovate, restore, repair, reconstruct, remodel, refurbish; *informal* do up, revamp.

reconnaissance ▸ noun =**survey**, exploration, observation, investigation, examination, inspection; patrol, search; *informal* recce.

reconnoitre ▸ verb =**survey**, explore, scout (out), find out the lie of the land; investigate, examine, scrutinize, inspect, observe, take a look at; patrol; *informal* recce, check out.

reconsider ▸ verb =**rethink**, review, revise, re-examine, re-evaluate, reassess, reappraise; have second thoughts, change one's mind.

reconsideration ▸ noun =review, rethink, re-examination, reassessment, re-evaluation, reappraisal.

reconstruct ▸ verb **1** *the building had to be reconstructed* =**rebuild**, restore, renovate, recreate, remake, reassemble, remodel, refashion, revamp, recondition, refurbish. **2** *reconstructing the events of that day* =**recreate**, piece together, re-enact.

record ▸ noun **1** *written records* =**account(s)**, document(s), data, file(s), dossier(s), evidence, report(s); annal(s), archive(s), chronicle(s); minutes, transactions, proceedings, transcript(s); certificate(s), instrument(s), deed(s); register, log. **2** *listening to records* =**album**, vinyl; *dated* LP, single. **3** *his previous good record* =**previous conduct/performance**, (life) history, reputation. **4** *a new British record* =**best performance**, highest achievement; best time, fastest time. **5** *a lasting record of what they have achieved* =**reminder**, memorial, souvenir, memento, remembrance, testament.
▸ adjective *record profits* =**record-breaking**, best ever, unsurpassed, unparalleled, unequalled, second to none.
▸ verb **1** *the doctor recorded her blood pressure* =**write down**, take down, note, jot down, put down on paper; document, enter, minute, register, log. **2** *the thermometer recorded a high temperature* =**indicate**, register, show, display. **3** *the team recorded their fourth win* =**achieve**, accomplish, chalk up, notch up; *informal* clock up. **4** *the recital was recorded live* =**tape**, tape-record; video-record, videotape.
■ **off the record 1** *his comments were off the record* =**unofficial**, confidential. **2** *they admitted, off the record, that they had made a mistake* =**unofficially**, privately, confidentially, between ourselves.

recount ▸ verb =**tell**, relate, narrate, describe, report, outline, delineate, relay, convey, communicate, impart.

recoup ▸ verb =**get back**, regain, recover, win back, retrieve, redeem, recuperate.

recourse ▸ noun =**option**, possibility, alternative, resort, way out, hope, remedy, choice, expedient.
■ **have recourse to** =**resort to**, make use of, avail oneself of, turn to, call on, look to, fall back on.

recover ▸ verb **1** *he's recovering from a heart attack* =**recuperate**, get better, convalesce, get stronger; be on the mend, pick up, rally, respond to treatment, improve, heal, pull through, bounce back. **2** *later, shares recovered* =**rally**, improve, pick up, rebound, bounce back. **3** *the stolen material has been recovered* =**retrieve**, regain (possession of), get back, recoup, reclaim, repossess, redeem, recuperate, find (again), track down. **4** *gold coins recovered from a wreck* =**salvage**, save, rescue, retrieve.
–OPPOSITES deteriorate.
■ **recover oneself** =**pull oneself together**, regain one's composure, regain one's self-control; *informal* get a grip (on oneself).

recovery ▸ noun **1** *her recovery may be slow* =**recuperation**, convalescence. **2** *the economy was showing signs of recovery* =**improvement**, rallying, picking up, upturn, upswing. **3** *the recovery of stolen goods* =**retrieval**, repossession, reclamation, recouping, redemption, recuperation.
–OPPOSITES relapse, deterioration.

recreation ▸ noun **1** *she cycles for recreation* =**pleasure**, leisure, relaxation, fun, enjoyment, entertainment, amusement; *informal* R and R. **2** *his favourite recreations* =**pastime**, hobby, leisure activity.
–OPPOSITES work.

recrimination ▸ noun =**accusation(s)**, countercharge(s), counter-attack(s), retaliation(s).

recruit ▸ verb **1** *more soldiers were recruited* =**enlist**, call up, conscript; *US* draft, muster in. **2** *the king recruited an army* =**muster**, form, raise, mobilize. **3** *the company is recruiting staff* =**hire**, employ, take on; enrol, sign up, engage.
–OPPOSITES disband, dismiss.
▸ noun **1** *new recruits were enlisted* =**conscript**, new soldier; *US* draftee; *N. Amer. informal* yardbird. **2** *top-quality recruits* =**new member**, newcomer, initiate, beginner, novice; *N. Amer.* tenderfoot; *informal* rookie, newbie; *N. Amer. informal* greenhorn.

rectify ▸ verb =**correct**, (put) right, sort out, deal with, amend, remedy, repair, fix, make good, resolve, settle; *informal* patch up.

rectitude ▸ noun =**righteousness**, goodness, virtue, morality, honour, integrity, principle, probity, honesty, trustworthiness, decency, good character.

recumbent ▸ adjective =lying, flat, horizontal, stretched out, sprawled (out), reclining, prone, prostrate, supine.
–OPPOSITES upright.

recuperate ▸ verb **1** *he went to France to recuperate* =**get better**, recover, convalesce, get well, regain one's strength/health, get over something. **2** *he recuperated the money* =**get back**, regain, recover, recoup, retrieve, reclaim, repossess, redeem.

recur ▸ verb =**happen again**, reoccur, repeat (itself); come back (again), return, reappear; *formal* recrudesce.

recurrent ▸ adjective =**repeated**, repetitive, periodic, cyclical, seasonal, perennial, regular, frequent; intermittent, sporadic, spasmodic.

recycle ▸ verb =**reuse**, reprocess, reclaim, recover.

red ▸ adjective **1** *a red dress* =scarlet, vermilion, ruby, cherry, cerise, cardinal, carmine, wine; *literary* damask, vermeil, sanguine. **2** *he was red in the face* =**flushed**, pink, florid, rubicund; ruddy, rosy. **3** *red hair* =auburn, Titian, chestnut, carroty, ginger.

red-blooded ▸ adjective =**manly**, masculine, virile, macho.

redden ▸ verb =**go/turn red**, blush, flush, colour (up), burn.

redeem ▸ verb **1** *one feature redeems the book* =**save**, vindicate. **2** *he fully redeemed himself next time* =**vindicate**, absolve. **3** *you cannot redeem their sins* =**atone for**, make amends for, make restitution for. **4** *redeeming sinners* =**save**, deliver from sin. **5** *Billy redeemed his drums from the pawnbrokers* =**retrieve**, regain, recover, get back, reclaim, repossess; buy back. **6** *this voucher can be redeemed at any branch* =(give in) exchange, cash in, convert, trade in.

redeeming ▸ adjective =**compensating**, extenuating, redemptive.

redemption ▸ noun **1** *God's redemption of his people* =**saving**, freeing from sin, absolution. **2** *the redemption of their possessions* =**retrieval**, recovery, reclamation, repossession, return. **3** *the redemption of vouchers* =**exchange**, cashing in, conversion. **4** *the redemption of the mortgage* =**paying off/back**, discharge, clearing, honouring. **5** *the redemption of his obligations* =**fulfilment**, carrying out, discharge, performing, honouring, meeting.

red-handed ▸ adjective =**in the act**, in flagrante delicto; *Brit. informal* with one's trousers down.

redolent ▸ adjective =**evocative**, suggestive, reminiscent.

redoubtable ▸ adjective =**formidable**, awe-inspiring, fearsome, daunting; impressive, commanding, indomitable, invincible, doughty, mighty.

redress ▸ verb **1** *we redressed the problem* =**rectify**, correct, right, compensate for, amend, remedy, make good, resolve, settle. **2** *we aim to redress the balance* =**even up**, regulate, equalize.
▸ noun *your best hope of redress* =**compensation**, reparation, restitution, recompense, repayment, indemnity, retribution, satisfaction.

reduce ▸ verb **1** *the aim to reduce pollution* =**lessen**, make smaller, lower, bring down, decrease, diminish, minimize; shrink, narrow, contract, shorten; *informal* chop. **2** *he reduced her to tears* =**bring to**, drive to. **3** *he was reduced to the ranks* =**demote**, downgrade, lower (in rank).
–OPPOSITES increase, put up.
■ **in reduced circumstances** =impoverished, ruined, bankrupted; poor, indigent, impecunious, poverty-stricken, destitute; needy, badly off, hard up; *informal* flat (broke), strapped for cash; *Brit. informal* stony broke, skint; *formal* penurious.

reduction ▸ noun **1** *a reduction in pollution* =**lessening**, lowering, decrease, diminution. **2** *a reduction in staff* =**cut**, cutback, scaling down, trimming, pruning, axing, chopping. **3** *a reduction in inflationary pressure* =**easing**, lightening, moderation, alleviation. **4** *a reduction in status* =**demotion**, downgrading, lowering. **5** *substantial reductions* =**discount**, markdown, deduction, (price) cut, concession.

redundancy ▸ noun **1** *redundancy in language* =**superfluity**, unnecessariness, excess. **2** *redundancies are in the offing* =**sacking**, dismissal, lay-off, discharge; unemployment.

redundant ▸ adjective **1** *many churches are redundant* =**unnecessary**, not required, unneeded, uncalled for, surplus (to requirements), superfluous. **2** *2,000 workers were made redundant* =**sacked**, dismissed, laid off, discharged;

unemployed, jobless, out of work.
−OPPOSITES employed.

reef ▸ noun =**shoal**, bar, sandbar, sandbank.

reek ▸ verb *the whole place reeked* =**stink**, smell (bad).
▸ noun *the reek of cattle dung* =**stink**, bad smell, stench, malodour; *Brit. informal* niff, pong, whiff.

reel ▸ verb **1** *he reeled as the ship began to roll* =**stagger**, lurch, sway, rock, stumble, totter, wobble, falter. **2** *we were reeling from the crisis* =**be shaken**, be stunned, be in shock, be taken aback, be staggered, be aghast, be upset. **3** *the room reeled* =**go round (and round)**, whirl, spin, revolve, swirl, twirl, turn, swim.

refer ▸ verb **1** *he referred to errors in the article* =**mention**, allude to, touch on, speak of/about, talk of/about, write about, comment on, deal with, point out, call attention to. **2** *the matter has been referred to my insurers* =**pass**, hand on/over, send on, transfer, remit, entrust, assign. **3** *these figures refer only to 2001* =**apply to**, be relevant to, concern, relate to, be connected with, pertain to, appertain to, be pertinent to, have a bearing on, cover. **4** *the name refers to a Saxon village* =**denote**, describe, indicate, mean, signify, designate. **5** *the constable referred to his notes* =**consult**, turn to, look at, have recourse to.

referee ▸ noun **1** *the referee blew his whistle* =**umpire**, judge; *informal* ref. **2** *include the names of two referees* =**supporter**, character witness, advocate.
▸ verb **1** *he refereed the game* =**umpire**, judge. **2** *they asked him to referee in the dispute* =**arbitrate**, mediate.

reference ▸ noun **1** *his journal contains many references to railways* =**mention of**, allusion to, comment on, remark about. **2** *references are given in the bibliography* =**(information) source**, citation, authority, credit. **3** *reference to a higher court* =**referral**, transfer, remission. **4** *a glowing reference* =**testimonial**, recommendation; credentials.
■ **with reference to** =**apropos**, with regard to, with respect to, on the subject of, re; in relation to, in connection with.

referendum ▸ noun =**(popular) vote**, ballot, poll, plebiscite.

refine ▸ verb **1** *refining our cereal foods* =**purify**, process, treat. **2** *helping students*

to refine their skills =**improve**, perfect, polish (up), hone, fine-tune.

refined ▸ adjective **1** *refined sugar* =**purified**, processed, treated. **2** *a refined lady* =**cultivated**, cultured, polished, stylish, elegant, sophisticated, urbane; polite, gracious, well mannered, well bred. **3** *a person of refined taste* =**discriminating**, discerning, fastidious, exquisite, impeccable, fine.
−OPPOSITES crude, coarse.

refinement ▸ noun **1** *writing needs endless refinement* =**improvement**, polishing, honing, fine-tuning, touching up, finishing off, revision, editing. **2** *a woman of refinement* =**style**, elegance, finesse, polish, sophistication, urbanity; politeness, grace, good manners, good breeding, gentility.

reflect ▸ verb **1** *the snow reflects light* =**send back**, throw back, cast back. **2** *their expressions reflected their feelings* =**indicate**, show, display, demonstrate, be evidence of, register, reveal, betray, disclose; express, communicate; *formal* evince. **3** *he reflected on his responsibilities* =**think about**, consider, review, mull over, contemplate, cogitate about/on, meditate on, muse on, brood on/over.
■ **reflect badly on** =**discredit**, disgrace, shame, damage, bring into disrepute.

reflection ▸ noun **1** *her reflection in the mirror* =**(mirror) image**, likeness. **2** *your hands are a reflection of your well-being* =**indication**, display, demonstration, manifestation; expression, evidence. **3** *a sad reflection on society* =**slur**, aspersion, imputation, reproach, shame, criticism. **4** *after some reflection, he turned it down* =**thought**, consideration, contemplation, deliberation, pondering, meditation, musing, rumination; *formal* cogitation. **5** *write down your reflections* =**opinion**, thought, view, belief, feeling, idea, impression, conclusion, assessment; comment, observation, remark.

reflex ▸ adjective =**instinctive**, automatic, involuntary, impulsive, intuitive, spontaneous, unconscious, unconditioned, untaught, unlearned.
−OPPOSITES conscious.

reform ▸ verb **1** *a plan to reform the system* =**improve**, (make) better, ameliorate, refine; alter, change, adjust, adapt, amend, revise, reshape, refashion, re-

design, restyle, revamp, rebuild, reconstruct, remodel, reorganize. **2** *after his marriage he reformed* =**mend one's ways**, change for the better, turn over a new leaf, improve.
▶ noun *the reform of the prison system* =**improvement**, amelioration, refinement; alteration, change, adaptation, amendment, revision, reshaping, refashioning, redesigning, restyling, revamp, renovation, rebuilding, reconstruction, remodelling, reorganization.

refractory ▶ adjective *(formal)* =**obstinate**, stubborn, mulish, pig-headed, obdurate, headstrong, self-willed, wayward, wilful, perverse, contrary, recalcitrant, obstreperous, disobedient; *Brit. informal* bloody-minded, bolshie, stroppy.
−OPPOSITES obedient.

refrain ▶ verb =**abstain**, desist, hold back, stop oneself, forbear, avoid, eschew, shun, renounce; *informal* swear off; *formal* forswear, abjure.

refresh ▶ verb **1** *the cool air will refresh me* =**reinvigorate**, revitalize, revive, restore, fortify, enliven, perk up, stimulate, freshen, energize, exhilarate, reanimate, wake up, revivify, inspirit; *blow away the cobwebs; informal* buck up, pep up. **2** *let me refresh your memory* =**jog**, stimulate, prompt, prod. **3** *(N. Amer.) I refreshed his glass* =**refill**, top up, replenish, recharge.
−OPPOSITES weary.

refreshing ▶ adjective **1** *a refreshing drink* =**invigorating**, revitalizing, reviving, restoring, bracing, fortifying, enlivening, inspiriting, stimulating, energizing, exhilarating. **2** *a refreshing change of direction* =**welcome**, stimulating, fresh, imaginative, innovative.

refreshment ▶ noun **1** *refreshments were available* =**food and drink**, sustenance, provender; snacks, titbits; *informal* nibbles, eats, grub, nosh; *formal* comestibles. **2** *spiritual refreshment* =**invigoration**, revival, stimulation, reanimation, revivification, rejuvenation, regeneration, renewal.

refrigerate ▶ verb =**cool (down)**, chill.
−OPPOSITES heat.

refuge ▶ noun **1** *homeless people seeking refuge* =**shelter**, protection, safety, security, asylum, sanctuary. **2** *a refuge for mountain gorillas* =**sanctuary**, shelter, (safe) haven, sanctum; retreat, bolt-hole,

hiding place, hideaway, hideout.

refugee ▶ noun =**displaced person**, DP, fugitive, asylum seeker, exile, émigré.

refund ▶ verb **1** *we will refund your money if you're not satisfied* =**repay**, give back, return, pay back. **2** *they refunded the subscribers* =**reimburse**, compensate, recompense, remunerate, indemnify.
▶ noun *a full refund* =**repayment**, reimbursement, rebate.

refurbish ▶ verb =**renovate**, recondition, rehabilitate, revamp, overhaul, restore, renew, redevelop, rebuild, reconstruct; redecorate, spruce up, upgrade, refit; *informal* do up.

refusal ▶ noun **1** *we had one refusal to our invitation* =**non-acceptance**, no, dissent, demurral, negation, turndown. **2** *you have first refusal* =**option**, choice, opportunity to purchase. **3** *the refusal of planning permission* =**withholding**, denial, turndown.

refuse[1] ▶ verb **1** *he refused the invitation* =**decline**, turn down, say no to; reject, spurn, rebuff, dismiss; *informal* pass up. **2** *the Council refused planning permission* =**withhold**, deny.
−OPPOSITES accept, grant.

refuse[2] ▶ noun *piles of refuse* =**rubbish**, waste, debris, litter, detritus, dross; *N. Amer.* garbage, trash; *informal* dreck, junk.

refute ▶ verb **1** *attempts to refute Einstein's theory* =**disprove**, prove wrong/false, controvert, rebut, give the lie to, explode, debunk, discredit, invalidate; *informal* shoot full of holes; *formal* confute. **2** *she refuted the allegation* =**deny**, reject, repudiate, rebut; contradict; *formal* gainsay.

regain ▶ verb **1** *government troops regained the capital* =**recover**, get back, win back, recoup, retrieve, reclaim, repossess; take back, retake, recapture, reconquer. **2** *they regained dry land* =**return to**, get back to, reach again, rejoin.

regal ▶ adjective **1** *a regal feast. See* SPLENDID *sense* 1. **2** *his regal forebears* =**royal**, kingly, queenly, princely.

regale ▶ verb **1** *they were lavishly regaled* =**entertain**, wine and dine, fête, feast, serve, feed. **2** *he regaled her with stories* =**entertain**, amuse, divert, delight, fascinate, captivate.

regard ▶ verb **1** *we regard the results as encouraging* =**consider**, look on, view, see, think of, judge, deem, estimate, assess, reckon, adjudge, rate, gauge. **2** *he regarded her coldly* =**look at**, contemplate, eye, gaze at, stare at; watch, observe, view, study, scrutinize; *literary* behold.

▶ **noun 1** *he has no regard for life* =**consideration**, care, concern, thought, notice, heed, attention. **2** *doctors are held in high regard* =**esteem**, respect, acclaim, admiration, approval, approbation, estimation. **3** *Jamie sends his regards* =**best wishes**, greetings, felicitations, salutations, respects, compliments, best, love. **4** *his steady regard* =**(fixed) look**, gaze, stare; observation, contemplation, study, scrutiny. **5** *in this regard I disagree* =**respect**, aspect, point, item, particular, detail, specific; matter, issue, topic, question.

■ **with regard to.** *See* REGARDING.

regarding ▶ preposition =**concerning**, as regards, with/in regard to, with respect to, with reference to, relating to, respecting, re, about, apropos, on the subject of, in connection with, vis-à-vis.

regardless ▶ adverb *he decided to go, regardless* =**anyway**, anyhow, in any case, nevertheless, nonetheless, despite everything, even so, all the same, in any event, come what may; *informal* irregardless.

■ **regardless of** =**irrespective of**, without reference to, without consideration of, discounting, ignoring, notwithstanding, no matter; *informal* irregardless of.

regenerate ▶ verb =**revive**, revitalize, renew, restore, breathe new life into, revivify, reanimate, resuscitate; *informal* give a shot in the arm to.

regime ▶ noun **1** *the Communist regime* =**(system of) government**, rule, authority, control, command, administration, leadership. **2** *a health regime* =**system**, arrangement, scheme; order, pattern, method, procedure, routine, course, plan, programme.

regiment ▶ noun =**unit**, outfit, force, corps, division, brigade, battalion, squadron, company, platoon.

▶ verb =**organize**, order, systematize, control, regulate, manage, discipline.

regimented ▶ adjective =**strictly regulated**, organized, disciplined, controlled, ordered, systematic.

region ▶ noun =**district**, province, territory, division, area, section, sector, zone, belt, part, quarter; *informal* parts.

■ **in the region of.** *See* APPROXIMATELY.

regional ▶ adjective **1** *regional variation* =**geographical**, territorial. **2** *a regional parliament* =**local**, provincial, district, parochial.

−OPPOSITES national.

register ▶ noun **1** *the register of electors* =**official list**, roll, roster, index, directory, catalogue, inventory. **2** *the parish register* =**record**, chronicle, log, ledger, archive; annals, files. **3** *the lower register of the piano* =**range**, reaches; notes, octaves.

▶ verb **1** *I wish to register a complaint* =**record**, enter, file, lodge, write down, submit, report, note, minute, log. **2** *it is not too late to register* =**enrol**, put one's name down, enlist, sign on/up, apply. **3** *the dial registered 100mph* =**indicate**, read, record, show, display. **4** *her face registered anger* =**display**, show, express, exhibit, betray, evidence, reveal, manifest, demonstrate, bespeak; *formal* evince. **5** *the content of her statement did not register* =**make an impression**, get through, sink in, penetrate, have an effect, strike home.

regress ▶ verb =**revert**, retrogress, relapse, lapse, backslide, slip back; deteriorate, decline, worsen, degenerate; *informal* go downhill.

−OPPOSITES progress.

regret ▶ verb **1** *they came to regret their decision* =**be sorry about**, feel contrite about, feel remorse about/for, rue, repent (of). **2** *regretting the passing of youth* =**mourn**, grieve for/over, weep over, sigh over, lament, sorrow for, deplore.

−OPPOSITES welcome.

▶ noun **1** *both players expressed regret* =**remorse**, sorrow, contrition, repentance, penitence, guilt, compunction, remorsefulness, ruefulness. **2** *please give your mother my regrets* =**apologies**; refusal. **3** *they left with genuine regret* =**sadness**, sorrow, disappointment, unhappiness, grief.

−OPPOSITES satisfaction.

regretful ▶ adjective =**sorry**, remorseful, contrite, repentant, rueful, penitent, conscience-stricken, apologetic, guilt-ridden, ashamed, shamefaced.

−OPPOSITES unrepentant.

regrettable ▶ adjective =**undesirable**, unfortunate, unwelcome, sorry, woeful, disappointing.

regular ▶ adjective **1** *plant them at regular intervals* =**uniform**, even, consistent, constant, unchanging, unvarying, fixed. **2** *a regular beat* =**rhythmic**, steady, even, uniform, constant, unchanging, unvarying. **3** *the subject of regular protests* =**frequent**, repeated, continual, recurrent, periodic, constant, perpetual, numerous. **4** *regular methods of business* =**established**, conventional, orthodox, proper, official, approved, bona fide, standard, usual, traditional, tried and tested. **5** *a regular procedure* =**methodical**, systematic, structured, well ordered, well organized, orderly, efficient. **6** *his regular route to work* =**usual**, normal, customary, habitual, routine, typical, accustomed, established.
−OPPOSITES erratic, occasional.

regulate ▶ verb **1** *the flow has been regulated* =**control**, adjust, manage. **2** *a new act regulating businesses* =**supervise**, police, monitor, check (up on), be responsible for; control, manage, direct, guide, govern.

regulation ▶ noun **1** *EC regulations* =**rule**, order, directive, act, law, by-law, statute, edict, canon, pronouncement, dictate, decree. **2** *the regulation of blood sugar* =**adjustment**, control, management, balancing. **3** *the regulation of financial services* =**supervision**, policing, superintendence, monitoring, inspection; control, management, responsibility for.
▶ adjective *regulation dress* =**official**, prescribed, set, fixed, mandatory, compulsory, obligatory.
−OPPOSITES unofficial.

regurgitate ▶ verb *regurgitating facts* =**repeat**, restate, reiterate, recite, parrot; *informal* trot out.

rehabilitate ▶ verb **1** *efforts to rehabilitate patients* =**reintegrate**, readapt; *N. Amer. informal* rehab. **2** *former dissidents were rehabilitated* =**reinstate**, restore, bring back; pardon, absolve, exonerate, forgive; *formal* exculpate. **3** *rehabilitating vacant housing* =**recondition**, restore, renovate, refurbish, revamp, overhaul, redevelop, rebuild, reconstruct; *N. Amer. informal* rehab.

rehearsal ▶ noun =**practice (session)**, trial performance, read-through, run-through; *informal* dry run.

rehearse ▶ verb **1** *I rehearsed the role* =**prepare**, practise, read through, run

through/over, go over. **2** *he rehearsed the Vienna Philharmonic* =**train**, drill, prepare, coach. **3** *the document rehearsed all the arguments* =**enumerate**, list, itemize, detail, spell out, catalogue, recite, rattle off; restate, repeat, reiterate, recapitulate, go over, run through; *informal* recap.

reign ▶ verb **1** *Robert II reigned for nineteen years* =**be king/queen**, be monarch, be sovereign, sit on the throne, wear the crown, rule. **2** *chaos reigned* =**prevail**, exist, be present, be the case, occur, be prevalent, be current, be rife, be rampant, be the order of the day; *formal* obtain.
▶ noun *during Henry's reign* =**rule**, sovereignty, monarchy.

reigning ▶ adjective **1** *the reigning monarch* =**ruling**, regnant; on the throne. **2** *the reigning champion* =**incumbent**, current.

reimburse ▶ verb **1** *they will reimburse your costs* =**repay**, refund, return, pay back. **2** *we'll reimburse you* =**compensate**, recompense, repay.

rein ▶ noun *there is no rein on his behaviour* =**restraint**, check, curb, constraint, restriction, limitation, control, brake.
▶ verb *they reined back costs* =**restrain**, check, curb, constrain, hold back/in, keep under control, regulate, restrict, control, curtail, limit.
■ **free rein** =**freedom**, a free hand, leeway, latitude, flexibility, liberty, independence, free play, licence, room to manoeuvre, carte blanche.
■ **keep a tight rein on** =**regulate**, discipline, regiment, keep in line.

reinforce ▶ verb **1** *troops reinforced the dam* =**strengthen**, fortify, bolster up, shore up, buttress, prop up, underpin, brace, support. **2** *reinforcing links between colleges and companies* =**strengthen**, fortify, support; cement, boost, promote, encourage, deepen, enrich, enhance, intensify, improve. **3** *the need to reinforce NATO troops* =**augment**, increase, add to, supplement, boost, top up.

reinforcement ▶ noun **1** *the reinforcement of our defences* =**strengthening**, fortification, bolstering, shoring up, buttressing, bracing. **2** *they returned with reinforcements* =**additional troops**, auxiliaries, reserves; support, backup, help.

reinstate ▶ verb =**restore**, put back, bring back, reinstitute, reinstall.

reiterate ▶ verb =**repeat**, restate, recapitulate, go over (and over), rehearse.

reject ▶ verb **1** *the miners rejected the offer* =**turn down**, refuse, decline, say no to, spurn; *informal* give the thumbs down to. **2** *Jamie rejected her* =**rebuff**, spurn, shun, snub, repudiate, cast off/aside, discard, abandon, desert, turn one's back on, have nothing (more) to do with, wash one's hands of; *literary* forsake.
−OPPOSITES accept.

▶ noun **1** *it is only a reject* =**substandard article**, discard, second. **2** *what a reject!* =**failure**, loser, incompetent.

rejection ▶ noun **1** *a rejection of the offer* =**refusal**, declining, turning down, dismissal, spurning. **2** *Madeleine's rejection of him* =**repudiation**, rebuff, spurning, abandonment, desertion; *informal* brush-off; *literary* forsaking.

rejoice ▶ verb **1** *they rejoiced when she returned* =**be joyful**, be happy, be pleased, be glad, be delighted, be elated, be ecstatic, be euphoric, be overjoyed, be as pleased as Punch, be cock-a-hoop, be jubilant, be thrilled, be on cloud nine; celebrate, make merry; *informal* be over the moon. **2** *he rejoiced in their success* =**take delight**, find/take pleasure, feel satisfaction, find joy, enjoy, revel in, glory in, delight in, relish, savour.
−OPPOSITES mourn.

rejoicing ▶ noun =**happiness**, pleasure, joy, gladness, delight, elation, jubilation, exuberance, exultation, celebration, revelry, merrymaking.

rejoin[1] ▶ verb *the path rejoins the road further on* =**return to**, be reunited with, join again, reach again, regain.

rejoin[2] ▶ verb *Eugene rejoined that you couldn't expect much* =**answer**, reply, respond, return, retort, riposte, counter.

rejoinder ▶ noun =**answer**, reply, response, retort, riposte, counter; *informal* comeback.

rejuvenate ▶ verb =**revive**, revitalize, regenerate, breathe new life into, revivify, reanimate, resuscitate, refresh, reawaken; *informal* give a shot in the arm to, pep up, buck up.

relapse ▶ verb **1** *a few patients relapse* =**get ill/worse again**, deteriorate, degenerate. **2** *she relapsed into silence* =**revert**, lapse; regress, retrogress, slip back, slide back, degenerate.
−OPPOSITES improve.

relate ▶ verb **1** *he related stories* =**tell**, recount, narrate, report, chronicle, out-

line, delineate, retail, recite, repeat, communicate, impart. **2** *mortality is related to unemployment levels* =**connect (with)**, associate (with), link (with), correlate (with), ally (with), couple (with). **3** *the charges relate to offences committed in August* =**apply**, be relevant, concern, pertain to, be pertinent to, have a bearing on, appertain to, involve. **4** *she cannot relate to her father* =**have a rapport**, get on (well), feel sympathy, feel for, identify with, empathize with, understand; *informal* hit it off with.

related ▶ adjective **1** *related ideas* =**connected**, interconnected, associated, linked, coupled, allied, affiliated, concomitant, corresponding, analogous, kindred, parallel, comparable, homologous, equivalent. **2** *are you two related?* =**of the same family**, kin, kindred, consanguineous.
−OPPOSITES unconnected.

relation ▶ noun **1** *the relation between church and state* =**connection**, relationship, association, link; correlation, correspondence, parallel, alliance, bond, interrelation, interconnection. **2** *this had no relation to national security* =**relevance**, applicability, reference, pertinence, bearing. **3** *are you a relation of his?* =**relative**, member of the family, kinsman, kinswoman; (**relations**) family, (kith and) kin, kindred. **4** *improving relations with India* =**dealings**, communication, relationship, connections, contact, interaction. **5** *sexual relations.* See SEX sense 1.

relationship ▶ noun **1** *the relationship between diet and diabetes* =**connection**, relation, association, link; correlation, correspondence, parallel, alliance, bond, interrelation, interconnection. **2** *evidence of their relationship to a common ancestor* =**family ties/connections**, blood relationship, kinship, affinity, consanguinity, common ancestry/lineage. **3** *the end of their relationship* =**romance**, (love) affair, love, liaison, amour.

relative ▶ adjective **1** *the relative importance of each factor* =**comparative**, respective, comparable, correlative, parallel, corresponding. **2** *the food required is relative to body weight* =**proportionate**, commensurate, corresponding. **3** *relative ease* =**moderate**, reasonable, a fair degree of, considerable, comparative.

▶ noun *he's a relative of mine* =**relation**,

member of someone's/the family, kinsman, kinswoman; (**relatives**) family, (kith and) kin, kindred, kinsfolk.

relatively ▶ adverb =comparatively; quite, fairly, reasonably, rather, somewhat, to a certain extent/degree, to an extent, to a degree, tolerably, passably; *informal* pretty, kind of, sort of.

relax ▶ verb **1** *yoga is helpful in learning to relax* =unwind, loosen up, ease up/off, slow down, de-stress, unbend, rest, put one's feet up, take it easy; *informal* unbutton; *N. Amer. informal* hang loose, chill out. **2** *a walk will relax you* =calm (down), unwind, loosen up, make less tense/uptight, soothe, pacify, compose. **3** *he relaxed his grip* =loosen, slacken, unclench, weaken, lessen. **4** *her muscles relaxed* =become less tense, loosen, slacken, unknot. **5** *they relaxed the restrictions* =moderate, modify, temper, ease (up on), loosen, lighten, dilute, weaken, reduce, decrease; *informal* let up on.
–OPPOSITES tense, tighten.

relaxation ▶ noun **1** *a state of relaxation* =(mental) repose, calm, tranquillity, peacefulness, loosening up, unwinding. **2** *I just play for relaxation* =recreation, enjoyment, amusement, entertainment, fun, pleasure, leisure; *informal* R and R. **3** *relaxation of censorship rules* =moderation, easing, loosening, lightening; alleviation, mitigation, dilution, weakening, reduction; *informal* letting up.

relay ▶ noun *a live relay of the performance* =broadcast, transmission, showing.
▶ verb *I'd relayed the messages* =pass on, hand on, transfer, repeat, communicate, send, transmit, disseminate, spread, circulate.

release ▶ verb **1** *all prisoners were released* =(set) free, let go/out, liberate, set at liberty. **2** *Burke released the animal* =untie, undo, loose, let go, unleash, unfetter. **3** *this released staff for other duties* =make available, free (up), supply, furnish, provide. **4** *she released Stephen from his promise* =excuse, exempt, discharge, deliver, absolve; *informal* let off. **5** *police released the news yesterday* =make public, make known, issue, break, announce, declare, report, reveal, divulge, disclose, publish, broadcast, circulate, communicate, disseminate. **6** *the film has been released on video* =launch, put on sale, bring out, make available.
–OPPOSITES imprison, tie up.
▶ noun **1** *the release of political prisoners*

=freeing, liberation, deliverance; freedom, liberty. **2** *the release of the news* =issuing, announcement, declaration, reporting, revealing, divulging, disclosure, publication, communication, dissemination. **3** *a press release* =announcement, bulletin, newsflash, dispatch, proclamation. **4** *the group's last release* =CD, album, single, record; video, film; book.

relegate ▶ verb =downgrade, lower (in rank/status), put down, move down; demote, degrade.
–OPPOSITES upgrade.

relent ▶ verb **1** *the government relented* =change one's mind, do a U-turn, backpedal, back down, give way/in, capitulate; *Brit.* do an about-turn; *formal* accede. **2** *the rain relented* =ease (off/up), slacken, let up, abate, drop, die down, lessen, decrease, subside, weaken, tail off.

relentless ▶ adjective **1** *their relentless pursuit of quality* =persistent, constant, continual, non-stop, never-ending, unabating, interminable, incessant, unceasing, endless, unremitting; unfaltering, unflagging, untiring, unwavering, dogged, single-minded, tireless, indefatigable; *formal* pertinacious. **2** *a relentless taskmaster* =harsh, grim, cruel, severe, strict, remorseless, merciless, pitiless, ruthless, unmerciful, heartless, hardhearted, unforgiving.

relevant ▶ adjective =pertinent, applicable, apposite, material, apropos, to the point, germane; connected, related, linked.

reliable ▶ adjective **1** *reliable evidence* =dependable, good, well founded, authentic, valid, genuine, sound, true. **2** *a reliable friend* =trustworthy, dependable, good, true, faithful, devoted, steadfast, staunch, constant, loyal, trusty, dedicated, unfailing. **3** *reliable brakes* =dependable, safe, fail-safe. **4** *a reliable firm* =reputable, dependable, trustworthy, honest, responsible, established, proven.
–OPPOSITES untrustworthy.

reliance ▶ noun **1** *reliance on the state* =dependence. **2** *reliance on his judgement* =trust, confidence, faith, belief, conviction.

relic ▶ noun **1** *a Viking relic* =artefact, historical object, antiquity. **2** *a saint's relics* =remains, corpse, bones, reliquiae.

relief ▶ noun **1** *it was a relief to share my worries* =reassurance, consolation, comfort, solace. **2** *pain relief* =alleviation, relieving, assuagement, palliation, allaying, soothing, easing, lessening, reduction. **3** *relief from her burden* =freedom, release, liberation, deliverance. **4** *a little light relief* =respite, amusement, diversion, entertainment, jollity, recreation. **5** *bringing relief to the starving* =help, aid, assistance, succour, sustenance; charity, gifts, donations. **6** *his relief arrived to take over* =replacement, substitute, deputy, reserve, cover, stand-in, supply, locum (tenens), understudy. –OPPOSITES intensification.

relieve ▶ verb **1** *this helps relieve pain* =alleviate, mitigate, assuage, ease, dull, reduce, lessen, diminish. **2** *relieving the boredom* =counteract, reduce, alleviate, mitigate; interrupt, vary, stop, dispel, prevent. **3** *the helpers relieved us* =replace, take over from, stand in for, fill in for, substitute for, deputize for, cover for. **4** *this relieves the teacher of a heavy load* =(set) free, release, exempt, excuse, absolve, let off, discharge. –OPPOSITES aggravate.

relieved ▶ adjective =glad, thankful, grateful, pleased, happy, easy/easier in one's mind, reassured. –OPPOSITES worried.

religion ▶ noun =faith, belief, worship, creed; sect, cult, church, denomination.

> WORD LINKS
> *study of religion:* **divinity, theology**

religious ▶ adjective **1** *a religious person* =devout, pious, reverent, godly, God-fearing, churchgoing, practising, faithful, devoted, committed. **2** *religious beliefs* =spiritual, theological, scriptural, doctrinal, ecclesiastical, church, holy, divine, sacred. **3** *religious attention to detail* =scrupulous, conscientious, meticulous, sedulous, punctilious, strict, rigorous, close. –OPPOSITES atheistic, secular.

relinquish ▶ verb **1** *he relinquished control of the company* =renounce, give up/away, hand over, let go of. **2** *he relinquished his post* =leave, resign from, stand down from, bow out of, give up; *informal* quit, chuck. –OPPOSITES retain, continue.

relish ▶ noun **1** *he dug into his food with relish* =enjoyment, gusto, delight, pleasure, glee, rapture, satisfaction, contentment, appreciation, enthusiasm, appetite; *humorous* delectation. **2** *a hot relish* =condiment, sauce, dressing. –OPPOSITES dislike.

▶ verb **1** *he was relishing his moment of glory* =enjoy, delight in, love, adore, take pleasure in, rejoice in, appreciate, savour, revel in, luxuriate in, glory in. **2** *I don't relish the drive* =look forward to, fancy.

reluctance ▶ noun =unwillingness, disinclination; hesitation, wavering, vacillation; doubts, second thoughts, misgivings.

reluctant ▶ adjective **1** *her parents were reluctant* =unwilling, disinclined, unenthusiastic, resistant, opposed; hesitant. **2** *a reluctant smile* =shy, bashful, coy, diffident, reserved, timid, timorous. **3** *he was reluctant to leave* =loath, unwilling, disinclined, indisposed. –OPPOSITES willing, eager.

rely ▶ verb **1** *we can rely on his discretion* =depend, count, bank, place reliance, reckon; be confident of, be sure of, believe in, have faith in, trust in; *informal* swear by; *N. Amer. informal* figure on. **2** *we rely on government funding* =be dependent, depend.

remain ▶ verb **1** *the problem will remain* =continue to exist, endure, last, abide, carry on, persist, stay (around), prevail, survive, live on. **2** *he remained in hospital* =stay (behind/put), wait (around), be left, hang on; *informal* hang around/round. **3** *union leaders remain sceptical* =continue to be, stay, keep. **4** *the few minutes that remain* =be left (over), be still available, be unused; have not yet passed.

remainder ▶ noun =residue, balance, rest, others, those left, remnant(s), surplus, extra, excess, overflow.

remaining ▶ adjective **1** *the remaining workers* =residual, surviving, left (over). **2** *his remaining jobs* =unsettled, outstanding, unfinished, incomplete, to be done, unattended to. **3** *my only remaining memories* =surviving, lasting, enduring, continuing, persisting, abiding, (still) existing.

remains ▶ plural noun **1** *the remains of her drink* =remainder, residue, rest, remnant(s). **2** *Roman remains* =antiquities, relics, reliquiae. **3** *the saint's remains* =corpse, (dead) body, carcass; bones, skeleton.

remark ▸ verb 1 *'You're quiet,' he remarked* =**comment**, say, observe, mention, reflect, state, declare, announce, pronounce, assert; *formal* opine. 2 *many critics remarked on their rapport* =**comment**, mention, refer to, speak of, pass comment on.
▸ noun 1 *his remarks have been misinterpreted* =**comment**, statement, utterance, observation, declaration, pronouncement. 2 *worthy of remark* =**attention**, notice, comment, mention, observation, acknowledgement.

remarkable ▸ adjective =**extraordinary**, exceptional, amazing, astonishing, astounding, marvellous, wonderful, sensational, stunning, incredible, unbelievable, phenomenal, outstanding, momentous; *informal* fantastic, terrific, tremendous, stupendous, awesome; *literary* wondrous.
−OPPOSITES ordinary.

remediable ▸ adjective =**curable**, treatable, operable; solvable, reparable, rectifiable, resolvable.
−OPPOSITES incurable.

remedy ▸ noun 1 *herbal remedies* =**treatment**, cure, medicine, medication, medicament, drug. 2 *a remedy for all kinds of problems* =**solution**, answer, cure, antidote, curative, nostrum, panacea, cure-all.
▸ verb 1 *remedying the situation* =**put/set right**, rectify, solve, sort out, straighten out, resolve, correct, repair, mend, make good. 2 *anaemia can be remedied by iron tablets* =**cure**, treat, heal, make better; relieve, ease, alleviate, palliate.

remember ▸ verb 1 *remembering happy times* =**recall**, call to mind, recollect, think of; reminisce about, look back on. 2 *can you remember all that?* =**memorize**, retain; learn off by heart. 3 *you must remember she's only five* =**bear/keep in mind**, be mindful of the fact; take into account, take into consideration. 4 *remember to feed the cat* =**be sure**, be certain; mind that you, make sure that you. 5 *remember me to Alice* =**send one's best wishes to**, send one's regards to, give one's love to, send one's compliments to, say hello to. 6 *the nation remembered those who gave their lives* =**commemorate**, pay tribute to, honour, salute, pay homage to.
−OPPOSITES forget.

remembrance ▸ noun 1 *an expression of remembrance* =**recollection**, reminiscence; recalling, recollecting, reminiscing. 2 *she smiled at the remembrance* =**memory**, recollection, reminiscence, thought. 3 *we sold poppies in remembrance* =**commemoration**, memory, recognition. 4 *a remembrance of my father* =**memento**, reminder, keepsake, souvenir, memorial, token.

remind ▸ verb 1 *I left a note to remind him* =**jog someone's memory**, prompt. 2 *the song reminded me of my sister* =**make one think of**, cause one to remember, put one in mind of, bring/call to mind, evoke.

reminder ▸ noun =**prompt**, aide-memoire.

reminisce ▸ verb =**remember (with pleasure)**, cast one's mind back to, look back on, be nostalgic about, recall, recollect, reflect on, call to mind.

reminiscences ▸ plural noun =**memories**, recollections, reflections.

reminiscent ▸ adjective =**similar to**, comparable with, evocative of, suggestive of, redolent of.

remiss ▸ adjective =**negligent**, neglectful, irresponsible, careless, thoughtless, heedless, lax, slack, slipshod, lackadaisical; *N. Amer.* derelict; *informal* sloppy.
−OPPOSITES careful.

remission ▸ noun 1 *the cancer is in remission* =**respite**, abeyance. 2 *the wind howled without remission* =**respite**, lessening, abatement, easing, decrease, reduction, diminution, dying down, slackening, lull; *informal* let-up. 3 *the remission of sins* =**forgiveness**, pardoning, absolution, exoneration; *formal* exculpation.

remit ▸ verb 1 *they remit funds to head office* =**send**, dispatch, forward, hand over; pay. 2 *their sins were remitted* =**pardon**, forgive; excuse.
▸ noun *that is outside his remit* =**area of responsibility**, sphere, orbit, scope, ambit, province; brief, instructions, orders; *informal* bailiwick.

remittance ▸ noun 1 *send the form with your remittance* =**payment**, money, fee; cheque; *formal* monies. 2 *a monthly remittance* =**allowance**, sum of money.

remnant ▸ noun 1 *the remnants of the picnic* =**remains**, remainder, leftovers, residue, rest. 2 *remnants of cloth* =**scrap**, piece, bit, fragment, shred, offcut, oddment.

remonstrate ▶ verb **1** *'I'm not a child!' he remonstrated* =**protest**, complain, expostulate. **2** *we remonstrated against this proposal* =**object strongly to**, protest against, argue against, oppose strongly, make a fuss about, challenge; deplore, condemn, denounce, criticize; *informal* kick up a fuss/stink about.

remorse ▶ noun =**contrition**, deep regret, repentance, penitence, guilt, compunction, remorsefulness, ruefulness, contriteness.

remorseful ▶ adjective =**sorry**, regretful, contrite, repentant, penitent, guilt-ridden, conscience-stricken, chastened, self-reproachful.
−OPPOSITES unrepentant.

remorseless ▶ adjective **1** *a remorseless killer* =**heartless**, pitiless, merciless, ruthless, callous, cruel, hard-hearted, inhumane, unmerciful, unforgiving, unfeeling. **2** *remorseless cost-cutting* =**relentless**, unremitting, unabating, inexorable, unstoppable.
−OPPOSITES compassionate.

remote ▶ adjective **1** *areas remote from hospitals* =**faraway**, distant, far (off), far removed. **2** *a remote village* =**isolated**, out of the way, off the beaten track, secluded, lonely, in the back of beyond, godforsaken, inaccessible; *N. Amer.* in the backwoods, lonesome; *informal* in the sticks, in the middle of nowhere. **3** *events remote from modern times* =**irrelevant to**, unrelated to, unconnected to, unconcerned with, not pertinent to, immaterial to, unassociated with; foreign to, alien to. **4** *a remote possibility* =**unlikely**, improbable, implausible, doubtful, dubious; faint, slight, slim, small, slender. **5** *she seems very remote* =**aloof**, distant, detached, withdrawn, reserved, uncommunicative, unforthcoming, unapproachable, unresponsive, unfriendly, unsociable, introspective, introverted; *informal* stand-offish.
−OPPOSITES close, central.

removal ▶ noun **1** *the removal of church treasures* =**taking away**, moving, carrying away, transporting. **2** *his removal from office* =**dismissal**, ejection, expulsion, ousting, displacement, deposition, unseating; *N. Amer.* ouster; *informal* sacking, firing. **3** *the removal of customs barriers* =**withdrawal**, elimination, abolition, taking away. **4** *her removal to France* =**move**, transfer, relocation.
−OPPOSITES installation.

remove ▶ verb **1** *remove the plug* =**detach**, unfasten; pull out, take out, disconnect. **2** *she removed the lid* =**take off**, undo, unfasten. **3** *he removed a note from his wallet* =**take out**, produce, bring out, get out, pull out, withdraw. **4** *police removed boxes of documents* =**take away**, carry away, move, transport; confiscate; *informal* cart off. **5** *Henry removed his coat* =**take off**, pull off, slip out of; *Brit. informal* peel off. **6** *he was removed from his post* =**dismiss**, discharge, get rid of, dislodge, displace, expel, oust, depose; *informal* sack, fire, kick out; *Brit. informal* turf out. **7** *tax relief was removed* =**withdraw**, abolish, eliminate, get rid of, do away with, stop, cut, axe. **8** *Gabriel removed two words* =**delete**, erase, rub out, cross out, strike out, score out.
−OPPOSITES attach, insert, replace.

removed ▶ adjective =**distant**, remote, disconnected; unrelated, unconnected, alien, foreign.

remunerate ▶ verb =**pay**, reward, reimburse, recompense.

remuneration ▶ noun =**payment**, pay, salary, wages; earnings, fee(s), reward, recompense, reimbursement; *formal* emolument(s).

remunerative ▶ adjective =**lucrative**, well paid, financially rewarding; profitable.

renaissance ▶ noun =**revival**, renewal, resurrection, reawakening, re-emergence, rebirth, reappearance, resurgence, regeneration; *formal* renascence.

rend ▶ verb =**tear/rip apart**, split, rupture, sever.

render ▶ verb **1** *her fury rendered her speechless* =**make**, cause to be/become, leave. **2** *rendering assistance* =**give**, provide, supply, furnish, contribute; offer, proffer. **3** *paintings rendered in vivid colours* =**paint**, draw, depict, portray, represent, execute. **4** *the characters are vividly rendered* =**act**, perform, play, depict, interpret. **5** *the phrase was rendered into English* =**translate**, put, express, rephrase, reword.

rendezvous ▶ noun *Edward was late for their rendezvous* =**meeting**, appointment, assignation; *informal* date; *literary* tryst.
▶ verb *the bar where they had agreed to rendezvous* =**meet**, come together, gather, assemble.

rendition ▶ noun **1** *our rendition of Beet-*

hoven's *Fifth* =**performance**, interpretation, presentation, execution, delivery. **2** *the artist's rendition of Adam and Eve* =**depiction**, portrayal, representation. **3** *an interpreter's rendition of the message* =**translation**, interpretation, version.

renegade ▶ noun **1** *he was denounced as a renegade* =**traitor**, defector, deserter, turncoat, rebel, mutineer.
▶ adjective **1** *renegade troops* =**treacherous**, traitorous, disloyal, treasonous, rebel, mutinous. **2** *a renegade monk* =**apostate**, heretic, heretical, dissident.
–OPPOSITES loyal.

renege ▶ verb =**default on**, fail to honour, go back on, break, back out of, withdraw from, retreat from, welsh on, backtrack on; break one's word/promise.
–OPPOSITES honour.

renew ▶ verb **1** *I renewed my search* =**resume**, return to, take up again, come back to, begin again, start again, restart, recommence; continue (with), carry on (with). **2** *they renewed their vows* =**reaffirm**, reassert; repeat, reiterate, restate. **3** *something to renew her interest in life* =**revive**, regenerate, revitalize, reinvigorate, restore, resuscitate, breathe new life into. **4** *the hotel was completely renewed* =**renovate**, restore, refurbish, modernize, overhaul, redevelop, rebuild, reconstruct, remodel; *informal* do up; *N. Amer. informal* rehab. **5** *they renewed Jack's contract* =**extend**, prolong. **6** *I renewed my supply of paper* =**replenish**, restock, resupply, top up, replace.

renewal ▶ noun **1** *the renewal of our friendship* =**resumption**, recommencement, re-establishment; continuation. **2** *spiritual renewal* –**regeneration**, revival, reinvigoration, revitalization. **3** *the renewal of older urban areas* =**renovation**, restoration, modernization, reconditioning, overhauling, redevelopment, rebuilding, reconstruction.

renounce ▶ verb **1** *Edward renounced his claim to the throne* =**give up**, relinquish, abandon, abdicate, surrender, waive, forego; *formal* abnegate. **2** *Hungary renounced the agreement* =**reject**, refuse to abide by, repudiate. **3** *she renounced her family* =**repudiate**, deny, reject, abandon, wash one's hands of, turn one's back on, disown, spurn, shun; *literary* forsake. **4** *he renounced alcohol* =**abstain from**, give up, desist from, refrain from, keep off, eschew; *informal* quit, pack in, lay off; *formal* forswear.

–OPPOSITES assert, accept.
■ **renounce the world** =become a recluse, cloister oneself, hide oneself away.

renovate ▶ verb =**modernize**, restore, refurbish, revamp, recondition, rehabilitate, overhaul, redevelop; update, upgrade, refit; *informal* do up; *N. Amer. informal* rehab.

renown ▶ noun =**fame**, distinction, eminence, prominence, repute, reputation, prestige, acclaim, celebrity, notability.

renowned ▶ adjective =**famous**, celebrated, famed, eminent, distinguished, acclaimed, illustrious, prominent, great, esteemed, of note, of repute, well known.
–OPPOSITES unknown.

rent¹ ▶ noun *I can't afford to pay the rent* =**hire charge**, rental.
▶ verb **1** *she rented a car* =**hire**, lease, charter. **2** *why don't you rent it out?* =**let (out)**, lease (out), hire (out); sublet, sublease.

rent² ▶ noun *the rent in his trousers* =**rip**, tear, split, hole, slash, slit.

renunciation ▶ noun **1** *Henry's renunciation of his throne* =**relinquishment**, giving up, abandonment, abdication, surrender, waiving, foregoing. **2** *his renunciation of luxury* =**abstention**, refraining, going without, giving up, eschewal; *formal* forswearing. **3** *their renunciation of terrorism* =**repudiation**, rejection, abandonment.

reorganize ▶ verb =**restructure**, change, alter, adjust, transform, shake up, rationalize, rearrange, reshape, overhaul.

repair¹ ▶ verb **1** *the car was repaired* =**mend**, fix (up), put/set right, restore (to working order), overhaul, service; *informal* patch up. **2** *they repaired the costumes* =**mend**, darn; *informal* patch up. **3** *repairing relations with other countries* =**put/set right**, mend, fix, straighten out, improve; *informal* patch up. **4** *she sought to repair the wrong she had done* =**rectify**, make good, (put) right, correct, make up for, make amends for, make reparation for.
▶ noun **1** *in need of repair* =**restoration**, fixing (up), mending, renovation. **2** *an invisible repair* =**mend**, darn. **3** *in good repair* =**condition**, working order, state, shape, fettle; *Brit. informal* nick.
■ **beyond repair** =**irreparable**, irreversible, irretrievable, irremediable,

irrecoverable, past hope.

repair² ▸ verb *(formal) we repaired to the sitting room* =**go to**, head for, adjourn, wend one's way; *formal* remove.

reparable ▸ adjective =**rectifiable**, remediable, curable, restorable, recoverable, retrievable, salvageable.

reparation ▸ noun =**amends**, restitution, redress, compensation, recompense, repayment, atonement.

repartee ▸ noun =**banter**, badinage, bantering, raillery, witticism(s), ripostes, sallies, quips, joking, jesting, chaff; *formal* persiflage.

repay ▸ verb **1** *repaying customers who have been cheated* =**reimburse**, refund, pay back/off, recompense, compensate, indemnify. **2** *the grants have to be repaid* =**pay back**, return, refund, reimburse. **3** *I'd like to repay her generosity* =**reciprocate**, return, requite, recompense, reward. **4** *interesting books that would repay further study* =**be well worth**, be worth one's while.

repayment ▸ noun **1** *the repayment of tax* =**refund**, reimbursement, paying back. **2** *repayment for all they have done* =**recompense**, reward, compensation.

repeal ▸ verb *the Act was repealed* =**revoke**, rescind, cancel, reverse, annul, nullify, quash, abolish; *formal* abrogate.
−OPPOSITES enact.
▸ noun *the repeal of the law* =**revocation**, rescinding, cancellation, reversal, annulment, nullification, quashing, abolition; *formal* abrogation.

repeat ▸ verb **1** *she repeated her story* =**say again**, restate, reiterate, go/run through again, recapitulate; *informal* recap. **2** *children can repeat chunks of text* =**recite**, quote, parrot, regurgitate; *informal* trot out. **3** *Steele was invited to repeat his work* =**do again**, redo, replicate, duplicate. **4** *the episodes were repeated* =**rebroadcast**, rerun, reshow.
▸ noun **1** *a repeat of the previous year's final* =**repetition**, replication, duplicate. **2** *repeats of his TV show* =**rerun**, rebroadcast, reshowing.
■ **repeat itself** =**reoccur**, recur, happen again.

repeated ▸ adjective =**recurrent**, frequent, persistent, continual, incessant, constant; regular, periodic, numerous, (very) many.
−OPPOSITES occasional.

repeatedly ▸ adverb =**frequently**, often, again and again, over and over (again), time and (time) again, many times; persistently, recurrently, constantly, continually, regularly; *N. Amer.* oftentimes; *informal* 24-7; *literary* oft.

repel ▸ verb **1** *the rebels were repelled* =**fight off**, repulse, drive back/away, force back, beat back, push back; hold off, ward off, keep at bay; *Brit.* see off. **2** *the coating will repel water* =**be impervious to**, be impermeable to, keep out, resist. **3** *the thought of kissing him repelled me* =**revolt**, disgust, repulse, sicken, nauseate, turn someone's stomach, be distasteful, be repugnant; *informal* turn off; *N. Amer. informal* gross out.

repellent ▸ adjective **1** *a repellent stench* =**revolting**, repulsive, disgusting, repugnant, sickening, nauseating, stomach-turning, vile, nasty, foul, horrible, awful, dreadful, terrible, obnoxious, loathsome, offensive, objectionable; abhorrent, despicable, reprehensible, contemptible, odious, hateful, execrable; *N. Amer.* vomitous; *informal* ghastly, horrid, gross, yucky, icky; *literary* noisome. **2** *a repellent coating* =**impermeable**, impervious, resistant; -proof.
−OPPOSITES delightful.

repent ▸ verb =**feel remorse**, regret, be sorry, rue, reproach oneself, be ashamed, feel contrite; be penitent, be remorseful.

repentance ▸ noun =**remorse**, contrition, penitence, regret, ruefulness, shame, guilt.

repentant ▸ adjective =**penitent**, contrite, regretful, rueful, remorseful, apologetic, chastened, ashamed, shamefaced.
−OPPOSITES impenitent.

repercussion ▸ noun =**consequence**, result, effect, outcome; reverberation, backlash, aftermath, fallout.

repertoire ▸ noun =**collection**, stock, range, repertory, reserve, store, repository, supply.

repetition ▸ noun **1** *the statistics bear repetition* =**reiteration**, restatement, retelling. **2** *the repetition of the words* =**repeating**, echoing, parroting. **3** *a repetition of the scene in the kitchen* =**recurrence**, reoccurrence, rerun, repeat. **4** *there is some repetition* =**repetitiousness**, repetitiveness, redundancy, tautology.

repetitious ▶ adjective. *See* REPETITIVE.

repetitive ▶ adjective =monotonous, tedious, boring, humdrum, mundane, dreary, tiresome; unvaried, unchanging, recurrent, repeated, repetitious, routine, mechanical, automatic.

rephrase ▶ verb =reword, paraphrase.

replace ▶ verb 1 *Adam replaced the receiver* =put back, return, restore. 2 *a new chairman came in to replace him* =take the place of, succeed, take over from, supersede; stand in for, substitute for, deputize for, cover for, relieve; *informal* step into someone's shoes/boots. 3 *she replaced the spoon with a fork* =substitute, exchange, change, swap.
–OPPOSITES remove.

replacement ▶ noun 1 *we have to find a replacement* =successor; substitute, stand-in, locum, relief, cover. 2 *the wiring was in need of replacement* =renewal.

replenish ▶ verb 1 *she replenished their glasses* =refill, top up, fill up, recharge; *N. Amer.* freshen. 2 *their supplies were replenished* =stock up, restock, restore, replace.
–OPPOSITES empty, exhaust.

replete ▶ adjective 1 *the guests were replete* =well fed, sated, satiated, full (up); *informal* stuffed. 2 *a sumptuous environment replete with antiques* =filled, full, well stocked, well supplied, crammed, packed, jammed, teeming, overflowing, bursting; *informal* jam-packed, chock-a-block.

replica ▶ noun 1 *is it real or a replica?* =(carbon) copy, model, duplicate, reproduction, replication; dummy, imitation, facsimile. 2 *a replica of her mother* =perfect likeness, double, lookalike, (living) image, twin, clone; *informal* spitting image, (dead) ringer.

replicate ▶ verb =copy, reproduce, duplicate, recreate, repeat, perform again; clone.

reply ▶ verb 1 *Rachel didn't reply* =answer, respond, come back, write back. 2 *he replied defensively* =respond, answer, rejoin, retort, riposte, counter, come back.
▶ noun *he waited for a reply* =answer, response, rejoinder, retort, riposte; *informal* comeback.

report ▶ verb 1 *the company reported a loss* =announce, describe, detail, outline, communicate, divulge, disclose, reveal, make public, publish, broadcast, proclaim, publicize. 2 *the newspapers reported on the scandal* =investigate, look into, inquire into; write about, cover, describe, give details of, commentate on. 3 *I reported him to the police* =inform on, tattle on; *informal* shop, tell on, squeal on, rat on; *Brit. informal* grass on. 4 *Juliet reported for duty* =present oneself, arrive, turn up, clock in, sign in; *Brit.* clock on; *N. Amer.* punch in; *informal* show up.
▶ noun 1 *a full report on the meeting* =account, review, record, description, statement; transactions, proceedings, transcripts, minutes. 2 *reports of drug dealing* =news, information, word, intelligence; *literary* tidings. 3 *newspaper reports* =story, account, article, piece, item, column, feature, bulletin, dispatch. 4 *(Brit.) a school report* =assessment, evaluation, appraisal; *N. Amer.* report card. 5 *reports of his imminent resignation* =rumour, whisper; *informal* buzz. 6 *the report of a gun* =bang, blast, crack, shot, gunshot, explosion, boom.

reporter ▶ noun =journalist, correspondent, newsman, newswoman, columnist; *Brit.* pressman; *N. Amer.* legman, wireman; *Austral.* roundsman; *informal* news hound, hack, stringer, journo; *N. Amer. informal* newsy.

repose ▶ noun 1 *a face in repose* =rest, relaxation, inactivity; sleep, slumber. 2 *they found true repose* =peace, quiet, calm, tranquillity. 3 *he lost his repose* =composure, serenity, equanimity, poise, self-possession, aplomb.
▶ verb 1 *the diamond reposed on a bed of velvet* =lie, rest, be placed, be situated. 2 *the beds where we reposed* =lie (down), recline, rest, sleep; *literary* slumber.

repository ▶ noun =store, storehouse, depository; reservoir, bank, cache, treasury, fund, mine.

reprehensible ▶ adjective =deplorable, disgraceful, discreditable, despicable, blameworthy, culpable, wrong, bad, shameful, dishonourable, objectionable, opprobrious, repugnant, inexcusable, unforgivable, indefensible, unjustifiable.
–OPPOSITES praiseworthy.

represent ▶ verb 1 *a character representing a single quality* =symbolize, stand for, personify, epitomize, typify, embody, illustrate. 2 *the initials which represent her qualification* =stand for, designate, denote. 3 *Hathor is represented as a*

representation | reproach

woman with cow's horns =**depict**, portray,
render, picture, delineate, show, illustrate. **4** ageing represents a threat to one's
independence =**constitute**, be, amount
to, be regarded as. **5** a panel representing
a cross section of the public =**be a typical
sample of**, be representative of, typify.
6 his solicitor represented him in court =**appear for**, act for, speak on behalf of.
7 the Queen was represented by Lord Lewin
=**deputize for**, substitute for, stand in
for.

representation ▶ noun **1** Rossetti's
representation of women =**portrayal**, depiction, delineation, presentation, rendition. **2** representations of the human form
=**likeness**, painting, drawing, picture,
illustration, sketch, image, model,
figure, statue. **3** (formal) making representations to the council =**statement**, deposition, allegation, declaration, exposition, report, protestation.

representative ▶ adjective **1** a representative sample =**typical**, prototypical,
characteristic, illustrative, archetypal.
2 a female figure representative of Britain
=**symbolic**, emblematic. **3** representative
government =**elective**, democratic, popular.
  –OPPOSITES atypical, totalitarian.
▶ noun **1** a representative of the Royal Society
=**spokesperson**, spokesman, spokeswoman, agent, official, mouthpiece. **2** a
sales representative =**(commercial)
traveller**, (travelling) salesman, saleswoman, agent; informal rep; N. Amer. informal drummer. **3** the Cambodian representative at the UN =**delegate**, commissioner,
ambassador, attaché, envoy, emissary,
chargé d'affaires, deputy. **4** our representatives in parliament =**Member (of Parliament)**, MP; councillor; N. Amer. Member
of Congress, senator. **5** he acted as his
father's representative =**deputy**, substitute, stand-in, proxy.

repress ▶ verb **1** the rebellion was repressed =**suppress**, quell, quash, subdue,
put down, crush, extinguish, stamp out,
defeat, conquer, rout, overwhelm, contain. **2** the peasants were repressed =**oppress**, subjugate, keep down, tyrannize,
crush. **3** these emotions may well be repressed =**restrain**, hold back/in, keep
back, suppress, keep in check, control,
curb, stifle, bottle up; informal button up,
keep the lid on.

repressed ▶ adjective **1** a repressed
country =**oppressed**, subjugated, sub-

dued, tyrannized. **2** repressed feelings =**restrained**, suppressed, held back/in,
kept in check, stifled, pent up, bottled
up. **3** emotionally repressed =**inhibited**,
frustrated, restrained; informal uptight,
hung up.
  –OPPOSITES democratic, uninhibited.

repression ▶ noun **1** the repression of
the protests =**suppression**, quashing,
subduing, crushing, stamping out.
2 political repression =**oppression**, subjugation, suppression, tyranny, despotism, authoritarianism. **3** the repression of sexual urges =**restraint**, holding
back, keeping back, suppression, keeping in check, control, stifling, bottling
up.

repressive ▶ adjective =**oppressive**,
authoritarian, despotic, tyrannical, dictatorial, fascist, autocratic, totalitarian,
undemocratic.

reprieve ▶ verb **1** she was reprieved
=**pardon**, spare, amnesty; informal let off
(the hook). **2** the project has been reprieved
=**save**, rescue; informal take off the hit
list.

reprimand ▶ verb he was publicly rep-
rimanded =**rebuke**, admonish, chastise,
chide, upbraid, reprove, reproach,
scold, berate, take to task, haul over the
coals, lecture, criticize, censure; informal
tell off, give someone a talking-to, dress
down, give someone a roasting, rap over
the knuckles, slap someone's wrist,
bawl out; Brit. informal tick off, carpet, tear
off a strip, give someone what for, give
someone a rollicking; N. Amer. informal
chew out, ream out; formal castigate.
  –OPPOSITES praise.
▶ noun a severe reprimand =**rebuke**, reproach, scolding, admonition, reproof,
criticism, censure; informal telling-off,
dressing-down, talking-to; Brit. informal
rocket, ticking-off; formal castigation.
  –OPPOSITES praise.

reprisal ▶ noun =**retaliation**, counter-
attack, comeback; revenge, vengeance,
retribution, requital; informal a taste of
one's own medicine.

reproach ▶ verb & noun See REPRIMAND.
■ **beyond/above reproach** =**perfect**,
blameless, above suspicion, without
fault, flawless, irreproachable, exemplary, impeccable, immaculate, unblemished, spotless, untarnished, stainless, unsullied, whiter than white;
informal squeaky clean.

reproachful ▶ adjective =disapproving, reproving, critical, censorious, disparaging, withering, accusatory, admonitory; *formal* castigatory.
−OPPOSITES approving.

reprobate ▶ noun *a hardened reprobate* =**rogue**, rascal, scoundrel, miscreant, good-for-nothing, villain, wretch, rake, degenerate, libertine, debauchee.
▶ adjective *reprobate behaviour* =**unprincipled**, bad, roguish, wicked, rakish, shameless, immoral, degenerate, dissipated, debauched, depraved.

reproduce ▶ verb 1 *each artwork is reproduced in colour* =**copy**, duplicate, replicate; photocopy, xerox, photostat, print. 2 *this work has not been reproduced in other laboratories* =**repeat**, replicate, re-create, redo; simulate, imitate, emulate, mirror, mimic. 3 *some animals reproduce prolifically* =**breed**, procreate, propagate, multiply.

reproduction ▶ noun 1 *colour reproduction* =**copying**, duplication; photocopying, xeroxing, photostatting, printing. 2 *a reproduction of the original* =**print**, copy, reprint, duplicate, facsimile, photocopy; *trademark* Xerox. 3 *the process of reproduction* =**breeding**, procreation, multiplying, propagation.

reproductive ▶ adjective =**generative**, procreative, propagative; sexual, genital.

reproof ▶ noun =**rebuke**, reprimand, reproach, admonishment, admonition; disapproval, censure, criticism, condemnation; *informal* telling-off, dressing down; *Brit. informal* ticking-off; *dated* rating.

reprove ▶ verb =**reprimand**, rebuke, reproach, scold, admonish, chastise, chide, upbraid, berate, take to task, haul over the coals, criticize, censure; *informal* tell off, give someone a talking-to, dress down, give someone a roasting, rap over the knuckles, slap someone's wrist; *Brit. informal* tick off, carpet, tear off a strip; *formal* castigate.

reptile ▶ noun

WORD LINKS

study of reptiles and amphibians:
  herpetology

reptilian ▶ adjective *a reptilian smirk* =**unpleasant**, distasteful, nasty, disagreeable, unattractive, off-putting, horrible; unctuous, ingratiating, oily, oleaginous; *informal* smarmy, slimy, creepy.

repudiate ▶ verb 1 *she repudiated communism* =**reject**, renounce, abandon, give up, turn one's back on, disown, cast off, lay aside; *formal* forswear, abjure; *literary* forsake. 2 *Cranham repudiated the allegations* =**deny**, refute, contradict, controvert, rebut, dispute, dismiss, brush aside; *formal* gainsay. 3 *Egypt repudiated the treaty* =**cancel**, revoke, rescind, reverse, overrule, overturn, invalidate, nullify; disregard, flout, renege on; *Law* disaffirm; *formal* abrogate.
−OPPOSITES embrace, confirm.

repudiation ▶ noun 1 *the repudiation of one's religion* =**rejection**, renunciation, abandonment, forswearing, giving up. 2 *his repudiation of the allegations* =**denial**, refutation, rebuttal, rejection. 3 *a repudiation of the contract* =**cancellation**, revocation, rescindment, reversal, invalidation, nullification; *formal* abrogation.

repugnance ▶ noun =**revulsion**, disgust, abhorrence, repulsion, loathing, hatred, detestation, aversion, distaste, antipathy, contempt.

repugnant ▶ adjective =**abhorrent**, revolting, repulsive, repellent, disgusting, offensive, objectionable, vile, foul, nasty, loathsome, sickening, nauseating, hateful, detestable, execrable, abominable, monstrous, appalling, insufferable, intolerable, unacceptable, contemptible, unsavoury, unpalatable; *informal* ghastly, gross, horrible; *literary* noisome.
−OPPOSITES pleasant.

repulse ▶ verb 1 *the rebels were repulsed* =**repel**, drive back/away, fight back/off, put to flight, force back, beat off/back; ward off, hold off; *Brit.* see off. 2 *her advances were repulsed* =**rebuff**, reject, spurn, snub, cold-shoulder; *informal* give someone the brush-off, freeze out; *Brit. informal* knock back; *N. Amer. informal* give someone the bum's rush. 3 *his bid for the company was repulsed* =**reject**, turn down, refuse, decline. 4 *the brutality repulsed her* =**revolt**, disgust, repel, sicken, nauseate, turn someone's stomach, be repugnant to; *informal* turn off; *N. Amer. informal* gross out.
▶ noun =**rebuff**, rejection, snub, slight; *informal* brush-off, knock-back.

repulsion ▶ noun =**disgust**, revulsion, abhorrence, repugnance, nausea, horror, aversion, abomination, distaste.

repulsive ▶ adjective =revolting, disgusting, hateful, repellent, repugnant, offensive, objectionable, vile, foul, nasty, loathsome, sickening, nauseating, hateful, detestable, execrable, abominable, monstrous, noxious, horrendous, awful, terrible, dreadful, frightful, obnoxious, unsavoury, unpleasant, disagreeable, distasteful; ugly, hideous, grotesque; *informal* ghastly, horrible, gross; *literary* noisome.
–OPPOSITES attractive.

reputable ▶ adjective =well thought of, highly regarded, (well) respected, respectable, of (good) repute, prestigious, established; reliable, dependable, trustworthy.
–OPPOSITES untrustworthy.

reputation ▶ noun =(good) name, character, repute, standing, stature, status, position, renown, esteem, prestige.

repute ▶ noun 1 *a woman of ill repute* =reputation, name, character. 2 *a firm of international repute* =fame, renown, celebrity, distinction, high standing, stature, prestige.

reputed ▶ adjective 1 *they are reputed to be very rich* =thought, said, reported, rumoured, believed, held, considered, regarded, deemed, alleged. 2 *his reputed father* =supposed, putative. 3 *a reputed naturalist* =well thought of, (well) respected, highly regarded.

reputedly ▶ adverb =supposedly, by all accounts, so I'm told, so people say, allegedly.

request ▶ noun 1 *requests for assistance* =appeal, entreaty, plea, petition, application, demand, call. 2 *Charlotte spoke, at Ursula's request* =bidding, entreaty, demand, insistence. 3 *indicate your requests on the form* =requirement, wish, desire; choice.
▶ verb 1 *the government requested aid* =ask for, appeal for, call for, seek, solicit, plead for, apply for, demand. 2 *I requested him to help* =call on, beg, entreat, implore; *literary* beseech.

require ▶ verb 1 *the child required hospital treatment* =need. 2 *a situation requiring patience* =necessitate, demand, call for, involve, entail. 3 *unquestioning obedience is required* =demand, insist on, call for, ask for, expect. 4 *she was required to pay costs* =order, instruct, command, en-

join, oblige, compel, force. 5 *do you require anything else?* =want, desire; lack, be short of.

required ▶ adjective 1 *required reading* =essential, vital, indispensable, necessary, compulsory, obligatory, mandatory, prescribed. 2 *cut it to the required length* =desired, preferred, chosen; correct, proper, right.
–OPPOSITES optional.

requirement ▶ noun =need, wish, demand, want, necessity, essential, prerequisite, stipulation.

requisite ▶ adjective *he lacks the requisite skills* =necessary, required, prerequisite, essential, indispensable, vital.
–OPPOSITES optional.
▶ noun 1 *toilet requisites* =requirement, need, necessity, essential. 2 *a requisite for a successful career* =necessity, essential (requirement), prerequisite, precondition, sine qua non; *informal* must.

requisition ▶ noun 1 *requisitions for staff* =order, request, call, application, claim, demand; *Brit.* indent. 2 *the requisition of cultural treasures* =appropriation, commandeering, seizure, confiscation, expropriation.
▶ verb 1 *the house was requisitioned by the army* =commandeer, appropriate, take over, take possession of, occupy, seize, confiscate, expropriate. 2 *she requisitioned statements* =request, order, call for, demand.

requital ▶ noun 1 *in requital of your kindness* =repayment, return, payment, recompense. 2 *personal requital* =revenge, vengeance, retribution, redress.

requite ▶ verb 1 *requiting their hospitality* =return, reciprocate, repay. 2 *Drake had requited the wrongs inflicted on them* =avenge, revenge, pay someone back for; take reprisals, settle the score, get even.

rescind ▶ verb =revoke, repeal, cancel, reverse, overturn, overrule, annul, nullify, void, invalidate, quash, abolish; *formal* abrogate.
–OPPOSITES enforce.

rescue ▶ verb 1 *an attempt to rescue the hostages* =save, come to the aid of; (set) free, release, liberate. 2 *Boyd rescued his papers* =retrieve, recover, salvage, get back.
▶ noun *the rescue of 10 crewmen* =saving, rescuing; release, freeing, liberation, deliverance, redemption.

■**come to someone's rescue** =help, assist, lend a (helping) hand to, bail out; *informal* save someone's neck/skin.

research ▸ noun 1 *medical research* =investigation, experimentation, testing, analysis, fact-finding, examination, scrutiny. 2 *he continued his researches* =experiments, tests, inquiries, studies.
▸ verb 1 *the phenomenon has been widely researched* =investigate, study, inquire into, look into, probe, explore, analyse, examine, scrutinize, review. 2 *I researched all the available material* =study, read (up on), sift through; *informal* check out.

resemblance ▸ noun =similarity, likeness, similitude, correspondence, congruence, coincidence, conformity, agreement, equivalence, comparability, parallelism, uniformity, sameness.

resemble ▸ verb =look like, be similar to, remind one of, take after, favour, have the look of; approximate to, smack of, have (all) the hallmarks of, correspond to, echo, mirror, parallel.

resent ▸ verb =begrudge, feel aggrieved at/about, feel bitter about, grudge, be annoyed at/about, be resentful of, dislike, take exception to, object to, take amiss, take offence at, take umbrage at.
–OPPOSITES welcome.

resentful ▸ adjective =aggrieved, indignant, irritated, piqued, put out, in high dudgeon, dissatisfied, disgruntled, discontented, offended, bitter, jaundiced; envious, jealous; *informal* miffed, peeved; *Brit. informal* narked; *N. Amer. informal* sore.

resentment ▸ noun =bitterness, indignation, irritation, pique, dissatisfaction, disgruntlement, discontentment, bad/feelings, ill will, acrimony, rancour, animosity, jaundice.

reservation ▸ noun 1 *grave reservations* =doubt, qualm, scruple; misgivings, scepticism, unease, hesitation, objection. 2 *the reservation of the room* =booking, ordering, securing. 3 *an Indian reservation* =reserve, enclave, sanctuary, territory, homeland.
■**without reservation** =wholeheartedly, unreservedly, without qualification, fully, completely, totally, entirely, wholly, unconditionally.

reserve ▸ verb 1 *ask your newsagent to reserve you a copy* =put aside, set aside,

keep (back), save, hold back, keep in reserve, earmark. 2 *he reserved a table* =book, order, arrange for, secure. 3 *the management reserves the right to alter the programme* =retain, keep, hold. 4 *reserve your judgement until you know him better* =defer, postpone, put off, delay, withhold.
▸ noun 1 *reserves of petrol* =stock, store, supply, stockpile, pool, hoard, cache. 2 *the army are calling up reserves* =reinforcements, extras, auxiliaries. 3 *a nature reserve* =national park, sanctuary, preserve, conservation area. 4 *his natural reserve* =reticence, detachment, distance, remoteness, coolness, aloofness, constraint, formality; shyness, diffidence, timidity, taciturnity, inhibition; *informal* stand-offishness. 5 *she trusted him without reserve* =reservation, qualification, condition, limitation, hesitation, doubt.
▸ adjective *a reserve goalkeeper* =substitute, stand-in, relief, replacement, fallback, spare, extra.
■**in reserve** =available, to/on hand, ready, in readiness, set aside, at one's disposal.

reserved ▸ adjective 1 *Sewell is rather reserved* =reticent, quiet, private, uncommunicative, unforthcoming, undemonstrative, unsociable, formal, constrained, cool, aloof, detached, distant, remote, unapproachable, unfriendly, withdrawn, secretive, silent, taciturn; shy, retiring, diffident, timid, self-effacing, inhibited, introverted; *informal* stand-offish. 2 *that table is reserved* =booked, taken, spoken for, pre-arranged.
–OPPOSITES outgoing.

reservoir ▸ noun 1 *sailing on the reservoir* =lake, pool, pond. 2 *an ink reservoir* =receptacle, container, holder, repository, tank. 3 *the reservoir of managerial talent* =stock, store, stockpile, reserve(s), supply, bank, pool, fund.

reshuffle ▸ verb *the prime minister reshuffled his cabinet* =reorganize, restructure, rearrange, change (around), shake up, shuffle.
▸ noun *a management reshuffle* =reorganization, restructuring, change, rearrangement; *informal* shake-up.

reside ▸ verb 1 *most students reside in flats* =live in, occupy, inhabit, stay in, lodge in; *formal* dwell in, be domiciled in. 2 *the paintings reside in a vault* =be situated, be found, be located, lie. 3 *executive power* *resides in the president* =**be vested in**, be bestowed on, be conferred on, be in the hands of. **4** *the qualities that reside within each individual* =**be inherent**, be present, exist.

residence ▶ noun **1** *(formal) her private residence* =**home**, house, address; quarters, lodgings; *informal* pad; *formal* dwelling (place), domicile, abode. **2** *his place of residence* =**occupancy**, habitation; *formal* abode.

resident ▶ noun **1** *the residents of New York City* =**inhabitant**, local, citizen, native; householder, homeowner, occupier, tenant; *formal* denizen. **2** *(Brit.) the bar is open to residents only* =**guest**, lodger.
▶ adjective **1** *resident in the UK* =**living**, residing; *formal* dwelling. **2** *a resident nanny* =**live-in**. **3** *the resident registrar in obstetrics* =**permanent**, incumbent.

residual ▶ adjective **1** *residual heat* =**remaining**, leftover, unused, unconsumed. **2** *residual affection* =**lingering**, enduring, abiding, surviving, vestigial.

residue ▶ noun =**remainder**, rest, remnant(s); surplus, extra, excess; remains, leftovers.

resign ▶ verb **1** *the manager resigned* =**leave**, give notice, stand down, step down; *informal* quit. **2** *19 MPs resigned their seats* =**give up**, leave, vacate, stand down from; *informal* quit, pack in. **3** *we resigned ourselves to a wait* =**reconcile oneself to**, come to terms with.

resignation ▶ noun **1** *his resignation from his post* =**departure**, leaving, standing down, stepping down; *informal* quitting. **2** *she handed in her resignation* =**notice (to quit)**. **3** *he accepted his fate with resignation* =**patience**, forbearance, stoicism, fortitude, fatalism, acceptance, acquiescence, compliance, passivity.

resigned ▶ adjective =**patient**, long-suffering, uncomplaining, forbearing, stoical, philosophical, fatalistic, acquiescent, compliant.

resilient ▶ adjective **1** *resilient materials* =**flexible**, pliable, supple; durable, hard-wearing, stout, strong, sturdy, tough. **2** *young and resilient* =**strong**, tough, hardy; quick to recover, buoyant, irrepressible.

resist ▶ verb **1** *built to resist cold winters* =**withstand**, be proof against, combat, weather, endure, be resistant to, keep out. **2** *they resisted his attempts to change things* =**oppose**, fight against, object to,

defy, set one's face against, kick against; obstruct, impede, hinder, block, thwart, frustrate; *informal* be anti. **3** *I resisted the urge to retort* =**refrain from**, abstain from, forbear from, desist from, not give in to, restrain oneself from, stop oneself from. **4** *she tried to resist him* =**struggle with/against**, fight (against), stand up to, withstand, hold off; fend off, ward off.
–OPPOSITES welcome, submit.
■ **cannot resist** =**love**, adore, relish, have a weakness for, be very keen on, like, delight in, enjoy, take great pleasure in; *informal* be mad about, get a kick/thrill out of.

resistance ▶ noun **1** *resistance to change* =**opposition**, hostility. **2** *a spirited resistance* =**opposition**, fight, stand, struggle. **3** *the body's resistance to disease* =**immunity from**, defences against. **4** *the French resistance* =**freedom fighters**, underground, partisans.

resistant ▶ adjective **1** *resistant to water* =**impervious**, unsusceptible, immune, invulnerable, proof against, unaffected by. **2** *resistant to change* =**opposed**, averse, hostile, inimical, against; *informal* anti.

resolute ▶ adjective =**determined**, purposeful, resolved, adamant, single-minded, firm, unswerving, unwavering, steadfast, staunch, stalwart, unfaltering, unhesitating, persistent, indefatigable, tenacious, strong-willed, unshakeable; *informal* gutsy, spunky; *formal* pertinacious.
–OPPOSITES half-hearted.

resolution ▶ noun **1** *her resolution not to smoke* =**intention**, resolve, decision, intent, aim, plan; commitment, pledge, promise. **2** *the committee passed the resolution* =**motion**, proposal, proposition; *N. Amer.* resolve. **3** *she handled the work with resolution* =**determination**, purpose, resolve, single-mindedness, firmness (of purpose); *informal* guts, spunk; *formal* pertinacity. **4** *a satisfactory resolution of the problem* =**solution**, answer, end, settlement, conclusion.

resolve ▶ verb **1** *this matter cannot be resolved overnight* =**settle**, sort out, solve, fix, straighten out, deal with, put right, rectify; *informal* hammer out, thrash out, figure out. **2** *Charity resolved not to wait any longer* =**determine**, decide, make up one's mind, take a decision. **3** *the committee resolved that the project should pro-*

ceed =**vote**, rule, decide formally, agree. **4** *the compounds were resolved into their active constituents* =**break down/up**, separate, reduce, divide.
▶ noun **1** *their intimidation merely strengthened his resolve. See* RESOLUTION *sense 3.* **2** *(N. Amer.) he made a resolve not to go again* =**decision**, resolution, commitment.

resolved ▶ adjective =**determined**, hell bent, intent, set.

resonant ▶ adjective **1** *a resonant voice* =**deep**, low, sonorous, full, full-bodied, vibrant, rich, clear, ringing; loud, booming, thunderous. **2** *valleys resonant with the sound of church bells* =**reverberant**, resounding, echoing, filled. **3** *resonant words* =**evocative**, suggestive, expressive, redolent.

resort ▶ noun **1** *settle the matter without resort to legal proceedings* =**recourse to**, turning to, the use of, utilizing. **2** *strike action is our last resort* =**expedient**, measure, step, recourse, alternative, option, choice, possibility, hope.
■ **in the last resort** =**ultimately**, in the end, in the long run, when all is said and done.
■ **resort to** =**have recourse to**, fall back on, turn to, make use of, use, employ, avail oneself of.

resound ▶ verb **1** *the explosion resounded round the street* =**echo**, reverberate, ring out, boom, thunder, rumble. **2** *resounding with the clang of hammers* =**reverberate**, echo, resonate, ring. **3** *nothing will resound like their earlier achievements* =**be acclaimed**, be celebrated, be renowned, be famed, be glorified, be trumpeted.

resounding ▶ adjective **1** *a resounding voice* =**reverberating**, resonating, echoing, ringing, sonorous, deep, rich, clear; loud, booming. **2** *a resounding success* =**enormous**, huge, very great, tremendous, terrific, colossal; emphatic, decisive, conclusive, outstanding, remarkable, phenomenal.

resource ▶ noun **1** *use your resources efficiently* =**assets**, funds, wealth, money, capital; staff; supplies, materials, store(s), stock(s), reserve(s). **2** *your tutor is there as a resource* =**facility**, amenity, aid, help, support. **3** *tears were her only resource* =**expedient**, resort, course, scheme, stratagem; trick, ruse, device. **4** *a person of resource* =**initiative**, resourcefulness, enterprise, ingenuity, inventiveness; talent, ability, capability; *informal* gumption.

resourceful ▶ adjective =**ingenious**, enterprising, inventive, creative; clever, talented, able, capable.

respect ▶ noun **1** *the respect due to a great artist* =**esteem**, regard, high opinion, admiration, reverence, deference, honour. **2** *he spoke to her with respect* =**due regard**, politeness, courtesy, civility, deference. **3** *paying one's respects* =**(kind) regards**, compliments, greetings, best/good wishes, felicitations, salutations. **4** *the report was accurate in every respect* =**aspect**, regard, facet, feature, way, sense, particular, point, detail.
–OPPOSITES contempt.
▶ verb **1** *he is highly respected for his industry* =**esteem**, admire, think highly of, have a high opinion of, look up to, revere, honour. **2** *they respected our privacy* =**show consideration for**, have regard for, observe, be mindful of, be heedful of; *formal* take cognizance of. **3** *father respected her wishes* =**abide by**, comply with, follow, adhere to, conform to, act in accordance with, defer to, obey, observe, keep (to).
–OPPOSITES despise, disobey.
■ **with respect to/in respect of** =**concerning**, regarding, in/with regard to, with reference to, re, about, apropos, on the subject of, in connection with, vis-à-vis.

respectable ▶ adjective **1** *a respectable middle-class background* =**reputable**, upright, honest, honourable, trustworthy, decent, good, well bred, clean-living. **2** *a respectable salary* =**fairly good**, decent, fair, reasonable, moderately good.
–OPPOSITES disreputable, paltry.

respectful ▶ adjective =**deferential**, reverent, dutiful; polite, well mannered, civil, courteous, gracious.
–OPPOSITES rude.

respective ▶ adjective =**separate**, personal, own, particular, individual, specific, special, appropriate, different, various.

respite ▶ noun =**rest**, break, breathing space, interval, intermission, interlude, recess, lull, pause, time out; relief, relaxation, repose; *informal* breather, let-up.

resplendent ▶ adjective =**splendid**, magnificent, brilliant, dazzling, glittering, gorgeous, impressive, imposing, spectacular, striking, stunning, majestic; *informal* splendiferous.

respond ▶ verb **1** *they do not respond to*

questions =**answer**, reply, make a rejoin-der. **2** '*No,' she responded* =**answer**, reply, rejoin, retort, riposte, counter. **3** *they were slow to respond* =**react**, reciprocate, retaliate.

response ▸ noun **1** *his response to the question* =**answer**, reply, rejoinder, re-tort, riposte; *informal* comeback. **2** *an angry response* =**reaction**, reply, retali-ation; *informal* comeback.
–OPPOSITES question.

responsibility ▸ noun **1** *it was his re-sponsibility to find witnesses* =**duty**, task, function, job, role, business; *Brit. informal* pigeon. **2** *they denied responsibility for the attack* =**blame**, fault, guilt, culpability, liability. **3** *a sense of responsibility* =**trust-worthiness**, (common) sense, maturity, reliability, dependability. **4** *managerial responsibility* =**authority**, control, power, leadership.

responsible ▸ adjective **1** *who is re-sponsible for prisons?* =**in charge of**, in control of, at the helm of, accountable for, liable for. **2** *I am responsible for the mis-take* =**accountable**, answerable, to blame, guilty, culpable, blameworthy, at fault, in the wrong. **3** *a responsible job* =**important**, powerful, executive. **4** *a re-sponsible tenant* =**trustworthy**, sensible, mature, reliable, dependable.

responsive ▸ adjective =**reactive**, re-ceptive, open to suggestions, amenable, flexible, forthcoming.

rest[1] ▸ verb **1** *he needed to rest* =**relax**, ease up/off, let up, slow down, have/take a break, unbend, unwind, recharge one's batteries, be at leisure, take it easy, put one's feet up; lie down, go to bed; *informal* take five, have/take a breather; *N. Amer. informal* chill out. **2** *his hands rested on the rail* =**lie**, be laid, repose, be placed, be positioned, be supported by. **3** *she rested her basket on the ground* =**support**, prop (up), lean, lay, set, stand, position, place, put. **4** *the film script rests on an improbable premise* =**be based**, depend, rely, hinge, turn on, be contingent, revolve around.
▸ noun **1** *get some rest* =**repose**, relaxation, leisure, respite, time off, breathing space; *informal* lie-down. **2** *a short rest from work* =**holiday**, vacation, break, breath-ing space, interval, interlude, intermis-sion, time off/out; *informal* breather. **3** *she took the poker from its rest* =**stand**, base, holder, support, rack, frame, shelf. **4** *we came to rest 100 metres lower* =**a standstill**, a halt, a stop.

rest[2] ▸ noun *the rest of the board are ap-pointees* =**remainder**, residue, balance, others, those left, remnant(s), surplus, excess.
▸ verb *you may rest assured that he is there* =**remain**, continue to be, stay, keep, carry on being.

restful ▸ adjective =**relaxing**, quiet, calm, tranquil, soothing, peaceful, pla-cid, reposeful, leisurely, undisturbed, untroubled.
–OPPOSITES exciting.

restitution ▸ noun **1** *restitution of the land seized* =**return**, restoration, hand-ing back, surrender. **2** *restitution for the damage caused* =**compensation**, recom-pense, reparation, damages, indemni-fication, reimbursement, repayment, remuneration, redress.

restive ▸ adjective **1** *Edward is getting restive. See* RESTLESS *sense 1.* **2** *the militants are increasingly restive* =**unruly**, disor-derly, uncontrollable, unmanageable, wilful, recalcitrant, insubordinate; *Brit. informal* bolshie; *formal* refractory.

restless ▸ adjective **1** *Maria was restless* =**uneasy**, ill at ease, restive, fidgety, edgy, tense, worked up, nervous, nervy, agitated, anxious, on tenterhooks, keyed up; *informal* jumpy, jittery, twitchy, uptight; *Brit. informal* like a cat on hot bricks. **2** *a restless night* =**sleepless**, wakeful; fitful, broken, disturbed, troubled, unsettled.

restlessness ▸ noun =**unease**, rest-iveness, edginess, tenseness, nervous-ness, agitation, anxiety, fretfulness, apprehension, disquiet; *informal* jitteri-ness.

restoration ▸ noun **1** *the restoration of democracy* =**reinstatement**, reinstitu-tion, re-establishment, reimposition, re-turn. **2** *the restoration of derelict housing* =**repair**, fixing, mending, refurbish-ment, reconditioning, rehabilitation, rebuilding, reconstruction, overhaul, re-development, renovation; *N. Amer. infor-mal* rehab.

restore ▸ verb **1** *the aim to restore democ-racy* =**reinstate**, bring back, reinstitute, reimpose, reinstall, re-establish. **2** *he re-stored it to its rightful owner* =**return**, give back, hand back. **3** *the building has been restored* =**repair**, fix, mend, refurbish, recondition, rehabilitate, rebuild, re-construct, remodel, overhaul, re-develop, renovate; *informal* do up; *N. Amer.*

informal rehab. **4** *a good sleep can restore you* =**reinvigorate**, revitalize, revive, refresh, energize, fortify, revivify, regenerate, stimulate, freshen.
−OPPOSITES abolish.

restrain ▸ verb **1** *Charles restrained his anger* =**control**, check, curb, suppress, repress, contain, dampen, subdue, rein back/in; *informal* keep the lid on. **2** *she could barely restrain herself from swearing* =**prevent**, stop, keep, hold back. **3** *the insane used to be restrained* =**tie up**, bind, tether, chain (up), fetter, shackle, manacle, put in irons.

restrained ▸ adjective **1** *Julie was quite restrained* =**self-controlled**, not given to excesses, sober, steady, unemotional, undemonstrative. **2** *restrained elegance* =**muted**, soft, discreet, subtle, quiet, unobtrusive, unostentatious, understated, tasteful.

restraint ▸ noun **1** *a restraint on their impulsiveness* =**constraint**, check, control, restriction, limitation, curtailment; rein, bridle, brake, damper, impediment, obstacle. **2** *the customary restraint of the police* =**self-control**, self-discipline, control, moderation, prudence, judiciousness. **3** *the room has been decorated with restraint* =**subtlety**, understatedness, taste, tastefulness, discretion, discrimination.

restrict ▸ verb **1** *a busy working life restricted his leisure activities* =**limit**, keep within bounds, regulate, control, moderate, cut down. **2** *the cuff supports the ankle without restricting movement* =**hinder**, interfere with, impede, hamper, obstruct, block, check, curb. **3** *he restricted himself to a 15-minute speech* =**confine**, limit.

restricted ▸ adjective **1** *restricted space* =**cramped**, confined, constricted, small, narrow, tight. **2** *a restricted calorie intake* =**limited**, controlled, regulated, reduced. **3** *a restricted zone* =**out of bounds**, off limits, private, exclusive. **4** *restricted information* =**(top) secret**, classified; *informal* hush-hush.
−OPPOSITES unlimited.

restriction ▸ noun **1** *there is no restriction on the number of places* =**limitation**, constraint, control, check, curb; condition, proviso, qualification. **2** *the restriction of personal freedom* =**reduction**, limitation, diminution, curtailment. **3** *restriction of movement* =**hindrance**, im-

pediment, slowing, reduction, limitation.

result ▸ noun **1** *stress is the result of overwork* =**consequence**, outcome, upshot, sequel, effect, reaction, repercussion, ramification, conclusion, culmination. **2** *what is your result?* =**answer**, solution; sum, total, product. **3** *exam results* =**mark**, score, grade. **4** *the result of the trial* =**verdict**, decision, outcome, conclusion, judgement, findings, ruling.
−OPPOSITES cause.
▸ verb **1** *differences between species could result from their habitat* =**follow**, ensue, develop, stem, spring, arise, derive, evolve, proceed; occur, happen, take place, come about; be caused by, be brought about by, be produced by, originate in, be consequent on. **2** *the shooting resulted in five deaths* =**end in**, culminate in, finish in, terminate in, lead to, prompt, precipitate, trigger; cause, bring about, occasion, effect, give rise to, produce, engender, generate; *literary* beget.

resume ▸ verb **1** *the government resumed negotiations* =**restart**, recommence, begin again, start again, reopen; renew, return to, continue with, carry on with. **2** *the priest resumed his kneeling posture* =**return to**, come back to, take up again, reoccupy.
−OPPOSITES suspend, abandon.

résumé ▸ noun =**summary**, precis, synopsis, abstract, outline, summarization, summation, epitome; abridgement, digest, condensation, abbreviation, overview, review.

resumption ▸ noun =**restart**, recommencement, reopening; continuation, carrying on, renewal, return to.

resurgence ▸ noun =**renewal**, revival, recovery, comeback, reawakening, resurrection, reappearance, re-emergence, regeneration; resumption, recommencement, continuation; *formal* renascence.

resurrect ▸ verb *an attempt to resurrect his career* =**revive**, restore, regenerate, revitalize, breathe new life into, reinvigorate, resuscitate, rejuvenate, stimulate, re-establish, relaunch.

resuscitate ▸ verb **1** *medics resuscitated him* =**bring round**, revive, bring back to consciousness; give artificial respiration to, give the kiss of life to. **2** *measures to resuscitate the economy* =**revive**, resurrect, restore, regenerate, revitalize, breathe new life into, reinvigorate, rejuvenate, stimulate.

retain ▸ verb **1** *the government retained a share in the industries* =**keep (possession of)**, keep hold of, hang on to. **2** *existing footpaths are to be retained* =**maintain**, keep, preserve, conserve. **3** *some students retain facts easily* =**remember**, memorize, keep in one's mind/memory. **4** *solicitors can retain a barrister* =**employ**, contract, keep on the payroll.
–OPPOSITES give up, abolish.

retainer ▸ noun **1** *they're paid a retainer* =**(retaining) fee**, periodic payment, advance, standing charge. **2** *a faithful retainer.* See SERVANT sense 1.

retaliate ▸ verb =**fight back**, hit back, respond, react, reply, reciprocate, counter-attack, get back at someone, give tit for tat; have/get/take one's revenge, avenge oneself, take reprisals, get even, pay someone back; *informal* get one's own back.

retaliation ▸ noun =**revenge**, vengeance, reprisal, retribution, requital, recrimination, repayment; response, reaction, reply, counter-attack.

retard ▸ verb =**delay**, slow down/up, hold back/up, set back, postpone, put back, detain, decelerate; hinder, hamper, obstruct, inhibit, impede, check, restrain, restrict, trammel.
–OPPOSITES accelerate.

retch ▸ verb **1** *the taste made her retch* =**gag**, heave; *informal* keck. **2** *he retched all over the table.* See VOMIT verb sense 1.

reticence ▸ noun =**reserve**, restraint, inhibition, diffidence, shyness; unresponsiveness, quietness, taciturnity.

reticent ▸ adjective =**reserved**, withdrawn, introverted, inhibited, diffident, shy; uncommunicative, unforthcoming, unresponsive, tight-lipped, quiet, taciturn, silent.
–OPPOSITES expansive.

retinue ▸ noun =**entourage**, escort, company, court, staff, personnel, household, train, suite, following, bodyguard.

retire ▸ verb **1** *he has retired* =**give up work**, stop work. **2** *we've retired him on full pension* =**pension off**, force to retire. **3** *Gillian retired to her office* =**withdraw**, go away, take oneself off, decamp, shut oneself away; *formal* repair. **4** *everyone retired early* =**go to bed**, call it a day; *informal* turn in, hit the hay/sack.

retired ▸ adjective *a retired schoolteacher* =**former**, ex-, past, elderly.
▸ noun *apartments for the retired* =**(old-age) pensioners**, OAPs, senior citizens, the elderly; *N. Amer.* seniors.

retirement ▸ noun **1** *they are nearing retirement* =**giving up work**, stopping work. **2** *retirement in an English village* =**seclusion**, retreat, solitude, isolation, obscurity.

retiring ▸ adjective **1** *the retiring president* =**departing**, outgoing. **2** *a retiring man* =**shy**, diffident, self-effacing, unassuming, unassertive, reserved, reticent, quiet, timid, modest.
–OPPOSITES incoming, outgoing.

retort ▸ verb *'Oh, sure,' she retorted* =**answer**, reply, respond, return, counter, rejoin, riposte, retaliate.

retract ▸ verb **1** *the sea otter can retract its claws* =**pull in/back**, draw in. **2** *he retracted his allegation* =**take back**, withdraw, recant, disavow, disclaim, repudiate, renounce, reverse, revoke, rescind, go back on, backtrack on; *formal* abjure.

retreat ▸ verb **1** *the army retreated* =**withdraw**, retire, draw back, pull back/out, fall back, give way, give ground. **2** *the tide was retreating* =**go out**, ebb, recede, fall, go down. **3** *the government had to retreat* =**change one's mind**; back down, climb down, do a U-turn, backtrack, back-pedal, give in, concede defeat; *Brit.* do an about-turn.
–OPPOSITES advance.
▸ noun **1** *the retreat of the army* =**withdrawal**, pulling back. **2** *the President's retreat* =**climbdown**, backdown, aboutface; *Brit.* about-turn. **3** *her rural retreat* =**refuge**, haven, sanctuary; hideaway, hideout, hiding place; *informal* hidey-hole. **4** *a period of retreat from the world* =**seclusion**, withdrawal, retirement, solitude, isolation, sanctuary.

retrench ▸ verb **1** *we have to retrench* =**economize**, cut back, make savings, make economies, be economical, be frugal, tighten one's belt. **2** *services have to be retrenched* =**reduce**, cut (back/down), pare (down), slim down, trim, prune; *informal* slash.

retribution ▸ noun =**punishment**, penalty, one's just deserts; revenge, reprisal, requital, retaliation, vengeance, an eye for an eye (and a tooth for a tooth), tit for tat; redress, reparation, restitution, recompense, repayment, indemnification, atonement, amends.

retrieve ▸ verb **1** *I retrieved our ball from their garden* =**get back**, bring back, recover, regain (possession of), recoup, reclaim, repossess, redeem, recuperate. **2** *they were trying to retrieve the situation* =**put/set right**, rectify, remedy, restore, sort out, straighten out, resolve.

retrograde ▸ adjective **1** *a retrograde step* =**for the worse**, regressive, negative, downhill, unwelcome. **2** *retrograde motion* =**backward(s)**, reverse, rearward.
–OPPOSITES positive.

retrospect ■ **in retrospect** =**looking back**, on reflection, in/with hindsight.

retrospective ▸ adjective =**backdated**, retroactive, ex post facto.

return ▸ verb **1** *he returned to London* =**go back**, come back, arrive back, come home. **2** *the symptoms returned* =**recur**, reoccur, repeat (itself); reappear. **3** *he returned the money* =**give back**, hand back; pay back, repay. **4** *Peter returned the book to the shelf* =**restore**, put back, replace, reinstall. **5** *he returned the volley* =**hit back**, throw back. **6** *she returned his kiss* =**reciprocate**, requite, repay, give back. **7** *'Later,' returned Isabel* =**answer**, reply, respond, counter, rejoin, retort. **8** *the jury returned a unanimous verdict* =**deliver**, bring in, hand down. **9** *the club returned a profit* =**yield**, earn, realize, net, gross, clear.
–OPPOSITES depart, disappear, keep.
▸ noun **1** *the return of hard times* =**recurrence**, reoccurrence, repeat, repetition, reappearance, revival, resurrection, re-emergence, resurgence. **2** *I requested the return of my books* =**giving back**, handing back, replacement, restoration, reinstatement, restitution. **3** *a quick return on investments* =**yield**, profit, gain, revenue, interest, dividend. **4** *a census return* =**statement**, report, submission, record, dossier; document, form.
–OPPOSITES departure, disappearance.
■ **in return for** =**in exchange for**, as a reward for, as compensation for.

revamp ▸ verb =**renovate**, redecorate, refurbish, recondition, rehabilitate, overhaul, make over; upgrade, refit, reequip; remodel, refashion, redesign, restyle; *informal* do up, give something a facelift, vamp up; *Brit. informal* tart up; *N. Amer. informal* rehab.

reveal ▸ verb **1** *the police can't reveal his whereabouts* =**divulge**, disclose, tell, let slip/drop, give away/out, blurt (out), release, leak; make known, make public, broadcast, publicize, circulate, disseminate; *informal* let on. **2** *he revealed his new car* =**show**, display, exhibit, disclose, uncover; *literary* unmask. **3** *the data reveal a good deal of information* =**bring to light**, uncover, lay bare, unearth, unveil; *formal* evince; *literary* unmask.
–OPPOSITES hide.

revel ▸ verb **1** *they revelled all night* =**celebrate**, make merry, carouse, roister, go on a spree; *informal* party, live it up, whoop it up, make whoopee, rave, paint the town red. **2** *he revelled in the applause* =**enjoy**, delight in, love, like, adore, take pleasure in, appreciate, relish, lap up, savour; *informal* get a kick out of.
▸ noun *late-night revels* =**celebration**, festivity, jollification, merrymaking, carousal, carouse, spree; party, jamboree; *informal* rave, shindig, bash; *Brit. informal* rave-up, knees-up; *N. Amer. informal* wingding, blast.

revelation ▸ noun **1** *revelations about his personal life* =**disclosure**, announcement, report; admission, confession. **2** *the revelation of a secret* =**divulgence**, disclosure, letting slip/drop, giving away/out, leak, betrayal, unveiling, making known, making public, broadcasting, publicizing, dissemination, report, declaration.

reveller ▸ noun =**merrymaker**, partygoer, carouser, roisterer.

revelry ▸ noun =**celebration(s)**, parties, festivity, jollification, merrymaking, carousal, roistering; *informal* partying.

revenge ▸ noun **1** *she is seeking revenge* =**vengeance**, retribution, retaliation, reprisal, requital, recrimination, an eye for an eye (and a tooth for a tooth), redress, satisfaction. **2** *they were filled with revenge* =**vengefulness**, vindictiveness, vitriol, spite, malice, malevolence, ill will, animosity, hate, rancour, bitterness.
▸ verb **1** *he revenged his brother's murder* =**avenge**, exact retribution for, take reprisals for, get redress for, get satisfaction for. **2** *I'll be revenged on the whole pack of you* =**avenge oneself on**, take vengeance on, get even with, settle a/the score with, pay back, take reprisals against; *informal* get one's own back on.

revenue ▶ noun =income, takings, receipts, proceeds, earnings; profit(s). –OPPOSITES expenditure.

reverberate ▶ verb =resound, echo, resonate, ring, boom, rumble.

reverberation ▶ noun 1 *natural reverberation* =resonance, echo, resounding, ringing, booming, rumbling. 2 *political reverberations* =repercussions, ramifications, consequences, shock waves; aftermath, fallout, backlash.

revere ▶ verb =respect, admire, think highly of, esteem, look up to. –OPPOSITES despise.

reverence ▶ noun =high esteem, high regard, great respect, acclaim, admiration, appreciation, estimation, favour. –OPPOSITES scorn.

reverent ▶ adjective =respectful, admiring, devoted, devout, dutiful, awed, deferential.

reverie ▶ noun =daydream, trance, musing; inattention, inattentiveness, wool-gathering, preoccupation, absorption, abstraction.

reversal ▶ noun 1 *there was no reversal on this issue* =turnaround, turnabout, about-face, volte-face, change of heart, U-turn, backtracking; Brit. about-turn. 2 *a reversal of roles* =swap, exchange, change, interchange. 3 *the reversal of the decision* =alteration, changing; countermanding, undoing, overturning, overthrow, disallowing, overriding, overruling, veto, revocation, repeal, rescinding, annulment, nullification, voiding, invalidation; formal rescission, abrogation. 4 *they suffered a reversal* =setback, upset, failure, misfortune, mishap, disaster, blow, disappointment, adversity, hardship, affliction, vicissitude, defeat.

reverse ▶ verb 1 *the car reversed* =back, move back/backwards. 2 *reverse the bottle in the ice bucket* =turn upside down, turn over, upend, upturn, invert. 3 *reverse your roles* =swap (round), change (round), exchange, interchange, switch (round). 4 *the umpire reversed the decision* =alter, change; overturn, overthrow, disallow, override, overrule, veto, revoke, repeal, rescind, annul, nullify, void, invalidate; Brit. do an about-turn on; formal abrogate.

▶ adjective *in reverse order* =backward(s), inverted, transposed.

▶ noun 1 *the reverse is the case* =opposite, contrary, converse, inverse, obverse, antithesis. 2 *successes and reverses*. See REVERSAL sense 4. 3 *the reverse of the page* =other side, back, underside, wrong side, verso.

revert ▶ verb 1 *life will soon revert to normal* =return, go back, change back, default; fall back, regress, relapse. 2 *the property reverted to the landlord* =be returned.

review ▶ noun 1 *the Council undertook a review* =analysis, evaluation, assessment, appraisal, examination, investigation, inquiry, probe, inspection, study. 2 *the rent is due for review* =reconsideration, reassessment, re-evaluation, reappraisal; change, alteration, modification, revision. 3 *book reviews* =criticism, critique, assessment, evaluation, commentary; Brit. informal crit. 4 *a scientific review* =journal, periodical, magazine, publication. 5 *their review of the economy* =survey, report, study, account, description, statement, overview.

▶ verb 1 *I reviewed the evidence* =survey, study, research, consider, analyse, examine, scrutinize, explore, look into, probe, investigate, inspect, assess, appraise; informal size up. 2 *the referee reviewed his decision* =reconsider, re-examine, reassess, re-evaluate, reappraise, rethink; change, alter, modify, revise. 3 *he reviewed the day* =remember, recall, reflect on, think through, go over in one's mind, look back on. 4 *she reviewed the play* =comment on, evaluate, assess, appraise, judge, critique, criticize.

reviewer ▶ noun =critic, commentator, judge, observer, pundit, analyst.

revile ▶ verb =criticize, censure, condemn, attack, inveigh against, rail against, lambaste, denounce; slander, libel, malign, vilify, besmirch, abuse; informal knock, slam, pan, crucify, roast, bad-mouth; Brit. informal slate, rubbish, slag off; N. Amer. informal pummel; formal excoriate. –OPPOSITES praise.

revise ▶ verb 1 *she revised her opinion* =reconsider, review, re-examine, reassess, re-evaluate, rethink; change, alter, modify. 2 *the editor revised the text* =amend, emend, correct, alter, change, edit, rewrite, redraft, rephrase, rework. 3 (Brit.) *revise your lecture notes* =go over, reread, memorize; cram; infor-

mal bone up on; *Brit. informal* swot up (on), mug up (on).

revision ▸ noun 1 *a revision of the Prayer Book* =**emendation**, correction, alteration, adaptation, editing, rewriting, redrafting. 2 *a major revision of the system* =**reconsideration**, review, re-examination, reassessment, re-evaluation, reappraisal, rethink; change, alteration, modification. 3 *(Brit.) he was doing some revision* =**rereading**, memorizing, cramming; *Brit. informal* swotting.

revitalize ▸ verb =**reinvigorate**, reenergize, boost, regenerate, revive, revivify, rejuvenate, reanimate, resuscitate, refresh, stimulate, breathe new life into; *informal* give a shot in the arm to, pep up, buck up.

revival ▸ noun 1 *a revival in the economy* =**improvement**, rallying, picking up, amelioration, turn for the better, upturn, upswing, resurgence. 2 *the revival of traditional crafts* =**comeback**, reestablishment, reintroduction, restoration, reappearance, resurrection, regeneration, rejuvenation.
−OPPOSITES downturn, disappearance.

revive ▸ verb 1 *attempts to revive her failed* =**resuscitate**, bring round, bring back to consciousness. 2 *the man soon revived* =**regain consciousness**, come round, wake up. 3 *a cup of tea revived her* =**reinvigorate**, revitalize, refresh, energize, reanimate, resuscitate, revivify, rejuvenate, regenerate, enliven, stimulate. 4 *reviving old traditions* =**reintroduce**, re-establish, restore, resurrect, bring back, regenerate, resuscitate.

revoke ▸ verb =**cancel**, repeal, rescind, reverse, annul, nullify, void, invalidate, countermand, retract, withdraw, overrule, override; *formal* abrogate.

revolt ▸ verb 1 *the people revolted* =**rebel**, rise (up), take to the streets, riot, mutiny. 2 *the smell revolted him* =**disgust**, sicken, nauseate, turn someone's stomach, be repugnant to, be repulsive to, put off, be offensive to; *informal* turn off; *N. Amer. informal* gross out.
▸ noun *an armed revolt* =**rebellion**, revolution, insurrection, mutiny, uprising, riot, insurgence, seizure of power, coup (d'état).

revolting ▸ adjective =**disgusting**, sickening, nauseating, stomach-turning, repulsive, repellent, repug-

nant, appalling, abominable, hideous, horrible, awful, dreadful, terrible, obnoxious, vile, nasty, foul, loathsome, offensive, objectionable; *N. Amer.* vomitous; *informal* ghastly, putrid, horrid, gross, yucky; *literary* noisome.
−OPPOSITES attractive, pleasant.

revolution ▸ noun 1 *the French Revolution* =**rebellion**, revolt, insurrection, mutiny, uprising, riot, insurgence, coup (d'état). 2 *a revolution in printing techniques* =**dramatic change**, sea change, metamorphosis, transformation, innovation, reorganization, restructuring; *informal* shake-up; *N. Amer. informal* shakedown. 3 *one revolution of a wheel* =**(single) turn**, rotation, circle, spin; circuit, lap. 4 *the revolution of the earth* =**turning**, rotation, circling; orbit.

revolutionary ▸ adjective 1 *revolutionary troops* =**rebellious**, insurgent, rioting, mutinous, renegade, insurrectionary, seditious, subversive, extremist. 2 *revolutionary change* =**thoroughgoing**, complete, total, absolute, utter, comprehensive, sweeping, far-reaching, extensive, profound. 3 *a revolutionary kind of wheelchair* =**new**, novel, original, unusual, unconventional, unorthodox, newfangled, innovatory, modern, state-of-the-art, futuristic, pioneering.
▸ noun *political revolutionaries* =**rebel**, insurgent, mutineer, insurrectionist, agitator, subversive.

revolutionize ▸ verb =**transform**, shake up, turn upside down, restructure, reorganize, transmute, metamorphose; *humorous* transmogrify.

revolve ▸ verb 1 *a fan revolved slowly* =**go round**, turn round, rotate, spin. 2 *the moon revolves around the earth* =**circle**, travel, orbit. 3 *his life revolves around cars* =**be concerned with**, be preoccupied with, focus on, centre around.

revulsion ▸ noun =**disgust**, repulsion, abhorrence, repugnance, nausea, horror, aversion, abomination, distaste.
−OPPOSITES delight.

reward ▸ noun *a reward for its safe return* =**recompense**, prize, award, honour, decoration, bonus, premium, bounty, present, gift, payment; *informal* pay-off, perk; *formal* perquisite.
▸ verb *they were well rewarded* =**recompense**, pay, remunerate; give an award to.
−OPPOSITES punish.

rewarding ▸ adjective =satisfying, gratifying, pleasing, fulfilling, enriching, edifying, beneficial, illuminating, worthwhile, productive, fruitful.

reword ▸ verb =rewrite, rephrase, recast, redraft, revise; paraphrase.

rewrite ▸ verb =revise, recast, reword, rephrase, redraft.

rhetoric ▸ noun **1** *a form of rhetoric* =oratory, eloquence, command of language, way with words. **2** *empty rhetoric* =bombast, turgidity, grandiloquence, magniloquence, pomposity, extravagant language, purple prose; wordiness, verbosity, prolixity; *informal* hot air.

rhetorical ▸ adjective **1** *rhetorical devices* =stylistic, oratorical, linguistic, verbal. **2** *rhetorical hyperbole* =extravagant, grandiloquent, magniloquent, high-flown, orotund, bombastic, grandiose, pompous, pretentious, overblown, oratorical, turgid, flowery, florid; *informal* highfalutin.

rhyme ▸ noun =poem, verse; (**rhymes**) poetry, doggerel.

rhythm ▸ noun **1** *the rhythm of the music* =beat, cadence, tempo, time, pulse, throb, swing. **2** *poetic features such as rhythm* =metre, measure, stress, accent, cadence. **3** *the rhythm of daily life* =pattern, flow, tempo.

rhythmic ▸ adjective =rhythmical, measured, throbbing, beating, pulsating, regular, steady, even.

rib ▸ noun

> WORD LINKS
>
> *relating to ribs:* **costal**
> *between ribs:* **intercostal**

ribald ▸ adjective. See CRUDE sense 3.

rich ▸ adjective **1** *rich people* =wealthy, affluent, moneyed, well off, well-to-do, prosperous, opulent; *N. Amer.* silkstocking; *informal* rolling in money, loaded, well heeled, made of money. **2** *rich furnishings* =sumptuous, opulent, luxurious, de luxe, lavish, gorgeous, splendid, magnificent, costly, expensive, fancy; *informal* posh, plush, ritzy, swanky, classy; *Brit. informal* swish; *N. Amer. informal* swank. **3** *a garden rich in flowers* =abounding, well provided, well stocked, crammed, packed, teeming, bursting; *informal* jam-packed, chock-a-block; *Austral./NZ informal* chocker. **4** *a rich supply of restaurants* =plentiful, abun-

dant, copious, ample, profuse, lavish, liberal, generous, bountiful; *literary* plenteous, bounteous. **5** *rich soil* =fertile, productive, fecund, fruitful. **6** *a rich sauce* =creamy, fatty, heavy, full-flavoured. **7** *a rich wine* =full-bodied, heavy, fruity. **8** *rich colours* =strong, deep, full, intense, vivid, brilliant. **9** *her rich voice* =sonorous, full, resonant, deep, clear, mellow, mellifluous.
–OPPOSITES poor, light.

riches ▸ plural noun **1** *his new-found riches* =money, wealth, funds, (hard) cash, (filthy) lucre, wherewithal, means, (liquid) assets, capital, resources, reserves; opulence, affluence, prosperity; *informal* dough, bread, loot, readies; *Brit. informal* dosh, brass, lolly, spondulicks; *N. Amer. informal* bucks; *US informal* greenbacks, rocks. **2** *underwater riches* =resources, treasure(s), bounty, jewels, gems.

richly ▸ adverb **1** *the richly furnished chamber* =sumptuously, opulently, luxuriously, lavishly, gorgeously, splendidly, magnificently; *informal* poshly, plushly, ritzily, swankily, classily; *Brit. informal* swishly. **2** *the joy she richly deserves* =fully, thoroughly, in full measure, well, completely, wholly, totally, entirely, absolutely, amply, utterly.
–OPPOSITES meanly.

rickety ▸ adjective =shaky, unsteady, unsound, unsafe, tumbledown, brokendown, dilapidated, ramshackle; *informal* shambly; *N. Amer. informal* shacky.

rid ▸ verb =clear, free, purge, empty, strip.
■ **get rid of 1** *we must get rid of some stuff* =dispose of, throw away/out, clear out, discard, scrap, dump, bin, jettison; *informal* chuck (away), ditch, junk, get shut of; *Brit. informal* get shot of; *N. Amer. informal* trash. **2** *the cats got rid of the rats* =destroy, eliminate, annihilate, obliterate, wipe out, kill.

riddle[1] ▸ noun =puzzle, conundrum, brain-teaser, (unsolved) problem, question, poser, enigma, mystery; *informal* stumper.

riddle[2] ▸ verb **1** *his car was riddled by gunfire* =perforate, hole, pierce, puncture, pepper. **2** *he was riddled with cancer* =permeate, suffuse, fill, pervade, spread through, imbue, saturate, overrun, beset.

ride ▸ verb **1** *she can ride a horse* =sit on,

mount, bestride; manage, handle, control. **2** *riding round the town on bikes* =**travel**, move, proceed; drive, cycle; trot, canter, gallop.
▸ **noun** *he took us for a ride* =**trip**, journey, drive, run, excursion, outing, jaunt; lift; *informal* spin.

ridicule ▸ **noun** *he was subjected to ridicule* =**mockery**, derision, laughter, scorn, scoffing, contempt, jeering, sneering, jibes, teasing, taunts, ragging, chaffing; *informal* kidding, ribbing, joshing.
–OPPOSITES respect.
▸ **verb** *his theory was ridiculed* =**deride**, mock, laugh at, heap scorn on, jeer at, jibe at, sneer at, scorn, make fun of, scoff at, satirize, lampoon, burlesque, caricature, parody, tease, taunt, rag, chaff; *informal* kid, rib, josh, take the mickey out of.

ridiculous ▸ **adjective 1** *that looks ridiculous* =**laughable**, absurd, comical, funny, hilarious, risible, droll, amusing, farcical, silly, ludicrous. **2** *a ridiculous suggestion* =**senseless**, silly, foolish, foolhardy, stupid, inane, fatuous, half-baked, hare-brained, ill-thought-out, crackpot, idiotic. **3** *a ridiculous exaggeration* =**absurd**, preposterous, ludicrous, laughable, risible, nonsensical, senseless, outrageous.
–OPPOSITES sensible.

rife ▸ **adjective 1** *violence is rife* =**widespread**, general, common, universal, extensive, ubiquitous, omnipresent, endemic, inescapable, insidious, prevalent. **2** *the village was rife with gossip* =**overflowing**, bursting, alive, teeming, abounding.
–OPPOSITES unknown.

riff-raff ▸ **noun** =**rabble**, scum, the lowest of the low, good-for-nothings, undesirables; *informal* peasants.
–OPPOSITES elite.

rifle ▸ **verb 1** *she rifled through her wardrobe* =**rummage**, search, hunt, forage. **2** *a thief rifled her home* =**burgle**, rob, steal from, loot, raid, plunder, ransack.

rift ▸ **noun 1** *a deep rift in the ice* =**crack**, fault, flaw, split, break, breach, fissure, fracture, cleft, crevice, cavity, opening. **2** *the rift between them* =**breach**, division, split; quarrel, squabble, disagreement, falling-out, row, argument, dispute, conflict, feud; *informal* spat, scrap; *Brit. informal* bust-up.

rig[1] ▸ **verb 1** *the boats were rigged with a single sail* =**equip**, kit out, fit out, supply, furnish, provide, arm. **2** *I rigged myself out in black* =**dress**, clothe, attire, robe, garb, array, deck out, drape, accoutre, outfit, get up; *informal* doll up. **3** *he will rig up a shelter* =**set up**, erect, assemble; throw together, cobble together, put together, whip up, improvise, contrive; *Brit. informal* knock up.
▸ **noun 1** *a CB radio rig* =**apparatus**, appliance, machine, device, instrument, contraption, system. **2** *the rig of the American Army Air Corps* =**uniform**, costume, ensemble, outfit, livery, attire, clothes, garments, dress, garb, regimentals, regalia, trappings; *Brit.* strip; *informal* get-up, gear, togs; *Brit. informal* kit; *formal* apparel.

rig[2] ▸ **verb** *they rigged the election* =**manipulate**, engineer, distort, misrepresent, pervert, tamper with, doctor; falsify, fake, trump up; *informal* fix; *Brit. informal* fiddle.

right ▸ **adjective 1** *it wouldn't be right to do that* =**just**, fair, proper, good, upright, righteous, virtuous, moral, ethical, honourable, honest; lawful, legal. **2** *the right answer* =**correct**, accurate, exact, precise; proper, valid, conventional, established, official, formal; *Brit. informal* spot on. **3** *the right person for the job* =**suitable**, appropriate, fitting, correct, proper, desirable, preferable, ideal. **4** *you've come at the right time* =**opportune**, advantageous, favourable, propitious, good, lucky, happy, fortunate, providential, felicitous. **5** *he's not right in the head* =**sane**, lucid, rational, balanced, compos mentis; *informal* all there. **6** *on my right side* =*Nautical* starboard; *Heraldry* dexter.
–OPPOSITES wrong, insane, left, port.
▸ **adverb 1** *she was right at the limit of her patience* =**completely**, fully, totally, absolutely, utterly, thoroughly, quite. **2** *right in the middle of the village* =**exactly**, precisely, directly, immediately, just, squarely, dead; *informal* (slap) bang, smack, plumb. **3** *keep going right on* =**straight**, directly, as the crow flies. **4** *I think I heard right* =**correctly**, accurately, properly, precisely, perfectly. **5** *make sure you're treated right* =**well**, properly, justly, fairly, equitably, impartially, honourably, lawfully, legally. **6** *things will turn out right* =**well**, for the best, favourably, happily, advantageously, profitably, providentially, luckily, conveniently.

−OPPOSITES wrong, badly.

▶ **noun 1** *the difference between right and wrong* =**goodness**, righteousness, virtue, integrity, rectitude, propriety, morality, truth, honesty, honour, justice, fairness, equity. **2** *you have the right to say no* =**entitlement**, prerogative, privilege, advantage, due, birthright, liberty, authority, power, licence, permission, dispensation, leave, sanction.
−OPPOSITES wrong.

▶ **verb 1** *the way to right a capsized dinghy* =**set upright**, turn back over. **2** *we must right the situation* =**remedy**, rectify, retrieve, fix, resolve, sort out, settle, square; straighten out, correct, repair, mend, redress, make good, ameliorate, better.

■ **by rights** =**properly**, correctly, technically, in fairness.

■ **in the right** =**justified**, vindicated.

■ **put something to rights**. *See* RIGHT *verb sense 2*.

■ **right away** =**at once**, straight away, (right) now, this (very) minute, this instant, immediately, instantly, directly, forthwith, without further ado, promptly, quickly, without delay, a.s.a.p., as soon as possible; *N. Amer. informal* in short order, straight off, p.d.q., pretty damn quick, pronto.

■ **within one's rights** =**entitled**, permitted, allowed, at liberty, empowered, authorized, qualified, licensed, justified.

righteous ▶ **adjective 1** *righteous living* =**good**, virtuous, upright, upstanding, decent; ethical, principled, moral, high-minded, law-abiding, honest, honourable, blameless, irreproachable, noble. **2** *righteous anger* =**justifiable**, legitimate, defensible, supportable, rightful.
−OPPOSITES sinful, unjustifiable.

rightful ▶ **adjective 1** *the car's rightful owner* =**legal**, lawful, real, true, proper, correct, recognized, genuine, authentic, acknowledged, approved, licensed, valid, bona fide; *informal* legit, kosher. **2** *their rightful place in society* =**deserved**, merited, due, just, right, fair, proper, fitting, appropriate, suitable.
−OPPOSITES wrongful.

right-wing ▶ **adjective** =**conservative**, rightist, blimpish, diehard; reactionary, traditionalist, conventional, unprogressive.
−OPPOSITES left-wing.

rigid ▶ **adjective 1** *a rigid container* =**stiff**, hard, firm, inflexible, unbending, un-

yielding, inelastic. **2** *a rigid routine* =**fixed**, set, firm, inflexible, unalterable, unchangeable, immutable, unvarying, invariable, hard and fast, cast-iron. **3** *a rigid approach to funding* =**strict**, severe, stern, stringent, rigorous, inflexible, uncompromising, intransigent.
−OPPOSITES flexible, lenient.

rigmarole ▶ **noun 1** *the rigmarole of dressing up* =**fuss**, bother, trouble, folderol, ado; *informal* palaver, song and dance, performance, to-do, pantomime, hassle; *Brit. informal* carry-on. **2** *that rigmarole about the house being haunted* ⩲**tale**, saga, yarn, shaggy-dog story; *informal* spiel.

rigorous ▶ **adjective 1** *rigorous attention to detail* =**meticulous**, conscientious, punctilious, careful, diligent, attentive, scrupulous, painstaking, exact, precise, accurate, thorough, particular, strict, demanding, exacting; *informal* pernickety. **2** *the rigorous enforcement of rules* =**strict**, severe, stern, stringent, tough, harsh, rigid, relentless, unsparing, inflexible, draconian, intransigent, uncompromising, exacting. **3** *rigorous conditions* =**harsh**, severe, bad, bleak, extreme, inclement; unpleasant, disagreeable, foul, nasty, filthy.
−OPPOSITES slapdash, lax, mild.

rigour ▶ **noun 1** *a mine operated under conditions of rigour* =**strictness**, severity, stringency, toughness, harshness, rigidity, inflexibility, intransigence. **2** *intellectual rigour* =**meticulousness**, thoroughness, carefulness, diligence, scrupulousness, exactness, exactitude, precision, accuracy, correctness, strictness. **3** *the rigours of the journey* =**hardship**, harshness, severity, adversity; ordeal, misery, trial.

rim ▶ **noun 1** *the rim of her cup* =**brim**, edge, lip. **2** *the rim of the crater* =**edge**, border, side, margin, brink, fringe, boundary, perimeter, circumference, limits, periphery.

rind ▶ **noun** =**skin**, peel, zest, integument.

ring¹ ▶ **noun 1** *a ring round the moon* =**circle**, band, halo, disc; *technical* annulus. **2** *a circus ring* =**arena**, enclosure, field, ground. **3** *a spy ring* =**gang**, syndicate, cartel, mob, band, circle, organization, association, society, alliance, league, coterie, cabal.

▶ **verb** *police ringed the building* =**surround**, circle, encircle, encompass, girdle, enclose, hem in, confine, seal off.

ring² ▶ verb **1** *church bells rang* =**toll**, sound, peal, chime, clang, bong; *literary* knell. **2** *the room rang with laughter* =**resound**, reverberate, resonate, echo. **3** *I'll ring you tomorrow* =**telephone**, phone (up), call (up); *informal* give someone a buzz; *Brit. informal* give someone a bell, give someone a tinkle, get on the blower to.

■ **ring something in** =**herald**, signal, announce, proclaim, usher in, introduce; mark, signify, indicate.

rinse ▶ verb =**wash (out)**, clean, cleanse, bathe; dip, drench, splash, swill, sluice, hose down.

riot ▶ noun **1** *a riot in the capital* =**uproar**, commotion, upheaval, disturbance, furore, tumult, melee, scuffle, fracas, fray, brawl, free-for-all; violence, fighting, lawlessness. **2** *the garden was a riot of colour* =**mass**, sea, splash, show, exhibition.

▶ verb *the miners rioted* =**(go on the) rampage**, run wild, run amok, go berserk; *informal* raise hell.

■ **run riot 1** *the children ran riot* =**(go on the) rampage**, run amok, go berserk, go out of control; *informal* raise hell. **2** *the vegetation has run riot* =**grow profusely**, spread uncontrolled, burgeon, multiply, rocket.

riotous ▶ adjective **1** *a riotous demonstration* =**unruly**, rowdy, disorderly, uncontrollable, unmanageable, undisciplined, uproarious, tumultuous; violent, wild, ugly, lawless, anarchic. **2** *a riotous party* =**boisterous**, lively, loud, noisy, unrestrained, uninhibited, uproarious; *Brit. informal* rumbustious.

–OPPOSITES peaceable.

rip ▶ verb **1** *he ripped the posters down* =**tear**, wrench, wrest, pull, snatch, tug, prise, heave, drag, peel, pluck; *informal* yank. **2** *she ripped Leo's note into pieces* =**tear**, claw, hack, slit, cut; *literary* rend.

ripe ▶ adjective **1** *a ripe tomato* =**mature**, full grown. **2** *the dock is ripe for development* =**ready**, fit, suitable, right. **3** *the ripe old age of ninety* =**advanced**, hoary, venerable, old. **4** *the time is ripe for his return* =**opportune**, advantageous, favourable, auspicious, propitious, promising, good, right, fortunate, benign, providential, felicitous, seasonable.

–OPPOSITES unsuitable, young.

ripen ▶ verb =**mature**, mellow.

riposte ▶ noun =**retort**, counter, rejoinder, sally, return, answer, reply, response; *informal* comeback.

ripple ▶ noun =**wavelet**, wave, undulation, ripplet, ridge, ruffle.

rise ▶ verb **1** *the sun rose* =**move up/upwards**, come up, arise, ascend, climb, mount, soar. **2** *the mountains rising above us* =**loom**, tower, soar, rear (up). **3** *prices rose* =**go up**, increase, soar, shoot up, surge, leap, jump, rocket, escalate, spiral. **4** *living standards have risen* =**improve**, get better, advance, go up, soar, shoot up. **5** *his voice rose* =**get higher**, grow, increase, become louder, swell, intensify. **6** *he rose from his chair* =**stand up**, get to one's feet, get up, jump up, leap up; *formal* arise. **7** *he rises at dawn* =**get up**, rouse oneself, stir, bestir oneself, be up and about; *informal* surface; *formal* arise. **8** *the court rose at midday* =**adjourn**, recess, be suspended, pause, take a break; *informal* knock off, take five. **9** *he rose through the ranks* =**make progress**, climb, advance, get on, work one's way, be promoted. **10** *he wouldn't rise to the bait* =**react**, respond; take. **11** *the dough started to rise* =**swell**, expand, enlarge, puff up. **12** *the nation rose against its oppressors* =**rebel**, revolt, mutiny, riot, take up arms. **13** *the Rhine rises in the Alps* =**originate**, begin, start, emerge; issue from, spring from, flow from, emanate from. **14** *her spirits rose* =**brighten**, lift, cheer up, improve, pick up; *informal* buck up. **15** *the ground rose gently* =**slope upwards**, go uphill, incline, climb.

–OPPOSITES fall, descend, drop, sit, retire, resume, die, shelve.

▶ noun **1** *a price rise* =**increase**, hike, leap, upsurge, upswing, climb, escalation. **2** *he got a rise of 11%* =**raise**, pay increase; hike, increment. **3** *a rise in standards* =**improvement**, amelioration, upturn, leap. **4** *his rise to power* =**progress**, climb, promotion, elevation, aggrandizement. **5** *we walked up the rise* =**slope**, incline, acclivity, hillock, hill.

risible ▶ adjective =**laughable**, ridiculous, absurd, comical, amusing, funny, hilarious, humorous, droll, farcical, silly, ludicrous, hysterical; *informal* rib-tickling, priceless.

risk ▶ noun **1** *there is a certain amount of risk* =**chance**, uncertainty, unpredictability, precariousness, instability, insecurity, perilousness. **2** *the risk of fire* =**possibility**, chance, probability, like-

lihood, danger, peril, threat, menace, fear, prospect.
–OPPOSITES safety, impossibility.
▶ verb *he risked his life to save them* =**endanger**, imperil, jeopardize, hazard, gamble (with), chance; put on the line, put in jeopardy.
■ **at risk** =**in danger**, in peril, in jeopardy, under threat.

risky ▶ adjective =**dangerous**, hazardous, perilous, unsafe, insecure, precarious, parlous, touch-and-go, treacherous; uncertain, unpredictable; *informal* chancy, dicey, hairy; *N. Amer. informal* gnarly.

risqué ▶ adjective =**ribald**, rude, bawdy, racy, earthy, indecent, suggestive, improper, naughty, locker-room; vulgar, dirty, smutty, crude, coarse, obscene, lewd, X-rated; *informal* blue, raunchy; *Brit. informal* fruity, off colour, saucy; *euphemistic* adult.

rite ▶ noun =**ceremony**, ritual, ceremonial; service, sacrament, liturgy, worship, office; act, practice, custom, tradition, convention.

ritual ▶ noun *an elaborate civic ritual* =**ceremony**, rite, observance; service, sacrament, liturgy, worship; act, practice, custom, tradition, convention, formality, protocol.
▶ adjective *a ritual burial* =**ceremonial**, prescribed, set, formal; sacramental, liturgical; traditional, conventional.

rival ▶ noun 1 *his rival for the nomination* =**opponent**, challenger, competitor, contender; adversary, antagonist, enemy; *literary* foe. 2 *the tool has no rival* =**equal**, match, peer, equivalent, counterpart, like.
–OPPOSITES ally.
▶ verb *few countries can rival it for scenery* =**match**, compare with, compete with, vie with, equal, measure up to, be in the same league as, be on a par with, touch, challenge; *informal* hold a candle to.
▶ adjective *rival candidates* =**competing**, opposing, contending.

rivalry ▶ noun =**competitiveness**, competition, contention, vying; opposition, conflict, feuding, antagonism, friction, enmity; *informal* keeping up with the Joneses.

river ▶ noun 1 =**watercourse**, waterway, tributary, stream, rivulet, brook, inlet; *Scottish & N. English* burn; *N. English* beck; *S. English* bourn; *N. Amer. & Austral./NZ* creek;

Austral. billabong. 2 *a river of molten lava* =**stream**, torrent, flood, deluge, cascade.

WORD LINKS

relating to rivers: **fluvial, fluvio-, riparian**
study of rivers: **potamology**
fear of rivers: **potamophobia**

riveted ▶ adjective 1 *she stood riveted to the spot* =**fixed**, rooted, frozen, unable to move. 2 *he was riveted by the newsreels* =**fascinated**, engrossed, gripped, captivated, enthralled, spellbound, mesmerized, transfixed. 3 *their eyes were riveted on the teacher* =**fixed**, fastened, focused, concentrated, locked.
–OPPOSITES bored.

riveting ▶ adjective =**fascinating**, gripping, engrossing, interesting, intriguing, absorbing, captivating, enthralling, compelling, spellbinding, mesmerizing; *informal* unputdownable.
–OPPOSITES boring.

road ▶ noun 1 *the roads were crowded* =**street**, thoroughfare, roadway, avenue, broadway, bypass, ring road, trunk road, byroad; *Brit.* dual carriageway, clearway, motorway; *N. Amer.* highway, freeway, parkway, throughway, expressway; *US* turnpike, interstate. 2 *a step on the road to recovery* =**way**, path, route, course.
■ **on the road** =**on tour**, travelling.

roam ▶ verb =**wander**, rove, ramble, drift, walk, traipse; range, travel, tramp, traverse, trek; *Scottish & Irish* stravaig; *informal* cruise, mosey; *formal* perambulate.

roar ▶ noun 1 *the roars of the crowd* =**shout**, bellow, yell, cry, howl; clamour; *informal* holler. 2 *the roar of the sea* =**boom**, crash, rumble, roll, thundering. 3 *roars of laughter* =**guffaw**, howl, hoot, shriek, gale, peal.
▶ verb 1 *'Get out!' roared Angus* =**bellow**, yell, shout, bawl, howl; *informal* holler. 2 *thunder roared* =**boom**, rumble, crash, roll, thunder. 3 *the movie left them roaring* =**guffaw**, laugh, hoot; *informal* split one's sides, be rolling in the aisles, be doubled up, crack up, be in stitches; *Brit. informal* crease up, fall about.

roaring ▶ adjective *a roaring fire* =**blazing**, burning, flaming.

roast ▶ verb =**cook**, bake, grill; *N. Amer.* broil.

rob ▶ verb 1 *the gang robbed a bank* =**bur-**

gle, steal from, hold up, break into; raid, loot, plunder, pillage; *N. Amer.* burglarize; *informal* do, turn over, knock off, stick up. **2** *he robbed an old woman* =**steal from**; *informal* mug, jump; *N. Amer. informal* clip. **3** *he was robbed of his savings* =**cheat**, swindle, defraud; *informal* do out of, con out of, fleece. **4** *defeat robbed him of his title* =**deprive**, strip, divest; deny.

robber ▸ noun =**burglar**, thief, housebreaker, mugger, shoplifter; stealer, pilferer, raider, looter, plunderer, pillager; bandit, highwayman; *Brit. informal* tea leaf.

robbery ▸ noun *they were arrested for the robbery* =**burglary**, theft, stealing, breaking and entering, housebreaking, larceny, shoplifting; embezzlement; fraud; hold-up, break-in, raid; *informal* mugging, smash-and-grab, stick-up; *Brit. informal* blag; *N. Amer. informal* heist.

robe ▸ noun **1** *the women wore black robes* =**cloak**, kaftan, djellaba, wrap, mantle, cape; *N. Amer.* wrapper. **2** *coronation robes* =**garb**, regalia, costume, finery; garments, clothes; *formal* apparel. **3** *priestly robes* =**vestment**, surplice, cassock. **4** *a towelling robe* =**dressing gown**, bathrobe, housecoat; *N. Amer.* wrapper.
▸ verb *he robed for Mass* =**dress**, clothe oneself; *formal* enrobe.

robot ▸ noun =**automaton**, android, golem; *informal* bot, droid.

robust ▸ adjective **1** *a robust man* =**strong**, vigorous, sturdy, tough, powerful, solid, muscular, sinewy, rugged, hardy, strapping, brawny, burly, husky; healthy, (fighting) fit, hale and hearty; *informal* beefy, hunky. **2** *these knives are robust* =**durable**, resilient, tough, hard-wearing, long-lasting, sturdy, strong. **3** *her usual robust view of things* =**down-to-earth**, practical, realistic, pragmatic, common-sense, matter-of-fact, businesslike, sensible, unromantic, unsentimental; *informal* no-nonsense.
−OPPOSITES frail, fragile, romantic, insipid.

rock[1] ▸ verb **1** *the ship rocked on the water* =**move to and fro**, sway, see-saw; roll, pitch, plunge, toss, lurch, reel, list. **2** *the building began to rock* =**shake**, vibrate, quake, tremble. **3** *Wall Street was rocked by the news* =**stun**, shock, stagger, astonish, startle, surprise, shake (up), take aback, throw, unnerve, disconcert.

rock[2] ▸ noun **1** *a gully strewn with rocks* =**boulder**, stone, pebble. **2** *a castle built on a rock* =**crag**, cliff, outcrop. **3** *he was the rock on which they relied* =**foundation**, cornerstone, support, prop, mainstay; tower of strength, bulwark, anchor.

> **WORD LINKS**
>
> relating to rock: **litho-, petro-**
> study of rocks: **petrology, petrography**

rocket ▸ verb **1** *prices have rocketed* =**shoot up**, soar, increase, rise, escalate, spiral; *informal* go through the roof. **2** *they rocketed into the alley* =**speed**, zoom, shoot, whizz, tear, career; *Brit. informal* bomb.
−OPPOSITES plummet.

rocky[1] ▸ adjective *a rocky path* =**stony**, pebbly, shingly; rough, bumpy; craggy, mountainous.

rocky[2] ▸ adjective **1** *that table's rocky* =**unsteady**, shaky, unstable, wobbly, tottery, rickety. **2** *a rocky marriage* =**difficult**, problematic, precarious, unstable, unreliable; *informal* iffy, up and down.
−OPPOSITES steady, stable.

rococo ▸ adjective =**ornate**, fancy, elaborate, extravagant, baroque; fussy, busy, ostentatious, showy; *informal* highfalutin.
−OPPOSITES plain.

rod ▸ noun **1** *an iron rod* =**bar**, stick, pole, baton, staff; shaft, strut, rail, spoke. **2** *the ceremonial rod* =**staff**, mace, sceptre. **3** *instruction was accompanied by the rod* =**corporal punishment**, the cane, the lash, the birch; beating, flogging.

rogue ▸ noun **1** *a rogue without ethics* =**scoundrel**, villain, miscreant, reprobate, rascal, good-for-nothing, ne'er-do-well, wretch; *informal* rat, dog, louse, crook. **2** *your boy's a little rogue* =**rascal**, imp, devil, monkey; *informal* scamp, scallywag, monster, horror, terror, tyke.

roguish ▸ adjective **1** *a roguish character* =**unprincipled**, dishonest, deceitful, unscrupulous, untrustworthy, shameless; wicked, villainous; *informal* shady. **2** *a roguish grin* =**mischievous**, playful, teasing, cheeky, naughty, wicked, impish, devilish; *informal* waggish.

roister ▸ verb =**enjoy oneself**, celebrate, revel, carouse, frolic, romp, make merry, rollick; *informal* party, live it up, whoop it up, have a ball.

role ▸ noun **1** *a small role in the film* =**part**; character. **2** *his role as President* =**capacity**, position, job, post, office, duty, responsibility, mantle, place.

roll ▸ verb **1** *the bottle rolled down the table* =**bowl**, turn over and over, spin, rotate. **2** *waiters rolled in the trolleys* =**wheel**, push, trundle. **3** *we rolled past fields* =**travel**, go, move, pass, cruise, sweep. **4** *the months rolled by* =**pass**, go by, slip by, fly by, elapse, wear on, march on. **5** *tears rolled down her cheeks* =**flow**, run, course, stream, pour, spill, trickle. **6** *the mist rolled in* =**billow**, undulate, tumble. **7** *he rolled his handkerchief into a ball* =**wind**, coil, fold, curl; twist. **8** *they rolled about with laughter* =**stagger**, lurch, reel, totter, teeter, wobble. **9** *the ship began to roll* =**lurch**, toss, rock, pitch, plunge, sway, reel, list, keel. **10** *thunder rolled* =**rumble**, reverberate, echo, resound, boom, roar, grumble.
▸ noun **1** *a roll of wrapping paper* =**cylinder**, tube, scroll. **2** *a roll of film* =**reel**, spool. **3** *a roll of notes* =**wad**, bundle. **4** *a roll of the dice* =**throw**, toss, turn, spin. **5** *crusty rolls* =**bun**, bagel; *Brit.* bap, muffin; *N. English* barm; *N. Amer.* hoagie. **6** *the electoral roll* =**list**, register, directory, record, file, index, catalogue, inventory. **7** *a roll of thunder* =**rumble**, reverberation, echo, boom, clap, crack, roar, grumble.
■ **roll something out** =**unroll**, spread out, unfurl, unfold, open (out), unwind, uncoil.
■ **roll something up** =**fold (up)**, furl, wind up, coil (up), bundle up.

rollicking ▸ adjective =**lively**, boisterous, exuberant, spirited; riotous, noisy, wild, rowdy; *Brit. informal* rumbustious.

romance ▸ noun **1** *their romance blossomed* =**love**, passion, ardour, adoration, devotion. **2** *he's had many romances* =**love affair**, relationship, liaison, courtship, attachment. **3** *an author of historical romances* =**love story**; *informal* tear jerker. **4** *the romance of the Far East* =**mystery**, glamour, excitement, exoticism, mystique; appeal, allure, charm.
▸ verb **1** *(dated) he was romancing Meg* =**woo**, chase, pursue; go out with, pay court to; *informal* see, go steady with, date. **2** *I am romancing the past* =**romanticize**, idealize, paint a rosy picture of.

romantic ▸ adjective **1** *he's so romantic* =**loving**, amorous, passionate, tender, affectionate; *informal* lovey-dovey. **2** *romantic songs* =**sentimental**, hearts-and-flowers; mawkish, sickly, saccharine, syrupy; *informal* slushy, mushy, sloppy, schmaltzy, gooey; *Brit. informal* soppy. **3** *a*

romantic setting =**idyllic**, picturesque, fairy-tale; beautiful, lovely, charming, pretty. **4** *romantic notions of rural communities* =**idealistic**, unrealistic, fanciful, impractical; head-in-the-clouds, starry-eyed, optimistic, hopeful, visionary, utopian, fairy-tale.
–OPPOSITES unsentimental, realistic.
▸ noun *an incurable romantic* =**idealist**, sentimentalist, romanticist; dreamer, visionary, utopian, Don Quixote, fantasist.
–OPPOSITES realist.

Romeo ▸ noun =**ladies' man**, Don Juan, Casanova, Lothario, womanizer, playboy, lover, seducer, philanderer, flirt; gigolo; *informal* ladykiller, stud.

romp ▸ verb **1** *two fox cubs romped playfully* =**play**, frolic, frisk, gambol, skip, prance, caper, cavort, rollick. **2** *South Africa romped to a win* =**sail**, coast, sweep; win hands down, run away with it; *informal* walk it.

room ▸ noun **1** *there isn't much room* =**space**; headroom, legroom; area, expanse, extent. **2** *room for improvement* =**scope**, capacity, leeway, latitude, freedom. **3** *he had rooms in the Pepys building* =**lodgings**, quarters; accommodation; *informal* a pad, digs.

roomy ▸ adjective =**spacious**, capacious, sizeable, generous, big, large, extensive; voluminous, ample; *formal* commodious.
–OPPOSITES cramped.

root ▸ noun **1** *the root of the problem* =**source**, origin, germ, beginnings, genesis; cause, reason, basis, foundation, bottom, seat; core, heart, nub, essence. **2** *he rejected his roots* =**origins**, beginnings, family, ancestors, predecessors, heritage.
▸ verb **1** *has the shoot rooted?* =**take root**, establish itself, strike, take. **2** *he rooted around in the cupboard* =**rummage**, hunt, search, rifle, delve, forage, dig, nose, poke.
■ **put down roots** =**settle**, establish oneself, set up home.
■ **root and branch 1** *the firm should be eradicated, root and branch* =**completely**, entirely, wholly, totally, thoroughly. **2** *a root-and-branch reform* =**complete**, total, thorough, radical.
■ **root something out 1** *the hedge was rooted out* =**uproot**, deracinate, pull up, grub out. **2** *root out corruption* =**eradicate**, eliminate, weed out, destroy, wipe out, stamp out, extirpate, abolish, end,

put a stop to. **3** *he rooted out a dark secret* =**unearth**, dig up, bring to light, uncover, discover, dredge up, ferret out, expose.

■**take root 1** *leave the plants to take root* =**germinate**, sprout, establish, strike, take. **2** *Christianity took root in Persia* =**become established**, take hold.

> WORD LINKS
> *relating to roots:* **radical**

rooted ▸ adjective **1** *views rooted in Indian culture* =**embedded**, fixed, established, entrenched, ingrained. **2** *Neil was rooted to the spot* =**frozen**, riveted, paralysed, glued, fixed.

rootless ▸ adjective =**itinerant**, unsettled, drifting, roving, footloose; homeless, of no fixed abode.

rope ▸ noun =**cord**, cable, line, hawser; string.
▸ verb =**tie**, bind, lash, truss; secure, moor, fasten, attach; hitch, tether, lasso.

> WORD LINKS
> *relating to ropes:* **funicular**

ropy ▸ adjective =**stringy**, thready, fibrous, filamentous; viscous, sticky.

roster ▸ noun =**schedule**, list, register, agenda, calendar; *Brit.* rota.

rostrum ▸ noun =**dais**, platform, podium, stage; soapbox.

rosy ▸ adjective **1** *a rosy complexion* =**pink**, roseate, reddish; glowing, healthy, fresh, radiant, blooming; blushing, flushed; ruddy, high-coloured, florid. **2** *his future looks rosy* =**promising**, optimistic, auspicious, hopeful, encouraging, favourable, bright, golden; *informal* upbeat.
−OPPOSITES pale, bleak.

rot ▸ verb **1** *the floorboards rotted* =**decay**, decompose; disintegrate, crumble, perish. **2** *the meat began to rot* =**go bad**, go off, spoil; moulder, putrefy, fester. **3** *poor neighbourhoods have been left to rot* =**deteriorate**, degenerate, decline, decay, go to seed, go downhill; *informal* go to pot, go to the dogs.
−OPPOSITES improve.
▸ noun **1** *the leaves turned black with rot* =**decay**, decomposition, mould, mildew, blight, canker. **2** *traditionalists said the rot had set in* =**deterioration**, decline; corruption, cancer.

rota ▸ noun (*Brit.*). See ROSTER.

rotary ▸ adjective =**rotating**, revolving, turning, spinning, gyratory.

rotate ▸ verb **1** *the wheels rotate continually* =**revolve**, go round, turn (round), spin, gyrate, whirl, twirl, swivel, circle, pivot. **2** *many nurses rotate jobs* =**alternate**, take turns, change, switch, interchange, exchange, swap.

rotation ▸ noun **1** *the rotation of the wheels* =**revolving**, turning, spinning, gyration, circling. **2** *a rotation of the Earth* =**turn**, revolution, orbit, spin. **3** *each member is chair for six months in rotation* =**sequence**, succession; alternation, cycle.

> WORD LINKS
> *relating to rotation:* **gyro-**

rote ■ **by rote** =**mechanically**, automatically, parrot-fashion, unthinkingly, mindlessly; from memory, by heart.

rotten ▸ adjective **1** *rotten meat* =**decaying**, bad, off, decomposing, putrid, putrescent, perished, mouldy, rancid, festering, fetid; addled. **2** *rotten teeth* =**decayed**, carious, black. **3** *he's rotten to the core* =**corrupt**, unprincipled, dishonest, dishonourable, unscrupulous, untrustworthy, immoral; villainous, bad, wicked, evil, iniquitous, venal; *informal* crooked, warped; *Brit. informal* bent.
−OPPOSITES fresh, honourable.

rotund ▸ adjective **1** *a small, rotund man* =**plump**, chubby, fat, stout, portly, dumpy, round, chunky, overweight, heavy, paunchy, ample; flabby, fleshy, bulky, corpulent, obese; *informal* tubby, roly-poly, pudgy, beefy, porky; *Brit. informal* podgy. **2** *rotund cauldrons* =**round**, bulbous, spherical.
−OPPOSITES thin.

roué ▸ noun =**libertine**, rake, debauchee, degenerate, profligate; lecher, seducer, womanizer, philanderer, adulterer, Don Juan, Lothario; *informal* lady-killer, lech, dirty old man.

rough ▸ adjective **1** *rough ground* =**uneven**, irregular, bumpy, stony, rocky, rugged, rutted, pitted. **2** *the terrier's rough coat* =**coarse**, bristly, scratchy, prickly; shaggy, hairy, bushy. **3** *rough skin* =**dry**, leathery, weather-beaten; chapped, calloused, scaly, scabrous. **4** *his voice was rough* =**gruff**, hoarse, harsh, rasping, husky, throaty, gravelly, guttural. **5** *he gets rough when he's drunk* =**violent**, brutal, vicious; **aggressive**, belligerent, pugnacious, thuggish; boisterous, rowdy, disorderly, unruly, riotous. **6** *a machine that can take rough handling* =**careless**, clumsy, inept, unskilful. **7** *rough manners* =**boorish**, loutish, oafish, brutish, coarse, crude, uncouth, vulgar, unrefined, unladylike, ungentlemanly, uncultured. **8** *rough seas* =**turbulent**, stormy, tempestuous, violent, heavy, heaving, choppy. **9** *a rough draft* =**preliminary**, hasty, quick, sketchy, cursory, basic, crude, rudimentary, raw, unpolished; incomplete, unfinished. **10** *a rough estimate* =**approximate**, inexact, imprecise, vague, estimated, hazy; *N. Amer. informal* ballpark.

−OPPOSITES smooth, sleek, soft, dulcet, sweet, gentle, careful, refined, calm, exact.

▸ noun **1** *the artist's initial roughs* =**sketch**, draft, outline, mock-up. **2** *(Brit.) a bunch of roughs attacked him* =**ruffian**, thug, lout, hooligan, hoodlum, rowdy; *informal* tough, roughneck, bruiser; *Brit. informal* yob.

■ **rough something out** =draft, sketch out, outline, block out, mock up.

rough and ready ▸ adjective − basic, simple, crude, unrefined, unsophisticated; makeshift, provisional, stopgap, improvised, extemporary, ad hoc.

roughly ▸ adverb **1** *he shoved her roughly* =**violently**, forcefully, forcibly, abruptly, unceremoniously. **2** *they treated him roughly* =**harshly**, unkindly, unsympathetically; brutally, savagely, mercilessly, cruelly, heartlessly. **3** *roughly £2.4 million* =**approximately**, (round) about, around, circa, in the region of, something like, of the order of, or so, or thereabouts, more or less, give or take; nearly, close to, approaching; *Brit.* getting on for.

round ▸ adjective **1** *a round window* =**circular**, disc-shaped, ring-shaped, hoop-shaped; spherical, globular, orb-shaped; cylindrical; bulbous, rounded, rotund. **2** *a short, round man* =**plump**, chubby, fat, stout, rotund, portly, dumpy, chunky, overweight, pot-bellied, paunchy; flabby, corpulent, fleshy, bulky, obese; *informal* tubby, roly-poly, pudgy, beefy, porky; *Brit. informal* podgy. **3** *his deep, round voice* =**sonorous**, resonant, rich, full, mellow, mellifluous, orotund. **4** *a round dozen* =**complete**, entire, whole, full. **5** *she berated him in round*

terms =**candid**, frank, direct, honest, truthful, straightforward, plain, blunt, forthright, bald, explicit, unequivocal.

−OPPOSITES thin, reedy.

▸ noun **1** *mould the dough into rounds* =**ball**, sphere, globe, orb, circle, disc, ring, hoop. **2** *a policeman on his rounds* =**circuit**, beat, route, tour. **3** *the first round of the contest* =**stage**, level; heat, game, bout, contest. **4** *an endless round of parties* =**succession**, sequence, series, cycle. **5** *the gun fires thirty rounds a second* =**bullet**, cartridge, shell, shot.

▸ preposition & adverb **1** *the alleys round the station* =**around**, about, encircling; near, in the vicinity of; orbiting. **2** *casinos dotted round France* =**throughout**, all over.

▸ verb *the ship rounded the point* =**go round**, travel round, skirt, circumnavigate, orbit.

■ **round about** =approximately, around, circa, roughly, of the order of, something like, more or less, close to, near to, practically; or so, or thereabouts, give or take a few; not far off, nearly, almost, approaching; *Brit.* getting on for.

■ **round the clock 1** *we're working round the clock* =**day and night**, all the time, {morning, noon, and night}, continuously, non-stop, steadily, unremittingly; *informal* 24-7. **2** *round-the-clock supervision* =**continuous**, constant, non-stop, uninterrupted.

■ **round something off 1** *the square edges were rounded off* =**smooth off**, plane off, sand off, level off. **2** *the party rounded off a successful year* =**complete**, finish off, crown, cap, top; conclude, close, end.

■ **round someone/something up** =gather together, herd together, muster, marshal, rally, assemble, collect, group; *N. Amer.* corral.

roundabout ▸ adjective **1** *a roundabout route* =**circuitous**, indirect, meandering, serpentine, tortuous. **2** *I asked in a roundabout sort of way* =**indirect**, oblique, circuitous, circumlocutory, periphrastic, digressive, long-winded.

−OPPOSITES direct.

▸ noun *(Brit.)* **1** *go straight on at the roundabout* =N. Amer. rotary, traffic circle. **2** *a roundabout with wooden horses* =**merry-go-round**, carousel.

roundly ▸ adverb **1** *he was roundly condemned* =**vehemently**, emphatically, fiercely, forcefully, severely; plainly, frankly, candidly. **2** *she was roundly de-*

feated =**utterly**, completely, thoroughly, decisively, conclusively, heavily, soundly.

round-up ▶ noun **1** *a cattle round-up* =**assembly**, muster, rally; *N. Amer.* rodeo. **2** *the sports round-up* =**summary**, synopsis, overview, review, outline, digest, precis; *N. Amer.* wrap-up; *informal* recap.

rouse ▶ verb **1** *he roused Ralph at dawn* =**wake (up)**, awaken, arouse; *Brit. informal* knock up; *formal* waken. **2** *she roused and looked around* =**wake up**, awake, come to, get up, rise, bestir oneself; *formal* arise. **3** *he roused the crowd* =**stir up**, excite, galvanize, electrify, stimulate, inspire, inspirit, move, inflame, agitate, goad, provoke; *informal* light a fire under. **4** *he's got a temper when he's roused* =**provoke**, annoy, anger, infuriate, madden, incense, vex, irk; *informal* aggravate. **5** *her disappearance roused my suspicions* =**arouse**, awaken, prompt, provoke, stimulate, pique, trigger, spark off, touch off, kindle, elicit.
−OPPOSITES calm, pacify, allay.

rousing ▶ adjective =**stirring**, inspiring, exciting, stimulating, moving, electrifying, invigorating, energizing, exhilarating; enthusiastic, vigorous, spirited.

rout ▶ noun **1** *the army's ignominious rout* =**retreat**, flight. **2** *Newcastle scored 13 tries in the rout* =**trouncing**, annihilation, decisive defeat; *informal* licking, hammering, thrashing, pasting, drubbing, massacre.
−OPPOSITES victory.

▶ verb **1** *his army was routed* =**put to flight**, drive off, scatter; defeat, beat, conquer, vanquish, crush, overpower. **2** *he routed the defending champion* =**trounce**, defeat decisively, get the better of; *informal* lick, hammer, clobber, thrash, paste, demolish, annihilate, drub, cane, wipe the floor with, walk all over, make mincemeat of, massacre, slaughter; *Brit. informal* stuff.
−OPPOSITES lose.

route ▶ noun =**way**, course, road, path, direction.

▶ verb =**direct**, send, convey, dispatch, forward.

routine ▶ noun **1** *his morning routine* =**procedure**, practice, pattern, drill, regime, regimen; programme, schedule, plan. **2** *a stand-up routine* =**act**, performance, number, turn, piece; *informal* spiel, patter.

▶ adjective **1** *a routine health check* =**standard**, regular, customary, normal, usual, ordinary, typical; everyday, common, conventional, habitual. **2** *a routine action movie* =**boring**, tedious, tiresome, wearisome, monotonous, humdrum, run-of-the-mill, prosaic, dreary, pedestrian; predictable, hackneyed, stock, unimaginative, unoriginal, banal, trite.
−OPPOSITES unusual.

rove ▶ verb =**wander**, roam, ramble, drift, meander; range, travel; *Scottish* stravaig.

rover ▶ noun =**wanderer**, traveller, globetrotter, drifter, roamer, itinerant, transient; nomad, gypsy, Romany; tramp, vagrant, vagabond; *N. Amer.* hobo.

row¹ ▶ noun **1** *rows of children* =**line**, column, file, queue; procession, chain, string, succession; *informal* crocodile. **2** *the middle row of seats* =**tier**, line, rank, bank.
■ **in a row** *three days in a row* =**consecutively**, in succession; running, straight; *informal* on the trot.

row² (*Brit. informal*) ▶ noun **1** *have you two had a row?* =**argument**, quarrel, squabble, fight, contretemps, dispute, clash, shouting match; *informal* tiff, set-to, run-in, slanging match, spat; *Brit. informal* barney, bust-up. **2** *I couldn't hear for the row* =**din**, noise, racket, uproar, hubbub, rumpus, babel; *informal* hullabaloo.

▶ verb *they rowed about money* =**argue**, quarrel, squabble, bicker, fight, fall out, disagree, have words; *informal* scrap.

rowdy ▶ adjective =**unruly**, disorderly, obstreperous, riotous, undisciplined, uncontrollable, ungovernable, disruptive, out of control, rough, wild, lawless; boisterous, uproarious, noisy, loud, clamorous; *Brit. informal* rumbustious.
−OPPOSITES peaceful.

royal ▶ adjective **1** *the royal prerogative* =**regal**, kingly, queenly, princely; sovereign, monarchical. **2** *a royal welcome* =**excellent**, fine, magnificent, splendid, superb, wonderful, first-rate; *informal* fantastic, great, tremendous.

rub ▶ verb **1** *Polly rubbed her arm* =**massage**, knead; stroke, pat. **2** *he rubbed sun lotion on her back* =**apply**, smear, spread, work in. **3** *my shoes rub painfully* =**chafe**, pinch.

▶ noun **1** *she gave his back a rub* =**massage**, rub-down. **2** *I gave my shoes a rub* =**polish**, wipe, clean. **3** *it's too complicated —*

rubbish | ruin

that's the rub =**problem**, difficulty, trouble, drawback, hindrance, impediment; snag, hitch, catch.

■ **rub something down** =**clean**, sponge, wash.

■ **rub off on** =**be transferred to**, be passed on to, be transmitted to, be communicated to; affect, influence.

■ **rub something out** =**erase**, delete, remove, efface, obliterate, expunge.

■ **rub something up** =**polish**, buff up, burnish, shine, wax; clean, wipe.

rubbish ▸ noun **1** *throw away that rubbish* =**refuse**, waste, litter, debris, detritus, scrap, dross; *N. Amer.* garbage, trash; *informal* dreck, junk. **2** *she's talking rubbish* =**nonsense**, balderdash, gibberish, claptrap, blarney, moonshine, garbage; *informal* hogwash, baloney, tripe, drivel, bilge, bunk, piffle, poppycock, phooey, twaddle, gobbledegook; *Brit. informal* codswallop, cobblers, tosh, cack.

rubble ▸ noun =**debris**, remains, ruins, wreckage.

ruddy ▸ adjective *a ruddy complexion* =**rosy**, red, pink, roseate, rubicund; healthy, glowing, fresh; flushed, blushing; florid, high-coloured.
–OPPOSITES pale.

rude ▸ adjective **1** *a rude man* =**ill-mannered**, bad-mannered, impolite, discourteous, uncivil, mannerless; impertinent, insolent, impudent, disrespectful, cheeky; churlish, curt, brusque, brash, offhand, short, sharp; offensive, insulting, derogatory, disparaging, abusive. **2** *rude jokes* =**vulgar**, coarse, smutty, dirty, filthy, crude, lewd, obscene, off colour, offensive, indelicate, tasteless; risqué, naughty, ribald, bawdy, racy; *informal* blue; *Brit. informal* near the knuckle; *euphemistic* adult. **3** *a rude awakening* =**abrupt**, sudden, sharp, startling; unpleasant, nasty, harsh.
–OPPOSITES polite, clean.

rudimentary ▸ adjective **1** *rudimentary carpentry skills* =**basic**, elementary, primary, fundamental, essential. **2** *the equipment was rudimentary* =**primitive**, crude, simple, unsophisticated, rough (and ready), makeshift. **3** *a rudimentary thumb* =**vestigial**, undeveloped, incomplete.
–OPPOSITES advanced, sophisticated, developed.

rudiments ▸ plural noun =**basics**, fundamentals, essentials, first principles,

foundation; *informal* nuts and bolts, ABC.

rue ▸ verb =**regret**, be sorry about, feel remorseful about, repent of, reproach oneself for; deplore, lament, bemoan, bewail.

rueful ▸ adjective =**regretful**, apologetic, sorry, remorseful, shamefaced, sheepish, hangdog, contrite, repentant, penitent, conscience-stricken, self-reproachful; sorrowful, sad.

ruffian ▸ noun =**thug**, lout, hooligan, hoodlum, vandal, delinquent, rowdy, scoundrel, villain, rogue, bully boy, brute; *informal* tough, bruiser; *Brit. informal* rough, yob.

ruffle ▸ verb **1** *he ruffled her hair* =**disarrange**, tousle, dishevel, rumple, mess up; *N. Amer. informal* muss up. **2** *don't let him ruffle you* =**annoy**, irritate, vex, nettle, anger, exasperate; disconcert, unnerve, fluster, agitate, harass, upset, disturb, discomfit, put off, perturb, unsettle, bother, worry, trouble; *informal* rattle, faze, throw, get to, rile, needle, aggravate, bug, peeve; *Brit. informal* wind up, nark.
–OPPOSITES smooth, soothe.
▸ noun *a shirt with ruffles* =**frill**, flounce, ruff, ruche.

rug ▸ noun **1** *they sat on the rug* =**mat**, carpet, drugget, runner; *N. Amer.* floorcloth. **2** *he was wrapped in a tartan rug* =**blanket**, coverlet, throw, wrap; *N. Amer.* lap robe.

rugged ▸ adjective **1** *the rugged path* =**rough**, uneven, bumpy, rocky, stony, pitted, jagged, craggy. **2** *a rugged vehicle* =**robust**, durable, sturdy, strong, tough, resilient. **3** *rugged manly types* =**well built**, burly, strong, muscular, muscly, brawny, strapping, husky, hulking; tough, hardy, robust, sturdy, solid; *informal* hunky, beefy. **4** *his rugged features* =**strong**, craggy, rough-hewn; manly, masculine.
–OPPOSITES smooth, flimsy, weedy, delicate.

ruin ▸ noun **1** *the buildings were saved from ruin* =**disintegration**, decay, disrepair, dilapidation; destruction, demolition, wreckage. **2** *the ruins of a church* =**remains**, remnants, fragments, relics; rubble, debris, wreckage. **3** *electoral ruin for Labour* =**downfall**, collapse, defeat, undoing, failure, breakdown; Waterloo. **4** *shopkeepers are facing ruin* =**bankruptcy**, insolvency, penury, poverty,

destitution, impoverishment, indigence.
–OPPOSITES preservation, triumph, wealth.

▶ **verb 1** *don't ruin my plans* =**wreck**, destroy, spoil, mar, blight, shatter, dash, torpedo, scotch, mess up; sabotage; *informal* screw up, foul up, put the kibosh on, do for; *Brit. informal* scupper. **2** *the bank's collapse ruined them* =**bankrupt**, make insolvent, impoverish, pauperize, wipe out, break, cripple; bring someone to their knees. **3** *a country ruined by civil war* =**destroy**, devastate, lay waste, ravage; raze, demolish, wreck, wipe out, flatten.
–OPPOSITES save, rebuild.

■ **in ruins 1** *the abbey is in ruins* =**derelict**, in disrepair, falling to pieces, dilapidated, tumbledown, ramshackle, decrepit, decaying. **2** *his career is in ruins* =**destroyed**, in pieces, in ashes; over, finished; *informal* in tatters, on the rocks, done for.

ruined ▶ adjective =**derelict**, dilapidated, tumbledown, ramshackle, decrepit, falling to pieces, crumbling, decaying, disintegrating; *informal* shambly.

ruinous ▶ adjective **1** *a ruinous trade war* =**disastrous**, devastating, catastrophic, calamitous, crippling, crushing, damaging, destructive, harmful; costly. **2** *ruinous interest rates* =**extortionate**, exorbitant, excessive, sky-high, outrageous, inflated; *Brit.* over the odds; *informal* criminal, steep.

rule ▶ noun **1** *health and safety rules* =**regulation**, directive, order, act, law, statute, edict, canon, mandate, command, dictate, decree, fiat, injunction, commandment, stipulation, requirement, guideline, direction; *formal* ordinance. **2** *church attendance on Sunday was the general rule* =**procedure**, practice, protocol, convention, norm, routine, custom, habit, wont; *formal* praxis. **3** *moderation is the golden rule* =**precept**, principle, standard, axiom, truth, maxim. **4** *under British rule* =**control**, jurisdiction, command, power, dominion; government, administration, sovereignty, leadership, supremacy, authority.

▶ verb **1** *El Salvador was ruled by Spain* =**govern**, preside over, control, lead, dominate, run, head, administer, manage. **2** *Mary ruled for six years* =**be in power**, be in control, be in command, be in charge, govern; reign, be monarch, be sovereign. **3** *the judge ruled that they be set*

free =**decree**, order, pronounce, judge, adjudge, ordain; decide, find, determine, resolve, settle. **4** *subversion ruled* =**prevail**, predominate, be the order of the day, reign supreme; *formal* obtain.

■ **as a rule** =**usually**, in general, normally, ordinarily, customarily, for the most part, on the whole, by and large, in the main, mostly, commonly, typically.

■ **rule something out** =**exclude**, eliminate, disregard; preclude, prohibit, prevent, disallow.

ruler ▶ noun =**leader**, sovereign, monarch, potentate, king, queen, emperor, empress, prince, princess; crowned head, head of state, president, premier, governor.
–OPPOSITES subject.

ruling ▶ noun *the judge's ruling* =**judgement**, decision, adjudication, finding, verdict; pronouncement, resolution, decree, injunction.

▶ adjective **1** *the ruling monarch* =**reigning**, sovereign, regnant. **2** *Japan's ruling party* =**governing**, controlling, commanding, supreme, leading, dominant, ascendant. **3** *football was their ruling passion* =**main**, chief, principal, major, prime, dominating, foremost; predominant, central, focal; *informal* number-one.

rumble ▶ verb =**boom**, thunder, roll, roar, resound, reverberate, echo, grumble.

ruminate ▶ verb *we ruminated on life* =**think about**, contemplate, consider, meditate on, muse on, mull over, ponder on/over, deliberate about/on, chew over, puzzle over; *formal* cogitate about.

rummage ▶ verb =**search**, hunt, root about/around, ferret about/around, fish about/around, poke around in, dig, delve, go through, explore, sift through, rifle through.

rumour ▶ noun =**gossip**, hearsay, talk, tittle-tattle, speculation, word; (**rumours**) reports, stories, whispers, canards; *informal* the grapevine, the word on the street, the buzz.

rump ▶ noun **1** *a smack on the rump* =**rear** (**end**), backside, seat; buttocks, cheeks; *Brit.* bottom; *informal* behind, BTM, sit-upon, derrière; *Brit. informal* bum, botty, jacksie; *N. Amer. informal* butt, fanny, tush, tail, buns, booty, heinie; *humorous* fundament, posterior, stern. **2** *the rump of the army* =**remainder**, rest, remnant, remains.

rumple ▸ verb **1** *the sheet was rumpled* =**crumple**, crease, wrinkle, crinkle, ruck (up), scrunch up; *Brit.* ruckle. **2** *Ian rumpled her hair* =**ruffle**, disarrange, tousle, dishevel, riffle; mess up; *N. Amer. informal* muss up.
−OPPOSITES smooth.

rumpus ▸ noun =**disturbance**, commotion, uproar, furore, brouhaha, hue and cry, ruckus; fracas, melee, tumult, noise, racket, din; *informal* to-do, hullabaloo, hoo-ha, kerfuffle; *Brit. informal* row, carry-on.

run ▸ verb **1** *she ran across the road* =**sprint**, race, dart, rush, dash, hasten, hurry, scurry, scamper, hare, bolt, fly, gallop, career, charge, shoot, hurtle, speed, zoom, go like lightning, go hell for leather, go like the wind; jog, trot; *informal* tear, pelt, scoot, hotfoot it, leg it, belt, zip, whip; *Brit. informal* bomb. **2** *the robbers turned and ran* =**flee**, take flight, make off, take off, take to one's heels, make a break for it, bolt, make one's getaway, escape; *informal* beat it, clear off/out, vamoose, skedaddle, split, leg it, scram; *Brit. informal* do a runner, scarper, do a bunk. **3** *he ran in the marathon* =**compete**, take part, participate. **4** *a shiver ran down my spine* =**go**, pass, slide, move, travel. **5** *he ran his eye down the list* =**cast**, pass, skim, flick. **6** *the road runs the length of the valley* =**extend**, stretch, reach, continue. **7** *water ran from the eaves* =**flow**, pour, stream, gush, flood, cascade, roll, course, spill, trickle, drip, dribble, leak. **8** *a bus runs to Sorrento* =**travel**, shuttle, go. **9** *I'll run you home* =**drive**, take, bring, ferry, chauffeur, give someone a lift. **10** *he runs a transport company* =**be in charge of**, manage, direct, control, head, govern, supervise, superintend, oversee. **11** *it's expensive to run a car* =**maintain**, keep, own, possess, have. **12** *they ran some tests* =**carry out**, do, perform, execute. **13** *he left the engine running* =**operate**, function, work, go; tick over, idle. **14** *the lease runs for twenty years* =**be valid**, last, be in effect, be operative, continue. **15** *the show ran for two years* =**be staged**, be performed, be on, be mounted, be screened. **16** *he ran for president* =**stand for**, be a candidate for, be a contender for. **17** *the paper ran the story* =**publish**, print, feature, carry, put out, release, issue. **18** *they run drugs* =**smuggle**, traffic in, deal in.
▸ noun **1** *his morning run* =**sprint**, jog, dash,

gallop, trot. **2** *she did the school run* =**route**, journey; circuit, round, beat. **3** *a run in the car* =**drive**, ride, turn; trip, excursion, outing, jaunt, airing; *informal* spin, tootle. **4** *an unbeaten run of victories* =**series**, succession, sequence, string, chain, streak, spell, stretch, spate. **5** *a run on sterling* =**demand for**, rush on. **6** *the usual run of cafes* =**type**, kind, sort, variety, class. **7** *against the run of play, he scored again* =**trend**, tendency, course, direction, movement, drift, tide. **8** *a chicken run* =**enclosure**, pen, coop. **9** *a ski run* =**slope**, track, piste; *N. Amer.* trail. **10** *a run in her tights* =**ladder**, rip, tear, snag, hole.
■ **in the long run** =**eventually**, in the end, ultimately, when all is said and done, in the fullness of time; *Brit. informal* at the end of the day.
■ **on the run** =**on the loose**, at large; running away, fleeing, fugitive; *informal* AWOL.
■ **run across** =**meet (by chance)**, come across, run into, chance on, stumble on, happen on; *informal* bump into.
■ **run away 1** *her attacker ran away. See* RUN *verb sense 2.* **2** *she ran away with the championship* =**win easily**; *informal* win by a mile, walk it, romp home.
■ **run down** =**decline**, degenerate, go downhill, go to seed, decay, go to rack and ruin; *informal* go to pot, go to the dogs.
■ **run someone down 1** *he was run down by joyriders* =**run over**, knock down/ over; hit, strike. **2** *she ran him down in front of other people* =**criticize**, denigrate, belittle, disparage, deprecate, find fault with; *informal* put down, knock, badmouth; *Brit. informal* rubbish, slag off; *formal* derogate.
■ **run for it.** *See* RUN *verb sense 2.*
■ **run high** *feelings were running high* =**be strong**, be fervent, be passionate, be intense.
■ **run in** *heart disease runs in the family* =**be common in**, be inherent in.
■ **run into 1** *a car ran into his van* =**collide with**, hit, strike, crash into, smash into, plough into, ram, impact. **2** *I ran into Hugo the other day* =**meet (by chance)**, run across, chance on, stumble on, happen on; *informal* bump into. **3** *we ran into a problem* =**experience**, encounter, meet with, be faced with, be confronted with. **4** *his debts run into six figures* =**reach**, extend to, be as much as.
■ **run low** *supplies were running low*

=**dwindle**, diminish, become depleted, be used up, be in short supply, be tight.
■ **run off** *the youths ran off. See* RUN verb sense 2.

■ **run something off 1** *would you run off that list for me?* =**copy**, photocopy, xerox, duplicate, print, produce, do. **2** *run off some of the excess water* =**drain**, bleed, draw off, pump out.

■ **run on 1** *the call ran on for hours* =**continue**, go on, carry on, last, keep going, stretch. **2** *your mother does run on* =**talk incessantly**, go on, chatter on, ramble on; *informal* yak, gab, yabber; *Brit. informal* rabbit on, witter on, chunter on, talk the hind leg off a donkey; *N. Amer. informal* run off at the mouth.

■ **run out 1** *supplies ran out* =**be used up**, dry up, be exhausted, be finished, peter out. **2** *they ran out of cash* =**be out of**; use up, consume, eat up; *informal* be fresh out of, be cleaned out of. **3** *her contract ran out* =**expire**, end, terminate, finish; lapse.

■ **run over 1** *the bathwater ran over* =**overflow**, spill over, brim over. **2** *the project ran over budget* =**exceed**, go over, overshoot, overreach. **3** *he quickly ran over the story* =**recapitulate**, repeat, run through, go over, reiterate, review; look over, read through; *informal* recap on.

■ **run someone over.** *See* RUN SOMEONE DOWN *sense 1.*

■ **run through 1** *they quickly ran through their money* =**squander**, spend, fritter away, dissipate, waste, go through, consume, use up; *informal* blow. **2** *the attitude that runs through his writing* =**pervade**, permeate, suffuse, imbue, inform. **3** *he ran through his notes. See* RUN OVER *sense 3.* **4** *let's run through scene three* =**rehearse**, practise, go over, repeat; *N. Amer.* run down; *informal* recap on.

■ **run to 1** *the bill ran to £2,000* =**amount to**, add up to, total, come to, equal, reach, be as much as. **2** *we can't run to champagne* =**afford**, stretch to, manage.

> WORD LINKS
> place for running or racing: **-drome**

runaway ▶ noun *a teenage runaway* =**fugitive**, escaper; refugee; truant; absconder, deserter.
▶ adjective **1** *a runaway horse* =**out of control**, escaped, loose. **2** *a runaway victory* =**easy**, effortless. **3** *runaway inflation* =**rampant**, out of control, unchecked, unbridled.

rundown ▶ noun =**summary**, synopsis, precis, run-through, summarization, review, overview, briefing, sketch, outline; *informal* low-down, recap.

run down ▶ adjective **1** *a run-down area of London* =**dilapidated**, tumbledown, ramshackle, derelict, ruinous, crumbling; neglected, uncared-for, depressed, seedy, shabby, slummy, squalid; *informal* shambly; *Brit. informal* grotty. **2** *she was feeling rather run down* =**unwell**, ill, poorly, unhealthy, peaky; tired, drained, exhausted, fatigued, worn out, below par, washed out; *Brit.* off colour; *informal* under the weather; *Brit. informal* off, ropy, knackered; *Austral./NZ informal* crook.

runner ▶ noun **1** =**athlete**, sprinter, hurdler, racer, jogger. **2** *a strawberry runner* =**shoot**, offshoot, sprout, tendril. **3** *the bookmaker employed runners* =**messenger**, courier, errand boy; *informal* gofer.

running ▶ noun **1** *his running was fast* =**sprinting**, racing, jogging. **2** *the running of the school* =**administration**, management, organization, coordination, orchestration, handling, direction, control, regulation, supervision. **3** *the smooth running of her department* =**operation**, working, function, performance.
▶ adjective **1** *running water* =**flowing**, gushing, rushing, moving. **2** *a running argument* =**ongoing**, sustained, continuous, incessant, ceaseless, constant, perpetual. **3** *she was late two days running* =**in succession**, in a row, in sequence, consecutively; straight, together; *informal* on the trot.

■ **in the running** *he's in the running for a prize* =**likely to get**, a candidate for, in line for, on the shortlist for, up for.

runny ▶ adjective =**liquefied**, liquid, fluid, melted, molten; watery, thin.
–OPPOSITES solid.

run-of-the-mill ▶ adjective =**ordinary**, average, middle-of-the-road, commonplace, humdrum, mundane, standard, nondescript, characterless, conventional; unremarkable, unexceptional, uninteresting, dull, boring, routine, bland, lacklustre; *N. Amer.* garden-variety; *informal* bog-standard, nothing special, a dime a dozen; *Brit. informal* common or garden.
–OPPOSITES exceptional.

rupture ▶ noun **1** *pipeline ruptures* =**break**, fracture, crack, burst, split, fissure. **2** *a rupture due to personal differences* =**rift**, estrangement, falling-out, break-up, breach, split, separation, parting, division, schism; *informal* bust-up.

▶ verb **1** *the reactor core might rupture* =**break**, fracture, crack, breach, burst, split; *informal* bust. **2** *the problem ruptured their relationships* =**sever**, break off, breach, disrupt; *literary* sunder.

rural ▶ adjective =**country**, bucolic, rustic, pastoral; agricultural, agrarian; *literary* sylvan.
–OPPOSITES urban.

ruse ▶ noun =**ploy**, stratagem, tactic, scheme, trick, gambit, dodge, subterfuge, machination, wile; *Brit. informal* wheeze.

rush ▶ verb **1** *she rushed home* =**hurry**, dash, sprint, run, race, sprint, bolt, dart, gallop, career, charge, shoot, hurtle, hare, fly, speed, zoom, scurry, scuttle, scamper, hasten; *informal* tear, belt, pelt, scoot, zip, whip, hotfoot it, leg it; *Brit. informal* bomb. **2** *water rushed along gutters* =**flow**, pour, gush, surge, stream, cascade, run, course. **3** *the tax was rushed through parliament* =**push**, hurry, hasten, speed, hustle, press, force. **4** *they rushed the cordon of troops* =**attack**, charge, run at, assail, storm.

▶ noun **1** *Tim made a rush for the exit* =**dash**, run, sprint, dart, bolt, charge, scramble, break. **2** *the lunchtime rush* =**hustle and bustle**, commotion, hubbub, hurly-burly, stir. **3** *a last minute rush for flights* =**demand**, clamour, call, request; run on. **4** *he was in no rush to leave* =**hurry**, haste, urgency. **5** *a rush of adrenalin* =**surge**, flow, flood, spurt, stream; dart, thrill, flash. **6** *a rush of cold air* =**gust**, draught, flurry. **7** *I made a sudden rush at him* =**charge**, onslaught, attack, assault, onrush.

▶ adjective *a rush job* =**urgent**, high-priority, emergency; hurried, hasty, fast, quick, swift.

rushed ▶ adjective **1** *a rushed divorce* =**hasty**, fast, speedy, quick, swift, rapid, hurried. **2** *he was too rushed to enjoy his stay* =**pushed for time**, busy, in a hurry, run off one's feet.

rust ▶ verb =**corrode**, oxidize, tarnish.

> **WORD LINKS**
>
> containing rust: **ferruginous**

rustic ▶ adjective **1** *a rustic setting* =**rural**, country, pastoral, bucolic; agricultural, agrarian; *literary* sylvan. **2** *rustic wooden tables* =**plain**, simple, homely, unsophisticated; rough, rude, crude. **3** *rustic peasants* =**unsophisticated**, uncultured, unrefined, simple; artless, unassuming, guileless, naive, ingenuous; coarse, rough, uncouth, boorish; *N. Amer. informal* hillbilly, hick.
–OPPOSITES urban, ornate, sophisticated.

▶ noun =**peasant**, countryman, countrywoman, bumpkin, yokel, country cousin; *N. Amer. informal* hillbilly, hayseed, hick; *Austral./NZ informal* bushy.

rustle ▶ verb **1** *her dress rustled as she moved* =**swish**, whoosh, whisper, sigh. **2** *he was rustling cattle* =**steal**, thieve, take; abduct, kidnap.

rusty ▶ adjective **1** *rusty wire* =**rusted**, rust-covered, corroded, oxidized; tarnished, discoloured. **2** *a rusty colour* =**reddish-brown**, chestnut, auburn, tawny, russet, coppery, Titian, red. **3** *my French is a little rusty* =**out of practice**, below par.

rut ▶ noun **1** *the car bumped across the ruts* =**furrow**, groove, trough, ditch, hollow, pothole, crater. **2** *he was stuck in a rut* =**boring routine**, humdrum existence, groove, dead end.

ruthless ▶ adjective =**merciless**, pitiless, cruel, heartless, hard-hearted, cold-hearted, cold-blooded, harsh, callous, unmerciful, unforgiving, uncaring, unsympathetic, uncharitable; remorseless, unbending, inflexible, implacable.
–OPPOSITES merciful.

sabotage ▶ noun =vandalism, wrecking, destruction, incapacitation, damage; subversion, obstruction, disruption, spoiling, undermining; *Brit. informal* a spanner in the works.
▶ verb =vandalize, wreck, damage, destroy, incapacitate; obstruct, disrupt, spoil, ruin, undermine, subvert.

saccharine ▶ adjective =sentimental, sickly, mawkish, cloying, sugary, sickening, nauseating; *informal* schmaltzy, cheesy, corny, toe-curling; *Brit. informal* soppy, twee; *N. Amer. informal* cornball.

sack ▶ noun =bag, pouch, pocket, pack.
▶ verb *(informal)* =dismiss, discharge, lay off, make redundant, let go, throw out; *Military* cashier; *informal* fire, give someone the sack, give someone their marching orders; *Brit. informal* give someone their cards.
■ **the sack** *(informal)* =dismissal, discharge, redundancy; *informal* the boot, the axe, the heave-ho, one's marching orders, the elbow, the push.

sackcloth ▶ noun =hessian, sacking, burlap; *N. Amer.* gunny.
■ **wearing sackcloth and ashes** =penitent, contrite, remorseful, apologetic, ashamed.

sacred ▶ adjective 1 *a sacred place* =holy, hallowed, blessed, consecrated, sanctified. 2 *sacred music* =religious, spiritual, devotional, church, ecclesiastical.
−OPPOSITES secular, profane.

sacrifice ▶ noun 1 *the sacrifice of animals* =(ritual) slaughter, (votive) offering. 2 *the sacrifice of privileges* =surrender, giving up, abandonment, renunciation, forfeiture, relinquishment.
▶ verb 1 *two goats were sacrificed* =offer up, slaughter. 2 *he sacrificed his principles* =give up, abandon, renounce, relinquish; betray. 3 *he sacrificed his life* =give (up), lay down; surrender, forfeit.

sacrilege ▶ noun =desecration, profanity, blasphemy, irreverence, disrespect.
−OPPOSITES piety.

sacrilegious ▶ adjective =profane, blasphemous, impious, sinful, irreverent, unholy, disrespectful.

sacrosanct ▶ adjective =sacred, hallowed, inviolable, inalienable; off limits, protected.

sad ▶ adjective 1 *we felt sad* =unhappy, sorrowful, depressed, downcast, miserable, down, despondent, wretched, glum, gloomy, doleful, melancholy, mournful, forlorn, heartbroken; *informal* blue, down in the mouth, down in the dumps. 2 *a sad story* =tragic, unhappy, miserable, wretched, sorry, pitiful, pathetic, heartbreaking, heart-rending. 3 *a sad state of affairs* =unfortunate, regrettable, sorry, deplorable, lamentable, pitiful, shameful, disgraceful.
−OPPOSITES happy, cheerful, fortunate.

sadden ▶ verb =depress, dispirit, deject, dishearten, grieve, discourage, upset, get down, break someone's heart.

saddle ▶ verb =burden, encumber, lumber; land, charge; impose something on.

sadism ▶ noun =cruelty, viciousness, callousness, cold-bloodedness, brutality; perversion; sadomasochism.

sadistic ▶ adjective =cruel, vicious, brutal, fiendish, callous; perverted; sadomasochistic.

sadness ▶ noun =unhappiness, sorrow, dejection, depression, misery, despondency, wretchedness, gloom, gloominess, melancholy, mournfulness, woe, heartache, grief.

safe ▶ adjective 1 *the jewels are safe in the bank* =secure, protected, out of harm's way. 2 *the children are all safe* =unharmed, unhurt, uninjured, unscathed, all right, fine, well, in one piece, out of danger; *informal* OK. 3 *a safe place* =secure, sound, impregnable, invulnerable; secret. 4 *a safe driver* =cautious, circumspect, prudent, careful; unadventurous, conservative. 5 *the drug is safe* =harmless, innocuous, benign, non-toxic, non-poisonous.

—OPPOSITES insecure, dangerous, reckless, harmful.

safeguard ▸ noun =**protection**, defence, buffer, provision, security; surety, cover, insurance.
▸ verb =**protect**, preserve, conserve, save, secure, shield, guard, keep safe.
—OPPOSITES jeopardize.

safety ▸ noun **1** *the safety of the residents* =**welfare**, well-being, protection, security. **2** *the safety of ferries* =**security**, soundness, dependability, reliability. **3** *the safety of the shore* =**shelter**, sanctuary, refuge.

sag ▸ verb **1** *he sagged back in his chair* =**sink**, slump, loll, flop, crumple. **2** *the floors all sag* =**dip**, droop; bulge, bag.

saga ▸ noun **1** *Icelandic sagas* =**epic**, legend, (folk) tale, romance, narrative, myth. **2** *the saga of how they met* =**story**, tale, yarn.

sage ▸ noun =**wise man/woman**, philosopher, scholar, guru; prophet, mystic.

sail ▸ verb **1** *we sailed across the Atlantic* =**voyage**, travel, navigate, cruise. **2** *we sail tonight* =**set sail**, put to sea, leave, weigh anchor. **3** *who is sailing the ship?* =**steer**, pilot, captain; *informal* skipper. **4** *clouds were sailing past* =**glide**, drift, float, flow, sweep, skim, coast, flit, scud. **5** *a pencil sailed past his ear* =**whizz**, speed, streak, shoot, whip, zoom, flash; fly; *informal* zip.
■ **sail through** =**succeed/pass easily**, romp/walk through.

sailor ▸ noun =**seaman**, seafarer, mariner; yachtsman, yachtswoman; hand; *Brit. informal* matelot; merchant seaman.

saint ▸ noun

> **WORD LINKS**
>
> *writing about saints:* **hagiography**
> *fear of saints:* **hagiophobia**

saintly ▸ adjective =**holy**, godly, pious; religious, devout, spiritual, prayerful; virtuous, righteous, good, pure.
—OPPOSITES ungodly.

sake ▸ noun **1** *for the sake of clarity* =**purpose(s)**, reason(s). **2** *for her son's sake* =**benefit**, advantage, good, well-being, welfare.

salacious ▸ adjective =**pornographic**, obscene, indecent, crude, lewd, vulgar, dirty, filthy; erotic, titillating, arousing, suggestive, sexy, risqué, ribald, smutty; X-rated; *informal* porn, porno, blue; euphemistic adult.

salary ▸ noun =**pay**, wages, earnings, payment, remuneration, fee(s), stipend, income; *formal* emolument.

sale ▸ noun **1** *the sale of firearms* =**selling**; dealing, trading. **2** *they make a sale every minute* =**deal**, transaction, bargain.
—OPPOSITES purchase.
■ **for/on sale** =**on the market**, on offer, available, obtainable.

salesperson ▸ noun =**(sales/shop) assistant**, salesman, saleswoman, agent; shopkeeper, trader, merchant, dealer; *N. Amer.* clerk; *informal* rep.

salient ▸ adjective =**important**, main, principal, major, chief, primary; noteworthy, outstanding, conspicuous, striking, noticeable, obvious, prominent, dominant; key, crucial, vital, essential.
—OPPOSITES minor.

saliva ▸ noun =**spit**, spittle, dribble, drool, slaver, slobber, sputum.

sallow ▸ adjective =**yellowish**, jaundiced; unhealthy, sickly, washed out, peaky.

salon ▸ noun =**shop**, establishment, premises; boutique, store.

salty ▸ adjective =**salt**, salted, saline, briny, brackish.

salubrious ▸ adjective =**pleasant**, agreeable, nice, select, high-class; *Brit.* upmarket; *informal* posh, swanky, classy; *Brit. informal* swish; *N. Amer. informal* swank.

salutary ▸ adjective =**beneficial**, advantageous, good, profitable, productive, helpful, useful, valuable, worthwhile; timely.
—OPPOSITES unwelcome.

salutation ▸ noun =**greeting**, salute, address, welcome.

salute ▸ noun =**tribute**, testimonial, homage, honour; celebration (of), acknowledgement (of).
▸ verb =**pay tribute to**, pay homage to, honour, celebrate, acknowledge, take one's hat off to.

salvage ▸ verb =**rescue**, save, recover, retrieve, reclaim.

salvation ▸ noun **1** *praying for salvation* =**redemption**, deliverance. **2** *that man was her salvation* =**lifeline**; means of escape; saviour.
—OPPOSITES damnation.

salve ▸ noun =**ointment**, cream, balm, unguent; embrocation, liniment.

salver ▶ noun =**platter**, plate, dish, tray.

same ▶ adjective **1** *we both stayed at the same hotel* =**identical**, selfsame, very same. **2** *they had the same symptoms* =**matching**, identical, alike, carbon-copy, twin; indistinguishable, inter-changeable, corresponding, equivalent, parallel, like, comparable, similar. **3** *it happened that same month* =**selfsame**; very.
–OPPOSITES another, different, dissimilar, varying.
■ **the same 1** *Louise said the same* =**the (very) same thing**, that. **2** *their menu is the same worldwide* =**unchanging**, unvarying, unvaried, consistent, uniform.

> WORD LINKS
> *of the same kind:* **homogeneous**

sample ▶ noun **1** *a sample of the fabric* =**specimen**, example, bit, snippet, swatch; taste, taster. **2** *a representative sample* =**cross section**, selection.
▶ verb *we sampled the food* =**try (out)**, taste, test, put to the test; appraise, evaluate; *informal* check out.
▶ adjective *a sample copy* =**specimen**, test, trial, pilot, dummy.

sanctimonious ▶ adjective =**self-righteous**, holier-than-thou, pious, churchy, moralizing, smug, superior, priggish, hypocritical, insincere; *informal* goody-goody.

sanction ▶ noun **1** *trade sanctions* =**penalty**, punishment, deterrent; restriction; embargo, ban, prohibition, boycott. **2** *the scheme has the sanction of the court* =**authorization**, consent, leave, permission, authority, dispensation, assent, acquiescence, agreement, approval, approbation, endorsement, blessing; *informal* the go-ahead, the thumbs up, the OK, the green light.
–OPPOSITES reward, prohibition.
▶ verb *the rally was sanctioned by the government* =**authorize**, permit, allow, endorse, approve, accept, back, support; *informal* OK.
–OPPOSITES prohibit.

sanctity ▶ noun =**importance**, primacy; centrality.

sanctuary ▶ noun **1** *the garden is our sanctuary* =**refuge**, haven, oasis, shelter, retreat, bolt-hole, hideaway. **2** *he was given sanctuary in the embassy* =**safety**, protection, shelter, immunity, asylum. **3** *a bird sanctuary* =**reserve**, park.

sand ▶ noun =**beach**, sands, (sea)shore; (sand) dunes.

sane ▶ adjective **1** *he is presumed to be sane* =**of sound mind**, in one's right mind, compos mentis, lucid, rational, balanced, stable, normal; *informal* all there. **2** *a sane suggestion* =**sensible**, practical, realistic, prudent, reasonable, rational, level-headed.
–OPPOSITES mad, foolish.

sanguine ▶ adjective =**optimistic**, bullish, hopeful, buoyant, positive, confident, cheerful, cheery; *informal* upbeat.
–OPPOSITES gloomy.

sanitary ▶ adjective =**hygienic**, clean, antiseptic, aseptic, sterile.

sanitized ▶ adjective =**censored**, doctored, expurgated, airbrushed, revised, edited.

sanity ▶ noun **1** *she was losing her sanity* =**mental health**, reason, rationality, stability, lucidity; sense, wits, mind. **2** *sanity has prevailed* =**(common/good) sense**, wisdom, prudence, rationality.

sap ▶ noun =**juice**, secretion, fluid, liquid.
▶ verb =**erode**, wear away/down, deplete, reduce, lessen, undermine, drain, bleed.

sarcasm ▶ noun =**irony**; derision, mockery, ridicule, scorn.

sarcastic ▶ adjective =**ironic**; sardonic, derisive, scornful, contemptuous, mocking; caustic, scathing, trenchant, acerbic; *Brit. informal* sarky; *N. Amer. informal* snarky.

sardonic ▶ adjective =**mocking** cynical, scornful, derisive, sneering, jeering; scathing, caustic, trenchant, cutting, acerbic.

sash ▶ noun =**belt**, cummerbund, waistband, girdle.

satanic ▶ adjective =**diabolical**, fiendish, devilish, demonic, ungodly, hellish, infernal, wicked, evil, sinful.

sate ▶ verb. *See* SATIATE.

satiate ▶ verb =**fill**, satisfy, sate; slake, quench; gorge, stuff, surfeit, glut, sicken, nauseate.

satire ▶ noun =**parody**, burlesque, caricature, irony; lampoon, skit; *informal* spoof, take-off, send-up.

satirical ▶ adjective =**mocking**, ironic, sardonic; acerbic; critical, irreverent, disparaging, disrespectful.

s

satirize ▸ verb =mock, ridicule, deride, make fun of, parody, lampoon, caricature, take off; criticize; *informal* send up, take the mickey out of.

satisfaction ▸ noun 1 *he derived great satisfaction from his work* =contentment, content, pleasure, gratification, fulfilment, enjoyment, happiness, pride. 2 *investors turned to the courts for satisfaction* =compensation, recompense, redress, reparation, restitution, repayment, reimbursement.

satisfactory ▸ adjective =adequate, all right, acceptable, good enough, sufficient, reasonable, competent, fair, decent, average, passable; fine, in order, up to scratch, up to the mark.
–OPPOSITES inadequate, poor.

satisfied ▸ adjective 1 *a satisfied smile* =pleased, contented, happy, proud, triumphant; smug, self-satisfied. 2 *I am satisfied that this is true* =convinced, certain, sure, positive, persuaded.
–OPPOSITES discontented, unhappy.

satisfy ▸ verb 1 *a chance to satisfy his lust* =fulfil, gratify, meet, fill; indulge; appease, assuage; quench, slake, satiate. 2 *she satisfied herself that it was an accident* =convince, assure; reassure. 3 *products which satisfy EC law* =comply with, meet, fulfil, answer, conform to; measure up to, come up to.
–OPPOSITES frustrate.

satisfying ▸ adjective =fulfilling, rewarding, gratifying, pleasing, enjoyable, pleasurable.

saturate ▸ verb 1 *rain had saturated the ground* =soak, drench, waterlog. 2 *the company has saturated the market* =flood, glut, oversupply, overfill, overload.

saturated ▸ adjective 1 *his trousers were saturated* =soaked, soaking (wet), wet through, sopping (wet), sodden, dripping, wringing wet, drenched; soaked to the skin. 2 *the saturated pitch* =waterlogged, flooded, boggy; awash.
–OPPOSITES dry.

sauce ▸ noun =relish, condiment, ketchup; dip, dressing; jus, coulis, gravy.

saucepan ▸ noun =pan, pot, casserole, skillet; billy, billycan.

saunter ▸ verb =stroll, amble, wander, meander, walk; *informal* mosey, tootle; *formal* promenade.

savage ▸ adjective 1 *savage dogs* =ferocious, fierce, vicious; wild, feral. 2 *a savage assault* =vicious, brutal, cruel, sadistic, ferocious, fierce, violent. 3 *a savage attack on free trade* =fierce, blistering, scathing, searing, stinging, devastating, withering, virulent, vitriolic.
–OPPOSITES tame, mild, civilized.
▸ noun *she described her assailants as savages* =brute, beast, monster, barbarian, sadist, animal.
▸ verb 1 *savaged by a dog* =maul, attack, lacerate, claw, bite. 2 *critics savaged the film* =criticize, attack, lambaste, condemn, denounce, pillory, revile; *informal* pan, tear to pieces, hammer, slam; *Brit. informal* slate, rubbish; *N. Amer. informal* trash; *Austral./NZ informal* bag, monster.

save ▸ verb 1 *the captain was saved by his crew* =rescue; set free, free, liberate, deliver, extricate; bail out; *informal* save someone's bacon/neck/skin. 2 *the house was saved from demolition* =preserve, keep, protect, safeguard; salvage, retrieve, reclaim, rescue. 3 *start saving old newspapers* =put/set aside, put by/to one side, keep, retain, reserve, conserve, stockpile, store, hoard; *informal* squirrel/stash away, hang on to. 4 *asking her saved a lot of trouble* =prevent, obviate, forestall, spare; stop; avoid, avert.
▸ preposition & conjunction *(formal) no one save herself* =except, apart from, but, other than, besides, aside from, bar.

saving ▸ noun 1 *a considerable saving in development costs* =reduction, cut, decrease, economy. 2 *I'll have to use my savings* =nest egg; capital, assets, funds, resources, reserves.

saviour ▸ noun 1 *the country's saviour* =rescuer, liberator, deliverer; champion, knight in shining armour, good Samaritan. 2 *the Saviour* =Christ, Jesus (Christ), Our Lord, the Son of God, the Son of Man.

savoir faire ▸ noun =social skill(s), social grace(s), urbanity, suavity, finesse, sophistication, poise, aplomb, polish, style, smoothness; *informal* savvy.
–OPPOSITES gaucheness.

savour ▸ verb *she savoured every moment* =relish, enjoy (to the full), appreciate, delight in, revel in, luxuriate in.
▸ noun *the subtle savour of wood smoke* =smell, aroma, fragrance, scent, perfume, bouquet; taste, flavour, tang, smack.

savoury ▸ adjective 1 *sweet or savoury dishes* =salty; spicy, tangy, meaty. 2 *one of the less savoury aspects of the affair* =acceptable, pleasant, appealing, palatable.

–OPPOSITES sweet, unappetizing.

▸ noun *cocktail savouries* =**canapé**, hors d'oeuvre, appetizer, titbit.

say ▸ verb 1 *he said her name* =**speak**, utter, voice, pronounce, vocalize. 2 *'I must go,' she said* =**declare**, state, announce, remark, observe, mention, comment, note, add; reply, respond, answer. 3 *he says he's innocent* =**claim**, maintain, assert, hold, insist, contend; allege. 4 *more than I can say* =**express**, put into words, articulate, communicate, make known, put/get across, convey, verbalize; reveal, divulge, impart, disclose; imply, suggest. 5 *they said a prayer* =**recite**, repeat, utter, deliver, perform. 6 *her watch said one twenty* =**indicate**, show, read. 7 *I'd say it's about five miles* =**estimate**, judge, guess, hazard a guess, predict, speculate, surmise, conjecture, venture; *informal* reckon. 8 *let's say you'd won a million pounds* =**suppose**, assume, imagine, presume.

▸ noun 1 *everyone had their say* =**chance/turn (to speak)**; *informal* twopenn'orth. 2 *don't I have any say in the matter?* =**influence**, sway, weight, voice, input.

saying ▸ noun =**proverb**, maxim, aphorism, axiom, adage, saw, tag, motto, epigram, dictum; expression, phrase, formula; slogan, catchphrase; platitude, cliché, commonplace, truism.

scalding ▸ adjective =**hot**, burning, blistering, searing, red-hot; piping hot; *informal* boiling (hot), sizzling.

scale ▸ noun 1 *the Celsius scale* =**system (of measurement)**. 2 *opposite ends of the social scale* =**hierarchy**, ladder, ranking, pecking order, order, spectrum. 3 *the scale of the map* =**ratio**, proportion. 4 *the scale of the disaster* =**extent**, size, scope, magnitude, dimensions, range, breadth, degree, reach.

▸ verb *thieves scaled an 8ft high fence* =**climb**, ascend, clamber/scramble up, shin (up); mount; *N. Amer.* shinny (up).

■ **scale something down** =**reduce**, cut (down/back), decrease, lessen, lower, trim, slim down, prune.

■ **scale something up** =**increase**, expand, augment, build up; step up, boost, escalate.

scaly ▸ adjective =**dry**, flaky, flaking, rough, scabrous, mangy.

scamper ▸ verb =**scurry**, scuttle, dart, run, rush, race, dash, hurry; *informal* scoot.

scan ▸ verb 1 *Adam scanned the horizon* =**scrutinize**, examine, study, inspect, survey, search, scour, sweep; look/stare/gaze at, eye, watch; *informal* check out; *N. Amer. informal* scope. 2 *I scanned the papers* =**glance/look through**, have a look at, run/cast one's eye over, skim/flick/flip/leaf through.

▸ noun 1 *a quick scan through the report* =**glance**, look, flick, browse. 2 *a brain scan* =**examination**, screening.

scandal ▸ noun 1 *a scandal that led him to resign* =**affair**, issue, incident, outrage; skeleton in the closet; *informal* -gate. 2 *it's a scandal* =**disgrace**, outrage; (crying) shame, sin. 3 *a name tarnished by scandal* =**(malicious) gossip**, (malicious) rumour(s), slander, libel, calumny, aspersions, muckraking; *informal* dirt.

scandalize ▸ verb =**shock**, appal, outrage, horrify, disgust; offend, affront, cause raised eyebrows.

–OPPOSITES impress.

scandalous ▸ adjective 1 *a scandalous waste of money* =**disgraceful**, shocking, outrageous, monstrous, criminal, wicked, shameful, appalling, deplorable, inexcusable, intolerable, unforgivable, unpardonable. 2 *a series of scandalous affairs* =**discreditable**, disreputable, dishonourable, improper, unseemly, sordid. 3 *scandalous rumours* =**scurrilous**, malicious, slanderous, libellous, defamatory.

scant ▸ adjective =**little**, little or no, minimal, limited, negligible, meagre; insufficient, inadequate.

–OPPOSITES abundant, ample.

scanty ▸ adjective 1 *their scanty wages* =**meagre**, scant, minimal, limited, modest, restricted, sparse, tiny, small, paltry, negligible; scarce, in short supply, thin on the ground, few and far between; *informal* measly, piddling, mingy, pathetic. 2 *her scanty nightdress* =**skimpy**, revealing; short, brief; low, low-cut.

–OPPOSITES ample, plentiful.

scapegoat ▸ noun =**whipping boy**, Aunt Sally; *informal* fall guy; *N. Amer. informal* patsy.

scar ▸ noun 1 *the scar on his arm* =**mark**, blemish, disfigurement, discoloration; pockmark, pit; lesion; stitches. 2 *psychological scars* =**trauma**, damage, injury.

▸ verb 1 *scarred for life* =**disfigure**, mark,

blemish. **2** *a landscape scarred by mining* =**damage**, spoil, mar, deface, injure. **3** *she was deeply scarred* =**traumatize**, damage, injure; distress, disturb, upset.

scarce ▸ adjective **1** *food was scarce* =**in short supply**, scant, meagre, sparse, hard to find, hard to come by, insufficient, deficient, inadequate. **2** *wading birds are now scarce* =**rare**, few and far between, thin on the ground.
–OPPOSITES plentiful.

scarcely ▸ adverb **1** *she could scarcely hear him* =**barely**, only just. **2** *I scarcely see her* =**rarely**, seldom, infrequently, not often, hardly ever; *informal* once in a blue moon. **3** *this could scarcely be an accident* =**surely not**, not, hardly.
–OPPOSITES often.

scarcity ▸ noun =**shortage**, dearth, lack, undersupply, insufficiency, paucity, poverty; deficiency, inadequacy; unavailability, absence.

scare ▸ verb *stop it, you're scaring me* =**frighten**, startle, alarm, terrify, unnerve, worry, intimidate, terrorize, cow; put the fear of God into, make someone's blood run cold; *informal* freak out, make someone's hair stand on end, make someone jump out of their skin; *Brit. informal* put the wind up; *N. Amer. informal* spook.
▸ noun *you gave me a scare* =**fright**, shock, start, turn, jump.

scared ▸ adjective =**frightened**, afraid, fearful, nervous, panicky; terrified, petrified, panic-stricken, scared stiff; *Scottish* feart; *informal* in a cold sweat, in a (blue) funk; *Brit. informal* funky, windy; *N. Amer. informal* spooked.

scaremonger ▸ noun =**alarmist**, prophet of doom, doom-monger; *informal* doom (and gloom) merchant.

scarf ▸ noun =**muffler**, headscarf; mantilla, stole, tippet; *N. Amer.* babushka.

scarper ▸ verb (*Brit. informal*). See RUN verb *sense 2.*

scary ▸ adjective (*informal*) =**frightening**, alarming, terrifying, hair-raising, spine-chilling, blood-curdling, horrifying, nerve-racking, unnerving, eerie, sinister; *informal* creepy, spine-tingling, spooky, hairy.

scathing ▸ adjective =**withering**, blistering, searing, devastating, fierce, ferocious, savage, severe, stinging, biting, cutting, virulent, vitriolic, scornful, bitter, harsh.

–OPPOSITES mild.

scatter ▸ verb **1** *scatter the seeds evenly* =**throw**, strew, toss, fling; sprinkle, spread, distribute, sow. **2** *the crowd scattered* | *onlookers were scattered in all directions* =**disperse**, break up, disband, separate, dissolve; drive, send, chase. **3** *the floor was scattered with books* =**cover**, dot, sprinkle, stipple, spot, pepper, litter.
–OPPOSITES gather, assemble.

scatterbrained ▸ adjective =**absent-minded**, forgetful, disorganized; dreamy, feather-brained, giddy; *informal* scatty, with a mind/memory like a sieve, dizzy, dippy.

scavenge ▸ verb =**search**, hunt, look, forage, rummage, root about/around, grub about/around.

scenario ▸ noun **1** *Walt wrote scenarios for various studios* =**plot**, outline, storyline, framework; screenplay, script. **2** *consider every possible scenario* =**situation**, course/chain of events; possibility, option.

scene ▸ noun **1** *the scene of the accident* =**location**, site, place, position, point, spot. **2** *the scene is London in the 1890s* =**background**, setting, context, milieu, backdrop. **3** *scenes of violence* =**incident**, event, episode, happening. **4** *an impressive mountain scene* =**view**, vista, outlook, panorama; landscape, scenery. **5** *she made a scene* =**fuss**, exhibition of oneself, performance, tantrum, commotion, disturbance, row, upset, furore; *informal* to-do; *Brit. informal* carry-on. **6** *the political scene* =**arena**, stage, sphere, world, milieu, realm, domain; field. **7** *a scene from a movie* =**clip**, section, segment, part, sequence, extract.

scenery ▸ noun **1** *beautiful scenery* =**landscape**, countryside, country, terrain, setting, surroundings, environment; view, vista, panorama. **2** *scenery and costumes* =**(stage) set**, backdrop; *technical* mise en scène.

scenic ▸ adjective =**picturesque**, pretty, pleasing, attractive, lovely, beautiful, charming; impressive, striking, spectacular, breathtaking; panoramic.

scent ▸ noun **1** *the scent of freshly cut hay* =**smell**, fragrance, aroma, perfume, savour, odour; bouquet, nose. **2** *a bottle of scent* =**perfume**, fragrance, eau de toilette; (eau de) cologne. **3** *the hounds picked up the scent* =**spoor**, trail, track.
▸ verb *a shark can scent blood from far away*

=**smell**, detect, pick up, register, sense, discern, recognize.

scented ▸ adjective =**perfumed**, fragranced, perfumy; sweet-smelling, fragrant, aromatic.

sceptic ▸ noun =**cynic**, doubter; pessimist, prophet of doom; unbeliever, doubting Thomas.

sceptical ▸ adjective =**dubious**, doubtful, taking something with a pinch of salt, doubting; cynical, distrustful, suspicious, disbelieving, unconvinced; pessimistic, defeatist, negative.
–OPPOSITES certain, convinced.

scepticism ▸ noun =**doubt**, a pinch of salt; disbelief, cynicism, distrust, suspicion, incredulity; pessimism, defeatism.

schedule ▸ noun **1** *our production schedule* =**plan**, programme, timetable, scheme. **2** *I have a busy schedule* =**timetable**, agenda, diary, calendar; itinerary.
▸ verb *a meeting has been scheduled* =**arrange**, organize, plan, programme, timetable, set up, line up; *N. Amer.* slate.
■ **ahead of schedule** =**early**, ahead of time; prematurely.
■ **behind schedule** =**late**, overdue, behind time.

scheme ▸ noun **1** *fund-raising schemes* =**plan**, project, programme, strategy, stratagem, tactic; system, procedure, design, formula, recipe; *Brit. informal* wheeze. **2** *his schemes and plots* =**plot**, intrigue, conspiracy; ruse, ploy, stratagem, manoeuvre, subterfuge; machinations; *informal* game, racket, scam. **3** *the poem's rhyme scheme* =**arrangement**, system, organization, configuration, pattern, format.
▸ verb *he schemed endlessly* =**plot**, conspire, intrigue, connive, manoeuvre, plan.

scheming ▸ adjective =**cunning**, crafty, calculating, devious, conniving, wily, sly, tricky, artful, slippery, manipulative, Machiavellian, unscrupulous; duplicitous, deceitful, underhand, treacherous.
–OPPOSITES ingenuous, honest.

schism ▸ noun =**division**, split, rift, breach, rupture, break, separation; chasm, gulf; discord, disagreement, dissension.

schismatic ▸ adjective =**separatist**, heterodox, dissident, dissenting, heret-

ical; breakaway, splinter.
–OPPOSITES orthodox.

scholar ▸ noun =**academic**, intellectual, learned person, man/woman of letters; authority, expert; *informal* egghead; *N. Amer. informal* pointy-head.

scholarly ▸ adjective =**learned**, erudite, academic, well read, widely read, intellectual; literary, lettered, educated, highbrow; studious, bookish, donnish, cerebral; *N. Amer. informal* pointy-headed.
–OPPOSITES uneducated, illiterate.

scholarship ▸ noun **1** *a centre of scholarship* =**learning**, knowledge, erudition, education, letters, culture, academic study/achievement. **2** *a scholarship of £2000* =**grant**, award, endowment, payment; *Brit.* bursary.

scholastic ▸ adjective =**academic**, educational, school, scholarly.

school ▸ noun **1** *the village school* =**educational institution**; academy, college; alma mater. **2** *the university's School of English* =**department**, faculty, division. **3** *the evolutionary school in linguistics* =**way of thinking**, persuasion, creed, credo, doctrine, belief, opinion, point of view; strand, approach, method, style.
▸ verb **1** *he was schooled in Paris* =**educate**, teach, instruct. **2** *he schooled her in horsemanship* =**train**, teach, tutor, coach, instruct, drill, discipline; prepare, groom; prime, verse.

> **WORD LINKS**
>
> relating to schools: **scholastic**

schooling ▸ noun =**education**, teaching, tuition, instruction, tutoring, tutelage; lessons.

schoolteacher ▸ noun =**teacher**, schoolmaster, schoolmistress, tutor; *Brit.* master, mistress; *N. Amer. informal* schoolmarm; *Austral./NZ informal* chalkie, schoolie; *formal* pedagogue.

science ▸ noun **1** *a science teacher* =**physics**, chemistry, biology; physical sciences, life sciences. **2** *the science of criminology* =**branch of knowledge**, body of knowledge/information, area of study, discipline, field.

scientific ▸ adjective **1** *scientific research* =**technological**, technical; evidence-based, empirical. **2** *a more scientific approach* =**systematic**, methodical, organized, ordered, orderly, meticulous, rigorous; exact, precise, accurate, math-

s

ematical; analytical, rational.

scintillating ▶ adjective =**brilliant**, dazzling, exciting, exhilarating, stimulating; sparkling, lively, vivacious, vibrant, animated, effervescent; witty, clever.
–OPPOSITES dull, boring.

scoff[1] ▶ verb =**mock**, deride, ridicule, sneer, jeer, laugh at, dismiss, belittle; *informal* pooh-pooh.

scoff[2] ▶ verb (Brit. informal) =**eat**, devour, consume, guzzle, gobble, wolf down, bolt; *informal* put away, nosh, polish off, demolish, shovel down, pig oneself on; *N. Amer. informal* scarf (down/up), snarf (down/up).

scold ▶ verb =**rebuke**, reprimand, reproach, reprove, admonish, chastise, chide, upbraid, berate, haul over the coals; *informal* tell off, dress down, give someone an earful, give someone a roasting, bawl out, give someone hell; *Brit. informal* tick off, have a go at, carpet, tear someone off a strip, give someone what for, give someone a rollicking/rocket/row; *N. Amer. informal* chew out, ream out; *Austral. informal* monster; *formal* castigate.
–OPPOSITES praise.

scoop ▶ noun 1 *a measuring scoop* =**spoon**, ladle, dipper. 2 *a scoop of ice cream* =**spoonful**, ladleful, portion, lump, ball; *informal* dollop.
▶ verb 1 *a hole was scooped out in the ground* =**hollow out**, gouge out, dig, excavate. 2 *cut the tomatoes in half and scoop out the flesh* =**remove**, take out, spoon out, scrape out. 3 *she scooped up armfuls of clothes* =**pick up**, gather up, lift, take up; snatch up, grab.

scope ▶ noun 1 *the scope of the investigation* =**extent**, range, breadth, width, reach, sweep, span; area, sphere, realm, compass, orbit, ambit, terms/field of reference, remit; limit. 2 *the scope for change is limited* =**opportunity**, freedom, latitude, leeway, capacity, room (to manoeuvre); possibility, chance.

scorch ▶ verb 1 *trees were scorched by the fire* =**burn**, sear, singe, char, blacken, discolour. 2 *grass scorched by the sun* =**dry up**, parch, wither, shrivel.

scorching ▶ adjective =**hot**, red-hot, blazing, flaming, fiery, burning, blistering, searing, sweltering, torrid; *N. Amer.* broiling; *informal* boiling (hot), baking (hot), sizzling.

–OPPOSITES freezing, mild.

score ▶ noun 1 *the final score was 4–3* =**result**, outcome; total, sum total, tally, count. 2 *an IQ score of 161* =**rating**, grade, mark, percentage.
▶ verb 1 *he's scored 13 goals this season* =**get**, gain, chalk up, achieve, make; record, rack up, notch up; *informal* bag, knock up. 2 *the piece was scored for flute* =**orchestrate**, arrange, set, adapt; write, compose. 3 *score the wood in criss-cross patterns* =**scratch**, cut, notch, incise, scrape, nick, gouge; mark.
■ **score points off** =**get the better of**, gain the advantage over, outdo, have the edge over; make a fool of, humiliate; *informal* get/be one up on, get one over on.
■ **score something out/through** =**cross out**, strike out, put a line through; delete, obliterate, expunge.

scorn ▶ noun *the scorn in his voice* =**contempt**, derision, disdain, mockery, sneering.
–OPPOSITES admiration, respect.
▶ verb 1 *critics scorned the talks* =**deride**, treat with contempt, pour/heap scorn on, mock, scoff at, sneer at, jeer at, laugh at; disparage; dismiss. 2 *they scorned my offers of help* =**spurn**, rebuff, reject, ignore, shun, snub.
–OPPOSITES admire, respect.

scornful ▶ adjective =**contemptuous**, derisive, withering, mocking, sneering, jeering, scathing, snide, disparaging, supercilious, disdainful.
–OPPOSITES admiring, respectful.

scotch ▶ verb =**put an end to**, put a stop to, nip in the bud, put the lid on; ruin, wreck, destroy, smash, shatter, demolish; frustrate, thwart; *informal* put paid to, put the kibosh on; *Brit. informal* scupper.

scot-free ▶ adverb =**unpunished**, without punishment.

Scotland ▶ noun =**Caledonia**; *Brit.* north of the border.

scoundrel ▶ noun =**rogue**, rascal, miscreant, good-for-nothing, reprobate; cheat, swindler, fraudster, trickster, charlatan; *informal* villain, rat, louse, swine, dog, skunk, heel, wretch, scumbag; *Irish informal* sleeven, spalpeen; *N. Amer. informal* rat fink; *informal, dated* rotter; *dated* cad; *archaic* blackguard, knave.

scour[1] ▶ verb *the saucepan needs scouring* =**scrub**, rub, clean, wash, cleanse, wipe;

polish, buff (up), shine, burnish; abrade.

scour² ▸ verb *Christine scoured the shops* =**search**, comb, hunt through, rummage through, go through with a fine-tooth comb, look high and low in; ransack, turn upside-down; *Austral./NZ informal* fossick through.

scourge ▸ noun =**affliction**, bane, curse, plague, menace, evil, misfortune, burden; blight, cancer, canker.
−OPPOSITES blessing, godsend.

scout ▸ noun **1** *scouts reported that the Romans were advancing* =**lookout**, outrider; spy. **2** *a lengthy scout round the area* =**reconnaissance**, reconnoitre; exploration, search, expedition; *informal* recce; *Brit. informal* shufti; *N. Amer. informal* recon. **3** *a record company scout* =**talent spotter**, talent scout; *N. Amer. informal* bird dog.

▸ verb **1** *I scouted around for some logs* =**search**, look, hunt, ferret about/around, root about/around. **2** *a patrol was sent to scout out the area* =**reconnoitre**, explore, inspect, investigate, spy out, survey; examine, scan, study, observe; *informal* check out, case; *Brit. informal* take a shufti round; *N. Amer. informal* recon.

scowl ▸ verb =**glower**, frown, glare, grimace, lour, look daggers at; *informal* give someone a dirty look.
−OPPOSITES smile, grin.

scraggy ▸ adjective =**scrawny**, thin, skinny, skin-and-bones, gaunt, bony, angular, gawky, raw-boned.
−OPPOSITES fat.

scramble ▸ verb **1** *we scrambled over the boulders* =**clamber**, climb, crawl, claw one's way, scrabble, struggle; *N. Amer.* shinny. **2** *the alcohol has scrambled his brains* =**muddle**, confuse, mix up, jumble (up), disarrange, disorganize, disorder, disturb, mess up.

▸ noun **1** *a short scramble over the rocks* =**clamber**, climb. **2** *the scramble for a seat* =**tussle**, jostle, scrimmage, scuffle, struggle, free-for-all, competition, jockeying; muddle, confusion, melee.

scrap ▸ noun **1** *a scrap of paper* =**fragment**, piece, bit, snippet, shred; offcut, oddment, remnant. **2** *there wasn't a scrap of evidence* =**bit**, speck, iota, particle, ounce, whit, jot, shred, scintilla. **3** *the foxes ate all our scraps* =**leftovers**, crumbs, remains, remnants, residue, odds and ends, bits and pieces. **4** *a sculpture made from scrap* =**waste (metal)**; rubbish, refuse, debris, detritus; *N. Amer.* garbage,

trash; *informal* junk.

▸ verb **1** *old computers are scrapped* =**throw away**, throw out, dispose of, get rid of, discard, dispense with, bin; decommission, break up, demolish; *informal* chuck (away/out), ditch, dump, junk, get shut of; *Brit. informal* get shot of; *N. Amer. informal* trash. **2** *MPs called for the plans to be scrapped* =**abandon**, drop, abolish, withdraw, do away with, put an end to, cancel, axe; *informal* ditch, dump, junk.
−OPPOSITES keep, preserve.

scrape ▸ verb **1** *we scraped all the paint off the windows* =**abrade**, sand, sandpaper, scour, scratch, rub, file. **2** *their boots scraped along the floor* =**grate**, creak, rasp, grind, scratch. **3** *Ellen scraped her shins on the wall* =**graze**, scratch, scuff, rasp, skin, cut, lacerate, bark, chafe.

▸ noun **1** *the scrape of her key in the lock* =**grating**, creaking, grinding, rasp, scratch. **2** *there was a long scrape on his shin* =**graze**, scratch, abrasion, cut, laceration, wound. **3** *(informal) he's always getting into scrapes* =**predicament**, plight, tight corner/spot, ticklish/tricky situation, problem, crisis, mess, muddle; *informal* jam, fix, stew, bind, hole, hot water; *Brit. informal* spot of bother.

■ **scrape by** =**manage**, cope, survive, muddle through/along, make ends meet, get by/along, make do, keep the wolf from the door, keep one's head above water, eke out a living; *informal* make out.

scrappy ▸ adjective =**disorganized**, untidy, disjointed, unsystematic, uneven, bitty, sketchy; piecemeal; fragmentary, incomplete, unfinished.

scratch ▸ verb **1** *the paintwork was scratched* =**score**, abrade, scrape, scuff. **2** *thorns scratched her skin* =**graze**, scrape, abrade, skin, cut, lacerate, bark, chafe; wound. **3** *many names had been scratched out* =**cross out**, strike out, score out, delete, erase, remove, expunge, obliterate. **4** *she was forced to scratch from the race* =**withdraw**, pull out of, back out of, bow out of, stand down.

▸ noun **1** *he had scratches on his cheek* =**graze**, scrape, abrasion, cut, laceration, wound. **2** *a scratch on the paintwork* =**score**, mark, line, scrape.

■ **up to scratch** =**good enough**, up to the mark, up to standard, up to par, satisfactory, acceptable, adequate, passable, sufficient, all right; *informal* OK, up to snuff.

scrawl ▸ verb =**scribble**, write hurriedly/untidily, dash off.
▸ noun =**scribble**, squiggle(s), hieroglyphics.

scrawny ▸ adjective =**skinny**, thin, as thin as a rake, skin-and-bones, gaunt, bony, angular, gawky, scraggy.
−OPPOSITES fat.

scream ▸ verb =**shriek**, screech, yell, howl, shout, bellow, bawl, cry out, call out, yelp, squeal, wail, squawk; *informal* holler.
▸ noun =**shriek**, screech, yell, howl, shout, bellow, bawl, cry, yelp, squeal, wail, squawk; *informal* holler.

screech ▸ verb & noun. See SCREAM.

screen ▸ noun 1 *he dressed behind the screen* =**partition**, (room) divider; windbreak. 2 *a computer with a 15-inch screen* =**display**, monitor, visual display unit, VDU; cathode ray tube, CRT. 3 *every window has a screen because of mosquitoes* =**mesh**, net, netting. 4 *the hedge acts as a screen against the wind* =**buffer**, protection, shield, shelter, guard.
▸ verb 1 *the end of the hall had been screened off* =**partition off**, divide off, separate off, curtain off. 2 *the cottage was screened by the trees* =**conceal**, hide, veil; shield, shelter, shade, protect. 3 *the prospective candidates will have to be screened* =**vet**, check, investigate; *informal* check out. 4 *all blood is screened for the virus* =**check**, test, examine, investigate. 5 *the programme is screened on Thursday* =**show**, broadcast, transmit, televise, put out, air.

screw ▸ noun 1 *four steel screws* =**bolt**, fastener. 2 *the handle needs a couple of screws to tighten it* =**turn**, twist, wrench. 3 *the ship's twin screws* =**propeller**, rotor.
▸ verb 1 *he screwed the lid back on the jar* =**tighten**, turn, twist, wind. 2 *the bracket was screwed in place* =**fasten**, secure, fix, attach. 3 *(informal) she intended to screw more money out of them* =**extort**, force, extract, wrest, wring, squeeze; *informal* bleed.
■ **screw something up** 1 *Christina screwed up her face in disgust* =**wrinkle (up)**, pucker, crumple, crease, furrow, contort, distort, twist. 2 *(informal) they'll screw up the whole thing* =**wreck**, ruin, destroy, damage, spoil; dash, shatter, scotch, mess up; *informal* louse up, foul up, put the kibosh on, banjax, do for; *Brit. informal* scupper, cock up.

scribble ▸ verb =**scrawl**, write hurriedly, write untidily, scratch, dash off, jot (down); doodle, sketch.
▸ noun =**scrawl**, squiggle(s), jottings; doodle, doodlings.

scrimp ■ **scrimp and save** =**economize**, skimp, save; be thrifty, be frugal, tighten one's belt, cut back, draw in one's horns, watch one's pennies; *N. Amer.* pinch the pennies.

script ▸ noun 1 *her neat, tidy script* =**handwriting**, writing, hand. 2 *the script of the play* =**text**, screenplay; libretto, score; lines, dialogue, words.

scripture ▸ noun =**the Bible**, the Holy Bible, Holy Writ, the Gospel, the Good Book, the Word of God; sacred text(s).

Scrooge ▸ noun =**miser**, pennypincher, niggard; *informal* skinflint, meanie, money-grubber, cheapskate; *N. Amer. informal* tightwad.
−OPPOSITES spendthrift.

scrounge ▸ verb =**beg**, borrow; *informal* cadge, sponge, bum, touch someone for; *N. Amer. informal* mooch; *Austral./NZ informal* bludge.

scrounger ▸ noun =**beggar**, parasite, cadger; *informal* sponger, freeloader; *N. Amer. informal* mooch, moocher, schnorrer; *Austral./NZ informal* bludger.

scrub¹ ▸ verb 1 *he scrubbed the kitchen floor* =**scour**, rub; clean, cleanse, wash, wipe. 2 *(informal) the plans were scrubbed* =**abandon**, scrap, drop, cancel, call off, axe, jettison, discard, discontinue, abort; *informal* ditch, dump, junk.

scrub² ▸ noun *there the buildings ended and the scrub began* =**brush**, brushwood, scrubland, undergrowth.

scruffy ▸ adjective =**shabby**, worn, down at heel, ragged, tattered, mangy, dirty; untidy, unkempt, bedraggled, messy, dishevelled, ill-groomed; *informal* tatty, the worse for wear; *N. Amer. informal* raggedy.
−OPPOSITES smart, tidy.

scrumptious ▸ adjective *(informal)* =**delicious**, delectable, mouthwatering, tasty, appetizing, toothsome; succulent, luscious; *informal* scrummy, yummy; *Brit. informal* moreish; *N. Amer. informal* finger-licking, nummy.
−OPPOSITES unpalatable.

scrunch ▸ verb =**crumple**, crunch, crush, rumple, screw up, squash, squeeze, compress; *informal* squidge.

scruples ▶ plural noun =**qualms**, compunction, hesitation, reservations, second thoughts, doubt(s), misgivings, uneasiness, reluctance.

scrupulous ▶ adjective =**careful**, meticulous, painstaking, thorough, assiduous, sedulous, attentive, conscientious, punctilious, searching, close, minute, rigorous, particular, strict.
–OPPOSITES careless.

scrutinize ▶ verb =**examine**, inspect, survey, study, look at, peruse; investigate, explore, probe, inquire into, go into, check.

scrutiny ▶ noun =**examination**, inspection, survey, study, perusal; investigation, exploration, probe, inquiry; *informal* going-over.

scud ▶ verb =**speed**, race, rush, sail, shoot, sweep, skim, whip, whizz, flash, fly, scurry, flit.

scuff ▶ verb =**scrape**, scratch, rub, abrade; mark.

scuffle ▶ noun =**fight**, struggle, tussle, fracas, rough and tumble, scrimmage; *informal* scrap, dust up, set-to, shindy; *N. Amer. informal* rough house; *Law, dated* affray.
▶ verb =**fight**, struggle, tussle, clash; *informal* scrap.

sculpt ▶ verb =**carve**, model, chisel, sculpture, fashion, form, shape, cut, hew.

sculpture ▶ noun =**model**, carving, statue, statuette, figure, figurine, effigy, bust, head, likeness; construction, form.

scum ▶ noun =**film**, layer, covering, froth; filth, dross, dirt.

scupper ▶ verb (*Brit. informal*) =**ruin**, wreck, destroy, sabotage, torpedo, spoil.

scurrilous ▶ adjective =**defamatory**, slanderous, libellous, scandalous, insulting, offensive; abusive, malicious; *informal* bitchy.

scurry ▶ verb =**hurry**, hasten, run, rush, dash; scamper, scuttle, scramble; *informal* scoot, beetle.
–OPPOSITES amble.

scuttle ▶ verb. *See* SCURRY.

sea ▶ noun **1** *the sea sparkled in the sun* =**(the) ocean**, the waves; *informal* the drink; *literary* the briny; *literary* the deep. **2** *the boat overturned in the heavy seas* =**waves**, swell, breakers. **3** *a sea of roofs and turrets* =**expanse**, stretch, area, tract, sweep, carpet, mass; multitude,

host, profusion, abundance, plethora.
–OPPOSITES land.
▶ adjective *sea creatures* =**marine**, ocean, oceanic; saltwater, seawater; oceangoing, seagoing, seafaring; maritime, naval, nautical; *technical* pelagic.
■ **at sea** =**confused**, perplexed, puzzled, baffled, mystified, bemused, bewildered, nonplussed, disconcerted, disoriented, dumbfounded, at a loss, at sixes and sevens; *informal* flummoxed, bamboozled, fazed; *N. Amer. informal* discombobulated.

> **WORD LINKS**
>
> *relating to the sea:* **marine, maritime, nautical**
> *under the sea:* **submarine**
> *surveying of the sea:* **hydrography**
> *fear of the sea:* **thalassophobia**

seafaring ▶ adjective =**maritime**, nautical, naval, seagoing, sea.

seal¹ ▶ noun **1** *the seal round the bath* =**sealant**, adhesive, mastic. **2** *the royal seal* =**emblem**, symbol, insignia, device, badge, crest, coat of arms, monogram, stamp.
▶ verb **1** *seal each bottle while it is hot* =**stop up**, seal up, cork, stopper, plug. **2** *he held out his hand to seal the bargain* =**clinch**, secure, settle, conclude, complete, establish, confirm, guarantee.
■ **seal of approval** =**ratification**, approval, blessing, consent, agreement, permission, sanction, endorsement, clearance.
■ **seal something off** *police sealed off the High Street* =**close off**, shut off, cordon off, fence off, isolate.

seal² ▶ noun

> **WORD LINKS**
>
> *male:* **bull**
> *female:* **cow**
> *young:* **pup, calf**
> *collective noun:* **rookery**

seam ▶ noun **1** *the seam was coming undone* =**join**, stitching. **2** *a seam of coal* =**layer**, stratum, vein, lode.

seaman ▶ noun =**sailor**, seafarer, mariner, boatman, hand; *Brit. informal* matelot.
–OPPOSITES landlubber.

seamy ▶ adjective =**sordid**, disreputable, seedy, sleazy, squalid, insalubrious, unwholesome, unsavoury, rough, unpleasant.
–OPPOSITES salubrious.

sear ▸ verb **1** *the heat of the blast seared his face* =**scorch**, burn, singe, char. **2** *sear the meat before adding the other ingredients* =**flash-fry**, seal, brown.

search ▸ verb **1** *I searched for the key* =**hunt**, look, seek, forage, fish about/around, look high and low, ferret about/around, root about/around, rummage about/around. **2** *he searched the house* =**look through**, scour, go through, sift through, comb, go through with a fine-tooth comb; turn upside down, turn inside out; *Austral./NZ informal* fossick through. **3** *the guards searched him* =**examine**, inspect, check, frisk.
▸ noun *we continued our search* =**hunt**, look, quest.
■ **in search of** =**searching for**, hunting for, seeking, looking for, on the lookout for, in pursuit of.

searching ▸ adjective =**penetrating**, piercing, probing, keen, shrewd, sharp, intent.

searing ▸ adjective **1** *the searing heat* =**scorching**, blistering, sweltering, blazing (hot), burning, fiery; *informal* boiling (hot), baking (hot), sizzling, roasting. **2** *searing pain* =**intense**, excruciating, agonizing, sharp, severe, extreme, racking.

seaside ▸ noun =**coast**, shore, seashore; beach, sand, sands; *technical* littoral.

season ▸ noun =**period**, time, time of year, spell, term.
▸ verb =**flavour**, add salt/pepper to, spice.
■ **in season** =**available**, obtainable, to be had, on offer, on the market; plentiful, abundant.

seasonable ▸ adjective =**usual**, expected, predictable, normal.

seasoned ▸ adjective =**experienced**, practised, well versed, knowledgeable, established, habituated, veteran, hardened, battle-scarred.
–OPPOSITES inexperienced.

seasoning ▸ noun =**flavouring**, salt and pepper; herbs, spices, condiments.

seat ▸ noun **1** *a wooden seat* =**chair**, bench, stool; (**seats**) seating, room; *Brit. informal* pew. **2** *the seat of government* =**headquarters**, base, centre, nerve centre, hub, heart; location, site, whereabouts, place. **3** *the family's country seat* =**residence**, (ancestral) home, mansion; *formal* abode.
▸ verb **1** *they seated themselves round the table*

=**position**, put, place; ensconce, install, settle; *informal* plonk, park. **2** *the hall seats 500* =**have room for**, contain, take, sit, hold, accommodate.

seating ▸ noun =**seats**, room, places, chairs, accommodation.

secede ▸ verb =**withdraw from**, break away from, break with, separate (oneself) from, leave, split with, split off from, disaffiliate from, resign from, pull out of; *informal* quit.
–OPPOSITES join.

secluded ▸ adjective =**sheltered**, private, concealed, hidden, unfrequented, sequestered, tucked away.
–OPPOSITES busy.

seclusion ▸ noun =**isolation**, solitude, retreat, privacy, retirement, withdrawal, purdah, concealment, hiding, secrecy.

second[1] ▸ adjective **1** *the second day of the trial* =**next**, following, subsequent. **2** *a second pair of glasses* =**additional**, extra, alternative, another, spare, backup; *N. Amer.* alternate. **3** *second prize* =**secondary**, subordinate, subsidiary, lesser, inferior. **4** *the conflict could turn into a second Vietnam* =**another**, new; repeat of, copy of, carbon copy of.
–OPPOSITES first.
▸ noun *Eva had been working as his second* =**assistant**, attendant, helper, aide, supporter, auxiliary, right-hand man/woman, girl/man Friday, second in command, number two, deputy, understudy, subordinate; *informal* sidekick.
▸ verb *George seconded the motion* =**(formally) support**, vote for, back, approve, endorse.
■ **second to none** =**incomparable**, matchless, unrivalled, inimitable, beyond compare/comparison, unparalleled, without equal, in a class of its own, peerless, unsurpassable; unique; perfect, consummate, transcendent, superlative, supreme.

second[2] ▸ noun *I'll only be gone for a second* =**moment**, bit, little while, short time, instant, split second; *informal* sec, jiffy; *Brit. informal* mo, tick, two ticks.
■ **in a second** =**very soon**, in a minute, in a moment, in a trice, shortly, any minute (now), in the twinkling of an eye, in (less than) no time, in no time at all; *N. Amer.* momentarily; *informal* in a jiffy, in two shakes (of a lamb's tail), before you can say Jack Robinson, in the blink of

an eye; *Brit. informal* in a tick, in two ticks, in a mo; *N. Amer. informal* in a snap.

second[3] ▸ verb *he was seconded to the Welsh office* =**assign (temporarily)**, lend; transfer, move, shift, relocate, send.

secondary ▸ adjective **1** *a secondary issue* =**less important**, subordinate, lesser, minor, peripheral, incidental, ancillary, subsidiary. **2** *secondary infections* =**accompanying**, attendant, concomitant, consequential, resulting, resultant.
–OPPOSITES primary, main.

second-class ▸ adjective =**second-rate**, second-best, inferior, lesser, unimportant.

second-hand ▸ adjective **1** *second-hand clothes* =**used**, old, worn, pre-owned, handed-down, hand-me-down, cast-off. **2** *second-hand information* =**indirect**; vicarious, mediated.
–OPPOSITES new, direct.
▸ adverb *I heard this second-hand* =**indirectly**; *informal* on the grapevine.
–OPPOSITES directly.

second in command ▸ noun =**deputy**, number two, subordinate, right-hand man/woman; understudy.

secondly ▸ adverb =**furthermore**, also, moreover; second, in the second place, next.

second-rate ▸ adjective =**inferior**, substandard, low-quality, below par, bad, poor, deficient, defective, faulty, shoddy, inadequate, insufficient, unacceptable; *Brit. informal* ropy, duff, rubbish.
–OPPOSITES first-rate, excellent.

secrecy ▸ noun **1** *the secrecy of the material* =**confidentiality**. **2** *a government which thrived on secrecy* =**secretiveness**, covertness, furtiveness, stealth.

secret ▸ adjective **1** *a secret plan* =**confidential**, top secret, classified, undisclosed, unknown, private, under wraps; *informal* hush-hush. **2** *a secret drawer in the table* =**hidden**, concealed, disguised. **3** *a secret campaign* =**clandestine**, covert, undercover, underground, surreptitious, cloak-and-dagger; *informal* hush-hush. **4** *a secret message* | *a secret code* =**cryptic**, encoded, coded; mysterious, abstruse, recondite, arcane, esoteric. **5** *a secret place* =**secluded**, private, concealed, hidden, out of the way, tucked away. **6** *a very secret person.* See SECRETIVE.
–OPPOSITES public, open.
▸ noun **1** *he just can't keep a secret* =**confi-**

dential matter; confidence; skeleton in the cupboard. **2** *the secrets of the universe* =**mystery**, enigma. **3** *the secret of their success* =**recipe**, (magic) formula, blueprint, key, answer, solution.
■ **in secret** =**secretly**, in private, privately, behind closed doors, behind the scenes, in camera, under cover, under the counter, discreetly, behind someone's back, furtively, stealthily, on the sly, on the quiet, conspiratorially, covertly, clandestinely, on the side; *informal* on the q.t.

secretary ▸ noun =**assistant**, personal assistant, PA, administrator, girl/man Friday.

secrete[1] ▸ verb *a substance secreted by the liver* =**produce**, discharge, emit, excrete, release, send out.
–OPPOSITES absorb.

secrete[2] ▸ verb *we secreted ourselves in the bushes* =**conceal**, hide, stow away; bury, cache; *informal* stash away.
–OPPOSITES reveal.

secretive ▸ adjective =**uncommunicative**, secret, unforthcoming, playing one's cards close to one's chest, reticent, reserved, silent, tight-lipped.
–OPPOSITES open, communicative.

secretly ▸ adverb **1** *they met secretly* =**in secret**, in private, privately, behind closed doors, in camera, behind the scenes, under cover, under the counter, behind someone's back, furtively, stealthily, on the sly, on the quiet, covertly, clandestinely, on the side; *informal* on the q.t. **2** *he was secretly jealous of Bart* =**privately**, in one's heart (of hearts), deep down.

sect ▸ noun =**(religious) cult**, (religious) group; denomination, order; splinter group, faction.

sectarian ▸ adjective =**factional**, separatist, partisan; doctrinaire, dogmatic, illiberal, intolerant, bigoted, narrow-minded.
–OPPOSITES tolerant, liberal.

section ▸ noun **1** *the separate sections of the box* =**part**, bit, segment, compartment, module, area. **2** *the last section of the questionnaire* =**subdivision**, part, subsection, portion, bit, chapter, passage, clause. **3** *the reference section of the library* =**department**, area, part, division.

sector ▸ noun **1** *every sector of the industry is affected* =**part**, branch, arm, division, area, department, field, sphere.

2 *the north-eastern sector of the town* =**district**, quarter, part, section, zone, region, area, belt.

secular ▸ adjective =**non-religious**, lay, temporal, worldly, earthly, profane.
–OPPOSITES holy, religious.

secure ▸ adjective **1** *check that all bolts are secure* =**fastened**, fixed, secured, done up; closed, shut, locked. **2** *a place where children feel secure* =**safe**, protected from harm/danger, safe and sound, out of harm's way, in a safe place, in safe hands, invulnerable; at ease, unworried, relaxed, happy, confident. **3** *a secure future* =**certain**, assured, reliable, dependable, settled, fixed.
–OPPOSITES loose, vulnerable, uncertain.
▸ verb **1** *secure the handle to the main body* =**fix**, attach, fasten, affix, connect, couple. **2** *the doors had not been properly secured* =**fasten**, close, shut, lock, bolt, chain, seal. **3** *he leapt out to secure the boat* =**tie up**, moor, make fast; anchor. **4** *efforts to secure the country against attack* =**protect**, make safe, fortify, strengthen. **5** *a written constitution would secure our rights* =**assure**, ensure, guarantee, protect, confirm, establish; enshrine. **6** *the division secured a major contract* =**obtain**, acquire, gain, get; *informal* land.

security ▸ noun **1** *the security of our citizens* =**safety**, protection. **2** *he could give her security* =**peace of mind**, stability, certainty. **3** *security at the court was tight* =**safety measures**, safeguards, surveillance, defence, protection, policing. **4** *additional security for your loan* =**guarantee**, collateral, surety, pledge, bond.
–OPPOSITES vulnerability, danger.

sedate[1] ▸ verb *the patient had to be sedated* =**tranquillize**, put under sedation, drug.

sedate[2] ▸ adjective **1** *a sedate pace* =**slow**, steady, dignified, unhurried, relaxed, measured, leisurely, slow-moving, easy, easy-going, gentle. **2** *he had lived a sedate life* =**calm**, placid, tranquil, quiet, uneventful; boring, dull.
–OPPOSITES exciting, fast.

sedative ▸ adjective =**tranquillizing**, calming, calmative, relaxing, soporific.
▸ noun =**tranquillizer**, sleeping pill; narcotic, opiate.

sedentary ▸ adjective =**sitting**, seated, desk-bound; inactive.

–OPPOSITES active.

sediment ▸ noun =**dregs**, lees, precipitate, deposit, grounds, residue, remains; silt; *technical* residuum.

sedition ▸ noun =**rabble-rousing**, subversion, troublemaking, provocation; rebellion, insurrection, mutiny, insurgence, civil disorder.

seditious ▸ adjective =**rabble-rousing**, provocative, inflammatory, subversive, troublemaking; rebellious, mutinous, insurgent.

seduce ▸ verb **1** *he tried to seduce her* =*euphemistic* have one's (wicked) way with, take advantage of. **2** *customers are seduced by the advertising* =**attract**, allure, lure, tempt, entice, beguile, inveigle, manipulate.

seductive ▸ adjective =**alluring**, tempting, beguiling, attractive; manipulative.

sedulous ▸ adjective =**diligent**, careful, meticulous, thorough, assiduous, attentive, industrious, conscientious, punctilious, scrupulous, painstaking, rigorous, particular.

see ▸ verb **1** *he saw her in the street* =**discern**, spot, notice, catch sight of, glimpse, make out, pick out, spy, distinguish, detect, perceive, note; *informal* clap/lay/set eyes on, clock; *literary* behold, espy. **2** *I saw a programme about it* =**watch**, look at, view; catch. **3** *would you like to see the house?* =**inspect**, view, look round, tour, survey, examine, scrutinize; *informal* give something a/the once-over. **4** *I finally saw what she meant* =**understand**, grasp, comprehend, follow, realize, appreciate, recognize, work out, get the drift of, perceive, fathom (out); *informal* get, latch on to, cotton on to, catch on to, tumble to, savvy, figure out, get a fix on; *Brit. informal* twig, suss (out). **5** *I must see what Victor is up to* =**find out**, discover, learn, ascertain, determine, establish. **6** *see that no harm comes to him* =**ensure**, make sure/certain, see to it, take care, mind. **7** *I see trouble ahead* =**foresee**, predict, forecast, prophesy, anticipate, envisage, picture, visualize. **8** *later, I saw him in town* =**encounter**, meet, run into/across, come across, stumble on/across, happen on, chance on; *informal* bump into. **9** *they see each other from time to time* =**meet**, meet up with, get together with, socialize with. **10** *you'd better see a doctor* =**consult**, confer with, talk to, speak to, have recourse to, call in, turn to, ask. **11** *he's seeing someone else now* =**go out with**, date, take out, be involved with; *informal* go steady with; *N. Amer. informal, dated* step out with; *dated* court. **12** *he saw her to her car* =**escort**, accompany, show, walk, conduct, lead, take, usher.

■ **see someone through** =**sustain**, encourage, buoy up, keep going, support, comfort, help (out), stand by, stick by.
■ **see something through** =**persevere with**, persist with, continue (with), carry on with, keep at, follow through, stay with; *informal* stick at, stick it out.
■ **see to** =**attend to**, deal with, see about, take care of, look after, sort out, fix, organize, arrange.

seed ▸ noun =**pip**, stone, kernel.
■ **go/run to seed** =**deteriorate**, degenerate, decline, decay, fall into decay, go to rack and ruin, moulder, rot; *informal* go to pot, go to the dogs, go down the toilet.

> **WORD LINKS**
>
> *relating to seeds:* **seminal**

seedy ▸ adjective **1** *the seedy world of prostitution* =**sordid**, disreputable, seamy, sleazy, squalid, unsavoury. **2** *a seedy part of town* =**dilapidated**, tumbledown, ramshackle, decrepit, gone to rack and ruin, run down, down at heel, shabby, dingy, slummy, insalubrious, squalid; *informal* crummy; *Brit. informal* grotty.
–OPPOSITES high-class.

seek ▸ verb **1** *he is seeking work* =**search for**, try to find, look for, be after, hunt for. **2** *the company is seeking a judicial review* =**try to obtain**, work towards, be intent on, aim at/for. **3** *he sought help from a motorist* =**ask for**, request, solicit, call for, appeal for, apply for, put in for. **4** *we constantly seek to improve the service* =**try**, attempt, endeavour, strive, work, do one's best.

seem ▸ verb =**appear (to be)**, have the appearance/air of being, give the impression of being, look; come across as, strike someone as, sound.

seeming ▸ adjective =**apparent**, ostensible, supposed, outward, surface, superficial.
–OPPOSITES actual, genuine.

seemingly ▸ adverb =**apparently**, on the face of it, to all appearances, as far as one can see/tell, on the surface, to all

intents and purposes, outwardly, superficially, supposedly.

seemly ▸ adjective =**decorous**, proper, decent, becoming, fitting, suitable, appropriate, in good taste, the done thing, right, correct, acceptable.
–OPPOSITES unseemly, unbecoming.

seep ▸ verb =**ooze**, trickle, exude, drip, dribble, flow, issue, escape, leak, drain, bleed, filter, percolate, soak.

see-saw ▸ verb =**fluctuate**, swing, go up and down, rise and fall, oscillate, alternate, yo-yo, vary.

seethe ▸ verb **1** *the water seethed with fish* =**teem**, swarm, boil, swirl, churn, surge, bubble, heave. **2** *I seethed at the injustice of it all* =**be angry**, be furious, be enraged, be incensed, be beside oneself, boil, simmer, rage, rant, rave, storm, fume, smoulder; *informal* be livid, foam at the mouth, be steamed up, be hot under the collar; *Brit. informal* do one's nut, throw a wobbly.

see-through ▸ adjective =**transparent**, translucent, clear; thin, lightweight, flimsy, sheer, diaphanous, filmy, gauzy.
–OPPOSITES opaque.

segment ▸ noun =**piece**, bit, section, part, chunk, portion, division, slice; fragment, wedge, lump, tranche.
▸ verb =**divide (up)**, subdivide, separate, split, cut up, carve up, slice up, break up.
–OPPOSITES amalgamate.

segregate ▸ verb =**separate**, set apart, keep apart, isolate, quarantine, closet; partition, divide.
–OPPOSITES amalgamate.

seize ▸ verb **1** *she seized the microphone* =**grab**, grasp, snatch, take hold of. **2** *rebels seized the air base* =**capture**, take, overrun, occupy, conquer, take over. **3** *the drugs were seized by customs* =**confiscate**, impound, commandeer, requisition, appropriate, expropriate. **4** *terrorists seized his wife* =**kidnap**, abduct, take captive, take prisoner, take hostage; *informal* snatch.
–OPPOSITES relinquish, release.

■ **seize on** *they seized on the opportunity* =**take advantage of**, exploit, grasp with both hands, leap at, jump at, pounce on.

seizure ▸ noun **1** *Napoleon's seizure of Spain* =**capture**, takeover, annexation, invasion, occupation, colonization. **2** *the seizure of defaulters' property* =**confiscation**, appropriation, expropriation, sequestration. **3** *the seizure of UN staff* =**kidnapping**, kidnap, abduction. **4** *the baby suffered a seizure* =**convulsion**, fit, spasm, paroxysm; *Medicine* ictus.

seldom ► adverb =**rarely**, infrequently, hardly (ever), scarcely (ever); *informal* once in a blue moon.
–OPPOSITES often.

select ► verb *select the correct tool for the job* =**choose**, pick (out), single out, sort out, take.
► adjective **1** *a small, select group* =**choice**, hand-picked, elite; *informal* top-flight. **2** *a very select area* =**exclusive**, privileged; wealthy; *informal* posh.
–OPPOSITES inferior.

selection ► noun **1** *Jim made his selection* =**choice**, pick; option, preference. **2** *a wide selection of dishes* =**range**, array, diversity, variety, assortment, mixture. **3** *a selection of his poems* =**anthology**, assortment, collection, assemblage; miscellany, medley.

selective ► adjective =**discerning**, discriminating, exacting, demanding, particular; fussy, fastidious, faddish; *informal* choosy, pernickety, picky.

self ► noun =**ego**, I, oneself, persona, person, identity, character, personality, psyche, soul, spirit, mind, inner self.
–OPPOSITES other.

> **WORD LINKS**
>
> *relating to oneself:* **auto-**
> *story of one's own life:* **autobiography**
> *obsession with oneself:* **egomania**
> *killing oneself:* **suicide**

self-assembly ► adjective =**flat-pack**, kit, self-build, do-it-yourself, DIY.

self-assurance ► noun =**self-confidence**, confidence, assertiveness, self-reliance, self-possession, composure.
–OPPOSITES diffidence.

self-assured ► adjective =**self-confident**, confident, assertive, assured, authoritative, self-possessed, poised.

self-centred ► adjective =**egocentric**, egotistic, self-absorbed, self-obsessed, self-seeking, self-interested, self-serving; narcissistic, vain; inconsiderate, thoughtless; *informal* looking after number one.

self-confidence ► noun =**morale**, confidence, self-assurance, assurance, composure.

self-conscious ► adjective =**embarrassed**, uncomfortable, uneasy, nervous.
–OPPOSITES confident.

self-contained ► adjective **1** *a self-contained unit* =**complete**, independent, separate, free-standing, stand-alone, autonomous. **2** *a very self-contained child* =**independent**, self-sufficient, self-reliant.

self-control ► noun =**self-discipline**, restraint, self-possession, will power, composure; moderation, temperance, abstemiousness; *informal* cool.

self-denial ► noun =**self-sacrifice**, selflessness, unselfishness; asceticism, abstemiousness, abstinence, abstention.
–OPPOSITES self-indulgence.

self-discipline ► noun =**self-control**; restraint, self-restraint; will power, strong-mindedness, moral fibre.

self-employed ► adjective =**freelance**, independent, casual; consultant.

self-esteem ► noun =**self-respect**, pride, dignity, self-regard, faith in oneself; morale, self-confidence, confidence, self-assurance.

self-evident ► adjective =**obvious**, clear, plain, evident, apparent, manifest, patent.
–OPPOSITES unclear.

self-explanatory ► adjective =**easily understood**, comprehensible, intelligible, straightforward, unambiguous, accessible, crystal clear, self-evident, obvious.
–OPPOSITES impenetrable.

self-governing ► adjective =**independent**, sovereign, autonomous, free; self-determining.
–OPPOSITES dependent.

self-important ► adjective =**conceited**, arrogant, bumptious, full of oneself, puffed up, pompous, overbearing; presumptuous, sententious.
–OPPOSITES humble.

self-indulgent ► adjective =**hedonistic**, pleasure-seeking, sybaritic, indulgent, luxurious, epicurean; intemperate, immoderate, overindulgent, excessive, extravagant, licentious, dissolute, decadent.
–OPPOSITES abstemious.

self-interest ► noun =**self-seeking**, self-regard; selfishness; *informal* looking

after number one.
–OPPOSITES altruism.

self-interested ▸ adjective = self-seeking, self-serving, selfish.

selfish ▸ adjective = egocentric, egotistic, self-centred, self-absorbed, self-obsessed, self-seeking, self-serving, wrapped up in oneself; inconsiderate, thoughtless, unthinking, uncaring; mean, miserly, grasping, greedy, mercenary, acquisitive, opportunistic; *informal* looking after number one.
–OPPOSITES altruistic.

selfless ▸ adjective = unselfish, altruistic; considerate, compassionate, kind, noble, generous, magnanimous, ungrudging.
–OPPOSITES inconsiderate.

self-possessed ▸ adjective = assured, self-assured, calm, cool, composed, at ease, unperturbed, unruffled, confident, self-confident, poised; *informal* together, unfazed, unflappable.
–OPPOSITES unsure.

self-reliant ▸ adjective = self-sufficient, self-contained, able to stand on one's own two feet; independent.

self-respect ▸ noun = self-esteem, self-regard, pride, dignity, morale, self-confidence.

self-restraint ▸ noun = self-control, restraint, self-discipline, will power, moderation, temperance, abstemiousness.
–OPPOSITES self-indulgence.

self-righteous ▸ adjective = sanctimonious, holier-than-thou, self-satisfied, smug, priggish, complacent, pious, moralizing, superior, hypocritical; *informal* goody-goody.
–OPPOSITES humble.

self-sacrifice ▸ noun = self-denial, selflessness, unselfishness.

self-satisfied ▸ adjective = complacent, self-congratulatory, smug, superior, pleased with oneself.

self-seeking ▸ adjective = self-interested, self-serving, selfish; *informal* looking after number one.
–OPPOSITES altruistic.

self-styled ▸ adjective = would-be, so-called, self-appointed, professed; supposed, alleged.

self-sufficient ▸ adjective = self-supporting, self-reliant, self-sustaining, able to stand on one's own two

feet; independent.

self-willed ▸ adjective = wilful, contrary, perverse, uncooperative, wayward, headstrong, stubborn, obstinate, obdurate, pig-headed, intransigent, recalcitrant, intractable; *Brit. informal* bloody-minded; *formal* refractory.
–OPPOSITES biddable.

sell ▸ verb 1 *they are selling their house* = **put up for sale**, put on the market, get rid of, auction (off); trade in. **2** *he sells cakes* = **trade in**, deal in, traffic in, stock, carry, offer for sale, peddle, retail, market. **3** *the book should sell well* = **go**; move, be in demand. **4** *it sells for £70* = **cost**, be priced at, retail at, go for, be.
–OPPOSITES buy.

■ **sell out 1** *we've sold out of petrol* = **have none left**, be out of, have run out (of). **2** *the book sold out quickly* = **be bought (up)**, go. **3** *the band has sold out* = **abandon one's principles**, prostitute oneself, sell one's soul, betray one's ideals.

■ **sell someone out = betray**, inform on; be unfaithful to, double-cross, stab in the back; *informal* tell on, sell down the river, stitch up, do the dirty on; *Brit. informal* grass on, shop; *N. Amer. informal* finger.

seller ▸ noun = vendor, retailer, purveyor, supplier, stockist, trader, merchant, dealer; salesperson, salesman, saleswoman, pedlar; auctioneer.

semblance ▸ noun = (outward) **appearance**, air, show, facade, front, veneer, guise, pretence.

seminal ▸ adjective = influential, formative, groundbreaking, pioneering, original, innovative; major, important.

seminar ▸ noun 1 *a seminar for education officials* = **conference**, symposium, meeting, convention, forum, summit. **2** *a history seminar* = **study group**, workshop, tutorial, class.

send ▸ verb 1 *they sent a message to HQ* = **dispatch**, post, mail, consign, direct, forward; transmit, convey, communicate; broadcast. **2** *we sent for a doctor* = **call**, summon; ask for, request, order. **3** *the pump sent out a jet of petrol* = **propel**, project, eject, deliver, discharge, spout, fire, shoot, release; throw, let fly, spew. **4** *it's enough to send one mad* = **make**, drive, turn.
–OPPOSITES receive.

■ **send someone down** *(informal)* = **send to prison**, imprison, jail, incarcerate, lock up, confine, detain, intern; *informal*

s

put away; *Brit. informal* bang up.

■ **send someone off** *(Sport)* =**order off**, dismiss; show the red card; *informal* red-card, send for an early bath.

■ **send someone/something up** *(informal)* =**satirize**, ridicule, make fun of, parody, lampoon, mock, caricature, imitate, ape; *informal* take off, spoof, take the mickey out of.

send-off ▶ noun =**farewell**, goodbye, adieu, leave-taking, valediction; funeral.
–OPPOSITES welcome.

send-up ▶ noun *(informal)* =**satire**, lampoon, pastiche, caricature, imitation, impression, impersonation; *informal* spoof, take-off.

senile ▶ adjective =**doddering**, decrepit, senescent, infirm, feeble; (mentally) confused, having Alzheimer's (disease), having senile dementia; *informal* gaga.

senior ▶ adjective **1** *senior school pupils* =**older**, elder. **2** *a senior officer* =**superior**, higher-ranking, more important; *N. Amer.* ranking. **3** *Albert Stone Senior* =**the Elder**; *Brit.* major; *N. Amer.* I.
–OPPOSITES junior, subordinate.

senior citizen ▶ noun =**retired person**, (old-age) pensioner, OAP; old person, elderly person, geriatric; *N. Amer.* senior, retiree, golden ager; *informal* old stager, old-timer, oldie, wrinkly, crumbly.

seniority ▶ noun =**rank**, superiority, standing, primacy, precedence, priority; age.

sensation ▶ noun **1** *a sensation of heaviness* =**feeling**, sense, perception, impression. **2** *she caused a sensation* =**commotion**, stir, uproar, furore, scandal, impact; *informal* splash, to-do, hullabaloo.

sensational ▶ adjective **1** *a sensational murder trial* =**shocking**, scandalous, appalling; amazing, startling, astonishing; fascinating, interesting, noteworthy, significant, remarkable, momentous, historic, newsworthy. **2** *sensational stories* =**overdramatized**, melodramatic, exaggerated, sensationalist; graphic, explicit, lurid; *informal* shock-horror, juicy. **3** *(informal) she looked sensational* =**gorgeous**, stunning, wonderful, exquisite, lovely, radiant, delightful, charming, enchanting, captivating; superb, excellent, first-class; *informal* great, terrific, tremendous, fantastic, fabulous, fab, heavenly, divine, knockout, awesome,

magic, wicked, out of this world; *Brit. informal* smashing, brilliant, brill.
–OPPOSITES dull, understated, unremarkable.

sense ▶ noun **1** *the sense of touch* =**(sensory) faculty**, sensation, perception; sight, hearing, touch, taste, smell. **2** *a sense of guilt* =**feeling**, awareness, sensation, recognition. **3** *a sense of humour* =**appreciation**, awareness, understanding, comprehension, discernment. **4** *she had the sense to leave* =**wisdom**, common sense; wit, intelligence, cleverness, shrewdness, judgement, reason, logic, brain(s); *informal* gumption, nous, horse sense, savvy; *Brit. informal* loaf, common; *N. Amer. informal* smarts. **5** *I can't see the sense in this* =**purpose**, point, reason, object, motive; use, value, advantage, benefit. **6** *different senses of the word 'dark'* =**meaning**, definition; nuance; drift, gist, thrust, tenor, message.
–OPPOSITES stupidity.

▶ verb *she sensed their hostility* =**discern**, feel, observe, notice, recognize, pick up, be aware of, distinguish, make out, identify; suspect, have a hunch, divine, intuit; *informal* catch on to; *Brit. informal* twig.

senseless ▶ adjective **1** *they found him senseless on the floor* =**unconscious**, insensible, comatose, knocked out, out cold, out for the count; numb; *informal* dead to the world; *Brit. informal* spark out. **2** *a senseless waste* =**pointless**, futile, useless, needless, purposeless, meaningless, unprofitable; absurd, foolish, insane, stupid, idiotic, mindless, illogical.
–OPPOSITES conscious, wise.

sensibility ▶ noun =**(finer) feelings**, emotions, sensitivities, moral sense.

sensible ▶ adjective =**practical**, realistic, responsible, reasonable, commonsensical, rational, logical, sound, balanced, sober, no-nonsense, level-headed, thoughtful, down-to-earth, wise.
–OPPOSITES foolish.

sensitive ▶ adjective **1** *she's sensitive to changes in temperature* =**responsive to**, reactive to, sensitized to; aware of, conscious of; susceptible to, affected by, vulnerable to; attuned to. **2** *sensitive skin* =**delicate**, fragile; tender, sore. **3** *the matter needs sensitive handling* =**tactful**, careful, thoughtful, diplomatic, delicate, subtle, kid-glove. **4** *he's sensitive about his bald patch* =**touchy**, oversensi-

tive, hypersensitive, easily offended, thin-skinned, defensive; paranoid, neurotic; *informal* uptight. **5** *a sensitive issue* =**difficult**, delicate, tricky, awkward, problematic, ticklish, precarious; controversial, emotive.
–OPPOSITES impervious, resilient, clumsy, thick-skinned, uncontroversial.

sensitivity ▶ noun **1** *the sensitivity of the skin* =**responsiveness**, sensitiveness, reactivity. **2** *the job calls for sensitivity* =**tact**, diplomacy, delicacy, subtlety; understanding, empathy; insight. **3** *her sensitivity on the subject* =**touchiness**, oversensitivity, hypersensitivity, defensiveness. **4** *the sensitivity of the issue* =**delicacy**, trickiness, awkwardness, ticklishness.

sensual ▶ adjective **1** *sensual pleasure* =**physical**, carnal, bodily, fleshly, animal. **2** *a very sensual woman* =**passionate**, sexual, physical, tactile; hedonistic.
–OPPOSITES spiritual, passionless.

sensualist ▶ noun =**hedonist**, pleasure-seeker; epicure, gastronome; bon vivant, bon viveur.

sensuality ▶ noun =**sexuality**, (sexual) pleasure, eroticism; physicality, carnality.

sensuous ▶ adjective **1** *big sensuous canvases* =**rich**, sumptuous, luxurious. **2** *sensuous lips* =**voluptuous**, sexy, seductive, luscious, lush, ripe.

sentence ▶ noun =**prison term**; punishment; *informal* time, stretch, stint.
▶ verb *they were sentenced to death* =**condemn**, doom; punish, convict.

sententious ▶ adjective =**moralistic**, moralizing, sanctimonious, self-righteous, pious, priggish, judgemental; pompous, self-important.

sentient ▶ adjective =(capable of) feeling, living, live; conscious, aware, responsive, reactive.

sentiment ▶ noun **1** *the comments echo my own sentiments* =**view**, feeling, attitude, thought, opinion, belief. **2** *there's no room for sentiment* =**sentimentality**; emotion, softness; *informal* schmaltz, mush, slushiness, corniness, cheese; *Brit. informal* soppiness; *N. Amer. informal* sappiness.

sentimental ▶ adjective **1** *she kept the vase for sentimental reasons* =**nostalgic**, tender, emotional. **2** *the film is too sentimental* =**mawkish**, overemotional, cloying, sickly, saccharine, sugary; roman-

tic; *Brit.* twee; *informal* slushy, mushy, tear-jerking, schmaltzy, gooey, drippy, cheesy, corny; *Brit. informal* soppy; *N. Amer. informal* cornball, sappy, hokey. **3** *she is very sentimental* =**soft-hearted**, soft; *informal* soppy.
–OPPOSITES practical, gritty.

sentry ▶ noun =**guard**, sentinel, lookout, watch, watchman.

separate ▶ adjective **1** *his personal life was separate from his job* =**unconnected**, unrelated, different, distinct, discrete; detached, divorced, disconnected, independent, autonomous. **2** *the infirmary was separate from the school* =**set apart**, detached; fenced off, cut off, segregated, isolated; free-standing, self-contained.
–OPPOSITES linked, attached.
▶ verb **1** *they separated the two youths* =**split (up)**, break up, part, pull apart. **2** *the connectors can be separated* =**disconnect**, detach, disengage, uncouple; split, divide, sever; disentangle. **3** *the wall that separated the two estates* =**partition**, divide, keep apart; bisect, intersect. **4** *the south aisle was separated off* =**isolate**, partition off, section off; close off, shut off, cordon off, fence off. **5** *they separated at the airport* =**part (company)**, go their separate ways, split up; say goodbye; disperse, scatter. **6** *the road separated* =**fork**, divide, branch, bifurcate, diverge. **7** *her parents separated* =**split up**, break up, part, divorce. **8** *separate fact from fiction* =**isolate**, set apart, tell; distinguish, differentiate; sort out. **9** *those who separate themselves from society* =**break away from**, break with, secede from, withdraw from, leave, quit, dissociate oneself from, drop out of, reject.
–OPPOSITES unite, join, link, meet, merge, marry.

separately ▶ adverb =**individually**, one by one, one at a time, singly, severally; apart, independently, alone, by oneself, on one's own.

separation ▶ noun **1** *the separation of the two companies* =**disconnection**, splitting, dividing up, disaffiliation, breaking up. **2** *her parent's separation* =**break-up**, split, estrangement; divorce; *Brit. informal* bust-up. **3** *the separation between art and life* =**distinction**, difference, division, dividing line; gulf, gap, chasm.

septic ▶ adjective =**infected**, festering, suppurating, putrid, putrefying, poisoned; *Medicine* purulent.

S

sepulchral ▸ adjective =**gloomy**, lugubrious, sombre, melancholy, mournful, dismal.
–OPPOSITES cheerful.

sepulchre ▸ noun =**tomb**, vault, burial chamber, crypt; grave.

sequel ▸ noun *a sequel to the riots* =**consequence**, result, upshot, postscript; after-effect; *informal* follow-on.

sequence ▸ noun 1 *the sequence of events* =**succession**, order, course, series, chain, train, progression, chronology; pattern, flow. 2 *a sequence from his film* =**excerpt**, clip, extract, section.

sequester ▸ verb 1 *he sequestered himself from the world* =**isolate oneself**, hide away, shut oneself away, seclude oneself, cut oneself off, segregate oneself; closet oneself, withdraw, retire. 2 *the government sequestered his property. See* SEQUESTRATE.

sequestrate ▸ verb =**confiscate**, seize, take, sequester, appropriate, expropriate, impound, commandeer.

serendipitous ▸ adjective =**chance**, accidental, coincidental; lucky, fortuitous; unexpected.

serendipity ▸ noun =(happy) **chance**, (happy) accident; luck, good luck, good fortune, providence; happy coincidence.

serene ▸ adjective 1 *on the surface she seemed serene* =**calm**, composed, tranquil, peaceful, untroubled, relaxed, at ease, unperturbed, unworried; placid; *N. Amer.* centered; *informal* together, unflappable. 2 *serene valleys* =**peaceful**, tranquil, quiet, still.
–OPPOSITES agitated, turbulent.

series ▸ noun =**succession**, sequence, string, chain, run, round; spate, wave, rash; set, course, cycle; row, line.

serious ▸ adjective 1 *a serious expression* =**solemn**, earnest, grave, sombre, sober, unsmiling, poker-faced, stern, grim, dour, humourless, stony-faced. 2 *serious decisions* =**important**, significant, consequential, momentous, weighty, far-reaching, major, grave. 3 *give serious consideration to this* =**careful**, detailed, in-depth. 4 *a serious play* =**intellectual**, highbrow, heavyweight, deep, profound, literary, learned, scholarly; *informal* heavy. 5 *serious injuries* =**severe**, grave, bad, critical, acute, terrible, dire, dangerous; *formal* grievous. 6 *we're serious about equality* =**(in) earnest**, sincere, wholehearted, genuine; committed,

resolute, determined.
–OPPOSITES light-hearted, trivial, superficial, lowbrow, minor, half-hearted.

seriously ▸ adverb 1 *Faye nodded seriously* =**solemnly**, earnestly, gravely, soberly, sombrely, sternly, grimly, dourly, humourlessly. 2 *seriously injured* =**severely**, gravely, badly, critically, dangerously; *formal* grievously. 3 *do you seriously expect me to come?* =**really**, actually, honestly. 4 *seriously, I'm very pleased* =**really**, honestly, truthfully, truly, I mean it; *informal* Scout's honour; *Brit. informal* straight up. 5 *(informal) seriously rich. See* EXTREMELY.

sermon ▸ noun 1 *he delivered a sermon* =**homily**, address, speech, talk, discourse, oration; lesson. 2 *a lengthy sermon about drugs* =**lecture**, speech, monologue.

serpentine ▸ adjective =**winding**, zigzag, twisty, twisting and turning, meandering, sinuous, snaky, tortuous.
–OPPOSITES straight.

serrated ▸ adjective =**jagged**, sawtoothed, zigzag, notched, toothed; *technical* crenulated.
–OPPOSITES smooth.

servant ▸ noun 1 *servants were cleaning the hall* =**attendant**, retainer; lackey, flunkey, minion; maid, housemaid, footman, page (boy), valet, butler, manservant; housekeeper, steward, drudge, slave. 2 *a servant of the Labour Party* =**helper**, supporter, follower.

serve ▸ verb 1 *they served their masters faithfully* =**work for**; obey; do the bidding of. 2 *this job serves the community* =**be of service to**, be of use to, help, assist, aid, make a contribution to, do one's bit for, do something for, benefit. 3 *she served on the committee* =**be a member of**, work on, be on, sit on, have a place on. 4 *he served his apprenticeship in Scotland* =**carry out**, perform, do, fulfil, complete, discharge; spend. 5 *serve the soup hot* =**dish up/out**, give out, distribute; present, provide, supply; offer. 6 *she served another customer* =**attend to**, deal with, see to; **assist**, help, look after. 7 *they served him with a writ* =**present**, deliver, give, hand over. 8 *a saucer serving as an ashtray* =**act as**, function as, do the work of, be a substitute for. 9 *official forms will serve in most cases* =**suffice**, be adequate, be good enough, fit/fill the bill, do, meet requirements, suit.

service ▶ noun **1** *conditions of service* =**work**, employment, labour. **2** *he has done us a service* =**favour**, kindness, good turn, helping hand; (**services**) assistance, help, aid. **3** *the service was excellent* =**waiting**, serving, attendance. **4** *products which give reliable service* =**use**, usage; functioning, operation. **5** *he took his car in for a service* =**overhaul**, (preventive) maintenance. **6** *a marriage service* =**ceremony**, ritual, rite; liturgy. **7** *a range of local services* =**amenity**, facility, resource, utility. **8** *soldiers leaving the services* =**(armed) forces**, military; army, navy, air force.

▶ verb *the appliances are serviced regularly* =**overhaul**, check, go over, maintain.

■ **be of service** =**help**, assist, be of assistance, be useful, be of use; do someone a good turn.

■ **out of service** =**out of order**, broken (down), out of commission, unserviceable, faulty, defective, inoperative; down; *informal* conked out, bust, kaput, on the blink, acting up, shot; *Brit. informal* knackered.

serviceable ▶ adjective **1** *a serviceable heating system* =**in working order**, working, functioning, operational; usable, workable, viable. **2** *serviceable lace-up shoes* =**functional**, utilitarian, sensible, practical; **hard wearing**, durable, tough, robust.
–OPPOSITES unusable, impractical.

servile ▶ adjective =**obsequious**, sycophantic, deferential, subservient, fawning, ingratiating, unctuous, grovelling, toadyish; *informal* slimy, bootlicking, smarmy; *N. Amer. informal* apple-polishing.
–OPPOSITES assertive.

serving ▶ noun =**portion**, helping, plateful, plate, bowlful.

servitude ▶ noun =**slavery**, enslavement, bondage, subjugation, domination.
–OPPOSITES liberty.

session ▶ noun **1** *a session of the committee* =**meeting**, sitting, assembly, conclave, plenary, hearing; *N. Amer. & NZ* caucus. **2** *training sessions* =**period**, time; class, lesson, meeting. **3** *the next college session begins in August* =**academic year**, school year; term, semester; *N. Amer.* trimester.

set[1] ▶ verb **1** *Beth set the bag on the table* =**put (down)**, place, lay, deposit, position, settle, leave, stand, plant; *informal* stick, dump, bung, park, plonk, pop. **2** *the cottage is set on a hill* =**be situated**, be located, lie, stand, be sited. **3** *the fence is set in concrete* =**fix**, embed, insert; mount. **4** *a ring set with precious stones* =**adorn**, ornament, decorate, embellish. **5** *I'll go and set the table* =**lay**, prepare, arrange, fix. **6** *we set them some work* =**assign**, allocate, give, allot. **7** *they set a date for the election* =**decide on**, select, choose, arrange, schedule; fix (on), settle on, determine, designate, name, appoint, specify, stipulate. **8** *his jump set a new record* =**establish**, create, institute. **9** *he set his watch* =**adjust**, regulate, synchronize; calibrate; put right, correct. **10** *remember to set the alarm* =**put/turn/switch on**, activate; programme. **11** *the adhesive will set in an hour* =**solidify**, harden, stiffen, thicken, gel; cake, congeal, coagulate, clot. **12** *the sun was setting* =**go down**, sink, dip; vanish, disappear.
–OPPOSITES melt, rise.

■ **set about 1** *Mike set about raising £5000* =**begin**, start, commence, go about, get to work on, get down to, embark on, tackle, address oneself to, undertake. **2** *the youths set about him* =**attack**, assault, hit, strike, beat, thrash, pummel, wallop, set upon, fall on; *informal* lay into, lot someone have it, do/work over, rough up, knock about/around; *Brit. informal* duff up, have a go at; *N. Amer. informal* beat up on.

■ **set someone/something apart** =**distinguish**, differentiate, mark out, single out, separate, demarcate.

■ **set something aside 1** *set aside some money each month* =**save**, put by/aside/away, keep, reserve; store, stockpile, hoard; *informal* squirrel/stash away. **2** *he set aside his cup* =**put down**, put aside, discard, abandon. **3** *set aside your differences* =**disregard**, put aside, ignore, forget, bury. **4** *the Appeal Court set aside the decision* =**overrule**, overturn, reverse, revoke, nullify, quash, dismiss, reject.

■ **set someone/something back** =**delay**, hold up/back, slow down/up, retard; hinder, impede, obstruct, hamper, inhibit.

■ **set someone free** =**release**, free, let go, turn loose, let out, liberate, deliver.

■ **set off** =**set out**, start out, sally forth, leave, depart, embark, set sail; *informal* hit the road.

■ **set something off 1** *a bomb was set*

off =**detonate**, explode, blow up, touch off, trigger; ignite. **2** *it set off a wave of protest* =**give rise to**, cause, lead to, set in motion, occasion, bring about, initiate, precipitate, prompt, trigger (off), spark (off), provoke, incite. **3** *the blue dress set off her hair* =**enhance**, bring out, emphasize, show off; complement.

■ **set on/upon** =**attack**, assault, hit, set about, fall on; *informal* lay into, let someone have it, get stuck into, work over, rough up, knock about/around; *Brit. informal* duff up, have a go at; *N. Amer. informal* beat up on.

■ **set out 1** *he set out early. See* SET OFF. **2** *you've done what you set out to achieve* =**aim**, intend, mean, seek; hope, aspire, want.

■ **set something out 1** *the gifts were set out on tables* =**arrange**, lay out, put out, array, dispose, display, exhibit. **2** *they set out some guidelines* =**present**, set forth, detail; state, declare, announce; submit, put forward, advance, propose, propound.

■ **set someone up** =**establish**; finance, fund, back, subsidize.

■ **set something up 1** *a monument was set up* =**erect**, put up, construct, build. **2** *she set up her own business* =**establish**, start, begin, institute, found, create. **3** *set up a meeting* =**arrange**, organize, fix (up), schedule, timetable, line up.

set² ▸ noun **1** *a set of postcards* =**group**, collection, series; assortment, selection, batch, number; arrangement, array. **2** *the literary set* =**clique**, coterie, circle, crowd, group, crew, band, company, ring, camp, fraternity, school, faction; *informal* gang, bunch. **3** *a chemistry set* =**kit**, pack, outfit. **4** *a set of cutlery* =**canteen**, box, case. **5** *he's in the bottom set at school* =**class**, form, group; stream, band.

set³ ▸ adjective **1** *a set routine* =**fixed**, established, predetermined, hard and fast, prearranged, prescribed, specified, defined; unvarying, unchanging, invariable, rigid, inflexible, strict, settled; routine, standard, customary, regular, usual, habitual, accustomed, wonted. **2** *she had very set ideas* =**inflexible**, rigid, fixed; entrenched. **3** *he had a set way of doing it* =**stock**, standard, routine, rehearsed, well worn, formulaic. **4** *I was all set for the evening* =**ready**, prepared, organized, equipped, primed; *informal* geared up, psyched up.

–OPPOSITES variable, flexible, original, unprepared.

setback ▸ noun =**problem**, difficulty, hitch, complication, upset; blow, stumbling block, hindrance, impediment, obstruction, hold-up; *informal* glitch, hiccup.

–OPPOSITES breakthrough.

settee ▸ noun =**sofa**, couch, divan, chaise longue, chesterfield; *Brit.* put-you-up; *N. Amer.* davenport, day bed.

setting ▸ noun =**surroundings**, position, situation, environment, background, backdrop, milieu; spot, place, location, locale, site, scene.

settle ▸ verb **1** *they settled the dispute* =**resolve**, sort out, clear up, end, fix, work out, iron out, set right, reconcile; *informal* patch up. **2** *she settled her affairs* =**put in order**, sort out, tidy up, arrange, organize, order, clear up. **3** *they settled on a date for the wedding* =**decide on**, set, fix, agree on, name, establish, arrange, appoint, designate, assign; choose, pick. **4** *she went to settle her bill* =**pay**, square, clear. **5** *they settled for a 4.2% pay rise* =**accept**, agree to, assent to; *formal* accede to. **6** *he settled in London* =**make one's home**, set up home, take up residence, put down roots, establish oneself; live. **7** *immigrants settled much of Australia* =**colonize**, occupy, populate. **8** *Catherine settled down to her work* =**apply oneself to**, get on with, set about, attack; concentrate on, focus on, devote oneself to, immerse oneself in. **9** *the class wouldn't settle down* =**calm down**, quieten down, be quiet, be still; *informal* shut up. **10** *a brandy will settle your nerves* =**calm**, quieten, quiet, soothe, pacify, quell. **11** *he settled into an armchair* =**sit down**, seat oneself, install oneself, ensconce oneself, plant oneself; *informal* park oneself. **12** *a butterfly settled on the flower* =**land**, come to rest, alight, perch; *archaic* light. **13** *sediment settles at the bottom* =**sink**, fall, gravitate; accumulate, concentrate, gather.

–OPPOSITES agitate, rise.

settlement ▸ noun **1** *a pay settlement* =**agreement**, deal, arrangement, resolution, understanding, pact. **2** *the settlement of the dispute* =**resolution**, settling, solution, reconciliation. **3** *a frontier settlement* =**community**, colony, outpost, encampment, post; village. **4** *the settlement of the area* =**colonization**, settling, populating.

settler ▶ noun =**colonist**, colonizer, frontiersman, frontierswoman, pioneer; immigrant, newcomer, incomer.
–OPPOSITES native.

seven ▶ cardinal number =**septet**, septuplets.

> **WORD LINKS**
>
> relating to seven: **hepta-**, **sept-**
> seven-sided figure: **heptagon**

sever ▶ verb 1 *the head was severed from the body* =**cut off**, chop off, detach, separate; amputate. 2 *a knife had severed the artery* =**cut (through)**, rupture, split, pierce. 3 *they severed diplomatic relations* =**break off**, discontinue, suspend, end, cease, dissolve.
–OPPOSITES join, maintain.

several ▶ adjective =**some**, a number of, a few; various, assorted.

severe ▶ adjective 1 *severe injuries* =**acute**, very bad, serious, grave, critical, dreadful, terrible, awful; dangerous, life-threatening; *formal* grievous. 2 *severe storms* =**fierce**, violent, strong, powerful. 3 *a severe winter* =**harsh**, bitter, cold, freezing, icy, arctic. 4 *a severe headache* =**excruciating**, agonizing, intense, dreadful, awful, terrible, unbearable; *informal* splitting, pounding. 5 *a severe test of their stamina* =**difficult**, demanding, tough, arduous, formidable, exacting, rigorous, punishing, gruelling. 6 *severe criticism* =**harsh**, scathing, sharp, strong, fierce, savage, devastating, withering. 7 *a severe training programme* =**harsh**, stern, hard, uncompromising, unrelenting; brutal, cruel, savage. 8 *his severe expression* =**stern**, dour, grim, forbidding, disapproving, unsmiling, unfriendly, sombre, grave, serious, stony, steely; cold, frosty. 9 *a severe style of architecture* =**plain**, simple, austere, unadorned, stark, spartan, ascetic; clinical, uncluttered.
–OPPOSITES minor, gentle, mild, easy, lenient, friendly, ornate.

severely ▶ adverb 1 *he was severely injured* =**badly**, seriously, critically. 2 *she was severely criticized* =**sharply**, roundly, soundly, fiercely, savagely. 3 *murderers should be treated more severely* =**harshly**, strictly, sternly, rigorously. 4 *she looked severely at Harriet* =**sternly**, grimly, dourly, disapprovingly. 5 *she dressed severely in black* =**plainly**, simply, austerely.

sew ▶ verb *she sewed the seams of the tunic* =**stitch**, tack; seam, hem; embroider.

sewing ▶ noun =**stitching**, needlework, needlecraft.

sex ▶ noun 1 *they talked about sex* =**(sexual) intercourse**, lovemaking, making love, the sex act, (sexual) relations; mating, copulation; *informal* nooky; *Brit. informal* bonking, rumpy pumpy; *formal* fornication; *technical* coitus; *dated* carnal knowledge. 2 *teach your children about sex* =**the facts of life**, reproduction; *informal* the birds and the bees. 3 *adults of both sexes* =**gender**.
■ **have sex** =have sexual intercourse, make love, sleep with, go to bed; mate, copulate; seduce, rape; *informal* do it, go all the way, know in the biblical sense; *Brit. informal* bonk; *N. Amer. informal* get it on; *euphemistic* be intimate; *formal* fornicate.

> **WORD LINKS**
>
> relating to sex: **carnal**
> obsession with sex: **erotomania**,
>   **nymphomania**
> fear of sex: **erotophobia**

sex appeal ▶ noun =**sexiness**, seductiveness, (sexual) attractiveness, desirability, sensuality, sexuality.

sexism ▶ noun =**sexual discrimination**, chauvinism, prejudice, bias.

sexless ▶ adjective =**asexual**, nonsexual, neuter; androgynous, epicene.

sexual ▶ adjective 1 *the sexual organs* =**reproductive**, genital, sex, procreative. 2 *sexual activity* =**carnal**, erotic; *formal* venereal; *technical* coital.

sexual intercourse ▶ noun. See SEX sense 1.

sexuality ▶ noun 1 *she had a powerful sexuality* =**sensuality**, sexiness, seductiveness, desirability, eroticism, physicality, lusciousness; sexual appetite, passion, desire, lust. 2 *I'm open about my sexuality* =**(sexual) orientation**, sexual preference, leaning, persuasion; heterosexuality, homosexuality, lesbianism, bisexuality.

sexy ▶ adjective 1 *she's so sexy* =**(sexually) attractive**, seductive, desirable, alluring, sensual, sultry, slinky, provocative, tempting, tantalizing; nubile, voluptuous, luscious; *informal* fanciable, beddable; *Brit. informal* fit; *N. Amer. informal* foxy, cute; *Austral. informal* spunky. 2 *sexy videos* =**erotic**, (sexually) explicit, arousing, exciting, stimulating, hot, titillating, racy, naughty, risqué, X-rated; rude, pornographic, crude, lewd, graphic; *informal* raunchy, steamy, porno, blue, skin; *euphemistic* adult. **3** *they weren't feeling sexy* =**(sexually) aroused**, sexually excited, amorous, lustful, passionate; *informal* horny, hot, turned on; *Brit. informal* randy. **4** *(informal) a sexy sales promotion* =**exciting**, stimulating, interesting, appealing.

shabby ▸ adjective **1** *a shabby little bar* =**run down**, scruffy, dilapidated; seedy, slummy, insalubrious, squalid, sordid; *informal* crummy, scuzzy, shambly; *Brit. informal* grotty; *N. Amer. informal* shacky. **2** *a shabby grey coat* =**scruffy**, old, worn out, threadbare, ragged, frayed, tattered, battered, faded, moth-eaten, mangy; *informal* tatty, ratty; *N. Amer. informal* raggedy. **3** *her shabby treatment of Ben* =**contemptible**, despicable, dishonourable, discreditable, mean, low, dirty, hateful, shameful, ignoble, unfair, unworthy, unkind, shoddy, nasty; *informal* rotten, low-down.
–OPPOSITES smart, honourable.

shack ▸ noun =**hut**, shanty, cabin, lean-to, shed; hovel; *Scottish* bothy.
■ **shack up with** *(informal)* =**cohabit**, move in with, live with; *informal, dated* live in sin.

shackle ▸ verb **1** *he was shackled to the wall* =**chain**, fetter, manacle; secure, tie (up), bind, tether, hobble; put in chains, clap in irons, handcuff. **2** *journalists were shackled by a new law* =**restrain**, restrict, limit, constrain, handicap, hamstring, hamper, hinder, impede, obstruct, inhibit.

shackles ▸ plural noun =**chains**, fetters, irons, leg irons, manacles, handcuffs.

shade ▸ noun **1** *they sat in the shade* =**shadow(s)**, shelter, cover; cool. **2** *shades of blue* =**colour**, hue, tone, tint, tinge. **3** *shades of meaning* =**nuance**, gradation, degree, difference, variation, variety, nicety, subtlety; undertone, overtone. **4** *her skirt was a shade too short* =**a little**, a bit, a trace, a touch, a modicum, a tinge; slightly, rather, somewhat; *informal* a tad, a smidgen. **5** *the window shade* =**blind**, curtain, screen, cover, covering; awning, canopy. **6** *(informal) he was wearing shades* =**sunglasses**, dark glasses; *Austral. informal* sunnies.
–OPPOSITES light.
▸ verb **1** *vines shaded the garden* =**cast a shadow over**, shadow, shelter, cover,

screen. **2** *she shaded in the picture* =**darken**, colour in, pencil in, block in, fill in; cross-hatch.
■ **put someone/something in the shade** =**surpass**, outshine, outclass, overshadow, eclipse, cap, top, outstrip, outdo, put to shame, beat hollow, upstage; *informal* run rings around, be a cut above, leave standing.
■ **shades of** =**echoes of**, a reminder of, memories of, suggestions of, hints of.

shadow ▸ noun **1** *he saw her shadow in the doorway* =**outline**, shape, contour, profile. **2** *he emerged from the shadows* =**shade**, darkness, twilight; gloom. **3** *the shadow of war* =**(black) cloud**, pall; spectre; threat. **4** *a shadow of a smile* =**trace**, hint, suggestion, suspicion, ghost, glimmer.
▸ verb *he is shadowing a suspect* =**follow**, trail, track, stalk, pursue; *informal* tail, keep tabs on.

> **WORD LINKS**
>
> *fear of shadows:* **sciophobia**

shadowy ▸ adjective **1** *a shadowy corridor* =**dark**, dim, gloomy, murky, shady, shaded. **2** *a shadowy outline* =**indistinct**, hazy, indefinite, vague, ill-defined, faint, blurred, blurry, unclear; ghostly, spectral, wraithlike. **3** *a shadowy figure* =**mysterious**, enigmatic.
–OPPOSITES bright, clear, high-profile.

shady ▸ adjective **1** *a shady garden* =**shaded**, shadowy, dim, dark; sheltered; leafy. **2** *(informal) shady deals* =**suspicious**, suspect, questionable, dubious, doubtful, irregular; *N. Amer.* snide; *informal* fishy, murky; *Brit. informal* dodgy; *Austral./NZ informal* shonky.
–OPPOSITES bright, honest.

shaft ▸ noun **1** *the shaft of a golf club* =**pole**, shank, stick, rod, staff; handle, hilt, stem. **2** *shafts of sunlight* =**ray**, beam, gleam, streak. **3** *a ventilation shaft* =**tunnel**, passage; borehole, bore; duct, well, flue, vent.

shaggy ▸ adjective =**hairy**, bushy, thick, woolly; tangled, tousled, unkempt, dishevelled, untidy; *formal* hirsute.
–OPPOSITES sleek.

shake ▸ verb **1** *the building shook* =**vibrate**, tremble, quiver, quake, shiver, shudder, judder, jiggle, wobble, rock, sway; convulse. **2** *she shook the bottle* =**jiggle**, agitate; *informal* wiggle, waggle. **3** *he*

shook his stick =**brandish**, wave, flourish, swing, wield; *informal* waggle. **4** *what she saw shook her* =**upset**, distress, disturb, unsettle, disconcert, discompose, unnerve, trouble, throw off balance, agitate, fluster; shock, alarm, frighten, scare, worry; *informal* rattle. **5** *this will shake their confidence* =**weaken**, undermine, damage, impair, harm.
–OPPOSITES soothe, strengthen.

▶ noun **1** *he gave his coat a shake* =**jiggle**, joggle; *informal* waggle. **2** *a shake of his fist* =**flourish**, wave.

■ **shake someone off** =**get away from**, escape, elude, dodge, lose, leave behind, get rid of, give someone the slip, throw off the scent; *Brit. informal* get shot of.

■ **shake something off** =**recover from**, get over; get rid of, free oneself from; *Brit. informal* get shot of; *N. Amer. informal* shuck off.

■ **shake someone/something up**
1 *the accident shook him up.* See SHAKE verb sense 4. **2** *plans to shake up the legal profession* =**reorganize**, restructure, revolutionize, alter, change, transform, reform, overhaul.

shake-up ▶ noun *(informal)* =**reorganization**, restructuring, reshuffle, change, overhaul, makeover; *N. Amer. informal* shakedown.

shaky ▶ adjective **1** *shaky legs* =**trembling**, shaking, tremulous, quivering, unsteady, wobbly, weak; doddery; *informal* trembly. **2** *I feel a bit shaky* =**faint**, dizzy, light-headed, giddy; weak, wobbly; in shock, upset. **3** *a shaky table* =**unsteady**, unstable, wobbly, rickety; *Brit. informal* wonky. **4** *the evidence is shaky* =**unreliable**, untrustworthy, questionable, dubious, doubtful, tenuous, suspect, flimsy, weak; *informal* iffy; *Brit. informal* dodgy.
–OPPOSITES steady, stable, sound.

shallow ▶ adjective =**superficial**, facile, insubstantial, lightweight, empty, trivial, trifling; surface, skin-deep; frivolous, foolish, silly.
–OPPOSITES profound.

sham ▶ noun =**pretence**, fake, act, fiction, simulation, fraud, feint, lie, counterfeit; humbug.

▶ adjective *sham concern* =**fake**, pretended, feigned, simulated, false, artificial, bogus, insincere, affected, make-believe; *informal* pretend, put-on, phoney.
–OPPOSITES genuine.

▶ verb =**pretend**, fake, dissemble; malin-

ger; *informal* put it on; *Brit. informal* swing the lead.

shaman ▶ noun =**witch doctor**, medicine man/woman, healer.

shamble ▶ verb =**shuffle**; lumber, totter; hobble, limp.

shambles ▶ plural noun **1** *we have to sort out this shambles* =**chaos**, mess, muddle, confusion, disorder, havoc; *Brit. informal* dog's dinner/breakfast. **2** *the room was a shambles* =**mess**, pigsty; *informal* disaster area; *Brit. informal* tip.

shambolic ▶ adjective *(Brit. informal)*. See CHAOTIC.

shame ▶ noun **1** *her face was scarlet with shame* =**humiliation**, mortification, chagrin, ignominy, embarrassment, indignity, discomfort. **2** *a sense of shame* =**guilt**, remorse, contrition. **3** *he brought shame on the family* =**disgrace**, dishonour, discredit, ignominy, disrepute, infamy, scandal, opprobrium. **4** *it's a shame she never married* =**pity**, sad thing; bad luck; *informal* bummer, crime, sin.
–OPPOSITES pride, honour.

▶ verb **1** *you shamed your family* =**disgrace**, dishonour, discredit, taint, sully, tarnish, besmirch, blacken, drag through the mud. **2** *he was shamed in public* =**humiliate**, embarrass, humble, take down a peg or two, cut down to size; *informal* show up; *N. Amer. informal* make someone eat crow.
–OPPOSITES honour.

■ **put someone/something to shame**
=**outshine**, outclass, eclipse, surpass, excel, outstrip, outdo, put in the shade; *informal* run rings around, leave standing; *Brit. informal* knock spots off.

shamefaced ▶ adjective =**ashamed**, abashed, sheepish, guilty, contrite, sorry, remorseful, repentant, penitent, regretful, rueful, apologetic; *informal* with one's tail between one's legs.
–OPPOSITES unrepentant.

shameful ▶ adjective **1** *shameful behaviour* =**disgraceful**, deplorable, despicable, contemptible, dishonourable, discreditable, reprehensible, low, unworthy, ignoble, shabby; shocking, scandalous, outrageous, abominable, atrocious, appalling; inexcusable, unforgivable. **2** *a shameful secret* =**embarrassing**, mortifying, humiliating, ignominious.
–OPPOSITES admirable.

shameless ▶ adjective =**flagrant**, bla-

tant, barefaced, overt, brazen, undisguised, unconcealed; unabashed, unashamed, unblushing, unrepentant.
–OPPOSITES modest.

shanty ▶ noun =**shack**, hut, cabin, lean-to, shed; hovel; *Scottish* bothy.

shape ▶ noun **1** *the shape of the dining table* =**form**, appearance, configuration, structure; figure, build, physique, body; contours, lines, outline, silhouette, profile. **2** *a spirit in the shape of a fox* =**guise**, likeness, semblance, form, appearance, image. **3** *in good shape* =**condition**, health, trim, fettle, order; *Brit. informal* nick.
▶ verb **1** *the metal is shaped into tools* =**form**, fashion, make, mould, model; sculpt, carve, cut, whittle, bend. **2** *attitudes shaped by his report* =**determine**, form, fashion, mould, develop; influence, affect.
■ **take shape** =**become clear**, become definite, become tangible, crystallize, come together, fall into place.

WORD LINKS

study of the shapes of things:
  morphology

shapeless ▶ adjective **1** *shapeless lumps* =**formless**, amorphous, unformed, indefinite. **2** *a shapeless dress* =**baggy**, saggy, ill-fitting, oversized, unshapely, formless.

shapely ▶ adjective =**well proportioned**, clean-limbed, curvaceous, voluptuous, full-figured, Junoesque; attractive, sexy; *informal* curvy.

shard ▶ noun =**fragment**, sliver, splinter, chip, piece, bit.

share ▶ noun *her share of the profits* =**portion**, part, division, quota, allowance, ration, allocation, measure, due; percentage, commission, dividend; helping, serving; *informal* cut, slice, rake-off; *Brit. informal* whack.
▶ verb **1** *we share the bills* =**split**, divide, go halves on; *informal* go fifty-fifty. **2** *they shared out the peanuts* =**apportion**, divide (up/out), allocate, portion out, measure out; carve up; *Brit. informal* divvy up. **3** *we all share in the learning process* =**participate in**, take part in, play a part in, be involved in, contribute to, have a hand in, partake in.

sharp ▶ adjective **1** *a sharp knife* =**keen**, razor-edged; sharpened, well-honed. **2** *a sharp pain* =**excruciating**, agonizing, intense, stabbing, shooting, severe, acute, keen, fierce, searing. **3** *a sharp taste* =**tangy**, piquant; **acidic**, acid, sour, tart, pungent, acrid. **4** *a sharp cry* =**loud**, piercing, shrill, high-pitched, penetrating, harsh, strident, ear-splitting, deafening. **5** *a sharp wind* =**cold**, chilly, chill, brisk, keen, penetrating, biting, icy, bitter, freezing, raw. **6** *sharp words* =**harsh**, bitter, cutting, spiteful, hurtful, nasty, cruel. **7** *a sharp sense of loss* =**intense**, acute, keen, strong, bitter, fierce, heartfelt, overwhelming. **8** *her nose is sharp* =**pointed**, tapering, tapered; *informal* pointy. **9** *the lens brings it into sharp focus* =**distinct**, clear, crisp; stark, obvious, marked, definite, pronounced. **10** *a sharp increase* =**sudden**, abrupt, rapid; steep, precipitous. **11** *a sharp corner* =**tight**, blind. **12** *a sharp drop* =**steep**, sheer, abrupt, precipitous, vertical. **13** *sharp eyes* =**keen**, perceptive, observant, acute, beady. **14** *she was sharp and witty* =**perceptive**, incisive, keen, acute, quick-witted, shrewd, canny, astute, intelligent, intuitive, bright, alert, smart, quick off the mark; *informal* on the ball, quick on the uptake, savvy; *Brit. informal* suss; *N. Amer. informal* heads-up.
–OPPOSITES blunt, mild, sweet, soft, kind, rounded, indistinct, gradual, slow, weak, stupid, naive.
▶ adverb =**precisely**, exactly, on the dot; promptly, prompt, punctually, dead on; *informal* on the nose; *N. Amer. informal* on the button.
–OPPOSITES roughly.

sharpen ▶ verb =**hone**, whet, strop, grind, file.

shatter ▶ verb **1** *the glasses shattered* =**smash**, break, splinter, crack, fracture, fragment, disintegrate. **2** *the announcement shattered their hopes* =**destroy**, wreck, ruin, dash, crush, devastate, demolish, torpedo, scotch; *informal* put the kibosh on, do for, put paid to; *Brit. informal* scupper. **3** *we were shattered by the news* =**devastate**, shock, stun, daze, traumatize; *informal* knock sideways; *Brit. informal* knock for six.

shattered ▶ adjective **1** *he was shattered by the reviews* =**devastated**, shocked, stunned, dazed, traumatized. **2** *(informal) I feel too shattered to move.* See EXHAUSTED sense 1.
–OPPOSITES thrilled.

shave ▶ verb **1** *he shaved his beard* =**cut off**; crop, trim, barber. **2** *shave off excess* *wood* =**plane**, pare, whittle, scrape.

sheaf ▶ noun =**bundle**, bunch, stack, pile, heap, mass; *Brit. informal* wodge.

sheath ▶ noun **1** *put the sword in its sheath* =**scabbard**, case. **2** *the wire has a plastic sheath* =**covering**, cover, case, casing, sleeve.

shed¹ ▶ noun *the rabbit lives in the shed* =**hut**, lean-to, outhouse, outbuilding; shack; *Brit.* lock-up.

shed² ▶ verb **1** *the trees shed their leaves* =**drop**, spill. **2** *the caterpillar shed its skin* =**slough off**, cast off, moult. **3** *we shed our clothes* =**take off**, remove, discard, climb out of, slip out of; *Brit. informal* peel off. **4** *much blood has been shed* =**spill**, discharge. **5** *the firm is to shed ten workers* =**make redundant**, dismiss, let go, discharge, get rid of, discard; *informal* sack, fire. **6** *the moon shed a watery light* =**cast**, radiate, diffuse, disperse, give out.
−OPPOSITES don, hire, keep.

sheen ▶ noun =**shine**, lustre, gloss, patina, shininess, burnish, polish, shimmer, brilliance, radiance.

sheep ▶ noun

> **WORD LINKS**
>
> *male:* **ram**
> *female:* **ewe**
> *young:* **lamb**
> *relating to sheep:* **ovine**
> *collective noun:* **flock, herd**

sheepish ▶ adjective =**embarrassed**, uncomfortable, hangdog, self-conscious; shamefaced, ashamed, abashed, mortified, chastened, remorseful, contrite, apologetic, penitent, repentant.

sheer¹ ▶ adjective **1** *the sheer audacity of the plan* =**utter**, complete, absolute, total, pure, downright, out-and-out; *Austral./NZ informal* fair. **2** *a sheer drop* =**precipitous**, steep, vertical, perpendicular, abrupt, sharp. **3** *a sheer dress* =**diaphanous**, gauzy, thin, translucent, transparent, see-through, insubstantial.
−OPPOSITES gradual, thick.

sheer² ▶ verb *the boat sheered off along the coast* =**swerve**, veer, slew, skew, swing.

sheet ▶ noun **1** *she changed the sheets* =**(bed) linen**, bedclothes. **2** *a sheet of ice* =**layer**, stratum, covering, blanket, coat, film, skin. **3** *a sheet of glass* =**pane**, panel, piece, plate. **4** *a fresh sheet of paper* =**piece**, leaf, page. **5** *a sheet of water* =**expanse**, area, stretch, sweep.

shelf ▶ noun =**ledge**, sill.

shell ▶ noun **1** *a crab shell* =**carapace**, exterior; armour; *Zoology* exoskeleton. **2** *peanut shells* =**pod**, husk, hull, casing, case, covering; *N. Amer.* shuck. **3** *shells passing overhead* =**projectile**, bomb, missile; bullet. **4** *the metal shell of the car* =**hull**, body.
▶ verb **1** *they were shelling peas* =**hull**, pod, husk; *N. Amer.* shuck. **2** *rebel artillery shelled the city* =**bombard**, fire on, attack, bomb, blitz, strafe.

> **WORD LINKS**
>
> *study or collection of shells:* **conchology**

shellfish ▶ noun =**crustacean**, bivalve, mollusc.

shelter ▶ noun **1** *the trees provide shelter for animals* =**protection**, cover, shade; safety, security, refuge. **2** *a shelter for abandoned cats* =**sanctuary**, refuge, home, haven, safe house.
−OPPOSITES exposure.
▶ verb **1** *the hut sheltered him from the sun* =**protect**, shield, screen, cover, shade, defend, cushion, guard, insulate. **2** *where the convoy sheltered* =**take shelter**, take refuge, take cover; *informal* hole up.
−OPPOSITES expose.

sheltered ▶ adjective **1** *a sheltered stretch of water* =**protected**, tranquil, still; shady. **2** *a sheltered life* =**protected**, cloistered; privileged, secure, safe, quiet.

shelve ▶ verb =**postpone**, put off, delay, defer, put back, reschedule, hold over/off, put to one side, suspend, stay, mothball; *N. Amer.* put over, table, take a rain check on; *informal* put on ice, put on the back burner.
−OPPOSITES execute.

shepherd ▶ verb *we shepherded them away* =**usher**, steer, herd, lead, take, escort, guide, conduct, marshal, walk, show, see.

shield ▶ noun *a shield against radiation | a gum shield* =**protection**, guard, defence, cover, screen.
▶ verb *he shielded his eyes* =**protect**, cover, screen, shade.
−OPPOSITES expose.

shift ▶ verb **1** *he shifted some chairs* =**move**, transfer, transport, switch, relocate, reposition, rearrange. **2** *she shifted*

her position =**change**, alter, adjust; modify, revise, reverse. **3** *the cargo has shifted* =**move**, slide, slip, be displaced, subside. **4** *the wind shifted* =**veer**, alter, change, turn. **5** *(Brit.) this brush really shifts the dirt* =**get rid of**, remove, get off, budge, lift.
—OPPOSITES keep.

▶ noun **1** *a shift in public opinion* =**change**, alteration, adjustment, variation, modification, revision, reversal, U-turn; *Brit.* about-turn. **2** *they worked three shifts* =**stint**, stretch, spell. **3** *the night shift went home* =**workers**, crew, gang, team, squad, patrol.

shiftless ▶ adjective =**lazy**, idle, indolent, slothful, lethargic, feckless, good-for-nothing, worthless.

shifty ▶ adjective *(informal)* =**devious**, evasive, slippery, duplicitous, deceitful, untrustworthy; *N. Amer.* snide; *Brit. informal* dodgy; *Austral./NZ informal* shonky.
—OPPOSITES honest.

shimmer ▶ verb =**glint**, glisten, twinkle, sparkle, flash, gleam, glow, glimmer, glitter, wink.
▶ noun =**glint**, twinkle, sparkle, flash, gleam, glow, glimmer, lustre, glitter.

shin ▶ verb =**climb**, clamber, scramble, swarm; mount, ascend, scale; descend; *N. Amer.* shinny.

shine ▶ verb **1** *the sun shone* =**beam**, radiate, gleam, glow, glint, glimmer, sparkle, twinkle, glitter, glisten, shimmer, flash, glare. **2** *she shone her shoes* =**polish**, burnish, buff, rub up. **3** *they shone at university* =**excel**, stand out.
▶ noun *linseed oil restores the shine* =**polish**, gleam, gloss, lustre, sheen, patina.

shining ▶ adjective **1** *a shining expanse of water* =**gleaming**, bright, brilliant, lustrous, glowing, glinting, sparkling, twinkling, glittering, glistening, shimmering, dazzling, luminous, incandescent. **2** *a shining face* =**glowing**, beaming, radiant, happy. **3** *shining chromium tubes* =**shiny**, bright, polished, gleaming, glossy, lustrous.
■ **a shining example** =**paragon**, model, epitome, archetype, ideal, exemplar, paradigm.

shiny ▶ adjective =**glossy**, glassy, bright, polished, gleaming, satiny, sheeny, lustrous.
—OPPOSITES matt.

ship ▶ noun =**boat**, vessel, craft.

WORD LINKS

relating to ships: **marine, maritime, nautical, naval**

shirk ▶ verb =**evade**, dodge, avoid, get out of, sidestep, shrink from, shun, skip; neglect; *informal* duck (out of), cop out of; *Brit. informal* skive off; *N. Amer. informal* cut; *Austral./NZ informal* duck-shove.

shirker ▶ noun =**dodger**, truant, absentee, layabout, loafer, idler; *informal* slacker; *Brit. informal* skiver.

shiver ▶ verb *she was shivering with fear* =**tremble**, quiver, shake, shudder, quake.
▶ noun *she gave a shiver as the door opened* =**shudder**, twitch, start.

shock¹ ▶ noun **1** *the news came as a shock* =**blow**, upset; surprise, revelation, a bolt from the blue, rude awakening, eye-opener. **2** *you gave me a shock* =**fright**, scare, start; *informal* turn. **3** *suffering from shock* =**trauma**; collapse, breakdown. **4** *the first shock of the earthquake* =**vibration**, reverberation, shake, jolt; impact, blow.
▶ verb *the murder shocked the nation* =**appal**, horrify, outrage, revolt, disgust; traumatize, distress, upset, disturb, disquiet, unsettle; stun, rock, shake, take aback, throw, unnerve.

shock² ▶ noun *a shock of red hair* =**mass**, mane, mop, thatch, head, bush, tangle, cascade, halo.

shocking ▶ adjective =**appalling**, horrifying, horrific, dreadful, awful, frightful, terrible; scandalous, outrageous, disgraceful, abominable, atrocious, disgusting; distressing, upsetting, disturbing, startling, surprising.

shoddy ▶ adjective **1** *shoddy goods* =**poor-quality**, inferior, second-rate, third-rate, jerry-built; *Brit. informal* rubbish. **2** *shoddy workmanship* =**careless**, slapdash, sloppy, slipshod; negligent.
—OPPOSITES quality, careful.

shoot ▶ verb **1** *they shot him in the street* =**gun down**, mow down, hit, wound, injure; kill; *informal* blast, pump full of lead, plug. **2** *they shot at the police* =**fire**, open fire, snipe, let fly; bombard, shell. **3** *it can shoot bullets or grenades* =**discharge**, fire, launch, release. **4** *a car shot past* =**race**, speed, flash, dash, dart, rush, hurtle, streak, whizz, go like lightning, go hell for leather, zoom; career, fly; *informal* belt, tear, zip, whip; *Brit. informal*

bomb, bucket; *N. Amer. informal* clip, high-tail it, barrel. **5** *the film was shot in Tunisia* =**film**, photograph, take, make, record.
▶ noun *new shoots* =**sprout**, bud, runner, tendril.

shop ▶ noun **1** *a shop selling gloves* =**store**, (retail) outlet, boutique, emporium, department store, supermarket, hypermarket, superstore, chain store; *N. Amer.* minimart. **2** *he works in the machine shop* =**workshop**, plant, factory, works.

shopkeeper ▶ noun =**shop-owner**, vendor, retailer, dealer, trader, salesperson; *N. Amer.* storekeeper.

shopper ▶ noun =**buyer**, purchaser, customer, consumer, client, patron.

shore¹ ▶ noun *he swam to the shore* =**seashore**, beach, sand(s), shoreline, coast.

> **WORD LINKS**
> *relating to a shore:* **littoral**

shore² ▶ verb *we had to shore up the building* =**prop up**, hold up, bolster, support, brace, buttress, strengthen, reinforce, underpin.

short ▶ adjective **1** *a short piece of string* =**small**, little, tiny. **2** *short people* =**small**, little, petite, tiny, diminutive, elfin; *Scottish* wee. **3** *a short report* =**concise**, brief, succinct, compact, pithy, abridged, abbreviated, condensed. **4** *a short visit* =**brief**, fleeting, lightning, quick. **5** *money is a bit short* =**scarce**, scant, meagre, sparse, insufficient, deficient, inadequate, lacking, wanting. **6** *he was rather short with her* =**curt**, sharp, abrupt, blunt, brusque, terse, offhand, gruff, surly, rude.
−OPPOSITES long, tall, plentiful, courteous.
▶ adverb *she stopped short* =**abruptly**, suddenly, sharply, all of a sudden, unexpectedly, without warning.
■ **in short** =**briefly**, in a word, in a nutshell, in essence.
■ **short of** =**deficient in**, lacking, wanting, in need of, low on, short on, missing; *informal* strapped for, pushed for, minus.

shortage ▶ noun =**scarcity**, dearth, poverty, insufficiency, deficiency, inadequacy, famine, lack, want, deficit, shortfall.
−OPPOSITES abundance.

shortcoming ▶ noun =**defect**, fault, flaw, imperfection, deficiency, limitation, failing, drawback, weakness, weak point.
−OPPOSITES strength.

shorten ▶ verb =**make shorter**, abbreviate, abridge, condense, contract, compress, reduce, shrink, diminish, cut (down); trim, pare down, prune; curtail, truncate.
−OPPOSITES extend.

short-lived ▶ adjective =**brief**, short, temporary, impermanent, fleeting, fugitive, transitory, transient, ephemeral.

shortly ▶ adverb **1** *she will be with you shortly* =**soon**, presently, in a little while, at any moment, in a minute, in next to no time, before long, by and by; *N. Amer.* momentarily; *informal* anon, any time now, in a jiffy; *Brit. informal* in a mo. **2** *'I know,' he replied shortly* =**curtly**, sharply, abruptly, bluntly, brusquely, tersely.

short-sighted ▶ adjective **1** *I'm a little short-sighted* =**myopic**, near-sighted; *informal* as blind as a bat. **2** *short-sighted critics* =**narrow-minded**, unimaginative, small-minded.
−OPPOSITES long-sighted, imaginative.

short-staffed ▶ adjective =**understaffed**, short-handed, undermanned, below strength.

short-tempered ▶ adjective =**irritable**, irascible, hot-tempered, quick-tempered, touchy, volatile, on a short fuse; *Brit. informal* narky, ratty.
−OPPOSITES placid.

shot ▶ noun **1** *a shot rang out* =**report**, crack, bang, blast; (**shots**) gunfire, firing. **2** *a winning shot* =**stroke**, hit, strike; kick, throw. **3** *Mike was an excellent shot* =**marksman**, markswoman, shooter. **4** *a shot of us on holiday* =**photograph**, photo, snap, snapshot, picture, print, slide, still. **5** *(informal) it's nice to get a shot at driving* =**attempt**, try; turn, chance, opportunity; *informal* go, stab, crack, bash. **6** *tetanus shots* =**injection**, inoculation, immunization, vaccination, booster; *informal* jab.
■ **like a shot** *(informal)* =**without hesitation**, unhesitatingly, eagerly; immediately, at once, right away/now, straight away, instantly, instantaneously, without delay; *informal* in/like a flash, before one can say Jack Robinson.

shoulder ▶ verb **1** *I shouldered the responsibility* =**take on (oneself)**, undertake, accept, assume; bear, carry. **2** *an-*

other lad shouldered him aside =**push**, shove, thrust, jostle, force, bulldoze, bundle.

■ **shoulder to shoulder** =**united**, (working) together, jointly, in partnership, in collaboration, in cooperation, side by side, in alliance.

shout ▶ verb =**yell**, cry (out), call (out), roar, howl, bellow, bawl, clamour, shriek, scream; raise one's voice. –OPPOSITES whisper.

▶ noun =**yell**, cry, call, roar, howl, bellow, bawl, shriek, scream.

shove ▶ verb 1 *she shoved him back* =**push**, thrust, propel, drive, force, ram, knock, elbow, shoulder; jostle, bundle, hustle, manhandle. 2 *she shoved past him* =**push (one's way)**, force one's way, barge (one's way), elbow (one's way), shoulder one's way.

▶ noun *a hefty shove* =**push**, thrust, bump, jolt.

■ **shove off** *(informal)* =**go away**, get out (of my sight); get going, take oneself off, be off (with you); *informal* scram, make yourself scarce, be on your way, beat it, get lost, push/clear/buzz off; *Brit. informal* hop it, bog off, naff off; *N. Amer. informal* bug off, haul off, take a hike; *Austral. informal* nick off; *Austral./NZ informal* rack off; *literary* begone.

shovel ▶ verb *he was shovelling snow* =**scoop (up)**, dig, excavate, shift, move.

show ▶ verb 1 *the stitches do not show* =**be visible**, be seen, be in view, be obvious. 2 *he wouldn't show the picture* =**display**, exhibit, put on show/display/view. 3 *Frank showed his frustration* =**manifest**, exhibit, reveal, convey, communicate, make known; express, make plain, make obvious, disclose, betray. 4 *I'll show you how to cook* =**demonstrate**, explain, describe, illustrate, teach, instruct. 5 *events show this to be true* =**prove**, demonstrate, confirm; substantiate, corroborate, verify, establish, attest, bear out. 6 *she showed them to their seats* =**escort**, accompany, take, conduct, lead, usher, guide, direct, steer, shepherd. –OPPOSITES conceal.

▶ noun 1 *a spectacular show of bluebells* =**display**, array. 2 *the motor show* =**exhibition**, fair, festival, parade; *N. Amer.* exhibit. 3 *they took in a show* =**musical**, play. 4 *she's only doing it for show* =**appearance**, display, image. 5 *Drew made a show of looking busy* =**pretence**, outward appearance, (false) front, guise, semblance, pose.

■ **show off** *(informal)* =**put on airs**, put on an act, swank, strut, grandstand, posture; draw attention to oneself; *N. Amer. informal* cop an attitude.

■ **show something off** =**display**, show to advantage, exhibit, demonstrate, parade, draw attention to, flaunt.

■ **show up 1** *cancers show up on X-rays* =**be visible**, be obvious, be seen, be revealed, appear. 2 *only two waitresses showed up.* =**turn up**, appear, arrive, come, get here/there, put in an appearance, materialize.

■ **show someone/something up 1** *the sun showed up the shabbiness of the room* =**expose**, reveal, make visible/obvious, highlight, emphasize, draw attention to. 2 *(informal) they showed him up in front of his friends.* See HUMILIATE.

showdown ▶ noun =**confrontation**, clash, face-off.

shower ▶ noun 1 *a shower of rain* =**fall**, drizzle, sprinkling. 2 *a shower of missiles* =**volley**, hail, salvo, barrage.

▶ verb 1 *confetti showered down on us* =**rain**, fall, hail. 2 *she showered them with gifts* =**deluge**, flood, inundate, swamp, engulf; overwhelm, overload, snow under.

showing ▶ noun 1 *another showing of the series* =**presentation**, broadcast, airing. 2 *the party's present showing* =**performance**, (track) record, results, success, achievement(s).

showman ▶ noun 1 *a travelling showman* =**impresario**; ringmaster, host, compère, master of ceremonies, MC; presenter; *N. Amer. informal* emcee. 2 *he is a great showman* =**entertainer**, performer, virtuoso; *informal* show-off.

show-off ▶ noun *(informal)* =**exhibitionist**, extrovert, poser, poseur, swaggerer, self-publicist; *informal* pseud.

showy ▶ adjective =**ostentatious**, conspicuous, flamboyant, gaudy, garish, brash, vulgar, loud, extravagant, fancy, ornate; *informal* flash, flashy, glitzy, ritzy, swanky; *N. Amer. informal* superfly. –OPPOSITES restrained.

shred ▶ noun 1 *her dress was torn to shreds* =**tatter**, ribbon, rag, fragment, sliver, (tiny) bit/piece. 2 *not a shred of evidence* =**scrap**, bit, speck, iota, particle, ounce, whit, jot, crumb, fragment, grain, drop, trace, scintilla, spot.

▸ verb *shredding vegetables* =**chop finely**, cut up, grate, mince, grind.

shrewd ▸ adjective =**astute**, sharp, smart, acute, intelligent, clever, canny, perceptive, wise; *informal* on the ball, savvy; *N. Amer. informal* heads-up.
–OPPOSITES stupid.

shrewdness ▸ noun =**astuteness**, acuteness, acumen, intelligence, cleverness, smartness, wit, insight, understanding, perception, perceptiveness; *informal* savvy.

shriek ▸ verb & noun =**scream**, screech, squeal, squawk, roar, howl, shout, yelp.

shrill ▸ adjective =**high-pitched**, piercing, high, sharp, ear-piercing, ear-splitting, penetrating.

shrine ▸ noun =**tomb**, sanctuary, memorial, monument.

shrink ▸ verb **1** *the number of competitors shrank* =**get/grow smaller**, contract, diminish, lessen, reduce, decrease, dwindle, decline, fall/drop off. **2** *he shrank back against the wall* =**draw back**, recoil, back away, retreat, withdraw, cringe, cower. **3** *he doesn't shrink from naming names* =**recoil**, shy away, flinch, be averse, be afraid, hesitate.
–OPPOSITES expand, increase.

shrivel ▸ verb =**wither**, shrink; wilt; dry up, dehydrate, parch, frazzle.

shroud ▸ noun =**covering**, cover, cloak, mantle, blanket, layer, cloud, veil.
▸ verb =**cover**, envelop, veil, cloak, blanket, screen, conceal, hide, mask, obscure.

shrug ■ **shrug something off** =**disregard**, dismiss, take no notice of, ignore, play down, make light of.

shudder ▸ verb =**shake**, shiver, tremble, quiver; judder.
▸ noun =**shake**, shiver, tremor, trembling, quivering, vibration; judder.

shuffle ▸ verb **1** *they shuffled along the passage* =**shamble**, drag one's feet. **2** *she shuffled her feet* =**scrape**, drag, scuffle. **3** *he shuffled the cards* =**mix (up)**, rearrange, jumble (up).

shun ▸ verb =**avoid**, evade, eschew, steer clear of, shy away from, give a wide berth to, have nothing to do with; snub, give someone the cold shoulder, cold-shoulder, ignore, cut (dead), look right through; reject, rebuff, spurn, ostracize; *informal* give someone the brush-off, freeze out; *Brit. informal* send to Coventry.

–OPPOSITES welcome.

shut ▸ verb *please shut the door* =**close**, pull/push to, slam, fasten; put the lid on, lock, secure.
–OPPOSITES open, unlock.
■ **shut down** =**cease activity**, close (down), cease trading; *informal* fold.
■ **shut someone/something in** =**confine**, enclose, shut up, pen (in/up), fence in, lock up/in, cage, imprison; *N. Amer.* corral.
■ **shut someone/something out 1** *he shut me out of the house* =**lock out**, keep out. **2** *she shut out the memories* =**block**, suppress.
■ **shut up** *(informal)* =**be quiet**, keep quiet, hold one's tongue; stop talking, quieten (down); *informal* button it, cut the cackle, shut it, shut your face/mouth/trap, belt up, put a sock in it, give it a rest; *Brit. informal* shut your gob; *N. Amer. informal* save it.
■ **shut someone/something up 1** *I haven't shut the hens up yet. See* SHUT SOMEONE/SOMETHING IN. **2** *(informal) that should shut them up* =**quieten (down)**, silence, hush, quiet, gag, muzzle.

shuttle ▸ verb =**ply**, run, commute, go/travel back and forth; ferry.

shy ▸ adjective *I was painfully shy* =**bashful**, diffident, timid, reserved, reticent, introverted, retiring, self-effacing, withdrawn.
–OPPOSITES confident.
■ **shy away from** =**flinch**, recoil, hang back; be loath, be reluctant, be unwilling, be disinclined, be hesitant, hesitate, baulk at; *informal* boggle at.

shyness ▸ noun =**bashfulness**, diffidence, reserve, introversion, reticence, timidity, coyness.

sibling ▸ noun =**brother**, sister.

sick ▸ adjective **1** *the children are sick* =**ill**, unwell, poorly, ailing, indisposed, not oneself; *Brit.* off colour; *informal* laid up, under the weather; *Austral./NZ informal* crook. **2** *he was feeling sick* =**nauseous**, queasy, bilious, green about the gills; seasick, carsick, airsick, travel-sick. **3** *I'm sick of this music* =**fed up**, bored, tired, weary. **4** *(informal) a sick joke | sick humour* =**macabre**, tasteless, ghoulish, black, perverted, gruesome, gallows, cruel.
–OPPOSITES well.
■ **be sick** *(Brit.)* =**vomit**, throw up, heave; *informal* chunder, chuck up, hurl,

spew; *Brit. informal* honk; *N. Amer. informal* spit up, barf, upchuck.

sicken ▸ verb **1** *the stench sickened him* =**cause to feel sick/nauseous**, make sick, turn someone's stomach, revolt, disgust; *informal* make someone want to throw up; *N. Amer. informal* gross out. **2** *she sickened and died* =**become/fall ill**, catch something.
−OPPOSITES recover.

sickening ▸ adjective =**nauseating**, stomach-turning, stomach-churning; repulsive, revolting, disgusting, repellent, vile, nasty, foul, loathsome, offensive, objectionable, off-putting, distasteful, obscene, gruesome, grisly; *N. Amer.* vomitous; *informal* gross.

sickly ▸ adjective **1** *a sickly child* =**unhealthy**, in poor health, delicate, frail, weak. **2** *sickly faces* =**pale**, wan, pasty, sallow, pallid, ashen, anaemic. **3** *sickly love songs* =**sentimental**, mawkish, cloying, sugary, syrupy, saccharine; *informal* mushy, slushy, schmaltzy, cheesy, corny; *Brit. informal* soppy; *N. Amer. informal* cornball, sappy, hokey.
−OPPOSITES healthy.

sickness ▸ noun **1** *she was absent through sickness* =**illness**, disease, ailment, infection, malady, infirmity; *informal* bug, virus; *Brit. informal* lurgy; *Austral. informal* wog. **2** *a wave of sickness* =**nausea**, biliousness, queasiness. **3** *sickness and diarrhoea* =**vomiting**, retching; travelsickness, seasickness, carsickness, airsickness, motion sickness; *informal* throwing up, puking.

side ▸ noun **1** *the side of the road* =**edge**, border, verge, boundary, margin, fringe(s), flank, bank, perimeter, extremity, periphery, (outer) limit, limits. **2** *the wrong side of the road* =**half**, part; carriageway, lane. **3** *the east side of the city* =**district**, quarter, area, region, part, neighbourhood, sector, section, zone, ward. **4** *one side of the paper* =**surface**, face. **5** *his side of the argument* =**point of view**, viewpoint, perspective, opinion, way of thinking, standpoint, position, outlook, slant, angle. **6** *the losing side* =**faction**, camp, bloc, party. **7** *the players in their side* =**team**, squad, line-up.
−OPPOSITES centre, end.

▸ adjective **1** *elaborate side pieces* =**lateral**, wing, flanking. **2** *a side issue* =**subordinate**, lesser, lower-level, secondary, minor, peripheral, incidental, ancillary, subsidiary, extraneous.

−OPPOSITES front, central.

▸ verb *siding with the underdog.* See TAKE SOMEONE'S SIDE.

■ **side by side** =**alongside** (each other), beside each other, abreast, shoulder to shoulder.

■ **take/be on someone's side** =**support**, take someone's part, side with, stand by, back, give someone one's backing, be loyal to, defend, champion, ally (oneself) with, sympathize with, favour.

WORD LINKS

relating to the side of something: **lateral**

sideline ▸ noun =**secondary occupation**, second job; hobby, leisure activity/pursuit, recreation.

▸ verb =**overlook**, marginalize, ignore, forget (about), leave behind/out, exclude, discount.

sidelong ▸ adjective *a sidelong glance* =**indirect**, oblique, sideways, sideward; surreptitious, furtive, covert, sly.
−OPPOSITES overt.

sidestep ▸ verb =**avoid**, evade, dodge, circumvent, skirt round, bypass; *informal* duck.

sidetrack ▸ verb =**distract**, divert, deflect, draw away.

sideways ▸ adverb **1** *I slid sideways* =**to the side**, laterally. **2** *the expansion slots are mounted sideways* =**edgewise**, sidewards, side first, edgeways, end on.

▸ adjective **1** *sideways force* =**lateral**, sideward, on the side, side to side. **2** *a sideways look.* See SIDELONG adjective.

sidle ▸ verb =**creep**, sneak, slink, slip, slide, steal, edge, inch.

siege ▸ noun =**blockade**, encirclement; stand-off.
−OPPOSITES relief.

siesta ▸ noun =**afternoon sleep**, nap, catnap, doze, rest; *informal* snooze, liedown, forty winks, shut-eye; *Brit. informal* kip.

sieve ▸ noun =**strainer**, sifter, filter, screen.

▸ verb =**strain**, sift, screen, filter, riddle; *archaic* bolt.

sift ▸ verb **1** *sift the flour into a large bowl* =**sieve**, strain, screen, filter. **2** *we sift out unsuitable applications* =**separate out**, filter out, sort out, weed out, get rid of, remove. **3** *sifting through the wreckage* =**search through**, look through, examine, inspect, scrutinize, pore over, investigate, analyse, dissect.

sigh ▸ verb **1** *she sighed with relief* =**breathe (out)**, exhale; groan, moan. **2** *the wind sighed in the trees* =**rustle**, whisper, murmur.

sight ▸ noun **1** *she has excellent sight* =**eyesight**, vision, eyes. **2** *her first sight of it* =**view**, glimpse, glance, look. **3** *within sight of the enemy* =**range/field of vision**, view. **4** *historic sights* =**landmark**, place of interest, monument, spectacle, view, marvel, wonder.

▸ verb *one of the helicopters sighted wreckage* =**glimpse**, catch/get a glimpse of, catch sight of, see, spot, spy, make out, pick out, notice, observe; *literary* espy.

> **WORD LINKS**
>
> *relating to sight:* **optical, visual**

sightseer ▸ noun =**tourist**, visitor, tripper, holidaymaker.

sign ▸ noun **1** *a sign of affection* =**indication**, signal, symptom, pointer, suggestion, intimation, mark, manifestation, demonstration, token. **2** *a sign of things to come* =**portent**, omen, warning; promise, threat. **3** *at his sign they attacked* =**gesture**, signal, wave, cue, nod. **4** *signs saying 'danger'* =**notice**, signpost, road sign. **5** *the dancers were daubed with signs* =**symbol**, cipher, letter, character, figure, hieroglyph, ideogram, rune, emblem, device, logo.

▸ verb *he signed the letter* =**write one's name on**, autograph, initial, countersign. **2** *the government signed the treaty* =**endorse**, validate; agree to, approve, ratify, adopt. **3** *he signed his name* =**write**, inscribe, pen. **4** *we have signed a new player* =**recruit**, engage, employ, take on, appoint, sign on/up, enlist. **5** *she signed to Susan to leave* =**gesture**, signal, motion; wave, beckon, nod.

■ **sign on/up** =**enlist**, take a job, join (up), enrol, register, volunteer.

■ **sign someone on/up.** *See* SIGN *verb sense 4.*

signal¹ ▸ noun **1** *a signal to stop* =**gesture**, sign, wave, cue, indication, warning. **2** *a clear signal that we're in trouble* =**indication**, sign, symptom, hint, pointer, intimation, clue, demonstration, evidence, proof. **3** *at his signal, they attacked* =**cue**, prompt.

▸ verb **1** *the driver signalled to her* =**gesture**, sign, indicate, motion; wave, beckon,

nod. **2** *they signalled their displeasure* =**indicate**, show, express, communicate. **3** *his death signals the end of an era* =**mark**, signify, mean, be a sign of, be evidence of.

signal² ▸ adjective *the campaign was a signal failure* =**notable**, striking, glaring, significant, momentous, obvious, conspicuous.

significance ▸ noun **1** *a matter of significance* =**importance**, import, consequence, seriousness, gravity, weight, magnitude; *formal* moment. **2** *the significance of his remarks* =**meaning**, sense, signification, import, thrust, drift, gist, implication, message, essence, substance, point.

significant ▸ adjective **1** *a significant fact* =**notable**, noteworthy, remarkable, important, of consequence; *formal* of moment. **2** *a significant increase* =**sizeable**, considerable, appreciable, conspicuous, striking; meaningful, obvious, large, sudden. **3** *a significant look* =**meaningful**, expressive, eloquent, suggestive, knowing, telling.

significantly ▸ adverb **1** *significantly better* =**notably**, remarkably, materially, appreciably; markedly, considerably, obviously, conspicuously, strikingly. **2** *he paused significantly* =**meaningfully**, expressively, eloquently, revealingly, suggestively, knowingly.

signify ▸ verb **1** *this signified a change* =**be evidence of**, be a sign of, mark, signal, be symptomatic of, herald, indicate. **2** *the egg signifies life* =**mean**, denote, designate, represent, symbolize, stand for. **3** *signify your agreement by signing below* =**express**, indicate, show, declare.

silence ▸ noun **1** *the silence of the night* =**quietness**, quiet, still, stillness, hush, tranquillity, noiselessness, soundlessness, peacefulness, peace (and quiet). **2** *she was reduced to silence* =**speechlessness**, wordlessness, dumbness, muteness.

–OPPOSITES sound.

▸ verb **1** *he silenced her with a kiss* =**quieten**, quiet, hush. **2** *dissidents have been silenced* =**gag**, muzzle, censor. **3** *this would silence their complaints* =**stop**, put an end/stop to.

silent ▸ adjective **1** *the night was silent* =**(completely) quiet**, still, hushed, inaudible, noiseless, soundless. **2** *the right to remain silent* =**speechless**, quiet, un-

speaking, dumb, mute, taciturn, un-communicative, tight-lipped. **3** *silent thanks* =**unspoken**, wordless.
−OPPOSITES audible, noisy.

silently ▸ adverb **1** *Nancy crept silently up the stairs* =**quietly**, inaudibly, noiselessly, soundlessly, in silence. **2** *they drove on silently* =**without a word**, saying nothing, in silence.
−OPPOSITES audibly, out loud.

silhouette ▸ noun =**outline**, contour(s), profile, form, shape.
▸ verb =**outline**, delineate, define.

silk ▸ noun

> WORD LINKS
>
> *farming of silk:* **sericulture**

silky ▸ adjective =**smooth**, soft, sleek, fine, glossy, silken.

silly ▸ adjective **1** *don't be so silly* =**foolish**, stupid; scatterbrained; frivolous, giddy, inane, immature, childish, puerile, empty-headed; *informal* dotty, scatty. **2** *that was a silly thing to do* =**unwise**, imprudent, thoughtless, foolish, stupid, unintelligent, idiotic, brainless, senseless, mindless, rash, reckless, foolhardy, irresponsible, injudicious; *informal* crazy, mad; *Brit. informal* daft. **3** *he would worry about silly things* =**trivial**, trifling, frivolous, petty, small, insignificant, unimportant; *informal* piffling, piddling; *N. Amer. informal* small-bore.
−OPPOSITES sensible.

silt ▸ noun =**sediment**, deposit, alluvium, mud.
▸ verb =**become blocked**, become clogged, fill up.

silver ▸ noun **1** *freshly polished silver* =**silverware**, (silver) plate; cutlery. **2** *a handful of silver* =**coins**; (small) change, loose change. **3** *she won three silvers* =**silver medal**.
▸ adjective **1** *silver hair* =**grey**, greying, white. **2** *the silver water* =**silvery**, shining, lustrous, gleaming.

similar ▸ adjective **1** *you two are very similar* =**alike**, (much) the same, homogeneous; *informal* much of a muchness. **2** *northern India and similar areas* =**comparable**, like, corresponding, equivalent, analogous. **3** *other parts were similar to Wales* =**like**, much the same as, comparable to.
−OPPOSITES different, unlike.

similarity ▸ noun =**resemblance**, likeness, sameness, comparability, corres-

pondence, parallel, equivalence, homogeneity, uniformity.

similarly ▸ adverb =**likewise**, in similar fashion, comparably, correspondingly, in the same way.

simmer ▸ verb **1** *the soup was simmering on the stove* =**boil (gently)**, cook (gently), bubble. **2** *she was simmering with resentment* =**seethe**, fume, smoulder.
■ **simmer down** =**become less angry**, cool off/down, calm down.

simple ▸ adjective **1** *it's really pretty simple* =**straightforward**, easy, uncomplicated, uninvolved, undemanding, elementary, child's play; *informal* as easy as falling off a log, as easy as pie, as easy as ABC, a piece of cake, a cinch, no sweat, a doddle, a pushover, money for old rope, kids' stuff, a breeze; *Brit. informal* easy-peasy; *N. Amer. informal* duck soup, a snap; *Austral./NZ informal* a bludge, a snack. **2** *simple language* =**clear**, plain, straightforward, accessible; *informal* user-friendly. **3** *a simple white blouse* =**plain**, unadorned, basic, unsophisticated, no-frills; classic, understated, uncluttered, restrained. **4** *the simple truth* =**candid**, frank, honest, sincere, plain, absolute, bald, stark, unadorned, unvarnished. **5** *simple country people* =**unpretentious**, unsophisticated, ordinary, unaffected, unassuming, natural, straightforward; *N. Amer.* cracker-barrel. **6** *he's a bit simple* =**with learning difficulties**, with special (educational) needs.
−OPPOSITES difficult, complex, fancy.

simpleton ▸ noun. *See* FOOL *noun sense* 1.

simplicity ▸ noun **1** *the simplicity of the recipes* =**straightforwardness**, ease, easiness, simpleness. **2** *the simplicity of the language* =**clarity**, clearness, plainness, simpleness, intelligibility, comprehensibility, straightforwardness, accessibility. **3** *the building's simplicity* =**plainness**, lack/absence of adornment, lack/absence of decoration, austerity, spareness, clean lines. **4** *the simplicity of their lifestyle* =**plainness**, modesty, naturalness.

simplify ▸ verb =**make simple/simpler**, make easy/easier to understand, make plainer, clarify; paraphrase, put in words of one syllable.
−OPPOSITES complicate.

simplistic ▸ adjective =**facile**, superficial, oversimplified.

simply ▸ adverb **1** *he spoke simply and*

forcefully =**straightforwardly**, directly, clearly, plainly, lucidly, unambiguously. **2** *she was dressed simply* =**plainly**, soberly, unfussily, classically. **3** *they lived simply* =**modestly**, plainly, quietly. **4** *they are welcomed simply because they are rich* =**merely**, just, purely, solely, only. **5** *she was simply delighted* =**utterly**, absolutely, completely, positively, just; *informal* plain.

simulate ▶ verb **1** *they simulated pleasure* =**feign**, pretend, fake, affect, put on. **2** *simulating conditions in space* =**imitate**, reproduce, replicate, duplicate, mimic.

simulated ▶ adjective **1** *simulated fear* =**feigned**, fake, mock, affected, sham; *informal* pretend, put-on, phoney. **2** *simulated leather* =**artificial**, imitation, fake, mock, synthetic, man-made, ersatz.
–OPPOSITES real.

simultaneous ▶ adjective =**concurrent**, happening at the same time, contemporaneous, concomitant, coinciding, coincident, synchronous, synchronized.

simultaneously ▶ adverb =**at (one and) the same time**, at the same instant/moment, at once, concurrently, concomitantly; (all) together, in unison, in concert, in chorus.

sin ▶ noun **1** *a sin in the eyes of God* =**immoral act**, wrong, wrongdoing, act of evil/wickedness, transgression, crime, offence, misdeed, misdemeanour; *archaic* trespass. **2** *the human capacity for sin* =**wickedness**, wrongdoing, evil, evildoing, sinfulness, immorality, iniquity, vice, crime.
–OPPOSITES virtue.
▶ verb *I have sinned* =**transgress**, do wrong, misbehave, go astray.

sincere ▶ adjective **1** *our sincere gratitude* =**heartfelt**, wholehearted, profound, deep; true, honest. **2** *a sincere person* =**honest**, genuine, truthful, direct, frank, candid; *informal* straight, upfront, on the level; *N. Amer. informal* on the up and up.

sincerely ▶ adverb =**genuinely**, honestly, really, truly, truthfully, wholeheartedly, earnestly.

sincerity ▶ noun =**honesty**, genuineness, truthfulness, integrity, openness, candour.

sinewy ▶ adjective =**muscular**, muscly, strong, powerful, athletic.
–OPPOSITES puny.

sinful ▶ adjective =**immoral**, wicked, (morally) wrong, evil, bad, iniquitous.
–OPPOSITES virtuous.

sinfulness ▶ noun =**immorality**, wickedness, sin, wrongdoing, evil, evildoing, iniquitousness, corruption, depravity, degeneracy, vice; *formal* turpitude.
–OPPOSITES virtue.

sing ▶ verb **1** *he began to sing* =**croon**, trill, chant, intone, chorus. **2** *the birds were singing* =**warble**, trill, chirp, chirrup, cheep.

singe ▶ verb =**scorch**, burn, sear, char.

singer ▶ noun =**vocalist**, soloist, songster, songstress, cantor.

single ▶ adjective **1** *a single red rose* =**one** (only), sole, lone, solitary, unaccompanied, alone. **2** *every single word* =**individual**, separate, distinct. **3** *is she single?* =**unmarried**, unwed, unattached, free, a bachelor, a spinster.
–OPPOSITES double, multiple, married.
■ **single someone/something out** =**select**, pick out, choose, decide on; target, earmark, mark out, separate out, set apart/aside.

WORD LINKS

relating to a single thing: **uni-, mono-**
obsession with a single thing: **monomania**

single-handed ▶ adverb =**by oneself**, alone, on one's own, solo, unaided, unassisted, without help.

single-minded ▶ adjective =**determined**, committed, unswerving, unwavering, resolute, purposeful, devoted, dedicated, uncompromising, tireless, tenacious, persistent, dogged.
–OPPOSITES half-hearted.

singly ▶ adverb =**one by one**, one at a time, one after the other, individually, separately.
–OPPOSITES together.

singular ▶ adjective =**remarkable**, extraordinary, exceptional, outstanding, signal, notable, noteworthy.

singularly ▶ adverb. See EXTREMELY.

sinister ▶ adjective **1** *there was a sinister undertone in his words* =**menacing**, threatening, ominous, forbidding, frightening, alarming, disturbing, disquieting, dark. **2** *a sinister motive* =**evil**, wicked, criminal, nefarious, villainous,

base, malicious; *informal* shady.
–OPPOSITES innocent.

sink ▶ verb **1** *the coffin sank below the waves*
=**become submerged**, be engulfed,
drop, fall, descend. **2** *the cruise liner sank
yesterday* =**founder**, go down. **3** *they sank
their ships* =**scuttle**; *Brit.* scupper. **4** *the sun
was sinking* =**set**, go down. **5** *Loretta sank
into an armchair* =**lower oneself**, flop,
collapse, drop down, slump; *informal*
plonk oneself. **6** *her voice sank to a whisper*
=**fall**, drop; become/get quieter, be-
come/get softer. **7** *she would never sink to
your level* =**stoop**, lower oneself, descend. **8** *sink the pots into the ground*
=**embed**, insert, drive, plant. **9** *sinking a
well* =**dig**, excavate, bore, drill. **10** *they
sank their life savings in the company* =**invest**, venture, risk.
–OPPOSITES float, rise.
■ **sink in** =**register**, be understood, be
comprehended, be grasped, get
through.

sinner ▶ noun =**wrongdoer**, evil-doer,
transgressor, miscreant, offender, criminal.

sinuous ▶ adjective **1** *a sinuous river*
=**winding**, windy, serpentine, curving,
twisting, meandering, snaking, zigzag,
curling, coiling. **2** *sinuous grace* =**lithe**,
supple, graceful, loose-limbed, lissom.
–OPPOSITES straight, awkward.

sip ▶ verb =**drink (slowly)**; *dated* sup.
▶ noun =**mouthful**, swallow, drink, drop,
dram, nip; *informal* swig.

siren ▶ noun =**alarm (bell)**, warning
(bell), (danger) signal, horn, hooter;
trademark klaxon.

sister ▶ noun **1** *I have two sisters* =**sibling**.
2 *our European sisters* =**comrade**, partner,
colleague; counterpart. **3** *the sisters in the
convent* =**nun**, novice; abbess, prioress.

> **WORD LINKS**
>
> relating to a sister: **sororal**
> killing of one's sister: **fratricide**

sit ▶ verb **1** *you'd better sit down* =**take a
seat**, seat oneself, be seated, perch, ensconce oneself, plump oneself, flop; *informal* take the load/weight off one's feet,
plonk oneself; *Brit. informal* take a pew.
2 *she sat the package on the table* =**put
(down)**, place, set (down), lay, deposit,
rest, stand; *informal* stick, park. **3** *she sat
for Picasso* =**pose**, model. **4** *a hotel sitting
on the bank of the River Dee* =**be situated**,

be located, be sited, stand. **5** *the committee sits on Saturday* =**be in session**, meet,
be convened. **6** *she sits on the tribunal*
=**serve on**, have a seat on, be a member
of. **7** *his shyness doesn't sit easily with Hollywood tradition* =**be harmonious**, go, fit
in, harmonize.
–OPPOSITES stand.
■ **sit back 1** *sit back and enjoy the music*
=**relax**, take it easy, lie back; *informal* chill
out. **2** *we can't just sit back and wait* =**do
nothing**, walk away, keep one's distance, stand (idly) by.
■ **sit in for** =**stand in for**, fill in for,
cover for, substitute for, deputize for.
■ **sit in on** =**attend**, be present at, observe; *N. Amer.* audit.
■ **sit tight** *(informal)* **1** *just sit tight* =**stay
put**, wait there. **2** *we're advising our clients
to sit tight* =**take no action**, wait, hold
back, bide one's time.

site ▶ noun =**location**, place, position,
situation, locality, whereabouts; *technical*
locus.
▶ verb =**place**, put, position, situate, locate.

sitting ▶ noun =**session**, meeting, assembly; hearing.
▶ adjective =**sedentary**, seated.
–OPPOSITES standing.

sitting room ▶ noun =**living room**,
lounge, front room, drawing room, reception room; *dated* parlour.

situate ▶ verb =**locate**, site, position,
place, station.

situation ▶ noun **1** *their financial situation* =**circumstances**, (state of) affairs,
state, condition. **2** *I'll fill you in on the situation* =**the facts**, how things stand, the
lie of the land, what's going on; *Brit.* the
state of play; *N. Amer.* the lay of the land;
informal the score. **3** *the hotel's pleasant situation* =**location**, position, spot, site, setting, environment. **4** *he was offered a situation in America* =**job**, post, position,
appointment; employment.

six ▶ cardinal number =**sextet**, sextuplets.

> **WORD LINKS**
>
> relating to six: **hexa-, sexi-**
> six-sided figure: **hexagon**

size ▶ noun =**dimensions**, measurements, proportions, magnitude, largeness, area, expanse; breadth, width,
length, height, depth; immensity, hugeness, vastness.

s

▶ verb =**sort**, categorize, classify.
■ **size someone/something up** (*informal*) =**assess**, appraise, get the measure of, judge, take stock of, evaluate; *Brit. informal* suss out.

sizeable ▶ adjective =**fairly/pretty large**, substantial, considerable, respectable, significant, largish, biggish, goodly.
−OPPOSITES small.

sizzle ▶ verb =**crackle**, frizzle, sputter, spit.

sizzling ▶ adjective (*informal*) **1** *sizzling temperatures* =(**extremely**) **hot**, unbearably hot, blazing, burning, scorching, sweltering; *N. Amer.* broiling; *informal* boiling (hot), baking (hot). **2** *a sizzling affair* =**passionate**, torrid, ardent, lustful, erotic; *informal* steamy, hot.
−OPPOSITES freezing.

skeletal ▶ adjective =**emaciated**, painfully thin, as thin as a rake, cadaverous, skin-and-bones, skinny, bony, gaunt; *informal* anorexic.
−OPPOSITES fat.

skeleton ▶ noun **1** *the human skeleton* =**bones**; *technical* endoskeleton, exoskeleton. **2** *a wire skeleton* =**framework**, frame, shell.
▶ adjective *a skeleton staff* =**minimum**, minimal, basic, essential.

sketch ▶ noun **1** *a sketch of the proposed design* =(**preliminary**) **drawing**, outline; diagram, design, plan; *informal* rough. **2** *she gave a brief sketch of what had happened* =**outline**, brief description, rundown, main points, thumbnail sketch, (bare) bones; summary, synopsis, summarization, precis, résumé; *N. Amer.* wrap-up. **3** *a hilarious sketch* =**skit**, scene, piece, act, item, routine.
▶ verb **1** *he sketched the garden* =**draw**, make a drawing of, draw a picture of, pencil, rough out, outline. **2** *the company sketched out its plans* =**describe**, outline, give a brief idea of, rough out; summarize, precis.

sketchily ▶ adverb =**perfunctorily**, cursorily, incompletely, patchily, vaguely, imprecisely; hastily, hurriedly.

sketchy ▶ adjective =**incomplete**, patchy, fragmentary, cursory, perfunctory, scanty, vague, imprecise; hurried, hasty.
−OPPOSITES detailed.

skilful ▶ adjective =**expert**, accomplished, skilled, masterly, master, virtuoso, consummate, proficient, talented, adept, adroit, deft, dexterous, able, good, competent, capable, handy; *informal* mean, wicked, crack, ace, wizard; *N. Amer. informal* crackerjack.

skill ▶ noun **1** *his skill as a politician* =**expertise**, skilfulness, expertness, adeptness, adroitness, deftness, dexterity, ability, prowess, mastery, competence, capability, aptitude, artistry, virtuosity, talent. **2** *bringing up a family demands many skills* =**accomplishment**, strength, ability.
−OPPOSITES incompetence.

skilled ▶ adjective =**experienced**, trained, qualified, proficient, practised, accomplished, expert, skilful, adept, adroit, deft, dexterous, able, good, competent; *informal* crack; *N. Amer. informal* crackerjack.
−OPPOSITES inexperienced.

skim ▶ verb **1** *skim off the fat* =**remove**, scoop off. **2** *the boat skimmed over the water* =**glide**, move lightly, slide, sail, skate. **3** *he skimmed the pebble across the water* =**throw**, toss, cast, pitch. **4** *she skimmed through the newspaper* =**glance**, flick, flip, leaf, thumb, read quickly, scan, run one's eye over. **5** *Hannah skimmed over this part of the story* =**mention briefly**, pass over quickly, skate over, gloss over.
−OPPOSITES elaborate on.

skimp ▶ verb =**stint on**, scrimp on, economize on, cut back on, be sparing, be frugal, be mean, cut corners; *informal* be stingy, be mingy, be tight.

skimpy ▶ adjective =**revealing**, short, low, low-cut.

skin ▶ noun **1** *these chemicals could damage the skin* =**epidermis**, dermis, derma. **2** *Mary's fair skin* =**complexion**, colouring, pigmentation. **3** *leopard skins* =**hide**, pelt, fleece. **4** *a banana skin* =**peel**, rind. **5** *milk with a skin on it* =**film**, layer, membrane. **6** *the plane's skin was damaged* =**casing**, exterior, membrane.
▶ verb **1** *skin the tomatoes* =**peel**, pare, hull. **2** *he skinned his knee* =**graze**, scrape, abrade, bark, rub something raw, chafe.
■ **it's no skin off my nose** (*informal*) =**I don't care**, I don't mind, I'm not bothered, it doesn't bother me, it doesn't matter to me; *informal* I don't give a damn, I don't give a monkey's.

WORD LINKS

relating to the skin: **cutaneous, dermato-**
under the skin: **subcutaneous**
branch of medicine concerning the skin: **dermatology**

skin-deep ▶ adjective =**superficial**, (on the) surface, external, outward, shallow.

skinflint ▶ noun *(informal). See* MISER.

skinny ▶ adjective. *See* THIN adjective sense 3.

skip ▶ verb **1** *skipping down the path* =**caper**, prance, trip, dance, bound, bounce, gambol. **2** *we skipped the boring stuff* =**omit**, leave out, miss out, dispense with, pass over, skim over, disregard; *informal* give something a miss. **3** *I skipped school* =**play truant from**, miss; *N. Amer.* cut; *Brit. informal* skive off; *N. Amer. informal* play hookey from; *Austral./NZ informal* play the wag from. **4** *I skipped through the magazine* =**have a quick look at**, flick through, flip through, leaf through.

skirmish ▶ noun **1** *the unit was caught up in a skirmish* =**fight**, battle, clash, conflict, encounter, engagement, firefight. **2** *a skirmish over the budget* =**argument**, quarrel, squabble, contretemps, disagreement, difference of opinion, falling-out, dispute, clash, altercation, tussle; *informal* tiff, spat; *Brit. informal* row, barney, ding-dong.
▶ verb *they skirmished with enemy soldiers* =**fight**, (do) battle with, engage with, close with, combat, clash with.

skirt ▶ verb **1** *he skirted the city* =**go round**, walk round, circle. **2** *the fields that skirt the park* =**border**, edge, flank, line, lie alongside/next to. **3** *he carefully skirted round the subject* =**avoid**, evade, sidestep, dodge, pass over, gloss over; *informal* duck; *Austral./NZ informal* duck-shove.

skit ▶ noun =(comedy) **sketch**, parody, pastiche, satire; *informal* spoof, take-off, send-up.

skittish ▶ adjective **1** *she grew increasingly skittish* =**playful**, lively, high-spirited, frisky; *literary* frolicsome. **2** *his horse was skittish* =**restive**, excitable, nervous, jumpy, highly strung.

skive ▶ verb *(Brit. informal)* =**malinger**, play truant, truant, shirk, idle; *Brit. informal* bunk off, swing the lead; *N. Amer. informal* gold-brick, play hookey, goof off; *Austral./NZ informal* play the wag.

skulduggery ▶ noun =**trickery**, sharp practice, underhandedness, chicanery; *informal* shenanigans, funny business, monkey business; *Brit. informal* jiggery-pokery; *N. Amer. informal* monkey-shines.

skulk ▶ verb =**lurk**, loiter, hide; creep, sneak, slink, prowl.

skull ▶ noun

WORD LINKS

relating to the skull: **cranial**
study of skull shape as supposed indicator of character: **phrenology**

sky ▶ noun *the sun was shining in the sky* =**the upper atmosphere**; *literary* the heavens, the firmament, the blue, the (wide) blue yonder.
■ **to the skies** =**effusively**, profusely, very highly, very enthusiastically, unreservedly, fervently, fulsomely, extravagantly.

WORD LINKS

relating to the sky: **celestial**

slab ▶ noun =**piece**, block, hunk, chunk, lump; cake, tablet, brick.

slack ▶ adjective **1** *the rope went slack* =**loose**, limp. **2** *slack skin* =**flaccid**, flabby, loose, sagging, saggy. **3** *business is slack* =**sluggish**, slow, quiet, slow-moving, flat, depressed, stagnant. **4** *slack accounting procedures* =**lax**, negligent, careless, slapdash, slipshod; *informal* sloppy, slap-happy.
–OPPOSITES tight, taut.
▶ noun **1** *the rope had some slack in it* =**looseness**, play, give. **2** *foreign demand will help pick up the slack* =**surplus**, excess, spare capacity.
▶ verb *(Brit. informal)* =**idle**, shirk, be lazy, be indolent, waste time, lounge about; *Brit. informal* skive; *N. Amer. informal* goof off.

slacken ▶ verb **1** *he slackened his grip* =**loosen**, release, relax, loose, lessen, weaken. **2** *he slackened his pace* =**slow (down)**, become/get/make slower, decelerate. **3** *the rain is slackening* =**decrease**, lessen, subside, ease up/off, let up, abate, diminish, die down, fall off.
–OPPOSITES tighten.

slake ▶ verb =**quench**, satisfy, sate, satiate, relieve, assuage.

slam ▶ verb **1** *he slammed the door behind him* =**bang**, shut/close with a bang. **2** *the car slammed into a lamp post* =**crash into**, smash into, collide with, hit, strike, ram, plough into, run into, bump into; *N. Amer.* impact.

slander ▶ noun =defamation (of character), character assassination, calumny, libel; malicious gossip, disparagement, denigration, aspersions, vilification; lie, slur, smear; *informal* mudslinging, bad-mouthing.

▶ verb =defame (someone's character), blacken someone's name, tell lies about, speak ill/evil of, libel, smear, cast aspersions on, besmirch, tarnish; malign, vilify, disparage, denigrate, run down; *N. Amer.* slur.

slanderous ▶ adjective =defamatory, denigrating, disparaging, libellous, pejorative, false, misrepresentative, scurrilous, scandalous, malicious.
–OPPOSITES complimentary.

slang ▶ noun =informal language, colloquialisms, patois, argot, cant.

slant ▶ verb 1 *the floor was slanting* =slope, tilt, incline, be at an angle, tip, lean, dip, pitch, shelve, list, bank. **2** *their findings were slanted in our favour* =bias, distort, twist, skew, weight.

▶ noun 1 *the slant of the roof* =slope, incline, tilt, gradient, pitch, angle, camber, inclination. **2** *a feminist slant* =point of view, viewpoint, standpoint, stance, angle, perspective, approach, view, attitude, position; bias, leaning.

slanting ▶ adjective =oblique, sloping, at an angle, inclined, tilting, tilted, slanted, diagonal.

slap ▶ verb 1 *he slapped her hard* =hit, strike, smack, clout, cuff, spank; *informal* whack, wallop, biff, bash; *Brit. informal* slosh; *Austral./NZ informal* dong, quilt. **2** *he slapped down a £10 note* =fling, throw, slam, bang; *informal* plonk. **3** *slap on a coat of paint* =daub, plaster, throw. **4** *(informal) they slapped a huge tax on imports* =impose, levy, put on.

▶ noun *a slap across the face* =smack, blow, cuff, clout; *informal* whack, thwack, wallop, clip.

■ **a slap in the face** =rebuff, rejection, snub, insult, put-down, humiliation.

■ **a slap on the back** =congratulations, commendation, approbation, approval, accolades, compliments, tributes, a pat on the back, praise, acclaim.

■ **a slap on the wrist** =reprimand, rebuke, reproof, scolding, admonishment; *informal* telling-off, rap over the knuckles,

dressing-down; *Brit. informal* ticking-off; *Austral./NZ informal* serve.

slapdash ▶ adjective =careless, slipshod, hurried, haphazard, unsystematic, untidy, messy, hit-or-miss, negligent, neglectful, lax; *informal* sloppy, slap-happy; *Brit. informal* shambolic.
–OPPOSITES meticulous.

slash ▶ verb 1 *her tyres had been slashed* =cut (open), gash, slit, split open, lacerate, knife. **2** *(informal) the company slashed prices* =reduce, cut, lower, bring down, mark down. **3** *(informal) they have slashed 10,000 jobs* =get rid of, axe, cut, shed.

▶ noun 1 *a slash across his temple* =cut, gash, laceration, slit, incision; wound. **2** *sentence breaks are indicated by slashes* =solidus, oblique; forward slash, backslash.

slate ▶ verb *(Brit. informal)*. See CRITICIZE.

slaughter ▶ verb 1 *the cattle were slaughtered* =kill, butcher; cull, put down. **2** *civilians are being slaughtered* =massacre, murder, butcher, kill (off), annihilate, exterminate, decimate, wipe out, put to death; *literary* slay.

▶ noun 1 *the slaughter of 20 demonstrators* =massacre, murdering, (mass) murder, (mass) killing, (mass) execution, annihilation, extermination, liquidation, decimation; *literary* slaying. **2** *a scene of slaughter* =carnage, bloodshed, bloodletting, bloodbath.

slaughterhouse ▶ noun =abattoir; *archaic* shambles.

slave ▶ noun 1 *the work was done by slaves* =historical serf, vassal; *archaic* bondsman, bondswoman. **2** *he treats her like a slave* =servant, lackey; *informal* gofer; *Brit. informal* skivvy, dogsbody, poodle.
–OPPOSITES freeman, master.

▶ verb *slaving away* =toil, labour, grind, sweat, work one's fingers to the bone, work like a Trojan/dog; *informal* kill oneself, sweat blood, slog away; *Brit. informal* graft; *Austral./NZ informal* bullock.

┌─────────────────────┐
│ **WORD LINKS** │
└─────────────────────┘
like a slave: **servile**

slaver ▶ verb =drool, slobber, dribble, salivate.

slavery ▶ noun =bondage, enslavement, servitude, serfdom.
–OPPOSITES freedom.

slavish ▶ adjective =unoriginal, uninspired, unimaginative, uninventive, imitative, mindless.

slay ▸ verb (literary) =kill, murder, put to death, butcher, cut down, slaughter, massacre, shoot down, gun down, mow down, eliminate, annihilate, exterminate, liquidate; informal wipe out, bump off.

slaying ▸ noun (literary) =murder, killing, butchery, slaughter, massacre, extermination, liquidation.

sleazy ▸ adjective 1 sleazy politicians =corrupt, immoral. 2 a sleazy bar =squalid, seedy, seamy, sordid, insalubrious, mean, cheap, low-class, run down; informal scruffy, scuzzy, crummy; Brit. informal grotty.
−OPPOSITES reputable, upmarket.

sledge ▸ noun =toboggan, bobsleigh, sleigh; N. Amer. sled.

sleek ▸ adjective 1 his sleek dark hair =smooth, glossy, shiny, shining, lustrous, silken, silky. 2 the car's sleek lines =streamlined, elegant, graceful. 3 sleek young men in city suits =well groomed, stylish.

sleep ▸ noun =nap, doze, siesta, catnap, beauty sleep; informal snooze, forty winks, a bit of shut-eye; Brit. informal kip; literary slumber.
▸ verb =be asleep, doze, take a siesta, take a nap, catnap; informal snooze, snatch forty winks, get some shut-eye; Brit. informal (have a) kip, get one's head down; N. Amer. informal catch some Zs; humorous be in the land of Nod; literary slumber.
−OPPOSITES wake up.
■ go to sleep =fall asleep, get to sleep; informal drop off, nod off, drift off, crash out, flake out; N. Amer. informal sack out, zone out.
■ put something to sleep =put down, destroy, slaughter; N. Amer. euthanize.

> [!NOTE] **WORD LINKS**
> causing sleep: **sedative, hypnotic, soporific, somnolent**
> fear of sleep: **hypnophobia**

sleepiness ▸ noun =drowsiness, tiredness, somnolence, languor, doziness; lethargy, sluggishness, lassitude, enervation.

sleepless ▸ adjective =wakeful, restless, insomniac; (wide) awake, tossing and turning.

sleeplessness ▸ noun =insomnia, wakefulness.

sleepwalker ▸ noun =somnambulist.

sleepy ▸ adjective 1 she felt very sleepy =drowsy, tired, somnolent, heavy-eyed, asleep on one's feet; lethargic, enervated, torpid; informal dopey. 2 a sleepy little village =quiet, peaceful, tranquil, placid, slow-moving; dull, boring.
−OPPOSITES awake, alert.

sleight of hand ▸ noun 1 impressive sleight of hand =dexterity, adroitness, deftness, skill. 2 financial sleight of hand =deception, deceit, chicanery, trickery, sharp practice.

slender ▸ adjective 1 her tall slender figure =slim, lean, willowy, sylphlike, svelte, lissom, graceful; slight, thin, skinny. 2 slender evidence =meagre, limited, slight, scanty, scant, sparse, paltry, insubstantial. 3 the chances seemed slender =faint, remote, flimsy, tenuous, fragile, slim; unlikely, improbable.
−OPPOSITES plump.

slice ▸ noun 1 a slice of fruitcake =piece, portion, slab, rasher, sliver, wafer. 2 a huge slice of public spending =share, part, portion, tranche, piece, proportion, allocation, percentage.
▸ verb slice the cheese thinly =cut (up), carve.

slick ▸ adjective 1 a slick advertising campaign =efficient, smooth, smooth-running, polished, well organized, well run, streamlined. 2 his slick use of words =glib, smooth, fluent, plausible. 3 a slick salesman =suave, urbane, polished, assured, self-assured, smooth-talking, glib; informal smarmy. 4 her slick brown hair =shiny, glossy, shining, sleek, smooth.
▸ verb his hair was slicked down =smooth, sleek, grease, oil, gel.

slide ▸ verb 1 the glass slid across the table =glide, slip, slither, skim, skate; skid, slew. 2 tears slid down her cheeks =trickle, run, flow, pour, stream. 3 four men slid out of the shadows =creep, steal, slink, slip, tiptoe, sidle. 4 the country is sliding into recession =sink, fall, drop, descend; decline, degenerate.
▸ noun 1 the current slide in house prices =fall, decline, drop, slump, downturn, downswing. 2 a slide show =transparency.
−OPPOSITES rise.

slight ▸ adjective 1 the chance of success is slight =small, modest, tiny, minute, negligible, insignificant, minimal, remote, slim, faint; informal minuscule. 2 the book *is a slight work* =**minor**, inconsequential, trivial, unimportant, lightweight. **3** *Elizabeth's slight figure* =**slim**, slender, petite, diminutive, small, delicate, dainty.

–OPPOSITES considerable.

▶ verb *he had been slighted* =**insult**, snub, rebuff, spurn, give someone the cold shoulder, cut (dead), scorn.

–OPPOSITES respect.

▶ noun *an unintended slight* =**insult**, affront, snub, rebuff; *informal* put-down.

–OPPOSITES compliment.

slightly ▶ adverb =**a little**, a bit, somewhat, rather, moderately, to a certain extent, faintly, vaguely, a shade.

–OPPOSITES very.

slim ▶ adjective **1** *tall and slim* =**slender**, lean, thin, willowy, sylphlike, svelte, lissom, trim. **2** *a slim silver bracelet* =**narrow**, slender. **3** *a slim chance* =**slight**, small, slender, faint, poor, remote.

–OPPOSITES plump.

▶ verb **1** *I'm trying to slim* =**lose weight**, get into shape; *N. Amer.* slenderize. **2** *the number of staff had been slimmed down* =**reduce**, cut (down/back), scale down, decrease, diminish, pare down.

slime ▶ noun =**ooze**; *informal* goo, gunk, gook, gloop; *Brit. informal* gunge; *N. Amer. informal* guck, glop.

slimy ▶ adjective **1** *the floor was slimy* =**slippery**, slithery, greasy; *informal* slippy, gunky, gooey, gloopy. **2** *(informal) her slimy press agent. See* OBSEQUIOUS.

sling ▶ noun *she had her arm in a sling* =**(support) bandage**, support, strap.

▶ verb **1** *a hammock was slung between two trees* =**hang**, suspend, string, swing. **2** *(informal) she slung her jacket on the sofa. See* THROW *verb sense* 1.

slink ▶ verb =**creep**, sneak, steal, slip, slide, sidle, tiptoe.

slinky ▶ adjective *(informal)* **1** *a slinky black dress* =**tight-fitting**, close-fitting, figure-hugging, sexy. **2** *her slinky elegance* =**sinuous**, feline, willowy, sleek.

slip¹ ▶ verb **1** *she slipped on the ice* =**slide**, skid, slither; fall (over), lose one's balance, tumble. **2** *the envelope slipped through Luke's fingers* =**fall**, drop, slide. **3** *we slipped out by a back door* =**creep**, steal, sneak, slide, sidle, slope, slink, tiptoe. **4** *standards have slipped* =**decline**, deteriorate, degenerate, worsen, get worse, fall (off), drop; *informal* go downhill, go to the dogs, go to pot. **5** *the bank's*

shares slipped 1.5p =**drop**, go down, sink, slump, decrease, depreciate. **6** *she slipped the map into her pocket* =**put**, tuck, shove; *informal* pop, stick, stuff. **7** *Sarah slipped into a black skirt* =**put on**, pull on, don, dress/clothe oneself in; change into.

8 *she slipped out of her clothes* =**take off**, remove, pull off, doff; *Brit. informal* peel off.

▶ noun **1** *a single slip could send them plummeting down* =**false step**, slide, skid, fall, tumble. **2** *a careless slip* =**mistake**, error, blunder, gaffe; oversight, omission, lapse; *informal* slip-up, boo-boo, howler; *Brit. informal* boob, clanger, bloomer; *N. Amer. informal* goof, blooper, bloop. **3** *a silk slip* =**underskirt**, petticoat.

▪ **give someone the slip** *(informal)* =**escape from**, get away from, evade, dodge, elude, lose, shake off, throw off (the scent), get clear of.

▪ **let something slip** =**reveal**, disclose, divulge, let out, give away, blurt out; *informal* let on, blab.

▪ **slip up** *(informal)* =**make a mistake**, (make a) blunder, get something wrong, make an error, err; *informal* make a boo-boo; *Brit. informal* boob, drop a clanger; *N. Amer. informal* goof up.

slip² ▶ noun *a slip of paper* =**piece of paper**, scrap of paper, sheet, note; chit.

slippery ▶ adjective **1** *the roads are slippery* =**slithery**, greasy, oily, icy, glassy, smooth, slimy, wet; *informal* slippy. **2** *a slippery customer* =**evasive**, unreliable; devious, crafty, cunning, wily, tricky, artful, slick, sly, sneaky, scheming, untrustworthy, deceitful, duplicitous, dishonest, treacherous, two-faced; *N. Amer.* snide; *informal* shady, shifty; *Brit. informal* dodgy; *Austral./NZ informal* shonky.

slipshod ▶ adjective =**careless**, lackadaisical, slapdash, disorganized, haphazard, hit-or-miss, untidy, messy, unsystematic, casual, negligent, neglectful, lax, slack; *informal* sloppy, slaphappy.

–OPPOSITES meticulous.

slip-up ▶ noun *(informal)* =**mistake**, slip, error, blunder, oversight, omission, gaffe, inaccuracy; *informal* boo-boo, howler; *Brit. informal* boob, clanger, bloomer; *N. Amer. informal* goof, blooper, bloop.

slit ▶ noun **1** *three diagonal slits* =**cut**, incision, split, slash, gash, laceration. **2** *a slit in the curtains* =**opening**, gap, chink, crack, aperture, slot.

▶ verb *he threatened to slit her throat* =**cut**,

slash, split open, slice open.

slither ▶ verb =**slide**, slip, glide, wriggle, crawl; skid.

sliver ▶ noun =**splinter**, shard, chip, flake, shred, scrap, shaving, paring, piece, fragment.

slob ▶ noun (informal) =**layabout**, good-for-nothing, sluggard, laggard; informal slacker, couch potato.

slobber ▶ verb =**drool**, slaver, dribble, salivate.

slog ▶ verb **1** they were all slogging away =**work hard**, toil, labour, work one's fingers to the bone, work like a Trojan/dog, exert oneself, grind, slave, plough, plod, peg; informal beaver, plug, work one's guts out, work one's socks off, sweat blood; Brit. informal graft; Austral./NZ informal bullock. **2** they slogged around the streets =**trudge**, tramp, traipse, toil, plod, trek.
−OPPOSITES relax.
▶ noun **1** 10 months' hard slog =**hard work**, toil, labour, effort, exertion, grind; informal sweat; Brit. informal graft; Austral./NZ informal (hard) yakka. **2** a steady uphill slog =**trudge**, tramp, traipse, plod, trek.
−OPPOSITES leisure.

slogan ▶ noun =**catchphrase**, catchline, jingle; N. Amer. informal tag line.

slop ▶ verb =**spill**, flow, overflow, run, slosh, splash.

slope ▶ noun **1** the slope of the roof =**gradient**, incline, angle, slant, inclination, pitch, decline, fall, tilt, tip, downslope, upslope; N. Amer. grade, downgrade, upgrade. **2** a grassy slope =**hill**, hillside, hillock, bank, escarpment, scarp. **3** the ski slopes =**piste**, run; N. Amer. trail.
▶ verb the garden sloped down to a stream =**slant**, incline, tilt; drop/fall away, descend, shelve, lean; rise, ascend, climb.
■ **slope off** (informal) =**leave**, go away, slip away, steal away, slink off, creep off, sneak off; informal push off.

sloping ▶ adjective =**at a slant**, at an angle, slanting, slanted, leaning, inclining, inclined, angled, cambered, tilting, tilted, dipping.
−OPPOSITES level.

sloppy ▶ adjective **1** sloppy chicken curry =**runny**, watery, thin, liquid, semi-liquid, mushy; informal gloopy. **2** their defending was sloppy =**careless**, slapdash, slipshod, lackadaisical, haphazard, lax,

slack, slovenly; informal slap-happy; Brit. informal shambolic. **3** sloppy letters =**sentimental**, mawkish, cloying, sugary, syrupy; romantic; informal slushy, schmaltzy, lovey-dovey; Brit. informal soppy; N. Amer. informal cornball, sappy, hokey.

slosh ▶ verb **1** beer sloshed over the side of the glass =**spill**, slop, splash, flow, overflow. **2** workers sloshed round in boots =**splash**, squelch, wade; informal splosh. **3** she sloshed more wine into her glass =**pour**, slop, splash.

slot ▶ noun **1** he slid a coin into the slot =**aperture**, slit, crack, hole, opening. **2** a mid-morning slot =**spot**, time, period, niche, space; informal window.
▶ verb he slotted a cassette into the machine =**insert**, put, place, slide, slip.

sloth ▶ noun =**laziness**, idleness, indolence, slothfulness, inactivity, inertia, sluggishness, shiftlessness, apathy, listlessness, lassitude, lethargy, languor.
−OPPOSITES industriousness.

slothful ▶ adjective =**lazy**, idle, indolent, work-shy, inactive, sluggish, apathetic, lethargic, listless, languid, torpid; informal bone idle.

slouch ▶ verb =**slump**, hunch; loll, droop.

slovenly ▶ adjective **1** his slovenly appearance =**scruffy**, untidy, messy, unkempt, ill-groomed, dishevelled, bedraggled, tousled, rumpled, frowzy; informal slobbish, slobby; N. Amer. informal raggedy, raunchy. **2** his work is slovenly =**careless**, slapdash, slipshod, haphazard, hit-or-miss, untidy, messy, negligent, lax, lackadaisical, slack; informal sloppy, slap-happy.
−OPPOSITES tidy, careful.

slow ▶ adjective **1** their slow walk home =**unhurried**, leisurely, steady, sedate, plodding, dawdling. **2** a slow process =**long-drawn-out**, time-consuming, lengthy, protracted, prolonged, gradual. **3** he's a bit slow =**obtuse**, stupid, unperceptive, insensitive, dull-witted, unintelligent, witless; informal dense, dim, dim-witted, thick, slow on the uptake, dumb, dopey; Brit. informal dozy. **4** they were slow to voice their opinions =**reluctant**, unwilling, disinclined, loath, hesitant, afraid. **5** the slow season =**sluggish**, slack, quiet, inactive, flat, depressed, stagnant, dead. **6** a slow narrative =**dull**,

boring, uninteresting, unexciting, uneventful, tedious, tiresome, wearisome,
monotonous, dreary.
−OPPOSITES fast.
▸ verb **1** *the traffic forced him to slow down*
=**reduce speed**, go slower, decelerate,
brake. **2** *you need to slow down* =**take it
easy**, relax, ease up/off, take a break, let
up; *N. Amer. informal* chill out, hang loose.
3 *this would slow down economic growth*
=**hold back/up**, delay, retard, set back;
restrict, check, curb, inhibit, impede,
obstruct, hinder, hamper.
−OPPOSITES accelerate.

slowly ▸ adverb **1** *Rose walked off slowly*
=**without hurrying**, unhurriedly, steadily, at a leisurely pace, at a snail's pace;
Music adagio, lento, largo. **2** *her health is
improving slowly* =**gradually**, bit by bit,
little by little, slowly but surely, step by
step.
−OPPOSITES quickly.

sludge ▸ noun =**mud**, muck, mire,
ooze, silt, alluvium; *informal* gunk, crud,
gloop, gook, goo; *Brit. informal* gunge, grot;
N. Amer. informal guck, glop.

sluggish ▸ adjective **1** *Alex felt tired and
sluggish* =**lethargic**, listless, lacking in
energy, lifeless, inactive, slow, torpid,
languid, apathetic, weary, tired, fatigued, sleepy, drowsy; lazy, idle, indolent, slothful, sluggardly; *N. Amer. logy;*
informal dozy, dopey. **2** *the economy is sluggish* =**inactive**, quiet, slow, slack, flat,
depressed, stagnant.
−OPPOSITES vigorous.

sluice ▸ verb =**wash (down)**, rinse,
clean.

slum ▸ noun =**hovel**; (**slums**) ghetto,
shanty town.

slump ▸ verb **1** *he slumped into a chair*
=**sit heavily**, flop, collapse, sink, fall;
informal plonk oneself. **2** *houses prices
slumped* =**fall steeply**, plummet, tumble, drop, go down; *informal* crash, nosedive. **3** *reading standards have slumped*
=**decline**, deteriorate, degenerate,
worsen, slip; *informal* go downhill.
▸ noun **1** *a slump in profits* =**steep fall**, drop,
tumble, downturn, downswing, slide,
decline, decrease; *informal* nosedive. **2** *an
economic slump* =**recession**, economic
decline, depression, slowdown.
−OPPOSITES rise, boom.

slur ▸ verb =**mumble**, speak unclearly,
garble.

▸ noun =**insult**, slight, slander, smear,
allegation.

sly ▸ adjective **1** *she's very sly* =**cunning**,
crafty, clever, wily, artful, guileful,
tricky, scheming, devious, deceitful, duplicitous, dishonest, underhand,
sneaky. **2** *a sly grin* =**roguish**, mischievous, impish, playful, wicked, arch,
knowing. **3** *she took a sly sip of water* =**surreptitious**, furtive, stealthy, covert.

smack[1] ▸ noun **1** *she gave him a smack*
=**slap**, clout, cuff, blow, rap, swat, crack,
thump, punch; *informal* whack, thwack,
clip, biff, wallop, belt, bash. **2** *(informal)
a smack on the lips* =**kiss**, peck; *informal*
smacker.
▸ verb **1** *he tried to smack her* =**slap**, hit,
strike, spank, cuff, clout, thump, punch,
swat; box someone's ears; *informal* whack,
clip, wallop, belt, bash; *Scottish & N. English informal* skelp. **2** *the waiter smacked a
plate down* =**bang**, slam, crash, thump;
sling, fling; *informal* plonk; *N. Amer. informal*
plunk.
▸ adverb *(informal) smack in the middle*
=**exactly**, precisely, straight, right, directly, squarely, dead, plumb, point-
blank; *informal* slap, bang; *N. Amer. informal*
smack dab.

smack[2] ■ **smack of 1** *the tea smacked
of tannin* =**taste of**, have the flavour of.
2 *the plan smacked of self-promotion* =**suggest**, hint at, have overtones of, give the
impression of, have the stamp of, seem
like; smell of, reek of.

small ▸ adjective **1** *a small flat* =**little**,
compact, tiny, miniature, mini; minute,
microscopic, minuscule; toy; baby;
poky, cramped, boxy; *Scottish* wee; *informal* tiddly, teeny, pocket-sized, half-pint,
dinky; *Brit. informal* titchy; *N. Amer. informal*
little-bitty. **2** *a very small man* =**short**, little, petite, diminutive, elfin, tiny; puny,
undersized, stunted; *Scottish* wee; *informal*
teeny, pint-sized. **3** *a few small changes*
=**slight**, minor, unimportant, trifling,
trivial, insignificant, inconsequential,
negligible, infinitesimal; *informal* minuscule, piffling, piddling. **4** *small helpings*
=**inadequate**, meagre, insufficient, ungenerous; *informal* measly, stingy, mingy,
pathetic. **5** *they made him feel small* =**foolish**, stupid, insignificant, unimportant;
embarrassed, humiliated, uncomfortable, mortified, ashamed; crushed. **6** *a
small farmer* =**small-scale**, small-time;
modest, unpretentious, humble.

−OPPOSITES big, tall, major, ample, substantial.

WORD LINKS

prefixes meaning 'small': **micro-, mini-, nano-**

small change ▶ noun =**coins**, change, coppers, silver, cash.

small-minded ▶ adjective =**narrow-minded**, petty, mean-spirited, uncharitable.
−OPPOSITES tolerant.

small-time ▶ adjective =**minor**, small-scale; petty, unimportant, insignificant, inconsequential; *N. Amer.* minor-league; *informal* penny-ante, piddling; *N. Amer. informal* two-bit, bush-league, picayune.
−OPPOSITES major.

smarmy ▶ adjective (*informal*) =**unctuous**, ingratiating, slick, oily, greasy, obsequious, sycophantic, fawning; *informal* slimy.

smart ▶ adjective 1 *you look very smart* =**well dressed**, stylish, chic, fashionable, modish, elegant, neat, spruce, trim, dapper; *N. Amer.* trig; *informal* snazzy, natty, snappy, sharp, cool; *N. Amer. informal* sassy, spiffy, fly, kicky. 2 *a smart restaurant* =**fashionable**, stylish, high-class, exclusive, chic, fancy; *Brit.* upmarket; *N. Amer.* high-toned; *informal* trendy, posh, ritzy, plush, classy, swanky, glitzy; *Brit. informal* swish; *N. Amer. informal* swank. 3 (*informal*) *he's very smart* =**clever**, bright, intelligent, sharp-witted, quick-witted, shrewd, astute; perceptive; *informal* brainy, savvy, quick on the uptake. 4 *a smart pace* =**brisk**, quick, fast, rapid, swift, lively, energetic, vigorous; *informal* cracking. 5 *a smart blow on the snout* =**sharp**, severe, forceful, violent.
−OPPOSITES untidy, downmarket, stupid, slow, gentle.
▶ verb 1 *her eyes were smarting* =**sting**, burn, tingle, prickle; hurt. 2 *she smarted at the accusations* =**feel annoyed**, feel upset, take offence, feel aggrieved, feel indignant, be put out, feel hurt.

smarten ▶ verb =**spruce up**, clean up, tidy up, neaten; groom, freshen, preen, primp, beautify; redecorate, refurbish, modernize; *informal* do up, titivate, doll up; *Brit. informal* tart up; *N. Amer. informal* gussy up.

smash ▶ verb 1 *he smashed a window* =**break**, shatter, splinter, crack; *informal* bust. 2 *she's smashed the car* =**crash**, wreck; *Brit.* write off; *Brit. informal* prang; *N. Amer. informal* total. 3 *they smashed into a wall* =**crash into**, collide with, hit, strike, ram, smack into, slam into, plough into, run into, bump into; *N. Amer.* impact. 4 *Don smashed him over the head* =**hit**, strike, thump, punch, smack; *informal* whack, bash, bop, clout, wallop, crown; *Brit. informal* slosh; *N. Amer. informal* slug.
▶ noun 1 *the smash of glass* =**breaking**, shattering, crash. 2 *a motorway smash* =**crash**, collision, accident, road traffic accident, bump; *Brit.* RTA; *N. Amer.* wreck; *informal* pile-up; *Brit. informal* prang, shunt. 3 (*informal*) *a box-office smash* =**success**, sensation, sell-out, triumph; *informal* (smash) hit, winner, crowd-puller, biggie.

smattering ▶ noun =**bit**, little, modicum, touch, soupçon; nodding acquaintance; rudiments, basics; *informal* smidgen, smidge, tad.

smear ▶ verb 1 *the table was smeared with grease* =**streak**, smudge, mark. 2 *smear the meat with olive oil* =**cover**, coat, grease. 3 *she smeared sunblock on her skin* =**spread**, rub, daub, slap, smother, plaster, slick. 4 *they are trying to smear our reputation* =**sully**, tarnish, blacken, drag through the mud, taint, damage, defame, discredit, malign, slander, libel; *N. Amer.* slur; *informal* do a hatchet job on; *literary* besmirch.
▶ noun 1 *smears of blood* =**streak**, smudge, daub, dab, spot, patch, blotch, mark; *informal* splotch, splodge. 2 *press smears about his closest aides* =**(false) accusation**, lie, untruth, slur, slander, libel, defamation.

smell ▶ noun *the smell of the kitchen* =**odour**, aroma, fragrance, scent, perfume, redolence; bouquet, nose; stench, stink, reek; *Brit. informal* pong, niff, whiff, hum; *Scottish informal* guff; *N. Amer. informal* funk.
▶ verb 1 *he smelled her perfume* =**scent**, get a sniff of, detect. 2 *the dogs smelled each other* =**sniff**, nose. 3 *the cellar smells* =**stink**, reek, have a bad smell; *Brit. informal* pong, hum, niff, whiff.

WORD LINKS

relating to the sense of smell: **olfactory**

smelly ▶ adjective =**foul-smelling**, stinking, reeking, fetid, malodorous, pungent, rank, noxious; off; musty, fusty; *informal* stinky; *Brit. informal* pongy, whiffy, humming; *N. Amer. informal* funky; *literary* noisome.

smile ▸ verb *he smiled at her* =**beam**, grin (from ear to ear); smirk, simper; leer. —OPPOSITES frown.

▸ noun *the smile on her face* =**beam**, grin; smirk, simper; leer.

smirk ▸ verb =**smile smugly**, simper, snigger; leer.

smitten ▸ adjective **1** *smitten with cholera* =**struck down**, laid low, suffering, affected, afflicted. **2** *Jane's smitten with you* =**infatuated**, besotted, in love, obsessed, head over heels; enamoured of, attracted to, taken with; captivated, enchanted, under someone's spell; *informal* bowled over, swept off one's feet, crazy about, mad about, keen on; *Brit. informal* potty about.

smog ▸ noun =**fog**, haze; fumes, smoke, pollution; *Brit. informal* pea-souper.

smoke ▸ verb **1** *the fire was smoking* =**smoulder**. **2** *he smoked his cigarette* =**puff on**, draw on, pull on; inhale; *informal* drag on.

▸ noun *the smoke from the bonfire* =**fumes**, exhaust, gas, vapour; smog.

smoky ▸ adjective =**smoke-filled**, sooty, smoggy, hazy, foggy, murky, thick; *Brit. informal* fuggy.

smooth ▸ adjective **1** *the smooth flat rocks* =**even**, level, flat, plane; featureless; glassy, glossy, silky, polished. **2** *his face was smooth* =**clean-shaven**, hairless. **3** *a smooth sauce* =**creamy**, velvety. **4** *a smooth sea* =**calm**, still, tranquil, undisturbed, unruffled, even, flat, waveless, like a millpond. **5** *the smooth running of the equipment* =**steady**, regular, uninterrupted, unbroken; straightforward, easy, effortless, trouble-free. **6** *a smooth wine* =**mellow**, velvety. **7** *a smooth, confident man* =**suave**, urbane, sophisticated, polished, debonair; courteous, gracious; glib, slick, ingratiating, unctuous; *informal* smarmy.

—OPPOSITES uneven, rough, hairy, lumpy, irregular, gauche.

▸ verb **1** *she smoothed the soil* =**flatten**, level (out/off), even out/off; press, roll, iron, plane. **2** *a plan to smooth the way for the agreement* =**ease**, facilitate, clear the way for, pave the way for, expedite, assist, aid, help, oil the wheels of, lubricate.

smoothly ▸ adverb **1** *her hair was combed smoothly back* =**evenly**, level, flat, flush. **2** *the door closed smoothly* =**fluidly**,

fluently, steadily, easily; quietly. **3** *the plan had gone smoothly* =**without a hitch**, like clockwork, without difficulty, easily, according to plan, swimmingly, satisfactorily, very well; *informal* like a dream.

smooth-talking ▸ adjective *(informal)* =**persuasive**, glib, plausible, silver-tongued, slick, eloquent, fast-talking; ingratiating, flattering, unctuous, obsequious, sycophantic; *informal* smarmy. —OPPOSITES blunt.

smother ▸ verb **1** *she tried to smother her baby* =**suffocate**, asphyxiate, stifle, choke. **2** *we smothered the flames* =**extinguish**, put out, snuff out, dampen, douse, stamp out. **3** *we smothered ourselves with suncream* =**smear**, daub, spread, cover. **4** *she smothered a sigh* =**stifle**, muffle, strangle, repress, suppress, hold back, fight back, bite back, swallow, conceal, hide; bite one's lip; *informal* keep a/the lid on.

smoulder ▸ verb **1** *the bonfire still smouldered* =**smoke**, glow, burn. **2** *smouldering with resentment* =**seethe**, boil, fume, burn, simmer, be boiling over, be beside oneself; *informal* be livid.

smudge ▸ noun *a smudge of blood* =**streak**, smear, mark, stain, blotch, blob, dab; *informal* splotch, splodge.

▸ verb **1** *her face was smudged with dust* =**streak**, mark, dirty, soil, blotch, blacken, smear, blot, daub, stain; *informal* splotch, splodge. **2** *she smudged her make-up* =**smear**, streak, mess up.

smug ▸ adjective =**self-satisfied**, self-congratulatory, complacent, pleased with oneself.

smuggle ▸ verb =**import/export illegally**, traffic in, run.

smuggler ▸ noun =**runner**, courier, bootlegger; *informal* mule.

smutty ▸ adjective =**vulgar**, rude, crude, dirty, filthy, salacious, coarse, obscene, lewd, pornographic, X-rated; risqué, racy, earthy, bawdy, suggestive, naughty; *informal* blue, raunchy; *Brit. informal* near the knuckle, saucy; *N. Amer. informal* gamy; *euphemistic* adult.

snack ▸ noun *she made herself a snack* =**light meal**, sandwich, refreshments, nibbles, titbit(s); *informal* bite (to eat).

▸ verb *don't snack on sugary foods* =**eat between meals**, nibble, munch; *informal* graze.

snag ▸ noun =**complication**, difficulty,

catch, hitch, obstacle, stumbling block, pitfall, problem, impediment, hindrance, inconvenience, setback, hurdle, disadvantage, downside, drawback.
▸ verb =**catch**, get caught, hook.

snake ▸ noun =*literary* serpent; *Austral./NZ rhyming slang* Joe Blake.
▸ verb *the road snakes inland* =**twist**, wind, meander, zigzag, curve.

> **WORD LINKS**
>
> *relating to snakes:* **colubrine, ophidian, serpentine**
> *study of snakes:* **ophiology**
> *fear of snakes:* **ophidiophobia**

snap ▸ verb 1 *the ruler snapped* =**break**, fracture, splinter, come apart, split, crack; *informal* bust. 2 *she snapped after years of violence* =**flare up**, lose one's self-control, go to pieces; *informal* crack up, freak out, lose one's cool, blow one's top, fly off the handle; *Brit. informal* throw a wobbly. 3 *a dog was snapping at him* =**bite**, gnash its teeth, snarl. 4 *'Shut up!' Anna snapped* =**say (roughly/angrily)**, bark, snarl, growl; retort; *informal* jump down someone's throat. 5 *photographers snapped the royals* =**photograph**, picture, take, shoot, film, capture.
▸ noun 1 *she closed her purse with a snap* =**click**, crack, pop. 2 *a cold snap* =**period**, spell, time, interval, stretch; *Brit. informal* patch. 3 (*informal*) *holiday snaps* =**photograph**, picture, photo, shot, snapshot, print; slide.
■ **snap something up** =**buy eagerly**, accept eagerly, jump at, take advantage of, grab, seize (on), pounce on.

snappy ▸ adjective (*informal*) 1 *a snappy mood* =**irritable**, irascible, short-tempered, touchy; cross, crabby, crotchety, cantankerous, grumpy, bad-tempered, testy, tetchy; *informal* grouchy, cranky; *Brit. informal* narky, ratty. 2 *a snappy catchphrase* =**concise**, succinct, memorable, catchy, neat, clever, crisp, pithy, witty, incisive, brief, short. 3 *a snappy dresser* =**smart**, fashionable, stylish, chic, modish, elegant, neat, spruce, dapper; *informal* snazzy, natty, sharp, nifty, cool; *N. Amer. informal* sassy, spiffy, fly.
−OPPOSITES peaceable, long-winded, slovenly.

snare ▸ noun 1 *a fox caught in a snare* =**trap**; gin, net, noose. 2 *the snares of the new law* =**pitfall**, trap, catch, danger,

hazard, peril.
▸ verb 1 *game birds were snared* =**trap**, catch, net, bag. 2 *he snared an heiress* =**ensnare**, catch, get hold of, bag, hook, land; marry.

snarl[1] ▸ verb 1 *the wolves are snarling* =**growl**, gnash one's teeth. 2 *'Shut it!' he snarled* =**say (roughly)**, bark, snap, growl; *informal* jump down someone's throat.

snarl[2] ▸ verb 1 *the rope got snarled up in a bush* =**tangle**, entangle, entwine, enmesh, ravel, knot, foul. 2 *this case has snarled up the court process* =**complicate**, confuse, muddle, jumble; *informal* mess up.

snarl-up ▸ noun (*informal*) =**traffic jam**, tailback, gridlock.

snatch ▸ verb 1 *she snatched the microphone* =**grab**, seize, take hold of, take, pluck; grasp at, clutch at. 2 (*informal*) *someone snatched my bag.* See STEAL verb sense 1. 3 (*informal*) *she snatched the baby from the hospital.* See ABDUCT. 4 *he snatched victory* =**seize**, pluck, wrest, achieve, secure, obtain; scrape.
▸ noun 1 *brief snatches of sleep* =**period**, spell, time, fit, bout, interval, stretch. 2 *a snatch of conversation* =**fragment**, snippet, bit, scrap, part, extract, excerpt, portion.

sneak ▸ verb 1 *I sneaked out* =**creep**, slink, steal, slip, slide, sidle, edge, tiptoe, pad, prowl. 2 *she sneaked a camera in* =**bring/take (secretly)**, smuggle, spirit, slip. 3 *he sneaked a doughnut* =**take (secretly)**; steal; *informal* snatch.
▸ adjective *a sneak preview* =**furtive**, secret, stealthy, sly, surreptitious, clandestine, covert; private, quick, exclusive.

sneaking ▸ adjective 1 *she had a sneaking admiration for him* =**secret**, private, hidden, concealed, unvoiced, undisclosed. 2 *a sneaking feeling* =**niggling**, nagging, lurking, insidious, lingering, gnawing, persistent.

sneaky ▸ adjective =**sly**, crafty, cunning, wily, artful, scheming, devious, deceitful, duplicitous, underhand; furtive, secretive, secret, stealthy, surreptitious, clandestine, covert.
−OPPOSITES honest.

sneer ▸ noun 1 *a sneer on her face* =**smirk**, curled lip. 2 *the sneers of others* =**jibe**, jeer, taunt, insult; *informal* dig.
▸ verb 1 *he looked at me and sneered* =**smirk**, curl one's lip. 2 *it is easy to sneer at them*

=scoff at, scorn, disdain, mock, laugh at, ridicule, deride; *N. Amer.* slur.

snicker ▶ verb *they all snickered at her* =**snigger**, titter, giggle, chortle, simper.
▶ noun *he could not suppress a snicker* =**snigger**, titter, giggle, chortle, simper.

snide ▶ adjective =**disparaging**, derogatory, deprecating, insulting, contemptuous; mocking, taunting, sneering, scornful, derisive, sarcastic, spiteful, nasty, mean.

sniff ▶ verb **1** *she sniffed and blew her nose* =**inhale**; snuffle. **2** *Tom sniffed the fruit* =**smell**, scent, get a whiff/smell of.
▶ noun **1** *she gave a loud sniff* =**snuffle**, snort. **2** *a sniff of fresh air* =**smell**, scent, whiff; lungful. **3** *(informal) the first sniff of trouble* =**indication**, hint, whiff, inkling, suggestion, whisper, trace, sign, suspicion.
■ **sniff at** =**scorn**, disdain, look down on, sneer at, scoff at; *informal* turn one's nose up at.
■ **sniff something out** *(informal)* =**detect**, find, discover, bring to light, track down, dig up, hunt/root out, uncover, unearth.

snigger ▶ verb *they snigger at him behind his back* =**snicker**, titter, giggle, chortle, laugh; sneer, smirk.
▶ noun *the joke got a snigger* =**snicker**, titter, giggle, chortle, laugh; sneer, smirk.

snip ▶ verb **1** *she snipped my fringe* =**cut**, clip, trim, tidy (up). **2** *snip off the faded flowers* =**cut off**, trim (off), clip, prune, chop off, sever, detach, remove, take off.
▶ noun **1** *make snips along the edge* =**cut**, slit, snick, nick, notch, incision. **2** *snips of wallpaper* =**scrap**, snippet, cutting, shred, remnant, fragment, sliver, bit, piece. **3** *(Brit. informal) the book was a snip.* See BARGAIN noun sense 2. **4** *(informal) the job was a snip.* See CINCH sense 1.

snippet ▶ noun =**piece**, bit, scrap, fragment, particle, shred; excerpt, extract.

snivel ▶ verb =**sniffle**, snuffle, whimper, whine, weep, cry; *Scottish* greet; *informal* blubber; *Brit. informal* grizzle.

snobbery ▶ noun =**affectation**, pretension, pretentiousness, arrogance, haughtiness, airs and graces, elitism; disdain, condescension; *informal* snootiness, uppitiness.

snobbish ▶ adjective =**elitist**, snobby, superior, supercilious; arrogant, condescending; pretentious, affected; *informal* snooty, uppity, high and mighty, la-di-da, stuck-up, snotty; *Brit. informal* toffee-nosed.

snoop *(informal)* ▶ verb =**pry**, inquire, poke about/around, be a busybody, poke one's nose into; root about/around; *informal* be nosy; *Austral./NZ informal* stickybeak.
▶ noun =**search**, nose, look, prowl, ferret, root, poke.

snooper ▶ noun =**meddler**, busybody, eavesdropper; *informal* nosy parker, snoop; *Austral./NZ informal* stickybeak.

snooty ▶ adjective *(informal)* =**arrogant**, proud, haughty, conceited, aloof, superior, self-important, disdainful, supercilious, snobbish, snobby; *informal* uppity, high and mighty, la-di-da, stuck-up; *Brit. informal* toffee-nosed.
−OPPOSITES modest.

snooze *(informal)* ▶ noun =**nap**, doze, sleep, rest, siesta, catnap; *informal* forty winks; *Brit. informal* kip.
▶ verb =**nap**, doze, sleep, rest, take a siesta, catnap; *informal* snatch forty winks, get some shut-eye; *Brit. informal* kip, get one's head down; *N. Amer. informal* catch some Zs.

snout ▶ noun =**muzzle**, nose, proboscis, trunk; *Scottish & N. English* neb.

snow ▶ noun =**snowflakes**, flakes, snowfall, snowstorm, blizzard, sleet, snowdrift.

> **WORD LINKS**
>
> *relating to snow:* **niveous, nival**
> *fear of snow:* **chionophobia**

snub ▶ verb =**rebuff**, spurn, cold-shoulder, give the cold shoulder to, keep at arm's length; cut (dead), ignore; insult, slight; *informal* freeze out, knock back; *N. Amer. informal* stiff.
▶ noun =**rebuff**, slap in the face; *informal* brush-off, put-down.

snuff ▶ verb =**extinguish**, put out, douse, smother, choke, blow out, quench, stub out.

snug ▶ adjective **1** *our tents were snug* =**cosy**, comfortable, warm, homely, sheltered, secure; *informal* comfy. **2** *a snug dress* =**tight**, skintight, close-fitting, figure-hugging, slinky.
−OPPOSITES bleak, loose.

snuggle ▶ verb =**nestle**, curl up, huddle (up), cuddle up, nuzzle, settle; *N. Amer.* snug down.

soak ▶ verb **1** *soak the beans in water* =immerse, steep, submerge, dip, dunk, bathe, douse, marinate, souse. **2** *we got soaked outside* =**drench**, wet through, saturate, waterlog, deluge, inundate, submerge, drown, swamp. **3** *the sweat soaked through his clothes* =**permeate**, penetrate, percolate, seep, spread through, infuse, impregnate. **4** *use towels to soak up the water* =**absorb**, suck up, blot (up), mop (up), sponge up.

soaking ▶ adjective =**drenched**, wet (through), soaked (through), sodden, soggy, waterlogged, saturated, sopping wet, dripping wet, wringing wet.
−OPPOSITES parched.

soar ▶ verb **1** *the bird soared into the air* =**fly**, wing, ascend, climb, rise; take off, take flight. **2** *the gulls soared on the winds* =**glide**, plane, float, drift, wheel, hover. **3** *the cost of living soared* =**increase**, escalate, shoot up, rise, spiral; *informal* go through the roof, skyrocket.
−OPPOSITES plummet.

sob ▶ verb =**weep**, cry, shed tears, snivel, whimper; howl, bawl; *Scottish* greet; *informal* blubber; *Brit. informal* grizzle.

sober ▶ adjective **1** *the driver was clearly sober* =**not drunk**, clear-headed; teetotal, abstinent, dry; *informal* on the wagon. **2** *a sober view of life* =**serious**, solemn, sensible, grave, sombre, staid, level-headed, businesslike, down-to-earth. **3** *a sober suit* =**sombre**, subdued, severe; conventional, traditional, quiet, drab, plain.
−OPPOSITES drunk, frivolous, sensational, flamboyant.
▶ verb **1** *I ought to sober up* =**become sober**; *informal* dry out. **2** *sobered by her experience* =**make serious**, subdue, calm down, quieten, steady; bring down to earth, make someone stop and think, give someone pause for thought.

sobriety ▶ noun =**seriousness**, solemnity, gravity, dignity, level-headedness, self-control, self-restraint, conservatism.

so-called ▶ adjective =**inappropriately named**, supposed, alleged, presumed, ostensible, reputed, self-styled, professed, self-appointed.

sociable ▶ adjective =**friendly**, affable, companionable, gregarious, convivial, clubbable, amicable, cordial, warm, genial.
−OPPOSITES unfriendly.

social ▶ adjective **1** *a major social problem*

=**communal**, community, collective, group, general, popular, civil, public. **2** *a social club* =**recreational**, leisure, entertainment, amusement. **3** *a social animal* =**gregarious**, collective; pack, herd.
−OPPOSITES individual.
▶ noun *the club has a social once a month* =**party**, gathering, function, get-together; celebration; *informal* bash, shindig, do; *Brit. informal* rave-up, knees-up, beano, bunfight, jolly.

socialism ▶ noun =**leftism**; communism, Marxism, Leninism, Maoism; *historical* Bolshevism.

socialist ▶ adjective *the socialist movement* =**left-wing**, leftist, Labour; communist, Marxist, Leninist, Maoist; *informal, derogatory* lefty, Commie.
▶ noun *a well-known socialist* =**left-winger**, leftist; communist, Marxist, Leninist, Maoist; *informal, derogatory* lefty, red, Commie.

socialize ▶ verb =**interact**, converse, be sociable, mix, mingle, get together, meet, fraternize, consort; entertain, go out; *informal* hobnob.

society ▶ noun **1** *a danger to society* =**the community**, the (general) public, the people, the population; civilization, humankind, mankind, humanity. **2** *an industrial society* =**culture**, community, civilization, nation, population. **3** *Lady Angela will help you enter society* =**high society**, polite society, the upper classes, the elite, the smart set, the beautiful people; *informal* the upper crust, the top drawer. **4** *a local history society* =**association**, club, group, circle; fellowship, guild, lodge, fraternity, brotherhood, sisterhood, sorority, league, union, alliance. **5** *the society of others* =**company**, companionship, fellowship, friendship.

> **WORD LINKS**
> *study of society:* **sociology**

sodden ▶ adjective **1** *his clothes were sodden* =**soaking**, soaked (through), wet (through), saturated, drenched, sopping wet, wringing wet. **2** *sodden fields* =**waterlogged**, soggy, saturated, boggy, swampy, miry, marshy; squelchy.
−OPPOSITES arid.

sofa ▶ noun =**settee**, couch, divan, chaise longue, chesterfield; *Brit.* put-you-up; *N. Amer.* davenport, day bed.

soft ▶ adjective **1** *soft fruit* =**mushy**, squashy, pulpy, slushy, squelchy,

squishy, doughy; *informal* gooey; *Brit. informal* squidgy. **2** *soft ground* =**swampy**, marshy, boggy, miry, oozy; heavy, squelchy. **3** *a soft cushion* =**squashy**, spongy, supple, springy, pliable, pliant, resilient, malleable. **4** *soft fabric* =**velvety**, smooth, fleecy, downy, furry, silky, silken, satiny. **5** *a soft wind* =**gentle**, light, mild, moderate. **6** *soft light* =**dim**, low, faint, subdued, muted, mellow. **7** *soft colours* =**pale**, pastel, muted, restrained, subdued, subtle. **8** *soft voices* =**quiet**, low, gentle; faint, muted, subdued, muffled, hushed, whispered, murmured, dulcet. **9** *soft outlines* =**blurred**, vague, hazy, misty, foggy, nebulous, fuzzy, blurry, indistinct, unclear. **10** *soft words* =**kind**, gentle, sympathetic, soothing, tender, sensitive, affectionate, loving, warm, sweet, sentimental. **11** *she's too soft with her pupils* =**lenient**, easy-going, tolerant, forgiving, forbearing, indulgent, clement, permissive, liberal, lax. **12** *(informal) he's soft in the head* =**foolish**, stupid, simple; slow, weak, feeble; *informal* dopey, dippy, dotty, scatty, loopy; *Brit. informal* daft; *Scottish & N. English informal* glaikit.
−OPPOSITES hard, firm, rough, strong, harsh, lurid, strident, sharp, strict, sensible.

soften ▸ verb =**alleviate**, ease, relieve, soothe, take the edge off, assuage, cushion, moderate, mitigate, palliate, diminish, blunt, deaden.
■ **soften someone up** =**charm**, win over, persuade, influence, weaken, disarm, sweeten, butter up, soft-soap.

softly-softly ▸ adjective =**cautious**, circumspect, discreet, gentle, patient, tactful, diplomatic.

soggy ▸ adjective =**mushy**, squashy, pulpy, slushy, squelchy, squishy; swampy, marshy, boggy; soaking, soaked through, wet, saturated, drenched; *Brit. informal* squidgy.

soil[1] ▸ noun **1** *acid soil* =**earth**, loam, dirt, clay, sod, turf; ground. **2** *British soil* =**territory**, land, domain, dominion, region, country.

soil[2] ▸ verb *he soiled his tie* =**dirty**, stain, spot, spatter, splatter, smear, smudge, sully, spoil, foul.

sojourn *(formal)* ▸ noun =**stay**, visit, stop, stopover; holiday, vacation.
▸ verb =**stay**, live, put up, stop (over), lodge, room, board; holiday, vacation.

solace ▸ noun =**comfort**, consolation, cheer, support, relief.

soldier ▸ noun =**fighter**, trooper, serviceman, servicewoman; warrior; *US* GI; *Brit. informal* squaddie; *archaic* man-at-arms.
■ **soldier on** *(informal)*. See PERSEVERE.

> **WORD LINKS**
> relating to soldiers: **military**

sole ▸ adjective =**only**, one (and only), single, solitary, lone, unique, exclusive.

solecism ▸ noun =(grammatical) mistake, error, blunder; *informal* howler, blooper; *Brit. informal* boob.

solely ▸ adverb =**only**, simply, just, merely, uniquely, exclusively, entirely, wholly; alone.

solemn ▸ adjective **1** *a solemn occasion* =**dignified**, ceremonial, stately, formal, courtly, majestic; imposing, splendid, magnificent, grand. **2** *he looked very solemn* =**serious**, grave, sober, sombre, unsmiling, stern, grim, dour, humourless. **3** *a solemn promise* =**sincere**, earnest, honest, genuine, firm, heartfelt, wholehearted, sworn.
−OPPOSITES frivolous, light-hearted, insincere.

solemnize ▸ verb =**perform**, celebrate; formalize, officiate at.

solicit ▸ verb **1** *Phil tried to solicit his help* =**ask for**, request, seek, apply for, put in for, call for, beg for, plead for. **2** *they are solicited for their opinions* =**ask**, approach, appeal to, lobby, petition, importune, call on, press.

solicitor ▸ noun *(Brit.)* =**lawyer**; legal representative, advocate, attorney; *Brit.* articled clerk; *Scottish* law agent; *informal* brief.

solicitous ▸ adjective =**concerned**, caring, considerate, attentive, mindful, thoughtful, interested; anxious, worried.

solid ▸ adjective **1** *the plaster was solid* =**hard**, rock-hard, rigid, firm, solidified, set; frozen. **2** *solid gold* =**pure**, unadulterated, genuine. **3** *a solid line* =**continuous**, uninterrupted, unbroken, undivided. **4** *solid houses* =**well built**, sound, substantial, strong, sturdy, durable. **5** *a solid argument* =**well founded**, valid, sound, logical, authoritative, convincing, cogent. **6** *a solid friendship* =**firm**, unshakeable, stable, steadfast. **7** *solid citizens* =**sensible**, dependable, trust-

worthy, decent, law-abiding, upright, upstanding, worthy. **8** *solid support from their colleagues* =**unanimous**, united, consistent, undivided.
–OPPOSITES liquid, alloyed, broken, flimsy, untenable, unreliable.

solidarity ▶ noun =**unanimity**, unity, agreement, accord, harmony, consensus, concurrence; *formal* concord.

solidify ▶ verb =**harden**, set, thicken, stiffen, congeal, cake; freeze, ossify, fossilize, petrify.
–OPPOSITES liquefy.

solitary ▶ adjective **1** *a solitary man* =**lonely**, unaccompanied, by oneself, on one's own, alone, friendless; unsociable, withdrawn, reclusive; *N. Amer.* lonesome. **2** *solitary farmsteads* =**isolated**, remote, lonely, out of the way, in the back of beyond, outlying, off the beaten track, godforsaken, obscure, inaccessible, cut-off; secluded, private, sequestered; *N. Amer.* in the backwoods; *literary* lone. **3** *a solitary piece of evidence* =**single**, lone, sole; only, one, individual.
–OPPOSITES sociable, accessible.

solitude ▶ noun =**loneliness**, solitariness, isolation, seclusion, privacy, peace.

> WORD LINKS
> *fear of solitude:* **eremophobia**

solo ▶ adjective =**unaccompanied**, single-handed, unescorted, unattended, independent, solitary; alone, on one's own, by oneself.
–OPPOSITES accompanied.
▶ adverb =**unaccompanied**, alone, on one's own, single-handed(ly), by oneself, unescorted, unattended, unaided, independently.
–OPPOSITES accompanied.

solution ▶ noun **1** *a solution to the problem* =**answer**, result, resolution, way out; key, formula, explanation, interpretation. **2** *a solution of salt and water* =**mixture**, blend, compound; tincture, infusion.

solve ▶ verb =**resolve**, answer, work out, find a solution to, find the key to, puzzle out, fathom, decipher, decode, clear up, straighten out, get to the bottom of, unravel, explain; *informal* figure out, crack; *Brit. informal* suss out.

solvent ▶ adjective =**(financially) sound**, in the black, in credit, creditworthy, solid, secure.

sombre ▶ adjective **1** *sombre clothes* =**dark**, drab, dull, dingy; restrained, subdued, sober, funereal. **2** *a sombre expression* =**solemn**, earnest, serious, grave, sober, unsmiling, stern, grim, dour, humourless; gloomy, sad, melancholy, dismal, doleful, mournful, lugubrious.
–OPPOSITES bright, cheerful.

somebody ▶ noun *she wanted to be a somebody* =**important person**, VIP, public figure, notable, dignitary, worthy; someone, (big/household) name, celebrity, star, superstar, luminary; *informal* celeb, bigwig, big shot, big cheese, hotshot, megastar.
–OPPOSITES nonentity.

somehow ▶ adverb =**one way or another**, no matter how, by fair means or foul, by hook or by crook, come what may.

sometime ▶ adverb **1** *I'll visit sometime* =**some day**, one day, one of these (fine) days, at a future date, sooner or later, by and by, in due course, in the fullness of time, in the long run. **2** *sometime on Sunday* =**at some time/stage/point**; during, in the course of.
–OPPOSITES never.
▶ adjective *my sometime editor* =**former**, past, previous, erstwhile, one-time, ex-.

sometimes ▶ adverb =**occasionally**, from time to time, now and then, every so often, once in a while, on occasion, at times, off and on, at intervals, periodically, sporadically, spasmodically, intermittently.

somewhat ▶ adverb **1** *matters have improved somewhat* =**a little**, a bit, to some extent, (up) to a point, in some measure, rather, quite; *informal* kind of, sort of; *N. Amer. informal* some. **2** *a somewhat longer book* =**slightly**, relatively, comparatively, moderately, fairly, rather, quite, marginally.
–OPPOSITES greatly.

son ▶ noun =**male child**, boy, heir; descendant, offspring; *informal* lad.

> WORD LINKS
> *relating to a son or daughter:* **filial**
> *killing of one's son or daughter:* **filicide**

song ▶ noun **1** *a beautiful song* =**air**, strain, ditty, melody, tune, number, track. **2** *the song of the birds* =**call(s)**, chirping, cheeping, chirruping, warbling, trilling, twitter; birdsong.

■ **song and dance** (informal). See FUSS noun sense 1.

sonorous ▸ adjective =**resonant**, rich, full, round, booming, deep, clear, mellow, strong, resounding, reverberant.

soon ▸ adverb 1 we'll be there soon =**shortly**, presently, in the near future, before long, in a little while, in a minute, in a moment, before you know it, any minute (now), any day (now), by and by; informal anon; Brit. informal sharpish, in a tick, in two ticks. 2 how soon can you get here? =**early**, quickly, speedily.

sooner ▸ adverb 1 he should have done it sooner =**earlier**, before (now). 2 I would sooner stay =**rather**, preferably, given the choice.

soothe ▸ verb 1 Rachel tried to soothe him =**calm (down)**, pacify, comfort, hush, quiet, settle (down); appease, mollify; Brit. quieten (down). 2 an anaesthetic to soothe the pain =**alleviate**, ease, relieve, take the edge off, assuage, allay, lessen, reduce.
−OPPOSITES agitate, aggravate.

soothing ▸ adjective 1 soothing music =**relaxing**, restful, calm, calming, tranquil, peaceful. 2 soothing ointment =**palliative**, gentle.

sophisticated ▸ adjective 1 sophisticated technology =**advanced**, modern, state of the art, the latest, new, up to the minute; cutting-edge, trailblazing; complex, complicated, intricate. 2 a sophisticated woman =**worldly**, worldly-wise, experienced, cosmopolitan; urbane, cultured, cultivated, polished, refined; elegant, stylish.
−OPPOSITES crude, naive.

sophistication ▸ noun =**worldliness**, experience, urbanity, culture, polish, refinement; elegance, style, poise, finesse, savoir faire.

soporific ▸ adjective =**sleep-inducing**, sedative, somnolent; narcotic; drowsy, sleepy.
−OPPOSITES invigorating.

soppy ▸ adjective (Brit. informal) See SENTIMENTAL sense 2.

sorcerer, sorceress ▸ noun =**wizard**, witch, magician, warlock, enchanter, enchantress, magus; shaman, witch doctor; archaic mage.

sorcery ▸ noun =**(black) magic**, the black arts, witchcraft, wizardry, enchantment, spells; voodoo; shamanism; Irish pishogue.

sordid ▸ adjective 1 a sordid love affair =**sleazy**, seedy, seamy, unsavoury, tawdry, cheap, disreputable, discreditable, ignominious, shameful, wretched. 2 a sordid little street =**squalid**, slummy, dirty, filthy, shabby, scummy; informal cruddy, grungy, crummy, scuzzy; Brit. informal grotty.
−OPPOSITES respectable, immaculate.

sore ▸ adjective 1 a sore leg =**painful**, hurting, hurt, aching, throbbing, smarting, stinging, agonizing, excruciating; inflamed, sensitive, tender, raw, bruised, injured. 2 (N. Amer. informal) they were sore at us =**upset**, angry, annoyed, cross, vexed, displeased, disgruntled, dissatisfied, irritated, galled, irked, put out, aggrieved, offended, affronted, piqued, nettled; informal aggravated, miffed, peeved, hacked off, riled; Brit. informal narked, cheesed off, brassed off; N. Amer. informal teed off, ticked off.
▸ noun a sore on his leg =**inflammation**, swelling, lesion; ulcer, boil, abscess.

sorrow ▸ noun 1 he felt sorrow at her death =**sadness**, unhappiness, misery, despondency, regret, despair, desolation, dejection, wretchedness, gloom, woe, heartache, grief. 2 the sorrows of life =**trouble**, difficulty, problem, adversity, misery, woe, affliction, trial, tribulation, misfortune, setback, reverse, blow, failure, tragedy.
−OPPOSITES joy.

sorrowful ▸ adjective =**sad**, unhappy, dejected, regretful, downcast, miserable, downhearted, despondent, despairing, disconsolate, desolate, glum, gloomy, doleful, dismal, mournful, woeful, forlorn, heartbroken.
−OPPOSITES joyful.

sorry ▸ adjective 1 I was sorry to hear about his accident =**sad**, moved, sorrowful, distressed; regretful. 2 he felt sorry for her =**full of pity**, sympathetic, compassionate, moved, empathetic, concerned. 3 I'm sorry I was rude =**regretful**, remorseful, contrite, repentant, rueful, penitent, apologetic, guilty, ashamed. 4 a sorry sight =**pitiful**, pathetic, wretched.
−OPPOSITES glad, unsympathetic, unrepentant.

sort ▸ noun what sort of book is it? =**type**, kind, manner, variety, class, category, style; quality, form, genre, species, make, model, brand, ilk; N. Amer. stripe.
▸ verb 1 they sorted the books alphabetically

=**classify**, class, group; organize, arrange, order. **2** *the problem was soon sorted* =**resolve**, settle, solve, fix, work out, straighten out, deal with, put right, set right, rectify, iron out.

■ **out of sorts 1** *I'm feeling out of sorts* =**unwell**, ill, poorly, sick, peaky, run down, below par; *Brit.* off colour; *informal* under the weather, funny, rough; *Brit. informal* off, ropy; *Scottish informal* wabbit, peely-wally; *Austral./NZ informal* crook. **2** *I've been out of sorts and I'd like a chat* =**unhappy**, sad, down, depressed, melancholy, gloomy, glum, dispirited, despondent, forlorn, woebegone, fed up, low, in the doldrums; *informal* blue, down in the dumps, down in the mouth.

■ **sort of** (*informal*) **1** *you look sort of familiar* =**slightly**, faintly, vaguely; somewhat, quite, rather, fairly, reasonably, relatively; *informal* pretty, kind of. **2** *he sort of pirouetted* =**as it were**, kind of, virtually.

■ **sort something out 1** *she sorted out the clothes. See* SORT *verb sense 1.* **2** *they must sort out their problems. See* SORT *verb sense 2.*

sortie ▶ noun **1** *a sortie against their besiegers* =**foray**, charge, offensive, attack, assault, onslaught, thrust, drive. **2** *a bombing sortie* =**raid**, flight, mission, operation.

so-so ▶ adjective (*informal*) =**mediocre**, indifferent, average, middle-of-the-road, middling, moderate, ordinary, adequate, fair; uninspired, undistinguished, unexceptional, unremarkable, run-of-the-mill, lacklustre; *informal* bog-standard, no great shakes, not up to much; *NZ informal* half-pie.

soul ▶ noun **1** *his soul cried out* =**spirit**, psyche, (inner) self. **2** *the soul of discretion* =**embodiment**, personification, incarnation, epitome, essence; model. **3** *not a soul in sight* =**(single) person**, individual, man, woman, mortal, creature. **4** *their music lacked soul* =**feeling**, emotion, passion, animation, intensity, warmth, energy, vitality, spirit.

soulful ▶ adjective =**emotional**, heartfelt, sincere, passionate; moving, stirring; sad, mournful, doleful.

soulless ▶ adjective =**characterless**, featureless, bland, dull, colourless, dreary, drab, impersonal.
–OPPOSITES exciting.

sound¹ ▶ noun **1** *the sound of a car* =**noise**, din, racket, row, hubbub; resonance, reverberation. **2** *she did not make a sound* =**utterance**, cry, word, noise, peep. **3** *the sound of the flute* =**music**, tone, timbre; call, song, voice. **4** *I don't like the sound of that* =**idea**, thought, prospect. **5** *we're within sound of the sea* =**earshot**, hearing (distance), range.
–OPPOSITES silence.

▶ verb **1** *the buzzer sounded* =**make a noise**, resonate, resound, reverberate, go off; ring, chime, ping. **2** *drivers must sound their horns* =**blow**, blast, toot, ring; use, operate, activate, set off. **3** *do you sound the 'h'?* =**pronounce**, verbalize, voice, enunciate, articulate, vocalize, say. **4** *she sounded a warning* =**utter**, voice, deliver. **5** *it sounds a crazy idea* =**appear**, look (like), seem, give every indication of being.

> **WORD LINKS**
>
> *relating to sound:* **acoustic, sonic, aural, audio**
> *fear of sound:* **acoustiphobia**

sound² ▶ adjective **1** *your heart is sound* =**healthy**, in good condition/shape, fit, hale and hearty, in fine fettle; undamaged, unimpaired. **2** *a sound building* =**well built**, solid, substantial, strong, sturdy, durable, stable, intact, unimpaired. **3** *sound advice* =**well founded**, valid, reasonable, logical, weighty, authoritative, reliable. **4** *a sound judge of character* =**reliable**, dependable, trustworthy, fair; good. **5** *financially sound* =**solvent**, debt-free, in the black, in credit, creditworthy, secure. **6** *a sound sleep* =**deep**, undisturbed, uninterrupted, untroubled, peaceful. **7** *a sound thrashing* =**thorough**, proper, real, complete, unqualified, out-and-out, thoroughgoing, severe; *informal* right (royal).
–OPPOSITES unhealthy, unsafe, unreliable, insolvent, light.

sound³ ■ **sound someone/something out** =**investigate**, test, check, examine, probe, research, look into; canvass, survey, poll, question, interview; *informal* pump.

soup ▶ noun =**broth**; potage, consommé, bouillon, chowder, bisque.

sour ▶ adjective **1** *sour wine* =**acid**, acidic, tart, bitter, sharp, vinegary, pungent; *N. Amer.* acerb; *technical* acerbic. **2** *sour milk* =**bad**, off, turned, curdled, rancid, high, fetid. **3** *a sour old man* =**embittered**, resentful, jaundiced, bitter; irrit-

able, peevish, fractious, cross, crabby, crotchety, cantankerous, disagreeable, ill-humoured; *informal* grouchy.
–OPPOSITES sweet, fresh, amiable.
▸ verb *the dispute soured relations between the two towns* =**spoil**, mar, damage, harm, impair, wreck, upset, poison, blight.
–OPPOSITES improve.

source ▸ noun **1** *the source of the river* =**spring**, origin. **2** *the source of the rumour* =**origin**, starting point; derivation, root; author, originator, initiator, inventor. **3** *historical sources* =**reference**, authority, informant; document.

souse ▸ verb =**drench**, douse, soak, steep, saturate, plunge, immerse, submerge, dip, sink, dunk.

south ▸ adjective =**southern**, southerly, meridional, austral.

souvenir ▸ noun =**memento**, keepsake, reminder, remembrance, token, memorial; trophy, relic.

sovereign ▸ noun =**ruler**, monarch, potentate, overlord; king, queen, emperor, empress, prince, princess.
▸ adjective *a sovereign state* =**independent**, autonomous, self-governing, self-determining; non-aligned, free.

sovereignty ▸ noun **1** *their sovereignty over the islands* =**jurisdiction**, rule, supremacy, dominion, power, ascendancy, hegemony, domination, authority, control. **2** *full sovereignty was achieved in 1955* =**autonomy**, independence, self-government, self-rule, home rule, self-determination, freedom.

sow ▸ verb **1** *sow the seeds in April* =**plant**, broadcast, disperse, strew, distribute; seed. **2** *the new policy has sown confusion* =**cause**, bring about, create, lead to, produce, engender, generate, prompt, precipitate, trigger, provoke; foster, foment; *literary* beget.

space ▸ noun **1** *there was not enough space* =**room**, capacity, latitude, margin, leeway, play, clearance. **2** *green spaces in London* =**area**, expanse, stretch, sweep, tract. **3** *a space between the timbers* =**gap**, interval, opening, aperture, cavity, cranny, fissure, crack. **4** *write your name in the appropriate space* =**blank**, gap, box. **5** *a space of seven years* =**period**, span, time, duration, stretch, course, interval, gap. **6** *the first woman in space* =**outer space**, deep space; the universe, the galaxy, the solar system; infinity.
▸ verb *the chairs were spaced widely* =**position**, arrange, range, array, spread, lay out, set, stand.

WORD LINKS

study of space: **cosmology, astronomy**

spaceman, spacewoman
▸ noun =**astronaut**, cosmonaut, space traveller, space cadet.

spacious ▸ adjective =**roomy**, capacious, sizable, generous, large, big, vast, immense.
–OPPOSITES cramped.

span ▸ noun **1** *a six-foot wing span* =**extent**, length, width, reach, stretch, spread, distance, range. **2** *the span of one week* =**period**, space, time, duration, course, interval.
▸ verb **1** *an arch spanned the stream* =**bridge**, cross, traverse, pass over. **2** *his career spanned twenty years* =**last**, cover, extend, spread over.

spank ▸ verb =**smack**, slap, hit; *informal* wallop, belt, whack, give someone a hiding; *Scottish & N. English* skelp.

spar ▸ verb =**quarrel**, argue, fight, disagree, differ, be at odds, be at variance, dispute, squabble, wrangle, cross swords, lock horns; *informal* scrap.

spare ▸ adjective **1** *a spare set of keys* =**extra**, supplementary, additional, second, other, alternative; emergency, reserve, backup, relief; substitute; *N. Amer.* alternate. **2** *they sold off the spare land* =**surplus**, superfluous; excess, leftover; redundant, unnecessary, unneeded, unwanted; *informal* going begging. **3** *your spare time* =**free**, leisure, own. **4** *her spare, elegant form* =**slender**, lean, willowy, svelte, lissom, rangy; thin, skinny, gaunt, lanky, spindly.
▸ verb **1** *he couldn't spare any money* =**afford**, manage; part with, give, provide. **2** *they were spared by their captors* =**pardon**, let off, forgive, reprieve, release, free.
■ **to spare** =**left (over)**, remaining, unused, unneeded, not required, still available, surplus (to requirements), superfluous, extra; *informal* going begging.

sparing ▸ adjective =**thrifty**, economical, frugal, canny, careful, prudent, cautious; mean, miserly, niggardly, parsimonious, ungenerous.
–OPPOSITES lavish.

spark ▸ noun =**flash**, glint, twinkle, flicker, flare.
▸ verb =**cause**, give rise to, lead to, occasion, bring about, start, initiate, pre-

sparkle ▸ verb =**glitter**, glint, glisten, twinkle, flash, blink, wink, shimmer.
▸ noun =**glitter**, glint, twinkle, flicker, shimmer, flash.

sparkling ▸ adjective **1** *sparkling wine* =**effervescent**, fizzy, carbonated, aerated. **2** *a sparkling performance* =**brilliant**, dazzling, scintillating, exciting, exhilarating, stimulating, invigorating; vivacious, lively, vibrant.
−OPPOSITES still, dull.

sparse ▸ adjective =**scant**, scanty, scattered, scarce, infrequent, few and far between; meagre, paltry, limited, in short supply.
−OPPOSITES abundant.

spartan ▸ adjective =**austere**, harsh, hard, frugal, rigorous, strict, stern, severe; ascetic; bleak, joyless, grim, bare, stark, plain.
−OPPOSITES luxurious.

spasm ▸ noun **1** *a muscle spasm* =**contraction**, convulsion, cramp; twitch, jerk, tic, shudder, shiver, tremor. **2** *a spasm of coughing* =**fit**, paroxysm, attack, burst, bout, seizure, outburst.

spasmodic ▸ adjective =**intermittent**, fitful, irregular, sporadic, erratic, occasional, infrequent, scattered, patchy, isolated, periodic.

spate ▸ noun =**series**, succession, run, cluster, string, rash, epidemic, outbreak, wave, flurry.

spatter ▸ verb =**splash**, splatter, spray, sprinkle, shower, speckle, fleck, mark; *informal* splotch; *Brit. informal* splodge.

spawn ▸ verb =**give rise to**, bring about, occasion, generate, engender; lead to, result in, effect, initiate, start, set off, precipitate, trigger; breed, bear.

speak ▸ verb **1** *she refused to speak about it* =**talk**, say anything/something; utter, state, declare, tell, voice, express, pronounce, articulate, enunciate, vocalize, verbalize. **2** *we spoke the other day* =**converse**, have a conversation, talk, communicate, chat, have a word, gossip. **3** *the Minister spoke for two hours* =**give a speech**, talk, lecture, hold forth, discourse, expound, expatiate, pontificate; *informal* spout, spiel, sound off. **4** *he was spoken of as a promising student* =**mention**, talk about, discuss, refer to, remark on, allude to. **5** *you must speak to him about his rudeness* =**reprimand**, rebuke, admonish, chastise, chide, upbraid, reprove, reproach, scold, remonstrate with, take to task, pull up; *informal* tell off, dress down; *Brit. informal* tick off, have a go at, tear someone off a strip, give someone what for; *formal* castigate.

■ **speak against** =**oppose**, condemn, attack, criticize.

■ **speak for 1** *she speaks for the Liberal Democrats* =**represent**, act for, be spokesperson for. **2** *I spoke for the motion* =**advocate**, champion, uphold, defend, support, promote, recommend, back, endorse, sponsor.

■ **speak out** =**speak publicly**, speak openly, speak one's mind, sound off, stand up and be counted.

■ **speak up** =**speak loudly**, speak clearly, raise one's voice.

speaker ▸ noun =**speech-maker**, lecturer, talker, orator; spokesperson, spokesman/woman, mouthpiece; reader, commentator, broadcaster, narrator; *historical* demagogue.

spear ▸ noun =**javelin**, lance, harpoon; *historical* pike.

spearhead ▸ verb *we're spearheading a campaign* =**lead**, head, front.

special ▸ adjective **1** *a very special person* =**exceptional**, unusual, singular, remarkable, outstanding, unique. **2** *our town's special character* =**distinctive**, distinct, individual, particular, specific, peculiar. **3** *a special occasion* =**momentous**, significant, memorable, important, historic. **4** *a special tool for cutting tiles* =**specific**, particular, purpose-built, tailor-made, custom-built.
−OPPOSITES ordinary, general.

specialist ▸ noun =**expert**, authority, pundit, professional; connoisseur; master, maestro, adept, virtuoso; *informal* buff.
−OPPOSITES amateur.

speciality ▸ noun **1** *his speciality was watercolours* =**forte**, strong point, strength, métier, strong suit, talent, skill, bent, gift; *informal* bag, thing, cup of tea. **2** *a speciality of the region* =**delicacy**, specialty.

species ▸ noun =**type**, kind, sort; genus, family, order; breed, strain, variety, class, classification, category, set, bracket; style, manner, form, genre.

specific ▸ adjective **1** *a specific purpose* =**particular**, specified, fixed, set, determined, distinct, definite. **2** *I gave specific*

instructions =**detailed**, explicit, express, clear-cut, unequivocal, precise, exact.
−OPPOSITES general, vague.

specification ▸ noun **1** *clear specification of objectives* =**statement**, identification, definition, description, setting out, framing, enumeration; stipulation. **2** *a shelter built to their specifications* =**instructions**, guidelines, parameters, stipulations, requirements, conditions, order; description, details.

specify ▸ verb =**state**, name, identify, define, describe, set out, frame, itemize, detail, list, spell out, enumerate, cite, instance; stipulate.

specimen ▸ noun =**sample**, example, instance, illustration, demonstration.

specious ▸ adjective =**misleading**, deceptive, false, fallacious, unsound.

speck ▸ noun **1** *a mere speck in the distance* =**dot**, pinprick, spot. **2** *a speck of dust* =**particle**, grain, molecule; bit, trace.

speckled ▸ adjective =**flecked**, speckly, freckled, freckly, spotted, spotty, dotted, mottled, dappled.

spectacle ▸ noun **1** *his love of spectacle* =**display**, show, pageant(s), performance, exhibition; pomp and circumstance; extravaganza, spectacular. **2** *they were rather an odd spectacle* =**sight**, vision, scene, prospect, vista, picture. **3** *don't make a spectacle of yourself* =**exhibition**, laughing stock, fool.

spectacles ▸ plural noun =**glasses**, eyewear; *N. Amer.* eyeglasses; *informal* specs.

spectacular ▸ adjective **1** *a spectacular victory* =**impressive**, magnificent, splendid, dazzling, sensational, dramatic, remarkable, outstanding, memorable, unforgettable. **2** *a spectacular view* =**striking**, picturesque, eye-catching, breathtaking, arresting, glorious; *informal* out of this world.
−OPPOSITES unimpressive, dull.
▸ noun *a medieval spectacular.* See SPECTACLE sense 1.

spectator ▸ noun =**watcher**, viewer, observer, onlooker, bystander, witness; commentator, reporter; *literary* beholder.
−OPPOSITES participant.

spectral ▸ adjective =**ghostly**, phantom, wraithlike, shadowy, incorporeal, insubstantial, disembodied, unearthly, other-worldly; *informal* spooky.

spectre ▸ noun **1** *the spectres in the crypt* =**ghost**, phantom, apparition, spirit, wraith, presence; *informal* spook; *literary* phantasm, shade. **2** *the spectre of war* =**threat**, menace, shadow, cloud; prospect; danger, peril, fear, dread.

spectrum ▸ noun =**range**, gamut, sweep, scope, span; compass, ambit.

speculate ▸ verb **1** *they speculated about my private life* =**conjecture**, theorize, hypothesize, guess, surmise, wonder, muse. **2** *investors speculate on the stock market* =**gamble**, venture, wager; invest, play the market; *Brit. informal* punt.

speculative ▸ adjective **1** *any discussion is largely speculative* =**conjectural**, suppositional, theoretical, hypothetical; tentative, unproven, unfounded, groundless, unsubstantiated. **2** *a speculative investment* =**risky**, hazardous, unsafe, uncertain, unpredictable; *informal* chancy, dicey, iffy; *Brit. informal* dodgy.

speech ▸ noun **1** *the power of speech* =**speaking**, talking, (verbal) expression, (verbal) communication. **2** *her speech was slurred* =**diction**, elocution, articulation, enunciation, pronunciation, delivery; words. **3** *an after-dinner speech* =**talk**, address, lecture, discourse, oration, presentation; sermon, homily; monologue; *informal* spiel. **4** *in popular speech* =**language**, tongue, parlance, idiom, dialect, vernacular, patois; *informal* lingo, patter, -speak, -ese.

WORD LINKS

relating to speech: **lingual, oral, phonetic, phonic**

speechless ▸ adjective =**lost for words**, dumbstruck, tongue-tied, inarticulate, mute, dumb, voiceless, silent.
−OPPOSITES verbose.

speed ▸ noun **1** *the speed of their progress* =**rate**, pace, tempo, momentum. **2** *the speed with which they responded* =**rapidity**, swiftness, quickness, promptness, immediacy, briskness, sharpness; haste, hurry, precipitateness; acceleration, velocity; *informal* lick; *literary* celerity.
▸ verb **1** *I sped home* =**hurry**, rush, dash, run, race, sprint, gallop, career, shoot, hurtle, hare, fly, zoom, hasten; *informal* tear, belt, pelt, scoot, zip, whip, hotfoot it, leg it; *Brit. informal* bomb; *N. Amer. informal* hightail it. **2** *he was caught speeding*

=**drive too fast**, exceed the speed limit. **3** *a holiday will speed his recovery* =**hasten**, speed up, accelerate, advance, further, promote, boost, stimulate, aid, assist, facilitate.
–OPPOSITES slow, hinder.

■ **speed up** =**hurry up**, accelerate, go faster, get a move on, put a spurt on, pick up/gather speed; *informal* get cracking/moving, step on it, shake a leg; *Brit. informal* get one's skates on; *N. Amer. informal* get a wiggle on.

WORD LINKS

fear of speed: **tachophobia**

speedily ▶ adverb =**rapidly**, swiftly, quickly, fast, post-haste; promptly, immediately, briskly; hastily, hurriedly, precipitately; *informal* p.d.q. (pretty damn quick), double quick, hell for leather, at the double; *literary* apace.

speedy ▶ adjective =**rapid**, swift, quick, fast; prompt, immediate, expeditious, brisk, sharp; hasty, hurried, precipitate, rushed, snappy.
–OPPOSITES slow.

spell[1] ▶ verb *the drought spelled disaster* =**signal**, signify, mean, amount to, add up to, constitute.

■ **spell something out** =**explain**, make clear, make plain, elucidate, clarify; specify, itemize, detail, enumerate, list, expound, catalogue.

WORD LINKS

spelling system of a language: **orthography**

spell[2] ▶ noun **1** *the witch muttered a spell* =**incantation**, charm, formula; (**spells**) magic, sorcery, witchcraft; *N. Amer.* hex. **2** *she surrendered to his spell* =**influence**, (animal) magnetism, charisma, charm; magic.

■ **put a spell on** =**bewitch**, enchant, entrance; curse, jinx, witch; *N. Amer.* hex.

spell[3] ▶ noun **1** *a spell of dry weather* =**period**, time, interval, season, stretch, run, course, streak; *Brit. informal* patch. **2** *a spell of dizziness* =**bout**, fit, attack.

spellbinding ▶ adjective =**fascinat**ing, enthralling, entrancing, bewitching, captivating, riveting, engrossing, gripping, absorbing, compelling, compulsive, mesmerizing, hypnotic; *informal* unputdownable.
–OPPOSITES boring.

spellbound ▶ adjective =**enthralled**, fascinated, rapt, riveted, transfixed, gripped, captivated, bewitched, enchanted, mesmerized, hypnotized.

spend ▶ verb **1** *she spent £185 on shoes* =**pay out**; squander, waste, fritter away; *informal* blow, splurge. **2** *the morning was spent gardening* =**pass**, occupy, fill, take up, while away. **3** *I've spent hours on this essay* =**put in**, devote; waste.

spendthrift ▶ noun =**profligate**, prodigal, squanderer, waster; *informal* big spender.
–OPPOSITES miser.
▶ adjective =**profligate**, improvident, wasteful, extravagant, prodigal.
–OPPOSITES frugal.

spent ▶ adjective =**used up**, consumed, exhausted, finished, depleted, drained; *informal* burnt out.

spew ▶ verb **1** *factories spewed out smoke* =**emit**, discharge, eject, expel, belch/ pour out. **2** *(informal) he wanted to spew.* See VOMIT verb *sense* 1.

sphere ▶ noun **1** *a glass sphere* =**globe**, ball, orb; bubble. **2** *sphere of influence* =**area**, field, compass, orbit; range, scope, extent. **3** *the sphere of foreign affairs* =**domain**, realm, province, field, area, territory, arena, department.

spherical ▶ adjective =**round**, globular.

spice ▶ noun **1** *the spices in curry powder* =**seasoning**, flavouring, condiment. **2** *the risk added spice to their affair* =**excitement**, interest, colour, piquancy, zest; an edge.

■ **spice something up** =**enliven**, make more exciting, perk up, put some life into, galvanize, electrify, boost; *informal* pep up, jazz up, buck up.

spicy ▶ adjective =**piquant**, tangy, peppery, hot; spiced, highly seasoned; pungent.
–OPPOSITES bland.

spider ▶ noun

WORD LINKS

fear of spiders: **arachnophobia**

spiel ▶ noun *(informal)* =**speech**, patter, (sales) pitch, talk; monologue; rigmarole, story, saga.

spike ▶ noun =**prong**, barb, point; skewer, stake, spit; tine, pin; spur; *Mountaineering* piton.
▶ verb *(informal)* =**adulterate**, contaminate,

drug, lace; *informal* dope, doctor, cut.

spill ▸ verb 1 *Kevin spilled his drink*
=**knock over**, tip over, upset, overturn.
2 *the bath water spilled on to the floor*
=**overflow**, flow, pour, run, slop, slosh,
splash; leak. **3** *students spilled out of the
building* =**stream**, pour, surge, swarm,
flood, throng, crowd.
▸ noun *an oil spill* =**spillage**, leak, leakage,
overflow, flood.
■ **spill the beans** (*informal*) =**reveal all**,
tell all, give the game away, talk; *informal*
let the cat out of the bag, blab, come
clean.

spin ▸ verb 1 *the wheels are spinning* =**revolve**, rotate, turn, go round, whirl.
2 *she spun round to face him* =**whirl**, wheel,
twirl, turn, swing, twist, swivel, pivot.
3 *her head was spinning* =**reel**, whirl, go
round, swim. **4** *she spun me a yarn* =**tell**,
recount, relate, narrate; weave, concoct, invent, fabricate, make up.
▸ noun **1** *a spin of the wheel* =**rotation**, revolution, turn, whirl, twirl. **2** *a positive
spin* =**slant**, angle, twist, bias. **3** *a spin in
the car* =**trip**, jaunt, outing, excursion,
journey; drive, ride, run, turn; *informal*
tootle.
■ **spin something out** =**prolong**, protract, draw out, drag out, string out,
extend, carry on, continue; fill out, pad
out.

spindle ▸ noun =**pivot**, pin, rod, axle,
capstan; axis.

spindly ▸ adjective **1** *he was pale and
spindly* =**lanky**, thin, skinny, lean, spare,
gangling, gangly, scrawny, bony, rangy,
angular. **2** *spindly chairs* =**rickety**, flimsy,
wobbly, shaky.
–OPPOSITES stocky.

spine ▸ noun **1** *he injured his spine* =**backbone**, spinal column; back. **2** *cactus
spines* =**needle**, quill, bristle, barb, spike,
prickle; thorn.

┌─────────────────┐
│ WORD LINKS   │
└─────────────────┘
relating to the spine: **vertebral**

spine-chilling ▸ adjective =**terrifying**, blood-curdling, petrifying, hair-
raising, frightening, chilling, horrifying; *informal* scary, creepy, spooky.
–OPPOSITES comforting, reassuring.

spineless ▸ adjective =**weak**, weak-
willed, feeble, soft, ineffectual; **cowardly**, timid, faint-hearted, pusillanimous, craven, lily-livered, chicken-

hearted; *informal* wimpish, wimpy, gutless.
–OPPOSITES bold, brave, strong-willed.

spiny ▸ adjective =**prickly**, spiky,
thorny, bristly, bristled, spiked, barbed,
scratchy, sharp.

spiral ▸ adjective *a spiral column* =**coiled**,
helical, curling, winding, twisting.
▸ noun *a spiral of smoke* =**coil**, helix, corkscrew, curl, twist, whorl, scroll.
▸ verb **1** *smoke spiralled up* =**coil**, wind,
swirl, twist, snake. **2** *prices spiralled*
=**soar**, shoot up, rocket, escalate, climb;
informal skyrocket, go through the roof.
3 *the economy is spiralling out of control*
=**veer**, shoot, lurch, swing, hurtle.
–OPPOSITES fall.

spirit ▸ noun **1** *body and spirit* =**soul**,
psyche, (inner) self, inner man/woman,
mind. **2** *a spirit haunts the island* =**ghost**,
phantom, spectre, apparition, presence.
3 *in good spirits* =**mood**, frame/state of
mind, humour, temper. **4** *team spirit*
=**morale**, esprit de corps. **5** *the spirit of
the age* =**ethos**, essence, quintessence;
atmosphere, mood, feeling, climate.
6 *they played with spirit* =**enthusiasm**,
liveliness, vivacity, animation, energy,
verve, vigour, dynamism, zest, dash,
elan, panache, sparkle, exuberance,
gusto, pep, fervour, zeal, fire, passion;
informal get-up-and-go. **7** *the spirit of the
law* =**real/true meaning**, essence, substance; idea. **8** *he drinks spirits* =**strong
liquor/drink**; *informal* (the) hard stuff,
firewater, hooch; *Brit. informal* short.
–OPPOSITES body, flesh.
■ **spirit someone/something away**
=**whisk away/off**, make someone/
something disappear, run away with,
carry off, steal someone/something
away, abduct, kidnap, snatch, seize.

spirited ▸ adjective =**lively**, vivacious,
vibrant, full of life, vital, animated,
sparkling, sprightly, energetic, active,
vigorous, dynamic, enthusiastic, passionate; *informal* feisty, spunky, have-a-go,
gutsy; *N. Amer. informal* peppy.
–OPPOSITES timid, apathetic, lifeless.

spiritual ▸ adjective **1** *your spiritual self*
=**non-material**, incorporeal; inner,
mental, psychological; transcendent,
ethereal, mystic, metaphysical. **2** *spiritual writings* =**religious**, sacred, divine,
holy, church, ecclesiastical, devotional.
–OPPOSITES physical, secular.

spit¹ ▸ verb **1** *Cranston coughed and spat*

s

=**expectorate**, hawk; *Brit. informal* gob. **2** *'Go to hell,' she spat* =**snap**, say angrily, hiss. **3** *the fat began to spit* =**sizzle**, hiss, crackle, sputter. **4** *(Brit.) it began to spit* =**rain lightly**, drizzle, spot; *N. English* mizzle; *N. Amer.* sprinkle.

▶ **noun** *spit dribbled from his mouth* =**spittle**, saliva, sputum, slobber, dribble; *Brit. informal* gob.

spit² ▶ **noun** *chicken cooked on a spit* =**skewer**, brochette, rotisserie.

spite ▶ **noun** *he said it out of spite* =**malice**, malevolence, ill will, vindictiveness, vengefulness, malignity; *informal* bitchiness, cattiness.
−OPPOSITES benevolence.

▶ **verb** *he did it to spite me* =**upset**, hurt, wound.
−OPPOSITES please.

■ **in spite of** =**despite**, notwithstanding, regardless of, for all; in defiance of, in the face of; even though, although.

spiteful ▶ **adjective** =**malicious**, malevolent, vindictive, vengeful, mean, nasty, hurtful, mischievous, cruel, unkind; *informal* bitchy, catty.
−OPPOSITES benevolent.

splash ▶ **verb 1** *splash your face with water* =**sprinkle**, spray, shower, wash, squirt; daub; wet. **2** *his boots were splashed with rain* =**spatter**, splatter, speck, smear, stain, mark. **3** *waves splashing on the beach* =**wash**, break, lap; pound. **4** *children splashed in the water* =**paddle**, wade; wallow. **5** *the story was splashed across the front pages* =**blazon**, display, spread, plaster, trumpet.

▶ **noun 1** *a splash of rain* =**spot**, blob, smear, speck. **2** *a splash of lemonade* =**drop**, dash, bit, spot, soupçon, dribble; *Scottish informal* scoosh. **3** *a splash of colour* =**patch**, burst, streak.

■ **splash out** *(Brit. informal)* =**be extravagant**; *informal* lash out, splurge; *Brit. informal* push the boat out.

spleen ▶ **noun** =**bad temper**, ill humour, anger, wrath, vexation, annoyance, irritation, displeasure, dissatisfaction, resentment; spite, malice, bitterness, animosity, venom, bile.
−OPPOSITES good humour.

splendid ▶ **adjective 1** *splendid costumes* =**magnificent**, sumptuous, grand, imposing, superb, spectacular, opulent, luxurious, de luxe, rich, fine, costly, expensive, lavish, ornate, gorgeous, glorious, dazzling, handsome, beautiful;

informal plush, posh, swanky, ritzy, splendiferous; *Brit. informal* swish; *N. Amer. informal* swank. **2** *(informal) a splendid holiday* =**excellent**, wonderful, marvellous, superb, glorious, sublime, lovely, delightful, first-class, first-rate; *informal* super, great, amazing, fantastic, terrific, tremendous, phenomenal, sensational, heavenly, gorgeous, grand, fabulous, fab, awesome, magic, ace, cool, mean, out of this world; *Brit. informal* smashing, brilliant, brill; *dated* divine, capital; *Brit. informal, dated* champion, wizard, ripping, cracking, spiffing, top-hole; *N. Amer. informal, dated* swell.
−OPPOSITES modest, awful.

splendour ▶ **noun** =**magnificence**, sumptuousness, grandeur, opulence, luxury, richness, fineness, lavishness, ornateness, glory; majesty, stateliness; *informal* ritziness.
−OPPOSITES ordinariness, simplicity, modesty.

splenetic ▶ **adjective** =**bad-tempered**, ill-tempered, peevish, petulant, irritable, irascible, dyspeptic, testy, tetchy, waspish, crotchety, crabby, querulous, resentful, bilious.
−OPPOSITES good-humoured.

splice ▶ **verb** =**interweave**, braid, plait, intertwine, interlace.

splinter ▶ **noun** =**sliver**, chip, shard; fragment, piece, bit, shred; *Scottish* skelf.
▶ **verb** =**shatter**, smash, break into smithereens, fracture, split, crack, disintegrate.

split ▶ **verb 1** *the force split the wood* =**break**, cut; snap, crack. **2** *the ice cracked and split* =**break (apart)**, fracture, rupture, snap, come apart, splinter. **3** *her dress was split* =**tear**, rip, slash, slit. **4** *the issue could split the Party* =**divide**, separate, sever; *literary* tear asunder. **5** *they split the profit* =**share (out)**, divide (up), distribute, dole out, parcel out, measure out; carve up, slice up. **6** *the path split* =**fork**, divide, bifurcate, diverge, branch. **7** *the band split up last year* =**break up**, separate, part, part company, go their separate ways.
−OPPOSITES mend, join, unite, pool, converge, get together, marry.

▶ **noun 1** *a split in the rock face* =**crack**, fissure, cleft, crevice, break, fracture, breach. **2** *a split in the curtain* =**rip**, tear, cut, rent, slash, slit. **3** *a split in the Party* =**division**, rift, breach, schism, rupture, partition. **4** *the acrimonious split with his*

wife =**break-up**, split-up, separation, parting, estrangement, rift.
–OPPOSITES join, merger, marriage.

WORD LINKS

easily split: **fissile**
relating to splitting: **schizo-**

spoil ▸ verb 1 *smoking spoils your complexion* =**damage**, ruin, impair, blemish, disfigure, blight, deface, harm; destroy, wreck. 2 *rain spoiled my plans* =**ruin**, wreck, upset, undo, mess up, sabotage, scotch, torpedo; *informal* foul up, louse up, muck up, screw up, put the kibosh on, do for; *Brit. informal* cock up, scupper. 3 *his sisters spoil him* =**overindulge**, pamper, indulge, mollycoddle, cosset, wait on hand and foot. 4 *stockpiled food may spoil* =**go bad**, go off, go rancid, turn, go sour, rot, perish.
–OPPOSITES improve, enhance, further, help, neglect, be strict with, keep.
■ **spoiling for** =**eager for**, itching for, looking for, keen to have, after, bent on, longing for.

spoils ▸ plural noun =**booty**, loot, plunder, haul, pickings.

spoilsport ▸ noun =**killjoy**, dog in the manger, misery; *informal* wet blanket, party-pooper.

spoken ▸ adjective *spoken communication* =**verbal**, oral, vocal; unwritten; by word of mouth.
–OPPOSITES non-verbal, written.
■ **spoken for** =**reserved**, set aside, claimed, booked.

spokesman, spokeswoman ▸ noun =**spokesperson**, representative, agent, mouthpiece, voice, official; *informal* spin doctor.

sponge ▸ verb 1 *I'll sponge your face* =**wash**, clean, wipe, swab; mop, rinse, sluice, swill. 2 *(informal) he lived by sponging off others* =**scrounge**, be a parasite, beg; live off; *informal* freeload, cadge, bum; *N. Amer. informal* mooch; *Austral./NZ* bludge.

sponger ▸ noun *(informal)* =**parasite**, hanger-on, leech, scrounger; *informal* freeloader; *N. Amer. informal* mooch, moocher, schnorrer; *Austral./NZ informal* bludger.

spongy ▸ adjective =**soft**, squashy, cushioned, yielding; springy; porous, absorbent, permeable; *Brit. informal* squidgy.
–OPPOSITES hard, solid.

sponsor ▸ noun =**backer**, patron, promoter, benefactor, supporter, contributor, subscriber, friend, guarantor, underwriter.
▸ verb =**finance**, fund, subsidize, back, promote, support, contribute to, underwrite; *N. Amer. informal* bankroll.

sponsorship ▸ noun =**backing**, support, promotion, patronage, subsidy, funding, financing, aid, (financial) assistance.

spontaneous ▸ adjective 1 *a spontaneous display of affection* =**unplanned**, unpremeditated, unrehearsed, impulsive, impromptu, spur-of-the-moment, extempore; unprompted, unbidden, unsolicited; *informal* off-the-cuff. 2 *a spontaneous reaction to danger* =**reflex**, automatic, knee-jerk, involuntary, unthinking, unconscious, instinctive. 3 *a spontaneous kind of person* =**natural**, uninhibited, relaxed, unselfconscious, unaffected, open, genuine; impulsive, impetuous.
–OPPOSITES planned, calculated, conscious, voluntary, inhibited.

spontaneously ▸ adverb 1 *they applauded spontaneously* =**without being asked**, of one's own accord, voluntarily, on impulse, impulsively, on the spur of the moment, extemporaneously; *informal* off the cuff. 2 *he reacted spontaneously* =**without thinking**, automatically, instinctively.

spooky ▸ adjective *(informal)* =**eerie**, sinister, ghostly, uncanny, weird, unearthly, mysterious; *informal* creepy, scary.

sporadic ▸ adjective =**occasional**, infrequent, irregular, periodic, scattered, patchy, isolated, odd; intermittent, spasmodic, fitful, desultory, erratic, unpredictable.
–OPPOSITES frequent, steady, continuous.

sport ▸ noun =**games**; (physical) recreation.
▸ verb =**wear**, have on, dress in; display, exhibit, show off, flourish, parade, flaunt.

sporting ▸ adjective =**sportsmanlike**, generous, considerate; fair, just, honourable; *Brit. informal* decent.
–OPPOSITES dirty, unfair.

sporty ▸ adjective *(informal)* 1 *he's quite a sporty type* =**athletic**, fit, active, energetic. 2 *a sporty outfit* =**stylish**, smart;

casual, informal; *informal* trendy, cool, snazzy; *N. Amer. informal* sassy.
−OPPOSITES unfit, lazy, formal, sloppy.

spot ▶ noun **1** *a grease spot* =**mark**, patch, dot, fleck, smudge, smear, stain, blotch, splash; *informal* splotch, splodge. **2** *a spot on his nose* =**pimple**, pustule, blackhead, boil, swelling; **(spots)** acne; *informal* zit; *Scottish informal* plook. **3** *a secluded spot* =**place**, location, site, position, situation, setting, locale; venue.
▶ verb **1** *she spotted him* =**notice**, see, observe, detect, make out, recognize, identify, locate; catch sight of, glimpse; *Brit. informal* clock; *literary* behold, espy. **2** *spotted with grease* =**stain**, mark, fleck, speckle, smudge, streak, splash, spatter; *informal* splotch, splodge.
■ **spot on** *(Brit. informal)* =**accurate**, correct, right, perfect, exact, unerring; *Brit. informal* bang on; *N. Amer. informal* on the money, on the nose.

spotless ▶ adjective =**clean**, pristine, immaculate, shining, shiny, gleaming, spick and span.
−OPPOSITES filthy.

spotlight ▶ noun =**public eye**, glare of publicity, limelight.
▶ verb =**focus attention on**, highlight, point up, draw/call attention to, give prominence to, throw into relief, bring to the fore.

spotted ▶ adjective =**polka-dot**, spotty, dotted.
−OPPOSITES plain.

spotty ▶ adjective **1** *a spotty dress* =**polka-dot**, spotted, dotted. **2** *(Brit.) his spotty face* =**pimply**, pimpled, acned; *Scottish informal* plooky.

spouse ▶ noun =**partner**; mate, consort; *informal* better half; *Brit. informal* other half. *See also* HUSBAND *noun*, WIFE.

spout ▶ verb **1** *lava spouting from the crater* =**spurt**, gush, spew, erupt, shoot, squirt, spray; discharge, emit, belch. **2** *he spouted about morality* =**hold forth**, sound off, go on; *informal* mouth off.
▶ noun *a can with a spout* =**nozzle**, lip.

sprawl ▶ verb **1** *he sprawled on the sofa* =**stretch out**, lounge, loll, lie, recline, drape oneself, slump, flop, slouch. **2** *the town sprawled ahead of them* =**spread** (out), stretch (out), extend, spill.

spray[1] ▶ noun **1** *a spray of water* =**shower**, sprinkle, jet, mist, drizzle; spume; foam, froth. **2** *a perfume spray* =**atomizer**, vaporizer, aerosol.

▶ verb **1** *we sprayed water on the soil* =**sprinkle**, dribble, drizzle. **2** *spray the plants with weedkiller* =**water**, mist; coat, soak, douse. **3** *water sprayed into the air* =**spout**, jet, gush, spurt, shoot, squirt.

spray[2] ▶ noun **1** *a spray of holly* =**sprig**, twig. **2** *a spray of flowers* =**bouquet**, bunch, posy, nosegay; corsage, buttonhole.

spread ▶ verb **1** *he spread the map out* =**lay out**, open out, unfurl, unroll, roll out; straighten out, fan out; stretch out, extend. **2** *the landscape spread out below* =**extend**, stretch, open out, be displayed; sprawl. **3** *papers spread all over his desk* =**scatter**, strew, disperse, distribute. **4** *he's spreading rumours* =**disseminate**, circulate, put about, communicate, purvey, broadcast, publicize, propagate, promulgate; repeat. **5** *the disease spread rapidly* =**travel**, move, be borne, sweep; develop, diffuse; reproduce, thrive, be passed on, be transmitted. **6** *she spread sun cream on her arms* =**smear**, daub, plaster, slather, lather, apply, put; rub. **7** *he spread his toast with jam* =**cover**, coat, smear, daub, smother; butter.
−OPPOSITES fold up, suppress.
▶ noun **1** *the spread of learning* =**expansion**, proliferation, extension, growth; dissemination, diffusion, transmission, propagation. **2** *a spread of six feet* =**span**, width, extent, stretch, reach. **3** *a wide spread of subjects* =**range**, span, spectrum, sweep; variety. **4** *(informal) his mother laid on a huge spread* =**meal**, feast, banquet; *informal* blowout; *Brit. informal* nosh-up.

spree ▶ noun **1** *a shopping spree* =**bout**, orgy; *informal* binge, splurge. **2** *a drinking spree* =**bout**; *informal* binge, bender, session.

sprig ▶ noun =**stem**, spray, twig.

sprightly ▶ adjective =**spry**, lively, agile, nimble, energetic, active, vigorous, spirited, animated, vivacious, frisky.
−OPPOSITES doddery, lethargic.

spring ▶ verb **1** *the cat sprang off her lap* =**leap**, jump, bound, vault. **2** *the branch sprang back* =**fly**, whip, flick, whisk, kick, bounce. **3** *all art springs from feelings* =**originate**, derive, arise, stem, emanate, proceed, issue, evolve, come. **4** *he sprang from nowhere* =**appear (suddenly/unexpectedly)**, materialize, pop up, sprout; proliferate, mushroom.

▶ noun **1** *with a sudden spring he leapt up* =**leap**, jump, bound. **2** *the mattress has lost its spring* =**springiness**, bounciness, bounce, resilience, elasticity, flexibility, stretch, stretchiness, give. **3** *there was a spring in his step* =**buoyancy**, bounce, energy, liveliness, jauntiness, sprightliness, confidence. **4** *a mineral spring* =**well (head)**; spa, geyser.

> **WORD LINKS**
>
> *relating to the season of spring:* **vernal**

springy ▶ adjective =**elastic**, stretchy, tensile; flexible, pliable; bouncy, resilient.
–OPPOSITES rigid, squashy.

sprinkle ▶ verb **1** *he sprinkled water on the cloth* =**splash**, trickle, spray, shower; drip. **2** *sprinkle sesame seeds over the top* =**scatter**, strew. **3** *sprinkle the cake with icing sugar* =**dredge**, dust.

sprinkling ▶ noun **1** *a sprinkling of nutmeg* =**scattering**, sprinkle, dusting; pinch, dash. **2** *mainly women, but a sprinkling of men* =**few**, one or two, couple, handful, small number, trickle, scattering.

sprint ▶ verb =**run**, race, rush, dash, hurry, bolt, fly, gallop, charge, shoot, speed, zoom, go hell for leather, go like the wind; *informal* tear, pelt, scoot, hotfoot it, leg it, belt, zip, whip; *Brit. informal* bomb; *N. Amer. informal* hightail it.
–OPPOSITES walk.

sprite ▶ noun =**fairy**, elf, pixie, imp.

sprout ▶ verb **1** *the seeds begin to sprout* =**germinate**, put/send out shoots, bud. **2** *he had sprouted a beard* =**grow**, develop. **3** *parsley sprouted from the pot* =**spring (up)**, come up, grow, develop, appear.

spruce ▶ adjective =**neat**, well groomed, well turned out, well dressed, smart, trim, dapper; *informal* natty, snazzy; *N. Amer. informal* spiffy, trig.
–OPPOSITES untidy.

■**spruce up 1** *the flat had been spruced up* =**smarten up**, tidy up, clean; *informal* do up; *Brit. informal* tart up; *N. Amer. informal* gussy up. **2** *Sarah had spruced herself up* =**groom**, tidy, smarten, preen, primp; *N. Amer. trig*; *informal* titivate, doll up; *Brit. informal* tart up.

spry ▶ adjective =**sprightly**, lively, agile, nimble, active; spirited, animated, vivacious, frisky.
–OPPOSITES doddery, lethargic.

spume ▶ noun =**foam**, froth, surf, spindrift, bubbles.

spur ▶ noun **1** *the spur of competition* =**stimulus**, incentive, encouragement, inducement, impetus. **2** *a spur of bone* =**projection**, spike, point; *technical* process.
–OPPOSITES disincentive.
▶ verb *the thought spurred him into action* =**stimulate**, encourage, prompt, propel, prod, induce, impel, motivate, move, galvanize, inspire, drive, stir; incite, goad, provoke, sting.
–OPPOSITES discourage.

spurious ▶ adjective =**bogus**, fake, false, fraudulent, sham, artificial, imitation, simulated, feigned; *informal* phoney.
–OPPOSITES genuine.

spurn ▶ verb =**reject**, rebuff, scorn, turn down, treat with contempt, disdain, look down one's nose at; snub, slight, jilt, brush off, turn one's back on; give someone the cold shoulder; *informal* turn one's nose up at, give someone the brush-off; *Brit. informal* knock back.
–OPPOSITES welcome, accept.

spurt ▶ verb *water spurted from the tap* =**squirt**, shoot, jet, erupt, gush, pour, stream, pump, surge, spew, course, well, spring, burst; discharge, emit, expel, eject.
▶ noun **1** *a spurt of water* =**squirt**, jet, spout, gush, stream, rush, surge; flood, cascade, torrent. **2** *a spurt of energy* =**burst**, fit, bout, rush, spate, surge.

spy ▶ noun *a foreign spy* =**agent**, mole, plant; *N. Amer. informal* spook.
▶ verb **1** *he spied for the West* =**be a spy**, gather intelligence. **2** *officials spied on them* =**observe**, keep under surveillance/observation, watch. **3** *she spied a coffee shop* =**notice**, observe, see, spot, sight, catch sight of, glimpse, make out, discern, detect; *literary* espy, behold.

spying ▶ noun =**espionage**, intelligence gathering, surveillance, infiltration.

squabble ▶ noun =**quarrel**, disagreement, row, argument, contretemps, falling-out, dispute, clash, altercation, shouting match, exchange, war of words; *informal* tiff, set-to, run-in, slanging match, shindig, spat, scrap, dust-up; *Brit. informal* barney, ding-dong; *N. Amer. informal* rhubarb.
▶ verb =**quarrel**, row, argue, bicker, fall out, disagree, have words; *informal* scrap.

squad ▸ noun **1** *a maintenance squad* =**team**, crew, gang, force. **2** *a squad of marines* =**detachment**, detail, unit, platoon, battery, troop, patrol, squadron, cadre, commando.

squalid ▸ adjective **1** *a squalid flat* =**dirty**, filthy, grubby, grimy, slummy, foul, poor, sorry, wretched, miserable, mean, seedy, shabby, sordid, insalubrious; **neglected**, run down, down at heel, dilapidated, ramshackle, tumbledown, crumbling, decaying; *informal* scruffy, crummy; *Brit. informal* grotty; *N. Amer. informal* shacky. **2** *a squalid deal* =**improper**, sordid, unseemly, unsavoury, sleazy, shoddy, cheap, base, low, corrupt, dishonest, dishonourable, disreputable, discreditable, contemptible, shameful.
–OPPOSITES clean, pleasant, smart, upmarket, proper, decent.

squall ▸ noun =**gust**, storm, blast, flurry, shower, gale.

squally ▸ adjective =**stormy**, gusty, blustery, windy, blowy; wild, tempestuous, rough.

squalor ▸ noun =**dirt**, filth, grubbiness, grime, muck, foulness, poverty, wretchedness, shabbiness, sordidness; **neglect**, decay, dilapidation; *informal* scruffiness, crumminess, grunge; *Brit. informal* grottiness.
–OPPOSITES cleanliness, pleasantness, smartness.

squander ▸ verb =**waste**, misspend, misuse, throw away, fritter away, spend (like water); *informal* blow, go through, splurge, pour down the drain.
–OPPOSITES manage, make good use of, save.

square ▸ noun *a shop in the market square* =**marketplace**, plaza, piazza.
▸ adjective **1** *a square table* =**quadrilateral**, rectangular, oblong, right-angled, at right angles, perpendicular; straight, level, parallel, horizontal, upright, vertical, true. **2** *the sides were square at half-time* =**level**, even, drawn, equal, tied; neck and neck, level pegging, nip and tuck, side by side, evenly matched; *informal* even-steven(s).
–OPPOSITES crooked, underhand, trendy.
▸ verb **1** *this does not square with the data* =**agree**, tally, be in agreement, be consistent, match up, correspond, fit, coincide, accord, conform, be compatible.

2 *his goal squared the match 1–1* =**level**, even (up), make equal. **3** *Tom squared things with his boss* =**resolve**, sort out, settle, clear up, work out, iron out, straighten out, deal with, set right, rectify, remedy; *informal* patch up.

squash ▸ verb **1** *the fruit got squashed* =**crush**, squeeze, flatten, compress, distort, pound, trample, stamp on; pulverize. **2** *she squashed her clothes inside the bag* =**force**, ram, thrust, push, cram, jam, stuff, pack, squeeze, wedge, press.

squashy ▸ adjective =**mushy**, pulpy, slushy, squelchy, squishy, oozy, doughy, soft; *Brit. informal* squidgy.
–OPPOSITES firm, hard.

squat ▸ verb =**crouch (down)**, hunker (down), sit on one's haunches, sit on one's heels.
▸ adjective =**stocky**, thickset, dumpy, stubby, stumpy, short, small.

squawk ▸ verb & noun =**screech**, squeal, shriek, scream, croak, crow, caw, cluck, cackle, hoot, cry, call.

squeak ▸ noun & verb **1** *the vole's squeak | the rat squeaked* =**peep**, cheep, squeal, tweet, yelp, whimper. **2** *the squeak of the hinge | the hinges squeaked* =**squeal**, creak, scrape, grate, rasp, groan.

squeal ▸ noun & verb =**screech**, scream, shriek, squawk.

squeamish ▸ adjective =**easily nauseated**, nervous; (**be squeamish about**) be put off by, cannot stand the sight of, … makes one feel sick.

squeeze ▸ verb **1** *I squeezed the bottle* =**compress**, press, crush, squash, pinch, nip, grasp, grip, clutch. **2** *squeeze the juice from both oranges* =**extract**, press, force, express. **3** *Sally squeezed her feet into the sandals* =**force**, thrust, cram, ram, jam, stuff, pack, wedge, press, squash. **4** *we all squeezed into Steve's van* =**crowd**, crush, cram, pack, jam, squash, wedge oneself, shove, push, force one's way.
▸ noun **1** *he gave her hand a squeeze* =**press**, pinch, nip; grasp, grip, clutch, hug. **2** *it was quite a squeeze* =**crush**, jam, squash; congestion. **3** *a squeeze of lemon* =**few drops**, dash, splash, dribble, trickle, spot, hint, touch.

squint ▸ verb **1** *the sun made them squint* =**screw up one's eyes**, narrow one's eyes, peer, blink. **2** *he has squinted from birth* =**be cross-eyed**, have a squint.
▸ noun *does he have a squint?* =**cross-eyes**, strabismus; *informal* boss-eye.

squirm ▶ verb **1** *I tried to squirm away* =**wriggle**, wiggle, writhe, twist, slither, fidget, twitch, toss and turn. **2** *he squirmed as everyone laughed* =**wince**, shudder.

squirrel ■ **squirrel something away** =**save**, put aside, put by, lay by, set aside, lay aside, keep in reserve, stockpile, accumulate, stock up with/on, hoard; *informal* salt away, stash away.

> WORD LINKS
>
> *relating to squirrels:* **sciurine**
> *home:* **drey**

squirt ▶ verb **1** *a jet of ink squirted out of the tube* =**spurt**, shoot, spray, jet, erupt; gush, rush, pump, surge, stream, spew, well, issue, emanate; emit, belch. **2** *she squirted me with scent* =**splash**, spray, shower, sprinkle.
▶ noun *a squirt of water* =**spurt**, jet, spray, fountain, gush, stream, surge.

stab ▶ verb **1** *he stabbed him in the stomach* =**knife**, run through, skewer, spear, gore, spike, impale, transfix, pierce, prick, puncture. **2** *she stabbed at the earth with a fork* =**lunge**, thrust, jab, poke, prod, dig.
▶ noun **1** *a stab in the leg* =**(knife) wound**, puncture, incision, prick, cut, perforation. **2** *a stab of pain* =**twinge**, pang, throb, spasm, cramp, prick, flash, thrill. **3** *(informal) a stab at writing* =**attempt**, try; *informal* go, shot, crack, bash.
■ **stab someone in the back** =**betray**, desert, double-cross, sell out.

stability ▶ noun **1** *the stability of the equipment* =**firmness**, solidity, steadiness. **2** *his mental stability* =**balance (of mind)**, (mental) health, sanity, reason. **3** *the stability of their relationship* =**strength**, durability, lasting/enduring nature, permanence.

stable ▶ adjective **1** *a stable vehicle* =**firm**, solid, steady, secure. **2** *a stable person* =**well balanced**, of sound mind, compos mentis, sane, normal, rational. **3** *a stable relationship* =**secure**, solid, strong, steady, firm, sure, steadfast; established, enduring, lasting.
−OPPOSITES loose, wobbly, unbalanced, rocky, lasting, changeable.

stack ▶ noun **1** *a stack of boxes* =**heap**, pile, mound, mountain, pyramid, tower. **2** *(informal) a stack of money. See* LOT *pronoun.*
−OPPOSITES few, little.
▶ verb **1** *Leo was stacking plates* =**heap (up)**, pile (up); assemble, put together, collect. **2** *they stacked the shelves* =**load**, fill (up), pack, charge, stuff, cram; stock.
−OPPOSITES clear.

stadium ▶ noun =**arena**, field, ground, pitch; track, course, racetrack, racecourse, speedway, velodrome.

staff ▶ noun **1** *we'll take on new staff* =**employees**, workers, workforce, personnel, human resources, manpower, labour. **2** *a wooden staff* =**stick**, stave, pole, crook. **3** *a staff of office* =**rod**, mace, wand, sceptre, crozier.
▶ verb *the centre is staffed by teachers* =**man**, people, crew, work, operate, occupy.

stage ▶ noun **1** *this stage of the development* =**phase**, period, juncture, step, point, time, moment, instant, level. **2** *the last stage of the race* =**part**, section, portion, stretch, leg, lap, circuit. **3** *a raised stage* =**platform**, dais, stand, rostrum, podium. **4** *she has written for the stage* =**theatre**, drama, dramatics, thespianism; *informal* the boards.
▶ verb **1** *they staged two plays* =**put on**, present, produce, mount, direct; perform, act, give. **2** *workers staged a protest* =**organize**, arrange, set up; orchestrate, engineer; take part in, participate in, join in.

stagger ▶ verb **1** *he staggered to the door* =**lurch**, reel, sway, teeter, totter, stumble. **2** *I was absolutely staggered* =**amaze**, astound, astonish, surprise, stun, confound, stupefy, daze, take aback, leave open-mouthed; *informal* flabbergast; *Brit. informal* knock for six, gobsmack. **3** *meetings are staggered* =**spread (out)**, space (out).

stagnant ▶ adjective **1** *stagnant water* =**still**, standing, dead; foul, stale, putrid. **2** *a stagnant economy* =**inactive**, sluggish, slow-moving, lethargic, static, flat, depressed, moribund, dead, dormant.
−OPPOSITES flowing, fresh, active, vibrant.

stagnate ▶ verb =**languish**, decline, deteriorate, fall, become stagnant, do nothing, stand still, be sluggish.
−OPPOSITES boom.

staid ▶ adjective =**sedate**, respectable, serious, steady, conventional, traditional, unadventurous, set in one's ways, sober, formal, stuffy, stiff; *informal* starchy, stick-in-the-mud.
−OPPOSITES frivolous, daring, informal.

stain ▶ verb **1** *her clothing was stained with blood* =**discolour**, soil, mark, muddy, spot, spatter, splatter, smear, splash, smudge, blotch. **2** *the wood was stained* =**colour**, tint, dye, pigment.

▶ noun **1** *a mud stain* =**mark**, spot, blotch, smudge, smear. **2** *a stain on his character* =**blemish**, taint, blot, smear, dishonour; damage.

stake¹ ▶ noun *a stake in the ground* =**post**, pole, stick, spike, upright, support, prop, strut, pale, cane.

▶ verb *the plants have to be staked* =**prop up**, tie up, support, hold up, brace, truss.
■ **stake something out 1** *builders staked out the plot* =**mark off/out**, demarcate, measure out. **2** *(informal) the police staked out his flat* =**observe**, watch, keep an eye on, keep under observation/surveillance, keep watch on, monitor.

stake² ▶ noun **1** *playing dice for high stakes* =**bet**, wager, ante. **2** *they are racing for record stakes* =**prize money**, purse, pot, winnings. **3** *low down in the popularity stakes* =**competition**, contest, battle, challenge, race, running, struggle, scramble. **4** *a 40% stake in the business* =**share**, interest, ownership, involvement.

▶ verb *he staked his week's pay* =**bet**, wager, lay, put on, gamble.

stale ▶ adjective **1** *stale food* =**old**, past its best; off, dry, hard, musty, rancid. **2** *stale air* =**stuffy**, close, musty, fusty, stagnant; *Brit.* fuggy. **3** *stale beer* =**flat**, spoiled, off, insipid, tasteless. **4** *stale jokes* =**hackneyed**, tired, worn out, overworked, threadbare, banal, clichéd; out of date, outdated, outmoded, passé, archaic, obsolete; *N. Amer.* played out.
–OPPOSITES fresh, original.

stalemate ▶ noun =**deadlock**, impasse, stand-off, gridlock; draw, tie, dead heat.

stalk¹ ▶ noun *the stalk of a plant* =**stem**, shoot; trunk.

stalk² ▶ verb **1** *he was stalking a deer* =**trail**, follow, shadow, track, go after, hunt; *informal* tail. **2** *she stalked out* =**strut**, stride, march, flounce, storm, stomp, sweep.

stall ▶ noun **1** *a market stall* =**stand**, table, counter, booth, kiosk. **2** *stalls for larger animals* =**pen**, coop, sty, corral, enclosure, compartment. **3** *(Brit.) theatre stalls* =*N. Amer.* orchestra, parterre.

▶ verb **1** *the Government has stalled the project* =**block**, impede, hinder, hamper, interrupt, hold up, hold back, thwart, delay, stonewall, check, stop, halt; *informal* stymie; *N. Amer. informal* bork. **2** *quit stalling* =**delay**, play for time, procrastinate, hedge, drag one's feet, filibuster, stonewall. **3** *stall him for a bit* =**delay**, divert, distract, hold off.

stalwart ▶ adjective =**staunch**, loyal, faithful, committed, devoted, dedicated, dependable, reliable, steady, constant, trusty, steadfast, unwavering.
–OPPOSITES disloyal, unfaithful, unreliable.

stamina ▶ noun =**endurance**, staying power, tirelessness, fortitude, strength, energy, toughness, determination, tenacity, perseverance, grit.

stammer ▶ verb =**stutter**, stumble (over one's words), hesitate, falter, pause, splutter.

▶ noun *he had a stammer* =**stutter**, speech impediment, speech defect.

stamp ▶ verb **1** *he stamped on my toe* =**trample**, step, tread, tramp; **crush**, squash, flatten. **2** *John stamped off, muttering* =**stomp**, stump, clump. **3** *the name is stamped on the cover* =**imprint**, print, impress, punch, inscribe, emboss. **4** *his face was stamped on Martha's memory* =**fix**, inscribe, etch, carve, imprint, impress. **5** *his style stamps him as a player to watch* =**identify**, characterize, brand, distinguish, classify, mark out, set apart, single out.

▶ noun *the stamp of authority* =**mark**, hallmark, sign, seal, (sure/telltale) sign, smack, savour, air.
■ **stamp something out** =**put an end/stop to**, end, stop, crush, put down, crack down on, curb, nip in the bud, scotch, quash, quell, suppress, extinguish, stifle, abolish, get rid of, eliminate, eradicate, destroy, wipe out.

stampede ▶ noun =**charge**, panic, rush, flight, rout.

▶ verb =**bolt**, charge, flee, take flight; race, rush, career, run.

stance ▶ noun **1** *a natural golfer's stance* =**posture**, (body) position, pose, attitude. **2** *a liberal stance* =**attitude**, stand, point of view, viewpoint, standpoint, position, angle, perspective, approach, line, policy.

stand ▶ verb **1** *he was standing in the doorway* =**be on one's feet**, be upright. **2** *the men stood up* =**rise**, get/rise to one's feet,

get up, pick oneself up, find one's feet; *formal* arise. **3** *today a house stands on the site* =**be**, be situated, be located, be positioned, be sited, have been built. **4** *he stood the vase on the shelf* =**put**, set, erect, place, position, prop, lean, stick, install, arrange; *informal* park. **5** *my decision stands* =**remain in force**, remain in operation, hold, hold good, apply, be the case, exist. **6** *his heart could not stand the strain* =**withstand**, endure, bear, put up with, take, cope with, handle, sustain, resist, stand up to. **7** *(informal) I won't stand cheek* =**put up with**, endure, tolerate, accept, take, abide, stand for, support, countenance; *formal* brook.
−OPPOSITES sit, lie, sit down, lie down.

▸ noun **1** *the party's stand on immigration* =**attitude**, stance, point of view, viewpoint, opinion, way of thinking, outlook, standpoint, position, approach, thinking, policy, line. **2** *a stand against tyranny* =**opposition**, resistance. **3** *a mirror on a stand* =**base**, support, platform, rest, plinth; tripod, rack, trivet. **4** *a newspaper stand* =**stall**, counter, booth, kiosk.
■ **stand by** =**wait**, be prepared, be in (a state of) readiness, be ready for action, be on full alert, wait in the wings.
■ **stand by someone/something 1** *she stood by her husband* =**remain/be loyal to**, stick with/by, remain/be true to, stand up for, support, back up, defend, stick up for. **2** *the government must stand by its pledges* =**abide by**, keep (to), adhere to, hold to, stick to, observe, comply with.
■ **stand down** =**relax**, stand easy, come off full alert.
■ **stand for 1** *V stands for volts* =**mean**, be short for, represent, signify, denote, indicate, symbolize. **2** *(informal) I won't stand for any nonsense. See* STAND *verb sense* 7. **3** *we stand for animal welfare* =**advocate**, champion, uphold, defend, stand up for, support, back, endorse, be in favour of, promote.
■ **stand in** =**deputize**, act (as deputy/stand-in), substitute, fill in, sit in, take over, cover, hold the fort, step into the breach; replace, relieve, take over from; *informal* sub, fill someone's shoes, step into someone's shoes; *N. Amer.* pinch-hit.
■ **stand out 1** *his veins stood out* =**project**, stick out, bulge (out), be proud, jut (out). **2** *she certainly stood out* =**be noticeable**, be visible, be obvious, be conspicuous, stick out, attract attention, catch the eye, leap out; *informal* stick/stand out a mile, stick/stand out like a sore thumb.
■ **stand up** =**remain/be valid**, be sound, be plausible, hold water, hold up, bear examination/scrutiny, be verifiable.
■ **stand someone up** =**let down**, fail to meet, jilt.
■ **stand up for someone/something** =**support**, defend, back, stick up for, champion, promote, uphold, take someone's part, take the side of, side with.
■ **stand up to someone/something** =**defy**, confront, challenge, resist, take on, argue with, take a stand against.

standard ▸ noun **1** *the standard of her work* =**quality**, level, calibre, merit, excellence. **2** *a safety standard* =**guideline**, norm, yardstick, benchmark, measure, criterion, guide, touchstone, model, pattern. **3** *a standard to live by* =**principle**, ideal; (**standards**) code (of behaviour/honour), morals, ethics. **4** *the regiment's standard* =**flag**, banner, ensign, colour(s).
▸ adjective **1** *the standard way of doing it* =**normal**, usual, typical, stock, common, ordinary, customary, conventional, wonted, established, settled, set, fixed, traditional, prevailing. **2** *the standard work on the subject* =**definitive**, established, classic, recognized, accepted.
−OPPOSITES unusual, special.

standardize ▸ verb =**systematize**, make consistent, make uniform, regulate, normalize, bring into line, equalize, homogenize.

stand-in ▸ noun =**substitute**, replacement, deputy, surrogate, proxy, understudy, locum, cover, relief, stopgap; *informal* temp; *N. Amer. informal* pinch-hitter.
▸ adjective =**substitute**, replacement, deputy, fill-in, stopgap, surrogate, relief, acting, temporary, provisional, caretaker; *N. Amer. informal* pinch-hitting.

standing ▸ noun **1** *his standing in the community* =**status**, ranking, position; reputation, stature. **2** *a person of some standing* =**seniority**, rank, eminence, prominence, prestige, repute, stature, esteem, importance, account, consequence, influence, distinction; *informal* clout.

stand-off ▸ noun =**deadlock**, stalemate, impasse.

standpoint ▸ noun =**point of view**, viewpoint, vantage point, attitude, stance, view, opinion, position, way of thinking, outlook, perspective.

standstill ▶ noun =**halt**, stop, dead stop; gridlock.

staple ▶ adjective =**main**, principal, chief, major, primary, leading, foremost, first, most important, predominant, dominant, basic, standard, prime, premier; *informal* number-one.

star ▶ noun **1** *the sky was full of stars* =**celestial/heavenly body**; sun; planet. **2** *the stars of the film* =**principal**, leading lady/man, (female/male) lead, hero, heroine. **3** *a star of the world of chess* =**celebrity**, superstar, big/famous name, household name, someone, somebody, leading light, VIP, personality, luminary; *informal* celeb, big shot, big noise, megastar.
–OPPOSITES nobody.
▶ adjective **1** *a star pupil* =**outstanding**, exceptional. **2** *the star attraction* =**top**, leading, best, greatest, foremost, major, pre-eminent.
–OPPOSITES poor, minor.

WORD LINKS

relating to stars: **astral, sidereal, stellar**
study of stars: **astronomy**
measurement of stars: **astrometry**

starchy ▶ adjective *(informal)*. See STAID.

stare ▶ verb =**gaze**, gape, goggle, glare, ogle, peer; *informal* gawk; *Brit. informal* gawp.

stark ▶ adjective **1** *a stark silhouette* =**sharp**, crisp, distinct, clear, clear-cut. **2** *a stark landscape* =**desolate**, bare, barren, empty, godforsaken, bleak, arid. **3** *a stark room* =**austere**, severe, plain, simple, bare, unadorned. **4** *stark terror* =**sheer**, utter, absolute, total, pure, downright, out-and-out, outright. **5** *the stark facts* =**blunt**, bald, bare, simple, basic, plain, unvarnished, harsh, grim.
–OPPOSITES fuzzy, indistinct, pleasant, ornate, disguised.
▶ adverb *stark naked* =**completely**, totally, utterly, absolutely, entirely, wholly, fully, quite, altogether, thoroughly, truly.

start ▶ verb **1** *the meeting starts at 7.45* =**begin**, commence, get under way, go ahead, get going; *informal* kick off. **2** *this was how her illness started* =**come into being/existence**, begin, commence, be born, arise, originate, develop. **3** *she*

started her own charity =**establish**, set up, found, create, bring into being, institute, initiate, inaugurate, introduce, open, launch. **4** *we had better start on the work* =**make a start**, begin, commence, get going, set things moving, start/get/ set the ball rolling, buckle to/down; *informal* get moving/cracking, get stuck in, get down to business. **5** *he started across the field* =**set off/out**, depart, leave, get under way, make a start, embark; *informal* hit the road. **6** *you can start the machine* =**activate**, switch/turn on, start up, fire up; boot up. **7** *the machine started* =**begin working**, start up, get going, spring into life. **8** *'Oh my!' she said, starting* =**flinch**, jerk, jump, twitch, recoil, shrink, wince.
–OPPOSITES finish, stop, clear up, wind up, hang about, give up, arrive, stay, close down.
▶ noun **1** *the start of the event* =**beginning**, commencement, inception. **2** *the start of her illness* =**onset**, commencement, emergence. **3** *a quarter of an hour's start* =**lead**, head start, advantage. **4** *she awoke with a start* =**jerk**, twitch, spasm, jump.
–OPPOSITES end, finish.

startle ▶ verb =**surprise**, frighten, scare, alarm, give someone a shock/ fright/jolt, make someone jump.
–OPPOSITES put at ease.

startling ▶ adjective =**surprising**, astonishing, amazing, unexpected, unforeseen, shocking, stunning; frightening, alarming, scary.
–OPPOSITES predictable, ordinary.

starvation ▶ noun =**hunger**, lack of food, famine, undernourishment, malnourishment, fasting.

starving ▶ adjective =**hungry** undernourished, malnourished, starved, half-starved; ravenous, famished.
–OPPOSITES full.

stash *(informal)* ▶ verb =**store**, stow, pack, load, cache, hide, conceal, secrete; hoard, save, stockpile.
▶ noun =**cache**, hoard, stock, stockpile, store, supply, reserve.

state[1] ▶ noun **1** *the state of the economy* =**condition**, shape, position; predicament, plight. **2** *(informal) don't get into a state* =**fluster**, frenzy, fret, panic; *informal* flap, tizzy, stew; *N. Amer. informal* twit. **3** *(informal) your room is in a state* =**mess**, chaos, disarray, muddle, shambles. **4** *an autonomous state* =**country**, nation, land, sovereign state, nation state, kingdom, realm, power, republic. **5** *the country is divided into thirty-two states* =**province**, region, territory, canton, department, county, district; *Brit.* shire. **6** *the power of the state* =**government**, parliament, administration, regime, authorities.

▶ **adjective** *a state visit to China* =**ceremonial**, official, formal, public.

–OPPOSITES unofficial, private, informal.

state² ▶ verb =**express**, voice, utter, put into words, declare, announce, make known, put across/over, communicate, air, reveal, disclose, divulge, proclaim, present, expound.

stated ▶ adjective =**specified**, agreed, declared, designated.

–OPPOSITES undefined, irregular, tacit.

stately ▶ adjective =**dignified**, majestic, ceremonious, courtly, imposing, solemn, regal, grand; slow-moving, measured, deliberate.

statement ▶ noun =**declaration**, expression, affirmation, assertion, announcement, utterance, communication, proclamation, presentation, account, testimony, evidence, report, bulletin, communiqué.

state-of-the-art ▶ adjective =**modern**, the latest, new, up to the minute; advanced; sophisticated.

static ▶ adjective **1** *prices remained static* =**unchanged**, fixed, stable, steady, unchanging, constant. **2** *a static display* =**stationary**, motionless, immobile, unmoving, still, fixed.

–OPPOSITES variable, mobile, dynamic.

station ▶ noun **1** *a railway station* =**stop**; terminus, terminal, depot. **2** *a research station* =**establishment**, base, camp; post, depot; mission; site, facility, installation, yard. **3** *a police station* =**office**, depot, base, headquarters; *N. Amer.* precinct, station house. **4** *a radio station* =**channel**; wavelength.

▶ verb *the regiment was stationed at Woolwich* =**base**, post; establish, install; deploy, garrison.

stationary ▶ adjective =**static**, parked, motionless, immobile, unmoving, still, stock-still, at a standstill, at rest; not moving a muscle, like a statue, rooted to the spot, inactive, inert, lifeless, inanimate.

–OPPOSITES moving, shifting.

statue ▶ noun =**sculpture**, figure, effigy, statuette, figurine, idol; carving, bronze, graven image, model; bust.

statuesque ▶ adjective =**imposing**, striking, stately, majestic, noble, magnificent, regal.

stature ▶ noun **1** *small in stature* =**height**, tallness; size, build. **2** *an architect of international stature* =**reputation**, repute, standing, status, position, prestige, distinction, eminence, preeminence, prominence, importance, influence, fame, renown, acclaim.

status ▶ noun **1** *the status of women* =**standing**, rank, position, level, place; *dated* station. **2** *wealth and status* =**prestige**, kudos, cachet, standing, stature, regard, fame, note, renown, honour, esteem, image, importance.

statute ▶ noun =**law**, regulation, act, bill, decree, edict, rule, ruling, resolution, dictum, command, order, directive, by-law; *N. Amer.* formal ordinance.

staunch¹ ▶ adjective =**stalwart**, loyal, faithful, committed, devoted, dedicated, steadfast, redoubtable, unwavering.

–OPPOSITES disloyal, unfaithful, unreliable.

staunch² ▶ verb =**stem**, stop, halt, check; block, dam; *N. Amer.* stanch; *archaic* stay.

stave ■ **stave something off** =**avert**, prevent, avoid, counter, preclude, forestall, nip in the bud; ward off, fend off, head off, keep off, keep at bay.

stay¹ ▶ verb **1** *he stayed where he was* =**remain (behind)**; wait, linger, stick, be left, hold on, hang on; *informal* hang around/round; *Brit. informal* hang about. **2** *they won't stay hidden* =**continue (to be)**, remain, keep, carry on being, go on being. **3** *our aunt is staying with us* =**visit**, stop (off/over); holiday, lodge, be housed, be accommodated, be billeted; *N. Amer.* vacation; *formal* sojourn.

–OPPOSITES leave.

▶ noun *a stay at a hotel* =**visit**, stop, stop-off, stopover, break, holiday; *N. Amer.* vacation; *formal* sojourn.

stay² ▶ noun =**strut**, wire, brace, tether, guy, prop, rod, support, truss.

steadfast ▶ adjective **1** *a steadfast friend* =**loyal**, faithful, devoted, dedicated, dependable, reliable, steady, true, constant, staunch, trusty. **2** *steadfast policy* =**firm**, determined, resolute, relentless, implacable, single-minded.

−OPPOSITES disloyal, irresolute.

steady ▸ adjective **1** *the ladder must be steady* =**stable**, firm, fixed, secure, fast, safe; anchored, moored. **2** *keep the camera steady* =**motionless**, still, static, stationary, unmoving. **3** *a steady gaze* =**fixed**, intent, unwavering, unfaltering. **4** *a steady income* =**constant**, regular, consistent, reliable. **5** *steady rain* =**continuous**, continual, unceasing, ceaseless, perpetual, unremitting, unwavering, unfaltering, unending, endless, round-the-clock. **6** *a steady boyfriend* =**regular**, settled, firm; committed, long-term.
−OPPOSITES unstable, loose, shaky, darting, fluctuating, sporadic, occasional.
▸ verb **1** *he steadied the rifle* =**stabilize**, hold steady; brace, support; balance, rest. **2** *she needed to steady her nerves* =**calm**, soothe, quieten, compose, settle; subdue, quell.

steal ▸ verb **1** *burglars stole the TV* =**purloin**, thieve, take, help oneself to, pilfer, run off with, carry off, shoplift; embezzle; have one's fingers/hand in the till; *informal* walk off with, swipe, nab, rip off, lift, 'liberate', 'borrow', filch, snaffle; *Brit. informal* nick, pinch, whip, knock off; *N. Amer. informal* heist. **2** *his work was stolen by his tutor* =**plagiarize**, copy, pirate; *informal* rip off, lift, borrow, pinch, nick, crib. **3** *he stole a kiss* =**snatch**, sneak. **4** *he stole out of the room* =**creep**, sneak, slink, slip, slide, glide, tiptoe, slope.

> WORD LINKS
> *compulsion to steal:* **kleptomania**

stealing ▸ noun =**theft**, thieving, robbery, larceny, burglary, shoplifting, pilfering; embezzlement.

> WORD LINKS
> *compulsive stealing:* **kleptomania**
> *fear of stealing:* **kleptophobia**

stealth ▸ noun =**furtiveness**, secretiveness, secrecy, surreptitiousness.
−OPPOSITES openness.

stealthy ▸ adjective =**furtive**, secretive, secret, surreptitious.
−OPPOSITES open.

steam ▸ noun *steam from the kettle* =**water vapour**, condensation, mist, haze, fog, moisture.
■ **steamed up** (*informal*) **1** *he got steamed*

up *about forgetting his papers.* See AGITATED. **2** *they get steamed up about the media.* See ANGRY *sense* 1.
■ **steam up** =**mist (up/over)**, fog (up), become misty/misted.

steamy ▸ adjective **1** *the steamy jungle* =**humid**, muggy, sticky, moist, damp, clammy, sultry, sweaty, steaming. **2** (*informal*) *a steamy love scene.* See EROTIC.

steel ■ **steel oneself** =**brace oneself**, summon (up) one's courage, screw up one's courage, gear oneself up, prepare oneself; fortify oneself, harden oneself; *informal* psych oneself up; *literary* gird (up) one's loins.

steely ▸ adjective **1** *his steely gaze* =**piercing**, penetrating; merciless, ruthless, pitiless, severe, unrelenting, unpitying, unforgiving; *literary* adamantine. **2** *steely determination* =**resolute**, firm, steadfast, single-minded; ruthless, iron, grim, gritty; unflinching, unswerving, unfaltering, untiring, unwavering.
−OPPOSITES flabby, half-hearted.

steep¹ ▸ adjective **1** *steep cliffs* =**precipitous**, sheer, abrupt, sharp, perpendicular, vertical, vertiginous. **2** *a steep increase* =**sharp**, sudden, dramatic, precipitous.
−OPPOSITES gentle, gradual, reasonable.

steep² ■ **steeped in** =**imbued with**, filled with, permeated with, suffused with, soaked in; pervade.

steeple ▸ noun =**spire**, tower; bell tower, belfry, campanile.

steer ▸ verb **1** *he steered the boat* =**guide**, direct, manoeuvre, drive, pilot, navigate. **2** *Luke steered her down the path* =**guide**, conduct, direct, lead, take, usher, shepherd, marshal, herd.
■ **steer clear of** =**keep away from**, keep one's distance from, keep at arm's length, give a wide berth to, avoid, have nothing to do with; shun, eschew.

stem¹ ▸ noun *a plant stem* =**stalk**, shoot, trunk.
■ **stem from** =**have its origins in**, arise from, originate from, spring from, derive from, come from, emanate from, flow from, proceed from.

stem² ▸ verb =**staunch**, stop, halt, check, hold back, restrict, control, contain, curb; *N. Amer.* stanch; *archaic* stay.

stench ▸ noun =**stink**, reek; *Brit. informal* niff, pong, whiff; *N. Amer. informal* funk; *literary* miasma.

step ▶ noun **1** *Frank took a step forward* =**pace**, stride. **2** *she heard a step on the stairs* =**footstep**, footfall, tread. **3** *it is only a step to the river* =**short distance**, stone's throw, spitting distance; *informal* {a hop, skip, and jump}. **4** *the top step* =**stair**, tread; (**steps**) stairs, staircase. **5** *resigning is a very serious step* =**course of action**, measure, move, act, action, operation. **6** *a significant step towards a cease-fire* =**advance**, development, move, movement; breakthrough.
▶ verb *she stepped forward* =**walk**, move, tread, pace, stride.
■ **in step with** =**in accord with**, in harmony with, in agreement with, in tune with, in line with, in keeping with, in conformity with.
■ **mind/watch one's step** =**be careful**, take care, step/tread carefully, exercise care/caution, mind how one goes, look/watch out, be wary, be on one's guard.
■ **out of step with** =**at odds with**, at variance with, in disagreement with, out of tune with.
■ **step by step** =**one step at a time**, bit by bit, gradually, in stages, by degrees, slowly, steadily.
■ **step down** =**resign**, stand down, give up one's post/job, bow out, abdicate; *informal* quit.
■ **step in** =**intervene**, intercede.
■ **step something up 1** *the army stepped up its offensive* =**increase**, intensify, strengthen, escalate; *informal* up, crank up. **2** *I stepped up my pace* =**speed up**, increase, accelerate, quicken, hasten.

stereotype ▶ noun =**standard/conventional image**, received idea, cliché, formula.
▶ verb =**typecast**, pigeonhole, conventionalize, categorize, label, tag.

stereotyped ▶ adjective =**stock**, conventional, stereotypical, standard, formulaic, predictable; hackneyed, clichéd, cliché-ridden; typecast.
−OPPOSITES unconventional, original.

sterile ▶ adjective **1** *sterile desert* =**unproductive**, infertile, unfruitful, barren. **2** *a sterile debate* =**pointless**, unproductive, useless, futile, vain, idle. **3** *sterile conditions* =**aseptic**, sterilized, germ-free, antiseptic, disinfected; uncontaminated, unpolluted, pure, clean; sanitary, hygienic.
−OPPOSITES fertile, productive, septic.

sterilize ▶ verb **1** *the scalpel was first sterilized* =**disinfect**, fumigate, decontamin-

ate, sanitize; pasteurize; clean, cleanse, purify. **2** *stray dogs are usually sterilized* =**neuter**, castrate, spay, geld; *N. Amer. & Austral.* alter; *Brit. informal* doctor.
−OPPOSITES contaminate.

sterling ▶ adjective (*Brit.*) =**excellent**, first-rate, first-class, exceptional, outstanding, splendid, superlative, laudable, commendable, admirable.
−OPPOSITES poor, unexceptional.

stern¹ ▶ adjective **1** *a stern expression* =**serious**, unsmiling, frowning, severe, forbidding, grim, unfriendly, austere, dour, stony, flinty, steely, unrelenting, unforgiving, unsympathetic, disapproving. **2** *stern measures* =**strict**, severe, stringent, harsh, drastic, hard, tough, extreme, ruthless, rigorous, uncompromising, unsparing, draconian.
−OPPOSITES genial, friendly, lenient, lax.

stern² ▶ noun *the stern of the ship* =**rear (end)**, back, poop, transom, tail.
−OPPOSITES bow.

stew ▶ noun **1** *a beef stew* =**casserole**, hotpot, ragout, goulash; *N. Amer.* burgoo. **2** (*informal*) *she's in a right old stew* =**panic**, fluster; *informal* flap, sweat, lather, tizzy, state; *N. Amer. informal* twit.
▶ verb **1** *stew the meat for an hour* =**braise**, casserole, simmer. **2** (*informal*) *there's no point stewing over it.* See WORRY verb sense 1.

steward ▶ noun **1** *an air steward* =**flight attendant**; stewardess, air hostess. **2** *the race stewards* =**official**, marshal. **3** *the steward of the estate* =**manager**, agent, overseer, custodian, caretaker.

stick¹ ▶ noun **1** *a fire made of sticks* =**piece of wood**, twig, branch. **2** *he walks with a stick* =**walking stick**, cane, staff, crook, crutch. **3** *the plants need supporting on sticks* =**cane**, pole, post, stake. **4** *he beat me with a stick* =**club**, cudgel; truncheon, baton; cane, switch, rod; *Brit. informal* cosh. **5** (*Brit. informal*) *he'll get some stick for this.* See CRITICISM sense 1.
−OPPOSITES praise, commendation.
■ **the sticks** (*informal*) =**the country**, the countryside, the provinces; the backwoods, the back of beyond, the wilds, the hinterland, a backwater; *N. Amer.* the backcountry, the backland; *Austral./NZ* the backblocks, the booay; *S. African* the backveld, the platteland; *informal* the middle of nowhere; *N. Amer. informal* the boondocks; *Austral./NZ informal* Woop Woop.

stick² ▶ verb **1** *he stuck his fork into the sausage* = **thrust**, push, insert, jab, poke, dig, plunge. **2** *the bristles stuck into his skin* = **pierce**, penetrate, puncture, prick, stab. **3** *the mug stuck to the mat* = **adhere**, cling. **4** *stick the stamp there* = **affix**, attach, fasten, fix; paste, glue, gum, tape. **5** *the wheels stuck fast* = **become/get trapped**, become/get jammed, jam, catch, become/get caught. **6** *that sticks in his mind* = **remain**, stay, linger, persist, continue, endure. **7** *the charges won't stick* = **be upheld**, hold, be believed; *informal* hold water. **8** (*informal*) *just stick it on my desk* = **put (down)**, place, set (down), lay (down), deposit; leave, stow; *informal* dump, bung, park, plonk, pop; *N. Amer. informal* plunk. **9** (*Brit. informal*) *I can't stick it* = **tolerate**, put up with, take, stand, stomach, endure, bear; *informal* abide.
■ **stick at** = **persevere with**, persist with, work at, continue with, carry on with, stay with; go the distance, stay the course; *informal* soldier on with, hang in there.
■ **stick by** = **be loyal to**, be faithful to, be true to, stand by.
■ **stick out 1** *his front teeth stuck out* = **protrude**, jut (out), project, stand out, extend, poke out; bulge. **2** *they stuck out in their new clothes* = **be conspicuous**, be obvious, stand out, attract attention, leap out; *informal* stick/stand out a mile, stick/stand out like a sore thumb.
■ **stick to** = **abide by**, keep, adhere to, hold to, comply with, fulfil, make good, stand by.
■ **stick up for** = **support**, take someone's side/part, side with, stand by, stand up for, defend.

sticky ▶ adjective **1** *sticky tape* = **(self-)adhesive**, gummed. **2** *sticky clay* = **glutinous**, viscous; gluey, tacky, gummy, treacly; *Brit.* claggy; *informal* gooey, gloopy. **3** *sticky weather* = **humid**, muggy, close, sultry, steamy, sweaty. **4** *a sticky situation* = **awkward**, difficult, tricky, ticklish, delicate, embarrassing, sensitive, uncomfortable; *informal* hairy.
−OPPOSITES dry, fresh, cool, easy.

stiff ▶ adjective **1** *stiff cardboard* = **rigid**, hard, firm. **2** *a stiff paste* = **semi-solid**, viscous, thick, firm. **3** *I'm stiff all over* = **aching**, achy, painful; arthritic. **4** *a rather stiff manner* = **formal**, reserved, wooden, forced, strained, stilted; *informal* starchy, uptight, stand-offish. **5** *a stiff fine* = **harsh**, severe, heavy, stringent, drastic, draconian; *Brit.* swingeing. **6** *stiff resistance* = **vigorous**, determined, strong, spirited, resolute, tenacious, steely, dogged, stubborn. **7** *a stiff climb* = **difficult**, hard, arduous, tough, strenuous, laborious, uphill, exacting, tiring, demanding, formidable, challenging, punishing, gruelling; *Brit. informal* knackering. **8** *a stiff breeze* = **strong**, fresh, brisk. **9** *a stiff drink* = **strong**, potent, alcoholic.
−OPPOSITES flexible, plastic, limp, runny, supple, relaxed, informal, lenient, mild, half-hearted, easy, gentle, weak.

stiffen ▶ verb **1** *stir until the mixture stiffens* = **become stiff**, thicken; set, become solid, solidify, harden, gel, congeal, coagulate, clot. **2** *she stiffened her muscles | without exercise, joints will stiffen* = **make/become stiff**, tense (up), tighten, tauten. **3** *intimidation stiffened their resolve* = **strengthen**, harden, toughen, fortify, reinforce.
−OPPOSITES soften, liquefy, relax, weaken.

stifle ▶ verb **1** *Eleanor stifled a yawn* = **suppress**, smother, restrain, fight back, check, swallow, curb, silence. **2** *cartels stifle competition* = **constrain**, hinder, hamper, impede, hold back, curb, prevent, inhibit, suppress.
−OPPOSITES let out, encourage.

stifling ▶ adjective = **airless**, suffocating, oppressive; sweltering; humid, close, muggy; *informal* boiling.
−OPPOSITES fresh, airy, cold.

stigma ▶ noun = **shame**, disgrace, dishonour, ignominy, humiliation.
−OPPOSITES honour, credit.

stigmatize ▶ verb = **condemn**, denounce; brand, label, mark out.

still ▶ adjective **1** *Polly lay still* = **motionless**, unmoving, stock-still, immobile, rooted to the spot, transfixed, static, stationary. **2** *a still night* = **quiet**, silent; calm, peaceful, serene, windless. **3** *the lake was still* = **calm**, flat, even, smooth, placid, waveless, glassy, like a millpond/mirror, unruffled.
−OPPOSITES moving, active, noisy, rough.
▶ noun *the still of the night* = **quiet**, silence, stillness, hush; calm, tranquillity, peace.
−OPPOSITES noise, disturbance, hubbub.
▶ adverb **1** *he's still here* = **even now**, yet.

2 *He's crazy. Still, he's harmless* =**nevertheless**, nonetheless, all the same, even so, but, however, despite that, in spite of that, for all that, be that as it may, in any event, at any rate.

▸ **verb 1** *he stilled the crowd* =**quieten**, quiet, silence, hush; calm, settle, pacify, subdue.
–OPPOSITES stir up, get stronger, get up.

stilted ▸ adjective =**strained**, forced, contrived, laboured, stiff, self-conscious, awkward, unnatural, wooden.
–OPPOSITES natural, effortless, spontaneous.

stimulate ▸ verb =**encourage**, act as a stimulus/incentive/impetus/fillip/spur to, prompt, prod, motivate, trigger, spark, spur on, galvanize, activate, fire, fuel; inspire, incentivize, rouse, excite, animate, electrify; *N. Amer.* light a fire under.
–OPPOSITES discourage.

stimulating ▸ adjective =**thought-provoking**, interesting, inspiring, inspirational, lively, exciting, stirring, rousing, refreshing, invigorating; provocative, challenging.
–OPPOSITES sedative, uninspiring, uninteresting, boring.

stimulus ▸ noun =**spur**, stimulant, encouragement, impetus, boost, prompt, prod, incentive, inducement, inspiration; motivation, impulse.
–OPPOSITES deterrent, discouragement.

sting ▸ noun **1** *a bee sting* =**prick**, wound, injury. **2** *this cream will take the sting away* =**smart**, pricking; pain, soreness, hurt, irritation.
▸ verb **1** *she was stung by a scorpion* =**prick**, wound; poison. **2** *the smoke made her eyes sting* =**smart**, burn, hurt, be irritated, be sore. **3** *the criticism stung her* =**upset**, wound, cut to the quick, hurt, pain, mortify. **4** *he was stung into action* =**provoke**, goad, incite, spur, prick, prod, rouse, drive, galvanize.
–OPPOSITES deter.

stingy ▸ adjective *(informal)* =**mean**, miserly, niggardly, close-fisted, parsimonious, penny-pinching, cheeseparing, Scrooge-like; *informal* tight-fisted, tight, mingy; *N. Amer. informal* cheap.
–OPPOSITES generous, liberal.

stink ▸ verb **1** *his clothes stank of sweat* =**reek**, smell disgusting. **2** *(informal) the whole idea stinks* =**be abhorrent**; *N. Amer. informal* suck.
▸ **noun 1** *the stink of sweat* =**stench**, reek; *Brit. informal* pong, niff; *N. Amer. informal* funk; *literary* miasma. **2** *(informal) she kicked up a stink* =**fuss**, commotion, trouble, outcry, uproar, furore; *informal* song and dance, to-do, kerfuffle, hoo-ha; *Brit. informal* row, carry-on.

stinking ▸ adjective =**foul-smelling**, smelly, reeking, fetid, malodorous, rank, noxious; *informal* stinky, reeky; *Brit. informal* niffy, pongy, whiffy; *N. Amer. informal* funky; *literary* noisome.
–OPPOSITES sweet-smelling, fragrant.

stint ▸ noun =**spell**, stretch, turn, session, term, shift, tour of duty.

stipulate ▸ verb =**specify**, set down/out, lay down; demand, require, insist on.

stipulation ▸ noun =**condition**, precondition, proviso, provision, prerequisite, specification; demand, requirement.

stir ▸ verb **1** *stir the mixture well* =**mix**, blend; beat, whip, whisk, fold in; *N. Amer.* muddle. **2** *Travis stirred in his sleep* =**move**, change one's position, shift. **3** *a breeze stirred the leaves* =**disturb**, rustle, shake, move, agitate. **4** *he finally stirred at ten o'clock* =**get up**, rouse oneself, rise; **wake (up)**; *informal* rise and shine, surface, show signs of life; *formal* arise; *literary* waken. **5** *I never stirred from here* =**move**, budge, shift; leave. **6** *a film that stirs the imagination* =**arouse**, rouse, fire, kindle, inspire, stimulate, excite, awaken, quicken. **7** *the war stirred him to action* =**spur**, drive, rouse, prompt, propel, prod, motivate, encourage; urge, impel; provoke, goad, sting, incite; *N. Amer.* light a fire under.
–OPPOSITES go to bed, retire, go to sleep, stultify, stay, stay put.
▸ **noun** *the news caused a stir* =**commotion**, disturbance, fuss, excitement, turmoil, sensation; *informal* to-do, hoo-ha, hullabaloo, flap, splash.
■ **stir something up** =**whip up**, work up, foment, fan the flames of, trigger, spark off, precipitate, excite, provoke, incite.

stirring ▸ adjective =**exciting**, thrilling, rousing, stimulating, moving, inspiring, heady.
–OPPOSITES boring, pedestrian.

stitch ▶ verb =sew, tack; seam, hem; darn.

stock ▶ noun **1** *the shop doesn't carry much stock* =**merchandise**, goods, wares; range, choice, variety. **2** *a stock of fuel* =**store**, supply, stockpile, reserve, hoard, cache, bank. **3** *farm stock* =**animals**, livestock, beasts; flocks, herds. **4** *his mother was of French stock* =**descent**, ancestry, origin(s), parentage, pedigree, lineage, heritage, birth, extraction, family, blood. **5** *chicken stock* =**bouillon**, broth. **6** *the stock of a weapon* =**handle**, butt, haft, grip, shaft, shank.
▶ adjective *the stock response* =**usual**, routine, predictable, set, standard, staple, customary, familiar, conventional, traditional, stereotyped, clichéd, hackneyed, unoriginal, formulaic.
−OPPOSITES non-standard, original, unusual.
▶ verb **1** *we do not stock GM food* =**sell**, carry, keep (in stock), offer, have, supply. **2** *the fridge was well stocked with milk* =**supply**, provide, furnish, provision, equip, fill.
■ **in stock** =**for/on sale**, available, on the shelf.
■ **stock up on/with** =**amass**, stockpile, hoard, cache, lay in, buy up/in, put away/by, put/set aside, collect, accumulate, save; *informal* squirrel away, salt away, stash away.
■ **take stock of** =**review**, assess, weigh up, appraise, evaluate; *informal* size up.

stockpile ▶ noun =**stock**, store, supply, collection, reserve, hoard, cache; *informal* stash.
▶ verb =**store up**, amass, accumulate, store (up), stock up on, hoard, cache, collect, lay in, put away, put/set aside, put by, stow away, save; *informal* salt away, stash away.

stocky ▶ adjective =**thickset**, sturdy, heavily built, chunky, burly, strapping, brawny, solid, heavy, hefty, beefy.
−OPPOSITES slender, skinny.

stodgy ▶ adjective **1** *a stodgy pudding* =**solid**, substantial, filling, hearty, heavy, indigestible. **2** *stodgy writing* =**boring**, dull, uninteresting, dreary, turgid, tedious, heavy going, unimaginative, uninspired, unexciting.
−OPPOSITES light, interesting, lively.

stoical ▶ adjective =**long-suffering**, uncomplaining, patient, forbearing, accepting, tolerant, resigned, phlegmatic, philosophical.
−OPPOSITES complaining, intolerant.

stoicism ▶ noun =**patience**, forbearance, resignation, fortitude, endurance, acceptance, tolerance, philosophicalness, phlegm.
−OPPOSITES intolerance.

stoke ▶ verb =**add fuel to**, mend, keep burning, tend.

stolid ▶ adjective =**impassive**, phlegmatic, unemotional, cool, calm, placid, unexcitable; dependable; unimaginative, dull.
−OPPOSITES emotional, lively, imaginative.

stomach ▶ noun **1** *a pain in my stomach* =**abdomen**, belly, gut, middle; *informal* tummy, tum, insides. **2** *his fat stomach* =**paunch**, belly, beer belly/gut, girth; *informal* pot, tummy, spare tyre, middle-aged spread; *N. Amer. informal* bay window. **3** *no stomach for a fight* =**appetite**, taste; inclination, desire, wish.
▶ verb *they couldn't stomach it* =**tolerate**, put up with, take, stand, endure, bear; *informal* hack, abide; *Brit. informal* stick.

> **WORD LINKS**
>
> *relating to the stomach:* **gastric**
> *branch of medicine concerning the stomach:* **gastroenterology**
> *inflammation of the stomach and intestines:* **gastro-enteritis**

stomach ache ▶ noun =**indigestion**, dyspepsia; colic; *informal* bellyache, tummy ache, gut ache, collywobbles.

stone ▶ noun **1** *someone threw a stone* =**rock**, pebble, boulder. **2** *a commemorative stone* =**tablet**, monument, monolith, obelisk; gravestone, headstone, tombstone. **3** *paving stones* =**slab**, flagstone, flag. **4** *a precious stone* =**gem**, gemstone, jewel; *informal* rock, sparkler. **5** *a peach stone* =**kernel**, seed, pip, pit.

> **WORD LINKS**
>
> *relating to stone:* **lithic, lapidary, lithos-**
> *study of precious stones:* **gemmology**

stony ▶ adjective **1** *a stony path* =**rocky**, pebbly, gravelly, shingly; rough. **2** *a stony stare* =**unfriendly**, hostile; hard, flinty, steely, stern, severe; expressionless, blank, poker-faced; unfeeling, uncaring, unsympathetic, indifferent.
−OPPOSITES smooth, friendly, sympathetic.

stooge ▶ noun =**underling**, minion, lackey, subordinate; henchman; **puppet**, pawn, cat's paw; *informal* sidekick;

Brit. informal dogsbody, poodle.

stoop ▸ verb **1** *she stooped to pick up the pen* =**bend (over/down)**, lean over/down, crouch (down). **2** *he stoops when he walks* =**hunch one's shoulders**, walk with a stoop, be round-shouldered.
▸ noun *a man with a stoop* =**hunch**, round shoulders; curvature of the spine; *Medicine* kyphosis.
■ **stoop to** =**lower oneself**, sink, descend, resort; go as far as, sink as low as.

stop ▸ verb **1** *we can't stop the decline* =**put an end/stop/halt to**, bring to an end/stop/halt/close/standstill, end, halt; finish, terminate, wind up, discontinue, cut short, interrupt, nip in the bud; deactivate, shut down. **2** *he stopped running* =**cease**, discontinue, desist from, break off; give up, abandon, cut out; *informal* quit, leave off, pack in, lay off; *Brit. informal* jack in. **3** *the car stopped* =**pull up**, draw up, come to a stop/halt, come to rest, pull in/over. **4** *the music stopped* =**come to an end/stop/standstill**, cease, end, finish, draw to a close, be over, conclude; pause, break off. **5** *divers stopped the flow of oil* =**stem**, staunch, check, curb, block, dam; *N. Amer.* stanch. **6** *the police stopped her leaving* =**prevent**, obstruct, impede, block, bar, preclude; dissuade from. **7** *the council stopped the scheme* =**thwart**, foil, frustrate, stand in the way of; scotch, derail; *informal* put paid to, put the kibosh on, do for, stymie; *Brit. informal* scupper. **8** *just stop the bottle with your thumb* =**block (up)**, plug, close (up), fill (up); seal, bung up; *technical* occlude.
−OPPOSITES start, begin, continue, allow, encourage, expedite, open.
▸ noun **1** *all business came to a stop* =**halt**, end, finish, close, standstill. **2** *a brief stop in the town* =**break**, stopover, stop-off, stay, visit. **3** *the next stop is Oxford Street* =**stopping place**, station.
−OPPOSITES start, beginning, continuation.
■ **put a stop to**. See STOP verb senses 1, 7.
■ **stop off/over** =**break one's journey**, take a break, pause; stay, remain, put up, lodge, rest; *formal* sojourn.

stopgap ▸ noun *the system is just a stopgap* =**temporary solution**, expedient, makeshift.
▸ adjective *a stopgap measure* =**temporary**, provisional, interim, short-term, working, makeshift, emergency.
−OPPOSITES permanent.

stopover ▸ noun =**break**, stop, stop-off, visit, stay; *formal* sojourn.

stoppage ▸ noun **1** *a stoppage over pay* =**strike**, walkout; industrial action. **2** *(Brit.) she got £10.00 an hour before stoppages* =**deduction**, subtraction.

stopper ▸ noun =**bung**, plug, cork, spigot, seal; *N. Amer.* stopple.

store ▸ noun **1** *a store of food* =**stock**, supply, stockpile, hoard, cache, reserve, bank, pool. **2** *a grain store* =**storeroom**, storehouse, repository, depository, stockroom, depot, warehouse; *informal* lock-up. **3** *ship's stores* =**supplies**, provisions, stocks; food, rations, provender; materials, equipment, hardware; *Military* materiel, accoutrements. **4** *a DIY store* =**shop**, (retail) outlet, boutique, department store, chain store, emporium; supermarket, hypermarket, superstore, megastore.
▸ verb *rabbits don't store food* =**keep**, stockpile, lay in, put/set aside, put away/by, save, collect, accumulate, hoard; *informal* squirrel away, salt away, stash away.
−OPPOSITES use, discard.

storehouse ▸ noun =**warehouse**, depository, repository, store, storeroom, depot.

storey ▸ noun =**floor**, level, deck.

storm ▸ noun **1** *battered by a storm* =**tempest**, squall; gale, hurricane, tornado, cyclone, typhoon; thunderstorm, rainstorm, monsoon, hailstorm, snowstorm, blizzard; *N. Amer.* williwaw, windstorm. **2** *there was a storm over his remarks* =**uproar**, outcry, fuss, furore, rumpus, trouble, hue and cry, controversy; *informal* to-do, hoo-ha, hullabaloo, ballyhoo, ructions, stink; *Brit. informal* row. **3** *a storm of protest* =**outburst**, outbreak, explosion, outpouring, surge, blaze; wave, flood.
▸ verb **1** *she stormed out* =**stride**, stomp, march, stalk, flounce, stamp, fling. **2** *police stormed the building* =**attack**, charge, rush; descend on, swoop on.

stormy ▸ adjective **1** *stormy weather* =**blustery**, squally, windy, gusty, blowy; rainy, thundery; wild, tempestuous, turbulent, violent, rough, foul. **2** *a stormy debate* =**angry**, heated, fiery, fierce, furious, passionate, 'lively', acrimonious.
−OPPOSITES calm, fine, peaceful.

story ▸ noun **1** *an adventure story* =**tale**,

narrative; account, anecdote; saga; *informal* yarn, spiel. **2** *the novel has a good story* = **plot**, storyline, scenario; *formal* diegesis. **3** *the story appeared in the papers* = **(news) item**, (news) report, article, feature, piece. **4** *there have been a lot of stories going round* = **rumour**, whisper, allegation; speculation, gossip; *Austral./NZ informal* furphy. **5** *Harper changed his story* = **testimony**, statement, report, account, version. **6** *Ellie never told stories.*
See FALSEHOOD *sense* 1.

stout ▶ adjective **1** *a short stout man* = **fat**, plump, portly, rotund, dumpy, chunky, corpulent; *informal* tubby, pudgy; *Brit. informal* podgy; *N. Amer. informal* zaftig, corn-fed. **2** *stout leather shoes* = **strong**, sturdy, solid, substantial, robust, tough, durable, hard-wearing. **3** *stout resistance* = **determined**, vigorous, forceful, spirited, committed; *informal* gutsy, spunky.
–OPPOSITES thin, flimsy, feeble.

stout-hearted ▶ adjective = **brave**, determined, courageous, bold, plucky, spirited, valiant, valorous, fearless, intrepid, stalwart; *informal* gutsy, spunky.

stove ▶ noun = **oven**, range, cooker, hob.

stow ▶ verb = **pack**, load, store, place, put (away), deposit, stash.
–OPPOSITES unload.
■ **stow away** = **hide**, conceal oneself.

straddle ▶ verb **1** *she straddled the motorbike* = **sit/stand astride**, bestride, mount, get on. **2** *a mountain range straddling the border* = **lie on both sides of**, lie/extend across, span.

strafe ▶ verb = **bomb**, shell, bombard, fire on, machine-gun, rake (with gunfire).

straggle ▶ verb = **trail**, lag, dawdle; fall behind, bring up the rear.

straggly ▶ adjective = **untidy**, messy, unkempt, straggling, dishevelled.

straight ▶ adjective **1** *a long, straight road* = **unswerving**, undeviating, linear. **2** *that picture isn't straight* = **level**, even, in line, aligned, square; vertical, upright, perpendicular; horizontal. **3** *we must get the place straight* = **in order**, tidy, neat, shipshape, orderly, organized, arranged, sorted out, straightened out. **4** *a straight answer* = **honest**, direct, frank, candid, truthful, sincere, forthright, straightforward, plain-spoken, blunt, unequivocal, unambiguous; *informal* upfront. **5** *three straight wins* = **successive**,

in succession, consecutive, in a row, running; *informal* on the trot. **6** *straight brandy* = **undiluted**, neat, pure; *N. Amer. informal* straight up.
–OPPOSITES winding, crooked, untidy, evasive.
▶ adverb **1** *he looked me straight in the eyes* = **right**, directly, squarely, full; *informal* smack, (slap) bang; *N. Amer. informal* spang, smack dab. **2** *she drove straight home* = **directly**, right. **3** *I'll call you straight back* = **right/straight away**, immediately, directly, at once. **4** *I told her straight* = **frankly**, directly, candidly, honestly, forthrightly, plainly, point-blank, bluntly, flatly, straight from the shoulder, without beating about the bush, without mincing words, unequivocally, unambiguously, in plain English, to someone's face; *Brit. informal* straight up. **5** *he can't think straight* = **logically**, rationally, clearly, lucidly, coherently, cogently.
■ **straight away** = **at once**, right away, (right) now, this/that (very) minute, this/that instant, immediately, instantly, directly, forthwith, without further/more ado, promptly, quickly, without delay, then and there, here and now; *N. Amer. informal* short order; *informal* straight off, in double quick time, pronto, before you can say Jack Robinson; *N. Amer. informal* lickety-split.

WORD LINKS

relating to straightness: **ortho-**
straightening of teeth: **orthodontics**

---

straighten ▶ verb **1** *Rory straightened his tie* = **make straight**, adjust, arrange, rearrange, (make) tidy. **2** *we must straighten things out with Viola* = **put/set right**, sort out, clear up, settle, resolve, put in order, rectify, remedy; *informal* patch up. **3** *he straightened up* = **stand up (straight)**, stand upright.

straightforward ▶ adjective **1** *the process was relatively straightforward* = **uncomplicated**, simple, easy, effortless, painless, plain sailing, child's play; *informal* a piece of cake, a cinch, a snip, a doddle, a breeze; *Brit. informal* easy-peasy, a doss; *N. Amer. informal* duck soup, a snap; *Austral./NZ informal* a bludge, a snack. **2** *a straightforward man* = **honest**, frank, candid, open, truthful, sincere, on the level; forthright, plain-speaking, direct; *informal* upfront; *N. Amer. informal* on the up and up.

−OPPOSITES complicated.

strain¹ ▶ verb 1 *take care that you don't strain yourself* =**overtax**, overwork, over-extend, overreach, overdo it; exhaust, wear out; *informal* knacker, knock oneself out. 2 *you have strained a muscle* =**injure**, damage, pull, wrench, twist, sprain. 3 *we strained to haul the guns up the slope* =**struggle**, labour, toil, make every effort, break one's back; *informal* pull out all the stops, go all out, bust a gut; *Austral. informal* go for the doctor. 4 *the flood of refugees is straining the relief services* =**make excessive demands on**, overtax, be too much for, test, tax, put a strain on. 5 *the bear strained at the chain* =**pull**, tug, heave, haul; *informal* yank. 6 *strain the mixture* =**sieve**, sift, filter, screen.
▶ noun 1 *the rope snapped under the strain* =**tension**, tightness, tautness. 2 *muscle strain* =**injury**, sprain, wrench, twist. 3 *the strain of her job* =**pressure**, demands, burdens; stress; *informal* hassle. 4 *Melissa was showing signs of strain* =**stress**, (nervous) tension; exhaustion, fatigue, pressure, overwork. 5 *the strains of Brahms's lullaby* =**sound**, music; melody, tune.

strain² ▶ noun *a different strain of flu* =**variety**, kind, type, sort; breed, genus.

strained ▶ adjective 1 *relations were strained* =**awkward**, tense, uneasy, uncomfortable, edgy, difficult, troubled. 2 *Jean's strained face* =**drawn**, careworn, worn, pinched, tired, exhausted, drained, haggard. 3 *a strained smile* =**forced**, unnatural; artificial, insincere, false, affected, put-on.
−OPPOSITES friendly.

strait ▶ noun 1 *a strait about six miles wide* =**channel**, sound, inlet, stretch of water. 2 *desperate/dire straits* =**a bad/difficult situation**, difficulty, trouble, crisis, a mess, a predicament, a plight; *informal* hot/deep water, a jam, a hole, a bind, a fix, a scrape.

straitened ▶ adjective =**impoverished**, poverty-stricken, poor, destitute, penniless, in penury, impecunious, unable to make ends meet, in reduced circumstances; *Brit.* on the breadline; *informal* on one's uppers.

strait-laced ▶ adjective =**prim (and proper)**, prudish, puritanical, prissy; conservative, old-fashioned, stuffy, staid; *informal* starchy, square, fuddy-duddy.

strand ▶ noun 1 *strands of wool* =**thread**, filament, fibre; length. 2 *the various strands of the ecological movement* =**element**, component, factor, ingredient, aspect, feature, strain.

stranded ▶ adjective 1 *a stranded ship* =**beached**, grounded, run aground, high and dry; shipwrecked, wrecked, marooned. 2 *stranded in a strange city* =**helpless**, abandoned, lost.

strange ▶ adjective 1 *strange things have been happening* =**unusual**, odd, curious, peculiar, funny, bizarre, weird, uncanny, queer, unexpected, unfamiliar, atypical, anomalous, out of the ordinary, puzzling, mystifying, mysterious, perplexing, baffling, inexplicable, singular, freakish; suspicious; eerie, unnatural; *informal* fishy, creepy, spooky. 2 *strange clothes* =**weird**, eccentric, odd, peculiar, funny, bizarre, unusual; unconventional, outlandish, quirky, zany; *informal* wacky, way out, freaky, kooky, offbeat, off the wall; *N. Amer. informal* screwy. 3 *visiting a strange house* =**unfamiliar**, unknown, new. 4 *Jean was feeling strange* =**ill**, unwell, poorly; *Brit.* off colour; *informal* under the weather, funny, peculiar; *Brit. informal* off, ropy, grotty; *Austral./NZ informal* crook. 5 *she felt strange with him* =**ill at ease**, uneasy, uncomfortable, awkward, self-conscious.
−OPPOSITES ordinary, familiar.

strangeness ▶ noun =**oddity**, eccentricity, peculiarity, curiousness, bizarreness, weirdness, unusualness, abnormality, unaccountability, inexplicability, incongruousness, outlandishness, singularity.

stranger ▶ noun =**newcomer**, new arrival, visitor, outsider; *Austral. informal* blow-in.
■ **a stranger to** =**unaccustomed to**, unfamiliar with, unused to, new to, fresh to, inexperienced in.

strangle ▶ verb =**throttle**, choke, garrotte.

strap ▶ noun *thick leather straps* =**thong**, tie, band, belt.
▶ verb 1 *a bag was strapped to the bicycle* =**fasten**, secure, tie, bind, make fast, lash, truss. 2 *his knee was strapped up* =**bandage**, bind.

strapping ▶ adjective =**big**, strong, well-built, brawny, burly, muscular;

informal hunky, beefy.
−OPPOSITES weedy.

stratagem ▸ noun =**plan**, scheme, tactic, manoeuvre, ploy, device, trick, ruse, plot, machination, dodge; subterfuge, artifice; *Brit. informal* wheeze; *Austral. informal* lurk.

strategic ▸ adjective =**planned**, calculated, tactical, judicious, prudent, shrewd.

strategy ▸ noun =**master plan**, grand design, game plan, plan (of action), policy, programme.

stratum ▸ noun **1** *a stratum of flint* =**layer**, vein, seam, bed. **2** *this stratum of society* =**level**, class, echelon, rank, grade, group, set; caste.

stray ▸ verb **1** *the gazelle had strayed from the herd* =**wander off**, get separated, get lost. **2** *we strayed from our original topic* =**digress**, deviate, wander, get sidetracked, go off at a tangent; get off the subject.
▸ adjective **1** *a stray dog* =**homeless**, lost, abandoned. **2** *a stray bullet* =**random**, chance, freak, unexpected.
▸ noun *wardens who deal with strays* =**homeless animal**, stray dog/cat, waif.

streak ▸ noun **1** *a streak of light* =**band**, line, strip, stripe, vein, slash, ray. **2** *green streaks on her legs* =**mark**, smear, smudge, stain, blotch; *informal* splotch. **3** *a streak of self-destructiveness* =**element**, vein, strain. **4** *a winning streak* =**period**, spell, stretch, run; *Brit. informal* patch.
▸ verb **1** *the sky was streaked with red* =**stripe**, band, fleck. **2** *overalls streaked with paint* =**mark**, daub, smear; *informal* splotch. **3** *Miranda streaked across the road.* See RUN verb sense 1.

streaky ▸ adjective =**striped**, stripy, streaked, banded, veined, brindled.

stream ▸ noun **1** *a mountain stream* =**brook**, rivulet; tributary; *Scottish & N. English* burn; *N. English* beck; *S. English* bourn; *N. Amer. & Austral./NZ* creek; *Austral.* billabong. **2** *a stream of boiling water* =**jet**, flow, rush, gush, surge, torrent, flood, cascade, outpouring, outflow; *technical* efflux. **3** *a steady stream of visitors* =**succession**, series, string.
▸ verb **1** *tears were streaming down her face* =**flow**, pour, course, run, gush, surge, flood, cascade, spill. **2** *children streamed out of the classrooms* =**pour**, surge, flood, swarm, pile, crowd. **3** *a flag streamed from the mast* =**flutter**, float, flap, fly,

blow, waft, wave.

streamer ▸ noun =**pennant**, pennon, flag, banner.

streamlined ▸ adjective **1** *streamlined cars* =**aerodynamic**, smooth, sleek. **2** *a streamlined organization* =**efficient**, smooth-running, well run.

street ▸ noun =**road**, thoroughfare, avenue, drive, boulevard, parade; side street/road, lane; *N. Amer.* highway.
■ **the man/woman in the street** =**the ordinary person**, Mr/Mrs Average; *Brit. informal* Joe Bloggs, Joe Public; *N. Amer. informal* John Doe, Joe Sixpack.
■ **on the streets** =**homeless**, sleeping rough, down and out.

strength ▸ noun **1** *enormous physical strength* =**power**, muscle, sturdiness, robustness, toughness, hardiness; vigour, force, might. **2** *Oliver began to regain his strength* =**health**, fitness, vigour, stamina. **3** *her great inner strength* =**fortitude**, resilience, spirit, backbone; courage, bravery, pluck, courageousness, grit; *informal* guts, spunk. **4** *the strength of the retaining wall* =**robustness**, sturdiness, firmness, toughness, soundness, solidity, durability. **5** *Europe's military strength* =**power**; influence; *informal* clout. **6** *strength of feeling* =**intensity**, vehemence, force, depth. **7** *the strength of their argument* =**cogency**, forcefulness, force, weight, power, persuasiveness, soundness, validity. **8** *what are your strengths?* =**strong point**, advantage, asset, forte, aptitude, talent, skill; speciality. **9** *the strength of the army* =**size**, extent, magnitude.
−OPPOSITES weakness.

strengthen ▸ verb **1** *calcium strengthens growing bones* =**make strong/stronger**, build up, give strength to. **2** *engineers strengthened the walls* =**reinforce**, make stronger, buttress, shore up, underpin. **3** *heat strengthens the glass* =**toughen**, temper, harden. **4** *the wind had strengthened* =**become strong/stronger**, gain strength, intensify, pick up. **5** *his insistence strengthened her determination* =**fortify**, bolster, make stronger, boost, reinforce, harden, stiffen, toughen, fuel. **6** *the argument is strengthened by this evidence* =**reinforce**, lend more weight to; support, back up, confirm, bear out, corroborate.
−OPPOSITES weaken.

strenuous ▸ adjective **1** *a strenuous*

climb =**arduous**, difficult, hard, tough, taxing, demanding, exacting, exhausting, tiring, gruelling, back-breaking; *Brit. informal* knackering. **2** *strenuous efforts* =**vigorous**, energetic, forceful, strong, spirited, intense, determined, resolute, dogged.
–OPPOSITES easy, half-hearted.

stress ▶ noun **1** *he's under a lot of stress* =**strain**, pressure, (nervous) tension, worry, anxiety, trouble, difficulty; *informal* hassle. **2** *laying greater stress on education* =**emphasis**, importance, weight. **3** *the stress falls on the first syllable* =**emphasis**, accent, accentuation; beat. **4** *the stress is uniform across the bar* =**pressure**, tension, compression; strain.
▶ verb **1** *they stress the need for reform* =**emphasize**, draw attention to, underline, underscore, point up, place emphasis on, highlight, accentuate, press home. **2** *the last syllable is stressed* =**place the emphasis on**, emphasize, accent. **3** *all the staff were stressed* =**overstretch**, overtax, pressurize, pressure, make tense, worry, harass; *informal* hassle.
–OPPOSITES play down.

stressful ▶ adjective =**demanding**, trying, taxing, difficult, hard, tough; fraught, traumatic, tense, frustrating.
–OPPOSITES relaxing.

stretch ▶ verb **1** *this material stretches* =**be elastic**, be stretchy, give, expand. **2** *he stretched the elastic* =**pull (out)**, draw out, extend, lengthen, elongate, expand. **3** *the court case stretched their finances* =**put a strain on**, overtax, overextend, drain, sap. **4** *stretching the truth* =**bend**, strain, distort, exaggerate, embellish. **5** *she stretched out her hand to him* =**reach out**, hold out, extend, proffer. **6** *he stretched his arms* =**extend**, straighten (out). **7** *she stretched out on the sofa* =**lie down**, recline, lean back, sprawl, lounge, loll. **8** *the desert stretches for miles* =**extend**, spread, continue, go on.
–OPPOSITES shorten.
▶ noun **1** *magnificent stretches of forest* =**expanse**, area, tract, belt, sweep, extent. **2** *a four-hour stretch* =**period**, time, spell, run, stint, session, shift.
▶ adjective *stretch fabrics* =**stretchy**, stretchable, elastic.

strew ▶ verb =**scatter**, spread, disperse, litter, toss.

stricken ▶ adjective =**troubled**, (deeply) affected, afflicted.

strict ▶ adjective **1** *a strict interpretation of the law* =**precise**, exact, literal, faithful, accurate, careful, meticulous, rigorous. **2** *strict controls on spending* =**stringent**, rigorous, severe, harsh, hard, rigid, tough. **3** *strict parents* =**stern**, severe, harsh, uncompromising, authoritarian, firm. **4** *in strict confidence* =**absolute**, utter, complete, total. **5** *a strict Roman Catholic* =**orthodox**, devout, conscientious.
–OPPOSITES loose, liberal.

stricture ▶ noun =**constraint**, restriction, limitation, restraint, curb, impediment, barrier, obstacle.
–OPPOSITES freedom.

stride ▶ verb =**march**, pace, step.
▶ noun =(long/large) **step**, pace.

strident ▶ adjective =**harsh**, raucous, rough, grating, jarring, loud, shrill, screeching, piercing, ear-piercing.
–OPPOSITES soft.

strife ▶ noun =**conflict**, friction, discord, disagreement, dissension, dispute, argument, quarrelling, wrangling, bickering, controversy; ill/bad feeling, falling-out, bad blood, hostility, animosity.
–OPPOSITES peace.

strike ▶ verb **1** *the teacher struck Mary* =**hit**, slap, smack, thump, punch, cuff; *informal* clout, wallop, belt, whack, thwack, bash, clobber, bop, biff; *Austral./NZ informal* quilt; *literary* smite. **2** *he struck the gong* =**bang**, beat, hit; *informal* bash, wallop. **3** *the car struck a tree* =**crash into**, collide with, hit, run into, bump into, smash into; *N. Amer.* impact. **4** *Jennifer struck the ball* =**hit**, drive; *informal* clout, wallop, swipe. **5** *she was asleep when the killer struck* =**attack**; act, descend, come. **6** *strike a balance* =**achieve**, reach, arrive at, find, attain, establish. **7** *we have struck a bargain* =**agree (on)**, come to, settle on; *informal* clinch. **8** *he struck a heroic pose* =**assume**, adopt, take on/up, affect; *N. Amer. informal* cop. **9** *they have struck oil* =**discover**, find, come upon/across. **10** *a thought struck her* =**occur to**, come to (mind), dawn on one, hit, spring to mind, enter one's head. **11** *you strike me as intelligent* =**seem to**, appear to; give someone the impression of being. **12** *train drivers are to strike* =**take industrial action**, go on strike, down tools, walk out.
▶ noun **1** *a 48-hour strike* =**industrial action**, walkout. **2** *a military strike* =(**air**)

attack, assault, bombing.

■ **strike something out** =delete, cross out, erase, rub out.

■ **strike something up 1** *the band struck up another tune* =begin to play, start playing, launch into. **2** *we struck up a friendship* =begin, start, commence, embark on, establish.

striking ▶ adjective **1** *a striking resemblance* =noticeable, obvious, conspicuous, evident, marked, notable, unmistakable, strong; remarkable, extraordinary, incredible, amazing, astounding, astonishing, staggering. **2** *Kenya's striking landscape* =impressive, imposing, grand, splendid, magnificent, spectacular, breathtaking, superb, marvellous, wonderful, stunning, staggering, sensational, dramatic.
–OPPOSITES unremarkable.

string ▶ noun **1** *a ball of string* =twine, cord, yarn, thread, strand. **2** *a string of brewers* =chain, group, firm, company. **3** *a string of convictions* =series, succession, chain, sequence, run, streak. **4** *a string of wagons* =queue, procession, line, file, column, convoy, train, cavalcade. **5** *a string of pearls* =strand, rope, necklace. **6** *a guaranteed loan with no strings* =conditions, qualifications, provisions, provisos, caveats, stipulations, riders, prerequisites, limitations, limits, constraints, restrictions; *informal* catches.
▶ verb **1** *lights were strung across the promenade* =hang, suspend, sling, stretch, run; thread, loop, festoon. **2** *beads strung on a silver chain* =thread, loop, link.

■ **string someone along** (*informal*) =mislead, deceive, take advantage of, dupe, hoax, fool, make a fool of.

■ **string something out** =spin out, drag out, lengthen.

stringent ▶ adjective =strict, firm, rigid, rigorous, severe, harsh, tough, tight, exacting, demanding.

stringy ▶ adjective **1** *stringy hair* =straggly, lank, thin. **2** *stringy meat* =fibrous, gristly, sinewy, chewy, tough.

strip¹ ▶ verb **1** *he stripped and got into bed* =undress, strip off, take one's clothes off, unclothe, disrobe. **2** *stripping the paint off the door* =peel, remove, take off, scrape, clean. **3** *they stripped him of his doctorate* =take away from, deprive, divest, relieve. **4** *I stripped down the engine* =dismantle, disassemble, take to bits/pieces, take apart. **5** *the house had been stripped* =empty, clear, clean out; plunder, rob, burgle, loot, pillage, ransack, despoil, sack.
–OPPOSITES dress.
▶ noun *the team's new strip* =outfit, dress, garb; *Brit.* kit; *informal* gear, get-up; *Brit. informal* rig-out.

strip² ▶ noun *a strip of paper* =(narrow) piece, bit, band, belt, ribbon, slip, shred.

stripe ▶ noun =line, band, strip, belt, bar, streak, vein, flash; *technical* stria, striation.

striped ▶ adjective. See STRIPY.

stripling ▶ noun =youth, youngster, boy, schoolboy, lad; *informal* kid, young 'un, nipper, whippersnapper, shaver.

stripy ▶ adjective =striped, barred, lined, banded; streaky, variegated; *technical* striated.

strive ▶ verb **1** *I shall strive to be fair* =try (hard), attempt, endeavour, aim, venture, make an effort, exert oneself, do one's best, do all one can, do one's utmost, labour, work; *informal* go all out. **2** *scholars must strive against bias* =struggle, fight, battle, combat.

stroke ▶ noun **1** *five hammer strokes* =blow, hit. **2** *light upward strokes* =movement, action, motion. **3** *broad brush strokes* =mark, line. **4** *he suffered a stroke* =thrombosis, seizure; *Medicine* ictus.
▶ verb *she stroked the cat* =caress, fondle, pat, pet, touch, rub, massage, soothe.

stroll ▶ verb *they strolled along the river* =saunter, amble, wander, meander, ramble, promenade, walk, stretch one's legs, get some air; *informal* mosey; *formal* perambulate.
▶ noun *a stroll in the park* =saunter, amble, wander, walk, turn, promenade; *informal* mosey; *dated* constitutional; *formal* perambulation.

strong ▶ adjective **1** *a strong lad* =powerful, sturdy, robust, athletic, tough, rugged, lusty. **2** *she isn't very strong* =well, healthy, fit. **3** *a strong character* =forceful, determined, spirited, self-assertive, tough, tenacious, formidable, redoubtable, strong-minded; *informal* gutsy, feisty. **4** *a strong fortress* =secure, well built, well fortified, well protected, solid. **5** *strong cotton bags* =durable, hard-wearing, heavy-duty, tough, sturdy, well made, long-lasting. **6** *the current is very strong* =forceful, powerful, vigorous, fierce, intense. **7** *a strong interest in literature* =keen, passionate, fervent. **8** *strong feelings* =intense, force-

ful, passionate, ardent, fervent, deep-seated. **9** *a strong supporter* =**keen**, eager, enthusiastic, dedicated. **10** *strong arguments* =**compelling**, cogent, forceful, powerful, convincing, sound, valid, well founded, persuasive. **11** *a need for strong action* =**firm**, forceful, drastic, extreme. **12** *she bore a very strong resemblance to Vera* =**marked**, noticeable, pronounced, distinct, definite, unmistakable, notable. **13** *a strong voice* =**loud**, powerful, forceful, resonant, sonorous, rich, deep, booming. **14** *strong language* =**bad**, foul, obscene, profane. **15** *a strong blue colour* =**intense**, deep, rich, bright, brilliant, vivid, vibrant. **16** *strong lights* =**bright**, brilliant, dazzling, glaring. **17** *strong coffee* =**concentrated**, undiluted. **18** *strong cheese* =**highly flavoured**, flavourful, flavoursome; mature, ripe; piquant, tangy, spicy. **19** *strong drink* =**alcoholic**, intoxicating, hard, stiff.
−OPPOSITES weak, gentle, mild.

stronghold ▶ noun **1** *the enemy stronghold* =**fortress**, fort, castle, citadel, garrison. **2** *a Tory stronghold* =**bastion**, centre, hotbed.

strong-minded ▶ adjective =**determined**, firm, resolute, purposeful, strong-willed, uncompromising, unbending, forceful, persistent, tenacious, dogged.

strong point ▶ noun =**strength**, strong suit, forte, speciality.
−OPPOSITES weakness.

strong-willed ▶ adjective =**determined**, resolute, stubborn, obstinate, wilful, headstrong, strong-minded, self-willed, unbending, unyielding.

structure ▶ noun **1** *a vast Gothic structure* =**building**, edifice, construction, erection. **2** *the structure of local government* =**construction**, form, formation, shape, composition, anatomy, make-up, constitution; organization, system, arrangement, design, framework, configuration, pattern.
▶ verb *the programme is structured around periods of study* =**arrange**, organize, design, shape, construct, build.

struggle ▶ verb **1** *they struggled to do better* =**strive**, try hard, endeavour, make every effort. **2** *James struggled with the raiders* =**fight**, grapple, wrestle, scuffle, brawl, spar; *informal* scrap. **3** *the teams struggled to be first* =**compete**, contend,

vie, fight, battle, jockey. **4** *she struggled over the dunes* =**scramble**, flounder, stumble, fight/battle one's way, labour.
▶ noun **1** *the struggle for justice* =**endeavour**, striving; campaign, battle, crusade, drive, push. **2** *no signs of a struggle* =**fight**, scuffle, brawl, tussle, skirmish, fracas; *informal* bust-up, ding-dong. **3** *many perished in the struggle* =**conflict**, fight, battle, confrontation, clash, skirmish; hostilities, fighting, war, warfare, campaign. **4** *a struggle within the leadership* =**contest**, competition, fight, clash; rivalry, friction, feuding, conflict. **5** *life has been a struggle for me* =**effort**, trial, trouble, stress, strain, battle; *informal* grind, hassle.

strut ▶ verb =**swagger**, swank, parade, stride, sweep; *N. Amer. informal* sashay.

stub ▶ noun **1** *a cigarette stub* =**butt**, (tail) end; *informal* dog-end. **2** *a ticket stub* =**counterfoil**, slip, tab. **3** *a stub of pencil* =**stump**, remnant, (tail) end.

stubble ▶ noun **1** *a field of stubble* =**stalks**, straw. **2** *grey stubble* =**bristles**, whiskers, facial hair; *informal* five o'clock shadow.

stubbly ▶ adjective =**bristly**, unshaven, whiskered; prickly, rough, coarse, scratchy.

stubborn ▶ adjective **1** *you're too stubborn to admit it* =**obstinate**, headstrong, wilful, strong-willed, pig-headed, obdurate, recalcitrant, inflexible, uncompromising, unbending; *informal* stiff-necked. **2** *stubborn stains* =**indelible**, permanent, persistent, tenacious, resistant.
−OPPOSITES compliant.

stubby ▶ adjective =**dumpy**, stocky, chunky, chubby, squat; short, stumpy.
−OPPOSITES slender, tall.

stuck ▶ adjective **1** *a message was stuck to his screen* =**fixed**, fastened, attached, glued, pinned. **2** *the gate was stuck* =**immovable**, jammed. **3** *if you get stuck, leave a blank* =**baffled**, beaten, at a loss, at one's wits' end; *informal* stumped, bogged down, flummoxed, fazed, bamboozled.
■ **stuck with** =**lumbered with**, left with, made responsible for.

studded ▶ adjective =**dotted**, scattered, sprinkled, covered, spangled; peppered.

student ▶ noun **1** *a university student* =**undergraduate**, postgraduate; *N. Amer.* sophomore; *Brit. informal* fresher. **2** *a for-*

mer student =**pupil**, schoolchild, school-boy, schoolgirl, scholar. **3** *a nursing student* =**trainee**, apprentice, probationer, novice.

studied ▶ adjective =**deliberate**, careful, considered, conscious, calculated, intentional; affected.

studio ▶ noun =**workshop**, workroom.

studious ▶ adjective **1** *a studious nature* =**scholarly**, academic, bookish, intellectual. **2** *studious attention* =**diligent**, careful, attentive, assiduous, painstaking, thorough, meticulous.

study ▶ noun **1** *two years of study* =**learning**, education, schooling, scholarship, tuition, research; *informal* swotting, cramming. **2** *a study of global warming* =**investigation**, enquiry, research, examination, analysis, review, survey. **3** *Bob was in the study* =**office**, workroom, studio.
▶ verb **1** *Anne studied hard* =**work**, revise; *informal* swot, cram. **2** *he studied maths* =**learn**, read, be taught. **3** *Thomas studied ants* =**investigate**, research, look at, examine, analyse. **4** *she studied him thoughtfully* =**scrutinize**, examine, inspect, consider, regard, look at, observe, watch, survey; *informal* check out; *N. Amer. informal* eyeball.

WORD LINKS

study of something: -ology
person who studies something: -ologist

stuff ▶ noun **1** *suede is tough stuff* =**material**, fabric, cloth; substance. **2** *first-aid stuff* =**items**, articles, objects, goods; *informal* things, bits and pieces, odds and ends. **3** *all my stuff is in the suitcase* =**belongings**, (personal) possessions, effects, paraphernalia; *informal* gear, things, kit; *Brit. informal* clobber.
▶ verb **1** *stuffing pillows* =**fill**, pack, pad, upholster. **2** *Robyn stuffed her clothes into a bag* =**shove**, thrust, push, ram, cram, squeeze, force, jam, pack, pile, stick. **3** *(informal) they stuffed themselves with chocolate* =**fill**, gorge. **4** *my nose was stuffed up* =**block**, bung, congest.

stuffing ▶ noun =**padding**, wadding, filling, packing.

stuffy ▶ adjective **1** *a stuffy atmosphere* =**airless**, close, musty, stale; *Brit. informal* fuggy. **2** *a stuffy young man* =**staid**, sedate, sober, prim, priggish, strait-laced, conformist, conservative, old-fashioned; *informal* straight, starchy, fuddy-duddy. **3** *a stuffy nose* =**blocked**, stuffed up,

bunged up.
–OPPOSITES airy, clear.

stumble ▶ verb **1** *he stumbled and fell* =**trip (over/up)**, lose one's balance, lose/miss one's footing, slip. **2** *he stumbled back home* =**stagger**, totter, trip, blunder, hobble. **3** *he stumbled during his speech* =**stammer**, stutter, hesitate, falter.
■ **stumble across/on** =**come across/upon**, chance on, happen on, light on; discover, find, unearth, uncover; *informal* dig up.

stump ▶ verb *(informal)* =**baffle**, perplex, puzzle, confuse, confound, nonplus, defeat, put at a loss; *informal* flummox, fox, throw, floor; *N. Amer. informal* discombobulate.

stun ▶ verb **1** *the force of the blow stunned him* =**daze**, stupefy, knock out, lay out. **2** *she was stunned by the news* =**astound**, amaze, astonish, dumbfound, stupefy, stagger, shock, take aback; *informal* flabbergast, knock sideways.

stunning ▶ adjective **1** *a stunning win* =**remarkable**, extraordinary, staggering, incredible, outstanding, amazing, astonishing, marvellous, phenomenal; *informal* fabulous, fantastic, tremendous. **2** *she looked stunning. See* BEAUTIFUL.
–OPPOSITES ordinary.

stunt¹ ▶ verb =**inhibit**, impede, hamper, hinder, restrict, retard, slow, curb, check.
–OPPOSITES encourage.

stunt² ▶ noun =**feat**, exploit, trick.

stunted ▶ adjective =**small**, undersize(d), diminutive.

stupefaction ▶ noun =**bewilderment**, confusion, perplexity, wonder, amazement, astonishment.

stupefy ▶ verb **1** *stupefied by alcohol* =**drug**, sedate, tranquillize, intoxicate, inebriate. **2** *his reply stupefied us* =**shock**, stun, astound, dumbfound, overwhelm, stagger, amaze, astonish, take someone's breath away; *informal* flabbergast, knock sideways, bowl over, floor; *Brit. informal* knock for six.

stupendous ▶ adjective =**amazing**, astounding, astonishing, extraordinary, remarkable, phenomenal, staggering, breathtaking; *informal* fantastic, mind-boggling, awesome; *literary* wondrous.
–OPPOSITES ordinary.

stupid ▶ adjective **1** *he's really stupid* =**un-**

intelligent, ignorant, dense, foolish, slow, vacuous, vapid, idiotic, obtuse; *informal* thick (as two short planks), dim, dumb, dopey, dozy, moronic, cretinous, pea-brained, half-witted, soft in the head; *Brit. informal* daft. **2** *a stupid mistake* =**foolish**, silly, unintelligent, idiotic, ill-advised, ill-considered, unwise, injudicious; mad; *informal* crazy, half-baked, cock-eyed, hare-brained, nutty, dotty, batty, loony, loopy; *Brit. informal* potty. **3** *he drank himself stupid* =**senseless**, into a stupor; unconscious.
–OPPOSITES intelligent, sensible.

stupidity ▶ noun =**foolishness**, folly, silliness, idiocy, senselessness, ineptitude, inanity, absurdity, ludicrousness, ridiculousness, fatuousness, madness, insanity, lunacy; *informal* craziness; *Brit. informal* daftness.

stupor ▶ noun =**daze**, torpor, insensibility, oblivion.

sturdy ▶ adjective **1** *a sturdy lad* =**strapping**, well built, muscular, strong, hefty, brawny, powerful, solid, burly; *informal* beefy. **2** *sturdy boots* =**robust**, strong, well built, solid, stout, tough, durable, long-lasting, hard-wearing.
–OPPOSITES feeble.

stutter ▶ verb =**stammer**, stumble, falter.
▶ noun =**stammer**, speech impediment, speech defect.

WORD LINKS

fear of stuttering: **lalophobia**

style ▶ noun **1** *differing styles of management* =**manner**, way, technique, method, approach, system, form. **2** *a non-directive style of counselling* =**type**, kind, variety, sort, school, brand, pattern, model. **3** *dressing with style* =**flair**, stylishness, elegance, grace, poise, polish, suaveness, sophistication, dash, panache, elan; *informal* class. **4** *Laura travelled in style* =**comfort**, luxury. **5** *modern styles* =**fashion**, trend, vogue.
▶ verb *sportswear styled by Karl* =**design**, fashion, tailor.

stylish ▶ adjective =**fashionable**, modish, modern, up to date; smart, sophisticated, elegant, chic, dapper, dashing; *informal* trendy, natty, classy, nifty, snazzy; *N. Amer. informal* fly, kicky, tony, spiffy.
–OPPOSITES unfashionable.

suave ▶ adjective =**charming**, sophisticated, debonair, urbane, polished,

refined, poised, self-possessed, gallant; smooth.
–OPPOSITES unsophisticated.

subconscious ▶ adjective =**unconscious**, latent, suppressed, repressed, subliminal, dormant, underlying, innermost.
▶ noun =**(unconscious) mind**, imagination, inner(most) self, psyche.

subdue ▶ verb =**conquer**, defeat, vanquish, overcome, overwhelm, crush, quash, beat, trounce, subjugate, suppress, bring someone to their knees.

subdued ▶ adjective **1** *Lewis's subdued air* =**sombre**, downcast, sad, dejected, depressed, gloomy, despondent, dispirited, disheartened, forlorn, woebegone; withdrawn. **2** *subdued voices* =**hushed**, muted, quiet, low, soft, faint, muffled, indistinct. **3** *subdued lighting* =**dim**, muted, soft, low.
–OPPOSITES cheerful, loud, bright.

subject ▶ noun **1** *the subject of this chapter* =**theme**, subject matter, topic, issue, question, concern. **2** *popular university subjects* =**branch of study**, discipline, field. **3** *six subjects did the trials* =**participant**, volunteer; *informal* guinea pig. **4** *British subjects* =**citizen**, national, taxpayer, voter.
▶ verb *subjected to violence* =**put through**, treat with, expose to.
■ **subject to** =**conditional on**, contingent on, dependent on.

subjection ▶ noun =**subjugation**, domination, oppression, repression, suppression.

subjective ▶ adjective =**personal**, individual, emotional; intuitive.
–OPPOSITES objective.

subjugate ▶ verb =**conquer**, vanquish, defeat, crush, quash, bring someone to their knees, enslave, subdue, suppress.
–OPPOSITES liberate.

sublime ▶ adjective **1** *sublime music* =**exalted**, elevated, noble, lofty, awe-inspiring, majestic, magnificent, glorious, superb, wonderful, marvellous, splendid; *informal* fantastic, fabulous, terrific, heavenly, divine, out of this world. **2** *the sublime confidence of youth* =**supreme**, total, complete, utter, consummate.

subliminal ▶ adjective =**subconscious**; hidden, concealed.
–OPPOSITES explicit.

submerge ▶ verb **1** *the U-boat submerged* =**go under (water)**, dive, sink. **2** *submerge the bowl in water* =**immerse**, plunge, sink. **3** *the farmland was submerged* =**flood**, deluge, swamp.
–OPPOSITES surface.

submission ▶ noun **1** *submission to authority* =**yielding**, capitulation, acceptance, consent, compliance. **2** *Tim raised his hands in submission* =**surrender**, capitulation, resignation, defeat. **3** *he wanted her total submission* =**compliance**, submissiveness, acquiescence, obedience, docility, subservience, servility, subjection. **4** *a report for submission to the Board* =**presentation**, presenting, proffering, tendering, proposing. **5** *his original submission* =**proposal**, suggestion, proposition, recommendation. **6** *the judge rejected his submission* =**argument**, assertion, contention, statement, claim, allegation.
–OPPOSITES defiance, resistance.

submissive ▶ adjective =**compliant**, yielding, acquiescent, passive, obedient, dutiful, docile, pliant; *informal* under someone's thumb.

submit ▶ verb **1** *she was forced to submit* =**give in/way**, yield, back down, cave in, capitulate; surrender. **2** *he refused to submit to their authority* =**be governed by**, abide by, comply with, accept, adhere to, be subject to, agree to, consent to, conform to. **3** *we submitted an application* =**put forward**, present, offer, tender, propose, suggest; put in, send in, register. **4** *they submitted that the judgement was incorrect* =**contend**, assert, argue, state, claim, posit.
–OPPOSITES resist, withdraw.

subordinate ▶ adjective =**lower-ranking**, junior, lower, supporting.
–OPPOSITES senior.
▶ noun =**junior**, assistant, second (in command), number two, deputy, aide, underling, minion.
–OPPOSITES superior.

subscribe ▶ verb **1** *we subscribe to 'Punch'* =**pay a subscription**, take. **2** *I can't subscribe to that theory* =**agree with**, accept, go along with, endorse, support; *formal* accede to.

subscriber ▶ noun =**(regular) reader**, member, patron.

subscription ▶ noun **1** *the club's subscription* =**membership fee**, dues, annual payment, charge. **2** *their subscription to capitalism* =**agreement**, belief, endorsement, backing, support.

subsequent ▶ adjective =**following**, ensuing, succeeding, later, future, coming, to come, next.
–OPPOSITES previous.

subsequently ▶ adverb =**later (on)**, at a later date, afterwards, in due course, following this/that; eventually; *informal* after a bit; *formal* thereafter.

subservient ▶ adjective **1** *subservient women* =**submissive**, deferential, compliant, obedient, dutiful, docile, passive, subdued, downtrodden; *informal* under someone's thumb. **2** *individual rights are subservient to the interests of the state* =**subordinate**, secondary, subsidiary.
–OPPOSITES independent.

subside ▶ verb **1** *wait until the storm subsides* =**abate**, let up, quieten down, calm, slacken (off), ease (up), relent, die down, diminish, decline, dwindle, fade, wane, ebb. **2** *the flood has subsided* =**recede**, ebb, fall, go down, get lower, abate. **3** *the house is gradually subsiding* =**sink**, settle, cave in, collapse, give way.
–OPPOSITES intensify.

subsidiary ▶ adjective =**subordinate**, secondary, ancillary, auxiliary, subservient, supplementary, peripheral.
–OPPOSITES principal.
▶ noun =**branch**, division, subdivision, derivative, offshoot.

subsidize ▶ verb =**give money to**, contribute to, invest in, sponsor, support, fund, finance, underwrite; *informal* shell out for, fork out for, cough up for; *N. Amer. informal* bankroll.

subsidy ▶ noun =**grant**, allowance, contribution, handout; backing, support, sponsorship, finance, funding.

subsist ▶ verb =**survive**, live, stay alive, exist, eke out an existence/living; support oneself, manage, get along/by, make (both) ends meet.

subsistence ▶ noun =**survival**, existence, living, life, sustenance, nourishment.

substance ▶ noun **1** *organic substances* =**material**, compound; matter, stuff. **2** *ghostly figures with no substance* =**solidity**, body; density, mass, weight. **3** *none of the objections has any substance* =**meaningfulness**, significance, importance, import, validity, foundation. **4** *the substance of the tale is very thin* =**content**, subject matter, theme, message, essence.

5 *Rangers are a team of substance* =**character**, backbone, mettle. **6** *men of substance* =**wealth**, fortune, riches, affluence, prosperity, money, means.

substandard ▶ adjective =**inferior**, second-rate, poor, below par, imperfect, faulty, defective, shoddy, shabby, unsound, unsatisfactory; *informal* tenth-rate, crummy, lousy; *Brit. informal* duff.

substantial ▶ adjective **1** *substantial progress had been made* =**considerable**, real, significant, important, major, valuable, useful. **2** *substantial damages* =**sizeable**, considerable, significant, large, ample, appreciable. **3** *substantial Victorian villas* =**sturdy**, solid, stout, strong, well built, durable, long-lasting, hardwearing. **4** *substantial agreement* =**fundamental**, essential, basic.

substantially ▶ adverb **1** *the cost has fallen substantially* =**considerably**, significantly, to a great/large extent, greatly, markedly, appreciably. **2** *the draft was substantially accepted* =**largely**, for the most part, by and large, on the whole, in the main, mainly, in essence, basically, fundamentally, to all intents and purposes.
−OPPOSITES slightly.

substantiate ▶ verb =**prove**, show to be true, support, justify, vindicate, validate, corroborate, verify, authenticate, confirm.
−OPPOSITES disprove.

substitute ▶ noun *substitutes for permanent employees* =**replacement**, deputy, relief, proxy, reserve, surrogate, cover, stand-in, understudy; *informal* sub.
▶ adjective *a substitute teacher* =**acting**, replacement, deputy, relief, reserve, surrogate, stand-in.
−OPPOSITES permanent.
▶ verb **1** *curd cheese can be substituted for yogurt* =**exchange**, replace with, use instead of, use as an alternative to, use in place of, swap. **2** *the Senate was empowered to substitute for the President* =**deputize**, stand in, cover.

substitution ▶ noun =**exchange**, change; replacement, replacing.

subterfuge ▶ noun **1** *the use of subterfuge by journalists* =**trickery**, intrigue, deviousness, deceit, deception, dishonesty, cheating, duplicity, guile, cunning, craftiness, chicanery, pretence, fraud, fraudulence. **2** *a disreputable subterfuge* =**trick**, hoax, ruse, wile, ploy, strata-gem, artifice, dodge, bluff, pretence, deception; *informal* con, scam.

subtle ▶ adjective **1** *subtle colours* =**understated**, muted, subdued; delicate, soft. **2** *subtle distinctions* =**fine**, nice. **3** *a subtle change* =**gentle**, slight, gradual.

subtlety ▶ noun =**delicacy**; understatedness, mutedness, softness.

subtract ▶ verb =**take away/off**, deduct, debit, dock; *informal* knock off, minus.
−OPPOSITES add.

suburb ▶ noun =**residential area**, commuter belt; suburbia.

suburban ▶ adjective **1** *a suburban area* =**residential**, commuter. **2** *her drab suburban existence* =**dull**, boring, uninteresting, conventional, ordinary, commonplace, unremarkable, unexceptional; bourgeois, middle-class.

subversive ▶ adjective =**disruptive**, troublemaking, insurrectionary; seditious, dissident.
▶ noun =**troublemaker**, dissident, agitator, renegade.

subvert ▶ verb **1** *a plot to subvert the state* =**destabilize**, unsettle, overthrow, overturn; bring down, topple; disrupt, wreak havoc on, sabotage, ruin, undermine, weaken, damage. **2** *attempts to subvert Soviet youth* =**corrupt**, pervert, deprave, contaminate, poison.

subway ▶ noun **1** *he walked through the subway* =**underpass**. **2** *Tokyo's subway* =**underground (railway)**, metro; *Brit. informal* tube.

succeed ▶ verb **1** *Darwin finally succeeded* =**triumph**, achieve success, be successful, do well, flourish, thrive; *informal* make it, make the grade, make a name for oneself. **2** *the plan succeeded* =**be successful**, turn out well, work (out), be effective; *informal* come off, pay off. **3** *he succeeded Gladstone as Prime Minister* =**replace**, take over from, follow, supersede.
−OPPOSITES fail, precede.

succeeding ▶ adjective =**subsequent**, successive, following, ensuing, later, future, coming.

success ▶ noun **1** *the success of the scheme* =**favourable outcome**, successfulness, triumph. **2** *the trappings of success* =**prosperity**, affluence, wealth, riches, opulence. **3** *a box-office success* =**triumph**, best-seller, sell-out; *informal* hit, smash,

winner.
−OPPOSITES failure.

successful ▶ adjective **1** *a successful designer* =**prosperous**, affluent, wealthy, rich; famous, eminent, top; respected. **2** *successful companies* =**flourishing**, thriving, booming, buoyant, doing well, profitable, moneymaking, lucrative.

succession ▶ noun **1** *a succession of exciting events* =**sequence**, series, progression, chain, string, train, line, run. **2** *his succession to the throne* =**accession**.
■ **in succession** =**one after the other**, in a row, consecutively, successively, in sequence; running; *informal* on the trot.

successive ▶ adjective =**consecutive**, in a row, sequential, in succession, running; *informal* on the trot.

successor ▶ noun =**heir (apparent)**, inheritor, next-in-line.
−OPPOSITES predecessor.

succinct ▶ adjective =**concise**, short (and sweet), brief, compact, condensed, crisp, laconic, terse, to the point, pithy.
−OPPOSITES verbose.

succour ▶ noun =**aid**, help, a helping hand, assistance; comfort, ease, relief, support.

succulent ▶ adjective =**juicy**, moist, luscious, soft, tender; choice, mouthwatering, appetizing, flavoursome, tasty, delicious; *informal* scrumptious, scrummy.
−OPPOSITES dry.

succumb ▶ verb **1** *she finally succumbed to temptation* =**yield**, give in/way, submit, surrender, capitulate, cave in. **2** *he succumbed to the disease* =**die from/of**.
−OPPOSITES resist.

suck ▶ verb **1** *they sucked orange juice through straws* =**sip**, sup, siphon, slurp, draw, drink. **2** *Fran sucked in a deep breath* =**draw**, pull, breathe, gasp. **3** *they got sucked into crime* =**involve in**, draw into; *informal* mix up in. **4** *(N. Amer. informal) this weather sucks* =**be very bad**, be awful, be terrible, be dreadful, be horrible; *informal* stink.
■ **suck up (to)** *(informal)* =**grovel**, creep, kowtow, bow and scrape; fawn on; *informal* lick someone's boots.

suckle ▶ verb =**breastfeed**, feed, nurse.

sudden ▶ adjective =**unexpected**, unforeseen; immediate, instantaneous, instant, precipitous, abrupt, rapid, swift, quick.

suddenly ▶ adverb =**all of a sudden**, all at once, abruptly, swiftly; unexpectedly, without warning, out of the blue.
−OPPOSITES gradually.

suds ▶ plural noun =**lather**, foam, froth, bubbles, soap.

sue ▶ verb **1** *he sued for negligence* =**take legal action**, take to court. **2** *suing for peace* =**appeal**, petition, ask; solicit, request, seek.

suffer ▶ verb **1** *I hate to see him suffer* =**hurt**, ache, be in pain; be in distress, be upset, be miserable. **2** *he suffers from asthma* =**be afflicted by**, be affected by, be troubled with, have. **3** *England suffered a humiliating defeat* =**undergo**, experience, be subjected to, receive, endure, face. **4** *our reputation has suffered* =**be impaired**, be damaged, decline.

suffering ▶ noun =**hardship**, distress, misery, wretchedness, adversity; pain, agony, anguish, trauma, torment, torture, hurt, affliction, sadness, unhappiness, sorrow, grief, woe, angst, heartache, heartbreak, stress.
−OPPOSITES pleasure, joy.

suffice ▶ verb =**be enough**, be sufficient, be adequate, do.

sufficient ▶ adjective & determiner =**enough**, adequate, plenty of, ample.
−OPPOSITES inadequate.

suffocate ▶ verb **1** *she suffocated her baby* =**smother**, asphyxiate, stifle; choke. **2** *she was suffocating in the heat* =**be breathless**, be short of air, struggle for air; be too hot, swelter; *informal* roast, bake, boil.

suffrage ▶ noun =**franchise**, the vote, enfranchisement, ballot.

suffuse ▶ verb =**permeate**, spread over, cover, bathe, pervade, wash, saturate, imbue.

sugary ▶ adjective **1** *sugary snacks* =**sweet**, sugared, sickly. **2** *sugary romance* =**sentimental**, mawkish, cloying, sickly (sweet), saccharine, syrupy; *informal* soppy, schmaltzy, slushy, mushy, corny.
−OPPOSITES sour.

suggest ▶ verb **1** *Ruth suggested a holiday* =**propose**, put forward, recommend, advocate; advise. **2** *evidence suggests that voters are unhappy* =**indicate**, lead to the belief, demonstrate, show. **3** *what exactly are you suggesting?* =**hint**, insinuate, imply, intimate.

suggestion ▶ noun **1** *some suggestions*

for tackling this problem =**proposal**, proposition, recommendation; advice, counsel, hint, tip, clue, idea. **2** *the suggestion of a smirk* =**hint**, trace, touch, suspicion; ghost, semblance, shadow, glimmer. **3** *a suggestion that he knew about the plot* =**insinuation**, hint, implication.

suggestive ▶ adjective **1** *suggestive remarks* =**indecent**, indelicate, improper, unseemly, sexual, sexy, smutty, dirty. **2** *an odour suggestive of a brewery* =**redolent**, evocative, reminiscent; characteristic, indicative, typical.

suicide ▶ noun =**self-destruction**, taking one's own life, self-immolation, hara-kiri; *informal* topping oneself.

suit ▶ noun **1** *a pinstriped suit* =**outfit**, ensemble. **2** *a medical malpractice suit* =**legal action**, lawsuit, (court) case, action, (legal/judicial) proceedings, litigation.
▶ verb **1** *blue really suits you* =**look attractive on**, look good on, become, flatter. **2** *savings schemes to suit all pockets* =**be convenient for**, be acceptable to, be suitable for, meet the requirements of; *informal* fit. **3** *recipes suited to students* =**be appropriate to/for**, tailor, fashion, adjust, adapt, modify, fit, gear, design.

suitable ▶ adjective **1** *suitable employment* =**acceptable**, satisfactory, fitting; *informal* right up someone's street. **2** *a drama suitable for all ages* =**appropriate**, fitting, fit, acceptable, right. **3** *music suitable for a dinner party* =**appropriate**, suited, befitting, in keeping with. **4** *they treated him with suitable respect* =**proper**, seemly, decent, appropriate, fitting, correct, due.
–OPPOSITES inappropriate.

suitcase ▶ noun =(travel) **bag**, case, valise, portmanteau; (**suitcases**) luggage, baggage.

suite ▶ noun =**apartment**, flat, (set of) rooms.

suitor ▶ noun =**admirer**, boyfriend, sweetheart, lover; *dated* beau.

sulk ▶ verb =**mope**, brood, be in a bad mood, be in a huff.
▶ noun =(**bad**) **mood**, fit of pique, pet, huff.

sulky ▶ adjective =**sullen**, surly, moody; petulant, disgruntled, put out; bad-tempered, grumpy.
–OPPOSITES cheerful.

sullen ▶ adjective =**surly**, sulky, morose, resentful, moody, grumpy, bad-tempered; uncommunicative.
–OPPOSITES cheerful.

sully ▶ verb =**taint**, defile, soil, tarnish, stain, blemish, pollute, spoil, mar; *literary* besmirch.

sultry ▶ adjective **1** *a sultry day* =**humid**, close, airless, stifling, oppressive, muggy, sticky, sweltering, tropical, heavy; hot; *informal* boiling, roasting. **2** *a sultry film star* =**passionate**, sensual, sexy, seductive.
–OPPOSITES refreshing.

sum ▶ noun **1** *a large sum of money* =**amount**, quantity. **2** *just a small sum* =**amount (of money)**, price, charge, fee, cost. **3** *the sum of two numbers* =(**sum**) **total**, grand total, tally. **4** *the sum of his wisdom* =**entirety**, totality, total, whole, beginning and end. **5** *we did sums at school* =(**arithmetical**) **problem**, calculation; (**sums**) arithmetic, mathematics; *Brit. informal* maths; *N. Amer. informal* math.
–OPPOSITES difference.
■ **sum someone/something up 1** *that just about sums him up* =**evaluate**, describe, encapsulate, summarize, put in a nutshell. **2** *he summed up his reasons* =**summarize**, make/give a summary of, precis, outline, recapitulate, review; *informal* recap.

summarily ▶ adverb =**immediately**, instantly, right away, straight away, at once, on the spot, promptly; speedily, swiftly, rapidly, without delay; arbitrarily, without formality, peremptorily.

summarize ▶ verb =**sum up**, abridge, condense, encapsulate, outline, put in a nutshell, recapitulate, give a synopsis of, precis, give a résumé of; *informal* recap.

summary ▶ noun *a summary of the findings* =**synopsis**, precis, résumé, abstract; outline, rundown, summing-up, overview, recapitulation; *informal* recap.
▶ adjective **1** *a summary financial statement* =**abridged**, abbreviated, shortened, condensed, concise, short. **2** *summary execution* =**immediate**, instant, instantaneous, on-the-spot; arbitrary, peremptory.

summer ▶ noun

WORD LINKS

relating to summer: **aestival**
---

summit ▶ noun **1** *the summit of Mont Blanc* =(**mountain**) **top**, peak, crest, crown, apex, tip, cap, hilltop. **2** *the next superpower summit* =**meeting**, conference, talk(s).

−OPPOSITES base.

summon ▶ verb **1** *he was summoned to the Embassy* =**send for**, call for, request the presence of; ask, invite. **2** *they were summoned as witnesses* =**summons**, subpoena. **3** *he summoned the courage to move closer* =**muster**, gather, collect, rally, screw up. **4** *they summoned an evil spirit* =**conjure up**, call up, invoke.

summons ▶ noun =**writ**, subpoena, warrant, court order.
▶ verb =**serve with a summons**, summon, subpoena.

sumptuous ▶ adjective =**lavish**, luxurious, opulent, magnificent, resplendent, gorgeous, splendid, grand, palatial, rich; *informal* plush, ritzy; *Brit. informal* swish.
−OPPOSITES plain.

sun ▶ noun =**sunshine**, sunlight, daylight, light, warmth; beams, rays.

> WORD LINKS
>
> *relating to the sun:* **solar, helio-**
> *fear of the sun:* **heliophobia**

sunbathe ▶ verb =**sun oneself**, bask, get a tan, tan oneself; *informal* catch some rays.

sunburnt ▶ adjective **1** *his sunburnt shoulders* =**burnt**, sunburned, red, pink. **2** *a handsome sunburnt face* =**tanned**, suntanned, brown, bronzed.
−OPPOSITES pale.

Sunday ▶ noun =**the Sabbath**.

> WORD LINKS
>
> *relating to Sunday:* **dominical**

sundry ▶ adjective =**various**, varied, miscellaneous, assorted, mixed, diverse, diversified; several, numerous, many, manifold, multifarious, multitudinous; *literary* divers.

sunken ▶ adjective =**hollowed**, hollow, depressed, deep-set, concave, indented, inset.

sunless ▶ adjective **1** *a sunless day* =**dark**, overcast, cloudy, grey, gloomy, dismal, murky, dull. **2** *a sunless wood* =**shady**, shadowy, dark, gloomy.

sunlight ▶ noun =**daylight**, sun, sunshine, the sun's rays, (natural) light.

sunny ▶ adjective **1** *a sunny day* =**bright**, sunshiny, sunlit, clear, fine, cloudless. **2** *a sunny disposition* =**cheerful**, cheery, happy, bright, merry, joyful, bubbly, jolly, jovial, animated, buoyant, ebullient, upbeat, vivacious.
−OPPOSITES dull, miserable.

sunrise ▶ noun =**(crack of) dawn**, daybreak, break of day, first light, (early) morning, cockcrow; *N. Amer.* sunup.

sunset ▶ noun =**nightfall**, twilight, dusk, evening; *N. Amer.* sundown; *literary* gloaming.

sunshine ▶ noun =**sunlight**, sun, sun's rays, daylight, (natural) light.

super ▶ adjective *(informal)* =**excellent**, superb, superlative, first-class, outstanding, marvellous, magnificent, wonderful, splendid, glorious; *informal* great, fantastic, fabulous, terrific, ace, divine, wicked, cool; *Brit. informal* smashing, brilliant, brill.
−OPPOSITES rotten.

superannuated ▶ adjective **1** *a superannuated civil servant* =**pensioned (off)**, retired; elderly, old. **2** *superannuated computing equipment* =**old**, old-fashioned, antiquated, out of date, outmoded, broken-down, obsolete, disused, defunct; *informal* clapped out.

superb ▶ adjective **1** *a superb goal* =**excellent**, superlative, first-rate, first-class, outstanding, marvellous, magnificent, wonderful, splendid, admirable, fine, exquisite, exceptional, glorious; *informal* great, fantastic, fabulous, terrific, super, awesome, ace, A1; *Brit. informal* brilliant, brill, smashing. **2** *a superb house* =**magnificent**, splendid, grand, impressive, imposing, awe-inspiring, breathtaking; gorgeous, beautiful.
−OPPOSITES poor, inferior.

supercilious ▶ adjective =**arrogant**, haughty, conceited, disdainful, overbearing, pompous, condescending, superior, patronizing, imperious, proud, snobbish, smug, scornful, sneering; *informal* high and mighty, snooty, stuck-up, snotty.

superficial ▶ adjective **1** *superficial burns* =**surface**, exterior, external, outer; slight. **2** *a superficial relationship* =**shallow**, artificial; empty, hollow, meaningless. **3** *a superficial investigation* =**cursory**, perfunctory, casual, sketchy, desultory, token, slapdash, offhand, rushed, hasty, hurried. **4** *a superficial resemblance* =**apparent**, seeming, outward, ostensible, cosmetic, slight. **5** *a superficial biography* =**trivial**, lightweight. **6** *a superficial person* =**facile**,

shallow, flippant, empty-headed, trivial, frivolous, silly, inane.
–OPPOSITES deep, thorough.

superficially ▸ adverb =apparently, seemingly, ostensibly, outwardly, on the surface, on the face of it, to all intents and purposes, at first glance, to the casual observer.

superfluity ▸ noun =surplus, excess, over-abundance, glut, surfeit, profusion, plethora.
–OPPOSITES shortage.

superfluous ▸ adjective 1 *superfluous material* =surplus (to requirements), redundant, unneeded, excess, extra, (to) spare, remaining, unused, left over, in excess, waste. 2 *words seemed superfluous* =unnecessary, unneeded, redundant, uncalled for, unwarranted.
–OPPOSITES necessary.

superhuman ▸ adjective 1 *a superhuman effort* =extraordinary, phenomenal, prodigious, stupendous, exceptional, immense, heroic. 2 *superhuman powers* =supernatural, preternatural, paranormal, other-worldly, unearthly.
–OPPOSITES mundane.

superintend ▸ verb =supervise, oversee, be in charge of, be in control of, preside over, direct, administer, manage, run, be responsible for.

superintendent ▸ noun =manager, director, administrator, supervisor, overseer, controller, chief, head, governor; *informal* boss.

superior ▸ adjective 1 *a superior officer* =higher-ranking, higher-level, senior, higher. 2 *the superior candidate* =better, worthier, fitter, preferred. 3 *superior workmanship* =finer, better, higher-grade; accomplished, expert. 4 *superior chocolate* =top-quality, choice, select, exclusive, prime, prize, fine, excellent, best, choicest, finest. 5 *a superior smile* =condescending, supercilious, patronizing, haughty, disdainful; *informal* high and mighty.
–OPPOSITES junior, inferior.
▸ noun *my immediate superior* =manager, chief, supervisor, senior, controller, foreman; *informal* boss.
–OPPOSITES subordinate.

superiority ▸ noun =supremacy, advantage, lead, dominance, primacy, ascendancy, eminence.

superlative ▸ adjective =excellent, magnificent, wonderful, marvellous,

supreme, consummate, outstanding, remarkable, first-rate, first-class, premier, prime, unsurpassed, unequalled, unparalleled, unrivalled, pre-eminent; *informal* crack, ace, wicked; *Brit. informal* brilliant.
–OPPOSITES mediocre.

supernatural ▸ adjective 1 *supernatural powers* =paranormal, psychic, magic, magical, occult, mystic, mystical, superhuman. 2 *a supernatural being* =ghostly, phantom, spectral, otherworldly, unearthly.

supersede ▸ verb =replace, take the place of, take over from, succeed; supplant, displace, oust, overthrow, remove, unseat.

superstition ▸ noun =myth, belief, old wives' tale.

supervise ▸ verb 1 *he had to supervise the loading* =superintend, oversee, be in charge of, preside over, direct, manage, run, look after, be responsible for, govern, organize, handle. 2 *you may need to supervise her* =watch, oversee, keep an eye on, observe, monitor, mind.

supervision ▸ noun 1 *the supervision of the banking system* =administration, management, control, charge; regulation, government, governance. 2 *keep your children under supervision* =observation, guidance, custody, charge, safe keeping, care, guardianship; control.

supervisor ▸ noun =manager, director, overseer, controller, superintendent, governor, chief, head; steward, foreman; *informal* boss; *Brit. informal* gaffer.

supine ▸ adjective 1 *she lay supine on the sand* =flat on one's back, face up, flat, stretched out. 2 *a supine media* =weak, spineless; docile, acquiescent, submissive, passive.
–OPPOSITES prostrate, strong.

supper ▸ noun =dinner, evening meal; snack, bite to eat.

supplant ▸ verb 1 *motorways supplanted the A-roads* =replace, supersede, displace, take over from. 2 *the man he supplanted as Prime Minister* =oust, usurp, overthrow, remove, topple, unseat, depose, dethrone; succeed.

supple ▸ adjective 1 *her supple body* =lithe, limber, lissom(e), willowy, flexible, loose-limbed, agile, acrobatic, nimble, double-jointed. 2 *supple leather* =pliant, pliable, flexible, soft, bendy, workable, stretchy, springy.
–OPPOSITES stiff, rigid.

supplement ▶ noun **1** *a dietary supplement* =**extra**, add-on, accessory, adjunct. **2** *a single room supplement* =**surcharge**, addition, increase. **3** *a supplement to the essay* =**appendix**, addendum, postscript, addition, coda. **4** *a special supplement with today's paper* =**pull-out**, insert.
▶ verb *he supplemented his income by teaching* =**augment**, increase, add to, boost, swell, amplify, enlarge, top up.

supplementary ▶ adjective =**additional**, supplemental, extra, more, further; add-on, subsidiary, auxiliary, ancillary.

supply ▶ verb **1** *they supplied money to the rebels* =**give**, contribute, provide, furnish, donate, bestow, grant, endow, impart; dispense, disburse, allocate, assign; *informal* fork out, shell out. **2** *the lake supplies the city with water* =**provide**, furnish, endow, serve, confer; equip, arm. **3** *windmills supply their power needs* =**satisfy**, meet, fulfil, cater for.
▶ noun **1** *a limited supply of food* =**stock**, store, reserve, reservoir, stockpile, hoard, cache; fund, bank. **2** *the supply of alcoholic liquor* =**provision**, dissemination, distribution, serving. **3** *go to the supermarket for supplies* =**provisions**, stores, rations, food, necessities; *informal* eats; *formal* comestibles.
▶ adjective *a supply teacher* =**substitute**, stand-in, fill-in, locum, temporary, stopgap.

support ▶ verb **1** *a roof supported by pillars* =**hold up**, bear, carry, prop up, keep up, brace, shore up, underpin, buttress, reinforce. **2** *he struggled to support his family* =**provide for**, maintain, sustain, keep, take care of, look after. **3** *she supported him to the end* =**stand by**, defend, back, stand/stick up for. **4** *evidence to support the argument* =**substantiate**, back up, bear out, corroborate, confirm, attest to, verify, prove, validate, authenticate, endorse, ratify. **5** *the money supports charitable projects* =**help**, aid, assist; contribute to, back, subsidize, fund, finance; *N. Amer. informal* bankroll. **6** *a candidate supported by local people* =**back**, champion, favour, encourage; vote for; sponsor, second, promote, endorse, sanction; *informal* throw one's weight behind. **7** *they support human rights* =**advocate**, promote, champion, back, espouse, be in favour of, recommend, subscribe to.
–OPPOSITES neglect, contradict, oppose.
▶ noun **1** *bridge supports* =**pillar**, post, prop, upright, brace, buttress; substructure, foundation, underpinning. **2** *I was lucky to have their support* =**encouragement**, friendship, backing, help, assistance. **3** *he was a great support* =**comfort**, help, assistance, tower of strength. **4** *thank you for your support* =**contributions**, backing, donations, money, subsidy, funding, funds, finance, capital. **5** *they voiced their support for him* =**endorsement**, approval; vote(s), patronage.

supporter ▶ noun **1** *supporters of gun control* =**advocate**, backer, adherent, promoter, champion, defender, upholder, proponent, campaigner, apologist. **2** *Labour supporters* =**backer**, helper, adherent, follower, voter, disciple; member. **3** *the charity relies on its supporters* =**contributor**, donor, benefactor, sponsor, backer, patron, subscriber, well-wisher. **4** *the team's supporters* =**fan**, follower, enthusiast, devotee, admirer; *informal* buff, addict.

supportive ▶ adjective =**encouraging**, caring, sympathetic, reassuring, understanding, concerned, helpful.

suppose ▶ verb **1** *I suppose he's used to it* =**assume**, presume, expect, dare say, take it (as read); guess. **2** *suppose you had a spacecraft* =**assume**, imagine, (let's) say; hypothesize, theorize, speculate.

supposed ▶ adjective **1** *the supposed phenomenon* =**alleged**, putative, reputed, rumoured, claimed, purported. **2** *I'm supposed to meet him at 8.30* =**meant**, intended, expected; required, obliged.

supposition ▶ noun =**belief**, surmise, idea, notion, conjecture, speculation, inference, theory, hypothesis, guess work, feeling, assumption, presumption.

suppress ▶ verb **1** *they will suppress any criticism* =**subdue**, repress, crush, quell, quash, squash, stamp out; put down, crack down on. **2** *she suppressed her irritation* =**conceal**, restrain, stifle, smother, check, curb, contain, keep a rein on, put a lid on. **3** *the report was suppressed* =**censor**, keep secret, conceal, hide, hush up, gag, withhold, cover up, stifle; sweep under the carpet.
–OPPOSITES incite, reveal.

suppurate ▶ verb =**fester**, discharge, run, weep.

supremacy ▸ noun =ascendancy, predominance, primacy, dominion, hegemony, authority, mastery, control, power, rule, sovereignty; dominance, superiority, the upper hand, the whip hand, the edge.

supreme ▸ adjective **1** *the supreme commander* =highest, chief, head, top, foremost, principal, superior, premier, first, prime. **2** *a supreme achievement* =extraordinary, remarkable, incredible, phenomenal, exceptional, outstanding, great, incomparable, unparalleled, peerless. **3** *the supreme sacrifice* =ultimate, final, last; utmost, extreme, greatest, highest.
–OPPOSITES subordinate, insignificant.

sure ▸ adjective **1** *I'm sure they knew* =certain, positive, convinced, confident, definite, satisfied, persuaded. **2** *someone was sure to find out* =bound; likely, destined, fated. **3** *a sure winner* =guaranteed, unfailing, infallible, unerring, assured, certain, inevitable; *informal* sure-fire. **4** *a sure sign that he's worried* =reliable, dependable, trustworthy, certain, unambiguous. **5** *the sure hand of the surgeon* =firm, steady, steadfast, unfaltering, unwavering.
–OPPOSITES uncertain, unlikely.
■ **be sure to** =remember to, don't forget to, see that you, mind that you, take care to, be certain to.
■ **for sure** (*informal*) =definitely, surely, certainly, without doubt, without question, undoubtedly, indubitably, absolutely, undeniably, unmistakably.
■ **make sure** =check, confirm, make certain, ensure, assure; verify, corroborate, substantiate.

surety ▸ noun **1** *she's a surety for his debts* =guarantor, sponsor. **2** *bail of £10,000 with a further £10,000 surety* =pledge, collateral, guarantee, bond, assurance, insurance, deposit; security, indemnity.

surface ▸ noun **1** *the surface of the wall* =outside, exterior; top, side; finish, veneer. **2** *the surface of polite society* =outward appearance, facade, veneer. **3** *a floured surface* =worktop, top, work surface.
–OPPOSITES inside, interior.
▸ adjective *surface appearances* =superficial, external, exterior, outward, ostensible, apparent, cosmetic.
–OPPOSITES underlying.
▸ verb **1** *a submarine surfaced* =come to the surface, come up, rise. **2** *the idea first surfaced in the sixties* =emerge, arise, ap-

pear, come to light, crop up, materialize, spring up.
–OPPOSITES dive.
■ **on the surface** =at first glance, to the casual eye, outwardly, to all appearances, apparently, ostensibly, superficially, externally.

surfeit ▸ noun =excess, surplus, abundance, oversupply, superabundance, superfluity, glut; overdose; too much; *informal* bellyful.
–OPPOSITES lack.

surge ▸ noun **1** *a surge of water* =gush, rush, outpouring, stream, flow. **2** *a surge in demand* =increase, rise, growth, upswing, upsurge, escalation, leap. **3** *a sudden surge of anger* =rush, storm, torrent, blaze, outburst, eruption.
▸ verb **1** *the water surged into people's homes* =gush, rush, stream, flow, burst, pour, cascade, spill, sweep, roll. **2** *the Dow Jones index surged 47.63 points* =increase, rise, grow, leap.

surly ▸ adjective =sullen, sulky, moody, unfriendly, unpleasant, scowling, unsmiling, bad-tempered, grumpy, gruff, churlish, ill-humoured.
–OPPOSITES pleasant.

surmise ▸ verb =guess, conjecture, suspect, deduce, infer, conclude, theorize, speculate, divine; assume, presume, suppose, understand, gather.

surmount ▸ verb **1** *he has surmounted many obstacles* =overcome, prevail over, triumph over, beat, vanquish; clear, cross. **2** *they surmounted the ridge* =climb over, top, ascend, scale, mount. **3** *the dome is surmounted by a statue* =cap, top, crown, finish.
–OPPOSITES descend.

surname ▸ noun =family name, last name, second name.

surpass ▸ verb =excel, exceed, transcend; outdo, outshine, outstrip, outclass, eclipse; improve on, top, trump, cap, beat, better, outperform.

surplus ▸ noun =excess, surfeit, superabundance, superfluity, oversupply, glut; remainder, residue, remains, leftovers.
–OPPOSITES dearth.
▸ adjective =excess, leftover, unused, remaining, extra, additional, spare; superfluous, redundant, unwanted, unneeded, dispensable, expendable.
–OPPOSITES insufficient.

surprise ▸ noun **1** *Kate looked at me in*

surprise =astonishment, amazement, wonder, bewilderment, disbelief. **2** *the test came as a big surprise* =**shock**, bolt from the blue, bombshell, revelation, rude awakening, eye-opener; *informal* turn up for the books.
▸ verb **1** *I was so surprised that I dropped it* =**astonish**, amaze, startle, astound, stun, stagger, shock; leave open-mouthed, take aback, shake up; *informal* bowl over, floor, flabbergast; *Brit. informal* knock for six. **2** *she surprised a burglar* =**take by surprise**, catch unawares, catch off guard, catch red-handed.

surprised ▸ adjective =**astonished**, amazed, astounded, startled, stunned, staggered, nonplussed, shocked, taken aback, dumbfounded, speechless, thunderstruck; *informal* bowled over, flabbergasted, floored, flummoxed.

surprising ▸ adjective =**unexpected**, unforeseen; astonishing, amazing, startling, astounding, staggering, incredible, extraordinary, breathtaking, remarkable; *informal* mind-blowing.

surrender ▸ verb **1** *the gunmen surrendered* =**capitulate**, give in, give (oneself) up, concede (defeat), submit, back down, crumble; lay down one's arms/weapons. **2** *they surrendered power to the government* =**give up**, relinquish, renounce, forswear; cede, abdicate, waive, forfeit, sacrifice; hand over, turn over, yield, transfer, grant.
–OPPOSITES resist, seize.
▸ noun **1** *the surrender of the hijackers* =**capitulation**, submission, yielding, succumbing, acquiescence. **2** *a surrender of power to the shop floor* =**relinquishment**, renunciation, cession, abdication, resignation, transfer.

surreptitious ▸ adjective =**secret**, secretive, stealthy, clandestine, sneaky, sly, furtive.
–OPPOSITES blatant.

surrogate ▸ noun =**substitute**, proxy, replacement; deputy, representative, stand-in.

surround ▸ verb =**encircle**, enclose, encompass, ring; fence in, hem in, confine, bound, circumscribe, cut off; besiege, trap.
▸ noun =**border**, edging, edge, perimeter, boundary.

surrounding ▸ adjective =**neighbouring**, nearby, near, local; adjoining, adjacent.

surroundings ▸ plural noun =**environment**, setting, milieu, background, backdrop; vicinity, locality, habitat.

surveillance ▸ noun =**observation**, scrutiny, watch, view, inspection, supervision; spying, espionage; *informal* bugging.

survey ▸ verb **1** *he surveyed his work* =**look at**, look over, view, contemplate, regard, gaze at, stare at, eye; scrutinize, examine, inspect, scan, study, consider, review, take stock of; *informal* size up. **2** *they surveyed 4000 drug users* =**interview**, question, canvass, poll, cross-examine, investigate, research, study. **3** *he was asked to survey the house* =**appraise**, assess, prospect; value.
▸ noun **1** *a survey of the current literature* =**study**, review, overview; examination, inspection, appraisal. **2** *a survey of sexual behaviour* =**poll**, review, investigation, inquiry, study, probe, questionnaire, census, research. **3** *a thorough survey of the property* =**appraisal**, assessment, valuation.

survive ▸ verb **1** *he survived by escaping through a hole* =**remain alive**, live, sustain oneself, pull through, hold out, make it. **2** *the theatre must survive* =**continue**, remain, persist, endure, live on, persevere, abide, go on, carry on. **3** *he was survived by his sons* =**outlive**, outlast.

susceptible ▸ adjective **1** *susceptible children* =**impressionable**, credulous, gullible, innocent, ingenuous, naive, easily led; defenceless, vulnerable. **2** *people susceptible to blackmail* =**open to**, vulnerable to; an easy target for. **3** *he is susceptible to ulcers* =**liable to**, prone to, subject to, inclined to, predisposed to, disposed to, given to.
–OPPOSITES sceptical, immune, resistant.

suspect ▸ verb **1** *I suspected she'd made a mistake* =**have a suspicion**, have a feeling, feel, (be inclined to) think, fancy, reckon, guess, surmise, conjecture, conclude, have a hunch; fear. **2** *he had no reason to suspect me* =**doubt**, distrust, mistrust, have misgivings about, have qualms about, be suspicious of.
▸ adjective *a suspect package* =**suspicious**, dubious, doubtful, untrustworthy; *informal* fishy, funny; *Brit. informal* dodgy.

suspend ▸ verb **1** *the court case was suspended* =**adjourn**, interrupt, break off; cut short, discontinue; *N. Amer.* table.

2 *he was suspended from college* =**exclude**, debar, remove; expel, eject. **3** *lights were suspended from the ceiling* =**hang**, sling, string; swing, dangle.

suspense ▶ noun *I can't bear the suspense* =**tension**, uncertainty, doubt, anticipation, excitement, anxiety, strain.

suspension ▶ noun **1** *the suspension of army operations* =**adjournment**, interruption, postponement, deferral, deferment, stay; cessation, halt, stoppage. **2** *his suspension from school* =**exclusion**, debarment, removal; expulsion, ejection.

suspicion ▶ noun **1** *she had a suspicion that he didn't like her* =**intuition**, feeling, impression, inkling, hunch, fancy, notion, idea, theory; presentiment, premonition; *informal* gut feeling, sixth sense. **2** *I confronted him with my suspicions* =**misgiving**, doubt, qualm, reservation, hesitation, question.

suspicious ▶ adjective **1** *she gave him a suspicious look* =**doubtful**, unsure, dubious, wary, chary, sceptical, distrustful, mistrustful, disbelieving, cynical. **2** *a suspicious character* =**disreputable**, unsavoury, dubious, suspect; *informal* shifty, shady; *Brit. informal* dodgy. **3** *in suspicious circumstances* =**questionable**, odd, strange, dubious, irregular, funny, doubtful, mysterious, murky; *informal* fishy; *Brit. informal* dodgy.
–OPPOSITES trusting, honest, innocent.

sustain ▶ verb **1** *her memories sustained her* =**comfort**, help, assist, encourage, support, give strength to, buoy up. **2** *they were unable to sustain a coalition* =**continue**, carry on, keep up, keep alive, maintain, preserve, perpetuate, retain. **3** *she had bread and cheese to sustain her* =**nourish**, feed, nurture; maintain, keep alive, keep going. **4** *she sustained slight injuries* =**undergo**, experience, suffer, endure. **5** *the allegation was not sustained* =**uphold**, validate, ratify, vindicate, confirm, endorse; verify, corroborate, substantiate, bear out, prove, authenticate, back up.

sustained ▶ adjective =**continuous**, ongoing, steady, continual, constant, prolonged, persistent, non-stop, perpetual, relentless, incessant, unceasing, ceaseless, round the clock.
–OPPOSITES sporadic.

sustenance ▶ noun =**nourishment**, food, nutrition, provisions, rations; *in-*

formal grub, chow; *Brit. informal* scoff; *literary* viands; *dated* victuals.

swagger ▶ verb =**strut**, parade, stride; walk confidently; *informal* sashay.
▶ noun =**strut**; confidence, arrogance, ostentation.

swallow ▶ verb =**eat**, gulp down, consume, devour, put away; drink, guzzle, quaff, imbibe, sup, slug; *informal* polish off, swig, swill, down; *Brit. informal* scoff.
■ **swallow someone/something up 1** *the darkness swallowed them up* =**engulf**, swamp, devour, overwhelm, overcome. **2** *the colleges were swallowed up by universities* =**take over**, engulf, absorb, assimilate, incorporate.

> **WORD LINKS**
>
> *fear of swallowing:* **phagophobia**

swamp ▶ noun *he got stuck in the swamp* =**marsh**, bog, quagmire; quicksand; *N. Amer.* bayou.
▶ verb **1** *the rain was swamping the boat* =**flood**, inundate, deluge, immerse. **2** *he was swamped by media attention* =**overwhelm**, inundate, flood, deluge, engulf, snow under, overload, overpower, weigh down, besiege, beset.

swampy ▶ adjective =**marshy**, boggy; soft, soggy, muddy, spongy, heavy, squelchy, waterlogged, sodden, wet.

swan ▶ noun

> **WORD LINKS**
>
> *male:* **cob**
> *female:* **pen**
> *young:* **cygnet**
> *collective noun:* **wedge** (in flight)

swap ▶ verb **1** *I swapped some food for a CD* =**exchange**, trade, barter; switch, change, replace. **2** *we swapped jokes* =**bandy**, exchange, trade.
▶ noun *a job swap* =**exchange**, trade, switch, trade-off, substitution.

swarm ▶ noun **1** *a swarm of bees* =**hive**, flock, collection. **2** *a swarm of reporters* =**crowd**, multitude, horde, host, mob, throng, mass, army, troop, herd, pack.
▶ verb *reporters were swarming all over the place* =**flock**, crowd, throng, surge, stream.
■ **be swarming with** =**be crowded with**, be thronged with, be overrun with, be full of, be teeming with, bristle with, be alive with, be crawling with, be infested with, overflow with.

S

swarthy ▶ adjective =dark-skinned, olive-skinned, dusky, tanned.
–OPPOSITES pale.

swashbuckling ▶ adjective =daring, heroic, daredevil, dashing, adventurous, bold, valiant, fearless, devil-may-care.
–OPPOSITES timid.

swathe ▶ verb =wrap, envelop, bind, swaddle, bandage, cover, shroud, drape, wind, enfold.

sway ▶ verb 1 *the curtains swayed in the breeze* =swing, shake, undulate, move to and fro, move back and forth. 2 *she swayed on her feet* =stagger, wobble, rock, lurch, reel, roll, list, stumble. 3 *we are swayed by the media* =influence, affect; manipulate, bend, mould.
▶ noun 1 *the sway of her hips* =swing, roll, shake, undulation. 2 *a province under the sway of the Franks* =jurisdiction, rule, government, sovereignty, dominion, control, command, power, authority.
■ **hold sway** =hold/wield power, rule, be in control, predominate.

swear ▶ verb 1 *they swore to protect each other* =promise, vow, pledge, give one's word, undertake, guarantee. 2 *she swore she would never go back* =insist, avow, pronounce, declare, proclaim, assert, profess, maintain, contend, emphasize, stress. 3 *Kate spilled her wine and swore* =curse, blaspheme, use bad language; *informal* cuss, eff and blind.
■ **swear by** *(informal)* =believe in, have faith in, trust; set store by, value; *informal* rate.

swearing ▶ noun =bad language, strong language, cursing, blaspheming; profanities, obscenities, curses, oaths, expletives, swear words; *informal* effing and blinding, four-letter words.

sweat ▶ noun *drenched with sweat* =perspiration, moisture, dampness, wetness.
▶ verb 1 *she was sweating heavily* =perspire; be damp, be wet, secrete. 2 *I've sweated over this for six months* =work (hard), labour, toil, slog, slave, work one's fingers to the bone; *informal* graft.

> **WORD LINKS**
>
> *relating to sweat:* **sudatory, sudorific**

sweaty ▶ adjective =perspiring, sweating, clammy, sticky; moist, damp.

sweep ▶ verb 1 *she swept the floor* =brush, clean, scrub, mop, scour; *informal* do. 2 *I swept the crumbs off* =remove, brush, clean, clear. 3 *he was swept out to sea* =carry, pull, drag, tow. 4 *riots swept the country* =engulf, overwhelm, flood. 5 *she swept down the stairs* =glide, sail, breeze, drift, flounce; stride. 6 *a limousine swept past* =glide, sail, rush, race, speed; *informal* whip.
▶ noun 1 *a sweep of his hand* =gesture, stroke, wave, movement. 2 *a security sweep* =search, hunt, probe. 3 *a long sweep of golden sand* =expanse, tract, stretch, extent. 4 *the broad sweep of our interests* =range, span, scope, compass, reach, spread, ambit, extent.
■ **sweep something aside** =disregard, ignore, take no notice of, dismiss, shrug off, brush aside.

sweeping ▶ adjective 1 *sweeping changes* =extensive, wide-ranging, global, broad, comprehensive, all-inclusive, all-embracing, far-reaching; thorough, radical; *informal* wall-to-wall. 2 *a sweeping victory* =overwhelming, decisive, thorough, complete, total, absolute, out-and-out, unqualified. 3 *sweeping statements* =wholesale, blanket, generalized, unqualified, indiscriminate, oversimplified. 4 *sweeping banks of heather* =broad, extensive, expansive, vast.
–OPPOSITES limited, narrow, focused, small.

sweet ▶ adjective 1 *sweet biscuits* =sugary, sweetened; sugared, honeyed, candied, glacé; sickly, cloying. 2 *the sweet scent of roses* =fragrant, aromatic, perfumed. 3 *her sweet voice* =dulcet, melodious, mellifluous, musical, tuneful, soft, harmonious, silvery, honeyed, mellow, golden. 4 *life was still sweet* =pleasant, pleasing, agreeable, delightful, nice, satisfying, gratifying, good; *informal* lovely, great. 5 *she has a sweet nature* =likeable, appealing, engaging, amiable, pleasant, agreeable, nice, kind, thoughtful, considerate; charming, enchanting, captivating, delightful, lovely. 6 *she looks quite sweet* =cute, lovable, adorable, endearing, charming. 7 *my sweet Lydia* =dear, dearest, darling, beloved, loved, cherished, precious.
–OPPOSITES sour, savoury, harsh, disagreeable.
▶ noun 1 *sweets for the children* =confectionery, chocolate, bonbon, toffee; *N. Amer.* candy; *informal* sweetie. 2 *a delicious sweet*

for the guests =**dessert**, pudding; *Brit. informal* afters, pud. **3** *happy birthday my sweet!* =**dear**, darling, dearest, love, sweetheart, beloved, honey, pet, treasure, angel.

sweeten ▸ verb **1** *sweeten the milk* =**make sweet**, add sugar to, sugar. **2** *he chewed gum to sweeten his breath* =**freshen**, refresh, purify, deodorize. **3** *(informal) a bigger dividend to sweeten shareholders* =**mollify**, placate, soothe, soften up, pacify, appease, win over.

sweetheart ▸ noun **1** *you look lovely, sweetheart* =**darling**, dear, dearest, love, beloved, sweet; *informal* honey, sweetie, sugar, baby, babe, poppet. **2** *my high-school sweetheart* =**lover**, love, girlfriend, boyfriend, beloved; *informal* steady, flame.

swell ▸ verb **1** *her lip swelled up* =**expand**, bulge, distend, inflate, dilate, bloat, puff up, balloon, fatten, fill out. **2** *the population swelled* =**grow**, enlarge, increase, expand, rise, escalate, multiply, proliferate, snowball, mushroom. **3** *she swelled with pride* =**be filled**, be bursting, brim, overflow. **4** *the graduate scheme swelled entry numbers* =**increase**, enlarge, augment, boost, top up, step up, multiply. **5** *the music swelled to fill the house* =**grow loud**, grow louder, intensify, heighten.
–OPPOSITES shrink, decrease, quieten.
▸ noun **1** *a brief swell in demand* =**increase**, rise, surge, boost. **2** *a heavy swell on the sea* =**surge**, wave, roll.
–OPPOSITES decrease, dip.

swelling ▸ noun =**bump**, lump, bulge, protuberance, protrusion, nodule, tumescence; boil, blister, bunion, carbuncle.

sweltering ▸ adjective =**hot**, stifling, humid, sultry, sticky, muggy, close, stuffy; tropical, torrid, searing, blistering; *informal* boiling (hot), baking, roasting, sizzling.
–OPPOSITES freezing.

swerve ▸ verb =**veer**, deviate, diverge, weave, zigzag, change direction; *Sailing* tack.
▸ noun =**curve**, curl, deviation, twist.

swift ▸ adjective **1** *a swift decision* =**prompt**, rapid, sudden, immediate, instant; abrupt, hasty, hurried. **2** *swift runners* =**fast**, rapid, quick, speedy, brisk, lively; fleet-footed.
–OPPOSITES slow, leisurely.

swill ▸ verb **1** *(informal) she was swilling*

pints =**drink**, quaff, swallow, down, gulp, drain, sup, slurp, consume, slug; *informal* swig, knock back, put away; *N. Amer. informal* chug. **2** *he swilled out a glass* =**wash**, rinse, sluice, clean, flush.
▸ noun *swill for the pigs* =**pigswill**, mash, slops, scraps, refuse, scourings, leftovers.

swim ▸ verb **1** *they swam in the pool* =**bathe**, take a dip, splash around; float. **2** *his food was swimming in gravy* =**be saturated in**, be drenched in, be soaked in, be steeped in, be immersed in, be covered in, be full of.

swimmingly ▸ adverb =**well**, smoothly, easily, effortlessly, like clockwork, without a hitch, as planned, to plan; *informal* like a dream, like magic.

swimsuit ▸ noun =**bathing suit**, (swimming) trunks, bikini; swimwear; *Brit.* bathing costume, swimming costume; *informal* cossie; *Austral./NZ informal* bathers.

swindle ▸ verb =**defraud**, cheat, trick, dupe, deceive, fool, hoax, hoodwink, bamboozle; *informal* fleece, do, con, diddle, swizzle, rip off, take for a ride, pull a fast one on, put one over on; *N. Amer. informal* stiff, euchre; *literary* cozen.
▸ noun =**fraud**, trick, deception, deceit, cheat, sham, artifice, ruse, dodge, racket; sharp practice; *informal* con, fiddle, diddle, rip-off, flimflam; *N. Amer. informal* bunco.

swindler ▸ noun =**fraudster**, fraud, (confidence) trickster, cheat, rogue, charlatan, impostor, hoaxer; *informal* con man, con artist, shark, hustler, phoney, crook.

swing ▸ verb **1** *the sign swung in the wind* =**sway**, move back and forth, move to and fro, wave, rock. **2** *Helen swung the bottle* =**brandish**, wave, flourish, wield, shake, twirl. **3** *the road swings to the left* =**curve**, bend, veer, turn, bear, wind, twist, deviate, slew, head. **4** *the balance swung from one party to the other* =**change**, fluctuate, shift, alter, alternate, see-saw, yo-yo, vary.
▸ noun **1** *a swing of the pendulum* =**oscillation**, sway, wave. **2** *the swing to the Conservatives* =**change**, move; turnaround, turnabout, reversal. **3** *mood swings* =**fluctuation**, change, shift, variation, oscillation.

swingeing ▸ adjective *(Brit.)* =**severe**, extreme, serious, substantial, drastic,

harsh, punishing, excessive, heavy.
–OPPOSITES minor.

swipe ▶ verb *(informal)* =**steal**, thieve, take, pilfer, purloin, snatch; *informal* filch, lift, snaffle, rob, nab; *Brit. informal* nick, pinch, whip; *N. Amer. informal* glom.

swirl ▶ verb =**whirl**, eddy, billow, spiral, circulate, revolve, spin, twist; flow, stream, surge, seethe.

switch ▶ noun **1** *the switch on top of the telephone* =**button**, lever, control. **2** *a switch from direct to indirect taxation* =**change**, move, shift, transition, transformation; reversal, turnaround, U-turn, changeover, transfer, conversion.
▶ verb **1** *he switched sides* =**change**, shift; *informal* chop and change. **2** *he managed to switch the envelopes* =**exchange**, swap, interchange, change round, rotate.
■ **switch something on** =**turn on**, put on, activate, start, set going, set in motion, operate, initiate, actuate, initialize, energize.
■ **switch something off** =**turn off**, shut off, stop, cut, halt, deactivate.

swivel ▶ verb =**turn**, rotate, revolve, pivot, swing; spin, twirl, whirl, wheel.

swollen ▶ adjective =**distended**, enlarged, bulging, inflated, dilated, bloated, puffed up, puffy, tumescent; inflamed.

swoop ▶ verb **1** *pigeons swooped down after the grain* =**dive**, descend, pounce, plunge, pitch, nosedive; rush, dart, speed, zoom. **2** *police swooped on the flat* =**raid**, descend on; pounce on, attack; *N. Amer. informal* bust.

sword ▶ noun =**blade**, foil, épée, cutlass, rapier, sabre, scimitar.
■ **cross swords** =**quarrel**, disagree, dispute, wrangle, bicker, be at odds, be at loggerheads, lock horns; fight, contend; *informal* scrap.

sycophant ▶ noun =**toady**, creep, crawler, flatterer, truckler; *informal* bootlicker, yes-man.

sycophantic ▶ adjective =**obsequious**, servile, subservient, grovelling, toadying, fawning, ingratiating, unctuous; *informal* smarmy, bootlicking.

syllabus ▶ noun =**curriculum**, course (of study), programme (of study); timetable, schedule.

symbol ▶ noun **1** *the lotus is the symbol of purity* =**emblem**, token, sign, represen-

tation, figure, image; metaphor, allegory. **2** *the chemical symbol for helium* =**sign**, character, mark, letter, ideogram. **3** *the Red Cross symbol* =**logo**, emblem, badge, stamp, trademark, crest, insignia, coat of arms, seal, device, monogram, hallmark, flag, motif.

symbolic ▶ adjective **1** *the Colosseum is symbolic of the Roman Empire* =**emblematic**, representative, typical, characteristic, symptomatic. **2** *symbolic poetry* =**figurative**, emblematic, metaphorical, allegorical, allusive, suggestive.
–OPPOSITES literal.

symbolize ▶ verb =**represent**, stand for, be a sign of, exemplify; denote, signify, mean, indicate, convey, express, imply, suggest; embody, epitomize, encapsulate, personify.

symmetrical ▶ adjective =**regular**, uniform, consistent; even, equal; balanced, proportional.

symmetry ▶ noun =**regularity**, evenness, uniformity, consistency, conformity, correspondence, equality; balance, proportion.

sympathetic ▶ adjective **1** *a sympathetic listener* =**compassionate**, caring, concerned, solicitous, understanding, sensitive, supportive, encouraging. **2** *the most sympathetic character in the book* =**likeable**, pleasant, agreeable, congenial. **3** *I was sympathetic to his cause* =**in favour of**, in sympathy with, pro, on the side of, supportive of, encouraging of; favourably disposed to, receptive to.
–OPPOSITES unfeeling, opposed.

sympathize ▶ verb **1** *I sympathized with her* =**pity**, feel sorry for, commiserate, offer condolences to, feel for, show concern; identify with, understand, relate to. **2** *they sympathize with the rebels* =**agree with**, support, be in favour of, favour, approve of, back, side with.

sympathizer ▶ noun =**supporter**, backer, well-wisher, advocate, ally, partisan; collaborator.

sympathy ▶ noun **1** *her sympathy for the unemployed* =**compassion**, care, concern, solicitude; commiseration, pity. **2** *their sympathy with the Republicans* =**agreement**, favour, approval, approbation, support, encouragement, partiality; association, alignment, affiliation.
–OPPOSITES indifference, hostility.

symptom ▶ noun **1** *the symptoms of the*

disease =**manifestation**, indication, indicator, mark, feature, trait. **2** *a symptom of the country's present turmoil* =**expression**, sign, indication, mark, token, manifestation; portent, warning, clue, hint; testimony, evidence, proof.

symptomatic ▸ adjective =**indicative**, characteristic, suggestive, typical, representative, symbolic.

synopsis ▸ noun =**summary**, precis, abstract, outline, rundown, round-up, abridgement.

synthesis ▸ noun =**combination**, union, amalgam, blend, mixture, compound, fusion, composite, alloy.

synthetic ▸ adjective =**artificial**, fake, imitation, mock, simulated, ersatz, substitute; pseudo, so-called; man-made, manufactured, fabricated; *informal* phoney, pretend.
—OPPOSITES natural.

system ▸ noun **1** *a system of canals* =**structure**, organization, arrangement, complex, network; *informal* set-up. **2** *a system for regulating sales* =**method**, methodology, technique, process, procedure, approach, practice; means, way, mode, framework; scheme, plan, policy, programme, regimen, formula, routine. **3** *there was no system in his work* =**order**, method, orderliness, planning, logic, routine. **4** *youngsters have no faith in the system* =**the establishment**, the administration, the authorities, the powers that be; bureaucracy, officialdom; the status quo.

systematic ▸ adjective =**structured**, methodical, organized, orderly, planned, systematized, regular, routine, standardized, standard; logical, coherent, consistent; efficient, businesslike, practical.
—OPPOSITES disorganized.

s

Tt

tab ▸ noun =**tag**, label, flap.

table ▸ noun **1** *he provides an excellent table* =**meal**, food, fare, menu, nourishment; *informal* spread, grub, chow, eats, nosh. **2** *the report has numerous tables* =**chart**, diagram, figure, graphic, graph, plan; list, tabulation.
▸ verb *she tabled a question in parliament* =**submit**, put forward, propose, suggest, move, lodge, file, introduce, air, moot.

tableau ▸ noun **1** *mythic tableaux* =**picture**, painting, representation, illustration, image. **2** *the first act is a series of tableaux* =**pageant**, parade, scene. **3** *a domestic tableau around the fireplace* =**scene**, arrangement, grouping; picture, spectacle, image, vignette.

tablet ▸ noun **1** *a carved tablet* =**slab**, stone, panel, plaque, plate, sign. **2** *a headache tablet* =**pill**, capsule, lozenge, pastille, drop; *informal* tab. **3** *a tablet of soap* =**bar**, cake, slab, brick, block.

taboo ▸ noun *the taboo against healing on the sabbath* =**prohibition**, proscription, veto, interdict, ban.
▸ adjective *taboo language* =**forbidden**, prohibited, banned, proscribed, interdicted, outlawed, illegal, unlawful, off limits; unmentionable, unspeakable, unutterable; *informal* no go.
–OPPOSITES acceptable.

tabulate ▸ verb =**chart**, arrange, order, organize, systematize, catalogue, list, index, classify, class, codify.

tacit ▸ adjective =**implicit**, understood, implied, inferred, hinted, suggested; unspoken, unstated, unsaid, unexpressed, unvoiced; taken for granted, taken as read.
–OPPOSITES explicit.

taciturn ▸ adjective =**untalkative**, uncommunicative, reticent, unforthcoming, quiet, secretive, tight-lipped, close-mouthed; silent, mute, dumb, inarticulate.
–OPPOSITES talkative.

tack ▸ noun **1** *tacks held the carpet down* =**pin**, nail, staple, rivet, stud. **2** *the brig bowled past on the opposite tack* =**heading**, bearing, course, track, path. **3** *the defender changed his tack* =**approach**, way, method; policy, procedure, technique, tactic, plan, strategy.
▸ verb **1** *a photo tacked to the wall* =**pin**, nail, staple, fix, fasten, attach, secure, affix. **2** *the dress was roughly tacked together* =**stitch**, baste, sew, bind. **3** *the yachts tacked back and forth* =**change course**, change direction, swerve, zigzag, veer. **4** *poems tacked on at the end of the book* =**add**, append, join, tag.

tackle ▸ noun **1** *fishing tackle* =**gear**, equipment, apparatus, kit, hardware; implements, instruments, accoutrements, paraphernalia, trappings; *informal* things, stuff, clobber. **2** *lifting tackle* =**pulleys**, gear, hoist, crane, winch. **3** *a tackle by the scrum half* =**interception**, challenge, block, attack.
▸ verb **1** *we must tackle the problems* =**get to grips with**, address, get to work on, approach, take on, attend to, see to; deal with, take care of, handle, manage; *informal* get stuck into, have a go at. **2** *I tackled Nina about it* =**confront**, speak to, interview, question, cross-examine. **3** *he tackled an intruder* =**confront**, face up to, take on, contend with, challenge; seize, grab, intercept, block, stop; bring down, floor, fell; *informal* have a go at. **4** *the winger got tackled* =**intercept**, challenge, block, stop, attack.

tacky[1] ▸ adjective *the paint was still tacky* =**sticky**, wet, gluey, viscous; *informal* gooey.

tacky[2] ▸ adjective *a tacky game show* =**tawdry**, tasteless, kitsch, vulgar, crude, garish, gaudy, trashy, cheap; *informal* cheesy; *Brit. informal* naff.
–OPPOSITES tasteful.

tact ▸ noun =**diplomacy**, sensitivity, understanding, thoughtfulness, consideration, delicacy, discretion, prudence, judiciousness, subtlety; *informal* savvy.

tactful ▸ adjective =**diplomatic**, discreet, considerate, sensitive, understanding, thoughtful, delicate, judicious, subtle; *informal* savvy.

tactic ▸ noun **1** *a tax-saving tactic* =**strategy**, scheme, plan, manoeuvre; method, expedient, gambit, tack; device, trick, ploy, dodge, ruse, machination; *informal* wangle. **2** *our fleet's superior tactics* =**strategy**, policy, campaign, game plans, manoeuvres, logistics.

tactical ▸ adjective =**calculated**, planned, strategic; prudent, politic, diplomatic, judicious, shrewd, cunning, artful.

tactless ▸ adjective =**insensitive**, inconsiderate, thoughtless, indelicate, undiplomatic, impolitic, indiscreet, unsubtle, inept, gauche; blunt, frank, outspoken, abrupt, crude.

tag ▸ noun **1** *a price tag* =**label**, ticket, badge, mark, tab, sticker, docket. **2** *his jacket was hung up by its tag* =**tab**, loop, label. **3** *he gained a 'bad boy' tag* =**designation**, label, description, characterization, identity; nickname, name, epithet, title, sobriquet; *informal* handle, moniker; *formal* denomination, appellation. **4** *tags from Shakespeare* =**quotation**, quote, phrase, platitude, cliché, excerpt; saying, proverb, maxim, adage, aphorism; slogan, catchphrase.
▸ verb **1** *bottles tagged with stickers* =**label**, mark, ticket, identify, flag, indicate. **2** *he is tagged as a 'thinking' actor* =**label**, class, categorize, characterize, designate, describe, identify, classify; mark, stamp, brand, pigeonhole, stereotype, typecast, compartmentalize, typify. **3** *a poem tagged on as an afterthought* =**add**, tack, join; attach, append. **4** *he was tagging along behind* =**follow**, trail; come after, shadow, dog; accompany, attend, escort; *informal* tail.

tail ▸ noun **1** *the tail of the queue* =**rear**, end, back, extremity; bottom. **2** *the tail of the hunting season* =**close**, end, conclusion.
−OPPOSITES head, front, start.
■ **on someone's tail** =**close behind**, (hard) on someone's heels.
■ **turn tail** =**run away**, flee, bolt, make off, take to one's heels, cut and run, beat a (hasty) retreat; *informal* scram, scarper.

WORD LINKS

relating to a tail: **caudal, cercal**

tailback ▸ noun =**traffic jam**, queue, line; congestion.

tailor ▸ noun =**outfitter**, dressmaker, couturier, (fashion) designer; clothier, costumier, seamstress.
▸ verb *services can be tailored to requirements* =**customize**, adapt, adjust, modify, change, convert, alter, attune, mould, gear, fit, cut, shape, tune.

WORD LINKS

relating to tailoring: **sartorial**

taint ▸ noun *the taint of corruption* =**trace**, touch, suggestion, hint, tinge; stain, blot, stigma.
▸ verb **1** *the wilderness is tainted by pollution* =**contaminate**, pollute, adulterate, infect, blight, spoil, soil, ruin. **2** *fraudulent firms taint our firm's reputation* =**tarnish**, sully, blacken, stain, blot, stigmatize, mar, corrupt, defile, soil, damage, hurt.
−OPPOSITES clean, improve.

take ▸ verb **1** *she took his hand* =**lay hold of**, get hold of; grasp, grip, clasp, clutch, grab. **2** *he took an envelope from his pocket* =**remove**, pull, draw, withdraw, extract, fish. **3** *a passage taken from my book* =**extract**, quote, cite, excerpt, derive, abstract, copy, cull. **4** *she took a little wine* =**drink**, imbibe; consume, swallow, eat, ingest. **5** *many prisoners were taken* =**capture**, seize, catch, arrest, apprehend, take into custody; carry off, abduct. **6** *someone's taken my car* =**steal**, remove, appropriate, make off with, pilfer, purloin; *informal* filch, swipe, snaffle; *Brit. informal* pinch, nick. **7** *take four from the total* =**subtract**, deduct, remove; discount; *informal* knock off, minus. **8** *all the seats had been taken* =**occupy**, use, utilize, fill, hold; reserve, engage; *informal* bag. **9** *I have taken a room nearby* =**rent**, lease, hire, charter; reserve, book, engage. **10** *I took the job* =**accept**, undertake. **11** *I'd take this over the other option* =**pick**, choose, select; prefer, favour, opt for, plump for, vote for. **12** *take, for instance, the English* =**consider**, contemplate, ponder, think about, weigh up, mull over, examine, study, meditate over, ruminate about. **13** *he takes 'The Observer'* =**subscribe to**, buy, read. **14** *she took his temperature* =**ascertain**, determine, establish, measure, find out, discover; calculate, compute, evaluate, rate, assess, appraise, gauge. **15** *he took notes* =**write**, note (down), jot (down), scribble, scrawl, record, register, document, minute. **16** *I took it back to London* =**bring**, carry, bear, transport, convey, move, transfer, shift, ferry; *informal* cart, tote. **17** *the priest took her home* =**escort**, ac-

company, help, assist, show, lead, guide, see, usher, convey. **18** *he took the train* =**travel on/by**, journey on, go via; use. **19** *the town takes its name from the lake* =**derive**, get, obtain, come by, acquire, pick up. **20** *she took the prize for best speaker* =**receive**, obtain, gain, get, acquire, collect, accept, be awarded; secure, come by, win, earn, pick up, carry off; *informal* land, bag, net, scoop. **21** *I took the chance to postpone it* =**act on**, take advantage of, capitalize on, use, exploit, make the most of, leap at, jump at, pounce on, seize, grasp, grab, accept. **22** *he took great pleasure in painting* =**derive**, draw, acquire, obtain, get, gain, extract, procure. **23** *Liz took the news badly* =**receive**, respond to, react to, meet, greet; deal with, cope with. **24** *do you take me for a fool?* =**regard as**, consider to be, view as, see as, believe to be, reckon to be, imagine to be, deem to be. **25** *I take it that you are hungry* =**assume**, presume, suppose, imagine, expect, reckon, gather, dare say, trust, surmise, deduce, guess, conjecture, fancy, suspect. **26** *I take your point* =**understand**, grasp, get, comprehend, apprehend, see, follow; accept, appreciate, acknowledge. **27** *Shirley was rather taken with him* =**captivate**, enchant, charm, delight, attract, beguile, enthral, entrance, infatuate, dazzle; *informal* tickle someone's fancy. **28** *I can't take much more* =**endure**, bear, tolerate, stand, put up with, abide, stomach, accept, allow, countenance, support, shoulder; *formal* brook. **29** *applicants must take a test* =**carry out**, do, complete, conduct, perform, execute, discharge, accomplish, fulfil. **30** *I took English and French* =**study**, learn, have lessons in; take up, pursue; *Brit.* read; *informal* do. **31** *the journey took six hours* =**last**, continue for, go on for, carry on for; require, call for, need, necessitate, entail, involve. **32** *it would take an expert to know that* =**require**, need, necessitate, demand, call for, entail, involve. **33** *I take size three shoes* =**wear**, use; require, need.
−**OPPOSITES** give, free, add, refuse, miss.
▶ **noun 1** *the whalers' take* =**catch**, haul, bag, yield, net. **2** *the state's tax take* =**revenue**, income, gain, profit; takings, proceeds, returns, receipts, winnings, pickings, earnings, spoils; purse. **3** *a clapperboard for the start of each take* =**scene**, sequence, (film) clip. **4** *a wry take on gender issues*

=**view of**, reading of, version of, interpretation of, understanding of, account of, analysis of, approach to.
■ **take after** =**resemble**, look like; remind one of, make one think of, recall, conjure up, suggest, evoke; *informal* favour, be a chip off the old block, be the spitting image of.
■ **take something apart** =**dismantle**, pull to pieces, pull apart, disassemble, break up; tear down, demolish, destroy, wreck.
■ **take someone back 1** *the dream took me back to Vienna* =**evoke**, remind one of, conjure up, summon up. **2** *I will never take that girl back* =**be reconciled to**, forgive, pardon, excuse, exonerate, absolve; let bygones be bygones, bury the hatchet.
■ **take something back 1** *I take back every word* =**retract**, withdraw, renounce, disclaim, unsay, disavow, recant, repudiate; *formal* abjure. **2** *I must take the keys back* =**return**, bring back, give back, restore.
■ **take something down** =**write down**, note down, jot down, set down, record, commit to paper, register, draft, document, minute, pen.
■ **take someone in 1** *she took in paying guests* =**accommodate**, board, house, feed, put up, admit, receive. **2** *you were taken in by a hoax* =**deceive**, delude, hoodwink, mislead, trick, dupe, fool, cheat, defraud, swindle, outwit, gull, hoax, bamboozle; *informal* con, put one over on.
■ **take something in 1** *she could hardly take in the news* =**comprehend**, understand, grasp, follow, absorb; *informal* get. **2** *this route takes in some great scenery* =**include**, encompass, embrace, contain, comprise, cover, incorporate, comprehend, hold.
■ **take it out of someone** =**exhaust**, drain, enervate, tire, fatigue, wear out, weary, debilitate; *informal* knacker, poop.
■ **take off 1** *the horse took off at speed* =**run away/off**, flee, abscond, decamp, leave, go, depart, make off, bolt, take to one's heels, escape; *informal* split, clear off. **2** *the plane took off* =**become airborne**, take to the air, take wing; lift off, blast off. **3** *the idea really took off* =**succeed**, do well, become popular, catch on, prosper, flourish, thrive, boom.
■ **take oneself off** =**withdraw**, retire, leave, exit, depart, go away, quit; *informal* clear off.
■ **take someone on 1** *there was no chal-*

lenger to take him on =**compete against**, oppose, challenge, confront, face, fight, vie with, contend with, stand up to. **2** *we took on extra staff* =**engage**, hire, employ, enrol, enlist, sign up.

■ **take something on 1** *he took on more responsibility* =**undertake**, accept, assume, shoulder, acquire, carry, bear. **2** *the study took on political meaning* =**acquire**, assume, come to have.

■ **take one's time** =**go slowly**, dally, dawdle, delay, linger, drag one's feet; *informal* dilly-dally.

■ **take someone out** *he asked if he could take her out* =**go out with**, escort, partner, accompany, go with; romance, woo; *informal* date, see, go steady with; *dated* court.

■ **take something over** =**assume control of**, take charge of, take command of, seize, hijack, commandeer.

■ **take to 1** *he took to carrying his money in his sock* =**make a habit of**, resort to, turn to, have recourse to; start, commence. **2** *Ruth took to him instantly* =**like**, get on with, be friendly towards; *informal* take a shine to. **3** *the dog has really taken to racing* =**become good at**, develop an ability for; like, enjoy.

■ **take something up 1** *he took up abstract painting* =**engage in**, practise; begin, start, commence. **2** *the meetings took up all her time* =**consume**, fill, absorb, use, occupy. **3** *her cousin took up the story* =**resume**, recommence, restart, carry on, continue, pick up, return to. **4** *he took up their offer of a job* =**accept**, say yes to, agree to, adopt; *formal* accede to. **5** *take the skirt up an inch* =**shorten**, turn up; raise, lift.

take-off ▸ noun =**departure**, lift-off, launch, blast-off; ascent, flight.
–OPPOSITES touchdown.

takeover ▸ noun =**buyout**, merger, amalgamation; purchase, acquisition.

takings ▸ plural noun =**proceeds**, returns, receipts, earnings, winnings, pickings, spoils; profit, gain, income, revenue.

tale ▸ noun **1** *a tale of witches* =**story**, narrative, anecdote, report, account, history; legend, fable, myth, parable, allegory, saga; *informal* yarn. **2** *she told tales to her mother* =**lie**, fib, falsehood, story, untruth, fabrication, fiction; *informal* tall story, fairy story/tale, cock and bull story.

talent ▸ noun =**flair**, aptitude, facility,

gift, knack, technique, touch, bent, ability, expertise, capacity, faculty; strength, forte, genius, brilliance.

talented ▸ adjective =**gifted**, skilful, accomplished, brilliant, expert, consummate, masterly, adroit, dexterous, able, deft, adept, proficient; *informal* ace.
–OPPOSITES inept.

talisman ▸ noun =**(lucky) charm**, fetish, amulet, mascot, totem, juju.

talk ▸ verb **1** *I was talking to a friend* =**speak**, chat, chatter, gossip, prattle, babble, rattle on; *informal* yak, gab, chew the fat; *Brit. informal* natter, rabbit, witter. **2** *you're talking rubbish* =**utter**, speak, say, voice, express, articulate, pronounce, verbalize, vocalize. **3** *they were able to talk in peace* =**converse**, communicate, speak, confer, consult; negotiate, parley; *informal* have a confab. **4** *he talked of suicide* =**mention**, refer to, speak about, discuss. **5** *I was able to talk English* =**speak (in)**, talk in, communicate in, converse in, express oneself in; use.
▸ noun **1** *he was bored with all this talk* =**chatter**, gossip, prattle, jabbering; *informal* yakking; *Brit. informal* nattering. **2** *she needed a talk with* Vi =**conversation**, chat, discussion, tête-à-tête, heart-to-heart, dialogue, parley, powwow; *informal* confab, chit-chat, gossip. **3** *peace talks* =**negotiations**, discussions; conference, summit, meeting, consultation, dialogue, symposium, seminar; mediation, arbitration; *informal* powwow. **4** *she gave a talk on her travels* =**lecture**, speech, address, discourse, oration, presentation, report, sermon; *informal* spiel.

■ **talk back** =**answer back**, be impertinent, be cheeky, be rude; contradict, argue with.

■ **talk something down** =**denigrate**, deprecate, disparage, belittle, diminish, criticize; *informal* knock, put down.

■ **talk down to** =**condescend to**, patronize, look down one's nose at, put down.

■ **talk someone into something** =**persuade into**, argue into, cajole into, coax into, bring round to, inveigle into, wheedle into, sweet-talk into, prevail on someone to; *informal* hustle, fast-talk.

talkative ▸ adjective =**chatty**, loquacious, garrulous, voluble, conversational, communicative; long-winded, wordy, verbose; *informal* mouthy.
–OPPOSITES taciturn.

tall ▸ adjective **1** *a tall man* =**big**, large,

huge, towering, colossal, gigantic, giant, monstrous; leggy; *informal* long. **2** *tall buildings* =**high**, big, lofty, towering, elevated, sky-high. **3** *she's five feet tall* =**in height**, high, from head to toe; from top to bottom. **4** *a tall tale* =**unlikely**, improbable, exaggerated, far-fetched, implausible, dubious, unbelievable, incredible, absurd, untrue; *informal* cock and bull. **5** *a tall order* =**demanding**, exacting, difficult; unreasonable, impossible.
–OPPOSITES short, low, wide, credible, easy.

tally ▶ noun **1** *a tally of the score* =**running total**, count, record, reckoning, register, account, roll. **2** *his tally of 816 wickets* =**total**, score, count, sum.
▶ verb **1** *these statistics tally with government figures* =**correspond**, agree, accord, concur, coincide, match, fit, be consistent, conform, equate, harmonize, dovetail, correlate, parallel; *informal* square. **2** *votes were tallied with abacuses* =**count**, calculate, add up, total, compute; figure out, work out, reckon, measure, quantify; *Brit.* tot up; *formal* enumerate.
–OPPOSITES disagree.

tame ▶ adjective **1** *a tame elephant* =**domesticated**, docile, broken, trained; gentle, mild; pet. **2** *a tame affair* =**unexciting**, uninteresting, uninspiring, dull, bland, flat, insipid, spiritless, pedestrian, colourless, humdrum, boring.
–OPPOSITES wild, exciting.
▶ verb **1** *wild rabbits can be tamed* =**domesticate**, break, train, master, subdue. **2** *she learned to tame her emotions* =**subdue**, curb, control, calm, master, moderate, discipline, suppress, temper, soften, bridle; *informal* lick.

tamper ▶ verb **1** *she saw them tampering with her car* =**interfere**, monkey around, meddle, tinker, fiddle, fool around, play around; *informal* mess about/around; *Brit. informal* muck about/around. **2** *the defendant tampered with the jury* =**influence**, get at, rig, manipulate, bribe, corrupt, bias; *informal* fix; *Brit. informal* nobble.

tan ▶ adjective =**yellowish-brown**, light brown, tawny.

tang ▶ noun =**flavour**, taste, savour, sharpness, zest, bite, edge, smack, piquancy, spice; smell, odour, aroma, fragrance; *informal* kick.

tangible ▶ adjective =**touchable**, palpable, material, physical, real, substantial, corporeal, solid, concrete; visible, noticeable; actual, definite, clear, distinct, perceptible, discernible.
–OPPOSITES abstract.

tangle ▶ verb **1** *the wool got tangled up* =**entangle**, snarl, catch, entwine, twist, ravel, knot, mat, jumble. **2** *he tangled with his old rival* =**come into conflict**, dispute, argue, quarrel, fight, wrangle, squabble, contend, cross swords, lock horns.
▶ noun **1** *a tangle of branches* =**snarl**, mass, knot, mesh, mishmash. **2** *the defence got into an awful tangle* =**muddle**, jumble, mix-up, confusion, shambles.

tangled ▶ adjective **1** *tangled hair* =**knotted**, ravelled, snarled (up), twisted, matted, messy; tousled, unkempt; *informal* mussed up. **2** *a tangled bureaucratic mess* =**confused**, jumbled, mixed up, messy, chaotic, complicated, involved, complex, intricate, knotty, tortuous.
–OPPOSITES simple.

tangy ▶ adjective =**zesty**, sharp, acid, tart, sour, bitter, piquant, spicy, tasty, flavoursome, pungent.
–OPPOSITES bland.

tank ▶ noun *a water tank* =**container**, receptacle, vat, cistern, repository, reservoir, basin.

tantalize ▶ verb =**tease**, torment, torture, bait; tempt, entice, lure, allure, beguile; excite, fascinate, titillate, intrigue.

tantamount ▶ adjective *this is tantamount to mutiny* =**equivalent to**, equal to, as good as, more or less, comparable to, on a par with, commensurate with.

tantrum ▶ noun =**fit of temper**, fit of rage, outburst, pet, paroxysm, frenzy, (bad) mood, huff; *informal* paddy, wobbly; *N. Amer. informal* hissy fit.

tap[1] ▶ noun **1** *she turned the tap on* =**valve**, stopcock, cock, spout; *N. Amer.* faucet, spigot. **2** *a phone tap* =**listening device**, wiretap, bug, microphone, receiver.
▶ verb **1** *several barrels were tapped* =**drain**, bleed, milk; broach, open. **2** *butlers were tapping ale* =**pour (out)**, draw off, siphon off, pump out, decant. **3** *their telephones were tapped* =**bug**, wiretap, monitor, overhear, eavesdrop on. **4** *the resources were to be tapped for our benefit* =**draw on**, exploit, milk, mine, use, utilize, turn to account.
■ **on tap** *beers on tap* =**on draught**, cask, keg.

tap² ▶ verb **1** *she tapped on the door* =**knock**, rap, strike, beat, drum. **2** *Dad tapped me on the knee* =**pat**, hit, strike, slap, jab, poke, dig.

tape ▶ noun **1** *a package tied with tape* =**binding**, ribbon, string, braid. **2** *they listened to tapes* =**(audio) cassette**, (tape) recording, reel, spool; video.
▶ verb **1** *a card was taped to the box* =**bind**, stick, fix, fasten, secure, attach. **2** *they taped off the area* =**cordon**, seal, close, shut, mark, fence; isolate, segregate. **3** *police taped his confession* =**record**, tape-record; video.

taper ▶ verb **1** *the leaves taper* =**narrow**, thin (out), come to a point, attenuate. **2** *the meetings soon tapered off* =**decrease**, lessen, dwindle, diminish, reduce, decline, die down, peter out, wane, ebb, slacken (off), fall off, let up, thin out.
−OPPOSITES thicken, increase.
▶ noun =**candle**, spill, sconce.

target ▶ noun **1** *targets at a range of 200 yards* =**mark**, bullseye, goal. **2** *eagles can spot their targets from half a mile* =**prey**, quarry, game, kill. **3** *their profit target* =**objective**, goal, aim, end; plan, intention, design, aspiration, ambition, ideal, desire, wish. **4** *she was the target for abuse* =**victim**, butt, recipient, focus, object, subject.
▶ verb **1** *he was targeted by a gunman* =**pick out**, single out, earmark, fix on; attack, aim at, fire at. **2** *the product is targeted at a specific market* =**aim**, direct, level, intend, focus.
■ **on target 1** *the striker was bang on target* =**accurate**, precise, unerring, sure, on the mark; *Brit. informal* spot on. **2** *the project was on target* =**on schedule**, on track, on course, on time.

tariff ▶ noun =**tax**, duty, toll, excise, levy, charge, rate, fee; price list.

tarnish ▶ verb **1** *gold does not tarnish easily* =**discolour**, rust, oxidize, corrode, stain, dull, blacken. **2** *it tarnished his reputation* =**sully**, blacken, stain, blemish, blot, taint, soil, ruin, disgrace, mar, damage, harm, hurt, undermine, dishonour, stigmatize.
−OPPOSITES polish, enhance.
▶ noun **1** *the tarnish on the candlesticks* =**discoloration**, oxidation, rust, verdigris; film. **2** *the tarnish on his reputation* =**smear**, stain, blemish, blot, taint, stigma.

tart¹ ▶ noun *a jam tart* =**pastry**, flan, quiche, pie.

tart² *(informal)* ▶ verb **1** *she tarted herself up* =**dress up**, make up, smarten up, preen oneself, beautify oneself, groom oneself; *informal* doll oneself up, titivate oneself. **2** *we must tart this place up a bit* =**decorate**, renovate, refurbish, redecorate, give something a makeover; smarten up; *informal* do up, fix up.

tart³ ▶ adjective **1** *a tart apple* =**sour**, sharp, acidic, zesty, tangy, piquant; lemony. **2** *a tart reply* =**acerbic**, sharp, biting, cutting, astringent, caustic, trenchant, incisive, barbed, scathing, sarcastic, acrimonious, nasty, rude, vicious, spiteful, venomous.
−OPPOSITES sweet, kind.

task ▶ noun =**job**, duty, chore, charge, assignment, detail, mission, engagement, occupation, undertaking, exercise, business, responsibility, burden, endeavour, enterprise, venture.

taste ▶ noun **1** *a distinctive sharp taste* =**flavour**, savour, relish, tang, smack. **2** *a taste of brandy* =**mouthful**, drop, bit, sip, nip, swallow, touch, soupçon, dash, modicum. **3** *it's too sweet for my taste* =**palate**, appetite, stomach. **4** *a taste for adventure* =**liking**, love, fondness, fancy, desire, preference, penchant, predilection, inclination, partiality. **5** *my first taste of prison* =**experience**, impression; exposure to, contact with, involvement with. **6** *the house was furnished with taste* =**judgement**, discrimination, discernment, refinement, finesse, elegance, grace, style. **7** *the photo was rejected on grounds of taste* =**decorum**, propriety, etiquette, politeness, delicacy, nicety, sensitivity, discretion.
−OPPOSITES dislike.
▶ verb **1** *Adam tasted the wine* =**sample**, test, try, savour; sip, sup. **2** *he could taste blood* =**perceive**, discern, make out, distinguish. **3** *a beer that tasted of cashews* =**have a flavour**, savour, smack, be reminiscent. **4** *it'll be good to taste real coffee again* =**consume**, drink, partake of; eat, have.

> **WORD LINKS**
> *relating to the sense of taste:* **gustative, gustatory**

tasteful ▶ adjective **1** *the decor is tasteful* =**aesthetically pleasing**, refined, cultured, elegant, stylish, smart, chic, attractive, exquisite. **2** *this video is erotic but tasteful* =**decorous**, proper, seemly, respectable, appropriate, modest.

−OPPOSITES tasteless, improper.

tasteless ▸ adjective **1** *the vegetables are tasteless* =**flavourless**, bland, insipid, unappetizing, savourless, watery. **2** *tasteless leather panelling* =**vulgar**, crude, tawdry, garish, gaudy, loud, trashy, showy, ostentatious, cheap, inelegant; *informal* flash, tacky, kitsch; *Brit. informal* naff. **3** *a tasteless remark* =**crude**, vulgar, indelicate, uncouth, crass, tactless, undiplomatic, indiscreet, inappropriate, offensive.

−OPPOSITES tasty, tasteful, seemly.

tasty ▸ adjective =**delicious**, palatable, luscious, mouth-watering, delectable, flavoursome; appetizing, tempting; *informal* yummy, scrumptious, scrummy, finger-licking, moreish.

−OPPOSITES bland.

tatters ▸ plural noun *the satin had frayed to tatters* =**rags**, scraps, shreds, bits, pieces, ribbons.

■ in tatters **1** *his clothes were in tatters* =**ragged**, torn, ripped, frayed, in pieces, worn out, moth-eaten, falling to pieces, threadbare. **2** *her marriage is in tatters* =**in ruins**, on the rocks, destroyed, finished, devastated.

taunt ▸ noun *the taunts of his classmates* =**jeer**, gibe, sneer, insult, barb, catcall; (**taunts**) teasing, provocation, goading, derision, mockery; *informal* dig, putdown.

▸ verb *she taunted him about his job* =**jeer at**, sneer at, scoff at, poke fun at, make fun of, get at, insult, tease, chaff, torment, goad, ridicule, deride, mock, heckle; *N. Amer.* ride; *informal* rib, needle.

taut ▸ adjective **1** *the rope was pulled taut* =**tight**, stretched, rigid. **2** *his muscles remained taut* =**flexed**, tense, hard, solid, firm, rigid, stiff. **3** *a taut expression* =**fraught**, strained, stressed, tense; *informal* uptight. **4** *a taut tale of gang life* =**concise**, controlled, crisp, pithy, sharp, succinct, compact, terse. **5** *he ran a taut ship* =**orderly**, tight, trim, neat, disciplined, tidy, spruce, smart.

−OPPOSITES slack, relaxed.

tavern ▸ noun =**bar**, inn, hostelry, taphouse; *Brit.* pub; *informal* watering hole; *Brit. informal* local, boozer; *dated* alehouse; *N. Amer. historical* saloon.

tawdry ▸ adjective =**gaudy**, flashy, showy, garish, loud; tasteless, vulgar, trashy, junky, cheap (and nasty), cheapjack, shoddy, shabby, gimcrack; *informal*

rubbishy, tacky, kitsch.

−OPPOSITES tasteful.

tax ▸ noun **1** *they have to pay tax* =**duty**, excise, customs, dues; levy, tariff, toll, tithe, charge, fee. **2** *a heavy tax on one's attention* =**burden**, load, weight, demand, strain, pressure, stress, drain, imposition.

−OPPOSITES rebate.

▸ verb **1** *they tax foreign companies more harshly* =**charge (duty on)**, tithe. **2** *his whining taxed her patience* =**strain**, stretch, overburden, overload, encumber, push too far; overwhelm, try, wear out, exhaust, sap, drain, weary, weaken.

WORD LINKS
relating to tax: **fiscal**

taxing ▸ adjective =**demanding**, exacting, challenging, burdensome, arduous, onerous, difficult, hard, tough, laborious, back-breaking, strenuous, rigorous, punishing; tiring, exhausting, enervating, wearing, stressful; *informal* murderous.

−OPPOSITES easy.

teach ▸ verb **1** *she teaches small children* =**educate**, instruct, school, tutor, coach, train. **2** *I taught English* =**give lessons in**, lecture in, be a teacher of. **3** *teach your teenager how to negotiate* =**train**, show, guide, instruct, demonstrate.

WORD LINKS
relating to teaching: **didactic, pedagogic, educational**

teacher ▸ noun =**educator**, tutor, instructor, schoolteacher, master, mistress, schoolmarm, governess, educationist, preceptor; coach, trainer; lecturer, professor, don; guide, mentor, guru; *formal* pedagogue.

team ▸ noun **1** *the sales team* =**group**, squad, company, party, crew, troupe, band, side, line-up; *informal* bunch, gang, posse. **2** *a team of horses* =**pair**, span, yoke, duo, set, tandem.

▸ verb **1** *the horses are teamed in pairs* =**harness**, yoke, hitch, couple. **2** *team a T-shirt with matching shorts* =**match**, coordinate, complement, pair up. **3** *you could team up with another artist* =**join (forces)**, collaborate, work together; unite, combine, cooperate, link, ally, associate, club together.

tear¹ ▸ verb **1** *I tore up the letter* =**rip up**,

pull to pieces, shred. **2** *his flesh was torn* =**lacerate**, cut (open), gash, slash, scratch, hack, pierce, stab. **3** *the trauma tore her family apart* =**divide**, split, sever, break up, disunite, rupture. **4** *Gina tore the book from his hands* =**snatch**, grab, seize, rip, wrench, wrest, pull, pluck; *informal* yank.
–OPPOSITES unite.
▶ noun *a tear in her dress* =**rip**, hole, split, slash, slit; ladder, snag.
■ **tear something down** =**demolish**, knock down, raze (to the ground), flatten, level, bulldoze.

tear² ▶ noun
■ **in tears** =**crying**, weeping, sobbing, wailing, howling, bawling, whimpering; *informal* weepy, blubbing.

WORD LINKS

relating to tears: **lachrymal**
causing tears: **lachrymose**

tearaway ▶ noun =**hooligan**, hoodlum, ruffian, lout, rowdy, roughneck; *informal* yahoo; *Brit. informal* yob; *Austral./NZ informal* roughie.

tearful ▶ adjective **1** *she was tearful* =**close to tears**, emotional, upset, distressed, sad, unhappy; in tears, crying, weeping, sobbing, snivelling; *informal* weepy; *formal* lachrymose. **2** *a tearful farewell* =**emotional**, upsetting, distressing, sad, heartbreaking, sorrowful; poignant, moving, touching, tear-jerking.
–OPPOSITES cheerful.

tease ▶ verb =**make fun of**, chaff, laugh at, guy, make a monkey (out) of; taunt, bait, goad, pick on; deride, mock, ridicule; *informal* take the mickey out of, rag, send up, rib, josh, have on, pull someone's leg; *Brit. informal* wind up.

technical ▶ adjective **1** *an important technical achievement* =**practical**, scientific, technological, high-tech. **2** *this might seem very technical* =**specialist**, specialized, scientific; complex, complicated, esoteric. **3** *a technical fault* =**mechanical**.

technique ▶ noun **1** *different techniques for solving the problem* =**method**, approach, procedure, system, modus operandi, way; means, strategy, tack, tactic, line; routine, practice. **2** *I was impressed with his technique* =**skill**, ability, proficiency, expertise, mastery, talent, genius, artistry, craftsmanship; aptitude, adroitness, deftness, dexterity,

facility, competence; performance, delivery; *informal* know-how.

technology ▶ noun

WORD LINKS

fear of technology: **technophobia**

tedious ▶ adjective =**boring**, dull, monotonous, repetitive, unrelieved, unvaried, uneventful; characterless, colourless, lifeless, insipid, uninteresting, unexciting, uninspiring, lacklustre, dreary, humdrum, mundane; mind-numbing, soul-destroying, wearisome; *informal* deadly, not up to much; *Brit. informal* samey; *N. Amer. informal* dullsville.
–OPPOSITES exciting.

tedium ▶ noun =**monotony**, boredom, ennui, uniformity, routine, dreariness, dryness, banality, vapidity, insipidity.
–OPPOSITES variety.

teem¹ ▶ verb *the pond was teeming with fish* =**be full of**, be alive with, be brimming with, abound in, be swarming with; be packed with, be crawling with, be overrun by, bristle with, seethe with, be thick with; *informal* be jam-packed with, be chock-a-block with.

teem² ▶ verb *the rain was teeming down* =**pour**, pelt, tip, beat, lash, sheet; come down in torrents, rain cats and dogs; *informal* be chucking it down; *Brit. informal* bucket down.

teenage ▶ adjective =**adolescent**, juvenile; *informal* teen.

teenager ▶ noun =**adolescent**, youth, young person, minor, juvenile; *informal* teen, teeny-bopper.

teeter ▶ verb **1** *Daisy teetered towards them* =**totter**, wobble, toddle, sway, stagger, stumble, reel, lurch, pitch. **2** *the situation teetered between tragedy and farce* =**see-saw**, veer, fluctuate, oscillate, swing, alternate, waver.

teetotal ▶ adjective =**abstinent**, abstemious; sober, dry; *informal* on the wagon.
–OPPOSITES alcoholic.

telepathic ▶ adjective =**psychic**, clairvoyant.

telepathy ▶ noun =**mind-reading**, thought transference; extrasensory perception, ESP; clairvoyance, sixth sense; psychometry.

telephone ▶ noun *Sophie picked up the telephone* =**phone**, handset, receiver; *informal* blower; *N. Amer. informal* horn.
▶ verb *he telephoned me* =**phone**, call, dial;

get, reach; *Brit.* ring (up); *informal* call up, give someone a buzz, get on the blower to; *Brit. informal* give someone a bell, give someone a tinkle; *N. Amer. informal* get someone on the horn.

telescope ▶ verb **1** *the front of the car was telescoped* =concertina, compact, compress, crush, squash. **2** *his experience can be telescoped into a paragraph* =condense, shorten, reduce, abbreviate, abridge, summarize, precis, abstract, shrink, consolidate; truncate, curtail.

televise ▶ verb =broadcast, screen, air, telecast; transmit, relay.

television ▶ noun =TV; *informal* the small screen; *Brit. informal* telly, the box; *N. Amer. informal* the tube.

tell ▶ verb **1** *why didn't you tell me?* =inform, notify, apprise, let know, make aware, acquaint with, advise, put in the picture, brief, fill in; alert, warn; *informal* clue in/up. **2** *she told the story slowly* =relate, recount, narrate, report, recite, describe, sketch, weave, spin; utter, voice, state, declare, communicate, impart, divulge. **3** *she told him to leave* =instruct, order, command, direct, charge, enjoin, call on, require; *literary* bid. **4** *I tell you, I did nothing wrong* =assure, promise, give one's word, swear, guarantee. **5** *the figures tell a different story* =reveal, show, indicate, be evidence of, disclose, convey, signify. **6** *promise you won't tell?* =give the game away, talk, tell tales, tattle; *informal* spill the beans, let the cat out of the bag, blab; *Brit. informal* blow the gaff. **7** *she was bound to tell on him* =inform on, tell tales on, give away, denounce, sell out; *informal* split on, blow the whistle on, rat on, peach on, squeal on; *Brit. informal* grass on, sneak on, shop; *N. Amer. informal* finger; *Austral./NZ informal* dob on. **8** *it was hard to tell what he said* =ascertain, determine, work out, make out, deduce, discern, perceive, see, identify, recognize, understand, comprehend; *informal* figure out; *Brit. informal* suss out. **9** *he couldn't tell one from the other* =distinguish, differentiate, discriminate. **10** *the strain began to tell on him* =take its toll, leave its mark; affect.

teller ▶ noun **1** *a bank teller* =cashier, clerk. **2** *a teller of tales* =narrator, raconteur; storyteller, anecdotalist.

telling ▶ adjective =revealing, significant, weighty, important, meaningful, influential, striking, potent, powerful, compelling.
–OPPOSITES insignificant.

telltale ▶ adjective =revealing, revelatory, suggestive, meaningful, significant; *informal* giveaway.
▶ noun =informer, whistle-blower; *N. Amer.* tattletale; *informal* snitch, squealer; *Brit. informal* sneak.

temerity ▶ noun =audacity, nerve, effrontery, impudence, impertinence, cheek, gall, presumption; daring; *informal* face, front, (brass) neck, chutzpah.

temper ▶ noun **1** *he walked out in a temper* =(fit of) rage, fury, fit of pique, tantrum, (bad) mood, pet, sulk, huff; *informal* grump, snit; *Brit. informal* strop, paddy; *N. Amer. informal* hissy fit. **2** *a display of temper* =anger, fury, rage, annoyance, vexation, irritation, irritability, ill humour, spleen, pique, petulance, testiness, tetchiness, crabbiness; *Brit. informal* stroppiness; *literary* ire, choler. **3** *she struggled to keep her temper* =composure, equanimity, self-control, self-possession, sangfroid, calm, good humour; *informal* cool.
▶ verb **1** *the steel is tempered by heat* =harden, strengthen, toughen, fortify, anneal. **2** *their idealism is tempered with realism* =moderate, modify, modulate, mitigate, alleviate, reduce, weaken, lighten, soften.
■ **lose one's temper** =get angry, fly into a rage, erupt, lose control, go berserk, breathe fire, flare up, boil over; *informal* go mad, go crazy, go bananas, have a fit, see red, fly off the handle, blow one's top, do one's nut, hit the roof, go off the deep end, go ape, flip, lose one's rag; *Brit. informal* go spare, throw a wobbly.

temperament ▶ noun =disposition, nature, character, personality, make-up, constitution, mind, spirit; stamp, mettle, mould; mood, frame of mind, attitude, outlook, humour.

temperamental ▶ adjective **1** *a temperamental chef* =volatile, excitable, emotional, mercurial, capricious, erratic, unpredictable, changeable, inconsistent; hot-headed, fiery, quick-tempered, irritable, irascible, impatient; touchy, moody, sensitive, highly strung. **2** *a temperamental dislike of conflict* =inherent, innate, natural, inborn, constitutional, deep-rooted, ingrained, congenital.
–OPPOSITES placid.

temperance ▸ noun =teetotalism, abstinence, abstention, sobriety, self-restraint; prohibition.
−OPPOSITES alcoholism.

temperate ▸ adjective 1 *temperate climates* =**mild**, clement, benign, gentle, balmy. 2 *he was temperate in his consumption* =**self-restrained**, moderate, self-controlled, disciplined; abstemious, self-denying; teetotal, abstinent.
−OPPOSITES extreme.

tempestuous ▸ adjective 1 *the day was tempestuous* =**stormy**, blustery, squally, wild, turbulent, windy, gusty, blowy, rainy. 2 *the tempestuous political environment* =**turbulent**, stormy, tumultuous, wild, lively, heated, explosive, feverish, frenetic, frenzied. 3 *a tempestuous woman* =**emotional**, passionate, impassioned, fiery, intense; temperamental, volatile, excitable, mercurial, capricious, unpredictable, quick-tempered.
−OPPOSITES calm, peaceful, placid.

temple ▸ noun =house of God, shrine, sanctuary; church, cathedral, mosque, synagogue, shul.

tempo ▸ noun 1 *the tempo of the music* =**cadence**, speed, rhythm, beat, time, pulse; measure, metre. 2 *the tempo of life in Western society* =**pace**, rate, speed, velocity.

temporal ▸ adjective =secular, non-spiritual, worldly, profane, material, mundane, earthly, terrestrial; non-religious, lay.
−OPPOSITES spiritual.

temporarily ▸ adverb 1 *the girl was temporarily placed with a foster-family* =**for the time being**, for the moment, for now, for the present, in the interim, for the nonce, in/for the meantime; provisionally, pro tem; *informal* for the minute. 2 *he was temporarily blinded by the light* =**briefly**, for a short time, momentarily, fleetingly.
−OPPOSITES permanently.

temporary ▸ adjective 1 *temporary accommodation | the temporary captain* =**non-permanent**, short-term, interim; provisional, pro tem, makeshift, stopgap; acting, fill-in, stand-in, caretaker. 2 *a temporary loss of self-control* =**brief**, short-lived, momentary, fleeting, passing.
−OPPOSITES permanent, lasting.

temporize ▸ verb =equivocate, pro-crastinate, play for time, stall, delay, hang back, prevaricate; *Brit.* hum and haw.

tempt ▸ verb 1 *the manager tried to tempt him to stay* =**entice**, persuade, convince, inveigle, induce, cajole, coax, woo; *informal* sweet-talk. 2 *more customers are being tempted by credit* =**allure**, attract, appeal to, whet the appetite of; lure, seduce, beguile, tantalize, draw.
−OPPOSITES discourage, deter.

temptation ▸ noun 1 *Mary resisted the temptation to answer back* =**desire**, urge, itch, impulse, inclination. 2 *the temptations of London* =**lure**, allurement, enticement, seduction, attraction, draw, pull. 3 *the temptation of travel to exotic locations* =**allure**, appeal, attraction, fascination.

tempting ▸ adjective 1 *tempting shops* =**enticing**, alluring, attractive, appealing, inviting, captivating, seductive, beguiling, fascinating, tantalizing. 2 *a plate of tempting cakes* =**appetizing**, mouth-watering, delicious, toothsome; *informal* scrumptious, yummy.
−OPPOSITES off-putting, uninviting.

temptress ▸ noun =seductress, siren, femme fatale, Mata Hari; *informal* vamp.

ten ▸ cardinal number =decade.

┌─────────────────┐
│ **WORD LINKS**   │
└─────────────────┘
relating to ten: **decimal, deca-, deci-**
ten-sided figure: **decagon**

tenable ▸ adjective =defensible, justifiable, supportable, sustainable, arguable, able to hold water, reasonable, rational, sound, viable, plausible, credible, believable, conceivable.
−OPPOSITES indefensible.

tenacious ▸ adjective 1 *his tenacious grip* =**firm**, tight, fast, clinging; strong, forceful, powerful, unshakeable, immovable, iron. 2 *a tenacious man* =**persevering**, persistent, determined, dogged, strong-willed, tireless, indefatigable, resolute, patient, purposeful, unflagging, staunch, steadfast, untiring, unwavering, unswerving, unshakeable, unyielding, insistent; *formal* pertinacious.
−OPPOSITES weak, irresolute.

tenacity ▸ noun =persistence, determination, perseverance, doggedness, strength of purpose, bulldog spirit, tirelessness, indefatigability, resolution, resoluteness, resolve, firmness, patience, purposefulness, staunchness, steadfastness, staying power, application; *formal* pertinacity.

tenancy ▸ noun =**occupancy**, occupation, residence, habitation, holding, possession; tenure, lease, rental, leasehold.

tenant ▸ noun =**occupant**, resident, inhabitant; leaseholder, lessee, renter; *Brit.* occupier.
−OPPOSITES owner, freeholder.

tend¹ ▸ verb **1** *I tend to get very involved in my work* =**be inclined**, be apt, be disposed, be prone, be liable, have a propensity. **2** *younger voters tended towards the tabloid press* =**incline**, lean, gravitate, move; prefer, favour; *N. Amer.* trend.

tend² ▸ verb *she tended her cattle* =**look after**, take care of, minister to, attend to, see to, wait on; watch over, keep an eye on, mind, protect, watch, guard.
−OPPOSITES neglect.

tendency ▸ noun **1** *his tendency to take the law into his own hands* =**propensity**, proclivity, proneness, aptness, likelihood, inclination, disposition, predisposition, bent, leaning, penchant, predilection, susceptibility, liability. **2** *this tendency towards cohabitation* =**trend**, movement, drift, swing, gravitation, direction, course; orientation, bias.

tender¹ ▸ adjective **1** *a gentle, tender man* =**caring**, kind, kind-hearted, soft-hearted, compassionate, sympathetic, warm, fatherly, motherly, maternal, gentle, mild, benevolent, generous, giving, humane. **2** *a tender kiss* =**affectionate**, fond, loving, emotional, warm, gentle, soft; *informal* lovey-dovey. **3** *tender love songs* =**romantic**, sentimental, emotional, emotive, touching, moving, poignant; *Brit. informal* soppy. **4** *simmer until the meat is tender* =**soft**, easy to chew, succulent, juicy; tenderized. **5** *her ankle was swollen and tender* =**sore**, painful, sensitive, inflamed, raw; hurting, aching, throbbing, smarting. **6** *the tender age of fifteen* =**young**, youthful; impressionable, inexperienced, immature, unsophisticated, unseasoned, juvenile, callow, green, raw; *informal* wet behind the ears.
−OPPOSITES hard-hearted, callous, tough.

tender² ▸ verb **1** *she tendered her resignation* =**offer**, proffer, present, put forward, propose, suggest, advance, submit, extend, give, render; hand in.

2 *firms tendered for the work* =**put in a bid**, quote, give an estimate.
▸ noun *contractors were invited to submit tenders* =**bid**, offer, quotation, quote, estimate, price; proposal, submission.

tenderness ▸ noun **1** *I felt an enormous tenderness for her* =**affection**, fondness, love, devotion, emotion, sentiment. **2** *with unexpected tenderness, he told her what had happened* =**kindness**, kind-heartedness, tender-heartedness, compassion, care, concern, sympathy, warmth, fatherliness, motherliness, gentleness, benevolence, generosity. **3** *abdominal tenderness* =**soreness**, pain, inflammation; ache, smarting, throbbing.

tenet ▸ noun =**principle**, belief, doctrine, precept, creed, credo, article of faith, dogma, canon; theory, thesis, conviction, idea, view, opinion, position, hypothesis, postulation; (**tenets**) ideology, code of belief, teaching(s).

tenor ▸ noun **1** *the general tenor of his speech* =**sense**, meaning, theme, drift, thread, import, purport, intent, intention, burden, thrust, significance, message; gist, essence, substance, spirit. **2** *the even tenor of life in the village* =**course**, direction, movement, drift, current, trend.

tense ▸ adjective **1** *tense muscles* =**taut**, tight, rigid, stretched, strained, stiff. **2** *Loretta was feeling tense* =**anxious**, nervous, on edge, edgy, strained, stressed, under pressure, agitated, ill at ease, uneasy, restless, worked up, keyed up, overwrought, jumpy, nervy, on tenterhooks, worried, apprehensive, panicky; *informal* a bundle of nerves, jittery, twitchy, uptight, stressed out; *N. Amer. informal* spooky, squirrelly. **3** *a tense moment* =**nerve-racking**, stressful, anxious, worrying, fraught, charged, strained, nail-biting, difficult, uneasy, uncomfortable; exciting.
−OPPOSITES slack, calm.
▸ verb *Hebden tensed his muscles* =**tighten**, tauten, flex, contract, brace, stiffen; screw up, knot, strain, stretch.
−OPPOSITES relax.

tension ▸ noun **1** *the tension of the rope* =**tightness**, tautness, rigidity; pull, traction. **2** *the tension was unbearable* =**strain**, stress, anxiety, pressure; worry, apprehensiveness, agitation, nervousness, jumpiness, edginess, restlessness; suspense, uncertainty, anticipation, excitement; *informal* butterflies (in one's stomach), collywobbles. **3** *months of tension between the military and the government* =**strained relations**, strain; ill feeling, friction, antagonism, antipathy, hostility, enmity.

tentative ▸ adjective **1** *tentative arrangements | a tentative conclusion* =**provisional**, unconfirmed, pencilled in, preliminary, to be confirmed, TBC; speculative, conjectural, untried, unproven, exploratory, experimental, trial, test, pilot. **2** *he took a few tentative steps* =**hesitant**, uncertain, cautious, timid, hesitating, faltering, shaky, unsteady, halting; wavering, unsure.
−OPPOSITES definite, confident.

tenterhooks ■ **on tenterhooks** =in **suspense**, waiting with bated breath; anxious, nervous, nervy, apprehensive, worried, on edge, edgy, tense, strained, stressed, agitated, restless, worked up, keyed up, jumpy; *informal* with butterflies in one's stomach, jittery, twitchy, in a state, uptight; *N. Amer. informal* spooky, squirrelly.

tenuous ▸ adjective **1** *a tenuous connection* =**slight**, insubstantial, flimsy, weak, doubtful, dubious, questionable, suspect; vague, nebulous, hazy. **2** *a tenuous thread* =**fine**, thin, slender, delicate, gossamer, fragile.
−OPPOSITES convincing, strong.

tenure ▸ noun **1** *residents should have security of tenure* =**tenancy**, occupancy, holding, occupation, residence; possession, title, ownership. **2** *his tenure as Secretary of State* =**incumbency**, term (of office), period (of/in office), time (in office).

tepid ▸ adjective **1** *tepid water* =**lukewarm**, warmish. **2** *a tepid response* =**unenthusiastic**, apathetic, half-hearted, indifferent, cool, lukewarm, uninterested.
−OPPOSITES hot, cold, enthusiastic.

term ▸ noun **1** *scientific terms* =**word**, expression, phrase, idiom, locution; name, title, designation, label; *formal* appellation, denomination. **2** *a protest in the strongest terms* =**language**, mode of expression, manner of speaking, phraseology, terminology; words, phrases, expressions. **3** *the terms of the contract* =**conditions**, stipulations, specifications, provisions, provisos; restrictions, qualifications. **4** *a policy offering favour-*

able terms =**rates**, prices, charges, costs, fees; tariff. **5** *the President is elected for a four-year term* =**period**, length of time, spell, stint, duration; stretch, run; period of office, incumbency. **6** *the summer term* =**session**; *N. Amer.* semester, trimester, quarter.
▸ verb *he has been termed the father of modern theology* =**call**, name, entitle, title, style, designate, describe as, dub, label, tag; nickname; *formal* denominate.
■ **come to terms 1** *the two sides came to terms* =**reach an agreement/understanding**, make a deal, reach a compromise, meet each other halfway. **2** *she eventually came to terms with her situation* =**accept**, reconcile oneself to, learn to live with, become resigned to, make the best of; face up to.

terminal ▸ adjective **1** *a terminal illness* =**incurable**, untreatable, inoperable; fatal, mortal, deadly. **2** *terminal patients* =**dying**, near death; incurable. **3** *a terminal bonus may be payable* =**final**, last, concluding, closing, end.
▸ noun **1** *a railway terminal* =**station**, last stop, end of the line; depot; *Brit.* terminus. **2** *a computer terminal* =**workstation**, VDU, visual display unit.

terminate ▸ verb **1** *treatment was terminated* =**bring to an end**, bring to a close/conclusion, close, conclude, finish, stop, wind up, discontinue, cease, cut short, abort, axe; *informal* pull the plug on. **2** *the train will terminate in Stratford* =**end its journey**, finish up, stop. **3** *the pregnancy was terminated* =**abort**, end.
−OPPOSITES begin, start, continue.

termination ▸ noun **1** *the termination of a contract* =**ending**, closing, conclusion, finish, stopping, winding up, discontinuance, discontinuation; cancellation, dissolution; *informal* wind-up. **2** *she had a termination* =**abortion**.
−OPPOSITES start, beginning.

terminology ▸ noun =**phraseology**, terms, expressions, words, language, parlance, vocabulary, nomenclature; usage, idiom; jargon, cant, argot; *informal* lingo, -speak, -ese.

terminus ▸ noun *(Brit.) the bus terminus* =**station**, last stop, end of the line, terminal; depot, garage.

terrain ▸ noun =**land**, ground, territory; topography, landscape, countryside, country.

terrestrial ▸ adjective =**earthly**, worldly, mundane, earthbound.

terrible ▸ adjective **1** *a terrible crime | terrible injuries* =**dreadful**, awful, appalling, horrific, horrifying, horrible, horrendous, atrocious, abominable, abhorrent, frightful, shocking, hideous, ghastly, grim, dire, unspeakable, gruesome, monstrous, sickening, heinous, vile; serious, grave, acute; *formal* grievous. **2** *a terrible smell* =**nasty**, disgusting, awful, dreadful, ghastly, horrid, horrible, vile, foul, abominable, frightful, loathsome, revolting, repulsive, odious, nauseating, repellent, horrendous, hideous, appalling, offensive, objectionable, obnoxious; *informal* gruesome, putrid, diabolical, yucky, sick-making, God-awful, gross. **3** *he was in terrible pain* =**severe**, extreme, intense, excruciating, agonizing, unbearable, intolerable, unendurable. **4** *that's a terrible thing to say* =**unkind**, nasty, unpleasant, foul, obnoxious, vile, contemptible, despicable, wretched, shabby; spiteful, mean, malicious, poisonous, mean-spirited, cruel, hateful, hurtful; *Brit. informal* beastly. **5** *the film was terrible* =**very bad**, dreadful, awful, frightful, atrocious, hopeless, poor; *informal* pathetic, pitiful, useless, lousy, appalling, abysmal, dire; *Brit. informal* duff, chronic, poxy, rubbish, (a load of) pants. **6** *(informal) you're a terrible flirt* =**incorrigible**, outrageous; real, awful, dreadful, frightful, shocking; *informal* impossible, fearful; *Brit. informal* right, proper. **7** *I feel terrible — I've been in bed all day* =**ill**, poorly, sick, green about the gills; *informal* rough, lousy, awful, dreadful; *Brit. informal* grotty, ropy. **8** *he still feels terrible about what he did* =**guilty**, conscience-stricken, remorseful, ashamed, chastened, contrite, sorry.
–OPPOSITES minor, slight, pleasant, wonderful.

terribly ▸ adverb **1** *he played terribly* =**very badly**, atrociously, awfully, dreadfully, appallingly, execrably; *informal* abysmally, pitifully, diabolically. **2** *(informal) I shall miss you terribly* =**very much**, greatly, a great deal, a lot; *informal* loads.

terrific ▸ adjective **1** *a terrific bang* =**tremendous**, huge, massive, gigantic, colossal, mighty, great, prodigious, formidable, sizeable, considerable; intense, extreme, extraordinary; *informal* mega, whopping great, humongous; *Brit. informal* whacking great, ginormous. **2** *(informal) a terrific game of top-quality football* =**marvellous**, wonderful, sensational, outstanding, superb, excellent, first-rate, first-class, dazzling, out of this world, breathtaking; *informal* great, fantastic, fabulous, fab, mega, super, ace, magic, cracking, cool, wicked, awesome; *Brit. informal* brilliant, smashing.

terrified ▸ adjective =**petrified**, frightened, scared, horrified, shaking in one's shoes.

terrify ▸ verb =**petrify**, horrify, frighten, scare, strike terror into, put the fear of God into; paralyse, transfix.

territory ▸ noun **1** *British overseas territories* =**area of land**, area, region, enclave; country, state, land, dependency, colony, dominion, protectorate, fief. **2** *mountainous territory* =**terrain**, land, ground, countryside. **3** *the territory of biblical scholarship* =**domain**, area of concern/interest/knowledge, province, department, field, preserve, sphere, arena, realm, world. **4** *Sheffield was his territory* =**sphere of operations**, area, section; *informal* turf; *Brit. informal* patch, manor.

terror ▸ noun **1** *she screamed in terror* =**extreme fear**, dread, horror, fright, alarm, panic, shock. **2** *the terrors of her own mind* =**demon**, fiend, devil, monster; horror, nightmare.

terrorist ▸ noun =**bomber**, arsonist; gunman, assassin; hijacker; revolutionary, anarchist, radical, guerrilla, freedom fighter.

terrorize ▸ verb =**persecute**, victimize, torment, tyrannize, intimidate, menace, threaten, bully, browbeat; scare, frighten, terrify, petrify; *Brit. informal* put the frighteners on.

terse ▸ adjective =**brief**, short, to the point, concise, succinct, crisp, pithy, incisive, laconic, elliptical; **brusque**, abrupt, curt, clipped, blunt.
–OPPOSITES long-winded, polite.

test ▸ noun **1** *a series of scientific tests* =**trial**, experiment, pilot study, try-out; check, examination, assessment, evaluation, appraisal, investigation, inspection, analysis, scrutiny, study, probe, exploration; screening. **2** *candidates may be required to take a test* =**exam**, examination; *N. Amer.* quiz. **3** *the test of a good wine* =**criterion**, proof, indication, yardstick, touchstone, standard, measure, litmus test, acid test.

▶ **verb 1** *a small-scale prototype was tested* =**try out**, trial, put through its paces, experiment with, pilot; check, examine, assess, scrutinize, study, probe, explore; sample; screen. **2** *such behaviour would test any marriage* =**put a strain on**, tax, try; make demands on, stretch, challenge.

testament ▶ noun *an achievement which is a testament to his professionalism* =**testimony**, witness, evidence, proof, attestation; demonstration, indication, exemplification.

testify ▶ verb **1** *you may be required to testify in court* =**give evidence**, bear witness, give one's testimony, attest. **2** *he testified that he had been threatened by a fellow officer* =**attest**, swear, state on oath, declare, assert, affirm; allege, submit, claim. **3** *the exhibits testify to the talents of the sculptors* =**be evidence/proof of**, attest to, confirm, prove, corroborate, substantiate, bear out; show, demonstrate, bear witness to, indicate.

testimonial ▶ noun =**reference**, letter of recommendation, commendation.

testimony ▶ noun **1** *Smith was in court to hear her testimony* =**evidence**, sworn statement, attestation, affidavit; statement, declaration, assertion, affirmation; allegation, submission, claim. **2** *the work is a testimony to his professional commitment* =**testament**, proof, evidence, attestation, witness; confirmation, corroboration; demonstration, indication.

testing ▶ adjective =**difficult**, challenging, tough, hard, demanding, taxing, stressful.
–OPPOSITES easy.

tetchy ▶ adjective =**irritable**, cantankerous, irascible, bad-tempered, grumpy, grouchy, crotchety, crabby, testy, crusty, curmudgeonly, ill-tempered, ill-humoured, peevish, cross, fractious, pettish, crabbed, prickly, waspish; Brit. informal shirty, stroppy, narky, ratty; N. Amer. informal cranky, ornery.
–OPPOSITES good-humoured.

tether ▶ verb *the horse was tethered to a post* =**tie (up)**, hitch, rope, chain; fasten, secure.
–OPPOSITES unleash.
▶ noun *a dog on a tether* =**rope**, chain, cord, lead, leash; restraint; halter.

text ▶ noun **1** *a text which explores pain and grief* =**book**, work. **2** *the pictures relate well to the text* =**words**; content, body. **3** *academic texts* =**textbook**, book. **4** *a text from the First Book of Samuel* =**passage**, extract, quotation, verse, line; reading. **5** *he took as his text the fact that Australia is a paradise* =**theme**, subject, topic, motif; thesis, argument.

textiles ▶ plural noun =**fabrics**, cloths, materials.

texture ▶ noun =**feel**, touch; appearance, finish, surface, grain.

thank ▶ verb =**express (one's) gratitude to**, say thank you to, show one's appreciation to.

thankful ▶ adjective =**grateful**, relieved, pleased, glad.

thankless ▶ adjective **1** *a thankless task* =**unenviable**, difficult, unpleasant, unrewarding; unappreciated, unrecognized, unacknowledged. **2** *her thankless children* =**ungrateful**, unappreciative.
–OPPOSITES rewarding, grateful.

thanks ▶ plural noun *they expressed their thanks* =**gratitude**, appreciation; acknowledgement, recognition, credit.
▶ exclamation *thanks for being so helpful* =**thank you**, much obliged, much appreciated, bless you; informal cheers; Brit. informal ta.
■ **thanks to** =**as a result of**, owing to, due to, because of, through, as a consequence of, on account of, by virtue of.

thaw ▶ verb =**melt**, unfreeze, soften, liquefy; defrost.
–OPPOSITES freeze.

theatre ▶ noun **1** =**playhouse**, auditorium, amphitheatre. **2** *what made you want to go into the theatre?* =**acting**, performing, the stage; drama, dramaturgy; show business; informal the boards, showbiz. **3** *a lecture theatre* =**hall**, room, auditorium. **4** *the theatre of war* =**scene**, arena, field/sphere/place of action.

theatrical ▶ adjective **1** *a theatrical career* =**stage**, dramatic, thespian, dramaturgical; show-business; informal showbiz. **2** *Henry looked over his shoulder with theatrical caution* =**exaggerated**, ostentatious, stagy, showy, melodramatic, overacted, overdone, histrionic, affected, mannered.

theft ▶ noun =**robbery**, stealing, larceny, shoplifting, burglary, embezzlement; raid, hold-up; informal smash and grab; *N. Amer. informal* heist, stick-up.

WORD LINKS
compulsive theft: **kleptomania**

theme ▸ noun 1 *the theme of her speech* =**subject**, topic, thesis, argument, text, burden, thrust; thread, motif, keynote. 2 *the first violin takes up the theme* =**melody**, tune, air; motif, leitmotif.

then ▸ adverb 1 *I was living in Cairo then* =**at that time**, in those days; at that point (in time), at that moment, on that occasion. 2 *she won the first and then the second game* =**next**, after that, afterwards, subsequently. 3 *and then there's another problem* =**in addition**, also, besides, as well, on top of that, moreover, furthermore, what's more, to boot; too. 4 *well, if that's what he wants, then he should leave* =**in that case**, that being so, it follows that.

theological ▸ adjective =**religious**, scriptural, ecclesiastical, doctrinal; divine, holy.

theoretical ▸ adjective =**hypothetical**, conjectural, academic, suppositional, speculative, notional, postulatory, assumed, presumed, untested, unproven, unsubstantiated. –OPPOSITES actual, real.

theorize ▸ verb =**speculate**, conjecture, hypothesize, postulate, propose, posit, suppose.

theory ▸ noun 1 *I reckon that confirms my theory* =**hypothesis**, thesis, conjecture, supposition, speculation, postulation, proposition, premise, surmise, assumption, presupposition; opinion, view, belief, contention. 2 *modern economic theory* =**principles**, ideas, concepts; philosophy, ideology, thinking.
■ **in theory** =**in principle**, on paper, in the abstract, in an ideal world; hypothetically.

therapeutic ▸ adjective =**healing**, curative, remedial, medicinal, restorative, health-giving, tonic. –OPPOSITES harmful.

therapist ▸ noun =**psychologist**, psychotherapist, analyst, psychoanalyst, psychiatrist; counsellor; *informal* shrink; *Brit. humorous* trick cyclist.

therapy ▸ noun 1 *complementary therapies* =**treatment**, remedy, cure. 2 *he's currently in therapy* =**psychotherapy**, psychoanalysis; counselling.

thereabouts ▸ adverb 1 *the land thereabouts* =**near there**, around there. 2 *they sold it for five million or thereabouts* =**approximately**, or so, give or take a bit, in round numbers, not far off; *Brit.* getting on for; *N. Amer. informal* in the ballpark of.

thereafter ▸ adverb =**after that**, following that, afterwards, subsequently, then, next.

therefore ▸ adverb =**consequently**, so, as a result, hence, thus, accordingly, for that reason, ergo, that being the case.

thesis ▸ noun 1 *the central thesis of his lecture* =**theory**, contention, argument, proposal, proposition, premise, assumption, hypothesis, postulation, surmise, supposition. 2 *a doctoral thesis* =**dissertation**, essay, paper, treatise, disquisition, composition, study; *N. Amer.* theme.

thick ▸ adjective 1 *the walls are five feet thick* =**in extent/diameter**, across, wide, broad, deep. 2 *his short, thick legs* =**stocky**, sturdy, chunky, hefty, thickset, beefy, meaty, big, solid; fat, stout, plump. 3 *a thick sweater* =**chunky**, bulky, heavy; woolly. 4 *the station was thick with people* =**crowded**, full, filled, packed, teeming, seething, swarming, crawling, crammed, thronged, bursting at the seams, solid, overflowing, choked, jammed, congested; *informal* jam-packed, chock-a-block, stuffed; *Austral./NZ informal* chocker. 5 *the thick vegetation* =**plentiful**, abundant, profuse, luxuriant, bushy, rich, riotous, exuberant; rank, rampant; dense, close-packed; *informal* jungly. 6 *a thick paste* =**semi-solid**, firm, stiff, heavy; clotted, coagulated, viscous, gelatinous. 7 *thick fog* =**dense**, heavy, opaque, impenetrable, soupy, murky. –OPPOSITES thin, slender, sparse.
▸ noun *in the thick of the crisis* =**midst**, centre, hub, middle, core, heart.

thicken ▸ verb =**become thick/thicker**, stiffen, condense; solidify, set, gel, congeal, clot, coagulate.

thicket ▸ noun =**copse**, coppice, grove, brake, covert, clump; wood; *Brit.* spinney.

thickness ▸ noun 1 *the gateway is several feet in thickness* =**width**, breadth, depth, diameter. 2 *several thicknesses of limestone* =**layer**, stratum, stratification, seam, vein.

thickset ▸ adjective =**stocky**, sturdy, heavily built, well built, chunky, burly,

strapping, brawny, solid, beefy.
–OPPOSITES slight.

thick-skinned ▸ adjective =**insensitive**, unfeeling, tough, impervious, hardened.
–OPPOSITES sensitive.

thief ▸ noun =**robber**, burglar, housebreaker, shoplifter, pickpocket, mugger; kleptomaniac; *informal* crook; *Brit. rhyming slang* tea leaf.

thieve ▸ verb =**steal**, take, purloin, help oneself to, snatch, pilfer; embezzle, misappropriate; *informal* rob, swipe, nab, lift, filch, snaffle; *Brit. informal* nick, pinch, knock off; *N. Amer. informal* heist.

thin ▸ adjective **1** *a thin white line* =**narrow**, fine, attenuated. **2** *a thin cotton nightdress* =**lightweight**, light, fine, delicate, floaty, flimsy, diaphanous, gossamer, insubstantial; sheer, gauzy, filmy, chiffony, transparent, see-through. **3** *a tall, thin woman* =**slim**, lean, slender, rangy, willowy, svelte, sylphlike, spare, slight; **skinny**, underweight, scrawny, scraggy, bony, gaunt, sticklike, emaciated, skeletal, wasted, pinched; lanky, spindly, gangly; *informal* anorexic. **4** *thin soup* =**watery**, weak, dilute; runny, sloppy.
–OPPOSITES thick, broad, fat, abundant.
▸ verb **1** *some paint must be thinned down* =**dilute**, water down, weaken. **2** *the crowds were beginning to thin out* =**disperse**, dissipate, scatter; decrease, diminish, dwindle.

thing ▸ noun **1** *the room was full of strange things* =**object**, article, item, artefact, commodity; device, gadget, instrument, utensil, tool, implement; *informal* doo-dah, whatsit, whatchamacallit, thingummy, thingy; *Brit. informal* gubbins. **2** *I'll collect my things* =**belongings**, possessions, stuff, property, worldly goods, (personal) effects, paraphernalia, bits and pieces; luggage, baggage; *informal* gear, junk; *Brit. informal* clobber. **3** *his gardening things* =**equipment**, apparatus, gear, kit, tackle, stuff; implements, tools, utensils; accoutrements. **4** *I've got several things to do* =**activity**, act, action, deed, undertaking, exploit, feat; task, job, chore. **5** *I've got other things on my mind* =**thought**, notion, idea; concern, matter, worry, preoccupation. **6** *the things he said* =**remark**, statement, comment, utterance, observation, declaration, pronouncement. **7** *a few odd things*

happened =**incident**, episode, event, happening, occurrence, phenomenon. **8** *how are things?* =**matters**, affairs, circumstances, conditions, relations; state of affairs, situation, life. **9** *one of the things I like about you* =**characteristic**, quality, attribute, property, trait, feature, point, aspect, facet. **10** *there's another thing you should know* =**fact**, piece of information, point, detail, particular, factor. **11** *the thing is, I'm not sure* =**fact of the matter**, point, issue, problem. **12** *you lucky thing!* =**person**, soul, creature, wretch; *informal* devil, beggar, bastard. **13** *she had a thing about men who wore glasses* =**penchant**, preference, taste, inclination, partiality, predilection, soft spot, weakness, fancy, fondness, liking, love, fetish. **14** *books aren't really my thing* =**what one likes**, what interests one; *informal* one's cup of tea, one's bag, what turns one on.

think ▸ verb **1** *I think he's gone home* =**believe**, be of the opinion, be of the view, be under the impression; expect, imagine, anticipate; surmise, suppose, conjecture, guess, fancy; *informal* reckon, figure. **2** *his family was thought to be enormously rich* =**deem**, judge, hold, reckon, consider, presume, estimate; regard as, view as. **3** *Jack thought for a moment* =**ponder**, reflect, deliberate, consider, meditate, contemplate, muse, ruminate, brood; concentrate, rack one's brains; *informal* put on one's thinking cap, sleep on it; *formal* cogitate. **4** *she thought of all the visits she had made* =**recall**, remember, recollect, call to mind. **5** *she forced herself to think of how he must be feeling* =**imagine**, picture, visualize, envisage.
■ **think better of** =have second thoughts about, think twice about, think again about, change one's mind about; reconsider, decide against; *informal* get cold feet about.
■ **think something over** =consider, contemplate, deliberate about, weigh up, consider the pros and cons of, mull over, ponder, reflect on, muse on, ruminate on.
■ **think something up** =devise, dream up, come up with, invent, create, concoct, make up; hit on.

thinker ▸ noun =**theorist**, ideologist, philosopher, scholar, savant, sage, intellectual, intellect, mind; *informal* brain.

thinking ▸ adjective *a thinking man* =**intelligent**, sensible, reasonable, rational;

logical, analytical; thoughtful, reflective, meditative, contemplative, pensive, philosophical.
–OPPOSITES stupid, irrational.
▶ noun *the thinking behind the campaign* =**reasoning**, idea(s), theory, thoughts, philosophy, beliefs; opinion(s), view(s), position, judgement, assessment, evaluation.

third-rate ▶ adjective =**substandard**, bad, inferior, poor, low-grade, inadequate, unsatisfactory, unacceptable.
–OPPOSITES excellent.

thirst ▶ noun *his thirst for knowledge* =**craving**, desire, longing, yearning, hunger, hankering, keenness, eagerness, lust, appetite; *informal* yen, itch.
▶ verb *she thirsted for power* =**crave**, want, covet, desire, hunger for, lust after, hanker after; wish for, long for.

thirsty ▶ adjective **1** *the boys were hot and thirsty* =**longing for a drink**, dry, dehydrated; *informal* parched, gasping; *Brit. informal* spitting feathers. **2** *the thirsty soil* =**dry**, arid, parched, baked, desiccated. **3** *she was thirsty for power* =**eager**, hungry, greedy, craving, longing, yearning, lusting, burning, desirous, hankering; *informal* itching, dying.

thirteen ▶ cardinal number

> WORD LINKS
> *fear of thirteen:* **triskaidekaphobia**

thorn ▶ noun =**prickle**, spike, barb, spine.

thorny ▶ adjective **1** *thorny undergrowth* =**prickly**, spiky, barbed, spiny, sharp. **2** *a thorny subject* =**problematic**, tricky, ticklish, delicate, controversial, awkward, difficult, knotty, tough; complicated, complex, involved, intricate; vexed; *informal* sticky.

thorough ▶ adjective **1** *a thorough investigation* =**rigorous**, in-depth, exhaustive, minute, detailed, close, meticulous, methodical, careful, complete, comprehensive, full, extensive, widespread, sweeping, all-embracing, all-inclusive. **2** *he is slow but thorough* =**meticulous**, scrupulous, assiduous, conscientious, painstaking, punctilious, methodical, careful, diligent, industrious, hard-working. **3** *the child is being a thorough nuisance* =**utter**, downright, absolute, complete, total, out-and-out, arrant, real, perfect, proper; *Brit. informal* right; *Austral./NZ informal* fair.

–OPPOSITES superficial, cursory, careless.

thoroughbred ▶ adjective =**purebred**, pedigree, pure-blooded.

thoroughfare ▶ noun **1** *the park is used as a thoroughfare* =**through route**, access route; *Brit. informal* rat run. **2** *the teeming thoroughfares of central London* =**street**, road, roadway, avenue, boulevard; *N. Amer.* highway, freeway, throughway.

thoroughly ▶ adverb **1** *we will investigate all complaints thoroughly* =**rigorously**, in depth, exhaustively, from top to bottom, minutely, closely, in detail, meticulously, scrupulously, assiduously, conscientiously, painstakingly, methodically, carefully, comprehensively, fully. **2** *she is thoroughly spoilt* =**utterly**, downright, absolutely, completely, totally, entirely, really, perfectly, positively, in every respect; *informal* plain, clean.

though ▶ conjunction *though she smiled bravely, she looked tired* =**although**, even though/if, despite the fact that, notwithstanding (the fact) that, for all that.
▶ adverb *You can't always do that. You can try, though* =**nevertheless**, nonetheless, even so, however, be that as it may, for all that, despite that, having said that; *informal* still and all.

thought ▶ noun **1** *what are your thoughts on the matter?* =**idea**, notion, opinion, view, impression, feeling, theory. **2** *he gave up any thought of taking a degree* =**hope**, aspiration, ambition, dream; intention, idea, plan, design, aim. **3** *it only took a moment's thought* =**thinking**, contemplation, musing, pondering, consideration, reflection, introspection, deliberation, rumination, meditation, brooding; *formal* cogitation. **4** *have you no thought for others?* =**compassion**, sympathy, care, concern, regard, solicitude, empathy; consideration, understanding, sensitivity, thoughtfulness, charity.

thoughtful ▶ adjective **1** *a thoughtful expression* =**pensive**, reflective, contemplative, musing, meditative, introspective, philosophical, ruminative, preoccupied; *formal* cogitative. **2** *how very thoughtful of you!* =**considerate**, caring, attentive, understanding, sympathetic, solicitous, concerned, helpful, obliging, accommodating, kind, compassionate, charitable.
–OPPOSITES vacant, inconsiderate.

thoughtless ▶ adjective **1** *I'm so*

sorry—how thoughtless of me =**inconsiderate**, uncaring, insensitive, uncharitable, unkind, tactless, undiplomatic, indiscreet, careless. **2** *thoughtless pleasure* =**unthinking**, heedless, careless, unmindful, absent-minded, injudicious, ill-advised, ill-considered, imprudent, unwise, foolish, silly, stupid, reckless, rash, precipitate, negligent, neglectful, remiss.
–OPPOSITES considerate, careful.

thousand ▸ cardinal number =*informal* k, thou.

WORD LINKS

relating to a thousand: **millenary, kilo-**
relating to a thousand or a thousandth: **milli-**
thousandth anniversary: **millennium**

thrash ▸ verb **1** =**hit**, beat, strike, batter, thump, hammer, pound; assault, attack; *informal* wallop, belt, bash, whack, clout, clobber, slug, tan, biff, bop, sock. **2** *he was thrashing around in pain* =**flail**, writhe, thresh, jerk, toss, twist, twitch.

thread ▸ noun **1** *a needle and thread* =**cotton**, yarn, filament, fibre. **2** *she lost the thread of the conversation* =**train of thought**, drift, direction, theme, motif, tenor.
▸ verb **1** *he threaded the rope through a pulley* =**pass**, string, work, ease, push, poke. **2** *she threaded her way through the tables* =**weave**, inch, squeeze, navigate, negotiate.

threadbare ▸ adjective =**worn**, old, holey, moth-eaten, mangy, ragged, frayed, tattered, battered; decrepit, shabby, scruffy; *informal* tatty, the worse for wear.

threat ▸ noun **1** *Maggie ignored his threats* =**threatening remark**, warning, ultimatum. **2** *a possible threat to aircraft* =**danger**, peril, hazard, menace, risk. **3** *the company faces the threat of liquidation* =**possibility**, chance, probability, likelihood, risk.

threaten ▸ verb **1** *how dare you threaten me?* =**menace**, intimidate, browbeat, bully, terrorize. **2** *these events could threaten the stability of Europe* =**endanger**, jeopardize, imperil, put at risk. **3** *the grey skies threatened snow* =**herald**, bode, warn of, presage, augur, portend, foreshadow, be a harbinger of, indicate, point to, be a sign of, signal, spell. **4** *rain threatened* =**seem likely**, seem immi-

nent, be on the horizon, be brewing, be gathering, be looming, be on the way, be impending.

threatening ▸ adjective **1** *a threatening letter* =**menacing**, intimidating, bullying, frightening; *formal* minatory. **2** *threatening black clouds* =**ominous**, sinister, menacing, dark, black.

three ▸ cardinal number =**trio**, threesome, triple, triad, trinity, troika, triumvirate, trilogy, triptych, trefoil.

WORD LINKS

relating to three: **triple, treble, ter-, tri-**
three-sided figure: **triangle**
group of three powerful people: **triumvirate**
relating to three years: **triennial**
three-hundredth anniversary: **tercentetary**

threesome ▸ noun =**trio**, triumvirate, triad, trinity, troika.

threshold ▸ noun **1** *the threshold of the church* =**doorstep**, entrance, entry, gate, portal. **2** *the threshold of a new era* =**start**, beginning, commencement, brink, verge, dawn, inception, day one, opening, debut; *informal* kick-off. **3** *the human threshold of pain* =**lower limit**, minimum.

thrift ▸ noun =**frugality**, economy, providence, prudence, saving, abstemiousness, parsimony, penny-pinching.
–OPPOSITES extravagance.

thriftless ▸ adjective =**extravagant**, profligate, spendthrift, wasteful, improvident, imprudent, prodigal, lavish.

thrifty ▸ adjective =**frugal**, economical, sparing, careful with money, provident, prudent, abstemious, parsimonious, penny-pinching.
–OPPOSITES extravagant.

thrill ▸ noun **1** *the thrill of jumping out of an aeroplane* =**(feeling of) excitement**, stimulation, pleasure, tingle; fun, enjoyment, amusement, delight, joy; *informal* buzz, kick; *N. Amer. informal* charge. **2** *a thrill of excitement ran through her* =**wave**, rush, surge, flash, blaze, stab, dart, throb, tremor, quiver, flutter, shudder.
▸ verb **1** *his words thrilled her* =**excite**, stimulate, arouse, rouse, inspire, delight, exhilarate, intoxicate, stir, electrify, galvanize, move, fire (with enthusiasm); *informal* give someone a buzz, give someone a kick; *N. Amer. informal* give someone

a charge. **2** *he thrilled at the sound of her voice* = **be/feel excited**, tingle; *informal* get a buzz out of, get a kick out of; *N. Amer. informal* get a charge out of.
−OPPOSITES bore.

thrilling ▶ adjective = **exciting**, stirring, action-packed, rip-roaring, gripping, riveting, fascinating, dramatic, hair-raising; rousing, stimulating, electrifying.
−OPPOSITES boring.

thrive ▶ verb = **flourish**, prosper, burgeon, bloom, blossom, do well, advance, succeed, boom.
−OPPOSITES decline, wither.

thriving ▶ adjective = **flourishing**, prospering, growing, developing, burgeoning, blooming, healthy, successful, booming, profitable, expanding; *informal* going strong.
−OPPOSITES moribund.

throat ▶ noun = **gullet**, oesophagus; windpipe, trachea.

WORD LINKS

relating to the throat: **guttural, jugular**
branch of medicine concerning the ears and throat: **otolaryngology**
branch of medicine concerning the ears, nose, and throat:
otorhinolaryngology

throaty ▶ adjective = **gravelly**, husky, rough, guttural, deep, thick, gruff, growly, hoarse, croaky, raspy.
−OPPOSITES high-pitched.

throb ▶ verb *her arms and legs throbbed with tiredness* = **pulsate**, beat, pulse, palpitate, pound, thud, thump, drum, vibrate, quiver.
▶ noun *the throb of the ship's engines* = **pulsation**, beat, pulse, palpitation, pounding, thudding, thumping, drumming.

throes ▶ plural noun *the throes of childbirth* = **agony**, pain, pangs, suffering, torture.
■ **in the throes of** = **in the middle of**, in the process of, in the midst of, busy with, occupied with, taken up with/by, involved in; struggling with, wrestling with, grappling with.

thrombosis ▶ noun = **blood clot**, embolism, thrombus, infarction.

throne ▶ noun = **sovereign power**, sovereignty, rule, dominion.

throng ▶ noun *throngs of people blocked her way* = **crowd**, horde, mass, multitude, host, army, herd, flock, drove, swarm, sea, troupe, pack, press, crush; *informal* gaggle, bunch, gang.
▶ verb **1** *the pavements were thronged with tourists* = **fill**, crowd, pack, cram, jam. **2** *people thronged to see the play* = **flock**, stream, swarm, troop. **3** *visitors thronged round him* = **crowd**, cluster, mill, swarm, congregate, gather.

throttle ▶ verb **1** *he tried to throttle her* = **choke**, strangle, garrotte. **2** *attempts to throttle the supply of drugs* = **suppress**, inhibit, stifle, control, restrain, check.

through ▶ preposition **1** *we drove through the tunnel* = **into and out of**, to the other/far side of. **2** *he got the job through an advertisement* = **by means of**, by way of, by dint of, via, using, thanks to, by virtue of, as a result of, as a consequence of, on account of, owing to. **3** *he worked through the night* = **throughout**, for the duration of, until/to the end of, all.
▶ adverb **1** *as soon as we opened the gate they came streaming through* = **from one side to the other**, from one end to another. **2** *I woke up, but Anthony slept through* = **the whole time**, from start to finish, without a break, without an interruption, non-stop, continuously; throughout.
▶ adjective *a through train* = **direct**, non-stop.
■ **through and through** = **in every respect**, to the core; thoroughly, utterly, absolutely, completely, totally, wholly, fully, entirely, unconditionally, out-and-out.

throughout ▶ preposition **1** *it had repercussions throughout Europe* = **all over**, in every part of, everywhere in. **2** *Rose had been very fit throughout her life* = **all through**, for the duration of, for the whole of, until the end of.

throw ▶ verb **1** = **hurl**, toss, fling, pitch, cast, lob, launch; *informal* chuck, heave, sling, bung; *dated* shy. **2** *he threw the door open* = **push**, thrust, fling, bang. **3** *a chandelier threw its light over the walls* = **cast**, send, give off, emit, radiate, project. **4** *he threw another punch* = **deliver**, give, land. **5** *she threw him a quick glance* = **direct**, cast, send, dart, shoot. **6** *his question threw me* = **disconcert**, unnerve, fluster, ruffle, put off, throw off balance, unsettle, confuse; *informal* rattle, faze; *N. Amer. informal* discombobulate.
▶ noun = **lob**, pitch; bowl, ball.
■ **throw something away** *she hated throwing old clothes away* = **discard**, throw out, dispose of, get rid of, do away with, scrap, dump, jettison; *informal* chuck

(away/out), ditch, bin, junk; *Brit. informal* get shot of.

■ **throw someone out** =expel, eject, evict, drive out, force out, oust, remove; get rid of, depose, topple, unseat, overthrow; *informal* boot out, kick out, give someone the boot; *Brit. informal* turf out.

■ **throw something out 1** See THROW SOMETHING AWAY. **2** *his case was thrown out by the magistrate* =reject, dismiss, turn down, refuse, disallow. **3** *a thermal light bulb throws out a lot of heat* =radiate, emit, give out/off, send out.

thrust ▶ verb **1** =shove, push, force, plunge, stick, drive, ram. **2** *fame had been thrust on him* =force, foist, impose, inflict. **3** *he thrust his way past her* =push, shove, force, elbow, shoulder, barge.
▶ noun **1** *a hard thrust* =shove, push, lunge, poke. **2** *a thrust by the Third Army* =advance, push, drive, attack, assault, onslaught, offensive, charge. **3** *only one engine is producing thrust* =force, propulsion, power, impetus. **4** *the thrust of the speech* =gist, substance, drift, burden, message, import, tenor.

thud ▶ noun & verb =thump, clunk, clonk, crash, smack, bang; *informal* wham.

thug ▶ noun =ruffian, hooligan, bully boy, hoodlum, gangster, villain; *informal* tough, bruiser, heavy; *Brit. informal* rough, bovver boy; *N. Amer. informal* hood, goon.

thumb ▶ verb **1** *he thumbed through his notebook* =leaf, flick, flip, riffle. **2** (**thumbed**) *his dictionaries were thumbed and ink-stained* =soiled, marked, dog-eared. **3** *he was thumbing his way across France* =hitch-hike; *informal* hitch, hitch/thumb a lift.

■ **thumbs down** (*informal*) =rejection, refusal, veto, no, rebuff; *informal* red light.

■ **thumbs up** (*informal*) =approval, seal of approval, endorsement; permission, authorization, consent, yes, leave, authority, nod, assent, blessing, rubber stamp, clearance; *informal* go-ahead, OK, green light, say-so.

thump ▶ verb **1** =hit, strike, smack, cuff, punch; *informal* whack, wallop, bash, biff, bop, lam, clout, clobber, sock, swipe, crown, belt; *Brit. informal* stick one on, slosh; *N. Amer. informal* slug, boff; *literary* smite. **2** *her heart thumped with fright* =throb, pound, thud, hammer, pulsate, pulse, pump, palpitate.
▶ noun **1** =blow, punch, box, cuff, smack; *informal* whack, thwack, wallop, bash,

belt, biff, clout; *Brit. informal* slosh; *N. Amer. informal* boff, slug. **2** *she put the box down with a thump* =thud, clunk, clonk, crash, smack, bang.

thunder ▶ noun =rumble, boom, roar, pounding, thud, crash, reverberation.
▶ verb **1** *below me the surf thundered* =rumble, boom, roar, pound, thud, thump, bang. **2** *'Answer me!' he thundered* =roar, bellow, bark, bawl; *informal* holler.

> **WORD LINKS**
>
> *fear of thunder:*
> **brontophobia/tonitrophobia/**
> **keraunophobia**

thunderous ▶ adjective =very loud, tumultuous, booming, roaring, resounding, reverberating, ringing, deafening, ear-splitting.

thunderstruck ▶ adjective =astonished, amazed, astounded, staggered, stunned, shocked, aghast, dumbfounded, dumbstruck; *informal* flabbergasted; *Brit. informal* gobsmacked, knocked for six.

thus ▶ adverb **1** *the studio handled production, thus cutting its costs* =consequently, so, therefore, ergo, accordingly, hence, as a result. **2** *legislation forbids such data being held thus* =like that, in that way, so, like so.

■ **thus far** =so far, (up) until now, up to now, up to this point, hitherto.

thwart ▶ verb =foil, frustrate, baulk, forestall, derail, dash; stop, check, block, prevent, defeat, impede, obstruct; *informal* put paid to, put the kibosh on, do for, stymie; *Brit. informal* scupper.
−OPPOSITES facilitate.

tic ▶ noun =twitch, spasm, jerk, tremor.

tick ▶ noun *put a tick against your choice* =mark, stroke; *N. Amer.* check.
▶ verb *tick the box* =put a tick in/against, mark, check off, indicate; *N. Amer.* check.

ticket ▶ noun **1** *a bus ticket* =pass, authorization, permit; token, coupon, voucher. **2** *a price ticket* =label, tag, sticker, tab.

tickle ▶ verb **1** =stroke, pet, chuck. **2** *something tickled his imagination* =stimulate, interest, appeal to, arouse, excite. **3** *the idea tickled Lewis* =amuse, entertain, divert, please, delight.

ticklish ▶ adjective =difficult, problematic, tricky, delicate, sensitive, awkward, prickly, thorny, tough; vexed; *informal* sticky.

tide ▸ noun 1 = **tidal flow**, ebb and flow, ebb, current. 2 *the tide of history* = **course**, movement, direction, trend, current, drift, run.

tidy ▸ adjective 1 *a tidy room* = **neat**, orderly, well ordered, well kept, shipshape (and Bristol fashion), in apple-pie order, uncluttered, straight. 2 *a very tidy person* = **neat**, trim, spruce, dapper, well groomed, well turned out; organized, methodical, meticulous; *informal* natty. –OPPOSITES messy.
▸ verb 1 *I'd better tidy up the living room* = **put in order**, clear up, sort out, straighten (up), clean up, spruce up. 2 *she tidied herself up in the bathroom* = **groom oneself**, spruce oneself up, freshen oneself up, smarten oneself up; *informal* titivate oneself.

tie ▸ verb 1 = **bind**, tie up, tether, hitch, strap, truss, fetter, rope, make fast, moor, lash. 2 *he bent to tie his shoelaces* = **do up**, lace, knot. 3 *women can feel tied by childcare responsibilities* = **restrict**, restrain, limit, tie down, constrain, trammel, confine, cramp, hamper, handicap, hamstring, encumber, shackle. 4 *a pay deal tied to a productivity agreement* = **link**, connect, couple, relate, join, marry. 5 *they tied for second place* = **draw**, be equal, be even.
▸ noun 1 *he tightened the ties of his robe* = **lace**, string, cord, fastening. 2 *a collar and tie* = **necktie**, bow tie. 3 *family ties* = **bond**, connection, link, relationship, attachment, affiliation. 4 *pets can be a tremendous tie* = **restriction**, constraint, curb, limitation, restraint, hindrance, encumbrance, handicap; obligation, commitment. 5 *a tie for first place* = **draw**, dead heat. 6 (*Brit.*) *Turkey's World Cup tie against Holland* = **match**, game, contest, fixture.
■ **tie in** = **be consistent**, tally, agree, be in agreement, accord, concur, fit in, harmonize, be in tune, dovetail; *informal* square; *N. Amer. informal* jibe.
■ **tie someone/something up** 1 *robbers tied her up and ransacked her home* = **bind**, fasten together, truss (up). 2 *he is tied up in meetings all morning* = **occupy**, engage, keep busy. 3 *they were anxious to tie up the contract* = **finalize**, conclude, complete, finish off, seal, settle, secure, clinch; *informal* wrap up.

tie-in ▸ noun = **connection**, link, association, correlation, tie-up, relationship.

tier ▸ noun 1 *six tiers of seats* = **row**, rank, bank, line; layer, level. 2 *a tier of management* = **grade**, gradation, echelon, rung on the ladder.

tight ▸ adjective 1 *a tight grip* = **firm**, fast, secure. 2 *the rope was pulled tight* = **taut**, rigid, stiff, tense, stretched, strained. 3 *tight jeans* = **close-fitting**, narrow, figure-hugging, skintight; *informal* sprayed on. 4 *a tight mass of fibres* = **compact**, compressed, dense, solid. 5 *a tight space* = **small**, tiny, narrow, limited, restricted, confined, cramped, constricted. 6 *a tight joint* = **impervious**, impenetrable, sealed, sound, hermetic. 7 *tight limits* = **strict**, rigorous, stringent, tough, rigid, firm. 8 *he's in a tight spot* = **difficult**, tricky, delicate, awkward, problematic; *informal* sticky; *Brit. informal* dodgy. 9 *a tight piece of writing* = **succinct**, concise, pithy, incisive, crisp, to the point. 10 *money is a bit tight just now* = **limited**, restricted, in short supply, scarce, depleted, diminished, low. –OPPOSITES slack, loose.

tighten ▸ verb 1 = **make tighter**, make fast, screw up. 2 *he tightened his grip* = **strengthen**, harden. 3 *she tightened the rope* = **tauten**, stretch, strain, stiffen, tense. 4 *he tightened his lips* = **narrow**, constrict, contract, compress, screw up, pucker, purse; *N. Amer.* squinch. 5 *security has been tightened up* = **increase**, make stricter, toughen up, heighten, scale up. –OPPOSITES loosen, slacken, relax.

tight-lipped ▸ adjective = **reticent**, uncommunicative, unforthcoming, close-mouthed, silent, taciturn; *informal* mum. –OPPOSITES forthcoming.

till[1] ▸ preposition & conjunction See UNTIL.

till[2] ▸ noun *the money in the till* = **cash register**, cash box, cash drawer; checkout, cash desk.

till[3] ▸ verb *he went back to tilling the land* = **cultivate**, work, farm, plough, dig.

tilt ▸ verb *the ground seemed to tilt* = **slope**, tip, lean, list, bank, slant, incline, pitch, cant, angle.
▸ noun *a tilt of some 45°* = **slope**, list, camber, gradient, bank, slant, incline, pitch, cant, bevel, angle.

timber ▸ noun 1 *houses built of timber* = **wood**; *N. Amer.* lumber. 2 *the timbers of wrecked ships* = **beam**, spar, plank, batten, lath, board, joist, rafter.

timbre ▸ noun = **tone**, sound, voice, colour, tonality.

time ▶ noun **1** *what time is it?* =**hour**; dated *o'clock*. **2** *the best time to leave* =**moment**, point (in time), occasion, instant, juncture, stage. **3** *he worked there for a time* =**while**, spell, stretch, stint, season, interval, period, length of time, duration, phase. **4** *the time of the dinosaurs* =**era**, age, epoch, period, years, days. **5** *tunes in waltz time* =**rhythm**, tempo, beat; metre, measure, cadence, pattern.
▶ verb =**schedule**, set, arrange, organize, fix, book, line up, timetable, plan; *N. Amer.* slate.

■ **all the time** =**constantly**, the entire time, around the clock, day and night, night and day, {morning, noon, and night}, {day in, day out}, at all times, always, without a break, ceaselessly, endlessly, incessantly, perpetually, permanently, continuously, continually, eternally; *informal* 24-7.

■ **at one time** =**formerly**, previously, once, in the past, at one point, once upon a time, time was when, in days/times gone by, in times past, in the (good) old days; *literary* in days/times of yore.

■ **at the same time 1** *they arrived at the same time* =**simultaneously**, at the same instant/moment, together, all together, as a group, as one. **2** *I can't really explain it, but at the same time I'm not convinced* =**nonetheless**, even so, however, but, still, yet, though; in spite of that, despite that, be that as it may, for all that, that said; anyhow; *informal* still and all.

■ **at times** =**occasionally**, sometimes, from time to time, now and then, every so often, once in a while, on occasion, off and on, at intervals, periodically.

■ **for the time being** =**for now**, for the moment, for the present, in the interim, in the meantime; temporarily, provisionally, pro tem.

■ **from time to time**. See AT TIMES above.

■ **in good time** =**punctually**, on time, early, with time to spare, ahead of time/schedule.

■ **in time 1** *I came back in time for the party* =**early enough**, in good time, punctually, on time, not too late, with time to spare, on schedule. **2** *in time, she forgot about it* =**eventually**, in the end, in due course, by and by, finally; one day, some day, sometime, sooner or later.

■ **on time** =**punctually**, in good time, to/on schedule, when expected; *informal* on the dot.

■ **time after time** =**repeatedly**, frequently, often, again and again, over and over (again), time and (time) again; persistently, recurrently, constantly, continually; *N. Amer.* oftentimes; *literary* oft, oft-times.

WORD LINKS

relating to time: **chronological, horological, temporal**
study of time: **horology**
measurement of time: **chronometry, horology**
fear of time: **chronophobia**

timeless ▶ adjective =**lasting**, enduring, classic, ageless, permanent, perennial, abiding, unfailing, unchanging, unvarying, never-changing, changeless, unfading, eternal, everlasting.
−OPPOSITES ephemeral.

timely ▶ adjective =**opportune**, well timed, convenient, appropriate, expedient, seasonable.
−OPPOSITES ill-timed.

timetable ▶ noun =**schedule**, programme, agenda, calendar.
▶ verb =**schedule**, arrange, programme, organize, fix, time, line up; *N. Amer.* slate.

timid ▶ adjective =**easily frightened**, fearful, afraid, faint-hearted, timorous, nervous, scared, frightened; shy, diffident, self-effacing.
−OPPOSITES bold.

tinge ▶ verb **1** *white blossom tinged with pink* =**tint**, colour, stain, shade, wash. **2** *his optimism is tinged with realism* =**influence**, affect, touch, flavour, colour.
▶ noun **1** *a blue tinge* =**tint**, colour, shade, tone, hue. **2** *a tinge of cynicism* =**trace**, note, touch, suggestion, hint, flavour, element, streak, suspicion, soupçon.

tingle ▶ verb =**prickle**, pricking, sting.
▶ noun =**prickle**, pricking, sting.

tinker ▶ verb =**fiddle with**, adjust, try to mend, play about with, mess about with; *informal* rearrange the deckchairs on the Titanic; *Brit. informal* muck about with.

tinkle ▶ verb **1** *the bell tinkled* =**ring**, jingle, jangle, chime, ding, ping. **2** *cool water tinkled in the stone fountain* =**splash**, purl, babble; *literary* plash.
▶ noun **1** *the tinkle of the doorbell* =**ring**, chime, ding, ping, jingle, jangle. **2** *the faint tinkle of water* =**splash**, purl, babble, burble; *literary* plash.

tinny ▸ adjective **1** *tinny music* =**jangly**, jingly. **2** *a tinny little car* =**cheap**, poor-quality, inferior, low-grade, gimcrack, shoddy, jerry-built; *informal* tacky, tatty, rubbishy.

tint ▸ noun **1** *an apricot tint* =**shade**, colour, tone, hue, tinge, cast, flush, blush. **2** *a hair tint* =**dye**, colourant, colouring, wash.

tiny ▸ adjective =**minute**, minuscule, microscopic, very small, mini, diminutive, miniature, baby, toy, dwarf; *Scottish* wee; *informal* teeny, teensy, itsy-bitsy, tiddly; *Brit. informal* titchy; *N. Amer. informal* little-bitty.
–OPPOSITES huge.

tip[1] ▸ noun **1** *the tip of the spear* =**point**, end, extremity, head, spike, prong. **2** *the tips of the mountains* =**peak**, top, summit, apex, crown, crest, pinnacle. **3** *the sticks have tips fitted to protect them* =**cap**, cover, ferrule.
▸ verb *mountains tipped with snow* =**cap**, top, crown.

tip[2] ▸ verb **1** *the boat tipped over* =**overturn**, turn over, topple (over), fall (over); keel over, capsize, turn turtle. **2** *a whale could tip over a small boat* =**upset**, overturn, topple over, turn over, push over, upend, capsize; *informal* roll; *archaic* overset. **3** *the car tipped to one side* =**lean**, tilt, list, slope, bank, slant, incline, pitch, cant. **4** *she tipped the water into the trough* =**pour**, empty, drain, dump, discharge; decant.
▸ noun *(Brit.) rubbish must be taken to the tip* =**dump**, rubbish dump, landfill site.

tip[3] ▸ noun **1** *a generous tip* =**gratuity**, baksheesh; present, gift, reward. **2** *useful tips* =**piece of advice**, suggestion, word of advice, pointer; clue, hint; *informal* wrinkle.

tip-off ▸ noun *(informal)* =**piece of information**, warning, lead; hint, clue; advice.

tippler ▸ noun =**drinker**, imbiber; alcoholic, drunk, drunkard, dipsomaniac; *informal* boozer, alky, barfly, sponge, dipso, wino, soak; *Austral./NZ informal* hophead; *archaic* toper.
–OPPOSITES teetotaller.

tipsy ▸ adjective =**merry**, mellow, slightly drunk; *Brit. informal* tiddly, squiffy.
–OPPOSITES sober.

tirade ▸ noun =**diatribe**, harangue, rant, attack, polemic, broadside, fulmination, tongue-lashing; *informal* blast; *literary* philippic.

tire ▸ verb **1** *he began to tire* =**get tired**, weaken, flag, droop. **2** *the journey had tired him* =**fatigue**, tire out, exhaust, wear out, drain, weary, wash out, enervate; *informal* knock out, take it out of, do in, fag out, wear to a frazzle; *Brit. informal* knacker. **3** *they tired of his difficult behaviour* =**weary**, get tired, get fed up, get sick, get bored.

tired ▸ adjective **1** *tired from travelling* =**exhausted**, worn out, weary, fatigued, dog-tired, bone-tired, ready to drop, drained, enervated; *informal* done in, all in, dead beat, shattered, bushed, knocked out, wiped out; *Brit. informal* knackered, whacked, jiggered; *N. Amer. informal* pooped, tuckered out; *Austral./NZ informal* stonkered. **2** *are you tired of having him here?* =**fed up with**, weary of, bored with/by, sick (and tired) of; *informal* up to here with. **3** *tired jokes* =**hackneyed**, overused, overworked, worn out, stale, clichéd, predictable, unimaginative, unoriginal, dull, boring; *informal* corny, played out.
–OPPOSITES energetic, lively, fresh.

tiredness ▸ noun =**fatigue**, weariness, exhaustion, enervation; sleepiness, drowsiness, somnolence.
–OPPOSITES energy.

tireless ▸ adjective =**vigorous**, energetic, industrious, determined, enthusiastic, keen, zealous, spirited, dynamic, stout, untiring, unwearying, indefatigable, unflagging.
–OPPOSITES lazy.

tiresome ▸ adjective =**boring**, dull, tedious, wearisome, wearing; annoying, irritating, trying; *informal* aggravating, pesky.
–OPPOSITES interesting, pleasant.

tiring ▸ adjective =**exhausting**, wearying, taxing, fatiguing, wearing, enervating, draining; hard, heavy, arduous, strenuous, onerous, demanding, gruelling; *informal* killing; *Brit. informal* knackering.

tissue ▸ noun **1** *living tissue* =**matter**, material, substance; flesh. **2** *a box of tissues* =**paper handkerchief**, paper towel; *trademark* Kleenex. **3** *a tissue of lies* =**web**, complex, mass, set, series, chain.

titbit ▸ noun **1** *tasty titbits* =**delicacy**, tasty morsel, bonne bouche, treat; nibble, savoury, appetizer; *informal* goody; *N. Amer.* tidbit. **2** *a fascinating titbit* =**piece**

of gossip, bit of scandal, piece of information.

titillate ▶ verb =arouse, excite, tantalize, stimulate, stir, thrill, interest, attract, fascinate; *informal* turn on.
–OPPOSITES bore.

titillating ▶ adjective =arousing, exciting, stimulating, sexy, thrilling, provocative, tantalizing, interesting, fascinating; suggestive, salacious, lurid; *Brit. informal* saucy.
–OPPOSITES boring.

title ▶ noun 1 *the title of the book* =name. 2 *the cartoon title* =caption, legend, inscription, label, heading, subheading. 3 *the company publishes 40 titles a year* =publication, work, book, newspaper, paper, magazine, periodical. 4 *the title of Duke of Marlborough* =designation, name, form of address; epithet, style; rank, office, position; *informal* moniker, handle; *formal* appellation, denomination. 5 *an Olympic title* =championship, crown, first place; laurels. 6 *the vendor is obliged to prove his title to the land* =ownership, proprietorship, possession, holding, freehold, entitlement, right, claim.
▶ verb *a policy paper titled 'Law and Order'* =call, entitle, name, dub, designate, style, term; *formal* denominate.

titter ▶ verb & noun =giggle, snigger, snicker, tee-hee, chuckle, laugh; *informal* chortle.

tittle-tattle ▶ noun *she would never listen to tittle-tattle* =gossip, rumour(s), idle talk, hearsay, whispers, titbits; scandal; *Brit. informal* goss.
▶ verb *he was tittle tattling all over the village* =gossip, spread rumours, talk, tell tales.

titular ▶ adjective 1 *the titular head of a university* =nominal, in title/name only, ceremonial; token, puppet. 2 *the work's titular song* =eponymous, identifying.

toady ▶ noun =sycophant, fawner, flatterer, creep, crawler; *informal* bootlicker, yes-man.
▶ verb =grovel to, ingratiate oneself with, be obsequious to, kowtow to, pander to, crawl to, truckle to, bow and scrape to, make up to, fawn on/over; *informal* suck up to, lick someone's boots, butter up.

toast ▶ noun 1 *he raised his glass in a toast* =tribute, salutation. 2 *he was the toast of the West End* =darling, favourite, pet, heroine, hero; talk; *Brit. informal* blue-eyed boy/girl.
▶ verb 1 *she toasted her hands in front of the fire* =warm (up), heat. 2 *we toasted the couple with champagne* =drink (to) the health of, salute, honour, pay tribute to.

today ▶ adverb 1 *the work must be finished today* =this (very) day. 2 *the complex tasks demanded of computers today* =nowadays, these days, at the present time, in these times, in this day and age, now, currently, at the moment; in the present climate; *N. Amer.* presently.

toddle ▶ verb =totter, teeter, wobble, falter, waddle, stumble.

together ▶ adverb 1 *friends who work together* =with each other, in conjunction, jointly, in cooperation, in collaboration, in partnership, in combination, in league, side by side, hand in hand, shoulder to shoulder, cheek by jowl; in collusion, hand in glove; *informal* in cahoots. 2 *they both spoke together* =simultaneously, at the same time, at once, all together, as a group, in unison, in chorus. 3 *I was not able to get up for days together* =in succession, in a row, at a time, successively, consecutively, running, straight, on end, one after the other; *informal* on the trot.
–OPPOSITES separately.
▶ adjective *(informal) a very together young woman.* See LEVEL-HEADED.

toil ▶ verb 1 *she toiled all night* =work hard, labour, exert oneself, slave (away), grind away, strive, work one's fingers to the bone, work like a Trojan/slave, keep one's nose to the grindstone; *informal* slog away, plug away, peg away, beaver away; *Brit. informal* graft. 2 *she began to toil up the path* =struggle, trudge, tramp, traipse, slog, plod, trek, footslog, drag oneself; *N. Amer. informal* schlep.
–OPPOSITES rest, relax.
▶ noun *a life of toil* =hard work, labour, exertion, slaving, drudgery, effort, industry, {blood, sweat, and tears}; *informal* slog, elbow grease; *Brit. informal* graft.

toilet ▶ noun 1 =lavatory, WC, water closet, (public) convenience, cloakroom, powder room, urinal, privy, latrine, jakes; *N. Amer.* washroom, bathroom, rest room, men's/ladies' room, commode, comfort station; *informal* little girls'/boys' room, smallest room; *Brit. informal* loo, bog, the Ladies, the Gents, khazi, lav; *N. Amer. informal* can, john; *Austral./NZ informal* dunny. 2 *she had always taken a long time over her toilet* =washing, bathing, showering; grooming; *formal or humorous* ablutions.

token ▶ noun **1** *a token of our appreciation* =**symbol**, sign, emblem, badge, representation, indication, mark, manifestation, expression, pledge, demonstration. **2** *he kept the menu as a token of the wedding* =**memento**, souvenir, keepsake, reminder. **3** *a book token* =**voucher**, coupon. **4** *a telephone token* =**counter**, disc, jetton, chip.
▶ adjective **1** *a one-day token strike* =**symbolic**, emblematic, indicative; peppercorn. **2** *the practice now meets only token resistance* =**perfunctory**, slight, nominal, minimal, minor, mild, superficial.

tolerable ▶ adjective **1** *a tolerable noise level* =**bearable**, endurable, supportable, acceptable. **2** *he had a tolerable voice* =**fairly good**, passable, adequate, all right, acceptable, satisfactory, not (too) bad, average, fair; mediocre, middling, ordinary, unexceptional; *informal* OK, so-so, nothing to write home about, no great shakes.
−OPPOSITES unacceptable.

tolerance ▶ noun **1** *an attitude of tolerance towards people* =**acceptance**; open-mindedness, broad-mindedness, forbearance; patience, charity, understanding. **2** *the plant's tolerance of pollution* =**endurance**, resilience, resistance, immunity. **3** *a 1% maximum tolerance in measurement* =**deviation**, variation, play; inaccuracy, imprecision.

tolerant ▶ adjective =**open-minded**, forbearing, broad-minded, liberal, unprejudiced, unbiased; patient, long-suffering, understanding, charitable, lenient, easy-going.
−OPPOSITES intolerant.

tolerate ▶ verb **1** *a regime unwilling to tolerate dissent* =**allow**, permit, condone, accept, swallow, countenance; *formal* brook. **2** *he couldn't tolerate her moods any longer* =**endure**, put up with, bear, take, stand, support, stomach; *informal* hack, abide; *Brit. informal* stick, wear, be doing with.

toleration ▶ noun =**acceptance**, endurance; forbearance, open-mindedness, broad-mindedness; patience, charity, understanding.

toll¹ ▶ noun **1** *a motorway toll* =**charge**, fee, payment, levy, tariff, tax. **2** *the toll of dead and injured* =**number**, count, tally, total, sum. **3** *the toll on the environment has been high* =**adverse effect(s)**, detriment, harm, damage, injury, hurt; cost, price, loss, disadvantage.

toll² ▶ verb *I heard the bell toll* =**ring (out)**, chime, strike, peal; sound, clang, resound, reverberate; *literary* knell.

tomb ▶ noun =**burial chamber**, sepulchre, mausoleum, vault, crypt, undercroft, catacomb; grave.

> **WORD LINKS**
>
> *relating to a tomb:* **sepulchral**

tombstone ▶ noun =**gravestone**, headstone; memorial, monument.

tome ▶ noun =**volume**, book, work, opus, publication, title.

tomfoolery ▶ noun =**silliness**, clowning, capers, antics, pranks, tricks, buffoonery, nonsense, horseplay, mischief; *informal* larks, shenanigans.

tone ▶ noun **1** *the tone of the tuba* =**timbre**, sound, voice, colour, tonality. **2** *his friendly tone* =**intonation**, modulation, accentuation. **3** *the impatient tone of his letter* =**mood**, air, feel, flavour, note, attitude, character, temper; tenor, vein, drift, gist. **4** *a dialling tone* =**note**, signal, bleep. **5** *tones of lavender and rose* =**shade**, colour, hue, tint, tinge.
▶ verb *the shirt toned well with her cream skirt* =**harmonize**, go, blend, coordinate, team; match, suit, complement.
■ **tone something down 1** *the colour needs to be toned down a bit* =**soften**, lighten, mute, subdue. **2** *the papers refused to tone down their criticism* =**moderate**, modify, modulate, mitigate, temper, dampen, soften.

tongue ▶ noun **1** *a foreign tongue* =**language**, dialect, patois, vernacular; *informal* lingo. **2** *her sharp tongue* =**way/manner of speaking**, speech, parlance.

> **WORD LINKS**
>
> *relating to the tongue:* **lingual**

tongue-tied ▶ adjective =**lost for words**, speechless, dumbstruck; mute, silent; *informal* mum.
−OPPOSITES loquacious.

tonic ▶ noun **1** *ginseng can be used as a tonic* =**stimulant**, restorative, refresher; *informal* pick-me-up, bracer. **2** *the change of scene was a tonic* =**stimulant**, boost, fillip; *informal* shot in the arm, pick-me-up.

too ▶ adverb **1** *invasion would be too risky* =**excessively**, overly, unduly, immoderately, inordinately, unreasonably, extremely, very. **2** *he was unhappy, too, you know* = **also**, as well, in addition, into the bargain, besides, furthermore, moreover.

tool ▶ noun **1** *garden tools* = **implement**, utensil, instrument, device, apparatus, gadget, appliance, machine, contrivance, contraption; *informal* gizmo. **2** *the beautiful Estella is Miss Havisham's tool* = **puppet**, pawn, creature; minion, lackey; *informal* stooge.

▶ verb *red leather, tooled in gold* = **ornament**, embellish, decorate, work.

tooth ▶ noun = **fang**, tusk; *informal* gnasher; *Brit. informal* pearly white.

> **WORD LINKS**
>
> *relating to teeth:* **dental**
> *study of teeth:* **odontology**

top ▶ noun **1** *the top of the cliff* = **summit**, peak, pinnacle, crest, crown, brow, head, tip, apex, vertex. **2** *the top of the table* = **upper part**, upper surface. **3** *the top of the coffee jar* = **lid**, cap, cover, stopper. **4** *a short-sleeved top* = **sweater**, jumper, jersey, sweat shirt; T-shirt, shirt, blouse. **5** *he was at the top of his profession* = **high point**, height, peak, pinnacle, zenith, acme, culmination, climax, crowning point; prime.
– OPPOSITES bottom, base.

▶ adjective **1** *the top floor* = **highest**, topmost, uppermost. **2** *top scientists* = **foremost**, leading, principal, pre-eminent, greatest, best, finest, elite; *informal* topnotch. **3** *the organization's top management* = **chief**, principal, main, leading, highest, ruling, commanding, most powerful, most important. **4** *a top hotel* = **prime**, excellent, superb, superior, choice, select, first-rate, grade A, best, finest, premier; *informal* A1, top-notch. **5** *they are travelling at top speed* = **maximum**, greatest, utmost.
– OPPOSITES bottom, lowest, minimum.

▶ verb **1** *sales are expected to top £1 billion* = **exceed**, surpass, go beyond, better, beat, outstrip, outdo, outshine, eclipse. **2** *their CD is currently topping the charts* = **lead**, head. **3** *mousse topped with cream* = **cover**, cap, coat; finish, garnish.
■ **top something up** = **fill**, refill, refresh, freshen, replenish, recharge, resupply.

topic ▶ noun = **subject**, theme, issue, matter, point, question, concern, argu-

ment, thesis, text, keynote.

topical ▶ adjective = **current**, up to date, up to the minute, contemporary, recent, relevant; in the news.
– OPPOSITES out of date.

topmost ▶ adjective **1** *the tree's topmost branches* = **highest**, top, uppermost. **2** *the topmost authority on the subject* = **foremost**, leading, principal, premier, prime, top, greatest, best, supreme, pre-eminent, outstanding, main, chief; *N. Amer.* ranking; *informal* number-one.

topple ▶ verb **1** *she toppled over* = **fall**, tumble, overbalance, overturn, tip, keel; lose one's balance. **2** *protesters toppled a statue* = **knock over**, upset, push over, tip over, upend. **3** *a plot to topple the government* = **overthrow**, oust, unseat, overturn, bring down, defeat, get rid of, dislodge, eject.

torch ▶ noun **1** *an electric torch* = **flashlight**. **2** *(historical) a flaming torch* = **firebrand**, brand.

torment ▶ noun **1** *emotional torment* = **agony**, suffering, torture, pain, anguish, misery, distress, affliction, trauma, wretchedness. **2** *it was a torment to see him like that* = **ordeal**, affliction, scourge, curse, plague, bane; sorrow, tribulation.

▶ verb **1** *she was tormented by shame* = **torture**, afflict, rack, harrow, plague, haunt, distress, agonize. **2** *she began to torment the boys* = **tease**, taunt, bait, harass, provoke, goad, plague, bother, trouble, persecute; *informal* needle.

torn ▶ adjective **1** *a torn shirt* = **ripped**, rent, cut, slit; ragged, tattered. **2** *she was torn between the two options* = **wavering**, vacillating, irresolute, dithering, uncertain, unsure, undecided, in two minds.

tornado ▶ noun = **whirlwind**, cyclone, typhoon, storm, hurricane, windstorm; *N. Amer. informal* twister.

torrent ▶ noun **1** *a torrent of water* = **flood**, deluge, inundation, spate, cascade, rush, stream, current, flow, overflow, tide. **2** *a torrent of abuse* = **outburst**, outpouring, stream, flood, volley, barrage, tide, spate.
– OPPOSITES trickle.

torrential ▶ adjective = **copious**, heavy, teeming, severe, relentless.

torrid ▶ adjective **1** *a torrid summer* = **hot**, dry, scorching, searing, blazing, blistering, sweltering, burning; *informal* boiling,

baking. **2** *a torrid affair* =**passionate**, ardent, lustful, amorous; *informal* steamy, sizzling.
–OPPOSITES cold.

tortuous ▸ adjective **1** *a tortuous route* =**twisting**, winding, zigzag, sinuous, snaky, meandering, serpentine. **2** *a tortuous argument* =**convoluted**, complicated, complex, labyrinthine, involved, Byzantine, lengthy.
–OPPOSITES straight, straightforward.

torture ▸ noun **1** *the torture of political prisoners* =**abuse**, ill-treatment, maltreatment, cruel treatment or punishment. **2** *the torture of losing a loved one* =**torment**, agony, suffering, pain, anguish, misery, distress, heartbreak, trauma, wretchedness.
▸ verb **1** *the forces routinely tortured suspects* =**abuse**, ill-treat, mistreat, maltreat, persecute; *informal* work over. **2** *he was tortured by grief* =**torment**, rack, afflict, harrow, plague, agonize.

toss ▸ verb **1** *he tossed his tools into the boot* =**throw**, hurl, fling, sling, cast, pitch, lob, propel, project, launch; *informal* heave, chuck, bung. **2** *he tossed a coin* =**flip**, flick, spin. **3** *the ship tossed about on the waves* =**pitch**, lurch, rock, roll, plunge, reel, list, keel, sway. **4** *toss the ingredients together* =**shake**, stir, turn, mix, combine.

tot¹ ▸ noun **1** =**infant**, baby, toddler, child, little one, mite; *Scottish* bairn. **2** *a tot of rum* =**dram**, drink, nip, drop, slug; *informal* shot, finger, snifter.

tot² ▸ verb **1** *he totted up some figures* =**add**, total, count, calculate, compute, reckon, tally. **2** *we've totted up 8 victories* =**accumulate**, build up, amass, accrue.

total ▸ adjective **1** *the total cost* =**entire**, complete, whole, full, comprehensive, combined, aggregate, gross, overall. **2** *a total disaster* =**complete**, utter, absolute, thorough, perfect, downright, out-and-out, outright, sheer, unmitigated; *Brit. informal* right.
–OPPOSITES partial.
▸ noun *a total of £16* =**sum**, aggregate; whole, entirety, totality.
▸ verb **1** *the prize money totalled £33,050* =**add up to**, amount to, come to, run to, make, work out as. **2** *he totalled up his score* =**add (up)**, count, reckon, tot up, compute, work out.

totalitarian ▸ adjective =**autocratic**, undemocratic, one-party, dictatorial,

tyrannical, despotic, fascist, oppressive; authoritarian, absolutist.
–OPPOSITES democratic.

totality ▸ noun =**entirety**, whole, total, aggregate, sum.

totally ▸ adverb =**completely**, entirely, wholly, thoroughly, fully, utterly, absolutely, perfectly, unreservedly, unconditionally, downright; in every way, one hundred per cent, every inch, to the hilt, all the way; *informal* dead.
–OPPOSITES partly.

totter ▸ verb **1** *he tottered off down the road* =**teeter**, stagger, wobble, stumble, shuffle, shamble, toddle; reel. **2** *the foundations began to heave and totter* =**shake**, sway, tremble, quiver, teeter, shudder, judder, rock, quake.

touch ▸ verb **1** *his shoes were touching the bed* =**be in contact with**, meet, join, connect with, converge with, be contiguous with, be against. **2** *he touched her cheek* =**press lightly**, tap, pat; feel, stroke, fondle, caress, pet; brush, graze. **3** *sales touched twenty grand* =**reach**, attain, come to, make; rise to, soar to; sink to, plummet to; *informal* hit. **4** *nobody can touch him when he's on form* =**compare with**, be on a par with, equal, match, be in the same class/league as, parallel, rival, come/get close to, measure up to; better, beat; *informal* hold a candle to. **5** *you're not supposed to touch the computer* =**handle**, hold, pick up, move, use; meddle with, play about with, fiddle with, interfere with, tamper with, disturb, lay a finger on. **6** *Lisa felt touched by her kindness* =**affect**, move.
▸ noun **1** *her touch on his shoulder* =**tap**, pat; stroke, caress; brush, graze. **2** *his political touch* =**skill**, expertise, dexterity, deftness, adroitness, adeptness, ability, talent, flair, facility, proficiency, knack. **3** *there was a touch of bitterness in her voice | add a touch of vinegar* =**trace**, bit, suggestion, suspicion, hint, scintilla, tinge, overtone, undertone; dash, taste, spot, drop, dab, soupçon. **4** *the gas lights are a nice touch* =**detail**, feature, point; addition, accessory. **5** *have you been in touch with him?* =**contact**, communication, correspondence.
■ **touch down** =**land**, alight, come down, put down, arrive.
■ **touch on/upon 1** *many television programmes have touched on the subject* =**refer to**, mention, comment on, remark on, bring up, raise, broach, allude to; cover,

deal with. **2** *a self-confident manner touching on the arrogant* =**come close to**, verge on, border on, approach.

■ **touch something up 1** *these paints are handy for touching up small areas* =**repaint**, retouch, patch up, fix up; renovate, refurbish, revamp; *informal* do up. **2** *touch up your CV and improve your interview skills* =**improve**, enhance, make better, refine; *informal* tweak.

> **WORD LINKS**
>
> *relating to touch:* **tactile**

touch-and-go ▸ adjective =**uncertain**, precarious, risky, hazardous, dangerous, critical, suspenseful, cliffhanging.
–OPPOSITES certain.

touched ▸ adjective =**affected**, moved.

touching ▸ adjective =**moving**, affecting, heart-warming, emotional, emotive, tender, sentimental; poignant, sad, tear-jerking.

touchstone ▸ noun =**criterion**, standard, yardstick, benchmark, barometer, litmus test; measure, point of reference, norm, gauge, test, guide, exemplar, model, pattern.

touchy ▸ adjective **1** *she can be touchy* =**sensitive**, oversensitive, hypersensitive, easily offended, thin-skinned, highly strung, tense; irritable, tetchy, testy, crotchety, peevish, querulous, bad-tempered, petulant; *informal* snappy, ratty; *N. Amer. informal* cranky. **2** *a touchy subject* =**delicate**, sensitive, tricky, ticklish, embarrassing, awkward, difficult; contentious, controversial.
–OPPOSITES affable.

tough ▸ adjective **1** *tough leather* =**durable**, strong, resilient, sturdy, rugged, solid, stout, robust, hard-wearing, long-lasting, heavy-duty, well built, made to last. **2** *the steak was tough* =**chewy**, leathery, gristly, stringy, fibrous. **3** *he'll survive—he's pretty tough* =**robust**, resilient, strong, hardy, rugged, fit; *informal* hard; *dated* stalwart. **4** *tough sentencing for offenders* =**strict**, stern, severe, stringent, rigorous, hard, firm, hard-hitting, uncompromising. **5** *the training was pretty tough* =**arduous**, onerous, strenuous, gruelling, exacting, difficult, demanding, hard, heavy, taxing, tiring, exhausting, punishing, laborious. **6** *tough questions* =**difficult**, hard, knotty, thorny, tricky.

–OPPOSITES soft, weak, easy.

▸ noun *a gang of toughs* =**ruffian**, thug, hoodlum, hooligan, bully boy; *Brit.* rough; *informal* roughneck, heavy, bruiser; *Brit. informal* yob.

toughen ▸ verb **1** *the process toughens the wood fibres* =**strengthen**, fortify, reinforce, harden, temper, anneal. **2** *measures to toughen up discipline* =**make stricter**, make more severe, stiffen, tighten up.

tour ▸ noun **1** *a three-day walking tour* =**trip**, excursion, journey, expedition, jaunt, outing; trek, safari. **2** *a tour of the factory* =**visit**, inspection, walkabout. **3** *his tour of duty in Ulster* =**stint**, stretch, spell, turn, assignment, period of service.

▸ verb **1** *this hotel is well placed for touring Devon* =**travel round**, explore, holiday in; *informal* do. **2** *the prince toured a local factory* =**visit**, go round, walk round, inspect.

tourist ▸ noun =**holidaymaker**, traveller, sightseer, visitor, backpacker, globetrotter, tripper; *N. Amer.* vacationer, out-of-towner.
–OPPOSITES local.

tournament ▸ noun =**competition**, contest, championship, meeting, meet, event, match, fixture.

tousled ▸ adjective =**untidy**, dishevelled, wind-blown, messy, disordered, disarranged, messed up, rumpled, uncombed, ungroomed, tangled, wild, unkempt; *informal* mussed up.
–OPPOSITES neat, tidy.

tout ▸ verb **1** *street merchants were touting their wares* =**peddle**, sell, hawk, offer for sale; *informal* flog. **2** *minicab drivers were touting for business* =**solicit**, seek, drum up; ask, petition, appeal, canvas. **3** *he's being touted as the next Scotland manager* =**recommend**, speak of, talk of; predict; *Brit.* tip.

tow ▸ verb =**pull**, haul, drag, draw, tug, lug.
■ **in tow** =**in attendance**, by one's side, in one's charge; accompanying, following.

towards ▸ preposition **1** *they were driving towards her flat* =**in the direction of**, to; on the way to, on the road to, en route for. **2** *towards evening dark clouds gathered* =**just before**, shortly before, near, around, approaching, close to, coming to, getting on for. **3** *her attitude* towards politics =**with regard to**, in/with regard to, respecting, in relation to, concerning, about, apropos. **4** *a grant towards the cost* =**as a contribution to**, for, to help with.

tower ▸ noun *a church tower* =**steeple**, spire; minaret; turret; bell tower, belfry, campanile.
▸ verb **1** *snow-capped peaks towered over the valley* =**soar**, rise, rear; overshadow, overhang, hang over, dominate. **2** *he towered over most other theologians* =**dominate**, overshadow, outshine, eclipse, be head and shoulders above.

towering ▸ adjective **1** *a towering sky-scraper* =**high**, tall, lofty, soaring, sky-high, sky-scraping, multi-storey; giant, gigantic, enormous, huge, massive; *informal* ginormous. **2** *a towering intellect* =**outstanding**, pre-eminent, leading, foremost, finest, top, surpassing, supreme, great, incomparable, unrivalled, unsurpassed, peerless. **3** *a towering rage* =**extreme**, fierce, terrible, intense, overpowering, mighty, violent, vehement, passionate.

town ▸ noun =**urban area**, conurbation, municipality; city, metropolis; *Brit.* borough; *Scottish* burgh.
–OPPOSITES country.

> WORD LINKS
>
> *relating to a town:* **municipal, urban**

toxic ▸ adjective =**poisonous**, virulent, noxious, dangerous, harmful, injurious, pernicious.
–OPPOSITES harmless.

toy ▸ noun **1** *a cuddly toy* =**plaything**, game. **2** *an executive toy* =**gadget**, device; trinket, knick-knack; *informal* gizmo.
▸ adjective **1** *a toy gun* =**model**, imitation, replica; miniature. **2** *a toy poodle* =**miniature**, small, tiny, diminutive, dwarf, midget, pygmy.
■ **toy with 1** *I was toying with the idea of writing a book* =**think about**, consider, flirt with, entertain the possibility of; *informal* kick around. **2** *Adam toyed with his glasses* =**fiddle with**, play with, fidget with, twiddle; finger. **3** *she toyed with her food* =**nibble**, pick at, peck at.

trace ▸ verb **1** *police hope to trace the owner* =**track down**, find, discover, detect, unearth, turn up, hunt down, ferret out, run to ground. **2** *she traced a pattern in the sand* =**draw**, outline, mark. **3** *the analysis traces out the consequences of such beliefs* =**outline**, map out, sketch out, delineate, depict, show, indicate.
▸ noun **1** *no trace had been found of the missing plane* =**vestige**, sign, mark, indication, evidence, clue; remains, remnant. **2** *a trace of bitterness crept into her voice* =**bit**, touch, hint, suggestion, suspicion, shadow, whiff; drop, dash, tinge; *informal* smidgen, tad. **3** *the ground was hard and they left no traces* =**trail**, tracks, marks, prints, footprints; spoor.

track ▸ noun **1** *a gravel track* =**path**, pathway, footpath, lane, trail, route, way, course. **2** *the final lap of the track* =**course**, racecourse, racetrack; velodrome; *Brit.* circuit. **3** *he found the tracks of a fox* =**traces**, marks, prints, footprints, trail, spoor. **4** *commuters had to walk along the tracks* =**rail**, line. **5** *the album's title track* =**song**, recording, number, piece.
▸ verb *he tracked a bear for 40 km* =**follow**, trail, trace, pursue, shadow, stalk; *informal* tail.
■ **keep track of** =**monitor**, follow, keep up with, keep an eye on; keep in touch with, keep up to date with; *informal* keep tabs on.
■ **track someone/something down** =**discover**, find, detect, hunt down/out, unearth, uncover, turn up, dig up, ferret out, bring to light, run to ground.

tract¹ ▸ noun *large tracts of land* =**area**, region, expanse, sweep, stretch, extent, belt, swathe, zone.

tract² ▸ noun *a political tract* =**treatise**, essay, article, paper, work, monograph, disquisition, dissertation, thesis; pamphlet, booklet, leaflet.

tractable ▸ adjective =**malleable**, manageable, amenable, pliable, governable, yielding, complaisant, compliant, persuadable, accommodating, docile, biddable, obedient, submissive, meek.
–OPPOSITES recalcitrant.

traction ▸ noun =**grip**, purchase, friction, adhesion.

trade ▸ noun **1** *the illicit trade in stolen cattle* =**commerce**, buying and selling, dealing, traffic, business, marketing, merchandising; dealings, transactions. **2** *the glazier's trade* =**craft**, occupation, job, career, profession, business, line (of work), métier, walk of life, field; work, employment.
▸ verb **1** *he made his fortune trading in diamonds* =**deal**, buy and sell, traffic, market, merchandise, peddle; *informal* hawk,

flog. **2** *the business is trading at a loss* =**operate**, run, do business. **3** *I traded the old machine for a newer model* =**swap**, exchange, switch; barter.
■ **trade on** =**exploit**, take advantage of, capitalize on, profit from, use; milk; *informal* cash in on.

WORD LINKS

relating to trade: **mercantile**

trademark ▸ noun **1** *the company's trademark* =**logo**, emblem, sign, mark, stamp, symbol, device, badge, crest, monogram, colophon; trade name, brand name, proprietary name. **2** *it had all the trademarks of a Mafia hit* =**characteristic**, hallmark, sign, trait, quality, attribute, feature.

trader ▸ noun =**dealer**, merchant, buyer, seller, marketeer, merchandiser, broker, agent; distributor, vendor, purveyor, supplier, trafficker; shopkeeper, retailer, wholesaler.

tradesman, tradeswoman
▸ noun **1** *tradesmen standing outside their stores* =**shopkeeper**, retailer, vendor, wholesaler; *N. Amer.* storekeeper. **2** *a qualified tradesman* =**craftsman**, workman, artisan.

tradition ▸ noun **1** *during a maiden speech, by tradition, everyone keeps absolutely silent* =**historical convention**, unwritten law; oral history, lore, folklore. **2** *an age-old tradition* =**custom**, practice, convention, ritual, observance, way, usage, habit, institution; *formal* praxis.

traditional ▸ adjective **1** *traditional Christmas fare* =**long-established**, customary, time-honoured, established, classic, wonted, accustomed, standard, regular, normal, conventional, usual, orthodox, habitual, ritual; age-old. **2** *traditional beliefs* =**handed-down**, folk, unwritten, oral.

traffic ▸ noun **1** *they might be stuck in traffic* =**traffic jams**, congestion, gridlock, tailbacks, hold-ups, queues; *informal* snarl-ups. **2** *the increased use of railways for goods traffic* =**transport**, freight, conveyancing, shipping. **3** *the illegal traffic in stolen art* =**trade**, dealing, commerce, business, buying and selling; smuggling, bootlegging, black market; dealings, transactions.
▸ verb *he confessed to trafficking in ivory* =**trade**, deal, do business, buy and sell; smuggle, bootleg; *informal* run.

tragedy ▸ noun =**disaster**, calamity, catastrophe, cataclysm, misfortune, reverse, vicissitude, adversity.

tragic ▸ adjective **1** *a tragic accident* =**disastrous**, calamitous, catastrophic, cataclysmic, devastating, terrible, dreadful, awful, appalling, horrendous; fatal. **2** *a tragic tale* =**sad**, unhappy, pathetic, moving, distressing, painful, harrowing, heart-rending, piteous, wretched, sorry. **3** *a tragic waste of talent* =**dreadful**, terrible, awful, deplorable, lamentable, regrettable; *formal* grievous.
–OPPOSITES fortunate, happy.

trail ▸ noun **1** *a trail of clues | a trail of devastation* =**series**, string, chain, succession, sequence; aftermath. **2** *wolves on the trail of their prey* =**track**, spoor, path, scent; traces, marks, signs, prints, footprints. **3** *the plane's vapour trail* =**wake**, tail, stream. **4** *a trail of ants* =**line**, column, train, file, procession, string, chain, convoy; queue. **5** *country parks with nature trails* =**path**, pathway, way, footpath, track, course, route.
▸ verb **1** *her robe trailed along the ground* =**drag**, sweep, be drawn; dangle, hang (down). **2** *the roses grew wild, their stems trailing over the banks* =**hang**, droop, fall, spill, cascade. **3** *Sharpe suspected they were trailing him* =**follow**, pursue, track, shadow, stalk, hunt (down); *informal* tail. **4** *the defending champions were trailing 10–5* =**lose**, be down, be behind, lag behind. **5** *I hate trailing round the shops* =**trudge**, plod, drag oneself, traipse, trek; *N. Amer. informal* schlep. **6** *her voice trailed off* =**fade**, tail off/away, grow faint, die away, dwindle, subside, peter out, fizzle out.

train ▸ verb **1** *an engineer trained in remote-sensing techniques* =**instruct**, teach, coach, tutor, school, educate, prime, drill, ground. **2** *she's training to be a hairdresser* =**study**, learn, prepare, take instruction. **3** *with the Olympics in mind, athletes are training hard* =**exercise**, work out, get into shape, practise. **4** *she trained the gun on him* =**aim**, point, direct, level, focus.
▸ noun **1** *a minister and his train of attendants* =**retinue**, entourage, cortège, following, staff, household, court, suite, retainers. **2** *a train of elephants* =**procession**, line, file, column, convoy, cavalcade, caravan, succession. **3** *a bizarre train of events* =**chain**, string, series, sequence, succession, set, course.

trainer ▸ noun =**coach**, instructor, teacher, tutor; handler.

training ▸ noun **1** *in-house training for staff* =**instruction**, teaching, coaching, tuition, tutoring, schooling, education. **2** *four months' hard training before the match* =**exercise**, working out; practice, preparation.

traipse ▸ verb =**trudge**, trek, tramp, trail, plod, drag oneself, slog; *N. Amer. informal* schlep.

trait ▸ noun =**characteristic**, attribute, feature, quality, property; habit, custom, mannerism, idiosyncrasy, peculiarity, quirk, oddity, foible.

traitor ▸ noun =**betrayer**, back-stabber, double-crosser, renegade, Judas, quisling, fifth columnist; turncoat, defector; *informal* snake in the grass.

traitorous ▸ adjective =**treacherous**, disloyal, treasonous, back-stabbing; double-crossing, unfaithful, two-faced, duplicitous, false.
–OPPOSITES loyal.

trajectory ▸ noun =**course**, path, route, track, line, orbit.

tramp ▸ verb **1** *men were tramping through the shrubbery* =**trudge**, plod, stamp, trample, lumber, clomp, stomp; *informal* traipse. **2** *he spent ten days tramping through the jungle* =**trek**, slog, footslog, trudge, drag oneself, walk, hike, march; *informal* traipse; *Brit. informal* yomp; *N. Amer. informal* schlep.
▸ noun **1** *a dirty old tramp* =**vagrant**, vagabond, homeless person, down-and-out; traveller, drifter; beggar, mendicant; *N. Amer.* hobo; *N. Amer. informal* bum. **2** *the tramp of boots* =**footstep**, step, footfall, tread, stomp. **3** *a tramp round York* =**trek**, slog, trudge, hike, march, walk; *Brit. informal* yomp; *N. Amer. informal* schlep.

trample ▸ verb **1** *someone had trampled on the tulips* =**tread**, stamp, walk over; squash, crush, flatten. **2** *he trampled over their feelings* =**treat with contempt**, ride roughshod over, disregard, set at naught, show no consideration for.

trance ▸ noun =**daze**, stupor, hypnotic state, dream.

tranquil ▸ adjective **1** *a tranquil village* =**peaceful**, calm, restful, quiet, still, relaxing, undisturbed. **2** *Martha smiled, perfectly tranquil* =**calm**, serene, relaxed, unruffled, unperturbed, unflustered, untroubled, composed; equable, placid;

informal unflappable.
–OPPOSITES busy, excitable.

tranquillity ▸ noun **1** *the tranquillity of the countryside* =**peace**, restfulness, repose, calm, quiet, stillness. **2** *the incident jolted her out of her tranquillity* =**composure**, calmness, serenity; equanimity, equability, placidity; *informal* cool.

tranquillize ▸ verb =**sedate**, narcotize, drug.

tranquillizer ▸ noun =**sedative**, barbiturate, calmative, narcotic, opiate; *informal* trank, downer.
–OPPOSITES stimulant.

transact ▸ verb =**conduct**, carry out, negotiate, do, perform, execute.

transaction ▸ noun **1** *property transactions* =**deal**, undertaking, arrangement, bargain, negotiation, agreement, settlement; proceedings. **2** *the transactions of the Historical Society* =**proceedings**, report, record(s), minutes, account. **3** *the transaction of government business* =**conduct**, carrying out, negotiation, performance, execution.

transcend ▸ verb **1** *an issue that transcended party politics* =**go beyond**, rise above, cut across. **2** *his military exploits far transcended those of his predecessors* =**surpass**, exceed, beat, top, cap, outdo, outclass, outstrip, leave behind, outshine, eclipse, overshadow.

transcendence ▸ noun =**excellence**, supremacy, incomparability, matchlessness, peerlessness, magnificence.

transcendent ▸ adjective **1** *a transcendent level of knowledge* =**mystical**, spiritual; metaphysical. **2** *a transcendent genius* =**incomparable**, matchless, peerless, unrivalled, inimitable, unparalleled, unequalled, second to none, unsurpassed, nonpareil; *formal* unexampled.

transcribe ▸ verb **1** *each interview was taped and transcribed* =**write out**, copy out, put on paper. **2** *a person who can take and transcribe shorthand* =**transliterate**, interpret, translate.

transcript ▸ noun =**written version**, printed version, text, transliteration, record.

transfer ▸ verb **1** *the hostages were transferred to a safe house* =**move**, convey, take, bring, shift, remove, carry, transport. **2** *the property was transferred to his* *wife* = **hand over**, pass on, make over, turn over, sign over, consign, devolve, assign.

▸ noun *his transfer to hospital* = **move**, conveyance, relocation, removal.

transfigure ▸ verb = **transform**, transmute, change, alter, metamorphose; *humorous* transmogrify.

transfix ▸ verb 1 *he was transfixed by the images* = **mesmerize**, hypnotize, spellbind, bewitch, captivate, entrance, enthral, fascinate, enrapture, grip, rivet. 2 *a mouse is transfixed by the owl's talons* = **impale**, stab, spear, pierce, spike, skewer, gore, stick, run through.

transform ▸ verb = **change**, alter, convert, metamorphose, transfigure, transmute; revolutionize, overhaul; remodel, reshape, remould, redo, reconstruct, rebuild, reorganize, rearrange, rework, revamp; *humorous* transmogrify.

transformation ▸ noun = **change**, alteration, conversion, metamorphosis, transfiguration, transmutation; revolution, overhaul; remodelling, reshaping, remoulding, redoing, reconstruction, rebuilding, reorganization, rearrangement, reworking, revamp; *humorous* transmogrification.

transgress ▸ verb 1 *if they transgress the punishment is harsh* = **misbehave**, break the law, err, fall from grace, sin, do wrong, go astray; *archaic* trespass. 2 *she had transgressed an unwritten law* = **infringe**, breach, contravene, disobey, defy, violate, break, flout.

transgression ▸ noun 1 *a punishment for past transgressions* = **offence**, crime, sin, wrong, wrongdoing, misdemeanour, misdeed, lawbreaking; error, lapse; *archaic* trespass. 2 *Adam's transgression of God's law* = **infringement**, breach, contravention, violation, defiance, disobedience, non-observance.

transgressor ▸ noun = **wrongdoer**, offender, miscreant, lawbreaker, criminal, villain, felon, malefactor, culprit; sinner; *archaic* trespasser.

transient ▸ adjective = **transitory**, temporary, short-lived, short-term, ephemeral, impermanent, brief, short, momentary, fleeting, passing. –OPPOSITES permanent.

transit ▸ noun = **transport**, movement, conveyance, shipment, haulage, freightage, carriage. ■ **in transit** = **en route**, on the journey,

on the way, along/on the road.

transition ▸ noun = **change**, passage, move, transformation, conversion, metamorphosis, alteration, changeover, shift, switch.

transitional ▸ adjective 1 *a transitional period* = **intermediate**, interim, changeover; changing, fluid, unsettled. 2 *the transitional government* = **interim**, temporary, provisional, pro tem, acting, caretaker.

transitory ▸ adjective = **transient**, temporary, brief, short, short-lived, short-term, impermanent, ephemeral, momentary, fleeting, passing. –OPPOSITES permanent.

translate ▸ verb 1 *the German original had been translated into English* = **render**, put, express, convert, change; transcribe, transliterate. 2 *translate the jargon into normal English* = **render**, paraphrase, reword, rephrase, convert, decipher, decode, gloss, explain. 3 *ideas cannot always be translated into movies* = **change**, convert, transform, alter, adapt, turn, transmute; *humorous* transmogrify.

translation ▸ noun 1 *the translation of the Bible into English* = **rendition**, conversion; transcription, transliteration. 2 *the translation of these policies into practice* = **conversion**, change, transformation, alteration, adaptation, transmutation; *humorous* transmogrification.

translucent ▸ adjective = **semi-transparent**, pellucid, limpid, clear; diaphanous, gossamer, sheer. –OPPOSITES opaque.

transmission ▸ noun 1 *the transmission of knowledge* = **transference**, communication, conveyance; dissemination, spreading, circulation. 2 *the transmission of the film* = **broadcasting**, relaying, airing, televising. 3 *a live transmission* = **broadcast**, programme, show.

transmit ▸ verb 1 *the use of computers to transmit information* = **transfer**, pass on, hand on, communicate, convey, impart, channel, carry, relay, dispatch; disseminate, spread, circulate. 2 *the programme will be transmitted on Sunday* = **broadcast**, relay, send out, air, televise.

transmute ▸ verb = **change**, alter, adapt, transform, convert, metamorphose, translate; *humorous* transmogrify.

transparency ▸ noun 1 *the transparency of the glass* = **translucency**, limpidity, glassiness, clearness, clarity. 2 *colour* *transparencies* =**slide**, diapositive.

transparent ▶ adjective **1** *transparent blue water* =**clear**, see-through, translucent, pellucid, limpid, glassy. **2** *fine transparent fabrics* =**see-through**, sheer, filmy, gauzy, diaphanous. **3** *the symbolism of this myth is transparent* =**obvious**, unambiguous, unequivocal, clear, plain, apparent, unmistakable, manifest, conspicuous, patent, indisputable, evident, undisguised.
–OPPOSITES opaque, obscure.

transpire ▶ verb **1** *it transpired that her family had moved* =**become known**, emerge, come to light, be revealed, turn out, come out, be discovered. **2** *I'm going to find out exactly what transpired* =**happen**, occur, take place, arise, come about, turn up, befall; *literary* come to pass.

transplant ▶ verb **1** *it was proposed to transplant the club to the vacant site* =**transfer**, move, remove, shift, relocate, take. **2** *the seedlings should be transplanted in pots* =**replant**, repot, relocate. **3** *kidneys must be transplanted within 48 hours of removal* =**transfer**, implant.

transport ▶ verb **1** *the blocks were transported by lorry* =**convey**, carry, take, transfer, move, shift, send, deliver, bear, ship, ferry; *informal* cart. **2** *he was convicted of theft and transported* =**banish**, exile, deport, expatriate, extradite. **3** *she was completely transported by the excitement* =**thrill**, delight, carry away, enrapture, entrance, enchant, enthral, electrify, captivate, bewitch, fascinate, spellbind, charm.
▶ noun **1** *alternative forms of transport* =**conveyance**; vehicle. **2** *the transport of crude oil* =**conveyance**, carriage, freight, shipment, haulage; transit. **3** *transports of delight* =**rapture**, ecstasy, elation, exaltation, exhilaration, euphoria, bliss, (seventh) heaven, paradise, high; *informal* cloud nine.

transpose ▶ verb **1** *the blue and black plates were transposed* =**interchange**, exchange, switch, swap (round), reverse. **2** *the themes are transposed from the sphere of love to that of work* =**transfer**, shift, relocate, transplant, move, displace.

transverse ▶ adjective =**crosswise**, horizontal, diagonal, oblique.

trap ▶ noun **1** *an animal caught in a trap* =**snare**, net, mesh, gin; *N. Amer.* deadfall.

2 *the question was set as a trap* =**trick**, ploy, ruse, deception, subterfuge; *informal* set-up.
▶ verb **1** *police trapped the men* =**snare**, entrap; capture, catch, corner, ambush. **2** *a rat trapped in a barn* =**confine**, cut off, corner, shut in, pen in, hem in; imprison, hold captive. **3** *I hoped to trap him into an admission* =**trick**, dupe, deceive, lure, inveigle, beguile, fool, hoodwink.

trappings ▶ plural noun =**accessories**, accoutrements, appurtenances, trimmings, frills, accompaniments, extras, ornamentation, adornment, decoration; regalia, panoply, paraphernalia, finery.

trash ▶ noun **1** *(N. Amer.) the entrance was blocked with trash* =**rubbish**, refuse, waste, litter, junk, detritus; *N. Amer.* garbage. **2** *(informal) they read trash* =**rubbish**, nonsense, trivia, pulp (fiction), pap; *N. Amer.* garbage; *informal* drivel, dreck.
▶ verb *(informal) the apartment had been trashed* =**wreck**, ruin, destroy, wreak havoc on, devastate; vandalize; *informal* total.

trauma ▶ noun **1** *the trauma of divorce* =**shock**, upheaval, distress, stress, strain, pain, anguish, suffering, upset, agony, misery, sorrow, grief, heartache; ordeal, trial, tribulation. **2** *trauma to the liver* =**injury**, damage, wound.

traumatic ▶ adjective =**disturbing**, shocking, distressing, upsetting, heartbreaking, painful, agonizing, hurtful, stressful, awful, terrible, devastating, harrowing.

travel ▶ verb **1** *he spent much of his time travelling* =**journey**, tour, take a trip, voyage, go sightseeing, globetrot, backpack; *informal* gallivant. **2** *we travelled the length and breadth of the island* =**journey through**, cross, traverse, cover; roam, rove, range, trek. **3** *light travels faster than sound* =**move**, be transmitted.
▶ noun **(travels)** =**journeys**, expeditions, trips, tours, excursions, voyages, treks, explorations, wanderings, odysseys, pilgrimages, jaunts; *informal* gallivanting.

┌─────────────────────┐
│ **WORD LINKS**   │
└─────────────────────┘
fear of travel: **hodophobia**

traveller ▶ noun **1** *thousands of travellers were stranded* =**tourist**, tripper, holidaymaker, sightseer, visitor, globetrotter, backpacker; passenger, commuter; *N. Amer.* vacationer. **2** *a travellers' site*

=**gypsy**, Romany, tzigane; nomad, migrant, wanderer, itinerant; *dialect* didicoi; *Brit. derogatory* tinker.

travelling ▶ adjective **1** *the travelling population* =**nomadic**, itinerant, peripatetic, wandering, roaming, roving, wayfaring, migrant; gypsy, Romany. **2** *a travelling clock* =**portable**, lightweight, compact.

traverse ▶ verb **1** *he traversed the deserts* =**travel over/across**, cross, journey over/across, pass over; cover; ply; wander, roam, range. **2** *a ditch traversed by a bridge* =**cross**, bridge, span; extend across, lie across, stretch across.

travesty ▶ noun *a travesty of justice* =**misrepresentation**, distortion, perversion, corruption, mockery, parody; farce, charade, pantomime, sham; *informal* apology for.

treacherous ▶ adjective **1** *her treacherous brother* =**traitorous**, disloyal, unfaithful, duplicitous, deceitful, false, back-stabbing, double-crossing, two-faced, untrustworthy, unreliable; apostate, renegade. **2** *treacherous driving conditions* =**dangerous**, hazardous, perilous, unsafe, precarious, risky; *informal* dicey, hairy.
–OPPOSITES loyal, faithful, reliable.

treachery ▶ noun =**betrayal**, disloyalty, unfaithfulness, infidelity, breach of trust, duplicity, deceit, back-stabbing, double-dealing, untrustworthiness; treason.

tread ▶ verb **1** *he trod purposefully down the hall* =**walk**, step, stride, pace, go; march, tramp, plod, stomp, trudge. **2** *the snow had been trodden down by the horses* =**crush**, flatten, press down, squash; trample on, stamp on.
▶ noun *we heard his heavy tread on the stairs* =**step**, footstep, footfall, tramp.

treason ▶ noun =**treachery**, lese-majesty; disloyalty, betrayal, faithlessness; sedition, subversion, mutiny, rebellion.
–OPPOSITES allegiance, loyalty.

treasonable ▶ adjective =**traitorous**, treacherous, disloyal; seditious, subversive, mutinous, rebellious.
–OPPOSITES loyal.

treasure ▶ noun **1** *a casket of treasure* =**riches**, valuables, jewels, gems, gold, silver, precious metals, money, cash; wealth, fortune. **2** *art treasures* =**valuable object**, work of art, objet de virtu, masterpiece. **3** *(informal) she's a real treasure* =**paragon**, gem, angel, nonpareil; find, prize; *informal* star, one of a kind, one in a million.
▶ verb *I treasure the photographs* =**cherish**, hold dear, prize, set great store by, value greatly.

treasury ▶ noun **1** *the national treasury* =**exchequer**, purse; bank, coffers. **2** *the area is a treasury of fossils* =**rich source**, repository, storehouse, treasure house; fund, mine, bank. **3** *a treasury of stories* =**anthology**, collection, miscellany, compilation, compendium.

treat ▶ verb **1** *Charlotte treated him badly* =**behave towards**, act towards, use; deal with, handle. **2** *police are treating the fires as arson* =**regard**, consider, view, look on; put down as. **3** *the book treats its subject with insight* =**deal with**, tackle, handle, discuss, explore, investigate; consider, study, analyse. **4** *she was treated in hospital* =**give medical care to**, nurse, tend, attend to. **5** *the plants may prove useful in treating cancer* =**cure**, heal, remedy. **6** *he treated her to lunch* =**buy**, take out for, stand, give; pay for; entertain, wine and dine; *informal* foot the bill for. **7** *delegates were treated to dance performances* =**regale with**, entertain with/by, fête with, amuse with, divert with.
▶ noun **1** *a birthday treat* =**celebration**, entertainment, amusement; surprise. **2** *I bought you some chocolate as a treat* =**present**, gift; titbit, delicacy, luxury, indulgence, extravagance; *informal* goody. **3** *it was a real treat to see them* =**pleasure**, delight, thrill, joy.

treatise ▶ noun =**disquisition**, essay, paper, work, exposition, discourse, dissertation, thesis, monograph, study, critique.

treatment ▶ noun **1** *the company's treatment of its workers* =**behaviour towards**, conduct towards; handling of, dealings with. **2** *she's responding well to treatment* =**medical care**, therapy, nursing; medication, drugs, medicaments. **3** *her treatment of the topic* =**discussion**, handling, investigation, exploration, consideration, study, analysis, critique.

treaty ▶ noun =**agreement**, settlement, pact, deal, entente, concordat, accord, protocol, compact, convention, contract, covenant, bargain, pledge; *formal* concord.

tree ▶ noun

> **WORD LINKS**
>
> *relating to trees:* **arboreal**
> *study of trees:* **dendrology**
> *farming of trees:* **forestry, agroforestry, arboriculture, silviculture**

trek ▶ noun =**journey**, trip, expedition, safari, odyssey; hike, march, slog, tramp, walk; *Brit. informal* yomp.

trellis ▶ noun =**lattice**, framework, espalier; network, mesh, tracery.

tremble ▶ verb **1** *Joe's hands were trembling* =**shake**, quiver, twitch. **2** *the entire building trembled* =**shake**, shudder, judder, wobble, rock, vibrate, move, sway. **3** *she trembled at the thought of what he had in store for her* =**be afraid**, be frightened, be apprehensive, worry; quail, shrink, blench; *informal* be in a blue funk.

tremendous ▶ adjective **1** *tremendous sums of money* =**huge**, enormous, immense, colossal, massive, prodigious, stupendous, monumental, mammoth, vast, gigantic, giant, mighty, epic, titanic, towering, king-size(d), gargantuan, Herculean; substantial, considerable; *informal* whopping, astronomical, humongous; *Brit. informal* whacking, ginormous. **2** *a tremendous explosion* =**very loud**, deafening, ear-splitting, booming, thunderous, resounding.
–OPPOSITES tiny, small.

tremor ▶ noun **1** *the sudden tremor of her hands* =**tremble**, shake, quiver, twitch, tic. **2** *a tremor of fear ran through her* =**frisson**, shiver, spasm, thrill, tingle, stab, dart, shaft; wave, surge, rush, ripple. **3** *the epicentre of the tremor* =**earthquake**, shock; *informal* quake.

> **WORD LINKS**
>
> *relating to tremors:* **seismic**

tremulous ▶ adjective **1** *a tremulous voice* =**shaky**, trembling, unsteady, quavering, wavering, quivering, quaking, weak. **2** *a tremulous smile* =**timid**, diffident, shy, hesitant, uncertain, nervous, timorous, fearful, frightened, scared.
–OPPOSITES steady, confident.

trench ▶ noun =**ditch**, channel, trough, excavation, furrow, rut, conduit, cut, drain, watercourse; earthwork, moat.

trenchant ▶ adjective =**incisive**, penetrating, sharp, keen, acute, shrewd, razor-sharp, rapier-like, piercing.

–OPPOSITES vague.

trend ▶ noun **1** *an upward trend in unemployment* =**tendency**, movement, drift, swing, shift, course, current, direction, inclination, leaning. **2** *the latest trend in music* =**fashion**, vogue, style, mode, craze, mania, rage; *informal* fad, thing.
▶ verb *interest rates are trending up* =**move**, go, head, drift, gravitate, swing, shift, turn, incline, tend, lean, veer.

trendy ▶ adjective (*informal*). See FASHIONABLE.

trepidation ▶ noun =**fear**, apprehension, dread, agitation, anxiety, worry, nervousness, tension, misgivings, unease, foreboding, disquiet, dismay, consternation, alarm, panic; *informal* butterflies, the jitters, a cold sweat, a blue funk, collywobbles.
–OPPOSITES equanimity, composure.

trespass ▶ verb **1** *he was trespassing on railway property* =**intrude on**, encroach on, enter without permission, invade. **2** *I must not trespass on your good nature* =**take advantage of**, impose on, play on, exploit, abuse; encroach on, infringe. **3** (*archaic*) *he would be the last among us to trespass* =**sin**, transgress, offend, do wrong, err, go astray, fall from grace.
▶ noun **1** *his alleged trespass on council land* =**unlawful entry**, intrusion, encroachment, invasion. **2** (*archaic*) *he asked forgiveness for his trespasses* =**sin**, wrong, wrongdoing, transgression, crime, offence, misdeed, misdemeanour, error, lapse, fall from grace.

trespasser ▶ noun **1** *a high wall discouraged trespassers* =**intruder**, interloper, unwelcome visitor, encroacher. **2** (*archaic*) *trespassers asking for forgiveness* =**sinner**, transgressor, wrongdoer, evildoer, malefactor, offender, criminal.

tresses ▶ plural noun =**hair**, mane; locks, curls, ringlets.

trial ▶ noun **1** *the trial is expected to last several weeks* =**court case**, lawsuit, suit, hearing, inquiry, tribunal, litigation, (legal/judicial) proceedings, legal action; court martial. **2** *the drug is undergoing clinical trials* =**test**, try-out, experiment, pilot study; examination, check, assessment, evaluation, appraisal; *informal* dry run. **3** *she could be a bit of a trial at times* =**nuisance**, pest, bother, irritant, problem, inconvenience, plague, thorn in one's flesh; *informal* pain, headache, drag, nightmare. **4** *an account of her trials and tribulations* =**trouble**, anxiety, worry, burden, affliction, ordeal, tribulation, adversity, hardship, tragedy, trauma, difficulty, problem, misfortune, bad luck, mishap, misadventure; *informal* hassle.

▸ **adjective** *a three-month trial period* =**test**, experimental, pilot, exploratory, probationary, provisional.

▸ **verb** *the cash card has been trialled by several banks* =**test**, try out, put through its paces; pilot.

tribe ▸ **noun 1** *the nomadic tribes of the Sahara* =**ethnic group**, people; family, dynasty, house; nation, clan. **2** *a tribe of children trailed after her* =**group**, crowd, gang, company, body, band, host, bevy, party, pack, army, herd, flock, drove, horde; *informal* bunch, crew, gaggle, posse.

tribulation ▸ **noun 1** *the tribulations of her life* =**trouble**, difficulty, problem, worry, anxiety, burden, cross to bear, ordeal, trial, adversity, hardship, tragedy, trauma; *informal* hassle. **2** *his time of tribulation was just beginning* =**suffering**, distress, trouble, misery, wretchedness, unhappiness, sadness, heartache, woe, grief, pain, anguish, agony.

tribunal ▸ **noun 1** *a rent tribunal* =**arbitration board/panel**, board, panel, committee. **2** *an international war-crimes tribunal* =**court**; court of inquiry; *N. Amer.* forum.

tributary ▸ **noun** =**headwater**, branch, feeder, side stream, influent; *N. Amer. & Austral./NZ* creek.

tribute ▸ **noun 1** *tributes flooded in from colleagues* =**accolade**, praise, commendation, salute, testimonial, homage, eulogy, paean; congratulations, compliments, plaudits; gift, present, offering; *informal* bouquet; *formal* laudation. **2** *it is a tribute to his determination that he ever played again* =**testimony**, indication, manifestation, evidence, proof, attestation. **3** *the Vikings demanded tributes in silver* =**payment**, contribution, dues, levy, tax, duty, impost.
−OPPOSITES criticism, condemnation.

■ **pay tribute to** =**praise**, speak highly of, commend, acclaim, take one's hat off to, applaud, salute, honour, recognize, acknowledge, pay homage to, extol; *formal* laud.

trick ▸ **noun 1** *he's capable of any mean trick* =**stratagem**, ploy, ruse, scheme, device,

manoeuvre, contrivance, machination, artifice, wile, dodge; deceit, subterfuge, chicanery, sharp practice; swindle, hoax, fraud; *informal* con, set-up, game, scam, sting; *Brit. informal* wheeze. **2** *I think he's playing a trick on us* =**practical joke**, prank, jape; *informal* leg-pull, spoof, put-on. **3** *conjuring tricks* =**feat**, stunt; (**tricks**) **sleight of hand**, legerdemain, prestidigitation; magic. **4** *it was probably a trick of the light* =**illusion**, figment of the imagination; mirage. **5** *the tricks of the trade* =**knack**, art, skill, technique; secret.

▸ **verb** *many people have been tricked by villains with false identity cards* =**deceive**, delude, hoodwink, mislead, take in, dupe, fool, double-cross, cheat, defraud, swindle, catch out, hoax; *informal* con, diddle, rook, pull a fast one on, take for a ride, shaft, do; *N. Amer. informal* sucker.

trickery ▸ **noun** =**deception**, dishonesty, cheating, duplicity, double-dealing, legerdemain, sleight of hand, guile, craftiness, deviousness, subterfuge, skulduggery, chicanery, fraud, swindling, sharp practice; *informal* jiggery-pokery.
−OPPOSITES honesty.

trickle ▸ **verb** *blood was trickling from two cuts* =**drip**, dribble, ooze, leak, seep, spill.
−OPPOSITES pour, gush.

▸ **noun** *trickles of water* =**dribble**, drip, thin stream, rivulet.

trickster ▸ **noun** =**swindler**, cheat, fraud; charlatan, mountebank, quack, impostor, sham, hoaxer; rogue, villain, scoundrel; *informal* con man, sharp; *Brit. informal* twister; *dated* confidence man.

tricky ▸ **adjective 1** *a tricky situation* =**difficult**, awkward, problematic, delicate, ticklish, sensitive, embarrassing, touchy; risky, uncertain, precarious, touch-and-go; *informal* sticky, dicey; *N. Amer. informal* gnarly. **2** *a tricky and unscrupulous politician* =**cunning**, crafty, wily, guileful, artful, devious, sly, scheming, calculating, designing, sharp, shrewd, astute, canny; duplicitous, dishonest, deceitful; *informal* foxy.
−OPPOSITES straightforward, honest.

trifle ▸ **noun 1** *we needn't bother the headmaster over such trifles* =**unimportant thing**, triviality, thing of no consequence, bagatelle, inessential, nothing; technicality; (**trifles**) trivia, minutiae. **2** *he bought it for a trifle* =**next to nothing**, very small amount; pittance; *infor-*

mal peanuts. **3** *he went to buy a few trifles for Christmas* =**bauble**, trinket, knick-knack, gimcrack, gewgaw.

■ **a trifle** =**a little**, a bit, somewhat, a touch, a spot, a mite, a whit; *informal* a tad.

■ **trifle with** =**play with**, amuse oneself with, toy with, dally with, flirt with; *informal* mess about with.

trifling ▶ adjective =**trivial**, unimportant, insignificant, inconsequential, petty, minor, of little/no account, footling, incidental; silly, idle, superficial, small, tiny, inconsiderable, nominal, negligible; *informal* piffling, piddling; *formal* exiguous.

–OPPOSITES important.

trigger ▶ verb **1** *the incident triggered an acrimonious debate* =**precipitate**, prompt, set off, spark (off), touch off, provoke, stir up; cause, give rise to, lead to, set in motion, occasion, bring about, generate, engender, begin, start, initiate. **2** *burglars triggered the alarm* =**activate**, set off, trip.

trill ▶ verb =**warble**, sing, chirp, chirrup, tweet, twitter, cheep.

trim ▶ verb **1** *his hair had been trimmed* =**cut**, barber, crop, bob, shorten, clip, snip, shear. **2** *trim off the lower leaves* =**cut off**, remove, take off, chop off, lop off; prune. **3** *costs need to be trimmed* =**reduce**, decrease, cut down, scale down, prune, slim down, pare down, dock. **4** *the story was trimmed for the film version* =**shorten**, abridge, condense, abbreviate, telescope, truncate. **5** *a pair of gloves trimmed with fake fur* =**decorate**, adorn, ornament, embellish; edge, pipe, border, fringe.

▶ noun **1** *white curtains with a blue trim* =**decoration**, ornamentation, adornment, embellishment; border, edging, piping, fringe, frill. **2** *an unruly mop in need of a trim* =**haircut**, cut, barbering, clip, snip; pruning.

▶ adjective **1** *a fitted jacket looks trim with a long-line skirt* =**smart**, stylish, chic, spruce, dapper, elegant, crisp; *informal* natty, sharp. **2** *a trim little villa* =**neat**, tidy, orderly, uncluttered, well kept, well maintained, immaculate, spick and span. **3** *her trim figure* =**slim**, slender, lean, sleek, willowy, lissom, sylphlike, svelte; streamlined.

–OPPOSITES untidy, messy.

■ **in trim** =**fit**, in good health, in fine fettle; slim, in shape.

trimming ▶ noun **1** *a black dress with lace trimming* =**decoration**, ornamentation, adornment, embroidery; border, edging, piping, fringing, frills. **2** *roast turkey with all the trimmings* =**accompaniments**, extras, frills, accessories, accoutrements, trappings, paraphernalia; garnishing. **3** *hedge trimmings* =**cuttings**, clippings, parings, shavings.

trinket ▶ noun =**knick-knack**, bauble, ornament, bibelot, curio, trifle, toy, novelty, gimcrack, gewgaw.

trio ▶ noun =**threesome**, three, triumvirate, triad, troika, trinity, trilogy, triptych.

trip ▶ verb **1** *he tripped on the stones* =**stumble**, lose one's footing, catch one's foot, slip, lose one's balance, fall (down), tumble, topple, take a spill. **2** *taxpayers often trip up by not declaring taxable income* =**make a mistake**, miscalculate, blunder, go wrong, make an error, err; *informal* slip up, screw up; *Brit. informal* boob; *N. Amer. informal* goof up. **3** *the question was intended to trip him up* =**catch out**, trick, outwit, outsmart; throw off balance, disconcert, unsettle, discountenance, discomfit; *informal* throw, wrong-foot; *Brit. informal* catch on the hop. **4** *they tripped up the steps* =**skip**, run, dance, prance, bound, spring, scamper. **5** *Hoffman tripped the alarm* =**set off**, activate, trigger; turn on, switch on, throw.

▶ noun **1** *a trip to Paris* =**excursion**, outing, jaunt; holiday, visit, tour, journey, expedition, voyage; drive, run, day out; *informal* junket, spin. **2** *trips and falls cause nearly half such accidents* =**stumble**, slip, misstep.

triple ▶ adjective **1** *a triple alliance* =**threeway**, tripartite; threefold. **2** *they paid him triple the going rate* =**three times**, treble.

trite ▶ adjective =**banal**, hackneyed, clichéd, platitudinous, vapid, commonplace, stock, conventional, stereotyped, overused, overdone, overworked, timeworn, tired, hoary, hack, unimaginative, unoriginal; *informal* old hat, corny, played out.

–OPPOSITES original, imaginative.

triumph ▶ noun **1** *Napoleon's triumphs* =**victory**, win, conquest, success; achievement. **2** *his eyes shone with triumph* =**jubilation**, exultation, elation, delight, joy, happiness, glee, pride, satisfaction. **3** *a triumph of Victorian engineering* =**tour de force**, masterpiece,

crowning example, coup, wonder, master stroke.
−OPPOSITES defeat, disappointment.
▶ verb **1** *he triumphed in the Grand Prix* =**win**, succeed, come first, be victorious, carry the day, prevail, take the honours. **2** *they had no chance of triumphing over the Nationalists* =**defeat**, beat, conquer, trounce, vanquish, worst, overcome, overpower, overwhelm, get the better of; *informal* lick, best. **3** *'You can't touch me,' she triumphed* =**crow**, gloat; rejoice, exult.
−OPPOSITES lose.

triumphant ▶ adjective **1** *the triumphant team* =**victorious**, successful, winning, conquering. **2** *a triumphant expression* =**jubilant**, exultant, elated, rejoicing, joyful, delighted, gleeful, proud, cock-a-hoop; gloating.
−OPPOSITES unsuccessful, despondent.

trivia ▶ plural noun =(petty) **details**, minutiae, niceties, technicalities, trifles, non-essentials.

trivial ▶ adjective **1** *trivial problems* =**unimportant**, insignificant, inconsequential, minor, of no account, of no importance; incidental, inessential, petty, trifling, footling, small, slight, little, negligible, paltry; *informal* piddling, piffling. **2** *a trivial person* =**frivolous**, superficial, shallow, unthinking, emptyheaded, feather-brained, lightweight.
−OPPOSITES important, significant, serious.

triviality ▶ noun **1** *the triviality of the subject matter* =**unimportance**, insignificance, inconsequence, pettiness. **2** *he need not concern himself with such trivialities* =**minor detail**, petty detail, thing of no importance/consequence, trifle, non-essential; technicality; (**trivialities**) trivia, minutiae.

trivialize ▶ verb =**treat as unimportant**, minimize, play down, underestimate, underplay, make light of, treat lightly, dismiss; *informal* pooh-pooh.

troop ▶ noun **1** *a troop of tourists* =**group**, party, band, gang, bevy, body, company, crowd, throng, horde, pack, drove, flock, swarm, multitude, host, army; *informal* bunch, gaggle, crew, posse. **2** *British troops were stationed here* =**soldiers**, armed forces, service men/women.
▶ verb **1** *we trooped out of the hall* =**walk**, march, file; flock, crowd, throng, stream, swarm, surge, spill. **2** *Caroline*

trooped wearily home =**trudge**, plod, traipse, trail, drag oneself, tramp; *N. Amer. informal* schlep.

trophy ▶ noun **1** *a swimming trophy* =**cup**, medal; prize, award. **2** *trophies from his travels* =**souvenir**, memento, keepsake; spoils, booty.

tropical ▶ adjective *tropical weather* =**very hot**, sweltering, humid, sultry, steamy, sticky, oppressive, stifling; *informal* boiling.
−OPPOSITES cold, arctic.

trot ▶ verb =**run**, jog; scuttle, scurry, bustle, scamper.

trouble ▶ noun **1** *you've caused enough trouble* =**problems**, difficulty, bother, inconvenience, worry, anxiety, distress, stress, agitation, harassment, unpleasantness; *informal* hassle. **2** *she poured out all her troubles* =**problem**, misfortune, difficulty, trial, tribulation, trauma, burden, pain, woe, grief, heartache, misery, affliction, suffering. **3** *he's gone to a lot of trouble* =**bother**, inconvenience, fuss, effort, exertion, work, labour; pains, care. **4** *I wouldn't want to be a trouble to her* =**nuisance**, bother, inconvenience, irritation, problem, trial, pest; *informal* headache, pain, drag. **5** *you're too gullible, that's your trouble* =**shortcoming**, weakness, failing, fault, imperfection, defect, blemish; problem, difficulty. **6** *he had heart trouble* =**disease**, illness, sickness, ailments, complaints, problems; disorder, disability. **7** *the crash was due to engine trouble* =**malfunction**, dysfunction, failure, breakdown. **8** *a match marred by crowd trouble* =**disturbance**, disorder, unrest, fighting, ructions, fracas, breach of the peace.
▶ verb **1** *this matter had been troubling her for some time* =**worry**, bother, concern, disturb, upset, agitate, distress, perturb, annoy, irritate, vex, irk, nag, niggle, prey on someone's mind, weigh down, burden; *informal* bug. **2** *he was troubled by ill health* =**afflict**, burden; suffer from, be cursed with. **3** *there is nothing you need trouble about* =**worry**, upset oneself, fret, be anxious, be concerned. **4** *don't trouble to see me out* =**bother**, exert oneself, go out of one's way. **5** *I'm sorry to trouble you* =**inconvenience**, bother, impose on, disturb, put out, disoblige; *informal* hassle; *formal* discommode.

■ **in trouble** =**in difficulty**, in a mess, in a bad way, in a predicament; *informal* in a tight corner/spot, in a fix, in a hole, in hot water, in a pickle, up against it; *Brit. informal* up a gum tree.

troubled ▸ adjective **1** *Joanna looked troubled* = **anxious**, worried, concerned, perturbed, disturbed, bothered, uneasy, unsettled, agitated; distressed, upset, dismayed. **2** *we live in troubled times* = **difficult**, problematic, unsettled, hard, tough, stressful, dark.

troublemaker ▸ noun = **mischief-maker**, rabble-rouser, firebrand, agitator, agent provocateur, ringleader, incendiary; scandalmonger, gossip-monger, meddler; *informal* stirrer.

troublesome ▸ adjective **1** *a troublesome problem* = **annoying**, irritating, exasperating, maddening, infuriating, irksome, vexatious, bothersome, tiresome, worrying, disturbing, upsetting, niggling, nagging; difficult, awkward, problematic, taxing; *informal* aggravating; *N. Amer. informal* pesky. **2** *a troublesome child* = **difficult**, awkward, trying, demanding, uncooperative, rebellious, unmanageable, unruly, obstreperous, disruptive, disobedient, naughty, recalcitrant; *formal* refractory.
–OPPOSITES simple, cooperative.

trough ▸ noun **1** *a large feeding trough* = **manger**, feedbox, feeder, fodder rack, crib. **2** *a thirty-yard trough* = **channel**, conduit, trench, ditch, gully, drain, culvert, cut, flume, gutter.

trounce ▸ verb = **defeat utterly**, beat hollow, rout, crush, overwhelm; *informal* hammer, clobber, thrash, drub, demolish, destroy, annihilate; *Brit. informal* stuff.

troupe ▸ noun = **group**, company, band, ensemble, set; cast.

trousers ▸ plural noun = **slacks**; *N. Amer.* pants; *Brit. informal* trews, strides, kecks, breeches; *Austral. informal* daks.

truant ▸ noun = **absentee**; *Brit. informal* skiver; *Austral./NZ informal* wag.
■ **play truant** = **stay away from school**, truant; *Brit. informal* skive (off), bunk off; *N. Amer. informal* play hookey; *Austral./NZ informal* play the wag.

truce ▸ noun = **ceasefire**, armistice, peace; respite, lull; *informal* let-up.

truck[1] ▸ noun *a heavily laden truck* = **lorry**, heavy goods vehicle, juggernaut; van, pickup; *Brit.* HGV; *dated* pantechnicon.

truck[2] ▸ noun *we are to have no truck with him* = **dealings**, association, contact, communication, connection, relations; business, trade.

truculent ▸ adjective = **defiant**, aggressive, antagonistic, belligerent, pugnacious, confrontational, obstreperous, argumentative, quarrelsome, uncooperative; bad-tempered, short-tempered, cross, snappish; *informal* feisty; *Brit. informal* stroppy, bolshie.
–OPPOSITES cooperative, amiable.

trudge ▸ verb = **plod**, tramp, drag oneself, walk heavily/slowly, plough, slog, toil, trek; *informal* traipse; *Brit. informal* trog.

true ▸ adjective **1** *what I say is true* = **correct**, accurate, right, verifiable, in accordance with the facts, the case, so; faithful, literal, factual, unelaborated. **2** *true craftsmanship* = **genuine**, authentic, real, actual, bona fide, proper; *informal* honest-to-goodness, kosher, pukka, legit. **3** *the true owner* = **rightful**, legitimate, legal, lawful, authorized, bona fide. **4** *the necessity for true repentance* = **sincere**, genuine, real, unfeigned, heartfelt. **5** *a true friend* = **loyal**, faithful, constant, devoted, staunch, steadfast, unswerving, unwavering; trustworthy, reliable, dependable. **6** *a true reflection of life* = **accurate**, faithful, telling it like it is, fact-based, realistic, close, lifelike.
–OPPOSITES untrue, false, disloyal, inaccurate.

truism ▸ noun = **platitude**, commonplace, cliché, stock phrase, banality, old chestnut, bromide.

truly ▸ adverb **1** *tell me truly what you want* = **truthfully**, honestly, frankly, candidly, openly; *informal* pulling no punches. **2** *I'm truly grateful* = **sincerely**, genuinely, really, indeed, heartily, profoundly; very, extremely, dreadfully, immensely, tremendously, most; *informal* awfully, terribly; *Brit. informal* jolly, ever so. **3** *a truly dreadful song* = **really**, absolutely, simply, utterly, totally, perfectly, thoroughly, completely. **4** *this is truly a miracle* = **without (a) doubt**, unquestionably, certainly, surely, definitely, undeniably; really, actually, in fact. **5** *the programme truly reflected jazz at the sharp end* = **accurately**, correctly, exactly, precisely, faithfully.

trump ▸ verb *by wearing the simplest of dresses, she had trumped them all* = **outshine**, outclass, outdo, upstage, put in the shade, eclipse, surpass, outdo, outperform; beat; *informal* be a cut above, leave standing; *Brit. informal* knock spots off.

trumped-up ▶ adjective =bogus, spurious, specious, false, fabricated, invented, manufactured, contrived, made-up, fake, factitious; *informal* phoney.
–OPPOSITES genuine.

trumpet ▶ verb 1 *'come on!' he trumpeted* =shout, bellow, roar, yell, cry out, call out; *informal* holler. 2 *companies trumpeted their enthusiasm for the multimedia revolution* =proclaim, announce, declare, noise abroad, shout from the rooftops.
■ **blow one's own trumpet** =boast, brag, sing one's own praises, show off, swank, congratulate oneself.

truncate ▶ verb =shorten, cut, curtail, bring to an untimely end; abbreviate, condense, reduce.
–OPPOSITES lengthen, extend.

truncheon ▶ noun (*Brit.*) =club, baton, cudgel, bludgeon; stick, staff; *Brit.* life preserver; *N. Amer.* billy, blackjack, nightstick; *Brit. informal* cosh.

trunk ▶ noun 1 *the trunk of a tree* =main stem, bole, stock. 2 *his powerful trunk* =torso, body. 3 *an elephant's trunk* =proboscis, nose, snout. 4 *an enormous tin trunk* =chest, box, crate, coffer; case, portmanteau. 5 (*N. Amer.*) *the trunk of his car* =luggage compartment; *Brit.* boot.

truss ▶ noun 1 *the bridge is supported by three steel trusses* =support, buttress, joist, brace, prop, strut, stay, stanchion, pier. 2 *a hernia truss* =surgical appliance, support, pad.
▶ verb *they trussed us up with ropes* =tie up, bind, chain up; pinion, fetter, tether, secure.

trust ▶ noun 1 *good relationships are built on trust* =confidence, belief, faith, certainty, assurance, conviction, credence; reliance. 2 *a position of trust* =responsibility, duty, obligation. 3 *the money is to be held in trust* =safe keeping, protection, charge, care, custody; trusteeship, guardianship.
–OPPOSITES distrust, mistrust, doubt.
▶ verb 1 *I should never have trusted her* =have faith in, have (every) confidence in, believe in, pin one's hopes/faith on. 2 *he can be trusted to carry out an impartial investigation* =rely on, depend on, bank on, count on, be sure of. 3 *I trust we shall meet again* =hope, expect, take it, assume, presume. 4 *they don't like to trust their money to anyone outside the family* =entrust, consign, commit, give, hand over, turn over, assign; *formal* commend.

–OPPOSITES distrust, mistrust, doubt.

WORD LINKS

relating to trust: **fiduciary**

trustee ▶ noun =administrator, agent; custodian, keeper, steward, depositary; executor.

trusting ▶ adjective =trustful, unsuspecting, unquestioning, unguarded, unwary; naive, innocent, childlike, ingenuous, wide-eyed, credulous, gullible, easily taken in.
–OPPOSITES distrustful, suspicious.

trustworthy ▶ adjective =reliable, dependable, honest, honourable, upright, principled, true, truthful, as good as one's word, ethical, virtuous, incorruptible, unimpeachable, above suspicion; responsible, sensible, level-headed; loyal, faithful, staunch, steadfast; safe, sound, reputable; *informal* on the level; *N. Amer. informal* straight-up.
–OPPOSITES unreliable.

trusty ▶ adjective =reliable, dependable, trustworthy, unfailing; loyal, faithful, true, staunch, steadfast, constant.
–OPPOSITES unreliable.

truth ▶ noun 1 *he doubted the truth of her statement* =veracity, verity, sincerity, candour, honesty; accuracy, correctness, validity, factuality, authenticity. 2 *it's the truth, I swear it* =what actually happened, the case, so. 3 *truth is stranger than fiction* =fact(s), reality, real life, actuality. 4 *scientific truths* =fact, verity, certainty, certitude; law, principle.
–OPPOSITES lies, fiction, falsehood.
■ **in truth** =in (actual) fact, in reality, really, actually.

truthful ▶ adjective 1 *a truthful answer* =honest, sincere, trustworthy, genuine; candid, frank, open, forthright, straight; *informal* upfront, on the level. 2 *a truthful account* =true, accurate, correct, factual, faithful, reliable; unvarnished, unembellished; *formal* veracious.
–OPPOSITES deceitful, untrue.

try ▶ verb 1 *try to help him* =attempt, endeavour, make an effort, exert oneself, strive, do one's best, do one's utmost, move heaven and earth; undertake, aim, take it on oneself; *informal* have a go, give it one's best shot, go all out; *formal* essay. 2 *try it and see what you think* =test, sample, taste, inspect, investigate, examine, appraise, evaluate, assess; *informal* check out, give something a whirl. 3 *Mary tried* *everyone's patience* =**tax**, strain, test, stretch, sap, drain, exhaust, wear out. **4** *the case is to be tried by a jury* =**adjudicate**, consider, hear, examine.

▶ **noun** *I'll have one last try* =**attempt**, effort, endeavour; *informal* go, shot, crack, stab, bash, whack; *formal* essay.

■ **try something out** =**test**, trial, experiment with, pilot; put through its paces; assess, evaluate.

trying ▶ **adjective 1** *a trying day* =**stressful**, taxing, demanding, difficult, tough, challenging, hard, pressured, frustrating, fraught; arduous, gruelling, tiring, exhausting; *informal* hellish. **2** *Steve was very trying* =**annoying**, irritating, exasperating, maddening, infuriating; tiresome, irksome, troublesome, bothersome; *informal* aggravating.

–OPPOSITES easy, accommodating.

tub ▶ **noun 1** *a wooden tub* =**container**, butt, barrel, cask, drum, keg. **2** *a tub of yogurt* =**pot**, carton.

tuck ▶ **verb 1** *he tucked his shirt into his trousers* =**push**, insert, slip; thrust, stuff, stick, cram; *informal* pop. **2** *the dress was tucked all over* =**pleat**, gather, fold, ruffle. **3** *he tucked the knife behind his seat* =**hide**, conceal, secrete; store, stow; *informal* stash.

■ **tuck someone in/up** =**make comfortable**, settle down, cover up; put to bed.

tuft ▶ **noun** =**clump**, bunch, knot, cluster, tussock, tuffet; lock, wisp; crest, topknot; tassel.

tug ▶ **verb 1** *Ben tugged at her sleeve* =**pull**, pluck, tweak, twitch, jerk, wrench; catch hold of; *informal* yank. **2** *she tugged him towards the door* =**drag**, pull, lug, draw, haul, heave, tow, trail.

tuition ▶ **noun** =**instruction**, teaching, coaching, tutoring, tutelage, lessons, education, schooling; training, drill, preparation, guidance.

tumble ▶ **verb 1** *he tumbled over* =**fall (over/down)**, topple over, lose one's balance, keel over, take a spill, go headlong, go head over heels, trip (up), stumble; *informal* come a cropper. **2** *they all tumbled from the room* =**hurry**, rush, scramble, scurry, bound, pile, bundle. **3** *a brook tumbled over the rocks* =**cascade**, fall, flow, pour, spill, stream. **4** *oil prices tumbled* =**plummet**, plunge, fall, dive, nosedive, drop, slump, slide, decrease, decline; *informal* crash.

–OPPOSITES rise.

tumbledown ▶ **adjective** =**dilapidated**, ramshackle, decrepit, neglected, run down, decaying, derelict, crumbling; rickety, shaky.

tumour ▶ **noun** =**cancerous growth**, cancer, malignancy; lump, swelling; *Medicine* carcinoma, sarcoma.

> **WORD LINKS**
>
> *relating to tumours:* **onco-, -oma**
> *branch of medicine concerning tumours:* **oncology**

tumult ▶ **noun 1** *she added her voice to the tumult* =**clamour**, din, noise, racket, uproar, commotion, ruckus, pandemonium, babel, melee, frenzy; *informal* hullabaloo; *Brit. informal* row. **2** *years of political tumult* =**turmoil**, confusion, disorder, disarray, unrest, chaos, turbulence, mayhem, havoc, upheaval.

–OPPOSITES tranquillity.

tumultuous ▶ **adjective 1** *tumultuous applause* =**loud**, deafening, thunderous, uproarious, noisy, clamorous, vociferous. **2** *a tumultuous crowd* =**disorderly**, unruly, rowdy, turbulent, boisterous, excited, agitated, restless, wild, riotous.

–OPPOSITES soft, orderly.

tune ▶ **noun** *she hummed a tune* =**melody**, air, strain, theme; song, jingle, ditty.

▶ **verb** *a body clock tuned to the tides* =**attune**, adapt, adjust; regulate, modulate.

■ **in tune** =**in accord**, in keeping, in agreement, in harmony, in step, in line, in sympathy.

tuneful ▶ **adjective** =**melodious**, musical, mellifluous, dulcet, euphonious, harmonious, lyrical, lilting, sweet.

–OPPOSITES discordant.

tuneless ▶ **adjective** =**discordant**, unmelodious, dissonant, harsh, cacophonous.

–OPPOSITES melodious.

tunnel ▶ **noun** =**underground passage**, underpass, subway; shaft; burrow, hole.

▶ **verb** =**dig**, burrow, mine, bore, drill.

turbid ▶ **adjective** =**murky**, opaque, cloudy, muddy, thick.

–OPPOSITES clear.

turbulent ▶ **adjective 1** *the country's turbulent past* =**tempestuous**, stormy, unstable, unsettled, tumultuous, chaotic; violent, anarchic, lawless. **2** *turbulent seas* =**rough**, stormy, tempestuous, heavy, violent, wild, seething, choppy,

agitated, boisterous.
–OPPOSITES peaceful, calm.

turf ▸ noun **1** *they walked across the turf* =**grass**, lawn, sod; *literary* sward. **2** *devotees of the turf* =**horse racing**; racecourses.

turgid ▸ adjective *turgid prose* =**bombastic**, pompous, overblown, inflated, tumid, high-flown, affected, pretentious, grandiose, florid, ornate, magniloquent, grandiloquent, orotund; *informal* highfalutin.
–OPPOSITES simple.

turmoil ▸ noun =**confusion**, upheaval, turbulence, tumult, disorder, disturbance, agitation, ferment, unrest, trouble, disruption, chaos, mayhem; uncertainty.
–OPPOSITES peace.
■ **in turmoil** =**confused**, in a whirl, at sixes and sevens; reeling, disorientated; *informal* all over the place.

turn ▸ verb **1** *the wheels were still turning* =**go round**, revolve, rotate, spin, roll, circle, wheel, whirl, gyrate, swivel, pivot. **2** *I turned and headed back* =**change direction**, change course, make a U-turn, turn about/round, wheel round. **3** *the car turned the corner* =**go round**, negotiate, take. **4** *the path turned to right and left* =**bend**, curve, wind, twist, meander, snake, zigzag. **5** *he turned his pistol on Liam* =**aim at**, point at, level at, direct at, train on. **6** *he turned his ankle* =**sprain**, twist, wrench. **7** *their honeymoon turned into a nightmare* =**become**, develop into, turn out to be; be transformed into, metamorphose into. **8** *Emma turned red* =**become**, go, grow, get. **9** *he turned the house into flats* =**convert**, change, transform, make; adapt, modify, rebuild, reconstruct. **10** *I've just turned forty* =**reach**, get to, become; *informal* hit. **11** *the milk had turned* =**(go) sour**, go off, curdle, become rancid, go bad, spoil.
▸ noun **1** *a turn of the wheel* =**rotation**, revolution, spin, whirl, gyration, swivel. **2** *a turn to the left* =**change of direction**, veer, divergence. **3** *we're approaching the turn* =**bend**, corner, dog-leg, junction, crossroads; *N. Amer.* turnout; *Brit.* hairpin bend. **4** *you'll get your turn in a minute* =**opportunity**, chance, say; stint, time; try; *informal* go, shot, stab, crack. **5** *a comic turn* =**act**, routine, performance, number, piece. **6** *a turn around the garden* =**stroll**, walk, saunter, amble, wander, airing, promenade; outing, excursion,

jaunt; *informal* mosey, tootle, spin; *Brit. informal* pootle. **7** *you gave me quite a turn!* =**shock**, start, surprise, jolt; fright, scare. **8** *she did me some good turns* =**service**, deed, act; favour, kindness; disservice, wrong.
■ **at every turn** =**repeatedly**, recurrently, all the time, always, constantly, again and again.
■ **in turn** =**one after the other**, one by one, one at a time, in succession, sequentially.
■ **turn of events** =**development**, incident, occurrence, happening, circumstance.
■ **turn against someone** =**become hostile to**, take a dislike to.
■ **turn someone away** =**send away**, reject, rebuff, repel, cold-shoulder; *informal* send packing.
■ **turn back** =**retrace one's steps**, go back, return; retreat.
■ **turn someone/something down 1** *his novel was turned down* =**reject**, spurn, rebuff, refuse, decline; *Brit. informal* knock back. **2** *Pete turned the sound down* =**reduce**, lower, decrease, lessen; muffle, mute.
■ **turn someone in** =**betray**, inform on, denounce, sell out, stab someone in the back; *informal* split on, blow the whistle on, rat on; *Brit. informal* grass on, shop.
■ **turn off** *they turned off the road* =**leave**, branch off; *informal* take a left/right; *N. Amer. informal* hang a left/right.
■ **turn something off** =**switch off**, shut off, put off, extinguish, deactivate; *informal* kill, cut.
■ **turn something on** =**switch on**, put on, start up, activate, trip.
■ **turn on someone** =**attack**, set on, fall on, let fly at, lash out at, hit out at, round on; *informal* lay into, tear into; *Brit. informal* have a go at; *N. Amer. informal* light into.
■ **turn out 1** *a huge crowd turned out* =**come**, be present, attend, appear, turn up, arrive; assemble, gather; *informal* show up. **2** *it turned out that she had been abroad* =**transpire**, emerge, come to light, become apparent. **3** *things didn't turn out as I'd intended* =**happen**, occur, come about; develop, work out, come out, end up; *informal* pan out; *formal* eventuate.
■ **turn someone out** =**throw out**, eject, evict, expel, oust, drum out, banish; *informal* kick out, send packing, boot out, show someone the door, turf out.
■ **turn something out 1** *turn out the*

light. See TURN SOMETHING OFF. **2** *they turn out a million engines a year* =**produce**, make, manufacture, fabricate, put out, churn out. **3** *she turned out the cupboards* =**clear out**, clean out, empty (out).

■ **turn over** =**overturn**, upturn, capsize, keel over, turn turtle, be upended.

■ **turn something over 1** *I turned over a few pages* =**flip over**, flick through, leaf through. **2** *she turned the proposal over in her mind* =**think about/over**, consider, weigh up, ponder, contemplate, reflect on, chew over, mull over, muse on, ruminate on. **3** *he turned over the business to his brother* =**transfer**, hand over, pass on, consign, commit.

■ **turn someone's stomach** =**nauseate**, sicken, make someone's gorge rise.

■ **turn to someone/something** =**seek help from**, have recourse to, approach, apply to, appeal to; take to, resort to.

■ **turn up 1** *the documents turned up* =**be found**, be discovered, be located, reappear. **2** *the police turned up* =**arrive**, appear, present oneself; *informal* show (up). **3** *something better will turn up* =**present itself**, occur, happen, crop up.

■ **turn something up 1** *she turned up the volume* =**increase**, raise, amplify, intensify. **2** *they turned up lots of information* =**discover**, uncover, unearth, find, dig up, ferret out, root out, expose. **3** *I turned up the hem* =**take up**, raise; shorten.

turncoat ▶ noun =**traitor**, renegade, defector, deserter, betrayer, Judas.

turning ▶ noun =**turn-off**, side road, exit; *N. Amer.* turnout.

turning point ▶ noun =**watershed**, critical moment, decisive moment, moment of truth, crossroads, crisis.

turnout ▶ noun **1** *the lecture attracted a good turnout* =**attendance**, audience, house; crowd, gathering, throng, assembly. **2** *his turnout was very elegant* =**outfit**, clothing, dress, garb, attire, ensemble; *informal* get-up, gear, togs; *Brit. informal* clobber, kit; *formal* apparel.

turnover ▶ noun **1** *an annual turnover of £2 million* =**(gross) revenue**, income, yield; sales. **2** *a high turnover of staff* =**rate of replacement**, change, movement.

tussle ▶ noun *his glasses were smashed in the tussle* =**scuffle**, fight, struggle, skirmish, brawl, scrum, rough and tumble, free-for-all, fracas, fray, rumpus, melee; *informal* scrap, dust-up, spat; *Brit. informal* ding-dong, bust-up.

▶ verb *demonstrators tussled with police* =**scuffle**, fight, struggle, brawl, grapple, wrestle, clash; *informal* scrap.

tutor ▶ noun *a history tutor* =**teacher**, instructor, educator, lecturer, trainer, mentor; *formal* pedagogue.

▶ verb *he was tutored at home* =**teach**, instruct, educate, school, coach, train, drill.

tutorial ▶ noun =**lesson**, class, seminar.

tweak ▶ verb =**pull**, jerk, tug, twist, pinch, squeeze.

twee ▶ adjective *(Brit.)* **1** *twee little shops* =**quaint**, sweet, dainty, pretty; *informal* cute. **2** *the lyrics are too twee in places* =**sentimental**, mawkish, sickly; *Brit. informal* soppy.

twelve ▶ cardinal number =**dozen**.

WORD LINKS

relating to twelve: **duodecimal, dodeca**-
twelve-sided figure: **dodecagon**

twenty ▶ cardinal number =**score**.

twiddle ▶ verb =**turn**, twist, swivel, twirl; adjust, move, jiggle; fiddle with, play with.

■ **twiddle one's thumbs** =**be idle**, kick one's heels, kill time; *informal* hang around/round.

twig ▶ noun *leafy twigs* =**stick**, sprig, withy, shoot, stem, branchlet.

twilight ▶ noun **1** *we arrived at twilight* =**dusk**, sunset, sundown, nightfall, evening, close of day; *literary* eventide. **2** *it was scarcely visible in the twilight* =**half-light**, semi-darkness, gloom. **3** *the twilight of his career* =**decline**, waning, ebb; autumn, final years. –OPPOSITES dawn.

▶ adjective *a twilight world* =**shadowy**, dark, shady, dim, gloomy, obscure.

WORD LINKS

relating to twilight: **crepuscular**

twin ▶ noun *a sitting room that was the twin of her own* =**duplicate**, double, carbon copy, exact likeness, mirror image, replica, lookalike, clone; counterpart, match, pair; *informal* spitting image, dead ringer.

▶ adjective **1** *the twin towers of the stadium* =**matching**, identical, paired. **2** *the twin aims of conservation and recreation* =**twofold**, double, dual; related, linked, connected; corresponding, parallel, complementary, equivalent.

▶ verb *the company twinned its brewing with distilling* =**combine**, join, link, couple, pair.

twine ▶ noun =**string**, cord, thread, yarn.
▶ verb **1** *she twined her arms around him* =**wind**, entwine, wrap, wreathe. **2** *convolvulus twined around the tree* =**entwine itself**, coil, loop, twist, spiral, curl. **3** *a bloom was twined in her hair* =**weave**, interlace, intertwine, braid, twist.

twinge ▶ noun **1** *twinges in her stomach* =**pain**, spasm, ache, throb; cramp, stitch. **2** *a twinge of guilt* =**pang**, prick, dart.

twinkle ▶ verb **1** *lights twinkled* =**glitter**, sparkle, shine, glimmer, shimmer, glint, gleam, glisten, flicker, flash, wink; *literary* coruscate, glister. **2** *his feet twinkled over the ground* =**dart**, dance, skip, flit, glide.

twinkling ▶ adjective =**sparkling**, glistening, glittering, glimmering, glinting, gleaming, flickering, winking, shining, scintillating; *literary* coruscating.

twirl ▶ verb **1** *she twirled her parasol* =**spin**, whirl, turn, gyrate, pivot, swivel, twist, revolve, rotate. **2** *she twirled her hair round her fingers* =**wind**, twist, coil, curl, wrap.
▶ noun *she did a quick twirl* =**pirouette**, spin, whirl, turn, twist, rotation, revolution, gyration.

twist ▶ verb **1** *the impact twisted the chassis* =**crumple**, crush, buckle, mangle, warp, deform, distort. **2** *her face twisted with rage* =**contort**, screw up. **3** *he twisted round in his seat* =**turn (round)**, swivel (round), spin (round), pivot, rotate, revolve. **4** *she twisted out of his grasp* =**wriggle**, squirm, worm. **5** *I twisted my ankle* =**sprain**, wrench, turn, rick, crick. **6** *you are twisting my words* =**distort**, misrepresent, change, alter, pervert, falsify, warp, skew, misinterpret, misconstrue, misstate, misquote. **7** *he twisted the knob* =**twiddle**, adjust, turn, rotate, swivel. **8** *she twisted her hair round her finger* =**wind**, twirl, coil, curl, wrap. **9** *the wires were twisted together* =**intertwine**, interlace, weave, plait, braid, coil, wind. **10** *the road twisted and turned* =**wind**, bend, curve, turn, meander, weave, zigzag, swerve, snake.
▶ noun **1** *the twist of a dial* =**turn**, twirl, spin. **2** *a personality twist* =**quirk**, idiosyncrasy, foible, eccentricity, peculiarity,

oddity, kink; aberration, fault, flaw, imperfection, defect, failing, weakness. **3** *(Brit.) a twist of tobacco* =**wad**, quid, plug, chew; *Brit.* screw. **4** *long twists of black hair* =**ringlet**, curl, corkscrew, coil; lock, hank. **5** *the twists of the road* =**bend**, curve, turn, zigzag, kink, dog-leg. **6** *the twists of the plot* =**convolution**, complication, complexity, intricacy. **7** *a new twist on an old theme* =**interpretation**, slant, outlook, angle, approach, treatment; variation.

twisted ▶ adjective **1** *twisted metal* =**crumpled**, bent, crushed, buckled, warped, misshapen, distorted, deformed. **2** *a twisted smile* =**crooked**, lopsided; contorted, wry. **3** *his twisted mind* =**perverted**, warped, deviant, depraved, corrupt, abnormal, unhealthy, aberrant, distorted, debauched, debased; *informal* sick, kinky, pervy.

twisty ▶ adjective =**windy**, bendy, zigzag, meandering, curving, sinuous, snaky, serpentine.
−OPPOSITES straight.

twitch ▶ verb **1** *he twitched and then lay still* =**jerk**, convulse, have a spasm, quiver, tremble, shiver, shudder. **2** *he twitched the note out of my hand* =**snatch**, tweak, pluck, pull, tug; *informal* yank.
▶ noun **1** *a twitch of her lips* =**spasm**, convulsion, quiver, tremor, shiver, shudder; tic. **2** *he gave a twitch at his moustache* =**pull**, tug, tweak; *informal* yank. **3** *he felt a twitch of annoyance* =**pang**, twinge, dart, stab, prick.

twitter ▶ verb **1** *sparrows twittered* =**chirp**, chirrup, cheep, tweet, peep, chatter, trill, warble. **2** *stop twittering about Francis* =**prattle**, babble, chatter, go on, yap, blether, ramble; *informal* yak; *Brit. informal* witter, rabbit, chunter, waffle.

two ▶ cardinal number =**pair**, duo, duet, double, dyad, duplet, tandem.

> **WORD LINKS**
>
> *relating to two:* **binary, dual, bi-, di-, duo-**
> *occurring twice a year:* **biannual**
> *occurring every two years:* **biennial**
> *two-hundredth anniversary:* **bicentenary**

two-faced ▶ adjective =**deceitful**, insincere, double-dealing, hypocritical, back-stabbing, false, untrustworthy, duplicitous, deceiving; disloyal, treacher-

ous, faithless.
—OPPOSITES sincere.

twosome ▸ noun =**couple**, pair, duo.

tycoon ▸ noun =**magnate**, mogul, businessman, captain of industry, industrialist, financier, entrepreneur; millionaire; *informal* big shot, honcho; *Brit. informal* supremo; *N. Amer. informal* big wheel; *derogatory* fat cat.

type ▸ noun **1** *a curate of the old-fashioned type* =**kind**, sort, variety, class, category, set, genre, species, order, breed, race; style, nature, manner, rank. **2** *(informal) sporty types* =**person**, individual, character, sort; *Brit. informal* bod. **3** *his sayings are the type of modern wisdom* =**epitome**, quintessence, essence, archetype, paradigm, model, embodiment. **4** *italic type* =**print**, typeface, characters, lettering; font; *Brit.* fount.

typhoon ▸ noun =**cyclone**, tropical storm, tornado, hurricane, whirlwind; *N. Amer. informal* twister.

typical ▸ adjective **1** *a typical example of art deco* =**representative**, classic, quintessential, archetypal, prototypical, stereotypical. **2** *a fairly typical day* =**normal**, average, ordinary, standard, regular, routine, run-of-the-mill, conventional, unremarkable; *informal* bog-standard. **3** *it's typical of him to forget* =**characteristic**, in keeping, usual, normal, par for the course, predictable, true to form.
—OPPOSITES unusual, exceptional, uncharacteristic.

typify ▸ verb **1** *he typified the civil servant* =**epitomize**, exemplify, characterize, be representative of; personify, embody. **2** *the sun typified the Greeks* =**symbolize**, represent, stand for, be emblematic of.

tyrannical ▸ adjective =**dictatorial**, despotic, autocratic, oppressive, repressive, totalitarian, undemocratic, illiberal; authoritarian, high-handed, imperious, iron-handed, severe, cruel, brutal, ruthless.
—OPPOSITES liberal.

tyrannize ▸ verb =**dominate**, dictate to, browbeat, intimidate, bully; persecute, victimize, torment; oppress, repress, crush, subjugate; *informal* push around.

tyranny ▸ noun =**despotism**, absolute power, autocracy, dictatorship, totalitarianism, fascism; oppression, repression, subjugation, enslavement.

tyrant ▸ noun =**dictator**, despot, autocrat, authoritarian, oppressor; slave-driver, martinet, bully.

WORD LINKS

killing of a tyrant: **tyrannicide**

Uu

ubiquitous ▶ adjective =omnipresent, everywhere, all over the place, all-pervasive; universal, worldwide, global.
–OPPOSITES rare.

UFO ▶ noun flying saucer, foo fighter.

> **WORD LINKS**
>
> study of UFOs: **ufology**

ugly ▶ adjective **1** =unattractive, ill-favoured, hideous, plain, unprepossessing, unsightly, horrible, ghastly, repellent, repugnant; grotesque, monstrous; N. Amer. homely; informal not much to look at; Brit. informal no oil painting. **2** things got pretty ugly =**unpleasant**, nasty, disagreeable, alarming, charged; dangerous, perilous, threatening, menacing, hostile, ominous, sinister. **3** an ugly rumour =**horrible**, despicable, reprehensible, nasty, appalling, offensive, obnoxious, vile, vicious, spiteful.
–OPPOSITES beautiful, pleasant.

ulcer ▶ noun =**sore**, abscess, boil, carbuncle, wen.

ulterior ▶ adjective =**underlying**, undisclosed, undivulged, concealed, hidden, covert, secret.
–OPPOSITES overt.

ultimate ▶ adjective **1** the ultimate collapse of the Empire =**eventual**, final, concluding, terminal, end; resulting, ensuing, consequent, subsequent. **2** ultimate truths =**fundamental**, basic, primary, elementary, absolute, central, key, crucial, essential, pivotal. **3** the ultimate gift for cat lovers =**best**, ideal, greatest, supreme, paramount, superlative, optimum, quintessential.
▶ noun the ultimate in luxury living =**utmost**, optimum, last word, height, epitome, peak, pinnacle, acme, zenith.

ultimately ▶ adverb **1** the cost will ultimately fall on us =**eventually**, in the end, in the long run, at length, finally, in time, one day; informal when push comes to shove; Brit. informal at the end of the day. **2** two ultimately contradictory reasons =**fundamentally**, basically, primarily, essentially, at heart, deep down.

ultra- ▶ combining form an ultra-conservative view =**extremely**, exceedingly, immensely, exceptionally; N. English right; informal mega, majorly; Brit. informal dead, well.
▶ noun ultras in the animal rights movement =**extremist**, radical, fanatic, zealot, diehard, militant.

umbrage ■ take umbrage =**take offence**, take exception, be aggrieved, be affronted, be annoyed, be indignant, be put out, be insulted, be piqued, go into a huff; informal be miffed; Brit. informal get the hump.

umbrella ▶ noun **1** =**parasol**, sunshade; Brit. informal brolly. **2** the groups worked under the umbrella of the Liberal Party =**aegis**, auspices, patronage, protection, guardianship, guidance, cover.

umpire ▶ noun the umpire reversed his decision =**referee**, linesman, adjudicator, arbitrator, judge, moderator; informal ref.
▶ verb he umpired a boat race =**referee**, adjudicate, arbitrate, judge, moderate, oversee; informal ref.

unabashed ▶ adjective =**unashamed**, shameless, unembarrassed, brazen, audacious, barefaced, blatant, flagrant, bold.
–OPPOSITES sheepish.

unable ▶ adjective =**powerless**, impotent, inadequate, incompetent, unfit, incapable.

unabridged ▶ adjective =**complete**, entire, whole, intact, uncut, unshortened, unexpurgated.

unacceptable ▶ adjective =**intolerable**, insufferable, unsatisfactory, inadmissible, inappropriate, unsuitable, undesirable, unreasonable, insupportable; informal not on, a bit much, out of order; Brit. informal a bit thick, a bit off; formal exceptionable.
–OPPOSITES satisfactory.

unaccompanied ▶ adjective =**alone**, on one's own, by oneself, solo, lone, solitary, single-handed; unescorted, unchaperoned; Brit. informal on one's tod.

unaccomplished ▶ adjective 1 *unaccomplished works* =**uncompleted**, unfinished, undone, half-done, unfulfilled. 2 *an unaccomplished poet* =**inexpert**, unskilful, amateur, unqualified, untrained; incompetent, maladroit.
–OPPOSITES complete, skilful.

unaccountable ▶ adjective 1 *for some unaccountable reason* =**inexplicable**, insoluble, incomprehensible, unfathomable, impenetrable, puzzling, perplexing, baffling, bewildering, mystifying, peculiar, strange, odd, obscure; *informal* weird. 2 *the Council is unaccountable to anyone* =**unanswerable**, not liable; unsupervised.

unaccustomed ▶ adjective 1 *she was unaccustomed to being bossed about* =**unused**, new, fresh; unfamiliar with, inexperienced in. 2 *he showed unaccustomed emotion* =**unusual**, unfamiliar, uncommon, unwonted, rare, surprising, atypical.
–OPPOSITES habitual.

unadorned ▶ adjective =**unembellished**, unornamented, undecorated, unfussy, no-nonsense, no-frills; plain, basic; bare, stark.
–OPPOSITES ornate.

unadventurous ▶ adjective =**cautious**, careful, circumspect, wary, hesitant, timid; conservative, conventional, unenterprising; *informal* square, straight, stick-in-the-mud.
–OPPOSITES enterprising.

unaffected ▶ adjective 1 *they are unaffected by the reshuffle* =**unchanged**, unaltered, uninfluenced; untouched, unmoved, unresponsive to. 2 *his manner was unaffected* =**unassuming**, unpretentious, down-to-earth, natural, easy, uninhibited, open, artless, guileless.
–OPPOSITES influenced, pretentious, false.

unafraid ▶ adjective =**undaunted**, unabashed, fearless, brave, courageous, plucky, intrepid, stout-hearted, bold, daring, confident, audacious; *informal* gutsy, spunky.
–OPPOSITES timid.

unanimous ▶ adjective 1 *doctors were unanimous about the effects* =**united**, in agreement, in accord, of one mind, in harmony, concordant, undivided. 2 *a unanimous vote* =**uniform**, consistent, united, congruent.
–OPPOSITES divided.

unanswerable ▶ adjective 1 *an unanswerable case* =**irrefutable**, indisputable, undeniable, incontestable, incontrovertible; conclusive, absolute, positive. 2 *unanswerable questions* =**insoluble**, unsolvable, inexplicable.
–OPPOSITES weak, obvious.

unanswered ▶ adjective =**unresolved**, undecided, unsettled, undetermined; pending, up in the air.

unappetizing ▶ adjective =**unpalatable**, uninviting, unappealing, unpleasant, off-putting, distasteful, unsavoury, insipid, flavourless; *informal* yucky, gross.
–OPPOSITES tempting.

unapproachable ▶ adjective *her boss appeared unapproachable* =**aloof**, distant, remote, detached, reserved, withdrawn, uncommunicative, unforthcoming, unfriendly, unsympathetic; cool, frosty, stiff; *informal* stand-offish.
–OPPOSITES friendly.

unarmed ▶ adjective =**defenceless**; unprotected, unguarded, unshielded, exposed.

unassailable ▶ adjective 1 *an unassailable fortress* =**impregnable**, invulnerable, impenetrable, invincible; secure, safe, strong, indestructible. 2 *his logic was unassailable* =**indisputable**, undeniable, unquestionable, incontestable, incontrovertible, irrefutable, indubitable, watertight.
–OPPOSITES defenceless.

unassertive ▶ adjective =**passive**, retiring, unforthcoming, submissive, humble, meek, unconfident, shy, timid; *informal* mousy.
–OPPOSITES bold.

unassuming ▶ adjective =**modest**, self-effacing, humble, meek, reserved, diffident; unobtrusive, unostentatious, unpretentious, unaffected, natural.

unattached ▶ adjective 1 *they were both unattached* =**single**, unmarried, unwed, partnerless, footloose and fancy free. 2 *we are unattached to any organization* =**unaffiliated**, unallied; autonomous, independent, non-aligned, separate, unconnected.
–OPPOSITES married.

unattended ▶ adjective 1 *his cries went unattended* =**ignored**, disregarded, neglected, passed over. 2 *an unattended vehicle* =**unguarded**, unwatched; abandoned. 3 *she had to walk there unattended* =**unaccompanied**, unescorted, partnerless, unchaperoned, alone, on one's own, by oneself, solo; Brit. informal on one's tod.

unattractive ▸ adjective =**plain**, ugly, ill-favoured, unappealing, unsightly, unlovely, unprepossessing, displeasing; N. Amer. homely; informal not much to look at; Brit. informal no oil painting.
−OPPOSITES beautiful.

unauthorized ▸ adjective =**unofficial**, unsanctioned, unaccredited, unlicensed, unwarranted, unapproved; disallowed, prohibited, banned, forbidden, outlawed, illegal, illicit, proscribed.
−OPPOSITES official.

unavoidable ▸ adjective =**inescapable**, inevitable, inexorable, assured, certain, predestined, predetermined, ineluctable; necessary, compulsory, required.

unaware ▸ adjective =**ignorant**, unknowing, unconscious, heedless, unmindful, oblivious, unsuspecting, uninformed, unenlightened, unwitting, innocent; informal in the dark.
−OPPOSITES conscious.

unawares ▸ adverb **1** brigands caught them unawares =**by surprise**, unexpectedly, without warning, suddenly, abruptly, unprepared, off-guard; informal with one's trousers down, napping; Brit. informal on the hop. **2** the roach approached the pike unawares =**unknowingly**, unwittingly, unconsciously; unintentionally, inadvertently, accidentally, by mistake.
−OPPOSITES prepared, knowingly.

unbalanced ▸ adjective **1** he is unbalanced and dangerous =**unstable**, mentally ill, deranged, demented, disturbed, unhinged, insane, mad; informal crazy, loopy, nuts, batty, dotty, bonkers, round the bend/twist; Brit. informal barmy, potty, crackers, barking (mad). **2** an unbalanced article =**biased**, prejudiced, one-sided, partisan, inequitable, unfair.
−OPPOSITES sane, unbiased.

unbearable ▸ adjective =**intolerable**, insufferable, insupportable, unendurable, unacceptable, unmanageable, overpowering; informal too much.
−OPPOSITES tolerable.

unbeatable ▸ adjective =**invincible**, unstoppable, unassailable, indomitable, unconquerable, unsurpassable,

matchless, peerless.

unbeaten ▸ adjective =**undefeated**, unconquered, unsurpassed, unequalled, unrivalled; triumphant, victorious, supreme, matchless, second to none.

unbecoming ▸ adjective **1** an unbecoming dress =**unflattering**, unattractive, unsightly. **2** conduct unbecoming to the Senate =**inappropriate**, unfitting, unsuitable, inapt, out of keeping, incorrect, unacceptable; unworthy, improper, unseemly, undignified.
−OPPOSITES flattering, appropriate.

unbelievable ▸ adjective =**incredible**, inconceivable, unthinkable, unimaginable; unconvincing, far-fetched, implausible, improbable; informal hard to swallow.
−OPPOSITES credible.

unbend ▸ verb I couldn't unbend my knees =**straighten (out)**, extend, flex, uncurl.

unbending ▸ adjective unbending attitudes =**uncompromising**, inflexible, unyielding, hard-line, tough, strict, firm, resolute, determined, unrelenting, inexorable, intransigent, immovable.

unbiased ▸ adjective =**impartial**, unprejudiced, neutral, non-partisan, disinterested, detached, dispassionate, objective, equitable, even-handed, fair.
−OPPOSITES prejudiced.

unblemished ▸ adjective =**impeccable**, flawless, faultless, perfect, pure, clean, spotless, unsullied, unspoilt, undefiled, untarnished; incorrupt, innocent; informal squeaky clean.
−OPPOSITES flawed.

unborn ▸ adjective your unborn child =**embryonic**, fetal, in utero.

unbreakable ▸ adjective =**shatterproof**, indestructible, imperishable, durable; toughened, sturdy, stout, resistant, hard-wearing, heavyduty.
−OPPOSITES fragile.

unbridled ▸ adjective =**unrestrained**, unconstrained, uncontrolled, uninhibited, unrestricted, unchecked, uncurbed, rampant, irrepressible, unstoppable.
−OPPOSITES restrained.

unbroken ▸ adjective **1** the last unbroken window =**undamaged**, unharmed, unscathed, untouched, sound, intact, whole. **2** an unbroken horse =**untamed**,

u

undomesticated, wild, feral. **3** *an un-broken chain of victories* =**uninterrupted**, continuous, endless, constant, unremitting, ongoing. **4** *his record is still unbroken* =**unbeaten**, undefeated, unsurpassed, unrivalled, unmatched, supreme.

unburden ▸ verb *she had a sudden wish to unburden herself* =**open one's heart**, confess, tell all; *informal* come clean.

uncalled ■ **uncalled for** =**gratuitous**, unnecessary, needless; undeserved, unmerited, unwarranted, unjustified, unreasonable, unfair, inappropriate; unsolicited, unprompted, unprovoked.

uncanny ▸ adjective **1** *the silence was uncanny* =**eerie**, unnatural, unearthly, other-worldly, ghostly, strange, abnormal, weird, bizarre; *informal* creepy, spooky. **2** *an uncanny resemblance* =**striking**, remarkable, extraordinary, exceptional, incredible, arresting.

unceasing ▸ adjective =**incessant**, constant, continual, unabating, interminable, endless, never-ending, everlasting, eternal, perpetual, continuous, non-stop, uninterrupted, unbroken, unremitting, persistent, unrelenting, unrelieved, sustained.
–OPPOSITES interrupted.

unceremonious ▸ adjective **1** *an unceremonious dismissal* =**abrupt**, sudden, hasty, hurried, summary, perfunctory, undignified; rude, impolite, discourteous, offhand. **2** *an unceremonious man* =**informal**, casual, relaxed, easy-going, familiar, natural, open; *informal* laid-back.
–OPPOSITES formal.

uncertain ▸ adjective **1** *the effects are uncertain* =**unknown**, debatable, open to question, in doubt, undetermined, unsure, in the balance, up in the air; unpredictable, unforeseeable, incalculable; *informal* iffy. **2** *Ed was uncertain about the decision* =**unsure**, doubtful, dubious, undecided, irresolute, hesitant, vacillating, vague, unclear, ambivalent, in two minds. **3** *an uncertain smile* =**hesitant**, tentative, faltering, unsure, unconfident.
–OPPOSITES predictable, sure, confident.

unchangeable ▸ adjective =**unalterable**, immutable, invariable, changeless, fixed, hard and fast, cast-iron, set in stone, established, permanent, enduring, abiding, lasting, indestructible, ineradicable, irreversible.

–OPPOSITES variable.

unchanging ▸ adjective =**consistent**, constant, regular, unvarying, predictable, stable, steady, fixed, permanent, perpetual, eternal.

uncharitable ▸ adjective =**mean**, unkind, selfish, self-centred, inconsiderate, thoughtless, insensitive, unfriendly, unsympathetic, uncaring, ungenerous, ungracious, unfair.

uncharted ▸ adjective =**unexplored**, undiscovered, unmapped, untravelled, unfamiliar, unplumbed, unknown, new.

uncivilized ▸ adjective =**uncouth**, coarse, rough, boorish, vulgar, philistine, uneducated, uncultured, benighted, unsophisticated; ill-bred; barbarian, primitive, savage.

unclear ▸ adjective =**uncertain**, unsure, unsettled, up in the air, debatable, in doubt; ambiguous, equivocal, indefinite, vague, mysterious, obscure, hazy, foggy, nebulous; *informal* iffy.
–OPPOSITES evident.

uncomfortable ▸ adjective **1** *an uncomfortable chair* =**painful**, confining, cramped. **2** *I felt uncomfortable in her presence* =**uneasy**, awkward, nervous, tense, strained, edgy, restless, embarrassed, anxious; *informal* rattled, twitchy.
–OPPOSITES relaxed.

uncommitted ▸ adjective **1** *uncommitted voters* =**floating**, undecided, nonpartisan, unaffiliated, neutral, impartial, independent, undeclared, uncertain; *informal* sitting on the fence. **2** *the uncommitted male* =**unmarried**, unattached, unwed, partnerless; footloose and fancy free, available, single, lone.
–OPPOSITES aligned, attached.

uncommon ▸ adjective **1** *an uncommon plant* =**unusual**, abnormal, rare, atypical, unconventional, unfamiliar, strange, odd, curious, extraordinary, singular, peculiar, bizarre; *informal* weird, oddball, offbeat. **2** *abductions are uncommon* =**rare**, scarce, few and far between, exceptional, abnormal, isolated, infrequent.

uncommonly ▸ adverb =**unusually**, remarkably, extraordinarily, exceptionally, singularly, particularly, especially, decidedly, notably, eminently, extremely, very; *N. English* right; *informal* awfully, terribly, seriously; *Brit. informal* jolly, dead.

uncommunicative ▶ adjective
=**taciturn**, quiet, unforthcoming, reserved, reticent, laconic, tongue-tied, silent, tight-lipped; guarded, secretive, close, private; distant, remote, aloof, withdrawn; *informal* mum, stand-offish.
–OPPOSITES talkative.

uncomplicated ▶ adjective =**simple**, straightforward, clear, accessible, undemanding, unchallenging, unsophisticated, trouble-free, painless, effortless, easy, elementary, idiot-proof, plain sailing; *informal* a piece of cake, child's play, a cinch, a doddle, a breeze; *Brit. informal* easy-peasy.
–OPPOSITES complex.

uncompromising ▶ adjective =**inflexible**, unbending, unyielding, unshakeable, resolute, rigid, hard-line, immovable, intractable, firm, determined, iron-willed, obstinate, stubborn, adamant, obdurate, intransigent, headstrong, pig-headed; *Brit. informal* bloody-minded.
–OPPOSITES flexible.

unconcerned ▶ adjective **1** *he is unconcerned about their responses* =**indifferent**, unmoved, apathetic, uninterested, incurious, dispassionate, heedless, unmindful. **2** *she tried to look unconcerned* =**untroubled**, unworried, unruffled, insouciant, nonchalant, blasé, carefree; *informal* laid-back.
–OPPOSITES interested, anxious.

unconditional ▶ adjective =**unquestioning**, unqualified, unreserved, unlimited, unrestricted, wholehearted; complete, total, entire, full, absolute, out-and-out, unequivocal.

unconnected ▶ adjective **1** *the earth wire was unconnected* =**detached**, disconnected, loose. **2** *unconnected tasks* =**unrelated**, dissociated, separate, independent, distinct, different, disparate, discrete. **3** *unconnected chains of thought* =**disjointed**, incoherent, rambling, wandering, diffuse, disorderly, garbled, mixed, muddled.
–OPPOSITES attached, related, coherent.

unconscious ▶ adjective **1** *she made sure he was unconscious* =**insensible**, senseless, insentient, comatose, inert, knocked out; *informal* out cold, out for the count. **2** *she was unconscious of the pain* =**heedless**, unmindful, disregarding, oblivious to, insensible to, impervious to, unaffected by; unaware, unknowing.

3 *an unconscious desire* =**subconscious**, latent, suppressed, subliminal, inherent, instinctive, involuntary, uncontrolled; *informal* gut.
–OPPOSITES aware, voluntary.
▶ noun *fantasies raging in the unconscious* =**subconscious**, psyche, ego, id, inner self.

uncontrollable ▶ adjective **1** *the crowds were uncontrollable* =**unmanageable**, ungovernable, wild, unruly, disorderly, recalcitrant, undisciplined; *formal* refractory. **2** *an uncontrollable rage* =**ungovernable**, irrepressible, unstoppable, unquenchable; wild, violent, frenzied, furious, mad, hysterical, passionate.
–OPPOSITES compliant.

unconventional ▶ adjective =**unusual**, irregular, unorthodox, unfamiliar, uncommon, unwonted, out of the ordinary, atypical, singular, alternative, different; new, novel, innovative, groundbreaking, pioneering, original, unprecedented; eccentric, idiosyncratic, quirky, odd, strange, bizarre, weird, outlandish, curious; extraordinary; nonconformist, bohemian, avant-garde; *informal* way out, far out, offbeat, wacky, madcap, zany; *Brit. informal* rum; *N. Amer. informal* kooky.
–OPPOSITES orthodox.

unconvincing ▶ adjective =**improbable**, unlikely, implausible, incredible, unbelievable, questionable, dubious, doubtful; strained, laboured, far-fetched, unrealistic, fanciful, fantastic; *informal* hard to swallow.
–OPPOSITES persuasive.

uncooperative ▶ adjective =**unhelpful**, awkward, disobliging, recalcitrant, perverse, contrary, stubborn, wilful, unyielding, unbending, inflexible, immovable, obstructive; *Brit. informal* bloody-minded.
–OPPOSITES obliging.

uncoordinated ▶ adjective =**clumsy**, awkward, blundering, bumbling, lumbering, graceless, gawky, ungainly, ungraceful; *informal* butterfingered, cack-handed, ham-fisted; *Brit. informal* all (fingers and) thumbs; *N. Amer. informal* klutzy.
–OPPOSITES dexterous.

uncouth ▶ adjective =**uncivilized**, uncultured, unrefined, unpolished, unsophisticated, rough, coarse, crude, loutish, boorish, uncivil, rude, impolite, discourteous, disrespectful, bad-

u

mannered, ill-bred, vulgar, crass.
–OPPOSITES refined.

uncover ▶ verb **1** *she uncovered the sand-wiches* =**expose**, reveal, lay bare; un-wrap, unveil. **2** *they uncovered a plot* =**de-tect**, discover, come across, stumble on, chance on, find, turn up, unearth, dig up; expose, bring to light, unmask, un-veil, reveal, lay bare, betray, give away; *informal* blow the whistle on.

unctuous ▶ adjective =**sycophantic**, ingratiating, obsequious, fawning, ser-vile, grovelling, subservient, insincere, gushing, effusive; glib, smooth, slick, oily, greasy; *informal* smarmy, slimy.

undaunted ▶ adjective =**unafraid**, un-dismayed, unflinching, unshrinking, unabashed, fearless, intrepid, bold, vali-ant, brave, courageous, plucky, mettle-some, gritty; *informal* gutsy, spunky.
–OPPOSITES fearful.

undecided ▶ adjective =**unresolved**, uncertain, unsure, unclear, unsettled, indefinite, undetermined, unknown, in the balance, up in the air, moot, open to question, doubtful, vague; indecisive, irresolute, hesitant, wavering, vacillat-ing, uncommitted, ambivalent, in two minds; *informal* iffy.
–OPPOSITES certain.

undefined ▶ adjective **1** *some matters are still undefined* =**unspecified**, unex-plained, unspecific, indeterminate, un-settled; unclear, woolly, imprecise, in-exact, indefinite, vague. **2** *undefined shapes* =**indistinct**, indefinite, indistin-guishable, vague, hazy, misty, shadowy, nebulous, blurred.
–OPPOSITES definite, distinct.

undemonstrative ▶ adjective =**un-emotional**, unaffectionate, impassive, dispassionate, restrained, reserved, un-responsive, stiff, guarded, aloof, distant, detached, remote, withdrawn; cool, frosty, frigid; *informal* stand-offish.
–OPPOSITES emotional, unrestrained.

undeniable ▶ adjective =**indisput-able**, indubitable, unquestionable, be-yond doubt, undebatable, incontrovert-ible, irrefutable, unassailable; certain, sure, definite, positive, conclusive, self-evident, patent, unequivocal.
–OPPOSITES questionable.

under ▶ preposition **1** *they hid under a bush* =**beneath**, below, underneath. **2** *the rent is under £250* =**less than**, lower than, below. **3** *branch managers are under the re-tail director* =**subordinate to**, junior to, inferior to, subservient to, answerable to, responsible to, subject to, controlled by. **4** *forty homes are under construction* =**undergoing**, in the process of. **5** *the town was under water* =**flooded by**, im-mersed in, submerged by, sunk in, en-gulfed by, inundated by.
–OPPOSITES above, over.

▶ adverb *coughing and spluttering she went under* =**down**, lower, below, under-neath, beneath; underwater.

undercover ▶ adjective =**covert**, se-cret, clandestine, underground, sur-reptitious, furtive, cloak-and-dagger, stealthy; *informal* hush-hush.
–OPPOSITES overt.

undercurrent ▶ noun **1** *dangerous undercurrents in the cove* =**undertow**, underflow, underswell. **2** *the undercur-rent of despair in his words* =**undertone**, overtone, suggestion, connotation, in-timation, hint, nuance, trace, whisper, tinge; feeling, atmosphere, aura, echo; *informal* vibes.

undercut ▶ verb **1** *the firm undercut their rivals* =**charge less than**, undersell, underbid. **2** *his authority was being under-cut* =**undermine**, weaken, impair, sap, threaten, subvert, destabilize.

underdog ▶ noun =**weaker party**, vic-tim, loser; *informal* little guy, fall guy, stooge.

underestimate ▶ verb =**underrate**, undervalue, do an injustice to; sell short, play down, understate; minim-ize, underemphasize, diminish, down-grade, gloss over, trivialize; miscalcu-late, misjudge.
–OPPOSITES exaggerate.

undergo ▶ verb =**go through**, experi-ence, undertake, face, submit to, be sub-jected to, come in for, receive, sustain, endure, brave, bear, tolerate, stand, withstand, weather; *Brit. informal* wear.

underground ▶ adjective **1** *an under-ground car park* =**subterranean**, buried, sunken, basement. **2** *underground or-ganizations* =**clandestine**, secret, sur-reptitious, covert, undercover, closet, cloak-and-dagger, sneaky, furtive; re-sistance, subversive; *informal* hush-hush. **3** *the underground art scene* =**alternative**, radical, revolutionary, unconventional, unorthodox, avant-garde, experimen-tal, innovative.

▶ adverb **1** *the insects live underground* =**below ground**, in the earth. **2** *the rebels*

went underground =**into hiding**, into seclusion, undercover.
▶ noun 1 he took the underground =**metro**;
N. Amer. subway; Brit. informal tube. 2 information from the French underground
=**resistance**; partisans, guerrillas, freedom fighters.

undergrowth ▶ noun =**shrubbery**,
vegetation, greenery, ground cover,
brush, scrub, covert, thicket, copse;
bushes, plants, brambles.

underhand ▶ adjective =**deceitful**,
dishonest, dishonourable, disreputable,
unethical, unprincipled, immoral, unscrupulous, fraudulent; treacherous,
duplicitous, double-dealing; devious,
artful, crafty, conniving, scheming, sly,
wily; clandestine, sneaky, furtive, covert, cloak-and-dagger; informal crooked,
shady, bent; Brit. informal dodgy.
–OPPOSITES honest.

underline ▶ verb 1 she underlined a
phrase =**underscore**, mark, pick out,
emphasize, highlight. 2 the programme
underlines the benefits of exercise =**emphasize**, stress, highlight, accentuate, accent, focus on, spotlight.

underling ▶ noun =**subordinate**, inferior, junior, minion, lackey, flunkey,
menial, retainer, vassal, servant, henchman, factotum; informal dogsbody, gofer;
Brit. informal skivvy.
–OPPOSITES boss.

underlying ▶ adjective 1 the underlying
aims =**fundamental**, basic, primary,
central, principal, chief, key, elementary. 2 an underlying feeling of irritation
=**latent**, repressed, suppressed, undisclosed, unexpressed, concealed, hidden.

undermine ▶ verb 1 their integrity is
being undermined =**subvert**, sabotage,
threaten, weaken, compromise, diminish, reduce, impair, mar, spoil, ruin,
damage, sap, shake. 2 the damp had so
undermined the wall that it collapsed
=**erode**, wear away, eat away at.
–OPPOSITES strengthen, support.

underrate ▶ verb =**undervalue**,
underestimate, do an injustice to, sell
short, play down, understate, trivialize.
–OPPOSITES exaggerate.

understand ▶ verb 1 he couldn't understand anything we said =**comprehend**,
grasp, take in, see, apprehend, follow,
make sense of, fathom; informal work out,
figure out, make head or tail of, take on
board, get the drift of, catch on to, get;

Brit. informal twig, suss. 2 she understood
how hard he'd worked =**appreciate**, recognize, realize, acknowledge, know, be
aware of, be conscious of; informal be wise
to; formal be cognizant of. 3 I understand
that you wish to go =**believe**, gather, take
it, hear (tell), notice, see, learn.

understandable ▶ adjective 1 make
it understandable to the layman =**comprehensible**, intelligible, coherent, clear,
explicit, unambiguous, transparent,
plain, straightforward. 2 an understandable desire =**unsurprising**, expected,
predictable, inevitable; reasonable, acceptable, logical, rational, normal, natural; justifiable, excusable, pardonable,
forgivable.

understanding ▶ noun 1 test your
understanding of the language =**comprehension**, apprehension, grasp, mastery, appreciation, assimilation, absorption; knowledge, awareness, insight,
skill, expertise, proficiency; informal
know-how; formal cognizance. 2 a young
man of brilliant understanding =**intellect**,
intelligence, brainpower, judgement,
reasoning, mentality; insight, intuition,
acumen, sagacity, wisdom; informal nous,
savvy. 3 it was my understanding that this
was free =**belief**, perception, view, conviction, feeling, opinion, intuition, impression, assumption, supposition. 4 he
treated me with understanding =**compassion**, sympathy, pity, feeling, concern,
consideration, kindness, sensitivity, decency, humanity, charity, goodwill. 5 we
had a tacit understanding =**agreement**,
arrangement, deal, bargain, settlement,
pledge, pact.
–OPPOSITES ignorance, indifference.
▶ adjective an understanding friend =**compassionate**, sympathetic, sensitive, considerate, tender, kind, thoughtful, tolerant, patient, forbearing, lenient,
forgiving, humane.

understate ▶ verb =**play down**,
underrate, underplay, trivialize, minimize, diminish, downgrade, brush
aside, gloss over; informal sell short.
–OPPOSITES exaggerate.

understudy ▶ noun =**stand-in**, substitute, replacement, reserve, fill-in,
locum, proxy, backup, relief, standby;
informal sub; N. Amer. informal pinch-hitter.

undertake ▶ verb =**tackle**, take on,
assume, shoulder, handle, manage, deal
with, be responsible for; engage in, take
part in, go about, get down to, get to

u

grips with, embark on; attempt, try, endeavour; *informal* have a go at; *formal* essay.

undertaker ▸ noun =funeral director; *N. Amer.* mortician.

undertaking ▸ noun **1** *a risky undertaking* =**enterprise**, venture, project, campaign, scheme, plan, operation, endeavour, effort, task, activity, pursuit, exploit, business, affair, procedure; mission, quest. **2** *sign this undertaking to comply with the rules* =**pledge**, agreement, promise, oath, covenant, vow, commitment, guarantee, assurance.

undertone ▸ noun **1** *he said something in an undertone* =**low voice**, murmur, whisper, mutter. **2** *the story's dark undertones* =**undercurrent**, overtone, suggestion, nuance, vein, atmosphere, aura, tenor, flavour.

undervalue ▸ verb =**underrate**, underestimate, play down, understate, diminish, minimize, downgrade, reduce, brush aside, gloss over, trivialize; *informal* sell short.

underwater ▸ adjective =**submerged**, immersed, sunken, subaqueous; undersea, submarine.

underwear ▸ noun =**underclothes**, undergarments, underthings, lingerie; *informal* undies, frillies; *Brit. informal* smalls.

underworld ▸ noun **1** *Osiris, god of the underworld* =**the netherworld**, hell, the abyss; eternal damnation; Gehenna, Tophet, Sheol, Hades. **2** *the violent underworld of Southwark* =**criminal world**, gangland; criminals, gangsters; *informal* mobsters.
–OPPOSITES heaven.

underwrite ▸ verb =**sponsor**, support, back, insure, indemnify, subsidize, pay for, finance, fund; *N. Amer. informal* bankroll.

undesirable ▸ adjective **1** *undesirable effects* =**unpleasant**, disagreeable, nasty, unwelcome, unwanted, unfortunate, infelicitous. **2** *undesirable people* =**unpleasant**, disagreeable, obnoxious, nasty, awful, terrible, dreadful, abhorrent, loathsome, hateful, detestable, deplorable, appalling, contemptible, odious, vile, unsavoury; *informal* ghastly, horrible.
–OPPOSITES pleasant, agreeable.

undignified ▸ adjective =**unseemly**, demeaning, unbecoming, unworthy, unbefitting, degrading, dishonourable, ignominious, discreditable, ignoble,

untoward, unsuitable; scandalous, disgraceful, indecent, low, base; *informal* infra dig.

undisciplined ▸ adjective =**unruly**, disorderly, disobedient, recalcitrant, wilful, wayward, delinquent, naughty, rebellious, insubordinate, disruptive, errant, out of control, wild; disorganized, unsystematic, unmethodical, lax, slapdash, sloppy; *Brit. informal* stroppy, bolshie; *formal* refractory.

undisguised ▸ adjective =**obvious**, evident, patent, manifest, transparent, overt, unconcealed, unhidden, unmistakable, undeniable, plain, clear, clearcut, explicit, naked, visible; blatant, flagrant, glaring, bold; *informal* standing/sticking out a mile.

undisputed ▸ adjective =**undoubted**, indubitable, uncontested, unchallenged, incontrovertible, unequivocal, undeniable, irrefutable, unmistakable, certain, definite, accepted, acknowledged, recognized.
–OPPOSITES doubtful.

undistinguished ▸ adjective =**unexceptional**, indifferent, run-of-the-mill, middle-of-the-road, ordinary, average, commonplace, mediocre, humdrum, lacklustre, uninspired, unremarkable, featureless, nondescript; *N. Amer.* garden-variety; *informal* nothing special, no great shakes, OK, so-so, bog standard; *Brit. informal* common or garden.
–OPPOSITES extraordinary.

undivided ▸ adjective =**complete**, full, total, whole, entire, absolute, unqualified, unreserved, unmitigated, unbroken, consistent, thorough, exclusive, dedicated; focused, engrossed, absorbed, attentive, committed.

undo ▸ verb **1** *he undid a button* =**unfasten**, unbutton, unhook, untie, unlace; unlock, unbolt; loosen, detach, free, open. **2** *they will undo a decision by the lords* =**revoke**, overrule, overturn, repeal, rescind, reverse, countermand, cancel, annul, nullify, invalidate, void, negate. **3** *she undid much of the good work* =**ruin**, undermine, subvert, overturn, scotch, sabotage, spoil, impair, mar, destroy, wreck; cancel out, neutralize, thwart; *informal* blow, muck up; *Brit. informal* scupper.
–OPPOSITES fasten, ratify, enhance.

undoing ▸ noun **1** *she plotted the king's undoing* =**downfall**, defeat, conquest, deposition, overthrow, ruin, failure, debasement; Waterloo. **2** *their complacency was their undoing* =**fatal flaw**, Achilles heel, weak point, failing, misfortune.

undoubted ▶ adjective =**undisputed**, unchallenged, unquestioned, indubitable, incontrovertible, irrefutable, incontestable, certain, unmistakable; definite, accepted, acknowledged, recognized.

undoubtedly ▶ adverb =**doubtless**, indubitably; unquestionably, indisputably, undeniably, incontrovertibly, clearly, obviously, patently, certainly, definitely, of course, indeed.

undress ▶ verb *he undressed and got into bed* =**strip (off)**, disrobe; *Brit. informal* peel off.

undue ▶ adjective =**excessive**, immoderate, intemperate, inordinate, disproportionate; uncalled for, unnecessary, unwarranted, unjustified, unreasonable; inappropriate, unmerited, unsuitable, improper.
−OPPOSITES appropriate.

undulate ▶ verb =**rise and fall**, surge, swell, heave, ripple, flow; wind, wobble, oscillate.

undying ▶ adjective =**abiding**, lasting, enduring, permanent, constant, infinite; unceasing, perpetual, incessant, unending; immortal, eternal.

unearth ▶ verb **1** *workmen unearthed an artillery shell* =**dig up**, excavate, exhume, disinter, root out, uncover. **2** *I unearthed an interesting fact* =**discover**, uncover, find, come across, hit on, bring to light, expose, turn up.

unearthly ▶ adjective **1** *an unearthly chill in the air* =**other-worldly**, supernatural, preternatural, alien; ghostly, spectral, phantom, mysterious, spine-chilling, hair-raising; uncanny, eerie, strange, weird, unnatural, bizarre; *informal* spooky, creepy, scary. **2** *(informal) they rose at some unearthly hour* =**unreasonable**, preposterous, abnormal, extraordinary, absurd, ridiculous; *informal* ungodly, unholy.
−OPPOSITES normal, reasonable.

uneasy ▶ adjective **1** *the doctor made him feel uneasy* =**worried**, anxious, troubled, disturbed, nervous, nervy, tense, overwrought, edgy, apprehensive, restless, discomfited, perturbed, fearful, uncomfortable, unsettled; *informal* jittery. **2** *he had an uneasy feeling* =**worrying**, disturbing, troubling, alarming, dismaying, disquieting, unsettling, disconcerting, upsetting. **3** *the victory ensured an uneasy peace* =**tense**, awkward, strained, fraught; precarious, unstable, insecure.
−OPPOSITES calm, stable.

uneconomic, uneconomical ▶ adjective =**unprofitable**, uncommercial, non-viable, loss-making, worthless; wasteful, inefficient, improvident.

uneducated ▶ adjective =**untaught**, unschooled, untutored, untrained, unread, unscholarly, illiterate, ignorant, ill-informed; uncouth, unsophisticated, uncultured, unaccomplished, unenlightened, philistine.
−OPPOSITES learned.

unemotional ▶ adjective =**reserved**, undemonstrative, sober, restrained, passionless, emotionless, unsentimental, unexcitable, impassive, phlegmatic, stoical, equable.

unemployed ▶ adjective =**jobless**, out of work, unwaged, redundant, laid off; on benefit; *Brit.* signing on; *N. Amer.* on welfare; *Brit. informal* on the dole, 'resting'.

unending ▶ adjective =**endless**, interminable, perpetual, eternal, incessant, unceasing, non-stop, uninterrupted, continuous, constant, persistent, unbroken, unabating, unremitting, relentless.

unenthusiastic ▶ adjective =**indifferent**, apathetic, half-hearted, lukewarm, casual, cool, lacklustre, offhand, unmoved.
−OPPOSITES keen.

unenviable ▶ adjective =**disagreeable**, nasty, unpleasant, undesirable, horrible, thankless; unwanted, unwished-for.

unequal ▶ adjective **1** *they are unequal in length* =**different**, dissimilar, unlike, disparate, unmatched, variable. **2** *the unequal distribution of wealth* =**unfair**, unjust, disproportionate, inequitable, biased. **3** *an unequal contest* =**one-sided**, uneven, unfair, ill-matched, unbalanced. **4** *she felt unequal to the task* =**inadequate for**, incapable of, unqualified for, unsuited to, incompetent at, not up to; *informal* not cut out for.
−OPPOSITES identical, fair.

unequalled ▶ adjective =**unbeaten**, unmatched, unrivalled, unsurpassed, unparalleled, peerless, incomparable, inimitable, second to none, unique.

unequivocal ▶ adjective =unambiguous, unmistakable, indisputable, incontrovertible, indubitable, undeniable; clear, plain, explicit, specific, categorical, straightforward, blunt, candid, emphatic.
–OPPOSITES ambiguous.

unerring ▶ adjective =unfailing, infallible, perfect, flawless, faultless, impeccable, unimpeachable; sure, true, assured, deadly; informal sure-fire.

unethical ▶ adjective =immoral, amoral, unprincipled, unscrupulous, dishonourable, dishonest, wrong, deceitful, unconscionable, fraudulent, underhand; unprofessional, improper.

uneven ▶ adjective 1 uneven ground =bumpy, rough, lumpy, stony, rocky, potholed, rutted. 2 uneven teeth =irregular, unequal, unbalanced, lopsided, askew, crooked, asymmetrical. 3 uneven quality =inconsistent, variable, fluctuating, irregular, erratic, patchy. 4 an uneven contest =one-sided, unequal, unfair, unjust, inequitable, ill-matched, unbalanced.
–OPPOSITES flat, regular, equal.

uneventful ▶ adjective =unexciting, uninteresting, monotonous, boring, dull, tedious, humdrum, routine, unvaried, ordinary, run-of-the-mill.
–OPPOSITES exciting.

unexceptional ▶ adjective =ordinary, average, typical, everyday, mediocre, run-of-the-mill, middle-of-the-road, indifferent; informal OK, so-so, nothing special, no great shakes, no big deal, nothing to write home about, forgettable; Brit. informal common or garden; N. Amer. informal ornery.

unexpected ▶ adjective =unforeseen, unanticipated, unpredicted, without warning; sudden, abrupt, surprising, out of the blue.

unfailing ▶ adjective his unfailing good humour =constant, reliable, dependable, steadfast, steady; endless, undying, unfading, inexhaustible, boundless, ceaseless.

unfair ▶ adjective 1 the trial was unfair =unjust, inequitable, prejudiced, biased, discriminatory; one-sided, unequal, uneven, unbalanced, partisan. 2 his comments were unfair =undeserved, unmerited, uncalled for, unreasonable, unjustified; Brit. informal out of order. 3 unfair play =unsporting, dirty, below the belt, underhand, dishonourable. 4 you're being very unfair =inconsiderate, thoughtless, insensitive, selfish, mean, unkind, unreasonable.
–OPPOSITES just, justified.

unfaithful ▶ adjective her husband had been unfaithful =adulterous, faithless, fickle, untrue, inconstant; informal cheating, two-timing.
–OPPOSITES loyal.

unfaltering ▶ adjective =steady, resolute, firm, steadfast, fixed, decided, unswerving, unwavering, tireless, indefatigable, persistent, unyielding, relentless, unremitting.
–OPPOSITES unsteady.

unfamiliar ▶ adjective 1 an unfamiliar part of the city =unknown, new, strange, foreign, alien. 2 unfamiliar sounds =unusual, uncommon, unconventional, novel, exotic, unorthodox, odd, peculiar, curious, uncharacteristic, out of the ordinary. 3 investors unfamiliar with the market =unacquainted, unused, unaccustomed, unconversant, inexperienced, uninformed, new to, a stranger to.

unfashionable ▶ adjective =out of fashion, outdated, old-fashioned, outmoded, dated, unstylish, passé; informal out, square, out of the ark, uncool, unhip, untrendy.

unfasten ▶ verb =undo, open, disconnect, remove, untie, unbutton, unzip, loosen, free, unlock, unbolt.

unfathomable ▶ adjective 1 unfathomable eyes =inscrutable, incomprehensible, enigmatic, indecipherable, obscure, esoteric, mysterious, deep, profound. 2 unfathomable water =deep, immeasurable, unplumbed, bottomless.
–OPPOSITES revealing.

unfavourable ▶ adjective 1 unfavourable comment =adverse, critical, hostile, inimical, unfriendly, unsympathetic, negative; discouraging, disapproving, uncomplimentary, unflattering. 2 the unfavourable economic climate =disadvantageous, adverse, inauspicious, unpropitious, gloomy; unsuitable, inappropriate, inopportune.
–OPPOSITES positive.

unfeeling ▶ adjective =uncaring, unsympathetic, unemotional, uncharitable; heartless, hard-hearted, harsh, austere, cold.
–OPPOSITES compassionate.

unfettered ▸ adjective =unrestrained, unrestricted, unconstrained, free, unbridled, unchecked, uncontrolled.
−OPPOSITES restricted.

unfinished ▸ adjective **1** *an unfinished essay* =incomplete, uncompleted; partial, half-done; unpolished, unrefined, sketchy, fragmentary, rough. **2** *the door can be supplied unfinished* =unpainted, unvarnished, untreated.
−OPPOSITES complete.

unfit ▸ adjective **1** *the film is unfit for children* | *unfit for duty* =unsuitable, inappropriate, unequipped, inadequate, not designed; incapable of, not up to, not equal to; *informal* not cut out for, not up to scratch. **2** *I am unfit* =unhealthy, out of condition/shape.
−OPPOSITES suitable, healthy.

unflattering ▸ adjective **1** *an unflattering review* =unfavourable, uncomplimentary, harsh, unsympathetic, critical, hostile, scathing. **2** *an unflattering dress* =unattractive, unbecoming, unsightly.
−OPPOSITES complimentary, becoming.

unflinching ▸ adjective =resolute, determined, single-minded, dogged, resolved, firm, committed, steady, unwavering, unflagging, unswerving, unfaltering, untiring, undaunted, fearless.

unfold ▸ verb **1** *May unfolded the map* =open out, spread out, flatten, straighten out, unroll. **2** *I watched the events unfold* =develop, evolve, happen, take place, occur, transpire, progress.

unforeseen ▸ adjective =unpredicted, unexpected, unanticipated, unplanned, unlooked for, not bargained for.
−OPPOSITES expected.

unforgettable ▸ adjective =memorable, haunting, catchy; striking, impressive, outstanding, extraordinary, exceptional.
−OPPOSITES unexceptional.

unforgivable ▸ adjective =inexcusable, unpardonable, unjustifiable, indefensible, inexpiable, irremissible.
−OPPOSITES venial.

unfortunate ▸ adjective **1** *unfortunate people* =unlucky, hapless, wretched, forlorn, poor, pitiful; *informal* down on one's luck. **2** *an unfortunate start to our holiday* =adverse, disadvantageous, unfavour-able, unlucky, unwelcome, unpromising, inauspicious, unpropitious; *formal* grievous. **3** *an unfortunate remark* =regrettable, inappropriate, unsuitable, infelicitous, tactless, injudicious.
−OPPOSITES lucky, auspicious.

unfortunately ▸ adverb =unluckily, sadly, regrettably, unhappily, alas, sad to say; *informal* worse luck.

unfounded ▸ adjective =groundless, baseless, unsubstantiated, unproven, unsupported, uncorroborated, unconfirmed, unverified, unattested, without basis, speculative, conjectural.
−OPPOSITES proven.

unfriendly ▸ adjective **1** *an unfriendly look* =hostile, disagreeable, antagonistic, aggressive; ill-natured, unpleasant, surly, unamicable, uncongenial; inhospitable, unneighbourly, unwelcoming; unsociable; *informal* stand-offish. **2** *unfriendly terrain* =unfavourable, disadvantageous, unpropitious, inauspicious, hostile.
−OPPOSITES amiable, favourable.

ungainly ▸ adjective =awkward, clumsy, ungraceful, inelegant, gawky, maladroit, gauche, uncoordinated.
−OPPOSITES graceful.

ungovernable ▸ adjective =uncontrollable, unmanageable, anarchic, intractable; unruly, disorderly, rebellious, riotous, wild, mutinous, undisciplined.

ungracious ▸ adjective =rude, impolite, uncivil, discourteous, ill-mannered, uncouth, disrespectful, insolent.
−OPPOSITES polite.

ungrateful ▸ adjective =unappreciative, unthankful, ungracious.
−OPPOSITES thankful.

unguarded ▸ adjective **1** *an unguarded frontier* =undefended, unprotected, unfortified; vulnerable, insecure. **2** *an unguarded remark* =careless, ill-considered, thoughtless, rash, foolhardy, indiscreet, imprudent, injudicious, ill-judged, insensitive; *literary* temerarious. **3** *an unguarded moment* =unwary, inattentive, off guard, distracted, absent-minded.

unhappiness ▸ noun =sadness, sorrow, dejection, depression, misery, downheartedness, despondency, despair, desolation, wretchedness, glumness, gloom, dolefulness; melancholy, low spirits, mournfulness, woe, heartache, distress, chagrin, grief; *informal* the blues.

unhappy ▶ adjective **1** *an unhappy child-hood* = **sad**, miserable, sorrowful, dejected, despondent, disconsolate, morose, heartbroken, down, dispirited, downhearted, depressed, melancholy, mournful, gloomy, glum, doleful, forlorn, woeful, long-faced; *informal* down in the mouth/dumps, fed up, blue. **2** *in the unhappy event of litigation* = **unfortunate**, unlucky; ill-starred, ill-fated, doomed; *informal* jinxed. **3** *I was unhappy with the service* = **dissatisfied**, displeased, discontented, disappointed, disgruntled.
–OPPOSITES cheerful.

unharmed ▶ adjective **1** *they released the hostage unharmed* = **uninjured**, unhurt, unscathed, safe, alive and well, in one piece, without a scratch. **2** *the tomb was unharmed* = **undamaged**, unbroken, unmarred, unspoiled, unsullied, unmarked; sound, intact, unblemished.
–OPPOSITES injured, damaged.

unhealthy ▶ adjective **1** *an unhealthy lifestyle* = **harmful**, detrimental, destructive, injurious, damaging, deleterious; noxious, poisonous, insalubrious. **2** *an unhealthy pallor* = **ill-looking**, unwell, ailing, sick, poorly, weak, frail, infirm, washed out, run down, peaky. **3** *an unhealthy obsession* = **unwholesome**, morbid, macabre, twisted, abnormal, warped, depraved, unnatural; *informal* sick.

unheard ■ **unheard of 1** *a game unheard of in the UK* = **unknown**, unfamiliar, new. **2** *such behaviour was unheard of* = **unprecedented**, exceptional, extraordinary, unthought of, undreamed of, unbelievable, inconceivable, unimaginable, unthinkable.

unheeded ▶ adjective = **disregarded**, ignored, neglected, overlooked, unnoted, unrecognized.

unholy ▶ adjective **1** *a grin of unholy amusement* = **ungodly**, irreligious, impious, blasphemous, sacrilegious, profane, irreverent; wicked, evil, immoral, sinful. **2** *(informal) an unholy row* = **shocking**, dreadful, outrageous, appalling, terrible, horrendous, frightful. **3** *an unholy alliance* = **unnatural**, unusual, improbable, made in Hell.

unhygienic ▶ adjective = **insanitary**, dirty, filthy, contaminated, unhealthy, unwholesome, insalubrious.
–OPPOSITES sanitary.

unidentified ▶ adjective = **unknown**, unnamed, anonymous, incognito, nameless, unfamiliar, strange.
–OPPOSITES known, familiar.

unification ▶ noun = **union**, merger, fusion, amalgamation, coalition, combination, confederation.

uniform ▶ adjective **1** *a uniform temperature* = **constant**, consistent, steady, invariable, unfluctuating, unchanging, stable, static, regular, fixed, even. **2** *pieces of uniform size* = **identical**, matching, similar, equal; same, like, homogeneous, consistent.
–OPPOSITES variable.
▶ noun *a soldier in uniform* = **costume**, livery, regalia, suit, ensemble, outfit; regimentals, colours; *informal* get-up, rig, gear.

uniformity ▶ noun **1** *uniformity in tax law* = **constancy**, consistency, conformity, invariability, stability, regularity, evenness, homogeneity. **2** *a dull uniformity* = **monotony**, tedium, dullness, dreariness, flatness, sameness.
–OPPOSITES variation, variety.

unify ▶ verb = **unite**, bring together, join (together), merge, fuse, amalgamate, coalesce, combine, consolidate.
–OPPOSITES separate.

unimaginable ▶ adjective = **unthinkable**, inconceivable, incredible, unbelievable, untold, beyond one's wildest dreams.

unimaginative ▶ adjective = **uninspired**, uninventive, unoriginal, uncreative, commonplace, pedestrian, mundane, ordinary, routine, humdrum, workaday, run-of-the-mill, hackneyed, trite.

unimpeded ▶ adjective = **unrestricted**, unhindered, unblocked, unhampered, free, clear.

unimportant ▶ adjective = **insignificant**, inconsequential, trivial, minor, trifling, of no account, irrelevant, peripheral, extraneous, petty, paltry; *informal* piddling.

uninhabited ▶ adjective **1** *much of this land was uninhabited* = **unpopulated**, unpeopled, unsettled. **2** *an uninhabited hut* = **vacant**, empty, unoccupied, untenanted.

uninhibited ▶ adjective **1** *uninhibited dancing* = **unrestrained**, unrepressed,

abandoned, wild, reckless; unrestricted, uncontrolled, unchecked, intemperate, wanton. **2** *I'm pretty uninhibited* =**unreserved**, unrepressed, liberated, unselfconscious, free and easy, relaxed, informal, open, outgoing, extrovert, outspoken; *informal* upfront.
–OPPOSITES repressed.

uninspired ▸ adjective =**unimaginative**, uninventive, pedestrian, mundane, unoriginal, commonplace, ordinary, routine, humdrum, run-of-the-mill, hackneyed, trite.

uninspiring ▸ adjective =**boring**, dull, dreary, unexciting, unstimulating; dry, colourless, bland, lacklustre, tedious, humdrum, run-of-the-mill.

unintelligent ▸ adjective =**stupid**, ignorant, dense, brainless, dull-witted, slow, simple-minded, idiotic; *informal* thick, dim, dumb, dopey, half-witted, dozy.

unintelligible ▸ adjective **1** *unintelligible sounds* =**incomprehensible**, indiscernible, mumbled, indistinct, unclear, slurred, inarticulate, incoherent, garbled. **2** *unintelligible graffiti* =**illegible**, indecipherable, unreadable.

unintentional ▸ adjective =**accidental**, inadvertent, involuntary, unwitting, unthinking, unpremeditated, unconscious.
–OPPOSITES deliberate.

uninterested ▸ adjective =**indifferent**, unconcerned, uninvolved, apathetic, lukewarm, unenthusiastic.

uninteresting ▸ adjective =**unexciting**, boring, dull, tiresome, wearisome, tedious, dreary, lifeless, humdrum, colourless, bland, insipid, banal, dry, pedestrian; *informal* samey.
–OPPOSITES exciting.

uninterrupted ▸ adjective =**unbroken**, continuous, undisturbed, untroubled.
–OPPOSITES intermittent.

uninvited ▸ adjective **1** *an uninvited guest* =**unasked**, unexpected; unwelcome, unwanted. **2** *uninvited suggestions* =**unsolicited**, unrequested.

uninviting ▸ adjective =**unappealing**, unattractive, unappetizing, off-putting; bleak, cheerless, dreary, dismal, depressing, grim, inhospitable.
–OPPOSITES tempting.

union ▸ noun **1** *the union of art and nature*

=**unification**, joining, merger, fusion, amalgamation, coalition, combination, synthesis, blend. **2** *the crowd moved in union* =**unity**, accord, harmony, agreement, concurrence; *formal* concord. **3** *representation by a union* =**association**, league, guild, confederation, federation.
–OPPOSITES separation, parting.

unique ▸ adjective **1** *each site is unique* =**distinctive**, individual, special, idiosyncratic; single, sole, lone, unrepeated, solitary, exclusive, rare, uncommon; *informal* one-off. **2** *a unique insight into history* =**remarkable**, special, singular, noteworthy, notable, extraordinary; unequalled, unparalleled, unmatched, unsurpassed, incomparable; *formal* unexampled. **3** *species unique to the island* =**peculiar**, specific.

unison ∎ **in unison 1** *they lifted their arms in unison* =**simultaneously**, at the same time, (all) at once, (all) together. **2** *we are in complete unison* =**in agreement**, in accord, in harmony, as one; *formal* in concord.

unit ▸ noun **1** *the family is the fundamental unit of society* =**component**, element, constituent, subdivision. **2** *a unit of currency* =**quantity**, measure, denomination. **3** *a guerrilla unit* =**detachment**, contingent, division, company, squadron, corps, regiment, brigade, platoon, battalion; cell, faction.

unite ▸ verb **1** *uniting the nation* =**unify**, join, link, connect, combine, amalgamate, fuse, weld, bond, bring together. **2** *environmentalists and activists united* =**join together**, join forces, combine, band together, ally, cooperate, collaborate, work together, pull together, team up. **3** *he sought to unite comfort with elegance* =**merge**, mix, blend, mingle, combine.
–OPPOSITES divide.

united ▸ adjective **1** *a united Germany* =**unified**, integrated, amalgamated, joined, merged; federal, confederate. **2** *a united response* =**common**, shared, joint, combined, communal, cooperative, collective, collaborative. **3** *they were united in their views* =**in agreement**, in unison, of the same opinion, like-minded, as one, in accord, in harmony.

United States of America
▸ noun =**America**; *informal* the States, the US of A, Uncle Sam; *literary* Columbia.

unity ▸ noun **1** *European unity* =**union**,

u

unification, integration, amalgamation; coalition, federation, confederation. **2** *unity between opposing factions* =**harmony**, accord, cooperation, collaboration, agreement, consensus, solidarity; *formal* concord. **3** *the organic unity of the universe* =**oneness**, singleness, wholeness, uniformity, homogeneity.
−OPPOSITES division, discord.

universal ▸ adjective =**general**, ubiquitous, comprehensive, common, omnipresent, all-inclusive; global, worldwide, international, widespread.

universally ▸ adverb =**invariably**, always, without exception, in all cases; everywhere, worldwide, globally, internationally; widely, commonly, generally.

universe ▸ noun **1** *the physical universe* =**cosmos**, macrocosm, totality; infinity, all existence. **2** *the universe of computer hardware* =**province**, world, sphere, preserve, domain, field.

WORD LINKS

relating to the universe: **cosmic**
study of the universe: **cosmology, astronomy**

university ▸ noun =**college**, academy, institute; *N. Amer.* school; *historical* polytechnic.

unjust ▸ adjective **1** *the attack was unjust* =**biased**, prejudiced, unfair, inequitable, discriminatory, partisan, one-sided. **2** *an unjust law* =**wrongful**, unfair, undeserved, unmerited, unwarranted, unreasonable, unjustifiable, indefensible.
−OPPOSITES fair.

unjustifiable ▸ adjective **1** *an unjustifiable extravagance* =**indefensible**, inexcusable, unforgivable, unpardonable, uncalled for; excessive, immoderate. **2** *an unjustifiable slur on his character* =**groundless**, unfounded, baseless, unsubstantiated, uncorroborated.
−OPPOSITES reasonable.

unkempt ▸ adjective =**untidy**, messy, scruffy, disordered, wild, dishevelled, disarranged, rumpled, wind-blown, ungroomed, bedraggled, messed up; tousled, uncombed.
−OPPOSITES tidy.

unkind ▸ adjective **1** *everyone was being unkind to him* =**uncharitable**, unpleasant, disagreeable, nasty, mean, cruel, vicious, spiteful, malicious, callous, un-

sympathetic, hard-hearted; unfriendly, uncivil, inconsiderate, insensitive, hostile; *informal* bitchy, catty. **2** *unkind weather* =**inclement**, intemperate, rough, severe, filthy.

unkindness ▸ noun =**nastiness**, unpleasantness, disagreeableness, cruelty, malice, meanness, viciousness, callousness, hard-heartedness; unfriendliness, hostility; *informal* bitchiness, cattiness.

unknown ▸ adjective **1** *the outcome was unknown* =**undisclosed**, unrevealed, secret; undetermined, undecided, unresolved, unsettled, unascertained. **2** *unknown country* =**unexplored**, uncharted, unmapped, untravelled, undiscovered. **3** *persons unknown* =**unidentified**, unnamed, anonymous. **4** *firearms were unknown to the Indians* =**unfamiliar**, unheard of, new, novel, strange. **5** *unknown artists* =**obscure**, unheard of, unsung, minor, undistinguished.
−OPPOSITES familiar.

unlawful ▸ adjective =**illegal**, illicit, illegitimate, against the law; criminal, felonious; prohibited, banned, outlawed, proscribed, forbidden.
−OPPOSITES legal.

unleash ▸ verb =**let loose**, release, (set) free, untie, untether, unchain.

unlike ▸ preposition **1** *England is totally unlike Jamaica* =**different from**, dissimilar to. **2** *unlike Lyn, Chris was a bit of a radical* =**in contrast to**, as opposed to.
−OPPOSITES similar to.

unlikely ▸ adjective **1** *it is unlikely they will recover* =**improbable**, doubtful, dubious. **2** *an unlikely story* =**implausible**, improbable, questionable, unconvincing, far-fetched, unrealistic, incredible, unbelievable, inconceivable; *informal* tall, cock and bull.
−OPPOSITES probable, believable.

unlimited ▸ adjective **1** *unlimited supplies of water* =**inexhaustible**, limitless, boundless, immeasurable, incalculable, untold, infinite, endless. **2** *unlimited travel* =**unrestricted**, unconstrained, unrestrained, unchecked, unbridled, uncurbed. **3** *unlimited power* =**total**, unqualified, unconditional, unrestricted, absolute, supreme.
−OPPOSITES finite, restricted.

unload ▸ verb **1** *we unloaded the van* =**unpack**, empty. **2** *they unloaded the cases from the lorry* =**remove**, offload, discharge. **3** *the state unloaded its 25 per cent* *stake* =**sell**, discard, jettison, offload, get rid of, dispose of; *informal* dump, get shot/shut of.

unlock ▸ verb =**unbolt**, unlatch, unbar, unfasten, open.

unloved ▸ adjective =**uncared-for**, unwanted, friendless, unvalued; rejected, unwelcome, shunned, spurned, neglected, abandoned.

unlucky ▸ adjective 1 *he was unlucky not to score* =**unfortunate**, hapless, ill-fated. 2 *an unlucky number* =**unfavourable**, inauspicious, unpropitious, ominous, cursed, ill-fated, ill-omened.
−OPPOSITES fortunate, favourable.

unmanageable ▸ adjective 1 *the huge house was unmanageable* =**troublesome**, awkward, inconvenient; cumbersome, bulky, unwieldy. 2 *his behaviour was becoming unmanageable* =**uncontrollable**, ungovernable, unruly, disorderly, out of hand control, difficult, disruptive, undisciplined, wayward.
−OPPOSITES docile.

unmanly ▸ adjective =**effeminate**, effete, unmasculine; weak, soft, timid, limp-wristed; *informal* sissy, wimpy.
−OPPOSITES virile.

unmarried ▸ adjective =**unwed(ded)**, single; spinster, bachelor; unattached, available, eligible, free.

unmatched ▸ adjective 1 *a talent for publicity unmatched by any other politician* =**unequalled**, unrivalled, unparalleled, unsurpassed. 2 *unmatched clarity and balance* =**peerless**, without equal, incomparable, inimitable, superlative, second to none, in a class of its own.

unmentionable ▸ adjective =**taboo**, censored, forbidden, banned, proscribed, prohibited, ineffable, unspeakable, unutterable, unprintable, off limits; *informal* no go.

unmerciful ▸ adjective =**ruthless**, cruel, harsh, merciless, pitiless, cold-blooded, hard-hearted, callous, brutal, severe, unforgiving, inhumane, inhuman, heartless, unsympathetic, unfeeling.

unmistakable ▸ adjective =**distinctive**, distinct, telltale, indisputable, indubitable, undoubted; plain, clear, definite, obvious, evident, manifest, patent, unequivocal, pronounced.

unmitigated ▸ adjective =**absolute**, unqualified, categorical, complete, total, downright, outright, utter, out-and-out, unequivocal, veritable, consummate, pure, sheer.

unmoved ▸ adjective 1 *he was totally unmoved by her outburst* =**unaffected**, untouched, unimpressed, undismayed, unworried; aloof, cool; unconcerned, uncaring, indifferent, impassive, unemotional, stoical, phlegmatic, equable; impervious (to), oblivious (to). 2 *he remained unmoved on the crucial issues* =**steadfast**, firm, unwavering, unswerving, resolute, decided, resolved, inflexible, unbending, implacable, adamant.

unnatural ▸ adjective 1 *the life of a battery hen is completely unnatural* =**abnormal**, unusual, uncommon, extraordinary, strange, unorthodox, exceptional, irregular, untypical. 2 *an unnatural colour* =**artificial**, man-made, synthetic, manufactured. 3 *unnatural vice* =**perverted**, warped, twisted, deviant, depraved, degenerate; *informal* kinky, pervy, sick. 4 *her voice sounded unnatural* =**affected**, artificial, stilted, forced, laboured, strained, false, fake, insincere; *informal* put on, phoney.
−OPPOSITES normal, genuine.

unnecessary ▸ adjective =**unneeded**, inessential, not required, uncalled for, useless, unwarranted, unwanted, undesired, dispensable, optional, extraneous, expendable, redundant, pointless, purposeless.
−OPPOSITES essential.

unnerve ▸ verb =**demoralize**, discourage, dishearten, dispirit, alarm, frighten, disconcert, perturb, upset, discomfit, take aback, unsettle, disquiet, fluster, shake, ruffle, throw off balance; *informal* rattle, faze, shake up; *Brit. informal* put the wind up; *N. Amer. informal* discombobulate.
−OPPOSITES hearten.

unobtrusive ▸ adjective 1 *she was unobtrusive and shy* =**self-effacing**, retiring, unassuming, quiet; shy, bashful, timid, reserved, withdrawn, introvert(ed), unforthcoming, unassertive. 2 *unobtrusive service* =**inconspicuous**, unnoticeable, low-key, discreet, circumspect, understated, unostentatious.
−OPPOSITES extrovert, conspicuous.

unoccupied ▸ adjective 1 *an unoccupied house* =**vacant**, empty, uninhabited; free, available, to let. 2 *an unoccupied territory* =**uninhabited**, unpopulated, un-

unofficial | unprincipled

peopled, unsettled. **3** *many young people were unoccupied* =**at leisure**, idle, free, at a loose end.
–OPPOSITES inhabited, populated, busy.

unofficial ▸ adjective **1** *unofficial figures* =**unauthenticated**, unconfirmed, uncorroborated, unsubstantiated, off the record. **2** *an unofficial committee* =**informal**, casual; unauthorized, unsanctioned, unaccredited.
–OPPOSITES confirmed, formal.

unorthodox ▸ adjective **1** *unorthodox views on management* =**unconventional**, unusual, radical, nonconformist, avant-garde, eccentric; *informal* off the wall, way out, offbeat. **2** *unorthodox religious views* =**heterodox**, heretical, nonconformist, dissenting.
–OPPOSITES conventional.

unpaid ▸ adjective **1** *unpaid bills* =**unsettled**, outstanding, owed, payable, undischarged. **2** *unpaid work* =**voluntary**, volunteer, honorary, unremunerative, unsalaried.

unpalatable ▸ adjective **1** *unpalatable food* =**unappetizing**, unappealing, unsavoury, inedible; disgusting, revolting, nauseating, tasteless, flavourless. **2** *the unpalatable truth* =**disagreeable**, unpleasant, regrettable, unwelcome, upsetting, distressing, dreadful.
–OPPOSITES tasty.

unparalleled ▸ adjective =**exceptional**, unique, singular, rare, unequalled, unprecedented; matchless, peerless, unrivalled, unsurpassed, incomparable, second to none.

unperturbed ▸ adjective =**untroubled**, undisturbed, unworried, unconcerned, unmoved, unflustered, unruffled; calm, composed, cool, collected, unemotional, self-possessed, self-assured, unfazed, laid-back.

unpleasant ▸ adjective **1** *a very unpleasant situation* =**disagreeable**, irksome, troublesome, annoying, irritating, vexatious, distressing, nasty, horrible, terrible, awful, dreadful, invidious, objectionable, repugnant, repellent, revolting, disgusting, distasteful, nauseating, unsavoury. **2** *an unpleasant man* =**unlikable**, unlovable, disagreeable; unfriendly, rude, impolite, obnoxious, nasty, spiteful, mean; insufferable, unbearable, annoying, irritating. **3** *an unpleasant taste* =**unappetizing**, unpalat-

able, unsavoury, unappealing; disgusting, revolting, nauseating, sickening.
–OPPOSITES agreeable, likable.

unpolished ▸ adjective **1** *unpolished wood* =**unvarnished**, unfinished, untreated, natural. **2** *his unpolished ways* =**unsophisticated**, unrefined, uncultured, coarse, vulgar, crude, rough, awkward, clumsy, gauche. **3** *an unpolished performance* =**slipshod**, rough, crude.
–OPPOSITES varnished, sophisticated.

unpopular ▸ adjective =**disliked**, friendless, unloved; unwelcome, avoided, ignored, rejected, shunned, spurned, cold-shouldered.

unprecedented ▸ adjective =**unparalleled**, unequalled, unmatched, unrivalled, out of the ordinary, unusual, exceptional, singular, remarkable, unique; unheard of, unknown, new, groundbreaking, revolutionary, pioneering.

unpredictable ▸ adjective **1** *unpredictable results* =**unforeseeable**, uncertain, doubtful, in the balance, up in the air. **2** *unpredictable behaviour* =**erratic**, moody, volatile, unstable, capricious, temperamental, mercurial, changeable, variable.

unprejudiced ▸ adjective **1** *unprejudiced observation* =**objective**, impartial, unbiased, neutral, non-partisan, detached, disinterested. **2** *unprejudiced attitudes* =**unbiased**, tolerant, non-discriminatory, liberal, broad-minded, unbigoted.
–OPPOSITES partisan, intolerant.

unprepared ▸ adjective **1** *we were unprepared for the new regime* =**unready**, off (one's) guard, surprised, taken aback; *informal* caught napping, caught on the hop. **2** *they are unprepared to support the reforms* =**unwilling**, disinclined, loath, reluctant, resistant, opposed.
–OPPOSITES ready, willing.

unpretentious ▸ adjective **1** *he was unpretentious* =**unaffected**, modest, unassuming, without airs, natural, straightforward, open, honest, sincere, frank. **2** *an unpretentious hotel* =**simple**, plain, modest, humble, unostentatious, homely, unsophisticated.

unprincipled ▸ adjective =**immoral**, unethical, unscrupulous, dishonourable, dishonest, deceitful, devious, corrupt, crooked, wicked, evil, villainous,

shameless, base, low.
−OPPOSITES ethical.

unproductive ▸ adjective **1** *unproductive soil* =**sterile**, barren, infertile, unfruitful, poor. **2** *unproductive meetings* =**fruitless**, futile, vain, idle, useless, worthless, valueless, pointless, ineffective, unprofitable, unrewarding.
−OPPOSITES fruitful.

unprofessional ▸ adjective **1** *unprofessional conduct* =**improper**, unethical, unprincipled, unscrupulous, dishonourable, disreputable; *informal* shady, crooked. **2** *he accused the detectives of being unprofessional* =**amateurish**, unskilful, inexpert, unqualified, inexperienced, incompetent, second-rate, inefficient.

unpromising ▸ adjective =**inauspicious**, unfavourable, unpropitious, discouraging, disheartening, gloomy, bleak, black, portentous, ominous, ill-omened.
−OPPOSITES auspicious.

unqualified ▸ adjective **1** *an unqualified accountant* =**uncertificated**, unlicensed, untrained. **2** *those unqualified to look after children* =**unsuitable**, unfit, ineligible, incompetent, incapable. **3** *unqualified support* =**unconditional**, unreserved, unlimited, categorical, unequivocal, unambiguous, wholehearted; complete, absolute, downright, undivided, total, utter.

unquestionable ▸ adjective =**indubitable**, undoubted, indisputable, undeniable, irrefutable, incontestable, incontrovertible, unequivocal; certain, definite, evident, manifest, obvious, apparent, patent.

unravel ▸ verb **1** *he unravelled the strands* =**untangle**, disentangle, separate out, unwind, untwist. **2** *detectives are trying to unravel the mystery* =**solve**, resolve, clear up, puzzle out, get to the bottom of, explain, clarify; *informal* figure out, suss.
−OPPOSITES entangle.

unreadable ▸ adjective **1** *unreadable writing* =**illegible**, indecipherable, unintelligible, scrawled. **2** *heavy, unreadable novels* =**dull**, tedious, boring, uninteresting, dry, wearisome, difficult, heavy. **3** *Nathan's expression was unreadable* =**inscrutable**, enigmatic, impenetrable, cryptic, mysterious, deadpan; *informal* poker-faced.
−OPPOSITES legible, accessible.

unreal ▸ adjective =**imaginary**, ficti-

tious, pretend, make-believe, made-up, dreamed-up, mock, false, illusory, mythical, fanciful; hypothetical, theoretical; *informal* phoney.

unrealistic ▸ adjective **1** *it is unrealistic to expect changes overnight* =**impractical**, unfeasible; unreasonable, irrational, illogical, senseless, silly, foolish, fanciful, idealistic, romantic, starry-eyed. **2** *unrealistic images* =**unlifelike**, unnatural, abstract.
−OPPOSITES pragmatic, lifelike.

unreasonable ▸ adjective **1** *an unreasonable woman* =**uncooperative**, unhelpful, disobliging, unaccommodating, awkward, contrary, difficult; obstinate, obdurate, wilful, headstrong, pig-headed, intractable, intransigent, inflexible. **2** *unreasonable demands* =**unacceptable**, preposterous, outrageous; excessive, immoderate, disproportionate, undue, inordinate, intolerable, unjustified, unwarranted.

unrecognizable ▸ adjective =**unidentifiable**; disguised.

unrefined ▸ adjective **1** *unrefined clay* =**unprocessed**, untreated, crude, raw, natural, unprepared, unfinished. **2** *unrefined men* =**uncultured**, uncultivated, uncivilized, uneducated, unsophisticated; boorish, oafish, loutish, coarse, vulgar, rude, uncouth.
−OPPOSITES processed.

unrelated ▸ adjective **1** *unrelated incidents* =**separate**, unconnected, independent, unassociated, distinct, discrete, disparate. **2** *a reason unrelated to my work* =**irrelevant**, immaterial, inapplicable, unconcerned, off the subject, not pertinent.

unrelenting ▸ adjective **1** *the unrelenting heat* =**continual**, constant, unremitting, unabating, unrelieved, incessant, unceasing, endless, persistent. **2** *an unrelenting opponent* =**implacable**, inflexible, uncompromising, unyielding, unbending, determined, dogged, tireless, unswerving, unwavering.
−OPPOSITES intermittent.

unreliable ▸ adjective **1** *unreliable volunteers* =**undependable**, untrustworthy, irresponsible, fickle, capricious, erratic, unpredictable, inconstant, faithless. **2** *an unreliable indicator* =**questionable**, doubtful, dubious, suspect, unsound, tenuous, fallible; risky, chancy, inaccurate; *informal* iffy, dicey.

u

unremitting ▸ adjective =**relentless**, continual, constant, unabating, unrelieved, sustained, unceasing, unending, persistent, perpetual, interminable.

unrepentant ▸ adjective =**impenitent**, remorseless, unashamed, unapologetic, unabashed.

unreserved ▸ adjective **1** *unreserved support* =**unconditional**, unqualified, unlimited, categorical, unequivocal, unambiguous; absolute, complete, thorough, wholehearted, total, utter, undivided. **2** *an unreserved man* =**uninhibited**, extrovert, outgoing, unrestrained, open, unselfconscious, frank, candid. **3** *unreserved seats* =**unbooked**, unallocated, unoccupied, free, empty, vacant.
−OPPOSITES qualified, reticent, booked.

unresolved ▸ adjective =**undecided**, unsettled, undetermined, uncertain, open, pending, open to debate/question, in doubt, up in the air.
−OPPOSITES decided.

unrest ▸ noun =**disruption**, disturbance, trouble, turmoil, disorder, chaos, anarchy; discord, dissent, strife, protest, rebellion, uprising, rioting.
−OPPOSITES peace.

unrestrained ▸ adjective =**uncontrolled**, unrestricted, unchecked, unbridled, unlimited, unfettered, uninhibited, unbounded, undisciplined.

unrestricted ▸ adjective =**unlimited**, open, free, clear, unhindered, unimpeded, unhampered, unchecked, unrestrained, unblocked, unbounded, unconfined, unqualified.
−OPPOSITES limited.

unripe ▸ adjective =**immature**, unready, green, sour.

unrivalled ▸ adjective =**unequalled**, unparalleled, unmatched, unsurpassed, unexcelled, incomparable, inimitable, second to none.

unruffled ▸ adjective =**calm**, composed, self-controlled, self-possessed, untroubled, unperturbed, at ease, relaxed, serene, cool, unemotional, stoical; *informal* unfazed.

unruly ▸ adjective =**disorderly**, rowdy, wild, unmanageable, uncontrollable, disobedient, disruptive, undisciplined, wayward, wilful, headstrong, obstreperous, difficult, intractable, out of hand, recalcitrant; *formal* refractory.
−OPPOSITES disciplined.

unsafe ▸ adjective **1** *the building was unsafe* =**dangerous**, risky, perilous, hazardous, high-risk, treacherous, insecure, unsound; harmful, injurious, toxic. **2** *the verdict was unsafe* =**unreliable**, insecure, unsound, questionable, doubtful, dubious, suspect; *informal* iffy; *Brit. informal* dodgy.
−OPPOSITES harmless, secure.

unsaid ▸ adjective =**unspoken**, unuttered, unstated, unexpressed, unvoiced, suppressed; tacit, implicit, understood, not spelt out, taken as read, implied.

unsanitary ▸ adjective =**unhygienic**, dirty, filthy, unclean, contaminated, unhealthy, germ-ridden, disease-ridden, infested.
−OPPOSITES hygienic.

unsatisfactory ▸ adjective =**disappointing**, undesirable, disagreeable, displeasing; inadequate, unacceptable, poor, bad, substandard, weak, mediocre, not up to par, defective, deficient, imperfect, inferior; *informal* leaving a lot to be desired.

unsavoury ▸ adjective **1** *unsavoury food* =**unpalatable**, unappetizing, distasteful, disagreeable, unappealing, unattractive; inedible, uneatable, disgusting, revolting, nauseating, sickening; tasteless, bland, flavourless; *informal* yucky. **2** *an unsavoury character* =**disreputable**, unpleasant, disagreeable, nasty, mean, rough; immoral, degenerate, dishonourable, dishonest, unprincipled, unscrupulous, low, villainous; *informal* shady, crooked.
−OPPOSITES tasty, appetizing.

unscathed ▸ adjective =**unharmed**, unhurt, uninjured, undamaged, in one piece, intact, safe, unmarked, untouched, unscratched.

unscrupulous ▸ adjective =**unprincipled**, unethical, immoral, shameless, reprobate, exploitative, corrupt, dishonest, dishonourable, deceitful, devious, underhand, unsavoury, disreputable, evil, wicked, villainous; *informal* crooked, shady.

unseat ▸ verb **1** *the horse unseated his rider* =**dislodge**, throw, dismount, upset, unhorse. **2** *an attempt to unseat the party leader* =**depose**, oust, topple, overthrow, bring down, dislodge, supplant, usurp, overturn, eject.

unseemly ▸ adjective =**indecorous**, improper, unbecoming, unfitting, unbe-

fitting, unworthy, undignified, indiscreet, indelicate, ungentlemanly, unladylike.
−OPPOSITES decorous.

unseen ▶ adjective =hidden, concealed, obscured, camouflaged, out of sight, imperceptible, undetectable, unnoticed, unobserved.

unselfish ▶ adjective =altruistic, disinterested, selfless, self-denying, self-sacrificing; generous, philanthropic, public-spirited, charitable, benevolent, noble.

unsettle ▶ verb =discompose, unnerve, upset, disturb, disquiet, perturb, discomfit, disconcert, alarm, dismay, trouble, bother, agitate, fluster, ruffle, shake (up), throw; *informal* rattle, faze.

unsettled ▶ adjective 1 *an unsettled life* =aimless, directionless, purposeless; rootless, nomadic. 2 *an unsettled child* =restless, restive, fidgety, anxious, worried, troubled, fretful; agitated, ruffled, uneasy, disconcerted, discomposed, unnerved, ill at ease, edgy, tense, nervous, apprehensive, disturbed, perturbed; *informal* rattled, fazed. 3 *unsettled weather* =changeable, variable, inconstant, inconsistent, erratic, unstable, undependable, unreliable, uncertain, unpredictable. 4 *unsettled areas* =uninhabited, unpopulated, unpeopled, desolate, lonely.

unshakeable ▶ adjective =steadfast, resolute, staunch, firm, decided, determined, unswerving, unwavering; unyielding, inflexible, dogged, obstinate, persistent, indefatigable, tireless, unflagging, unremitting, unrelenting.

unsightly ▶ adjective =ugly, unattractive, unprepossessing, unlovely, disagreeable, displeasing, hideous, horrible, repulsive, revolting, offensive, grotesque.
−OPPOSITES attractive.

unskilful ▶ adjective =inexpert, incompetent, inept, amateurish, unprofessional, inexperienced, untrained, unpractised; *informal* ham-fisted, cack-handed.

unskilled ▶ adjective =untrained, unqualified; manual, blue-collar, menial; inexpert, inexperienced, amateurish, unprofessional.

unsociable ▶ adjective =unfriendly, uncongenial, unneighbourly, unapproachable, introverted, reticent, reserved, withdrawn, retiring, aloof, distant, remote, detached; *informal* standoffish.
−OPPOSITES friendly.

unsolicited ▶ adjective =uninvited, unasked for, unrequested.

unsophisticated ▶ adjective 1 *she seemed unsophisticated* =unworldly, naive, simple, innocent, green, immature, callow, inexperienced, childlike, artless, guileless, ingenuous, natural, unaffected, unassuming, unpretentious. 2 *unsophisticated software* =simple, crude, basic, rudimentary, primitive, rough and ready.

unsound ▶ adjective 1 *structurally unsound* =rickety, flimsy, wobbly, unstable, crumbling, damaged, rotten, ramshackle, insubstantial, unsafe, dangerous. 2 *this submission appears unsound* =untenable, flawed, defective, faulty, ill-founded, flimsy, unreliable, questionable, dubious, tenuous, suspect, fallacious; *informal* iffy. 3 *of unsound mind* =disordered, deranged, disturbed, demented, unstable, unbalanced, unhinged, insane; *informal* touched.
−OPPOSITES strong.

unsparing ▶ adjective 1 *he is unsparing in his criticism* =merciless, pitiless, ruthless, relentless, remorseless, unmerciful, unforgiving, implacable, uncompromising; stern, strict, severe, harsh. 2 *unsparing approval* =ungrudging, unstinting, free, ready; lavish, liberal, generous, magnanimous, open-handed.

unspeakable ▶ adjective 1 *unspeakable delights* =indescribable, inexpressible, unutterable, indefinable, unimaginable, inconceivable, marvellous, wonderful. 2 *an unspeakable crime* =dreadful, awful, appalling, horrific, horrendous, abominable, frightful, shocking, ghastly, monstrous, heinous, deplorable, despicable, execrable, vile.

unspecified ▶ adjective =unnamed, unstated, unidentified, undesignated, undefined, undecided, undetermined, uncertain; unknown, indefinite, indeterminate, vague.

unspoilt ▶ adjective =unimpaired, perfect, pristine, immaculate, unblemished, unharmed, unflawed, undamaged, untouched, unmarked, untainted.

unspoken ▶ adjective =unstated, unexpressed, unuttered, unsaid, unvoiced, unarticulated, undeclared, not spelt out;

u

tacit, implicit, implied, understood, taken as read.
–OPPOSITES explicit.

unstable ▶ adjective **1** *icebergs are notoriously unstable* =**unsteady**, rocky, wobbly, rickety, shaky, unsafe, insecure, precarious. **2** *unstable coffee prices* =**changeable**, volatile, variable, fluctuating, irregular, unpredictable, erratic. **3** *he was mentally unstable* =**unbalanced**, of unsound mind, mentally ill, deranged, demented, disturbed, unhinged.
–OPPOSITES steady, firm.

unsteady ▶ adjective **1** *she was unsteady on her feet* =**unstable**, rocky, wobbly, rickety, shaky, doddery. **2** *an unsteady flow* =**irregular**, uneven, variable, erratic, spasmodic, changeable, fluctuating, inconstant, intermittent, fitful.
–OPPOSITES stable, regular.

unstinted, unstinting ▶ adjective =**lavish**, liberal, generous, openhanded, ungrudging, unsparing, ready, profuse, abundant.

unsubstantiated ▶ adjective =**unconfirmed**, unsupported, uncorroborated, unverified, unattested, unproven; unfounded, groundless, baseless.

unsuccessful ▶ adjective **1** *an unsuccessful attempt* =**failed**, abortive, ineffective, fruitless, profitless, unproductive; vain, futile, useless, pointless, worthless. **2** *an unsuccessful business* =**unprofitable**, loss-making. **3** *an unsuccessful candidate* =**failed**, losing, beaten; unlucky.

unsuitable ▶ adjective **1** *an unsuitable product* =**inappropriate**, ill-suited, inapt, inapposite, unacceptable, unfitting, incompatible, out of place/keeping. **2** *an unsuitable moment* =**inopportune**, infelicitous; *formal* malapropos.
–OPPOSITES appropriate, opportune.

unsullied ▶ adjective =**spotless**, untarnished, unblemished, unspoilt, untainted, impeccable, undamaged, unimpaired, immaculate, unflawed.
–OPPOSITES tarnished.

unsung ▶ adjective =**unacknowledged**, uncelebrated, unacclaimed, unapplauded, unhailed; neglected, unrecognized, overlooked, forgotten.
–OPPOSITES celebrated.

unsure ▶ adjective **1** *she felt very unsure* =**unconfident**, unassertive, insecure, hesitant, diffident, anxious, apprehensive. **2** *Sally was unsure what to do* =**undecided**, uncertain, irresolute, dither-

ing, equivocating, in two minds, in a quandary. **3** *some teachers are unsure about the proposed strike* =**dubious**, doubtful, sceptical, uncertain, unconvinced.
–OPPOSITES confident.

unsurpassed ▶ adjective =**unmatched**, unrivalled, unparalleled, unequalled, matchless, peerless, inimitable, incomparable, unsurpassable.

unsurprising ▶ adjective =**predictable**, foreseeable, to be expected, foreseen, anticipated, par for the course; *informal* inevitable, on the cards.

unsuspecting ▶ adjective =**unsuspicious**, unwary, unconscious, ignorant, unwitting; trusting, gullible, naive.
–OPPOSITES wary.

unswerving ▶ adjective =**unwavering**, unfaltering, steadfast, unshakeable, staunch, firm, resolute, stalwart, dedicated, committed, constant, single-minded, dogged, indefatigable, unyielding, unbending, indomitable.

unsympathetic ▶ adjective **1** *unsympathetic staff* =**uncaring**, unconcerned, unfeeling, insensitive, unkind, pitiless, heartless, hard-hearted. **2** *the government was unsympathetic to these views* =**opposed**, against, (dead) set against, antagonistic, ill-disposed; *informal* anti. **3** *an unsympathetic character* =**unlikeable**, disagreeable, unpleasant, objectionable, unsavoury.
–OPPOSITES caring.

unsystematic ▶ adjective =**unmethodical**, uncoordinated, disorganized, unplanned, indiscriminate; random, inconsistent, irregular, erratic, casual, haphazard, chaotic.

untangle ▶ verb **1** *I untangled the fishing tackle* =**disentangle**, unravel, unsnarl, straighten out, untwist, unknot. **2** *untangling a mystery* =**solve**, find the answer to, resolve, puzzle out, fathom, clear up, clarify, get to the bottom of; *informal* figure out; *Brit. informal* suss out.

untarnished ▶ adjective =**unsullied**, unblemished, untainted, impeccable, undamaged, unspoilt, spotless.

untenable ▶ adjective =**indefensible**, undefendable, insupportable, unsustainable, unjustifiable, flimsy, weak, shaky.

unthinkable ▶ adjective =**unimaginable**, inconceivable, unbelievable, incredible, implausible.

untidy ▸ adjective **1** *untidy hair* =**scruffy**, tousled, dishevelled, unkempt, messy, disordered, disarranged, rumpled, bedraggled, uncombed, ungroomed, straggly, ruffled, tangled, matted. **2** *the room was untidy* =**disordered**, messy, disorganized, cluttered, in chaos, haywire, in disarray; *informal* higgledy-piggledy.
−OPPOSITES neat, orderly.

untie ▸ verb =**undo**, unknot, unbind, unfasten, unlace, untether, unhitch; loose, free.

until ▸ preposition & conjunction **1** *I was working until midnight* =**(up) till**, up to, as late as; *N. Amer.* through. **2** *this did not happen until 1998* =**before**, prior to, previous to, up to, earlier than.

untimely ▸ adjective **1** *an untimely interruption* =**ill-timed**, mistimed; inopportune, inappropriate; inconvenient, unwelcome, infelicitous; *formal* malapropos. **2** *his untimely death* =**premature**, (too) early, too soon, before time.
−OPPOSITES opportune.

untiring ▸ adjective =**vigorous**, energetic, determined, resolute, enthusiastic, keen, zealous, spirited, dogged, tenacious, persistent, persevering, staunch; tireless, unflagging, unfailing, unfaltering, unwavering, indefatigable, unrelenting, unswerving.

untold ▸ adjective **1** *untold damage* =**boundless**, measureless, limitless, infinite, immeasurable, incalculable. **2** *untold billions* =**countless**, innumerable, endless, limitless, numberless, uncountable; numerous, many, multiple; *literary* multitudinous, myriad. **3** *the untold story* =**unreported**, uncounted, unrevealed, undisclosed, undivulged, unpublished.
−OPPOSITES limited.

untouched ▸ adjective **1** *the food was untouched* =**uneaten**, unconsumed, undrunk. **2** *one of the few untouched areas* =**unspoilt**, unmarked, unblemished, unsullied, undefiled, undamaged, unharmed; pristine, natural, immaculate, in perfect condition, unaffected, unchanged, unaltered.

untoward ▸ adjective =**unexpected**, unanticipated, unforeseen, unpredictable, unpredicted, surprising, unusual; unwelcome, unfavourable, adverse, unfortunate, infelicitous; *formal* malapropos.

untrained ▸ adjective =**unskilled**, untaught, unschooled, untutored, unpractised, inexperienced; unqualified, unlicensed, amateur, non-professional.

untried ▸ adjective =**untested**, unestablished, new, experimental, unattempted, trial, test, pilot, unproven.
−OPPOSITES established.

untroubled ▸ adjective =**unworried**, unperturbed, unconcerned, unruffled, undismayed, unbothered, unagitated, unflustered; insouciant, nonchalant, blasé, carefree, serene; *informal* laid-back.

untrue ▸ adjective *these suggestions are totally untrue* =**false**, fabricated, made up, invented, concocted, trumped up; erroneous, wrong, incorrect, inaccurate; fallacious.
−OPPOSITES correct.

untrustworthy ▸ adjective =**dishonest**, deceitful, double-dealing, treacherous, two-faced, duplicitous, dishonourable, unprincipled, unscrupulous, corrupt; unreliable, undependable.
−OPPOSITES reliable.

untruthful ▸ adjective **1** *the answers may be untruthful* =**false**, untrue, fabricated, made up, invented, trumped up; erroneous, wrong, incorrect, inaccurate, fallacious, fictitious. **2** *an untruthful person* =**lying**, mendacious, dishonest, deceitful, duplicitous, false, two-faced; *informal* crooked, bent.
−OPPOSITES honest.

untwist ▸ verb =**untwine**, disentangle, unravel, unsnarl, unwind, unroll, uncoil, unfurl, open (out), straighten (out).

unused ▸ adjective **1** *the notebook is unused | unused food* =**unutilized**, unemployed, unexploited, not in service; left over, remaining, uneaten, unconsumed, unneeded, not required, to spare, surplus (to requirements). **2** *he was unused to such directness* =**unaccustomed**, new, a stranger, unfamiliar, unconversant, unacquainted.
−OPPOSITES accustomed.

unusual ▸ adjective **1** *an unusual sight* =**uncommon**, abnormal, atypical, unexpected, surprising, unfamiliar, different; strange, odd, curious, extraordinary, unorthodox, unconventional, singular, peculiar, bizarre; rare, scarce, exceptional, isolated, occasional, infrequent; *informal* weird, offbeat, way out, freaky. **2** *a man of unusual talent* =**re-**

markable, extraordinary, exceptional, singular, particular, outstanding, notable, noteworthy, distinctive, striking, significant, special, unique, unparalleled, prodigious.
–OPPOSITES common.

unutterable ▶ adjective **1** *an existence of unutterable boredom* =**indescribable**, inexpressible, unspeakable, undefinable, inconceivable; extreme, great, overwhelming; dreadful, awful, appalling, terrible. **2** *unutterable joy* =**marvellous**, wonderful, superb, splendid, unimaginable, profound, deep.

unvarnished ▶ adjective **1** *unvarnished wood* =**bare**, unpainted, unpolished, unfinished, untreated. **2** *the unvarnished truth* =**straightforward**, plain, simple, stark; truthful, candid, honest, frank, forthright, direct, blunt.

unveil ▶ verb =**reveal**, present, disclose, divulge, make known, make public, communicate, publish, broadcast; display, show, exhibit; release, bring out.

unwanted ▶ adjective **1** *an unwanted development* =**unwelcome**, undesirable, unpopular, unfortunate, unlucky, unfavourable, untoward; unpleasant, disagreeable, displeasing, distasteful, objectionable; regrettable, deplorable; unacceptable, intolerable, awful, terrible, wretched, appalling. **2** *tins of unwanted food* =**unused**, left over, surplus, superfluous; uneaten, unconsumed, untouched. **3** *an unwanted guest* =**uninvited**, unbidden, unasked, unrequested, unsolicited. **4** *many ageing people feel unwanted* =**friendless**, unloved, forsaken, rejected, shunned; superfluous, useless, unnecessary.
–OPPOSITES welcome.

unwarranted ▶ adjective **1** *the criticism is unwarranted* =**unjustified**, indefensible, inexcusable, unforgivable, unpardonable, uncalled for, unnecessary, unjust, groundless. **2** *an unwarranted invasion of privacy* =**unauthorized**, unsanctioned, unapproved, uncertified, unlicensed; illegal, unlawful, illicit, illegitimate, criminal, actionable.
–OPPOSITES justified.

unwary ▶ adjective =**incautious**, careless, thoughtless, heedless, inattentive, unwatchful, off one's guard.

unwavering ▶ adjective =**steady**, fixed, resolute, resolved, firm, steadfast, unswerving, unfaltering, untiring, tireless, indefatigable, unyielding, relentless, unremitting, sustained.
–OPPOSITES unsteady.

unwelcome ▶ adjective **1** *I was made to feel unwelcome* =**unwanted**, uninvited. **2** *even a small increase is unwelcome* =**undesirable**, unpopular, unfortunate, unlucky; disappointing, upsetting, distressing, disagreeable, displeasing; regrettable, deplorable, lamentable.

unwell ▶ adjective =**ill**, sick, poorly, indisposed, ailing, not oneself, under/below par, peaky; *Brit.* off colour; *informal* under the weather, funny, lousy, rough; *Brit. informal* grotty; *Austral./NZ informal* crook.

unwieldy ▶ adjective =**cumbersome**, unmanageable, unmanoeuvrable; awkward, clumsy, massive, heavy, hefty, bulky.

unwilling ▶ adjective **1** *unwilling conscripts* =**reluctant**, unenthusiastic, hesitant, resistant, grudging, involuntary, forced. **2** *he was unwilling to take on that responsibility* =**disinclined**, reluctant, averse, loath; (**be unwilling to do something**) not have the heart to, baulk at, demur at, shy away from, flinch from, shrink from, have qualms about, have misgivings about, have reservations about.
–OPPOSITES keen.

unwillingness ▶ adjective =**disinclination**, reluctance, hesitation, diffidence, wavering, vacillation, resistance, objection, opposition, doubts, second thoughts, scruples, qualms, misgivings.

unwind ▶ verb **1** *Ella unwound the scarf* =**unroll**, uncoil, unravel, untwine, untwist, disentangle, open (out), straighten (out). **2** *unwinding after work* =**relax**, loosen up, ease up/off, slow down, de-stress, put one's feet up, take it easy; *informal* wind down, unbutton; *N. Amer. informal* hang loose, chill out, kick back.

unwise ▶ adjective =**injudicious**, illadvised, imprudent, foolish, silly, inadvisable, impolitic, misguided, foolhardy, irresponsible, rash, reckless.
–OPPOSITES sensible.

unwitting ▶ adjective **1** *an unwitting accomplice* =**unknowing**, unconscious, unsuspecting, oblivious, unaware, innocent. **2** *an unwitting mistake* =**unintentional**, inadvertent, involuntary, unconscious, accidental.

–OPPOSITES conscious.

unworldly ▶ adjective **1** *a gauche, unworldly girl* =**naive**, simple, inexperienced, innocent, green, raw, callow, immature, unsophisticated, gullible, ingenuous, artless, guileless. **2** *unworldly beauty* =**unearthly**, other-worldly, ethereal, ghostly, preternatural, supernatural, paranormal, mystical. **3** *an unworldly religious order* =**non-materialistic**, spiritualistic.

unworthy ▶ adjective **1** *he was unworthy of trust* =**undeserving**, ineligible, unqualified, unfit. **2** *unworthy behaviour* =**unbecoming**, unsuitable, inappropriate, unbefitting, unfitting, unseemly, improper; discreditable, shameful, dishonourable, despicable, ignoble, contemptible, reprehensible.
–OPPOSITES deserving, becoming.

unwritten ▶ adjective =**tacit**, implicit, unvoiced, taken for granted, accepted, recognized, understood; traditional, customary, conventional.

unyielding ▶ adjective **1** *unyielding spikes of cane* =**stiff**, inflexible, unbending, inelastic, firm, hard, solid, tough. **2** *an unyielding policy* =**resolute**, inflexible, uncompromising, unbending, unshakeable, unwavering, immovable, intractable, intransigent, determined, dogged, obstinate, stubborn, tenacious, relentless, implacable, single-minded.

up-and-coming ▶ adjective =**promising**, budding, rising, on the up and up, with potential; talented, gifted, able.

upbeat ▶ adjective *(informal)* =**optimistic**, cheerful, cheery, positive, confident, hopeful, sanguine, bullish, buoyant.
–OPPOSITES pessimistic, negative.

upbringing ▶ noun =**childhood**, early life, formative years, teaching, instruction, rearing.

update ▶ verb **1** *security measures are continually updated* =**modernize**, upgrade, improve, overhaul. **2** *I'll update him on developments* =**brief**, bring up to date, inform, fill in, tell, notify, apprise, keep posted; *informal* clue in, put in the picture, bring/keep up to speed.

upgrade ▶ verb **1** *there are plans to upgrade the system* =**improve**, modernize, update, make better, ameliorate, reform. **2** *he was upgraded to a seat in the cabinet* =**promote**, elevate, move up, raise.

–OPPOSITES downgrade, demote.

upheaval ▶ noun =**disruption**, disturbance, trouble, turbulence, disorder, confusion, turmoil, pandemonium, chaos, mayhem, cataclysm.

uphill ▶ adjective **1** *an uphill path* =**upward**, rising, ascending, climbing. **2** *an uphill job* =**arduous**, difficult, hard, tough, taxing, demanding, exacting, stiff, formidable, laborious, gruelling, onerous, Herculean; *informal* no picnic, killing.
–OPPOSITES downhill.

uphold ▶ verb **1** *the court upheld his claim* =**confirm**, endorse, sustain, approve, support, back (up), stand by, defend. **2** *they've a tradition to uphold* =**maintain**, sustain, continue, preserve, protect, keep, hold to, keep alive, keep going.
–OPPOSITES overturn, oppose.

upkeep ▶ noun **1** *the upkeep of the road* =**maintenance**, repair(s), service, care, preservation, conservation; running. **2** *the child's upkeep* =**(financial) support**, maintenance, keep, subsistence, care.

uplift ▶ verb *she needs something to uplift her spirits* =**boost**, raise, buoy up, cheer up, perk up, enliven, brighten up, lighten, stimulate, inspire, revive, restore; *informal* buck up.

uplifting ▶ adjective =**inspiring**, stirring, inspirational, rousing, moving, touching, affecting, cheering, heartening, encouraging.

upper ▶ adjective **1** *the upper floor* =**higher**, superior; top. **2** *the upper echelons of the party* =**senior**, superior, higher-level, higher-ranking, top.
–OPPOSITES lower.

■ **the upper hand** =**an advantage**, the edge, a lead, a head start, ascendancy, superiority, supremacy, sway, control, power, mastery, dominance, command.

upper-class ▶ adjective =**aristocratic**, noble, patrician, titled, blue-blooded, high-born, elite, landed, born with a silver spoon in one's mouth; *Brit.* county; *informal* upper-crust, top-drawer; *Brit. informal* posh.

uppermost ▶ adjective **1** *the uppermost branches* =**highest**, top, topmost. **2** *their own problems remained uppermost in their minds* =**predominant**, of greatest importance, to the fore, foremost, dominant, principal, chief, main, paramount, major.

upright ▶ adjective **1** *an upright position*

u

=**vertical**, perpendicular, plumb, straight (up), erect, on end; on one's feet. **2** *an upright member of the community* =**honest**, honourable, upstanding, respectable, high-minded, law-abiding, worthy, righteous, decent, good, virtuous, principled.
–OPPOSITES horizontal, dishonourable.

uprising ▶ noun =**rebellion**, revolt, insurrection, mutiny, revolution, insurgence, rioting; civil disobedience, unrest, anarchy; coup.

uproar ▶ noun **1** *the uproar in the kitchen continued* =**turmoil**, disorder, confusion, chaos, commotion, disturbance, rumpus, tumult, turbulence, mayhem, pandemonium, bedlam, noise, din, clamour, hubbub, racket; *informal* hullabaloo; *Brit. informal* row. **2** *there was an uproar when he was dismissed* =**outcry**, furore, fuss, commotion, hue and cry, rumpus; *informal* hullabaloo, stink, ructions; *Brit. informal* row.
–OPPOSITES calm.

uproarious ▶ adjective **1** *an uproarious party* =**riotous**, rowdy, noisy, loud, wild, unruly, rip-roaring, rollicking, boisterous. **2** *an uproarious joke* =**hilarious**, rib-tickling; *informal* priceless, side-splitting, a scream, a hoot.
–OPPOSITES quiet.

uproot ▶ verb **1** *don't uproot wild flowers* =**pull up**, root out, deracinate, grub out/ up. **2** *a revolution is necessary to uproot the social order* =**eradicate**, get rid of, eliminate, root out, destroy, put an end to, do away with, wipe out, stamp out.
–OPPOSITES plant.

upset ▶ verb **1** *the accusation upset her* =**distress**, trouble, perturb, dismay, disturb, discompose, unsettle, disconcert, disquiet, worry, bother, agitate, fluster, throw, ruffle, unnerve, shake; hurt, sadden, grieve. **2** *he upset a tureen of soup* =**knock over**, overturn, upend, tip over, topple; spill. **3** *the dam will upset the ecological balance* =**disrupt**, interfere with, disturb, throw into confusion, mess up.
▶ noun **1** *a legal dispute will cause worry and upset* =**distress**, trouble, perturbation, dismay, disquiet, worry, bother, agitation; hurt, grief. **2** *a stomach upset* =**disorder**, complaint, ailment, illness, sickness, malady; *informal* bug; *Brit. informal* lurgy.
▶ adjective **1** *I was upset by the news* =**distressed**, troubled, perturbed, dismayed,

disturbed, unsettled, disconcerted, worried, bothered, anxious, agitated, flustered, ruffled, unnerved, shaken; hurt, saddened, grieved; *informal* cut up, choked; *Brit. informal* gutted. **2** *an upset stomach* =**disturbed**, unsettled, queasy, bad, poorly; *informal* gippy.
–OPPOSITES unperturbed, calm.

upshot ▶ noun =**result**, consequence, outcome, conclusion; effect, repercussion, reverberations, ramification.
–OPPOSITES cause.

upside down ▶ adjective **1** *an upside-down canoe* =**upturned**, upended, wrong side up, overturned, inverted; capsized. **2** *they left the flat upside down* =**in disarray**, in disorder, jumbled up, in a muddle, untidy, disorganized, in chaos, in confusion; *informal* higgledy-piggledy.

upstanding ▶ adjective *an upstanding member of the community* =**honest**, honourable, upright, respectable, high-minded, law-abiding, worthy, righteous, decent, good, virtuous, principled, noble, incorruptible.
–OPPOSITES dishonourable.

upstart ▶ noun =**parvenu(e)**, arriviste, nouveau riche; status seeker, social climber; *informal* johnny-come-lately.

up to date ▶ adjective **1** *up-to-date equipment* =**modern**, contemporary, the latest, state-of-the-art, new, up to the minute; advanced. **2** *the newsletter will keep you up to date* =**informed**, up to speed, in the picture, in touch, au fait, conversant, familiar, knowledgeable, acquainted.
–OPPOSITES out of date, old-fashioned.

upturn ▶ noun =**improvement**, upswing; recovery, revival, rally, resurgence, increase, rise, jump, leap, upsurge, boost, escalation.
–OPPOSITES fall, slump.

upward ▶ adjective *an upward trend* =**rising**, ascending, climbing, mounting; uphill.
–OPPOSITES downward.

upwards ▶ adverb *he inched his way upwards* =**up**, upward, uphill; to the top.
–OPPOSITES downward.

■ **upward(s) of** =**more than**, above, over, in excess of, exceeding, beyond.

urban ▶ adjective =**town**, city, municipal, metropolitan, built-up, inner-city, suburban.
–OPPOSITES rural.

urbane ▶ adjective =**suave**, sophisti-

cated, debonair, worldly, cultivated, cultured, civilized; smooth, polished, refined, self-possessed; courteous, polite, civil, well mannered, mannerly, charming, gentlemanly, gallant.
−OPPOSITES uncouth, unsophisticated.

urchin ▶ noun =**ragamuffin**, waif, stray; imp, rascal; *derogatory* guttersnipe.

urge ▶ verb 1 *she urged him to try* =**encourage**, exhort, enjoin, press, entreat, implore, call on, appeal to, beg, plead with; egg on, spur; *formal* adjure; *literary* beseech. 2 *I urge caution in interpreting these results* =**advise**, counsel, advocate, recommend.
▶ noun *his urge to travel* =**desire**, wish, need, compulsion, longing, yearning, hankering, craving, appetite, hunger, thirst; *informal* yen, itch.

urgent ▶ adjective 1 *the urgent need for more funding* =**acute**, pressing, dire, desperate, critical, serious, grave, intense, crying, burning, compelling, extreme, high-priority; life-and-death. 2 *an urgent whisper* =**insistent**, persistent, importunate, earnest, pleading, begging.

urinate ▶ verb =**pass water**, relieve oneself; *informal* spend a penny, have/take a leak, pee, piddle, have a tinkle; *Brit. informal* wee, have a Jimmy (Riddle), have a slash; *N. Amer. informal* take a whizz; *formal* micturate.

usable ▶ adjective =**ready/fit for use**, disposable; working, functional, serviceable, operational, up and running.

usage ▶ noun 1 *energy usage* =**use**, consumption, utilization. 2 *the usage of equipment* =**use**, utilization, operation, manipulation, running, handling. 3 *the intricacies of English usage* =**phraseology**, parlance, idiom, way of speaking/writing, mode of expression; idiolect.

use ▶ verb 1 *she used her key to open the door* =**utilize**, avail oneself of, employ, work, operate, wield, ply, apply, manoeuvre, put into service. 2 *the court will use its discretion* =**exercise**, employ, bring into play, practise, apply. 3 *use your troops well and they will not let you down* =**manage**, handle, treat, deal with, behave/act towards, conduct oneself towards. 4 *I couldn't help feeling that she was using me* =**take advantage of**, exploit, manipulate, take liberties with, impose on, abuse; capitalize on, profit from, trade on, milk; *informal* cash in on, walk all over. 5 *we have used all the available*

funds =**consume**, get/go through, exhaust, deplete, expend, spend.
▶ noun 1 *the use of such weapons* =**utilization**, application, employment, operation, manipulation. 2 *his use of other people for his own ends* =**exploitation**, manipulation; abuse. 3 *what is the use of that?* =**advantage**, benefit, service, utility, help, good, gain, avail, profit, value, worth, point, object, purpose, sense, reason. 4 *composers have not found much use for the device* =**need**, necessity, call, demand, requirement.

used ▶ adjective *a used car* =**second-hand**, pre-owned, nearly new, old; worn, hand-me-down, cast-off.
−OPPOSITES new.
■ **used to** =**accustomed to**, no stranger to, familiar with, at home with, in the habit of, experienced in, versed in, conversant with, acquainted with.

useful ▶ adjective 1 *a useful tool* =**functional**, practical, handy, convenient, utilitarian, serviceable, of service; *informal* nifty. 2 *a useful experience* =**beneficial**, advantageous, helpful, worthwhile, profitable, rewarding, productive, constructive, valuable, fruitful. 3 *(informal) they had some very useful players* =**competent**, capable, able, skilful, talented, proficient, accomplished, good, handy; *informal* nifty.
−OPPOSITES useless, disadvantageous, incompetent.

useless ▶ adjective 1 *it was useless to try | useless knowledge* =**futile**, to no avail, vain, pointless, to no purpose, unavailing, hopeless, ineffectual, fruitless, unprofitable, unproductive; broken, kaput. 2 *(informal) he was useless at his job* =**incompetent**, inept, ineffective, incapable, inadequate, hopeless, bad; *informal* pathetic, a dead loss.
−OPPOSITES useful, beneficial, competent.

usher ▶ verb *she ushered him to a seat* =**escort**, accompany, take, show, see, lead, conduct, guide, steer, shepherd.
▶ noun *ushers showed them to their seats* =**guide**, attendant, escort.

usual ▶ adjective =**habitual**, customary, accustomed, wonted, normal, routine, regular, standard, typical, established, set, settled, stock, conventional, traditional, expected, predictable, familiar; average, general, ordinary, everyday.
−OPPOSITES exceptional.

usually ▶ adverb =**normally**, generally,

habitually, customarily, routinely, typically, ordinarily, commonly, conventionally, traditionally; as a rule, in general, more often than not, mainly, mostly.

usurp ▸ verb **1** *Richard usurped the throne* =**seize**, take over, take possession of, take, commandeer, assume. **2** *the Hanoverian dynasty had usurped the Stuarts* =**oust**, overthrow, remove, topple, unseat, depose, dethrone; supplant, replace.

utensil ▸ noun =**implement**, tool, instrument, device, apparatus, gadget, appliance, contrivance, contraption, aid; *informal* gizmo.

utilitarian ▸ adjective =**practical**, functional, serviceable, useful, sensible, efficient, utility, workaday; plain, unadorned, undecorative.
– OPPOSITES decorative.

utility ▸ noun =**usefulness**, use, benefit, value, advantage, help, profitability, practicality, effectiveness, avail, service; *formal* efficacy.

utilize ▸ verb =**use**, employ, avail oneself of, bring/press into service, bring into play, deploy, draw on, exploit.

utmost ▸ adjective **1** *a matter of the utmost importance* =**greatest**, highest, maximum, most; extreme, supreme, paramount. **2** *the utmost tip of Shetland* =**furthest**, farthest, extreme, very, outermost.

Utopia ▸ noun =**paradise**, heaven, Eden, Shangri-La, Elysium; idyll, nirvana; *literary* Arcadia.

Utopian ▸ adjective =**idealistic**, visionary, romantic, starry-eyed, fanciful, unrealistic; ideal, perfect, paradisal, heavenly, idyllic, blissful, Elysian; *literary* Arcadian.

utter[1] ▸ adjective *that's utter nonsense* =**complete**, total, absolute, thorough, perfect, downright, out-and-out, outright, sheer, arrant, positive, prize, rank, pure, real, veritable, consummate, categorical, unmitigated.

utter[2] ▸ verb **1** *he uttered an exasperated snort* =**emit**, let out, give, produce. **2** *he hardly uttered a word* =**say**, speak, voice, express, articulate, pronounce, enunciate, verbalize, vocalize.

utterance ▸ noun =**remark**, comment, word, statement, observation, declaration, pronouncement.

utterly ▸ adverb =**completely**, totally, absolutely, entirely, wholly, fully, thoroughly, quite, altogether, one hundred per cent, downright, really, to the hilt, to the core; *informal* dead.

U-turn ▸ noun *a complete U-turn in economic policy* =**volte-face**, turnaround, about-face, reversal, shift, change of heart, change of mind, backtracking, change of plan; *Brit.* about-turn.

Vv

vacancy ▶ noun **1** *there are vacancies for technicians* =**opening**, position, post, job, opportunity. **2** *Cath stared into vacancy* =**empty space**, emptiness, nothingness, void. **3** *a vacancy of mind* =**empty-headedness**, lack of intelligence, brainlessness, vacuity.

vacant ▶ adjective **1** *a vacant house* =**empty**, unoccupied, available, not in use, free, unfilled; uninhabited, untenanted. **2** *a vacant look* =**blank**, expressionless, unresponsive, emotionless, impassive, vacuous, empty, glazed.
–OPPOSITES full, occupied, expressive.

vacate ▶ verb **1** *he was forced to vacate the premises* =**leave**, move out of, evacuate, quit, depart from. **2** *he will be vacating his post next year* =**resign from**, leave, stand down from, give up, bow out of, relinquish, retire from; *informal* quit.
–OPPOSITES occupy, take up.

vacation ▶ noun **1** =**holiday**, trip, tour, break; leave, time off, recess; *formal* sojourn. **2** *the squatters' vacation of the land* =**departure**, evacuation, abandonment, desertion.

vacillate ▶ verb =**dither**, be indecisive, waver, hesitate, be in two minds, blow hot and cold; *Brit.* haver, hum and haw; *informal* dilly-dally.

vacillating ▶ adjective =**irresolute**, indecisive, dithering, hesitant, wavering, ambivalent, divided, uncertain, in two minds, blowing hot and cold; *informal* dilly-dallying.
–OPPOSITES resolute.

vacuous ▶ adjective =**silly**, inane, unintelligent, foolish, stupid, brainless, vapid, vacant, empty-headed; *informal* gormless, moronic, brain-dead.
–OPPOSITES intelligent.

vacuum ▶ noun **1** *people longing to fill the spiritual vacuum in their lives* =**emptiness**, void, nothingness, vacancy. **2** *the political vacuum left by the Emperor's death* =**gap**, space, lacuna, void.

vagary ▶ noun =**change**, fluctuation, variation, quirk, peculiarity, oddity, eccentricity, unpredictability, caprice, whim, fancy.

vagrant ▶ noun =**tramp**, drifter, down-and-out, beggar, itinerant, wanderer, nomad, traveller, vagabond, transient, homeless person; *N. Amer.* hobo; *N. Amer. informal* bum.
▶ adjective *vagrant beggars* =**homeless**, drifting, transient, roaming, itinerant, wandering, nomadic, travelling, vagabond.

vague ▶ adjective **1** *a vague shape* =**indistinct**, indefinite, indeterminate, unclear, ill-defined; hazy, fuzzy, misty, blurry, out of focus, faint, shadowy, dim, obscure. **2** *a vague description* =**imprecise**, rough, approximate, inexact, nonspecific, generalized, ambiguous, equivocal, hazy, woolly. **3** *vague plans* =**hazy**, uncertain, undecided, unsure, unclear, unsettled, indefinite, indeterminate, unconfirmed, up in the air, speculative. **4** *she was so vague in life* =**absent-minded**, forgetful, dreamy, abstracted; *informal* scatty, not with it.
–OPPOSITES clear, precise, certain.

vaguely ▶ adverb **1** *she looks vaguely familiar* =**slightly**, a little, a bit, somewhat, rather, in a way; faintly, obscurely; *informal* sort of, kind of. **2** *he fired his rifle vaguely in our direction* =**roughly**, more or less, approximately. **3** *he smiled vaguely* =**absent-mindedly**, abstractedly, vacantly.
–OPPOSITES very, exactly.

vain ▶ adjective **1** *their flattery made him vain* =**conceited**, narcissistic, self-loving, egotistic; proud, arrogant, boastful, cocky, immodest; *informal* big-headed. **2** *a vain attempt* =**futile**, useless, pointless; ineffective, fruitless, unproductive, unsuccessful, failed, abortive; thwarted, frustrated, foiled.
–OPPOSITES modest, successful.
■ **in vain** =**unsuccessfully**, to no avail, to no purpose, fruitlessly.

valedictory ▶ adjective =**farewell**, goodbye, leaving, parting; last, final.

valet ▶ noun =**manservant**, personal attendant, Jeeves.

valiant ▶ adjective =**brave**, courageous, plucky, intrepid, heroic, gallant, lion-

hearted, bold, fearless, daring, audacious; unflinching, unafraid, undaunted, doughty, indomitable, mettlesome, stout-hearted; *informal* game, gutsy.
–OPPOSITES cowardly.

valid ▸ adjective **1** *a valid criticism* =**well founded**, sound, reasonable, rational, logical, justifiable, defensible, viable, bona fide; cogent, credible, forceful, strong, weighty. **2** *a valid contract* =**legally binding**, lawful, official; in force, in effect.

validate ▸ verb **1** *clinical trials exist to validate this claim* =**prove**, substantiate, corroborate, verify, support, back up, bear out, confirm, authenticate. **2** *250 course proposals were validated* =**ratify**, endorse, approve, agree to, accept, authorize, legalize, legitimize, warrant, license, certify, recognize.
–OPPOSITES disprove.

valley ▸ noun =**dale**, vale; hollow, gully, gorge, ravine, canyon, rift; *Brit.* combe, dene; *N. English* clough; *Scottish* glen, strath; *literary* dell, dingle.

valour ▸ noun =**bravery**, courage, pluck, nerve, daring, fearlessness, audacity, boldness, stout-heartedness, heroism; *informal* guts; *Brit. informal* bottle.
–OPPOSITES cowardice.

valuable ▸ adjective **1** *a valuable watch* =**precious**, costly, high-priced, expensive, dear; worth its weight in gold, priceless. **2** *a valuable contribution* =**useful**, helpful, beneficial, invaluable, productive, worthwhile, worthy, important.
–OPPOSITES cheap, worthless, useless.

valuables ▸ plural noun =**precious items**, costly items, prized possessions, treasures.

value ▸ noun **1** *houses exceeding £250,000 in value* =**price**, cost, worth; market price. **2** *the value of adequate preparation* =**worth**, usefulness, advantage, benefit, gain, profit, good, help; importance, significance. **3** *society's values* =**principles**, ethics, morals, standards, code of behaviour.
▸ verb **1** *his estate was valued at £45,000* =**evaluate**, assess, estimate, appraise, price. **2** *she valued his opinion* =**think highly of**, have a high opinion of, rate highly, esteem, set (great) store by, respect.

valued ▸ adjective =**cherished**, treasured, dear, prized; esteemed, respected.

vanguard ▸ noun =**forefront**, van, advance guard, spearhead, front, fore, lead, cutting edge; leaders, founders, pioneers, trailblazers, groundbreakers.

vanish ▸ verb **1** *he vanished into the darkness* =**disappear**, be lost to sight/view, become invisible, recede from view. **2** *all hope vanished* =**fade (away)**, evaporate, melt away, end, cease to exist, pass away, die out.
–OPPOSITES appear, materialize.

vanity ▸ noun **1** *she had none of the vanity often associated with beautiful women* =**conceit**, narcissism, self-love, self-admiration, egotism; pride, arrogance, boastfulness, cockiness, swagger; *informal* big-headedness. **2** *the vanity of all desires of the will* =**futility**, uselessness, pointlessness, worthlessness, fruitlessness.
–OPPOSITES modesty.

vapid ▸ adjective =**insipid**, uninspired, colourless, uninteresting, feeble, dull, boring, tedious, unexciting, unimaginative, lifeless, tame, bland.
–OPPOSITES lively, colourful.

vapour ▸ noun =**haze**, mist, steam, condensation; fumes, exhalation, fog, smog, smoke.

variable ▸ adjective =**changeable**, shifting, fluctuating, irregular, inconstant, inconsistent, fluid, unstable, unsettled, protean, wavering, vacillating, capricious, fickle; *informal* up and down.
–OPPOSITES constant.

variance ▸ noun =**difference**, variation, discrepancy, dissimilarity, disagreement, conflict, divergence, deviation, contrast, contradiction.
■ **at variance 1** *his recollections were at variance with evidence* =**inconsistent**, at odds, not in keeping, out of line, out of step, in conflict, in disagreement, different, discrepant, dissimilar, contrary, incompatible, contradictory. **2** *they were at variance with their former allies* =**in disagreement**, at odds, at cross purposes, at loggerheads, in conflict, in dispute.

variant ▸ noun *there are a number of variants of the same idea* =**variation**, form, alternative, adaptation, alteration, modification, permutation.
▸ adjective *a variant spelling* =**alternative**, other, different, divergent.

variation ▸ noun **1** *regional variations in farming* =**difference**, dissimilarity;

disparity, contrast, discrepancy, imbalance. **2** *opening times are subject to variation* =**change**, alteration, modification. **3** *there was very little variation from the pattern* =**deviation**, variance, divergence, departure, fluctuation. **4** *hurling is an Irish variation of hockey* =**variant**, form; development, adaptation, alteration, modification.

varied ▶ adjective =**diverse**, assorted, miscellaneous, mixed, sundry, heterogeneous, wide-ranging, multifarious; disparate, motley.

variegated ▶ adjective =**multicoloured**, particoloured, polychromatic, prismatic, kaleidoscopic; mottled, marbled, streaked, speckled, flecked, dappled.
−OPPOSITES plain, monochrome.

variety ▶ noun **1** *the lack of variety in the curriculum* =**diversity**, variation, diversification, multifariousness, heterogeneity; change, difference. **2** *a wide variety of flowers* =**assortment**, miscellany, range, array, collection, selection, mixture, medley; mixed bag, motley collection, pot-pourri. **3** *fifty varieties of pasta* =**sort**, kind, type, class, category, style, form; make, model, brand; strain, breed, genus.
−OPPOSITES uniformity.

various ▶ adjective =**diverse**, different, differing, varied, a variety of, assorted, mixed, sundry, miscellaneous, heterogeneous, disparate, motley.

varnish ▶ noun & verb =**lacquer**, shellac, japan, enamel, glaze; polish.

vary ▶ verb **1** *estimates of the cost vary* =**differ**, be dissimilar. **2** *rates of interest vary over time* =**fluctuate**, rise and fall, go up and down, change, alter, shift, swing. **3** *the diaphragm is used for varying the aperture* =**modify**, change, alter, adjust, regulate, control, set; diversify. **4** *the routine never varied* =**change**, alter, deviate, differ, fluctuate.

vast ▶ adjective =**huge**, extensive, expansive, broad, wide, boundless, immeasurable, limitless, infinite; enormous, immense, great, massive, colossal, gigantic, gargantuan, mammoth; giant, towering, mountainous, titanic; *informal* jumbo, mega, whopping, humongous; *Brit. informal* ginormous.
−OPPOSITES tiny.

vat ▶ noun =**tub**, tank, cistern, barrel, butt, cask, tun, drum; vessel, receptacle, container, holder, reservoir.

vault[1] ▶ noun **1** *the highest Gothic vault in Europe* =**arched roof**, dome, arch. **2** *the vault under the church* =**cellar**, basement, underground chamber; crypt, undercroft, catacomb, burial chamber. **3** *valuables stored in the vault* =**strongroom**, safe deposit.

vault[2] ▶ verb *he vaulted over the gate* =**jump over**, leap over, spring over, bound over; hurdle, clear.

vaunt ▶ verb =**boast about**, brag about, make much of, crow about, parade, flaunt; *informal* show off about; *formal* laud.

veer ▶ verb =**turn**, swerve, swing, career, weave, wheel; change direction/course, deviate.

vegetate ▶ verb =**do nothing**, idle, languish, laze, lounge, loll; *informal* veg out, slob out.

vegetation ▶ noun =**plants**, flora; greenery, foliage, herbage, verdure.

> **WORD LINKS**
>
> *substance used to kill vegetation:* **herbicide**

vehemence ▶ noun =**passion**, force, ardour, fervour, violence, urgency, strength, vigour, intensity, keenness, enthusiasm, zeal.

vehement ▶ adjective =**passionate**, forceful, ardent, impassioned, heated, spirited, urgent, fervent, violent, fierce, strong, forcible, powerful, emphatic, vigorous, intense, earnest, keen, enthusiastic, zealous.
−OPPOSITES mild, apathetic.

vehicle ▶ noun **1** *a stolen vehicle* =**means of transport**, conveyance. **2** *a vehicle for the communication of ideas* =**channel**, medium, means, agent, instrument, mechanism, organ, apparatus.

> **WORD LINKS**
>
> *relating to vehicles:* **automotive**

veil ▶ noun *a thin veil of cloud* =**covering**, screen, curtain, mantle, cloak, mask, blanket, shroud, canopy, cloud, pall.
▶ verb *the peak was veiled in mist* =**envelop**, surround, swathe, enfold, cover, conceal, hide, screen, shield, cloak, blanket, shroud; obscure.

veiled ▶ adjective *veiled threats* =**disguised**, camouflaged, masked, covert, hidden, concealed, suppressed, under-

lying, implicit, indirect.
−OPPOSITES overt.

vein ▶ noun **1** =blood vessel. **2** *the veins in the rock* =layer, lode, seam, stratum, stratification, deposit. **3** *white marble with grey veins* =streak, mark, line, stripe, strip, band, thread, strand. **4** *he closes the article in a humorous vein* =mood, humour, disposition, attitude, tenor, tone, key, spirit, character, feel, flavour, quality, atmosphere; manner, way, style.

WORD LINKS

relating to veins: **vascular, venous**
incision into a vein: **phlebotomy**

velocity ▶ noun =speed, pace, rate, tempo, momentum, impetus; swiftness, rapidity; *literary* fleetness, celerity.

vendetta ▶ noun =feud, quarrel, argument, falling-out, dispute, fight, war; bad blood, enmity.

vendor ▶ noun =seller, retailer, purveyor, dealer, trader, merchant, supplier, stockist.

veneer ▶ noun **1** *cherry wood with a maple veneer* =surface, lamination, layer, overlay, facing, covering, finish, exterior. **2** *a veneer of sophistication* =facade, front, show, outward display, appearance, impression, semblance, guise, mask, pretence, camouflage, cover.

venerable ▶ adjective =respected, revered, honoured, esteemed, hallowed, august, distinguished, eminent, great.

venerate ▶ verb =revere, worship, hallow, hold sacred, exalt, adore, honour, respect, esteem.

veneration ▶ noun =reverence, worship, adoration, exaltation, devotion, honour, respect, esteem.

vengeance ▶ noun =revenge, retribution, retaliation, requital, reprisal, an eye for an eye.

vengeful ▶ adjective =vindictive, revengeful, unforgiving.
−OPPOSITES forgiving.

venom ▶ noun **1** *snake venom* =poison, toxin. **2** *his voice was full of venom* =rancour, malevolence, vitriol, spite, vindictiveness, malice, animosity, antagonism, hostility, bile, hate; *informal* bitchiness, cattiness.

venomous ▶ adjective **1** *a venomous snake* | *a venomous bite* =poisonous, toxic; dangerous, deadly, lethal, fatal. **2** *venomous remarks* =vicious, spiteful, rancorous, malevolent, vitriolic, vindictive, malicious, poisonous, virulent, hostile, cruel; *informal* bitchy, catty.
−OPPOSITES harmless, benevolent.

vent ▶ noun *an air vent* =outlet, inlet, opening, aperture, hole, gap, orifice, space; duct, flue, shaft, well, passage, airway.
▶ verb *the crowd vented their fury* =let out, release, pour out, express, air, voice.

ventilate ▶ verb **1** *the greenhouse must be ventilated* =air, aerate, oxygenate; freshen, cool. **2** *the workers ventilated their discontent* =express, air, bring into the open, communicate, voice, verbalize, discuss, debate, talk over.

venture ▶ noun *a business venture* =enterprise, undertaking, project, scheme, operation, endeavour, speculation.
▶ verb **1** *we ventured across the moor* =set out, go, travel, journey. **2** *may I venture an opinion?* =put forward, advance, proffer, offer, air, suggest, submit, propose, moot.

verbal ▶ adjective =oral, spoken, stated, said; unwritten.

verbatim ▶ adverb =word for word, letter for letter, literally, exactly, precisely, closely, faithfully.

verbose ▶ adjective =wordy, loquacious, garrulous, talkative, voluble; long-winded, lengthy, prolix, circumlocutory, circuitous, discursive, digressive, rambling; *informal* mouthy.
−OPPOSITES succinct, laconic.

verbosity ▶ noun =wordiness, loquacity, garrulity, talkativeness, volubility; long-windedness, verbiage, prolixity, circumlocution; *Brit. informal* waffle.

verdant ▶ adjective =green, leafy, grassy; lush, rich.

verdict ▶ noun =judgement, adjudication, decision, finding, ruling, resolution, pronouncement.

verge ▶ noun **1** *the verge of the lake* =edge, border, margin, side, brink, rim, lip; fringe, boundary, perimeter. **2** *Spain was on the verge of an economic crisis* =brink, threshold, edge, point.
▶ verb *a degree of caution that verged on the obsessive* =approach, border on, be close/near to, be tantamount to; tend towards, approximate to.

verification ▶ noun =confirmation, substantiation, proof, corroboration, support, attestation, validation, authentication, endorsement.

verify ▶ verb =**substantiate**, confirm, prove, corroborate, back up, bear out, justify, support, uphold, attest to, testify to, validate, authenticate, endorse.
–OPPOSITES refute.

vernacular ▶ noun =**everyday language**, colloquial language, conversational language, common parlance; dialect, regional language, patois; *informal* lingo.

versatile ▶ adjective =**adaptable**, flexible, all-round, multitalented, resourceful; adjustable, multi-purpose, all-purpose.

verse ▶ noun 1 *Elizabethan verse* =**poetry**, versification; balladry, lyrics. 2 *a verse he'd composed to mark my anniversary* =**poem**, lyric, ballad, sonnet, ode, limerick, rhyme, ditty, lay. 3 *a poem with sixty verses* =**stanza**, canto, couplet.
–OPPOSITES prose.

version ▶ noun 1 *his version of events* =**account**, report, statement, description, record, story, rendering, interpretation, explanation, understanding, reading, impression, side. 2 *the English version will be published next year* =**edition**, translation, impression. 3 *they have replaced coal-burning fires with gas versions* =**form**, sort, kind, type, variety.

vertical ▶ adjective =**upright**, erect, perpendicular, plumb, on end, standing.
–OPPOSITES horizontal.

vertigo ▶ noun =**dizziness**, giddiness, light-headedness, loss of balance.

verve ▶ noun =**enthusiasm**, vigour, energy, pep, dynamism, go, elan, vitality, vivacity, buoyancy, liveliness, animation, zest, sparkle, spirit, ebullience, brio, gusto, keenness, passion, zeal, relish, ardour; *informal* zing, zip, vim, pizzazz, oomph.

very ▶ adverb *that's very kind of you* =**extremely**, exceedingly, exceptionally, extraordinarily, tremendously, immensely, hugely, intensely, acutely, abundantly, singularly, unusually, decidedly, highly, remarkably, really; *informal* terrifically, awfully, terribly, majorly, seriously, mega, ultra, damn; *Brit. informal* ever so, well, dead, jolly; *N. Amer. informal* real, mighty, awful, darned.
–OPPOSITES slightly.
▶ adjective 1 *those were his very words* =**exact**, actual, precise. 2 *the very thought of food*

made her feel ill =**mere**, simple, pure; sheer.

vessel ▶ noun 1 *a fishing vessel* =**boat**, ship, craft; *literary* barque. 2 *pour the mixture into a heatproof vessel* =**container**, receptacle; basin, bowl, pan, pot.

vest ▶ verb *executive power is vested in the President* =**confer on**, entrust to, invest in, bestow on, grant to, give to; endow, lodge, lay, place.

vestibule ▶ noun =**entrance hall**, porch, portico, foyer, lobby, anteroom, antechamber, waiting room.

vestige ▶ noun 1 *the last vestiges of colonialism* =**remnant**, fragment, relic, echo, indication, sign, trace, mark, legacy, reminder. 2 *she showed no vestige of emotion* =**bit**, touch, hint, suggestion, suspicion, shadow, scrap, tinge, speck, shred, jot, iota, whit; *informal* smidgen, tad.

vestigial ▶ adjective 1 *vestigial limbs* =**rudimentary**, undeveloped; nonfunctional; *Biology* primitive. 2 *he felt a vestigial flicker of anger from last night* =**remaining**, surviving, residual, leftover, lingering.

vet ▶ verb =**check**, examine, scrutinize, investigate, inspect, look over, screen, assess, evaluate, appraise; *informal* check out.

veteran ▶ noun *a veteran of 16 political campaigns* =**old hand**, past master, doyen, doyenne; *informal* old-timer.
–OPPOSITES novice.
▶ adjective *a veteran diplomat* =**long-serving**, seasoned, old, hardened; adept, expert, practised, experienced; *informal* battle-scarred.

veto ▶ noun *parliament's right of veto* =**rejection**, dismissal; prohibition, proscription, embargo, ban, interdict; *informal* thumbs down, red light.
–OPPOSITES approval.
▶ verb *the president vetoed the bill* =**reject**, turn down, throw out, dismiss; prohibit, forbid, interdict, proscribe, disallow, embargo, ban; *informal* kill, put the kibosh on, give the thumbs down to, give the red light to.
–OPPOSITES approve.

vex ▶ verb =**annoy**, irritate, irk, pique; *informal* aggravate, peeve, miff, rile, nettle, needle, get (to), bug, hack off, get up someone's nose; *Brit. informal* wind up, nark; *N. Amer. informal* tee off, rankle.

vexed ▶ adjective 1 *a vexed expression* =**annoyed**, irritated, cross, angry, infuriated, exasperated, irked, piqued, displeased, put out, disgruntled; *informal* aggravated, peeved, nettled, miffed, riled, hacked off; *Brit. informal* narked, shirty; *N. Amer. informal* teed off. **2** *the vexed issue of immigration* =**disputed**, contested, contentious, debated, at issue, controversial, contentious, moot; problematic, difficult, knotty, thorny.

viable ▶ adjective =**feasible**, workable, practicable, practical, usable, possible, realistic, achievable, attainable; *informal* doable.
−OPPOSITES impracticable.

vibrant ▶ adjective **1** *a vibrant woman* =**spirited**, lively, energetic, vigorous, vital, animated, sparkling, effervescent, vivacious, dynamic, passionate, fiery; *informal* peppy, feisty. **2** *vibrant colours* =**vivid**, bright, striking, brilliant, strong, rich. **3** *his vibrant voice* =**resonant**, sonorous, reverberant, resounding, ringing, echoing; strong, rich.
−OPPOSITES lifeless, pale.

vibrate ▶ verb **1** *the floor vibrated* =**quiver**, shake, tremble, shiver, shudder, throb, pulsate. **2** *a low rumbling sound began to vibrate through the car* =**reverberate**, resonate, resound, ring, echo.

vibration ▶ noun =**tremor**, shaking, quivering, quaking, shuddering, throb, pulsation.

vicar ▶ noun =**minister**, rector, priest, parson, clergyman, clergywoman, cleric, churchman, churchwoman, ecclesiastic, pastor, man/woman of the cloth, curate, chaplain, preacher; *informal* reverend, padre, Holy Joe.

vicarious ▶ adjective =**indirect**, secondary, derived, surrogate, substitute; empathic.

vice ▶ noun **1** *youngsters may be driven to vice* =**immorality**, wrongdoing, wickedness, badness, evil, iniquity, villainy, corruption, misconduct; sin, ungodliness; depravity, degeneracy, dissolution, dissipation, debauchery, decadence; *formal* turpitude. **2** *smoking is my only vice* =**shortcoming**, failing, flaw, fault, defect, weakness, deficiency, foible, frailty.
−OPPOSITES virtue.

vice versa ▶ adverb =**conversely**, inversely; reciprocally.

vicinity ▶ noun =**neighbourhood**, surrounding area, locality, area, district, region, quarter, zone; environs, surroundings, precincts; *informal* neck of the woods.
■ **in the vicinity of** =**around**, about, nearly, circa, approaching, roughly, something like, more or less; in the region of, near to, close to; *Brit.* getting on for.

vicious ▶ adjective **1** *a vicious killer* =**brutal**, ferocious, savage, violent, dangerous, ruthless, merciless, heartless, callous, cruel, harsh, cold-blooded, inhuman, barbaric, bloodthirsty, sadistic. **2** *a vicious hate campaign* =**malicious**, malevolent, malign, spiteful, vindictive, venomous, rancorous, cruel, bitter, acrimonious, hostile; *informal* catty.
−OPPOSITES gentle, kindly.

victim ▶ noun **1** *a victim of crime* =**sufferer**, injured party, casualty; fatality, loss; survivor. **2** *the victim of a confidence trick* =**dupe**, stooge, gull; target, prey, quarry, object, subject, focus, recipient; *informal* sucker, fall guy; *N. Amer. informal* patsy, pigeon, sap.
■ **fall victim to** =**fall ill with**, be stricken with, catch, develop, contract, pick up; succumb to; *informal* go down with.

victimize ▶ verb =**persecute**, pick on, bully, abuse, discriminate against, illtreat, terrorize; exploit, prey on, take advantage of, dupe, cheat, double-cross; *informal* get at, have it in for, hassle, lean on.

victorious ▶ adjective =**triumphant**, conquering, vanquishing, winning, champion, successful.

victory ▶ noun =**success**, triumph, conquest, win, landslide, coup; mastery, superiority, supremacy; *informal* walkover, thrashing, trouncing.
−OPPOSITES defeat.

vie ▶ verb =**compete**, contend, contest, struggle, fight, battle, cross swords, lock horns, jockey; war, feud.

view ▶ noun **1** *the view from her flat* =**outlook**, prospect, panorama, vista, scene, aspect; scenery, landscape. **2** *we agree with this view* =**opinion**, viewpoint, belief, judgement, thinking, notion, idea, conviction, persuasion, attitude, feeling, sentiment; stance, standpoint, approach. **3** *the church came into view* =**sight**, perspective, vision, visibility.
▶ verb **1** *they viewed the landscape* =**look at**, eye, observe, gaze at, contemplate, regard, scan, survey, inspect, scrutinize;

informal check out, gawp at; *Brit. informal* clock; *N. Amer. informal* eyeball; *literary* espy, behold. **2** *the law was viewed as a last resort* =**consider**, regard, look on, see, perceive, judge, deem, reckon.

■ **in view of** =**considering**, bearing in mind, on account of, in the light of, owing to, because of, as a result of.

■ **on view** =**on display**, on exhibition, on show.

viewer ▶ noun =**watcher**, spectator, onlooker, observer; (**viewers**) audience, crowd; *literary* beholder.

vigilant ▶ adjective =**watchful**, observant, attentive, alert, eagle-eyed, on the lookout; on one's guard, cautious, wary, heedful, mindful; *informal* beady-eyed.
–OPPOSITES inattentive.

vigorous ▶ adjective **1** *the child was vigorous* =**robust**, healthy, hale and hearty, strong, sturdy, fit; hardy, tough; bouncing, thriving, flourishing; energetic, lively, active, perky, spirited, vibrant, vital; *informal* peppy. **2** *a vigorous defence* =**strenuous**, powerful, forceful, spirited, mettlesome, determined, aggressive, zealous, ardent, fervent, vehement, passionate; tough, hard-hitting; *informal* punchy.
–OPPOSITES weak, feeble.

vigorously ▶ adverb =**strenuously**, strongly, powerfully, forcefully, energetically, heartily, for dear life, all out, fiercely, hard; *informal* like mad; *Brit. informal* like billy-o.

vigour ▶ noun =**robustness**, health, hardiness, strength, sturdiness, toughness; bloom, radiance, energy, life, vitality, verve, spirit; zeal, passion, determination, dynamism, zest, pep, drive; *informal* oomph, get-up-and-go.
–OPPOSITES lethargy.

vile ▶ adjective =**foul**, nasty, unpleasant, bad, horrid, dreadful, abominable, atrocious, offensive, obnoxious, odious, repulsive, disgusting, hateful, nauseating; disgraceful, appalling, shocking, shameful, dishonourable, execrable, heinous, abhorrent, deplorable, monstrous, wicked, evil, iniquitous, depraved, debased; contemptible, despicable, reprehensible; *informal* gross, low-down.
–OPPOSITES pleasant.

vilify ▶ verb =**disparage**, denigrate, defame, run down, revile, abuse, speak ill of, criticize, condemn; malign, slander, libel; *N. Amer.* slur; *informal* pull apart, bad-

mouth; *Brit. informal* rubbish, slate; *formal* derogate.
–OPPOSITES commend.

villain ▶ noun =**criminal**, lawbreaker, offender, felon, convict, miscreant, wrongdoer; rogue, scoundrel, reprobate, hoodlum; *informal* crook, con, baddy.

villainous ▶ adjective =**wicked**, evil, iniquitous, sinful, nefarious, heinous, egregious, fiendish, vicious, murderous; criminal, illicit, unlawful, illegal, lawless; immoral, corrupt, degenerate, sordid, depraved, dishonest, unscrupulous, unprincipled; *informal* crooked, bent, lowdown, dirty, shady.
–OPPOSITES virtuous.

villainy ▶ noun =**wickedness**, badness, evil, iniquity, wrongdoing, dishonesty, roguery, delinquency; crime, vice, criminality, lawlessness, corruption; *formal* turpitude.

vindicate ▶ verb **1** *he was vindicated by the jury* =**acquit**, clear, absolve, exonerate; discharge, free; *informal* let off; *formal* exculpate. **2** *I had fully vindicated my request* =**justify**, warrant, substantiate, ratify, authenticate, verify, confirm, corroborate, prove, defend, support, back, endorse.

vindictive ▶ adjective =**vengeful**, unforgiving, resentful, acrimonious, bitter; spiteful, mean, rancorous, venomous, malicious, malevolent, nasty, cruel; *informal* catty.
–OPPOSITES forgiving.

vintage ▶ noun **1** *the best vintage for years* =**(grape) harvest**, crop, yield. **2** *furniture of Louis XV vintage* =**period**, era, epoch, time, origin; genre, style, kind, sort, type.
▶ adjective **1** *vintage French wine* =**high-quality**, quality, choice, select, superior, best. **2** *vintage motor vehicles* =**classic**, ageless, timeless; old, antique, heritage, historic. **3** *his reaction was vintage Francis* =**characteristic**, typical, pure.

violate ▶ verb **1** *this violates human rights* =**contravene**, breach, infringe, break, transgress, overstep, disobey, defy, flout; disregard, ignore. **2** *the tomb was violated* =**desecrate**, profane, defile, degrade, debase; damage, vandalize, deface, destroy. **3** *he drugged and violated her* =**rape**, assault, force oneself on, abuse, molest, interfere with; *dated* deflower, defile; *literary* ravish.

−OPPOSITES respect.

violation ▸ noun **1** *a violation of human rights* =**contravention**, breach, infringement, infraction, transgression, defiance. **2** *a violation of their private lives* =**invasion**, breach, infraction; trespass, intrusion, encroachment. **3** *she was threatened with violation* =**rape**, sexual assault, sexual abuse, molestation, interference; *dated* defloration, defilement.

violence ▸ noun **1** *police violence* =**brutality**, ferocity, savagery, cruelty, barbarity. **2** *the violence of the blow* =**force**, power, strength, might, savagery, ferocity, brutality. **3** *the violence of his passion* =**intensity**, severity, strength, force, vehemence, power, potency, ferocity, fury.

violent ▸ adjective **1** *a violent alcoholic* =**brutal**, vicious, savage, rough, aggressive, threatening, fierce, ferocious; barbaric, thuggish, cut-throat, homicidal, murderous, cruel. **2** *a violent blow* =**powerful**, forceful, hard, sharp, smart, strong, vigorous, mighty, hefty; savage, ferocious, brutal, vicious. **3** *violent jealousy* =**intense**, extreme, strong, powerful, intemperate, unbridled, uncontrollable, ungovernable, consuming, passionate.
−OPPOSITES gentle, weak, mild.

VIP ▸ noun =**celebrity**, famous person, very important person, personality, big name, star; dignitary, luminary, worthy, grandee, notable; *informal* heavyweight, celeb, bigwig, big shot, big cheese, honcho, top dog.

virago ▸ noun =**harridan**, shrew, dragon, vixen; fishwife, witch, she-devil, martinet, spitfire, ogress; *informal* battle-axe.

virgin ▸ adjective **1** *virgin forest* =**untouched**, unspoilt, untainted, pristine, flawless, spotless, unsullied, unpolluted, undefiled, perfect; unchanged, intact; unexplored, uncharted. **2** *virgin girls* =**chaste**, celibate, abstinent; pure, uncorrupted, undefiled, unsullied, innocent; *literary* vestal.

virginity ▸ noun =**chastity**, maidenhood, honour, purity, innocence; celibacy, abstinence; *informal* cherry.

virile ▸ adjective =**manly**, masculine, male; strong, tough, vigorous, robust, muscly, brawny; red-blooded, fertile; *informal* macho, laddish, butch, beefy, hunky.

−OPPOSITES effeminate.

virtual ▸ adjective =**effective**, near (enough), essential, practical, to all intents and purposes; indirect, implied, unacknowledged, tacit.

virtually ▸ adverb =**effectively**, all but, more or less, practically, almost, nearly, close to, verging on, just about, as good as, essentially, to all intents and purposes; roughly, approximately; *informal* pretty much/well; *literary* well nigh.

virtue ▸ noun **1** *the simple virtue of peasant life* =**goodness**, righteousness, morality, integrity, dignity, rectitude, honour, decency, respectability; principles, ethics. **2** *promptness was not one of his virtues* =**good point**, good quality, strong point, asset, forte, attribute, strength, talent. **3** *I can see no virtue in this* =**merit**, advantage, benefit, usefulness, strength.
−OPPOSITES vice, failing, disadvantage.
■ **by virtue of** =**because of**, on account of, by dint of, by means of, by way of, via, through, as a result of, as a consequence of, on the strength of, owing to, thanks to, due to, by reason of.

virtuosity ▸ noun =**skill**, mastery, expertise, prowess, proficiency, ability, aptitude; excellence, brilliance, talent, genius, artistry, flair, panache, finesse, wizardry; *informal* know-how.

virtuoso ▸ noun *the pianist is a virtuoso* =**genius**, expert, (past) master, maestro, artist, prodigy, marvel, adept, professional, doyen, doyenne, veteran; star, champion; *informal* hotshot, wizard, pro, ace; *Brit. informal* dab hand.
−OPPOSITES duffer.
▸ adjective *a virtuoso violinist* =**skilful**, expert, accomplished, master, consummate, proficient, talented, gifted, adept, good, competent; impressive, outstanding, exceptional, magnificent, supreme, first-rate, brilliant, excellent; *informal* superb, mean, ace.
−OPPOSITES incompetent.

virtuous ▸ adjective =**righteous**, good, moral, ethical, upright, upstanding, high-minded, principled, exemplary; irreproachable, honest, honourable, reputable, decent, respectable, worthy; pure, whiter than white, saintly, angelic; *informal* squeaky clean.

virulent ▸ adjective **1** *virulent herbicides* =**poisonous**, toxic, venomous, noxious, deadly, lethal, fatal, mortal, pernicious,

damaging, destructive; *literary* deathly, noxious. **2** *a virulent epidemic* =**infectious**, contagious, communicable, transmittable, spreading, pestilential; *informal* catching. **3** *a virulent attack on morals* =**vitriolic**, malicious, malevolent, hostile, spiteful, venomous, vicious, vindictive, bitter, rancorous, acrimonious, scathing, caustic, withering, nasty, savage, harsh.
–OPPOSITES harmless, amicable.

viscous ▸ adjective =**sticky**, gummy, gluey, adhesive, tacky, treacly, syrupy; glutinous, gelatinous, thick, mucous; *informal* gooey, gloopy.

visible ▸ adjective =**perceptible**, seeable, observable, noticeable, detectable, discernible; in sight, in/on view, on display; evident, apparent, manifest, transparent, plain, clear, conspicuous, obvious, patent, unmistakable, prominent.

vision ▸ noun **1** *her vision was blurred* =**eyesight**, sight, observation, (visual) perception; eyes; view, perspective. **2** *visions of the ancestral pilgrims* =**apparition**, spectre, phantom, ghost, wraith, manifestation; hallucination, illusion, mirage; *informal* spook. **3** *visions of a better future* =**dream**, reverie; plan, hope; fantasy, delusion. **4** *his speech lacked vision* =**imagination**, creativity, inventiveness, innovation, inspiration, intuition, perception, insight, foresight, prescience. **5** *Melissa was a vision in lilac* =**beautiful sight**, feast for the eyes, pleasure to behold, delight, dream, beauty, picture, sensation; *informal* sight for sore eyes, stunner, knockout, peach.

> WORD LINKS
> *relating to vision:* **visual, optical**

visionary ▸ adjective =**inspired**, imaginative, creative, inventive, ingenious, enterprising, innovative; insightful, perceptive, intuitive, prescient, discerning; idealistic, romantic, quixotic, dreamy; *informal* starry-eyed.
▸ noun **1** *a visionary pictured him in hell* =**seer**, mystic, oracle, prophet, soothsayer, augur, diviner, clairvoyant. **2** *a visionary can't run a business effectively* =**dreamer**, idealist, romantic, fantasist, utopian.

visit ▸ verb **1** *I visited my uncle* =**call on**, go to see, look in on; stay with, holiday with; stop by, drop by; *informal* pop in on, drop in on, look up. **2** *Alex was visiting*

America =**stay in**, stop over in, spend time in, holiday in, vacation in; tour, explore, see; *informal* do.
▸ noun **1** *she paid a visit to her mum* =**(social) call**. **2** *a visit to the museum* =**trip to**, tour of, look round; stopover, stay; holiday, break, vacation; *formal* sojourn.

visitation ▸ noun *a visitation from God* =**apparition**, vision, appearance, manifestation, materialization.

visitor ▸ noun **1** *I am expecting a visitor* =**guest**, caller; company. **2** *the monument attracts many visitors* =**tourist**, traveller, holidaymaker, tripper, vacationer, sightseer; pilgrim; foreigner, outsider, stranger, alien.

vista ▸ noun =**view**, prospect, panorama, aspect, sight; scenery, landscape.

visual ▸ adjective **1** *visual defects* =**optical**, ocular, eye; vision, sight. **2** *a visual indication that the alarm works* =**visible**, perceptible, discernible.

visualize ▸ verb =**envisage**, conjure up, picture, call to mind, see, imagine, evoke, dream up, conceptualize.

vital ▸ adjective **1** *it is vital that action is taken* =**essential**, critical, crucial, indispensable, all-important, imperative, mandatory, high-priority; *informal* earth-shattering, world-shaking. **2** *the vital organs* =**major**, main, chief; essential, necessary. **3** *he is young and vital* =**lively**, energetic, active, sprightly, spirited, vivacious, exuberant, bouncy, zestful, dynamic, vigorous, lusty; *informal* peppy, full of beans.
–OPPOSITES unimportant, minor, listless.

vitality ▸ noun =**liveliness**, life, energy, spirit, vivacity, exuberance, buoyancy, bounce, verve, vim, pep, brio, zest, sparkle, dynamism, vigour, drive; *informal* get-up-and-go.

vitriolic ▸ adjective =**acrimonious**, rancorous, bitter, caustic, acerbic, trenchant, spiteful, savage, venomous, malicious; nasty, cruel, unkind, harsh, vindictive, scathing, cutting, withering; *informal* bitchy, catty.

vivacious ▸ adjective =**lively**, spirited, bubbly, ebullient, buoyant, merry, happy, jolly, full of fun, cheery, perky, sunny, breezy, enthusiastic, vibrant, dynamic; *informal* peppy, bouncy, upbeat, chirpy.
–OPPOSITES dull.

vivid ▸ adjective **1** *a vivid blue* =**bright**,

colourful, brilliant, radiant, vibrant, strong, bold, deep, intense, rich, warm. **2** *a vivid account* =**graphic**, evocative, realistic, lifelike, faithful, authentic, clear, lucid, striking, arresting, colourful, rich, dramatic, stimulating; memorable, powerful, stirring, moving, haunting.
–OPPOSITES dull, vague.

viz. ▶ adverb =**namely**, that is to say, in other words, to wit, specifically; such as, like, for instance, for example; *formal* videlicet.

vocal ▶ adjective **1** *vocal sounds* =**vocalized**, voiced, uttered, articulated, oral; spoken, said. **2** *a vocal critic* =**vociferous**, outspoken, forthright, plain-spoken, blunt, frank, candid, open; vehement, vigorous, emphatic, insistent.

vocation ▶ noun =**calling**, life's work, mission, purpose; profession, occupation, career, job, employment, trade, craft, business, line (of work), métier.

vociferous ▶ adjective. See VOCAL *sense 2.*

vogue ▶ noun *the skirt is enjoying a new vogue* =**fashion**, trend, fad, fancy, craze, rage, enthusiasm, passion; fashionableness, popularity, currency, favour; *informal* trendiness.
■ **in vogue** =**fashionable**, stylish, modish, up to date, modern, current; prevalent, popular, in favour, in demand, sought-after, all the rage; chic, smart, le dernier cri; *informal* trendy, hip, cool, happening, now, in, with it.

voice ▶ noun **1** *he gave voice to his anger* =**expression**, utterance, verbalization, vocalization. **2** *the voice of the people* =**opinion**, view, feeling, wish, desire, vote. **3** *a powerful voice for conservation* =**mouthpiece**, representative, spokesperson, intermediary; forum, vehicle, instrument, channel, organ, agent.
▶ verb *they voiced their opposition* =**express**, vocalize, communicate, declare, state, assert, reveal, proclaim, announce, air, vent; utter, say, speak, articulate; *informal* come out with.

void ▶ noun *the void of space* =**vacuum**, emptiness, nothingness, blankness, vacuity; (empty) space, gap, cavity, chasm, abyss, gulf.
▶ verb *the contract was voided* =**invalidate**, annul, nullify; negate, quash, cancel, countermand, repeal, revoke, rescind, retract, withdraw, reverse, undo, abol-

ish; *formal* abrogate.
–OPPOSITES validate, fill.
▶ adjective **1** *vast void spaces* =**empty**, vacant, blank, bare, clear, free, unfilled, unoccupied, uninhabited. **2** *a country void of man or beast* =**devoid of**, empty of, vacant of, bereft of, free from; lacking, without. **3** *the election was void* =**invalid**, null, ineffective, non-viable, worthless, nugatory.
–OPPOSITES full, occupied, valid.

volatile ▶ adjective **1** *a volatile personality* =**unpredictable**, changeable, variable, inconstant, erratic, irregular, unstable, turbulent, varying, shifting, fluctuating, fluid; mercurial, capricious, whimsical, fickle, impulsive, temperamental, excitable, emotional, fiery, moody. **2** *the atmosphere is too volatile for an election* =**tense**, strained, fraught, uneasy, uncomfortable, charged, explosive, inflammatory, turbulent; *informal* nailbiting. **3** *a volatile organic compound* =**evaporative**, vaporous; explosive, inflammable; unstable, labile.
–OPPOSITES stable, calm.

volition ■ **of one's own volition** =**of one's own free will**, of one's own accord, by choice, by preference; voluntarily, willingly, readily, freely, intentionally, consciously, deliberately, on purpose.

volley ▶ noun =**barrage**, cannonade, battery, bombardment, salvo; storm, hail, shower, deluge, torrent.

volume ▶ noun **1** *a volume from the library* =**book**, publication, tome, hardback, paperback, title. **2** *a syringe of known volume* =**capacity**, size, magnitude, mass, bulk, extent; dimensions, proportions, measurements. **3** *a huge volume of water* =**quantity**, amount, proportion, measure, mass, bulk. **4** *she turned the volume down* =**loudness**, sound, amplification.

voluminous ▶ adjective =**capacious**, roomy, spacious, ample, full, big, large, generous; billowing, baggy, loosefitting; *formal* commodious.

voluntarily ▶ adverb =**of one's own free will**, of one's own accord, of one's own volition, by choice, by preference; willingly, readily, freely, purposely, spontaneously.

voluntary ▶ adjective **1** *attendance is voluntary* =**optional**, discretionary, elective, non-compulsory, volitional. **2** *voluntary work* =**unpaid**, unsalaried, for free, without charge, for nothing; honorary. –OPPOSITES compulsory, paid.

volunteer ▸ verb **1** *I volunteered my services* =**offer**, tender, proffer, put forward, put up, venture. **2** *he volunteered as a driver* =**offer one's services**, present oneself, make oneself available.
▸ noun *each volunteer was tested three times* =**subject**, participant, case, client, patient; *informal* guinea pig.

voluptuous ▸ adjective **1** *a voluptuous model* =**curvaceous**, shapely, ample, buxom, full-figured, Junoesque, Rubenesque; *informal* curvy, busty. **2** *she was voluptuous by nature* =**hedonistic**, sybaritic, epicurean, pleasure-loving, self-indulgent; decadent, intemperate, immoderate, dissolute.
–OPPOSITES scrawny, ascetic.

vomit ▸ verb **1** *he needed to vomit* =**be sick**, spew, fetch up; heave, retch, gag; *informal* throw up, puke, chunder, chuck up; *Brit. informal* honk; *N. Amer. informal* barf, upchuck. **2** *I vomited my breakfast* =**regurgitate**, bring up, spew up; *informal* chuck up, throw up, puke; *Brit. informal* sick up.
▸ noun *a coat stained with vomit* =**sick**; *informal* chunder, puke, spew; *N. Amer. informal* barf.

WORD LINKS

fear of vomiting: **emetophobia**

voracious ▸ adjective =**insatiable**, unquenchable, unappeasable, prodigious, uncontrollable, compulsive, gluttonous, greedy, rapacious; enthusiastic, eager, keen, avid, desirous; *informal* piggish.

vortex ▸ noun =**whirlwind**, whirlpool, gyre, maelstrom, eddy.

vote ▸ noun **1** *a rigged vote* =**ballot**, poll, election, referendum, plebiscite; show of hands. **2** *in 1918 women got the vote* =**suffrage**, franchise; voice, say.
▸ verb *I vote we have one more game* =**suggest**, propose, recommend, advocate, move, table, submit.
■ **vote someone in** =**elect**, return, select, choose, pick, adopt, appoint, designate, opt for.

WORD LINKS

study of elections and voting: **psephology**

vouch ■ **vouch for** =**attest to**, confirm, verify, swear to, testify to, bear out, back up, support, stick up for, corroborate, substantiate, prove, uphold, endorse, certify, validate.

voucher ▸ noun =**coupon**, token, ticket; chit, slip, stub, docket; *Brit. informal* chitty.

vow ▸ noun *a vow of silence* =**oath**, pledge, promise, bond, covenant, commitment, profession, affirmation, attestation; word (of honour); *formal* troth.
▸ verb *I vowed to do better* =**swear**, pledge, promise, undertake, make a commitment, give one's word, guarantee.

WORD LINKS

relating to a vow: **votive**

voyage ▸ noun *the voyage lasted 12 days* =**journey**, trip, expedition, excursion, tour; hike, trek; pilgrimage; cruise, passage.
▸ verb *he voyaged through Peru* =**travel**, journey, tour; sail, steam, cruise.

vulgar ▸ adjective **1** *a vulgar joke* =**rude**, indecent, indelicate, offensive, distasteful, coarse, crude, ribald, risqué, racy, earthy, off colour, bawdy, obscene, lewd, salacious, smutty, dirty, filthy; *informal* sleazy, raunchy, blue, lockerroom; *Brit. informal* saucy. **2** *the decor was lavish but vulgar* =**tasteless**, crass, tawdry, ostentatious, flamboyant, showy, gaudy, garish, brassy, kitsch; *informal* flash, tacky. **3** *it was vulgar for a woman to whistle* =**impolite**, ill-mannered, indecorous, unseemly, boorish, uncouth, crude; unsophisticated, unrefined.
–OPPOSITES tasteful, decorous.

vulnerable ▸ adjective **1** *a vulnerable city* =**in danger**, in peril, in jeopardy, at risk, unprotected, unguarded; open to attack, assailable, exposed; undefended, unfortified, unarmed, pregnable. **2** *he is vulnerable to criticism* =**exposed to**, open to, liable to, prone to, prey to, susceptible to, subject to.
–OPPOSITES resilient.

v

wad ▶ noun **1** *a wad of cotton wool* =**lump**, clump, mass, plug, pad, wedge, ball, cake, nugget; *Brit. informal* wodge. **2** *a wad of dollar bills* =**bundle**, roll, pile, stack, sheaf; *N. Amer.* bankroll. **3** *a wad of tobacco* =**quid**, twist, plug, chew.

wadding ▶ noun =**stuffing**, filling, packing, padding, cushioning, quilting.

waddle ▶ verb =**toddle**, totter, wobble, shuffle; duckwalk.

wade ▶ verb **1** *they waded in the water* =**paddle**, wallow; *informal* splosh. **2** *I had to wade through some hefty documents* =**plough**, plod, trawl, labour, toil.

waffle (*Brit. informal*) ▶ verb *they waffled on about the baby* =**prattle**, chatter, babble, ramble, jabber, gabble; *informal* blather; *Brit. informal* rabbit, witter, natter.
▶ noun *my panic reduced the interview to waffle* =**prattle**, drivel, nonsense, twaddle, gibberish, mumbo-jumbo; *informal* hot air, gobbledegook.

waft ▶ verb **1** *smoke wafted through the air* =**drift**, float, glide, whirl, travel. **2** *a breeze wafted the smell* =**convey**, carry, transport, bear; blow.

wag[1] ▶ verb **1** *the dog's tail wagged* =**swing**, swish, switch, sway, shake; *informal* waggle. **2** *he wagged his stick at them* =**shake**, wave, wiggle, flourish, brandish.

wag[2] ▶ noun (*informal*) *he's a bit of a wag.* See JOKER.

wage ▶ noun **1** *the workers' wages* =**pay**, remuneration, salary, stipend, fee, honorarium; income; earnings; *formal* emolument. **2** *the wages of sin is death* =**reward**, recompense, retribution; returns, deserts.
▶ verb *they waged war on the guerrillas* =**engage in**, carry on, conduct, execute, pursue, prosecute, proceed with.

wager ▶ noun *a wager of £10* =**bet**, gamble, speculation; stake, pledge, ante; *Brit. informal* flutter.
▶ verb *I'll wager a pound on the home team* =**bet**, gamble, lay odds, put money on; stake, pledge, risk, venture, hazard, chance; *informal* punt.

waif ▶ noun =**ragamuffin**, urchin; foundling, orphan, stray.

wail ▶ noun *a wail of anguish* =**howl**, bawl, cry, moan, groan; shriek, scream, yelp.
▶ verb *the children began to wail* =**howl**, weep, cry, sob, lament, yowl, snivel, whimper, whine, bawl, shriek, scream, yelp, caterwaul; *Scottish* greet.

wait ▶ verb **1** *we'll wait in the airport* =**stay (put)**, remain, rest, stop, halt, pause; linger, loiter; *informal* stick around. **2** *she had to wait until her bags arrived* =**stand by**, hold back, bide one's time, hang fire, mark time, kill time, waste time, kick one's heels, twiddle one's thumbs; *informal* hold on, hang around, sit tight. **3** *they were waiting for the kettle to boil* =**await**; anticipate, expect, be ready. **4** *that job will have to wait* =**be postponed**, be delayed, be put off, be deferred; *informal* be put on the back burner, be put on ice.
▶ noun *a long wait* =**delay**, hold-up, interval, interlude, pause, break, suspension, stoppage, halt, interruption, lull, respite, recess, moratorium, hiatus, gap.

waiter, waitress ▶ noun =**server**, stewardess, steward, attendant, garçon; butler, servant, page; *N. Amer.* waitperson.

waive ▶ verb **1** *he waived his right to a hearing* =**relinquish**, renounce, give up, abandon, surrender, yield, dispense with, sacrifice, turn down. **2** *the manager waived the rules* =**disregard**, ignore, overlook, set aside, forgo.

wake[1] ▶ verb **1** *at 4.30 a.m. Mark woke up* =**awake**, waken, rouse oneself, stir, come to, come round; *formal* arise. **2** *she woke her husband* =**rouse**, waken. **3** *a shock woke him up a bit* =**activate**, stimulate, galvanize, enliven, stir up, spur on, ginger up, buoy up, invigorate, revitalize; *informal* perk up. **4** *they woke up to what we were saying* =**realize**, become aware of, become conscious of, become mindful of.
–OPPOSITES sleep.
▶ noun =**vigil**, watch; funeral.

wake[2] ▶ noun *the cruiser's wake* =**backwash**, slipstream; trail, path.

■ **in the wake of** =in the aftermath of, after, subsequent to, following, as a result of, as a consequence of, on account of, because of.

Wales ▸ noun =Cambria; *Brit.* the Principality.

walk ▸ verb 1 *they walked along the road* =**stroll**, saunter, amble, trudge, plod, hike, tramp, trek, march, stride, troop, wander, ramble, promenade, traipse; *informal* mosey, hoof it; *formal* perambulate. **2** *he walked her home* =**accompany**, escort, guide, show, see, take, chaperone.
▸ noun 1 *her elegant walk* =**gait**, step, stride, tread. **2** *the riverside walk* =**pathway**, footpath, track, walkway, promenade, footway, pavement, trail, towpath.
■ **walk of life** =class, status, rank, caste, sphere, arena; profession, career, vocation, job, occupation, employment, business, trade.
■ **walk out 1** *he walked out in a temper* =**leave**, depart, storm off/out, flounce out, absent oneself; *informal* take off. **2** *teachers walked out in protest* =(**go on**) **strike**, stop work; protest, mutiny, revolt; *Brit. informal* down tools.
■ **walk out on someone** =desert, abandon, leave, betray, jilt, run out on; *informal* chuck, dump, ditch.

walker ▸ noun =hiker, rambler, stroller; pedestrian; *literary* wayfarer.

walkout ▸ noun =strike, stoppage, industrial action.

walkover ▸ noun =easy victory, rout, landslide; *informal* piece of cake, doddle, pushover, cinch, breeze, picnic, whitewash, massacre.

wall ▸ noun 1 =**fortification**, rampart, barricade, bulwark. **2** *break down the walls that stop trade* =**obstacle**, barrier, fence; impediment, hindrance, block.
▸ verb 1 *tenements walled in the courtyard* =**enclose**, bound, encircle, confine, hem, close in, fence in. **2** *the doorway had been walled up* =**block**, seal, close, brick up.

wallet ▸ noun =purse; *N. Amer.* billfold, pocketbook.

wallow ▸ verb 1 *buffalo wallowed in the lake* =**loll about**, lie around, splash about; slosh, wade, paddle. **2** *she seems to wallow in self-pity* =**luxuriate**, bask, take pleasure, take satisfaction, indulge (oneself), delight, revel, glory; *informal* get a kick out of.

wan ▸ adjective 1 *she looked wan and frail* =pale, ashen, white, grey; anaemic, colourless, waxen, pasty, peaky, sickly, washed out, ghostly. **2** *the wan light of the moon* =**dim**, faint, weak, feeble, pale, watery.
−OPPOSITES flushed, bright.

wand ▸ noun =baton, stick, staff, dowel, rod; twig, cane, birch.

wander ▸ verb 1 *I wandered around the estate* =**stroll**, amble, saunter, walk, potter, ramble, meander; roam, rove, range, drift; *Scottish & Irish* stravaig; *informal* traipse, mosey. **2** *we are wandering from the point* =**stray**, depart, diverge, veer, swerve, deviate, digress, drift, get sidetracked. **3** *the child wandered off* =**get lost**, go astray.

wanderer ▸ noun =traveller, rambler, hiker, migrant, roamer, rover; itinerant, rolling stone, nomad; tramp, drifter, vagabond, vagrant; *Brit. informal* dosser; *N. Amer. informal* hobo, bum; *literary* wayfarer.

wane ▸ verb 1 *the moon is waning* =**decrease**, diminish, dwindle. **2** *their support was waning* =**decline**, diminish, decrease, dwindle, shrink, tail off, ebb, fade, lessen, peter out, fall off, recede, slump, weaken, wither, evaporate, die out.
−OPPOSITES wax, grow.
■ **on the wane** =declining, decreasing, diminishing, dwindling, shrinking, contracting, tapering off, subsiding, ebbing, fading away, dissolving, petering out, falling off, on the way out, receding, flagging, melting away, crumbling, withering, disintegrating, evaporating, dying out.

want ▸ verb =desire, wish for, hope for, fancy, care for, like; long for, yearn for, crave, hanker after, hunger for, thirst for, cry out for, covet; *informal* have a yen for, be dying for.
▸ noun 1 *his want of vigilance* =**lack**, absence, non-existence; dearth, deficiency, inadequacy, insufficiency, paucity, shortage, scarcity, deficit. **2** *a time of want* =**need**, austerity, privation, deprivation, poverty, penury, destitution. **3** *her wants would be taken care of* =**wish**, desire, demand, longing, yearning, fancy, craving, hankering; need, requirement; *informal* yen.

wanting ▸ adjective 1 *the defences were found wanting* =**deficient**, inadequate, lacking, insufficient, imperfect, unacceptable, flawed, unsound,

substandard, inferior, second-rate; *Brit. informal* not much cop. **2** *the kneecap is wanting in amphibians* =**absent**, missing, lacking, non-existent. **3** *millions were left wanting for food* =**without**, lacking, deprived of, devoid of, bereft of, in need of; deficient in, short on; *informal* minus.
–OPPOSITES sufficient, present.

wanton ▸ adjective **1** *wanton destruction* =**deliberate**, wilful, malicious, spiteful, wicked, cruel; gratuitous, unprovoked, motiveless, arbitrary, groundless, unjustifiable, needless, unnecessary, uncalled for, senseless, pointless, purposeless. **2** *a wanton seductress* =**promiscuous**, immoral, immodest, indecent, shameless, unchaste, fast, impure, abandoned, lustful, lecherous, lascivious, libidinous, licentious, dissolute, debauched, degenerate, disreputable; *dated* loose.
–OPPOSITES justifiable, chaste.

war ▸ noun **1** *the Napoleonic wars* =**conflict**, warfare, combat, fighting, action, bloodshed, struggle; battle, skirmish, fight, clash, engagement, encounter; offensive, attack, campaign; hostilities; jihad, crusade. **2** *the war against drugs* =**campaign**, crusade, battle, fight, struggle.
–OPPOSITES peace.
▸ verb *rival Emperors warred against each other* =**fight**, battle, combat, wage war, take up arms; feud, quarrel, struggle, contend, wrangle, cross swords; attack, engage, take on, skirmish with.

WORD LINKS

relating to war: **belligerent, martial**

warble ▸ verb =**trill**, sing, chirp, chirrup, cheep, twitter, tweet, chatter, peep.

ward ▸ noun **1** *the surgical ward* =**room**, department, unit, area. **2** *the most marginal ward in Westminster* =**district**, constituency, division, quarter, zone, parish. **3** *the boy is my ward* =**dependant**, charge, protégé.

warden ▸ noun **1** *the flats have a resident warden* =**superintendent**, caretaker, janitor, porter, custodian, watchman, concierge, doorman. **2** *a game warden* =**ranger**, custodian, keeper, guardian, protector. **3** *he was handcuffed to a warden* =**prison officer**, guard, jailer, warder, keeper, sentry; *informal* screw. **4** (*Brit.*) *the college warden* =**principal**, head, governor, master, mistress, rector, provost, president, director, chancellor.

wardrobe ▸ noun **1** =**cupboard**; *N. Amer.* closet. **2** *her wardrobe has an outfit for every mood* =**collection of clothes**; garments, attire, outfits.

warehouse ▸ noun =**storeroom**, depot, depository, stockroom; magazine; granary; *informal* lock-up.

wares ▸ plural noun =**merchandise**, goods, products, produce, stock, commodities; lines, range.

warfare ▸ noun =**fighting**, war, combat, conflict, action, hostilities; bloodshed, battles, skirmishes.

warlike ▸ adjective =**aggressive**, belligerent, warring, bellicose, pugnacious, combative; hostile, threatening; militaristic; *informal* gung-ho.

warlock ▸ noun =**sorcerer**, wizard, (black) magician, enchanter.

warm ▸ adjective **1** *a warm kitchen* =**hot**, cosy, snug; *informal* toasty. **2** *a warm day* =**balmy**, summery, sultry, hot, mild, temperate. **3** *warm water* =**heated**, tepid, lukewarm. **4** *a warm sweater* =**thick**, chunky, thermal, winter, woolly. **5** *a warm welcome* =**friendly**, cordial, amiable, genial, kind, pleasant, fond; welcoming, hospitable, benevolent, benign, charitable; sincere, genuine, heartfelt, enthusiastic, eager, hearty.
–OPPOSITES cold, chilly, light, hostile.
▸ verb *warm the soup in that pan* =**heat (up)**, reheat, cook.
–OPPOSITES chill.
■ **warm to/towards 1** *everyone warmed to him* =**like**, take to, get on (well) with, hit it off with. **2** *he couldn't warm to the notion* =**be enthusiastic about**, be supportive of, be excited about.
■ **warm up** *the players were warming up* =**limber up**, loosen up, stretch; prepare, rehearse.
■ **warm someone up** *the compère warmed up the crowd* =**enliven**, liven, stimulate, rouse, stir, excite; *informal* get going.

warmed-up ▸ adjective =**reheated**; *N. Amer.* warmed-over.

warmonger ▸ noun =**militarist**, hawk, jingoist, sabre-rattler, aggressor, belligerent.

warmth ▸ noun **1** *the warmth of the fire* =**heat**; cosiness. **2** *the warmth of their welcome* =**friendliness**, amiability, geniality, cordiality, kindness, tenderness, fondness; benevolence, charity; enthusiasm, eagerness.

warn ▸ verb **1** *David warned her that it was too late* =**notify**, alert, apprise, inform, tell, make someone aware, remind; *informal* tip off, put wise. **2** *police are warning galleries to be alert* =**advise**, exhort, urge, counsel, caution.

warning ▸ noun **1** *the earthquake came without warning* =(**advance**) **notice**, alert; hint, signal, sign, alarm bells; *informal* a tip-off. **2** *a health warning* =**caution**, notification, information; exhortation, injunction; advice. **3** *a warning of things to come* =**omen**, premonition, foreboding, prophecy, prediction, forecast, token, portent, signal, sign. **4** *his sentence is a warning to other drunk drivers* =**example**, deterrent, lesson, caution, exemplar, message, moral. **5** *a written warning* =**admonition**, caution, remonstrance, reprimand, censure; *informal* dressing-down, talking-to, telling-off.

warp ▸ verb **1** *timber which is too dry will warp* =**buckle**, twist, bend, distort, deform, curve, bow, contort. **2** *he warped the mind of her child* =**corrupt**, twist, pervert, deprave.
−OPPOSITES straighten.

warrant ▸ noun **1** *a warrant for his arrest* =**authorization**, order, licence, permit, document; writ, summons, subpoena; mandate, decree, edict. **2** *a travel warrant* =**voucher**, chit, slip, ticket, coupon, pass. **3** *there's no warrant for this assumption* =**justification**, grounds, cause, rationale, basis, authority, licence, sanction, vindication.
▸ verb **1** *the charges warranted a severe sentence* =**justify**, vindicate, call for, sanction, validate; permit, authorize; deserve, excuse, account for, legitimize; support, license, approve of; merit, qualify for, rate, be worthy of, be deserving of. **2** *we warrant that the texts do not infringe copyright* =**guarantee**, affirm, swear, promise, vow, pledge, undertake, state, assert, declare, profess, attest; vouch, testify.

warranty ▸ noun =**guarantee**, assurance, promise, commitment, undertaking, agreement.

warring ▸ adjective =**opposing**, conflicting, fighting, battling, quarrelling; competing, hostile, rival.

warrior ▸ noun =**fighter**, soldier, serviceman, combatant.

wary ▸ adjective **1** *he was trained to be wary* =**cautious**, careful, circumspect, on one's guard, chary, alert, on the lookout; attentive, heedful, watchful, vigilant, observant. **2** *we are wary of strangers* =**suspicious**, chary, leery, careful, distrustful.
−OPPOSITES inattentive, trustful.

wash ▸ verb **1** *he washed in the bath* =**clean oneself**, bathe, shower; *formal* perform one's ablutions. **2** *she washed her hands* =**clean**, cleanse, scrub, wipe; shampoo, lather; sluice, swill, douse, swab, disinfect. **3** *she washed off the blood* =**remove**, expunge, eradicate; sponge off, scrub off, wipe off, rinse off. **4** *the women were washing clothes* =**launder**, clean, rinse. **5** *waves washed against the hull* =**splash**, lap, dash, break, beat, surge, ripple, roll. **6** *the wreckage was washed downriver* =**sweep**, carry, convey, transport; deposit. **7** *guilt washed over her* =**affect**, rush through, surge through, course through, flood over, flow over.
−OPPOSITES dirty, soil.
▸ noun **1** *that shirt should go in the wash* =**laundry**, washing. **2** *antiseptic skin wash* =**lotion**, salve, preparation, rinse, liquid; liniment, embrocation. **3** *the wash of a motor boat* =**backwash**, wake, trail, path.
■ **wash something away** =**erode**, abrade, wear away, eat away, undermine.
■ **wash up** –wash the dishes, do the dishes, do the washing-up.

waste ▸ verb **1** *he doesn't like to waste money* =**squander**, misspend, misuse, fritter away, throw away, lavish, dissipate; *informal* blow, splurge. **2** *kids are wasting away in the streets* =**grow weak**, grow thin, shrink, wilt, fade, flag, deteriorate. **3** *the disease wasted his legs* =**emaciate**, atrophy, wither, shrivel, shrink, weaken.
−OPPOSITES conserve, thrive.
▸ adjective **1** *waste material* =**unwanted**, excess, superfluous, left over, scrap; unusable, unprofitable. **2** *waste ground* =**uncultivated**, barren, desert, arid, bare; desolate, uninhabited, unpopulated; wild.
▸ noun **1** *a waste of money* =**misuse**, misapplication, misemployment, abuse; extravagance, lavishness. **2** *household waste* =**rubbish**, refuse, litter, debris, dross, junk, detritus, scrap; sewage, effluent; *N. Amer.* garbage, trash. **3** *the frozen wastes of the South Pole* =**desert**, wasteland, wilderness, emptiness, wilds.

w

wasted ▸ adjective **1** *a wasted effort* =squandered, misspent, misdirected, dissipated; pointless, useless, unnecessary. **2** *a wasted opportunity* =missed, lost, forfeited, neglected, squandered; *informal* down the drain. **3** *I'm wasted in this job* =underemployed, underused, too good for. **4** *his wasted legs* =emaciated, atrophied, withered, shrunken, skeletal, scrawny, wizened.

wasteful ▸ adjective =prodigal, profligate, uneconomical, extravagant, lavish, excessive, imprudent, improvident; thriftless, spendthrift; needless, useless. –OPPOSITES frugal.

wasteland ▸ noun =wilderness, desert; wilds, wastes, badlands.

watch ▸ verb **1** *she watched him as he spoke* =observe, view, look at, eye, gaze at, peer at; contemplate, survey, keep an eye on; inspect, scrutinize, scan, examine, study, ogle, regard, mark; *informal* check out, get a load of, recce, eyeball; *Brit. informal* have a butcher's at; *literary* behold. **2** *he was being watched by the police* =spy on, keep in sight, track, monitor, survey, follow; *informal* keep tabs on, stake out. **3** *will you watch the kids?* =look after, mind, keep an eye on, take care of, supervise, tend; guard, protect. **4** *we stayed to watch the boat* =guard, protect, shield, defend; cover, patrol, police. **5** *watch what you say* =be careful, mind, be aware of, pay attention to, consider. –OPPOSITES ignore, neglect.
▸ noun **1** *Bill looked at his watch* =timepiece, chronometer. **2** *we kept watch on the yacht* =guard, vigil, lookout, an eye; observation, surveillance.
∎ **watch out/it/yourself** =be careful, be on your guard, beware, be wary, be cautious, mind out, look out, pay attention, take care, keep an eye open/out, keep one's eyes peeled, be vigilant.

watchdog ▸ noun =ombudsman, monitor, scrutineer, inspector, supervisor.

watcher ▸ noun =onlooker, spectator, observer, viewer, fly on the wall; witness, bystander; spy; voyeur; *informal* rubberneck; *literary* beholder.

watchful ▸ adjective =observant, alert, vigilant, attentive, aware, sharp-eyed, eagle-eyed; on the lookout, wary, cautious, careful.

watchman ▸ noun =security guard, custodian, warden; sentry, guard, patrolman, lookout, sentinel, scout.

watchword ▸ noun =guiding principle, motto, slogan, maxim, mantra, catchword, byword; *informal* buzzword.

water ▸ noun *a house down by the water* =sea, ocean; lake, loch, river.
▸ verb **1** *water the plants* =sprinkle, moisten, dampen, wet, spray, splash. **2** *my mouth watered* =moisten, become wet; salivate.
∎ **water something down 1** *staff had watered down the drinks* =dilute, thin (out), weaken. **2** *the proposals were watered down* =moderate, temper, mitigate, tone down, soften, tame; understate, play down, soft-pedal.

WORD LINKS

relating to water: **aqueous, aqua-, hydro-**
fear of water: **hydrophobia**

waterfall ▸ noun =cascade, cataract, rapids.

waterproof ▸ adjective =watertight, water-repellent, water-resistant, dampproof; impermeable, impervious.
▸ noun *(Brit.)* =raincoat, cagoule; *Brit.* mackintosh; *Brit. informal* mac.

watertight ▸ adjective **1** *a watertight container* =impermeable, impervious, (hermetically) sealed; waterproof, water-repellent, water-resistant, dampproof. **2** *a watertight alibi* =indisputable, unquestionable, incontrovertible, irrefutable, unassailable; foolproof, sound, flawless, airtight, conclusive. –OPPOSITES leaky, flawed.

watery ▸ adjective **1** *a watery discharge* =liquid, fluid, aqueous. **2** *watery porridge* =thin, runny, weak, sloppy, dilute; tasteless, insipid, bland. **3** *watery light* =pale, wan, faint, weak, feeble; *informal* wishy-washy. **4** *watery eyes* =tearful, weepy, moist; *formal* lachrymose. –OPPOSITES thick, bright.

wave ▸ verb **1** *he waved his flag* =move up and down, move to and fro, wag, shake, swish, swing, brandish, flourish, wield. **2** *the grass waved in the breeze* =ripple, flutter, undulate, stir, flap, sway, shake, quiver, move. **3** *the waiter waved them closer* =gesture, gesticulate, signal, beckon, motion.
▸ noun **1** *she gave him a friendly wave* =gesticulation; signal, sign, motion. **2** *he surfs the big waves* =breaker, roller, comber, boomer, ripple; **(waves)** swell,

surf, froth. **3** *a wave of emigration* =**flow**, rush, surge, flood, stream, tide, deluge, spate. **4** *a wave of self-pity* =**surge**, rush, stab, dart, upsurge; feeling. **5** *his hair grew in thick waves* =**curl**, kink, twist, ringlet. **6** *electromagnetic waves* =ripple, vibration, oscillation.

■ **wave something aside** =**dismiss**, reject, brush aside, shrug off, disregard, ignore, discount, play down; *informal* pooh-pooh.

■ **wave someone/something down** =**flag down**, hail, stop, summon, call, accost.

waver ▸ verb **1** *the candlelight wavered in the draught* =**flicker**, quiver. **2** *his voice wavered* =**falter**, wobble, tremble, quaver. **3** *he wavered between the choices* =**be undecided**, be irresolute, hesitate, dither, equivocate, vacillate; think twice, change one's mind, blow hot and cold; *Brit.* haver, hum and haw; *informal* shilly-shally, sit on the fence.

wavy ▸ adjective =**curly**, curvy, undulating, squiggly, rippled, crinkly, zigzag.

wax ▸ verb =**get bigger**, increase, enlarge.
–OPPOSITES wane.

way ▸ noun **1** *a way of reducing the damage* =**method**, process, procedure, technique, system; plan, strategy, scheme; means, mechanism, approach. **2** *she kissed him in her brisk way* =**manner**, style, fashion, mode. **3** *I've changed my ways* =**practice**, wont, habit, custom, convention, routine; trait, attribute, peculiarity, idiosyncrasy; conduct, behaviour, manner, style. **4** *which way leads home?* =**route**, course, direction; road, street, track, path. **5** *I'll go out the back way* =**door**, gate, exit, entrance; route. **6** *a short way downstream* =**distance**, length, stretch, journey; space, interval, span. **7** *April is a long way away* =**time**, stretch, term, span, duration. **8** *a car coming the other way* =**direction**, bearing, course, orientation, line, tack. **9** *in some ways, he may be better off* =**respect**, regard, aspect, facet, sense; detail, point, particular. **10** *the country is in a bad way* =**state**, condition, situation, circumstances, position; predicament, plight; *informal* shape.

■ **give way 1** *the government gave way and passed the bill* =**yield**, back down, surrender, concede defeat, give in, submit, succumb; acquiesce, agree, assent; *informal* throw in the towel/sponge, cave in. **2** *the door gave way* =**collapse**, give, cave in,

fall in, come apart, crumple. **3** *grief gave way to guilt* =**be replaced by**, be succeeded by, be followed by, be supplanted by.

■ **on the way** =**coming**, imminent, forthcoming, approaching, impending, close, near, on us; proceeding, en route, in transit.

waylay ▸ verb **1** *we were waylaid and robbed* =**ambush**, hold up, attack, assail, rob; *informal* mug, stick up. **2** *several people waylaid her to chat* =**accost**, detain, intercept, take aside, pounce on, importune; *informal* buttonhole.

wayward ▸ adjective =**wilful**, headstrong, stubborn, obstinate, obdurate, perverse, contrary, disobedient, undisciplined; rebellious, defiant, recalcitrant, unruly, wild; *formal* refractory.
–OPPOSITES docile.

weak ▸ adjective **1** *they are too weak to move* =**frail**, feeble, delicate, fragile; infirm, sick, debilitated, incapacitated, ailing, indisposed, decrepit; tired, fatigued, exhausted; *informal* weedy. **2** *bats have weak eyes* =**inadequate**, poor, feeble; defective, faulty, deficient, imperfect, substandard. **3** *a weak excuse* =**unconvincing**, tenuous, implausible, unsatisfactory, poor, inadequate, feeble, flimsy, lame, hollow; *informal* pathetic. **4** *I was too weak to be a rebel* =**spineless**, craven, cowardly, timid; irresolute, indecisive, ineffectual, meek, tame, soft, faint-hearted; *informal* yellow, gutless. **5** *a weak light* =**dim**, pale, wan, faint, feeble, muted. **6** *a weak voice* =**indistinct**, muffled, muted, hushed, faint, low. **7** *weak coffee* =**watery**, dilute, watered down, thin. **8** *a weak smile* =**unenthusiastic**, feeble, half-hearted, lame.
–OPPOSITES strong, powerful, convincing, resolute, bright, loud.

weaken ▸ verb **1** *the virus weakened him* =**enfeeble**, debilitate, incapacitate, sap, tire, exhaust. **2** *our morale weakened* =**decrease**, dwindle, diminish, wane, ebb, subside, peter out, fizzle out, tail off, decline, falter. **3** *the move weakened her authority* =**impair**, undermine, compromise; invalidate, negate.

weakling ▸ noun =**milksop**, namby-pamby, coward, pushover; *informal* wimp, weed, sissy, drip, softie, doormat, chicken, yellow-belly; *N. Amer. informal* wuss.

weakness ▸ noun **1** *with old age came*

weakness =**frailty**, feebleness, fragility, delicacy; infirmity, debility, incapacity, indisposition, decrepitude; *informal* weediness. **2** *he has worked on his weaknesses* =**fault**, flaw, defect, deficiency, failing, shortcoming, imperfection, Achilles heel. **3** *a weakness for champagne* =**fondness**, liking, partiality, love, penchant, predilection, inclination, taste; enthusiasm, appetite. **4** *the President was accused of weakness* =**timidity**, cravenness, cowardliness; indecision, irresolution, ineffectuality, ineptitude, meekness, ineffectiveness, impotence. **5** *the weakness of this argument* =**untenability**, implausibility, poverty, inadequacy, transparency; flimsiness, hollowness.

> **WORD LINKS**
>
> *fear of weakness:* **asthenophobia**

weak-willed ▶ adjective =**spineless**, irresolute, indecisive; impressionable, persuasible, submissive, unassertive, compliant; *informal* wimpish.

weal ▶ noun =**welt**, wound, lesion, swelling; scar.

wealth ▶ noun **1** *a gentleman of wealth* =**affluence**, prosperity, riches, means, fortune; money, cash, lucre, capital, treasure, finance; *informal* wherewithal, dough, bread. **2** *a wealth of information* =**abundance**, profusion, plethora, mine, store, treasury, bounty, cornucopia; *informal* load, mountain, stack, ton; *Brit. informal* shedload; *formal* plenitude.
　–OPPOSITES poverty, dearth.

wealthy ▶ adjective =**rich**, affluent, moneyed, well off, well-to-do, prosperous; of substance; *informal* well heeled, rolling in it, made of money, loaded, flush, quids in.
　–OPPOSITES poor.

wear ▶ verb **1** *he wore a suit* =**dress in**, be clothed in, have on, sport. **2** *Barbara wore a smile* =**bear**, have (on one's face), show, display, exhibit; give, put on, assume. **3** *the bricks have been worn down* =**erode**, abrade, rub away, grind away, wash away, crumble (away); corrode, eat away (at), dissolve. **4** *the tyres are wearing well* =**last**, endure, hold up, bear up.
　▶ noun **1** *you won't get much wear out of that* =**use**, service, utility, value; *informal* mileage. **2** *evening wear* =**clothes**, garments, dress, attire, garb, wardrobe; *informal* getup, gear, togs; *Brit. informal* kit, clobber;

formal apparel. **3** *the varnish will withstand wear* =**damage**, friction, erosion, attrition, abrasion.
　■ **wear something down** *he wore down her resistance* =**gradually overcome**, slowly reduce, erode, exhaust, undermine.
　■ **wear off** *the novelty soon wore off* =**fade**, diminish, lessen, dwindle, decrease, wane, ebb, peter out, fizzle out, pall, disappear, vanish.
　■ **wear out** =**deteriorate**, become worn, fray, become threadbare, go into holes.
　■ **wear someone out** =**fatigue**, tire out, weary, exhaust, drain, sap, overtax, enervate, jade; *informal* whack, poop, shatter, do in; *Brit. informal* knacker.

wearing ▶ adjective =**tiring**, exhausting, wearying, fatiguing, enervating, draining, sapping; demanding, exacting, taxing, arduous, gruelling, punishing, laborious, strenuous, rigorous.

weary ▶ adjective **1** *he was weary after cycling* =**tired**, worn out, exhausted, fatigued, sapped, spent, drained; *informal* done in, dead beat, ready to drop, bushed, shattered; *Brit. informal* knackered, whacked; *N. Amer. informal* pooped. **2** *she was weary of the arguments* =**tired of**, fed up with, bored by, sick of; *informal* have had it up to here with. **3** *a weary journey* =**tiring**, exhausting, fatiguing, enervating, draining, sapping, wearing, trying, demanding, taxing, arduous, gruelling.
　–OPPOSITES fresh, keen, refreshing.

weather ▶ noun *what's the weather like?* =**forecast**, outlook; meteorological conditions, climate, atmospheric pressure, temperature; elements.
　▶ verb *we weathered the recession* =**survive**, come through, ride out, pull through; withstand, endure, rise above, surmount, overcome, resist; *informal* stick out.

weathered ▶ adjective =**weather-beaten**, worn; tanned, bronzed; lined, creased, wrinkled.

weave[1] ▶ verb **1** *flowers were woven into their hair* =**entwine**, lace, twist, knit, braid, plait. **2** *he weaves colourful plots* =**invent**, make up, fabricate, construct, create, contrive, spin.

weave[2] ▶ verb *he had to weave his way through the crowds* =**thread**, wind, wend; dodge, zigzag.

web ▶ noun **1** *a spider's web* =**mesh**, net, lattice, lacework; gauze, gossamer. **2** *a web of friendships* =**network**, nexus, complex, set, chain.

wedded ▶ adjective **1** *wedded bliss* =**married**, matrimonial, marital, conjugal, nuptial. **2** *he is wedded to his work* =**dedicated to**, devoted to, attached to, fixated on, single-minded about.

wedding ▶ noun =**marriage (service/rites)**, nuptials, union.

WORD LINKS

relating to a wedding: **nuptial**

wedge ▶ noun **1** *the door was secured by a wedge* =**chock**, stop. **2** *a wedge of cheese* =**triangle**, segment, slice, section; chunk, lump, slab, hunk, block, piece.
▶ verb *she wedged her case between two bags* =**squeeze**, cram, jam, ram, force, push, shove; *informal* stuff, bung.

weed ▪ **weed something/someone out** =**isolate**, separate out, sort out, sift out, winnow out, filter out, set apart, segregate; eliminate, get rid of, remove; *informal* lose.

weep ▶ verb *even the toughest soldiers wept* =**cry**, shed tears, sob, snivel, whimper, wail, bawl, keen; *Scottish* greet; *informal* boohoo, blub.

weepy ▶ adjective =**tearful**; in tears, crying, snivelling; *formal* lachrymose.
–OPPOSITES cheerful.

weigh ▶ verb **1** *she weighs the vegetables* =**measure the weight of**, put on the scales. **2** *he weighed 118 kg* =**have a weight of**, tip the scales at. **3** *the situation weighed heavily on him. See* WEIGH SOMEONE DOWN *sense 2.* **4** *he has to weigh up the possibilities* =**consider**, contemplate, think about, mull over, chew over, reflect on, ruminate about, muse on; assess, appraise, analyse, examine, review, explore, take stock of. **5** *they need to weigh benefit against risk* =**balance**, evaluate, compare, juxtapose, contrast.
▪ **weigh someone down 1** *my fishing gear weighed me down* =**burden**, saddle, overload, overburden, encumber. **2** *the silence weighed me down* =**oppress**, depress, lie heavy on, burden, cast down, hang over; trouble, worry, bother, disturb, upset, haunt, torment, afflict, plague.

weight ▶ noun **1** *the weight of the book* =**heaviness**, mass, load, burden. **2** *his recommendation will carry great weight* =**influence**, force, leverage, sway, pull, importance, significance, value, substance, power, authority; *informal* clout. **3** *a weight off her mind* =**burden**, load, millstone, albatross, encumbrance; trouble, worry, strain. **4** *the weight of the evidence is against him* =**preponderance**, majority, bulk, body, lion's share, predominance; most.

weighty ▶ adjective **1** *a weighty tome* =**heavy**, thick, bulky, hefty, cumbersome, ponderous. **2** *a weighty subject* =**important**, significant, momentous, consequential, far-reaching, key, major, vital, critical, crucial; serious, grave, solemn. **3** *a weighty responsibility* =**burdensome**, onerous, heavy, oppressive, taxing, troublesome. **4** *weighty arguments* =**compelling**, cogent, strong, forceful, powerful, potent, effective, sound, valid, persuasive, convincing.
–OPPOSITES light, trivial, weak.

weird ▶ adjective *weird apparitions* =**uncanny**, eerie, unnatural, supernatural, unearthly, other-worldly, ghostly, mysterious, strange, abnormal, unusual; *informal* creepy, spooky, freaky.
–OPPOSITES normal, conventional.

welcome ▶ noun *a welcome from the vicar* =**greeting**, salutation; reception, hospitality; the red carpet.
▶ verb **1** *welcome your guests in their own language* =**greet**, salute, receive, meet, usher in. **2** *we welcomed their decision* =**be pleased by**, be glad about, approve of, appreciate, embrace; *informal* give the thumbs up to.
▶ adjective *welcome news* =**pleasing**, agreeable, encouraging, gratifying, heartening, promising, favourable, pleasant.

weld ▶ verb =**fuse**, bond, stick, join, attach, seal, splice, melt, solder.

welfare ▶ noun **1** *the welfare of children* =**well-being**, health, comfort, security, safety, protection, success; interest, good. **2** *we cannot claim welfare* =**social security**, benefit, public assistance; pension, credit, support; sick pay, unemployment benefit; *Brit. informal* the dole.

well¹ ▶ adverb **1** *please behave well* =**satisfactorily**, nicely, correctly, properly, fittingly, suitably, appropriately. **2** *they get on well together* =**harmoniously**, agreeably, pleasantly, nicely, happily, amicably, amiably, peaceably; *informal*

famously. **3** *he plays the piano well* =**skilfully**, ably, competently, proficiently, adeptly, deftly, expertly, excellently. **4** *treat your employees well* =**decently**, fairly, kindly, generously. **5** *mix the ingredients well* =**thoroughly**, completely; effectively, rigorously, carefully. **6** *I know her quite well* =**intimately**, thoroughly, deeply, profoundly, personally. **7** *they studied the car market well* =**carefully**, closely, attentively, rigorously, in depth, exhaustively, in detail, meticulously, scrupulously, methodically, comprehensively, fully, extensively. **8** *they speak well of him* =**admiringly**, highly, approvingly, favourably, appreciatively, warmly, enthusiastically, glowingly. **9** *she makes enough money to live well* =**comfortably**, in luxury, prosperously. **10** *you may well be right* =**quite possibly**, conceivably, probably; undoubtedly, certainly, unquestionably. **11** *he is well over forty* =**considerably**, very much, a great deal, substantially, easily, comfortably, significantly. **12** *she could well afford it* =**easily**, comfortably, readily, effortlessly.
–OPPOSITES badly, negligently, disparagingly, barely.

▶ **adjective 1** *she was completely well again* =**healthy**, fine, fit, robust, strong, vigorous, blooming, thriving, in fine fettle; *informal* in the pink. **2** *all is not well* =**satisfactory**, all right, fine, in order, as it should be, acceptable; *informal* OK, hunky-dory.
–OPPOSITES poorly, unsatisfactory.

■ **as well** =**too**, also, in addition, into the bargain, besides, furthermore, moreover, to boot.
■ **as well as** =**together with**, along with, besides, plus, and, with, on top of, not to mention, to say nothing of, let alone.

well² ▶ **noun 1** *she drew water from the well* =**borehole**, spring, waterhole. **2** *he's a bottomless well of forgiveness* =**source**, supply, fount, reservoir, mine, fund, treasury.

▶ **verb** *tears welled from her eyes* =**flow**, spill, stream, run, rush, gush, roll, cascade, flood, spout; burst, issue.

well behaved ▶ **adjective** =**orderly**, obedient, disciplined, peaceable, docile, controlled, restrained, cooperative, compliant; mannerly, polite, civil, courteous, respectful, proper, decorous, refined.

–OPPOSITES naughty.

well-being ▶ **noun.** *See* WELFARE *sense* 1.

well bred ▶ **adjective** =**well brought up**, polite, civil, mannerly, courteous, respectful; ladylike, gentlemanly, genteel, cultivated, urbane, proper, refined.

well built ▶ **adjective** =**sturdy**, strapping, brawny, burly, hefty, muscular, strong, rugged, Herculean; *informal* hunky, beefy.
–OPPOSITES puny.

well dressed ▶ **adjective** =**smart**, fashionable, stylish, chic, modish, elegant, neat, spruce, trim, dapper; *informal* snazzy, natty, snappy, sharp.
–OPPOSITES scruffy.

well founded ▶ **adjective** =**justifiable**, warranted, legitimate, defensible, valid, understandable, excusable, acceptable, reasonable, sensible, sound.
–OPPOSITES groundless.

well known ▶ **adjective 1** *well-known principles* =**familiar**, popular, common, everyday, established. **2** *a well-known family of architects* =**famous**, famed, prominent, notable, renowned, distinguished, eminent, illustrious, acclaimed.
–OPPOSITES obscure.

well off ▶ **adjective 1** *her family's very well off. See* WEALTHY. **2** *the prisoners were relatively well off* =**fortunate**, lucky, comfortable. **3** *the island is not well off for harbours* =**well supplied with**, well stocked with, well furnished with.

well read ▶ **adjective** =**knowledgeable**, erudite, scholarly, literate, educated, cultured, bookish, studious.
–OPPOSITES ignorant.

well spoken ▶ **adjective** =**articulate**; refined, polite; *Brit. informal* posh.

welter ▶ **noun** =**confusion**, jumble, tangle, mess, hotchpotch, mishmash, mass.

wend ▶ **verb** =**meander**, wind one's way, wander, amble, stroll, saunter, drift, roam, traipse, walk; *informal* mosey, tootle.

west ▶ **adjective** =**western**, westerly; occidental.

wet ▶ **adjective 1** *wet clothes* =**damp**, moist, soaked, drenched, saturated, sopping, dripping, soggy; waterlogged, squelchy. **2** *it was cold and wet* =**rainy**, pouring, teeming, showery, drizzly; damp. **3** *the paint is still wet* =**sticky**,

tacky. **4** *a wet mortar mix* =**aqueous**, watery, sloppy.
–OPPOSITES dry, fine.

▶ verb *wet the clothes before ironing them* =**dampen**, moisten; sprinkle, spray, splash; soak, saturate, flood, douse, drench.
–OPPOSITES dry.

▶ noun **1** *the wet of his tears* =**wetness**, damp, moisture, moistness, sogginess. **2** *the race was held in the wet* =**rain**, drizzle, precipitation; spray, dew, damp.

whale ▶ noun

> **WORD LINKS**
>
> *male:* **bull**
> *female:* **cow**
> *young:* **calf**
> *collective noun:* **school, pod**

wharf ▶ noun =**quay**, pier, dock, berth, landing, jetty; harbour, dockyard, marina.

wheedle ▶ verb =**coax**, cajole, inveigle, induce, entice, charm, tempt, beguile, flatter, persuade, influence, win someone over, bring someone round, convince, prevail on, get round; *informal* sweet-talk, soft-soap.

wheel ▶ noun *a wagon wheel* =**disc**, hoop, ring, circle.
▶ verb **1** *she wheeled the trolley away* =**push**, trundle, roll. **2** *the flock of doves wheeled round* =**turn**, go round, circle, orbit.
 ■ **at/behind the wheel** =**driving**, steering.

wheeze ▶ verb *the illness left her wheezing* =**breathe noisily**, gasp, whistle, hiss, rasp, croak, pant, cough.
▶ noun **1** *she still had a slight wheeze* =**rasp**, croak, whistle, hiss, pant, cough. **2** *(Brit. informal) I've thought of a brilliant wheeze.* See RUSE.

whereabouts ▶ noun =**location**, position, site, place, situation, spot, point; home, address, locale, neighbourhood; bearings, orientation.

wherewithal ▶ noun =**money**, cash, capital, finance(s), funds; resources, means, ability, capability; *informal* dough, bread, loot, readies, the necessary; *Brit. informal* dosh, brass, lolly; *N. Amer. informal* bucks.

whet ▶ verb **1** *he whetted his knife on a stone* =**sharpen**, hone, strop, grind, file. **2** *something to whet your appetite* =**stimulate**, excite, arouse, rouse, kindle, trigger, spark, quicken, stir, inspire,

animate, fuel, fire, activate, tempt, galvanize.
–OPPOSITES blunt.

whiff ▶ noun **1** *I caught a whiff of perfume* =**faint smell**, trace, sniff, scent, odour, aroma. **2** *the faintest whiff of irony* =**trace**, hint, suggestion, impression, suspicion, soupçon, nuance, intimation, tinge, vein, shred, whisper, overtone.

while ▶ noun *we chatted for a while* =**time**, spell, stretch, stint, span, interval, period; duration, phase; *Brit. informal* patch.
▶ verb *tennis helped to while away the time* =**pass**, spend, occupy, use up, kill.

whim ▶ noun **1** *she bought it on a whim* =**impulse**, urge, notion, fancy, foible, caprice, conceit, vagary, inclination. **2** *human whim* =**capriciousness**, caprice, volatility, fickleness, idiosyncrasy.

whimper ▶ verb =**whine**, cry, sob, moan, snivel, wail, groan; *Brit. informal* grizzle.

whimsical ▶ adjective **1** *a whimsical sense of humour* =**fanciful**, playful, mischievous, waggish, quaint, curious, droll; eccentric, quirky, idiosyncratic, unconventional, outlandish; *informal* offbeat. **2** *the whimsical arbitrariness of autocracy* =**volatile**, capricious, fickle, changeable, unpredictable, variable, erratic, mercurial, mutable, inconstant, inconsistent, unstable, protean.

whine ▶ verb **1** *a child was whining* =**wail**, whimper, cry, mewl, moan, howl, yowl. **2** *the lift began to whine* =**hum**, drone. **3** *he's always whining about something* =**complain**, grouse, grouch, grumble, moan, carp; *informal* gripe, bellyache, whinge.

whip ▶ noun *he used a whip on his dogs* =**lash**, scourge, strap, belt.
▶ verb **1** *he whipped the boy* =**flog**, scourge, flagellate, lash, strap, belt, thrash, beat, tan someone's hide. **2** *whip the cream* =**whisk**, beat. **3** *he whipped his listeners into a frenzy* =**rouse**, stir up, excite, galvanize, electrify, stimulate, inspire, fire up, get someone going, inflame, agitate, goad, provoke.

whippersnapper ▶ noun *(informal)* =**upstart**, stripling; *informal* pipsqueak, squirt.

whirl ▶ verb **1** *leaves whirled in the wind* =**rotate**, circle, wheel, turn, revolve, orbit, spin, twirl. **2** *they whirled past* =**hurry**, race, dash, rush, run, sprint,

W

bolt, dart, gallop, career, charge, shoot, hurtle, hare, fly, speed, scurry; *informal* tear, belt, pelt, scoot; *Brit. informal* bomb. **3** *his mind was whirling* =**spin**, reel, swim.
▶ **noun 1** *a whirl of dust* =**swirl**, flurry, eddy. **2** *the mad social whirl* =**hurly-burly**, activity, bustle, rush, flurry, merry-go-round; *informal* to-do. **3** *Laura's mind was in a whirl* =**spin**, daze, stupor, muddle, jumble; confusion; *informal* dither.

whirlpool ▶ **noun 1** *a river full of whirlpools* =**eddy**, vortex, maelstrom. **2** *the health club has a whirlpool* =**spa bath**, hot tub; *trademark* jacuzzi.

whirlwind ▶ **noun 1** *the building was hit by a whirlwind* =**tornado**, hurricane, typhoon, cyclone, vortex; *N. Amer. informal* twister. **2** *a whirlwind of activity* =**maelstrom**, welter, bedlam, mayhem, babel, swirl, tumult, hurly-burly, commotion, confusion; *N. Amer.* three-ring circus.
▶ **adjective** *a whirlwind romance* =**rapid**, lightning, headlong, impulsive, breakneck, meteoric, sudden, swift, fast, quick, speedy.

whisk ▶ **verb 1** *the cable car will whisk you to the top* =**speed**, hurry, rush, sweep, hurtle, shoot. **2** *she whisked the cloth away* =**pull**, snatch, pluck, tug, jerk; *informal* whip, yank. **3** *he whisked out of sight* =**dash**, rush, race, bolt, dart, gallop, career, charge, shoot, hurtle, hare, fly, speed, zoom, scurry, scuttle, scamper; *informal* tear, belt, pelt, scoot, zip, whip. **4** *whisk the egg yolks* =**whip**, beat, mix.
▶ **noun** =**beater**, mixer, blender.

whisper ▶ **verb** *Alison whispered in his ear* =**murmur**, mutter, mumble, speak softly, breathe.
–OPPOSITES shout.
▶ **noun 1** *she spoke in a whisper* =**murmur**, mutter, mumble, low voice, undertone. **2** *I heard a whisper that he's left town* =**rumour**, story, report, speculation, insinuation, suggestion, hint; *informal* buzz.
–OPPOSITES shout.

whit ▶ **noun** =**scrap**, bit, speck, iota, jot, atom, crumb, shred, grain, mite, touch, trace, shadow, suggestion, whisper, suspicion, scintilla; *informal* smidgen.

white ▶ **adjective 1** *a white bandage* =**colourless**, unpigmented, bleached, natural; snowy, milky, chalky, ivory. **2** *her face was white with fear* =**pale**, pallid, wan, ashen, bloodless, waxen, chalky, pasty, peaky, washed out, ghostly, deathly. **3** *white hair* =**snowy**, grey, silver, hoary,

grizzled. **4** *the early white settlers* =**Caucasian**, European. **5** *a whiter than white government* =**virtuous**, moral, ethical, good, righteous, honourable, reputable, wholesome, honest, upright, upstanding, irreproachable; decent, worthy, noble; blameless, spotless, impeccable, unsullied, unblemished, uncorrupted, untainted; *informal* squeaky clean.
–OPPOSITES black, florid, immoral.

white-collar ▶ **adjective** =**clerical**, professional, executive, office.
–OPPOSITES blue-collar.

whiten ▶ **verb** =**make white**, make pale, bleach, blanch, lighten, fade.

whitewash ▶ **noun 1** *the report was a whitewash* =**cover-up**, camouflage, deception, facade, veneer, pretext. **2** *a four-match whitewash* =**walkover**, rout, landslide; *informal* pushover, cinch, breeze.
–OPPOSITES exposé.
▶ **verb** *don't whitewash what happened* =**cover up**, sweep under the carpet, hush up, suppress, draw a veil over, conceal, veil, obscure, keep secret; gloss over, downplay, soft-pedal.
–OPPOSITES expose.

whittle ▶ **verb 1** *he sat whittling a piece of wood* =**pare**, shave, trim, carve, shape, model. **2** *his powers were whittled away* =**erode**, wear away, eat away, reduce, diminish, undermine, weaken, subvert, impair, impede, hinder, sap. **3** *the ten teams have been whittled down to six* =**reduce**, cut down, prune, trim, slim down, pare down, decrease, decrease, diminish.

whole ▶ **adjective 1** *the whole report* =**entire**, complete, full, unabridged, uncut. **2** *a whole marble mantelpiece* =**intact**, in one piece, unbroken; undamaged, flawless, unmarked, perfect.
–OPPOSITES incomplete.
▶ **noun 1** *a single whole* =**entity**, unit, body, ensemble. **2** *the whole of the year* =**all**, every part, the lot, the sum.
■ **on the whole** =**overall**, all in all, all things considered, for the most part, in the main, in general, by and large; normally, usually, more often than not, almost always, typically, ordinarily.

wholehearted ▶ **adjective** =**committed**, positive, emphatic, devoted, dedicated, enthusiastic, unshakeable, unswerving; unqualified, unreserved, unconditional, unequivocal, unmitigated; complete, full, total, absolute.

w

–OPPOSITES half-hearted.

wholesale ▸ adverb *the images were removed wholesale* =**extensively**, on a large scale, comprehensively; indiscriminately, without exception.
–OPPOSITES selectively.

▸ adjective *wholesale destruction* =**extensive**, widespread, large-scale, wide-ranging, comprehensive, total, mass; indiscriminate.
–OPPOSITES partial.

wholesome ▸ adjective **1** *wholesome food* =**healthy**, health-giving, good, nutritious, nourishing; natural, uncontaminated, organic. **2** *wholesome fun* =**moral**, ethical, good, clean, virtuous, pure, innocent, chaste; uplifting, edifying; *informal* squeaky clean.

wholly ▸ adverb **1** *the measures were wholly inadequate* =**completely**, totally, absolutely, entirely, fully, thoroughly, utterly, downright, in every respect; *informal* one hundred per cent. **2** *they rely wholly on me* =**exclusively**, only, solely, purely, alone.

whore ▸ noun *the whores on the street. See* PROSTITUTE *noun.*

▸ verb *she spent her life whoring* =**work as a prostitute**, sell one's body, sell oneself, be on the streets; *informal* be on the game.

wicked ▸ adjective **1** *wicked deeds* =**evil**, sinful, immoral, wrong, bad, iniquitous, corrupt, base, mean, vile; villainous, nefarious, erring, foul, monstrous, shocking, outrageous, atrocious, abominable, reprehensible, detestable, despicable, odious, contemptible, heinous, execrable, fiendish, barbarous; criminal, dishonest, unscrupulous; *informal* crooked. **2** *a wicked sense of humour* =**mischievous**, playful, naughty, impish, roguish, arch, puckish, cheeky.
–OPPOSITES virtuous.

wickedness ▸ noun =**evil**, sin, iniquity, vileness, baseness, badness, wrongdoing, dishonesty, unscrupulousness, roguery, villainy, degeneracy, depravity, immorality, vice, corruption, devilry, fiendishness; *formal* turpitude.

wide ▸ adjective **1** *a wide river* =**broad**, extensive, spacious, vast, spread out. **2** *their mouths were wide with shock* =**fully open**, agape. **3** *a wide range of opinion* =**comprehensive**, ample, broad, extensive, large, exhaustive, all-inclusive. **4** *his shot was wide* =**off target**, off the mark, inaccurate.

–OPPOSITES narrow.

▸ adverb **1** *he opened his eyes wide* =**fully**, to the fullest/furthest extent, as far/much as possible. **2** *he shot wide* =**off target**, wide of the mark/target, inaccurately.

wide-eyed ▸ adjective **1** *the whole class was wide-eyed* =**goggle-eyed**, open-mouthed, dumbstruck, amazed, astonished, astounded, stunned, staggered; *informal* flabbergasted; *Brit. informal* gobsmacked. **2** *wide-eyed visitors* =**innocent**, naive, impressionable, ingenuous, childlike, credulous, trusting.

widen ▸ verb **1** *a proposal to widen the motorway* =**broaden**, open up/out, expand, extend, enlarge. **2** *the Party must widen its support* =**increase**, augment, boost, swell, enlarge.

wide open ▸ adjective **1** *his eyes were wide open* =**fully open**, agape. **2** *the championship is wide open* =**unpredictable**, uncertain, in the balance, up in the air; *informal* anyone's guess. **3** *they were wide open to attacks* =**vulnerable**, exposed, unprotected, defenceless, undefended, at risk, in danger.

widespread ▸ adjective =**general**, extensive, universal, common, global, worldwide, omnipresent, ubiquitous, across the board, predominant, prevalent, rife, broad.
–OPPOSITES limited.

width ▸ noun **1** *the width of the river* =**breadth**, thickness, span, diameter, girth. **2** *the width of experience required* =**range**, breadth, compass, scope, span, scale, extent, extensiveness, comprehensiveness.
–OPPOSITES length, narrowness.

wield ▸ verb **1** *he was wielding a sword* =**brandish**, flourish, wave, swing; use, employ, handle. **2** *he has wielded power since 1972* =**exercise**, exert, hold, maintain, command, control.

wife ▸ noun =**spouse**, partner, mate, consort, woman, helpmate, bride; *informal* old lady, better half, missus; *Brit. informal* other half, her indoors, trouble and strife.

> WORD LINKS
>
> *relating to a wife:* **uxorial**
> *killing of one's wife:* **uxoricide**

wiggle ▸ verb =**jiggle**, wriggle, twitch, shimmy, wag, squirm, writhe; *informal* waggle.

wild ▸ adjective **1** *wild animals* =**un-**

tamed, undomesticated, feral; fierce, ferocious, savage. **2** *wild flowers* =**uncultivated**, native, indigenous. **3** *wild hill country* =**uninhabited**, unpopulated, uncultivated; rugged, rough, inhospitable, desolate, barren. **4** *a wild night* =**stormy**, squally, tempestuous, turbulent, boisterous. **5** *her wild black hair* =**dishevelled**, tousled, tangled, windswept, untidy, unkempt. **6** *wild behaviour* =**uncontrolled**, unrestrained, undisciplined, unruly, rowdy, disorderly, riotous. **7** *wild with excitement* =**very excited**, delirious, in a frenzy; tumultuous, passionate, vehement, unrestrained. **8** *Bill's wild schemes* =**madcap**, ridiculous, ludicrous, foolish, stupid, foolhardy, idiotic, absurd, silly; impractical, impracticable, unworkable; *informal* crazy, crackpot. **9** *a wild guess* =**random**, arbitrary, haphazard, uninformed.
−OPPOSITES tame, cultivated, calm, disciplined.
■ **run wild 1** *the garden had run wild* =**grow unchecked**, grow profusely, run riot. **2** *the children are running wild* =**run amok**, run riot, get/be out of control, be undisciplined.

wilderness ▸ noun **1** *the Siberian wilderness* =**wilds**, wastes; desert. **2** *a litter-strewn wilderness* =**wasteland**.

wildlife ▸ noun =**(wild) animals**, creatures, fauna.

wilds ▸ plural noun =**remote areas**, wilderness; backwoods; *N. Amer.* backcountry; *Austral./NZ* outback, bush; *N. Amer. informal* boondocks.

wiles ▸ plural noun =**tricks**, ruses, ploys, schemes, dodges, manoeuvres, subterfuges, artifices; guile, artfulness, cunning, craftiness.

wilful ▸ adjective **1** *wilful destruction* =**deliberate**, intentional, premeditated, planned, conscious. **2** *a wilful child* =**headstrong**, strong-willed, obstinate, stubborn, pig-headed, recalcitrant, uncooperative, obstreperous; *Brit. informal* bloody-minded, bolshie; *formal* refractory.
−OPPOSITES accidental, amenable.

will¹ ▸ verb *accidents will happen* =**have a tendency to**, are bound to, do.

will² ▸ noun **1** *the will to succeed* =**determination**, strength of character, resolve, single-mindedness, drive, commitment, dedication, doggedness, tenacity, staying power. **2** *they stayed against their will* =**desire**, wish, preference, inclination, intention. **3** *God's will* =**wish**, desire, decision, choice; decree, command.
▸ verb **1** *do what you will* =**want**, wish, please, see/think fit, think best, like, choose, prefer. **2** *God willed it* =**decree**, order, ordain, command. **3** *she willed the money to her husband* =**bequeath**, leave, hand down, pass on.
■ **at will** =**as one pleases**, as one thinks fit, to suit oneself.

willing ▸ adjective **1** *I'm willing to give it a try* =**ready**, prepared, disposed, inclined, minded; happy, glad, pleased, agreeable, amenable; *informal* game. **2** *willing help* =**readily given**, ungrudging.
−OPPOSITES reluctant.

willingly ▸ adverb =**voluntarily**, of one's own free will, of one's own accord; readily, without reluctance, ungrudgingly, cheerfully, happily, gladly, with pleasure.
−OPPOSITES reluctantly.

willingness ▸ noun =**readiness**, inclination, will, wish, desire.
−OPPOSITES reluctance.

willy-nilly ▸ adverb **1** *cars were parked willy-nilly* =**haphazardly**, at random, all over the place. **2** *we are, willy-nilly, in a new situation* =**whether one likes it or not**, of necessity; *informal* like it or lump it; *formal* perforce.

wilt ▸ verb **1** *the roses had begun to wilt* =**droop**, sag, become limp, flop; wither, shrivel (up). **2** *wilting in the heat* =**languish**, flag, droop, become listless. **3** *Shelley's happy mood wilted* =**fade**, ebb, wane, evaporate, melt away.
−OPPOSITES flourish.

wily ▸ adjective =**shrewd**, clever, sharp, astute, canny, smart; crafty, cunning, artful, sly, scheming, calculating, devious; *informal* tricky, foxy.
−OPPOSITES naive.

win ▸ verb **1** *Steve won the race* =**be the victor in**, come first in, take first prize in, triumph in, be successful in. **2** *she was determined to win* =**come first**, be victorious, carry/win the day, come out on top, succeed, triumph, prevail. **3** *he won a cash prize* =**secure**, gain, collect, pick up, walk away/off with, carry off; *informal* land, net, bag, scoop. **4** *Ilona won his heart* =**captivate**, steal.

–OPPOSITES lose.

▶ noun *a 3–0 win* =**victory**, triumph, conquest.

–OPPOSITES defeat.

■ **win someone round/over** =**persuade**, talk round, convince, sway.

wince ▶ verb *he winced at the pain* =**grimace**, pull a face, flinch, blench, start.

wind[1] ▶ noun 1 *the trees were swaying in the wind* =**breeze**, current of air; gale, hurricane; *informal* blow; *literary* zephyr. **2** *Jez got his wind back* =**breath**; *informal* puff. **3** *no, thanks, it gives me wind* =**flatulence**, gas; *formal* flatus.

■ **in the wind** =**on the way**, coming, about to happen, in the offing, in the air, on the horizon, approaching, looming, brewing, afoot; *informal* on the cards.

WORD LINKS

instrument for measuring wind speed: **anemometer**

wind[2] ▶ verb 1 *the road winds up the mountain* =**twist (and turn)**, bend, curve, loop, zigzag, weave, snake. **2** *he wound a towel around his waist* =**wrap**, furl, entwine, lace. **3** *Anne wound the wool into a ball* =**coil**, roll, twist, twine.

■ **wind down** *the campaign was winding down* =**draw to a close**, come to an end, tail off, slack(en) off, slow down.

■ **wind something down** =**bring to a close/end**, wind up, close down.

■ **wind something up 1** *Richard wound up the meeting* =**conclude**, bring to an end/close, terminate; *informal* wrap up. **2** *the company has been wound up* =**close (down)**, dissolve, put into liquidation.

winded ▶ adjective =**out of breath**, breathless, panting, puffing.

windfall ▶ noun =**bonanza**, jackpot, pennies from heaven.

winding ▶ noun *the windings of the stream* =**twist**, turn, turning, bend, loop, curve, zigzag, meander.

▶ adjective *the winding country roads* =**twisting and turning**, meandering, twisty, bending, curving, zigzag, serpentine, sinuous, snaking.

–OPPOSITES straight.

windswept ▶ adjective 1 *the windswept moors* =**exposed**, bleak, bare, desolate. **2** *his windswept hair* =**dishevelled**, tousled, unkempt, wind-blown, untidy.

windy ▶ adjective 1 *a windy day* =**breezy**, blowy, fresh, blustery, gusty; wild, stormy, squally, tempestuous. **2** *a windy*

hillside =**windswept**, exposed, open to the elements, bare, bleak.

–OPPOSITES still, sheltered.

wine ▶ noun =*informal* plonk, vino, the grape; *literary* vintage.

WORD LINKS

relating to wine: **vinous, oeno-**
wine production: **viniculture**
study of wine: **oenology**

wing ▶ noun 1 *the east wing of the house* =**part**, section, side; annexe, extension. **2** *the radical wing of the party* =**faction**, camp, caucus, arm, branch, group, section, set, coterie, cabal.

▶ verb 1 *a seagull winged its way over the sea* =**fly**, glide, soar. **2** *the bomb winged past* =**hurtle**, speed, shoot, whizz, zoom, streak, fly. **3** *she was shot at and winged* =**wound**, graze, hit.

WORD LINKS

related prefix: **ptero-**

wink ▶ verb 1 *he winked an eye at her* =**blink**, flutter, bat. **2** *the diamond winked in the moonlight* =**sparkle**, twinkle, flash, glitter, gleam, shine, scintillate.

■ **wink at** =**turn a blind eye to**, close one's eyes to, ignore, overlook, disregard; connive at, condone, tolerate.

winkle ■ **winkle something out** =**worm out**, prise out, dig out, extract, draw out.

winner ▶ noun =**victor**, champion, conqueror, vanquisher, hero; medallist; *informal* champ, top dog.

–OPPOSITES loser.

winning ▶ adjective 1 *the winning team* =**victorious**, successful, triumphant, vanquishing, conquering; first, top. **2** *a winning smile* =**engaging**, charming, appealing, endearing, sweet, cute, winsome, attractive, prepossessing, fetching, disarming, captivating.

winnings ▶ plural noun =**prize money**, gains, booty, spoils; proceeds, profits, takings, purse.

winsome ▶ adjective. See WINNING *sense 2.*

wintry ▶ adjective 1 *wintry weather* =**bleak**, cold, chilly, frosty, freezing, icy, snowy, arctic, glacial, bitter, raw; *informal* nippy; *Brit. informal* parky. **2** *a wintry smile* =**unfriendly**, unwelcoming, cool, cold, frosty, frigid.

–OPPOSITES summery, warm.

WORD LINKS

relating to winter: **hibernal**

wipe ▶ verb **1** *Beth wiped the table* =**rub**, mop, sponge, swab; clean, dry, polish. **2** *he wiped the marks off the window* =**rub off**, clean off, clear up, remove, get rid of, take off, erase, efface. **3** *she wiped the memory from her mind* =**obliterate**, expunge, erase, blot out, blank out.
■ **wipe someone/something out** =**destroy**, annihilate, eradicate, eliminate; slaughter, massacre, kill, exterminate; demolish, raze to the ground; *informal* take out, zap; *N. Amer. informal* waste; *literary* slay.

wire ▶ noun =**cable**, lead, flex.

wiry ▶ adjective **1** *a wiry man* =**sinewy**, tough, athletic, strong; lean, spare, thin, stringy, skinny. **2** *wiry hair* =**coarse**, rough, strong.
−OPPOSITES flabby, smooth.

wisdom ▶ noun **1** *we questioned the wisdom of the decision* =**sagacity**, intelligence, sense, common sense, shrewdness, astuteness, smartness, judiciousness, judgement, prudence, circumspection; logic, rationale, soundness, advisability. **2** *the wisdom of the East* =**knowledge**, learning, erudition, scholarship, philosophy; lore.
−OPPOSITES folly.

wise ▶ adjective *a wise old man* =**sage**, sagacious, intelligent, clever, learned, knowledgeable, enlightened; astute, smart, shrewd, sharp-witted, canny, knowing; sensible, prudent, discerning, judicious, perceptive, insightful; rational, logical, sound, sane; *Brit. informal* fly; *formal* sapient.
−OPPOSITES foolish.
■ **wise to** *(informal)* =**aware of**, familiar with, acquainted with; *formal* cognizant of.

wish ▶ verb **1** *I wished for power* =**desire**, want, hope for, covet, dream of, long for, yearn for, crave, hunger for, lust after; aspire to, set one's heart on, seek, fancy, hanker after; *informal* have a yen for. **2** *they can do as they wish* =**want**, desire, feel inclined, feel like, care; choose, please, think fit. **3** *I wish you to send them a message* =**want**, desire, require.
▶ noun **1** *his wish to own a Mercedes* =**desire**, longing, yearning, inclination, urge, whim, craving, hunger; hope, aspiration, aim, ambition, dream; *informal*

hankering, yen. **2** *her parents' wishes* =**request**, requirement, bidding, instruction, direction, demand, order, command; want, desire; will; *literary* behest.

wisp ▶ noun =**strand**, tendril, lock; scrap, shred, thread.

wispy ▶ adjective =**thin**, fine, feathery, flyaway.

wistful ▶ adjective =**nostalgic**, yearning, longing; plaintive, regretful, rueful, melancholy, mournful; pensive, reflective, contemplative.

wit ▶ noun **1** *he needed all his wits to escape* =**intelligence**, shrewdness, astuteness, cleverness, canniness, sense, wisdom, sagacity, judgement, acumen, insight; brains, mind; *informal* nous, gumption, savvy. **2** *my sparkling wit* =**wittiness**, humour, drollery; repartee, badinage, banter, wordplay; jokes, witticisms, quips, puns. **3** *she's such a wit* =**comedian**, humorist, comic, joker; *informal* wag; *informal, dated* card.

witch ▶ noun **1** *the witch cast a spell* =**sorceress**, enchantress, hex; Wiccan. **2** *(informal)* *she's a right old witch* =**hag**, crone, harpy, harridan, she-devil; *informal* battle-axe.

witchcraft ▶ noun =**sorcery**, (black) magic, wizardry, spells, incantations, necromancy; Wicca.

witch doctor ▶ noun =**medicine man**, shaman, healer.

with ▶ preposition =**accompanied by**, escorted by; alongside, in addition to, as well as.

withdraw ▶ verb **1** *she withdrew her hand from his* =**remove**, extract, pull out, take out; take back. **2** *the ban on advertising was withdrawn* =**abolish**, cancel, lift, set aside, end, stop, remove, reverse, revoke, rescind, repeal, annul, void. **3** *she withdrew the allegation* =**retract**, take back, go back on, recant, disavow, disclaim, repudiate, renounce; back down, climb down, backtrack, back-pedal, do a U-turn, eat one's words. **4** *the troops withdrew from the city* =**leave**, pull out of, evacuate, quit, retreat from. **5** *his partner withdrew from the project* =**pull out of**, back out of, bow out of; get cold feet. **6** *they withdrew to their rooms* =**retire**, retreat, adjourn, decamp; leave, depart, absent oneself; *formal* repair; *dated* remove; *literary* betake oneself.
−OPPOSITES insert, introduce, deposit, enter.

withdrawal ▶ noun **1** *the withdrawal of subsidies* =**removal**, abolition, cancellation, discontinuation, termination, elimination. **2** *the withdrawal of the troops* =**departure**, pull-out, exit, exodus, evacuation, retreat.

withdrawn ▶ adjective =**introverted**, unsociable, inhibited, uncommunicative, unforthcoming, quiet, reticent, reserved, retiring, private, reclusive; shy, timid; aloof; *informal* stand-offish.
–OPPOSITES outgoing.

wither ▶ verb **1** *the flowers withered in the sun* =**shrivel (up)**, dry up; wilt, droop, go limp, fade, perish. **2** *the muscles in his leg withered* =**waste (away)**, shrivel (up), shrink, atrophy. **3** *her confidence withered* =**diminish**, dwindle, shrink, lessen, fade, ebb, wane; evaporate, disappear.
–OPPOSITES thrive, grow.

withering ▶ adjective =**scornful**, contemptuous, scathing, stinging, devastating; humiliating, mortifying.
–OPPOSITES admiring.

withhold ▶ verb **1** *he withheld the information* =**hold back**, keep back, refuse to give; retain, hold on to; hide, conceal, keep secret; *informal* sit on. **2** *she could not withhold her tears* =**suppress**, repress, hold back, fight back, choke back, control, check, restrain, contain.

within ▶ preposition **1** *within the prison walls* =**inside**, in, enclosed by, surrounded by. **2** *within a few hours* =**in less than**, in under, in no more than, after only.
–OPPOSITES outside.

without ▶ preposition **1** *thousands were without food* =**lacking**, short of, deprived of, in need of, wanting, requiring. **2** *I don't want to go without you* =**unaccompanied by**, unescorted by; in the absence of.

withstand ▶ verb =**resist**, weather, survive, endure, cope with, stand, tolerate, bear, defy, brave, hold out against; stand up to, face, confront.

witness ▶ noun **1** *witnesses claimed that he started the fight* =**observer**, onlooker, eyewitness, spectator, viewer, watcher; bystander, passer-by. **2** *a whisky bottle was the only witness of his mood* =**evidence**, indication, proof, testimony.
▶ verb **1** *who witnessed the incident?* =**see**, observe, watch, view, notice, spot; be present at, attend; *literary* behold. **2** *the will is correctly witnessed* =**countersign**, sign,

endorse, validate. **3** *his writings witness an inner toughness* =**attest to**, testify to, confirm, evidence, prove, verify, corroborate, substantiate; show, demonstrate, indicate, reveal, bespeak.

witticism ▶ noun =**joke**, quip, jest, pun, play on words, bon mot; *informal* one-liner, gag, funny, crack, wisecrack.

witty ▶ adjective =**humorous**, amusing, droll, funny, comic; jocular, facetious, waggish; sparkling, scintillating, entertaining; clever, quick-witted.

wizard ▶ noun **1** *the wizard cast a spell* =**sorcerer**, warlock, magus, (black) magician, enchanter. **2** *a financial wizard* =**genius**, expert, master, virtuoso, maestro, marvel, Wunderkind; *informal* hotshot, demon, whizz-kid, buff, pro, ace; *Brit. informal* dab hand; *N. Amer. informal* maven.

wizardry ▶ noun =**sorcery**, witchcraft, (black) magic, enchantment; spells, charms.

wizened ▶ adjective =**wrinkled**, lined, creased, shrivelled (up), withered, weather-beaten, shrunken, gnarled.

wobble ▶ verb **1** *the table wobbled* =**rock**, teeter, jiggle, sway, see-saw, shake. **2** *he wobbled across to the door* =**teeter**, totter, stagger, lurch. **3** *his voice wobbled* =**tremble**, shake, quiver, quaver, waver. **4** *for a few days the minister wobbled* =**hesitate**, vacillate, waver, dither, shilly-shally, blow hot and cold.

wobbly ▶ adjective **1** *a wobbly table* =**unsteady**, unstable, shaky, rocky, rickety; unsafe, precarious; *informal* wonky. **2** *her legs were a bit wobbly* =**shaky**, quivery, weak, unsteady; *informal* trembly, like jelly. **3** *I feel so wobbly* =**faint**, dizzy, light-headed, giddy, weak (at the knees), groggy, muzzy; *informal* woozy.
–OPPOSITES stable.

woe ▶ noun **1** *a tale of woe* =**misery**, sorrow, distress, wretchedness, sadness, unhappiness, heartache, heartbreak, despondency, despair, depression, gloom, melancholy; adversity, misfortune, disaster, suffering, hardship; *literary* dolour. **2** *financial woes* =**trouble**, difficulty, problem, trial, tribulation, misfortune, setback, reverse.
–OPPOSITES joy.

woeful ▶ adjective **1** *a woeful tale* =**tragic**, sad, miserable, cheerless, gloomy, sorry, pitiful, pathetic, traumatic, depressing, heartbreaking, heart-rending,

w

tear-jerking. **2** *the team's woeful performance* =**dreadful**, awful, terrible, atrocious, disgraceful, deplorable, shameful, hopeless, lamentable; *informal* rotten, appalling, crummy, pathetic, pitiful, lousy, abysmal, dire; *Brit. informal* duff, chronic, rubbish.

–OPPOSITES cheerful, excellent.

wolf ▶ verb =**devour**, gobble (up), guzzle, gulp down, bolt; *informal* put away, demolish, shovel down, scoff (down), get outside of; *N. Amer. informal* snarf (down/up).

> WORD LINKS
>
> *male:* **dog**
> *female:* **bitch**
> *young:* **cub**
> *relating to wolves:* **lupine**
> *collective noun:* **pack**

woman ▶ noun **1** *a woman got out of the car* =**lady**, female; matron; *Scottish & N. English* lass; *Irish* colleen; *informal* chick, girlie, filly; *Brit. informal* bird; *N. Amer. informal* sheila; *literary* damsel. **2** *he found himself a new woman* =**girlfriend**, sweetheart, partner, significant other, lover, mistress; fiancée; wife, spouse; *informal* bird, fancy woman, missus, better half; *Brit. informal* other half, trouble and strife; *N. Amer. informal* squeeze; *dated* lady friend.

> WORD LINKS
>
> *relating to women:* **female, feminine, gynaeco-**
> *branch of medicine concerning women:* **gynaecology**
> *fear of women:* **gynophobia**
> *hatred of women:* **misogyny**

womanhood ▶ noun **1** *she was on the brink of womanhood* =**adulthood**, maturity. **2** *she's an ideal of womanhood* =**womanliness**, femininity. **3** *the stereotype of Soviet womanhood* =**women**, womenfolk; womankind; the female sex.

womanizer ▶ noun =**philanderer**, Casanova, Don Juan, Romeo, Lothario, ladies' man, playboy, seducer; *informal* skirt-chaser, ladykiller, lech.

womankind ▶ noun =**women**, the female sex.

womanly ▶ adjective **1** *womanly virtues* =**feminine**, female. **2** *her womanly figure* =**voluptuous**, curvaceous, shapely, ample, Junoesque, Rubenesque, buxom, full-figured; *informal* curvy, busty.

–OPPOSITES manly, boyish.

wonder ▶ noun **1** *she was speechless with wonder* =**awe**, admiration, fascination; surprise, astonishment, amazement. **2** *the wonders of nature* =**marvel**, miracle, phenomenon, sensation, spectacle, beauty; curiosity.

▶ verb **1** *I wondered what was on her mind* =**ponder**, think about, meditate on, reflect on, muse on, speculate about, conjecture; be curious about. **2** *people wondered at such bravery* =**marvel**, be amazed, be astonished, stand in awe, be dumbfounded, gape, goggle; *informal* be flabbergasted.

wonderful ▶ adjective =**marvellous**, magnificent, superb, glorious, sublime, lovely, delightful; *informal* super, great, fantastic, terrific, tremendous, sensational, incredible, fabulous, awesome, magic, wicked; *Brit. informal* smashing, brilliant; *N. Amer. informal* peachy, dandy, neat; *Austral./NZ informal* beaut, bonzer.

wont ▶ noun *(formal or humorous) Paul drove fast, as was his wont* =**custom**, habit, way, practice, convention, rule.

▶ adjective *(literary) he was wont to arise at 5.30* =**accustomed**, used, given, inclined.

wonted ▶ adjective *(literary)* =**customary**, habitual, usual, accustomed, familiar, normal, conventional, routine, common.

woo ▶ verb **1** *Richard wooed Joan* =**pay court to**, pursue, chase (after); *dated* court, romance, seek the hand of, set one's cap at, make love to. **2** *the party wooed voters with promises* =**seek**, pursue, curry favour with, try to win, try to attract, try to cultivate. **3** *an attempt to woo him out of retirement* =**entice**, tempt, coax, persuade, wheedle, seduce; *informal* sweet-talk.

wood ▶ noun **1** *polished wood* =**timber**, planks; logs; *N. Amer.* lumber. **2** *a walk through the woods* =**forest**, woodland, trees; copse, coppice, grove; *Brit.* spinney.

> WORD LINKS
>
> *relating to wood:* **ligneous**
> *farming of wood:* **forestry, agroforestry, arboriculture, silviculture**

wooded ▶ adjective =**forested**, afforested, tree-covered; *literary* sylvan.

wooden ▶ adjective **1** *a wooden door*

=**wood**, timber; *technical* ligneous.
2 *wooden acting* =**stilted**, stiff, unnatural, awkward, leaden; dry, flat, stodgy, lifeless, passionless, spiritless, soulless.
3 *her face was wooden* =**expressionless**, impassive, poker-faced, emotionless, blank, vacant, unresponsive.

woodland ▶ noun =**woods**, forest, trees.

woodwork ▶ noun =**carpentry**, joinery.

wool ▶ noun *sheep's wool* =**fleece**, hair, coat.

woolly ▶ adjective **1** *a woolly hat* =**woollen**, fleecy. **2** *a sheep's woolly coat* =**fleecy**, shaggy, hairy, fluffy, flocculent. **3** *woolly generalizations* =**vague**, ill-defined, hazy, unclear, fuzzy, blurry, foggy, nebulous, imprecise, inexact, indefinite; confused, muddled.

word ▶ noun **1** *the Italian word for 'ham'* =**term**, name, expression, designation, locution, vocable; *formal* appellation.
2 *his words were meant kindly* =**remark**, comment, observation, statement, utterance, pronouncement. **3** *I've got three weeks to learn the words* =**script**, lyrics, libretto. **4** *I give you my word* =**promise**, assurance, guarantee, undertaking; pledge, vow, oath, bond; *formal* troth. **5** *I want a word with you* =**talk**, conversation, chat, tête-à-tête, heart-to-heart, one-to-one; discussion; *informal* confab, powwow. **6** *there's no word from the hospital* =**news**, information, communication, intelligence; message, report, communiqué, dispatch, bulletin; *informal* info, gen; *literary* tidings. **7** *word has it he's turned over a new leaf* =**rumour**, hearsay, talk, gossip; *informal* the grapevine. **8** *I'm waiting for the word from HQ* =**instruction**, order, command; signal, prompt, cue, tip-off; *informal* go-ahead, thumbs up, green light. **9** *his word was law* =**command**, order, decree, edict; bidding, will.

▶ verb *the question was carefully worded* =**phrase**, express, put, couch, frame, formulate, style.

■ **in a word** =**briefly**, in short, in a nutshell, to come to the point, to cut a long story short, not to put too fine a point on it; to sum up.

■ **word for word 1** *they took down the speeches word for word* =**verbatim**, letter for letter; exactly, faithfully. **2** *a word-for-word translation* =**verbatim**, literal, exact, direct, accurate, faithful; unadul-

terated, unabridged.

WORD LINKS

relating to words: **verbal, lexical, logo-**

wording ▶ noun =**phrasing**, phraseology, language, expression, terminology.

wordplay ▶ noun =**punning**, play on words; wit, witticisms, repartee.

wordy ▶ adjective =**long-winded**, verbose, prolix, lengthy, protracted, rambling, circumlocutory, periphrastic; loquacious, garrulous, voluble; *informal* windy; *Brit. informal* waffly.
–OPPOSITES succinct.

work ▶ noun **1** *a day's work in the fields* =**labour**, toil, slog, drudgery, exertion, effort, industry; *informal* grind, sweat, elbow grease; *Brit. informal* graft; *literary* travail. **2** *I'm looking for work* =**employment**, a job, a post, a position, a situation; occupation, profession, career, vocation, calling. **3** *haven't you got any work?* =**tasks**, jobs, duties, assignments, projects; chores. **4** *works of literature* =**composition**, piece, creation; opus. **5** *this is the work of a radical faction* =**handiwork**, doing, act, deed. **6** *a lifetime spent doing good works* =**deeds**, acts, actions. **7** *the complete works of Shakespeare* =**writings**, oeuvre, canon, output. **8** *a car works* =**factory**, plant, mill, foundry, workshop, shop. **9** *the works of a clock* =**mechanism**, machinery, workings, parts, movement, action; *informal* insides.
–OPPOSITES leisure.

▶ verb **1** *staff worked late into the night* =**toil**, labour, exert oneself, slave (away); keep at it, keep one's nose to the grindstone; *informal* slog (away), beaver away, put one's back into it, sweat blood; *Brit. informal* graft; *literary* travail. **2** *he worked in education for years* =**be employed**, have a job, earn one's living, do business. **3** *farmers worked the land* =**cultivate**, farm, till, plough. **4** *his car was working perfectly* =**function**, go, run, operate; *informal* behave. **5** *how do I work this machine?* =**operate**, use, handle, control, manipulate, run. **6** *their ploy worked* =**succeed**, turn out well, go as planned, get results, be effective; *informal* come off, pay off, do the trick. **7** *blusher can work miracles* =**bring about**, accomplish, achieve, produce, perform, create, engender, contrive, effect. **8** *he worked the crowd into a frenzy* =**stir (up)**, excite,

drive, move, rouse, fire, galvanize; whip up, agitate. **9** *work the mixture into a paste* =**knead**, squeeze, form; mix, stir, blend. **10** *he worked the blade into the padlock* =**manoeuvre**, manipulate, guide, edge. **11** *he worked his way through the crowd* =**manoeuvre**, make, thread, wind, weave, wend, elbow.
–OPPOSITES rest, fail.

■ **work on someone** =**persuade**, manipulate, influence; coax, cajole, wheedle, soften up; *informal* twist someone's arm, lean on.

■ **work out 1** *the bill works out at £50* =**amount to**, add up to, come to, total; *Brit.* tot up to. **2** *my idea worked out. See* WORK *verb sense* 6. **3** *things didn't work out the way she planned* =**end up**, turn out, go, come out, develop; happen, occur; *informal* pan out. **4** *he works out at the local gym* =**exercise**, train.

■ **work something out 1** *work out what you can afford* =**calculate**, compute, reckon up, determine. **2** *I'm trying to work out what she meant* =**understand**, comprehend, puzzle out, sort out, make sense of, get to the bottom of, make head or tail of, unravel, decipher, decode; *informal* figure out; *Brit. informal* suss out. **3** *they worked out a plan* =**devise**, formulate, draw up, put together, develop, construct, arrange, organize, contrive, concoct; hammer out, negotiate.

■ **work something up** =**stimulate**, rouse, raise, arouse, awaken, excite.

╭─────────────╮
│ **WORD LINKS** │
╰─────────────╯
fear of work: **ergophobia**

workable ▶ adjective =**practicable**, feasible, viable, possible, achievable; realistic, reasonable, sensible, practical; *informal* doable.
–OPPOSITES impracticable.

worker ▶ noun **1** *a strike by workers* =**employee**, member of staff; workman, labourer, hand, operator; proletarian; wage-earner, breadwinner. **2** *(informal) I got a reputation for being a worker* =**hard worker**, toiler, workhorse; *informal* busy bee, eager beaver, workaholic.

workforce ▶ noun =**employees**, staff, personnel, workers, labour force, manpower; human resources; *informal* liveware.

working ▶ adjective **1** *working mothers* =**employed**, in work, waged. **2** *a working waterwheel* =**functioning**, operating,

running, active, in working order, operational, functional, serviceable; *informal* up and running. **3** *a working knowledge of contract law* =**sufficient**, adequate, viable; useful, effective.
–OPPOSITES unemployed, faulty.

▶ noun **1** *the working of a carburettor* =**functioning**, operation, running, action, performance. **2** *the workings of a watch* =**mechanism**, machinery, parts, movement, action, works; *informal* insides.

workman ▶ noun =(**manual) worker**, labourer, hand, operative, operator; employee.

workmanship ▶ noun =**craftsmanship**, artistry, craft, art, artisanship, handiwork; skill, expertise, technique.

workout ▶ noun =**exercise session**, keep-fit session, training session, drill; warm-up; exercises, aerobics.

workshop ▶ noun **1** *a car repair workshop* =**factory**, works, plant; industrial unit, garage. **2** *the craftsmen had a chilly workshop* =**workroom**, studio, atelier. **3** *a workshop on combating stress* =**study group**, discussion group, seminar, forum, class.

world ▶ noun **1** *he travelled the world* =**earth**, globe, planet, sphere. **2** *life on other worlds* =**planet**, satellite, moon, star, heavenly body, orb. **3** *the academic world* =**sphere**, society, circle, arena, milieu, province, domain, preserve, realm, field, discipline, area. **4** *she would show the world that she was strong* =**everyone**, people, mankind, humankind, humanity, the public, all and sundry, {every Tom, Dick, and Harry}. **5** *a world of difference* =**huge amount**, good deal, abundance; wealth, profusion, mountain; plenty; *informal* heap, lot, load, ton, masses; *Brit. informal* shedload.

worldly ▶ adjective **1** *worldly pursuits* =**earthly**, terrestrial, temporal, mundane; mortal, human, material, physical, carnal, fleshly, bodily, corporeal, sensual. **2** *a worldly man* =**sophisticated**, experienced, worldly-wise, knowledgeable, knowing, enlightened, shrewd, mature, seasoned, cosmopolitan, urbane, cultured.
–OPPOSITES spiritual, naive.

worldwide ▶ adjective =**global**, international, intercontinental, universal; ubiquitous, extensive, widespread, far-reaching, wide-ranging.
–OPPOSITES local.

worm ▸ noun

WORD LINKS

relating to worms: **vermi-**
worm-shaped: **vermiform**
worm-eating: **vermivorous**
substance used to kill worms: **vermicide**
fear of worms: **helminthophobia**

worn ▸ adjective **1** *his hat was worn*
=**shabby**, worn out, threadbare, in tatters, holey, falling to pieces, ragged,
frayed, moth-eaten, scruffy, having
seen better days. **2** *her face looked worn.*
See WORN OUT *sense* 2.
–OPPOSITES smart, fresh.

worn out ▸ adjective **1** *a worn-out shirt.*
See WORN *sense* 1. **2** *by evening they looked
worn out* =**exhausted**, fatigued, tired
(out), weary, drained, worn, drawn,
wan, sapped, spent; careworn, haggard,
hollow-eyed, pinched, pale, peaky; *informal* all in, done in, dog-tired, dead beat,
fit to drop, shattered; *Brit. informal* knackered; *N. Amer. informal* pooped. **3** *worn-out
ideas* =**obsolete**, antiquated, old, stale,
hackneyed, trite, overused, overworked,
clichéd, unoriginal, commonplace, pedestrian, prosaic, stock, conventional; *informal* played out, old hat.
–OPPOSITES smart, fresh.

worried ▸ adjective =**anxious**, perturbed, troubled, bothered, concerned,
disquieted, uneasy, fretful, agitated,
nervous, edgy, tense, overwrought,
worked up, keyed up, jumpy, stressed;
apprehensive, fearful, afraid, frightened, scared; *informal* uptight, a bundle of
nerves, on tenterhooks, jittery, twitchy,
in a stew, all of a dither, in a flap, in a
sweat, het up; *Brit. informal* having kittens;
N. Amer. informal antsy.
–OPPOSITES carefree.

worry ▸ verb **1** *she worries about his health*
=**fret**, be concerned, be anxious, agonize, brood, panic, lose sleep, get worked
up; *informal* get stressed, get in a flap, get
in a state, stew, torment oneself. **2** *is
something worrying you?* =**trouble**,
bother, make anxious, disturb, distress,
upset, concern, disquiet, fret, agitate,
unsettle, perturb, scare, fluster, stress,
torment, plague; prey on one's mind,
weigh down, gnaw at; *informal* bug, get to.
3 *a dog worried his sheep* =**attack**, savage,
maul, mutilate, mangle; molest, tor-
ment, persecute.
▸ noun **1** *I'm beside myself with worry* =**anxiety**, perturbation, distress, concern, un-

ease, disquiet, fretfulness, restlessness,
nerves, agitation, edginess, tension,
stress; apprehension, fear, dread, trepidation, misgiving, angst; *informal* butterflies, the willies, the heebie-jeebies. **2** *the
rats are a worry* =**problem**, cause for concern; nuisance, pest, plague, trial,
trouble, vexation, bane, bugbear; *informal*
pain, headache, hassle.

worrying ▸ adjective =**alarming**, worrisome, daunting, perturbing, niggling,
bothersome, troublesome, unsettling,
nerve-racking; distressing, disquieting,
upsetting, traumatic, problematic; *informal* scary, hairy.

worsen ▸ verb **1** *insomnia can worsen a
patient's distress* =**aggravate**, exacerbate,
compound, add to, intensify, increase,
magnify, heighten, inflame, augment;
informal add fuel to the fire. **2** *the recession
worsened* =**deteriorate**, degenerate, decline; *informal* go downhill, go to pot, go
to the dogs.
–OPPOSITES improve.

worship ▸ noun **1** *the worship of saints*
=**reverence**, veneration, adoration,
glorification, exaltation; devotion,
praise, thanksgiving, homage, honour;
formal laudation. **2** *morning worship* =**service**, religious rite, prayer, praise, devotion, religious observance; matins,
vespers, evensong. **3** *he contemplated her
with worship* =**admiration**, adulation,
idolization, lionization, hero-worship.
▸ verb *they worship pagan gods* =**revere**, venerate, pay homage to, honour, adore,
praise, pray to, glorify, exalt, extol; hold
dear, cherish, treasure, esteem, adulate,
idolize, deify, hero-worship, lionize; *informal* put on a pedestal; *formal* laud.

worth ▸ noun **1** *evidence of the rug's worth*
=**value**, price, cost; valuation, quotation, estimate. **2** *the intrinsic worth of education* =**benefit**, advantage, use, value,
virtue, utility, service, profit, help, aid;
desirability, appeal; significance, sense;
informal mileage, percentage. **3** *a sense of
personal worth* =**worthiness**, merit,
value, excellence, calibre, quality, stature, eminence, consequence, importance, significance, distinction.

worthless ▸ adjective **1** *the item was
worthless* =**valueless**; inferior, second-
rate, low-grade, cheap, shoddy, tawdry;
informal crummy, rubbishy, ten a penny;
N. Amer. informal nickel-and-dime. **2** *your
conclusions are worthless* =**useless**, ineffective, ineffectual, fruitless, unproduct-

ive, unavailing, pointless, nugatory, valueless, inadequate, deficient, meaningless, senseless, insubstantial, inconsequential; *informal* a dead loss. **3** *his worthless son* =**good-for-nothing**, ne'er-do-well, useless, despicable, contemptible, low, ignominious, degenerate; *informal* no-good, lousy.
–OPPOSITES valuable, useful.

worthwhile ▶ adjective =**valuable**, useful, of service, beneficial, rewarding, advantageous, positive, helpful, profitable, gainful, fruitful, productive, constructive, effective.

worthy ▶ adjective *a worthy citizen* =**virtuous**, righteous, good, moral, ethical, upright, upstanding, high-minded, principled, exemplary; law-abiding, irreproachable, unimpeachable, honest, honourable, reputable, decent, respectable, noble; *informal* squeaky clean.
–OPPOSITES disreputable.
▶ noun *local worthies* =**dignitary**, personage, grandee, VIP, notable, notability, pillar of society, luminary, leading light, big name; *informal* heavyweight, bigwig, top dog, big shot, big cheese.
–OPPOSITES nobody.
■ **be worthy of** =**deserve**, merit, warrant, rate, justify, earn, be entitled to, qualify for.

would-be ▶ adjective =**aspiring**, budding, promising, prospective, potential, hopeful, keen, eager, ambitious; *informal* wannabe.

wound ▶ noun **1** *a chest wound* =**injury**, lesion, cut, gash, laceration, tear, slash; graze, scratch, abrasion; *Medicine* trauma. **2** *the wounds inflicted by the media* =**insult**, blow, slight, offence, affront; hurt, damage, injury, pain, distress, grief, anguish, torment.
▶ verb **1** *he was critically wounded* =**injure**, hurt, harm; maim, mutilate, disable, incapacitate, cripple; lacerate, cut, graze, gash, stab, slash. **2** *her words had wounded him* =**hurt**, scar, damage, injure; insult, slight, offend, affront, distress, disturb, upset, trouble; grieve, sadden, pain, sting.

wrangle ▶ noun *a wrangle over money* =**argument**, dispute, disagreement, quarrel, falling-out, fight, squabble, altercation, war of words, shouting match, tiff; *informal* set-to, run-in, slanging match; *Brit. informal* barney, row, bust-up.
▶ verb *we wrangled over the details* =**argue**,

quarrel, bicker, squabble, fall out, have words, disagree, be at odds, fight, battle, feud, clash; *informal* scrap; *Brit. informal* row.

wrap ▶ verb **1** *she wrapped herself in a towel* =**swathe**, bundle, swaddle, muffle, cloak, enfold, envelop, encase, cover, fold, wind. **2** *I wrapped the vase carefully* =**parcel up**, package, pack, bundle (up); gift-wrap.
▶ noun *he put a wrap round her* =**shawl**, stole, cloak, cape, mantle, scarf, poncho, serape.
■ **wrap up** *wrap up well — it's cold* =**dress warmly**, muffle up.

wrapper ▶ noun **1** *a sweet wrapper* =**wrapping**, packaging, paper, cover, covering; jacket, sheath. **2** *(N. Amer.) she wore a cotton wrapper* =**housecoat**, bathrobe, dressing gown, robe, kimono, peignoir.

wrath ▶ noun =**anger**, rage, fury, outrage, spleen, vexation, (high) dudgeon, crossness; *literary* ire, choler.
–OPPOSITES happiness.

wreak ▶ verb =**inflict**, bestow, mete out, administer, deliver, impose, exact, create, cause, result in, effect, engender, bring about, perpetrate, unleash, vent; *formal* effectuate.

wreath ▶ noun =**garland**, circlet, chaplet, crown, festoon, lei; ring, loop, circle.

wreathe ▶ verb **1** *a pulpit wreathed in holly* =**festoon**, garland, drape, cover, deck, decorate, ornament, adorn. **2** *blue smoke wreathed upwards* =**spiral**, coil, loop, wind, curl, twist, snake, curve.

wreck ▶ noun **1** *salvage teams landed on the wreck* =**shipwreck**, sunken ship, derelict; shell, hull. **2** *the wreck of a stolen car* =**wreckage**, debris, ruins, remains.
▶ verb **1** *he had wrecked her car* =**demolish**, crash, smash up, damage, destroy; vandalize, deface, desecrate, write off; *N. Amer. informal* trash, total. **2** *his ship was wrecked* =**shipwreck**, sink, capsize, run aground. **3** *the crisis wrecked his plans* =**ruin**, spoil, disrupt, undo, put a stop to, frustrate, blight, crush, quash, dash, destroy, scotch, shatter, devastate, sabotage; *informal* mess up, screw up, foul up, put paid to, stymie, put the kibosh on; *Brit. informal* scupper.

wrench ▶ noun **1** *she felt a wrench on her shoulders* =**tug**, pull, jerk, jolt, heave; *informal* yank. **2** *hold the piston with a wrench* =**spanner**. **3** *a wrench in his arm* =**sprain**, twist, strain, rick, crick. **4** *leaving was an*

immense wrench =**painful parting**, traumatic event; pang, trauma.
▶ **verb 1** *he wrenched the gun from her* =**tug**, pull, jerk, wrest, heave, twist, pluck, grab, seize, snatch, force, prise; *N. Amer.* pry; *informal* yank. **2** *she wrenched her ankle* =**sprain**, twist, turn, strain, rick, crick, pull; injure, hurt.

wrest ▶ **verb** =**wrench**, snatch, seize, grab, prise, pluck, tug, pull, jerk, dislodge; *N. Amer.* pry; *informal* yank.

wrestle ▶ **verb** =**grapple**, fight, struggle, contend, vie, battle, wrangle; scuffle, tussle, brawl; *informal* scrap.

wretch ▶ **noun 1** *the wretches killed themselves* =**poor creature**, poor soul, poor thing; *informal* poor devil. **2** *I wouldn't trust the old wretch* =**scoundrel**, villain, ruffian, rogue, rascal, reprobate, miscreant, good-for-nothing; *informal* heel, creep, louse, rat, swine, dog, lowlife, scumbag; *informal, dated* rotter, blighter.

wretched ▶ **adjective 1** *I felt so wretched without you* =**miserable**, unhappy, sad, heartbroken, grief-stricken, sorrowful, distressed, desolate, devastated, despairing, disconsolate, downcast, dejected, crestfallen, cheerless, depressed, melancholy, morose, gloomy, mournful, doleful, dismal, forlorn, woebegone; *informal* blue; *literary* dolorous. **2** *I feel wretched* =**ill**, unwell, poorly, sick, below par; *Brit.* off colour; *informal* under the weather, out of sorts. **3** *their living conditions are wretched* =**harsh**, hard, grim, stark, difficult; poor, impoverished; pitiful, pathetic, miserable, cheerless, dilapidated; *informal* scummy; *Brit. informal* grotty. **4** *the wretched dweller in the shanty town* =**unfortunate**, unlucky, ill-starred, blighted, hapless, poor, pitiable, downtrodden, oppressed. **5** *he's a wretched coward* =**despicable**, contemptible, reprehensible, base, vile, loathsome, detestable, odious, ignoble, shameful; *informal* dirty, rotten, low-down, lousy. **6** *wretched weather* =**terrible**, awful, dire, atrocious, dreadful, bad, poor, lamentable, deplorable; *informal* God-awful. **7** *I don't want the wretched money* =*informal* damn, blasted, blessed, flaming, confounded, rotten; *Brit. informal* flipping, blinking, bloody.
−OPPOSITES cheerful, well, comfortable, fortunate, excellent.

wriggle ▶ **verb 1** *she tried to hug him but he wriggled* =**squirm**, writhe, wiggle, jiggle, jerk, thresh, flounder, flail, twitch, twist and turn; snake, worm, slither. **2** *he wriggled out of his responsibilities* =**avoid**, shirk, dodge, evade, elude, sidestep; escape from; *informal* duck.

wring ▶ **verb 1** *wring out the clothes* =**twist**, squeeze, screw, scrunch, knead, press, mangle. **2** *concessions were wrung from the government* =**extract**, elicit, force, exact, wrest, wrench, squeeze, milk; *informal* bleed. **3** *his expression wrung her heart* =**rend**, tear at, harrow, pierce, stab, wound, rack; distress, pain, hurt.

wrinkle ▶ **noun** *fine wrinkles around her mouth* =**crease**, fold, pucker, line, crinkle, furrow, ridge, groove; *informal* crow's feet.
▶ **verb** *his coat tails wrinkled up* =**crease**, pucker, gather, line, crinkle, crumple, rumple, ruck up, scrunch up.

writ ▶ **noun** =**summons**, subpoena, warrant, arraignment, indictment, citation, court order.

write ▶ **verb 1** *he wrote her name in the book* =**put in writing**, put down, jot down, note (down), take down, record, register, log, list; inscribe, sign, scribble, scrawl, pencil. **2** *I wrote a poem* =**compose**, draft, think up, formulate, compile, pen, dash off, produce. **3** *he had her address and promised to write* =**correspond**, communicate, get in touch, keep in contact; *informal* drop someone a line.
■ **write someone/something off 1** *they have had to write off loans* =**forget about**, disregard, give up on, cancel, annul, wipe out. **2** *he wrote off his new car* =**wreck**, smash up, crash, destroy, demolish, ruin; *N. Amer. informal* total. **3** *who would write off a player of his stature?* =**disregard**, dismiss, ignore.

writer ▶ **noun** =**author**, wordsmith, man/woman of letters, penman; novelist, essayist, biographer; journalist, columnist, correspondent; scriptwriter, playwright, dramatist; poet; *informal* scribbler, scribe, pen-pusher, hack.

writhe ▶ **verb** =**squirm**, wriggle, thrash, flail, toss, twist.

writing ▶ **noun 1** *I can't read his writing* =**handwriting**, hand, script, print; penmanship, calligraphy, chirography; *informal* scribble, scrawl. **2** *the writings of Gertrude Stein* =**works**, compositions, books, publications, oeuvre; papers, articles, essays.

w

WORD LINKS

study of handwriting: **graphology**
study of ancient writing systems:
  palaeography
fear of writing: **graphophobia**

wrong ▶ adjective **1** *the wrong answer*
=**incorrect**, mistaken, in error, erroneous, inaccurate, inexact, imprecise, fallacious, wide of the mark; *informal* off
beam, out. **2** *he knew he had said the wrong
thing* =**inappropriate**, unsuitable, inapt,
inapposite, undesirable; ill-advised, ill-
considered, ill-judged, impolitic, injudicious, infelicitous, unfitting, improper;
informal out of order. **3** *I've done nothing
wrong* =**illegal**, unlawful, illicit, criminal, dishonest, dishonourable, corrupt;
unethical, immoral, bad, wicked, sinful,
iniquitous, nefarious, reprehensible; *informal* crooked. **4** *there's something wrong
with the engine* =**amiss**, awry, out of
order, not right, faulty, defective.
−OPPOSITES right, correct, appropriate,
legal.
▶ adverb *she guessed wrong* =**incorrectly**,
wrongly, inaccurately, erroneously,
mistakenly.
▶ noun **1** *the difference between right and
wrong* =**immorality**, sin, wickedness,
evil; unlawfulness, crime, corruption,
villainy, dishonesty, injustice, misconduct, transgression. **2** *an attempt to make
up for past wrongs* =**misdeed**, offence, injury, crime, transgression, peccadillo,
sin; injustice, outrage, atrocity.
−OPPOSITES right.
▶ verb *she was determined to forget the man
who had wronged her* =**ill-use**, mistreat,
do an injustice to, ill-treat, abuse, harm,
hurt, injure; *informal* do the dirty on.
■ **get someone/something wrong**
=**misunderstand**, misinterpret, misconstrue, mistake, misread, take amiss;
get the wrong idea/impression; *informal*
get the wrong end of the stick, be barking up the wrong tree.
■ **go wrong 1** *I've gone wrong somewhere*
=**make a mistake**, make an error, blunder, miscalculate, trip up; *informal* slip up,
screw up, make a boo-boo; *Brit. informal*
boob. **2** *their plans went wrong* =**go awry**,
go amiss, go off course, fail, be unsuccessful, fall through, come to nothing;
backfire, misfire, rebound; *informal* come
to grief, come a cropper, go up in smoke;
Brit. informal go adrift. **3** *the radio's gone
wrong* =**break down**, malfunction, fail,
stop working, crash, give out; *informal* be
on the blink, conk out, go kaput; *Brit. informal* play up, pack up.
■ **in the wrong** =**to blame**, at fault, reprehensible, responsible, culpable, answerable, guilty.

wrongdoer ▶ noun =**offender**, lawbreaker, criminal, felon, delinquent, villain, culprit, evil-doer, sinner, transgressor, malefactor, miscreant, rogue,
scoundrel; *informal* crook, wrong 'un.

wrongdoing ▶ noun =**crime**, lawbreaking, lawlessness, criminality, misconduct, misbehaviour, malpractice,
corruption, immorality, sin, wickedness, evil, vice, iniquity, villainy; offence, felony, misdeed, misdemeanour,
fault, peccadillo, transgression.

wrongful ▶ adjective =**unjustified**, unwarranted, unjust, unfair, undue, undeserved, unreasonable, groundless, indefensible, inappropriate, improper,
unlawful, illegal.
−OPPOSITES rightful.

wrought up ▶ adjective =**agitated**,
tense, stressed, overwrought, nervous,
edgy, keyed up, worked up, jumpy, anxious, nervy, flustered, fretful; *informal* in
a state, in a stew, het up, wound up, uptight, in a tizz; *Brit. informal* strung up.
−OPPOSITES calm.

wry ▶ adjective **1** *his wry humour* =**ironic**,
sardonic, satirical, mocking, sarcastic;
dry, droll, witty, humorous. **2** *a wry expression* =**unimpressed**, displeased, annoyed, irritated, irked, vexed, piqued,
disgruntled, dissatisfied; *informal* peeved.

w

Xx

xenophobic ▶ adjective =jingoistic, chauvinistic, flag-waving, nationalistic, isolationist; prejudiced, bigoted, intolerant.

Xerox ▶ noun *(trademark)* =photocopy, copy, duplicate, reproduction; *trademark* photostat.

Xmas ▶ noun *(informal)*. *See* CHRISTMAS.

X-ray ▶ noun =radiograph, radiogram.

> **WORD LINKS**
>
> *making images using X-rays:*
>   **radiography**
> *study of X-rays:* **radiology**

Yy

yank ▶ verb (informal) =**jerk**, pull, tug, wrench.

yap ▶ verb *the dogs yapped about his heels* =**bark**, yelp, snap.

yardstick ▶ noun =**standard**, measure, gauge, scale, guide, guideline, indicator, test, touchstone, barometer, criterion, benchmark.

yarn ▶ noun =**thread**, cotton, wool, fibre, filament.

yawning ▶ adjective =**gaping**, wide, cavernous, deep; huge, great, big.

year ▶ noun *literary* summer, winter; *archaic* twelvemonth.

> **WORD LINKS**
>
> occurring once a year or lasting a year: **annual**

yearly ▶ adjective =**annual**.
▶ adverb =**annually**, once a year, per annum, each/every year.

yearn ▶ verb =**long**, pine, crave, desire, want, wish, hanker, covet, hunger, thirst, ache, eat one's heart out; *informal* have a yen, itch.

yearning ▶ noun =**longing**, craving, desire, want, wish, hankering, urge, hunger, thirst, ache; *informal* yen, itch.

yell ▶ verb *he yelled in agony* =**cry out**, shout, howl, wail, scream, shriek, screech, yelp, squeal; roar, bawl.
▶ noun *a yell of rage* =**cry**, shout, howl, scream, shriek, screech, yelp, squeal; roar.

yellow ▶ adjective =**flaxen**, golden, gold, blonde, fair.

yelp ▶ noun & verb =**squeal**, shriek, howl, yell, cry, shout.

yen ▶ noun (informal) =**hankering**, yearning, longing, craving, urge, desire, want, wish, hunger, thirst, ache; *informal* itch.

yes ▶ adverb =**all right**, very well, of course, by all means, sure, certainly, absolutely, indeed, affirmative, agreed, roger; *Scottish, N. English, & archaic* aye; *Nautical* aye aye; *informal* yeah, yep, uh-huh, okay, OK, okey-dokey; *Brit. informal* righto, righty-ho; *N. Amer. informal* surely.
–OPPOSITES no.

yes-man ▶ noun (informal) =**sycophant**, toady, creep; *informal* bootlicker; *N. Amer. informal* suck-up.

yet ▶ adverb **1** *he hasn't made up his mind yet* =**so far**, as yet, up till/to now. **2** *don't celebrate just yet* =**(right) now**, at this time; already, so soon. **3** *he did nothing, yet he seemed happy* =**nevertheless**, nonetheless, even so, but, however, still, notwithstanding, despite that, in spite of that, for all that, all/just the same, at the same time. **4** *yet more advice* =**even**, still.

yield ▶ verb **1** *such projects yield poor returns* =**produce**, bear, give, provide, afford, return, bring in, earn, realize, generate, deliver, pay out. **2** *Duke was forced to yield* =**surrender**, capitulate, submit, admit defeat, back down, give in. **3** *he yielded to her demands* =**give in to**, give way to, submit to, comply with, agree to, consent to, go along with; grant, permit, allow; *informal* cave in to; *formal* accede to. **4** *the floorboards yielded underfoot* =**bend**, give.
–OPPOSITES withhold, resist, defy.
▶ noun *we expected a higher yield* =**profit**, gain, return, dividend, earnings.

yob, yobbo ▶ noun (Brit. informal). See **HOOLIGAN**.

yokel ▶ noun =**bumpkin**, peasant, provincial; *Irish informal* culchie; *N. Amer. informal* hayseed, hillbilly, hick; *Austral. informal* bushy.

young ▶ adjective **1** *young people* =**youthful**; junior, adolescent, teenage. **2** *she's very young for her age* =**immature**, childish, juvenile, inexperienced, unsophisticated, naive; *informal* wet behind the ears. **3** *the young microbrewery industry* =**fledgling**, developing, budding, in its infancy, emerging.
–OPPOSITES old, elderly, mature.
▶ noun **1** *a robin feeding its young* =**offspring**, progeny, family, babies. **2** *the young don't care nowadays* =**young people**, children, boys and girls, youngsters, youth, the younger generation,

juveniles, minors; *informal* kids.

youngster ▸ noun =child, teenager, adolescent, youth, juvenile, minor, junior; boy, girl; *Scottish & N. English* lass, lassie; *informal* lad, kid, whippersnapper, teen.

youth ▸ noun **1** *he was a fine athlete in his youth* =early years, teens, teenage years, adolescence, boyhood, girlhood, childhood; minority. **2** *she had kept her youth* =youthfulness, freshness, bloom, vigour, energy. **3** *local youths* =young man, boy, juvenile, teenager, adolescent, junior, minor; *informal* lad, kid. **4** *the youth of the nation* =young people, young, younger generation, next generation; *informal* kids.
−OPPOSITES adulthood, old age.

youthful ▸ adjective =young-looking, spry, sprightly, vigorous, active; young, boyish, girlish; fresh-faced.
−OPPOSITES old, elderly.

Zz

zany ▸ adjective =**eccentric**, odd, unconventional, bizarre, weird; mad, crazy, comic, madcap, funny, quirky, idiosyncratic; *informal* wacky, screwy, nutty, oddball, off the wall; *Brit. informal* daft; *N. Amer. informal* kooky, wacko.
−OPPOSITES conventional, sensible.

zeal ▸ noun =**passion**, ardour, love, fervour, fire, devotion, enthusiasm, eagerness, keenness, relish, gusto, vigour, energy, intensity; fanaticism.
−OPPOSITES apathy.

zealot ▸ noun =**fanatic**, enthusiast, extremist, radical, diehard, activist, militant; *informal* fiend, maniac, nut.

zealous ▸ adjective =**fervent**, ardent, fanatical, passionate, impassioned, devout, devoted, committed, dedicated, enthusiastic, eager, keen, avid, vigorous, energetic, intense, fierce.
−OPPOSITES apathetic.

zenith ▸ noun =**high point**, crowning point, height, top, acme, peak, pinnacle, apex, apogee, crown, crest, summit, climax, culmination, prime.
−OPPOSITES nadir.

zero ▸ noun **1** *you've left off a zero* =**nought**, nothing, nil, 0. **2** *I rated my chances as zero* =**nothing (at all)**, nil, none; *N. English* nowt; *informal* zilch, not a dicky bird; *Brit. informal* damn all, not a sausage; *N. Amer. informal* zip, nada, diddly-squat; *archaic* nought.
■ **zero in on** =**focus on**, focus attention on, centre on, concentrate on, home in on, fix on, pinpoint, highlight, spotlight; *informal* zoom in on.

zest ▸ noun **1** *her zest for life* =**enthusiasm**, gusto, relish, appetite, eagerness, keenness, zeal, fervour, passion. **2** *the zest of an orange* =**rind**, peel, skin.
−OPPOSITES apathy, indifference, blandness.

zigzag ▸ verb =**twist**, meander, snake, wind.

zip ▸ verb *(informal)*. *See* SPEED verb *sense* 1.

zone ▸ noun =**area**, sector, section, belt, stretch, region, territory, district, quarter, precinct, locality, neighbourhood, province.

zoom ▸ verb *(informal)*. *See* SPEED verb *sense* 1.

Wordfinder lists
1. Food and drink

Alcoholic drinks

absinthe
advocaat
alcopop
ale
amaretto
anisette
applejack
aquavit
Armagnac
arrack/arak
barley wine
beer
bitter
Bloody Mary
bourbon
brandy
Buck's Fizz
Calvados

cava
champagne
chartreuse
cherry brandy
cider
cognac
crème de
 menthe
curaçao
daiquiri
gimlet
gin
ginger wine
grappa
Harvey
 Wallbanger
highball
kirsch

kümmel
kvass
lager
liqueur
Madeira
malmsey
malt (whisky)
maraschino
marc
margarita
Marsala
mead
mild
ouzo
pastis
perry
Pils
pina colada

pink gin
pombe
port
porter
poteen
pulque
punch
raki
rum
St Clements
sake
sambuca
sangria
schnapps
screwdriver
scrumpy
shandy
sherry

slivovitz
sloe gin
snowball
spritzer
stout
tej
tequila
tequila sunrise
Tom Collins
vermouth
vodka
whisky/
 whiskey
whisky mac
whisky sour
wine

Bread

bagel
baguette
bannock
bap
bara brith
barmbrack
barm cake
barracouta
bialy
billy-bread
bloomer

boxty
bridge roll
brioche
bun
challah
chapatti
ciabatta
cob
cottage loaf
damper
farl

farmhouse
 loaf
flatbread
focaccia
French stick
granary bread
hoagie
injera
johnnycake
kaiser
kulcha

malt loaf
matzo
milk loaf
muffin
nan
pan dulce
panettone
panino
pan-loaf
paratha
petit pain

pitta
pone
poppadom
pumpernickel
puri
roti
soda bread
sourdough
split tin
spoon bread
stotty

Fruit

apple
apricot
Asian pear
avocado
banana

bilberry
blackberry
blackcurrant
blood orange
blueberry

boysenberry
breadfruit
cantaloupe
Cape
 gooseberry

carambola
cherry
Chinese
 gooseberry
citron

clementine
cloudberry
coconut
crab apple
cranberry

currant
damson
date
dewberry
elderberry
fig
galia melon
gooseberry
gourd
granadilla
grape
grapefruit
greengage
guava

honeydew
 melon
huckleberry
jackfruit
jujube
kiwi fruit
kumquat
lemon
lime
lingonberry
loganberry
lychee
mandarin
mango
mangosteen

melon
minneola
mulberry
muscat
musk melon
navel orange
nectarine
Ogen melon
olive
orange
ortanique
papaya
passionfruit
pawpaw

peach
pear
persimmon
physalis
pineapple
plantain
plum
pomegranate
pomelo
prickly pear
pumpkin
quince
rambutan
raspberry

redcurrant
roseapple
satsuma
sharon fruit
sloe
starfruit
strawberry
tangerine
tayberry
tomato
Ugli fruit
 (*trademark*)
watermelon
white currant
whortleberry

Herbs See also **Spices**.

anise
basil
bay leaf
bergamot
borage
camomile
chervil

chicory
chives
comfrey
coriander
dill
dittany
fennel

hyssop
lavender
lemon balm
lemon grass
lovage
marjoram
mint

oregano
parsley
peppermint
rosemary
rue
saffron
sage

savory
sorrel
spearmint
sweet cicely
tarragon
thyme
vervain

Meat

bacon
baron of beef
beef
belly
best end
brisket
chateaubriand
chine
chop
chuck
collar

cutlet
entrecôte
escalope
fillet
flank
fricandeau
game
gammon
gigot
ham
hand

hock
knuckle
leg
loin
mince
mutton
neck
noisette
pork
porterhouse
 steak

rack
rib
rump
saddle
shank
shoulder
shin
side
silverside
sirloin
skirt

spare rib
steak
T-bone
tenderloin
topside
tournedos
veal
venison

Nuts

almond
areca nut
beechnut
betel nut
Brazil nut

cashew
chestnut
cobnut
coco-de-mer
coconut

cola nut
earthnut
filbert
groundnut
hazelnut

macadamia
monkey nut
palm nut
peanut
pecan

pine nut
piñon
pistachio
walnut
water chestnut

Pasta

agnolotti	farfalle	macaroni	rigatoni	taglioni
angel hair	farfalline	manicotti	rotelle	tortellini
annellini	fettuccine	orecchiette	rotini	tortelloni
bucatini	fusilli	orzo	spaghetti	tortiglioni
cannelloni	gemelli	paglia e fieno	spaghettini	trenette
cappelletti	gramigna	pappardelle	stelline	vermicelli
conchiglie	lasagne	penne	tagliatelle	ziti
ditalini	linguine	ravioli	tagliolini	

Spices *See also* **Herbs.**

allspice	chilli	fennel seeds	juniper berries	pepper
capers	cinnamon	fenugreek	mace	pimento
caraway seeds	cloves	garlic	mustard	star anise
cardamom	coriander	ginger	nutmeg	turmeric
cayenne pepper	cumin	ginseng	paprika	vanilla

Vegetables

adzuki/adukl bean	cannellini bean	cucumber	jicama	plantain
alfalfa	capsicum	curly kale	leek	potato
artichoke	cardoon	cush-cush	lentil	puha
asparagus	carrot	custard marrow	lettuce	pumpkin
aubergine	cassava	dishcloth gourd	lima bean	radish
avocado pear	cauliflower	eggplant	mangetout	radicchio
bamboo shoots	celeriac	endive	manioc	runner bean
bean	celery	fennel	marrow	rutabaga
beet	chard	flageolet	marrow squash	salsify
beetroot	chayote	French bean	mizuna	savoy cabbage
black bean	chervil	garden pea	mung bean	scallion
black-eyed bean	chickpea	garlic	mustard	scorzonera
borlotti bean	chicory	gherkin	okra	sea kale
butter bean	Chinese artichoke	globe artichoke	onion	shallot
breadfruit	Chinese cabbage	gobo	orache	snap bean
broad bean	Chinese leaves	gourd	oyster plant	spinach
broccoli	choko	gumbo	pak choi	spinach beet
Brussels sprout	collard	haricot bean	parsnip	spring onion
butter bean	corn on the cob	kale	pattypan	squash
butternut squash	cos lettuce	kidney bean	pea	string bean
cabbage	courgette	kohlrabi	pea bean	succory
calabrese	cress	Jerusalem artichoke	pepper	sugar bean
			petits pois	sugar-snap peas
			pimiento	swede
			pinto bean	

sweetcorn
sweet potato
taro

tomato
turnip
turnip greens

vegetable
  spaghetti
water chestnut

watercress
waxpod
yam

yam bean
zucchini

....

2. Animals

Birds

adjutant bird
albatross
auk
avocet
bald eagle
barnacle
  goose
barn owl
bateleur
bearded tit
bee-eater
Bewick's
  swan
bird of
  paradise
bittern
blackbird
blackcap
black grouse
black kite
black swan
bluebird
bluethroat
blue tit
booby
bowerbird
brambling
brent goose
bronzewing
brown owl
budgerigar
bullfinch
bunting
burrowing owl
bustard
butcher-bird
buzzard

Canada goose
canary
capercaillie
caracara
cardinal
cassowary
chaffinch
chat
chickadee
chicken
chiffchaff
chough
coal tit
cockatiel
cockatoo
cock-of-the-
  rock
collared dove
condor
coot
cormorant
corncrake
crane
crested tit
crossbill
crow
cuckoo
curlew
currawong
dabchick
dipper
diver
diving duck
dodo
dotterel
dove

duck
dunnock
eagle
eagle owl
egret
eider duck
elephant bird
emperor
  penguin
emu
erne
fairy penguin
fairy tern
falcon
fantail
ferruginous
  duck
fieldfare
finch
firecrest
fish eagle
flamingo
flycatcher
frigate bird
fulmar
galah
gannet
gentoo
  penguin
goldcrest
golden eagle
golden oriole
golden
  pheasant
goldfinch
goose
goshawk

great auk
great crested
  grebe
great tit
grebe
greenfinch
green
  woodpecker
greylag goose
grey parrot
griffon vulture
grouse
guillemot
guineafowl
gull
gyrfalcon
harpy eagle
harrier
Harris' hawk
Hawaiian
  goose
hawfinch
hawk
hawk owl
hedge
  sparrow
hen
hen harrier
heron
herring gull
hobby
honey buzzard
honeyeater
honeyguide
hooded crow
hoopoe
hornbill

horned owl
house martin
house
  sparrow
hummingbird
ibis
jackdaw
jay
junglefowl
kea
kestrel
kingbird
kingfisher
king penguin
kite
kittiwake
kiwi
kookaburra
lammergeier
lanner
lapwing
lark
laughing
  jackass
lily-trotter
linnet
little owl
long-tailed tit
loon
lorikeet
lovebird
lyrebird
macaroni
  penguin
macaw
magpie
mallard

malleefowl
mandarin duck
marabou stork
marsh harrier
martin
meadowlark
meadow pipit
merlin
mistle thrush
moa
mockingbird
moorcock
moorfowl
moorhen
Mother Carey's chicken
Muscovy duck
mute swan
mynah bird
nightingale
nightjar
noddy
nuthatch
oriole
ortolan
osprey
ostrich
ouzel
owl
oystercatcher
parakeet
parrot

partridge
passenger pigeon
peacock
peafowl
peewit
pelican
penguin
peregrine falcon
petrel
phalarope
pheasant
pied wagtail
pigeon
pilot bird
pipit
plover
pochard
prairie chicken
pratincole
ptarmigan
puffin
quail
quetzal
rail
raven
razorbill
red kite
redpoll
redstart
redwing
reed-bird

reed bunting
reed warbler
rhea
rhinoceros bird
ringed plover
ring ouzel
roadrunner
robin
rockhopper
rook
roseate tern
ruddy duck
ruddy shelduck
ruff
sacred ibis
sandgrouse
sand martin
sandpiper
sandwich tern
screech owl
sea eagle
seagull
secretary bird
sedge warbler
shag
shearwater
shelduck
shoveler
shrike
siskin
skua

skylark
snakebird
snipe
snow bunting
snow goose
snowy owl
song thrush
sooty tern
sparrow
sparrowhawk
spoonbill
spotted flycatcher
starling
stilt
stonechat
stone curlew
stork
storm petrel
sunbird
sunbittern
sungrebe
swallow
swan
swift
tawny owl
teal
tern
thrush
tit
titlark
titmouse
toucan

treecreeper
tree pipit
tree sparrow
tufted duck
turkey
turkey vulture
turtle dove
umbrellabird
vulture
wagtail
wallcreeper
warbler
water rail
waxwing
weaver bird
wheatear
whimbrel
whippoorwill
whooping crane
wigeon
willow warbler
woodchat
woodcock
wood duck
woodgrouse
wood ibis
woodlark
woodpecker
wood pigeon
wren
yellowhammer
zebra finch

Butterflies

Adonis blue
alpine
angle wings
apollo
arctic
argus
azure
birdwing
blue
brimstone
brown
buckeye

cabbage white
Camberwell Beauty
chalkhill blue
checkerspot
cleopatra
clouded yellow
comma
copper
diana
dog face
dryad

Duke of Burgundy
dusky wing
elfin
emperor
festoon
fritillary
gatekeeper
grayling
hairstreak
julia
map butterfly

marbled white
mazarine blue
meadow brown
metalmark
milkweed
monarch
morpho
mourning cloak
nettle-tree butterfly

nymph
orange tip
owl butterfly
painted lady
peacock butterfly
pearly eye
plain tiger
purple emperor
red admiral
ringlet

satyr
Scotch argus
silver-studded blue
skipper
snout butterfly
speckled wood
sulphur
swallowtail
tortoiseshell
two-tailed pasha
wall brown
white admiral
wood nymph
zebra

Deer and antelopes

addax
blackbuck
blesbok
bongo
bontebok
brocket
caribou
chamois
chevrotain
chital
dik-dik
duiker
eland
elk
fallow deer
gazelle
gemsbok
gerenuk
gnu
goat-antelope
goral
hartebeest
impala
klipspringer
kudu
lechwe
marsh deer
moose
mountain goat
mouse deer
mule deer
muntjac
musk deer
musk ox
nilgai
nyala
okapi
oribi
oryx
Père David's deer
pronghorn antelope
puku
red deer
reedbuck
reindeer
rhebok
roan antelope
roe deer
royal stag
rusa
sable antelope
saiga
sika
sitatunga
springbok
steenbok
suni
swamp deer
topi
wapiti
waterbuck
water deer
white-tailed deer
wildebeest

Fish

albacore
alewife
amberjack
anchovy
angelfish
angel shark
anglerfish
arapaima
archerfish
argus fish
balloonfish
bandfish
barbel
barracouta
barracuda
barramundi
basking shark
bass
beluga
bib
bitterling
black durgon
blackfish
blenny
bloodfin
blowfish
bluefin
bluefish
bluegill
bluehead
blue shark
bonefish
bonito
bonnethead
bonnetmouth
bowfin
boxfish
bream
brill
brisling
brown trout
bullhead
bummalo
burbot
butterfish
butterfly fish
cabezon
callop
candiru
candlefish
capelin
cardinal fish
carp
carpet shark
catfish
cat shark
cavefish
charr
chimera
chinook salmon
chub
clownfish
coalfish
cod
coelacanth
coley
comber
combfish
conger eel
cornetfish
cowfish
cow shark
cutlassfish
dab
dace
damselfish
darter
devil ray
discus
dogfish
dorado
dory
Dover sole
dragonet
dragonfish
drumfish
eel
eelpout
electric eel
electric ray
espada
fighting fish
filefish
flatfish
flathead
flounder
fluke
flying fish
frogfish
gaper
garden eel
garfish
garpike
glassfish
globefish
goatfish
goby
goldfish
goosefish
gourami
grayling
great white shark
grey mullet
grouper
grunion
grunt
gudgeon
guitarfish

gulper eel
gunnel
guppy
gurnard
haddock
hagfish
hake
halfbeak
halibut
hammerhead
  shark
harlequin fish
hatchetfish
hawkfish
herring
hogfish
hoki
horse
  mackerel
houndfish
huss
icefish
jackfish
jackknife fish
jawfish
jewelfish
John Dory
kingfish
koi carp
lamprey
lancetfish
lanternfish
leatherjacket
lemon sole
ling
lionhead
lizardfish
loach
lumpsucker
lungfish
lyrefish
mackerel
mako
manta
marlin
medusa fish

megrim
midshipman
milkfish
minnow
mirror carp
monkfish
moonfish
Moorish idol
moray eel
morwong
mudfish
mudminnow
mudskipper
mullet
muskellunge
musselcracker
needlefish
neon tetra
Nile perch
nurse shark
oarfish
orfe
paddlefish
paradise fish
parrotfish
perch
pike
pikeperch
pilchard
pilotfish
pipefish
piranha
plaice
platy
pollack
pollan
pomfret
porbeagle
porcupine fish
porgy
pout
prowfish
puffer fish
rabbitfish
ragfish
rainbow trout

rascasse
ratfish
ray
razorfish
redfin
red mullet
red snapper
remora
requiem shark
ribbonfish
roach
rock bass
rockfish
rockling
rock snapper
ronquil
rouget
roughy
rudd
ruffe
sablefish
sailfish
saithe
salmon
salmon trout
sand dab
sand eel
sandfish
sand shark
sardine
sawfish
scabbardfish
scad
scat
scorpionfish
sea bass
sea bream
sea horse
sea perch
sea trout
sergeant fish
sergeant
  major
shad
shark
shark-sucker

shovelhead
shubunkin
sild
silverside
skate
skilfish
skipjack tuna
skipper
smelt
smooth hound
snaggle-tooth
snailfish
snakehead
snapper
snipe eel
snipefish
snook
soapfish
sockeye
  salmon
soldierfish
sole
spadefish
sparling
spearfish
sprat
square-tail
squawfish
squirrelfish
stargazer
stickleback
stingaree
stingray
stockfish
stonefish
striped bass
sturgeon
sucker
sunfish
surfperch
surgeonfish
sweetlips
swordfish
swordtail
tai
tailorfish

tarpon
tench
tetra
thornback
threadfin
thresher shark
tiger fish
tiger shark
tilapia
toadfish
tope
topminnow
torpedo ray
triggerfish
trout
trumpeter
trumpetfish
trunkfish
tubesnout
tuna
tunny
turbot
unicorn fish
vendace
walleye
warbonnet
weakfish
weatherfish
weever
whale shark
whitebait
white bass
whitefish
whiting
wobbegong
wolf fish
wormfish
wrasse
wreckfish
wrymouth
X-ray fish
yellowfin
yellowtail
zander
zebra fish

Insects

ant
ant-lion
aphid
army ant
assassin bug
bedbug
bee
beetle
blackfly
bloodworm
blowfly
bluebottle
bombardier
  beetle
bookworm
botfly
bristletail
bumblebee
butterfly
cabbage root
  fly
caddis fly
cardinal beetle
carpenter bee
carpet beetle
carrion beetle
carrot fly
chafer

chigger
cicada
click beetle
cockchafer
cockroach
Colorado
  beetle
crab louse
crane fly
cricket
cutworm
daddy-long-
  legs
damselfly
death-watch
  beetle
demoiselle
devil's coach-
  horse
dor beetle
dragonfly
drosophila
dung beetle
earwig
elm bark
  beetle
fire ant
firefly

flea
flour beetle
fly
froghopper
fruit fly
furniture
  beetle
gadfly
gall wasp
glow-worm
gnat
goliath beetle
grasshopper
greenbottle
greenfly
honeybee
hornet
horsefly
housefly
hoverfly
ichneumon
katydid
lacewing
lac insect
ladybird
leafcutter ant
leaf insect

leaf miner
leatherjacket
locust
longhorn
  beetle
louse
mantis
mason bee
mason wasp
May bug
mayfly
meal beetle
mealworm
mealy bug
midge
mining bee
mosquito
moth
paper wasp
phylloxera
pond skater
praying mantis
red ant
rhinoceros
  beetle
root fly
sawfly
scale insect

scarab
sexton beetle
shield bug
silverfish
Spanish fly
springtail
stag beetle
stick insect
stink bug
stonefly
termite
thrips
thunderbug
thunderfly
tsetse fly
tumblebug
warble fly
wasp
water
  boatman
weevil
whirligig
whitefly
wireworm
witchetty grub
woodworm
woolly bear

Marsupials

antechinus
bandicoot
bettong
brushtail
cuscus
dunnart

glider
kangaroo
koala
kowari
mulgara
numbat

opossum
pademelon
phalanger
possum
potoroo
quokka

quoil
rat-kangaroo
ringtail
Tasmanian
  devil
Tasmanian
  tiger/wolf

thylacine
wallaby
wallaroo
wombat
yapok

Monkeys and apes

baboon
Barbary ape
capuchin
  monkey
chimpanzee

colobus
douroucouli
gelada
gibbon
gorilla

green monkey
grivet
guenon
hamadryas

hanuman
  langur
howler
  monkey
langur

lar gibbon
leaf monkey
macaque
mandrill
marmoset

orang-utan
proboscis
  monkey

rhesus
  monkey
spider monkey

squirrel
  monkey
tamarin

vervet
woolly monkey

Moths

angle shades
atlas moth
bagworm
bogong
brimstone
brown-tail
buff-tip
burnet
burnished
  brass
cabbage moth
cecropia
cinnabar
clearwing
Clifden
  nonpareil
clothes moth
codling/codlin
  moth
common
  heath
corn borer
crescent

dagger
death's head
  hawkmoth
diamondback
  moth
drinker
dun-bar
eggar
emerald
emperor
ermine
festoon
flour moth
footman
forester
fox moth
garden carpet
garden tiger
ghost moth
goat moth
gypsy moth
hawkmoth
heath

hooktip
hornet moth
io moth
Kentish moth
kitten
lackey
lappet
leaf miner
leaf roller
leopard moth
lobster moth
luna moth
magpie moth
meal moth
merveille du
  jour
minor
moon moth
Mother
  Shipton
noctuid
oak eggar
old lady

owlet
peach
  blossom
peppered
  moth
pine beauty
pink bollworm
plume moth
processionary
prominent
pug
puss moth
pyralid
rivulet
rustic
sallow
saturniid
shark
silk moth
silver-line
silver Y
snout
sphingid

swallow-tailed
  moth
swift
tabby
tapestry moth
thorn
tiger moth
tortrix
triangle
turnip moth
tussock moth
tussore moth
umber
underwing
vapourer
wainscot
wax moth
white spot
winter moth
yellow-tail
yellow
  underwing
yucca moth

Reptiles *See also* **Snakes**.

alligator
basilisk
bearded
  dragon
blindworm
caiman

chameleon
crocodile
gecko
gharial
Gila monster
goanna

hawksbill
iguana
Komodo
  dragon
leatherback
lizard

loggerhead
  turtle
marine iguana
moloch
monitor lizard
skink

slow-worm
terrapin
tortoise
turtle
whiptail

Rodents

acouchi
agouti
beaver
capybara
cavy
chinchilla

chipmunk
coypu
degu
desert rat
dormouse
field mouse

gerbil
gopher
groundhog
guinea pig
hamster

harvest
  mouse
house mouse
jerboa
kangaroo rat
lemming

mara
marmot
mole rat
mouse
muskrat
paca

pacarana | rat | swamp rat | vole | woodchuck
porcupine | springhare | tuco-tuco | water rat | wood mouse
prairie dog | squirrel | viscacha | water vole | wood rat

Snakes

adder | colubrid | garter snake | night adder | sidewinder
anaconda | copperhead | gopher snake | pine snake | smooth snake
asp | coral snake | grass snake | pit viper | spitting cobra
black mamba | corn snake | green snake | puff adder | taipan
blind snake | diamondback | horned snake | python | tiger snake
boa | diamond | indigo snake | rat snake | tree snake
  constrictor | python | king cobra | rattlesnake | viper
brown snake | egg-eating | krait | reticulated | water snake
bushmaster | snake | mamba | python | whip snake
carpet snake | fer de lance | massasauga | rinkhals | wolf snake
coachwhip | flying snake | milk snake | rock python |
cobra | Gaboon viper | | sea snake |

Spiders and other arachnids

baboon spider | cardinal spider | harvestman | orb-web | trapdoor
bird-eating | cobweb spider | hunting spider | spider | spider
  spider | crab spider | jumping spider | raft spider | violin spider
black widow | diadem spider | katipo | redback | wolf spider
button spider | funnel-web | money spider | sun spider | zebra spider
camel spider | spider | | tarantula |

Whales and dolphins

Amazon dolphin | dusky dolphin | minke whale | sei whale
baleen whale | finback whale | narwhal | sperm whale
beaked whale | fin whale | orca | spinner dolphin
beluga | grampus | pilot whale | toothed whale
blue whale | Greenland right | porpoise | tucuxi
bottlenose dolphin | whale | right whale | whalebone whale
bottlenose whale | grey whale | Risso's dolphin | white whale
bowhead whale | humpback whale | river dolphin |
cachalot | killer whale | rorqual |

Wild cats

bobcat | clouded | jaguarundi | margay | puma
caracal | leopard | leopard | mountain lion | serval
cheetah | cougar | lion | ocelot | snow leopard
 | jaguar | lynx | panther | tiger

Countries

country	related adjective/noun	currency unit
Afghanistan	Afghan	afghani = 100 puls
Albania	Albanian	lek = 100 qindarka
Algeria	Algerian	dinar = 100 centimes
America (*see* United States of America)		
Andorra	Andorran	euro = 100 cents (formerly French franc, Spanish peseta)
Angola	Angolan	kwanza = 100 lwei
Antigua and Barbuda	Antiguan, Barbudan	dollar = 100 cents
Argentina	Argentine *or* Argentinian	peso = 10,000 centavos
Armenia	Armenian	dram = 100 luma
Australia	Australian	dollar = 100 cents
Austria	Austrian	euro = 100 cents (formerly schilling = 100 groschen)
Azerbaijan	Azerbaijani	manat = 100 gopik
Bahamas	Bahamian	dollar = 100 cents
Bahrain	Bahraini	dinar = 1,000 fils
Bangladesh	Bangladeshi	taka = 100 poisha
Barbados	Barbadian	dollar = 100 cents
Belarus	Belarusian	rouble
Belgium	Belgian	euro = 100 cents (formerly franc = 100 centimes)
Belize	Belizian	dollar = 100 cents
Benin	Beninese	African franc
Bhutan	Bhutanese	ngultrum = 100 chetrum
Bolivia	Bolivian	boliviano = 100 centavos
Bosnia–Herzegovina	Bosnian	dinar = 100 paras
Botswana	Botswanan / Tswana	pula = 100 thebe
Brazil	Brazilian	real = 100 centavos
Brunei	Bruneian	dollar = 100 sen
Bulgaria	Bulgarian	lev = 100 stotinki
Burkina Faso	Burkinese	African franc
Burma (officially called Myanmar)	Burmese	kyat = 100 pyas
Burundi	Burundian	franc = 100 centimes
Cambodia	Cambodian	riel = 100 sen
Cameroon	Cameroonian	African franc
Canada	Canadian	dollar = 100 cents
Cape Verde Islands	Cape Verdean	escudo = 100 centavos
Central African Republic	–	African franc
Chad	Chadian	African franc
Chile	Chilean	peso = 100 centavos
China	Chinese	yuan = 10 jiao or 100 fen
Colombia	Colombian	peso = 100 centavos

country	related adjective/noun	currency unit
Comoros	Comoran	African franc
Congo	Congolese	African franc
Congo, Democratic Republic of (Zaire)	Congolese	franc = 100 centimes
Costa Rica	Costa Rican	colón = 100 centimos
Croatia	Croat or Croatian	kuna = 100 lipa
Cuba	Cuban	peso = 100 centavos
Cyprus	Cypriot	pound = 100 cents
Czech Republic	Czech	koruna = 100 haleru
Denmark	Danish/Dane	krone = 100 øre
Djibouti	Djiboutian	franc = 100 centimes
Dominica	Dominican	dollar = 100 cents
Dominican Republic	Dominican	peso = 100 centavos
Ecuador	Ecuadorean	sucre = 100 centavos
Egypt	Egyptian	pound = 100 piastres or 1,000 milliemes
El Salvador	Salvadorean	colón = 100 centavos
Equatorial Guinea	Equatorial Guinean	African franc
Eritrea	Eritrean	nakfa = 100 cents
Estonia	Estonian	kroon = 100 sents
Ethiopia	Ethiopian	birr = 100 cents
Fiji	Fijian	dollar = 100 cents
Finland	Finnish / Finn	euro = 100 cents (formerly markka = 100 penniä)
France	French	euro = 100 cents (formerly franc = 100 centimes)
Gabon	Gabonese	African franc
Gambia, the	Gambian	dalasi = 100 butut
Georgia	Georgian	lari = 100 tetri
Germany	German	euro = 100 cents (formerly Deutschmark = 100 pfennigs)
Ghana	Ghanaian	cedi = 100 pesewas
Greece	Greek	euro = 100 cents (formerly drachma = 100 leptae)
Grenada	Grenadian	dollar = 100 cents
Guatemala	Guatemalan	quetzal = 100 centavos
Guinea	Guinean	franc = 100 centimes
Guinea-Bissau	–	peso = 100 centavos
Guyana	Guyanese	dollar = 100 cents
Haiti	Haitian	gourde = 100 centimes
Holland (see Netherlands)		
Honduras	Honduran	lempira = 100 centavos
Hungary	Hungarian	forint = 100 filler
Iceland	Icelandic / Icelander	krona = 100 aurar
India	Indian	rupee = 100 paisa
Indonesia	Indonesian	rupiah = 100 sen
Iran	Iranian	rial = 100 dinars
Iraq	Iraqi	dinar = 1,000 fils

country	related adjective/noun	currency unit
Ireland, Republic of	Irish	euro = 100 cents (formerly pound [punt] = 100 pence)
Israel	Israeli	shekel = 100 agora
Italy	Italian	euro = 100 cents (formerly lira = 100 centesimos)
Ivory Coast	Ivorian	African franc
Jamaica	Jamaican	dollar = 100 cents
Japan	Japanese	yen = 100 sen
Jordan	Jordanian	dinar = 1,000 fils
Kazakhstan	Kazakh	tenge = 100 teins
Kenya	Kenyan	shilling = 100 cents
Kiribati	–	dollar = 100 cents
Kuwait	Kuwaiti	dinar = 1,000 fils
Kyrgyzstan	Kyrgyz	som = 100 tiyin
Laos	Laotian	kip = 100 ats
Latvia	Latvian	lat = 100 santims
Lebanon	Lebanese	pound = 100 piastres
Lesotho	Lesothan / Mosotho, pl. Basotho	loti = 100 lisente
Liberia	Liberian	dollar = 100 cents
Libya	Libyan	dinar = 1,000 dirhams
Liechtenstein	–/ Liechtensteiner	Swiss franc
Lithuania	Lithuanian	litas = 100 centas
Luxembourg	–/ Luxembourger	euro = 100 cents (formerly franc = 100 centimes)
Macedonia	Macedonian	denar = 100 deni
Madagascar	Malagasay or Madagascan	franc = 100 centimes
Malawi	Malawian	kwacha = 100 tambala
Malaysia	Malaysian	ringgit = 100 sen
Maldives	Maldivian	rufiyaa = 100 laris
Mali	Malian	African franc
Malta	Maltese	lira = 100 cents
Marshall Islands	Marshallese	US dollar
Mauritania	Mauritanian	ouguiya = 5 khoums
Mauritius	Mauritian	rupee = 100 cents
Mexico	Mexican	peso = 100 centavos
Micronesia, Federated States of	Micronesian	US dollar
Moldova	Moldovan	leu = 100 bani
Monaco	Monegasque or Monacan	euro = 100 cents (formerly franc = 100 centimes)
Mongolia	Mongolian	tugrik = 100 mongos
Montenegro	Montenegrin	dinar = 100 paras
Morocco	Moroccan	dirham = 100 centimes
Mozambique	Mozambican	metical = 100 centavos
Myanmar (see Burma)		
Namibia	Namibian	rand = 100 cents
Nauru	Nauruan	Australian dollar

country	related adjective/noun	currency unit
Nepal	Nepalese	rupee = 100 paisa
Netherlands, the	Dutch	euro = 100 cents (formerly guilder = 100 cents)
New Zealand	– / New Zealander	dollar = 100 cents
Nicaragua	Nicaraguan	cordoba = 100 centavos
Niger	Nigerien	African franc
Nigeria	Nigerian	naira = 100 kobo
North Korea	North Korean	won = 100 jun
Norway	Norwegian	krone = 100 øre
Oman	Omani	rial = 1,000 baiza
Pakistan	Pakistani	rupee = 100 paisa
Panama	Panamanian	balboa = 100 centésimos
Papua New Guinea	Papua New Guinean or Guinean	kina = 100 toea
Paraguay	Paraguayan	guarani = 100 centimos
Peru	Peruvian	nuevo sol = 100 cents
Philippines	Filipino or Philippine	peso = 100 centavos
Poland	Polish / Pole	zloty = 100 groszy
Portugal	Portuguese	euro = 100 cents (formerly escudo = 100 centavos)
Qatar	Qatari	riyal = 100 dirhams
Romania	Romanian	leu = 100 bani
Russia	Russian	rouble = 100 copecks
Rwanda	Rwandan	franc = 100 centimes
St Kitts and Nevis	–	dollar = 100 cents
St Lucia	St Lucian	dollar = 100 cents
St Vincent and the Grenadines	Vincentian, Grenadian	dollar = 100 cents
Samoa	Samoan	tala = 100 sene
San Marino	–	euro = 100 cents (formerly Italian lira)
São Tomé and Principe	–	dobra = 100 centavos
Saudi Arabia	Saudi Arabian or Saudi	riyal = 20 qursh or 100 halalas
Senegal	Senegalese	African franc
Serbia	Serbian	dinar = 100 paras
Seychelles, the	Seychellois	rupee = 100 cents
Sierra Leone	Sierra Leonean	leone = 100 cents
Singapore	Singaporean	dollar = 100 cents
Slovakia	Slovak or Slovakian	koruna = 100 haleru
Slovenia	Slovene or Slovenian	tolar = 100 stotins
Solomon Islands	– / Solomon Islander	dollar = 100 cents
Somalia	Somali or Somalian	shilling = 100 cents
South Africa	South African	rand = 100 cents
South Korea	South Korean	won = 100 jeon
Spain	Spanish / Spaniard	euro = 100 cents (formerly peseta = 100 centimos)
Sri Lanka	Sri Lankan	rupee = 100 cents
Sudan	Sudanese	dinar = 10 pounds

country	related adjective/noun	currency unit
Suriname	Surinamese	guilder = 100 cents
Swaziland	Swazi	lilangeni = 100 cents
Sweden	Swedish / Swede	krona = 100 öre
Switzerland	Swiss	franc = 100 centimes
Syria	Syrian	pound = 100 piastres
Taiwan	Taiwanese	New Taiwan dollar = 100 cents
Tajikistan	Tajik	somoni = 100 dirams
Tanzania	Tanzanian	shilling = 100 cents
Thailand	Thai	baht = 100 satangs
Togo	Togolese	African franc
Tonga	Tongan	pa'anga = 100 seniti
Trinidad and Tobago	Trinidadian, Tobagonian	dollar = 100 cents
Tunisia	Tunisian	dinar = 1,000 milliemes
Turkey	Turkish / Turk	lira = 100 kurus
Turkmenistan	Turkmen *or* Turkoman	manat = 100 tenge
Tuvalu	Tuvaluan	dollar = 100 cents
Uganda	Ugandan	shilling = 100 cents
Ukraine	Ukrainian	hryvna = 100 kopiykas
United Arab Emirates	—	dirham = 100 fils
United Kingdom	British / Briton	pound = 100 pence
United States of America	American	dollar = 100 cents
Uruguay	Uruguayan	peso = 100 centésimos
Uzbekistan	Uzbek	som
Vanuatu	Vanuatuan	vatu = 100 centimes
Vatican City	—	euro = 100 cents (formerly Italian lira)
Venezuela	Venezuelan	bolivar = 100 centimos
Vietnam	Vietnamese	dong = 10 hao or 100 xu
Yemen	Yemeni	riyal = 100 fils
Zaire (*see* Congo, Democratic Republic of)		
Zambia	Zambian	kwacha = 100 ngwee
Zimbabwe	Zimbabwean	dollar = 100 cents

Supplement contents

LONGLEY PARK SIXTH FORM COLLEGE
HORNINGLOW ROAD
SHEFFIELD
S5 6SG